GLOBAL HEALTH CARE

Issues and Policies

SECOND EDITION

The Pedagogy

Global Health Care: Issues and Policies, Second Edition drives comprehension through various strategies that meet the learning needs of students while also generating enthusiasm about the topic. This interactive approach addresses different learning styles, making this the ideal text to ensure mastery of key concepts. The pedagogical aids that appear in most chapters include the following:

2

Global Health in Developed Societies: Examples in the United States, Sweden, Japan, and the United Kingdom

Carol Holtz

> *"It is health that is real wealth and not pieces of gold and silver."*
> Mohandas K. Gandhi

OBJECTIVES

After completing this chapter, the reader will be able to:

1. Compare and contrast population health statistics for the United States, Sweden, Japan, and the United Kingdom.
2. Compare and contrast the major health issues and healthcare systems of the United States, Sweden, Japan, and the United Kingdom.
3. Relate healthcare disparities within and among the countries of the United States, Sweden, Japan, and the United Kingdom.
4. Discuss the high rates of longevity for residents of Japan and Sweden.

INTRODUCTION

This chapter gives examples of developed countries and their major health issues and health issues will be reviewed in greater detail within other chapters of this text. T chosen because they vary in terms of their healthcare systems and geographic areas.

Many of the developed countries are currently working on controversial legal, issues that directly relate to health care and healthcare systems of delivery. Specificall ics are being addressed:

- Access to health care for all residents
- Issues of funding for nonlegal residents (illegal aliens) and healthcare services ment and nongovernment organizations
- Options for termination of an unwanted pregnancy

CHAPTER OBJECTIVES

These objectives provide instructors and students with a snapshot of the key information they will encounter in each chapter. They serve as a checklist to help guide and focus study. Objectives can also be found on the companion website at **http://go.jblearning.com/holtz**.

19

This chapter has examined the health and health care of the countries of the United States, Sweden, Japan, and the United Kingdom. Included in this comparison were population statistics, types of government healthcare programs, economics and healthcare spending, and healthcare personnel.

STUDY QUESTIONS

1. Why do you think that the United States has the world's highest rate of obesity? How does this problem relate to chronic health diseases such as cardiovascular disease, hypertension, and diabetes?
2. In spite of the country having the highest level of per capita expenditures, why does the United States still have a relatively high rate of infant mortality as compared to other developed countries?
3. What are some reasons that contribute to Japan and Sweden having the world's best longevity rates? Even though it spends the most dollars per capita on health care, why is the United States so far behind in terms of longevity?
4. What are some health disparities within the United Kingdom, and how might they be solved?

CASE STUDY

The mortality rate for American Indians, which includes Alaskan Nat[...] has increased primarily due to the effects of type 2 diabetes. The U[...] Health Service has provided a Special Diabetes Program for Indian[...] spending for health care, however, the rate for age-adjusted deaths[...] pared to white Americans.

Infectious diseases are decreasing while chronic diseases, s[...] are increasing in this population. Data collected was mainly from [...] the western part of the United States. Other major health issues [...] vascular diseases, smoking, and hypertension. Also discussed was the high rate of sedentary lifestyles as compared to historically much greater daily physical activities.

Reference

Kunitz, S. (2008). Changing patterns of mortality among American Indians. *American Journal of Public Health, 98*(3), 404–411.

Case Study Questions

1. Create a culturally congruent plan for reduction[...] diabetes among American Indians/Alaskan Nativ[...]
2. Why do American Indians have higher levels of [...] entary life styles, which contribute to the type 2 [...]
3. Why is the Indian Health Service an important [...] "owed" to American Indians/Alaskan Natives?

STUDY QUESTIONS

Review key concepts from each chapter with these questions at the end of each chapter. More questions can be found at **http://go.jblearning .com/holtz**, where students can submit their answers and instantly review their results.

CASE STUDIES

Read and analyze real-life situations dealing with global health and apply what you have learned from the text to answer critical thinking questions. Case studies can also be found on the companion website at **http://go.jblearning .com/holtz.**

GLOBAL
HEALTH CARE

Issues and Policies

SECOND EDITION

EDITED BY

CAROL HOLTZ, PhD, RN

Professor of Nursing
WellStar School of Nursing
Kennesaw State University
Kennesaw, Georgia

JONES & BARTLETT
LEARNING

World Headquarters
Jones & Bartlett Learning
5 Wall Street
Burlington, MA 01803
978-443-5000
info@jblearning.com
www.jblearning.com

Jones & Bartlett Learning books and products are available through most bookstores and online booksellers. To contact Jones & Bartlett Learning directly, call 800-832-0034, fax 978-443-8000, or visit our website, www.jblearning.com.

Substantial discounts on bulk quantities of Jones & Bartlett Learning publications are available to corporations, professional associations, and other qualified organizations. For details and specific discount information, contact the special sales department at Jones & Bartlett Learning via the above contact information or send an email to specialsales@jblearning.com.

Global Health Care: Issues and Policies, Second Edition is an independent publication and has not been authorized, sponsored, or otherwise approved by the owners of the trademarks or service marks referenced in this product.

Some images in this book feature models. These models do not necessarily endorse, represent, or participate in the activities represented in the images.

The authors, editor, and publisher have made every effort to provide accurate information. However, they are not responsible for errors, omissions, or for any outcomes related to the use of the contents of this book and take no responsibility for the use of the products and procedures described. Treatments and side effects described in this book may not be applicable to all people; likewise, some people may require a dose or experience a side effect that is not described herein. Drugs and medical devices are discussed that may have limited availability controlled by the Food and Drug Administration (FDA) for use only in a research study or clinical trial. Research, clinical practice, and government regulations often change the accepted standard in this field. When consideration is being given to use of any drug in the clinical setting, the health care provider or reader is responsible for determining FDA status of the drug, reading the package insert, and reviewing prescribing information for the most up-to-date recommendations on dose, precautions, and contraindications, and determining the appropriate usage for the product. This is especially important in the case of drugs that are new or seldom used.

Production Credits

Publisher: Kevin Sullivan
Acquisitions Editor: Amanda Harvey
Editorial Assistant: Sara Bempkins
Associate Production Editor: Cindie Bryan
Senior Marketing Manager: Elena McAnespie
V.P., Manufacturing and Inventory Control:
   Therese Connell
Composition: Arlene Apone

Cover Design: Kristin E. Parker
Cover Images: Clockwise from top left:
   © Konstantin Sutyagin/ShutterStock, Inc.,
   © Sascha Burkard/ShutterStock, Inc.,
   © Ermek/ShutterStock, Inc.,
   © Kuzma/ShutterStock, Inc.
Printing and Binding: Edwards Brothers Malloy
Cover Printing: Edwards Brothers Malloy

To order this product, use ISBN: 1-978-1-4496-7959-0

Library of Congress Cataloging-in-Publication Data
Global health care : issues and policies / [edited by] Carol Holtz. -- 2nd ed.
   p. ; cm.
 Includes bibliographical references and index.
  ISBN 978-0-7637-9964-9 (pbk.) -- ISBN 0-7637-9964-5 (pbk.)
 I. Holtz, Carol.
 [DNLM: 1. World Health. 2. Cross-Cultural Comparison. 3. Delivery of Health Care. 4. Health Policy. WA 530.1]
 362.1--dc23

              2012002459

6048

Printed in the United States of America
16 15 14 13 12   10 9 8 7 6 5 4 3 2 1

"*The health of the people is really the foundation upon which all their happiness and all their powers as a State depend.*"

Benjamin Disraeli

"*It is health that is the real wealth, and not pieces of gold and silver.*"

Mahatma Gandhi

CONTENTS

14 Global Perspectives on Nutrition   355

Carol Holtz, Kathy Plitnick, and Marvin Friedman

15 Global Perspectives on Mental Health   385

Mary Ann Camann

The main purpose of this textbook is to provide a better understanding of global health and health care with its related issues and policies. As stated by the Institute of Medicine in "America's Vital Interest in Global Health" (2012, p. 1), "The failure to engage in the fight to anticipate, prevent, and ameliorate global health problems would diminish America's stature in the realm of health and jeopardize our own health, economy, and national security." One cannot argue the need to have a global perspective, and many have stated this need so eloquently. Kofi Annan, Ghanaian, diplomat, seventh secretary-general of the United Nations, and 2001 Nobel Peace Prize recipient noted, "It has been said that arguing against globalization is like arguing against the laws of gravity." He also observed, "We have different religions, different languages, different-colored skin, but we all belong to one human race."

This textbook was written to give a basic perspective on world health issues, policies, and selected healthcare systems. While it is impossible to be timely and inclusive of all world health issues, geographical regions, or world events, the book is meant to give a background and summary of representative issues at the time the chapters were written.

WHAT IS GLOBAL HEALTH?

Global health refers to health problems, such as infectious and insect-borne diseases, that transcend national borders and spread from one country to another. It also includes health problems that have a global, political, and economic impact. Global health encompasses health problems that are best addressed by cooperative actions and whose solutions involve more than one country. Because global health problems can move across national borders, countries can learn from one another's experiences, in terms of both how diseases spread and how they can be treated and controlled. Cooperation across countries is essential to effectively address those health problems that transcend borders. Working to solve global health problems will help avert the needless suffering and preventable deaths of millions of adults and children. Approximately 90% of the world's healthcare resources are spent on diseases that affect 10% of the world's population. Working to solve global health problems will help ensure that money and resources are distributed more fairly across the globe. In an increasingly connected world, diseases can move as freely as people and products. Infectious diseases can easily cross national borders and pose immediate threats in the United States and other developed countries—diseases such as severe acute respiratory syndrome (SARS), avian flu, and drug-resistant tuberculosis (Institute of Medicine, 2012).

As defined by the World Health Organization (2012, p. 1), "Health is a state of complete physical, mental, and social well-being and not merely the absence of disease or infirmity." Global health takes into account the health of populations in a worldwide context and includes perspectives and health issues of all individual nations. Health problems transcend national borders and have a global political and economic impact.

The U.S. government's Global Health Initiative, based on the conduct of global health activities, is building successful bipartisan leadership in global health and expanding these activities' impact in achieving sustainable results around the world. Fighting global disease directly protects the health not only of people living in the United States, but also of people living all over the world, because infectious diseases recognize no border. Global health is also vital to U.S. national security. Investing in the health of people in developing countries reduces the instability that fuels war and conflict and drives the economic growth that strengthens families, communities, and countries (USAID, 2012).

References

Institute of Medicine. (2012). America's vital interest in global health. Retrieved from http://www.familiesusa.org/issues/global-health/matters/

USAID. (2012). Global Health Initiative. Retrieved from http://www.usaid.gov/ghi/

World Health Organization. (2012). Definition of health. Retrieved from www.who.int/en/

ACKNOWLEDGMENTS

This textbook represents the combined efforts of numerous well-educated, very dedicated, experienced, and hard-working contributors. The administrators of Kennesaw State University, located in greater Atlanta, Georgia, including the dean of the College of Health and Human Services, Dr. Richard Sowell, gave me tremendous support and encouragement to complete this textbook. I wish to thank the outstanding editors of Jones & Bartlett Learning, located in Burlington, Massachusetts, who supported my ideas and assisted me, as well as the many chapter contributors, for their help in organizing, writing, and editing this textbook.

I wish to thank my husband of 44 years, Dr. Noel Holtz, a neurologist, and medical director at WellStar Health System, for his love, devotion, and consistent support. To my children, Pamela Gilmore, Aaron and Stacy Holtz, and Daniel and Maggie Holtz, and my grandchildren, Andrew, Brandon, Caroline, Ben, Eva, and William Holtz, and Sarah and Meryl Gilmore, I give you this legacy of scholarship, hard work, and perseverance that I learned from my grandparents and my parents, Barbara Smith Weinberg and the late William Smith, and my late in-laws, Irving and Lillian Holtz, who always believed in me and encouraged me to achieve my scholarly pursuits.

CONTRIBUTORS

Kathie Aduddell, EdD, MSN, BSN, RN
Associate Professor of Nursing
Kennesaw State University
Kennesaw, GA

Linda G. Alley, PhD, RN
Health Research Scientist
Department of Community Health
 and Health Studies
Lehigh Valley Health Network
Allentown, PA

Barbara J. Blake, PhD, ACRN
Associate Professor of Nursing
Kennesaw State University
Kennesaw, GA

Mary Ann Camann, PhD, RN
Associate Professor of Nursing
Kennesaw State University
Kennesaw, GA

Kimberly A. Crawford, MSN, MPH, NP-C
Professor of Nursing
School of Nursing
University of Georgia, Sakartvelo University
Tbilisi, Georgia

Bowman O. Davis, Jr., PhD
Professor Emeritus of Biology
Kennesaw State University
Kennesaw, GA

Richard B. Davis, MSFS
Centers for Disease Control and Prevention
Atlanta, GA

Ibrahim Elsawy, PhD
Regional Director of Arab World Projects,
 Institute for Global Initiatives
Associate Professor
Kennesaw State University
Kennesaw, GA

Jeff Etchason, MD
Senior Vice President, Health Systems Research
 and Innovation
Chairman, Department of Community Health
 and Health Studies
Lehigh Valley Health Network
Allentown, PA

Michelle D. Flores, BSN, RN
Population Health Nurse
Department of Community Health
 and Health Studies
Lehigh Valley Health Network
Allentown, PA

Marvin A. Friedman, PhD, DABT, DATS, SNF
Scientific Advisor
Oviedo, FL

Govind Hariharan, PhD
Chair, Department of Economics, Finance and
 Quantitative Analysis and Professor of Economics
Kennesaw State University
Kennesaw, GA

Carol S. Holtz, PhD, RN
Professor of Nursing
Kennesaw State University
Kennesaw, GA

Ping Hu Johnson, MD, PhD
Associate Professor of Health, Physical Education
    and Sport Science
Kennesaw State University
Kennesaw, GA

Janice Long, PhD, RN
Associate Professor of Nursing
Kennesaw State University
Kennesaw, GA

David B. Mitchell, PhD
Distinguished Scholar in Gerontology and
    Professor of Health, Physical Education
    and Sport Science
Kennesaw State University
Kennesaw, GA

Hannah D. Paxton, MPH, RN
Population Health & Health Systems Scientist
Department of Community Health
    and Health Studies
Lehigh Valley Health Network
Allentown, PA

Kenneth D. Phillips, PhD, RN
Professor and Associate Dean for Research
    and Evaluation
College of Nursing
University of Tennessee
Knoxville, TN

Kathy Plitnick, PhD, RN, CNS, CCRN
Assistant Professor of Nursing
Georgia State University
Atlanta, GA

Larry Purnell, PhD, RN, FAAN
Professor Emeritus, University of Delaware,
    and Adjunct Professor, Florida International
    University, Consulting Faculty Excelsior
    College, Professor Universita de Moderna, Italy
Newark, DE

Lois R. Robley, PhD, RN
Professor Emeritus
Kennesaw State University
Kennesaw, GA

Gregory Simone, MD, MBA
Health Initiatives LLC
Marietta, GA

Richard L. Sowell, PhD, RN, FAAN
Dean, WellStar College of Health
    and Human Services
Kennesaw State University
Kennesaw, GA

Gloria A. Taylor, DNS, RN
Professor of Nursing
Kennesaw State University
Kennesaw, GA

Orly Toren, PhD, RN
Associate Director for Development and Research
    in Nursing
Hadassah Medical Center
Jerusalem, Israel

Judith L. Wold, PhD, RN
Clinical Professor, Lillian Carter Center for
    Global Health & Social Responsibility
Emory University
Atlanta, GA

Michelle Zebich-Knos, PhD
Chair, Department of International Studies
Department of Political Science &
    International Affairs
Kennesaw State University
Kennesaw, GA

Rick D. Zoucha, PhD, APRN-BC, CT
Associate Professor of Nursing
Duquesne University
Pittsburgh, PA

I

Global Health Issues, Policy, and Healthcare Delivery

1

Global Health: An Introduction

Carol Holtz

"The health of the people is really the foundation upon which all their happiness and their powers as a state depend."

Benjamin Disraeli, British politician
and author (1804–1881)

OBJECTIVES

After completing this chapter, the reader will be able to:

1. Define global health.
2. Identify global health terminology, agencies, and significant historical events.
3. Relate the state of the world's population growth and relevance to world health.
4. Discuss the Millennium Developmental Goals and the latest progress made toward their attainment.
5. Relate reasons for health and healthcare disparities worldwide.
6. Define indices of health.
7. Compare and contrast the universal "right to health care" and realistic global healthcare access.
8. Relate global health and healthcare priorities.

GLOBAL HEALTH

Tarantola (2005) states that global health, as applied to human development, is a political variable that relates to the health of the whole planet, which moves beyond geographical and political boundaries. These include both governmental agencies and nongovernmental organizations (NGOs). During the 1960s, the World Bank first advocated global thinking in relation to health issues with the phrase, "Think globally and act locally."

    Beaglehole and Yach (2003) report that the term "globalization" is now frequently used to describe the increasing global "interconnectedness" or global interdependence of humanity, which includes the health of all on the earth. Economic globalization has been affected by the last two decades of international trade, financial investments, human migration, travel, and tourism. The marketing and sales strategies of international tobacco companies, pharmaceutical companies, and international travel have had a huge influence on global health issues.

Negative aspects of globalization include global warming, cross-border pollution, financial crises, the spread of human immunodeficiency virus (HIV)/acquired immune deficiency syndrome (AIDS), and international crime. The globalization of disease began with the European explorers and conquerors who came to the Americas and spread smallpox, measles, and yellow fever among the various indigenous populations. They also brought typhus, influenza, and the plague. The poorest were most vulnerable, with the small elite, wealthier groups having better nutrition, access to better health care, and better sanitary (hygienic) conditions. More recently, the spread of HIV/AIDS, tuberculosis (TB), severe acute respiratory syndrome (SARS), West Nile virus, Ebola virus, and other infectious diseases has emerged as a global concern. Rapid movement of people and food products by travel has also resulted in new health problems such as "mad cow" disease and avian influenza. Globalization has recently changed the lifestyles of developing countries, resulting in new chronic diseases from the importation of high-sodium, high-fat fast foods, along with the more sedentary lifestyles promoted by newer technologies (e.g., TV, appliances). Moreover, in developing countries today, populations are rapidly acquiring chronic diseases (such as heart disease, cancer, stroke, and obesity leading to diabetes), which are adding a double burden given the still challenging acute infectious diseases (Beaglehole & Yach, 2003).

HISTORY OF GLOBAL HEALTH

The World Health Organization (WHO) was established just after World War II as an intergovernmental agency for the purpose of leading and coordinating worldwide health activities. Its activities are initiated when consensus regarding world health priorities is reached. Today's world health is improved when the economic development of nations is improved with the cooperation of governmental and nongovernmental agencies. In the last decade, numerous efforts directed at global health have been initiated, such as the Global Alliance for Vaccines and Immunizations, the Global Tuberculosis Partnership, and the Global Fund on HIV/AIDS (Ruger, 2005).

The World Bank began in 1946. Although it was originally established to finance European reconstruction after World War II, today it serves as a major resource for the health, nutrition, and population (HNP) of developing countries. A few examples of the historical activities of the World Bank include the 1968 appointment of Robert McNamara as president of the organization. His term as president resulted in the initiation of a Population Control program, which provided funding for family planning. In 1971, McNamara emphasized the need to combat malnutrition. Additionally, in 1974, the Onchocerciasis Control Program was developed in cooperation with the United Nations Development Program, Food and Agriculture Organization, and the World Health Organization. This program was created to eliminate river blindness in West Africa. After 30 years, the onchocerciasis program had protected an estimated 34 million people and also cleared an estimated 25 million hectares of land for agricultural use (Ruger, 2005).

In 1985, WHO gave $3 million in grants for the World Food Program for emergency food supplies to sub-Saharan Africa. This effort was followed by the WHO and the United Nations co-sponsoring, in 1987, a Safe Motherhood Project in the same region—the first of global initiatives for this area. In addition, in 1998, WHO lent $300 million to India's Women and Child Development Program (Ruger, 2005).

At present, the World Bank is the world's largest financial contributor to health projects throughout the world, having an annual budget of $1 billion for HNP programs. In addition, it gives $1.3 billion for HIV/AIDS treatment and prevention, 50% of which goes to sub-Saharan Africa. When making loans, it allows repayment periods up to 35–40 years and a 10-year grace period. Although one of the main purposes of the World Bank is to generate and disseminate knowledge, its main advantage over other global healthcare agencies is its ability to generate and mobilize healthcare resources. One of the criticisms of the World Bank focuses on its reliance on user fees, which are said to cause a disproportionate burden on the poor and sick people of the world (Ruger, 2005).

In 1978, in Alma-Ata, Kazakhstan (formerly part of the Soviet Union), leaders within the world community assembled to discuss and solve the issue of primary care for all world inhabitants. The Alma-Ata Declaration stated that governments have the responsibility for the health of their people, which can be fulfilled only by the provision of adequate health and social measures. According to this document, a main social target of governments, international organizations, and the whole world community in coming decades was to be the attainment by all peoples of the world, by the year 2000, of a level of health care that would permit them to lead a socially and economically productive life. Primary health care is the key to attaining this target as part of development of social justice (Hixon & Maskarinec, 2008).

The Alma-Ata Declaration states that citizens cannot always provide primary health care by themselves, so governments must include everyone, not just those who can afford health care, in their health-related programs. This document urges member states:

(1) To ensure political commitment at all levels to the values and principles of the Declaration of Alma-Ata, keep the issue of strengthening health systems based on the primary health care approach high on the international political agenda, and take advantage, as appropriate, of health-related partnerships and initiatives relating to this issue, particularly to support achievement of the Millennium Development Goals.

(2) To accelerate action towards universal access to primary health care by developing comprehensive health services and by developing national equitable and sustainable financing mechanisms, mindful of the need to ensure social protection and protect health budgets in the context of the current international financial crisis.

(3) To put people at the center of health care by adopting, as appropriate, delivery models focused on the local and district levels that provide comprehensive primary health-care services, including health promotion, disease prevention, curative care and end-of-life services, that are integrated and coordinated according to need. (Hixon & Maskarinec, 2008)

In 2005, WHO established a Commission on Social Determinants of Health: A Renewal of the Alma-Ata Declaration. In 2008, this commission completed its report recommending a renewal of the goal of primary health care for all and new attention to the need for addressing health disparities worldwide. The Renewal of the Alma-Ata Declaration addressed the following issues:

1. The aging of the world population
2. The plight of indigenous populations
3. Food and nutrition
4. The impact of conflicts and violence
5. The environment and health
6. Global and national inequalities
7. The impact of health on the global economy, social standing, and hierarchy
8. Health disparities among and within nations
9. Best practices and country studies
10. The importance of expanding social determinants of health studies (Hixon & Maskarinec, 2008)

STATE OF THE WORLD POPULATION

Worldwide, a child born in 1955 had an average life expectancy at birth of only 48 years. By 2000, the average life expectancy at birth had increased to 66 years and, if past trends continue, the global life expectancy at birth is projected to rise to 73 years by 2025. These improvements in longevity have resulted from improved living conditions overall, advances in medical science, and a number of population-level interventions. However, major disparities persist. During the past decade, in low-income countries, average life expectancy at birth increased from 55 to 57 years (3.6%), while increasing from 78 to 80 years (2.6%) in high-income countries. The world's population as of October 31, 2011 reached 7 billion. While women are on average are having fewer children than they were in the 1960s, the world population continues to rise. At present, there are more people who are younger and also more people who are older than ever before. In some of the poorest countries, high fertility rates hamper the infrastructure development and perpetuate poverty, while in some of the richest countries, there are great concerns regarding low fertility rates and too few people entering the job market. The unemployed people of many nations who wish to migrate from developing countries to developed countries are finding more national borders closed to them. Gaps between rich and poor are widening in almost every location worldwide (UNFPA, 2011).

In 2050, the world population is projected to total 9.15 billion. It is expected that in developing countries, most families will have two or fewer children per family. The largest increases in population growth rates will occur in Africa. Many countries are facing a shrinking pool of working-age individuals (ages 15–64 years), who are needed to support the older adult population. This imbalance may jeopardize pension guarantees and long-term healthcare programs for the elderly. Within the United States, the largest population growth is expected to come from immigration and from growth of the older adult population (Bremner, Frost, Haub, Mather, Ringheim, & Zuehlke, 2010).

The countries with the largest populations are China (1.338 billion), India (1.189 billion), and the United States (310 million). By 2050, India is expected to have the largest population (1.748 billion), followed by China (1.437 billion) and the United States (423 million). The countries with the youngest populations include Niger and Uganda, whereas those with the oldest populations include Japan, Germany, Italy, and Sweden ("World Population Data Sheet," 2010).

The United Nations Family Planning Association (UNFPA, 2011) has validated, across nations, the inadequate resources, gender bias, and gaps in serving the world's poor. Many developing countries have initiated population projects to reduce poverty, develop laws and policies to protect the rights of women and girls, introduce reproductive health services as part of primary health care, increase the skills of birth attendants, and provide more prevention and treatment of HIV/AIDS. Many couples today continue to lack access to birth control. Birth complications remain the leading cause of death of women worldwide, with 5 million new fatalities per year from this cause. Every minute, a woman dies in pregnancy or childbirth and another 20–30 women suffer serious injury or disability; most of these women die in developing countries of preventable or treatable complications. A wide disparity in global survival rates among the rich and poor women within countries is evident (UNFPA, 2011).

In addition, unsustainable consumption and rapid population growth have created serious problems related to the world environment, resulting in clean water becoming scarce in many countries. Land is being deforested, and fish stocks are being harvested beyond sustainable limits. These problems are further compounded by people moving from rural to urban environments, resulting in overcrowded cities that burden the caring capacity of government agencies.

The current global birth rate is 19.15 births/1000 population which results in about 252 worldwide births per minute or 4.2 births every second (2011 est.) (Indexmundi birth rate, 2011). The birth rate is usually the dominant factor in determining the rate of population growth. It depends on both the level of fertility and the age structure of the population. In addition the world death rate is 8.12 deaths/1000 population which results in about 107 worldwide deaths per minute or 1.8 deaths every second (July 2011 est.) (Indexmundi death rate, 2011).

The death rate, while only a rough indicator of the mortality situation in a country, accurately indicates the current mortality impact on population growth. This indicator is significantly affected by age distribution, and most countries will eventually show a rise in the overall death rate, in spite of continued decline in mortality at all ages, as declining fertility results in an aging population (Indexmundi death rate, 2011).

MILLENNIUM DEVELOPMENT GOALS

The Millennium Development Goals (MDGs) are the most broadly supported, comprehensive, and specific development goals worldwide. Collectively, they provide benchmarks for resolving extreme poverty and include goals and targets related to income, poverty, hunger, maternal and child mortality, disease, inadequate shelter, gender inequality, environmental degradation, and the Global Partnership for Development. Adopted by world leaders in 2000 and set to be achieved by 2015, the MDGs are both global and local, adapted by each country to address its specific development needs. They provide a framework for the entire international community to work together toward a common end for everyone.

The eight goals are summarized here:

1. Eradicate extreme poverty and hunger: Reduce by half the proportion of people living on less than a dollar a day; achieve full and productive employment and decent work for all, including women and young people; and reduce by half the proportion of people who suffer from hunger.

PROGRESS

The goal of cutting in half the proportion of people in the developing world living on less than $1 per day by 2015 remains within reach. This achievement will be mainly due to extraordinary economic success in most of Asia. In contrast, previous estimates suggested that little progress was made in reducing extreme poverty in sub-Saharan Africa. In western Asia, poverty rates are relatively low but increasing.

2. Achieve universal primary education: Ensure that all children complete a full course of primary schooling.

PROGRESS

In most regions, primary school enrollment rates in 2006 exceeded 90%, and universal enrollment was achieved in many countries. The number of children of primary school age who were not in school dropped from 103 million in 1999 to 73 million in 2006 despite an overall increase in children of that age group. In sub-Saharan Africa, net enrollment only reached 71%, with 38 million children in that region still out of school. In southern Asia, enrollment reached 90%, with 18 million children still not enrolled.

3. Promote gender equality and empower women. Eliminate gender disparity in primary and secondary education by 2005 and at all levels by 2015.

PROGRESS

For girls in some regions, education remains elusive. Poverty is a major barrier to education, especially among older girls. Women are slowly rising to political power, but mainly when boosted by quotas and other special measures.

4. Reduce child mortality: Reduce the mortality rate of children under age 5 by two-thirds.

PROGRESS

In 2006, the annual number of deaths among children younger than age 5 dropped below 10 million. A child born in a developing country is 13 times more likely to die within the first five years of life than a child born in a developed country. Sub-Saharan Africa accounts for half of all under-five deaths in the developing world. In eastern Asia, Latin America, and the Caribbean, child mortality rates are approximately four times higher than in developed regions. Mortality rates are higher for children from rural areas and poor families whose mothers lack basic education.

5. Improve maternal health: Reduce by three-fourths the maternal mortality ratio; achieve by 2015 universal access to reproductive health.

PROGRESS

Maternal mortality remains high across most of the developing world. In 2005, more than 500,000 women died during pregnancy, childbirth, or within six weeks after delivery. Ninety-nine percent of these deaths occurred in developing regions, with sub-Saharan Africa and southern Asia accounting for 86% of them. In sub-Saharan Africa, a woman's chance of dying from pregnancy or childbirth complications is 1 in 22, compared to 1 in 7300 in developed regions.

6. Combat HIV/AIDS, malaria, and other diseases: Halt and reverse the spread of HIV/AIDS; achieve by 2010 universal access to treatment; halt and reverse the incidence of malaria and other diseases.
7. Ensure environmental sustainability: Halve by 2015 the proportion of people without access to sustainable drinking water and sanitation.
8. Develop a global partnership for development: Develop further an open, rule-based predictable, nondiscriminating trading and financial system; address the special needs of the least developed countries; deal with landlocked developing countries and small island countries; deal comprehensively with the debt problems of developing countries.

Source: "United Nations Millennium Development Goals Report 2009," 2010.

PREDICTIONS OF GLOBAL HEALTH PATTERNS

WHO (2005) predicted that the following issues will dominate the world health conversation in the future:

1. Tobacco will cause chronic obstructive pulmonary diseases (e.g., emphysema and lung cancer) and will kill more people than the HIV epidemic.
2. Males living in the former USSR and socialist economies in Europe will have poor and deteriorating health status, including a 28% risk of death in the 15–60 age groups.
3. Mental health diseases (depression, alcoholism, and schizophrenia), which have long been underestimated in significance, will be responsible for 1% of deaths and 11% of the total world disease burden.
4. Communicable diseases, maternal and perinatal problems, and nutritional diseases will continue to be major problems in developing countries, while noncommunicable diseases such as depression and heart diseases will also cause premature death and disability.
5. Deaths from noncommunicable diseases will increase by 77% due to the aging of the world population and the decrease in birth rate.
6. Accidents and violence mortality (death) rates may compete with mortality rates of infectious diseases.

PREDICTIONS OF THE LEADING CAUSES OF DISEASES OR INJURY WORLDWIDE

In rank order, the following issues are expected to be major sources of morbidity and mortality:

1. Ischemic heart disease
2. Unipolar major depression
3. Road traffic accidents
4. Cerebrovascular disease (stroke)
5. Chronic obstructive pulmonary disease (COPD)
6. Lower respiratory infections
7. Tuberculosis
8. War
9. Diarrhea diseases
10. HIV
11. Perinatal conditions
12. Violence
13. Congenital anomalies
14. Self-inflicted injuries
15. Trachea, bronchus, and lung cancer (WHO, 2005)

Greater investments in scientific research and technology will be needed in developing countries to meet the increasing demand for the challenges of treatment of illness and disease prevention. The UNFPA (2011) indicates that world population challenges will include the following issues:

1. Migration from rural areas to urban cities. Half the world's population lived in urban areas by 2007—a pattern that creates a greater need for social services, including reproductive health, especially in poor urban areas.
2. Stress on the global environment. Global warming, population growth, resource consumption, deforestation, and decreases in water and cropland will further negatively impact health outcomes.
3. Increased demand for family planning. More than 350 million couples still lack family planning services; by 2025, the demand for such services will increase by 40%.
4. Pregnancy and childbirth complications. These issues continue to cause illness and death in women in developing countries, resulting in 8 million women having life-threatening complications and 529,000 deaths from this cause.

5. Lack of prenatal care. Thirty-three percent of all pregnant women in the world receive no prenatal care and 60% of all deliveries occur outside a hospital.
6. Skilled birth attendants. Only 50% of all pregnant women will be delivered by a skilled birth attendant.
7. HIV/AIDS. Thirty-eight million people have HIV/AIDS.

According to the U.S. Implementation of the Global Health Initiative Consultation Document (2009, p. 3), global health needs include the problems identified by the following global statistics:

1. Almost 3 million people are affected by HIV each year, and AIDS is the leading cause of death for women of reproductive age.
2. Malaria kills 900,000 people yearly—mostly children younger than age 5 years—with 300 million more people affected annually.
3. More than 9 million people are infected with tuberculosis on an annual basis, and 1.7 million people die each year from this disease.
4. More than 1 billion people suffer each year from neglected tropical diseases (NTD), and 400,000 die each year from these causes.
5. More than 530,000 women die each year from preventable pregnancy or childbirth complications.
6. At least 8.8 million children die yearly from easily treatable or vaccine preventable diseases or malnutrition.
7. In developing countries, more than 150 million children younger than age 5 years and 1 out of 3 women are undernourished.

The goals of the Global Health Initiative Consultation Document (2009) are to contribute to major improvements and health outcomes with a special emphasis on women, newborns, and children. The Global Health Initiative was proposed in 2009 by President Barack Obama as a six-year (2009–2014), $63 billion initiative to develop a comprehensive U.S. government strategy for global health, which builds on the President's Emergency Plan for AIDS Relief (PEPFAR) as well as efforts to combat malaria; TB; neglected tropical diseases; maternal, newborn, and child health; family planning and reproductive health; and nutrition and health systems strengthening. The countries targeted by the Global Health Initiative include 80 lower-income to middle-income countries with high levels of burden of diseases. These countries are mainly located in Africa, but also include nations in other world regions, such as Guatemala, Bangladesh, Malawi, and Nepal.

HEALTH DISPARITIES

A health disparity is a statistically significant difference in health indicators that persists over time. Health disparities are comparative measurements of the burden of disease, and morbidity and mortality rates, in specific populations. Healthcare disparities, by comparison, are differences in access to appropriate healthcare services by various groups because of a multitude of factors; they are mainly associated with social inequalities. Health disparities are differentiated from healthcare disparities, although both concepts are intimately linked. Disparities in access to quality and timely healthcare services contribute to the disparities in health status. Poorer health status compromises the ability of some groups to obtain timely and appropriate health services. Health and healthcare disparities exist worldwide, affecting both developed and developing countries. Population groups both in one nation and across different countries are affected by health disparities. In contrast to developed countries, developing nations have a lower level of material well-being based on per capita income, life expectancy, and rate of literacy. These nations are also referred to as less economically developed, Third World, lower-income nations, or resource-poor countries. In contrast, developed nations are also called industrialized societies, advanced economies, and higher-income nations ("United Nations Developmental Project Report"

[UNDP], 2009). These terms should be used with caution because they may imply inferiority–superiority relationships among nations.

Indices of Health Disparities

1. Burden of disease: the impact of a health problem in an area measured by financial cost, mortality, morbidity, or other indicators. It is often quantified in terms of quality-adjusted life-years (QALYs), which allows for comparison of disease burden due to various risk factors or diseases. It also makes it possible to predict the possible impact of health interventions. WHO provides a detailed explanation of how disease burden is measured at local and national levels for various environmental contexts. The global burden of disease is shifting from infectious diseases to noncommunicable diseases, including chronic conditions such as heart disease and stroke, which are now the chief causes of death globally.

2. Mortality rate: the number of deaths in some population, scaled to the size of that population, per unit of time. This rate is expressed in units of deaths per 1000 people per year; thus a mortality rate of 9.5 in a population of 100,000 would mean 950 deaths per year in that entire population.

3. Infant mortality rate (IMR): the number of deaths of infants (one year of age or younger) per 1000 live births. The IMR is a useful indicator of a country's level of health or development.

4. Morbidity rate: the number of individuals in poor health during a given time or number who currently have that disease (prevalence rate), scaled to the size of the population. This rate takes into account the state of poor health, the degree or severity of a health condition, and the total number of cases in a particular population during a particular point in time irrespective of cause.

5. Life expectancy: the average number of years of life remaining at a given age or average life span or average length of survival in a specified population; the expected age to be reached before death for a given population in a country, based on the year of birth or other demographic variables.

6. Birth rate: the number of childbirths per 100,000 people per year. As of 2011 the current global birth rate is 19.15 births/1000 population which results in about 252 worldwide births per minute or 4.2 births every second (2011 est.)

7. Total fertility rate: the average number of children born to each woman over the course of her life. Fertility rates tend to be higher in developing countries and lower in more economically developed countries. The government of China has developed a mandatory "one child per family" policy with some exceptions, which is still valid at present and represents an attempt to cap China's total fertility rate.

8. Disability: the lack of ability relative to a personal or group standard or spectrum. It may involve physical, sensory, cognitive, or intellectual impairment, or a mental disorder; it may occur during a person's lifetime or be present from birth.

9. Nutritional status: a factor influenced by diet, levels of nutrients in the body, and ability to maintain normal metabolic integrity. Body fat may be estimated by measuring skin fold thickness and muscle diameter; levels of vitamins and minerals are measured based on their serum levels, through urine concentration of nutrients and their metabolites, or by testing for specific metabolic responses (Centers for Disease Control and Prevention [CDC], 2003; UNFPA, 2011).

Health Disparities in the United States

Health disparities may be defined more narrowly as persistent gaps between the health status of minorities and nonminorities that continue despite advances in health care and technology. In the United States, ethnic minorities have higher rates of disease, disability and premature deaths than nonminorities. African Americans, Hispanics/Latinos, American Indians and Alaska Natives, Asian Americans, Native Hawaiians, and Pacific Islanders all have higher rates of infant mortality, cardiovascular diseases, diabetes, HIV/AIDS, and cancer, as well as lower rates of immunizations and cancer screenings, than nonminority groups. Such disparities arise for a number of reasons:

■ Inadequate access to health care—caused by economic, geographic, and linguistic factors; lack of or decrease in health insurance and education; and poorer quality of health care
■ Substandard quality of care/lower quality of care—caused by patient–provider miscommunication, provider discrimination, and stereotyping or prejudice (Agency of Healthcare Research and Quality, 2006; "National Healthcare Disparities Report 2009," 2010)

POPULATION GROWTH ISSUES

As of October 2011, the global population of 7 billion continues to grow rapidly at a rate of approximately 76 million per year. The average family size has declined from 6 children per woman in 1960 to 3 children per woman today, mainly due to family planning. Countries that have significant decreases in fertility will have increases in the aging population. Ninety-six percent of the world population growth will be attributable to growth in developing countries. Europe and Japan will have declining populations, whereas the North American population will increase by 1% due to immigration. Actual population sizes and growth patterns today are somewhat lower than those predicted 10 years ago, mainly due to the impact of the HIV/AIDS epidemic. The 38 African countries most affected by HIV/AIDS are projected to have 823 million people by 2015—a population that includes 91 million fewer people than if no AIDS deaths had occurred (UNFPA, 2011).

EQUALITY IN HEALTH CARE

The world collectively lacks an equal rights-based approach in the distribution of health care. Disparities in health care are now a major challenge for healthcare agencies around the world. As former South African President Nelson Mandela (1998) stated, "The greatest single challenge facing our globalized world is to combat and eradicate its disparities." The burden of disease is growing disproportionately within certain regions of the world, especially in areas commonly affected by "brain drain." Some doctors and nurses from Africa, Asia, and Latin America are leaving the rural areas for cities, while many others are leaving their countries altogether and relocating in developed nations. The irony is that more healthcare providers in developed countries are now working, at least for part of their working lives, in developing countries, even as the "brain drain" pulls some of the most competent healthcare providers out of their home countries, where they are most needed. Regardless of the causes, many developing countries with the least amount of human and economic resources are confronted with the largest burden in public health. In the developed world, the most affluent 15% of the world's population consumes more than 60% of the world's total energy—much more than the developing world (Farmer, Furin, & Katz, 2004).

There is still major evidence that socioeconomic as well as health inequalities exist within and among nations. Although the health of the world population has improved considerably, some countries of the world still have inadequate and inequitable health care within their borders and among their citizens. For example, in 2010, there was an estimated 22.9 million people living with HIV in Sub-Saharan Africa. This has increased since 2009, when an estimated 22.5 million people were living with HIV, including 2.3 million children. The increase in people living with HIV could be partly due to a decrease in AIDS-related deaths in the region. There were 1.2 million deaths due to AIDS in 2010 compared to 1.3 million in 2009. Almost 90% of the 16.6 million children orphaned by AIDS live in sub-Saharan Africa (Avert.org, 2011).

The disappearance of an entire generation of productive men and women (ages 18–45) is evidence that healthcare services have been inadequate in this region, resulting in children and grandparents left behind (Ruger, 2005).

Adequate health care promotes social stability and economic growth. Countries that do not have adequate health care often have inadequate funding, poor government organization, and inadequate access for healthcare services for all of their populations (Go & Given, 2005). Go and Given (2005) report that although developing countries such as India, Mexico, and China would like to expand their healthcare systems and have more high technology, they first must restructure their systems to devote more expenditures to, and place greater emphasis on, education and preventive medicine, rather than trying to first invest in high-technology health care. The three main criteria for an adequate healthcare system include (1) equitable access to quality care in the form of both prevention and treatment services for rural and urban populations; (2) affordability, which means that even if people have no income or health insurance they may receive services; and (3) sustainability, which means that the system has long-term political and financial support.

For example, Mexico, China, and India are emerging economies that are rapidly industrializing and embracing global markets; each has its own unique culture, geography, and history as well. All three countries are working to improve access to their healthcare systems for all of their citizens, and are emphasizing preventive health care as a major priority. Ninety percent of Mexicans now have access to preventive care and basic public health services, although some indigenous Indians in isolated rural areas still have no coverage. Sixty-seven percent of India's population is now immunized, although many rural areas have less basic health care than urban areas. In the past, the Indian government paid the entire cost of health care for individuals, but now a shift in healthcare costs has placed greater burden on individuals to cover their own healthcare needs. The Indian government is now spending less and expects that individuals will pay for part of the services that were once completely funded by the government. At present, new medical treatments and medications are becoming more expensive and many people must also pay out-of-pocket for health care because they lack health insurance. For example, the percentages of people in Mexico, China, and India with healthcare insurance are 53%, 60–70%, and 82–85%, respectively (Go & Given, 2005). The World Health Report (WHO, 2003) states that a key responsibility of any government's healthcare system is to decrease the health disparities. Lack of political power and basic education represent barriers to accessing the healthcare system for all. The majority of the populations in Mexico, China, and India has equal access, yet only a small elite group has access to state-of-the-art health care.

UNIVERSAL RIGHT TO HEALTH CARE

The right to health care under international law is found in 1948 under the 1948 Universal Declaration of Human Rights ("the Declaration"), which was unanimously accepted by the UN General Assembly as a common standard for the entire world's population. This declaration sets forth each person's right to "a standard of living adequate for the health and well-being of himself and his family . . . including medical care and . . . the right to security in the event of . . . sickness, disability . . . or other lack of livelihood in circumstances beyond his control." The Declaration does not define the components of a right to health, but they are included in the statement regarding medical care. Health is considered to extend beyond health care to include basic preconditions for health, such as potable water and adequate sanitation and nutrition. In addition, the right to health includes freedoms from nonconsensual medical treatment and experimentation.

Historically, the United States has not wanted to accept international human rights standards or pass the laws necessary to meet them. The United States is currently the only developed country in the world that does not have a plan for universal healthcare coverage and some type of legal right to health care for all its residents (Yamin, 2005).

EMERGING HEALTH THREATS

The WHO Report of 2010 indicates that public health issues evolve over time. As a result of planned and unplanned activities or changing environments, humans may come in contact with many different organisms that have the capacity to cause disease. Thanks to the development of antibiotics, people are now able to survive many bacterial infections, which previously would have been the cause of certain death. Even so, infectious diseases continue to cause both new epidemics, such as those linked to HIV/AIDS or the Ebola virus, or reoccurring epidemics, such as those involving tuberculosis or cholera. Many of the emerging health threats around the world today are caused by resistance to antibiotics, new strains of drug-resistant bacteria, or poor adherence to medical regimens (WHO, 2011).

Preventable diseases and injuries are seen more often as humans migrate from rural to urban areas. Also seen more often are unintentional injuries such as traffic accidents, poisonings, and intentional injuries, such as war and street violence. More than 40% of the total disease burden due to urban air pollution occurs in developing countries, and children are most vulnerable to these environmental hazards, because they do not have the ability to detoxify pollutants related to their bodies' immaturity. More than 90% of all deaths due to injuries occurred in low- and middle-income countries. Although tobacco use is declining in developed countries, it is increasing in developing countries (WHO, 2011).

Mental health, neurological disorders, and substance abuse are causing a great amount of disability and human suffering. Many people do not receive any health care for these problems because of inadequate infrastructures, and widely prevalent stigma and discrimination may prevent them from seeking care even when it is available. Many countries lack mental healthcare policies, facilities, or budgets within their healthcare systems. Cost-effective services are available, and research clearly demonstrates that depression, schizophrenia, and alcohol- and drug-related problems can be treated at primary care centers with inexpensive medications and basic training of healthcare personnel. Intentional (suicide, violence, and war) and unintentional (traffic accidents) injuries, which primarily affect young adults, accounted for more than 14% of the adult disease burden of the world, yet in parts of Europe and the Eastern Middle East region, these causes were responsible for more than 30% of the disease burden. In males, violence, traffic injuries, and self-inflicted injuries are within the top 10 disease burdens in the 15- to 44-year-old groups (WHO, 2011).

MEASURES OF POPULATION HEALTH

In order to evaluate the health of a population, one needs to examine four aspects of that population:

1. Life expectancy: a measure of mortality rates across the developmental life span, which is expressed in years of life.
2. Healthy life expectancy (HLE): years of active life, reflecting a person's ability to perform tasks that reflect self-care, called the activities of daily living. HLE is a way of measuring not just years of life, but expected years of life divided into healthy and unhealthy life. It is a way to more accurately measure the current health of a population, measuring the extent of morbidity and mortality of a population.
3. Mortality: the number of deaths within a specific population, which has often been used as a basic indicator of health.
4. Disability: a situation in which a person's abilities or limitations are determined by physical, mental, or cognitive status within society, which is itself determined by how well the personal environment accommodates the loss of functioning.

GLOBAL HEALTH INDICATORS

Global monitoring of health changes across world populations requires global health indicators. The indicators provide estimates of a country's state of health and may reflect either direct measurements of health phenomena, such as diseases and deaths, or indirect measurements, such as education and poverty. With population statistics available regarding education, access to safe water and sanitation, and rates of diseases, it is possible to fairly accurately measure a population's burden of disease and designate it as low, medium, or high. Unfortunately, few developing countries are able to measure their health statistics accurately; therefore, numbers of births, deaths, persons with specific diseases, and so on may be only estimates—and may not be truly representative of the population. Criteria for good health indicators include the following:

1. Definition. The indicator must be well defined and be able to be used internationally.
2. Validity. The indicator must accurately measure what it is supposed to measure and must be reliable so that it can be replicable and consistent in different settings, and be easy to interpret.
3. Feasibility. Obtaining the information must be easily affordable and not overburden the system.
4. Utility. The indicator must provide useful information for various levels of health decision makers (Larson & Mercer, 2004).

GLOBAL HEALTH AND MORAL VALUES

The creation of global initiatives requires a review of ethical and moral values. In 2003, Lee Jong-Wook, the Director General of the WHO, stated that global health must be guided by an ethical vision. According to Lee, technical excellence and political commitment have no value unless they have an ethically sound purpose. The following are different schools of thought used to justify global initiatives:

1. Humanitarianism: acting virtuously toward those in need. It is often the response to social problems. Humanitarianism is incorporated within all religions, based on compassion, empathy, or altruism. It is the ethical basis of philanthropy by NGOs; it is also the basic philosophy behind U.S. governmental foreign aid policy.
2. Utilitarianism: maximizing happiness for many people. Improving the health of individuals living within a society will be in the best interest for all the people of a society.
3. Equity by achieving a fair distribution of health capabilities: ensuring that all people in a society have a fair and equal chance to achieve good health.
4. Rights: fulfilling obligations so others are dignified; ensures that health care respects human rights and dignity for all people living in a society.
5. Knowledge and institutions: supports the basis for research and development of new health technologies and medications. For example, the development of HIV/AIDS antiretroviral drugs created a new moral dilemma by emphasizing the differences in the drugs' affordability among nations. Corporations have realized what are perceived as "huge" profits by producing and selling the drugs; however, the cost of development and use of resources must be recouped.
6. Consensus and advocacy groups: people who are usually in powerful political positions who wish to have health policies established for others in the society.

THEORETICAL SOLUTION PLANS

At the United Nations Millennium Summit in 2000, representatives of 189 countries met to develop a road map with goals for improvement in the areas of peace, security and disarmament, poverty eradication, environmental protection, human rights, democracy and good governance protecting the vulnerable populations, assisting with the special needs of Africa, and strengthening the United Nations. These goals were established to be achieved by 2015. While governments made commitments to work toward these millennium goals, practical solutions have yet to be fully identified or implemented (WHO, 2003).

CONCLUSION

This introduction, which serves as a gateway to the rest of this textbook, has sought to provide an overall perspective on various global health issues. Definitions of key terms and a brief discussion of global health history, the state of the world population, predictions of global health patterns, population growth issues, equity in accessing health care, emerging health threats, global health indicators, and global health and its relationship to moral values were briefly addressed. Within the following chapters, these and many more issues pertaining to global health are addressed.

DEFINITION OF KEY TERMS

1. Population: total number of people
2. Education level: percentage of the population 20 years and older with no education
3. Unemployment rate: percentage of the population age 15–64 who do not have jobs
4. Energy source for cooking: percentage of households using electricity, wood, paraffin, and other sources for cooking
5. Water and sanitation: percentage of households with refuse removal, access to piped water, no toilet

Burden of Disease

1. Infant mortality rate: the number of children younger than one year old who die in one year, per 1000 live births
2. Under-five mortality rate: the probability of a child dying before age 5 years per 1000 live births per year (percentage of children who die before the age of 5 years)
3. Adult mortality: the probability of dying between the ages of 15 and 60 (percentage of 15-year-olds who die before their 60th birthday)
4. Life expectancy: the average number of years a person could expect to live if current mortality trends were to continue for the rest of that person's life
5. Cause of death profile: percentage of deaths in the population caused by a specific disease from the Nation Burden of Disease List
6. Years of life lost: the number of years lost based on the standard life expectancy for the age of death, with future years discounted at 3% and age weighting
7. Prevalence of a disability: percentage of people with moderate to severe disability, which is a physical or mental handicap that has lasted for at least six months, or is expected to last at least six months, which prevents the person from carrying out the activities of daily living independently, or participating fully in educational, economic, or social activities

Source: CDC, 2003.

STUDY QUESTIONS

1. What are some of the major health issues regarding the world population growth?
2. What are some causes of the numerous global health disparities?
3. Why it is necessary for wealthier developed countries to share needed funds and technology to assist with developing countries' major health and healthcare problems?
4. What are the Millennium Health Goals and why is important to note their progress worldwide?

CASE STUDY: UNFORESEEN COSTS OF CUTTING MOSQUITO SURVEILLANCE BUDGETS

A recent budget proposal to stop the funding for the U.S. Centers for Disease Control and Prevention (CDC) surveillance and research for a mosquito-borne diseases program was found to have the potential to leave a country poorly-prepared to handle mosquito trans-mitted diseases. Their study showed that decreasing this type of program can signifi-cantly increase the management costs of epidemics and total costs of preparedness. The authors' findings demonstrated a justification for the reassessment of a current proposal to slash the budget of the CDC vector-borne diseases program, and emphasized the need for improved and sustainable systems for vector-borne disease surveillance.

Case Study Questions

1. What do you think about the U.S. Centers for Disease Control and Prevention (CDC) making budget cuts for surveillance and research for countries with mosquito-borne diseases?
2. Is money really saved for the long-term for prevention and control of diseases, such as dengue and West Nile virus, by cutting the surveillance budget? What else could be done to save money?

Reference

Vazquez-Prokopec, G., Chaves, L., Ritchie, S., Davis, J., & Kitron, U. (2010). *Neglected Tropical Diseases, 4*(10), 1–4.

REFERENCES

Agency of Healthcare Research and Quality (AHRQ). (2006). National healthcare disparities report 2009. Retrieved from http://www.ahrq.gov/qual/nhdr09/nhdr09.pdf

Avert.org. (2011). HIV/AIDS statistics for sub-Saharan Africa. Retrieved from http://www.avert.org/africa-hiv-aids-statistics.htm

Beaglehole, R., & Yach, D. (2003). Globalisation and the prevention and control of non-communicable disease: The neglected chronic disease of adults. *Lancet, 362,* 903–908.

Bremner, J., Frost, A., Haub, C., Mather, M., Ringheim, K., & Zuehlke, E. (2010). World population high-lights: Key findings from PRB's 2010 world population data sheet. *Population Reference Bureau, 65*(2). Retrieved from www.prb.org

Centers for Disease Control and Prevention (CDC). (2003). Summary measures of population health: Report of findings on methodologic and data issues. Retrieved from http://www.cdc.gov/nchs/data/misc/pophealth.pdf

Farmer, P., Furin, J. J., & Katz, J. T. (2004). Global health equity. *Lancet, 363,* 1832.

Global Health Initiative consultation document. (2009). Retrieved from http://www.usaid.gov/bd/files/GHI _Consultation_Document.pdf

Go, R., & Given, R. (2005). Sustainable healthcare. Deloitte Research. Tuck Executive Education of Dartmouth. Retrieved from http://www.publicservice.co.uk/pdf/em/issue_3/EM3Robert%20Go%20Ruth %20Given%20ATL.pdf

Hixon, A., & Maskarinec, G. (2008). The declaration of Alma Ata on its 30th anniversary: Relevance for family medicine today. *Family Medicine, 40*(8), 585–589.

Indexmundi birth rate (2011). Retrieved from http://www.indexmundi.com/world/birth_rate.html

Indexmundi death rate (2011). Retrieved from http://www.indexmundi.com/world/death_rate.html

Larson, C., & Mercer, A. (2004). Global health indicators: An overview. *Canadian Medical Association, 171*(10), 1.

Mandela, N. (1998). Transcript of the speech at the special convocation of an honorary doctoral degree, Harvard University, Cambridge, Massachusetts, September 18, 1998. Retrieved from http://www .cambridgeforum.org/cfmandela/13_nelson_mandela.html

National healthcare disparities report 2009. (2010). Retrieved from http://www.healthpolicy.ucla.edu/pubs /Publication.aspx?pubID=406; retrieved from http://NHRQ.gov National Healthcare Disparities Report 2008

Ruger, J. P. (2005). The changing role of the World Bank in global health. *American Journal of Public Health, 95,* 60–90.

Tarantola, D. (2005). Global health and national governance. *American Journal of Public Health Association, 95*(1), 8.

UNFPA (2011). State of the World Population 2011. Retrieved from www.unfpa.org

United Nations Developmental Project Report 2009 (UNDP). (2009) Retrieved from http://www.undp .org/publicationsannualreport.2009/index.shtml

United Nations Millennium Development Goals report 2009. (2010). Retrieved from http://www.un.org /millenniumgoals/reports.shtml

Universal Declaration of Human Rights. United Nations General Assembly Resolution 217 A (III). (1947). New York: United Nations.

United States implementation of Global Health Initiative. (2009). Retrieved from http://www.pepfar.gov /documents/organization/129504.pdf

Vazquez-Prokopec, G., Chaves, L., Ritchie, S., Davis, J., & Kitron, U. (2010). *Neglected Tropical Diseases, 4*(10), 1–4.

World Health Organization (WHO). (2003). World health report 2003: Shaping the future. Retrieved from http://www.who.int/whr/2003/en

World Health Organization (WHO). (2005). Integrated chronic disease prevention and control. Retrieved from http://www.who.int/chp/about/integrated_cd/en

World Health Organization (WHO). (2011). World health statistics. Retrieved from http://www.who.int /whosis/whostat/2011/en/

World population data sheet. (2010). Retrieved from www.prb.org

Yamin, A. (2005). The right to health under international law and its relevance to the United States. *American Journal of Public Health, 95*(7), 1156–1161.

For a full suite of assignments and additional learning activities, use the access code located in the front of your book to visit this exclusive website: http://go.jblearning.com/holtz. If you do not have an access code, you can obtain one at the site.

2

Global Health in Developed Societies: Examples in the United States, Sweden, Japan, and the United Kingdom

Carol Holtz

> *"It is health that is real wealth and not pieces of gold and silver."*
>
> Mohandas K. Gandhi

OBJECTIVES

After completing this chapter, the reader will be able to:

1. Compare and contrast population health statistics for the United States, Sweden, Japan, and the United Kingdom.
2. Compare and contrast the major health issues and healthcare systems of the United States, Sweden, Japan, and the United Kingdom.
3. Relate healthcare disparities within and among the countries of the United States, Sweden, Japan, and the United Kingdom.
4. Discuss the high rates of longevity for residents of Japan and Sweden.

INTRODUCTION

This chapter gives examples of developed countries and their major health issues and trends. Many of the health issues will be reviewed in greater detail within other chapters of this text. These countries were chosen because they vary in terms of their healthcare systems and geographic areas.

Many of the developed countries are currently working on controversial legal, religious, and ethical issues that directly relate to health care and healthcare systems of delivery. Specifically, the following topics are being addressed:

- Access to health care for all residents
- Issues of funding for nonlegal residents (illegal aliens) and healthcare services provided by government and nongovernment organizations
- Options for termination of an unwanted pregnancy

- A woman's right to determine what happens to her body (birth control, abortion, contraception, genital mutilation, sexual assault and/or abuse, sterilization, child molestation, prostitution)
- Sex education in schools, clinics, and public health facilities

UNITED STATES

Location

The United States is located in North America, bordering both the Atlantic and Pacific Oceans, between Canada in the north and Mexico in the south. It includes 50 states, the District of Columbia, and several territories and possessions.

Population Statistics

The U.S. population as of 2010 was 303,500,000. In 2050, it is projected that the U.S. population will be third largest in the world, after China and India (U.S. Census Bureau, 2010).

Economy

The United States has the largest and most technologically powerful economy in the world, with a per capita gross domestic product (GDP) of $47,000 annually in 2007 ($2.2 trillion in total), ranking tenth in world income (Central Intelligence Agency [CIA], 2009). In this market-oriented economy, 12% of the population lives below the poverty line. The unemployment rates vary among ethnic groups, gender, socioeconomic groups, and geographic locations.

The United States is the leading industrial power of the world, highly diversified and technologically advanced. Its products include steel, petroleum, motor vehicles, aerospace, telecommunications, chemicals, electronics, food processing, consumer goods, lumber, and mining. Products include wheat, corn, other grains, fruits, vegetables, cotton, beef, pork, poultry, dairy products, forest products, and fish.

Health Trends and Issues

Monitoring the health of any country is essential for identifying and prioritizing public health and research needs. It is necessary for identifying important information such as diseases and conditions and for determining new health policy priority areas, funding, and programs. The overall health of the United States is improving because of funding devoted to health education, public health programs, health research, and health care. In 2007, U.S. men could expect to live 3.5 years longer and U.S. women 1.6 years longer than their counterparts in 1990. Longer life expectancies are considered desirable with healthy aging, but aging often is accompanied with an increase in chronic diseases such as hypertension, diabetes, renal disease, cancer, and Alzheimer's disease and other dementias (Centers for Disease Control and Prevention [CDC], 2009).

In 2007, the U.S. infant mortality rate was 6.77 infant deaths per 1000 live births, 27% lower than 1990. Yet there remains a disparity in infant mortality based on race and ethnicity: Infant mortality was highest among non-Hispanic African Americans, with a rate of 13.63 deaths per 1000 live births (CDC, 2009).

During the past 50 years, many diseases have been eradicated or greatly controlled in the United States. Heart disease deaths have declined because of public health education emphasizing healthy lifestyles, such as decreasing cigarette smoking, lowering cholesterol through medications and diet, and new technology in heart procedures and surgery. Despite the fact that the 1964 U.S. Surgeon General's report was published more than 45 years ago, 25% of men and 20% of women in the United States continue to smoke. With respect to infectious diseases, HIV/AIDS rates have declined because of the introduction of antiretroviral medications. Home, workplace, and motor vehicle safety have also helped to extend lives by lowering unintentional injuries for adults and children. Rates of acute infectious diseases of children such as measles, mumps, and rubella have decreased due to immunizations (CDC, 2009).

The U.S. healthcare system is not cost-effective given the amount of money spent yearly. The United States spends more on health care than any other developed country ($1.7 trillion annually) in the world—approximately $5267 per person per year. Neither public nor private funding at this level can be sustained indefinitely.

The United States clearly is the leader in healthcare spending as a percentage of GDP. **Figure 2-1** shows per capita health expenditures for 2008 in U.S. dollars purchasing power parity. Health spending per capita in the United States is much higher than in other developed country.

In spite of these large expenditures on health care, a growing number of Americans—often referred to as the working poor—are "caught in the middle," earning too much money to be eligible for Medicaid, not being old enough for Medicare, yet not earning enough to pay for a private healthcare policy. In addition to these cost issues, accessing health care presents a problem in the United States. The life expectancy in the United States is lower than in many other developed countries. For example, the life expectancy in Japan is 82.1 years, the life expectancy in Germany is 79 years, the life expectancy in Switzerland is 81.3 years, and the life expectancy in the United Kingdom is 79 years. By comparison, the life expectancy in the United States is 78 years (Organisation for Economic Co-operation and Development [OECD], 2010).

U.S. infant mortality in 2011 was 6.06 deaths per 1000 live births, which is not an especially good rate, considering that other developed countries—such as Sweden, Japan, France, Italy, Spain, Finland, Norway, and many others—have much lower rates (CIA, 2011). The United States also has one of the

FIGURE 2-1

Total Health Expenditure per Capita, U.S. and Selected Countries, 2008

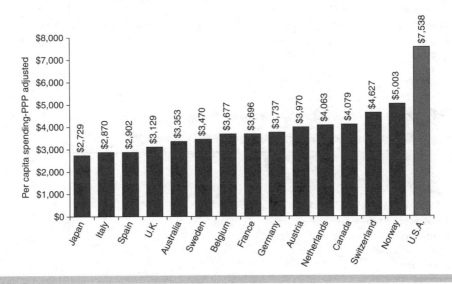

Source: Organisation for Economic Co-operation and Development (2010), "OECD Health Data", OECD Health Statistics (database).

highest rates of all types of cancers and one of the highest obesity rates. Medical errors injure 1.5 million people annually (Institute of Medicine, 2011).

Population Characteristics

The racial and ethnic composition of the United States has changed in recent decades. Notably, the Hispanic (Latino) population and Asian and Pacific Islander ethnic groups have grown rapidly. In 2012, the Hispanic population became the largest ethnic minority, representing 16.3 % of the total population, and the Asian subpopulation accounted for 5.6% of the total U.S. population. During the past 50 years, the U.S. population of adults age 75 and older grew from 3% to 6%, and by 2050, the older adult population is projected to make up 12% of the total population. In 2002, more than 50% of African American and Hispanic children and those older than 65 years lived at or near poverty levels (CDC, 2004a; Pew Hispanic Center, 2012; U.S. Census Bureau, 2011a).

Health Risk Factors

Obesity increases the risk of heart disease, diabetes, and stroke. Alcohol consumption and illicit drugs increase the risk of disease and injuries, whereas cigarette smoking increases the risk of lung cancer, heart disease, emphysema, and other diseases. Regular exercise can reduce the risk for many diseases and enhance mental health functioning. Nevertheless, the rates of overweight and obesity can be seen to have more than doubled among U.S. school-aged children, 6–11 years, and more than tripled among adolescents, when comparing the periods 1976–1980 and 2005–2006. Also, among adults 20–74 years of age, the obesity rates have more than doubled for similar-year differences (CDC, 2009).

The rates of nonfatal workplace injuries and illnesses were 50% lower in 2007 as compared to the corresponding rates in 1989. In 2007, there were 36,000 new HIV/AIDS cases in the United States. Males 13 years and older accounted for 70% of all cases and African American males accounted for 31% of all new cases; African American females accounted for 17% of all new cases. Adults living below the poverty level were four times more likely to have serious psychological stress as compared to those living at twice the poverty level or higher (CDC, 2009).

Table 2-1 shows the leading U.S. health indicators as indicated by the CDC in its *Healthy People 2010* goals (CDC, 2010b). **Table 2-2** summarizes the leading causes of death in the United States in 2009 (CDC, 2010c).

TABLE 2-1

Leading U.S. Health Indicators According to *Healthy People 2010*

1. Physical activity
2. Overweight and obesity
3. Tobacco use
4. Substance abuse
5. Responsible sexual behavior
6. Mental health
7. Injury and violence
8. Immunization
9. Access to health care

Source: CDC, 2010b.

TABLE 2-2

Leading Causes of Death in the United States, 2009

1. Heart disease: 616,067 deaths
2. Cancer: 562,875 deaths
3. Stroke (cerebrovascular diseases): 135,952 deaths
4. Chronic lower respiratory diseases: 127,924 deaths
5. Accidents (unintentional injuries): 123,706 deaths
6. Alzheimer's disease: 74,632 deaths
7. Diabetes: 71,382 deaths
8. Influenza and pneumonia: 52,717 deaths
9. Nephritis, nephrotic syndrome, and nephrosis: 46,448 deaths
10. Septicemia: 34,828 deaths

Source: CDC, 2010c.

Utilization of Health Care

According to the CDC (2004b), the U.S. healthcare system has undergone a dramatic change over the last decade. New technology, drugs, procedures, and tests have changed the manner in which care is delivered. The growth of ambulatory surgery has been influenced by improvements in noninvasive and minimally invasive techniques. The growth of managed care and limits on payment by insurers and other payers represent an attempt to control healthcare costs, which has also had a major impact on healthcare utilization.

The following are factors that decrease the utilization of health care (CDC, 2004a):

- Decreased supply of hospitals and healthcare providers
- Improvement in public health and sanitation, such as cleaner water
- Better public health education of risk factors and methods to make behavioral changes to reduce risks
- New treatments or cures for diseases
- Public policy or guidelines that recommend decreased utilization
- Shifts of care sites, such as from inpatient to outpatient surgery
- Payer pressures to decrease costs
- Changes in practice patterns, such as those that emphasize more self-care, alternative sites, or alternative medicine

The following are factors that increase the utilization of health care (CDC, 2004a):

- Increased supply of healthcare facilities and providers
- Population growth
- Aging of the population
- New procedures and technologies
- Guidelines or policies that recommend increased utilization
- New threats, such as HIV or bioterrorism
- New drugs
- Increased healthcare coverage
- More aggressive treatments for patients
- Changes in consumer demand, such as for cosmetic surgery and hip replacements

Many types of preventive care or treatment of illnesses are performed at an increasing rate in outpatient clinics or physicians' offices. For example, the use of prenatal care services, which begins in the first trimester of pregnancy, has been steadily rising. The percentage of children receiving their childhood immunizations is at a high level. The chickenpox vaccine (varicella) has been widely distributed as well. Women are getting Pap smears and mammograms at increasing rates, and older adults are increasingly getting vaccines for influenza and pneumonia (CDC, 2004a).

At the same time, inpatient healthcare utilization has been declining. Admissions and length of hospitalization stays have decreased. Many procedures that were traditionally done within the hospital are now performed in clinics, physicians' offices, outpatient surgery centers, and rehabilitation centers, leaving more complex procedures and illnesses to be treated within the hospital. Inpatients now have higher acuity levels whereas inpatient mental health treatment has significantly declined (CDC, 2004a).

Healthcare Resources

Use of healthcare resources is partially determined by the quantity of healthcare providers and the infrastructure. Although the number of healthcare providers in the United States has increased, they are unequally distributed, with most often being found in large urban centers rather than isolated rural areas. Proportionately, there were a higher percentage of healthcare specialists in 2006 as compared to 1993. Since 1990, the number of inpatient mental health hospital beds has decreased by 45%, compared to the number available in 2004 (CDC, 2009).

Healthcare Access Disparities

The best health care in the world is meaningless to those who do not have access to health insurance coverage or who cannot afford it. The continued increases in healthcare costs combined with economic changes have caused a number of U.S. residents to go without any health insurance, giving them less access to health care.

A health disparity is a statistically significant difference in health indicators that persists over time, between groups—for example, maternal and infant mortality. A health disparity also comprises an unequal burden of disease morbidity and mortality often found in racial, ethnic, or socioeconomic groups as compared to the dominant group. Examples of U.S. health disparities include the following:

- Infant mortality: Mortality rates for African American babies remain nearly 2.5 times higher than the corresponding rates for white babies.
- Life expectancy: African American men and women have nearly 10 fewer years of life than their white counterparts.
- Death rates attributable to heart disease, stroke, prostate and breast cancer: Rates are significantly higher for the African American population, and diabetes rates are more than 30% higher among Native Americans and Hispanics than among whites (CDC, 2004a, 2010a; Smedley, Stith, & Nelson, 2003; Sridhar, 2005).

Healthcare disparities exist across racial, ethnic, and socioeconomic groups. Racial and ethnic minorities and low-socioeconomic groups tend to receive lower-quality health care than whites, even when insurance status, income, age, and illness severity are comparable. To decrease these healthcare disparities, the United States needs to increase the awareness of the problems among providers, insurers, and policy makers; promote consistency and equity of care; and strengthen the culturally competent healthcare approach and improve diversity of the healthcare workforce to increase patients' choices for healthcare providers. Measurement of health and healthcare quality includes the following considerations: (1) clinical performance measures of how well healthcare providers deliver specific services; (2) assessment by patients of how well providers meet their healthcare needs; and (3) outcome measures that may be affected by the quality of health care received, such as death rates from cancers preventable by screening (CDC, 2004a, 2010a; Smedley et al., 2003; Sridhar, 2005).

Causes of healthcare disparities in the United States include unequal and inadequate access to insurance coverage. Health insurance directly affects access to health care regardless of race, ethnicity, or socioeconomic status. When they lack insurance, many people will go without medical care because they cannot afford to pay out-of-pocket for care. Minority groups and persons without a regular source of health care are less likely to access care. Low-income and uninsured individuals are particularly unlikely to access health care. Low-income immigrant minorities, in particular, may be unable to obtain health insurance through programs such as Children's Insurance Program (CHIP).

Physical barriers to accessing health care include inadequate or no transportation to healthcare services and long waiting times for seeing a healthcare provider. Scarcity of healthcare providers and pharmacy services in inner-city and isolated rural areas where there are higher concentrations of minority populations are major issues as well.

Language barriers create additional barriers. Persons with limited or no English speaking and understanding abilities are less likely to be able to set up an appointment for medical care and, therefore, tend to rely on emergency rooms for care when vitally needed (CDC, 2004a, 2010a; Smedley et al., 2003; Sridhar, 2005). Lack of English skills also inhibits comprehension of healthcare advice and contributes to lack of health literacy. Health literacy is the ability to obtain, process, and understand basic health information so as to make appropriate health decisions; it is needed to access healthcare systems. A larger number of minority patients have challenges in health literacy.

Lack of diversity in healthcare providers can also be a problem. Minority patients, when given a choice, tend to be more comfortable with healthcare providers who are more like themselves and know their culture and language, as well as their health beliefs and practices. Collectively, minority groups in the United States represent 25% of the population, yet members of minorities account for less than 9% of nurses, 6% of physicians, and only 5% of dentists (CDC, 2004a, 2010a; Smedley et al., 2003; Sridhar, 2005).

In its 2004 report, the Sullivan Commission noted that racial and ethnic disparities in healthcare delivery are related to differences in treatment by healthcare providers. Minority groups are less likely than whites to be given appropriate cardiac medicines or to undergo cardiac bypass surgery when necessary. Compared to whites, they are less likely to receive renal dialysis or transplants, the best diagnostic tests, treatment for a stroke or cancer, or the best treatment for HIV/AIDS. Moreover, they often distrust healthcare providers (the majority of whom are white), receive care from less adequate health facilities, and are treated by lower-quality (in terms of education and experience) healthcare providers than whites. African Americans are more likely than whites to seek care from hospitals that have fewer resources and up-to-date technology, have higher surgical mortality rates, and have higher neonatal mortality rates. African Americans are also more likely to receive care from physicians with less training, have less access to specialist physicians, have higher rates of breast and prostate cancer due to less screening, and receive later care and have less access to care. Perhaps not surprisingly, the cancer incidence for African Americans is 10% higher than for whites.

The overall health statistics for all ethnic and socioeconomic groups in the United States have, in many cases, improved, yet some health statistics indicate worsening situations. Based on CDC (2010a) data, **Table 2-3** compares U.S. health statistics from 2000 (left column) with more recent statistics (middle and right columns) for 2006–2009.

The United States has also been growing more racially and ethnically diverse, and its residents are living longer. The National Center for Health Statistics (CDC, 2004a) has pointed out major areas where disparities exist between race and ethnicity and socioeconomic status. Those residents who live in poverty are more likely to be in poor health and less likely to receive adequate health care. Poor people are four times more likely to have psychological stress. There are large disparities in infant mortality rates and life expectancy rates between those persons living in poverty and the remainder of the population. In addition, adults younger than 64 years who are Latino or Native American (American Indian) are more likely to be uninsured than members of other racial or ethnic groups. Diseases and medical conditions

TABLE 2-3			

U.S. Health Statistics, 2000 and 2006–2009

	2000	*2006–2009*	
Life Expectancy (Years)			
At birth	76.8 (2000)	77.7 (2006)	77.9 (2007)
At age 65 years	17.6 (2000)	18.5 (2006)	18.6 (2007)
Infant Deaths per 1000 Live Births			
All infants	6.91 (2000)	6.69 (2006)	6.75 (2007)
Heart disease	257.6 (2000)	200.2 (2006)	190.9 (2007)
Cancer	199.6 (2000)	180.7 (2006)	178.4 (2007)
Stroke	60.9 (2000)	43.6 (2006)	42.2 (2007)
Chronic lower respiratory diseases	44.2 (2000)	40.5 (2006)	40.8 (2007)
Unintentional injuries	34.9 (2000)	39.8 (2006)	40.0 (2007)
Motor-vehicle collision	15.4 (2000)	15.0 (2006)	14.4 (2007)
Diabetes	25.0 (2000)	23.3 (2006)	22.5 (2007)
Obesity (BMI at or Above Sex- and Age-Specific 95th Percentile)			
2–5 years	10.3 (1999–2000)	11.0 (2005–2006)	10.4 (2007–2008)
6–11 years	15.1 (1999–2000)	15.1 (2005–2006)	19.6 (2007–2008)
12–19 years	14.8 (1999–2000)	17.8 (2005–2006)	18.1 (2007–2008)
Cigarette Smoking (Percent)			
18 years and older	23.2 (2000)	20.6 (2008)	20.6 (2009)
Healthcare Utilization: No Healthcare Visit in Past 12 Months (Percent)			
Younger than 18 years	12.3 (2000)	10.1 (2008)	9.1 (2009)
18–44 years	23.5 (2000)	22.7 (2008)	22.7 (2009)
45–64 years	15.0 (2000)	14.4 (2008)	15.4 (2009)
65 years and older	7.5 (2000)	5.6 (2008)	4.7 (2009)

Source: CDC, 2010a.

such as diabetes or obesity increase with age and are more likely to occur in non-Hispanic blacks and Latinos than in non-Hispanic whites. Some of these disparities may be the result of differences in socio-economic status, culture and health practices, stress, environmental exposures, discrimination, and access to health care (CDC, 2004a).

Peterson, Wright, and Peterson (2002) studied the utilization of interventional cardiac procedures among African American and Caucasian patients; their findings revealed that African Americans had far fewer cardiac interventions and procedures. Dr. David Satcher (former U.S. Surgeon General) and colleagues (2005) reported that from 1960 to 2000, the United States made progress in decreasing the black–white gap in civil rights, housing, education, and income, but inequality still exists in health care and general health status.

A study conducted by Callahan and Cooper (2005) revealed that young adults, 19–24 years old, are the most likely to be uninsured in the United States. These researchers collected data from 11,866 subjects. Their results indicated that 27% of women and 33% of men had no health insurance. Thus almost one-third of the young adults in the United States are uninsured. Only half of the employers of this group pay any health insurance for their employees. As a consequence, these young adults are more likely to be uninsured—even though they are at the highest risk of all age cohorts for unintended pregnancy, sexually transmitted diseases, substance abuse, injuries, and other chronic medical diseases. Lack of insurance in adults is related to less frequent healthcare screenings, delayed diagnosis of illnesses such as cancer, poor care for chronic diseases, and higher rates of mortality when hospitalized. According to Callahan and Cooper (2005), Latino young adults are more likely to be uninsured than any other ethnic group.

Clearly, there are significant disparities in accessing health care in the United States based on race, ethnicity, and socioeconomic status. Those living in poverty are significantly less likely to access health care and are generally in poorer health than others. In addition, those in poverty are four times more likely to have serious mental health problems. Infant mortality rates and life expectancy rates also differ among racial and ethnic groups (CDC, 2004a). In essence, the United States rations health care by not providing universal coverage to its entire population. Ultimately, the United States provides less access to health care to more people than any other developed country. Those who get charity treatment are most likely to get less than adequate health care (Lamm & Blank, 2005).

Reschovsky and Staiti (2005) conducted a study that addressed both physicians' and patients' perspectives on quality of health care in rural America as compared to urban America. Data were collected from 12,406 physicians and 59,725 patients, representing 48 U.S. states. Results of the study indicated that rural areas had far fewer physicians than urban areas, but the overall perception was that health care was adequate for the rural areas. A decreased rural supply of healthcare providers did not necessarily mean lower quality of care. Because of the lower population density and smaller number of physicians available, patients in rural areas often had to travel longer distances for care, wait longer for appointments, and wait longer in doctors' offices—yet there were no perceived differences in unmet medical needs within the two groups. Nevertheless, physicians in rural areas reported greater difficulty in helping patients (by referral) receive specialty medical care, when needed, owing to a lack of qualified medical specialists in rural areas. Rural residents were also poorer and more likely to lack adequate insurance or be able to pay out-of-pocket expenses for health care (CDC, 2004a).

Healthcare Expenditures

Healthcare expenses in the United States are the highest in the world, and continue to rise, due to both the cost of services and the greater number of services provided, made necessary by the country's increasingly older population. In 2010, the United States spent 16% of its GDP on health care, compared to 11% of GDP in Switzerland, the second highest spender. Medicaid is funded by federal and state governments to provide medical care for low-income people. In 2007, 36% of health care was paid by private insurance, 14% was paid out-of-pocket, and 45% was covered by public funds (CDC, 2010a).

Overall Quality and Future Needs of U.S. Health Care

The quality of U.S. health care is less than desirable. There is a substantial gap between the best of health care that can be provided to some individuals and that which is routinely delivered to many people. Reports indicate that 95% of hospice patients receive the right amount of pain medications, yet only 8% of alcoholic patients needing treatment receive care in a special facility. The median level of receipt of needed services is 58%. In spite of efforts to focus on effective prevention and chronic illness care, the U.S. healthcare system performs better in making patient diagnoses and treating acute illnesses, such as myocardial infarctions (heart attacks), than in providing outpatient treatments for chronic diseases such as cancer and diabetes. For those without health insurance, the healthcare situation is even worse. The median level of receipt of health care for the uninsured is 50% compared to 65% among people with health insurance. Persons 65 years and older are excluded from these statistics because most have Medicare. In addition, the data do not take into account the current recession (CDC, 2010a).

Patient safety remains a major healthcare problem and clearly needs improvement. In 2008, approximately one of every seven hospitalized Medicare patients experienced one or more adverse events. Nosocomial infections (infections acquired during hospital care) are, by far, the most serious problem.

Health care varies not only with types of health insurance, but also with geographic location. There are wide variations in the quality of care provided throughout the country. The upper Midwest and New England regions have the highest quality of health care, while the Southwest and South Central regions of the country tend to have lower-quality health care. Quality of health care appears to be improving, albeit at a very slow rate. Outcome measures related to quality health care are also improving (CDC, 2010a).

Infectious diseases remain a great cause of morbidity and mortality. The numbers of measles and rubella cases have decreased because of an increase in vaccinations, but some communicable diseases such as chlamydia have increased. In addition, the incidence of new infectious diseases such as H1N1, SARS, H5N1, avian influenza, and some drug-resistant bacteria strains, such as methicillin-resistant *Staphylococcus aureus* (MRSA), has increased. Influenza and pneumonia remain major causes of death, and HIV/AIDS continues to spread (CDC, 2010a).

The removal of barriers to receiving health care is greatly needed in the United States. Lack of health insurance continues to represent the major barrier to quality health care. The Office of Healthcare Reform is leading the government effort to improve healthcare access and quality for all residents of the country. Health information technology is needed to support these quality improvements (CDC, 2010a).

Medication Usage

Utilization of medications differs according to third-party coverage (insurance) and availability. Nearly half of the U.S. population takes at least one prescription medication, and almost one in six takes three or more medications. These medications are predominately prescribed for lowering cholesterol to reduce the risk of heart disease, controlling depression, and/or controlling diabetes. The number of people taking medications and the number of medications taken both increase with age, with five out of six people who are 65 years or older taking at least one medication and nearly half taking three or more (CDC, 2004d).

Fertility

Teenage mothers and their children are more likely to be disadvantaged and have less adequate health status than older mothers and their children. In 2002, birth rates for teenagers declined to 43 births per 1000 women, while birth rates for women aged 35–44 increased. More women are postponing birth for education and careers, and infertility interventions make it more possible for women to give birth at later ages (CDC, 2004a). From 2005 to 2007, however, birth rates rose 5% among teenagers from 40.5 to 42.5 live births per 1000 females (CDC, 2009).

Other trends differ by racial and ethnic groups. In 2002, the birth rates for Hispanic (Latina) women ages 15–44 years was 64% higher than for non-Hispanic white women, with 94.4 births per 1000 Hispanic women as compared to 57.4 births per 1000 white women (CDC, 2004a).

Health Behaviors

Rates of cigarette smoking have declined in the United States, with 22% of men and 17% of women remaining smokers (CDC, 2009). Between 1997 and 2003, the rate of teenage smoking also decreased from 36% to 22%. The rate of smoking during pregnancy, which causes a higher incidence of preterm and low-birth-weight babies, declined from 20% in 1989 to 11% in 2002 for all women, yet teenage smoking during pregnancy for 2002 was higher at 18%. Low-birth-weight babies, who have higher risks for death or disability, have also increased as a proportion of all newborns, from 7% of all births in 1990 to 7.8% in 2002 (CDC, 2004a).

Overweight and obesity have become nationwide problems among children and adults in all age groups. Obesity causes approximately 300,000 deaths per year in the United States and is perhaps second only to smoking as a preventable cause of death. Estimates of deaths from obesity are based on body mass index (BMI), which is defined as weight in kilograms divided by height in meters squared. BMI is correlated with body fat and is the measure recommended by the National Heart, Lung, and Blood Institute for use in clinical practice. Much of the overweight/obesity problem relates to trends toward inactivity and overeating, especially of the high-fat "junk" foods. In 2003, 33.3% of high school students had no moderate or vigorous physical activity, with females reporting less activity than males. Within the adult population 20–74 years of age, obesity increased from 47% in 1976–1980 to 65% in 1999–2002.

Obesity across the life span also varies by race and ethnicity. In 2002, 50% of non-Hispanic African Americans, 39% of Mexican Americans, and 31% of non-Hispanic white adults were obese. From the period 1976–1980 to the period 1999–2002, the rates of overweight and obesity in children, 6–11 years of age, rose from 7% to 16%, and for adolescents 12–19 years, the obesity rate more than tripled from 5% to 16% (CDC, 2004a, 2010a; Flegal, Williamson, Pamuk, & Rosenberg, 2004).

Alcohol use among those 18 years and older is reported by 41% of males and 20% of females, with the most common usage by 18- to 24-year-olds. The rate of illegal drug use among 12- to 17-year-olds was reported to be 12% in 2002. Males 26–34 years had a rate of 222 cocaine-related visits to emergency rooms per 100,000 (CDC, 2004a).

Morbidity and Mortality

Morbidity (disease rate) includes the limitation of activities due to chronic illness. The morbidity rate was 6–7% for U.S. children younger than 18 years during 1997–2002. As adults age, morbidity caused by chronic illness increases. In 2002, 14% of those persons 65 years and older were limited in at least one ADL (CDC, 2004a).

Mortality (death rate) reflects the statistics of life expectancy and infant mortality—the key measures to evaluate the overall health standard of a population. In the United States, there is an upward trend in life expectancy. State variations in infant mortality range from 12.6 deaths per 100,000 live births in Mississippi to 4.9 deaths per 100,000 live births in Massachusetts. Infant mortality rates (IMRs) also differ greatly by race, with highs of 20.9 deaths per 100,000 in non-Hispanic African Americans in Hawaii and 18.5 deaths per 100,000 in the District of Columbia, as compared to 2.7 deaths per 100,000 non-Hispanic whites in Hawaii and 3.2 deaths per 100,000 non-Hispanic whites in the District of Columbia. In Massachusetts, the IMR is 10.3 deaths per 100,000 live births among non-Hispanic whites (Kaiser Family Foundation, 2011).

Despite the fact that Americans smoke less, they have lowered their cholesterol levels, and deaths from heart disease and stroke are declining in the general population, deaths are not declining within specific racial and ethnic groups in the United States. Those groups who have not experienced any positive changes in their health statistics include African Americans, Hispanics (Latinos), persons who are poor, and persons with less than a high school education. African American men and women have the highest rates of hypertension, diabetes, and hospitalizations for stroke. African American women also have higher rates of obesity. Hispanics (Latinos) are most likely to lack health insurance, are less likely to receive influenza or pneumonia vaccines, and have the poorest rates of good health. Native Americans (American Indians) have the highest rates of cigarette smoking and alcohol use. Reasons for these disparities include inadequate access to health care, distrust of the healthcare providers, cultural and language barriers, and genetic predisposition to heart diseases and stroke (CDC, 2008).

American Indians/Alaskan Natives represent 1.5 percent of the total U.S. population. More than 538,000 of American Indian/Alaskan Natives (representing one third of the total American Indian/Alaskan Native population) live on reservations or other trust lands where the climate is challenging, the roads are often impassable, transportation is scarce, and healthcare facilities are difficult to access. In some areas, health services and facilities have not kept up with services and facilities in areas with white populations. In the Navajo area, the numbers of hospital beds have declined steadily; the proportion of doctors and nurses to patients has not kept up with that of the general U.S. population. About 60 percent of American Indians nationwide, rely on the Indian Health Service (IHS) to provide access to health care. Addressing barriers of access to health care is a large part of the overall IHS goal, which strives to assure that comprehensive, culturally acceptable, personal and public health services are available and accessible to American Indian and Alaskan Native persons. Diabetes and liver diseases within this population are greater than twice that of all other adults in the United States. The greatest mortality rates are due to direct and indirect effects of type 2 diabetes despite special federal expenditure programs. Compared with whites, Indians of all cultural groups, have higher levels of obesity, diabetes, and spend less time in doing physical activities than whites. A special Diabetes Program for American Indians has provided funds for prevention and treatment of diabetes, yet rates are still higher than those of whites. Compared with whites, Indians of all cultural groups have higher levels of smoking and heart disease than whites; have higher death rates of fetuses, infants, children, adolescents and young adults than other groups; have higher preterm deaths and fetal alcohol syndrome (FAS) than other groups; and have lower rates of prenatal care. Infant mortality is 1.7 times higher, and they have twice the rate of sudden infant death syndrome compared to all other US population groups. Their rates of sexually transmitted diseases are 5.5 times higher than for non-Hispanic whites. Unintentional injuries are the third leading cause of death for the 1–44 age group. Death rates for unintentional injuries and motor vehicle accidents are 1.7 to 2 times higher than rates for all other groups in the US. Suicide rates are 3 times greater than for whites of similar ages (CDC, 2008).

African-Americans have twice the uninsured rates as non-Hispanic whites. Non-Hispanic African-Americans bear a disproportionate burden of disease, injury, death, and disability. The risk factors, incidence and morbidity rates for diseases and injuries are greater than for non-Hispanic whites. Three of the 10 leading causes of deaths for non-Hispanic African-Americans are not among those listed among the 10 leading causes of deaths for non-Hispanic whites. They are homicide (sixth), HIV virus (seventh) and septicemia (ninth). The infant mortality rate for African-Americans is 13.9 per 1,000 live births as compared to 6.9 per 1,000 live births for non-Hispanic white Americans. Today, an African American baby is 2.5 times more likely to die before reaching one year of age than a non-Hispanic white American baby. Preterm birth is the leading cause of death for African-American infants. Higher pregnancy-related mortalities are found among African-American women compared to white women of similar socioeconomic status including rates of preeclampsia, eclampsia, abruptio placenta, placenta previa, and postpartal hemorrhage, leading to death. Non-Hispanic African-American women are at a higher risk for having low and very low birth weight babies. There are lower numbers of females receiving prenatal care during the first trimester of pregnancy. Compared to white American women, middle class African-American women have access to fewer financial resources, more restricted opportunities for wealth accumulation, are more likely to reside in racially segregated areas, and more are affected by lifelong legacies of childhood poverty and psychological stress due to discrimination (CDC, 2008).

Child Health

Wise (2004) revealed the following about the determinants of child health in the United States. In 2002, approximately 17% of all children and 18.5% of those younger than 6 years lived in poverty—that is, in households with incomes below 100% of the federal poverty level ($14,348 in 2002). Half of those living in poverty live at 50% of the federal poverty level, placing them within the "severely poor" group. Children who are poor disproportionately suffer more problems with low birth weight and overall higher infant and child mortality and morbidity rates. Medicaid eligibility expansion for poor children and the State Children's Health Insurance Program (SCHIP) for poor children eligible for Medicaid have made a significant difference in facilitating access to health care for poor children.

Almost 60% of all deaths in childhood occur during the first year of life, and 40% of all deaths in childhood occur during the first month of life. Death in newborns is usually from prematurity, low birth weight, congenital anomalies, or other genetic disorders. The United States has increased the survival rates of premature babies mainly through advances in technology and establishment of neonatal intensive care units. In spite of this advanced technology, however, the United States still does not rank among the best in infant mortality rates among developed countries, mainly because of the high rate of premature births in the United States. With the ever-increasing rates of survival of premature babies also comes long-term health problems. African-American babies continue to have at least twice the infant mortality rates as white babies, a difference that is attributed to the higher rates of low-birth-weight and premature babies of African-American women who live in poverty (Wise, 2004).

The U.S. mortality rates for children have fallen sharply during the past few decades. The greatest reduction is attributable to prevention and treatment of acute infectious diseases. Unintentional injury remains the leading cause of childhood death at present in the United States, but children having complex chronic conditions have the second highest death rates. Hospitalization costs for children ages 1–18 are typically related to the following causes (ranked from highest to lowest in cost): asthma, mental disorders, trauma, respiratory infections, ear infections, other infections, epilepsy, diabetes, and congenital anomalies. Mortality rates for African-American male adolescents (15–19) have risen dramatically in recent years, mainly because of homicide and suicide. In addition, African-American children experience significant death rates from sickle cell disease (Wise, 2004).

Child health outcome trends (according to a study by the National Health Interview Survey of 40,000 households) revealed that little changed from the years 1962 to 2000 in terms of the rate of children with acute illnesses (defined as any disease that requires restriction of activity for less than 3 months). For young children, this rate remained stable; it declined slightly for school-aged children. For chronic illnesses such as asthma, type 2 diabetes, and behavioral disorders, an increase in rates has been seen during the past several decades. Obesity is now considered a chronic problem with children, and also causes other problems, such as type 2 diabetes (Wise, 2004).

The CDC reported that more children than ever had health insurance in 2003, but their parents often had less coverage (CDC, 2004c). More than 70% of indigent children younger than 18 years are covered by some form of public insurance, either federal or state. Even so, approximately 3.9 million children did not have any form of health care in 2003. More specifically, 12% of Hispanic (Latino) children, 5% of non-Hispanic African American children, and 3% of Caucasian children had no health care in that year. Also, more than 4 million children aged 2 to 17 years lacked dental care.

Blumberg, Halfon, and Olson (2004) report that the first 3 years of a child's life are critical for development. Early exposure to malnutrition, viral infections, drugs, and environmental toxins can have harmful consequences for children's neurological development, resulting in alterations in cognitive and emotional development. These effects are not always recognized immediately and may not be discovered until the child is older. Exposure to a compromised environment may also result in cardiovascular disease or diabetes later in adulthood. Ideally, a child who has a positive caring relationship with parents and other caregivers will have opportunities for learning skills needed throughout the child's life. Today, however, there are great obstacles that impede many children's progress toward a safe and healthy life. Children need regular health checkups that include immunizations and treatment for illnesses, intellectual stimulation, good nutrition, and a safe and caring home environment to ensure the best long-term outcomes.

Health Care for Older Adults

According to Lamm and Blank (2005, p. 23), "One of the challenges in America's future is to retire the baby boomer without bankrupting the country or unduly burdening future generations." Ways to provide health care and services to the elderly include society (the government) funding of health care or social insurance. The U.S. healthcare retirement system is now unsustainable, in part because healthcare expenditures have grown in the past 40 years at 2.5 times the rate of inflation, which is now greater than 15% of the GDP. Approximately 3 times more funds are spent on health care for the elderly than for children in the United States.

The most rapidly growing segment of the U.S. population during the past decade has been the group of people ages 65 and older. With the increases in life expectancy, more health care is needed for maintaining and improving quality of life. The United States has made progress in vaccinating 90% of children by the time they are 2 years old, but immunization rates for adults 65 years and older range from 23% to 49%, and are characterized by great racial and ethnic disparities. Influenza and pneumonia vaccines can be given in the traditional sites of physician offices or health clinics, as well as in nontraditional sites, such as grocery stores and senior centers. Recommendations from the CDC for immunizations for older adults include the following (Weber, 2004):

- Tetanus–diphtheria vaccine: all adults, every 10 years
- Influenza vaccine: adults 50 and older, annually
- Hepatitis A vaccine: adults at risk
- Hepatitis B vaccine: adults at risk
- Measles, mumps, and rubella vaccine: susceptible adults
- Varicella (chickenpox) vaccine: susceptible adults
- Meningococcal polysaccharide vaccine: susceptible adults

For older adults, oral health care is not covered by Medicare, and many have difficulty in accessing this care. The well elderly as well as the chronically ill elderly will need good oral care for routine cleaning, problems with tooth loss, dental caries, and periodontal diseases. Periodontal diseases are chronic and can carry organisms and spread endotoxins that cause other problems, such as systemic infections. At present, there are not enough dentists trained to meet the needs of the elderly in the United States, and many residents do not have sufficient funds to pay for these services on an out-of-pocket basis (CDC, 2004e; Lamster, 2004).

In addition to providing medical care benefits, the federal government operates a federal food and nutrition program for older adults who qualify. The U.S. government appropriates approximately $1 billion annually for all food and nutrition assistance programs for older adults, funded through the Older Americans Act (OAA). OAA nutrition programs, which are run by the U.S. Department of Health and Human Services and the U.S. Department of Agriculture, reach only 6% to 7% of the people who need them, however. By comparison, the federal government's special Supplemental Nutrition Program for Women, Infants and Children (WIC) is funded at $5 billion and reaches approximately 50% of eligible women, infants, and children; this program began in the 1970s (Friedland, 2005a; Wellman, 2004).

Occupational Health

The total recordable cases of nonfatal occupational injury and illness incidence rate among private industry employers declined in 2010 to 3.5 cases per 100 workers—its lowest level since 2003, when estimates from the Survey of Occupational Injuries and Illnesses were first published. The preliminary count of fatal work injuries in the U.S. in 2010 was 4547. Overall, fatal work injuries are down 22 percent since 2006. Fatal work injuries due to fires and explosions increased by 65% in 2010 (U.S. Department of Labor, 2011).

Overall, much progress has been made in decreasing work-related diseases and deaths. Nevertheless, muscular and skeletal disorders remain the biggest sources of problems reported; these disorders typically come from repetitive motion injuries, which create medical problems such as carpel tunnel syndrome and back injuries. Occupations with the most repetitive motion injuries are as follows (Seminario, 2003):

- Truck drivers
- Nursing aids, orderlies, and attendants
- Laborers, nonconstruction

- Assemblers
- Janitors
- Registered nurses
- Stock handlers and baggers
- Construction workers
- Supervisors, sales jobs
- Carpenters
- Cashiers
- Maids and housemen
- Sales workers
- Clerks
- Welders
- Cooks

Vallarejo (2003) reported that of U.S. hired farm workers, who are mostly Mexican immigrants, two-thirds are living in poverty. Very few data have been collected related to their health issues. At least half of these individuals are undocumented immigrants; only 20% have any health insurance either from the government or from their employer. The Federal Migrant Health Program serves approximately 13% of all workers plus their dependent families. Only 10% receive food stamps or WIC benefits, and 13% receive Medicaid services (these federal health benefits are available for those persons deemed eligible because of their low income and number of family members, age younger than 65 years, and ineligibility to receive Medicare). Half of these workers are younger than age 29, 80% are male, and many earn less than $10,000 per year. Most migrant farm workers have only 6 years of education, and the majority have access to health care only when absolutely necessary—for example, by visiting hospital emergency rooms or clinics. Fewer than half of the workers have ever been to a dentist. The infectious diseases most often reported among these individuals typically come from parasites from poor drinking water in work camps, and the rate of tuberculosis in this group is six times greater than the rate in the general U.S. population. In addition, HIV/AIDS and sexually transmitted diseases rates among farm workers are much higher than the rates among the general U.S. population.

Complementary and Alternative Medicine

The CDC (2004f) reports that 158 million people in the United States use complementary and alternative medicine (CAM) medical interventions for health, at a cost of $230 million. One study of 31,000 adults conducted by the CDC (2004f) revealed that 36% of the U.S. adult population uses CAM. If prayer for health is also considered, the percentage rises to 62%.

CAM is defined as a group of diverse medical and healthcare systems, practices, and products that are not at present considered to be part of conventional medicine. When used with conventional medicine, such measures are considered complementary; when used alone or in place of conventional medicine, they are considered alternative. Types of CAM include services offered by providers, such as acupuncture and chiropractic, plus others that do not require a provider, such as yoga, message, special diets, vitamins, herbs, and botanical products. In addition, prayer for health is classified as a type of CAM. CAM interventions are most often used to treat back pain, colds, neck pain, joint pain or stiffness, depression, or anxiety. Fifty-five percent of U.S. residents use CAM with conventional methods, 26% use CAM at the suggestion of their conventional medical care providers, and 13% use CAM because they believe it is less expensive than conventional medicine. In addition, 28% use CAM because they believe that their conventional medicine is not helping them.

The CDC (2004f) has reported that some strong scientific evidence from randomized clinical trials supports the use of acupuncture and some herbal medicines and manual therapies. More research is necessary to prove the safety and efficacy of other practices and medicinal plants. Unregulated or inappropriate use of some CAM (traditional) medicines or practices can sometimes have harmful effects. For example, the herb ephedra (ma huang in Chinese) is traditionally used to treat respiratory congestion in China, but in the United States it has been marketed as a diet additive—a usage that has caused some deaths from heart attacks or strokes. Twenty-five percent of modern medicines are made from plants that were first used in traditional medicine. Many other traditional medicines from plants or herbs are currently being tested for prospective modern use—for example, for malaria, HIV, and sickle cell anemia.

The National Center for Complimentary and Alternative Medicine (NCCAM) of the National Institutes of Health recommends that people who are considering the use of CAM review the following key points:

■ As an informed consumer, review the scientific studies (published in refereed journals) done of the products that are being considered for use.

■ Consult a conventional healthcare provider before starting any use.

■ Learn more about the background and competency of a healthcare provider who is practicing a therapy such as acupuncture.

■ Check for health insurance coverage before starting treatments or care.

■ Check about the components or ingredients that make the products and where they come from.

■ Check about the safety of the manufacturing process. How does the manufacturer avoid contamination?

The U.S. Food and Drug Administration (FDA) does not require testing of dietary supplements. If dietary supplements claim to diagnose, treat, cure, or prevent disease, they are considered "unapproved new drugs" that are being sold illegally.

Payment for Health Care

Healthcare costs have been rising for several years. Expenditures in the United States on health care surpassed $2.3 trillion in 2008, more than three times the $714 billion spent in 1990, and over eight times the $253 billion spent in 1980. Controlling this growth has become a major policy priority, as the government, employers, and consumers increasingly struggle to keep up with healthcare costs (Kaiser Family Foundation, 2011). In 2008, U.S. healthcare spending was about $7,681 per resident and accounted for 16.2% of the nation's Gross Domestic Product (GDP); this is among the highest of all developed countries. Total healthcare expenditures grew at an annual rate of 4.4 percent in 2008, a slower rate than recent years, yet still outpacing inflation and the growth in national income. Without healthcare reform, there is general agreement that health costs are likely to continue to rise in the foreseeable future. President Obama has made cost control a focus of health reform efforts under way (Kaiser Family Foundation, 2011).

Although Americans benefit from many of the investments in health care, the recent rapid cost growth, coupled with an overall economic slowdown and rising federal deficit, places great strains on the systems used to finance health care, including private employer-sponsored health insurance coverage and public insurance programs such as Medicare and Medicaid. Since 1999, family premiums for employer-sponsored health coverage have increased by 131 percent, placing increasing cost burdens on employers and workers. Workers' wages growing at a much slower pace than healthcare costs are causing many people to face difficulty in affording out-of-pocket spending (Kaiser Family Foundation, 2011).

Government programs have been growing. For example, Medicare and Medicaid account for a significant share of healthcare spending, but have increased at a slower rate than private insurance. Medicare per capita spending has grown at a slightly lower rate, on average, than private health insurance spending, at about 6.8 vs. 7.1% annually respectively between 1998 and 2008. Medicaid expenditures, similarly, have grown at a slower rate than private spending, though enrollment in the program has increased during the current economic recession, which may result in increased Medicaid spending figures soon (Kaiser Family Foundation, 2011).

Methods to control healthcare expenditures are needed. Factors driving the growth in spending are:

- Technology and prescription drugs—New medical technology and prescription drugs are leading contributors to the increase in overall health spending. Some analysts state that the availability of more expensive, state-of-the-art technological services and new drugs fuel healthcare spending not only because the development costs of these products must be recouped by industry, but also because they generate consumer demand for more intense, costly services even if they are not necessarily cost-effective.
- Chronic disease—Health care in the United States has changed dramatically over the past century with longer life spans and greater chronic illnesses causing increased demands on the healthcare system, particularly treatment of ongoing illnesses and long-term care services such as nursing homes; it is estimated that healthcare costs for chronic disease treatment account for over 75% of national health expenditures.
- Aging of the population—Health expenses have increased as the baby boomers began qualifying for Medicare in 2011 and many of the costs are shifted to the public sector. Yet the aging of the population contributes minimally to the high growth rate of healthcare spending.
- Administrative costs—It is estimated that at least 7% of healthcare expenditures are for administrative costs (e.g., marketing, billing) and this portion is much lower in the Medicare program (<2%), which is operated by the federal government. The mixed public-private system creates overhead costs and large profits that are causing increases in healthcare spending.

(Kaiser Family Foundation, 2011)

Four major factors make up the healthcare system: (1) healthcare purchasers, which include employers, governments, and individuals; (2) medical insurance groups, which receive money from the purchasers and reimburse the providers; (3) governments, which are both insurers and purchasers through the Medicare and Medicaid programs; and (4) payers, which are both purchasers and insurers. Healthcare providers include physicians, nurses, and other healthcare professionals, along with hospitals, nursing homes, home care agencies, and pharmacies. Healthcare suppliers include the pharmaceutical, medical suppliers, and computer industries. Each dollar spent on healthcare services is an expense to payers and a source of income to providers and suppliers. Payers would like to reduce healthcare costs, whereas providers and suppliers generally resist cost containment (Bodenheimer, 2005).

Seventy-five percent of people in the United States who are younger than age 65 have private health insurance, which is mainly obtained through their place of work. Health insurance is usually provided through a managed care organization such as a health maintenance organization (HMO), preferred provider organization (PPO), or point-of-service plan (POS). For those persons who are older than 65 years, and for those who are disabled, Medicare—a federally funded program—provides health care. Medicaid—a program jointly funded by federal and state governments—provides health care for low-income individuals and families (CDC, 2004a). In 2010, the percentage of people without health insurance was 16.3 percent of the total U.S. population. Among the non-elderly, 18.4% of individuals were uninsured in 2010. During 2010, 49.9 million people were without insurance. Young adults are the age group least likely to have health insurance. However, 18–24 year olds were the only age group to experience a significant increase in the percentage with health insurance over the past year, from 70.7% in 2009 to 72.8% in 2010. This is a two percentage point increase in the share of adults 18–24 with coverage and represents 500,000 more young adults with health insurance. The Affordable Care Act allows children to remain on their parents' plans until age 26, and this policy took effect for insurance plan renewals beginning on September 23, 2010. The percentage of children under age 18 without health insurance in 2010 was 9.8%. The uninsured rate for children has decreased significantly from 12.0% in 1999, due to the substantial expansion of coverage in response to the Children's Health Insurance Program (CHIP). Employer-sponsored insurance continues to be the largest source of health insurance coverage in 2010, covering 55.3% of the population, a decline from 56.1% in 2009 and 64.1% in 1999. Uninsured rates for Hispanics (30.7%) and blacks (20.8%) are higher than for non-Hispanic whites (11.7%) (U.S. Census Bureau, 2011b).

SWEDEN

The kingdom of Sweden is a Nordic country in Scandinavia, in Northern Europe. The present king is Carl XVI Gustaf, and the prime minister is Goran Persson. This country, having a subarctic climate, has light all summer, but very little light during the winter. It is divided into 21 different counties, each with a county administration board and a county council. Each council, in turn, is divided into many municipalities. In 2004, there were 290 municipalities in Sweden. Sweden has a very high standard of living because of its high-tech capitalism and an extensive social welfare system (Government Offices of Sweden, Ministry of Health and Social Affairs, 2004).

Sweden has one of the highest levels of health care in the world, a very low infant mortality rate, and a high average life expectancy. Those in the population who have chronic illnesses have a good quality of life due to the country's excellent health care. Death rates from diseases such as diabetes and heart disease are declining. The older adult population is growing, and more people are able to live a higher quality of life than in previous years (Government Offices of Sweden, Ministry of Health and Social Affairs, 2004).

Healthcare System

The goal of the Swedish healthcare system is for the entire population to have equal access to good health care, which is provided to all citizens based on need, and funded by the Swedish government. The government health welfare system includes health and medical care, care of the elderly, pharmaceutical care, psychiatric care, and dental care. The healthcare system is directed by the Medical Responsibility Board, the Pharmaceutical Benefits Board, the Medical Products Agency, the National Board of Health and Welfare, the Swedish Council on Technology Assessment in Health Care, and the state-owned National Corporation of Swedish Pharmacies (Government Offices of Sweden, Ministry of Health and Social Affairs, 2004).

Health care is administered by 21 different county councils throughout the country. Eighty-nine percent of the councils' budgets is used for health and dental care. Municipalities are responsible for care of the elderly and psychiatric care. For those needing psychiatric care, the municipalities also take care of their housing, employment, and financial support. Healthcare agencies within Sweden consist of 9 regional hospitals, 70 county and provincial hospitals, and 1000 health centers. Expenditures on health care amount to 9.1% of the GDP, which is equal to $196.8 billion. The out-of-pocket costs paid by patients represent 15% of the total healthcare expenditures (Government Offices of Sweden, Ministry of Health and Social Affairs, 2004).

There are different categories of charges for health care within the Swedish healthcare system:

■   Outpatient healthcare charges. Charges are applied to visits to a district nurse, doctor, or specialist. Costs vary among the different councils and depend on the type of healthcare provider used. The maximum that any one person pays for health visits per year is 900 SEK ($115); this maximum cost also includes children younger than age 18 within the same family.
■   Pharmaceutical charges. The maximum cost per year for medications is 1800 SEK ($230). After this cost is reached, a free pass is given, which is good for 12 months from the date of the first purchase.

- Charges for a portion of dental treatments. These charges vary depending on the type of treatment and materials used. This category also includes orthodontia work.
- Costs for inpatient care. When a patient is admitted to a hospital, the local council can charge the patient a maximum of 80 SEK ($10.24) per day (Government Offices of Sweden, Ministry of Health and Social Affairs, 2004).

Sweden has an extensive social welfare system in which the government pays for child care, maternity and paternity leave, healthcare costs above a ceiling amount, retirement pensions, and sick leave. Parents get 480 days paid leave of absence from their jobs from the time of the birth of a child to his or her eighth year. Child care is free and guaranteed for all children 1–5 years old. For the aging adult, the Swedish Social Security Insurance Agency provides an old-age pension. It also provides for loss of income if a person is unable to work because of illness or because of caring for a child (Government Offices of Sweden, Ministry of Health and Social Affairs, 2004).

During the 1990s, Sweden's welfare state was in crisis due to economic challenges and lack of political support. Some spending cuts and reforms were made, but the healthcare system was left mostly intact. For the first time, however, the private healthcare sector competed with the public healthcare providers. The new private healthcare services (which represent 5% to 15% of all health care) began to somewhat undermine the egalitarian system of equal quality health care for all the citizens. At present there are choices of health services, and wealthier citizens often use private healthcare services while lower-income individuals use the public health services (Government Offices of Sweden, Ministry of Health and Social Affairs, 2004).

Statistics

The country of Sweden has a population of 9.5 million people. Its gross national product per capita is $27,271, which is ranked as the 26th highest in the world. Life expectancy at birth is 78 years for males and 83 years for females. Healthy life expectancy is 71.9 years for men and 74.8 years for females. The infant mortality rate (prior to 12 months of age) is 3 deaths per 100,000 live births, which is among the lowest in the world. The child mortality rate (prior to 5 years of age) is 5 deaths per 100,000 males and 3 deaths per 100,000 females. Total health expenditures per capita amount to $2512. The total fertility rate is 1.6. Because Sweden has socialized medicine, the government pays 85.3% of the total health expenditures incurred by the country's citizens. The remaining 14.7% of healthcare expenditures is paid privately in the form of out-of-pocket payments. Approximately 23% of the Swedish population is 60 years old or older (WHO, 2005).

Dental Care

The dental health of Sweden has improved considerably for all age groups over the last few decades. The number of children who need tooth fillings has declined, as has the number of older adults who need total tooth extractions. Many differences persist in the level of dental care among county councils, however. The criteria for good dental care are as follows:

- Having high standards with a particular emphasis on preventive care
- Satisfying safety concerns
- Being easily accessible
- Respecting patients' rights
- Having good communication between patients and dental healthcare personnel (WHO, 2005)

Mental Health

The Swedish government takes responsibility for providing mental health care as a part of basic health and medical care. Patients with slight or moderate mental health needs can get care from primary care healthcare providers. Compulsory mental health care is regulated by the Compulsory Mental Care Act.

Under this act, patients with serious mental health problems are treated in a special psychiatric care setting, even if they refuse care. This is especially true if the individual threatens the personal safety, physical safety, or mental health of others. Forensic mental health care includes care for people who have committed serious crimes and for those who suffer from mental illness (Government Offices of Sweden, Ministry of Health and Social Affairs, 2004).

Sex Education

Sweden is a pioneer country in terms of family planning. In Sweden, attitudes toward teenage sex education are considered liberal. Sex education is a high priority and has been taught in schools since the 1950s. Since 1975, abortion has been free and given on demand. Contraceptive counseling is free, and Planned Parenthood services are available in youth clinics. Screening for sexually transmitted diseases is included in these services as well. Contraception and emergency contraception are low in cost and sold over the counter. Teenage pregnancy is rare. Since the 1990s, however, the Swedish economy has been stagnant and rates of teen abortions, sexually transmitted diseases, smoking, and drug use have increased (Edgargth, 2002).

JAPAN

Background

Japan (also known as "Nippon") is an island-nation, made up of four main islands and 4000 smaller islands located in the Pacific Ocean, east of the Sea of Japan, China, North Korea, South Korea, and Russia, and north of Taiwan. The four largest islands—Honshu, Hokkaido, Kyushu, and Shikoku—account for 97% of Japan's area. Most of the islands are mountainous, and many are volcanic. Approximately 70% to 80% of the country is covered with forests and mountains and, therefore, is unsuitable for agriculture, industry, or residential use; as a consequence, the habitable areas, which are mainly located on the coasts, have very high population density. The population of Japan exceeds 127 million—making Japan home to the world's tenth largest population. Tokyo, the capital city, in combination with its surrounding smaller cities, has a population of more than 30 million, making it the largest metropolitan area in the world.

Japan is organized into 47 prefectures, each of which is overseen by an elected governor, legislature, and administrative bureaucracy. Each prefecture is divided into cities, towns, and villages. Japan has a constitutional monarchy with very little power, and an elected parliament, called the Diet. The prime minister of Japan is the head of state.

Until recently, Japan had the world's second largest economy, but China has now taken its place in the number 2 spot, making Japan the third largest economy. (The United States remains the largest economy.) Japan is the world's fourth largest exporter and fifth largest importer. It is the only Asian country in the G8 (Group of Eight) and currently serves as a nonpermanent member of the UN Security Council. Japan officially renounced its right to declare war but still maintains a large military for peacekeeping and self-defense purposes. It is a developed country with a very high standard of living.

Japan has the world's highest life expectancy and the third lowest infant mortality rate. The country's unemployment rate is at 4%, and Japan's workers get the highest salary per hour in the world. Some of the largest businesses in Japan include Toyota, Nintendo, Canon, Honda, Sony Panasonic, Sharp, and Japan Oil. In addition, Japan is one of the world's leaders in scientific research, including technology, machinery and biomedical research.

Population

Within Japan's population of 127.3 million, the largest group comprises the Yamoto people, the main ethnic groups are the Ainu and Ryukyuan peoples, and the main social ethnic group is the Burakumin.

Today many young Japanese choose not to marry and have children, and the population is expected to drop to 100 million by 2050. As of 2008, Japan's per capita GDP was $34,200. Approximately 84% to 96% of the population practice both Buddhism and Shintoism; a small minority practice Christianity, Taoism, Confucianism, or Buddhism. Most people speak Japanese, and most children today learn both Japanese and English in school. Approximately 75.9% of Japanese children finish high school and attend a university or trade school. The educational system is very competitive, particularly for entrance into universities (CIA, 2010; WHO, 2010).

Health and Health Care

Japan has the highest life expectancy rates in the world: 79 years for males and 86 years for females. The leading cause of death in people younger than age 30 is suicide; in 2009, the number of suicides in Japan exceeded 30,000 for the twelfth straight year. The infant mortality rate is 2.8 deaths per 1000 live births, also one of the lowest rates in the world. The number of physicians per 10,000 people is 21.

Government health expenditures represent 17.9% of total government expenditures. In 2006, total per capita expenditures for health amounted to $2514, compared to a gross national income per capita of $32,840. Mandatory universal healthcare coverage is provided to all residents by a national, employer-based insurance system. Medical care is based on cost sharing, but is free for those on welfare support and living below the poverty line. Long-term care for everyone older than age 65 covers home care, respite care, or institutional care, which is financed by public and private buyers, with premiums based on income and ability to pay. Cash payments are given to mothers to cover pregnancy care because there is no maternity care health insurance coverage.

Japan provides universal coverage to all residents through three broad categories of insurance: employer-based insurance, national insurance, and insurance for the elderly. These programs are financed primarily by the national government, private employers, and individual coinsurance payments, but the services are delivered through a mostly privately operated hospital and clinic system. All programs cover a broad range of services, including inpatient and outpatient care, dental care, and some pharmaceuticals. The programs cover little preventive care, however. All programs place a cap on the amount of out-of-pocket spending health consumers may incur in a year (CIA, 2010; NationMaster.com, 2010; WHO, 2010).

Healthcare System

Japan's healthcare system is characterized by universal coverage; free choice of healthcare providers for patients; a multi-payer, employment-based system of financing; and a predominant role for private hospitals and fee-for-service practices. Virtually all residents of Japan are covered without regard to any medical problems; that is, predisposing conditions or risks for illnesses do not affect coverage. Premiums are based on income and ability to pay. Control of the delivery of care is left largely to medical professionals, and there appears to be no public concern about healthcare rationing (CIA, 2010; WHO, 2010).

The healthcare system in Japan provides healthcare services, including screening examinations for particular diseases. Patients pay 30% of the cost of prenatal care and infectious disease control, and the government pays the remaining 70%. Payment for personal medical services is offered through a universal healthcare insurance system that provides relative equality of access, with fees set by a government committee. People who do not have insurance through their employers can participate in a national health insurance program administered by local governments. Patients are free to select physicians or facilities of their choice and cannot be denied coverage. Hospitals, by law, must be run as nonprofit entities and be managed by physicians (CIA, 2010; WHO, 2010).

Japan has 15.8 inpatient hospital beds per 1000 persons. In contrast to the high number of hospital beds, the country has only 21 physicians per 10,000 people. In 2007, Japan had 95 nurses per 10,000 people.

The country has a low rate of hospital admissions; once hospitalized, however, patients tend to spend comparatively long periods of time in the hospital, notwithstanding low hospital staffing ratios. In Japan, the average hospital stay is 36 nights, compared to 6 nights in the United States (CIA, 2010; WHO, 2010).

All residents of Japan are required to be enrolled in one of the Japanese insurance programs. In contrast, foreigners living in Japan are recommended to join the national health scheme but are not forced to do so. There are a total of eight health insurance systems divided into two categories, Employee Health Insurance and National Health Insurance. National Health Insurance is generally reserved for self-employed people and students, whereas social insurance is normally for corporate employees. National Health Insurance can be broken down into two groups: National Health Insurance for each city, town, or village, and the National Health Insurance Union (CIA, 2010).

Services are provided either through regional/national public hospitals or through private hospitals/clinics, and patients have universal access to any facility, although hospitals tend to charge higher fees to those patients who arrive without a referral. Compared to the United States, Japan has about three times as many hospitals per capita. Japanese patients visit the hospital 14 times per year, on average, more than four times as often as Americans do. Due to large numbers of people visiting hospitals and doctors for relativity minor problems, space can be an issue in some regions (CIA, 2010).

Japan Nuclear Concerns

According WHO (2011), radiation-related health consequences remain a serious concern for the Japanese people. These health risks are dependent upon exposure, which takes into account factors such as amount and type of radiation, weather conditions, proximity to nuclear power plants, and amount of time spent in irradiated areas. The Fukushima Daiichi nuclear power plant experienced serious leakage from the tsunami and earthquake of March 11, 2011. Those persons living between 20 and 30 kilometers from the plant were asked to evacuate the area, and risks of exposure included food contamination (WHO, 2011).

UNITED KINGDOM

The United Kingdom of Great Britain and Northern Ireland is a country located in Western Europe. A member of the European Union, the nation is usually known as the United Kingdom, or inaccurately known as Great Britain, Britain, or England. The United Kingdom has four parts consisting of England, Wales, and Scotland (all located on the Island of Great Britain) and Northern Ireland (located on the island of Ireland). The capital and largest city is London. As of January 2012, England's government was headed by Prime Minister David Cameron (the leader of the Conservative Party) and Queen Elizabeth II. The queen's role is mainly ceremonial; the U.K. government is a constitutional monarchy with executive power given to the prime minister.

Population

In 2010, the population of the United Kingdom totaled approximately 63 million. Life expectancy is 78 years for men and 82 years for females. Total expenditures on health as a percentage of the GDP amounted to 9.3% in 2009. On a per capita basis, $3399 is spent on health care annually.

The United Kingdom is a leading world financial power and trading center, with a capitalist economy. The country's economy is ranked fourth largest in the world, with a per capita income of $36,240. During the past 20 years, the government has decreased private ownership and has continued the growth in the direction of a welfare state. The United Kingdom produces 60% of its food and needs through the efforts of only 1% of its labor force. It has coal, natural gas, and oil supplies available from domestic sources. Insurance, banking, and other business services provides for the high per capita incomes in the country. The United Kingdom is Europe's largest manufacturer of cars, armaments, computers, petroleum products, televisions, and mobile phones. It is ranked sixth in the world for tourism. Languages spoken are mainly English, but other indigenous languages include Welsh, Scottish Gaelic, Irish Gaelic, Cornish, Lowland Scots, Romany, and British Sign Language.

Healthcare System

The National Health System (NHS) was established in 1948 to provide free health care for all residents of the United Kingdom. It was designed to be free at the point of need, meaning that every time a resident needs to go to the doctor or receive inpatient hospital treatment, it is provided free of charge. This system is funded by federal taxation and run by the Department of Health. In addition, private healthcare providers are available; people pay for such services either through their insurance or as out-of-pocket expenses at the time of use (BBC, 2005).

Funding for health care comes from direct taxation. The 2008–2009 budget equated to £1980 ($3.11) for every person in the United Kingdom (NHS, 2009). As of 2009, the prescription charge for medication in England was £7.20 ($11.31); the equivalent charge was £4 ($6.28) in Scotland, and prescription medications in Wales and Northern Ireland were free. All people older than 60 years; children 16 years or younger, or younger than 19 years if in a full-time educational program; those who have certain medical conditions; and those who are considered very low income are exempt from all healthcare payments. NHS dental services had been reduced as of 2008. Optical exams are free for everyone and there are vouchers for free glasses for those who qualify (NHS, 2009).

The basic concepts underlying the U.K. healthcare system are as follows (Light, 2003):

- Health care should be "free at the point of service." No copayments are needed for services.
- Health care is funded through income taxes. The U.K. people believe that income taxes are more equitable and cost-effective than insurance-based health care as in the United States.
- A strong primary healthcare base should be established for the NHS. Every U.K. resident should be able to choose a physician or healthcare service. The system also provides general practitioners (physicians) with incentives to practice in underserved areas.
- Reductions in the inequalities of health care have been made. Areas that have greater health problems and are poorer are now getting more funding.
- Bonuses are given to general practitioners who reach population-based targets for health prevention.
- All subspecialists are paid on the same salary scale.
- Basic prescription drugs are price controlled, while research that produces new drugs is rewarded. The government works out an agreement with the private pharmaceutical companies to create price controls for drugs.

In October 2006, the number of primary healthcare trusts (PCTs) in the United Kingdom was reduced from 303 to 152 in an attempt to bring services closer together and cut costs. PCTs oversee 29,000 general practitioners and 18,000 NHS dentists, and they control 80% of the total NHS budget. As of April 2008, every adult in the United Kingdom was eligible for a free health screening to check for heart disease, stroke, diabetes, and kidney disease under a new government plan (NHS, 2009).

During the last few years, the private sector has funded some of the buildings and structures within the NHS, and in addition some local communities are currently making some of their own healthcare decisions. Since 1997, a change in philosophy toward healthcare management has emphasized more partnerships and comprehensive planning. Although there are differences in the healthcare system within each country in the United Kingdom, there is a single secretary of state for health, who must answer to the U.K. parliament. The Department of Health is responsible for local planning, regulation, inspection, and policy development. There are also 28 strategic health authorities who manage the health care of their respective regions and are considered the link between the Department of Health and the NHS (BBC, 2005).

Healthcare services are classified as either primary or secondary, and are managed by the local NHS organizations called trusts. The primary trusts are often outsourced to private companies. Primary care is delivered by local general practitioners, surgeons, dentists, and opticians (i.e., PCTs). The PCTs, who decide the amount and quality of services provided by hospitals, receive approximately 75% of the overall NHS budget. In addition, the PCTs control hospital funding. Hospitals and specialized services, such as mental health, are managed by organizations called acute trusts. Usually, outpatient services such as surgery and ophthalmology have long waiting lists.

Private health care offers similar services, and patients who use this system of care generally pay through private health insurance. Insurance premiums are paid by either employers or individuals who pay out of pocket by themselves. There are more than 300 private hospitals in the United Kingdom (BBC, 2005).

The U.K. healthcare system is currently far from ideal. Regarding the current situation of the NHS, Light (2003) reports that the current system is no longer sustainable and no longer affordable. If services were limited to only emergency and welfare service, however, the NHS approach would be economically feasible. In the future, specialty care services are likely to be united with primary care services. Muller (2002) states that the system is failing to meet expectations because of underfunding and the fact that it is centrally controlled.

Stevens (2004) reports that the NHS operates with outdated old buildings and inadequate equipment. Health professionals are in short supply, with 2 physicians available per 1000 people in the United Kingdom, as compared to 2.8 in the United States and 3.3 in France and Germany. Long waiting lists are the norm for routine surgery.

In 2003, U.K. taxes increased and policy makers began to pay more attention to improving the healthcare system. Recently some especially pressing issues were identified, and the following changes were made as a result (Stevens, 2004):

■ The supply of physicians and nurses was increased by 55%.
■ The infrastructure was modernized. Hospitals were rebuilt and record keeping, prescriptions, and scheduling were transferred to an electronic system.
■ In-service learning help for doctors, nurses, and other health professionals was increased, leading to great improvements in the new knowledge and technology of healthcare delivery.
■ National standards were developed for the types of care given to patients. Goals were set to improve health statistics for specific illnesses, such as reductions in rates of heart and cancer disease, increased access to care for all residents, and reductions in infant mortality rates.
■ Physicians are now subject to mandatory relicensing every five years. Quality assurance is used to upgrade standards of care.
■ Healthcare providers are individually rated by performance and the results are published as public information.
■ Financial bonuses are given to healthcare providers who are doing an excellent job.
■ Healthcare funding now goes to PCTs directly, which purchase some managed care for patient care.
■ Patients are given a choice of any provider, which may be public, private, or not for profit.
■ The NHS has begun using the diagnosis-related group (DRGs) system to regulate pricing for services.
■ The NHS is being held accountable to local citizens for its budget, spending, and services.

Medicines are the most frequently and widely used NHS treatment and account for more than 12% of total NHS expenditures. A pilot program involving half of the PCTs in England is testing out individual budgets for health care, including medications. In this program, patients are offered more choice and control over their health care through the country's first direct payment scheme. Direct payments for health care are given to individual patients to allow them to purchase the care they need (NHS, 2009).

Health Issues

Within the United Kingdom, there is a persistent disparity in health care and health issues. Scotland has the lowest life expectancy among the U.K. countries, at 74.6 years for men and 77.2 years for women, compared with 77.2 years for men and 81.5 years for women in England. The rate of hospital inpatient admissions varies from 205 per 1000 population in Northern Ireland, to 135 per 1000 population in Scotland. The death rate from heart disease is highest in Scotland and lowest in England. From 1996 to 2006, smoking rates among teens and young adults dropped 18% in England, 15% in Scotland, and 12% in Wales. A greater number of women are breastfeeding, with the highest rates (77%) seen in England and Wales; in contrast, only 64% of women breastfeed their children in Northern Ireland. The infant mortality rate in the United Kingdom is 1.8 deaths per 1000 live births, which is higher than the IMR in many countries in the European Union, yet lower than the rate in the United States. The HIV rate within the general population is 2 cases per 1000 adults (13–49 years) (NHS, 2009).

Within the United Kingdom, the major health issues are cancer, coronary heart disease, stroke, accidents, and mental illness. Newer health problems include HIV/AIDs and Creutzfeldt-Jacob disease (Sproston & Primatesta, 2003). Cardiovascular disease (CVD) and stroke are two of the major causes of death or disability on an annual basis.

A goal was set to reduce CVD and stroke death rates for people younger than age 75 by two-fifths by 2010. In a study conducted by the U.K. government, 13.6% of males and 13% of females reported a CVD or stroke diagnosis. Incidence increased as household income decreased (poorer people had greater incidence).

Heart attack deaths have decreased by 50% in less than a decade, according to a major study of over 800,000 patients in England. The research has been extensively reported, with news sources suggesting a range of possible reasons, such as better treatments and a reduction in numbers of people smoking. A recent study found that in England the death rate from heart attacks halved between 2002 and 2010. The researchers calculated that just over half this decline was caused by fewer people having heart attacks and just under half by more people who had heart attacks surviving (NHS, 2012).

Deaths from heart and circulatory disease are falling, but it remains the UK's biggest killer. In 2009, over 180,000 people died from cardiovascular disease (CVD) in the UK—one in three of all deaths. Twenty-eight percent of premature deaths in men and almost 20% of premature deaths in women were from CVD in 2009. (British Heart Foundation, 2010).

Stroke is the single largest cause of severe disability and the third most common cause of death in the United Kingdom. Each year 11,000 people die of stroke in England and Wales. Most people diagnosed with CVD or stroke take aspirin and lipid-reducing medications (Sproston & Primatesta, 2003; Youman, Wilson, Harraf, & Kalra, 2003).

There are 2.6 million people who have been diagnosed with diabetes in the UK (2009). By 2025, there will be more than four million people with diabetes in the UK. It is estimated that there are up to half a million more people in the UK who have diabetes, but have not been diagnosed. This gives a UK average prevalence of 4%. The rate is also increasing in children. There are over 22,000 people under the age of 17 with diabetes in England with 97% having type 1 diabetes, 1.5 percent have type 2 and 1.5 percent have another type of diabetes (Diabetes in the UK, 2010).

Hypertension (high blood pressure) was diagnosed in those people with a systolic blood pressure of 140 mm Hg or greater and a diastolic blood pressure of 90 mm Hg or more. Uncontrolled hypertension is the greatest cause of stroke (Sproston & Primatesta, 2003). Lloyd, Schmieder, and Marchant (2003) report that in the United Kingdom approximately 5.7 million adults, or 12% of the population older than age 16 years, have a blood pressure exceeding 160/95 mm Hg. In addition, 10.3 million (21%) have a blood pressure of 140/90 mm Hg. An estimated 58,000 cardiovascular problems occur in these patients because of hypertension, which would not exist if their blood pressure were within normal limits. Failure to control blood pressure contributes to huge monetary costs to the NHS for treating cardiovascular problems.

Cancer causes problems for one in four people, with the most common form (one third) being lung cancer. Eighty percent to 90% of all lung cancers are attributable to smoking. In women, 20% of all cancer cases involve breast cancer: England has one of the highest rates of breast cancer in all of Western Europe. Cancer in the United Kingdom is one of the three leading causes of death for people of all ages, except for preschool children. Cancer causes approximately 62,000 deaths per year (Sproston & Primatesta, 2003).

Smoking has been identified as the single greatest preventable cause of illness and premature death in the United Kingdom. In this country, the overall smoking rates for all ages are 27% of men and 24% of women, though these rates are higher among younger adults and lower among persons 75 years or older. Cigarette smoking in the United Kingdom has been found to increase as household income decreases (Sproston & Primatesta, 2003).

Alcohol consumption has been reported by 42% of men and 26% of women in the United Kingdom, who stated that they consumed alcohol at least three days per week. Statistics on alcohol reveal that in 2002, 47% of men drank more than four units of alcohol at least one day in the previous week, and 22% of women drank at least three units of alcohol one day in the past week. Total expenditures on alcohol amounted to 5.7% of family income in 2003 (Sproston & Primatesta, 2003).

Overweight and obesity have been diagnosed in 65.4% of men and 55.5% of women in the United Kingdom. Overweight is defined as 25 kg/mm^2 and obesity as more than 30 kg/mm^2. Obesity rates are higher in lower-income households (Sproston & Primatesta, 2003).

Accidents account for 10,000 deaths per year in England. England has lower death rates from car accidents than anywhere else in Europe, but rates of death of children from pedestrian accidents are among the highest in Europe. Road accident rates are higher in rural areas than in larger cities. Older adults are at risk for death and disability from falls. Osteoporosis affects more women and contributes to the number of broken bones, especially wrists and hips, incurred by this population (Sproston & Primatesta, 2003).

Infant and Child Health

In 2010 the infant mortality rate was 4.2 deaths per 1000 live births, the lowest ever recorded for England and Wales. Infant mortality rates were high among babies of mothers aged under 20 years and over 40 years at 5.6 and 5.8 deaths per 1000 live births respectively. Perinatal mortality rates were also higher for mothers in the "under 20" and "40 and over" age groups, at 8.3 and 10.2 deaths per 1000 live births respectively. Very low birthweight babies (under 1500 grams) had the highest infant and perinatal mortality rates, at 164.7 and 250.9 deaths per 1000 live births respectively. Infant mortality rates were highest for babies registered jointly by parents living at different addresses and those registered solely by their mother, at 5.5 and 5.4 deaths per 1000 live births respectively (Office of National Statistics UK, 2011).

Herbal Supplements Use by Adults

The use of herbal extracts in the United Kingdom, especially by older adults, has been increasing. A recent survey found that 15% of those persons older than 65 years used over-the-counter herbal medicine during the last 12 months. The herbs are used to treat existing health problems, prevent illness, and promote general health. Older adults should report the use of herbs to their doctors, of course, and doctors should have good information about potential herb and drug interactions (Canter & Ernst, 2004).

CONCLUSION

Table 2-4 compares population and health statistics for Japan, Sweden, the United Kingdom, and the United States (Kaiser Family Foundation, 2011).

| TABLE 2-4 |

Healthcare Statistics for Japan, Sweden, the United Kingdom, and the United States

Indicator	Date/ Date Range	Data Type	Data Japan	Sweden	United Kingdom	United States
Demography and Population						
Population	2011	Number	126,475,664	9,088,728	62,698,362	313,232,044
Adult sex ratio	2011	Number	1.02	1.02	1.03	1.00
Median age	2011	Number	44.8	42.0	40.0	36.9
Population younger than age 15	2010	%	13%	17%	18%	20%
Urban population	2010	%	86%	84%	80%	79%
Birth rate	2011	Rate per 1000	7.31	10.18	12.29	13.83
Total fertility rate	2011	Number	1.21	1.67	1.91	2.06
Contraceptive prevalence rate	2000– 2010	%	54.3%	NA	84.0%	78.6%
Death rate	2011	Rate per 1000	10.09	10.20	9.33	8.38
Infant mortality rate	2011	Rate per 1000	2.78	2.74	4.62	6.06
Female infant mortality rate	2011	Rate per 1000	2.58	2.57	4.15	5.37
Male infant mortality rate	2011	Rate per 1000	2.98	2.90	5.07	6.72
Under-five mortality rate	2009	Rate per 1000	3	3	6	8
Maternal mortality ratio	2008	Rate per 100,000	6	5	12	24
Life expectancy: female	2009	Number	86	83	82	81
Life expectancy: male	2009	Number	80	79	78	76
Population growth rate	2011	%	-0.28%	0.16%	0.56%	0.96%
Income and the Economy						
GDP per capita	2009	U.S. dollars	$32,418	$37,377	$35,155	$45,989
GNI per capita	2009	U.S. dollars	$33,440	$38,050	$35,860	$45,640
Country income classification	As of July 2011	Text	High income	High income	High income	High income

(continues)

TABLE 2-4

Healthcare Statistics for Japan, Sweden, the United Kingdom, and the United States (continued)

			Data			
Indicator	*Date/ Date Range*	*Data Type*	*Japan*	*Sweden*	*United Kingdom*	*United States*
HIV/AIDS						
People living with HIV/AIDS	Data from most recent year available	Number	8100	8100	85,000	1,200,000
Adults living with HIV/AIDS	2009	Number	8100	8100	85,000	1,200,000
Adult HIV/AIDS prevalence rate	2009	%	<0.1%	0.1%	0.2%	0.6%
Women living with HIV/AIDS	Number of women living with HIV/AIDS and women as a percentage of adults living with HIV/AIDS, 2009	%	33%	31%	31%	26%
Men living with HIV/AIDS	Number of men living with HIV/AIDS and men as a percentage of adults living with HIV/AIDS, 2009	%	65%	69%	69%	77%
Children living with HIV/AIDS	2009	Number	NA	NA	NA	NA
AIDS deaths	2009	Number	<100	<100	<1000	17,000
AIDS orphans	2009	Number	NA	NA	NA	NA
Tuberculosis						
New TB cases	2009	Number	26,000	580	7400	13,000
People living with TB	2009	Number	33,000	750	9100	14,000
TB prevalence rate	2009	Rate per 100,000	26	8	15	5
TB death rate	2009	Rate per 100,000	1	0	1	0
TB incidence in HIV+ people	2009	Number	110	14	260	1300
TB incidence in HIV+ people per 100,000 population	2009	Rate per 100,000	0	0	0	0
HIV prevalence in incident TB cases	2009	%	0.4%	2.4%	3.5%	10.0%

TABLE 2-4

Healthcare Statistics for Japan, Sweden, the United Kingdom, and the United States *(continued)*

Indicator	Date/ Date Range	Data Type	Japan	Sweden	United Kingdom	United States
Other Diseases, Conditions, and Risk Indicators						
DTP3 immunization coverage rate	2009	%	98%	98%	93%	95%
Percent with water	2008	%	100%	100%	100%	99%
Access to sanitation	2008	%	100%	100%	100%	100%
Population undernourished	2005–2007	%	NA	NA	NA	NA
Low-birth-weight babies	2000–2009	%	8%	NA	8%	8%
Child malnutrition	2000–2009	%	NA	NA	NA	1.3%
Female prevalence of obesity	2005	%	2%	11%	24%	42%
Male prevalence of obesity	2005	%	2%	12%	22%	37%
Female prevalence of smoking	2006	%	13%	23%	24%	19%
Male prevalence of smoking	2006	%	42.4%	17.3%	26.1%	25.4%
Programs, Funding, and Financing						
Health expenditures per capita	2008	$	$2817	$3622	$3222	$7164
Total expenditures on health	2008	%	8.3%	9.4%	8.7%	15.2%
Government health expenditures as a percentage of total government expenditures	2008	%	17.9%	13.8%	15.1%	18.7%
Government health expenditures as a percentage of total health expenditures	2008	%	80.5%	78.1%	82.6%	47.8%
Social security expenditures on health	2008	%	81.5%	0.0%	0.0%	27.8%
Out-of-pocket expenditures on health	2008	%	80.6%	92.8%	63.7%	24.4%
Health Workforce and Capacity						
Physicians	2000–2010	Rate per 10,000	21	36	27	27
Nurses and midwives	2000–2010	Rate per 10,000	41	116	103	98
Community health workers	2000–2010	Rate per 10,000	NA	NA	NA	NA
Births attended by skilled health personnel	2000–2010	%	100%	NA	NA	99%
Hospital beds	2000–2009	Rate per 10,000	139	NA	39	31

This chapter has examined the health and health care of the countries of the United States, Sweden, Japan, and the United Kingdom. Included in this comparison were population statistics, types of government healthcare programs, economics and healthcare spending, and healthcare personnel.

STUDY QUESTIONS

1. Why do you think that the United States has the world's highest rate of obesity? How does this problem relate to chronic health diseases such as cardiovascular disease, hypertension, and diabetes?
2. In spite of the country having the highest level of per capita expenditures, why does the United States still have a relatively high rate of infant mortality as compared to other developed countries?
3. What are some reasons that contribute to Japan and Sweden having the world's best longevity rates? Even though it spends the most dollars per capita on health care, why is the United States so far behind in terms of longevity?
4. What are some health disparities within the United Kingdom, and how might they be solved?

CASE STUDY

The mortality rate for American Indians, which includes Alaskan Natives (Native Americans), has increased primarily due to the effects of type 2 diabetes. The U.S. Department of Indian Health Service has provided a Special Diabetes Program for Indians resulting in increased spending for health care, however, the rate for age-adjusted deaths has increased as compared to white Americans.

Infectious diseases are decreasing while chronic diseases, such as type 2 diabetes are increasing in this population. Data collected was mainly from Navaho Indians living in the western part of the United States. Other major health issues include obesity, cardiovascular diseases, smoking, and hypertension. Also discussed was the high rate of sedentary lifestyles as compared to historically much greater daily physical activities.

Reference

Kunitz, S. (2008). Changing patterns of mortality among American Indians. *American Journal of Public Health, 98*(3), 404–411.

Case Study Questions

1. Create a culturally congruent plan for reduction of exceptionally high levels of type 2 diabetes among American Indians/Alaskan Natives.
2. Why do American Indians have higher levels of increased smoking, obesity, and sedentary life styles, which contribute to the type 2 diabetes rates than whites?
3. Why is the Indian Health Service an important part of health care that is historically "owed" to American Indians/Alaskan Natives?

REFERENCES

BBC. (2005). Guide: How the healthcare system works in England. Retrieved from http://www.bbc.co.uk /dna/ocam/A2454978

Blumberg, S., Halfon, N., & Olson, L. (2004). National survey of early childhood health. *Pediatrics, 113*(6), 1899–1906.

Bodenheimer, T. (2005). High and rising health care costs. Part 1: Seeking an explanation. *Annals of Internal Medicine, 142*(10), 847–854.

British Heart Foundation (2010). CVD in the UK. Retrieved from http://www.bhf.org.uk/heart-health /statistics/mortality.aspx

Callahan, S. T., & Cooper, W. (2005). Uninsurance and health care access among young adults in the United States. *Pediatrics, 116*(1), 88–95.

Canter, P., & Ernst, E. (2004). Herbal supplement use by persons over 50 years in Britain. *Drugs and Aging, 21*(9), 597–605.

Centers for Disease Control and Prevention (CDC). (2004a). National Center for Health Statistics. Retrieved from http://www.cdc.gov/nchs/pubs/pubd/other/atlas/atlas.htm

Centers for Disease Control and Prevention (CDC). (2004b). National Center for Health Statistics. New chartbook examines health care utilization in America. Retrieved from www.cdc.gov/nchs /pressroom/04facts/healthcare.htm

Centers for Disease Control and Prevention (CDC). (2004c). National Center for Health Statistics. More children than ever had health insurance in 2003, but coverage for working-age adults declined. Retrieved from http://www.cdc.gov/nchs/pressroom/04news/insur2003.htm

Centers for Disease Control and Prevention (CDC). (2004d). National Center for Health Statistics. Almost half of Americans use at least one prescription drug, annual report on nation's health shows. Retrieved from http://www.cdc.gov/nchs/pressroom/04news/hus04.htm

Centers for Disease Control and Prevention (CDC). (2004e). National Center for Health Statistics. The state of aging and health in America 2004. Retrieved from http://www.cdc.gov/aging/pdf/State_of_ Aging_and_Health_in_America_2004.pdf

Centers for Disease Control and Prevention (CDC). (2004f). More than one third of U.S. adults use complementary and alternative medicine, according to new government survey. Retrieved from http://www .cdc.gov/nchs/pressroom/04news/adultsmedicine.htm

Centers for Disease Control and Prevention (CDC). (2008). Healthy People 2010. Retrieved from www .healthypeople.gov/

Centers for Disease Control and Prevention (CDC). (2009). Health, United States. Retrieved from http://cdc .gov/nchs/hus.htm

Centers for Disease Control and Prevention (CDC). (2010a). National healthcare disparities report 2010. Retrieved from http://www.ahrq.gov/qual/nhdr10/nhdr10.pdf

Centers for Disease Control and Prevention (CDC). (2010b). Healthy people 2010. Retrieved from http://www .cdc.gov/nchs/healthy_people/hp2010.htm

Centers for Disease Control and Prevention (CDC). (2010c). Leading causes of death in the United States. Retrieved from http://www.cdc.gov/nchs/fastats/lcod.htm

Central Intelligence Agency (CIA). (2009). The world factbook—United States. Retrieved from http://www .cia.gov/cia/publications/factbook/index.html

Central Intelligence Agency (CIA). (2010). The world factbook—Japan. Retrieved from http://www.cia.gov /cia/publications/factbook/index.html

Central Intelligence Agency (CIA). (2011). The world factbook: Infant mortality rate–country comparison. Retrieved from http://www.indexmundi.com/g/r.aspx?c=us&v=29

Diabetes in the U.K. (2010). Retrieved from http://www.diabetes.org.uk/Documents/Reports/Diabetes_in_the_UK_2010.pdf

Edgargth, K. (2002). Adolescent sexual health in Sweden. *Sexually Transmitted Infections, 78*(5), 352.

Flegel, K., Williamson, D., Pamuk, E., & Rosenberg, H. (2004). Estimating deaths attributable to obesity in the United States. *American Journal of Public Health, 94*(9), 1486–1489.

Friedland, R. (2005a, Spring). How Medicare works. *Generations,* 30–34.

Government Offices of Sweden, Ministry of Health and Social Affairs. (2004). Retrieved from http://www.sweden.gov.se/sb/d/2061

Institute of Medicine. (2011). Medication errors injure 1.5 million people and cost billions of dollars annually. Retrieved from http://www8.nationalacademies.org/onpinews/newsitem.aspx?RecordID=11623

Kaiser Family Foundation. (2011). State health facts. Retrieved from http://statehealthfacts.org/

Kunitz, S. (2008). Changing patterns of mortality among American Indians. *American Journal of Public Health, 98*(3), 404–411.

Lamm, R. & Blank. (2005). The challenge of an aging society. *The Futurist, July–August,* 23–27.

Lamster, I. (2004). Oral health care services for older adults: A looming crisis. *American Journal of Public Health, 94*(5), 699–701.

Light, D. (2003). Universal health care: Lessons from the British experience. *American Journal of Public Health, 93*(1), 25–30.

Lloyd, A., Schmieder, C., & Marchant, N. (2003). Financing and health costs of uncontrolled blood pressure in the United Kingdom. *Pharmacoeconomics, 21,* 33–34.

Muller, R. (2002). Enabling prospective health care: Great Britain's efforts to provide comprehensive health care. Retrieved from http://conferences.mc.duke.edu/privatesector/dpsc2002/bj.html

National Health Service (NHS). (2012). Massive decline in deadly heart attacks. Retrieved from http://www.nhs.uk/news/2012/01January/Pages/heart-attack-death-rate-reduction.aspx

National Health Service (NHS). (2009). About the NHS: Overview. Retrieved from http://www.nhs.uk/aboutNHSChoices/aboutnhschoices/Aboutus/Pages/improved-homepage.aspx

NationMaster.com. (2010). Retrieved from http://www.nationalmaster.com/country/ja-japan/hea-health

Office of National Statistics UK. (2011). Infant and perinatal mortality in England and Wales by social and biological factors, 2010. Retrieved from http://www.ons.gov.uk/ons/rel/child-health/infant-and-perinatal-mortality-in-england-and-wales-by-social-and-biological-factors/2010/index.html

Organisation for Economic Co-operation and Development (OECD). (2010). OECD health data. *OECD Health Statistics* [Database]. doi: 10.1787/data-00350-enped countries.

Peterson, L., Wright, S., & Peterson, E. (2002). Impact of race on cardiac care and outcomes in veterans with acute myocardial infarction. *Medical Care, 40*(suppl 1), 186–196.

Pew Hispanic Center (2011). Hispanics account for more than half of the nation's growth in a decade. Retrieved from http://www.pewhispanic.org/2011/03/24/hispanics-account-for-more-than-half-of-nations-growth-in-past-decade/

Reschovsky, J., & Staiti, A. (2005). Access and quality: Does rural America lag behind? *Health Affairs, 24*(4), 1128–1139.

Satcher, D., Fryer, G., McCann, J., Troutman, A., Woolf, S., & Rust, G. (2005). What if we were equal? A comparison of the black–white mortality gap in 1960 and 2000. *Health Affairs, 24*(2), 459–463.

Seminario, M. (2003, June). Workers at risk. The dangers on the job when the regulators don't try very hard. *Multinational Monitor,* 21–26.

Smedley, B., Stith, A., & Nelson, A. (Eds.). (2003). *Unequal treatment: Confronting racial and ethnic disparities in health care.* Institute of Medicine. Washington, DC: National Academies Press.

Sproston, K., & Primatesta, P. (Eds). (2003). *Health survey for England.* London: The Stationary Office.

Sridhar, D. (2005). *Inequality in the United States healthcare system: Human development report. 2005.* UNDP, pp. 1–42.

Stevens, S. (2004). Reform strategies for the English NHS. *Health Affairs, 23*(3), 37–44.

Sullivan Commission. (2004). Missing persons: Minorities in health professions. In *The Sullivan report*, pp. 1–208.

U.S. Census Bureau. (2010). Population profile. Retrieved from http://www.census.gov/population/www/pop-profile/natproj.html

U.S. Census Bureau. (2011a). Profile America facts for features. Retrieved from http://www.census.gov/newsroom/releases/archives/facts_for_features_special_editions/cb11-ff06.html

U.S. Census Bureau. (2011 b). Overview of the uninsured in the United States: A summary of the 2011 current population survey. Retrieved from http://aspe.hhs.gov/health/reports/2011/CPSHealthIns2011/ib.shtml

U.S. Department of Labor. (2011). U.S. Injuries, illnesses, and fatalities. Retrieved from www.bls.gov/IIF/

Vallarejo, D. (2003). The health of the U.S. farm workers. *Annual Review of Public Health, 24,* 175–193.

Weber, C. (2004). Update on immunizations for older adults. *Urologic Nursing, 24*(4), 352–353.

Wellman, N. (2004, Fall). Federal food and nutrition assistance programs for older people. *Generations,* 78–85.

Wise, P. (2004). The transformation of child health in the United States. *Health Affairs, 21*(3), 9–25.

World Health Organization (WHO). (2005). Sweden. Retrieved from http://www.who.int/countries

World Health Organization (WHO). (2010). Japan. Retrieved from http://www.who.int/countries/jpn/en/

World Health Organization (WHO). (2011). Japan nuclear concerns. Retrieved from http://www.who.int/hac/crises/jpn/faqs/en/index.html

Youman, P., Wilson, K., Harraf, F. & Kalra, L. (2003). The economic burden of stroke in the United Kingdom. *Pharmacoeconomics, 21*(Suppl. 1), 43–50.

*For a full suite of assignments and additional learning activities, use the access code located in the front of your book to visit this exclusive website: **http://go.jblearning.com/holtz**. If you do not have an access code, you can obtain one at the site.*

3

Developing Countries: Egypt, China, India, and South Africa

Carol Holtz
Ibrahim Elsawy

> *"It's immoral that people in Africa die like flies of diseases that no one dies of in the United States. And the more disease there is, the more political unrest there will be, leading to more Darfurs."*
>
> Former President Bill Clinton

OBJECTIVES

After completing this chapter, the reader will be able to:

1. Discuss family planning, infertility, abortion, and sterilization practices in Egypt, China, India, and South Africa.
2. Explain how communism affects health and health care in China.
3. Discuss women's rights issues in South Africa.
4. Compare the health and healthcare systems of Egypt, China, India, and South Africa.

INTRODUCTION

This chapter addresses the health conditions of four developing countries: Egypt, China, India, and South Africa. These countries were selected for examination because they differ in culture, economics, politics, geographic regions, and types of health care and health issues.

EGYPT

Background

Egypt (the Arab Republic of Egypt) is located in the far northeastern part of the African continent, bordered on the north by the Mediterranean Sea, on the east by the Red Sea, on the west by Libya, on the south by Sudan, and on the northeast by the Gaza Strip and Israel. Egypt is traversed by the Suez Canal, which is located between its Asian and African territories. The country's total land area is 1,002,450 square kilometers. Most of Egypt is located in Africa, but part of its land, the Sinai Peninsula, is located in Asia. The majority of its population of approximately 83 million people lives on the banks of the Nile River or on the coasts of the Mediterranean Sea, the Red Sea, and the Suez Canal. The largest defined landmass within Egypt is the Sahara Desert, which is very sparsely populated. The largest cities include Cairo (the capital), Alexandria, and other cities in the Nile Delta. Ninety-eight percent of the Egyptian population lives on just 4% of the country's land (Arab Republic of Egypt, Ministry of Foreign Affairs, 2010).

Most of Egypt's rainfall occurs during the winter months, with only 0.1 to 0.2 inches of precipitation falling each year. Before the construction of the Aswan Dam, the Nile River flooded annually, producing good soils and good harvests in its floodplains.

Arabic is the official language; English and French are the most commonly used foreign languages. The majority ethnic groups are Egyptian, Bedouin Arab, and Nubian. Education is compulsory for children aged 6–15 years, and the literacy rate is 58% ("About Egypt," 2010).

Egypt has a distinguished cultural heritage, accumulated over the thousands of years of its history. Each of the Egyptian successive civilizations (Pharaonic, Greco-Roman, Coptic, and Islamic) contributed to the areas of philosophy, literature, and the arts. Because of its long-held ties with Europe, Egypt has been a cultural pioneer in the modern Arab world. In 2002, with the support of the United Nations Educational, Scientific and Cultural Organization (UNESCO), the new Bibliotheca Alexandrina was inaugurated. This world-recognized special historical site is located in Alexandria. The goal of the reconstruction of the ancient Library of Alexandria was to revive the legacy of this universal center for science and knowledge ("About Egypt," 2010).

In terms of religion, the Egyptian population consists of 94% Muslims and 6% Christians. The two main Islamic institutions in Egypt are the oldest and the most important Islamic institutions in the country:

■ Al-Azhar, which was built by the Fatimids to spread the Shiite sect in North Africa. Later Salah El-Din converted it to Sunni University, which became one of the main pillars of Sunni Islam in the world.

■ Dar el Eftaa, founded in 1895 and headed by the Grand Mufti of Egypt.

The Coptic Orthodox Church, one of the oldest Christian churches in the world, and the Roman Orthodox Church of the Arab Republic of Egypt are located in Alexandria (Arab Republic of Egypt, Ministry of Foreign Affairs, 2010).

Economy

Table 3-1 presents statistics on Egypt's current economy.

TABLE 3-1

Egypt's Economy

GDP	$218.91 billion
GDP growth	5.2%/year
Inflation, GDP deflator	10.1%/year
Agriculture, value added	10% of GDP
Industry, value added	29% of GDP
Services and other revenue sources, value added	61% of GDP
Exports of goods and services	21% of GDP
Imports of goods and services	28% of GDP
Gross capital formation	19% of GDP

Source: World Bank, 2010.

Health

Table 3-2 presents population health statistics for Egypt.

Healthcare Systems

The majority of Egyptians have access to health care for basic health services, managed by the Ministry of Health and Population (MOHP), the Health Insurance Organization (HIO), private health practitioners, and nongovernmental organizations (NGOs). The HIO covers 45% of the population, and there is a growing and unregulated private healthcare sector. Pharmaceuticals account for nearly one-third of all healthcare costs (World Health Organization [WHO], 2011).

TABLE 3-2

Egypt's Population Health Statistics, 2011

Birth rate	28.9 per 1000
Underweight children	7.5%
Population younger than age 15 years	31.7%
Population 65 years or older	3.7%
Total births per woman	3
Adult literacy rate (among persons 15 years or older)	71%
Population with sustainable access to improved water sources	94%
Population with sustainable access to improved sanitation	94%
Smoking rate of adults	19%
Total government expenditure per capita on health	$124
Total government expenditure on health as a percentage of GDP	6.4%
Out-of-pocket expenditure on health per capita	58.7%
Human Resources (per 10,000)	
Physicians	28.3
Dentists	4.2
Pharmacists	16.7
Nurses and midwives	35.2
Hospital beds	17.3
Primary healthcare units and centers	0.7
Primary Health Care (per 100)	
Population with access to healthcare services	88
Contraception prevalence	57.6
Prenatal care	52
Births attended by skilled personnel	84
Health Status	
Life expectancy	72.3 years
Infant mortality rate (per 1000 live births)	17
Under-five mortality rate	21.8 per 1000
Maternal mortality rate	55 per 100,000
Probability of not reaching 40 years of age	10.3%
Smoking prevalence (among males 15 years or older)	40%

Source: WHO, 2011.

Communicable Diseases

Within the last decade there has been a huge decline in deaths from communicable diseases in Egypt, largely due to the high rate of vaccinations for preventable diseases. Hepatitis B and C continue to be problems, however. Schistosomiasis (a parasitic disease caused by flatworms), hepatitis C (affecting 9.8% of the general population), and tuberculosis are the top three infectious diseases found in Egypt today (WHO, 2011).

A study conducted in Egypt and supported by USAID to prevent typhoid fever in rural communities used the intervention of hand washing with soap. Studies indicate that 9000 to 42,000 cases of typhoid are reported in this country each year. Typhoid fever is transmitted by the fecal–oral route, so it is appropriate to build prevention strategies against this infection—yet only 40% of all households in Egypt had soap and water available for hand washing at the time the intervention was undertaken. The scarcity of water and problems with waste disposal are related issues for hand washing. As part of the intervention, proper hand washing techniques were taught and general education of disease transmission was performed. Results indicated improvement in hand washing rates in the rural Fayoum region of Egypt (Lohinivak, El-Sayeed, & Talaat, 2008).

Maternal and Infant Health

Despite health clinics that are accessible to the general public, maternal and infant mortality rates in Egypt are high, with an infant mortality rate of 17 deaths per 1000 live births and a maternal mortality rate of 55 deaths per 1000 live births. In addition, the 21.8 per 1000 death rate for children younger than age five is considered high. These rates reflect exceptionally high mortality rates among women and children in rural Upper Egypt. Child survival initiatives, such as cord care, delivery instrument antisepsis, and infant warming have reduced the rate of mortality of children younger than five years.

As is true in most developing countries, most births in Egypt take place in the home. A major contributing factor to maternal and infant morbidity and mortality is unhygienic conditions, which increase the likelihood of infections within both the mother and the newborn. Tetanus typhoid immunization is one method of reducing deaths due to tetanus, but many other infections can occur at the time of birth. Infection ranks third among the causes of maternal mortalities in Egypt. A cohort study explored the use of a clean delivery kit as a means of reducing infant and maternal infections. Kits were distributed from primary health facilities, and birth attendants received training on how to use the kits. Results from the study of 334 women indicated that neonates of mothers who had the use of the kits were less likely to develop sepsis from cord infection and mothers had fewer postpartum infections (Darmstadt et al., 2009).

Pregnancy outcomes in Egypt are poorer as compared to those in other developing nations with similar per capita gross national products (GDPs). The national rate of low birth weight in Egypt is 12% of all live births, but for 30% of low-birth-weight infants in Egypt, the mortality rate is 2.5 times that of full-term infants. These increased risks of mortality for low-birth-weight children persist throughout the first year of life and beyond, with this risk factor also being associated with increased cognitive disabilities. A special antenatal nutrition project in Al-Minia, in Upper Egypt, demonstrated an ability to improve birth weight in newborns. Women in this project received food supplements and nutrition education as well as prenatal care and home visits. Results indicated that infant birth weights increased, which ultimately resulted in healthier babies who were less likely to contribute to the infant mortality rate (Ahrani et al., 2006).

Noncommunicable Diseases

Neuropsychiatric (19.8%), digestive diseases (11.5%), chronic respiratory diseases (6.9%), cardiovascular diseases (6.7%), and diabetes are major noncommunicable diseases whose incidence continues to increase in Egypt. Smoking, substance abuse, failure to use car seats and seat belts, lack of exercise, and consumption of fatty and salty foods are major contributors to the disease burden. Diabetes mellitus affects

TABLE 3-3

Top Five Cancers in Egypt

Males	*Females*	*Both Sexes*
1. Bladder	1. Breast	1. Breast
2. Liver	2. Non-Hodgkins lymphoma	2. Bladder
3. Non-Hodgkins lymphoma	3. Ovary	3. Non-Hodgkins lymphoma
4. Lung	4. Colorectal	4. Liver
5. Leukemia	5. Leukemia	5. Leukemia

Source: WHO, 2011.

nearly 3.9 million people in Egypt, and its prevalence is expected to increase to 9 million by 2025. A study conducted in 2011 in Cairo indicated that type 1 diabetes mellitus care needs to be carefully monitored, as complication rates were nearly 50% among patients in the study. Regular exercise for patients in this study demonstrated a significant positive effect for children and adolescents (Ismail, 2011).

Table 3-3 lists the top five most frequently occurring cancers in Egypt. Breast cancer accounts for 38% of all new cancer cases among women living in this country. The age-standardized rate (ASR) for breast cancer incidence in Egypt is 37.3 per 100,000, and the mortality rate is 20.1 per 100,000. Incidence of breast cancer is lower in Egyptian women than in U.S. women, possibly due to a lower rate of cancer screening, and mortality rates for Egyptian women are higher than those for U.S. women (International Agency for Research on Cancer, 2010).

Mortality and Burden of Disease

Table 3-4 provides child mortality data for Egypt in 2009 and 2010. Table 3-5 lists adult mortality rates, defined as the probability of dying between 15 and 60 years of age per 1000 population; a breakout is provided for the maternal mortality rate. Table 3-6 identifies age-standardized mortality rates by cause. Table 3-7 gives causes of death for Egyptian children younger than age five. Table 3-8 provides mortality data related to HIV/AIDS, tuberculosis, and malaria.

TABLE 3-4

Child Mortality in Egypt, 2009 and 2010

	Year	*Rates*
Under-five mortality rate (probability of dying by age 5 per 1000 live births)	2010	22
Number of under-five deaths (thousands)	2010	41
Infant mortality rate (probability of dying between birth and age 1 per 1000 live births)	2010	19
Number of infant deaths (thousands)	2010	35
Neonatal mortality rate (per 1000 live births)	2010	9
Number of neonatal deaths (thousands)	2010	18
Stillbirth rate (per 1000 total births)	2009	13

Source: WHO, 2011.

TABLE 3-5

Adult Mortality in Egypt, 2008 and 2009

	Year	*Number of Deaths Among Persons Aged 15–60 Years per 1000 Population*
Male	2009	215
Female	2009	130
Both sexes	2009	174
Maternal mortality ratio (per 100,000 live births; interagency estimates)	2008	82 (range: 51–130)

Source: WHO, 2011.

Female Circumcision

Female circumcision has been a tradition in Egypt since the Pharaonic period. The prevalence of female circumcision is widespread in Egypt; 91% of all women age 15–49 have been circumcised. The female circumcision rate among women younger than age 25 is lower than the corresponding rate in the 25–49 age group, in which 94% to 96% of women have been circumcised. The rate also is lower among never-married than ever-married women (81% and 95%, respectively). Urban women are less likely to be circumcised than rural women (85% and 96%, respectively). The likelihood that a woman is circumcised also declines with the woman's education level and is markedly lower among women in the highest wealth quintile than in other quintiles (78% versus 92% or higher). The majority of circumcised women (63%) report that (midwives) were responsible for performing the procedure. Trained medical personnel (primarily doctors) performed most of the remaining circumcisions (Egypt Demographic and Health Survey, 2008).

Spousal Violence in Egypt

Nearly three-fourths of women visiting family health centers in Alexandria, Egypt, have experienced spousal violence in their lifetimes. Approximately half of the women experienced physical violence ("Spousal Violence in Egypt," 2010).

Mental Health

A national household survey of prevalence of disorders in five governorates, using the Mini International Neuropsychiatric Interview–Plus (MINI-Plus) instrument, indicated that almost 17% (range: 11% to 25.4%

TABLE 3-6

Age-Standardized Mortality Rates by Cause, 2008 (per 100,000 population)

Mortality rate from communicable disease	76
Mortality rate from noncommunicable disease	749
Mortality rate from injuries	34

Source: WHO, 2011.

TABLE 3-7

Causes of Death Among Children Younger Than Age Five Years, 2008 (percentage of all deaths)

Prematurity	30
Pneumonia	11
Diarrhea	6
Birth asphyxia	5
Injuries	5
Neonatal sepsis	1
HIV/AIDS	0
Measles	0
Malaria	0
Other	23

Source: WHO, 2011.

in different governorates) of adults in Egypt had mental disorders, with the common being mood disorders (6.4%), anxiety disorders (4.9%), and somatoform disorders (0.6%). Psychoses were seen in 0.3% of the population (WHO, 2005).

Environmental Problems

Air pollution, especially in Cairo and Alexandria, is a major source of chronic respiratory diseases (WHO, 2006). According to the Country Cooperation Study, Egypt receives 98% of its fresh water from the Nile River; unfortunately, there is excessive water pollution in the Nile due to large discharges of pesticides, nutrients, and heavy metals from industry in Cairo, making obtaining clean water a major health challenge for the country's population. Tap water assessments indicate that lead levels are at a high risk level as well. A recommendation by the WHO suggested that lead and other heavy metal residuals should be lowered for health safety of the population (Lasheen, El-Kholy, Sharaby, Elsherif, & El-Wakeel, 2008).

TABLE 3-8

HIV/AIDS, Malaria, and Tuberculosis in Egypt, 2008 and 2009

	Year	*Data (Range)*
Deaths due to HIV/AIDS (per 100,000 population per year)	2009	0.6 (0.5–0.9)
Deaths due to malaria (per 100,000 population per year)	2008	0.2 (0.1–0.2)
Deaths due to tuberculosis among HIV-negative people (per 100,000 population per year)	2009	1.10 (0.74–1.50)
Prevalence of HIV among adults aged 15 to 49 (%)	2009	<0.1
Incidence of tuberculosis (per 100,000 population per year)	2009	19.0 (16.0–22.0)
Prevalence of tuberculosis (per 100,000 population)	2009	30.0 (13.0–49.0)

Source: WHO, 2011.

Egypt's Response to the Millennium Development Goals

The tables presented in this subsection profile Egypt's responses to WHO's Millennium Development Goals (WHO Global Health Observatory Data Repository, 2011):

■ MDG 1: Poverty and hunger (**Table 3-9**)

TABLE 3-9

Egypt: Hunger Indicators, 2008

	Male	*Female*	*Both Sexes*
Percentage of children younger than 5 years who are underweight	8.1	5.4	6.8
Percentage of children younger than 5 years who are stunted	33	28.4	30.7

Source: WHO, 2011.

■ MDG 4: Child mortality (**Table 3-10**)

TABLE 3-10

Egypt: Child Mortality Indicators, 2009 and 2010

	Year	*Data*
Under-five mortality rate (probability of dying by age 5 per 1000 live births)	2010	22
Number of under-five deaths (thousands)	2010	41
Infant mortality rate (probability of dying between birth and age 1 per 1000 live births)	2010	19
Number of infant deaths (thousands)	2010	35
Measles (MCV) immunization coverage among 1-year-olds (%)	2009	95

Source: WHO, 2011.

■ MDG 5: Maternal health

  • Maternal mortality (**Table 3-11**)

  • Births attended by skilled health personnel, 2008: 79%

  • Reproductive health (**Table 3-12**)

TABLE 3-11

Egypt: Maternal Mortality Indicators, 2008

Maternal mortality ratio (per 100,000 live births; interagency estimates)	82 (range: 51–130)
Births attended by skilled health personnel	79%

Source: WHO, 2011.

TABLE 3-12

Egypt: Reproductive Health Indicators, 2006 and 2008

	Year	Data
Contraceptive prevalence	2008	60.3%
Contraceptive prevalence, among women aged 15–19	2008	23.4%
Adolescent fertility rate (per 1000 girls aged 15–19 years)	2006	50
Antenatal care coverage: at least one visit	2008	74%
Antenatal care coverage: at least one visit, among women aged 15–19	2008	76.5%
Antenatal care coverage: at least four visits	2008	66%
Unmet need for family planning	2008	9.2%
Unmet need for family planning: women aged 15–19	2008	7.9%
Births attended by skilled health personnel, among women aged 15–19	2008	78.8%

Source: WHO, 2011.

■ MDG 6: HIV/AIDS, malaria, and other diseases (**Table 3-13**)

TABLE 3-13

Egypt: HIV/AIDS, Malaria, and Tuberculosis Indicators, 2008 and 2009

	Year	Data
Prevalence of HIV among adults aged 15–49 (%)	2009	<0.1
Deaths due to malaria (per 100,000 population per year)	2008	0.2 (0.1–0.2)
Incidence of tuberculosis (per 100,000 population per year)	2009	19.0 (16.0–22.0)
Prevalence of tuberculosis (per 100,000 population)	2009	30.0 (13.0–49.0)
Deaths due to tuberculosis among HIV-negative people (per 100,000 population per year)	2009	1.10 (0.74–1.50)
Case detection rate for all forms of tuberculosis	2009	63 (54–75)
Smear-positive tuberculosis treatment: success rate (%)	2008	89

Source: WHO, 2011.

■ MDG 7: Environment sustainability (**Table 3-14**)

TABLE 3-14

Egypt: Water and Sanitation Indicators, 2008

	Urban	Rural	Total
Population using improved drinking-water sources	100%	98%	99%
Population using improved sanitation facilities	97%	92%	94%

Source: WHO, 2011.

■ Not a MDG. The following is a table relating nutrition in Egypt (**Table 3-15**).

TABLE 3-15

Egypt: Nutrition Indicators, 2008

	Male	*Female*	*Both Sexes*
Children younger than 5 years: overweight	19.8%	21.2%	20.5%
Children younger than 5 years: stunted	33%	28.4%	30.7%
Children younger than 5 years: underweight	8.1%	5.4%	6.8%
Children younger than 5 years: wasted for age	8.8%	7.1%	7.9%

Source: WHO, 2011.

Traditional Health

In the Arab Republic of Egypt, a national policy on traditional medicine/complementary alternative medicine (TM/CAM) is part of the national drug policy that was issued in 2001. Herbal medicine regulation in Egypt began in 1955, and is achieved through the same laws as are applied to conventional pharmaceuticals. Herbal medicines are regulated in the forms of prescription medicines, over-the-counter medicines, self-medication, and dietary supplements. Control mechanisms exist for both manufacturing and safety assessment requirements. There are 600 registered herbal medicines, though no herbal medicines are included on the national essential drugs list. In Egypt, herbal medicines are sold in pharmacies by licensed practitioners, as over-the-counter products, and as prescription medicines (WHO, 2011).

CHINA

Description

China is the world's fourth largest country in area (after the countries of Russia, Canada, and the United States), and is located in east Asia, bordering numerous countries, including the Russian Federal Republic, India, Pakistan, Vietnam, and Mongolia. China, which is slightly smaller than the United States, has climates varying from tropical in the south to subarctic in the north. At present it has a great amount of air pollution—mostly greenhouse gases and sulfur dioxide particles from use of coal and other carbon-based fuels. It also has water pollution, hazardous waste, deforestation, and soil erosion problems (Central Intelligence Agency [CIA], 2011a).

Population

China currently has 1.3 billion people. A graph of China's aging population and the forecast for the increased percentage of the total population represented by people 65 and older can be seen in **Figure 3-1**. **Table 3-16** provides a breakdown of China's health and vital statistics.

Ethnic Groups in China

The Han ethnic group makes up 91.9% of the population, with the remainder being Zhaung, Uygur, Hui, Yi, Tibetan, Miao, Manchu, Mongol, Buyi, Korean, and other nationalities. The official religion of China

FIGURE 3-1

China's Aging Population

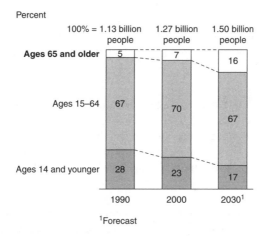

¹Forecast

Source: Quoted from the website of the National Bureau of Statistics of the People's Republic of China, www.stats.gov.cn

TABLE 3-16

China's Population, 2010

Total population	1.330 billion people
Birth to 14 years	17.9%
15–64 years	73.4%
65+ years	8.6%
Population growth rate	0.494%
Birth rate	12.17 per 1000 people
Death rate	6.89 per 1000 people
Gender ratio	1.08 males per 1 female
Infant mortality rate	16.51 deaths per 1000 live births
	Males: 21.21 deaths per 1000 live births
	Females: 27.5 deaths per 1000 live births
Life expectancy at birth (ranks 92nd in world)	Males: 72.54 years
	Females: 76.77 years
Fertility rate	1.54 children per woman
HIV rate	0.1% (700,000 persons already have the disease)
Education (average)	11 years
Literacy (can read and write)	91.6%

Source: CIA, 2011a.

is atheist, but 1% to 2% is Daoist, Buddhist, or Muslim, and 3% to 4% is Christian. The standard language is Mandarin; other dialects spoken in the country include Cantonese, Shanghaiese, Fuzhou, Hokkien-Taiwanese, Xiang, Gan, and Hakka. China has a 91.6% literacy rate (CIA, 2011a).

Government

The government of China (also called the People's Republic of China [PRC]) is communist, and the capital is in Beijing. China has 23 provinces and 5 autonomous regions (CIA, 2011a).

Economy

Since 1978, the Chinese economy has moved from a centrally run and planned Soviet-style of government to a market economy. Business and agriculture are now more locally run, rather than being controlled by the central communist government. The overall economic system continues to function within strict communist political control, however. The change in management style of business has increased the GDP four times and boosted per capita income to $8288 in 2011 (CIA, 2011a).

China has now moved beyond Japan to become the world's second-largest economy, and it may overtake the United States in terms of national income within the next 10 years, though it remains far behind in per capita income. The country now has hundreds of millions of people who have moved out of poverty and has a large group of students and tourists who visit the West. In spite of China now having many billionaires, as well as numerous millionaires, the average income for most of its residents is still among the world's lowest ("China Surges Past Japan," 2010).

Healthcare System

History

China has one of the longest historical records of medicine of any existing civilization in the world. Both traditional medicine and new technology are components of the Chinese healthcare system.

In 1949, Chairman Mao Zedong established a rural preventive healthcare program, emphasizing disease prevention. At that time, the ministry of public health was made responsible for all health care. Large numbers of more sophisticated urban physicians were sent to the countryside to practice. In addition, less trained "barefoot doctors" were sent to small rural communities to help supply the needs for local rural health care. They worked out of village medical centers, providing preventive and primary medical care. In addition, township health centers that had 10–30 bed hospitals were established as part of the so-called rural collective health system. Only seriously ill patients went to county hospitals, which served a much larger population base. In large urban areas, health care was provided by paramedical personnel, who were assigned to factories and neighborhood health stations. Patients with serious illnesses went to the district or municipal hospitals.

In the 1950s, China was isolated by the Western powers, and the Soviet Union was its only ally. During this era, medical schools and hospitals in China were built with the help of Russians. There was an emphasis on public health and prevention of illness. The government mobilized the people to begin massive patriot health campaigns aimed at environmental sanitation and preventing disease. An example was the assault on the "four pests" (rats, sparrows, flies, and mosquitoes), as well as the efforts directed toward eradicating snails that carried schistosomia disease. Other health campaigns were devoted to water quality and waste management (CIA, 2011a). Unfortunately, much of the country's agricultural sector was ignored or handled poorly by overplanting and not harvesting all the crops, leaving them to rot. Thus many of the agricultural programs failed. As many as 20 to 30 million people starved to death, and infant mortality rose to 300 per 1000 (Hesketh & Zhu, 2002).

In the 1960s, campaigns to prevent sexually transmitted diseases, such as syphilis, were successful. By the 1970s, China was able to set up affordable primary health care in the rural areas. During the 1980s, its health policy was restructured based on market-driven reforms. The barefoot doctors were then less needed, as a more sophisticated system of health care was established. With a 1% growth rate and a population of 1.3 billion people, China became very concerned about population growth and began restricting family size by implementing the "one child per family" policy. Diseases such as tuberculosis, hepatitis, hookworm, and schistosomiasis still remained problems. Later, other, more chronic diseases such as HIV/AIDS, cancer, cardiovascular disease, and heart diseases became frequent causes of mortality, similar to the situation in other developed societies (CIA, 2011a).

According to Freedom House (an organization that judges how much freedom citizens of various countries have), China is near the bottom of the list of countries for limiting freedom. It is possible that these restrictions actually helped the healthcare system in China, however. From the 1950s to the 1970s, health care in China improved greatly under a very strict authoritarian rule. Brothels and opium dens were officially closed, the four pests (flies, mosquitoes, rats, and sparrows) were greatly reduced, and the training of a million barefoot (lay) doctors by urban doctors was accomplished. Health care through prevention was promoted. The communist government claimed that incidence of sexually transmitted diseases, schistosomiasis, and leprosy decreased, access to health care for all was promoted, and infant mortality decreased. It is almost impossible to verify all of these claims, however, because China was a closed system that allowed few outsiders to document facts. The irony today is that as China becomes freer and turns toward a more market-driven economy, some advances in health care have actually been reversed. For example, universal access to health care for all is gone, and poor rural Chinese have great difficulty today getting prevention and treatment under the current partial out-of-pocket payment system (Hesketh & Zhu, 2002).

China, through its market reforms, has experienced tremendous economic growth. One of the results of the economic upturn has been the establishment of a fee-for-service private medical practice with few governmental restrictions. Private medical practice was not allowed during the Cultural Revolution, but it reemerged in the 1980s after the dissolving of the Cooperative Medical System (CMS) during the Maoist times, when many people lived in communes. At present, rural families must pay out-of-pocket fees for medical services; these often prohibitive costs render health care inaccessible for many (Lim, Yang, Zhang, Feng, & Zhou, 2004).

The Chinese barefoot doctors today in the small remote villages of the far west are often supported by a very small government salary each month and typically work out of their homes rather than a clinic, which enables them to maintain their farms when there are no patients. The doctors charge a small fee to the patients for their services, and the remainder of their salaries comes from drug sales. Often doctors overprescribe medicines simply to increase their incomes. Village doctors have inadequate training and often do not take patient histories or keep medical records as part of China's economic reforms. The Chinese government has increasingly cut the funds made available for health care, so by 2000, 60% of all healthcare costs were paid for by the individual. The typical city doctor earns $600 to $1200 per month and sees 60 to 80 patients per day. The government has recently budgeted $350 million dollars to establish disease control and prevention centers in poor areas. Many poor areas had difficulty treating severe acute respiratory syndrome (SARS) cases when this disease emerged in China because of the inadequate resources ("Life as a Village Doctor," 1997).

Access to Health Care and Costs

Since the 1980s, the Chinese government has had a laissez-faire policy for health care in rural areas. As part of that policy, it reverted to a self-pay system for clinic visits and hospitalization, which are now both very expensive relative to income. One average hospitalization costs 50% more than the average annual income. Access to health care in many areas is now priced on a sliding scale based on the ability to pay, yet many people are still unable to afford health care. In urban areas, medical care includes the use of high technology. The government health insurance program has given more equal access to health care, but cost inflation is now a major governmental concern. Copayments were first started to make the users more aware of health costs when accessing medical care. Medications and high-tech tests are now charged to patients and not covered by the government insurance.

The majority of China's population lives in rural areas. Those who live in urban areas are in many ways advantaged. The distinction between rural and urban subpopulations is reinforced by a system of population registration that limits migration from rural to urban areas (Zimmer & Kwong, 2004).

In recent years, China has made great efforts to improve its public health system. Funds have been expended to modify and enlarge the disease prevention and control centers and to establish emergency centers and hospitals throughout the country. The major infrastructure has been improved. The ministry of health set up 10 national medical teams for disaster relief and disease prevention in some of the major cities. The SARS epidemic was controlled rapidly with through this new infrastructure (Zheng, 2005).

China has the most hospitals (60,784) and the most doctors (1.97 million) of any country in the world. In 1949 when the Communists came to power there were only 2,600 hospitals in China. There are now 17 doctors per 10,000 people which compares to 25 doctors per 10,000 people in the United States. About 4.5 percent of the gross domestic product (GDP) is allocated to health care, half of which comes from the private sector. By comparison the average healthcare expenditure of countries in the European Union is 9 percent of GDP, while in the United States, it is closer to 16 percent (Hays, 2011).

Government insurance programs have been expanded in recent years to decrease the out-of-pocket payments and lack of equity in healthcare availability and quality. With China's strong economic growth and huge financial reserves, it has the potential of decreasing the health disparities and improving access to and quality of healthcare nationwide (Hu, Tang, Liu, & Zhao, 2008). The Chinese government is hoping to establish a universal healthcare plan and plans to overhaul most of its inadequate hospitals by 2011; the government also approved a plan to spend $124.3 billion by 2012 on healthcare improvements. The plan is to provide annual health subsidies to citizens as well as to implement a system to provide drugs and vaccines. In 2007, WHO ranked the healthcare system of China as number 144 out of 190 nations, well below the systems found in far poorer countries such as Haiti (Wang, 2009).

The makeup of the current healthcare workforce in China differs from that in many other nations. China has more doctors than nurses. In 2005, there were 1.9 million licensed doctors and 1.4 million licensed nurses. The density of healthcare providers is much greater in urban as compared to rural areas—specifically, a 3:1 ratio. Most doctors and nurses have only a junior college or high school level of education. Approximately one-third of physicians and nurses have been educated at the college level or higher. The majority of the higher-educated healthcare workers can be found in the urban areas, which creates a great disparity in the quantity and quality of healthcare providers in urban versus rural areas (Anand, Fan, & Zhang, 2008).

Health Priorities

China has experienced rapid growth in social and economic development that has created a demand for high-quality health care within the country. The life expectancy of the average person has increased, and this trend is expected to create an aging population with chronic health problems. The leading cause of death in those 1–44 years is injury. Approximately 750,000 deaths and 3.5 million hospitalizations occur each year. More people are now using motorcycles and cars, and fewer people are walking or using bicycles. As a result of changes in diet and activity, cardiovascular disease is increasing rapidly. Nearly 2.6 million deaths occur annually from this problem, but by 2020 it is projected that 13 million people will die each year from cardiovascular disease (George Institute for International Health, 2003).

Environmental Health Issues and Respiratory Problems

China's movement toward a market economy has increased incomes and improved health indicators for its population but created some difficult environmental problems. Biomass fuel and coal are burned in most of China for cooking and heating in most rural areas and a significant number of urban areas, which contributes to a major problem with indoor air pollution. In addition, the country has intense pollution from coal combustion for industry, which is damaging the air, water, and ultimately the agriculture, which in turn affects the residents' health. Of the 10 most polluted cities of the world, China is home to 7 of them. China is also the world's second highest emitter (after the United States) of carbon dioxide pollution, mainly from industry. With the help of the United Nations and the United States, China hopes to develop a multimillion-dollar energy strategy to combat pollution (Zhang & Cai, 2003).

Respiratory diseases are now a widespread and serious issue. Driven by China's tremendous industrial growth, the pollution that causes these diseases is taking a heavy toll on both the environment and public health. High rates of smog from industrial and traffic pollution are associated with very high rates of respiratory infections and chronic illnesses. China relies heavily on coal that contains high levels of sulfur; this fuel is used to satisfy 70% of the country's domestic energy needs (Zhang & Cai, 2003).

Water pollution is another major problem. Half of all of China's water sources are considered too polluted for human consumption. Air and water pollution in China is estimated to cause 2.4 million premature deaths per year from cardiopulmonary and gastrointestinal diseases. Increases in the use of fossil fuels in industrial and residential use increases the country's production of greenhouse gases, which in turn poses significant health risks to the population. Significant health disparities exist between poor and wealthy populations, related to the exposure to polluted air and water in poorer households (Zhang, Mauzerall, Zhu, Liang, Ezzati, & Remais, 2010).

Lead poisoning is a concern among many residents. In 2009, approximately 2000 children living near zinc and manganese smelting plants in two provinces were found with unsafe levels of lead in their blood—a revelation that provoked riots (Watts, 2009).

A major food safety incident in China was made public in 2008. An estimated 300,000 infants and young children were made ill and 6 died after melamine was deliberately added to diluted raw milk as well as other food and feed products. This additive led to formation of kidney stones and renal failure. Twenty-two manufacturers of infant formula sold this contaminated product, in what is considered one of the largest ever food contamination incidents—which also had implication for international food safety (Gossner et al., 2009).

Tobacco smoking, especially among adult males, is another growing environmental problem in China that has caused many respiratory diseases and deaths. China makes and sells more cigarettes than any other country in the world and has more than 350 million smokers, which represents about one-third of the population. Rates are highest among adult men, who have a 67% smoking rate; in contrast, only 4% of all females smoke. Cigarette smoking is now the leading cause of preventable deaths in China (and the rest of the world). It seems inevitable that China will see a tremendous increase in mortality from smoking-related diseases such as chronic obstructive pulmonary disease (COPD), lung cancer, and pulmonary tuberculosis. The China National Tobacco Corporation is the largest tobacco manufacturer in the world. As part of an effort to stem the tide of smoking, the Minister of Health publishes an annual tobacco control report and campaigns have been launched to increase tobacco taxes and put health warnings on the tobacco products beginning in January 2009 (Gonghuan, 2010).

Mental Health

Mental health is a major issue in China today because of the rapid social and economic changes. Changes that some members of the population face today include financial losses from bad business deals and gambling; higher rates of extramarital affairs, family violence, and divorce; rising rates of substance use and abuse; weakening of traditional family values and relationships; large numbers of rural migrants seeking employment in larger urban environments; a widening gap between the rich and poor; work-related stress; and a faster pace of life. Eighty percent of the country's healthcare budget goes to the urban residents, even though they represent only 30% of the total population. Funds for mental health are very limited for the rural population, most of whom cannot afford the out-of-pocket costs for mental health care. Shanghai, the largest population in China, boasts having the most comprehensive mental healthcare system in the country (Chang & Kleinman, 2002).

According to 2003 WHO data, 13% of the Chinese population has psychological problems, and 16 million people in China suffer from serious mental illness. Every year in China, some 280,000 people commit suicide, accounting for 25% of the entire world's suicide statistics. Another 20 to 50 million people attempt suicide each year. Suicide is the fifth leading cause of death for Chinese people 15–35 years of age. The suicide rate in China is three times higher in rural areas as compared to urban areas. This rate is 25% higher among women than men, a trend that is the opposite of that found in many other nations of the world. The higher rates of female suicides in rural areas are primarily due to poverty, the low status of rural women, forced marriages, family violence and conflict, chronic stress, and no hope for the future. Men in rural areas are often absent from the homes for long periods of time, leaving the women to work in the fields, take care of children, cook, and care for the house (Pochagina, n.d.).

Nutrition

Throughout China, there has been a change in diet and physical activity and overall body composition patterns. During the past 10 years, the number of people living in China in absolute poverty has significantly declined. The proportion of those considered extremely poor decreased from 20% to 6% of the total population during the same period. As a result of this change in economic status, the prevalence of obesity and diet-related noncommunicable diseases has increased more rapidly in China than in other developed societies. Diets have shifted from high-carbohydrate to high-fat and high-density energy foods, leading to overweight and obesity—and their associated diseases, such as diabetes, stroke, cancer, and cardiovascular diseases (Du, Mroz, Zhai, & Popkin, 2004).

Cardiovascular Disease

Cardiovascular disease is the leading cause of mortality in the world, including in China and other developing countries. China and other developing nations have been experiencing an epidemic in cardiovascular disease during the last few decades mainly because of lifestyle and diet changes. Currently, there is a growing prevalence of metabolic syndrome and overweight individuals among adults in China. Metabolic syndrome is characterized by a cluster of problems that consists of abdominal obesity, increased blood pressure and glucose concentration, and elevated cholesterol levels. Obesity is a risk factor not only for cardiovascular disease but also type 2 diabetes, hypertension, and cancer. Excess weight is also a cause for osteoarthritis and gallbladder disease (Dang, Yan, Yamamoto, Wang, & Zeng, 2004; Gu et al., 2005).

Infectious Diseases

Major infectious diseases in China include the following (CIA, 2011a):

- Food- and water-borne diseases (bacterial diarrhea, hepatitis A, and typhoid fever)
- Vector-borne diseases (Japanese encephalitis and dengue fever)
- Soil-contact diseases (hantaviral hemorrhagic fever and renal syndrome)
- Animal contact diseases (rabies)

HIV/AIDS

HIV/AIDS entered China in 1985, and more than 20 years later the epidemic continues to spread at an alarming rate. The CIA (2011a) has estimated that 0.1% of the total Chinese population is infected with HIV; this rate, compared to that found in other parts of the world, ranks 115th worldwide. It translates into 700,000 adults living with HIV/AIDS, which ranks as the 17th largest population with this disease in the world. The estimated number of deaths from this cause—39,000 per year—places China at 15th world-wide in AIDS deaths (Kanabus, 2005).

The general population of China knows little about the sexual practices that increase the risk of contracting HIV infection. HIV/AIDS prevention in the general population has been rare. Those now living in China with HIV/AIDS face severe discrimination and have limited access to healthcare services, especially in the rural areas (Chen, Han, & Holzemer, 2004). The government has promised to provide free HIV tests to anyone who wants one and fully cover treatment costs for poorer patients (Kanabus, 2005).

Tuberculosis

China reported the worldwide second-highest number of new tuberculosis (TB) cases (1.31 million) and the second-highest number of TB deaths (201,000 TB cases) in 2007, behind only India. China has 4.5 million TB cases currently, and each year 1.4 million people fall ill with the disease. TB killed 160,000 people in China in 2008, according to WHO. TB also represents a big drain on China's health budget because of the high incidence of people with a drug-resistant strain of the disease, which is much more difficult and expensive to treat; these patients need to take drugs for up to two years. This worst type of TB, for which there is no cure, kills one out of every two patients. Regular TB costs 1000 Yuan ($158.60) to treat in China, whereas drug-resistant TB costs range from 100,000 to 300,000 Yuan ($15,900 to $47,600) per person. China spent $225 million on tackling TB in 2008, up from $98 million in 2002, according to WHO. (These figures do not take into account the amounts that patients pay out of their pockets, which typically amounts to between 47% and 62% of their hospital bills.) The World Bank funded the first TB survey in China, which was followed by a new program that aimed to treat the cases and prevent new ones ("China Fights Growing Problem of Tuberculosis," 2010).

Population Control

China has only 7% of the world's arable land, yet 22% of the world's population. To feed, house, and promote good health care for this country's citizens despite the relatively scarce resources, the "one child per family" policy was established by Chinese leader Deng Xiaoping in 1979 to limit China's population growth. The advantages of such a policy are that each child will have a healthier life, family costs will be lower, and the child will get a better education. Women will be able to focus on their careers as well as on care for their families. The government claims that this policy has prevented mass starvation.

Fines, pressures to abort a pregnancy, and even forced sterilization occur with subsequent pregnancies after the first. The policy includes ethnic Han Chinese living in urban areas. Citizens living in rural areas and minorities living in China are not subject to the law. The "one child" policy has estimated to have reduced the population of the country by as much as 300 million people in the past 20 years. A new law in addition to the "one child" regulation states that if both parents have no siblings, they may have two children, thus preventing too dramatic a population decrease.

One problem with this population control policy is that Chinese parents usually rely on their children—especially their sons—for support in their old age. The result is that most couples want a male child if they can have only one child (Population—China, 2004). In turn, sex selection during pregnancy (e.g., through ultrasound and subsequent abortion of female fetuses) has resulted in a ratio of 114 males to 100 females among children from birth to 4 years old. Over time, the population control policies have caused serious problems for female infants such as abortion, neglect, abandonment, and even infanticide (Rosenberg, 2011).

Internal Migration and Its Healthcare Implications

China has a highly mobile population of 140 million rural-to-urban migrants representing 10% of the total population. Migrants move between cities and provinces in search of improved living conditions. Most are young, single males, who have a socioeconomic status above rural groups but below urban populations. Migrants are excluded from urban healthcare services, including access to public health facilities, and they do not qualify for public medical insurance and other assistance programs. They must pay out-of-pocket for medical services in the cities. Within this population are individuals who pose special concerns given their spread of communicable diseases such as sexually transmitted diseases (STDs), respiratory infections such as TB, diarrheal infections, and parasitic infections. A second concern is maternal and infant health for members of migrant groups; such care is also not covered by public insurance to migrants. Lastly, occupational diseases and injuries have become a significant problem among this group, given their lack of public insurance coverage (Hu, Cook, & Salazar, 2008).

Traditional Medicine

The practice of traditional Chinese medicine was strongly promoted by Chinese leaders, and it has remained a major part of health care. Western medicine gained acceptance in the 1970s and 1980s. The goal of China's medical personnel is to synthesize the use of both Western and traditional Chinese medicine, yet this practice has not always worked seamlessly. Physicians trained in traditional medicine and those trained in Western medicine are very separate groups with different basic ideas. Traditional Chinese medicine uses herbal treatments, acupuncture, acupressure, moxibustion, and cupping of skin with heated bamboo. These approaches are very effective in treating minor ailments and chronic diseases, and they produce far fewer side effects. Some more serious and acute problems are also treated with traditional medicine. For more information regarding this topic see the chapter entitled, "Global Use of Complementary and Alternative Medicine."

INDIA

History

The Indus Valley civilization, one of the world's oldest, was a vibrant presence during the second and third millennia B.C.E. Aryan tribes from the northwest came to the Indian subcontinent in 1500 B.C.E., merging with the earlier Dravidian people and creating the classical Indian culture. Many years later in the nineteenth century, India came under British rule. Nonviolent resistance to British rule, led by Ghandi and Nehru, brought India to independence in 1947. Violence in the new state eventually led to a partition of the nation, creating two countries, India and Pakistan. Later, a war in 1971 resulted in East Pakistan becoming the country of Bangladesh (CIA, 2011b).

Geography

The country of India is located in southern Asia, bordering the Arabian Sea and the Bay of Bengal, between Burma and Pakistan. It has a large land area, ranking seventh in the world. The climate includes monsoons in the south and a more temperate climate in the north. The country's natural resources include coal (India has the fourth largest reserves in the world), iron ore, manganese, mica, titanium ore, natural gas, diamonds, and petroleum, among others. Within this country there is an abundance of deforestation, soil erosion, overgrazing, air pollution from industry and vehicle emission, and water pollution from raw sewage and agricultural pesticides, making water nonpotable throughout the country (CIA, 2011b).

Population

India is home to 1.173 billion people, ranking the country second in the world in terms of population size. The population is growing at a rate of 2% annually, which will create the world's largest population—surpassing China—by 2030. By 2050, India's population is expected to reach 1.6 billion people. The population increase is due to increases in life expectancy, decreases in infant mortality, and emphasis on eradication of diseases such as hepatitis, tetanus, and polio among infants. The median age is 25.9 years, with approximately 30% of the population being younger than 14 years, 64.6% being between the ages of 14 and 64 years, and 5.3% being 65 years or older. The birth rate is 21.34 births per 1000 population; the death rate is 7.53 deaths per 1000 population. The infant mortality rate is 49.13 deaths per 1000 live births. Life expectancy is 66.46 years, ranking 159th in the world.

The majority of India's people live in a rural agrarian economy and have incomes of less than $1 per day (CIA, 2011b). Only 29% of the total population lives in urban areas.

Infectious Diseases

The HIV/AIDs rate in India is 0.3% (2007 estimate) of the total population, with 2.4 million (2007 estimate) people living with HIV/AIDS, and 310,000 deaths occurring from this cause (2001 estimate). Food- and water-borne diseases cause a high rate of bacterial diarrhea, hepatitis A and E, and typhoid fever. Vector-borne diseases include chikugunya, dengue fever, Japanese encephalitis, and malaria. Rabies is caused from animal contact, and leptospirosis is caused from water contact. India's malaria and TB rates are ranked third in the world (CIA, 2011b).

Chronic Diseases

India is now faced with a double burden of long-term chronic illnesses and serious acute illnesses. Cardiovascular diseases, cancer, degenerative diseases, and diabetes have become major health issues in addition to the acute communicable diseases mentioned previously.

Culture

Indians practice a number of different religions: Hindu (80.5%), Muslim (13.4%), Christian (2.3%), Sikh (1.9%), other (1.8%), and unspecified (0.1%). English is the official language, yet Indians use many other languages as well. Hindi is the most widely used of these languages (used by 41% of the population), but 14 other languages are also spoken. Approximately 61% of the population is literate, being able to read and write, and the average education level is 10 years. Inequality of opportunity has caused the lower-caste Hindus, Muslims, tribal people, and other minority populations to be disproportionately represented within the poor, the uneducated, and those with most health problems (CIA, 2011b).

Government and Economy

India is a federal republic with New Delhi as its capital city. The country contains 28 states and 7 union territories. The economy is developing into an open-market economy, which encompasses traditional village farming, modern agriculture, handicrafts, and a wide range of services, including information technology and software workers. India's annual per capita income is $3100 (2009 estimate). The country has a significant labor force of 467 million people (second largest in the world) and has 81 million people using the Internet (the fourth largest group of users in the world). The unemployment rate is 10.7%. The Indian pharmaceutical market has grown rapidly in the past few years and the federal government uses price controls to ensure that vital drugs are available to the general population (CIA, 2011b).

Health Care

Health care is the responsibility of each state or territory of India. Each state is expected to pay for 80% of healthcare facilities, and the federal government pays 15%, mainly through national healthcare programs. Health care in India can be traced back 3500 years to the inception of Ayurvedic traditional medicine, which is still used today. India has historically suffered from great famines, which have been eradicated, yet continues to experience significant problems with malnutrition, starvation, and disease, especially in the rural areas.

Undernutrition rates in children in India are higher than sub-Saharan Africa. Approximately 46% of children from birth to 3 years are undernourished (Rao, 2009). A preference for male babies has led to an imbalanced ratio of 93.5 girls per 100 boys, in contrast to the natural gender ratio at birth of 105 males to 100 females. Maternal and infant death rates remain high. The vast majority of the Indian population suffers from waterborne and airborne infections. Most of the country lacks a basic infrastructure, as its development has not kept up with the growing economy. Almost 1 million people die each year due to inadequate health care, and 700 million people lack access to specialist care, which mainly exists in large urban areas. Forty percent of the healthcare facilities in India are understaffed (Rao, 2009).

The number of hospital beds is low—only 0.7 per 1000 population, compared to the world average of 3.96 hospital beds per 1000 population. In addition, India lacks an adequate number of trained healthcare personnel for its growing healthcare industry. Rural healthcare services are mainly provided by smaller primary healthcare centers, which rely on trained paramedics for most of the care. Serious cases are sent to urban areas, where specialists and acute care facilities are available. Skilled birth attendants are needed, yet are still not provided in adequate numbers to decrease the high rates of maternal and infant mortality (Rao, 2009).

Indigenous traditional medicine is practiced throughout the country. The main forms are Ayurvedic medicine, which addresses mental and spiritual well-being as well as physical well-being. In addition, Unani herbal medicine is practiced. Today only 25% of the Indian population has access to Western medicine (Rao, 2009).

The government has made a major commitment to telemedicine to reach the majority of the poor, rural, underserved population. Health insurance is inaccessible to the majority of Indians, and 75% of healthcare expenses are paid on an out-of-pocket basis, which is very challenging for the many people who live in poverty. Emergency and specialty care is well beyond the reach of most of the poor lower-class residents. Among those in the urban middle and upper classes, approximately 50% have private health insurance.

The National Rural Health Mission was begun in 2005 to provide major improvements in health care for the rural population. Primary healthcare clinics, which have social activist leanings, help support public health priorities such as childhood immunizations and compliance with TB treatments. The National Rural Health Mission program was established to address issues of poverty and provide 100 days of work at minimal wage to one family member per household. In addition, an increase in primary school enrollment, particularly among girls, was established as a goal.

SOUTH AFRICA

Geography

South Africa is located at the southern tip of the continent of Africa. It is bordered by Botswana, Lesotho, Mozambique, Namibia, Swaziland, and Zimbabwe, as well as the Atlantic and Indian Oceans. Its climate is mostly arid, with a subtropical region found along the country's east coast. Natural resources include gold, chromium, antimony, coal, iron ore, manganese, nickel, phosphates, tin, uranium, gem diamonds, platinum, copper, vanadium, salt, and natural gas (CIA, 2012).

Population

South Africa's population as of 2010 was approximately 47 million. The country is currently experiencing the world's highest rate of people with HIV/AIDS, as well as the world's highest mortality rate from this disease (see **Table 3-17**).

Ethnic groups in South Africa include the following (CIA, 2012):

- Black African (79.6%)
- White (9.1%)
- Colored (8.9%)
- Indian/Asian (2.5%)

Religions practiced include the following:

- Zion Christian (11.1%)
- Pentecostal/Charismatic (8.2%)
- Catholic (7.1%)
- Methodist (6.8%)
- Dutch Reformed (6.7%)
- Anglican (3.8%)
- Other Christian (36%)
- Islam (1.5%)
- Other (2.3%)
- Unspecified (1.4%)
- None (15.1%)

Languages spoken in South Africa include the following:

- IsiZulu (23.8%)
- IsiXhosa (17.6%)
- Afrikaans (13.3%)
- Sepedi (9.4%)
- English (8.2%)
- Setswana (8.2%)
- Sesotho (7.9%)
- Xitsonga (4.4%)
- Other (7.2%)

The literacy rate of the total population is 86.4%.

South Africa has the largest population of people of European descent in Africa, the largest Indian population in Africa, and the largest colored (mixed European and African) group in Africa. It is one of the most ethnically diverse countries in Africa. The country has had a long history of racial problems between the black majority and the white minority. The country's Apartheid policy, which was introduced in 1948, ended in 1990. Crime remains a major problem in South Africa, which ranks first in the world in terms of number of murders by firearms, manslaughter, rape, and assault cases. It also ranks fourth in the world in terms of robbery incidence, according to a survey done by the United Nations during 1998–2000. Problems also persist with illegal drug transportation and sales (CIA, 2012).

TABLE 3-17

South Africa: Rates of HIV/AIDS

Population	47 million (2010 data)
Birth–14 years	30.3%
15–64 years	64.5%
65+ years	5.2%
Population growth rate	−0.31%
Death rate	21.32 per 1000 people
Infant mortality	61.81 per 1000 live births
Life expectancy	43.27 years
HIV/AIDS adult prevalence rate	21.5 % (2003 estimate)
	Approximately 5 million people (20% of 15- to 49-year-old population and 35% of all women of childbearing age)

Source: Adapted from U.S. Department of State, Bureau of African Affairs, 2005.

The South African population is relatively young, with approximately one-third younger than age 15. Fertility is declining, and there is an increase in persons older than 60 years. The country's healthcare services include not only services for obstetrics, pediatrics, and adolescents, but also those for the aging population. A large proportion of the population (18% in some areas) is illiterate. Half of all households use electricity for cooking (Bradshaw & Nannan, 2004).

Since 1994, life expectancy in South Africa has declined by 20 years, mainly because of the increase in HIV/AIDS incidence. The average life expectancy at birth is now 50 years for men and 54 years for women. The global burden of disease is quite high, and morbidity and mortality rates are very high due to HIV/AIDS, violence and injury, chronic diseases, mental health disorders, and maternal, neonatal, and child mortality (Chopra et al., 2009).

Government

The government is a republic, formally named the Republic of South Africa (RSA), with a legal system based on Roman-Dutch law and English common law. The system of government is also called a parliamentary democracy. South Africa has three capital cities: Cape Town, the largest, is the legislative capital; Pretoria is the administrative capital; and Bloemfontein is the judicial capital. The country comprises nine provinces (CIA, 2005; U.S. Department of State, Bureau of African Affairs, 2005).

Economy

South Africa has a two-tiered economy. One segment is similar to other economically strong developed countries, and the other is more like developing countries with only the basic infrastructure. South Africa has well-developed financial, legal, communication, energy, and transportation systems. It has the world's tenth largest stock exchange and a modern infrastructure. It has the best telecommunications system in Africa. At the same time, South Africa has a very high unemployment rate (25%) and most of the country's citizens live on less than $1.25 per day.

The country's wealth is unevenly distributed, with the minority whites having a much larger portion of the wealth and the majority blacks having a very challenging existence with difficulty finding well-paying jobs. The country has an overall per capita GDP of $11,100 (2004 estimate). Its industries include mining (South Africa is the world's largest producer of platinum, gold, and chromium), auto assembly, metalworking, machinery, textile, iron and steel, chemicals, fertilizers, ship repair, and foods (CIA, 2005; U.S. Department of State, Department of African Affairs, 2005). The main agricultural products are corn, wheat, sugarcane, fruits, vegetables, beef, poultry, mutton, wool, and dairy products (CIA, 2005; U.S. Department of State, Department of African Affairs, 2005).

Healthcare System

South Africa's healthcare system consists of a large public sector and a smaller, yet fast-growing private sector. Basic primary health care is offered free to all residents of the country, but is highly specialized; high-tech care is limited to only those who can afford private care. The dilemma is that the government contributes approximately 40% of healthcare costs for the public health, yet 80% of the population uses the services. The number of public hospitals continues to grow, and companies in the mining industry operate their own 60 hospitals and clinics in different locations within the country (U.S. Department of State, Department of African Affairs, 2005; Coovadia, Jewkes, Barron, Sanders, & McIntyre, 2009).

Since 1978, the country has had a decentralized basic primary healthcare system, instead focusing on a district healthcare system run by local governments. Disparities exist between municipalities, depending on the funding from the local area. Poor municipalities with little funding have little allocated for their healthcare budgets. Rural areas are poorly funded as compared to urban areas. Poor women, especially in rural areas, are often seen by a nurse or nurse–midwife for prenatal care and delivery, whereas urban women more often receive prenatal care and delivery from a physician (Harrison, 2004).

The South African healthcare system faces many challenges. The country's history of very high rates of communicable and noncommunicable diseases, combined with the legacy of colonialism, Apartheid, and post-Apartheid turmoil, have led to major racial and gender discrimination, a migrant labor system, destruction of family life, great disparities in family incomes, and extreme violence, which have all affected the health and healthcare system of the nation. For many decades, black people were forced to work for the white minority for very low wages. Before 1994, politics restricted health and healthcare for blacks. The public healthcare system has now been transformed into an integrated national service, but is plagued by a lack of management and leadership. Some of the main problems related to health include poverty-related illnesses such as infectious diseases (HIV/AIDS, TB, and malaria), maternal mortality, malnutrition, and high rates of noncommunicable diseases. HIV/AIDS accounts for 31% of the disability-adjusted life-years, and violence and injury continue to cause premature deaths (Coovadia et al., 2009).

South Africa is considered a middle-income country because of its economy, yet its disease rates are higher than those in many low-income countries. It is one of only 12 countries in the world where child mortality has increased, rather than decreased, since the 1990 Millennium Developmental Goals were established (Coovadia, Jewkes, Barron, Sanders, & McIntyre, 2009). There are great disparities between the country's public and private healthcare systems. Less than 15% of the population uses private health care, yet 46% of all healthcare expenditures are devoted to private healthcare services. There is also a disparity in funding among the provinces within South Africa's healthcare system.

State of Health in South Africa

The general state of health in South Africa reflects the huge burden of disease, particularly the tremendous impact of HIV/AIDS. HIV rates have reached as high as 31% of all pregnant women being HIV positive, and 25% of the general population being HIV positive. Approximately 5 million people in South Africa are living with HIV/AIDS at present. The link between high risk sexual behaviors, IV drug use, and transfer of HIV virus from mother to child (vertical transmission) which resulted in HIV disease was long denied by both former president Thabo Mbeki and former Prime Minister Kgalema Motlanthe. In 2008, Mbeki resigned, and by 2009 a new government administration was committed to increasing the funding for HIV/AIDS treatment. Only 12% to 13% of patients who need antiretroviral drugs actually receive them, however. Approximately 60% to 70% of all hospital admissions are HIV/AIDS related, which is creating a huge burden on the healthcare system, with concomitant challenges related to financing of health care and availability of trained healthcare personnel. At present there are 1.2 million orphans in South Africa, In addition, many elderly have lost their financial support due to the early deaths of their adult children from HIV/AIDS (Coovadia et al., 2009).

Healthcare spending in South Africa averages $748 per capita. Solutions to the problems facing the healthcare system need to include the integration of services, including maternal and child health, at the primary care level. The average life expectancy at birth is low—53.4 years (2005)—in South Africa, mainly due to HIV rates, which are exceptionally high among the 15- to 49-year-old age group. Maternal mortality is 150 deaths per 100,000 live births, and child mortality is 55 deaths per 1000 live births (Coovadia et al., 2009).

Violence and Injury

South Africa also has many disturbing social issues that have proved challenging to manage. It is estimated that 500,000 women are raped each year in the country. Approximately 28% of men state that they have committed rape. Gender-based violence is especially high, with South African female homicide rates being six times the global average; 50% of the female victims are killed by their spouses or partners. In addition, this country is ranked by the United Nations as second in the world for murder and first for assaults and rape. Violence and injury are the second leading cause of death, and the injury rate is almost twice the global average. Approximately 16,000 road-related (motor vehicle collision) deaths occur yearly. Children also are subject to very high rates of sexual, physical, and emotional abuse and neglect (Coovadia et al., 2009).

Maternal and Infant Health

South Africa has a major problem with maternal and infant health. The infant mortality rate is 42.5 per 1000 live births. Each year approximately 75,000 children die, and 23 die within their first month of life. In addition, 23,000 babies are stillborn, a factor closely associated with the 1660 maternal deaths that occur annually. The major causes of maternal deaths are HIV/AIDS infections. Strengthening HIV/AIDS health care will require at least a 2.4% increase in funding for HIV prevention and treatment programs (Coovadia et al., 2009).

Major Health Issues

As noted previously, South Africa is challenged by very high rates of injury, the problem of underdevelopment of the country as a whole, and numerous residents with chronic diseases. The largest rise in death rates for adults has occurred among the young adult group, who are dying in increasing numbers from HIV/AIDS. Deaths from tuberculosis, pneumonia, and diarrhea are also increasing rapidly. The leading cause of death in South Africa is HIV/AIDS (infants and young adults), followed by homicide (young adult men), tuberculosis, road traffic accidents, and diarrhea. Large numbers of deaths from noncommunicable diseases occur in the 60 and older group of the population. Causes of death for children younger than 5 years are ranked as follows (Bradshaw & Nannan, 2004):

1. HIV/AIDS
2. Low birth weight
3. Diarrhea
4. Lower respiratory infections

5. Protein-energy malnutrition
6. Neonatal infections
7. Birth asphyxia and birth trauma
8. Congenital heart disease
9. Road traffic accidents
10. Bacterial meningitis

There is a significant increase in the use of tobacco in South Africa, which in turn is causing more lung diseases, especially lung cancer. Campaigns to deter youth from smoking and encourage smokers to stop are being led by healthcare organizations in increasing numbers.

Throughout South Africa, there is a major change in diet in terms of types and quantity of foods consumed, with movement away from traditional plant foods to high-fat and high-sugar foods with low fiber. As a result of this change, overweight and obesity are now chronic problems among South African people. Urban people are more likely to be obese than rural people, and those older than 65 years are less likely to be obese. South Africans are now more sedentary than they previously were as well.

Alcohol consumption is also increasing, especially among males. It not only is causing chronic diseases such as liver and esophageal cancer, but also is contributing to homicides, violence, and motor vehicle accidents (Bradshaw & Nannan, 2004).

Racial/Ethnic Inequalities

Numerous racial inequalities continue to exist in the wake of Apartheid. Significant disparities in standards of living persist, with most blacks continuing to lack adequate public health services, such as clean water, a proper sewage system, and access to health care, making them much more vulnerable to disease. Unemployment is much higher within the black or African populations compared to the other ethnic groups. Whites are the most employed group. Half of all Africans live in formal housing (solid structures with indoor plumbing and electricity), compared with 95% of whites. Poverty-related health problems such as infectious diseases, maternal and infant deaths, and malnutrition remain widespread (Kon & Lackan, 2008).

Healthcare Personnel

There is a shortage of nursing and other healthcare personnel in South Africa, as well as a problem of maldistribution of resources. The majority of trained nursing and allied health professionals work in the private sector, which serves much less of the general population than does the public sector. In addition, more trained health personnel work in urban areas than in rural areas. Doctors, especially those with more subspecialty training, are more likely to work in the private sector and in urban areas (79%) as well. Moreover, there has been a trend of skilled health personnel leaving South Africa for other countries, such as the United States, Canada, New Zealand, the United Kingdom, and Australia. South Africa is actively trying to recruit nurses and doctors, especially to work in the underserved areas. In addition to healthcare personnel trained in Western medicine, there are 200,000 traditional healers who practice in South Africa (Coovadia et al., 2009; Padarath, Ntuli, & Berthiaume, 2004).

Chronic Diseases

South Africa, a developing country, currently is experiencing a vast increase in the prevalence of chronic diseases, which historically were more associated with developed countries. Health problems such as hypertension, elevated cholesterol, alcohol and tobacco use, and obesity are now being observed in South

Africa in greater frequencies. Risks for chronic diseases reflect individuals' age, gender, tobacco and alcohol use, diet, and physical activity. Other risk factors include family history and genetic background. Most chronic diseases are preventable with modification of lifestyle behaviors, and changes in activity and diet can greatly influence the risk for numerous chronic diseases.

The leading causes of deaths in South Africa include the following:

- HIV/AIDS
- Heart disease
- Homicide and violence
- Stroke
- Tuberculosis
- Lower respiratory infections
- Road traffic accidents
- Diarrhea diseases
- Hypertension
- Diabetes

All of these conditions are chronic diseases, with the exception of homicide and violence and traffic accidents (Coovadia et al., 2009; Padarath, Ntuli, & Berthiaume, 2004).

Communicable Diseases

Sexually transmitted infections (STIs) remain one of the most common problems in adolescents and young adults in South Africa. Approximately 10% of all adults who visit a health clinic have concerns about a STI. Nearly 4 million people develop these diseases each year. Healthcare workers are involved in treatments and prevention measures, such as counseling, condom promotion, and partner notification (Shabalala et al., 2002).

Tuberculosis is a chronic pulmonary and extrapulmonary disease characterized by positive acid-fast stains or cultures of *Mycobacterium tuberculosis*. A TB skin test provides evidence of the infection, if positive. A chest X-ray is taken to confirm shadowing, reflecting lung invasions from TB. Cervical lymph node swelling may also be present.

Tuberculosis is a huge problem in South Africa. South Africa ranks fifth in the world in number of TB cases, with 948 cases per 100,000 population, and cure rates remain at 60%. Part of the reason for the high prevalence in this country is improved case detection brought on by the HIV/AIDS epidemic, especially among young adults. The high rate also reflects South Africa's poor standard of living, which is characterized by poverty and overcrowding. Other factors include the increase and extent of drug resistance, particularly multidrug resistance (MDR) (Mwinga & Fourie, 2004). A recent study reported that 55% of the people with TB were also HIV positive. Those affected by HIV/AIDS are five times more likely to develop TB. One-third of the 40 million people in all of Africa with HIV/AIDS also have TB; in sub-Saharan Africa, the rate is even higher. The South African Medical Research Council predicted that there would be 300,000 cases of TB and 30,000 deaths from this cause in the country—a fatality rate of 10%, in a nation that once had one of the lowest TB death rates in Africa before the advent of HIV/AIDS (Bamford, Loveday, & Verkuijl, 2004; Nullis-Kapp, 2005). The Eastern Cape, a very poor rural area with limited resources, has an extremely high incidence of TB, with 675 cases per 100,000 population (Bamford et al., 2004).

Cholera is an intestinal illness caused by the *Vibrio cholerae* organism. Cholera results in loss of large volumes of watery stool (excrement), leading to rapid dehydration and shock, and often resulting in death without treatment. The fatality rate for untreated cholera is 50%. Persons with cholera develop rapid breathing, vomiting, and painless diarrhea, and they go into metabolic acidosis. Appropriate oral or intravenous rehydration therapy is needed to replace lost fluids and electrolytes.

Cholera is one of the diseases requiring notification of the WHO. Nevertheless, cholera epidemics remain common in Asia, Africa, India, and South America (Sack, Sack, Nair, & Siddique, 2005). In South Africa, cholera represents a significant burden. In 2000–2001, a cholera epidemic occurred, with 106,389 reported cases. Cholera deaths result from poor sanitation and poor-quality water supplies—and an estimated 18 million South Africans have no basic sanitation. Of this group, 75.8% live in rural areas. Almost 50% of those children go to schools where there is only a pit for toilet use. By 2002, after initiatives were undertaken to help those persons without water and sanitation, the number of persons in South Africa with cholera infection was reduced to 7 million (Duse, da Silva, & Zeitsman, 2003; Mudzanani, Ratsaka-Mathokoa, Mahlasela, Netshidzivhani, & Mugero, 2004).

Across the continent of Africa, more than 38% of all people have no access to safe water—a percentage higher than that found in any other place in the world. In South Africa, some 12 million people lack safe water and 20 million lack sanitation facilities. By the year 2020, South Africa's population demands will exceed its water supply by 6%. Health maintenance is dependent on an adequate water supply and adequate sanitation facilities (toilets). It is vital in hospitals and healthcare clinics to have adequate clean water and sanitation for prevention and treatment of diseases and illnesses. A clean and adequate supply is necessary for simple hand washing in patient care. In short supply areas, it is necessary for healthcare workers to disinfect water if unclean and teach similar techniques to patients. Example techniques include boiling, use of chlorine tablets, filtration, and clean storage (Duse et al., 2003).

Malaria is a serious disease transmitted to humans by the bite of the *Anopheles* mosquito. Symptoms include fever and a flulike illness characterized by chills, headache, muscle aches, and fatigue. Malaria can also cause anemia and jaundice. If not treated promptly, this infection can lead to kidney failure, coma, and death. Malaria can be prevented by antimalarial drugs, such as atovaquone/proguanil, doxycycline, and mefloquine. Chloroquine is not effective for malaria prevention in South Africa. Protection from mosquito bites is also very important (Centers for Disease Control and Prevention [CDC], 2004).

Malaria is a major health problem in sub-Saharan Africa and affects great numbers of young children and pregnant women. It is the main cause of 20% of all deaths of young children in Africa. Approximately 95% of the infections in South Africa are due to *Plasmodium falciparum,* a microbe that lives in the gut of the *Anopheles* mosquito. Transmission is seasonal, with October to February seeing the emergence of the largest number of cases. Use of drugs for treatment and vector control by spraying has proved effective in deterring infection. South Africa, along with five other countries, was given permission by the United Nations Environmental Programme to use DDT for public health use only. The application of DDT in 2000 led to significant improvements in the mortality and morbidity associated with this disease. It should be noted, however, that DDT is a banned pesticide in the United States and most developed and developing countries (Moonasar et al., 2004).

South Africa has an estimated 4–6 million people living with HIV/AIDS. The national prevalence of HIV in pregnant women is 26.2%. A study by the South African Medical Research Council concluded that for 2000–2001, the prevalence of HIV/AIDS was almost three times as high in reality as that listed in a government statistical report. In 80% of AIDS-related deaths in men, and 70% in women, the cause of death listed on the death certificate as TB or lower respiratory tract infection. In children, three times as many AIDS-related deaths were identified as due to lower respiratory tract infections, diarrheal disease, and protein-energy malnutrition, rather than AIDS ("South Africa Needs to Face the Truth," 2005).

The highest rates of disease transmission occur among newborns and breastfed children. Poverty increases the vulnerability to HIV infection somewhat, because poor people usually have less education and less access to information about safe sex practices. High unemployment rates and lack of support may deny mothers access to care in clinics. Access to antiretroviral therapy (ART) drugs for HIV/AIDS patients in South Africa is very limited. In 2002, of the 500,000 who could immediately benefit from such medications, only 20,000 to 40,000 were receiving treatment; of those who were receiving treatment, most were receiving care in the private sector. In 2003, the government made ART more widely available to the public sector. One problem in providing these drugs is the very high costs for the medications and tests (Doherty & Colvin, 2004).

In 2005 in South Africa, where less than 3% of people who need ART actually receive it, private companies began supplying drugs directly to employees who are HIV positive. The corporate sector is presently taking more responsibility for care of workers with this disease than ever before (Venter, 2005).

Some of the social factors that make South African women vulnerable to HIV/AIDS relate to the position of women in society and practice of safe sex. Women are often born into a low social status in South Africa. Physiologically men are able to pass the virus to women more easily than women pass the virus to men, making a woman twice as likely to become infected. Women are also vulnerable to contracting the HIV virus and many other STIs because of the greater mucosal surface exposed to pathogens in females during sexual activity, particularly in young girls, who are not fully mature.

Another HIV/AIDS risk factor is the very high rate of violence against women in South Africa. The incidence of rape in South Africa is considered to be among the highest in the world, yet these crimes are seldom reported. Rates of rapes of female children are exceptionally high. A myth that "having sex with a virgin will cure AIDS" remains to blame for part of the increase in child rape. In addition, a very high incidence of husband/boyfriend violence occurs. Women can be beaten if they refuse to have sex with their partners. Women often remain in abusive relationships for financial dependency reasons. No matter why it occurs, violence against women increases the risk of HIV and STI infections.

In South Africa, 30% of women are heads of households; these individuals are often poor, have no financial aid from men, and consequently have a very unfavorable economic position and little power. Selling sex can often be a survival strategy for these women, albeit one that makes them even more vulnerable to HIV. Young girls may trade sex for money, clothes, or food (Ackerman & de Klerk, 2001).

Another problem in South Africa is the increasing number of orphans who are left behind when both of their parents die of AIDS. Some grandparents are trying to provide care for as many as 10 to 20 grandchildren after they have lost their children. Other AIDS orphans are left alone to care for themselves. There is a lost generation of street children who have no education and have few economic resources. Some sell themselves for sex to keep themselves and siblings fed. Some are HIV infected and some are not, but many will die regardless of their situation (Sowell, 2000).

Aging

The South African population is aging because of declining fertility rates and decreases in life expectancy among those persons infected with HIV. In 2001 those in their 70s represented 3.2% of the population, and those in their 80s represented 1%. Elderly adults are expected to account for 30 people per 100 population in 2015. Even with the AIDS epidemic there will be a large number of adults 65 and older, as compared to the number of children—AIDS affects the older adult population to the least extent (Joubert & Bradshaw, 2004).

The older black adults of South Africa are among the poorest people in the country and often lack credit or employment. Most have lived through the Apartheid years and have been poor all their lives. Fifty-eight percent of older adult Africans have no education; in Limpopa the rate is 74%, and in Mpurmalanga the rate is 66%. Many older adults, especially the Africans who live in poverty and have little or no formal education, are now taking care of their children and/or grandchildren, which is a very difficult burden. Their main source of income is Social Protection (Old Age Pension), which is provided for men 65 and older and for women 60 and older (Joubert & Bradshaw, 2004).

Traditional Medicine

The Alma-Ata Declaration on primary health care, in conjunction with WHO and the United Nations International Children's Emergency Fund (UNICEF), gave international recognition to the positive role of traditional indigenous healthcare providers. Traditional practitioners and birth attendants are recognized as important people in the primary healthcare team, but not as part of the public health service. Historically Western-style health practitioners, such as Dr. David Livingston, consulted with indigenous healers on drug treatment for fevers. Within South Africa, many traditional healers believe that illness cannot be directly explained in physical terms, and some believe in supernatural entities, such as spirits, that bring about illness. Some also believe in direct causal connections comparable to Western medicine. Different healthcare ideologies and systems have stood side by side together in South Africa for many years. Patients may want to use both types of medicine "just to play it safe." As many as 80% of the indigenous African people are accustomed to using traditional medicine as a first means for treatment of illness. Their faith in this system may not necessarily be misplaced: Noristan Laboratories, a large pharmaceutical company, tested 350 herbs used by indigenous healers and found that 80% had some medicinal properties. In any event, patients are faced with two healthcare system perspectives and will most likely continue to seek care from either as they see fit. At present, there is limited cooperation between the two systems (Muller & Steyn, 1999).

The indigenous flora of South Africa include 23,404 higher plant species, and the use of many of these species for medicinal use dates back to the San people in the region more than 20,000 years ago. Traditional medicine use in South Africa is often unacknowledged by the Western-style healthcare system, yet pharmacists are often well equipped to bridge the gap between indigenous medicines and Western ones (Scott, Springfield, & Coldrey, 2004).

CONCLUSION

Table 3-18 compares and contrasts a variety of health statistics for the developing countries covered in this chapter—Egypt, China, India, and South Africa. It identifies the health indicator or type of health issue, the date of data collection, data type, and then the various data collected from each country.

This chapter has addressed the health and health care of four developing countries. Although Egypt, China, India, and South Africa are located in different regions of the world, and they have a variety of languages, customs, values, health practices, types of government, and health care per capita allocations, they also share some commonalities and similar health challenges. Although the data presented here can be used for cross-country comparisons, the definitions of health problems and data collection methodology may greatly differ, so that these comparisons, at best, may be only a good estimate for a certain time and geographical location.

TABLE 3-18

Healthcare Statistics for Egypt, China, India, and South Africa

Indicator	Date/ Date Range	Data Type	Data			
			China	Egypt	India	South Africa
HIV/AIDS						
People living with HIV/AIDS	Data from most recent year available	Number	740,000	11,000	2,400,000	5,600,000
Adults living with HIV/AIDS	2009	Number	730,000	10,000	2,300,000	5,300,000
Adult HIV/AIDS prevalence rate	2009	%	0.1%	<0.1%	0.3%	17.8%
Women living with HIV/AIDS	Number of women living with HIV/AIDS and women as a percentage of adults living with HIV/AIDS, 2009	%	32%	24%	38%	62%
Men living with HIV/AIDS	Number of men living with HIV/AIDS and men as a percentage of adults living with HIV/AIDS, 2009	%	NA	81%	61%	38%
Children living with HIV/AIDS	2009	Number	NA	NA	NA	330,000
AIDS deaths	2009	Number	26,000	<500	170,000	310,000
AIDS orphans	2009	Number	NA	NA	NA	1,900,000
ARV need	2009	Number	NA	3,300	NA	2,600,000
ARV treatment	2009	Number	65,481	359	320,074	971,556
ARV coverage Rate	2009	%	NA	11%	NA	37%
Tuberculosis						
Tuberculosis HBCs	2010	Text	Yes	No	Yes	Yes
New TB cases	2009	Number	1,300,000	15,000	2,000,000	490,000
New TB smear-positive cases	2008	Number	640,000	6500	890,000	200,000
New TB case rate	2009	Rate per 100,000	96	19	168	971
People living with TB	2009	Number	1,900,000	25,000	3,000,000	400,000
TB prevalence rate	2009	Rate per 100,000	138	30	249	808
TB death rate	2009	Rate per 100,000	12	1	23	52
TB prevalence in HIV-positive people per 100,000 population	2007	Rate per 100,000	1	0	4	345

TABLE 3-18

Healthcare Statistics for Egypt, China, India, and South Africa (continued)

Indicator	Date/ Date Range	Data Type	Data			
			China	Egypt	India	South Africa
Malaria						
Malaria cases	2009	Number	14,491	94	1,563,344	6072
Malaria deaths	2009	Number	12	2	1133	45
Other Diseases, Conditions, and Risk Indicators						
Yellow fever cases	2009	Number	NA	NA	NA	0
Yellow fever deaths	2004	Number	0	0	0	0
Diphtheria cases	2009	Number	0	0	NA	1
Measles cases	2009	Number	52,461	608	NA	5857
Polio cases	2009	Number	0	0	752	0
DTP3 immunization coverage rate	2009	%	97%	97%	66%	69%
Vitamin A supplementation coverage rate	2009	%	NA	NA	66%	NA
Percentage with water	2008	%	89%	99%	88%	91%
Access to sanitation	2008	%	55%	94%	31%	77%
Population undernourished	2005–2007	%	10%	NA	21%	NA
Low-birth-weight babies	2000–2009	%	3%	13%	28%	NA
Child malnutrition	2000–2009	%	6.8%	6.8%	43.5%	NA
Female prevalence of obesity	2005	%	2%	46%	1%	35%
Male prevalence of obesity	2005	%	2%	22%	1%	7%
Female prevalence of smoking	2006	%	4%	1%	4%	9%
Male prevalence of smoking	2006	%	59.5%	27.6%	33.2%	29.5%
Programs, Funding, and Financing						
Financial development assistance for health per capita	2007	U.S. dollars	$0.18	$1.23	$0.50	$6.60
USAID NTD program countries	Fiscal year 2010	Text	No	No	Yes	No
USAID maternal assistance	Fiscal year 2010	Text	No	Yes	Yes	No
U.S. food assistance program countries	Fiscal year 2008	Text	No	No	Non-emergency	No
USAID nutrition program countries	Fiscal year 2010	Text	No	Yes	Yes	No
Health expenditure per capita	2008	U.S. dollars	$265	$261	$122	$843
Total expenditure on health	2008	%	4.3%	4.8%	4.2%	8.2%
Government health expenditures as a percentage of total government expenditures	2008	%	10.3%	5.9%	4.4%	10.4%
Government health expenditures as a percentage of total health expenditures	2008	%	47.3%	42.2%	32.4%	39.7%
Social security expenditures on health	2008	%	66.3%	21.6%	17.2%	3.0%
Out-of-pocket expenditures on health	2008	%	82.6%	97.7%	74.4%	29.7%

(continues)

TABLE 3-18

Healthcare Statistics for Egypt, China, India, and South Africa *(continued)*

Indicator	Date/ Date Range	Data Type	China	Egypt	India	South Africa
Health Workforce and Capacity						
Physicians	2000–2010	Rate per 10,000	14	28	6	8
Nurses and midwives	2000–2010	Rate per 10,000	14	35	13	41
Community health workers	2000–2010	Rate per 10,000	8	NA	1	NA
Births attended by skilled health personnel	2000–2010	%	96%	79%	47%	91%
Hospital beds	2000–2009	Rate per 10,000	30	21	9	28
Demography and Population						
Population	2011	Number	1,336,718,015	82,079,636	1,189,172,906	49,004,031
Adult sex ratio	2011	Number	1.17	1.03	1.07	1.02
Median age	2011	Number	35.5	24.3	26.2	25.0
Population younger than age 15	2010	%	18%	33%	32%	31%
Urban population	2010	%	47%	43%	29%	52%
Land area	2009	Number	9,560,981	1,001,449	3,287,263	1,221,037
Population density	2010	Number	140	80	362	41
Birth rate	2011	Rate per 1000	12.29	24.63	20.97	19.48
Total fertility rate	2011	Number	1.54	2.97	2.62	2.30
Adolescent fertility rate	2000–2008	Rate per 1000	5	50	45	54
Contraceptive prevalence rate	2000–2010	%	84.6%	60.3%	56.3%	59.9%
Death rate	2011	Rate per 1000	7.03	4.82	7.48	17.09
Infant mortality rate	2011	Rate per 1000	16.06	25.20	47.57	43.20
Female infant mortality rate	2011	Rate per 1000	16.57	23.52	49.14	39.14
Male infant mortality rate	2011	Rate per 1000	15.61	26.80	46.18	47.19
Under-five mortality rate	2009	Rate per 1000	19	21	66	62
Maternal mortality ratio	2008	Rate per 100,000	38	82	230	410
Life expectancy: female	2009	Number	76	73	66	55
Life expectancy: male	2009	Number	72	69	63	54
Population growth rate	2011	%	0.49%	1.96%	1.34%	-0.38%

TABLE 3-18

Healthcare Statistics for Egypt, China, India, and South Africa *(continued)*

Indicator	Date/ Date Range	Data Type	Data China	Egypt	India	South Africa
Income and the Economy						
GDP per capita	2009	$	$6828	$5673	$3296	$10,278
GNI per capita	2009	$	$6890	$5680	$3280	$10,050
Population living on less than $1.25 per day	Data from most recent year available	%	4.0% (2005)	0.4% (2005)	10.5% (2005)	3.3% (2006)
Unemployment rate	Data from most recent year available	%	4.3% (2005)	9.7% (2010)	10.8% (2010)	23.3% (2010)
Country income classification	As of July 2011	Text	Upper middle income	Lower middle income	Lower middle income	Upper middle income
External country debt	2009	U.S. dollars	$428,442	$33,257	$237,692	$42,101

ARV: antiretroviral therapy.

Source: Kaiser Family Foundation, n.d.

STUDY QUESTIONS   www

1. How are the health issues of infant mortality and nutrition similar for the countries of Egypt, China, India, and South Africa?
2. Compare and contrast the health beliefs and practices of traditional medicine in China with those in India. How do cultural influences affect health and health care differently? What are some basic commonalities?
3. What are some contributory factors leading to the exceptionally high rate of HIV/AIDS in South Africa?

CASE STUDY

Smoking and health concerns vs. tobacco production in China

"As the health impact of smoking, including rising heart disease and lung cancer, gradually emerges, unless there is effective government intervention, it will affect China's overall economic growth due to lost productivity," said Yang Gonghuan, deputy director of the Chinese Center for Disease Control and Prevention. Lost productivity from smoking-related health problems will hamper China's economic growth, and related costs incurred by smoking far exceed the tobacco industry's contribution in terms of profits and jobs it generates. China's addiction to huge revenues from the state-owned tobacco monopoly is hindering anti-smoking measures, potentially costing millions of lives in the country with the world's largest number of smokers. The warnings, issued in a report prepared by a group of prominent public health experts and economists, came amid growing calls for the government to give stronger support to tobacco-control measures. China is the world's largest tobacco producing and consuming country, with more than 300 million smokers on the mainland. Each year, about 1.2 million people die from smoking-related diseases on the mainland and the figure will increase to 3.5 million by 2030, according to estimates from the World Health Organization (WHO). The report underscores increasing concern that the country's economic potential will be jeopardized due to escalating medical costs and lost productivity if the government fails to take serious action to combat smoking.

Reference

Shan, J. (2012). Report: Smoking industry harming economic health. *China Daily.*

Case Study Questions

1. What are some major health risks related to smoking and what is the impact on health for the Chinese people?
2. Why do you think that government owned tobacco production in China continues in spite of knowledge about health risks?
3. How would you suggest that smoking in China be decreased?

REFERENCES

About Egypt: General information (2010). Retrieved from http://cabinet.gov.eg/AboutEgypt/GeneralInfo
.aspx

Ackerman, L., & de Klerk, G. (2002). Social factors that make South African women vulnerable to HIV infection. *Health Care for Women International, 23,* 163–172.

Ahrani, M., Houser, R., Yassin, S., Mogheez, M., Hussaini, Y., Crump, P. . . . Levinson, F. J. (2006). A positive deviance-based antenatal nutrition project improves birth-weight in Upper Egypt. *Journal of Health, Population, and Nutrition, 24*(4), 498–509.

Anand, S., Fan, V., & Zhang, J. (2008). Health care reform in China 5. China's human resources for health: Quantity, quality, and distribution. *Lancet, 372*(9651), 1774–1782.

Arab Republic of Egypt, Ministry of Foreign Affairs. (2010). Retrieved from http://www.mfa.gov.eg/English /insideegypt/history/Pages/default.aspx

Bamford, L., Loveday, M., & Verkuijl, S. (2004). Tuberculosis. In P. Ijumba, C. Day & A. Ntuli (Eds.), *South African Health Review* (pp. 213–228). Durban, South Africa: Health Systems Trust.

Bradshaw, D., & Nannan, N. (2004). Health status. In P. Ijumba & C. Day (Eds), *South African Health Review* (pp. 45–58).Durban, South Africa: Health Systems Trust.

Centers for Disease Control and Prevention (CDC). (2004). Malaria information for travelers to South Africa. Retrieved from http://www.cdc.gov/travel/regionalmalaria/safrica.htm

Central Intelligence Agency (CIA). (2005). The world factbook: South Africa. Retrieved from http://www .cia.gov/cia/publications/factbook/geos/sf.html

Central Intelligence Agency (CIA). (2012). The world factbook: South Africa. Retrieved from https://www .cia.gov/library/publications/the-world-factbook/geos/sf.html

Central Intelligence Agency (CIA). (2011a). The world factbook: China. Retrieved from http://www.cia.gov /cia/publications/factbook/goes/ch.html

Central Intelligence Agency (CIA). (2011b). The world factbook: India. Retrieved from http://www.cia.gov /cia/publications/factbook/goes/ind.html

Chang, D., & Kleinman, A. (2002). Growing pains: Mental health care in a developing China. In A. Cohen, A. Kleinman, & B. Saraceno (Eds.), *The World Mental Health Casebook* (pp. 85–97). New York: Kluwer.

Chen, W., Han, M., & Holzemer, W. (2004). Nurse's knowledge, attitudes, and practice related to HIV transmission in Northeastern China. *AIDS Patient Care and STDs, 18*(7), 417–422.

China fights growing problem of tuberculosis. (2010). Retrieved from http://www.reuters.com/article/2010 /01/06/idUSTOE5BG085

China surges past Japan as number 2 economy. (2010, August 17). *Atlanta Journal-Constitution*, p. 1.

Chopra, M., Lawn, J. E., Sanders, D., Barron, P., Abdool Karim, S. & Jewkes, R. (2009). Health in South Africa. *Lancet*. doi: 10.1016/S0140-6736(9).

Coovadia, H., Jewkes, R., Barron, P., Sanders, D., & McIntyre, D. (2009). Health in South Africa. *Lancet*. Retrieved from http://www.thelancet.com/series/health-in-south-africa

Dang, S., Yan, H., Yamamoto, S., Wang, X., & Zeng, L. (2004). Poor nutritional status of younger Tibetan children living at high altitudes. *European Journal of Clinical Nutrition, 58*, 938–946.

Darmstadt, G., Hasaan, M., Balsaran, Z., Winch, P., Darmstadt,G., Gipson, M. & Santosham M. (2009). Impact of clean delivery-kit use on newborn umbilical cord and maternal puerperal infections in Egypt. *Journal of Health, Population and Nutrition, 27*(6), 746–755.

Doherty, T., & Colvin, M. (2004). HIV/AIDS. In P. Ijumba & C. Day (Eds.), *South African Health Review* (pp. 191–212). Durban, South Africa: Health Systems Trust.

Du, S., Mroz, T., Zhai, F., & Popkin, B. (2004). Rapid income growth adversely affects diet quality in China—particularly the poor. *Social Science and Medicine, 59*, 1505–1515.

Duse, A., da Silva, M., & Zeitsman, I. (2003). Coping with hygiene in South Africa, a water scarce country. *International Journal of Environmental Research, 13*, S95–S105.

Egypt Demographic and Health Survey. (2008). Retrieved from http://www.measuredhs.com/pubs/pdf /FR220/FR220.pdf

George Institute for International Health. (2003). *China program: Factsheet*.

Gonghuan, Y. (2010). China wrestles with tobacco control. *Bulletin of the World Health Organization, 88*, 251–252.

Gossner, C., Schlundt, J., Embarek, P., Hird, S., Lo-FoWong, D., Beltran, J., . . . Tritscher, A. (2009). The melamine incident: Implications for international food and feed safety. *Environmental Health Perspectives, 117*(12), 1803–1808.

Gu, D., Reynolds, K., Wu, X., Chen, J., Duan, X., Reynolds, R., . . . He, J. (2005). Prevalence of the metabolic syndrome and overweight among adults in China. *Lancet, 365*, 1398–1405.

Harrison, S. (2004). Medical schemes. In P. Ijumba & C. Day (Eds.), *South African Health Review* (pp. 291–293). Durban, South Africa: Health Systems Trust.

Hays, J. (2011). Health Care in China: Doctors, insurance and costs. Retrieved from http://factsanddetails .com/china.php?itemid=335&catid=13&subcatid=83

Hesketh, T., & Zhu, W. (2002). *Health in China: From Mao to market reform.* China: United Nations Development Programme.

Hu, S., Tang, S., Liu, Y., & Zhao, Y. (2008). Reform of which health care is paid for in China: Challenges and opportunities. *Lancet, 372*(9652), 1846–1854.

Hu, X., Cook, S., & Salazar, M. (2008). Internal migration in China. *Lancet, 372,* 117–120.

International Agency for Research on Cancer. (2010). Cancer in Egypt. Retrieved from http://www.iarc.fr /en/publications/scientific-papers/2010/index.php

Ismail, H. (2011). Self-related health and factors influencing responses among young Egyptian type 1 diabetes patients. *BioMedCentral, 11,* 216–223.

Joubert, J., & Bradshaw, D. (2004). Health of older persons. In P. Ijumba & C. Day (Eds.), *South African Health Review* (pp. 147–162). Durban, South Africa: Health Systems Trust.

Kaiser Family Foundation. (n.d.). Customized data sheet. Retrieved from http://www.globalhealthfacts .org/data/factsheet.aspx?loc=59, 76,105, 195&ind=1,2

Kanabus, A. (2005). HIV and AIDS in China. Retrieved from http://www.avert.org/aidschina.htm

Kon, Z. R., & Lackan, N. (2008). Ethnic disparities in access to care in post-Apartheid South Africa. *American Journal of Public Health, 98*(12), 2272–2277.

Lasheen, M. R., El-Kholy, G., Sharaby, C. M., Elsherif, I. Y., & El-Wakeel, S. T. (2008). Assessment of selected heavy metals in some water treatment plants and household tap water in greater Cairo, Egypt. *Management of Environmental Quality, 19*(3), 367.

Life as a village doctor in southwest China. (1997). *Newsweek/Healthweek.* Retrieved from http://www .nurseweek.com/features/dispatches/China/971023.html

Lim, M., Yang, H., Zhang, T., Feng, W., & Zhou, Z. (2004, November/December). Public perceptions of private health care in socialist China. *Data Watch, 222–234.*

Lohinivak, A., El-Sayeed, N., & Talaat, M. (2008). Clean hands: Prevention of typhoid fever in rural communities in Egypt. *International Quarterly of Community Health Education, 28*(3), 215–227.

Moonasar, D., Johnson, C., Maloba, B., Kruger, P., le Grange, K., Mthembu, J., & van den Ende, J. (2004). Malaria. In P. Ijumba & C. Day (Eds.), *South African Health Review* (pp. 243–256). Durban, South Africa: Health Systems Trust.

Mudzanani, L., Ratsaka-Mathokoa, M., Mahlasela, L., Netshidzivhani, P., & Mugero, C. (2004). Cholera. In P. Ijumba & C. Day (Eds.), *South African Health Review* (pp. 257–264). Durban, South Africa: Health Systems Trust.

Muller, A., & Steyn, M. (1999). Culture and the feasibility of a partnership between Westernized medical practitioners and traditional healers. *Society in Transition, 30*(2), 142–156.

Mwinga, A., & Fourie, B. (2004). Prospects for new tuberculosis treatment in Africa. *Tropical Medicine and International Health, 9*(7), 827–832.

Nullis-Kapp, C. (2005). Africa is worst hit by dual epidemic. *Bulletin of the World Health Organization, 83*(3), 165–166.

Padarath, A., Ntuli, A., & Berthiaume, L. (2004). Human resources. In P. Ijumba & C. Day (Eds.), *South African Health Review* (pp. 299–318). Durban, South Africa: Health Systems Trust.

Pochagina, O. (n.d.). Suicide in present day China. *Far Eastern Affairs.*

Population—China. (2004, December). Putting on the brakes on reproduction. *Canada and the World,* 18–21.

Rao, M. (2009). Tackling health inequalities in India. *Perspectives in Public Health, 129*(5).

Rosenberg, M. (2011). China's one child policy. Retrieved from http://geography.about.com

Sack, D., Sack, R. B., Nair, G. B., & Siddique, A. K. (2005). Cholera. *Lancet, 363,* 223–33.

Scott, G., Springfield, E. P., & Coldrey, N. (2004). A pharmacognostical study of 26 South African plant species used in traditional medicine. *Pharmaceutical Biology, 42*(3), 186–213.

Shabalala, N., Strebel, A., Shefer, T., Simbayi, L., Wilson, T., Ratele, K., . . . Potgieter, C. (2002). Evaluation of the quality of care for sexually transmitted infections in primary care centers in South Africa. *South African Journal of Psychology, 32*(4), 33–40.

Shan, J. (2012). Report: Smoking industry harming economic health. *China Daily.* Retrieved from http://www.chinadaily.com.cn/china/2011-01/07/content_11805846.htm

South Africa needs to face the truth about HIV mortality. (2005). *Lancet, 365,* 546.

Sowell, R. (2000). AIDS orphans: The cost of doing nothing. *Journal of the Association of Nurses in AIDS Care, 11*(6), 15–16.

Spousal violence in Egypt. (2010). Retrieved from http://www.prb.org/pdf10/spousalviolence-egypt.pdf

U.S. Department of State, Bureau of African Affairs. (2005). South Africa. Retrieved from http://www.state.gov.r/pa/ei/bgn/2898.htm

Venter, L. (2005). Firms fill antiretroviral gap in South Africa. *Lancet, 365,* 1215–1216.

Wang, T. (2009). China takes a stab at universal health care. Retrieved from http://www.forbes.com/2009/01/22/china-health-care-markets-econ-cx_twdd_0122markets04.html

Watts, J. (2009). Lead poisoning cases spark riots in China. *Lancet, 374*(9693), 868.

World Health Organization (WHO). (2005). Mental health atlas. Retrieved from http://www.who.int/mental_health/evidence/atlas

World Health Organization (WHO). (2006). *Egypt: Country cooperation study for WHO and Egypt 2005–2009,* pp. 1–81. Geneva, Switzerland: Author.

World Health Organization (WHO). (2011). Egypt: Country health profile. Retrieved from http://www.who.int/gho/countries/egy/country_profiles/en/

World Health Organization (WHO) Global Health Observatory Data Repository. (2011). Retrieved from http://apps.who.int/ghodata/?vid=710

World Bank. (2010). Arab Republic of Egypt. Retrieved from http://worldbank.org/WBSITE/EXTERNAL/COUNTRIES/MENEXT/EGYPTEXTN/),menuPK:287182~pagePK:141132~piPK:141109~thesitePK:256307,00.html

Zhang, H., & Cai, B. (2003). The impact of tobacco on lung health in China. *Respirology, 8,* 17–21.

Zhang, J., Mauzerall, D., Zhu, T., Liang, S., Ezzati, M., & Remais, J. (2010). Environmental health in China: Progress towards clean air and safe water. *Lancet, 375,* 1110–1119.

Zheng, C. (2005). China making big progress in public health care. *China Education and Research Network.* Retrieved from http://www.edu.cn/20050114/3126783.shtml

Zimmer, Z., & Kwong, J. (2004). Socioeconomic status and health among older adults in rural and urban China. *Journal of Aging and Health, 16*(1), 44–70.

4

Global Perspectives of Economics and Health Care

Govind Hariharan
Gregory Simone

> *The lives of far too many people in the world are being blighted and cut short by chronic diseases such as heart disease, stroke, cancer, chronic respiratory diseases, and diabetes. This is no longer only happening in high income countries. Four out of five chronic disease deaths today are in low and middle income countries. People in these countries tend to develop diseases at younger ages, suffer longer—often with preventable complications—and die sooner than those in high income countries.*
>
> Lee Jon Wook, Director General,
> World Health Organization, 2005

OBJECTIVES

After reading this chapter the reader will be able to:

1. Compare and contrast the health economics of five countries: Canada, India, Japan, Ukraine, and the United States.
2. Discuss the greatest economic challenges in the United States' healthcare system.
3. Explain how the health economic systems of Canada and Japan differ from those of the United States.
4. Relate commonalities in economic challenges of the healthcare systems in India and the Ukraine.

INTRODUCTION

Across the world there is tremendous variation in the way health care is provided and funded and, most importantly, in healthcare outcomes. Despite these differences, concern about the financing of health care has become a matter of great concern in every economy. In developed countries, rapid growth in medical innovations and technology and the cost of caring for an aging population have combined to make soaring healthcare costs a primary concern. Developing countries, which are typically plagued with struggling economies, find themselves hard-pressed to find sources of funding for providing even basic medical care for a growing population.

Economics is the study of how to allocate scarce resources across unlimited wants and needs. It is no wonder, then, that in a world faced with the problem of ever-growing demands on its healthcare resources amid tightening budgets, the field of health economics has grown exponentially more important in academic and policy settings. Health economists are often interested in analyzing whether healthcare resources are utilized efficiently and whether the proper incentives and healthcare systems exist or can be created to ensure efficiency. The current system for the provision of health care in countries such as the United States is rather complex, with the patient often receiving care from providers who are paid by a third party such as a private or public health insurance organization. Unfortunately, more than 45 million people in the United States currently lack insurance coverage. Providing unpaid medical care for these uninsured segments of the population results in cost shifting that makes health insurance more expensive. Since the early 1970s, the emergence of managed care organizations in the United States (often centered on health insurance companies), with their emphasis on cost-effectiveness, return on investment, and proper alignment of incentives, highlighted the importance of utilizing economic principles in health care.

In this chapter, we compare and contrast five countries—Canada, India, Japan, Ukraine, and the United States—in terms of health economics. The choice of these particular countries for analysis was driven by the stark differences in their systems for providing health care and in their economic strength. Of these five countries, Canada, Japan, and the United States are highly industrialized countries with high per capita gross domestic product (GDP) levels and high levels of expenditure on health care, as shown in **Table 4-1**. Nevertheless, there are significant differences between them in the levels of public and private expenditures on health care, the type of health systems they use, and, by some measures, the levels of health of their population. India, by comparison, has a rapidly growing economy and the second largest population in the world, but faces enormous problems of health inequality. Ukraine is a newly independent former Soviet republic recovering from an economic recession; it has an archaic healthcare system.

The first section of this chapter briefly describes the history and structure of the healthcare systems in each country, pointing out some of the critical problems in each. It is followed by a comparative analysis of these countries on the basis of health care. The next section develops the economic concept of productivity, explains the various techniques for applying it in healthcare settings, and analyzes the productivity of healthcare resources in each country. Finally, we discuss some of the key issues in the development of an ideal healthcare system.

TABLE 4-1

Basic Economic and Demographic Characteristics, 2009 (or Latest Available Data)

Indicator	Canada	India	Japan	Ukraine	United States
Population (in thousands)	33,573	1,198,003	127,156	45,708	314,659
Gross national income per capita (international $)	38,710	2930	35,190	7210	46,790
Total health expenditure per capita (international $)	2883	132	2713	445	7410

Source: WHO, 2011.

PROFILES OF FIVE HEALTHCARE SYSTEMS

The five countries highlighted here show a wide range of healthcare structures, from the predominantly private system in Japan to the central universal program in Canada, from a health insurance-based system in the United States to a Ukrainian system with no health insurance. In this section, we begin with a profile of each country's healthcare system and then briefly conduct a comparatives study. The data for the profiles are derived from various sources at the Organization for Economic Cooperation and Development (OECD) and the Global Health Observatory Data Repository (GHODR) at the World Health Organization (WHO).

Profile of the Canadian Healthcare System

Canada is the second largest country in terms of land area in the world, but has a relatively small population of slightly more than 33.5 million. Prior to 1971, the Canadian healthcare system was very similar to that found in the United States; that is, it was predominantly based on employer-provided health insurance with a smaller role played by various government programs. Both hospitals and physicians operated privately, with physicians' fees determined by the market and hospitals paid on a negotiated fee-for-service basis. During this period, a little more than 7% of the country's GDP was spent on health care.

In 1971, Canada adopted a system of universal health insurance (Canadian Medicare System) provided by the government and funded by value-added taxes and income tax. All basic services are covered and patient copayments are nominal. Physicians are paid on the basis of a fee schedule determined by the government, and hospitals are allocated a budget by the provincial government, with the overall budget set nationally. Although health insurance is provided to all by the government, the provision of health care remains largely in private hands. Private health providers in Canada are heavily regulated, however, with price controls placed on most activities, services, and products. Hospitals also are restricted from raising funds on their own for capital investments and instead must obtain funds from the provincial government. Although there are significant differences in overall spending on health care between Canada and the United States, Canadian health expenditures have not grown as rapidly as those in the United States, mostly as a result of the government regulation of prices and the government setting the budget allocation for health care.

In the early 1990s, Canada went through an economic recession that resulted in significant cost-cutting measures. The cuts significantly affected healthcare expenditures, as these expenses represented the largest single item in the provincial government budgets. As a result, between 1992 and 1997, total health expenditure (THE) as a percentage of GDP declined significantly. Since then, it has continued to increase and, according to the OECD, was 11.4% in 2009. Public expenditure on health accounted for 70.6% of THE, while private expenditure represented 31.3% of this total. Hospitals occupy an important role in the Canadian health system, and inpatient costs represented 20% of THE in 2009 while outpatient services accounted for 33%. Payments to physicians account for approximately 13% of THE, with the vast majority of the physician payments being of the fee-for-service variety. Much of the increase in healthcare costs can be attributed to pharmaceutical costs; such costs account for 1.8% of Canada's GDP and have almost tripled since the late 1970s. The average per capita expenditure on drugs was $692 in 2009, with close to 90% of that amount being devoted to prescribed medication. In 2009, there were 2.4 physicians per 1000 people and 9.4 nurses per 1000 people. The number of hospital beds on a percentage basis decreased marginally during the 2000s, reaching a level of 3.3 beds per 1000 population in 2008. Canada has the longest waiting times for medical care among OECD countries, with 59% of patients waiting for four weeks or more for a specialty appointment.

Canadians have enjoyed significant improvements in life expectancy over the last four decades. Canadian life expectancy is among the highest in the countries belonging to the OECD (2001): 78.3 years for men and 83.0 years for women in 2007. The interesting aspect of Canadian life expectancy patterns recently has been the narrowing of the gap between men and women. According to Or (2000), per capita GDP and tobacco, alcohol, and fat consumption are all strongly correlated with premature mortality. Over the last three decades, there has been a 31% reduction in smoking rates (especially among men), with overall smoking rates in Canada dropping to 16.2% in 2009. Similarly, alcohol consumption has declined by 23% over the last 30 years. However, obesity, especially among women, remains a problem, with 40.3% of Canadian females and 55.5% of males classified as being obese. The reduction in male smoking and the higher rates of female obesity may be responsible for the narrowing gap in life expectancy across gender.

Canada has often been cited as an example of the type of system the United States should adopt to provide universal coverage, though its healthcare system has at least as many critics.

Profile of the Indian Healthcare System

With a population of more than 1 billion, India is the world's second largest country (after China) in terms of population. It is a country with sharp distinctions between "haves" and "have-nots," in which significant proportions of the population live in poverty while other segments are extremely well off. The Indian economy grew very rapidly during the 1990s and in the 2000s, with some years seeing double-digit growth rates. While the economy has continued on the fast track in this century, there has been a recent slowdown. Like China, India has benefited greatly from participating in the global economy and is fast approaching the status of an economic superpower.

India obtained its independence in 1947 from Great Britain and has, for much of its post-independent life, adopted a socialist approach to the provision of most services. Healthcare services, however, have to a large extent been provided and funded by private entities. More than 50% of all inpatient services and 60% of outpatient services are provided by the private sector. Many of the newer private hospitals are staffed by Western-educated medical personnel and equipped with the latest medical technologies available. Health care for the poorer and disadvantaged segments of the population, in contrast, is primarily provided in government-owned and ill-equipped health facilities. Public ownership of these institutions is divided between central (national), state, municipal, and *panchayat* (village) governments. Public facilities own and operate many teaching hospitals, secondary hospitals, rural referral hospitals, primary health centers, and clinics or dispensaries.

In 1951, Indian life expectancy at birth was only 36.7 years. It increased steadily over the second half of the twentieth century, reaching 64.1 years by 2009. Similarly, infant mortality was 146 deaths per 1000 live births in 1950, but declined to 50.3 deaths per 1000 births by 2009. On the positive side, only 2.1% of adults reported being obese in 2009 (self-reported data with attendant errors), alcohol consumption was only 0.7 liter per capita, and only 14.3% of the population older than age 15 smoked daily—all of which are among the lowest rates reported by OECD. On the negative side, although significant progress has been made since India won its independence, communicable diseases such as tuberculosis continue to affect large segments of the population. In addition, HIV/AIDS has assumed virulent proportions, and problems of access to clean drinking water and access to infant and maternal health care remain major barriers to advancement in health care.

According to WHO data, THE in India was 4.16% of GDP in 2010, with government expenditures accounting for 30.27% of total spending and private expenditures on health accounting for close to 70%. Health care is financed mostly with out-of-pocket payments, as private health insurance remains a very nascent industry in India. Out-of-pocket expenditures (which include fees paid by employers, which are mostly self-insured) accounted for 86.35% of private health expenditures on health and 60.21% of THE. The high out-of-pocket payments often pose a problem for the Indian population given that, according to a World Bank report by Peters and colleagues (2002), almost one-fourth of all hospitalizations push people into poverty because of the loss of jobs and the high cost of private medical facilities. In regard to public expenditures, the central government's allocation of funds for health as a component of its total budget remained stagnant in the 1990s and 2000s, while state allocations actually declined.

Health insurance covers approximately 10% of the population, with government employees covered under government plans and some private-sector employees covered under employer-provided plans. Since 2000, various plans have been rolled out by the government to provide affordable health insurance for the needy, but coverage for those insured by such plans is often restricted to delivery of services in ill-equipped public health facilities.

In 2009, India had approximately 0.7 physician per 1000 population and 0.9 nurse per 1000 population. Primary care physicians working in the public sector are paid a low and fixed salary, which is set at the national level. As a result most physicians work in their own clinics, where fees are determined in competitive factors. During the 1990s, with liberalization of controls, many private hospitals and hospital chains that had made large capital investments in advanced technology and with highly trained staff began to grow rapidly. These new facilities are providing care for the many beneficiaries of the booming economy. In addition, these new facilities have made significant inroads into providing services for the health tourists from Western economies attracted by the lower cost of advanced care in these facilities.

The stark disparity in healthcare utilization between different socioeconomic classes and rural–urban regions in India has been a matter of great concern for the government of India for many decades. The best indicator of this inequity is the disparity in infant mortality rates. The under-five mortality rate for the lowest wealth quintile is triple that of the highest quintile; it is also twice as high for rural regions compared to urban, and for mothers with no education compared to mothers with higher education. Similar disparities also exist with immunizations (see **Table 4-2**). Such disparities in health care at young ages are undoubtedly likely to result in widening disparities at older ages.

TABLE 4-2

Inequities in Health in India, 2010 (or Latest Available Data)

Indicator	Value
Under-five mortality rate (per 1000 live births)—rural	82
Under-five mortality rate (per 1000 live births)—urban	51.7
Under-five mortality rate (per 1000 live births)—lowest wealth quintile	64.3
Under-five mortality rate (per 1000 live births)—highest wealth quintile	30.6
Under-five mortality rate (per 1000 live births)—mother with no education	124.4*
Under-five mortality rate (per 1000 live births)—mother with higher education	50.5*
Measles immunization coverage among one-year-olds (%)—rural	45.3*
Measles immunization coverage among one-year-olds (%)—urban	69.2*
Measles immunization coverage among one-year-olds (%)—lowest wealth quintile	28.4*
Measles immunization coverage among one-year-olds (%)—highest wealth quintile	81.2*
Measles immunization coverage among 1-year-olds (%)—mother with no education	34*
Measles immunization coverage among 1-year-olds (%)—mother with higher education	75.8*

*Data are for 2005.
Sources: WHO, 2011; WHOSIS, 2006.

In addition to the inequalities between rural and urban regions, significant variations exist across states in India in every aspect of income and health, as shown in **Table 4-3**. The state of Punjab has the highest per capita income and the lowest percentage of its population living below the poverty level. The best-performing state in terms of health is Kerala; it also has the highest literacy rate (especially for women) and density of physicians and healthcare facilities per capita. Excluding Kerala, a positive relationship between high incomes and better health appears to hold in India.

As one of the fastest-growing economies in the world, India has to take urgent steps to address the huge disparities in healthcare provision that characterize the country. Sustained growth in the economy, however, will require a source of healthy human resources.

Profile of the Japanese Healthcare System

Since the end of World War II, Japan has evolved from being an economy devastated by war to the second largest economy in the world. In 2010 the gross domestic product per capita in Japan was 42,783 U.S. dollars [Japan: Gross domestic product (GDP) per capita in respective prices from 2001 to 2011 (in U.S. dollars), 2011]. It has a population of approximately 125 million, of which 20% are 65 years or older. By 2020, this segment is expected to account for more than one-fourth of the Japanese population. The rapid aging of the population is a matter of great concern, especially for healthcare provision and funding. Japan has some of the best health outcomes in the world, and it continues to improve the health status of the population. There is also very little disparity within the country in healthcare access.

At the end of World War II, life expectancy in Japan was 50 years for men and 54 years for women. It has since increased to become the highest life expectancy among developed countries, at 83 years at birth. Infant mortality is very low, with only 2.4 deaths per 1000 live births. The leading cause of death in Japan is malignant neoplasm, followed by cardiovascular disease. High stress levels have been blamed for the very high levels of suicides (19.7 deaths per 100,000 population), especially among working men. Although the prevalence of smoking is decreasing, this rate is still high—26.2% of the population aged 15 and older smokes—compared to other developed countries. Nearly 40% of Japanese men smoke, and this behavior is becoming increasingly prevalent among women as well.

The Japanese population enjoys universal healthcare coverage and free access to all health facilities. Enrollment in an insurance plan was made mandatory for all Japanese in 1961. Most people (approximately 75 million) obtain their insurance through employer-related groups; the rest are covered under a national health insurance plan. Employers contribute approximately 4.5% of their revenues and employees

---

TABLE 4-3

Health Disparity Across States in India

State	Per Capita Net State Domestic Product (Rupees)	Life Expectancy at Birth	Infant Mortality Rate per 1000 Live Births	Share of the Population Below the Poverty Line (%)
Andhra Pradesh	9982	63.1	55	15.77
Bihar	4123	60.2	62	42.6
Gujarat	12,975	62.8	62	14.07
Kerala	10,627	73.5	14	12.72
Punjab	15,310	68.1	52	6.16

Source: Government of India, 2005.

contribute 3.5% of their pay toward the insurance premium. Both the employer groups and the national plans have copayments and catastrophic caps on out-of-pocket payments. Balance billing—the practice of charging full fees and billing the patient for the amount unpaid by insurer—is prohibited, and prices to providers are set by the government. The fees for physicians are lower than those found in the Medicare Relative Value Scale used in the United States, a factor that explains a great deal of the lower health costs in Japan (Phelps, 2003). Hospitals are mostly private, but the large hospitals and teaching hospitals are public. Most doctors work in private clinics and earn much more than the specialists working in the hospitals. Members of the Japanese public visit their physicians regularly, at an average rate of 15 times per year (Phelps, 2003). However, the number of minutes spent with the doctor is lower than in the United States. The existence of a fee-for-service system makes high usage levels palatable to physicians and patients alike, as the patient does not bear much additional cost for frequent visits. For much the same reason, pharmaceutical spending is very high in Japan, accounting for 20% of total spending on health.

Total health expenditure in Japan has increased considerably since the 1990s, and now accounts for 8.5% of the country's GDP, according to OECD data. The rapid aging of the population has been a primary cause of high health expenditures in Japan, as in many other countries. A sizable portion of THE (approximately one-third) is devoted to care for the aged. Likewise, per capita expenditure for the aged was three times the average per-patient expenditure of $2046. In 2000, in response to the large increase in demand for long-term nursing care, the government introduced long-term care insurance. Although rates of hospital admission in Japan are lower than the United States, the average length of stay is much longer in Japan—more than 3 weeks. This factor explains why 32% of total health spending in 2009 was for inpatient care, with hospitals providing more than 90% of it. Outpatient care expenditure accounted for 34% of THE.

Public funds were used for 80% of total health expenditure, with the majority coming from the Social Security Fund. Private expenditure accounted for 18.5% of THE in 2009, with most of it being in the form of household copayments (80.6% in 2009). The low levels of private payment often result in patients going directly to specialists even for minor ailments. The fee-for-service system also results in overtreatment and has been blamed for the high average length of stay in hospitals. In 2006, there were 264,515 physicians in Japan, or 20.63 physicians per 10,000 population, and 41.4 nurses per 10,000 population.

Profile of the Ukrainian Healthcare System

Ukraine is the second largest country in Europe. It is a newly independent state formed as a result of the breakup of the Soviet Union in 1991. In the 2001 census, it had a population of 48.4 million, of whom 67% lived in urban areas. During the era of the Soviet republic, Ukraine was severely affected by major disasters including civil wars, famines, German invasion, and World War II. The Chernobyl nuclear accident in 1986 was a major catastrophe with significant consequences to life. The Ukrainian economy similarly suffered through a major economic recession from which it has only recently begun to recover. Since obtaining independence, Ukraine has developed the foundations for a more democratic system, but its healthcare system continues to be shackled by Soviet-style incentive systems.

Since the country gained its independence, the population of Ukraine has fallen by 3.6 million, or approximately 7.5%. In 2009, the population was estimated at 45,708,000. The country finds itself faced with the unfortunate situation of poor economic health and a shrinking and aging population. Its fertility rate is the lowest in Europe, and its birth rate fell by 40% during the 1990s. This trend has been attributed by some to the increased rates of abortion. For example, in 2002, there were 82.8 abortions for every 100 live births. As a result of the low birth rates, the proportion of the population younger than age 15 has declined over the last 10 years.

Ukraine faced a severe health crisis in the early 1990s when life expectancy actually fell by 4.4 years for men and 2.4 years for women. Although it has recovered from that crisis, in 2002 life expectancy was still only 62.2 years for men and 73.3 years for women. In 2009, life expectancy at birth in Ukraine was 68 years according to GHODR data. Cardiovascular disease is the primary cause of death in Ukraine. Because smoking is very prevalent (67% among men), alcohol consumption is very high, and 1% of adults have HIV/AIDS, the potential for significant health improvements is bleak.

Between 1990 and 1999, the GDP in Ukraine fell by 62%. During this period, declining incomes were accompanied by hyperinflation. Economic recovery since that time has been very slow. In 2000, only 66% of the adult population was actively employed, and more than one-fourth of the population lives in poverty. Thus the ability of the government to finance the growing demand for health care is very limited.

In the postwar Soviet state, healthcare services with universal access to care were provided in a multitier structure, with much of the responsibility for care being handled at the district (*rayon*) and regional (*oblasts*) levels. The republic provided more of the guidelines and norms governing the lower tiers. Healthcare services were provided at hospitals, sanitary and epidemiological stations, polyclinics, and specialized healthcare facilities. Size and staffing of these facilities were determined by population size. Much of the provision of care was initiated at the clinics and by primary physicians. During the 1970s and 1980s, there was considerable growth in the network of specialized facilities and units. This shifted priority away from primary care and physicians to specialists (WHO, 1999). The goal of the planning authorities was to increase capacity as measured by beds and personnel, and as a result Ukraine had the highest number of beds and physicians per capita in the world. The incentive structure was such that 80% of healthcare expenditure went toward inpatient care, and long hospital stays were common even for minor disorders. During the waning years of the Soviet Republic, a new economic mechanism (NEM) was introduced to transform the system to a performance-based system rather than a capacity-based system.

After Ukrainian independence in 1991, the economy experienced a painful restructuring stage in which the country had very little ability to fund the increasing need for health care. This phase of transition to a free market economy, as with many other former Soviet economies saw dramatic increases in prices of pharmaceuticals as well as basic necessities such as energy. The Ukrainian Constitution in 1996 stated that the function of the state was to "create conditions for effective medical services accessible to all citizens." Although Ukraine has universal access to health care for its citizens, most medical expenses are not covered except for children and other socially vulnerable groups. Thus out-of-pocket payments are quite high, as shown in **Table 4-4**.

Even by 2009, private insurance accounted for only slightly more than 2% of private health care spending in Ukraine. The structure of the present-day system remains similar to that of the Soviet system. Most of the primary health clinics (PHCs; there were 6456 of them in 2000) are funded and operated at the district (*rayon*) level. The regions fund and operate both the multispecialty and specialized

TABLE 4-4

Source of Finance (Percentage of Total Health Expenditure)

Source of Finance	1996	2000	2009*
Public (tax, nontax revenue)	81.4%	66.4%	55.03%
Private (out of pocket)	18.3%	32.1%	44.97%
Private health insurance	0.3%	0.7%	2.0%

*Data from GHODR.

Source: Lekhan, Rudiy, & Nolte, 2004.

hospitals. They also establish the number of beds and staffing levels. The area serviced by a PHC is broken up into catchment areas (*uchastok*), each with a certain number of residents and a primary care physician. Although on paper patients have free choice of physicians, there are many obstacles to realization of that freedom. Patients can also go to a specialist directly, and more 60% do so. The incentive system is such that this practice is even lucrative for primary care physicians, who get paid for referrals. More than 80% of the total public healthcare expenditure is funded locally, which results in significant inequalities across regions in the level of healthcare provision. In 2001, a system of interbudget transfers was set up to eliminate such regional imbalances. The budget allocation is based on the number of beds for hospitals and the number of visits for clinics. There is very little incentive to be efficient, and the system encourages use of consultants upon admissions.

Since 1991, healthcare expenditure in Ukraine has declined by 60%. The vast majority of healthcare facilities are publicly owned (24,166 such facilities in 2000) (WHO, 2000). Since 2000, there has been an attempt to increase the role played by privately owned facilities, but such a development is still in the nascent stages. The share of THE accounted for by inpatient care has dropped since independence, but remains high—more than 60% of THE—mostly as a result of reductions in the number of beds. By 2006, there were approximately 87 hospital beds per 10,000 population in the country. Capital investments in health care, while increasing during the 1990s, remain low, at only 7% of THE. The rate of replacement of outdated medical technology and equipment has been very low, consuming approximately 2% of THE.

Private health insurance remains very limited, with only 2% of the population covered by such policies in 2000. This meager rate is primarily a result of the high cost of such insurance and the inability of much of the population to afford it. In 1998, Ukraine developed a plan to provide mandatory state social insurance. This insurance was expected to cover the entire population, with insurance premiums being paid by employers and employees equally, and employee premium levels set at a fixed proportion of income. Ultimately, the high rates of unemployment and a poor state revenue base made this approach impractical, and the plan was rejected by parliament in 2003.

Ukraine has a very large number of physicians per capita. In 2006, there were 31.254 physicians per 10,000 people, according to WHO. Of this number, only 26.6% are primary care physicians; the remainder are specialists. The staffing model and low remuneration resulted in approximately 1300 vacant positions for physicians in 2000. The number of medical graduates rose by 20% from 1996 to 2001, but the supply of nurses has been falling steadily. In 1991, it reached its highest point, at 11.9 nurses per 1000 population, but had fallen to 7.8 nurses per 1000 population by 2002. This trend primarily reflects the low pay and low social prestige accorded to nurses. Healthcare professionals are paid fixed salaries based on a national pay scale. Since 2000, the government has been making efforts to provide performance-based salary increments.

Profile of the United States Healthcare System

The United States is the richest country in the world and is a leader in technological innovation. It is no wonder, then, that it has evolved into a leader in the provision of sophisticated health care. According to OECD data, in 2009, total health spending as a share of GDP was 17.4%, and health expenditures per capita were $7410. These rates were higher than those of any other country. The United States also has one of the fastest growth rates in real health expenditures per capita (exceeding 5% for most of the last two decades) and spends the most on pharmaceuticals among OECD member countries—$947 per capita in 2004. Despite these vast sums, over the past four decades the increase in life expectancy at birth of 7.6 years in the United States is less than the 14 years gained in Japan and the 8.6 years gained in Canada over the same time period. This finding has resulted in the claim by many that the United States has reached a level of production of health care at which further improvements in health care will require very large increases in expenditure, an issue explored further in the next section.

The U.S. healthcare system relies extensively on private insurance to provide financial coverage for its people. More than 70% of all U.S. residents younger than age 65 are enrolled in private health insurance plans, mostly through their employers. The American health system is also distinguished by the unique role of managed care organizations. Managed care organizations evolved in the early 1970s primarily as a response to the rapidly growing cost of care in the United States. In the previously common practice known as *fee for service,* providers charged a fee per unit of service rendered. Such reimbursement method resulted in significant overprovision of services: The provider was paid more for delivering more services. In managed care organizations, payment for services rendered by providers of care is usually based on a negotiated capitation or per-enrollee rate. In the early days of managed care, health maintenance organizations, in which the same organization that provided insurance itself provided care, were the norm. Since then, numerous other variants with different types of contractual arrangements between the insurance company and healthcare providers have emerged.

Government provision of health insurance in the United States is undertaken through Medicare and Medicaid, both of which were initiated in 1966. Medicare provides health insurance for the population aged 65 and older. Part A of Medicare covers hospitalization and some skilled nursing facility charges, and the supplemental Part B covers physician and laboratory charges and medical supplies. Most prescription drugs are not covered under Medicare, but the passage of the Prescription Drug Act in 2005 provided some relief from the soaring costs of pharmaceutical products. The working population pays a Medicare tax to pay for the benefits received by the elderly. The rapid growth in the elderly population caused by the aging of the baby-boom generation and their longer life spans, coupled with low birth rates and smaller working populations, has made the financial viability of such a program a matter of immediate and great concern. The Medicare system has been unable to meet its current obligations with current revenue since approximately 1995, and it is expected to deplete all of its accumulated funds within the next decade. Numerous attempts have been made to rein in the growth of Medicare expenditures, including contracting with managed care organizations and stricter controls on charges by hospitals and physicians.

Medicaid is a "safety net" program for people with low income—mostly women, children, and the elderly and disabled—who receive federal or state financial assistance. The program typically covers charges for physician visits, inpatient and outpatient hospital stays, and nursing home stays. Each state has tremendous discretion in determining benefits covered, however. As a result, significant variations exist across states in the level of benefits provided by Medicaid. Although initially it was a federal–state program with matching federal funds, Medicaid has become increasingly reliant on state tax revenues. As a result of escalating healthcare costs, Medicaid programs have become the largest single item in many states' budgets. As with Medicare, attempts to control growing Medicaid expenditures have included contracting with managed care organizations.

A potentially significant recent development has been the passage of the Affordable Care Act in 2010 (White House, 2011). This act attempts to overhaul health care provision in the United States by, among other things, prohibiting insurance coverage denial due to preexisting conditions and banning (restricting) use of lifetime (annual) limits on expenditure. The more significant and controversial aspects of the act take effect in 2014 with the creation of state-run medical insurance exchanges and mandatory insurance coverage. Because many aspects of this act are still under litigation, it is too early to include a detailed analysis of it in this edition.

In 2002, there were 5794 hospitals in the United States, and 3025 of them were nongovernment owned. Most of these hospitals are nonprofit organizations, with only about 766 of them being investor owned. Hospital charges account for more than one-third of all healthcare costs in the United States, racking up a total bill of $650 billion in 2002. Medicare paid 43.5% of this bill, private insurance paid 31.2%, Medicaid paid 18.3%, and the uninsured accounted for 3.8%. Persons aged 65 years and older make up about 13% of the total U.S. population but account for approximately 35% of all hospital stays. The top three principal diagnoses for this age group are hardening of the heart arteries, pneumonia, and congestive heart failure. The mean charge per stay was $17,300 in 2002, with infant respiratory distress syndrome having the highest average charge at $91,400 (see **Table 4-5**).

In the United States, unlike in most other OECD countries, private expenditure on health is larger than public expenditure, as health care is mostly financed through private insurance. The share of the population with private insurance is, therefore, higher than in any other country in the OECD. Nevertheless, approximately 15% of the U.S. population does not have any form of insurance and often must rely on emergency rooms for medical care. Emergency rooms are required by law to provide essential care regardless of insurance status. The cost of providing uncompensated care to uninsured patients is recovered by hospitals when feasible by charging more for their insured patients. Faced with the strong forces of competition from other providers, healthcare facilities in locations where such uncompensated care represents a large portion of the caseload often face an inability to pass on much of the costs; hospital bankruptcies are quite prevalent in these situations. The high cost of inefficiency to the hospitals under the newer reimbursement mechanisms has also resulted in significant reductions in the number of hospital beds. The United States now has the fewest number of hospital beds per capita among OECD countries, at 3.1 beds per 1000 population in 2009.

The United States has fewer physicians and nurses per capita than the OECD average (OECD, 2006). In 2009, there were 2.4 practicing doctors and 10.8 nurses per 1000 population. Because of the increasing prevalence of managed care organizations and the adoption of the relative value fee schedule for physician reimbursement rates, the number of general practitioners has been growing while the number of some specialists (anesthesiologists, for example) has been declining.

Smoking prevalence among U.S. adults has been estimated at 15.5% of the population aged 15 and older in 2009, a rate that is lower than that in Japan but higher than that in Canada. The obesity rate among adults was 33.8% in 2009—the highest in the OECD.

TABLE 4-5

Mean Hospital Charges

Principal Diagnoses with the Highest Mean Charges	Mean Charges*	Mean Length of Stay (days)
1. Infant respiratory distress syndrome	$91,400	24.2
2. Premature birth and low birth weight	$79,300	24.2
3. Spinal cord injury	$76,800	12.8
4. Leukemia (cancer of blood)	$74,500	14.1
5. Intrauterine hypoxia and birth asphyxia (lack of oxygen to baby in uterus or during birth)	$72,800	15.6
6. Cardiac and circulatory birth defects	$71,400	8.9
7. Heart valve disorders	$70,900	8.8
8. Polio and other brain or spinal infections	$63,200	13.0
9. Aneurysm (ballooning or rupture of an artery)	$55,300	7.7
10. Adult respiratory failure or arrest	$48,500	10.0

Source: Agency for Healthcare Research and Quality (AHRQ), 2003.

The question of why the United States, despite the prevalence of managed care and other cost-control mechanisms, finds its healthcare costs soaring has puzzled many. Three reasons are often cited for the rapid increase in healthcare costs: pharmaceutical price increases, utilization of new technology, and healthcare costs associated with aging.

Expenditures on pharmaceuticals accounted for 2.1% of the U.S. GDP in 2009—the highest rate as a percentage and in absolute amount per capita in the world, according to OECD data. Retail prescription drugs accounted for approximately 11% of national health expenditures in 2003, according to Smith et al. (2003). According to a study done by the American Association of Retired Persons (AARP, 2006), during the 2000–2005 period manufacturer's prices for the most widely used brand-name prescription drugs grew at an average annual rate of 6%. Without exception, prescription drug prices have increased more rapidly than the overall inflation rate during the last two decades. The growth in utilization of expensive new technology has been another key driver of the rising costs of health care in the United States, according to many studies (Hay, 2003; PricewaterhouseCoopers, 2002). According to Rothenberg (2003), "Changes in medical technology accounted for 20–40% of the yearly rise in healthcare spending in the late 1990s."

As pointed out in the discussion of hospital costs earlier, the elderly (defined as persons aged 65 and older) make up 13% of the U.S. population but consume 36% of all health care in the country. According to Stanton and Rutherford (2005), the elderly had an average healthcare expenditure of $11,089 compared to $3352 for working-age people in 2002. **Figure 4-1** shows that 43% of the highest spenders are in the 65 and older age group—which is also the fastest-growing cohort in the U.S. population. In 2010, the United States had by far the world's largest number of centenarians (70,490), more than even Japan (44,449), according to the Population Division of the United Nations. The number of centenarians in the United States grew by more than 6% during the 1990s, according to Krach and Velkoff (1999). There were 120 centenarians per 10,000 population aged 85 and older in 1990 in the United States; during that same year, Japan had 29 centenarians per 10,000 "very old" population. Manton and Vaupal (1995) found that life expectancy at age 85 is significantly higher in the United States than in the United Kingdom, France, Japan, or Sweden. Although this achievement can be seen as a feather in the cap for the U.S. healthcare system, it is also a cause for great concern due to the associated high costs of caring for older individuals.

FIGURE 4-1

Distribution of Top 5% of Healthcare Spenders

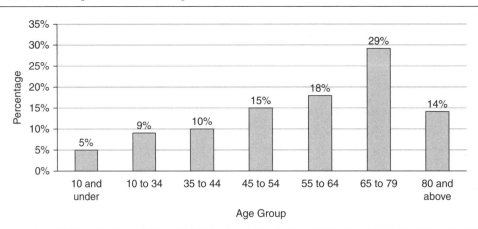

Source: Conwell & Cohen, 2005.

COMPARATIVE ANALYSIS OF HEALTHCARE SYSTEMS

The five countries under study here show tremendous variation in the size of their healthcare expenditures, role of government in healthcare provision, and health insurance (see **Figure 4-2** and **Table 4-6**). For consistency, we have used the same data source extracted from the World Health Organization Statistical Information System (WHOSIS) for our analysis. WHOSIS is one of the few data sets that collects comparable data for these five countries. While WHOSIS has been subsumed into a new Global Health Observatory Data Repository (GHODR) system, some of the key data that are utilized here for cost impact studies are not yet readily available to the public; hence we have refrained from updating the data in this section from the last edition of this text. The OECD has much more detailed data on some variables, but it does not collect data on Ukraine and India and, therefore, is of limited value here.

The United States leads the world in healthcare spending, and spends about seven times as much on total health expenditure per capita as does India. The government's share of the total health expenditure is also very different across countries. While the government in India spends only $20 per capita annually on health care, the U.S. government spends more than 100 times as much (see Table 4-6). Canada has a universal healthcare system, and private spending accounts for only 30% of total spending in that country. In the United States, the majority (55%) is private spending; in India, three-fourths of all healthcare spending is private. Ukraine, which has universal coverage, still has a high share of private spending, as the benefits provided are so limited that patients are forced to make sizable out-of-pocket payments. In India, where private provision of health care dominates but private health insurance is at a nascent stage, out-of-pocket expenditures account for almost all of private spending on health care. By comparison, out-of-pocket expenditures account for only 25% of all private spending on health care in the more developed private-pay system in the United States. Private health insurance pays for more than 65% of private spending in the United States, but less than 1% of such spending in India. Thus India is the most private in terms of healthcare financing, and the United States is the most privately insured economy.

FIGURE 4-2

Per Capita Health Expenditure Shares

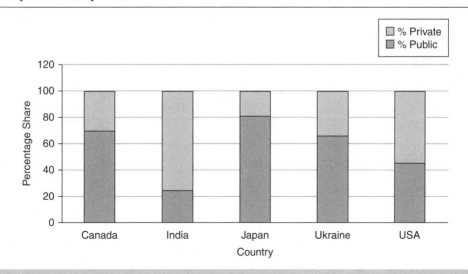

TABLE 4-6

Expenditure Breakdown, 2004

Country	Per Capita Total Health Expenditure ($)	Per Capita Government Health Expenditure ($)	Private Expenditure as a Percentage of Total Health Spending (%)	Out-of-Pocket Expenditure as a Percentage of Private Expenditure on Health (%)	Private Prepaid Plans as a Percentage of Private Expenditure on Health (%)
Canada	2989	2090	30	49.6	42.3
India	82	20	76	97	0.9
Japan	2244	1818	19	90.1	1.7
Ukraine	305	201	34	78.6	1.6
United States	5711	2548	55	24.3	65.9

Source: WHOSIS, 2006.

The next question we can ask is about the relationship between the type of healthcare financing system and national healthcare outcomes. Measures of health outcomes that are commonly used to assess country-level health include life expectancy and infant mortality rates; their values for the five countries under study are shown in **Table 4-7**. The mostly public health financing system in Japan appears to do the best under either measure, followed by Canada, which is also the second most in public financing of health care. In addition to the health system, lifestyle and other differences often play a big role in determining national health, as discussed later in this chapter.

Because measures of life expectancy do not always reflect the true health of the person, an alternative measure called healthy life expectancy (HALE) has recently been developed. HALE attempts to measure the number of healthy life years the person can expect to live. In **Table 4-8**, HALE numbers are

TABLE 4-7

Health Outcomes

Country	Life Expectancy in Years		Infant Mortality Rate (per 1000 Live Births)
	Males at Birth	Females at Birth	
Canada	68.2	71.6	5
India	51.5	51.3	62
Japan	71.4	75.8	3
Ukraine	52.9	61.8	14
United States	66.4	68.8	6

Source: WHOSIS, 2006.

TABLE 4-8

Healthy Life Expectancy (HALE) in Years

	Population at Birth		Males		Females	
	2000	2001	At Birth	At Age 60	At Birth	At Age 60
Canada	69.7	69.9	68.2	15.3	71.6	17.9
India	51.2	51.4	51.5	9.7	51.3	10.2
Japan	73.5	73.6	71.4	17.1	75.8	20.7
Ukraine	57.5	57.4	52.9	8.8	61.8	12.2
United States	67.4	67.6	66.4	14.9	68.8	16.6

Source: WHO, 2006a.

shown for the comparison countries at birth and at age 60 for males and females. They follow the same ranking as life expectancy measures. It is difficult to argue that this hierarchy is a result of the financing system employed in each country, however.

The structure of the healthcare system and the reimbursement arrangements (capitation versus fee for service) can influence how much health care is provided per dollar spent. A crude illustration of this notion is displayed in **Table 4-9**; a more accurate investigation is undertaken in the next section. We compute the number of expected years of life at birth per dollar of per capita health expenditure by dividing life expectancy at birth and infant mortality rates by per capita health expenditure. Life expectancy per dollar spent (and HALE per dollar spent) is lowest in the United States across both genders. Canada has the lowest outcome per dollar spent on infant mortality rate. The huge disparity in healthcare expenditures

TABLE 4-9

Health Outcome per Dollar of per Capita Health Expenditure

	Life Expectancy per Capita Dollar		Infant Mortality Rate per Capita Dollar	Healthy Life Expectancy per Capita Dollar			
	At Birth			At Birth		At Age 60	
Country	Males	Females		Males	Females	Males	Females
Canada	0.02	0.02	0.01	0.02	0.01	0.02	0.01
India	0.63	0.63	0.76	0.63	0.12	0.63	0.12
Japan	0.03	0.03	0.01	0.03	0.01	0.03	0.01
Ukraine	0.17	0.20	0.01	0.17	0.03	0.20	0.04
United States	0.01	0.01	0.01	0.01	0.01	0.01	0.01

Source: Computations by authors.

per capita across countries without an equally large disparity in outcomes is what drives this result, but the point still remains.

A good deal of evidence in the literature indicates that lifestyle factors play a major role in determining the level of health. The Japanese diet rich in fish has often been argued to be a principal reason for the healthier Japanese population. **Table 4-10** displays prevalence rates for some key lifestyle risk factors across the five countries under study. No clear pattern emerges from these data, however. Smoking is highly prevalent among Japanese males, with their smoking rate being second only to that of Ukrainian males. Obesity is most prevalent in the United States, and given the links between obesity, diabetes, and heart disease it is a cause for major concern. India has very low levels of obesity but high levels of smoking prevalence among males.

Thus it is clear that there are wide variations in healthcare systems, expenditures, and outcomes across this selection of countries. In the following section, we describe and analyze production and productivity of health care in these countries.

HEALTHCARE PRODUCTIVITY AND COSTS

This section describes the concepts of productivity and costs in health care and explains how they are used in making healthcare expenditure decisions. Cross-country data are then used to estimate the production and cost of health improvements. We also compare the productivity and cost of health care across the sample of five countries.

Why does the United States have such high levels of medical expenditure per capita compared to the other countries but not much better outcomes? Phelps (2003), using data on perinatal mortality rates for five developed nations including Canada, Japan, and the United States, points out that the United States with higher medical spending than any other country is closer to the 'flat of the curve' because additional spending on medical care is less likely to produce increases in health outcomes. **Figure 4-3** plots per capita healthcare spending versus male life expectancy at birth for the sample of five countries. As per capita healthcare spending increases from a low of $82 in India to $2244 in Japan, life expectancy increases rapidly from 61 years to 79 years. Further increases in spending, such as for Canada at $2989 and the United States at $5711, are actually associated with lower life expectancies of 78 and 75 years, respectively. This relationship could be taken to suggest that healthcare spending in Canada and United States has

TABLE 4-10

Selected Risk Factors

Country	Prevalence of Obese Adult Males (%)	Prevalence of Obese Adult Females (%)	Prevalence of Adult Male Tobacco Smokers (%)	Prevalence of Adult Female Tobacco Smokers (%)
Canada	15.9	13.9	22	18
India	0.3	0.5	42.25	8.62
Japan	—	—	47.9	12.2
Ukraine	—	—	54.06	10.24
United States	19.7	21.4	24.1	19.2

Source: WHOSIS, 2006.

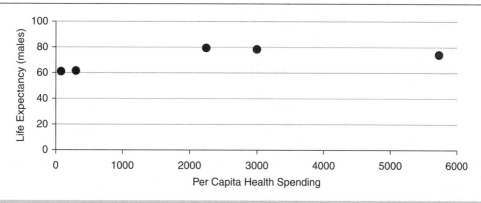

FIGURE 4-3

Health Spending and Life Expectancy

gone beyond the stage of effectiveness in increasing medical outcomes, which is an issue that we explore further in this section. The association depicted here must be viewed with great caution, however, because of the very small number of observations and other factors such as lifestyle that play a role in determining both healthcare spending and life expectancy.

Economists often describe the production of health care using the concept of a production function. A production function describes the relationship between inputs and outcomes. It specifies, for any given technology of production, the maximum amount of output that could be produced by a given combination of amounts of inputs. Outputs or outcomes could be cancer detection, mortality rates, length of hospital stay, or other measures of morbidity, and inputs could be tests, treatment procedures, and expenditures. With better technology, methods, and processes, the same amount of inputs, such as physician time, can produce more outputs. The average product of an input (often referred to as productivity of an input) is the amount of output produced per unit of input, whereas the marginal product of an input refers to the amount of additional output produced using an additional unit of that input. At very low levels of health care, every additional test (unit of treatment) has a large and positive effect in improving health outcome. As the number of tests and procedures performed on the patient increases, each additional test has a smaller and smaller effect on outcomes. Such a tendency is referred to as diminishing marginal productivity. Across disease groups, across countries, and across patients, this pattern often tends to occur, and it may explain why the United States does not do much better in some measures of health outcomes while spending significantly more than many other developed countries.

Neuhauser and Lewicki (1975) were among the first researchers to use economic analysis in medical decision making; they looked at the use of stool guaiac tests for detecting colon cancer cases. The stool guaiac test can be repeated in an effort to detect more cases because of the existence of false positives or negatives in each round of testing. **Table 4-11** shows the number of tests performed and the resulting number of cases detected. As can be seen, while more cases are detected with more tests, each additional test detects fewer and fewer additional cases of colon cancer. Moving from the fifth to the sixth test, almost no additional cases are detected. **Figure 4-4** plots the production function for cancer detection using the sixth stool guaiac test. The curve flattens out from the third test onward, indicating that very few additional cases are detected through more testing beyond this point. **Figure 4-5** plots the marginal product of the sixth stool guaiac test showing the number of additional cases detected through additional tests.

TABLE 4-11

Cancer Detection

Number of Tests	Number of Cancer Cases Detected	Additional Cases Detected
1	65.9469	65.9469
2	71.4425	5.4956
3	71.9005	0.458
4	71.9387	0.0382
5	71.9419	0.0032
6	71.9422	0.0003

Many studies, such as those carried out by Pritchett and Summers (1996) and by Bhargava, Jamison, and Murray (2001), have found evidence that higher incomes permit individuals to afford better nutrition and better health care, and thereby achieve better health. Similarly, studies (McGinnis & Foege, 2004) have shown that education and lifestyle factors play an important role in many dimensions of health. At a cross-country level, the production of health (as measured by HALE) should depend on the country's income (per capita gross national income [GNI]) and education (literacy rate) as well as lifestyle factors (smoking prevalence). In our analysis, we extracted data from WHO's World Health Statistics database for 58 countries (the reduction in sample size is due to the lack of data on smoking prevalence in many countries). Our regression result indicates that not only does HALE increase with literacy rate and GNI, but the effect of GNI on HALE also gets smaller as GNI increases, suggesting that it becomes less and less effective at generating higher HALE. Smoking prevalence was not significant probably because GNI already captures most of its effect.

$$HALE = 35.6 + 0.186 \text{ ALR} + 0.00141 \text{ GNI} - 0.0000003 \text{ GNI2}$$

FIGURE 4-4

Production Function for Cancer Detection

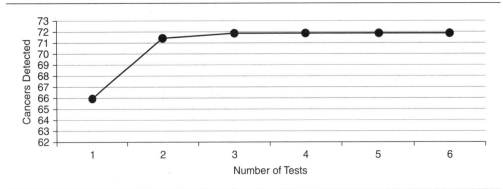

FIGURE 4-5

Additional Cases Detected

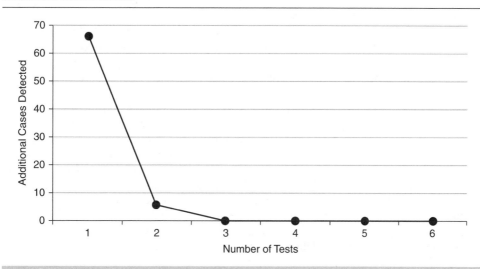

Figure 4-6 shows the position of each of the sample countries in this relationship (with literacy rate fixed at a mean value of 80%). As can be seen, the United States, Japan, and Canada are at the stage where further increases in gross national income is not likely to bring about any increase in HALE, whereas India and Ukraine are likely to see significant improvements in HALE as their economy grows. These results should be regarded with great caution and are intended for illustrative purposes only, as there are potentially multiple directions of causality between income and health (Chapman & Hariharan, 1994) that are not controlled for in this analysis. Bloom, Canning, and Sevilla (2004) also provide evidence that

FIGURE 4-6

Health Activity Life Expectancy vs. GNP (Literacy Rate Fixed at Mean Value of 80%)

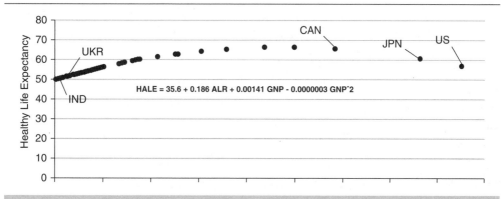

improvements in health have a significant positive effect on the rate of growth of GDP per capita. There are also problems associated with using cross-country regressions that we have not addressed.

Although productivity studies can characterize which tests or treatments are most effective, or which countries are most effective in providing health care, the cost of treatments must play a central role in the decision-making process for allocation of scarce resources. In a world faced with growing demands on its scarce healthcare budgets, the most pressing and controversial decisions are often associated with the question of how much health care to provide. Whether it is governments, healthcare providers, or private individuals making such decisions, cost considerations invariably become critical in addressing them.

Economists and other sources have developed many methods to include cost considerations so as to make better decisions. The most controversial of these is benefit–cost analysis (BCA). In BCA, the monetized value of all the benefits (better or longer life, for example) is compared with the cost of obtaining such a benefit. The controversy in the use of BCA to allocate healthcare resources is often centered on the methods for monetization of health benefits. For example, one commonly used dollar value for increases in life expectancy is the value of a statistical life (VSL) (Viscusi & Aldy, 2003). The VSL is often arrived at by using the amount individuals have been willing to accept as appropriate compensation for a reduction in life expectancy (for example, accepting a wage premium for jobs with a higher risk of death). **Table 4-12** lists some estimates of VSL for a sample of countries. For example, the value of a statistical life in India is $3.3 million compared to $9.7 million in Japan.

Critics of this approach point to the difficulty of extrapolating results from a small increase in risk of death to a large increase, as well as the wide range of these estimates and measurement errors in these studies. In a recent report (Jamison, 2006), the author calculated the value of investments in health by comparing changes in annual healthcare costs to changes in annual population health outcomes monetized using VSL. In the United States, the cost per disability-adjusted life-year ranges from as little as $3 for taxing tobacco products to more than $25,000 for performing coronary artery bypass surgery. In a

TABLE 4-12

International Estimates of Value of Statistical Life (VSL)

Country	Estimated VSL (millions of US$)
United Kingdom	5.7–74.1
Canada	5.1–5.3
India	4.1
Taiwan	0.7
Japan	9.7
Hong Kong	1.7
Australia	11.3–19.1
South Korea	0.8
Austria	3.9– 6.5
United States	5–12
Ukraine	3.3

Sources: Viscusi & Aldy, 2003; Wallsten & Kosec, 2005.

study on the effects of technological change on cost and care, Cutler and McClellan (2001) identified two channels through which improved medical technology affects health: substitution of newer technology for older, less effective technology, and expansion, in which more people are treated with the new technology. Their results suggest that while improved technology comes at a higher cost, its benefit outweighs the extra cost.

As a result of some of these criticisms and the difficulties in identifying all of the costs and benefits across generations, other approaches have become popular in healthcare decision making. Perhaps the most popular method for advising decision making in the allocation of scarce medical resources is cost-effectiveness analysis (CEA). CEA measures the cost per additional or incremental unit of health outcome and uses that metric to guide decisions on which procedure or test should be used and how much of it should be employed. The greater popularity of CEA relative to BCA reflects the lack of a need to monetize health outcomes or benefits in the former methodology. CEA can be used for both the decision of which test or intervention to use and the decision of how much of any given test or treatment to administer. In the Neuhauser and Lewicki (1975) study, the cost per additional case detected increases rapidly with each additional test (**Table 4-13**). The first screening test is highly cost-effective: it detects an additional cancer case for only $1175. Further tests detect fewer and fewer cases, however, and thus entail progressively higher costs per case detected. The additional cost per cancer case detected gained due to the sixth test exceeds $40 million, making that last test highly cost-ineffective. To decide on the number of tests that is reasonable to conduct, it becomes necessary to draw a subjective line. One attempt to do so can be found in the work of Chapman and Hariharan (1994, 1996), in which the value of statistical life provides the cutoff.

International Comparisons of Cost

Because of a lack of comparable data across countries, especially for developing countries, international comparisons of healthcare productivity have until recently been difficult. In 1998, WHO began an elaborate study to compute the costs of health care for a wide range of countries using a standardized metric. Researchers computed the unit cost of care for primary, secondary, and tertiary care bed-days and outpatient visits as well as for health centers at different levels of population coverage. **Table 4-14** lists the unit cost of care for hospitalization (bed-days), outpatient visits, and health center visits for the five countries profiled in this chapter. As might be expected, the differences are quite stark. While Canada and Japan have similar unit costs, the United States has inpatient and outpatient costs that are approximately seven

TABLE 4-13

Stool Guaiac Test Cost-Effectiveness

Number of Tests	Total Cost of Diagnosis ($)	Additional Cost of Detection ($)	Cost per Cancer Detected ($)	Marginal Cost per Cancer Detected ($)
1	77,511	77,511	1175.35	1175.35
2	107,690	30,179	1507.37	5491.48
3	130,199	22,509	1810.82	49,146.29
4	148,116	17,917	2058.92	469,031.41
5	163,141	15,025	2267.68	4,695,312.50
6	176,331	13,190	2451.01	43,966,666.67

TABLE 4-14

Unit Cost for Health Care

	Canada	*India*	*Japan*	*Ukraine*	*United States*
Cost per Bed-Day					
Primary	140.09	14.71	138.85	30.11	906.64
Secondary	182.76	19.19	181.14	39.29	1182.81
Tertiary	249.64	26.21	247.42	53.66	1615.58
Cost per Outpatient Visit					
Primary	55.43	3.96	54.85	9.16	366.17
Secondary	78.62	5.62	77.80	12.99	519.38
Tertiary	116.30	8.31	115.09	19.22	768.31
Cost per Health Center Visit					
50%	29.05	6.43	28.95	6.79	30.46
80%	29.05	6.43	28.95	6.79	30.46
95%	31.58	6.99	31.47	7.38	33.11

Source: Adapted from WHO, 2006b.

times as high. India has the lowest unit costs across the board, followed by Ukraine. Unlike inpatient and outpatient costs, health center care costs across the three wealthier countries are not significantly different, indicating that the major cost difference between the United States and other developed countries must be found in hospitals.

To make any reasonable statements, sample sizes much larger than our five countries are required. We therefore extracted a set of 58 countries from the WHO-Choice data for which recent information on HALE and unit cost per primary bed-day was available. If the higher unit costs in developed countries are attributable to better quality of care, that fact should be reflected in higher HALE in those countries. We used unit cost per bed-day rather than per outpatient or health center visit because hospitalization is more often required for treating ailments with a high risk of death. **Figure 4-7** is a scatter plot of healthy life expectancy and unit costs of primary bed care for the 58 countries. The United States is an extreme outlier here because of its very high unit cost of inpatient care. When the United States is omitted from this data set owing to its outlier status, the results do show that higher unit costs result in higher healthy life expectancy.

We also regressed healthy life expectancy on unit cost and unit cost squared to see if the increase in HALE gets progressively smaller as unit costs increase. We found that supposition to be true:

$$\text{HALE} = 41.4 + 0.454 \text{ UnitCosts} - 0.00194 \text{ UnitCost2}$$

Figure 4-8 shows the positive relationship between unit costs and health outcomes (as measured by healthy life expectancy). Thus there is some evidence that higher unit costs do translate into better health outcomes.

To summarize, some evidence suggests that the United States may be at a stage where additional improvements in health are more difficult to achieve, whereas countries such as India and Ukraine may find it easier and less expensive to achieve improvements in health.

FIGURE 4-7

Healthy Life Expectancy vs. Unit Costs (Health)

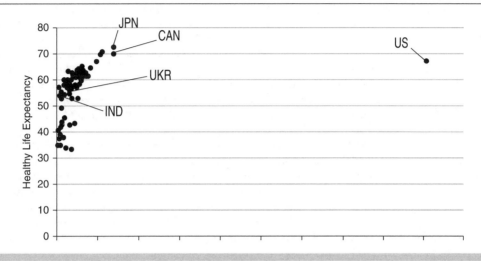

FIGURE 4-8

Unit Costs and Health Outcomes

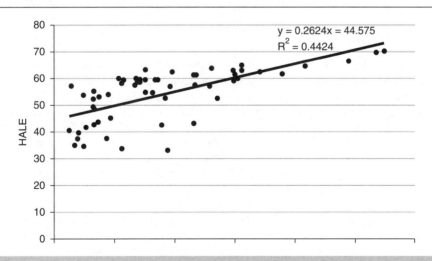

KEY COMPONENTS OF AN IDEAL HEALTHCARE SYSTEM

After exploring the healthcare systems of several countries, examining the differences and similarities among them, and comparing certain outcomes and costs, can we now identify the attributes of an effective healthcare system? An effective system would provide the best value for the healthcare of each inhabitant of that country.

Value has many definitions. Economists define value as either "the utility of goods or services" or "the power of goods or services to command other goods, services, or money in voluntary exchange." These definitions lead to the concepts of value in use or value in exchange. We can consider health care to be a collection of particular goods and services, and, as with all goods and services, there is a cost to acquire and use them. Taking cost into consideration, we can now define value as the healthcare benefits obtained minus the cost of acquisition.

Cost of acquisition includes the easily recognized accounting expenses measured in monetary terms, but also includes the more subtle opportunity cost—namely, the amount of return sacrificed by choosing one investment over another. Economists also recognize the concept of social cost, in which a transaction may adversely affect society as a whole. An example might make these various costs more understandable. Imagine a cancer patient who takes off time from work, goes to a doctor's office, and is treated with a chemotherapy agent. This event is associated with a charge for the office visit and professional fee, which is an accounting or monetary cost; a loss of income from missing work, which is an opportunity cost; and the disposal of a toxic substance, which has a social cost both in financial terms and in the potential for creating an environmental hazard. The total cost of acquisition must be deducted from the benefits accrued to determine the true value of health care.

The benefits of health care can be considered in terms of the product or services, the relationship with the consumer, and the image of the organization in the eyes of the consumer. Healthcare products and services are defined by their quality, accessibility, and the breadth of options available. Relationships include customer service and sustainable partnerships with consumers. Image is the perception of the organization by the consumer in comparison to other organizations. If healthcare value represents the prioritized benefits obtained less the costs, then it is abundantly clear that value may be defined differently by each individual and will certainly differ among various countries. An effective healthcare system for any nation must arise within the intersection of its unique culture, available resources, and finances to produce a combination of products and relationships that uniquely suit that country.

Cultural Considerations

If we define culture as a common set of beliefs, customs, values, and languages within a given group of people, then it is clear that different countries have different cultures and, further, that there may be different cultures within a single country. Given that individuals compose the cultural group, there will be variation even within a single cultural group. Individual variation can manifest itself as differences in patient expectations from one person to the next. The same outcomes or results for different patients may or may not meet their individual expectations, so the levels of satisfaction for the individuals may be different. An effective healthcare system is not expected to meet all of the expectations of each individual, but rather should meet the collective reasonable expectations of the group as a whole. These group expectations reflect the dominant social philosophy of that culture.

One important consideration within social philosophy is the relative reliance on individual responsibility versus governmental responsibility. This distinction manifests itself not only in healthcare policy, but in a vast spectrum of issues and social behaviors. At one end of the spectrum is a totalitarian regime that makes all economic, social policy, and political decisions; at the other end is totally free market, laissez-faire, and pure democracy. Neither extreme of the spectrum represents a sustainable situation, so most countries accept a combination of governmental and individual responsibilities.

Certain European countries tend toward a very high reliance on governmental activity to provide for social welfare. In this setting, individuals must relinquish some of their individual expectations in deference to the common societal good. This philosophy extends into healthcare policy, which relies on governmental guidance regarding utilization of available resources. Individual expectations and needs are prioritized based on the expectations and needs of the country and the population as a whole. In such countries, the healthcare system may given a higher priority to prenatal care and vaccinations than to futile end-of-life care, thus placing societal needs above individual expectations. We can label such systems as nationalized healthcare systems.

In many developing nations, even basic survival relies on individual actions and responsibilities, and that perspective is reflected in their social philosophies. Instead of government-administered healthcare, these countries depend on the interactions between individuals to provide services. There may be wide variations in health care available and in individual expectations for those services. The common and societal welfare is placed secondary to the demands of the individuals. For the sake of discussion, we can label such countries as having emerging healthcare systems.

The U.S. social philosophy is a chimera of the primacy of the individual and the entitlement of social structure. The American individual defends his or her right to health care that meets his or her expectations with little or no external restraints, but simultaneously demands increasing benefits from employers, payers, and government. We can designate such situations as evolving healthcare systems.

Realizing that there is a great disparity in social philosophies among nations, we can explore various aspects of culture and how they may be addressed differently, resulting in very different healthcare systems that nevertheless represent an effective system for a given country.

Individual and personal responsibility for wellness, health, and self care are extremely important considerations. Let us assume that a patient has a medical condition that can be cured or controlled by adherence to a specific medical regimen and lifestyle modifications such as stopping smoking, weight loss, and regular exercise. If that patient does not take the prescribed medications and does not alter his or her lifestyle, and subsequently suffers a recurrence of the same medical problem, in the process of treatment consuming huge resources, yet develops significant permanent disability, then how much of the unnecessary burden should society shoulder? In some cultures, it would be unthinkable for individuals to be so irresponsible; in other countries, this may represent a common scenario and, therefore, may have to be addressed with deterrents to inappropriate behavior. The type of deterrents would have to be culture specific and might range from financial contribution to social stigma. In emerging systems where society bears little of the burden, this issue is irrelevant. If an individual exercises little or no self-responsibility, he or she may unconsciously ascribe his or her health status to the responsibility of others, such that failures to meet expectations are considered the failures of others. This mindset can result in litigation. An effective healthcare system must work in tandem with an effective legal system to protect the rights of both patients and providers. In an effective healthcare system, individuals must bear significant responsibility for their own health and care, and each system must use whatever incentives or deterrents are needed to achieve that goal.

The obverse of individual responsibility is social responsibility for a nation's health care. The first consideration is who receives care. In national healthcare systems, everyone is entitled to care and to a standard of quality, whereas in emerging systems, care is far from universal or consistent. In an evolving healthcare system, the question is still debated and hinges on pragmatic considerations rather than on pure social commitment. An effective system for any country must address the important question of who is entitled to healthcare based on the culture and social philosophy of the time. The system must be designed to meet the practical implications of meeting the needs of the covered group.

Once it is determined who should receive care, then the next consideration is how much care each individual is entitled to and how to provide it. The economic conundrum is how to allocate limited resources in the face of unlimited demand.

Resource Considerations

The first and most important resources in any healthcare system are trained medical professionals. An effective system must have sufficient personnel to meet the needs of the population. Individual and societal expectations must match up with the pool of available personnel. Each healthcare professional should function at the top of his or her level of expertise, and there should be a pyramidal distribution of professionals along a skill continuum. This distribution is the most efficient and cost-effective approach to meeting population and individual needs. For example, after an initial evaluation, blood pressure control could be delegated to specialty trained medical personnel who utilize a treatment protocol. Under certain conditions, a more highly trained individual, such as an advanced practitioner, may become involved in the care plan, and if necessary, a physician would then add to the team expertise. This approach would result in high-quality, cost-effective care, but would require a convergence of patient and societal expectations with the healthcare delivery system.

Further, because the needs of emerging countries are substantially different than the needs of highly developed countries, the stratified team approach can be tailored to very specific local needs. For example, in an emerging healthcare system, a very large cadre of personnel with very basic training can address sanitation and prenatal counseling in rural communities with a major impact on population health. By comparison, the need for medical specialists in that setting is minimal.

Once the specific healthcare needs are determined, then the team structure can be designed and the appropriate number of professionals and trained personnel can be sought. An effective system must match personnel presently available with the desired structure, develop a plan to train additional professionals for the future, and supplement any current shortages with professionals trained elsewhere.

If medical professionals are the first resource needed, then tools needed for them to do their job are the next essentials. An effective healthcare system must have sufficient facilities for diagnosis and treatment, including hospitals, testing locations, and adequate supplies and technology. Both physical facilities and technology must meet the needs of the population, and an effective system would ensure that these needs are met, whether by free market forces, by governmental direction, or by a combination of approaches. The best approach will vary from nation to nation, but each system should be effective for that particular country. A system of medical professionals working in adequate facilities with sufficient supplies and technology depends on a functioning infrastructure.

Basic infrastructure includes roads and transportation, communication, power, water, sanitation, and other functions that are considered part of normal life in developed countries, but may be woefully lacking in emerging countries. These basics must be in place for an effective healthcare system to operate, but responsibility for them primarily resides in the realm of government. Infrastructure specific to health care includes computer technology, data and information storage and retrieval, and outcome tracking. The mode of providing healthcare specific infrastructure may vary, but must be part of an effective system. As noted previously, value is defined as benefit obtained minus cost of acquisition, so an effective system must make decisions with finances clearly in mind.

Financial Considerations

Health care must be paid for. Payment may come directly from individuals; may pass through intermediaries including employers, insurance companies, and government; or may result from a combination of sources. In reality, all money comes from individuals, either directly for services, indirectly through healthcare costs embedded in consumer prices, or through taxes administered by the government. The indirect costs are very difficult to measure, so most countries compare the amount spent directly on health care compared to the total wealth created by that country in a given year—that is, healthcare spending as a percentage of GDP. These values vary widely from country to country, but what is the significance of a high ratio? If more is spent on health care, it means that less wealth of either a country or an individual can be spent on other goods or services, which in turn limits discretionary spending. There is also an opportunity cost that makes the actual total much greater if indirect costs are considered. Because health care is provided to individuals, we can explore a simplified concept of demand curves for consumers.

A demand curve is a graphic representation of the relationship between price and volume of goods or services demanded by a consumer. In essence, the more something costs, the less of that product a consumer is willing to buy; conversely, the lower the price, the more of the product that is bought. In our simple example, we will ignore other important concepts such as elasticity of demand, but it is intuitive that demand for goods or services is sensitive to price. If prices for health care are high, consumers do not demand less if they feel they are receiving adequate value, or if they rely on the instructions of their healthcare providers to obtain additional goods or services in the form of diagnostic or therapeutic activities. There are two important considerations here: the concept of value and fee-for-service (FFS) payment.

The FFS payment methodology is common, and not limited to health care; in particular, it is also used for lawyers, accountants, consultants, and other professionals whose expertise is needed to solve specific problems of a given individual. With this financing strategy, the consumer pays for time and talent, not for outcomes. A consultant expects payment whether his or her best efforts result in spectacular results for the client or in mundane outcomes. Physicians who work in a FFS setting may order additional tests or services for various reasons, thereby increasing costs without any guarantee of obtaining the best possible outcome for the cost—that is, without providing the best value. Tactics to address the potential shortcomings of the FFS approach include salaried physicians, capitation, bundled payment systems, high deductible plans with health savings accounts, pay-for-performance, and global payment systems. An effective healthcare system must utilize a payment mechanism or combination of methods to maximize healthcare value in conjunction with the culture and resources of that nation. Any payment system can only distribute available funds, so the next issue is to determine the pool of available funds.

When the government pays a majority of the healthcare costs, then the government acts as the major consumer with market power to determine how much it will pay, to whom, and for which services. This is clearly the case in nationalized healthcare systems and is becoming a reality in evolving systems such as the U.S. healthcare system. Medicare and Medicaid have long established prices and payments for medical goods and services, and in the era of healthcare reform, evolutionary questions continue to focus on who will be covered and what will be paid for. Measures of quality are beginning to drive reimbursement in efforts to define and reward value.

Global Perspectives

As we have seen, there can be no one ideal healthcare system that can possibly suit the needs of every country. The culture of each country must devise a system that balances individual expectations against societal expectations, and decides which members of its society will have access to and coverage for health care. The value of care will be determined by providing the greatest benefit to the nation paid for by the financial resources that country can or decides to dedicate to health care. It will be characterized by the quality, access, and breadth of services available to the population, rendered in a customer-friendly relationship. An effective system must have sufficient resources to meet the needs of the population, including medical professionals, physical facilities, technology, infrastructure, and an efficient organizational structure to deliver the care. Finally, the government of an evolving or nationalized system must raise money from the taxpayers to fund a functional administrative organization to act as the major consumer of goods and services, in conjunction with private payers in certain settings, and distribute payment to the care providers in an effective and equitable manner.

U.S. Healthcare Evolution

Many measures of health care rank the United States among the best places in the world to receive care, as can be attested to by the rich and powerful from other nations who come to the country for care; many other measures, however, place the United States low on the list of developed countries. It is this wide dispersion of outcomes superimposed on the highest per capita spending and highest national healthcare costs as a percentage of GDP that is driving the reexamination of the U.S. healthcare system during the ongoing healthcare reform debate and legislation.

As we look at innovative ways to improve the value of health care—that is, prioritized benefit minus cost—we must remember that any changes must evolve from the intersection of the unique American culture, resources, and finances. It is clear that Americans, as a whole, would support changes that improve the system, but even basic questions such as who is eligible for care remain unsettled. Should the U.S. system provide health care only for its citizens and legal residents, or should everyone, including illegal aliens, receive the same benefits? The recognition that two-thirds of all Medicare spending goes for care rendered in the final stages of life has opened up the volatile topic of controlling costs for end-of-life care and futile care. How to handle those issues has yet to be determined and has raised concerns of healthcare rationing. Nationalized healthcare systems have recognized the necessity of having some controls over which procedures will be paid for. Countries such as the United Kingdom have empowered panels to review tests and treatments to select which give the best outcomes at the lowest cost, with only those approved procedures being deemed eligible to receive payment. This payment approval methodology is still being debated in the United States. Payment to medical providers is being shifted to a system based on incentives for quality, but which metrics should be tracked remains controversial. The medical education component of the healthcare system is under scrutiny, and several proposals for overhaul have been cited as well. Finally, the question of how to pay for health care is far from settled. The original foundation for the Patient Protection and Affordable Care Act (PPACA)—the mandate for every individual to purchase healthcare insurance—is so controversial that several states have sued the federal government challenging its constitutionality. The ultimate status of the health insurance exchanges outlined by PPACA is uncertain and is under consideration. Payment cuts to medical professionals and hospitals are part of the plan, but it is uncertain how they might affect access to care, and whether operating cost reductions would reduce the workforce, which would have a hugely deleterious effect on consumer spending and thus reduce GPD.

Besides governmental efforts, the private sector is also working diligently to make the U.S. healthcare system more effective. Insurance companies are becoming more active in chronic care management, and employers are offering employee wellness programs. Professional organizations and medical specialty groups are developing hosts of disease-specific, evidence-based best practice guidelines. The ascendency of integrated healthcare networks promises a coordinated and seamless approach to care, with those networks assuming clinical and fiscal responsibility for their patients.

It is clear that the healthcare system in the United States is undergoing a dramatic evolution, but it is equally clear that to attempt change that is too rapid and too sweeping and would have drastic and many unanticipated consequences. The best approach would be a measured melding of free market forces and governmental policy to drive toward an effective system that reflects the culture, resources, and finances of the United States.

ACKNOWLEDGMENTS

This chapter is dedicated to the memory of Dr. Robert Lipson, a healthcare visionary, leader, and mentor.

STUDY QUESTIONS

1. Define economics and explain the role that economists play in analyzing healthcare systems.
2. Why do you think that the United States spends more money per capita on health care and does not have the greatest return for the money as compared to other developed countries such as Japan?
3. Define production function and give an example in terms of cost of care and outcomes.
4. Explain, with an example, the difficult decisions of how much and what types of health care can be provided with a limited budget.

CASE STUDY: FINANCIAL CHALLENGES OF RURAL U.S. RESIDENTS IN A DIFFICULT ECONOMY

Background:

Many rural communities have faced long-term challenges related to healthcare access and costs, which are persistent problems and have exacerbated by the recent economic downturn. This case study describes the current healthcare environment within a rural community in North Carolina, U.S.A. that is characterized by:

- an aging population with relatively high rates of poverty
- a vulnerable local economy
- substantial healthcare access barriers

These cost issues are fueled by increases in both uninsurance and under-insurance. Health providers have noticed a jump in the number of patients with very high deductible health plans. Many of these patients cannot afford to meet their deductibles, forcing them to forgo care or rely on charity from local providers. This includes many on Medicare, who cannot afford their copayments and have dropped supplemental coverage because they cannot afford the premiums.

Health Implications:

Many residents are going without recommended care. According to local healthcare providers, there has been a marked decline in rates of preventive care and elective procedures over the past 8 months. Outpatient diagnostic care at the local hospital has decreased somewhere between 8% to 12% in the first quarter of 2009 as some patients have skipped recommended screenings because they lacked the ability to pay for treatment; they do not see the point in getting screened. A local leader told of another patient who did not have the money to receive care for a newly diagnosed cancer. Fortunately, a foundation was able to fund the needed care for this person, but leaders feel that there are hundreds of patients who are falling through the cracks.

Reference

Rural Health Policy and Health and Analysis Research Center. (2010.). A Case Study of Rural Health Care in the Economic Downturn.

REFERENCES

Agency for Healthcare Research and Quality (AHRQ). (2003). Hospitalization in the United States. *HCUP Fact Book*, 6.

American Association of Retired Persons (AARP). (2006). Trends in manufacturer prices of brand name prescription drugs used by older Americans—2005 year end update. *AARP Public Policy Institute Data Digest*, 134.

Bhargava, A. D. T., Jamison Lau, L. J., & Murray, C. J. L. (2001). Modeling the effects of health on economic growth. *Journal of Health Economics, 20*, 423–440.

Bloom, D., Canning, D. & Sevilla, J. (2004). The effect of health on economic growth: A production function approach to world development. *World Development, 32*(1) 1–13.

Chapman, K. S., & Hariharan, G. (1994). Controlling for causality in the link from income to mortality. *Journal of Risk and Uncertainty, 8*(1), 85–94.

Chapman, K. S., & Hariharan, G. (1996). Do poor people have a stronger relationship between income and mortality than the rich: Implications of panel data for health—health analysis. *Journal of Risk and Uncertainty, 12*, 51–63.

Conwell, L., & Cohen, J. (2005). Characteristics of persons with high medical expenditures in the U.S. civilian noninstitutional population, 2002. *MEPS Statistical Brief* No. 73. Retrieved from https://meps.ahrq.gov/mepsweb/data_files/publications/st73/stat73.pdf

Cutler, D. M., & McClellan, M. (2001). Is technological change in medicine worth it? *Health Affairs, 20*, 11–29.

Government of India. (2005). *Financing and delivery of health care services in India* (Background Papers, table 1, p. 7). New Delhi, India: National Commission on Macroeconomics and Health.

Hay, J. W. (2003). Hospital cost drivers: An evaluation of 1998–2001 state-level data. *American Journal of Managed Care, 9*, 13–24.

Jamison, D. T. (2006). *Economics and cost effectiveness: Disease Control Priorities Project.* International Bank for Reconstruction and Development/World Bank.

Japan: Gross domestic product (GDP) per capita in respective prices from 2001 to 2011 (in U.S. dollars). (2011). Retrieved from http://www.statista.com/statistics/14439/gross-domestic-product-per-capita-in-japan/

Krach, C. A., & Velkoff, V. A. (1999). *Centenarians in the United States. Current population report: Special studies.* Washington, DC: U.S. Census Bureau.

Lekhan, V., Rudiy, V., & Nolte, E. (2004). *Health care systems in transition: Ukraine.* WHO Regional Office for Europe, European Observatory on Health Systems and Policies.

Manton, K. J., & Vaupal, E. W. (1995). Survival after the age of 80 in the United States, England, France, Japan and Sweden. *New England Journal of Medicine, 333*(18), 1232–1235.

McGinnis, J. M., & Foege, W. H. (2004). Actual causes of death in the United States, 2000. *Journal of the American Medical Association, 291*(10), 1238–1245.

Neuhauser, D., & Lewicki, A. M. (1975). What do we gain from the sixth stool guaiac? *New England Journal of Medicine, 293*, 226–228.

Or, Z. (2000). Determinants of health in industrialized countries: A pooled cross-country time series analysis," *OECD Economic Studies, 30*, 53–77.

Organization for Economic Cooperation and Development (OECD). (2001, October). *OECD health a glance: How Canada compares.* OECD Policy Brief.

Organization for Economic Cooperation and Development (OECD). (2006). OECD health data 2006: How does the United States compare? Retrieved from http://www.oecd.org/dataoecd/29/52/36960035.pdf

Peters, D. H., Yazbeck, A. S., Sharma, R. P., Ramana, G. N. V., Pritchett, L. H., & Wagstaff, A. (2002). *Better health systems for India's poor: Findings, analysis, and options.* Washington, DC: World Bank.

Phelps, C. E. (2003). *Health economics* (3rd ed.). Boston: Addison Wesley.

PricewaterhouseCoopers. (2002). *The factors fueling rising healthcare costs.* Washington, DC: Author.

Pritchett, L., & Summers, L. H. (1996). Wealthier is healthier. *Journal of Human Resources, 31*, 841–868.

Rothenberg, B. M. (2003). Medical technology as a driver of healthcare costs: Diagnostic imaging. Blue Cross and Blue Shield Association. Retrieved from http://www.bcbs.com/betterknowledge/cost/diagnostic-imaging.html

Rural Health Policy and Health and Analysis Research Center. (2010). A Case Study of Rural Health Care in the Economic Downturn. Retrieved from http://www.shepscenter.unc.edu/rural/pubs/other/AsheProfile.pdf

Smith, C., Cowan, C., Sensenig, A., Catlin, A., & Health Accounts Team. (2003). Health spending growth slows in 2003. *Health Affairs, 24*(1), 185–194.

Stanton, M. W., & Rutherford, M. K. (2005). The high concentration of US healthcare expenditures (Agency for Healthcare Quality and Research Pub. No. 06-0060). *Research in Action, 19*.

Viscusi, K. W., & Aldy, J. E. (2003). The value of a statistical life: A critical review of market estimates throughout the world. *Journal of Risk and Uncertainty, 27*(1), 5–76.

Wallsten, S., & Kosec, K. (2005). *The economic cost of the war in Iraq* (Working Paper 05-19). AEA-Brookings Joint Center for Regulatory Studies.

White House. (2011). Affordable Care Act. Retrieved from http://www.whitehouse.gov/healthreform/healthcare-overview#healthcare-menu

WHOSIS. (2006). *Statistical information system.* World Health Organization.

World Health Organization (WHO). (1999). *Ukraine country health report.* Kiev, Ukraine: WHO Liaison Office.

World Health Organization (WHO). (2000). Highlights on health in Ukraine. Retrieved from http://www.euro.who.int/document/e72372.pdf

World Health Organization (WHO). (2006a). *World health statistics 2006.* Geneva, Switzerland: Author.

World Health Organization (WHO). (2006b). Choosing interventions that are cost effective (WHO-CHOICE). Retrieved from http://www.who.int/choice/publications/discussion_papers/en/index.html

World Health Organization (WHO). (2011). Global health data repository. Retrieved from http://www.who.int/gho/en/

*For a full suite of assignments and additional learning activities, use the access code located in the front of your book to visit this exclusive website: **http://go.jblearning.com/holtz**. If you do not have an access code, you can obtain one at the site.*

5

Global Perspectives on Politics and Public Health Policy: The Case of Tobacco

Michele Zebich-Knos
Richard B. Davis

> *The poorest of the poor, around the world, have the worst health. Those at the bottom of the distribution of global and national wealth, those marginalized and excluded within countries, and countries themselves disadvantaged by historical exploitation and persistent inequity in global institutions of power and policy-making present an urgent moral and practical focus for action. But focusing on those with the least, on the 'gap' between the poorest and the rest, is only a partial response (WHO, 2008).*

OBJECTIVES

After completing this chapter the reader will be able to:

1. Relate examples of health policies at local, state, provincial, or national levels within developed and developing countries.
2. Discuss WHO's health policies and implications for health within nations.
3. Explain the need for governments to collaborate with nongovernment organizations to improve health care.
4. Explain the global perspectives on politics and health policy as it relates to tobacco.

INTRODUCTION

The creation of public health policy, like other policies such as foreign policy or education policy, requires that ideas about problem identification and problem solving be transformed into measurable standards that require government involvement. Sometimes the need for creating a policy evolves from societal movements or nongovernmental actors advocating for government to set policies or standards that affect the society in an equitable and efficient manner. This chapter introduces one avenue for discussing the role of government and politics in policy making—that of tobacco policy in a multilateral setting rather than simply within U.S. borders.

This example illustrates the difference between several prime actors in the policy-making process— both official and unofficial. The dynamics of what is generally a very slow multilateral process will also become evident as some states (meaning "countries" in this context) are shown to move in tandem with their own domestic political situation that may be more or less beholden to specific business interests or ideological viewpoints. Such viewpoints may prefer less government intervention, rather than more, and become particularly influential during electoral campaigns. Sometimes this influence is enough to derail even the best intentions to cooperate on a global level. The United States is a good example of this kind of wavering. In the first edition of this book, we noted that the United States had signed the World Health Organization's (WHO's) Framework Convention on Tobacco Control (FCTC) on May 10, 2004. As of this edition's writing, however, the United States had still not ratified the treaty (WHO, 2011, "Country Profile: United States of America," p. 1). Additionally, policy can be significantly influenced by current events, which are often unpredictable and create a dynamic, and oftentimes challenging environment within which to implement global health objectives.

To understand how the global arena approaches health concerns such as smoking, this chapter explores the tobacco example to describe how policy is set in a multilateral organization. In this chapter, the United Nations' (UN's) WHO agency is seen as the primary driver in proactively developing and instituting public health policies on a global scale. To understand how policy is created by a multilateral organization, we will describe how WHO operates and how WHO was successful in gaining enough worldwide support to have a treaty ratified on the control of tobacco products, all the while mitigating conflicting values among member countries.

Before we delve further into the tobacco case, it is helpful to note that tobacco fits into the "global health agenda" because it is openly accepted by major stakeholders—that is, states, international governmental organizations, nongovernmental organizations (NGOs), and the general public—as a health problem that merits action. To this end, world leaders have expressed their concern through the formal adoption of agreements or treaties, and the creation of projects within WHO. The FCTC, or tobacco treaty, and WHO's Tobacco Free Initiative clearly illustrate that this issue is part of the global health agenda. This agenda, according to Shiffman et al. (2009), serves as a "steering mechanism for collective action and strategic plans of the national and international stakeholders toward the achievement of specific agreed-on goals" (p. 3). Indeed, it appears that the global anti-tobacco agenda is now highly institutionalized. As WHO proudly notes, "As of May 2011, the WHO FCTC has 173 Parties covering 87% of the world's population, making it one of the most rapidly embraced treaties in United Nations history" (WHO, 2011, p. 8).

A MULTILATERAL PERSPECTIVE

In this era of expanding global trade and interdependence, travel, and international awareness of domestic events within countries, international health has become an increasingly important policy issue. Disease is a transnational phenomenon that knows no borders and, for this reason, has become especially worrisome as busy executives fly, for example, from Europe to Asia and Africa, with the United States as their final destination—all in a matter of days.

News of infectious disease outbreaks in the developing world (e.g., severe acute respiratory syndrome [SARS]) and newly emerging diseases such as avian influenza (pandemic flu) now attracts great attention in the European, Canadian, and U.S. media. Such attention typically focuses more on the fear of spreading disease to the developed world, often called the "North," than it does on the well-being of persons in Africa, Asia, or Latin America who contract debilitating or even deadly diseases. As the global "South," or developing world, expands its connections within the global marketplace, health issues once relegated to populations of the developed North (e.g., cancer, diabetes, obesity) are also emerging as real health concerns. With increased disposable income in the developing world comes access to products such as cigarettes, which are linked to cancer in humans. As a consequence, global policy makers must now confront the burdens imposed by both communicable, or infectious, diseases, and noncommunicable, or chronic, diseases.

The policy debate continues to revolve around whether to stress issues related to the communicable diseases prevalent among the South's poor or those related to the noncommunicable diseases that are responsible for most deaths in the developed world ("A Manipulated Dichotomy," 2000). Many in the developing world argue, as Reddy and colleagues (2005) do, that we should emphasize both communicable and noncommunicable diseases rather than solely targeting those infectious diseases that commonly afflict the poorest 20% of the developing world. Reddy et al. point out that India has the most oral cancers in the world attributed to the use of chewing tobacco as well as the highest number of diabetics. Even in far-off locations like Bolivia, communicable diseases account for only 12% of all deaths (Pan-American Health Organization, 2002).

Reddy et al. (2005) urge us not to forget that noncommunicable, chronic diseases such as cancer or cardiovascular disease afflict the middle 60% of those who live in the global South. Because of his status as a respected Indian cardiologist, and a proponent of dealing with chronic diseases, Reddy achieved the status of an innovator within WHO's Network of Innovators, an organization intended to encourage the diffusion of new ideas for disease prevention. Scarce resources also influence this policy debate. Put simply, how should countries allocate their money toward communicable or noncommunicable diseases? This same question applies in the global arena when WHO makes decisions within the UN's own budgetary constraints.

We know that health policy can be made within countries at the local, provincial or state, and national levels. However, policy can also be made in international organizations by member countries. One very important international organization responsible for health policy making that influences countries around the globe is WHO. In this section, we examine how WHO member countries strive to create effective global health policies that meet the needs of many countries both in the developed North and the developing South. This is not an easy task because member countries maintain sovereignty within their own borders and have a final say over whether to accept and implement a WHO policy.

One recent example of a successful WHO creation is the Framework Convention on Tobacco Control, an international treaty that has been signed by many developed and developing countries. The FCTC is the first public health treaty currently in force that globally addresses a major health issue. Expansion of such wellness-related treaties narrows the health gap worldwide and contributes to a rapidly evolving relationship between North and South that reflects a new health paradigm (i.e., model). This paradigm's major objective is the improvement of health worldwide, but it also reflects a two-way path between the developed and developing world as a means to achieve that objective. One way to achieve this objective is through the expansion of global health policies by means of international treaties, agreements, and conventions. Such documents possess greater legal clout than a global health program or regulation; the latter forms were how WHO functioned until the FCTC came into force.

This chapter treats WHO as the primary catalyst driving this paradigm shift to a proactive, multilateral treaty-based method of improving global health. To better understand how WHO operates, we should ask ourselves which factors contribute to making the FCTC an innovative global health initiative within the UN umbrella. By asking this question, we will gain a deeper appreciation of how WHO operates and what that organization values in the global health policy-making process. Arriving at an organization's values, however, is a complex task and involves not only agreement, but also struggles and conflict among member countries—some of which do not share a similar approach to solving health problems.

WORLD HEALTH ORGANIZATION: OBJECTIVES AND GOVERNANCE STRUCTURES

Before examining programs, treaties, and activities, it behooves us to understand what WHO is and how it operates. The World Health Organization was founded on April 7, 1948, as a specialized agency within the United Nations designed to deal with health issues. Its constitution recognizes the totality of health, defined as ranging from physical and mental aspects to social well-being, rather than simply disease eradication. In fact, its comprehensive approach aspires to the "attainment by all peoples of the highest possible level of health" (WHO, 1948a).

The WHO constitution emphasizes cooperation by individuals and states in its promotion of health and wellness, and also recognizes unequal development patterns among states, asserting that "Governments have a responsibility for the health of their peoples which can be fulfilled only by the provision of adequate health and social measures." From its inception, WHO has operated on the premise that health is a public good requiring governmental action to achieve its objectives. To achieve its objectives, WHO engages in coordinating international health work and enabling governments to strengthen their own health systems. Its functions also include supplying technical assistance and emergency aid when requested by host governments. In addition, WHO functions as a statistical clearinghouse for epidemiological information and assists in disease eradication. Its Weekly Epidemiological Record (WHO, 2006e), for example, is an outcome of its information dissemination function and is a useful tool for health policy makers worldwide, as is its annual publication, *World Health Statistics* (WHO, 2006g). WHO also promotes international standards for food and biological and other products.

WHO is actively involved in data gathering, research, and policy applications that contribute to the goal of improved health for the world's peoples. Its first notable project, the creation of international sanitary regulations, was unveiled in 1951 and later renamed the International Health Regulations (IHR). The IHR are a binding legal instrument on all WHO members that have not specifically lodged a reservation about or rejection of these regulations. The 1969 regulations are currently in force and aim to stop the international spread of disease. Revised IHR were adopted in May 2005 and entered into force on June 15, 2007 (WHO, 2005, 2006d). In moving to establish uniform world standards, the new regulations create a "single code of procedures and practices for routine public health measures at international airports and ports and some ground crossings" (WHO, 2006d).

So emotionally charged is the global spread of infectious disease that it becomes less controversial and acts as a unifying force among states. Regardless of their political beliefs or systems, afflicted states share one commonality—a fear of disease. This is not the case for product-induced illnesses such as the link between tobacco and chronic diseases—especially cancer. Because tobacco products such as cigarettes or cigars are commercially produced and sold globally, their health ramifications may become mired in a trade-related debate. This is not the case for infectious diseases such as malaria or dengue fever. Moreover, while the avian flu does involve the poultry industry worldwide, the poultry industry does not willfully produce a product it knows will harm people's health; thus avian flu is not considered a product-induced illness in the same sense as tobacco-related chronic diseases.

To manage its numerous programs and achieve its objectives, WHO relies on what some consider a vast bureaucracy. However, as the most recent IHR reveal, this organizational structure has shown itself capable of rapid response. The latest regulations represent a post–September 11, 2001, recognition of global health security and incorporate standards not only for natural occurrences but also for "accidental release or deliberate use of biological and chemical agents or radionuclear material that affect health" (WHO, 2005).

WHO's administrative headquarters is located in Geneva, Switzerland, and the World Health Assembly (WHA) is its main decision and policy-making body. Each May WHA holds an annual meeting for delegates from all 192 member countries with the goal of policy and financial review. WHA appoints the director-general and also approves the budget. The 32-member executive board meets in January each year to discuss current issues and concerns, which the board then formulates into a formal agenda for WHA's annual meeting in May. The executive board elects its members, who serve 3-year terms (WHO, 2006f).

The WHO Secretariat includes a 3500-employee team of health experts and support personnel who work at the organization's Geneva headquarters, in WHO's six regional offices worldwide (Africa, Eastern Mediterranean, Europe, Latin America, Southeast Asia, and Western Pacific), or as needed throughout the world. Reflecting the unavoidably political nature of this specialized agency, WHO also maintains offices at the African Union (AU) and Economic Commission for Africa (Addis Ababa, Ethiopia), the European Union (Brussels), the United Nations (New York), and the World Bank and International Monetary Fund (Washington, D.C.).

COLLABORATION WITH NONGOVERNMENTAL ORGANIZATIONS

Although the WHO's current Civil Society Initiative encourages working relations between itself and nongovernmental organizations, it is the constitution that delineates this relationship (WHO, 2006a). One appendix to the WHO's Basic (Constitutional) Text is called the "Principles Governing Relations Between the World Health Organization and Nongovernmental Organizations." This constitutional appendix states that NGOs play a vital role in support of international health needs especially as they harmonize various interests within countries and regions (WHO, 1948b). WHO's desire to collaborate with NGOs stems from its constitutional beginnings and appears on its website: "The objectives of WHO's relations with NGOs are to promote the policies, strategies, and activities of WHO and, where appropriate, to collaborate with NGOs in jointly agreed activities to implement them" (WHO, 2000a).

WHO recognizes that informal or ad hoc contacts with NGOs can develop into an official relationship sanctioned by the executive board. Privileges awarded to officially sanctioned NGOs are outlined in the "Principles" text and include the following rights:

▪ The right to appoint a nonvoting representative to WHO meetings and conferences
▪ The right to provide statements upon request by the meeting chairperson
▪ The right to request that the director-general make documentation available
▪ The right to access nonconfidential documents that the director-general makes available to NGOs (WHO, 1948a)

The relevance of these governance structures and collaborative relationship with NGOs becomes apparent when moving to the next step—that of examining how WHO transitioned from relatively politically risk-free health policies to a bolder, more innovative approach that tackles not only tobacco-related diseases, but also the tobacco companies themselves.

POLITICIZATION OF GLOBAL HEALTH

WHO has faced allegations of politicization of the global health agenda in the past, which manifested itself primarily as Cold War or Arab-Israeli cleavages, and in the post–Cold War era as a North–South cleavage. Amid the Cold War–era impasse and in an effort to accomplish what it set out to do in its constitutional objectives—to deal with health issues—many of WHO's policies shied away from aggressively tackling social or commerce-related health issues. Siddiqi (1995) reminds us that such allegations span the breadth of WHO's history and go as far back as 1949, when the Soviet Union walked out from WHO meetings in protest over accusations of politicization.

As mentioned earlier, its constitution put WHO philosophically at odds with the United States from its inception in 1948 because of its view that health is a public good and that government has an inherent responsibility for the health of its citizens. While providing some of the world's best health care and demonstrating a strong commitment to public health issues such as creation of a sanitary infrastructure (e.g., clean drinking water, sewage control, disease control), the United States has long regarded personal health care as a private matter—not as a defined right over which government has responsibility. Only as medical costs rose dramatically and the pool of uninsured increased did the United States' domestic policy debate expand to consider whether Americans have a right to universal health care.

The role of government as having a responsibility for every American's health then entered the national debate in the United States, but it remains just that—a debate. However, very real fears of socialized medicine tainted WHO's constitutional preamble from the beginning as it clearly stated that "governments have a responsibility for the health of their peoples" (WHO, 1948a).

Siddiqi (1995) notes that, as early as 1946 and prior to the actual creation of WHO, a rift among UN member states occurred over the new organization's responsibilities. Its opposition to socialized medicine from an insurance standpoint put the United States at odds with the Soviet Union, the Scandinavian countries, and most European countries. Objections over health insurance issues in this new health body delayed U.S. ratification of the WHO-creation proposal by 2 years (Siddiqi, 1995). The notion of political blocs is not new to the UN in the General Assembly or the Security Council, and WHO is certainly not immune to such political maneuvering. Indeed, WHA members have occasionally split their votes over North–South issues. WHA's one state/one vote policy means that African states, for example, can "produce as many as 30 or 35 votes, compared to the 1 vote for the United States or even some 20 votes for the major, developed states that supply most of the funds of the WHO" (Siddiqi, 1995). The voting structure within the main policy-making and legislative body of WHO provides the South with an inherent advantage when formulating policies.

Given that European, socialist, and developing countries share a broader interpretation of what public health should encompass and how to solve related health problems, WHO voting practices offer yet another structural advantage for pushing the innovative envelope—and expanding the global health agenda to include the negative effects of commercially produced tobacco products. It is not surprising that, within this environment, a more comprehensive interpretation of health issues eventually made it to the forefront of the global health agenda in the form of the FCTC.

The evolution of Eastern European countries into one European bloc has strengthened the argument in favor of government responsibility for health care because both Eastern and Western Europe share a belief in the "health as a public good" position. Both are also prone to accept greater government regulation as a means of achieving a health objective. This stance puts Europe in greater harmony with the global South, which also favors adopting a regulatory approach in dealing with the tobacco industry.

By 1978, WHO had become noticeably bolder in its assertions that health is a totality of aspects, not merely the absence of disease. The WHO-sponsored International Conference on Primary Health Care produced the Declaration of Alma-Ata in September 1978, which called health a "fundamental human right" and clarified WHO's position that optimal health requires "the action of many other social and economic sectors in addition to the health sector" (WHO, 1978). Further emboldened by the global South to move beyond health into the economic realm, this declaration went on to state:

> Economic and social development, based on a New International Economic Order, is of
> basic importance to the fullest attainment of health for all and to the reduction of the
> gap between the health status of the developing and developed countries. (WHO, 1978)

The Alma-Ata Declaration wrote of health as a human right, but WHO's publication, *Health for All in the Twenty-First Century* (WHO, 1998), went a step further by affirming a "global public health good" within the context of trade liberalization. This document urged "greater compatibility in policy objectives to be developed between international and intergovernmental agencies and multinationals involved in trade and health" (p. A51/5). A first step toward linking multinational companies to health, it would later prove useful in formulating a tobacco treaty.

In support of the 2000 UN Millennium Declaration, WHO set about implementing a series of global health-related goals by the year 2015. The Millennium Development Goals (MDGs) are development oriented and seek to eradicate poverty and hunger, achieve universal primary education, promote gender equality, reduce child mortality, improve maternal health, combat disease, promote environmental sustainability, and develop a global partnership for development (UN Millennium Project, 2006). WHO interprets the MDGs as a means for developed countries to contribute money and expertise to developing countries so as to improve global health. The link reflects an expanded approach to health "through trade, development assistance, debt relief, access to essential medicines, and technology transfer" (WHO, 2006c). While *Health for All* set the stage for making multinational organizations be responsible health actors in WHO policies, the MDGs closed the loop around economic and global trade as a means to improving health ends. Debt relief and technology transfer were now linked to health policy. Naturally, the creation of a global tobacco treaty seeking to curb the economic activity of a major industry would not be unanimously received by all states, especially a major tobacco exporter such as the United States.

GLOBAL ENVIRONMENTAL POLICY: A MODEL FOR HEALTH POLICY MAKING?

Policy makers often examine other policies and policy mechanisms to help enhance their own specific policy needs. One place where global health policy makers look for inspiration is within the realm of environmental policy and its many treaties. The similarity between global environmental and health issues is striking because, as Sands and Peel (2005) assert, states cannot act single-handedly within their own borders and expect to adequately address such environmental problems. This is evident in the example of air pollution, where one country's carbon dioxide or sulfur dioxide emissions often affect its neighbors. Just as many environmental problems are "transboundary" by nature (i.e., they cross boundaries), so, too, are many health problems—one nation's avian flu outbreak can quickly become a cross-border problem and leap from one country to another.

International cooperation becomes the norm in such circumstances, and most states are apt to increase cooperation if spread of a feared disease is imminent. Unfortunately, the same degree of cooperation is not always as rapidly forthcoming for noncommunicable, or chronic, diseases resulting from tobacco or alcohol use, for example, or from the adverse effects of poverty. In these cases, states might be tempted to regard such health issues as largely domestic and nonthreatening to their own populations.

Although lung cancer and malnutrition are clearly health problems, they do not evoke fear of cross-border contamination in the same manner as avian flu or SARS, for example. Also, when a disease such as lung cancer implicates a globally sold product such as cigarettes, solutions become highly charged and more controversial as the discussion shifts from the health sector to free trade. Accomplishing meaningful change becomes all the more difficult, which in turn makes the use of treaties with binding components increasingly more attractive. Binding components are those parts of a treaty that countries are obligated to obey, provided they ratify the treaty.

Since World War II, the world has seen the proliferation of many environmental treaties brokered by the UN, yet only one treaty exists for global health policy. Today there are approximately 200 multilateral environmental agreements (MEAs) of global importance (Axelrod, Downie, & Vig, 2005). However, as the FCTC illustrates, this situation is changing. Countries can ultimately use international law in the form of multilateral treaties as a mechanism with which to expand their impact on health issues in a legally binding manner. Developing countries stand to gain the most from treaties that are written in a manner that recognizes "common, but differentiated responsibilities"—to borrow a term from global environmental policy and law. In other words, while both developed and developing countries agree upon the objectives of a given treaty, both groups also recognize that each other's contributions will vary over time based on levels of development and economic viability.

Although sources of international law include treaties, binding acts of international organizations, rules of customary international law, and judgments from international courts or tribunals, the treaty is the most important mechanism available in the global arena (Sands & Peel, 2005). A framework convention or treaty, such as the FCTC, does not contain binding obligations and is usually negotiated with the idea that a binding protocol will follow at a later date (Steel, Clinton, & Lovrich, 2003). For example, the 1997 Kyoto Protocol creates binding obligations for the UN Framework Convention on Climate Change signatories, much as the 1987 Montreal Protocol on Substances That Deplete the Ozone Layer did for the 1985 Vienna Convention for the Protection of the Ozone Layer. Presumably the FCTC will also have its own binding protocol at a later date.

In the meantime, several principles of international environmental law serve as applicable strategies to health issues. These environmental principles include the following:

- "Cause no harm," which calls upon states to be "good neighbors" to other states.
- "Common but differentiated responsibility," or the recognition that all states share common responsibility for protecting the environment. Differences among states mean that not all of them are required to simultaneously pursue identical solutions to the problem, however.
- The "precautionary principle," or understanding that lack of full information should not prevent preemptive cooperation before the problem gets worse.
- "Polluter pays," or the idea that pollution costs should be the responsibility of those who cause the pollution. A similar concept, known as "producer pays," is often applied to the disposal of European waste packaging.
- "Sustainable development," which in its strict sense implies that humans must preserve our natural resources for the benefit of present and future generations (World Commission on Environment and Development, 1987, p. 8). *Our Common Future* (discussed next) also expanded this definition to include the notion of equitable resource use while inferring that economic and general development planning must incorporate environmental concerns into the process.

As we will see upon closer examination in this tobacco treaty case, both European and developing states saw the relevance of applying such principles to WHO policy. They also found an ally in Gro Harlem Brundtland, who is both an environmentalist and a global health advocate. A former Norwegian prime minister and physician, Brundtland chaired the 1987 World Commission on Environment and Development—commonly known as the Brundtland Commission—which produced the historic document *Our Common Future*. *Our Common Future* introduced the world to an environmentally conscious way of thinking and inspired the creation of two major international treaties on climate change and biodiversity as well as the Agenda 21 action plan for sustainable development. Implementation of this sustainable development goal occurred at the famous UN Conference on Environment and Development (UNCED), commonly called the Earth Summit, which was held in Rio de Janeiro, Brazil (Axelrod et al., 2005). These efforts created the realization among policy makers that development and environmental issues cannot be solved in a vacuum. Instead, they must be viewed as goals into which economic and social aspects must be incorporated in a manner that harnesses the strengths of the North for the good of the entire planet with a special focus on the needs of the global South.

Brundtland served as the WHO's fifth director-general from 1998 to 2003 and set the tone for policy priorities that would include both communicable and noncommunicable diseases. During this period, the FCTC was being refined in working group sessions; it was ultimately signed in 2003. Early in her term as director-general, Brundtland (1998) made her support of the global South clear when she stated, "I envisage a world where solidarity binds the fortunate with those less favoured. . . . Where our collective efforts will help roll back all diseases of the poor." Brundtland believes that the role of developed countries must be to help developing countries achieve their health objectives, even if that means going beyond financial assistance and actually curbing the North's commercial interests in harmful products such as tobacco. Brundtland was not shy about attacking the behemoth tobacco industry. Indeed, in 2003, she described the FCTC as an avenue for developing "efforts to build legal and regulatory protection against marketing efforts of the large tobacco companies."

CHANGE AGENTS

As described earlier in this chapter, members of both the global North and South are proponents of global health governance through treaties. Nation states from the North and South that propose new ways to conceptualize global health policy become what Rogers and Shoemaker (1971) call "change agents." A change agent is a person or group "who influences innovation decisions in a direction deemed desirable by a change agency" (Rogers & Shoemaker, 1971, p. 227). In this case, the change agency is WHO and the change agents are its members (i.e., nation states).

Political learning gained from environmental treaty successes has spilled over into the global health arena and made the developing South, in particular, a driving force, a primary innovator for a paradigm shift toward the use of multilateral treaties in global health policy. Hinrichs (2002) reminds us that "the prospects of successfully 'learning from others' are better the more it is possible to construct a direct link between a unanimously defined problem and a concrete policy." While existing WHO programs, such as the Malaria Program, attempt to overcome a unanimously defined problem of malaria's often-deadly effects through the creation of a concrete malaria policy, the global weight of a program is not the same as that of a treaty. Thus expanded global cooperation to achieve health policy goals is more likely to occur if such policy problems, goals, and solutions are couched in a formal treaty having the status of hard international law.

TACKLING BIG TOBACCO: A BOLD NEW PATH TOWARD IMPLEMENTING GLOBAL HEALTH STANDARDS?

The WHO-initiated tobacco treaty known as the Framework Convention on Tobacco Control represents a response to the increasing use of tobacco products worldwide. The increased usage rate for tobacco in the developing world was a particular cause for alarm among WHO member states that sought to reduce the incidence of smoking by opening negotiations on a global treaty in October 1999. These negotiations culminated in the first-ever global health treaty, which was adopted in June 2003 and which came into force on February 27, 2005.

WHO acknowledged the harmful effects of tobacco as early as 1970 when the 23rd WHA passed Resolution 23.32, "Health Consequences of Smoking." This quiet start recognized the serious health effects of smoking, which can lead to pulmonary and cardiac disease, including cancer and chronic bronchitis. Despite this known linkage, recommendations at the time fell far short of an international treaty, were fairly benign, and lacked authority. Instead, the WHA resolution called for WHO representatives to refrain from smoking at assembly meetings and for WHO to generally discourage smoking in all countries especially through education of young people. The WHO resolution also called on the Food and Agriculture Organization (FAO) to study crop-substitution alternatives in tobacco-producing countries (WHO, 1970).

In May 1992, WHO initiated a serious tobacco campaign at the 45th WHA, which took shape in Resolution 45.20. This resolution encouraged collaboration among international organizations to deal with the issue that WHO called "tobacco or health." In 1992, WHO sought to balance health concerns against the economic objectives to this policy raised by tobacco-growing countries of the global South. Although the WHO (1992) recognized the health effects of tobacco use, it was "concerned about the economic effects of reduced production in the tobacco-producing countries that are still unable to develop a viable economic alternative to tobacco." In order of importance, economic and health issues were equally divided.

In May 1995, however, the 48th WHA officially shifted its position on the tobacco issue by identifying control of tobacco's negative-health ramifications as the primary objective (WHO, 1995). The Ninth World Conference on Tobacco and Health held in Paris in October 1994 resulted in the first international strategy for tobacco control. This strategy was later adopted by the WHA in May 1995 in the form of Resolution 48.11, "An International Strategy for Tobacco Control." This resolution called for the creation of an international instrument—guidelines, a declaration, or international convention—on tobacco control to be adopted by the United Nations. The 49th WHA in May 1996 called for the fast-track creation of a tobacco treaty.

The Resolution 48.11 and its subsequent 1996 fast-tracking marked the starting point for a tobacco control treaty, but it was not until 1999 that negotiations within the intergovernmental working group actually addressed the content of the Framework Convention on Tobacco Control. Once the working group began its treaty-making task, a clear shift toward use of environmental techniques also became evident.

SETTING THE STAGE

The Report of the First Meeting of the Working Group recognized that not only is tobacco a cross-border issue, but it also transcends the "bounds of public health" (WHO, 1999). This recognition made it easier for WHO to create a treaty that emphasized trade and regulatory controls as well as financial sharing of the enforcement burden. This latter point was also linked to the recognition that tobacco-growing countries of the South may need financial support for crop substitution. Fears about this policy's adverse economic impact on developing countries were assuaged by World Bank findings in the book *Curbing the Epidemic: Governments and the Economics of Tobacco Control* (1999).

The World Bank findings pointed to tobacco control as more economically cost-effective in the long term due to the millions of lives saved by relieving the disease burden imposed by this addictive substance. According to World Bank (1999) estimates, tobacco was expected to kill nearly 4 million people around the globe by 2000. While one in ten deaths is currently attributed to tobacco's harmful effects, by 2030 this ratio is expected to be one in six—equivalent to 10 million deaths annually. Moreover, use of tobacco is increasing in the developing world and especially in China, where 25% of the world's smokers reside. Chinese smoking rates in the 1990s were comparable to those of the United States in 1950 (World Bank, 1999). The World Bank's call for action reminded readers of *Curbing the Epidemic,* including working group members, that the prevalence of only two causes of death is growing worldwide—human immunodeficiency virus (HIV) infection and tobacco. While fighting HIV is universally accepted, the global response to tobacco has been limited at best and largely focused within developed countries.

Curbing the Epidemic suggested that the need for tobacco controls is most acute in developing countries. According to the World Bank, the impact of reduced tobacco production on the economy of developing countries would be negligible or have little impact on employment or revenue. Any impact would be gradual and nearly inconsequential. The conclusions drawn in *Curbing the Epidemic* thus gave WHO the green light to proceed with a comprehensive treaty that incorporates an environmental approach to treaty making. In fact, the book explicitly recognized the successes of the environmental approach and urged its application to tobacco: "The framework convention-protocol approach has been used to address other global problems, for example, the Vienna Convention for the Protection of the Ozone Layer and the Montreal Protocol."

The one difference between environmental issues and tobacco use is that the World Bank urged actions to curb demand rather than to restrict or ban supply. This strategy is markedly different from the phase-out approach to harmful pollutants adopted in many environmental treaties. Neither the World Bank nor the WHO working group called for the phase-out of tobacco products—just a reduction in consumer use through various means. Perhaps a phase-out will become acceptable in the future, but it is not presently an option under discussion, nor was it in the working group meetings leading up to the FCTC.

The working group felt that "treaties make a difference" and can take the form of a framework convention and subsequent amendments and protocols. While a framework convention has as its objective to garner widespread global support, the subsequent protocol will elaborate upon the details and binding obligations at a later date. This is so similar in approach to the environmental arena that the working group report specifically acknowledged that "this type of instrument had proved its worth in disarmament and environmental protection" (WHO, 1999). Moving even closer to the environmental tactics, the working group went so far as to recognize the principle of "polluter pays" and urged that it be "explored as a means of holding the tobacco industry accountable for the harm it causes."

While the working group met to formulate the treaty, concomitant tobacco-control projects were undertaken simultaneously by WHO's Tobacco Free Initiative. These projects ranged from advice on the policy effects of scientific aspects of the tobacco problem to better understanding of regulation and media as tobacco-limiting tools. The Tobacco Free Initiative also explored anti-tobacco legislative capacity, youth activities, and improved data gathering and surveillance in collaboration with the U.S. Centers for Disease Control and Prevention (CDC), which is a U.S. government agency within the Department of Health and Human Services (WHO, 2000c). The utility of these parallel projects was considered to be complementary to the treaty process.

The Tobacco Free Initiative projects reinforced the notion that tobacco was a high priority for WHO. In other words, WHO prepared the world incrementally through these various projects for, and facilitated global acceptance of, a controversial and groundbreaking health treaty that painted commercially marketed tobacco products as a grave health risk. In essence, WHO prepared potentially reticent countries for the FCTC by creating a link from tobacco initiative projects to a treaty having the force of international law behind it.

Director-General Brundtland was also a strong treaty supporter and, at every opportunity, smoothed the transition to its eventual entry into force in February 2005. In her 2000 report on noncommunicable diseases, Brundtland reminded the 53rd WHA of the link between cancer, diabetes, and chronic pulmonary disease and lifestyle factors such as diet, physical inactivity, and tobacco use (WHO, 2000b). Brundtland did not shy away from innovation and mentioned the need for "innovative organizational models" throughout her report. Her report was essentially a call to action that spurred the development of the tobacco treaty.

By May 11, 2000, the framework convention was ready in draft form (WHO, 2000c). The idea was to create a treaty that would set standards while not discouraging countries with harsh rhetoric and obligations—those measures could come later in a protocol. The draft treaty received WHA approval for the negotiation phase to begin in October 2000, and an intergovernmental negotiating body was formed to begin the task of finalizing the document.

Between 2000 and May 21, 2003, WHO continually revisited the tobacco issue in its assembly. In May 2001, for example, WHA addressed the issue of transparency in the tobacco control process and used stronger language to portray the role of big tobacco interests: "The tobacco industry has operated for years with the expressed intention of subverting the role of government and of WHO in implementing public health policies to combat the tobacco epidemic." The tobacco industry was thus portrayed as a formidable public enemy. WHO member states were encouraged to be mindful should tobacco interests attempt to infiltrate their midst. Any member delegation affiliated with the tobacco industry was encouraged to be forthcoming with this relationship (WHO, 2001).

FRAMEWORK CONVENTION ON TOBACCO CONTROL

The final product was adopted on May 21, 2003, in Geneva and contained most of the important elements discussed in preliminary working group sessions. The treaty was a victory for developing countries, and its preamble reinforced the serious concern posed by the increase in global tobacco product consumption, "particularly in developing countries" (WHO, 2003). Thus, although the FCTC was aimed at empowering countries worldwide, it gave special emphasis to the global South. Part VII, Article 20, calls for parties to provide financial and technical resources for the purpose of helping developing countries as well as countries in transition (e.g., former communist countries).

Article 22 of the treaty is more explicit in its assertion that parties should take into account developing country needs and "promote the transfer of technical, scientific and legal expertise and technology, as mutually agreed, to establish and strengthen national tobacco control strategies" (WHO, 2003). With the FCTC, WHO made a groundbreaking contribution to the body of international law in the form of the world's first global health treaty and reinforced the understanding that tobacco consumption and exposure to tobacco smoke cause disease and death, a relationship "unequivocally established" by the scientific community (WHO, 2003).

Harsh words were reserved for the industry's use of carcinogenic chemicals in cigarettes to foster human dependence on tobacco, and any attempt by the tobacco industry to undermine or subvert tobacco control efforts was identified as an ongoing concern for signatory states (WHO, 2003). In short, the treaty demonstrated its acceptance of the premise that tobacco is harmful to health, and the tobacco industry was to blame. Unlike the Vienna Convention for the Protection of the Ozone Layer, the FCTC did not call for such drastic action as a total ban on tobacco—only its control. The phase-out of the most harmful ozone-depleting chemicals was possible because more ozone-friendly substitutes were created. Perhaps industry will respond to the FCTC by creating a harmless cigarette that meets health standards; unfortunately, this appears unlikely as long as the product contains tobacco.

Although chlorofluorocarbon (CFC) manufacturers were encouraged to create safer alternatives as part of the Vienna Convention, the global community does not encourage the development of safer cigarettes. Instead, the treaty's ultimate intent is to stamp out tobacco entirely, from a health perspective, although WHO is unable to state this objective explicitly at this time. The "polluter pays" concept indirectly appears in Part VI, Article 19, of the treaty, where liability is seen as a tactic to achieve the goal of decreasing tobacco use:

> For the purpose of tobacco control, the Parties shall consider taking legislative action
> or promoting their existing laws, where necessary, to deal with criminal and civil lia-
> bility, including compensation where appropriate. (WHO, 2003)

Reference to appropriate compensation is a generalized attempt to recognize the "polluter pays" concept without implying a cause-and-effect relationship between tobacco manufacturers and end users—or victims.

Article 19 encourages member states to pursue product liability as a means of bringing attention to the problem. The FCTC focuses on the need to take measures to protect everyone from tobacco's harmful effects. To achieve this goal, the treaty urges member states to take concrete steps such as reducing demand through price and tax measures, regulation of packaging and labeling, educational and public awareness campaigns, cessation of tobacco advertising where constitutionally feasible, and reduction in illegal supply. It encourages member states to take appropriate measures in this regard, but does not require them to do so. Creating specific and required benchmarks related to tobacco control (i.e., binding obligations) will come at a later date in a protocol.

TOBACCO-RELATED HEALTH POLICY DEVELOPMENT: AN ONGOING PROCESS

The momentum created by the first-ever global health treaty represents an innovative start to tackling health problems—especially those caused by lifestyle choices. The treaty was a result of cooperative efforts among actors from the North and South and benefited from strong guidance of WHO's Director-General

Gro Brundtland, who vigorously lobbied for its creation. While the United States, the world's second-leading tobacco-producing state (after China), signed the treaty as mentioned earlier in this chapter, it has yet to ratify the document (WHO, 1999). At first glance, the U.S. reluctance may appear detrimental to global anti-tobacco goals, but is less troublesome than one might think because 84% of the world's smokers live in developing and transitional, or formerly communist, countries (2006b). These countries overwhelmingly ratified the treaty and should thus reap its benefits with or without U.S. participation.

Unlike transboundary greenhouse gas pollution from a major emitter nation, to which anyone may fall victim regardless of his or her country of residence, tobacco use is largely a self-contained lifestyle issue. It is more easily controlled through lifestyle changes resulting from education and personal decisions not to smoke. The FCTC thus provides tools and facilitates individuals' ability to say no to smoking.

Future protocols could go further by pressing for mandatory reductions in tobacco production or manufacture. The FCTC creates a future avenue for global health policy that leads the way toward more aggressive options to deal with tobacco—even to the extent of calling for a gradual phase-out of its manufacture into cigarettes, smokeless tobacco, or tobacco chewing products.

Health innovation continues to evolve toward international cooperative efforts that take a proactive approach to the disease burden. Pandemic spread of avian flu is one problem that WHO and other regional health organizations take seriously and are tackling as of this writing. Yet, innovation within the global health agenda will have a greater impact if it takes the form of the hard law that a treaty provides. In the meantime, WHO's tobacco-related activities continue. In November 2011, for example, the WHO Center for Tobacco Control in Africa opened in Kampala, Uganda. Its purpose is to build "regional capacity" for what WHO calls tobacco control interventions, the first of which is a no-smoking music video in which a singer vocalizes about "smoking up my cash for a tiny piece of trash" ("WHO Opens Centre for Tobacco Control in Africa," 2012).

While Africa may be associated more with malaria than with smoking, as its residents' disposable income increases, the purchase of tobacco products is sure to rise—and many Africans will inevitably fall victim to "diseases of development." Focus on developing areas such as Africa is a key part of WHO's capacity-building campaign. Capacity building also appears to be taking hold within domestic policy arenas of the developing world. Recognizing that tobacco is a main contributor to the increase in noncommunicable diseases in Mauritius, for example, that country's government adopted a graphic tobacco-warning on cigarette packs. Since 2008, tobacco regulations in Mauritius have required visual health warnings on cigarette packs that reinforce the adage "A picture is worth a thousand words." One such photo depicts a dying man with an oxygen mask over his face and carries the tag line in French and English, "Smoking causes a long and painful death" ("Fumer cause une mort lente et douloureuse") (WHO, 2011, p. 59).

CONCLUSION

This chapter presented an important example—that of tobacco and the role of a multilateral organization, WHO—of how public health policy making can be accomplished. As illustrated in this case, global health policy making is influenced by domestic and global political actors, the news media, interest groups, and, oftentimes, the unpredictable collusion of current events and public opinion. There are many routes to influencing and overseeing the implementation of policies affecting public health policy, all of which make for a dynamic, oftentimes slow, and certainly tumultuous policy process.

WHO as a multilateral organization seems to illustrate that health innovation continues to evolve toward international cooperative efforts that take a proactive approach to the burden of disease. A pandemic threat, such as the spread of avian flu, is one problem that WHO and other regional health organizations take seriously and are currently tackling, along with controlling the reemergent threats of diseases once thought to be eradicated. Yet, innovation in the global health arena will have a greater impact if it takes the form of "hard" law that a treaty provides, instead of guidelines, or "soft" law, that can be ignored or only partially instituted in those member states that chose to implement them. The bold first step was taken thanks to a North–South coalition that recognized that a treaty would attract global attention like no other WHO documents or pronouncements had done previously. In short, this action goes beyond a "business as usual" approach and can strengthen WHO's ability to address global health inequalities.

STUDY QUESTIONS

1. Explain how a tobacco control policy affects the health of a nation.
2. How can WHO's health policies make a difference in global health care?
3. Discuss how treaties between nations of the "North" and "South" can work together as change agents to improve worldwide health.

CASE STUDIES

Background: In 2005, fewer than 11,000 cases of Guinea worm were reported in the nine countries and the majority of the cases were in Sudan, where civil war has restricted progress. Before 1986, an estimated 3.5 million people in Africa and Asia were infected with Guinea worm, and 120 million were at risk.

Intervention Program: With the technical and financial support of the a global coalition of organizations led by the Carter Center, the United Nations Children's Fund, the U.S. Centers for Disease Control and Prevention, and the World Health Organization, 20 countries implemented national Guinea Worm Eradication Programs, organized and implemented through the ministries of health. The primary interventions of the campaign included:

- the provision of safe water (through deep well digging, applying larvicide, and purifying water through cloth filters);
- health education;
- case containment, management, and surveillance.

Results: The eradication efforts have led to a 99.7 percent drop in Guinea worm prevalence. In 2005, fewer than 11,000 cases were reported, compared with an estimated 3.5 million infected people in 1986. The campaign has prevented more than 63 million cases of Guinea worm disease, reduced the number of endemic villages by 91 percent, and stopped the transmission of the disease in 11 of the 20 endemic countries. The total cost of the program between 1986 and 1998 was $87.4 million. The estimated cost per case was $5 to $8. The World Bank determined that the campaign has been highly cost-effective and cost-beneficial. The economic rate of return based on agricultural productivity alone has been estimated at 29 percent.

(The Carter Center, 2012)

REFERENCES

Axelrod, R. S., Downie, D. L., & Vig, N. J. (2005). *The global environment: Institutions, law, and policy.* Washington, DC: CQ Press.

Brundtland, G. H. (1998, May 13). Speech to the Fifty-First World Health Assembly, A51/DIV/6, Geneva, Switzerland.

Hinrichs, K. (2002). What can be learned from whom? Germany's employment problem in comparative perspective. *Innovation, 15*(2), 89–97.

A manipulated dichotomy in global health policy. (2000). *Lancet, 355*(9219), 1923.

Pan-American Health Organization. (2002, September). Basic country health profiles for the Americas, Bolivia. Retrieved from http://www.paho.org

Reddy, S. K., Shah, B., Varghese, C., & Ramadoss, A. (2005). Responding to the threat of chronic diseases in India. *Lancet, 366*, 1746–1751.

Rogers, E. M., & Shoemaker, F. F. (1971). *Communication of innovations: A cross-cultural approach.* New York, NY: Free Press.

Sands, P., & Peel, J. (2005). Environmental protection in the twenty-first century: Sustainable development and international law. In R. S. Axelrod, D. L. Downie, & N. J. Vig (Eds.), *The global environment: Institutions, law, and policy* (pp. 43–63). Washington, DC: CQ Press.

Shiffman, J., Berlan, D., Abou Assi, K., Elberger, B., Cordero, A., & Soper, T. (2009). *What is the "global health agenda" and how would we know if an issue is on it?* Paper presented at the International Studies Association Conference, New York City.

Siddiqi, J. (1995). *World health and world politics: The World Health Organization and the UN system.* Columbus, SC: University of South Carolina Press.

Steel, B. S., Clinton, R. L., & Lovrich, N. P. (2003). *Environmental politics and policy: A comparative approach.* Boston: McGraw-Hill.

The Carter Center (2012). CASE 11: Reducing guinea worm in Asia and sub-Saharan Africa. Retrieved from http://www.cgdev.org/section/initiatives/_archive/millionssaved/studies/case_11

UN Millennium Project. (2006). UN Millennium Project. Retrieved from http://www.unmillennium project.org/

WHO opens Centre for Tobacco Control in Africa. (2012). Retrieved from www.who.int/tobacco /communications/events/who_centre_tobacco_control_africa/en/

World Bank. (1999). *Curbing the epidemic: Governments and the economics of tobacco control.* Washington, DC: Author.

World Commission on Environment and Development. (1987). *Our common future.* New York: Oxford University Press.

World Health Organization (WHO). (1948a). *Constitution of the World Health Organization.* Geneva, Switzerland: Author. Retrieved from http://www.who.int/about/en/

World Health Organization (WHO). (1948b). *Principles governing relations between the World Health Organization and nongovernmental organizations.* Geneva, Switzerland: Author. Retrieved from http://www.who.int/about/en/

World Health Organization (WHO). (1970, May 19). *Health consequences of smoking.* WHA23.32. Geneva, Switzerland: Author.

World Health Organization (WHO). (1978, September 6–12). *Declaration of Alma-Ata.* International Conference on Primary Health Care, Alma-Ata, USSR.

World Health Organization (WHO). (1992, May 13). *Multisectoral collaboration on WHO's programme on tobacco or health.* WHA45.20. Geneva, Switzerland: Author.

World Health Organization (WHO). (1995, May 12). *An international strategy for tobacco control.* WHA48.11. Geneva, Switzerland: Author.

World Health Organization (WHO). (1998, May 7–16). *Health for all in the twenty-first century.* A51/5. Geneva, Switzerland: Author.

World Health Organization (WHO). (1999, October 28). *WHO Framework Convention on Tobacco Control: Report of the first meeting of the working group.* A/FCTC/WG1/7. Geneva, Switzerland: Author.

World Health Organization (WHO). (2000a, May 20). *Framework Convention on Tobacco Control.* WHA53.16. Geneva, Switzerland: Author.

World Health Organization (WHO). (2000b, March 22). *Global strategy for the prevention and control of noncommunicable diseases: Report by the director-general.* A53/14. Geneva, Switzerland: Author.

World Health Organization (WHO). (2000c, March 10). *Tobacco Free Initiative: Report by the director-general.* A53/13. Geneva, Switzerland: Author.

World Health Organization (WHO). (2001, May 22). *Transparency in tobacco control process.* WHA54.18. Geneva, Switzerland: Author.

World Health Organization (WHO). (2003, May 21). *WHO Framework Convention on Tobacco Control.* Geneva, Switzerland: Author.

World Health Organization (WHO). (2005, May 23). *Revision of the International Health Regulations.* WHA58.3.

World Health Organization (WHO). (2006a). The Civil Society Initiative. Retrieved from http://www.who.int/civilsociety/en/

World Health Organization (WHO). (2006b, February 6–17). The first session of the conference of the parties to the WHO Framework Convention on Tobacco Control, Geneva, Switzerland. Retrieved from www.who.int/tobacco/fctc/cop/en

World Health Organization (WHO). (2006c). Health and the MDGs: Background. Retrieved from http://www.who.int/mdg/background/en/index.html

World Health Organization (WHO). (2006d). International Health Regulations. Retrieved from http://www.who.int/csr/ihr/en/

World Health Organization (WHO). (2006e). *Weekly Epidemiological Record.* Retrieved from www.who.int/wer

World Health Organization (WHO). (2006f). WHO executive board members. Retrieved from www.who.int/governance/eb/eb_members/en/print.html

World Health Organization (WHO). (2006g). World health statistics. Retrieved from http://www.who.int/gho/publications/world_health_statistics/2006/en/index.html

World Health Organization (WHO). (2008). *WHO Commission on Social Determinants of Health.* Geneva, Switzerland: Author.

World Health Organization (WHO). (2011). *WHO report on the global tobacco epidemic, 2011.* Geneva, Switzerland: Author.

*For a full suite of assignments and additional learning activities, use the access code located in the front of your book to visit this exclusive website: **http://go.jblearning.com/holtz**. If you do not have an access code, you can obtain one at the site.*

6

Ethics of End-of-Life Care from a Global Perspective

Lois R. Robley

> *"And in the end, it's not the years in your life that count.
> It's the life in your years."*
>
> Abraham Lincoln

OBJECTIVES

1. Explain the rationale and moral foundations for palliative care.
2. Identify the scope of patient/family needs at the end of life.
3. Identify similarities and differences in palliative care among selected countries.
4. Cite the barriers to adequate palliative care in regions around the world.
5. Develop a plan for participating in international efforts to improve palliative care.

DEFINITIONS

Palliative Care

The goal of palliative care is to prevent and relieve suffering, and to support the best possible quality of life for patients and their families, regardless of their stage of disease or the need for other therapies, in accordance with their values and preferences. Palliative care is both a philosophy of care and an organized, highly structured system for delivering care. It expands traditional disease-model medical treatments to include the goals of enhancing quality of life for the patient and family, optimizing function, helping with decision making, and providing opportunities for personal growth. As such, it can be delivered concurrently with life-prolonging care or as the main focus of care (American Academy of Hospice and Palliative Medicine, 2011; Lynch, Dahlin, Hultman, & Coakley, 2011; National Quality Forum, 2006).

Hospice Care

Hospice is a type of palliative care. The term "hospice" (from the same linguistic root as "hospitality") can be traced back to medieval times, when it referred to a place of shelter and rest for weary or ill travelers on a long journey. Hospice is a program of care provided across settings that assists "patients and their families deal with life-limiting illnesses and caregiving so that they may (1) live each day with comfort and dignity, (2) retain control over their lives, and (3) discover renewed meaning and purpose in this time of their lives" (Egan & Labyak, 2006, p. 13). This multidisciplinary care is delivered by physicians, nurses, social workers, chaplains, and volunteers and employs compassion and skill that address the physical, psychological, social, and spiritual needs of a patient and family at the end of life.

ETHICS AND END-OF-LIFE CARE FROM A GLOBAL PERSPECTIVE

With approximately 57 million persons dying each year around the world, the need for community-level, basic end-of-life care is both urgent and enormous in scope (Rajagopal, 2007; World Health Organization [WHO], 2003). Many people, both young and old, die without pain and symptom management, let alone spiritual, social, and psychological support. The suffering of these patients and their loved ones is incalculable. The lack of access to relatively simple analgesic methods using morphine and other inexpensive medication is decried as a major and significant global problem. In fact, as Joranson, Ryan, and Maurer (2010) point out, the "vast majority of cancer and AIDS patients in the developing world, and many in developed countries, still lack access to these essential medications" (p. 1). As the pain and symptom burden increases toward the end of life, particularly with cancer and HIV/AIDS, adherence to the WHO guidelines for palliative and comfort care becomes critical.

Palliative care addresses quality of life for those suffering life-threatening illness as well as for their families. It is designed to address pain and symptom management, along with psychological, social, and spiritual concerns. It is estimated that as many as 100 million persons would benefit from palliative care, yet less than 8% of the world's population of dying patients receives it (Economist Intelligence Unit, 2010). Only "6% of all palliative care services are located in Asia or Africa, the regions where the majority of the world's population lives and dies" (Shanmugasundaram & O'Connor, 2009, p. 84). **Figure 6-1** outlines the levels of palliative care development in countries around the world (Wright, Wood, Lynch, & Clark, 2006).

Palliative care is considered a good, a service with noble origins, and a process that addresses the needs of those individuals who are most vulnerable—namely, those with life-threatening illness. In the Western world, it is often identified as a basic human right and an extension of the ethics of care (Brennan, Carr, & Cousins, 2007; Human Rights Watch, 2009). Best practice standards in palliation are not universal, however, but rather are situated within the context of a society's culture and patient/family variables (Barazzetti, Borreani, Miccinesi, & Toscani, 2010).

SOCIAL DETERMINANTS OF HEALTH

The health of individuals and nations is determined in great part by social factors. Differences of extraordinary dimensions are seen depending on the social environment where people are born, live, develop, work, age, and die. WHO (2008) has declared that social inequities are the cause of unnecessary death across the globe and that leadership is needed in many countries to address those elements of public policy, economics, and politics that influence health. Grassroots efforts, intersectoral cooperation, and transglobal assistance are needed to effect change in the basic areas of prevention, treatment, and delivery of health services (Exworthy, 2008).

In their historical perspective on social determinants of health (SDH), Irwin and Scali (2007) claim that forward movement on SDH depends "heavily on the extent to which civil society organizations are engaged on the issue, working to drive action in the political arena, and holding decision-makers accountable" (p. 252). In theory, and in practice in developing nations, there has been a fundamental shift in focus away from urban centers and toward mobilization of community members as health workers, as

FIGURE 6-1

Levels of Palliative Care Development

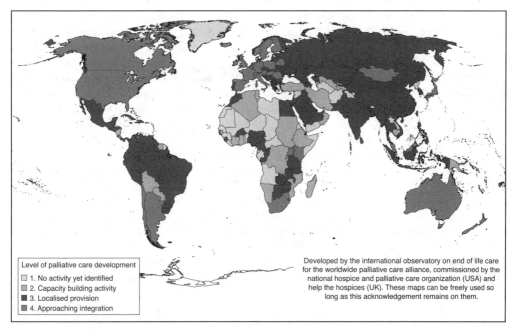

Level of palliative care development
☐ 1. No activity yet identified
☐ 2. Capacity building activity
■ 3. Localised provision
■ 4. Approaching integration

Developed by the international observatory on end of life care
for the worldwide palliative care alliance, commissioned by the
national hospice and palliative care organization (USA) and
help the hospices (UK). These maps can be freely used so
long as this acknowledgement remains on them.

Source: Hanks et al., 2011.

part of a trend toward locating all health services where people live (Irwin & Scali, 2007). In the arena of end-of-life health care, there is a concomitant shift in the same direction. In Uganda, where a national priority for palliative care has existed since 2000, the focus of charitable institutions, at least in one region, has been on teaching all healthcare professionals about end-of-life and palliative care. Educating and empowering nurses in distant communities to prescribe opioids for comfort is one successful action toward the delivery of palliative care (Economist Intelligence Unit, 2010).

ETHICS OF SOCIAL JUSTICE

Significant inequalities in care for the chronically ill and dying are being given serious attention by the ethics research and scholarship community because they are of quantitatively greater importance than discussions of highly technical interventions (cessation of life support) that affect only a minority of individuals across the globe (Rennie & Mupenda, 2008). Attention to end-of-life disparities is related to the human values of health, human flourishing, and respect (Ruger, 2006). People in impoverished, developing communities lack the basic human rights of life (disparities in life expectancy and well-being), health (inadequate access to illness prevention), and comfort (even until death). The relief of suffering (physical, social, psychological, and spiritual) is a moral imperative for healthcare professionals (Amoah, 2011), and efforts to reduce disparities are motivated by moral concern for justice.

Justice, from the global perspective, derives from collective self-interest and security as nations as well as from the prevention of harm and the fostering of human agency (Ruger, 2006). The concept of justice means fairness or equality; the concept of social justice—a preeminent idea that guides public health policy and service—addresses social equity or balance. Social justice ascribes the fair distributions of benefits and burdens to all members of a society, paying close attention to those who are most vulnerable and least well off (Gostin & Powers, 2006; Tochon & Karaman, 2009). From another perspective, a just society is one that provides at least a modicum of healthcare services to the disadvantaged (Daniels, 2008).

Attention is being directed toward intercultural education with a focus on social justice in the United States (Belknap, 2008), and cooperative inroads have been made to address concerns about health disparities and the ethics of social justice internationally (Anderson, et al., 2009). One such entity focusing on international bioethics is the consortium formed by the University of North Carolina–Chapel Hill, the University of Louvain (Belgium), and the Kinshasa School of Public Health (Rennie & Mupenda, 2008). Ventures such as this lead to cooperative ethics scholarship, research, and advocacy.

Even so, there are those who maintain that caution needs to be applied to the issue of enhancing global palliative care, thereby responding to the call of the suffering. Although much needs to be done to provide nations with models, support, and encouragement in their development of palliative care programs, such efforts should not be undertaken to the detriment or in lieu of wellness and treatment programs. As Krakauer (2008) states, "acceptance of unequal access for the poor to life-saving medical services that are badly needed and potentially feasible is unjust" (p. 505). It would be unethical to deny life-saving treatments such as immunizations and cancer treatments merely because they are less costly. Palliative care warrants incorporation into public health systems rather than being singled out as having higher value.

BARRIERS TO PALLIATIVE CARE

There are practical barriers to even minimal palliative and end-of-life care in many societies. Inadequate availability of opioids to relieve pain and dyspnea creates diminished quality of life for patients across the world (Cherny, Baselga, de Conno, & Radbruch, 2009). This is particularly true for patients in developing nations, where diagnoses are more often made in the late stages of disease. In addition, many countries lack public or government will to fund the work of palliation, pay little attention to palliation as part of the public health agenda, lack education for health providers regarding palliative care, and must deal with the cultural stigma of dying. In some countries, the morbidity and mortality of healthcare workers is an additional issue (Selman et al., 2011).

It is widely acknowledged that relief of pain and suffering is a professional moral obligation and is part of compassionate, competent medical and nursing care of all patients (Ashley, 2008; Brennan et al., 2007). Opioids are the hallmark medications for relief of pain and dyspnea and are required at stage 2 (moderate) and stage 3 (severe) level of pain as reflected on the WHO Pain Relief Ladder (**Figure 6-2**; WHO, 2011).

When compared to opioid consumption in 2008 in the United States (66.56 mg/person) and Canada (73.98 mg/person), the mean African consumption is very low (0.5548 mg/person), as is that in Southeast Asia (0.3288 mg/person) (University of Wisconsin, 2010). In fact, "only six countries together accounted for 79% of worldwide consumption of morphine . . . developing countries (with almost 80% of the world population) accounted for only 6%" (Mosoiu, Ryan, Joranson, & Garthwaite, 2006, p. 3). In low- and middle-income countries, 50% to 90% of the population pays for their medication on an out-of-pocket basis (Mendis et al., 2007). As Taylor (2007) states, "availability of effective pain medications

FIGURE 6-2

WHO Three-Step Anaglesic Ladder

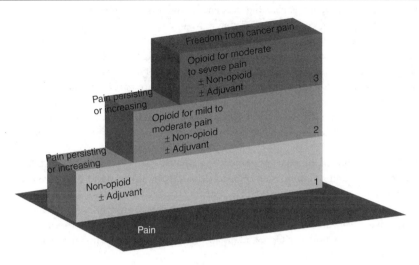

Source: WHO, 2011.

is undoubtedly one of the most neglected realms of global public health" (p. 556). Barriers to the use of opioids are numerous:

> Fear of addiction to opioids; lack of training of health care professionals about the use of opioids; laws or regulations that restrict the manufacturing, distribution, prescribing, or dispensing of opioids; reluctance to prescribe or stock opioids stemming from fear of legal consequences; overly burdensome administrative requirements related to opioids; insufficient amount of opioids imported or manufactured in the country; fear of diversion; cost of opioids; inadequate health care resources, such as facilities and health care professionals; lack of national policy or guidelines related to opioids. (Joranson et al., 2010, p. 199)

Integration of pain management in the education of doctors, nurses, and other healthcare providers is essential to dispelling the fears about opioids, concern about legal consequences, and anxiety related to illicit drug use and diversion.

The world community, through international treaty, created the Single Convention that outlined four "schedules" of plant-based controlled substances. The purpose of this measure was to control illegal use and trafficking while making the drugs available for medicinal and scientific purposes. Emphasis on control has, according to some, made it more difficult to assure access for patients who need pain relief (Taylor, 2007). Irrational fear of addiction causes inappropriate dosing and reluctance on the part of patients to use such drugs. There is no scientific evidence that the use of opioids prescribed for acute and cancer pain causes addiction, yet the fallacy persists among both policy makers and the general public. Although there is legitimate concern about the risk of addiction in certain patients with a history of substance abuse, only 0.27% of patients receiving opioid treatment for chronic noncancer pain develop addiction or use these medications inappropriately (Ballantyne & Mao, 2003; Dickinson, Altman, Nielsen, & Williams, 2000; Harrison, 2010). Wise use of opioids includes determining a definitive diagnosis, establishing the inadequacy of non-opioid and nonmedical treatments, calculating the balance of risk and benefit that favors treatment, explaining the benefits and risks and monitoring to the patient, establishing goals, and requesting consent (Ballantyne & Mao, 2003). Even when these issues are managed correctly, however, the cost of opioids may be a problem: In developing nations, this cost unnecessarily exceeds the cost incurred in developed nations such as the United States (Mendis et al., 2007).

Funding for palliative and hospice care within nations comes from a variety of sources. In the Catalonia region of Spain, for example, palliative care services are part of the state-supported regional public health services (Economist Intelligence Unit, 2010). In the United States, both Medicare and Medicaid fund palliative care if it is delivered by board-certified palliative care consultants. Medicare and Medicaid provide for hospice care in the last six months of life, but only if the patient or family forgoes curative treatments.

One shining example of national investment in palliative care can be found in Romania. In 2003, the Minister of Health and a Commission of Specialists in Pain Therapy and Palliative Care addressed 35-year-old regulations on opioid availability, drafted changes in the laws and regulations, piloted changes through the Romanian Parliament, and supported national guidelines for education and palliative care. This advocacy by the palliative care community and the government was accomplished with the assistance of WHO, international criteria, and organizations such as the National Hospice and Palliative Care Organization of the United States and the Pain and Policy Studies Group from the University of Wisconsin (Mosoiu et al., 2006). Casa Sperantei has become a model hospice for Romania as well as other countries in Eastern Europe; this hospice was created by U.K. philanthropist Graham Perolls (Economist Intelligence Unit, 2010). In most countries, governments are not the main source of financial support for hospice care; instead, such programs are typically funded by churches, philanthropic organizations, or international aid programs.

PALLIATIVE CARE IN CHINA

While there is a moral commitment by the Chinese government to improve palliative and hospice care, improved state funding is recognized as necessary to do so. Moreover, palliative care is a relatively new philosophy and venture in the country. In China:

> [N]inety percent of cancer patients in the terminal phase will not have pain relief or relief from distressing symptoms because palliative care services are still lacking in most of the country. The family unit has become smaller due to policy, and the historical care giving function of the family has been reduced. Traditionally, the children cared for their parents but at present many are not able to do so. Many patients and their relatives request euthanasia. A few even commit suicide to avoid excruciating cancer pain or because of poorly controlled spiritual and emotional distress. (Li, Davis, & Gamier, 2011, p. 290)

Nevertheless, long life is valued in Chinese culture and there is a cultural taboo against thinking and talking about death. Deeply embedded within it is the belief that elders are a font of knowledge, wisdom, and respect. With 149 million individuals older than the age of 60, there is enormous need for palliative and hospice care in China. The reasons for lack of palliative care, such as inadequate numbers of educated professionals, opioid fear, and a bent toward life-saving treatment even in the terminal stages of illness, are being revealed publicly (Han, 2011; Li et al., 2011; Yujie, 2011). Throughout China, there are just 30 hospices and 120 palliative care facilities; most are located within hospitals, make visits to patients in their homes, and are funded by charitable entities, notably the Li Ka-Shing Foundation (Becker, 2008).

The hospice movement is supported by physicians and nurses who see the need for care, compassion, and comfort at the end of life. It is also the focus of young people who are unable to care for their elders. The Li Ka-Shing Foundation assists in rapidly developing hospice and palliative care programs by donating HK $16 million ($2,063,335) annually to expand the earlier established programs in 16 major hospitals throughout China (Law, 2011).

In Hong Kong's regional Tuen Mun Hospital Palliative Care Unit, the multidisciplinary professional team adapted a clinical pathway created in Liverpool, England, by incorporating cultural and situational modifications to structure service delivery. Specific quality indicators were adapted that are being used to guide treatments such as removing inappropriate interventions, managing pain, and meeting religious needs (Lo et al., 2009). This effort demonstrates the role of developed countries leading the way in education and project management.

PALLIATIVE CARE IN INDIA

India ranks last out of 40 countries on the Quality of Death Index (Economic Intelligence Unit, 2010). This Index "scores countries across four categories: basic end-of-life healthcare environment, availability of end-of-life care, cost of end-of-life care, and quality of end-of-life care" (p. 11). Health care in general accounts for only 6% of the gross domestic product (GDP) of India and is logically focused on acute care. The average household pays 98.4% of healthcare expenses out of pocket; for many families, this means selling off possessions and incurring lifelong—indeed, generational—debt (PricewaterhouseCoopers, 2007). As the family structure changes with the movement of young people to urban centers, the need for palliative care clinics and hospices is growing (Shubha, 2007).

Eighty percent of patients in India present with late-stage disease. Families traditionally take on the responsibility of caring for the ill and dying, and frequently are distressed when symptoms are uncontrolled. The principles of palliative care involve the use of alternative therapies as adjunctive measures; they are incorporated with opioids and other medications and treatments to relieve symptoms, thereby bringing peace and comfort to the chronically ill and dying. Because of the lack of access to medical treatment in general, most people in India seek traditional Indian alternatives as the mainstay of end-of-life care. Ayurveda, naturopathy, pranic healing, reiki, and homeopathy are popular and are often mainstay healing modalities. According to the University of Maryland's (2011) online overview of complementary therapies, such treatment has the following goals:

> [To] prevent and treat illness by maintaining balance in the body, mind, and consciousness through proper drinking, diet, and lifestyle, as well as herbal remedies. There are two main types of Ayurveda: traditional and Maharishi. Maharishi is a version of traditional Ayurveda based on translations from the classical texts by Maharishi Mahesh Yogi. Both types of Ayurvedic practitioners prescribe herbs, believe that disease results from an imbalance . . . and use many of the same remedies for treating illness. Maharishi Ayurveda, however, emphasizes the role of supreme consciousness in maintaining good health, and promotes transcendental meditation (TM) as a way to experience the pure consciousness of the universe. It also highlights the expression of positive emotions and the need to attune your life to the natural rhythms of the body.

Despite these many and varied traditional therapies, in India most people die silently and in pain.

Naturopathy includes such treatments as nutritional counseling, herbal medicine, acupuncture, hydrotherapy, physical medicine, detoxification, spirituality, and lifestyle and psychological counseling. Pranic healing is a no-touch invocation of life forces to promote healing using energy from the sun, earth, and air (Pranic Healing Center, 2011). Reiki is a stress-reduction therapy that involves the "laying on of hands." It is a spiritual—though not religious—technique using "life force energy" that is designed to improve health and well-being (International Center for Reiki Training, 2011).

Hydrotherapy is water therapy including drinking natural spring water, taking baths, alternating hot and cold applications, and water exercise, all of which are thought to stimulate healing and strengthen the immune system. Physical medicine uses touch, hot and cold compresses, electric currents, and sound waves to manipulate the muscles, bones, and spine. Detoxification removes toxins from the body by fasting, using enemas, and drinking volumes of water. Personal spiritual development is sought as well. Lifestyle and psychological counseling includes the use of hypnosis, guided imagery, or other counseling methods as part of a treatment plan.

Homeopathy derives from the principle of similars (or "like cures like"). It is founded upon the belief that a disease can be cured by a substance that produces similar symptoms in healthy people. Therefore, herbal and natural substances from plants, minerals, and animals are used in diluted form for treatment. Common remedies of homeopathy include red onion, arnica (mountain herb), and stinging nettle plant (National Center for Complementary and Alternative Medicine, 2011).

Spiritual and existential well-being is an important facet to quality of life for the dying and their families. Each of the world's religions has influence upon end-of-life care with its own perspectives and practices surrounding the period before death, during the dying process, with care of the body, intern-ment, and bereavement (Bauer-Wu, Barrett, & Yeager, 2007). Tested spiritual, social, and psychological therapies are provided in India as part of holistic care. Ministrations through hospice in India include prayer, devotion, yoga, meditation, and philosophical dialogue (Chaturvedi, 2007). Hospice is in keeping with the predominant Buddhist beliefs espoused by Indians: concern for a good death, death as sub-sumed as a part of life, values of compassion and wisdom, willingness to serve, inclusion of meditation and reminiscence, and the duty to do no harm (Shubha, 2007).

Only 3% of the Indian population has access to palliative care (100 programs compared with 4050 in North America), and these programs are concentrated in the state of Karala. There, a network of 33 palliative care clinics serves approximately 6000 new persons per year, reaching out to rural areas with home care even where access is difficult for nurses and physicians (Shanmugasundaram, Chapman, & O'Connor, 2006). There are glimmers of hope that such care might be made available in other areas of India, though the movement's progress is slow. A pioneering home care program in New Delhi, started by a patient and supported by charitable funds, provides palliative care in North India, and the Tamil Nadu state government relaxed rules about morphine that makes pain management more available (Shanmugasundaram et al., 2006). Indian physicians report that they are more knowledgeable about palliation and are ready to learn the practical elements of good palliative care (Bharadwaj, Vidyasagar, Kakria, & Tanvir Alam, 2007).

When Indians locate to another country, it may be difficult to receive culturally appropriate pal-liative care. Highly educated families of Indians in Australia reported that they were not provided with information about the status of their dying loved one. They also found healthcare services insensitive to their cultural needs, such as the provision of meat and eggs instead of vegetarian meals, absence of wash-ing facilities before praying, and lack of privacy (Shanmugasundaram & O'Connor, 2009).

PALLIATIVE CARE IN AFRICA

Africa's experience and development in palliative care have left the region with much to share with the rest of the world. In Africa, there is no boundary between hospice and palliative care: Both are part of the con-tinuum of care and no prognosis (such as "terminally ill" or "six months to live") is necessary to establish a referral. Palliative care is integrated into "existing home-based care, clinics, hospitals and academic institu-tions where professionals are trained" rather than in designated beds or institutions such as in the United

States (Di Sorbo, 2011, p. 129). In Africa, cultural values are integrated into care and are truly respected: Tribal, ancestral and extended family concepts are ingrained into the healthcare systems. African professionals also place great value on their connectedness to the world family of hospice and palliative care providers as seen from the African philosophy: The whole is greater than its parts (Di Sorbo, 2011).

A recent report (Selman et al., 2011) of a study on multidimensional quality of life among patients receiving palliative care in South Africa and Uganda (two of the countries with the most advanced palliative care programs in Africa) concluded that close relationships, feeling at peace, a sense of meaning, and spiritual well-being were more important than physical activity or comfort to the seriously ill. The overall total Quality of Life (QOL) score as measured with the Missoula Vitas Quality of Life Index, though, was relatively poor at 17.32 (possible range: 0–30). The study authors indicated that "these findings show that it is vital to meet the psychological and spiritual care needs of patients as well as to rigorously assess and treat pain and other symptoms" (p. 11).

Among the cancer centers in Africa, only 17% have a fully developed national cancer control program (Sharma et al., 2010). Quality of life suffers in part because of the relative lack of palliative treatments available for late-stage disease. A case in point is the clinical practice of palliative radiotherapy for esophageal cancers. This treatment is effective in alleviating dysphagia and pain, but there is great variability among centers in the indications for and characteristics of treatment (Sharma et al., 2010). Furthermore, the cancer centers are located in major cities and often are not accessible to the much larger rural populations of each state. In Egypt, the opioid needs of patients with cancer (again, usually late-stage disease) are not met because of prescribing and dispensing regulations (Alsirafy et al., 2011). Alsirafy and colleagues provided research evidence that the Egyptian Narcotics Control Law permits physicians to prescribe only enough morphine to manage 26% of the patients with moderate to severe pain.

Citing the monumental burden of incurable illness in sub-Saharan Africa due to HIV/AIDS, cancer, and malaria, Dr. Anne Merriman (Merriman & Harding, 2010), the founder of Hospice Africa and Hospice Africa Uganda, called for improved pain management. She discussed pain relief as a public health and human rights issue as well as a mandate of the moral principle "Do no harm." Merriman states, "Leaving my patient in pain in the era when pain relief and symptom control is affordable is breaking our ethical code" (p. 1). The pain control method used in her clinics relies upon the importation of morphine powder, which is then mixed with boiled water to reach the desired oral concentration, bolstered by addition of a preservative, and dispensed in carefully washed, recycled-plastic water bottles. A bottle will last a patient as many as 10 days, and the cost is roughly equivalent to the price of a loaf of bread. As many as 11 countries in Africa, with governmental blessing, now have oral morphine available to patients. As this example demonstrates, it took the advocacy of a few to improve care for many on the continent.

While home-based care is desirable and the reality in many sub-Saharan countries (Harding, Stewart, Marconi, O'Neill, & Higginson, 2003), in Rwanda—the site of the horrific 1994 war that led to genocide—67% of the people with life-threatening HIV/AIDS would elect to receive palliative care in the hospital (Uwimana & Struthers, 2008). These people believe in-hospital settings are more secure and trustworthy, and have personnel and expertise available. Also, many families have been decimated by war, leaving few to provide care in the home. Rwandans and healthcare ministers have learned from a trip to Uganda that relaxing regulation and access to opioids, establishing palliative care units, and educating health professionals and the public can have monumental effects in realizing the goal of provision of high-quality, affordable palliative care services by 2020. Rwanda's first adult palliative care unit was established in 2010 and its pediatric unit in 2009. Enthusiasm for the promise of quality palliative care is growing, and hope for the future is gaining strength (Vogel, 2011).

In their comprehensive review of qualitative research on end-of-life care in sub-Saharan Africa, Gysels, Pell, Straus, and Pool (2011) identified the culturally specific information about end of life that ought to guide policy, clinical care, and further research. These researchers found that while the provision of specific end-of-life care is scarce in Africa, a variety of models do exist: home-based care, hospital units, free-standing inpatient hospices, day care, and hospital support teams (Gysels et al., 2011). Four African countries (out of 57) have end-of-life care integrated into their public health systems: Uganda, South Africa, Kenya, and Zimbabwe. Research conducted on the continent has been done primarily with HIV/AIDS victims in South Africa and demonstrated "significant financial, physical, or social burden for caregivers," including personal pain, lack of self-care, stigma and its resulting abuse, loneliness, depression, and isolation (p. 3). Exhaustion often occurred due to the additional circumstances of poverty, age, and the illnesses of the caregiver. For these individuals, seeking food, water, shelter, and livelihood production were activities often required beyond caregiving. Grief was a luxury, usurped by the needs of daily survival. Moreover, the researchers once again found that barriers to pain management included a lack of practice standards, knowledge on the part of providers, and inadequate resources.

In an effort to address the issues of clinical standards and knowledge while lending colleagueship and support to nurses in Tanzania and neighboring countries, Paice, Ferrell, Coyle, Coyne, and Smith (2010) provided a three-day end-of-life education curriculum in 2007. Under way since February 2000, and spearheaded by the American Association of Colleges of Nursing (AACN) and the City of Hope (AACN, 2010a), the End-of-Life Nursing Education Consortium (ELNEC) has long provided education in palliative care for undergraduate and graduate nursing faculty, continuing education providers, staff development educators, specialty nurses in pediatrics, oncology, critical care and geriatrics, and other nurses in the United States. Its work has since been adapted for international audiences (Paice, Ferrell, Coyle, Coyne, & Callaway, 2007). The program's implementation follows a train-the-trainer model: The recipients of ELNEC education teach this essential information to nursing students and practicing nurses in their own locales (ELNEC, 2010). The program comprises nine modules: nursing care at the end of life; pain management; symptom management; ethical/legal issues; cultural considerations; communication; grief, loss, and bereavement; achieving quality care; and preparation and care at the time of death (AACN, 2010b). To date, more than 11,375 nurses and other healthcare professionals, representing all 50 U.S. states plus 65 international countries, have received ELNEC training (ELNEC, 2010). The Tanzania program was carefully adapted for the realities of the environment, the cultural and political state, and funding realities of nurses in the field (Paice et al., 2010).

PALLIATIVE CARE IN EUROPE

There is wide variability in the provision of palliative care to the seriously ill and dying in Europe. The term "hospice" was first envisioned there and applied to specialized care for dying patients in 1967 by physician Dame Cicely Saunders, who founded the first modern hospice—St. Christopher's Hospice—in a residential suburb of south London. Today, more than 1,000 palliative care physician experts can be found in the United Kingdom, many of whom belong to the Association for Palliative Medicine (Grogan et al., 2009). In 2006–2007 in England, Wales, and Northern Ireland, there were 210 palliative care specialist inpatient units with 2774 beds, of which 20% were National Health Service (NHS) beds; 295 home care services, including both advisory services delivered by hospice or NHS-based community palliative care teams and other more sustained care provided in the patient's home; 314 hospital-based services; 234 daycare services; and 314 bereavement support services (Higginson & Costantini, 2008; National Council for Palliative Care, 2011). In London, St. Christopher's Hospice serves 850 patients on any given day and six palliative care teams care for patients from all socioeconomic and ethnic groups (Monroe & Hansford, 2010). Across the United Kingdom, as many as 46% of all patients enrolled in hospices die in their homes, as compared to 25% in the United States. Palliative care core standards have been developed, audits of hospice care are conducted routinely, and research in end-of-life care is in full flower.

As in the United States, there remain challenges in delivering palliative care in the United Kingdom. Funding for such care is provided in part by the NHS (45%); the rest comes from charitable donations. Always having to work within budget constraints has prompted some hospices to combine forces and personnel. A lack of a defined and universal pathway to palliative care education and credentialing has left some clinical nurse specialists who lead the palliative care teams without the full array of skills and competencies needed for the work; establishment of a registry linked to specialist education is seen as a solution to this problem. Another problem associated with an aging population is the undesirable frequency of hospitalizations at the end of life. Education of "care home" staff is identified as important to the resolution of these frequent transfers. Monroe and Hansford (2010) have also called for improved early assessment and management of the needs of those with dementia, particularly pain, discomfort, and psychiatric symptoms. Bereavement support for families after death—an integral part of hospice services—suffers in both the United Kingdom and the United States from inadequate numbers of paid staff, variations in the education of professionals, insufficient levels of funding, and inconsistent use of bereavement assessment tools (O'Connor, Abbott, Payne, & Demmer, 2009). The hesitancy of the populace in both countries as well as in Australia to discuss death and dying leaves many families unprepared for decisions at the end of life.

Ethical issues surrounding death and dying that are vigorously discussed and periodically appear in the literature from developed countries are euthanasia and assisted suicide (see, for example, Seale, 2009). Assisted dying, as the two practices are collectively called, is codified in the Netherlands and Belgium. Assisted suicide (but not euthanasia) is not illegal and is practiced in Switzerland. In an era of increased public acceptance of assisted dying in Europe, some physicians have argued that such practices are the antithesis of good medical care and violate the basic principles of medical codes of ethics. Indeed, an "Assisted Dying for the Terminally Ill" bill proposed in the United Kingdom in 2005 met with great scrutiny and eventual failure (Bosshard, Broeckaert, Clark, Materstvedt, Gordijn, & Muller-Busch, 2008). Bosshard and colleagues argue that "if society is willing to make assisted death an available option, the responsibility for such decisions must be spread as widely as possible" (p. 31). They call for second opinions from those other than physicians on elements of the process that do not lie within the expertise of the practicing physician: determining whether the patient has the capacity to make such a decision, ascertaining whether the decision was thoughtfully considered, and ensuring that the decision was made without undue influence by others.

In their review of palliative care for cancer victims of Europe, Higginson and Costantini (2008) cite the fact that the median number of symptoms for those entering palliative care services is 11. These authors maintain that "pain, breathlessness, fatigue, anorexia, constipation and insomnia are especially common . . . In around one third of patients this pain will be severe, requiring complex treatment" (pp. 234–235). While these symptoms are not unique to Europeans, nor to cancer patients, research in Europe has shown the effectiveness of dedicated multidisciplinary teams to symptom relief and reduction of inpatient days (Higginson & Costantini, 2008). Nevertheless, countries in Europe demonstrate wide variability in the services offered, with anywhere from 0 to 20 providers available per million population. They include hospice and palliative care units, hospital-based care teams, home care teams (either in advisory or actual hands-on caregiving as in Italy), and day care (in the United Kingdom). Those countries with lower socioeconomic status have fewer services (Higginson & Costantini, 2008).

Despite the ability to demonstrate the effectiveness of palliative care programs, challenges continue to be encountered by palliative care professionals in Europe. Because there is a longer period of illness and treatment with cancer today, WHO recommends earlier-onset palliative care. Changing the culture of referral is a daunting task, however. Concerns have also arisen regarding standardized assessment and outcome measures with the Palliative Care Outcome Scale (Hearn & Higginson, 1999), a validated instrument recommended for use.

There are also concerns about suboptimal pain control (Phillips, 2009), given that only one of five patients receives opioid therapy (Breivik, 2009). Pain management varies tremendously across Europe, and the reasons for this inconsistency are unclear. It is surmised that even though few patients require high doses of opioids, "clinical traditions, price, education and legal or cultural barriers to the use of opioids are the culprits" (Klepstad, Kaasa, Cherny, Hanks, & de Conno, 2005). The European Association for Palliative Care is instrumental in recording services, enhancing education, and advocating for the rights of patients who have serious illness. Doing needs assessments to match services and their design with the needs of the community, investment in coordinated end-of-life care research (Sigurdardottir et al., 2010), improved education in palliative care for professionals, and assessment of programs are all required (Higginson & Costantini, 2008).

In contrast to the more highly developed palliative care programs in countries such as the United Kingdom, Germany, France, and Italy, some countries in Eastern Europe are in earlier stages of development. Hungary is one. As Csikos, Albanese, Busa, Nagy, and Radwany (2008) state, "Death and dying are taboo topics in Hungary." The hospice movement started for the first time in the 1990s in Hungary, and minimum qualifications for professionals and services were established in 2004. Also in 2004, financing for such care began, including funding for the wider palliative care team. Problems associated with dying are not yet well addressed, although some 52 organizations now provide hospice/palliative care in the country. Physicians are uncomfortable providing full disclosure, pain and symptom management are less than efficacious, and there is a lack of home hospice care, however. Hungarians fear loss of autonomy, are concerned about the experience of pain and suffering, and want end-of-life care available in the home instead of the hospital, where currently 60% die (Csikos et al., 2008).

THE ROLE OF NURSES IN PALLIATIVE CARE

Nurses across the globe are urged to advocate for the best possible care of patients who need comfort or are reaching the end of their lives (Lynch et al., 2011; Seal, 2007; Thacker, 2008). In their role as advocates, nurses desire to be well informed, astute, culturally sensitive, creative, skillful at communication, and caring. They are present at the pivotal times in patients' lives when the acute disease becomes chronic, serve as witness to the effect of symptoms on quality of life, and acknowledge when the psychosocial and spiritual perspectives of life take precedence. Nurses are, and will continue to be, influential in the early identification of those patients and families who need the expertise of palliative care practitioners. They seek improved pain and symptom management for their patients and acknowledge their own need to learn more about the science and art of palliative care. Nurses serve on palliative care and hospice teams as innovators, advocates, and counselors. They are central to the work of palliation and end-of-life care.

STUDY QUESTIONS

1. Select two countries and compare ethical and legal differences in caring for the dying patient.
2. What are some advantages of hospice care vs. hospital critical care for the dying patient?
3. Compare and contrast pain management in end-of-life care within a selected developing country vs. a developed country.

CASE STUDY

Julie Shulty, a palliative care nurse in the United States, wishes to participate in international education. Her specific area of expertise is pain management using medications and complementary and alternative therapies. She responds to the stories told by missionaries at her church who are seeking volunteers for their next trip. Julie could, they say, help the dying patients in Kenya by teaching a course on palliative care and pain management to nurses in the country. Julie responds to the very real need and emotionally reacts to the scenes of dying children who have little pain relief. Which steps ought to be part of Julie's planning for such a venture?

REFERENCES

Alsirafy, S. A., El-Mesidi, S. M., Le-Sherief, W. A., Galal, K. M., Abou-Elela, E. N., & Aklan, N. A. (2010). Opioid needs of patients with advanced cancer and the morphine dose-limiting law in Egypt. *Journal of Palliative Medicine, 14*(1), 51–55. doi: 10.1089/jpm.2010.0220

American Academy of Hospice and Palliative Medicine. (2011) Statement on clinical practice guidelines for quality palliative care. Retrieved from http://www.aahpm.org/Practice/default/quality.html

American Association of Colleges of Nursing (AACN). (2010a). End of life care. Retrieved from http://www.aacn.nche.edu/elnec/

American Association of Colleges of Nursing (AACN). (2010b). ELNEC core curriculum. Retrieved from http://www.aacn.nche.edu/elnec/curriculum.htm

Amoah, C. F. (2011). The central importance of spirituality in palliative care. *International Journal of Palliative Nursing, 17*(7), 353–358.

Anderson, J. M., Rodney, P., Reimer-Kirkham, S., Browne, A. J., Kahn, K. B., & Lynam, M. J. (2009). Inequities in health and healthcare viewed through the ethical lens of critical social justice: Contextual knowledge for the global priorities ahead. *Advances in Nursing Science, 32*(4), 282–294. doi: 10.1097/ANS.obo13e3181bd6955

Ashley, J. L. (2008). Pain management: Nurses in jeopardy. *Oncology Nursing Forum, 35*(5), E70–E75.

Ballantyne, J. D., & Mao, J. (2003). Opioid therapy for chronic pain. *New England Journal of Medicine, 349*, 1943–1953.

Barazzetti, G., Borreani, C., Miccinesi, G., & Toscani, F. (2010). What "best practice" could be in palliative care: An analysis of statements on practice and ethics expressed by the main health organizations. *BMC Palliative Care, 9*(1). Retrieved from http://www.biomedcentral.com/1472-684X/9/1

Bauer-Wu, S., Barrett, R., & Yeager, K. (2007). Spiritual perspectives and practices at the end-of-life: A review of the major world religions and application to palliative care. *Indian Journal of Palliative Care, 13*(2), 53–58.

Becker, R. (2008). Attitudes to death and dying in China. *International Journal of Palliative Nursing, 14*(10), 471.

Belknap, R. A. (2008). Teaching social justice using a pedagogy of engagement. *Nurse Educator, 33*(1), 9–226.

Bharadwaj, P., Vidyasagar, M. S., Kakria, A., & Tanvir Alam, U. A. (2007). Survey of palliative care concepts among medical students in India. *Journal of Palliative Medicine, 10*(3), 651–653.

Bosshard, G., Broeckaert, B., Clark, D., Materstvedt, L. J., Gordijn, B., & Muller-Busch, H. C. (2008). A role for doctors in assisted dying? An analysis of legal regulations and medical professional positions in six European countries. *Journal of Medical Ethics, 34*, 28–32. doi: 10.1136/jme.2006.018911

Breivik, H. (2009). Analgesia without boundaries: Removing barriers to care. *Journal of Pain & Palliative Care Pharmacotherapy, 23*(1), 74–76.

Brennan, F., Carr, D. B., & Cousins, M. (2007). Pain management: A fundamental human right. *Pain Medicine, 105*(1), 205–221.

Chaturvedi, S. K. (2007). Spiritual issues at the end of life. *Indian Journal of Palliative Care, 13*(2), 48–52.

Cherny, N. A., Baselga, J., de Conno, F., & Radbruch, L. (2009). Formulary availability and regulatory barriers to accessibility of opioids for cancer pain in Europe: A report from the ESMO/EAPC Opioid Policy Initiative. *Annals of Oncology, 21*(3), 615–626. doi: 10.1093/annonc/mdp581

Csikos, A., Albanese, T., Busa, C., Nagy, L., & Radwany, S. (2008). Hungarians' perspectives on end-of-life care. *Journal of Palliative Medicine, 11*(8), 1083–1087. doi: 10.1089/jpm.2008.0094

Daniels, N. (2008). *Just health: Meeting health needs fairly.* New York: Cambridge University Press.

Dickinson, B. D., Altman, R. D., Nielsen, N. H., & Williams, M. A. (2000). Use of opioids to treat chronic, noncancer pain. *Western Journal of Medicine, 172*, 107–115.

Di Sorbo, P. G. (2011). What Africa has to teach the United States about hospice and palliative care. *Journal of Palliative Medicine, 14*(2), 129–131. doi: 10.1089/jpm.2010.9732

Economist Intelligence Unit. (2010). *The quality of death: Ranking end-of-life care across the world.* London: Lien Foundation.

Egan, K. A., & Labyak, M. J. (2006). Hospice palliative care: A model for quality end-of-life care. In B. R. Ferrell & N. Coyle (Eds.), *Textbook of palliative nursing* (pp. 13–46). New York: Oxford University Press.

End of Life Nursing Education Consortium (ELNEC). (2010). Fact sheet. Retrieved from http://www.aacn.nche.edu/elnec/about/factsheet

Exworthy, M. (2008). Policy to tackle the social determinants of health: Using conceptual models to understand the policy process. *Health Policy and Planning, 23*, 318–327.

Gostin, L. O., & Powers, M. (2006). What does social justice require for the public's health? Public health ethics and policy imperatives. *Health Affairs, 25*(4), 1053–1060.

Grogan, E., Beattie, R., Campbell, C., George, R., Harlow, T., MacGregor, B., . . . Noble, B. (2009). End-of-life decisions in the United Kingdom involving medical practitioners and legalization of euthanasia or physician-assisted suicide: Survey of doctors' attitudes. *Palliative Medicine, 23,* 569. doi: 10.1177/0269216309106458

Gysels, M., Pell, C., Straus, L., & Pool, R. (2011). End of life care in sub-Saharan Africa: A systematic review of the qualitative literature. *BMC Palliative Care, 10*(6), 1–11. Retrieved from www.biomedcentral.com/1472-684X/10/6

Han, H. (2011). Barriers in palliative care in current mainland China. Retrieved from www.articlebiz.com/article/427716-1barriers-in-palliativecare-in-current-mainland-china/

Hanks, G., Cherny, N. I., Christakis, N. A., Fallon, M., Kaasa, S. & Portenoy, R. K. (2011). Level of palliative care development. *Oxford Textbook of Palliative Medicine.* Oxford, UK: Oxford University Press.

Harding, R., Stewart, K., Marconi, K., O'Neill, J. F., & Higginson, I. J. (2003). Current HIV/AIDS end-of-life care in sub-Saharan Africa: A survey of models, services, challenges and priorities. *BMC Public Health, 3*(33). Retrieved from www.biomedcentral.com/1471-2458/3/33

Harrison, P. (2010). Little risk for addiction from long-term opioid use in select chronic pain patients. *Cochrane Review.* Retrieved from www.medscape.com/viewarticle/715452

Hearn, J., & Higginson, I. J. (1999). Development and validation of a core outcome measure for palliative care: The palliative care outcome scale. *Quality in Health Care, 8,* 219–227.

Higginson, I. J., & Costantini, M. (2008). Dying with cancer, living well with advanced cancer. In M. P. Coleman, D. Alexe, T. Albreht, & M. McKee (Eds.), *Responding to the challenge of cancer in Europe* (pp. 231–252). Republic of Slovenia: Institute of Public Health.

Human Rights Watch. (2009). *"Please, do not make us suffer any more": Access to pain treatment as a human right.* New York: Human Rights Watch.

International Center for Reiki Training. (2011). Reiki: How does it work? Retrieved from http://www .reiki.org/FAQ/FAQHomepage.html

Irwin, A., & Scali, E. (2007). Action on the social determinants of health: A historical perspective. *Global Public Health, 2*(3), 235–256.

Joranson, D. E., Ryan, K. M., & Maurer, M. A. (2010). Opioid policy, availability, and access in developing and nonindustrialized countries. University of Wisconsin, Pain and Policies Studies Group. In *Bonica's management of pain* (4th ed., pp. 196–208). Retrieved from http://www.bonicasmanagementofpain .com/...1]/TXTBKBD[1]/DIVISIONA[2]/CHAPTER[6]&highlightTo=&printPreview=yes#gohere

Klepstad, P., Kaasa, S., Cherny, N., Hanks, G., & de Conno, F. (2005). Pain and pain treatments in European palliative care units: A cross sectional survey from the European Association for Palliative Care Research Network. *Palliative Medicine, 19,* 477–484. doi: 10.1191/0269216305pm1054oa

Krakauer, E. L. (2008). Just palliative care: Responding responsibly to the suffering of the poor. *Journal of Pain and Symptom Management, 36*(5), 505–512.

Law, F. (2011). National hospice service program in mainland China sponsored by Li Ka Shing Foundation. Retrieved from http://www.paxforum.org/2090/4_program/text/frieda.pdf

Li, J., Davis, M. P., & Gamier, P. (2011). Palliative medicine: Barriers and developments in mainland China. *Current Oncology Report, 13,* 290–294.

Lo, S. H., Chan, C. Y., Chan, C. H., Sze, W.-K., Yuen, K. K., Wong, C.S.,. . . Tung, Y. (2009). The implementation of an end-of-life integrated care pathway in a Chinese population. *International Journal of Palliative Nursing, 15*(8), 384–388.

Lynch, M., Dahlin, C., Hultman, T., & Coakley, E. E. (2011). Palliative care nursing. *Journal of Hospice and Palliative Nursing, 13*(2), 106–111. doi: 10.1097/NJH.0b013e3182075b6e

Mendis, S., Fukino, K., Cameron, A., Laing, R., Filipe Jr., A., Khatib, O., . . . Ewen, M. (2007). The availability and affordability of selected essential medicines for chronic diseases in six low- and middle-income countries. *Bulletin of the World Health Organization, 85*(4), 279–289. doi: 10.2471/BLT .06.033647

Merriman, A., & Harding, R. (2010). Pain control in the African context: The Ugandan introduction of affordable morphine to relieve suffering at the end of life. *Philosophy, Ethics and Humanities in Medicine, 5*(10). doi: 10.1186/1747-5341-5-10

Monroe, B., & Hansford, P. (2010). Challenges in delivering palliative care in the community: A perspective from St Christopher's Hospice, London, UK. *Progress in Palliative Care, 18*(1), 9–13. doi: 10.1179 /096992610X12624290276115

Mosoiu, D., Ryan, K. M., Joranson, D. E., & Garthwaite, J. P. (2006). Reform of drug control policy for palliative care in Romania. *Lancet, 367*(9528), 2110–2117.

National Center for Complementary and Alternative Medicine. (2011). Homeopathy. Retrieved from http://nccam.nih.gov/health/homeopathy/

National Council for Palliative Care. (2011). Palliative care explained. Retrieved from http://www.ncpc .org.uk/site/professionals/explained

National Quality Forum. (2006). *A national framework and preferred practices for palliative and hospice care quality.* Washington, DC: Author.

O'Connor, M., Abbott, J., Payne, S., & Demmer, C. (2009). A comparison of bereavement services provided in hospice and palliative care settings in Australia, the UK and the USA. *Progress in Palliative Care, 17*(2), 69–74. doi: 10.1179/096992609X392240

Paice, J. A., Ferrell, B. R., Coyle, N., Coyne, P., & Callaway, M. (2007). Global efforts to improve palliative care: The International End-of-Life Nursing Education Consortium Training Programme. *Journal of Advanced Nursing, 61*(2), 173–180. doi: 10.1111/j.1365-2648.2007.04475.x

Paice, J. A., Ferrell, B., Coyle, N., Coyne, P., & Smith, T. (2010). Living and dying in east Africa: Implementing the End-of-Life Nursing Education Consortium Curriculum in Tanzania. *Clinical Journal of Oncology Nursing, 14*(2), 161–166.

Phillips, S. (2009). The pain story study: Improving our understanding of patients with chronic pain. *Journal of Pain & Palliative Care Pharmacotherapy, 23*(1), 72–73

Pranic Healing Center. (2011). What is pranic healing? Retrieved from http://pranichealing.com /what-pranic-healing

PricewaterhouseCoopers. (2007). Healthcare in India: Emerging market report. Retrieved from www .pwc.com/globalhealthcare

Rajagopal, M. R. (2007). Palliative care: An urgent need for most of the world. *International Journal of Environmental Studies, 64*(3), 301–307.

Rennie, S., & Mupenda, B. (2008). Living apart together: Reflections on bioethics, global inequity and social justice. *Philosophy, Ethics, and Humanities in Medicine, 3*(25), Para 2. doi: 10.1186/1747-5341-3-25. Retrieved from http://www.peh-med.com/content/pdf/1747-5341-3-25.pdf

Ruger, J. P. (2006). Ethics and governance of global health inequalities. *Journal of Epidemiological Community Health, 60*, 998–1002. doi: 10.1136/jech.205.041947

Seal, M. (2007). Patient advocacy and advance care planning in the acute hospital setting. *Australian Journal of Advanced Nursing, 24*(4), 29–36.

Seale, C. (2009). Legalisation of euthanasia or physician-assisted suicide: Survey of doctors' attitudes. *Palliative Medicine, 00*, 1–8. doi: 10.1177/0269216308102041

Selman, L. E., Higginson, I. J., Agupio, G., Dinat, N., Downing, J., Gwyther, L., . . . Harding, R. (2011). Quality of life among patients receiving palliative care in South Africa and Uganda: A multicentered study. *Health and Quality of Life Outcomes, 9*(21). doi:10.1186/1477-7525-9-21

Shanmugasundaram, S., Chapman, Y., & O'Connor, M. (2006). Development of palliative care in India: An overview. *International Journal of Nursing Practice, 12*, 241–246.

Shanmugasundaram, S., & O'Connor, M. (2009). Palliative care services for Indian migrants in Australia: Experiences of the family of terminally ill patients. *Indian Journal of Palliative Care, 15*(1), 76–83. doi: 10.4103/0973-1075.53589

Sharma, V., Gaye, P. M., Wahab, S. A., Ndlovu, N., Ngoma, T., & Vanderpuye, V., . . . Jeremic, B. (2010). Palliative radiation therapy practice for advanced esophageal carcinoma in Africa. *Diseases of the Esophagus, 23*, 240–243. doi: 10.1111/j.1442-2050.2009.00997

Shubha, R. (2007). End of life care in the Indian context: The need for cultural sensitivity. *Indian Journal of Palliative Care, 13*(2), 59–64.

Sigurdardottir, K. R., Haugen, D. F., Bausewein, C., Higginson, I. J, Harding, R., & Rosland, J. H., . . . Project PRISMA. (2010). A pan-European survey of research in end-of-life cancer care. *Support are Cancer* [Advance online publication]. doi: 10.1007/s00520-010-1048-x

Taylor, A. L. (2007). Addressing the global tragedy of needless pain: Rethinking the United Nations Single Convention on narcotic drugs. *Journal of Law, Medicine & Ethics, 35*(4), 556–570.

Thacker, K. S. (2008). Nurses' advocacy behavior in end-of-life nursing care. *Nursing Ethics, 15*(2), 174–185.

Tochon, F. V., & Karaman, A. C. (2009). Critical reasoning for social justice: Moral encounters with the paradoxes of intercultural education. *Intercultural Education, 20*(2), 135–149. doi: 10.1080 /14675980902922168

University of Maryland. (2011). Ayurveda: Overview. Retrieved from http://www.umm.edu/altmed/articles/ayurveda-000348.htm

University of Wisconsin, Pain & Policy Studies Group. (2010). Opioid consumption data. Retrieved from http://www.painpolicy.wisc.edu/internat/opioid_data.html

Uwimana, J., & Struthers, P. (2008). What is the preferred place of care at the end of life for HIV/AIDS patients in countries affected by civil war and genocide: The case of Rwanda. *Progress in Palliative Care, 16*(3), 129–134.

Vogel, L. (2011). Rwanda moving to provide "good deaths" for terminally ill. *Canadian Medical Association Journal.* Retrieved from http://www.cmaj.ca/content/early/2011/09/12/cmaj.109-3963.long

World Health Organization (WHO). (2003). Global cancer rates could increase by 50% to 15 million by 2020. Retrieved from http://www.who.int/mediacentre/news/releases/2003/pr27/en/

World Health Organization (WHO). (2008). Inequities are killing people on a "grand scale" reports WHO's Commission [Press release]. Retrieved from http://www.who.int/mediacentre/news/releases/2008/pr29/en/

World Health Organization (WHO). (2011). WHO's pain relief ladder. Retrieved from http://www.who.int/cancer/palliative/painladder/en/

Wright, M., Wood, J., Lynch, T., & Clark, D. (2006). *Mapping levels of palliative care development: A global view.* Lancaster, UK: International Observatory on End of Life Care. Retrieved from http://www.ncbi.nlm.nih.gov/pubmed/18243637

Yujie, L. (2011, March 29). Families lament lack of palliative care centers. *China Daily.* Retrieved from http://www.chinadaily.com.cn/cndy/2011-03/29/content_12240782.htm

For a full suite of assignments and additional learning activities, use the access code located in the front of your book to visit this exclusive website: http://go.jblearning.com/holtz. If you do not have an access code, you can obtain one at the site.

II

Special Global Health and Healthcare Issues

7

Infectious Diseases from a Global Perspective

Barbara J. Blake
Gloria A. Taylor

> *"As to diseases, make a habit of two things—to help, or at least to do no harm."*
>
> Hippocrates

OBJECTIVES

www

After completing this chapter, the reader will be able to:

1. Relate the historical aspects of selected infectious diseases.
2. Discuss the need for global infectious disease surveillance.
3. Compare and contrast the causes, transference patterns, and treatments of diseases such as typhoid, T.B., HIV/AIDS, severe acute respiratory syndrome (SARS), dengue fever, West Nile virus, hepatitis A, B, and C, avian influenza, malaria, Ebola fever, and influenza.

INTRODUCTION

During the twentieth century, the race to combat infectious diseases made great strides in saving millions of lives as nations became more developed through industrialization, advances in prevention and health promotion education, and pharmacological innovation. Despite such gains, viral, bacterial, fungal, and parasitic diseases continue to cause one-fourth of all deaths in the world. Moreover, this number does not account for the impact of infectious diseases resulting in disabilities, devastated economies, demographic changes, and social and physical environmental influences that can range from stigma felt by individuals living with HIV/AIDS to regions ravaged through vector-control measures, such as the eradication of mosquitoes to control malaria. Many complex issues surround infectious diseases, including those related to geography, environment, economics, population characteristics, infrastructure, and health conditions.

As the world becomes "smaller" as a result of air travel, population growth, and transnational commerce, existing, emerging, or reemerging infectious diseases continue to pose complex challenges and threats to systems of healthcare delivery, regional and national policies, security, disease surveillance, and research. Because of the enormous variety of infectious diseases endemic to some nations and regions of the world, this chapter cannot hope to describe, characterize, and define the hundreds of viral, bacterial, fungal, and parasitic diseases that coexist with humans throughout the world. Rather, this chapter selectively describes some of the most common infectious diseases that manifest themselves globally and discusses the challenges that nations routinely confront in their battle to coexist with their invisible neighbors.

Recent estimates from the World Health Organization (WHO, 2011a) indicate that the leading causes of deaths from infectious diseases globally are HIV/AIDS, tuberculosis, lower respiratory infections (influenza, pneumonia), and diarrheal diseases, especially in low- to middle-income countries. Although these infectious diseases wreak havoc on nations, regions, and communities, it is best, at times, to distinguish between people and their environment, which takes into account a host of other coexisting diseases. For example, persons with HIV/AIDS are more likely to acquire tuberculosis and malaria.

■ HISTORICAL APPROACHES TO INFECTIOUS DISEASES

According to philosopher George Santayana, "Those who cannot remember the past are condemned to repeat it." This saying is quite appropriate in the context of infectious diseases. As societies evolved from primitive hunters and gatherers and formed larger civilizations, acute infectious diseases became manifest as populations expanded outward. When small, nomadic tribes began bartering resources between Asia and Europe, contact among these civilizations increased. Just within the past six centuries, the bubonic plague ("The Black Death"), which killed almost half of the European population, was carried by crusaders and merchant traders from central Asia to Western Europe. As time, travel, and migration progressed, the 1500s and 1600s witnessed smallpox being carried by European migrants to the Americas, which further spread death and disease to the indigenous peoples of the New World.

Although many historical examples can be cited to characterize the link between people and their environment, none is more telling to examine than how cholera spread throughout London in the 1800s. In the mid-1850s, Dr. John Snow, a physician in London, spent a great deal of time trying to convince his colleagues that cholera was a waterborne disease. His assertion contradicted the current theory of the time, which stated that cholera, caused by the bacterium *Vibrio cholerae,* was transmitted through the air in the form of mists or miasmas (noxious atmosphere). It was not until 1854 when Snow began mapping the location of all well-water pumps and the location of every case of cholera that a pattern began to emerge. Through his geospatial mapping of cholera incidence and deaths and the city's well-water pumps, Snow was able to link the well on Broad Street, which tended to mix with the city's sewage system, to the cholera outbreak. Snow used this evidence to persuade officials to remove the Broad Street pump handle. Afterward, cholera was contained and decreased in London (Magner, 2009; Sherman, 2007).

Another historical snapshot that links international travel and migration to infectious diseases, people, and their environment entails the story of Mary Mallon. Mallon was an Irish immigrant to the United States at the turn of the 1900s who eventually became known as "Typhoid Mary." She became the first healthy carrier of the typhoid bacterium *Salmonella typhi* in the United States. During this time, Mallon was employed as a domestic cook, from which position she infected more than 50 people with the disease, of whom 3 died. However, given the many years she worked as a cook in domestic settings, it was never clearly determined just how many people became infected by Mallon preparing their meals. As the typhoid bacteria were expelled through Mallon's feces, improper hand washing was probably to blame for the further spread of the contamination through her food preparation (Hasian, 2000).

These examples reflect the variable nature of how infectious diseases spread between people and their environment. As one continues to examine the global infectious diseases most common throughout the world, it becomes clear how the sciences of clinical and molecular epidemiology, virology, bacteriology, mycology, and public health can have global, regional, national, and local effects on the detection, prevention, or eradication of various infectious diseases. Differences within countries—such as political instability, economic unrest, and limited healthcare infrastructure—can, in turn, affect a community's response to the threat of infectious diseases.

CHOLERA

Cholera is an acute diarrheal disease caused by the bacterium *Vibrio cholerae* (subgroups O-group 1 and O-group 139 are responsible for the majority of outbreaks worldwide). It remains one of the most feared enteric diseases, often affecting poor and vulnerable populations. Persons are typically infected by consuming water or eating food that has been contaminated with the organism. Each year 3 to 5 million cases are identified globally and more than 100,000 deaths occur, the vast majority in sub-Saharan Africa. This disease is endemic in many countries across Asia and Africa. A lack of basic infrastructure (access to clean water, sanitation, and hygiene) plays a predominate role in disease transmission. Once persons are infected, they continue to shed the organism in their feces for 7 to 14 days, thereby creating new opportunities for the infection to spread to others in environments that lack adequate basic hygiene (Centers for Disease Control and Prevention [CDC], 2010a; WHO, 2011b, 2011c).

Persons affected may experience mild to severe symptoms characterized by profuse watery diarrhea, vomiting, and abdominal and leg cramps. Symptoms can appear as soon as two hours to as long as five days after exposure. Approximately 80% of persons affected will develop mild to moderate symptoms, and 20% will have severe dehydration. Symptoms can develop quickly, and the disease has been known to kill healthy adults within hours. Dehydration is the primary factor contributing to mortality. Most people can be successfully treated with oral rehydration salts, if readily available. Severely dehydrated individuals, however, require treatment with intravenous (IV) fluids. In addition to IV fluids, antibiotics can be helpful in diminishing the duration of diarrhea and reducing the amount of IV fluids needed for recovery. Use of IV fluids and antibiotics shortens the excretion time of the organism from the body. If immediate response measures are instituted (e.g., safe/clean water, proper sanitation, hygiene education, and safe food handling), the mortality rate will typically remain less than 1% in an outbreak (CDC, 2010a; WHO, 2011b, 2011c).

In areas of the world where cholera is endemic, WHO recommends the use of vaccines to assist in controlling the spread of the disease. In addition, vaccination is recommended in complex emergency situations such as a natural disaster, internally displaced people, or refugees due to famine or war. Currently, two vaccines are available: Dukoral (WHO prequalified and licensed in more than 60 countries) and Shanchol (pending WHO requalification). Both vaccines are administered orally in 150 mL of safe/clean water (two doses, six weeks apart). These vaccines provide protection for as long as two years in endemic settings and have demonstrated efficacy of 85% to 90%; however, such vaccines do not take the place of adequate environmental controls (CDC, 2010a; WHO, 2011b).

Recognizing that cholera remains a global concern, WHO launched the Global Task Force on Cholera Control in 1992. The aim of this initiative was to reduce morbidity and mortality related to cholera and to address the social and economic consequences of the disease. The WHO-supported group brings together government agencies and nongovernmental organizations (NGOs) and institutions from around the world to address epidemics, develop technical reports, and develop training guidelines to minimize the spread of cholera, thereby decreasing the number of epidemics worldwide. Priority activities currently focus on improved surveillance, support to communities to reduce the risk of spread during an outbreak, and environmental controls, such as access to clean water to diminish the incidence of waterborne diseases in general (WHO, 2011d). Overall, cholera continues to be a global infectious disease, and is considered to be endemic in many parts of the world, and a reemerging infectious disease where the incidence has been low.

DENGUE AND DENGUE HEMORRHAGIC FEVER

Dengue is the most common mosquito-borne infection in the world and is a global public health problem. Four serotypes of Flaviviridae viruses cause dengue: DENV 1, DENV 2, DENV 3, and DENV 4. More than 2.5 billion people worldwide (two-fifths of the world's population) live in areas where these viruses are transmitted. Dengue is the leading cause of morbidity and mortality in tropical and subtropical areas, and an estimated 50 million infections occur annually. As urban areas and newly emerging urban environments continue to extend their reach, the prevalence of dengue has expanded to more than 100 countries throughout Africa, the Americas, the Eastern Mediterranean, Southeast Asia, and the Western Pacific (CDC, 2011a; WHO, 2009a, 2011e).

Dengue is a vector-borne illness caused by the bite of the *Aedes aegypti* or *Aedes albopictus* mosquito, which spreads the infection from person to person. Many people who are infected may be asymptomatic or experience only a mild form of the disease; however, dengue can progress to very severe states, including dengue hemorrhagic fever (DHF), dengue shock syndrome (DSS), and death. The disease typically presents as a flulike illness (high fever, headache, exhaustion, severe joint and muscle pain, swollen lymph nodes, and rash) affecting persons of all ages. In general, symptoms of the illness usually begin 4 to 7 days after the mosquito bite and last for 3 to 10 days. In recent years, there has been an increase in incidence of DHF (characterized by abdominal pain and hemorrhage—petechiae, ecchymosis, thrombocytopenia—leading to circulatory collapse), which was first identified in the 1950s during an outbreak in the Philippines and Thailand. Since that time, there has been a fourfold increase in DHF on a worldwide basis. Currently, DHF is a leading cause of morbidity and mortality among children in Asian countries, where the burden of disease is greatest. Severe hemorrhage can lead to DSS, which consists of circulatory failure leading to a critical state of shock and death within 12 to 24 hours. There is no specific treatment for dengue, although supportive therapy saves lives, decreasing mortality to less than 1% (CDC, 2011a; WHO, 2005, 2009a, 2011e).

Currently, there is no vaccine for dengue, although progress is occurring on this front and two vaccines are being tested with human subjects. A major hurdle in vaccine development is finding a preparation that is effective against all four dengue serotypes, as infection from one strain does not confer immunity to the others. Persons affected by one serotype will have a milder form of the disease when exposed to the other variants (CDC, 2011a; WHO, 2009a).

Given the lack of a vaccine, the first line of defense against dengue is prevention, environmental controls, and health education. Approaches for prevention should be addressed within the context of the environment, as mosquitoes breed in different habitants based on the community. In Asia and the Americas, mosquitoes breed in human-made vessels for water storage (e.g., jars, metal drums, concrete cisterns); in contrast, in Africa, mosquitoes breed in natural habitats. Communities can benefit from the use of insecticides to help control this vector population. In addition, the community can be educated regarding proper waste disposal and water storage practices (i.e., covering containers to prevent mosquito access for breeding). During outbreaks, the broad application of insecticides can be helpful, but the effect is not long lasting. In general, active monitoring and surveillance of dengue illness and the mosquito populations represent basic control measures. Their implementation allows for immediate tracking of new cases so as to strengthen and recommend prevention strategies that affect and alter the behavior of individuals, households, and community infrastructures (CDC, 2011a; WHO, 2005, 2009a, 2011e).

Dengue is considered an emerging infectious disease given its spread around the world since the early 1950s and its appearance in the Americas in 1981. Moreover, due to immature surveillance and reporting systems in some countries where dengue is endemic, its true incidence is unknown (Vong et al., 2010).

MALARIA

A disease resembling malaria was described in ancient Chinese medical writings, making it one of the oldest-known diseases. However, the causative organism was not identified until 1880, by Charles Louis Alphonse Laveran. This parasitic, mosquito-borne disease is caused by four different forms of *Plasmodium* parasites: *falciparum, malariae, ovale,* and *vivax*. Of these, the most common types are *falciparum* and *vivax*; however, *falciparum* is associated with the highest mortality among persons affected. These organisms are transferred to humans through the bites of *Anopheles* mosquitoes, which predominantly feed at night (CDC, 2011b; WHO, 2010a).

Currently, 3.3 billion people (approximately half the world's population) live in areas at risk of malaria transmission (109 countries and territories); 35 countries (30 in sub-Saharan Africa and 5 in Asia) account for 98% of global malaria deaths. The most vulnerable and greatest number of victims of malaria are children, especially those who have not developed protective immunity against the infection. Recent estimates indicate that in 2008 malaria was responsible for 190 to 311 million cases of illness and 708,000 to 1,003,000 deaths. Epidemics can occur in areas where climatic conditions are favorable to the survival of mosquitoes—that is, in areas with high levels of rainfall, temperature, and humidity. Therefore, outbreaks of disease can be seasonal or occur in areas where people have little or no immunity to malaria. These same variables apply in areas where malaria is endemic. Malaria is the second leading cause of death in Africa and the fifth leading cause of death from infectious diseases globally (CDC, 2011b; WHO, 2010a).

Early symptoms of malaria include fever, headache, chills, and vomiting. Because these symptoms can be mild and resemble a flulike illness, malaria may be misdiagnosed or go undiagnosed. A delay in recognizing and initiating treatment for *falciparum* malaria can lead to death within a short period of time. Effective treatment is key; however, *P. falciparum* has become resistant to conventional (monotherapy) antimalarial drugs (chloroquine, sulfadoxine–pyrimethamine, and amodiaquine), especially in endemic areas of the world. A long history of inappropriate use of these drugs has rendered them ineffective due to resistance, especially in Africa. Each country, therefore, needs to determine the level of resistance in each community; if monotherapy drug resistance is high, then artemisinin-based combination medication should be used (CDC, 2011b; WHO, 2006a, 2010a).

In high-endemic areas, mosquito control represents the best strategy to reduce malaria transmission. A two-pronged approach is best, consisting of mosquito nets and indoor spraying with residual insecticides. Insecticide-impregnated mosquito nets should be distributed communitywide so that everyone sleeps under an appropriate mosquito net. Indoor household spraying should be routine (the results last for three to six months depending on the agent used) and achieved at the 80% level within the community. This action has proved to be the most powerful way to reduce malaria transmission. For persons traveling to areas of the world where malaria is endemic, several drugs have been found to be effective prophylactic agents: chloroquine, proguanil, mefloquine, and doxycycline (CDC, 2011b; WHO, 2006a, 2010a).

Malaria continues to be a public health concern related to infectious disease. In countries where the disease is rampant, many interventions are being tried to reduce the number and severity of seasonal malaria cases (which account for 80% to 90% of all cases). In Mali, in western Africa, healthcare providers reduced the number of seasonal malaria cases (by 22% to 59%) among infants by administering sulfadoxine–pyrimethamine at 2, 3 and 9 months of age. Senegal, also in western Africa, was able to reduce seasonal malaria cases by 86% through a program of administering three doses of sulfadoxine-pyrimethamine (at 1-month intervals) plus one dose of artesunate during the peak season for mosquitoes. Employing these types of strategies, along with environmental controls, is helping to lower the incidence of malaria on a broad scale (Dicko et al., 2011).

AVIAN (BIRD) FLU

Avian influenza (H5N1), commonly referred to as "bird flu," manifests its presence primarily in birds and poultry. The world community saw a new virus emerge from one that historically did not infect humans when the virus crossed over from birds to humans and caused severe respiratory disease, leading to respiratory failure in many persons affected. This virus was considered to be highly pathogenic. Persons who became ill had experienced close contact with infected poultry or inanimate objects contaminated with their feces (although data also suggest human-to-human spread may occur in some selected/special situations of close contact—that is, with an infected person and an unprotected caregiver).

The H5N1 virus was first isolated in a domestic goose in China and later associated with an outbreak in Hong Kong where 18 cases among humans (6 fatalities) were identified, representing the first evidence of human infection. No additional cases were identified until 2003, when 3 new cases were recognized in China; the epidemic then continued through March 2009. During the epidemic, 15 countries reported human cases of H5N1 infection. The four countries with the highest number of affected persons were Indonesia, Vietnam, Egypt, and China. Among birds, between 1996 and 2009, the disease quickly spread across three continents (Asia, Europe, and Africa) and involved 67 countries. This outbreak represented the first time avian influenza virus had been transferred directly to humans and was found to cause severe respiratory illness. To break the chain of transmission, millions of chickens were killed. This approach may have served a valuable purpose and saved many lives (CDC, 2008; WHO, 2009b, 2011h, 2011i).

Symptoms of H5N1 infection include high fever, sore throat, muscle aches, diarrhea, vomiting, abdominal pain, chest pain, neurological changes, and bleeding from the nose and gums. This illness can progress into the lower respiratory system and cause shortness of breathing, respiratory distress, a hoarse voice, and crackling on inhaling. Effective treatment entails the use of antiviral medications, with the preferred drug of choice being oseltamivir. For this drug to be efficacious, it must be initiated within 48 hours of the onset of symptoms. Unfortunately, oseltamivir has not demonstrated effectiveness if early treatment is delayed.

Several H5N1 viruses are now circulating worldwide, and there have been some reports of possible drug resistance to oseltamivir. Drugs used to treat infectious diseases are classified as antimicrobial agents. Organisms can develop resistance to such therapies by mutating to a different strain, thereby rendering the medication ineffective. This possibility is a huge concern for managing future outbreaks to minimize loss of life. From a prevention perspective, careful attention to hand washing and adhering to strict food-handling procedures (avoiding cross-contamination) are paramount in minimizing the spread from poultry. As some cases can be passed from person to person, healthcare workers should use appropriate personal protective equipment when H5N1 disease is suspected. Any exposed persons should be carefully observed for symptoms for at least seven days following contact (CDC, 2008; WHO, 2011i).

WEST NILE VIRUS

West Nile virus, which is a member of the Flaviviridae family, is maintained in nature in a cycle involving transmission between birds and mosquitoes. However, this virus is also known to infect humans, horses, and other mammals. Birds of many varieties serve as its primary reservoir, with mosquitoes being the transmission vector.

West Nile virus is virulent enough to cross species, nations, and continents, and it has had a long history of traversing Africa, parts of Europe, west and central Asia, the Middle East, and Australia. It was first isolated in 1937 from a Ugandan woman in the West Nile province of the country—hence the name. However, it has only been in the past 50 years that the virus was reported in many countries. This virus was imported into the United States in 1999, when it produced a large-scale outbreak for the first time; since that time West Nile cases have been reported across the United States. Epidemiologically, this phenomenon represents a classic case of importation and the establishment of a pathogen outside of its normal habitat, to the point that the organism now represents a potential global threat. In the western hemisphere, cases of West Nile virus infection have been reported in many geographical regions since its introduction via New York City in 1999: Canada, Mexico, the Caribbean islands, Central America, Venezuela, Columbia, and Argentina (CDC, 2011c; Chakarova, Dimitrov, & Chenchev, 2011; WHO, 2011f).

West Nile virus is carried in mosquitoes' salivary glands; when they bite humans or other animals, the virus is transferred to the target. Eighty percent of persons infected with the virus will remain asymptomatic, the other 20% will become ill, and only a small percentage of these individuals will develop severe disease—neuroinvasive disease—in the form of West Nile encephalitis, West Nile meningitis, or West Nile poliomyelitis. Symptoms associated with uncomplicated West Nile infection include fever, headache, fatigue, body aches, nausea, vomiting, skin rash (occasionally), and swollen lymph glands. Neuroinvasive West Nile disease is characterized by high fever, headache, stiffness of the neck, involuntary movements, stupor, disorientation, tremors, convulsions, coma, muscle weakness, and paralysis. The areas of the brain most often affected by West Nile Virus are the cerebral cortex, thalamus, basal ganglia, brain stem, cerebellum, and spinal cord. Persons older than the age of 50 and individuals with weakened immune systems are at greatest risk for severe disease (CDC, 2011c; Government of Alberta, Health and Wellness, 2011; Lim, Koraka, Osterhaus, & Martina, 2011; WHO, 2011f, 2011g).

There is no vaccine for West Nile virus, so environmental mosquito control measures, monitoring and disease surveillance (human and veterinary), and prevention education are paramount to decreasing transmission. Mosquito control entails insecticide spraying during peak mosquito seasons, use of insecticide mosquito nets, and use of repellents. Monitoring and surveillance are best achieved by maintaining an active animal health surveillance system (birds and horses) to provide early warning of the presence of West Nile virus. It is also important to report dead birds to local authorities, as their demise may be an early warning sign. Use of insect repellents and wearing long-sleeve garments during peak mosquito seasons can also lower the risk of infection, especially in endemic environments (Government of Alberta, Health and Wellness, 2011; WHO, 2011f, 2011g).

West Nile virus is an emerging infectious disease that has made its way around the globe in just a few decades. Expansion of the virus across the western hemisphere within a decade indicates a rapid spread. There will be much to learn about this pathogen in the years ahead.

SEVERE ACUTE RESPIRATORY SYNDROME

Severe acute respiratory syndrome (SARS) is a viral respiratory illness that is caused by a coronavirus (SARS-CoV). These viruses have been found to infect cattle, pigs, horses, turkeys, cats, dogs, rats, and mice. In addition, coronaviruses are the second leading cause of the common cold (after the rhinoviruses). SARS-CoV was first recognized in Asia in March 2003, as a highly infectious disease that rapidly progressed across other environmental settings (North America, South America, and Europe). Following its identification, SARS spread to more than 25 other countries before it was deemed contained on July 5, 2003. During this outbreak, 8098 persons worldwide became ill and 774 died. The vast majority of the SARS cases occurred in mainland China, with the epidemic starting in Guangdong Province and three months later reaching Beijing, bringing the country to almost a standstill and creating significant social and economic disruption. China and Hong Kong (the epicenter) were heavily affected by this outbreak, accounting for 87% of all cases worldwide. SARS was characterized as a "superspreading event" because of its rapid spread internationally—to the United States, Canada, Taiwan, the People's Republic of China, the Hong Kong Special Administrative Region of China, Singapore, and Vietnam. During this outbreak, much of the rapid spread was associated with international travel, in which persons visiting China imported the disease to their countries of residence (Cao, de Vlas, & Richardus, 2011; CDC, 2005; WHO, 2003, 2004).

Symptoms of SARS include fever, headache, general malaise, and diarrhea—which collectively affect 10% to 20% of patients—and body aches, dry cough, and pneumonia—which are found in most patients. During the epidemic, especially in China, many patients were treated with systemic corticosteroids. A recent longitudinal study of 71 patients identified long-term consequences related to this treatment approach. Specifically, 58% of persons who received such therapy developed avascular necrosis of the hip, which was directly attributed to treatment (CDC, 2005; Lv et al., 2009).

The reservoir for SARS-CoV has not been clearly identified, but it is speculated that a number of species can serve as hosts. In particular, domestic cats were found to be infected with the SARS virus, and other species were identified with being infected with a related coronavirus. SARS appears to be primarily transmitted on a person-to-person basis through droplets expelled by way of coughing or sneezing. When an infected person touches his or her mouth, nose, or eyes, further spread can occur by means of others touching contaminated surfaces in the affected person's environment. Also, there is a possibility of airborne spread. In addition, there may be other methods of transmission that have not yet been identified (CDC, 2005; WHO, 2004).

SARS is an emerging infectious disease and has the potential for reemergence. Since 2003, three breaches of laboratory biosafety have produced cases in Singapore, Taipei, and Beijing. A fourth laboratory incident (in Guandong Province, China) spawned four community-acquired cases. To date, it has proved extraordinarily difficult to predict where SARS will reemerge in epidemic proportion. However, countries should remain vigilant regarding surveillance of suspicious respiratory illnesses and have preparedness response plans in place (WHO, 2004).

EBOLA (HEMORRHAGIC FEVER)

The Ebola virus is part of the Filoviridae family of viruses. It was named after the Ebola River Valley in the Democratic Republic of the Congo (formally Zaire)—the site of the first outbreak in 1976, where 318 human cases were identified, leading to the first recognition of the disease. During this outbreak, 280 people died, for an 88% case fatality rate.

Five species of Ebola virus have been identified: Zaire, Sudan, Côte d'Ivoire, Bundibugyo, and Reston. Of these species, only Zaire, Sudan, and Bundibugyo have been associated with large outbreaks with high case fatality rates. Reston and Côte d'Ivoire have been associated with animal-related cases; when exposed to these variants, humans do not suffer catastrophic disease events.

Since Ebola infection was first recognized, sporadic outbreaks of the disease have occurred. The largest recorded outbreak was in Uganda (from 2000 to 2001, species Ebola-Sudan), where 425 persons were infected and 224 died from the virus. The most recent case of Ebola infection (a single case in May 2011) involved a 12-year-old Ugandan female with a recent history of fever and hemorrhagic manifestations. A national task force was convened by the Ugandan Ministry of Health, and representatives from WHO and CDC were sent to conduct a detailed epidemiological investigation in conjunction with the Ministry of Health. To date, all human fatalities associated with Ebola virus have occurred in Africa. Overall, approximately 1850 cases and 1200 deaths have been associated with the Ebola virus since its discovery in 1976 (CDC, 2011d; Tyagi, Kumar, & Singla, 2010; WHO, 2008a, 2011j).

Ebola infection is characterized by fever, intense weakness, muscle pain, headache, and sore throat. These symptoms are typically followed by vomiting, diarrhea, rash, impaired kidney and liver function, and sometimes internal and external bleeding. The disease has an incubation period ranging from 2 to 21 days. By the tenth day of the infection, fever subsides and a person who has been infected either improves or dies. Organ necrosis signals the end stage of the disease.

Ebola infection is diagnosed by blood tests that can identify antigens or genes of the virus. New testing techniques can identify the organism using a blood or urine sample. Currently the only treatment for this disease is supportive: electrolyte and fluid replacement, maintaining good oxygen saturation and blood pressure, and treating any complicating infections. There is no vaccine, although several potential vaccines are in the testing stage. Finding a suitable vaccine that will be effective against the more virulent strains of Ebola may take years (CDC, 2010b; Tyagi et al., 2010; WHO, 2008a).

The natural reservoir for the Ebola virus seems to be in the rain forests of Africa and the Philippines; however, essentially it remains unknown. There have been documented Ebola cases in which persons developed the disease from direct contact with infected gorillas, chimpanzees, monkeys, forest antelope, and porcupines found dead in the rainforest. Ecological studies are currently being conducted to identify the virus's natural reservoir (WHO, 2008a).

Ebola continues to be an emerging infectious disease. Due to the high case fatality rate associated with outbreaks, preparedness is a key factor in minimizing the impact on a community. Containment is the priority, as evidenced by the following recommendations: isolation of suspected cases; strict barrier protection during care; good contact tracing; effective environmental controls—disinfection of clothing and bed linens; and careful and appropriate handling (safe burial) of the deceased (WHO, 2008a).

ESCHERICHIA COLI

Escherichia coli (*E. coli*) comprises a large and diverse group of bacteria that live in the intestines of healthy humans and warm-bloodied animals. Most of these bacteria are harmless, but one strain (*E. coli* O157:H7) produces a powerful toxin that can cause serious illness. Known as Shiga toxin-producing *Escherichia coli (STEC),* this pathogenic organism has been isolated from the feces of cattle, sheep, pigs, deer, and poultry, and produces toxins (verotoxins) similar to those made by the *Shigella dysenteriae* organism. STEC was first identified in 1982 during an outbreak of diarrheal disease—hemorrhagic colitis—in the United States. People generally become infected by consuming contaminated food or water; hence *E. coli* is considered to be a foodborne illness. Worldwide, it is difficult to estimate the number of people affected each year by foodborne disease; however, one estimate from 2005 indicates that 1.8 million people died from diarrheal diseases. In resource-poor countries, the incidence is even higher and suggests there may be underlying issues with food safety in the affected region (CDC, 2011e; Rangel, Sparling, Crowe, Griffin, & Swerdlow, 2004; WHO, 2011k).

E. coli O157:H7 symptoms include abdominal cramps, diarrhea that can progress to bloody diarrhea (hemorrhagic colitis), and sometimes fever and vomiting. Most persons affected recover within 10 days. However, a small percentage of people will develop hemolytic uremic syndrome (HUS), especially vulnerable populations such as the children and the elderly. Other populations at risk include persons with compromised immune systems and multiple chronic diseases. HUS is associated with acute renal failure and can cause other problems, such as seizure, stroke, and coma. The incidence of HUS associated with outbreaks has been as high as 20% (CDC, 2011e; Rangel et al., 2004; WHO, 2011k).

The primary source of transmission of the bacteria is consumption of undercooked meats, raw milk (unpasteurized), fecal contamination of water and other foods (water spread being associated with fecal polluted drinking and recreational waters), cross-contamination during food preparation (using the same food surface to prepare raw meats and uncooked foods without proper disinfection between types of food preparation tasks), and person-to-person spread. The world's worst outbreak of hemorrhagic *E. coli* (O104:H4) occurred in Germany in 2011; as of June 18, 2011, there had been 3200 cases reported and 39 deaths. This foodborne organism moved through the food chain to the dinner table and produced a large number of HUS cases in adults, with the majority occurring in women. The most likely cause was contaminated raw sprouts from a farm in Germany (Frank et al., 2011; WHO, 2011k).

Prevention education related to food safety is important to prevent *E. coli* infection. Also, improving surveillance efforts can lower the response time by public health officials when new cases are identified.

Controls at all stages of the food chain (agriculture, processing and manufacturing, and food preparation—commercial and domestic) can make a difference in the number of cases identified each year (CDC, 2011e; WHO, 2011k).

INFLUENZA

Influenza (flu) is a respiratory illness caused by influenza viruses that infect the nose, throat, and lungs of people. Three types influenza viruses are distinguished: A, B, and C. Human influenza viruses A and B cause seasonal epidemics of disease almost every fall and winter in temperate regions of the world. Globally, these annual epidemics result in approximately 3 to 5 million cases of severe illness and 250,000 to 500,000 deaths. Influenza type C infection causes a mild respiratory illness and is not thought to lead to epidemics. Current subtypes of influenza A virus found in people include H1N1 and H3N2. Influenza B viruses are not divided into subtypes. In spring 2009, influenza A (H1N1) caused the first influenza pandemic in more than 40 years (CDC, 2011f; WHO, 2009c, 2010b).

Flu virus can be transmitted when someone who is infected coughs, sneezes, or talks; infected droplets travel through the air, and another person may then inhale them. People with flu can spread the virus to others up to 6 feet away. Less often, a person might become infected from touching surfaces or objects that have the flu virus on them and then touching his or her own mouth or nose. Transmission of the virus can occur one day before symptoms become evident and as long as seven days after someone gets sick (CDC, 2011f; WHO, 2009c, 2010b).

Flu cases are typically diagnosed based on clinical symptoms, but laboratory tests that confirm infection are available. Rapid testing can detect influenza viruses within 15 minutes. Some rapid tests are approved for use in outpatient settings, whereas others must be performed in a moderately complex clinical laboratory. These tests detect influenza A only or both influenza A and B viruses. However, rapid tests do not provide information about subtypes. Rapid testing during an acute respiratory disease outbreak can help determine whether influenza virus is the underlying cause of the illnesses. For surveillance purposes and development of vaccines, collecting and culturing nasal and throat specimens are important because only culture isolates can provide specific information about circulating strains and subtypes of influenza viruses (CDC, 2011f; WHO, 2010b).

Seasonal flu is characterized by a sudden onset of high fever, cough (usually dry), headache, muscle and joint pain, fatigue, sore throat, and runny nose. Most people recover from fever and other symptoms within a week without requiring medical attention, but among high-risk individuals, the flu can cause severe illness and death. The highest risks of complications occur among children younger than 2 years of age, adults age 65 or older, and people with certain medical conditions such as chronic heart, lung, kidney, liver, blood, and metabolic diseases such as diabetes, or with weakened immune systems. The time from infection to the development of symptoms (i.e., the incubation period) is approximately two days (CDC, 2011f; WHO, 2010b).

The single best way to prevent flu and possible severe outcomes is to get a flu vaccination. Safe and effective flu vaccines have been available for more than 60 years. Seasonal flu vaccines are updated every year based on information about which influenza viruses are causing illness and how well the previous season's vaccine protects against the newly identified virus. Currently, 136 national influenza centers in 106 countries collaborate to conduct year-round surveillance for influenza viruses and disease activity. WHO recommends specific vaccine viruses for influenza vaccine production, and each country then makes a decision about licensing the vaccines (CDC, 2011f; WHO, 2009c, 2010b).

Two types of flu vaccines are available: flu shots and nasal spray flu. Traditional flu vaccine contains inactivated (killed) virus and is given by injection into the muscle. It is recommended for people 6 months of age and older and makes up the majority of the vaccine supply. A high-dose vaccine for people 65 years of age and older was first made available in the United States during the 2010–2011 flu season.

In the 2011–2012 flu season, an intradermal (microinjection under the skin) vaccine for people 18 to 64 years of age was also made available in the United States. This type of microinjection system has previously been approved and used in more than 40 countries (Sanofi Pasteur, 2011). The nasal spray flu vaccine is made with live, weakened flu viruses and is approved for use in healthy people 2 to 49 years of age and for women who are not pregnant. Antibodies that protect against influenza viruses usually develop about two weeks after receiving the vaccine. Other prevention measures to decrease transmission of the flu virus include frequent hand washing, using hand sanitizers, and covering the mouth and nose when coughing or sneezing (CDC, 2011f; WHO, 2009c, 2010b).

▌ HEPATITIS A, B, AND C

The first WHO World Hepatitis Day was held on July 28, 2011. It was established to increase awareness and understanding of viral hepatitis, the diseases that hepatitis viruses can cause, and hepatitis immunization programs. Hepatitis is a general term meaning inflammation of the liver. Five main hepatitis viruses exist, referred to as types A, B, C, D and E; however, the most common types are A, B, and C. These three types of hepatitis are of greatest concern because of the burden of illness and death they cause and the potential for outbreaks and epidemic spread (WHO, 2011l).

Hepatitis A virus (HAV) is usually spread from person to person when an uninfected person ingests a food or beverage that has been contaminated with stool of an infected person (fecal–oral route). Waterborne outbreaks can occur when there is inadequate sanitation or water is not treated properly. Depending on the environmental conditions, HAV can live outside of the human body for months (CDC, 2011g; Sharapov & Hu, 2010; WHO, 2008b).

WHO estimates that 1.4 million cases of HAV infection occur annually. In resource-poor countries with poor sanitation systems and hygienic practices, the lifetime risk of infection with HAV is 90%. Most infections occur in early childhood, and symptoms of the disease are minimal or nonexistent. After infection, immunity to the virus develops; therefore, epidemics in these parts of the world are less likely to occur. Because HAV infection is less common in developed countries, however, communitywide outbreaks can occur in these areas (Sharapov, 2011; WHO, 2008b).

The symptoms of hepatitis A range from mild to severe and can include fever, fatigue, loss of appetite, diarrhea, nausea, abdominal discomfort, dark-colored urine, and a yellowing of the skin and whites of the eyes (jaundice). Adults develop symptoms more often than children, and not everyone who is infected will have all symptoms. There is no specific treatment for HAV infection. Most people recover within weeks or months without complications. A diagnosis of hepatitis A requires laboratory testing of blood and/or stool. Vaccination with the HAV vaccine is the best way to prevent the disease. Because HAV is transmitted primarily through the fecal–oral route, good personal hygiene is important in preventing transmission of the virus. Recommended measures include good hand washing or use of a hand sanitizer after using the bathroom, changing diapers, and before preparing or eating food (CDC, 2011g; Sharapov & Hu, 2010; WHO, 2008b).

Hepatitis B virus (HBV) causes a potentially life-threatening liver infection that is transmitted through contact with infected blood or other body fluids (i.e., semen, vaginal fluids, and saliva). Modes of transmission include having sex with an infected partner; sharing needles, syringes, or other drug paraphernalia; acquiring needle sticks or sharp instrument exposures; sharing items such as razors or toothbrushes with an infected person; and vertical transmission from mother to baby at birth. The virus is not transmitted through casual contact. HBV is 50 to 100 times more infectious than HIV; it can survive outside the body for at least seven days and still be capable of causing infection. HBV infection is considered an occupational hazard for healthcare workers (CDC, 2011g; WHO, 2008c).

HBV infection can cause both acute and chronic disease. Symptoms of acute disease include jaundice, dark-colored urine, fatigue, nausea, vomiting, and abdominal pain. People can take several months to a year to recover. The likelihood that HBV infection will become chronic depends on the age at which a person becomes infected; young children are the most likely to develop a chronic infection. Approximately 90% of healthy adults who become infected with HBV will recover and be completely rid of the virus in six months. Complications of chronic HBV infection include cirrhosis of the liver and liver cancer. To diagnose hepatitis B and determine the phase of infection (acute versus chronic), blood testing is required. For acute HBV infections, there are no medications available that can affect a cure; instead, treatment is supportive and is based on symptoms. Persons with chronic HBV infection require long-term follow up-to assess progression of the disease and can be treated with medications that include interferon and antiviral drugs (CDC, 2010c; Sharapov & Hu, 2010; WHO, 2008c).

Worldwide, an estimated 2 billion people have been infected with HBV and more than 350 million have chronic infections. An estimated 600,000 people die each year from the disease. HBV is endemic in China and other parts of Asia. High rates of chronic infection are also found in the Amazon and southern parts of eastern and central Europe. Less than 1% of the population in Western Europe and North America is chronically infected (Sharapov & Hu, 2010; WHO, 2008c).

Hepatitis B vaccine is the mainstay of HBV prevention. Any unvaccinated individual who is seeking protection from this infection should receive the vaccination, especially persons traveling to parts of the world where HBV is prevalent or working in healthcare settings where exposure to HBV-infected body fluids can occur. Implementation of universal vaccination for infants has lowered the prevalence of hepatitis B in most countries. As of 2007, HBV vaccine had been introduced to 171 countries and an estimated 65% of the world's population, compared to 3% in 1992. Coverage is highest in the Americas (88%) and lowest in Southeast Asia (30%) (Te & Jensen, 2010; WHO, 2008c).

Similar to HBV infection, hepatitis C virus (HCV) infection is a contagious liver disease that can range in severity from a mild illness to a serious, lifelong disease. HCV is usually spread when blood from a person who is infected enters the body of someone who is not infected. The most common forms of transmission include receiving a contaminated blood transfusion, blood product, or organ transplant; injection with a contaminated syringe, needle-stick injuries in healthcare settings, or injection drug use; and being born to an HCV-infected mother. The virus is less commonly transmitted through sexual exposure and sharing of personal items contaminated with infected blood (CDC, 2011g; WHO, 2011m).

During the acute phase of HCV disease, most people (80%) have no symptoms. When symptoms do occur, they can include loss of appetite, vague abdominal discomfort, nausea and vomiting, fever, fatigue, dark-colored urine, joint pain, and jaundice. As many as 70% to 90% of HCV-infected persons develop a chronic infection. As is true of acute-phase disease, most people with chronic hepatitis C have no symptoms. When symptoms develop, their manifestation usually indicates advanced liver disease—that is, fibrosis, cirrhosis, or liver cancer. Just as in HBV infection, determining the phase of HCV infection (acute versus chronic) requires blood testing. Combination drug therapy using interferon and ribavirin is the backbone of treatment. Unfortunately, interferon is not widely available globally, is not always well tolerated, and may not be effective in treating the infection. In resource-rich countries, hepatitis C is the most common reason for liver transplantation (CDC, 2011g; Lavanchy, 2009; Sharapov & Hu, 2010; WHO, 2011m).

Since its discovery in 1989, HCV has been recognized as a major global health problem. WHO estimates that 3 to 4 million people around the world are infected with HCV each year and that 130 to 170 million people are chronically infected. Annually, more than 350,000 people die from HCV-related liver disease. Countries with high rates of infection include Egypt (22%), Pakistan (4.8%), and China (3.2%). The primary mode of transmission in these countries is sharing of contaminated injection-drug paraphernalia (WHO, 2011m).

Currently, there is no vaccine available that can prevent HCV infection. Therefore, prevention of HCV infection relies on education to alter risk factors associated with contracting the disease (e.g., injection drug use) and universal HCV screening of blood and organ donors. In persons already infected, education should focus on changing or modifying behaviors (e.g., alcohol consumption) that can lead to liver disease and subsequent liver failure (Sharapov & Hu, 2010; WHO, 2011m).

SYPHILIS

Despite the existence of effective prevention measures and relatively inexpensive treatment options, syphilis remains a global problem, with an estimated 12 million people becoming infected each year. Syphilis is a systemic disease that is caused by the bacterium *Treponema pallidum*. Because of the enormous variation in the disease symptoms, it is sometimes called the "Great Imitator" (Sherman, 2007; WHO, 2007).

Depending on the stage of the disease, syphilis can be characterized as primary, secondary, or tertiary (late). In the primary stage of syphilis, a painless, spontaneously resolving sore (called a chancre) appears. The chancre appears where syphilis entered the body. If syphilis is not treated in the primary stage, it becomes a chronic disease (Blencowe, Cousens, Kamb, Berman, & Lawn, 2011; CDC, 2007).

The development of a rash on one or more parts of the body characterizes the secondary stage. The rash usually does not cause itching, and it may be so faint that it is not noticed. Other signs and symptoms of secondary syphilis can include fever, swollen lymph glands, sore throat, patchy hair loss, headaches, weight loss, muscle aches, and fatigue. The symptoms of secondary syphilis will also resolve without treatment.

Tertiary syphilis begins after the primary and secondary symptoms of syphilis disappear. Complications during this stage occur in 15% to 40% of persons and can appear years after the infection was first acquired. These complications can damage the brain, nervous system, blood vessels, liver, bones, and joints. Signs and symptoms of late-stage syphilis include difficulty in coordinating muscle movements, paralysis, numbness, gradual blindness, and dementia.

Syphilis can be diagnosed by examining material from a chancre under a special microscope or through blood testing. Having syphilis makes an individual more susceptible to HIV if exposed to the virus; thus, if an individual tests positive for syphilis, he or she should also be tested for HIV and other sexually transmitted infections (CDC, 2010c).

Syphilis is primarily transmitted through vaginal, anal, or oral sexual contact, but a pregnant woman who is infected can transmit the infection to her fetus, causing congenital syphilis and adverse pregnancy outcomes. WHO estimates that 2 million pregnancies around the world are affected by syphilis annually. Approximately 25% of these pregnancies end in stillbirth or spontaneous abortion. The seroprevalence of syphilis among women attending antenatal (prenatal) clinics is estimated to be highest in Central and South America, parts of Africa, and Southeast Asia (Schmid, Stoner, Hawkes, & Broutet, 2007; WHO, 2007). In 2007, WHO launched a campaign seeking the global elimination of syphilis through mobilization and strengthening of existing maternal and newborn health systems (Kamb et al., 2010). Point-of-care (at the site of healthcare service) rapid testing of pregnant women for syphilis and same-day treatment have been found to be cost-effective measures in resource-poor regions of the world (Blandford, Gift, Vasaikar, Mwesigwa-Kayongo, Diali, & Bronzan, 2007; Sen_a, White, & Sperling, 2010).

For the purposes of treatment, syphilis is divided into early syphilis (less than one year's duration) and late syphilis. A single intramuscular injection of penicillin (an antibiotic) will cure a person who has had syphilis for less than a year. Additional doses are needed to treat someone who has had syphilis longer than a year. For people who are allergic to penicillin, other antibiotics are available (CDC, 2010c). The best way to avoid transmission of syphilis is to abstain from sexual contact or to be in a long-term mutually monogamous relationship with a partner who has been tested and is known to be uninfected. In lieu of abstinence or monogamy, using male or female condoms properly and consistently can reduce the risk of contracting syphilis (Beksinska, Smit, Joanis, Userher-Patel, & Potter, 2011; CDC, 2010c, 2011h).

TUBERCULOSIS

Tuberculosis (TB) has often been considered a disease of poverty. This airborne illness is caused by the bacterium *Mycobacterium tuberculosis* (Mtb). The acid-fast bacilli are spread through infected, aerosolized droplets from people who cough, sneeze, or talk with vigor. Other people may then breathe in the aerosolized droplets and become infected. The bacteria usually attack the lungs, but can attack other parts of the body such as the kidney, spine, or brain (CDC, 2010d).

It is important to differentiate between being infected with TB and having TB disease. Someone who has been infected with TB has the bacteria in his or her body, but the immune system is protecting the person from the bacteria so the individual is not sick. This condition is called latent TB. In contrast, someone with TB disease is sick and can spread the disease to others. Persons with TB disease may develop a persistent cough, fatigue, weight loss, decreased appetite, fever, bloody sputum, and night sweats.

TB infection can be detected through a skin or blood test. If someone has a positive test for TB, it means that the individual has been infected with the TB pathogen, but does not indicate that a person has an active disease. Additional tests, including chest X-rays and sputum that is cultured for the TB bacteria, are needed to confirm a diagnosis of TB disease (CDC, 2010d).

Approximately one-third of the world's population is infected with the TB bacillus. Some 5% to 10% of people who are infected with TB become sick or infectious at some time in their lives. In 2009, there were an estimated 9.4 million incident cases of TB disease globally, most of which occurred in Asia (55%) and Africa (30%). Women accounted for an estimated 3.3 million of these cases; the disease is one of the top three causes of death among women aged 15–44. Among the 9.4 million TB cases reported, approximately 1.0 to 1.2 million occurred in people who were also HIV positive. TB is a leading cause of death among people infected with HIV. People living with HIV (the virus that causes AIDS) are more likely than uninfected people to get sick with infections such as TB. Even though TB is preventable and curable, among HIV-negative TB cases reported, approximately 1.3 million deaths occurred in 2009 (WHO, 2010c).

Treatment for TB depends on whether a person has latent TB or TB disease. The most common treatment for latent TB is 6 to 9 months of isoniazid (INH). This regimen kills the bacteria that are currently not causing any damage, but could do so in the future. In contrast, if an individual has TB disease, a combination of medications is used. The most common treatment is INH plus two or three other drugs (rifampicin, pyrazinamide, ethambutol, and streptomycin). Unfortunately, strains of TB that are resistant to the major anti-TB medications have developed over time (WHO, 2009d).

Multidrug-resistant TB (MDR-TB) is defined as the disease caused by TB bacilli that are resistant to at least INH and rifampicin, the two most powerful anti-TB medications. It is estimated that 3.3% of all new TB cases involve MDR-TB. Resistance strains develop when TB disease is not treated appropriately. MDR-TB is treatable, but it requires extensive pharmacological treatment (up to two years) with second-line TB medications that are more expensive than the first-line drugs. Almost 50% of the global burden of MDR-TB is found in India and China (Gandhi et al., 2010). Extensively drug-resistant TB (XDR-TB) is a subset of MDR-TB in which the strains of TB bacteria are resistant to several of the best second-line drugs. XDR-TB cases account for approximately 10% of all MDR-TB cases (WHO, 2009d).

TB is largely a preventable disease, with adequate ventilation being the most important measure to prevent its transmission. In countries that have adequate financial resources, hospitals and clinics take precautions to prevent the spread of TB by using ultraviolet light to sterilize the air, special filters, and special respirators and masks. In hospitals, people with TB are isolated in special rooms with controlled ventilation and air flow until they can no longer spread the TB bacteria (CDC, 2010d; WHO, 2010c).

In parts of the world where TB is more prevalent, WHO recommends that infants receive a vaccine called bacille Calmette-Guérin (BCG), which is made from a live weakened bacterium related to Mtb. BCG vaccine prevents Mtb from spreading within the body, thereby preventing TB from developing. Recently, the safety of this vaccine has been questioned. There is a concern that use of the vaccine in immunocompromised persons (i.e., individuals with weakened immune systems) may result in an infection caused by the vaccine itself. Also, among immunocompetent (i.e., having a normal immune system) persons, local reactions, including ulceration at the site of vaccination, may result in shedding of live organisms, which could infect others who may be immunocompromised. Furthermore, BCG may interfere with the TB skin test, producing a positive skin test reaction in people who have received the vaccine. In countries where BCG vaccine is used, the ability of skin testing to identify people infected with Mtb is limited. Because of these concerns, U.S. health experts do not recommend BCG for general use (CDC, 2011i; WHO, 2011n).

Directly observed treatment—short course (DOTS) is the internationally recommended strategy for TB control and is recognized as being highly efficient and cost-effective. It was launched in 1994 after WHO declared the TB epidemic to be a global public health emergency. DOTS was created based on five key elements: (1) sustained political and financial commitment; (2) diagnosis by quality-ensured sputum-smear technology; (3) use of a standardized short course of anti-TB treatment given under direct and support observation; (4) provision of a regular and uninterrupted supply of high-quality anti-TB drugs; and (5) use of standardized recording and reporting. Between 1995 and 2009, a total of 41 million TB patients were successfully treated in DOTS programs and an estimated 6 million lives were saved. The DOTS program has since been expanded, further clarified, and implemented in 182 countries worldwide (Glaziou et al., 2010; WHO, 2006b, 2010c).

The "Stop TB Strategy" is a global movement that was built on the DOTS program. It was established in 2000 to help eliminate TB as a public health problem and ultimately eradicate the disease on a worldwide basis. The six principal components of the strategy are as follows: (1) sustain, improve, and accelerate quality DOTS; (2) address TB-HIV, MDR-TB, and other special challenges; (3) contribute to health system strengthening; (4) engage all providers (private and public); (5) empower patients and communities; and (6) enable and promote research. The Stop TB Global Partnership is a network of more than 400 international organizations, countries, donors from the public and private sectors, governmental agencies and NGOs, and individuals committed to achieving the "Stop TB Strategy" goals. One of its targets is to decrease the global incidence of TB disease to less than 1 per million persons, which has the potential to virtually eliminate TB as a global public health problem (WHO, 2006b, 2010c).

HUMAN IMMUNODEFICIENCY VIRUS/ACQUIRED IMMUNODEFICIENCY SYNDROME

Human immunodeficiency virus (HIV) is a retrovirus that infects cells of the immune system, destroying or impairing their function. There are two forms of the virus: HIV-1 and HIV-2. Compared to HIV-1, HIV-2 is much less prevalent and is found primarily among people living in West Africa and India. The most advanced stage of HIV infection is acquired immunodeficiency syndrome (AIDS). During this stage of infection, the immune system becomes extremely weak and is unable to fight off other infections and diseases (CDC, 2011j).

HIV is transmitted through unprotected sexual intercourse (anal or vaginal), contaminated blood, and sharing of contaminated injecting-drug equipment, and between a mother and her infant during pregnancy, childbirth, and breastfeeding (CDC, 2006; Cohen, Hellmann, Levy, DeCock, & Lange, 2008). Globally, the majority of new HIV infections occur through sexual transmission (Global HIV Prevention Working Group, 2009a, 2009b). However, in many countries throughout Eastern Europe and parts of Asia, the sharing of contaminated drug-injecting equipment is the primary mode of transmission (Institute of Medicine, 2006).

In 2009, approximately 33.3 million people around the world were living with HIV infection. Slightly more than half of these were women and children. Fortunately, the number of new HIV infections has been declining. In 1999, there were approximately 3.1 million new infections, compared to 2.6 million in 2009. This represents one-fifth (19%) fewer new infections. The number of new infections peaked in 1997 at 3.2 million. In sub-Saharan Africa, where the highest number of new HIV infections occurs, HIV incidence in 22 countries fell by more than 25% between 2001 and 2009. The rate of new infections in Western, Central, and Eastern Europe and North America has been stable for the past five years (UNAIDS, 2010).

Prior to 1996, scientists estimated that half of all HIV-positive people would develop AIDS within 10 years after becoming infected with HIV. This time varied greatly from person to person and depended on many factors, including a person's health status and health-related behaviors. Since 1996, however, the introduction of powerful antiretroviral therapy (ART) regimens has dramatically changed the progression of HIV infection to AIDS and transitioned AIDS from a death sentence to a chronic illness (UNAIDS, 2010). More than 30 medications are currently available for treatment, although not all countries have access to these drugs. In addition, medical treatments are available that can prevent or cure some of the illnesses associated with HIV/AIDS, although such treatments do not cure AIDS. As with other diseases, early detection allows for more treatment options and preventive healthcare measures (Boyd, 2011; CDC, 2006).

The number of annual AIDS-related deaths worldwide has also been steadily decreasing. In 2004, the number of deaths peaked at approximately 2.1 million, but has since declined to 1.8 million in 2009. Between 2004 and 2009, there were 20% fewer AIDS-related deaths in sub-Saharan Africa. In Asia and Central and South America, the number of deaths has stabilized, but there has been an increase in AIDS-related mortality in Eastern Europe. The overall decline in number of deaths reflects the increased availability of ART on a worldwide basis (UNAIDS, 2010).

To improve access to HIV prevention and care, WHO and UNAIDS issued a guidance on provider-initiated testing and counseling (PITC) for HIV infection at all healthcare encounters. The recommendation for PITC was based on worldwide evidence suggesting that many opportunities to provide HIV testing and counseling (HTC) are being missed. Because HTC is a critical entry point to care for people infected with HIV and essential for prevention of mother-to-child HIV transmission, the guidance recommends an "opt-out" approach. Opt-out testing means performing an HIV test after notifying the person that the test is normally performed, unless the patient chooses to decline testing. However, opt-out testing has been criticized because of the risk that people may not be fully informed about the purpose of testing (Gruskin, Ahmed, & Ferguson, 2008; Njeru, Blystad, Shayo, Nyamongo, & Fylkesnes, 2011; WHO & UNAIDS, 2007).

In recent years, HIV testing has become quicker and less invasive. Rapid testing allows clients to receive results on the same day as the testing takes place, which is important in urgent medical situations and settings where clients do not to return for HIV test results. These tests use oral fluid, urine, and finger-stick blood samples versus the collection of blood by venipuncture (CDC, 2009).

Access to treatment, care, and support services has improved significantly around the world. In 2009, an estimated 5.2 million people in resource-poor countries were able to obtain ART. This represents an increase of 30% (1.2 million people) in the number of people receiving ART compared to the previous year. The percentage of HIV-infected pregnant women who received ART to prevent vertical transmission (i.e., from mother to baby) increased from 35% in 2007 to 53% in 2009. Unfortunately, according to UNAIDS, some 10 million people around the world do not have access to HIV care and treatment. Furthermore, the revision of WHO treatment guidelines in 2010, which recommended initiation of ART earlier in the disease process, increased the number of people who are medically eligible for ART by 50%—from 10 million persons to 15 million persons (UNAIDS, 2010; WHO, 2010d).

Preventing new HIV infections is an urgent global priority, but there is no single solution to this problem. A combination of biomedical, behavioral, and structural strategies that promote risk reduction among both HIV-positive and HIV-negative individuals and that work at individual, group, and societal levels is needed. According to the Global HIV Prevention Working Group, expanded access to evidence-based prevention strategies could avert half of the 62 million new HIV infections projected to occur between 2005 and 2015. This group advocates for a comprehensive response to HIV/AIDS that integrates prevention, treatment, care and support (Global HIV Prevention Group, 2009a, 2009b).

Despite global efforts to address HIV-related stigma and discrimination, these issues continue to be challenging. To address these problems, countries have been urged to scale up their stigma and discrimination laws, build the capacity of their HIV-related service providers, and empower those individuals who are infected with and affected by HIV. Decriminalization of sex workers, people who use drugs, men who have sex with men, and transgendered individuals will also help to break down obstacles to effective worldwide HIV prevention strategies (UNAIDS, 2010).

INFECTIOUS DISEASE SURVEILLANCE

An effective and comprehensive global disease surveillance and response capability is required to identify and control infectious diseases. Global disease surveillance includes disease detection through a mature information collection system that can ensure data quality, analyze and interpret data, get information to those individuals who can act on it, and then facilitate the response that will deal with the problem effectively. To achieve these goals, surveillance and response capabilities must be developed based on a foundation of skills in areas such as case detection, epidemiology, data analysis and interpretation, laboratory diagnostic confirmation, and appropriate response (USAID, 2009).

The crux of infectious disease surveillance is to identify disease occurrence and undertake activities to prevent those diseases from becoming a threat to global health. Disease surveillance is an essential prerequisite for establishing local, national, regional, and global priorities; planning, mobilizing, and allocating resources; detecting epidemics early; and monitoring and evaluating disease prevention and control programs. WHO has long-term data on numerous infectious disease epidemics and has the mandate to lead and coordinate the international effort in global surveillance and response (Castillo-Salgado, 2010; WHO, 2011o).

SUMMARY

This chapter provided an overview of the more common infectious diseases that are found around the world. These descriptive summaries serve as a foundation for understanding how infectious diseases fit into the context of global health. Learning about infectious diseases can potentially improve global health and better prepare the world to cope with future epidemics.

STUDY QUESTIONS

1. Discuss, giving examples, how infectious diseases can spread worldwide in a rapid manner.
2. How do the diagnoses and treatments of infectious diseases differ globally and culturally within different regions of the world?
3. How does economics affect a country's ability to prevent and treat infections?
4. Why is it necessary for developed countries to share their knowledge and technology with developing countries?
5. Relate the role of climate and the global spread of infectious diseases.

CASE STUDY 1

Mr. S., a recently retired 67-year-old male living in an urban area, has decided to become more involved in his passion, home renovations. This summer he has been spending many hours on several external home projects, repairing siding, and performing other home-related tasks. The weather had been unusually hot and wet this year, so, he was really grateful for the bright sunny days. To feel comfortable while working, Mr. S. wore short-sleeve shirts and on many occasions removed his shirt while working. In late September, he started to feel fatigued for no apparent reason, but kept this information from his wife. One Saturday afternoon while his friend was visiting for his birthday, he noticed that he was having difficulty walking and was experiencing some involuntary movements. Mr. S. admitted that he had a stiff neck and occasionally had headaches. His friend offered to take him to the hospital, where he was evaluated and admitted. After two days, the doctors concluded that Mr. S. probably had a stroke due to problems with walking and involuntary movements; however, the diagnostic data did not clearly support this conclusion. What was suspicious was that Mr. S. had a low-grade fever. Two days later, an infectious disease specialist was consulted; she ordered additional tests, and a diagnosis of West Nile virus was confirmed.

Case Study Questions

1. What may have put this 67-year-old male at risk for West Nile virus infection?
2. Which preventive measures could Mr. S. have taken to decrease his risk of disease?
3. What are some important facts about the epidemiology of West Nile disease?

CASE STUDY 2

Parsi is 25-year-old Indian female working on a graduate degree at the local university in southern India. She is upset because recently she has been recovering from a second bout of diarrhea illness within the past two months. Her doctor recommended over-the-counter medications for the diarrhea. Parsi was feeling frustrated because she really needed to return to her studies. During her most recent episode of illness, she experienced a weight loss of 15 pounds. Also, she had a low-grade fever and was feeling fatigued most of the time. In the past week she noticed neck pain and some swelling of the glands in her neck. At night she had a slight cough, which she found annoying. Parsi became exasperated and returned to the doctor, who did a chest x-ray and noted the swelling in her neck. The x-ray was positive for a problem in the upper portion of the left lung and a tuberculin skin test was performed. Two days later, the skin test was positive. Tuberculosis disease was confirmed by the laboratory, which found tuberculosis organisms in Parsi's sputum specimens. Parsi was started on medication.

Case Study Questions

1. What is important for Parsi and her family to be aware of now that she has been diagnosed with TB?
2. Why is it likely that Parsi developed TB?
3. What are some important facts related to taking TB medication?

CASE STUDY 3

Myra, a 26-year-old female, has been working in advertising at a local firm for the past two years and has recently moved from her parents' home to a small apartment. She is delighted at finally being on her own. A male colleague at work had been asking her out on a date for several weeks and she finally consented. Myra was very impressed with this young man and felt they had a lot in common. Over the next few months, the relationship became very serious and there was talk of marriage in the near future. Their relationship progressed to a sexual level. Myra felt that she had found her soul mate. Discussions about marriage became deeper, with couple talking about starting a family soon after getting married.

Myra was having lunch with her best friend recently, when her friend informed Myra that she had seen Myra's boyfriend with another woman, and even disclosed the person's name. That evening Myra searched Facebook and discovered that her boyfriend and the other person were sharing intimate information with each other. Myra was devastated. She called her best friend and revealed that her relationship with the boyfriend had reached a sexual level, but noted that they were not using condoms. Her friend encouraged her to see a doctor, as the "rumor mill" was suggesting that Myra's boyfriend was also having a sexual relationship with the other woman. Taking her friend's advice, Myra saw her doctor immediately. Following the exam, the doctor informed Myra that syphilis was suspected because of a small lesion near Myra's vaginal opening. A blood specimen was taken and the diagnosis of syphilis confirmed. Myra was immediately treated.

Case Study Questions

1. What should Myra keep in mind when engaging in a sexual relationship in the future?
2. What could have been the possible long-term consequences for Myra if her syphilis had not been diagnosed?
3. If Myra not been diagnosed, had married, and become pregnant, would there be concerns regarding the health of the unborn child?

REFERENCES

Beksinska, M., Smit, J. Joanis, C., Usher-Patel, M., & Potter, W. (2011). Female condom technology: New products and regulatory issues. *Contraception, 83*(4), 316–321. doi:10.1016/j.contraception.2010.07.022

Blandford, J. M., Gift, T. L., Vasaikar, S., Mwesigwa-Kayongo, D., Diali, P., & Bronzan, R. N. (2007). Cost-effectiveness of on-site antenatal screening to prevent congenital syphilis in rural eastern Cape Province, Republic of South Africa. *Sexually Transmitted Diseases, 34*(suppl 7), S61–S66. doi: 10.1097/01.olq.0000258314.20752.5f

Blencowe, H., Cousens, S., Kamb, M., Berman, S., & Lawn, J. E. (2011). Lives Saved Tool supplement detection and treatment of syphilis in pregnancy to reduce syphilis related stillbirths and neonatal mortality. *BioMed Central Public Health, 11*(suppl 3), S3–S9. doi:10.1186/1471-2458-11-S3-S9

Boyd, S. D. (2011). Management of HIV infection in treatment-naïve patients: A review of the most current recommendations. *American Journal of Health-System Pharmacy, 68,* 991–1001. doi: 10.2146/ajhp100156

Cao, W., de Vlas, S. J., & Richardus, J. H. (2011). The severe acute respiratory syndrome epidemic in mainland China dissected. *Infectious Disease Reports, 3*(e2), 3–6. doi: 10.4081/idr.2011.e2

Castillo-Salgado, C. (2010). Trends and directions of global public health surveillance. *Epidemiological Reviews, 32,* 93–109. doi: 10.1093/epirev/mxq008

Centers for Disease Control and Prevention (CDC). (2005). Basic information about SARS. Retrieved from http://www.cdc.gov/ncidod/sars/factsheet.htm

Centers for Disease Control and Prevention (CDC). (2006). HIV/AIDS basics. Retrieved from http://www.cdc.gov/hiv/resources/qa/definitions.htm

Centers for Disease Control and Prevention (CDC). (2007). Syphilis. Retrieved from http://www.cdc.gov/std/syphilis/syphilis-Fact-Sheet.pdf

Centers for Disease Control and Prevention (CDC). (2008). Avian influenza virus infections of humans. Retrieved from http://www.cdc.gov/flu/avian/gen-info/avian-flu-humans.htm

Centers for Disease Control and Prevention (CDC). (2009). HIV testing. Retrieved from http://www.cdc.gov/hiv/topics/testing/index.htm

Centers for Disease Control and Prevention (CDC). (2010a). Cholera. Retrieved from http://www.cdc.gov/cholera/index.html

Centers for Disease Control and Prevention (CDC). (2010b). Ebola hemorrhagic information packet. Retrieved from http://www.cdc.gov/ncidod/dvrd/spb/mnpages/dispages/Fact_Sheets/Ebola_Fact_Booklet.pdf

Centers for Disease Control and Prevention. (2010c). Sexually transmitted diseases treatment guidelines, 2010. *Morbidity and Mortality Weekly Report, 59*, 1–110. Retrieved from http://www.cdc.gov/std/treatment/2010/STD-Treatment-2010-RR5912.pdf

Centers for Disease Control and Prevention (CDC). (2010d). Tuberculosis. Retrieved from http://www.cdc.gov/tb

Centers for Disease Control and Prevention (CDC). (2011a). Dengue. Retrieved from http://www.cdc.gov/dengue/

Centers for Disease Control and Prevention (CDC). (2011b). Malaria. Retrieved from http://www.cdc.gov/malaria/

Centers for Disease Control and Prevention (CDC). (2011c). West Nile virus. Retrieved from http://www.cdc.gov/ncidod/dvbid/westnile/index.htm

Centers for Disease Control and Prevention (CDC). (2011d). Ebola hemorrhagic fever. Retrieved from http://www.cdc.gov/ncidod/dvrd/spb/mnpages/dispages/ebola/ebolatable.htm

Centers for Disease Control and Prevention (CDC). (2011e). *Escherichia coli* O157:H7 and other Shiga toxin-producing *Escherichia coli* (STEC). Retrieved from http://www.cdc.gov/nczved/divisions/dfbmd/diseases/ecoli_o157h7/

Centers for Disease Control and Prevention (CDC). (2011f). Seasonal influenza (flu). Retrieved from http://www.cdc.gov/flu/

Centers for Disease Control and Prevention (CDC). (2011g). Viral hepatitis. Retrieved from http://www.cdc.gov/hepatitis/

Centers for Disease Control and Prevention (CDC). (2011h). Condoms and STDs: Fact sheet for public health personnel. Retrieved from http://www.cdc.gov/condomeffectiveness/latex.htm

Centers for Disease Control and Prevention (CDC). (2011i). Tuberculosis fact sheet: BCG vaccine. Retrieved from http://www.cdc.gov/tb/publications/factsheets/prevention/BCG.htm

Centers for Disease Control and Prevention (CDC). (2011j). Basic information about HIV and AIDS. Retrieved from http://www.cdc.gov/hiv/topics/basic/index.htm

Chakarova, S. R., Dimitrov, K. M., & Chenchev, I. I. (2011). Etiology, epidemiology, clinical features and laboratory diagnostics of West Nile fever: A review. *Bulgarian Journal of Veterinary Medicine, 14*(2), 71–79. Retrieved from http://tru.uni-sz.bg/bjvm/BJVM%20June%202011%20p.71-79.pdf

Cohen, M. S., Hellmann, N., Levy, J. A., DeCock, K., & Lange, J. (2008). The spread, treatment, and prevention of HIV-1: Evolution of a global epidemic. *Journal of Clinical Investigation, 118*(4), 1244–1254. doi: 110.1172/JCI34706

Dicko, A., Diallo, A. I., Tembine, I., Dicko, Y., Dara, N., Sidibe, Y., . . . Greenwood, B. (2011). Intermittent preventive treatment of malaria provides substantial protection against malaria in children already protected by an insecticide-treated bednet in Mali: A randomized, double-blind, placebo-controlled trial. *PLoS Medicine, 8*(2), 1–14. Retrieved from http://www.plosmedicine.org/article/info%3Adoi%2F10.1371%2Fjournal.pmed.1000408

Frank, C., Werber, D., Cramer, J. P., Askar, M., Faber, M., an der Heiden, M., . . . Krause, G. (2011). Epidemic profile of Shiga-toxin–producing *Escherichia coli* outbreak in Germany: Preliminary report. *New England Journal of Medicine,* 1–11. doi: 10.1056/NEJMoa1106483. Retrieved from http://www.nejm.org/doi/full/10.1056/NEJMoa1106483

Gandhi, N. R., Nunn, P., Dheda, K., Schaaf, H. S., Zignol, M., van Soolingen, D., . . . Bayona, J. (2010). Multi-drug resistant and extensively drug-resistant tuberculosis: A threat to global control of tuberculosis. *Lancet, 375,* 1830–1843. doi: 10.1016/S0140-6736(10)60410-2

Glaziou, P., Floyd, K., Korenromp, E. L., Sismanidis, C., Bierrenbach, A. L., Williams, B. G., . . . Raviglione, M. (2011). Lives saved by tuberculosis control and prospects for achieving the 2015 global target for reducing tuberculosis mortality. *Bulletin of the World Health Organization, 89,* 573–582. doi: 10.2471/BLT.11.087510

Global HIV Prevention Working Group. (2009a). Proven HIV prevention strategies. Retrieved from http://www.globalhivprevention.org/pdfs/HIV_Prevention_Strategies_0604.pdf

Global HIV Prevention Working Group. (2009b). Global HIV prevention: The access, funding, and leadership gaps. Retrieved from http://www.globalhivprevention.org/pdfs/PWG_Access_Funding_and_Leadership_Gaps_Final.pdf

Government of Alberta, Health and Wellness. (2011). West Nile virus. Retrieved from http://www.health.alberta.ca/health-info/west-nile-virus.html

Gruskin, S., Ahmed, S., & Ferguson, L. (2008). Provider-initiated HIV testing and counseling in health facilities: What does this mean for the health and human rights of pregnant women? *Developing World Bioethics, 8*(1), 23–32. doi: 10.1111/j.1471-8847.2007.00222.x

Hasian, M. A. (2000). Power, medical knowledge, and the rhetorical invention of "Typhoid Mary." *Journal of Medical Humanities, 21*(3), 123–139. doi: 10.1023/A:1009074619421

Institute of Medicine. (2006). Preventing HIV infection among injection drug users in high risk countries. Retrieved from http://books.nap.edu/openbook.php?record_id=11731

Kamb, M. L., Newman, L. M., Riley, P. L., Mark, J., Hawkes, S., Malik, T., & Brooutet, N. (2010). A roadmap for the global elimination of congenital syphilis. *Obstetrics and Gynecology International.* doi: 10.155/2010/312798

Lavanchy, D. (2009). The global burden of hepatitis C. *Liver International, 29*(s1), 74–81. doi: 10.1111/j.1478-3231.2008.01934.x

Lim, S. M., Koraka, P., Osterhaus, A. D. M. E., & Martina, B. E. E. (2011). West Nile virus: Immunity and pathogenesis. *Viruses, 3,* 811–828. doi: 10.3390/v3060811

Lv, H., de Vlas, S. J., Liu, W., Wang, T., Cao, Z., Li, C., . . . Richardus, J. H. (2009). Avascular osteonecrosis after treatment of SARS: A 3-year longitudinal study. *Tropical Medicine and International Health, 14,* 79–84. doi: 10.1111/j.1365-3156.2008.02187.x

Magner, L. N. (2009). *A history of infectious diseases and the microbial world.* Westport, CT: Praeger.

Njeru, M. K., Blystad, A., Shayo, E. H., Nyamongo, I. K., & Fylkesnes, K. (2011). Practicing provider-initiated HIV testing in high prevalence settings: Consent concerns and missed preventive opportunities. *BMC Health Services Research, 11*(87). doi: doi:10.1186/1472-6963-11-87

Rangel, J. M., Sparling, P. H., Crowe, C., Griffin, P. M., & Swerdlow, D. L. (2004). Epidemiology of *Escherichia coli* O157:H7 outbreaks, United States, 1982–2002. *Emerging Infectious Diseases, 11*(4). Retrieved from http://wwwnc.cdc.gov/eid/article/11/4/04-0739.htm

Sanofi Pasteur. (2011). FDA licenses Sanofi Pasteur's new influenza vaccine delivered by intradermal micro-injection. Retrieved from http://sanofipasteurus.mediaroom.com/index.php?s=11069&item=34882

Schmid, G. O., Stoner, B. P., Hawkes, S., & Broutet, N. (2007). The need and plan for global elimination of congenital syphilis. *Sexually Transmitted Diseases, 34*(7), S5–S10. doi: 10.1097/01.olq.0000261456.09797.1b

Sen_a, A. C., White, B. L., & Sparling, P. F. (2010). Novel *Treponema pallidum* serologic tests: A paradigm shift in syphilis screening for the 21st century. *Clinical Infectious Diseases, 51*(6), 700–708. doi: 10.1086.655832

Sharapov, U. M. (2011). Infectious diseases related to travel: Hepatitis A. In G. W. Brunette (Ed.), *CDC health information for international travel 2012: The yellow book.* Retrieved from http://wwwnc.cdc.gov/travel/yellowbook/2012/chapter-3-infectious-diseases-related-to-travel/hepatitis-a.htm

Sharapov, U. M., & Hu, D. J. (2010). Viral hepatitis A, B, C: Grown-up issues. *Adolescent Medicine, 21*(2), 265–286.

Sherman, I. W. (2007). *Twelve diseases that changed our world.* Washington, DC: American Society of Microbiology Press.

Te, H. S., & Jensen, D. M. (2010). Epidemiology of hepatitis B and C: A global overview. *Clinics in Liver Disease, 14*(1), 1–21. doi: 10.1016/j.cld2—9.11.009

Tyagi, S., Kumar, S., & Singla, M. (2010). Clinical aspects of Ebola hemorrhagic fever: A review. *International Journal of Pharma and Bio Sciences, 1*(3), 1–9. Retrieved from http://www.ijpbs.net/issue-3/62.pdf

UNAIDS. (2010). UNAIDS global report on the global epidemic: 2010. Retrieved from http://www.unaids.org/globalreport/global_report.htm

USAID. (2009). Infectious diseases. Disease surveillance: Overview. Retrieved from http://www.usaid.gov/our_work/global_health/id/surveillance/#

Vong, S., Khieu, V., Glass, O., Ly, S., Duong, V., Huy, R., . . . Buchy, P. (2010). Dengue incidence in urban and rural Cambodia: Results from population-based active fever surveillance, 2006–2008. *PLoS Neglected Tropical Diseases, 4*(11), 1–10. Retrieved from http://www.plosntds.org/article/info%3Adoi%2F10.1371%2Fjournal.pntd.0000903

World Health Organization (WHO). (2003). Alert, verification and public health management of SARS in the post-outbreak period. Retrieved from http://www.who.int/csr/sars/postoutbreak/en/

World Health Organization (WHO). (2004). SARS risk assessment and preparedness framework. Retrieved from http://www.who.int/csr/resources/publications/CDS_CSR_ARO_2004_2.pdf

World Health Organization (WHO). (2005). Dengue, dengue haemorrhagic fever and dengue shock syndrome in the context of the integrated management of childhood illness. Retrieved from http://whqlibdoc.who.int/hq/2005/WHO_FCH_CAH_05.13_eng.pdf

World Health Organization (WHO). (2006a). Facts on ACTs (artemisinin-based combination therapies). Retrieved from http://www.rbm.who.int/cmc_upload/0/000/015/364/RBMInfosheet_9.htm

World Health Organization (WHO). (2006b). The stop TB strategy. Retrieved from http://www.who.int/tb/strategy/en/index.html

World Health Organization (WHO). (2007). The global elimination of congenital syphilis: Rationale and strategy for action. Retrieved from http://whqlibdoc.who.int/publications/2007/9789241595858_eng.pdf

World Health Organization (WHO). (2008a). Ebola haemorrhagic fever. Retrieved from http://www.who.int/mediacentre/factsheets/fs103/en/

World Health Organization (WHO). (2008b). Hepatitis A. Retrieved from http://www.who.int/mediacentre/factsheets/fs328/en/index.html

World Health Organization (WHO). (2008c). Hepatitis B. Retrieved from http://www.who.int/mediacentre/factsheets/fs204/en/index.html

World Health Organization (WHO). (2009a). Dengue and dengue haemorrhagic fever. Retrieved from http://www.who.int/mediacentre/factsheets/fs117/en/

World Health Organization (WHO). (2009b). H5N1 avian influenza: Timeline of major events. Retrieved from http://www.who.int/csr/disease/avian_influenza/Timeline_09_03_23.pdf

World Health Organization (WHO). (2009c). Influenza (seasonal). Retrieved from http://www.who.int/mediacentre/factsheets/fs211/en/index.html

World Health Organization (WHO). (2009d). Treatment of TB: Guidelines. Retrieved from http://whqlibdoc.who.int/publications/2010/9789241547833_eng.pdf

World Health Organization (WHO). (2010a). Malaria. Retrieved from http://www.who.int/mediacentre/factsheets/fs094/en/index.html

World Health Organization (WHO). (2010b). Use of influenza rapid diagnostic tests. Retrieved from http://whqlibdoc.who.int/publications/2010/9789241599283_eng.pdf

World Health Organization (WHO). (2010c). Global tuberculosis control 2010. Retrieved from http://whqlibdoc.who.int/publications/2010/9789241564069_eng.pdf

World Health Organization (WHO). (2010d). Antiretroviral therapy for HIV infection in adults and adolescents: Recommendations for a public health approach, 2010 revision. Retrieved from http://whqlibdoc.who.int/publications/2010/9789241599764_eng.pdf

World Health Organization (WHO), Global Health Observatory. (2011a). Causes of deaths in 2008. Retrieved from http://www.who.int/gho/mortality_burden_disease/causes_death_2008/en/index.html

World Health Organization (WHO). (2011b). Cholera. Retrieved from http://www.who.int/mediacentre/factsheets/fs107/en/index.html

World Health Organization (WHO). (2011c). Prevention and control of cholera outbreaks: WHO policy and recommendations. Retrieved from http://www.who.int/cholera/technical/prevention/control/en/

World Health Organization (WHO). (2011d). The Global Task Force on Cholera Control. Retrieved from http://www.who.int/cholera/en/

World Health Organization (WHO). (2011e). Dengue/dengue haemorrhagic fever. Retrieved from http://www.who.int/csr/disease/dengue/en/index.html

World Health Organization (WHO). (2011f). West Nile virus. Retrieved from http://www.who.int/mediacentre/factsheets/fs354/en/index.html

World Health Organization (WHO). (2011g). West Nile virus infection (WNV) in Europe. Retrieved from http://www.who.int/csr/don/2011_08_16/en/

World Health Organization (WHO). (2011h). Avian influenza. Retrieved from http://www.who.int/topics/avian_influenza/en/

World Health Organization (WHO). (2011i). Avian influenza. Retrieved from http://www.who.int/mediacentre/factsheets/avian_influenza/en/index.html

World Health Organization (WHO). (2011j). Ebola in Uganda. Retrieved from http://www.who.int/csr/don/2011_05_18/en/index.html

World Health Organization (WHO). (2011k). *Escherichia coli* infections. Retrieved from http://www.who.int/topics/escherichia_coli_infections/en/

World Health Organization (WHO). (2011l). Global alert and response. Retrieved from http://www.who.int/csr/disease/hepatitis/world_hepatitis_day/en/

World Health Organization (WHO). (2011m). Hepatitis C. Retrieved from http://www.who.int/mediacentre/factsheets/fs164/en/index.html

World Health Organization (WHO). (2011n). BCG: The current vaccine for tuberculosis. Retrieved from http://www.who.int/vaccine_research/diseases/tb/vaccine_development/bcg/en/

World Health Organization (WHO). (2011o). Global alert and response. Retrieved from http://www.who.int/csr/en/

World Health Organization & UNAIDS. (2007). Guidance on HIV testing and counseling in health facilities. Retrieved from http://whqlibdoc.who.int/publications/2007/9789241595568_eng.pdf

*For a full suite of assignments and additional learning activities, use the access code located in the front of your book to visit this exclusive website: **http://go.jblearning.com/holtz**. If you do not have an access code, you can obtain one at the site.*

8

HIV/AIDS, Stigma, and Disclosure: A Need for a Human Rights Perspective

Richard L. Sowell
Kenneth D. Phillips

> *"Living with all the infections, diarrhea, and physical pain of HIV/AIDS is overwhelming, but the emotional pain I experience when people find out I am HIV infected is almost worse than the physical pain of the disease"*
>
> (personal communication, April 13, 1994, cited in Sowell & Phillips, 2010).

OBJECTIVES

After completing this chapter, the reader will be able to:

1. Define stigma.
2. Discuss the historical evolution of the concept of HIV/AIDS stigma.
3. Identify the consequences of stigma on persons with HIV/AIDS and on society.
4. Identify the effects of prevention efforts on stigma and discrimination for HIV/AIDS.
5. Discuss the phenomenon of multiple stigma or layer stigma.
6. Discuss the relationships among stigma, discrimination, and disclosure in HIV/AIDS.
7. Compare the manifestations of HIV/AIDS stigma in resource-rich and resource-limited countries and regions.
8. Discuss HIV/AIDS stigma and discrimination in the context of a human rights framework.

Some content included in this chapter was previously published in: Sowell, R. L., & Phillips, K. D. (2010). Understanding and responding to HIV/AIDS stigma and disclosure: An international challenge for mental health nurses. *Issues in Mental Health Nursing, 31,* 394–402. Referenced and used with permission.

INTRODUCTION

Acquired immunodeficiency syndrome (AIDS) has reached pandemic levels worldwide (UNAIDS, 2007a). AIDS is the final stage of a protracted illness caused by the human immunodeficiency virus (HIV). HIV selectively attacks the immune system and, if unchecked, it completely destroys the T-helper lymphocytes, resulting in severe cellular immune deficiency. These lymphocytes are important in defending the body against a variety of pathogens, virally infected cells, and malignant cells.

Since it was first identified in the early 1980s (Centers for Disease Control and Prevention [CDC], 1981a, 1981b), HIV/AIDS has been associated with fear, progressive physical deterioration, and suffering resulting in death (Feller & Lemmer, 2007). Yet, despite the devastating physical manifestations for individuals infected with the virus, the consequences of HIV/AIDS are far more complex and far-reaching. Closely tied to HIV/AIDS is a secondary pandemic of stigma and discrimination that negatively affects persons with HIV/AIDS, their families and communities, and the global society (Bogart et al., 2008; Herek, Gillis, Glunt, Lewis, Welton, & Capitanio, 1998; Holzemer & Uys, 2004). Even in resource-rich countries where access to advanced treatments has resulted in HIV/AIDS becoming a more chronic disease, HIV/AIDS stigma and varying degrees of discrimination remain pervasive (Chandra, Deepthivarma, & Manjula, 2003; Dlamini et al., 2007; Herek, Capitanio, & Widaman, 2002; Kohi et al., 2006). Persons with HIV/AIDS, as well as persons associated with HIV-infected individuals, are routinely subjected to fear, rejection, ostracism, hostility, and potential physical and economic violence (Balabanova, Coker, Atun, & Drobniewski, 2006; Cao, Sullivan, Xu, Wu, & China CIPRA Project 2 Team, 2006; McNeil, 1998; Sowell, Seals, Moneyham, Guillory, & Mizuno, 1997).

The stigma associated with HIV/AIDS can have severe consequences both physically and psychologically for the person with HIV infection. Fear of rejection and social isolation are frequent outcomes of a known HIV/AIDS diagnosis (Bos, Kok, & Dijker, 2001; Carr & Gramling, 2004; Herek, Capitanio, & Widaman, 2003; Kilewo et al., 2001). Individuals can lose their housing, their employment, and social relationships if their HIV-infected status becomes known (Kohi et al., 2006; Lee, Wu, Rotheram-Borus, Detels, Guan, & Li, 2005). Research has demonstrated that HIV-related stigma and the discrimination that follows decrease quality of life (Fuster & Molero, 2010). In countries where health insurance exists, insurance and access to treatment are often linked to employment. Because of HIV/AIDS stigma and related discrimination, there are great incentives to keeping an HIV/AIDS diagnosis secret. A reluctance to disclose being HIV-infected in both resource-rich and resource-limited countries, as well as across cultures, has been well documented (Akani & Erhabor, 2006; Chandra et al., 2003; Gray, 1999; Kilewo et al., 2001). Such nondisclosure can have dire consequences for both the individual and society. When individuals are not willing to disclose their infection or even be tested for HIV infection, that factor limits their ability to access treatment and support (Allen et al., 2006; Anderson & Doyal, 2004; Carr & Gramling, 2004; Greeff & Phetlhu, 2007). Additionally, lack of willingness to disclose the presence of HIV infection can negatively affect HIV/AIDS prevention efforts both on individual and community levels (Babalola, 2007; Buseh & Stevens, 2006; Hasnain, 2005). Therefore, HIV/AIDS-related stigma and its related actions represent a psychosocially based pandemic that profoundly affects individuals and communities across cultures and feeds the ever-increasing global HIV/AIDS pandemic.

STIGMA

Stigma is a social phenomenon that has been defined as "an attribute that is deeply discrediting" (Goffman, 1963, p. 3). The standards by which individuals or groups are categorized as ordinary in the course of daily interactions are established by society and its related culture (Goffman, 1963). Stigma results when there is the presence of attributes that are not viewed as being within acceptable norms for an individual or a group. It denotes a difference or departure from the norm in a negative context. Such variance from normal expectations is frequently met with prejudice, discrimination, stereotyping, and distancing (Goffman, 1963; Jones, Farina, Hastorf, Markus, Miller, & Scott, 1984). Jones and associates (1984, p. 6) define individuals who are stigmatized as "the bearer of the 'mark' that indicates they are somehow deviant, flawed, spoiled, or generally undesirable." The ancient Greeks used the term "stigma" to refer to bodily signs designed to expose something unusual and bad about the moral status of the signifier. The sign (mark) was cut or burned into the body and advertised that the bearer was a slave, a criminal, or a traitor—that is, a blemished person, ritually polluted, to be avoided, especially in public places (Goffman, 1963, p. 1). Therefore, the basic concept of bearing the mark or being stigmatized has its origin in the very term "stigma."

The negative responses to individuals who are assessed as different or unworthy remain a reality and can be identified globally transcending cultures and geographic borders. The act of stigmatizing focuses on assigning blame to an individual or group, which not only allows for the discrediting and devaluing of an individual or a group, but also provides the basis for behaviors that would otherwise be unacceptable. By stigmatizing the individual or group, it becomes acceptable to blame the individual or group for processing the stigmatizing attribute, which in turn supports the concept of punishment (Abler, Henderson, Wang, & Avery, 2010; Laryea & Gien, 1993). Ekstrand, Bharatand, and Ramkrishna (2010) report that blame and inaccurate information concerning HIV/AIDS transmission were found to be associated with coercive public policies and intent to discriminate targeted persons living with HIV/AIDS (PLWHA).

Stigma is often rooted in fear, and it can validate avoidance, discrimination, and economic and social violence toward the stigmatized. Individuals and groups can be stigmatized for a variety of reasons, including lifestyle choices, physical characteristics, ethnic or racial group membership, socioeconomic status, and medical conditions. In examining stigma within the context of HIV/AIDS, it becomes clear that HIV/AIDS stigma is complex and multifaceted. HIV/AIDS stigma not only results from fear of a contagious, life-threatening illness, but also is layered with negative attitudes and beliefs toward groups or lifestyles believed to be associated with the disease (Logie, James, Tharao, & Loutfy, 2010).

HIV/AIDS STIGMA

Stigma and discrimination have been closely related with HIV infection since HIV/AIDS was first identified. Homosexual men, intravenous drug users, hemophiliacs, and people of color were the groups in whom HIV/AIDS was first recognized (CDC, 1981a, 1981b). These groups represent individuals who were the targets of stigma and discrimination prior to the advent of HIV/AIDS. Prior to the identification of its causative virus, HIV/AIDS was initially referred to by many as gay-related immune deficiency (GRID) or the "gay plague" (Shilts, 1987). The GRID designation for a new and deadly syndrome serves as evidence that individuals in the general society sought to place blame for the disease on a stigmatized group, as well as distance themselves from the disease and the deviant behavior that was proposed as the source of its spread. Sontag (1998) suggests that the term "plague" represents a metaphor that indicates that an illness is inflicted on a group and often is a punishment from "God." This idea that HIV/AIDS is a punishment from "God" transcends religions and represents a threat that facilitates discrimination against persons with HIV/AIDS, and also acts as a barrier to HIV/AIDS prevention efforts (Adebajo, Bamgbala, & Oyediran, 2003; Dorozynski, 1996; Hess & McKinney, 2007; Huy, Johansson, & Long, 2007; Kaldjian, Jekel, & Friedland, 1998; Kopelman, 2002; Odebiyi, 1992; Oorjitham, 1999; Wang, 1997). HIV/AIDS's association with gay men has transferred the negative attitudes toward homosexuality to a disease thought to be the result of immoral and deviant behavior of this group. Further, as the HIV/AIDS pandemic has evolved, the disease has become associated with other marginalized groups such as drug users, the poor, and people of color (Logie et al., 2010). The role of stigmatizing behaviors and attitudes is to distance oneself from the illness and its associated negative consequences and attributes, thereby supporting the contention that "those individuals with HIV/AIDS are different from me."

Although those individuals who contracted HIV infection through blood or blood component transfusions were not viewed as directly responsible for their infection (i.e., guilty of immoral behavior), these persons—especially hemophiliacs—were viewed as being flawed or were considered imperfect. Having a chronic health condition or illness predisposed these individuals to some level of stigma that was further compounded by a diagnosis of HIV/AIDS. Further, the rapid spread of HIV/AIDS among ethnic and racial minorities, people of color, and the poor continues to support the global stereotyping of persons with or at risk for HIV/AIDS as individuals and groups that are immoral, unworthy, devalued, and responsible for their disease (Balabanova et al., 2006; Cao et al., 2006; Muthuswamy, 2005; Pittam & Gallois, 1997; Rao, 2002). Such stigma can be so strong and pervasive that individuals who are HIV infected or who engage in high-risk behaviors may accept and internalize negative feelings and stereotypes, resulting in their feelings of unworth and shame (Goffman, 1963; Jones et al., 1984).

Petros and colleagues (2006) identified the concept that they called "othering" among South Africans. It was noted that blame for HIV/AIDS was most often imputed based on race, culture, homophobia, and xenophobia. Black Africans blamed whites, and whites blamed black Africans (Petros et al., 2006). HIV-infected women are viewed by some as sexually promiscuous, as loose, as prostitutes, and as dirty and immoral. Through this process of "gender othering," men absolve themselves from blame (Petros et al., 2006). Another means of distancing oneself from HIV/AIDS is by blaming "outsiders." In the Petros et al. study, for example, South African participants held people from Zimbabwe, Mozambique, and Botswana responsible for bringing HIV/AIDS disease to the people of South Africa.

The phenomenon of othering has been described in other cultures as well, and is often based on racism, sexism, or homophobia (Gilmore & Somerville, 1994; Singer, 1994; Ungphakorn & Sittitrai, 1994). Attributing negative attributes to others, as well as to individuals with HIV/AIDS, provides an excuse for majority groups, those with economic resources, and local, national, and international leaders to not fully engage in responding to the ever-growing HIV/AIDS pandemic.

While specific groups, lifestyles, and individual attributes may carry varying degrees of stigma within different cultures and geographic regions, HIV/AIDS stigma, in most cases, has an additive effect to stigma already experienced by individuals and groups experiencing the highest rates of HIV infection. This situation makes HIV/AIDS stigma and the resultant discrimination a complex phenomenon that can drastically increase the social isolation, physical pain, and psychological distress of individuals fighting to survive after a HIV/AIDS diagnosis. The complexity of such layered stigma and potential discrimination, in turn, influences the type and level of healthcare and support services that is required to adequately respond to the individual's situation and needs.

CHARACTERISTICS OF THE ILLNESS AND STIGMA

Jones and colleagues (1984) described six dimensions of stigma that determine the degree of stigma that is associated with a particular characteristic, as well as the ability to conceal or minimize stigma resulting from the characteristic. These dimensions are *concealability* (the degree to which the characteristic is hidden or obvious), *course* (the degree to which the change occurs over time and the ultimate outcome), *disruptiveness* (the degree to which the characteristic hampers communication), *aesthetic qualities* (the degree to which the characteristic makes the person repellent, ugly, or upsetting), *origin* (the degree to which the person is to blame for the characteristic), and *peril* (the degree of danger that results from the characteristic).

HIV/AIDS progresses through several stages, which over time, increasingly limits the person's ability to conceal the disease. *Stage 1,* the primary infection, may begin weeks or months after infection and lasts for approximately 1 to 2 weeks. This first stage of illness is characterized by flu-like or mononucleosis-like symptoms. Often HIV is overlooked as the diagnosis. Because no major symptoms are apparent during *Stage 2,* this phase is called the asymptomatic stage; it lasts for an average of 10 years. During the first two stages, HIV-infected persons may not know that they are infected. Moderate unexplained weight loss, recurrent respiratory infections, shingles, skin and nail lesions, and oral conditions may occur in this phase. Persistent generalized lymphadenopathy may begin in this phase as well.

In *Stage 3*, the symptomatic stage, immunity progressively declines and the person may begin to experience a variety of symptoms, such as severe weight loss (more than 10% of the total body weight), diarrhea, persistent fever, thrush, oral hairy leukoplakia, skin lesions, or mouth conditions that worsen over the course of time. Even during this stage, however, it is often possible for a person to hide the fact that he or she has HIV/AIDS, although nondisclosure becomes more difficult in the symptomatic stage. Thus, for the majority of the time that a person is living with HIV/AIDS, it is possible to conceal his or her illness.

In *Stage 4*, with a decline of the T-helper lymphocyte count to less than 200 cells/mm^3, the person advances to the stage known as AIDS, in which he or she suffers from a variety of opportunistic infections (e.g., *Pneumocystis jiroveci* pneumonia) and malignancies (e.g., Kaposi's sarcoma) that are very difficult to hide (Weeks & Alcamo, 2008; World Health Organization [WHO], 2005).

Not only does the increasing symptomatology of HIV infection identify an individual as having HIV/AIDS, thereby subjecting the person to the overall stigma associated with the disease, but many of the symptoms exhibited (wasting syndrome, profound diarrhea, and open lesions) can, in themselves, also result in distancing and social isolation. Examining the continuum of symptoms and opportunistic infections resulting from HIV/AIDS in relation to Jones et al.'s (1984) dimensions that determine the degree of stigma, it is easily seen that characteristics of HIV/AIDS support the severe stigmatization of individuals contracting the illness. HIV progression and resultant symptoms makes *concealing* HIV/AIDS almost impossible. A number of physical symptoms cause a change in physical appearance, making the individual *unattractive or repellent*. HIV/AIDS remains a life-threatening illness that across its *course* adversely affects physical and psychological well-being, *disrupting* social relationships and quality of life. Individuals with HIV/AIDS are in *peril* of facing psychological stress and physical deterioration.

Collectively, these factors make HIV/AIDS one of the most stigmatizing illnesses in history. HIV/AIDS is an illness that has devastating consequences for PLWHA, their families, communities, and society.

CONSEQUENCES OF HIV/AIDS STIGMA

The global response to HIV/AIDS can be said to represent discrimination and devaluing of the "humanness" of the poor and the disenfranchised. HIV/AIDS is most frequently transmitted through heterosexual sex and places the greatest hardship on women and children (UNAIDS, 2008c; UNICEF, 2006).

The diminished rights of women and young girls is a major factor in fueling the continued spread of HIV/AIDS on a worldwide basis (Kehler, 2010; Kehler & Crone, 2010; Moreno, 2007; Nyanzi, 2010). In some regions, women can be considered property and are subjected to the will of men (Foster, Makufa, Drew, Kambeu, & Saurombe, 1997; Mendenhall et al., 2007; Seeley, Grellier, & Barnett, 2004). In some African cultures, a woman becomes the property of a male member of her husband's family if her husband dies. She has no rights to her husband's property and is often expected to become sexually active with the male relative who inherits her (Nyanzi, 2010). In countries such as Nepal, the spread of HIV/AIDS can be related to the trafficking of young girls to Indian brothels (Kaiser, 2000; Miramontes, 2000), while African girls frequently become HIV infected between the ages of 15 and 19 years of age. In both of these examples, young girls become HIV infected as a result of sexual exploitation.

Globally, more than 15 million children are believed to have been orphaned by HIV/AIDS (UNAIDS, 2008a). These children live in a variety of settings, ranging from the streets of large cities to orphanages. Children who have been orphaned as a result of their parents dying from AIDS suffer the triple stigma of an association with parents who died because of their "immoral behavior," the fear that the children may carry HIV infection, and their status as "the poorest of the poor" (Coursen-Neff, 2004; UNAIDS, 2004;

UNICEF, 2006). The result of such stigma and discrimination is that the vast majority of AIDS orphans are viewed as "throwaway children" and left to fend for themselves. This situation promotes sexual exploitation of both young boys and girls and further spread of HIV infection within communities (Sowell & Phillips, 2010, pp. 395–396; Wenani, 2010).

In Latin cultures, a major influence in the lives of women is machismo, which refers to male dominant behavior and excessive masculinity. In Mexico, machismo essentially defines the father of the family as the head of the household, who is often feared by both the wife and children. The wife is expected to handle childrearing and household responsibilities without questioning her husband's authority (Galanti, 2003; Moreno, 2007). A study of Mexican migrant workers (Sowell, Holtz, & Velasquez, 2008) found that women were willing to accept unrealistic explanations of how their husbands contracted HIV as a strategy to maintain their families and avoid conflict. In many resource-limited countries, women's dependence on men is formalized in culture and/or law (UNAIDS, 2004). Of course, this dominance of men over their female partners is not limited to Latin cultures. The societal view of women as family caregivers and as submissive to their husbands is prevalent in many cultures and regions of the world (Anderson, 2010; Beaulleu, Adrien, & Lebounga Vouma, 2010; Pharris, Tishelman, Huyen, Chuc, & Thorson, 2010). Research findings revealed that even in the United States women often remain in relationships where their partners put them at risk for HIV/AIDS. Women reported feelings of dependence on the male partner and needing him to provide for them and/or their children (Moser, Sowell, & Phillips, 2001; Sowell, Phillips, Seals, Murdaugh, & Rush, 2002; Timmons & Sowell, 1999). Yet, despite the lack of status of many women and the unequaled hardship that HIV/AIDS has placed on women, women have frequently been the innovators in taking leadership in community development efforts around HIV/AIDS care and prevention (Demarco, Lynch, & Board, 2002; McGovern, 2006; Romero, Wallerstein, Lucero, Fredine, Keefe, & O'Connell, 2006; Sowell et al., 2002).

Globally, fear, prejudice, and misinformation related to HIV/AIDS, and the way in which the infection is transmitted and prevented, continue to be widespread and form the basis for stigma, discrimination, and punitive behaviors (Ekstrand et al., 2010; Herek, 1999; Kehler & Crone, 2010; Mykhalovskiy, 2010). In Western countries, stigma and discrimination associated with HIV/AIDS have generally become somewhat more subtle, but remain a significant challenge for PLWHA and those associated with HIV/AIDS (Blake, Jones Taylor, Reid, & Kosowski, 2008; Mann, Tarantola, & Netter, 1992). Both the United States and Canada have enacted legislative protections for person with HIV/AIDS (Elliott & Gold, 2005). Nevertheless, such legislative actions were not instigated until a number of high-profile cases occurred in which individuals experienced extreme consequences because they were believed to have HIV/AIDS or were at high risk for the disease (Botnick, 2000; Sowell & Phillips, 2010, p. 396).

Even where such protection has been enacted, punitive sanctions or restrictions have sometimes been placed on persons with HIV/AIDS (Lambda Legal, 2009; Liski, 1998). For example, it was not until 2010 that the United States lifted travel restrictions targeting potential visitors with HIV/AIDS (Oh, 2010). Despite WHO's declaration that travel restrictions and sanctions against persons with HIV/AIDS are not effective, 66 countries maintain their restrictions on HIV-infected persons entering and/or residing in their countries, thereby targeting noncitizens with HIV/AIDS. Additionally, migrants and refugees who test HIV seropositive frequently face governmental-level discrimination and deportation (Human Rights Watch, 2009). Governments that take immigration detainees into custody have the obligation to ensure that those detainees receive adequate medical care that is equivalent to the care available to the general population during the resolution of their cases. For detainees who have HIV/AIDS, evidence indicates that systems are not in place to ensure adequate treatment of their disease (Human Rights Watch, 2004, 2007). Migrant workers and refugees fleeing political persecution or war, for example, represent not just the most vulnerable members of society, but also the groups at high risk for HIV infection and/or need for treatment.

In reality, HIV/AIDS stigma and discrimination are not limited to noncitizens. Verbal and physical abuse (beatings), including denial of food and basic care, remain a consequence of being identified as having HIV/AIDS in a number of countries (Abler et al., 2010; Tran Huy & Nguyen, 2010). In recent years, there has been an increase in the criminalization of groups or behaviors associated with HIV/AIDS (Galletly & Pinkerton, 2004; Lambda Legal, 2002; Liski, 1998), even though there is no evidence that criminalization of behaviors is an effective deterrent to the spread of HIV/AIDS. Numerous international groups have expressed human rights concerns about the effects of such criminalization and efforts to prevent the spread of HIV/AIDS (Kazatchkine, 2010; UNICEF, 2010). It is likely that such criminalization will disproportionately affect women including sex workers, drug users, and men who have sex with men, resulting in these marginalized groups retreating further underground—thereby decreasing their access to prevention efforts, leading them to avoid HIV testing and treatment, and increasing the likelihood of the spread of HIV infection (Baral et al., 2010; Horter, Nkhoma, Baradaran, Baggaley, & Stedwick, 2010; Molina & Lainez, 2010; Poteat et al., 2010; Thomas, Lalu, Mukambetov, Odhiambo, & Williams, 2010).

DISCLOSURE

HIV testing has been touted as one of the most important strategies in the prevention of HIV transmission (Thompson et al., 2010). Nevertheless, a raft of consequences must be considered in "testing," including the ability to keep test results confidential and manage the disclosure of an HIV seropositive result. Knowing one's HIV status and sharing an HIV seropositive status is important for a number of reasons, including the need to access health care and social support services. The advances made in treatment of HIV infection in recent years allow individuals who have access to appropriate antiretroviral therapy to remain healthy and slow the progression of their illness (Thompson et al., 2010). Additionally, research findings indicate that persons with HIV/AIDS who receive social support and/or mental health services have more positive outcomes (Andrews, 1995; Black, Nair, & Harrington, 1994; Moneyham, Hennessy, Sowell, Demi, Seals, & Mizuno, 1998). A second potential outcome that supports the value of disclosure is the ability to negotiate with potential sex partners, thereby making the implementation of "safe sex" strategies more likely and preventing HIV transmission. For individuals who have decided to publicly disclose their HIV status, such disclosures can provide the foundation for an open dialogue within communities that can support a change of social norms that demonize and discriminate against persons with HIV/AIDS (Macintyre et al., 2004).

Disclosure of an HIV seropositive status is a serious step, and one that should be thoughtfully considered and based on factual information. The stigma and potential discrimination associated with HIV/AIDS make the disclosure of being HIV positive a complex and risky decision. Factors that may influence the decision to disclose and the response to such disclosure can include culture, access to HIV/AIDS treatment, region, community size, beliefs about HIV/AIDS, and economic considerations (Hossain, Islam, Islam, & Kabir, 2010; Ibekwe & Agbo, 2010; Muchenje et al., 2010; Pedrotti, Bishop, & Dunhma, 2010; Tenkorang, Obeng-Gyimah, Maticka-Tyndale, & Adjei, 2010). Numerous researchers have documented that the fear of being stigmatized and facing discrimination is a primary factor that prevents many individuals from accessing HIV testing and counseling services, as well as disclosing their status when HIV infection is identified (Adeneye et al., 2006; Akani & Erhabor, 2006; Brown, Macintyre, & Trujillo, 2003; Parker & Aggleton, 2003; UNAIDS, 2003). For women, this fear may be compounded by concerns that their families, especially children, will be stigmatized or face discrimination (Moneyham et al., 1998; UNAIDS, 2004). Until HIV/AIDS stigma and its consequences are effectively addressed, it is likely that the secrecy surrounding and HIV/AIDS diagnosis will continue to fuel the pandemic.

One of the key concepts related to disclosure of HIV infection is that of "damage control." As well as managing the disease itself, individuals with HIV/AIDS have to manage the concern regarding who knows about their HIV infection (Bairan, Taylor, Blake, Akers, Sowell, & Mediola, 2007; Moneyham, Seals, Demi, Sowell, Cohen, & Guillory, 1996; Sowell, Seals, Phillips, & Julious, 2003). Disclosure of a HIV/AIDS diagnosis is not an "all or nothing" decision, but rather a series of decisions about to how to disclose, to whom, and when to disclose. Trust issues and concerns about confidentiality are paramount in deciding to whom to disclose this status. Lazarus and Folkman's (1984) theory of stress and coping provides a framework for HIV/AIDS disclosure decision making. In this framework, HIV-infected individuals cognitively assess the potential value of disclosing their HIV-positive status against the potential negative consequences that may result from disclosure. Based on the outcome of this evaluation, disclosure either will or will not occur. It is well documented that PLWHA frequently disclose their HIV infection to some groups, such as healthcare workers and sex partners, while not disclosing this information to some members of their family, friends, and casual acquaintances (Bairan et al., 2007; Sowell & Phillips, 2010, p. 397; Sowell et al., 2003).

Sowell and associates (2003), in a study of women with HIV/AIDS, found that participants in their study had specific criteria for deciding to whom to disclose their infection. These criteria were based on one or more factors that included the following: (1) their relationship to the individuals to whom they disclosed (healthcare provider, sex partner, or family member); (2) the quality of their relationship with the individual (accepting versus rejecting); and (3) the perceived ability or likelihood of the other person to keep the information confidential. Even then, many individuals report that disclosing their HIV infection is based on a "need to know" basis. This can result in partial disclosure to healthcare providers, employers, and family, based on the assessment of whether there is any reason for that individual to know about their HIV infection. Therefore, an individual with HIV infection who is seeing a healthcare provider who is not treating him or her for an HIV-related condition and/or will not be placed at risk of contracting the virus as a result of the care delivered, may not be informed that the individual is HIV infected. Likewise, insisting on condom use during casual sexual encounters may be used by PLWHA to prevent HIV transmission rather than telling the sex partner that they are HIV infected. This selective disclosure is an important aspect of managing the disclosure experience and limiting the negative consequences that can result from becoming known as having HIV/AIDS (Sowell & Phillips, 2010, p. 398).

Bairan and associates (2007) proposed a model of selective disclosure of HIV status based on the quality of relationships. This model identifies two primary types of relationships that influence disclosure decisions: sexual relationships and nonsexual relationships. The second tenet of the model is the concept that the attributes of the relationship (quality of the relationship, the level of intimacy in the relationship, and the length of the relationship) significantly influence the likelihood of disclosure or nondisclosure. This model may be useful in understanding factors that influence disclosure, thereby helping healthcare and social services providers to assist and support PLWHA in their disclosure decisions. Nevertheless, a question remains about the responsibility of healthcare and social services providers who are aware of an individual's nondisclosure of his or her HIV infection to inform or protect those who are being placed at risk. There is obviously no easy answer to this ethical dilemma. The obligation to maintain confidentiality must be weighed against the potential harm that may result from nonintervention, as well as the question of whether breaking confidentiality will actually prevent harm or result in even greater negative consequences. A harm reduction framework may be helpful to healthcare and social services providers in determining the most effective way to meet their professional standards while maintaining the confidentiality and trust of clients. The philosophical perspective of that framework supports actions that decrease the negative outcomes of a situation without having to eliminate all negative results, which is often unrealistic (Hasnain, 2005; Riley & O'Hare, 2000).

Clearly, supportive strategies that assist HIV-infected individuals to disclose their status, as well as community development efforts that change attitudes related to HIV stigma and discrimination, offer the greatest promise for positive outcomes. Despite the continued pandemic of stigma and discrimination targeting PLWHA, a limited number of research-based interventions have proved successful in decreasing HIV/AIDS stigma and facilitating dialogue concerning HIV/AIDS, including personal disclosure of HIV status. **Table 8-1** provides an overview of interventions that have been tested to reduce stigma and promote disclosure at the individual level, the specific group level, and the community/societal level (Sowell & Phillips, 2010, pp. 398–400).

TABLE 8-1

Examples of Interventions and Strategies to Reduce the Stigma of HIV/AIDS

Type and Levels of the Intervention/Strategy	Intervention/Strategy Description	Results	Reference
Issue Addressed: Stigma **Type:** Educational intervention **Primary Level:** Individual **Secondary Level:** Group	**Sample:** 217 mothers participating in a WIC program. **Purpose:** To compare a videotape and a one-on-one, face-to-face educational intervention to improve attitudes toward PLHWA.	At the first post-test, both experimental groups showed higher tolerance for PLWHA when compared to the control group. By the second post-test, the tolerance level for PLWHA was the same for all three groups. The results suggested that both interventions were successful in this sample.	Ashworth, DuRant, Gaillard, & Rountree, 1994
Issue Addressed: Stigma **Type:** Media simulation **Primary Level:** Individual **Secondary Level:** Group	**Sample:** 96 young women enrolled in an introductory psychology course. **Purpose:** To test whether a mock pilot radio broadcast could increase empathy toward PLWHA. The broadcast consisted of testimonials by a female PLWHA who had acquired HIV through either a blood transfusion (victim not responsible) or through sexual behavior (victim responsible).	The empathy scores were higher in the high-empathy group than in the low-empathy group. The empathy scores were higher for the victim-not- responsible group than for the victim-responsible group. The results demonstrated that inducing empathy for a stigmatized individual can also induce empathy for a stigmatized group.	Batson et al., 1997
Issue Addressed: Stigma **Type:** Role-play. The intervention compared two role-playing strategies (improvisational or controlled role play) **Primary Level:** Individual	**Sample:** 53 psychology students and volunteers, of whom 22 were men and 31 were women. **Purpose:** To reduce AIDS anxiety/fear and to improve attitudes toward PLWHA.	Participants in the improvisational groups reported a more positive attitude toward PLWHA and were more willing to grant rights to PLWHA. However, the intervention did not reduce fear. Stronger role-play effects were seen when the experimenter was the same gender as the participants.	Bean, Keller, Newburg, & Brown, 1989

(continues)

TABLE 8-1

Examples of Interventions and Strategies to Reduce the Stigma of HIV/AIDS *(continued)*

Type and Levels of the Intervention/Strategy	Intervention/Strategy Description	Results	Reference
Issue Addressed: Stigma **Type:** Multi-method educational intervention. An HIV/AIDS education intervention was delivered in six weekly sessions. Each session included lectures, film, role-plays, stories, songs, debates, and essays. **Primary Level:** Individual **Secondary Level:** Group	**Sample:** 240 secondary school students in urban Ibadan, Nigeria. **Purpose:** To improve knowledge, attitudes, and behaviors of secondary school students.	Students in the intervention group were more likely to be tolerant of PLWHA when compared to controls.	Fawole, Asuzu, Oduntan, & Brieger, 1999
Issue Addressed: Stigma **Type:** Multi-method intervention. The intervention combined factual information, student-created posters, songs, poetry, small-group discussions, plays, and role-play. **Primary Level:** Individual **Secondary Level:** Group	**Sample:** 814 students who were recruited from two school districts in Tanzania. **Purpose:** The purpose was to test the effectiveness of an educational program to reduce children's risk of HIV infections and to improve their tolerance of and willingness to care for a PLWHA.	Attitudes toward PLWHA significantly improved in the treatment group, when compared to the control group.	Klepp, Ndeki, Leshabari, Hannan, & Lyimo, 1997
Issue Addressed: Stigma **Type:** Acceptance by high-profile Individuals. **Primary Level:** Societal	**Target Population:** The country of Cambodia. **Purpose:** Cambodian Prince Ranariddh gave flowers to a PLWHA at a national AIDS conference to demonstrate care and compassion for a PLWHA.	Anecdotal evidence shows a reduction in stigma.	Busza, 2001

TABLE 8-1

Examples of Interventions and Strategies to Reduce the Stigma of HIV/AIDS *(continued)*

Type and Levels of the Intervention/Strategy	Intervention/Strategy Description	Results	Reference
Issue Addressed: Stigma **Type:** Emotional writing disclosure **Primary Level:** Individual	**Sample:** 11 HIV-positive women living in a large metropolitan area. **Purpose:** The researchers tested the effects of an emotional writing disclosure intervention on stigma and other health outcomes. Participants were asked to write for 20 minutes on 3 consecutive days about their deepest thoughts and feelings about the most traumatic event they ever experienced.	This pilot study tested the feasibility and acceptability of this intervention. In this small sample, the researchers found that stigma scores increased for the control group and decreased for the experimental group. The changes did not achieve significance.	Abel, Rew, Gortner, & Delville, 2004
Issue Addressed: Stigma **Type:** Community participatory intervention **Primary Level:** Community/societal	**Sample:** 199 PLWHA, 31 caregivers, and 195 randomly selected community members who were heads of household. **Purpose:** To test an intervention developed from a community participatory perspective and process.	A significant reduction in HIV/AIDS stigma scores was observed for the intervention group when compared to the control group.	Apinundecha, Laohasiriwong, Cameron, & Lim, 2007
Issue Addressed: Stigma **Type:** Sex workers were trained as peer educators and workshops were offered on self-care **Primary Level:** Individual **Secondary Level:** Group	**Sample:** The sample included women, men, and transsexual sex workers. **Purpose:** To describe educational interventions presented in two programs: "In the Battle for Health" and "Get Friendly with Her."	Anecdotal evidence shows a reduction in stigma	Chacham, Diniz, Maia, Galati, & Mirim, 2007

(continues)

TABLE 8-1

Examples of Interventions and Strategies to Reduce the Stigma of HIV/AIDS *(continued)*

Type and Levels of the Intervention/Strategy	Intervention/Strategy Description	Results	Reference
Issue Addressed: Stigma **Type:** Diffusion of positive messages about HIV/AIDS such as (1) advocating for universal precautions, (2) advocating that PLWHA receive the same level of care as everyone else, (3) advocating that PLWHA should not be discriminated against, and (4) advocating for protecting the confidentiality of PLWHA. **Primary Level:** Group **Secondary Level:** Community/society	**Sample:** Healthcare providers currently working at 89 general healthcare facilities. **Purpose:** To describe characteristics of popular opinion leaders and investigate factors associated with the diffusion of AIDS care messages by healthcare providers.	Female providers, members of the Han ethnic group, providers with less education, personnel at larger provincial hospitals, and personnel with HIV training were more likely to diffuse positive messages about HIV/AIDS.	Li, Cao, Wu, Wu, & Xiao, 2007

Sources: Brown, Macintyre, & Trujillo, 2003; Busza, 2001.

HUMAN RIGHTS FRAMEWORK

There is a growing call for the response to HIV/AIDS as well as other public health issues to be addressed within the context of a human rights framework. This perspective was highlighted by the theme of the 2010 International AIDS Conference: "Rights Here, Right Now." This titling of the conference represented the explicit declaration of the International AIDS Society of the global need to bring attention to the disregard for basic human rights that fuels the spread of HIV/AIDS, as well as issues related to the allocation of resources, access to preventive education, access to treatment, and ability of PLWHA to live their lives with dignity, free of stigma and discrimination. Worldwide, PLWHA or those who represent groups at high risk for HIV infection (i.e., males having sex with males, sex workers, drug users, migrants, refugees) have not just faced stigma and discrimination, but have actually been criminalized. Criminalizing behaviors (and individuals) that are viewed as immoral has frequently been a strategy applied to control the spread of HIV/AIDS. In reality, however, evidence consistently shows that such strategies have not been effective in promoting public health, but instead have fueled the spread of HIV infection by driving such behaviors underground and decreasing potential access to HIV prevention information and programs (UNAIDS, 2008b).

In the closing session of the 2010 International AIDS Conference, Barrett (2010), in summarizing the research and programmatic presentation related to human rights and HIV/AIDS, proposed that human rights represent a necessary framework to inform any effective public health program. Some have been argued that, to protect the masses, individual rights may have to be suspended (Human Rights

Watch, 2008). We would propose that the suspension of individual rights is a short-sighted strategy, and that the appropriate approach is based on a respect of individual and group human rights. This view challenges practitioners and policy makers to find a balanced approach that engages at-risk individuals or targeted groups in determining effective solutions. It is important to be clear about the public health objective that is trying to be achieved. The goal of public health is to decrease the spread of disease in populations; it is not to stigmatize, disenfranchise, or criminalize individuals or groups. The failure of such a punitive approach can be easily seen in the failure of criminalization of drug use, sex work, and same-sex sexual relationships to deter or eliminate these behaviors or the negative health risks associated with these behaviors. To the contrary, research shows that positive health and societal outcomes can be effectively achieved by respecting the individual's right to self-determination and engaging individuals in finding solutions to negative outcomes such as the spread of HIV/AIDS (UNAIDS, 2010). Jonathan Mann, WHO Director (as cited in Beyrer & Pizer, 2000), proposed that health and human rights (incorrectly) have rarely been linked in an explicit manner. Building on the framework of explicitly linking human rights and public health provided by Mann, there has been recognition that human rights and the concept of human dignity must be at the center of any response to any major public health challenge (Rubenstein, 2000).

It may be important for the reader of this chapter to engage in values clarification. Do individuals have the right to self-determination, the right to have access to health education and medical treatment and/or nursing care? Is freedom to live without fear of stigma, discrimination, and violence a right that should be expected and protected? What, if any, obligation do resource-rich countries and governments have to respond to disease and poverty in resource-limited regions? Acknowledging the overwhelming data that link HIV/AIDS-related stigma, discrimination, and punitive sanctions to the spread of HIV infection (UNAIDS, 2007b, 2008c), does the need to stigmatize and isolate those who are viewed as "other" serve the global public health? When prejudice, moral intolerance, and fear interfere with public policy, the result will consistently be increased morbidity and mortality. The HIV/AIDS pandemic may well have provided the definitive exemplar of this linkage and underscores the need for a reconceptualization of the relationship between human rights, human dignity, and health policy and practice.

CONCLUSION

In this chapter, the authors have provided a global overview of stigma and discrimination and the devastating consequences of stigma at both individual and societal levels. While the focus of the chapter is on HIV/AIDS-related stigma and its consequences, it provides insight into the sources and effects of stigma that can be applied internationally to a large number of stigmatizing conditions, including illness, economic status, gender, sexual orientation, and any physical or psychological trait or characteristic that makes a person different or deviates from the norm. HIV/AIDS can be seen as representing a model case of stigma and resulting discrimination that, in reality, encompasses a variety of conditions. HIV/AIDS-related discrimination is a complex phenomenon that is rooted in fear of a life-threatening disease and deviation from social standards or codes.

This chapter has also provided an overview of selected strategies that have been used globally to combat HIV/AIDS stigma and to support appropriate HIV/AIDS disclosure across a variety of cultures and settings. The authors propose that HIV/AIDS and their related stigma and discrimination may be best viewed in a human rights context. They challenge the reader to explore how HIV/AIDS stigma can be layered on other stigmatizing traits or conditions to form the basis for discrimination. Additionally, the authors suggest that freedom from stigma and discrimination and access to health care are basic human rights; public health strategies should be based on a balance between social welfare and respect for individual human rights.

STUDY QUESTIONS

1. Why do stigma and discrimination continue to be a challenge for HIV/AIDS patients and their families?
2. What remedies to you suggest for decreasing HIV/AIDS stigma and discrimination.
3. Name five reasons why HIV/AIDS patients hesitate to disclose their diagnosis.

CASE STUDY: STIGMA AND DISCRIMINATION

The XIII International AIDS Conference was held in Durban, South Africa, during July 2000. This conference was significant for a number of reasons, including the fact that it marked the first time that the International AIDS Conference had been held in the southern hemisphere in a region that has been disproportionately affected by the HIV/AIDS epidemic. As delegates (scientists, HIV/AIDS care/service providers, researchers, educators, political and public figures, and persons living with HIV/AIDS) arrived in Durban, a renewed sense of challenge surrounded this conference that hosted more than 12,000 delegates. I (Sowell) had the privilege of being one of those delegates. There was an understanding that the conference would profoundly affect the region by focusing attention on HIV/AIDS, bringing it out of the shadows and confronting the devastating stigma and discrimination associated with HIV/AIDS in much of the world. To that end, the theme of the XIII International AIDS Conference was "Breaking the Silence." This theme sought to encourage persons infected and affected with HIV/AIDS to speak out and educate their communities concerning persons with HIV/AIDS and the transmission of the virus. Testing and counseling have long been important strategies in preventing the spread of HIV infection. However, being diagnosed with HIV/AIDS carries many social consequences that can be increased if this diagnosis becomes known. To openly admit to being HIV infected in many regions of the world can lead to physical danger from violence, as well as social isolation, rejection, and discrimination. This situation weighed heavy on the minds of the delegates to the XIII International AIDS Conference, in light of the murder of a South African woman in December 1998 after she publicly revealed that she was HIV infected.

Gugu Dlamini was a 36-year-old, single mother living in KwaMashu, KwaZulu Natal. Unlike the conference delegates, who enjoyed the nice hotels and conference center of Durban, Gugu lived in a poor township in KwaZulu Natal. Wilson (2000) reported that "the poverty in KwaMashu attacks the soul" (p. 1). It is a place of pain and despair where the devastation and silence surrounding HIV/AIDS add to the misery of the people. The vast majority of black South Africans live in poverty and in townships that surround major urban centers. While Gugu Dlamini was honored as a hero in the fight to decrease the ignorance and fear surrounding HIV/AIDS in resource-limited regions of the world, her brutal murder provided evidence that the stigma of HIV/AIDS can be fatal.

In 1998, the South African National Association of People Living with HIV or AIDS and the KwaZulu Natal Department of Health encouraged persons with HIV/AIDS to disclose their HIV infection and urged local communities to become informed and to accept their neighbors. Gugu Dlamini became a volunteer in the provincial Department of Health Campaign (Beat It, 2011; McNeil, 1998). She publicly acknowledged her HIV infection to the press and worked to support others to disclose their own illness in an acceptance

CASE STUDY: STIGMA AND DISCRIMINATION

campaign in her township. She was one of the brave individuals who were willing to break the silence surrounding HIV/AIDS in an effort to try to make things better (South African Government Information, 1998). It is often women who step to the forefront in responding to HIV/AIDS, both by disclosing their own HIV status and by working to support and educate their communities. Over time, Gugu evolved into an outspoken AIDS activist. She began to meet and support other persons with HIV/AIDS in her township and believed that disclosure would be beneficial to her and to her community. However, she did not receive the support of her neighbors, but rather was the target of threats. Her family reported that Gugu often called them crying, saying that she was being threatened and people were coming for her. Many people in the community believed that she had brought shame on the community and that her openness about her HIV status would negatively affect the community, as other community members would be viewed as likely having the disease. Jabulani, Gugu's boyfriend, reported that people did not like her and were afraid for her to touch them or even drink with them (Beat It, 2011).

Gugu reported that she was threatened repeatedly. On December 12, 1998, she was attacked twice. In the afternoon, a man struck her and threatened her. Witnesses to the assault reported the incident to the local police, but they did nothing. Gugu was reported to be afraid to go home alone and went to a local *shebeen* (tavern) to tell people about the incident and publicly identified the man who had attacked her. Later that evening, Gugu was confronted by a man about her disclosure of her HIV status in the shebeen. She was dragged outside and beaten to unconsciousness by men from the community (McNeil, 1998). It was reported that after the men had beaten Gugu to unconsciousness, they sent a note to her boyfriend: "You can come fetch your dog. We are finished with her." It took four hours for an ambulance to come to take Gugu to the hospital where she died (Beat It, 2011). While many members of the community know who attacked and killed Gugu Dlamini, there has been little follow-up by the local police. Her family has been threatened, and many who might speak out about this murder fear for their own safety (Beat It; Wilson, 2000).

However, Gugu's legacy did not end in KwaMashu, KwaZulu Natal, on the evening of December 12, 1998. Gugu became a symbol of the potential extreme psychosocial and physical consequences related to the stigma and discrimination associated with HIV/AIDS. Her murder forced AIDS activists both in South Africa and globally to reevaluate their strategies in addressing HIV/AIDS stigma and related discrimination. Gugu represents only one of the many individuals who have suffered and died due to ignorance and stigma related to HIV/AIDS globally. Her death underscored and provided new urgency to the XIII International AIDS Conference theme of time to *Break the Silence*.

Case Study Questions

1. Was Gugu Dlamini's public disclosure of her HIV-positive status worth the outcome for herself, her family, her community, and her country? Why or why not?
2. What responsibility do the organizations and groups that encouraged Gugu Dlamini to disclose her HIV-positive status have in her death?
3. Is disclosure of stigmatizing conditions always the best step to take? What are the advantages and disadvantages of such disclosure?

(continues)

CASE STUDY: STIGMA AND DISCRIMINATION *(continued)*

4. Discuss why women are more likely to respond to educate and address HIV/AIDS in their communities than men. Why was it men in this case study who instituted the violence against Gugu Dlamini?
5. Could (has) such terrible violence seen in the Gugu case study occur (occurred) in more resource-rich countries such as the United States and Europe?
6. Which types of discrimination and stigmatizing acts do persons living with HIV/AIDS continue to encounter today in different regions of the world?
7. What are the human rights implications of a woman being killed by her neighbors for disclosing her HIV/AIDS status? Why was no one willing to protect her? Would this situation have been different if Gugu had been a man?
8. What have you done in your community to ensure that persons with stigmatizing conditions do not face discrimination, including violence?

REFERENCES

Abel, E., Rew, L., Gortner, E. M., & Delville, C. L. (2004). Cognitive reorganization and stigmatization among persons with HIV. *Journal of Advanced Nursing, 47*(5), 510–525. Retrieved from PM:15312114

Abler, L., Henderson, G., Wang, X., & Avery, M. (2010). Factors associated with HIV stigma in an urban area in China: Results from the 2008 population survey [Abstract TUPE0565]. *Proceedings of the XVIII International AIDS Conference: Rights Here, Right Now.* Vienna, Austria.

Adebajo, S. B., Bamgbala, A. O., & Oyediran, M. A. (2003). Attitudes of health care providers to persons living with HIV/AIDS in Lagos State, Nigeria. *African Journal of Reproductive Health, 7*(1), 103–112. Retrieved from PM:12816317

Adeneye, A. K., Brieger, W. R., Mafe, M. A., Adeneye, A. A., Salami, K. K., Titiloye, M. A., . . . Agomo, P. U. (2006). Willingness to seek HIV testing and counseling among pregnant women attending antenatal clinics in Ogun State, Nigeria. *International Quarterly of Health Education, 26*(4), 337–353. Retrieved from PM:17890180

Akani, C. I., & Erhabor, O. (2006). Rate, pattern and barriers of HIV serostatus disclosure in a resource-limited setting in the Niger delta of Nigeria. *Tropical Doctor, 36*(2), 87–89. Retrieved from PM:16611440

Allen, C. F., Edwards, M., Williamson, L. M., Kitson-Piggott, W., Wagner, H. U., Camara, B., & Hospedales, C. J. (2006). Sexually transmitted infection service use and risk factors for HIV infection among female sex workers in Georgetown, Guyana. *Journal of Acquired Immune Deficiency Syndromes, 43*(1), 96–101. Retrieved from PM:16885774

Anderson, E. L. (2010). How gender leaves women vulnerable to HIV infection: Lessons from Malawi [Abstract TUPE 0670]. *Proceedings of the XVIII International AIDS Conference: Rights Here, Right Now.* Vienna, Austria.

Anderson, J., & Doyal, L. (2004). Women from Africa living with HIV in London: A descriptive study. *AIDS Care, 16*(1), 95–105. Retrieved from PM:14660147

Andrews, S. (1995). Social support as a stress buffer among human immunodeficiency virus–seropositive urban mothers. *Holistic Nursing Practice, 10*(1), 36–43. Retrieved from PM:7593365

Apinundecha, C., Laohasiriwong, W., Cameron, M. P., & Lim, S. (2007). A community participation intervention to reduce HIV/AIDS stigma, Nakhon Ratchasima Province, Northeast Thailand. *AIDS Care, 19*(9), 1157–1165. Retrieved from PM:18058400

Ashworth, C. S., DuRant, R. H., Gaillard, G., & Rountree, J. (1994). An experimental evaluation of an AIDS educational intervention for WIC mothers. *AIDS Education and Prevention, 6*(2), 154–162. Retrieved from PM:7517156

Babalola, S. (2007). Readiness for HIV testing among young people in northern Nigeria: The roles of social norm and perceived stigma. *AIDS and Behavior, 11*(5), 759–769. Retrieved from PM:17191141

Bairan, A., Taylor, G. A., Blake, B. J., Akers, T., Sowell, R., & Mediola, R. Jr. (2007). A model of HIV disclosure: Disclosure and types of social relationships. *Journal of the American Academy of Nurse Practitioners, 19*(5), 242–250. Retrieved from PM:17489957

Balabanova, Y., Coker, R., Atun, R. A., & Drobniewski, F. (2006). Stigma and HIV infection in Russia. *AIDS Care, 18*(7), 846–852. doi: W614R5550L10MJ00 [pii]; 10.1080/09540120600643641 [doi]. Retrieved from PM:16971297

Baral, S., Semugoma, P., Diouf, D., Trapence, G., Poteat, T., Ndaw, M., . . . Bayrer, C. (2010). Criminalization of same sex practices as a structural driver of HIV risk among men who have sex with men (MSM): The cases of Senegal, Malawi, and Uganda [Abstract MOPE0951]. *Proceedings of the XVIII International AIDS Conference: Rights Here, Right Now.* Vienna, Austria.

Barrett, D. (2010). Track F rapporteur report. *Proceedings of the XVIII International AIDS Conference: Rights Here, Right Now.* Vienna, Austria.

Batson, C. D., Polycarpou, M. P., Harmon-Jones, E., Imhoff, H. J., Mitchener, E. C., Bednar, L. L., . . . Highberger, L. (1997). Empathy and attitudes: Can feeling for a member of a stigmatized group improve feelings toward the group? *Journal of Personality & Social Psychology, 72*(1), 105–118. Retrieved from PM:9008376

Bean, J., Keller, L., Newburg, C., & Brown, M. (1989). Methods for the reduction of AIDS social anxiety and social stigma. *AIDS Education and Prevention, 1*(3), 194–221. Retrieved from PM:2641241

Beat It. (2011). Special report: Gugu Dlamini. *Siyayinoqoba: Beat It.* Retrieved from http://www.beatit.co.za/archive-events/1-december-1998-gugu-dlamini

Beaulleu, M., Adrien, A., & Lebounga Vouma, J. I. (2010). How gender roles influence HIV-STI risk among young Quebecers of Haitian origin [Abstract TUPE0670]. *Proceedings of the XVIII International AIDS Conference: Rights Here, Right Now.* Vienna, Austria.

Beyrer, C., & Pizer, H. F. (2000). *Public health and human rights: Evidence-based approaches.* Baltimore, MD: Johns Hopkins University Press.

Black, M. M., Nair, P., & Harrington, D. (1994). Maternal HIV infection: Parenting and early child development. *Journal of Pediatric Psychology, 19*(5), 595–615. Retrieved from PM:7807292

Blake, B. J., Jones Taylor, G. A., Reid, P., & Kosowski, M. (2008). Experiences of women in obtaining human immunodeficiency virus testing and healthcare services. *Journal of the American Academy of Nurse Practitioners, 20*(1), 40–46. Retrieved from PM:18184164

Bogart, L. M., Cowgill, B. O., Kennedy, D., Ryan, G., Murphy, D. A., Elijah, J., & Schuster, M. A. (2008). HIV-related stigma among people with HIV and their families: A qualitative analysis. *AIDS and Behavior, 12*(2), 244–254. Retrieved from PM:17458691

Bos, A. E., Kok, G., & Dijker, A. J. (2001). Public reactions to people with HIV/AIDS in the Netherlands. *AIDS Education and Prevention, 13*(3), 219–228. Retrieved from PM:11459358

Botnick, M. R. (2000). Part 1: HIV as "the line in the sand." *Journal of Homosexuality, 38*(4), 39–76. Retrieved from PM:10807028

Brown, L., Macintyre, K., & Trujillo, L. (2003). Interventions to reduce HIV/AIDS stigma: What have we learned? *AIDS Education and Prevention, 15*(1), 49–69. Retrieved from PM:12627743

Buseh, A. G., & Stevens, P. E. (2006). Constrained but not determined by stigma: Resistance by African American women living with HIV. *Women & Health, 44*(3), 1–18. Retrieved from PM:17255063

Busza, J. R. (2001). Promoting the positive: responses to stigma and discrimination in Southeast Asia. *AIDS Care, 13*(4), 441–456. Retrieved from PM:11454265

Cao, X., Sullivan, S. G., Xu, J., Wu, Z., & China CIPRA Project 2 Team. (2006). Understanding HIV-related stigma and discrimination in a "blameless" population. *AIDS Education and Prevention, 18*(6), 518–528. Retrieved from PM:17166078

Carr, R. L., & Gramling, L. F. (2004). Stigma: A health barrier for women with HIV/AIDS. *Journal of the Association of Nurses in AIDS Care, 15*(5), 30–39. Retrieved from PM:15358923

Centers for Disease Control and Prevention (CDC). (1981a). Kaposi's sarcoma and *Pneumocystis* pneumonia among homosexual men—New York City and California. *Morbidity and Mortality Weekly Report, 30,* 305–308.

Centers for Disease Control and Prevention (CDC). (1981b). *Pneumocystis* pneumonia—Los Angeles. *Morbidity and Mortality Weekly Report, 30,* 250–252.

Chacham, A. S., Diniz, S. G., Maia, M. B., Galati, A. F., & Mirim, L. A. (2007). Sexual and reproductive health needs of sex workers: Two feminist projects in Brazil. *Reproductive Health Matters, 15*(29), 108–118. Retrieved from PM:17512382

Chandra, P. S., Deepthivarma, S., & Manjula, V. (2003). Disclosure of HIV infection in south India: Patterns, reasons and reactions. *AIDS Care, 15*(2), 207–215. Retrieved from PM:12856342

Coursen-Neff, Z. (2004). Future forsaken: Abuses against children affected by HIV/AIDS in India. *Human Rights Watch.* Retrieved from http://hrw.org/reports/2004/india0704

Demarco, R., Lynch, M. M., & Board, R. (2002). Mothers who silence themselves: A concept with clinical implications for women living with HIV/AIDS and their children. *Journal of Pediatric Nursing, 17*(2), 89–95. Retrieved from PM:12029602

Dlamini, P. S., Kohi, T. W., Uys, L. R., Phetlhu, R. D., Chirwa, M. L., Naidoo, J. R., . . . Makoae, L. N. (2007). Verbal and physical abuse and neglect as manifestations of HIV/AIDS stigma in five African countries. *Public Health Nursing, 24*(5), 389–399. Retrieved from PM:17714223

Dorozynski, A. (1996). French bishops ease ban on condoms. *British Medical Journal, 312*(7029), 462. Retrieved from PM:8597670

Ekstrand, M., Bharat, S., & Ramakrishna, J. (2010). Blame and HIV misconceptions are associated with endorsement of coercive policies and intent to discriminate against PLHAs in two urban sites in India: Implications for stigma reduction interventions [Abstract TUPE0556]. *Proceedings of the XVIII International AIDS Conference: Rights Here, Right Now.* Vienna, Austria.

Elliott, R., & Gold, J. (2005). Protection against discrimination based on HIV/AIDS status in Canada: The legal framework. *HIV/AIDS Policy & Law Review, 10*(1), 20–31. Retrieved from PM:15991367

Fawole, I. O., Asuzu, M. C., Oduntan, S. O., & Brieger, W. R. (1999). A school-based AIDS education programme for secondary school students in Nigeria: A review of effectiveness. *Health Education Research, 14*(5), 675–683. Retrieved from PM:10510075

Feller, L., & Lemmer, J. (2007). Aspects of immunopathogenic mechanisms of HIV infection. *Journal of the South African Dental Association, 62*(10), 432–4, 436. Retrieved from PM:18500104

Foster, G., Makufa, C., Drew, R., Kambeu, S., & Saurombe, K. (1997). Perceptions of children and community members concerning the circumstances of orphans in rural Zimbabwe. *AIDS Care, 9*(4), 391–405. Retrieved from PM:9337884

Fuster, M. J. & Molero, F. (2010). The relationship between HIV related stigma and quality of life among people with HIV. [Abstract TUADO203]. Proceedings of the XVIII International AIDS Conference. July 18-23, 2010, Vienna, Austria.

Galanti, G. A. (2003). The Hispanic family and male–female relationships: An overview. *Journal of Transcultural Nursing, 14*(3), 180–185. Retrieved from PM:12861920

Galletly, C. L., & Pinkerton, S. D. (2004). Toward rational criminal HIV exposure laws. *Journal of Law Medicine & Ethics, 32*(2), 327–337. Retrieved from PM:15301197

Gilmore, N., & Somerville, M. A. (1994). Stigmatization, scapegoating and discrimination in sexually transmitted diseases: Overcoming "them" and "us." *Social Science and Medicine, 39*(9), 1339–1358. Retrieved from PM:7801170

Goffman, E. (1963). *Stigma: Notes on the management of spoiled identity*. Englewood Cliffs, NJ: Prentice-Hall.

Gray, J. J. (1999). The difficulties of women living with HIV infection. *Journal of Psychosocial Nursing & Mental Health Services, 37*(5), 39–43. Retrieved from PM:10340228

Greeff, M., & Phetlhu, R. (2007). The meaning and effect of HIV/AIDS stigma for people living with AIDS and nurses involved in their care in the North West Province, South Africa. *Curationis, 30*(2), 12–23. Retrieved from PM:17703819

Hasnain, M. (2005). Cultural approach to HIV/AIDS harm reduction in Muslim countries. *Harm Reduction Journal, 2*, 23. Retrieved from PM:16253145

Herek, G. M. (1999). AIDS and stigma. *American Behavioral Scientist, 42*(7), 1102–1112.

Herek, G. M., Capitanio, J. P., & Widaman, K. F. (2002). HIV-related stigma and knowledge in the United States: Prevalence and trends, 1991–1999. *American Journal of Public Health, 92*(3), 371–377. Retrieved from PM:11867313

Herek, G. M., Capitanio, J. P., & Widaman, K. F. (2003). Stigma, social risk, and health policy: Public attitudes toward HIV surveillance policies and the social construction of illness. *Health Psychology, 22*(5), 533–540. Retrieved from PM:14570537

Herek, G. M., Gillis, J. R., Glunt, E. K., Lewis, J., Welton, D., & Capitanio, J. P. (1998). Culturally sensitive AIDS educational videos for African American audiences: Effects of source, message, receiver, and context. *American Journal of Community Psychology, 26*(5), 705–743. Retrieved from PM:9861691

Hess, R. F., & McKinney, D. (2007). Fatalism and HIV/AIDS beliefs in rural Mali, West Africa. *Journal of Nursing Scholarship, 39*(2), 113–118. Retrieved from PM:17535310

Holzemer, W. L., & Uys, L. R. (2004). Managing AIDS stigma. *Journal of Social Aspects of HIV/AIDS Research Alliance, 1*(3), 165–174. Retrieved from PM:17601004

Horter, S., Nkhoma, H., Baradaran, S., Baggaley, R., & Stedwick, R. (2010). Proposed HIV and HIDSS bill in Malawi: Benefit or barrier to improving the HIV response? [Abstract THPE0903]. *Proceedings of the XVIII International AIDS Conference: Rights Here, Right Now*. Vienna, Austria.

Hossain, M. B., Islam, M. R., Islam, M. A., & Kabir, M. A. (2010). HIV-related stigmatized attitude and its predictors among the general population in Bangladesh [Abstract TUPE 0554]. *Proceedings of the XVIII International AIDS Conference: Rights Here, Right Now*. Vienna, Austria.

Human Rights Watch. (2004). Bad dreams: Exploitation and abuse of migrant workers in Saudi Arabia. *Human Rights Watch, 16*(5E).

Human Rights Watch. (2007). Chronic indifference: HIV/AIDS services for immigrants detained by the United States. *Human Rights Watch, 19*(5G).

Human Rights Watch. (2008). A testing challenge. *Human Rights Watch*. Retrieved from http://www.hrw.org/en/node/75974/section/5

Human Rights Watch. (2009). 2009 a bad year for migrants: Deaths, labor exploitation, violence, and poor treatment in detention. Retrieved from http://www.hrw.org/news/2009/12/16/2009-bad-year-migrants

Huy, T. Q., Johansson, A., & Long, N. H. (2007). Reasons for not reporting deaths: A qualitative study in rural Vietnam. *World Health and Population, 9*(1), 14–23. Retrieved from PM:18270497

Ibekwe, N., & Agbo, L. (2010). HIV and AIDS related stigma and discrimination in the rural Eastern Nigeria [Abstract TUPE0550]. *Proceedings of the XVIII International AIDS Conference: Rights Here, Right Now*. Vienna, Austria.

Jones, E. E., Farina, A., Hastorf, A. H., Markus, H., Miller, D. T., & Scott, R. A. (1984). *Social stigma: The psychology of marked relationships*. New York, NY: W. H. Freeman.

Kaiser. (2000). Kaiser daily HIV/AIDS update. Kaiser-newsupdate@kff.org.

Kaldjian, L. C., Jekel, J. F., & Friedland, G. (1998). End-of-life decisions in HIV-positive patients: The role of spiritual beliefs. *AIDS, 12*(1), 103–107. Retrieved from PM:9456260

Kazatchkine, C. (2010). Criminalizing HIV transmission or exposure: The context of francophone West and Central Africa. *HIV/AIDS Policy & Law Review, 14*(3), 1–11.

Kehler, J. (2010). Women's sexual and reproductive rights in national strategic plans: Are women's rights at the centre of the AIDS response? [Abstract THPE0996]. *Proceedings of the XVIII International AIDS Conference: Rights Here, Right Now.* Vienna, Austria.

Kehler, J., & Crone, E. T. (2010). Addressing the implications of HIV criminalization for women [Abstract THPE1024]. *Proceedings of the XVIII International AIDS Conference: Rights Here, Right Now.* Vienna, Austria.

Kilewo, C., Massawe, A., Lyamuya, E., Semali, I., Kalokola, F., Urassa, E., . . . Biberfeld, G. (2001). HIV counseling and testing of pregnant women in sub-Saharan Africa: Experiences from a study on prevention of mother-to-child HIV-1 transmission in Dar es Salaam, Tanzania. *Journal of Acquired Immune Deficiency Syndromes, 28*(5), 458–462. Retrieved from PM:11744835

Klepp, K. I., Ndeki, S. S., Leshabari, M. T., Hannan, P. J., & Lyimo, B. A. (1997). AIDS education in Tanzania: Promoting risk reduction among primary school children. *American Journal of Public Health, 87*(12), 1931–1936. Retrieved from PM:9431279

Kohi, T. W., Makoae, L., Chirwa, M., Holzemer, W. L., Phetlhu, D. R., Uys, L., . . . Greeff, M. (2006). HIV and AIDS stigma violates human rights in five African countries. *Nursing Ethics, 13*(4), 404–415. Retrieved from PM:16838571

Kopelman, L. M. (2002). If HIV/AIDS is punishment, who is bad? *Journal of Medicine and Philosophy, 27*(2), 231–243. Retrieved from PM:11961699

Lambda Legal. (2002). State criminal statutes on HIV transmission. Retrieved from http://www.lambdalegal.org/our-work/publications/general/state-criminal-statutes-hiv.html

Lambda Legal. (2009). State criminal statutes on HIV exposure. Retrieved from http://www.lambdalegal.org/our-work/publications/general/state-criminal-statutes-hiv.html

Laryea, M., & Gien, L. (1993). The impact of HIV-positive diagnosis on the individual, Part 1: Stigma, rejection, and loneliness. *Clinical Nursing Research, 2*(3), 245–263, discussion. Retrieved from PM:8401240

Lazarus, R. S., & Folkman, S. (1984). *Stress, appraisal, and coping.* New York: Springer.

Lee, M. B., Wu, Z., Rotheram-Borus, M. J., Detels, R., Guan, J., & Li, L. (2005). HIV-related stigma among market workers in China. *Health Psychology, 24*(4), 435–438. Retrieved from PM:16045380

Li, L., Cao, H., Wu, Z., Wu, S., & Xiao, L. (2007). Diffusion of positive AIDS care messages among service providers in China. *AIDS Education and Prevention, 19*(6), 511–518. Retrieved from PM:18190275

Liski, E. A. (1998). Legal implications of study results showing continued failure to disclose HIV status to sexual partners. Retrieved from http://www.law.uh.edu/healthlaw/perspectives/HIVAIDS/980213LegalImplications.html

Logie, C., James, L., Tharao, W., & Loutfy, M. (2010). The intersection of race, gender, sexual orientation, and HIV: Understanding multi-dimensional forms of stigma and discrimination experienced by women living with HIV in Ontario, Canada [Abstract WEAD0102]. *Proceedings of the XVIII International AIDS Conference: Rights Here, Right Now.* Vienna, Austria.

Macintyre, K., Rutenberg, N., Brown, L., & Karim, A. (2004). Understanding perceptions of HIV risk among adolescents in KwaZulu-Natal. *AIDS and Behavior, 8,* 237–250.

Mann, J., Tarantola, D. J. M., & Netter, T. W. (1992). *AIDS in the world.* Cambridge, MA: Harvard University Press.

McGovern, T. M. (2006). Models of resistance: "Victims" lead. *Health and Human Rights, 9*(2), 234–255. Retrieved from PM:17265762

McNeil, D. J., Jr. (1998, December 28). Neighbors kill an HIV-positive AIDS activist in South Africa. *New York Times,* p. 28.

Mendenhall, E., Muzizi, L., Stephenson, R., Chomba, E., Ahmed, Y., Haworth, A., & Allen, S. (2007). Property grabbing and will writing in Lusaka, Zambia: An examination of wills of HIV-infected cohabiting couples. *AIDS Care, 19*(3), 369–374. Retrieved from PM:17453571

Miramontes, H. M. (2000). The global challenges of the HIV/AIDS pandemic. *Journal of the Association of Nurses in AIDS Care, 11*(4), 11–12. Retrieved from PM:10911590

Molina, E., & Lainez, H. (2010). Criminalization of sex work as an obstacle for access to integral attention on HIV/AIDS [Abstract TUPE1004]. *Proceedings of the XVIII International AIDS Conference: Rights Here, Right Now.* Vienna, Austria.

Moneyham, L., Hennessy, M., Sowell, R., Demi, A., Seals, B., & Mizuno, Y. (1998). The effectiveness of coping strategies used by HIV-seropositive women. *Research in Nursing & Health, 21*(4), 351–362. Retrieved from PM:9679811

Moneyham, L., Seals, B., Demi, A., Sowell, R., Cohen, L., & Guillory, J. (1996). Perceptions of stigma in women infected with HIV. *AIDS Patient Care and STDS, 10*(3), 162–167. Retrieved from PM:11361616

Moreno, C. L. (2007). The relationship between culture, gender, structural factors, abuse, trauma, and HIV/AIDS for Latinas. *Qualitative Health Research, 17*(3), 340–352. Retrieved from PM:17301342

Moser, K. M., Sowell, R. L., & Phillips, K. D. (2001). Issues of women dually diagnosed with HIV infection and substance use problems in the Carolinas. *Issues in Mental Health Nursing, 22*(1), 23–49. Retrieved from PM:11885060

Muchenje, M., Tharao, W., Mehes, M., Njeri, R., Ndungu, M., Hove, P., . . . Hintzen, D. (2010). To disclose or not to disclose? The factors influencing HIV disclosure among African and Caribbean women [Abstract WEPE0602]. *Proceedings of the XVIII International AIDS Conference: Rights Here, Right Now.* Vienna, Austria.

Muthuswamy, V. (2005). Ethical issues in HIV/AIDS research. *Indian Journal of Medical Research, 121*(4), 601–610. Retrieved from PM:15817966

Mykhalovskiy, E. (2010). HIV non-disclosure and the criminal law: Effects of Canada's significant risk test on people living with HIV/AIDS and health and social services providers [Abstract THLBF102]. *Proceedings of the XVIII International AIDS Conference: Rights Here, Right Now.* Vienna, Austria.

Nyanzi, S. (2010). Contesting diverse widow inheritance customs in Uganda, Kenya, and Tanzania [Abstract MOAD0104]. *Proceedings of the XVIII International AIDS Conference: Rights Here, Right Now.* Vienna, Austria.

Odebiyi, A. I. (1992). Conception of AIDS and its prevention among students in a Nigerian university. *Journal of the Royal Society of Health, 112*(2), 59–63. Retrieved from PM:1573623

Oh, K. (2010). The past, present and future of HIV-related travel restrictions in the United States and the Republic of Korea [Abstract WEPE0884]. *Proceedings of the XVIII International AIDS Conference: Rights Here, Right Now.* Vienna, Austria.

Oorjitham, S. (1999). A spirited response: Malaysia's AIDS activists woo Muslim clerics. *Asiaweek, 37.* Retrieved from PM:12295478

Parker, R., & Aggleton, P. (2003). HIV and AIDS-related stigma and discrimination: A conceptual framework and implications for action. *Social Science and Medicine, 57*(1), 13–24. Retrieved from PM:12753813

Pedrotti, C., Bishop, A., & Dunhma, S. (2010). HIV, human rights and social inclusion: The experience of HIV oost-clubs over the life of the "reducing community vulnerability to HIV and AIDS program" in Kenya, Zambia, and Zimbabwe [Abstract MOPE0640]. *Proceedings of the XVIII International AIDS Conference: Rights Here, Right Now.* Vienna, Austria.

Petros, G., Airhihenbuwa, C. O., Simbayi, L., Ramlagan, S., & Brown, B. (2006). HIV/AIDS and "othering" in South Africa: The blame goes on. *Culture, Health, & Sexuality, 8*(1), 67–77. Retrieved from PM:16500826

Pharris, A., Tishelman, C., Huyen, D. T., Chuc, N. T. K., & Thorson, A. (2010). The "infected innocent": Gender roles and stigma among women living with HIV in Vietnam [Abstract WEPE0656]. *Proceedings of the XVIII International AIDS Conference: Rights Here, Right Now.* Vienna, Austria.

Pittam, J., & Gallois, C. (1997). Language strategies in attribution of blame for HIV and AIDS. *Communication Monographs, 64,* 201–208.

Poteat, T., Diouf, D., Baral, S., Ndaw, M., Drame, F., Traore, C., . . . Beyrer, C. (2010). The impact of criminalization of same sex practices on HIV risk among men who have sex with men (MSM) in Senegal:

Results of a qualitative rapid assessment [Abstract TUPE0709]. *Proceedings of the XVIII International AIDS Conference: Rights Here, Right Now.* Vienna, Austria.

Rao, K. S. (2002). Live and let live. *Journal of the Indian Medical Association, 100*(12), 712, 714, 716. Retrieved from PM:12793638

Riley, D., & O'Hare, P. (2000). Harm reduction: History, definition, and practice. In J. Inciardi & L. D. Hanson (Eds.), *Harm reduction: National and international perspectives* (pp. 1–26). Thousand Oaks, CA: Sage.

Romero, L., Wallerstein, N., Lucero, J., Fredine, H. G., Keefe, J., & O'Connell, J. (2006). Woman to woman: Coming together for positive change—using empowerment and popular education to prevent HIV in women. *AIDS Education and Prevention, 18*(5), 390–405. Retrieved from PM:17067251

Rubenstein, L. S. (2000). Foreword. In C. Beyrer & H. F. Pizer (Eds.), *Public health and human rights: Evidence-based approaches.* Baltimore, MD: Johns Hopkins University Press.

Seeley, J., Grellier, R., & Barnett, T. (2004). Gender and HIV/AIDS impact mitigation in sub-Saharan Africa: Recognising the constraints. *Journal of Social Aspects of HIV/AIDS Research Alliance, 1*(2), 87–98. Retrieved from PM:17601014

Shilts, R. (1987). *And the band played on: Politics, people, and the AIDS epidemic.* New York: St. Martin's Press.

Singer, M. (1994). The politics of AIDS. Introduction. *Social Science and Medicine, 38*(10), 1321–1324. Retrieved from PM:8023183

Sontag, S. (1998). *AIDS and its metaphors.* New York: Vintage Books.

South African Government Information. (1998). Press release issued by the Department of Health on the killing of Ms. Gugu Dlamini (AIDS campaign worker).

Sowell, R. L., Holtz, C., & Velasquez, G. (2008). Bringing HIV/AIDS home to Mexico: Perspectives of migrant workers and their wives. *Journal of the Association of Nurses in AIDS Care, 19*(4), 267–282.

Sowell, R. L., & Phillips, K. D. (2010). Understanding and responding to HIV/AIDS stigma and disclosure: An international challenge for mental health nurses. *Issues in Mental Health Nursing, 31*(6), 394–402. doi: 10.3109/01612840903497602. Retrieved from PM:20450341

Sowell, R. L., Phillips, K. D., Seals, B., Murdaugh, C., & Rush, C. (2002). Incidence and correlates of physical violence among HIV-infected women at risk for pregnancy in the southeastern United States. *Journal of the Association of Nurses in AIDS Care, 13*(2), 46–58. Retrieved from PM:11936064

Sowell, R. L., Seals, B. F., Moneyham, L., Guillory, J., & Mizuno, Y. (1997). Experiences of violence in women infected with HIV. *Proceedings of the Ninth International Nursing Research Congress,* 141.

Sowell, R. L., Seals, B. F., Phillips, K. D., & Julious, C. H. (2003). Disclosure of HIV infection: How do women decide to tell? *Health Education Research, 18*(1), 32–44. Retrieved from PM:12608682

Tenkorang, E., Obeng-Gyimah, S., Maticka-Tyndale, E., & Adjei, J. (2010). Superstition, witchcraft, and HIV/AIDS prevention in sub-Saharan Africa: The case of Ghana [Abstract MOPE 0508]. *Proceedings of the XVIII International AIDS Conference: Rights Here, Right Now.* Vienna, Austria.

Thomas, R., Lalu, V., Mukambetov, A., Odhiambo, T., & Williams, J. (2010). Arrest the violence and halt HIV: Strategies for reducing police abuse against sex workers [Abstract TUAF0401]. *Proceedings of the XVIII International AIDS Conference: Rights Here, Right Now.* Vienna, Austria.

Thompson, M. A., Aberg, J. A., Cahn, P., Montaner, J. S., Rizzardini, G., Telenti, A., . . . Schooley, R. T. (2010). Antiretroviral treatment of adult HIV infection: 2010 recommendations of the International AIDS Society—USA panel. *Journal of the American Medical Association, 304*(3), 321–333. doi: 304/3/321 [pii]; 10.1001/jama.2010.1004 [doi]. Retrieved from PM:20639566

Timmons, S. M., & Sowell, R. L. (1999). Perceived HIV-related sexual risks and prevention practices of African American women in the southeastern United States. *Health Care for Women International, 20*(6), 579–591. Retrieved from PM:10889636

Tran Huy, D., & Nguyen, T. H. (2010). Discrimination: A major barrier in Vietnam [Abstract WEBP0663]. *Proceedings of the XVIII International AIDS Conference: Rights Here, Right Now.* Vienna, Austria.

UNAIDS. (2003). UNAIDS report for 2003: Most deaths and new infections ever; some good news. *AIDS Treatment News, 396,* 3. Retrieved from PM:14717110

UNAIDS. (2004). *2004 report on the global AIDS epidemic* (4th ed.). Geneva, Switzerland: UNAIDS Joint United Nations Programme on HIV/AIDS.

UNAIDS. (2007a). AIDS epidemic update: December 2007. Retrieved from http://data.unaids.org/pub/EPISlides/2007/2007_epiupdate_en.pdf

UNAIDS. (2007b). *Reducing HIV stigma and discrimination: A critical part of national AIDS programmes.* Geneva, Switzerland: UNAIDS Joint United Nations Programme on HIV/ADS.

UNAIDS. (2008a). 2008 report on the global AIDS epidemic. Retrieved from http://www.unaids.org/en/KnowledgeCentre/HIVData/GlobalReport/2008/2008_Global_report.asp

UNAIDS. (2008b). International consultation on the criminalization of HIV transmission. Retrieved from http://data.unaids.org/pub/Report/2008/20080919_hivcriminalization_meetingreport_en.pdf

UNAIDS. (2008c). Stigma and discrimination. Retrieved from http://www.unaids.org/en/PolicyAndPractice/StigmaDiscrim/default.asp

UNAIDS. (2010). Human rights and HIV. UNAIDS: Joint United Nations Programme on HIV/AIDS. Retrieved from http://www.unaids.org/en/PolicyAndPractice/HumanRights/default.asp

Ungphakorn, J., & Sittitrai, W. (1994). The Thai response to the HIV/AIDS epidemic. *AIDS, 8*(suppl 2), S155–S163. Retrieved from PM:7857559

UNICEF. (2006). Africa's orphaned and vulnerable generations: Children affected by AIDS. Retrieved from http://www.unicef.org/publications/index_35645.html

UNICEF. (2010). *Blame and banishment: The underground HIV epidemic affecting children in Eastern Europe and Central Asia.* United Nations Children's Fund.

Wang, Y. G. (1997). AIDS, policy and bioethics: Ethical dilemmas facing China in HIV prevention: A report from China. *Bioethics, 11*(3–4), 323–327. Retrieved from PM:11654786

Weeks, B. S., & Alcamo, I. E. (2008). Defining and recognizing AIDS. In B.S. Weeks & I. E. Alcamo (Eds.), *AIDS: The biologic basis* (4th ed., pp. 84–113). Sudbury, MA: Jones and Bartlett Publishers.

Wenani, T. (2010). Violence, neglect and abuse of children affected by AIDS at the Dandora Dumping Site, Nairobi, Kenya [Abstract TUPE0578]. *Proceedings of the XVIII International AIDS Conference: Rights Here, Right Now.* Vienna, Austria.

Wilson, P. (2000). Perspective: Seeing the true surroundings. *HIV Plus.* Retrieved from http://aidsinfonyc.org/hivplus/issue10/columns/perspective.html

World Health Organization (WHO). (2005). Interim WHO clinical staging of HIV/AIDS and the HIV/AIDS case definition for surveillance, 2005. Retrieved from http://www.who.int/hiv/pub/guidelines/casedefinitions/en/index.html

9

Global Use of Complementary and Alternative Medicine and Treatments

Ping Hu Johnson

"The highest ideal of cure is the speedy, gentle, and enduring restoration of health by the most trustworthy and least harmful way."

Samuel Hahnemann (1755-1844), Founder of Homeopathy

OBJECTIVES

After completing this chapter, the student will be able to:

1. Describe complementary and alternative medicine (CAM) and its main categories.
2. Discuss the trends of CAM use in both developing and developed countries, and explain the reasons behind the increased popularity of CAM use.
3. Identify the predictors, reasons, patterns, and cost of CAM use in the United States.
4. Discuss the theories and practices of different types of complementary and alternative therapies being used in the United States today.
5. Describe the major types of CAM providers.
6. Discuss the current status and challenges of CAM research.
7. Identify the impact of technology on the use of and research in CAM.
8. Discuss the legal and ethical issues surrounding CAM treatments and research.
9. Describe the influence of politics, economics, culture, and religion on complementary and alternative medicine and treatments.
10. Compare the use of complementary and alternative medicine and treatments between developing and developed societies.

INTRODUCTION

In recent years, we have seen an increased interest in complementary and alternative medicine (CAM) and treatments in the United States and worldwide. It appears to be a trend that more people are seeking holistic healthcare approaches and using natural products to treat their health problems, prevent diseases, and promote wellness. Although CAM is becoming increasingly popular, the conventional modern Western medicine remains predominant in the developed world, and the majority of those people continue to seek conventional medical care most of the time (Eisenberg et al., 2001). In contrast, what Americans and others in the developed world label as CAM treatments and practices are considered to be traditional medicine and have been used by the majority of the global population for hundreds to thousands of years. In the past decade, CAM treatments and practices have spread rapidly in the developed countries (World Health Organization [WHO], 2011a).

CAM DEFINED: COMPLEMENTARY AND ALTERNATIVE *OR* TRADITIONAL?

According to the World Health Organization (WHO, 2011a) and the United States National Center for Complementary and Alternative Medicine (NCCAM, 2011a), complementary and alternative medicine refers to a broad set of diverse medical and healthcare systems, practices, and products that are not part of that country's own tradition and are not integrated into the dominant healthcare system. Based on this definition, it is clear that the conventional modern Western medicine and treatments are considered traditional in the United States and other developed countries. Also, those entities that Americans and others in the Western world consider to be CAM treatments and practices have mostly originated from other countries and cultures and are considered traditional medicine in those countries. WHO (2011a) defines traditional medicine as "the sum total of the knowledge, skills, and practices based on the theories, beliefs, and experiences indigenous to different cultures, whether explicable or not, used in the maintenance of health as well as in the prevention, diagnosis, improvement or treatment of physical and mental illness."

Although the terms *alternative medicine* and *complementary medicine* have been used interchangeably in the literature, they mean different things. According to NCCAM (2011a), alternative medicine is used *in place of* conventional medicine, and complementary medicine is used *together with* conventional medicine. Using a special diet to treat cancer instead of surgery, radiation, or chemotherapy recommended by a conventional doctor is an example of alternative medicine, while using aromatherapy to help lesson a patient's discomfort following surgery is an example of complementary medicine.

In this chapter, the term *CAM* is used to refer to the medical and healthcare systems, practices, and products that are not part of and are not integrated into the dominant conventional modern Western healthcare system in the United States and other developed countries. The term *traditional medicine* is used to denote the indigenous medical and healthcare systems, practices, and products that are used in developing countries.

CAM IN THE UNITED STATES

Unlike many countries in the world, allopathic medicine is the mainstream medical practice and considered conventional medicine in the United States, even though Native American folk medical practices existed long before the early settlers from Europe migrated to the United States. In the past decade, there has been an upsurge of CAM use in the United States due to the increasing demand for such therapies from U.S. consumers. According to the 2005 *Institute of Medicine Report on Complementary and Alternative Medicine in the United States,* the use of CAM will continue to be present in the United States (Institute of Medicine, 2005). Several surveys of nationally representative samples of U.S. adults have revealed that the proportion of adults who used at least one CAM therapy in a given year increased from 33.8% in 1990 to 42.1% in 1997 (Eisenberg et al., 1998) and again to 62% in 2002 (Barnes, Powell-Griner, McFann, & Nahin, 2004). CAM usage seems even more prevalent among health educators and patients. When daily vitamins excluding megavitamins or vitamins prescribed by a doctor and exercise not for the purpose of weight management were included as forms of CAM therapy, nearly 90% of health educators in the United States reported having used at least one form of CAM in the 12 months prior to the survey

(Johnson, Priestly, Porter, & Petrillo, 2010). Similarly, as many as 85% of cancer patients reported having used at least one form of CAM (Morris, Johnson, Homer, & Walts, 2000).

A recent report of a nationally representative sample of U.S. adults found that nearly 38.3% had used some form of CAM therapy in the past 12 months (Barnes, Bloom, & Nahin, 2008). The frequencies of CAM use by category are as follows, in order of prevalence:

- Biologically based therapies include chelation therapy; nonvitamin, nonmineral, natural products; and diet-based therapies (19.9%).
- Mind–body therapies include biofeedback, meditation, guided imagery, progressive relaxation, deep breathing exercises, hypnosis, yoga, tai chi, and qi gong (19.2%).
- Manipulative and body-based therapies include chiropractic or osteopathic manipulation, massage, and movement therapies (15.2%).
- Alternative medical systems include acupuncture, Ayurveda, homeopathic treatment, naturopathy, and traditional healers (3.4%).
- Energy healing therapies (0.5%).

Table 9-1 compares the age-adjusted percentages of U.S. adults who used the most commonly used CAM therapies between 2002 (Barnes et al., 2004) and 2007 (Barnes et al., 2008). Based on these data, it seems that the overall CAM use decreased over the five-year period between 2002 and 2007. In reality, this "drop" in the CAM use prevalence is due to the narrower definition of CAM used in later years. Some forms of therapies included in CAM in the past, such as prayer for health reasons, daily vitamins, and exercise not for the purpose of weight management, are no longer considered CAM and are not included in the more recent study on CAM use among general U.S. population.

The increased popularity of CAM therapies has been accompanied by increased out-of-pocket expenditures on CAM therapies and services. Based on the most current estimates (Nahin, Barnes, Stussman, & Bloom, 2009), U.S. adults spent a total of $33.9 billion on an out-of-pocket basis on visits

---

TABLE 9-1

Comparison of Commonly Used CAM Therapies Among U.S. Adults According to Adjusted Percentages

Therapy	2002	2007	Difference	p
Used at least one form of CAM in the past 12 months	62%	38.3%	*	—
Nonvitamin, nonmineral, natural products	18.9%	17.7%	†	—
Deep breathing exercises	11.6%	12.7%	1.1	<.01
Meditation	7.6%	9.4%	1.8	<.0001
Chiropractic care	7.5%	—	‡	—
Chiropractic/osteopathic manipulation	—	8.6%	‡	—
Massage	5.0%	8.3%	3.3	<.0001
Yoga	5.1%	6.1%	1.0	<.001

*The data are not comparable between 2002 and 2007 because prayer for health reasons, daily vitamins, and exercise not for the purpose of weight management were not included in the 2007 survey.

†The data are not comparable between 2002 and 2007 due to question order and the specific nonvitamin, nonmineral, natural products covered.

‡The data are not comparable because respondents were asked about chiropractic care in 2002 and chiropractic or osteopathic manipulation in 2007.

to CAM providers and purchases of CAM products and services. Almost two-thirds of these expenses ($22.0 billion) were devoted to self-care CAM products and services during the past 12 months, whereas the rest ($11.9 billion) were spent by 38.1 million adults on more than 354 million visits to CAM providers.

With the increasing popularity and use of CAM, it is crucial to understand the nature and extent of CAM use. Studies have identified the following people as being more likely to use CAM:

- Women (Barnes et al., 2004; Barnes et al., 2008; Eisenberg et al., 1998).
- People with higher household income, almost certainly attributable to the reality that most CAM therapies are not covered by health insurance policies and require cash payments at the time of service (Eisenberg et al., 1998; Palinkas & Kabongo, 2000).
- People with higher levels of education, private health insurance, more health conditions, and more visits to doctor's office (Barnes et al., 2008).
- Older adults (Barnes et al., 2004; Barnes et al., 2008).
- Ethnic minorities (Barnes et al., 2004) and low-income individuals (Barnes et al., 2008; Dessio, Wade, Chao, Kronenberg, Cushman, & Kalmuss, 2004).
- People with lower level of emotional functioning and perceived general health (Palinkas & Kabongo, 2000).
- People who have been hospitalized in the last year, indicating that health status is a significant predictor of CAM utilization (Barnes et al., 2004; Barnes et al., 2008).
- People with a holistic orientation to health and who have had a transformational experience that changed their worldview.
- People with certain health problems, such as anxiety, back problems, headaches, chronic pain, and urinary tract problems (Astin, 1998).

The most common reasons cited for using CAM include the following:

- Users believed CAM therapies integrated with conventional therapies would yield better results (54.9%).
- They thought trying CAM therapies would be interesting (50.1%).
- CAM therapies were recommended by a medical professional (26%).
- Individuals felt allopathic therapies were not effective (28%).
- They felt CAM therapies would be more cost-effective (13%) (Barnes et al., 2004).
- They believed CAM therapies can boost the immune system, treat cancer, and help them live longer (Astin, 1998).

Results from those studies indicate that the high prevalence of CAM use in the United States cannot be attributed solely to the perceived dissatisfaction with conventional medical care or caregivers, or to a societal rejection of allopathic medical care (Eisenberg et al., 2001). Instead, such trends may indicate that more Americans have taken personal responsibility for their health and appreciate the choices they have between conventional and CAM care.

Although a large proportion of the U.S. adult population uses at least one of the CAM therapies, only 28% to 37% communicated such use to their doctors (Eisenberg et al., 2001). The most common reason for nondisclosure of CAM use was that patients believed "it was not important for their doctor to know," followed by "the doctor never asked," "it was not the doctor's business," and "the doctor would not understand." These views reveal a trend within the broader society toward increased individual autonomy and taking greater personal responsibility for one's own health. In addition, among the U.S. adults who reported seeing both a conventional doctor and a CAM provider in a given year, the majority (70%) saw a conventional doctor before or concurrent with their visits to a CAM provider, whereas only 15% saw a CAM provider before seeing a conventional medical care provider. Such a visit presents an excellent opportunity for the conventional medical care provider to advise patients on the use or avoidance of certain CAM therapies. It also presents a challenge, however, in that conventional healthcare providers need to understand what the common CAM therapies are and whether they are safe or effective.

CAM IN THE WORLD

Throughout history, different cultures in different parts of the world have developed and used various types of traditional medicine or CAM. People residing in Africa, Asia, and Latin America, for example, have used traditional medicine for hundreds and thousands of years to meet their primary healthcare needs. In African countries, as much as 80% of the population uses traditional medicine for primary health care. In recent years, many forms of traditional medicine have been adapted by more and more developed countries and are considered "complementary" or "alternative" medicine (CAM) depending on how the traditional medicine is used (WHO, 2011a).

In the last decade, we have seen a global increase in the use of both traditional medicine and CAM in both developed and developing countries. Many types of traditional, complementary, and alternative medicines are playing a more important role in health care and healthcare reform worldwide. Several countries—for example, China, the Democratic People's Republic of Korea, the Republic of Korea, and Vietnam—have fully integrated traditional medicine into their formal healthcare systems (Robinson & Zhang, 2011). Several other countries, such as the United States, are collecting standardized data on CAM therapies and encourage the integration of CAM into their mainstream medical care system. Many other countries, however, have yet to collect and integrate standardized evidence on this type of health care.

The following facts provide a better view of CAM's increased use and popularity:

- In China, traditional herbal preparations account for 30% to 50% of the total medicinal consumption.
- In Ghana, Mali, Nigeria, and Zambia, the first line of treatment for 60% of children with high fever resulting from malaria is the use of herbal medicines at home.
- The World Health Organization (WHO) estimates that traditional birth attendants in several African countries assist in the majority of births.
- In Canada, 70% of the population has used complementary medicine at least once.
- In the United Kingdom, annual expenditures on alternative medicine total $230 million.
- The global market for herbal medicines currently stands at more than $60 billion annually and is growing steadily (WHO, 2005).
- In Asia and Africa, as much as 80% of the population depend on traditional medicine for their health care.
- Traditional medicine is becoming increasingly more popular in many developed countries. For example, 80% of Germans, 70% of Canadians, 49% of French citizens, and 48% of Australians have used some form of CAM at least once.
- In Europe, sales of herbal medicine reached €3.7 billion, ($4.8 billion) with Germany responsible for 39% of these sales.
- At least 75% of AIDS patients use some form of CAM to treat various conditions and relieve symptoms in Africa, North America, and Europe.
- Thirty-one percent of WHO member states have established a national policy on traditional medicine/CAM, and 51 member countries have national policies pending.
- Sixty-five percent of WHO member states that participated in the 2005 WHO Global Survey have established herbal medicines law or regulation, and 42 countries (49%) are in the process of developing herbal medicine regulations.
- In 2005, sales of traditional Chinese medicine reached $14 billion, a 23.81% increase from the 2004 level.

- In 2006, sales of Kampo medicine (i.e., the practice of Chinese medicine in Japan) totaled nearly $1.1 billion in Japan.
- In 2007, sales of herbal medicine totaled $160 million in Brazil (WHO, 2008).
- WHO recently called upon African governments to recognize traditional medicine, create an environment that supports and encourages its practice, and integrate it into their national health systems (WHO, 2011b).
- Approximately 80% of the world population uses traditional systems of medicines for primary health care, with plants (rather than other natural resources) being the dominant components of such medicines (Mukherjee & Wahile, 2006).
- There are more than 800 Chinese medicine pharmaceutical factories with an annual production of more than 400,000 tons, spread among more than 5000 drug varieties (Johnson & Johnson, 2002).
- An estimated $83 billion was spent on traditional medicine in 2008, with an exponential rate of increase being observed worldwide (Robinson & Zhang, 2011).
- In Singapore, more than 80% of the population has used some form of CAM in their lifetime (Koh, Ng, & Teo, 2004).
- In Brazil, as many as 89% of cancer patients use CAM (Samano et al., 2005).

It is clear that traditional medicine has maintained its popularity in developing countries and is used more frequently in developed countries. The global expansion of traditional medicine and CAM use in the developed world can in part be explained by these modalities' holistic approach to health and life; their belief in equilibrium between the mind, body and environment; their emphasis on health rather than on disease; and their treatment focus on the overall condition of the individual patient, rather than on the ailment or disease (WHO, 2005).

MAJOR FORMS OF CAM

In response to the increasing demand for CAM, the U.S. Congress passed legislation in 1992 to establish an office within the National Institutes of Health (NIH), known as the Office of Alternative Medicine (OAM), to investigate and evaluate potentially beneficial unconventional medical practices (NIH, 2005). In 1999, this office was elevated to a center within NIH, to be known as the National Center of Complementary and Alternative Medicine (NCCAM), with the specific intent of exploring complementary and alternative healing practices in the context of rigorous science, to train CAM researchers, and to inform the public and health professionals about the results of CAM research studies (NIH, 2005).

According NCCAM, CAM therapies are grouped into the following categories, with some perhaps fitting into more than one category: natural products, mind and body medicine, manipulative and body-based practices, and other CAM practices (NCCAM, 2011a). Generally speaking, therapies in each category were developed over different time periods in different places and have been used to deal with different health problems. Their therapeutic effects, efficacy, and side effects have been studied to different extents as well. While some CAM therapies are backed by scientific evidence of their safety and effectiveness, most need to be examined for their safety, effectiveness, and efficacy.

Natural Products

In the past, NCCAM referred this area of CAM as "biologically based therapies," and defined it as including natural and biologically based practices, interventions, and products such as herbs, whole diets, functional foods, animal-derived extracts, vitamins, minerals, fatty acids, amino acids, proteins, prebiotics and probiotics, and other dietary supplements. Because taking a multivitamin to meet daily nutritional requirements or taking calcium to promote bone health are no longer considered as CAM, natural products are currently considered to include a variety of herbal products (i.e., botanicals), and beneficial microorganisms (i.e., probiotics) that are similar to those normally found in the human digestive tract (NCCAM, 2011a). Many herbal products are sold as dietary supplements on an over-the-counter (OTC) basis, whereas individuals obtain probiotics from foods such as yogurts or dietary supplements.

Before manufactured drugs came into widespread use, herbal medicines played an important role in human health. A review of the history of the development of medicines reveals that many herbal medicines were originally derived from foods and that many manufactured drugs were developed from medicinal plants. A single medicinal plant may be defined as a food, a functional food, a dietary supplement, or an herbal medicine in different countries, depending on the regulations applied to foods and medicines in each country. The influences of culture and history on the use of herbal medicines differ from country to country and from region to region, and these factors continue to have a major impact on the use of herbal medicines in modern societies (WHO, 2005).

In the past two decades, we have seen a considerable increase in the interest in and use of dietary supplements. In 2011, overall sales of dietary supplements increased to $28.1 billion, of which nearly one-fifth came from sales of herbs/botanical supplements in the United States (U.S. Nutrition Industry, 2011). According to a recent national survey, a large proportion of U.S. adults used at least one nonvitamin, nonmineral, natural product in a given year for health reasons. Of those natural products, fish oil (also known as omega-3 or DHA) was the most commonly used product (37.4%) among the U.S. adult population, followed by Echinacea (19.8%), flaxseed oil or pills (15.9%), ginseng (14.1%), combination herb pills (13.0%), ginkgo biloba (11.3%), chondroitin (11.2%), garlic supplements (11.0%), and coenzyme Q-10 (8.7%) (Barnes et al., 2008).

Because of their widespread use and long history (often spanning several centuries), and because the products are "natural," many people assume that dietary supplements are harmless. Unfortunately, this is not always the case. Some herbal products have proved to be quite harmful. For example, the herb "ma huang" (ephedra) has been used in traditional Chinese medicine to treat respiratory congestion and certain illnesses for thousands of years. In the United States, ma huang was marketed as a dietary aid whose use led to at least a dozen deaths, heart attacks, and strokes. On April 12, 2004, the Food and Drug Administration (FDA) banned the sale of dietary supplements that contain ephedra after it determined that this product posed an unreasonable risk to those who used it (FDA, 2004). One recent FDA consumer update, "Beware of Fraudulent 'Dietary Supplements'," alerts consumers that nearly 300 fraudulent dietary supplements that have been promoted mostly for weight loss, body building, or sexual enhancement contain hidden or deceptively labeled ingredients. So far, FDA has received numerous reports of harm caused by consuming those products, including heart palpitations, stroke, liver injury, kidney failure, and even death (FDA, 2011a).

It is important to recognize that many plants are poisonous, some are toxic if ingested in large doses, others are dangerous when used with prescription or OTC drugs, and still others decrease the effectiveness of the prescription or OTC drugs. One good example is the popular herbal remedy known as St. John's wort. This supplement has a significant negative interaction with Indinavir, a protease inhibitor used to treat HIV infection, and may also potentially interact with prescription drugs used to treat conditions such as heart disease, depression, seizures, and certain cancers. St. John's wort may also potentially interact with prescription drugs used to prevent conditions such as transplant rejection or pregnancy (i.e., oral contraceptives) (FDA, 2000). To review FDA warnings and safety information related to dietary supplements, visit the FDA Warnings and Safety Information website: http://www.cfsan.fda.gov/~dms/ds-warn.html. For information on how to use dietary supplements wisely, visit the NCCAM's Get the Facts website: http://nccam.nih.gov/health/supplements/wiseuse.htm.

Unlike prescription or OTC drugs, which are all regulated by FDA, dietary supplements are largely free of FDA oversight (FDA, 2011b). The 1994 Dietary Supplement Health and Education Act (DSHEA) allows dietary supplement manufacturers to produce and promote their products without going through the stringent FDA approval process. Thus it is up to consumers to decide which products they will use or not use. Given this fact, it is important that healthcare consumers talk to their healthcare providers and/or obtain information from reliable websites sponsored by FDA, NCCAM, or other nonprofit health organizations before they take any dietary supplements.

Mind–Body Medicine

Mind–body interventions focus on the interactions among the brain, mind, body, and behavior as well as the powerful ways in which emotional, mental, social, spiritual, and behavioral factors directly affect health. The importance of mind in the development and treatment of diseases has been reflected in the diagnostic and healing approaches employed in traditional Chinese medicine and Ayurveda for thousands of years. The moral and spiritual aspects of healing were noted by Hippocrates, who believed that attitude, environmental influences, and natural remedies must be considered in treating patients (NCCAM, 2011a).

Currently, mind–body therapies represent a major part of the overall use of CAM by the public. In 2002, prayer for health reasons was used by 55% of the U.S. adult population, and relaxation techniques (e.g., meditation, progressive relaxation, deep breathing exercises, yoga), guided imagery, biofeedback, and hypnosis, taken together, were used by approximately 40% of the population (Barnes et al., 2004). Although prayer for health reasons, which was included in the 2002 survey, was removed from the 2007 survey, the use of several types of mind–body therapies, including deep breathing exercises, meditation, and yoga, increased significantly between 2002 and 2007 (Table 9-1) (Barnes et al., 2008).

Mind–body medicine employs different techniques to enhance the mind's capacity to affect bodily function and symptoms. Examples include meditation and yoga.

Meditation

Several meditation techniques exist, including mindfulness meditation, Transcendental Meditation, mantra meditation, relaxation response, and Zen Buddhist meditation, with the first two being the most commonly practiced forms. Meditation has been used for many reasons. For example, it has been employed to enhance health and well-being, to reduce stress and anxiety, and to cope with pain and certain illnesses such as depression, insomnia, heart disease, HIV/AIDS, and cancer. Recent studies have confirmed the effects of meditation in altering intrinsic functional brain connectivity after 8 weeks of mindfulness meditation training (Kilpatrick et al., 2011), along with functional changes in brain regions related to internalized attention as a result of long-term meditation (Jang et al., 2011). Some recent NCCAM-funded studies examined the effects of meditation in relieving stress in caregivers for elderly patients with dementia, reducing the frequency and intensity of hot flashes in menopausal women, relieving the symptoms of chronic back pain, improving attention-related abilities, and relieving asthma symptoms (NCCAM, 2010a). Once those studies are completed, the role of meditation in improving health and well-being should be clearer.

Yoga

Yoga, which originated in India, has been used for health and fitness purposes for thousands of years. Although various styles of yoga are available, they all typically include physical postures, breathing techniques, and meditation to help the individual reach a state of increased relaxation and balanced mind, body, and spirit. One recent review study suggests that yoga may be as effective as or better than exercise at improving a variety of health-related outcomes among both healthy and diseased populations (Ross & Thomas, 2010). Other studies have found that yoga seems to be effective in relieving menopause symptoms (Lee, Kim, Ha, Boddy, & Ernst, 2009), helping children through the rehabilitation process

(Galantino, Galbavy, & Quinn, 2008), improving subjective and objective outcome in bronchial asthma patients (Vempati, Bijlani, & Deepak, 2009), improving mood and reducing anxiety (Streeter et al., 2010), alleviating pain (Posadzki, Ernst, Terry, & Lee, 2011), increasing sense of well-being, reducing stress, decreasing heart rate and blood pressure, increasing lung capacity, improving overall physical fitness, and positively influencing certain brain or blood chemicals (NCCAM, 2008).

Although yoga is generally considered safe in healthy individuals when practiced properly, people with certain medical conditions should not use certain types of yoga. Instead, they should consult with their healthcare provider first if they are considering yoga. In addition, yoga should not be used as a replacement for conventional medical care or to postpone seeing a doctor about a health problem (NCCAM, 2008). Because certain types of yoga require a minimum physical fitness level, not everyone can practice all types of yoga. Most importantly, one should use a well-trained and experienced yoga instructor.

Manipulative and Body-Based Practices

Manipulative and body-based practices are based on manipulation and/or movement of one or more parts of the body. They focus primarily on the systems and structures of the body, including the bones and joints, soft tissues, and circulatory and lymphatic systems. Spinal manipulation and massage therapy are the two commonly used therapies within this category (NCCAM, 2011a). As noted in Table 9-1, 8.6% of U.S. adults have used spinal manipulation and 8.3% of U.S. adults have received some form of massage therapy (Barnes et al., 2008).

Manipulative and body-based therapies focus mainly on the structures and systems of the body, including the bones and joints, the soft tissues, and the circulatory and lymphatic systems. Some practices were derived from traditional medical systems, such as those from China, India, or ancient Greece, whereas others were developed within the last 150 years, such as chiropractic and osteopathic manipulation. Although many providers have formal training in the anatomy and physiology of humans, there is considerable variation in the training and the approaches of these providers both across and within therapies (NCCAM, 2011a). For example, osteopathic and chiropractic practitioners, who primarily use manipulations that involve rapid movements, may have a very different treatment approach from massage therapists, whose techniques involve slower applications of force. Despite this heterogeneity, manipulative and body-based practices share some common characteristics, such as the principles that the human body is self-regulating, has the ability to heal itself, and has body parts that are interdependent. Practitioners in all these therapies also tend to tailor their treatments to the specific needs of each patient.

Chiropractic Medicine

Chiropractic medicine is a form of spinal manipulation, which is one of the oldest healing practices. Spinal manipulation was described by Hippocrates in ancient Greece. In 1895, Daniel David Palmer founded the modern profession of chiropractic in Davenport, Iowa. Based on his observations, he developed a chiropractic theory that describes the nervous system as the most important determinant of health and posits that most diseases are caused by spinal subluxations that respond to spinal manipulation (Ernst, 2008). In turn, manipulation or adjustment of the spine is the core procedure used by chiropractic doctors, who are also called chiropractors or chiropractic physicians. Manipulation is the passive joint movement beyond the normal range of motion; chiropractic medicine prefers the term "adjustment" for this practice (NCCAM, 2010b).

Chiropractic training is a 4-year academic program consisting of both classroom and clinical instruction. At least 3 years of preparatory college work is required for admission to chiropractic schools. Students who graduate receive a doctor of chiropractic (DC) degree and are eligible to take the state licensure board examinations to practice in this field. Some schools also offer postgraduate courses, including 2- to 3-year residency programs in specialized fields (NCCAM, 2010b).

In addition to manipulation, most chiropractors use other treatments such as mobilization, massage, and nonmanual therapies. Examples of nonmanual chiropractic treatments include the following:

- Heat and ice
- Ultrasound
- Electrical stimulation
- Rehabilitative exercise
- Magnetic therapy
- Mobilization, a technique in which a joint is passively moved within its normal range of motion
- Counseling (i.e., counseling about diet, weight loss, and other lifestyle factors)
- Dietary supplements
- Homeopathy
- Acupuncture

Massage

Massage therapies manipulate muscle and connective tissue to enhance the function of those tissues and promote relaxation and well-being. Massage was first practiced thousands of years ago in ancient Greece, ancient Rome, Japan, China, Egypt, and the Indian subcontinent. In the United States, massage therapy first became popular and was promoted for a variety of health purposes starting in the mid-1800s; interest in this modality has greatly increased since the 1970s (NCCAM, 2010c).

The term "massage therapy" covers a group of more than 80 types of massage therapy practices and techniques. In all of them, therapists press, rub, and otherwise manipulate the muscles and other soft tissues of the body, often varying pressure and movement. They most often use their hands and fingers, but may use their forearms, elbows, or feet. Typically, the intent is to relax the soft tissues, increase delivery of blood and oxygen to the massaged areas, warm them, and decrease pain. Based on firsthand experience of receiving Chinese massage, a massage therapist trained in the United States indicated that massage therapies practiced in the United States today are much milder in their forces and different as compared to those practiced in traditional Chinese medicine.

To learn massage, most therapists attend a school or training program, and a much smaller number receive training from an experienced practitioner. After they complete 500 hours of training, they can be certified to be massage therapists. Massage therapy appears to have few serious risks if appropriate cautions are followed (**Table 9**-2). A very small number of serious injuries have been reported, but they appear to have occurred mostly because cautions were not followed or a massage was given by a person who was not properly trained (NCCAM, 2010c).

Energy Fields

Two types of energy fields are distinguished: veritable and putative. The veritable energies employ mechanical vibrations (such as sound) and electromagnetic forces, including visible light, magnetism, monochromatic radiation (such as laser beams), and rays from other parts of the electromagnetic spectrum. They involve the use of specific, measurable wavelengths and frequencies to treat patients. For example, different degrees of heat produced by various heat lamps have been used in treating many disorders in China. In contrast, putative energy fields (also called biofields) are believed to surround and penetrate the human body, but their existence has yet to be measured. Therapies involving putative energy fields are based on the belief that human beings are permeated with a subtle form of energy, called vital

TABLE 9-2

Things You Should Know When Considering Massage Therapy

Do not use massage therapy to replace your regular medical care or as a reason to postpone seeing a healthcare provider about a medical problem.

If you have a medical condition and are unsure whether massage therapy would be appropriate for you, discuss your concerns with your healthcare provider. Your healthcare provider may also be able to help you select a massage therapist. You might also look for published research articles on massage therapy for your condition.

Before deciding to begin massage therapy, ask about the therapist's training, experience, and credentials. Also ask about the number of treatments that might be needed, the cost, and insurance coverage.

If a massage therapist suggests using other CAM practices (for example, herbs or other supplements, or a special diet), discuss these measures first with your regular healthcare provider.

Tell all your healthcare providers about any complementary and alternative practices you use. Give them a full picture of what you do to manage your health. This will ensure coordinated and safe care.

If you have one or more of the following conditions, do not use massage therapy:

- Deep vein thrombosis (a blood clot in a deep vein, usually in the legs)
- A bleeding disorder or use of blood-thinning drugs such as warfarin
- Damaged blood vessels
- Weakened bones from osteoporosis, a recent fracture, or cancer
- A fever
- Any of the following in an area that would be massaged:
  - An open or healing wound
  - A tumor
  - Damaged nerves
  - An infection or acute inflammation
  - Inflammation from radiation treatment
- If you have one or more of the following conditions, be sure to consult your healthcare provider before having massage:
  - Pregnancy
  - Cancer
  - Fragile skin, as from diabetes or a healing scar
  - Heart problems
  - Dermatomyositis, a disease of the connective tissue
  - A history of physical abuse
- Side effects of massage therapy may include the following:
  - Temporary pain or discomfort
  - Bruising
  - Swelling
  - A sensitivity or allergy to massage oils

Source: NCCAM, 2010c.

energy (NCCAM, 2011a). Energy field therapists assert that they can work with this subtle energy, see it with their bare eyes, and use it to cause changes in the physical body and influence health.

Energy field practitioners believe that illness is caused by disturbances of the biofields. For instance, ancient Asian practitioners believed that the flow and balance of life energies are necessary for maintaining health and described tools to restore them more than 2000 years ago. Many therapies in traditional Chinese medicine, such as herbal medicine, acupuncture, acupressure, moxibustion, and cupping, are believed to act by correcting imbalances in the internal biofield, and by restoring the flow of *qi* through meridians to reinstate health. Some therapists are believed to emit or transmit the vital energy (external qi) to a recipient to restore health (Chen & Turner, 2004). A recent systematic review of 66 clinical trials involving a variety of biofield therapies in different populations, however, revealed mixed results of biofield therapies in reducing pain, decreasing anxiety, and improving quality of life (Shamini & Mills, 2010). Thus the effectiveness and efficacy of biofield therapies have not been established, and more well-designed studies are needed to determine their usefulness.

Examples of practices involving putative energy fields include Reiki of Japanese origin and *qi gong* of Chinese origin. Each practice relies on "healing touch," in which the therapist is purported to identify imbalances and correct a client's energy by passing his or her hands over the patient, and intercessory prayer, in which a person intercedes through prayer on behalf of another. These approaches are among the most controversial of CAM therapies because neither the external energy fields nor their therapeutic effects have been confirmed by any biophysical means. Yet, energy medicine is gaining popularity in the American marketplace and has become a subject of investigations at some academic medical centers. A recent national survey revealed that about 0.5% of the U.S. adult population had used Reiki and 0.3% had used qi gong (Barnes et al, 2008).

Qi Gong

Qi gong is a type of energy therapy that supposedly can restore health. It has been practiced widely in China for more than 2000 years. One study examined more than 2000 records in qi gong therapy and found that this modality has health benefits for conditions ranging from high blood pressure to asthma (Sancier & Holman, 2004). Several small randomized clinical trials have revealed the therapeutic effects of qi gong in improving psychological measures (Hui, Wan, Chan, & Yung, 2006), reducing pain and long-term anxiety (Wu et al., 1999), implementing heroin detoxification (Li, Chen, & Mo, 2002), and improving heart rate variability (Lee, Kim, & Lee, 2005). A recent meta-analysis of 77 published peer-reviewed articles that reported the results of randomized controlled trials of qi gong or tai chi interventions found that these practices are associated with consistent, significant results demonstrating a number of positive health benefits in the areas of bone density, cardiopulmonary effects, physical function, falls and related risk factors, quality of life, self-efficacy, patient-reported outcomes, psychological symptoms, and immune function (Jahnke, Larkey, Rogers, Etnier, & Lin, 2010). A review of 36 clinical trials of qi gong and tai chi in older adults found that qi gong and tai chi may help older adults improve their physical function, lower blood pressure, reduce fall risk, and decrease depression and anxiety (Rogers, Larkey, & Keller, 2009).

Reiki

Reiki means "universal life energy" in Japanese. This modality relies on the belief that the patient's spirit and physical body are healed when spiritual energy is channeled through a Reiki practitioner. While this healing method is widely used for a variety of psychological and physical symptoms, there is scarce and conflicting evidence supporting its effectiveness. Most of the existing research studies have been found to have serious limitations in research methods and result reporting, making it difficult to confirm this therapy's effectiveness (Lee, Pittler, & Ernst, 2008; vanderVaart, Gijsen, de Wildt, & Koren, 2009). For more information on Reiki, one can read NCCAM's article, "Backgrounder: Reiki: An Introduction," at http://nccam.nih.gov/health/reiki/introduction.htm.

Therapeutic Touch

Therapeutic touch, another form of energy therapy, is derived from the laying on of hands. It is founded on several ancient healing practices. Since its introduction in 1972 by Dr. Dolores Krieger and Dora Kunz (The Nurse Healers, 2006), the use of therapeutic touch has increased significantly. A 1997 national survey found that approximately 4% of the U.S. adults used therapeutic touch in a given year and that nearly 40 million visits were made to therapeutic touch practitioners, ranking it fifth among the 16 CAM therapies assessed (Eisenberg et al., 1998).

According to advocates of therapeutic touch, each person has a unique energy field (sometimes visible as an "aura") that is simultaneously inside and surrounding the person's physical body. For an individual to be healthy, his or her energy field must be flowing freely or balanced. One or more blockages in a person's energy field will prevent the free flow of energy, causing illness. Therapeutic touch is used to balance or retain the free flow of life energy in an individual, thereby restoring good health (Brewer, 2006).

Therapeutic touch is a deliberately directed process during which a therapeutic touch practitioner moves his or her hands approximately 4 inches above the patient's body to detect the energy imbalance and repair any "holes" where the energy escapes from the body. During the process of restoring the energy balance, the practitioner assists the healing process.

To date, there has been little rigorous scientific research in this area, with few high-quality articles on this modality having been published. A meta-analysis of 11 controlled therapeutic touch studies found that eight controlled studies demonstrated positive outcomes from such treatment, and three showed no effect (Winstead-Fry & Kijekm, 1999). Another meta-analysis of research-based literature on therapeutic touch published in a 10-year period found that although therapeutic touch appears to have a positive, medium effect on physiological and psychological variables, no substantive claims can be made because of the limited published studies and problems with research methods that could seriously bias the reported results (Peters, 1999). A review of 30 studies on therapeutic touch did not yield any generalizable results (Wardell & Weymouth, 2004).

Due to the lack of well-designed research on the effects of therapeutic touch, the efficacy of this therapy cannot be determined until sufficient scientific evidence becomes available. However, the therapist's individual attention and the passing of his or her hands over the patient's body may lead the patient to feel a sense of well-being (Brewer, 2006).

Whole Medical Systems

Whole medical systems are based on complete systems of theory and practice and often evolved prior to, and independently of, the conventional biomedical approach used in the United States (NCCAM, 2011a). They can be categorized into systems developed in Asian (Oriental), Western, and other cultures. Systems developed in Asian cultures include traditional Chinese medicine and Ayurveda (traditional Indian medicine). Systems developed in Western cultures include homeopathic medicine and naturopathic medicine. Systems developed in other cultures include Native American, aboriginal, Middle Eastern, Tibetan, and South American medicine (Donatelle, 2012). This section briefly introduces the more commonly practiced whole medical systems.

Ayurvedic Medicine

Ayurvedic medicine (or Ayurveda) originated in India and has been practiced primarily in the Indian subcontinent for more than 5000 years (Mukherjee & Wahile, 2006). Ayurveda medicine literally means "the science of life," with *ayur* meaning "life" and *veda* meaning "science" (White, 2000). This branch of medicine is based on the Hindu belief that everyone is born in a state of balance within themselves and in relation to the universe (interconnectedness). Thus a person will experience good health if he or she has an effective and wholesome relationship with the immediate universe, whereas disease occurs when the person is out of harmony with the universe. Ayurveda also emphasizes the importance of the body's constitution. "Constitution" is thought to be a unique combination of physical and psychological features and the way in which the body functions. Its characteristics are determined by three *doshas* (*vata*, *pitta*, and *kapha*). Each dosha is associated with a certain body type, a certain personality type, and a greater chance of certain types of illnesses. Therefore, the imbalance of doshas, the state of physical body, and mental or lifestyle factors increases a person's chances of developing certain types of diseases (NCCAM, 2009).

To determine what is wrong with the person, an Ayurvedic practitioner seeks to identify the primary dosha and the balance of doshas by asking the person about his or her diet, behavior, lifestyle practices, and the reasons for the most recent health problem and symptoms the patient had; by observing the person's teeth, tongue, eyes, skin, and overall appearance; by checking the person's bodily sounds, urine, and stool; and by feeling the person's pulse. The practitioner may prescribe diagnostic treatment to restore the balance of one particular dosha. Because of the emphasis on removing the cause of the disease, Ayurvedic doctors prescribe many changes in diet and lifestyle of the patient. After these changes have been made, the doctor will then prescribe a combination of therapies that may include herbs, metals, massage, yoga, breathing exercises, and meditation to balance the body, mind, and spirit (Sharma, Chandola, Singh, & Basisht, 2007).

In India, Ayurvedic doctors are trained in a formal academic setting that includes 4½ years of coursework, a 1-year internship in Ayurveda, and advanced postgraduate training. Ayurvedic practitioners in the United States have various types of training. Some study Ayurveda after they are trained in Western medical or nursing schools. Others may undergo training in naturopathy either before or after their Ayurvedic training. Still others receive training in India. Students who complete their Ayurvedic training in India receive either a bachelor's or doctoral degree and may go to the United States or other countries to practice. Some practitioners are trained in a particular aspect of Ayurvedic practice such as massage or meditation (NCCAM, 2009).

Some Ayurvedic medications have the potential to be toxic because of the high level of heavy metals (lead, mercury, and arsenic) used in these preparations (Saper et al., 2004; van Schalkwyk, Davidson, Palmer, & Hope, 2006). There is also a potential for interactions between Ayurvedic treatments and other medicines. For patients, it is important to tell their healthcare providers if they are using Ayurveda therapy and any associated dietary supplements or medications. Patients who plan to use Ayurvedic remedies should do so under the guidance of an experienced Ayurvedic practitioner. In the United States, there is no national standard for certifying Ayurvedic practitioners at the present time, although several states have approved Ayurvedic schools as educational institutions (NCCAM, 2009). Consumers interested in Ayurveda should be aware that many persons claiming to practice Ayurvedic medicine have had little formal training in this modality (White, 2000). For example, Ayurvedic services offered at spas and salons may not be provided by well-trained Ayurvedic practitioners. Anyone who is interested in Ayurvedic treatment should ask about the practitioner's training and experience and inform his or her healthcare provider about these Ayurvedic medications to ensure there is no conflict with medications or treatments prescribed by the conventional healthcare provider (NCCAM, 2009).

Homeopathic Medicine

Homeopathic medicine, also known as homeopathy, was developed in Germany during the late 1700s by Samuel Hahnemann, a physician, chemist, and linguist. It was introduced to the United States in 1825 by a Boston-born doctor, Hans Burch Gram. Homeopathy is based on the similia principle ("Like cures like"), "potentialization," and the concept that treatment should be selected based on a total picture of the patient including the patient's physical symptoms, emotions, mental state, lifestyle, nutrition, and other aspects (Ballard, 2000; Merrell & Shalts, 2002; Tedesco & Cicchetti, 2001).

The principle of "Like cures like" considers that the symptoms are part of the body's attempt to heal itself, such that an appropriately selected homeopathic remedy will support this self-healing process (Scheiman-Burkhardt, 2001). According to this concept, the symptoms caused by a large dose of a substance can be alleviated by the extremely diluted small amount of the same substance. The concept of "potentialization" holds that systematically diluting a substance, with vigorous shaking at each step of dilution, makes the remedy more effective by extracting the vital essence of the substance. Homeopathy believes that even when the substance is diluted to the point where no single molecule exists in the remedy, the remedy may still be effective because the substance's molecules have exerted their effects on the surrounding water molecules (NCCAM, 2010d).

To select the appropriate homeopathic remedies, a homeopathic provider conducts an in-depth assessment of the patient during the patient's first visit. Based on how the patient responds to the remedy or remedies, the practitioner determines whether to prescribe any additional treatment.

In the United States, training in homeopathy is offered through diploma programs, certificate programs, short courses, and correspondence courses. Medical education in naturopathy includes homeopathic training. Most homeopathy in the United States is practiced along with another health practice for which the practitioner is licensed, such as conventional medicine, naturopathy, chiropractic, dentistry, acupuncture, or veterinary medicine when homeopathy is used to treat animals. In Europe, training in homeopathy is usually pursued as a primary professional degree completed after 3 to 6 years of formal training or as a postgraduate training for doctors.

Homeopathic remedies do not have to undergo any testing or review by the FDA, so some researchers question their effectiveness. Because they are extremely diluted solutions of natural substances that come from plants, mineral, or animals, and are given under the supervision of trained professionals, homeopathic remedies are considered safe and unlikely to cause severe adverse reactions (Dantas & Rampes, 2000). Although homeopathic remedies are not known to interfere with conventional drugs, patients should discuss with their healthcare providers that they are considering using these therapies. As when taking any medications, if patients are taking a homeopathic remedy, they should contact the healthcare provider if their symptoms have not improved in 5 days and keep remedies out of reach for children. Pregnant women and women who are nursing a baby should consult a healthcare provider before using any homeopathic remedies.

Naturopathic Medicine

Naturopathic medicine, or naturopathy, is an eclectic system of health care originating in Germany. Although many of its principles have been used in various healing traditions such as Chinese, Ayurvedic, Native American, and Hippocratic medicine for thousands of years, the term "naturopathy" was coined by a German-born doctor, John Scheel, in 1895 and was popularized by Dr. Benedict Lust, a hydrotherapist from Germany who in 1905 founded the American School of Naturopathy in New York. Because of the influence of various traditional healing principles, naturopathy has elements of complementary and conventional medicine that are used to support and enhance self-healing processes and works with natural healing forces within the body (NCCAM, 2010e).

The term "naturopathy" literally means "nature disease." Naturopaths seek to treat disease by stimulating an individual's innate healing capacities through the use of organic, nontoxic therapies such as fresh air, pure water, bright sunlight, natural food, proper sleep, water therapies, homeopathic remedies, herbs, acupuncture, spinal and soft-tissue manipulation, hydrotherapy, lifestyle counseling, and psychotherapy to heal ailments of body and mind (White, 2000). Naturopaths strive to treat the underlying cause of the condition and see illness as an opportunity to educate and empower patients to develop healthy lifestyles and to take responsibility for their lives.

Today, naturopathic medicine is practiced throughout Europe, Australia, New Zealand, Canada, and the United States. Naturopathic physicians are trained in the art and science of natural health care at accredited naturopathic medical schools. Five major naturopathic schools in the United States and Canada award naturopathic doctor (ND) degrees to students who have completed a 4-year graduate program that focuses on holistic principles, natural therapies, and an orientation to patients as partners in their own healing (NCCAM, 2010e).

Traditional Chinese Medicine

Traditional Chinese medicine (TCM) has gained worldwide popularity. Although it sometimes seems to be foreign and mysterious to many in the Western world, more Westerners are now embracing it. TCM is a complete medical system that has been used to diagnose, treat, and prevent illness for more than 2500 years. Inscriptions on bones and tortoise shells outline TCM treatments for health problems dating from 1500 to 1000 B.C. The earliest TCM books date back to 221 B.C. (Johnson & Johnson, 2002). Korea, Japan, and Vietnam have developed their own unique versions of traditional medicine based on practices originated from China.

TCM is based on the ancient Chinese philosophical theory of *yin* and *yang*. In this view, all of creation is born from the marriage of the two polar principles in the body, yin and yang, which are opposing forces. These forces stand for earth and heaven, winter and summer, night and day, inner and outer, cold and hot, wet and dry, body and mind. Human beings, like everything else in the universe, have two opposite aspects, yin and yang, that are interrelated and interdependent (White, 2000). Interactions of yin and yang regulate the flow of qi (vital energy) throughout the body. Qi is believed to regulate a person's mental, physical, spiritual, and emotional, balance. If yin and yang become imbalanced, the flow of qi is disrupted and disease occurs (NCCAM, 2010f).

TCM diagnosis involves taking a history; inspecting facial complexion, body build, posture, and motion; examining the tongue and its coating; listening to the sound of voice, respiration, and cough; smelling the odor of the patient; interrogating the patient; and palpating the pulses. The TCM interrogation includes the "ten askings": Question one asks about chill and fever, question two about perspiration, question three about the head and trunk, question four about stool and urine, question five about food intake, and question six about the chest. Deafness and thirst are covered in questions seven and eight, question nine asks about past history, and question ten covers causes. Experienced TCM practitioners can make a diagnosis based solely on the examination of the tongue and palpation of the pulse (Johnson & Johnson, 2002).

Based on the philosophy of TCM, the purpose of treatment is to restore yin and yang harmony. The TCM doctor uses acupuncture, tui na (Chinese massage, a more powerful and stronger form of massage than that practiced in the United States), herbal therapy, moxibustion (applying cones of herbal substances to the skin and igniting them to make smoke, or igniting prepared strip of herbs to cause smoke and holding the smoking strip of herbs close to certain parts of the body), cupping (attachment of a small cup to the skin of the patient that creates a vacuum after the heated air inside the cup cools), energetic exercises (e.g., tai chi, qi gong), and diet (adjusting the food based on *its yin and yang properties*) to recover and sustain the patient's health (Johnson & Johnson, 2002).

Traditionally, TCM practitioners are trained within the family. Typically, the father would train the son to be a TCM practitioner, who would then carry on the family tradition and extend the rich first-hand experiences in TCM diagnosis and practices. Many such experiences were to be kept secret and within the family. Since 1949, the Chinese government has encouraged many of such family-trained TCM practitioners to share their secret experiences. Many of them have been employed as clinical faculty members in various TCM colleges, passing on their rich experiences in TCM to their students. A modern TCM doctor typically receives 5 years of academic training in one of the TCM colleges in China or several Western countries. After 4 years of coursework in basic science and TCM subjects, the student completes a 1-year internship in a TCM hospital or a TCM department in a major comprehensive teaching hospital. Students who complete the formal academic training receive a bachelor's or doctoral degree. After they graduate from a TCM college, the TCM doctors can be employed by TCM hospitals or TCM departments in any comprehensive teaching hospitals where they receive advanced clinical training. Many TCM colleges in China also offer postgraduate training in TCM.

TCM is generally safe if it is administered under the supervision of a well-trained and experienced TCM practitioner. It is important that you tell your healthcare provider if you are using any TCM treatments, as some herbal preparations may interact with other medications you are taking.

RESEARCH AND TECHNOLOGY

Scientific evidence from randomized clinical trials is strong for many uses of acupuncture, for some herbal medicines, and for some of the manipulative therapies (such as chiropractic and massage therapy) (Robinson & Zhang, 2011). For most CAM approaches, however, there is an insufficient amount of valid and reliable randomized controlled data to demonstrate their mechanisms of action, efficacy, and applicability. In addition, many studies in CAM are flawed by insufficient statistical power, poor controls, inconsistent treatment, or lack of comparisons (Nahin & Straus, 2001).

Nevertheless, there exist significant challenges in applying research methods for CAM. The current model of research evaluation of CAM is based on the methodology of Western medicine (i.e., quantitative research methods), which cannot quantify the impact of profound traditional philosophy, culture, and religion. In this regard, qualitative research may be more appropriate. In the Western world, many researchers question the efficacy of many CAM therapies because "science has not provided sufficient evidence." However, history reveals that several traditional healing systems (e.g., traditional Chinese medicine and Ayurveda) have been practiced and used in treating diseases and promoting health for thousands of years. The long history of field-tested human experiments, long-term observations, and clinical trials may have proved the value of those ancient healing systems.

Perhaps the currently available science and technology are simply unable to measure the effects of many CAM therapies, or perhaps we do not have the appropriate research methodologies available to perform such studies. As new knowledge is discovered and technologies are developed, it may become possible to detect the effects of many CAM therapies, especially those that have been practiced for thousands of years. The historical process of discovering the mind–body connection best illustrates this possibility. For example, the connection between the mind and the body was first believed to be in existence in ancient times. Early technological advances (e.g., microscopy, the stethoscope, the blood pressure cuff, and refined surgical techniques) separated the mind from the physical body. The discovery of bacteria and antibiotics further dispelled the notion of belief influencing health. Later science discovered the link between the mind and the body. Nowadays, with functional connectivity magnetic resonance imaging (fMRI) and other modern technologies, we are able to confirm the connection between mind and body.

The U.S. government has placed significant emphasis on CAM research. In recent years, NCCAM has supported studies in various therapies in each of the major categories to different extents. It regularly examines and redefines its research priorities to fill gaps in the research, capitalize on emerging opportunities, and leverage resources. The recently released NCCAM *Third Strategic Plan: 2011–2015* presents the following five objectives to guide NCCAM in determining future research priorities in CAM (NCCAM, 2011b):

1. Advance research on mind and body interventions, practices, and disciplines
2. Advance research on CAM natural products
3. Increase understanding of "real-world" patterns and outcomes of CAM use and its integration into health care and health promotion
4. Improve the capacity of the field to carry out rigorous research
5. Develop and disseminate objective, evidence-based information on CAM interventions

In 2011, there were 54 active program announcements including research projects (R01, R03, and other R awards), exploratory/developmental research projects (all R21), health disparity/minority research, and others. Although NCCAM funds a wide range of research topics, the current areas of special interest focus on CAM interventions used often by the public and on health conditions in which CAM modalities are most frequently used, including investigations of the impact of CAM interventions in relieving chronic pain syndromes and inflammatory processes, and improving health and wellness (NCCAM, 2011c).

To develop skilled investigators in CAM research, NCCAM offers funding to support predoctoral, postdoctoral, and career awards through several funding channels. To encourage clinicians interested in pursuing careers as investigators, NCCAM offers them Clinical Research Curriculum Awards and training in the skills needed for conducting rigorous research in CAM (NIH, 2011). With the support from the U.S. government and many professional organizations along with the commitment and contributions from the scientists, significant progress in CAM research has been made in the last decade.

Biomedical science and technology have advanced CAM treatment and research significantly. For example, standardizing the "dose" of acupuncture through the use of an electrical apparatus to simulate the acupuncture needles makes quantitative research on acupuncture possible. Cells isolated and cultured in the laboratory have been used to study the effect of qi in TCM. Biomedical laboratory techniques have been used to assess the benefits of music (Chikahisa et al., 2006) and humor (Christie & Moore, 2005). Biopharmacology has contributed to the research on the effects of various herbal therapies on cancer (Richardson, 2001). fMRI has been used to study the effects of acupuncture on the human brain among normal persons (K. Li et al., 2006) and among stroke patients (Li, Jack, & Yang, 2006), as well as to measure the effects of electroacupuncture versus manual acupuncture on the human brain (Napadow, Makris, Liu, Kettner, Kwong, & Hui, 2005).

In addition, information technology has been used to support collaborative research, monitor clinical trials, and provide educational information to medical students, fellows, faculty, and community-based care providers who work with people and CAM (Monkman, 2001; Whelan & Dvorkin, 2003). NCCAM has also used the Internet to disseminate authoritative information to the public and professionals (NIH, 2011).

With the advancement of biomedical science, computer technology, and human genome, we can expect to see more applications of science and technology in CAM treatment and research. It is hoped that one day we will be able to provide scientific evidence that demonstrates the effects of the ancient traditional medicines.

LEGAL AND ETHICAL ISSUES

Many countries face major challenges in the development and implementation of regulations aimed at traditional, complementary, alternative, and herbal medicines. These challenges are related to these treatments' regulatory status, assessment of safety and efficacy, quality control, safety monitoring, and lack of knowledge about traditional, complementary, alternative, and herbal medicines by national drug regulatory authorities. According to a recent WHO report (Robinson & Zhang, 2011), the number of WHO member states reporting to have regulations or laws governing herbal medicine increased significantly from 14 prior to 1986 to 110 in 2007, while slightly more than one-third of WHO member countries reported to have laws or regulations focused on traditional medicine or complementary alternative medicine (38% or 54 of 141 countries) (WHO, 2005).

Currently, the United States does not have a regulatory process to ensure the safety and efficacy of various CAM therapies except for homeopathic remedies and dietary supplements. In 1938, the U.S. Congress passed a law allowing homeopathic remedies to be regulated by the FDA in the same manner as nonprescription, OTC drugs. As a consequence, people can purchase homeopathic remedies in any drugstore without a prescription from a doctor. In addition, homeopathic remedies do not need to meet the FDA's requirements for conventional prescription drugs and other OTC drugs. Specifically, FDA requires that all conventional prescription drugs must go through thorough testing and systematic review that proves their safety and effectiveness before they can be licensed for sale as prescription drugs. Only those prescription drugs that have been marketed as prescription medications for at least 3 years, have a relatively high use, and have not had any alarming adverse drug reactions and increased side effects during the time they were available as prescription drugs can be switched from prescription to OTC status. However, the FDA does require homeopathic remedies to meet certain legal standards for strength, quality, purity, and packaging (Junod, 2000).

The FDA regulates dietary supplements under a different set of regulations than those that apply to conventional prescription and OTC drugs. Under the Dietary Supplement Health and Education Act of 1994 (DSHEA), dietary supplements are considered products (other than tobacco) intended to supplement the diet and are not "drugs" from an official standpoint. Dietary supplement manufacturers are responsible for ensuring that a dietary supplement is safe and the product label information is truthful and not misleading before it is marketed. They are required by the Bioterrorism Act of 2002 to register with the FDA before they can make or sell supplements. However, these manufacturers do not have to prove the safety and effectiveness of any dietary supplements, nor do their products need FDA approval before they are marketed. The FDA is responsible for monitoring product information (such as package inserts and labeling claims) and taking action against any unsafe dietary supplement products after they reach the market (FDA, 2011b).

A large proportion of patients who use CAM therapies do not inform their conventional doctors about their use of such products and services. This omission, combined with the possibility of adverse reactions with prescription drugs, is placing the lives of many Americans in danger. Ethically, consumers have the right to use CAM therapies as a matter of autonomy, but they also have the duty not to harm themselves. Ethically, manufacturers must ensure that their products are not harmful and have the claimed effect(s), but there are no laws or regulations that require manufacturers to prove that their products work as stated. When patients are experiencing problems related to health and illness, ineffective products, although not necessarily harmful on their own, may mask the signs and symptoms that would allow for accurate diagnosis, delay appropriate treatment, and jeopardize patients' lives. This, in effect, not only causes physical and emotional harm to patients, but also brings added costs to patients and society in terms of money and resources.

To ensure patients' safety, CAM therapies must be evaluated with regard to safety and efficacy. The FDA has the ethical responsibility to take the lead in this area. To protect the common good, there is a need to know not only what CAM can do *for* us, but also what it can do *to* us. In addition, the U.S. government has the ethical responsibility to develop specific regulations that require manufacturers of CAM devices, remedies, and dietary supplements to follow the requirements for devices and prescription drugs used in conventional medicine. Unless a device or remedy is proved to be safe and effective, no products with the potential to alter health should be allowed in the market. Achieving this goal may take a long time, however. Since its passage, the 1994 DSHEA has been intensely debated in the U.S. Congress. Until such regulations are developed, approved, and implemented, we need to educate consumers on how to select qualified CAM practitioners and therapies and how to evaluate CAM information from the Internet and other sources. **Table 9-3**, **Table 9-4**, and **Table 9-5** provide useful information offered by the NCCAM.

TABLE 9-3

Are You Considering Using CAM?

- Take charge of your health by being an informed consumer. Find out and consider which scientific studies have been done on the safety and effectiveness of the CAM therapy that interests you. Discuss the information with your healthcare provider before making a decision.

- If you decide to use a CAM therapy provided by a practitioner, such as acupuncture or chiropractic, choose the practitioner with care.

- If you decide to use a dietary supplement, such as an herbal product, find out about any potential side effects or interactions with medications or other dietary supplements you may be taking.

- Tell all your healthcare providers about any complementary and alternative practices you use. Give them a full picture of what you do to manage your health. This will help ensure coordinated and safe care.

Source: National Center for Complementary and Alternative Medicine (NCCAM). (n.d.). CAM basics: Are you considering using CAM? Retrieved from http://nccam.nih.gov/health/decisions/consideringcam.htm

TABLE 9-4

Key Issues to Consider When Selecting a CAM Practitioner

Selecting a qualified healthcare provider is an important decision and can be the key to ensuring that you are receiving the best health care. The following key points are provided by the National Center for Complementary and Alternative Medicine (NCCAM) to assist you when making a decision about selecting a CAM provider.

- Talk to your primary healthcare providers if you are considering a CAM therapy. They may be able to answer questions and/or refer you to a practitioner. Also, be aware that there are other resources for locating a CAM practitioner, such as professional organizations for specific practitioner groups.

- Gather basic information on the CAM practitioners whom you are considering, such as their education, experience, and cost, and interview them in person or by telephone. Make your selection based on their answers to your questions, and your level of comfort during the interview.

- Evaluate your practitioner after the initial treatment visit—including what you have been told to expect in terms of therapy outcomes, time, and costs—and decide whether the practitioner is right for you.

- Tell all of your healthcare providers about any complementary and alternative practices you use. Give them a full picture of what you do to manage your health. This will help ensure coordinated and safe care.

Source: National Center for Complementary and Alternative Medicine (NCCAM). (n.d.). CAM basics: Selecting a complementary and alternative medicine practitioner. Retrieved from http://nccam.nih.gov/health/decisions /practitioner.htm

TABLE 9-5

Ten Things to Know About Evaluating Medical Resources on the Web

The number of websites offering health-related resources grows every day. Many sites provide valuable information, whereas others may have information that is unreliable or misleading. This short guide contains important questions you should consider as you look for health information online. Answering these questions when you visit a new site will help you evaluate the information you find.

1. Who runs the web-based health resource site?	Any good health-related website should make it easy for you to learn who is responsible for the site and its information. On this site, for example, the National Center for Complementary and Alternative Medicine (NCCAM) is clearly marked on every major page of the site, along with a link to the NCCAM homepage.
2. Who pays for the health website?	It costs money to run a website. The source of a website's funding should be clearly stated or readily apparent. For example, web addresses ending in ".gov" indicate government-sponsored sites, ".edu" denotes an educational institution, ".org" a noncommercial organization, and ".com" a commercial organization. You should know how the site pays for its existence. Does it sell advertising? Is it sponsored by a drug company? The source of funding can affect which content is presented, how the content is presented, and what the site owners want to accomplish on the site.
3. What is the purpose of the online health resource?	The site's purpose is related to who runs and pays for it. Look for an "About This Site" link on the home page. There you should find a clear statement of purpose, which will help you evaluate the trustworthiness of the information.
4. What are the health information sources?	Many health/medical sites post information collected from other websites or sources. If the person or organization in charge of the site did not create the information, the original source should be clearly labeled.
5. What is the basis of the health information?	In addition to identifying who wrote the material you are reading, the site should describe the evidence (such as articles in medical journals) upon which the material is based. Also, opinions or advice should be clearly set apart from information that is "evidence-based" (that is, based on research results).
6. How is the health information selected and reviewed?	If a website is presenting medical information, people with credible professional and scientific qualifications should review the material before it is posted. Check for the presence of an editorial board, or other indications of how information is selected and reviewed.
7. Is the health information current?	Websites should be reviewed and updated on a regular basis. It is particularly important that medical information be current—outdated content can be misleading or even dangerous. The most recent update or review date should be clearly posted.
8. How does the site choose links to other sites?	Websites usually have a policy about establishing links to other sites. Some medical sites take a conservative approach and do not link to any other sites. Some link to any site that asks, or pays, for a link. Others only link to sites that have met certain criteria.
9. How does the site collect your personal health information and why?	Websites routinely track visitors' paths to determine which pages are being viewed. A health website may ask you to "subscribe" or "become a member." In some cases, this may be so that it can collect a user fee or select information for you that is relevant to your concerns. In all cases, this will give the site personal information about you.

(continues)

TABLE 9-5	

Ten Things to Know About Evaluating Medical Resources on the Web *(continued)*

9. *(continued)*	Any credible site asking for this kind of information should tell you exactly what it will and will not do with it. Many commercial sites sell "aggregate" (collected) data about their users to other companies—information such as what percentage of their users are women older than 40, for example. In some cases, they may collect and reuse information that is "personally identifiable," such as your ZIP code, gender, and birth date. Be sure to read any privacy policy or similar language on the site, and do not sign up for anything you do not fully understand.
10. How does the site manage interactions with visitors?	You should always be able to contact the site owner if you run across problems, have questions or feedback. If the site hosts chat rooms or other online discussion areas, it should explain the terms of using this service. Is it moderated? If so, by whom, and why? Spend some time reading the discussion before joining in, to see whether you feel comfortable with the environment.

Source: National Center for Complementary and Alternative Medicine (NCCAM). (n.d.). CAM basics: Evaluating web-based health resources. Retrieved from http://nccam.nih.gov/health/webresources/

Ethical issues related to CAM research remain to be resolved. The current clinical trials of acupuncture have examined its efficacy by administering a fixed course of treatment sessions based on biomedical diagnosis. This standardized approach conflicts with the traditional means of delivering holistic TCM treatments that are customized to the individual's level of strength or weakness of yin and yang (Hammerschlag, 1998). A similar ethical challenge exists in evaluating the effects of Ayurvedic therapies that are determined, based on the individual's constitution (Sharma et al., 2007). Likewise, homeopathic remedies are highly individualized (White, 2000). Because many traditional medicines are deeply rooted in cultural traditions and religion, the interactions between the practitioner and the patient, and the influence of the family, religion, cultural and personal belief systems are important factors in the success of those traditional therapies. When patients are taken out of their traditional, social, and cultural context, and placed in a scientifically controlled treatment environment, the question becomes, "Are we serving the best interests of our patients?"

With the current scientific research methods available, researchers continue to debate which research mythologies are most appropriate. Some researchers argue against the use of placebo and sham controls (patients in the control group receive no treatment or fake treatment), while others favor wait lists (patients receive the treatment once the study is completed) and standard care (patients receive routine care) designs. The former group believes withholding treatment to be inappropriate, and the latter group considers testing a treatment prior to demonstrating its efficacy against a placebo to be just as inappropriate.

From these examples, we can see that there are many legal and ethical challenges in CAM treatment and research. It is hoped that we will be able to meet these challenges as we learn more about CAM and develop more appropriate research methods.

INFLUENCES OF POLITICS, ECONOMICS, CULTURE, AND RELIGION

Politics: The Role of Government

Government has always played a major and an important role in CAM treatments and research. For example, the Indian government has undertaken systematic research of Ayurvedic practices since 1969. In China, TCM has gone through several waves of challenges and has a long history of regulation.

Between 1911 and 1949, the Chinese government embraced Western medicine with the goal of modernizing the Chinese medical care system. This movement forced TCM go underground and nearly wiped out TCM. Since 1949, however, the Chinese government has promoted the integration of Western and Chinese medicine, established major colleges of TCM, reprinted many older TCM-related works, and worked with WHO and other interested organizations and countries to promote TCM globally. In the last three decades, international training centers have been established in Beijing, Shanghai, Guangzhou, Nanjing, and Xiamen to train TCM personnel from all over the world. Multiple TCM colleges have been established in many Western countries, and many cooperative research projects have been conducted between China and developed countries (Johnson & Johnson, 2002).

The influence of politics and government is significant in the United States as well. One politician, U.S. Senator Tom Harkins, played a key role in the establishment of the Office of Alternative Medicine (OAM) within the National Institutes of Health (NIH) in 1992 and the National Center for Complementary and Alternative Medicine (NCCAM) in 1999. Since the establishment of OAM and NCCAM, government funding for NCCAM has increased from $2 million in 1990 to $127.7 million in 2011 (**Figure 9-1**). The support by the U.S. government has allowed NCCAM to explore CAM practices in the context of rigorous science, training of CAM researchers, and dissemination of authoritative information to the public and professionals (NCCAM, 2011d; NIH, 2011).

Worldwide, however, two-thirds of the countries that participated in a WHO survey on national policy on traditional medicine and regulations of herbal medicines reported that they do not have such a national policy (68%, or 96 of 141 countries). Based on the definition provided by WHO (2005), a national policy on traditional medicine or CAM may include a definition of traditional medicine/CAM, provision for the creation of laws and regulations, consideration of intellectual property issues, and strategies for achieving the objectives of the policy. For those countries that do have such a national policy, most of them established it recently. Less than one-third of the participating countries (28%, or 40 of 141) reported having issued a national program on traditional medicine/CAM, slightly more than half of the countries (53%, or 75 of 141) reported having a national office in charge of traditional medicine/CAM,

FIGURE 9-1

NCCAM Funding Appropriations History

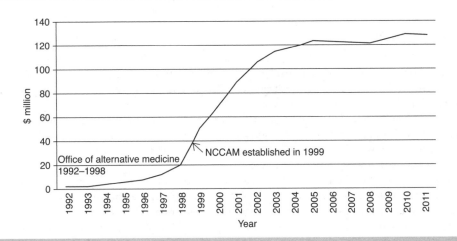

Source: NCCAM, 2011b.

and 58 countries (41%) indicated having at least one national institute on traditional medicine, CAM, or herbal medicines (WHO, 2005). The United States did not participate in this survey.

The limited scientific evidence regarding the safety and efficacy of traditional medicine/CAM and the widespread use of traditional medicine/CAM worldwide makes it important for governments to take the following steps (WHO, 2011a):

- Formulate national policy and regulation for the proper use of traditional medicine/CAM and its integration into national healthcare systems in line with the provisions of the WHO strategies on traditional medicines
- Establish regulatory mechanisms to control the safety and quality of products and of traditional medicine/CAM practice
- Create awareness about safe and effective traditional medicine/CAM therapies among the public and consumers
- Cultivate and conserve medicinal plants to ensure their sustainable use

Economics

The widespread use of traditional medicine and CAM in developing countries partly reflects the impact of each country's economy. Because traditional and herbal medicines are less expensive and more widely accessible than Western medicine, many developing countries, especially those in Africa, Asia, and Latin America, use traditional medicine to help meet some of the primary healthcare needs of their citizens. It is estimated that 80% of the African population uses traditional medicine for primary health care (WHO, 2008). The poorer economic conditions in developing countries limit their residents' access to modern Western medicine, which is typically characterized by expensive consultations provided by doctors who are expensively trained, using expensive procedures, laboratory equipment, and pharmaceuticals. One of WHO's priorities is to promote safe and effective traditional medicine/CAM therapies to increase access to health care in developing countries (WHO, 2008).

In contrast, the economic conditions in developed countries have actually promoted the use of CAM. In developed countries, most CAM therapies are not covered by health insurance plans. Because of the better economies found in developed countries, however, the people who live there are generally better off and are financially able to pay for various CAM services and treatments on an out-of-pocket basis (Eisenberg et al., 1998; Palinkas & Kabongo, 2000).

Culture and Religion

The evolution of traditional medicines has been influenced by the different religious, cultural, and historic conditions in which they were first developed (WHO, 2005). For example, traditional Chinese medical care and practice are strongly influenced by Chinese tradition and religion including Confucian principles, Taoism, the theory of yin and yang, and Buddhism (Chen, 2001; Zhang & Cheng, 2000). The ideas from Hinduism, one of the world's oldest and largest religions, as well as ancient Persian thoughts about health and healing shaped the core principles of Ayurveda. Mexican American folk medicine, curanderismo, mainly draws from the combination of Mayan and Aztec teachings and the Mexican heritage of Spanish Catholicism (Krippner, 1995).

Religious and cultural beliefs also influence the practice and use of traditional medical healings. Mexican American healers often attribute an illness to an agent whose existence must be taken on faith because it cannot be detected with medical instruments. For instance, Mexican American healers use prayers and songs to treat an illness caused by an inappropriate salute to an owl. This illness is characterized by heart palpitations, anxiety, sweating, and shaking. It is believed that this disease can lead to suicide if left untreated. Many Native American healings are considered spiritual in nature and, in turn, rituals and magic such as medicine wheels and sand paintings are used to treat these supernatural disorders. Native Americans' imitative magic treatment is based on the belief that what happened to an image or drawing of a person did happen in reality (Krippner, 1995). Such beliefs were also prevalent among Chinese in the old times and still exist among many older Chinese.

Cultural beliefs significantly predict the use of traditional medical practices. For instance, in Chinese culture, it is believed that the mother loses a significant amount of yang during the delivery of a baby and must preserve any yang left so that her yin will not be too strong. Therefore, a new mother must stay indoors for an entire month, regardless of the season, after delivering the baby; cannot touch or eat anything cold (yin); cannot take a bath; and cannot go outdoors without covering all of the exposed body parts to avoid cold air. All of those activities are considered yin, so the traditional practices are believed to help promote the yang and maintain yin–yang balance. If the new mother failed to follow those practices, her yang could not be restored and her yin would be too strong, which is believed to cause joint pain, lower back pain, lost teeth, and headaches later in her life. Also, ancient Chinese beliefs hold that animal organs correspond to human organs. If a particular human organ is weak, the same organ of an animal should be consumed. For example, a new mother is believed to have "weakened" blood caused by losing blood during and after the delivery, so she might eat cooked pig's blood to strengthen her own blood.

CAM IN DEVELOPING VERSUS DEVELOPED SOCIETIES

Traditional medicine and CAM use is more prevalent in developing countries as compared to developed countries. In the developing world, traditional medicine has been used largely for primary health care. In India, Ayurveda has been the main healthcare system and is still used today by 80% of the population (NCCAM, 2009). A 2008 WHO report revealed that as much as 90% of African populations uses traditional medicine to meet their primary care needs, and TCM is available to 75% of the areas in China and has been fully integrated into its healthcare system.

In contrast to the developing countries, the developed world perceives traditional medicine and CAM as a choice because the number of well-educated and well-informed patients is increasing. These individuals are often attracted by the holistic and natural approaches employed by various CAM therapies. Well-educated and well-informed healthcare consumers want to become more involved in their overall health care, take a more natural and holistic approach to achieving personal well-being, and are willing to pay for CAM therapies out of pocket (Astin, 1998; Eisenberg et al., 1998; Palinkas & Kabongo, 2000).

STUDY QUESTIONS

1. What are some of the potential benefits and risks of traditional medicine/CAM? Why do you think these practices and products have maintained their popularity in the developing countries and are becoming so popular in the Western world?
2. What role do you believe governments should play in promoting traditional medicine/CAM?
3. Should the use of CAM in the United States and other developed countries be regulated? If use of CAM should be regulated, by whom and how should it be regulated? If use of CAM should not be regulated, why and what would be the consequences?
4. What do you believe to be the major challenges in CAM use and CAM research? What would you do to address such challenges?

CASE STUDIES

Homeopathic Remedy Treating Anxiety and Depression After Conventional Therapies Failed (Wember, 1997)

John had a relatively long history of depression. In the past, his anxiety and depression would dissipate over time after he took psychotropic drugs. His present depression started a year ago, in the wake of an incident at work where he felt betrayed. Even after John had taken six different antidepressant and antianxiety drugs and suffered from the side effects of the drugs, his depressive symptoms remained. He became more and more dysfunctional at work, to the point where he was on sick leave for the month prior to seeking homeopathic care. At the time he saw the homeopathic practitioner, he was extremely upset and still angry and aggressive. He received a single dose of Staphysagria IM. At the next appointment, 3 weeks later, John said he was "much better." His appetite had returned, and he had started to gain back the weight he had lost. He was calmer and sleeping better. He was working full-time at home and would go back to the office that next week. He said, "I decided to change my priorities. I will do more things for myself and enjoy life a little more."

Homeopathy Treating Postpartum Depression (White, 2000)

A 28-year-old woman with postpartum depression revealed to her psychologist fantasies and impulses of throwing her 14-week-old daughter off of a cliff. Envying her friends without children and feeling distant and angry toward her husband as well as her infant, she was mired in a severe clinical depression that had been unresponsive to two trials of antidepressant medication. The psychologist referred the patient to a homeopath, a practitioner of the German-born form of medicine that uses a minute dose of an herb, plant, or other substance to effect healing, reportedly by stimulating a patient's "vital force." Within 4 days of beginning treatment with a remedy called sepia, the woman's depression lifted, and she began bonding with her infant. Homeopaths explain such rapid cures by saying that the energy of the remedy repairs the "leakage" in the patient's "energy balloon" that has been created by particular traumas or life events. The specific remedy used in this case, sepia, is made from the ink of the cuttlefish. It reportedly is indicated when a woman is exhausted physically and emotionally from a myriad of responsibilities and work or from too many pregnancies, abortions, or miscarriages. A classic sign of its indication, according to homeopaths, is a person's indifference or aversion to loved ones. "The change was astounding!" her psychologist told the homeopath. "Now she loves the baby and is taking all kinds of photographs and videotapes of her child, and her marital relationship has improved considerably."

Traditional Chinese Medicine Treating Infertility

A Chinese couple in their early 30s went to see a TCM doctor, hoping the practitioner could help them conceive a child. This couple had been married for 3 years and had gone through extensive clinical examinations and laboratory tests, including ultrasound. Nothing appeared to be wrong with their reproductive organs and functions, but they just could not conceive a child. The TCM doctor checked the pulse, examined the tongue, and took the history from the couple. The TCM diagnosis was that both the husband and the wife had *yin xu* (meaning weak yin) caused by weak "kidney"; the TCM doctor prescribed

CASE STUDIES

Chinese herbal medicine for the couple to strengthen the kidney, which would enhance yin and balance the yin–yang harmony. After 3 months of treatment, the wife was pregnant. The TCM doctor checked the wife's pulse at 5 weeks' gestation and informed the wife that she was carrying a boy. Nine months later, a healthy baby boy was born to the couple. Now the baby boy is in his third year in a medical school in China.

Qi Therapy Used to Relieve Symptoms of Cancer in a Terminally III Cancer Patient (Lee & Jang, 2005)

Jane suffered from late-stage ovarian cancer and was experiencing unbearable abdominal discomfort and pain, depression, and fatigue. Four sessions of qi therapy on alternate days was given to Jane over a 7-day period. After 20 minutes of qi therapy, she experienced improvements in mood and alertness, and a reduction in pain, anxiety, depression, discomfort, and fatigue, on both the first and last days of the interventions. Furthermore, the scores recorded on the last day for most symptoms were improved relative to those recorded on the first day. Although the result of this case study does not constitute conclusive evidence, the data suggest that qi therapy may have some beneficial effects on some symptoms of cancer.

Case Study Questions (related to the previous case studies)

1. Why do you think that complementary or alternative medicine (CAM) can be highly effective in the above described scenarios when Western medicine was not able to produce positive results?
2. What are the reasons that many people will not believe in, nor try to use complementary or alternative medicines (CAM) as a first intervention for a health problem?
3. What are the legal/ethical issues (if they exist) for prescribing CAM in your area of residence?

REFERENCES

Astin, J. A. (1998). Why patients use alternative medicine. *Journal of the American Medical Association, 279*, 1548–1553.

Ballard, R. (2000). Homeopathy: An overview. *Australian Family Physician, 29*, 1145–1148.

Barnes, P. M., Bloom, B., & Nahin, R. (2008). Complementary and alternative medicine use among adults and children: United States, 2007. CDC National Health Statistics Report #12. Retrieved from http://nccam.nih.gov/news/2008/nhsr12.pdf

Barnes, P. M., Powell-Griner, E., McFann, K., & Nahin, R. L. (2004). *Complementary and alternative medicine use among adults: United States, 2002. Advance data from vital and health statistics, No. 343.* National Center for Health Statistics. Retrieved from http://www.cdc.gov/nchs/data/ad/ad343.pdf

Brewer, A. V. (2006). *Energy healing.* In J. Brewer & K. King (Eds.), *Complementary and alternative medicine: A physician guide* [Electronic book]. Retrieved from http://medicine.wustl.edu/~compmed/cam_toc.htm

Chen, K. W., & Turner, F. D. (2004). A case study of simultaneous recovery from multiple physical symptoms with medical qigong therapy. *Journal of Alternative and Complementary Medicine, 10*, 159–162.

Chen, Y. C. (2001). Chinese values, health and nursing. *Journal of Advanced Nursing, 36*, 270–273.

Chikahisa, S., Sei, H., Morishima, M., Sano, A., Kitaoka, K., Nakaya, Y., . . . Morita, Y. (2006). Exposure to music in the perinatal period enhances learning performance and alters BDNF/TrkB signaling in mice as adults. *Behavioral Brain Research, 169*, 312–319.

Christie, W., & Moore, C. (2005). The impact of humor on patients with cancer. *Clinical Journal of Oncology Nursing, 9*, 211–218.

Dantas, F., & Rampes, H. (2000). Do homeopathic medicine provoke adverse effects? A systematic review. *British Homeopathic Journal, 89*, S35–S38.

Dessio, W., Wade, C., Chao, M., Kronenberg, F., Cushman, L. E., & Kalmuss, D. (2004). Religion, spirituality, and healthcare choices of African-American women: Results of a national survey. *Ethnicity & Disease, 14*, 189–197.

Donatelle, R. J. (2012). *Access to health* (12th ed.). San Francisco, CA: Benjamin Cummings, Pearson Education.

Eisenberg, D. M., Davis, R. B., Ettner, S. L., Appel, S., Wilkey, S., Van Rompay, M., & Kessler, R. C. (1998). Trends in alternative medicine use in the United States, 1990–1997: Results of a follow-up national survey. *Journal of the American Medical Association, 280*, 1569–1575.

Eisenberg, D. M., Kessler, R. C., Van Rompay, M. I., Kaptchuk, T. J., Wilkey, S. A., Appel, S., & R. B. Davis. (2001). Perceptions about complementary therapies relative to conventional therapies among adults who use both: Results from a national survey. *Annals of Internal Medicine, 135*, 344–351.

Ernst, E. (2008). Chiropractic: A critical evaluation. *Journal of Pain and Symptom Management, 35*(5), 544–562.

Food and Drug Administration (FDA). (2000). Risk of drug interactions with St John's wort and Indinavir and other drugs. Retrieved from http://www.fda.gov/Drugs/DrugSafety/PostmarketDrug SafetyInformationforPatientsandProviders/DrugSafetyInformationforHealthcareProfessionals /PublicHealthAdvisories/ucm052238.htm

Food and Drug Administration (FDA). (2004). FDA announces rule prohibiting sale of dietary supplements containing ephedrine alkaloids effective April 12. Retrieved from http://www.fda.gov/NewsEvents /Newsroom/PressAnnouncements/2004/ucm108281.htm

Food and Drug Administration (FDA). (2011a). Beware of fraudulent "dietary supplements." Retrieved from http://www.fda.gov/downloads/ForConsumers/ConsumerUpdates/UCM247107.pdf

Food and Drug Administration (FDA). (2011b). Dietary supplements. Retrieved from http://www.fda.gov /Food/DietarySupplements/default.htm

Galantino, M. L., Galbavy, R., & Quinn, L. (2008). Therapeutic effects of yoga for children: A systematic review of the literature. *Pediatric Physical Therapy, 20*(1), 66–80.

Hammerschlag, R. (1998). Methodological and ethical issues in clinical trials of acupuncture. *Journal of Alternative And Complementary Medicine, 4*, 159–171.

Hui, P. N., Wan, M., Chan, W. K., & Yung, P. M. (2006). An evaluation of two behavioral rehabilitation programs, qigong versus progressive relaxation, in improving the quality of life in cardiac patients. *Journal of Alternative and Complementary Medicine, 12*, 373–378.

Institute of Medicine. (2005). *Institute of Medicine report on complementary and alternative medicine in the United States*. Washington, DC: National Academies Press.

Jahnke, R., Larkey, L., Rogers, C., Etnier, J., & Lin, F. (2010). A comprehensive review of health benefits of qigong and tai chi. *American Journal of Health Promotion, 24*(6), e1–e25. Retrieved from http://www .ncbi.nlm.nih.gov/pmc/articles/PMC3085832/?tool=pubmed

Jang, J. H., Jung, W. H., Kang, D. J., Byun, M. S., Kwon, S. J., Chio, C. H., & Kwon, J. S. (2011). Increased default mode network connectivity associated with meditation. *Neuroscience Letter, 487*(3), 358–362.

Johnson, P. H., & Johnson, R. D. (2002). *Looking to the East: The theory and practice of traditional Chinese medicine*. Paper presented at the 130th American Public Health Association (APHA) Annual Meeting, Philadelphia, PA.

Johnson, P. H., Priestley, J., Johnson, K. M., & Petrillo, J. (2010). Complementary and alternative medicine: Attitudes and use among health educators in the United States. *American Journal of Health Education, 41*(3), 167–177.

Junod, S. W. (2000). Alternative drugs: Homeopathy, Royal Copeland, and federal drug regulation. *Pharmacy in History, 42*, 13–35.

Kilpatrick, L. A., Suyenobu, B. Y., Smith, S. R., Bueller, J. A., Goodman, T., Creswell, J. D., . . . Naliboff, B. D. (2011). Impact of mindfulness-based stress reduction training on intrinsic brain connectivity. *Neuroimage, 56*(1), 299–298.

Koh, H. L., Ng, H. L., & Teo, H. H. (2004). A survey on knowledge, attitudes and usage of complementary and alternative medicine in Singapore. *Asia Pacific Biotech News, 8*, 1266–1270.

Krippner, S. (1995). A cross-cultural comparison of four healing models. *Alternative Therapies in Health and Medicine, 1*, 21–29.

Lee, M. S., & Jang, H. S. (2005). Two case reports of the acute effects of qi therapy (external qigong) on symptoms of cancer: Short report. *Complement Therapy in Clinical Practice, 11*, 211–213.

Lee, M. S., Kim, J. I., Ha, J. Y., Boddy, K., & Ernst, E. (2009). Yoga for menopausal symptoms: A systematic review. *Menopause, 16*(3), 602–608.

Lee, M. S., Kim, M. K., & Lee, Y. H. (2005). Effects of qi-therapy (external qigong) on cardiac autonomic tone: A randomized placebo controlled study. *International Journal of Neuroscience, 115*, 1345–1350.

Lee, M. S., Pittler, M. H., & Ernst, E. (2008). Effects of Reiki in clinical practice: A systematic review of randomised clinical trials. *International Journal of Clinical Practice, 62*(6), 947–954.

Li, G., Jack, C. R., Jr., & Yang, E. S. (2006). An fMRI study of somatosensory-implicated acupuncture points in stable somatosensory stroke patients. *Journal of Magnetic Resonance Imaging, 24*(5), 1018–1024.

Li, K., Shan, B., Xu, J., Wang, W., Zhi, L., Li, K., . . . Tang, X. (2006). Changes in FMRI in the human brain related to different durations of manual acupuncture needling. *Journal of Alternative and Complementary Medicine, 12*, 615–623.

Li, M., Chen, K., & Mo, Z. (2002). Use of qigong therapy in the detoxification of heroin addicts. *Alternative Therapies in Health and Medicine, 8*, 50–54, 56–59.

Merrell, W. C., & Shalts, E. (2002). Homeopathy. *Medical Clinics of North America, 86*, 47–62.

Monkman, D. (2001). Educating health professionals about how to use the Web and how to find complementary and alternative medicine (CAM) information. *Complementary Therapies in Medicine, 9*, 258.

Morris, K. T., Johnson, N., Homer, L., & Walts, D. (2000). A comparison of complementary therapy use between breast cancer patients and patients with other tumors. *American Journal of Surgery, 179*, 407–411.

Mukherjee, P. K., & Wahile, A. (2006). Integrated approaches towards drug development from Ayurveda and other Indian system of medicines. *Journal of Ethnopharmacology, 103*, 25–35.

Nahin, R. L., Barnes, P. M, Stussman, B. J., & Bloom, B. (2009). Costs of complementary and alternative medicine (CAM) and frequency of visits to CAM practitioners: United States, 2007. CDC National Health Statistics Report #18. Retrieved from http://nccam.nih.gov/sites/nccam.nih.gov/files/nhsrn18.pdf

Nahin, R. L., & Straus, S. E. (2001). Research into complementary and alternative medicine: Problems and potential. *British Journal of Medicine, 322*, 161–163.

Napadow, V., Makris, N., Liu, J., Kettner, N. W., Kwong, K. K., & Hui, K. K. (2005). Effects of electroacupuncture versus manual acupuncture on the human brain as measured by fMRI. *Human Brain Mapping, 24*, 193–205.

National Center for Complementary and Alternative Medicine (NCCAM). (2008). Backgrounder: Yoga for health: An introduction (NCCAM Publication No. D412). Retrieved from http://nccam.nih.gov/health/yoga/introduction.htm

National Center for Complementary and Alternative Medicine (NCCAM). (2009). Backgrounder: Ayurvedic medicine: An introduction (NCCAM Publication No. D287). Retrieved from http://nccam.nih.gov/health/ayurveda/introduction.htm

National Center for Complementary and Alternative Medicine (NCCAM). (2010a) Backgrounder: Meditation: An introduction (NCCAM Publication No. D308). Retrieved from http://nccam.nih.gov/health/meditation/overview.htm

National Center for Complementary and Alternative Medicine (NCCAM). (2010b). Backgrounder: Chiropractic: An introduction (NCCAM Publication No. D403). Retrieved from http://nccam.nih.gov/health/chiropractic/introduction.htm

National Center for Complementary and Alternative Medicine (NCCAM). (2010c). Backgrounder: Massage therapy: An introduction (NCCAM Publication No. D327). Retrieved from http://nccam.nih.gov/health/massage/massageintroduction.htm

National Center for Complementary and Alternative Medicine (NCCAM). (2010d). Backgrounder: Homeopathy: An introduction (NCCAM Publication No. D439). Retrieved from http://nccam.nih.gov/health/homeopathy/

National Center for Complementary and Alternative Medicine (NCCAM). (2010e). Backgrounder: Naturopathy: An introduction (NCCAM Publication No. D372). Retrieved from http://nccam.nih.gov/health/naturopathy/naturopathyintro.htm

National Center for Complementary and Alternative Medicine (NCCAM). (2010f). Backgrounder: Traditional Chinese medicine: An introduction (NCCAM Publication No. 428). Retrieved from http://nccam.nih.gov/health/whatiscam/chinesemed.htm

National Center for Complementary and Alternative Medicine (NCCAM). (2011a). CAM basics: What is complementary and alternative medicine? Retrieved from http://nccam.nih.gov/health/whatiscam/

National Center for Complementary and Alternative Medicine (NCCAM). (2011b). Exploring the science of complementary and alternative medicine: Third strategic plan: 2011–2015. Retrieved from http://nccam.nih.gov/about/plans/2011/

National Center for Complementary and Alternative Medicine (NCCAM), (2011c). NCCAM active funding announcements (Pas, RFAs, RPFs). Retrieved from http://nccam.nih.gov/cgi-bin/grants/funding.php

National Center for Complementary and Alternative Medicine (NCCAM). (2011d). NCCAM funding: Appropriations history. Retrieved from http://nccam.nih.gov/about/budget/appropriations.htm

National Institutes of Health (NIH). (2005). The NIH almanac—organizations: National Center for Complementary and Alternative Medicine. Retrieved from http://www.nih.gov/about/almanac/archive/2001/organization/NCCAM.htm

National Institutes of Health (NIH). (2011). The NIH almanac—appropriations. Retrieved from http://www.nih.gov/about/almanac/appropriations/part2.htm

Palinkas, L. A., & Kabongo, M. L. (2000). The use of complementary and alternative medicine by primary care patients. *Journal of Family Practice, 49*, 1121–1130.

Peters, R. M. (1999). The effectiveness of therapeutic touch: A meta-analytic review. *Nursing Science Quarterly, 12*, 52–61.

Posadzki, P., Ernst, E., Terry, R., & Lee, M. S. (2011). Is yoga effective for pain? A systematic review of randomized clinical trials. *Complementary Therapies in Medicine, 19*(5), 281–287.

Richardson, M. A. (2001). Biopharmacologic and herbal therapies for cancer: Research update from NCCAM. *Journal of Nutrition, 131*, 3037S–3040S.

Rogers, C. E., Larkey, L. K., & Keller, C. (2009). A review of clinical trials of tai chi and qigong in older adults. *Western Journal of Nursing Research, 31*(2), 245–279.

Robinson, M. M., & Zhang, X. R. (2011). *The world medicines situation 2011: Traditional medicines: Global situations, issues, and challenges.* Geneva, Switzerland: World Health Organization. Retrieved from http://www.who.int/medicines/areas/policy/world_medicines_situation/WMS_ch18_wTraditionalMed.pdf

Ross, A., & Thomas, S. (2010). The health benefits of yoga and exercise: A review of comparison studies. *Journal of Alternative and Complementary Medicine, 16*(1), 3–12

Samano, E. S. T., Ribeiro, L. M., Campos, A. S., Lewin, F., Filho, E. S. V., Goldenstein, P. T., . . . Del Giglio, A. (2005). Use of complementary and alternative medicine by Brazilian oncologists. *European Journal of Cancer Care, 14,* 143–148.

Sancier, K. M., & Holman, D. (2004). Commentary: Multifaceted health benefits of medical qigong. *Journal of Alternative and Complementary Medicine, 10,* 163–165.

Saper, R. B., Kales, S. N., Paquin, J., Burns, M. J., Eisenberg, D. M., Davis, R. B., & Phillips, R. S. (2004). Heavy metal content of Ayurvedic herbal medicine products. *Journal of the American Medical Association, 292,* 2868–2873.

Scheiman-Burkhardt, Z. (2001). Homeopathic treatment in a polluted world. *Natural Life, 81,* 10–11.

Shamini, J., & Mills, P.J. (2010). Biofield therapies: Helpful or full of hype? A best evidence synthesis. *International Journal of Behavioral Medicine, 17*(1), 1–16.

Sharma, H., Chandola, H. M., Singh, G., & Basisht, G. (2007). Utilization of Ayurveda in health care: An approach for prevention, health promotion, and treatment of disease. Part 1—Ayurveda, the science of life. *Journal of Alternative and Complementary Medicine, 13*(9), 1011–1019.

Streeter, C. C., Whitfield, T. H., Owen, L., Rein, T., Karri, S. K., Yakhkind, A., . . .Jensen, J. E. (2010). Effects of yoga versus walking on mood, anxiety, and brain GABA levels: A randomized controlled MRS study. *Journal of Alternative and Complementary Medicine, 16*(11), 1145–1152.

Tedesco, P., & Cicchetti, J. (2001). Like cures like: Homeopathy. *American Journal of Nursing, 101,* 43–49.

The Nurse Healers: Professional Associates International. (2006). *Therapeutic touch facts.* Retrieved from http://www.therapeutic-touch.org/newsarticle.php?newsID=18

U.S. Nutrition Industry. (2011). *Nutrition Business Journal's* Supplement business report 2011. Retrieved from http://newhope360.com/2010-supplement-business-report-0

vanderVaart, S., Gijsen, V. M., de Wildt, S. N., & Koren, G. (2009). A systematic review of the therapeutic effects of Reiki. *Journal of Alternative and Complementary Medicine, 15*(11), 1157–1169.

van Schalkwyk, J., Davidson, J., Palmer, B., & Hope, V. (2006). Ayurvedic medicine: Patients in peril from plumbism. *New Zealand Medical Journal, 119,* U1958.

Vempati, R., Bijlani, R. L., & Deepak, K. K. (2009). The efficacy of a comprehensive lifestyle modification programme based on yoga in the management of bronchial asthma: A randomized controlled trial. *BMC Pulmonary Medicine, 9,* 37.

Wardell, D. W., & Weymouth, K. F. (2004). Review of studies of healing touch. *Journal of Nursing Scholarship, 36,* 147–154.

Wember, D. (1997). The heart and soul of homeopathy. *Journal of the American Institute of Homeopathy, 90,* 36–40.

Whelan, J. S., & Dvorkin, L. (2003). HolisticKids.org: Evolution of information resources in pediatric complementary and alternative medicine projects: From monographs to Web learning. *Journal of the Medical Library Association, 91,* 411–417.

White, K. P. (2000). Psychology and complementary and alternative medicine. *Professional Psychology: Research and Practice, 31,* 671–681.

Winstead-Fry, P., & Kijekm, J. (1999). An integrative review and meta-analysis of therapeutic touch research. *Alternative Therapies in Health and Medicine, 5,* 58–67.

World Health Organization (WHO). (2005). *National policy on traditional medicine and regulations of herbal medicines: Report of a WHO global survey.* Geneva, Switzerland: Author. Retrieved from http://apps.who.int/medicinedocs/en/d/Js7916e/

World Health Organization (WHO). (2008). *Global review challenges and future direction for traditional medicine.* Geneva, Switzerland: Author. Retrieved from http://www.who.int/medicines/technical_briefing/tbs/traditionalmedicines_rdg_prs/en/

World Health Organization (WHO). (2011a). *Traditional medicine.* Geneva, Switzerland: Author. Retrieved from http://www.who.int/medicines/areas/traditional/definitions/en/

World Health Organization (WHO). (2011b). *Press release: WHO calls African governments to formally recognize traditional medicine*. Geneva, Switzerland: Author. Retrieved from http://www.afro.who .int/en/component/content/article/1318-press-releases/515-who-calls-on-african-governments-to-formally-recognize-traditional-medicine.html

Wu, W. H., Bandilla, E., Ciccone, D. S., Yang, J., Cheng, S. C., Carner, N., . . . Shen, R. (1999). Effects of qigong on late-stage complex regional pain syndrome. *Alternative Therapies in Health and Medicine, 5*, 45–54.

Zhang, D., & Cheng, Z. (2000). Medicine is a humane art: The basic principles of professional ethics in Chinese medicine. *Hastings Center Report, 30*, S8–S12.

*For a full suite of assignments and additional learning activities, use the access code located in the front of your book to visit this exclusive website: **http://go.jblearning.com/holtz**. If you do not have an access code, you can obtain one at the site.*

10

Global Perspectives on Selected Chronic Cardiovascular Diseases

Bowman O. Davis, Jr.

> *"The real tragedy is that more hasn't been done to avoid this epidemic, as overweight and obesity, and their related chronic diseases, are largely preventable. Approximately 80% of heart disease, stroke, and type 2 diabetes, and 40% of cancer could be avoided through healthy diet, regular physical activity and avoidance of tobacco use."*
>
> *"Low-cost, simple approaches are the key to saving 36 million lives by 2015."*
>
> Dr. Robert Beaglehole, Director,
> Chronic Diseases and Health Promotion

OBJECTIVES

Upon completion of this chapter, the learner will be able to:

1. Compare and contrast cardiovascular disease risks, disease screening, and treatments available within developed and developing countries.
2. Discuss metabolic syndrome and its relationship to chronic diseases in both developed and developing countries.
3. Explain why developing countries have a "double burden of disease."

INTRODUCTION

As people of the world saw their calendars roll over to a new millennium, few realized that the twenty-first century would be greeted differently by different human populations around the globe. Technologically developed, industrialized countries anxiously awaited the prospect of some undetected Y2K glitches that threatened to corrupt databases on systems ranging from those of major financial institutions to individual home computers and jeopardize cherished financial security or personal convenience. By comparison, individuals in developing nations saw the day as one of continuing poverty and the struggle to acquire adequate nourishment and to survive disease. The dawn of the new millennium revealed a persistent disparity in relative prosperity among the diverse human populations of the world. Converted to U.S. dollars, people of developed nations averaged approximately 18 times the per capita gross domestic product (GDP) of their developing nation counterparts (World Health Organization [WHO], 1996).

In this age of global economic trade and global communication, the rapid spread of technology has not had equitable impact on everyone. Not only has there not been equitable sharing of technological advances and socioeconomic prosperity, but the assumption that all technological advances are good is subject to serious debate. Close examination reveals both positive and negative influences of technological advances. Paradoxically, as developed nations export beneficial advances in technology, including health care, they also export popular culture and lifestyles, such as alcohol and tobacco use, stressful work environments, sedentary lifestyles, and calorie-dense diets high in salt, sugar, and saturated fat, that can have negative effects on the health of persons influenced by these trends. Disease burdens around the world often reflect this paradox. Developing nations struggle under the burden of infectious and communicable diseases, while socioeconomically developed nations see their disease burden shift toward one involving chronic and noncommunicable diseases. This shift is primarily due to the fact that infant mortality decreases as a country's economic development accelerates, allowing life expectancy at birth to increase sufficiently for chronic diseases to become prevalent. From the most developed nation to the least, the gap in average life expectancy can be as much as 37 years. Unfortunately, the path from developing to developed status leads through a transitional phase during which the disease burden on the population may be dual in nature, such that both infectious and chronic diseases have nearly equal mortality impact.

Accurately assessing the disease burden among populations around the world is a daunting task complicated by factors such as the need to account for migratory segments of the population, inaccurate diagnoses of medical conditions, and inconsistent reporting and recording of disease incidences and causes of death. Within these constraints, the United Nations' WHO agency collects and publishes in its annual World Health Report a yearly compilation of causes of death among its member states around the world. The availability of this comprehensive database reveals emerging trends in disease burdens and allows for analyses of health needs and of the effectiveness of healthcare measures, as well as for the redirection and prioritization of healthcare efforts and resources.

Specific methods are used to measure and characterize the overall health status of a given population, and specific terminology is used to reference these data. For example, prevalence of a given disease is the total number of cases, both previously existing and newly diagnosed, present within a population at any given time, whereas incidence or morbidity refers to the number of new cases of a given disease reported each year. The mortality rate reflects the actual deaths due to a specific, identifiable cause. For this discussion of chronic diseases, mortality rate is used as the index of disease burden within a population.

DEMOGRAPHIC AND SOCIOECONOMIC TRANSITION

Biologists often represent the developmental status of a population by means of graphic "age pyramids," as shown in **Figure 10-1**. Growing populations have fertility rates greater than basic replacement levels (more than two offspring per female of reproductive age) and exhibit a typical upright pyramid with the number of individuals declining, primarily due to mortality, as they move vertically through the various age groups. Populations with fertility rates approaching replacement level show a loss of the pyramid shape as stability is reached. If fertility rates drop below replacement levels, the age structure pyramid becomes inverted as the population moves into decline. Human populations fit this model very closely, but to consider only age structure would give an incomplete picture with no insight into the other aspects of population dynamics that might be causing the growth, decline, or stability.

WHO groups its member states by geographic regions and mortality strata to give a more complete picture of population status. Mortality strata range from A, which is characterized by very low child mortality and very low adult mortality, to E, where child mortality is high and adult mortality is very high. Based on these criteria, a majority of United Nations member states fall into the "developing" category with comparatively few having attained "developed" status.

Although causes of death due to disease can be conveniently reduced to either infectious or chronic disease categories, the demographic and socioeconomic contexts within which these deaths occur are not as simply described. Demographically, a population can be described by certain characteristics such as age composition, immigration and emigration rates, fertility rate, life expectancy at birth, death rate, and so on. Although these properties are generally objective and quantifiable, they convey little about the actual lifestyles experienced by members of the population. Socioeconomic aspects of a population, such as per capita GDP, literacy rate, percent urbanization, and so on, give a better picture of the overall quality of life within the population. Interestingly, as populations transition from undeveloped or developing toward developed status, they undergo changes in both demographic and socioeconomic aspects that can be generally reflective of their stage of development and its characteristic causes of death.

It is important to emphasize the "generally reflective" descriptor here to avoid the pitfall of imposing stereotypic benchmarks on the progress of a population through its development. In reality, populations do undergo demographic and socioeconomic changes as they progress, but rather the characteristics of this developmental process are inevitably directed by geographical, political, cultural, and religious influences present within the population. Because these influences can be dramatically different from one population to another, each developing nation experiences this process within its own unique set of circumstances. Therefore, each nation must be considered individually if a truly accurate assessment of its developmental progress is desired. It is not the purpose of this discussion to analyze in detail every aspect influencing this developmental transition in every country undergoing it. Instead, it is more important to begin with broader generalizations to develop an appreciation of the general complexities involved in the progression toward developed status.

It is important to realize the lack of universal application of every aspect of population transition. It is equally important to realize that complex interactions occur among the various demographic, socioeconomic, cultural, and political factors, many of which are poorly understood and appreciated. In a

FIGURE 10-1

Population Age Structures

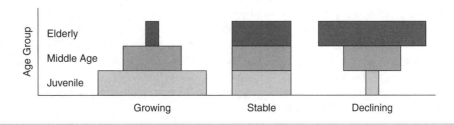

purely hypothetical example, fertility rate may be high in a rural, agricultural population where per capita income is low and access to medical care is limited. As a result, infant mortality is high and life expectancy is low. The high fertility rate is a positive factor in this population, where large families are essential to maintain an agrarian lifestyle. In contrast, a high fertility rate in a different population might be a negative factor because it might increase child dependency stress on constituent families. Because literacy is of little perceived value, in this hypothetical population, literacy rates are low. Thus preventive healthcare measures are difficult to communicate, and resultant communicable disease avoidance is also low. Such a population would be vulnerable to infectious diseases, circuitously making high fertility even more advantageous to offset disease losses. Cultural and religious factors can figure into the equation if they permit promiscuity, impose restrictions on family planning practices, or reinforce gender preferences of offspring. Such practices could keep family size large but enforce inequitable distribution of family resources to one gender. At the same time there may be increased risk of spreading infectious sexually transmitted diseases within and among family units.

Typically, high fertility and mortality combined with low income and literacy rates are characteristic of developing states. Nevertheless, such a characterization does not address the population's stability. In fact, the population may be quite stable and in equilibrium with its geographic, demographic, cultural, and socioeconomic environment. The question then becomes one of humanitarian concern—namely, whether to intervene in an attempt to raise the standard of living of individuals at the potential risk of disturbing the population's equilibrium.

Although the preceding example is purely hypothetical, it clearly illustrates that there can be no universal set of standards for assessing population development if the unique circumstances within which that group is developing are not considered as well. With those precautionary notes emphasized, the following characterization of population transition identifies major transitional phases. It also describes some of their demographic and socioeconomic characteristics, with the understanding that they may not be universally applicable.

By applying the phases of demographic transition described by Lee and Cyrus Chu (2000) as a basic framework and adding certain socioeconomic factors as appropriate, it is possible to generate a more descriptive model of population development within which the causes of death can be examined more specifically.

Beginning with a hypothetical, undeveloped population, the people are often widely dispersed in individual family units across a basically rural environment. With the primary livelihood being agriculture, the labor force is small and per capita income is low. Financial savings are virtually nonexistent because any family income is devoted to living essentials. Families often reside in primitive, unsanitary living conditions and are exposed to contaminated indoor air from fuels used for heating and cooking. Clean water for drinking and food storage capability may be inadequate, as investment in infrastructure is minimal. Fertility rate is high but perinatal health care is substandard for both mothers and their children, leading to an increased child mortality rate. Fertility rate may also be affected by the cultural preference for large families and the benefit of having large families to share the agricultural workload. Literacy levels are low, because literacy has little perceived value in this agrarian lifestyle. The status of women in the population is often low, as women have little incentive to improve either their literacy or their participation in the workforce. The combination of primitive living conditions, poor sanitation, illiteracy, and limited access to health care increases the prevalence of infectious diseases and results in a low life expectancy at birth because both child and adult mortality rates are high. With high fertility rates helping to offset the high mortality rates, the population may be transiently stable. At the same time, it is extremely vulnerable to environmental disasters such as drought or infectious disease epidemics that could tip the delicate balance toward decline.

Phase One Transition: Reducing Child Mortality

The first phase of transition usually begins with a decline in child mortality. This decline may be the result of internal healthcare measures within the population structure or attributable to external humanitarian efforts. Many developed nations export medical technology such as vaccination programs in an effort to reduce child mortality on a global basis. A decline in child mortality increases the proportion of children in a developing country's population and raises the child dependency stress on individual family units and on the population as a whole. This increased dependency stress can result in continued low per capita income with all of its consequences, including continued low expenditure on healthcare practice and infrastructure. With minimal healthcare access and continued low literacy rates, infectious diseases remain the primary cause of death among adults as life expectancy remains low. The rural, agrarian lifestyle persists, and the unsanitary living conditions and female status within the population show little change.

Phase Two Transition: Fertility Decline

In the second phase of transition, the most distinguishing feature is the beginning of a decline in fertility. A number of factors may influence this trend (Poston, 2000), and it may take two or three generations, or approximately 50 years, to go to completion. Completion is considered to be the attainment of a replacement level of about two children per reproductive female. For example, the People's Republic of China and Taiwan serve as examples of how socioeconomic and political factors can curtail fertility rate. In 1950, both China and Taiwan had fertility rates of approximately six children per reproductive female. By 1995, both countries' fertility levels had declined to fewer than two child per reproductive female. However, Taiwan's fertility decline resulted from voluntary reductions in family size as a possible result of socioeconomic development, whereas the decline in China reflected the combination of socioeconomic development and government intervention in family planning (Poston, 2000).

Socioeconomically speaking, as livelihood gradually shifts from an agricultural base to one of an industrial or service labor force, large family size is no longer an asset and, indeed, can be a liability. Under these conditions, adequate food can no longer be grown to feed a large family and most living essentials must now be purchased. To be competitive in the new work environment, literacy is of greater value than large family size. Literacy rate and educational level negatively correlate with fertility rate especially when the educational level of females is considered. Additionally, female value within the population may trend upward as more women move into the workforce, which can also negatively impact fertility rate. During this phase, the labor force grows rapidly and boosts the per capita income, assuming the economy grows sufficiently to provide jobs for the growing workforce. Because a workforce tends to locate close to a work source, migration from rural to urban environments may be evident. Urbanization of the population has a positive impact by increasing access to both education and health care and a negative impact on fertility as literacy improves. However, the shift from the physical labor of agriculture to the more stressful structured work environment can increase the mental stress on working adults. As actual work becomes more structured and less physically demanding, leisure time also increases and more sedentary lifestyles may become the norm.

Total dependency stress is low in this phase of transition, as the generally healthy, middle-aged segment of the population predominates with very few dependent children and few dependent elderly members. With low dependency stress, financial savings may increase along with consumption as labor becomes more lucrative and the overall standard of living increases. Unfortunately, exposure to popular cultural promotions also increases as businesses perceive the population with its improving standard of living as a potential market for goods and services, some of which may be accompanied by behavioral practices and lifestyles that may not be conducive to good health. The glamorization of alcohol, tobacco, and drug use have negative impacts on health and longevity, as does ready access to prepared foods that are dense in calories and high in salt, sugar, and fats; the convenience of these foods may encourage the population to substitute these widely available options for healthy diets. The resulting dietary changes can increase the prevalence of obesity within a population whose members are following an increasingly sedentary lifestyle. Such lifestyle practices can exacerbate existing risk factors for chronic diseases, especially those of a cardiovascular nature. Thus the mortality rates resulting from these chronic diseases increase at about the same time as, or even before, infectious diseases have been adequately controlled. In this case, socioeconomic improvement may simply change the nature of a population's overall disease burden instead of reducing it.

With increased per capita income, expenditure on healthcare services and infrastructure is now an affordable option. Easier access to improved health care further reduces mortality rates from infectious diseases and increases life expectancy. As life expectancy increases, individuals now live long enough to develop chronic diseases, especially if unhealthy lifestyles have become the cultural norm. In fact, the population may pass through a time period where infectious and chronic diseases have a dual impact on mortality rates. Eventually, the population may progress beyond the dual disease burden stage toward one where chronic diseases predominate as the major cause of death.

Figure 10-2 shows a global perspective of the causes of death worldwide (WHO, 2009). Examination of these data shows a shift away from an infectious disease burden and toward one characterized by chronic diseases as the mortality stratum trends from E (high child, very high adult) to A (very low child, very low adult). Interestingly, the D mortality stratum of the geographic regions of Southeast Asia, Eastern Mediterranean, South America, and Eastern Europe shows a significant dual disease burden. Also important is the recognition that chronic diseases now account for more deaths worldwide than infectious diseases. This point is both a testament to the effectiveness of infectious disease eradication measures and an indication of the need to direct more effort toward the emerging chronic disease problem.

Phase Three Transition: Increasing Age Dependency

To appreciate the final phase of population development, selected aspects of the second phase must be considered as contributing to the major characteristic of third-phase development—namely, emerging age dependency. Increased life expectancy combined with the declining infant mortality and the shift to a more gender-diverse, urban labor force generates a comparatively large "balloon" of persons moving both into the labor force and into the older age strata of the population. As this ballooned middle-aged population stratum grows older, age dependency stress on the population increases. Interestingly, as this aging occurs, the total dependency stress increases on the population until the total dependency stress is now similar to that experienced during phase one. The only difference is that age dependency now replaces child dependency.

Age is a primary, irreversible risk factor for chronic disease development, and the prevalence of these diseases inevitably increases within any aging population. The extent to which they increase in prevalence depends on the number of risk factors occurring simultaneously. Unfortunately, a past history of substance abuse, tobacco and alcohol use, sedentary lifestyle, and unhealthy diet serves to exacerbate the chronic disease burden of the susceptible aging population segment. Additionally, the prolonged psychological stress of urban living and genetic predisposition, should it exist, can be contributing factors to the rise in chronic disease burden. This increase in chronic disease is particularly evident as an increase in cardiovascular disorders with ischemic heart disease and hypertension being the general manifestations.

Up to this point, hypothetical situations have been used to provide a basic awareness of the complexities of population development. They also provide a context within which to assess the importance of chronic disease burdens around the world. The next step in a logical progression is to examine in more detail the major contributing factors to this emerging global chronic disease burden.

FIGURE 10-2

Comparison of Deaths Due to Infectious Versus Chronic Diseases by UN/WHO Mortality Strata and Geographic Regions for the Year 2000

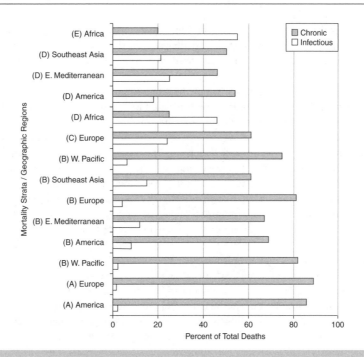

Source: Adapted from WHO World Health Report, 2001.

THE UNDERLYING ROLE OF POVERTY

Although people around the world die from a variety of causes, ranging from accidental deaths and political conflicts to infectious and chronic diseases, the age at which they die is somewhat more predictable. The old adage, "The rich die old while the poor die young," appears to have a factual basis. Nations with higher per capita GDPs also have longer life expectancies. This relationship should come as no surprise, given that a higher GDP leads to greater expenditure on healthcare infrastructure and greater individual access to health care. The impact of literacy can be seen across the entire age spectrum. Infant mortality is negatively correlated with literacy level for the obvious reasons that literate parents are more likely to be aware of disease prevention measures and to have the necessary personal income to access and practice them. For example, the WHO's Global Immunization Program, begun in 1974, helped to eradicate smallpox and increase the level of child immunization globally from 5% to 80% by 1995 (WHO, 1997). Although the reduction of childhood diseases was significant by the end of the last century, efforts to achieve these goals were least effective in underdeveloped countries. This lack of child immunization combined with substandard or total absence of adequate peripartum care drives the child mortality rates high and drives life expectancy at birth low in developing nations.

In the middle and elderly age strata, the role of literacy is more individual in nature, as these age groups are less directly dependent on care from others to protect them from diseases and unhealthy practices. Their receptivity to publicly communicated health warnings and their vulnerability to unhealthy cultural and lifestyle practices depend in part on their literacy level and the ease with which sound health practices can be communicated to them.

The WHO World Health Report (1995) devoted much of its narrative to the role of poverty in global mortality rates. In 1990, it was estimated that 20% of the world's human population lived in poverty. This estimate was accompanied by an observed 37-year gap in life expectancy between richer and poorer nations.

Poverty affects longevity and subjects people to disease in a variety of ways: It destines people to drink unclean water and to live in unsanitary conditions; it forces people to breathe air polluted by industrial emissions as well as unclean fuels used for home heating and cooking; and it can be a contributing factor to mental stress, family unit disintegration, and substance abuse. More importantly, it excludes people from the educational process, thereby depriving them of the essential knowledge needed to prevent diseases that could be avoided by lifestyle changes. This educational deficiency leaves vulnerable populations with only cultural or religious practices for protection, which very often may not be adequate.

It is easy to make an erroneous leap in generalization by assuming that wealthier, developed nations are devoid of poverty. Conversely, a variant impact of poverty can be seen to be the result of industrialization. A developing industrial economy can entice people to migrate from rural to urban environments in search of higher incomes and better lifestyles. Their lack of adequate marketable skills or periods of economic depression, however, may then leave them stranded in isolated pockets of poverty within the urban environment. Similarly, it is a mistake to assume that everyone within a population will "catch the wave" of industrialization and be swept equally toward personal financial improvement. As the United States underwent industrialization during the 1800s and 1900s, some people in rural environments were not included in the transition. Although many migrated to the industrialized urban environments, others remained behind—for example, those subpopulations in pockets of central Appalachia. In this geographic area, poverty rates approach 35% compared to the U.S. national rate of 14% (Phipps, 2006). Regardless of the circumstances that produced them, these pockets of poverty are not unique to either a rural or an urban environment; indeed, they can be seen in both. Unfortunately, the people living in them, as with those in underdeveloped nations, may be subject to a dual threat from both infectious and chronic diseases.

THE CHRONIC DISEASE BURDEN

Increasing life expectancy of a population has both positive and negative effects on disease burden. Clearly, reducing child mortality and controlling infectious diseases to enable a longer life expectancy is, without doubt, a positive aspect. Nevertheless, if a longer life expectancy increases the risk of developing chronic diseases, the population's disease burden is not eliminated but rather just changed in character Life expectancy at birth for the total world population is 67.07 years. For males, it is 65.21 years; for females, 69.05 years (2011 est.) (Infoplease, 2011). Developed nations with greater average life expectancies, however, present a different mortality profile. As individuals within a population survive to adulthood and live longer, chronic diseases, which can be age dependent, emerge and prevail as the major cause of deaths.

Chronic diseases can occur with any organ system, but typically include a variety of malignancies, as well as respiratory, cardiovascular, renal, and neuropsychiatric disorders. In recognition of the fact that renal and neuropsychiatric diseases combined account for only about 3% of the total deaths during any one year, the major emphasis here will be on cardiovascular diseases. **Figure 10-3** illustrates the prevalence of these chronic diseases and their effects on mortality data for the decade between 1993 and 2003.

FIGURE 10-3

Percentage of Total Deaths Due to Selected Chronic Diseases Among WHO Member States

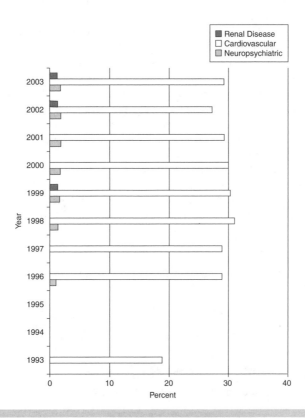

Source: Data compiled from WHO World Health Reports, 1995, 1996, 1997, 1998, 1999, 2000, 2001, 2002, 2003, 2004.

Cardiovascular diseases far outweigh the distant second (neuropsychiatric) and third (renal disease) causes of death. Interestingly, when available data were plotted, cardiovascular diseases could be seen to increase until the middle 1990s, then remained high but relatively stable through the remainder of the observation period. During the same time interval, renal disease remained low in prevalence and unchanging while neuropsychiatric disorders, although low in prevalence compared to cardiovascular disease, almost doubled in prevalence from 1996 to 2003. Although this point is somewhat speculative, the prevalence of neuropsychiatric disorders may prove to be an index of societal stress experienced by a population.

The Cardiovascular Disease Burden

Cardiovascular disease (CVD) is a broad category of generally chronic diseases affecting the heart and blood vessels. This category includes conditions ranging from pericardial disorders, to heart valve and rhythm abnormalities, to elevated blood pressure values, to inflammatory disease states affecting the walls of arteries. From a global health perspective, detailed and specific diagnoses are not readily available, but generalized mortality data are. Such data are collected by the WHO and grouped categorically into ischemic heart disease (diminished blood supply to the myocardium), cerebrovascular disease (cerebrovascular accident [CVA], stroke), and rheumatic heart disease. Synonyms for ischemic heart disease are commonly used within medical literature and require notation here to avoid confusion. These synonyms are coronary heart disease (CHD or coronary artery disease) and atherosclerotic coronary heart disease (ACHD). Data pertaining to the prevalence of these three major cardiovascular disorders are summarized in **Figure 10-4** for the decade ending in 2003.

A cursory examination of the data reveals that ischemic heart disease and cerebrovascular strokes far exceed the prevalence of rheumatic heart disease, and their combined percentages accounted for about 25% of the total annual deaths worldwide by the end of the 1900s. Rheumatic heart disease is an acute inflammatory disorder that follows a group A streptococcal (GAS) infection of the throat in 3% to 5% of these pharyngitis cases. During the acute inflammatory phase of the disease (rheumatic fever), valve leaflets of the heart become inflamed and thicken from scar tissue formation. The diseased valves do not close properly, leading to regurgitation (murmur) with the danger of congestive failure and death (Howson, Reddy, Ryan, & Bale, 1998; Porth, 2005). Rheumatic heart disease is epidemiologically interesting because it is a chronic disease caused by an infectious microorganism that can be successfully treated with antibiotics when and where they are available. In developed, industrialized countries with access to antibiotic therapy, the prevalence of rheumatic heart disease dramatically declined in the last half of the

FIGURE 10-4

Percentage of Total Deaths Due to Selected Cardiovascular Diseases Among UN/WHO Member States

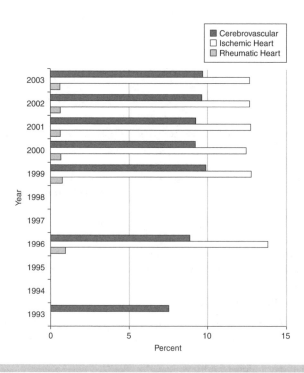

Source: Data compiled from WHO World Health Reports, 1995, 1996, 1997, 1998, 1999, 2000, 2001, 2002, 2003, 2004.

twentieth century. Although it ranked a distant third to ischemic heart disease and CVA globally, this condition was still responsible for 500,000 deaths worldwide in 1998 (WHO, 1998). Rheumatic heart disease can be part of the dual disease burden of developing nations where access to antibiotic therapy may be limited.

It is not just the prevalence of rheumatic heart disease that differs globally when the epidemiology of cardiovascular disease is examined. In fact, the mortality profile of major cardiovascular diseases differs with the particular country and its developmental status. In developed nations, CVD is the major cause of death within the populations, but the specific ranking of individual types of CVD shows atherosclerosis and hypertension to be the most prevalent. In developing states, CVD can be a part of the dual disease burden along with high mortality rates from a variety of infectious diseases. For example, rheumatic heart disease is the most prevalent CVD in Asia, but hypertension and related ischemic heart diseases are more ubiquitous in the Americas, in the Caribbean, and in more urbanized areas of Africa (Akinkugbe, 1990). This trend suggests that urbanization or the exposure to Western lifestyles may correlate positively with the prevalence of ischemic heart disease and cerebrovascular strokes.

Akinkugbe (1990) provided more supportive evidence of this trend. It has long been observed that blood pressure tends to rise with age in human populations. However, this age-dependent hypertension trend is not seen in developing populations of Africa that are isolated from Western influence and show relative freedom from known CVD risk factors. Among the examples cited for future study were the pygmies of northeastern Zaire, the bushmen of Botswana, and the Koma people of northeastern Nigeria. Additionally, a study of Kenyans showed a rise in blood pressure with migration into more urbanized areas of the country. Apparently, improvement in socioeconomic status along with exposure to Western lifestyle can yield a population within which the chronic disease profiles reflect an increased probability of developing cardiovascular disease.

Cardiovascular Disease Risk Factors

Factors that increase the risk of developing chronic cardiovascular disease may be demographic (age and gender), behavioral (lifestyle patterns), or genetic (familial). The presence of any given risk factor is considered to increase the likelihood of developing CVD, and the concurrence of multiple risk factors seriously compound this probability.

Chronological Age

Age, along with gender and familial inheritance, make up the irreversible risk factors predisposing individuals to develop CVD. Because CVDs are classed as chronic diseases, it is logical to expect them to increase in prevalence in the older age strata of a population. In fact, males who are older than 45 years of age are at increased risk, as are women who are older than 55 or who have undergone premature menopause without exogenous estrogen (estradiol) replacement therapy (Porth, 2005). The gender differences in age susceptibility are poorly understood but may involve dietary and/or hormonal differences. For example, testosterone in males can mobilize body lipid reserves and increase blood lipid levels, while estrogen seems to protect against early onset of CVD and increase body fat stores. Female fertility depends in part upon adequate body fat stores, and the proportion of body fat to lean muscle mass increases in both sexes with advancing age.

Regardless of the underlying physiological mechanisms, phases two and three of population transition are characterized, in part, by increased life expectancy. This factor alone predisposes individuals to increased risk of CVD, as individuals may now be living long enough to develop these chronic diseases. However, many transitional populations also develop unhealthy lifestyles, which expose them to multiple other risk factors in addition to simple aging.

Genetic Predisposition and Hyperlipidemia

Because lipids, including cholesterol and triglycerides, are insoluble in the water of blood plasma, they must be transported in minute chylomicron forms and in combination with water-soluble proteins as blood lipoproteins. These blood lipoproteins include the common low-density lipoproteins (LDL), which are high in fat and cholesterol components, and the beneficial high-density lipoproteins (HDL), which are high in protein including the cholesterol-destroying enzyme, cholesterol esterase. Additionally, a typical blood lipid profile includes metabolic intermediates such as very-low-density lipoproteins (VLDL) and intermediate-density lipoproteins (IDL), which are also controlled through metabolic activity of the liver. The processing of these lipid fractions involves metabolic pathways with enzymes or receptors that are produced by inherited genes of the human genome (Porth, 2005). Consequently, familial inheritance of hyperlipoproteinemia patterns constitutes a major irreversible risk factor for CVD.

Although familial inheritance is irreversible, unhealthy lipid profiles can often be controlled by medication. Yet, because of the cost of these medications, many developing populations do not have this option. Genetic predisposition is often compounded in its risk severity by dietary intake of saturated fats, trans fats, and cholesterol. These compounding factors are reversible with education regarding sound dietary practices. Again, developing populations may not have high literacy levels or may not have access to this dietary information. Making matters worse are the existence of cultural dietary preferences and societal pressures to resort to convenience foods, which may exacerbate the lipid problem. Regardless of whether the high-risk blood lipid profile is caused by genetics or behavior, such a condition can predispose individuals to develop CVD, especially atherosclerosis.

Atherosclerosis is a type of arteriosclerosis, or "hardening of the arteries." Some arterial hardening is a normal consequence of aging. More ominously, the often premature hardening due to atheromatous, fibrofatty, inflammatory lesions developing within and beneath the inner intimal layer of arteries leads to an acceleration of the sclerotization process. This inflammatory, atheromatous reaction in arteries can weaken the artery wall while occluding the vessel lumen and providing a site for platelet aggregation. Because atherosclerosis commonly affects the aorta, arteries of coronary circulation, and the arterial supply to the brain, it can result in aneurysms as well as thromboembolic ischemic events leading to angina pectoris, myocardial infarction, transient ischemic attacks (TIA), or more serious cerebrovascular strokes (CVA).

Clearly, genetic predisposition and/or diets rich in saturated fats and cholesterol can lead to a variety of cardiovascular and cerebrovascular disorders. The current trend for developing populations to adopt Western lifestyles—that is, lifestyles characterized by stressful, sedentary jobs and diets consisting mainly of convenience foods that are calorie rich and contain high salt, fat, and sugar content—acts to exacerbate any genetic predisposition to develop CVD. Unfortunately, unhealthy lifestyles can act independently to increase the risk for CVD in individuals without an inherited risk.

Hypertension

Hypertension can be defined as a persistent increase in systolic and diastolic arterial pressures, and the condition can present as either essential or secondary elevation in blood pressure. Secondary hypertension results from some concurrent pathophysiological condition and is commonly seen in renal disease as a consequence of fluid and salt retention with resultant blood volume expansion. In contrast, essential hypertension is a chronic elevation of blood pressure, either systolic or diastolic, above 140/90 mm Hg with no identifiable secondary cause. The actual causes of essential hypertension are unknown, but a number of risk factors, such as age, sodium retention, and anxiety, have been identified and correlated with the condition. Mood and anxiety disorders are more prevalent in city dwellers, and urban stress has been shown to increase activity in brain regions associated with social stress processing (Lederbogen et al., 2011). In contrast, sporadic anxiety episodes seem to cause acute hypertensive events but have not been convincingly correlated with chronic hypertension (Porth, 2005).

Blood pressure is known to increase with age, rising from an average of 50/40 mm Hg at birth to about 120/80 mm Hg by adolescence (Porth, 2005). Systolic pressure continues to increase slowly throughout life, ultimately increasing the risk of cerebrovascular stroke in later life as high pulse pressure (systolic minus diastolic) stresses aging arteries. Because this phenomenon is not seen in isolated African populations distantly removed from Western influence, it is speculated that lifestyle changes during population transition may be a contributing factor to its emergence. People of African descent in developing or developed populations tend to show hypertension earlier in life, and they are statistically more susceptible to cardiovascular and renal damage compared to Caucasians. This observation is not completely understood and may have a genetic component. People of African descent do not respond readily to increased dietary sodium with an increased renal salt excretion (Porth, 2005). This tendency to retain salt may have had evolutionary survival value in a hot, sodium-deficient environment, but can have negative survival value in an environment with excessive dietary salt availability, such as exists with the convenience diets of many developed and some developing nations.

Nicholas, Agodoa, and Norris (2004) reported very little difference in prevalence of early-stage chronic kidney disease (CKD) among Caucasian, Hispanic, and African people in the United States. However, people of African descent were twice as likely as Hispanics and four times more likely than Caucasians to progress to end-stage renal disease (ESRD). This racial/ethnic disparity in disease prevalence may reflect low levels of educational experience, income, and access to health care. Any or all of these factors could contribute to the observed high rates of prerenal disorders, such as hypertension and diabetes, in these minorities. These risk factors for ESRD can be controlled if detected and treated early, but both actions require educational awareness and adequate income to ensure healthcare access.

Additionally, it is not uncommon to see several risk factors for hypertension occurring in the same individual. An example of this phenomenon, the *insulin resistance syndrome* (metabolic syndrome), is a situation in which a cluster of risk factors occur simultaneously in one individual (Porth, 2005). For example, obesity, particularly abdominal fat accumulation, and type 2 diabetes (non-insulin-dependent diabetes mellitus [NIDDM]) lead to hyperinsulinemia due to insulin insensitivity, or insulin resistance, in body cells. This elevated insulin level results in an increase in sympathetic nervous system activity, which in turn leads to an elevated heart rate and increased vasoconstriction. Because both cardiac output and peripheral resistance are increased simultaneously, blood pressure increases accordingly with hyperinsulinemia.

Dietary salt intake can affect blood pressure as well. High-sodium diets can expand blood volume through fluid retention and increase blood pressure. Because high-salt diets are usually high in either sodium or potassium, but rarely both, a high-sodium diet would likely be low in potassium. Low potassium can increase blood pressure, possibly by suppression of the renin–angiotensin–aldosterone (RAA) mechanism (Porth, 2005).

Regardless of its causative factors, chronic hypertension is extremely dangerous for the simple reason that it is often asymptomatic and can exist for years undetected in persons who do not receive regular medical exams. Uncorrected elevated arterial blood pressure has negative effects on retinal, cardiac, cerebral, and renal blood vessels, as well as a direct effect on heart workload. Specifically, high blood pressure distends flexible vessel walls, creating small lesions that predispose the individual to development of aneurysms and atheromatous plaque. Simultaneously, high systemic arterial pressure increases the workload (afterload) on the left ventricle, leading to hypertrophy and, ultimately, ischemic heart disease. Myocardial ischemia evolves gradually as the enlarged muscle mass increases in its metabolic requirements for blood oxygen and nutrient delivery beyond that which the partially occluded vessels can provide. However, a sudden cardiac ischemic event (infarction) can occur should an embolus originating from an atheromatous artery totally block a smaller arterial branch of coronary circulation.

Finally, the increased renal perfusion as a result of elevated arterial blood pressure causes a concomitant increase in glomerular filtration. Chronically elevated glomerular filtration leads to an inflammatory thickening of the glomerular membrane and subsequent renal dysfunction or failure. Failing kidneys can expand blood volume by fluid retention and constrict arteries via activation of the RAA mechanism, both of which would increase pressure further and produce an unfavorable positive feedback situation leading to more progressive damage. Unfortunately, the large renal reserve in the human requires approximately 75% loss of the total renal capacity before symptoms appear. Consequently, both hypertension and its associated renal damage can progress unnoticed until serious damage is done.

It is not difficult to see how a transitioning population, which is experiencing a changing lifestyle with longer life expectancy, would be susceptible to marketing of convenience foods and might value a more leisurely life with a sedentary type of employment. Should these lifestyle modifications be accorded a high value in the changing culture, it is easy to understand the observed high levels of CVD and CVA in populations as they progress through the phases of this demographic transition.

Obesity

Obesity has become a major public health problem of global significance, with its prevalence increasing in countries around the world regardless of their developmental status. The fact that obesity is currently responsible for twice as many deaths as malnutrition worldwide is not surprising given that the global food supply has generally increased as a result of enhanced productivity and distribution.

By definition, obesity results when excess fat accumulates in adipose cells to the extent of endangering the individual's health. It is easier to define obesity than it is to quantify it, however. More specifically, at what point does energy storage as body fat cease to be an advantage and become detrimental to health, given that there are cultural, racial, and gender differences that influence the perception of the ideal body type? In some cultures, excess body fat is viewed as an index of good health or prosperity. Strauss and Duncan (1998) found that even in the United States, earned wages increased with body mass up to a peak within the normal body mass index (BMI) range and then declined as the BMI range approached obesity. In terms of racial characteristics, populations in colder climates, for example, tend to be shorter in stature with greater amounts of body fat serving physiologically for heat energy conservation. Likewise, the human female tends to have a higher proportion of subcutaneous fat; because of its role in body contouring, this aspect of anatomy can be considered a secondary sex characteristic. Physiologically, female fertility depends on the presence of a certain amount of body fat, which may possibly be an adaptive mechanism ensuring that the mother's nutritional status is adequate to support dependent children. In the United States, minority females of African and Hispanic descent show a greater prevalence of obesity than do Caucasians (Porth, 2005). This observation suggests roles of genetics and socioeconomic status in the prevalence of obesity. Obesity is known to run in families, which indicates a genetic component of the disorder. Additionally, the diets consumed by lower-income individuals are often more dense in caloric content, which serves to increase the risk of obesity in persons in the lower socioeconomic strata. Thus, when people genetically predisposed to obesity occur in lower socioeconomic strata, the risk of developing obesity is compounded.

In light of these complicating factors, WHO has attempted to quantify obesity by means of the BMI, which is calculated by dividing an individual's weight in kilograms by his or her height in meters squared; the resulting ratio value is considered reflective of obesity level. By this standard, BMIs between 18.5 and 24.9 are considered normal, while values greater than 30 represent obesity (WHO, 1998). However, caution must be exercised when applying these standards across racial and ethnic lines, as the relationship between BMI and actual body fat varies with body build and may require adjustment for these variables. For instance, Americans of African and Polynesian descent have higher average BMIs, while Asians and Indonesians tend toward lower BMIs than Caucasians (Deurenberg, Yap, & van Staveren, 1998).

Moreover, it is important to realize that central fat (abdominal or upper-torso fat) is more indicative of health risk than is subcutaneous fat. This realization has led to the use of waist circumference or waist/hip circumference ratio as a measure of unhealthy obesity levels. These alternative indices correlate more closely with increased risk for CVD, such that waist circumferences greater than 102 cm (40.2 in.) for men and 88 cm (34.6 in.) for women are associated with substantially increased risk of obesity-related metabolic complications. From a health perspective, the risk of premature death more than doubles in a population when the mean BMI increases from 25 to 35 (Antipatis & Gill, 2001).

The primary reason for the effect of obesity on premature death involves the negative impact of excessive central fat on workload of the heart and on organ perfusion in general. Obese individuals with excessive central fat deposits are at greater risk of type 2 diabetes mellitus and hypertension leading to premature ischemic heart disease. It has been estimated that 2–3 mL of blood per minute is required to perfuse every 100 g of adipose tissue. This increased workload can lead to myocardial hypertrophy and increased heart muscle metabolism. Yet, the required increased blood supply through coronary circulation to support this increased metabolism may be impaired by premature atherosclerosis resulting from chronic hypertension, type 2 diabetes mellitus, and hyperlipidemia. This medley of pathophysiological disorders, referred to as metabolic syndrome, is generally more prevalent in obese individuals. Additionally, general inflammation, as indicated by C-reactive protein (CRP) levels, is elevated with central obesity while platelet aggregation is enhanced, contributing further to vascular damage and increased risk of thrombotic events in obese individuals. CRP level has become a useful indicator of systemic inflammation and risk of myocardial infarction and can be assessed by simple blood tests. In fact, the American Heart Association has established indices of CRP levels that correlate with risk levels (less than 1 mg/L = low risk, 1–3 mg/L = average risk, and more 3 mg/L = high risk).

Central obesity with elevated BMI is a modifiable risk factor for CVD that can be controlled by nutrition education intervention (Kelley-Hedgepeth et al., 2008). Furthermore, obesity in combination with hypertension might predictably increase in prevalence in aging populations who have chronically exhibited these risk factors (Tiengo & Avogaro, 2001).

The WHO/MONICA Project (Monitoring of Trends and Determinants in Cardiovascular Disease) collected data from randomly selected participants from different nations and found, with few exceptions, general increases in levels of obesity approaching epidemic status among United Nations member states over a five-year observation interval during the 1980s. Mean BMI demonstrably increases with socioeconomic transition and is a greater problem in urban populations with more sedentary lifestyles. For each single-point increase in average BMI, obesity prevalence increases by 5% within a population (Seidell, 2001). Obesity has been known to increase with age but now shows a progressively earlier age of onset, a factor that increases the time of chronic exposure for affected individuals and poses a significant child health problem. In developing populations, women are more frequently obese than men. Interestingly, men in developed countries are more likely to be obese than are either their female cohorts or males in developing countries (Antipatis & Gill, 2001; Gutzwiller, 1994). Apparently, socioeconomic status, which is reflective of income level, occupational physical activity, educational level, and place of residence, correlates with obesity prevalence. However, the correlations are not the same across different populations. In developed countries, these socioeconomic factors correlate negatively with obesity levels. In contrast, in developing countries, the correlation is positive, with early improvements in lifestyle appearing to increase obesity levels (Antipatis & Gill, 2001). This reverse correlation in developing countries may reflect exposure to Western culture with its convenience foods and sedentary lifestyles too early in their transition and before healthy lifestyles can be adopted. This same Western popular culture places more emphasis on the stereotypic "ideal" female body type than it does on that of males, which may help account for the gender difference in obesity observed in developed countries.

Although increased BMI has been found to be the major risk factor for CVD, a recent study of premenopausal and postmenopausal women in the United States showed definite ethnic differences in risk levels as well. African American women had the highest risk of CVD, while Asian Americans had the lowest.

Because of the complex interactions among demographic, socioeconomic, cultural, and genetic factors that contribute to obesity prevalence, obesity may prove to be the most difficult CVD risk factor to control. Further complicating this challenge is the awareness that preventing obesity is easier than correcting it once it has developed. Preventing obesity requires early intervention with identification of at-risk individuals and subsequent application of preventive public health measures including educational awareness. Any control strategy becomes less likely to be effective as the number of obese individuals increases progressively over time—a relationship that is likely to occur if the condition continues to appear at progressively earlier ages. Yet, without correction, the trend will merely increase in negative economic impact through increasing healthcare costs and continued lost productivity.

Diabetes Mellitus and Metabolic Syndrome

Diabetes mellitus, or sugar diabetes, is characterized by elevated blood sugar (hyperglycemia), increased urine output (polyuria) with excessive thirst (polydipsia), and glucose in the urine (glucosuria). It may have a variety of pathophysiological causes, all related to either the availability of or the sensitivity to the hormone insulin produced by beta pancreatic islet cells. Type 1 diabetes (formerly called juvenile or insulin-dependent diabetes) is thought to result from insulin deficiency caused by autoimmune (type 1A) or idiopathic (type 1B) destruction of pancreatic beta cells. Type 2 diabetes (non-insulin-dependent diabetes [NIDDM]) exhibits a range of pathophysiology from insulin resistance to insulin deficiency, or a combination of the two.

Type 2 diabetes is the most prevalent form (accounting for approximately 95% of all diabetes cases) and is part of the metabolic syndrome risk factor for CVD. It is also the most common form of diabetes occurring with obesity. The etiology of type 2 diabetes and metabolic syndrome in obese people shows an initial resistance to insulin peripherally. Increased body fat is accompanied by increased macrophages within adipose tissue. These macrophages produce pro-inflammatory cytokines that increase generalized inflammation, as evidenced by C-reactive protein levels, and decrease cellular sensitivity to insulin. Macrophages can also produce a hormone, resistin, which further increases insulin resistance as the diabetes evolves (Maizels & Allen, 2011). This early insulin resistance raises the blood sugar level (hyperglycemia) and increases lipid lysis in adipocytes as an alternative energy source, which in turn can lead to ketosis and ketoacidosis. Also, the elevated blood sugar increases beta cells' secretion of insulin, leading to hyperinsulinemia, and can ultimately lead to loss of beta cell function. This cluster of pathophysiological signs predisposes people to atherosclerosis and ultimately to ischemic heart disease and cerebrovascular stroke (Porth, 2005).

At this point, a dangerous disease sequela emerges. Obesity leads to peripheral insulin resistance and hyperglycemia, which in turn leads to hyperinsulinemia. Excess blood insulin levels produce metabolic syndrome, culminating in CVD or CVA. Because central body fat increases with both advancing age and dietary caloric excess, it is reasonable to expect a higher prevalence of chronic cardiovascular and cerebrovascular diseases in populations during the second phase of the demographic and socioeconomic transition as improvements in life expectancy and personal income occur. This relationship would be particularly evident if changes in general lifestyle lead to unhealthy diets and more sedentary lives. Similarly, in phase three of the demographic and socioeconomic transition, in which the proportion of elderly individuals in the overall population increases, age-related obesity alone would be expected to increase the risk for CVD and CVA. When this trend is combined with an earlier onset of obesity in the population age structure, risks for CVD and CVA can be chronically exacerbated.

The risk of death among diabetics is twice that of nondiabetic people of similar age. In the United States, nearly 2 million people 20 years of age or older were diagnosed with diabetes in 2010 alone, with approximately 35% of that age group showing signs of prediabetes. In fact, the prevalence of diabetes has doubled globally since 1980, with the United States, Saudi Arabia, and Samoa showing the greatest increases in their populations with this disease. This epidemic increase in obesity and diabetes constitutes a significant economic burden, given that healthcare expenditures for diabetics are double those for persons without diabetes (Centers for Disease Control and Prevention [CDC], 2011).

Alcohol and Tobacco Use

Alcohol and tobacco use have long been correlated with chronic hepatic, gastrointestinal, respiratory, and cardiovascular diseases, but the detailed pathophysiology of their effects remains poorly understood. Because alcohol and tobacco use are often seen in conjunction with obesity, hypertension, and diabetes, it is often difficult to separate out the true causes and effects of these conditions. In fact, a major effect of alcohol and tobacco use is known to be the exacerbation of existing cardiovascular risk factors. Moreover, because of their addictive properties, alcohol and tobacco pose unique challenges for control efforts.

Alcohol consumption in excess of three drinks per day increases blood levels of catecholamines, leading to increased blood pressure; systolic values are more dramatically affected than diastolic pressures. This effect becomes quite serious when seen in elderly or obese individuals with sedentary lifestyles and constitutes a significant health risk in these people. Alcohol use decreases hepatic gluconeogenesis, a major mechanism of hepatic glucose production, and can lead to hypoglycemia. This effect is dangerous for people with diabetes who are on insulin therapy and at risk of hypoglycemia through their treatment regimens. Cerebrovascular stroke (CVA) risk increases with alcohol consumption because of three known physiological effects. First, cardiac arrhythmias—particularly atrial fibrillation (the "holiday heart" phenomenon)—can transiently retard blood flow, causing thrombi to form on the atrial walls or heart valve leaflets. Such thrombotic events may give rise to emboli that can obstruct brain circulation and cause a thromboembolic stroke. Second, the tendency for alcohol to exacerbate existing hypertension can contribute to accelerated atherosclerosis with resultant thromboembolic events. Third, an enhanced effect on blood coagulation further increases thromboembolic risks (Massie & Amidan, 1998; Porth, 2005).

With chronic tobacco use, components of cigarette smoke may be toxic to the extent of causing inflammatory damage to vascular endothelium, increasing the likelihood of thrombotic events. Additionally, nicotine increases the incidence of vascular spasms while increasing plasma norepinephrine levels and lowering HDL levels. These effects would predispose a smoker to hypertension, atherosclerosis, and CHD (Massie, 1998; Porth, 2005). In populations with a high underlying risk for cardiovascular disease, such as South Asia, India, and former USSR countries, tobacco consumption has been shown to exacerbate their risk levels (Howson et al., 1998). The WHO World Health Report (1999) presented disturbing statistics on the prevalence of tobacco use globally. Estimates were that at the end of the 1900s approximately 4 million deaths per year were caused by tobacco use. This number was extrapolated to reach 10 million per year by 2030. It is easy to speculate that this mortality rate is primarily attributable to tobacco use in more developed nations, as their per capita GDP would be high enough to permit significant tobacco use. In reality, smoking is increasing by 3.4% per year in developing countries, a level declared by the WHO to be an epidemic. Because people in these developing nations must contend with infectious diseases as well, tobacco use and related chronic diseases may prove to be a significant part of their dual disease burden.

Because chronic diseases resulting from tobacco use can also be caused by other inherent or environmental risk factors, it is difficult to single out tobacco as the solitary causative agent. Consequently, it is difficult to get a reliable estimate of the true impact of tobacco use on health. Ezzati and Lopez (2004) attempted to factor out statistically any background disease rates caused by environmental factors other than smoking. They found that in developing countries cardiovascular diseases were the major smoking-attributable causes of death, representing 27.8% of total smoking-related deaths. Contrastingly, in developed countries, the portion of cardiovascular deaths that were deemed tobacco related jumped to 42.1%.

The disproportionately high percentage of tobacco-related cardiovascular deaths in developed nations may be due to the fact that, in these populations, other risk factors for chronic diseases have been minimized by their level of socioeconomic development. A corollary to this conclusion might be that developing populations have to contend with both tobacco-related risks and other chronic disease risks inherent in their developmental status.

Although tobacco use is increasing in developing nations, there is an overall decline in this habit in developed nations, led primarily by North America and Western Europe. This decline occurred after a peak in tobacco consumption in the early 1980s. It may reflect the efficacy of antismoking campaigns in developed nations in raising awareness of the hazards of smoking. Unfortunately, it may also reflect the recognition by tobacco manufacturers and marketers of the large potential market afforded by developing nations. As the per capita income in these developing nations increases and they are exposed to Western popular culture, they could be seen to represent an opportunity to extend tobacco sales.

After examining all of the risk factors for CVD, it is noteworthy that only chronological age and genetic inheritance represent irreversible risks over which individuals have no control. The remaining risks, which are considered to be behavioral in nature, can be reduced or eliminated entirely by behavioral modification. To do so, however, requires first that people be made aware of potential health risks through education and, second, that through personal choice, they avoid behaviors that predispose them to CVD. Unfortunately, these lifestyle behaviors can be acquired during adolescence or early adulthood, which further compounds the problems. Adolescents and young adults often are perceived as being more susceptible to peer pressure and mass marketing of glamorized behaviors. In addition, they may lack the experience and maturity to fully appreciate the risks that certain behaviors might pose because the immediate negative effects of these behaviors rarely appear early in their indulgence. Additionally, alcohol, tobacco, and substance use can be psychologically and physiologically addictive, making behavioral change in addicted individuals more difficult to achieve. Adopting these high-risk behaviors early in life increases the time of exposure as life expectancies increase within a population. In such situations, the unavoidable age risk factor eventually occurs in conjunction with the results of behavioral risks, leading to multiple risk factors and an increased probability of contracting chronic cardiovascular diseases.

CONCLUSIONS

At the beginning of the twenty-first century, only 22% of the United Nations/WHO member states had attained developed status. More than 150 nations around the globe are in some phase of demographic or socioeconomic transition. Of these developing nations, 68 countries in Africa, the Americas, Southeast Asia, and the Eastern Mediterranean regions are experiencing high mortality levels at both ends of the population age strata; that is, they are contending with high child mortality and high adult mortality with generally low average life expectancies. Poverty is prevalent in these developing countries and is sustained by poor health and high fertility rates, both of which serve to keep per capita income low. Breaking this cycle of poverty is a meaningful goal of intervention efforts for this century. Interrupting this cycle requires an intervention stimulus to any or all of the following (Bloom, Canning, & Malaney, 2000):

- Income level
- Health status
- Fertility rate

Income Level Versus Health Status Improvements

It has long been known that economic and financial conditions affect access to food supply and have a direct impact on mortality. Child mortality is of particular concern because it correlates positively with high fertility rates, correlates negatively with per capita income, and, where prevalent, impedes socioeconomic development. Prevalent childhood diseases and poor perinatal health care influence socioeconomic development by reducing the number of individuals surviving, thriving, and moving into the economically productive labor force of the middle-aged demographic strata. It would be logical to expect that improvements in economic status of a population would decrease child mortality and increase life expectancy through better living conditions and better access to health care. Although effective as a short-term emergency measure, financial aid alone without concomitant economic expansion is controversial and may be ineffective in some cases. Simple money infusion increases the cost burden on donor countries and carries the inherent risk of the funds being diverted by corrupt regimes away from targeted peoples. Additionally, a simple, short-term boost in economic activity can have the reverse effect of causing a surge in population growth, increasing dependency stress, and driving the population back to baseline per capita income levels. For an economic stimulus to have a long-term effect on the economic status of a population, it must involve sustainable measures that will perpetuate further economic growth.

Preston (1975) suggests that, during the twentieth century, mortality became increasingly dissociated from economic level. This dissociation occurred primarily because of the tendency for advances in medical care and health technologies to spread from developed nations to their lesser-developed neighbors. As a result of this trend, underdeveloped populations benefit from a reduction in mortality without having a concomitant remarkable improvement in their per capita incomes. In these situations, mortality is more responsive to health interventions than it is to boosts in per capita income. When comparing per capita income with life expectancy in 30 countries during the 1930s and 1960s, Preston (1975) noted that average per capita incomes between $100 and $600 (in 1963 U.S. dollars) were associated with dramatic increases in life expectancy. By comparison, incomes greater than $600 resulted in little improvement in life expectancy.

It can be speculated that the observed initial economic-related improvements in life expectancy may have resulted from decreased rates of child mortality and other deaths caused by infectious disease. Because of the relative low cost of antibiotics and vaccines, child mortality and infectious diseases can be relatively inexpensively managed through minimal peripartum care, vaccination programs, and easy access to antibiotics. Thus these initial improvements in life expectancy would require minimal financial resources. However, the chronic disease burden that inevitably occurs with an aging population created through increasing life expectancy poses a different long-term problem, and one that requires substantially more income for health management. For example, many chronic cardiovascular diseases cannot be "cured" in the traditional sense of the word. Instead, people afflicted with these diseases undergo comparatively expensive health management regimens involving costly surgical procedures or expensive, long-term drug therapy. These treatment regimens may continue or recur throughout their life spans and can extend their life expectancies only within certain limits. Consequently, it may be that slight improvements in economic status will prove effective in minimizing the mortality from infectious diseases, but significantly larger economic expansion may be required to make the extended health management of chronic diseases affordable. Additionally, the simple ability to afford chronic disease management does not always guarantee a significantly longer life expectancy when compared to that of disease-free individuals.

Developed nations can and do export antibiotics, immunization vaccines, and other healthcare technologies as a humanitarian commitment to lesser-developed countries. Such exports should raise child survival rates and can give recipient populations a boost along the path of socioeconomic development. Within the context of typical population development, this practice should increase the number of people moving into the middle-aged labor force and eventually break the poverty cycle, providing sufficient income growth to manage the eventual chronic disease burden as the population ages. However, this scenario requires that the developing economy grow at a rate capable of providing jobs for the growing labor force. Should this not be the case, the danger exists that subsequent generations may slip back into a low per capita income situation.

Further complicating the preceding scenario is the fact that, in addition to the export of medical technology, cultural practices may be exported. This potential activity is enhanced by the rapid growth of global communication. In such an environment, the improving lifestyles and personal income levels of developing nations may make them targets for marketing strategies undertaken to expand business consumer bases and overall profits. The impact of exporting these marketing strategies can be mixed. It may encourage people to strive toward better lifestyles through the pursuit of jobs that lead them to safer work environments and higher educational achievements, but it can also result in the adoption of lifestyles that include less physical activity and greater dependence on convenience diets and other unhealthy behaviors. The combination of sedentary lifestyles with unhealthy diets and behaviors predisposes people to increased risk of chronic cardiovascular disease later in life as multiple risk factors begin to accrue along with normal aging. Moreover, as adoption of these unhealthy practices occurs progressively earlier in life, the likelihood of developing chronic disease will increase.

Tobacco use and obesity serve as examples of this trend. Tobacco-related deaths occur at nearly equal levels—approximately 2.4 million deaths per year—in both developed and developing countries (Ezzati & Lopez, 2004). Nearly 7% of the world's population has a BMI greater than 30, and obesity is occurring at earlier ages (Seidell, 2001). In children, increases in BMI correlate with increased blood pressure (Raj, Sundaram, Paul, Sudhakar, & Kumar, 2010); if this situation is not corrected, it will yield a generation of adult individuals with extended exposures to CVD risk factors. This increasing prevalence of obesity is occurring in both developed and developing countries and is likely related to unhealthy dietary practices in populations with increasingly more sedentary lifestyles.

Fertility Rate Improvements

Poston (2000) considered four specific factors to have influential effects on fertility:

- Advances in economic development through participation in a nonagricultural labor force
- Improvement in general health conditions with reduction in infant mortality
- Improvement in social conditions particularly in educational attainment
- Absolute and relative improvement in female status within the population

These four factors may also interact with one another. For example, movement from an agricultural to an industrial labor force can generate higher per capita income. Higher incomes relate to better access to health care and education. Better education, especially among females, leads to improved female status within the population. Better education can also lead circuitously back to improved jobs and better health conditions. More affluent and better educated populations with improved health conditions show lower fertility rates, as large families become more of a liability in a nonagrarian lifestyle. Thus improvements in any or all of these factors should lead naturally to a decline in fertility. Such a decline in fertility correlates with elevated socioeconomic status and can contribute to breaking the poverty cycle of a developing population by relieving the child dependency stress while increasing per capita GDP.

All of these fertility influences can occur naturally in the typical developmental process of a population. However, fertility declines can be accelerated over and above the decreases that would occur naturally, such as by governmental mandate—for example, as was done in the People's Republic of China (mainland China). In the 1970s, China instituted a coercive fertility control program as discussed earlier in this chapter. Although it was successful in dropping the fertility rate below replacement levels, Taiwan was able to accomplish a similar reduction in fertility without direct government intervention. In Taiwan, the natural socioeconomic development process was effective in diminishing the fertility rate, presumably by affecting the perceived or actual economic costs and social value of children (Poston, 2000). Because both approaches were effective in reducing fertility rates below replacement levels, these examples illustrate how different social and political climates in two separate populations can produce similar outcomes.

Future Considerations

Even in developed countries, high prevalence levels of chronic diseases pose a significant economic threat through lost productivity from afflicted workers, along with increased healthcare costs. If this economic impact can be significant in developed market economies, it would be considerably more damaging to the fragile, fledgling economies of developing nations. Thus a major problem confronting both developed and developing economies is deciding how to prioritize expenditures for chronic disease risk avoidance compared to the expenditures required for the expansion of healthcare infrastructure to sufficiently manage increasing levels of chronic disease. Both approaches require a significant, though not necessarily equal, financial commitment. Chronic health care has historically proved to be more costly than education. Regardless of the priority, the costs must come from the overall GDP generated through a population's economic activity, and its economy must be strong enough to withstand the added stress. As a larger percentage of GDP is diverted into risk management and health care for the chronically ill, less will be available for economic expansion, and the risk of economic stagnation or decline increases. The decision is not a simple one and, in reality, both probably will have to be dealt with simultaneously. Moreover, the combined actions will take a financial toll on a population's economy.

STUDY QUESTIONS

1. Discuss the impact of expanding technology in developing countries upon the increased burden of chronic diseases such as diabetes, cardiovascular diseases, and hypertension.
2. Explain the role of obesity and its influence on metabolic syndrome both in developed and developing countries.
3. Compare and contrast the impact of polysubstance abuse (alcohol, drugs, and tobacco) on chronic diseases within developed and developing countries.

CASE STUDY

The prevalence of obesity is increasing worldwide. Obesity, the result of chronic positive energy balance, is associated with many chronic diseases, including diabetes, heart disease, hypertension, and some forms of cancer. Determining those factors that influence the prevalence of obesity in developing countries is important, since these countries generally lack the infrastructure to adequately treat the chronic diseases associated with obesity. As developing countries' economies improve and the population becomes urban, changes in dietary habits and physical activity create an environment in which a person predisposed to weight gain could become obese. Ironically, nutritional stunting early in life has been associated with obesity in later years. Those countries that have had traditionally high prevalences of under-nutrition and stunting may be faced with a double burden of under- and over-nutrition. These countries are already poorly equipped to handle acute and chronic diseases. In the future, they will face the increased economic burden of supporting an overweight or obese population, together with the associated and costly chronic diseases.

Reference

Hoffman, D.J. (2001). Obesity in developing countries: Causes and implications. *Food, Nutrition and Agriculture*, 28.

(continues)

CASE STUDY

Case Study Questions

1. Explain why obesity in a developing country creates a "double burden" to its society.
2. How does urbanization of a population affect increase rates of obesity and more chronic diseases?
3. What are some ways that developing countries could decrease the rate of obesity while maintaining costs within a limited budget?

REFERENCES

Akinkugbe, O. O. (1990). Epidemiology of cardiovascular disease in developing countries. *Journal of Hypertension, 8*(7), S233–S237.

Antipatis, V. J., & Gill, T. P. (2001). Obesity as a global problem. In P. Bjorntorp (Ed.), *International textbook of obesity* (pp. 2–22). New York, NY: John Wiley & Sons.

Bloom, D. E., Canning, D., & Malaney, P. N. (2000). Population dynamics and economic growth. In C. Y. Cyrus Chu & R. Lee (Eds.), *Population and development review: A supplement to volume 26* (p. 257). New York: Population Council.

Centers for Disease Control and Prevention (CDC). (2011) *National diabetes fact sheet: National estimates and general information on diabetes and prediabetes in the United States.* Atlanta, GA: U.S. Department of Health and Human Services, Centers for Disease Control and Prevention.

Deurenberg, P., Yap, M., & van Staveren, W. A. (1998). Body mass index and percent body fat: A meta analysis among different ethnic groups. *International Journal of Obesity, 22,* 1164–1171.

Ezzati, M., & Lopez, A. D. (2004). Regional, disease specific patterns of smoking-attributable mortality in 2000. *Tobacco Control, 13,* 388–395.

Gutzwiller, F. (1994). Monitoring of cardiovascular disease and risk factor trends: Experiences from the WHO/MONICA project. *Annals of Medicine, 26*(1), 61–65.

Hoffman, D. J. (2001). Obesity in developing countries: Causes and implications. *Food, Nutrition and Agriculture.* No. 28. Retrieved from http://www.fao.org/ag/agn/publications/fna/article.jsp?lang=en&myURI=id497

Howson, C. P., Reddy, K. S., Ryan, T. J., & Bale, J. R. (1998). *Control of cardiovascular diseases in developing countries: Research, development, and institutional strengthening* (p. 237). Washington, DC: National Academy Press.

Infoplease. Profile of the World. (2011). Retrieved from http://www.infoplease.com/ipa/A0004373.html

Kelly-Hedgepeth, A., Lloyd-Jones, D. M., Calvin, A., Matthews, K. A., Johnston, J., Sowers, M. R., . . . Chae, C. U. (2008). Ethnic differences in C-reactive protein concentrations. *Clinical Chemistry, 54,* 1027–1037.

Lederbogen, F., Kirsch, P., Haddad, L., Streit, F., Test, H., Shuch, P., . . . Meyer-Lindenberg, A. (2011). City living and urban upbringing affect neural social stress processing in humans. *Nature, 474,* 498–501. doi: 10.1038/nature10190

Lee, R., & Cyrus Chu, C. Y. (2000). Introduction. In C. Y. Cyrus Chu & R. Lee (Eds.), *Population and development review: A supplement to volume 26* (pp. 1–9). New York, NY: Population Council.

Maizels, R. M., & Allen, J. E. (2011). Eosinophils forestall obesity. *Science, 332,* 186–187.

Massie, B. M. (1998). Systemic hypertension. In L. M. Tierney, Jr., S. J. McPhee, & M. A. Papadakis (Eds.), *Current medical diagnosis and treatment* (37th ed., pp. 429–447). Stamford, CT: Appleton and Lange.

Massie, B. M., & Amidan, T. M. (1998). Heart. In L. M. Tierney, Jr., S. J. McPhee, & M. A. Papadakis (Eds.), *Current medical diagnosis and treatment* (37th ed., pp. 333–348). Stamford, CT: Appleton and Lange.

Nicholas, S., Agodoa, L., & Norris, K. (2004, November). Ethnic disparities in the prevalence and treatment of kidney disease. *Nephrology News and Issues,* 29–36.

Phipps, S. R. (2006). Settlement and migration. In R. Abramson & J. Haskell (Eds.), *Encyclopedia of Appalachia* (pp. 285–292). Knoxville, TN: University of Tennessee Press.

Porth, C. M. (2005). *Pathophysiology: Concepts of altered health states* (7th ed., p. 1582). Philadelphia: Lippincott Williams and Wilkins.

Poston, D. L. Jr. (2000). Social and economic development and the fertility transitions in mainland China and Taiwan. In C. Y. Cyrus Chu & R. Lee (Eds.), *Population and development review: A supplement to volume 26* (pp. 40–41). New York: Population Council.

Preston, S. H. (1975). The changing relation between mortality and level of economic development. *Population Studies, 29,* 213–248.

Raj, M., Sundaram, K. R., Paul, M., Sudhakar, A., & Kumar, R. K. (2010). Body mass index trend and its association with blood pressure distribution in children. *Journal of Hypertension, 24,* 652–658.

Seidell, J. C. (2001). The epidemiology of obesity. In P. Bjorntorp (Ed.), *International textbook of obesity* (pp. 23–29). New York, NY: John Wiley & Sons.

Strauss, J., & Duncan, T. (1998, June). Health, nutrition and economic development. *Journal of Economic Literature, 36,* 766–817.

Tiengo, A., & Avogaro, A. (2001). Cardiovascular disease. In P. Bjorntorp (Ed.), *International textbook of obesity* (pp. 365–377). New York, NY: John Wiley & Sons.

World Health Organization (WHO). (1995). *World health report 1995: Bridging the gaps.* Geneva, Switzerland: Author.

World Health Organization (WHO). (1996). *World health report 1996: Fighting disease, fostering development.* Geneva, Switzerland: Author.

World Health Organization (WHO). (1997). *World health report 1997: Conquering suffering, enriching humanity.* Geneva, Switzerland: Author.

World Health Organization (WHO). (1998). World health report 1998: *Life in the 21st century: A vision for all.* Geneva, Switzerland: Author.

World Health Organization (WHO). (1999). *World health report 1999: Making a difference.* Geneva, Switzerland: Author.

World Health Organization (WHO). (2009). Chronic diseases and risk factors. Retrieved from http://www.smartglobalhealth.org/issues/entry/chronic-diseases

*For a full suite of assignments and additional learning activities, use the access code located in the front of your book to visit this exclusive website: **http://go.jblearning.com/holtz**. If you do not have an access code, you can obtain one at the site.*

11

Global Perspectives on Diabetes, Respiratory Diseases, and Orthopedic Chronic Diseases

Janice Long

> *"It is not only individuals who get sick from noncommunicable diseases, but whole societies."*
>
> Roger S. Magnusson, PhD

> *"Health is not everything, but without health, everything is nothing."*
>
> Schopenhauer, 1788–1860, German philosopher

OBJECTIVES

After completing this chapter, the reader will be able to:

1. Recognize the impact of globalization on health.
2. Discuss three major chronic noncommunicable diseases affecting global population health.
3. State the major risk factors for chronic noncommunicable diseases.
4. List the major implications of chronic noncommunicable diseases related to social and economic demographics of various regions of the world.
5. Identify global and local strategies for prevention and treatment of chronic noncommunicable diseases.

THE GLOBAL BURDEN OF CHRONIC (NONCOMMUNICABLE) DISEASES

Globalization—the increasing interdependency of countries and the openness of borders to ideas, people, commerce, and finances—has both beneficial and harmful effects on the health of people worldwide. Historically, globalization has influenced the control and treatment of infectious diseases in addition to national security threats, provision of affordable medicines, and public policy changes for international trade and financial agreements. In contrast to the attention paid to acute (including infectious) diseases, noncommunicable diseases (NCDs), such as cardiovascular disease, cancers, chronic respiratory diseases, and diabetes, were neglected. Today, the global impact of NCDs is readily evident, as the world faces a growing prevalence of chronic, long-term, debilitating, and costly diseases. The growth of NCDs is fueled in part by population growth, aging, and unhealthy lifestyle behaviors. As the world's greatest cause of mortality, NCDs result in an estimated 38 million deaths annually (World Health Organization [WHO], 2010).

In 2008, of the estimated 57 million deaths worldwide, 60% were caused by chronic NCDs. Deaths caused by chronic diseases are expected to increase by 17% over the next decade, with an increase from 38 million deaths from these causes to 44 million deaths by 2020 (WHO, 2010). This increase in mortality from lifestyle-dependent diseases, such as diabetes, cancers, cardiovascular diseases, and respiratory diseases is projected to affect people from all countries in the world, although its impact may be felt to the greatest extent among the poorest populations.

Eighty percent of NCD deaths occur in low- and middle-income countries, placing the burden of chronic disease disproportionately higher on low-income countries (WHO, 2011). The age of those affected by NCDs is younger in developing countries than in developed countries, though people of all ages and in all countries suffer from chronic NCDs. The poorer populations of the world tend to bear the greatest risk for chronic illnesses, paralleling the social determinants of these diseases. This creates a cycle of poverty and chronic disease that poor families and communities may be powerless to break. The impact of the increase of NCDs on the disadvantaged populations of the world contributes to the global widening gap in health.

CAUSES OF NCDs

While genetics contribute to chronic diseases, the primary cause of chronic NCDs is thought to be related to four behavioral risk factors that are secondary to economic changes, urbanization, and variations in lifestyles (WHO, 2011). Specifically, tobacco use, unhealthy diets, inactivity, and excessive alcohol use are factors that contribute to the lifestyle behavior risks.

Tobacco Use

WHO estimates that by 2015 approximately 6.4 million deaths worldwide will be due to tobacco-related diseases annually, or 10% of all worldwide deaths. If trends continue, more than 70% of these lives will be lost in developing countries. While tobacco companies have experienced increasing difficulty in marketing their products in developed countries, they have been able to aggressively promote the use of tobacco products in developing countries. "Tobacco is the only consumer product, that when used as recommended by its manufacturers, eventually kills half of its regular users" (Beaglehole & Yach, 2003, p. 904).

Despite what we know about tobacco use today, the use of tobacco products continues to increase worldwide, but especially in low- and middle-income countries. In these countries, the tobacco industry has a large potential market that is not rigidly governed, thereby allowing tobacco manufacturers to collect a great number of new customers (WHO, 2006). An example of the impact of tobacco marketing and use can be seen in India, where death rates from tobacco use are forecasted to be similar to the tobacco use in China. Families in China where smoking is practiced spend less money on education, food, housing, education, and clothing than on tobacco products.

Unhealthy Diets

Unhealthy diets are the second factor contributing to the worldwide burden of NCDs. Global trade and marketing promote consumption of diets containing higher proportions of saturated fats and sugars, thereby placing consumers at risk for atherosclerosis and other cardiovascular illnesses. Even though inadequate nutrition or malnutrition remains a problem for some developing countries, the major nutritional risk factors for NCDs are increasing due to widespread adoption of diets high in fats and carbohydrates. In many of these countries, diets with saturated fats and less natural carbohydrates, such as fruits and vegetables, may be more readily accessible at a cost that is affordable.

Successful marketing campaigns by fast-food chains are able to influence the purchase of products by people of all ages and reach a young population where the result can change a lifestyle of eating habits. In 2009, the fast-food industry spent more than $4.2 billion on television media and other marketing to children. Children of all ethnic groups in developed countries, where television is available, are target audiences for these campaigns; however, African American and Hispanic children are more likely to view the television ads (Rudd Center, 2011). While popular fast-food chains now offer healthier options on the menus and include these items in their advertising, the ads do not encourage consumption of healthier options. Consequently, the sales of the healthier choice products remain lower than the sales of the historically more popular food options, which are higher in saturated fats. The impact of campaigns such as those in the fast-food industry reaches children and adults across the world. In the United States, approximately 84% of parents report taking their child to a fast-food restaurant at least once a week (Rudd Center, 2011). These eating habits that are learned early in life can have a long-standing and profound effect across the life span. Notably, one outcome of such unhealthy eating habits that leads to several chronic illnesses is obesity.

The worldwide prevalence of obesity ranges from less than 5% in rural China, Japan, and some African countries to levels as high as 75% of the adult population in urban Samoa. The rate of childhood obesity in the United States was approximately 32% in 2008 (Ogden, Carroll, Curtin, Lamb, & Flegal, 2010), with increasing rates of prevalence seen in second-generation immigrants and native-born African American and Hispanic American children. In China, obesity rates in children younger than the age of 15 years increased from 15% in 1982 to 27% in 2004 (Lau, 2004). Although the overall prevalence of obesity in China remains low compared with Western countries such as the United States, a rapid increase of obesity is now being seen among children. Data from Chinese national surveys on the constitution and health of school children reveal that the prevalence of overweight and obesity in children aged 7 to 18 years increased 28 times and obesity increased 4 times between 1985 and 2000 (Wu, 2006). One explanation for this obesity epidemic in China is related to culture: Some Chinese subpopulations believe that excess body fat represents health and prosperity—a view shaped in part by the history of famine and chronic malnutrition that resulted in millions of people dying in China in the 1950s.

By the year 2020, with chronic diseases becoming the leading contributors to early death and disability in many areas of the world, the obesity epidemic is expected to parallel the development of NCDs. With more than 1.1 billion of the world's adults overweight, the incidences of cardiovascular disease and diabetes are expected to double over the period of 2000–2030. Although the impact of these increases will be felt across all countries, 70% of the burden will be borne by developing countries (Nikolic, Stanciole, & Zaydman, 2011). The factors contributing to this epidemic are related in large part to a lack of exercise and physical activity.

Physical Inactivity

In addition to tobacco use and poor nutrition, decreased physical activity has placed many people of the world at risk for obesity and its accompanying health challenges. Physical inactivity is associated with increased risk for chronic diseases, including cardiovascular disease, diabetes, and osteoporosis. Physical inactivity is estimated to cause almost one-third of all cases of diabetes and cardiovascular diseases. Despite the clear benefits of physical activity, more than half of all adults in the United States have adopted inactivity and sedentary lifestyles. Physical inactivity is not just a U.S. problem, however: the same trend can be seen among most developed and developing countries. One difference across high- and low-income countries is seen in the timing of physical activity and may reflect the type and number of occupations where either high or low physical activity is required. For people living in high-income countries, most of their activity occurs during leisure time, whereas people in low-income countries are more active during working hours.

Physical activity reduces the risk of cardiovascular disease, some cancers, and type 2 diabetes. It can also improve musculoskeletal health, control body weight, and improve overall quality of life. As a result, WHO has identified increasing physical activity as a challenge and a responsibility for all countries.

THE COST OF NCDs

Because of the increasing burden of chronic diseases, the world faces a continuing financial and health crisis. According to WHO, approximately 80% of premature cardiovascular disease and diabetes cases could be prevented by three interventions: smoking cessation, a healthy diet, and adequate physical activity.

Over the past few decades, global alliances and funding have helped in research and treatment of many communicable diseases, particularly HIV/AIDS, malaria, tuberculosis, and vaccine-preventable diseases. Now, similar attention is provided to the challenge and global response for NCDs. "As the response to NCDs matures and the number of global initiatives and partnerships increases, it becomes increasingly important to map their respective functions, to identify gaps, and to evaluate progress overall" (Magnusson, 2010, p. 491).

Increases in funding with investments in public health prevention programs are necessary to combat the ever-increasing numbers of people with chronic illnesses (Katz, 2004). In 2004, WHO published a global strategy on diet, physical activity, and health. This comprehensive approach to chronic disease prevention and control directed at governments was followed several years later by the Global Recommendations on Physical Activity for Health (WHO, 2010). In 2010, the WHO published its Global Status Report on Noncommunicable Diseases to call all countries to action to prevent or control NCDs.

Few chronic diseases take a toll on the world's population equal to the burden of cardiovascular, musculoskeletal, diabetes, and asthma disorders. These conditions are common chronic conditions affecting adults and children in every country. Lifestyle, environmental, and social risk factors—many of which are controllable—contribute to the development or worsening of these chronic conditions despite advances in science and technology that make the conditions avoidable or controllable. Expert panels have made recommendations for their diagnosis and treatment, with many guidelines and protocols available over the Internet in many languages for each of the conditions. Although numerous chronic global health issues have engendered significant worldwide concern, this chapter addresses the global burden imposed by three common NCDs—musculoskeletal disorders, asthma, and diabetes.

MUSCULOSKELETAL DISORDERS

In both developed and developing countries, the most frequent cause of disability severely affecting individuals' daily lives is musculoskeletal conditions. Although the diseases that cause the greatest mortality may draw the most public attention, musculoskeletal diseases are the major cause of morbidity throughout the world. Longer life expectancy, which has had the effect of increasing the average age of the population in all countries, has caused a corresponding increase in prevalence of diseases of the musculoskeletal system.

Not only are diseases of the musculoskeletal system a problem for the elderly, but musculoskeletal conditions are also responsible for more functional limitations in the adult population than any other group of disorders. Specifically, they are responsible for loss of days of work, loss of years of life quality, disability, and rising healthcare costs in all continents. Studies from Canada, the United States, and Western Europe indicate that the prevalence of physical disabilities caused by musculoskeletal disorders in the past was 4% to 5% of the adult population (Woolf & Pfleger, 2003). In 2000 in both Europe and the United States, the point prevalence of musculoskeletal disorders involving low back pain, osteoarthritis, or tendonitis in the population older than age 45 was greater than 5.5% (Felson, 2000). In 2001, approximately 33% of U.S. adults were thought to be affected by musculoskeletal signs or symptoms, including limitation of motion or pain in a joint or extremity (Helmick et al., 2008). While these kinds of disorders occur in people of all races and ethnicities and in both men and women, the prevalence of musculoskeletal disorders is higher among women, particularly with increased age.

Musculoskeletal conditions include more than 150 diseases and syndromes. It is believed that musculoskeletal disorders represent a major cause of loss of work and life quality on a worldwide basis. The European Agency for Safety and Health Report (2010) reported that musculoskeletal disorders were responsible for the most occupational diseases in the European Union, with workers from all sectors and occupations being affected by these conditions. Reports from Austria, Germany, and France indicate that musculoskeletal disorders have a considerable impact on costs. Not only are wages lost when workers miss days of work due to chronic illnesses, such as musculoskeletal disorders, but the losses incurred from workers who are unable to work may also be passed on to consumers, causing an increase in the costs of consumer goods and products.

The primary types of musculoskeletal disorders include rheumatoid arthritis, osteoarthritis, osteoporosis, spinal disorders, major limb trauma, gout, and fibromyalgia. Limb trauma is increasing rapidly, especially in developing countries due to road traffic accidents. Rheumatoid arthritis leads to work disability and limitation of movement approximately 10 years after disease onset. Those persons who are diagnosed with musculoskeletal diseases frequently have difficulty with activities of daily living, such as eating, walking, toileting, and bathing. Forty percent of people older than 70 years suffer from osteoarthritis of the knee; of those having this disease, 80% experience some degree of limitation of movement. Treatment and recovery are often unsatisfactory especially for more chronic causes. The end result in these circumstances can be permanent disability, chronic pain, and loss of employment. Musculoskeletal disorders are the second most common reason for consulting a doctor in many countries, accounting for 10% to 20% of all medical consultations (Health Safety Executive [HSE], 2010).

The costs associated with such conditions, as reflected in treatment and loss of work resulting from musculoskeletal diseases, can be staggering. Musculoskeletal diseases were the most expensive disease category in a Swedish cost-of-illness study, representing 22.6% of the total cost of illness. In the United Kingdom, work-related musculoskeletal disorders were responsible for 11 million days lost from work in 1995; in 2009–2010, however, an estimated 9.3 million working days were lost through work-related musculoskeletal disorders. The newer data suggest an improvement overall, but confirm that musculoskeletal diseases continue to affect the lives of many U.K. workers (HSE, 2010).

Pain is the most prominent symptom in people with musculoskeletal disorders. Low back pain has reached epidemic proportions around the world. A 2005 European survey revealed that 25% of workers reported work-related low back pain and another 23% experienced other types of muscular pain (De Broeck & Verjans, 2010). In the United States, almost everyone in the workforce experiences back pain at some point in time. In fact, back pain is the second most common neurological complaint after headaches. Americans spend more than $50 billion annually on treatment for back pain (National Institute of Neurological Disorders and Stroke [NINDS], 2011).

In 1990 an estimated 1.7 million people had hip fractures caused by osteoporosis, and by 2050 the number of people affected by this disease will exceed 6 million worldwide. The greatest incidence of musculoskeletal diseases is expected to be found in countries such as Brazil, Chile, China, Pakistan, the Philippines, India, Indonesia, Malaysia, Mexico, and Thailand. Among the developed countries of the world, the United States, European countries, Japan, New Zealand, and Australia all have high rates of such diseases (WHO, 2008).

The following are types of musculoskeletal disorders that are classified as chronic NCDs:

■ Rheumatoid arthritis: A chronic systemic disease that affects the joints, connective tissue, muscle, tendons, and fibrous tissue, with an onset mainly in the 20- to 40-year age range. It is a chronic disability causing pain and deformity.

■ Osteoarthritis: A non-inflammatory joint disease affecting the articular cartilage, associated with aging, and attacking stressed joints such as the knees, hips, finger joints, and lower back.

- Osteoporosis: A disease characterized by reduction in bone mass resulting in fractures. It may be caused by genes, inadequate intake of calcium and vitamin D, physical inactivity, or decrease in ovary function at menopause in women.
- Spinal disorders: Specific diseases of the spine, including trauma, mechanical injury, spinal cord injury, inflammation, infection, or tumors. These disorders may involve muscles, nerves, intervertebral disks, joints, cartilage, tendons, and ligaments.
- Severe limb trauma: Results from permanent disability from fractures, crushing injuries, dislocations, open wounds, amputation, and blood and nerve vessel injuries.

Rheumatoid Arthritis

Rheumatoid arthritis is the most frequent cause of disability in the United States, affecting more than 70 million people, or 1 out of every 3 adults. The direct costs of this disease exceed $16 billion annually in the United States. Another $80 billion is lost in productivity and wages as a result of pain and disability from this condition. Pain, together with functional limitations and dependence on others, is an increasing problem for persons with rheumatoid arthritis. This chronic, autoimmune, inflammatory disease of the joints has unknown etiology and no cure, and is characterized by periods of exacerbation (very active state) followed by periods of remission (inactive state). Besides the physiological problems, the effects of rheumatoid arthritis may include psychological outcomes such as depression and anxiety (Chui, Lau, & Yau, 2004).

Twice as many women as men are affected by this disease. It occurs most often in the United States and northern European countries, and more rarely in developing countries. Very few cases are found in Africa, but of those in African countries, more are found in urban areas. Smoking and obesity as well as family genetics are known risk factors (Woolf & Pfleger, 2003).

Many self-management programs for rheumatoid arthritis have been established worldwide, including in the United States, Australia, Canada, and England. These programs focus on relaxation techniques, exercise, joint protection, pain and stress coping strategies, and self-management skills. In Hong Kong, a community-based rehabilitation program offers knowledge and skill information. In a study examining a rheumatoid arthritis self-management program in Hong Kong, researchers found that the program of exercise, self-management skills, and communication with doctors enhanced positive self-help behavior and reduced visits to the general physician (Chui et al., 2004).

Acupuncture therapy for rheumatoid arthritis is currently being tested in studies in Tel Hashomer, Israel. Acupuncture is a therapeutic method in which thin needles are inserted into specific points (assisting energy flow); for each treatment, specific points are manipulated. According to traditional Chinese medicine philosophy, illness results from an imbalance of energy flow, so the acupuncture needle insertions are connected to precise locations or "meridians" that are certain sites for channels of energy. Although medications are widely prescribed for treatment of rheumatoid arthritis, complementary medicine has been found to be useful as a treatment for many patients. In the United States, 26.7% of the population uses some form of complementary medicine, such as acupuncture, for treatment for rheumatoid arthritis in addition to seeing a medical doctor for treatment (Zan-Bar, Aron, & Shoenfeld, 2004).

Many patients with rheumatoid arthritis who have muscle and joint pain are able to reduce their pain by doing physical exercise in heated pools. Since the 1960s, Swedish patients with inflammatory joint disease have been prescribed intensive physiotherapy in a subtropical climate, called "climate therapy." Patients who were treated in the Mediterranean regions with warmer climates were found to have significant improvement over earlier treatments in Sweden. In a study in 1996, patients treated in Tiberias, Israel's hot springs, for 4 weeks, returned to Sweden significantly improved. The improvements were short-lived, however, as the symptoms returned after 3 and 6 months following treatment (Hafstrom & Hallengren, 2003).

Osteoarthritis

Osteoarthritis is a disease characterized by a loss of articular cartilage within the synovial joints, which is associated with hypertrophy (thickening) of the bone. People with this disease often have joint pain, tenderness, limitation of movement, crepitus, and local inflammation. Osteoarthritis can occur in any joint, but most often affects the hip, knee, joints of the hand, foot, and spine. This disease causes great pain, loss of height, and a significant number of bone fractures. On a worldwide basis among persons age 60 or older, it affects 9.6% of all men and 18% of all women. Research reveals that this condition is more prevalent in the United States and other European countries than elsewhere in the world, and the most commonly affected area is the knee (Chui et al., 2004).

Osteoporosis

Osteoporosis is a disease characterized by low bone mass and a deterioration of the bone tissue. These effects result in bone fragility and vulnerability to bone fractures. In osteoporosis, the bone mineral density is greater than 2.5 standard deviations below the mean bone mineral density of young women. In addition, osteopenia (low bone mass) is between 1 to 2.5 standard deviations below the mean bone mass of young adult women. Those affected often develop hip, vertebrae, and forearm bone fractures. Osteoporosis often occurs in postmenopausal Caucasian women living in the northern parts of the United States. In the United Kingdom, 23% of women age 50 or older have osteoporosis. This disease affects more than 75 million people in Europe, Japan, and Latin and North America. In the United States alone, approximately 15% of the population has osteoporosis. The prevalence increases with age, and the condition is not reversible. Physical activity and adequate diet intake of especially calcium and vitamin D are vital for maintaining healthy bones and preventing this disease (Chui et al., 2004).

In Western Ontario, Canada, a medical study found leech therapy to be helpful in treating arthritis of the knee. Leech therapy was widely used in ancient times, but its popularity declined rapidly in Europe and the United States with the use of modern surgery and medicine. The polypeptide hirudin, an active substance in leech saliva, was found to be effective for relieving pain in the knee in osteoarthritis (Michalsen, Klotz, Ludtke, Moebus, Spahn, & Dobos, 2003).

Hip Fracture

The National Center for Injury Prevention and Control states that 3% to 4% of older adults experience falls each year, leading to more than 400,000 hip fractures in the United States annually. Within this group, 4% die during their initial hospitalization, and 10% to 35% die within the first year after the fracture. Of those who do survive, many never regain their prefracture level of functioning. Most hip fractures result from underlying chronic musculoskeletal conditions, such as arthritis, osteoporosis, or a bone malignancy (Centers for Disease Control and Prevention [CDC], 2004).

DIABETES

The word "diabetes" is derived from the Greek word meaning "going through" and the Latin word "mellitus" means "honey" or "sweet." The disease of diabetes mellitus can be traced to the first century A.D., when Aretaeus the Cappadocian described the disorder as a chronic affliction characterized by intense thirst and voluminous, honey-sweet urine (Porth, 2009). This devastating disease affects nearly every system of the body. As a disorder of the metabolism of carbohydrates, proteins, and fats, diabetes mellitus results from alterations in insulin development and use in the body. Uncontrolled diabetes occurs when the body is unable to regulate the way glucose is transported into fat and muscle cells. Without the ability to move the glucose to the cells where it can be broken down into energy, the body becomes starved and fat and proteins are broken down. As a result, the effects of the disease can be seen across nearly all organs and functions of the body.

Types of Diabetes Mellitus

Diabetes is classified as type 1 diabetes, type 2 diabetes, or gestational diabetes. Types 1 and 2 affect both genders, whereas gestational diabetes occurs only in pregnant women. Each type of diabetes has the characteristic of glucose elevation, but each differs in the type of population affected and the treatment protocols.

Type 1 Diabetes

Type 1 diabetes is characterized by the destruction of the beta cells of the pancreas and is thought to be mediated by immune factors; it may also be idiopathic (National Institute of Diabetes, and Digestive and Kidney Disorders [NIDDK], 2011). Type 1 diabetes is rare in occurrence, affecting only 5% to 10% of people within the United States and Europe. Most individuals with type 1 diabetes are thought to have the immune-mediated form of the condition (Porth, 2009). In the past, type 1 diabetes was referred to as juvenile diabetes because it occurs most often in young persons, but it is now recognized as being able to present at any age. This condition is characterized by the complete inability of the pancreas to produce insulin, which results in high blood glucose and muscle and fat cell catabolism. Without insulin administration, body cells will starve and die.

Type 2 Diabetes

Type 2 diabetes occurs when there is a decreased amount of insulin or the cells of the body are resistant to the insulin produced and a relative loss of insulin is present. This form of diabetes accounts for 90% to 95% of all persons with diabetes. Most people with type 2 diabetes are adults older than 40 years of age and have some degree of obesity. The symptoms of type 2 diabetes—fatigue, frequent urination, and slow-healing sores—can be difficult to detect and often go unnoticed for years before a person is formally diagnosed. As a result, persons with type 2 diabetes often learn they have the condition when they are diagnosed with a diabetes complication. Complications often found in type 2 diabetes include microvascular disorders that can cause visual loss, renal disease, or peripheral vascular disease. Although obesity and physical activity are the chief factors contributing to the condition, genetic links are also implicated.

A younger population has more recently been identified with type 2 diabetes, and this disease appears to be increasing in prevalence. Over the next 10 years, type 2 diabetes is expected to become the predominant form of diabetes in younger members of some ethnic groups worldwide (International Diabetes Federation Consensus Workshop, 2004). Mohan and colleagues (2006) reported that in 2005, in Chennai, India, the age-standardized prevalence of diabetes increased 72% from 1989 to 2005. Among those persons who were 40–49 years of age, 20% have diabetes (Mohan et al., 2006). A study conducted by Tseng and colleagues (2006) found that incidence of diabetes in Taiwan increased across all age groups but was highest in the youngest groups (younger than 35 years of age and including children). The study reported that obesity was an increasing problem in this country, particularly in the school children.

A study of more than 10,000 individuals in one region in the United Kingdom also found a rising prevalence of diabetes by age, with the prevalence of diabetes in females increasing above that in males, beginning at age 30. Also noted in this study was a decrease in diabetes incidence in persons older than 80 years (Morgan, Currie, Stott, Smithers, Butler, & Peters, 2000). Another study conducted in Fukuoka, Japan, found that in both men and women, changes in lifestyle to a more Western diet and increases in dietary fat consumption were contributing factors to the increased prevalence of diabetes (Ohmura et al., 1993).

A study conducted in Italy produced similar results, including increases in prevalence of type 2 diabetes, particularly in groups older than 44 years; greater diabetes incidence was also associated with increased rates of obesity. This suggests a lifestyle-related contribution to the burden of diabetes (Garancini et al., 1995). As a result of lifestyle behaviors that lead to obesity, many people worldwide are at high risk for the cascade of symptoms that often follows overweight and obesity and leads to diabetes. Obesity is one of the most difficult risk factors to change once it is present, so intervening before over-weight occurs is the best strategy for preventing diabetes in all age groups.

Gestational Diabetes Mellitus

As its name indicates, gestational diabetes mellitus (GDM) occurs during pregnancy. It involves an intol-erance to glucose that may be found in 2% to 14% of pregnancies and in particular in those women who have a prior history of gestational diabetes, have a family history of diabetes, are obese, had a high-birth-weight baby in the past, or have had more than five pregnancies. With gestational diabetes, early diag-nosis is critical, as is early intervention with careful medical management to prevent maternal and fetal complications (Masharani, Karam, & German, 2004). Treatment of GDM includes close monitoring for the mother and fetus and maintenance of low blood glucose levels in the mother with frequent maternal glucose monitoring.

In 1995, WHO estimated the prevalence rate of diabetes (all types) in participating coun-tries to be approximately 135 million. The International Diabetes Federation (IDF) regions found a much higher prevalence in 2003, when the organization reported global estimates of 194 mil-lion people living with diabetes. Of those persons with diabetes, approximately 85% to 95% have type 2 diabetes in developed countries and an even higher rate of people in developing countries have this disease (IDF, 2009). Although type 1 diabetes is less frequent in global occurrence, there are variations among the patterns of prevalence of this condition. In particular, the prevalence of type 1 diabetes is highest in North America (0.25%), followed by Europe (0.19%). The IDF findings reported an even more worrisome fact—namely, that public awareness about diabetes is quite low.

If the current global growth rate of diabetes mellitus continues, the prevalence of this condition will increase to much more serious levels over the next two decades. The IDF (2009) projects that the global prevalence of diabetes by the year 2025 will approach 6.3% for adults between 20 and 79 years of age. Education and care interventions are needed to forestall the disease, especially given how strongly its incidence is influenced by lifestyle (IDF, 2009).

The highest regional prevalence of diabetes was seen in North America, followed by the European Union, in 2003; these regions are projected to maintain these positions in 2025. The Southeast Asian region has the highest prevalence of impaired glucose tolerance over all regions.

Treatment Recommendations

The cornerstone of treatment for diabetes has been the active participation in care by the individual who has the condition (Funnell et al., 2011). To assume responsibility for one's own care, a diagnosis must first be made. Given the findings of the IDF suggesting that one of the greatest barriers to treatment is the lack of public awareness of the disease, campaigns to educate the public must become the priority global intervention. Education on diabetic symptoms in concert with screening campaigns for those at risk for diabetes could offer a first stage of awareness to the populations of the world where diabetes or impaired glucose tolerance is most prevalent.

Early intervention with diabetes education and dietary and lifestyle adjustments before complica-tions are present could provide for improved overall outcomes of the disease. Self-monitoring for blood glucose—a process that can easily be performed in the home—offers promise in helping individuals to manage their disease on a daily basis by knowing their blood sugar levels. Tests for the average blood glucose level over a 3-month period (hemoglobin A_{1c} [HbA_{1c}]) are also available, albeit more costly. Research in the United Kingdom indicates that for type 2 diabetes, every 1-point reduction of the HbA_{1c} toward normal levels brings a reduction in the risk for many of the complications that lead to the morbidity and mortality associated with diabetes (Stratton, Cull, Adler, Matthews, Neil, & Holman, 2006).

The American Diabetes Association (ADA) and the European Union–International Diabetes Federation (EUIDF) both recognize that lifestyle changes alone are inadequate in the long term to achieve and maintain weight loss. Exercise and medical and nutrition adjustments are needed to attain the HbA_{1c} levels sought (Nathan et al., 2006). The ADA recommends that individuals try to maintain HbA_{1c} levels below 7.0%, and the EUIDF recommends a level at or below 6.5%, which is closer to the normal level. Even with global advances in pharmacologic therapy included in current-day management, reduction and maintenance of near-normal levels of glycemia have not always been possible. The consensus of the ADA and the EUIDF supports the position that any reduction of HbA_{1c} offers a reduction in risk for the complications of diabetes. The complex nature of diabetes makes treatment quite problematic, and morbidity is particularly high in relationship to cardiovascular disease.

The United Kingdom Prospective Diabetes Study (Stratton et al., 2006) found that hypertension and glycemia have additive effects in the development of cardiovascular mortality, and that by treating both together, the risk for diabetes-related cardiovascular complications could be markedly reduced. Unfortunately, studies suggest that hypertension control is not consistently well achieved (Liebl, Mata, & Eschwege, 2002). Many factors must be considered in the treatment of diabetes, from socioeconomic implications and lifestyle factors to complex comorbid conditions that may accompany diabetes. Research is ongoing on strategies to prevent diabetes and to reduce the seriousness of the complications. The greatest effect on diabetes outcomes is thought to be achieved through the prevention of the condition via changes in the lifestyle factors that predispose individuals to the disease.

Cost of Diabetes Care

The concern for the world in terms of diabetes is not only the human cost and loss of life, but also the economic burden the disease causes. The evidence of this burden was reported by Koster, von Ferer, Ihle, Schubert, and Hauner (2006), who noted that diabetes mellitus is a "public health issue of significant economic importance with a globally increasing prevalence . . . And one that has complications that contribute to long-term disease duration" (p. 1498). Studies from the United States and Europe suggest that the economic burden of diabetes is high (Liebl, Neiß, Spannheimer, Reitberger, Wagner, & Gortz, 2001). Age and type of treatment contribute to the overall cost of treatment, with the highest costs being observed when treatment of the complications of diabetes becomes necessary. As one of the most common global noncommunicable diseases, diabetes ranks as the fourth or fifth leading cause of death in developed countries (IDF, 2009). Complications from diabetes range from coronary artery and peripheral vascular disease, stroke, neuropathy, renal failure, and visual impairment to increased disability and reduced life quality and expectancy. This health issue "results in enormous health costs for virtually every society" (IDF, 2009, p. 7). Although it is important to remember that prevention of diabetes would contribute the greatest cost savings, prevention of complications through tight glycemic control and hypertension management is needed to reduce the economic burden of costly complications once diabetes is diagnosed.

Diabetes Prevention

With advances in transportation and technology, survival in the modern world is much different than that of years ago. Exercise has little by little been taken out of the daily life of the world's population. "In their struggle for longevity, modern-day humans are dying because of lack of physical exercise" (Erikssen,

2001, p. 571). Automobiles carry people directly from the interior of their home to their destination, and parking lots for work and school often offer convenience for parking near the building entrances. Technology also has offered more advances in communication so that children and adults alike have access to friends and family via phones or the Internet, which means the need to physically meet may be lessened. Even recreational activities in a virtual environment makes playtime something that occurs in a chair or on a sofa in the confines of the private residence, and running and playing are less often chosen as alternates as compared to the appeal of an online game or TV show. Fast food and vending machines with high-calorie, high-fat drinks and foods offer quick treats to all age groups and increase the diabetes risk, particularly for those who infrequently exercise.

Overweight in children is a growing worldwide concern that has drawn the attention of WHO as the implications and severity of obesity are assessed in this organization's member countries (Schoenborn, Adams, & Barnes, 2002). In the United States, the CDC has placed the problem of obesity in the forefront of national efforts after studies and trends have revealed that the burden of this condition on the U.S. population is growing (Ogden et al., 2010). The National Health and Nutrition Examination Survey (NHANES) from 1988 to 1994 showed rates of overweight in children and adolescents at about 10%, rising to 14.4% by 1999–2000; the 2001–2002 survey findings indicated that 16% of children between 6 and 11 years of age were overweight (Hedley, Ogden, Johnson, Carroll, Curtin, & Flegal, 2004). The childhood overweight impact varies by U.S. region, as evidenced by one study conducted in a rural region of a southern U.S. state where risk for overweight was found to be 36.2% compared to the national rate at 31.2% (Lewis et al., 2006). These trends indicate a rapid growth in the prevalence of overweight in the United States, with this problem being paralleled by growth in the rate of chronic health conditions, particularly diabetes (Hedley et al., 2004).

Since 1990, physical inactivity has been among the leading risk factors for the global burden of disease, according to the Global Burden of Disease Study (Murray & Lopez, 1996). While many governments around the world are implementing laws to legislate smoking in public places as a deterrent to one of the health risks, legislation of exercise would be very difficult to conceive and enforce in any country (Erikssen, 2001). In a unique move in the United States, a law implemented in July 2006 charges public school systems with the responsibility of improving outcomes in child health through healthy food options in cafeterias and vending machines and through physical exercise programs while the child is in school (S. 2507). The hopes are that through interventions in public schools children can learn many healthy messages, and that the future of diabetes in the United States will not be so grim.

ASTHMA

"When you cannot breathe—nothing else matters."

American Lung Association

Asthma is a serious public health problem that affects the lives of people from all countries, races, and ages. As a condition that causes loss of life, life quality, and productivity when it is not controlled, asthma limits daily life activities and can be fatal (Global Initiative for Asthma [GINA], 2010). Asthma is a significant global burden, sparing no region or country from its effects.

Despite new knowledge, treatments, and environmental innovations, asthma continues to take its toll on the lives of the people of the world. The National Heart Lung and Blood Institute (NHLBI) of the National Institutes of Health (NIH), Expert Panel Report 3 suggests that in the United States, the number of deaths due to asthma have declined, even though the prevalence of asthma is still on the rise (National Health Interview Survey [NHIS], 2007).

Definition

Asthma is a chronic episodic inflammatory disease of the airways that causes recurrent episodes of wheezing, breathlessness, chest tightness, and coughing, particularly at night or in the early morning (NHLBI, 2010). It is one of the most common diseases of childhood and continues to afflict individuals throughout the life span. Asthma's symptoms result from inflammation that occurs from environmental factors and leads to airway hyperresponsiveness and airflow limitation (NHLBI, 2010). The asthmatic lung seems to overreact to stimuli such as airborne allergens and cold, dry air. Over time, the airways or bronchial tubes become inflamed and sensitive; this sensitivity, if not treated, may lead to an asthma "attack." Three major factors related to the airways contribute to the symptoms of asthma:

- Mucus plug formation: Changes in the airways take place once a trigger occurs and an immediate complex inflammatory response follows, resulting in a hypersecretion of mucus from the lining of the airway. The mucus formation also may form plugs of mucus that limit airflow further.
- Acute bronchoconstriction: Immune complexes are released as a result of the allergen/trigger that activates the asthmatic exacerbation. These immune complexes directly contract the smooth muscle of the airways. As a result of the narrowing of the airways from the smooth muscle contraction, the airways become narrowed and airflow is limited (Park, Kim, Kim, & Lee, 2010).
- Airway edema: Airway wall edema limits the airflow through the airways even further, resulting in diminished flow of air in asthma. The mucosa of the airway walls swell and become less compliant to changes in airflow.

The symptoms of asthma may occur either alone or in combination. The frequency and complexity of symptoms determines the degree of severity of asthma, which ranges from mild to severe. In severe cases, the attack may be fatal if no treatment is available. Although asthma symptoms cannot be completely avoided, they can for the most part be controlled. The symptoms of asthma are usually recognizable in advance of an impending exacerbation through the use of a peak flow meter that can be purchased and used in the home. Peak flow meters are available from several manufacturers and are marketed worldwide.

Diagnosis

To diagnose asthma, a thorough history and physical assessment are performed. A spirometer is used to measure the amount of air inhaled and exhaled with each breath. The spirometer readings provide data on the level of pulmonary function and airway obstruction (NHLBI, 2010). Using the history, assessment results, and spirometry readings, asthma is then categorized into one of three levels—mild, moderate, or severe—and treatment recommendations are made to address each level.

Asthma Prevalence

Asthma is one of the most common NCDs in the world, with an estimated 300 million people being affected by the condition. The pattern of asthma prevalence in the world is not explained by the current knowledge of causation. Asthma has become more common in both children and adults in recent decades as communities become increasingly urbanized. WHO projections suggest that the urban population will increase from 45% to 59% by 2025 (NHLBI, 2010). Given this increase, a corresponding increase in asthma worldwide can be anticipated.

The prevalence of asthma has increased globally, but particularly affects people within disadvantaged groups, urban residents, poorly educated persons, individuals of low socioeconomic status, and those who live in large cities. While asthma accounts for about 1 in 250 deaths worldwide (GINA, 2008), mortality is actually much lower in countries where the prevalence is the highest, such as Scotland (prevalence 18.4%, mortality 3.0%), England (prevalence 15.3%, mortality 3.2%), New Zealand (prevalence 15.1%, mortality 4.6%), Costa Rica (prevalence 11.9%, mortality 3.9%), and the United States (prevalence 10.9%, mortality 5.2%). Conversely, countries with lower prevalence rates of asthma have higher mortality, such as China (prevalence 2.1%, mortality 26.7%), Russia (prevalence 2.2%, mortality 28.6%), and Mexico (prevalence 3.3%, mortality 14.5%). Asthma is less common in low-income countries than in high-income countries (Stewart, Mitchell, Pearce, Strachan, & Weilandon, 2001). The reasons for these gaps in prevalence and mortality may be accounted for by the lack of resources, treatments, and pharmaceutical agents in countries where poverty and poor access to care are present.

Asthma Triggers

Factors that create an exacerbation of asthma are known as triggers. Numerous environmental factors or triggers contribute to the development of asthma. They may be from an inhaled irritant or other sources. The following discussion highlights some of the triggers.

Inhaled Factors

More than half the world's population still cooks with wood, coal, or dung on simple stoves or open fires. Because adequate ventilation is not always present, the risk for inhalation irritants is high in these settings, especially in women and children. Exposure to indoor air pollutants is responsible for more than 1.6 million premature worldwide deaths and accounts for approximately 3% of the global burden of disease (Ezzati, 2004). Biomass-type fuels (e.g., wood, charcoal, crop residues, animal dung, and coal) are primary sources for cooking, heating, and other household needs, such as food preservation, in most developing countries. More than 3 billion people use these sources of energy, and the resulting pollutants cause chronic and acute conditions such as asthma and other respiratory conditions that affect the poor more often than individuals who reside in higher socioeconomic conditions. Emissions of the pollutants are most worrisome when solid fuels are used in open or poorly ventilated stoves (Smith, Mehta, Maeusezahl-Feuz, 2004; Zhao, Zhang, Wang, Ferm, Liang, & Norbäck, 2008).

Residents of China bear a high risk for asthma, as coal is the major source of energy in that country, providing about 75% of all energy used. Found within the coal smoke, respiratory contaminants of suspended particulate matter and sulfur dioxide pose a trigger for asthma and other respiratory conditions (Chen, Hong, & Kan, 2004).

Although stoves with improved ventilation have been developed to reduce the risk posed by burning the biomass-type fuels, their use has not been widely accepted. Preprocessing of biomass fuels may potentially decrease this risk by providing for cleaner burning of the fuels (Barnes, Openshaw, Smith, & van der Plas, 2002).

Tobacco smoke exposure ranks highest as an indoor air irritant that can trigger worsening symptoms of asthma. People with known asthma should not smoke or be exposed to environmental smoke in any form because smoking reduces lung function, increases the need for medications, and increases missed days from work. Infants of mothers who smoke have higher rates of infant and childhood asthma (Arshad, Bateman, & Matthews, 2003).

In 2003, WHO reported that 1 in 10 adult deaths could be related to tobacco smoke and estimated that by the year 2030 this number might be closer to 1 in 6. Health promotion activities and smoking cessation treatments for tobacco dependence are needed in most developing and developed countries. Although more than 30% of smokers try to quit at least annually, studies show that only 1% to 3% succeed without the help of smoking cessation programs or pharmaceutical support (Schneider Shafey, Dolwick, & Guindon, 2003).

Other Environmental Factors

Other factors that may trigger asthma attacks include indoor dampness and humidity. Indoor dampness occurs within Nordic countries at a rate of 17–24% of all homes, within the Netherlands at a rate of 25%, and within Canada at a 37% rate. Home indoor dampness can often be detected from signs of water leakage or visible mold on walls, floors, or ceilings (Masoli, Fabian, Holt, & Beasley, 2004). Molds and fungi are produced by the humid indoor environment and are present in homes that have dampness problems. Children who live in homes where these high humid conditions exist are at greater risk for respiratory conditions such as asthma (Tham, Zurainmi, Koh, Chew, & Ooi, 2007).

Another factor that must be considered when assessing asthma triggers is the common house dust mites and animal and cockroach allergens. House dust mites are universal in areas of high humidity (most areas of the United States are included), but are not usually present at high altitudes or dry climates unless moisture is added to the indoor atmosphere (NHLBI, 2010). Dust mites can be found in high concentrations in pillows, mattresses, carpets, upholstered furniture, clothes, and stuffed toys. Pet dander comes from all warm-blooded pets, including small rodents and birds. These animals produce dander, urine, and feces that can cause allergic reactions.

Factors that cause individuals to have regular exposure to allergens or asthma triggers, such as in a work setting, may worsen the condition. Exposure to fluorides and other respiratory irritants has been suggested as an environmental factor that can result in asthma (Taiwo et al., 2006). In Australia and New Zealand, asthma has been found among workers in aluminum smelters and is referred to as "potroom" asthma. Individuals who had exposure improved in pulmonary function once they were removed from the potroom worksite; however, the longer the worker had been exposed, the lower the level of improvement. These kinds of studies offer hope as preventive measures are identified and implemented in the worksite (Arnaiz, Kaufman, Daroowalla, Quigley, Farin, & Checkoway, 2003).

Asthma Treatment

The treatment of asthma includes controlling the environmental factors (triggers) that make asthma worse, pharmacologic therapy geared toward quick relief, and long-term control of symptoms using a stepwise approach with self-management. By reducing the environmental factors that trigger an asthma episode, and by ensuring use of essential medications, control of asthma attacks is possible. For example, data from WHO's *Access to Essential Drugs* report (GINA, 2007) suggest that countries in which more than 95% of the population has access to the essential drugs for NCDs fare better than countries offering less access to these medications. The United States, Canada, New Zealand, and Ireland reported that more than 95% of their populations had access to essential drugs for asthma, while Russia, China, and Mexico reported that between 50% and 80% of their populations had such access (GINA, 2007). Having access to essential treatments for asthma can save the lives of the individuals who suffer with the disease and can offer improved quality of life.

Pharmacologic Treatments for Asthma

Pharmacologic management of asthma is broken into two components—relievers and controllers. Medications for relieving the symptoms of asthma that are delivered through inhalers include products that relax and open the airway to improve the movement of air; these therapies are short term in their action. Controller medications are long term in action and include steroids and nonsteroidal medications that must be taken on a regular basis to be effective. Medications for treating asthma can be costly, and they may not be available in developing countries. Immunotherapy may be considered when specific allergens are present and cannot be avoided. Allergens such as grass or trees, for example, can pose as a major irritant for asthma (NHLBI, 2010).

Cost of Asthma Treatment

The cost of asthma management varies based on the severity and extent of the exacerbation and the need for hospitalization versus self-management to control episodes of the disease. Some episodes require emergency room visits, but they are successfully treated and hospitalization is not required. More severe exacerbations may require hospitalization, with costs being correspondingly higher. Through the use of the peak flow meter, which is a lower-cost alternative to pulmonary function tests, individuals in low-income countries could be provided with a measure of evaluation on which basis to offer early intervention, thereby preventing serious exacerbations. A group of lower-priced generic drugs, delivered by both the oral and inhalation routes of administration, can keep the cost of the government-provided health services to a minimum. With lower-cost asthma medications, a greater benefit could be realized for the population who suffer with asthma.

GINA (2010) recommends that countries identify low-cost drugs that can be made available for those who suffer with asthma. Otherwise, the cost of treatment for countries where the burden for maintaining the health of the population falls on the government will be far greater than can be provided. According to GINA, as much as 30% of the entire health-related expenditures in some countries would have to be spent on asthma medication alone if only 5% of the population had asthma and the cost of asthma treatment was approximately $30. Guidelines for medications should include what is available as well as what is affordable for treatment of asthma.

CONCLUSION

WHO has endorsed a global strategy to address NCDs and the common preventable risk factors related to lifestyle. While such a global strategy may seem ambitious, a global campaign will be necessary to reduce the burden of chronic NCDs on all regions of the world. One recommendation from WHO (2010) is for countries to develop activities that focus on five areas: (1) advocacy, (2) policy, (3) health promotion, (4) prevention, and (5) management of chronic conditions such as diabetes, chronic respiratory diseases, cardiovascular disease, blindness and visual impairment, and musculoskeletal diseases. This chapter has offered suggestions for addressing chronic NCDs globally; however, for a comprehensive public health approach, the strategies for interventions must include a broad-brush approach guided by the five major categories identified by WHO.

Efforts designed to improve the world's health and reduce the incidence and prevalence of NCDs must address improvements in several areas:

1. Monitoring and surveillance of chronic health conditions and their cost and impact
2. Health system changes to address the services needed for patients with NCDs, including addressing the need for cost-effective recommended pharmaceutical agents
3. Policies to support health system changes that are needed and for public health safety
4. Education for healthcare providers on screening, diagnosis, and management of NCDs
5. Public health campaigns to educate the public on NCD recognition and prevention
6. Health promotion and disease prevention programs such as worksite, faith-based, and other alternate site programs
7. Funding of grassroots programs that offer innovative practices in reduction of NCDs
8. Increased research and strategies for applying evidence-based findings to practice

Through such a coordinated approach to NCD prevention and treatment, a significant impact may be achieved in reducing the incidence and prevalence of NCDs.

STUDY QUESTIONS

1. Discuss diabetes prevention strategies within developing countries. What can be accomplished with limited funds?
2. Discuss environmental cause and treatment remedies for asthma in adults and children.
3. Relate the types, causes, and treatments associated with arthritis. Which geographic areas of the world are most likely to have the greatest number of people with osteoarthritis?

CASE STUDY

C. Jones is a 63-year-old female with a 5-year history of type 2 diabetes and worsening symptoms of chronic asthma with dyspnea and cough. She smoked 2 packs of cigarettes per day for 30 years, although she has not smoked since she was diagnosed with asthma 2 years ago.

Ms. Jones lives alone on a farm in rural Georgia, U.S.A., where she has an ample supply of oak, elm, and fruit trees as well as a large wooded area of mixed firs and other foliage nearby. She maintains several farm animals, including cattle that provide milk and meat. She raises chickens, sheep, and goats for food, milk, and to sell at the market in town. Ms. Jones has two dogs, both of which live in the house with her. For heat in the winter, she uses a wood-burning stove, but loves to use it for cooking as often as possible. Her husband died 2 years ago, so she is responsible for the upkeep and maintenance of the farm. A farmhand, Mr. Ramirez, works for her 2 to 3 days per week during nonharvest seasons. During harvest seasons, he works full-time planting and maintaining the fields where Ms. Jones grows cotton, corn, and an assortment of vegetables. Mr. Ramirez arranges for migrant workers to supply labor to harvest the vegetables that she raises on the substantial farmland.

For control and management of her asthma symptoms, Ms. Jones has been on inhalers since she was diagnosed, but today she is having increased wheezing and is struggling to breathe. She is overweight at 5 ft. 6 in. in height and 180 pounds. She has managed her type 2 diabetes with diet and exercise, but more recently has seen her blood sugars in the 200 range. Her most recent glycosylated hemoglobin test (performed last week) was 7.0% (normal is 4% to 6%).

On physical exam, Ms. Jones is anxious. Her blood pressure is 136/90 mm Hg, pulse 120, and respiratory rate at 28. Her lungs have wheezes bilaterally. No accessory muscles are being used and she is not cyanotic. Her lab values reveal the following: ABG 7.48; pO_2: 58; pCO_2: 40; O_2 sat: 90%. On the chest X-ray, her diaphragm is hyperinflated and no infiltrates are seen.

Ms. Jones is treated with albuterol and Atrovent nebulizer and started on a course of prednisone at 40 mg/day for 3 days, to be tapered over 2 weeks. On day 2 of her prednisone, she calls you to say that her blood sugar is 350 mg/dL.

Case Study Questions

1. What are the risk factors for diabetes that Ms. Jones has?
2. What are the triggers for asthma in Ms. Jones's environment?
3. Which actions could be taken to treat her emergently?
4. Which actions could be taken for long-term effect?

REFERENCES

Arnaiz, N. O., Kaufman, J. D., Daroowalla, F. M., Quigley, S., Farin, F., & Checkoway, H. (2003). Genetic factors and asthma in aluminum smelter workers. *Archives of Environmental Health, 58*(4), 197–200.

Arshad, S., Bateman, B., & Matthews, S. (2003). Primary prevention of asthma and atopy during childhood by allergen avoidance in infancy: A randomized controlled study. *Thorax, 58,* 489–493.

Barnes, D., Openshaw, K., Smith, K., & van der Plas, R. (2002). *What makes people cook with improved biomass stoves? A comparative international review of stove programs* (World Bank Technical Paper No. 242. Energy Series). Washington, DC: World Bank.

Beaglehole, R., & Yach, D. (2003). Globalisation and the prevention and control of non-communicable disease: The neglected chronic disease of adults. *Lancet, 362,* 903–908.

Centers for Disease Control and Prevention (CDC). (2004). Chronic disease prevention. Retrieved June 13, 2005, from http://www.cdc.gov/programs/chronic.htm

Chen, B., Hong, C., & Kan, H. (2004). Exposures and health outcomes from outdoor air pollutants in China. *Toxicology, 198*(1–3), 291–300.

Chui, D., Lau, J. S. K., & Yau, I. T. Y. (2004). An outcome evaluation study of the Rheumatoid Arthritis Self-Management Programme in Hong Kong. *Psychology, Health & Medicine, 9*(3), 286–291.

De Broeck, V., & Verjans, M. (2010). Work related musculoskeletal disorders: Facts and figures. National report: Europe. Retrieved from http://osha.europa.eu/en/resources/tero09009enc-resources/europe.pdf

Erikssen, G. (2001). Physical fitness and changes in mortality: The survival of the fittest. *Sports Medicine, 31*(8), 571–576.

European Agency for Safety and Health Report (2010). Retrieved from http://osha.europa.eu/en/publications/annual_report/ar_summary_2010/view

Ezzati, M. (2004). Indoor air pollution and health in developing countries. *Lancet, 366,* 104–106.

Felson, D. T. (2000). Epidemiology of the rheumatic diseases. In W. Koopman (Ed.), *Arthritis and allied conditions.* (pp. 2015–2025). New York: Lippincott, Williams and Collens.

Funnell, M. M., Brown, T. L., Childs, B. P., Haas, L. B., Hosey, G. M., Jensen, B., . . . Weiss, M. A. (2011). National standards for diabetes self-management education. *Diabetes Care, 34,* S89–S96.

Garancini, M. P., Calori, G., Ruotolo, G., Manara, E., Izzo, A., Ebbli, E., . . . Gallus, G. (1995). Prevalence of NIDDM and impaired glucose tolerance in Italy: An OGTT–based population study. *Diabetologia, 38,* 306–313.

Genetic Information Nondiscrimination Act (GINA). (2008). Retrieved from http://www.genome.gov/24519851

Global Initiative for Asthma (GINA). (2010). Global strategy for asthma management and prevention. Retrieved from http://www.ginasthma.org/

Hafstrom, I., & Hallengren, M. (2003). Physiotherapy in subtropic climate improves functional capacity and health-related quality of life in Swedish patients with rheumatoid arthritis and spondylarthropathies still after 6 months. *Scandinavian Journal of Rheumatology, 32,* 108–113.

Health Safety Executive (HSE). (2010). The health and safety executive statistics 2009/2010. Retrieved from http://www.hse.gov.uk/statistics/overall/hssh0910.pdf

Hedley, A., Ogden, C., Johnson, C., Carroll, M., Curtin, L., & Flegal, K. (2004). Prevalence of overweight and obesity among US children, adolescents, and adults (1999–2002). *Journal of the American Medical Association, 291*(23), 2847–2850.

Helmick, C. G., Felson, D. T., Lawrence, R. C., Gabriel, S., Hirsch, R., Kwoh, C. K., . . . Stone, J. H. (2008). Estimates of the prevalence of arthritis and other rheumatic conditions in the United States. *Arthritis & Rheumatism, 58*(1), 15–25. doi: 10.1002/art.23177

International Diabetes Federation (IDF). (2009). Diabetes atlas: Executive summary (4th ed.). Retrieved from http://www.idf.org/diabetesatlas/executive-summary

International Diabetes Federation Consensus Workshop. (2004). Type 2 diabetes in the young: The evolving epidemic. *Diabetes Care, 27,* 1798–1811.

Katz, D. (2004). The burden of chronic disease: The future is prevention [Electronic version]. *Public Health Research, Practice, and Policy, 1*(2), 1.

Koster, I., von Ferber, L., Ihle, P., Schubert, I., & Hauner, H. (2006). The cost burden of diabetes mellitus: The evidence from Germany—the CoDIM Study. *Diabetologia, 49,* 1498–1504.

Lau, X., (2004). Lazy lifestyle a weighty issue. *Beijing Review, 47*(6), 28–29.

Lewis, R. D., Meyer, M. C., Lehman, S. C., Trowbridge, F. L., Bason, J. J., Yurman, K. H., . . . Yin, Z. (2006). Prevalence and degree of childhood and adolescent overweight in rural, urban, and suburban Georgia. *Journal of School Health, 76*(4), 126.

Liebl, A., Mata, M., & Eschwege, E. (2002). Evaluation of risk factors for development of complications in type II diabetes in Europe. *Diabetología, 45,* S23–S28.

Liebl, A., Neiß, A., Spannheimer, A., Reitberger, U., Wagner, T., & Gortz, A. (2001). Costs of type 2 diabetes in Germany: Results of the Code-2 study. *Dutsch Medical Wochenschr, 126,* 585–589.

Magnusson, R. (2010). Global health governance and the challenge of chronic, non-communicable disease. *Journal of Law, Medicine and Ethics, 38*(3), 490–507.

Masharani, U., Karam, J. H., & German, M. S. (2004). Pancreatic hormones and diabetes. In F. S. Greenspan & D. G. Garner (Eds.), *Basic and clinical endocrinology* (7th ed., pp. 658–746). New York: Lange Medical Books/McGraw-Hill.

Masoli, M., Fabian, D., Holt, S., & Beasley, R. (2004). The global burden of asthma. Developed for the global initiative for asthma. *Allergy, 59*(5), 469–478.

Michalsen, A., Klotz, S., Ludtke, R., Moebus, S., Spahn, G., & Dobos, G. (2003). Effectiveness of leech therapy in osteoarthritis of the knee. *Annals of Internal Medicine, 139,* 724–730.

Mohan, V., Deepa, M., Deepa, R., Shanthirani, C. S., Farooq, S., Ganesan, A., & Datta, M. (2006). Secular trends in the prevalence of diabetes and impaired glucose tolerance in urban South India: The Chennai Urban Rural Epidemiology Study (CURES-17). *Diabetologia, 49,* 1175–1178.

Morgan, C. L., Currie, C. J., Stott, N. C. H., Smithers, M., Butler, C. C., & Peters, J. R. (2000). Estimating the prevalence of diagnosed diabetes in a health district of Wales: The importance of using primary and secondary care sources of ascertainment with adjustment for death and migration. *Diabetic Medicine, 17,* 141–145

Murray, C. J., & Lopez A. D. (1996). The Global Burden of Disease: a comprehensive assessment of mortality and disability from diseases, injuries and risk factors in 1990 and projected to 2020. Cambridge, MA: Harvard School of Public Health. Global Burden of Disease and Injury Series. Vol. I.

Nathan, D. M., Buse, J. B., Davidson, M. B., Heine, R. J., Holman, R. R., Sherwin, R., & Zinman, B. (2006). Management of hyperglycaemia in type 2 diabetes: A consensus algorithm for the initiation and adjustment of therapy. *Diabetologia, 49,* 1711–1721.

National Health Interview Survey (NHIS). (2007). Lifetime asthma population estimates. Retrieved from http://www.cdc.gov/asthma/nhis/05/table1-1.htm

National Heart, Lung, and Blood Institute (NHLBI). (2010). Global Initiative for Asthma. (GINA). *Global strategy for asthma management and prevention* (NHLBI/WHO Workshop Report No. 02-3659). Bethesda, MD: NLBHI.

National Institute of Diabetes, and Digestive and Kidney Disorders (NIDDK). (2011). Diabetes overview. Retrieved from http://diabetes.niddk.nih.gov/dm/pubs/overview/

National Institute of Neurological Disorders and Stroke (NINDS). (2011). Low back pain fact sheet. Retrieved from http://www.ninds.nih.gov/disorders/backpain/detail_backpain.htm

Nikolic, I. A., Stanciole, A. E., & Zaydman, M. (2011). *Chronic emergency: Why NCDs matter. Health Nutrition and Population Discussion Paper.* Washington, DC: World Bank.

Ogden, C. L., Carroll, M. D., Curtin, L. R., Lamb, M. M., & Flegal, K. M. (2010). Prevalence of high body mass index in US children and adolescents, 2007–2008. *Journal of the American Medical Association, 303,* 242–249.

Ohmura, T., Ueda, K., Kiyohara, Y., Kato, I., Iwanoto, H., Nakayama, K., . . . Shinkawu, A. (1993). Prevalence of type 2 (non-insulin dependent) diabetes mellitus and impaired glucose tolerance in the Japanese general population: The Hisayama study. *Diabetologia, 36*, 1198–1203.

Park, H. S., Kim, S. Y., Kim, S. R., & Lee, Y. C. (2010). Targeting abnormal airway vascularity as a therapeutical strategy in asthma. *Journal of the Asian Pacific Society of Respirology, 15*, 459–471. doi: 10.1111/j.1440-1843.2010.01723.x

Porth, C. M. (2009). *Essentials of pathophysiology: Concepts of altered health states.* Philadelphia: Lippincott Williams & Wilkins.

Rudd Center. (2011). Fast food f.a.c.t.s.: Food advertising to children and teens score. Retrieved from http://fastfoodmarketing.org/

Schneider Shafey, O., Dolwick, S., & Guindon, G. (2003). Tobacco control country. Retrieved May 28, 2007, from http://www.wpro.who.int/NR/rdonlyres/437C3114-24FE-45CA-9A62-8E119BC66CC6/0/TCCP2.pdf

Schoenborn, C. A., Adams, P. F., & Barnes, P. M. (2002). *Body weight status of adults: United States, 1997–98.* Advance data from *Vital and Health Statistics, 330.* Hyattsville, MD: National Center for Health Statistics.

Smith, K. R., Mehta, S., & Maeusezahl-Feuz, M. (2004). Indoor air-pollution from household solid fuel use. In M. Ezzati, A. D. Lopez, A. Rodgers, & C. J. L. Murray (Eds.), *Comparative quantification of health risks: Global and regional burden of disease attributable to selected major risk factors* (pp. 1435–1493). Geneva, Switzerland: World Health Organization.

Stewart, A. W., Mitchell, E. A., Pearce, N., Strachan, D. P., & Weilandon, S. K. (2001). The relationship of per capita gross national product to the prevalence of symptoms of asthma and other atopic disease in children. *International Journal of Epidemiology, 30*, 173–179.

Stratton, I. M., Cull, C. A., Adler, A. I., Matthews, D. R., Neil, H. A. W., & Holman, R. R. (2006). Additive effects of glycaemia and blood pressure exposure on risk of complications in type 2 diabetes: A prospective observational study (UKPDS 75). *Diabetologia, 49*, 1761–1769.

Taiwo, O. A., Sircar, K. D., Slade, M. D., Cantley, L. F., Vegso, S. J. L, Rabinowitz, P. M., . . . Cullen, M. R. (2006). Incidence of asthma among aluminum workers. *Journal of Occupational and Environmental Medicine, 48*(3), 275–282.

Tham, K. W., Zuraimi, M. S., Koh, D., Chew, F. T., & Ooi, P. L. (2007). Associations between home dampness and presence of molds with asthma and allergic symptoms among young children in the tropics. *Pediatric Allergy Immunology, 18*, 418–424. doi: 10.1111/j.139903038.2007.00544.x

Tseng, C. H., Tseng, C. P., Chong, C. K., Huang, T. P., Song, Y. M., Chou, C. W., . . . Cheng, J. C. (2006). Increasing incidences of diagnosed type 2 diabetes in Taiwan: Analysis of data from a national cohort. *Diabetologia, 49*, 1755–1760.

Woolf, A., & Pfleger, B. (2003). Burden of major musculoskeletal conditions. *Bulletin of the World Health Organization, 81*(9), 646–656.

World Health Organization (WHO). (2004). *Global strategy on diet, physical activity and health.* France: WHO Press.

World Health Organization (WHO). (2006). Tobacco: deadly in any form or disguise. Retrieved from http://www.who.int/tobacco/communications/events/wntd/2006/Report_v8_4May06.pdf

World Health Organization (WHO). (2008, April 18). *Action plan for the global strategy for the prevention and control of noncommunicable diseases.* World Health Assembly Document A61/8.

World Health Organization (WHO). (2010). *Global recommendations on physical activity for health.* Geneva, Switzerland: Author.

World Health Organization (WHO). (2011). Global status report on noncommunicable diseases 2010. Retrieved from http://www.who.int/nmh/publications/ncd_report2010/en/

Wu, Y. (2006). Overweight and obesity in China. *British Medical Journal, 333*, 362. doi: 10.1136/bmj.333.7564.362.

Zan-bar, T., Aron, A., & Shoenfeld, Y. (2004). Acupuncture therapy for rheumatoid arthritis. *APLar Journal of Rheumatology, 7,* 207–214.

Zhao, Z., Zhang, Z., Wang, Z., Ferm, M., Liang, Y. & Norbäck, D. (2008). Asthmatic symptoms among pupils in relation to winter indoor and outdoor air pollution in schools in Taiyuan, China. *Environmental Health Perspectives,* 116:90–97. Retrieved from http://dx.doi.org/10.1289/ehp.10576

*For a full suite of assignments and additional learning activities, use the access code located in the front of your book to visit this exclusive website: **http://go.jblearning.com/holtz**. If you do not have an access code, you can obtain one at the site.*

12

Cancer as a Public Health Problem: An Overview for Allied Healthcare Professionals

Linda G. Alley

Hannah D. Paxton

Michelle D. Flores

Jeff Etchason

> *Cancer is an enormous global health burden, touching every region and socioeconomic level.*
>
> American Cancer Society [ACS], 2012, p. 53

> *The worldwide application of existing cancer control knowledge according to the capacity and economic development of countries or regions could lead to the prevention of even more cancer deaths in the next 2 or 3 decades. In order to achieve this, however, national and international public health agencies, governments, donors, and the private sectors must play major roles in the development and implementation of national or regional cancer control programs worldwide.*
>
> Brawley, 2011, p. 68

OBJECTIVES

After reading this chapter the reader will be able to:

1. Compare and contrast global cancer statistics, including types, risks, geographic locations, and treatments in developed and developing nations.
2. Relate economic, personal, and physiological costs of cancers worldwide.
3. Discuss cancer survivorship and palliative and end-of-life care for cancer patients worldwide.
4. Compare and contrast disparities in cancer statistics for vulnerable populations.
5. Discuss the role of cancer registries worldwide.
6. Compare and contrast cancer prevention, control and education strategies.
7. Explain how public policy changes can decrease cancer risks in various global populations.

INTRODUCTION

The fight to eliminate cancer as a major health problem extends around the world (ACS, 2012). Although better prevention, early detection, and advances in treatment have helped some developed nations lower their incidence and mortality rates for certain types of cancers, in most parts of the world cancer is a growing problem (ACS, 2011b). Worldwide, the number of new cancer cases is expected to grow by 50% to a total of 15 million by the year 2020 (Stewart & Kleihues, 2003). By the year 2030, the expected numbers reveal a continuing rise in global burden, with approximately 21.4 million new cancer cases and 13.2 million cancer deaths expected to occur yearly, due *only* to the growth and aging of the population (ACS, 2012). The future burden may be further increased by the adoption of some specific, unhealthy behaviors and lifestyles associated with economic development and urbanization in low-and middle-income countries (ACS, 2011e, 2012). According to *The Cancer Atlas,* the global epidemic of cancer is shifting from developed to developing nations (Mackay, Jemal, Lee, & Parkin, 2006), where approximately 85% of the world population resides (ACS, 2012).

This chapter is written from a public health perspective, and is intended to introduce allied health-care professionals to important issues and concepts related to cancer and cancer patient care, both within the United States and in other parts of the world. The four sections address the following aspects of this topic: (1) key cancer and public health concepts and definitions; (2) cancer prevention; (3) early detection, screening, and education; and (4) cancer care considerations, including treatment, survivorship, palliative care, and end-of-life care. Efforts have been made throughout the chapter to highlight cancer-related topics that undergraduate students and healthcare professionals in a variety of disciplines (e.g., nurses, physician assistants, physical and occupational therapists, dieticians) may encounter early in their clinical work. Global perspectives are also provided to highlight both similarities of some issues as well as different challenges that countries throughout the world encounter in addressing cancer.

For detailed information on cancer-related topics presented in this chapter, readers are encouraged to refer to the numerous high-quality national reports, guidelines, textbooks, journal articles, and other current resources cited here. Websites of national organizations that are frequently updated to reflect changes in current knowledge about cancer and cancer care are also highlighted.

KEY CANCER AND PUBLIC HEALTH CONCEPTS AND DEFINITIONS

Cancer and the Comprehensive Cancer Control Approach

An often-cited definition of cancer is provided by the ACS (2012): "Cancer is a group of diseases characterized by uncontrolled growth and spread of abnormal cells" (p. 1). More than 100 different diseases are covered by the term "cancer," and each of these diseases has a unique profile in terms of the population at risk, symptoms, and prognosis (Curry, Byers, & Hewitt, 2003). If the spread of abnormal cells is not controlled, it can lead to death of the individual affected (ACS, 2012). Cancer can be caused by external factors (e.g., tobacco, chemicals, radiation, infectious organisms) or internal factors (e.g., inherited mutations, hormones, immune conditions, mutations that occur from metabolism); these causal factors, acting together or in sequence, may initiate or promote the development of a cancer (ACS, 2012). A period of 10 or more years often passes between exposure to such factors and the onset of detectable cancer (ACS, 2012). The resulting time period between cancer development, detection, diagnosis, treatment, and possible progression can be quite long, ranging from months to decades, depending on the type of cancer.

For this reason, cancer prevention and control efforts must take a coordinated, long-term perspective (Centers for Disease Control and Prevention [CDC], 2011c; Miller, Hager, Lopez, Salinas, & Shepherd, 2009). The comprehensive cancer control (CCC) process was developed to support the long-term perspective. Through this process, a community pools its resources to reduce the burden of cancer by reducing risk, facilitating early detection, ensuring better treatment, and enhancing survivorship; these efforts, in turn, encourage healthy lifestyles, promote recommended cancer screening guidelines and tests, increase access to high-quality cancer care, and improve quality of life for cancer survivors (CDC, 2011b). One example of a far-reaching, public health–oriented collaboration is the National Comprehensive Cancer Control Program (NCCCP), which is supported by the CDC. The NCCCP is a national collaborative initiative that seeks to create the necessary conditions for dramatically reducing the burden of cancer incidence and mortality and improving the quality of life for cancer survivors (Black, Cowens-Alvarado, Gershman, & Weir, 2005; CDC, 2011b).

In the United States, the NCCCP conducts its work by supporting the development and implementation of state CCC plans (Black et al., 2005). Since 1998, the number of member CCC programs participating in NCCCP has grown from 6 to 65; currently, member programs include all 50 states and the District of Columbia, 7 tribes and tribal organizations, and 7 United States associated Pacific Islands/territories (CDC, 2011b). The CDC's Division of Cancer Prevention and Control works with national organizations, state health agencies, and other key groups to develop, implement, and promote effective cancer prevention and control practices within the NCCCP.

Internationally, cancer prevention and control initiatives are taking place on every continent. Canada, China, France, and Chile are currently implementing national cancer control programs, for example. According to the World Health Organization (WHO, 2008), the basic principles of cancer control include the following:

- Leadership to create clarity and unity of purpose
- Involvement of stakeholders
- Creation of partnerships
- Responding to the needs of people at risk
- Decision making based on evidence, social values, and efficient and cost-effective use of resources
- Application of a systematic approach
- Seeking continuous improvement
- Planning and implementing cancer control using a stepwise approach

Cancer Burden

Burden refers to the size of a health problem in a specified area, as measured by several statistics, such as incidence, mortality, rates, and prevalence, as well as other indicators such as cost, morbidity ("any departure from physiological or psychological well-being" [Mackay et al., 2006, p. 17]), and risk factors (Black et al., 2005; Stewart & Kleihues, 2003). "Cancer is an enormous global health burden, touching every region and socioeconomic level" (ACS, 2012, p. 53). Knowledge of the burden of a disease can help determine where investments in time, money, and other resources may be most effective in reducing the burden.

Recognizing the growing global cancer crisis, the ACS (2011b, 2011e) has established three integrated priorities aimed at reducing the burden of cancer: (1) increasing funding for the control of cancer and other noncommunicable diseases, including making cancer control a political and public health priority; (2) reducing tobacco use; and (3) increasing awareness about the burden of cancer and its leading risk factor, tobacco. *The Worldwide Cancer Burden Report* (ACS, 2006) described factors that contribute to the burden in developed countries versus those that contribute to the burden in developing countries. Contributing factors include regional differences in age structure, prevalence of major risk factors, availability of detection services, and completeness of reporting data to cancer registries. A 2007 Institute of Medicine (IOM) report on cancer control opportunities in low- and middle-income countries provided an excellent review of the significant burden of cancer in both low- and middle-income countries, and identified major opportunities for such countries to achieve better cancer control, including cancer planning, cancer prevention and early detection/screening, cancer management, and psychosocial support for patients and families (Sloan & Gelband, 2007). Despite the ever-increasing evidence of the growing burden of cancer, far too little continues to be spent globally to manage this growing crisis (Economist Intelligence Unit, 2009).

Regarding the U.S. cancer burden, a decade ago, Colditz, Samplin-Salgado, Ryan, Dart, Fisher, Tokuda, and Rockhill (2002) wrote that sufficient knowledge of cancer causes and prevention was available, at that time, to reduce cancer burden in the United States by more than 50% in the coming decades, *if* public policies relying on the current scientific knowledge were implemented. Unfortunately, this knowledge has not been translated into systematic action across the country, and the failure to take this step presents a major challenge to current CCC efforts (Black et al., 2005).

In the 2006 *Cancer Atlas* (Mackay et al., 2006), the burden associated with this disease is discussed within the context of three related topics outlined briefly here: the risk of getting cancer, the incidence of major cancers worldwide, and geographical diversity in the risks of developing cancers.

The Risk of Getting Cancer

Cancer risk is commonly expressed either as lifetime risk (the probability that a person will develop or die from cancer over the course of his or her lifetime) or relative risk (a measure of the strength of the relationship between risk factors and a particular cancer) (ACS, 2012). Although anyone can develop cancer, most cases occur in adults who are middle-aged or older, as the risk of being diagnosed with cancer increases as people age (ACS, 2012). The most common cancers involve epithelial tissues (linings of the airways, gastrointestinal, and urinary systems); the risk of developing these types of cancer increases rapidly with age, as does the overall risk of cancer (Mackay et al., 2006).

> Cancer develops when a sequence of mutations occurs in critical genes in one cell of the body, as a result of exposure to carcinogens, such as tobacco, infectious organisms, and chemicals, and internal factors such as inherited mutations, hormones, and immune conditions. Cumulative exposure to such agents increases with time, so that the probability of cancer increases as we age. (Mackay et al., 2006, p. 42)

All cancers involve the malfunction of genes that control cell growth and division, with approximately 5% of cancers being strongly hereditary, meaning that an inherited genetic alteration confers a very high risk of developing one or more specific types of cancer (ACS, 2012). In children, leukemias and cancers of connective tissue are more common than epithelial tissue cancers (Mackay et al., 2006). Information regarding the differences between childhood and adult cancers can be found in the 2007 IOM report on cancer control (Sloan & Gelband, 2007).

Most cancers can be linked to a few controllable factors, including tobacco use, poor diet, lack of exercise, and infectious diseases (ACS, 2011b; Curry et al., 2003); these factors are discussed in the "Prevention" section later in this chapter. Tobacco use is the number one cause of cancer and the number one cause of preventable death throughout the world (ACS, 2012; Shafey, Eriksen, Ross, & Mackay, 2009), and reduction in tobacco use offers the greatest opportunity to reduce the global incidence, morbidity, and mortality of cancer (Curry et al., 2003). In fact, all cancers caused by cigarette smoking and heavy use of alcohol could be prevented completely (ACS, 2012). The most important modifiable risk factors (i.e., risk factors that can be changed), as outlined in *The Cancer Atlas* (Mackay et al., 2006), include an unhealthy diet (high in saturated fats with an insufficient intake of fresh fruits and vegetables), physical inactivity, infections with viruses or bacteria that cause cancer, and ultraviolet radiation exposure. Other modifiable risk factors are alcohol use, occupational exposures to carcinogens such as asbestos and secondhand tobacco smoke (also referred to as passive smoking), socioeconomic status, environmental pollution, obesity, food contaminants, and ionizing radiation (Mackay et al., 2006). Modifying some risk factors requires individual behavior changes, while modifying other risk factors requires changes at the population level (e.g., by employers or communities); often, improvement in risk factors is best accomplished by employing both individual and population level efforts (Mackay et al., 2006).

Additional perspectives on cancer risk and outcomes, on the continuum from prevention to palliative care, can be gained by reviewing current reports focused on specific racial and ethnic groups. *Cancer Facts & Figures for African Americans 2011–2012* (ACS, 2011c) and *Cancer Facts & Figures for Hispanics/Latinos 2009–2011* (ACS, 2009) reveal how cancer occurrence and survival are influenced by cultural values and beliefs as well as by the aforementioned risk factors.

Incidence of Major Cancers Worldwide

Cancer incidence refers to the number of newly diagnosed cases of cancer that occur in a defined population during a specified period of time, such as a year (Mackay et al., 2006; Menck & Bolick-Aldrich, 2007). The cancer incidence rate is the rate at which new cases occur in a population and is calculated by dividing the number of new cases that occur during a specified time period by the total number of people who were at risk for the given cancer in the defined population; this rate is generally expressed as the number of cancers per 100,000 people (Mackay et al., 2006; Menck & Bolick-Aldrich, 2007). Cancer incidence differs from cancer prevalence, which refers to how many cases of a particular cancer are present in a defined population at a given point in time (Hutchison, Menck, Burch, & Gottschalk, 2004).

The most common cancers worldwide are lung, breast, colorectal, stomach, and prostate (Mackay et al., 2006; World Cancer Research Fund International, 2011). Liver cancer is the most common cancer for men in several African countries, although Kaposi's sarcoma is the most common cancer in 13 of these African countries that are severely affected by the HIV/AIDS epidemic. Either breast or cervical cancer is the most common malignancy for women in almost all countries, except for in some East Asian countries, where stomach cancer is more frequent (Mackay et al., 2006). The cancer that causes the most deaths worldwide is lung cancer, followed by stomach and liver cancer, although the pattern is quite different in males and females (Mackay et al., 2006). Cancer affects people of all races, ethnicities, genders, and ages. The cancers that are common in developing countries are those that have a poor prognosis, including cancers of the lung, stomach, liver, and esophagus (Mackay et al., 2006).

Geographical Diversity

The risk of developing different cancers varies widely by world region, as noted by the examples that follow. Studies of migrants or populations who move from one location to another confirm that differences in the risk of various cancers are largely environmental in origin (not due to ethnic or genetic differences) and especially are a product of different lifestyles (Mackay et al., 2006). Liver cancer incidence reflects the prevalence of infection by hepatitis viruses, especially hepatitis B virus. Esophageal cancer rates are high in east Africa and Asia, including China and Central Asia, whereas testicular cancer is rare in African and Asian men (Mackay et al., 2006). Although not rare anywhere in the world, breast cancer is primarily a disease of affluent countries (Mackay et al., 2006). In contrast, the burden of disease from cervical cancer is highest in the poorer southern countries in Africa, Latin America, and South and Southeast Asia (Sloan & Gelband, 2007). Worldwide, lung cancer is the most common cancer, both in terms of new cases and of deaths; approximately 80% of cases in men and 50% of cases in women are caused by tobacco smoking (Mackay et al., 2006). International variations in cancer incidence and mortality have been described for the most common cancers (i.e., lung, female breast, colon and rectum, stomach, prostate, liver, and cervical) in both economically developed and developing regions of the world (ACS, 2006, 2011e). The bacterium *Helicobacter pylori* (*H. pylori*) is a major cause of stomach cancer, which is poorly responsive to treatment (Sloan & Gelband, 2007). The prevalence of *H. pylori*, as well as that of stomach cancer, has declined dramatically even without the implementation of targeted measures in much of the world; this trend suggests the possibility of developing interventions for geographic regions where *H. pylori* is not declining, which includes most low-income countries (Mackay et al., 2006; Sloan & Gelband, 2007).

In the United States, cancer overall is the second leading cause of death, exceeded only by heart disease (ACS, 2012). One of every four deaths in the United States is due to cancer (ACS, 2012). In 2012, more than 1.6 million Americans are predicted to receive a new diagnosis of invasive cancer and more than a half million Americans are expected to die of this disease—more than 1500 people per day (ACS, 2012). The 2012 new cancer case estimate does not include carcinoma in situ (noninvasive cancer) of any site (except for urinary bladder cancer) or basal and squamous cell skin cancers (which are not required to be reported to cancer registries).

Men in the United States are most often diagnosed with or die from prostate, lung, and colorectal cancers, whereas women are most often diagnosed or die from female breast, lung, and colorectal cancers (United States Cancer Statistics Working Group [USCSWG], 2006). Variations in the incidence and mortality of various cancers, examined according to race and ethnicity and to geographic area in the United States, are complex to explain and have been well described (ACS, 2011b). Such variations may be the result of regional differences in exposure to known or unknown risk factors such as sociodemographic population characteristics (e.g., age, race and ethnicity, geographic region, urban or rural residence), use of screening activities, health-related behaviors (e.g., behaviors related to tobacco use, diet, physical activity), exposure to cancer-causing agents, or cancer registry operations factors (e.g., completeness and timeliness of data collection; specificity in coding data collected for various cancer sites) (CDC, 2005; Devesa, Grauman, Blot, Pennello, & Hoover, 1999; Howe, Keller, & Lehnherr, 1993).

Cancer Mortality

Cancer mortality refers to "the numbers of deaths from cancer that occur in a population during a specified period of time" (Mackay et al., 2006, p. 17). The mortality rate is the rate at which deaths occur in a population and is calculated by dividing the number of deaths that occur during a specified period of time by the number of people at risk for the given cancer in the specified population (Mackay et al., 2006; Menck & Bolick-Aldrich, 2007). Overall, the probability of an individual dying from cancer during his or her lifetime does not differ appreciably between the developed and developing world (Mackay et al., 2006). At the same time, although the risk of getting cancer is higher in the developed world, cancers in the developing world are more likely to prove fatal (Mackay et al., 2006). Evidence regarding the influence of gender on mortality is seen in data from U.S. government research, which indicates that men who are diagnosed with cancer are more likely to die from the disease than are women, due to a higher initial risk and later detection (Beasley, 2011). Other investigators have found that male-to-female mortality rate ratios (MRR) differ markedly, while cancer survival disparities are much less pronounced, suggesting that sex-related cancer disparities are more strongly related to etiology than to prognosis (Cook, McGlynn, Devesa, Freedman, & Anderson, 2011).

The Expanding Role of Cancer Registries

Cancer registries serve as important links between high-quality cancer data collection and high-quality patient care. Despite the enormous contributions made by registries, registry staff often work in fairly low-visibility positions in clinical settings, so healthcare professionals working in hospitals may be unaware of the time- and labor-intensive, and highly technical, work of these cancer surveillance leaders. Thus highlights of cancer registries and the registration process are provided here.

Cancer registries are data collection systems that assess the occurrence and characteristics of reportable cancers. They are designed for the collection, management, and analysis of data on persons who have been diagnosed with cancer (Hutchison et al., 2004). The organized and systematic cancer registration process involves the collection of five items in the fundamental data set: (1) occurrence of cancer, (2) type of cancer (site, morphology, and behavior), (3) extent of disease at the time of diagnosis (stage), (4) types of treatment received by the patient, and (5) treatment outcomes (survival) (Hutchison et al., 2004). Cancer registries exist in a wide range of settings and function within varying organizational structures, such as hospitals, physicians' offices, radiation facilities, freestanding surgical centers, research centers, and pathology laboratories (Hutchison et al., 2004; USCSWG, 2006). The status of cancer registration in other countries has been addressed by Menck (2004).

Cancer registries may collect details of new cancer cases and their follow-up, either for a defined population (e.g., a geographical area; a particular cancer diagnosis) or for a hospital (Mackay et al., 2006). Registries that seek to collect and maintain data on all possible patients within a defined geographic area (such as a state, province, or city) are referred to as population-based (Hutchison et al., 2004). Because the reader may hear the term "cancer registry" in the course of daily business, two main types of registries are briefly noted here. Hospital-based cancer registries provide detailed information about cancer patients receiving care at the hospital, the nature of their tumors (including the precise histological types and stage of disease), the treatment received, and the outcome of the disease to date (Mackay et al., 2006). Central cancer registries collect cancer information from more than one facility (typically including hospitals, as well as other healthcare facilities such as radiation therapy clinics) and consolidate multiple reports from the various facilities on a single patient into one record (Hutchison et al., 2004). If a patient has multiple primary cancers, special attention is given so that this information is properly captured. Hospital and central registries are unified in a synergistic and complex effort to help reduce the burden of cancer through the common use of cancer patient data (Menck, Deapen, Phillips, & Tucker, 2007).

Two national cancer data surveillance systems from which a healthcare provider will find useful publications when seeking updated U.S. cancer statistics are the Surveillance, Epidemiology, and End Results (SEER) Program and the National Program of Cancer Registries (NPCR). Together, NPCR and SEER collect data for the entire U.S. population (CDC, 2011d).

The Surveillance, Epidemiology, and End Results Program is a federally funded program of the National Cancer Institute (NCI), comprising 20 population-based cancer registries in various parts of the United States (NCI, 2011d). The member registries have been included based on their ability to operate and maintain a high-quality reporting system and for their epidemiologically significant population subgroups (NCI, 2011d). SEER covers approximately 28% of the U.S. population. Established in 1973, it includes population-based information on stage of disease at diagnosis and patient survival data. It is the only comprehensive source of population-based information in the United States that includes stage of cancer at the time of diagnosis and patient survival data (NCI, 2011d).

The National Program of Cancer Registries is a federally funded CDC program that supports central registries and promotes the use of high-quality registry data in 45 states, the District of Columbia, Puerto Rico, and the U.S. Pacific Island jurisdictions (CDC, 2011d). Established in 1995, it covers 96% of the U.S. population (CDC, 2011d; Intlekofer & Michaud, 2007). The NPCR data collected by state cancer registries enable public health professionals to understand and address the cancer burden more effectively in their states; NPCR data are critical to planning state-specific cancer control activities that meet the needs of residents of the participating NPCR states.

Each year, CDC and NCI combine their high-quality cancer incidence data from NPCR and SEER, respectively, to produce an important set of official federal cancer statistics, in collaboration with the North American Association of Central Cancer Registries (NAACCR). The resulting collaborative effort, the annual *United States Cancer Statistics* (USCS) report, provides state-specific, regional, and national data for cancer cases diagnosed for a single year. The most currently available statistics can be found at http://www.cdc.gov/cancer/dcpc/data (CDC, 2011e).

When registries were first established about six decades ago, they focused primarily on describing cancer patterns and trends and sometimes calculating survival. In the last 20 years, however, their roles have been significantly expanded so that they now play an increasingly important role in planning and evaluation of cancer control activities and in improving the care of individual cancer patients (Hutchison et al., 2004; Mackay et al., 2006; Menck et al., 2007; Parkin, 2006). Cancer registries serve as the "eyes and ears" of cancer control around the world, and the statistics they produce are essential in planning and evaluating activities of comprehensive cancer control programs (Mackay et al., 2006). Some cancer registries continue to follow patients throughout their lifetimes to identify those who have recurring cancer or a second cancer, have received additional treatments, have had progression or remission of disease, and/or have died (Clive, 2004).

Cancer registries have increasingly important public health and research functions (Mackay et al., 2006). For example, NPCR cancer registry data were recently used in CDC's first multistate, patterns of care (PoC) cancer research study, designed to assess the completeness and quality of NPCR cancer registry data collected in seven participating states and to determine the extent to which guidelines-based, stage-specific treatments were provided to patients with specific cancer diagnoses residing in those states (Alley et al., 2007; Alley et al., 2008). Such studies provide information that can be used to continue to improve the quality of NPCR registry data and to identify groups of patients (e.g., by age, race, ethnicity) who may be receiving less than adequate care. This type of work can thereby help researchers and clinicians develop a better understanding of treatment disparities and ways to correct them. Obtaining high-quality data—which lies at the core of cancer registry surveillance work—is an important step toward motivating action to reducing the burden of cancer, whether through prevention, screening, treatment, and/or survivorship-related activities (Black et al., 2005). In other parts of the world, cancer registries are active and experienced in some countries, while still in nascent stages in others. The reader is referred to interesting references that trace the development of registries in other countries over the last 65 years (Mackay et al., 2006; Menck, 2004; Parkin, 2006). The International Association of Cancer Registries (IARC) has a global membership and sponsors a variety of publications, including an every-five-years publication in collaboration with IARC, entitled *Cancer Incidence in Five Continents*. This publication contains statistical data from all the best-quality registries worldwide (Mackay et al., 2006).

Cancer Costs

"The costs of cancer pose an economic burden on both the individual and society" (Mackay et al., 2006, p. 57), regardless of the country being considered. According Harvard University economist David E. Bloom, newly diagnosed cancer cases cost the global economy $300 billion in 2010; the increase in tobacco use, alcohol intake, obesity, and decreased physical activity in poorer countries, according to Bloom, also led to an increase in cancer and diabetes cases (Renick, 2011). Although data limitations do not allow for a worldwide comparison of the economic costs of cancer (Mackay et al., 2006), *The Cancer Atlas* (2006) has published data from selected countries and described the diverse and significant costs incurred for selected cancers. Three categories of cost domains especially relevant to cancer are often discussed in the literature: (1) direct costs, including both medical costs (e.g., hospitalizations and treatments) and associated nonmedical costs (e.g., transportation to hospital or physician's office); (2) indirect costs, such as time spent seeking medical care or economic productivity lost due to premature death; and (3) intangible/psychosocial costs, such as pain, suffering, or grief (Brown & Yabroff, 2006). Recent research has shown that cancer has the most devastating economic impact of any cause of death in the world (ACS & Livestrong, 2010). Pointedly, Mackay and colleagues (2006) note that cancer prevention may be the best way to save money for many countries, given that the costs associated with cancer continue to increase.

Not surprisingly, in the United States, the financial costs of cancer are both staggering and rising. All of the cancer-related costs will likely continue to increase because of the anticipated growth and aging of the U.S. population (USCSWG, 2006). Currently, lack of health insurance and other cost barriers prevent many people living in the United States from receiving optimal health care (ACS, 2012). As examples, consider that approximately almost 51 million Americans were uninsured in 2009 (according to U.S. Census Bureau figures), and that almost one-third of Hispanics and one in 10 children (ages 17 years and younger) had no health insurance coverage (ACS, 2012). Such cost barriers are significant, given that uninsured patients and those from ethnic minorities are substantially more likely to be diagnosed with cancer at a later stage, when treatment can be more extensive and more costly (ACS, 2012).

PREVENTION

Cancer, the world's second biggest killer after cardiovascular disease, is one of the most preventable, noncommunicable, chronic diseases (ACS, 2012; WHO, 2008). This section and the "Cancer Prevention" appendix at the end of this chapter focus on concepts and definitions related to the broad area of cancer prevention, including key actions such as reducing tobacco use and exposure to secondhand smoke; maintaining optimal nutrition, physical activity, and body weight; and minimizing exposure to infectious disease agents. These health-promoting actions can contribute to reducing the global cancer burden over the long term.

Prevention, sometimes described as primary prevention, refers to activities directed toward avoiding the occurrence of disease (ACS, 2011e; Menck & Bolick-Aldrich, 2007). Cancer prevention represents the most beneficial population-based public health approach to reducing morbidity and mortality from cancer. Its ultimate goal is to promote health and potentially eliminate disease risk. Cancer prevention strategies generally focus on known, modifiable risk factors such as exposure to infectious agents, specific lifestyle behaviors, and environmental carcinogens (ACS, 2011d). Some risk factors, such as age, gender, and genetic predisposition, cannot be altered (ACS, 2011d), although these factors can be considered in developing screening strategies. Public health measures that incorporate prevention strategies are meant to benefit people at the individual, community, and environmental levels. Globally, one of the most important mechanisms for implementing these public health prevention measures has been the development and enforcement of policies and/or systems changes. Examples of such policies and systems changes include laws (e.g., controlling tobacco and alcohol use), education and awareness activities (e.g., World Cancer Day), resolutions (e.g., WHO's *Cancer Prevention and Control Report*), and clinical care–oriented, preventive services guidelines (e.g., ACS, 2011a).

The "Cancer Prevention" appendix includes a detailed discussion focused on the three examples of key cancer prevention actions, mentioned previously, and the positive changes in lifestyle factors that have the potential to reduce a large proportion of the cancer burden. Although specific research methods and results of analyses related to cancer prevention and early detection activities vary, studies cited are consistent in pointing to the potential benefits of reducing tobacco use, improving nutrition, increasing physical activity, maintaining a healthy body weight, keeping alcohol consumption at low to moderate levels, and getting screened regularly for cancer (Curry et al., 2003).

EARLY DETECTION, SCREENING, AND EDUCATION

Early detection is one of the central components of cancer control and the complementary strategy to cancer prevention. The two core components of early detection of cancer are screening and education (Curry et al., 2003; Gullatte, Phillips, & Gibson, 2006; Mackay et al., 2006). The two primary strategies for early detection are (1) early diagnosis, which is often triggered by the patient's discovery of early signs and symptoms, leading to an appointment with a healthcare provider, and (2) screening of asymptomatic and apparently healthy individuals to detect precancerous lesions or an early stage of cancer, leading to referral for diagnosis and treatment (WHO, 2006a). It is important to note that screening and treatment services for most cancers may not be available in developing countries because of limited resources.

Given these limitations, countries that cannot afford to implement the infrastructure required to organize screening programs are encouraged to focus on increasing awareness of signs and symptoms of cancer in the general population, thereby leading to early diagnosis and treatment (Sloan & Gelband, 2007).

A high proportion of cancers that are relatively curable in developed countries (because such cancers are often screened for/diagnosed early, and treated successfully) are often not managed as successfully in developing countries due to resource limitations (WHO, 2006b). Variations in cancer burden in developed and developing countries may result in part from differences in access to effective screening and treatment programs. For example, in 2008, more than 85% ($n = 530,232$) of the new cases of cervical cancer diagnosed worldwide occurred in developing countries that lacked organized screening programs (ACS, 2011e; Ferlay, Shin, Bray, Forman, Mathers, & Parkin, 2010). In the same year, cervical cancer was the fourth leading cause of cancer-related deaths in women worldwide, with 90% of these deaths occurring in developing countries. In more developed nations, cervical cancer estimates have generally declined over the past few decades (ACS, 2011e), likely due to the availability of broadly available screening programs. The prognosis for cervical cancer is generally better and treatment usually more successful if the disease is detected and treated early (WHO, 2006b). Declining death rates worldwide for many cancers in developed nations prove that cancer can be controlled with aggressive intervention.

The "Early Detection, Screening, and Education" appendix at the end of this chapter outlines the general principles governing the introduction of early detection programs and provides a definition of and key concepts related to cancer screening. Specific information regarding screening for breast cancer, cervical cancer, colon and rectal cancers, and prostate cancer is also presented. Also included in this appendix is a discussion of the importance of public and healthcare professional education programs related to cancer screening and early detection efforts.

CANCER CARE CONSIDERATIONS

Cancer Treatment

Employing effective treatment is the single most important strategy to ensure optimal life following a cancer diagnosis, and advances in treatments have enhanced survival for many patients (Mackay et al., 2006). Statistics that show a continuing improvement in 5-year relative survival rate for all cancers (i.e., cancers diagnosed between 2001 and 2007 as compared with cancers diagnosed between 1975 and 1977) reflect the progress being made in diagnosing certain cancers at an earlier stage and the improvements in treatment (ACS, 2012). "Survival statistics vary greatly by cancer type and stage at diagnosis" (ACS, 2012, p. 2). According to NCI (2006), although approximately one-third of all cancers are avoidable through lifestyle changes and early detection, and despite available information that could permit the early diagnosis and effective treatment of an additional one-third of cancer cases, millions of cancer cases worldwide still cannot currently be prevented or cured. Thus new and effective treatments must continue to be urgently be sought (NCI, 2006).

According to WHO (2008), the primary goals of cancer treatment throughout the world, depending on extent of disease and other key variables, are threefold: (1) cure, (2) prolongation of useful life, and (3) improvement of quality of life. WHO (2008) has acknowledged that although the basic principles of cancer treatment are the same throughout the world, the specific treatment approaches adopted in each country should take into account cost-effectiveness, affordability, and social and ethical aspects of care. Services should, however, always be provided in an equitable and sustainable manner. WHO (2002, 2008) has long held that the primary aim for treatment is multidisciplinary management, which is more effective than sequential independent management of patients; such a treatment plan should be linked to an early detection program so that cases are detected at an early stage, when treatment is more effective and there is a greater chance of cure. Careful cancer diagnosis and cancer staging are key steps in providing adequate cancer management, wherever a person receives cancer care in the world; these steps aid in selecting the most appropriate therapies, determining prognosis, and standardizing the design of research treatment protocols (ACS, 2011e).

The main methods of treatment for cancer are surgery, radiotherapy, and chemotherapy, with each of the three effecting cures in certain cancers (ACS, 2011e, 2012). Biologic therapy, targeted therapy, and hormone treatment (sometimes classified as chemotherapy) are other important treatments (ACS, 2012; NCI, 2011b). The three principal modes of therapy may be given alone or in combination for best success, depending upon key patient-related considerations (ACS, 2011e; Stewart & Kleihues, 2003). For detailed information on various therapies and rehabilitation considerations, refer to recently published documents on state-of-the-art treatments, immediate side effects, possible long-term and late-appearing side effects, and treatments that are best suited for particular cancers (e.g., ACS, 2012; NCCN, 2011a; NCI, 2011a).

Two frequently updated sources for cancer treatment information are the National Comprehensive Cancer Network (NCCN) Clinical Practice Guidelines in Oncology and the NCI PDQ (Physician Data Query) Comprehensive Cancer Database. Both are known for maintaining highly interactive websites with frequently updated content on an impressive number of topics. The NCCN Clinical Practice Guidelines are a recognized standard for clinical policy in the oncology community, providing easy access to continually updated guidelines based upon evaluation of scientific data integrated with expert judgment (NCCN, 2011b). Included in the NCCN Clinical Practice Guidelines are clinical trials information, available in versions tailored for patients, clinicians, and industry. Interested readers can also access the NCCN Drugs & Biologics Compendium and information about a physician-oriented Cancer Resource Line (for selected cancers) (NCCN, 2011b). The adult treatment and pediatric treatment summaries available on the NCI PDQ cancer information website contain evidence-based summaries of prognostic and treatment information for the major types of cancer in both adults and children, as well as for unusual childhood cancers in the pediatric summaries; summaries are available in professional and patient versions as well as in Spanish (NCI, 2011e). The NCI PDQ houses a comprehensive list of cancer clinical trials, containing more than 8000 abstracts of clinical trial protocols that are accepting patients (NCI, 2011e). A wide-ranging array of other cancer-related topics are covered as well, including subjects such as genetics, complementary and alternative medicine, and supportive care.

Innovative approaches that use the main treatment methods in novel ways are continually under development; thus studying up-to-date literature is invaluable in learning about state-of-the-science approaches to treating cancer. A reported 30% of cancer patients worldwide use complementary and alternative medicine (Mackay et al., 2006). PDQ summaries on complementary and alternative medicine are available; these summaries contain background information about the treatments, a brief history of their development, information about their proposed mechanism(s) of action, and information about relevant laboratory, animal, and clinical studies (NCI, 2011e). In addition to summaries written for healthcare professionals, summaries available for patients use language appropriate for laypeople and include glossary links to scientific terms (NCI, 2011e). Also instructive are reviews of medical and psychological concerns of cancer survivors following cancer treatment and barriers to care (Stewart & Kleihues, 2003). Information on coping with cancer concerns and resources focused on living with and after cancer are also available (NCCN, 2011a; NCI, 2011c, 2011f). A resource featuring tools to help both clinicians and cancer patients prevent infections has recently been made available online by CDC (2011a).

Particularly in developed parts of the world (e.g., in northern and western Europe and the United States), advances in treatment modalities (such as improved forms of chemotherapy) have increased survival for many patients (Mackay et al., 2006). In many developing countries, however, patients' ability to receive prompt treatment care is hampered by poor availability of treatments and delays in seeking cancer care, both of which contribute to lower survival rates (WHO, 2008). WHO (2008) described this challenge, observing:

> [I]n many countries, particularly low-income countries, diagnostic and treatment services are not planned rationally. Treatment technologies and infrastructure are not linked to early detection strategies, and there is usually an excessive reliance on costly procedures that serve mainly the wealthy who can afford them. Consequently, a high proportion of patients having cancers that are curable if detected early are diagnosed in advanced stages, at which point a small number receive costly, but ineffective and incomplete treatment. In such settings, the same resources would be better employed, and would benefit a greater number of patients, if they were to be used to fund low-cost palliative care. The development of good quality diagnostic and treatment services to address curable cancers is therefore imperative, especially in the great majority of low-income countries. This would help to save lives, avoid unnecessary suffering and make more efficient use of limited resources. (p. 6)

Even in developed nations, problems in accessing treatment care can vary according to the patient's geographic location, socioeconomic status, and age (Mackay et al., 2006). ACS (2011e) recently observed that there is increasing emphasis worldwide on the development of specialized cancer centers that apply evidence-based multimodal therapies and provide rehabilitation and palliative care. WHO (2008) has emphasized the importance of guarding against neglecting early detection and palliative care in favor of treatment-oriented approaches, regardless of whether these treatment approaches are cost-effective or whether they improve patients' quality of life. WHO (2008) further suggested that treatment guidelines should emphasize the importance of avoiding the offering of curative therapy when a cancer is incurable; in such situations, patients with incurable cancers should be offered palliative care instead.

Survivorship, Palliative Care, and End-of-Life Care

More people are surviving cancer and living longer because of advances in early detection, treatment, and supportive care options (Hewitt, Greenfield, & Stovall, 2006; Wingo et al., 2005). Cancer is often experienced as a chronic illness (ACS, 2011e; Foley & Gelband, 2001), and the patient may require specialized care for months and often years. Such specialized care may involve a range of professional services that extends beyond the discipline of oncology (Stewart & Kleihues, 2003). Some experts have noted that improvements in the development and delivery of symptom control throughout all stages of cancer and in other aspects of palliative care needed in the late stages of cancer have not kept pace with the medical advances that have allowed people to live longer (Foley & Gelband, 2001; WHO, 2004). At the same time, the growing body of literature addressing survivorship, palliative care, and end-of-life care attests to the fact that these topics are viewed by many as subjects equal in importance to more cure-oriented topics.

Allied healthcare professionals, such as nurses, physician assistants, physical and occupational therapists, and dieticians, can benefit from developing a working knowledge of survivorship, palliative care, and end-of-life care issues, all of which are pertinent to understanding the patients' and families' experience of cancer. Knowledge in these three areas can inform healthcare providers' clinical practice, helping to improve their ability to deliver high-quality care to patients. Because allied healthcare professionals working in both inpatient and outpatient settings routinely spend many hours each day in service to cancer patients, these skilled healthcare providers often have invaluable and in-depth knowledge of the everyday problems and needs of cancer patients and their families. Armed with up-to-date knowledge about the issues that patients and families face, healthcare professionals can add meaningful information to the patients' care plans and improve care for patients.

A brief overview of three broad topics—survivorship, palliative care, and end-of-life care—is presented here, along with definitions of selected terms and short descriptions of some key issues. National and international reports, position papers, and guidelines, cited throughout the chapter, can provide detailed discussions of the topics for the reader needing more information.

Survivorship

The risk of developing cancer in one's lifetime is more than one in three; as a result, each of us is likely to experience cancer or know someone who has survived cancer (Hewitt et al., 2006). In the United States, men have slightly less than a one in two lifetime risk of developing cancer; for women, the corresponding risk is a little more than one in three (ACS, 2012). Nearly 12 million people in the United States (based on statistics from January 2008) are living with a history of cancer (ACS, 2012; Reuben, 2006), with this number representing a tripling of the number of survivors since 1971 (Hewitt et al., 2006). Cancer survivors constitute 3.5% of the U.S. population (Travis, Rabkin, & Brown, 2006), and 68% of cancer survivors (diagnosed between 1999 and 2006) are expected to live at least 5 years after diagnosis (ACS, 2011b). From an international perspective, more than 25 million people throughout the world are cancer survivors, and their number grows daily (NCI, 2006). Although most people eventually die from their cancer, treatment advances are allowing many patients with cancer to live much longer than ever before, with periods of adaptation to cancer as a chronic disease (Foley & Gelband, 2001; WHO, 2004).

Among healthcare providers, patients, families, and the general public, the topic of cancer survivorship is of great interest (Ferrell & Coyle, 2010; Kolata, 2004; NCI, 2011a; Riddle & Boeshaar, 2006). However, the terms "cancer survivor" and cancer "survivorship" have different meanings to different people (Reuben, 2006), and the means by which to refer to this growing population has stirred some controversy (Hewitt et al., 2006). Also, some different views continue regarding who is considered to be a survivor. For the purpose of this discussion, the survivor definition supported by CDC, NCI, and the National Coalition for Cancer Survivorship is used: An individual is considered a cancer survivor from the time of diagnosis through the balance of his or her life; family members, friends, and caregivers are also affected by the survivorship experience and, therefore, are included in this definition (CDC, 2011b; NCI, 2011d). Survivorship care has been described as a distinct phase of care for cancer survivors that includes four components: (1) prevention and detection of recurrent and new cancers and of late effects; (2) surveillance for cancer spread or recurrence, or second cancers; (3) intervention for consequences of cancer and its treatment; and (4) coordination between specialists and primary care providers to ensure that all of the survivor's health needs are met (Hewitt et al,, 2006). The fourth component, involving development of a detailed plan of coordinated care created by a multidisciplinary team, can help ensure that the survivorship plan is as high quality as the earlier plan that guided the diagnosis and treatment phases of care.

Physical, psychosocial, employment-related, educational, financial, and legal issues may affect cancer survivors across the life span (Reuben, 2004). The diagnosis and treatment of cancer pose a threat to a person's physical, psychological, social, spiritual, and economic well-being (CDC, 2011b). Using a public health approach, entitled "A National Action Plan for Cancer Survivorship," a joint effort led by Livestrong (formerly the Lance Armstrong Foundation) and the CDC distinguished between living with cancer (referring to the experience of receiving a cancer diagnosis and treatment that may follow), living through cancer (referring to the extended stage following treatment), and living beyond cancer (referring to post-treatment and long-term survivorship (CDC, 2011b). Although these distinctions are meant to signify the experience of survivorship as a progression, the process is unique for each patient, and movement from one phase to the next may not be clearly delineated (CDC, 2011b), adding to the complexity of providing comprehensive care for cancer survivors.

Securing effective, long-term care is an important strategy for ensuring optimal living following a cancer diagnosis. There is growing agreement among healthcare providers and cancer patients and their families that the transition from active treatment to the post-treatment period is critical to the cancer patient's long-term health (Hewitt et al., 2006). In addition, cancer survivors need lifelong care to (1) monitor for and treat late effects of cancer therapies, recurrences, and second cancers, and (2) address psychosocial, nutritional, rehabilitation, and other needs that may arise years after treatment ends (Reuben, 2006). Although the medical and psychological effects of cancer and its treatment have been recognized for many years, survivorship has only recently come to be recognized as a distinct phase of the cancer trajectory (Hewitt et al., 2006). Despite the heartening fact that nearly 12 million cancer survivors currently live in the United States (CDC, 2011b), being a survivor comes at a cost: Nearly 75% of people who survive cancer live long enough to develop significant sequelae, in the form of late-appearing or long-term side effects (Haylock, Mitchell, Cox, Temple, & Curtiss, 2007).

Various follow-up care guidelines (e.g., covering screening, evaluation, psychosocial services) to assist healthcare providers in delivering care to survivors have been proposed as a result of advances in knowledge of how to manage conditions that arise in this patient group. In addition, as people with cancer live longer as a result of improved access to effective screening, diagnosis, and treatments (making cancer a chronic condition in many cases), another issue that has begun to generate an increased amount of attention is how to produce and use comprehensive guidelines that adequately address the possible long-term and late effects of a particular cancer diagnosis and treatment (Hewitt et al., 2006). Although no specific care guidelines are widely accepted and followed in many clinical settings, the President's Cancer Panel (Reuben, 2006) urges the acceleration of efforts to develop and disseminate survivorship follow-up clinical guidelines that are based on the best available evidence (including best practices and expert opinions) until the evidence base is further developed through targeted outcomes and related research. Improving access to care and insurance coverage for healthcare services needed by survivors is another important survivor issue drawing increased attention (Reuben, 2004).

Readers wanting detailed information about the process for creating guidelines for survivorship care are referred to the in-depth discussion by Haylock and colleagues (2007) regarding their work in progress called "Prescription for Living"; an included template provides clinicians with a concise guide to treatment and follow-up care planning while also offering survivors a guide for planning healthful lifestyles. NCI (2011c) provides detailed, online information regarding follow-up care after cancer therapy, including links to guidelines and care plans created by national organizations. An important theme repeated throughout the current survivorship literature is that the care of survivors encompasses the entire cancer control continuum, from prevention, detection, diagnosis, and treatment, through what some refer to as a survivorship phase, with end-of-life care completing the continuum (Pollack et al., 2005).

Palliative Care

In the last 50 years, there have been amazing advances in the treatment and early detection of a few types of cancer and at least modest gains in many other cancer diagnoses. However, some have observed that in our society's aggressive pursuit of cures for cancer, symptom control and comfort care have been neglected. Recent literature suggests that acute care settings generally focus primarily on curative treatments and are less well equipped to provide palliative care (Hewitt et al., 2006; Wingo et al., 2005). At the same time, the growing recognition of the importance of symptom control and other aspects of palliative care, from diagnosis through the dying process, has been documented (Foley & Gelband, 2001; Hewitt et al., 2006; Patrizi, Thompson, & Spector, 2011). The notion that "patients should not have to choose between treatment with curative intent or comfort care" is still very relevant, more than a decade after palliative care leaders offered that thought (Foley & Gelband, 2001, p. 9). Further, "[t]here is a need for both [treatment with curative intent and comfort care], in varying degrees, throughout the course of cancer, whether the eventual outcome is long-term survival or death" (Foley & Gelband, 2001, p. 9). WHO (2004) has engaged in an in-depth discussion of why palliative care for older people is a public health priority.

Multiple definitions of palliative care highlight the complexity inherent in this term. *A National Action Plan for Cancer Survivorship: Advancing Public Health Strategies,* jointly produced by CDC, Livestrong, and other partners, defined palliative care, in accordance with the NCI, as follows: "Care given to improve the quality of life of patients who have a serious or life-threatening disease. Also called comfort care, supportive care, and symptom management" (CDC, 2004, p. 65; 2010). Palliative care is also defined as "treatment of symptoms associated with the effects of cancer and its treatment" (Hewitt et al., 2006, p. 481). WHO (2011a) has defined palliative care in cancer as "an approach that improves the quality of life of patients and their families facing the problem associated with life-threatening illness, through the prevention and relief of suffering by means of early identification and impeccable assessment and treatment of pain and other problems, physical, psychosocial and spiritual." Palliative care may begin at the time of a cancer diagnosis and increase in amount and intensity, as needed, throughout the course of a patient's illness until death (Foley & Gelband, 2001). Comprehensive care should proceed concurrently with anticancer treatment, whether with curative or palliative intent (Stewart & Kleihues, 2003). Treating symptoms is of the utmost importance, as symptoms can influence not only quality of life but also the course of disease (WHO, 2002).

From a global perspective, WHO (2011b) has observed that palliative care measures can relieve physical psychosocial, and spiritual problems in almost all (i.e., more than 90%) patients with advanced cancer. WHO also asserts that global improvements in palliative care do not depend so much upon the creation of specialized palliative care services separate from mainstream health care but rather "upon the permeation of the whole health care system by the principles of palliative care" (Stewart & Kleihues, 2003, p. 299). In addition, because palliative care can be provided relatively simply and inexpensively, such services should be made available in every country (Stewart & Kleihues, 2003).

In its recommendations to member governments, WHO has stated that any national cancer control program should address the needs of its citizens for palliative care. Within such a program, six major skill sets are part of complete palliative care: (1) communication, (2) decision making, (3) management of complications of treatment and the disease, (4) symptom control, (5) psychosocial care of patient and family, and (6) care of the dying (Foley & Gelband, 2001). Some of these skills—such as communication, decision making, and psychosocial care of patient and family—are important throughout the trajectory of illness, whereas other skills emerge and recede in importance at different times. Physical symptoms of cancer can be both acute and chronic, can occur at various times throughout the disease trajectory, and may include pain, fatigue, nausea, hair loss, and others, depending on the cancer site and the types of treatments being used (CDC, 2004). WHO has outlined three specific issues that should be addressed in the context of palliative care for any patient: (1) relief of major symptoms in all stages of disease, especially cancer-related pain relief; (2) comprehensive care of patients who are close to death; and (3) support for the family during the course of the illness and after the patient's death (cited in Stewart & Kleihues, 2003).

The "pain of surviving cancer"—pain that may be caused by a variety of reasons—is one of the most challenging aspects of achieving quality palliative care for the patient coping with cancer (Kaplan, 2011). Considerable evidence in the healthcare literature indicates that inadequate treatment of pain continues to be a frequent problem, both in countries with few resources and as in technologically advanced countries with adequate resources (ACS, 2011c, 2011e; American Pain Society [APS], 2008; Hill, 1990; Max, 1990; Stewart & Kleihues, 2003; WHO, 2002). WHO (2002) has long asserted that freedom from cancer pain must be regarded as a human rights issue, and unrelieved pain in cancer patients is unacceptable because it is generally avoidable with proper treatment. Paice and Ferrell (2011) summarized current, published U.S. statistics on cancer-related pain, indicating that the prevalence of cancer pain is estimated at 25% for patients newly diagnosed, 33% for patients undergoing active treatment, and greater than 75%

for cancer patients with advanced disease. The needed analgesics to relieve most cancer-related pain have been available for decades, and 85% of cancer patients could obtain satisfactory relief using only simple, inexpensive, "low-technology" oral analgesics (Andima, Gulati, & Cubert, 2009; Grossman & Nesbit, 2004; Sloan & Gelband, 2007), with the remaining 15% of patients achieving satisfactory relief using more sophisticated pain control measures (Andima et al., 2009; Cleeland, 1990; Grossman & Nesbit, 2004).

New healthcare professionals who expect to have contact with patients dealing with cancer pain can better appreciate the numerous clinical challenges and issues that are faced by patients and care providers by reviewing current cancer pain publications (e.g., APS, 2008; NCCN, 2011b; Paice & Ferrell, 2011; Sloan & Gelband, 2007). Covered therein are topics such as principles of cancer pain management, techniques related to pain assessment and simple tools to use in communicating with patients regarding pain levels, barriers to cancer pain relief, pharmacologic and nonpharmacologic treatments used for cancer pain, and considerations for special populations. It has been suggested that the implementation of a well-developed, organizational policy approach to managing patients' pain could be instrumental in changing clinical practice patterns and building institutional commitment to improving pain management (Alley, 2001; Gordon, Dahl, & Stevenson, 2000; Pasero, Gordon, McCaffery, & Ferrell, 1999). Consistent with this deliberate organizational commitment, optimal management of pain requires adequate infrastructure (e.g., sufficient personnel, facilities, drugs) and effective methodology (e.g., modes of drug delivery; dose adjustment by the patient) (Stewart & Kleihues, 2003). Neither a formal, effective organizational commitment to pain relief nor the necessary infrastructure is routinely in place in many healthcare settings.

From a global perspective, quality-of-life outcomes such as adequate pain relief and freedom from nausea are universally accepted as valuable (NCI, 2006), although these outcomes are often not fully achieved. Conceptually, quality of life encompasses not only the physical aspects of well-being but also the cognitive, spiritual, emotional, and social aspects of life; further, it is important to note that a "good" quality of life as viewed by a cancer patient in central Africa may be very different from that defined by a cancer patient in the suburbs of an American city (NCI, 2006). For the interested reader, the topic of pain as a public health challenge is discussed in *Relieving Pain in America: A Blueprint for Transforming Prevention, Care, Education, and Research* (Committee on Advancing Pain Research, Care, and Education, IOM, 2011).

End-of-Life Care

A key aspect of palliative care for dying patients is end-of-life care. At the end of life, only a few people (i.e., less than 10%) die suddenly and unexpectedly (Emanuel, Ferris, von Gunten, & Von Roenn, 2010). Most people die after a long period of illness, with gradual deterioration until an active dying phase at the end (Coyle, 2010; Field & Cassel, 1997). Thus providing end-of-life care is an important responsibility for health professionals caring for patients at this stage of life; for such providers, there is an established and growing body of knowledge to guide this care (Ellershaw & Ward, 2003; Ferris, von Gunten, & Emanuel, 2003; Twycross & Lichter, 1998).

End-of-life care is defined as "care provided during the period of time in which an individual copes with declining health from an ultimately terminal illness" (Hewitt et al., 2006, p. 478). The goal of end-of-life care is to achieve the best possible quality of life for cancer patients by controlling pain and other symptoms and addressing psychological and spiritual needs (CDC, 2011b). The previously mentioned, public health–focused National Action Plan for Cancer Survivorship stated that "end-of-life care affirms life and regards dying as a normal process, neither hastening nor postponing death while providing relief from distress and integrating psychological and spiritual aspects of survivor care" (CDC, 2004, p. 4; 2010).

End-of-life care as a healthcare issue continues to grow in prominence, with both patients and healthcare professionals advocating for improvements (American Medical Association [AMA], 1996; Holland & Chertkov, 2001; Patrizi et al., 2004; WHO, 2004). From a public health perspective, end of life has three characteristics (also present in other public health priorities): high burden, major impact, and a potential for preventing suffering associated with illness (Rao, Anderson, & Smith, 2002). Unfortunately, most clinicians have received little or no formal training in managing the dying process or death, and families usually have even less experience and knowledge in these areas (Emanuel et al., 2010). Although principles of end-of-life care are well discussed in the literature, it appears that established standards of care are not universally followed, especially in institutional settings, where an estimated 85% of Americans die (Rummans, Bostwick, and Clark, 2000). In a study by Coyle (2010), 70% of Americans said they would prefer to die at home, but only 25% die at home and half die in hospitals. In many European countries, despite the preference of many people to be cared for and die at home, death in the hospital remains common (WHO, 2004). Writing from a highly positive perspective, Patrizi, Thompson, and Spector (2011) provided updates on work being done in the United States to establish and promote national palliative care standards and quality measures. In institutions whose cultures are not focused on end-of-life care, however, challenges remain relative to ensuring good end-of-life care and a comfortable death (Ferris, Hallward, Ronan, & Billings, 1998; WHO, 2004).

People with cancer suffer from a variety of symptoms at all stages of disease and cancer treatment, though symptoms are often more frequent and severe in advanced stages (Foley & Gelband, 2001; WHO, 2004). A WHO paper (2004) addressing palliative care for aging populations reported that a growing body of evidence indicates that older people, in particular, suffer unnecessarily because of widespread under-assessment and undertreatment of problems at the end of life. There is support for the idea that much suffering could be alleviated if available symptom control measures were used more widely (ACS, 2011e; Foley & Gelband, 2001; WHO, 2004). Some authors writing in the public health realm have observed that it is unclear as to whether the trend toward aggressive care in acute care hospitals is occurring in response to patient care preferences or to the culture of acute care hospitals (Wingo et al., 2005). In either case, allied health professionals can benefit from being aware of barriers in the healthcare and medical research systems that can stand in the way of the delivery of effective palliative care and end-of-life care. These barriers, along with conclusions and recommendations to address them, have been outlined by palliative care experts (Ferrell & Coyle, 2010; Foley & Gelband, 2001). The American College of Surgeons, Commission on Cancer's (CoC) "Cancer Program Standards (CPS) 2011 Project" resulted in publication of standards in 2012; their goal is to ensure that key elements of quality cancer care are provided to all people with cancer treated in a CoC-accredited facility. The CoC standards address patient care needs throughout the diagnosis and treatment process, including psychosocial support, care for cancer-related pain, palliative care, and hospice care (Commission on Cancer, 2011).

Interface Between Palliative Care and Hospice Care

In the United States, some healthcare experts have described the institutionalization of a healthcare system that focuses on either active therapy or palliative or hospice care and does not allow for the appropriate interface between these two approaches (Foley & Gelband, 2001; Holland & Chertkov, 2001; Lynn & O'Mara, 2001; Payne, 2001). Coyle (2010) has stated that hospice may best be described as "a program through which palliative care is intensified as an individual moves closer to death" (p. 5). Hospice care is widely considered to be the most substantial innovation to serve the dying, although many end-of-life patients do not receive hospice care, even in technologically advanced countries (Center for Bioethics, 2005; Coyle, 2010; Foley & Gelband, 2001).

The term *hospice* has at least three somewhat different uses that can be confusing and misleading (Field & Cassel, 1997). First, a hospice may be a discrete site of care in the form of an inpatient hospital or nursing home unit or a freestanding facility. Second, a hospice may be an organization or program that provides, arranges, and advises on a wide range of medical and supportive services for dying patients and their families and friends, with care based in the patient's home. The third and most culturally sweeping meaning of hospice refers to an approach to caring for dying patients that is based on clinical, social, and spiritual principles (Field & Cassel, 1997). To gain a better understanding of issues related to evaluating the adequacy of end-of-life care, the reader is directed to the detailed IOM report entitled *Approaching Death* (Field & Cassel, 1997), which offers a blueprint for change at the global level in end-of-life care practices (Stewart & Kleihues, 2003).

Compilations of Cancer Information with Additional Features

High-quality cancer-related reports, guidelines, books, journal articles, and online resources have been cited throughout this chapter. Some resources provide, in addition to the typical narrative format, additional helpful features. Two examples are *The Cancer Atlas* (Mackay et al., 2006) and *The Tobacco Atlas* (Shafey et al., 2009). *The Cancer Atlas* (2006), which is jointly produced by ACS, CDC, and Union for International Cancer Control (UICC), uses graphic and colorful atlas map formats for making visual points relative to each two-page topic. The atlas also provides a detailed timeline on the history of cancer starting 70–80 million years ago up to the present; tables of risk factors for cancers in various countries; extensive statistics on cancer, indexed by country; information on sources used in the figures, tables, and graphs; and a listing of useful contacts at WHO headquarters and regional offices, WHO cancer programs, and key cancer organizations, indexed by specific countries (Mackay et al., 2006). The latest (third) edition of the groundbreaking report entitled *The Tobacco Atlas,* which is produced in a collaborative effort by the ACS, the International Tobacco Control Research Program, Georgia State University, and the World Lung Foundation, gives shape and meaning to statistics about tobacco use and control, using a novel, user-friendly format. The atlas uses full-color maps and graphics to illustrate a wide range of tobacco issues, revealing similarities and differences between countries and exposing behavior of tobacco companies (Shafey et al., 2009). The small volume addresses in a detailed manner topics such as types of tobacco use; prevalence of tobacco use among various populations (including health professionals!) and smoking health risks; the costs of tobacco; and an overview of the tobacco trade and the promotion of tobacco. The atlas also details numerous activities under way to curtail, ban, or otherwise limit tobacco usage and availability. The fourth edition of *The Tobacco Atlas* was released in March 2012 at the 15th World Conference on Tobacco or Health in Singapore (ACS, 2012).

CONCLUSIONS

"Cancer is a major public health problem in the United States and many other parts of the world" (Siegel, Naishadham, & Jemal, 2012, p. 10). In this chapter, the reader has been introduced to a public health perspective on key cancer and cancer patient care issues, both within the United States and in other countries in the world. The goal of this chapter has been to provide allied healthcare professionals with an introductory overview of selected cancer-related topics. Also discussed in this chapter were common challenges experienced as well as varied challenges faced by developed and developing countries of the world as they work to decrease cancer-related morbidity and mortality. Although predicted increases in the number of new cases of cancer are mostly due to a steadily increasing proportion of elderly people in the world, the rate of increase will be even greater if current levels of smoking and the high prevalence of unhealthy lifestyles persist (Mackay et al., 2006).

The content discussed in this chapter includes background information that can be helpful to healthcare providers and public health professionals who provide patient services and/or conduct research with an eye toward improving some aspect of cancer care. Regardless of future advances in high-technology medicine, any major reduction in deaths and disability from cancer will come from efforts directed toward cancer prevention, not from cancer cures (Mackay et al., 2006). One of the primary goals of this chapter has been to raise awareness of the importance of cancer prevention activities and to promote cancer prevention efforts among new healthcare providers, with a major focus placed on patient and professional education. If successful, such cancer prevention efforts could result in 2 million lives per year being saved by 2020, and 6.5 million lives per year by 2040 (Mackay et al., 2006). Cancer care considerations briefly outlined in the chapter—specifically, cancer treatment and palliative, end-of-life, and survivorship care—are all important in considering how best to provide high-quality patient care.

ACKNOWLEDGMENTS

Appreciation is expressed to Temeika Fairley, PhD, Division of Cancer Prevention and Control, CDC, for her contributions to the "Prevention" and "Early Detection, Screening, and Education" sections of this chapter.

The findings and conclusions in this report are those of the authors and do not necessarily represent the views of the Centers for Disease Control and Prevention.

STUDY QUESTIONS

1. What are some reasons for the disparity of cancer incidence, treatments, and survivorship among vulnerable populations worldwide?
2. Compare and contrast global methods of pain control and palliative care.
3. Discuss examples of economic and political restrictions for cancer care worldwide.
4. Using a social justice lens or framework, how do you think cancer treatments could be more equalized worldwide?

CASE STUDY

A population-based case-control interview study of 309 childhood leukemia cases and 618 healthy population control children was conducted in urban Shanghai, China. Excess risks for both acute lymphocytic leukemia (ALL) and acute non-lymphocytic leukemia (ANLL) were associated with intrauterine and paternal preconception diagnostic X-ray exposure, and with maternal employment in the chemical and agricultural industries during pregnancy. ANLL was linked to maternal occupational exposure to benzene during pregnancy, whereas both ALL and ANLL were significantly associated with maternal exposure to gasoline and the patient's prior use of chloramphenicol. Excess risks included ANLL among children whose mothers were employed in metal refining and processing and ALL associated with maternal occupational exposure to pesticides.

Reference
Ou Shu, X., Gao, Y., Tu, J., Zheng, Y., Brinton, L., Linet, M., & Fraumeni, J. (2006).

Case Study Questions
1. What do you think could be done to decrease the rate of ALL to Chinese children in Shanghai? What policies would be needed?
2. Do you think that the Chinese government would want to make policy changes? What would be reasons for changes and what would be reasons not to make changes?

REFERENCES

Alley, L. G. (2001). The influence of an organizational pain management policy on nurses' pain management practices. *Oncology Nursing Forum, 28*, 867–874.

Alley, L. G., Chen, V. W., Wike, J. M., Schymura, M. J., Rycroft, R. K., Shen, T., . . . Fulton, J. P. (2007). CDC-NPCR's breast, colon, and prostate cancer data quality and patterns of care study: Overview and methodology. *Journal of Registry Management, 34*(4), 148–157.

Alley, L. G., Wike, J. M., Chen, V. W., Kahn, A. R., Roshala, W., Fulton, J., . . . Snodgrass, J. (2008). Challenges and lessons learned in examining patterns of cancer care in National Program of Cancer Registries (NPCR) states. *Journal of Registry Management, 35*(1), 27–33.

American Cancer Society (ACS). (2006). *The worldwide cancer burden report.* Atlanta, GA: Author.

American Cancer Society (ACS). (2009). *Cancer facts & figures for African Americans 2011–2012.* Atlanta, GA: Author.

American Cancer Society (ACS). (2011a). ACS guidelines on nutrition and physical activity for cancer prevention. Retrieved from http://www.cancer.org/Healthy/EatHealthyGetActive/ACSGuidelineson NutritionPhysicalActivityforCancerPrevention/index

American Cancer Society (ACS). (2011b). *Cancer facts & figures 2011.* Atlanta, GA: Author.

American Cancer Society (ACS). (2011c). *Cancer facts & figures for Hispanics/Latinos 2009–2011.* Atlanta, GA: Author.

American Cancer Society (ACS). (2011d). *Cancer prevention & early detection facts & figures 2011.* Atlanta, GA: Author.

American Cancer Society (ACS). (2011e). *Global cancer facts & figures* (2nd ed.). Atlanta, GA: Author.

American Cancer Society (ACS). (2012). *Cancer facts & figures 2012.* Atlanta, GA: Author.

American Cancer Society (ACS) & Livestrong. (2010). *The global economic cost of cancer.* Atlanta: ACS.

American Medical Association (AMA). (1996). Good care of the dying. *Journal of the American Medical Association, 275*, 474–478.

American Pain Society (APS). (2008). *Principles of analgesic use in the treatment of acute pain and cancer pain* (6th ed.). Glenview, IL: Author.

Andima, L., Gulati, A., & Cubert, K. (2009). Interventional pain management in the patient with cancer (pp. 437–516). In M. D. Stubblefield & M. O'Dell (Eds.), *Cancer rehabilitation: Principles and practice.* New York, NY: Demos Medical.

Beasley, D. (2011). American men with cancer more likely to die than women. Reuters. Retrieved from http://www.reuters.com/article/2011/07/12/us-cancer-genderidUSTRE76B4W220110712

Black, B. L., Cowens-Alvarado, R., Gershman, S., & Weir, H. K. (2005). Using data to motivate action: The need for high quality, an effective presentation, and an action context for decision-making. *Cancer Causes and Control, 16*(suppl 1), 15–25.

Brawley, O. (2011). Avoidable cancer deaths globally. *CA: A Cancer Journal for Clinicians, 61*(2), 67–68.

Brown, M. L., & Yabroff, K. R. (2006). Economic impact of cancer in the United States. In D. Schottenfeld & J. F. Fraumeni (Eds.), *Cancer epidemiology and prevention* (3rd ed., pp. 202–216). Oxford, UK: Oxford University Press.

Center for Bioethics. (2005). End of life care: An ethical overview. University of Minnesota's Center for Bioethics. Retrieved from www.ahc.umn.edu/img/assets/26104/End_of_Life.pdf

Centers for Disease Control and Prevention (CDC). (2004). *A national action plan for cancer survivorship: Advancing public health strategies.* Atlanta, GA: CDC & Lance Armstrong Foundation.

Centers for Disease Control and Prevention (CDC). (2005). *Behavioral risk factor surveillance system operational and user's guide.* Version 3.0. Atlanta, GA: Author.

Centers for Disease Control and Prevention (CDC). (2010). The national action plan for cancer survivorship. Retrieved from http://www.cdc.gov/cancer/survivorship

Centers for Disease Control and Prevention (CDC). (2011a). About the Preventing Infections in Cancer Patients program. Retrieved from http://www.cdc.gov/cancer/preventinfections/about.htm?source= govdelivery

Centers for Disease Control and Prevention (CDC). (2011b). Cancer survivorship. Retrieved from http://cdc .gov/cancer/survivorship

Centers for Disease Control and Prevention (CDC). (2011c). National Comprehensive Cancer Control Program (NCCCP). Retrieved from http://www.cdc.gov/cancer/ncccp

Centers for Disease Control and Prevention (CDC). (2011d). National Program of Cancer Registries (NPCR). Retrieved from http://www.cdc.gov/cancer/npcr

Centers for Disease Control and Prevention (CDC). (2011e). United States cancer statistics. Retrieved from http://www.cdc.gov/cancer/dcpc/data

Cleeland, C. S. (1990). Pain assessment. *Advances in Pain Research and Therapy, 13,* 287–291.

Clive, R. E. (2004). Introduction to cancer registries. In C. L. Hutchinson, H. R. Menck, M. Burch, & R. Gottschalk. (Eds.), *Cancer registry management principles and practice* (2nd ed., pp. 31–49). Alexandria, VA: National Cancer Registrars Association.

Colditz, G. A., Samplin-Salgado, M., Ryan, C. T., Dart, H., Fisher, L., Tokuda, A., & Rockhill, B. (2002). Harvard report on cancer prevention: Vol. 5, Fulfilling the potential for cancer prevention: Policy approaches. *Cancer Causes & Control, 13,* 199–212.

Commission on Cancer (CoC). (2011). *Cancer program standards 2012: Ensuring patient-centered care, v. 1.0.* Chicago, IL: American College of Surgeons. Retrieved from www.facs.org/cancer/coc/cocprogram standards2012.pdf

Committee on Advancing Pain Research, Care, and Education, Institute of Medicine. (2011). *Relieving pain in America: A blueprint for transforming prevention, care, education, and research.* Washington, DC: National Academies Press.

Cook, M. B., McGlynn, K. A., Devesa, S. S., Freedman, N. D., & Anderson, W. F. (2011). Sex disparities in cancer mortality and survival. *Cancer Epidemiology, Biomarkers, and Prevention, 20,* 629.

Coyle, N. (2010). Introduction to palliative nursing care. In B. R. Ferrell & N. Coyle (Eds.), *Oxford textbook of palliative nursing* (3rd ed., p. 3). New York: Oxford University Press.

Curry, S. J., Byers, T., & Hewitt, M. (Eds.). (2003). *Fulfilling the potential of cancer prevention and control.* Washington, DC: National Academies Press.

Devesa, S. S., Grauman, D. J., Blot, W. J., Pennello, G. A., & Hoover, R. N. (1999). *Atlas of cancer mortality in the United States, 1950–1994.* Bethesda, MD: National Cancer Institute.

Economist Intelligence Unit. (2009). *Breakaway: The global burden of cancer— challenges and opportunities.* Commissioned by Livestrong.

Ellershaw, J., & Ward, C. (2003). Care of the dying patient. *British Medical Journal, 326,* 30–34.

Emanuel, L., Ferris, F. D., von Gunten, C. F., & Von Roenn, J. H. (2010). The last hours of living: Practical advice for clinicians. Retrieved from http://www.medscape.org/viewarticle/716874

Ferlay, J., Shin, H. R., Bray, F., Forman, D., Mathers, C., & Parkin, D. M. (2010). GLOBOCAN 2008 v1.2: Cancer incidence and mortality worldwide. IARC CancerBase No. 10. Lyon, France: International Agency for Research on Cancer. Retrieved from http://globocan.iarc.fr

Ferrell, B. R., & Coyle, N. (2010). *Oxford textbook of palliative nursing* (3rd ed.). New York: Oxford University Press.

Ferris, T. G., Hallward, J. A., Ronan, L., & Billings, J. A. (1998). When the patient dies: A survey of medical housestaff about care after death. *Journal of Palliative Medicine, 1,* 231–239.

Ferris, F. D., von Gunten, C. F., & Emanuel, L. L. (2003). Competency in end of life care: The last hours of living. *Journal of Palliative Medicine, 6,* 605–613.

Field, M. J., & Cassel, C. K. (Eds.). (1997). *Approaching death: Improving care at the end of life.* Washington, DC: National Academy Press.

Foley, K. M., & Gelband, H. (Eds.). (2001). *Improving palliative care for cancer: Report by the Institute of Medicine and National Research Council.* Washington, DC: National Academy Press.

Gordon, D. B., Dahl, J. L., & Stevenson, K. K. (2000). *Building an institutional commitment to pain management* (2nd ed.). Madison, WI: University of Wisconsin–Madison, UW Board of Regents.

Grossman, S. A., & Nesbit, S. (2004). Symptom management and palliative care. In M. D. Abeloff, J. O. Armitage, J. E. Niederhuber, M. B. Kastan, & W. G. McKenna (Eds.), *Clinical oncology* (pp. 180–185). Philadelphia: Elsevier.

Gullatte, M. M., Phillips, J. M., & Gibson, L. M. (2006). Factors associated with delays in screening of self-detected breast changes in African-American women. *Journal of the National Black Nurses Association, 17,* 45–50.

Haylock, P. J., Mitchell, S. A., Cox, T., Temple, S. V., & Curtiss, C. P. (2007). The cancer survivor's prescription for living. *American Journal of Nursing, 107*(4), 58–70.

Hewitt, M., Greenfield, S., & Stovall, E. (Eds.). (2006). *From cancer patient to cancer survivor: Lost in transition.* Washington, DC: National Academies Press.

Hill, C. S. (1990). Relationship among cultural, educational, and regulatory agency influences on optimum cancer pain treatment. *Journal of Pain and Symptom Management, 5,* S37–S45.

Howe, H. L., Keller, J. E., & Lehnherr, M. (1993). Relation between population density and cancer incidence, Illinois, 1986–1990. *American Journal of Epidemiology, 138,* 29–36.

Holland, J. C., & Chertkov, L. (2001). Clinical practice guidelines for the management of psychosocial and physical symptoms of cancer. In K. M. Foley & H. Gelband (Eds.), *Improving palliative care for cancer: Report by the Institute of Medicine and National Research Council* (pp. 7–60). Washington, DC: National Academy Press.

Hutchison, C. L., Menck, H. R., Burch, M., & Gottschalk, R. (Eds.). (2004). *Cancer registry management: Principles and practice* (2nd ed.). Dubuque, IA: Kendall/Hunt.

Intlekofer, R., & Michaud, F. (2007). The National Program of Cancer Registries. In H. R. Menck, L. Deapen, J. L. Phillips, & T. Tucker (Eds.), *Central cancer registries: Design, management and use* (2nd ed., pp. 357–369). Dubuque, IA: Kendall/Hunt.

Kaplan, B. W. (2011, May/June). The pain of surviving cancer: Coping with the lasting effects of chemotherapy treatment. *Oncology Nurse Advisor, 30,* 32.

Kolata, G. (2004, June 1). New approach about cancer and survival. *New York Times,* pp. A1, A14.

Lynn, J., & O'Mara, A. (2001). Reliable, high-quality, efficient end-of-life care for cancer patients: Economic issues and barriers. In K. M. Foley & H. Gelband (Eds.), *Improving palliative care for cancer: Report by the Institute of Medicine and National Research Council* (pp. 65–95). Washington, DC: National Academy Press.

Mackay, J., Jemal, A., Lee, N. C., & Parkin, D. M. (2006). *The cancer atlas.* Atlanta, GA: American Cancer Society.

Max, M. B. (1990). Improving outcomes of analgesic treatment: Is education enough? *Annals of Internal Medicine, 113,* 885–889.

Menck, H. R. (2004). Cancer registries in other countries. In C. L. Hutchinson, H. R. Menck, M. Burch, & R. Gottschalk (Eds.), *Cancer registry management principles and practice* (2nd ed., pp. 403–439). Alexandria, VA: National Cancer Registrars Association.

Menck, H. R., & Bolick-Aldrich, S. (2007). Glossary of terms and concepts. In H. R. Menck, L. Deapen, J. L. Phillips, & T. Tucker (Eds), *Central cancer registries: Design, management and use* (2nd ed., pp. 421–439). Dubuque, IA: Kendall/Hunt.

Menck, H. R., Deapen, D., Phillips, J. L., & Tucker, T. (Eds.). (2007). *Central cancer registries: Design, management and use* (2nd ed.). Dubuque, IA: Kendall/Hunt.

Miller, S. E., Hager, P., Lopez, K., Salinas, J., & Shepherd, W. L. (2009). The past, present, and future of Comprehensive Cancer Control from the state and tribal perspective. *Preventing Chronic Disease, 6*(4), A112, Retrieved from http://www.ncbi.nlm.nih.gov/pmc/articles/PMC2774626

National Cancer Institute (NCI). (2006). *NCI international portfolio: Addressing the global challenge of cancer* (Publication No. 06-6650). Bethesda, MD: Author.

National Cancer institute (NCI). (2011a) Cancer survivorship research. Retrieved from http://cancer control.cancer.gov/ocs/office-survivorship.html

National Cancer Institute (NCI). (2011b). Fact sheets: Cancer therapy. Retrieved from http://www.cancer .gov/cancertopics/factsheet/Therapy

National Cancer Institute (NCI). (2011c). Follow-up care after cancer treatment. Retrieved from http://www .cancer.gov/cancertopics/factsheet/Therapy/followup

National Cancer Institute (NCI). (2011d). Overview of the SEER program. Retrieved from http://seer .cancer.gov

National Cancer Institute (NCI). (2011e). PDQ (Physician Data Query) comprehensive cancer database. Retrieved from http://www.cancer.gov/cancertopics/pdq/cancerdatabase

National Cancer Institute (NCI). (2011f). Survivorship: Living with and beyond cancer. Retrieved from http://www.cancer.gov/cancertopics/coping/survivorship

National Comprehensive Cancer Network (NCCN). (2011a). Living with cancer. Retrieved from http://www .nccn.com/living-with-cancer.html

National Comprehensive Cancer Network (NCCN). (2011b). National Comprehensive Cancer Network (NCCN) clinical practice guidelines in oncology. Retrieved from http://www.nccn.org

Ou Shu, X., Gao, Y., Tu, J., Zheng, Y., Brinton, L., Linet, M., & Fraumeni, J. (2006). A population-based case-control study of childhood leukemia in Shanghai. *Cancer, 62*(3), 635–644.

Paice, J. A. & Ferrell, B. (2011). The management of cancer pain. *CA: A Cancer Journal for Clinicians, 61,* 157–182. (Originally published May 4, 2011, at http://caonline.amcancersoc.org/cgi/content/full /61/3/157)

Parkin, D. M. (2006). The evolution of the population-based cancer registry. *Nature Reviews Cancer, 6,* 603–612.

Pasero, C., Gordon, D. B., McCaffery, M., & Ferrell, B. R. (1999). Building an institutional commitment to improving pain management. In M. McCaffery & C. Pasero (Eds.), *Pain: Clinical manual* (2nd ed., pp. 711–744). St. Louis: Mosby.

Patrizi, P., Thompson, E., & Spector, A. (2011). *Robert Wood Johnson Foundation (RWJF) retrospective series: Improving care at the end of life.* Princeton, NJ: Robert Wood Johnson Foundation.

Payne, R. (2001). Palliative care for African Americans and other vulnerable populations: Access and quality issues. In K. M. Foley & H. Gelband (Eds.), *Improving palliative care for cancer: Report by the Institute of Medicine and National Research Council,* (pp. 153–160). Washington, DC: National Academy Press.

Pollack, L. A., Greer, G. E., Rowland, J. H., Miller, A., Doneski, D., Coughlin, S. S., . . . Ulman D. (2005). Cancer survivorship: A new challenge in comprehensive cancer control. *Cancer Causes & Control, 16*(suppl 1), 51–59.

Rao, J. K., Anderson, L. A., & Smith, S. M. (2002). End of life is a public health issue. *American Journal of Preventive Medicine, 23,* 215–220.

Renick, O. (2011). Global rise in cancer cost $300 billion in 2010, Harvard economist says. Retrieved from http://www.bloomberg.com/news/2011-06-20/global-rise-in-cancer-cost-300-billion-in-2010-harvard-economist-says.html

Reuben, S. H. (2004). *Living beyond cancer: Finding a new balance. President's Cancer Panel, 2003–2004 annual report.* Bethesda, MD: National Cancer Institute.

Reuben, S. H. (2006). *Assessing progress, advancing change. President's Cancer Panel, 2005–2006 annual report.* Bethesda, MD: National Cancer Institute.

Riddle, B. L., & Boeshaar, D. K. (2006). Event driven data set for cancer surveillance. *Journal of Registry Management, 33,* 57–62.

Rummans, T. A., Bostwick, J. M., & Clark, M. M. (2000). Maintaining quality of life at the end of life. *Mayo Clinic Proceedings, 75,* 1305–1315.

Shafey, O, Eriksen, M., Ross, H, & Mackay, J. (2009). *The tobacco atlas* (3rd ed.). Atlanta, GA: American Cancer Society.

Siegel, R., Naishadham, D., & Jemal, A. (2012). Cancer statistics, 2012. *CA: A Journal for Clinicians, 62*(1), 10–29.

Sloan, F. A., & Gelband, H. (2007). *Cancer control opportunities in low- and middle-income countries.* Washington, DC: National Academies Press.

Stewart, B. W., & Kleihues, P. (2003). *World cancer report.* Lyon, France: IARC Press.

Travis, L. B., Rabkin, C. S., & Brown, L. M. (2006). Cancer survivorship—genetic susceptibility and second primary cancers: Research strategies and recommendations. *Journal of the National Cancer Institute, 98,* 15–25.

Twycross, R., & Lichter, I. (1998). The terminal phase. In D. Doyle, G. W. C. Hanks, & N. MacDonald (Eds.), *Oxford textbook of palliative medicine* (2nd ed., pp. 977–992). Oxford, England: Oxford University Press.

United States Cancer Statistics Working Group (USCSWG). (2006). *United States cancer statistics 2003 incidence and mortality.* Atlanta, GA: Centers for Disease Control and Prevention & National Cancer Institute.

Wingo, P. A., Howe, H. L., Thun, M. J., Ballard-Barbash, R., Ward, E., Brown, M. L., . . . Edwards, B. K. (2005). A national framework for cancer surveillance in the United States. *Cancer Causes and Control, 16,* 151–170.

World Cancer Research Fund International. (2011). Top five most common cancers worldwide. Retrieved from http://www.wcrf.org/cancer_facts/5-most-common-cancers.php

World Health Organization (WHO). (2002). *National cancer control programmes: Policies and managerial guidelines* (2nd ed.). Geneva, Switzerland: Author.

World Health Organization (WHO). (2004). *Better palliative care for older people.* Edited by E. Davies & I. J. Higginson. Copenhagen, Denmark: Author.

World Health Organization (WHO). (2006a). *Cancer control: Knowledge into action. WHO guide for effective programmes.* Geneva, Switzerland: Author.

World Health Organization (WHO). (2006b). *Non-communicable diseases: Cancer.* Retrieved from http://www.emro.who.int/ncd/cancer.htm

World Health Organization (WHO). (2008). *Cancer control: Knowledge into action: WHO guide for effective programmes. Module 4: Diagnosis and treatment.* Geneva, Switzerland: Author.

World Health Organization (WHO). (2011a). WHO definition of palliative care. Retrieved from http://www.who.int/cancer/palliative/definition/en/

World Health Organization (WHO). (2011b). Cancer, fact sheet no. 297. Retrieved from http://www.who.int/mediacentre/factsheets/fs297/en

For a full suite of assignments and additional learning activities, use the access code located in the front of your book to visit this exclusive website: http://go.jblearning.com/holtz. If you do not have an access code, you can obtain one at the site.

Appendix A

Cancer Prevention

REDUCING TOBACCO USE AND EXPOSURE TO SECONDHAND SMOKE

Cigarette smoking and other forms of tobacco, which are collectively the largest single contributor to cancer mortality, are responsible for a large and growing global public health burden (Sloan & Gelband, 2007). Tobacco consumed in any form, but particularly when smoked, is carcinogenic (Viswanath, Herbst, Land, Leischow, Shields, Writing Committee for the AACR Task Force on Tobacco and Cancer, 2010). Tobacco is the only consumer product proven to kill half of its regular users as well as nonsmoking bystanders and is responsible for approximately 6 million deaths worldwide every year (Shafey, Eriksen, Ross, & Mackay, 2009; Warren, Asma, Lee, Lea, & Mackay, 2009). Almost three-fourths of these tobacco-related deaths occur in middle- and low-income countries (Shafey et al., 2009). As of 2004, the U.S. Surgeon-General had identified 10 cancers (lung/bronchial, pharyngeal, laryngeal, esophageal, stomach, pancreatic, kidney/renal, urinary bladder, cervical, and myeloid leukemia) for which "the evidence is sufficient to infer a causal relationship" between tobacco use and disease onset (U.S. Department of Health and Human Services [USDHHS], 2004). Building on decades of studies dating back to the 1950s, researchers have now identified the specific mechanisms by which tobacco causes disease (USDHHS, 2010).

By the year 2030, tobacco use is expected to become *the* leading cause of death and disability, if current trends persist. Thus, not surprisingly, the biggest single impact on cancer worldwide could be made solely by reducing tobacco use (Mackay, Jemal, Lee, & Parkin, 2006). Substantial health benefits accrue to smokers who quit, with the cessation of tobacco use reducing the risk of many cancers over time (ACS, 2011b). Passive smoking, also known as exposure to secondhand smoke or environmental tobacco smoke, causes a variety of adverse health effects in nonsmokers, and the growing evidence about the health risks related to passive smoking has led to a ban on smoking in public areas in many countries (USDHHS, 2010; WHO, 2009). In addition to public smoking bans, education/awareness activities and policy changes are being implemented worldwide, with their goal being to decrease tobacco use and thereby protect nonsmokers from passive smoking (Sloan & Gelband, 2007; WHO, 2009).

The WHO's Framework Convention on Tobacco Control (FCTC), which was developed in response to the globalization of the tobacco epidemic, is the first treaty negotiated by the member states of WHO (WHO, 2003a). It is also the world's first internationally binding, global health treaty designed to reduce noncommunicable diseases (Mackay et al., 2006; WHO, 2003a, 2006a). This treaty was put into effect in 2003 in response to the global tobacco pandemic, with the objective of substantially reducing the world-wide prevalence of tobacco use and exposure to tobacco smoke (ACS, 2011d). The FCTC includes provisions for both reduction of the demand for tobacco and reduction of the supply of tobacco, along with the evidence of the impact of the key interventions. The key provisions of the framework are related to the following issues (WHO, 2009, 2011g):

- Advertising, sponsorship, and promotion of tobacco products
- Packaging and labeling of tobacco products
- Protection from exposure to tobacco smoke
- Illicit trade in tobacco products

From a global health perspective, the most important step toward decreasing the burden of cancer relative to tobacco is ratification of the FCTC. As of October 2010, most eligible countries (168 out of 195) had ratified the treaty (ACS, 2011d; FCTC Convention Secretariat, 2009). In response to the FCTC, the U.S. Congress passed the Family Smoking Prevention & Tobacco Control Act of 2009, which imposes strict regulation of the tobacco industry and aims to prevent smoking among youth (Carvajal, Clissold, & Shapiro, 2009). In accordance with the FCTC, the CDC's Office on Smoking and Health developed the Global Tobacco Surveillance System (GTSS) to assess smoking prevalence and evaluate tobacco control initiatives across the world (CDC, 2011c). Experts believe that interventions to reduce tobacco use will have much broader benefits beyond the reduction of tobacco-related cancers, resulting in significant decreases in other illnesses as well, such as cardiovascular and respiratory diseases (Sloan & Gelband, 2007). The Global Tobacco Surveillance System Atlas (Warren et al., 2009) provides an overview of trends in prevalence, consumption, attitudes, and actions related to tobacco use in various parts of the world.

MAINTAINING OPTIMAL NUTRITION, PHYSICAL ACTIVITY, AND BODY WEIGHT

Nutrition, physical activity, and body weight have been linked to almost one-third of all cancer deaths (Kushi et al., 2006), with a substantial proportion of these deaths occurring in low- and middle-income countries (Sloan & Gelband, 2007). Diet, activity levels, and body weight are interrelated, and research suggests that these three factors act in complex ways to either promote or reduce the risk of cancer (Sloan & Gelband, 2007; World Cancer Research Fund [WCRF] & American Institute for Cancer Research [AICR], 2007). "For the great majority of Americans who do not use tobacco, the most important modifiable determinants of cancer risk are weight control, dietary choices, and levels of physical activity" (Kushi et al., 2012, p. 30). Worldwide, studies have suggested that the state of nutrition and extent of physical activity, along with level of alcohol consumption, may be the most important modifiable causes of cancer or cancer risk (Mackay et al., 2006).

Regarding nutrition, research to date has uncovered few definite or causal relationships between diet and cancer risk (WHO, 2011b). However, poor diet has been linked to some cancers, with the most consistent evidence connecting increased consumption of fruits and vegetables with a lower risk of developing cancers of the colon and rectum, lung, stomach, esophagus, mouth, and pharynx (Curry, Byers, & Hewitt, 2003; Sloan & Gelband, 2007; WCRF & AICR, 2007). There is also limited evidence of probable risk reduction for cancers of the larynx, pancreas, breast, and bladder (WCRF & AICR, 2007). Correspondingly, excess consumption of red and processed meat and preserved fish has been associated with an increased risk of colorectal and nasopharyngeal cancers, respectively (WCRF & AICR, 2007).

As with many other cancer risk factors, it is important that health interventions related to diet be implemented throughout a person's life. For example, breastfeeding—a central component of most mainstream public health nutrition policy—has been shown to protect nursing mothers against breast cancer at all ages (WCRF & AICR, 2007). Exclusive breastfeeding for the first 6 months after a child's birth is a recommended strategy in the United Nations' document *Strategy for Infant and Young Child Feeding Recommendations* (WHO & United Nations Children's Fund, 2003). It is important to note that implementation of this recommendation worldwide may be influenced by a variety of factors, such as the rising prevalence of HIV (Dop, 2002) as well as famine and/or diminishing availability of food sources. Countries affected by these two issues may need to consider alternative mechanisms for reducing cancer.

Alcohol consumption is one of the most important known risk factors for human cancers and, next to smoking, one of the largest modifiable risk factors (WHO, 2011c). Despite being a known carcinogen and dietary source of energy, alcohol is rarely discussed as a dietary risk factor for cancer (International Agency for Research on Cancer [IARC], 2011; USDHHS, 2011). Alcohol consumption is believed to increase risk of cancers of the oral cavity, pharynx, larynx, esophagus, liver, colon/rectum, and breast (Boffetta et al., 2006), with the risk varying by cancer site and increasing for all sites with greater alcohol consumption (ACS, 2011d; Baan, Straif, Grosse, Secretan, & El Ghissassi, 2007; Boffetta et al., 2006; Rehm et al., 2009; Sloan & Gelband, 2007; WCRF & AICR, 2007). The interested reader can access the literature to learn about similarities between the problems of excessive alcohol use and tobacco use, along with potentially powerful strategies to reduce individual consumption and provide public education about the harmful effects of these substances on health (Global Health Information System on Tobacco and Health, 2011, WHO, 2003a, 2011c, 2011h).

Physical activity is closely associated with nutrition and body weight factors, as it protects against overweight, weight gain, and obesity. Physical activity also protects against cancers for which the risk is increased by being overweight or having poor nutrition. Engaging in regular physical activity allows the body to function more efficiently; it complements healthy dietary practices in this sense. Urbanization, mechanization, and industrialization have significantly contributed to an increasingly sedentary lifestyle around the world. Although a sedentary lifestyle has been a public health problem in developed nations for many years, developing nations are also now experiencing this phenomenon. Given the known benefits of regular sustained physical activity, shifts in whole populations from being active to sedentary may be the most ominous public health phenomena in recent history (WCRF & AICR, 2007).

Physical activity is defined as any body movement that works a person's muscles and uses more energy than a person uses when resting (National Heart, Lung, and Blood Institute [NHLBI], 2011). Regular, sustained physical activity appears to be protective, or may be protective, against cancers of the colon, breast (postmenopausal), and, endometrial cancers (WCRF & AICR, 2007). Research investigating a possible relationship between physical activity and cancer has focused largely on cancer of the colon, endometrium, testes, prostate, lung, pancreas, and breast. Notably, numerous studies have demonstrated an association between physical activity and colon, breast (postmenopausal), and endometrial cancers (Lund Nilsen & Vatten, 2002; Matthews et al., 2005; McTiernan et al., 2003; WCRF & AICR, 2007). There is limited evidence from prospective studies suggesting an association between physical activity and premenopausal breast cancer, lung, pancreatic, rectal, or prostate cancer (Howard, Leitzmann, Linet, & Freedman, 2009; WCRF & AICR, 2007; Yang, Berstein, & Wu, 2003).

Body weight, the third factor discussed here, is closely associated with the nutrition and physical activity factors. Excess body weight—by being either overweight or obese—is a global public health crisis affecting all age groups, races, and ethnicities, and both sexes. Obesity and overweight are distinguished from each other, as follows: Obesity is defined as having a body mass index (BMI) greater than or equal to 30.0, whereas being overweight is defined as having a BMI of 25.0 to 29.9. BMI is calculated as weight in kilograms divided by height in meters squared (kg/m^2) (Garrow & Webster, 1985). Obesity is caused primarily by a combination of a sedentary lifestyle that lacks physical activity and excessive consumption of high-calorie, high-fat, and low-nutrient foods. Overweight and obesity both increase the risk of colorectal, breast (postmenopausal), endometrial, kidney, pancreas, and gallbladder cancers (WCRF &

AICR, 2007). Excess body fat has also been linked to esophageal, ovarian, and gallbladder cancers (ACS, 2011c; NCI, 2004; WCRF & AICR, 2007; Wolin & Colditz, 2008).

Once considered a problem only in high-income countries, rates of overweight and obesity are now dramatically on the rise in low- and middle-income countries, particularly in urban settings (WHO, 2011d). The availability of adequate and even excess food sources coupled with reduced physical activity has led to epidemics of overweight and obesity in developed nations. As food resources have become more available in middle- and low-resource countries, the issues of obesity and overweight have emerged as major global public health concerns. Social, economic, and nutritional transitions experienced by these countries have led to changes in the health of their people. The nutritional transition, characterized by a shift from "traditional" diets that are low in fat and high in fiber to high-energy 'Western "diets, which are high in fat and low in fiber (WCRF & AICR, 2007), has contributed substantially to the global epidemic of obesity and overweight. The full impact of this transition may not be fully understood for years; however, many of the nations now experiencing it are already reporting increases in chronic diseases related to obesity and overweight. Global recognition of these changes and their impact on resources needed to combat disease in middle- and low-resource countries has, in part, led to the development of resolutions and new plans and strategies by the United Nations and WHO to address issues of noncommunicable diseases such as cancer (United Nations, 2011; WHO, 2008).

Addressing the global obesity crisis will be essential to controlling the pandemic of chronic disease, which includes cancer. This pandemic must be addressed at every stage of life, primarily by modifying eating habits and regularly engaging in physical activity. Although diet and physical activity are clearly documented as very important determinants of cancer, interventions that are known to have a substantial effect on diet and exercise habits are not well established in high-income countries (Sloan & Gelband, 2007). The WHO report entitled *Global Strategy on Diet, Physical Activity, and Health* makes a series of recommendations related to establishing stronger evidence for policy, advocating for policy changes, fostering stakeholder involvement, and developing a strategic framework tailored for specific countries (Sloan & Gelband, 2007; WHO, 2004). From a global perspective, highly consistent evidence indicates that excessive calorie intake relative to an individual's level of physical activity increases the risk of many cancers—this is the second most important avoidable cause of cancer mortality in many countries, after cigarette smoking (Willett, 2006). Given that many of the cancers linked to obesity have also been linked to diet or physical activity, it is difficult to clearly determine whether improved cancer outcomes are due solely to diet, obesity, physical activity, or a combination of these factors. For a thorough discussion of the interrelatedness of these risk factors and effects impacts on cancer, the reader is referred to the WCRF and AICR (2007) report titled *Food, Nutrition, Physical Activity, and the Prevention of Cancer: A Global Perspective* and the overview of "The ACS Guidelines on Nutrition and Physical Activity for Cancer Prevention" (Kushi et al., 2012).

MINIMIZING EXPOSURE TO INFECTIOUS DISEASE AGENTS

Worldwide, infectious agents, such as the hepatitis B and C viruses (liver cancer), human papillomaviruses (cervical and anogenital cancers), and *Helicobacter pylori* (stomach cancers), are linked to approximately 15% to 20% of cancers (ACS, 2011d; De Flora & Bonanni, 2011). In developing countries, infections can account for as many as one in five (20%) of all cancers. In 2008, two of the four leading cancers in men (stomach and liver) and women (cervix and stomach) in developing countries were related to infection (ACS, 2011d). In contrast, in the United States and other developed countries, less than 10% of all cancers are thought to be linked to infectious agents (ACS, 2011d). Preventive measures for these infections include known interventions such as vaccination, antibiotics, improved sanitation, or education (ACS, 2011d; WHO, 2011b).

H. pylori Infection

Over the past two decades, epidemiological studies have established a strong causal relationship between *H. pylori* infection and gastric cancer (Cheung, Xia, & Wong, 2007; NCI, 2011d). Approximately two-thirds of the world's population is infected with this bacterium, with infection rates being much higher in developing countries than in developed nations (CDC, 2011d; NCI, 2011d). More than 50% of all new stomach cancer cases can be attributed to *H. pylori* infection (Parkin, 2006).

H. pylori colonizes the stomach lining and causes chronic inflammation of and damage to the gastric mucosa, with the resulting infection placing an individual at three to six times greater risk for developing gastric cancer (Bornschein, Kandulski, Selgrad, & Malfertheiner, 2010; Sepulveda & Graham, 2003; Stewart & Kleihues, 2003). The exact mode of transmission for this infection is unclear but is thought to follow a fecal–oral or oral–oral transmission route. Improvement in hygienic conditions and treatment with antibiotics have been used to prevent or reduce infection. In developing countries and those with high rates of stomach cancer, calls for the eradication of this bacterial infection from the human stomach using antibiotics have been tempered by a concern about possible development of antibiotic resistance in *H. pylori* (ACS, 2011d; Suzuki, Iwasaki, & Hibi, 2009). It is important to note that while *H. pylori* infection is very common, most people who are colonized with these bacteria will never develop cancer (WHO, 2011b).

HPV Infection and Cervical Cancer

Persistent infections due to human papillomavirus (HPV), a common sexually transmitted virus, lead to all types of cervical cancers as well as 90% of cancers of the anus and external genitalia; to a lesser extent, HPV also causes cancers of the mouth and oropharynx and possibly also respiratory cancers (Chaturvedi, 2010; Kreimer, Clifford, Boyle, & Franceschi, 2005; Parkin & Bray, 2006; Walboomers et al., 1999). While all cases of cervical cancer are caused by oncogenic strains of HPV, 90% of women infected with HPV will clear their infections with no intervention. HPV persists in the remaining 10%, who make up the population at risk of cervical cancer (Bosch & Munoz, 2002; NCI, 2011c; Sloan & Gelband, 2007).

Based on the nearly absolute causal link between oncogenic HPV and cervical cancer, two new approaches for cervical cancer prevention have emerged: (1) primary prevention via HPV vaccination to prevent HPV infection and (2) secondary prevention via carcinogenic HPV detection for identifying and treating women with cervical precancerous lesions and early-stage cancers (Scarinci et al., 2010). Vaccines developed to prevent infection with the most prevalent oncogenic strains of HPV, types 16 and 18 (associated with 70% of cervical cancers), have shown complete efficacy in preventing persistent infection by both HPV types (Sloan & Gelband, 2007). In addition, one of the vaccines developed by Merck was also designed to protect against HPV types 6 and 11, the most common agents of genital warts (Joura, Leodolter, Hernandez-Avila, Wheeler, & Perez, 2007; Sloan & Gilband, 2007).

Cervical cancer incidence rates have historically been low in developed nations; however, several countries have experienced increases in cervical cancer incidence among younger women (ACS, 2011d). These increases were likely due in part to increases in HPV infection rates among adolescent girls. The higher rates of disease in this group have prompted many developed nations to aggressively implement HPV vaccination programs for this population. Developing nations have implemented such vaccination programs on a much smaller scale, however, because the HPV vaccine is very expensive and is not yet widely accepted (ACS, 2011d; Sankaranarayanan, 2009).

Hepatitis B and C and Liver Cancer

Chronic infection with either hepatitis B virus (HBV) or hepatitis C virus (HCV) increases the risk of liver cancer 20-fold or more (ACS, 2011d; Chuang et al., 1992; IARC, 1994; Mackay et al., 2006). Together these two infections are responsible for more than 85% of the liver cancer in the world (Mackay et al., 2006). In developing countries, 58% of liver cancers are attributable to HBV and 33% are attributable to HCV; in contrast, only 23% (HBV) and 20% (HCV) of liver cancers in developed countries are attributable to these viruses (Parkin, 2006). Globally, 350 million people have chronic (lifelong) HBV infections and are at high risk of death from liver cirrhosis and hepatocellular carcinoma; these liver conditions kill more than 1 million people each year (WHO, 2008). While inexpensive HBV vaccines have been available for 20 years, they are still not being used in areas with some of the highest liver cancer rates (CDC, 2008; Sloan & Gelband, 2007). Increasing the worldwide coverage and usage of the HBV vaccine has the potential to save lives both now and in the future and to build cancer control capacity in geographic areas where it is currently limited (CDC, 2009; Chang et al., 2009; Sloan & Gelband, 2007).

Liver cancer incidence is increasing in developed countries, which have historically had low rates of disease, likely due to increases in HCV infection or possibly obesity (El-Serag, 2007). Hepatitis C virus infection is the most common chronic, blood-borne infection in the United States; approximately 3.2 million persons are chronically infected with this pathogen (CDC, 2011e). There is currently no vaccine available to prevent hepatitis C transmission. In 2001, CDC implemented the National Hepatitis C Prevention Strategy (NHCPS) to lower the incidence of acute HCV in the United States and reduce the disease burden from chronic HCV infection (CDC, 2001). The proposed strategy includes a combination of education of healthcare providers and members of the public, counseling and testing of at-risk persons, community outreach prevention activities, and surveillance and monitoring. Copies of the strategy can be downloaded from the CDC website (CDC, 2001).

Other infection-related risk factors for liver cancer have been identified and are of particularly high interest in developing countries. These include parasitic infections (schistosomiasis and liver flukes), viruses (Epstein-Barr virus, human immunodeficiency virus [HIV], human T-cell lymphotrophic virus type 1, and human herpesvirus-8), and fungal infections (e.g., aflatoxin B) (ACS, 2011d; Liao, 2006). Epstein-Barr, HIV, and human herpesvirus-8 are each responsible for approximately 100,000 new cancer cases each year, while schistosomes, human T-cell lymphotrophic virus type 1, and liver flukes are infectious organisms that less frequently cause cancer (Mackay et al., 2006).

Positive changes in lifestyle factors have the potential to reduce a large proportion of the world's cancer burden (Curry et al., 2003). Although specific research methods and results of analyses related to cancer prevention and early detection activities vary, the studies are all remarkably consistent in pointing to the potential benefits of reducing tobacco use, improving nutrition, increasing physical activity, maintaining a healthy body weight, keeping alcohol consumption at low to moderate levels, and getting screened regularly for cancer (Curry et al., 2003). For health professional-oriented summaries of current data on prevention for particular disease sites, the reader is referred to NCI's Physician Data Query (PDQ) Comprehensive Cancer Database series of detailed summaries (NCI, 2011e). All of the PDQ prevention summaries are also available in patient versions, written in easy-to-understand, nontechnical language.

Appendix B

Early Detection, Screening, and Education

GENERAL PRINCIPLES GOVERNING INTRODUCTION OF EARLY CANCER DETECTION PROGRAMS

The implementation of early cancer detection programs requires considerable resources. Thus it is important that national cancer control programs avoid imposing the "high technology" of the developed world on countries that lack the infrastructure and resources to use such technology appropriately or to achieve adequate coverage of their populations (WHO, 2011f). For these reasons, population-level screening programs should be undertaken as a component of early detection only in the following circumstances (WHO, 2003d, 2011g):

1. Effectiveness of the screening programs has been demonstrated.
2. Resources (e.g., personnel, equipment) are sufficient to cover a majority of the target group.
3. An effective treatment is available.
4. Facilities exist for confirming diagnoses and for treatment and follow-up of those persons with abnormal results.
5. The target disease is a common form of cancer, with high associated morbidity or mortality.
6. Testing procedures are acceptable, safe, and relatively inexpensive.

SCREENING

Some cancers can be detected before they cause symptoms. The process of checking for cancer in people who have no symptoms is called screening (Curry, Byers, & Hewitt, 2003; NCI, 2011g; Zapka, 2003). Appropriately implemented screening can help doctors find and treat certain cancers earlier and, in many cases, improve cancer outcomes. Population-level cancer screening is generally recommended only for cancers for which there is sufficient evidence that the screening test used reduces morbidity and mortality in the population being screened. To this end, population-level cancer screening is recommended only for breast, cervical, and/or colorectal cancer (NCI, 2011b, 2011g; WHO, 2011f).

Most developed and medium-resource countries have programs and/or national policies for cervical cancer screening (cytology tests) and breast cancer screening (mammography); few have programs and policies for colorectal cancer screening, specifically, the fecal occult blood test (FOBT), sigmoid-oscopy, and colonoscopy (ACS, 2011d). For example, in 2009, CDC implemented the Colorectal Cancer Control Program (CRCCP), which provides funding to 25 states and 4 tribes across the United States with the goal of increasing colorectal (colon) cancer screening rates among men and women aged 50 years and older (CDC, 2011a). This program was implemented only after considerable research and sufficient demonstration that population-level screening for colon cancer was feasible and effective (CDC, 2011b). WHO recommends only cervical and breast cancer screening programs that require little technology for low-resource countries (WHO, 2011g); it does not recommend screening for colorectal cancer in resource-limited countries.

While screening methods are in use or being studied for specific cancers (e.g., lung, stomach, and prostate), the ability of the screening methods to reduce cancer mortality has not been established. Despite the lack of evidence to support full implementation of these screening methods at the population level, countries with high rates of these diseases sometimes still proceed with implementation. For example, since 1983, Japan has conducted nationwide screening for gastric cancer among all people 40 years of age and older (Hamashima et al., 2008). To learn more about the development and testing of these newer screening programs, visit the National Cancer Institute's website: http://www.cancer.gov/cancertopics/screening/othercancers.

To be widely effective, education and screening should be accessible to all members of the population at risk. However, research indicates that members of minority ethnic groups, people living in deprived areas, and those with less education are often prevented from accessing services (von Wagner et al., 2009). Disparities in access to early detection resources contribute to differences in cancer burden. This lack of equity in terms of healthcare access is a challenge for people living in developed as well as developing countries. In the United States, issues of health disparities that plague the cancer community are, in part, associated with access to cancer screening and follow-up care. Programs such as the National Breast and Cervical Cancer Early Detection Program (NBCCEDP), created in 1991 by the CDC, were implemented to help improve access to cancer screening for at-risk populations (CDC, 2011f). Lack of access to screening and care in developing countries is caused primarily by a lack of available resources for noncommunicable diseases and fragile health infrastructures (Sloan & Gelband, 2007). Thus considerable attention must be given to implementing cancer screening programs in developing nations.

Studies show that primary care physicians do not always comply with cancer screening guidelines (Meissner et al., 2011). One reason is that recommendations for cancer detection and screening are often fragmented, in the sense that they are developed by various medical organizations, which may make decision making more confusing regarding which recommendations to follow (Geiger & Ricciardi, 2009). Numerous national and international guidelines on cancer screening have been promulgated, including those proposed by the American College of Surgeons, American Academy of Family Physicians, U.S. Preventive Services Task Force (USPSTF), American Cancer Society, and various specialty-specific medical organizations, to name a few (Geiger & Ricciardi, 2009). Variations in recommendations developed by each organization are due to factors such as differences in interpretation of research findings (Meissner et al., 2011).

Screening for Breast Cancer

Breast cancer is the most common malignancy affecting women worldwide, with more than 1 million new cases and 400,000 deaths from this cause occurring annually (ACS, 2011d). Nearly half of these cancers occur in the developing world (ACS, 2011d; Curado et al., 2007). Worldwide, the incidence of breast cancer is increasing, with 1.7 million women predicted to be diagnosed with this disease in 2020, mostly in developing countries ("Breast Cancer in Developing Countries," 2009). The

"Westernization" of developing countries is often cited as the principal cause of this increase (Porter, 2008). This Westernization is often related to social factors such as smoking, alcohol, and obesity; also considered are hormonal risk factors such as early menarche, delayed parity, and reduced breastfeeding (Anyanwu, 2008; Porter, 2008). These factors, which are often observed in developing nations, have been related to the adoption of Western culture, diets, and lower exercise levels (Tfayli, Temraz, Abou Mrad, & Shamseddine, 2010).

Recent studies have described declines in breast cancer incidence in several developed nations. These changes have been attributed to factors such as the declining use of menopausal hormone replacement therapy and/or declines in mammography use in the age-eligible population (Banks & Canfell, 2010; Canfell, Banks, Moa, & Beral, 2008; Kumle, 2008; Ravdin et al., 2007). In North America, Western Europe, and Australia, breast cancer mortality rates have also started to decline (ACS, 2011d; IACR, 2011), likely due to improvements in early detection, treatment, and/or healthcare management (Jorgensen, Zahl, & Gotzsche, 2010).

It is important to note that debate has arisen regarding the relative contributions of screening and therapy to the decrease in mortality rates in developed countries. While this debate is ongoing, several large, observational studies in Europe have directly measured the effects of mammographic screening in large general populations, finding that most of the decrease in deaths from breast cancer is due to screening (Kopans, Smith, & Duffy, 2011). In terms of survival, rates vary but are generally higher than 70% in most developed countries. Five-year survival rates are nearly 60% in middle-income countries, but less than 40% in low-income countries (Coleman et al., 2008). These estimates generally reflect the availability of breast cancer early detection programs and access to high-quality treatment for women diagnosed with disease. The absence of these resources often results in a high proportion of women presenting with late-stage disease, and is exacerbated by the lack of adequate breast cancer diagnosis and treatment facilities (Coleman et al., 2008).

The public health impact of breast cancer has been acknowledged by members of the international community, many of which have implemented population-based mammography education and screening programs (Okonkwo, Draisma, derKinderen, Brown, & deKoning, 2008; WHO, 2011a). The United States, for example, implemented a national breast cancer screening program in the 1980s with the aim of reducing rates of breast cancer mortality (CDC, 2011f). Similar programs exist in other developed countries in North America and Europe, as well as in Japan and Australia (Okonkwo et al., 2008). In most developing countries (where breast cancer incidence rates are low and access to state-of-the-art treatment is limited), the number of deaths attributable to breast cancer is double the number in high-income countries (ACS, 2011d; Mathers, Lopez, & Murray, 2006).

Breast cancer is characterized by systemic dissemination; thus presentation of symptoms and diagnosis may not occur until the disease is advanced or metastatic. Screening tests for breast cancer include clinical breast examination and mammography (i.e., an X-ray examination of the breast) (NCI, 2011h). Mammography is the primary screening tool for early detection because it can detect a tumor before it is felt or causes symptoms. This screening tool is associated with a reduction of as much as 20% in breast cancer mortality in women at greatest risk for developing breast cancer (e.g., women aged 50–64 years) (NCI, 2011a; WHO, 2011a). Population-based screening for breast cancer occurs primarily through mammographic examination, at prescribed intervals, of all women within a specified age range (WHO, 2011a). Mammography screening is expensive, as it requires special machinery and well-trained staff to implement. Thus population-based screening programs should be undertaken only in countries with high rates of breast cancer and the infrastructure in place to provide services to eligible women (WHO, 2011a). Ideally, implementation of breast cancer screening programs should reduce the proportion of women who are diagnosed with late-stage cancer because screening should identify cancers before they progress to late stage.

Each country determines the specific age range and appropriate screening interval for its breast cancer screening program. At the minimum, programs worldwide screen all women 50 or more years of age every one to three years. Screening of women ages 40 to 49 is performed in several developed countries (e.g., United States, Australia, and Sweden). However, in 2009, the USPSTF issued new controversial guidelines regarding the appropriate screening of this population. Instead of recommending that women aged 40–49 be screened for breast cancer, the new recommendation suggested that "the decision to start regular, biennial screening mammography before the age of 50 years should be an individual one and take patient context into account, including the patient's values regarding specific benefits and harm" (USPSTF, 2009). Concerns that this recommendation would confuse physicians and women at risk for breast cancer prompted health officials to refrain from fully implementing these recommendations.

It is important to note that breast cancer risk is higher among women with a family history of breast or ovarian cancer (ACS, 2011c). Thus screening is initiated earlier and often in more frequent intervals for these women (ACS, 2011c). While not currently recommended at the population level, some women who are at higher risk for developing breast cancer (e.g., women of Ashkenazi Jewish descent) may also consider genetic testing to determine their risk for developing the disease. Genetic testing for breast cancer involves a blood test that looks for mutation within the BRCA1 and BRCA2 genes (breast cancer–associated tumor suppressor genes). These tests are usually reserved for women at high risk for breast cancer.

Screening for Cervical Cancer

Cervical cancer is the third most commonly diagnosed cancer and the fourth leading cause of cancer death in women worldwide (ACS, 2011a). The highest incidence rates occur in Central and South America, the Caribbean, sub-Saharan Africa, and Southern Asia (ACS, 2011a). In developing countries, cervical cancer is the leading cause of cancer death in women (Ferlay, Shin, Bray, Forman, Mathers, & Parkin, 2010). Nearly 90% of cervical cancer deaths occur in the developing part of the world, including Africa, Latin America, and Asia (ACS, 2011a). Although developing nations are reporting increasing cervical cancer rates, most developed countries have reported a decline in cervical cancer incidence and mortality in the last 30 years (ACS 2011d; WHO, 2011f). U.S. cervical cancer mortality rates declined steadily from 1975 to 2003 due to prevention and early detection due to screening with the Papanicolaou test (Pap test); since 2003, however, rates have remained stable (ACS, 2011b).

Estimates suggest as many as 80% of cervical cancer cases can be prevented through comprehensive screening programs (ACS, 2011c; Sankaranarayanan, 2009). When the disease is detected in the earliest stage, the five-year survival rate for cervical cancer is 91%; when it is detected late, the rate drops to 17% (Howlader et al., 2011). The prevention and early detection of cervical cancer is accomplished largely through timely screening using the Pap test, which identifies abnormal (cancerous or precancerous) cell changes in the cervix and is considered the gold standard. The importance of being screened regularly for cervical cancer cannot be underestimated, as survival declines rapidly when women are diagnosed in later stages (NCI, 2011b).

Many developed countries now have cervical cancer screening programs. However, the Pap test is not practical in all settings, as it requires a trained cytologist, laboratory facilities, and multiple clinical visits (WHO, 2011f). Thus, in low-resource countries, increased emphasis has been placed on increasing access to, and improvement of the quality of, screening programs for at-risk populations (ACS, 2011d). Fortunately, more cost-effective screening methods are gaining prominence in low-resource settings; these options include visual inspection using either acetic acid (VIA) or Lugol's iodine (VILI) and DNA testing for HPV in cervical cell samples (Sherris et al., 2009). Current HPV tests may be cost prohibitive for developing nations; as a consequence, developed countries may consider implementation of these tests only as an adjunct to cytological screening (i.e., Pap test).

Screening for Colon and Rectal Cancers

Cancer of the colon and rectum is the third most common cancer in men and the second most common cancer in women worldwide (ACS, 2011d). Colon and rectal cancers are the fourth leading cause of cancer death in men and the third leading cause of cancer death in women (ACS, 2011d; Ferlay et al., 2010). Colon and rectal cancers are one of the few internal cancers that are amenable to early detection—more specifically, prevention by detection of preclinical lesions. Screening can prevent colorectal cancer and reduce the number of deaths due to disease by detecting and removing precancerous colorectal polyps (ACS, 2011c; Alberts et al., 2005). Although a small proportion of colorectal cancers occur among persons with a genetic or family history of the disease (ACS, 2011c), the primary objective of colorectal cancer screening is to detect the 90% of cases of colorectal cancer that occur sporadically, most often in patients older than the age of 50 (WHO, 2003b).

The approved screening tests for colorectal cancer are the fecal occult blood test (FOBT), flexible sigmoidoscopy, colonoscopy, and double-contrast barium enema. Colonoscopy, often considered the gold standard of screening methods, is expensive, requires a skilled examiner, is less convenient, and carries more risk for the patient (Winawer, 2007). FOBT is easy to perform and is considered the optimal screening strategy in terms of cost-effectiveness (Center, Jemal, Smith, & Ward, 2009).

Screening recommendations and guidelines for colorectal cancer vary by country, with most countries using an opportunistic approach to screening. Several nations have implemented national screening program (e.g., Japan, Germany, United States, and the Czech Republic) (CDC, 2011a; Parkin, Tappenden, Olsen, Patnick, & Sasieni, 2008). Other developing nations are conducting pilot studies to assess the feasibility of implementing colorectal cancer screening programs on a national level. Colorectal cancer screening is scarce in developing countries (ACS, 2011b) due to resource limitations.

Screening for Prostate Cancer

Prostate cancer is the second most commonly diagnosed cancer among males and the sixth leading cause of cancer mortality in men (ACS, 2011b; Ferlay et al., 2010). Prostate cancer generally develops slowly, and the risk for the disease increases with age (ACS, 2011c). Screening modalities for prostate cancer include digital rectal examination (DRE), the prostate-specific antigen (PSA) test, and transrectal ultrasound. While several developed nations use prostate cancer screening tests, it is not yet clear whether any of these screening modalities reduce the mortality from the disease.

Prostate cancer screening efficacy is currently under review by numerous organizations, and experts in major medical organizations disagree on the specifics of prostate cancer screening recommendations (National Guideline Clearinghouse [NGC], 2010). While screening tests are able to detect prostate cancer at an early stage, the lack of clarity as to whether earlier detection and treatment can lead to any change in the natural history and outcome of the disease (NCI, 2011f) continues to fuel the debate over screening for this disease. According to the USPSTF (2002), there is insufficient research evidence to recommend either using or abstaining from using PSA and DRE as prostate cancer screening modalities. The USPSTF concluded that the current evidence was insufficient to assess the balance of benefits and harms of prostate cancer screening in men younger than age 75 years (USPSTF, 2008).

Early detection of prostate cancer often hinges on clinicians and patients jointly deciding to screen for disease. The American Urological Association (AUA) recommends screening for specific groups of men (AUA, 2009). The AUA, like the American Cancer Society, believes that deciding whether to be screened for prostate cancer is a personal decision that should be made by each patient after consulting with his physician and becoming informed about the advantages and disadvantages of early detection and treatment options (ACS, 2011c; AUA, 2009). Although multiple organizations in the United States and parts of Europe recommend prostate cancer screening for certain groups, the broader international cancer control community does not yet formally do so (WHO, 2011e).

PUBLIC AND HEALTHCARE PROFESSIONAL EDUCATION

The Institute of Medicine of the National Academies recommends that low-resource countries that cannot afford the infrastructure required for organized screening programs focus on increasing awareness of signs and symptoms of diagnosis in the general population, which can lead to earlier diagnosis and treatment (Sloan & Gelband, 2007). Increased education and awareness among physicians and allied healthcare workers in developing countries, in addition to increased availability of effective therapy, could have a major impact on cancer incidence, mortality, and survival (WHO, 2006b). Public health education campaigns teach people to recognize early signs of the disease and urge them to seek prompt medical attention. Health professionals, especially primary health workers who are at the forefront of the initial contact between possible cancer patients and the medical care system, should be trained to identify suspicious cases and refer them for rapid diagnosis (WHO, 2002). Professional education is essential to primary healthcare workers whose initial training may have exposed them only to advanced and often untreatable cancers. Further, it may be necessary to improve accessibility to trained healthcare workers who are competent in performing the necessary examinations (including female health workers for women) (WHO, 2002).

Cancer education programs can educate people to recognize the early signs and symptoms of cancer and emphasize the fact that cancer diagnosed early is more likely to be treatable and to respond to effective treatment. These efforts can also promote public awareness of early signs of certain cancers (e.g., those affecting the oral cavity, larynx, colon, rectum, skin, breast, cervix, urinary bladder, and prostate) as well as proper follow-up with healthcare providers if individuals experience unexplained symptoms (WHO, 2006b).

CONCLUSIONS

Early detection of cancer is part of a broad strategy that includes diagnosis, treatment of the condition detected, and follow-up. These components must work together to produce the desired outcomes (e.g., decreased mortality). Cancer screening or education programs in the absence of suitable treatment and follow-up will fail. When deciding whether to implement such programs, policy makers and cancer control planners should factor in the impact of the cancer burden in the population and the cost-effectiveness of such programs.

For interested readers, up-to-date health professional-oriented summaries containing current screening and detection information are available online from the NCI PDQ (Physician Data Query) Comprehensive Cancer Database for many cancer diagnoses (NCI, 2011e). These summaries contain current information related to screening and detection for particular disease sites, the levels of evidence for the statements included in the summaries and the significance of and evidence of benefit for the stated positions included in the summaries; supporting references to current literature are also offered. Many screening and detection summaries are also available in patient versions that are written in easy-to-understand, nontechnical language (NCI, 2011e).

The health infrastructure of each country also affects the implementation of screening and detection programs. Early detection of cancer undoubtedly contributes to increased disease burden. Thus more resources to support the health services infrastructure may be required to address the additional disease burden. Decisions to implement early screening and detection programs should be evidence based and take into account the public health importance of the specific cancer, characteristics of early-detection tests, efficacy and cost-effectiveness of early detection, personnel requirements, and the level of development of health services in a given setting.

REFERENCES

Alberts, D. S., Martínez, M. E., Hess, L. M., Einspahr, J. G., Green, S. B., Bhattacharyya, A. K., . . . Lance, P. (2005). Phase III trial of ursodeoxycholic acid to prevent colorectal adenoma recurrence. *Journal of the National Cancer Institute, 97,* 846–853.

American Cancer Society (ACS). (2011a). ACS guidelines on nutrition and physical activity for cancer prevention. Retrieved from http://www.cancer.org/Healthy/EatHealthyGetActive/ACSGuidelineson NutritionPhysicalActivityforCancerPrevention/index

American Cancer Society (ACS). (2011b). *Cancer facts & figures 2011.* Atlanta, GA: Author.

American Cancer Society (ACS). (2011c). *Cancer prevention & early detection facts & figures 2011.* Atlanta, GA: Author.

American Cancer Society (ACS). (2011d). *Global cancer facts & figures* (2nd ed.). Atlanta, GA: Author.

American Urological Association (AUA). (2009). *Prostate-specific antigen best practice statement: 2009 update.* Linthicum, MD: American Urological Association Education and Research.

Anyanwu, S. N. C. (2008). Temporal trends in breast cancer presentation in the third world. *Journal of Experimental and Clinical Cancer Research, 27*(1), 17.

Baan, R, Straif, K, Grosse, Y, Secretan, B, & El Ghissassi, F, 2007). Carcinogenicity of alcoholic beverages. *Lancet Oncology, 8*(4), 292–293.

Banks, E., & Canfell, K. (2010). Recent declines in breast cancer incidence: Mounting evidence that reduced use of menopausal hormones is largely responsible. *Breast Cancer Research, 12*(1), 103.

Boffetta, P., Hashibe, M., La Vecchia, C., Zatonski, W., & Rehm, J. (2006). The burden of cancer attributable to alcohol drinking. *International Journal of Cancer, 119*(4), 884–887.

Bornschein, J., Kandulski, A., Selgrad, M., & Malfertheiner, P. (2010). From gastric inflammation to gastric cancer. *Digestive Disease, 28*(4–5), 609–614.

Bosch, F. X., & Munoz N. (2002). The viral etiology of cervical cancer. *Virus Research, 89*(2), 183–190.

Breast cancer in developing countries. (2009). *Lancet, 374*(9701), 1567–2131.

Canfell, K., Banks, E., Moa, A., & Beral, V. (2008). Decrease in breast cancer incidence following a rapid fall in use of hormone replacement therapy in Australia. *Medical Journal of Australia, 188,* 641–644.

Carvajal, R., Clissold, D., & Shapiro, J. (2009). The Family Smoking Prevention and Tobacco Control Act: An overview. *Food and Drug Law Journal, 64*(4), 717–732.

Center, M. M., Jemal, A., Smith, R. A., & Ward, E. (2009). Worldwide variations in colorectal cancer. *CA: A Cancer Journal for Clinicians, 59*(6), 366–378.

Centers for Disease Control and Prevention (CDC). (2001). National prevention strategy: A comprehensive strategy for the prevention and control of hepatitis C virus infection and its consequences. Retrieved from http://www.cdc.gov/hepatitis/HCV/Strategy/NatHepCPrevStrategy.htm

Centers for Disease Control and Prevention (CDC). (2008, November 21). Implementation of newborn Hepatitis B vaccination—worldwide, 2006. *Morbidity and Mortality Weekly Report, 57*(46), 1249–1252.

Centers for Disease Control and Prevention (CDC). (2009). Surveillance for acute viral hepatitis—United States, 2007. Surveillance summaries, May, 2009. *Morbidity and Mortality Weekly Report, 58*(SS-3), 1–27.

Centers for Disease Control and Prevention (CDC). (2011a). Colorectal cancer control program. Retrieved from http://www.cdc.gov/cancer/crccp/index.htm

Centers for Disease Control and Prevention (CDC). (2011b). Colorectal cancer screening demonstration program. Retrieved from http://www.cdc.gov/cancer/crccp/demonstration.htm

Centers for Disease Control and Prevention (CDC). (2011c). Global tobacco surveillance system. Retrieved from http://www.cdc.gov/tobacco/global/gtss/

Centers for Disease Control and Prevention (CDC). (2011d). *Helicobacter pylori* and peptic ulcer disease: The key to cure. Retrieved from http://www.cdc.gov/ulcer/keytocure.htm

Centers for Disease Control and Prevention (CDC). (2011e). Hepatitis C information for health professionals. Retrieved from http://www.cdc.gov/hepatitis/HCV/index.htm

Centers for Disease Control and Prevention (CDC). (2011f). National Breast and Cervical Cancer Early Detection Program (NBCCEDP). Retrieved from http://cdc.gov/cancer/nbccedp/

Chang, M. H., You, S. L., Chen, C. J., Liu, C. J., Lee, C. M., Lin, S. M., . . . Chen, D. S. (2009, October 7). Decreased incidence of hepatocellular carcinoma in hepatitis B vaccines: A 20-year follow up study. *Journal of the National Cancer Institute, 101*(19), 1348–1355.

Chaturvedi, A. K. (2010). Beyond cervical cancer: Burden of other HPV-related cancers among men and women. *Journal of Adolescent Health, 46*(4 suppl), S20–S26.

Cheung, T. K., Xia, H. H., & Wong, B. C. (2007). *Helicobacter pylori* eradication for gastric cancer prevention. *Journal of Gastroenterology, 42*(suppl 17), 10–15.

Chuang, W. L., Chang, W. Y., Lu, S. N., Su, W. P., Lin, Z. Y., Chen, S. C., . . . Chen, C. J. (1992). The role of hepatitis B and C viruses in hepatocellular carcinoma in a hepatitis B endemic area: A case-control study. *Cancer, 69,* 2052–2054.

Coleman, M. P., Quaresma, M., Berrino, F., Lutz, J. M., De Angelis, R., Capocaccia, R., . . . Young J. L.; CONCORD Working Group. (2008). Cancer survival in five continents: A worldwide population-based study (CONCORD). *Lancet Oncology, 9*(8), 730–756.

Curado, M., Edwards, B., Shin, H., Storm, H., Ferlay, J., Heanue, M., & Boyle, P. (Eds.). (2007). *Cancer incidence in five continents.* IARC Scientific Publications No. 160. Lyon, France: IARC.

Curry, S. J., Byers, T., & Hewitt, M. (Eds.). (2003). *Fulfilling the potential of cancer prevention and control.* Washington, DC: National Academies Press.

De Flora, S., & Bonanni, P. (2011, June). The prevention of infection-associated cancers. *Carcinogenesis, 32*(6), 787–795.

Dop, M. C. (2002). Breastfeeding in Africa: Will positive trends be challenged by AIDS epidemic? *Sante, 12,* 64–72.

El-Serag, H. B. (2007, September). Epidemiology of hepatocellular carcinoma in USA. *Hepatology Research, 37*(suppl 2), S88–S94.

FCTC Convention Secretariat. (2009). 2009 summary report on global progress in implementation of the WHO Framework Convention on Tobacco Control. Retrieved from http://www.who.int/fctc/FCTC-2009-1-en.pdf

Ferlay, J., Shin, H. R., Bray, F., Forman, D., Mathers, C., & Parkin, D. M. (2010). GLOBOCAN 2008 v1.2: Cancer incidence and mortality worldwide: IARC CancerBase No. 10. Lyon, France: International Agency for Research on Cancer. Retrieved from http://globocan.iarc.fr

Garrow, J. S., & Webster, J. (1985). Quetlet's index (W/H2) as a measure of fatness. *International Journal of Obesity, 9,* 147–153.

Geiger, T. M., & Ricciardi, R. (2009, November). Screening options and recommendations for colorectal cancer. *Clinics in Colon and Rectal Surgery, 22*(4), 209–217.

Hamashima, C., Shbuya, D., Yamazaki, H., Inoue, K., Fukao, A., Saito, H., & Sobu, T. (2008). The Japanese guidelines for gastric cancer screening. *Japan Journal of Clinical Oncology, 38*(4), 259–267.

Howard, R. A., Leitzmann, M. F., Linet, M. S., & Freedman, D. M. (2009). Physical activity and breast cancer risk among pre- and postmenopausal women in the U.S. Radiologic Technologists cohort. *Cancer Causes Control, 20*(3), 323–333.

Howlader, N., Noone, A. M., Krapcho, M., Neyman, N., Aminou, R., Waldron, W., . . . Edwards, B. K. (Eds.). (2011). *SEER cancer statistics review, 1975–2008.* Bethesda, MD: National Cancer Institute. Retrieved from http://seer.cancer.gov/csr/1975_2008/

International Agency for Research on Cancer (IARC). (1994). *Hepatitis viruses: Monographs on the evaluation of carcinogenic risks to humans.* IARC Scientific Publication No. 59. Lyon, France: IARC.

International Agency for Research on Cancer (IARC). (2011). Agents classified by the *IARC Monographs,* Volumes 1–100. Retrieved from http://monographs.iarc.fr/ENG/Classification/ClassificationsGroup Order.pdf

Jorgensen, K. J., Zahl, P., & Gotzsche, P. C. (2010). Breast cancer mortality in organized mammography screening in Denmark: Comparative study. *British Medical Journal, 340.*

Joura, E. A., Leodolter, S., Hernandez-Avila, M., Wheeler, C. M., & Perez, G. (2007). Efficacy of a quadrivalent prophylactic human papillomavirus (types 6, 11, 16, and 18) L1 virus-like-particle vaccine against high-grade vulval and vaginal lesions: A combined analysis of 3 randomised clinical trials. *Lancet, 369,* 1693–1702.

Kopans, D. B., Smith, R. A., Duffy, S. W. (2011). Mammographic screening and "overdiagnosis." *Radiology, 260,* 616–620.

Kreimer, A. R., Clifford, G. M., Boyle, P., & Franceschi, S. (2005). Human papillomavirus types in head and neck squamous cell carcinomas worldwide: A systematic review. *Cancer Epidemiology, Biomarkers, & Prevention, 14*(2), 475–476.

Kumle, M. (2008). Declining breast cancer incidence and decreased HRT use. *Lancet, 372,* 608–610.

Kushi, L. H., Byers, T., Doyle, C., Bandera, E. V., McCullough, M., Gansler, T., . . . Thun, M. J. (2006), American Cancer Society guidelines on nutrition and physical activity for cancer prevention: Reducing the risk of cancer with healthy food choices and physical activity. *CA: A Cancer Journal for Clinicians, 56,* 254–281. doi: 10.3322/canjclin.56.5.254

Kushi, L. H., Doyle, C., McCullough, M., Rock, C. L., Demark-Wahnefried, W., Bandera, E. V., . . . American Cancer Society 2010 Nutrition and Physical Activity Guidelines Advisory Committee. (2012). American Cancer Society guidelines on nutrition and physical activity for cancer prevention: Reducing the risk of cancer with health food choices and physical activity. *CA: A Cancer Journal for Clinicians, 62*(1), 30–67.

Liao, J. B. (2006, December). Viruses and human cancer. *Yale Journal of Biology and Medicine, 79*(3–4), 115–122.

Lund Nilson, T. I., & Vatten, L. J. (2002). Colorectal cancer associated with BMI, physical activity, diabetes, and blood glucose. *IARC Science Publications, 156,* 257–258.

Mackay, J., Jemal, A., Lee, N. C., & Parkin, D. M. (2006). *The cancer atlas.* Atlanta, GA: American Cancer Society.

Mathers, C. D., Lopez, A. D., & Murray, C. J. L. (2006). The burden of disease and mortality by condition: Data, methods and results for 2001. In A. D. Lopez, C. D. Mathers, M. Ezzati, D. T. Jamison, & C. J. L. Murray (Eds.), *Global burden of disease and risk factors* (pp. 45–240). New York, NY: Oxford University Press.

Matthews, C. E., Xu, W. H., Zheng, W., Gao, Y. T., Ruan, Z. X., Cheng, J. R., . . . Shu, X. O. (2005). *Cancer Epidemiology, Biomarkers, & Prevention, 14,* 779–785.

McTiernan, A., Kooperberg, C., White, E., Wilcox, S., Adams-Campbell, L. L., Woods, N., . . . Ockene, J. (2003). Recreational physical activity and the risk of breast cancer in postmenopausal women: The Women's Health Initiative Cohort Study. *Journal of the American Medical Association, 290,* 1331–1336.

Meissner, H. I., Klabunde, C. N., Han, P. K., Benard, V. B. & Breen, N. (2011, January 18). Breast cancer screening beliefs, recommendations and practices: Primary care physicians in the United States. *Cancer 117*(14), 3101–3111.

National Cancer Institute (NCI). (2004). Cancer facts: Obesity and cancer. Retrieved from http://cis.nci.nih.gov/fact/pdfdraft/3_risk/fs3_70.pdf

National Cancer Institute (NCI). (2011a). Breast cancer screening (PDQ®): Effect of screening on breast cancer mortality. Retrieved from http://www.cancer.gov/cancertopics/pdq/screening/breast/healthprofessional/page5

National Cancer Institute (NCI). (2011b). Cervical cancer screening (PDQ®). Retrieved from http://www.cancer.gov/cancertopics/pdq/screening/cervical/healthprofessional/allpages

National Cancer Institute (NCI). (2011c). Fact sheet: Human papillomavirus (HPV) vaccine. Retrieved from http://www.cancer.gov/cancertopics/factsheet/prevention/HPV-vaccine

National Cancer Institute (NCI). (2011d). *Helicobactor pylori* and cancer. Retrieved from http://www.cancer.gov/cancertopics/factsheet/risk/h-pylori-cancer

National Cancer Institute (NCI). (2011e). Physician data query (PDQ®) comprehensive cancer database. Retrieved from http://www.cancer.gov/cancertopics/pdq/cancerdatabase

National Cancer Institute (NCI). (2011f). Prostate cancer screening (PDQ®). Retrieved from http://www .cancer.gov/cancertopics/pdq/screening/prostate/HealthProfessional

National Cancer Institute (NCI). (2011g). Screening and testing to detect cancer. Retrieved from http://www .cancer.gov/cancertopics/screening

National Cancer Institute (NCI). (2011h). Screening and testing to detect cancer: Breast cancer. Retrieved from http://www.cancer.gov/cancertopics/screening/breast

National Guideline Clearinghouse (NGC). (2011). Guideline synthesis: Screening for prostate cancer [Originally published December 1998; revised May 2010]. Retrieved from http://www.guideline.gov

National Heart, Lung, and Blood Institute (NHLBI). (2011). Retrieved from http://www.nhlbi.nih.gov /health/health-topics/topics/phys

Okonkwo, Q. L., Draisma, G., derKinderen, A., Brown, M. L., & deKoning, H. J. (2008). Breast cancer screening policies in developing countries: A cost-effectiveness analysis for India. *Journal of the National Cancer Institute, 100,* 1290–1300.

Parkin, D. M. (2006). The global health burden of infection-associated cancers in the year 2002. *International Journal of Cancer, 118,* 3030–3044.

Parkin, D. M., & Bray, F. (2006). HPV vaccines and screening in the prevention of cervical cancer. Chapter 2: The burden of HPV-related cancers. *Vaccine, 24*(suppl 3), S11–S25.

Parkin, D. M., Tappenden, P., Olsen, A. H., Patnick, J., & Sasieni, P. (2008). Predicting the impact of the screening programme for colorectal cancer in the UK. *Journal of Medical Screening, 15*(4), 163–174.

Porter, P. (2008). "Westernizing" women's risks? Breast cancer in lower-income countries. *New England Journal of Medicine, 358*(3), 213–216.

Ravdin, P. M., Cronin, K. A., Howlader, N., Berg, C. D., Chlebowski, R. T., Feuer, E. J., . . . Berry, D. A. (2007). The decrease in breast-cancer incidence in 2003 in the United States. *New England Journal of Medicine, 356,* 1670–1674.

Rehm, J., Mathers, C., Popova, S., Thavorncharoensap, M., Teerawattananon, Y., & Patra, J. (2009). Global burden of disease and injury and economic cost attributable to alcohol use and alcohol-use disorders. *Lancet, 373*(9682), 2223–2233.

Sankaranarayanan, R. (2009). HPV vaccination: The promise and problems. *Indian Journal of Medical Research, 130*(3), 322–326.

Scarinci, I. C., Garcia, F. A., Kobetz, E., Partridge, E. E., Brandt, H. M., Bell, M. C., . . . Castle, P. E. (2010, June 1). Cervical cancer prevention: New tools and old barriers. *Cancer, 116*(11), 2531–2542.

Sepulveda, A. R., & Graham, D. Y. (2003). Role of *Helicobacter pylori* in gastric carcinogenesis. *Hematology Oncology Clinics of North America, 17,* 505–523.

Shafey, O., Eriksen, M., Ross, H., & Mackay, J. (2009). *The tobacco atlas* (3rd ed.). Atlanta, GA: American Cancer Society.

Sherris, J., Wittet, S., Kleine, A., Sellors, J., Luciani, S., Sankaranarayanan, R., & Barone, M. A. (2009). Evidence-based alternative cervical cancer screening approaches in low-resource settings. *International Perspectives on Sexual and Reproductive Health, 35*(3), 147–154.

Sloan, F. A., & Gelband, H. (2007). *Cancer control opportunities in low- and middle-income countries.* Washington, DC: National Academies Press.

Stewart, B. W., & Kleihues, P. (2003). *World cancer report.* Lyon, France: IARC Press.

Suzuki, H., Iwasaki, E., & Hibi T. (2009). *Helicobacter pylori* and gastric cancer. *Gastric Cancer, 12*(2), 79–87.

Tfayli, A., Temraz, S., Abou Mrad, R., & Shamseddine, A. (2010, December 15). Breast cancer in low- and middle-income countries: An emerging and challenging epidemic. *Journal of Oncology, 2010,* 490631.

U.S. Department of Health and Human Services (USDHHS). (2004, May–June). The 2004 United States Surgeon General's report: The health consequences of smoking. *New South Wales Public Health Bulletin, 15*(5–6), 107.

U.S. Department of Health and Human Services (USDHHS). (2010). The 2010 United States Surgeon General's report: How tobacco smoke causes disease: The biology and behavioral basis for smoking-attributable disease: A report of the Surgeon General. Rockville, MD: Author.

U.S. Department of Health and Human Services (USDHHS). (2011). Public Health Service, National Toxicology Program: Report on carcinogens (12th ed.). Retrieved from http://ntp.niehs.nih.gov/ntp/roc/twelfth/roc12.pdf

U.S. Preventive Services Task Force (USPSTF). (2002). Screening for prostate cancer: Recommendations and rationale. *Annals of Internal Medicine, 137*(11), 915–916.

U.S. Preventive Services Task Force (USPSTF). (2008). Screening for prostate cancer. Retrieved from http://www.uspreventiveservicestaskforce.org/uspstf/uspsprca.htm

U.S. Preventive Services Task Force (USPSTF). (2009). Screening for breast cancer: U.S. Preventive Task Force recommendation statement. *Annals of Internal Medicine, 151*, 716–726.

United Nations (UN). (2011). Prevention and control of non-communicable diseases. Report of the Secretary-General. Retrieved from http://www.un.org/ga/search/view_doc.asp?symbol=A/RES/64/265&Lang=E

Viswanath, K., Herbst, R. S., Land, S. R., Leischow, S. J., Shields, P. G., & Writing Committee for the AACR Task Force on Tobacco and Cancer. (2010, May 1). Tobacco and cancer: An American Association for Cancer Research policy statement. *Cancer Research, 70*, 3419.

von Wagner, C., Good, A., Wright, D., Rachet, B., Obichere, A., Bloom, S., & Wardle, J. (2009). Inequalities in colorectal cancer screening participation in the first round of the national screening programme in England. *British Journal of Cancer, 101*, S60–S63.

Walboomers, J. M. M., Jacobs, M. V., Manos, M. M., Kummer, J. A., Shah, K. V., Snijders, P. J. F., . . . Munoz, N. (1999). Human papillomavirus is a necessary cause of invasive cervical cancer worldwide. *Journal of Pathology, 189*(1), 12–19.

Warren, C. W., Asma, S., Lee, J., Lea, V., & Mackay, J. (2009). *Global Tobacco Surveillance System: The GTSS atlas.* Atlanta, GA: CDC Foundation.

Willett, W. C. (2006). Diet and nutrition. In D. Schottenfeld, & J. F. Fraumeni, Jr. (Eds.), *Cancer epidemiology and prevention* (3rd ed., pp. 405–421). New York: Oxford University Press.

Winawer, S. J. (2007). The multidisciplinary management of gastrointestinal cancer: Colorectal cancer screening. *Best Practice & Research Clinical Gastroenterology, 21*(60), 1031–1048.

Wolin, K. Y., & Colditz, G. A. (2008, October 7). Can weight loss prevent cancer? *British Journal of Cancer, 99*(7), 995–999.

World Cancer Research Fund (WCRF) & American Institute for Cancer Research (AICR). (2007). *Food, nutrition, physical activity, and the prevention of cancer: A global perspective.* Washington, DC: AICR.

World Health Organization (WHO). (2002). *National cancer control programmes: Policies and managerial guidelines* (2nd ed.). Geneva, Switzerland: Author.

World Health Organization (WHO). (2003a). Framework Convention on Tobacco Control. Retrieved from http://www.who.int/tobacco/framework/WHO_FCTC_english.pdf

World Health Organization (WHO). (2003b). *World cancer report.* Geneva, Switzerland: Author. Retrieved from http://www.who.int/cancer/prevention/en/

World Health Organization (WHO). (2004). Global strategy on diet, physical activity and health. Retrieved from http://www.who.int/dietphysicalactivity/goals/en

World Health Organization (WHO). (2006a). *Cancer control: Knowledge into action. WHO guide for effective programmes.* Geneva, Switzerland: Author.

World Health Organization (WHO). (2006b). Non-communicable diseases: Cancer. Retrieved from http://www.emro.who.int/ncd/cancer.htm

World Health Organization (WHO). (2008). Prevention and control of non-communicable diseases: Implementation of the global strategy. Report by the Secretariat. Retrieved from http://apps.who.int /gb/ebwha/pdf_files/A61/A61_8-en.pdf

World Health Organization (WHO). (2009). Report on the global tobacco epidemic, 2009: Implementing smoke-free environments. Retrieved from http://whqlibdoc.who.int/publications/2009/9789241563918_ eng_full.pdf

World Health Organization (WHO). (2011a). Breast cancer: Prevention and control. Retrieved from http://www.who.int/cancer/detection/breastcancer/en/index3.html

World Health Organization (WHO). (2011b). Cancer prevention. Retrieved from http://www.who.int /cancer/prevention/en/

World Health Organization (WHO). (2011c). Global status report on alcohol and health 2011. Retrieved from http://www.who.int/substance_abuse/publications/global_alcohol_report/msbgsruprofiles.pdf

World Health Organization (WHO). (2011d). Obesity. Retrieved from http://www.who.int/topics/obesity/en

World Health Organization (WHO) (2011e). Prostate cancer. Retrieved from http://www.who.int/cancer /detection/prostatecancer/en/index.html

World Health Organization (WHO). (2011f). Screening for various cancers. Retrieved from http://www .who.int/cancer/detection/variouscancer/en/index.html

World Health Organization (WHO). (2011g). WHO report on the global tobacco epidemic, 2011: Warning about the dangers of tobacco. Retrieved from http://www.who.int/tobacco/global_report/2011 /en/index.html

World Health Organization (WHO) & United Nations Children's Fund. (2003). *Global strategy for infant and young children feeding.* Geneva, Switzerland: Authors.

Yang, D., Berstein, L., & Wu, A. H. (2003). Physical activity and breast cancer risk among Asian American women in Los Angeles: A case-control study. *Cancer, 97,* 2565–2575.

Zapka, J. (2003). A framework for improving the quality of cancer care: The case of breast and cervical cancer screening. *Cancer Epidemiology, Biomarkers, & Prevention, 12,* 4–13.

13

Global Perspectives on Violence, Injury, and Occupational Health

Carol Holtz

> *"So I take a blanket and I spend the night with my children out in the cold because he is hitting me too much and I have to take the kids to stop him hitting them too. I would go up the mountain, and sleep there all night. I've done that more than ten times."*
>
> Woman interviewed in Peru (WHO, 2005b)

OBJECTIVES

After completing this chapter, the reader will be able to:

1. Compare and contrast types of violence, including physical, sexual, psychological, and neglect.
2. Discuss differences in global and U.S. violence statistics.
3. Explain causes of violence against women including intimate-partner violence and violence during pregnancy.
4. Discuss culture and honor killings.
5. Examine issues of school violence including bullying and cyberbullying.
6. Characterize violence in war and related issues of post-traumatic stress disorder.
7. Compare and contrast U.S. and global statistics regarding injuries.
8. Discuss passenger and pedestrian road traffic injuries and fatalities in developed versus developing countries.
9. Discuss issues regarding injuries and fatalities related to drugs, alcohol, poisoning, and drowning worldwide.
10. Explain the need for protection from injury for populations worldwide within the workplace.
11. Discuss how public policy can promote occupational health both in the United States and globally.
12. Explain the special needs for health protection of healthcare workers.
13. Examine the issues of job stress and its relationship to an individual's general health.
14. Discuss special health issues of agricultural workers worldwide.
15. Discuss suicide in women in China.

INTRODUCTION

The United Nations' *World Report on Violence and Health* defines violence as "the intentional use of physical force or power, threatened or actual, against oneself, another person, or against a group or community, that either results in or has a high likelihood of resulting in injury, death, psychological harm, maldevelopment, or deprivation" (United Nations, 2005, p. 1). Worldwide, there are many different opinions regarding the definition of violence.

Violence is a world health issue that includes child abuse and neglect by caregivers, violence by youth (ages 10 to 29 years), intimate-partner violence, sexual violence, elder abuse, self-inflicted violence, and collective violence, such as war or terrorism. Worldwide, an average of 4500 people die a violent death every day (Krug, Dahlberg, Mercy, Zwi, & Lozano, 2002).

What is acceptable in one geographic region of the world and one specific culture may vary greatly from what is acceptable in another geographic region and culture. This includes what is acceptable behavior, what is unacceptable behavior, and what constitutes harm. For example, beating a child's arm, leg, or buttock in public school was a regular part of discipline generations ago, but today would be considered a crime in the United States or Great Britain, and a teacher who committed such acts could be considered for criminal prosecution (Krug et al., 2002).

Categories of violence include physical, sexual, psychological, or deprivation or neglect. These categories can be broken down further into the subcategories listed in **Table 13-1**.

To decrease world violence, a political commitment within nations must be made and it must be recognized that change is possible. Recommendations to decrease violence in a nation from the *World Report on Violence and Health* (Krug et al., 2002) include the following:

1. Create, implement, and monitor a national action plan for violence prevention.
2. Enhance the capacity for collecting data on violence. Many acts are hidden and unreported.
3. Define priorities and support research on causes, consequences, costs, and prevention of violence.
4. Promote primary prevention responses. Make improvements in parental training, family functioning, and measures to reduce firearms and firearm safety, and implement media campaigns to change attitudes, behaviors, and social norms.
5. Strengthen responses to victims of violence. Improve emergency responses, recognition of signs of violence situations, and referral of victims to agencies; support prevention programs; and increase reporting mechanisms and legal processes for victims.
6. Promote and monitor adherence to international treaties, laws, and other mechanisms to protect human rights.
7. Seek practical internationally agreed upon responses to the global drug trade and global arms trade.

TABLE 13-1

Types of Violence

Physical	*Self Abuse* *Suicide*	*Interpersonal* *Family/Partner* *Child/Partner/Spouse* *Elder*	*Community* *Acquaintance* *Stranger*	*Collective* *Social* *Political* *Economic*
Sexual		✓	✓	✓
Psychological	✓	✓	✓	✓
Deprivation and neglect	✓	✓	✓	✓

Source: Adapted from Krug et al., 2002.

According to NationMaster (2010) statistics, the following countries have the highest rates of murders per capita (the statistics are per 1000 people):

1. Colombia (0.6)
2. South Africa (0.496)
3. Jamaica (0.34)
4. Venezuela (0.316)
5. Russia (0.2)
6. Mexico (0.13)

The United States ranks twenty-fourth with a rate of 0.04 murder per 1000 residents. World homicide rates by region or subregion (per 100,000 population) are as follows:

- South Africa (37.3)
- Central America (29.3)
- South America (25.9)
- West and Central Africa (21.6)
- East Africa (20.8)

The least violent regions are Europe with a rate of 5.4 homicides per 100,000 population and the Near and Middle East/Southwest Asia with 4.4 homicides per 100,000 population.

In 2002, 1.2 million violent deaths occurred around the world; half of them were from suicide, one-third were from homicide, and one-fifth were from war-related injuries (World Health Organization [WHO], 2002). The World Bank and the Inter-American Development Bank consider violence and insecurity to be major health obstacles. In the Americas (the United States, Canada, Mexico, and Central and South America), 14.2% of the gross national product (GNP), or the equivalent of $168 billion, is lost or transferred because of violence. The human capital loss in GNP from this cause is 1.9%. Intentional violence is the leading cause of death in many countries, and there are approximately 120,000 homicides worldwide per year. The majority of the victims are persons living in poverty and young males. Thirty percent to 60% of all hospital emergency visits are the result of violence of some kind. For all kinds of violent acts, such as murder, child abuse, family abuse, assaults, or felonies, most are associated with alcohol consumption. Research indicates that children exposed to family violence have a higher risk of engaging in violent behavior in their adolescent years.

In the United States, violence was declared a public health emergency in 1992 by then–Surgeon General C. Everett Koop. In Latin American countries, the ministers of public health made the prevention of violence a public health priority in 1993. Later in 1996, the Pan American Health Organization and the World Health Assembly made similar resolutions (Guerro, 2002; Mercy, Krugberg, Dahlberg, & Zwi, 2003).

The United States has high rates of homicide and deaths related to firearms as compared to other developed countries, but when considering all countries of the world, the United States has lower rates of such fatalities than many other countries, including developing countries. Homicide rates for Africa, Central America, and South America are three times the U.S. rate. The U.S. suicide rate of 10.6 deaths per 100,000 population in 2000 was also lower than the global rate of 14.5 deaths per 100,000 population. Suicide rates for Europe and the Western Pacific regions were twice the U.S. rate. Suicide was considered the thirteenth leading cause of death in the world for 2000, and homicide was the twenty-second leading cause of death. By comparison, in the United States, suicide was the eleventh leading cause of death and homicide the fourteenth leading cause of death for 2000 (Guerro, 2002; Mercy et al., 2003).

Domestic violence reduces the health of millions of women throughout the world. The American Psychiatric Association reports that 4 million American women experience a serious assault by an intimate partner each year. In the United States, one study revealed that 22.1% of women reported physical assault by an intimate partner. The rate of sexual assault by an intimate partner in the United States has been estimated to be approximately 7.7%. In addition, 4% to 6% of elderly have experienced some form of abuse.

Parental abuse also has a severe impact on child health worldwide. Some research studies have revealed a 50% rate of children who have been hit, kicked, or beaten by their parents. Approximately 20% of women and 5% of men reported being sexually abused during their childhoods. Exposure to violence during childhood may result in later-life consequences such as mental illness, depression, smoking, obesity, high-risk sexual behaviors, unintended pregnancies, alcohol, and drug use (Guerro, 2002; Mercy et al., 2003).

Violence related to war may result in increased health services costs, reduction in productivity, and decreased property values. Violence may cross international borders, especially when it is associated with illegal drug trade, small arms trade, sexual slavery, or terrorism.

Sometimes violence is contained within cultural practices, such as violence against women and female genital mutilation. A unique preventive method for curtailing domestic violence exists in some communities in India. A dharna is a public shaming and protest done in front of the home or workplace of abusive men. In countries where there are huge differences in incomes, such that some people are vastly wealthy in comparison to people living in extreme poverty, rates of violence are much higher.

Today, a variety of violence prevention programs are promoted by the Centers for Disease Control and Prevention (CDC), and many U.S. state and city health departments (Guerro, 2002; Mercy et al., 2003) (**Figure 13-1**). The U.S. public health approach recommends the following four steps to prevent violence:

1. Define the violence problem through systematic data collection.
2. Conduct research to find out why it occurs and who it affects.
3. Find out what works to prevent violence by designing, implementing, and evaluating interventions.
4. Promote effective and promising interventions in a wide range of settings and evaluate their impact and cost-effectiveness.

How people are raised in childhood affects their vulnerability and likelihood of becoming either a victim or a perpetrator. Examples of factors that play a role in this sense include alcohol abuse, being a victim of child maltreatment, or a psychological or personality disorder. Close relationships with others also influence the possibility of becoming a victim or perpetrator when faced with the following issues (United Nations, 2005):

- Poor parenting practices
- Marital discord and having friends who engage in violence
- Social, economic, and gender inequalities
- Weak economic safety nets
- Poor law enforcement
- Cultural norms about toleration of violence

CHILD MALTREATMENT AND NEGLECT

Child maltreatment is a serious problem that can have long-term harmful effects. The main goal of public health efforts is prevention by supporting families with skills and resources. One method of prevention is by teaching and supporting parental nurturing skills (National Center for Injury Prevention and Control, 2005a):

- Giving physical signs of affection such as in hugging
- Fostering self-esteem in children such as with positive reinforcement
- Recognizing and understanding children's feelings
- Engaging in effective communication with children
- Learning alternative methods to shaking, hitting, and spanking

Parents are also encouraged to take a break from a situation if they feel they are losing control.

FIGURE 13-1

Homicide Rates Per State, 1999

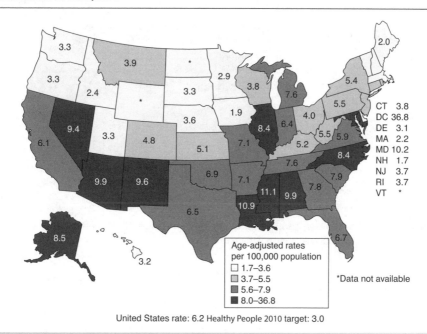

CT	3.8
DC	36.8
DE	3.1
MA	2.2
MD	10.2
NH	1.7
NJ	3.7
RI	3.7
VT	*

Age-adjusted rates
per 100,000 population
□ 1.7–3.6
▢ 3.7–5.5
▤ 5.6–7.9
■ 8.0–36.8

*Data not available

United States rate: 6.2 Healthy People 2010 target: 3.0

Source: National Vital Statistics System, National Center for Health Statistics, CDC.

The benefits of community support can significantly and positively affect previous parental behavioral practices. Volunteers from nongovernmental organizations and corporations can also provide family support services. Through such partnerships, parents and teachers can teach children how to be safe (National Center for Injury Prevention and Control, 2005a).

A 2002 CDC report on child maltreatment documented 906,000 maltreated children. Within this group, 61% of the children experienced neglect, 19% were physically abused, 10% were sexually abused, and 5% were emotionally (psychologically) abused (**Figure 13-2**). Moreover, shaken baby syndrome is a form of child abuse that affects 1200 to 1600 children per year, and that may result in serious permanent damage or death. Twenty-five percent to 30% of shaken babies die from their injuries. Effects of child maltreatment may result in brain maldevelopment, sleep disturbances, panic disorder, and attention-deficit/hyperactivity disorder (ADHD). Long-term consequences of child maltreatment may also result in problematic behavior as adults, including smoking, alcoholism, drug abuse, eating disorders, severe obesity, depression, suicide, and sexual promiscuity. Victims of child maltreatment are twice as likely to be physically assaulted as adults. As many as one-third of parents who are maltreated as children are likely to maltreat their own children. The children who are most likely to suffer severe injury or death from such maltreatment are those younger than age 4.

A study conducted in the Netherlands identified child abuse and neglect as important causes of child morbidity and death. In this research, infants aged 6 months who were crying had been smothered, slapped, or shaken at least once. The study results suggested that clinicians should be aware of babies who cry a lot, and target interventions to parents to help them cope with the crying (Reijneveld, Brugman, Sing, & Verloove-Vanhorick, 2004). See **Table 13-2**.

FIGURE 13-2

Percentage of Child Abuse and Neglect Victims by Type of Maltreatment, 2000

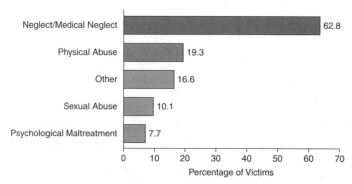

Note: Percentage totals more than 100% because children may have been victims of more than one type of maltreatment. Includes victims in 49 states.

Source: US Department of Health and Human Resources.

TABLE 13-2

Risk Factors That Can Contribute to the Need for Protective Factors for the Child

Risk Factors	*Protective Factors Needed for the Child*
Disabilities or mental retardation, increasing caregiver burden	Supportive family environment
Social isolation of families	Nurturing parental skills
Parents' lack of knowledge of child development and needs	Stable family relationships
Poverty and unemployment	
Family disorganization and/or violence	
Substance abuse in family members	
Young and single parents	
Poor parent–child relationships	
Parental thoughts and emotions that support child maltreatment	
Parental stress and/or mental health issues	
Community violence	

SEXUAL VIOLENCE

Sexual violence is defined as any act or attempt to obtain a sexual act, unwanted sexual comments or advances, or acts to traffic by any person regardless of the relationship to the victim, in any setting, including but not limited to home or work. Coercion may involve physical force or psychological intimidation, blackmail, or other forms of physical threats. It may also occur when the victim is unable to give consent, such as while drunk, asleep, or mentally incapable of understanding the situation. In addition, sexual violence may include denial of the right to use contraception or to use other protection against sexually transmitted diseases, or forced abortion. It includes coerced sex in marriage and dating relationships, rape by strangers, rape during armed conflict, sexual harassment (including demands for sexual favors in return for jobs or school grades), sexual abuse of children, forced prostitution and sexual trafficking, child marriage, and violent acts against the sexual integrity of women, including female genital mutilation and obligatory inspections for virginity (CDC, 2010d).

Sexual trafficking involves physical coercion, deception, and bondage incurred by forced debt. Trafficked women and children are often promised work in domestic or service industries, but then are instead taken to brothels.

Sexual violence has a tremendous impact on physical and mental health. As well as causing physical injury, it leads to a variety of short- and long-term reproductive health problems. The impact on mental health can be as serious as the physical impact and equally long-lasting. Deaths following sexual violence may come as a result of suicide, HIV infection, or murder. Murder can occur either during a sexual assault or later, such as in "honor" killings from family members. People who have been sexually assaulted may be stigmatized and ostracized by their family or other community members. Coerced sex may result in sexual gratification of the perpetrator, although it is generally the result of the need for power and control over the person assaulted. Rape of either men or women is often used as a weapon of war as a form of attack on the enemy (CDC, 2010d).

Honor Killings

An honor killing is the murder of a family member or member of a social group by other members, due to a belief of the perpetrators and possibly other members of the community that the victim has brought dishonor to the family or the community. Dishonorable behavior is often identified as the manner of dressing, wanting to terminate an arranged marriage, wanting to marry someone of the individual's own choice, engaging in homosexual acts, engaging in heterosexual acts outside of marriage, or engaging in a nonsexual act that is considered inappropriate. Women who are targeted for honor killings may also be the victim of rape, or perhaps seeking a divorce from an abusive husband. Honor crimes are acts of violence, usually murder, committed by male family members against female family members, whom the perpetrators perceive as having brought "dishonor" to their family.

Sometimes people will commit suicide if they perceive themselves as dishonoring their family. For example, more than 80 women chose to become suicide bombers because they had previously been raped. In 2002, an 18-year-old unwed pregnant woman was a suicide bomber in a Jerusalem market, for example.

Honor killings have been reported in countries such as Egypt, Syria, Jordan, Turkey, Lebanon, Morocco, Pakistan, Syria, and Yemen, as well as in immigrant communities in France, Germany, and the United Kingdom. Some countries, such as Jordan, Syria, and Morocco, have laws stating that men are allowed to kill female relatives who commit illegitimate sexual acts. Countries where such acts are not legal, but honor killings continue to occur, include Turkey and Pakistan. According to *The New York Times* ("A Killing Sets Honor Above Love," 2010), in Dokan, Iraq, more than 12,000 women were victims of honor killings from 1991 to 2007. Since 2008, Kurdish law has stated that honor killings are to be treated like any other murder, but the practice continues and crime is often disguised to look like a suicide.

According to WHO (2005b), sexual violence occurs in all cultures and in every part of the world. As many as 20% of all women experience an attempted or completed rape by an intimate partner during their lifetime. As many as one-third of women experience rape as their first sexual experience. More than 50% of all rapes occur in women younger than age 18, and 22% of these crimes occur in girls younger than age 12. In 80% of all rape cases, the victim knows the perpetrator.

Although the majority of victims are women, men and children of both sexes also experience sexual violence. Sexual violence has a significant effect on the health of the population owing to its consequences such as depression, unwanted pregnancy, sexually transmitted diseases, HIV/AIDS, and risk of development of high-risk sexual behaviors through sexual promiscuity. One longitudinal study estimated that in the United States more than 32,000 pregnancies resulted from rape of women aged 12 to 45 years. Of the rape victims, 4% to 30% contract HIV or STDs. Post-traumatic stress disorder is often identified in victims within 3 months after the rape, and victims can experience one or more of the chronic symptoms of anxiety, guilt, nervousness, phobias, substance abuse, sleep disturbances, depression, and sexual dysfunction. Rape victims are also more likely than the general population to commit suicide (WHO, 2005b).

Violence Against Women

An interview-based study of women and violence conducted in 10 countries by WHO (2005b), known as the Multi-country Study on Women's Health and Domestic Violence Against Women, revealed the prevalence, outcomes, and women's responses to such violence. Women older than the age of 15 reported experiences with violence both by partners and by nonpartners throughout the world. The incidence of such violence ranged from 5% in Ethiopia to 65% in Samoa. Women reported higher levels of violence in urban settings than in rural settings, with the exception of Peru. When respondents were asked about forced sex by nonpartners after the age of 15, rates were highest (10% to 12%) in Peru, Samoa, and urban United Republic of Tanzania and lowest (1%) in Bangladesh and Ethiopia. Perpetrators included strangers, boyfriends, and male family members (not fathers) or male friends of the family. The WHO data revealed that women are more likely to experience acts of violence from people whom they know than from strangers. In 34% to 59% of all cases of physical violence against women, women who reported the act of violence had no one who responded by helping them.

To prevent and respond to such violence against women, WHO (2005b) made the following recommendations:

1. Promote gender equality and women's human rights. Violence against women is an extreme result of gender inequality. Improving women's legal and socioeconomic status is a key intervention in reducing women's vulnerability to violence.
2. Establish, implement, and monitor action plans to address violence against women. Governments need to publicly acknowledge that a problem exists, make a commitment to act upon it, and plan and implement programs to address the violence against women.
3. Elicit social, political, religious, and other leaders in speaking out against violence against women. Men in positions of authority and influence can raise awareness of the problem of violence against women and challenge misconceptions and norms within a society.
4. Establish systems for data collection to monitor violence against women.
5. Develop, implement, and evaluate primary prevention programs against violence.
6. Prioritize the prevention of child sexual abuse.
7. Integrate programs to prevent violence into existing programs, such as those treating women for HIV/AIDS.
8. Make environments safer for women. For example, improve lighting and increase police vigilance.

9. Make schools safe for girls. Eradicate physical and sexual violence against girls in schools.
10. Include referral services for violence in established reproductive health services.
11. Strengthen formal and informal support systems with social workers and shelters for women living with violence.
12. Encourage the legal and justice systems to protect women from violence.
13. Support research on causes, consequences, and costs of violence against women.

INTIMATE-PARTNER VIOLENCE

Domestic or intimate-partner violence comprises a range of sexually, psychologically, and physically coercive acts used against adult and adolescent women or men by current or former intimate partners. A CDC report on intimate-partner violence indicated that 5.3 million intimate partners are victims of violence each year (National Center for Injury Prevention and Control, 2005b), with such violence resulting in more than 2 million injuries and 1300 deaths per year. Intimate-partner violence occurs in all populations regardless of culture, socioeconomic status, or geographic location. Young women and those living at federal poverty levels are disproportionately more likely to be victims. As many as 324,000 women each year in the United States experience intimate-partner violence during their pregnancy. According to the CDC data, 44% of women murdered by their intimate partners had visited an emergency room within the last 2 years of the homicide, and 93% had at least one injury visit. Firearms were the most common type of weapon used in such murders. In the United States, approximately 40% to 70% of female murder victims were killed by their husbands or boyfriends and had a history of an abusive relationship.

The consequences of intimate-partner violence include a 60% higher rate of health problems among these women as compared to women with no history of abuse. Examples of these health issues include chronic pain, gastrointestinal disorders, and irritable bowel syndrome. Reproductive health problems may include unwanted pregnancy, premature labor and birth, sexually transmitted diseases, and HIV/AIDS. In addition, women often experience mental health problems such as anxiety and low self-esteem. They are also more likely to abuse alcohol and make suicide attempts. Women subjected to such abuse are more likely to be unemployed and to be recipients of public assistance (CDC, 2010d).

Both men and women experience intimate-partner violence, but women are 2–3 times more likely to report their situations. Hispanic women and women of American Indian/Native Alaskan descent also have a lower rate of reporting victimizations than non-Hispanic white women.

According to the CDC (2010d), characteristics of perpetrators of intimate-partner violence include the following:

- Young age
- Heavy drinking
- Depression
- Personality disorders
- Low academic achievement
- Low income/poverty
- Witnessing or experiencing violence as a child
- Marital conflict or instability
- Male dominance in the family
- Economic stress
- Poor family functioning
- Weak community sanctions against domestic violence
- Traditional gender norms
- Social norms supportive of violence

The relationships of the perpetrators and the victims often featured the following characteristics (National Center for Injury Prevention and Control, 2004a):

■ Marital conflict
■ Marital instability
■ Male dominance in the family
■ Poor family functioning
■ Emotional dependence and insecurity
■ Belief in strict gender roles
■ Desire for power and control of a relationship, and exhibiting anger and hostility toward the partner

Low socioeconomic status and poverty are often linked to the causes of violence. Although domestic violence cuts across race, socioeconomic status, education, and income, African Americans experience a disproportionate amount of domestic violence compared with non-Hispanic white Americans. In recognition of this fact, the National Black Women's Health Project has identified domestic violence as the health issue of highest priority for African American women. African American women also are at a greater risk than non-Hispanic white women for contracting HIV as a result of domestic violence, and the number of deaths and serious injuries from such violence is greater in African American communities. African American women are more likely to kill a partner and are twice as likely to be killed because of domestic violence compared to white women. Possible explanations for this imbalance in the rates of intimate-partner violence are that African American women do not always see themselves as being in danger and are less likely to seek assistance for violence. Moreover, African Americans are more likely to live in poverty and to have less access to transportation to geographically convenient shelters. In addition, lack of culturally competent healthcare providers has resulted in hesitancy of African American women to seek counseling and assistance for domestic violence (Bent-Goodley, 2004).

In a study of domestic violence in the Rakai District of Uganda, 30% of women had experienced physical threats or physical abuse from their current partner. Of those who had experienced domestic violence, more than 50% reported injuries. In this study, the perpetrators' main characteristics included alcohol consumption and HIV-positive status. Unfortunately, most of the study's participants (70% of men and 90% of females) reported that beating a wife or female partner was considered justifiable in some circumstances, which creates a challenge for prevention in some settings. One explanation for the relationship between domestic violence and HIV-positive status is that women who believe that their partner is at high risk or is diagnosed with HIV may not want to have sexual relations with that partner; their resistance may, in turn, be met by physical violence (Koenig et al., 2003).

Watts and Mayhew (2004) relate that in sub-Saharan Africa, 13% to 49% of women have been hit or otherwise physically assaulted by an intimate male partner, with only 5% to 29% reporting their experience of physical violence. In Zimbabwe and in Ethiopia, 26% and 59% of women, respectively, have been forced to have sex with their intimate partners. For women who experience violence, such abuse continues and is often intensified during pregnancy.

A study conducted in Finland using open-ended questions with battered women found that women who had been maltreated in their parental home also experienced violence from their spouses. The researchers concluded that intimate-partner violence was associated with childhood experience of maltreatment, their partners' weak identities, and conflicts between individualism and familism. These results suggest that nurses and other healthcare providers need to be more aware of symptoms of violence and have the skills necessary to discuss intimate moral and spiritual issues (Flinck, Paavilainen, & Astedt-Kurki, 2005).

In 2004, 67 women in Spain were murdered by their husbands or boyfriends. Spain's medical community has long ignored the problems of domestic violence. Through the passage of new laws, the minister of health has developed a program to help doctors and other healthcare professionals recognize signs of domestic violence, such as eating disorders or depression, and develop special training programs for counseling abused women (Loewenberg, 2005).

A study in Fuzhou, China, of 600 women at a gynecological clinic 43% revealed that they had experienced intimate-partner violence. Such violence is highly prevalent in China, where it is strongly associated with male patriarchal values. Efforts to reduce this problem should be given a high priority in healthcare settings where woman can be seen (Xu, Zhu, O'Campo, Koenig, Mock, & Campbell, 2005). Notwithstanding the unique characteristics of developed and developing nations, intimate-partner violence is associated with consistent patterns and characteristics of perpetrators and of those who are abused.

Intimate-Partner Violence and Pregnancy

Domestic violence against women who are pregnant is a special case of intimate-partner violence. The true incidence of physical abuse in pregnancy is not known, but is suspected to range from 0.9% to 26% in developing countries. Most victims are reluctant to report such abuse. The effects of violence during pregnancy, which may include a blow to the abdomen, can be adverse outcomes such as preterm labor and delivery, chorioamnionitis (infection of the amniotic fluid), premature rupture of membranes, low-birth-weight babies, intrauterine growth retardation, hemorrhage, fetal injury, and death of the mother and fetus. Indirectly, psychological stress and lack of access to prenatal care can also cause poor outcomes. Related responses to domestic violence include polysubstance (alcohol, drugs, and tobacco) abuse, which can harm the developing fetus (CDC, 2010d).

In a study of 522 Nigerian pregnant women, 47.1% reported abuse from their intimate partner. Of those abused, 11.7% experienced such violence for the first time during pregnancy. The majority of women (99%) refused to report the abuse to the police. The conclusion of the study was that healthcare workers need to be alert to the clues of abuse so as to protect these women from further abuse (Ezechi, Kalu, Ezechi, Nworkoro, Ndububa, & Okeke, 2004).

In another study of 991 pregnant women in northern India, violence was higher when the husband/partner was less educated and when the man consumed opium, tobacco, and/or alcohol. The perpetrators in such cases included the intimate partner, the husband's mother, and the husband's brother (Khosla, Dua, Devi, & Sud, 2005).

SEXUAL VIOLENCE AGAINST MEN AND BOYS

Sexual violence against men and boys is a significant problem that takes place in a variety of settings, including in the home, in the workplace, in schools, on the streets, in the military, during war, in prisons, and in police custody. Studies conducted mainly in developed countries indicate that men report a 5% to 10% rate of sexual abuse experienced while they were children. In developing countries, rates of child sexual abuse in men have been reported as ranging from 3.6% in Namibia, to 13.4% in the United Republic of Tanzania, to 20% in Peru. Official statistics usually greatly underestimate the actual number of male rapes (CDC, 2010d).

SCHOOL VIOLENCE

Violence is taking an increasing toll on American society. School violence is now a major problem that inhibits learning and causes physical and psychological harm to students. Homicide and suicide cause 25% of all deaths of people ages 10 to 24 years in the United States. The potential for being threatened or injured by a weapon on school property has increased in recent years (Brener, Lowry, & Barrios, 2005). In addition, children may be bullied both at home and in their school environments. Victimized children often experience symptoms of withdrawal, anxiety, or depression, and many remain unhappy within their school environment. Prevention and intervention programs have been proven to reduce mental health problems during childhood.

Risk factors for perpetrators and victims for school violence include the following:

1. Substance abuse
2. Experiencing or witnessing violence and/or abuse within the home—physical, mental, and/sexual abuse/neglect
3. Depression
4. Low IQ and higher levels of aggression
5. Living in high-crime neighborhoods with gangs and exposure to community violence
6. School achievement problems such as ADHD, poor reading, and poor motor skills (CDC, 2010c)

Approximately 30% of U.S. school children are exposed to bullying at school in grades 6 through 10. School bullying and cyberbullying are increasingly viewed as important contributors to youth violence, including homicides and suicides. Studies of shootings at Columbine High School (Colorado) and other U.S. schools indicate that bullying was a factor in these situations. Each day 160 U.S. children miss school because of the fear of being bullied. An estimated 100,000 children carry guns to schools each year. Of those who carry weapons to school, 285 have witnessed violence at home. Playground statistics reveal that every 7 minutes a child is bullied and that responses from bystanders include adult intervention (4%), peer intervention (11%), and no intervention (85%). School bullying statistics reveal that 87% of school shootings are motivated by a desire to get back at those who have hurt them ("Bullying Statistics/ Cyberbullying Statistics/School Bullying," n.d.).

In the United States, 11.1% of youths (15.1% of males and 6.7% of females) in grades 9 through 12 reported in a 2009 survey by the CDC that, within the past 12 months, they had been in a physical fight on school property. Five percent of students did not go to school on one or more days in the past 30 days because they felt unsafe at school or on their way to school. Also in 2009, in a national survey of youths in grades 9 through 12, 19.9% reported that they had experienced bullying on school property within the past 12 months (CDC, 2010c). Youth violence harms not only its victims but also their families, their friends, and entire communities.

Violent young people are also associated with other problems such as truancy, school dropouts, substance abuse, reckless driving, and high rates of sexually transmitted diseases. Youth who witness physical or sexual abuse of other individuals in their homes or neighborhoods often get the idea that violence is an acceptable means of resolving problems (CDC, 2010c).

ELDER ABUSE

Elder abuse includes violence against individuals who are 60 and older, usually committed by a caregiver or a person whom the victim trusts. It may continue to occur because the older person is afraid to tell others or the police.

Types of elder abuse include the following:

1. Physical: Hitting, kicking, pushing, slapping, burning or other means of force
2. Sexual: Forcing an elder to have sex without consent
3. Emotional: Behaviors that hurt the elder's self-worth or emotional well-being such as name calling, embarrassing the person, or not letting him or her see friends or family
4. Neglect: Failure to meet the person's basic needs, including food, housing, clothing, and medical care
5. Abandonment: Leaving the elder alone and no longer providing care
6. Financial: Misusing the person's money, property, or assets

Prevention strategies for elder abuse include these recommendations:

1. Listening to the elders and their caregivers
2. Reporting abuse to Adult Protective Services
3. Education about signs of elder abuse
4. Getting help from adult day care programs and caregivers who need help seeking counseling and treatment for psychological problems (CDC, 2010b)

VIOLENCE AND WAR

Today, people in many parts of the world face the prospect of violence as a result of war and terrorism. These situations affect large groups of civilians who are confronted with civil strife, food shortages, and population displacements. Worldwide, there is about 1 death from war-related violence per day per 10,000 people. Some countries with greater violence, such as the Democratic People's Republic of the Congo, have a mortality rate as high as 3.5 deaths per 1000 people per month (Waldman, 2005). Efforts to address the high rates of violent deaths need to promote human security by taking the following measures ("A New Vision for Human Security," 2003):

- Protect people in violent conflict.
- Protect people from the proliferation of arms.
- Support migrants, refugees, and internally displaced persons.
- Establish funds for post-conflict situations.
- Encourage fair trade to benefit the poor.
- Provide minimum living standards everywhere.
- Give high priority to universal access to basic health care.
- Develop an equitable global system for patient rights.
- Provide basic education.

Within nations, violence reduction efforts can also be directed toward religious and political leaders, who can work toward developing systems of openness and opportunity for their own constituents.

Bioterrorism also relates to war and poses a major threat to world health. Safeguarding the public's health, safety, and security became a high priority after the terrorist attacks on New York's World Trade Center and Washington, D.C.'s Pentagon on September 11, 2001. A few weeks later, on October 4, 2001, a Florida man was diagnosed with inhalation anthrax. His illness was traced to an anthrax agent that was dispersed throughout the U.S. postal system in New York, Washington, D.C., and other locations. This act of bioterrorism resulted in five deaths, thousands more people being tested, and many hundreds being treated for this illness.

As part of the U.S. response to these events, the Model State Emergency Health Powers Act, or Model Act, was developed. The Model Act provides states with power to detect and contain bioterrorism or a naturally occurring disease outbreak. Included are the following elements (Gostin et al., 2002):

- Preparedness: Preparing for a public health emergency
- Surveillance: Measures to detect and track public health emergencies
- Management of property: Ensuring adequate availability of vaccines, pharmaceuticals, and hospitals
- Protection of persons: Powers to compel vaccination, testing, treatment, isolation, and quarantine when clearly necessary
- Communication: Providing clear and authoritative information to the public

POST-TRAUMATIC STRESS DISORDER

Post-traumatic stress disorder (PTSD) is a chronic anxiety disorder triggered by traumatic events. As part of their symptoms, victims may reexperience the event through flashbacks, bad dreams, or frightening thoughts. They may engage in avoidance behaviors such as staying away from places or objects that serve as reminders of the bad experiences, may feel numb and lose interest in things that they normally enjoy, or may have trouble remembering the event. They may also be hyper-aroused and easily startled, feel tense, have difficulty sleeping, or have angry outbursts. Signs and symptoms usually begin around 3 months after an event, but in some cases, may not occur until a year after the event. Triggering events may include rape, war, natural disasters, traumatic accidents or illnesses, or abandonment. Treatments include medication and psychological therapy. Unresolved problems can lead to permanent mental health disability or suicide.

In a study conducted by the U.S. Department of Veteran Affairs, National Center for PTSD, between 2001 and 2003, the lifetime prevalence of PTSD among men was 3.6% and among women was 9.7%. Lifetime global prevalence of PTSD ranges from 0.3% in China to 6.1% in New Zealand (Gradus, 2007).

INJURY

Injuries cause approximately 10% of all deaths worldwide, with traffic accidents, self-inflicted injuries, violence, and war being the most common causes of traumatic deaths. All types of injuries are predicted to increase by the year 2020. Historically, global health-related problems tended to derive from infectious disease, pollution, and malnutrition; today, however, injury is attracting more attention as a major global health problem. A study comparing mortality from serious blunt trauma showed that the rates of these fatalities decreased as income increased; in this study, the examples cited to prove this point included a low-income country, Ghana; a middle-income country, Mexico; and a high-income country, the United States. The higher rates of death in poorer countries were due to the increased time necessary to transport patients to a hospital emergency room setting and the less advanced care given in transit to the hospital (Leppaniemi, 2004; Mock, Joshipura, & Goosen, 2004; Mock, Quansah, Krishnan, Arreola-Risa, & Rivara, 2004).

The World Bank and WHO report that almost 12 million people die in traffic accidents each year, and this number is predicted to increase by 65% in the next 20 years. Most of this increase will be attributable to deaths in developing countries. In the United States, the estimated cost of serious trauma care for a single person is far greater than the cost of care for cancer and cardiovascular diseases. Thus reducing the number of deaths and injuries from trauma could have a major worldwide positive economic impact.

Significant advances in prehospital care in the form of advanced life support (ALS) and basic life support (BLS) have improved mortality rates for serious injuries. Likewise, advances in technology in hospital emergency rooms and operative care, as well as intensive care unit (ICU) hospital care, have significantly improved patients' chances of survival in these scenarios. Unfortunately many seriously injured patients who live in developing countries may not have the benefit of such care, owing to a lack of technology, lack of funds, or lack of transportation to healthcare facilities (Hyder & Peek-Asa, 2010; Leppaniemi, 2004; Mock, Joshipura, & Goosen, 2004; Mock, Quansah, et al., 2004).

Injuries have traditionally been considered to be random and unavoidable accidents, yet today intentional and unintentional injuries are considered to be preventable events. Injuries are among the world's leading causes of death, disability, or disease and affect people of all races, ages, and socioeconomic status. Worldwide, road traffic accidents and self-inflicted injuries are the leading causes of injury deaths.

In children 5 to 14 years of age, falls are the leading health injury problems. Among persons aged 15 to 29 years, road traffic accidents, self-inflicted injuries, interpersonal violence, war injuries, drowning, poisonings, and fire exposures are the leading causes of death. China is the only region for which drowning is one of the 15 leading causes of death and burden of disease. Low- and middle-income countries in Europe cite poisonings as the leading cause of death for injuries (Hyder, 2004; Silcock, 2003; WHO, 2005a).

There is a significant gap in the burden imposed by trauma and injury in low- and middle-income countries of the world as compared to high-income countries. Fifteen percent of the world's population resides in high-income countries, with 60% of this high-income population having life spans exceeding 70 years. In contrast, the remaining 85% of the world's population lives in middle- and low-income countries, where only 25% of the population live past 70 years. The newly independent countries of Eastern Europe, which are classified as middle-income countries, have the highest overall injury mortality rates. Countries in North America, Western Europe, Australia, and New Zealand, have the lowest injury rates. The main reasons for the higher rates of trauma and injury in low- and middle-income countries are inadequate systems of hospital and community-based emergency care. Roads used to transport trauma patients to hospitals are often unpaved and have few safety regulations. In addition, there is often little recognition of the need for road safety and public education on these issues in middle- and low-income countries. To bridge this significant gap, it is essential that trauma care services, research in trauma and injury, and comprehensive training programs for preventing injuries and violence that are unique to the specific demographic and environmental influences be developed (Hofman, Primack, Keusch, & Hrynkow, 2005; Zhang, Norton, Tang, Lo, Zhuo, & Wenkui, 2004).

Injuries and violence are also a great problem for U.S. older adults. To protect older Americans, many programs are being developed that address the following issues (National Center for Injury Prevention and Control, 2003):

- Elder abuse and maltreatment
- Falls
- Traffic accidents with injuries
- Residential fire injuries
- Sexual abuse
- Suicide
- Traumatic brain injury

The CDC, in partnership with the U.S. National Highway Traffic Safety Administration, is also working to reduce deaths caused by alcohol-related road traffic injuries (CDC, 2004).

Road Traffic Injuries and Fatalities

A road traffic injury is a fatal or nonfatal injury that occurred as a result of a road traffic crash. A road traffic crash is a collision or incident that may or may not lead to injury, which occurs on a public road and involves at least one moving vehicle (WHO, 2004). In 1990 road accidents were the ninth leading cause of death in the world, and by 2020 they are expected to be the third leading cause of death if nothing is done to stop the trend. Every year, more than 1.3 million people around the world are killed in traffic accidents. Ninety percent of these deaths occur in poorer countries. Such injuries are the single largest cause of death among persons 15 to 19 years of age. For each death from road traffic crashes, there are another 50 people who are injured or disabled from this cause. The majority of these deaths and injuries occur in developing countries where more people are now using cars, trucks, motorcycles, and mopeds, and where more pedestrians are vulnerable to injury and death from motor vehicles.

Wealthier countries are making significant progress in decreasing the numbers of traffic-related deaths and injuries. In developed nations, most of the victims of road accidents are drivers or passengers in vehicles. In contrast, most of those who die or are injured in road traffic accidents in developing countries are too poor to own a vehicle, and are pedestrians. The child pedestrian injury is highest in South Asia and sub-Saharan Africa (WHO, 2004).

In places such as India, far more health spending is devoted to HIV/AIDS than to road traffic injuries, yet more people die from road traffic accidents than HIV/AIDS. In addition to the losses due to injuries and deaths, many families lose the value of that person's earning potential, dramatically cutting household income, which is needed to help the household survive. Moreover, road traffic injuries place a huge strain on healthcare budgets. For example, in Kenya, road traffic injuries account for 45% to 60% of all hospital admissions to surgical units (Watkins & Sridhar, 2009; WHO, 2009a).

Since 1990, for example, traffic fatalities have increased 237.1% in Colombia. China and Botswana had increases of 243% and 383.8% in their traffic-related mortality rates, respectively. So far, nothing appears to be impeding this trend. Indeed, since 1990, China has quadrupled its rate of motor vehicle usage, to 55 million vehicles. Since its implementation of economic reform policies, China has also made great progress in development of its road infrastructures (WHO, 2004).

In developing countries, road crashes are more likely to result in death than in developed countries, because crashes in developing countries often involve pedestrians or people on unprotected mopeds or motorcycles. The good news is that most of these injuries and mortalities are preventable (Silcock, 2003; "Vehicular Manslaughter," 2004; WHO, 2004).

In Mexico, road traffic injuries and pedestrian injuries are a major public health problem. During 2000, 17,500 deaths occurred from traffic accidents in this country. Pedestrians have the highest rates of deaths from traffic accidents in Mexico City. Baja California Sur has a death rate from traffic injuries of 28.7 fatalities per 100,000 people—the highest in Mexico—as compared to Chiapas, with a rate of 7.9 deaths per 100,000 population (Hijar, Vazquez-Vela, & Arreola-Risa, 2002).

In the United States, teen drivers are especially vulnerable to traffic deaths. Forty percent of all deaths of teens are attributable to motor vehicle accidents. Teens aged 16 to 19 are four times more likely than older drivers to have traffic accidents. Specifically, teenagers represent 10% of the U.S. population, but account for 14% of all motor vehicle accidents. Moreover, the presence of other teen passengers increases the risk of accidents for teen drivers. Male teens have double the number of deaths from car accidents as female teens. The risk of such accidents is particularly high during the first years that teenagers are eligible to drive. Teens are more likely than older drivers to do the following:

■ Underestimate the dangers in hazardous situations
■ Have less experience coping with difficult driving situations
■ Speed
■ Run red lights
■ Make illegal turns
■ Ride with an intoxicated driver
■ Drive while using alcohol and drugs
■ Not use a seat belt

Male teens are less likely to use a seat belt than female teens (National Center for Injury Prevention and Control, 2004c).

U.S. drivers older than age 65 have higher rates of traffic accidents than all other drivers except teen drivers. In 2002, the majority of fatal traffic accidents of older drivers occurred during daytime (81%) and on weekdays (72%). Although older drivers are more likely than younger drivers to use a seat belt, drivers 65 and older are more likely to die from injuries than younger drivers. Injury rates are twice as high among older men than among older women. Factors related to injury and deaths for older drivers include problems with vision, hearing, cognitive functions, and physical impairments (National Center for Injury Prevention and Control, 2004b, c).

Child Passenger Safety

Motor vehicle injuries are the leading cause of death among children in the United States. In 2008, 968 children, 14 years and younger, died as occupants in motor vehicle accidents and another 168,000 were injured; many of these fatalities and injuries could have been prevented.

Of the children's deaths attributable to road crashes, 15% were a result of a drinking driver, and more than two-thirds of the children who died were in a vehicle with a drinking driver. In addition to children who are conveyed in vehicles with drinking drivers, many children are not restrained properly in the vehicles. Child restraint use is dependent upon the driver's use of restraints; that is, nearly 40% of children riding with unbelted drivers were also unrestrained in the vehicles. Moreover, nearly 75% of car and booster seats are not used properly, increasing a child's risk of dying in a car accident (CDC, 2010a).

Prevention of injuries to children in motor vehicles can be prevented by the following measures:

1. Children should be put into a child safety seat, which reduces deaths in cars by 71%.
2. Adult drivers should not use alcohol when driving.
3. Booster seats should be used for all children younger than 8 years or less than 4 ft 9 in. tall.
4. Children 12 years and younger should ride in the back seat of a vehicle, which reduces injury by 40%. (CDC, 2010a).

Other Injuries (Poisoning, Alcohol, Burns, and Drowning)

Poisoning

In 2000, U.S. poison control centers reported that 2.2 million poison exposures occurred. More than 90% of these exposures happened in the home, and 52.7% occurred in children younger than age 6 years. The most common exposures of children were ingestion of household products such as cosmetics and personal care products, cleaning substances, pain relievers, foreign objects, and plants. For adults, the most common exposures were pain relievers, sedatives, cleaning substances, antidepressants, and bites or stings (National Center for Injury Prevention and Control, 2002).

Lead poisoning in children is a very preventable problem, yet millions of children are subjected to this exposure. Elevated levels of lead in the blood cause problems in child cognitive growth and development (National Center for Injury Prevention and Control, 2002).

Alcohol-Related Injuries

In the United States, excessive alcohol consumption causes more than 10,000 deaths per year, and between 20% and 30% of the patients seen in all emergency rooms have alcohol-related problems. Half of all alcohol-related deaths are the result of injuries from motor vehicle accidents, falls, fires, drowning, homicides, and suicides. Thirty percent of Americans will at some stage in their lives be involved in an alcohol-related crash (CDC, 2004).

Preventable actions and programs can be developed, such as the following (CDC, 2004):

■ Suspend driver's licenses of those who drive intoxicated.
■ Lower the blood alcohol level concentration for U.S. adults to 0.08% in all states.
■ Establish a "zero tolerance" policy for drivers younger than age 21 who consume alcohol.
■ Establish sobriety check points and have community education about drinking and driving.
■ Raise state and federal alcohol excise taxes.
■ Have compulsory blood alcohol testing for all traffic accidents with injuries.

Burns

Burns are injuries of the skin and sometimes of the underlying tissue, muscle, nerves, and organs. They can be caused by hot liquids, flames, hot surfaces, sunlight or radiation, electricity, or chemicals. Primary prevention is the most effective means of combating burns. Fire-related burns were responsible for 322,000 deaths worldwide in 2002, with the majority of these fatalities occurring in developing countries. More than half of all the worldwide deaths were in Southeast Asia, where 66% of the victims were females.

Prevention of injurious fires can be achieved by taking the following measures (WHO, 2003):

- Enclose open fires, and limit the height of fires in homes, especially in developing countries.
- Promote use of safe stoves and fuels.
- Have housing fire safety regulations and inspections.
- Educate the public.
- Establish and comply with industrial safety regulations.
- Promote the use of smoke detectors, fire alarms, and escape systems for fires.
- Avoid smoking in bed.
- Promote the use of nonflammable children's pajamas.
- Lower the temperature of hot water taps in homes.

In the United States in 2002, four of every five fires occurred in the home, with cooking as the main cause of residential fires and smoking as the second leading cause of fires. Most fire-related deaths are attributable to smoke or toxic gas inhalation. Those persons at greatest risk from fires are children younger than 5 years of age, adults older than 65 years, African Americans and Native Americans, persons living in poverty, those living in rural areas, and those living in substandard housing (National Center for Injury Prevention and Control, 2003).

Fires occur more in the winter season, and more deaths occur among those persons without home smoke detectors (National Center for Injury Prevention and Control, 2003). However, homes in developing nations do not tend to have smoke detectors, and more residents of these countries tend to cook by fire within their homes.

Drowning

Drowning is the process of experiencing respiratory impairment from submersion or immersion in liquid resulting in death or morbidity. One-third of all drownings occur in the western Pacific region of the world, yet Africa has the highest world rate for a specific continent. In 2000, China reported 129,000 drowning deaths, and India had 86,000 drowning deaths. Both China and India have very high drowning death rates and together account for 43% of the world's deaths by drowning. Drowning in younger children generally results from a lapse of supervision by parents or caregivers. Males drown twice as often as females (WHO, 2001).

In 2000, approximately 409,272 people drowned worldwide. Drowning is the second leading cause of unintentional injury deaths, second only to traffic accidents. Ninety percent of all drownings occur in low- and middle-income countries. Large numbers of drowning deaths are associated with major floods, unsafe or overcrowded boats, alcohol use, and epilepsy.

Prevention intervention strategies include the following (WHO, 2001):

- Drain unnecessary accumulations of water in baths, ponds, buckets, and so on.
- Build a fence around swimming pools, ponds, lakes, and rivers, if possible.
- Teach people to swim.
- Train people to perform CPR when needed.

OCCUPATIONAL HEALTH

Work-related injuries and illnesses are events or exposures in the work environment that cause or contribute to a health condition or significantly aggravate a preexisting condition. These illnesses or injuries may result in death, loss of consciousness, time away from work, restricted work activity, or medical treatment beyond first aid. Significant work-related injuries or illnesses may be diagnosed by a physician or other healthcare professional.

Occupational illnesses may consist of any of the following (Bureau of Statistics, 2004):

■ Skin diseases or disorders caused by exposure to chemicals, plants, or other substances. The worker may get problems such as contact dermatitis, eczema, rash, ulcers, chemical burns, or inflammations.

■ Respiratory problems associated with breathing hazardous biological products, chemicals, dust, gases, vapors or fumes. Examples include pneumonitis, pharyngitis, rhinitis, tuberculosis (TB), occupational asthma, toxic inhalation injury, and chronic bronchitis.

■ Poisoning, which can occur from exposure to lead, mercury, arsenic, carbon monoxide, or hydrogen sulfide or other gases.

■ Other occupational illnesses, such as heatstroke, sunstroke, heat exhaustion, freezing, frostbite, decompression sickness, anthrax, HIV, and hepatitis B.

Occupational injuries could include broken bones, cuts, or fractured eardrums. Injuries may result in sick days away from work, a transfer to another location or assignment, or permanent job loss (Bureau of Statistics, 2004).

Workplace injuries, illnesses, and fatalities continue to occur at very high rates worldwide, contributing to the worldwide burden of health. In 2000, there were 2 million work-related deaths, and only 10% to 15% of workers worldwide have basic standard occupational health services. WHO is implementing a global strategy to provide evidence for policy legislation and support of decision makers to estimate the burden of occupational diseases and injuries. It also disseminates information to promote workers' health. In addition, WHO assists countries in developing or upgrading their national occupational health plans and implementing these plans (WHO, 2005a).

The movement of capital and technology and changes in the organization of work have outpaced development of the system for protecting workers' health. Women, in particular, have been affected by these revised employment patterns. They have taken on more jobs and begun to work longer hours, due to the double workload of household work and employment in formal or informal sectors, and they often fill low-skilled, low-paid jobs where rates of union membership are low. The work is often strenuous and monotonous, and they may have little control over the job pace or content. For both men and women who work in agriculture, manufacturing, and mining sectors, there are associated high rates of injury from mechanical, electrical, and physical hazards. In African countries, the injury rates in forestry, electricity production, mining, and manufacturing are all greater than 30 injuries per 1000 workers. In addition to the traditional problems of traumatic injury, respiratory disease, occupational dermatitis, and musculoskeletal injuries, workers are now suffering from asthmatic disorders and psychological stress. By some accounts, the burden of occupational health diseases in southern Africa may be underestimated 50-fold (Loewenson, 2001).

Noise-induced hearing loss is a significant problem among workers in a variety of settings. This hearing loss is irreversible. Workers in heavy industry, factories, coal and iron mining, construction, and airports are among the many employees who can become partially or completely deaf from occupational hazards of noise production at the workplace. In addition, exposure to excessive noise at the workplace may produce hearing problems in the newborns of pregnant women. Workers need to use hearing protection devices at work whenever they are exposed to harmful noise (Azizi, 2010).

In the United States in 2002, 14.6 million workers made visits to physicians' offices for worker's compensation, and in 2003, 40.1 million workers went to hospital emergency rooms for work-related problems (National Institute for Occupational Safety and Health [NIOSH], 2005c). The U.S. Occupational Safety and Health Administration (OSHA) calculates that 6000 employees die each year in the United States from injuries in the workplace, and another 50,000 die from illnesses caused by exposure to workplace hazards. This burden costs U.S. businesses more than $125 billion annually. Within the United States, federal criteria (OSHA standards) used to address worker safety consist of the following requirements (OSHA, 2002):

■ Provide well-maintained tools and equipment.
■ Provide medical examinations.
■ Provide training to OSHA standards.
■ Report accidents or fatalities within 8 hours.
■ Keep records of work-related accidents, injuries, or illnesses.
■ Post prominently employee rights and responsibilities.
■ Provide employees with access to their medical and exposure records.
■ Do not discriminate against employees who exercise their rights under the OSHA Act.
■ Post citations and violations at or near the worksite.
■ Respond to survey requests.

Acute trauma at work is a leading cause of death and disability among workers in the United States; it can occur with a sudden application of force or violence that causes injury or death. In 2000, there were 5915 workplace deaths in the United States from acute traumatic injury. NIOSH is currently conducting research to identify and prioritize the problems with injury surveillance studies, quantify and prioritize risk factors with analytic injury research, identify existing or new strategies to prevent occupational injuries through prevention and control research, and implement the most effective injury control measures with communication and dissemination of recent information and technology (NIOSH, 2005c).

Occupational health is often neglected in developing countries because of competing social, economic, and political issues. Indeed, the majority of developing countries lack the ability to establish new occupational health policies and regulations (Nuwayhid, 2004). In recent decades, however, many U.S. manufacturing jobs have moved to developing countries where labor and taxes are much more economical. Thus much of U.S. manufacturing has made a dramatic shift from well-regulated, high-wage, often unionized plants to low-wage, and unregulated, non-union plants in the developing world. In turn, workers in developing countries have often been subjected to high noise and temperature levels, unguarded machinery, and other safety hazards. In countries such as in Indonesia and Guatemala, limited or no safety regulations exist within occupational settings. Other countries such as China or Mexico may have safety regulations, but they may not be fully enforced. One problem in Mexico, and some other countries, is the nation's level of international indebtedness to private banks, the World Bank, and the International Monetary Fund. This results in a level of national dependency on foreign investment, which discourages the host country from pushing for occupational health policies (Nuwayhid, 2004).

In a study of the occupational health of workers in South Africa, results indicated that the most common work-related problems were musculoskeletal diseases and respiratory diseases. Of the 8 to 9 million employed South Africans, approximately 792,000 consult healthcare services every year for conditions related to or aggravated by their work (Kielkowski, Rees, & Bradshaw, 2004).

Working children in Nigeria often have health-related problems. They tend to work in unregulated industries, especially in the informal sector, such as on the streets, in markets, and in other public places. These working children can be exposed to environmental hazards that result in accidents and communicable diseases (Omokhodion & Omokhodion, 2004).

Municipal solid waste handling and disposal has become a great public health concern for workers employed in this area as well as for the general environment of a community. Because these workers are exposed to many pathogens and toxic substances from the waste itself and from its decomposition, they suffer significant rates of occupational diseases. A study conducted in Athens, Greece, concluded that respiratory diseases are significantly increased in these workers (Athanasiou, Makrynos, & Dounias, 2010).

Safety of Healthcare Providers

Nurses have one of the highest job-related injury rates of any occupation worldwide—even higher than the injury rates in construction and agriculture jobs. In the United States as of 2000, there were 2.7 million registered nurses and 700,000 licensed practical/vocational nurses. Major safety hazards in their work setting include biological and infectious risks, chemical risks, environmental and mechanical risks, physical risks, and psychological risks. Respiratory illnesses and other communicable diseases, such as severe acute respiratory syndrome (SARS) and TB, are examples of some of the health risks that confront healthcare providers on a daily basis. Healthcare workers are also subjected to the risk of blood-borne infections such as hepatitis B, hepatitis C, and HIV. Disinfectants and cold sterilants used to disinfect instruments can cause reactive airway problems and skin problems. Chemotherapy agents also can cause problems for nurses who administer them. Latex gloves can produce allergies, leading to dermatitis or even anaphylaxis. Lifting heavy patients or equipment can induce significant musculoskeletal injuries, especially in the lower back. Psychiatric patients can cause physical and psychological trauma as well (Foley, 2004).

In the United States, needlestick injuries have decreased from 1 million exposures in 1996 to 385,000 exposures in 2000. This decline has resulted from the development and application of OSHA's blood-borne pathogens standard. The success in decreasing needlesticks may largely be attributed to the elimination of needle recapping and the use of safer needle devices, sharps collection boxes, gloves and personal protective gear, and universal precautions. Increased risk for HIV from needlesticks can result from deep injury, visible blood on the device, high viral titer status of the patient (especially a newly infected patient), a patient in the terminal state, and the device being used to access an artery or vein. The U.S. surveillance for healthcare workers identified the following devices as being responsible for most needlestick injuries:

- Hypodermic needles (32%)
- Suture needles (19%)
- Winged steel needles (butterflies) (12%)
- Scalpel blades (7%)
- IV and catheter needles (6%)
- Phlebotomy needles (3%)

The most common circumstances that cause injuries involve hollow-bore needles, which can be filled with blood (Wilburn, 2004).

Job Stress

In the American workplace, 25% of employees view their jobs as the number one stressor in their lives. Job stress can be defined as the harmful physical and emotional responses that happen when the requirements of the job do not match the capabilities or resources or needs of the worker, leading to poor health or injury (**Figure 13-3**).

Job stress is not the same as job challenge, which often energizes workers. Possible causes of job stress include differences in the individual personality and coping styles as well as certain working conditions of the job itself. Certain jobs may be more likely to lead to stress than other jobs. Factors that lead to stress on the job include the following:

■ Heavy workloads
■ Infrequent rest breaks
■ Long working hours
■ Shift work
■ Routine tasks that have little inherent meaning
■ Having little or no participation in decision making
■ Poor communication in the organization
■ Insensitivity to family needs
■ Conflicting or uncertain job expectations
■ Too much responsibility
■ Job insecurity
■ Unpleasant or dangerous physical conditions such as crowding, noise, or air pollution

Healthcare expenses are 50% greater for workers who report high levels of job stress. An increase in job stress may result in an increase in risk for any or several of the following conditions (NIOSH, 2004):

■ Cardiovascular disease
■ Musculoskeletal disorders
■ Psychological disorders
■ Workplace injuries
■ Suicide
■ Cancer
■ Ulcers
■ Impaired immune function

Some employers assume that stressful working conditions are expected and that companies must constantly increase the pressure on workers so that they will remain productive and profitable. In reality, stress in the workplace is often associated with greater absenteeism, tardiness, and job quitting. Low morale, health and job complaints, and employee turnover often are the first signs of job stress. Remedies for job stress include stress management and employee assistant programs to help employees cope with difficult work, personal stressors, and organizational change. Employers also need to work with their employees to solve problems early before they become too large, causing greater damage to workers or the company (NIOSH, 2004).

Reproductive Health

Job stress and workplace hazards can cause problems related to reproductive health in employees. Such reproductive disorders may include developmental disorders, spontaneous abortion, low birth weight, preterm birth, and congenital anomalies. Other potential disorders include reduced fertility, infertility, impotence, and menstrual disorders (NIOSH, 2005c).

FIGURE 13-3

NIOSH Model of Job Stress

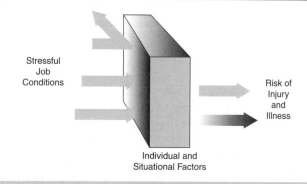

Source: NIOSH, 2004.

Occupational Lung Disease

Occupational lung disease is the most common work-related illness in the United States. Lung diseases attributable to the workplace are usually caused by extended exposure to irritating toxic substances, which in turn trigger acute or chronic respiratory problems. Even a severe single exposure can cause chronic lung problems, and smoking can exacerbate such problems. In the United States in 2002, there were 294,500 newly reported cases of occupational illness in private industry, including 22,000 new respiratory conditions. Workers had a 2.5 per 10,000 rate of developing nonfatal respiratory conditions. These diseases are preventable but often not curable. Prevention measures include improving ventilation, wearing protective equipment, changing work procedures, and educating workers about prevention. Common work-related lung diseases worldwide include the following (American Lung Association, 2005):

■ Occupational lung cancer: Approximately 20% to 30% of males and 5% to 20% of females may have been exposed during their working years to agents that cause lung cancer.

■ Occupational asthma: This is the most common form of occupational lung disease. In the United States, 15% to 23% of new adult asthma cases are caused by occupational exposures. Exposures in the workplace can also exacerbate preexisting asthma.

■ Asbestosis: This progressive disease, which causes scarring on lung tissue, is caused by exposure to asbestos. In the United States, 1.3 million employees in construction and industry have had exposures to asbestos on the job, and in 2002 there were 6343 deaths from asbestosis.

■ Black lung disease (pneumoconiosis): This chronic occupational lung disease is caused by the prolonged breathing of coal mine dust, which contains silica and carbon. Approximately one of every 20 miners studied in the United States has X-ray evidence of black lung disease. For some miners, the disease evolves into a more severe form, called progressive massive fibrosis. Black lung disease is not reversible, and there is no specific treatment for it.

■ Brown lung disease (byssinosis): This is a chronic obstruction of the small airways in the lungs, causing impaired lung function. It occurs when a worker breathes dust from hemp, flax, and cotton processing. In the United States, more than 30,000 textile workers have been affected by this problem.

■ Silicosis: This disease results from exposure to free crystalline silica in mines, in blasting operations, and in stone, clay, and glass manufacturing. The silica causes scar tissue in the lungs and increases the risk of TB.

■ Hypersensitivity pneumonitis—This disease results from exposure to fungus spores from moldy hay, bird droppings, or other organic dust. These contaminants inflame the lung sacs, creates scar tissue, and decreases lung functioning.

All forms of asbestos are now banned in 52 countries worldwide, with safer products having replaced them. Even so, a significant number of countries continue to use, import, and export asbestos. All forms of asbestos cause asbestosis, a fibrotic lung disease, as well as malignant mesothelioma, lung and laryngeal cancers, and potentially ovarian, gastrointestinal, and other cancers. Approximately 125 million people globally are exposed to asbestos in their working environments today, and many more have had such exposures in previous years. NIOSH has estimated that current rate of exposure to asbestos will lead to five deaths from lung cancer and two deaths from asbestosis for every 1000 workers who are exposed to asbestos during their lifetime. In the United Kingdom, at least 3500 people die each year from this exposure, and this number may increase to 5000 deaths per year in the future (LaDou et al., 2010).

In Asian countries such as China and India, there is ongoing use of asbestos despite substantial evidence of a link, even at low-level exposure, between this substance and the development of pulmonary fibrosis and lung cancer in humans. The continued use of this toxic material is allowed by these countries' poor occupational health and safety systems. The International Labour Organisation (ILO) reports that more than 100,000 deaths each year occur from asbestos-related disease. The number of cases is expected to increase and finally peak in 2020, with approximately 1 million deaths from this cause occurring in this time period. Other studies have reported that there is sufficient evidence to infer a causal relationship between particulate air pollution and respiratory deaths in infants up to one month of age (Joshi & Gupta, 2005; Radim, Binkova, Dejmek, & Bobak, 2005).

Occupational Cancer

In Canada, fetal exposure to chemical agents via maternal exposure at work has been shown to have a direct effect on the production of acute lymphoblastic leukemia in children. Exposures to industrial solvents (alkalines and mononuclear aromatic hydrocarbons) in this study ranged from 2 years prior to pregnancy up to the time of birth (Infante-Rivard, Siemiatycki, Lakhani, & Nadon, 2005). In the United States, approximately 20,000 cancer deaths and 40,000 new cases occur each year due to occupational exposures.

When a known or suspected cancer-causing agent is present and types of cancer have been linked with exposure, especially for a group of people working in the same place, it is possible that the particular job or workplace may be polluted with carcinogens. The time from exposure to the carcinogens to diagnosis of cancer may vary. Diagnosis of cancer may occur anytime from less than 1 year up to 15 or 20 years after exposure (NIOSH, 2005a).

Highway Work Zones

Globally, highway workers continue to be at high risk for injuries. Workers in highway construction work zones may potentially be injured by construction vehicles, vehicles and equipment within the work zones, and passing motor vehicles. These individuals often work in conditions of low lighting, low visibility, inclement weather, and congested areas with exposure to high traffic. Within the United States from 1980 to 1995, at least 17,000 construction workers died from injuries on the job (NIOSH, 2005b).

Here are some tips drivers should follow to reduce injuries in highway work zones (U.S. Federal Highway Administration, 2000):

- Dedicate full attention to the roadway.
- Disengage from distracting activities while driving, such as changing radio stations and using mobile phones.
- Pay close attention to merge signs and flaggers, and do not change lanes within the work zone.
- Watch out—not only for workers in the zone, but also for their equipment.
- Turn on vehicle headlights to become more conspicuous to workers and other motorists.

Agricultural Safety

Agriculture is among the world's most hazardous industries. Farmers are at high risk for both fatal and nonfatal injuries. Leading causes of agricultural machinery injuries include entanglements, being pinned or stuck by machinery, falls, and runovers. Nonmachinery injuries include falls from heights, animal-related trauma, and being stuck against objects. Frequently encountered injuries include limb fractures, open wounds, intracranial (head) injuries, and spinal cord injuries, as reported in a Canadian study of hospitalized farm workers (Pickett et al., 2001). Workers in agriculture have double the mortality rates because of inadequate training and safety systems. In the United States, agriculture workers make up only 3% of the workforce, but account for almost 8% of all work-related accidents. In Italy, 9% of the workforce are farm workers, but they account for 28.9% of work-related injuries. In this setting, the greatest dangers are posed by cutting tools and machinery such as tractors and harvesters, and exposure to pesticides and other chemicals (International Labour Organisation [ILO], 1997).

There were approximately 1,859,000 full-time workers in agriculture in the United States in 2003. In addition, approximately 1.08 million children and adolescents younger than 20 years of age resided on the farms, and 593,000 were performing work on the farm. Some 103 children are killed annually on U.S. farms, and 40% of these deaths are work related. In 2001, 22,600 children were injured on farms. Each year, 110 farm workers in the United States are crushed to death by tractor rollovers. Every day, about 228 farm workers have work-related injuries, and 5% of these injuries are permanent (Frank, McKnight, Kirkhorn & Gunderson, 2004).

In 1990, the U.S. Congress developed extensive agricultural safety and health programs to address the high risk of injuries and preventable deaths in these work environments. These programs conduct research and make recommendations for prevention of injuries and death from pesticide exposure, lung disease, musculoskeletal disorders, hearing loss, and stress (Frank, McKnight, Kirkhorn, & Gunderson, 2004).

STUDY QUESTIONS

1. How do culture, politics, geography, and economics play roles in violence within a community?
2. Why do populations in developing countries as compared to developed countries have higher death rates from road traffic accidents?
3. What is the relationship between domestic violence and school violence for an individual child?
4. What are some occupational health hazards related to mining and manufacturing?
5. Explain why farming can be hazardous to a person's health.
6. How do "honor" killings and female genital mutilation relate to culture and health for women?

CASE STUDY: WOMEN AND SUICIDE IN CHINA

Background

China accounts for 26% of all suicides worldwide. Suicide is the fifth leading cause of death in the country overall, and is the leading cause of death for young women in the country. Suicide is four to five times more frequent in rural settings than urban ones. Suicide rates are higher among women than among men in China (WHO, 2009b).

Situation

Zhang Xihuan, a 45-year-old woman with hepatitis B, was building a new home and needed to borrow extra money for the project. Her debt from her out-of-pocket health expenditures, as well as from her house loan, gave her great anxiety and depression. The shame of not being able to pay her bills and owing money caused her to make a quick decision to end her life by drinking a bottled pesticide. The cultural shame of owing money and the overwhelming burden of her disease both contributed to her decision to take her life.

Reference

WHO, 2009b.

Case Study Questions

1. Explain the contributing factors in Mrs. Zhang's behavior.
2. Which types of political, social, economic, and cultural-based interventions are needed to decrease this sort of violence in China?
3. Why are rural women more prone to suicide than urban men?
4. Why is China a higher risk area for suicide than other areas of the world?

REFERENCES

American Lung Association. (2005). Occupational lung disease fact sheet. Retrieved from http://www .lungusa.org/site/pp.as[?c=dv:IL9O0E&b=35334

Athanasiou, M., Makrynos, G., & Dounias, G. (2010). Respiratory health of municipal solid waste workers. *Occupational Medicine* [Advance access publication on September 5, 2010]. doi: 10.1093/occmed/ Kqq127

Azizi, M. H. (2010). Occupational noise-induced hearing loss. *The International Journal of Occupational and Environmental Medicine 1*(3), 118–123.

Bent-Goodley, T. (2004). Perceptions of domestic violence: A dialogue with African American women. *Health and Social Work, 29*(4), 307–316.

Brener, N., Lowry, R., & Barrios, L. (2005). Violence-related behaviors among high school students—United States, 1991–2003. *Journal of School Health, 75*(3), 81–85.

Bullying statistics/cyber bullying statistics/school bullying. (n.d.). Retrieved from http//www.how-to-stop-bullying.com/bullyingstatistics.html

Bureau of Statistics. (2004). Occupational safety and health definitions. Retrieved from http://www.bls .gov/iif/oshdef.htm

Centers for Disease Control and Prevention (CDC). (2004). Preventing alcohol-related injuries. Retrieved from http://www.cdc.gov/program

Centers for Disease Control and Prevention (CDC). (2010a). Child passenger safety: Fact sheet. Retrieved from http://www.cdc.gov/MotorVehicleSfety/Child_Passenger_Safety/CPS-Factsheet.html

Centers for Disease Control and Prevention (CDC). (2010b). Elder maltreatment fact sheet. Retrieved from http://www.cdc.gov/violenceprevention

Centers for Disease Control and Prevention (CDC). (2010c). Understanding school violence: Fact sheet. Retrieved from http://www.cdc.gov/ViolencePrevention/pdf/SchoolViolence_FactSheet-a.pdf

Centers for Disease Control and Prevention (CDC). (2010d). World report on violence and health. Retrieved from http://www.cdc.gov/violenceprevention

Ezechi, O. C., Kalu, B., Ezechi, L. O., Nwokoro, C., Ndububa, V., & Okeke, G. C. E. (2004). Prevalence and pattern of domestic violence against pregnant Nigerian women. *Journal of Obstetrics and Gynecology, 24*(6), 652–656.

Flinck, A., Paavilainen, E., & Astedt-Kurki, P. (2005). Survival of intimate partner violence as experienced by women. *Journal of Clinical Nursing, 14*, 383–393.

Foley, M. (2004). Caring for those who care: A tribute to nurses and their safety. *Online Journal of Issues in Nursing, 9*(3), 91–101.

Frank, A., McKnight, R., Kirkhorn, S., & Gunderson, P. (2004). Issues of agricultural safety and health. *Annual Review of Public Health, 25*, 225–245.

Gostin, L., Sapssin, J., Teret, S., Burris, S., Mair, J., Hodge, J., & Vernick, J. (2002). The model state emergency health powers act: Planning for and response to bioterrorism and naturally occurring infectious diseases. *Journal of the American Medical Association, 288*(5), 622–628.

Gradus, J. (2007). Epidemiology of PTSD. National Center for PTSD, U.S. Department of Veteran Affairs. Retrieved from http://www.ptsd.va.gov/professional/pages/epidemiological-facts-ptsd.asp

Guerro, R. (2002). Violence is a health issue. *Bulletin of the World Health Organization, 80*(10), 767.

Hijar, M., Vazquez-Vela, E., & Arreola-Risa, C. (2002). Pedestrian traffic injuries in Mexico: A country update. *Injury Control and Safety Promotion, 10*(1–2), 37–43.

Hofman, K., Primack, A., Keusch, G., & Hrynkow, S. (2005). Addressing the growing burden of trauma and injury in low- and middle-income countries. *American Journal of Public Health, 95*(1), 13–17.

Hyder, A. (2004). Road safety is no accident: A call for global action. *Bulletin of the World Health Organization, 82*(4), 240–240A.

Hyder, A., & Peek-Asa, C. (2010). The global burden of unintentional injuries and an agenda for progress. *Epidemiologic Review, 32*, 110–120.

Infante-Rivard, C., Siemiatycki, J., Lakhani, R., & Nadon, L. (2005). Maternal exposure to occupational solvents and childhood leukemia. *Environmental Health Perspectives, 113*(6), 787–792.

International Labour Organisation (ILO). (1997). ILO warns on farm safety. Retrieved from http://ilo.org/public/English/bureau/inf/pr/1997/23.htm

Joshi, T., & Gupta, R. (2005). Asbestos in developing countries: Magnitude of risk and its practical implications. *Human and Ecological Risk Assessment, 11*, 239–247.

Khosla, A., Dua, D., Devi, L., & Sud, S. (2005). Domestic violence in pregnancy in North Indian women. *Indian Journal of Medical Science, 59*(5), 195–199.

Kielkowski, D., Rees, D., & Bradshaw, D. (2004). Burden of occupational morbidity in South Africa: Two large field surveys of self-reported work-related and work-aggravated disease. *South African Journal of Science, 100*, 399–402.

A killing sets honor above love. (2010, November 21). *The New York Times*, p. 9.

Koenig, M., Lutalo, T., Zhao, F., Nalugoda, F., Wab-Wire-Mangen, F., Kiwanuka, N., . . . Gray, R. (2003). Domestic violence in rural Uganda: Evidence from a community-based study. *Bulletin of the World Health Organization, 81*, 53–60.

Krug, E. G., Dahlberg, L. L., Mercy, J. A., Zwi, A. B., & Lozano, R. (2002). Summary. In *World report on violence and health* (pp. 1–37). Geneva, Switzerland: World Health Organization.

LaDou, J., Castleman, B., Frank, A., Gochfeld, M., Greenberg, M., Huff, J., . . . Watterson, A. (2010). The case for global ban on asbestos. *Environmental Health Perspectives, 118*(7), 897–901.

Leppaniemi, A. K. (2004). Global trends in trauma. *Trauma, 6,* 193–203.

Loewenberg, S. (2005). Domestic violence in Spain. *Lancet, 365,* 464.

Loewenson, R. (2001). Globalization and occupational health: A perspective from southern Africa. *Bulletin of the World Health Organization, 79*(9), 863–868.

Mercy, J., Krugberg, E. G., Dahlberg, L., & Zwi, A. (2003). Violence and health: The United States in a global perspective. *American Journal of Public Health, 92*(12), 256–261.

Mock, C., Joshipura, M., & Goosen, J. (2004). Global strengthening of care for the injured. *Bulletin of the World Health Organization, 82*(4), 241.

Mock, C., Quansah, R., Krishnan, R., Arreola-Risa, C., & Rivara, F. (2004). Strengthening the prevention and care of injuries worldwide. *Lancet, 363,* 2172–2179.

National Center for Injury Prevention and Control. (2002). Poisonings: Fact sheet. Retrieved from http://www.cdc.gov/ncipc/factsheets/poisoning.htm

National Center for Injury Prevention and Control. (2003). Fires deaths and injuries: Fact sheet. Retrieved from http://www.cdc.gov/ncipc/factsheets/fire.htm

National Center for Injury Prevention and Control. (2004a). Intimate partner violence: Fact sheet. Retrieved from http://www.cdc.gov/ncipc/factsheets/ipvfacts.htm

National Center for Injury Prevention and Control. (2004b). Older adult drivers: Fact sheet. Retrieved from http://www.cdc.gov/ncipc/factsheets/older.htm

National Center for Injury Prevention and Control. (2004c). Teen drivers: Fact sheet. Retrieved from http://www.cdc.gov/ncipc/factsheets/teenmvh.htm

National Center for Injury Prevention and Control. (2005a). Child maltreatment: Fact sheet. Retrieved from http://www.cdc.gov/ncipc/factsheets/cmfacts.htm

National Center for Injury Prevention and Control. (2005b). Sexual violence: Fact sheet. Retrieved from http://www.cdc.gov/ncipc/factsheets/svfacts.htm

National Institute for Occupational Safety and Health (NIOSH). (2004). Stress at work. Retrieved from http://www.cdc.gov/niosh/docs/99-101/

National Institute for Occupational Safety and Health (NIOSH). (2005a). Occupational cancer. Retrieved from http://www.cdc.gov/niosh/topics/cancer

National Institute for Occupational Safety and Health (NIOSH). (2005b). Occupational: Highway work zones. Retrieved from http://www.cdc.gov/niosh/topics/highwayworkzones/default.html

National Institute for Occupational Safety and Health (NIOSH). (2005c). Occupational: Traumatic occupational injuries. Retrieved from http://www.cdc.gov/niosh/injury

NationMaster. (2010). Crime statistics: Murders per capita most recent by country. Retrieved from http://www.nationmaster.com/graph/cri_mur;erca;-crime-murders-per-capita

A new vision for human security. (2003). *Lancet, 361*(9370), 1665.

Nuwayhid, I. (2004). Occupational health research in developing countries: A partner for social justice. *American Journal of Public Health, 94*(11), 1916–1921.

Occupational Safety and Health Administration (OSHA). (2002). OSHA fact sheet. Retrieved from http://www.osha.gov

Omokhodion, F., & Omokhodion, S. (2004). Health status of working and nonworking school children in Ibadan, Nigeria. *Annals of Tropical Paediatrics, 24,* 175–178.

Pickett, W., Hartling, L., Dimich-Ward, H., Guernsey, J. R., Hagel, L., Voaklander, D. C., & Brison, R. J. (2001). Surveillance of hospitalized farm injuries in Canada. *Injury Prevention, 7,* 123–128.

Radim, R., Binkova, B., Dejmek, J., & Bobak, M. (2005). Ambient air pollution and pregnancy outcomes: A review of the literature. *Environmental Health Perspectives, 113*(4), 375–382.

Reijneveld, S., Brugman, E., Sing, R., & Verloove-Vanhorick, S. (2004). Infant crying and abuse. *Lancet, 364,* 1340–1342.

Silcock, D. (2003). Preventing death and injury on the world's roads. *Transport Reviews, 23*(3), 263–273.

United Nations. (2005). *Global campaign for violence prevention.* New York, NY: Author.

U.S. Federal Highway Administration. (2000). National work zone safety awareness. Retrieved from http://safety.fhwa.dot.gov/wz/index.htm

Vehicular manslaughter: The global epidemic of traffic deaths. (2004). *Environmental Health Perspectives, 112*(11), 629–631.

Waldman, R. (2005, Spring). Public health in war. *Harvard International Review,* 1283–1284.

Watkins, K., & Sridhar, D. (2009). *Road traffic injuries: The hidden development crisis: Making roads safe.* First Ministerial Conference on Road Safety. Moscow.

Watts, C., & Mayhew, S. (2004). Reproductive health services and intimate partner violence: Shaping a pragmatic response in sub-Saharan Africa. *International Family Planning, 30*(4), 207–213.

Wilburn, S. (2004). Needlestick and sharps injury prevention. *Online Journal of Issues of Nursing, 9*(3). Retrieved from http://web16.epnet.com/citation.asp?tb=1&_ug=sid+5/co5B185%2D3FD4%2D4CIA%2D

World Health Organization (WHO). (2001). Injuries and violence prevention: Facts about drowning. Retrieved from http://www.who.int/entity/violence_injury_prevention/publications/other_injury/en/drowning_factsheet.pdf

World Health Organization (WHO). (2002). Global burden of disease estimates—2002 rev. Retrieved from http://www.who.int/healthinfo/global_burden_disease/en/index.html

World Health Organization (WHO). (2003). Injuries and violence prevention: Facts about burns. Retrieved from http://www.who.int/entity/violence_injury_prevention/publications/other_injury/en/burns_factsheet.pdf

World Health Organization (WHO). (2004). Road safety: A public health issue. Retrieved from http://www.who.int/features/2004/road_safety/en

World Health Organization (WHO). (2005a). The injury chartbook: A graphical overview of the global burden of injuries. Retrieved from http://www.who.int/violence_injury_prevention/publications/other_injury/chartb/en

World Health Organization (WHO). (2005b). *Multi-country study on women's health and domestic violence against women* (pp. 1–28). Geneva, Switzerland: Author.

World Health Organization (WHO). (2009a). *Global status report on road safety* (pp. 1–43). Geneva, Switzerland: Author.

World Health Organization (WHO). (2009b). Women and suicide in rural China. *Bulletin of the WHO.* 87(12). 885–964.

Xu, X., Zhu, F., O'Campo, P., Koenig, M., Mock, V., & Campbell, J. (2005). Prevalence and risk factors of intimate partner violence in China. *American Journal of Public Health, 95*(1), 78–85.

Zhang, J., Norton, R., Tang, K. C., Lo, S., Zhuo, J., & Wenkui, G. (2004). Motorcycle ownership and injury in China. *Injury Control and Safety Promotion, 11*(3), 159–163.

*For a full suite of assignments and additional learning activities, use the access code located in the front of your book to visit this exclusive website: **http://go.jblearning.com/holtz**. If you do not have an access code, you can obtain one at the site.*

14

Global Perspectives on Nutrition

Carol Holtz
Kathy Plitnick
Marvin Friedman

> *"To live a life without malnutrition is a human right. The persistence of malnutrition, especially among children and mothers in this world of plenty is immoral. Nutrition improvement anywhere in the world is not a charity but a societal, household, and individual right. It is the world community's responsibility to find effective ways and means to invest for better livelihood and to avoid future unnecessary social and economic burdens. With collective efforts at international, national, and community levels, ending malnutrition is both a credible and achievable goal."*
>
> James et al., 2000

OBJECTIVES

After completing this chapter, the reader will be able to:

1. Compare and contrast good and poor nutrition in developed and developing nations.
2. Discuss the "human right to food."
3. List the nutritional challenges for the twenty-first century.
4. Discuss types of nutritional deficiencies, including iron-deficiency anemia and niacin, vitamin A, vitamin B, iodine, and zinc micronutrient deficiencies.
5. Explain protein–energy malnutrition.
6. Discuss obesity in developing and developed countries.
7. Discuss the role of fiber in good nutrition.
8. Compare and contrast food safety and security worldwide in developed and developing countries.
9. Discuss the worldwide relationship between poverty and nutrition levels.
10. Define and discuss food emergencies.

11. Compare and contrast nutritional challenges among developed and developing countries.
12. Describe the worldwide nutritional challenges of childbearing women.
13. Discuss the worldwide challenges of nutrition in older adults.
14. Discuss the clinical examples regarding nutritional challenges.

INTRODUCTION

Good nutrition is the basis for health and for infant and children's growth and development. In addition, it is correlated to a more effective immune system and reduction of a number of diseases. In considering nutritional status, two classes of nutrients are distinguished: macronutrients and micronutrients. Macronutrients make up the bulk of the diet and consist of fats, starches, and protein (amino acids); they primarily provide energy. Micronutrients are frequently enzyme cofactors or catalyze other reactions; they are required in much smaller amounts than macronutrients.

The primary source of energy in the U.S. and European diet is the potato, while Latin Americans prefer beans, and Asians prefer rice. Noodles and rice are the major global macronutrients. The selection of macronutrients is as much cultural as economic. When Europeans migrate from their native countries, they continue to prefer potatoes.

Traditionally the World Health Organization (WHO) focused on the issue of deficiencies induced by disease as part of its global outreach efforts. Now included in the agenda for both developing and developed countries, however, is the improvement of global nutrition related to overnutrition and, most notably, obesity. Worldwide, obesity and malnutrition are leading causes of such chronic diseases as cardiovascular disease, cancer, hypertension, and diabetes. Deficiency diseases include scurvy, a vitamin C deficiency; blindness that results from vitamin A deficiency; kwashiorkor, a protein deficiency; goiter, an iodine deficiency; pellagra, a niacin deficiency; anemia that results from an iron deficiency; vitamin B_{12}, or folic acid, deficiency; and many more. Significant morbidity, mortality, and economic costs are associated with these kinds of nutritional imbalances (WHO, 2006a).

Malnutrition is considered to be the world's leading threat to life and health today. The following is a common scenario: An infant has marginal macronutrient intake, usually as a result of maternal milk supply drawing to an end. The infant then develops diarrhea from an intestinal parasite or other infectious agent. This disease is promoted by low immune response from macronutrient deficiency. Unable to stop the consequent water/sodium imbalance, the infant dies of dehydration. Even if the infant survives, the long-term consequences of this bout with disease can be catastrophic.

It is difficult to imagine living on less than $1 per day, yet 1.2 billion people in the world do so. With this limited amount of income, it is very difficult to maintain a healthy and adequate diet. Every day 24,000 people worldwide die from hunger and malnutrition, the majority of whom are young children as described in the preceding scenario. In addition to macronutrient deficiency, nearly 33% of the world suffers from micronutrient malnutrition, which results in the following problems:

■ Decreased mental and physical development
■ Poor pregnancy outcomes
■ Decreased work capacity for adults
■ Increased illness
■ Premature death
■ Diseases
■ Deficiencies in zinc, leading to immune deficiency, growth retardation, and diarrhea
■ Bone loss
■ Blindness

(WHO, 2006a)

FREEDOM FROM HUNGER: A HUMAN RIGHT

In the International Covenant on Economic, Social and Cultural Rights (ICESCR), freedom from hunger is described as a human right. More specifically it was agreed, "The right to food is a human right inherent in all people, to have regular permanent and unrestricted access, either directly or by means of financial purchases, to have quantitatively and qualitatively adequate and sufficient food corresponding to the cultural traditions of people to which the consumer belongs, is one that ensures a physical and mental, individual and collective fulfilling and dignified life free of fear" (United Nations, 1999, p. 3). The signatory parties to this agreement concluded that the right to adequate food is linked to the inherent dignity of the human person. Furthermore, "the right to adequate food is realized with every man, woman and child, alone or in community with others, having physical access at all times to adequate food or means for its procurement" (United Nations, 1999, p. 3).

In addition, a human rights framework was addressed by the Universal Declaration of Human Rights, which was adopted by the United Nations in 1948. According to this document, to fulfill the right to food is to not interfere with one's ability to acquire food. To protect the right to food is to make sure that others do not interfere with the right to food. The right to food and the right to be free from hunger are outlined in article 25 of the Universal Declaration of Human Rights, which describes a minimum standard of living that includes the right to housing, clothing, health care, and social services. To fulfill the right to food, it is necessary to facilitate social and economic environments that foster human development and to provide food to people in an emergency or in circumstances when they are unable to provide for food by themselves (United Nations, 1999).

Today, not only are there problems from lack of quantity and quality of food to satisfy the dietary needs of individuals—that is, food that is both free from adverse substances and acceptable—but there are also worldwide issues with overnutrition (obesity). Overweight or obesity are prevalent global problems, and increasing numbers from emerging or transition economy nations are now facing health challenges related to these issues similar to the problems encountered by the developed world. Overweight and obesity in both developed and developing nations are creating chronic health problems and costing these countries' economies hundreds of millions of dollars (Centers for Disease Control and Prevention [CDC], 2003; WHO, 2006a). This is an even more extreme problem among individuals migrating from global areas where food is not available to developed countries where overeating is easy.

On the other side of this equation, WHO estimates that malnutrition is a contributing factor in at least 49% of the world's total death burden. Half of all malnourished children and a large proportion of malnourished adult women reside in Bangladesh, India, and Pakistan, and in many other countries in Africa and middle Asia (Underwood, 2002).

WHO's Nutrition for Health Development Department established major goals at the World Summit for Children in 1990 and the International Conference on Nutrition in 1992, which with some modification in 2003, were still relevant in 2012. They include the elimination of the following:

- Famine and related deaths
- Starvation and nutritional deficiency diseases caused by natural and human-made disasters
- Iodine and vitamin A deficiency

In addition, these goals called for reduction of the following:

- Starvation and widespread hunger
- Undernutrition, especially in women, children, and the aged
- Other micronutrient deficiencies, such as iron deficiency
- Diet-related communicable and noncommunicable diseases
- Barriers to breastfeeding
- Poor sanitation, hygiene, and unclean drinking water

Strategies for implementing these goals include the following measures (WHO, 2006a):

- Developing new nutritional health policies and programs
- Improving household food security
- Improving food quality and safety
- Preventing and treating infectious diseases
- Promoting breastfeeding
- Promoting diets with micronutrient supplements
- Assessing and monitoring nutritional programs

Stunting and low body weight problems are due to persistent undernutrition. In 2002, there were 180 million stunted children and 150 million underweight children in the world. Ninety million of these underweight children live in Asia. During the past two decades, progress in remedying this problem has been made in Asia, but has not yet occurred in sub-Saharan Africa (*Merck Manual,* 2002).

The combination of food distribution imbalance, rising fuel costs, and the global financial crisis beginning in 2007 has had negative impacts on global nutrition. The question is how long these crises will last and how they will affect food availability. Of particular interest is the U.S. Environmental Protection Agency's (USEPA's) and Brazilian government's requirement that a percentage of corn production be allocated for ethanol production, which will likely result in a substantial increase in food and livestock costs (USEPA, 2010).

NUTRITIONAL CHALLENGES FOR THE TWENTY-FIRST CENTURY

The following statistics highlight some of the challenges related to nutrition facing both developed and developing countries (Dangour & Uauy, 2006):

1. Thirty million infants (representing 25% of all newborns) are born each year in developing countries with intrauterine growth retardation (IUR) as a result of maternal malnutrition.
2. There are 150 million underweight preschool children and almost 200 million stunted children worldwide.
3. High proportions of pregnant women in Asia and Africa are undernourished.
4. Approximately 243 million adults in developing countries are severely undernourished.
5. Maternal malnutrition causes anemia during pregnancy, may cause maternal mortality, and causes poor fetal brain development, leading to decreased cognitive functioning in infants and children.
6. The prevalence of severe vitamin A deficiency is declining, yet this condition continues to affect 140 to 250 million preschool children in developing countries, where it is associated with high rates of morbidity and mortality.
7. Maternal and child malnutrition is linked to increased incidence of noncommunicable diseases such as diabetes, heart disease, some forms of cancer, and hypertension.
8. Overweight and obesity are increasing worldwide in both developing and developed countries. Obesity in adults—especially abdominal obesity—is linked to early infant and childhood malnutrition.
9. There is an increase in emergency nutrition problems due to food challenges among refugees and internally displaced persons.
10. Transmission and progression rates of HIV/AIDS are higher in malnourished populations, which is particularly problematic in sub-Saharan Africa.
11. Zinc deficiency is a worldwide problem specifically targeting pregnant women and children, and is associated with higher rates of pulmonary diseases and diarrhea.
12. The world's population is collectively consuming more saturated fats, sugars, salt, and highly dense, processed low-fiber foods.
13. Worldwide, people are living longer with chronic diseases and many nutritional challenges.

TYPES OF NUTRITIONAL CHALLENGES

Micronutrient Deficiencies

Micronutrient deficiencies are widespread among 2 billion people worldwide. These are silent epidemics of vitamin and mineral deficiencies affecting people globally of all genders, races, and geographic locations. Not only do they cause specific diseases, but they also exacerbate infectious and chronic diseases, thereby affecting morbidity, mortality, and quality of life. Deficiencies related to chronic diseases include osteoporosis, osteomalacia, thyroid deficiency, colorectal cancer, and cardiovascular disease. Consumption of folic acid and fortified foods by pregnant women is well known to prevent many congenital malformations and cognitive impairments. Deficiencies in micronutrients increase the severity of illnesses such as HIV/AIDS and tuberculosis (Tulchinsky, 2010).

Micronutrient deficiencies include deficiencies of iron, iodine, and vitamin A as well as zinc, folate, and other B vitamins. In many settings, more than one micronutrient deficiency exists, which necessitates interventions that address multiple micronutrient deficiencies. Areas of prevalence are especially extensive in Southeast Asia and sub-Saharan Africa. These deficiencies are mainly caused by inadequate food intake, poor quality of foods, poor bioavailability because of inhibitors, types of preparation, and presence of infections, especially as a result of poor water quality (Ramakrishnan, 2002).

Iron-Deficiency Anemia

Iron deficiency is the most widespread nutrient deficiency in the world, affecting more than 2 billion people. It is best known in causing anemia, a condition in which the body manufactures an inadequate number of red blood cells. Although iron deficiency is the main cause of anemia, other causes may be related to nutrient deficiencies such as vitamin B_{12} and folic acid, as well as non-nutritional causes such as malaria, genetic abnormalities (thalassemia), and chronic disease. Iron deficiency, which is diagnosed based on low hemoglobin or hematocrit levels, develops over time. Populations especially vulnerable to iron-deficiency anemia are young children and women of childbearing age.

When a person experiences decreased numbers of red blood cells, which normally carry oxygen throughout the body, the individual has a decreased oxygen level and develops symptoms of weakness and fatigue. This problem has profound effects on infants and children by limiting learning capacity and impairing the immune system.

Within the region of Southeast Asia, millions of people are affected by this problem, mainly adolescent girls and childbearing-age women (due to menstruation) and young children. Pregnant women with iron-deficiency anemia are more likely to die in childbirth as a result of postpartum hemorrhage, or to have their fetus or newborn die as a result of decreased oxygen levels in the tissues. Research indicates that children who have this problem have a 5- to 7-point reduction in IQ score (Gleason, 2002).

The main contributing factors to iron-deficiency anemia include inadequate intake of iron, poor iron availability from cereal-based diets, and high intestinal worm infections. According to WHO, iron-deficiency anemia is second only to tuberculosis as the world's most prevalent and costly health problem. In India and parts of Africa, more than 80% of the population has this condition (Ramakrishnan, 2002; Ulrich, 2005; WHO, 2004).

WHO (2004) estimates that anemia affects 47.4% of the global population younger than the age of 5, 25.4% of school-age children, 30.2% of nonpregnant women, 41.8% of pregnant women, 12.7% of men, and 23.9% of the elderly. Fifty percent of all cases of anemia worldwide are due to iron deficiency.

Iron supplementation improves iron status during pregnancy and the postpartum period, and infants born to mothers who take iron during pregnancy benefit by being protected from iron-deficiency anemia. Iron-deficiency disorders in pregnant women cause fetal and infant thyroid function alterations.

Countries such as China, Pakistan, India, Indonesia, and Ethiopia continue to have insufficient dietary iron intake (Boy et al., 2009).

Signs and symptoms of iron-deficiency anemia include pallor, fatigue, and weakness. Adaptation occurs such that the disease may go unrecognized for a long period of time. In severe cases, difficulty in breathing may occur. In addition, unusual obsessive cravings, know as pica, may be evident; dirt, white clay, or ice may be consumed. Also, hair loss and lightheadedness may be evident. Other symptoms may include mouth ulcers, sleepiness, constipation, tinnitus (ringing in the ears), fainting, depression, missed menstrual cycle, heavy menstrual cycle, itching, or poor appetite (National Institutes of Health [NIH], 2010).

The presence of overweight among children and adolescents has been increasing at a rapid rate in the United States and throughout the world. In the United States, more than 1 in 7 children is overweight. Results from the CDC's research study of 9698 U.S. children (2–16 years of age), conducted from 1988 to 1994, demonstrated that iron-deficiency anemia may be linked to overweight and obesity in children. The researchers who conducted this study concluded that children and adolescents who were overweight or at risk for overweight were almost twice as likely to be iron deficient than normal-weight children (Nead, Halterman, Kaczorowski, Auinger, & Weitzman, 2004). It is important to recognize that body weight alone is not a good index of nutritional status, however, as water retention from poor kidney function can result in misleading body weights.

The 2000 Global Burden of Disease Project, a study funded by WHO and the World Bank, ranked iron deficiency ninth among the risk factors that contribute to human death and disability. This deficiency affects approximately one-fifth of the world's population, or 1.4 billion people. In the United States since the 1940s, iron-fortified foods, most notably bread, have been widely adopted as a means to prevent iron deficiency (WHO, 2004).

Adding micronutrients to such products such as table salt has been practiced for many years to replenish deficient levels of iodine; a form of table salt with iron fortification has also been manufactured to help combat iron-related anemia. Researchers working in North Africa have demonstrated that iron added to salt causes the color to change to a yellow brown, and the salt may also sometimes have a rusty taste. Working in northern Morocco, researchers gave this new product to 75 children for 10 months. Results indicate that the children receiving the fortified salt had a reduction in anemia rates in the range of 5–30% (Harder, 2004). Iron is found primarily in meats, with liver being the best source of iron.

Niacin Deficiency (Pellagra)

Pellagra, also known as "black tongue," is found among populations who consume corn as the main staple of their diet, a practice often seen in Mexico, Northern Italy, and South America. Because corn is deficient in the amino acid tryptophan, and because tryptophan is required for biosynthesis of niacin, these populations are particularly sensitive to niacin deficiency. Signs of niacin deficiency include photosensitivity, red skin lesions, and dementia, and the condition can lead to mortality. Pellagra is easily treated with niacin supplements. Genetically engineered maize that has a high tryptophan content and does not cause pellagra is also available; a Nobel Prize was awarded for the development of this bioagricultural product.

Vitamin A Deficiency

Vitamin A deficiency (VAD) occurs because of inadequate storage of vitamin A, caused by either inadequate intake of food rich in vitamin A or severe and repeated illnesses. Approximately 2 billion people in the world are at risk for vitamin A deficiency along with iodine or iron deficiencies. This problem is especially prevalent in Southeast Asia and sub-Saharan Africa, and pregnant women and young children are at greatest risk. In many of these areas, more than one micronutrient deficiency exists, so that interventions must address multiple micronutrient deficiencies. Severe vitamin A deficiency is usually associated with signs of night blindness and decreased levels of vitamin A (less than 0.35/dL). Serum retinol is the biochemical indicator of vitamin A status (Ramakrishnan, 2002). Vitamin A is available from raw, colored foods such as carrots or tomatoes.

Vitamin A deficiency most commonly occurs in regions around the equator, and in poor urban and semi-urban settings. It causes people to have more frequent infections, and is associated with high infant mortality rates, usually exceeding 70 per 1000 live births. Basic interventions include improved diet, food fortification, and vitamin supplementation (Boy et al., 2009).

Vitamin D Deficiency

This nutritional deficiency is unique among vitamin deficiencies. Vitamin D is required for the absorption of calcium and translocation to bones and teeth. Deficiency of this micronutrient in children results in rickets, which is failure of the long bones to mature. In adults, it causes osteoporosis (fragile bones), and osteomalacia (bone thinning). Chronic vitamin D deficiency eventually also causes dermal lesions.

What makes this vitamin unique is that the body easily produces a large amount of vitamin D from the reaction of sunlight and sterol (a cholesterol derivative). In the absence of sunlight, the body cannot get enough vitamin D from diet alone. This disease was first seen among nuns in Europe who were always completely covered by their habits and generally worked inside. Now, vitamin D is added to milk, which is the major source of dietary calcium.

Rickets is a disease widely recognized in many developing countries today. Its origin was identified only in the early part of the twentieth century with the discovery of vitamin D, and the advent of ultraviolet light irradiation therapy meant that rickets could be eradicated. Today rickets is still found in some breastfed African American infants, and in Europe it is often found in children of recent immigrants from India, Pakistan and Bangladesh, North Africa, and the Middle East. In the Middle East, vitamin D deficiency and rickets continue to be problems despite abundant all-year sunshine. Infants, adolescent females, and pregnant women are particularly at risk, especially in areas where social and religious customs prevent adequate sunlight exposure of pregnant women and their adolescent daughters (Pettifor, 2008).

Iodine-Deficiency Disorder

Iodine deficiency is the leading cause of preventable brain damage in childhood. Iodine deficiency is found in populations with no access to saltwater fish (seawater is high in iodine) or as a result of consuming vegetables such as broccoli that bind with iodine and make iodine unavailable for absorption. During the last decade, worldwide improvement in the prevalence of this micronutrient deficiency has been realized through low-cost prevention measures such as the iodization of salt.

Under normal conditions the body has small amounts of iodine, housed mainly in the thyroid gland and utilized for the synthesis of thyroid hormones. Iodine deficiency causes hypothyroidism (goiter), which can lead to the syndrome called iodine-deficiency disorder (IDD). In developed countries, iodine intake correlates with obesity and basal metabolic rate because the hormone requiring iodine, thyroxin, regulates basal metabolism rate. Symptoms of IDD are listed in **Table 14-1**.

Worldwide data on urinary iodine levels and goiter are monitored via the WHO's Global Database on Iodine Deficiency Disorders. These disorders comprise deficiencies resulting from decreased intake of the element iodine, which is essential in minute amounts for normal growth and development. Thyroid failure causing irreversible brain damage can occur if the iodine deficiency occurs in the period ranging from fetal life to 3 months after birth. Iodine deficiency causes a decreased mean IQ loss of 13.5 points in children (Andersson, Takkouche, Egli, & de Benoist, 2003).

TABLE 14-1

Iodine-Deficiency Disorders at Various Stages of Development

Developmental Stage	Disorders
Fetus	Abortion (miscarriage)
	Stillbirth
	Congenital abnormalities
	Increased perinatal mortality
Neonate	Neonatal goiter
	Neonatal hypothyroidism
	Mental retardation
Child and adolescent	Goiter
	Hypothyroidism
	Decreased mental function
	Impaired physical development
Adult	Goiter and complications
	Hypothyroidism
	Impaired mental function
	Spontaneous hyperthyroidism in the elderly
	Iodine-induced hyperthyroidism

Source: Adapted from Andersson, Takkouche, Egli, & de Benoist, 2003.

During the past century, iodine fortification has been implemented into foods such as bread, milk, water, and salt. Salt has been the most commonly fortified product because it is widely used and available. WHO recommends the addition of 20–40 mg of iodine per kilogram of salt to meet daily iodine requirements, assuming that the average consumption is 10 g per day. It is necessary that the iodine content of iodine-fortified foods be monitored during manufacturing to ensure that the prescribed levels are maintained. Iodine fortification is safe, but excessive intake may produce hyperthyroidism (Andersson, Takkouche, Egli, & de Benoist, 2003).

Problems caused by iodine deficiency include goiter, psychomotor defects, impaired mental function, and slow cognitive development. The universal iodization of salt has been very successful in bringing the prevalence of these conditions down in many countries. Nevertheless, in Southeast Asia, 172 million people have goiter, and 599 million people are at risk for this condition (Center for Global Development, 2006; WHO, 2003).

Nuclear events, such as occurred in Chernobyl, USSR, cause the production of I^{131}, the radioactive form of iodine. Consumption of this isotope results in thyroid cancer. Similarly, irradiation of the head and neck, as was common in acne therapy in the 1950s, also caused conversion of iodine to I^{131} and a consequent epidemic of thyroid cancer.

Zinc Deficiency

Dietary zinc deficiency is unlikely in healthy persons. Secondary zinc deficiency can develop in the following individuals:

- Some patients with hepatic insufficiency (because the ability to retain zinc is lost)
- Patients taking diuretics

- Patients with diabetes mellitus, sickle cell disease, chronic renal failure, or malabsorption problems
- Patients with stressful conditions (e.g., sepsis, burns, head injury)
- Elderly institutionalized and homebound patients (common)

Maternal zinc deficiency may cause fetal malformations and low birth weight. Zinc deficiency in children causes impaired growth and impaired taste (hypogeusia). Other symptoms and signs in children include delayed sexual maturation and hypogonadism. In children or adults, symptoms include alopecia, impaired immunity, anorexia, dermatitis, night blindness, anemia, lethargy, and impaired wound healing. Zinc deficiency should be suspected in undernourished people with typical symptoms or signs. However, because many of these symptoms and signs are nonspecific, low albumin levels, which are also common in zinc deficiency, make serum zinc levels difficult to interpret. Diagnosis usually requires the combination of low levels of zinc in serum and increased urinary zinc excretion. If available, isotope studies can measure zinc status more accurately. Treatment consists of elemental zinc 15 to 120 mg/day, given orally, until symptoms and signs resolve (Boy et al, 2009; Johnson, 2008).

Hypozincemia is usually a nutritional deficiency, but can also be associated with malabsorption, diarrhea, chronic liver disease, chronic renal disease, sickle cell disease, diabetes, and malignancies. Zinc deficiency, however, is typically the result of inadequate dietary intake of zinc. Decreased vision, smell, and memory are also connected with zinc deficiency. Moreover, a deficiency in zinc can cause malfunctions of organs and their related functions. One sign that may be caused by zinc deficiency is white spots, bands, or lines on the fingernails (Boy et al, 2009; Johnson, 2008).

One-third of the world population is at risk of zinc deficiency, with the percentage of the population at risk ranging from 4% to 73% depending on the country. Zinc deficiency is the fifth leading risk factor for disease in the developing world. Providing micronutrients, including zinc, has been identified as one of the four quick positive solutions to major global problems. Zinc food fortification and supplementation to children in developing countries have been proven to decrease diarrhea, pneumonia, and childhood mortality (Boy et al., 2009; Johnson, 2008).

Protein–Energy Malnutrition

Protein–energy malnutrition (kwashiorkor) is a global health problem and is potentially fatal, often causing death in children, mainly in developing countries where the environment is characterized by unsafe water, reductions in macronutrients, and deficiencies in many micronutrients. Kwashiorkor is an example of various levels of inadequate protein or energy intake. Although it mainly occurs in infants and children, it can be found in persons of any age in the life cycle. In the United States, secondary protein–energy malnutrition is seen in elderly people who live in nursing homes and in children in poverty. Such malnutrition may result from AIDS, cancer, kidney failure, inflammatory bowel disease, and other disorders. It usually appears in people who have chronic disease or chronic semi-starvation, and takes three forms:

- *Dry (thin, desiccated).* Marasmus results from near-starvation with a deficiency of protein and calories. The marasmic child consumes little food, usually because the mother is unable to breastfeed, and appears very thin as a result of loss of body muscle and fat. This is the predominant form of protein–energy malnutrition in most developing countries. It occurs when energy intake is insufficient for the body's requirements and the body uses up its own reserves. Marasmic infants have hunger, weight loss, growth retardation, and wasting of fat and muscle. The chronic phase of this disease is made acute when an incident of diarrhea takes place. This diarrhea usually takes on fatal consequences.
- *Wet (edematous, swollen).* Kwashiorkor is an African word meaning first child–second child; it refers to the fact that a first child may develop protein–energy malnutrition when a second child is born and replaces the first child at the breast. In many poor areas of the world, the weaned child is then

fed a thin gruel of poor nutritional quality and has organic failure to thrive. Edema results because the protein deficiency is greater than the energy deficiency. Increased carbohydrate intake is accompanied with decreased protein intake, and a decrease in albumin causes the edema. Those affected get thinning and discoloration of the hair and have an increased vulnerability to infections. The body weight increases due to edema.

▪ *Combined form (between the two extremes).* In marasmic kwashiorkor, children have some edema and more body fat than marasmus.

Treatment of these conditions includes the following measures:

▪ Correcting fluid and electrolyte imbalances
▪ Treating infections (causing diarrhea) with antibiotics
▪ Supplying macronutrients (primarily milk-based formulas) by diet therapy

Mortality from protein–energy malnutrition ranges from 5% to 49% (*Merck Manual*, 2002).

Obesity

WHO estimates that within the next few years, noncommunicable diseases may become the main cause of mortality and morbidity worldwide. Elimination of childhood deaths, particularly as a result of poor water quality, is key to this estimate. Much of the world's population has shifted toward consumption of highly refined foods of animal origin and toward dietary intake of meat and dairy products containing high levels of saturated fats. With reduced energy expenditure and more available food stuffs as a result of better food preservation, there has been a concomitant rise in obesity and noncommunicable diseases. The prevalence of obesity is growing worldwide, not only in most developed countries, but also in developing countries, mainly from the influx of modern technology and economic growth. These factors result in both more inactivity and greater availability of food. Despite the use of diets and exercise plans for combating obesity, this problem continues to increase. One-third of the world's population age 15 or older is overweight or obese (U.S. Department of Agriculture [USDA], 2005b).

Overweight and obesity are ranges of weight greater than what is considered healthy for a specific height. In addition, these conditions are associated with specific likelihoods of chronic diseases and health problems. Overweight is defined as a body mass index (BMI) of 25–29.9; obesity is defined as a BMI of 30 or greater. BMI is calculated as weight (in kilograms) divided by height squared (in square meters). A BMI ranging from 18.5 to 24.9 is within the healthy weight range (U.S. Department of Agriculture [USDA], 2005b).

The BMI metric correlates the amount of body fat with height, but does not directly measure body fat. Other modes of measuring body fat include skinfold thickness and waist circumference, calculation of waist-to-hip circumference ratios, and other diagnostic measurements such as ultrasound, computed tomography (CT), and magnetic resonance imaging (MRI). For children and adolescents, the BMI ranges are defined taking into account normal male and female variations of body fat for specific ages (CDC, 2006a).

U.S. government surveys show that the average adult man age 20–74 weighs 191 pounds, and the average adult woman of the same age weighs 164 pounds. Approximately three-fourths of all Americans age 15 years and older were overweight or obese in 2005. The average U.S. adult currently weighs 24 pounds more than an adult did in the early 1960s. The United States is the world leader in percentage of the population who are obese. Approximately 60% of the U.S. population is overweight and 21% is obese. The rate of obesity is increasing approximately 5% per year (Marvin & Medd, 2004).

China, where 19% of the total population is overweight or obese, leads the world in numbers of people with these conditions. In China, the urbanization process has been linked to changes in diet, increased television viewing in homes, and reduced physical activity. The majority of the population is thin, but there are millions who are overweight, though generally not obese (Chopra, Galbraith, & Darnton-Hill, 2002; Johnson, 2006).

The function of fat is to provide a cushion, insulation, and energy storage, but excess fat causes numerous problems. When persons become obese, they are more likely to have problems such as the following:

- Diabetes
- Gallbladder disease
- Hypertension
- Dyslipidemia
- Breathlessness
- Apnea
- Heart disease
- Osteoarthritis
- Gout
- Increased risk for some cancers
- Reproductive hormone abnormalities
- Impaired fertility
- Low back pain
- Fetal defects

Obesity and overweight are chronic conditions attributable to energy imbalance, created by eating too many calories and not getting enough physical activity. The body weight is the sum of genetic makeup, metabolism, behavior, environment, culture, and socioeconomic status. Genetics and environment may influence overweight and obesity, but personal choices of eating and physical activity can be modified. The United States has experienced a number of changes in food options within grocery stores and restaurants that have contributed to the rising obesity/overweight rates. For example, a large percentage of the packaged foods and fast foods found in the United States are very high in salt, fat, sugar, and calories. In addition, portion size today is much larger compared to 20 years ago (CDC, 2006a).

Physical activity—the other half of the energy imbalance issue—is beneficial for overall health. It helps to decrease the risk of colon cancer, diabetes, and hypertension; helps in weight control; contributes to healthy bones, muscles, and joints; reduces falls in the elderly; and helps relieve the pain of arthritis. Exercise is particularly important to menopausal women to combat osteoporosis. Moderate activity of 30 minutes per day for five or more times per week will enhance overall fitness and help combat overweight and obesity (CDC, 2006a).

The economic cost of overweight and obesity in the United States and throughout the world is quite significant. Within the United States, obesity problems contribute to 12% of total U.S. healthcare costs, or $100 billion. Medical costs include preventive, diagnostic, and treatment services. Decreased productivity, restricted activity, and absenteeism further increase costs. Loss of future income due to premature death is also a cost of overweight and obesity (CDC, 2006b).

Within developing nations, there is also a growing trend toward overweight and obesity, especially among individuals of high socioeconomic status (SES) within these populations. Obesity is now increasing worldwide and is increasingly found in larger numbers within the lower-SES populations of developing countries as well (Monteiro, Moura, Conde, & Popkin, 2004).

Childhood obesity is also now considered a global epidemic problem even in developing nations. Approximately 10% of the world's children, ages 5–17 years, are now considered overweight, and 2–3% of children are obese. These rates correspond to 155 million overweight children and 30–45 million obese children on a worldwide basis (Stettler, 2004).

Why are children becoming obese? One factor is that children who consume high-fat and carbohydrate-rich foods produce high levels of circulating insulin, enabling the body to store extra calories as fat. On the South Pacific island of Nauru, both children and adults have access to cheap and easily accessible high-density, high-caloric foods and have become diabetes prone. In China, the one-child-per-family policy has produced millions of spoiled and overnourished children (the "little emperor" syndrome), leading to rising rates of both childhood obesity and type 2 diabetes in children (Nash, 2003). Dramatic shifts in food consumption and physical activity patterns are occurring. In the last 10 years, the traditional low-fat diet now seems to be more of a reflection of poverty than of concern for good nutrition and health (Monteiro et al., 2004).

Overweight and obesity affect children globally with problems such as type 2 diabetes, hypercholesterolemia, and hypertension—once seen mainly in adults, these conditions are now common among children. An inverse relationship has been revealed between the level of socioeconomic status and the prevalence of obesity in adults (low SES equates to higher obesity levels), and the same relationship is now becoming evident among children as well. In addition, ethnic differences may increase the risk of obesity during infancy, childhood, and adolescence. Data demonstrate that low-SES populations of adults and children consume more refined grains and added fats, whereas lean meats, fish, whole grains, low-fat dairy products, and fresh fruits and vegetables are more likely consumed by higher-SES populations. The cost of a healthy diet is very expensive. Energy-dense foods are the least expensive and do not seem to be as affected by inflation, which explains one of the possible reasons behind the highest rates of obesity among lower-SES groups (Costarelli & Manios, 2009).

Fiber Consumption

Dietary fiber, also known as food roughage or bulk, is found mainly in fruits, vegetables, whole grains, and legumes. It is best known for its ability to relieve constipation, but is also known to lower the risk of type 2 diabetes, heart disease and diverticular disease. There are two types of fiber:

■ *Insoluble fiber* promotes movement of material through the gastrointestinal system, increasing bulk in stool. Examples include whole-wheat flour, wheat bran, and numerous vegetables.
■ *Soluble fiber* dissolves in water, making a gel-like material, which aids in lowering blood cholesterol and glucose levels. It is found in oats, beans, peas, apples, citrus fruits, carrots, and barley.

Low-fiber foods include refined or processed foods such as canned fruits and vegetables, pulp-free juice, white breads and pastas, and non-whole-grain foods. Since the low-carbohydrate fad has passed, whole grains are making a comeback as part of the mainstream diet in the developed world. Eating a diet rich in whole grains has been associated with significant benefits, such as reduction in the rates of certain types of cancers, heart disease, type 2 diabetes, and weight management. The 2005 International Food Information Council (IFIC) Foundation guideline calls for at least three servings of whole grains per day, and particularly for young children, the servings need to be gradually increased (IFIC Foundation, 2005).

The fiber content of different whole-grain foods varies between 0.5 and 4 grams of fiber per serving, depending on the food category and serving size. Whole grains are the entire seed of plants, which contains all of the parts—the bran, germ, and endosperm—found in the original grain seed. They can take the form of a single food such as oatmeal, brown rice, barley, or popcorn, or can be an ingredient in another food such as bread or cereal. Examples include whole wheat, whole oats, whole-grain corn, popcorn, brown rice, whole rye, whole-grain barley, wild rice, buckwheat, bulgur (cracked wheat), millet, quinoa, and sorghum (IFIC Foundation, 2005). Oats are a good source of dietary fiber and particularly helpful in the treatment of diabetes and cardiovascular disorders. Oat bran, in particular, is a good source of B-complex vitamins, protein, fat, and minerals, as well as soluble fiber (Butt, Tahir-Nadeem, Kashif Iqbal Khan, Shabir, & Butt, 2008).

When grain is refined, most of the bran and some of the germ is removed, which results in loss of fiber, B vitamins, vitamin E, trace minerals, unsaturated fat, and other nutrients. In the United States, by law, enriched fortified grains must also contain folic acid (IFIC Foundation, 2005).

In a study of 5686 American preschoolers, Kranz (2006) noted that children are not likely consuming fiber at the recommended level, and even less likely to do so as their age increases. The reason is that the children have increased independence in food selection as they age. Medium-income non-Hispanic white children were less likely to have adequate daily fiber intake than low-income non-Hispanic white children. Although low-income families were more likely to consume fewer processed and refined foods because of financial restrictions, higher-income families bought and consumed more fresh fruits, vegetables, and whole-grain products than middle-income families.

FOOD SAFETY AND SECURITY

Food prevents illness and maintains normal growth and development. Food security may be defined as steady access to sufficient nutritious foods to maintain an active healthy life. Those who have food security have access to clean, safe, and nutritious food at all times. They are able to acquire necessary foods without having to scavenge or steal. In contrast, food insecurity exists when there is limited or uncertain availability of safe and nutritious food. In this situation, food may not be easily acquired in safe and socially acceptable ways. The long-term effects of food insecurity are ill health, reduction in physical and cognitive growth and development, disease vulnerability, and, if untreated, eventually death (Hall & Brown, 2005).

Food insecurity is a state in which there is a nonsustainable food supply that interferes with optimal self-reliance and social justice. People who lack nutritionally adequate and safe food in their diet must often utilize severe coping strategies to obtain food, such as scavenging, stealing, and going to food banks. Those most susceptible to food insecurity are single heads of households, older adults, children without parents or guardians, landless people, those living in war zones, migrants, and immigrants. Persons with food insecurity are living with unhealthy diets and poor health status.

"Hunger," "famine," and "starvation" are commonly used terms when addressing people with food insecurity. They are defined as follows (Kregg-Byers & Schlenk, 2010):

- Hunger: lethal, recurrent, and involuntary experiences of uneasy or painful sensations caused by lack of food. Hidden hunger is associated with deficiencies in micronutrients, may be less recognized and reported, and can be deadly. Hunger related to food insecurity leads to malnutrition.
- Famine: a sudden decrease in the level of food consumption for a large number of people. Lack of nutrients over at least several days can lead to starvation.
- Starvation: a severe lack of food that can occur without famine. For example, starvation may result from an inequitable social system, poverty, landlessness, civil disturbance, political injustice, government greed, or incompetency. Starvation is a severe reduction in vitamin, nutrient, and energy intake. It is the most extreme form of malnutrition.

Food insecurity in the United States affected 11.7% of married couple households in 2003, and was present in 32.3% of families with a female head of the household and no spouse. Today in the United States, women are more likely to live in poverty than men, which greatly increases their risk of experiencing food insecurity. In households with food insecurity, often the first foods to be eliminated are fruits and vegetables, causing the family members to lack essential vitamins and minerals. This population is more likely to become overweight or obese from diets that include more energy-dense foods than fruits and vegetables, and that contain more refined grain, sugars, and fats, which cost less per calorie. Food-insecure women and children are ultimately at greater risk for chronic illnesses, including cancers and cardiovascular diseases (Olson, 2005). National survey data indicate that more than 50% of all Americans are overweight based on BMI, and 22% of adults are classified as obese. Surveys also indicate those people most likely to be overweight or obese have less formal education, have lower family income, are African American or Latino, and are female (Stallings, Wolman, & Goodner, 2001).

In 2008, more than 14% of all U.S. households—49 million people—were food insecure. Most adults living in food-insecure households are not able to afford balanced meals, and worry about the adequacy of their food supply, running out of food, cutting the size of their meals, or skipping meals. Common responses to food insecurity include food budget adjustments, reduced food intake, and consumption of energy-dense foods (including refined grains, foods with added saturated trans fats, and foods with added sugar), which are of poor nutritional quality and less expensive calorie-for-calorie than alternatives. In addition, U.S. adults living in food-insecure homes tend to eat fewer weekly servings of fruits, vegetables, and dairy, and lower levels of micronutrients, including B-complex vitamins, magnesium, iron, zinc, and calcium. These diet patterns are linked to the development of chronic diseases such as diabetes, hypertension, and hyperlipidemia. Nutritional problems, which may also occur in children within these households, include iron-deficiency anemia, acute infection, chronic illness, and developmental and mental health problems. In addition, overweight and obesity are found in both adults and children who experience food insecurity (Seligman, Laraia, & Kushel, 2010).

In addition to the previously voiced concerns about food security, the term "food security" now has a new meaning that may differ from its traditional definition—that is, it may be defined in terms of food safety. Put simply, food has become a weapon of bioterrorism. Besides having terrorism-related concerns about disease threats such as anthrax and smallpox, the world population now has major concerns relating to the safety of food and water supplies, which could be a source of intentional spread of illness. Toxic substances might be put into the food and water supply that could include radioactive particles, microorganisms (e.g., *E. coli* 0517:H7, *Salmonella, Shigella*), or botulism toxin (a very deadly substance) (Hall & Brown, 2005).

National policies and programs can promote food safety and improve the capacity for monitoring, assessing, and controlling food quality. Training is also needed for food- borne disease surveillance and control, as well as assessing for food contamination. Public education about food safety issues is essential. In the United States, the food supply is considered reasonably safe, yet each year 76 million Americans get sick, 300,000 are hospitalized, and 5000 people die from food contamination. Contamination sources may be biological or chemical. The role of the U.S. Food and Drug Administration (FDA) is to protect and inspect the U.S. food supply. The Department of Agriculture protects the meat supply as well as fish and unusual species, such as snakes, alligators, and ostriches as food stuffs. The CDC may investigate a disease outbreak or a cluster if it does not fall within the FDA's or USDA's area of responsibility (CDC, 2003).

The International Food Safety Authorities Network (INFOSAN) was developed by WHO in cooperation with the Food and Agriculture Organization (FAO) of the United Nations to promote the exchange of food safety information and to improve collaboration among international food authorities. Its goal is preventing the international spread of contaminated food. This organization has 143 members representing most countries of the world (WHO, 2005b).

One example of a global concern related to the world food supply is bird flu, a disease that infected chickens in Southeast Asia as a result of failure to segregate these animals from wild birds. Once the chickens entered the commerce pathway, they had the potential to transmit the disease

Following natural disasters, food in affected areas may become contaminated and be at risk for outbreaks of food-borne diseases such as diarrhea, dysentery, cholera, and typhoid fever. Poor sanitation and lack of clean drinking water have caused massive epidemics of food-borne diseases. Contaminated water may be considered to be an unclean food and should be boiled or given additives (biocides) to be made safe before it is consumed or added to foods. Some examples of food and water issues after a major flood include the following (WHO, 2005a):

■ Agriculture harvested from an area that has been flooded may be contaminated with microorganisms from raw sewage or microorganisms and chemicals in the flood water.
■ Produce that was stored in the affected areas may be contaminated by flood waters.
■ Foods that have not been contaminated need to be protected against sources of contamination.
■ All foods distributed with mass feeding programs should be fit for human consumption and be nutritionally and culturally appropriate.
■ Consumers need education in food preparation in more primitive conditions to promote food safety.

NUTRITION AND POVERTY

The significance of poverty relates not only to low income. Perhaps more significant components of poverty include limited or no access to health services, safe water, literacy, and education. There is a two-way association between poverty and health—that is, poverty is one of the main factors related to poor health, and poor health can lead to poverty. Poverty causes people to be exposed to environmental risks such as poor sanitation, unhealthy food, violence, and natural disasters. Those in poverty are less prepared to cope with their problems, putting them at greater risk for illness and disability.

Nutritional status depends on both food and nonfood factors. The nonfood factors include education and hygiene. As of 2010, 925 million people in the world experienced significant hunger. This includes: 19 million in developed countries, 37 million in the Near East and North Africa, 53 million in Latin America and the Caribbean, and 239 million in sub-Saharan Africa (World Hunger and Poverty Fact and Statistics, 2012).

Poverty affects nutrition throughout the life span, causing both infectious and noncommunicable diseases and leading to a reduced learning capacity. Beginning in pregnancy, the fetus, when compromised with malnutrition, has slower intrauterine growth and as a result is small for gestational age. After being born, these low-birth-weight children do not respond to environmental stresses as well as their larger counterparts. Lifetime challenges from malnutrition affect the normal cognitive, psychomotor, and affective behavior in children, and later as they become adults, they have less resistance to infection (a weaker immune system) throughout the life span. Pregnant teens in poverty are more likely to have malnutrition and again expose the fetus and newborn to even greater risks. Low height for age (stunting) is the most frequently seen manifestation of malnutrition worldwide, with more than 30% of the world's children manifesting stunting. Poor quality and quantity of milk during the first 2 years of life results in shorter and more disease-prone individuals. Adults in poverty often use their money to buy more high-energy (calories) foods of low nutritional quality, which may not resolve nutritional deficiencies in vitamins or protein, but contribute to overweight and obesity. Older adults affected by poverty often suffer a long history of poor nutrition and frequent illnesses (both infectious and noncommunicable). Many have to continue working to help their adult children and grandchildren (Pena & Bacallao, 2002).

The most common scenario of food-related disease among poverty-stricken populations in developing countries is one in which children, aged 2–5, get bacterial infections from unsafe drinking water. This results in diarrhea, which, without antibiotics, is virtually impossible to cure. The child with diarrhea develops an electrolyte imbalance and protein and calorie deficits. Because poor children are not equipped with any reserve to fight this infection, the consequences of this diarrhea are more often fatal. Antibiotic treatment along with oral rehydration therapy (ORT) early in the disease will save numerous lives on a global basis.

NUTRITIONAL EMERGENCIES

WHO assists with worldwide nutritional emergencies through numerous projects developed to provide assistance as needed. Some of its projects include the development of the following (WHO, 2006b):

- A manual that provides an explanation or how-to guide for managing nutritional needs of a community in an emergency, including the estimation of energy, protein, and nutrient requirements for a specific population
- A field guide to determine nutritional requirements, current nutritional status, and methods for prevention and treatment of protein–energy malnutrition and micronutrient deficiency diseases
- Specific guides for prevention and control of scurvy, pellagra, and thiamine deficiency
- Guides for feeding infants and young children
- Training modules for humanitarian aid workers
- Guides for caring for the nutritionally vulnerable people of a population
- Training modules for management of severe malnutrition

Burundi, a sub-Saharan African nation, has a significant problem with acute malnutrition in the general population, which is especially acute in children younger than 5 years. This outcome is a consequence of armed conflicts resulting in displacement of people, the inability of people to work their land, and changes in weather patterns that have caused severe agricultural problems. To combat this situation, International Medical Corp (IMC), an emergency nongovernmental organization (NGO), has implemented a comprehensive program for treatment and prevention of malnutrition in three Burundian provinces (Muyinga, Rutana, and Kirundo) since 1998. The program consists of three therapeutic feeding centers, one in each province, and 38 supplementary feeding centers, 12–14 in each province. The therapeutic feeding centers provide inpatient, high-intensity treatment to the severely malnourished, and the supplementary feeding centers provide rations and treatment in an ambulatory (outpatient) center. UNICEF, USAID, and other NGOs have partnered with IMC to make a more dramatic impact in combating the acute malnutrition (Mach, n.d.).

NUTRITIONAL SUPPORT PROGRAMS

Programs to assist in improving the nutritional health of developing nations are urgently needed to provide opportunities for health promotion by education as well as diet changes reflecting specific local community cultural and health needs. In response to this need, the United States is presently supplying monetary funds via USAID to support nutritional programs. Recently, additional vitamins and minerals (food fortification) were added to common foods such as wheat flour, sugar, and cooking oil in Bangladesh, Central America, Eritrea, Ghana, Mali, Morocco, the Philippines, Uganda, Zambia, Bolivia, the Dominican Republic, Pakistan, and Uzbekistan. This kind of vitamin A supplementation, for example, can reduce infant mortality by 30% (International Nutrition Foundation, n.d.; USAID, 2005).

In September 2006, the Global Alliance for Improved Nutrition (GAIN) signed an agreement with the United Nations International Children's Emergency Fund (UNICEF) to support flour fortification in Central and Eastern Europe in an effort to improve maternal, infant, and child health. GAIN is an organization that was created to fight vitamin and mineral deficiency. This type of malnutrition affects more than 2 billion people globally, and produces major health problems such as limited cognitive and psychomotor function, blindness, and death (GAIN, 2006).

The International Micronutrient Malnutrition Prevention and Control Program (IMMpaCT) was established by the CDC in 2000 to eliminate vitamin and mineral deficiencies—the "hidden hunger." The CDC provides funding and technical assistance directly through cooperative agencies such as UNICEF, WHO, GAIN, USAID, and the Micronutrient Initiative (Gerberding, 2006).

Within the United States, the Women, Infants and Children (WIC) program was established in 1974 to safeguard low-income women, infants, and children up to age 5 who are at nutritional risk. This program provides nutritious foods to supplement diets, nutrition counseling, and healthcare referrals to low-income pregnant, breastfeeding, and nonbreastfeeding postpartum women, and to infants and children who are at nutritional risk. It is administered by the Food and Nutrition Service of the USDA. The majority of states provide vouchers that participants use at authorized food stores. Women who participate in the WIC program during their pregnancies have been shown to have lower Medicaid costs, longer gestational periods, higher birth weights, and lower infant mortality for their babies and lower mortality for themselves compared to women who do not participate in the program (USDA, 2005a).

NUTRITIONAL CHALLENGES IN VULNERABLE POPULATIONS

Infants and Children

The vast majority of children who die today of hunger will not die in a high-profile emergency, but rather will die unnoticed by anyone other than their families and neighbors. There are approximately 400 million hungry children in the world, including an estimated 146 million who are younger than age 5 years. These children will most likely die or have long-term disabilities unless the following occurs (Gerberding, 2006):

- The children are identified and support from local organizations can reach them in their local communities.
- Local organizations are able to initiate interventions.
- Water purification and transport systems are established.
- Antibiotics can be made available.
- Complementary interventions such as childhood immunizations, education, and food security are also given.

Each year undernutrition contributes to the deaths of approximately 5.6 million children younger than 5 years of age. In the least developed countries of the world, 42% of children are stunted in growth and 36% are underweight. Insufficient folic acid among childbearing-age women contributes to 200,000 babies being born with birth defects worldwide. Iron deficiency contributes to 60,000 deaths among women in pregnancy and childbirth and decreases cognitive development in 40–60% of the children of the developing world. Food fortification, supplementation, and dietary improvements have been successful in eliminating most of these problems in the developed world and could result in similar improvements in the developing world (Gerberding, 2006).

As stated earlier, children younger than 5 years of age are generally much more vulnerable and have higher mortality rates during major emergencies such as earthquakes or tidal waves because of increased rates of communicable diseases and diarrhea as well as very high rates of undernutrition. During major emergencies, donations of infant formula and other powdered milk products can actually do more harm than good among these children. Infants and small children do better if they are breastfed only. Mothers and infants need to be kept together during such crises, and mothers should continue breastfeeding. In addition, maternal nutrition cannot be ignored and must be addressed. Any breastmilk substitutes for feeding infants and young children should be given only after needs are carefully assessed and under strict medical supervision and hygienic conditions; there should be no general distribution of such products. Children older than 6 months should also be given fortified foods or micronutrient supplements under supervised programs (Labbok, Clark, & Goldman, 2004; Morris, 2006; WHO & UNICEF, 2005).

Safe water is also essential for nutrition. In settings with poor access to safe water and hygiene, children experience diarrhea and malnutrition. Diarrheal infections kill almost 2 million children younger than age 5 annually, and cause short- and long-term morbidity among millions more. Children with diarrhea frequently lose their appetites and do not absorb food, leading to nutritional deficiencies. In addition, malnourished children are at higher risk for diarrheal diseases. These children commonly have poor height and weight gains. Foods prepared with unsafe water or unclean hands expose children to diarrhea, causing illnesses and further promoting malnutrition (Gerberding, 2006). A significant percentage of infants anywhere from 4 to 6 months of age can be given complementary feedings, which usually consist of cereals or gruels (WHO, 2004).

Undernutrition and infectious diseases, both individually and in combination, have dramatic effects on children worldwide, with more than half of all deaths of children being due to the infectious diseases of pneumonia, diarrhea, malaria, measles, and AIDS. Undernutrition is a very important cause of these deaths—as many as 35% of all child deaths worldwide are a result of undernutrition. Undernutrition is a form of malnutrition that encompasses stunting (low height for age), wasting (low weight for age), and micronutrient deficiencies. As noted earlier, micronutrient deficiencies are common in children worldwide. A variety of interventions for undernutrition are available, including fortifications of condiments and other foods (Peterson, 2009).

As stated in Global Childhood Malnutrition (2006), in the developing world there are 146 million children younger than 5 years who are underweight. Undernutrition is the cause of 5.6 million deaths per year. In countries such as India, Bangladesh, and Pakistan, many children also have iron-deficiency anemia and iodine deficiency. From 1990 to 2002, China reduced the number of underweight children from 19% to 8% ("Global Childhood Malnutrition," 2006). Low birth weight (LBW) correlates with nutrition-related early childhood mortality. Thirty million newborns each year in developing countries (24% of the 126 million births per year) suffer from intrauterine growth retardation (IUGR). The world prevalence for of IUGR/LBW is 11% of all newborns in developing countries (13.7 million babies annually). Incidence in Asia (excluding Japan) is highest in the world with 28.3% (accounting for 80% of all newborns worldwide); next in line are middle and Western Africa with incidence of 14.9% and 11.4%, respectively. Almost 30% of South Asian women are moderately or severely underweight and do not gain a sufficient amount of weight during pregnancy to allow for fetal growth (Underwood, 2002). In rural areas of Southeast Asia, breastfeeding is common for infants and young children, but this practice is decreasing in urban areas. A very interesting social structure has evolved in which the poor and the wealthy perform breastfeeding, while the middle class, due to problems with the mothers having to work, use bottle feeding.

In Pakistan, for example, protein and calorie malnutrition is a significant health problem and contributes greatly to the morbidity and mortality in children. This area has been identified as a region with sex bias and female discrimination, including violence towards women. Boys are sent to school and given more nutrients when food is scarce. Preschool children, particularly girls, receive fewer calories than male children. In a study of 1878 children younger than 3 years old, protein–energy malnutrition remained an important cause of death among preschool children in Pakistan. Female illiteracy, poverty, and overcrowding were found to be important risks for stunting (Shah, Selwyn, Luby, Merchant, & Bano, 2003).

South African children younger than age 5 have a relatively high mortality rate and high prevalence of stunting. HIV and diarrheal disease are the leading causes of childhood morbidity and death. One way to reduce the high rates of diarrhea and mortality is by micronutrient supplementation. A study conducted by Chagan et al. (2009) of the effect of micronutrient supplementation on children with diarrheal disease, some of whom had HIV, demonstrated the efficacy of zinc combined with multiple micronutrients in reducing diarrhea morbidity in rural South African children.

Childbearing Women

Maternal malnutrition is disproportionately high in Asia and Africa and contributes to 87% of the 585,000 approximate maternal mortalities per year. The rate is highest in Africa, with 1 woman per

100 dying during birth, followed by the rate of 0.56 maternal death per 100 live births in Central Asia. Efforts to reduce the maternal mortality have focused on improvements in nutrition as well as other non-nutritional causes. Notably, iron-deficiency anemia is responsible for 15–20% of all maternal deaths (Underwood, 2002).

Another nutritional issue specific to childbearing-age women is folic acid deficiency. Folic acid is readily available from green leafy vegetables, but many populations' diets are marginally deficient in these components. Folic acid is necessary for nucleic acid production (i.e., DNA and RNA synthesis). A population marginally deficient in folic acid will appear normal at first glance. However, this deficiency results in numerous birth defects, particularly cleft lip and palate and spina bifida. Because most populations are marginally deficient in this vitamin, it is logical that folic acid supplements should be taken during pregnancy. This may be a problem, as most developmental anomalies are induced in the first 3 months of pregnancy, and for at least half of that time most women do not know they are pregnant. Folic acid is an essential water-soluble B vitamin that is used in the prevention of folate-deficiency anemia. In 1998, the United States mandated that all enriched flour be fortified with folic acid. Canada and Chile enacted similar laws for fortification of folic acid in wheat flour. At present, such fortification is mandatory in more than 50 countries. Where folic acid is fortified in flour, it has been shown to decrease neural tube defects in newborns.

Vitamin B_{12} deficiency is also widespread and the supplement (a safe additive) can also be added to flour to prevent pernicious anemia (Oakley & Tulchinsky, 2010).

Older Adults

National estimates reveal that there are more than 36 million older adults in the United States, 58% of whom are females. Among this group, the rate of food insecurity ranges from 6% to 16%. Good nutrition is particularly important for older adults because inadequate diets may contribute to or exacerbate diseases, or delay recovery from illnesses. This group consistently has lower intakes of nutrients such as protein, iron, zinc, vitamins B_6 and B_{12}, riboflavin, and niacin. Of particular note is the incidence of scurvy in elderly men. Many of these individuals eat primarily canned food, and the heat processing used during the canning process destroys ascorbic acid (vitamin C.)

Poverty in older adults frequently causes them to do the following:

- Consume fewer than 3 meals per day
- Have a lower intake of energy, vitamin C, iron, zinc, and calcium
- Have iron-deficiency anemia
- Have reduced bone density or osteoporosis
- Have oral health problems (tooth decay and gum disease)

Strategies to assist older U.S. adults by enhancing their food security include an increase in dieticians and health professionals and federal nutrition programs for elders such as the Older Americans Act Nutrition Program (meals-on-wheels program) and the Food Stamp Program (Hall & Brown, 2005).

Aging adults often get anorexia of aging, a physiological process in which a decrease in appetite and food intake results in undesirable weight loss. In addition, the senses of smell and taste decline with age, which can result in the consumption of a less varied and more monotonous diet, leading to micronutrient deficiencies that decrease nutritional status and immune function. In one study, older adult males and females who lost 10 pounds or more within a 10-year period of time had a higher adjusted mortality rate as compared to those with stable weight or weight gain. In addition, hospitalized older adults with a BMI less than 18.5 have increased mortality rates. Undernutrition in the older adult has been shown to increase respiratory and cardiac complications, infections, and pressure ulcers. Nutritional supplemental liquids have been shown to reduce hospitalization, complications, and mortality. Specific micronutrient (vitamins and trace metals) or macronutrient (protein or cholesterol) supplementation may be quite useful. Evidence also suggests that vitamin supplementation increases cognitive functioning and ulcer healing. In addition, research indicates that in some situations the consumption of some alcohol with meals may increase food intake. For frail older adults, delivery of food, such as through a meals-on-wheels program, may help increase food intake as well (Visvanathan, 2003).

STUDY QUESTIONS

1. Discuss the causes and possible remedies of childhood and adult hunger and malnutrition in both developed and developing countries.
2. Explain the human right "freedom from hunger." Do you believe that all people living in the world should have this right? Why?
3. Why is having good nutrition during pregnancy especially important for women throughout the world?
4. Compare and contrast nutritional deficiencies, such as iron-deficiency anemia, niacin, vitamin A, vitamin B, iodine, and zinc micronutrient deficiencies.
5. Describe some nutritional challenges and relate potential solutions for older adults worldwide.
6. Explain why obesity is a major health problem in both developed and developing nations.

NUTRITION CASE STUDIES

CASE STUDY: MICRONUTRIENT: IODINE DEFICIENCY

Prior to the initiation of a nationwide program in China to eliminate iodine deficiency in 1995, more than 20% of Chinese children between the ages of 8 and 10 years were found to have enlarged thyroid glands. In addition, there were approximately 400 million people living in China at risk for developing a disorder associated with iodine deficiency.

The National Iodine Deficiency Disorders Elimination Program was introduced by the Chinese government in an effort to combat this national health problem. The focus of the program was to produce, package, and distribute iodized salt nationwide. One challenge that had to be overcome for the program to be successful was that many people lived in salt-producing areas and on salt hills and consumed only raw salt; thus they were reluctant to pay for commercially produced salt.

The efforts of the program were primarily supported by the World Bank, UNICEF, and WHO. At its beginning, a nationwide health campaign was initiated to inform the public of the ill effects of iodine deficiency and to explain how essential it was to purchase only the fortified salt. Ensuring that the people across the nation would have access to the iodized salt, salt-producing factories were instructed to improve and increase their technology for production. New centers were also built for iodation and packaging. Licensing regulations, including quality control, were put into place by the government in an attempt to ban the sale of noniodized salt (Center for Global Development, 2006).

Five years after the initiation of the program, 94% of the country was receiving iodized salt as compared to only 80% at the start of the program. The quality of the product had

CASE STUDY: MICRONUTRIENT: IODINE DEFICIENCY *(continued)*

also dramatically improved. The health of schoolchildren has shown a significant improvement. Total goiter rates declined to 6.5% in 2002 (Center for Global Development, 2006).

An Essential Micronutrient: Iodine

Iodine is a trace element that participates in the synthesis of thyroxine, a hormone secreted by the thyroid gland. Thyroxine stimulates cell oxidation and regulates the basal metabolic rate. It also helps regulate protein synthesis in the brain and other organs. The majority of iodine found in the body is contained in the thyroid gland. The recommended daily intake of iodine is 90 micrograms (mcg) for preschool children, 120 mcg for school children, 150 mcg for adults, and 200 mcg for pregnant and lactating women. Iodine is naturally found in seafood and in soil and water around the world.

Iodine deficiency results when intake falls below the recommended levels. The principal disorder associated with deficient levels is enlargement of the thyroid gland, or goiter. Gland enlargement occurs as a result of continuous secretion of thyroid-stimulating hormone (TSH) despite low blood levels of thyroid hormone and the increase in the amount of thyroglobulin that accumulates in thyroid follicles. The gland thus increases in size; in some cases, it may weigh up 700 grams or more. Iodine deficiency can also cause profound damage to the developing brain in utero and during the growing years of infancy and childhood. Stillbirths and miscarriages can result during pregnancy (Williams & Schlenker, 2003).

CASE STUDY: MICRONUTRIENT: VITAMIN A

To reduce vitamin A deficiency in sub-Saharan Africa, the International Potato Center, supported by the Department for International Development, has developed a sweet potato variety that is enhanced with the provitamin A form known as beta-carotene. This orange-fleshed sweet potato is being promoted to alleviate vitamin A deficiency among children and pregnant and lactating women. In a project led by South African scientists, school children between the ages of 5 and 10 years old were given a portion of boiled, mashed orange-fleshed sweet potato, weighing 125 grams, each day over 53 school days. A similar group of children received the same portion of white-fleshed sweet potato. Blood tests showed that the orange-fleshed sweet potato provided 2.5 times the recommended dietary allowance of vitamin A for that age group. The vitamin A stored in the liver in this group of children increased by 10% as compared to a 5% decline in vitamin A liver stores in those children consuming the white variety of sweet potatoes (South African Medical Research Council, 2004).

(continues)

CASE STUDY: MICRONUTRIENT: VITAMIN A *(continued)*

An Essential Nutrient: Vitamin A

Vitamin A is a fat-soluble vitamin that has many physiological functions:

- It helps with visual adaptation to light and darkness and prevention of night blindness.
- It is essential for optimal growth of soft tissues and bones.
- It maintains the integrity of epithelial cells such as the mucous membranes.
- It maintains normal skin.
- It supports the immune system in the formation of T lymphocytes.

The recommended daily allowance for vitamin A is 300 mcg for children 1 to 3 years of age, 400 mcg for children 4 to 8 years of age, 600 mcg for children 9 to 13 years of age, and 700 mcg for women and 900 mcg for men ages 14 and older. Two dietary sources of vitamin A exist. Retinol, or preformed vitamin A, is the natural form that can be found in animal food sources and is associated with fats. Beta-carotene is the provitamin A form and is found in orange-yellow and dark green leafy vegetables. The clinical signs of vitamin A deficiency include conditions such as xerophthalmia, an abnormally dry and thickened surface of the cornea and conjunctiva; night blindness; and keratinization, where epithelial cells become dry, flat, and hard (National Institutes of Health, 2006b).

CASE STUDY: MICRONUTRIENT: IRON

Iron-deficiency anemia has been a major health problem for more than four decades in Sri Lanka. Women of childbearing age and those who are pregnant are at highest risk, as are preschool children and children in primary school. The rate of anemia is especially high among groups of low socioeconomic status living in crowded environmental conditions and those prone to recurrent infections. A national survey found that 58% of children in primary school were identified as anemic (International Nutrition Foundation, n.d.).

A research study was conducted in Colombo, Sri Lanka, using 453 school children between the ages of 5 and 10 years, who presented with and without infection. The study examined the effects of iron supplementation on both iron status and morbidity and was designed as a longitudinal, randomized, controlled, double-blind supplementation trial. Baseline information was collected on each child that consisted of a detailed medical history, height and weight, venous blood sample, socioeconomic status, and morbidity from respiratory and gastrointestinal illness (deSilva, Atukorala, Weerasinghe, & Ahluwalia, 2003).

The intervention consisted of iron supplementation for 8 weeks. The children were given 60 mg of elemental iron (ferrous sulfate) every day. The control group received placebo capsules of lactose. Field investigators followed up with each of the children

CASE STUDY: MICRONUTRIENT: IRON *(continued)*

at their homes every 2 weeks to ensure high compliance. After supplementation was completed, all children were reassessed according to the preintervention parameters (deSilva et al., 2003).

Of the 363 children who completed the 8-week iron supplementation, 52.6% of the children had anemia. After the children took iron supplements, there was a significant improvement in iron status as indicated by the serum hemoglobin and ferritin concentrations in both groups of children with and without infections. In addition, those children who received the iron had a lower number of upper respiratory tract infections and total number of sick days (deSilva et al., 2003).

An Essential Nutrient: Iron

Iron is found in the body bound to protein; it is present in blood as the heme portion of hemoglobin and in muscle as myoglobin, bound to a transport protein as transferrin, and stored as a protein–iron compound as ferritin. It has many functions, such as the following:

- Participates in the transportation of oxygen from the lungs to the tissues as a component of hemoglobin
- Acts as a catalyst of oxidative enzyme systems for energy production
- Converts beta-carotene to vitamin A
- Synthesizes collagen
- Removes lipids from the bloodstream
- Detoxifies drugs in the liver
- Helps in the production of antibodies

The recommended daily allowance for iron for the following age groups is as follows:

- Infants 7 to 12 months: 11 mg per day
- Children 4 to 8 years: 10 mg per day
- Children 9 to 13 years: 8 mg per day
- Children 14 to 18 years: 11 mg per day for males; 15 mg per day for females
- Women aged 19 to 50 years: 18 mg per day
- Men aged 19 to 50 years: 8 mg per day
- Women aged 51 and older: 8 mg per day
- Men aged 51 and older: 8 mg per day

Iron can be found in organ meats such as liver, dark green vegetables, and grains. The principal disorder associated with iron deficiency is anemia. Anemia can lead to various symptoms such as fatigue, pale skin, difficulty maintaining body temperature, glossitis, slow cognitive and social development, and decreased immune function. Common causes of iron-deficiency anemia are increased iron losses, inadequate dietary intake, and inadequate absorption of iron usually secondary to diarrhea (National Institutes of Health, 2006a).

CASE STUDY: PROTEIN–ENERGY

Mr. Williams, a 70-year-old man with long-standing insulin-dependent diabetes mellitus, renal insufficiency, and heart failure, was admitted to the hospital with fatigue, weakness, and weight loss. The nursing staff discovered a 4-inch-diameter decubitus ulcer located over his sacrum. His caretaker gave a detailed history of his eating patterns over the previous 3 months, indicating a progressive decline in his food intake. Mr. Williams is 5 feet 11 inches tall (180 cm) and his present weight is 125 pounds (56 kg). His calculated body mass index (BMI) is 17.2.

Causes of Unintentional Weight Loss in the Elderly

Unintentional weight loss often occurs in the elderly. There are many causes and situations that can signal and alert one to malnutrition, especially in the elderly population. Many chronic disorders of the cardiovascular, endocrine, gastrointestinal, and neurological systems can play a role in weight loss, along with infections and malignancy. Psychiatric and eating disorders such as anorexia nervosa and bulimia also predispose an individual to weight loss. As a person ages, grief and depression can result from separation from family or loss of a spouse, which may leave a person living and eating alone. The side effects of many medications can also cause an individual to be anorexic and interfere with the utilization of food nutrients. Variables that actually interfere with the ability to eat include ill-fitting dentures, loss of teeth, problems with swallowing, and decreased sensation of taste and smell. All of these factors play a role in nutritional intake. Economic factors may also place the elderly at risk for malnutrition, including low socioeconomic status, insufficient income to purchase food, and inadequate living conditions such as the lack of heating or cooling and the lack of appliances to prepare meals (Jensen, Friedmann, Coleman, & Smiciklas-Wright, 2001; Williams & Schlenker, 2003).

Physical features of protein–energy malnutrition include the following:

- Reduction in body weight
- Muscle wasting with loss of strength
- Reduction in cardiac and respiratory muscular capacity
- Thinning of skin
- Decreased basal metabolic rate
- Hypothermia
- Edema
- Immunodeficiency
- Apathy

Treatment of Protein–Energy Malnutrition

Nutritional therapy for Mr. Williams is aimed at improving tissue integrity, muscle function, and immune function by providing enhanced amounts of protein and energy intake. Optimal dietary protein should be supplemented to the patient to ensure that an adequate supply of necessary amino acids is obtained for tissue synthesis. Calories need to be provided in amounts that will meet his energy output demands (Akner & Cederholm,

CASE STUDY: PROTEIN–ENERGY MALNUTRITION *(continued)*

2001). Mr. Williams will also benefit from enhanced oral supplements to aid in healing of his pressure sore (European Pressure Ulcer Advisory Panel, n.d.). In addition, supplementation of arginine, vitamin C, vitamin A, and zinc has been shown to be beneficial for the treatment of pressure sores (Langer, Schloemer, Knerr, Kuss, & Behrens, 2003; Schmidt, n.d.).

Essential Nutrition: Protein

Proteins are made up of amino acids that are necessary for the body to function properly, for growth, and for maintenance of body tissue. Proteins are the principal source of nitrogen and are essential for many body functions, including the following:

- Building new body tissues and repairing old ones
- Supplying amino acids for making enzymes and hormones
- Regulating fluid and acid–base balance
- Providing resistance from disease
- Providing transport mechanisms
- Providing energy

Protein requirements are influenced by the rate of growth, body size, rate of protein synthesis, quality of the protein, and dietary intake of fats and carbohydrates. The recommended dietary allowance (RDA) for both men and women is 0.80 gram per kilogram of body weight per day (Institute of Medicine, 2005). Additional protein is needed during illness and disease, trauma, prolonged immobilization, pregnancy, and lactation. Protein needs of infants and children vary according to their age and patterns of growth.

Sources of proteins can be described as either complete proteins or incomplete proteins. A food that supplies a sufficient amount of the nine indispensable (essential) amino acids is called a complete protein. All proteins from animal sources are considered to be complete proteins. Foods from this group include chicken, beef, pork, fish, shellfish, eggs, and the milk food groups. Incomplete proteins are foods that lack one or more essential amino acids; they include foods such as some fruits, grains, and vegetables (National Library of Medicine, 2006).

The following are the nine indispensable (essential) amino acids (Institute of Medicine, 2005):

- Histidine
- Isoleucine
- Leucine
- Lysine
- Methionine
- Phenylalanine
- Threonine
- Tryptophan
- Valine

CASE STUDY: OBESITY

Dorothy is a 36-year-old female who has been diagnosed with hypertension by her family doctor. Her other significant medical history includes insulin-dependent diabetes mellitus. She reports that she has always had a sedentary job and lifestyle. Dorothy's weight is 204 pounds, her height is 66 inches, and she has a waist circumference of 38 inches. Her blood pressure is 170/95 mm Hg and her heart rate is 86. She has acknowledged that she has been taking her blood pressure at home and it has been at least 156/95 mm Hg on several occasions.

According to the USDA's Dietary Guidelines for Americans (2005b), Dorothy's BMI is 33, indicating that she is considered obese (see **Figure 14-1**). Another index that can be useful to identify obesity is the measurement of waist and waist/hips circumference.

There are two recommendations for overweight and obesity: calorie reduction and exercise promotion. The best choice that is indicated for weight loss is to undergo a change in diet and physical activity patterns. Recommendations include a reduction in total calories consumed initially by 500 or more calories per day while maintaining appropriate proportions of protein, carbohydrates, and fats in the diet, typically resulting in a loss of approximately 1 to 2 pounds per week—a common goal of most weight-loss programs (USDA, 2005b). Increasing energy expenditure is also very important in the reduction of weight. Exercise has many beneficial effects on nearly every system in the body. Regular physical activity helps reduce the risk of death from heart disease and decreases the risk for developing diabetes, hypertension, stroke, and colon cancer. Physical activity contributes to weight loss; assists in controlling weight; maintains healthy bones, muscles, and joints; reduces the incidence of falls among the elderly; assists in relieving pain associated with arthritis; and reduces the symptoms related to anxiety and depression (American Heart Association, 2006). Recommendations from the CDC and the American College of Sports Medicine state that adults should engage in moderate-intensity physical activities for at least 30 minutes on 5 or more days of the week (CDC, 2006a).

Obesity risk factors include the following (Williams & Schlenker, 2003):

- Cardiovascular disease
- Hyperlipidemia
- Hypertension
- Stroke
- Diabetes mellitus
- Cancer
- Surgical complications
- Pregnancy complications

FIGURE 14-1

Adult BMI Chart

BMI	19	20	21	22	23	24	25	26	27	28	29	30	31	32	33	34	35
Height							**Weight in Pounds**										
4'10"	91	96	100	105	110	115	119	124	129	134	138	143	148	153	158	162	167
4'11"	94	99	104	109	114	119	124	128	133	138	143	148	153	158	163	168	173
5'	97	102	107	112	118	123	128	133	138	143	148	153	158	163	158	174	179
5'1"	100	106	111	116	122	127	132	137	143	148	153	158	164	169	174	180	185
5'2"	104	109	115	120	126	131	136	142	147	153	158	164	169	175	180	186	191
5'3"	107	113	118	124	130	135	141	146	152	158	163	169	175	180	186	191	197
5'4"	110	116	122	128	134	140	145	151	157	163	169	174	180	186	192	197	204
5'5"	114	120	126	132	138	144	150	156	162	168	174	180	186	192	198	204	210
5'6"	118	124	130	136	142	148	155	161	167	173	179	186	192	198	204	210	216
5'7"	121	127	134	140	146	153	159	166	172	178	185	191	198	204	211	217	223
5'8"	125	131	138	144	151	158	164	171	177	184	190	197	203	210	216	223	230
5'9"	128	135	142	149	155	162	169	176	182	189	196	203	209	216	223	230	236
5'10"	132	139	146	153	160	167	174	181	188	195	202	209	216	222	229	236	243
5'11"	136	143	150	157	165	172	179	186	193	200	208	215	222	229	236	243	250
6'	140	147	154	162	169	177	184	191	199	206	213	221	228	235	242	250	258
6'1"	144	151	159	166	174	182	189	197	204	212	219	227	235	242	250	257	265
6'2"	148	155	163	171	179	186	194	202	210	218	225	233	241	249	256	264	272
6'3"	152	160	168	176	184	192	200	208	216	224	232	240	248	256	264	272	279
	Healthy Weight						**Overweight**					**Obese**					

Locate the height of interest in the leftmost column and read across the row for that height to the weight of interest. Follow the column of the weight up to the top row that lists the BMI. BMI of 19 to 24 is the healthy weight range, BMI of 25 to 29 is the overweight range, and BMI of 30 and above is in the obese range. Due to rounding, these ranges vary slightly from the NHLBI values.

Source: US Department of Agriculture, 2005.

REFERENCES

Akner, G., & Cederholm, T. (2001). Treatment of protein–energy malnutrition in chronic nonmalignant disorders [Electronic version]. *American Journal of Clinical Nutrition, 74,* 6–24.

American Heart Association (2006). Physical activity. Retrieved from http://americanheart.org

Andersson, M., Takkouche, B., Egli, I., & de Benoist, B. (2003). The WHO global database on iodine deficiency disorders: The importance of monitoring iodine nutrition. *Scandinavian Journal of Nutrition, 47*(4), 162–166.

Boy, E., Mannar, V., Pandav, C., de Benoist, B. Viteri, F., Fontaine, O., & Hotz, C. (2009). Achievements, challenges, and promising new approaches in vitamin and mineral deficiency control. *Nutrition Reviews, 67*(suppl 1), S24–S30.

Butt, M., Tahir-Nadeem, M., Kashif Iqbal Khan, M., Shabir, R., & Butt, M. (2008). Oat: Unique among the cereals. *European Journal of Nutrition, 4,* 68–69.

Center for Global Development. (2006). Case 14: Preventing iodine deficiency disease in China. Retrieved from http://www.cgdev.org

Centers for Disease Control and Prevention (CDC). (2003). Food safety and nutrition. Retrieved from http://www.cdc.gov/nceh/globalhealth/priorities/foodnutrition.htm

Centers for Disease Control and Prevention (CDC). (2006a). Overweight and obesity: Contributing factors. Retrieved from http://www.cdc.gov/needphp/obesity/contributing_factors.htm

Centers for Disease Control and Prevention (CDC). (2006b). Overweight and obesity: Economic consequences. Retrieved from http://www.cdc.gov/needphp/obesity/economic_consequences.htm

Chagan, M. K., Van den Broeck, J., Luabeya, K., Mpontshane, N., Tucker, K. L., & Bennish, M. L. (2009). Effect of micronutrient supplementation on diarrhoeal disease among stunted children in rural South Africa. *European Journal of Clinical Nutrition, 63,* 850–857.

Chopra, M., Galbraith, S., & Darnton-Hill, I. (2002). A global response to a global problem: The epidemic of overnutrition. *Bulletin of the World Health Organization, 80*(12), 952–958.

Costarelli, V., & Manios, Y. (2009). The influence of socioeconomic status and ethnicity on children's excess body weight. *Nutrition and food Science, 39*(6), 676.

Dangour, A., & Uauy, R. (2006). Nutrition challenges for the twenty-first century. *British Journal of Nutrition, 96*(suppl 1), S2–S7.

deSilva, A., Atukorala, S., Weerasinghe, I., & Ahluwalia, N. (2003). Iron supplementation improves iron status and reduces morbidity in children with or without upper respiratory tract infections: A randomized controlled study in Colombo, Sri Lanka [Electronic version]. *American Journal of Clinical Nutrition, 77,* 234–241.

European Pressure Ulcer Advisory Panel. (n.d.). Nutritional guidelines for pressure ulcer prevention and treatment. Retrieved from http://www.epuap.org

Gerberding, J. (2006). Initiative to combat child hunger. FDCH Congressional Testimony: 9/26/2006. Committee name: Senate Foreign Relations. Accession number: 32Y1742177555. Retrieved from http://wf2la7.webfeat.org/ WSvZG1118/url=http://web.ebscohost.com/ehost/delivery?vid

Gleason, G. (2002). Iron deficiency anemia finally reaches the global stage of public health. *Nutrition in Clinical Care, 5*(5), 217–219.

Global Alliance for Improved Nutrition (GAIN). (2006). GAIN signs grant agreement with UNICEF to support flour fortification in the CEE/CIS region. Retrieved from http://www.gainhealth.org/ch/FN /index.cfm?contentid=fp5C67729.1143.F7CC.3

Global childhood malnutrition. (2006). *Lancet, 367,* 1459.

Hall, B., & Brown, L. (2005). Food security among older adults in the United States. *Topics in Clinical Nutrition, 20*(4), 329–338.

Harder, B. (2004). Double credit. *Science News, 166*(18), 276–277.

IFIC Foundation. (2005, March/April). Whole grains on the rise. *Food Insight,* 4–6.

Institute of Medicine. (2005). Protein and amino acids. In *Dietary reference intakes for energy, carbohydrates, fiber, fat, fatty acids, cholesterol, protein, and amino acids (macronutrients).* Retrieved from http://www.nap.edu/catalog/10490.html

International Nutrition Foundation. (n.d.). Case studies on successful micronutrient programs: The Sri Lankan experience. Retrieved from http://www.inffoundation.org

James, W. P. T., Simitasiri, S., Hag, U., Tagwirery, J., Norum, K., Uauy, R., & Swaminathan, M. S. (2000). Ending malnutrition by 2020: An agenda for change in the millennium. *WHO Food and Nutrition Bulletin, 21S,* 1S–76S.

Jensen, G. L., Friedmann, J. M., Coleman, C. D., & Smiciklas-Wright, H. (2001). Screening for hospitalization and nutritional risks among community-dwelling older persons [Electronic version]. *American Journal of Clinical Nutrition, 74,* 201–205.

Johnson, B. (2006). The not-so-skinny: U.S. population weighs in as the world's most obese. *Advertising Age, 77*(20), 43.

Johnson, L. (2008). Zinc deficiency. In *Merck manual.* Whitehouse State, NJ: Merck and Company.

Kranz, S. (2006). Meeting the dietary reference for fiber: Sociodemographic characteristics of preschoolers with high fiber intakes. *American Journal of Public Health, 96*(9), 1538–1541.

Kregg-Byers, C., & Schlenk, E. (2010). Implications of food insecurity on global health policy and nursing practice. *Journal of Nursing Scholarship, 42*(3), 278–285.

Labbok, M., Clark, D., & Goldman, A. (2004). Breast-feeding: Maintaining an irreplaceable immunological resource. *Nature Reviews, 4,* 565–572.

Langer, G., Schloemer, G., Knerr, A., Kuss, O., & Behrens, J. (2003). Nutritional interventions for preventing and treating pressure ulcers. *Cochrane Database of Systematic Review, 4,* CD003216.

Mach, O. (n.d.). Improving nutrition in Burundi. Global Health Council, International Medical Corp. Retrieved from http://www.globalhealth.org/reports/printview-report.php3?id=53

Marvin, S., & Medd , W. (2004). Fat city. *World Watch, 18*(5), 10–14.

Merck manual. (2002). Protein–energy malnutrition. Retrieved from http://www.merck.com/mrkshared /mmanual/section1/chapter2/2c.jsp

Monteiro, C. A., Moura, E. C., Conde, W. L., & Popkin, B. M. (2004). Socioeconomic status and obesity in adult populations of developing countries: A review. *Bulletin of the World Health Organization, 82*(12), 940–946.

Morris, J. (2006, September 26). World Food Programme. Statement by James T. Morris, Executive Director World Food Program to the United States Senate, Foreign Relations Committee. Hearing: Ending Child Hunger and Undernutritional Initiative.

Nash, M. (2003). Obesity goes global. *Time, 162*(8), 53–54.

National Institutes of Health. (2006a). Dietary supplement fact sheet: Vitamin A and carotenoids. Retrieved from http://ods.od.nih.gov

National Institutes of Health. (2006b). Dietary supplement fact sheet: Iron. Retrieved from http://ods .od.nih.gov

National Institutes of Health. (2010). Dietary supplement fact sheet: Iron. Retrieved from http://www .ncbi.nlm.nih.gov/pubmedhealth/PMH0001610

National Library of Medicine. (2006). Medline Plus. Medical encyclopedia: Protein in diet. Retrieved from http://www.nlm.nih.gov

Nead, K., Halterman, J., Kaczorowski, Auinger, P., & Weitzman, M. (2004). Overweight children and adolescents: A risk for iron deficiency. *Pediatrics, 114*(1), 104–108.

Oakley, G., & Tulchinsky, T. (2010). Folic acid and vitamin B_{12} fortification of flour: A global basic food security requirement. *Public Health Reviews, 32*(1), 284–296.

Olson, C. (2005). Food insecurity in women. *Topics in Clinical Nutrition, 20*(4), 321–328.

Pena, M., & Bacallao, J. (2002). Malnutrition and poverty. *Annual Reviews of Nutrition, 22,* 241–253.

Peterson, K. (2009). Childhood undernutrition: A failing global priority. *Journal of Public Health Policy, 30*(4), 455–464.

Pettifor, J. (2008). Vitamin D & or calcium deficiency rickets in infants & children: A global perspective. *Indian Journal of Medical Research, 127,* 245–249.

Ramakrishnan, U. (2002). Prevalence of micronutrient malnutrition. *Nutrition Review, 60*(5), S46–S52.

Schmidt, T. R. (n.d.). What's new in nutrition: Wound care in long-term care. Retrieved from http://www .novartisnutrition.com

Seligman, H., Laraia, B., & Kushel, M. (2010). Food insecurity is associated with chronic disease among low-income NHANES participants 1,2. *Journal of Nutrition, 140*(2), 304–311.

Shah, S., Selwyn, B., Luby, S., Merchant, A., & Bano, R. (2003). Prevalence and correlates of stunting among children in rural Pakistan. *Pediatrics International, 45,* 49–53.

South African Medical Research Council. (2004). Not an ordinary sweet potato. Retrieved from http://www .mrc.ac.za/mrcnews/sep2004/sweetpotato.htm

Stallings, S., Wolman, P., & Goodner, C. (2001). Contribution of food intake patterns and number of daily food encounters to obesity in low-income women. *Topics in Clinical Nutrition, 16*(4), 51–60.

Stettler, N. (2004). Comment: The global epidemic of childhood obesity: Is there a role for the paediatrician? *Obesity Reviews, 5*(suppl 1), 1–3.

Tulchinsky, T. (2010). Micronutrient deficiency conditions: Global health issues. *Public Health Reviews, 32*(1), 243–256.

Ulrich, C. (2005). Iron plays a major role in nutrition. *Human Ecology, 32*(3), 7–11.

Underwood, B. (2002). Health and nutrition in women, infants, and children: Overview of the global situation and the Asia enigma. *Nutrition Reviews, 60*(5), S7–S13.

United Nations. (1999). The right to adequate food (Art.11). Committee on Economic, social, and Cultural Rights.

USAID. (2005). USAID announces contribution to global nutrition. Retrieved from http://www.usaid.gov/our_work/global_health/home/News/nutrition_program.html

U.S. Department of Agriculture (USDA). (2005a). About WIC. Retrieved from http://www.fns.usda.gov/wic/aboutwic/mission.htm

U.S. Department of Agriculture (USDA). (2005b). Dietary guidelines for Americans. Weight management (Ch. 3). Retrieved from http://www.health.gov/dietaryguidelines/dga2005/document/html/chapter3.htm

U.S. Environmental Protection Agency (USEPA). (2010). EPA finalizes regulations for national renewable fuel standard program for 2010 and beyond. Retrieved from http://www.epa.gov/otaq/renewablefuels/420f10007.pdf

Visvanathan, R. (2003). Under-nutrition in older people: A serious and growing global problem! *Journal of Postgraduate Medicine, 49,* 352–360.

Williams, S. R., & Schlenker, E. D. (2003). *Essentials of nutrition & diet therapy* (8th ed.). St. Louis, MO: Mosby.

World Health Organization (WHO). (2003). Goals: Nutrition for health development. Retrieved from http://w3.whosea.org/nhd/goal.htm

World Health Organization (WHO). (2004). Challenges for the 21st century. *Nutrition in Southeast Asia,* 74–80.

World Health Organization (WHO). (2005a). Ensuring food safety in the aftermath of natural disasters. Retrieved from http://www.who.int/foodsafety/foodborne_disease/emergency/en/print.html

World Health Organization (WHO). (2005b). INFOSAN: Building a food safety network to prevent foodborne disease. Retrieved from http://www.who.int/foodsafety/fs_management/flyer_info_eng.pdf

World Health Organization (WHO). (2006a). Challenges. Retrieved from http://who.int/nutrition/challenges/en/print.html

World Health Organization (WHO). (2006b). Nutrition in emergencies. Retrieved from http://who.int/nutrition/topics/emergencies_collaboration/en/print.html

World Health Organization (WHO) & United Nations Children's Emergency Fund (UNICEF). (2005). Call for support for appropriate infant and young child feeding in the current Asian emergency, and caution about unnecessary use of milk products. Retrieved from http://www.who.int/maternal_child_adolescent/documents/asian_support/en/index.html

World Hunger and Poverty Facts and Statistics (2012). Retrieved from http://www.worldhunger.org/articles/Learn/world%20hunger%20facts%202002.htm

*For a full suite of assignments and additional learning activities, use the access code located in the front of your book to visit this exclusive website: **http://go.jblearning.com/holtz**. If you do not have an access code, you can obtain one at the site.*

15

Global Perspectives on Mental Health

Mary Ann Camann

> *"Mental health problems do not affect three or four out of
> every five persons but one out of one."*
>
> Dr. William Menninger

OBJECTIVES

After completing this chapter, the reader will be able to:

1. Analyze the implications of mental health for overall health in a population or geopolitical area.
2. Compare the policies and programs that support mental health treatment across countries and areas.
3. Identify factors that result in client-centered services that are culturally appropriate and build on health and move an individual toward recovery.
4. Describe factors that are barriers to mental health care.
5. Discover the effect of crisis on mental health.
6. Evaluate case examples related to delivery of mental health services and recovery.

OVERVIEW

The importance of mental health and mental illness as components of population health is increasingly being recognized as vital to the overall health of a country. Additionally, lack of mental health care is a known factor in the economic burden placed on individuals and their families facing mental health issues, which simply adds to the personal burden of suffering and disability associated with such conditions. In a follow-up to the 2001 World Health Organization (WHO) report *Investing in Mental Health* (WHO, 2003a), action plans were developed and then later reported in the *Mental Health Global Action Programme: Close the Gap, Dare to Care* (WHO, 2002b). This ongoing program has stressed the importance of direction of adequate financial and human resources so as to provide more effective and humane treatment that will contribute to a healthier and more dignified life for those persons who experience mental illness.

WHO (2003a) defines mental health as "a state of well-being in which the individual realized his or her own abilities, can cope with the natural stresses of life, can work productively and fruitfully, and is able to make a contribution to his or her community" (p. 4). Also emerging is a concept of recovery from mental illness that goes beyond treatment to include an individual's sense of hope, sense of meaning, and opportunities for satisfying material needs, social relationship, meaningful activities and ability to use services of the mental health care system (Onken, Dumont, Ridgway, Dornan, & Ralph, 2002). Recovery concepts challenge assumptions about chronicity and the need to remove persons with mental illness from the population.

In this chapter, current issues related to the global understanding of mental health and mental illness are presented in a policy-making and policy implementation context. The extent of the effects of mental illness on health worldwide is explored, along with an overview of the prevalence of mental illness and application of the concept of disease burden to community health and recovery status. Issues related to mental health and illness, such as cultural variations in understanding of the course and treatment and related stigma, are discussed. A review of current global mental health issues and the policy, belief structure, and resource allocation that underpin program development in various parts of the world are presented. Finally, the most recent findings on mental illness as compiled in WHO's *Mental Health Atlas* project are presented as they point toward issues that will need continued attention.

GLOBAL PERSPECTIVE: THE INFLUENCE OF RESEARCH AND TECHNOLOGY

The first annual World Mental Health Day, initiated by the World Federation for Mental Health (WFMH), was held nearly two decades ago to call attention to the lives of persons who experience mental illness. World Mental Health Day was a public acknowledgment of the effects of mental health and illness on overall health and productivity worldwide. However, it would take much work to increase awareness of mental health issues before the landmark publication of the *World Health Report 2001: New Understanding, New Hope*. This landmark report gave mental health the place it deserves on the world health agenda (Levav & Rutz, 2002). On World Health Day, 2001, the WHO Director General Dr. Gro Harlen Brudtland proclaimed:

> We focus on mental health in recognition of the burden that mental and brain disorders pose on people and families. An estimated 400 million people suffer from mental or neurological disorders and psychosocial problems and those related to alcohol and drug abuse. The simple truth is that we have the means to treat many disorders. We have the means and scientific knowledge to help people with their suffering. (WFMH, 2004)

This time span also marked the culmination of the "Decade of the Brain" declared by the National Institute of Mental Health (NIMH) in the United States, which proclaimed the years 1990–1999 to be a decade focusing on continued study of the brain so as to expand upon the growing knowledge of brain neuroanatomy and physiology. The increasing knowledge shed light on the needs of millions of Americans affected each year by disorders of the brain, ranging from neurogenetic diseases to degenerative disorders such as Alzheimer's disease, stroke, schizophrenia, autism, and impairments of speech language and hearing. These efforts drew attention to the mapping of the brain's biochemical circuitry; study of how the brain's cells and chemicals develop, interact, and communicate with the rest of the body; and breakthroughs in molecular genetics and understanding of the connection between the body's nervous and immune system (White House, 1990). The emerging science provided a new foundation upon which to build new understanding of mental illness as well as understanding of the various factors that support mental health. Philosophical and religious leaders as well as the general public had the opportunity to learn a new paradigm for understanding of mental illness that was based on the visualization of brain activity through advanced imaging such as positron emission tomography (PET) scans, and begin to reconcile this biological view with long-held beliefs about human identity and understanding of the self (Boyle, 2001).

The acceptance of the developing neuroscience had implications around the world for the subsequent development of mental health policy and programs. The work that was done during the Decade of the Brain also brought together many public and private entities in the United States and abroad for discussion about the science of brain function as well as the economic implications of health and diseases. During this time, WHO, the World Bank, and Harvard University also worked on development of a single measure of disease burden to capture the effects of various illnesses on daily life—specifically, the disability-adjusted life-year (DALY), which expresses years of life lost to premature death and years lived with a disability. The DALY measure "provided a comparative tool to analyze and prioritize health challenges worldwide, regionally, and nationally" (Magee, 2000). "The results of the WHO study confirmed what many health workers in mental health promotion and injury prevention had suspected for some time: that neuropsychiatric disorders and injuries were major causes of lost years of healthy life" (Lopez, 2005, p. 1186).

In 1999, the Surgeon General's *Report on Mental Illness in the United States* was issued as the first such report in the nation's history and heralded an "understanding of the importance of mental health in the overall health and well-being and to the strength of a nation and its people" (U.S. Department of Health and Human Services [USDHHS], 1999, p. 1). Donna Shalala, Secretary of Health and Human Services, noted in the introduction to the report that "We are coming to realize . . . that mental health is absolutely essential to achieving prosperity . . . [and there is] an opportunity to dispel the myths and stigma surrounding mental illness" (USDHHS, 1999, p. I). The report marked the beginnings of more inclusive, population-based mental health policies. It also focused on the disparities in the availability of, and access to, services in the mental health field, and the stigma and hopelessness that often surrounded the issue. It set the tone for national policy and echoed the themes of WHO's (1999) *World Health Report*.

Closely following the Surgeon General's report, *World Health Report 2001: Mental Health: New Understanding, New Hope* was issued and firmly placed mental health in the arena of global health. This report marked the continuation of a collaborative effort to develop a global campaign focused on depression management, suicide prevention, schizophrenia, and epilepsy (WHO, 2001a). In keeping with the emphasis on disease burden, it was acknowledged that most illnesses—both mental and physical—are influenced by a combination of biological, psychological, and social factors, setting the stage for advocacy for the cause of mental health and treatment of mental illness all over the world. Following that groundbreaking report came WHO's (2002b) Mental Health Global Action Programme (mhGAP), which sought to "provide a clear and coherent strategy for closing the gap between what is urgently needed and what is currently available to reduce the burden of mental disorders, worldwide" (p. 1).

LEGAL AND ETHICAL ISSUES
Global Burden of Disease

The 1996 Global Burden of Disease study was created to measure the burden of disease and injury in a manner that could also assess the cost-effectiveness of interventions, in terms of the cost per unit of disease burden prevented. Disease burden represents the gap between a population's actual health status and a reference point—that is, the expected years of healthy life. The measure of disease burden takes into consideration egalitarian principles of how long a person should live regardless of socioeconomic status, race, or level of education. Disease burden also addresses the time lived with disability as well as lost healthy time due to death. Most people can agree that some disabilities are more serious than others and produce variations in the effects of the illness on the healthy days of individuals (Murray & Lopez, 1996).

The Global Burden of Disease findings demonstrated that disability plays an important role in determination of the overall health status of a population, and so placed disability on the public health agenda, in addition to morbidity and mortality. In doing so, the study illustrated the long-underestimated burden of psychiatric conditions:

> Of the 10 leading causes of disability worldwide in 1990, measured in years lived with a disability, five were psychiatric conditions: unipolar depression, alcohol use, bipolar affective disorder, schizophrenia, and obsessive–compulsive disorder. Altogether psychiatric and neurological conditions accounted for 28% of all disability adjusted years. (Murray & Lopez, 1996, p. 300).

The Global Burden of Disease findings that focused on mental illness in terms of loss of productivity cut across world regions and economic status levels, thereby setting the stage for worldwide health officials to address mental health as an important and economically significant public health issue. WHO's mhGAP built on these concepts and provided a direction for member states in developing programs of care for "priority mental health conditions within the context of overall health system strengthening, with a particular focus on low and middle income countries" (WHO, 2008a). Under this program, new efforts were directed toward building national capacities that involved analysis of need, establishment of policies, legislative frameworks, and systems of care delivery to respond to the needs of individuals with mental health conditions (WHO, 2008a).

Demographics of Mental Illness

The picture of global mental health and illness is complicated. At the time of the mental health–oriented *WHO Global Action Program Report 2002*, it was reported that 25% of individuals develop one or more mental disorders at some stage in life, with such disorders affecting 450 million people in both developed and developing countries (WHO, 2002a). Mental disorders are truly universal, and can be found in people of all regions, all countries, and all societies.

Mental and behavioral disorders are common among persons seeking care in primary healthcare settings, accounting for approximately 24% of all such individuals. The most common mental health diagnoses made in primary care settings are depression, anxiety, and substance abuse disorder. These disorders may be present either alone or in addition to one or more physical disorders. There are no consistent differences in prevalence between developed and developing countries (WHO, 2001a, chap. 2, p. 1).

It is estimated that one in four families has at least one member currently suffering from a mental or behavioral disorder. Very often families must also provide physical and emotional support and pay the expense of treatment, even as they also bear the impact of stigma and discrimination associated with mental illness worldwide (WHO, 2001a). The economic costs also affect the population in proportionally different manners. Mental and behavioral disorders are believed to cause considerable disruption in the lives of those who are affected and their families, which in turn increases the overall cost of health care and contributes to a loss of productivity and quality of life.

In a report commissioned by the WHO mhGAP, the vulnerability of persons with mental health conditions was addressed. The researchers found that persons with mental health conditions are likely to be subjected to stigma and discrimination on a daily basis, and that they experience extremely high rates of physical and sexual victimization. Moreover, they are restricted in ability to access essential health and social care, including emergency relief services, and may also have limited access to work and schooling. Collectively, these effects result in increased likelihood of disability and premature death (WHO, 2010).

Conflicts such as "war and civil strife and disasters additionally affect a large number of people and result in mental health problems. In 2000, it was estimated that about 50 million people were refugees or internally displaced. . . . Millions are also affected by natural disasters that take a heavy toll on the mental health of the people involved, many of whom live in developing countries, where capacity to take care of these problems is limited" (WHO, 2001a, chap. 2, p. 19). In 2009, the World Psychiatric Association (WPA), in response to global disasters, joined with WHO to initiate a series of "train the trainer" workshops to train psychiatrists from the various regions of the world to deal with the mental health consequences of disaster so that they, in turn, can become resources for their countries (WPA, 2011).

Development of Mental Health Policy

Health policy is always developed within the context of the larger social and political environment. All health policy is a work in progress that acknowledges the current state of health, invites discussion, focuses attention on specific issues, and at its best creates a sense of priority and encourages development of services and evaluation of effectiveness of the impact of services on human life. The *World Health Report 2001* on mental illness made available new knowledge about the understanding of mental and behavioral disorders. It also offered possible solutions and policy options to governments and policy makers that could influence strategic decision making and point toward positive changes in the acceptance and treatment of mental disorders (WHO, 2001c). It is beyond the scope of this chapter to explore all policy issues and the ramification of policy directions, but suffice it to say that policy development is a slow process that is affected by many internal and external issues, as well as by available resources and public understanding and will.

Appearing in *World Health Report 2001,* and reinforced in the mhGAP (WHO, 2002a), were broadly conceived recommendations for action as well as plans for follow-up. They included the following measures:

- *Provide treatment in primary care,* as it enables the largest number of people to get easier and faster access to services. This recommendation implies that general health personnel should be trained in the essential skills of mental health care, which in turn has implications for education and training programs.
- *Make psychotropic drugs available.* Include essential psychotropic drugs in every country's essential drugs list, as such medications can ameliorate symptoms, reduce disability, shorten the course of many disorders, and prevent relapse.
- *Give care in the community,* as community care has a better effect on quality of life of individuals with chronic mental disorders than does institutional treatment. Such care is also cost-effective, respects human rights, and can lead to early interventions and limit the stigma of seeking treatment.
- *Educate the public.* Educational and awareness campaigns on mental health should be launched in all countries to reduce barriers to treatment and care by increasing awareness of the frequency of mental disorders, their treatability, the recovery process, and the human rights of people with mental disorders.
- *Involve communities, families, and consumers in the development and decision making regarding policies, programs, and services,* taking into account factors such as age, sex, culture, and social conditions.
- *Establish national policies, programs, and legislation for sustained action* based on current knowledge and human rights considerations. Mental health reforms, including budgetary allocations, should be part of larger health system reforms.
- *Develop human resources,* especially in developing countries, to increase and improve the training of mental health professionals, who will provide specialized care as well as support the primary health-care programs. Specialist mental healthcare teams ideally should include medical and nonmedical professionals, such as psychiatrists, clinical psychologists, psychiatric nurses, psychiatric social workers, and occupational therapists, who can work together toward the total care of individuals in the community.

- *Link with other sectors.* Sectors such as education, labor, welfare, and law and nongovernmental organizations should be involved in improving the mental health of communities.
- *Monitor community mental health* through the inclusion of mental health indicators in health information and reporting systems to determine trends, detect mental health changes resulting from external events such as disasters, and assess the effectiveness of mental health prevention and treatment programs, all the while building the case for the provision of resources.
- *Support more research.* Increase research on an international basis to elucidate variations across communities; to identify factors that influence the cause, course, and outcomes of mental disorders; and to increase understanding of the biological and psychosocial aspects of mental health as a method of understanding mental disorders and the development of more effective interventions.

These recommendations provided the foundation for further work in global mental health policies and programs. The recommendations were also addressed in WHO's *Project Atlas* and *Mental Health Atlas,* which reports on progress made in each area on a regular basis (WHO, 2001b, 2005). While there has been some improvement, 78.0% of countries accounting for 69.1% of the world's total population have passed laws for including mental health care, for those in need, within their health care systems. However, when policy is put in action, the reality is that the amount of financial resources allocated to programs ultimately determines the availability of services. Among low-income countries, 29.2%, accounting for a population in excess of 0.5 billion people, spend less than 1% of their national health budget on mental health care. By comparison, among high-income countries, only 0.7%, accounting for a population of about 5 million people, spend less than 1% of their health budget on mental health care. In the area of therapeutic drug availability, 89.3% of countries in the world, covering 91.1% of the world's total population, reported the existence of a therapeutic drug policy or essential list of drugs (WHO, 2001b; 2005).

While goals related to provision of care in community settings are well developed, community care facilities are present in only 51.7% of low-income countries and in 97.4% of high-income countries. Some types of community mental health services—such as day centers, therapeutic residential services, crisis residential services, clubhouse programs, and rehabilitation—are generally found only in high-income countries (WHO, 2005). Recent data highlight differences in mental health policy and programs related to the economic situations of the countries. Competing priorities for general healthcare financing and lagging priorities related to mental health care point out that much work still needs to be done.

To better focus on regional issues, a selected review of examples of mental health programs is presented here. These examples include analysis of the scope, effectiveness, and cultural and economic issues related to such programs in various countries within larger regions. The greatest work accomplished has been in the integration of mental health care and primary care, an approach that combines financial resources, increases access, and mitigates some stigma associated with mental illness.

REGIONAL MENTAL HEALTH ISSUES AND OUTCOMES

There are no specific worldwide groups that can address all cultural and ideological issues that affect mental health care. The thrust of WHO's efforts is to focus on scientific research and good practices, while acknowledging that many cultures base local policies and programs on religious or ideological beliefs. The WHO efforts shed light on the role of stigma and exclusion, both of which represent barriers to care on an individual and population basis. The various action plans described also acknowledge the fear factor and stigma that promotes delivery of care in institutions rather than in communities. The descriptions highlight programs that have been successful when community-based care is developed (Levav & Rutz, 2002). In the following sections, regional mental health policies, programs, and outcomes are examined. Exemplar programs are presented when available, and examples are used to illustrate problems as well as successes.

North America

United States

In the United States, the prevalence of self-reported mental health disability is 2 million adults, representing 2.7% of all respondents to the U.S. National Health Interview Survey. (Mojtabai, 2011). Both trends are rather discouraging considering the more than 20-year history of mental health care in the United States since the 1999 publication of *Report of the Surgeon General on Mental Health*. In that report, the directors of the Substance Abuse and Mental Health Services Administration (SAMHSA), the National Institute of Mental Health (NIMH), and the Center for Mental Health Services issued a challenge to the nation as a whole, to U.S. communities, and to health and social services, policy makers, employers, and citizens to take action and collaborate on generating needed knowledge about the brain and behavior and then translating that knowledge into service systems and action by citizens. The Surgeon General at that time, Dr. David Satcher, called for a social resolve to make the needed investment to change attitudes about mental health and usher in a healthy era of mind and body for the nation (USDHHS, 1999). The fact that this 1999 report was the first Surgeon General's report ever issued on the topic of mental health and mental illness was significant. The report emphasized two main findings: (1) the well-documented efficacy of mental health treatments and the range of treatment that exists for most mental disorders and (2) the view of mental health and mental illness as points on a continuum, which suggested efforts were needed along the entire continuum.

The Surgeon General's report (USDHHS, 1999) heralded the inclusion of mental health care in the overall healthcare schema for the United States, created a vision for the future that encouraged good access to a range of mental health treatment programs, and continued to build on the scientific bases of neuroscience, molecular genetics, and pharmacotherapies. The report urged the reduction of stigma attached to mental illness by dispelling myths with accurate knowledge and improving public awareness of effective treatment. Further, it called for the supply of mental health services and providers to be developed in different venues, ensuring that state-of-the-art treatment would be delivered in a manner that considered age, gender, race, and culture by facilitating entry into treatment and by reduction of financial barriers to treatment. The report was greeted with enthusiasm by consumers and mental health advocates alike. Indeed, it did mark a major emphasis on the essential inclusion of mental health care in healthcare discussions, but unfortunately few direct-care programs resulted from the report.

In 2001, the New Freedom Commission on Mental Health was convened to conduct a comprehensive study of the U.S. mental health service delivery system and issue advice on methods to improve the system and fill the gaps in the mental health system. By 2003, the commission had issued its report, which confirmed that "recovery from mental illness is now a real possibility. . . yet for too many Americans with mental illness, the mental health services and supports they need remain fragmented and disconnected—often frustrating the opportunity for recovery. Today's mental healthcare system is a patchwork relic—the result of disjointed reforms and policies" (USDHHS, 2003, p. 4). While not painting a pretty picture, the report incorporated the views of consumers, families, and professionals.

In 2003, the New Freedom Commission focused on creating a transformed mental health system. As part of this effort, the goals listed in **Table 15-1** were established. The commission also noted that "the system (of mental health care) was not oriented to the single most important goal of the people it serves— the hope of recovery. Even though treatments are available, they are not being transferred to community settings" (p. 3).

The National Alliance on Mental Illness (NAMI) grades the states on a regular basis as a way to address needs and recognize achievement and to evaluate how policy is being implemented. *Grading the States: Report on America's Health Care System for Serious Mental Illness* was published in 2006 and 2009. Unfortunately, many of the states that had worked hard since the first report saw their initial gains wiped

---

TABLE 15-1

Goals: In a Transformed Mental Health System . . .

Goal 1	Americans understand that mental health is essential to overall health.
Goal 2	Mental health care is consumer and family driven.
Goal 3	Disparities in mental health services are eliminated.
Goal 4	Early mental health screening, assessment, and referral to services are common practice.
Goal 5	Excellent mental health care is delivered and research is accelerated.
Goal 6	Technology is used to access mental health care and information.

Source: USDHHS, 2003.

---

out with the economic crisis: Budget shortfalls meant cuts to mental health services. In the 2009 analysis, the states assigned "D" grades remained the same as in the first study. Fourteen states had improved their grades since 2006, but not enough to raise the national average. Twelve states had fallen back. Twenty-three states stayed the same (NAMI, 2009).

There are some areas where innovation and excellence exist in mental health care. The recovery movement has been a significant motivator toward reform and inclusiveness in care delivery. Many of the NAMI programs are designed around education and peer support. NAMI's Peer Support Center offers programs to families, providers, and peers who have experienced mental illness. Its programs also include those focused on understanding of mental illness and treatment, and the importance of living a healthy life (NAMI, 2011). Nationally, NAMI sponsors nine programs of education and support that address the needs of families, peer support for persons living with a mental illness, providers, parents of children and adolescents living with mental illness, and the general public (NAMI, 2011).

Many recovery-focused programs have emerged from the work conducted at Boston University, Center for Psychosocial Rehabilitation, Sargent College of Health and Rehabilitation Sciences. The center, which was founded in 1979, has been innovative in both assisting in the design of programs and evaluating their outcomes. Its Hope and Health program, Training for the Future program, individual services in recovery and research, and evaluation projects are directed toward "increasing knowledge in the field of psychiatric rehabilitation and applying the knowledge to train treatment personnel, to develop effective rehabilitation programs, and to assist in organizing both personnel and programs into efficient and coordinated service delivery systems" (Center for Psychiatric Rehabilitation, 2006, p. 4). The Center for Psychiatric Rehabilitation has evolved into a "think tank" for development of recovery-focused psychosocial programs. William Anthony, the center's executive director, in his book *Toward a Vision of Recovery* (2007), states emphatically that "I am more convinced than ever that recovery from severe mental illness is possible for many more people than was previously believed. I believe that much of the chronicity in severe mental illness is due to the way the mental health system and society treat mental illness and not the nature of the illness itself" (p. 3).

One such program is the St. Louis Empowerment Center, a peer-run drop-in center that emphasizes participatory decision making, self-help, and mutual assistance. Peer support workers are matched via a "buddy" system, and the pair participates in recreational and social activities. The center also operates a "friendship line" to combat feelings of social isolation. A multisite study of such programs noted specific positive effects of consumer-driven programs when compared with traditional programs (Rogers et al., 2007).

Another peer-focused program is the Georgia Peer Specialist Program, which pioneered a certificate program in which persons are trained in providing services, engaging in advocacy, and influencing mental health policy. What is unique about this program is that services were made eligible for funding through the Medicaid program. The stated aim of this billable peer support program is to "provide an opportunity for consumers to direct their own recovery and advocacy process and to teach and support each other in the acquisition and exercise of skills needed for management of symptoms and for utilization of natural resources within the community" (Sabin & Daniels, 2003, p. 497).

Another developing trend is integration of mental health programs with primary care services. "Integrating mental health services into a primary care setting offers a promising, viable, and efficient way of ensuring that people have access to needed mental health services. Additionally, mental health care delivered in an integrated setting can help to minimize stigma and discrimination, while increasing opportunities to improve overall health outcomes" (Collins, Hewson, Munger, & Wade, 2010). The Milbank Memorial Fund studied many programs built on various types of integration models. One such model—the unified primary care and behavioral health model—has been implemented by the Cherokee Health Systems in Tennessee, which expanded community mental health centers at 22 sites to become federally qualified general health centers. At these sites, case managers work with adults and children with serious mental illness, as well as patients with chronic physical health problems. Co-location enables collaborative practice where treatment teams can work together with those individuals who have complex problems. Brief intervention methods are used as the behavioral health model (Collins et al., 2010).

Advances in programs utilizing recovery, peer participation, and integrated care models provide a promising direction for future development, but are unlikely to compensate for the overall scarcity of programs to serve the mentally ill in the United States. However, accumulating evidence on their efficacy and efficiency may spur mental health policy to mend the mind–body schism and provide meaningful programs that are more easily accessed and acceptable to both individuals and communities.

Canada

Canada established a Mental Health Commission in 2005 "to provide leadership to make mental health a long-term priority of governments: facilitating the exchange of research and best practices, reducing fragmentation of mental health and illness policies and programs, and developing a strategy to increase awareness and reduce stigma around mental illness" (Canadian Collaborative Mental Health Initiative, 2005a). The Canadian Collaborative Mental Health Initiative was funded for 2 years by Health Canada's Primary Health Care Transition Fund.

As the funding model suggests, the Canadian healthcare system focused on the primary care model (Canadian Psychiatric Association [CPA]/College of Family Physicians of Canada [CFPC], 2003). When reviewing patterns of use, it was found that one in every five Canadians experience a mental illness during their lifetime, and the integration model offered the best options for greater access to mental health care. The Canadian Collaborative Mental Health Initiative addressed the complex interplay between physical and mental illnesses. It sought to maximize the shared care focus in mental health care through evaluation of various initiatives undertaken by a consortium of 12 national organizations representing mental health consumers, families, caregivers, community providers, dietitians, family physicians, nurses, occupational therapists, pharmacists, psychologists, psychiatrists, and social workers. One of the first activities of the initiative was to conduct a survey to obtain "buy-in" of the various groups, resulting in an engaged community of interest that provides ongoing advice. The initiative produced 10 research papers and 12 toolkits to ensure dissemination of the information (Canadian Collaborative Mental Health Initiative, 2006). In a follow-up report issued by the Mental Health Commission of Canada (MHCC) in

2009, efforts were directed toward recovery and well-being along the continuum of the seven goals articulated in the work of the commission and called for a social movement that puts mental health policy and programs in the forefront of health care.

Several initiatives developed out of the intentional collaborative efforts focused on integration of mental health services within primary care as a method of delivering mental health care, in recognition of the fact that the traditional models that expected persons to come to mental health services were not working (Kates, Crave, Crustola, Nikolaou, & Allen, 1997). A collaborative process was developed that resulted in mental health professionals being paired as consultants, either on-site or in shared space. The details of how the process worked varied. One project focused on knowledge exchange at a family medicine clinic in Nova Scotia, providing an academic teaching environment for family medicine residents and clinical staff, including family physicians, nurses, social workers, and psychiatrists. This program addressed knowledge transfer via use of electronic patient records, weekly rounds, monthly case discussions, and three shared care retreats held annually (Kates, Crustolo, Farrar, & Nikolaou, 2001).

These programs continue today, and have since been joined by Mental Health First Aid projects, in which connections are provided for a person developing a mental health problem or experiencing a mental health crisis. This program provides a point of access and considerable training to improve mental health literacy while increasing recognition of signs and symptoms of mental health problems. The Mental Health First Aid program provides initial help and guides persons toward appropriate professional mental health services. Nearly 50,000 Mental Health First Aid personnel have been trained, thereby expanding the outreach of the healthcare system (MHCC, 2011b).

Another initiative developed a geriatric psychiatry outreach team bringing together psychiatrists, registered nurses, social workers, and a neuropsychologist to provide consultation to two family practice clinics and one community health center as well as home-based assessment when appropriate. The collaborative also sponsors a shared care conference annually (MHCC, 2011a).

In 2010, a Peer Project was launched that targeted peer-based education strategies aimed at youth in schools and adults in workplaces. The commission is developing national standards of practice but also encourages innovation in program development geared toward mental health. The concept of psychological safety in the workplace is designed to begin a conversation on occupational health that includes mental health (MHCC, 2011c).

All of these activities were based on a shared belief that Canadians are entitled to a health system with the capacity to help them meet both their physical and mental health needs, whether those needs comprise illness prevention, early detection, treatment, rehabilitation, or recovery. The consortium produced a general toolkit for providers and policy makers on planning and implementing collaboration between mental health and primary care services; additionally, the consortium produced a two-volume report on emerging trends in mental health care, including descriptions of more than 90 Canadian initiatives (Canadian Collaborative Mental Health Initiative, 2005b, p. 25). In all, 61% (55 programs) of long-term mental health initiatives were started during the years of the collaboration (2000–2004) (Canadian Collaborative Mental Health Initiative, 2005b, p. 28). The work of the Canadian Collaborative Mental Health Initiative and the MHCC laid the ground for launching a Partners of Mental Health Initiative in 2012 that is expected to spur a social movement to position mental health on the national agenda by making use of the voices of ordinary Canadians (MHCC, 2011a).

There is considerable agreement in North America on the scope of mental health problems and a growing focus on the efficacy of recovery, community, and social change as being the route forward to providing mental health services. Although outstanding examples exist, the Canadian system's main focus is on keeping the care system working with the consumer as the focus and streamlining access to care. Much work remains to be done, which is made more difficult by the challenging economy.

Latin America

The Latin American region includes many different cultural groups. In geopolitical terms, there are 13 countries in South America, 5 in Central America, plus Mexico, and 13 other countries in the Caribbean basin (Pan American Health Organization [PAHO], 2005). In 2001, the PAHO began a process to consider new priorities for mental health care. In November 2005, a regional conference was held in Brazil convening governmental mental health officers, organizations from civil society, and consumers and family members to the Regional Conference on Mental Health Services Reform. The conference focused on the state of mental health care in the Americas and on improvement of mental health care through replacement of the service model based on the psychiatric hospital with community alternative care; it also addressed actions to safeguard the human rights and the social inclusion of persons affected by mental disorders. The main thrust of the discussion revolved around the use of the primary healthcare strategy adopted by PAHO (2005). Collectively, the conference participants declared the importance of preserving human rights and linking psychiatric care to primary health care. They also declared that the training of mental healthcare workers should be based on a community-based service model that includes psychiatric inpatient care, when necessary, in community hospitals.

Studies conducted jointly by the PAHO and WHO found that "around 30% of the total population of Latin America and the Caribbean was partially or totally excluded from access to health goods and services" (Acuna & Bolis, 2005, p. 3). Exclusion from health care was a particularly difficult issue for persons with mental illness and made them even more vulnerable through stigmatization. Stigmatization can be viewed as a social variable or as self-exclusion based on belief that there is no effective treatment (Acuna & Bolis, 2005). In the 2010 *Annual Report of the Director of the Pan American Sanitary Bureau,* mental health was viewed in the context of personal security. The report noted that mental health problems continue to be a major concern in Latin America and the Caribbean. It is estimated that more than 125 million people in this region suffer from some form of mental illness but that fewer than half have access to treatment.

In Cuba, El Salvador, and Guatemala, policies on mental health have been integrated and focused on community-based care versus the traditional cure models. These policies mandated decentralization of mental health services, moving them from a hospital setting to community-level primary care (PAHO, 2010).

Policies that focus on access to services and community-based care are necessary to meet the growing demand for mental health services in Latin America (PAHO, 2005). Today, 64.5% of Latin American countries have specific mental health policies and 80.6% have plans and programs—rates that are higher than those in many other regions (Alarcon, 2003). Consequently, actions geared toward dissemination of knowledge about mental health and the effective treatment of mental illness, as well as protection of human rights, are important to the success of future policy and program development. Efforts are being directed toward both legislation and policy implementation. Workshops are being held for mental health leaders, with the desired end point being comprehensive legislation that reflects the WHO human rights norms.

Chile has reported that it has experienced improvements in social indicators since the 1990s but that only 39% of persons with mental illness receive treatment. Efforts since 2000 have focused on increasing the role of primary health care in delivery of mental health services and access to psychotropic medications. There were still few mental health professionals per capita in the country, however, and this is an issue for future development (WHO, 2008b). In addition, there is a lack of mental health services designed specifically for the indigenous people of Latin America despite PAHO goals (Incayawar & Maldonado-Bourchard, 2009).

Other programs have focused on development of mental health worker capacity. In one training program in Panama, primary care nurses were trained to recognize depression, provide notification to primary physicians, and provide supportive interventions. This program had its greatest impact on the detection of moderate cases of depressive disorders, indicating that more education may be necessary (Moreno, Saravanan, Levav, Kohn, & Miranda, 2003). A program in Dominica addressed understanding of mental illness by calling attention to attitudes toward mental illness. In this program, case vignettes depicting persons experiencing psychosis, alcoholism, depression, and childhood hyperactivity were viewed by community leaders, nurses, teachers, police officers, and community members. The person in the psychosis vignette was identified by 84% of the leaders and by 71% of the community members; fewer than 30% identified the other situations as involving mental illness, but said that they would refer someone with mental health problems to a medical practitioner if it was identified (Kohn, Sharma, Camilleri, & Lavav, 2000).

Another program expanded on the recommendation of primary care interventions through a program that enrolled women in three primary care clinics in Santiago, Chile. The women were randomly assigned to either a stepped-care program or usual care. The stepped-care improvement program consisted of structured psychoeducation, systematic monitoring of clinical progress, and a pharmacotherapy program that was delivered for 7 weeks, with booster sessions at weeks 9 and 12. This program demonstrated far greater improvement among those randomized to stepped care, with 70% of these patients recovering at 6 months compared with 30% of those given standard care (Araya, Rojas, Fritsch, Gaete, Rojas, & Simon, 2003). This program provided a cost-effective intervention that was suitable for low-socioeconomic-status population groups.

In Argentina, mental healthcare reform was implemented on a state/provincial level. In the Rio Negro province, beds in a psychiatric hospital were replaced by beds in general hospitals, and a network of community-based services such as mental health centers and psychosocial rehabilitation programs was set up throughout the province (Caldas de Almedia & Horvitz-Lennon, 2010).

Based on the broad policy recommendations and the demonstration programs, it would seem that mental health programs would most likely be effective if they addressed increasing understanding of mental health issues and treatment and if they could be provided along with mental health care as part of the primary care system. These efforts will require development of trained healthcare workers who can identify mental health issues and direct individuals to primary care or community resources, as appropriate. There remain huge gaps in both stated policies and implemented programs in Latin America, especially for those addressing vulnerable groups. Recent policy initiatives have been developed that focus on the connection between mental health and economic development, but stretching limited resources will continue to challenge individual countries.

Europe

Countries in the WHO European Region face continued challenges with mental health problems, with 27% of persons in the European Union experiencing at least one mental disorder. Depression is the leading chronic condition in Europe, where the suicide prevalence rate is 13.9 deaths per 100,000 population. In Lithuania, this rate is 30.7 suicides per 100,000 population (WHO, 2009a).

Mental health policies and services vary greatly across the region. Community care has been shown to offer a better quality of life and greater satisfaction to consumers and family caregivers. Across Europe, the number of institutional beds is decreasing. Unfortunately, many European countries have limited services available in the community, and more than 50% of all patients are still treated in large mental hospitals. A recent publication, *Policies and Practices for Mental Health in Europe*, noted that 42 countries have adopted or updated their mental health policies since 2005 (WHO, 2011c). However, the establishment of such policies does not necessarily mean advancement of programs given the economic constraints and reduction in public spending related to the economic crisis that started in 2007 and continues to offer a challenging atmosphere (WHO, 2011b). The United Kingdom leads in the percentage of health spending earmarked for mental health at 13.5%, with Bulgaria, Romania, and Portugal all allocating less than 4% of their health expenditures to mental health services.

Some of the ongoing policy issues relate to the availability of mental health professionals. In some countries, care is delivered by doctors and nurses in institutional settings; in others, mental health care is provided as part of primary care. This practice varies considerably. In Malta, a relatively small county, there are no community-based services and the highest rate of hospital beds per capita—more than 180 beds per 100,000 population. In France, in contrast, mental health services include those provided at day hospitals, part-time therapeutic welcome centers, and therapeutic workshops (WHO, 2011c). Although the mental health Declaration for Europe emphasized the role of primary care as part of mental health service delivery, this role remains underdeveloped in many parts of Europe. In some countries, diagnosing mental disorders or prescribing related medication is illegal for family doctors. This policy often reflects a lack of training, but also results from longstanding stigma against persons with mental health problems (WHO, 2011c).

Efforts to improve or increase training since the 2005 report have resulted in inclusion of mental health training in the education of general practitioners in Austria; additional training for family doctors in Germany; development of courses in psychiatry, protocols on disease management, and standards of providing medicine in psychiatry in Russia; and establishment of improved access to evidence-based psychological therapy focused on anxiety and depression in the United Kingdom (WHO, 2011c). Activities generally support the defined scope of mental health policy and practice related to promoting mental well-being in the population; tackling stigma, discrimination, and social exclusion; prevention of mental health problems; and providing comprehensive and effective care for those who experience mental health disorders. These services also include recovery-focused programs for caregivers and patients that involve choice, including rehabilitation (WHO, 2011c).

Mental Health Europe carried out the project known as Good Practices for Combating Social Exclusion of People with Mental Health Problems, and worked on evaluation of which practices were transferable to other European countries, taking into account the major existing socioeconomic and cultural differences among these nations. The project addressed coordination and cooperation around the issues of health and social services in communities, employment, education, housing, transport, leisure, and civil and human rights (Mental Health Europe, 2005). Another program established a school aimed at parents of children with mental health problems; its aim was to assist parents to develop their own solutions, to make informed decisions, and to reduce the intensity of the burden of care. In the program, the parents received support and information on improving relationships and creating effective methods of communication, as well as assistance in creating independent self-help groups (European Commission, 2003).

In the United Kingdom, a five-year initiative was undertaken to deal with stigma and discrimination around mental health issues. Project SHIFT works with young people, public services and professional and private organizations, and the media to promote communication and disability rights. Another program, Our Choice in Mental Health, encourages the exercise of choice among people who use mental health services and their caregivers; it also provides best-practices models to be used as a basis for developing future programs (WHO, 2011c). Addressing the need for an educated mental health workforce, a three-year program on innovations in community-based mental health nursing was developed to include sites in the United Kingdom, Germany, and Italy. The training also focused on developing non-institutional approaches to mental health (Leonardo da Vinci Pilot Projects, 2007).

In Europe, there are islands of hope in a region that has much institutional history and stigma to overcome. Plans are well under way to make changes in the types of care provided, the accessibility of care, and delivery models for mental health care. The dissemination of evidence-based practices remains a challenge. Nevertheless, the gap is narrowing between policy and practice among some countries. The move toward greater community focus and away from institutional care is an economic issue as well as a social and political issue. Innovations and demonstrations provide a pathway to future success.

Africa

Africa is a vast land that encompasses many diverse peoples and has been the site of much strife and war. "Most of its countries also are characterized by low incomes, high prevalence of communicable diseases and malnutrition, low life expectancy, and poorly staffed services" (Gureje & Alem, 2000). Mental health most often ranks low on the list of policy priorities. In 1988 and 1990, the African Region of WHO adopted two resolutions to improve mental health services, and each state was expected to formulate mental health policies, programs, and action plans. When progress was addressed two years later, some modest achievements had been made. The current goals are directed toward changing the negative perception of mental disorders by the public and reducing the incidence and prevalence of mental disorders while providing adequate care for persons with mental illness (Gureje & Alem, 2000).

In a presentation titled "Mental Health and Poverty: Challenges in Service Delivery in Sub-Saharan Africa" (2011), Dr. Fred Kigozi, Executive Director of Butabika Nation Hospital, noted that Africa is the second largest continent in the world, with a population of more than 1 billion. There is a low life expectancy related to the fact that 60% of the population lives on less than $1 per day. Adding to the difficulties faced by this region are civil strife, unemployment, the HIV/AIDS epidemic, and an overall shortage of resources. There is only 0.05 psychiatrist per 100,000 population across Africa, few countries have clinical psychologists or social workers, and 79% of the African countries spend less than 1% of their health budget on mental health. Further, poverty often aggravates the stigma about mental illness and delays help-seeking. In most countries, services are limited to a central large mental hospital, a few beds in regional general hospitals, and very little community care. Generally needs are focused on development of policies that will guide development of services and counter stigma, as well as development of training for general health workers in the districts. The region embraces the principles of integration of mental health into primary health care and is focused on meeting structural needs to make that happen (Kigozi, 2011).

The HIV pandemic persists in some African communities, and the mental health consequences of AIDS contribute to overall psychiatric morbidity in the region, exacerbating the consequences of hunger, displacement, and lack of material resources. Compounding the fear of mental illness is the lack of mental health workers in most countries and the existence of only a limited drug formulary. Nearly half of the countries in Africa have just one hospital for the mentally ill. Further, because many families do not understand the manifestation of mental illness in their family members, they may chain or tie patients up and administer beatings (Kaplan, 2006).

Clearly, there are many challenges to providing mental health care in Africa that cannot be overcome by policy statement and goal setting. Several programs, however, provide beacons of hope for the future. In the WHO Mental Health Improvement for Nations Development (MIND) country summary series in 2007, Ghana reported that mental health services are available at most levels of care but the majority of care is provided through specialized psychiatric hospitals with less funding for general hospital– and primary care–based services. The current laws support institutional care to keep mentally ill people off the streets and protect their assets. In Ghana, 5.74% of the total health budget is dedicated to administration and mental health services. The national healthcare system provides community psychiatric nurses who report to the coordinator of community psychiatry, and some primary healthcare workers have received on-site mental health training. In addition, Ghana has many traditional healers, with 70% to 80% of the population using traditional medicine as their primary care. Ideally, more of the traditional healers will be integrated into the formal healthcare system and provided with standard accreditation and practice guidelines to provide mental health care (WHO, 2007).

In one project in Nigeria, traditional mental health practitioners (TMHPs) were included in a program to foster working relationships between orthodox mental health practitioners and traditional mental health practitioners. The project involved pre- and post-training evaluations and training on the types of mental illness and treatment of mental illness, including follow-up, aftercare, relapse prevention, and other primary prevention measures. The post-training evaluation revealed that a higher percentage of TMHPs could recognize all the symptoms of mental illness listed in the program. The post-intervention evaluation also noted a change in the attitude of the TMHPs toward persons with mental illness, including the belief that persons should not be sent out of the community and new ideas about how they should be treated. Beating of the mentally ill had been a long-time practice in Nigeria, where caning was seen as an effective treatment for the mentally ill. After the intervention, beating was less likely to occur. Another outcome was that traditional mental health professionals were more likely to refer patients to orthodox mental health providers (Adelekan, Makanjuola, & Ncom, 2001).

In another program conducted in Uganda—a site of war and rebellion for nearly two decades—local people were recruited to implement a program to treat depression in adults. Dr. Paul Bolton led the program, in which 250 persons from 30 villages were assessed as suffering from major depression and assigned to one of 30 groups. Fifteen of the groups received psychotherapy sessions for 16 weeks, and the other half received none. At the end of the period, those patients who received the therapy were significantly less depressed than the control group. Moreover, 14 of the 15 therapy groups continued to meet 6 months later, having transformed themselves into economic support groups so that members could help one another by lending money and helping one another develop small businesses (McNeil, 2005–2006). Another program led by Dr. Bolton was implemented with Ugandan teenagers in refugee camps and produced similar results. In all of the programs, Bolton began by asking participants open-ended questions about how they view mental health, and then went on to develop a sustainable program utilizing a relatively inexpensive and simple intervention. Also in Uganda, Bolton utilized a system and function assessment for depression to increase the likelihood that understanding of the impairment of depression would build justification for the allocation of scarce resources to mental health issues (Bolton, Wilk, & Ndogoni, 2004).

Elsewhere on the African continent, Zimbabwe launched mental health treatment guidelines for mental health care within its primary care system. They describe how a mentally ill patient should be managed holistically from history taking through diagnosis and delivery of the appropriate treatment and management (WHO, 2011a).

Where poverty is endemic, low-cost integrated public mental health programs are vital, as are programs that train and involve community workers. Culturally sensitive programs that include significant local involvement are important to change attitudes and offer hope to persons with mental illness. The vastness of Africa makes it important that individual countries and provinces make efforts to better the life of persons with mental illness within the constraints of few limited financial resources and much civil strife.

Asia and the Western Pacific

In 2003 in Beijing, Dr. Henk Bekedam spoke at the Second International Mental Health Development Conference, and noted that "While many aspects of physical health have improved in the region of the past 50 years, mental health has worsened." He also acknowledged that the burden of mental health goes hand-in-hand with rapid urbanization and social changes such as poverty and physical illness. To address these difficult realities, the region adopted three basic goals related to mental health:

1. Reduce the human, social, and economic burden produced by mental and neurological disorders, including intellectual disability and substance abuse and dependence.
2. Promote mental health.
3. Give appropriate attention to psychosocial aspects of health care and the improvement of quality of life.

Bekedam (2003) further called for the integration of mental health into general health care and primary care systems. As in Europe and largely as the lingering result of past European colonization, mental health activities in the countries of WHO's South East Asia Region have been concentrated on hospital-based psychiatry. A report on the work of WHO in this region called for mental health services that could be integrated into the primary healthcare system, and the development of innovative community-based programs. As in Africa, considerable attention in Asia has been paid to crisis situations such as tsunami relief efforts, provision of basic health care, and the demands of bird flu outbreaks. Additionally, some areas in Asia have been marked by war and insurgent activities that contribute to human suffering and mental illness. Mental health has been a low priority in such circumstances. In most of the countries in southeast Asia, mental health spending represents less than 2% of the total health budget, with 80% to 90% of those funds going to hospitals (Maramis, Nguyen, & Minas, 2011). A notable exception to the trend of hospital-based care is found in Cambodia, because of the necessity for the country to start from the beginning in creating a healthcare system following the Pol Pot regime. Cambodia has focused on development of a primary care and community-focused care model. Capacity is still limited in these programs, but they are growing as there was no hospital-based system to disassemble before their adoption (Maramis et al., 2011).

One project examined factors that influence Asian communities' access to mental health care and noted that both health professionals and the general public have considerable knowledge deficits regarding mental illness and mental health. Shame and stigma were commonly reported. "The sense of shame was significant, and it was noted that the shame connected with mental illness for Chinese people meant that 'you can't go out and face other people'" (Wynaden, Chapman, Org, McGowan, Zeeman, & Yeak, 2005, p. 90). Another commonly reported barrier to seeking care was the level of knowledge about mental illness, which was related to the level of education, country of origin, and religion. Karma, the law of cause and effect in Eastern spirituality, and beliefs about reincarnation are important concepts in many Eastern religions. Consequently, having a child with mental illness often results in the parents feeling as if they are being punished for conduct in their past lives. Others might believe that a mentally ill person is possessed by evil spirits, or that bad blood is passed down from the child from the mother. Even if a general practitioner asks about mental illness, concern about family reputation and shame may prohibit discussion of the illness. These beliefs often result in mental illness being hidden from the community, and family members not doing anything about the illness, or simply hoping that it will go away. Seeking help for mental illness is often seen as a last resort (Wynaden et al., 2005).

On a more positive note, the Pacific Island Mental Health Network (PIMHnet) was launched in March 2007. It includes 18 members: American Samoa, Australia, Commonwealth of the Northern Mariana Islands, Cook Islands, Federated States of Micronesia, Fiji, Kiribati, Marshall Islands, Nauru, New Zealand, Niue, Palau, Papua New Guinea, Samoa, Solomon Islands, Tokelau, Tonga, and Vanuatu. There has been considerable progress made in raising awareness of mental health issues within these countries. The government of each PIMHnet member country has nominated a leader to direct national activities in collaboration with a specially designated in-country mental health team. Acknowledging the many challenges faced in providing mental health services, there has been some progress in development of human resources and expansion of the use of primary health workforce to build services for people with mental health problems. One such program that came out of the partnership was developed in Vauatu, where two Australian family physicians with expertise in mental health were engaged to provide training of local health workers, who included doctors, nurses, and community health workers. The training consisted of classroom sessions, interactive activities, and visits to hospitals. The participants were also engaged in setting up a prevalence study for mental health problems that utilized a cultural awareness tool translated into Bislama, the local language. Outcomes have included using the new skills to identify and manage mental health problems and developing a series of educational activities for young people to raise understanding of mental illness. Other activities undertaken by PIMHnet include newsletters as well as teleconferences with member countries every six months to provide updates and opportunities to request assistance. Contacts have also been established with academic organizations, professional organizations, and church and spiritual organizations to add to the network's resources (Hughes, 2009).

WHO has focused on training and education as important first steps in developing mental health services. For example, it has supported activities such as training nurses in Fiji to detect symptoms of mental illness in primary care and to provide treatment. In China, workshops to train trainers were conducted to increase recognition and management of common mental disorders in general practice. In the Republic of Korea, a workshop was held on the development of a model for community-based mental health services. In Vietnam and Mongolia, projects were developed to produce a community-based mental healthcare text and to use an ICD-10 coding system to diagnose and manage common mental health disorders at the primary healthcare level (WHO, 2004). Efforts have been made to change understanding and reduce reliance on institutional care in other countries as well, but much still needs to be accomplished. In Jakarta, the Lawang mental hospital has reduced its patient population from more than 4200 to 700 patients, and the atmosphere has been changed to reflect changes in therapy and nonchemical approaches; nevertheless, Indonesian police continue to get calls to remove mentally ill people from the highways where they have been put out by their relatives because they are too ashamed to seek help ("Mental Illness Is Not Divine Retribution," 2006).

One project is attempting to provide services for basic mental health needs by encouraging effective community-based care, including treatment and support, and by addressing the issues of poverty and stigma through the creation of partnerships with governments and community groups to create sustainable programs. The program links medical model mental health treatment with community development approaches such as programs on how to earn a living and creation of small-scale horticultural projects that provide a family livelihood and reduce the stigma associated with mental illness (Kaplan, 2006).

In response to the recent earthquakes and tsunami in Japan, physicians and research fellows went to the University of California, San Francisco, to learn how to provide mental health counseling dealing with crisis. They were especially focused on the response for children in the face of disaster; thus psychologists taught the guiding principles for parents and other caregivers—listen, protect, and connect. In Japan, the stigma associated with mental health concerns often leads to guilt and shame, so training is being organized to help Japanese physicians and others improve their response to individuals who may be vulnerable to post-traumatic stress disorder (PTSD) (Norris, 2011).

To erase long-held stigma and promote delivery of mental health services in community settings, innovations such as the mood disorders center in Hong Kong have been developed. When the center opened, a hotline was established to bypass the taboos about talking about depression. The center's phone lines were heavily used by people asking for help and provided a point of contact regarding reports of chronic fatigue, headaches, and poor memory, which are often correlates of depression. The mood disorders center, developed by the Chinese University of Hong Kong, also trained family doctors to better recognize and treat anxiety disorders and depression as a face-saving way for people to seek treatment (Saywell & McManus, 2001). The government and a private organization plan to open one-stop centers in all 18 districts in Hong Kong, but face considerable community resistance linked to continued community stigma and fear (Bayron, 2010). In China, the scope of the taboos regarding mental illness has prompted the Chinese government to draft the country's first mental health law formally recognizing that mental health care is both a legal issue and a medical matter. Often hospitalization of mentally ill persons is sought for political reasons, whereas other individuals with mental health issues avoid care because of stigma; thus human rights issues are being discussed in the public comment period related to the law (Pumin, 2011).

Much effort is necessary to overcome centuries of cultural beliefs and political propaganda about the causes and treatment of mental illness. Small, locally developed programs delivered as part of a health system are likely to produce the best results for treatment if personal stigma and fear can be overcome by individuals and families.

SUMMARY

It is clear that considerable attention to mental health and mental illness issues needs to be paid by, and involve more, government entities and community agencies. There is increased evidence of the biopsy-chosocial nature of both mental illness and mental health, as well as evidence that mental illness has a profound impact on the lives of persons with such illness, their families, and their communities. The publication of such evidence has increased the global profile of international mental health, but sustained and sustainable action remains limited. Mental disorders have clear economic costs, as persons experiencing mental illness often experience reduced productivity at home and in the workplace. "Mental disorders also have a range of consequences on the course and outcomes of comorbid chronic conditions, such as cancer, heart disease, diabetes, and HIV/AIDS, and persons with untreated mental disorders are at heightened risk for poor health behaviors, noncompliance with prescribed medical regimens, diminished immune functioning, and unfavorable disease outcomes" (WHO, 2002a, p. 3).

Understanding of the importance of mental health and the treatment of mental illness does not necessarily instantly produce needed resources and programs. WHO's *Mental Health Atlas*, a compendium of global data from 192 countries, was updated in 2005; it "shows no substantial change in global mental health resources since 2001. There continues to be marked and growing differences in availability between high- and low-income countries. Only 62% of all regions have mental health policies, with the Western Pacific 48%, South-East Asia 54.5%, and Africa 50% falling behind in planning and implementation of mental health services" (WHO, 2005, p. 15). As discussed earlier, competing priorities in the form of serious health problems, natural disasters, and war may push mental health issues aside, to be considered a low priority, despite increased understanding of the effects of mental illness on the population.

Community care for mentally ill persons continues to be a high priority, but is available in only 68.1% of the WHO member countries, covering 83.3% of the world's population. In the Americas and Europe, more areas have community care programs but considerable variations in geographic access are apparent. Community care is also highly correlated to income level, with only 51.7% of low-income countries having it versus 97.4% of high-income countries (WHO, 2005, p. 19).

On a more positive note, 89.3% of countries have a therapeutic drug policy and essential list of drugs. The drugs list comprises basic and traditional psychotropic drugs that can be produced in generic formulations. This coverage is most likely related to the increased integration of mental health care within primary care, which has been an important health policy direction. Eighty-seven percent of the world reports having mental health as a component of primary care, but only 61% has treatment facilities for severe mental disorders in primary care. Psychiatric beds account for only 19.8% of all beds in general hospitals worldwide. Consequently, there is continued reliance on large mental hospitals in 68% of the world, which often also results in questions related to human rights in many countries (WHO, 2005).

When available personnel and training of primary care workers are considered, the deficits in mental health care become obvious. Worldwide, there are only 1.2 psychiatrists per 100,000 population and only 2 psychiatric nurses per 100,000 population. The state of mental health care is most evident in the 2.8% decrease in the number of countries stating that they had a specific budget line for mental health in their health budgets (WHO, 2005). "One fifth of the countries reported spending less than 1% of their health budget on mental health, in contrast to the estimate that 13% of all disease burden is caused by neuropsychiatric disorders" (Patel, Saraceno, & Kleinman, 2005, p. 1313).

Addressing many of the barriers to care, WHO's report titled *Improving Health Systems and Services for Mental Health* makes the case for improved laws and policies but also considers that primary care for mental health "is fundamental but must be supported by other levels of care including community-based and hospital services, informal services and self care to meet the full spectrum of mental health needs of the population" (2009c, p. 21). Such integration of services also serves to reduce stigma and support worker training and improved access to services.

There is much work to be done in educating healthcare providers and the general population about mental illness and its effective treatment. Major policy changes related to including mental health care in primary care and providing such care in community settings will come about only when governments and individuals demand such care and see the benefit of the outcomes for individuals and populations. Opportunities are present for developing countries to apply current knowledge and the lessons of exemplar programs to their developing healthcare policies and programs. Development of culturally congruent programs illustrates that major mental disorders can be treated in an efficient and cost-effective manner with low-cost and technically simple treatment. Community and primary care treatment programs need the support of philanthropic organizations as well as government entities to increase understanding of their effectiveness. WHO (2009b) has produced checklists for evaluating mental health plans, but it will take a greater community will to address implementation of mental health services in a meaningful fashion. Psychiatric drug availability can be increased if mental illness is included as an exemption category in the trade-related intellectual property rights international agreement; this would make it possible for developing countries to produce generic versions of drugs patented after 2005 (Patel et al., 2005).

In keeping with the spirit of the first Global Mental Health Day, mental health needs to have a larger presence on the world health agenda. The case needs to continue to be made that good mental health care enhances overall health and the prosperity of the population. The mhGAP program (WHO, 2008a) makes the case that more effort is required to change policy, practice, and services delivery systems to ensure that mental health needs are assigned the level of priority necessary to guarantee that they are addressed. There should be no more excuses for marginalizing funding and people who suffer from mental illness.

STUDY QUESTIONS

1. Relate the barriers to receiving mental health care as compared to physical health services, in both developed and developing countries.
2. Describe WHO policies which favor mental health services worldwide.
3. Discuss the social and economic loss of persons with mental health problems.
4. Do you believe that mental health care should be a "right" or entitlement for all residents of a nation, within developing as well as developed countries? Why?

CASE STUDY: CANADA

As a Chinese immigrant survivor of bipolar disorder living in Toronto, I would like to highlight two issues. People with mental health condition are subject to stigma and discrimination. It exists because of the lack of mental health education and the traditional notion that mental illness is a loss of face for the family.

I was new to Toronto and did not know of any social or mental health support services after my hospitalization. I was lost and isolated in the cold winter. Our world today has many people suffering from mental illness and it is my sincere hope that more services and programs will address our needs and those of our families.

Source: Adapted from WHO, 2010.

CASE STUDY: ZAMBIA

I was 28, married, and the father of two daughters when a terrifying life came in front of me. After my wife had an extramarital affair, I began a six-year roller-coaster ride through despair. I spent 28 days on my blankets, the meaning of life escaped out of me, with plenty of self-guilt, loss of sleep and appetite. I had suicidal thoughts. By the grace of God, I was diagnosed and hospitalized to save me from suicide. The hospital appeared more like a prison than a place for clinical attention. The experience was too harsh and turned my life upside down. I was isolated and often wandered in the wilderness with no food, shelter, and clothes.

Through a hard-fought empowerment program with the hospital, I started by own business for my livelihood. I became an advocate by talking about injustices in the hospital. Eventually my colleagues came on board to do away with an outdated and oppressive system. Upon seeing our determination in our quest for justice, the government requested that we register as a nongovernment organization. That is how the Mental Health Users Network of Zambia was born in 2001.

Source: Testimony at the WHO International Forum on Mental Health, Human Rights, and Legislation, Geneva, Switzerland 2003.

CASE STUDY: NEW ZEALAND

After my first episode I found my way home to the far north where I'm from. Back to my whanau (extended family). I had what I choose to call a healing crisis because it brought to my attention things in my life I need to change to heal and move on.

I was in hospital many times—the first time I went home on a lot of medication with a 7-year-old child and I was just left to my own devices. I was in and out of hospitals. The key question my whanau asked me had me look at what I was doing when illness first happened. After a while I was lucky enough to be around people who had survived trauma and distress. They gave me some hope—not like the messages I got through the hospital.

I have changed by life for the better. I had a healing crisis and I need to reconnect.

Source: New Zealand Mental Health Commission, 2000.

REFERENCES

Acuna, C., & Bolis, M. (2005). *Stigmatization and access to health care in Latin America: Challenges and perspectives.* Washington, DC: Pan American Health Organization.

Adelekan, M. I., Makanjuola, A. B., & Ncom, R. J. E. (2001). Traditional mental health practitioners in Kwara State, Nigeria. *East African Medical Journal, 78*(4), 190–196.

Alarcon, R. (2003). Mental health and mental health in Latin America. *World Psychiatry, 2*(1), 54–56.

Anthony, W. A. (2007). *Toward a vision of recovery for mental health and psychiatric rehabilitation services* (2nd ed.). Boston, MA: Center for Psychiatric Rehabilitation, Boston University.

Araya, R., Rojas, G., Fritsch, R., Gaete, J., Rojas, M., & Simon, G. (2003). Treating depression in primary care among low-income women in Santiago, Chile: A randomised controlled trial. *Lancet, 361,* 995–1000.

Bayron, H. (2010, September 14). Hong Kong undertakes first mental health survey in wake of violent cases. *Voice of America News: Asia.* Retrieved from http://www.voanews.com/english/news/asia /Hong-Kong-Undertakes-First-Mental-Health-Survey-in-Wake-of-Violent-Cases-102901909.html

Bekedam, H. (2003). *Speeches: WHO representative in China on the occasion of the second international mental health development conference.* China: World Health Organization.

Bolton, P., Wilk, C., & Ndogoni, L. (2004). Assessment of depression prevalence in rural Uganda using symptom and function criteria. *Social Psychiatry and Psychiatric Epidemiology, 39,* 442–447.

Boyle, P. (2001). Bulletin: Religion and the brain: The decade of the brain. *Park Ride Center, 19,* 1–6.

Caldas de Almeida, J., & Horvitz-Lennon, M. (2010, March). Mental health care reforms in Latin America. *Psychiatric Services, 61*(3), 218–221.

Canadian Collaborative Mental Health Initiative. (2005a, November 28). Canadian Collaborative Mental Health Initiative applauds the establishment of landmark commission. *Canada NewsWire.*

Canadian Collaborative Mental Health Initiative. (2005b). *A review of Canadian initiatives, Vol. I: Analysis of initiatives.* Mississauga, Ontario, Canada: Author.

Canadian Collaborative Mental Health Initiative. (2006). Health Canada primary care transition fund, 2006 Canadian Collaborative Mental Health Initiative, final report. Retrieved from http://www .ccmhi.ca

Canadian Psychiatric Association (CPA)/College of Family Physicians of Canada (CFPC), 2003. Collaborative mental health care initiative. Retrieved from http://www.cpa-apc.org/browse/documents/78

Center for Psychiatric Rehabilitation. (2006). About the Center for Psychiatric Rehabilitation. Retrieved from http://cpr.bu.edu/about

Collins, C., Hewson, D., Munger, R., & Wade, T. (2010, May). Evolving models of behavioral health integration in primary care, Miliband reports. Retrieved from http://www.milbank.org/reports/10430 EvolvingCare/1043EvolvingCare.html

European Commission. (2003). Included in society: Results and recommendations of the European research initiative on community-based residential alternatives for disabled people. Retrieved from http://www.community-living.info/contentpics/226/Included_in_Society.pdf

Gureje, O., & Alem, A. (2000). Mental health policy development in Africa. *Bulletin of the World Health Organization, 78*(4), 475–481.

Hughes, F. (2009). Mental health in the Pacific: The role of the Pacific Island Mental Health Network. *Pacific Health Dialog, 15*(1), 177–180.

Incayawar, M., & Maldonado-Bourchard, S. (2009). The forsaken mental health of the indigenous peoples: A moral case of outrageous exclusion in Latin America. *BMC International Health and Human Rights, 9,* 27.

Kaplan, A. (2006). Basic needs: Helping the mentally ill live productively. *Psychiatric Times, 23*(7), 51.

Kates, N., Crustolo, A., Farrar, S., & Nikolaou, L. (2001). Integrating mental health services into primary care: lessons learnt. *Family Systems & Health, 19*(1), 5–12.

Kates, N., Craves, M., Crustolo, A., Nikolaou, L., & Allen, C. (1997). Integrating mental health services within primary care: A Canadian program. *General Hospital Psychiatry, 19*(5), 324–332.

Kigozi, R. (2011, August). *Mental health and poverty: Challenges in service delivery in sub-Saharan Africa.* Presentation at Mbarara University, Uganda. Retrieved from http://www.slideshare.net /jasonharlow/kigozi-mental-health-service-delivery-in-africa

Kohn, R., Sharma, D., Camilleri, C. P., & Lavav, I. (2000). Attitudes towards mental illness in the Commonwealth of Dominica. *Pan American Journal of Public Health, 7*(3), 148–154.

Leonardo da Vinci Pilot Projects. (2007). WAP vocational training community based mental health nursing. Retrieved from http://www.bcu.ac.uk/_media/docs/ccmh_wap_report.pdf

Levav, I., & Rutz, W. (2002). The WHO world health report 2001: New understanding, new hope. *Israel Journal of Psychiatry Related Science, 39*(1), 50–56.

Lopez, A. D. (2005). The evolution of the global burden of disease framework for disease, injury and risk factor quantification: Developing the evidence based for national, regional and global public health action. *Globalization and Health, 1*(5), 1144–1186.

Magee, M. (2000). The global burden of disease: Health politics. Pfizer Medical Humanities Initiative. Retrieved from http://www.healthpolitics.org/archives.asp?previous=prog_01

Maramis, A., Nguyen, V., & Minas, H. (2011, February). Mental health in Southeast Asia. *Lancet, 377*(9767), 700–702.

McNeil, T. (2005–2006, Winter). An offer of hope: A pioneering BU effort bring mental health programs to the developing world. *The Bostonian*, 20–25.

Mental Health Commission of Canada (MHCC). (2009, November). *Toward recovery and well-being: A framework for a mental health strategy for Canada: Summary.* Retrieved from http://www.mentalhealth commission.ca/SiteCollectionDocuments/Key_Documents/en/2009/Mental_Health_ENG.pdf

Mental Health Commission of Canada (MHCC). (2011a). Annual report 2010–2011. Retrieved from http://www.mentalhealthcommission.ca/annualreport/

Mental Health Commission of Canada (MHCC). (2011b). Mental Health First Aid Canada. Retrieved from http://www.mentalhealthfirstaid.ca/EN/about/Pages/default.aspx

Mental Health Commission of Canada (MHCC). (2011c). Mental health in the workplace. Retrieved from http://www.mentalhealthcommission.ca/English/Pages/Mentalhealthintheworkplace.aspx

Mental Health Europe. (2005). *EU project: Good practices for combating social exclusion of people with mental health problems.* Brussels: Sante Mentale Europe.

Mental illness is not divine retribution. (2006, April 19). *Jakarta Post*, p. 17.

Mojtabai, R. (2011, September 22). National trends in mental health disability, 1997–2009. *American Journal of Public Health First Look.* Retrieved from http://ajph.aphapublications.org/cgi/content /abstract/AJPH.2011.300258v2

Moreno, P., Saravanan, Y., Levav, I., Kohn, R., & Miranda, C. T. (2003). Evaluation of the PAHO/WHO training program on the detection and treatment of depression for primary care nurses in Panama. *Acta Psychiatrica Scandinavica, 108*, 61–65.

Murray, C. J. L., & Lopez, A. D. (Eds.). (1996). *The global burden of disease: A comprehensive assessment of mortality and disability from diseases, injuries and risk facts in 1990 and projected to 2020.* Cambridge, MA: Harvard University Press on behalf of the World Health Organization and the World Bank.

National Alliance on Mental Illness (NAMI). (2006). Grading the states report, 2006. Retrieved from http://www.nami.org/content/navigationmenu/grading_the_states/project_overview/overview.htm

National Alliance on Mental Illness (NAMI). (2009). Grading the states report, 2009. Retrieved from http://www.nami.org/gtsTemplate09.cfm?Section=Overview1&Template=/ContentManagement /ContentDisplay.cfm&ContentID=75090

National Alliance on Mental Illness (NAMI). (2011). Treatment and services. Retrieved from http://www .nami.org/template.cfm?section=About_Treatments_and_Supports

New Zealand Mental Health Commission. (2000). Mental health commission. Retrieved from http://www .mhc.govt.nz/media-and-publications/publications/results/field_published_date%3A2000

Norris, J. (2011). UCSF experts aim to provide mental health services in Japan, UCSF new. Retrieved from http://www.ucsf.edu/news/2011/04/9702/ucsf-experts-aim-provide-mental-health-services-japan

Onken, S. J., Dumont, J. M., Ridgway, P., Dornan, D., & Ralph, R. O. (2002). Development of recovery facilitating system performance indicators. In *Mental health recovery: What helps and what hinders? A national research project for the National Association of State Mental Health Program Directors.* Alexandria, VA: National Technical Assistance Center.

Pan American Health Organization (PAHO). (2005). Mental disorders in Latin America and the Caribbean forecast to increase [Press release]. Retrieved from http://www.paho.org/English/DD/PIN/pr051209.htm

Pan American Health Organization (PAHO). (2010). Annual report of the director of the Pan American Sanitary Bureau: Promoting health, well-being, and human security in the Americas. Retrieved from http://scm.oas.org/pdfs/2011/PAHO/CP25544E.pdf

Patel, V., Saraceno, B., & Kleinman, A. (2005). Beyond evidence: The moral case for international mental health. *American Journal of Psychiatry.*163. 1312–1315.

Pumin, Y. (2011). A mental challenge: New law in the works to improve care for mentally ill persons. *Beijing Review.* Retrieved from http://www.bjreview.com.cn/print/txt/2011-09/30/content_395352.htm#

Rogers, E. S., Teague, G., Lichenstein, C., Campbell, J., Lyass, A., Chen, R., & Banks, S. (2007, November 6). Effects of participation in consumer-operated service programs on both personal and organizationally mediated empowerment: Results of a multisite study. *Journal of Rehabilitation Research & Development, 44,* 785–799.

Sabin, J., & Daniels, D. (2003, April). Strengthening the consumer voice in managed care: VII. The Georgia peer specialist program. *Psychiatric Services, 54*(4), 497–498.

Saywell, T., & McManus, J. (2001). Behind the smile: Silent suffering. *Far Eastern Economic Review, 9,* 26–31.

U.S. Department of Health and Human Services (USDHHS). (1999). Mental health: A report of the Surgeon General. Executive summary. Retrieved from http://www.surgeongeneral.gov/library/mentalhealth/home.html

U.S. Department of Health and Human Services (USDHHS). (2003). *President's new freedom commission on mental health, 2001.* DHHS Publication No. SMA-03-3832.

White House. (1990). Presidential Proclamation 615, Decade of the Brain: 1990–1999, by the President of the United States of America. Retrieved from http://www.loc.gov/loc/brain/proclaim.html

World Federation for Mental Health (WFMH). (2004). World Mental Health Day: The relationship between physical and mental health. Retrieved from http://www.wfmh.org/PDF/wmhday%202004English.pdf

World Health Organization (WHO). (1999). *The world health report 1999: Making a difference.* Geneva, Switzerland: Author.

World Health Organization (WHO). (2001a). Burden of mental and behavioural disorders. In *The world health report 2001: Mental health: New understanding, new hope* (pp. 1–169). Geneva, Switzerland: Author.

World Health Organization (WHO). (2001b). Fact sheet: Project Atlas: Mapping mental health resources around the world. Retrieved from http://www.who.int/entity/whr/2001/media_centre/en/whr01_fact_sheet3_en.pdf

World Health Organization (WHO). (2001c). *Mental disorders affect one in four people* [Press release]. Geneva, Switzerland: Author.

World Health Organization (WHO). (2002a). Mental health global action programme. Retrieved from http://www.who.int/mental_health/actionprogramme/en/index.html

World Health Organization (WHO). (2002b). *Mental Health Global Action Programme mhGAP: Close the gap, dare to care.* Geneva, Switzerland: Author.

World Health Organization (WHO). (2003a). Investing in mental health. Retrieved from http://www.who.int/entity/mental_health/media/investing_mnh.pdf

World Health Organization (WHO). (2004). The work of WHO in the South-East Asia region, 2004. Retrieved from http://www.searo.who.int/EN/Section898/Section1447.htm

World Health Organization (WHO). (2005). *Mental health atlas 2005.* Geneva, Switzerland: Author.

World Health Organization (WHO). (2007). *Mental health improvements for nations development, the country summary series: Ghana, October, 2007.* Geneva, Switzerland: Author.

World Health Organization (WHO). (2008a). *Mental Health Global Action Programme mhGAP: Close the gap, dare to care*. Geneva, Switzerland: Author.

World Health Organization (WHO). (2008b). *WHO Mind: Mental health improvement for nations' development: The country summary series, Chile*. Geneva, Switzerland: Author.

World Health Organization (WHO). (2009a). Europe mental health facts and figures: Prevalence of mental disorders. Retrieved from http://www.euro.who.int/en/what-we-do/health-topics/noncommunicable-diseases/mentalhealth

World Health Organization (WHO). (2009b). Growing mental health services in the Pacific. *NZ Aid*. Retrieved from http://www.who.int/mental_health/policy/pimhnet/NZAid_PIMHnetArticle_3June2009.pdf

World Health Organization (WHO). (2009c). Improving health systems and services for mental health. Retrieved from http://whqlibdoc.who.int/publications/2009/9789241598774_eng.pdf

World Health Organization (WHO). (2010). *Mental health and development: Targeting people with mental health conditions as a vulnerable group. Mental Health and Poverty Project*. Geneva, Switzerland: Author.

World Health Organization (WHO). (2011a, April). *Health Harare: An information bulletin of the SCO Zimbabwe, Vol. 7*.

World Health Organization (WHO). (2011b). *Impact of economic crises on mental health*. Copenhagen, Denmark: Regional Office for Europe.

World Health Organization (WHO). (2011c). *Policies and practices for mental health in Europe*. Copenhagen, Denmark: Regional Office for Europe.

World Psychiatric Association (WPA). (2011). WPA contribution to the management of mental health consequences of major disasters. Retrieved from http://www.wapnet.org/detail.php?section_id=20&conten_id=1049

Wynaden, D., Chapman, R., Org, A., McGowan, S., Zeeman, Z., & Yeak, S. (2005). Factors that influence Asian communities' access to mental health care. *International Journal of Mental Health Nursing, 14*(2), 88–92.

For a full suite of assignments and additional learning activities, use the access code located in the front of your book to visit this exclusive website: http://go.jblearning.com/holtz. If you do not have an access code, you can obtain one at the site.

16

Global Perspectives on Environmental Health

Marvin Friedman

> *All substances are poisons; there is none which is not a poison*
> *The right dose differentiates a poison from a remedy.*

Paracelsus, 1567

> *Toxicology is the study of the adverse effects of chemical, physical or biological agents on people, animals, and the environment. . . . Toxicologists are scientists trained to investigate, interpret, and communicate the nature of those effects.*

Society of Toxicology, 2011

OBJECTIVES

Upon completing this chapter, the reader will be able to:

1. Discuss the basic principles of the science of toxicology.
2. Relate the sources, pathways, receptors, and controls of toxicants.
3. Explain processes and endpoints in the human body associated with exposure to toxic agents.
4. Relate various responses associated with different routes of toxic exposure, metabolic pathways, mechanisms of distribution within the body, and elimination processes as they relate to potential pharmacological responses.
5. Describe risk assessment and risk management as they are applied to toxic agents in the environment.
6. Explain the relationship of major aspects of environmental toxicology and chemistry.
7. Discuss the significance of the dose and response to noxious substances.
8. Describe the occurrence and significance of major classes of environmental toxicants.
9. Compare and contrast different populations at risk for environmental health problems based on past history, age, geography, and occupational and environmental exposures.
10. Discuss environmental quality, public health, sustainability, regulatory science, and public communication related to environmental pollution and contamination.

INTRODUCTION

Environmentally induced diseases can result from lack of knowledge about the adverse effects of electromagnetic, ionizing, and non-ionizing radiation and environmental chemicals, or from intentional or ethical decisions that weigh the pros and cons of competing alternatives resulting in population exposure to toxic chemicals. This chapter relates examples of how epidemics have resulted from a failure to know and understand environmental risks from both human-made stimuli and natural contaminants as well as environmental risks that resulted from societal, economic, or ethical decisions. In addition, a moral or ethical framework to assess environmental decisions based on risk is described. The regulatory framework under which many governments implement these decisions will be explained as well. Upon completion of this chapter, the reader will have a broader and deeper understanding of how humans interact with their environment.

GLOBAL ISSUES: LESSONS IN ENVIRONMENTAL HEALTH

Much has been written and speculated on the issue of global health and sustainable development. Explanations will be provided regarding how to evaluate eco-disasters such as tsunamis, reactor meltdowns, and air contamination. This chapter is not a compendium of possibilities, however, but rather a development of how to think about and evaluate new scenarios. Speculation about problems for which there are no hard data is difficult and unreliable. However, environmental problems can be solved through application of diligent scientific procedures.

What Happened to the Mink?

In the early 1980s, reproductive complications were observed in mink (Aulerich & Ringer, 1977). Several dietary components were evaluated to determine whether they were the cause of this failure for mink to reproduce. Neither the Coho salmon, which made up the major component of their diet, nor other species of Great Lakes fish appeared to cause this response in experimental mink. Diets and carcasses were evaluated for mercury and chlorinated pesticides, and there was no correlation. Analysis of the pathological signs suggested that PCBs (polychlorinated biphenyls) might be the causative agent. However, no other species was presenting with these signs. With feeding of groups of mink on 30 ppm PCB diets or salmon from the Great Lakes, the signs were identical to those of wild mink. It turned out that mink are extremely sensitive to the reproductive effects of PCBs and there were enough PCBs in Great Lakes Coho salmon to induce the detrimental reproductive effects.

The next issue was to determine the source of the PCBs. It was determined that the major use of PCBs was as a heat transfer agent in electrical transformers (International Agency for Research on Cancer [IARC], 1978). At first glance, this use would not suggest an etiology for the high levels of PCBs that were observed in the mink and Coho salmon. However, PCBs are not metabolized to any large extent and, therefore, were stable in the environment. Because they were fat soluble and only marginally water soluble, the PCBs accumulated in the fat of the fish, which then accumulated in the fat of the mink. During the winter, as the mink lost their fat, their blood levels of PCBs would increase sharply. The PCBs caused increased drug metabolism that was reflected in alteration of circulating sex hormone levels that then adversely affected mink reproduction.

The science did not end here. It turned out that PCBs were contaminated with another chlorinated, environmentally stable hydrocarbon, TCDD (tetrachlorodibenzodioxin, more simply known as dioxin), which was three orders of magnitude more toxic than PCBs (Mandal, 2005). This substance was even more widely distributed and was found not only associated with PCBs but also in landfills associated with paper mills that chlorinated their waste at elevated temperatures. This discovery led to a change in the paper-making process in which chlorine dioxide—rather than chlorine—is used. Chlorine replacement due to environmental contamination will be a continuing theme in this chapter; it is a costly step that does not necessarily translate to developing countries.

Parenthetically, the PCB toxic response was replicated in humans when a Japanese family used PCBs for cooking instead of cooking oil; the signs of toxicity were the same. This chapter evaluates what makes one species more sensitive than another, how we characterize the toxicity of materials, and how we can extrapolate risk to environmental exposures. Although there was no human reproductive toxicity observed in these studies, the studies did cause a careful evaluation by regulatory agencies of the safety of Great Lakes fish, particularly to the Canadian aboriginal population, who consume large quantities of these animals.

What About the Cats in Japan?

In the 1950s, the domestic house cat population in Japan demonstrated a highly unusual central neuro-toxicity characterized by staggered gait and other signs—a condition referred to as Minimata disease, after the Japanese seaside town where the phenomenon was observed (Takeuchi, D'Itri, Fischer, Annett, & Okabe, 1977). A chemical plant had initiated manufacture of acetaldehyde and dumped waste methyl mercury in Minimata Bay. Methyl mercury, being fat soluble and not metabolized by fish, accumulated in fish in the bay. The cats ate these fish exclusively in their diet. Subsequently, people living in Minimata began to show the same neurological signs, which also included tunnel vision and learning deficits.

Methyl mercury is a well-known neurotoxin that causes neuropathies in experimental animals and has been studied as a pesticide. In the 1960s, grain was shipped to Iraq for planting that was treated with methyl mercury as a pesticide (Rustam & Hamdi, 1994). This pesticide was purple in color, and it was not expected that people would eat the grain; rather, they were instructed to plant it. They prepared it as bread, however, and a clear dose-response was noted between bread consumption and tunnel vision, peripheral neuropathies, terata, and other forms of methyl mercury toxicity.

Methyl mercury is a component of sea water and accumulates in pelagic (oceangoing) fish. Considerable debate has arisen about the safety of pelagic fish due to methyl mercury contamination. Island populations consuming diets consisting almost exclusively of fish have been studied, but to date these results are incon-clusive (Board on Environmental Science and Toxicology, 2000).

When methyl mercury is used as an herbicide, such as on golf courses, where the water is not free flowing like the ocean, its concentration can become excessive and the fish in the local waters can repre-sent a source of toxicity.

Why Do We Discuss Selenium?

The biological effects of selenium represent the best example of environmental health and toxicology. Selenium is a metal that is found in abundance in many parts of the world and concentrates in some plants. Most selenium is consumed as the sulfur amino acids methionine and cysteine, as the selenium can replace the sulfur in these compounds. There is a nutritional requirement for selenium in several biochemical pathways. In New Zealand, China, and Finland, for example, selenium deficiency has been a major public health problem; in these countries, selenium intake is less than 50 mcg/day. Selenium deficiency is characterized by cardiomyopathy and muscle pain (Dodig & Cepelak, 2004; Rederstorff, Krol, & Lescure, 2006). In contrast, in other areas of the world, selenium is present in excess (Dodig & Cepelak, 2004). In these areas, a characteristic neurotoxicity is observed when levels exceed 250 mcg/day. Consideration of selenium deficiency or excess in the absence of knowledge of the other biological prop-erties might lead to other toxic effects.

Vitamin A

Vitamin A, α-tocopherol, is a necessary component of the human diet. Vitamin A, which is needed for vision, is a fat-soluble vitamin that becomes concentrated in the liver (Fishman, 2002; Russell, 1967). Vitamin A, like selenium, also has toxic properties when consumed in excess. This toxicity has been documented among arctic explorers and Eskimos who consume polar bear. Polar bears live on a diet rich in fish, which in turn are rich in vitamin A. When arctic explorers consumed polar bear liver, their dose of vitamin A was enormous. As this example demonstrates, a nutrient that receives little attention in the Western diet can be a serious toxin in other conditions. A deficiency of vitamin A is characterized by night blindness, which is then followed by development of connective tissue disorders. Chronic toxicity affects the skin, the mucous membranes, and the musculoskeletal and neurological systems. Vitamin A toxicity is not necessarily restricted to polar bear consumption, however, as megadose vitamins are becoming popular.

Lessons to Be Learned

All materials have toxicity when their exposure reaches high enough doses. In the case of methyl mercury and PCBs, those animals with the highest consumption of these materials were harbingers of human exposure. With selenium and vitamin A, toxicities arise from both deficiencies and excesses. As they demonstrate, just because a material is required as part of the human diet does not mean it has no toxicity.

PRINCIPLES OF ENVIRONMENTAL HEALTH

Definitions

For the purposes of this chapter, infectious agents are excluded from the discussion to the extent possible. Very frequently, there is a trade-off between infectious agents and chemicals: Examples include food preservatives and water purification, not to mention antibiotics and other pharmaceuticals and antiseptics. Due to the ability of microorganisms to reproduce, infectious disease almost always represents a greater public health concern than chemical contamination.

Assessment of environmental health is couched in technical terms that have clear definitions. Sometimes these definitions have connotations that public health professionals must ignore. For example, workplace exposure to toxic substances is different from environmental exposure. However, contamination of rivers with pharmaceutical agents is an environmental event. The use of estrogens as birth controls agents in women would not be considered environmental. These hormones are excreted in urine, however, and may end up in river water (Shore, Gurevitz, & Semesh, 1993). In one case, this phenomenon resulted in developmental and reproductive problems in striped bass that almost killed the species. Prior to delineating the impact of environmental chemicals on public health, it is important to clarify these terms.

Environment

The environment is defined as the air we breathe, the water we drink, and the food we eat. None of these environmental components is pure in the chemical sense. That is, there is no chemical definition of air, water, or food, as each is a mixture and has both major and minor components contributed by natural sources. For example, the air in the forest contains chemical substances (e.g., terpenes) that volatilize from trees in the forest. Although these substances are natural components of the forest air, they are intentional additives in cleaning products, and in some cases have pesticidal and biocidal activity. The same caveat applies to food. Although a synthetic diet can be constructed from purified starches, proteins, and fatty acids, no one consumes this diet. Therefore, a qualifier is usually appropriate with an environmental component, such as "forest air" or "Great Lakes water."

Environmental Agent

An environmental agent is the chemical or infectious agent or radiation source that is alleged to induce an environmental health incident. Such an agent is associated with two critical characteristics.

First, the quality of data linking the agent with the effect is important. Although Koch's postulates can be applied to infectious agents, it is more difficult to apply them directly to environmental health. Koch's postulates are as follows:

1. The pathogen must be present in all hosts diagnosed with the disease.
2. The pathogen must be isolatable from the diseased host.
3. The pathogen must be purifiable.
4. The purified pathogen must cause the specific disease.
5. The pathogen must be isolated from the host used in step 4.
6. The pathogen in step 5 must be shown to be the same pathogen purified in step 3.

To do this, one would have to demonstrate that the environmental agent was present in the affected population, that the agent could cause the environmental outcome, and that it was present in sufficient quantities to account for the effects.

Second, there must exist an analytical technique for the agent in question. Of course, that requires a detailed definition of the environmental agent. For example, it is not sufficient to suggest that the neurological behavior observed in the cats at Minimata Bay was caused by methyl mercury. Instead, the neurological signs must be demonstrated in experimental animals following methyl mercury treatment. Methyl mercury had to be isolated from the cats at doses that would cause the disease. The first step in any environmental evaluation is always the development of an analytical method.

Adverse Health Effect

An adverse health effect is usually defined in preclinical toxicology as any significant deviation from the norm. In the human environment, applying this definition is not always easy. The best example of such difficulty in defining adverse health effects lies in the manufacture of hypnotics. These substances are safe and effective in people even when used in large doses. Sleep induction is a therapeutic response. However, in the manufacturing environment, they may cause workers to fall asleep on the job; this is an adverse outcome. As this example demonstrates, the definition of adverse health effect is subjective: It is the induction of an effect that the exposed population does not intend or want. This has already been demonstrated with environmental exposure to estrogens that can also inhibit reproduction in the environment.

Risk

Risk is the probability that an adverse outcome will occur. Individual risk is the probability that an individual will suffer from an adverse outcome. The opposite of individual risk is population risk—the expected number or percentage of adversely affected individuals in a population who will suffer an adverse outcome. Obviously, exposure of three people to a material that will cause one adverse event in a million is different from exposing 300 million people to that risk.

Risk has three components: exposure, causation, and dose-response. The calculation and interpretation of risk will be dealt with in great detail later.

Ecology

Receptors for adverse events are not restricted to humans but are also present in wildlife, including fish. Due to the varied spectrum of species and their different physiologies, a substantial difference in sensitivity has been observed. Subtle questions can be asked with regard to protection of the environment. For example, are environmental evaluations performed by protecting most of the species exposed or by protecting the total population?

Toxicology

Toxicology is the study of the adverse effects of materials, chemicals, or radiation on living organisms. Although not explicit in the definition, what makes a toxicologist different from other scientists is that a toxicologist relates dose and response rather than just studying response. The terms "adverse effects" and "toxicological effects" are used interchangeably in this chapter.

Physiologically or Toxicologically Significant Adverse Health Effects

Although the issue of what qualifies as a significant adverse effect might seem easily resolved, it is actually very difficult to state with clarity. For example, an environmental substance that causes weight loss at a specific dose is considered to be inducing an adverse effect. However, when that same substance is evaluated as a pharmaceutical for that purpose, it is considered therapeutic. Looking at the same situation in reverse, one can look at a material that can be used safely and effectively as a hypnotic. The dose at which it manifests the hypnotic response is not a toxic dose but rather a dose that produces a pharmacologically beneficial event. However, when this material is manufactured in the workplace and exposure takes place at a level sufficient to induce a hypnotic dose, the workers fall asleep, and there are substantial problems thereafter.

To put matters in perspective, one can consider how to evaluate additives for food that decrease calorie availability or promote weight loss. When a manufacturer evaluates an inert ingredient such as a nonmetabolizable starch for use in breads, cookies and cakes, the U.S. Food and Drug Administration (FDA) requires at least a 100-fold safety margin be maintained. Of course, adding 100 times the amount to be used in breads, cakes, and cookies will result in body weight loss, as the test animals do not eat enough food to compensate for the starch. It then appears that there is a toxic response characterized by weight loss. Because such components are food additives and not drugs, a margin of safety is required before they can be included in foods for the general public. Thus the definition of "adverse effect" is not always obvious.

Similarly, with large sample sizes or sensitive assays, small effects that have no physiological significance can be detected even while the response has no physiological significance. The terms "statistical significance" and "toxicological significance" relate to different findings: The former is dependent on characteristics of the assay and the sample size, while the latter deals with hazards. It is important to evaluate whether effects observed in populations around the world are real adverse health effects or just statistical anomalies caused by large sample sizes or sensitive assays.

Global Catastrophic Risk

There are a few risks whose consequences can be so significant that normal considerations of cost, benefit, weight of the evidence, and concentration dependency are not considered. The most obvious of these is global warming, which results from destruction of the ozone layer of the atmosphere and consequent warming of the surface of the earth by a few degrees Celsius. The postulate underlying the theory of global warming is that release of carbon dioxide or fully halogenated hydrocarbons (to be discussed later in this chapter) into the atmosphere can decrease the density and effectiveness of the stratospheric filter for radiation. Although the data are poor and the effects immeasurable, if true, this outcome would mean a global catastrophe. Therefore, the threat must be dealt with as if it were absolutely true. Such mega-events are not common, but when present require an entirely different way of thinking about risk. Treatment of drinking water, safety of vaccines, and contamination of foodstuffs all fit into this global catastrophic risk.

PRINCIPLES OF TOXICOLOGY

A detailed and comprehensive treatise on toxicology is beyond the scope of this chapter. However, there are some very critical concepts that can be covered here.

Intrinsic Activity

Intrinsic activity can be defined as the maximum response that can be induced by a material. It can be seen in **Figure 16-1**, which is an idealized schematic. Of the four curves, two have the same intrinsic activity and two have the same potency. For intrinsic activity, the maximum response is 40 at both high and low potency, whereas the maximum at the low dose is 8. Intrinsic activity is a biological property of a substance. For example, the diuretic properties of a substance such as melamine and the porphyrin-modifying properties of lead and iron are intrinsic activities; they may be considered as a physical property of the substance. Such activities are generally determined in animal experiments or in vitro studies, but sometimes are identified in humans first as anecdotal observations, such as the observation that vinyl chloride was a human carcinogen. In the European Union, a classification system for intrinsic activity

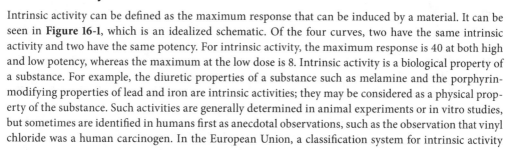

FIGURE 16-1

Comparison of Potency and Intrinsic Activity

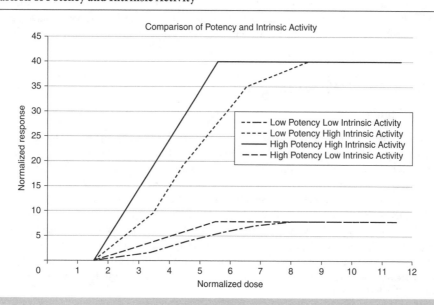

has been developed, where category 1 is an activity known to occur in humans, category 2 is an activity that will probably occur in humans, and category 3 is an activity that has been identified only in animals.

Intrinsic activity does have degrees of effectiveness associated with it. That is, the maximum effect of a substance can differ between two substances. For example, one substance may induce more chromosomal anomalies than another at the maximum dose tested.

One can compare the bladder cancer–inducing activity of chemicals as an example. Several materials such as melamine or cyclamate will precipitate in the bladder. This precipitate can irritate the walls of the bladder and cause tumors to be produced. Very seldom does the incidence of tumors produced by this mechanism exceed 15% even at doses such as 6000 ppm in the diet (Heck & Tyl, 1985; Melnick, Boorman, Haseman, Montali, & Huff, 1984). In contrast, some aromatic amines cause bladder cancer in rats in 50% of the animals ("Bioassay of 4,4′-Methylenebis-(*N,N*-dimethyl)benzeneamine," 1979).

Potency

Potency relates to the dose at which an effect is observed. The units of expression of potency are either expressions of doses where no responses occur or expressions of doses where a 50% response occurs. In the case of the doses with no response, the "no observed adverse effect" level (NOAEL) is used; it depends on the dose spacing and sensitivity of the assay to detect responses. The NOAEL is the experimental dose at which no adverse effect has been observed, but this experimental point is highly dependent on the protocol, quality of data, experimental design, and sample size. The poorer the design, the lower the quality of the data, or the smaller the sample size, the higher the NOAEL.

In the case of measuring a 50% response, the ED_{50} (effective dose in 50% of the population), LD_{50} (lethal dose in 50% of the population), or benchmark dose (BMD; a curve-fitting exercise) is used ("Bioassay of 4,4′-methylenebis-(*N,N*-dimethyl)benzeneamine," 1979). These metrics are the most reproducible experimental observations. Finally, a mathematical curve fitting can be used that will generate the best-fitting curve—that is, the curve that takes into account all of the data points. This mathematical expression can then be used to generate a theoretical 10% dose-response, which is the BMD. Because this is a mathematical curve fitting, virtually any dose can be used or the statistical bounds could also be used. In Figure 16-1, the ED_{50} for the higher-potency material is 4; for the lower-potency material, it is 6.

The concepts of potency and intrinsic activity underscore the inability to compare the adverse effects of substances. Either potency or intrinsic activity can be a variable.

LEGAL AND ETHICAL ISSUES

Laws and Regulations

Government of democratic nations is accomplished in two ways. First, laws are passed by an elected legislature that provides direction for governance. Second, within these laws is the delegation of responsibility to or establishment of an executive agency for implementation and enforcement of these laws.

The executive agencies deal with the details of management of nations. As an example, the U.S. Congress passed the Federal Insecticide, Pesticide and Rodenticide Act, which gave the U.S. Environmental Protection Agency (EPA) control over the labeling of pesticides and the FDA responsibility for establishing limits (tolerances) for pesticides in food. This separation of authority between legislative and executive branches is not unique to the United States, but rather is global in nature. Serious abuses in this system occur when there is no legislative branch to write the laws, such that the executive branch writes the laws, establishes the regulations, and performs the enforcement. This system typically leads to corruption and environmental deterioration.

Legal challenges to regulations, which make for interesting news, deal with whether the regulatory agency has the authority to perform a specific task as identified by legislation, or whether the regulatory agency has acted as described by law. Citizens may then challenge the regulatory enforcement on the basis that it was either not correctly carried out by law or that the law did not authorize the agency to act the way it did.

Perhaps the best example of the difference between regulation and legislation can be seen in the failed attempts of the FDA to regulate cigarette smoking. Clearly, the FDA is responsible for a major component of public health, and clearly cigarette smoking is detrimental to public health. However, there was no authorization in the Food, Drug, and Cosmetic Act that would allow the FDA to regulate smoking. Cigarette smoke is neither a food nor a food additive, and Congress chose not to change the legislation so as to authorize FDA regulation of tobacco products. Tobacco is also not considered a drug, as manufacturers do not make any health-related claims for cigarette smoke. It was only recently that the FDA embarked on regulating cigarette smoke by declaring cigarettes to be a drug delivery system, delivering nicotine as a drug (Centers for Disease Control and Prevention [CDC], 2007; FDA, 1995). This allegation brought cigarettes under the Food, Drug, and Cosmetics Act and, therefore, made them subject to FDA regulation. Otherwise, independent of the adverse health effects of cigarettes, the FDA was powerless to regulate tobacco smoke.

Regulation Versus Ethics

Ethics becomes an issue when there are no laws or regulations to be enforced. The critical issue associated with ethical decisions lies in the values involved. Values have many varied definitions, and can be parsed into moral values, ethical values, family values, religious values, and so on. Based on the soft and personal nature of values, interpreting them for environmental decision making is virtually impossible. Ethical considerations must either be converted to some form of regulation or cannot be major decision criteria for environmental issues.

An example of an ethical decision is Proposition 6 in California, a regulation to ban consumption of horse meat (CDC, 2007; Prohibition of Horse Slaughter, 1998). There was no public health issue involved in this proposition and no laws under which to regulate horse meat. Thus the state made a decision that it was unethical to slaughter horses for the purpose of human consumption.

WHAT IS THE ENVIRONMENT?

As noted earlier, the environment consists of the air we breathe, the water we drink, and the food we eat. Public health concerns about each of these aspects of the environment are very different.

Air Pollution

There are four major classes of air-polluting gases: irritating chemicals, asphyxiating chemicals, air toxics, and atmospheric reactants.

Irritants

Irritants damage the surface of the respiratory tract. Highly water-soluble irritants such as formaldehyde cause irritation of the upper respiratory tract, whereas less water-soluble irritants such as nitrogen oxides cause lower respiratory tract irritation.

Hydrogen chloride is very water soluble and is an upper respiratory tract irritant. Its inhalation causes effects in the nose, for example. As a response to contact with upper respiratory tract irritants, individuals will hold their breath or breathe more shallowly. The major chronic effect of upper respiratory tract irritants is loss of the sense of smell through toxicity to the olfactory epithelium. Sulfur dioxide is another example of an upper respiratory tract irritant.

Oxides of nitrogen such as nitrogen dioxide are lower respiratory tract irritants; exposure to these substances is accompanied by chest pains. The other major environmental irritant gases are ozone and chlorine, which oxidize in the lower respiratory tract. In each case, the result is fibrotic/scarring lesions in the irritated portion of the lung with an accompanying loss of function. Lower respiratory tract irritants can also cause emphysema and other typical pulmonary lesions.

It is extremely import to differentiate irritants from foul-smelling materials. Odor is not necessarily a characteristic of toxic vapors. Foul smells are designed to elicit an avoidance response.

Asphyxiates

Asphyxiates cause suffocation or lack of oxygen transport to the body. The major asphyxiate is carbon monoxide; overexposure to this gas leads to a chemical asphyxiation. Carbon dioxide induces a similar response but at markedly higher concentrations.

Toxics

The third class of pollutant gases comprises toxics—gases that are absorbed through the lungs and have adverse systemic effects. For example, hydrogen cyanide has direct effects on the blood, but not on the lungs. A wide variety of other materials, when inhaled, produce systemic toxicity. Anesthetic and neurotoxic gases, such as ether and toluene, are in this class. Virtually any material when inhaled can be absorbed into the lung to some extent.

High-molecular-weight polymers and water-insoluble chemicals are not absorbed into the bloodstream, but rather are deposited into the lungs and remain there. These materials may be removed by a system that moves them up the trachea for excretion or to be swallowed. The body defenses against these materials may have a side effect of irritating the adjacent lung tissue. Macrophages are designed to kill bacteria in the lungs by producing peroxide. An effect of some particulates is to kill the macrophages, thereby causing peroxide buildup in the lungs, which eventually proves toxic. Finally, exercise can accentuate lung toxicity through increase in the respiratory rate. With increased respiration, the dosage increases.

Atmospheric Reactants

Chemical reaction of pollutants with atmospheric constituents can induce serious environmental degradation. The two major classes of these air pollutants are smog and greenhouse gases.

Smog.   Photochemical smog is a concern in most major urban centers. Smog is caused by a reaction between sunlight and emissions, mainly from human activity such as automobile exhaust and fireplaces. Photochemical smog is the chemical reaction of sunlight, nitrogen oxides (NOx), and volatile organic compounds (VOCs) in the atmosphere, which leaves behind airborne particles (called particulate matter) and ground-level ozone. Nitrogen oxides are released in the exhaust of fossil fuel–burning engines in cars, trucks, coal power plants, and industrial manufacturing factories. VOCs are vapors released from gasoline, paints, solvents, pesticides, and other chemicals.

Greenhouse Gases.   Some organic substances—the most notable and avoidable being fully halogenated substances such as chlorofluorocarbons (CFCs)—decrease the atmospheric filter for sunshine. The greenhouse gases may interact with ozone, which filters sunlight and provides a stable temperature on Earth. Perhaps the most significant of these gases is carbon dioxide, which is produced by burning fossil fuels and by the setting of concrete. Methane is produced by livestock farming and rice paddies. Sunlight and other radiation turn methane and carbon dioxide into free radicals, which then interact with ozone.

Water Pollution

Pollution of drinking water can take the form of either chemical or microbial contamination. Microbial contamination is beyond the context of this chapter, except to note that it necessitates chemical treatment of water. In the absence of chemical treatment, epidemics of cholera and typhus can occur, as well as *E. coli* infection. On a global basis water contamination is a leading cause of death as an inducer of diarrhea.

Treatment of microbial contamination is not difficult, but it is costly. It generally involves killing the organisms with chlorine, chlorine dioxide, or ozone. The costly part is not only the treatment phase, but also the transport of the water to the site of use. In developing countries without water purification plants, boiling water is effective as a microbial decontamination measure. In general, chemical oxidants are added to the water to sterilize it. Historically the most popular of these compounds has been chlorine. Chlorine is an inexpensive and effective agent for this purpose. The downside of chlorine use is twofold: It is difficult and risky to transport, and the chemical reaction between chlorine and the biological agents in water results in the production of chloroform and other trihalomethanes that are carcinogens at high doses in experimental animals. Chemical reaction rate constants show that the bromine analogues—bromoforms—are also produced from this process. For this reason, newer water treatment facilities tend to use either peroxide or chloramine. Peroxide is very effective at eliminating other chlorination by-products such as TCDD, which is among the most toxic of all organic chemicals and is highly persistent in the environment. Paper mills, which may have a very high organic content waste, use the more costly peroxide process to avoid TCDD production. Chloramine is not without its disadvantages, however, as it appears to increase the level of nitrosamines in the water. Nitrosamines are highly carcinogenic chemicals more commonly found in nitrite-preserved meats.

The issues involved in the evaluation and trade-off of these treatment methods are closely analogous to the ethical decisions discussed previously. Possibly the worst alternative is microbiological contamination, but only peroxide is without a potentially toxic sequela. Yet the concentrations of halogenated contaminants are very low following water treatment, and the nitrosamine concentration resulting from this process amounts to less than 0.5% of dietary intake of these compounds. Regulatory risk assessment methods assume that there is no risk-free dose.

Radiation

Radiation represents an electromagnetic spectrum that covers many facets from visible light, to ultraviolet light, to infrared to radio waves, to microwaves, and so forth. From a health viewpoint, radiation can be condensed into three facets: ionizing, non-ionizing, and thermal radiation.

Ionizing Radiation

Ionizing radiation consists of high-energy radiation such as gamma rays, X-rays, and other high-energy particles. These forms of radiation penetrate the skin and are not stopped by most boundaries. Biologically, they ionize chemicals in the body, which has two effects. First, the ionization mutates DNA. Dividing cells with damaged DNA either will be repaired, will die, or will be transformed into cancer cells. Approximately 1 million DNA lesions per cell per day are produced as a result of background radiation. In the case of other cellular components, contact with ionizing radiation causes them to become oxidized. The resulting oxidative stress has many sequelae, such as aging and many diseases. The most significant lesion entails chromosome breakage, a nonrepairable phenomenon. However, it appears to be at least a second-order reaction; thus, at low levels of radiation, the risk of chromosome breakage is exponentially less than at high doses.

Non-ionizing Radiation

Non-ionizing radiation (UV radiation) is responsible for suntans and other dermal responses. It does not penetrate the skin to any great depth. While the chemical reaction resulting in tanning is not deleterious, non-ionizing radiation can cross-link dermal DNA, thereby inducing mutagenic reactions. This results in severe dermatological responses such sunburns and melanomas.

Thermal Radiation

Long-wave radiation such as microwave or radar causes water molecules to heat up and produce a thermal effect. This effect is usually not a concern in the environment.

PERSISTENT ORGANICS

Water contamination results in pollution from two sources. First and most obvious is drinking the water itself. Second, and not as obvious, is consumption of fish and seafood harvested from the water. The ability of materials to accumulate and persist in wildlife is a measurable characteristic of organic and inorganic chemicals. Some of the most recognizable of these persistent chemicals are DDT, PCBs, and TCDD. The environmental concern is not that these compounds are toxic at ambient concentrations, but rather that they can accumulate in biota to reach toxic levels as discussed earlier with methyl mercury. On a global basis, these persistent organic pollutants are being banned with the same aggressiveness as those that cause global warming.

Clearly, low-cost chlorination will continue to predominate in countries where the social costs of its elimination cannot be borne by the economy. In the Western world, one of the other water treatment methods will be selected.

Toxics

In the same way that there are toxic substances in the air, so there can also be toxic substances in water. Toxics are defined as materials in water that exert toxic effects through systemic absorption. Establishing an acceptable dose for materials in water is difficult. In addition, estimating consumption of water toxics is complicated. In the United States, individuals move frequently and their exposure to any particular drinking water source is, on average, limited to 10 years. Most individuals have an average consumption of 3 liters of water per day.

Toxics in drinking water may include pesticides, heavy metals, nitrosamines, halogenated materials from chlorination, and other pollutants, depending on the area, groundwater source, purification methods, and so on. There is currently no way to remove metals from drinking water, so these components represent a special problem. Symptomatology in a population exposed to chemically contaminated drinking water will not be restricted to a single individual, but rather will appear in large numbers of the overall population. For example, contamination of water with large amounts of iron salts will result in liver and blood problems in many people. If only a single individual is found to have a problem, the causative agent is not likely present in the community's drinking water.

A special subset within the general population when it comes to water pollution is people who have wells. Because the well can be contaminated in its construction, use, or the water supply it accesses, a family deriving its water from that source can have toxic symptoms separate from the overall population.

For example, one family in Japan lined its well with an acrylamide polymer that had not sufficiently polymerized to remove the acrylamide (Igisu, Glote, Kawamura, Kato, & Izumi, 1975). The entire family then came down with acrylamide neurotoxicity, while the rest of the population remained healthy.

Biological Oxygen Demand

When microorganisms in water metabolize pollutants to nontoxic carbon dioxide, they utilize oxygen in this process. As a side note, the degradability of an organic chemical is measured in terms of the demand it presents on oxygen. Such oxygen depletion can be disastrous to animals in the water that require oxygen, such as fish. Fish kills can be caused by adding to water various nutrients that microorganisms metabolize, thereby depleting the available oxygen. Another way to stimulate growth of oxygen-depleting organisms is to add a cofactor to the water that had previously been growth limiting. Runoff of phosphate from agricultural and suburban land, for example, provides much needed phosphate to algae, which then grow and deplete the oxygen in the water in which they live. This reaction is ruinous to many lakes and estuaries such as the Everglades. Globally, this problem has become more extensive as the equation for the value of conservation versus agricultural production has shifted to favor agricultural production in the developing world.

FOOD

The inclusion of food in this chapter is not meant to imply that food is toxic. However, food can serve as a source of pharmacologically active substances that must be considered in disease causation. These substances can arise through food storage, manufacture, or cooking, or they can be integral parts of the food being consumed. For example, some Guam inhabitants chew on cycad nuts ("The Cycad Story Extended," 1970). As a result, these individuals may develop a disease similar to amyotrophic lateral sclerosis (ALS, also known as Lou Gehrig's disease).

There are two ways of looking at food contamination. Historically, epidemiologists have been primarily concerned with low levels of very potent contaminants. In reality, there may be an even higher risk associated with high levels of low-potency substances.

For example, the presence of nitrosamines in nitrite-preserved foodstuffs has been the subject of extensive research. These substances cause cancer at low doses in virtually every species tested, including humans. Nevertheless, their presence in foodstuffs appears so low that they do not represent a public health risk. Nitrosamines are generally the result of food preservation using nitrites or are produced by the conversion of nitrate to nitrite in the stomachs of neonates and subsequent in vivo nitrosation. They are found in low levels in drinking water as a result of chloramine purification as well.

In contrast, polyunsaturated fatty acids are another cancer risk, albeit one with very little animal data to support their carcinogenic role. These chemicals are present in very high levels in many foods, delivering very significant doses to people who consume these foodstuffs. Even though they appear to have low potency, they may represent a much greater risk than the much more potent nitrosamines, simply because of the volumes in which they are consumed.

The argument about "risk versus potency" of components in foods approaches absurdity when nitrosamines are compared with the use of salt. Salt represents a real public health problem, even though it is a naturally occurring substance (Hussein & Brasel, 2001).

Food Storage

Contamination of food during storage can be a major source of toxic substances. Peanuts provide a perfect example of this problem. Peanuts, being approximately 50% fat, are an excellent substrate for mold growth. The mold *Aspergillus flavus* has been particularly well studied (Hussein & Brasel, 2001). This mold produces a unique metabolite, aflatoxin, which is among the most carcinogenic substances known. In many areas of the world, such as central Africa, this mold growth results in a substantial increase in liver cancer cases. Some areas of China also exhibit the same increased cancer incidence from aflatoxin consumption. Peanuts are not the only aflatoxin substrate, however; *Aspergillus* can also grow on corn, wheat, and so on. The FDA monitors aflatoxin contamination very closely, and foodstuffs are carefully assayed for aflatoxin content.

Many storage molds produce very potent toxins (Howlett, 1996). A laundry list will not be provided here, as this list grows continually with the discovery of new molds.

Food Manufacture

Contamination of food and beverages by chemicals during manufacture is a heavily regulated issue in the developed world. Many developing nations follow FDA or European Union (EU) regulations for their internal food manufacture industries. The United States and the EU have different approaches to this issue, however ("Evaluation of Certain Food Contaminants," 2006; Hattan & Kahl, 2002).

In the United States, industry must supply FDA not only with safety information that is correlated with expected exposure, but also with efficacy data in the case of direct food additives. Chemicals are evaluated on a single-use basis; that is, if a chemical is used in more than one process, each process is evaluated independently. Each chemical is also evaluated independent of the foodstuff. For example, the fortification of breakfast cereals does not consider the presence of these nutrients in the milk added to the cereal.

In contrast, the EU has developed a list of substances that are considered acceptable for food use. In addition, the EU has created a list of chemicals that are not allowed for use in foods. Efficacy is not an issue in the EU when it comes to food additives.

Consider the example of the addition of calcium to breakfast cereal. The FDA would consider the nutrient properties of calcium and set a standard for addition of calcium in breakfast cereal. It would not consider the calcium level in milk added to the breakfast cereal, arguing that cereal can be consumed without milk. In the EU, calcium salts are approved for use in foodstuffs, so calcium may be added to cereal or even milk by any food manufacturer.

Cooking

The most readily apparent cooking contaminants are associated with grilling food at high temperatures. The charred surfaces of meats and other grilled foodstuffs are rich in polynucleated aromatic hydrocarbons (PAHs). These materials are carcinogenic and mutagenic, and they induce reproductive disorders when present at elevated concentrations. The chemistry that produces PAHs occurs at elevated temperatures from all organics. For example, smoke from fires or automobile exhaust may contain high levels of these materials. Once highly significant air pollutants, PAHs are now tightly regulated in the developed world.

In contrast, heating amino acids—the major component of proteins—causes the production of heterocyclic amines (HCAs). The major source of these chemicals is cooking of muscle meat. Epidemiologists have linked this cooking process with cancer of the stomach. Frying, broiling, and barbequing cause much more HCA production than baking or microwaving, as they induce higher temperatures in the foodstuff.

In the same fashion as HCAs are produced by heating muscle meat at high temperatures, acrylamide is produced by heating starchy foods in excess of 230 °F. Acrylamide has long been established as a human neurotoxin due to its mishandling in industry. An industrial intermediate, it is used in the manufacture of polymers for water treatment, mining, paper manufacture, and sludge dewatering. Excessive heating of the amino acid asparagine in the presence of reducing sugars also produces acrylamide. In the mid-1980s, acrylamide was found to cause cancer in laboratory rats and to influence chromosomal segregation in male reproductive tissue. It is found in greatest quantities in those starchy foods cooked at the highest temperatures, such as potato chips. This elevated cooking process is used to drive out the water in the food product so that the temperature can exceed the boiling point of water. For example, acrylamide has been found in the crust of bread but not in the middle.

Saturated fatty acids have been found in low levels in meats. To increase their shelf life, some foodstuffs are treated with antioxidants to keep the unsaturated fatty acids from going rancid, which in turn elevates the saturated fatty acid content. Saturated fatty acids have been associated with many maladies, including memory loss and cancer.

Intrinsic Pharmacologically Active Chemicals

There is no end of naturally occurring chemicals in food that have pharmacological activity. For example, the puffer fish—considered a delicacy in Japan—is rich in tetrodotoxin, an extremely potent neurotoxin. Consequently, preparation of puffer fish must be done by a licensed individual who can remove the poisonous gland. Some mushrooms contain α-amanitin, which was developed into the anticancer drug amantadine. The existence of such potent agents has spawned an effort by the pharmaceutical industry to seek biological substances that occur naturally and develop them into commercial medications.

The presence of these substances in foodstuffs does not have a large impact on the Western world, where diets are relatively standard. In the developing world, however, it is a different story. As noted earlier, consumption of cycad nuts in Guam (and the Philippines) has resulted in amyotrophic lateral sclerosis. In the Western world, concern about foodstuffs focuses on those materials that are present in large amounts and have low potency, such as cholesterol. In the developing world, the more potent contaminants become more important. That is not to say that there is not also toxicity from low-potency chemicals. For example, iron toxicity is rampant in some areas of China and Africa as a result of cooking in rusty pots.

Food allergies are another area where intrinsic properties of food represent serious medical hazards. To some individuals, peanuts are extremely toxic. The incidence of this allergy is low, perhaps 1 person per million population. However, with 300 million inhabitants in America, it is questionable whether this risk can be economically regulated (Schoessler, 2005).

SUSTAINABLE DEVELOPMENT

According to the United Nations, sustainable development is the process of developing land, cities, business, communities, and so on, so that the result "meets the needs of the present without compromising the ability of future generations to meet their own needs" ("The Environment Becomes a Political Issue," 1988). One of the factors that sustainable development must overcome is environmental degradation, but it must do so without foregoing the needs related to economic development, social equality, and justice. To accomplish this goal, a balance must be struck between industrial development, pollution control with an absence of environmental degradation, and attention to the needs for the future. We have discussed air pollution with its toxics and oxidants, water pollution with its toxics and persistent organic chemicals, and the protection of our food supply. An unsustainable situation occurs when natural capital (the sum total of nature's resources) is used up faster than it can be replenished. Sustainability requires that human activity, at a minimum, use nature's resources only at a rate at which they can be replenished naturally. Implicit in this concept is the idea that pollution prevention is as important or more important than pollution development.

STUDY QUESTIONS

1. Explain, with examples, why it is important to human health to pay attention to environmental incidents caused by chemicals, infectious agents, or radiations. How do these agents cause global environmental health incidents?
2. Relate the problems of selenium deficiency and excess. What are some contributing factors in the environment which can cause these abnormalities? What solutions can correct these abnormal conditions? What other substances also have potential problems with excess and deficiency?
3. What is meant by dose and potency?
4. Explain how food can be contaminated during storage. What are the health implications? What are the important factors to consider while protecting our food supply?
5. Discuss how some methods of cooking food can cause harm to the body.
6. Explain, compare, and contrast examples of sustainable and unsustainable developments.

CASE STUDY: MICRONUTRIENT: AFLATOXIN B1

In 1960, more than 100,000 young turkeys on poultry farms in England died from an apparently new liver disease that was termed "Turkey X disease." It was soon found that ducklings and young pheasants were also affected, and heavy mortality among these fowl populations was experienced. This disease became associated with feed, particularly peanut meal from Brazil. Subsequently it was found that a potent toxin, aflatoxin B1, was present in the feed. Aflatoxin B1 was produced by a storage mold that grew on the peanuts because of the relative humidity on the surface of the peanuts. Visual selection of peanuts for human consumption could eliminate the aflatoxin contamination.

Chronic toxicology studies in rats revealed that aflatoxin B1 is among the most potent carcinogens known, causing liver cancer in rats (**Figure 16-2**). However, there are some geographic areas in the world where aflatoxin exposure causes no increase in liver cancer. Confounding environmental factors involved in aflatoxin-related liver cancer based on the global distribution of liver cancer and aflatoxin exposure can be present in some world locations, such as central Africa. Within central Africa, hemosiderosis, produced by iron toxicity from using rusty cooking utensils, causes liver cancer (Mandishona et al., 1998).

In China, there is a high rate of hepatitis B virus, which acts synergistically with aflatoxicosis. Knowledge of this phenomenon is enormously significant in preventing liver cancer. Specifically, the same techniques that are useful in Africa will not have utility in China. In both cases, hygienic food storage will be effective. In Africa, upgrading the cooking utensils will produce a sharp drop in liver cancer; in China, an upgrade in cooking utensils could prevent hepatitis B (Chen & Zhang, 2011; Yu & Yuan, 2004). An important lesson to be learned here is the same one that was presented with methyl mercury—namely, that domestic or wild animals can be a sentinel of human disease.

Case Study Questions

1. Earlier in this chapter, the presence of aflatoxin in peanuts was discussed. Are there any other foods that might be contaminated by aflatoxin?
2. As there may have been two factors required for the appearance of human cancer, is the risk from aflatoxin overestimated?

FIGURE 16-2

Correlation Between Populations with High Liver Cancer Rates and High Risk of Chronic Exposure to Aflatoxin Contamination

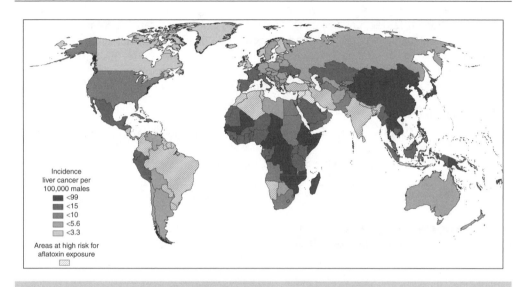

Incidence
liver cancer per
100,000 males

- <99
- <15
- <10
- <5.6
- <3.3

Areas at high risk for
aflatoxin exposure

Source: National Institute of Environmental Health Sciences. Liver cancer data from the GLOBOCAN 2002 database (http://www-dep.iarc.fr/GLOBOCAN_frame.htm). Aflatoxin data from Williams et al. (2004). Human Aflatoxicosis in Developing Countries. *American Journal of Clinical Nutrition, 80*, 1106–1122.

CASE STUDY: BALKAN NEPHROPATHY

Balkan nephropathy is an interstitial nephropathy first identified in the 1920s in people living along the Danube River (Cosyns, 2003). It was not a typical nephropathy, from a morphological standpoint, and was restricted to adults—that is, no children presented with the disease. Chronic exposure to dietary aristocholic acid appears to be a major causative risk factor for this nephropathy. Aristocholic acid may come from *Aristolochia clematitis,* a plant native to the endemic region, and its seeds may comingle with wheat used for bread. According to the International Agency for Research on Cancer, several *Aristolochia* species have been used in traditional Chinese medicine as antirheumatics, as diuretics, and in the treatment of edema. Aristolochic acids are constituents of these plant species.

After the recognition of these acids' role of Balkan nephropathy, the American Public Health Service tested aristocholic acid in rats and mice for chronic toxicity. This substance caused tumors at the site of application as well as kidney tumors in rats. Based on these toxicology studies, follow-up studies were done on individuals with nephropathy. High rates of urethral cancer, primarily of the upper urinary tract, among individuals with renal disease who had consumed botanical products containing aristocholic acids were found.

The human carcinogenicity of aristocholic acids was first identified in studies of Belgian patients with nephropathy (progressive interstitial renal fibrosis) related to the

(continues)

CASE STUDY: BALKAN NEPHROPATHY *(continued)*

consumption of herbal medicines. More than 100 cases have been reported in Belgium and more than 170 cases in other locations, including the United States, the United Kingdom, Japan, Taiwan, and China. Clinical studies found significantly increased risks of transitional-cell carcinoma of the urinary bladder and upper urinary tract among Chinese renal-transplant or dialysis patients who had consumed Chinese herbs or drugs containing aristocholic acids, using non-exposed patients as the reference population. This is the first "known human carcinogen" that was first discovered in animals.

Case Study Questions

1. Should FDA regulate the import and use of herbal medicines? If so, how should the FDA do so?
2. How would you compare the risk and hazards from aristocholic acid and aflatoxin?

REFERENCES

Aulerich, R. J., & Ringer, R. K. (1977). Current status of PCB toxicity to mink, and effect on their reproduction. *Archives of Environmental Contamination and Toxicology, 6*(2–3), 279–292.

Bioassay of 4,4'-methylenebis-(*N,N*-dimethyl) benzeneamine for possible carcinogenicity (CAS No. 101-61-1). (1979). *National Toxicology Program Technical Report Service, 186,* 1–11.

Board on Environmental Science and Toxicology. (2000). *Toxicological effects of methylmercury.* Washington, DC: National Research Council.

Centers for Disease Control and Prevention (CDC). (2007). *Selected actions of the U.S. government regarding the regulation of tobacco sales, marketing, and use.* Atlanta, GA: Author.

Chen, J. G., & Zhang, S. W. (2011). Liver cancer epidemic in China: Past, present and future. *Seminars in Cancer Biology, 21*(1), 59–69.

Cosyns, J. (2003). Aristolochic acid and "Chinese herbs nephropathy": A review of the evidence to date. *Drug Safety, 26*(1), 33–48.

The cycad story extended. (1970). *Food, Cosmetics, and Toxicology, 8*(2), 217–218.

Dodig, S., & Cepelak, I. (2004). The facts and controversies about selenium. *Acta Pharmacopeia, 54*(4), 261–276.

The environment becomes a political issue: Highlights of the Brundtland Commission Report. (1988). *UN Chronicles, 25*(1), 38–39.

Evaluation of certain food contaminants. (2006). *World Health Organization Technical Reporting Service, 930.*

Fishman, R. A. (2002). Polar bear liver, vitamin A, aquaporins, and pseudotumor cerebri. *Annals of Neurology, 52*(5), 531–533.

Food and Drug Administration (FDA). (1995). Regulations restricting the sale and distribution of cigarettes and smokeless tobacco products to protect children and adolescents: Proposed rule regarding FDA's jurisdiction over nicotine-containing cigarettes and smokeless tobacco products: Notice. *Federal Register,* pp. 41314–41787.

Hattan, D. G., & Kahl, L. S. (2002). Current developments in food additive toxicology in the USA. *Toxicology, 181–182,* 417–420.

Heck, H. D., & Tyl, R. W. (1985). The induction of bladder stones by terephthalic acid, dimethyl terephthalate, and melamine (2,4,6-triamino-*S*-triazine) and its relevance to risk assessment. *Regulatory Toxicology and Pharmacology, 5*(3), 294–313.

Howlett, J. (1996). ILSI Europe Workshop on Food Additive Intake: Scientific assessment of the regulatory requirements in Europe, 1995. Brussels summary report. *Food Additives and Contaminants, 13*(4), 385–395.

Hussein, H. S., & Brasel, J. M. (2001). Toxicity, metabolism, and impact of mycotoxins on humans and animals. *Toxicology, 167*(2), 101–134.

Igisu, H., Goto, I., Kawamura, Y., Kato, M. & Izumi, K. (1975). Acrylamide encephaloneuropathy due to well water pollution. *Journal of Neurology, Neurosurgery, and Psychiatry, 38*(6), 581–584.

International Agency for Research on Cancer (IARC). (1978). IARC monographs on the evaluation of the carcinogenic risk of chemicals to humans. Polychlorinated biphenyls and polybrominated biphenyls. *IARC Monograph Programme on the Evaluation of the Carcinogenic Risk of Chemicals to Humans,* 18.

Mandal, P. K. (2005). Dioxin: A review of its environmental effects and its aryl hydrocarbon receptor biology. *Journal of Comparative Physiology, 175*(4), 221–230.

Mandishona, E., MacPhail, A. P., Gordeuk, V. R., Kedda, M. A., Paterson, A. C., Rouault, T. A., & Kew, M. C. (1998). Dietary iron overload as a risk factor for hepatocellular carcinoma in black Africans. *Hepatology, 27*(6), 1563–1566.

Melnick, R. L., Boorman, G. A., Haseman, J. K., Montali, R. J., & Huff, J. (1984). Urolithiasis and bladder carcinogenicity of melamine in rodents. *Toxicology and Applied Pharmacology, 72*(2), 292–303.

Paracelsus. (1567). *Theiohratus ex Hohenheim Eremita: Von de Besucht.* Dilogen.

Prohibition of Horse Slaughter and Sale of Horse Meat for Human Consumption Act of 1998. (1998). California Proposition 6.

Rederstorff, M., Krol, A., & Lescure, A. (2006). Understanding the importance of selenium and selenoproteins in muscle function. *Cellular and Molecular Life Sciences, 63*(1), 52–59.

Russell, F. E. (1967). Vitamin A content of polar bear liver. *Toxicon, 5*(1), 61–62.

Rustam, H., & Hamdi, T. (1994). Methyl mercury poisoning in Iraq: A neurological study. *Brain, 97*(3), 500–510.

Schoessler, S. Z. (2005). The perils of peanuts. *School Nurse News, 22*(4), 22–26.

Shore, L. S., Gurevitz, M., & Semesh, M. (1993). Estrogen as an environmental pollutant. *Bulletin of Environmental Contamination and Toxicology, 51*(3), 361–366.

Society of Toxicology. (2011). Toxicology definition. Retrieved from http://toxicology.org

Takeuchi, T., D'Itri, F. M., Fischer, P. V., Annett, C. S., & Okabe, M. (1977). The outbreak of Minamata disease (methyl mercury poisoning) in cats on Northwestern Ontario reserves. *Environmental Research, 13*(2), 215–228.

Yu, M. C., & Yuan, J. M. (2004). Environmental factors and risk for hepatocellular carcinoma. *Gastroenterology, 127*(5 suppl 1), S72–S78.

*For a full suite of assignments and additional learning activities, use the access code located in the front of your book to visit this exclusive website: **http://go.jblearning.com/holtz**. If you do not have an access code, you can obtain one at the site.*

III

Life Span Health Issues

17

Global Health in Reproduction and Infants

Carol Holtz

> *In my country, the time of birth is associated with fear because so many mothers and babies die . . . It seems that no one notices women and children dying. Are we invisible? It feels that way to us.*
>
> Reverend Agnes Mukandoli of Rwanda, Partnership for Safe Motherhood and Newborn Health, 2004

OBJECTIVES

After completing this chapter, the reader will be able to:

1. Define *reproductive health* and *reproductive rights*.
2. Discuss the international health issues related to male and female reproduction, including human rights and public policy, infertility, family planning (contraception), pregnancy, childbirth, and infant health.
3. Discuss the history and background related to global reproduction and infant health.
4. Compare and contrast adolescent and adult reproductive issues, challenges, and rights.
5. Compare and contrast global perspectives, laws, and practices of legal and illegal abortions and maternal mortality consequences.
6. Relate the global progress of development toward Millennium Development Goal 5: Reduce the maternal mortality ratio as defined by the number of maternal deaths per 100,000 live births by three quarters between 1990 and 2015.
7. Discuss HIV status and reproductive health consequences.

BACKGROUND

According to the Alan Guttmacher Institute (2004), sustained and increased investment in reproductive health services increases benefits to women, families, and societies. In addition, it contributes to general economic growth of a nation, equality in gender, and democratic governance. Poor or inadequate sexual and reproductive health contributes to one-third of the world's burden of disease for women of childbearing age and one-fifth of the total world population. The greatest need for reproductive health services is among the poorest people in the developing countries. Improved contraception in developing countries could prevent 52 million unintended pregnancies.

Alam and Ashraf, within the United Nations, plead for better reproductive health in poor nations. They reveal the reproductive health challenges of today in developing countries as where they state, "Today in developing countries, poor reproductive health is responsible for one fifth of the burden of disease and 40% in sub-Saharan Africa. Poverty, poor health, and fertility are still the highest in the least developed countries where the population has tripled since 1955 and will triple again in the next 50 years" (Alam & Ashraf, 2003, p. 1843).

The Global Burden of Disease Initiative, which was developed by the World Health Organization (WHO), the World Bank, and the Harvard School of Public Health, began the estimation of world health impact from major diseases and behaviors, including reproduction and sexual behavior. Other efforts focused on the economic costs and benefits of health interventions. Sexual and reproductive health issues represent 18% of the world's total burden of disease and 32% of the burden of women of childbearing age (15–44 years). Medical benefits of health interventions can be measured in terms of disability-adjusted life-years (DALYs)—a measure developed by the Global Burden of Disease project to evaluate potential health interventions. Maternal causes, such as hemorrhage or sepsis, problems with labor, or abortion, cause 13% of all DALYs lost by childbearing-age women. Perinatal causes, such as low birth weight or birth trauma, are responsible for 7% of all DALYs lost. For example, the increased use of contraception from 0% to 20% in sub-Saharan Africa is highly cost-effective in preventing many maternal and infant health problems and deaths (Alan Guttmacher Institute, 2004).

Germain (2004, p. 65) states, "One of the greatest disparities between rich and poor countries is maternal mortality." The risk of dying from pregnancy in sub-Saharan Africa is 1 in 16, whereas the corresponding risk in many European countries is 1 in 4000. Seventy percent of the world's maternal mortality occurs in only 13 countries. More than 500,000 women of childbearing age die every year from causes related to pregnancy and childbirth. In addition, 3.9 million babies die within the first month of life. Countries with poor maternal and infant health generally have weak healthcare systems, are in a social crisis, or both. Sex discrimination and lack of healthcare services, lack of equal rights, and lack of power for women all contribute to this health problem. Violence against women, rape, and sexual coercion threaten women's human rights and reproduction (Germain, 2004).

Progress has been made in various areas of reproductive health. The global population growth rate has slowed to 77 million people per year. Nevertheless, while fertility rates have decreased in some countries, such as Mexico, they remain very high in other countries, such as Ethiopia. Contraceptive use has increased, but now an estimated 201 million women in developing countries have unmet needs for birth control, and 60 million unplanned pregnancies occur annually. Approximately 19 million unsafe abortions occur each year. More people are aware of sexually transmitted diseases (STDs) on a global basis, yet some 340 million people worldwide still have great concerns about such infections. Infant mortality rates have improved somewhat, yet at least 529,000 women die each year from pregnancy or childbirth complications. The highest rates are for those women living in sub-Saharan Africa, where 920 maternal deaths per 100,000 live births occur each year—a rate much higher than the corresponding rate of 24 deaths per 100,000 live births in Europe (Feki, 2004).

DEFINITION OF REPRODUCTIVE HEALTH

At the 21st session of the United Nations General Assembly in 1999, an overall plan for reproductive health and rights, called the Programme of Action, was created. Governments were asked to work in cooperation with nongovernmental organizations (NGOs) and to increase investments to improve quality of reproductive health. According to the United Nations Conference on Population and Development, the following is a definition of reproductive health:

> Reproductive health is a state of complete physical, mental, and social well-being and not merely the absence of disease or infirmity, in all matters relating to the reproductive system and to its functions and processes. Reproductive health therefore implies that people are able to have a satisfying and safe sex life and that they have the capability to reproduce and freedom to decide if, when, and how often to do so. Implicit in the last condition are the rights of men and women to be informed and to have access to safe, effective, affordable, and acceptable methods of family planning of their choice, as well as other methods of their choice for regulation of fertility that are not against the law, and the right of access to appropriate healthcare services that will enable women to go safely through pregnancy and childbirth and provide couples with the best chance of having a healthy infant. In line with the above definition of reproductive health, reproductive health care is defined as the constellation of methods, techniques, and services that contribute to reproductive well-being by preventing and solving reproductive health problems. It also includes sexual health, the purpose of which is the enhancement of life and personal relations and not merely counseling and care related to reproduction and sexually transmitted diseases. (United Nations, 2004; United Nations Family Planning Association [UNFPA], 2011).

Murphy (2003) suggests that gender inequality results in poor reproductive and mental health outcomes, including unwanted pregnancy, unsafe abortions, maternal mortality, STDs, and depression. In poor countries with strong male dominance, women usually have little control of their sex lives, are rarely able to choose whom to marry, when to have sex, how many children to have, or whether to use contraception or protection against STDs. Men are often permitted to have multiple sex partners, and women remain ignorant and passive about sexuality, which increases their risk of exposure to human immunodeficiency virus (HIV) and other STDs. Women often internalize the local cultural norm that they are inferior to males, an attitude that may be reflected in the patterns of female feticide and infanticide in some countries. Women's greater rate of malnutrition contributes to maternal and infant mortality. Pregnant women who are also malnourished have low-birth-weight babies. During pregnancy, the women may have anemia, making them vulnerable to postpartum hemorrhage, leading to shock and death.

REPRODUCTIVE RIGHTS

According to the United Nations' Programme of Action of the International Conference on Population and Development, 1995, para. 7.3, as cited in *World Population Monitoring 2002* (United Nations, 2004: UNFPA, 2011):

> Reproductive rights embrace certain human rights that are already recognized in national laws, international human rights documents, and other consensus documents. These rights rest on the recognition of the basic right of all couples and individuals to

decide freely and responsibly the number, spacing, and timing of their children and to have the information and means to do so, and the right to attain the highest standard of sexual and reproductive health. It also includes their right to make decisions concerning reproduction free of discrimination, coercion, and violence, as expressed in human rights documents. . . . The promotion of the responsible exercise of these rights for all people should be the fundamental basis for government and community-supported policies and programs in the area of reproductive health, including family planning. As part of their commitment, full attention should be given to the promotion of mutually respectful and equitable gender relations and particularly to meeting the educational and service needs of adolescents to enable them to deal in a positive and responsible way with their sexuality.

Reflecting upon this UN document, the key issues of reproductive human rights consist of the following: (1) family planning, (2) adolescent issues, (3) reproductive rights, (4) HIV/AIDS, and (5) violence against women.

An example of lack of personal reproductive rights is reflected by a law established in China. On June 1, 1995, the Chinese government passed the Maternal and Infant Health Care Law to decrease the number of congenital anomalies (birth defects) in the country. This law requires that couples obtain a premarital exam for serious genetic diseases and "relevant medical disorders," as well as prenatal testing. If a serious disorder is found, the law dictates that long-term contraception or sterilization must take place or the couple may not marry. People who have diseases or problems such as schizophrenia, psychoses, leprosy, HIV/AIDS, and STDs are subject to this law. Within this law is also a mandated right for all pregnant women to have the right to prenatal care, which includes education about pregnancy and general health care, and health care for the newborn. Encouragement is given to the couple to electively abort a pregnancy in which a fetus is known to have a serious genetic disorder or a serious defect, or a pregnancy in which the life of the mother may be jeopardized from the pregnancy (Law of the People's Republic of China on Maternal and Infant Care, 1995).

In China, women also lack personal rights to bear more than one child without permission from the government. Rural women are allowed one or two children, and ethnic minority women have fewer restrictions. For women of the majority Han ethnicity, if a second child is permitted, it is usually to be spaced 4 to 5 years after the first child is born. In some rural communities, if the first child is a girl, permission is given for a second child. Pregnant women who do not have permission from the government for the birth of a child may go outside their residential area to give birth and hide this birth. These women do not get any prenatal care or have a skilled birth attendant. They expect to pay a fine, but they are able to avoid being forced to terminate the pregnancy against their wishes (Short & Zhang, 2004).

Human rights are also needed for breastfeeding mothers. Workplace barriers contribute to low breastfeeding rates in the United States as well as other global locations. The American Academy of Pediatrics recommends breastfeeding through the first 6 months of an infant's life, and continued breastfeeding until at least 12 months of life. Of the children born in the United States in 2006, 73.9% were breastfed initially, but only 43.4% continued breastfeeding for at least 6 months, and only 13.6% continued exclusive breastfeeding for at least 6 months. *Healthy People 2010* established a goal of 75% of new mothers breastfeeding their babies. As mentioned previously, one of the causes of the continued low breastfeeding rates in the United States is workplace barriers. Of the 50 states, only 23 states have adopted laws to encourage breastfeeding (if mothers wish to do so) in the workplace. Federal law did not provide any protection to working mothers until the 2010 enactment of the reasonable "break time" provision of the Patient Protection and Affordable Care Act, which required that new mothers be given time to pump breastmilk for (not feed) children younger than 1 year of age; the law exempts from this requirement employers that demonstrate hardship (Murtagh & Moulton, 2011).

ADOLESCENT REPRODUCTIVE HEALTH

Across the globe, adolescents and young adults often face a transition into adulthood with insufficient knowledge and experience. It is important to educate them for effective health promotion and prevention of diseases and unwanted pregnancies. Menarche (the age at which reproduction is physically possible) varies greatly across societies. In a recent study of 67 countries, researchers concluded that menarche is reached early in developed societies as compared to developing societies. It is associated with socioeconomic class, literacy rates, and nutrition. The onset of sexual activity today typically takes place during adolescence, a period of growth, experimentation, and identity search. Lack of access to health information among adolescents may be due to social, cultural, and sometimes legal barriers. It results in adolescents who are often poorly informed and do not make responsible choices, which may lead to sexual and reproductive health problems (United Nations, 2004).

In the United States, approximately 1 million adolescents, ages 11–19, become pregnant every year, and 500,000 give birth. These pregnancies account for 13% of all births. Data show a decline in teen pregnancies and births in recent years. Even so, teen childbirth rates in the United States are at least five times greater than the rates for teens in other Western countries. Increases in rates of teen pregnancies contribute to the overall increased rates of premature labor, low-birth-weight babies, and perinatal mortality. In the United States, African American teens have the highest rates of pregnancy complications when compared to other racial groups. In addition, African American pregnant women (20–29) have higher rates of prematurity, low birth weights, and infant mortality when compared to similarly aged Caucasian women (Gilbert, Jandial, Field, Bigelow, & Danielsen, 2004).

Sexual activity in the United States among younger teenage girls and boys has declined in recent years, and contraception use among teenagers has increased. According to a study by the U.S. Department of Health and Human Services, sexual activity rates for females who have never married, ages 15–17, dropped from 38% in 1995 to 30% in 2002. More teenagers are avoiding or postponing sexual activity, which can lead to STDs, unwanted pregnancy, or emotional experiences that they are not prepared to handle. Today sexually active teens are also more likely to use contraception, which has led to decreases in teen pregnancy and birth rates (National Center for Health Statistics, 2004).

The decline in the U.S. teen birth rates has been attributed to delayed initial sexual activity, increased use of contraception, and education about the HIV virus and pregnancy prevention. Compared to nonpregnant teenagers, teenage mothers are less likely to graduate from high school, are more likely to score below average in language and reading skills, have lower self-esteem, and have more symptoms of depression. Children of adolescent mothers are at greater risk for prematurity, low birth weight, child abuse, neglect, and poverty. Seventy-five percent of teenage mothers receive public assistance within 5 years of delivering a baby. Costs to the larger society to provide health care, food, housing, employment training, and foster care for babies born to teenagers are estimated at $7 billion per year. Many prevention programs have been initiated to reduce the number of pregnancies and STD rates among adolescents. They attempt to increase social skills, promote educational goals, and support open communication between parents and teens. Abstinence-only programs teach that abstinence is the only certain way to avoid unmarried pregnancy, STDs, and other health problems. However, most abstinence-only programs have failed to show significant improvement in rates of either sexual intercourse or pregnancy (As-Sanie, Gantt, & Rosenthal, 2004).

Jones and Boonstra (2004) reported the results of a study regarding confidential reproductive health services for minors. They concluded that recent legislative efforts to mandate parental involvement for minor adolescents seeking birth control may contribute to increased rates of teenage pregnancy. According to these researchers, voluntary parental involvement is needed instead of mandatory programs.

On a worldwide basis, an estimated 14 million young women, ages 15 to 19, gave birth each year from 1995 to 2000; 12.8 million of those adolescent women were from developing countries. Adolescent women in developed countries give birth at a rate of 29 per 1000 women, while in developing countries the corresponding rate is 133 per 1,000 women, with adolescent women in Africa having the highest rates. In many countries in Asia, increases in age at marriage and low incidence of premarital sexual activity have resulted in low rates of adolescent pregnancies (United Nations, 2004).

In most developed countries of the world, the majority of teenagers become sexually active, and at least 75% have had sexual intercourse by the time they are 20 years old. Teenagers in the United States are becoming sexually active with more partners, as compared to teenagers of other developed countries such as Canada, Sweden, France, and the United Kingdom. Teenagers in the United States also have high rates of pregnancy, childbearing, and abortion as compared to their peers in other developed countries. A major factor explaining the last point is that the U.S. teenagers use fewer types of contraception than teens in other developed countries. This decrease in use is due to negative attitudes toward teen sexual activity, restriction of access to reproductive health services, and lack of motivation to prevent pregnancy (Alan Guttmacher Institute, 2004).

Teenage pregnancy rates have declined during the last 25 years in developed countries due to high motivation to complete education and get employment experience before having a baby. In general, teens in such countries have more extensive sex education and better access to contraception. Adolescent pregnancy rates vary greatly among countries, with an exceptionally high rate of 102 pregnancies per 1000 teenagers (15 to 19 years old) in the Russian Federation and a lower rate of 12 pregnancies per 1000 teens in the Netherlands. The United States, Belarus, Bulgaria, Romania, and the Russian Federation have a teen pregnancy rate of 70 or more pregnancies per 1000 teens. Childbearing (birthing) rates in developed countries vary from a low of 3.9 per 1000 in Japan, to a high of 54.4 per 1000 in several countries, including the United States (Alan Guttmacher Institute, 2004).

Abortion rates for teenagers in developed countries also vary greatly, from a rate of 10–20 abortions per 1000 teenagers (15 to 19 years old) in the Czech Republic, Denmark, England, Wales, Finland, Norway, and Sweden, to a high rate of 56 per 1000 in the Russian Federation. The youngest adolescents are more likely than older ones to have an abortion (Alan Guttmacher Institute, 2004).

Sexually transmitted diseases disproportionately affect teenagers as compared to older women of childbearing age. Syphilis, gonorrhea, and chlamydia are the most common STDs in teens. The United States has higher rates of STDs than other developed countries such as the United Kingdom, France, Canada, and Sweden, owing to lower use of condoms and higher numbers of sexual partners among U.S. teenagers (Alan Guttmacher Institute, 2004).

Cultural Influences

Muslim culture directly affects programs and policies involving adolescent reproductive health. Islamic law condemns prostitution, homosexuality, and premarital sex. The interpretation of the Koran presents challenges in establishing reproductive health programs for teenagers. For example, some religions in Morocco—a mostly Muslim country in northern Africa—oppose sex education and condom promotion for unmarried adolescent use, while others stress that the Hadith includes clear guidelines for sex education. In Iran in the late 1980s, fatwas declared that family planning methods were allowed. In Egypt since the 1960s, all major family planning and reproduction health programs have worked with religious leaders and supported family planning. Morocco and Tunisia tend to encourage NGOs to target the population's adolescent health issues and problems (Beamish & Abderrazik, 2003).

FERTILITY

Age of childbearing varies greatly among countries. In Africa, ages of women who are bearing children are evenly distributed between younger and older women; in most other major areas of the world, however, the majority (two-thirds) of childbearing takes place before age 30. In many developed countries today, the age at which women have their first child has increased. Women are having children later in life and having fewer children than previous generations, which has resulted in a below-replacement-level fertility rate in many developed countries. Lower fertility rates in developed countries are attributable to factors such as industrialization, urbanization, modernization of societies, improved access to education, improved survival of children, and increased use of contraception (United Nations, 2004).

Men are physiologically capable of reproducing longer than women and often marry later and become fathers at older ages than women. Women who have children closely spaced in age and who give birth at ages less than 18 years, or older than 34 years, have higher risks of morbidity and mortality for both themselves and their babies (United Nations, 2004).

Cultural Influences

In the Arab culture, the bride's status in her husband's household is unstable until she gives birth to her first baby and proves that she is fertile; she is then obligated to have a second child because of the fear that an only child may die and leave the parents childless. After the second child is born, the pressure to continue having children exists if there are only female children. Women are expected to continue having children until at least one son is born. The need to have a male child is great, so as to preserve the family name. Muslims believe that their religion requires them "to be fruitful and multiply" (Kridli, 2002).

Infertility

Infertility is the biological failure to conceive by normal sexual activity without contraception or to carry a pregnancy to full term; it affects both men and women of reproductive age. This definition contrasts with intentional childlessness, which may be due to cultural, social, economic, or psychological factors. Infertility rates are especially high in sub-Saharan Africa, where many individuals have reproductive tract infections caused by STDs, particularly gonorrhea, and HIV infections. Unsafe abortions may also be responsible for infertility problems among residents of countries with transition economies. In developed countries, infertility rates are higher than might be expected in spite of available legal abortions and treatment of STDs, mainly due to significant delays in childbearing. In many cultures, infertility causes stress, social exclusion, and stigma. In some cultures, women who are infertile may be divorced, neglected, abused, and given lower social status. Universally, infertility usually results in serious psychological stress for the couple. Approximately 8% to 12% of couples worldwide experience infertility problems of some type (United Nations, 2004).

In the United States, approximately 6.1 million Americans (10% of all people of reproductive age) are affected by this problem. Testing for infertility in men begins with an analysis of the semen, looking at the number, shape, and movement of sperm. Sometimes hormones are also tested. For women, checks for ovulation may be done. Depending on the test results, different types of treatments can be performed. Between 85% and 90% of infertile couples can be treated with drugs or surgery. Assisted reproductive therapy (ART) uses special methods to help infertile couples, involving the woman's eggs and the male sperm. These procedures are often very expensive and are not usually covered by health insurance. Donor eggs or frozen embryo are sometimes used as well (United Nations, 2004).

Cultural and Religious Issues

Religion and culture are often major influences on sexuality and reproduction, including fertility treatments. According to Jewish law, an infertile couple should undergo diagnosis and treatment. Christianity states that marriage does not confer upon spouses the duty to have a child, but the right to have intercourse. Sterility can be an occasion for other important services to humanity such as adoption, educational work, assistance to families, and assistance to disadvantaged children.

Polygamy is practiced today in many Islamic societies, which creates more opportunities for fertility within a family structure. According to the Jewish culture and religion, most infertile couples may do almost anything to have a child, including the use of reproductive technology. In fact, Israel, a predominately Jewish country, is one of the leading countries of the world in the research and development of reproductive technology. Insemination of husband's sperm is permitted, and some groups of Jews permit insemination of another man's sperm if absolutely necessary. In vitro fertilization and embryo transfer are also permitted by most groups of Jewish people. In contrast, the Roman Catholic Church states that assisted reproduction—including artificial insemination, in vitro fertilization (IVF), and embryo transfer—is not allowed. Most religious groups have more liberal attitudes toward infertility interventions and treatments. Islam allows all treatments for infertility as long as they involve only the husband and the wife; adoption is not permitted (Schenker, 2005).

Within Judaism, fetal reduction for multiple-gestation pregnancies is allowed by most Jews. Catholics consider this practice to be an abortion, which is not permitted. In Islam, fetal reduction is allowed if the other fetuses or the mother's life is in jeopardy (Schenker, 2005).

The status of the human embryo is quite controversial in the United States. Not all embryos created in IVF clinics are used for pregnancy implantation. Clinics may put "extra" created embryos in cryopreservation, to be donated for reproductive use for couples, research, or disposal. Disposal of excess embryos creates many moral and ethical issues, which continue to be widely debated. Currently some 400,000 embryos are frozen in storage in the United States, and many others exist in other countries as well. Depending on the culture, religion, and geographic location, human embryos are considered to be anything from a cluster of cells to an actual human being (Gurmankin & Caplan, 2004).

FAMILY PLANNING AND CONTRACEPTION

Family planning allows people to decide the number, spacing, and timing of the births of their children. Research clearly links adequate spacing of the birth of children with decreased maternal and infant morbidity and mortality. At present, 60% of the world's individuals or couples use family planning as compared to 10% in the 1960s (**Table 17-1**). Contraception is the intentional prevention of a pregnancy by natural or artificial methods. Family planning and contraception use are closely correlated to women or couple's urbanization, education, socioeconomic status, and approval by culture.

TABLE 17-1

Worldwide Contraceptive Use

Country	Percentage of Population Using Contraceptives (%)
Africa	<10
Eastern Europe	35
Russian Federation	70–74
Western Europe	71–77
Latin America	73
United States	82
China	83

Source: United Nations, 2004.

According to a survey of women 15–44 years of age in the United States, the most common forms of contraception are as follows:

- Oral contraceptive pill
- Female sterilization
- Male condom
- Male sterilization
- Injectable Depo-Provera

Nearly 98% of all U.S. women who have had sexual intercourse have used at least one type of contraception (National Center for Health Statistics, 2004).

A recent study of five European countries—France, Germany, Italy, Spain, and the United Kingdom—was conducted to determine contraceptive use in those nations. Results indicated that oral contraceptives were the most frequently used method. Male and female sterilization were the most widely used methods among the 40 years and older age groups, while 23% of the subjects did not practice contraception at all (Skouby, 2004).

Family planning services should be integrated within primary healthcare services, which should include education and counseling for informed contraception decision making for the couple. In addition, care for STDs, cervical cancer screening, and breast cancer screening need to be included as part of primary health care. Family planning serves the following purposes (WHO, 2010):

- It promotes gender equality and empowers women and families.
- It can reduce maternal deaths by 32% and deaths of newborns and children by 10%.
- It can potentially decrease unwanted pregnancies by 71%.
- It can decrease HIV transmission by as much as 80% with the promotion of consistent and correct condom use.
- It slows population growth, thereby significantly reducing poverty and hunger.

According to a United Nations report, in China premarital sex is no longer taboo, and norms and behaviors are changing. Most sexually active people do not want a pregnancy, yet many lack knowledge of contraception. Many unmarried women are embarrassed about obtaining contraception and do not want their sexual activity to be revealed. Many believe that family planning centers are for married women only, yet the government has made these services available to all (United Nations, 2004).

In Diandong County within the Yunnan province of China, the population is predominately Han Chinese, and 94% work in agriculture. The current population policy permits rural couples to have two children, with a spacing of 4 to 5 years between children. Couples who exceed the birth quota may be fined $374 to $500. Women with "unapproved by government" births are less likely to get adequate prenatal and postpartum care compared to women with "approved by government" births (Li, 2004). The majority of women in Li's study believed that having a son is extremely important. Female infants are much more likely to die than male infants in such areas, with deaths of female infants often being unrelated to illness or disease.

According to a Muslim jurist who uses the Koran, under a fatwa (ruling) related to family planning in Islam, family planning is permitted. There is a wide variation in opinion of Muslim authorities regarding family planning, however. Some Muslims do not believe in family planning and state that children are a great asset: The larger the number of Muslims, the greater the power. The higher courts in Jordan have stated that family planning is acceptable in Islam, but decisions on this issue are left to the couple (Hasna, 2003).

Mogilevkina and Odlind (2003) report that historically in Ukraine, as in other countries of the former Soviet Union (now known as the Commonwealth of Independent States), abortion was used as a method of birth control. This policy reflected negative attitudes toward contraception. These researchers' data from 1999 showed that the abortion rate was 121 abortions per 100 deliveries, and 36.7 abortions per 1000 women of reproductive age. Today, contraception services are increasing in Ukraine, yet abortion remains common and 32.5% of women do not use any form of contraception.

Emergency Contraception

One example of a moral dilemma regarding emergency contraception was reported by Zwillich (2005). In the United States, a small group of conservative pharmacists refuse to fill prescriptions for the emergency contraception medication called levonorgestrel (Barr Pharmaceuticals), which prevents pregnancy when taken within 72 hours of unprotected sex. The drug works by inhibiting ovulation, interfering with fertilization, and blocking implantation in the wall of the uterus.

Abortion

Definition

Elective abortion is the voluntary termination of a pregnancy, which in most cases, is done prior to viability of the fetus. In 1973, the U.S. Supreme Court ruled that induced abortions must be legal in all states as long as the pregnancy is less than 12 weeks' gestation. Individual states can regulate abortion in a second-trimester pregnancy and prohibit abortion that is not life threatening after 12 weeks' gestation. Some states have established additional regulations regarding use of the procedure in the third trimester of pregnancy, such as requiring a 24-hour waiting period for counseling or requiring parental approval for minors (Childbirth by Choice Trust, 1999).

Grimes et al. (2006) state that abortion is a persistent and preventable epidemic. According to WHO, an unsafe abortion, which represents a human rights issue, is a procedure for terminating an unintended and unwanted pregnancy either by people without necessary skills or in an environment that does not conform to minimum medical standards. It endangers women, the majority of whom live in developing countries, where abortion is highly restricted by law, or in countries where, although legally permitted, abortions are not easily accessible. In these settings women often obtain secret abortions from medical practitioners, paramedical workers, or traditional healers. Legal abortions by trained healthcare providers are a safe procedure with minimum morbidity and mortality.

According to WHO's (2010) *Packages of Interventions for Family Planning, Safe Abortion Care, Maternal, Newborn, and Child Health,* women should be provided safe abortion services to the full extent of the local law within a specific geographic location. In addition, women need access to treatment for complications due to spontaneous or unsafe abortion, as well as information and counseling services. In some parts of the world, women are forbidden to have any information, counseling, or procedure related to an elective abortion.

History of Elective Abortion

According to the Childbirth by Choice Trust (1999), abortion has been practiced in almost all regions throughout the world since the earliest times. Women have been faced with unwanted pregnancies and have chosen to abort a fetus regardless of religious or legal sanction, often risking their lives in the process. In primitive societies, abortions were induced by poisons, herbs, sharp sticks, and pressure on the abdomen, causing vaginal bleeding. Ancient Chinese and Egyptians used surgical instruments, much like modern ones of today. Socrates, Plato, and Aristotle were known to suggest abortion, while Hippocrates recommended it on occasion. St. Augustine (354–430 A.D.) related that the animation and sensation of pregnancy occurred at 40 days after conception; prior to the first 40 days, abortion was not considered homicide. Pope Innocent III wrote that quickening—the time of perception of fetal movement—was the moment that abortion became homicide. In 1869, Pope Pius IX declared excommunication for those who had an abortion at any stage of fetal development. From the late 1800s until World War II, abortion was restricted almost everywhere in the world. Later, countries in Eastern and Central Europe relaxed some of the laws, followed by most of the developed countries during the 1960s and 1970s (Childbirth by Choice Trust, 1999).

World Perspectives

At present, two-thirds of the world's population allows abortion upon request. In reality, abortions are carried out in every country in the world, regardless of the law. In places where it is prohibited (such as Muslim Asia, Latin America, and Africa), hidden abortions are a significant health problem to women. Maternal deaths occur as a result of hidden abortions that can cause hemorrhage, bleeding, infection, and damage to reproductive organs (Childbirth by Choice Trust, 1999).

Worldwide, nations have different ways of addressing the rules and regulations regarding abortion. In 1997, South Africa established a woman's right to an abortion upon request up to 12 weeks' gestation. This country allows abortion through 20 weeks of pregnancy if the mother's physical or mental health is endangered. A program was established to train licensed registered midwives to perform abortions at primary care facilities (Dickson-Tetteh & Billings, 2002).

In Mexico, elective abortion is a well-publicized issue and is punishable by law, dating back to 1931. Exceptions are made for saving a mother's life, or if the pregnancy was a result of rape. In some states, if a fetus is severely malformed, an abortion can be performed legally. The state of Yucatan accepts economic reasons as a valid basis for having a legal abortion. In spite of the public and government attitudes toward elective abortion, as many as 850,000 induced abortions are performed each year, both legally and illegally (Castaneda, Billings, & Blanco, 2003; Erviti, Castro, & Collado, 2004).

The availability and accuracy of statistics regarding abortion depend on the legal status that the country assigns to this procedure. In many countries throughout the world, including the United States, where abortion is legal, reporting of statistics is not always required, so data collection and reporting may be very difficult (see **Table 17-2**). Nevertheless, it appears that approximately 15 million legal abortions occur annually, with China, the Russian Federation, the United States, and Vietnam performing 80% of the world's legal abortions (United Nations, 2004).

Greater numbers of women from North America, Western Europe, Australia, New Zealand, and Latin America (with the exception of Brazil) who have elective abortions are unmarried, as compared to women from Eastern Europe and the former Soviet Union, who are mostly married when they have abortions. In countries such as Germany, Hungary, Israel, Italy, and the Netherlands, approximately half of women who undergo elective abortions are married and half are unmarried. In some societies, abortion is used as a method of family planning, especially among married women. In most countries, women in their twenties have the highest pregnancy rates as well as the highest rates of abortions.

According to a study conducted by Lofstedt, Shusheng, and Johansson (2004), in China high male-to-female ratios at birth are due to abortion practices. Between 1984 and 1987, rates of abortions for female fetuses in Huaning County, Yunnan Province, increased, creating a ratio of 107 males to 100 females born; between the period from 1988 to 2000, the ratio rose again to 110 males to 100 females born.

Abortion is legal in many areas of the world, yet the criteria for permitting it vary. Some countries permit abortions only to save the woman's life. The laws are generally more restrictive in the developing world than in the developed nations.

In countries where abortion is strictly illegal or very restrictive, unsafe abortions are performed against the law and can cause unnecessary morbidity and mortality. Globally, 1 in 8 maternal deaths is due to an unsafe abortion. The highest rates of maternal death by unsafe abortion are found in Africa, with a rate of 7 deaths per 1000 unsafe abortions, followed by Asia, with 4 deaths per 1000 unsafe abortions.

The most frequent complications from unsafe abortions are sepsis, incomplete abortion, hemorrhage, and abdominal cavity injury (United Nations, 2004).

An estimated 19 to 20 million elective abortions take place every year, with 97% of these procedures occurring in developing countries (**Table 17-3**). These procedures are among the most neglected of global health challenges. An estimated 68,000 women die each year worldwide from unsafe abortions, and many millions more are permanently injured. The leading causes of death in such cases are hemorrhage, infection, and poisoning. Legal abortions, by contrast, have a mortality rate of 1 per 100,000 procedures.

Deaths from abortions are very difficult to report with any accuracy because many of the procedures are illegal and secret, and there are powerful disincentives for reporting such data. Approximately half of such deaths occur in Asia, and most of the remainder occur in Africa. Unsafe abortion is estimated to cause approximately 13% of all maternal deaths worldwide, yet accounts for 17% of such mortality in Latin America and 19% in Asia.

Examples of unsafe elective abortion methods used worldwide include the following (Grimes et al., 2006):

- Toxic solutions:
  - Turpentine
  - Laundry bleach
  - Detergent solutions
  - Acid
  - Laundry bluing
  - Cottonseed oil
  - Arak (strong liquor)
  - Teas and herbal drinks
  - Boiled avocado or basil leaves
  - Drugs such as Pitosin
- Objects placed through the cervix:
  - Sticks
  - Rubber catheter
  - Knitting needle
  - Coat hanger
  - Pen
  - Air through a turkey baster
- Enemas
- Trauma

PRENATAL CARE

Prenatal care includes the following measures, all of which are recommended by WHO (2010):

- Information and counseling on self-care at home, including nutrition, safer sex, HIV prevention and care during pregnancy, breastfeeding, family planning, and the harmful effects of drugs, alcohol, and tobacco use during pregnancy
- Childbirth preparation and danger signs of pregnancy
- Support and care for women with HIV/AIDS
- Assessment and assistance with domestic violence
- Confirmation of pregnancy
- Monitoring pregnancy progress, including maternal and fetal well-being
- Detection and treatment of pregnancy complications
- In some situations, antimalaria treatment, assessment of female genital mutilation, and deworming

TABLE 17-2

Abortion Rates Among 14- to 44-Year-Olds, 1999

Country	*Abortion Rate (%)*
Soviet Union (Russian Federation, Belarus, and the Ukraine)	> 60
Estonia, Romania, Bulgaria, and Latvia	50–59
Republic of Moldova, Vietnam, Hungary, and Kazakhstan	40–49
Lithuania, Slovenia, Czech Republic, Armenia, Georgia, China, Slovakia, Sweden, Croatia, Turkmenistan, and Canada	30–39
Macedonia, Singapore, Australia, United States, Japan, New Zealand, United Kingdom, Italy, Denmark, Norway, and France	20–29
Germany, Spain, Israel, Tajikistan, Netherlands, Belgium, and Uzbekistan	10–19
Brazil	4.1
Chile	5
Colombia	3.6
Dominican Republic	4.7
Peru	5.6
Mexico	2.5

Source: United Nations, 2004.

TABLE 17-3

Unsafe Elective Abortion Procedures

Region	*Number*	*Number per 1000 Live Births*
World	19 million	14
Developed countries	500,000	2
Developing countries	18.5 million	16
Africa	4.2 million	24
Asia	10.5 million	13
Europe	500,00	3
Latin America/Caribbean	3.7 million	29
North America	Negligible	Negligible

DELIVERY AND NEWBORN CARE

Childbirth care increases safety and decreases complications for both mother and baby. It includes care from the onset of labor to at least 24 hours after childbirth, and can potentially reduce maternal mortality due to labor complications by as much as 95%, and asphyxia-related newborn complications by as much as 40%. Ideal childbirth situations should include the following.

- Skilled healthcare professionals
- Services accessible and available 24 hours a day for 7 days a week
- Essential medicines and equipment available
- Care during labor and delivery:
  - Diagnosis and monitoring of progress of labor
  - Infection prevention and treatment
  - Pain relief
  - Detection and treatment of complications
  - Delivery and immediate newborn care
  - Newborn resuscitation
  - Initiation of breastfeeding
  - Referrals, counseling, and family support for complications and/or death of mother and/or baby
- A referral system for complications (WHO, 2010).

POSTPARTUM CARE

Postpartum and immediate newborn care reduces maternal and newborn morbidity and mortality. These services should include the following (WHO, 2010):

- Skilled healthcare professionals
- Early identification and treatment of complications of mother and baby
- Family planning counseling services
- Care for HIV/AIDS mothers
- Support for breastfeeding

MATERNAL MORTALITY AND MORBIDITY

Maternal mortality is a major global problem that affects families and society as a whole. Obstetrical complications are the leading cause of death for women of reproductive age in developing countries today. Ninety-nine percent of these deaths occur in developing countries, and most could be prevented. Maternal health services and maternal mortality rates are very specific indicators of the general functioning of healthcare systems of a country (UNFPA, 2011).

A maternal death is defined as the death of a woman while pregnant or within 42 days after the termination of a pregnancy, irrespective of the duration, site, cause, or management of the pregnancy. Direct maternal deaths may be caused by obstetrical complications during pregnancy, labor and delivery, or postpartum. They may be related to interventions, omissions, incorrect treatment, or other events; examples include sepsis, pregnancy-induced hypertension, or delivery complications. Indirect maternal deaths are due to a previous existing disease or a disease that developed during pregnancy, yet not directly due to obstetrical causes. The disease may have been exacerbated during pregnancy. Examples include malaria, HIV/AIDS, and cardiovascular disease (United Nations, 2004; UNFPA, 2011).

A common indicator of national health is the maternal mortality rate, which is the number of maternal deaths per 100,000 women of reproductive age for a specific period of time, usually one year. Obtaining accurate data on maternal mortality is problematic because many countries do not indicate on the death certificate that a woman was pregnant or recently pregnant. In addition, a significant amount of underreporting and misclassification of actual deaths occurs. The causes of maternal mortality worldwide are ranked in the following list (see also **Table 17-4**).

1. Hemorrhage
2. Sepsis
3. Hypertensive disorders
4. Abortion complications
5. Obstructive labor (UNFPA, 2011).

In addition to deaths, many women suffer pregnancy-related complications that have long-term effects. For example, a woman could develop an amniotic fluid embolism or a cerebrovascular disorder causing a chronic disability, or a hemorrhage necessitating a hysterectomy, resulting in early loss of fertility. Family planning, good nutrition, and prenatal care have been shown to reduce maternal mortality (Horon, 2005; United Nations, 2004; UNFPA, 2011).

Skilled care has contributed to lowering of the maternal mortality rate, but in sub-Saharan Africa the maternal mortality rate is not improving. Access to prenatal care and high-quality delivery and postpartum care are needed for all women who give birth. As mentioned earlier, complications from pregnancy and childbirth remain the leading causes of death and disability for all women of reproductive age. The worldwide maternal mortality rate is 515,000 women per year. In addition, for each woman who dies, approximately 30 more experience injuries, infection, and disabilities (UNFPA, 2011; USAID, 2008).

In sub-Saharan Africa, women face a 1 in 13 chance of dying during pregnancy, in childbirth, or during the postpartum period; this risk is 200 times greater than the corresponding risk in the United States. **Table 17-5** provides global rates of death from pregnancy and childbirth (WHO, 2006).

TABLE 17-4

Causes of Global Maternal Mortality

Cause	Rate
Hemorrhage	31%
Indirect	14%
Sepsis	11%
Hypertension in labor (pregnancy-induced hypertension [PIH])	10%
Anemia	8%
Unclassified	6%
Other direct causes	5%
Unsafe abortion	5%

Source: Adapted from WHO, 2006.

TABLE 17-5

Global Rates of Death from Pregnancy or Childbirth

Region	Lifetime Risk of Dying from Pregnancy or Childbirth
Sub-Saharan Africa	1 in 13
South Asia	1 in 55
Middle East/North Africa	1 in 55
Latin America/Caribbean	1 in 150
East Asia/Pacific	1 in 280
Central and Eastern Europe and the Commonwealth of Independent States CEE/CIS	1 in 800
Least developed countries	1 in 16
Developing countries	1 in 60
Developed countries	1 in 4100
World	1 in 75

Source: Modified from USAID, Child Survival and Maternal Health Program, 2008.

Efforts to Reduce Maternal Mortality and Morbidity

WHO estimates that more than 500,000 women die annually of pregnancy complications. Maternal mortality in sub-Saharan African is very high, with an estimated 900 maternal deaths per 100,000 live births. Reasons for this high rate in sub-Saharan Africa are due to delays in the following actions:

■ Recognizing danger signs during pregnancy
■ Deciding to seek care
■ Reaching a healthcare facility
■ Receiving appropriate care when once at the healthcare facility

Most complications of pregnancy can be prevented or well managed if the danger signs are well known and transportation is available. In the region of northern Tanzania, the Mwanza Region, Care-Tanzania, along with the U.S. Centers for Disease Control and Prevention (CDC) and the local Ministry of Health and Social Welfare, implemented a community reproductive health project focused on improving the quality of maternal health care. Twenty-nine villages were involved in this project, which included intensive training of local healthcare providers; increasing the amount of hospital equipment and blood for transfusion; improving the water and electrical supply; administering HIV counseling, testing, and medical interventions; and establishing a community patient transport system. Specific educational programs addressed family planning, information about STDs, education about danger signs in pregnancy, and advice about labor and delivery and postpartum needs. These programs resulted in a decrease in maternal mortality from 2002 to 2005 in the Kwimba region (Ahluwalia, Robinson, Vallely, Gieseker, & Kabakama, 2010).

A close relationship exists between the maternal mortality rate and the proportion of births attended by skilled health personnel. A skilled health person can be a midwife, physician, or nurse who has skills needed to manage normal (uncomplicated) pregnancies, deliveries, and postpartum care. Worldwide, 63.3% of all births are attended by a skilled healthcare worker. However, traditional birth attendants, whether trained or not, are not counted in this category of healthcare workers (WHO, 2005a).

According to Graham and Hussein (2004), women who die as a result of pregnancy or childbirth are often not counted in statistics. Underreporting of these deaths ranges from 17% to 63% in developing countries, yet even in developed nations such as the United Kingdom, 19% of the maternal death reports did not cite causes. In most developed countries, misclassification—rather than total omission—is the major problem.

One example of a country that has achieved a significant drop in its maternal mortality rate is Egypt. A 52% decrease in such deaths occurred from 1992 to 2000. In addition to their prenatal care education about birth, self-care during pregnancy, and danger signs, many of the Egyptian women also received higher education during the same time period. This also allowed them to get better jobs and, in turn, receive better health benefits (Campbell et al., 2005).

Recently, Canada began a multibillion-dollar initiative on nutrition to help fight maternal and newborn mortality. The Canadian plan called for nations to adopt a Framework for Action on Nutrition, which was developed through the cooperative efforts of USAID, the World Bank, the United Nations, and Bread for the World (an NGO). The Canadian International Development Agency, a food security program, states that nutrition is often overlooked as a high priority to promote maternal and newborn well-being. The plan calls for government and international agencies to spend an additional $10.3 billion per year from public resources to benefit 360 million children in 36 countries in a campaign against malnutrition and prevent more than 1.1 million child deaths (Canadian Medical Association, 2010).

Cambodia also has attempted to decrease its exceptionally high maternal mortality rate. In this country, many mothers needlessly die from unsanitary water, poor sanitation, and lack of basic health care. Cambodia has a maternal mortality rate of 450 maternal deaths per 100,000 live births—one of the highest rates in the world. The infant mortality rate is also high, at 166 deaths per 1000 live births. Life expectancy at birth is 47.5 years. As of 2005, only 9% of pregnant Cambodian women received more than four prenatal checkups, and 44% had only one. The majority (68%) of deliveries still take place without any birth attendants. A special program by the Reproductive and Child Health Alliance (an NGO) has worked to increase the skills of lay birth attendants and to encourage births at health centers (Chatterjee, 2005).

After 20 years of war and conflict, women in Afghanistan have tremendous needs related to reproductive health. According to 2000 estimates, the maternal mortality rate in Afghanistan is the second highest in the world, 1600 deaths per 100,000 live births (Sierra Leone has the highest rate, 1900 maternal deaths per 100,000 live births). Women in Afghanistan have limited access to quality health services, adequate food, shelter, and clean water. In addition, women lack the ability to choose their marriage partners, access to birth control, or rights to not be beaten by their husbands when disobeying them. Causes of the high rate of maternal mortality in Afghan women include early marriage and childbirth, frequent childbirth with lack of spacing between births, and lack of power to seek health care; however, women with more education have a higher rate of skilled birth attendants at delivery and better rates of survival (Egmond, Naeem, Verstraelen, Bosmans, Claeys, & Temmerman, 2004).

ACCESSING REPRODUCTIVE HEALTH CARE

Prenatal care reduces maternal and newborn complications through regular checkups by a trained nurse midwife or physician. This care includes risk assessment, treatment for medical conditions or risk reduction, and education. In the United States, access to prenatal care has increased through the availability of Medicaid coverage for pregnancy-related services. An important element in reducing health risks for mothers and children is increasing the numbers of births with assistance by medically qualified people. Proper medical attention and hygienic conditions during delivery can reduce the risk of complications and infections that cause serious illness or death to either mother or baby. Women who do not receive prenatal care are more likely to deliver at home with no medically qualified birth attendant (CDC, 2004).

Two United Nations Millennium Development Goals (MDGs) relate to drastically improving maternal and child health by the year 2015. Currently, public health expenditures in the 75 countries with the highest maternal and child health problems total approximately $97 billion dollars per year ("WHO Calls for New Approach," 2005).

The likelihood of mothers entering prenatal care increases with age and education, and decreases with number of children. The risk of poor birth outcomes is greatest in women ages 15 and younger. Prenatal care needs to begin with the initial pregnancy and continue throughout pregnancy. The American College of Obstetricians and Gynecologists recommends at least 13 visits for a full-term low-risk pregnancy. More frequent visits are needed for a high-risk pregnancy (a pregnancy with complications such as diabetes or hypertension). In the United States, more than three-fourths of women receive adequate prenatal care; however, this rate varies with race and ethnicity. In addition to the prenatal visits to a healthcare provider, women are encouraged to attend with their spouse/partner/friend a series of childbirth education classes. Classes include education on fetal development, physiology of labor and birth, exercises and self-help techniques for labor, role of support persons, care of the newborn, and opportunities for questions (CDC, 2004).

In a U.S. study, women who received no prenatal care had more preterm births (less than or equal to 37 weeks' gestation), and their babies had lower birth weights. The women in the study were also more likely to be uninsured, have more children, be older, be less educated, and be more likely to use alcohol, tobacco, and drugs. Syphilis and HIV were also found in 5% of the women studied. The results indicated that intensive encouragement is needed to get women to use more prenatal care and, thereby, decrease many of the poor birth outcomes (Maupin et al., 2004).

China has more than 345 million women of reproductive age. Since the economic reforms that began in the late 1970s and early 1980s, the national government has gradually shifted responsibility for health care to local units, such as counties, townships, and villages. This change has resulted in people in poor rural areas having to pay for at least half of their health care out of pocket. Thus women must pay for half of their prenatal care visits, even though they often have no insurance coverage. In China, current birth control and family planning regulations require most women to seek permission to conceive and carry a child to term. Under the one-child-per-family policy, regulations may vary for women living in rural areas (Short & Zhang, 2004).

MATERNAL AND NEWBORN CARE DURING A HUMANITARIAN CRISIS

In any crisis, people must have access to shelter, nutrition, water, sanitation, and essential health care, including treatment of injuries. At the same time, special care must be given to pregnant women and newborn babies who are most vulnerable during a crisis period. Special considerations include the following (WHO, n.d.):

■ The crude birth rate (births per 1,000 population) will increase to a greater rate during humanitarian crises. As the situation gets worse, the rate will increase further.

■ Of the pregnant women within a crisis-affected population, 15% will have a spontaneous abortion (miscarriage), and the rate will increase further with the intensity of the crisis.

■ Emergency kits that contain medications and supplies should ideally be given to all birth attendants or women who are at least 6 months pregnant.

INFANT HEALTH

The following is a list of terms useful for discussing infant mortality (Kochanek & Martin, 2005):

■ Infant mortality rate: Deaths of infants aged younger than 1 year per 1000 or 100,000 live births. It is the sum of the neonatal and postneonatal mortality rates.

■ Neonatal mortality rate: Deaths of infants aged 0–27 days per 1000 live births.

■ Early neonatal mortality rate: Deaths of infants aged 0–6 days per 1000 live births.

■ Late neonatal mortality rate: Deaths of infants aged 7–27 days per 1000 live births.

■ Late fetal mortality rate: Fetal deaths of 28 or more weeks of gestation per 1000 live births.

■ Perinatal mortality rate: Late fetal deaths plus early neonatal deaths per 1000 live births plus fetal deaths.

■ Low-birth-weight rate: Births with weight at delivery of less than 2500 grams per 100 live births.

■ Moderately low-birth-weight rate—Births with weight at delivery of 1500 grams to 2499 grams per 100 live births

■ Very low-birth-weight rate: Births with a rate at delivery of 1500 grams or less per 100 live births.

■ Term: Births at 37–41 weeks of gestation.

■ Preterm: Births at less than 37 completed weeks of gestation per 100 live births.

Infant mortality worldwide differs greatly between and within developing and developed countries. The highest rate areas are found in sub-Saharan Africa. **Table 17-6** identifies some of the unusually high infant mortality rates worldwide, defined as number of deaths per 100,000 live births. Compared to developing countries, developed countries have much lower infant mortality rates and higher life expectancies (**Table 17-7**).

TABLE 17-6

Developing Countries: World's Highest Infant Mortality Rates with Accompanying Life Expectancies, 2004

Country	Infant Mortality Rate (per 1000 Live Births)	Life Expectancy (Years)
Afghanistan	161	42
Angola	192.5	36.8
Bangladesh	64.3	—
China	25.3	—
Egypt	33.9	—
Guatemala	36.9	—
India	57.9	—
Iran	42.9	—
Kenya	62.9	44.9
Mexico	21.7	—
Mozambique	137.1	37.1
Russian Federation	17	66.4
South Africa	62.2	44.2
Zimbabwe	67.1	37.8

Source: CIA, 2005.

TABLE 17-7

Developed Countries with Lower Rates of Infant Mortality and Higher Life Expectancies

Country	Infant Mortality Rate (per 1000 Live Births)	Life Expectancy (Years)
Australia	4.8	80.3
Austria	4.7	—
Canada	4.8	—
Finland	3.6	—
Israel	7.2	79.2
Sweden	2.8	80.3
United States	6.6	77.4

Source: CIA, 2005.

As can clearly be seen from Table 17-6 and Table 17-7, the United States does not have the lowest infant mortality rate in the world, even though more money per capita is spent on health care in the United States than anywhere else in the world. Within the United States, the infant mortality rates also differ greatly depending on the state, being influenced by education, income, cultures, geography, and politics (U.S. Census Bureau, 2001). As can be seen in **Table 17-8**, the northern states clearly have lower infant mortality rates than many of the southern states.

The U.S. Department of Health and Human Services has established a wide range of programs to prevent infant mortality. These programs include efforts to improve access to prenatal and newborn care,

TABLE 17-8

Selected U.S. Infant Mortality Rates by State

State or District	Infant Mortality Rate (per 1000 Live Births)
Delaware	10.7
District of Columbia (Washington, DC)	10.6
Mississippi	10.5
Louisiana	9.8
Alabama	9.4
South Carolina	8.9
New Hampshire	3.8
Utah	4.8
Massachusetts	5
Minnesota	5.3

Source: U.S. Census Bureau, 2001.

such as Healthy Start, Medicaid, and State Children's Health Insurance (SCHIP). The Department of Health and Human Services also supports educational programs teaching infant care and prevention of malnutrition, and research to prevent birth defects, premature births, and sudden infant death syndrome (Central Intelligence Agency [CIA], 2005). Birth defects are the leading cause of infant mortality in the United States, accounting for 20% of infant deaths each year. Approximately 150,000 babies are born annually with congenital abnormalities. Many who survive have long-term morbidities and disabilities (United Nations, 2004).

Infant mortality rates differ greatly in the United States within the categories of race and ethnicity. **Figure 17-1** compares various rates within selected groups.

As stated in the *World Health Report 2005*, hundreds of millions of women and children have no access to health care, and mortality rates could substantially be reduced by increasing access to prenatal and child care. Worldwide, approximately 530,000 babies die each year, more than 1 million are stillborn, and more than 4 million newborns die within the first days or weeks of life. In addition, 10.6 million children die before their fifth birthday. Approximately 90% of the children who die before age 5 deaths die from preterm birth, birth asphyxia, or infection, such as lower respiratory infection, diarrhea, malaria, measles, and HIV/AIDS (WHO, 2005b; "WHO Calls for New Approach," 2005).

The majority of neonatal deaths take place in low-income and middle-income countries, and approximately half occur at home. In many poor countries, infants die unnamed and unrecorded. "The availability of good medical care tends to vary inversely with the need for it in the population served" (Lawn,

FIGURE 17-1

Infant Mortality Rates,* By Selected Racial and Ethnic Populations, United States, 2002

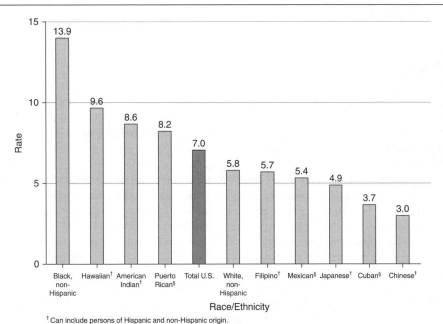

† Can include persons of Hispanic and non-Hispanic origin.
§ Persons of Hispanic origin might be any race.

Source: National Center for Health Statistics, 2005.

Cousens, & Zupan, 2005, p. 891). Challenges in these settings include HIV/AIDS, pneumonia, diarrhea, malaria, and vaccine-preventable infections, as well as increasing poverty.

In the period 1996–2005, an increase in neonatal deaths occurred in sub-Saharan Africa (5%). Elsewhere, decreases in rates were recorded, such as in the Americas, and especially in Latin America (Lawn, Cousens, & Zupan, 2005):

■ Latin American countries: −40%
■ Eastern Mediterranean countries: −9%
■ European countries: −18%
■ Southwest Asian countries: −21%
■ Western Pacific: −39%
■ Overall world: −16%

Mortality is greatest in the first 24 hours after birth (25–45%). Approximately 75% of all neonatal deaths worldwide occur during the first week of life. As many as 70% of deaths could be prevented if good neonatal care were implemented. Ideally a woman could choose to have a skilled birth attendant present during a delivery; if a complication should occur, she and the newborn would then have a much greater chance of receiving better care. Women in Asia and sub-Saharan Africa most often do not have this opportunity. Rates for cesarean section deliveries are low in the countries with the highest mortality, such as much of Africa. Within the poorest countries, the richest women have 2 to 3 times greater rates of antepartal care and about 6 times the rate of skilled birth attendants as compared to the poorest women (Knippenberg et al., 2005).

In developed nations that keep accurate statistics, the rate of neonatal death is less than 3%. In many developing countries, the vital statistics may come from verbal reports. Causes of neonatal deaths include the following:

■ Preterm birth (low birth weight)
■ Severe infection (sepsis, pneumonia, tetanus, and diarrhea)
■ Asphyxia
■ Congenital abnormalities

In many developing countries, babies are not weighed at birth and often gestational age in unknown. Eighteen million babies worldwide are estimated to be low birth weight, with half of the low-birth-weight babies born in Southeast Asia (Lawn, Cousens, & Zupan, 2005; Lawn, Shibuya, & Stein, 2005).

The infant mortality in the United States increased from 6.8 deaths per 1000 live births in 2001 to 7 deaths per 1000 live births in 2002. It was the first increase in the U.S. infant mortality rate in 40 years. Included in this increased rate were low-birth-weight, preterm, and "very preterm" infants. The main factor increasing infant mortality from 2001 to 2002 was related to the increase in infants born weighing less than 759 grams (1 pound, 10.5 ounces). These deaths were exclusively due to newborns dying in the first 4 weeks of life. The majority of these very-low-birth-weight infants die within the first year of life. Multiple-gestation (e.g., twins, triplets) births, more than half of which are born preterm or low birth weight, have contributed greatly to the recent increases in preterm and low birth weights. The preterm rate for singleton births (one baby per pregnancy) alone increased 7 percent during the 2001–2002 time period (MacDorman, Martin, Mathews, Hoyert, & Ventura, 2005).

Infant mortality for African American babies is still a poorly understood and unresolved problem in the United States. Although progress has been made to lower infant mortality among all ethnic and racial groups, a significant disparity persists between African American and non-Hispanic White American infant mortality rates. Regardless of maternal age, education, income, or marital status, an African American infant is twice as likely to die as a non-Hispanic White infant. This disparity is often associated with high rates of preterm delivery, as well as low-birth-weight and very-low-birth-weight neonates. Despite many efforts, the rate of preterm delivery remains high—18.4%—for African-American births, as compared to 9.1% of non-Hispanic White American births. Some interventions, such as treatment of urinary tract infections, cerclage, and treatment of bacterial vaginosis, have led to improvements in rates, but overall the preterm delivery rate among African American women remains twice as high as that among non-Hispanic White women. The risk of infant mortality increases greatly as birth weight decreases (Professional Education, 2000).

PROGRESS TOWARD MILLENNIUM DEVELOPMENTAL GOALS 4 AND 5 IN BRAZIL

Global progress toward MDG 4 (reducing child mortality) has been inadequately accomplished, but MDG 5 (improving maternal health) has been the subject of the least progress worldwide. Diverse economic and political conditions have affected all nations worldwide, but have had a severe effect on many countries, including Brazil. Brazil's north and northeast regions are the least developed and poorest parts of the country. The northeast region has a population of 54 million, representing 28.2% of the total population. Significant health interventions implemented in these poorer regions of Brazil include the following: piped water to households; increased use of contraception; prenatal care; delivery attendance by a medically trained person; options for cesarean delivery; diphtheria–pertussis–tetanus (DPT) vaccinations; measles vaccinations; care for pneumonia; and oral rehydration. Results of a study in Brazil indicate that, as a result of these interventions, infant mortality dropped from 47.1 deaths per 1000 live births in 1990 to 20.0 deaths per 1000 live births in 2007. Neonatal mortality also dropped from 23.1 deaths per 1000 live births in 1990 to 13.6 deaths per 1000 live births in 2007. Information regarding maternal mortality in Brazil was difficult to obtain due to underreporting of actual deaths. Nevertheless, overall progress was made in terms of infant and maternal health, with a significant reduction in the gap between the rich and poor regions of the country. Brazil has significantly met the issues of undernutrition (MDG 1), and is doing well in reduction of child mortality (MDG 4), yet its progress toward improving maternal mortality (MDG 5) remains unclear (Barros et al., 2010).

INFANT ABANDONMENT IN CHINA

New research on the abandonment of children in China reveals that some of the country's population policies may lead to abandonment of "excess" daughters so that couples may have a son. Among 237 families who abandoned their daughters, most did so because of the gender of their child; 90% of the children affected were girls and 86% were healthy. In contrast, 60% of the abandoned boys were disabled or severely ill. Other couples who were infertile emerged spontaneously to adopt these abandoned girls. Those who already had a son were also willing to adopt an abandoned girl (Johnson, Huang, & Wang, 1998).

DIARRHEA IN CHILDREN IN DEVELOPING COUNTRIES

Diarrheal diseases remain an important cause of infant and childhood morbidity and mortality in developing countries. Deaths from this cause have significantly declined in recent years due to wider availability of oral rehydration therapy (fluids and electrolytes). Most of the diarrheal problems in children in developing countries are infectious in origin, stemming from contaminated water supplies from various municipal and open-water sources (e.g., rivers, streams, creeks, and wells). Most episodes of diarrhea resolve within a week, whereas infectious diarrhea lasts more than 14 days. Significantly high mortality rates are associated with diarrhea that lasts more than 2 weeks. Persistent diarrhea is often associated with poor nutritional status, and this combination results in a significant risk for death.

Breastfeeding should be continued and even encouraged during episodes of diarrhea. Special diets and vitamins are recommended for nutritional management. Antimicrobial agents are not usually prescribed, except in the case of specific infections such as *Shigella, Salmonella,* and *Vibrio* species (Alam & Ashraf, 2003).

SEXUALLY TRANSMITTED DISEASES

The highest rates of STDs are found within urban populations, among men and women between 15 and 35 years of age. Women generally become infected earlier than men. Of particular concern are adolescents who may have unplanned sexual relations without adequate information about these diseases, their treatment, and their prevention. Sexual intercourse prior to menarche, such as in the cases of child brides, causes even greater vulnerability. Rape and incest victims are especially vulnerable to STDs. Those who are most vulnerable are of childbearing age, live in poverty, abuse drugs, and are uneducated, institutionalized, or living within an unstable social environment. Although most of the 20 or more pathogens transmitted by sexual intercourse can be treated with antibiotics, STDs remain a large problem in developing as well as developed countries (United Nations, 2004). **Table 17-9** gives examples of classic STDs with a worldwide prevalence.

Prevention and Treatment Care

Prevention helps stop the spread of STDs by interrupting the transmission path, reducing the infection duration, and preventing complications. Primary prevention begins with sex education about the diseases and prevention methods related to safe sex behavior, such as abstinence and condom use. Treatment care involves access to healthcare practitioners, making an accurate diagnosis based on laboratory tests,

TABLE 17-9

Classic Sexually Transmitted Diseases, Bacterial and Viral

Disease (Classification)	Pathogen	Signs and Symptoms
Syphilis (bacterial)	*Treponema pallidum*	Anogenital ulcers, swelling, skin rash
Gonorrhea (bacterial)	*Neisseria gonorrhoea*	Urethral discharge, cervicitis, lower abdominal pain in women, newborn conjunctivitis, may be asymptomatic
Chlamydia (bacterial)	*Chlamydia trachomatis*	Urethral discharge, cervicitis, lower abdominal pain in women, neonatal conjunctivitis, may be asymptomatic
HIV/AIDS (viral)	Human immunodeficiency	Lymph node swelling, fever, weight loss, skin rash, may be asymptomatic
Herpes genitalis (viral)	Herpes simplex virus type 2 (HSV-2)	Anogenital vesicular (genital herpes) lesions and lacerations (HSV-2)
Genital warts (viral)	Human papillomavirus (HPV)	Anogenital warts, cervical warts, cervical cancer
Viral hepatitis (viral)	Hepatitis B virus (HBV)	Nausea, malaise, fever, enlarged liver, jaundice, liver cancer, cirrhosis

Source: United Nations, 2004.

and giving the appropriate medication and education. Lack of treatment can cause mortality and morbidity (United Nations, 2004).

HIV Infection and Reproduction

Approximately 700,000 children younger than 15 years of age are infected with HIV every year in the world, and more than 90% of them reside in sub-Saharan Africa. Adding HIV to pregnancy causes an increase in numerous risk factors, which in turn can cause an increase in maternal mortality rates. HIV-infected pregnant women are at an increased risk of having HIV-positive children, stillbirth, low-birth-weight neonates, and preterm babies. Children of HIV-positive mothers (irrespective of the child's HIV status) also have a higher mortality due to maternal ill health or death.

Options for contraception are limited in many developing countries, which increases the risk of transmission of HIV to unborn children. HIV-infected women should use male or female latex condoms to protect their partners from STDs. In addition to condoms, contraception can take oral, injectable, and implantable forms. One potential problem with oral contraception is the possibility that it may interfere with antiretroviral medications; special consideration must be made for these situations (Duerr, Hurst, Kourtis, Rutenberg, & Jamieson, 2005).

An increasing number of men and women in the United States and elsewhere in the world are faced with the fact that they are HIV positive and wish to have children. As many as 28% of HIV-infected people in the United States wish to have children, and many in sub-Saharan Africa and Europe also have a desire to reproduce. Pregnancy seems to have little effect on HIV disease progression if women are receiving antiretroviral therapy. Male and female condoms are suggested for protection against unwanted pregnancy and STDs. In some countries, such as those in sub-Saharan Africa, the social stigma of not having children may be equal to or greater than the stigma of having the HIV infection itself. Concerns about having an HIV-infected child and the stigma attached to the combination of HIV and pregnancy are also problematic. Artificial insemination is often used as a means of conception without fear of transfer of the disease to the partner or spouse (WHO, 2000b).

WHO recommends exclusive breastfeeding for infants from birth to 6 months of age. In the general population, exclusive breastfeeding for the first 6 months of life protects against infant morbidity and mortality from gastrointestinal and respiratory infections. Unfortunately, breastfeeding causes more transmission of the HIV virus from mother to child, and avoidance of breastfeeding by HIV-positive mothers has been recommended in developed countries. In contrast, in developing countries, infants who are breastfed and have the HIV virus are better off with breastfeeding alone than with mixed feedings. In 1999 there were 620,000 children who were HIV positive, living mainly in sub-Saharan Africa. Antiretroviral medications have clearly reduced the rates of mother-to-child transmission of the HIV virus. In developing countries, however, children cannot be assured safe, feasible, affordable, and sustained breastmilk substitutes (Bland, Rollins, Coutsoudis, & Coovadia, 2002; Papathakis & Rollins, 2003).

VIOLENCE AGAINST WOMEN

According to the United Nations' Declaration on the Elimination of Violence Against Women of 1993, as cited in *World Population Monitoring 2002,* "Violence against women is any act of gender-based violence that results in, or is likely to result in, physical, sexual, or psychological harm or suffering to women, including threats of such acts, coercion or arbitrary deprivation of liberty, whether occurring in public or private life" (United Nations, 2004, p. 123). Such problems often arise in societies that give a higher recognition or value to males. Preferential treatment to males may affect the health and education of children. In societies where the husband is recognized as the dominant person with the most power in the relationship, women may be married without their consent and may be subject to domestic violence. In many cultures, women are often vulnerable because of their economic dependence on men. Violence against women also includes sexual exploitation of women refugees, rape as a weapon of war, and trafficking of women in prostitution. Violence against women needs to be considered a legal crime, and women need to get support and/or assistance in helping to protect themselves and their children (United Nations, 2004).

On a worldwide basis, many women are subjected to violence from intimate partners and sexual violence from strangers. Men who were abused or who witnessed marital violence in their homes are more likely to abuse their wives or partners and their children. Each year in the United States, 1.5 million women are physically abused or raped by an intimate partner. Rape and other acts of violence are common in refugee camps and by enemies in war. In many cultures, women who have been raped, or even who have been in the company of a nonrelative male, are killed by family member males, to preserve the "honor" of the family; these murders are known as "honor killings" (Murphy, 2003).

FEMALE GENITAL MUTILATION

Female genital mutilation (also called female circumcision) is experienced by some girls and sometimes young women prior to marriage, as part of cultural practices conducted outside the medical system. This procedure involves the partial or complete removal of the external female genitalia or other injury to female genital organs. The majority of these procedures also include the removal of the clitoris and labia minora. The following list describes the different types of female mutilation:

■   Type I: Excision of the prepuce, with or without excision of part or the entire clitoris
■   Type II: Excision of the clitoris with partial or total excision of the labia minora
■   Type III: Excision of part or all of the external genitalia and stitching/narrowing of the opening (infibulation)
■   Type IV: Pricking, piercing, or incision of the clitoris and/or labia; stretching of the clitoris and labia; cauterization by burning of the clitoris and surrounding tissue; scraping of tissue surrounding the vaginal orifice or cutting of the vaginal cuts; introduction of corrosive substances or herbs into the vagina causing it to bleed, or tightening or narrowing the vaginal cavity

The most common type of female genital mutilation is excision of the clitoris and the labia minora (80% of all cases); the most extreme form is infibulation (15% of all cases). The health consequences of these procedures vary according to the type and severity of the procedure. Long-term consequences include cysts, abscesses, keloid scars, damage to the urethra causing urinary incontinence, dyspareunia (painful sexual intercourse), sexual dysfunction, and painful childbirth. In addition, women may suffer anxiety and depression. An estimated 100 to 140 million girls and women have undergone this procedure, and each year 2 million girls are subjected to it. Reasons for these procedures include the following (WHO, 2000a):

■   Reduce or eliminate sexual desire in the female
■   Maintain chastity or virginity before marriage and fidelity during marriage
■   Increase male sexual pleasure
■   Promote female hygiene and external sexual appeal

Approximately 30 countries in Africa, some in Asia, and some immigrants to Europe, North America, Australia, and New Zealand report this issue within their populations. In these countries, cultural norms dictate that women undergo this procedure so that they can be pure for marriage. Often women who had this procedure done to them support having the procedure done to their daughters because of community pressure within the culture (United Nations, 2004). Amnesty International and WHO consider female genital mutilation to be an infringement of human rights. In the United States, these procedures became a crime in 1997, with the enactment of the Female Genital Mutilation Act of 1996 (Ellwood, 2005).

MALE REPRODUCTIVE HEALTH

The Alan Guttmacher Institute (2004) addresses global perspectives of male reproductive health needs and issues. Most men in the world wish for intimate and sexual relationships and a stable family. The reproductive health needs of men have historically received little attention, however. Unplanned pregnancies, infertility, and STDs, including HIV, can all have a major impact on men's lives. The outlook for men who assume a male traditional role can be gloomy due to poverty and lack of job perspectives, which can make many men fatalistic about their futures. Presently, men in sub-Saharan Africa have a significant reduction in life span, which may also decrease their motivation for adhering to preventive health measures. Fewer than half of these men aged 15–24 use any form of contraception, compared to 63–93% of their counterparts in developed countries. Urbanization may weaken support systems and also decrease the desire for large numbers of children. Many men are increasing their education, yet job opportunities are often not available, which leaves poor urban men with great frustrations.

Men between the ages of 15 and 24 typically become more independent and begin to initiate sexual relationships. In most countries of the world, men have their first sexual encounter by age 20. Few men in their teens marry and/or have children; instead, most marry and become fathers in their late 20s and 30s and begin to settle down during that period of their lives. The more educated a man is, the more likely he will consider and use a method of family planning with his spouse or partner. Fifty percent of men in the world become fathers in their mid- to late 20s. Men in their 40s and 50s usually have had all the children they wish. Male and female sterilization is common in both males and females in developed countries, as well as in China (The Alan Guttmacher Institute, 2004).

STD rates are highest in men in sub-Saharan Africa, Latin America, and the Caribbean areas. On a worldwide basis, HIV/AIDS rates are the highest among sub-Saharan African men and women. In many regions of the world, men migrate to other areas to find work, living at times away from their families for several years before returning to their homes. During this time away from home, they may have sexual relations with other women, contract STDs, and subsequently bring these diseases back to their sexual partners in their home communities (The Alan Guttmacher Institute, 2004).

CONCLUSION

This chapter has provided a worldwide perspective on male and female reproductive health issues, and cultural beliefs and practices related to pregnancy, childbirth, postpartum health, and infant health. Disparities in statistics demonstrate much of the perpetual inequality of health status, access to health care, available resources, research data collection, and health reporting worldwide. These health disparities exist not only between developing and developed nations, but also within both developed and developing nations, especially in those countries with populations that are heterogeneous in income, race, ethnicity, and socioeconomic status.

STUDY QUESTIONS

1. Explain the need for prenatal care and its relationship to better birth outcomes.
2. Relate causes of global maternal and infant mortality.
3. What is meant by "reproductive rights"?
4. Explain the relationship of skilled birth attendants, cleanliness at delivery, and better birth outcomes.
5. Give examples of cultural influences and reproductive health for men and women.
6. What are some causes of violence against women and what do you think can be done to decrease it?
7. Discuss the need for global male reproductive health.

CASE STUDY

An obstetrical fistula crisis in sub-Saharan Africa in the country of Niger (and other nearby countries as well) is an ongoing struggle for many women. An obstetrical fistula is a structurally abnormal passageway from the vagina to the bladder and/or rectum, as a postpregnancy consequence of bearing a child at a very young age with an inadequately sized pelvis. This condition results from a cultural practice of very early marriage of young girls, aged 9–15, to older men to ensure a virgin bride and to financially help the girl's family through the dowry given to her family by the groom. The women involved are young and often malnourished, having incomplete growth of the pelvis at the time of their first pregnancy. This situation may result in a cephalo-pelvic disproportion leading to obstructed labor, and eventually causing maternal and/or infant morbidity or mortality. Frequently the young woman is left without a surviving infant as well as urinary and/or bowel incontinence. Her life without a surviving child, the constant incontinence of urine and feces, and an inability to obtain adequate clean water for personal hygiene often leaves her unable to maintain her hygiene, which in turn leaves her unable to meet the sexual expectations of her marriage. Such a woman may become a social outcast, having tremendous stigma and shame. She has a difficult time surviving in her community without bearing a live child, without keeping clean, and without being unable to have sexual relations with her spouse. If she is unable to produce more children, she may be divorced by her husband. In addition, she typically has difficulty finding and paying for a surgical repair of her fistula. This scenario results in "blaming the victim" because others believe that the cause of her dilemma is one or more of the following:

- Her own bad behavior
- Witchcraft
- Sexually transmitted disease
- Sexual promiscuity

Source: Naracisi, Tieniber, Andriani, & McKinney, 2010.

Case Study Questions

1. Explain the relationship between culture and obstetrical fistula.
2. How can education and financial assistance prevent this situation?
3. How can maternal and infant mortality be improved?
4. How does this situation affect the local community?

REFERENCES

Ahluwalia, I., Robinson, D., Vallely, L., Gieseker, K., & Kabakama, A. (2010). Maternal health: Interagency youth working group. *Global Health Promotion, 17*(1), 39–49.

Alam, N., & Ashraf, H. (2003). Treatment of infectious diarrhea in children. *Therapy in Practice, 5*(3), 151–165.

Alan Guttmacher Institute. (2004). In their own right: Addressing the sexual and reproductive health needs of men worldwide. Retrieved from http://www.guttmacher.org

As-Sanie, S., Gantt, A., & Rosenthal, M. (2004). Pregnancy prevention in adolescents. *American Family Physician, 70*(8), 1517–1524.

Barros, F., Barros, A., Villar, J., Matijasevich, A., Domingues, M., & Victora, C. (2010). How many low birthweight babies in low- and middle-income countries are preterm? Retrieved from http://www .scielo.br/pdf/rsp/2011nahead/2289.pdf

Beamish, J., & Abderrazik (2003, January). Adolescent and youth reproductive health in Morocco. *Policy Project,* 1–30.

Bland, R., Rollins, N., Coutsoudis, A., & Coovadia, H. (2002). Breastfeeding practices in an area of high HIV prevalence in rural South Africa. *Acta Paediatrics, 91,* 704–711.

Campbell, O., Gipson, R., Issa, A., Matta, N., El Deeb, B., El Mohandes, A., . . . Mansour, E. (2005). National maternal mortality ratio in Egypt halved between 1992–1993 and 2000. *Bulletin of the World Health Organization, 83*(6), 462–471.

Canadian Medical Association (2010). Nutrition and integrated health care to highlight Canadian plan to fight child and maternal mortality, minister says. *Canadian Medical Association, 182*(9), E397–E398.

Castaneda, X., Billings, D., & Blanco, J. (2003). Abortion beliefs and practices among midwives (parteras) in a rural Mexican township. *Women and Health, 37*(2), 73–87.

Centers for Disease Control and Protection (CDC). (2004). Healthy people 2010: Maternal, infant, and child health. Retrieved from http://www.healthypeople.gov/Document/HTML/Volume2/16MICH.htm

Central Intelligence Agency (CIA). (2005). World factbook: United States infant mortality rate. Retrieved from http://www.indexmundi.com/united_states/infant_mortality_rate.html

Chatterjee, P. (2005). Cambodia tackles high maternal mortality. *Lancet, 366,* 281–282.

Childbirth by Choice Trust. (1999). Abortion in law, history and religion. Retrieved from http://www .cbctrust.com/abortion.html

Dickson-Tetteh, K., & Billings, D. (2002). Abortion care services provided by registered midwives in South Africa. *International Family Planning Perspectives, 28*(3), 144–150.

Duerr, A., Hurst, S., Kourtis, A., Rutenburg, N., & Jamieson, D. (2005). Integrating family planning and prevention of mother-to-child HIV transmission in resource-limited settings. *Lancet, 366,* 261–263.

Egmond, K., Naeem, A., Verstraelen, H., Bosmans, M., Claeys, P., & Temmerman, M. (2004). Reproductive health in Afghanistan: Results of a knowledge, attitudes and practices survey among Afghan women in Kabul. *Disasters, 28*(3), 269–282.

Ellwood, A. (2005). Female genital cutting, "circumcision" and mutilation: Physical, psychological and cultural perspectives. *Contemporary Sexuality, 39*(1).

Erviti, J., Castro, R., & Collado, A. (2004). Strategies used by low-income Mexican women to deal with miscarriage and spontaneous abortion. *Qualitative Health Research, 14*(8), 1058–1068.

Feki, S. (2004). The birth of reproductive health: A difficult delivery. *PLOS Medicine, 1*(1), 10–13.

Germain, A. (2004). Reproductive health and human rights. *Lancet, 363,* 65–66.

Gilbert, W., Jandial, D., Field, N., Bigelow, P., & Danielsen, B. (2004). Birth outcomes in teenage pregnancies. *Journal of Maternal–Fetal and Neonatal Medicine, 16,* 265–270.

Graham, W., & Hussein, J. (2004). The right to count. *Lancet, 363,* 67–68.

Grimes, D., Benson, J., Singh, S., Romero, M., Ganatra, B., Okonofua, F., & Shah, I. (2006). Unsafe abortion: the preventable pandemic. *Lancet, 368,* 1908–1919.

Gurmankin, A., & Caplan, A. (2004). Embryo disposal practices in IVF clinics in the United States. *Politics and the Life Sciences, 22*(2), 4–8.

Hasna, F. (2003). Islam, social traditions and family planning. *Social Policy & Administrative Issues, 37*(2), 181–197.

Horon, I. (2005). Underreporting of maternal deaths on death certificates and the magnitude of the problem of maternal mortality. *American Journal of Public Health, 95*(3), 478–482.

Johnson, K., Huang, B., & Wang, L. (1998). Infant adoption and abandonment in China. *Population and Development Review, 24*(3), 469–510.

Jones, R., & Boonstra, H. (2004). Confidential reproductive health services for minors: The potential impact of mandated parental involvement for contraception. *Perspectives on Sexual and Reproductive Health, 36*(5), 182–191.

Knippenberg, R., Lawn, J., Darmstadt, G., Begkoyian, G., Fogstad, H., Walelign, N., & Paul, V. (2005). Neonatal survival: 3 Systematic scaling up of the neonatal care in countries. Retrieved from http://www .mendeley.com/research/systematic-scaling-neonatal-care-countries-4/

Kochanek, K., & Martin, J. (2005). Supplemental analyses of recent trends in infant mortality. *International Journal of Health Services, 35*(1), 101–115.

Kridli, S. (2002). Health beliefs and practices among Arab women. *Maternal and Child Nursing, 27*(3), 178–182.

Law of the People's Republic of China on maternal and infant care. (1995). Population and family planning: Law on maternal and infant health care. Retrieved from http://www.unescap.org/esid/psis /population/database/poplaws/law_china/ch_record006.htm

Lawn, J., Cousens, S., & Zupan, J. (2005). 4 million neonatal deaths: When? Where? Why? *Lancet, 365*(9462), 89–900.

Lawn, J., Shibuya, K., & Stein, C. (2005). No cry at birth: Global estimates of intrapartum stillbirths and intrapartum-related neonatal deaths. *Bulletin of the World Health Organization, 83*(6), 409–417.

Li, J. (2004). Gender inequality, family planning, and maternal and child care in a rural Chinese county. *Social Science and Medicine, 59,* 695–708.

Lofstedt, P., Shusheng, L., & Johansson, A. (2004). Abortion patterns and reported sex ratios at birth in rural Yunnan, China. *Reproductive Health Matters, 12*(24), 86–96.

MacDorman, M., Martin, J., Mathews, M., Hoyert, D., & Ventura, S. (2005). Supplemental analysis of recent trends in infant mortality: Explaining the 2001–02 infant mortality increase: Data from the linked birth/infant data set. *National Vital Statistics Report, 53*(12).

Maupin, R., Lyman, R., Fatsis J., Prystowiski, E., Nguyen, A., Wright, C., . . . & Miller, J .(2004). Characteristics of women who deliver with no prenatal care. *Journal of Maternal–Fetal and Neonatal Medicine, 16,* 45–50.

Mogilevkina, I., & Odlind, V. (2003). Contraceptive practices and intentions of Ukrainian women. *European Journal of Contraception and Reproductive Health Care, 8,* 185–196.

Murphy, E. (2003). Being born female is dangerous to your health. *American Psychologist, 58*(3), 205–210.

Murtagh, L., & Moulton, A. (2011). Working mothers, breastfeeding and the law. *American Journal of Public Health, 101*(2), 217–223.

Naracisi, L., Tieniber, A., Andriani, L., & McKinney, T. (2010). The fistula crisis in sub-Saharan Africa: An ongoing struggle in education and awareness. *Urologic Nursing, 30*(6), 341–346.

National Center for Health Statistics. (2004). Teens delay sexual activity: Using contraception more effectively. Retrieved from http://www.cdc.gov/nchs/pressroom/04news/teens.htm

Papathakis, P., & Rollins, N. (2003). Are WHO/UNAIDS/UNICEF-recommended replacement milks for infants of HIV-infected mothers appropriate in the South African context? *Bulletin of the World Health Organization, 82*(3), 164–171.

Partnership for Safe Motherhood and Newborn Health. (2004, May). *An expanded initiative to promote the health and survival of women and newborns in the developing world.* Geneva, Switzerland: Author. Retrieved from http://www.safemotherhood.org

Professional Education. (2000). Black infant mortality problem still unsolved. Retrieved from http://www .state.nj.us/health/bibs/education/1unsolved.html

Schenker, J. (2005). Assisted reproductive practice: Religious perspectives. *Reproductive BioMedicine Online.* Retrieved from http://www.rmonline.com

Skouby, S. (2004). Contraceptive use and behavior in the 21st century: A comprehensive study across five European countries. *European Journal of Contraception and Reproductive Health Care, 9,* 57–68.

Short, S. & Zang, F. (2004). Use of maternal health services in rural China. *Population Studies, 58*(1), 3–19.

United Nations (UN). (2004). *World population monitoring 2002: Reproductive rights and reproductive health.* New York: Author.

United Nations Family Planning Association (UNFPA). (2011). Stepping up Efforts to Save Mothers' Lives. Retrieved from http://www.unfpa.org/public/mothers

U.S. Agency for International Development's (USAID). (2008). Child survival and maternal health programs. Retrieved from http://www.usaid.gov/our_work/global_health/mch/publications/docs/mch08_overview.pdf

USAID. (2008). Child Survival and Maternal Health Program, 2008. Retrieved from http://pdf.usaid.gov/pdf_docs/PDACL707.pdf

U.S. Census Bureau. (2001). State rankings—statistical abstract of the United States. Infant mortality rate—2001. Retrieved from http://www.census.gov/statab/ranks/rank17.html

WHO calls for new approach to save lives of children. (2005). *Indian Journal of Medical Science, 59*(4), 173–174.

World Health Organization (WHO). (2000a). Female genital mutilation. Retrieved from http://www.who.int/mediacentre/factsheets/fs241/en/index.html

World Health Organization (WHO). (2000b). Pregnancy and HIV/AIDS. Retrieved from http://who.int/mediacentre/factsheets/fs250/en/index.html

World Health Organization (WHO). (2005a). Reproductive health and research: Skilled attendant at birth: 2005 estimates. Retrieved from http://www.who.int/reproductive-health/global_monitoring/skilled_attendant.html

World Health Organization (WHO). (2005b). World health report 2005. Retrieved from http://www.who.int/whr/2005/en/index.html

World Health Organization (WHO). (2006). Analysis of causes of maternal deaths: A systematic review. *Lancet, 267,* 1066–1075.

World Health Organization (WHO). (2010). *Packages of interventions for family planning, safe abortion care, maternal, newborn and child health.* Retrieved from http://www.who.int/maternal_child_adolescent/documents/fch_10_06/en/index.html

World Health Organization (WHO). (n.d.). *Key steps for maternal and newborn health during a humanitarian crisis.* Retrieved from http://www.who.int/maternal_child_adolescent/documents/keysteps.pdf

Zwillich, T. (2005). US pharmacies vow to withhold emergency contraception. *Lancet, 365,* 1677–1688.

*For a full suite of assignments and additional learning activities, use the access code located in the front of your book to visit this exclusive website: **http://go.jblearning.com/holtz**. If you do not have an access code, you can obtain one at the site.*

18

Global Health of Children

Kathie Aduddell

"Children are the living messages we send to a time we will not see."

Neil Postman, The Disappearance
of Childhood (introduction), 1982

"Children are one third of our population and all of our future."

Select Panel for the Promotion
of Child Health, 1981

OBJECTIVES

After completing this chapter, the reader be able to:

1. Describe the overall causes of death and illness in children in the world.
2. Examine specific strategies and interventions that may improve the global health of children.

INTRODUCTION

This chapter describes children's health in our world today as well as the strategies to alleviate specific health concerns for children. Included in the discussion is a historical perspective of how organizations such as the United Nations (UN) and the World Health Organization (WHO) began to call attention to children's health. In addition, the chapter provides current measurements of health and the leading causes of death in children. The final part of the chapter reviews the documented approaches and international strategies to alleviate these health concerns for children and addresses future challenges.

Current United Nations Children's Fund (UNICEF) data indicate that there are more than 1.2 billion children younger than 18 years of age in the world (UNICEF, 2011). According to various national and international organizations, children and adolescents account for approximately 30% to 40% of the world's population (UNICEF, 2011; U.S. Census Bureau, 2010; WHO, 2011a). Nearly 8 million children younger than the age of 5 die each year, which translates to 21,000 children each day or 15 children every minute (Hogan et al., 2010; UNICEF, 2011; You, Jones, & Wardlaw, 2011); this rate is equivalent to 12,000 fewer deaths per day than occurred in 1990 (UNICEF, 2011; You et al., 2011). Nevertheless, millions of children continue to suffer the consequences of illnesses, malnutrition, and injuries that affect their well-being and options in life, including educational opportunities and diminished economic prospects (Grantham-McGregor et al., 2007). Children not only bear an undue share of global disease, but also suffer disproportionately from the conditions that lead to disease and death. Although considerable progress has been made in many nations and countries toward improving the global health of children, children are still vulnerable to many health threats—and they continue to be exposed to various policies and practices that put them at risk for death, unhealthy conditions, and failure to develop properly. Because children are often the most vulnerable members of society, their health serves as a marker for the well-being of a society and its future potential.

Children require not only the basic survival needs of food, water, adequate shelter, and appropriate hygienic requirements, but also basic social interactions and safe, supportive environments that allow for nurturing, healthy play, and optimal growth and development. Foundations of health as well as healthy habits are established during childhood. These health habits, or lack thereof, then become part of an adult's methods to survive and flourish, leading to a healthy society and world. It thus becomes vital to acknowledge and understand the background and historical perspective on the global health of children as well as current health concerns for children and future challenges.

BACKGROUND AND HISTORICAL PERSPECTIVE

According to Kotch (2005), the understanding and concern for the health of the world's children is closely linked to the world's political history, wars, colonialism, and trade. For example, during the colonial period, schools of tropical medicine were established in Western Europe to understand and examine the nature, origin, and transmission of diseases from the colonies that were dangerous to Europeans; they did not necessarily examine the introduction of European diseases (e.g., measles and smallpox) to the colonies or the native population. Over time these schools grew in importance. In 1913, the Rockefeller Foundation established the International Health Commission, which focused on the control or elimination of specific diseases that affected trade and the productivity of workers. As Kotch (2005) explains, the growth in world trade led to concerns about transmission of diseases such as cholera or the plague between countries by way of trading vessels. These issues eventually led to the adoption of a common sanitary code—the Pan-American Sanitary Code—among countries, which sought to improve sanitation in ports and establish fair and consistent quarantine measures.

The United Nations was created after World War II as a vehicle for peace and conflict resolution among nations; specialized agencies of the UN were developed to focus on promotion and protection of health (Kotch, 2005; United Nations, 2011). Two such agencies that continue to have a major impact on children's health are the United Nations International Children's Emergency Fund, which was developed to assist the thousands of orphans and abandoned children that resulted from the war, and the World Health Organization, which began in 1948 as an intergovernmental institution to promote and protect global health.

Over the years WHO has called attention to the plight of children through such efforts as the World Summit of Children held in 1990, revision of the International Health Regulations in 2005, and *The World Health Report 2005: Make Every Mother and Child Count* (WHO, 2003). Major gains have been achieved in reducing child mortality, although there have also been periods of stagnation or even reversal of trends since the World Summit. For example, between 1970 and 1990, the under-five mortality rate dropped by 20% every decade, but between 1990 and 2000 it declined by only 12% (WHO, 2005). There does seem to be hope for more progress on this front, as the rate of decline in under-five mortality accelerated from 1.9% per year over the 1990–2000 span to 2.5% per year over the last 10 years, 2000–2010 (UNICEF, 2011).

Ever-increasing globalization is associated with profound health implications, such as increased disease transfer and mobility risks, increased exchange of goods and information between countries in response to health problems, and changing roles of national governments and international organizations in the health field (Kotch, 2005; WHO, 2011a). As a result of the globalization trend and its profound implications for the health of the world, the United Nations unanimously adopted the Millennium Declaration in 2000 (United Nations, 2000, 2011). This international-scope document provides an overall mission, a set of guiding principles, and a list of specific objectives that target issues, concerns, and problems related to the health and development of the world's population; each objective is also linked to a specific completion date. Included in this document are specific development goals, of which three target the health of children (United Nations, 2004, 2011). Although all eight Millennium Development Goals (MDGs) affect children in various ways, these three bring attention specifically to children's health (**Table 18-1**).

Other documents relevant to children's health have followed in the wake of the Millennium Declaration, such as the report from the UN's Special Session for Children (published in 2002), which recognized the growing need for a new social agenda for children and their families, and the report from the 2005 World Summit, which began to focus on the issue of inequity in our world (United Nations, 2002, 2011). In 2003, WHO's *Strategic Directions for Improving the Health and Development of Children and Adolescents* summarized seven priority areas for action and defined specific principles to guide their implementation. More recently, the Global Strategy for Women's and Children's Health established key areas where action is urgently required (WHO, 2010), and WHO's Six-Point Agenda outlined six strategies to respond to the increasingly complex and often blurred boundaries of public health (WHO, 2011b) The purpose of these documents, summits, and initiatives is to emphasize the importance of investing in children's and adolescents' health and development as a cost-effective strategy to secure future prosperity for countries and nations. Unfortunately, few of the high-mortality, high-priority countries today are on track to accomplish the goals and objectives outlined in the various documents and initiatives (UNICEF, 2011).

CHILDHOOD MORTALITY STATISTICS: MEASURING HEALTH IN CHILDREN

Health problems of children vary widely among countries of the world. In general, an acceptable measure of the health of children is the mortality rate. Some authors have identified it as the ultimate indicator of poor child health outcomes as well as an indicator of the implementation of child survival interventions,

TABLE 18-1

United Nations Millennium Health Goals

Goal	Target Deadline
MDG 4: Reduce child mortality	By 2015, reduce the mortality rate by two-thirds among children
MDG 5: Improve maternal health	By 2015, reduce the ratio of women dying in childbirth by three-fourths
MDG 6: Combat HIV/AIDS, malaria, and other diseases	By 2015, halt and begin to reverse the spread of HIV/AIDS and lower incidences of malaria and other major diseases

Source: United Nations, 2004.

and, more broadly, of social and economic development (You et al., 2011; You, Wardlaw, Salama, & Jones, 2009). The mortality rate is calculated as the number of deaths occurring in an age range divided by the number of children entering that particular age range in a given period of time. In 2010, there were 57 deaths per 1000 children younger than the age of five (WHO, 2011b; You et al., 2011).

Because it captures the entire high-risk period in high-mortality settings, the under-five mortality rate is the most widely used and critical indicator to summarize child health from an international perspective (UNICEF, 2011; WHO, 2011b). This information is obtained through samples from vital registration systems in some countries; in others, it is gleaned from population-based surveys such as the Demographic and Health Survey (DHS) from the U.S. Agency for International Development and UNICEF's Multiple Indicator Cluster Surveys (UNICEF, 2011; You et al., 2011).

Globally, child mortality declined 2.5% per year over the 2000–2010 period, though this decline remains insufficient to reach MDG 4 (UNICEF, 2011; You et al., 2011). Spectacular reductions in childhood mortality were achieved during the 1980s, reducing childhood mortality by one-third on a worldwide basis. The 1990 World Summit for Children set a goal of reducing childhood mortality by an additional one-third by the year 2000 (Global Health Council, 2006). Although the decline in the overall child mortality rate represents considerable progress made over the past 40 years, the gains have not been uniform, with certain areas of the world showing much less improvement (Global Health Council, 2006; UNICEF, 2011; You, Jones, & Wardlaw, 2010, 2011). In fact, the child mortality rate has slowed or even increased in some countries (You et al., 2010, 2011). Northern Africa and Eastern Asia have made the greatest strides in reducing mortality, whereas sub-Saharan Africa and southern Asia have demonstrated the slowest declines in this metric (UNICEF, 2011; You et al., 2010, 2011). Approximately half of all under-five deaths in the world occur in just five countries: India, Nigeria, Democratic Republic of the Congo, Pakistan, and China (You et al., 2011)

WHAT ARE THE HEALTH PROBLEMS FOR CHILDREN?

Globally, the four major causes of death in children younger than five years of age are pneumonia, diarrheal diseases, preterm birth complications, and birth asphyxia (**Table 18-2**) (You et al., 2011). Other major causes leading to death in children include undernutrition/malnutrition, malaria, measles, HIV/AIDS, and injuries (Global Health Council, 2011; You et al., 2011). Specific diseases, however, cause more deaths in some regions—for example, malaria is the most significant cause of death in sub-Saharan Africa and AIDS is the leading cause of death for children in east and southern Africa. As the mortality rate for children declines in specific regions, the major causes of death tend to shift from diarrhea, pneumonia, and vaccine-preventable diseases such as measles to neonatal causes such as birth asphyxia and low birth weight (Bryce, Boschi-Pinto, Shibuya, & Black, 2005; Global Health Council, 2011; Kotch, 2005). Generally, in regions with low child mortality rates, the leading cause of death comprises neonatal conditions such as congenital anomalies and injuries.

Neonatal Deaths

The Global Health Council (2011) indicates that approximately 41% of all child deaths occur during the neonatal period, defined as the first 28 days of life. The leading causes of death for these nearly 3.6 million neonates include severe infection, birth asphyxia, complications of prematurity and low birth weight, and congenital conditions (Global Health Council, 2011; You et al., 2010). The number of deaths during the perinatal period is likely underestimated, as the existence of incomplete records and underreporting in various regions of the world suggests that the actual death toll may be much higher.

According to the Global Health Council (2011), 98% of neonatal deaths occur in just four countries: India, China, Pakistan, and Nigeria. WHO indicates that malnutrition or undernutrition is the

TABLE 18-2

Causes of Child Mortality and Number of Deaths, 2008

Cause of Death	Share of All Child Mortality (%)	Number of Deaths (Millions)
Neonatal causes	41	3.575
Pneumonia	14	1.189
Diarrhea	14	1.257
Malaria	8	0.732
Other infections	9	0.753
Other noncommunicable diseases	4	0.228
Injury	3	0.279
AIDS	2	0.201
Pertussis	2	0.195
Meningitis	2	0.164
Measles	1	0.118
Congenital abnormalities	1	0.104

Source: Black et al., 2010.

single largest contributor to premature death in children. When infants are born weighing less than 2500 grams (5.5 pounds), they are at a greater risk of death and disease than infants at normal and above-normal birth weights. Many times malnutrition results from the mother having poor nutrition and being deficient of essential minerals and vitamins such as vitamin A or zinc, which in turn increases the risk of her child dying from diarrhea, pneumonia, measles, or malaria (Global Health Council, 2006, 2011; WHO, 2003). In addition, children born to unhealthy mothers are at risk for being underweight, which can lead to difficulty combating illness. These infants face a world that is less able to provide a safe and nurturing environment necessary for healthy growth and development (Global Health Council, 2011; WHO, 2003).

Pneumonia

Acute respiratory infections, primarily pneumonia, killed approximately 1.6 million children in 2008 (Black et al., 2010; Global Health Council, 2011). Many of the deaths from pneumonia were the result of the child already being weakened by malnutrition or other diseases. Pneumonia is the leading cause of death for children younger than the age of five, with 95% of the infections in this age group occurring in developing countries (UNICEF, 2008, 2009). The development of such disease is also associated with indoor pollution resulting from the use of certain types of fuel combined with poor ventilation (Global Health Council, 2006). Pneumonia, although serious, can be effectively treated with the appropriate health care and availability of antibiotics, especially given that most fatal childhood pneumonia is of bacterial origin (Global Health Council, 2006). The two main pathogens that cause pneumonia in children are *Streptococcus pneumoniae* and *Haemophilus influenzae* type b (Hib) (Global Health Council, 2011). Vaccines have been developed for both of these conditions, so prevention is possible. This fact raises serious questions about the availability of health resources in developing countries or nations—a dilemma that often acts to thwart the effectiveness of even important prevention tools.

Diarrheal Disease

Diarrheal diseases such as cholera, shigellosis, rotavirus, typhoid, dysentery, and other diarrheal diseases kill nearly 2 million children each year (Black et al., 2010; Global Health Council, 2011; WHO, 2009). Because children are more vulnerable to dehydration and electrolyte imbalances, diarrheal conditions may lead to death in children more quickly than in adults. Death can occur even more easily in children with preexisting vitamin deficiencies or nondiarrheal infections. When children are subject to poor sanitation conditions, such as unsafe drinking water or lack of proper food storage, food-borne and water-borne diarrheal infections can develop more easily, making prevention extremely difficult.

Death from diarrheal diseases is mostly preventable and can be avoided with the use of inexpensive oral rehydration solutions while the child has diarrhea. WHO and UNICEF have advocated zinc supplement tablets during diarrhea episodes to help prevent recurrences. Diarrhea can also be prevented through better nutritional practices in early childhood, particularly exclusive breastfeeding until the age of six months and the appropriate introduction of complementary foods during the weaning period (Global Health Council, 2006). Just through these two practices, child mortality can be reduced by 20%. Other interventions outside the health sector, such as the provision of safe drinking water and clean sanitation facilities, also play a major role in stopping needless diarrhea-related deaths in children. Children living in poor countries get diarrhea, on average, four times per year, with each episode being life-threatening (WHO, 2009).

Malaria and Measles

Approximately 732,000 children die each year from malaria, with 85% of these deaths occurring in children younger than the age of five (Black et al., 2010; WHO, 2008b). Malaria is the leading cause of hospitalization, mortality, and morbidity in children living in areas such as sub-Saharan Africa. This illness can be prevented by using insecticide-treated bed netting and spraying with insecticides to decrease the infestation of mosquitoes. According to the Global Health Council (2006, 2011), both this intervention and the successful treatment of malaria with artemisinin derivatives are relatively affordable interventions. Unfortunately, resistance to these efforts has presented some barriers in eradicating this deadly disease.

Measles kills nearly 900,000 children each year, even though this disease can be prevented by ensuring that children are vaccinated (Global Health Council, 2011). As the result of a recent WHO and UNICEF program, deaths from measles have declined by 74% since 2000 (Global Health Council, 2011; WHO, 2009). For example, in southern Africa, measles was almost eliminated as a cause of child death through an active vaccination campaign that cost only $1.10 per child (Levine & Kinder, 2004). Unfortunately, 95% of measles deaths, including complications from measles such as pneumonia and diarrhea, still occur in low-income or developing countries (Global Health Council, 2011).

HIV/AIDS

More than 2.1 million children younger than age 15 are currently infected with the human immunodeficiency virus (HIV); more than 200,000 children become infected with HIV each year (UNICEF, 2008). More than 95% of all HIV-infected infants acquired their infection before birth (in utero), during delivery, or through breastmilk, with approximately one-third of these infants dying within one year of infection (Global Health Council, 2011). In 2008, the children younger than the age of five who died from AIDS-related causes primarily resided in sub-Saharan Africa (Global Health Council, 2011; You et al., 2009). In addition, more than 12.1 million children, most living in sub-Saharan Africa, have lost one or both parents to AIDS (Global Health Council, 2011). Other regions identified as having the potential for emerging epidemics of HIV and its more serious sequela, acquired immunodeficiency syndrome (AIDS), include the Caribbean, China, India, central Asia, and eastern Europe (Kotch, 2005).

Antiretroviral drugs (ARVs) can make a difference in saving children by substantially reducing the risk of transmitting HIV from a mother to her child. A single dose of an ARV can cut the risk of mother-to-child transmission of HIV by 50% (Global Health Council, 2011). Worldwide efforts to expand access to treatment for children with HIV have reached new milestones through various initiatives undertaken by the UN, WHO, and the U.S. President's Emergency Plan for AIDS Relief (Kotch, 2005; WHO, 2010). Most of these initiatives focus on four main strategies: primary prevention of HIV in young women; avoidance of unintended pregnancies among HIV-infected women; provision of ARVs targeted at preventing HIV transmission from HIV-infected women to their infants, safe delivery, counseling, and support for safer infant feeding practices; and provision of care and support for mothers and their families.

The treatment of children with AIDS has encountered barriers because of the lack of availability and accessibility of pediatric formulations of ARVs. The costs of these drugs are slightly higher for children than for adults, and the administration is more complicated to regulate in pediatric patients because children must have their medications adjusted as they grow (Dawson, 2006; Global Health Council, 2006). Thus fewer children with HIV/AIDS in areas such as sub-Saharan Africa get antiretroviral therapy because it is easier and cheaper to give the medicines to adults (Dawson, 2006). Another concern is the heavy emphasis on one single disease within severely resource-limited areas of the world, which could draw resources away from other health issues and concerns (Claeson, Gillespie, Mshinda, Troedsson, & Victora, 2003; Walker, Schwartlander, & Bryce, 2002).

Injuries

Approximately 3% of child deaths per year are due to injuries (Black et al., 2010; Global Health Council, 2011). Around the world, children are killed or hospitalized each year because of injuries caused by traffic accidents, fires, drownings, falls, and poisonings. Globally, the three major injury-related causes of death in children younger than 5 years of age are drowning, road traffic accidents, and fire-related burns (WHO, 2008c; UNICEF, 2008). Most of these injuries and deaths can be prevented, but occur in low- and middle- income countries and are more often associated with environmental conditions and outbreaks of armed conflict (Global Health Council, 2011). Over a 10-year period from 1999 to 2000, more than 20 million children were displaced by disasters (Torjesen & Olness, 2004). WHO attributes more than 1 million deaths of children and adolescents to injuries and violence. Injuries are also among the leading causes of mortality and lifelong disability for those who survive in higher-income countries.

Proven prevention measures have been developed that can result in major changes in injury risks for children. Some of these measures include laws on child-appropriate seat belts and helmets; hot tap-water temperature regulations; child-resistant closures on medicine bottles, lighters, and household product containers; draining of unnecessary water from baths and buckets; redesigning of nursery furniture, toys, and playground equipment; and strengthening of emergency medical care and rehabilitation services (WHO, 2008c).

Other Causes of Death in Children

Approximately 10% of all deaths of children younger than five years of age are due to other causes such as infectious diseases (other than those mentioned previously), childhood cluster diseases such as pertussis and tetanus, and other nutritional deficiencies (Global Health Council, 2006). Additional factors may lead to disease, disability, or chronic poor health. For example, malnutrition among pregnant women may lead to stunted growth and impaired learning in children. In children younger than five years of age, more than 2 million deaths each year are directly attributed to stunting, severe wasting, and restricted intrauterine growth; approximately one-third of all children younger than age five, particularly those from Asia and Africa, show evidence of being stunted (Black et al., 2008; Global Health Council, 2011; WHO, 2003). Good nutrition is the foundation for healthy development and prevention of illness. Children in developing countries who are not breastfed are six times more likely to die by the age of one month than are children who receive at least some breastmilk. Children are also particularly vulnerable from the age of six months onward, when breastfeeding is no longer sufficient to meet all nutritional requirements (WHO, 2003). In addition, many children around the world face the prospect of losing one or both parents to death from AIDS, which leads to more homeless children and children in poverty—a condition that has many health problems associated with it. Globalization has created an abundance of opportunities for many, yet resulted in a deepening of socioeconomic disparities in some regions of the world.

LARGER RAMIFICATIONS OF CHILDREN'S HEALTH PROBLEMS

The major determinants of childhood mortality can be traced to specific global issues such as poverty, lack of essential public health resources such as safe water and proper sanitation, absence of prenatal care, inadequate diet, exposure to insect vectors of disease, and lack of basic health and preventive services (Global Health Council, 2006, 2011). These conditions and situations put children at a higher risk of death from numerous other conditions and diseases. For example, as already discussed, malnutrition from lack of an inadequate diet underlies and contributes to a majority of all child deaths (Global Health Council, 2006, 2011). These conditions also have larger ramifications, leading to unrealized human potential and negative effects on individuals, families, communities, and countries in terms of productivity, economics, and politics (Torjesen & Olness, 2004; WHO, 2008a, 2011a).

Impaired Learning and Other Disabilities

The effects of poor nutrition continue throughout a child's life by contributing to poor school performance, reduced productivity, and other measures of impaired intellectual and social development (Global Health Council, 2011; WHO, 2003). Children with undernutrition or malnutrition may drop out of school and have difficulty finding employment if they lack access to special education and training. Children who survive birth asphyxia may develop problems such as learning difficulties, cerebral palsy, and other disabilities (Global Health Council, 2011; WHO, 2005). Disabilities affect 1 in 10 children in developing countries, with the major causes of these disabilities being premature birth, malnutrition, infections, injuries, child neglect, and understimulation—all of which are preventable (WHO, 2003). These conditions can be prevented through early identification, early intervention, and rehabilitation for children who are either at risk of developing disabilities or already have them.

Disasters and Child Trafficking

Between 1999 and 2000, more than 20 million malnourished children were displaced by disasters (Torjesen & Olness, 2004). It is also vital to pay special attention to the rising numbers of orphans who have lost parents due to HIV infection, disasters, or violence. In 2000, more than 10 million children younger than 15 years had lost one or both parents to AIDS (Torjesen & Olness, 2004). Whether it is natural events such as the 2005 and 2010 tsunamis, industrial accidents such as the 1984 chemical disasters in Bhopal, or the world's many wars, including the ongoing Middle East conflict, children are greatly affected. Many of the children orphaned by these events live on the streets or are lost to institutionalization. Even if they have not lost their parents and other family members, they are still at risk for infectious diseases, malnutrition, and psychological trauma with the potential for lifelong damages. Children displaced from wars in Southeast Asia, central Africa, and Bosnia, for example, have shown a high prevalence of mental health problems that persist for years after resettlement (Torjesen & Olness, 2004).

Other problematic issues, such as trafficking, smuggling, physical and sexual exploitation, and economic exploitation, are realities for children in all regions of the world (WHO, 2003). It is estimated that more than 1 million children fall victim annually to child trafficking (Global Health Council, 2011; UNICEF, 2003). This problem occurs when children are exploited in agricultural and domestic service, as has been documented in sub-Saharan Africa, or forced into prostitution, as seen in Southeast Asia, the Republic of Moldova, Romania, and Ukraine. In addition, WHO (2003) estimates that 300,000 children in Africa have been coerced into military service as soldiers, porters, messengers, and other positions.

Health Issues Later in Life

Many of these health conditions and issues become lifelong problems for children. For example, children may survive injuries but live with a long-term disability. Victims of interpersonal violence, such as children who were subjected to sexual abuse, are twice as likely to become depressed and four times as likely to attempt suicide (WHO, 2003). Child undernutrition is associated with shorter adult height, lower levels of academic achievement, reduced adult income, and low birth weight of their progeny (Victora et al., 2008). Once affected, a child's health and development are permanently altered.

Adolescents

Unfortunately, adolescents are often thought to be healthy simply because they survived any early childhood health issues. This premise has led to a lack of attention to adolescents' health and social needs until recently. The adolescent population has more than doubled since 1950, with the vast majority of these youths living in developing countries (UNICEF, 2011). Deaths of adolescents are generally caused by injuries from unintentional causes, suicide, violence, pregnancy-related complications, and illnesses—all conditions that can be treated and prevented (UNICEF, 2011; WHO, 2003).

This age group also has some unique health problems. For example, as the highest rates of new sexually transmitted infections occur in youth 15 to 24 years of age. Adolescents are also vulnerable to use of psychoactive substances such as amphetamines, opioids, and cocaine. Undernutrition and micronutrient deficiencies in girls in this age cohort may lead to adverse pregnancy outcomes. Finally, unhealthy diets and lack of physical activity in adolescents are leading to unprecedented increases in obesity and risk for chronic diseases such as diabetes, hypertension, and cardiovascular disease (UNICEF, 2011; WHO, 2003). The choices and habits established during this period of life will greatly influence the future health status of these up-and-coming adults.

Mental Health

Approximately 10% to 20% of children have one or more mental or behavioral problems (WHO, 2003). Mental health problems account for a large proportion of the disease burden among young people (UNICEF, 2011). Depression is the major contributor to mental illness in this group and often leads to suicide, which represents one of the three leading causes of mortality among people aged 15–35. More than 70,000 adolescents commit suicide each year (UNICEF, 2011).

Conflict, poverty, forced migration, and nutritional deficiencies may all affect the intellectual and social development of children. These factors present challenges and barriers that have consequences for the affected children's well-being and productivity as it relates to mental health.

Marginalized and Vulnerable Groups

Overt or implicit discrimination results in marginalized groups of children and adolescents, which in turn leads to vulnerability (WHO, 2003). Examples of these vulnerable groups include children who are permanently disabled or seriously injured by armed conflict, children displaced as refugees, street children, children suffering from natural and human-made disasters, children of migrant workers and other socially disadvantaged groups, and children who are victims of racial discrimination, xenophobia, and intolerance. Other disadvantaged groups include the orphans of the world and children who have been exploited economically, sexually, or physically. Even children who live in rural areas are approximately 1.7 times as likely to die as those who live in urban areas; children from the poorest areas of the world are twice as likely to die compared to those from wealthier areas (You et al., 2011).

One example of this marginalization involves refugees from ongoing military conflict, such as that taking place in Sudan. The Nation's Health report (2004) provides some staggering statistics and facts about the more than 1 million people who were refugees from the military conflict in Sudan. Malnutrition rates were up to 39% among these individuals, with 58% of children aged six months to five years having diarrhea and measles outbreaks. As many as 200 children died every month from violent acts, starvation, and disease. Many of these children worked the streets and would eventually return home—but not to a protective, nurturing family. In every country, children who live or spend most of their lives on the street are at greater risk for malnutrition, HIV infection, drug abuse, and violence (UNICEF, 2003).

STRATEGIES TO IMPROVE CHILD HEALTH AROUND THE WORLD

Widespread introduction of simple, inexpensive, "low-tech" interventions, successfully targeting major killers of children, can allow for a majority of the children in this world to survive and thrive. Two-thirds of children's deaths can be successfully averted by existing preventive and therapeutic strategies (Global Health Council, 2006; WHO, 2008c). Many of these proven prevention and treatment interventions used to improve child survival—such as exclusive breastfeeding; immunizations; micronutrient supplementation (particularly vitamin A and zinc); complementary feeding; antibiotics for pneumonia, dysentery, and sepsis; oral rehydration therapy for diarrhea; antimalarial drugs; and insecticide-treated bed netting—can be implemented even in resource-poor environments (Global Health Council, 2011; Kotch, 2005; Lopez, Mathers, Ezzati, Jamison, & Murray, 2006; WHO, 2011a). With only four years left to achieve the Millennium Development Goals, particularly MDG 4, the world and the various agencies and organizations concerned with global child health have much to do in a short time frame.

The WHO Expanded Program on Immunizations as well as the Diarrheal Disease Control Program are examples of effective programs with measurable impacts on child health (Bryce, el Arifeen, Pariyo, Lanata, Gwatkin, & Habicht, 2003; Claeson et al., 2003; WHO, 2011a). Launched in 1974, these programs focused on immunizing children against six major infectious diseases (diphtheria, pertussis, tetanus, tuberculosis, polio, and measles) before their first birthday. Great success was documented in various countries, but specific regions still lagged behind (Bryce et al., 2003; WHO, 2011a).

Broader approaches, such as the WHO Integrated Management of Childhood Illnesses (IMCI), were launched in the 1990s to improve case management skills of health staff, make improvements in the health systems to support effective management skills, and enhance family and community practices (Kotch, 2005). The IMCI was a positive step toward providing higher-quality, comprehensive care for children in developing countries. It used healthcare algorithms written at or slightly above the level of a village health-care worker and targeted children younger than five years—the age group with the highest death rate from common childhood diseases (Torjesen & Olness, 2004). Complex analyses indicate that mortality from diarrheal diseases fell from 2.4 million deaths in 1990 to about 1.6 million deaths in 2001 as a result of efforts in diarrhea case management, including the use of oral rehydration therapy (Lopez et al., 2006).

WHO (2003) called for addressing priority areas of action in its report titled *Strategic Directions for Improving the Health and Development of Children and Adolescents*. These priority areas, as identified in **Table 18-3**, require focused attention because they affect the physical well-being as well as the psychosocial

TABLE 18-3

Priority Areas for Actions Identified by WHO

Priority Area	Specified Action
Maternal and newborn health	Reduce neonatal mortality, provide skilled birth attendants with adequate facility support, promote prenatal care, and tackle the mother-to-child transmission challenge.
Nutrition	Provide adequate nutrition to mothers and their children, promote breastfeeding, and implement the Global Strategy for Infant and Young Child Feeding.
Communicable diseases	Avert more than 50% of childhood deaths by preventing communicable disease—specifically, pneumonia, diarrhea, malaria, measles, and HIV infection. Also prevent other diseases that pose a greater risk to children than to adults, such as syphilis, tuberculosis, meningitis, dengue, Japanese encephalitis, leishmaniasis, and trypanosomiasis. Move beyond addressing single diseases and toward integrated approaches for prevention and management of common diseases.
Injury and Violence	Draw attention to the prevention of injury and violence, which lead to death or lifelong disability in more than 1 million children and adolescents. Modify environments, change designs or structures, apply and reinforce regulatory measures, provide parent training and social support to families, and change unsafe behaviors through education. For the greatest success, combine the three strategies of regulatory measures, environmental changes, and education.
Physical Environment	Use interventions to improve water supplies, sanitation, and hygiene, which can reduce child mortality by 65%. Also implement other interventions to improve indoor air pollution, prevent injuries, and minimize other environmental risk factors. Focus on the WHO's six priority issues—household water security, hygiene and sanitation, air pollution, disease vectors, chemical hazards, and injuries and accidents.
Adolescent Health	Focus attention on support for mental, sexual, and reproductive health; the rights of adolescents to information, skills, services, and protection from exploitative relationships; and support to develop responsible behavior.
Psychosocial development and mental health	Examine the long-term consequences for well-being to prevent these concerns. Implement early interventions in areas of feeding, play, and communication as appropriate.

Source: Adapted from WHO, 2003.

development of children and adolescents. In addition, the report includes three specific guiding principles to be used in implementing the strategic actions:

- Address inequities and facilitate the respect, protection, and fulfillment of human rights as outlined in the Convention on the Rights of the Child
- Take a life-course approach that recognizes the continuum from birth through childhood, adolescence, and adulthood
- Implement a public health approach by focusing on major health issues and applying a systematic development model to ensure the availability and accessibility of effective, relevant interventions

In 2009, WHO, through the Partnership for Maternal, Newborn, and Child Health Strategy and Workplan, identified the need to build consensus and promote evidence-based, high-impact interventions with a focus on knowledge management systems and a core package of interventions and essential commodities, to strengthen human resources and advocacy for these populations, and to track progress and commitment toward the MDGs that affect these populations (WHO, 2009).

More recently, WHO's Six-Point Agenda has emphasized six strategies to continue a forward direction in achieving the MDGs:

- Promoting health development by focusing on equity
- Fostering health security through strengthened international health regulations
- Strengthening the world's health systems so services reach all populations, especially poor and underserved populations
- Harnessing research, information, and evidence to set priorities, define strategies, and measure results
- Enhancing partnerships with UN agencies and other international organizations, donors, civil society, and private sector to achieve results
- Improving performance by concentrating on efficiency and effectiveness (WHO, 2011b)

By focusing on disease-specific interventions and broad community-based programs, marked advances in child survival and development have been achieved. When cost-effective interventions that aid the largest possible number of people are utilized, fewer children die. It is also understood that children who have educated mothers have a better survival and health outcome than children with non-educated mothers (You et al., 2011).

The obstacles to implementing general health strategies are similar to the obstacles associated with implementing child-survival strategies. They include high staff turnover, poor management and supervision, and inadequate funding, all which continue to cause problems over and above the difficulty of acquiring adequate services in specific areas and regions (Kotch, 2005). The loss of children due to avoidable or treatable conditions is unnecessary, and the drastic decline in childhood mortality rates confirms that interventions can be successful, especially if the global health community, political leaders, governments, foundations, and private citizens make commitments to providing needed resources (Global Health Council, 2006; UNICEF, 2011). In 2006, four major obstacles were identified by the Global Health Council; these obstacles, which are shown in **Table 18-4**, remain challenges today. Although the current response to the needless deaths of children and the implementation of strategies to prevent these deaths are sometimes fragmented and uncoordinated, the Global Health Council has proposed four major actions to address the salient issues: effective leadership, strengthened health systems, evidence-based health delivery system guidelines, and evaluation systems to monitor progress toward improved survival.

Another important focus for eliminating health problems and issues for children and adolescents is to establish a developmental approach. WHO (2003) has outlined five developmental phases, accompanied by possible health outcomes and examples of interventions. Implementing this approach within a public health strategy that already targets the aforementioned obstacles could achieve the highest possible

TABLE 18-4

Obstacles to Implementing Child Survival Strategies

- The highest rates of under-five mortality occur in a limited number of the poorest countries.
- Many of these countries have been involved in war or civil conflict.
- The government is unwilling to or incapable of providing health services effectively.
- The poor are marginalized and most difficult to reach.

levels of health and well-being. For example, a study in Uttar Pradesh, India, demonstrated a 50% decline in neonatal mortality through raising awareness in the community with such simple survival strategies as cleaning, drying, and warming the newborn; skin-to-skin contact with the mother; and exclusive breastfeeding for the first six months of the infant's life (Darmstadt et al., 2005).

Some key strategies to consider include empowering women in developing countries, removing financial and social barriers to accessing basic services, increasing local health systems' accountability, and developing innovative approaches to deliver critical services in specific areas of the world (You et al., 2011).

FUTURE CHALLENGES

How can professional healthcare providers help children around the world? Which types of skills and systems are still needed by these individuals and institutions? Millions of children die each year from preventable causes. If they had appropriate and timely access to basic and inexpensive health prevention and therapeutic inventions such as rehydration, vaccines, vitamin A and micronutrients, most of these children would survive (Rx for Child Survival, 2005).

The Global Health Council (2006) advocates these additional methods of improving children's chances of survival: (1) the continuance of breastfeeding through a child's first year, (2) sanitation including clean water and waste disposal, (3) prevention of mother-to-child transmission of HIV in countries with a high prevalence of HIV through the use of antiretroviral drugs, and (4) the use of zinc therapy for diarrhea. These types of inventions are not expensive and could eliminate much unnecessary childhood deaths. If these interventions were available, there would be major decreases in child death for a fairly low cost (Global Health Council, 2006).

RESEARCH AND TECHNOLOGY

The United States has done an extraordinary job of documenting events surrounding perinatal health using the vital records system. This effort needs to continue to support the health of children on a population basis (Kotch, 2005). Some states monitor blood lead levels, hospitalizations, and injuries, as well as school physical examinations, but these efforts are not uniform across the country (Kotch, 2005). A more centralized database is needed so that these data can be used to effectively monitor and explore trends and issues that affect children's health, thereby allowing for advocacy of policies, initiatives, and programs to promote and maintain children's health care. On a global scale, more efforts need to continue in moving toward population-wide surveys and surveillance of child health parameters. Some authors suggest that one-third of all births in the developing world are not registered (Torjesen & Olness, 2004).

WHO (2003) recommends adoption of a public health model imbued with a strong research and technical implementation perspective. Priority should be given to research and development activities relevant to the needs of children and adolescents that would inform policy, lead to new technologies, and improve delivery strategies. For example, the Global Forum for Health Research's Child Health and Nutrition Research Initiative (CHNRI) has established a research priority-setting framework that takes into account an intervention's effectiveness, deliverability, affordability, sustainability, and potential to relieve the disease burden (Rudan, Arifeen, Black, & Campbell, 2007).

OTHER INFLUENCES ON CHILDREN'S HEALTH: POLITICS, ECONOMICS, AND CULTURE

Not only do health problems differ in various areas of the world, but communities and countries also set priorities and deal with children's health differently owing to local concerns, resources, and needs. Myriad factors influence children's health, ranging from political instability and violence in a country to the economic conditions and family resources that determine the healthcare decisions and resources provided for the children within a family. Children still must depend on their parents, advocates, and policy makers to articulate appropriate child healthcare policies and implement relevant programs (Akukwe, 2000). Most of the people living in poverty in this world are children, with the legacy of this condition being transmitted from one generation to the next (UNICEF, 2011). WHO (2005) estimates that poverty is directly responsible for the deaths of 12 million children younger than the age of five each year. For example, in sub-Saharan Africa, most of the countries with stagnant or high child mortality rates also have the highest incidence of extreme poverty (WHO, 2005).

Many of the world's children come from diverse ethnic and cultural backgrounds that will need to be understood by their healthcare providers. Cultural and religious practices may limit or counteract the effectiveness of some medical and health practices (Torjesen & Olness, 2004). For example, the survival of an infant reflects more than just its health at birth; it is also dependent on the race and ethnic status of the mother, the socioeconomic status of the parents, the residence of the parents, the preconception health status of the mother, and the level of maternal education (Akukwe, 2000). In the United States, women with fewer than 12 years of education have higher rates of delayed prenatal care, infants with low birth weight, and neonatal deaths compared to the women with higher educational levels (Akukwe, 2000).

A recurrent theme that emerges in examining the health of children of the world is the inequality in health outcomes within and among countries worldwide. Although unfortunate health outcomes are seen in the poorer regions of the world, examination of data from the wealthiest countries also shows inequality within specific countries (Macinko, Shi, & Starfield, 2004). Numerous authors of national and international documents have identified three major factors that have significant salience for this inequality: socioeconomic status, gender, and education (Black et al., 2003; Kotch, 2005; Victora et al., 2003; WHO, 2003). **Table 18-5** lists some of the conditions associated with each of these factors. Education of women and their children, higher socioeconomic status, and greater value and respect of women lead to more favorable health outcomes for children in countries and regions throughout the world (Black et al., 2003; Kotch, 2005; Victora et al., 2003). Poverty and health are inextricably linked, so the world must work toward eliminating poverty if it is to improve health.

UNICEF (2004a) advocates four major goals to benefit children throughout the world. Accomplishing these goals would result in individual well-being and productivity for all children and adolescents, with the overall result of healthy global communities. Today, fostering healthy families is a necessary global imperative. To continue to move beyond simple survival to ensure health, growth, and full development for all children, adolescents, and their families requires strong commitments from political leaders, clear identification of children's health as a priority, and strategic investments from nations' budgets, followed by investments in comprehensive and integrated efforts that have proved cost-effective and able to produce outcomes leading to improved child and adolescent health (Kotch, 2005; WHO, 2003).

TABLE 18-5

Three Major Factors Related to Inequality in Health Outcomes

Factor	Associated Conditions
Lower socioeconomic status	▪ Less use of antenatal and delivery care.
	▪ Exposure to poor sanitation, crowding, and undernutrition.
	▪ Less preventive health or appropriate and timely treatment for illness.
Gender	▪ Low status for women in various global areas leads to greater exposure to health risks such as gender-based violence and exposure to HIV (Blanc, 2001; Dunkle et al., 2004; Shiffman, 2000; WHO, 2003).
	▪ Stronger preference for sons leads to infanticide and neglect of female children in areas of the world such as northern India, China, and parts of east Asia (Victora et al., 2003; WHO, 2003).
Education	▪ Educated women and their children are less likely to die than their less educated counterparts (Kotch, 2005).
	▪ An increase in education leads to improved domestic health care and hygiene and increased use of health services.

CONCLUSION

The majority of deaths in children can be prevented worldwide if children receive appropriate and timely access to health care and interventions (Bryce et al., 2003; Global Health Council, 2006, 2011; Jones, Steketee, Black, Bhutta, & Morris, 2003; Shiffman, 2000). Many children continue to die needless deaths because of stagnant progress, missed opportunities, and growing inequities in the provision of basic services. Although we have made tremendous progress over the last few years, serious issues continue to face children in the world today. The international Millennium Development Goals continue to provide a clear strategy for improving children's health, with specific international organizations providing guidance and implementation tactics that can be used to achieve these goals. The world needs to continue to seek creative and effective approaches to cross political, socioeconomic, and cultural barriers so that all children will be adequately served, supported, and protected. Ideally, the value of the world's children will be elevated with an increased effort to guide and protect the world's future.

STUDY QUESTIONS

1. Discuss two United Nations Children's organizations and relate how they promote global child health.
2. Compare and contrast the major childhood global diseases such as pneumonia, diarrheal disease, HIV/AIDS, malaria, and measles.
3. Why are child injuries a major global problem today?
4. Discuss the major issues in child trafficking.

CASE STUDY

Tanmayi was excited about studying abroad next year. As a four-year nursing student in a major university in the United States, she felt prepared and ready to provide nursing to the people of Bangladesh. It was very surprising to her when on her first day she became immediately immersed in the culture by trying to console a parent of a two-year-old child dying of pneumonia. When she wrote in her journal (a requirement for her course of study), she had to answer the following questions:

1. What is the leading cause of death in children younger than the age of five?

2. What is the difference between childhood mortality versus morbidity?

3. What would be the best practice for intervening to prevent further deaths in this area of the world?

REFERENCES

Akukwe, C. (2000). Maternal and child health services in the twenty-first century: Critical issues, challenges, and opportunities. *Health Care for Women International, 21,* 641–653.

Black, R., Allen, L., Bhutta, Z., Caulfield, L., de Onis, M., Ezzati, M., . . . Rivera, J. (2008). Maternal & child undernutrition: Global & regional exposures & health consequences. *Lancet,* 371, 243–260.

Black, R., Cousens, S., Johnson, H. L., Lawn, J. E., Rudan, I., Bassani, D. G., . . . Mathers, C. (2010). Global, regional, and national causes of child mortality in 2008: A systematic analysis. *Lancet, 375,* 1969–1987.

Blanc, A. K. (2001). The effect of power in sexual relationships on sexual and reproductive health: An examination of the evidence. *Studies in Family Planning, 32,* 189–213.

Bryce, J., el Arifeen, S., Pariyo, G., Lanata, C. F., Gwatkin, D., & Habicht, J. (2003). Reducing child mortality: Can public health deliver? *Lancet, 362,* 159–164.

Bryce, J., Boschi-Pinto, C., Shibuya, K., & Black, R. E. (2005). WHO estimates of the causes of death in children. *Lancet, 365,* 1147–1152.

Claeson, M., Gillespie, D., Mshinda, H., Troedsson, H., Victorsee, C. (2003). Knowledge into action for child survival. *Lancet, 362,* 323–327.

Darmstadt, G., Kumar, V., Yadav, R., Singh, V., Singh, P., & Mohanty, S. (2005). *Community mobilization and behaviour change communication promote evidence-based essential newborn care practices and reduce neonatal mortality in Uttar Pradesh, India* [Poster]. Countdown to 2015: Tracking Progress in Child Survival, London.

Dawson, D. (2006). New hope for children with HIV/AIDS. *AIDMatters.* Retrieved from http://www.talcuk .org/aidmatters

Dunkle, K. L., Jewkes, R. K., Brown, H. C., Gray, G. E., McIntyre, J. A., & Harlow, S. D. (2004). Gender-based violence, relationship power, and risk of HIV infection in women attending antenatal clinics in South Africa. *Lancet, 363,* 1415–1421.

Global Health Council. (2006). Child health. Retrieved from http://www.globalhealth.org/view_top.php3 ?id=226

Global Health Council. (2011). Annual report 2010. Retrieved from http://www.globalhealth.org/Annual_Report.html

Grantham-McGregor, S., Cheung, Y. B., Cueto, S., Glewwe, P., Richter, L., & Strupp, B. (2007). Developmental potential in the first 5 years for children in developing countries. *Lancet, 369,* 60–70.

Hogan, M., Lopez, A., Lozan, R., Murray, C., Naghavi, M., & Rajaratnam, J. (2010). *Building momentum: Global progress toward reducing maternal and child mortality.* Seattle, WA: Institute for Health Metrics & Evaluation.

Jones, G., Steketee, R. W., Black, R. E., Bhutta, Z. A., & Morris, S. S. (2003). How many child deaths can we prevent this year? *Lancet, 363,* 65–71.

Kotch, J. B. (2005). *Maternal and child health: Programs, problems, and policy in public health* (2nd ed.). Sudbury, MA: Jones and Bartlett.

Levine, R., & Kinder, M. (2004). *Millions saved: Proven successes in global health.* Washington, DC: Center for Global Development.

Lopez, A. D., Mathers, C. D., Ezzati, M., Jamison, D. T., & Murray, C. J. L. (2006). Global and regional burden of diseases and risk factors, 2001: Systematic analysis of population health data. *Lancet, 367,* 1747–1757.

Macinko, J. A., Shi, L. Y., & Starfield, B. (2004). Wage inequality, the health system, and infant mortality in wealthy industrialized countries, 1970–1996. *Social Science and Medicine, 58,* 279–292.

The Nation's Health. (2004, October). Malnutrition, violence threaten Sudanese refugees. Retrieved from http://www.apha.org/NR/rdonlyres/67FD0431-3590-42FF-A7BE-CAA0570C59CF/0/TNHOct04full.pdf

Rudan, I., Arifeen, S., Black, R. E., & Campbell, H. (2007). Childhood pneumonia & diarrhea: Setting our priorities right. *Lancet Infectious Diseases, 7,* 56–61.

Rx for Child Survival. (2005). Rx for child survival campaign: A global health challenge. Retrieved from http://www.pbs.org/wgbh/rxforsurvival/about-project.html

Shiffman, J. (2000). Can poor countries surmount high maternal mortality? *Studies in Family Planning, 31,* 274–289.

Torjesen, K., & Olness, K. (2004). Child health in the developing world. In R. E. Behrman, R. M. Kliegman, & H. B. Jenson, *Nelson textbook of pediatrics* (17th ed., pp. 12–14). Philadelphia: Saunders.

UNICEF. (2003). *State of the world's children.* Geneva, Switzerland: United Nations.

UNICEF. (2004a). End of the decade databases. Retrieved from http://www.childinfo.org/index2.htm

UNICEF. (2008). United Nations, Department of Economic and Social Affairs, Population Division: World population prospects: The 2008 revision. Retrieved from http://www.un.org/esa/population/publications/wpp2008/wpp2008_highlights.pdf

UNICEF. (2009). *The state of the world's children 2009.* New York: United Nations.

UNICEF. (2011). *The state of the world's children 2011.* New York: United Nations.

United Nations. (2000). The millennium declaration. Retrieved from http://www.un.org/millennium/declaration/ares552e.htm

United Nations. (2002). Special session on children. Retrieved from http://www.un.org/documents

United Nations. (2004). Millennium development goals. Retrieved from http://www.un.org/millenniumgoals/poverty.shtml

United Nations. (2011). Update on millennium goals. Retrieved from http://www.un.org

U.S. Census Bureau (2010). Children. Retrieved from: http://www.census.gov/hhes/socdemo/children/

Victora, C., Adair, L., Fall, C., Hallal, P., Martorell, R., Richter, L., & Sachdev, H. S.(2008). Maternal and child undernutrition: Consequences for adult health and human capital. *Lancet, 371,* 340–357.

Victora, C. G., Wagstaff, A., Schellenberg, J. A., Gwatkin, D., Claeson, M., & Habicht, J. P. (2003). Applying an equity lens to child health and mortality: More of the same is not enough. *Lancet, 362,* 233–241.

Walker, N., Schwartlander, B., & Bryce, J. (2002). Meeting international goals in child survival and HIV/AIDS. *Lancet, 360,* 284–289.

World Health Organization (WHO). (2003). *Strategic directions for improving the health and development of children and adolescents.* Geneva, Switzerland: Author. Retrieved from http://www.who.int /maternal_child_adolescent/documents/9241591064/en/

World Health Organization (WHO). (2005). *The world health report, 2005: Make every mother and child count.* Geneva, Switzerland: Author.

World Health Organization (WHO). (2008a). *Children and AIDS: Third stocking report, 2008.* Geneva, Switzerland: Author & UNICEF

World Health Organization (WHO). (2008b). *World malaria report 2008.* Geneva, Switzerland: Author.

World Health Organization (WHO). (2008c). *World report on child injury prevention.* Geneva, Switzerland: WHO & UNICEF.

World Health Organization (WHO). (2009). *The partnership for maternal, newborn, & child health strategy & workplan 2009–2011.* Geneva, Switzerland: Author.

World Health Organization (2010). WHO Agenda. Retrieved from http://www.who.int/about/agenda/en /index.html

World Health Organization (WHO). (2011a). Fact sheet: 10 facts—October, 2007. Retrieved from http ://www.who.int/features/factfiles/child_health2/en/index.html

World Health Organization (WHO). (2011b). General page. Retrieved from www.who.int

You, D., Jones, G., & Wardlaw, T. (2010). *Levels and trends in child mortality: Estimates developed by the UN Inter-agency Group for Child Mortality Estimation.* United Nations Inter-agency Group for Child Mortality Estimation. New York: UNICEF.

You, D., Jones, G., & Wardlaw, T. (2011). *Levels and trends in child mortality: Report 2011.* United Nations Inter-agency Group for Child Mortality Estimation. New York: UNICEF.

You, D., Wardlaw, T., Salama, P., & Jones, G. (2009). Levels and trends in under-5 mortality, 1990–2008. *Lancet, 9,* 61601–61609.le

For a full suite of assignments and additional learning activities, use the access code located in the front of your book to visit this exclusive website: ***http://go.jblearning.com/holtz****. If you do not have an access code, you can obtain one at the site.*

19

Global Health of the Older Adult

David B. Mitchell

> *Grow old along with me!*
> *The best is yet to be,*
> *The last of life, for which the first was made:*
> *Our times are in His hand . . .*
>
> Robert Browning,
> "Rabbi Ben Ezra," 1864

OBJECTIVES

After reading this chapter the reader will be able to:

1. Define gerontology.
2. Compare and contrast the health concerns of the older adult in a developed vs. developing country.
3. Explain the influences of culture and geographic location on aging in various parts of the world.
4. Discuss gender differences in aging.
5. Relate legal and ethical issues related to global aging.

INTRODUCTION

Who is the older adult? Is it a person who is elderly? When does one become old or—to put it another way—when does aging begin? Under normal circumstances, a newborn baby begins its life with the same biological and psychological apparatus regardless of where in the world it is born. However, older individuals are clearly not all equally equipped. Although it is often said that all generalizations are false, including this one, a major hallmark of aging is that there are a variety of life span developmental trajectories (Nesselroade, 2001). A key concept to understanding the older adult is an appreciation of individual differences in patterns of aging, because there is no prototypical older adult. For example, one 79-year-old may be frail, suffering from osteoporosis, and experiencing significant deficits in strength and hearing. Another older person—of the same chronological age—might be in peak physical and mental condition (see **Figure 19-1**). How do aging and the experiences of elderly individuals vary around the world, as

FIGURE 19-1

Two Individuals of the Same Chronological Age (79) with Significantly Different Aging Experiences

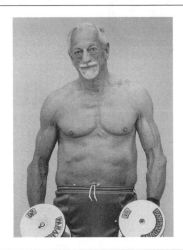

The image on the left is from the SPARHKS program at Kennesaw State University, courtesy of Dr. Angela Baldwin Lanier. The image on the right is a photo of Dr. John Turner by Etta Clark (1995).

Source: Clark, 1995.

a function of different environments, cultures, religions, and political landscapes? We will attempt to answer some of these questions in this chapter.

Gerontology (from *geron,* the Greek word for "old man") is most commonly defined as the scientific study of aging. The term was introduced by Élie Metchnikoff in 1903. A broader definition of gerontology also includes the following aspects: studies of the processes associated with aging; studies of mature and aged adults; studies of aging scholarship from the perspective of art, philosophy, history and literature; and applications for the benefit of older adults (Kastenbaum, 2006).

Not to be confused with gerontology, geriatrics is a subfield of gerontology concerned specifically with the medical aspects of aging. The American Geriatrics Society was established in 1942 (Rockwood, 2006).

In the field of gerontology, studies of older populations typically use the index of chronological age, starting at age 65. However, the passage of time per se does not cause the biological changes associated with age (Arking, 2006, p. 4). Because most biologists believe that aging begins at conception (Hayflick, 1996), the selection of the age of 65 is arbitrary and certainly not biologically precise. Furthermore, even though normative ages may be used to define specific stages of maturation, including adolescence and menopause, there is no such thing as a normative age at which a person "turns old." The historical reason for the use of 65 years as a cutoff is based on a story about German chancellor Otto von Bismarck, who lived from 1815 to 1898. Bismarck noted that his major political rivals were federal employees older than the age of 65. He succeeded in pushing through legislation that required retirement at age 65, and then "ascended to power with ease" when he was 56 years old (Hayflick, 1996, p. 108). Ironically, he held his position as chancellor until age 75.

The 65-plus criterion has long been the standard in most American (He, Sengupta, Velkoff, & DeBarros, 2005; Howden & Meyer, 2011) and European aging research, and is also used in studies of global aging (Haub & Kent, 2008; Kinsella & Phillips, 2005). However, this particular chronological milestone may not serve equally well for research conducted in developing countries, because, as discussed in the next section, a relatively smaller proportion of people in less developed countries survive past age 65 years.[1] Nevertheless, with a few exceptions (Lutz, Sanderson, & Scherbov, 2008; United Nations Programme on Aging, 2001) who prefer to use age 60-plus, the 65-plus criterion is the most commonly used index for defining the older adult category.

Chronological age is still the best marker available for making global comparisons of aging phenomena. We will start with data from the U.S. Census Bureau to describe the increase in the older portion of the population over the past century; we will then examine the same phenomenon across the globe. As **Figure 19-2** makes clear, the number of older people in the United States increased greatly during the past century. The population as a whole also grew substantially (from 76 million in 1900 to 281 million in the 2000 census[2]), so a simple count—even in millions—could be misleading. Perhaps the growth in the number of older people simply parallels the overall growth of the country as a whole. However, this is not the case. A more informative perspective is provided in **Figure 19-3**, where the number of older adults in America is plotted as a percentage of the total population. It is clear from this graph that the size of the older population has grown disproportionately, increasing at a much faster rate than the entire population. In other words, while the entire population increased almost fourfold, the older adult population increased more than tenfold. This phenomenon is called population aging, defined as "the process by which older individuals come to form a proportionately larger share of the total population"; it is "one of the most distinctive demographic events in the world today" (Chakraborti, 2004, p. 33). Indeed, global population aging is accelerating (Lutz et al., 2008).

The aforementioned demographic facts have led to an increased interest in the field of gerontology. Prior to 1974, the United States did not have a national health institute dedicated to aging; today, the National Institute on Aging has a budget of more than $1 billion and sponsors a number of important research projects aimed at increasing our understanding of aging and improving the lives of older Americans. The increased interest in gerontology is apparent on a global basis as well, as evidenced by the convening of the Second World Assembly on Aging in Madrid in 2002, 20 years after the United Nations convened the First World Assembly on Aging in Vienna in 1982. The International Association of Gerontology and Geriatrics will hold its 20th World Congress in 2013 in Seoul. In **Figure 19-4**, it is clear that although the percentage of older adults worldwide increased only slightly (2%) from 1950 to 2000, it is projected to increase dramatically during the first half of the twenty-first century (Lutz et al., 2008).

MORTALITY AND MORBIDITY STATISTICS

Old age is the most unexpected of all the things that happen to a man.

Leon Trotsky, *Diary in Exile*, entry for May 8, 1935

Before we consider life expectancy and mortality rates around the world, it is crucial to understand the distinction between two widely used measures: life expectancy and maximum life span (Hayflick, 1996). Life expectancy involves taking a statistical snapshot of a population during a particular year and calculating an arithmetic mean based on those persons' age at death. Although it is most commonly calculated

1. Various terms are used to differentiate national developments. In the United Nations usage, "more developed," "developed," and "industrialized" refer to countries in Europe and North America, and to Australia, New Zealand, and Japan. All other countries are referred to as "less developed," "developing," and "nonindustrialized" (Kinsella & Phillips, 2005). The terms "less developed" and "more developed" are used in this chapter.

2. The U.S. Census Bureau reported that the U.S. population was nearly 309 million in 2010 (Howden & Meyer, 2011).

FIGURE 19-2

Number of Older Adults in the United States in the Twentieth Century (in millions)

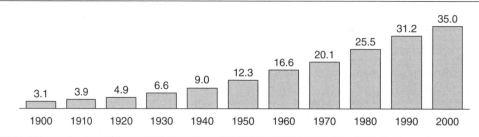

Source: He, Sengupta, Velkoff, & DeBarros, 2005.

from the time of birth, life expectancy can be calculated from any age. Maximum life span, in contrast, is simply the longest life span (or longevity) recorded. The human record is currently 122 years.

As before, we will start with data from the U.S. Census to describe how life expectancy has changed in the United States over the past century, and then we will examine the same phenomenon across the globe. **Figure 19-5** reveals the astonishing fact that the average life expectancy from birth has increased dramatically in the United States, from only 47 years in 1900 to 77 years in 2000. However, this increase in life expectancy is often misinterpreted. For example, one headline proclaimed, "New Health Statistics Show Americans Living Longer" ("New Health Statistics," 2011). Journalists such as *New York Times* columnist William Safire also make this mistake, saying, "When you look back over the last 50 or 75 years . . . you see these enormous advances in science where you are actually extending the life of a human being from 47 in 1900 to 77 today" (Morgan, 2006, p. 24). Although far less sensational, a more accurate headline stated: "U.S. Life Expectancy Up to 77.6" (2005). In other words, individuals are not setting new longevity records, but more people are surviving into the stage of old age, defined as older than 65 years.

Unlike life expectancy, the most compelling fact about the maximum life span is that it has not changed. That is, since these data have been recorded over the last few thousand years of human history, there have always been a few people who live to be older than 100 years, close to the maximum of approximately 120 years of age. One prominent biologist went so far as to say that "there is no evidence that the

FIGURE 19-3

Older Adults as a Percentage of Total US Population in the Twentieth Century

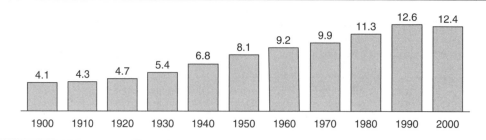

Source: He et al., 2005.

FIGURE 19-4

Older Adults (60+) as a Percentage of Total World Population

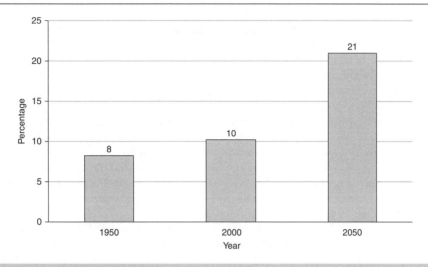

Source: Adapted from United Nations, 2002.

FIGURE 19-5

Changes in Mean Life Expectancy, United States, 1900–2000.

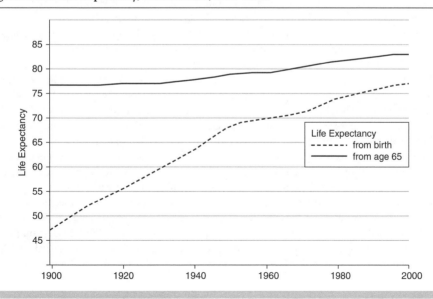

Note the dramatic change in life expectancy from birth, contrasted with much less change in remaining life expectancy for those who reached age 65.

Source: He et al., 2005; Hayflick, 1996.

maximum human life span has changed from what it was about a hundred thousand years ago" (Hayflick, 1996, p. 66). According to more recent history, the prophet Moses lived to exactly 120 years old, dying on his birthday in 1273 B.C.E. More than 1600 years ago (according to Athanasius, patriarch of Alexandria), Saint Anthony died in 356 C.E. at the age of 105 (Perls & Silver, 1999). In 1899, Mr. Geert Boomgaard of the Netherlands died at the age of 110. In England, Ann Pouder died in 1917 at the age of 110, and in the United States, Louisa Thiers lived to be 111 years old, passing away in 1926.[3] In 1906, the biologist Metchnikoff (1912) interviewed a certain Mme. Robineau who was age 106, and included her photograph in his book. Most recently, Jeanne Calment (**Figure 19-6**) died in 1997 at the age of 122 (Allard, Lèbre, & Robine, 1998). Although her life span may set a new record, a 2-year increase over the past 3279 years of recorded human history is not nearly as impressive as the changes seen in average life expectancy.

In addition, if life expectancy is calculated from ages beyond birth, very little change has occurred. As far back as 1693, Edmund Halley (famous for the comet bearing his name) reported that although life expectancy was only 33 years as calculated from birth (in the city of Breslau); those persons who made it to 80 years old, however, could expect to live an average of 6 more years (Hayflick, 1996). In the United States, life expectancy at age 65 increased only 6 years from 1900 to 2000 (from 11.9 to 17.9 years beyond 65, for a total of 76.9 to 82.9 years; see the top line in Figure 19-5). In the same time period, life expectancy increased only 1.7 years for those persons who reached age 85.

Yet another way to understand the changes in life expectancy is to plot the percentage of people surviving to a given age, according to calendar years. For example, in the United States in 1900, only 88% of newborn babies reached their first birthday; by 2000, that percentage was up to 99% (He et al., 2005). These changes are plotted on the left side of **Figure 19-7**. As more people survive into older age ranges, the survival curve starts to approximate the shape of a rectangle. If all of us survived to the maximum life span, the survival curve would become "rectangularized." As seen in Figure 19-7, the U.S. population is moving in that direction. The same phenomenon is happening globally, albeit at a much lower rate and slower pace.

Another type of rectangularization can be seen in the *population pyramids* in **Figure 19-8**. In 1900, these data did have a pyramidal shape, but by the year 2000, this demographic structure had grown fatter in the middle, so that it had what is called a midriff bulge, and now the upper tip is also widening. (This trend continued in 2010; the pyramid metaphor may have to be dropped in the future.)

It is estimated that there were more than 469 million people worldwide older than the age of 65 in 2008 (Haub & Kent, 2008), which represents 7% of the world's population. Paradoxically, because developed countries tend to have more elderly residents than developing countries, 59% of these older adults live in developing countries (He et al., 2005). These figures reveal a lopsided proportion of older adults in Africa, Asia, Central America, the Caribbean, and Oceania. As for the shape of the worldwide population structure, developing countries are still much more pyramidal, but in due course, the statistical prediction is that their population pyramids will also become rectangularized. This phenomenon is shown graphically in **Figure 19-9**, which compares more developed countries with less developed countries, with data from 1950 and 1990, and projections for 2030. The percentages of people 65 years of age and older are shown for different regions of the world in **Figure 19-10**. Sub-Saharan Africa is expected to experience the smallest increase over the next 30 years, due in large part to the HIV/AIDS epidemic. Of the 18.8 million people who died of AIDS by 2001, 79% resided in Africa (Kinsella & Phillips, 2005). Countries with the highest percentages of older adults are plotted in **Figure 19-11**. (The U.S. elderly population grew to 13% of the total population in 2010 [Howden & Meyer, 2011].) Based on 2001 and 2004 census data, the

---

3. The Gerontological Research Group, which includes Dr. Thomas Perls, director of the New England Centenarian Study (Perls, 2004), maintains a carefully validated list of supercentenarians, defined as anyone who has lived to be 110 years old or older. Boomgaard, Pouder, and Thiers top this list, which includes supercentenarians born in 29 different countries.

FIGURE 19-6

Madame Jeanne Calment (Arles, France), Photographed in 1995 at the Age of 120

She died in 1997 at the age of 122.

Source: Courtesy of the Gerontology Research Group, www.grg.org, 2006.

FIGURE 19-7

Percent of People Surviving to Certain Ages for Selected Years in the United States

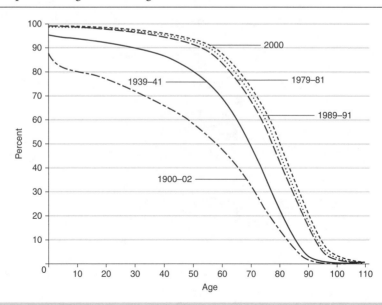

Source: He et al., 2005.

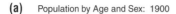

FIGURE 19-8

Population Pyramids Demonstrating the Changes in Structure of Age Groups in the United States

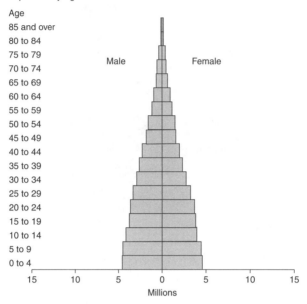

(a) Population by Age and Sex: 1900

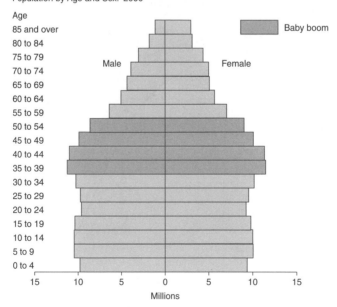

(b) Population by Age and Sex: 2000

Source: He et al., 2005.

populations with the longest life expectancies are Japanese females at 86 years and Swedish males at 78 years (He et al., 2005). The populations with the shortest life expectancies, only 33 years, are females in Botswana and males in Swaziland (Haub, 2006).

Disability-Adjusted Life Expectancy

Beyond basic life expectancy, the World Health Organization (WHO) uses a concept known as the disability-adjusted life expectancy (DALE), meaning the expected number of years to be lived in full health (Chakraborti, 2004). Japan has the highest DALE of 74.5 years, while the country of Sierra Leone has the lowest DALE of less than 26 years.

The Oldest-Old, Centenarians, and Supercentenarians

Among those persons older than 65 years, further distinctions are now recognized: young-old, oldest-old (more than 85 years old), and centenarians (100 years and older) (He et al., 2005). Centenarians account

FIGURE 19-9

Population Pyramids Comparing Less Versus More Developed Countries (Data from 1950 and 1990 with Projections for 2030)

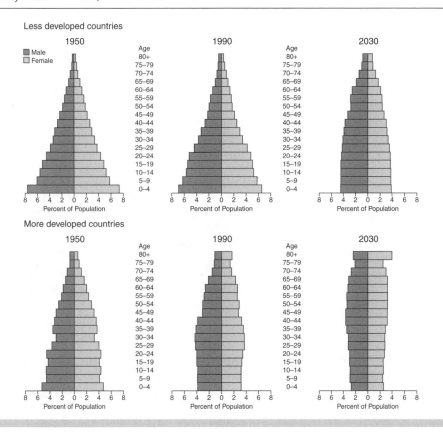

Source: Kinsella & Phillips, 2005.

FIGURE 19-10

Percent of the Population Aged 65 and Older in Various Regions (2000, Projected for the Year 2030)

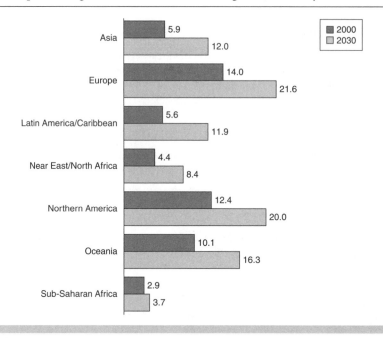

Source: He et al., 2005.

for the fastest-growing segment of the oldest-old. Surprisingly—given the age-related functional decline of people in their sixth, seventh, eighth, and ninth decades of life—approximately 25% of centenarians are in very good health (Perls, 2004). There are two centenarian research centers located in the United States, one in Massachusetts and the other in Georgia. The New England Centenarian Project is directed by Dr. Thomas Perls, and the Georgia Centenarian Study is directed by Dr. Leonard Poon. Although little information is available on the prevalence of centenarians around the world, Vaupel and Jeune (1995) estimated that in 1990 there were approximately 8800 people age 100 and older in Japan and the Western European countries combined.

Supercentenarians (age 110 and older) are a much smaller and even more elite group. According to the Gerontological Research Group, there are 82 validated supercentenarians alive in the world today (as of September 2011), only 4 of whom are men. This gender gap is discussed in the next section.

Gender Differences

Although males outnumber females at birth, by midlife this gender ratio is reversed. The relative proportion of females to males becomes even more exaggerated as age increases. This dramatic life span change is depicted graphically in **Figure 19-12**. The gender differential in life expectancy shown in Figure 19-12 is especially noticeable in more developed countries, where the average gender gap is about 7 years. Gender differences are typically smaller in less developed countries, and are even reversed in some south Asian and

FIGURE 19-11

Countries With the Greatest Percent of Older Population

Percentage age 65 or older

Italy	19.1
Japan	19.0
Greece	18.6
Germany	18.3
Spain	17.6
Sweden	17.3
Belgium	17.3
Bulgaria	17.1
Portugal	16.9
Estonia	16.5
France	16.4
Croatia	16.4
Austria	16.0
Latvia	15.8
United Kingdom	15.7
Finland	15.7
Georgia	15.5
Ukraine	15.4
Switzerland	15.3
Slovenia	15.1
United States	12.4

Note: United States ranks 38th.

Source: Kinsella & Phillips, 2005.

Middle Eastern countries. In some of these cultures, women have a lower social status, which, combined with a preference for male children, has a negative impact on female life expectancy. A sample of gender ratios in 20 countries is presented in **Table 19-1**. Some researchers have labeled this phenomenon as the "feminization of the elderly" (Chakraborti, 2004, p. 58). As mentioned earlier, the percentage of females increases with age, but gender ratios are less favorable for women living in developing countries. For example, among those persons 80 and older, women account for 71% of this group in Europe versus 59% in Africa.

RESEARCH AND TECHNOLOGY

In speaking of modern gerontology research, "it is more beneficial to opt for a healthy and vigorous, albeit finite, life than to search in vain for the elixir of immortality" (Arking, 2006, p. 5). As some gerontologists have suggested, we need to focus more on adding life to years, and less on adding years to life (Maddox, 1994). In both theory and practice, most current gerontological research and policy are committed to the goal of "successful aging" (Fernández-Ballesteros et al., 2010; Rowe & Kahn, 1998). Biologists have emphasized that "gerontology is committed not to a search for immortality but to the elimination of premature disability and death" (Arking, 2006, p. 5). Nowhere is this more true than in the arena of global aging, because life spans for the majority of people, at least in developing nations, fall far short of what can and should be expected.

FIGURE 19-12

Different Numbers of Males and Females as a Function of Age

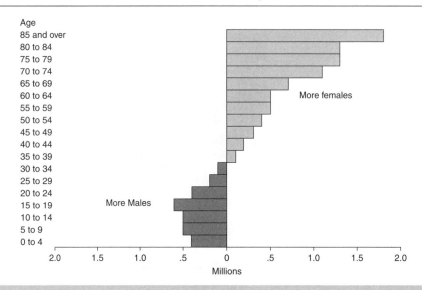

Source: He et al., 2005.

TABLE 19-1

Gender Ratios Among People Aged 65 and Older

More Developed Countries		Less Developed Countries	
Australia	79	Bangladesh	117
Bulgaria	72	Brazil	70
France	69	Ethiopia	84
Germany	68	Fiji	85
Italy	71	Ghana	89
Poland	62	Honduras	90
Russia	46	India	103
Ukraine	51	Iran	98
United Kingdom	74	Mexico	84
United States	71	Zambia	79

Note: Ratios are number of men per 100 women.

Source: Kinsella & Phillips, 2005.

The advances in communication and computer technologies "offer a promising future for older adults" (Mundorf, Mundorf, & Brownell, 2006, p. 242). More and more older adults are logging on to the Internet to use such sites as www.SeniorNet.org, which celebrated its 25th anniversary in 2011, and to use the worldwide web for e-mail, purchases, and medical information. U.S. Census Bureau data in 2005 revealed that 35% of older adults had a home computer, and 29% had Internet access (Greenberg, 2005). In 2009, home computer use was reported by 45% of older adults and use of the Internet by 41% (Greenberg, 2010; Keenan, 2009). New technologies are also playing a key role in new employment opportunities for older workers, at least in the United States (Riggs, 2004). Although no data are available, it is likely this trend is occurring in other developed countries (e.g., Japan and Europe) as well.

A significant portion of the research effort is to develop strategies and technology to help older adults age in place (Rogers & Fisk, 2006). Some of these initiatives involve providing good old-fashioned low-tech social support: "Birthday cards are one option being explored to keep health providers in contact with older clients" at the University of Auckland in New Zealand ("Helping Elderly Stay at Home," 2006). Other countries, such as Korea, have more ambitious plans involving robot maids for their elderly (Tae-gyu, 2006).

Work by Dr. Wendy Rogers and her colleagues (an interdisciplinary team of psychologists, engineers, and computer programmers at the Georgia Institute of Technology) has resulted in the creation of an "aware home," in which communication and control systems (involving cameras, sensors, and computers) maximize the independence of older adults living alone by monitoring many of their daily activities, ranging from providing recipe reminders during cooking to assisting in more complex tasks such as measuring insulin accurately (Rogers & Fisk, 2006; see awarehome.imtc.gatech.edu). The advantage of such a house is that the older person can function without requiring around-the-clock help from a nurse or other live-in assistant. Of course, expense is a serious obstacle, making this concept entirely impractical in developing countries at this time.

Another related innovation is telemedicine (see americantelemed.org), illustrated in the following vignette:

> Ruth, a functionally independent older adult, awakes and sits down at her computer. She helps manage her husband's chronic illness. Today, he has an appointment with a specialist. At 09:00, they have a live conversation with the specialist by videoconference, and the physician recommends a change in her husband's medications. After the appointment, Ruth checks her e-mail and receives a message from her online caregiver support group to schedule a chat later that afternoon. Ruth quickly responds that she is available and switches off the computer to begin her day. (Stronge, Rogers, & Fisk, 2007, p. 1)

The preceding scenario demonstrates how telemedicine can improve older adults' day-to-day lives. As Stronge et al. point out in their review, telemedicine systems have benefited older adults "by increasing peer support interactions, providing health-care access to older adults in rural communities, reducing the cost of health care, increasing exercise, reducing pain and depression, and, perhaps most important, improving functional independence" (Stronge et al., 2007, p. 1). Furthermore, family medicine physicians are also rediscovering the advantages of home care, "in light of the aging population, advances in portable medical technology, and changes in Medicare reimbursement" (Landers, 2006, p. 366). Recent studies have underscored the crucial need for the successful adoption of technology for the functional independence of older adults (Czaja et al., 2006). Again, the implementation of the previously mentioned technologies in developing countries will be dependent on significant increases in per capita income.

LEGAL AND ETHICAL ISSUES

Ethics of Aging Research

In the United States, the institutional review board (IRB) of any research institution considers all research on older adults to involve a vulnerable group, comparable to doing research with children or pregnant women. The IRB has to review all research done with older adults, such as basic cognitive aging research involving memory differences between young and older adults (Mitchell & Bruss, 2003). However, in practice, IRBs routinely grant permission to use the same consent forms used for younger adults with healthy older adults. When research participants have some degree of cognitive impairment, such as Alzheimer's disease (Mitchell & Schmitt, 2006), the participant's ability to understand and sign an informed consent form can be a significant issue (High & Doole, 1995). If the research participant is too cognitively impaired, the IRB will usually require a consent form signed by the participant's spouse (or other legal guardian or caregiver), as well as an assent provided verbally by the participant (Fazio & Mitchell, 2009).

IRBs were created through legislature in 1974 in the United States via the National Research Act, which established a National Commission for the Protection of Human Subjects of Biomedical and Behavioral Research. This act was based on the Declaration of Helsinki, made at the 18th World Medical Assembly in Helsinki, Finland in 1964, which was in turn based on the Nuremberg Code. The latter was an outcome of the Nuremberg war crimes trials in 1947, in which 23 Nazi German physicians were found guilty of "performing medical experiments upon concentration camp inmates and other living human subjects, without their consent, in the course of which the defendants committed murders, brutalities, cruelties, tortures, atrocities, and other inhuman acts." The court prescribed guidelines for permissible medical experiments, including voluntary consent, benefits outweighing risks, and the ability of subjects to terminate participation. The 1996 revision of the Helsinki declaration from the 48th General Assembly states: "Concern for the interests of the subject must always prevail over the interests of science and society."

WHO has established an international Research Ethics Review Committee and states that "all research involving human participants must be conducted in an ethical manner that respects the dignity, safety and rights of research participants" (WHO, 2006). Most of the current ethical concerns revolve around vaccines, cloning, and HIV. Although WHO singles out children, adolescents, and women as vulnerable populations, it has said little about research ethics specific to older adults. At the UN-sponsored World Conference on Human Rights in Vienna in 1993, it was determined that "neither ageing as a process, nor older persons as a group, are specifically mentioned in the text of the Convention" (Loza, 2001, p. 72). Clearly, different cultural and political systems and values affect the ethics of research procedures (and related legislation) followed in specific countries. At the same time, there is a growing interest in the establishment of universal standards for the concept of international elder law (Doron, 2005).

In "smart house" environments, "Big Brother" issues are raised, because the elderly person is being monitored 24 hours a day, 7 days a week. Rogers and Fisk (2006) asked their aware-home participants how they felt about the compromise of their privacy by the technology in their home. Among the nearly 3000 replies, they received the following comments (p. 29):

■ "If this [monitoring system] would keep me independent longer, I wouldn't mind as much."
■ "If it's only my daughter who monitors me, it's alright."
■ "If you really need it, privacy becomes secondary."

(As an aside, note that residents in nursing homes and even assisted-living arrangements already sacrifice a great deal of privacy.)

Euthanasia

Everybody has got to die, but I have always believed an exception would be made in my case. Now what?

William Saroyan, final statement
published after his death at age 72

Euthanasia is not specifically an aging issue, but is often addressed in a death and dying unit at the end of gerontology courses and textbooks. Assisted suicide is still illegal in most of the United States. Since the first edition of this book was published, two states—Washington and Montana—joined Oregon as exceptions. In 2009, Washington reported 36 such suicides. Assisted suicide has also been legalized in some countries. In the Netherlands, in 1995 alone, 3600 patients died via assisted suicide or euthanasia (Stern, 1998). In the field of "bioethics," this trend is viewed by many as a slippery slope (Foley & Hendin, 2002). The most visible proponent and conductor of assisted suicide, Dr. Jack Kevorkian, served a prison sentence from 1999 to 2007 for second-degree murder in the poisoning of a 52-year-old man in Michigan; he claimed to have assisted in the suicides of at least 130 other individuals. (Kevorkian died of thrombosis in 2011 at age 83.) Obviously, different countries and cultures have vastly differing views on euthanasia, but that is beyond the scope of this chapter.

INFLUENCES OF POLITICS, ECONOMICS, CULTURE, AND RELIGION

Ageism

Among the myriad topics covered in this book, one issue unique to the field of aging is *ageism*. Ageism is defined as "a process of systematic stereotyping and discrimination against people because they are old, just as racism and sexism accomplish this for skin color and gender" (Butler, 2006, p. 41). An entire *Encyclopedia of Ageism* (Palmore, Branch, & Harris, 2005) exists, with coverage of topics ranging from abuse to voice quality. For the purposes of this chapter, we consider whether ageism varies as a function of culture. Other than the United States, the encyclopedia entries include only Japan. However, at least one study found ageism to be prevalent among British physicians (Young, 2006). Given that the awareness of this issue and the phenomenon of ageism is relatively new in progressive countries (Butler, 1969; Palmore, 1990), it is likely to be widespread around the globe.

Elder Abuse

Elder abuse is an extreme version of ageism, involving both attitude and behavior. In the late 1970s, the issue of elder abuse and neglect began to receive more attention in the United States (Lantz, 2006). In 1999, the U.S. Administration on Aging published a report, the National Elder Abuse Incidence Study, which "identified more than 550,000 elderly persons who experienced abuse or neglect in community or institutional settings." Such abuse is thought to be "an extremely underreported crime" (Lantz, 2006, pp. 352–353). Recently, elder abuse in other cultures has also begun to receive more attention, both from researchers and from government policy makers. For example, Chakraborti (2004) reported that widows, in particular, constitute a disproportionately large number of the elderly in Asia, because women in those cultures tend to marry men who are 10 to 15 years older than themselves. As a result, they "have to endure longer periods of widowhood. Their conditions are worsened by the fact that they are unable to fend for themselves." Even worse, "abandonment of elderly widows, even from educated families, is on the rise" (Chakraborti, 2004, pp. 26–27).

Culture

The experiences of older adults vary widely around the world, not only because of individual differences in biological and psychological aging, but also because the "frameworks of social beliefs and values" (Wilson, 2000, p. 17) vary dramatically across different cultures.

Research in many non-Western cultures is lacking. For example, regarding Asia:

> Although aging research has been well developed and well documented in Europe and other developed countries, including Japan, it has yet to take shape in most other parts of Asia. To a great extent the lack of interest in aging research in Asia owes its origin to the belief that the family support system is and will continue to be foolproof insurance against all the problems faced during old age. (Chakraborti, 2004, pp. 25–26)

Family Support for the Elderly

A long-standing American myth is that *The Waltons* (a 1970s television show in which an extended family including parents, children, and grandparents live under one roof) was once the norm, and that now older adults are relegated to a lonely incarceration in nursing homes. Although only approximately 5% of those aged 65 or older are residents of any long-term institution (Palmore, 1998), frequent feelings of loneliness are reported in roughly 10% of older adults—especially those who live alone (Hughes, 2006).

Outside of America, "the family is an effective provider of old-age support in India and most other Asian countries." (Chakraborti, 2004, p. 26). In contrast to most countries in the Western world—where many programs have been developed specifically to support needs of older adults—"many Asian countries have barely begun to think about their elderly; and given the pace of population aging in Asia and the corresponding lack of adjustment mechanisms, a 'time bomb' or 'age quake' may not be very far" (Chakraborti, 2004, p. 27). Chakraborti goes on to say that glaciers might provide a more appropriate metaphor for rapid aging, "since a glacier moves at a slow pace but with enormous effects wherever it goes and with a long-term momentum that is unstoppable" (p. 29).

Developed countries, mostly in Europe and North America, have established institutions for dealing with older adults' health needs, in contrast to Asian countries, where family-based support of the elderly is the norm. Between these two extreme scenarios, Australia provides an interesting comparison, having the distinction of "a European tradition and an Asian future" (Kendig & Quine, 2006, p. 431). Ninety percent of the Australian population is concentrated in coastal urban areas. (For an interesting analysis of growing old in cities, specifically New York, London, Paris, and Tokyo, see Rodwin & Gusmano, 2006.) Australia's population aging profile is similar to that of the United States, in which older adults are projected to constitute 18% of the total population by 2021. Also similar to the United States, more than 90% of older adults live in private households, with the remainder living in nursing homes or boarding houses in 1998 (Kendig & Quine, 2006). Among older adults with disabilities, 77% have "some informal support from family or friends," and 53% receive some "formal support" in the form of community or private services (Kendig & Quine, 2006, p. 433). Although Australia—unlike most Asian countries—has formal community services available, "children have strong values of family obligation for frail older parents who wish to remain independent" (Kendig & Quine, 2006, p. 434). Thus Australia continues to provide a fascinating microcosm of the phenomenon of world population aging in the twenty-first century.

Respect and Status

Modernization theory—"a paradigm . . . to explain the diffusion of Western styles of individual, economic, and cultural development" (Achenbaum, 2006, p. 792)—has been applied to population aging. This theory predicts that "the status of elders . . . decline[s] with the degree of modernization" (Luborsky & McMullen, 1999, p. 83). Cowgill and Holmes (1972) found support for their modernization hypothesis by looking across 15 societies varying from preliterate to peasant to industrial. However, the relationship between cultural changes and the position of elderly is quite complex, as revealed by a summary of 10 key propositions listed in **Table 19-2**.

In the Jewish religion, there is great respect for older adults, regardless of the culture where the Jews are living. Instead of 65 years old, the operational definition of elder (*zaken* in Hebrew, which also means "wise") is age 70 and older. For example, Jewish law specifies that one should stand up when any person 70 years of age and older enters a room. In practice, children in religiously observant homes (i.e., Orthodox Jewish) stand up when either their parents or any other older person enters a room. In Israel, children and teenagers have been observed to leap to their feet to offer their seat on the bus to an older adult. This kind of respect is also true of many other religions and cultures, but even when this tenet is observed, does it translate into a lack of prejudice and discrimination in milieus such as the workplace, or treatment of patients? Unfortunately, respect for elders is not a characteristic of all cultures. For example, in India, it is not uncommon for older widows to be abandoned by their families (Chakraborti, 2004).

Cognitive Neuroscience and Aging

Cognitive neuroscience issues in aging and culture have begun to receive some attention (Park & Gutchess, 2006). Although the basic neurological and psychological mechanisms of perception, memory, and cognition—which by and large are affected negatively by normal aging—would not be expected to vary across cultures, some unusual phenomena (e.g., picture naming as a measure of semantic memory [Mitchell, 1989]) are being explored across different languages and cultures (Yoon, Feinberg, & Gutchess,

TABLE 19-2

Proposed Relationships Between Modernization and Aging

1. The concept of old age itself appears to be relative to the degree of modernization.

2. Longevity is directly and significantly related to the degree of modernization.

3. Modernized societies have a relatively high proportion of older people in their populations.

4. The aged are the recipients of greater respect in societies where they constitute a low proportion of the total population.

5. Societies that are in the process of modernizing tend to favor the young, while the aged are at an advantage in more stable, sedentary societies.

6. Respect for the aged tends to be greater in societies in which the extended family is prevalent, particularly if it functions as if they are part of the household unit. (The implication here is that modernization breaks down the extended family.)

7. In nonindustrial (developing) societies, the family is the basic social group providing economic security for dependent aged; in industrial societies, the responsibility tends to be partly or totally that of the state.

8. The proportion of aged who retain leadership roles in modern societies is lower than in industrial (developed) ones.

9. Religious leadership is more likely to be a continuing role of the aged in preindustrial societies than in modern societies.

10. Retirement is a modern invention found only in modernized, high-productivity societies.

Sources: Holmes & Holmes, 1995; Luborsky & McMullen, 1999.

2006). Indeed, one study found a positive correlation between attitude toward aging and explicit memory performance; older Chinese persons had both a more positive attitude and higher memory scores compared to a group of older Americans (Levy & Langer, 1994). Even something as fundamental as hearing loss (a ubiquitous aging phenomenon) has been found to be correlated with negative attitudes about hearing held by older adults ages 70 to 96 themselves (Levy, Slade, & Gill, 2006).

Aging Phenomena in South America

In South American countries, more attention is being focused on the lives of older women (Loza, 2001), who suffer from poverty and have disproportionate illiteracy rates. In Brazil, researchers have documented dramatic differences in aging cultures as a function of socioeconomic status, meaning those who are marginalized versus the well-to-do "self-sufficient" (Leibing & Py, 2005). Leibing (2005) examined historical changes in Brazilian culture and attitudes spanning from 1967 to 2002. Her investigation revealed a shift from an emphasis on old age to a "third age" label. Leibing describes third age as a phase between adulthood and old age, in which successful aging involves the "empowerment of elderly persons by fighting against aging stereotypes and for better living conditions" (Leibing, 2005, p. 18). This phenomenon was epitomized by Fernanda Montenegro, considered by many to be Brazil's most talented actress, who was nominated for an Academy Award at age 70. Although Montenegro called herself "the old lady from Ipanema" (Tom Jobim & Vinicius de Morae's song, "Garota de Ipanema") and did not try to conceal the visible effects of aging ("prominent wrinkles"), Leibing's analysis still portrays a class of people who use fame and financial power to transcend a more traditional life course (i.e., avoiding superficial signs of aging). Although positive aging stereotypes are welcome, in Brazil, it is only the rich and the famous who can afford to continue fighting and spending in the "struggle against becoming old" (Leibing, 2005, p. 22). In a country with significant poverty, the beautiful old lady is the exception, not the rule.

Religious Lifestyle in Israel

Bnei Brak, Israel's most religious city (Rosenblum, 2001), was found to have the highest global life expectancy in 2001: 81.1 years for women and 77.4 years for men (slightly higher records were held in 2006 by Japan and Iceland). What is most interesting about this small city's longevity record is that life is long in spite of other demographics: Bnei Brak is also Israel's poorest city, confounding the normal correlation between poverty and poor health (Rosenblum, 2001). In addition, the Orthodox Jewish residents are known neither for engaging in exercise nor for maintaining a low-fat diet. The most likely formula for long life in this community appears to be a highly engaged level of religious enthusiasm. Although the conclusions are not unequivocal, a majority of studies investigating the relationship between religious practice and health have found a positive correlation (Schaie, Krause, & Booth, 2004).

In Israel, a very exhaustive study ($N = 3900$ over a 16-year period) compared 11 religious versus 11 secular *kibbutzim* (best translated as egalitarian collectives). It was found that the mortality rate in the religious groups (3.9%) was less than of that in the secular groups (9.1%) (Kark et al., 1996). The authors ruled out potential confounds due to a variety of sociodemographic variables, including education, ethnic origin, and social support. The only explanation remaining was an "embracing protective effect of religious observance" (p. 346).

It will be interesting to see future studies of this relationship in other cultures around the world. To date, very few international or cross-national studies have been published (Schaie et al., 2004). In one notable exception (Musick, Traphagan, Koenig, & Larson, 2000), researchers compared religious and spiritual practices in the United States with those in Japan, and found a very different perspective on the relationship between spirituality and health. Older religious Japanese "employ religious activity in an attempt to avoid a decline into poor health as they grow older," including visits to *pokkuridera* (sudden death temples), "at which they pray for a sudden, peaceful, death devoid of excessive suffering" (p. 84).

CONCLUSION

La vejez no es una enfermedad, es una etapa de nuestra vida.

Betsie Hollants (cited in Loza, 2001)

Old age is not a disease and cannot be cured.

Élie Metchnikoff, biologist

Although Metchnikoff (1912) published his insights nearly a century ago, only a few biologists and even fewer gerontologists have grasped this message (Hayflick, 2006). According to Hayflick (2007), the best strategy at our disposal for slowing the rate of aging is to promote good health. Or, as many gerontologists have said—in light of some of the medical advances that can keep a person alive longer via artificial means—our goal should not be to add years to life, but rather, to add "life to years" (i.e., to improve people's health and decrease the proportion of old age spent in morbidity). James Fries (2006) has called for health policy promoting the compression of morbidity by shortening the period "between an increasing average age of the onset of disability and the age of death" (p. 257). This is certainly a worthwhile goal to pursue globally, particularly in developing countries.

STUDY QUESTIONS

1. Describe and give examples of ageism worldwide. How does ageism affect the life of older adults?
2. Describe the unique characteristics of the oldest-old.
3. Compare and contrast the influences of religion, politics, and culture on the aging adult worldwide.
4. Give examples of legal and ethical issues related to the older adult.

CASE STUDY: AGEISM

Dr. Robert Butler, a physician who founded the National Institute on Aging in the United States, related the following incident involving a centenarian friend. His 100-year-old friend had a pain in his left knee, so he went to see his internist about it. After examining the patient, the doctor concluded that it was just "old age." Dr. Butler's friend retorted, "But doc, my right knee is also 100 years old, and it doesn't hurt!" In this case, the physician's lack of knowledge (or at least inadequate diagnosis) resulted in a fairly benign outcome, although the patient's left knee did not receive treatment. However, it is difficult to imagine a 25-year-old being told that an ailment was the result of "youth."

Dr. Kevin Hendler specializes in geriatric dentistry at Emory Healthcare in Atlanta, Georgia, and related the following incident (Hendler, 2005). A 97-year-old woman presented with the need for some dental work. The patient and her family were not very enthusiastic about dental work, assuming that the older lady did not have much longer to live anyway, given her age. Dr. Hendler convinced her to go ahead with the dental work, and the lady went on to live to the age of 108. Imagine how different the last 11 years of her life would have been without the ability to chew food. If this dentist had succumbed to ageism, his patient would have lost many years of normal eating. At the other end of the life span, no one would suggest depriving a growing child of 11 years of normal life. As Dr. Hendler emphasizes, "Treatment decisions by patients or family members should

(continues)

CASE STUDY: AGEISM *(Continued)*

not be based solely on the number that represents age, but rather on health and quality of life" (personal communication, September 22, 2006). Older patients who decided not to have recommended dental work have subsequently told him that had they known they would live so long, they would have done things differently. Sometimes patients tell Dr. Hendler, "I don't know how much longer I have," and he replies, "That's right, you don't know, so you should be comfortable because it may be a while" (personal communication, September 22, 2006). Sometimes patients in their 70s will say they do not want better treatment because they will not need it for very long; Dr. Hendler's reply is, "How do you know?"

This case is only one concrete example of how attitudes toward the elderly can make such an enormous difference. Unfortunately, a number of studies (380 citations in a 2011 MEDLINE search) reveal that ageism is alive and well among health professionals. Dr. John Young (2006), head of the Academic Unit of Elderly Care and Rehabilitation at St. Luke's Hospital in England, writes that institutionalized ageism in his country is endemic, based on a number of recent medical studies. For example, a recent population-based study found that patients older than the age of 80 years with minor stroke and transient ischemic attacks were under-referred and undertreated (Fairhead & Rothwell, 2006). Nevertheless, Dr. Young expresses hope for the future, as the "UK government has recently been embarrassed into action" (Young, 2006, p. 509). Mortality rates from heart disease and cancer declined in the United Kingdom after a policy initiative called the National Service Framework for Older People was established. Perhaps other governments around the world will follow suit in the twenty-first century.

CASE STUDY: CENTENARIANS

Following are some vignettes of vibrant centenarians, taken from data gathered by volunteers at the Georgia Centenarian Study (University of Georgia, 2006):

- At 104, Mary Sims Elliott was working on her autobiography, writing poetry, and trying to influence her church's position on social issues. Now she is 105 and her autobiography, titled *My First One Hundred Years,* was just published.
- At 105, Geneva McDaniel taught aerobics daily at her senior citizens center. Now she is 107 and recruiting residents of her retirement community to exercise with her.
- At 106, former sharecropper Jessie Champion and his 86-year-old wife, Fronnie, were weeding and harvesting their garden. Recently, Fronnie passed away and Jessie, now 107, lives and gardens with his daughter.

The researchers at the Georgia Centenarian Study generally agree that the secret of longevity is still a mystery. First, according to Director Leonard Poon, no two centenarians are the same: "For as many optimistic people, we find as many who are grumpy" (University of Georgia, 2006). Furthermore, "centenarians are far more different than they are alike," according to Dr. Peter Martin, who codirects the centenarian study (University of Georgia, 2006). "There are many paths to longevity, and each situation is very different." As for a family history of longevity, Dr. Poon says: "People aren't likely to live long just because their

CASE STUDY: CENTENARIANS *(Continued)*

parents did. It seems the genetic contribution is important for some centenarians who come from a long line of long-lived people. But we have as many people who do not come from long-lived families" (University of Georgia, 2006). In contrast, other researchers have found a select group of centenarians living in Nova Scotia (Duenwald, 2003). This province has approximately 21 centenarians per 100,000 people, compared to a rate of 18 per 100,000 people in the United States and only 3 per 100,000 people worldwide. In Nova Scotia, it appears that longevity does run in families.

ACKNOWLEDGMENTS

Support for the preparation and writing of this chapter was provided by grants from the WellStar College of Health and Human Services and from the Foley Family Foundation. Thanks to Deborah Garfin for her unswerving logistical support and to Sandi Nelson for her invaluable bibliographic support.

REFERENCES

Achenbaum, W. A. (2006). Modernization theory. In R. Schulz (Ed.), *The encyclopedia of aging* (4th ed., Vol. II, pp. 792–794). New York: Springer.

Allard, M., Lèbre, V., & Robine, J.-M. (1998). Jeanne Calment: From Van Gogh's time to ours: 122 extraordinary years (B. Coupland, Trans.). New York: W. H. Freeman.

Arking, R. (2006). *The biology of aging: Observations and principles* (3rd ed.). New York: Oxford University Press.

Browning, R. (1942). Rabbi Ben Ezra. In P. Loving (Ed.), *The selected poems of Robert Browning* (pp. 260–266). Roslyn, NY: Walter J. Black.

Butler, R. N. (1969). Ageism: Another form of bigotry. *The Gerontologist, 9,* 243–246.

Butler, R. N. (2006). Ageism. In R. Schulz (Ed.), *The encyclopedia of aging* (4th ed., Vol. I, pp. 41–42). New York, NY: Springer.

Chakraborti, R. D. (2004). *The greying of India: Population ageing in the context of Asia.* New Delhi: Sage.

Clark, E. (1995). *Growing old is not for sissies II: Portraits of senior athletes.* Rohnert Park, CA: Pomegranate Artbooks.

Cowgill, D. O., & Holmes, L. D. (1972). *Aging and modernization.* New York, NY: Appleton-Century-Crofts.

Czaja, S. J., Charness, N., Fisk, A. D., Hertzog, C., Nair, S. N., Rogers, W. A., & Sharit, J. (2006). Factors predicting the use of technology: Findings from the Center for Research and Education on Aging and Technology Enhancement (CREATE). *Psychology and Aging, 21,* 333–352.

Doron, I. (2005). From national to international elder law. *Journal of International Aging, Law, & Policy, 1,* 43–67.

Duenwald, M. (2003, January). Puzzle of the century. *Smithsonian,* 73–80.

Fairhead, J. F., & Rothwell, P. M. (2006). Underinvestigation and treatment of carotid disease in elderly patients with transient ischaemic attack and stroke: Comparative population based study. *British Medical Journal, 333,* 525–534.

Fazio, S., & Mitchell, D. B. (2009). Persistence of self in individuals with Alzheimer's disease: Evidence from language and visual recognition. *Dementia, 8,* 39–59.

Fernández-Ballesteros, R., Garcia, L. F., Abarca, D., Blanc, E., Efklides, A., Moraitou, D., . . . Patricia, S. (2010). The concept of "ageing well" in ten Latin American and European countries. *Ageing & Society, 30*, 41–56.

Foley, K., & Hendin, H. (Eds.). (2002). *The case against assisted suicide: For the right to end-of-life care.* Baltimore, MD: Johns Hopkins University Press.

Fries, J. F. (2006). Compression of morbidity. In R. Schulz (Ed.), *The encyclopedia of aging* (4th ed., Vol. I, pp. 257–259). New York, NY: Springer.

Greenberg, S. (2005). A profile of older Americans 2005. Retrieved from http://www.aoa.gov/AoAroot /Aging_Statistics/Profile/2005/index.aspx

Greenberg, S. (2010). A profile of older Americans: 2010. Retrieved from http://www.aoa.gov/aoaroot /aging_statistics/Profile/2010/docs/2010profile.pdf

Haub, C. (2006). 2006 world population data sheet. Retrieved from http://www.prb.org

Haub, C., & Kent, M. M. (2008). *The 2008 world population data sheet.* Washington, DC: PRB.

Hayflick, L. (1996). *How and why we age.* New York, NY: Ballantine Books.

Hayflick, L. (2006). La dolce vita versus la vita sobria. *The Gerontologist, 46,* 413–416.

Hayflick, L. (2007). Biological aging is no longer an unsolved problem. *Annals of New York Academy of Science, 1100,* 1–13.

He, W., Sengupta, M., Velkoff, V. A., & DeBarros, K. A. (2005). *65+ in the United States: 2005.* Washington, DC: U.S. Census Bureau.

Helping elderly stay at home. (2006, 6 November). *Howick and Pakuranga Times* (New Zealand).

Hendler, K. (2005, June). *The relationship between oral health and general health: New research in health maintenance and promotion.* Paper presented at the Consortium on Active Retirement and Aging, Kennesaw State University, Kennesaw, GA.

High, D., & Doole, M. (1995). Ethical and legal issues in conducting research involving elderly subjects. *Behavioral Sciences and the Law, 13,* 319–335.

Holmes, E. R., & Holmes, L. (1995). *Other cultures, elder years.* Thousand Oaks, CA: Sage.

Howden, L. M., & Meyer, J. A. (2011). *Age and sex composition: 2010.* Washington, DC: U.S. Census Bureau.

Hughes, M. E. (2006). Loneliness. In R. Schulz (Ed.), *The encyclopedia of aging* (4th ed., Vol. II, pp. 674–675). New York, NY: Springer.

Kark, J. D., Shemi, G., Friedlander, Y., Martin, O., Manor, O., & Blondheim, S. H. (1996). Does religious observance promote health? Mortality in secular vs. religious kibbutzim in Israel. *American Journal of Public Health, 86,* 341–346.

Kastenbaum, R. (2006). Gerontology. In R. Schulz (Ed.), *The encyclopedia of aging* (4th ed., Vol. I, pp. 460–461). New York, NY: Springer.

Keenan, T. A. (2009). Internet use among midlife and older adults. Retrieved from http://assets.aarp.org /rgcenter/general/bulletin_internet_09.pdf

Kendig, H., & Quine, S. (2006). Community services for older people in Australia. In H. Yoon & J. Hendricks (Eds.), *Handbook of Asian aging* (pp. 431–451). Amityville, NY: Baywood.

Kinsella, K., & Phillips, D. R. (2005). Global aging: The challenge of success. *Population Bulletin, 60*(1), 3–42.

Landers, S. H. (2006). Home care: A key to the future of family medicine? *Annals of Family Medicine, 4,* 366–368.

Lantz, M. S. (2006). Elder abuse and neglect. In R. Schulz (Ed.), *The encyclopedia of aging* (4th ed., Vol. I, pp. 352–355). New York, NY: Springer.

Leibing, A. (2005). The old lady from Ipanema: Changing notions of old age in Brasil. *Journal of Aging Studies, 19,* 15–31.

Leibing, A., & Py, L. (2005). The new old: Aging and gerontology in Brasil. *AGHExchange, 28*(3), 1–19.

Levy, B., & Langer, E. (1994). Aging free from negative stereotypes: Successful memory in China and among the American deaf. *Journal of Personality and Social Psychology, 66,* 989–997.

Levy, B. R., Slade, M. D., & Gill, T. M. (2006). Hearing decline predicted by elders' stereotypes. *Journal of Gerontology: Psychological Sciences, 61B,* P82–P87.

Loza, M. D. (2001). Ageing in transition: Situation of older women in Latin America region. In United Nations Programme on Aging (Ed.), *The world ageing situation: Exploring a society for all ages* (pp. 70–98). New York, NY: United Nations.

Luborsky, M. R., & McMullen, C. K. (1999). Culture and aging. In J. C. Cavanaugh & S. K. Whitbourne (Eds.), *Gerontology: An interdisciplinary perspective* (pp. 65–90). New York, NY: Oxford University Press.

Lutz, W., Sanderson, W., & Scherbov, S. (2008). The coming acceleration of global population ageing. *Nature, 451,* 716–719.

Maddox, G. L. (1994). Social and behavioural research on ageing: An agenda for the United States. *Ageing and Society, 14,* 97–107.

Metchnikoff, É. (1912). *The prolongation of life: Optimistic studies* (P. C. Mitchell, Trans.). New York: G. P. Putnam's Sons & Knickerbocker Press.

Mitchell, D. B. (1989). How many memory systems? Evidence from aging. *Journal of Experimental Psychology: Learning, Memory, and Cognition, 15,* 31–49.

Mitchell, D. B., & Bruss, P. J. (2003). Age differences in implicit memory: Conceptual, perceptual, or methodological? *Psychology and Aging, 18,* 807–822.

Mitchell, D. B., & Schmitt, F. A. (2006). Short- and long-term implicit memory in aging and Alzheimer's disease. *Aging, Neuropsychology, and Cognition, 13,* 611–635.

Morgan, R. (2006, August). The medium is still the message. *Observer, 19,* 21–24.

Mundorf, N., Mundorf, J., & Brownell, W. (2006). Communication technologies and older adults. In R. Schulz (Ed.), *The encyclopedia of aging* (4th ed., Vol. I, pp. 242–247). New York, NY: Springer.

Musick, M. A., Traphagan, J. W., Koenig, H. G., & Larson, D. B. (2000). Spirituality in physical health and aging. *Journal of Adult Development, 7,* 73–86.

Nesselroade, J. R. (2001). Individual differences. In G. L. Maddox (Ed.), *The encyclopedia of aging* (3rd ed., Vol. I, pp. 532–533). New York, NY: Springer.

New health statistics show Americans living longer. (2011, March 17). Retrieved from http://uk.reuters .com/article/2011/03/17/us-statistics-idUKTRE72G00P20110317

Palmore, E. (1990). *Ageism.* New York, NY: Springer.

Palmore, E. (1998). *The facts on aging quiz* (2nd ed.). New York, NY: Springer.

Palmore, E., Branch, L., & Harris, D. K. (Eds.). (2005). *Encyclopedia of ageism.* Binghamton, NY: Haworth Pastoral Press.

Park, D., & Gutchess, A. (2006). The cognitive neuroscience of aging and culture. *Current Directions in Psychological Science, 15,* 105–108.

Perls, T. T. (2004). The oldest old. *Scientific American Special Edition, 14*(3), 6–11.

Perls, T. T., & Silver, M. H. (1999). *Living to 100: Lessons in living to your maximum potential at any age.* New York, NY: Basic Books.

Riggs, K. E. (2004). *Granny@work: Aging and new technology on the job in America.* New York, NY: Routledge.

Rockwood, K. (2006). Geriatric medicine. In R. Schulz (Ed.), *The encyclopedia of aging* (4th ed., Vol. I, pp. 452–455). New York, NY: Springer.

Rodwin, V. G., & Gusmano, M. K. (2006). *Growing older in world cities: New York, London, Paris, and Tokyo.* Nashville, TN: Vanderbilt University Press.

Rogers, W. A., & Fisk, A. D. (2006). Aware home technology: Potential benefits for older adults. *Public Policy and Aging Report, 15,* 28–30.

Rosenblum, J. (2001, February 16). L'chaim in Bnei Brak. *Jerusalem Post.*

Rowe, J. W., & Kahn, R. L. (1998). *Successful aging.* New York, NY: Pantheon.

Schaie, K. W., Krause, N., & Booth, A. (Eds.). (2004). *Religious influences on health and well-being in the elderly.* New York, NY: Springer.

Stern, Y. (1998, March). Hospice care: Can it have a Jewish heart? *The Jewish Observer,* 21–25.

Stronge, A. J., Rogers, W. A., & Fisk, A. D. (2007). Human factors considerations in implementing tele-medicine systems to accommodate older adults. *Journal of Telemedicine and Telecare, 13,* 1–3.

Tae-gyu, K. (2006, November 6). Robot maids for elderly to make debut in 2013. *The Korea Times.*

United Nations. (2002). *World populations ageing: 1950–2050*: United Nations publication, Sales No. E.02. XIII.3.

United Nations Programme on Aging. (2001). A society for all ages: Evolution and exploration. In United Nations Programme on Aging (Ed.), *The world ageing situation: Exploring a society for all ages* (pp. 1–12). New York, NY: United Nations.

University of Georgia, Institute of Gerontology, College of Public Health. (2006). Georgia centenarian study. Retrieved from http://www.publichealth.uga.edu/geron/research/centenarian-study

U.S. life expectancy up to 77.6. (2005, March 1). *The Boston Globe,* p. 1.

Vaupel, J. W., & Jeune, B. (1995). The emergence and proliferation of centenarians. In B. Jeune & J. Vaupel (Eds.), *Exceptional longevity: From prehistory to the present.* Odense, Denmark: Odense University Press.

Wilson, G. (2000). *Understanding old age: Critical and global perspectives.* London: Sage.

World Health Organization (WHO). (2006). Research ethics review committee. Retrieved from http://www.who.int/rpc/research_ethics/en

Yoon, C., Feinberg, F., & Gutchess, A. H. (2006). Pictorial naming specificity across ages and cultures: A latent class analysis of picture norms for younger and older Americans and Chinese. *Gerontology, 52,* 295–305.

Young, J. (2006). Ageism in services for transient ischaemic attack and stroke. *British Medical Journal, 333,* 507–508.

Appendix 19-A

20 Questions About Global Aging

1. True or false? In the year 2000, children younger than the age of 15 still outnumbered elderly people (aged 65 and over) in almost all nations of the world.

2. The world's elderly population is increasing by approximately how many people each month?
   a. 50,000   b. 300,000   c. 500,000   d. 800,000

3. Which of the world's developing regions has the highest aggregate percent elderly?
   a. Africa   b. Latin America   c. The Caribbean   d. Asia (excluding Japan)

4. China has the world's largest total population (more than 1.2 billion people). Which country has the world's largest elderly (65-plus) population?
   a. Japan   b. Germany   c. China   d. Nigeria

5. True or false? More than half of the world's elderly today live in the industrialized (developed) nations of Europe, North America, and Japan.

6. Of the world's major countries, which had the highest percentage of elderly people in the year 2000?
   a. Sweden   b. Turkey   c. Italy   d. France

7. True or false? Current demographic projections suggest that 35% of all people in the United States will be at least 65 years of age by the year 2050.

8. True or false? The number of the world's "oldest old" (people aged 80 and older) is growing more rapidly than that of the elderly as a whole.

9. More than one-third of the world's oldest old live in which three countries?
   a. Germany, the United States, and the United Kingdom
   b. India, China, and the United States
   c. Japan, China, and Brazil
   d. Russia, India, and Indonesia

10. Japan has the highest life expectancy at birth among the major countries of the world. How many years can the average Japanese baby born in 2000 expect to live?
    a. 70 years   b. 75 years   c. 81 years   d. 85 years

11. True or false? Today in some countries life expectancy at birth is less than 40 years.

12. What are the leading killers of elderly women in Europe and North America?
    a. Cancers   b. Circulatory diseases   c. Respiratory diseases   d. Accidents

13. True or false? Elderly women outnumber elderly men in all developing countries.

14. There are more older widows than widowers in virtually all countries because:
    a. Women live longer than men.
    b. Women typically marry men older than themselves.
    c. Men are more likely than women to remarry after divorce or the death of a spouse.
    d. All of the above.

15. In developed countries, recent declines in labor force participation rates of older (55 and older) workers are due almost entirely to changing work patterns of which group?
    a. Men   b. Women   c. Men and women

16. What proportion of the world's countries have a public old-age security program?
    a. All   b. Three-fourths   c. One-half   d. One-fourth

17. Approximately what percentage of the private-sector labor force in the United States is covered by a private pension plan (as opposed to, or in addition to, public Social Security)?
    a. 10%   b. 25%   c. 33%   d. 60%

18. In which country are elderly people least likely to live alone?
    a. Philippines   b. Hungary   c. Canada   d. Denmark

19. True or false? In developing countries, older men are more likely than older women to be illiterate.

20. True or false? In most nations, large cities have younger populations (i.e., a lower percentage of elderly persons) than the country as a whole.

ANSWERS

1. **True.** Although the world's population is aging, children still outnumber the elderly in all major nations except six: Bulgaria, Germany, Greece, Italy, Japan, and Spain.

2. **d.** The estimated change in the total size of the world's elderly population between July 1999 and July 2000 was more than 9.5 million people, an average of 795,000 each month.

3. **c.** The Caribbean, with 7.2% of all people aged 65 or older. The corresponding figures for the other regions are as follows: Asia (excluding Japan), 5.5%; Latin America, 5.3%; and Africa, 3.1%.

4. **c.** China also has the largest elderly population, numbering nearly 88 million in 2000.

5. **False.** Although industrialized nations have higher percentages of elderly people than do most developing countries, 59% of the world's elderly now live in the developing countries of Africa, Asia, Latin America, the Caribbean, and Oceania.

6. **c.** Italy, with 18.1% of all people aged 65 or older. Monaco, a small principality of about 32,000 people located on the Mediterranean, has more than 22% of its residents aged 65 and older.

7. **False.** Although the U.S. population will age rapidly when the baby boomers (people born between 1946 and 1964) begin to reach age 65 after the year 2010, the share of the population aged 65 and older in the year 2050 is projected to be slightly more than 20% (compared with approximately 13% today).

8. **True.** The oldest-old are the fastest-growing component of many national populations. The world's growth rate for the 80-plus population from 1999 to 2000 was 3.5%, while that of the world's elderly (65-plus) population as a whole was 2.3% (compared with 1.3% for the total [all ages] population).

9. **b.** India has roughly 6.2 million people aged 80 and older, China has 11.5 million, and the United States has 9.2 million. Taken together, these people constitute nearly 38% of the world's oldest-old.

10. **c.** 81 years, up from about 52 in 1947.

11. **True.** In some African countries (e.g., Malawi, Swaziland, Zambia, and Zimbabwe) where the HIV/AIDS epidemic has been particularly devastating, average life expectancy at birth may be as much as 25 years lower than it otherwise would be in the absence of HIV/AIDS.

12. **b.** Circulatory diseases (especially heart disease and stroke) typically are the leading cause of death as reported by WHO. In Canada in 1995, for example, 44% of all deaths of women at age 65 or older were attributed to circulatory disease. The percentage was virtually the same for elderly men.

13. **False.** Although there are more elderly women than elderly men in the vast majority of the world's countries, there are exceptions such as India, Iran, and Bangladesh.

14. **d.** All of the above.

15. **a.** From the late 1960s until very recently, labor force participation rates of older men in developed countries were declining virtually everywhere, whereas those for women were often holding steady or increasing. Because older men work in much greater numbers than do older women, however, increases in female participation were more than offset by falling male participation.

16. **b.** Of the 227 countries/areas of the world with populations of at least (74%) reported having some form of an old age/disability/survivors program circa 1999.

17. **d.** The share of the private-sector U.S. labor force covered by private pension plans was approximately 60% in the mid-1990s. However, not all employees who are covered by such plans actually participate in them.

18. **a.** Philippines. The percentage of elderly people living alone in developing countries is usually much lower than that in developed countries; levels in the latter may exceed 40%.

19. **False.** Older women are less likely to be literate. In China in 1990, for example, only 11% of women aged 60 and older could read and write, compared with half of men aged 60 and older.

20. **We do not know.** Some literature from developed countries suggests that the statement is false; evidence from certain developing countries suggests that it is true. Both the Census Bureau's International Programs Center and the National Institute on Aging's Behavioral and Social Research Program would be most interested in empirical input from interested parties. Understanding global aging is a dialectical process.

Source: Kinsella, K., & Velkoff, V. A. (2001). *An aging world: 2001* (No. P95/01-1): Washington, DC: U.S. Census Bureau.

For a full suite of assignments and additional learning activities, use the access code located in the front of your book to visit this exclusive website: **http://go.jblearning.com/holtz**. *If you do not have an access code, you can obtain one at the site.*

IV

Worldwide Health Issues and Trends by Specific Country

20

A Unique Perspective on Health Care in Panama

Larry Purnell

> *"In this time of globalization, with all its advantages, the poor are the most vulnerable to having their traditions, relationships and knowledge and skills ignored and denigrated, and experiencing development with a great sense of trauma, loss and social disconnectedness."*
>
> James D. Wolfensohn, World Bank President

OBJECTIVES

After reading this chapter the reader will be able to:

1. Compare and contrast the cultural background, history, economics, and geography of the people of the Republic of Panama and their relationships to health and health care.
2. Relate the status of technology and transportation to health care in Panama.
3. Compare and contrast the significant infectious diseases within Panama, such as Hantavirus pulmonary syndrome (HPS), malaria, Chagas disease, dengue fever, leishmaniasis, filariasis, and yellow fever.
4. Describe the traditional practitioners and the use of herbal medicine among the indigenous people of Panama.

OVERVIEW

To understand the healthcare system and health care in the Republic of Panama, one must be knowledgeable about (1) the people and their heritages, (2) the unique topography and biocultural ecology of the country, (3) the history of the Panama Canal, and (4) the relationship of Panama with the United States. The republic is a mixture of cosmopolitanism and traditionalism, wealth and poverty, advanced allopathic medicine and traditional medicine, biodiversity, and multiculturalism.

The Republic of Panama (Panama means "plenty of fish") is located on the narrowest and lowest part of the S-shaped Isthmus of Panama that links North America and South America. Panama is slightly smaller than South Carolina, approximately 77,082 km² (29,761 mi²). The country's two coastlines are the Caribbean on the north and the Pacific on the south. To the east is Colombia and to the west is Costa Rica. The highest point in the country, Volcán Barú near the Costa Rican border, rises to almost 3500 m (11,483 ft). The lowest elevation is in the middle of the country where the Panama Canal crosses. The estimated 2010 population of 3.4 million has a growth rate of 1.46%. The capital, Panama City, is home to one-third of the population. The unit of currency is the balboa, which is equal to the U.S. dollar. Balboas are available only in coins; otherwise, Panama uses the U.S. dollar. Spanish is the official language, although the U.S. influence in the Canal Zone reinforces the use of English as a second language. November 3 is celebrated as the official date of independence from Colombia; the country's independence was won from Spain in 1821.

Panama is divided into nine provinces and three provincial-level *comarcas,* which are similar to reserves. Each province is somewhat unique in its history, culture, and lifestyle. The more than 350 San Blas Islands, located near Colombia, are strung out for more than 160 km along the sheltered Caribbean coastline. Other principal islands are those of the Archipiélago de las Perlas in the middle of the Gulf of Panama, the penal colony on the Isla de Coiba in the Gulf of Chiriquí, and the decorative island of Taboga, a tourist attraction that can be seen from Panama City. In all, some 1,000 islands are found off the Pacific coast of Panama.

Panama has a tropical climate. Temperatures are uniformly high, as is the relative humidity, with little seasonal variation. Diurnal ranges are low; on a typical day during the dry season in the capital city, the early morning minimum may be 24 °C (75 °F) and the afternoon maximum 29 °C (84 °F). The temperature seldom exceeds 32 °C (90 °F) for more than a short time. Temperatures are markedly cooler in the mountain ranges in western Panama, where frosts occur. Panama's tropical environment supports an abundance of plants. Forests dominate, interrupted by grasslands, scrub, and crops. Although nearly 40% of Panama is still wooded, deforestation is a continuing threat to the rain-drenched woodlands.

Almost 500 rivers traverse Panama, with many originating as highland streams. The Río Chagres, one of the longest rivers, was dammed to create Gatun Lake, which forms a major part of the transit route between the locks near each end of the Panama Canal.

TRANSPORTATION

The only fully functioning railroad in Panama runs from Colon to Panama City. More than 9535 km (5925 mi) of roads twine through Panama. The Pan-American highway, running from Costa Rica through Panama, ends in Darien. Existing roads do not connect from Darien into Colombia. Sixty percent of the roadways are unpaved and not passable during parts of the rainy season. Of 105 airports, only 44 are paved. One international airport, Tocumen, is sited near Panama City. Buses are available between all major cities throughout Panama. Inexpensive intra-city bus lines are available but are not yet sufficient to meet the needs of outlying areas.

PEOPLE OF PANAMA

Panama has long enjoyed a measure of ethnic diversity, which has given rise to a number of distinct subcultures. Most Panamanians view their society as composed of three principal groups: the Spanish-speaking Roman Catholic mestizo majority, the English-speaking Protestant Antillean blacks, and indigenous Indians. The racial and ethnic divisions are 70% mestizo (mixed Amerindian and white), 14% West Indian (Amerindian and mixed), 10% white Spanish, and 6% Amerindian. Included in these groups are

Chinese, Middle Easterners, Swiss, Yugoslavian, and North American immigrants; all have contributed to the multiculturalism of Panama. Only 7% of the population is older than the age of 65 years and 28.9% is younger than the age of 14 years. Panama has a young population, with a median age of 27.2 years.

Panama is increasingly becoming a country for retirees, especially U.S. citizens who are mostly former Canal Zone employees. Small groups of Hispanic blacks (*playeros*) and Hispanic Indians (*cholos*) live along the Atlantic coast lowlands and in Darién. Their settlements date from the colonial era and are concentrated along waterways. They rely on farming and raising livestock that have adapted to the tropical forest environment.

The Guaymí, a vulnerable group related to the Nahatlan and Mayan Nations of Mexico and Central America, are concentrated in the western provinces. In the 1980s, the government began developing a copper mine, a highway, a pipeline, and a hydroelectric plant on Guaymi land in the province of Chiriquí. The Guaymi have attempted to protect their land and publicize their misgivings about the projects because of the impact on their lands and the effect of dam construction on fishing and water supplies. The matter has not been fully resolved.

ETHICAL ISSUE

An ethical principle of distributive justice is that basic goods should be distributed so that the least advantaged members of society are benefited. Distributive justice also means that the rights of one group are balanced against another. What is your opinion about the Panamanian government developing copper mines, traversing roads, and building pipelines through Guayamí Indian territory?

The Cuna, also referred to as the Kuna, are concentrated mainly along the Caribbean coast, on the San Blas Islands, which are small coral islands. The largest of these islands, Aligandí, is only 32 acres (13 hectares). Only native Kuna are allowed on the island overnight and only with prior permission from their independent government. Kuna homes are made with cane walls and guava-thatched roofs. Bathroom facilities are a short walk to the end of piers where outdoor toilets have the Atlantic Ocean as their automatic flushing system. Fresh water is piped from the mainland. In addition, a small number of Kuna are scattered in the remote mountains of western Panama and the interior of Darién.

The Bribri, part of the Talamanca tribe of Costa Rica, have substantial contact with outsiders. Many are employed on banana plantations. The Bókatá live in eastern Bocas del Toro and have little exposure to outsiders. Since the early 1980s, a small dirt road has served the area, though it is passable only in dry weather. The Chocó (or Embera) occupy the southeastern portion of Darién along the border with Colombia. Most are bilingual in Spanish and Chocó.

All tribes are under the jurisdiction of both the provincial and national governments. The indigenous policy section of the Ministry of Government and Justice bears primary responsibility for coordinating programs that affect Indians. The 1972 constitution required the government to establish reserves (*comarcas*) for indigenous tribes, but the extent to which this mandate had been implemented varies. Most settlements of any size have a primary school; a few also have secondary schools.

Urban society includes virtually all members of the elite. Centered mainly in Panama City, this group comprises old families of Spanish descent and newer families of immigrants. More established families think of themselves as aristocracy from birth. Newer families have less prestige and social status. Until the dominance of General Omar Torrijos, whose power base was the National Guard, an oligarchy of older elite families virtually controlled the country's politics under the auspices of the Liberal Party. Politics is considered the quintessential career for a young man of elite background. The old, aristocratic families have long provided the republic's presidents, cabinet ministers, and members of the legislature. Older elite families are closely interrelated and in the past were careful to avoid racially mixed unions.

Antillean blacks have had little success in attaining elite status, even when wealthy; however, Spanish-speaking Roman Catholic blacks are able to gain acceptance. An increasing degree of admixture with mestizo and more recent immigrants has been occurring in recent years, as many such families enter the elite and intermarry with members of the older families. Commercial success has become a substitute for an illustrious family background—a phenomenon acknowledged in the popular saying "Money whitens everyone."

Panama's middle socioeconomic class is predominantly mestizo. Like the elite, the middle class is largely urban, although many small cities and towns of the interior have their own middle-class families. Middle-class parents make great sacrifices to send their children to the best schools possible. Young men are encouraged to acquire a profession, and young women are steered toward office jobs in government or business. In contrast with the elite, the middle class views teaching and nursing as respected occupations for a young woman.

Ethnically, the lower socioeconomic classes have three principal components: mestizo migrants from the countryside, children and grandchildren of Antillean blacks, and Hispanicized blacks who are descendants of former slaves. The split between blacks and the rest of the populace is particularly marked. Although some social mixing and intermarriage occurs, religious and cultural differences tend to isolate Panama's black population. As a group, they are gradually becoming more Hispanicized, but the first generation usually remains oriented toward its Caribbean origins. The second and third generations are under North American influence through exposure to U.S. citizens in the former Canal Zone, where most blacks are employed.

Because the majority of rural migrants to metropolitan regions are women, women outnumber men in many larger urban areas. Many come in search of work as domestics. Young, single mothers constitute a significant proportion of the urban population.

HISTORY, POLITICS, AND GOVERNMENT

As early as 8000 B.C., people used the Isthmus of Panama to continue their southward migration and settle in South America. Whether they used land routes or sea routes or a combination of both to make their journeys is not known, but long before the arrival of Europeans, the Indians of North and South America established ocean routes for trade and cultural commerce along the Pacific coast. The Caribbean coast may also have had some maritime commerce among the Indians.

Columbus landed in Panama on his fourth voyage in 1502. In 1510, Vasco de Balboa crossed the isthmus and was the first European to see the Pacific Ocean. Pizarro used the isthmus for his subjugation of the Incas. Charles V ordered the first survey for a proposed canal in 1534. Although no construction was undertaken, a cobblestone mule trail, called Las Cruses, was built to support the conquest of South America's Pacific coast and to carry tons of gold being shipped to Spain from Peru. Parts of that trail are still visible today. Subsequently, the indigenous population of Panama was greatly reduced and Spanish control over the area was established. In 1821, under the leadership of Simon Bolivar, the Spanish colonies revolted against Spain; in the aftermath, Panama became a province of New Granada, which included Colombia, Ecuador, and Venezuela.

In 1882, the French began work on the Panama Canal; however, financial troubles, yellow fever, malaria, tuberculosis, cholera, diphtheria, smallpox, and bubonic plague among the workers ended the project. In 1885, the Republic of Colombia was formed with Panama as a Colombian province. Only in 1903, after Colombia's first civil war had killed nearly 100,000 people, did Panama gain independence with U.S. support. When Panama declared independence from Colombia, the new country and the United States entered into a treaty by which the United States undertook the construction of an interoceanic canal across the isthmus. Before any work could begin, indigenous Indians were relocated. The United States appointed an American physician, William Gorgas, to examine the area. Gorgas and his medical team eradicated yellow fever and brought malaria under control, making it possible to build a canal with international benefit.

ETHICAL ISSUE

The ethical principle respecting autonomy means that individuals are free to decide how they live their lives as long as their decisions do not negatively affect the lives of others. This principle is balanced with distributive justice. What are your thoughts and concerns about the forced relocation of people that has international implications?

The 1904 constitution gave the United States the right to intervene in any part of Panama and to reestablish public peace and constitutional order. This provision gave the United States the right to add more territory to the Canal Zone whenever it believed this step was necessary for defensive purposes. Later in the twentieth century, these grants of power to the United States caused increasing discontent in Panama, particularly in the 1950s and 1960s.

The 51-mile canal, completed in 1914, was originally operated exclusively by the United States. A 1977 agreement transferred the canal from the United States to Panama at the end of the century. The canal is to remain a neutral zone, and the United States is legally entitled to intervene to maintain its neutrality.

Because many of today's ships are larger than the original construction of the canal was designed to handle, the Panama Canal Commission is widening it to allow larger container vessels to pass through. This expansion is expected to be completed in 2014–2015.

The Panamanian government is divided into three branches: the executive, the legislative, and the judiciary. The executive branch has one president and two vice presidents, all elected by popular vote for 5-year terms. The legislative branch is the Unicameral National Assembly; its members are also elected by popular vote and serve 5-year terms. In the judiciary branch, the Supreme Court of Justice has nine appointed judges who serve 10-year terms.

In 1990, the Panamanian military was abolished and replaced with the Panamanian Public Forces. Four years later, the legislative assembly approved a constitutional amendment prohibiting the creation of a standing military force but allowed for the temporary establishment of special police units to counter acts of "external aggression."

Personalism—giving one's political loyalties to an individual rather than to a party—has influenced the political scene of Panama since its independence. Whereas government officials giving special privileges and positions to a family member is not unique to Panama, a high rate of nepotism occurs in Panama.

ETHICAL ISSUE

Balancing the rights of one individual against another is the ethical principle of justice. What concerns do you have with appointing and promoting family members over others who may be more qualified for a position?

ECONOMICS

With an estimated 2009 per capita income of $11,900 (up from $2509 in 1999), 28.6% of Panamanians still live in poverty, which is more prevalent in rural areas than in urban areas. The 2009 unemployment rate of 7% was significantly lower than it was in the early 1990s.

Panama's main crops are bananas, sugarcane, rice, corn, coffee, beans, tobacco, melons, and flowers. Livestock, forestry, and fishing are major commercial enterprises. Natural resources include copper, mahogany forests, shrimp, and hydropower. Major industries include construction, petroleum refining, brewing, manufacturing cement and other construction materials, and sugar milling. The country has an oversupply of nonskilled workers. International banking is also big business, as Panama operates as an offshore financial center.

Its extensive shoreline is responsible for Panama being a major transshipment point and primary laundering center for narcotic and money-laundering activities, especially in the Colon free trade zone. Most of the country's exports go to the United States and China, followed by Costa Rica, Germany, Belgium, the Netherlands, and Italy.

In addition to the substantial income generated by the Panama Canal, ecotourism is another major source of income. A land full of history, art, and culture, Panama's privileged geographical position shelters a rich and abundant natural flora and fauna, resulting in one of the most important natural areas of the world. More than 50% of the world's floral species can be found in Panama, consisting of vascular plant flowers, moss, lichens, algae, and fungi. Panama is also a destination for bird-watchers, as it is home to 940 species of birds; of these, 127 are migratory and 23 are endemic. The national bird of Panama, the harpy eagle, is considered the most powerful bird of prey in the world. Panama also claims 214 species of reptiles, 143 species of amphibians, 225 species of mammals, and 1500 species of butterflies. The maritime wealth is also fascinating, and includes 207 species of fish, algae, cetaceans, and coral reefs. Overall, Panama has 15 national parks that are major tourist attractions.

TECHNOLOGY

Until the early 2000s, Panama had only one telephone company, Cable and Wireless Panama, and it took Panamanians in some areas as long as 6 months to get telephone services. The impetus for improved services and competition started with the introduction of Radio Shack, where one could purchase a telephone and get immediate telephone service. Now the government has awarded new concessions for fixed-line and mobile services.

In October 2000, the Global Academy Institute for Integrative Medicine convened a conference called "Health Today: Realities, Obstacles and Perspectives" to offer the medical community and other constituencies of the healthcare sector of Panama a variety of health and medical perspectives. Cosponsors were the Foreign Ministry of Panama, the Health Ministry of Panama, the Global Academy Genome Institute, the Pan-American Health Organization, and the United Nations Development Program. The presentations and dialogues focused on two themes: (1) integrative medicine and its relevance in terms of the traditional healing systems of the Americas and its potential for low-cost medical services and (2) genetic technology and its impact on the future of health care. This conference demonstrated the importance Panamanians see for technology in their future.

In June 2003, Panama hosted Info Com 2003, a trade event aimed at promoting e-business and information technology in Panama and the Latin American region. Info Com 2003 was an initiative of the committee of technology of the American Chamber of Commerce and Industries of Panama. This event stimulated executives to find the most effective and efficient ways to administer resources, take advantage of new opportunities, and increase the use of the best technological options. Info Com 2003 had three major aims: (1) promoting the concept of the new Panama Canal; (2) offering technological solutions related to information systems, management, client relations, telecommunications, Internet access, electronic commerce, and network infrastructure; and (3) identifying new business opportunities that arise from technology.

The engineering and maintenance units in the Ministry of Public Health encourage health facilities to use common methods for procuring, installing, and maintaining biomedical equipment. They have also attempted to draft technical specifications for the procurement of biomedical equipment. Preventive maintenance continues to be problematic, however. The social security hospitals and clinics appear to have adequate and better equipment than the hospitals and clinics operated by the Ministry of Public Health. The few smaller, private hospitals appear to have adequate emergency equipment.

EDUCATION

Overview of Education

Public education began in Panama soon after independence from Colombia but presented an extremely paternalistic view of education. For example, a 1913 meeting of the First Panamanian Educational Assembly stated, "The cultural heritage given to the child should be determined by the social position he or she should occupy. For this reason, education should be different in accordance with the social class to which the student should be related" (Library of Congress, 2004).

This elitist focus changed under U.S. influence. Now, education has been recognized as a mark of status. Most people of elite status receive a university education, attend private schools either at home or abroad, and typically study a profession, with law and medicine being the most favored. Having a profession is viewed not as a means of livelihood, but as a status symbol and as an adjunct to a political career.

Since the 1920s, successive Panamanian governments have given high priority to developing a system of universal primary education. Adult literacy, which was only 30% in 1923, rose to 50% in less than a decade. By the early 1950s, adult literacy had increased to more than 70%, then to 87% in 1980, and is currently more than 91%. Men and women are equally represented among the literate, with more women than men attending college. The most notable disparity in education is between urban and rural Panamanians.

School attendance is compulsory for children from ages 6 to 15 years, or until the completion of primary school. However, some isolated areas of Panama still do not have a secondary school.

ETHICAL ISSUE

The principle of justice requires meaningful equality among individuals for those positions in society that bring greater economic and social rewards. What are your thoughts about the government not providing facilities for secondary education in some rural areas of Panama?

Secondary school programs follow an academic-oriented program or a vocational-type program. The academic program, which is followed by nearly three-fourths of all secondary-school enrollments, features a standard curriculum that includes Spanish, social studies, religion, art, and music. The upper cycle consists of two academic courses of study: arts and sciences, leading up to entrance to the university, or a less rigorous course of study, representing the end of a student's formal education.

Vocational secondary-school programs offer professional or technical courses aimed specifically at giving students the technical skills for employment following graduation. Like the more academic-oriented secondary school programs, the vocational-type programs are divided into two cycles. Students can choose their studies from a variety of specializations, including agriculture, art, commerce, and industrial trades.

The oldest, largest, and most highly regarded institution of higher education, the University of Panama, has produced many public figures—hence its nickname "the nest of eagles." Drawing most of its student body from upwardly mobile rather than long-established elements of the elite, students are well known for their political activism. Nearly three-fourths of all university students in the country attend the University of Panama. In addition to its main campus, the university operates regional centers and extensions. Other universities include the University of Santa Maria la Antigua, a private Roman Catholic institution established in 1965; Technical University, founded in 1981; and the Autonomous University of Chiriqui, which is rapidly expanding after separating from the University of Panama in 2000. In addition, some small, private universities with English as the language of instruction are located in Panama City.

Education for the Health Professions

Panama has one public medical school, which is located at the University of Panama, and two private ones. The university also has a master's program in health promotion geared toward multidisciplinary needs, which is located in the School of Public Health. Paramedic programs are provided at the baccalaureate level. Nurse–midwives work in many rural areas and inner-city clinics. The government finances higher education in public universities, but housing and books are not included in these subsidies.

Only baccalaureate nursing programs exist in Panama; there is one public program at the University of Panama, which affiliates with the University of South Florida in the United States, and one at the Autonomous University of Chiriqui in David. Baccalaureate nursing programs include 144 semester credits, which is equivalent to many master's degree programs in the United States. In their senior year, students provide health care to a community, sometimes in extremely remote areas where the student may travel 2 to 3 days on horseback to get to the destination, and then be the only healthcare provider in the area; their living arrangements may be in an elementary schoolhouse without heat or air conditioning. All nursing students complete a senior research thesis.

Panama has a master's degree program in nursing administration in which the author of this chapter consulted and taught for several years. Many nursing faculty have obtained their master's degrees and doctorates from U.S. universities. Others have master's degrees in nursing from Colombia, Costa Rica, and Mexico. The role of advanced practice nurses is being developed but has not been widely accepted to date.

■ COMMUNICATION

The official language of Panama is Spanish, but many members of the population are bilingual in Spanish and English. Some speak a third language, such as Chinese, Japanese, Portuguese, or Italian. Most of the indigenous populations are bilingual in their native languages and Spanish.

Contextual speech patterns among Panamanians can include a high-pitched, loud voice and a rate that seems extremely fast to the untrained ear. The language uses apocopation, which accounts for this rapid speech pattern. An apocopation occurs when one word ends with a vowel, and the next word begins with a vowel. This creates a tendency to drop the vowel ending of the first word and results in an abbreviated rapid-sounding form. For example, the Spanish phrase for "How are you?," *¿Cómo está usted?,* may become *¿Comestusted?* The last word, *usted,* is frequently dropped. Some may find this fast speech difficult to understand. However, if one asks the individual to enunciate slowly, the effect of the apocopation or truncation is less pronounced. For the first 3 days of each trip to Panama, this author has a mantra, *Habla mas despacio, por favor* ("Speak more slowly, please"), until becoming accustomed to the rapid speech patterns.

Using Spanish to communicate with Panamanian clients is important. The healthcare provider who assumes a total understanding of Panamanian Spanish, however, may negatively affect his or her interactions with these clients. Attempt speaking Spanish, but do not be overly confident; the idiomatic expressions are numerous and change from country to country.

Respect (*respeto*) is extremely important, especially when meeting a Panamanian for the first time. Always greet the person formally, unless told to do otherwise. Greeting the person with *Señorita* (Miss), *Señora* (Mrs.), *Señor* (Mister), *Doña* (Madam), *Don* (Sir), and *Doctor* or *Doctora* sets the stage for formal communication. Familism—the value of family—is also an important concept. For health teaching to be effective, the provider must engage the entire family.

Approaching the Panamanian client with personalism, being friendly, and directing questions to the family spokesperson (usually the male) may help to facilitate more open communication. However, one must remember that the spokesperson is not necessarily the decision maker. The woman may make the decision, but the culturally prescribed role is for the man to transmit the message. Personalism emphasizes people and family orientation and is essential for building confidence, promoting health, and establishing a cultural connection. On repeat visits, polite conversation includes briefly asking about family members. The concept of personalism may be difficult for some healthcare professionals because many are socialized to create rigid boundaries between the caregiver and the client and family.

Cultural Communication Patterns

While some topics such as income, salary, and investments are taboo, Panamanians generally like to express their inner beliefs, feelings, and emotions once they get to know and trust a person. Meaningful conversations are important, often becoming loud and seemingly disorganized. To the outsider, the situation may seem stressful or hostile, but this intense emotion means that the participants in the conversation are having a good time and enjoying one another's company.

Panamanians place great value on closeness and togetherness, including when they are in an inpatient facility. They frequently touch and embrace others and like to see relatives and significant others. Touch between a man and a woman, between two men, and between two women is acceptable. To demonstrate respect, compassion, and understanding, healthcare providers should greet the Panamanian client with a handshake. On establishing rapport, providers may further demonstrate approval and respect through backslapping, smiling, and affirmative nods of the head.

Many Panamanians consider sustained eye contact when speaking directly to an older person to be rude. Direct eye contact with teachers, physicians, nurses, and superiors may be interpreted as insolence. Avoiding sustained and direct eye contact with superiors is a sign of respect. This practice may or may not be seen in the younger generation, but it is imperative that healthcare providers take cues from the client and family. Many among the indigenous Indian populations do not maintain eye contact with persons older than themselves or people in hierarchical positions.

Out of respect for the healthcare provider, many Panamanians may avoid disagreeing, expressing doubts, or asking questions. Certainly, any negative feelings about the healthcare encounter would not be expressed. Nevertheless, encouraging patients to ask questions, even if it is through an interpreter, is considered polite behavior.

Temporal Relationships

Many Panamanians, especially those from lower socioeconomic groups, are focused on the present, out of choice and necessity. Many individuals do not consider it important or do not have the income to plan ahead financially. The trend is to live in the "more important" here and now, because *mañana* (tomorrow) cannot be predicted. With this emphasis on living in the present, preventive health care and immunizations may not be a priority. *Mañana* may or may not really mean tomorrow, but rather often means "not today" or "later."

Some Panamanians perceive time as relative, rather than categorically imperative. Deadlines and commitments are flexible, not firm. Punctuality is generally relaxed, especially in social situations. Because of their more relaxed concept of time, Panamanians may arrive late for appointments, although the current trend is toward greater punctuality. Healthcare facilities that use an appointment system for clients may need to make special provisions to see clients whenever they arrive. Healthcare providers must listen carefully for subtle cues when discussing appointments. Disagreeing with healthcare providers who set the appointment may be viewed as rude or impolite. Therefore, some Panamanians will not tell healthcare providers directly that they cannot make an appointment. In the context of the discussion, they may say something like, "My husband goes to work at 8:00 A.M. and the children are off to school, then I have to do the dishes . . ." The healthcare professional should ask: "Is 8:30 A.M. on Thursday okay for you?" The person might say "Yes," but the healthcare professional must still intently listen to the conversation and then possibly negotiate a new time for the appointment. Many Panamanians consider it rude to openly disagree in social situations. Because it might be seen as rude to directly say "No," the Panamanian may say "Yes." In reality, "Yes" may mean "I hear you, but I am not going to follow your instructions," "I hear you, and I do not agree," "I will think about it," "I am not sure what you mean, but I do not want to embarrass myself or you to explain it more," or "I understand you, agree with you, and will follow your instructions and advice."

Format for Names

Names in most Spanish-speaking populations seem complex to those unfamiliar with the culture. A typical name is La Señorita Olga Gaborra y Rodriguez. Gaborra is the name of this individual's father, and Rodriguez is her mother's surname. When she marries a man with the surname name of Guiterrez, she becomes La Señora (denotes a married woman) Olga de Guiterrez y Gaborra y Rodriguez. The word *de* is used to express possession, and the father's name, which is considered more important than the mother's name, comes first. However, this full name is rarely used except on formal documents and for recording the name in the family Bible. Out of respect, most Panamanians are more formal when addressing nonfamily members. Thus the best way to address Olga is not by her first name, but rather as Señora de Guiterrez. Use of titles such as *Don* and *Doña* for older respected members of the community and family is also common.

Healthcare providers must understand the role of older adults when providing care to people of Panamanian culture. To develop confidence and personalism, an element of formality must exist between healthcare providers and older adults. Becoming overly familiar by using physical touch or using first names may not be appreciated early in a relationship. As the healthcare professional develops confidence in the relationship, becoming familiar may be less of a concern. However, using the first name of an older adult client might never be appropriate.

SPIRITUALITY AND RELIGION

The religious affiliations of Panamanians are 85% Roman Catholic and 15% Protestant. Nevertheless, significant numbers of residents practice Islam and Judaism. Purnell's research (1999) reported a number of participants who self-identified as atheists. The Panamanian constitution prescribes that there shall be no prejudice with respect to religious freedom, and the practice of all forms of worship is authorized. At the same time, the constitution recognizes that the Roman Catholic faith is the country's predominant religion and contains a provision that it be taught in the public schools. Such instruction or other religious activity is not compulsory, however. The constitution does not specifically provide for the separation of church and state, but it implies the independent functioning of each entity.

Members of the clergy may not hold civil or military public office, excepting the posts that may be concerned with social welfare or public instruction. The constitution stipulates that senior officials of the church hierarchy in Panama must be native-born citizens.

ETHICAL ISSUE

> Respecting autonomy is an ethical principle that allows groups to make decisions about their lives and organization as long as they do not have a negative effect on the decisions of other groups. Do you think that requiring church officials in hierarchal positions to be native-born Panamanians violates this principle?

The devout Panamanians regard church attendance and the observance of religious duties as regular features of everyday life, and even the most casual or nominal Roman Catholics adjust their daily lives to the prevailing norms of the religious calendar. Although some sacraments are observed more scrupulously than others, baptism is almost universal; in fact, baptism is generally considered the most significant religious rite. Throughout the country, births and deaths are marked by religious rites observed by all but a very few individuals.

Virtually every town has its own Roman Catholic Church, but many do not have a priest in residence. Many rural inhabitants receive only an occasional visit from a busy priest who travels among a number of isolated villages. In rural areas, families often have to travel some distance to the nearest parish center. This trip is important and people willingly undertake it to practice religious rites.

The Antillean black community is largely Protestant. Indians follow their own indigenous belief systems, although both Protestant and Catholic missionaries are active among the various tribes. However, Roman Catholicism permeates the social environment culturally as well as religiously. Religious attitudes, customs, and beliefs differ between urban and rural areas, although many members of the urban working class and recent migrants from rural regions usually retain their folk beliefs.

Panamanians, regardless of their religious affiliation, take their religion seriously. Purnell's study (1999) reported that 81% of participants prayed for good health; however, the most important thing in their lives was family, followed by religion. If healthcare delivery is to be effective for Panamanians, care and health teaching must be delivered in the family context.

RESEARCH AND DEMONSTRATION PROJECTS

The National Geographic research station near Panama City and the American Institute of Biological Sciences conduct research on marine issues, fungal infections in frogs, and other environmental concerns. A cagelike steel gondola on top of a crane gives researchers a bird's-eye view of the jungle canopy where research studies are conducted. A number of archeological and anthropological sites are also being studied.

For many years, the Institute of Nutrition of Central America and Panama at the University of Panama has sponsored an ongoing research project on breastfeeding among diverse populations in Panama. One finding is a widespread belief that maternal milk plays a definite role in the etiology of diarrheal diseases. One of the explanatory models of diarrheal disease in children is the hot–cold theory of illness and disease causation: If the mother is too hot or too cold at the time of breastfeeding, the child will get diarrhea. Examples of this belief were explained to this author while teaching and taking nursing and dietetic students to Panama: (1) if ironing (a hot activity), wait a while before breastfeeding; (2) if the mother has been in the hot sun, she should cool off before breastfeeding, (3) if exposed to cold wind, the mother should wait until warm before breastfeeding, and (4) she should not immediately breastfeed if she has consumed cold liquids or been exposed to the open door of a cold refrigerator.

The City of Knowledge, created in 1995 and governed by a private, nonprofit organization, is an international complex for education, research, and innovation located at the former Fort Clayton military base in the Panama Canal Zone. The City of Knowledge offers facilities and support for establishing programs in education, research, and technological development and helps develop and strengthen the relationship between the academic, scientific, and business worlds with an international orientation. Current researchers at this complex come from the University of South Florida, University of Delaware, Purdue University, and Iowa State University, to name a few. The University of Florida Health Sciences Center is the only international foundation to participate in this venture to date.

Partners of the Americas: Delaware–Panama Partners of the Americas

Partners of the Americas has had a significant, sustained, and positive influence on people's lives in Panama and in the state of Delaware through Delaware–Panama Partners of the Americas. In 1963, President John F. Kennedy launched the Alliance for Progress, a program of government-to-government economic cooperation across the Western Hemisphere. At the same time, he called for a parallel people-to-people initiative, one that would allow private citizens to work together for the good of the Americas. These initiatives were established as part of the U.S. Agency for International Development.

Soon after its founding, the Alliance for Progress shifted to the private sector and changed its name to Partners of the Americas. In the following years, the organization expanded into the Caribbean and ultimately formed 120 volunteer chapters involved in 60 partnerships, of which Delaware–Panama Partners is one. This partnership developed because both Delaware and Panama are international banking centers, each has only one major university, both have a canal (Delaware Canal and the Panama Canal), and both have shared interests in farmer-to-farmer programs. Beekeeping for the production of honey and research on bee venom for allergies are also shared interests. Delaware–Panama Partners has engaged in numerous projects and conducted some noteworthy research.

Although Delaware–Panama Partners is not strictly a research-oriented organization, it has produced many noteworthy research projects. On the research side, faculty from the University of Delaware and the University of Panama have completed the following research studies and projects:

1. Young women's attitudes and involvement toward future needs of older adults for caregiving.
2. Panamanian health beliefs and the meaning of respect afforded them by healthcare providers.
3. Folic acid project financed by the March of Dimes to increase the awareness of the importance of folic acid in the diet of women of childbearing age in Panama and in Delaware, and the development of bilingual materials because of the increased risk of Hispanic populations for spina bifida and other neural tube defects that are related to folic acid deficiency.
4. Culturally appropriate material for tobacco use prevention geared toward a variety of age groups as well as material to aid teachers, physicians, and other health personnel with new approaches.
5. Environmental impact and cleanup of the Panama Canal Zone because of the effect that contamination has had on the environment and health of the people living in the Canal Zone.
6. Graduate student and faculty exchanges in pediatric oncology, disabilities studies, and disaster management. The U.S. Center for Disaster Management is located at the University of Delaware.
7. A family-life project to develop reproductive health education materials suitable for use in Panama and the Latin American community in Delaware.

8. Culturally relevant health information for emergency preparedness.
9. Higher education linkages to develop ongoing, self-sustaining programs in higher education.
10. Promotion of knowledge of women's rights to build awareness of the revised code of family law as it affects women's rights.
11. A service-learning program to promote and train participants in school and community leadership.

ETHICAL ISSUE

The ethical principle of nonmaleficence means that we as individuals, groups, or organizations should not engage in activities that run the risk of harming others. The U.S. military used the Panama Canal Zone as a dumping ground for biohazardous waste. What responsibility do you think the United States should have in cleaning up the Canal Zone, even though it is now under the control of the Panamanian government?

HEALTHCARE PRACTICES

Overview of the Healthcare System

The Panamanian constitution guarantees the right to medical and health care throughout the nation's territories. The public health sector comprises the Ministry of Health, which covers 60% of the population, and the Social Security Fund, which covers 40% of the population. The current government's health objectives are to offer universal access to comprehensive health programs, to improve the quality of the services, and to reduce gaps through a decentralized model of care that emphasizes primary health care. Private health insurance is available for those who can afford it.

The Department of Environmental Health is charged with administering rural health programs and maintaining a safe water supply for communities with fewer than 500 inhabitants, communities that make up roughly one-third of the total Panamanian population. The National Water and Sewage Institute and the Ministry of Public Works share responsibility for urban water supplies. Public health efforts are aimed at changing the emphasis from curative, hospital-based medical care to community-based preventive medicine. The Ministry of Health bears primary responsibility for public health programs. At the district and regional levels, medical directors are responsible for maintaining healthcare services at healthcare centers and hospitals and monitoring outreach programs for the communities surrounding these facilities.

The Social Security Institute maintains a medical fund for its members and operates a number of healthcare facilities, which members can use for free and nonmembers can use for a nominal fee. The Social Security Institute and the Ministry of Health have attempted, with limited success, to coordinate what in essence are two separate public healthcare systems in an effort to eliminate redundancy. Panama's social security system covers most permanent employees, with principal disbursements being for retirement and health care. Permanent employees pay taxes to the Social Security Institute, and the self-employed contribute on the basis of their income as reported on income tax returns.

The Ministry of Health and the Social Security Institute of Panama have signed a cooperative agreement to strengthen their coordination in the management of emergencies and disasters. This agreement is part of the Safe Hospitals global strategy and prioritizes a shared agenda to achieve the goal of keeping hospitals safe from disasters by the year 2015.

ETHICAL ISSUE

Which ethical principles have been violated with poor distribution of healthcare services in Panama? How is this different from the United States and other more- or less-developed countries?

Healthcare Workforce

The most recent data on the healthcare workforce are from 2004, so there may be questions about their accuracy. In 2004, there were 11.7 physicians, 2.4 dentists, and 10.7 nurses per 10,000 population. The number of nurses is inadequate to meet Panama's needs, and the supply is unevenly distributed between urban and rural areas. Nurses who are willing to practice in remote areas receive as much as a 50% increase in pay. The country is also short on laboratory technicians. All health professionals in the public sector are protected by union contracts, which set their pay scales.

ETHICAL ISSUE

Higher education is free in Panama. The health-sector distribution and statistics are not what one expects for a developing country. What do you suggest to address the ethical principles of justice, beneficence, autonomy, and nonmaleficence?

The birth rate of 19.71 births per 1000 population has been gradually decreasing over the past three decades. Infant mortality for males is 12.75 deaths per 1000 live births; for females, it is 11.97 deaths per 1000 live births. Most infant mortality is attributable to congenital abnormalities, pneumonia, intestinal infections, protein-calorie malnutrition, and accidental injuries. Rural Panama has disproportionately high infant and maternal mortality rates. Rural babies are roughly 20% more likely to die than their urban counterparts; childbearing is five times more likely to be fatal in rural Panama than in cities. The infant mortality rate of Panama Province is one-third that of Bocas del Toro and one-fourth that of Darién.

ETHICAL ISSUE

Which ethical principles are involved with health disparities in Panama? Can you make suggestions for addressing these disproportionate health disparities? How are these disparities different from or similar to wealthier nations?

The overall fertility rate of 2.48 per woman varies significantly from urban to rural areas. In his research, Purnell (1999) reported that nonuse of family planning services might be due in part to indigenous Indians' strong cultural values related to family. Female sterilization remains a prevalent method of birth control, followed by oral contraceptives (Warren, Monteith, Johnson, Santiso, Guerra, & Oberle, 1987). The crude death rate is 4.6%, with a maternal mortality rate of 6.4%. The life expectancy is 80.5 years for women and 74.85 years for men.

Service Facilities and Quality of Services

Panama has 22 hospitals, some of which are privately owned. The province of Panama has 12 hospitals, many of which are specialty specific, such as those geared toward psychiatry, maternal–child, pediatrics, or medical and surgical services. Chiriqui Province has three hospitals. The western provinces have only one hospital, and Bocas del Toro, Cocle, and Darien do not have any hospitals but do have clinics. Medical facilities, including nearly all laboratory and special-care facilities, are concentrated in the capital city. Roughly 87% of the hospital beds are in publicly owned facilities and are mostly located in Panama City. Hospital Punta Pacifica, which is affiliated with Johns Hopkins University, and Clinica Hospital San Fernando, which is affiliated with Miami Children's Hospital, Tulane University, and Miami Baptist Health Center, have English-trained and English-speaking physicians and staff.

Medical facilities and personnel are concentrated beyond what might reasonably be expected, even given the capital city's share of the country's total population. Panama City has roughly two and a half times the national average of hospital beds and doctors per capita and nearly three times the number of nurses per capita. The effect of this distribution is seen in continued regional disparities in health indicators.

ETHICAL ISSUE

Which ethical principles are involved with the maldistribution of healthcare facilities in Panama?

The overall perceptions of Panamanians regarding healthcare delivery are that (1) private care is best but too costly, (2) the Social Security facilities are better than those administered by the Ministry of Health, (3) the care is trusted and sophisticated despite long delays in accessing trusted providers, and (4) the rural, indigenous population have unmet basic needs without regard to quality (Moises, 2003). Sandiford and Salvetto (2002) reported that inequalities in health care in rural areas of Panama result from low utilization rates, which are related to the travel time to get to a facility and the perceived low quality when care is accessed.

Most hospitals have active infection-control programs. Specialty women's hospitals have active milk banks. In public hospitals that cater to the indigenous rural populations, facilities are available where one family member can stay in the hospital with the patient, while the rest of the family lives in adjacent facilities on hospital property.

ILLNESS, DISEASE, AND INJURY PROFILE

The illness, disease, and injury profile of Panama is changing from one of infectious diseases to one similar to the more developed nations. Nevertheless, some infectious diseases that were almost eliminated in the past are reemerging, and newer ones are arising. The leading causes of death are (1) malignant neoplasms; (2) accidents, self-inflicted injuries, assaults, and other acts of violence; (3) cerebrovascular diseases; (4) ischemic heart disease; (5) chronic diseases of the lower respiratory tract; and (6) diabetes mellitus. The rate for communicable diseases has decreased significantly over the last 15 years. Tuberculosis is on the rise, however, and diseases caused by the human immunodeficiency virus (HIV) represent 1 of 10 leading causes of death, with a rate of 15.2 per 100,000; rates are higher in men (23.3 per 100,000) than in women (7.0 per 100,000). All but one resident in the San Blas Islands have type B+ blood; testing for HIV does not exist in these islands. HIV in the rest of the country is on the rise, with 44% of such infections transmitted through heterosexual activity, 40% through homosexual or bisexual activity, 10% through intravenous drug use, 1% through blood transfusions, and 5% perinatally. The total number of Panamanians with HIV infection is less than 16,000.

The leading causes of morbidity treated at public health facilities are influenza, diarrhea and gastroenteritis, rhinopharyngitis, the common cold, and malnutrition. Health workers, nurses in urban areas, and either nurses or community health promoters in rural areas are trained to provide follow-through on mental health programs, control of vector-borne diseases, tuberculosis, and cervical cancer. The leading discharge diagnoses in public health hospitals are problems related to childbirth and the puerperium, diseases of the respiratory tract, multiple trauma, infectious parasitic diseases, and problems with the newborn and the perinatal process.

Although the country supposedly has an adequate blood supply, places in remote areas such as the San Blas Islands do not have storage facilities. When someone on these islands needs a transfusion, the donor and the recipient lie side by side on tables while the transfusion occurs.

A wide variety of medicines are available on an over-the-counter basis in Panama, as are herbal and traditional remedies. Family members may go to the pharmacy and purchase drugs, such as injectable diazepam, and then administer it to a relative or friend in the hospital.

Drug abuse is considered a priority health problem for younger groups and constitutes the leading cause of violence and crime in the country. Alcohol is the drug of choice for the population as a whole. Men are more likely to abuse illicit drugs and women are more likely to abuse less powerful tranquilizers. Cocaine use is on the rise, mainly in the young-adult population.

Infectious Diseases

The Gorgas Memorial Institute of Tropical and Preventive Medicine, founded in 1921, was named after William C. Gorgas, a U.S. Surgeon General known throughout the world as the conqueror of malaria and yellow fever. His pioneering efforts in halting an epidemic of yellow fever enabled the United States to complete the Panama Canal. The institute, which moved in 2002 to the University of Alabama, continues to focus on tropical and preventive medicine. After decades of healthcare and research projects, the hospital is now a specialty oncology hospital financed by Japanese investors.

Because of the Gorgas hospital, much research on infectious disease has been completed in Panama. Despite the progress made in eliminating many tropical and infectious diseases, Panama has recently seen a reemergence of cholera, classical dengue and dengue hemorrhagic fever, malaria, tuberculosis, and Venezuelan equine encephalitis.

Hantavirus pulmonary syndrome (HPS), transmitted by rodents, made its debut in Panama in 1999. HPS is an infectious disease typically characterized by fever, myalgia, and headache, followed by dyspnea, noncardiogenic pulmonary edema, hypotension, and shock. Common laboratory findings include elevated hematocrit, leukocytosis with the presence of immunoblasts, and thrombocytopenia. The case-fatality rate can be as high as 52%. Hantaviruses are most often transmitted to humans through the inhalation of infectious rodent feces, urine, or saliva. However, strain-specific virus transmission may occur from person-to-person contact. HPS was first recognized in 1993 in the Four Corners region of the United States. Since then, 363 cases of HPS have been confirmed in the United States. An outbreak of hantavirus pulmonary syndrome occurred in the province of Los Santos, Panama, in late 1999 and early 2000. Eleven cases were identified, three of which were fatal.

Arthropod-borne Diseases

Arthropod-borne diseases common in Panama include malaria, Chagas disease, dengue fever, leishmaniasis, filariasis, and yellow fever. A brief description of these diseases follows:

- Malaria, an infectious disease characterized by cycles of chills, fever, and sweating, is caused by a protozoan of the genus *Plasmodium* that takes up residence in red blood cells; the pathogen is transmitted to humans by the bite of an infected female anopheles mosquito. The period between the mosquito bite and the onset of malarial illness is usually 1 to 3 weeks. Prevention and treatment are frequently the same: Chloroquine phosphate and primaquine are the most commonly used medications, but other drugs are also used, such as artemether, artesunate, quinidine, doxycycline, mefloquine, and sulfa preparations.

- Chagas disease, also called trypanosomiasis, is caused by the parasite *Trypanosoma cruzi* and is transmitted by reduviid bugs (kissing bugs), which are primarily found in cracks and holes in substandard housing. Infection is spread to humans when an infected bug deposits feces on a person's skin, usually while the person is sleeping. The person may then accidentally rub the feces into the bite wound, in an open cut, the eyes, or mouth. An infected mother can pass infection to her baby during pregnancy, at delivery, or while breastfeeding. Chagas disease is characterized by fever and enlargement of spleen and lymph nodes. Acute symptoms occur only approximately 1% of the time; most people do not seek medical treatment.

- Dengue fever, a tropical disease transmitted by *Aedes aegypti* mosquitoes, is characterized by high fever, rash, headache, and severe muscle and joint pain. The disease usually occurs in 5-year cycles and strikes people who have low levels of immunity. The mosquito flourishes in rainy seasons and can breed year-round in water-filled flowerpots, plastic bags, and cans. The incubation period ranges from 3 to 15 days. Only supportive therapy is available, in the form of treating or preventing dehydration.

- Leishmaniasis, which is caused by a flagellate protozoan, is transmitted to humans by blood-sucking sand flies. The parasites, which can live in animals or in humans, affect white blood cells. The more serious type of infection affects internal organs, causing fever, anemia, splenomegaly, and discoloration of the skin. If left untreated, it can become fatal. Treatment relies on amphotericin B, drugs containing antimony, or the newest drug available, miltefosine, which had a 95% effectiveness in clinical trials in 2003.

- Yellow fever, a tropical disease caused by a bite from the female *Aedes aegypti* and *haemagogus* mosquitoes, is characterized by high fever, jaundice, and gastrointestinal hemorrhaging. In severe cases, prostration and renal failure may occur. Because there is no specific treatment for this infection, vaccination is important. Symptoms appear suddenly after an incubation period of 3 to 5 days.

- Filariasis, also called lymphatic filiariasis or elephantiasis, is caused by threadlike parasitic round worms (nematodes) and their larvae and is transmitted by mosquitoes. Acute episodes of local inflammation involving skin, lymph nodes and lymphatic vessels often accompany the chronic lymphedema or elephantiasis. Some of these symptoms are caused by the body's immune response to the parasite, but most are the result of bacterial infection of skin where normal defenses have been partially lost due to underlying lymphatic damage. In endemic communities, some 10% to 50% of men suffer from genital damage, especially hydrocele, and elephantiasis of the penis and scrotum. Elephantiasis of the entire leg, the entire arm, the vulva, or the breast swelling up to several times normal size affects as many as 10% of men and women with filariasis. The worst symptoms of the chronic disease generally appear in adults, and in men more often than in women. Treatment consists of albendazole and diethylcarbamazine.

The following are recommendations to help prevent arthropod-borne diseases:

■ Wear a long-sleeved shirt and long pants while outside to prevent illnesses carried by insects.
■ Use insect repellent containing DEET (diethylmethyltoluamide) in 30–35% strength for adults and 6–10% strength for children.
■ Use a bed net impregnated with the insecticide permethrin.
■ Properly dispose of household trash.
■ Do not leave water-filled flowerpots with standing water.
■ Eliminate other sources of standing water.

Food-borne and Waterborne Illnesses

Waterborne and food-borne diseases commonly identified in Panama include amoebiasis, brucellosis, cholera, hepatitis A, and typhoid fever. Other diseases include rabies and hepatitis B. Myiasis, a condition caused by a botfly, is endemic in Central America. A brief description of these illnesses follows:

■ Amoebiasis, an infection caused by pathogenic amebas, especially *Entamoeba histolytica,* is usually contracted by ingesting water or food contaminated by amoebic cysts. Symptoms include diarrhea, abdominal pain or discomfort, and fever. Symptoms take from a few days to a few weeks to develop and manifest themselves in approximately 2 to 4 weeks. This pattern is analogous to that seen with cardiovascular disease: It may take 5 years for cardiovascular disease to develop but symptoms do not become evident until many years later. Most infected people are asymptomatic, but amoebiasis has the potential to make the sufferer dangerously ill, especially if the individual is immunocompromised.

■ Brucellosis, a bacterial disease caused by the *Brucella* pathogen, is transmitted by contact with infected animals or through contaminated milk or milk products. The disease is also called undulant fever because of the rising and falling of fevers, sweats, malaise, weakness, anorexia, headache, and muscle and back pain.

■ Cholera, an infectious disease caused by the bacterium *Vibrio cholerae,* is characterized by profuse watery diarrhea, vomiting, muscle cramps, and severe dehydration. Some persons experience a mild version of cholera, with few to no symptoms.

■ Hepatitis A, also called infectious hepatitis, is an infection of the liver caused by an RNA virus that is transmitted by ingesting infected food and water or through contact with infected feces. Symptoms range from flulike symptoms to more severe symptoms such as nausea, poor appetite, abdominal pain, fatigue, jaundice, and dark urine. Recovery can be complete in a few weeks to months. Very few cases progress to death. Treatment is symptomatic, and includes rest and fluids.

■ Typhoid fever, a highly infectious disease caused by *Salmonella typhi,* is transmitted by contaminated food or water and is characterized by fever, headache, coughing, intestinal hemorrhaging, and rose-colored spots on the skin. Treatment includes antibiotics such as ampicillin, chloramphenicol, trimethoprim–sulfamethoxazole, or ciprofloxacin.

■ Myiasis, the condition caused by botfly, is endemic in Central America. It is caused by parasitic dipterous fly larvae feeding on the host's necrotic or living tissue. With this infection, botflies lay their larvae in open wounds. The larvae stage appears as maggots, which then live off the tissue. Treatment entails removing larvae through pressure or the maggots with forceps and then cleaning and disinfecting the wound.

The following are recommendations to prevent food-borne and waterborne illnesses:

■ Vaccinations for hepatitis A or immune globulin (IG)
■ Hepatitis B or immune globulin vaccination
■ Rabies vaccination, if you might be exposed to wild or domestic animals through your work or recreation

- Typhoid vaccination—particularly important because of the presence of *S. typhi* strains resistant to multiple antibiotics in Panama
- A booster for tetanus and diphtheria—if not vaccinated within the last 10 years
- Yellow fever vaccination

Also helpful is this overall general advice for staying healthy:

- Wash your hands often with soap and water.
- Drink only boiled water or water and carbonated (bubbly) drinks in cans.
- Avoid tap water, fountain drinks, and ice cubes.
- Eat only thoroughly cooked food or fruits and vegetables you have peeled yourself.
- Do not eat fruit purchased from street vendors.
- Boil it, cook it, peel it, or forget it.

Other Health Concerns

Other illnesses commonly found in Panama include contact dermatitis caused by pesticides and fungicides; it is observed among banana plantation workers, especially in the western provinces where Chiquita Banana and United Fruit Banana are major employers (Penagos, 2002). Efforts to teach workers how to protect themselves are being made, along with translating written materials into indigenous languages for those for whom Spanish and English are a second language.

In addition, drowning as a result of strong currents and undertows are common throughout Panama. One should always check with local authorities before attempting to swim in coastal areas. The problem is not the surf per se, but rather the unusual undertows from the surf.

TRADITIONAL PRACTITIONERS AND HERBAL MEDICINE

Traditional Practitioners

Panamanians from all socioeconomic levels rely on traditional care providers. Healers include curanderos(as), sobadores(as), espiritistas, brujos(as), masajistas, and (y)jerberos(as). Traditional practitioners, who are usually well known by the family, are often consulted before and during biomedical treatment. Although usually no contradictions or contraindications to traditional remedies arise, healthcare providers must always consider the client's use of these practitioners to prevent prescription of conflicting treatment regimens.

Curanderos receive their talents from God or serve an apprenticeship with an established practitioner. Curanderos are regarded with great respect by the community, accept no monetary payment (but may accept gifts), are usually a member of the extended family, and treat many traditional illnesses. These healers do not usually treat illnesses caused by witchcraft. Currently, curanderos prescribe drugs, a practice that physicians are trying to stop. However, because curanderos can prescribe only over-the-counter medicines, this practice is likely to continue. In Panama, one can purchase a wide variety of antibiotics and other medicines without a prescription.

Yerberos (also spelled jerberos) are folk healers with specialized training in growing herbs, teas, and roots, who prescribe these remedies for the prevention and cure of illnesses. A yerbero may suggest that the person go to a botanica (herb shop) for specific herbs. In addition, these traditional practitioners frequently prescribe the use of laxatives.

Sobadores subscribe to treatment methods similar to those of a chiropractor in the Western medicine tradition. The sobador treats illnesses that primarily affect the joints and musculoskeletal system by using massage and manipulation.

Brujos (witches) treat illnesses and conditions caused by witchcraft. Specific rituals are performed to eliminate the evils from the body.

Espiritistas, or spiritualists, work with clients in terms of their spiritual connections, including religious connections. They do not usually prescribe medications but might prescribe herbal remedies and religious icons.

Herbal Medicine

Multiple studies on herbal remedies have been completed on Mexican and Mexican American patients. However, the only research study found in the literature on herbal medicine of Panamanians was conducted by Purnell (1999). In this study, 61% of Panamanians reported that they regularly used herbs and herbal teas to maintain their health. Moreover, 74% used herbs and teas when they were ill. Many people grow such herbs in their yards. In the home in which this author stays when in Panama, the middle-class family grows a number of herbs. If they have an overabundance of herbs, they are sold to the local pharmacist, who dries and prepares them for sale to the general public. For some of the preparations, leaves are used; for others, the roots are used. **Table 20-1** lists these teas and their uses.

TABLE 20-1

Herbal Teas and Conditions for Use

Herbal Tea	*Conditions for Use*
Aguacate (avocado)	Hypertension, aphrodisiac
Ajo (garlic)	Bronchitis, respiratory conditions, hypertension, anti-inflammatory, infections, lower cholesterol
Canella con aniz (cinnamon)	Toothache, flu, coughs, pain, ulcers
Cebola (onion)	Bronchitis, respiratory conditions, flu
Cipres (cypress)	Whooping cough
Eucalyptus	Colds, coughs, allergies
Ginseng	Aphrodisiac, anemia, heart problems, diabetes, depression, hypertension, ulcers
Guanabano	Diarrhea, vomiting
Guava	Colds, diarrhea
Limon (lemon)	Colds, flu, calms nerves, sleep, headache, stomachache
Llanten (plantain)	Liver problems, stomachache
Malazana (tuberlike yam)	Colic
Manzanilla (chamomile)	Nerves, calms children, antispasmodic, diaphoretic, ulcers, aids digestion
Marano (mangrove)	Inflammation, edema
Mastranto	Colds, headache, stomachache, nerves, stress in children
Naranjo (orange)	Colds, flu, stomachache
Sabila (aloe)	Colds, gives strength, headache
Salvia (sage)	Worms, diabetes, ulcers, stomachache, headache, gives strength, strengthens nerves, stops sweating
Tilo (lime)	Colic, quiets nerves, flu, stomachache, ulcers
Toronjo (grapefruit)	Stomachache
Valleriana	Sleep, sedation, hypertension

STUDY QUESTIONS

1. Identify strategies for integrating allopathic healthcare providers and practices with traditional healthcare practices and providers.
2. How might churches and religious leaders assist healthcare providers in educating communities for health promotion and wellness, as well as illness, disease, and injury prevention?
3. What are some key elements that nurses should include in delivering educational programs to vulnerable populations in Panama with low literacy and with Spanish as a second language?
4. What are some positive and negative influences that the United States has had on the health of Panamanians?
5. What are the underlying cultural beliefs, values, and practices of Panamanians that have helped shape the country's healthcare delivery system?
6. What are the advantages and disadvantages of the Panamanian healthcare delivery system versus the healthcare delivery system of the United States (or another country) in meeting the healthcare needs of the population?

CASE STUDY: CROSS-CULTURAL LEARNING

McDowell Memorial Medical Center and a state university have joined forces to sponsor sending 10 nursing students and 10 nursing staff to Panama for a 2-week cross-cultural learning experience. Students and staff come from maternal–child, pediatric, medical–surgical, community, and psychiatric nursing. All students and staff identify with the dominant American culture. Only one student and two staff nurses have traveled outside the United States; their travel experiences were in Rio de Janeiro, Brazil; Ontario, Canada; and London, England. Three of the participants have limited experience with the Spanish language from high school; the remainder know only a few expressions in Spanish.

Brenda Polek, a nurse manager from the Medical Center, and Alan Hardy, a faculty member from the university, will accompany the group. Both feel they have a "fair" understanding of the Spanish language. The main reason for students to participate in this experience is to complete an elective course on international nursing. Multidisciplinary staff nurses are participating in the trip to specifically learn about the Panamanian culture because the medical center has increasing numbers of Panamanians on maternal–child, pediatric, and medical–surgical inpatient units and outpatient departments. All students and staff will be housed with Panamanian families throughout their travels.

All students in this cultural immersion experience will be able to attend classes in the nursing programs while in Panama. When in the clinical areas, staff and students will be accompanied with staff nurses in outpatient clinics and on inpatient units. Not all students and staff will get the same clinical rotations. They will be in formal learning experiences 4 days each week and have 3 days each week for traveling and sightseeing. Journaling, in which students and staff record their observations and experiences, will be a large part of this program.

Brenda Polek and Alan Hardy, in conjunction with faculty and staff in Panama, will arrange housing and clinical experiences; some of them will be with indigenous Indian groups. The students and staff nurses will plan any other details before they leave for Panama.

(continues)

CASE STUDY: CROSS-CULTURAL LEARNING (Continued)

Case Study Questions

1. How would you feel about staying with a family in Panama if you do not speak the Spanish language well?
2. How might you prepare to improve your Spanish language skills before you depart from home?
3. What are the passport and visa requirements for traveling to Panama? (These requirements will change depending on your country of origin.)
4. Which vaccinations or medications will you take before you leave home? Where will you go to find out what is currently recommended for traveling to Panama?
5. What do you need to know about verbal communication practices of Panamanians so as not to violate social taboos?
6. What do you need to know about nonverbal communication practices of Panamanians so as not to violate social taboos?
7. How might you go about visiting a traditional healer while in Panama?
8. A few Panamanians, especially the younger generation, are anti-American because of U.S. influence in the Canal Zone, the environmental concerns left by the military in the Canal Zone, and the Manuel Noriega experience. How might you handle negative comments from Panamanian students about Americans?
9. What do you need to know about arthropod-borne diseases and food-borne and waterborne illnesses you may encounter on your trip?
10. Make a list of at least 10 strategies to maintain your health, your personal safety, and the safety of your group while traveling in Panama.

CASE STUDY: PANAMANIAN CHALLENGES TO CARE

Leticia Maria de Isaacs Blancas y Chamorro, age 35, is married with four children, ages 15, 12, 10, and 6. Her husband, Omedo, works on a banana plantation distant from their small orange and banana farm in rural Panama; he makes it home only every other weekend. Leticia has been overweight since the birth of their first child and has never seen it as a problem. Approximately 3 months ago, she began losing weight, even though she was eating her usual diet and drinking a lot of carbonated beverages. She also has a rash on her arms and legs for which she has been using a poultice made from eucalyptus that helps the itching but does not clear up the rash.

Because going to the bathroom several times during the night was interfering with her sleep, Leticia sought advice from her mother. Her mother suggested a trip to the local botanica for herbs that a cousin used several years ago for the same condition. After trying the herbs for 2 weeks without improvement, she sought advice from a local curandera, who recommended guanabano and ginseng because Leticia was also having frequent bowel movements that she attributed to parasites. The curandera also recommended an antibiotic that did not require a prescription. Leticia obtained the antibiotic from the *farmacia* (pharmacist) and took it for 5 days, with no apparent improvement. In fact, her diarrhea and thirst worsened.

Leticia left her children with her younger sister and mother and took a bus 42 miles to a city with a physician. The physician wanted to admit Leticia to the hospital for a few days for a more complete health workup for diabetes mellitus. However, Leticia refused, saying that she needed to return home to her children. The physician reluctantly gave her an

CASE STUDY: PANAMANIAN CHALLENGES TO CARE *(Continued)*

oral hypoglycemic prescription and an instruction for a weight-reduction diabetic diet and encouraged her to return in one week. Leticia agreed to return if her husband came home that weekend with money so she could afford a second bus trip to the city. She also stated that if she could not return the following week, the curandera, whom she has know since she was an infant, would help her.

You are a public health nurse (health worker) who lives in the same town as Leticia and have heard of her health problems being discussed at local stores. You plan to make a visit to Leticia and offer advice if she will see you.

Case Study Questions

1. Leticia has a rather long name. What is her married name? What is the family name of her father? What is the family name of her mother?
2. What might you do to build a trusting relationship with Leticia before giving her health advice?
3. Which advantages might there be in visiting Leticia in her home?
4. Which disadvantages might there be in visiting Leticia in her home?
5. What do you think has caused the rashes on Leticia's arms and legs?
6. Would you encourage or discourage Leticia from using eucalyptus on the rashes?
7. Would you encourage her to take antibiotic and herbal medicine recommended by the curandera along with the hypoglycemic prescription?
8. What do you think might happen if you advised Leticia to refrain from taking the antibiotic and herbal medicine recommended by the curandera along with the hypoglycemic prescription?
9. How might you help Leticia integrate the care recommended by the physician and curandera?
10. Would you discourage Leticia from seeing the curandera completely?
11. Leticia tells you that she does not want to lose any more weight because her husband likes her being "stout." She eats a "traditional" Panamanian diet, which is high in fat but replete with fresh fruits and vegetables. Which dietary recommendations would you make to negotiate an acceptable weight and still maintain control of her diabetes?
12. If Leticia agrees to be admitted to a hospital for treatment, would she be admitted to a Social Security hospital or a Ministry of Health hospital?

REFERENCES

American Society of Tropical Medicine and Hygiene: The Gorges Memorial Institute. Retrieved from http://www.astmh.org/Gorgas_Memorial_Institute_Research_Award.htm

Business Panama. (2009). Panama at a glance. Retrieved from http://www.businesspanama.com/about_panama/glance.php

Central Intelligence Agency (CIA). (2010). World factbook: Panama country profile. Retrieved from https://www.cia.gov/library/publications/the-world-factbook/geos/pm.html

City of Panama. (2009). Information technology in Panama. Retrieved from http://www.e-panama.gob.pa/foro/forum_program.htm

El Ciudad del Saber. (2009). [The city of knowledge]. Retrieved from http://www.ciudaddelsaber.org/

Finding aid to the Gorgas Memorial Institute of Tropical and Preventive Medicine records. (1899–1992). Retrieved from http://oculus.nlm.nih.gov/cgi/f/findaid/findaid-idx?c=nlmfindaid;cc=nlmfindaid;view=text;rgn=main;didno=gorgas212

GlobalSecurity.Org. (2010). Fort Sherman. Retrieved from http://www.globalsecurity.org/military/facility /fort-sherman.htm

Hospital Punta Pacifica: Panama. (2010). Retrieved from http://www.hospitalpuntapacifica.com/

Hurtado, E. (1989). Breastfeeding in the etiology of diarrhea. *Archives of Latin American Nutrition, 39*(3), 278–291.

Library of Congress. (2004). Panama. Education. Retrieved from http://countrystudies.us/panama/39.htm

Meditz, S., & Hanratty, D. (1987). Panama: A country study. Retrieved from http://countrystudies.us/panama

Moises, L. (2003). Perceptions of health care quality in Central America. *International Journal for Quality in Health Care, 15*, 67–71.

Moreno, P., Saravanan, Y., Kohn, R., & Miranda, C. T. (2003). Evaluation of the PAHO/WHO training program on the detection and treatment of depression for primary care nurses in Panama. *Acta Psychiatrica Scandinavica, 108*(1), 61.

Native American tribes of Panama. (2009). Retrieved from http://www.native-languages.org/panama.htm

Outbreak of hantavirus pulmonary syndrome, Los Santos, Panama, 1999–2000. (2000, March). *Mortality and Morbidity Weekly Review, 17*(49), 205–207.

Panama. (2010). Pictures of Panama. Retrieved from http://www.info-panama.com/panama-gallery /index.php?lang=english

Panama Canal Authority. (2006). Welcome to the Panama Canal. Retrieved from http://www.pancanal .com/eng/index.html

Panama: Major infectious diseases. (2010). *Index Mundi.* Retrieved from http://www.indexmundi.com /panama/major_infectious_diseases.html

Pan-American Health Organization (PAHO). (2004). *Profile of the health services system of Panama.* Washington, DC: Author.

Pan-American Health Organization (PAHO). (2005). Information on health: Panama. Retrieved from http://www.paho.org/English/D/P39.pdf

Partners of the Americas. (2010). Retrieved from http://www.partners.net/partners/default.asp

Penagos, H. G. (2002). Contact dermatitis caused by pesticides among banana plantation workers in Panama. *International Journal of Occupational and Environmental Health, 8*(1), 14–18.

Purnell, L. (1999). Panamanian health beliefs and the meaning of respect afforded them by healthcare providers. *Journal of Transcultural Nursing, 14*(4), 331–340.

Sandiford, P., & Salvetto, M. (2002). Health inequities in Panama. *Gaceta Sanitaria, 16*(1), 70–81.

Universidad de Latina: Panama. (2010). Retrieved from http://www.medical-colleges.net/college/panama.htm

University of Panama. (2010). Retrieved from http://www.up.ac.pa

University of South Florida, Office of International Programs. (2010). Retrieved from http://health.usf .edu/intprog/panama/About_the_International_Foundation.htm

Warren, C. W., Monteith, R. S., Johnson, J. T., Santiso, E., Guerra, F., & Oberle, M. W. (1987). Use of maternal–child health services and contraception in Guatemala and Panama. *Journal of Biosocial Sciences, 19*(2), 229–243.

Where to get quality health care in Panama. (2009). Retrieved from http://www.costaricapages.com /panama/blog/where-to-get-quality-health-care-in-panama-city-panama-674

World Bank. (2010). Panama at a glance. Retrieved from http://web.worldbank.org/wbsite/external/countries /lacext/panamaextn/0,,menuPK:343567~pagePK:141159~piPK:141110~theSitePK:343561,00.html

World Health Organization (WHO). (2007). Country cooperation strategy: Panama. Retrieved from http://www.who.int/countryfocus.

*For a full suite of assignments and additional learning activities, use the access code located in the front of your book to visit this exclusive website: **http://go.jblearning.com/holtz**. If you do not have an access code, you can obtain one at the site.*

21

Health and Health Care in Mexico

Rick Zoucha

> *"An unprecedented collaboration between the federal and local governments created hundreds of mobile health units that deliver a basic health care package including: basic sanitation, diarrhea control, family planning, prevention and treatment of parasitic diseases, health and nutrition information, immunizations, child delivery, and prevention and control of tuberculosis and cervical cancer. Thanks to the five-year old program, basic public health services were extended to 8.2 million people, mostly in small communities, who previously had no access to basic health care."*
>
> The World Bank, 2002

OBJECTIVES

After completing this chapter the reader will be able to:

1. Relate a brief history of Mexico.
2. Discuss major health issues of the people of Mexico.
3. Compare and contrast the backgrounds and cultures of the people of Mexico.
4. Compare and contrast the Mexican healthcare system, including health facilities, to those of other developing nations.

INTRODUCTION

This chapter addresses health and health care in Mexico. The information presented here will be beneficial to healthcare professionals who may be interested in caring for people in Mexico, or those who may be caring for people who are either temporary residents of other countries or migrants from Mexico who cross between countries frequently. Appreciation of the health and health system in Mexico can provide a clearer understanding of the context for health, illness, and care for people from Mexico. Specific information is presented about the history of Mexico, along with a description of the country's people, including their cultural values and beliefs. Additional information about the health of the people in Mexico as well as the health system (professional and folk) and workforce is provided as well.

KEY TERMS AND DEFINITIONS

Padrino: godparent for sacraments (baptism, confirmation, communion and marriage) in the Catholic Church.

Compadres: joint father/mother, godfather/godmother, friend.

Quinceañera: the celebration of a girl's fifteenth birthday. This birthday is celebrated differently from any other birthday, as it marks the transition from childhood to young womanhood.

Damas: young women who serve as attendants for the girl celebrating her *quinceañera*.

Chambelanes: young men who serve as escorts for the attendants at the *quinceañera* celebration.

Seguro Popular: providers in Mexico offering healthcare services to the uninsured.

MEXICO AND ITS PEOPLE

Mexico is a country located on the North American continent, situated south of the United States and northwest of Guatemala. The land area occupied by Mexico is approximately 1,964,375 km^2 (761,600 mi^2), or roughly three times the size of Texas. The topography of the country includes coastal lowlands, mountains, and central-high plateaus, which have climates ranging from tropical to desert (U.S. Department of State, 2011).

The official name of the country is United Mexican States. Contemporary Mexico consists of 31 states and one federal district. Its capital, Mexico City, is located in the Federal district. The type of government is a federal republic comprising three branches: executive (the president is the chief of state and head of government), legislative (Senate and a Chamber of Deputies), and judicial (federal and state court systems). Several major political parties operate in Mexico, including the Institutional Revolutionary Party (PRI), National Action Party (PAN), Party of the Democratic Revolution (PRD), Green Ecological Party (PVEM), Labor Party (PT), and several small parties (U.S. Department of State, 2011).

Brief History of Mexico

The history and people of Mexico have been intertwined with the country's rich and diverse landscape dating back centuries before the Spanish conquest of Mexico in 1519. Prior to the Europeans' arrival, the land now known as Mexico was inhabited by several highly developed and organized cultures such as the Mayas, Toltecs, Aztecs, and Olmecs. After the conquest and in many cases the destruction of the people and their cultures, Spain established a colony that spanned three centuries.

On September 16, 1810, independence was declared through the efforts of Father Migel Hidalgo, who is known as the "Father of Mexican Independence." The struggle for independence lasted more than 10 years, until 1821. A treaty finally recognized the country's independence from Spain with the planned establishment of a constitutional monarchy. The attempt to proceed with this plan failed, however, and in 1822 a republic was proclaimed; it was firmly established in 1824.

The political context of Mexico was again challenged in 1862, when French forces invaded Mexico. The French invaders instituted a monarchy, with Hapsburg Archduke Ferdinand Maximilian of Austria serving as emperor of Mexico from 1864 to 1867. His reign came to an end in 1867 when liberal forces in Mexico overthrew and executed the emperor. Mexico then remained independent from foreign rule until the revolution of 1910. Severe social and economic problems led to a 10-year revolution and establishment of the new constitution in 1917. The new constitution set the stage for the present federal republic with three separate forms of power structure—executive, legislative, and judicial branches of the government (U. S. Department of State, 2011).

During the Mexican Revolution of the early twentieth century, many Mexicans left Mexico for its northern neighbor, the United States, to seek political, religious, and economic freedoms (Casa Historia, 2011). Following the Mexican Revolution, strict limits were placed on the activities of the Catholic Church, such that until recently clerics were not allowed to wear their church garb in public. For many residents, such rules restricted the expression of their faith and represented a minor factor in their immigration north to the United States (Meyer & Beezley, 2000). In the years since the "Great Migration," limited employment opportunities in Mexico, especially in rural areas, have encouraged Mexicans to migrate to the United States as immigrants or with undocumented status; the latter are often derogatorily referred to as *wetbacks* (*majodos*) by the white and Mexican American populations.

The People

The population of Mexico is estimated to number 133,724,226 (Central Intelligence Agency [CIA], 2011). The ethnic makeup of the people of Mexico includes Indian Spanish (mestizo), who represent 60% of the total population; Indian (Native American), 30%; Caucasian, 9%; and other, 1% (Census, 2000). The blend of Spanish white, Native American, Middle Eastern, and African heritage can be traced to descendants of Spanish and other European whites; Aztec, Mayan, and other Central American Indians; Inca and other South American Indians; and people from Africa (Schmal, 2007). Lesser-known ethnic groups whose members have historically immigrated to Mexico include Chinese and Jewish populations. Traditions and values of these cultures can still be seen in contemporary Mexico in music, food, and celebrations (Schmal, 2007).

Religion and Faith

The predominant religion in Mexico is Catholicism. The major religions in Mexico are Roman Catholic, 76.5%; Protestant, 6.3%; unspecified, 13.8%; and identified with no religion, 3.1% (Census, 2000). Since the mid-1980s, religious groups such as Mormons, Jehovah's Witnesses, Seventh Day Adventists, Presbyterians, and Baptists have been gaining in popularity in Mexico (CIA, 2011). Although many Mexicans may not appear to be practicing their faith on a daily basis, they may still consider themselves devout Catholics, and their religion has a major influence on daily living and beliefs. It is common to see religious symbols on public buses and taxis as well as in public squares.

Migration to Urban Areas

Historically, there has been consistent migration from the rural areas of Mexico to the urban areas due to lack of jobs and opportunities in underdeveloped sections of the country. It is estimated that 76% of the Mexican population resides in urban areas of the country. The population of Mexico City alone is estimated to exceed 22 million people, with sharp increases in population also occurring in other cities such as Guadalajara, Puebla, and Monterrey (U.S. Department of State, 2011).

Communication

Mexico is considered the most populous Spanish-speaking country in the world, with more than 80 million residents who speak the language. Although the dominant language of Mexicans is Spanish, the country also has 54 indigenous languages and more than 500 different dialects (Lewis, 2009). For example, major indigenous languages include Nahuatl and Otami, spoken in central Mexico; Mayan, in the Yucatan peninsula; Maya-Quiche, in the state of Chiapas; Zapotec and Mixtec, in the valley of Oaxaca; Tarascan, in the state of Michoacan; and Totonaco, in the state of Veracruz. Many of the Spanish dialects spoken by Mexicans have similar word meanings, but the dialects of Spanish spoken by other groups may not have the same meanings. Because of the rural nature of many ethnic groups and the influence of native indigenous languages, the dialects are so diverse in some regions that it may be difficult to understand the language, regardless of the degree of fluency in Spanish ("Language: About Spanish," 2007).

Education

The mean educational level in Mexico is five years. Until 1992, Mexican children were required to attend school through the sixth grade, but since the Mexican School Reform Act of 1992, a ninth-grade education has been required. In recent years, great strides have been made in improving educational standards in Mexico, which now reports an 86.1% literacy rate among its population (CIA, 2011). A common practice among parents in poor rural villages is to educate their children in what they need to know related to the immediate context of their lives. People from rural areas often find immigration to the United States to be a good option for both the individual and the family in terms of obtaining education. For many Mexicans, high school and a university education are unavailable and, in many cases, unattainable (Zoucha & Zamarripa, 2008).

Economy

The economy of Mexico is considered a free market economy in the trillion-dollar class. It is based on a mixture of modern and outmoded industry and agriculture, which is becoming more dominated by the private sector. In recent years, there has been an expansion of competition in seaports, railroads, telecommunications, electricity generation, natural gas distribution, and airports. Overall, per capita income is roughly one-third of that found in the United States, and overall income distribution remains highly unequal. Since the advent and implementation of the North American Free Trade Agreement (NAFTA) in 1994, Mexico's share of U.S. imports has increased from 7% to 12%, and its share of Canadian imports has doubled to 5% (U.S. Department of State, 2011).

Mexico is rich in natural resources such as petroleum, silver, copper, gold, lead, zinc, natural gas, and timber. Agriculture accounts for 5% of the country's gross domestic product (GDP), including such products as corn, wheat, soybeans, rice, beans, cotton, coffee, fruit, tomatoes, beef, poultry, dairy products, and wood products. Approximately 31% of the country's GDP is attributable to industrial production, including manufacture of such items as food and beverages, tobacco, chemicals, iron and steel, petroleum, mining, textiles, clothing, motor vehicles, and consumer durables. Services such as commerce and tourism, financial services, transportation, and communications provide 64% of the GDP (U.S. Department of State, 2011).

Family and Kinship

Historically and in contemporary society, family is an all-encompassing value among Mexicans, for whom the traditional family remains the foundation of the culture. Family takes precedence over work and all other aspects of life. In many Mexican families, it is often said, "God first, family, then self." The family is of foremost importance to most Mexicans, and individuals get strength from family ties and relationships. Individuals may speak in terms of a person's soul or spirit (*alma or espiritu*) when they refer to his or her inner qualities. These inner qualities represent the person's dignity and must be protected at all costs in times of both wellness and illness. In addition, Mexicans derive great pride and strength from their nationality, which embraces a long and rich history of traditions (Zoucha & Zamarripa, 2008).

In the Mexican culture, the concept of family moves beyond the nuclear family to incorporate a system of kinship that connects people as family without blood ties. In the Catholic faith, it is common to have godparents for an infant at baptism. Members of the Mexican culture may invite friends and or family to be godparents for other sacraments in the faith in addition to baptism, including *padrinos* for communion, confirmation, and marriage. When individuals are asked to be *padrinos,* then they become *compadres* or family. It is a great honor and responsibility to be invited to be a *padrino* in the Mexican culture (C. Zamarripa, personal communication, 2012).

Other important events in which people are invited to be a *padrino* include the *quinceañera*—a very special event in which the 15-year-old girl is presented as a young woman. The *quinceañera* celebration begins with a thanksgiving mass, which is followed by a dinner and dance. These events symbolically represent the movement from childhood to young adulthood. The *quinceañera* is a family and community celebration in which the young woman, wearing a ball gown, is presented at church by her parents and *padrinos* and accompanied by a court of honor. The young women in the court, called *damas,* are accompanied by young men called *chambelanes* (C. Zamarripa, personal communication, 2012).

Because family is the first priority for most Mexicans, activities that involve family members usually take priority over work and other issues. Putting up a tough business front may be seen as a weakness in the Mexican culture. Most Mexicans tend to shun confrontation for fear of losing face. Many are very sensitive to differences of opinion, which are perceived as disrupting harmony in the workplace. Mexicans find it important to keep peace in relationships in the workplace and family (Zoucha & Zamarripa, 2008).

For many Mexicans, truth is tempered by diplomacy and tact. When a service is promised for tomorrow, even when they know the service will not be completed tomorrow, the promise is intended to please, not to deceive. Thus, for many Mexicans, truth is seen as a relative concept. These conflicting perspectives about truth can complicate communication with non-Mexicans (Zoucha & Zamarripa, 2008).

For most Mexicans, work is viewed as a necessity for survival and may not be highly valued in itself, whereas money is for enjoying life. Many Mexicans place a higher value on other life activities. Material objects are usually necessities, rather than not ends in themselves. The concept of responsibility is based on values related to attending to the immediate needs of family and friends rather than on the work ethic. For most Mexicans, titles and positions may be more important than money (Zoucha & Zamarripa, 2008).

Many Mexicans believe that time is relative and fluid, so they set flexible deadlines, rather than stressing punctuality. In Mexico, shop hours may be posted but not rigidly respected. A business that is supposed to open at 8:00 A.M. may open when the owner arrives; a posted time of 8:30 A.M. may mean the business will open at 9:00 A.M., later, or not at all. The same attitude toward time is evidenced in reporting to work and in keeping social engagements and medical appointments. In some cases, if people believe that an exact time is truly important, such as the time a bus leaves, then they may keep to a schedule (Zoucha & Zamarripa, 2008).

Foods and Celebration

Mexicans often celebrate with food. Mexican foods are rich in color, flavor, texture, and spiciness depending on the state and region of the country. Any occasion—including births, birthdays, Sundays, religious holidays, official and unofficial holidays, and anniversaries of deaths—is seen as a time to celebrate with food and enjoy the togetherness of family and friends. Because food is a primary form of socialization in the Mexican culture, many Mexicans, from a health perspective, have difficulty adhering to a prescribed diet for illnesses such as diabetes mellitus and cardiovascular disease (Zoucha & Zamarripa, 2008).

The Mexican diet is varied, and its content may depend on the specific region in Mexico. The staples of the Mexican American diet are rice (*arroz*), beans, and tortillas, which are made from corn (*maíz*) treated with calcium carbonate. Popular Mexican American foods are eggs (*huevos*), pork (*puerco*), chicken (*pollo*), sausage (*chorizo*), lard (*lardo*), mint (*menta*), chili peppers (*chile*), onions (*cebollas*), tomatoes (*tomates*), squash (*calabaza*), canned fruit (*fruta de lata*), mint tea (*hierbabuena*), chamomile tea (*té de camomile* or *manzanilla*), carbonated beverages (*bebidas de gaseosa*), beer (*cerveza*), cola-flavored soft drinks, sweetened packaged drink mixes (*agua fresa*) that are high in sugar (*azucar*), sweetened breakfast cereals (*cereales de desayuno*), potatoes (*papas*), bread (*pan*), corn (*maíz*), gelatin (*gelatina*), custard (*flan*), and other sweets (*dulces*). Other commonly eaten dishes include chili, enchiladas, tamales, tostadas, chicken mole, arroz con pollo, refried beans, tacos, tripe soup (*menudo*), and other soups (*caldos*). Soups are varied in nature and may include chicken, beef, and pork with vegetables (Zoucha & Zamarripa, 2008).

Alcohol plays an important part in the Mexican culture, and many celebrations include alcohol consumption. Men overall may drink in greater proportion than women, but this trend is changing. Today, Mexican women are consuming more alcohol than their mothers or grandmothers (S. Bunting, personal communication, 2011). Because of these drinking patterns, alcoholism represents a crucial health problem for many Mexicans.

Health of the People

Many variables, ranging from violence to air pollution, affect the health and well-being of the people of Mexico. The life expectancy at birth is 74 years (*World Health Statistics,* 2008). In recent years, certain regions of Mexico have been plagued by extreme incidents of violence and death as the result of drug wars. The areas affected most are the northern states of Chihuahua, Coahuila, Nuevo Leon, and Tamaulipas, with recent spikes occurring in the Gulf state of Veracruz. According to a *Washington Post* report, 11,890 drug-related deaths were reported in Mexico in 2011 and a total of more than 50,000 drug-related deaths have been reported since 2006 (Booth, 2012).

In addition to violence related to drugs wars, a large number of people in Mexico are killed in road accidents. According to the Ministry of Health, 17,062 people were killed as a result of road traffic crashes in 2008 and a further 603,541 were injured. Most of those injured or killed on Mexico's roads are between the ages of 15 and 29 years—this group makes up 48% of the total population. Road traffic crashes are the leading cause of death for the group aged 10–29 years (World Health Organization [WHO], 2010). **Table 21-1** is a list of leading health issues in Mexico, including the ages, causes of mortality and mortality rates.

In addition to the list of health concerns previously mentioned, there are major problems regarding the health of Mexicans owing to the consistent increase in HIV/AIDS cases in Mexico. The estimated number of adults and children (ages 15 and older) living with HIV/AIDS rose from a range of 170,000 to 250,000 in 2001 to a range of 200,000 to 300,000 in 2007 (WHO & UNAIDS, 2008). However, the rate of increase in HIV/AIDS in Mexico is relatively low in comparison to other countries in Central America and the United States. In the past, the Mexican government acted quickly and formed an effective response to the epidemic through the creation of CONAIDA, a national AIDS council. In addition, the council created an effective surveillance system to track the spread of the virus. A series of interventions decreased the spread of the virus, including bans on private blood clinics, mandatory testing of

| TABLE 21-1 | | | |

Specific Health Problems in Mexico: Analysis by Population Group

Age	Mortality Rate	Leading Causes	Other Health Problems
0–4 years	15 per 1,000 live births (lb)	Conditions originating from the perinatal period Congenital malformations Infections from influenza and pneumonia	
5–14 years	34 per 100,000	Accidents (11 per 100,000) Malignant tumors (5 per 100,000) Congenital malformations (2 per 100,000)	
15–24 years		Accidents (31 per 100,000) Homicide (14 per 100,000) Malignant neoplasms (6 per 100,000) Intentional self-harm (6 per 100,000)	Male versus female mortality rates by gender: Males: 135 per 1,000 Females: 75 per 1,000 (all ages) Fertility rate: 70 per 1,000 women (aged 15–44)
20–59 years	283 per 100,000	Malignant neoplasms (40 per 100,000) Accidents (39 per 100,000) Diabetes mellitus (31 per 100,000) Heart diseases (29 per 100,000)	Hospitalizations related to: • Pregnancy, childbirth, and the puerperium (67%) • Disorders of the digestive system (6%) • Trauma from accidents (6%)
60 years and older	4,763 per 100,000	Heart disease (1106 per 100,000) Ischemic heart disease (706 per 100,000) Malignant neoplasms (612 per 100,000): • Trachea, bronchia, and lung (91 per 100,000) • Prostate (72 per 100,000) • Stomach (63 per 100,000) Diabetes mellitus (584 per 100,000) Cerebrovascular diseases (417 per 100,000)	

Source: Adapted from PAHO, 2010.

blood donations, and regulation of sex workers across the country. The AIDS council also promoted education on the use of condoms across Mexico as prevention for HIV/AIDS (Smallman, 2007). The threat of HIV/AIDS continues to be of great concern for Mexican health, however, and efforts aimed at decreasing the spread of the virus continue.

THE MEXICAN HEALTHCARE SYSTEM

The modern Mexican health system traces its origins to 1943, with the creation of three significant institutions: the Ministry of Health (MoH), the Mexican Institute for Social Security (IMSS), and Mexico's Children Hospital. These institutions were established to provide care to a variety of people. For example, the IMSS cared for the industrial workforce and the Ministry of Health was concerned with care for the urban and rural poor (Gomez-Dantes, 2010).

Between the inception of the Mexican health system in the 1940s and the 1980s, many changes occurred to bring about healthcare reform in Mexico. Because health care was delivered primarily in hospitals, its cost increased dramatically over the years. In addition, incidence of common infections and illness showed a sharp decline, while incidence of noncommunicable diseases and overall injuries showed dramatic increases.

In the mid-1980s, healthcare reform was launched to promote more efficiency in the system and decentralization of health services for the uninsured. The government built health centers and district hospitals to better serve the population. By the 1990s, however, at least half of the population was paying for health care out of pocket and lacked health insurance. The recognition of this problem prompted the Mexican legislature to enact reforms in 2003 that established the Social Protection in Health program (Gomez-Dantes, 2010). As a result of these historical struggles and evolution, Mexico's current health system includes care delivered by both the public and private sectors. The public sector encompasses the social security systems of: Instituto de Seguridad y Servicios Sociales de los Trabajadores del Estado (IMSS), which is a state health insurance system for workers of social service, the Mexican State Institute for Social Security Services (ISSTE), Petroleos Mexicanos (PEMEX), the social security institution for oil workers, Secretaría de la Defensa Nacional (Sedena), the insurance for people in the army armed services, SEDENA, Mexican Navy employees' insurance, SEMAR, and Seguro Popular, the healthcare services to the uninsured population in Mexico. The last institution includes services provided by the Ministry of Health, State Health Services (SESA), and IMSS–Oportunidades Program (Jaff, 2010).

The social security institutions are financed with contributions from employees, employers, and the government. The Ministry of Health and SESA are financed by the federal and state government as well as through a small fee charged to users when receiving care. The IMSS–Oportunidades Program is financed by the federal government and administered by the IMSS. Federal and state funding and family contributions fund the Seguro Popular, although families at the bottom 20% of the income levels are exempt from this contribution (Gomez-Dantes, 2010).

The private sector of the health system in Mexico includes hospitals, health centers, clinics, and health providers such as physicians and nurses who provide services mostly on a for-profit basis. Such services are financed mostly with out-of-pocket payments, with a small allocation coming from people who pay for private insurance (Gomez-Dantes, 2010).

Healthcare Facilities

The Mexican healthcare system consists of a total of 23,269 facilities. The majority of facilities comprise ambulatory clinics and 4103 hospitals. Of the total number of hospitals, 1121 are public; 628 are social security institutions and the remainder care for people who lack social security. Private hospitals in Mexico account for 3082 of the total number of hospitals in the system. In Mexico overall, there are 1.1 hospitals per 100,000 population. This ratio varies regionally, however. For example, Baja California has 3.2 hospitals per 100,000 population, whereas there is only 0.5 hospital per 100,000 population in the state of Mexico (Secretaria de Salud, 2007).

On a per capita basis, the healthcare workforce in Mexico is below the average of many South American countries. It is estimated that there were 1.8 doctors per 1000 population and 2.2 nurses per 1000 population in Mexico in 2005, although these ratios are expected to increase over the next 10 years. At the present time Mexico has a total of 82 medical schools and 593 nursing schools (Gomez-Dantes, 2010). There has been a movement in Mexico over the last 20 years to educate nurses in university-based settings and to increase the level of education for Mexican nurses. In the last 10 years, Mexico opened the first PhD program in nursing to promote education and research at an advanced level (Becerril Cardenas, Gandara Sanchez, Mejia Carmona, & Gomez Arana, 2009).

Mexican Folk Practices

In addition to following Western systems of health, many people in Mexico engage in folk medicine practices and use a variety of prayers, herbal teas, and poultices to promote health and treat illnesses. The folk beliefs and practices noted in Mexico vary according to the region of the country, as well as between and among families.

One such folk belief and practice focuses on the hot and cold theory, which suggests that many diseases and illness are caused by a disruption in the hot-and-cold balance of the body. The belief is that eating foods that have the opposite effect (i.e., if cold, eat hot food; if hot, eat cold food) may either cure or prevent specific hot-and-cold illnesses. Likewise, physical or mental illness may be perceived as being due to an imbalance between the person and the environment.

Cold diseases may be characterized by lower metabolic rate and may include menstrual cramps, *frio de la matriz*, rhinitis (*coryza*), pneumonia, *empacho*, cancer, malaria, earaches, arthritis, pneumonia and other pulmonary conditions, headaches, and musculoskeletal conditions and colic. Common hot foods used to treat cold diseases and conditions include cheeses, liquor, beef, pork, spicy foods, eggs, grains other than barley, vitamins, tobacco, and onions (Neff, 2011).

Hot diseases may be characterized by vasodilation and a higher metabolic rate and may include pregnancy, hypertension, diabetes, acid indigestion, *susto*, *mal de ojo* (bad eye or evil eye), *bilis* (imbalance of bile, which runs into the bloodstream), infection, diarrhea, sore throat, stomach ulcers, liver conditions, kidney problems, and fever. Cold foods used to treat hot diseases may include fresh fruits and vegetables, dairy products, barley water, fish, chicken, goat meat, and dried fruits (Neff, 2011).

A variety of folk healers are incorporated within Mexican culture, including *curanderos* (believed to be empowered by God), *yerberos* (herbalists), and *parteras* (lay midwives). At times families may consult a folk healer to cure illness or promote health. Folk healers in Mexico may also be called to treat a variety of illnesses commonly found in the culture—that is, culture-bound disorders (Holtz, 2008). For example, the ailment known as *mal de ojo* may occur when one person looks at another in an admiring fashion; its result may be fever, anorexia, and vomiting to irritability. This evil spell can be broken if the person doing the admiring touches the person admired while it is happening. Children seem to be more susceptible to this condition than women, and women are more susceptible than men. To prevent *mal de ojo*, the child may wear a bracelet with a seed (*ojo de venado*) or a bag of seeds pinned to the clothes (Kemp, 2001).

Susto (soul loss) is associated with epilepsy, tuberculosis, and other infectious diseases and is believed to be caused by a fright or by the soul being frightened out of the person. This culture-bound disorder may be psychological, physical, or physiological in nature. Symptoms can include anxiety, depression, loss of appetite, excessive sleep, bad dreams, feelings of sadness, and lack of motivation. Treatment some-times includes elaborate ceremonies at a crossroads with herbs and holy water to return the spirit to the body (R. Zamarripa, personal communication, April 2011).

Empacho (blocked intestines) is an illness that may be caused by a lump of food that sticks to the gastrointestinal tract. The healer may place a fresh egg on the abdomen to assess the problem. If the egg appears to stick to a particular area, this finding confirms the diagnosis. The folk healer treats the illness by administering herbal teas and by massaging the abdomen and back to dislodge the food and promote its passage through the body (Zoucha & Zamarripa, 2008).

Many other folk beliefs and practices contribute to the health and well-being of the people of Mexico. In some cases, specific folk healers are called upon to perform healing rituals, provide herbal medicines, and treat a variety of illness as well as promote health. In many communities, certain family members and neighbors are viewed as knowledgeable about healing and may perform the folk care locally.

CONCLUSION

Mexico is a country with a long and rich history dating back centuries. Its population comprises a mix-ture of many cultures including indigenous people with cultural roots connected to the Mayas, Toltecs, Aztecs, Olmecs, Spanish, French, and Africans, to name a few sources. The historical roots of these rich cultures come together to form the contemporary Mexican culture and people. Mexico is a rapidly devel-oping country with a fairly stable economy, whose growth is linked to both industry and petroleum.

The health of the Mexican people is in constant flux due to economic changes and ongoing violence in some parts of the country. Drug-related violence and homicides related to "turf wars" have resulted in record increases in the overall rate of violence and murder in Mexico. The potential for violence and actual violence has affected the health and well-being of the Mexican people. In addition, the incidence of HIV/AIDS in Mexico continues to increase, despite early efforts to monitor and control the spread of the virus.

The health system in Mexico has undergone several reforms since the 1940s, as the Mexican gov-ernment has sought to provide health care to all its citizens. Most Mexican citizens are provided with health care through several institutions run by the state and federal governments as well as by private insurance and institutions. Regardless of the individual's financial situation, some form of health care is provided through cooperation between the government, employer, employee, and social security and, in some cases, through private insurance.

STUDY QUESTIONS

1. Discuss the major health issues in Mexico. How do these problems compare to health concerns in other Latino countries, and other developed nations?
2. Compare and contrast strengths and weaknesses in the Mexican healthcare system.
3. What are major areas needed for improvement in the healthcare system? What do you suggest that can be accomplished within the economical constraints?
4. How do you think politics, economics, geography, and education affect the health of residents and the healthcare system of Mexico?

CASE STUDY

Dr. John Jones, a nursing professor at a local university, has accepted an invitation from a nurse colleague to assist with the health needs of people at a small urban clinic in Guanajuato, Mexico. He has gathered a total of 12 healthcare professionals, including four nursing students, four family nurse practitioners, two physicians, and two public health nurses, to assist at the clinic. The visiting healthcare professionals will be working in the clinic for about 3 weeks.

Guanajuato is a city of 100,000 people located in the center of Mexico, in a relatively high elevation surrounded by mountains. The climate is dry, with warm days and cool evenings. The health clinic serves an area of the city located near its outskirts. The clinic is funded by the government and is considered an IMSS institution.

Upon the group's arrival to the city and clinic, the nurse tells the team that the number one concern is health education regarding diabetes, followed by HIV/AIDS prevention. Other concerns include education about injury prevention such as auto accidents and treatment for influenza and pneumonia.

Case Study Questions

1. As a healthcare provider in Mexico, why is it important to know whether the people who will come to the clinic for services will pay out of pocket based on the type of institution?
2. What will the visiting healthcare provider need to know about HIV/AIDS prevention in Mexico? Will the interventions and education be the same as or different than the interventions and education delivered in the United States?
3. What does the visiting healthcare provider need to know about diabetic education and nutrition in Mexico?

REFERENCES

Becerril Cardenas, L., Gandara Sanchez, M., Mejia Carmona, B., & Gomez Arana, B. (2009). Nursing in Mexico. In K. Breda Lucas (Ed.), *Nursing and globalization in the Americas: A critical perspective* (p. 185). Amityville, NY: Baywood.

Booth, W. (2012, January 2). In Mexico, 12,000 killed in drug violence in 2011. *Washington Post*. Retrieved from http://www.washingtonpost.com/world/in-mexico-12000-killed-in-drug-violence-in-2011/2012/01/02/gIQAcGUdWP_story.html

Casa Historia. (2011, February 23). Mexican revolution and beyond. Retrieved from http://www.casahistoria.net/mexicorevolution.htm

Census. (2000). Mexico. Retrieved from http://www.census.gov/prod/2001pubs/c2kbr01-3.pdf

Central Intelligence Agency (CIA). (2011). The world factbook: North America: Mexico. Retrieved from https://www.cia.gov/library/publications/the-world-factbook/geos/mx.html

Gomez-Dantes, O. (2010). Mexico. In J. A. Johnson & C. H. Stoskopf (Eds.), *Comparative health systems: Global perspectives* (p. 337). Sudbury, MA: Jones & Bartlett Learning.

Holtz, C. (Ed.). (2008). *Global health care: Issues and policies.* Sudbury, MA: Jones and Bartlett.

Jaff, H. (2010, March 27). The right to health in Mexico: Seguro Popular. *World Poverty and Human Rights Online, 10/7/11.*

Kemp, C. (2001). Hispanic health beliefs and practices: Mexican and Mexican-Americans (clinical notes). Retrieved from http://www.nursingworld.org/MainMenuCategories/ANAMarketplace/ANAPeriodicals /OJIN/TableofContents/Volume112006/No3Sept06/ArticlePreviousTopics/CulturallyCompetent NursingCare.html

Lewis, M. Paul (Ed.). (2009). *Ethnologue: Languages of the World* (16th ed.). Dallas, TX: SIL International. Retrieved from http://www.ethnologue.com/

Meyer, M., & Beezley, W. (2000). *The Oxford history of Mexico.* Oxford, UK: Oxford University Press.

Neff, N. (2011). Folk medicine in Hispanics in the Southwestern United States. Retrieved from http://www .rice.edu/projects/HispanicHealth/Courses/mod7/mod7.html

Pan American Health Organization (PAHO). (2010). PAHO basic health indicators on Mexico. Retrieved from www.paho.org/English/DD/AIS/cp_484.htm

Schmal, J., (2007). Essays and research on indigenous Mexico. Retrieved from http://www.somosprimos .com/schmal/schmal.htm

Secretaria de Salud. (2007). *Programa nacional de salud 2007–2012.* Mexico City: Author.

Smallman, S. (2007). *The AIDS pandemic in Latin America.* Chapel Hill, NC: University of North Carolina Press.

Stanley Bunting, J. (2011). Chemical dependency within the Hispanic population: Considerations for diagnosis and treatment. In G. Lawson & A. Lawson (Eds.), *Alcoholism and substance abuse in diverse populations* (2nd ed., pp. 227–242). Austin, TX: Pro-Ed.

U.S. Department of State. (2011). Background notes: Mexico. Retrieved from http://www.state.gov/r/pa /ei/bgn/35749.htm

The World Bank. (2002). Retrieved from http://web.worldbank.org/WBSITE/EXTERNAL/NEWS /0,, contentMDK:20052226~menuPK:141310~pagePK:34370~piPK:34424~theSitePK:4607,00.html

World Health Organization (WHO). (2010). *Mexico road safety: Report on ten countries.* Geneva, Switzerland: WHO Department of Injuries and Violence Prevention and Disability.

World Health Organization (WHO) & UNAIDS. (2008). *Epidemiological fact sheet on HIV and AIDS, core data on epidemiology and response: Mexico 2008 update* (Update No. 089-735). Geneva, Switzerland: Author.

World health statistics. (2008). Geneva, Switzerland: WHO Press.

Zoucha, R.,& Zamarripa, C. (2008). People of Mexican heritage. In Larry D. Purnell & Betty J. Paulanka (Eds.). *Transcultural health care: A culturally competent approach* (3rd ed., pp. 309–324). Philadelphia, PA: F. A. Davis.

*For a full suite of assignments and additional learning activities, use the access code located in the front of your book to visit this exclusive website: **http://go.jblearning.com/holtz**. If you do not have an access code, you can obtain one at the site.*

22

Health and Health Care in Israel

Orly Toren

> *"Since by keeping the body in health and vigor one walks in the ways of God—*
>
> *—being impossible in sickness to have any understanding or knowledge of the Creator—*
>
> *it is a man's duty to avoid whatever is injurious to the body and cultivate habits conducive to health and vigor."*
>
> Maimonides (1135-1204 CE) Mishneh Torah:
> Laws Re: Moral Dispositions and Ethical Conduct

OBJECTIVES

After completing this chapter, the reader will be able to:

1. Relate a brief history of the establishment of the State of Israel and its healthcare system.
2. Compare and contrast population statistics for Israel.
3. Compare and contrast the healthcare system of Israel in the past to the current system.
4. Discuss the application of healthcare laws to the health of the various population groups in Israel.
5. Describe current healthcare goals in Israel.
6. Relate the state of nursing and medicine in Israel today.

INTRODUCTION

This chapter addresses the health and healthcare issues of Israel from a historical perspective as well as a current view. Numerous health and healthcare issues are examined within the cultural, economic, and legal systems of this country. A unique focus is the examination of the stress of anticipation of war and actual war, and its effects on the health of the population. The professions of nursing, medicine, and other healthcare professionals are also reviewed.

HISTORY

Israel, the land of the Jewish people, is located in the Middle East, in the midpoint of three continents (Asia, Europe, and Africa) and two seas (the Mediterranean and the Red Sea). Besides the Jewish people, it is home to many groups related to other cultures and religions. Among them are religious and secular groups, Christians and Muslims, Arabs, Druze, Bedouins, Cherkassy, and Samaritans.

During the last few centuries, its strategic geographic location has attracted many states to invest in Israel (e.g., by creating communication lines, through missionaries' organizations, by absorbing new immigrants), which promoted it to a leading position in the Middle East. This recognition of the land's strategic value was the basis for its occupation by Great Britain in 1917, at the end of World War I.

Israel gained its independence in 1948, when it became established as a Jewish democratic state. At that time, the founders of Israel declared that it would be open to all Jewish people around the world, would focus on the development of the country for the advantage of its citizens, and would be based on the principles of freedom, justice, and peace. Other goals were to provide freedom to practice any religion and to follow one's conscious language and culture, as well as to preserve the holy places of all nations.

The Israeli population now includes 7.4 million people (Israel Ministry of Tourism, 2009). The most important characteristic of this population is its diversity. The main population division is by Jewish people (80%) and Arabs (20%), but there are many other subdivisions and small ethnic and religious groups such as the Samaritans and the Cherkassy. **Table 22-1** summarizes some key demographic data for Israel.

Israel is a fairly young country compared to the Organization for Economic Cooperation and Development (OECD) countries, with a young population (median age: 28.3 years), low infant mortality

TABLE 22-1

Israel: Demographic and Economic Statistics

	Israel	*Average for OECD Countries*
GDP per capita (PPP$)	26,075	″ 29,292
Fertility rate (for women 15–49 years)	2.8	1.6
Dependency ratio	62	48.5
Percentage of the population older than 65 years	9.9	14.2
Percentage of the population older than 80 years	2.4	3.4
Life expectancy: men	77.4	75.5
Life expectancy: women	81.5	81.2
Number of hospital beds/1000 population	6.1	5.7
Number of general beds/1000 population	2.1	3.9
Occupancy rate: general beds	95.0%	75.4%
Out-of-pocket expenditures for health services (as a percentage of total healthcare expenditure)	23.7%	19.3%
Physicians/1000 population	3.6	3.0
Nurses/1000 population	5.9	8.7

Source: Kaidar & Bin Nun, 2007.

at birth rate (4.5 per 1000 deliveries), and long life expectancy (77.4 years) (Kaidar & Bin Nun, 2007). Elderly persons aged 65 and older account for one-tenth of the population. The number of elderly persons as a percentage of Jews and others (11.4%) was higher than the rate of older adults within the Arab population (3.5%) in 2008. Nevertheless, projected population data indicate that the Israeli population will continue to get older and the percentage of children will continue to decrease in coming years. In 2030, 25% of the population is expected to consist of children aged 14 and younger, while persons aged 65 and older are expected to account for 14% of the total population (Israel Ministry of Health, 2010c).

Israel's population is growing rapidly, partly related to major immigration waves coming to the country over the years. Since the country's establishment, the size of the population has grown almost 10-fold. The annual rate of population growth was 1.8% in 2009 (Israel Ministry of Health, 2010b). Largely owing to immigration, between 2000 and 2008 the population grew by 16%. The highest growth was among persons aged 55–64, whose number grew by 50%, and persons aged 75 and older, whose number grew by 25%.

The percentage of children aged 14 and younger in the total Israeli population has remained stable at 28% in the last decade. The percentage of Jewish and "other" children (26%) within those populations was lower than the percentage of children in the Arab population (39%) in 2008.

THE HEALTHCARE SYSTEM IN ISRAEL

History

Since the establishment of the State of Israel in 1948, health care has always been an important issue of the public agenda. The pluralistic nature of the healthcare system and its organization nowadays has deep roots in the period that preceded Israeli statehood (Bin Nun, Berlovitz, & Shani, 2010, p. 27). Many historical events, such as the waves of immigration to the region since the nineteenth century, along with epidemics of polio and malaria, have led to projects of economic aid through the donations of rich Jewish barons, thereby establishing a basis for social healthcare aid.

Prior to its establishment as an independent Jewish state, Israel was under an Ottoman occupation, a period that was characterized by missionary organizations treating the populations who came and went from Israel. The first hospital was built in 1854 by the Rothschild family; after it, many hospitals were established, mainly in Jerusalem, but also in Jaffa, Tiberias, and Zfat. With the first immigration wave at the end of the nineteenth century, many healthcare services were established to serve the healthcare needs of the newcomers, who were mainly farmers. The end of World War I brought many diseases to the people in the country, a situation that led to the founding of the Hadassah Zionist Women Organization—a group of volunteers who sought to build the Hadassah Organization in Israel so as to better organize health services. This organization offered health aid to the community mainly by treating infectious diseases and providing preventive medicine services to children. Its services included first aid treatment and hospitalization services.

After 1917 and until 1948, Israel was occupied by the British. Between the end of World War I and the establishment of the country of Israel, the trend for providing health care was to transfer the health services to other authorities such as local municipalities and other sick funds (e.g., health maintenance organizations [HMOs]). These organizations, which provided both preventive and first aid treatment, also developed hospitalization services. These sick funds have long served as organizations for mutual aid, providing health care to their members. Seven HMOs were operating by the evening of the declaration of the state of Israel. The largest in terms of its insured population (805,000) was Kupat Holim Clalit; the remainder of the population was served by several smaller sick funds. At the end of 1948, however, only 53% of the Jewish population was insured (Bin Nun et al., 2010, p. 37; Israel Ministry of Foreign Affairs, 1995).

The first two years after its establishment, the population of the state of Israel doubled to 1.2 million people due to the mass immigration of Holocaust survivors from Europe and Jewish refugees from Arab countries. Within a decade, the country's population reached 2.1 million. The percentage of those with health insurance increased dramatically during those years, to an estimated 90%. Both the Ministry of Health and Kupat Holim Clalit expanded their medical facilities to cope with the increasing demand for health services.

In 1953, all military hospital facilities were transferred to the control of the Ministry of Health to enhance financial and management efficiency, and the ministry became the major provider of hospitalization services. Kupat Holim Clalit also took steps to expand its services by building more hospitals and community clinics. Smaller sick funds tried to follow Kupat Holim Clalit's example and compete by opening more clinics in the community. **Table 22-2** presents data on hospital beds by ownership in the first two decades after the establishment of the State of Israel. The most noticeable trend is the growth of government-provided beds, from 12% of all hospital beds in 1948 to 42% in 1970.

The Current Healthcare System

Healthcare Coverage

With the establishment of the country in 1948, official institutions were formulated in Israel, including governmental offices and the Ministry of Health. The Ministry of Health is responsible for formulating health policy and, based on that policy, providing for citizens' health and health services. This office is responsible for planning, controlling, licensing, and coordinating health services and healthcare organizations (Israel Ministry of Health, 2010d). Two other roles of the ministry are as follows:

- Providing services—acute, chronic, prevention, research, rehabilitation, diagnosis, and treatment—either directly or through other organizations.
- Acting as an insurer. The ministry insures the whole population in the areas of mental health, geriatrics, public health, and rehabilitation and mobility appliances.

Israel has maintained a system of socialized health care since its establishment. Health care in the country is universally available, and participation in a medical insurance plan is compulsory through

TABLE 22-2

Number of Hospital Beds by Ownership, 1948–1970

Ownership	1948	1950	1960	1970
Government	689	2996	5785	10,063
Municipal	451	583	793	195
Kupat Holim Clalit	649	997	2636	3744
Hadassah	431	541	477	590
Private	1367	1449	3394	5606
Other	1039	461	2528	3529
Sum	5626	7627	15,613	23,727

Source: Bin Nun et al., 2010.

the National Health Insurance Act (legislated in 1995). Under this law, all Israeli citizens are entitled to the same uniform benefits package (a basic basket of services), regardless of the insurer organization. Treatment under this package is funded for all citizens regardless of their financial means. Before enactment of the National Health Insurance Act, the only HMO to accept members without discrimination based on age or medical situation was Kupat Holim Clalit. Today, however, healthcare coverage is administered by four not-for-profit sick funds (HMOs) guaranteeing healthcare services to all citizens, with additional funding provided by the government. The four sick funds are Kupat Holim Clalit (60% market share), Maccabi (20%), Meuchedet (10%), and Leumit (10%). Under the National Health Insurance Act, residents have the right to pick up their preferred sick fund, and transfer it to any of four other funds. Health care is provided to all insured citizens with no discrimination based on age, state of health, or other potential risk factors.

Laws Affecting the Healthcare System

The two major laws passed in Israel in the 1990s related to health care are the National Health Insurance Act and the Patient's Rights Act.

The *National Health Insurance Act* is a legal framework that enables and facilitates basic, compulsory universal health care. It was put into effect by the Knesset (Israeli parliament) on January 1, 1995. This legislation was adopted on the basis of the recommendations of a National Committee of Inquiry that examined the need for restructuring the healthcare system in Israel in the late 1980s. Prior to passage of the law, several major problems with the existing healthcare system were recognized:

- Membership in the largest fund (Kupat Holim Clalit) required one to belong to the Histadrut labor organization, even if a person did not wish to (or could not).
- Selection based on age and health status was used by some sick funds to determine acceptance of new members.
- Different funds provided different levels of benefit coverage or services to their members.
- Although their numbers were small, a certain percentage of the population did not have any health insurance coverage.

The National Health Insurance Act ensured that *all* citizens would have health coverage and identified a uniform benefits package for all citizens—that is, a list of medical services and treatments that each of the sick funds was required to cover for its members. The state is responsible for providing health services to all residents of the country, who can register with one of the four health service funds. To be eligible for such registration, a citizen must pay a health insurance tax. Coverage includes medical diagnosis and treatment, preventive medicine, hospitalization (general, maternity, psychiatric, and chronic), surgery and transplants, preventive dental care for children, first aid and transportation to a hospital or clinic, medical services at the workplace, treatment for drug abuse and alcoholism, medical equipment and appliances, obstetrics and fertility treatment, medication, treatment of chronic diseases, and paramedical services such as physiotherapy and occupational therapy. In addition to the uniform benefits package provided to all citizens, each sick fund is entitled to provide its members with supplementary services and treatments usually covered by private insurance, which may take the form of either a "supplementary insurance" offered by the sick fund or private insurance from any insurance company.

The National Health Insurance Act set out a system of public funding for healthcare services by means of a progressive health tax, administered by Israel's social security organization, which transfers funding to the sick funds according to a formula based on the number of members in each fund, the age distribution of those members, and a number of other indices. The sick funds also receive direct financing from the state. Although most of the services are covered by the law, certain services are administered and covered directly by the state.

While membership in one of the funds is now compulsory for all people, there is a free choice in moving among the sick funds, which compels the various sickness funds to compete for members among the populace. Each year, a committee appointed by the Ministry of Health publishes a "basket" or uniform package of medical services and drug formulary (list of prescription medications) that all funds must provide as a minimum service to all their members. Achieving this level of equality meant that all citizens are guaranteed to receive basic healthcare regardless of their fund affiliation, which was one of the principal aims of the law. An appeals process has also been put in place to handle rejection of treatments and procedures by the funds and to evaluate cases falling outside the "basket" of services or prescription formulary.

While the National Health Insurance Act is generally considered a success and Israeli citizens enjoy a high standard of medical care, with more competition having been introduced into the field of health care in the country, the law has some limitations:

- Some critics say that the "basket" is not large enough to provide coverage for any medical situation that is needed.
- So as to provide universal coverage to all, the tax income base amount (the maximum amount of yearly earnings that are subject to the tax) was set rather high; as a consequence, many high-income taxpayers have seen the amount they pay for their health premiums (now health tax) skyrocket.
- Some members complain about the constantly rising costs of copayments for certain services.

The *Patient's Right Act,* which was passed in 1996, aimed to establish the rights of every person who requests medical care or who is in receipt of medical care, and to protect his or her dignity and privacy (Israel Ministry of Health, 2010d). This act contains several parts:

- *The right to acquire care.* A major aspect of the act is the way that it outlines rights to medical care in Israel. Medical facilities and clinicians are not allowed to discriminate against patients on the basis of race, gender, religion, nationality, country of birth, or other similar grounds. Patients are required to get proper care, and everyone visiting an emergency medical facility is allowed to have an examination.
- *Privacy rights.* Physicians and other medical staff are required to maintain medical confidentiality; they cannot disclose any information about patients' medical conditions and treatments.
- *Informed consent rights.* Informed consent is required prior to any medical intervention. Physicians must explain treatment and other medical information to patients, including information about the diagnosis, prognosis, risks of treatment, risks of nontreatment, alternative treatments, and likelihood of treatment success. If an ethics committee determines that such medical information might cause a severe threat to a patient's mental or physical health, physicians may withhold information from the patient. Informed consent can be given verbally, in writing, or through another behavioral demonstration to the patient. Some situations are considered exceptional in terms of informed consent—for example, with patients whose mental state does not allow them to understand medical information. In these cases, an appointed legal guardian can make the medical decisions for the patient.
- *Medical records.* Physicians and medical staff are required to keep detailed medical records for patients. Patients may have access to their own medical records. Physicians can disclose medical information only to other medical professionals for treatment or when an ethics committee decides that disclosure of medical information is necessary for the health of the general public.

In many respects, the Israel Patient's Rights Act differs little from the policy and practice in other nations (Gross, 2005). Patients enjoy a wide range of rights, including access to the national healthcare system, the right of informed consent, privacy, confidentiality, and respect for dignity. Meaningful informed consent enjoins healthcare professionals to provide a wealth of information about risks, benefits, and alternative treatments.

Ministry of Health Policy to Promote Populations' Health

In January 2011, the Ministry of Health, guided by a new chief executive officer (CEO), issued a new work plan to promote Israel's national health. In the report introduction, Dr. Ronni Gamzu, head of the Ministry of Health, noted that "[The] Israeli health care system is one of the most qualitative in the western world. It appears with different and many health care indicators. The strongest points of the system are public infrastructures, with sick funds and other health care organizations caring for the citizens' health. However, the weakest point of the system is low investment for health, growing private expenditure for health care, health discrepancies between populations and geographical areas and the lack of national infrastructure to measure quality to assess outcomes" (Israel Ministry of Health, 2010d).

Based these issues, a "pillars of fire" strategic plan to reach the goals of the Ministry of Health for the Israeli health care system was developed. This plan focuses on five main goals:

1. *Promote public health.* This goal is geared toward decreasing hazardous behaviors, limiting the population exposure to external influences (mainly food and environment), and enhancing the ability to prevent diseases. Achieving this goal will involve promotions and campaigns to elevate public awareness about recommended nutrition and health activity, legislation against smoking, and improvements in immunization and child development programs.
2. *Decrease inequalities in health (geographically and socially).* This goal focuses on the reduction of economic inequalities that might prevent Israelis from purchasing health services, reduction of the cultural influence on healthcare services consumption, development of adequate human resources and infrastructures in the periphery of the country, and incentives for HMOs to invest in reducing inequalities.
3. *Strengthen the public nature of the healthcare system in Israel.* The focus is on expanding the public "healthcare basket" and reducing the importance of the private financial aspect of the system.
4. *Ensure the quality of health and the quality of the healthcare system.* The goal is to build a national database to measure quality and to select appropriate quality healthcare indicators for the different parties in the system (hospitals and community healthcare services).
5. *Adjust healthcare services to match future healthcare developments.* Israel hopes to develop a national strategic plan that will prepare its healthcare system to accommodate the country's healthcare needs in the short term and long run, reduce gaps among professional healthcare providers, and better match the infrastructure to healthcare needs. This goal will require the creating of an organizational structure for future policy planning.

Table 22-3 details selected health indicators for these goals for 2011–2012.

HEALTH IN ISRAEL: STATISTICS AND TRENDS

Israel has its own unique healthcare characteristics. Life expectancy at birth is increasing. In 2009, the expected life span in the country was 83.5 years for females and 79.7 years for males; 83.9 and 80.3 years among Jews and "other" females and males, respectively; and 80.7 and 76.3 years among Arab females and males, respectively. Maternal age at first birth is also increasing. In 2009, the median age of first-time mothers was 26.5 years compared with 25.3 years in 2000.

TABLE 22-3

Selected Health Indicators for Israel's National Healthcare Goals for 2011–2012

	Current Value	Date of Measure	Expected Value
Percentage of patients who waive healthcare services (general practitioner visits and medications)	22%	2012	20%
Percentage of patients paying out-of-pocket expenses for medications	33%	2012	28%
Specialist physicians/1000 population	3.2 (south) 2.8 (north)	2013	3.5 (south) 3.0 (north)
Percentage of the population older than 25 years who are overweight	23%	2015	20%
Number of hospital beds (general beds)	14,582	2016	15,542

Source: Israel Ministry of Health, 2010d.

The number of live births in 2009 was 161,000, of whom 72% were Jewish, compared with 67% in 2000. The total fertility rate was stable in the last decade: 3.0 births per woman in 2009. This rate was 2.9 births per Jewish woman and 3.7 births per Muslim woman during 2009, compared with 2.7 and 4.7 births for such women, respectively, in 2000.

The infant mortality rate is decreasing and was similar to the median for OECD countries in 2008. In 2009, 606 infants died in the first year of life, a rate of 3.8 deaths per 1000 live births—2.7 deaths per 1000 among Jews and 7.6 deaths per 1000 among Muslims. The rate among Muslims remained higher than among Jews, by a factor of between 2.0 and 2.9 during the last decade.

The main causes of infant mortality according to these data were congenital anomalies and other perinatal causes. The rate of mortality from congenital anomalies was four times higher among Arabs than among Jews and "others," and remained stable among both population groups in the last decade. The percentage of infants born weighing less than 2500 grams was stable in the last decade, estimated at 8.2% in 2009. The percentage was higher among mothers younger than age 20 or age 40 or older, at 10.6% and 10.2%, respectively, in 2009. The percentage of infants born at very low birth weight decreased in the last decade; 1.0% weighed less than 1500 grams and 0.3% weighed less than 1000 grams in 2009 compared with 1.2% and 0.5%, respectively, in 2000 (Israel Ministry of Health, 2010f).

The percentage of infants born preterm before 33 weeks' gestation decreased to 1.2% of all live births in 2009, compared with 1.9% in 2000, and the percentage of live births before 28 weeks gestation was 0.2% in 2009 and 0.5% in 2000. The percentage of infants born in multiple births was stable in the last decade, accounting for 4.7% of all live births in 2009. The percentage of infants born as triplets or greater multiples decreased to 0.16% in 2009, compared with 0.36% in 2000.

The crude mortality rate is decreasing, and is lower for Jews and "others" than for Arabs in all age groups. Most deaths occurred among those aged 65 and older—81% among Jews and "others" and 56% among the Arab population. By comparison, 1% of all deaths occurred in Jews and "other" children (age 14 and younger) and 11% in Arab children in 2008.

The age-adjusted suicide rate declined in 2005–2007 after remaining stable since the mid-1990s. The rate for males was 3.5 times that for females during this period. The highest rate was observed among persons aged 65 and older. The age-adjusted suicide rate in Israel is lower than the European Union's 15-member average.

Malignant neoplasms have been the leading cause of death in Israel since the end of the 1990s (**Figure 22-1**); by comparison, in the United States, the leading cause of death in the same period was cardiovascular disease (http://www.health.gov.il/Download/pages/v2_072010.pdf). In 2008, the leading causes of death in Israel were malignant neoplasms (25%), heart disease (18%), cerebrovascular disease (6%), diabetes (6%), and kidney disease (4%). The leading cause of death among males aged 15–44 and females aged 15–24 was accidents. In persons aged 75 and older, the leading cause of death was heart disease. Malignant neoplasms, however, were the leading cause of death for males aged 45–74 and females aged 25–74.

PREPARING FOR EMERGENCY SITUATIONS AND MASS-CASUALTY EVENTS

Israel is under threats of terror attacks and war from its surrounding borders. Part of the Ministry of Health's responsibility is to prepare the country's healthcare system for, and deploy it in, emergency situations. The Department of Emergency Situations and Mass-Casualty Events was created for this purpose, and is very active in preparing hospitals, HMOs, the Israeli Red Cross, and the general population for all kinds of attacks (conventional, chemical, biological, radiological, and atomic). In addition, this department works closely with other emergency services such as the fire department, police, and the army. Because the frequency of mass-casualty events is particularly high in Israel, the healthcare system must be prepare for any scenario, whether in quiet days or while at war (Rassin et al., 2007). The goal of this department is to prepare hospitals and community healthcare services to treat patients with injuries from conventional and unconventional sources in emergency situations and mass-casualty events (State of Israel, 2002). The Department of Emergency Situations and Mass-Casualty Events is responsible for

FIGURE 22-1

Leading Causes of Death

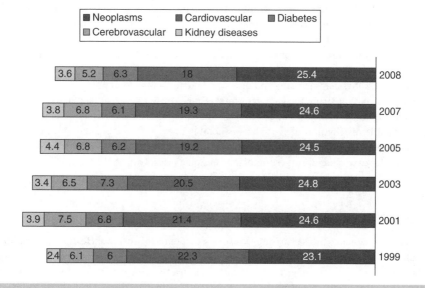

Source: Israel Ministry of Health, Death, 2010a.

writing standards and protocols for all kinds of situations, controlling and preparing for these situations, educating staff members from all levels of the healthcare system, developing technological infrastructures, adopting and verifying the availability of the right equipment in the adequate amount, performing live and simulated drills, and moving human resources and equipment among healthcare organizations as needed.

Israeli teams, owing to the country's past history of mass-casualty events, have gathered extensive data from these experiences. They continue to share this knowledge all over the world in different situations, from educating and preparing teams to deal with all kinds of mass-casualty events, to participating in real situations of life saving—for example, in the recent earthquakes in Haiti and Japan.

HEALTHCARE PROFESSIONALS IN ISRAEL

Overall, some 170,000 people worked in the Israeli healthcare system in 2009, of whom 94,000 were healthcare professionals (34% physicians and nurses, 24% allied healthcare professionals, and the rest from other occupations) (Israel Ministry of Health, 2010e). From 2000 to 2008, the number of nurses decreased by 5%, the number of other healthcare professionals increased by 5%, and the number of physicians increased by 1%. More than half of all physicians (58%) and 77% of all nurses work in hospitals; these percentages have remained the same during the past decade.

Physicians

The number of physicians in Israel in 2009 was 33,605. The ratio of physicians per 1000 population is still high compared to most of the OECD countries, but it has been decreasing in the last decade and the threat of a physician shortage now stands at the country's doorstep.

Until recently, the Israeli physician supply relied heavily on physicians trained in other countries—primarily immigrants from the former Soviet Union and Eastern Europe. Because the massive wave of immigration of the early 1990s has decreased dramatically, however, that source of physicians is now decreasing. To address the projected shortage, Israel is in the process of opening another medical school in the north, which will join the country's four other existing medical schools (Rosen & Merkur, 2009).

Many of the physicians in Israel are employed within governmental institutions financed by the sick funds, although private practices are becoming more common.

An increase in the rate of older physicians (age of 45 and older) has become apparent during the last decade; older physicians represented 50% of the total number of doctors in 2000 and 65% in 2008. The percentage of female physicians is rising and now stands at 40% of the total physician supply; the majority of the female physicians are from the younger group (Israel Ministry of Health, 2010e).

The percentage of specialists among the total number of physicians is rising (50% in 2008 compared to 37% in 1998). The distribution of specialists is notably uneven: Whereas there is an excessive supply of specialists in gynecology and ophthalmology, there is a shortage of physicians trained in the areas of geriatrics, intensive care, general surgery, and anesthesiology (Bin Nun et al., 2010).

Nurses

Overview of Nursing

Nursing in Israel is regulated by the Nursing Division, a part of the Ministry of Health. Its role is to develop nursing policy on the national level. The manager of the Nursing Division (head nurse) is a registered nurse, who serves both as a member of the Ministry of Health management and as a consultant to the Minister of Health for all aspects of nursing and nurses. This manager's responsibilities include nursing education, registration, standards, and development. In addition, the head nurse monitors patients' and the healthcare system's needs to accommodate the nursing profession to developing trends.

In Israel, three levels of nurses exist: practical nurses (LPN), registered nurses (diploma graduates), and nurses with academic degree (academic graduates). On a national level in Israel, it was decided to upgrade the education level of nursing personnel, such that a BSN (bachelor of sciences in nursing) became the entry-level requirement for admission into the profession (Toren & Picker, 2009). This level of training is available in Israel's four universities and several colleges. Since 2009, the track for LPN licensure has been closed, so that there have been no more entries of new LPNs into the system.

The ratio of registered nurses per 1,000 population in Israel has always been low and among the lowest in OECD countries: 5.5 nurses per 1000 population in 2009 as compared with the OECD average of 8.7 per 1000. Due to a severe nursing shortage in the 1980s, this field in Israel has been recognized as a "preferential profession," offering attractive remunerations and benefits. The shortage could have been more extensive, except that the large wave of immigration in the early 1990s brought with it many nurses who were recognized in Israel as practical nurses. Special training tracks to reach the diploma registered nurse level were opened for them, as well as second-career retraining tracks for university graduates. The many graduates from these tracks have been integrated into the country's healthcare system. Because of these measures, the global nursing shortage has been felt in Israel only in recent years. Despite the increasing number of nurses younger than the age of 60 years during that period, the population growth rate was slightly greater than the rate of increase in the number of nurses, resulting in a decreased rate of nurses per 1000 population. In recent years, the immigration waves have stopped, bringing a halt to the special training programs for this specific population, and resulting in a deeper shortage of nurses.

The majority of the nurses in Israel have academic degrees: 48% baccalaureate degrees and 18% graduate degrees. Nearly one-third of the nurses hold a diploma to practice nursing (**Figure 22-2**) (Nirel, Yair, Riba, Reicher, & Toren, 2010).

Nursing Development in Israel

In Israel, 1000 registered nurses are trained annually in various tracks (academic, diploma, and second-career programs for university graduates). In 2004, the government decided to increase the number of graduates of the BSN level by opening additional BSN training tracks in the country's colleges, replacing the diploma programs and LPN programs. One department in a college in the north of Israel was opened,

FIGURE 22-2

Distribution of Academic Degree of Nurses

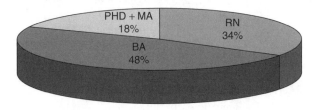

Source: Nirel et al., 2010.

replacing a diploma school in the area (Emek Israel College). In addition, three new academic departments opened without having closed their diploma programs—at Tzfat College, at Israel College, and at the Tal Institute in Jerusalem for orthodox and ultra-orthodox women.

There is a growing trend of accepting nursing students into academic schools and opening more colleges educating them in BSN degree programs. **Table 22-4** describes the universities, colleges, and nursing schools in Israel that offer nursing programs. In both universities and colleges, the education focuses on the academic level; at the end of their studies, the students acquire both an RN diploma and a baccalaureate degree in nursing science. A few schools (7 out of 20) continue to prepare candidates for the RN diploma.

Academic nursing schools are also responsible for teaching clinical courses in post-basic clinical practice. The courses in specialty clinical fields are mandatory for nurses who work in specialty clinical practices, providing them with the knowledge of and authority to perform specific clinical interventions. The courses come under the rubric of Post-Basic Education (PBE), a license-based training. Fifteen courses are offered to nurses, targeting education to specific clinical fields. The curriculum is designed by the Nursing Division in the Ministry of Health for the theoretical courses as well as the clinical practice. Examples of PBE courses include those dealing with pediatric intensive care, gerontology, psychiatry, oncology, neonatal intensive care, operating room nursing, community health, infection control, nephrology, and midwifery. The prerequisites for acceptance to these courses are a baccalaureate degree in nursing and a grade of 70 or higher on a general nursing test.

A PBE program lasts about one year (approximately 300 to 600 academic hours of learning), about half of it theoretical and the rest clinical hours. Students are required to take a national qualifying

TABLE 22-4

Distribution of Nursing Schools by Education Type

University (BSN)	College (BSN)	Nursing Schools (Diploma)
Ben Gurion University	Tal College	Laniado

Hebrew University:
  Asaf Harofe
  Hadassah
  Kaplan
	Zfat College	Shaare Zedek

Tel Aviv University:
  Beilinson
  Sheba
  Wolfson
  Sheinbron
  Hillel Yaffe
	Israel Valley College	Bnei Zion

	Israel College	
	Tel Aviv Yaffo College (in the planning stage)	Nazaret
	Rupin (in the planning stage)	Ziv
	Ariel (in the planning stage)	Ashkelon
		Meir

examination to obtain their certification. Success in this examination bestows upon the graduate a license to perform a series of nursing care interventions for which only the program's graduates are qualified (Toren, Kerzman, Kigli-shemes, & Kagan, 2011).

The nursing specialist field is in its preliminary stages of development, and the first area recognized in 2009 as appropriate for nursing specialization was palliative care (Israel Ministry of Health, 2009). To date, approximately 150 nurse specialists have obtained certification and are acting as pioneers in this clinical field. These nurses are authorized to train the next generation of new nurses who will acquire education in this particular field. In addition, nurses working in the community are authorized to treat and prescribe medication for specific conditions (under precise protocols).

Allied Healthcare Professionals

Besides nurses and physicians, a variety of other healthcare professionals work in the Israeli healthcare system. Some of these professionals, such as dentists, work mainly in the private sector (dental care is not covered by the national healthcare insurance). Others, such as pharmacists, physiotherapists, occupational health therapists, communication therapists, podiatrists, and radiation technologists, work both in the private and public sectors.

While legislation exists to regulate many healthcare professions, such as medicine, nursing, dentistry, and pharmacy, such legislation does not yet exist for many other allied healthcare professions (Rosen & Samuel, 2009).

CONCLUSION

Israel, as a relatively young modern democratic country, has made many accomplishments in terms of its healthcare system since it won independence in 1948. The country has a national healthcare system that has offered universal healthcare coverage for more than 15 years; this system is predominantly publicly financed, is government regulated, and features competition among providers (both health plans and hospitals). The healthcare system is based on health plans that apply to the Israeli population as a whole. It has succeeded in achieving above-average levels of health status despite the below-average level of resources allocated to the system (Rosen & Samuel, 2009).

Israel's small geographic size, combined with its good access to high-quality care services throughout the country, enables providers to deliver a relatively high level of care, both in the preventive realm and in the fields of curative and palliative care. This quality care relies in part on the strong academic training available for most levels of healthcare professionals in the nation. The impending shortage of physicians and nurses, however, threatens to derail this trend of success.

In addition, as a country absorbing immigrants from all around the world, Israel faces some challenges in caring for these new residents. For example, the large waves of immigration from the former Soviet Union and Ethiopia created a challenge in closing both cultural and health gaps among the various immigrant groups.

STUDY QUESTIONS

1. Discuss Israel's major health issues.
2. Compare and contrast Israel's healthcare system to other systems in developed countries worldwide.
3. Explain how the economics, politics, geographical location, technology, and cultures affect the health and healthcare of residents of Israel.
4. Discuss Israel's emergency preparedness needs and how they relate to the healthcare system.

CASE STUDY

Extending the Boundaries of the Declaration of Helsinki: A Case Study of an Unethical Experiment in a Non-Medical Setting

Richter, Barach, Berman, Ben-David, & Weinberger (2001)

Background

In 1993, the Israeli Ministry of Transportation initiated an "experiment" to raise the inter-urban speed limit from 90 to 100 kph. The "experiment" did not include a protocol and did not specify cut-off points for early termination in the case of adverse results. After the raise in the speed limit, the death toll on interurban roads rose as a result of a sudden increase in speeds and case fatality rates. The committee's decision was a case study which lacked an ethical framework. The case study states the case for extending Helsinki type safeguards for experimentation in non-medical settings.

The decision to continue with the "experiment" after the first high monthly death tolls was compared to the infamous Tuskegee experiment, in which physicians deliberately withheld penicillin from poor black sharecroppers with tertiary syphilis. The experiment to raise the speed limit differed from the Tuskegee experiment in two important respects. First, the raised speed limit did not require drivers to increase their speed. Second, the subjects were not a deprived minority, dependent on the doctors and nurses in a controlled medical setting, but an entire population of drivers. However, potential subjects were the entire population of drivers and passengers who could be injured or dead because of this policy change.

Case Study Questions

1. What lessons can be learned from this change in speed limits and its effect on road traffic injuries?
2. Discuss the ethical considerations that were disregarded in this study. What changes in the protocols could have made this study more ethical?

REFERENCES

Bin Nun, G., Berlovitz, Y., & Shani, M. (2010). *The health care system in Israel.* Tel Aviv: Am Oved.

Gross, M. L. (2005). Treating competent patients by force: The limits and lessons of Israel's Patient's Rights Act. *Journal of Medical Ethics, 31,* 29–34.

Israel Ministry of Foreign Affairs. (1995). National health insurance. Retrieved from http://www.mfa.gov .il/MFA/MFAArchive/1990_1999/1998/7/National+Health+Insurance.htm

Israel Ministry of Health (2009). Nurse specialist in palliative care. Nursing Standard No. 69. Retrieved from http://www.health.gov.il/download/forms/ a3526_ND-79int.pdf

Israel Ministry of Health. (2010a). Death causes in Israel 1999–2008. Retrieved from http://www.health .gov.il/Download/pages/Death_210711.pdf

Israel Ministry of Health. (2010b). Israel health 2010: Mortality. Retrieved from http://www.health.gov.il /Download/pages/Mortality2.pdf

Israel Ministry of Health. (2010c). Israel health: Population. Retrieved from http://www.health.gov.il /Download/pages/Population.pdf

Israel Ministry of Health. (2010d). Israel Ministry of Health, 2011 agenda. Retrieved from http://www .news1.co.il/uploadFiles/199001491069794.pdf

Israel Ministry of Health. (2010e). Manpower. Retrieved from .http://www.health.gov.il/download/docs /units/meida/manpower2009/1.pdf

Israel Ministry of Health. (2010f). Statistical abstract of Israel, CBS. Retrieved from http://www.health .gov.il/Download/pages/Vital__statistics2.pdf

Israel Ministry of Tourism. (2009). The Israel Ministry of Tourism: Discover Israel. Retrieved from http://www.goisrael.com/Tourism_Euk/Tourist+Information/Discover+Israel/Population.htm

Kaidar, N., & Bin Nun, G. (2007). International comparison of health care system: Israel and OECD member states 1970–2005. Retrieved from http://www.health.gov.il/download/pages/OECD2007.pdf

Nirel, N., Yair, Y., Riba, S., Reicher, S., & Toren, O. (2010). *Registered nurses in Israel: Workforce supply: Pattern and trends*. Jerusalem: Myers, JDC, Brookdale Institute.

Rassin, M., Avraham, M., Nasi-Bashari, A., Idelman, S., Peretz, Y., Morag, S., . . . Weiss, G. (2007). Emergency department staff preparedness for mass casualty events involving children. *Disaster Management Response, 5*(2), 36–44.

Richer, E., Barach, P., Berman,T., Ben-David, G., & Weinberger, Z. (2001). Extending the boundaries of the Declaration of Helsinki: a case study of an unethical experiment in a non-medical setting. *Journal of Medical Ethics, 1*(27), 126–129. doi:10.1136/jme.27.2.126

Rosen, B., & Merkur, S. (2009). Israel: Health system review. *Health Systems in Transition, 11*(2), 1–226.

State of Israel. (2002). Emergency Department. Retrieved from http://www.health.gov.il/emergency /yehud.htm

Toren, O., Kerzman, H., Kigli-shemes, R., & Kagan, I. (2011). The difference between professional image and job satisfaction of nurses who studied in a post basic education program and nurses with generic education: A questionnaire survey. *Journal of Professional Nursing, 27,* 28–34.

Toren, O., & Picker, O. (2009). Staff development in the national level. In O. Toren & O. Picker, *Nursing leadership and management in Israeli hospitals* (pp. 27–41). Jerusalem: Magness.

23

Establishing Medical and Nursing Education Programs in the Country of Georgia

Judith L. Wold
Kimberley A. Crawford

> "For fiscal years 1992 through 2000, the U.S. government has provided
> about $216 million in assistance to help the new independent states of the
> former Soviet Union develop the sustainable institutions, traditions, and
> legal foundations for establishing a strong rule of law. The United States
> has aimed its assistance at helping these countries (1) establish a modern
> legal basis for the administration of justice, (2) create a strong and inde-
> pendent judiciary, (3) strengthen legal education for legal professionals
> operating within the system, (4) improve law enforcement practices, and
> (5) broaden access and participation of civil society in the legal system."

OBJECTIVES

After completing this chapter the reader will be able to:

1. Describe the major health issues of the country of Georgia.
2. Describe the establishment process and major accomplishments of the medical and nursing education programs in the country of Georgia.
3. Relate the challenges of culture, economics and politics confronted in establishing the medical and
   nursing programs in the country of Georgia.

INTRODUCTION

A functional healthcare system is a critical cornerstone of any country. The health and well-being of a
country's population is vital to its economic progress. This chapter describes in detail the efforts of a
group of partners in Atlanta, Georgia, in the United States and in the country of Georgia, working to

This chapter was updated from the version in an earlier edition by Judith L. Wold, H. Kenneth Walker, and Natia
Partskhladze.

improve the healthcare system in this former republic of the Soviet Union. A vital goal of the partnership has been to elevate the profession of nursing in this country so as to improve the quality of health care and to have an impact upon other sectors. The nursing profession is particularly essential in developing countries that are in transition from totalitarian governments to democracy. The nursing profession in these countries, almost without exception, is at a very low professional level. Transitional countries make little use of the enormous potential that nurses have to influence every part of the healthcare sector. Nurses and the nursing profession form the foundation for the critical healthcare sector of any national healthcare system. Indeed, nurses are crucial caregivers and leaders in every facet of the healthcare sector, including rural areas, outpatient clinics, hospitals, primary care, and public health.

This chapter presents a guide that can be applied to other, similar transitional nations. The partnership has been engaged extensively in other areas of the healthcare sector, with the aim of revitalizing and modernizing the sector through capacity building, organizational development, and the institutionalization of contemporary practices. While nursing is the major focus, other health system activities are also outlined in this chapter.

GEORGIA: A COUNTRY PROFILE

The country of Georgia is located at the crossroads of the Western and the Eastern hemispheres. Technically located in southwest Asia, Georgia is bordered on the west by the Black Sea and Turkey, on the east by Azerbaijan, on the north by Russia (the longest of its land borders), and on the south by Armenia. The country is approximately the size of the U.S. state of South Carolina. Its capital is the city of Tbilisi. Located on the Silk Road, a well-known and historically significant Chinese trade route extending 7000 miles eastward from the Mediterranean Sea to the Yellow River, Georgia has been conquered innumerable times in its long history.

Rich in heritage, the people of Georgia are an intelligent, highly educated society with a literacy rate of almost 100% (Central Intelligence Agency [CIA], 2011). Although Georgia has been a Christian country for many centuries, a number of religious sects coexist peacefully in the area (see **Figure 23-1**). The people of Georgia, who now number fewer than 5 million, are warm and gracious to a fault, going above and beyond expectations to treat visitors to the country hospitably.

FIGURE 23-1

Old Tbilisi Mosque and Turkish Baths

While a republic of the Soviet Union, Georgia was quite prosperous by Soviet standards, serving as the wine capital and Black Sea summer playground of the Soviet elite. With the crumbling of the Soviet Union, however, Georgia suffered the same rapid economic decline that all of the former Soviet Union (FSU) republics suffered. Owing to its economic destabilization and the concomitant problems of providing social protection, poverty among its citizens has risen sharply. The poorer segments of the population are enduring the greatest hardships because of the lack of governmental spending on social services, infrastructure, and health (Hauschild & Berkhout, 2009). In 2010, there were still 258,000 internally displaced persons from the civil conflicts that Georgia had endured (Internal Displacement Monitoring Center [IDMC], 2011). Georgia currently ranks as number 74 on the human development index (HDI) among 169 countries—an improvement from its rank of 100 out of 177 countries in 2006 (United Nations Development Program [UNDP], 2011). The HDI is calculated from life expectancy, education, and gross domestic product indices, which are accurate human development measures of long and healthy life, knowledge, and a decent standard of living (UNDP, 2011).

During the country's transition from communism to democracy, Georgia's gross domestic product (GDP) fell by 75%, and in 1994 per capita healthcare expenditures fell from $95.50 to $0.90 (Skarbinski, Walker, Kobaladze, Kirtava, Baker, & Raffin, 2002). Georgia's economy has improved since the early 2000s, with a high GDP growth of more than 10% in 2006–2007. The GDP increase significantly slowed after the 2008 conflict with Russia, but then rebounded in 2010 with a growth rate of 6.4% (CIA, 2011). Aside from agriculture (arable land accounts for approximately 12% of the country's land), Georgia has few natural resources, making economic recovery for this country difficult. In a 2005 report, Brunnell, Hoover, Day, Yetter, and Dersham presented data suggesting that even though there is little interaction with governmental officials, Georgian communities still expect the government to take care of their needs—an unsurprising holdover attitude from the former Soviet era. Infrastructure deterioration in electricity, roads, gas, and water supply, especially in the rural areas, is a serious issue. An increasing number of people are leaving rural areas due to lack of employment opportunities (Brunnell et al., 2005). However, one positive action made by the government has been its attempt to decrease bureaucratic red tape and paperwork in an effort to make doing business in Georgia easier (International Finance Corporation, 2006). **Figure 23-2** depicts commerce in Georgia.

FIGURE 23-2

Commerce in Georgia

Environmental problems directly affecting health in Georgia include "air pollution; heavy pollution of Mtkvari River and the Black Sea; inadequate supplies of potable water; and soil pollution from toxic chemicals" (CIA, 2011). Georgia is a mountainous country, with the greater Caucasus Mountains in the north and the lesser Caucasus Mountains in the south (CIA, 2011). Although many of the roads in Georgia are in a state of disrepair, through the World Bank's Roads Rehabilitation program, Georgia was awarded more than $369 million for road projects. Such improvements have made travel less costly and more efficient on major roads throughout the country (World Bank, 2011a). Although major roads have been targeted for improvements, more than half of the population lives in rural, mountainous areas with poorly kept roads, making access to healthcare or other resources dangerous or not feasible.

Because of its location and the fact that it is a Christian country, Georgia has become a strategic ally of the United States. President Mikheil Saakashvili's courting of the Western world, among other issues, has kept the Georgia–Russia relationship in turmoil. In the past Georgia depended solely on Russia for much of its oil, but with the Baku–Tbilisi–Ceyhan oil pipeline Georgia's oil supplies are now increasingly coming from Azerbaijan (CIA, 2011). The construction of these pipelines has helped to bolster Georgia's economy. Although its ability to provide a constant supply of electricity is still a concern, Georgia is now utilizing more hydroelectric power, so power outages occur less frequently than in years past (CIA, 2011). Additionally, Russia has supported regional separatist activities in the areas of Abkhazia and South Ossetia, which has antagonized the Georgian government. This led to an armed conflict between Georgia and Russia over the separatist areas in August 2008 in which approximately 150 people were confirmed dead (Cornell, Popjanevski, & Nilsson, 2008). According to the Georgian Ministry of Labor Health and Social Affairs (MoLHSA) speaking at a large nursing conference in Tbilisi, nurses were commended for playing a vital role in providing care to the wounded in this conflict (MoLHSA deputy minister Nicoloz Pruidze, personal communication, 2009).

Following the 1991 collapse of the FSU, the American International Health Alliance (AIHA) was formed through the U.S. Agency for International Development (USAID) with the goal of advancing global health. Its work began in the newly independent states (NIS) in 1992 with a partnership model. The partnership model paired healthcare entities in the United States with hospitals and communities in the NIS in an attempt to address the problems experienced by the decimated NIS healthcare systems. The U.S. healthcare entities volunteered their expertise and committed to helping struggling nations through these partnerships, with AIHA providing the support services and management systems (AIHA, 2011). The only AIHA remuneration for the partners was essentially reimbursement of travel expenses for trips to and from the partnership countries. The time and expertise of the partners were considered in-kind funding. This partnership model proved extremely successful, and in turn AIHA broadened its scope of influence to the central and eastern European (CEE) countries and beyond.

AIHA's programmatic approach was based on the concept that all partnerships would most likely share common concerns and problems within their healthcare systems. With this concept instilled within the partnership philosophy, partners collaborated in a number of areas, including emergency medicine, nursing, women's health, health management, infection control, primary health care, and neonatal resuscitation, among others, to transform health care in the NIS and CEE countries (AIHA, 2011). Partnerships in most of the NIS ran for a specified length of time (three or four years) and then "graduated" from AIHA oversight and funding.

One of the longest-standing partnerships resulting from the original AIHA partnerships in the NIS was the Atlanta–Tbilisi healthcare partnership (ATHP). Also known as the "Georgia to Georgia" project, this endeavor, which started with a single partner hospital, has grown in scope and influence in both Georgias. Henry (2002) stated that through this partnership many "important relationships have been forged under the Fogarty Fellowships, the Muskie Fellowships, the World Bank health reform project, the Epidemic Intelligence Service programs of CDC, the World Health Organization (WHO) Collaborating Center in Maternal and Perinatal Health programs, USAID projects for infectious disease surveillance, and the Association of University Programs in Health Administration" (p. 9). In 2002, the Atlanta–Tbilisi project evolved into the nongovernmental organizations (NGO) known as Partners for International Development (PfID) and its in-country counterpart Partners for Health (PfH). The World Bank (2011b) provides a website outlining the many NGOs operations in Europe and Central Asia.

The World Bank defines NGOs as follows: "Private organizations that pursue activities to relieve suffering, promote the interests of the poor, protect the environment, provide basic social services, or undertake community development" (Operational Directive 14.70). In wider usage, the term NGO can be applied to any nonprofit organization that is independent from government. NGOs are typically value-based organizations, which depend, in whole or in part, on charitable donations and voluntary service. Although the NGO sector has become increasingly professional over the last two decades, principles of altruism and voluntarism remain key defining characteristics of all such organizations (Duke Libraries, 2011).

Georgia partners in the continuing Atlanta–Tbilisi coalition are the Government of Georgia (GOG), the Caucasus School of Business, Georgian Technical University, and Tbilisi State Medical University. The Atlanta institutions include Emory University, Georgia State University, Georgia Institute of Technology, Grady Memorial Hospital, and Morehouse School of Medicine. Although the partnership has received public-sector funding, sizable contributions by the U.S. partner institutions and their volunteer health professionals have more than matched the U.S. government's support.

The Atlanta–Tbilisi partnership has been involved in many aspects of the healthcare arena in Georgia over the span of this association. Assessment has been an ongoing task, with the partnership and priorities being changed as some of the more pressing problems have been addressed. After addressing the Georgian healthcare system and communicable diseases, this chapter discusses areas of assistance that include healthcare reform, nursing and nursing education, medical education, business education, healthcare management, emergency care, and other activities.

THE GEORGIAN HEALTHCARE SYSTEM

From 1921 until 1991, the Georgian healthcare system was part of the greater Soviet healthcare system. In this centralized system of health care, known as the Semashko model, health care for every Soviet citizen was provided by the government from general public revenues. The Semashko model was based on a hospital inpatient medical model, which was extremely costly and inefficient with little to no focus on prevention or primary care. This system included huge numbers of hospital beds, with equally huge numbers of doctors and other medical personnel staffing them. Governmental assessment of this system did not require reports on quality of care; rather, quantitative indicators such as number of beds, occupancy rates, or number of referrals were used as markers of achievement. Outcomes reported were usually congruent with goals the Soviet superiors wanted achieved.

With the collapse of the Soviet Union came economic blight for all of the countries of that entity— and Georgia was no exception. The healthcare system in Georgia declined rapidly because of the poor financial situation in the country resulting from civil war, a stagnant economy, and inflation. Although healthcare system reform has been on the table since 1995, the system is still not meeting the needs of its citizens, especially the poorer segment of the population. **Table 23-1** shows a partial representation of Georgian healthcare reform legislation, from the Law of Georgia on Health Care, Section 4, from December 10, 1997 (WHO, 2011b).

In principle, the legislation looks laudable, but economic circumstances have slowed forward movement. Healthcare-sector expenditures as a percentage of GDP have been increasing since 2000 and reached 8.2% in 2007, with public sources supplying 18.9% of total health expenditures (Chanturidze, Ugulava, Durán, Ensor, & Richardson, 2009). In that same year, 70.9% of total health expenditures were made as direct, out-of-pocket payments (Chanturidze et al., 2009). The reliance on out-of-pocket payments limits care to what the patient can afford and wants to spend and, therefore, limits services to the

TABLE 23-1

Georgian Healthcare Reform Legislation: Principles of State Policy in the Field of Health Care

1. To provide the population with universal and equal access to medical care within the framework of state-funded medical programs

2. To assure the protection of human rights and freedoms in the field of health care, as well as the recognition of the patient's dignity, honor, and autonomy

3. To recognize the independence of the physician and other medical personnel within the framework prescribed by Georgian legislation

4. To adapt the health system to the country's economic development strategy and ensure that the national health system is properly managed

5. To protect against discrimination, during the provision of medical care, toward detained or imprisoned persons, as well as persons suffering from certain disease

6. To implement and strengthen internationally recognized standards of medical ethics in the healthcare field

7. To provide the population with full information on all existing forms of medical care and the modalities of access to such care

8. To promote cooperation with international organizations working in the field of health care

9. To assign responsibility to the state for the extent and quality of the medical services determined by the compulsory health insurance program

10. To accord priority to primary health care and emergency medical care, with the participation of the public and private sectors

11. To assign responsibility to the state for the licensing and certification of medical personnel, health establishments, medical faculties, and medical training establishments

12. To ensure that the state, society, and every citizen participate in the adoption of a healthy lifestyle and also the protection of the working, home, and recreational environments

13. To assure the diversity of organizational and legal structures and forms of ownership in the field of medical service, as well as the equality of their rights

14. To apply administrative and legal sanctions against acts that are harmful to the population's health

15. To provide for state funding through an overall program and specific programs, and to assure the autonomy of the management system as well as financial and economic contractual relations in order to permit the self-management of state-funded health establishments, in accordance with the legislation

16. To provide for the state funding of biomedical and healthcare research in keeping with existing resources and to create, to this end, favorable conditions for attracting funds from the private sector

17. To ensure that professional and other nongovernmental organizations participate in the creation of a modern and efficient health system through consultations, scientific and professional discussions, the development of relevant projects, and participation in the protection of patients' rights

crisis of the moment rather than what is actually needed to keep a patient healthy or out of tertiary care. In particular, pharmaceuticals represent a major cost to the citizenry.

The MoLHSA is the lead agency in developing health policy in Georgia. MoLHSA's current strategy is decentralization of regulatory powers from the central MoLHSA to subordinate executive agencies. Healthcare reform since 2006 has mainly focused on making a complete transition to marketization and privatization of the health sector (Chanturidze et al., 2009). Despite the move toward privatization of health care in Georgia, poverty remains a major factor predictive of ill health. Because the privatization of care in Georgia has been characterized by a lack of strategy and visions, concerns have been expressed that such privatization will result in even greater inequality in access to care (Hauschild & Berkhout, 2009).

Currently, Georgian medical hospitals are accredited by the MoLHSA and only physicians are mandated to have a license to practice. Nurses are allowed to practice upon successful graduation from a nursing school but are not licensed.

The infrastructure of Georgia's healthcare system is antiquated and unable to meet the present needs of its citizenry in terms of both quality and geography (Hauschild & Berkhout, 2009). A study conducted by the Curatio International Foundation, based on a 2000 Tbilisi household survey, found that the poorest households spend almost one-fourth of their income on out-of-pocket healthcare expenses, compared to only 15% of income spent by wealthier families (Gotsadze, Bennett, Ranson, & Gzirishvili, 2005). Additionally, 55% of this money was spent on medicines that are not covered by government programs. More than half of the people in this survey reported that they self-treated their illnesses, and at least 11% did not seek treatment at all. When people do seek care, they turn to a specialist first, probably an acquaintance, which negates the country's push for less expensive primary care. Many seek emergency treatment because they wait too long to attend to their health in a less costly fashion; that is, they delay seeking care until their problems reach a more advanced—and expensive—stage. According to a 2009 Oxfam report, the Curatio 2000 findings are still valid (Hauschild & Berkhout, 2009). Because salaries of healthcare professionals are so low, out-of-pocket payments directly to healthcare personnel to receive better care (or any care at all) are commonplace (Hauschild & Berkhout, 2009; Nishiyama, Wold, & Partskhaladze, 2008). The current supply of healthcare professionals greatly exceeds demand, with physicians outnumbering nurses—4.09 per 1000 versus 2.92 per 1000, respectively, in 2009 (Chanturidze et al., 2009, p. 63; National Center for Disease Control and Public Health [NCDC], n.d.). **Figure 23-3** shows a typical Georgian intensive care unit.

FIGURE 23-3

A Typical Georgia Intensive Care Unit

HEALTH INDICATORS

According to the McGee and Bose (2009), Georgia is an economy in transition. Life expectancy at birth for Georgians is 73.8 years for males and 80.8 years for females (CIA, 2011), although healthy life expectancy is almost 10 years less than these figures (WHO, 2011d). Adult mortality rates are estimated to be 9.93 deaths per 1000 population (CIA, 2011). The life expectancy for males is 73.94 years and for females is 81 years. Total health expenditure per capita was $433 in 2008 (Kaiser Family Foundation, 2011). Health expenditures per capita in Georgia amounted to $499 in 2009, as compared to $7410 per capita in the United States (WHO, 2011d).

The health of nations is usually measured by its maternal and infant mortality rates. In 2011, the infant mortality rate (IMR) in Georgia was estimated at 15.2 deaths per 1000 population, and the under-5 child mortality rate was 43 per 1000. Although the IMR rate has decreased from the 2004 rate of 40 per 1000 (CIA, 2011), it compares unfavorably to the U.S. IMR of 6.1 per 1000 and the U.S. under-5 child mortality rate of 8 per 1000. The top two causes of under-5 deaths in Georgia are prematurity and pneumonia (World Bank, 2011b). Maternal mortality in Georgia is 50 per 100,000, versus 8 per 100,000 in the United States. The Georgian abortion-to-live birth ratio was down to 0.8:1 in 2010, which represented a significant improvement from the 2:1 ratio in 1999. Contraceptive prevalence in Georgia is at 40.5% versus 64.2% in the United States (Serbanescu, Egnatashvili, Ruiz, Suchdev, & Goodwill, 2011).

The deterioration of the healthcare system in Georgia is slowly being repaired under the auspices of many international aid agencies. John Snow International (JSI) is working with women in Georgia to improve reproductive health through the Sustain project and participation in a national reproductive health survey (JSI, 2011). UNICEF and other international organizations have worked with the Georgian government on maintaining the ability to refrigerate vaccines; in the past, the country's inability to maintain refrigeration all too often invalidated the vaccines' effectiveness. The number of reports on immunization coverage by WHO has increased in Georgia from 1993 to 2005 for bacille Calmette-Guérin (BCG), diphtheria–pertussis–tetanus 3 (DPT3), oral polio vaccine 3 (OPV3), measles containing vaccine 1 (MCV1), and hepatitis B 3 (HepB3) (WHO, 2011a). Immunization coverage has risen from 30–50% to more than 80–90% for BCG, DPT, OPV, and measles, but remains less impressive for hepatitis B, for which a vaccine was introduced only in 2001 (UNICEF, 2011). As a result of this initiative, in July 2002, Georgia received its polio-free certification, and it remains polio-free today.

HIV/AIDS

The first case of HIV in Georgia was diagnosed in 1989. The 2009 adult prevalence rate of HIV/AIDs was 0.1%, while the number of people living with AIDS was estimated at 3500 (CIA, 2011). Georgia is considered to have a low-prevalence HIV epidemic with the groups at the highest risk for transmission of the infection being men who have sex with men, IV drug users, and female sex workers (United Nations, 2010). The main factors contributing to HIV spread are a poor economic environment, increasing incidence of drug trafficking and use of illicit drugs, a large prison population, an increase in sexually transmitted infections (STIs), increased migration and internally displaced populations, rising incidence of HIV infection in frequently traveled, neighboring countries such as the Ukraine, and a burgeoning commercial sex trade. In addition, hepatitis C (HCV) is widespread and tuberculosis is epidemic, which could prove to be as destructive in Georgia as it is in Africa.

Treatment for HIV infection is typically initiated late because of the disease being diagnosed in the late stages due to the low coverage of interventions among the most at-risk people (MARP) (Tsertsavadze, 2011). Through the partnership of the AIDS International Training and Research Program (AITRP), the NCDC, and the Georgian government, the country has instigated a significant push to increase coverage to at least 80% through effective interventions and improved early diagnosis and initiation of antiretroviral therapy (ART). Currently the country has nine volunteer counseling and treatment centers (VCT) and four AIDS treatment centers (Tsertsavadze, 2011). HIV genotyping and real-time polymerase chain reaction (PCR) testing are among the many lab tests that have been utilized for HIV detection since 2005 in Georgia. Other measures include HIV resistance testing for low viral load and therapeutic drug monitoring. In 2004, Georgia became the first FSU country to ensure 100% access to antiretroviral therapy (Tsertsavadze, 2011). It is believed that through these interventions, Georgia was and is able to avoid a rapid growth rate of new HIV cases (Tsertsavadze, 2011)

The HIV-focused partnership has enabled promising young Georgians to come to Emory University for training. Many collaborative research projects have been undertaken, resulting in many publications and presentations. Eighteen Georgians have received short- and long-term training in the United States, and in-country training has been provided as well. Of particular importance was an Ethical Conduct of Research course, which helped Georgian scientists and institutions to improve their research practices so as to have their institutional review boards registered and approved by the U.S. Department of Health and Human Services, which is a prerequisite for applying for research funding from U.S. government agencies.

Other U.S. partners working with Georgia in the field of HIV/AIDS have included the Bloomberg School of Public Health of Johns Hopkins University, the State University of New York Downstate Medical Center, the Centers for Disease Control and Prevention (CDC), and the Sparkman Center of the University of Alabama. The U.S. partners have also collaborated with a successful Comprehensive International Research Program on AIDS (CIPRA) RO3 application and have worked closely on an U19 CIPRA application recently submitted to the National Institutes of Health. Each year a two-day conference, held by researchers and physicians from Georgia working with institutions that collaborate with NIH Fogarty programs, updates the recent research and changes made to treatment and prevention in Georgia.

Tuberculosis

Tuberculosis (TB) has emerged as a serious public health problem in Georgia (Lomtadze et al., 2009). The annual incidence of disease is approximately 100 cases per 100,000 people, and the prevalence is 116 per 100,000 (World Bank, 2011b). Georgia remains among the top 27 countries with high rates of multidrug-resistant TB (MDR-TB) (Tadumadze, 2011); MDR-TB accounts for 9.5% of new cases and 31.4% of retreated cases of TB in Georgia (Kalandadze, 2011; Lomtadze et al., 2009; WHO, 2011c). In 2008, Georgia had a significant increase in MDR-TB prevalence among both new (11.3%) and retreatment (40.3%) cases. The direct causes of this trend are unknown but are attributed to the programmatic availability of the second-line treatment since March 2008 on a countrywide basis. In 2009, the prevalence of drug resistance began to stabilize and returned to the 2007 level for retreatment cases. HIV coinfection appears to be low, but HCV coinfection is common, occurring in 18% of all TB patients (Avaliani, 2011).

Since 2005, the National Tuberculosis Program leadership has embraced the directly observed therapy short-course (DOTS) program, and limited pilot projects involving this treatment have been undertaken. DOTS implementation is greatly needed to improve TB control in Georgia and establish the infrastructure necessary for the treatment of patients with MDR-TB (i.e., through DOTS-plus). To date, nine DOTS spots have been established in Tbilisi. These sites report increased patient compliance with TB treatment therapy, ranging from 28% to 91%; the TB treatment success rate in Tbilisi reached 71% in 2005 compared with 60% in 2003 (USAID, 2006). In addition, several of the main TB hospitals and national centers have undergone renovations, including development of a new palliative care department for patients with Multi-Drug Resistant and Extensively Drug-Resistant M/XDR-TB treatment failure. A five-year TB control plan has also been created and includes the continual enhancement and strengthening of the DOTS program, aimed at enhancing surveillance and reducing the burden of M/XDR-TB (Kalandadze, 2011).

Collaborative research activities of the U.S.–Georgia partnership have focused on investigating the clinical and molecular epidemiology of tuberculosis in Georgia. Short-term trainees have come to the United States for laboratory or epidemiologic training for a duration of several months, and Emory University medical students have gone to Georgia to carry out collaborative research projects with the National Tuberculosis Program and AIDS Center colleagues. These projects have been supported by grants from the U.S. Civilian Research Development Foundation and the U.S. Department of Health and Human Services' Biotechnology Exchange Program. The NIH Fogarty International Center has funded the Emory–Georgia TB Research Training Program, which focuses on addressing the research needs and gaps in the current expertise in Georgia. The goal of the program is to help build human resources capacity for high-quality TB-related research in Georgia by providing long-, medium-, and short-term training to a diverse group of researchers with outstanding potential; it will build the in-country research capacity so it can support evidence-based translation of research into policy and practice in Georgia.

Health of Women and Children

Numerous exchanges have focused on perinatal medicine in Georgia, with an emphasis on public health problems. For example, an Emory medical student analyzed blood from 500 placentas and discovered a 60% incidence of hypothyroidism in Georgia newborns—a study that helped lead to corrective measures undertaken by the government and international organizations. Neonatal mortality in Georgia in the 1990s was five to seven times that in the European Union. Monitoring of the fetus during gestation by sonogram or during labor by electronic monitoring was rudimentary. A group of Emory physicians, composed of an obstetrician and several neonatologists, assessed care practices in the maternity houses throughout Georgia. Educational exchanges occurred, focusing on obstetric monitoring and neonatal care. The Neonatal Resuscitation Program of the American Academy of Pediatrics had 30 participants from the regions of Georgia. This group has now trained instructors throughout the Caucasus.

The Atlanta–Kutaisi Partnership was inaugurated in 1999, establishing the first Women's Wellness Center (WWC) in western Georgia. The Susan Komen Foundation provided $150,000 in grants for a project promoting breast health. In 2000, the WWC was opened in a renovated building, with Carelift International participating in furnishing the facility. The WWC provides screening and preventive health care, contraception, nutrition, prenatal care, breast health education, reproductive counseling, Pap smears, ultrasound, loop electrocautery excision procedures, and colposcopy. Moe than 36,000 women have been educated in breast self-examination. The partners established a community health council, a project in secondary schools on reproductive and psychiatric assessment of teenage girls, and community classes on childbirth, prenatal health, breast self-examination, and breastfeeding.

NURSING

Nursing has been a key presence in the work of the Georgia-to-Georgia partnership since its inception. Upgrading a culturally oppressed profession has proved to be no small task. The partners know that, on a worldwide basis, nurses at a modern professional level of education have enormous responsibility for patient care in hospitals, outpatient clinics, and rural areas. Research shows that patient outcomes suffer if nurses are not educated and prepared to meet the challenges of a modern system of health care (Van den Heede et al., 2009). In the villages of Georgia, a nurse often serves as a combination of nurse clinician and public health worker. Better education for Georgian nurses can produce better patient outcomes. Indeed, well-educated nurses are pivotal in executing the primary care, health promotion, and disease prevention model of health care desired by the country of Georgia. Prevention of disease in a time of scarce monetary resources is one way to reduce healthcare expenditures. Moreover, more comprehensively educated nurses will be able to provide the expert care at the bedside that will be required as Georgia acquires a more technologically advanced medical care system.

Acting as advisors to Georgian nursing leaders, the partnership has made an extensive effort to improve the knowledge level and professional acceptance of the profession of nursing in the country of Georgia largely through a "train the trainer" (TTT) model in an effort to build in-country capacity. The nurse participants from both sides of the partnership have put forth a great deal of effort in implementing a three-pronged approach to upgrade the nursing profession in Georgia. This plan has encompassed the enhancement of skills of practicing nurses (ongoing), strengthening of the political base of nursing within the country, and the implementation of a university-based program for nursing education.

Background of Nursing Activities

Over the years there have been many exchanges that featured nurses coming to the United States for observation and training in nursing leadership, education, and skills. In the early years of the partnerships, AIHA was very involved in developing nurse leaders in the NIS countries and held annual nurse leadership conferences that were attended by nurses from both partners. Numerous continuing education seminars were held on such topics as nursing triage, nursing assessment, infection control, intravenous therapy, pain management, preoperative and postoperative care, community-focused care, and other topics. Complete plans for setting up a modern nursing care system were provided for the partner hospitals, many of them translated into Georgian. This information included nursing structure standards (e.g., protocols, procedures, forms), infection control documents, hospital safety documents, a human resources policy manual, and a health system operational policy manual, among other items.

In 1993, a delegation of nurses, which included hospital nurse administrators and a university nursing educator, visited Tbilisi with the specific goal of assessing both the Georgian nursing education system and the level of nursing care and skills in the partner hospital, City Hospital #2. These objectives were accomplished, and were reported in their meetings with the Minister of Health. One of the most important features of this partnership was the regular and continuing U.S. interaction with the highest governmental officials for the country of Georgia.

By and large, nursing education in Georgia was and is carried out by both the government and private schools, and is called "middle and higher technical medical education." Currently, fewer than 20 nursing schools exist in Georgia. Although they were historically called nursing colleges, no nursing education has taken place in institutions of higher education; as a consequence, the graduates from these programs do not have a degree that would allow them to teach in a university-level baccalaureate nursing education program. Thus nursing is taught by physicians, and nursing education is carried out in schools with little funding, few learning resources, and, compared to nursing education in the United States, low expectations for their graduates (Nishiyama et al., 2008). Until very recently, students interested in pursuing a nursing career entered nursing school in their ninth or eleventh year of high school and spent two to three years in "nurse's training." Students took an examination designed by their nursing school at the end of their program, which, if they passed, qualified them to take a nursing position at a hospital or clinic. Georgia lacks a countrywide licensure examination for nursing, and a license is not mandated to practice nursing. To be accepted into a nursing school, students do not have to pass the national university examination. Those who do pass the national examination are allowed to enter a university and then obtain a nursing diploma as a second degree. To date, there has been little oversight of the quality of nursing education both because of the many private nursing schools and because of the economic situation in the country. The Ministry of Education and Science of Georgia (MOES) is responsible for the oversight and accreditation of schools but conducts only institutional accreditation.

In the past, medical students (who enter medical school immediately after high school) could practice as nurses in Georgia after two years of medical school. If these medical students decided to practice as nurses while attending medical school, they took positions from less well-prepared technical nurses.

Some physicians still practice as nurses today due to the over-abundant supply of physicians and the scarcity of jobs.

In Georgia, physicians outnumber nurses. In 2009, the NCDC reported that there were 20,962 physicians in the country (409 per 100,000 population) and 12,933 medical nurses (292.8 per 100,000 population). Midwives numbered 732 (16.5 per 100,000 population), and dentists numbered 1115 in total. Salaries for both physicians and nurses in Georgia are very low compared to U.S. standards. A nurse's salary on average is $210 per month, with a range of $24 to $1200 per month, and a physician's pay ranges between $400 and $5000 per month, with an average of $600—but with no guarantee that a paycheck will be delivered on time (Goshadze, personal communication, September 27, 2011). Of course, the out-of-pocket payments made by their patients can significantly raise healthcare providers' salaries.

During the initial and subsequent nursing delegation visits to Georgia, the level of hospital nursing has been assessed. Assessment revealed that nurses in Georgia are trained at a level somewhere between U.S. nursing assistants and licensed practical nurses (LPNs). Nurses in Georgia make few independent decisions regarding patient care, nor do they write in the medical records in the hospitals. Additionally, there are no written nursing standards of care. Historically, a nurse's primary role was to carry out the physician's medication orders and to assist with procedures.

Due to the desire of the MoLHSA, greater interest has been displayed in the nursing profession—specifically, in improving the current workforce. Even in the best hospitals in Georgia, nurses still do not complete assessments on their patients, but there is an increase in autonomy noted such that nurses are depended upon for procedures, medication administration, and general patient care for the day. Nurses are not taught procedures, such as taking vital signs, as part of their nursing diploma program; rather, procedures are taught via on-the-job training. Most nurses give medications without any formal pharmacology education. Often physicians hand orders to nurses that the nurses are obligated to complete if they want to keep their jobs. Throughout most of Georgia, the nurse's role is seen basically as "handmaiden" to the physician. As mentioned previously, there is no countrywide licensure for nurses, no countrywide registry, and no real mechanism or mandate for continuing nursing education.

For both political and educational reasons, the U.S. partners assisted the Georgian nurses in developing a nursing association. In 1996, the Georgian Nurses Association (GNA) was instituted as a mechanism to unite nurses in the country and to deliver continuing education under its auspices. A small fee for membership was assessed and the association began in earnest. At about the same time as the inauguration of the GNA, the Georgian parliament passed a law making nursing a distinct profession and the Minister of Health appointed a chief nursing officer (CNO) for the country. After the "Rose Revolution" in 2003, the CNO position was abolished and the GNA demonstrated little activity until December 2009. At that time, the GNA was revitalized. It now has active officers and board members, more than 1500 members, and regional representatives in 5 of the 11 Georgian regions. The dues are minimal (approximately $3.60 per year), so the GNA has little capital and no money for a paid position. Currently, the organization is working toward achieving ICN membership within the next year to gain linkage to the international nursing community. With no CNO position in existence at the MoLHSA, however, there is a lack of nursing advocacy at the top administrative levels of government.

Closely tied to continuing education was the quest to institute a university-based baccalaureate nursing education program. Because baccalaureate education of nurses in a U.S. model requires both sciences and liberal arts preparation, the partnership made the decision to align itself with a multipurpose institution instead of a medical university. It was felt that a medical university would continue with a heavy medical influence and limit nursing from becoming its own profession. In 1996, the partnership forged an agreement with Javakhishvili Tbilisi State University (TSU) to cooperate in instituting a bachelor of science nursing program. This arrangement was approved by the Minister of Health at that time, with the promise of start-up funding in the amount of 50.000 Lari (GEL) (approximately $25,000). The funding never materialized, however, as a result of both the dire financial straits of the government and the subsequent revolution.

Nevertheless, two delegations of Georgian physicians have been to the United States to be trained to conduct the baccalaureate program. Understanding the realities of teaching in a university system, the partnership knew there were no technically trained Georgian nurses qualified to teach in a university. Instead, the focus was on physicians who had worked as nurses or who had also taught in technical "colleges" of nursing. The first delegation of three physicians came to the United States for a month. They sat in on university nursing courses, visited clinical rotations in hospitals, and carried extensive course material and nursing texts back to their country. Hundreds of volumes of donated nursing texts were shipped to the TSU library. Negotiations continued in an attempt to implement the baccalaureate program, but government funding did not materialize.

After the partnership re-formed into Partners for International Development (PfID) and Partners for Health (PfH), implementing a university-based approach to nursing education continued to be a priority. A second attempt to prepare trainers to implement a BS program occurred in 2005 with funding from AIHA, the Soros Foundation, Open Society Georgia Foundation (OSGF), and the Nell Hodgson Woodruff School of Nursing (NHWSN) at Emory University (OSGF, 2006). From the group of Georgian nurses actively involved in this work, four nurse trainers were selected by the partnership to participate in the proposed project. In 2005, the nursing education director of the partnership had been leading the nursing education component of the partnership for 12 years and was very familiar with nursing, nursing education, and human resources in the country.

Four physicians spent an entire semester in the NHWSN at Emory. Not only were they enrolled in the Nursing Teaching Institute, but they were also guided in this teaching institute in developing a culturally specific 27-course baccalaureate nursing curriculum, completely translated into Georgian. Each course had an accompanying updated American text. Additionally, 40 continuing education (CE) courses were developed in the areas outlined in **Table 23-2**. The development of the CE courses was of prime importance because continuing education has always been a mainstay of the partnership and is a fallback approach in the ongoing efforts to undergird better nursing education. These trainers returned to Tbilisi in June 2005 to begin an ambitious CE plan for nurses in the partner hospitals and to continue to negotiate for the university-based program.

Nursing education centers, funded by AIHA through the PfID and PfH partners, were established at the Central Children's Hospital (CCH) in 2004 and at the National Medical Center in 2005 based on the model of the National Resource Learning Center, which was established early in the partnership. The nursing educators were hired by CCH at the continuous professional education (CPE) unit to provide continuous certificate courses and in-service nursing education to the partner hospitals and in other priority areas (e.g., primary healthcare) using the curricula developed at NHWSN. Follow-up of the CE activities with nurses who attended all sessions showed an overall knowledge retention rate of 84% and a skills usage rate of 75% among the 72 nurses sampled (Partskhladze, Gogashvili, Jashi, & Mindadze, 2006). Approximately 800 nurses were trained through partnership-sponsored CE courses from 2005 to 2009.

Current Activities

Building on the 2005 curriculum construction, in 2009 USAID and Emory University partnered to implement extensive continuing education courses for nurses as well as a further attempt to start a BSN program in Georgia. The objectives of this $2 million dollar grant were as follows:

1. Update the 2005 CE courses
2. Develop a new learning center
3. Establish a model nursing floor at a partnering hospital for clinical education
4. Establish a CE nursing program for practicing nurses
5. Establish a Western-model BSN nursing program
6. Develop nursing education models
7. Work with the government to create an appropriate regulatory environment for nursing

---

TABLE 23-2

Nursing Continuing Education Programs Developed in the Teaching Institute at Emory University, 2005

Course Title and Topics Covered

Nurses and Nursing: Nursing assessment

Fundamentals of Nursing: Vital signs, bed-making, hygiene, oral care, transferring patients, injections, transfusions, infection control

Infection Control

Trauma/Triage: Nursing skills

Cardiovascular–Lymphatic System: Pathology, pharmacology, skills, patient education

Respiratory System, TB: Pathology, pharmacology, skills, patient education

Gastrointestinal System: Pathology, pharmacology, skills, patient education

Neurological System: Pathology, pharmacology, skills, patient education

Endocrine System: Pathology, pharmacology, skills, patient education

Immune System: Pathology, pharmacology, skills, patient education

Renal and Urologic System: Pathology, pharmacology, skills, patient education

Preoperative Care: Nursing skills, patient education

Postoperative Care: Nursing skills, patient education

Musculoskeletal System: Pathology, pharmacology, skills, patient education

Integumentary System: Pathology, pharmacology, skills, patient education

Mental Health Conditions: Nursing skills, patient education

Care of Older Patients: Nursing skills, patient education

Critical Care: Pathology, pharmacology, skills, patient education

Cancer: Pathology, pharmacology, skills, patient education

Pain Management: Pathology, pharmacology, skills, patient education

Infectious Diseases, STDs: Pathology, pharmacology, skills, patient education

Reproductive/Pregnancy-Related Considerations: Pathology, pharmacology, skills, patient education

---

The grant included having a Western-trained, master's-level nurse on site for two years of the three-year grant. The Archil and Sergo Kobaladze Learning Resource Center has been developed through generous donations from the Atlanta–Tbilisi partnership as well as the staff of PfID. It currently has two classrooms, a simulation room, and a conference room, in addition to waiting areas and offices for the PfID faculty and staff. Additional classrooms, a practice clinic, and an apartment for guest lecturers are currently under construction. **Figure 23-4** shows a group of Georgian nurses at the partnership's newly furnished center. Additionally, a model nursing unit was developed at a partner hospital to educate nurses in clinical

FIGURE 23-4

Georgian Nurses at the Partnership's Newly Furnished Kobaladze Center

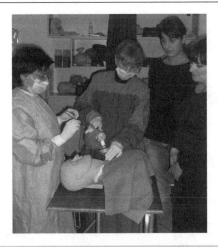

techniques learned in class. This model unit, while not up to Western standards, still allows student nurses more autonomy to practice their newly learned skills than in other hospitals throughout the country.

The new grant began with a three-month TTT program for carefully selected potential nursing faculty members consisting of both physicians and nurses. Faculty went through an extensive interview process and had to have at least a grade of 85%, a 90% attendance rate, and a grade of 90% on the comprehensive final exam. Sixteen faculty successfully completed the TTT program and to date have trained more than 1600 practicing nurses in either general nursing or one of the specialty nursing courses (see **Figure 23-5** for schematic of course implementation). The general nursing course must be taken prior to entering a specialty course; specialty courses include emergency, critical care, surgical nursing, and maternity nursing. The CE courses are conducted in a period from 3 to 5 weeks and are currently undergoing a major revision for the final year of the program. Most likely the time frame for classes and clinical experiences will be expanded because the level of current nursing education and ability to practice are limited. Students who have completed this course have shown a significant increase in knowledge and improvement in their skills and confidence levels.

A law has recently been passed in Georgia allowing university-based BSN programs. Three schools were slated to begin a BSN program in the fall of 2011: Tbilisi State Medical University (TSMU), Georgian University, and International Education in Rustavi. Throughout the 2010–2011 school year, PfID taught an elective recruitment course, titled Introduction to Nursing, at Ilia State University in Tbilisi; 58 students were enrolled in the course. However, PfID will be working with the newly established TSMU BSN program going forward.

As in the United States, the development of nursing as a respected profession in Georgia will take time and money. Georgia needs in-country nursing champions with political influence because upgrading the profession of nursing is a both a cultural change and an economic issue. It will require an investment and a commitment on the part of the Georgian government to upgrade nursing education in these university settings. Time will tell whether the newly implemented BSN programs are successful.

FIGURE 23-5

Schematic of Nursing Faculty Train the Trainer Schedule Cascade

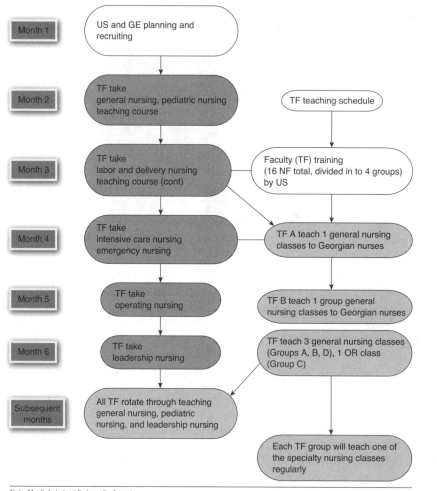

Note: Month 1 starts at first month of grant.

MEDICAL EDUCATION

Since 1991, medical education in Georgia has borne many similarities to the United States during the pre-Flexner era, with a plethora of private medical schools existing primarily to provide income for the teachers. In 2004, there were 69 higher level medical universities in Georgia graduating approximately 15,000 students per year in a country that has a population of fewer than 5 million. The number of medical schools had decreased to 34 in 2006 after the first round of accreditations. At the time of this chapter's writing, there were fewer than 20 accredited medical schools in the country (MoLHSA, 2011).

More than 75 medical students from Georgia have spent from 2 to 6 months doing clinical rotations at Emory, and many graduates have been accepted into residency programs at Emory in specialties such as internal medicine, psychiatry, radiation oncology, and neurology. More than 70 Emory medical students have also spent 1 to 2 months doing electives in Tbilisi. Each Emory student has undertaken a specific project, with some of these projects having an impact on public health policies in Georgia.

EMERGENCY MEDICAL CARE AND OTHER INITIATIVES

Although emergency medicine has long been practiced in the West, on-site resuscitation was unknown in the former Soviet Union. The U.S.–Georgia partnership opened an emergency medical services (EMS) training center in October 1995 for the purpose of training individuals in prehospital care. By 1998, 60 courses had been given to members of the public, including students, guards, mountain guides, and pipeline company workers; a total of 1492 people were trained. A webpage was produced, three manuals were published in Georgian, and a learning resource for emergency medicine was established.

A productive relationship evolved between pediatric emergency medicine faculty in Atlanta and a newly opened modern emergency room in Central Children's Hospital, the premier pediatric hospital in Georgia. The goal was to transition medical staff who were trained in pediatrics and critical care medicine into the role of emergency medicine practitioners. New concepts were introduced, including the role of an emergency medicine physician, nursing triage, patient tracking, and flow through an emergency department. A Western-style pediatric emergency facility was opened in 2005 at the Iashvili Pediatric Hospital in Tbilisi with the assistance of this partnership. **Figure 23-6** shows a Georgian child's drawing of an ambulance. The new emergency room served as a model for the country—indeed, the whole Caucasus—and has been instrumental in providing modern health care to hundreds of pediatric patients throughout Georgia.

In 2007, another start-up grant provided through World Learning and Emory University focused on the emergency nurses and physicians of Kipshidze Central Republican Hospital. This effort developed into a mini-emergency medicine residency program throughout the next three years. The initial effort was intended to develop and train the personnel to run a newly constructed emergency center that

FIGURE 23-6

Georgian Child's Drawing of an Ambulance

opened in May 2007. Kipshidze nurses were trained in continuing education and, through a TTT model conducted by an Emory-prepared emergency nurse, six nurses from the emergency department continued the training with other nurses.

The emergency medicine program was created and designed by the Emory Emergency Medicine Department at Emory University. It is an eight-month program that consists of both didactic and clinical components. The first group of 12 residents were interviewed and selected based on their English language ability and current jobs held in an emergency department. Training was provided through a TTT model, in which emergency medicine faculty came to Georgia for two to six weeks at a time to teach the classroom component and monitor the clinical components. The initial group graduated in the fall 2009, and those who successfully passed the course became instructors for the second round starting in spring 2010. The second group successfully completed the course after being reevaluated in spring 2011. Currently, the emergency medicine residency is seeking official government approval to be accepted as an official medical discipline.

BUSINESS EDUCATION

Early in the partnership, Georgia State University (GSU) of Atlanta began assisting with the establishment of business education programs in Tbilisi. This effort was followed by the establishment of the Caucasus School of Business (CSB) in 1998, in collaboration with the Georgian Technical University and Tbilisi State University. Funding for the project was obtained through the U.S. Department of State, Bureau of Educational and Cultural Affairs, and USAID, and through substantial cost sharing by Georgia State University. The Robinson College of Business at Georgia State University helped to develop the master of business administration (MBA) and bachelor of business administration (BBA) curricula, trained Georgian faculty and administrators, and developed computer and distance-learning facilities, as well as library and audiovisual facilities. More than 90% of the Georgian faculty members have been trained in Atlanta during semester-long faculty development programs and have been awarded certificates to teach specific courses. Furthermore, each year, five Georgian students are admitted to Georgia State University for one semester on a competitive basis. CSB has experienced dramatic growth: BBA and MBA, master of health administration (MHA) and doctor of philosophy (PhD) degrees are all now offered.

HEALTHCARE MANAGEMENT

Hospital management is a new and developing field in the country of Georgia. Under the Soviet-designed Semashko model, healthcare planning, financing, and management decisions were centralized. Chief doctors served as administrators. These doctors were clinicians by training, had no management education, and were held responsible only for volume indicators. Poor performance resulted in the application of administrative measures or removal. Since Georgian independence, however, hospital executives have struggled with multiple restructuring efforts to decentralize decision making, reduce costs, and improve efficiency. However, the old management structures are poorly prepared to manage resources and financial obligations.

Two Georgian partners with significant American hospital leadership experience have provided the new administrators with intensive instruction in budgeting, reimbursement, wage administration, performance monitoring and improvement, staffing, quality improvement programming, and service consolidation. Unfortunately, the learning curve is significant and the talent pool shallow. The partnership is now awarding a Certificate in Health Services Management to enhance middle-management capabilities and is in the process of designing academic-based master of health administration programs to broaden the base of individuals qualified to lead a financially sound and outcome-based health system.

DISCUSSION

The Georgia-to-Georgia partnership began when the American International Healthcare Alliance came to Atlanta in the spring of 1992 and invited the leaders of Emory University School of Medicine, Morehouse School of Medicine, and Grady Hospital to participate in a partnership with the country of Georgia. AIHA was formed in 1992 by a consortium of major healthcare provider associations and professional medical education organizations in response to a USAID initiative to develop healthcare partnerships between the United States and the former Soviet Union. AIHA guided the Georgia-to-Georgia partnership with wisdom and advice. In addition to providing direct funding and administrative support for the partnership, this organization provided substantial region-wide resources in support of many of the partnership's initiatives including emergency medical services, nursing, women's health care, infection control, evidence-based practice and informatics, and health management and administration.

The funds spent during the 18 years are estimated at approximately $15 million: $7 million from USAID, $7 million in in-kind contributions from the Atlanta partners, and $1 million in funds from other sources. The Atlanta–Tbilisi partnership has been formalized with the establishment of a nongovernmental organization, the Partners for International Development, and is becoming more productive with time. This richly collaborative relationship has coalesced into an effective unit of individuals and institutions from both countries, with its results spanning a surprisingly wide range of societal sectors. The Caucasus School of Business has educated many young Georgians in the methodology of a market-oriented economy, and they are having a pervasive effect upon business in Georgia. The school's efforts form the basis of education in healthcare administration. Georgian and U.S. medical students have benefited from cross-cultural medical and educational experiences. More than 30 Georgian medical school graduates are now fully trained and certified in specialties in the United States; three are on the faculty of Emory University. Their attempts in going back to practice in Georgia have not been successful due to the present lack of technology and financial uncertainty, so they are experimenting with how to best help Georgia without returning there. One has enlisted her U.S. colleagues in her efforts to establish a modern radiation oncology center in Georgia, which has only a few old cobalt units. Another graduate is working to establish modern cardiology practice in Georgia through equipment donation and training.

The Women's Wellness Center has introduced new concepts in the care of women and children. Collaborative research on AIDS and TB has produced new information that can be applied not only to Georgia but also to other transitioning countries, and has resulted in the establishment of a burgeoning modern research environment. Young Georgian scientists have been trained in current scientific rigor and methods, including ethics in science, making them eligible to compete for grants on the international scene. Ingrained societal behaviors and perceptions are also being transformed: The professional status of nurses is improving, albeit slowly due to the economic situation and the low status the culture has historically assigned to the nursing profession. Medical students and professionals continuously update their knowledge by reading current journals, and new concepts are taking root, such as measurement of patient satisfaction, evidence-based medicine, and the use of clinical practice guidelines.

Current activities include the development of a nursing school, a division of healthcare management in the Caucasus School of Business, and a pediatric radiation oncology center. The planning for a public health school is beginning. Plans for the next several years include reforming the current curriculum of medical schools, accreditation of the emergency medicine residency program, postgraduate residency training, and continuing medical education for practitioners. The launch of the BSN program in local universities and collaboration with the Georgian Nurses Association to give nurses a political voice are also in process. Continuing education for nurses will continue to improve the current nursing work force as well.

The changing nature and role of societal institutions shapes and is shaped by political, economic, and cultural changes already under way within the healthcare sector as well as more generally. The academic collaborations embraced by this partnership provide a vehicle for institution building and a model for future international development. Information technology remains crucial to providing access to electronic databases in the fields of health and business and to connecting sites in countries such as Georgia both with one another and with the West.

These results highlight the unique resources that academic institutions can bring to foreign aid and development. The universities of the West are replete with a vast amount of information that can be gainfully used by countries such as Georgia. Western scholars can collaborate with the scholars of developing countries to produce new information that can be used by all countries.

CRITCAL THINKING QUESTIONS

1. Discuss major health issues and the healthcare system in the country of Georgia,
2. Relate the financial, political, and cultural influences on the healthcare system of the country of Georgia.
3. Compare and contrast the health and healthcare system of the country of Georgia with other countries established from the former Soviet Union and other developing countries.
4. Describe the medical and nursing educational programs in the country of Georgia.

CASE STUDY

You are part of a local NGO that has been asked to help a regional general hospital and a clinic restructure their personnel and hospital administration model. Both were recently bought by an organization from Romania and this company wants your NGO to help develop this hospital.

The current information shown here:

- Hospital beds: 75
- Clinic beds: 8
- Physicians: 70 total
- Nurses: 95 total
- Auxiliary staff: 20 total

The number of beds will not change but the personnel mix may. Many of these people are the only members of their family with a job, and many have not been paid regularly by the hospital. The hospital and clinic are located in the rural region of Samtskhe-Javakheti (population 300,000) and are the only facilities within a 70-km radius. This hospital still resembles the Semashko system with the exception that people are turned away because supplies are not available.

Case Study Questions

1. What is your first concern?
2. Given that this hospital still operates under a Semashko model, what are some issues that must be overcome?

REFERENCES

American International Health Alliance (AIHA). (2011). AIHA web page. Retrieved from http://www.aiha.com/_content/3_What%20We%20Do/Archives/HealthcarePartnerships/TbilisiAtlanta.asp

Avaliani, M. V. (2011, June). *HCV/HBV surveillance in Georgia: Current status and future perspectives.* Presentation at the U.S.–Georgia Infectious Disease Research Conference: Building a Regional Research Agenda, Tbilisi, Georgia.

Brunnell, R., Hoover, B., Day, M., Yetter, S., & Dersham, L. (2005). Georgia employment and infrastructure initiative: Socioeconomic inventory assessment. Retrieved from http://pdf.usaid.gov/pdf_docs/PNADD296.pdf

Central Intelligence Agency (CIA). (2011). The world factbook: Georgia. Retrieved from https://www.cia.gov/library/publications/the-world-factbook/geos/gg.html

Chanturidze, T., Ugulava, T., Durán, A., Ensor, T., & Richardson, E. (2009). Georgia: Health system review. *Health Systems in Transition, 11*(8), 1–116.

Cornell, S. E., Popjanevski, J., & Nilsson, N. (2008). Russia's war in Georgia: Causes and implications for Georgia and the world. Central Asia Institute and Silk Road Studies Program. Retrieved from www.silkroadstudies.org

Duke Libraries. (2011). World Bank definition of NGOs. Retrieved from http://library.duke.edu/research/subject/guides/ngo_guide/igo_ngo_coop/ngo_wb.html

Gotsadze, G., Bennett, S., Ranson, K., & Gzirishvili, D. (2005). Health care seeking behaviour and out-of-pocket payments in Tbilisi, Georgia: Household survey findings. *Health Policy and Planning, 20*(4), 232–242.

Hauschild, T., & Berkhout, E. (2009, May). *Health-care reform in Georgia: A civil society perspective: Country case study.* Oxfam International Research Report.

Henry, A. (2002). *Proposal for capacity building to support health care reform in Georgia with emphasis on nursing, distance education, healthcare management and public health* [Unpublished grant document]. Atlanta, GA: Partners for International Development.

Internal Displacement Monitoring Center (IDMC). (2011). IDPs in Georgia still need attention. Retrieved from http://www.internal-displacement.org/8025708F004CE90B/%28httpCountries%29/F62BE07C33DE4D19802570A7004C84A3?opendocument&count=10000

International Finance Corporation. (2006). Doing business: Georgia is this year's top reformer. Retrieved from http://www.doingbusiness.org/documents/Press_Releases_07/DB07CISpressrelease.pdf

John Snow International (JSI). (2011). Sustain project. Retrieved from http://www.jsi.com/JSIInternet/Projects/ListProjects.cfm?Select=Region&ID=4&ProjectStatus=Active

Kaiser Family Foundation. (2011). Health Expenditure per Capita. Retrieved from http://www.globalhealthfacts.org/data/topic/map.aspx?ind=66

Kalandadze, I. (2011, June). *Updates on TB control in Georgia 2010–2011.* Presentation at the U.S.–Georgia Infectious Disease Research Conference: Building a Regional Research Agenda, Tbilisi, Georgia.

Lomtadze, N., Aspindzelashvili, R., Janjgava, M., Mirtskhulava, V., Wright, A., Blumberg, H. M., & Salakaia, A. (2009). Prevalence and risk factors for multidrug-resistant tuberculosis in Republic of Georgia: A population based study. *International Journal of Tuberculosis and Lung Disease, 13*(1), 68–73.

McGee, R. W., & Bose, S. (2009). Corporate governance in transition economies: A comparative study of Armenia, Azerbaijan and Georgia. *International Journal of Economic Policy in Emerging Economies, 2*(3), 228–240.

MoLHSA. (2011). Ministry of Labour, Health, and Social Affairs of Georgia. Retrieved from http://www.e-government.ge/uploads/GITI%202011/GITI2011(MOLHSA)ppt.pdf

National Center for Disease Control and Public Health, Georgia (NCDC). (n.d.). Health and healthcare in Georgia, 2009 statistical yearbook. Retrieved from http://www.ncdc.ge/index.php?do=fullmod&mid=234

Nishiyama, M., Wold, J. L., & Partskhladze, N. (2008). Building competencies for nurse administrators in the Republic of Georgia. *International Nursing Review, 55,* 179–186.

Open Society Georgia Foundation (OSGF). (2006). *Public health program: HealthCare system in Georgia* [Unpublished document].

Partskhladze, N., Gogashvili, M., Jashi, M., & Mindadze, S. (2006). *AIHA monitoring and evaluation—FY 2006 indicator: Percentage of targeted healthcare providers applying training (nurses)* [Unpublished report for the AIHA].

Serbanescu, F., Egnatashvili, V., Ruiz, A., Suchdev, D., & Goodwill, M. (2011). *Reproductive health survey, Georgia 2010: Summary report.* Atlanta, GA: Georgian National Center for Disease Control & Centers for Disease Control and Prevention.

Skarbinski, J., Walker, H. K., Kobaladze, A., Kirtava, Z., Baker, L. C., & Raffin, T. A. (2002). Ten years of transition: The burden of out-of-pocket payments for health care in Tbilisi, Republic of Georgia. *Journal of the American Medical Association, 287*(8), 1043–1049.

Tadumadze, N. (2011, June). *Priorities for tuberculosis research in Georgia.* Presentation at the U.S.–Georgia Infectious Disease Research Conference: Building a Regional Research Agenda, Tbilisi, Georgia.

Tsertsavadze, T. (2011, June). *Evidence-based decisions: Impact of Georgia health research on Georgian health policy.* Presentation at the U.S.–Georgia Infectious Disease Research Conference: Building a Regional Research Agenda, Tbilisi, Georgia.

UNICEF (2011). Georgia global health initiation strategy. Retrieved from http://www.ghi.gov/documents/organization/175130.pdf

United Nations (2010). United Nations General Assembly Special Session on HIV/AIDS. Retrieved from http://www.unaids.org/en/dataanalysis/monitoringcountryprogress/2010progressreportssubmittedbycountries/georgia_2010_country_progress_report_en.pdf

USAID. (2006). Europe and Eurasia. Tuberculosis profile. Retrieved from http://www.usaid.gov/our_work/global_health/id/tuberculosis/countries/eande/enade.pdf

United Nations Development Program (UNDP). (2011). Technical note 1: Calculating the human development indices. Retrieved from http://hdr.undp.org/en/humandev/indices/

Van den Heede, K., Lesaffre, E., Diya, L., Vleugels, A., Clarke, S. P., Aiken, L. H., & Sermeus, W. (2009). The relationship between inpatient cardiac surgery mortality and nurse numbers and educational level: Analysis of administrative data. *International Journal of Nursing Studies, 46*(6), 796–803.

World Bank. (2011a). Georgia country brief, 2010. Retrieved from http://web.worldbank.org/WBSITE/EXTERNAL/COUNTRIES/ECAEXT/GEORGIAEXTN/0,,menuPK:301755~pagePK:141132~piPK:141107~theSitePK:301746,00.html

World Bank. (2011b). International NGOs in Europe and central Asia. Retrieved from http://web.worldbank.org/WBSITE/EXTERNAL/COUNTRIES/ECAEXT/0,,contentMDK:20513289~pagePK:146736~piPK:146830~theSitePK:258599,00.html

World Health Organization (WHO). (2011a). Immunization Profile—Georgia. Retrieved from http://apps.who.int/immunization_monitoring/en/globalsummary/countryprofileresult.cfm?C=geo

World Health Organization (WHO). (2011b). Georgia: Law of Georgia on health care, December 10, 1997 (Sakartvelos k'anoni, 31 December 1997, No. 47–48, 126–145, Text No. 1139-Is). *WHO International Digest of Health Legislation.* Retrieved from http://apps.who.int/idhlrils/results.cfm?language=english&type=ByCountry&strRefCode=Geo&strTopicCode=IA

World Health Organization (WHO). (2011c). Georgia TB country profile. Retrieved from https://extranet.who.int/sree/Reports?op=Replet&name=/WHO_HQ_Reports/G2/PROD/EXT/TBCountryProfile&ISO2=GE&outtype=html

World Health Organization (WHO). (2011d). Global health observatory data repository. Retrieved from http://apps.who.int/ghodata/?vid=60610

For a full suite of assignments and additional learning activities, use the access code located in the front of your book to visit this exclusive website: http://go.jblearning.com/holtz. If you do not have an access code, you can obtain one at the site.

Figures and tables are indicated by f and t following the page number.

PRAISE FOR
One Woman, One Vote, Second Edition

One Woman, One Vote has been indispensable to me as I've worked to learn so much of the history that I'd not been taught about the nation and its centuries-long struggle toward full enfranchisement. I had been taught very little in school — shockingly little — about the lengthy, complex, fraught movement for woman suffrage in this country. When I began to learn about the movement, I turned to this compilation of academic perspectives over and over again, learning about the movement's horrifying racial politics, the many strategic approaches taken by different activists at different stages, the arguments about whether to create a proletariat coalition or appeal to elite women, and the domestic remaking of Susan B. Anthony. It's a terrific resource for those who want to know about suffrage from many different angles.

—**Rebecca Traister,** Author of
Good and Mad: The Revolutionary Power of Women's Anger

The study of the woman suffrage movement has flourished since the first edition of the anthology *One Woman, One Vote* appeared during the celebration of the Nineteenth Amendment's 75th anniversary. Marjorie Spruill's expanded second edition, published as part of the commemoration of the amendment's centennial, is a deeply satisfying and essential update, attending as it does to the campaign in the South, the international context, and the first hundred years of women voting. As with the first edition, the suffrage story told here will be compelling for both students and general readers.

—**Louise W. Knight,** Author of *Jane Addams: Spirit in Action*

Marjorie Spruill's new edition of *One Woman, One Vote* is a welcome and timely addition to the expanding body of literature on women›s gradual political empowerment. At a time when women have expanded their political influence, when the U.S. not only has its first and long overdue female vice president, Kamala Harris, when the organizing efforts of women of color, especially in Georgia, have shifted the balance of power in the U.S. Senate, and President Joseph R. Biden has appointed the first female-majority Cabinet in history, it's only appropriate that we have this updated re-examination of "how we got here," edited by Dr. Spruill, with the critical contributions of dozens of other scholars of the domestic and international woman›s movement.

—**Adele Logan Alexander,** Author of *Princess of the Hither Isles:*
A Black Suffragist's Story from the Jim Crow South

This engaging collection tackles the complexity of the mainstream movement head on. A timeless collection of classics that helped define the field, now revised and updated to help show us where we're headed. A great place to start or pick up your learning—with stories that will keep you thinking.

—**Lisa Tetrault,** Author of *The Myth of Seneca Falls:*
Memory and the Women's Suffrage Movement, 1848-1898.
Associate Professor of History, Carnegie Mellon University

The first edition of *One Woman, One Vote* was a key entry point into women's suffrage for me and many others. The now-classic essays by path- breaking scholars helped frame the complications and impact of the struggle for votes for women, spurring my own scholarly interests. The new edition maintains those key contributions and incorporates new insights from the diverse and exciting suffrage scholarship surrounding the recent centennial of the Nineteenth Amendment. The result is an invaluable collection for anyone interested in understanding this signal moment of democratization in American history.

—**Christina Wolbrecht,** Author of *A Century of Votes for Women.*
Professor of Political Science, University of Notre Dame

In recognition of the 100th anniversary of the Nineteenth Amendment in 2020 and the election of the country's first woman, first African American and South Asian American Vice President, the new edition of *One Woman One Vote* offers much needed perspectives on the history of U.S. women's suffrage. New essays foreground race, empire, global, and Southern regional perspectives that shed light not only on the passage of the Nineteenth Amendment but also the course of events after 1920.

—**Judy Tzu-Chun Wu,** Author of *Doctor "Mom" Chung of the Fair-Haired Bastards: The Life of a Wartime Celebrity.* Professor of Asian American Studies and Director of the Humanities Center, University of California, Irvine

This fascinating, meticulously researched, and clearly written anthology elevated the suffrage movement to its rightful stature as a central and continuing theme in American politics. Along with civil rights, the quest for women's inclusion in American political life becomes a crucial chapter in the ongoing re-definition of American democracy. Indispensable for women activists, historians, and anyone interested in women's contributions to our common past.

—**Edith Mayo,** Author of *The Smithsonian Book of the First Ladies: Their Lives, Times, and Issues.* Curator Emerita, Smithsonian Institution

One Woman, One Vote has been essential reading for students of the suffrage movement since it was first published in 1995. This revised and expanded edition provides an updated overview that incorporates the rich scholarship of the last twenty-five years. New chapters place the American movement in the context of international campaigns for woman suffrage and enhance our understanding of the role of race and racism in the suffrage movement. The book also offers more information about the impact of the 1918 influenza pandemic; expanded accounts of activism by women of color; and a concluding essay that brings the struggle for voting rights up through the 2020 elections. Scholars, teachers, students, and lay readers of American women's history and political history will enthusiastically welcome this new edition.

—**Catherine Rymph,** Author of *Republican Women: Feminism and Conservatism from Suffrage through the Rise of the New Right.* Professor and Chair, Department of History, University of Missouri

In this second edition of *One Woman, One Vote*, we are reminded not only of the long struggle of women to acquire the right to vote and how that struggle was shaped by issues of race and class, but also how women asserted that right on issues that spanned the political spectrum. Never a unified voting bloc, as many politicians feared would be the case, women proved that they could be as politically conservative, or liberal, as their male counterparts. Now expanded to include new chapters and a sweeping overview incorporating new scholarship, editor Marjorie J. Spruill brings the story of woman suffrage forward to include the historic election of Vice President Kamala Harris. Indispensable for classes in U.S. History and political science and for lay readers wanting to learn more about women and the vote.

—**Karen L. Cox**, Author of *Dixie's Daughters: The United Daughters of the Confederacy and the Preservation of Confederate Culture.* Professor of History, Director of Public History, University of North Carolina, Charlotte

No other single collection presents a more thorough account of woman suffrage. But more than that, *One Woman, One Vote* tells the story of women voters—not only White women voters, but Black women voters, and Native-American women voters, and Asian-American women voters—not just during the fight for the ratification of the Nineteenth Amendment but through the 2020 elections. *One Woman, One Vote* should be on the bookshelves and on the syllabi of every historian and political scientist in the country.

—**Angie Maxwell,** Author of *The Long Southern Strategy: How Chasing White Voters in the South Changed American Politics.* Diane D. Blair Professor of Southern Studies and Associate Professor of Political Science, University of Arkansas

The updated edition of *One Woman, One Vote* both builds on and expands the original content so that it clearly illustrates for students, historians and casual readers the undeniable work of women of color and also firmly places the U.S. suffrage efforts within the international women's equality movement. Not only is it an important historic narrative, but it also serves as an essential guide to understanding the link between enfranchisement, civil rights, the politicizing of women's equality efforts, and the unrelenting voter suppression that we still see today.

Page Harrington, Author of *Interpreting the Legacy of Women's Suffrage at Museums and Historic Sites*

Marjorie Spruill's *One Woman, One Vote* remains a model in how to address a single topic from a wide variety of angles that capture the complexities of American politics and activism. With new essays that complement the timeless scholarship from the collection's first printing, this updated edition moves a century beyond 1920 through the 2020 presidential election and that year's centennial celebrations of the Nineteenth Amendment. Readers can now draw connections from the roots of the suffrage movement through the ongoing struggle to allow all women to actually cast ballots and convert voting power into equal political power.

—**Stacie Taranto**, Co-Editor of *Suffrage at 100: Women in American Politics Since 1920* Associate Professor, Ramapo College of New Jersey

iii

Hundreds of women gave the accumulated possibilities of an entire lifetime, thousands gave years of their lives, hundreds of thousands gave constant interest, and such aid as they could. It was a continuous, seemingly endless, chain of activity. Young suffragists who helped forge the last links of that chain were not born when it began. Old suffragists who forged the first links were dead when it ended.

— CARRIE CHAPMAN CATT AND
NETTIE ROGERS SHULER
*Woman Suffrage and Politics: The Inner
Story of the Suffrage Movement*

On March 3, 1913, thousands of suffragists marched along Pennsylvania Avenue in support of woman suffrage. The procession took place the day before Woodrow Wilson's presidential inauguration to demonstrate women's exclusion from the democratic process. LIBRARY OF CONGRESS

ONE WOMAN, ONE VOTE

ONE WOMAN, ONE VOTE

REDISCOVERING THE WOMAN SUFFRAGE MOVEMENT

Edited by

MARJORIE J. SPRUILL

NEWSAGE PRESS
Oregon

One Woman, One Vote
Rediscovering the Woman Suffrage Movement

Edited by Marjorie J. Spruill

Second Edition copyright © 2021 by NewSage Press and Marjorie J. Spruill

Paperback Original ISBN 978-0939165-76-6
Library Edition ISBN 978-0-939165-78-0
E-Book ISBN 978-0939165-77-3

Address inquiries to:

NewSage Press
PO Box 610
Tillamook, OR 97141

503-695-2211

Designed and produced by Sherry Wachter,
Sherry Wachter Designs
Printed in the United States

Cover photos, clockwise from top left: Marie Louise Bottineau Baldwin; Dora Lewis; Rose Winslow, also known as Wenclawska; Nannie Helen Burroughs; Mabel Ping-Hua Lee; Fannie Barrier Williams; and *at center*, Susan B. Anthony. Additional information on page 524. Photos from the Library of Congress, except Susan B. Anthony, which is in the public domain.

Distributed by Publishers Group West

Library of Congress Cataloging-in-Publication Data Is Available

Names: Spruill, Marjorie J., 1951-

Title: One Woman, One Vote : rediscovering the
    Woman suffrage movement / edited by Marjorie J. Spruill
Description: Second Edition / Tillamook, Oregon : NewSage Press, 2021.

    Includes biographical references and index.
    ISBN 978-0-939165-76-6

Contents

Preface

The essays in this anthology focus on different aspects of the suffrage story, but presented in roughly chronological order, tell the intriguing story of women and the vote from the failure of the Constitution to enfranchise women to the participation of women in politics after 1920. A new concluding essay continues the story of woman suffrage past 1920 through the 2020 presidential election.

The authors of the essays—scholars in the fields of History, American Studies, Political Science, and Sociology—each advance our understanding of the movement's history, at times offering conflicting interpretations and challenging widely accepted theories from past and present. I begin the book with an overview of the woman suffrage movement that provides background for the essays that follow.

Together, the essays describe why a suffrage movement was necessary, how the movement began, and how it changed over time in response to changes in American history and politics. Through the essays, we are introduced to several generations of suffrage leaders and the supportive relationships as well as the tensions that developed among them. We learn more about the growing diversity of the suffrage constituency in terms of region, religion, race, class, ethnicity, and even attitude, and that the suffrage story includes both a record of harmony and cooperation between diverse groups of suffragists, and a record of discrimination and betrayal. The essays also offer insight as to why some American men and women opposed woman suffrage, and how suffragists finally prevailed.

After the Nineteenth Amendment was added to the U.S. Constitution, the diverse suffrage coalition did not turn into a united voting "bloc." However, women continued to be politically active in a wide range of organizations and movements, sometimes with conflicting agendas. Many women, including women in the U.S. territories, immigrant women, Native American women, and African American women living in the South, had to continue to fight for enfranchisement long after 1920.

Above all, these essays make it clear that the vote was not *given* to women when the Nineteenth Amendment was ratified. Generations of suffragists labored long and hard to establish woman's right to vote in the United States. Indeed, the fight for full voting rights and political equality continues to this day.

In the wake of the voting rights movement of the 1960s and the women's rights movement of the 1960s and 1970s, women turned out to vote in larger numbers, exceeding the turnout of men for the past forty years. Though not unified, the woman's vote is recognized as massive and highly influential in the outcome of elections. Women are a force in politics, not only as voters but as organizers, and increasingly, as elected officials.

After a century of woman suffrage, women have much to celebrate, even as they continue the fight to protect voting rights, to gain more equitable representation in American government, and to fully establish women's equality under the law.

—*Marjorie J. Spruill*
April 2021

xi

Generations of leaders of the long struggle for woman suffrage

PHOTOS FROM THE LIBRARY OF CONGRESS OR IN THE PUBLIC DOMAIN

One

HOW WOMEN WON:
The Long Road to the
Nineteenth Amendment
Marjorie J. Spruill

O N AUGUST 26, 1920, Secretary of State Bainbridge Colby signed a proclamation officially certifying the ratification of the Nineteenth Amendment to the U.S. Constitution. It declared that "the right of citizens of the United States to vote shall not be denied or abridged by the United States or by any state on account of sex."[1]

This victory was dearly won and long in coming. Between 1848, when reformers gathered in Seneca Falls, New York and endorsed a woman suffrage resolution, and 1920, when state legislators gathered in Nashville, Tennessee and ratified the Nineteenth Amendment, generations of suffragists labored tirelessly for the vote. As suffragists rejoiced, they recalled the sacrifices of their foremothers and the many thousands of women who had been a part of this "...continuous, seemingly endless, chain of activity." In the words of National American Woman Suffrage Association (NAWSA) leader Carrie Chapman Catt, "Old suffragists who forged the first links were dead when it ended," while "young suffragists who helped forge the last links of that chain were not born when it began."[2]

Why this long arduous struggle? In framing the Constitution, women were not explicitly excluded: the framers generally used the word "persons" when referring to American citizens and assigned the power to decide who would be allowed to vote to the individual states. But everywhere in the young republic the vote was restricted to White property owners on the theory that only they could exercise independent judgment. That automatically excluded married women, as state laws generally followed a concept borrowed from British common law in which a married woman's legal identify was "covered" by that of her husband, but states also excluded widows and unmarried women with property. The only exception was New Jersey, which, between 1776 and 1807, permitted all inhabitants who met property requirements to vote.[3]

Most people assumed women had no independent interests beyond the interests of their families, which were represented in politics by male heads of household. In addition, most considered women to be unsuitable as voters—too irrational and emotional. In the early nineteenth century, people increasingly spoke of women as

better than men in terms of morality and religiosity, but insisted they could inspire and influence male voters for good without being exposed to—and endangered by—the corrupt world of politics.[4]

Even as many states began to loosen restrictions on voting to allow all White men to qualify, including those without property, early advocates of woman suffrage found that ideas about gender and politics—along with laws stipulating qualifications for voting—were extremely resistant to change. Over time and through tremendous effort, and despite many defeats, suffragists managed to persuade many states to enfranchise women, however, some states, especially in the South, remained unwavering in their opposition. Full enfranchisement of women in the United States would ultimately depend on securing an amendment to the U.S. Constitution.

Amending the Constitution was difficult by design. Though the founding fathers intended for it to be a flexible document, they also wanted to forestall faddish changes that lacked broad, national support. To succeed, an amendment had to have the approval of two-thirds of each house of Congress and then three-fourths of the states. It followed that no reform regarded as radical by most citizens at a particular time could be added to the nation's founding document. And any proposed amendment that failed to gain at least some support in every part of the nation was destined to fail.

Thus, the story of how women won the vote in the United States of America is long and complicated. It is a tale of hard work and ingenuity; strategic adaptation to cope with changing circumstances; racial, regional, and generational tensions; struggles between ideals and political realities; and sheer perseverance. But at its core is a story about how a movement begun in one section of the nation by a small group of women considered to be radicals, managed to gain the strong, widespread support required to overcome the obstacles deliberately placed in its path.

The Beginning

The woman suffrage movement originated in the Northeastern United States in the context of antebellum reform. Women began speaking out for women's rights when their efforts to participate fully in the great reform movements of the day— most notably the movement to end slavery—were severely criticized as inappropriate for their sex. Agitation for women's rights preceded the start of a woman suffrage movement by almost two decades.

Maria W. Miller Stewart, an African American woman who grew up in Connecticut as an orphaned indentured servant, is considered the first American woman to speak in public about women's rights. While living in Boston in the early 1830s, she began lecturing and writing about racial and gender injustice. In her passionate speeches with frequent biblical references, Stewart denounced White Americans for enslaving African Americans and mistreating free Blacks in the North. Siding with abolitionist William Lloyd Garrison and other advocates of immediate and uncompensated emancipation, she denounced the more moderate critics of slavery who supported

colonization and were raising money to send freeborn and emancipated African Americans to Africa. This money, she insisted, should be spent on aiding and educating them. She also had sharp words for her fellow African Americans, especially women, demanding that they stand up for their rights.[5]

Stewart's audiences were often hostile, jeering her and even throwing rotten vegetables: she not only spoke in public, she addressed what were then called "promiscuous" audiences that included both men and women and were racially mixed. But Stewart bravely defied her critics, once stating, "Shall I, for fear of feeble man who shall die, hold my peace? Shall I for fear of scoffs and frowns, refrain my tongue? Ah, no!" Garrison, who supported women's rights and published her writings, encouraged her, but wrote that Stewart "encountered an opposition even from her Boston circle of friends that would have damped the ardor of most women." She soon moved to New York but continued to support the rights of women and African Americans.[6]

Sarah and Angelina Grimké also spoke out in the 1830s on behalf of women's rights and against slavery and racial prejudice. Though members of a prominent family in Charleston, South Carolina that enslaved African Americans, their opposition to slavery led them to leave behind lives of privilege to live among Quakers in the North. Their unique qualifications led the American Anti-Slavery Society to send them on speaking tours in New York and Massachusetts beginning in 1836. When their lectures began to attract huge audiences that included men, the Grimké sisters encountered tremendous criticism, including from the Congregational ministers of Massachusetts who denounced them for assuming "the place and tone of man as public reformer" and barred them from speaking in their churches.[7]

The controversy led many abolitionists to oppose hiring women as agents, fearing it would undermine the antislavery cause. But the criticism motivated the Grimkés to speak and write to promote women's freedom as well that of the enslaved. Each sister published a series of letters affirming women's right to participate in the great moral reforms of the day. Sarah Grimké also demanded equal pay and equal educational opportunities for women, insisting "Men and women are created equal." She wrote, "All I ask our brethren is that they take their feet off our necks and permit us to stand upright on the ground which God destined for us to occupy."[8]

In 1838, Angelina Grimké became the first woman in U.S. history to address a legislative body when she spoke to the Massachusetts legislature. However, exhaustion from dealing with all the controversy contributed to the sisters' decision to retire from public life. During Angelina's last public address in the brand-new Pennsylvania Hall erected by the Philadelphia Female Anti-Slavery Society, a howling mob of thousands threw stones through the windows and later that night burned the hall to the ground. Still, the Grimké sisters continued to support the struggle to end slavery, working with Angelina's husband, abolitionist Theodore Weld, in compiling a massive collection documenting the realities of slavery later used by Harriet Beecher Stowe in writing *Uncle Tom's Cabin*.[9]

Sarah Grimké

Angelina Grimké

The Grimké sisters' experience inspired yet another early advocate of women's rights, Abigail (Abby) Kelley Foster. Like them, she was a Quaker, fortified in her work by the Quakers' belief that women and men were equally led by an "inner light." Convinced that improving mankind was "the only object worth living for," she, too, became an agent for the American Anti-Slavery Society. In 1839, Foster began what proved to be a long and effective career as a traveling lecturer, converting many to the antislavery and women's rights causes. Facing hostile audiences and angry mobs, she became all the more committed to her work, stating, "We have good cause to be grateful to the slave. In striving to strike his irons off, we found most surely, that we were manacled ourselves."[10]

Foster's nomination to a leadership position in the American Anti-Slavery Society, however, prompted a heated debate that culminated in a permanent schism in the organization. In 1838, Garrison, who continued to support women's full participation, proclaimed in his newspaper, *The Liberator*, "As our object is universal emancipation, to redeem women as well as men from a servile to an equal condition—we shall go for the rights of women to their utmost extent." To the Grimkés, Foster, and other champions of women's rights and of the enslaved, it was impossible to work for the rights of one and deny the rights of the other. The goal was human rights.[11]

The Seneca Falls Convention

A year later, the controversy over women's role in the antislavery movement led indirectly to a fateful meeting of two women who later issued the call for the Seneca Falls Convention. Lucretia Mott, a revered Quaker minister and a co-founder of the Philadelphia Female Anti-Slavery Society in 1833, was an inspiration to the Grimkés and many other younger women reformers. In 1840, Mott arrived in London as a

Abby Kelley Foster
LIBRARY OF CONGRESS

Frederick Douglass
LIBRARY OF CONGRESS

delegate to the World Anti-Slavery Convention, only to find that women delegates were barred from participation. There she met Elizabeth Cady Stanton, a young woman who had come to London with her new husband, a delegate to the convention. The two women were disgusted by the exclusion of women delegates and spent their time in London discussing the status of women in the United States, vowing to do something to improve it. Forming a lasting friendship, they resolved to call a women's rights convention when back in the United States.[12]

In 1848, finding that Mott was visiting nearby, Stanton called on her, suggesting that they go forward with a plan for a convention. They were amazed that with little advance publicity, approximately three hundred people, mostly women, responded to the call. Frederick Douglass, editor of the antislavery newspaper, *The North Star*, published in nearby Rochester, New York, was among them. Having escaped from slavery in 1838, Douglass had become an agent for the American Anti-Slavery Society and in 1845, published his best-selling autobiography which made him famous in the United States and abroad. He was also devoted to the cause of women's rights.[13]

Meeting beforehand, Stanton and Mott drafted a "Declaration of Sentiments" to propose to the participants, using the Declaration of Independence as their model. In it they demanded a wide range of changes in women's social, legal, educational, and economic status, including reform of unjust marriage laws. Of the eleven Resolutions, the ninth would make this gathering iconic in the history of the woman suffrage movement: "Resolved, that it is the duty of the women of this country to secure to themselves their sacred right to the elective franchise."[14]

Ironically, at this conference, which would become famous as the start of the woman suffrage movement, the right to vote was not the initial focus. Indeed, those present at the Seneca Falls Convention regarded the resolution demanding the vote

as the most extreme of all the demands they put forward in the Declaration. Stanton, who had been inspired by the Chartist movement for universal manhood suffrage while she was in London, proposed the call for women's enfranchisement. The participants approved the woman suffrage resolution by a narrow margin due to the insistence of Stanton and Douglass.[15]

The Movement Grows

The first decade after the Seneca Falls Convention saw a tremendous amount of women's rights activism as reformers organized local, state, and "national" conventions in the Northeast and Midwest where they continued to debate the issues and work for change. The conventions stirred Americans to think anew about women's rights and women's place in the world.[16]

Though no formal state or national organizations were created, women's rights associations sprung up all over New England and the Midwest, as far west as Wisconsin. The frequent conventions attracted both women and men, some of whom were detractors. Having been forged in the crucible of abolitionism, the women's rights movement was firmly associated in the minds of most Americans with this cause, which was regarded by most as extremely radical. However, women's rights advocates continued to enjoy unconditional support from their allies in the antislavery movement, including Garrison, Douglass, and Wendell Phillips, a prominent abolitionist known for his oratorical skills and courage. At the World Anti-Slavery Convention in London in 1840, he had led the unsuccessful effort to have the women delegates seated.[17]

Lucretia Mott, Elizabeth Cady Stanton, Abby Kelley Foster, and others who had spoken out for women's rights before or during the Seneca Falls Convention, were soon joined by many promising newcomers, among them two women who would become some of the movement's most prominent leaders, Lucy Stone and Susan B. Anthony.[18]

Stone, who grew up on a farm in Massachusetts, was the daughter of abolitionists. She was one of the first American women to earn a B.A. degree, graduating from Oberlin College in Ohio in 1848. Oberlin, founded in 1833, was radically different from other American institutions of higher education; it began admitting women and African Americans in 1837. As a girl, Stone was inspired by Sarah and Angelina Grimké and Foster to devote her life to fighting against slavery and for women's rights. Stone began traveling as a speaker for the American Anti-Slavery Society in 1848. In 1850, she organized a convention in Worcester, Massachusetts billed as the first National Woman's Rights Convention. When she married Henry Blackwell in 1855, they wrote and published egalitarian marriage vows, and Stone made history by retaining her original name.[19]

Susan B. Anthony also became involved in the burgeoning women's rights movement, bringing her enormous talent as an organizer and campaigner to the cause. She grew up in a reform-minded family with parents committed to

abolition and temperance. They moved from Massachusetts to New York when she was young, living near Rochester, New York where she met many leading abolitionists, including Frederick Douglass, William Lloyd Garrison, and Wendell Phillips. Starting her career as a teacher and outraged by the vast discrepancy in the salaries of male and female teachers, Anthony was an early advocate of equal pay for equal work. She was also involved in the temperance movement, where she encountered the same hostility to women's public speaking and leadership that characterized much of the antislavery movement. In 1851, while in Seneca Falls to hear an antislavery lecture, Anthony met Elizabeth Cady Stanton and they began working together for women's rights; it was the beginning of a fruitful collaboration that would last the rest of their lives.[20]

African American women and men also attended these conventions throughout the 1850s and 1860s, committed to expanding women's rights while working to end slavery. African American and White women reformers often worked side by side, including organizing these conventions. Most African American women pioneers in these two movements were born free and were well educated and middle class, such as Harriet Forten Purvis and Margaretta Forten of a prominent family of reformers in Philadelphia. In 1833, along with their mother, Charlotte Forten, and Lucretia Mott, they co-founded the interracial Philadelphia Female Anti-Slavery Society, joined shortly thereafter by the Grimké Sisters. Purvis and her husband, Robert Purvis, played central roles in the Underground Railroad and worked with Harriet Tubman. He joined his wife in supporting women's

rights. Harriet Forten Purvis and Margaretta Forten helped organize the fifth National Women's Rights Convention in 1854. Sarah Remond, an antislavery speaker from a prominent African American family in Salem, Massachusetts, also took part in these conventions, winning acclaim as a speaker, notably at the 1858 National Women's Conference in New York.[21]

In addition, there was Sojourner Truth, who had escaped slavery in New York and went on to become an abolitionist and advocate for women's rights. Although Truth never learned to read or write, she dictated her memoirs, *The Narrative of Sojourner Truth: A Northern Slave*, to a friend, and they were published by William Lloyd Garrison in 1850. That same year, Truth began attending women's rights conventions, actively

Sojourner Truth

supporting woman suffrage and becoming one of the most renowned advocates for gender and racial equality of the nineteenth century. Her speech, often referred to as "Ain't I a Woman?" delivered at the 1851 Women's Rights Convention held in Akron, Ohio, is recognized as one of the most famous speeches in the history of the movement. Truth continued speaking for the rights of women and African Americans throughout the 1850s and beyond.[22]

As was the case at Seneca Falls, participants at these conventions addressed a wide array of issues and made recommendations for reform—then pressing legislatures to implement the reforms they recommended. The primary gain was the expansion of marital rights laws in some two dozen states. Women's rights activism in the United States cheered women's rights advocates in Britain and throughout Europe: women reformers in the United States, meanwhile, were inspired by the efforts of reformers abroad.[23]

During the Civil War, however, women's rights supporters in the United States put their nascent movement on hold to support the war effort. Along with their male allies, they worked to make it a war to end slavery as well as to save the Union. In 1863, Stanton and Anthony founded the Women's Loyal National League, which launched a massive petition drive to Congress calling for a constitutional amendment to permanently abolish slavery throughout the United States. This was necessary as the Emancipation Proclamation was a wartime measure freeing enslaved African Americans only in the states "still in rebellion." The League had five thousand members within the first year. By the end of the war, they had gathered signatures from almost four hundred thousand women and men—approximately four percent of the Union's population. Their ally, Senator Charles Sumner of Massachusetts, credited this "mighty army" as crucial to building public support for what became the Thirteenth Amendment.[24]

Dashed Hopes for Universal Suffrage

After the Civil War, women's rights leaders came to see enfranchisement as one of the most important—perhaps *the* most important—of their aims. It was essential, they believed, both as a symbol of equality and individuality, and as a means of improving one's legal and social condition. Their goal was universal suffrage, not just woman suffrage. Banding together with former antislavery movement allies, women's rights leaders formed a new group, the American Equal Rights Association (AERA) with the stated goal of securing "equal rights to all American citizens, especially the right of suffrage, irrespective of race, color or sex." Lucretia Mott served as president, and Elizabeth Cady Stanton and Frederick Douglass served as vice presidents. Other officers of this new organization included Susan B. Anthony, Lucy Stone, her husband Henry Blackwell, Harriet Forten Purvis, and Purvis's daughter Hattie Purvis. Frances Ellen Watkins Harper, a former abolitionist who was a poet, writer, and teacher, also joined the group.[25]

As Congress debated the legislation that eventually became the Fourteenth and Fifteenth Amendments, however, woman suffrage advocates found even former allies insisting that the demand for women's enfranchisement be postponed in the interest of securing suffrage for Black men. The Fourteenth Amendment, ratified in 1868, granted citizenship to all persons born or naturalized in the United States, including formerly enslaved people. But in the second section of the Fourteenth Amendment, which dealt with enforcement, Congress decreed that any state that denied the vote to "male" citizens would be punished by reduced representation. Woman suffrage advocates protested strenuously, aghast that the amendment did not call for universal suffrage for all and that the word "male" was added to the Constitution for the first time. When it appeared that further action, a Fifteenth Amendment, ratified in 1870, was required to secure the voting rights of the freedmen, women were again left out.[26]

Meanwhile, some former allies, particularly Wendell Phillips, aware there was considerable opposition to the proposed amendments, urged suffragists to desist campaigning for woman suffrage and work only to assure voting rights for the freedmen, stating, "One question at a time. This hour belongs to the Negro."[27]

Stanton and Anthony were incensed at Phillips's suggestion that the quest for woman suffrage be deferred for a generation, believing that, in Stanton's words, Reconstruction was "the opportunity, perhaps for the century," to press forward on full citizenship rights irrespective of race or sex. Anthony reportedly replied she "would rather cut off her right hand than ask for the ballot for the Black man and not for woman."[28]

Sojourner Truth was also distressed by Phillips's "Negro's hour" priority, and reminded her fellow reformers that "the Negro" included women also. Addressing the AERA, Truth said, "There is a great stir about colored men getting their rights, but not a word about the colored women, and if colored men get their rights and not colored women theirs, you see the colored men will be masters over the women, and it will be just as bad as it was before. So, I am for keeping the thing going while things are stirring."[29]

Douglass continued to affirm the desirability and justice of woman suffrage, but to him, enfranchisement of African American men—a claim made more viable by Black men's service to the Union during the Civil War—took priority. Moreover, he insisted that given the perils faced by newly freed African Americans in the South, enfranchising Black men was a matter of life and death.[30] Douglass and other advocates of Black male suffrage saw it as crucial that newly-freed African Americans be able to vote to protect themselves against Southern Whites' efforts to virtually re-enslave them.

Many Republican politicians also saw the enfranchisement of Black men as crucial for their party. Black men would almost certainly vote for Republicans, guaranteeing support for the party in the Southern states where the vast number of Whites were Democrats. Black male voters' support would enable the Republicans to maintain

their dominance of national politics and carry out their plans for Reconstruction of the South. Republicans reasoned that if women were enfranchised, not only Black women would vote, and in the South the far more numerous White women, who were likely to vote for Democrats, would gain the vote.[31]

Suffragists' former allies insisted that if the controversial issue of woman suffrage was included, the Fifteenth Amendment would not be ratified, and they begged suffragists to understand. The issue of how to respond split the woman suffrage movement in two. In 1869, women suffragists divided acrimoniously, largely over the issue of whether to support ratification of the Fifteenth Amendment or not.

Suffrage Strategies During "the Schism"

Harriet Forten Purvis, 1870s
LIBRARY OF CONGRESS

Frances Harper, 1872
LIBRARY OF CONGRESS

In 1869, suffragists founded two organizations with different positions on the Fifteenth Amendment and different ideas about how best to promote woman suffrage. The National Woman Suffrage Association (NWSA), headed by Elizabeth Cady Stanton and Susan B. Anthony, actively opposed the amendment. Given their background as antislavery activists and their staunch advocacy of universal suffrage, their opposition and public statements about the Fifteenth Amendment shocked and horrified long-time allies, including Frederick Douglass and Frances Harper. Stanton and Anthony bitterly denounced the enfranchisement of what they called "ignorant" and "degraded" former slaves and recent immigrants ahead of "educated White women" as a terrible injustice that would make the task of woman suffrage advocates harder than ever. Stanton was from an upper-class background and held elitist sentiments. She expressed outrage at the idea of suffragists having to go around the country begging "paupers, knaves, and drunkards" and every "Tom, Dick, Harry, Patrick, Hans, Yung-Tung, and Sambo" to accept them as political equals. Stanton declared that she, for one, refused to do so.[32]

When the Fifteenth Amendment was ratified in 1870, Stanton, Anthony, and their associates in the NWSA called for another federal amendment—hopefully the Sixteenth Amendment—that would enfranchise women. The New York based NWSA, led exclusively by women, focused on the enfranchisement of women through federal action

and promoted a wide variety of women's rights measures in its short-lived journal, *The Revolution*.[33]

The other organization founded in 1869 was the American Woman Suffrage Association (AWSA), with headquarters in Boston. Lucy Stone led the AWSA. Her husband, Henry Blackwell, played an active role in the organization, as did Antoinette Brown Blackwell, Stone's sister-in-law and a pioneering minister. Other AWSA members included Julia Ward Howe, author of the "Battle Hymn of the Republic"; Henry Ward Beecher, brother of Harriet Beecher Stowe and one of the nation's most prominent ministers; and Thomas Wentworth Higginson, White commander of African American troops during the Civil War and ardent supporter of women's rights. The AWSA supported ratification of the Fifteenth Amendment while working for woman suffrage as well. Stone explained, "I will be thankful in my soul if *any* body can get out of the terrible pit."[34]

Some African American suffrage supporters, including Harriet Forten Purvis—a close friend of Anthony—and journalist Mary Ann Shadd Cary, sided with the NWSA, however, the AWSA attracted more African American affiliates. For example, prominent businesswoman Caroline Remond Putnam helped found the Massachusetts Woman Suffrage Association under the auspices of the AWSA. Publisher and civil rights leader Josephine St. Pierre Ruffin, who was friends with Julia Ward Howe and Lucy Stone, was an early AWSA member. Frances Harper also chose the AWSA; speaking at the AWSA conference in 1873, she stated, "Much as White women need the ballot, colored women need it more." Sojourner Truth attended conferences sponsored by both groups.[35]

The AWSA endorsed adding a federal woman suffrage amendment to the U.S. Constitution, but recognizing how little backing the idea had at the time, concentrated on developing grassroots support for women's enfranchisement. The organization engaged in a massive educational campaign designed to make woman suffrage seem less radical and consistent with widely shared American values. It employed agents who traveled across the nation speaking and circulating literature, and reached a large audience through the AWSA's newspaper, *The Woman's Journal*. Members promoted state suffrage amendments and various forms of "partial suffrage" legislation, including bills giving women the right to vote on school or municipal issues, or in presidential elections. They believed that these measures were desirable in themselves and a means to the eventual end—full suffrage for women of the United States.[36]

The "New Departure"

Meanwhile, suffragists associated with the National Woman Suffrage Association (NWSA) were disheartened by the response to the proposed federal amendment and disdainful of the state-by-state approach as slow and cumbersome. Instead, they tried to win their rights by other approaches known collectively as the "New Departure." Invoking the equal protection clause of the Fourteenth Amendment,

these suffragists challenged women's exclusion from voting on the grounds that, as citizens, women were entitled to vote. Victoria Woodhull, a radical, iconoclastic, and charismatic figure who briefly gained the support of Elizabeth Cady Stanton and Susan B. Anthony, had made this argument before Congress in 1871.[37]

In the early 1870s, hundreds of women claimed the right to vote based on the equal protection clause of the Fourteenth Amendment and tried to register and vote, though most were turned away. In Hyde Park, Massachusetts, a group of forty-two women, led by Sarah Grimké and Angelina Grimké Weld, made their way through a heavy snowstorm to cast their votes. Sojourner Truth attempted to vote in Battle Creek, Michigan, and Mary Ann Shadd Cary was one of sixty-four women who tried to vote in Washington, D.C. In 1872, Anthony managed to cast a vote in Rochester, New York, hoping to be arrested and then test this new strategy in the courts. She was arrested and indicted for "knowingly, wrongfully and unlawfully vot[ing] for a representative to the Congress of the United States." Found guilty and fined, Anthony insisted she would never pay a dollar of it.[38]

Virginia Minor, a suffrage leader in St. Louis, succeeded in getting the issue before the U.S. Supreme Court, but in a key decision in 1875, *Minor v. Happersett*, the court ruled unanimously that citizenship did not automatically confer the right to vote. The decision forced suffragists to face a grim reality: woman suffrage would not come swiftly from an interpretation of the U.S. Constitution that accepted women's claim to the rights and privileges of all citizens. Instead, it would have to come about by state legislation or a constitutional amendment specially worded to enfranchise women.[39]

When a federal woman suffrage amendment was introduced in the Senate in 1878, it contained the same language as the bill that would become the Nineteenth Amendment, emphasizing the distinct claims of women and prohibiting denial of voting rights to citizens "on account of sex." It would take forty-two more years and a tremendous amount of work on the part of suffragists working at the state and national levels for it to become law.[40]

Pioneering Woman Suffrage States

Even as the National Woman Suffrage Association (NWSA) and the American Woman Suffrage Association (AWSA) competed for support and tried several strategies for winning female enfranchisement to no avail, woman suffrage was making headway in the West. While most politicians in Eastern states were dead set against woman suffrage, politicians and voters in several Western states enfranchised women and, at times, battled Congress for the right to do so.

In 1869, the very year that frustrated Eastern suffragists parted ways and formed the NWSA and the AWSA, the territory of Wyoming unexpectedly led the nation in the adoption of woman suffrage. In 1890, when it appeared that Congress would not approve its application for statehood as long as Wyoming allowed woman suffrage, the territorial legislature sent a telegram to Congress declaring that they

would remain out of the Union a hundred years rather than join without the women. Even the Mormon stronghold of Utah enacted woman suffrage in 1870 while still a territory; it came into the Union as a state with woman suffrage in 1896. Other pioneering suffrage states included Colorado, which enfranchised women in 1893, the first suffrage victory as a result of a state referendum, and Idaho, which enfranchised women by state constitutional amendment in 1896.[41]

Academic historians as well as proud Westerners have speculated at length about *why* the West was so precocious in its adoption of woman suffrage, putting forth a great variety of explanations. Western suffragists such as Esther Morris of Wyoming, who became a suffrage advocate after attending women's rights conferences back East, and Emmeline Wells, a Mormon suffrage leader and a "plural wife," certainly deserve part of the credit for these early victories. Credit must also be given to Eastern suffrage associations that aided suffragists in the West through speaking tours, funding, and organizational experience. Elizabeth Cady Stanton, Susan B. Anthony, Lucy Stone, and future national suffrage leaders Dr. Anna Howard Shaw and Carrie Chapman Catt all stumped for suffrage out West.[42]

However, the question remains: Why were woman suffrage advocates successful in the West when unable to make headway elsewhere in the United States? One theory is that frontier conditions undermined traditional gender roles and that women, having proven their ability to conquer difficult conditions and do "men's work," were rewarded with the vote. A related theory is that traditions and institutions in the West were less entrenched than in the East and people in the West were more open to new ideas. On the other hand, some have insisted that politicians in the West supported woman suffrage hoping that women voters would bring Eastern gender conventions along in their covered wagons and help to "civilize" as well as populate the West.[43]

Most historians stress practical politics rather than advanced thinking as the explanation, emphasizing that politicians in the West—whatever their views on woman suffrage—found it expedient to enfranchise women. For example, Wyoming was a brand-new territory, established only one year before adopting woman suffrage: Wyoming politicians hoped to gain publicity and to attract women migrants to the territory. The victory has also been attributed to Reconstruction-era politics with Republican and Democratic leaders both supporting woman suffrage, but for different reasons. Territorial Governor John Allen Campbell, a Union Army veteran appointed by President Ulysses Grant, was a Republican who believed in universal equal rights. The legislator who introduced the woman suffrage bill, William H. Bright, was a native of Virginia and a Democrat, who opposed the newly ratified Fourteenth Amendment. His wife, Julia Bright, was for woman suffrage and in his view, if African American men were going to vote, there was no reason to deny the vote to women. Bright and his Democratic colleagues also hoped that doubling the size of the White electorate might ensure White control of the territory and that grateful women would vote for the Democrats.[44]

In Utah, Mormons of both sexes believed that women's votes would aid in preserving Mormon traditions—including polygamy—and that enfranchising women would help dispel the idea widely accepted in the East that Mormon women were oppressed. More importantly, perhaps, Mormon leaders were confident that enfranchising women would tip the balance of power in their favor in their ongoing power struggle with the non-Mormon population, consisting largely of miners, railroad construction workers, cowboys, and prospectors, who tended not to have women with them.[45]

In Colorado and Idaho, two states with larger and more diverse populations, the issues were different and even more complex. Racial issues were brought into the debate over woman suffrage by people on both sides. African American women were involved in the campaign, particularly in Denver, but most suffrage supporters were White and middle class, and many of them argued that White, native-born American women should have at least equal political rights with African American men. Some White suffragists also objected to the fact that Native American men who, under an 1887 law, were allowed citizenship and voting rights if they moved off of reservations, and Chinese men, who were allowed to vote if born in the United States, were voting ahead of White American-born women. Many anti-suffragists railed against adding to the electorate what they called "Negro wenches" as well as Chinese and Native American women.[46]

Success came as local suffragists and their allies from Eastern suffrage associations became increasingly adept at building coalitions and finding ways to appeal to politicians. Suffragists in Colorado benefitted from alliances with a labor union, the Knights of Labor, and a new political movement, Populism, that aided them after they pledged to support silver as a currency basis, in addition to gold. In Idaho, all three parties—Populists, Democrats, and Republicans—endorsed woman suffrage, and in 1896 support from Populists, the labor movement, and Mormons, contributed to a victory for the woman suffrage referendum by a two-to-one margin.[47]

For whatever reasons, these four Western states were the only states to adopt woman suffrage in the nineteenth century. Many other campaigns were attempted in Western states, and in a few cases, suffragists came close to success. Most notably, back in 1854, the territory of Washington defeated a suffrage bill by a single vote. In 1868, Nevada passed an amendment eliminating the words "male" and "White" from the voting requirements in the state constitution, but Nevada law required that any constitutional change be approved by two successive legislative sessions and in 1871 the measure failed.[48]

Suffragists also made unsuccessful bids for enfranchisement in California, Oregon, and Washington. Oregon suffrage leader Abigail Scott Duniway and Susan B. Anthony made a two-thousand-mile journey through Washington and Oregon in 1871, and built considerable support for the suffrage cause. But in the 1870s and 1880s, Oregon legislatures defeated suffrage bills four times, and

Washington passed suffrage laws twice only to have the state Supreme Court invalidate them. A hard-fought referendum campaign in California in 1896 failed, despite the state's suffragists' tireless work, aided by Carrie Chapman Catt and Susan B. Anthony. Attempts in 1889 and 1898 to re-enfranchise women of Washington also failed. Suffragists in Arizona, Montana, and Nevada lobbied their legislatures repeatedly but without success. There were no other territorial or state victories in the United States for the rest of the century.[49]

Oregonians began another major push in the new century, and woman suffrage was on the ballot in 1900, 1904, 1906, 1908, and 1910, but lost each time. However, when the next round of state victories took place, beginning in 1910, the victories were all in the West: Washington in 1910 and California in 1911, soon followed by Oregon, Kansas, and Arizona in 1912, and Nevada and Montana in 1914.[50]

The West's precociousness on woman suffrage was reflected in Western women's early entry into elected office. In the 1890s, Idaho, Colorado, and Utah all elected women to their state legislatures. In a bizarre historical twist, Utah suffragist, physician, and plural wife, Dr. Martha Hughes Cannon, was elected to the state senate in 1896. Her victory gained considerable national attention as she was not only the first woman elected to a state senate but she ran against and defeated her husband. Montana elected Jeannette Rankin, a leading suffragist in the state, to the U.S. House of Representatives in 1916, making her the first woman to hold federal office in the United States.[51]

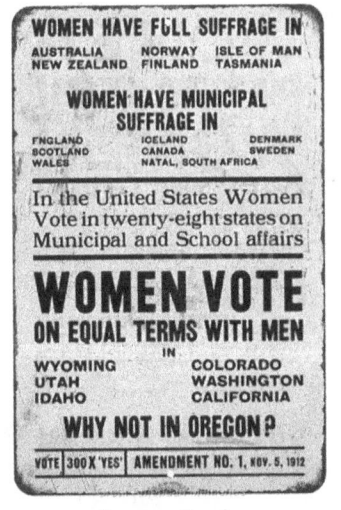

Oregon Poster
LIBRARY OF CONGRESS

Martha M. Hughes Cannon
LIBRARY OF CONGRESS

Meanwhile, Stanton and Anthony traveled to France and England in 1882 and 1883, where they found kindred spirits and instituted a committee of correspondence with the goal of establishing an international association for women's advancement. The goal was realized at the NWSA's 1888 conference in Washington, D.C. when representatives of many nations founded the International Council of Women (ICW).[52]

Suffrage sentiment was flourishing internationally, and in achieving full enfranchisement at the national level, suffragists outside the United States would be the first to taste success. In 1893, women in New Zealand won the vote, followed by Australia in 1902. These countries became the first in the world to enfranchise women, followed shortly by Finland in 1906 and Norway in 1913.[53]

Woman Suffrage and Temperance

The suffrage movement won a valuable ally when Frances Willard, as president of the Woman's Christian Temperance Union (WCTU), led thousands of otherwise quite traditional women to "convert" to the cause of woman suffrage as a means of protecting the home, women, and children. Following its official endorsement in 1881, the WCTU created a Department of Franchise under Zerelda Wallace and Dr. Anna Howard Shaw, which encouraged state WCTU chapters to endorse suffrage and distribute suffrage literature. African American suffragists also advanced the suffrage cause through the WCTU. Both Hattie Purvis and Frances Harper promoted woman suffrage in the role of WCTU Superintendent of Work Among Colored People.[54]

By 1890, the WCTU had grown into the largest woman's organization of the nineteenth century. It greatly aided the woman suffrage movement not only in the United States, but abroad. For example, the WCTU played a vital role in the victories for woman suffrage in New Zealand and Australia. In the United States, the WCTU was crucial to suffrage success both in attracting support among women who might have considered the existing suffrage organizations and their leaders eccentric or radical, and in expanding the suffrage movement's constituency to all parts of the United States. This included the South where the WCTU organized both White and Black women, though in segregated chapters.[55]

The WCTU endorsement, however, had serious repercussions for the suffrage movement; the politically powerful liquor industry concluded that woman suffrage was a threat to be stopped at all costs. At least one historian has argued that suffragists on the West Coast began to win their suffrage campaigns only after disassociating themselves from temperance. Looking back after 1920, Carrie Chapman Catt would denounce the liquor industry as "the Invisible Enemy" that "for forty years kept suffragists waiting for the woman's hour" through its corrupt manipulation of American politics.[56]

Unity Restored Through the NAWSA

One of the most important turning points in the history of the woman suffrage movement in the United States came in 1890 as the two national suffrage organizations reunited. At the instigation of younger suffragists, the movement's aging pioneers put aside their differences sufficiently to merge their rival organizations into the National American Woman Suffrage Association (NAWSA). Elizabeth Cady Stanton was chosen as president, Lucy Stone as head of the

Executive Committee, and Susan B. Anthony as Vice President, but it was Anthony who actually took command of the new organization, officially becoming president in 1892 and remaining in office until 1900.

While continuing to demand a federal amendment, NAWSA leaders concluded they must first build support within the states, eventually winning enough state suffrage amendments—and thus creating enough women voters—that Congress would be compelled to approve a federal amendment and three-fourths of the states would be sure to ratify. "I don't know the exact number of States we shall have to have," Anthony explained, "but I do know that there will come a day when that number will automatically and resistlessly [sic] act on the Congress of the United States to compel the submission of a federal suffrage amendment."[57]

Stanton continued to address a wide range of feminist issues and assert positions too radical for most suffragists; she became somewhat estranged from the movement after 1895 when she published *The Woman's Bible*, indicting Christianity for contributing to the subordination of women.[58] However, most NAWSA leaders, including Anthony, thought it imperative that the movement focus almost exclusively on winning the vote. While individual suffragists supported a wide variety of causes, they believed the national suffrage organization must work solely for enfranchisement, and as a single-issue group be able to attract the largest possible number of followers. In keeping with this strategy and influenced by the conservatism of new recruits, the suffragists went to great lengths to avoid association with radical causes.

Race, Region, and Suffrage Strategy

This new approach included attempts by White suffragists to shed the long-term association of women's rights with the rights of African Americans. Although the National American Woman Suffrage Association (NAWSA) never stopped using natural rights arguments for woman suffrage, many White suffragists were still indignant that Black men were enfranchised ahead of them and angry at the ease with which White immigrant men gained the vote. Increasingly, White suffragists departed from the movement's earlier emphasis on universal suffrage and employed racist and nativist rhetoric and tactics. Though individual friendships between White and African American suffragists continued and new ones developed, the interracial quality of woman suffrage movement in its earliest years when Blacks and Whites worked together for human equality was lost. As White suffragists no longer welcomed Black women's participation in their organizations and conferences, African American suffragists worked through their own organizations seeking to gain their own voting rights and to restore those of Black men.[59]

These changes resulted in part from the fact that the NAWSA now included thousands of younger White women from all parts of the nation who had not been a part of the earlier movements to end slavery and attain suffrage for all. Most of them shared the idea gaining currency at the time that voting should be a privilege

and a duty of the best qualified. Many White suffrage advocates favored literacy tests for voting, insisting that as long as the nation provided free public education, such a requirement was acceptable, even an incentive to self-improvement.[60]

The last three decades of the woman suffrage struggle coincided with an era in which support for universal suffrage waned across the country. Numerous factors contributed to this trend, including dramatic increases in the numbers of immigrants from Southern and eastern Europe and Asia, and imperialist ventures that left the U.S. government debating what rights could be claimed by people of color who inhabited territories under its control. In addition, the stubborn resistance of Southern White conservatives to the political equality of African Americans, along with distorted negative portrayals of Reconstruction-era governments that influenced public opinion outside the South, led many White, native-born voters to demand restriction rather than expansion of the electorate. In the 1890s, African American suffragists felt betrayed as NAWSA leaders crafted new strategies designed to succeed in this inhospitable climate, especially in the South.[61]

The historic connection between the woman's movement and the antislavery movement made advocacy of woman suffrage anathema to most White Southerners, and daunting to the Southern women that NAWSA leaders hoped to recruit. Southern White women who took up the suffrage cause were denounced as traitors to their region, accused of threatening the South's key institution—White supremacy. As one Alabama legislator put it, White Southern suffragists allowed themselves "to be misled by bold women who are the product of the peculiar social conditions of our Northern cities into advocating a political innovation the realization of which would be the undoing of the South."[62]

NAWSA leaders were aware, however, that a national victory would require support from at least some Southern states. Thus, in the 1890s they went to great lengths to, in Kentucky suffragist Laura Clay's words, "bring in the South." Using a strategy first suggested by Lucy Stone's husband, Henry Blackwell, Northern and Southern leaders began to argue that woman suffrage—far from endangering White supremacy in the South—could be a means of restoring it. Perhaps leading politicians in the South, like those in the West, might be persuaded that woman suffrage was expedient, a way to realize their political goals.[63]

At that point, Southern White politicians had yet to adopt the restrictions on voter eligibility they would soon put in place that disqualified most African American men, and were casting about for means other than the usual fraud and violence to solidify White control. NAWSA leaders and their Southern allies insisted that, as White women outnumbered Black women in the South, the adoption of woman suffrage would allow the South to restore White supremacy in politics *without* disfranchising Black men and risking congressional repercussions. When reminded that there were more African Americans than Whites in some parts of the South, White suffragists suggested that educational requirements, or even property requirements, could be

used to ensure that most of the new voters would be White.[64] The NAWSA spent considerable time and resources pursuing this "Southern strategy," locating suffrage sympathizers and organizing them, sending out recruiters, circulating literature, dispatching Carrie Chapman Catt and Susan B. Anthony on speaking tours through the region, and holding national conferences in Atlanta and New Orleans. However, by 1903 most suffragists recognized that the strategy had failed; the region's politicians had refused, in the words of one Mississippi politician, to "cower behind petticoats" and "use lovely women" to maintain White supremacy. Instead, these conservative men found other means to do so that did not involve the "destruction" of woman's traditional role. NAWSA leaders turned their attention elsewhere, and for a time, suffrage activity in the region declined.[65]

African Americans in the Struggle

African American suffragists were appalled by the racism White suffragists exhibited in the late nineteenth and early twentieth centuries. Still, they persisted, determined to gain the right to vote. For instance, the Rollin sisters, a family of activists in Columbia, South Carolina in the late 1860s and 1870s, were strong supporters of woman suffrage and well situated to promote it. Charlotte, Kathryn, and Louisa Rollin turned their home into a "salon" where movers and shakers in Reconstruction-era politics gathered. In addition, Frances was married to a state legislator, William J. Whipper, who promoted woman suffrage as a delegate to the 1868 South Carolina Constitutional Convention. In 1869, Charlotte "Lottie" Rollin addressed the state legislature on behalf of woman suffrage, insisting that "public opinion has had a tendency to limit woman's sphere to too small a circle" and asking for suffrage, "not as a favor, not as a privilege, but as a right."[66]

In 1870, the Rollins held a Woman's Rights Convention in Columbia attended by some of the state's most influential male Republicans, Black and White. With Lucy Stone's encouragement, in 1871 the sisters established a state suffrage organization affiliated with the American Woman Suffrage Association (AWSA) with Lottie Rollin representing South Carolina as an ex-officio member of the AWSA Executive Committee.[67]

Throughout the 1870s and 1880s, Mary Ann Shadd Cary continued to be involved in the National Woman Suffrage Association (NWSA). Cary, who became one of America's first female African American lawyers when she graduated from Howard University's school of law in 1870, joined other suffragists in testifying before the House Judiciary Committee in January 1874. Cary was disappointed when NWSA leaders rebuffed her request to include the names of ninety-four Black woman suffragists from Washington, D.C. on the Declaration of the Rights of the Women of the United States in 1876. Nevertheless, she remained a committed suffragist and attended all NWSA national conventions held in Washington, D.C.— giving an address at the 1878 convention. In 1880, Cary founded a Colored Woman's Franchise Association in Washington, D.C.

As noted, Frances Harper and Hattie Purvis promoted woman suffrage through their work with the Woman's Christian Temperance Union (WCTU) in the 1880s. Purvis, the daughter of Harriet Forten Purvis, had grown up in the suffrage movement. She was an officer in the Pennsylvania Woman Suffrage Association in 1884, and served as a delegate to NWSA meetings in that decade. When the International Council of Women (ICW) was created in 1888, African American women were involved from the beginning, including Frances Harper, who addressed the founding convention in Washington, D.C. A year later, Hattie Purvis accompanied Susan B. Anthony, a family friend, to London to attend the ICW meeting there.[68]

Even as White suffragists and suffrage groups distanced themselves from advocacy of the rights of African Americans in the late nineteenth and early twentieth centuries—a period that has been described as "the nadir" of race relations in the United States—the ranks of Black women working for the vote grew steadily. This rise in the number of African American suffragists reflected an increase in the number of educated, middle-class Black women in society and their eagerness to promote women's rights in tandem with racial uplift. The deterioration of race relations, including the rise of Jim Crow, a surge in the number of lynchings, and the Southern states' disfranchisement of Black men, made many Black women all the more determined to organize for collective self-help and resistance. Many worked through African American women's clubs affiliated with the National Association of Colored Women (NACW) founded in 1896.[69]

The NACW's first president, Mary Church Terrell, was an ardent suffragist. Born in Memphis to formerly enslaved parents who, after the Civil War, became affluent business owners, Terrell earned Bachelor's and Master's degrees at Oberlin College. She then spent several years in Europe where she became fluent in German, French, and Italian, and experienced what it was like to live free of the pervasive racism of life in the United States. Later, she settled in Washington, D.C. and became a teacher, principal, and a member of the District of Columbia Board of Education. As president of the NACW between 1896 and 1901, Terrell was a powerful advocate for woman suffrage and racial justice, and became one of the best-known African American women in the nation.[70]

When a horrific race riot in Ohio led a group of White liberals and African American leaders to issue a call for a meeting to discuss racial justice, Terrell was one of the signers. The 1909 meeting resulted in the founding of the National Association for the Advancement of Colored People (NAACP), which aimed to secure racial equality, including enforcement of the Fourteenth and Fifteenth Amendments. In the pages of the NAACP magazine, *The Crisis*, whose editor, W.E.B. DuBois, was a suffrage supporter, Terrell called on African Americans to support women's enfranchisment. Pointing out that the arguments against the Fifteenth Amendment mirrored those against women's right to vote, she wrote: "What could be more absurd and ridiculous than that one group of individuals who are trying to throw off the yoke of oppression themselves...should favor laws

and customs which impeded the progress of another unfortunate group and hinder them in every conceivable way."[71]

Likewise, as a member of the National American Suffrage Association (NAWSA), Terrell challenged White suffragists to support the struggles of African Americans, including the fights for equal suffrage and against lynching. At a time when few African American women were invited to speak at White suffragists' conferences, Terrell not only addressed NAWSA conferences but also represented American suffragists at an International Council of Women (ICW) conference in Berlin, where she spoke in fluent German and French about racial prejudice in the United States.[72]

Ida B. Wells-Barnett was also a nationally and internationally prominent advocate for gender and racial justice in the late nineteenth and early twentieth centuries. She became famous as a suffragist and as a passionate crusader against lynching. Born into slavery in Mississippi in 1862, she was freed six months later by the Emancipation Proclamation. As an adult, Wells-Barnett moved to Memphis where she was co-owner of a newspaper. Her crusade against lynching began in 1892 after three Memphis men, all friends of hers, were lynched after competing successfully with White businessmen. Afterward, she began investigating other lynchings and publishing the facts behind them, challenging the pervasive fiction that lynchings were committed by White men solely to avenge White women assaulted by Black men. In response, a White mob destroyed Wells-Barnett's newspaper office while she was away, and threatened to kill her if she ever returned to Memphis. She traveled extensively, founding anti-lynching societies and lecturing, including two trips to Great Britain in 1893 and 1894. Wells-Barnett settled in Chicago and founded many organizations and programs to serve the African American community, while continuing to travel and speak nationwide. Along with Terrell, Wells-Barnett was a co-founder of the NAACP and a member of the NAWSA.[73]

In 1913, after suffragists won the right to vote in presidential and municipal elections in Illinois, Wells-Barnett organized the Alpha Suffrage Club through which Black women played an influential role in Chicago politics. Outspoken and uncompromising, Wells-Barnett famously defied White suffragists' instructions that Black women march in a separate section at the back of the 1913 NAWSA suffrage parade in Washington, D.C. Instead, Wells-Barnett claimed her place in the middle of the parade with the Illinois delegation.[74]

Frances "Fannie" Barrier Williams was also a Chicago-based reformer, lecturer, and clubwoman who worked for women's rights and racial justice. Like Terrell, Barrier Williams was a co-founder of the NACW and a NAWSA member. A native of Brockport, New York, she spent most of her life in Chicago where, as a member of the city's Black elite, she used her considerable organizing ability and influence to expand services and create new institutions to aid African Americans and other residents of the city. Her efforts included an interracial hospital with a training school for nurses, a settlement house named the Frederick Douglass Center, and the Phillis Wheatley Home for Girls. In 1895, Barrier Williams became the first African American

Fannie Barrier Williams
LIBRARY OF CONGRESS

Adella Hunt Logan
LOGAN FAMILY COLLECTION

member of the prestigious Chicago Woman's Club. She gained national fame for her successful battle for representation of African Americans in the Columbia Exposition of 1893 in Chicago, where she delivered a famous address, "The Intellectual Progress of the Colored Women of the United States Since the Emancipation Proclamation." Barrier Williams was a supporter of W.E.B DuBois, and an early member of the NAACP. An avid supporter of woman suffrage and a friend of Susan B. Anthony, she was invited to eulogize Anthony at the 1907 NAWSA convention.[75]

Nannie Helen Burroughs, a Virginia-born woman whose parents had both been enslaved, became a prominent educator and church leader as well as a suffragist. When only thirty, she founded the National Training School for Women and Girls in Washington, D.C., one of the first vocational schools in the nation for African American girls and women. Burroughs first gained national recognition through a speech, "How the Sisters are Hindered from Helping," which she gave at the 1900 conference of the large and influential National Baptist Convention (NBC). For many decades thereafter, Burroughs promoted woman suffrage as an officer of the NBC's Women's Convention. She wrote and spoke extensively on the importance of enfranchisement for women of color in order to protect themselves against discrimination and injustice, and the need for African American and White women to work together to gain the vote.[76]

Adella Hunt Logan, a faculty member at the Tuskegee Institute in Alabama, was one of the beleaguered African American women supporting woman suffrage while remaining in the South. An active member of the NACW between 1900 and 1914, Logan spoke frequently at NACW conferences and headed the organization's department of suffrage. A life member of the NAWSA, she sometimes attended its conventions held in the South that excluded African American women. Logan looked like a White woman and on rare occasions such as these passed as White in order to

attend. After meeting privately with Carrie Chapman Catt at a conference in Atlanta, Logan explained (somewhat sarcastically) to a friend that she "could not resist the temptation to stay…a while, observing how the 'superior sister' does things."[77]

Logan was a great admirer of Anthony, though she deplored her concessions to racism in order to gain White support for the cause. In 1903, at Logan's invitation, Anthony and Catt visited Tuskegee, where, after an extended program, each female student "passed by in review before Miss Anthony and received each a hearty hand shake." Logan wrote articles about NACW activities for the NAWSA newspaper, the *Woman's Journal*, and promoted the suffrage cause through articles in the *Colored American* magazine and the NAACP magazine, *The Crisis*. One of her frequent themes was, if White women needed the vote to protect their rights, then Black women—victims of racism as well as sexism—needed the ballot even more.[78]

African American Suffragists' Crown of Thorns

White suffragists in this era varied in their attitudes toward African Americans and Black suffrage. Some shared the racism endemic in turn-of-the-century America; others were convinced they must cater to it in order to succeed. Some were sympathetic to Black suffrage, including Carrie Chapman Catt, who from the start of her career spoke in African American churches and clubs, published articles in the NAACP magazine, *The Crisis*, and spoke out against the discriminatory application of literacy tests. Mary Church Terrell praised Catt as being without race prejudice. However, in seeking the support of White Southerners, Catt catered to *their* racial prejudice and stated that White supremacy would be strengthened rather than weakened by woman suffrage.[79] Black suffragists accused White suffrage leaders—accurately—of being two-faced, of making concessions to White prejudice while making gestures of support to African Americans. But women's enfranchisement was also the Black suffragists' cause and they supported it regardless of the actions of White suffragists.

In 1903, Anthony and several NAWSA officials attending a Whites-only NAWSA conference in New Orleans, met separately with Black members of the Phillis Wheatley Club. The members welcomed Anthony's visit, but their leader, Sylvanie Williams, a *creole de couleur*, gently reminded her White guests of the poor treatment of Black women and the pain that it caused. According to the *History of Woman Suffrage*, Williams presented Anthony with a large bouquet tied with yellow satin ribbon and said:

> Flowers in their beauty and sweetness may represent the womanhood of the world. Some flowers are fragile and delicate, some strong and hardy, some are carefully guarded and cherished, others are roughly treated and trodden under foot. These last are the colored women. They have a crown of thorns continually pressed upon their brow, yet they are advancing and sometimes you find them further on than you would have expected. When women like you, Miss

Nannie Burroughs holding banner at Baptist convention
with church members, c. 1905
LIBRARY OF CONGRESS

Anthony, come to see us and speak to us it helps us to believe in the Fatherhood of God and the Brotherhood of Man, and at least for the time being in the sympathy of woman.[80]

Yet, White suffrage leaders' words and gestures of appeasement were but small comfort as NAWSA leaders sought to distance the suffrage movement from advocacy of the rights of Black Americans while African American suffragists watched in dismay. It was clear to them that White suffragists' main goals were to enlarge their White constituency and to cultivate White politicians whose support they deemed essential to a national victory—and they were willing to do what was necessary to achieve their goals.

At times, White suffragists reached out to African American suffragists for help, such as in cultivating Black support for state woman suffrage referenda in Northern states where Black men could vote. But White suffragists' discriminatory behavior would continue throughout the rest of the woman suffrage movement. In 1918, when a regional body of Black clubwomen, the Northeastern Federation of Women's Clubs, applied for affiliation with the NAWSA, White leaders rebuffed them. At that time, NAWSA leaders were desperate to convert at least a few of the Southern senators and congressmen who were blocking approval of the federal suffrage amendment. Believing it to be a "critical moment when our Federal Amendment hangs in the balance," NAWSA leaders felt they were 'justified" in making the request, and begged the Black clubwomen to temporarily withdraw their application. The NAWSA leaders expected the Black suffragists to understand and not take offense. However, the applicants, who had been testing the White

suffragists' commitment to the enfranchisement of African American women, understood all too well and were deeply offended.[81]

The situation was reminiscent of the Reconstruction era when it appeared that Black male suffrage could be attained if divorced from woman suffrage. At that time, former allies in a movement for universal suffrage had insisted that this was "the Negro's Hour" and that suffrage for women—White and Black—would have to wait. Now, half a century later, it appeared that "the Woman's Hour" had arrived, but White suffrage leaders were convinced that the federal woman suffrage amendment could not succeed it they defended Black suffrage. African American women were asked to *continue* to wait.

Rebuilding at the Turn of the Century

From the late 1890s to around 1910, the National American Woman Suffrage Association (NAWSA) went through a major period of change. Aging pioneers died or retired, and leadership shifted to younger women intent on modernizing NAWSA operations and bringing the movement to a successful conclusion. Historians have sometimes characterized this era as "the doldrums" of the woman suffrage movement owing to the lack of state victories. During these years, however, suffragists did much to expand the movement's constituency, retool its image, and adapt its strategy to fit current political conditions.[82]

The rebuilding effort commenced under the leadership of Susan B. Anthony's hand-picked successor, Carrie Chapman Catt, president of the NAWSA from 1900 to 1904. Catt was an early graduate of Iowa State University, the only woman in her graduating class. After a brief career in education in which she rose rapidly from teacher to principal to school superintendent, she married and moved to California, but after her husband's death in 1886, she returned to Iowa and began her crusade for woman suffrage. Catt married again, her new husband a wealthy engineer fully supportive of her suffrage work. In 1890, Catt attended the NAWSA's first convention, becoming a field organizer shortly thereafter, and soon proved to be exceptionally talented at organizing, speaking, and writing. Catt played a big role in the Colorado campaign, the first victory in which voters enfranchised women in a referendum. During the campaign, Catt traveled over a thousand miles, lecturing and establishing suffrage clubs. Her efforts extended even beyond national borders: between 1902 and 1904 she played a leading role in the creation of the International Woman Suffrage Alliance (IWSA), serving as its president from 1904 to 1923.[83]

Upon Anthony's retirement, Catt was elected to succeed the revered suffrage pioneer, but served only four years before her husband's illness led her to resign. One of Catt's earliest campaigns was the successful launch of what many called the "society plan"—an effort to recruit socially prominent and wealthy women. These included larger-than-life figures such as multi-millionaire and socialite Alva Smith (Vanderbilt) Belmont, philanthropist Katherine Dexter McCormick, and the daring and colorful newspaper publisher, Mrs. Frank Leslie (Miriam Folline Leslie legally

adopted her late husband's name), who later willed her fortune to the woman suffrage movement. An unspoken assumption among the NAWSA leadership was that the "society plan" was for Whites only.[84]

As suffragists attracted the support of women philanthropists of high social standing, it became more difficult for the press to dismiss the suffrage movement as radical. In fact, suffrage work was becoming quite fashionable at home and abroad. The International Council of Women (ICW), founded in 1888 by Elizabeth Cady Stanton and Susan B. Anthony, attracted what an American suffragist described as "the most eminent women" of their respective countries, including aristocrats. During ICW conferences in London in 1899 and Berlin in 1904, delegates were entertained by Queen Victoria and German Empress Augusta Victoria. The ICW did not formally endorse women's enfranchisement, but under Catt's leadership during the Berlin meeting, members who wanted to commit themselves to the suffrage cause created the spin-off organization, the International Woman Suffrage Alliance (IWSA).[85]

In the United States, the fact that Anthony's eightieth birthday celebration in 1900 took place at the White House at the invitation of President William McKinley, was proof that suffrage leaders' efforts to shed the movement's radical image had been a success—even though McKinley did not endorse it. Suffragists' success in converting so many women of wealth ensured that at least the last phase of the suffrage campaign would be well funded. In September 1909, the NAWSA moved its headquarters from the county courthouse in Warren, Ohio—the home of the organization's treasurer, Harriet Taylor Upton—to New York City where their wealthy benefactor, Alva Belmont, had leased an entire floor of a building on the corner of Fifth Avenue and 42nd Street.[86]

Leaders of the NAWSA also cultivated as allies well-respected and well-heeled men whose support meant a lot to the movement in its last years. In 1908, a group of prominent men from New York City established an organization called the Men's League for Woman Suffrage, which consisted of more than a hundred prominent and influential men in publishing, industry, finance, law, medicine, academia, the clergy, and the military. Their ranks included men such as Oswald Garrison Villard, a progressive editor and publisher; John Dewey, a philosopher and educational reformer; George Foster Peabody, a banker and philanthropist; and Stephen S. Wise, Reform rabbi and nationally prominent Jewish leader. These self-assured men marched proudly in woman suffrage parades, often ridiculed by observers who verbally assaulted their masculinity, calling them "Suffragents." The Men's League soon had thousands of members in thirty-five states, working closely with the NAWSA to persuade waffling politicians, the press, and the public to support the suffrage cause.[87]

A primary part of the NAWSA rebuilding effort involved convincing the growing numbers of White, middle- and upper-class members of women's clubs that woman suffrage would be a boon to their civic improvement efforts.

Local and state affiliates of the General Federation of Women's Clubs (GFWC) began to support woman suffrage, which would later culminate in its endorsement at the GFWC's national convention in 1914. NAWSA leaders also reached out to the new generation of college-educated women, many of them professionals, challenging them to take up the torch for woman suffrage, reminding them that their opportunities were owed to the pioneers of the women's rights movement.[88]

The movement profited greatly from the new ideas and energy of these younger leaders, such as Radcliffe College graduates Maud Wood Park and Inez Haynes Irwin who founded the College Equal Suffrage League (CESL) in 1900. Park, who would later emerge as one of the NAWSA's most prominent leaders, played a crucial role in bringing women of her generation into the suffrage fold. As Park explained:

> After hearing Miss Anthony speak, I came to realize what her life had been, the heroism of her service not for herself but for the sex, and so for the whole human race.... I promised myself then that I would try to make more women see these things as I have seen them. College women should realize their debt to the pioneers who have made our education and competence possible. They should be made to feel the obligation of their opportunities and to understand that one of the ways to pay that debt is to fight the battle for suffrage now in the quarter of the field in which it is still unwon.

"College Evenings" in which aging pioneers were lauded by an array of college deans and grateful graduates, came to be a regular feature at annual NAWSA conventions. College evenings were also effective for recruitment between conventions, and another useful tactic for making the suffrage movement less radical and more popular.[89]

Harriot Stanton Blatch, Elizabeth Cady Stanton's daughter, also had a major impact after returning from living in England for two decades. While the "society plan" and College Evenings brought more elite women into the woman suffrage movement, Blatch emphasized working women's need for the vote and the suffrage movement's need for them. Blatch admired self-supporting women, seeing them as exemplars to women like herself and partners in the fight. Having been impressed by the success of some British suffragists in organizing across class lines, she sought to do so in New York. In 1907, Blatch brought together working women—from professionals to trade unionists—into the Equality League of Self-Supporting Women, later called the Women's Political Union (WPU). The tactics she and her associates in New York borrowed from working-class political activists and British suffragists, including open-air meetings and parades, invigorated the suffrage movement and helped to diversify the movement's constituency.[90]

The NAWSA's increased membership, diversification, and heightened visibility were not accompanied by political victories in this era. When Catt resigned as NAWSA leader in 1904, Dr. Anna Howard Shaw inherited the

presidency. Though rebuilding efforts continued, under Shaw the organization became less centralized and provided little in the way of a national political strategy. She was undeniably a woman of incredible drive and ability. From a poor immigrant family on a struggling frontier farm in Michigan, Shaw overcame great obstacles to become both a Methodist minister and a physician before walking away from both professions to devote her life to woman suffrage. Shaw was also a gifted and witty orator who gave more than ten thousand speeches during her career. Catt praised Shaw as "the greatest orator among women the world has ever known." But from the late 1890s to 1910, few state campaigns were launched and all of them failed.[91]

The Suffrage Movement and Progressivism

By 1910, however, there were considerable grounds for optimism. The Progressive Movement, which had begun around 1900 at the grassroots level and swept both national political parties, was proving to be a tremendous boon to the cause of woman suffrage. Progressivism appealed especially to well-educated, middle- and upper-class women and men eager to reform government at all levels to better serve the needs of the people. Their aim was powerful, positive, and efficient government able to counter the malignant influence of giant corporations and "robber barons" that in the late nineteenth century corrupted the government and enriched themselves at the expense of consumers and workers.[92]

Progressives supported a wide variety of reforms such as pure food and drug legislation, expansion of public health programs, improvement of public schools, restrictions on child labor, and legislation to curb political corruption. They also advocated for a national income tax, believing that citizens who made the most money should pay at a higher rate than those who made less. This idea, which became known as "progressive taxation," was intended to curb the growing problem of inequality of wealth that many saw as a threat to the republic as well as to help fund the federal government.

Many Progressives were moral reformers with diverse goals ranging from stamping out prostitution to prohibiting the manufacture and sale of alcohol. Ultimately, the Progressive era would yield four amendments to the U.S. Constitution: The Sixteenth Amendment, establishing a tax on income; the Seventeenth Amendment, calling for senators to be directly elected by the people rather than by state legislators; the Eighteenth Amendment, prohibiting the manufacture and sale of alcohol; and the Nineteenth Amendment, enfranchising women.[93]

Progressives varied greatly in their attitudes on race. Some, such as the White and African American founders of the NAACP, were in the forefront of campaigns for racial justice. Other Progressives, including leading scholars and politicians— most notably President Woodrow Wilson—were profoundly racist. Particularly in the South, but in other regions of the United States as well, many White Progressives saw excluding racial minorities and illiterate Whites as Progressive reform, a

means of cleaning up politics. The Progressive impulse led Americans to try to improve conditions for immigrants, but also inspired efforts to "Americanize" them and to restrict further immigration.[94]

One of the most widely-shared goals of Progressives reformers was to improve conditions for workers. While labor unions sought improvements in wages, hours, and working conditions through collective bargaining, reformers from upper-class and middle-class backgrounds called on local and state governments to address these issues through "protective legislation." Reformers and unions often worked together for laws establishing a minimum wage or setting a limit on work hours. They sought protection for workers of both sexes, though after conservatives vigorously opposed these laws through the courts, reformers emerged with dearly-won protective legislation for women, but not for men.[95]

Regarding woman suffrage, Progressive politicians believed that women voters would provide vital support for reform and many women wanted the vote in order to do just that. Across the United States, countless Progressive women, many of them members of women's clubs, enlisted in the suffrage movement as they became frustrated with their inability to secure such reforms through "indirect influence" or lobbying.[96]

Reform-minded politicians were impressed by the argument that enfranchised women, as "municipal housekeepers" seeking to make government more honest, moral, and helpful to them in carrying out their traditional duties, would support them. Some suffragists disdained appealing for enfranchisement on the basis of "woman's nature" and its compatibility to progressive reform, instead insisting that women had a right to the vote regardless of what they chose to do with it.[97] Yet, Progressivism gave suffragists a new expediency argument that suffragists put to good use in the movement's final decade. Indeed, one could argue that the woman suffrage movement finally succeeded, not because of changes in Americans' ideas about "woman's nature," but because new ideas about the nature of government and what government should do were compatible with old ideas about the nature of woman.

In 1912, for the first time in its history woman suffrage was endorsed by a major national political party, Theodore Roosevelt's Progressive Party. Roosevelt invited leading suffragist and Progressive heroine Jane Addams, the founder of the famous Chicago settlement house, Hull House, to place his name in nomination at the Progressive's national convention.[98]

Diversity Strengthens the Movement for Woman Suffrage

During the Progressive Era, the woman suffrage movement grew dramatically in size and diversity. Even as many White suffrage leaders discriminated against African American suffragists, they reached out to women from diverse class and ethnic backgrounds who saw suffrage as crucial for enhancing the status of women and improving society.

Many prominent suffragists were women from elite backgrounds who founded or joined organizations dedicated to improving conditions for workers, especially women workers. For example, Maud Nathan and Florence Kelley were daughters of privilege who were determined to aid women who were not. Both were leaders of the National Consumers League, founded in 1899 by Jane Addams and other Progressives to harness the power of consumers to obtain fair wages and safe conditions for workers as well as reliable goods and services.[99]

Nathan was from a socially prominent, Sephardic Jewish family in New York, the descendent of a long line of prominent activists and leaders dating back to the American Revolution. A founding member of the New York Consumers League, Nathan served as its president from 1897 to 1927. During years of lobbying New York legislators, she became convinced that lawmakers cared little about the views of non-voters, leading Nathan to become an ardent suffragist—despite the fact that her sister, Annie Nathan Meyer, was a leading anti-suffragist. Maud Nathan's husband, Frederick, was a staunch suffrage supporter and headed the New York Men's League for Equal Suffrage. In 1913, Theodore Roosevelt appointed Maud Nathan to chair the Suffrage Committee of the National Progressive Party.[100]

Florence Kelley, a prominent suffragist born in Philadelphia, was a leading Progressive reformer as well as a scholar, lawyer, and socialist. She was also an activist for the rights of African Americans, strongly influenced by her father, an abolitionist, a founder of the Republican Party, a judge, and a congressman from Pennsylvania, and by Quaker relatives on her mother's side. In the 1890s, she lived at Jane Addams's Hull House in Chicago, writing and lecturing about child labor and "sweatshops," and successfully lobbying the Illinois legislature for reform. In 1899, she moved to New York where she became general secretary of the newly organized National Consumers League and henceforth one of the nation's leading advocates on behalf of industrial workers.[101]

Kelley was crucial to the successful defense of maximum hour laws for women, argued and won by Louis Brandeis in the landmark Supreme Court decision *Muller v. Oregon* in 1908. Kelley also played an important role in the founding of the National Association for the Advancement of Colored People (NAACP) in 1909 and afterward in its opposition to lynching and to racism in education. In 1912, she helped establish the Children's Bureau in the U.S. Department of Labor. As a vice president of the NAWSA, Kelley contributed greatly as an organizer, speaker, and writer, calling for woman suffrage as a means of protecting the most vulnerable members of society. In a well-known pamphlet "Woman Suffrage: Its Relation to Working Women and Children," she wrote:

> It is the daughters of the poor who chiefly fall victims to the basest crimes. Poor, young, ignorant, unorganized, they depend for protection upon laws framed and enforced by persons older than themselves. Is it safe or sane to exclude from a full share of power and responsibility the mothers and teachers, the older women whose first care is for the welfare of the young?[102]

Another prominent suffragist, Inez Milholland, a New Yorker from a wealthy background, was also a lawyer, a socialist, and reformer. From her days at Vassar, when she famously defied the college president's ban on woman suffrage activities on campus and organized a rally in the cemetery, Milholland was whole-heartedly engaged in the movement, lecturing, lobbying, and participating in public demonstrations and marches. Athletic and attractive, she became popular with the public for her role in leading suffrage parades on horseback. She was an early and enthusiastic member of the NAACP along with her father, John Milholland, a wealthy businessman and newspaper editor who served as the NAACP's first treasurer. Introduced to socialism as well as militant feminism while a student in London, Milholland became a fervent advocate for the rights of workers, especially women and children, and for unionization. It was natural for her to be drawn to the Women's Trade Union League (WTUL), founded in 1903 to unionize women to gain better wages and working conditions, and full citizenship.[103]

The WTUL was unusual for bringing women of different classes together. Florence Kelley and Harriot Stanton Blatch were members, as was wealthy NAWSA benefactor Alva Vanderbilt Belmont. WTUL members of all classes believed that politicians knew little and cared less about the needs of working women who needed the power of the ballot for their demands to be addressed. As a WTUL member, Milholland supported many strikes, such as the shirtwaist and laundry workers' strikes of 1910. She walked the picket lines, raised money from wealthy friends to support the strikers, and as a lawyer gave legal counsel to workers.[104]

While women like Nathan, Kelley, and Milholland sympathized with exploited workers and the injustices heaped upon them, there were many other women who were leaders in the fight for woman suffrage who had firsthand knowledge of these conditions. Leonora O'Reilly, Mary Kenney O'Sullivan, and Rose Schneiderman, for example, began working in factories at an early age. All were women of great courage and charisma who quickly rose to positions of leadership in labor organizations and in the WTUL.[105]

Many of the women workers in the WTUL were immigrants or the daughters of immigrants. O'Reilly and O'Sullivan, whose parents were poor Irish immigrants, were forced to leave school and begin work as young girls. O'Reilly started working in a clothing factory at age eleven in 1881 and became a union member at age sixteen. After she founded the Working Women's Society to promote fair wages and better working conditions, wealthy women philanthropists enabled her to take time off from her job to study factory conditions while living in the Henry Street Settlement house in New York. After helping establish the WTUL in 1903, O'Reilly spent twelve years as a member of its executive committee as well as an organizer and recruiter, often speaking in public for labor reform and woman suffrage. In 1909, O'Reilly signed the call leading up to the founding of the NAACP, then served on the organization's executive committee. That same year, she helped organize the famous New York City strike nicknamed the "Uprising of the 20,000." After the tragic 1911

Triangle Shirtwaist Factory Fire in which 146 workers, mostly young immigrant girls, died jumping from windows or being burned to death in locked rooms with no fire escapes, she worked to build support for occupational safety laws.[106]

O'Sullivan grew up in poverty in Hannibal, Missouri, left school after the fourth-grade, and started work as an apprentice dressmaker, later becoming a bookbinder. After working in Chicago bookbinderies, she organized a women bookbinders' union. Jane Addams invited O'Sullivan to hold union meetings at Hull House and paid for printing circulars that Addams personally helped distribute to workers during their lunch hours. Soon thereafter, Samuel Gompers, head of the American Federation of Labor (AFL), hired O'Sullivan as the federation's first woman organizer, and she began organizing in New York and Massachusetts. In 1903, O'Sullivan helped found the WTUL, becoming its first secretary and then vice president. An active suffragist, she addressed the U.S. House of Representatives on behalf of a federal suffrage amendment in 1906, insisting that women were producers in American society and that every producer deserves the right to vote.[107]

Rose Schneiderman was born in Poland to a Jewish family that moved to New York City's Lower East Side in 1890 when she was eight. At thirteen, she started working in a department store, which was considered more respectable than factory work, but as it paid less, Schneiderman became a capmaker. Still, wages were low and working conditions poor, leading her to organize a branch of a capmakers' union. While leading a strike, she became involved in the New York WTUL. By 1906, Schneiderman had become the WTUL's vice president, and by 1908, its chief organizer, focusing on New York's garment district. Schneiderman was legendary as a speaker; at only four feet nine inches tall and with flaming red hair, Schneiderman delivered powerful, militant speeches that many described as the most moving they had ever heard. Her "bread and roses" speech delivered in 1912 inspired many working women and touched the hearts of their wealthy "allies":

> What the woman who labors wants is the right to live, not simply exist—the right to life as the rich woman has the right to life, and the sun and music and art. You have nothing that the humblest worker has not a right to have also. The worker must have bread, but she must have roses, too. Help, you women of privilege, give her the ballot to fight with.

Schneiderman helped found the Wage Earner's League for Woman Suffrage in 1911. Although from different class backgrounds, Schneiderman and Maud Nathan helped carry heavily Jewish districts in New York for suffrage in the crucial 1917 referendum.[108]

All of this work had a major impact on the woman suffrage movement. Large numbers of working-class women joined the movement, urged on by suffragists from similar backgrounds and by middle-class and elite allies who sought to unite women of all classes into a revitalized suffrage movement that was also increasingly diverse.

LUISA
CAPETILLO

ROSE
SCHNEIDERMAN

FLORENCE
KELLEY

MARY KENNEY
O'SULLIVAN

MAUD
NATHAN

ADELINA
OTERO-WARREN

LEONORA
O'REILLY

INEZ
MILHOLLAND

MARIA GUADALUPE
EVANGELINA LOPÉZ

All photos are courtesy of the Library of Congress
or they are in the public domain.

Beyond the Northeast and Midwest, women from different economic, ethnic, and racial backgrounds were also working to gain the vote. Bilingual suffrage advocates reached out to potential supporters from various backgrounds and cultures. Some suffrage advocates who were important in expanding and diversifying the movement were immigrants unable to become citizens and voters themselves.

In New Mexico, Adelina "Nina" Otero-Warren, a descendent of elite "Hispanos" who had long ago settled in the area, cultivated support for women's enfranchisement among Spanish-speaking residents of her state. Aurora Lucero White, a bi-lingual educator, the daughter of New Mexico's first Secretary of State, gave suffrage speeches in Spanish. Recognizing that Spanish-speaking women made up at least half of the female population of New Mexico, they made sure that suffrage literature was published in Spanish as well as English.[109]

In California, suffragists narrowly won a state referendum in part by cultivating support from diverse immigrant communities in the state. They published suffrage articles in Spanish, Chinese, German, Portuguese, and Italian. Los Angeles suffragist, Maria Guadalupe Evangelina de Lopez, an instructor at the University of California, Los Angeles, reached out to Spanish-speaking residents of her city, translating at rallies, and working with other suffragists to distribute tens of thousands of pamphlets in Spanish. Though there was hostility to Chinese Americans among some White activists, others courted their support. When Californians voted on the suffrage referendum in 1911, a majority of Chinese voters supported it.[110]

In Oregon, as in California, suffragists finally won a referendum by putting together diverse coalitions; Jewish women were among the key leaders in Portland. The Colored Women's Equal Suffrage Association organized African American clubwomen, and Portland's Chinese neighborhoods were mobilized by the Chinese American Suffrage Club.[111]

Suffrage pamphlet of
L.A. Political Equality League
written by Maria de Lopéz
SCRIPPS COLLEGE, CLAREMONT

In New York, sixteen-year-old, Chinese-born Mabel Ping-Hua Lee supported the woman suffrage movement as a member of the New York Women's Political

Equality League. At the invitation of NAWSA leaders, Lee led a 1912 suffrage parade in New York City on horseback while behind her NAWSA president Dr. Anna Howard Shaw carried a banner that read "NAWSA Catching Up with China." Shaw sought to advertise the fact that the new Chinese Republic allowed women to vote when the United States did not. Lee, along with her mother and other Chinese immigrant women from New York, supported U.S. woman's suffrage, even though as Asian immigrants, they were ineligible to become citizens and one day vote.[112]

Marie Louise Bottineau Baldwin, a Native American suffragist, was a Chippewa born in North Dakota. She later lived in Washington, D.C. where her father was a lawyer working to defend the Chippewa's treaty rights. She worked in the Office of Indian Affairs (OIA), one of only two NativeAmerican employees in the OIA. In 1912 at age forty-nine, Baldwin entered the Washington College of Law, founded by women lawyers since few traditional law schools admitted women. She became the first woman of color and the first Native American to earn a law degree from the college. When she became involved in the suffrage movement, Baldwin reminded suffragists that Native American women had had "virtual suffrage, and the power of recall, since time immemorial" in their Native American communities. Baldwin marched with her classmates and teachers in the 1913 suffrage parade in Washington, D.C., joining a contingent of women lawyers. At a time when many Native Americans lacked citizenship, and therefore the right to vote, Baldwin was also a tireless advocate of voting rights for Native peoples. She testified before Congress and even met with President Wilson on behalf of Native Americans and voting rights.[113]

Puerto Rican-born Luisa Capetillo brought the suffrage message to Cuban American, African, African American, and Italian American workers, while she worked as a *lectora* (reader) in a Florida cigar factory. As a labor union leader who traveled back and forth between the United States and Puerto Rico, Capetillo was eager to address the problems facing the working conditions of women and children. Considered the first suffragist in Puerto Rico, she was also a writer, intellectual, freethinker, and feminist—remembered by some Puerto Ricans as the first woman to wear pants in public. She is also remembered as one of the most important advocates of woman suffrage in Puerto Rico.[114]

Mexican-born Teresa Villarreal in Texas, a revolutionary labor organizer, socialist, newspaper publisher, and activist for feminist causes, was an ardent suffragist. Forced to flee Mexico with her family, which opposed the dictatorship of President Porfirio Díaz, they found allies among unionists and socialists in the United States. In 1909, they settled in San Antonio. Together with her sister, Andrea Villarreal, Teresa Villarreal published *La Mujer Moderna* (*The Modern Woman*), the state's first feminist newspaper, as well as *El Obrero* (*The Worker*).[115]

Many converts to the suffrage movement in the United States were inspired by socialism and by socialist feminists abroad. Their efforts were crucial to the first

European victory for woman suffrage in Finland in 1906. In the United States, opponents of socialism and woman suffrage were quick to point out this connection, and in some cases, "mainstream" suffragists were less than welcoming of their socialist sisters. But socialist women made invaluable contributions during suffrage battles in several states, notably the victorious suffrage campaign in California in 1911.[116]

Often, socialist suffragists in the United States—who came from all classes— served as intermediaries between working-class women and middle-class and elite suffragists. They also helped win support from labor unions and working-class men. Though some socialists such as Emma Goldman disdained the suffrage movement, thinking it foolish to expect that real progress would come from female enfranchisement, many socialist feminists were convinced that gaining the vote was crucial in order for women to realize their goals.[117]

Anti-suffragists in the Progressive Era

As in the case of temperance and suffrage, however, the idea that women would support Progressive reforms inspired opposition. As the suffrage movement became more of a threat, its opponents became more organized. In 1911, the National Association Opposed to Woman Suffrage (NAOWS) was founded. The organization was based in New York City, later adding state branches, and in 1913 a second headquarters in Washington, D.C. Josephine Jewell Dodge, the NAOWS' founder and first president, was an educated and accomplished reformer well known as a pioneer in the American day nursery movement. When the suffrage fight shifted to Washington, D.C., Alice Hay Wadsworth, wife of a prominent anti-suffrage senator from New York, James W. Wadsworth, Jr., took over as NAOWS president.[118]

The NAOWS consisted of wealthy and influential women such as Dodge and Wadsworth, but also men eager to block the enfranchisement of women out of fear that their business interests or political power would suffer at the hands of women voters. In the South, the cotton textile industry that employed large numbers of child laborers joined the liquor industry as a formidable opponent of woman suffrage, and worked with a growing number of Southern anti-suffrage organizations to oppose state suffrage referenda.[119]

In the last ten years of the suffrage struggle, anti-suffragists continued to make extensive use of the race issue, particularly in the South, even as White Southern suffragists tried to dismiss it as irrelevant. While the suffragists insisted that the recently adopted laws that disfranchised African American men would apply to Black women as well, White Southern anti-suffragists insisted Black women would register and vote in even larger numbers than White women, who would be forced to associate with African Americans at the polls. Their racist tactics included publicizing the early association between the antislavery and the women's rights movements, and the continued friendship of White suffragists such as Susan B.

Anthony with Black suffrage leaders, including Frederick Douglass, whose late-life marriage to a White woman outraged many Americans. White Southern anti-suffragists also publicized Carrie Chapman Catt's supportive statements about Black suffrage, including comments that appeared in the NAACP magazine, *The Crisis*, as "proof" that Catt supported equal rights for African Americans and was an enemy of the South. The main anti-suffrage organization in the region, the Southern Women's League for the Rejection of the Susan B. Anthony Amendment, declared its opposition to "any measure that threatens the continuation of Anglo-Saxon domination of Social and Political affairs in each and every State of the Union."[120]

Anti-suffragists also opposed woman suffrage on the grounds that African American women supported it. For instance, suffrage opponents distributed reprints of "Negro Women's Resolutions for Enforcement of Federal Suffrage Amendments" adopted by the National Association of Colored Women (NACW). The document also noted that the retiring NACW president, Mary B. Talbert, would join Carrie Chapman Catt in the U.S. delegation to the International Council of Women in Norway, and called for a federal anti-lynching law. At times, anti-suffragists insisted that enfranchised African American women would be more demanding and difficult to deter than Black men. Moreover, as the suffragists became more focused on the federal woman suffrage amendment, White Southern politicians denounced it as an unacceptable extension of the Fifteenth Amendment, a measure that would inspire new demands for Black suffrage, which they insisted was "not dead but sleeping."[121]

Anti-suffrage rhetoric continued to present woman suffrage as a threat to home and family, warning that enfranchised womanhood would neglect children and saddle husbands with cooking and childcare. It is significant, however, that in the Progressive Era, female anti-suffragists like Josephine Dodge widely proclaimed that they *favored* women's involvement in public affairs, including nonpartisan political activity. Pointing to their own records of community service, anti-suffragists insisted that they opposed woman suffrage primarily out of the belief that involvement in partisan politics would dispel women's energies and dilute, rather than enhance, women's influence.[122]

As the suffrage movement entered what proved to be its last decade, a tradition of women's civic activism had developed—and had been accepted—to the point that the argument over suffrage was more often framed in terms of how women could be most effective, rather than if women should concern themselves with life outside a narrowly defined "woman's sphere."

Alice Paul and the National Woman's Party

Around 1912, the increased support for woman suffrage resulting from the Progressive Movement, together with the series of victories in the Western states, seemed to breathe new life into suffragists nationwide. The return of Alice Paul from England, where she was inspired by the energy and boldness of the

"militant" faction of British suffragists led by Emmeline Pankhurst, was also a major factor in the new suffrage activism. The Pankhursts, officially the Women's Social and Political Union (WSPU), embraced the derisive term coined by the press, "suffragettes," in part to distinguish themselves from the older, larger, and more moderate organization of British suffragists, the National Union of Women's Suffrage Societies led by Millicent Fawcett. While many American suffragists had been inspired by Pankhurst and her daughters during their speaking tours in the United States, Paul had become involved with them while a doctoral student in Britain. She participated in WSPU parades and demonstrations, and was arrested and jailed for the cause. Paul shared, as well as admired, the Pankhursts' militant spirit.[123]

Paul, along with her able associate Lucy Burns and the circle of women who gathered around them, many of them young, had no patience with the slow, state-by-state plodding that had consumed much of the National American Woman Suffrage Association's (NAWSA) energies. Paul and her cohort's militance and impatience to achieve what they considered a long-overdue victory also appealed to some older NAWSA leaders, including Harriot Stanton Blatch and the imperious NAWSA benefactor Alva Vanderbilt Belmont, who became a key financial backer and strategist.[124]

At first, these women worked through the Congressional Union, the group within the NAWSA charged with lobbying for a federal amendment. They urged the NAWSA to focus its attention almost exclusively on the federal route to enfranchisement. This infuriated some suffragists, particularly a small but vocal group of states' rights devotees led by Kate Gordon of New Orleans, who favored woman suffrage by state action only. The NAWSA did indeed step up its campaign for a federal amendment—but not before parting company with Paul and her associates who formed a separate organization, the National Woman's Party

First Picket line at the White House, 1917
LIBRARY OF CONGRESS

(NWP).[125]

The central issue in this new rift in the suffrage forces was Paul's advocacy of a strategy derived from the British suffragettes to oppose the "party-in-power"—in this case, the Democratic Party—until it compelled Congress to enfranchise women. This strategy, ill-suited to the divided party system in the United States, violated the NAWSA's longstanding policy of non-partisanship. Eventually, President Woodrow Wilson and the Democratic Party declared their support for woman suffrage by state action, but in keeping with their states' rights views, still refused to endorse a federal amendment. Paul and her associates employed a number of bold new tactics designed to force President Wilson and the Democrats to support the federal amendment, which the NWP members dubbed the "Susan B. Anthony Amendment." Their tactics ranged from mobilizing women voters in Western states to vote against all Democrats in the 1916 election—especially Wilson who was running for re-election—to publicly burning the president's war-time speeches in praise of democracy in front of the White House.[126]

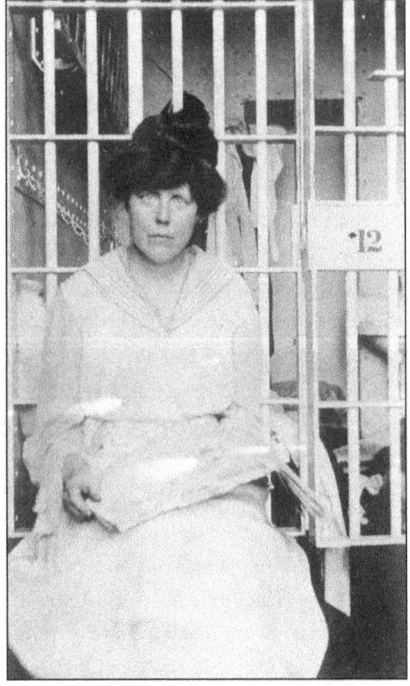

Suffragist Lucy Burns jailed at Occoquan Workhouse. Burns was arrested six times, sometimes spending months in jail.
LIBRARY OF CONGRESS

Paul proved to be brilliant at attracting and keeping the attention of the press and thereby forcing the issue of woman suffrage to the forefront of public debate. The massive, dramatic suffrage parade that she organized during Wilson's inaugural celebration in 1913 captured the attention of the nation. This spectacular event featured nine bands, four mounted brigades, and twenty-four floats. The striking Inez Milholland, already known for her role in New York suffrage campaigns and marches, led the parade dressed in flowing White robes and riding a White horse. Behind her came women from countries that had already enfranchised women, followed by the "Pioneers" who had worked for decades to gain the vote for women in the United States. Estimates varied, but around eight thousand suffragists—many dressed in White and representing every state plus a vast number of pro-suffrage organizations—participated in the march.[127]

Throngs of spectators, most of them men, many of them intoxicated, crowded

Pennsylvania Avenue sidewalks to watch the parade. Some men spit on the marchers, pelted them with lighted cigars and liquor bottles, and then began to attack them. About one hundred suffragists were injured and hospitalized as a result. The police failed to protect the marchers, either through indifference or in support of the mob's actions, which led to a congressional investigation. The whole affair attracted sympathy for the cause, not unlike the public outcry after the attacks on peaceful demonstrators during the civil rights movement of the 1960s.[128]

Paul and the NWP were among the first Americans to employ many of the tactics of civil disobedience, including being the first ever to picket the White House for a political cause. They held signs and banners designed to embarrass President Wilson and compel him to support a federal woman suffrage amendment. Nonviolent and dignified, the pickets were "silent sentinels," keeping up their demonstrations for nearly three years in every kind of weather, eventually winning the respect of many in the press who dubbed them the "Iron Jawed Angels." Many people were outraged when NWP members continued their demonstrations after the United States entered World War I in April 1917, at one point even carrying a sign calling the president "Kaiser Wilson."[129]

Crowds attacked the demonstrators as they protested in front of the White House, but the police arrested the suffragists—not their attackers. Charged with obstructing sidewalk traffic, the suffragists were sentenced to jail terms of up to six months. Most were imprisoned under deplorable conditions at the Occoquan Work House near Washington, D.C. Some of the prisoners, including elderly women,

Suffragists demonstrating against Woodrow Wilson in Chicago, 1916

NATIONAL WOMAN'S PARTY RECORDS, LIBRARY OF CONGRESS

protested this violation of their rights by going on hunger strikes, which led to forced feedings—a brutal and dangerous procedure—recorded in shocking detail in Doris Stevens's classic memoir of 1920, *Jailed for Freedom*.[130]

These horrific experiences only increased the suffragists' determination to expose the hypocrisy of a nation which, during World War I, proclaimed itself the leader of a crusade for democracy while at the same time jailing and abusing women in the United States for protesting their nation's denial of the vote to half of its adult citizens.

Carrie Chapman Catt and the "Winning Plan"

Carrie Chapman Catt was also eager for the National American Woman Suffrage Association (NAWSA) to bring the long struggle to a conclusion with the adoption of the federal suffrage amendment, but she pursued this end with a strategy that contrasted sharply with that of Alice Paul and the National Woman's Party (NWP). After stepping down as NAWSA president in 1904, Catt served as leader of the International Woman Suffrage Alliance (IWSA). But in 1915, responding to the NAWSA's call for a forceful general, Catt returned to the presidency and soon launched an initially top-secret "Winning Plan" to harness the power of the massive but sluggish NAWSA and initiate the final, victorious suffrage drive.[131]

Catt made it clear that the federal amendment was still the ultimate goal, while further state work was essential toward that end. The suffragists still had to have the support of key states on the East Coast, including "Mighty New York," which had one of the largest congressional delegations and did not adopt woman suffrage until 1917. Catt's plan called for suffragists in states that had not adopted woman suffrage—and where victories seemed possible—to launch campaigns immediately and simultaneously with strong NAWSA support. In states where defeat was likely, Catt insisted that suffragists refrain from state suffrage campaigns to avoid potential embarrassment to the cause but seek partial suffrage where possible, whether municipal, presidential, or primary suffrage. She urged suffragists in states where women already voted to pressure their national representatives to support the federal amendment.[132]

Meanwhile, Catt and key lieutenants, Maud Wood Park and Helen Gardener, worked hard to convince President Wilson to support woman suffrage by federal as well as state means, and conducted a massive lobbying effort to enlist congressional support. The press dubbed this effort the "Front Door Lobby" because of the contrast between suffragists' open and honest methods and those more common among Washington lobbyists.[133]

Women from all parts of the nation came in well-coordinated "relays" to reinforce those stationed at the NAWSA's Washington headquarters. They studied the congressmen with microscopic intensity, seeking the right words or arguments with which to persuade the politicians to support the federal amendment. It had long since become clear to the suffragists that "justice" arguments alone would not be

The first contingent of the Women's Overseas Hospitals, supported by the
National American Woman Suffrage Association

NATIONAL ARCHIVES

sufficient; politicians had to be convinced it was expedient for them personally as
well as for their party to support woman suffrage. Though some loved it and some
loathed it, suffragists found it necessary to learn the art of "practical politics."[134]

As Catt and Nettie Rogers Shuler later recalled in their book, *Woman Suffrage
and Politics,* this was an all-absorbing effort. "It is doubtful," they wrote, "if any
man, even among suffrage men, ever realized what the suffrage struggle came to
mean to women before the end was allowed in America. How much of time and
patience, how much work, energy and aspiration, how much faith, how much
hope, how much despair went into it. It leaves its mark on one, such a struggle."[135]

In these years, Catt, like Susan B. Anthony in the final decades of her life, set aside
other causes to focus exclusively on winning the suffrage battle. Catt had been a
founder of the Woman's Peace Party in 1915, but when the United States entered
World War I two years later, Catt urged suffragists to support the war effort—for
which she was expelled from the Woman's Peace Party and shunned by fellow
pacifists. The NAWSA even maintained a hospital in France for wounded soldiers.
Former NAWSA president Dr. Anna Howard Shaw chaired the Woman's Committee
of the Council of National Defense established by the Wilson administration to
coordinate the war efforts of American women. For her efforts, Shaw was awarded

the nation's Distinguished Service Medal, the first woman to receive it.[136]

Suffragists' war work enhanced the patriotic image of the movement with the public and powerful decision makers, including the president. When Wilson finally announced his support for the federal woman suffrage amendment in a September 30, 1918 speech to Congress, he stated: "We have made partners of the women in this war...Shall we admit them only to a partnership of suffering and sacrifice and toil and not to a partnership of privilege and right?"[137]

The 1918 Pandemic

At the time of Wilson's address, the House of Representatives had already approved the woman suffrage bill. The Senate would vote the next day. But even the president's plea failed to produce the last two votes from senators needed to clear the constitutional requirement of two-thirds of each chamber of Congress. Suffragists pressed on, looking toward the November mid-term elections and making plans for suffrage referenda in four states—striving for more state victories that would amplify the pressure on Congress. Suffragists were also determined to defeat four anti-suffrage senators whose challengers promised to vote for the federal amendment.[138]

Then calamity struck in the form of a massive outbreak of influenza, the deadliest in modern times. The 1918 flu pandemic lasted about fifteen months, ultimately killing up to 50 million people, including 675,000 in the United States. The death toll far exceeded that of World War I, horrific as it was. The first wave of the pandemic had come in the spring of 1918, but it roared back in the fall, worse than before. The flu killed almost 200,000 people in October alone. Washington, D.C. was hit especially hard. In a letter to supporters, Carrie Chapman Catt wrote, "These are sad times for the whole world, grown unexpectedly sadder by the sudden and sweeping epidemic of influenza. This new affliction is bringing sorrow into many suffrage homes and is presenting a serious new obstacle in our referendum campaigns and in the congressional and senatorial campaigns." Catt fell victim to the flu, described by frantic associates as "chained to her bed...and extremely ill." Nevertheless, she was determined that the suffrage movement would not lose momentum.[139]

It was a struggle. Suffragists' best-laid plans were wrecked. The U.S. Public Health Service issued a nationwide advisory prohibiting all large meetings and public gatherings. By late October of 1918, one suffragist wrote, the pandemic was "so bad that it was considered immoral for six women to meet in a parlor." Many National American Woman Suffrage Association (NAWSA) members who would have been campaigning for suffrage, instead volunteered as Red Cross workers or as nurses in hospitals. Alice Paul also faced setbacks. The National Woman's Party (NWP) had to postpone a cross-country train tour in which suffragists who had been imprisoned in their fight for suffrage, planned to don replicas of their prison uniforms and tell their story to large crowds along the way. To continue their work during the pandemic, suffragists had to be creative. They relied more heavily on

telephone calls, the press, and the mail: NAWSA headquarters provided over a million pamphlets for distribution door to door and hundreds of bulletins to be sent to local newspapers.[140]

The pandemic greatly suppressed voter turnout in the fall of 1918, but when the votes were counted, suffragists were thrilled that two senators they had targeted for defeat lost and several new pro-suffrage lawmakers were voted in. And though the referendum in Louisiana—the only one in the South—failed, the other referenda in Michigan, South Dakota, and Oklahoma, passed. The month brought more great news: on November 11, 1918, World War I came to an end.[141]

Gratitude for women's service during the war, and more recently, the epidemic, contributed to the growing support for women's enfranchisement in general, and to the success of these referenda in particular. The growing number of state victories and Woodrow Wilson's conversion, finally led Congress to approve the Nineteenth Amendment and submit it to the states.

Historians sometimes debate the relative contributions of Catt and the NAWSA versus Paul and the NWP to congressional endorsement of the Nineteenth Amendment, but most agree that their strategies were inadvertently complementary. Catt's careful coordination of suffragists nationwide and her skillful political maneuvering, together with Paul and the NWP's skill in focusing attention on the federal amendment and putting pressure on Wilson and members of Congress, all were major factors.

The Fight for Ratification

On June 4, 1919, when Congress approved the federal suffrage amendment, the final chapter in the long suffrage story was still ahead—the fight for ratification. The amendment had to be approved by three-fourths of the states, which at that time was thirty-six states, in order to be added to the Constitution. As the struggle began, Illinois and Wisconsin competed for the honor of being the first to ratify. Meanwhile, Georgia and Alabama scrambled to be the first to pass a "rejection resolution" in keeping with a scheme hatched by the governor of Louisiana for thirteen Southern states to formally reject the proposed amendment and ask for a "Proclamation of Defeat."[142]

Most states took longer to act and many battles were hard fought with suffragists and anti-suffragists using all the powers of persuasion at their command. By the end of 1919, twenty-two states had ratified and suffragists were confident that victory was on its way.[143] In February 1920, the National American Woman Suffrage Association (NAWSA) held a "Victory Convention" in Chicago to celebrate the impending victory and plot its course for the future. At that convention, the NAWSA officially changed its name to the League of Women Voters (LWV), confident that the federal suffrage amendment would be ratified before the November 1920 presidential election. Plans called for the LWV, which would continue the NAWSA's non-partisan policy, to promote good government and a more just society, and to

educate U.S. citizens, especially women, in becoming well-informed voters.[144]

During the spring of 1918, state ratifications continued though with more "rejection resolutions." When Mississippi voted against ratification of the amendment, the Jackson newspaper, the *Clarion-Ledger*, celebrated the defeat, proclaiming, "…the vile old thing is as dead as its author [Susan B. Anthony], the old advocate of social equality and intermarriage of the races, and Mississippi will never be annoyed with it again."[145]

By the summer of 1920, suffragists were dismayed to find that, while only one more state was needed, no further state legislative sessions were scheduled before the November 1920 election. Desperate, suffragists began working for special sessions. NAWSA leaders called on the chairs of the Republican and Democratic National Committees, insisting that women would soon be voting and the electorate would double in size: surely these leaders wanted a state controlled by their party to be "the Perfect 36." According to Catt and Shuler, "The Republican leaders were determined that their record should not be blackened at the eleventh hour, and Democratic leaders were equally sincere in the decision that defeat of final ratification not be laid at their door. So both national chairmen again issued statements and vied with each other in efforts to influence lagging states." Polls in Connecticut and Vermont, states with Republican majorities, indicated that their legislatures would ratify if called into special session, but the anti-suffrage governors refused.[146]

National Woman's Party (NWP) members picketed the Republican national convention, demanding that its nominee for president, Warren Harding, compel these GOP governors to call special sessions needed for ratification. When Harding declined, the NWP threatened to oppose all Republican candidates in 1920 as they had opposed all Democrats in 1916. Finally, President Wilson was able to pressure governors in North Carolina and Tennessee, states controlled by Democrats, into calling special sessions. North Carolina legislators refused to ratify, however, insisting they would not sacrifice their honor on the altar of political expediency, and urged Tennessee to do likewise.[147]

Armageddon

Thus, the final battle over woman suffrage took place in Nashville, Tennessee in the long, hot summer of 1920. In that final, dramatic contest, anti-suffragists as well as suffragists from across the nation descended upon the state in a bitter struggle over ideology and influence. As suffragists and their champions in the legislature began wearing yellow rose boutonnieres, and suffrage opponents donned red ones, the press began calling this unsavory struggle "The War of the Roses."[148]

Alice Paul wisely stayed away, aware that Southern Democrats were none too keen on the NWP's tactics, including opposing all Democrats back in 1916 and "harassing" their hero, President Woodrow Wilson; but she sent able lieutenants, including Sue Shelton White and Anita Pollitzer. White was a native Tennessean, well acquainted with state politics and with Tennessee suffragists affiliated with

the National Woman's Party (NWP) and the National American Woman Suffrage Association (NAWSA). Pollitzer, another Southerner who grew up in Charleston, South Carolina, was a talented NWP organizer. Also an experienced lobbyist with considerable charm, she traversed the state, seeking to find and persuade legislators to vote for ratification.[149]

Carrie Chapman Catt also sent deputies, notably Marjorie Shuler, who helped smooth out problematic rifts among Tennessee NAWSA members, which had complicated the ratification campaign. But when the battle heated up, Catt rushed to Nashville and remained for over a month, determined the fight would end successfully in Tennessee. However, that the suffrage movement's "Armageddon" would take place in the South, the region where the suffrage movement had encountered the most opposition, meant that the result was far from certain.[150]

Opponents of ratification urged Tennessee legislators to "Save the South from the Susan B. Anthony Amendment and Federal Force Bills." Anti-suffrage broadsides warned, "Remember that woman suffrage means a reopening of the entire negro suffrage question, loss of State rights, and another period of reconstruction horrors, which will introduce a set of female carpetbaggers as bad as their male prototypes of the sixties."[151]

Meanwhile, the liquor industry and its corporate allies, most notably the railroads, were clearly using all of their considerable power and resources to secure the proposed amendment's defeat. A year earlier in January 1919, the Eighteenth Amendment, banning the manufacture, sale, and transportation of liquor, had been ratified, making Prohibition the law of the land. Hardly willing to accept defeat, the liquor industry immediately began campaigning for repeal—more determined than ever to stop woman suffrage.[152]

Despite the glare of national publicity, the suffragists watched with dismay as a comfortable margin in favor of ratification gradually disappeared and they were quite uncertain of the result when the vote took place. On August 18, it appeared that Tennessee had ratified the amendment after an unexpected "aye" from Harry Burn, a twenty-four-year-old Republican legislator from the mountains who was wearing an anti-suffrage red rose. Burn had been sympathetic to the suffrage cause, but he was up for re-election and under intense pressure to vote against ratification. After the vote, he explained that he changed his position at the urging of his pro-suffrage, elderly mother, Febb King Ensminger Burn, whose letter urging him to support ratification he received just prior to the vote. He added, "A mother's advice is always safest for her boy to follow." Aware of the profound impact of his vote for ratification (though vastly underestimating the number of new women voters), Burn also stated that he "appreciated the fact that an opportunity such as seldom comes to a mortal man to free seventeen million women from political slavery was mine."[153]

After Burn's aye vote, both sides were stunned. The suffragists were jubilant, but the antis refused to accept defeat, moved to reconsider, and managed to delay official ratification through parliamentary tricks. While anti-suffrage legislators fled

the state to avoid a quorum, their associates held a "Mass Meeting…to Save the South" in Nashville's Ryman Auditorium and through more covert, under-the-table methods, attempted to pressure pro-suffrage legislators to change their votes.[154]

Finally, Tennessee reaffirmed its vote for ratification. Tennessee's governor, Albert H. Roberts, signed the bill and it was rushed to Washington, D.C. where Secretary of State Bainbridge Colby hastened to certify the Nineteenth Amendment in the wee hours of the morning and without ceremony, before the antis were able to gain an injunction or by any other means interfere with the ratification process.[155]

On August 26,1920, a week after the Tennessee legislature became the thirty-sixth state to ratify, the United States officially added the Nineteenth Amendment to the Constitution.

At last, the long suffrage movement had come to an end. It had taken over seventy-two years, but the U.S. Constitution finally prohibited denying citizens the vote "on account of sex." Defying all obstacles, including the high bar for amending the Constitution deliberately set by its authors, the movement begun by a small group of women's rights advocates in one corner of the nation had grown into the massive, diverse, powerful, national coalition required for victory.

Twenty-six million American women were now eligible to vote, the largest expansion of the electorate in the history of the nation. For many women of the United States, however, the fight was still not over. In 1920, many Native Americans, residents of U.S. overseas territories, immigrants from Asia who were barred from becoming citizens, and citizens disfranchised merely by residing in Washington, D.C., the struggle for voting rights would continue. African American women living in the Southern states now had the right to vote, but for almost half a century more, they would be kept from voting by the same discriminatory laws and policies that kept most African American men away from the polls. Only after the Voting Rights Act of 1965—the result of another prolonged struggle for equal suffrage in which African American women played leading roles—were they able to claim their right to vote established by the Nineteenth Amendment.[156]

Not a Gift but a Triumph

As news of the ratification of the Nineteenth Amendment spread across the nation, whistles blew and church bells rang. In towns and cities from coast to coast, there were processions, flag raisings, wreath-layings, toasts (some appropriate for the era of Prohibition and some not), and ceremonies transforming suffrage associations into the League of Women Voters (LWV). In Seneca Falls, suffragists draped a flag over a tablet marking the site of the women's rights convention where women had first demanded the vote in 1848.[157]

After hearing that Tennessee had ratified, Alice Paul sewed the thirty-sixth star on the National Woman's Party's (NWP) ratification banner and, with great fanfare, unfurled it from the balcony of the NWP headquarters, hailing the triumph of the

Alice Paul unfurling the suffrage flag upon ratification of the
Nineteenth Amendment in 1920

cause—a federal suffrage amendment—for which the NWP was founded. Earlier, Paul spoke of the emotional impact: "Women who have taken part in the long struggle for freedom feel today the full relief of the victory. Freedom has come not as a gift but as a triumph, and it is therefore a spiritual as well as political freedom which women receive."[158]

Back from Nashville, Carrie Chapman Catt was invited to the White House where she was congratulated by President Wilson, her former foe who had been, in the end, a formidable ally. Proceeding to New York City, she received a hero's welcome from Governor Al Smith who represented the Democratic Party, New York Senator William M. Calder, who represented the Republicans, and prominent New York suffragists, who presented her with an enormous victory bouquet. Catt then joined other suffragists for a final parade in which they marched together for the last time, accompanied by a regimental band and waving their worn suffrage banners.[159]

Catt and Paul often disagreed, but at this time of triumph, both rejected the rhetorical fancy that the vote had been "given" to American women. As a leader of the International Woman Suffrage Alliance (IWSA) as well as the National American Woman Suffrage Association (NAWSA), Catt found it "humiliating"

Victorious Carrie Chapman Catt receiving a hero's welcome from
Governor Al Smith as she returns to New York after ratification
LIBRARY OF CONGRESS

that so many other countries "had outdistanced America" in enfranchising women.
While thrilled that victory had come at last, as she later recalled, Catt's joy was
tempered by thoughts of its cost. The suffrage movement in the United States, Catt
wrote, "Engaged the lifelong energies of a longer list of women, called into action a
larger organization in proportion to population, and involved a greater cost in
money, personal sacrifice and ingenuity, than the suffrage campaign of any other
land." And when, in 1920, "the final victory came to the woman suffrage movement
in the land of its birth American suffragists knew that their victory had, even then,
been virtually wrung from hesitant and often resentful political leaders."[160]

In the prepared message Catt delivered on August 26, 1920, rather than thanking
the president, members of Congress, or state legislators, the NAWSA president
directed her remarks to the "women of America," reminding them of the seventy-
two years of struggle by generations of suffragists and the many sacrifices made so
that "you and your daughters might inherit political freedom. That vote has been
costly. Prize it!"[161]

Notes

1. This overview of the woman suffrage movement in the United States is meant to give readers a broad view of the movement from beginning to end as well as a solid background for the following essays in Marjorie J. Spruill, *One Woman, One Vote: Rediscovering the Woman Suffrage Movement*, Second edition, (NewSage Press, 2021).

2. Carrie Chapman Catt and Nettie Rogers Shuler, *Woman Suffrage and Politics: The Inner Story of the Suffrage Movement* (Seattle & London: University of Washington Press, 1923), 107-108.

3. Linda K. Kerber, "Ourselves and Our Daughters Forever: Women and the Constitution, 1787-1876," Chapter Two, in Spruill, *One Woman, One Vote*, Second edition.

4. Nancy F. Cott, 1997, *The Bonds of Womanhood: "Woman's Sphere" in New England, 1780-1835* (New Haven: Yale University Press, 1977, 1997).

5. Eleanor Flexner, "Maria W. Miller Stewart," in Edward T. James et al, *Notable American Women: A Biographical Dictionary* Vol. III, (Cambridge: Harvard University Press, 1975), 377-78.

6. Ibid. Erin Blakemore, "This Little-Known Abolitionist Dared to Speak in Public Against Slavery," *Time* January 24, 2017; Martha S. Jones, *All Bound Up Together: The Woman Question in African American Public Culture, 1830-1900* (Chapel Hill: University of North Carolina Press, 2007).

7. Gerda Lerner, *The Grimke Sisters from South Carolina: Pioneers for Women's Rights and Abolition* (University of North Carolina Press, 2004); Carol Berkin, *Civil War Wives: The Lives and Times of Angelina Grimké Weld, Varina Howell Davis, and Julia Dent Grant* (New York: Vintage Books, 2010); Nancy Woloch, *Women and the American Experience*, Fifth Edition (New York: McGraw-Hill, 2011), 180-95.

8. Ibid.; Sarah Moore Grimké. *Letters on the Equality of the Sexes and the Condition of Women* (Isaac Knapp, 1838).

9. Berkin, *Civil War Wives*; *The Grimké Sisters*; Woloch, *Women and the American Experience*, 180-95.

10. Ibid., 183.

11. Ibid. Keith Melder, "Abigail Kelley Foster," *Notable American Women*, Vol. I, 647-50.

12. Alice S. Rossi, "A Feminist Friendship: Elizabeth Cady Stanton and Susan B. Anthony," Chapter Four, in Spruill, *One Woman, One Vote*, Second Edition.

13. Sally G. McMillen, *Seneca Falls and the Origins of the Women's Rights Movement* (New York: Oxford University Press, 2009), 81-94; Leigh Fought, *Women in the World of Frederick Douglass*, (New York: Oxford University Press, 2019).

14. McMillen, *Seneca Falls*, 88-93

15. Elizabeth Cady Stanton, Susan B. Anthony, and Matilda Gage, eds. "The Seneca Falls Convention," from *History of Woman Suffrage*, 1881," Chapter Three; Rossi, Chapter Four; Katherine M. Marino, "The International History of the U.S. Suffrage Movement," Chapter Eleven, in Spruill, *One Woman, One Vote*, Second Edition; McMillen, *Seneca Falls*; Note: In *The Myth of Seneca Falls: Memory and the Women's Suffrage Movement, 1848-1898* (University of North Carolina Press, 2014), historian Lisa Tetrault emphasizes the multiplicity of events in the early stages of the women's rights movement. She argues that the myth that celebrates the Seneca Falls Convention rather than any other pre-war event as the origin was constructed to strengthen the movement as it "imposed a sense of order and inevitability onto the whole of nineteenth-century women's rights.

16. McMillen, *Seneca Falls*, 104-48; Woloch, *Women and the American Experience*, 192.

17. Ibid., 192-95; McMillen, *Seneca Falls*, 104-48.

18. Ibid.

19. Sally G. McMillen, *Lucy Stone: An Unapologetic Life* (New York: Oxford University Press, 2015).

20. Alma Lutz, "Susan Brownell Anthony," *Notable American Women*, Vol. I, 51-59.

21. Rosalyn Terborg-Penn, "African American Women and the Woman Suffrage Movement," Chapter Ten, in Spruill, *One Woman, One Vote*, Second Edition; Rosalyn Terborg-Penn, *African American Women in the Struggle for the Vote, 1850-1920* (Bloomington: Indiana Univ. Press, 1999); Sharon Harley, "African American Women and the Nineteenth Amendment,"

National Park Service nps.gov/articles/african-american-women-and-the-nineteenth-amendment.htm#_ednref1

22. Terborg-Penn, Chapter Ten; Harley, "African American Women and the Nineteenth Amendment"; Nell Irvin Painter, *Sojourner Truth: A Life, A Symbol* (New York, NY: Norton, 2007).

23. Rossi, Chapter Four; Terborg-Penn, *African American Women in the Struggle for the Vote*, 16, 18; Harley, "African American Women and the Nineteenth Amendment"; Marino, Chapter Eleven.

24. Andrea Moore Kerr, "White Women's Rights, Black Men's Wrongs, Free Love, Blackmail, and the Formation of the American Woman Suffrage Association," Chapter Five, in Spruill, *One Woman, One Vote*, Second Edition; Faye E. Dudden, *Fighting Chance: The Struggle Over Woman Suffrage and Black Suffrage in Reconstruction America* (Oxford University Press, 2014).

25. Kerr, Chapter Five; Terborg-Penn, Chapter Ten; Harley, "African American Women and the Nineteenth Amendment."

26. Dudden, *Fighting Chance*.

27. Ibid., 62.

28. Kerr, Chapter Five; Terborg-Penn, Chapter Ten; Dudden, *Fighting Chance*, 61-87; quotations Stanton 83, Anthony 86. Anthony reportedly said this to Wendell Phillips and Theodore Tilton in a private meeting in Tilton's office as the two men sought to convince her to wait for another generation to push for woman suffrage. Incident described in Ida Husted Harper, *Life and Work of Susan B. Anthony*, Vol. 1:261.

29. Truth quoted in Dudden, *Fighting Chance*, 96.

30. Ibid., 82.

31. Kerr, Chapter Five; Ellen Carol DuBois, "Taking the Law Into Our Own Hands: Bradwell, Minor, and Suffrage Militance in the 1870s, Chapter Six, in Spruill, *One Woman, One Vote*, Second Edition; Nell Irvin Painter, "Voices of Suffrage: Sojourner Truth, Frances Watkins Harper, and the Struggle for Woman Suffrage," in Jean H. Baker, *Votes for Women: The Struggle for Suffrage Revisited* (New York: Oxford University Press, 2002), 42-55; Dudden, *Fighting Chance*, 94-101, 161-66.

32. Kerr, Chapter Five; Dudden, *Fighting Chance*; On Harper, see Bettye Collier-Thomas, "Frances Ellen Watkins Harper: Abolitionist and Feminist Reformer, 1825-1911," in Ann D. Gordon and Betty Collier-Thomas, et al., *African American Women and the Vote* (Amherst: University of Massachusetts Press, 1998), 41-65; Lori D. Ginzberg, *Elizabeth Cady Stanton: An American Life* (New York: Hill and Wang, 2010).

33. Kerr, Chapter Five; DuBois, Chapter Six.

34. McMillen, *Lucy Stone*; Stone put aside previous opposition to the Fifteenth Amendment because it was crucial to the freedmen and a step toward universal suffrage. On Stone's decision, Stanton commented: "Mrs. Stone felt the slaves' wrongs more deeply than her own—my philosophy was more egotistical." Quotations, 178.

35. Kerr, Chapter Five; Terborg-Penn, *Women in the Struggle for the Vote*, 47.

36. Kerr, Chapter Five; McMillen, *Lucy Stone*.

37. Kerr, Chapter Five; DuBois, Chapter Six.

38. DuBois, Chapter Six; Terborg-Penn, Chapter Ten; Kerber, Chapter Two; Berkin, *Civil War Wives*, 99; Lynn Sherr, *The Trial of Susan B. Anthony* (New York: Humanity Books, 2003); Lynn Sherr and Susan B. Anthony, *Failure Is Impossible: Susan B. Anthony in Her Own Words* (New York: Times Books, 1996); Susan Ware, *Why They Marched: Untold Stories of the Women Who Fought for the Right to Vote* (Harvard University Press, 2019).

39. Ibid.

40. Kerber, Chapter Two; DuBois, Chapter Six.

41. Beverly Beeton, "How the West Was Won for Woman Suffrage," Chapter Seven, in Spruill, *One Woman, One Vote*, Second Edition.

42. Beeton, Chapter Seven; Beverly Beeton, *Women Vote in the West: The Woman Suffrage Movement, 1869-1896* (New York: Garland Publishing, 1986); Jad Adams, *Women and the Vote: A World History* (Oxford: Oxford University Press, 2016), 149-58; Susan Ware, *Why They Marched*; Rebecca J. Mead, *How the Vote Was Won: Woman Suffrage in the Western United States, 1868-1914* (New York University Press, 2006, 2004); Jennifer Helton, "Woman Suffrage in the West," nps.gov/articles/woman-suffrage-in-the-west.htm

43. For different views on woman suffrage in the West, see Beeton, Chapter Seven; Beeton, *Women Vote in the West: The Woman Suffrage Movement, 1869-1896* (New York: Garland Publishing, 1986); Alan Pendleton Grimes, *The Puritan Ethic and Woman Suffrage* (Westport, Conn: Greenwood Press, 1967, 1980); Adams, *Women and the Vote*, 149-58; Mead, *How the West Was Won*; Helton, "Woman Suffrage in the West."

44. Beeton, Chapter Seven; Adams, *Women and the Vote*, 149-56; Helton, "Woman Suffrage in the West"; Jennifer Helton, "To Pass Suffrage, Wyoming Embraced Radical Innovation," *Wyofile*, December 10, 2019, wyofile.com/to-pass-suffrage-wyoming-embraced-radical-innovation/; Tom Rea, "Right Choice, Wrong Reasons: Wyoming Women Win the right to Vote," WyoHistory.org, November 8, 2014 wyohistory.org/encyclopedia/right-choice-wrong-reasons-wyoming-women-win-right-vote

45. Beeton, Chapter Seven; Adams, *Women and the Vote*, 156-58; Susan Ware, *Why They Marched*. In 1887 Utah women lost the vote when the U.S. Congress passed the Edmunds-Tucker Anti-Polygamy Act. Though it mainly targeted plural marriage, it also took away women's voting rights in the Utah territory. As a result, Utah women, both Mormon and non-Mormon, founded suffrage organizations and began working to regain their voting rights. Woman suffrage was restored when Utah was admitted as a state in 1896.

46. Beeton, Chapter Seven.

47. Ibid.

48. Helton, "Woman Suffrage in the West."

49. Ibid.

50. Ibid.

51. Ibid.; For more information, see this extensive database: "Her Hat Was in the Ring! U.S. Women Who Ran for Political Office Before 1920," herhatwasinthering.org/about.php; Martha Cannon's 1884 marriage had to be held in secret. She was her husband's fourth wife and the U.S. government was actively prosecuting polygamists, especially men. When she had a child, the prosecutors took that as proof of the plural marriage she had to flee to England to avoid testifying against her husband as well as the husbands of other plural wives whose babies she personally delivered. She had to flee again when her second child was born. After she served in the Utah senate for four years, her public career ended when she had a third child, again showing evidence Mormons were continuing to practice polygamy, and again making national news. In 2018 the Utah legislature voted to place her statue in Statuary Hall of the U.S. Capitol beginning in 2020, the centennial of the Nineteenth Amendment; Jennifer Baker, "Martha Hughes Cannon," National Women's History Museum, 2019, www.womenshistory.org/education-resources/biographies/martha-hughes-cannon.

52. Marino, Chapter Eleven; Leila J. Rupp, *Worlds of Women: The Making of an International Women's Movement* (Princeton University Press, 1998).

53. Marino, Chapter Eleven; Adams, *Women and the Vote*, 106-34, 175-87.

54. Carolyn De Swarte Gifford, "Frances Willard and the Woman's Christian Temperance Union's Conversion to Woman Suffrage," Chapter Eight, in Spruill, *One Woman, One Vote*, Second Edition; Terborg-Penn, Chapter Ten; Harley, "African American Women and the Nineteenth Amendment."

55. Gifford, Chapter Eight; Marino, Chapter Eleven; Adams, *Women and the Vote*, 109-32; Glenda Elizabeth Gilmore, *Gender and Jim Crow: Women and the Politics of White Supremacy in North Carolina, 1896-1920*, (Chapel Hill: Univ. of North Carolina Press, 2006); Anastatia Sims, *The Power of Femininity in the New South: Women's Organizations and Politics in North Carolina, 1880-1930* (Columbia: University of South Carolina Press, 1997).

56. Helton, "Woman Suffrage in the West"; Catt and Shuler, *Woman Suffrage and Politics*, 132-59, 270-79.

57. Ibid., 266-69; Kerr, quotation from Maud Wood Park, "Campaigning State by State," in NAWSA, *Victory How Women Won It* (New York, 1940), 69-80. Anthony made this comment in the early 1880s after the New Departure and hopes for enfranchisement through an appeal to the Supreme Court had failed.

58. Elizabeth Cady Stanton, editor, *The Woman's Bible* (New York: European Publishing Company, 1895).

59. Marjorie J. Spruill, "Bringing in the South: Southern Ladies, White Supremacy, and States' Rights in the Fight for Woman Suffrage," Chapter Nine, and Judith N. McArthur, "Minnie Fisher Cunningham's Back Door Lobby in Texas: Political Maneuvering in a One-Party State," Chapter Twenty, in Spruill, *One Woman, One Vote*, Second Edition; Harley, "African American Women and the Nineteenth Amendment."

60. Spruill, "Bringing in the South," Chapter Nine; McArthur.

61. Aileen S. Kraditor, *The Ideas of Women Suffrage Movement 1890-1920* (New York: Columbia Univ. Press, 1965); Roger Daniels, *Guarding the Golden Door: American Immigration Policy and Immigrants Since 1882* (New York: Hill and Wang, 2005); David W. Blight, *Race and Reunion: The Civil War in American Memory* (Cambridge, Mass: Harvard University Press, 2002); Louise Michele Newman, *White Women's Rights: The Racial Origins of Feminism in the United States* (New York, N.Y.: Oxford Univ. Press, 2010); Spruill (Wheeler), *New Women of the New South: The Leaders of the Woman Suffrage Movement in the Southern States* (Oxford University Press, 1993).

62. Ibid., quotation, 25.

63. Ibid.

64. Ibid.; Spruill, "Bringing in the South," Chapter Nine.

65. Ibid.

66. Willard Gatewood, "The Rollin Sisters: Black Women in Reconstruction South Carolina," in Marjorie J. Spruill, Valinda Littlefield and Joan Marie Johnson, eds., *South Carolina Women: Their Lives and Times*, Vol. 2 (University of Georgia Press, 2010): 50-67; Terborg-Penn, Chapter Ten.

67. Gatewood, "The Rollin Sisters."

68. Ibid.; Megan Specia, "Overlooked No More: How Mary Ann Shadd Cary Shook Up the Abolitionist Movement," *New York Times*, June 6, 2018; Harley, "African American Women and the Nineteenth Amendment"; Terborg-Penn, Chapter Eleven; Nancy Santucci Cohen, "Biography of Harriet Hattie Purvis, 1839-1904," *Women and Social Movements of the United States* (Alexandria, VA: Alexander Street, 2018).

69. Rayford W. Logan, *The Negro in American Life and Thought: The Nadir, 1877-1901* (New York: Dial Press, 1954); Terborg-Penn, Chapter Ten; Paula Giddings, *When and Where I Enter: The Impact of Black Women on Race and Sex in America* (New York: Harper Collins, 2007); Jones, *All Bound Up Together*, 175-77.

70. Terborg-Penn, Chapter Ten; Mary Church Terrell, *A Colored Woman in a White World* (Washington, D.C.: Ransdell, 1940), 85-87; Marino, Chapter Eleven.

71. Terborg-Penn, Chapter Ten; Mary Church Terrell, "Woman Suffrage and the 15th Amendment," *The Crisis*, August 1915.

72. Alison M. Parker, Introduction to "What Was the Relationship between Mary Church Terrell's International Experience and Her Work against Racism in the United States?" Chapter Eleven, in Marino, *Women and the Vote*, Chapter Eleven; Terrell, *A Colored Woman in a White World*, 85-87; Marino, Chapter Ten.

73. Ibid.

74. Ibid.; Wanda A. Hendricks, "Ida B. Wells-Barnett and the Alpha Suffrage Club of Chicago," Chapter Seventeen, in Spruill, *One Woman, One Vote*, Second Edition.

75. Wanda A. Hendricks, *Fannie Barrier Williams: Crossing the borders of Region and Race* (Urbana: University of Illinois Press, 2014); Western New York Suffragists: Winning the Vote https://rrlc.org/winningthevote/biographies/fannie-barrier-williams/

76. Evelyn Brooks Higginbotham, *Righteous Discontent: The Women's Movement in the Black Baptist Church, 1880-1920* (Harvard University Press, 1994).

77. Adele Logan Alexander, "Adella Hunt Logan, The Tuskegee Woman's Club, and African Americans in the Suffrage Movement," in Marjorie Spruill (Wheeler), ed., *Votes for Women: The Woman Suffrage Movement in Tennessee, the South, and the Nation* (University of Tennessee Press, 1995): 71-104, quotation 88.

78. Ibid.; Adele Logan Alexander, *Princess of the Hither Isles: A Black Suffragist's Story from the Jim Crow South* (New Haven: Yale University Press, 2019).

79. For example, in an essay in a 1917 special woman suffrage issue of the NAACP magazine, Catt wrote: "Everybody counts

in applying democracy. And there will never be a true democracy until every responsible and law-abiding adult in it, without regard to race, sex, color or creed has his or her own inalienable and unpurchaseable voice in government." Carrie Chapman Catt, 1917, Votes for All: A Symposium, *The Crisis* (1917) 15 (1); Jane Cox, "Racism and Carrie Chapman Catt," *Iowa State Daily*, November 8, 1995, iowastatedaily.com/racism-and-carrie-chapman-catt-today/article_d052fd29-c606-5c29-883a-068f5bce3b30.html; Robbie Sequeira, "Catt Center Continues Efforts to Clear Namesake of Racism Allegation," July 27, 2019, *Ames Tribune*, amestrib.com/news/20190727/catt-center-continues-efforts-to-clear-namesake-of-racism-allegation ; Elaine F. Weiss, *The Woman's Hour: The Great Fight to Win the Vote* (Penguin, 2019),137-41.

80. Alexander, *Princess of the Hither Isles*; Terborg-Penn, Chapter Ten; Sylvanie Williams quoted in *History of Woman Suffrage*, Vol. 5, 115.

81. Terborg-Penn, Chapter Ten; Ida Husted Harper to Mary Church Terrell, March 18, 1919, Mary Church Terrell Papers: Correspondence, 1886-1954; 1919, Jan.-Mar., Manuscripts Division, Library of Congress .

82. Sara Hunter Graham, "The Suffrage Renaissance: A New Image for a New Century, 1896-1910," Chapter Twelve, in Spruill, *One Woman, One Vote*, Second Edition; Sara Hunter Graham, *Woman Suffrage and the New Democracy* (New Haven: Yale Univ. Press, 1996); Use of the term "doldrums" for this era began with historian Eleanor Flexner in her 1959 study, *Century of Struggle: The Woman's Rights Movement in the United States* (Cambridge, Mass., Belknap Press, 1959; Catt and Shuler, *Woman Suffrage and Politics*, 266-70).

83. Biographical sketch, Iowa State University Archives of Women's Political Communication, https://awpc.cattcenter.iastate.edu/directory/carrie-chapman-catt/; Helton, "Woman Suffrage in the West."

84. Graham, Chapter Twelve; Joan Marie Johnson, *Funding Feminism: Monied Women, Philanthropy, and the Women's Movement, 1870-1967* (Chapel Hill: University of North Carolina Press, 2017; Catt and Shuler, *Woman Suffrage and Politics*, 269-270.

85. Catt resigned as NAWSA president due to the illness of her husband who soon died. Afterwards she became heavily involved in promoting woman suffrage internationally through the IWSA. She served as its president from 1904 until 1923; Rupp, *Worlds of Women*, 22, 52. The quotation describing ICW participants is from suffragist Matilda Gage, 52. The Alliance began with six countries from Europe, Australia, and the United States, to twenty-six in 1913 to fifty-one in 1929, including South Africa, China, Argentina, Uruguay, Brazil, Egypt, India, Palestine, Jamaica, Bermuda, Cuba, Peru, Puerto Rico, Japan, Turkey, Ceylon, Dutch East Indies, Syria, and Rhodesia; *History of Woman Suffrage*, Stanton, Anthony, Gage, Harper, eds. (1881-1922), Vol. 6, pp. 805—11;

86. Graham, Chapter Twelve; Kathleen Barry, *Susan B. Anthony: A Biography of a Singular Feminist* (New York University Press, 1988), 331 - 32; Johnson, *Funding Feminism*, 56-58; Catt and Shuler, *Woman Suffrage and Politics*, 266, 269-70.

87. Brooke Kroeger, *The Suffragents: How Women Used Men to Get the Vote* (Albany: State University of New York Press, 2017), 1-5.

88. Graham, Chapter Twelve; *Susan Ware, Why They Marched*; Ellen Carol DuBois, *Harriot Stanton Blatch and the Winning of Woman Suffrage* (New Haven: Yale University Press, 1999).

89. Graham, Chapter Twelve; Park quotation in Graham, Elizabeth Miller NAWSA Suffrage Scrapbooks, 1897-1911, Rare Book and Special Collections Division, Library of Congress; Ellen Carol DuBois, "Working Women, Class Relations, and Suffrage Militance: Harriot Stanton Blatch and the New York Woman Suffrage Movement, 1894-1909," Chapter Fifteen, in Spruill, *One Woman, One Vote*, Second Edition.

90. Ibid.

91. Anna Howard Shaw, *The Story of a Pioneer*, 2011; Trisha Franzen, *Anna Howard Shaw: The Work of Woman Suffrage*. (University of Illinois Press, 2014); Graham, *Woman Suffrage and the New Democracy*; Quotation, Catt and Shuler, *Woman Suffrage and Politics*, 168.

92. Victoria Bissell Brown, "Jane Addams, Progressivism, and Woman Suffrage: An Introduction to 'Why Women Should Vote'," and Jane Addams, "Why Women Should Vote," Chapter

Thirteen, in Spruill, *One Woman, One Vote*, Second Edition.

93. Ibid.; Michael McGerr, *A Fierce Discontent: The Rise and Fall of the Progressive Movement in America, 1870-1920* (New York, Oxford University Press, 2005).

94. Ibid.; Patricia O'Toole, *The Moralist: Woodrow Wilson and the World He Made* (New York: Simon & Schuster, 2019); Eric Steven Yellin, *Racism in the Nation's Service: Government Workers and the Color Line in Woodrow Wilson's America* (Chapel Hill: University of North Carolina Press, 2016); William A. Link, *The Paradox of Southern Progressivism, 1880—1930* (Chapel Hill: University of North Carolina Press, 1992); Daniels, *Guarding the Golden Door*.

95. Brown, Chapter Thirteen; McGerr, *A Fierce Discontent*; Alice Kessler-Harris, *Out to Work: A History of Wage-Earning Women in the United States* (New York: Oxford University Press, 2003).

96. Brown, Chapter Thirteen.

97. Ibid.

98. Ibid.; Graham, *Woman Suffrage and the New Democracy*; Catt and Shuler, *Woman Suffrage and Politics*, 239.

99. DuBois, Chapter Fifteen; Brown, Chapter Thirteen; Kessler-Harris, *Out to Work*.

100. Elinor Lerner, "Jewish Involvement in the New York City Woman Suffrage Movement," Turning Point Suffragist Memorial, suffragistmemorial.org/jewish-suffragists/; Maud Nathan (1862-1946), Turning Point Suffragist Memorial, suffragistmemorial.org/maud-nathan-1862-1946/; Susan Ware, "Two Sisters," in Ware, *Why They Marched*.

101. Kathryn Kish Sklar, *Florence Kelley and the Nation's Work: The Rise of Women's Political Culture, 1830-1900* (New Haven: Yale University Press, 1995); Louise C. Wade, "Florence Kelley," *Notable American Women*, Vol. II, 316-19.

102. DuBois, Chapter Fifteen; Sklar, *Florence Kelley*; Wade, "Florence Kelley"; Quotation from, Kelley, "Woman Suffrage: Its Relation to Working Women and Children," [Circa 1913-1915]," Ann Lewis Women's Suffrage Collection, https://lewissuffragecollection.omeka.net/items/show/1597

103. DuBois, Chapter Fifteen; Paul S. Boyer, "Inez Milholland Boissevain," *Notable American Women*, Vol. I, 188-90; Linda Lumsden, *Inez: The Life and Times of Inez Milholland* (Bloomington: Indiana University Press, 2004).

104. DuBois, Chapter Fifteen; Nancy Schrom Dye, *As Sisters and As Equals: Feminism, the Labor Movement and the Women's Trade Union League of New York* (Columbia: University of Missouri Press, 1980).

105. Ibid.

106. Leonora O'Reilly, Iowa State University Archives of Women's Political Communication https://awpc.cattcenter.iastate.edu/directory/leonora-oreilly/

107. Eleanor Flexner, Janet Wilson James, "Mary Kenney O'Sullivan," *Notable American Women*, Vol. II, 655-56; Barbara Mayer Wertheimer, *"We Were There": The Story of Working Women in America* (Pantheon, 1977).

108. DuBois, Chapter Fifteen; Elinor Lerner, "Jewish Involvement in the New York City Woman Suffrage Movement"; Dye, *As Sisters and As Equals*; quotation from "Annie Schneiderman Valliere, "Rose Schneiderman," Turning Point Suffragists Memorial https://suffragistmemorial.org/rose-schneiderman-april-6-1882-august-11-1972/ ; Annelise Orleck, Rose Schneiderman," Jewish Women's Archive, jwa.org/encyclopedia/article/schneiderman-rose

109. Marino, Chapter Eleven; Nina Otero-Warren, National Park Service, nps.gov/people/nina-otero-warren.htm; Suffragists in New Mexico, Turning Point Suffragist Memorial suffragistmemorial.org/suffragists-in-new-mexico/; Helton, "Woman Suffrage in the West."

110. DuBois, Chapter Fifteen; Sherry J. Katz, "A Politics of Coalition: Socialist Women and the California Suffrage Movement, 1900-1911," Chapter Sixteen, in Spruill, *One Woman, One Vote*, Second Edition; Gayle Gullett, *Becoming Citizens: The Emergence and Development of the California Women's Movement, 1880-1911* (Urbana and Chicago: University of Illinois Press, 2000); Helton, "Woman Suffrage in the West."

111. Ibid.

112. Lee later acquired her Ph.D. in economics at Columbia University and became a lifetime supporter of girls and women, mobilizing the Chinese community. Cathleen D. Cahill, "Mabel Ping-Hua Lee: How Chinese-American Women Helped Shape the Suffrage Movement," Women's Vote Centennial,

womensvote100.org/the-suff-buffs-blog/2020/4/30/mabel-ping-hua-lee-how-chinese-american-women-helped-shape-the-suffrage-movement; Mabel Pink-Hua Lee, "More to the Movement," Library of Congress loc.gov/exhibitions/women-fight-for-the-vote/about-this-exhibition/more-to-the-movement/mabel-ping-hua-lee/

113. "Marie Louise Bottineau Baldwin," National Park Service, nps.gov/people/marie-louise-bottineau-baldwin.htm; Cathleen D. Cahill and Sarah Deer, "In 1920, Native Women Sought the Vote. Here's What's Next," New York Times, July 31, 2020.

114. Vicki L. Ruiz, Virginia E. Sánchez Korrol, Latina Legacies: Identity, Biography, and Community, (New York: Oxford University Press, 2005)

115. Ibid.; Marino, Chapter Eleven.

116. Ibid.; Katz, Chapter Sixteen.

117. Ibid.

118. Manuela Thurner, "'Better Citizens Without the Ballot': American Anti-suffrage Women and Their Rationale During the Progressive Era," Chapter Fourteen, in Spruill, One Woman, One Vote, Second Edition; Weiss, The Woman's Hour; Jo Freeman, A Room at a Time: How Women Entered Party Politics (New York: Rowman & Littlefield Publishers, Inc. 2000, 2002), 52; Catt and Shuler, Woman Suffrage and Politics, 271-79.

119. Ibid.; Spruill (Wheeler), New Women of the New South, 4, 11-13, 25, 27, 30, 35-36; Anastatia Sims, "Armageddon in Tennessee: The Final Battle Over the Nineteenth Amendment, Chapter Twenty-one, in Spruill, One Woman, One Vote, Second Edition.

120. See flyers and posters distributed by Southern anti-suffragists in Spruill (Wheeler), Votes for Women, 302-11; Sims, Chapter Twenty-one.

121. Ibid.; Spruill (Wheeler), Votes for Women, 303, 304; Terborg-Penn, Chapter Ten.

122. Sims, Chapter Twenty-one; Thurner, Chapter Fourteen; Spruill (Wheeler), Votes for Women, 300, 301.

123. Linda G. Ford, "Alice Paul and the Triumph of Militancy," Chapter Eighteen, and Robert Booth Fowler, "Carrie Chapman Catt, Strategist," Chapter Nineteen, in Spruill, One Woman, One Vote, Second Edition; Christine Bolt, "America and the Pankhursts," in Baker, Votes for Women, 143-58.

124. Fowler, Chapter Nineteen; Johnson, Funding Feminism, 67-69.

125. Ford, Chapter Eighteen; Spruill (Wheeler), New Women of the New South, 133-71; Spruill, "Bringing in the South," Chapter Nine.

126. Ford, Chapter Eighteen; Doris Stevens, Jailed for Freedom: American Women Win the Vote, 1920. New edition, Carol O'Hare, ed. (NewSage Press, 1995).

127. Sheridan Harvey, "Marching for the Vote: Remembering the Woman Suffrage Parade of 1913," Library of Congress https://guides.loc.gov/american-women-essays/marching-for-the-vote#note_3

128. Rebecca Boggs Roberts, Suffragists in Washington, D.C.: The 1913 Parade and the Fight for the Vote. (Charleston, SC: History Press, 2017); Ware, Why They Marched.

129. Ford, Chapter Eighteen; Linda Ford, "Alice Paul and the Politics of Nonviolent Protest," in Baker, Votes for Women, 174-88; Stevens, Jailed for Freedom; See also a film about Alice Paul and the National Woman's Party, Katja von Garnier, Director. Iron Jawed Angels: Lead, Follow or Get Out of the Way. Home Box Office, 2004.

130. Doris Stevens, Jailed for Freedom: The Story of the Militant American Suffragist Movement, ed. Marjorie J. Spruill (Chicago: Lakeside Press/R.R. Donnelley & Sons, 2008).

131. Fowler, Chapter Nineteen; McArthur, Chapter Twenty.

132. That "Mighty New York" had "finally caved in" was a line in a celebratory suffrage song. See "One Woman, One Vote," Educational Film Company, PBS documentary (1995, 2020); Fowler, Chapter Nineteen.

133. Catt and Shuler, Woman Suffrage and Politics, quotation, 316; McArthur, Chapter Twenty.

134. Ibid.

135. Catt and Shuler, Woman Suffrage and Politics, 462.

136. Ibid., 338-39; HWS, VI; Weiss, The Woman's Hour, 84; Fowler, Chapter Nineteen.

137. Catt and Shuler, Woman Suffrage and Politics, 325; Alisha Haridasani Gupta, "Everything Conspires Against Women (sic)

Suffrage. Now It Is the Influenza." New York Times, May 29, 2020; Catt and Shuler, Woman Suffrage and Politics, 294-96, 299, 337-39..

138. Ibid., 304-15, 324-28; Ellen Carol DuBois, A Pandemic Nearly Derailed the Women's Suffrage Movement, National Geographic, April 20, 2020.

139. Ibid.; Gupta, "Everything Conspires Against Women (sic) Suffrage"; Catt and Shuler, Woman Suffrage and Politics, 304, 314

140. Ibid.; Weiss, The Woman's Hour; DuBois, "A Pandemic Nearly Derailed the Women's Suffrage Movement."

141. Catt and Shuler, Woman Suffrage and Politics, 304-314, 328-29.

142. Spruill (Wheeler), New Women of the New South, 33,173-76;

143. Sims, Chapter Twenty-one; McArthur, Chapter Twenty; Spruill, "Bringing in the South," Chapter Nine.

144. Catt and Shuler, Woman Suffrage and Politics, Chapter Twenty-six, "Last of All Suffrage Conventions," 381-86; At the time of the Jubilee Convention, 31 states had ratified. Stanley Lemons, The Woman Citizen: Social Feminism in the 1920s (Urbana: University of Illinois Press, 1973, 1975), 50-51.

145. Spruill (Wheeler), New Women of the New South, quotation, 34.

146. Catt and Shuler, Woman Suffrage and Politics, 396-413, quotation, 398.

147. Ibid., 465, 476-80; Sims, Chapter Twenty-one; Freeman, A Room at a Time, 125; Spruill (Wheeler), New Women of the New South, 34-35.

148. Sims, Chapter Twenty-one; see also the vivid, detailed account of this final stage of the suffrage struggle in Weiss, The Woman's Hour.

149. On Tennessee Democrats' dislike of the NWP, on Sue White's role in the ratification battle, see Spruill (Wheeler), Votes for Women, 169-196; On Pollitzer, see Amy Thompson McCandless, "Anita Pollitzer: A South Carolina Advocate for Equal Rights," in Marjorie J. Spruill, Valinda W. Littlefield, and Joan Marie Johnson, South Carolina Women: Their Lives and Times Vol. 2, (Athens: University of Georgia Press, 2010), 172-74.

150. Sims, Chapter Twenty-one; Carrie Chapman Catt and Nettie Rogers Shuler, "Tennessee," their account of the suffrage battle taken from Woman Suffrage and Politics, in Spruill (Wheeler), Votes for Women, 243-74; See also the documentary produced by Nashville Public Television, "By One Vote: Woman Suffrage in the South," 2019, wnpt.org/suffrage

151. Spruill (Wheeler), Votes for Women, see anti-suffrage broadsides, 300-311, quotations, 305, 311.

152. Sims, Chapter Twenty-one.

153. Ibid.; Quotation from Harry Burn, Catt and Shuler, Woman Suffrage and Politics, 451. The number of women enfranchised was approximately 27 million.

154. Ibid., 449-55; Sims, Chapter Twenty-one; Tyler L. Boyd, Harry T. Burn: Tennessee Statesman, The History Press, 2019, 72-100.

155. Sims, Chapter Twenty-one; Catt and Shuler, Woman Suffrage and Politics, 455.

156. See Marjorie J. Spruill, "A Century of Woman Suffrage," Chapter Twenty-three in Spruill, One Woman, One Vote: Rediscovering the Woman Suffrage Movement, Second Edition.

157. Catt and Shuler, Woman Suffrage and Politics, 455-56.

158. Shall Not Be Denied: Women Fight for the Vote, Official Companion to the Library of Congress Exhibit, Rutgers University Press, 1919, 101; nps.gov/articles/celebrations-of-success.htm

159. Mary Gray Peck, Carrie Chapman Catt: A Biography (Westport, Conn: Hyperion Press, 1976), 339; Catt and Shuler, Woman Suffrage and Politics, 455-56.

160. Catt and Shuler, Woman Suffrage and Politics, 5.

161. Quotation from The Woman Citizen, September 4, 1920; Barbara Stuhler, For the Public Record: A Documentary History of the League of Women Voters (Westport, Connecticut: Greenwood Publishing Group, 2000), 26.

"OURSELVES AND OUR DAUGHTERS FOREVER":

Women and the Constitution
1787—1876

Linda K. Kerber

Editor's Introduction: In this essay, Linda K. Kerber, one of the leading scholars of women in the American Revolution and the early national period, discusses why women were excluded from the vote as the new nation was launched and remained disfranchised during the nation's first one hundred years. Kerber makes it clear why a woman suffrage movement was necessary, and why suffragists came to focus on an amendment to the Constitution.

After describing the dramatic protest against women's political and legal inferiority led by Susan B. Anthony and Elizabeth Cady Stanton at the 1876 celebration of the nation's centennial, Kerber examines the assumptions held by John Adams and the other Founding Fathers who implicitly excluded women from participation in the government of the new republic. These men, says Kerber, "Shared assumptions about women and politics so fully that they did not need to debate them," including the idea that women, like propertyless men, were dependent and "lacked a will of their own," and thus were appropriately excluded from suffrage. Significantly, the American Constitution did not *explicitly* exclude women from voting or other political rights. The states—assigned the task of establishing the requirements for voting—*could* have interpreted the Constitution to justify full enfranchisement of women, or the courts could have so ruled. "Women might have been absorbed fully into the American political community," writes Kerber, "without the necessity of constitutional amendment."

In the antebellum period, as the states dropped many of the restrictions on voting and extended the franchise to virtually all White men, however, no state moved to extend suffrage to women and the one state that had allowed women to vote rescinded this privilege. Thus, in the 1820s, 1830s, and 1840s, women began to protest publicly against their legal and political inferiority. In the Declaration of Sentiments adopted at the Seneca Falls Convention in 1848, participants demanded a wide range of constitutional, legal, and social reforms—including the right to vote.

After the Civil War, as the nation experienced a revolution in politics, and Congress amended the Constitution to address—for the first time—the issue of

voter qualifications, women's rights advocates hoped that universal suffrage for *all* would be the result. As Kerber describes, however, the Fourteenth and Fifteenth Amendments, adopted to enfranchise the freedmen, actually added new obstacles to woman suffrage; not only did the amendment fail to include sex as a protected category along with race, but in the Fourteenth Amendment the word "male" was added to the Constitution for the first time. Ironically, the fact that women were now demanding the vote led the authors of the amendment to believe it was necessary to specify that the amendment would *not* enfranchise women.

Initially dismayed by these events, suffragists then tried the "New Departure," claiming suffrage and other rights based on a broad interpretation of the Fourteenth Amendment. As citizens, they claimed all the "privileges and immunities" of citizens, but were rebuffed by the courts. Thus, by the centennial celebration in 1876, it had become clear that woman suffrage was not going to emerge from reinterpretations of existing laws, either state or federal. If women were to be enfranchised, said Kerber, they would have to have "either an explicit constitutional amendment or a series of revisions in the laws of the states." Suffragists now knew what they would have to do to establish their right to the vote. The long and difficult fight for enfranchisement had only begun.

★　★　★　★　★

I N 1876, THE UNITED STATES celebrated one hundred years as an independent nation dedicated to the proposition that all men are created equal. The capstone of the celebration was a public reading of the Declaration of Independence in Independence Square Philadelphia, by a descendant of a signer, Richard Henry Lee.

Elizabeth Cady Stanton, who was then president of the National Woman Suffrage Association (NWSA), asked permission to present silently a women's protest and a written women's Declaration of Rights. Her request was denied. "Tomorrow we propose to celebrate what we have done the last hundred years," replied the president of the official ceremonies, "not what we have failed to do."

Led by Susan B. Anthony, five women appeared nevertheless at the official reading, distributing copies of their own Declaration. After this mildly disruptive gesture, they withdrew to the other side of the symmetrical Independence Hall, where they staged a counter-Centennial. "With sorrow we come to strike the one discordant note, on this one-hundredth anniversary of our country's birth," Susan B. Anthony declared.

Although the rhythms of her speech echoed the Declaration of Independence, as was fitting for the day—"The history of our country the past hundred years has been a series of assumptions and usurpations of power over woman..."—the substance of her speech was built on references to the Constitution. Anthony and the women for whom she spoke were troubled by the discrepancy between the

universally applicable provisions of the Constitution and the specificity of the way in which these provisions were interpreted to exclude women. For example, since all juries excluded women, women were denied the right of trial by a jury of their peers. Although taxation without representation had been a rallying cry of the Revolution, single women and widows who owned property paid taxes although they could not vote for the legislators who set the taxes. A double standard of morals was maintained in law by which women were arrested for prostitution while men went free. The introduction of the word "male" into federal and state constitutions, Anthony asserted, functioned in effect as a bill of attainder, in that it treated women as a class, denying them the right of suffrage, and "thereby making sex a crime."

Anthony ended by calling for the impeachment of all officers of the federal government on the grounds that they had not fulfilled their obligations under the Constitution. Their "vacillating interpretations of constitutional law unsettle our faith in judicial authority, and undermine the liberties of the whole people," she declared.

> Special legislation for woman has placed us in a most anomalous position. Women invested with the rights of citizens in one section— voters, jurors, office holders—crossing an imaginary line, are subjects in the next. In some states a married woman may hold property and transact business in her own name; in others her earnings belong to her husband. In some states, a woman may testify against her husband, sue and be sued in the courts; in others she has no redress in case of damage to person, property, or character. In case of divorce on account of adultery in the husband, the innocent wife is held to possess no right to children or property, unless by special decrees of the court.... In some states women may enter the law school and practice in the courts; in others they are forbidden....

> These articles of impeachment against our rulers we now submit to the impartial judgment of the people.... From the beginning of the century, when Abigail Adams, the wife of one president and mother of another, said, "We will not hold ourselves bound to obey laws in which we have no voice or representation," until now, woman's discontent has been steadily increasing, culminating nearly thirty years ago in a simultaneous movement among the women of the nation, demanding the right of suffrage.... It was the boast of the founders of the republic, that the rights for which they contended were the rights of human nature. If these rights are ignored in the case of one half the people, the nation is surely preparing for its downfall. Governments try themselves. The recognition of a governing and a governed class is incompatible with the first principles of freedom....[1]

Abigail Adams
ENGRAVING BASED ON
ORIGINAL PORTRAIT BY GILBERT STUART

John Adams
ENGRAVING BY H.B. HALLS SONS,
LIBRARY OF CONGRESS

The Founding Generation

Let us stand with Susan B. Anthony at her vantage point of 1876 and review the constitutional issues that touched women's lives in the first hundred years of the republic. During those hundred years, basic questions were defined and strategies for affecting legislation were developed. Not until after the Centennial would women direct their energies primarily to constitutional amendment. In the first century, the challenge was to understand whether and to what extent women's political status was different from that of men, and to develop a rationale for criticizing that difference.

It is intriguing to speculate how the Founders might have responded to Anthony's challenge. Throughout the long summer of 1787 in Philadelphia, the role of women in the new polity went formally unconsidered. Whether they came from small or large states, whether they favored the New Jersey or Virginia Plan, whether they hoped for a gradual end to slavery or a strengthening of the system, the men who came to Carpenters' Hall in 1787 shared assumptions about women and politics so fully that they did not need to debate them. Indeed, John Adams had missed the point in his now-famous exchange with Abigail Adams to which Anthony referred in her Centennial Address: Abigail Adams clearly had domestic violence as well as political representation in mind as she wrote; that is, she was thinking in both practical and theoretical terms.[2] Her husband refused to deal with the issue:

Abigail Adams to John Adams
March 31, 1776
...in the new Code of Laws which I suppose it will be necessary for you to make, I desire you would Remember the Ladies, and be more generous

and favourable to them than your ancestors. Do not put such unlimited power into the hands of the Husbands. Remember all Men would be tyrants if they could. If perticular care and attention is not paid to the Laidies we are determined to foment a Rebelion, and will not hold ourselves bound by any Laws in which we have no voice, or Representation.

That your Sex are Naturally Tyrannical is a Truth so thoroughly established as to admit of no dispute…. Why then, not put it out of the power of the vicious and the Lawless to use us with cruelty and indignity with impunity….

John Adams to Abigail Adams
April 14, 1776
As to your extraordinary Code of Laws, I cannot but laugh. We have been told that our struggle has loosened the bonds of Government every where. That Children and Apprentices were disobedient—that schools and colleges were grown turbulent—that Indians slighted their guardians and Negroes grew insolent to their Masters. But your Letter was the first Intimation that another Tribe more numerous and powerfull than all the rest were grown discontented…. Depend upon it, We know better than to repeal our Masculine systems…. We have only the Name of Masters, and rather than give up this, which would compleatly subject Us to the Despotism of the Peticoat, I hope General Washington, and all our brave Heroes would fight….

Abigail Adams to John Adams
May 7, 1776
…Arbitrary power is like most other things which are very hard, very liable to be broken….[3]

The exclusion of married women from the vote was based on the same principle that excluded men without property from the vote. If the will of the people was in fact to be expressed by voting, it was important that each vote be independent and uncoerced. Men who had no property and were dependent on their landlords or employers for survival were understood to be vulnerable to pressure; they were, in John Adams's words, "too dependent upon other men to have a will of their own." Adams acknowledged, in fact, that excluding all women was somewhat arbitrary; but lines, as he explained in a thoughtful letter to the Massachusetts politician James Sullivan, had to be drawn somewhere.

John Adams to James Sullivan
May 26, 1776
It is certain, in theory, that the only moral foundation of government is, the consent of the people. But to what an extent shall we carry this principle?

Shall we say that every individual of the community, old and young, male and female, as well as rich and poor, must consent, expressly, to every act of legislation? No, you will say, this is impossible. How then, does the right arise in the majority to govern the minority, against their will? Whence arises the right of the men to govern the women, without their consent? Whence the right of the old to bind the young, without theirs?...

But why exclude women?

You will say, because their delicacy renders them unfit for practice and experience in the great businesses of life, and the hardy enterprises of war.... Besides, their attention is so much engaged with the necessary nurture of their children, that nature has made them fittest for domestic cares. And children have not judgment or will of their own. True, but will not these reasons apply to others? Is it not equally true, that men in general, in every society, who are wholly destitute of property, are also too little acquainted with public affairs to form a right judgment, and too dependent upon other men to have a will of their own?... They talk and vote as they are directed by some man of property....

Your idea that those laws which affect the lives and personal liberty of all, or which inflict corporal punishment, affect those who are not qualified to vote, as well as those who are, is just. But so they do women, as well as men; children, as well as adults. What reason should there be for excluding a man of twenty years eleven months and twenty-seven days old, from a vote, when you admit one who is twenty-one? The reason is, you must fix upon some period in life, when the understanding and will of men in general, is fit to be trusted by the public. Will not the same reason justify the state in fixing upon some certain quantity of property, as a qualification?

The same reasoning which will induce you to admit all men who have not property, to vote, with those who have, for those laws which affect the person, will prove that you ought to admit women and children; for, generally speaking, women and children have as good judgments, and as independent minds, as those men who are wholly destitute of property; these last being to all intents and purposes as much dependent upon others, who will please to feed, clothe and employ them, as women are upon their husbands, or children on their parents.

Depend upon it, Sire, it is dangerous to open so fruitful a source of controversy and altercations as would be opened by attempting to alter the qualifications of voters; there will be no end of it. New claims will arise; women will demand a vote; kids from twelve to twenty-one will think their rights not enough attended to; and every man who has not a farthing, will demand an equal voice with any other; in all acts of state. It

tends to confound and destroy all distinctions, and prostrate all ranks to one common level....[4]

John Adams spelled out with unusual frankness what most of his colleagues believed. If dependent men were to vote, the result would not be that the will of all individuals was counted; rather the result would be that landlords and employers would in effect exercise multiple votes. Married women were thought to be in much the same state as unpropertied men. Their property, according to the traditional British law of domestic relations, came under their husbands' power when they married, a practice known as coverture. The married woman, "covered" by her husband's civic identity, lost the power to manipulate her property independently. (She remained however, an independent moral being under the law, capable of committing crimes, even treason.) To give a vote to a person so dependent on another's will seemed to give a double vote to husbands, rather than to enfranchise wives. In a society in which it was assumed that the wife did the husband's bidding, it seemed absurd to give married men a political advantage over their unmarried brothers. Instead of revising the old law of domestic relations, and taking married women out from under the "cover" of their husbands' authority, virtually all the states denied the franchise to married women.

Roads Not Taken

The logic that excluded married women should not have, on the face of it, excluded unmarried women with property—including widows—who were not under the immediate influence of an adult man, who could buy and sell their property, and who paid taxes. Single adult women might have formed a substantial electorate, even in a system of coverture. But in practice custom rather than logic prevailed; single women were treated for the most part as were their married counterparts.

Only in New Jersey, where the state constitution of 1776 enfranchised "all free inhabitants" who could meet property and residence requirements did women vote; in 1790, possibly because of Quaker influence, an election law used the phrase "he or she" in referring to voters.

The New Jersey Constitution of 1776 provided that "All Inhabitants of this colony, of full age, who are worth fifty pounds proclamation money, clear estate in the same, and have resided within the county in which they claim a vote for twelve months immediately preceding the election, shall be entitled to vote for Representatives in Council and Assembly; and also for all other public officers, that shall be elected by the people of the county at large...."

In 1797, New Jersey law explicitly recognized that women voted: "No person shall be entitled to vote in any other township or precinct, than that in which he or she doth actually reside at the time of the election.... Every voter shall openly, and in full view deliver his or her ballot...."

The general tendency in suffrage law throughout the nineteenth century was to broaden the electorate by gradually eliminating property and racial qualifications; yet the New Jersey election statute did not become a model for other states. In 1797 the women's vote was thought to have been exercised as a bloc vote in favor of the Federalist candidate for Elizabethtown in the state legislature, and it was alleged to have made a real difference in the outcome of the election.

Faced with this gender gap, the defeated Democratic-Republicans launched a bitter campaign with two themes that were to appear and reappear as long as woman suffrage was debated in this country. First, they argued that women who appeared at the polls were unfeminine, forgetful of their proper place. Second, they asserted that women were easily manipulated, if not by husbands, then by fathers and brothers. It took ten years, but in 1807 New Jersey passed a new election law excluding all women from the polls, and no other state attempted New Jersey's 1776 experiment. In the absence of a collective political movement, no delegate came to Philadelphia in 1787 prepared to make an issue of woman suffrage or of any other distinctively female political concern; no one came prepared to engage in debate over the extent to which women were an active part of the political community.

With the benefit of hindsight, it is possible for historians to identify some substantive issues that politically empowered women might well have raised had

Women voting in New Jersey, c. 1800

the Constitution guaranteed their right to participate in a republican government. (Some of these issues would be addressed only a few years later, by Montagnards and Jacobins in France.) One obvious issue is divorce reform. In some states divorce was nearly impossible in 1787; in all it was extremely difficult. Since the majority of petitioners for divorce were women, the issue was one in which women had a distinctive interest. The language of republicanism, with its acknowledgment that the new order validated a search for happiness, was taken by a number of people to imply that divorce reform was a logical implication of republicanism. But the Constitution said nothing about it, and the states loosened restrictions only slowly. Two generations later women's rights activists would place divorce reform high on their political agenda; it is probable that it would also have been given priority on an agenda drafted in the 1780s.

A second concern might have been pensions for widows of soldiers. The Continental Congress authorized modest pensions for the widows of officers, but widows of soldiers would not be provided with pensions until 1832, by which time, of course, many of them were dead. It is easy to think of other issues: the right of mothers to child custody in the event of divorce, restrictions on wife abuse, the security of dower rights. But expressions of opinion on these issues remained the work of individuals; no collective feminist movement gave them articulate expression as was the case in France. No organized female political pressure was brought to bear at the Constitutional Convention; there do not seem to have been American predecessors of the female Jacobin clubs of Paris.

The Constitution reflected the experience of the White middle- and upper-class men who wrote it and the experience of their constituents, the men of the upper- and lower-middle classes, the farmers and artisans, who had, as historian Edward Countryman has observed, "established their political identity in the Revolution." Although their political choices were characterized by what the historian Michael Grossberg has called their "deep aversion to unaccountable authority," they retained the authority of husbands over wives intact.[5] All free men, rich or poor, continued to gain control of their wives' bodies and property when they married. Women had not yet, as a group, firmly established their political identity.

Gender and the Language of the Constitution

The Constitution did not explicitly welcome women as voters or take particular account of them as a class. However, what the Constitution left unsaid was as important as what it did say. The text of the Constitution usually speaks of "persons"; only rarely does it use the generic "he." Women as well as men were defined as citizens. The Constitution establishes no voting requirements, leaving it up to the states to set the terms by which people shall qualify to vote.

Article 1, Section 2: The House of Representatives shall be composed of Members chosen every Year by the People of the several States, and the

Electors in each State shall have the qualifications requisite for Electors of the most numerous Branch of the State Legislature.

Thus women were not explicitly excluded from Congress, nor even from the presidency. The Constitution, in fact, left an astonishing number of substantive matters open to the choices of individual states; every part of it was open to change by amendment. This flexibility is an important reason for the survival of the American Constitution, as contrasted to the other republican constitutions of the era, like the French, which were far more detailed and explicit, but also less resilient. Women might have been absorbed fully into the American political community without the necessity of constitutional amendment.

Yet this absorption did not occur automatically. No state imitated New Jersey's experiment with suffrage before the Civil War; only a few—Utah, Wyoming, Colorado, Idaho—did so after the war. No state moved to place non-voters on juries, although there was obvious common sense in the argument that in order for a woman to be tried by her peers a jury should include women, whether or not women voted in that state. Although the old argument that the proper voter was a person of property eroded as liberals steadily decreased property requirements for voting by men, women were not enfranchised.

Attempts at Reform

Still, even without the vote, effective political coalitions of feminists and legal reformers developed at the end of the 1830s. They were interested in the codification and simplification of state laws. They pressed for the passage of Married Women's Property Acts that would enable married women to control property without necessitating cumbersome trusteeship arrangements. Beginning with a severely limited statute passed in Mississippi in 1839 and continuing throughout the century, state Married Women's Property Acts gradually extended the financial independence of married women, making it possible for a few feminists to entertain a vision of a full range of women's political activity, even under the older requirements of property holding. However, the new control that women achieved over their own property was not accompanied by the extension of the franchise.

The New York State Married Women's Property Act provides an example of this type of legislation:

> The real and personal property of any female [now married and] who may here-after marry, and which she shall own at the time of marriage, and the rents, issues and profits thereof shall not be subject to the disposal of her husband, nor be liable for his debts, and shall continue her sole and separate property, as if she were a single female…. It shall be lawful for any married female to receive by gift, grant, devise or bequest, from any person other than her husband and hold to her sole and separate use, as if

she were a single female, real and personal property, and the rents, issues and profits thereof and the same shall not be subject to the disposal of her husband, nor be liable for his debts....

A married woman may bargain, sell, assign, and transfer her separate personal property, and carry on any trade or business, and perform any labor or services on her sole and separate account, and the earnings of any married woman from her trade...shall be her sole and separate property, and may be used or invested by her in her own name....

Any married woman may, while married, sue and be sued in all matters having relation to her ... sole and separate property...in the same manner as if she were sole....

Every married woman is hereby constituted and declared to be the joint guardian of her children, with her husband, with equal powers, rights, and duties in regard to them, with the husband....[6]

Elizabeth Cady Stanton, who had been a strong supporter of the New York Married Women's Property Acts, was also an energizing force behind the gathering of women in Seneca Falls in 1848. She and others who prepared and signed the Declaration of Sentiments at that meeting addressed forcefully the ways in which women had not been fully absorbed into the republican political order, although they were citizens. After a preface casting "Man" in a rhetorical role comparable to that played by King George III in the Declaration of Independence, the Declaration of Sentiments addressed constitutional and legal as well as social questions: trial by jury, the relationship between taxation and representation, the persistence of coverture.

He has compelled her to submit to laws, in the formation of which she had no voice....

He has made her, if married, in the eye of the law, civilly dead....

He has taken from her all right in property, even to the wages she earns....

After depriving her of all rights as a married woman, if single, and the owner of property, he has taxed her to support a government which recognizes her only when her property can be made profitable to it....[7]

The legislative gains of the early part of the century and the emergence of a women's movement at mid-century were not, however, followed by a wave of enfranchisement. In fact, women found themselves excluded from the debate about the extension of the franchise that was engendered by the Civil War.

The Civil War Amendments, the New Departure and Its Defeat

The Civil War was not only a military crisis but also a revolution in politics, which would be validated by the Thirteenth, Fourteenth, and Fifteenth Amendments. By now there was most emphatically, a collective women's public presence—in the

Sanitary Commission, the women's abolitionist societies, the Women's National Loyal League. But the "Woman Question" had not been central to the ideology of the Civil War, and once again, women found they could not claim the benefits. Abolitionist and Republican feminists had permitted themselves to anticipate that suffrage would be the appropriate reward for their sacrifices and support of the war effort. They also believed strongly that the authentic meaning of the expanded citizenship embedded in the Fourteenth Amendment was contradicted by its enforcement clauses. That is, if indeed "all persons, born or naturalized in the United States are citizens of the United States and the state in which they reside" then, they thought, women as well as men, Black and White, should have the vote as one of the "privileges and immunities of citizenship." Their resentment was therefore all the greater when woman suffrage was not made part of the post-war amendments. The inclusion of the word "male" in the second section of the Fourteenth Amendment—a section never enforced—rubbed salt in a raw wound. The Fifteenth Amendment, guaranteeing the vote to all men despite race or previous condition of servitude, made explicit what the Fourteenth Amendment had left implicit.

Fourteenth Amendment, 1868

Section One

All persons born or naturalized in the United States, and subject to the jurisdiction thereof, are citizens of the United States and of the State wherein they reside. No State shall make or enforce any law which shall abridge the privileges or immunities of citizens of the United States; nor shall any State deprive any person of life, liberty or property, without due process of law; nor deny to any person within its jurisdiction the equal protection of the laws.

Section Two

Representatives shall be apportioned among the several States according to their respective numbers, counting the whole number of persons in each State, excluding Indians not taxed. But when the right to vote at any election for the choice of electors for President and Vice-President of the United States, Representatives in Congress, the executive and judicial officers of a State, or the members of the legislature thereof, is denied to any of the male inhabitants of such State, being twenty-one years of age and citizens of the United States, or in any way abridged, except for participation in rebellion, or other crime, the basis of representation therein shall be reduced in the proportion which the number of such male citizens shall bear to the whole number of male citizens twenty-one years of age in such State....

Holding their tempers, suffragists embarked on a national effort to test the universal possibilities of the first section of the Fourteenth Amendment, a strategy

they called "the New Departure," only to discover that the Supreme Court rejected their arguments.[8] It was tested first in 1873 by Myra Bradwell, a Chicago woman who had studied law with her husband. She had been granted a special charter from the State of Illinois permitting her to edit and publish the *Chicago Legal News* as her own business, a business she carried on with distinction. (After the Chicago fire destroyed many law offices, it was the files of Bradwell's *Legal News* on which the city's attorneys relied for their records.) Bradwell claimed that one of the "privileges and immunities" of a citizen guaranteed by Section One was her right to practice law in the State of Illinois and to argue cases. The Illinois Supreme Court turned her down, on the ground that as a married woman, she was not a fully free agent.

In her appeal to the Supreme Court, Bradwell's attorney argued that among the "privileges and immunities" guaranteed to each citizen by the Fourteenth Amendment was the right to pursue any honorable profession. "Intelligence, integrity and honor are the only qualifications that can be prescribed.... The broad shield of the Constitution is over all, and protects each in that measure of success which his or her individual merits may secure." But the Supreme Court held that the right to practice law in any particular state was a right that might be granted by the individual state; it was not one of the privileges and immunities of citizenship. A concurring opinion added an ideological dimension:

> The natural and proper timidity and delicacy which belongs to the female sex evidently unfits it for many of the occupations of civil life. The constitution of the family organization, which is founded on the divine ordinance, as well as in the nature of things, indicates the domestic sphere as that which properly belongs to the domain and functions of womanhood. The harmony, not to say identity, of interests and views which belong or should belong to the family institution, is repugnant to the idea of a woman adopting a distinct and independent career from that of her husband. So firmly fixed was this sentiment in the founders of the common law that it became a maxim of that system of jurisprudence that a woman had no legal existence separate from her husband, who was regarded as her head and representative in the social state...many of the special rules of law flowing from and dependent upon this cardinal principal still exist in full force in most states. One of these is that a married woman is incapable, without her husband's consent, of making contracts which shall be binding on her or him. This very incapacity was one circumstance which the supreme court of Illinois deemed important in rendering a married woman incompetent fully to perform the duties and trusts that belong to the office of an attorney and counselor.[9]

Meanwhile, suffragists in a number of places attempted to test the other possibilities of the first section of the Fourteenth Amendment. In the presidential election of 1872, suffragist women in a number of districts appeared at the polls,

arguing that if all citizens had the right to the privileges of citizenship, they could certainly exercise the right to vote. Susan B. Anthony presented herself at a barber shop in the eighth ward in Rochester, New York, which was serving as a polling place, and convinced two out of the three polling inspectors to register her, on the grounds that the New York State Constitution made no sex distinctions in the qualifications for voters. By the end of the day, fifteen more women had registered. On November 5, having first assured the inspectors that if they were prosecuted for admitting unauthorized persons to the polls, she would pay their legal fees, Anthony and the other women voted. It would be Anthony and the other women who were arrested for an illegal attempt to vote, not the inspectors. When she was judged guilty, she refused to pay her bail, hoping to force the case to the Supreme Court. A supporter, however, thinking he was doing Anthony a favor, paid it. The case was set for trial; in the interlude she voted in the Rochester city elections, and no one made a fuss. When the trial was moved to another county, Anthony and her colleagues made a whirlwind tour, speaking in approximately twenty towns each, ensuring that public opinion would not be uniformly against them even in a strange locale.

Anthony reasoned that sex was a characteristic markedly different from youth or being an alien. Although aliens could not vote, an individual alien man could choose to become a naturalized citizen. Minors could not vote, but minors, in the nature of things, grew to adulthood. "Qualifications," she argued, "can not be in their nature permanent or insurmountable. Sex can not be a qualification any more than size, race, color, or previous condition of servitude."

The judge, wanting to deny Anthony the legal system as a forum, directed the jury to bring in a verdict of guilty, and immediately discharged the jury. He fined Anthony $100. When she announced that she would "never pay a dollar of your unjust penalty," he declined to enforce the punishment. "Madam, the Court will not order you to stand committed until the fine is paid." Thus he had it both ways; a verdict of guilty, which would dissuade others from following Anthony's path, but a refusal to punish, thus avoiding making Anthony a martyr and making it impossible for her to bring the case to the U.S. Supreme Court.[10]

The president of the Woman Suffrage Association of Missouri was able to do what Anthony could not. Observing that the "power to regulate is one thing, the power to prevent is an entirely different thing," Virginia Minor attempted to vote in St. Louis. When the registrar refused to permit her to register, she and her husband Francis, an attorney who had developed the distinction between regulation and prohibition of suffrage, sued him for denying her one of the privileges and immunities of citizenship. When they lost the case they appealed to the Supreme Court.

In *Minor v. Happersett*, decided in 1875, the Court ruled that change must happen as a result of explicit legislation or constitutional amendment, rather than by interpretation of the implications of the Constitution. In a unanimous opinion the Court observed that it was "too late" to claim the right of suffrage by implication;

the Founders had been men who weighed their words carefully. Nearly a hundred years of failure to claim inclusion by implication made a difference. What might have been gradual evolution in the founders' generation was avoidance of legal due process a hundred years later—"If suffrage was intended to be included... language better adapted to express that intent would most certainly have been employed." The Court was not prepared to interpret the Constitution freshly: "If the law is wrong it ought to be changed; but the power for that is not with us...." The decision meant that woman suffrage could not emerge from reinterpretation of the Constitution; it would require either an explicit constitutional amendment or a series of revisions in the laws of the states.

> ...For nearly ninety years the people have acted upon the idea that the Constitution, when it conferred citizenship, did not necessarily confer the right of suffrage. If uniform practice long continued can settle the construction of so important an instrument as the Constitution of the United States confessedly is, most certainly it has been done here. Our province is to decide what the law is, not to declare what it should be.[11]

Reluctant Realignment of Suffrage Strategy

In the years between 1848 and 1876, American women had created a collective movement. It is true that it did not include the entire female population; many women were unaware and more were hostile. But the activists had brought into being an articulate and politically sophisticated pressure group which was prepared to offer an explicit and detailed criticism of the American political system and to make direct demands for inclusion in it.

When Susan B. Anthony rose to speak on July 4, 1876, the strategies of feminist politics were being realigned. She had the court decisions in *Bradwell* and *Minor* in mind as she spoke. She addressed not only the issue of suffrage but also the exclusion of women from multiple aspects of the political community that the Constitution had created. The right to serve on a jury had been so precious to American men that some states had refused to ratify the Constitution until they were convinced it would be added; yet "the women of this nation have never been allowed a jury of their peers," even in crimes like infanticide or adultery, where women's perspective might well be different from that of men. Anthony decried the division of the community into a class of men, which governed, and a class of women, which was governed.

Anthony's generation of feminists would begin their campaign for suffrage to restore what the second section of the Fourteenth Amendment—with its introduction of the word male—had killed by implication. But as historian Ellen DuBois has shrewdly discerned, this strategy abandoned the healthier, more inclusive strategy of the pre-1876 period, when claims for the vote as part of the privileges of *all* citizens meant that women understood themselves to be part of a

Elizabeth Cady Stanton before the Senate Committee on
Privileges and Elections, *New York Daily Graphic*, January 16, 1878
LIBRARY OF CONGRESS

community that included men and women, Black and White. A suffrage
amendment would be introduced in the Senate in 1878, and a new chapter in the
political history of feminism would begin, one which emphasized the distinctive
claims of women.

It is important to recognize that Stanton and Anthony began with a definition of
equality under the Constitution that was considerably more inclusive than the vote
alone. It included a vision of egalitarianism in the process of lawmaking as well as
in the outcome. Ever since the 1848 Declaration of Sentiments, it had included a
vision of equality within the family, between husbands and wives, as well as social
equality, between male and female citizens, in the public realm. In her Centennial
Address, Anthony expressed the full range of this vision, attacking double
standards in moral codes, unequal pay scales, unequal treatment of adulterers. She
would not be surprised today to see wife abuse, female health, or the feminization
of poverty emerge as topics high on the contemporary feminist agenda. "It was the
boast of the founders of the republic, that the rights for which they contended were
the rights of human nature. If these rights are ignored in the case of one-half the
people, the nation is surely preparing for its downfall," she declared.

Anthony ended her Declaration of Rights with a ringing conclusion. If there are
any schoolchildren today who still—as children did in the nineteenth century—
memorize great moments in the oratorical tradition of this country like Webster's

reply to Hayne or Lincoln's Gettysburg Address, they should add this to their repertory:

And now, at the close of a hundred years, as the hour-hand of the great clock that marks the centuries points to 1876, we declare our faith in the principles of self government; our full equality with man in natural rights; that woman was made first for her own happiness, with the absolute right to herself—to all the opportunities and advantages life affords for her complete development; and we deny that dogma of the centuries, incorporated in the codes of all nations—that woman was made for man—her best interests ... to be sacrificed to his will. We ask of our rulers, at this hour, no special privileges, no special legislation. We ask justice, we ask equality, we ask that all the civil and political rights that belong to citizens of the United States be guaranteed to us and our daughters forever.

Notes

This essay is a slightly expanded version of "'Ourselves and Our Daughters Forever': Women and the Constitution, 1787-1876," reprinted from *This Constitution: A Bicentennial Chronicle*, Spring 1985, 25-34, published by Project '87, of the American Historical Association and the American Political Science Association.

1. This account of the July 4, 1876 protest and the text of Anthony's speech is drawn from *History of Woman Suffrage*, eds., Elizabeth Cady Stanton, Susan B. Anthony, and Matilda Joslyn Gage, (Rochester, N.Y., 1886), 3: 31-34.

2. On this point, see the shrewd comments of Nancy F. Cott, "Passionlessness: An Interpretation of Victorian Sexual Ideology, 1790-1850," *Signs: A Journal of Women in Culture and Society* 4 (1978): 228-29.

3. L.H. Butterfield, ed., *Adams Family Correspondence* (Cambridge, Mass., 1963: New York, 1965) 1: 369-70, 382, 402.

4. John Adams to James Sullivan, 26 May 1776, in Robert J. Taylor, et al, *Papers of John Adams* (Cambridge, Mass., 1979) 4: 208-213.

5. Michael Grossberg, *Governing the Hearth: Law and the Family in Nineteenth-Century America* (Chapel Hill, 1985), 5-6.

6. *Laws of the State of New-York, Passed at the Seventy-First Session of the Legislature...* (Albany, 1848), 307-8; *Laws of the State of New York, Passed at the Eighty-Third Session of the Legislature...* (Albany, 1860), 157-59.

7. The complete text of the Declaration of Sentiments can be found in "The Seneca Falls Convention," *One Woman, One Vote*, below.

8. See two brilliant essays by Ellen DuBois, "Outgrowing the Compact of the Fathers: Equal Rights, Woman Suffrage, and the United States Constitution, 1820-1878," *Journal of American History* 74 (1987): 836-62, and "Taking the Law Into Our Own Hands: *Bradwell, Minor* and Suffrage Militance in the 1870s," in *One Woman, One Vote*, below.

9. *Myra Bradwell v. State of Illinois*, 83 U.S. 130 (1873).

10. See Ida Husted Harper, ed. *The Life and Work of Susan B. Anthony* (Indianapolis, 1899), 1: 423-53.

11. *Minor v. Happersett*, 88 U.S. 162 (1875).

Three

THE SENECA FALLS CONVENTION

Editor's Introduction: In this passage from the six-volume suffrage classic, *History of Woman Suffrage*, (Volume 1, 1881), editors Elizabeth Cady Stanton, Susan B. Anthony, and Matilda J. Gage tell the story of the 1848 convention in Seneca Falls, New York. Though there were individuals including Abigail Adams, Frances Wright, Maria W. Stewart, Sarah and Angelina Grimké, Maria Weston Chapman, Abby Kelley Foster, Ernestine Rose, Lydia Maria Child, Margaret Fuller, and Lucy Stone, speaking out in favor of women's rights before 1848, the Seneca Falls Convention is usually cited as the origin of the woman suffrage movement. The site of the Wesleyan Chapel where the convention took place and Stanton's Seneca Falls home are now National Historic Sites.

The passage contains the famous "Declaration of Sentiments" adopted at the convention, one of the most important documents in American history. The suffragists modeled their Declaration after the United States Declaration of Independence, enlisting for their cause the powerful, revolutionary rhetoric still much in the public consciousness, and indirectly making the point that women had been left out of the freedoms gained by White men as a result of the Revolution.

The women who organized the convention and drafted the Declaration—all White, middle-class, married women—were, in the words of Stanton, Anthony, and Gage, "fortunately organized and conditioned," and "had not in their own experience endured the coarser forms of tyranny resulting from unjust laws or association with unscrupulous men." As they compiled their list of grievances to present to the world, these pioneering suffragists laughed at themselves for having to go to the books to find a list sufficient to make a good case! They nevertheless felt "the wrongs of others" as well as the "insults incident to sex" contained in law, religion, literature, and custom that were an affront to "every proud, thinking woman." Foreshadowing the elitism, nativism, and racism that was later manifested in the suffrage movement, however, they expressed indignation that man "has withheld from her [woman] rights which are given to the most ignorant and degraded men—both natives and foreigners."

The Declaration of Sentiments was a fitting document for the birth of the women's movement as it addressed a wide range of issues: moral, political, religious, legal, educational, occupational, and even psychological, issues that the women's movement continues to address. It comes as a surprise to most modern readers that

the ninth resolution calling for women to demand their "sacred right to the elective franchise" was the most controversial. It was adopted by a slender margin owing to the strenuous efforts of Elizabeth Cady Stanton and Frederick Douglass who insisted the vote was the means by which their other demands could be realized.

That so many people (three hundred, including forty men) responded to their "call" surprised the convention's organizers but made it clear that the time was right for their venture. That women like Stanton and Mott were daunted at the prospect of chairing such a large gathering and drafted James Mott for the job, indicates the degree to which women—even these extraordinary women—were affected by the nearly universal disdain for women speaking in public. Several of the resolutions reflect their frustration at being denied the right to participate fully in the great antebellum reform movements of their times including temperance and antislavery. Given the prevailing view that women were morally superior to men, these women found it absurd that so many men engaged in moral reforms were attempting to deny them and other women the right to preach and teach versus the social evils of their day. In fact, Stanton and Mott first met in London at the 1840 World Anti-Slavery Convention, where Mott and the other female delegates from America were rejected; rather than watch silently from the galleries, the two women took the opportunity to tour London "arm in arm" and talk of starting a women's rights movement in America.

As indicated by the concluding paragraph of the Declaration of Sentiments, the signers of the Declaration knew that they would be misrepresented and ridiculed, but they proclaimed that they would "use every instrumentality within our power to effect our object." All of this occurred as predicted. Outraged newspaper editors denounced the convention as shocking, unwomanly, monstrous, and unnatural, or ridiculed them as Amazons or love-starved spinsters. The ensuing storm of protest led some of the one hundred signers to retract their signatures. Frederick Douglass, one of their few champions in the press (and a supporter of women's rights until his death in 1895), defended the convention in *The North Star*. He was appalled that the women's rights advocates were abused and ridiculed even by those "who have at last made the discovery that negroes have some rights as well as other members of the human family." Indeed, said Douglass, "a discussion of the rights of animals would be regarded with far more complacency by many of what are called the wise and the good of our land."

However, the outraged editors inadvertently aided the movement; as word spread of the convention, women were inspired to call other conventions. In October 1850, the first National Woman's Rights Convention was held in Worcester, Massachusetts, and thereafter conventions took place every year (except 1857) until the Civil War led to a postponement of women's rights activities. Many of them were organized by a prominent antislavery orator and women's rights advocate Lucy Stone, who along with Susan B. Anthony, became fully engaged in this great movement soon after Seneca Falls.

★　★　★　★　★

Woman's rights convention—A Convention to discuss the social, civil, and religious condition and rights of woman, will be held in the Wesleyan Chapel, at Seneca Falls, N. Y., on Wednesday and Thursday, the 19th and 20th of July, current; commencing at 10 o'clock A.M. During the first day the meeting will be exclusively for women, who are earnestly invited to attend. The public generally are invited to be present on the second day, when Lucretia Mott, of Philadelphia, and other ladies and gentlemen, will address the convention.

This call, without signature, was issued by Lucretia Mott, Martha C. Wright, Elizabeth Cady Stanton, and Mary Ann McClintock ....

The eventful day dawned at last, and crowds in carriages and on foot, wended their way to the Wesleyan church. When those having charge of the Declaration, the resolutions, and several volumes of the Statutes of New York arrived on the scene, lo! the door was locked. However, an embryo Professor of Yale College was lifted through an open window to unbar the door; that done, the church was quickly filled. It had been decided to have no men present, but as they were already on the spot, and as the women who must take the responsibility of organizing the meeting, and leading the discussions, shrank from doing either, it was decided, in a hasty council round the altar, that this was an occasion when men might make themselves pre-eminently useful. It was agreed they should remain, and take the laboring oar through the Convention.

James Mott, tall and dignified, in Quaker costume, was called to the chair; Mary McClintock appointed Secretary, Frederick Douglass, Samuel Tillman, Ansel Bascom, E.W. Capron, and Thomas McClintock took part throughout in the discussions. Lucretia Mott, accustomed to public speaking in the Society of Friends, stated the objects of the Convention, and in taking a survey of the degraded condition of woman the world over, showed the importance of inaugurating some movement for her education and elevation. Elizabeth and Mary McClintock, and Mrs. Stanton, each read a well-written speech; Martha Wright read some satirical articles she had published in the daily papers answering the diatribes on woman's sphere. Ansel Bascom, who had been a member of the Constitutional Convention recently held in Albany, spoke at length on the property bill for married women, just passed the Legislature, and the discussion on woman's rights in that Convention. Samuel Tillman, a young student of law, read a series of the most exasperating statutes for women, from English and American jurists, all reflecting the tender mercies of men toward their wives, in taking care of their property and protecting them in their civil rights.

The Declaration having been freely discussed by many present, was re-read by Mrs. Stanton, and with some slight amendments adopted.

DECLARATION OF SENTIMENTS

When, in the course of human events, it becomes necessary for one portion of the family of man to assume among the people of the earth a position different from that which they have hitherto occupied, but one to which the laws of nature and of nature's God entitle them, a decent respect to the opinions of mankind requires that they should declare the causes that impel them to such a course.

We hold these truths to be self-evident: that all men and women are created equal; that they are endowed by their Creator with certain inalienable rights; that among these are life, liberty, and the pursuit of happiness; that to secure these rights governments are instituted, deriving their just powers from the consent of the governed. Whenever any form of government becomes destructive of these ends, it is the right of those who suffer from it to refuse allegiance to it, and to insist upon the institution of a new government, laying its foundation on such principles, and organizing its powers in such form, as to them shall seem most likely to effect their safety and happiness. Prudence indeed, will dictate that governments long established should not be changed for light and transient causes; and accordingly all experience hath shown that mankind are more disposed to suffer, while evils are sufferable, than to right themselves by abolishing the forms to which they were accustomed. But when a long train of abuses and usurpations, pursuing invariably the same object evinces a design to reduce them under absolute despotism, it is their duty to throw off such government, and to provide new guards for their future security. Such has been the patient sufferance of the women under this government, and such is now the necessity which constrains them to demand the equal station to which they are entitled.

The history of mankind is a history of repeated injuries and usurpations on the part of man toward woman, having in direct object the establishment of an absolute tyranny over her. To prove this, let facts be submitted to a candid world.

He has never permitted her to exercise her inalienable right to the elective franchise.

He has compelled her to submit to laws, in the formation of which she had no voice.

He has withheld from her rights which are given to the most ignorant and degraded men—both natives and foreigners.

Having deprived her of this first right of a citizen, the elective franchise, thereby leaving her without representation in the halls of legislation, he has oppressed her on all sides.

He has made her, if married, in the eye of the law, civilly dead.

He has taken from her all right in property, even to the wages she earns.

He has made her, morally, an irresponsible being, as she can commit many crimes with impunity, provided they be done in the presence of her husband. In the covenant of marriage, she is compelled to promise obedience to her husband, he becoming, to all intents and purposes, her master—the law giving him power to deprive her of her liberty, and to administer chastisement.

He has so framed the laws of divorce, as to what shall be the proper causes, and in case of separation, to whom the guardianship of the children shall be given, as to be wholly regardless of the happiness of women—the law, in all cases, going upon a false supposition of the supremacy of man, and giving all power into his hands.

After depriving her of all rights as a married woman, if single, and the owner of property, he has taxed her to support a government which recognizes her only when her property can be made profitable to it.

He has monopolized nearly all the profitable employments, and from those she is permitted to follow, she receives but a scanty remuneration. He closes against her all the avenues to wealth and distinction which he considers most honorable to himself. As a teacher of theology, medicine, or law, she is not known.

He has denied her the facilities for obtaining a thorough education, all colleges being closed against her.

He allows her in Church, as well as State, but a subordinate position, claiming Apostolic authority for her exclusion from the ministry, and, with some exceptions, from any public participation in the affairs of the Church.

He has created a false public sentiment by giving to the world a different code of morals for men and women, by which moral delinquencies which exclude women from society, are not only tolerated, but deemed of little account in man.

He has usurped the prerogative of Jehovah himself, claiming it as his right to assign for her a sphere of action, when that belongs to her con science and to her God.

He has endeavored, in every way that he could, to destroy her confidence in her own powers, to lessen her self-respect, and to make her willing to lead a dependent and abject life.

Now, in view of this entire disfranchisement of one-half the people of this country, their social and religious degradation—in view of the unjust laws above mentioned, and because women do feel themselves aggrieved, oppressed, and fraudulently deprived of their most sacred rights, we insist

that they have immediate admission to all the rights and privileges which belong to them as citizens of the United States.

In entering upon the great work before us, we anticipate no small amount of misconception , misrepresentation, and ridicule; but we shall use every instrumentality within our power to effect our object. We shall employ agents, circulate tracts, petition the State and Nation al legislatures, and endeavor to enlist the pulpit and the press in our behalf. We hope this Convention will be followed by a series of Conventions embracing every part of the country.

The following resolutions were discussed by Lucretia Mott, Thomas and Mary Ann McClintock, Amy Post, Catharine A. F. Stebbins, and others, and were adopted:

WHEREAS, The great precept of nature is conceded to be, that "man shall pursue his own true and substantial happiness." Blackstone in his Commentaries remarks, that this law of Nature being coeval with mankind, and dictated by God himself, is of course superior in obligation to any other. It is binding over all the globe, in all countries and at all times; no human laws are of any validity if contrary to this, and such of them as are valid, derive all their force, and all their validity, and all their authority, mediately and immediately, from this original; therefore,

Resolved, That such laws as conflict, in any way, with the true and substantial happiness of woman, are contrary to the great precept of nature and of no validity, for this is "superior in obligation to any other."

Resolved, That all laws which prevent woman from occupying such a station in society as her conscience shall dictate, or which place her in a position inferior to that of man, are contrary to the great precept of nature, and therefore of no force or authority.

Resolved, That woman is man's equal—was intended to be so by the Creator, and the highest good of the race demands that she should be recognized as such.

Resolved, That the women of this country ought to be enlightened in regard to the laws under which they live, that they may no longer publish their degradation by declaring themselves satisfied with their present position, nor their ignorance, by asserting that they have all the rights they want.

Resolved, That inasmuch as man, while claiming for himself intellectual superiority, does accord to woman moral superiority, it is pre eminently his duty to encourage her to speak and teach, as she has an opportunity, in all religious assemblies.

Resolved, That the same amount of virtue, delicacy, and refinement of behavior that is required of woman in the social state, should also be required of man, and the same transgressions should be visited with equal severity on both man and woman.

Resolved, That the objection of indelicacy and impropriety, which is so often brought against woman when she addresses a public audience, comes with a very ill-grace from those who encourage, by their attendance, her appearance on the stage, in the concert, or in feats of the circus.

Resolved, That woman has too long rested satisfied in the circumscribed limits which corrupt customs and a perverted application of the Scriptures have marked out for her, and that it is time she should move in the enlarged sphere which her great Creator has assigned her.

Resolved, That it is the duty of the women of this country to secure to themselves their sacred right to the elective franchise.

Resolved, That the equality of human rights results necessarily from the fact of the identity of the race in capabilities and responsibilities.

Resolved, therefore, That, being invested by the Creator with the same capabilities, and the same consciousness of responsibility for their exercise, it is demonstrably the right and duty of woman, equally with man, to promote every righteous cause by every righteous means; and especially in regard to the great subjects of morals and religion, it is self-evidently her right to participate with her brother in teaching them, both in private and in public, by writing and by speaking, by any instrumentalities proper to be used, and in any assemblies proper to be held; and this being a self-evident truth growing out of the divinely implanted principles of human nature, any custom or authority adverse to it, whether modern or wearing the hoary sanction of antiquity, is to be regarded as a self-evident falsehood, and at war with mankind.

At the last session Lucretia Mott offered and spoke to the following resolution:

Resolved, That the speedy success of our cause depends upon the zealous and untiring efforts of both men and women, for the overthrow of the monopoly of the pulpit, and for the securing to woman an equal participation with men in the various trades, professions and commerce.

The only resolution that was not unanimously adopted was the ninth, urging the women of the country to secure to themselves the elective franchise. Those who took part in the debate feared a demand for the right to vote would defeat others they deemed more rational, and make the whole movement ridiculous.

But Mrs. Stanton and Frederick Douglass seeing that the power to choose rulers and make laws, was the right by which all others could be secured, persistently

WOMAN'S RIGHTS
CONVENTION!

COOPER UNION

New York City, Wednesday, March 20th '56,

at 8 P. M.

A Convention to discuss the social, civil, and religious
rights of women.

SUSAN B. ANTHONY

LUCRETIA MOTT

and other ladies and gentlemen will address the convention.

JAMES MOTT, Sec'y.   ELIZABETH CADY STANTON, Chairman.

Each audience is requested to listen respectfully to the speeches but is invited to take part in the
discussion.

Poster announcing an
1856 Woman's Rights Convention
in New York

FRANK CORBEIL COLLECTION

advocated the resolution, and at last carried it by a small majority.

Thus it will be seen that the Declaration and resolutions in the very first Convention, demanded all the most radical friends of the movement have since claimed—such as equal rights in the universities, in the trades and professions; the right to vote; to share in all political offices, honors, and emoluments; to complete equality in marriage, to personal freedom, property, wages, children; to make contracts; to sue, and be sued; and to testify in courts of justice. At this time the condition of married women under the common law, was nearly as degraded as that of the slave on the Southern plantation. The Convention continued through two entire days, and late into the evenings. The deepest interest was manifested to its close.

The proceedings were extensively published, unsparingly ridiculed by the press, and denounced by the pulpit, much to the surprise and chagrin of the leaders. Being deeply in earnest, and believing their demands pre-eminently wise and just, they were wholly unprepared to find themselves the target for the jibes and jeers of the nation. The Declaration was signed by one hundred men, and women, many of whom withdrew their names as soon as the storm of ridicule began to break. The comments of the press were carefully preserved [and are in the Appendix to Volume I. of *History of Woman Suffrage*], and it is curious to see that the same old arguments, and objections rife at the start, are reproduced by the press of today. But the brave protests sent out from this Convention touched a responsive chord in the hearts of women all over the Country....

Four

A FEMINIST FRIENDSHIP:

Elizabeth Cady Stanton
and Susan B. Anthony

Alice S. Rossi

Editor's Introduction: In this classic essay, a favorite of suffrage scholars and students for many years, Alice Rossi brings these two suffrage leaders to life. The essay originally appeared in *The Feminist Papers: From Adams to de Beauvoir*, a collection of documents by major feminist writers edited by Rossi that was first published in 1973.

"A Feminist Friendship" describes Elizabeth Cady Stanton and Susan B. Anthony's extraordinary relationship, which lasted fifty-one years. Rossi explains how their contrasting but complementary skills and personalities empowered them both—making them such effective advocates for the cause of woman suffrage. In this essay, Rossi also offers an introduction to two of Stanton's writings: "Motherhood," and the Introduction to *The Woman's Bible*.

The two friends had quite different experiences and attitudes in regard to marriage and family. Married and the mother of seven children, Stanton took pleasure from her domestic life, but struggled to cope with the heavy burdens of housekeeping and children that left her little time to engage in the women's movement. Anthony, on the other hand, single and single-mindedly devoted to the cause of women's rights, resented the claims that marriage and childbearing exacted on other women's rights advocates. Yet she frequently came to Stanton's home and "stirred the pudding" and held the babies to free her hard pressed friend for writing.

This feminist friendship afforded Stanton moral support as well. Her women's rights activities were opposed vigorously by her conservative father and resented by her politically ambitious husband who feared her controversial activities would cost him votes. Henry Stanton actually left town on the eve of the Seneca Falls Convention when he learned the proposed Declaration of Sentiments would include a demand for the vote!

Rossi's essay also demonstrates the wide range of Stanton's and Anthony's interests regarding women's rights beyond suffrage, and discusses how their contrasting family backgrounds led to contrasting political perspectives. Rossi's analysis of the way Stanton's views changed over time—along with her personal circumstances—is intensely interesting, as is the fact that Stanton recognized that Anthony was growing more conservative while she grew more radical.

★　★　★　★　★

THE TWO WOMEN most closely associated with the emergence of the woman's rights movement in the nineteenth century are Elizabeth Cady Stanton and Susan B. Anthony. From the spring of 1851, when they first met, until Elizabeth's death in 1902 they were the most intimate of friends and the closest collaborators in the battle for women's rights in the United States. Together they were Lyceum lecturers in the 1850s, founders of equal rights and suffrage associations, organizers of annual conventions, hardy suffrage campaigners in the Western states, and coeditors of the massive first three volumes of the *History of Woman Suffrage;* the contributions of these two pioneers are so intertwined that it is nearly impossible to speak of one without the other. They were in and out of each other's personal lives and households for more than fifty years. Their friendship and shared commitment to the cause of women's rights were the solid, central anchor in both their lives. As Elizabeth wrote to Susan in 1869, "no power in heaven, hell or earth can separate us, for our hearts are eternally wedded together." [1]

It is fitting, therefore, to introduce these two remarkable women in one essay and to focus on their friendship and the nature of their collaboration. The key to their effectiveness lies in the complementary nature of their skills. It can truly be said in this instance that the sum was greater than its parts, for either woman by herself would have had far less impact on the history of women's rights than they had in combination. Elizabeth had the intellect and ability to organize thought and evidence in a pungent, punchy prose. Susan was a master strategist, the "Napoleon" of the movement, as [Unitarian minister and friend] William Channing described her, superb at managing large-scale campaigns, quick and nimble in handling the give-and-take of convention meetings, and an effective public speaker. Elizabeth had only average stage presence and delivery as a speaker, and Susan's ability to conceptualize and develop her ideas was poor. Between them, Elizabeth's effective prose found its perfect outlet in Susan's public speaking. Elizabeth summed up their complementarity very well:

> In writing we did better work together than either could alone. While she is slow and analytical in composition, I am rapid and synthetic. I am the better writer, she the better critic. She supplied the facts and statistics, I the philosophy and rhetoric, and together we have made arguments that have stood unshaken by the storms of thirty long years.[2]

Down through the years Susan turned to Elizabeth for help in drafting speeches, testimony, and letters for presentation to conventions on education, temperance, and women's rights. A good example of this pressure on Elizabeth is in a letter appealing for her help in preparing a speech for a convention of school teachers which Susan was invited to give in 1856:

> There is so much to say and I am so without constructive power to put in symmetrical order. So, for the love of me and for the saving of the

Elizabeth Cady Stanton and
Harriot, 1856. LIBRARY OF CONGRESS

Susan B. Anthony, 1848
LIBRARY OF CONGRESS

reputation of womanhood, I beg you, with one baby on your knee and another at your feet, and four boys whistling, buzzing, hallooing "Ma, Ma," set yourself about the work...Now will you load my gun, leaving me to pull the trigger and let fly the powder and ball? Don't delay one mail to tell me what you will do, for I must not and will not allow these school masters to say: "See, these women can't or won't do anything when we give them a chance." No, they sha'n't say that, even if I have to get a man to write it. But no man can write from my standpoint, nor no woman but you; for all, all would base their strongest argument on the unlikeness of the sexes.... And yet, in the schoolroom more than any other place, does the difference of sex, if there is any, need to be for gotten.... Do get all on fire and be as cross as you please.[3]

The letter captures several of Susan's qualities: blunt speech, a badgering of her associates to give her the help she needs (always in a hurry), a fighting spirit, and an ability to point to a central theme she wishes stressed. Elizabeth's response to this particular call for help came just five days later. She says in part:

Your servant is not dead but liveth. Imagine me, day in and day out, watching, bathing, dressing, nursing, and promenading the precious contents of a little crib in the corner of the room. I pace up and down these two chambers of mine, like a caged lioness longing to bring to a close nursing and housekeeping cares.... Is your speech to be exclusively on the point of educating the sexes together, or as to the best manner of educating women? I will do what I can to help you with your lecture.[4]

The "baby" referred to is five-month-old Harriot, Elizabeth's sixth child, and the speech, entitled "Co-education," was written by Elizabeth and delivered by Susan less than two months later.

This particular collaborative effort differed from most of their team work only in that it involved no face-to-face working out of the ideas to be developed in the speech. In most of their joint efforts they worked together more closely; Susan often visited the Stanton home in Seneca Falls for this purpose. Elizabeth described these occasions:

> Whenever I saw that stately Quaker girl coming across my lawn, I knew that some happy convocation of the sons of Adam were to be set by the ears, by one of our appeals or resolutions. The little portmanteau stuffed with facts was opened... Then we would get out our pens and write articles for papers, or a petition to the Legislature, letters to the faithful... call on *The Una, The Liberator,* and *The Standard,* to remember our wrongs as well as those of the slave. We never met without issuing a pronunciamento on some question.[5]

Thirty years later, when Elizabeth was no longer burdened with housekeeping and child-rearing responsibilities, she commented that in the 1850s, had it not been for Susan, who provided her with enough evidence of injustice to "turn any woman's thoughts from stockings and puddings," she might in time, "like too many women, have become wholly absorbed in a narrow family selfishness."

But a supportive friend who applied continual pressure to produce speeches and resolutions and articles for the press would hardly suffice to carry Elizabeth through the arduous years of child-rearing, from 1842 to the Civil War. During these years she not only bore seven children, but did a good deal of entertaining, produced reams of written material, served in temperance and abolition societies, lectured widely with the Lyceum circuit, and ran the household in Seneca Falls for long stretches of time without a man in the house. Elizabeth was clearly a woman of enormous physical energy coupled with a very strong will; these were needed to cope with such a regimen and to thrive on it. She was not a woman easily threatened by new experiences. Indeed, one of the best examples of her independence of mind and strength of body is the selection that follows, which describes her first experience of maternity. The reader will see how readily Elizabeth exercised her own judgment, even if it meant overriding medical advice. She seems to have given birth to all seven children with no aid beyond that of a friend and a nurse, commenting in a letter to Lucretia Mott after the fifth child's birth:

> Dear me, how much cruel bondage of mind and suffering of body poor woman will escape when she takes the liberty of being her own physician of both body and soul![6]

Among Elizabeth's prescriptions for a healthy womanhood was one she clearly followed herself, but which it would take many decades for medicine and psychiatry to learn: she insightfully put her finger on an important cause of hysteria and illness among the women of her day, in a 1859 letter to a Boston friend:

> I think if women would indulge more freely in vituperation, they would enjoy ten times the health they do. It seems to me they are suffering from repression.[7]

Elizabeth was not a woman to suffer from such repression herself. She showed none of the modern ambivalence about complaining when her responsibilities became onerous. One feels sure that in the intimacy of a friendly visit she let off steam in much the way she did in her letters during the 1850s, either by frankly admitting that she longed to be "free from housekeeping and children, so as to have some time to read and think and write" or by chafing at some affront to women and writing to Susan: "I am at a boiling point! If I do not find some day the use of my tongue on this question I shall die of an intellectual repression, a woman's rights convulsion .[8]

There was probably not another woman in the nineteenth century who put her tongue and pen to better use than Elizabeth Stanton. She and Susan clearly viewed themselves as rebels in a good fight for justice and equality for women. They wrote each other in martial terms full of "triggers," "powder and balls," "Thunderbolts." Locust Hill, Elizabeth 's home in Seneca Falls, was dubbed "the center of the rebellion" and from here Elizabeth "forged the thunderbolts" and Susan "fired them."

But even a close friend was no solution to the heavy family responsibilities Elizabeth carried throughout the 1850s. In the early years of her residence in Seneca Falls she was full of complaints about the unreliability of household servants falling back on a dream of some "cooperative housekeeping in a future time that might promise a more harmonious domestic life" for women. But from 1851 on she had the help of a competent housekeeper, Amelia Willard, a capable woman who could readily substitute for Elizabeth herself. It was unquestionably this household arrangement which released Elizabeth for at least periodic participation in lecture tours and convention speeches during the years of heavy family responsibilities.

> It was while living in Seneca Falls and at one of the most despairing periods of my young life, that one of the best gifts of the gods came to me in the form of a good, faithful housekeeper. She was indeed a treasure, a friend and comforter, a second mother to my children, and understood all life's duties and gladly bore its burdens. She could fill any department in domestic life, and for thirty years was the joy of our household. But for this noble, self sacrificing woman, much of my public work would have been quite impossible. If by word or deed I have made the journey of life easier for any struggling soul I must in justice share the meed of praise accorded me with my little Quaker friend Amelia Willard.[9]

It is curious that it maybe the help of a housekeeper and a friend that facilitates a woman's life's work, while the closest analogy to Elizabeth 's tribute one would find from the pen of a man is typically a tribute to his wife .

It is an interesting aspect of the friendship between Elizabeth and Susan that, while Susan was extremely critical of the energy her woman's rights friends gave to homemaking and "baby-making," as she put it, there is no written evidence that Elizabeth exerted any pressure on Susan to marry and have a family of her own, though Susan was only in her thirties during the first decade of their friendship. Elizabeth seems, in fact, to have been remarkably accepting of Susan exactly as she was; only a teasing quality in a few letters expressed any criticism of her. Susan, by contrast, showed little understanding of, and no hesitation in expressing herself strongly about, the diversion of her friends' energies away from reform causes. In the same 1856 letter in which she calls for Elizabeth's aid in writing a speech on coeducation Susan comments:

> Those of you who have the talent to do honor to poor womanhood, have all given yourself over to baby-making; and left poor brainless me to do battle alone. It is a shame . Such a body as I might be spared to rock cradles. But it is a crime for you and Lucy Stone and Antoinette Brown to be doing it.[10]

In response, Elizabeth urged her friend to let "Lucy and Antoinette rest awhile in peace and quietness," since "we cannot bring about a moral revolution in a day or year."[11] This advice from Elizabeth had no effect on Susan, however. Two years later, in learning of the birth of Antoinette Brown Blackwell's second child, she wrote the following revealing letter to Nettie (emphasis is by Susan):

> Dear Nettie: April 22, 1858
>
> A note from Lucy last night tells me that you have another *daughter*. Well, so be it. I rejoice that you are past the trial hour.
>
> Now Nettie, *not another baby* is my *peremptory command, two* will solve the problem whether a *woman can* be anything more than a *wife* and *mother* better than a half dozen or *ten even.*
>
> I am provoked at Lucy, just to think that she will attempt to speak in a course with such intellects as Brady, Curtis, and Chapin, and then as her special preparation, take upon herself in addition to baby cares, quite too absorbing for careful close and continued intellectual effort—the entire work of her house. A woman who is and must of necessity continue for the present at least, the representative woman, has no right to disqualify herself for such a representative occasion. I do feel it is so foolish for her to put herself in the position of *maid of all work and baby tender....*
>
> Nettie, I don't really want to be a downright scolder, but I can't help looking after the married sheep of the flock a wee bit.[12]

Three weeks later Susan sent another note to Nettie, this time adding a post script to report:

> Mrs. Stanton sends love, and says "if you are going to have a large family go right on and finish up at once," as she has done. She has only devoted 18 years out of the very heart of existence here to the great work. But I say stop now, once and for all. Your life work will be arduous enough with two.[13]

Elizabeth Stanton softened this message with her own warm congratulations in an undated letter to Nettie that must have been written during this same spring :

> How many times I have thought of you since reading your pleasant letter to Susan. I was so happy to hear that you had another daughter. In spite of all Susan's admonitions, I do hope you and Lucy will have all the children you desire. I would not have one less than seven, in spite of all the abuse that has been heaped upon me for such extravagance.[14]

Quite another aspect of the place their friendship held in their personal lives is suggested by their terms of address and reference to each other. They were not terms of "sisterhood" but of "marriage." Their hearts "are eternally wedded together," as Elizabeth put it. In 1870, when the press circulated rumors that their partnership was "dissolving," Elizabeth wrote her friend, half in jest:

> Have you been getting a divorce out in Chicago without notifying me? I should like to know my present status. I shall not allow any such proceedings. I consider that our relations are to last for life; so make the best of it.[15]

Two such passionate and committed women were bound to have differences of opinion, but once again, Elizabeth drew the analogy to marriage in explaining their conviction that differences should be confined to their private exchanges while they presented a united front in public:

> So entirely one are we, that in all our associations, ever side by side on the same platform, not one feeling of jealousy or envy has ever shad owed our lives. We have indulged freely in criticism of each other when alone, and hotly contended whenever we have differed, but in our friendship of thirty years there has never been a break of one hour. To the world we always seem to agree and uniformly reflect each other. Like husband and wife, each has the feeling that we must have no differences in public.[16]

During these years the two women were firm in their belief that the differences between men and women were rooted purely in social custom; it may be that the cultural model of differences between husband and wife made the complementarity of marital roles a closer analogy to the nature of their own relationship than the presumed similarity of sisterhood. There is nevertheless some psychological validity in the symbolic use of the marriage bond to describe their friendship.

Left: Susan B. Anthony (left) and Elizabeth Cady Stanton, c. 1870, c. 1888
SCHLESINGER LIBRARY, RADCLIFFE INSTITUTE, HARVARD UNIVERSITY / WYOMING STATE MUSEUM

Susan Anthony never married, and Elizabeth Stanton, though married for forty-six years, clearly received only shallow emotional support and no political support for her convictions from Henry Stanton. A warmth and effusiveness pervades Elizabeth's autobiography and her correspondence when she speaks of her children and of her close friends, but in hundreds of pages devoted to her personal life no comparable sentiment of warmth and mutuality appears in her rare references to her husband. It is not even clear whether Susan's frequent visits to the Stanton home coincided with Henry's stays at home. A politician, reformer, and journalist, he was clearly a traveling man. Seven children were born between 1842 and 1859, but there was a thinly disguised conflict between husband and wife on nonfamily matters. In 1855 Elizabeth wrote a few letters that permit a crack to show in the surface harmony. She had been developing plans that year to give a series of lectures on the Lyceum circuit and reports an exchange with her father concerning this plan in a letter to her cousin Elizabeth:

> We had a visit a little while ago from my venerable sire… As we sat alone one night, he asked me: "Elizabeth, are you getting ready to lecture before lyceums?" "Yes sir," I answered. "I hope," he continued, "you will never do it during my lifetime, for if you do, be assured of one thing, your first lecture will be a very expensive one." "I intend," I replied, "that it shall be a very profitable one."[17]

Her father did in fact disinherit her at this time, though he relented before his death and altered his will once again. Elizabeth does not give vent to her acute distress over this altercation with her father in writing to her cousin, but during the same month she wrote in quite a different vein to Susan. Referring to a "terrible scourging" on her last meeting with her father, she wrote:

> I cannot tell you how deep the iron entered my soul. I never felt more keenly the degradation of my sex. To think that all in me of which my father would have felt a proper pride had I been a man, is deeply mortifying to him because I am a woman. That thought has stung me to a fierce decision—to speak as soon as I can do myself credit. But the pres sure on me just now is

too great. Henry sides with my friends, who oppose me in all that is dearest to my heart. They are not willing that I should write even on the woman question. But I will both write and speak. I wish you to consider this letter strictly confidential. Some times, Susan, I struggle in deep waters.[18]

This letter is a revealing one concerning both men in her life. Elizabeth had deeply ambivalent feelings toward her father. On the one hand she admired him for his mental abilities, was grateful for the understanding he gave her of the law, and was indebted to him for his continual financial support of her and her family over the years after her marriage. On the other hand she deeply resented the fact that none of her abilities or successes either as a schoolgirl or an adult could gain any praise at all from him. The same profile seems to hold for her marriage to Henry Stanton. Though they were both active in temperance and abolition agitation, they were completely at odds on her ideas and political activity on the woman's rights issue. In the letter quoted above, the association of "father" and "husband" is immediate (Henry was ten years her senior), and Elizabeth feels herself a lone rebel in an unsympathetic social circle of family and neighbors, reaching out to the one sure friend who shares her commitments.

In this connection Henry Stanton's memoirs are interesting for what they leave unsaid. Though he wrote in the 1880s, when he was himself in his eighties, he seems unable even to mention the words "woman's rights." His wife is as absent from these pages as he is from her memoirs. The only reference in the entire book to Elizabeth's role in the woman's rights movement is the following passage, with its oblique reference to her leadership role "in another department."

> The celebrity in this country and Europe of two women in another department has thrown some-what into the shade the distin-nguished service they rendered to the slave in the four stormy years preceding the war and in the four years while the sanguinary con-flict was waged in the field. I refer to Elizabeth Cady Stanton and Susan B. Anthony.[19]

The submerged conflict in the Stan-ton household was not confined to the husband and wife, for the seven children were drawn in as well. It is interesting to compare their separate memoirs on this point. Of the seven, the first four and the last-born were boys; yet it was the fourth child, a fourth son, who was to be the closest of the sons to Elizabeth. In the kind of leap across time that is perhaps characteristic of women's memories of their children she wrote:

> I had a list of beautiful names for sons and daughters, from which to designate each newcomer; but, as yet, not one on my list had been used for my children. However, I put my foot down at number four, and named him Theodore, and, thus far, he has proved himself a veritable "gift of God," doing his uttermost, in every way possible, to fight the battle of freedom for woman.[20]

It was Theodore who studied the women's movement in Europe, where he lived for many years; he wrote a book entitled *The Woman Question in Europe*. In her autobiography Elizabeth noted:

> To have a son interested in the question to which I have devoted my life, is a source of intense satisfaction. To say that I have realized in him all I could desire, is the highest praise a fond mother can give.[21]

Theodore's daughter was named Elizabeth Cady Stanton Jr. That Elizabeth took pride in her two daughters and lived in close contact with them, particularly Harriot, is clear throughout her memoirs. Both Harriot and her own daughter Nora were active in the suffrage movement, carrying Elizabeth's lead into the third generation.

In contrast, Henry Stanton makes no reference at all to the three children Elizabeth talked about so warmly, though he mentions the remaining four sons with pride. Speaking of his life as a lawyer, he added:

> I have shown my regard for the profession by inducting four of my sons into its intricacies. Daniel Cady Stanton was for one year a supervisor of registration, and for two years a member of the legislature of Louisiana, in the turbulent era of reconstruction. Henry Stanton, a graduate of the law school of Columbia College, is now the official attorney of the Northern Pacific Railway Company. Gerrit Smith Stanton and Robert Livingston Stanton are also graduates of the Columbia School. The for mer cultivates the soil and dispenses the law in Iowa. The latter practices his profession in the city of New York.[22]

These are the only references Henry makes to any of his children. One senses a divisive line-up within the Stanton household that widened as the children grew up: Henry Sr. with sons Daniel, Henry, Gerrit, and Robert on the one side; Elizabeth with Theodore, Margaret, and Harriot on the other. The division, at least on the surface indications left to us, was rooted in Elizabeth's involvement in the "woman question."

It is little wonder that Elizabeth's friendship with Susan took on such intensity. While Elizabeth was torn between the love of her children and a sense of duty to home and spouse on the one hand, and the rebellious desire to be up and out fighting the battles dearest to her convictions on the other, Susan was a vital link that held these two worlds together in Elizabeth's heart and mind. Always the one to speak for both of them, and able to acknowledge tender sentiments to a far greater extent than the more purposive Susan, Elizabeth sums up the importance of their friendship:

> So closely interwoven have been our lives, our purposes, and experiences that, separated, we have a feeling of incompleteness—united, such strength of self-assertion that no ordinary obstacles, difficulties, or dangers ever appear to us insurmountable.[23]

The emotional quality of this assessment is one normally associated with the ideal, if not the reality, of a marital relationship; it is also a forerunner of the sisterly solidarity experienced in numerous feminist friendships in the 1970s.

It is much more difficult to gain a sense of Susan Anthony as a private person than it is of Elizabeth Stanton. Though she clearly reciprocated the deep friend ship Elizabeth described, her personal style was quite different. The pressures on Susan were far more of a public than a private nature throughout her life, nor did she experience the deeply ambivalent relationship to a parent as Elizabeth did. Since she did not marry, Susan had no adult conflict of loyalties between family and a public career. Indeed, she showed great impatience with her women friends in the reform movements as they married and took on family responsibilities. That reticence in an autobiographic sense may be rooted in a past of greater serenity and lack of conflict is an insight for which we are indebted to Gordon Allport:

> Autobiographical writing seems to be preoccupied with conflict... happy, peaceful periods of time are usually passed over in silence. A few lines may tell of many serene years whereas pages are devoted to a single humiliating episode or to an experience of suffering. Writers seem driven to elaborate on the conditions that have wrecked their hopes and deprived them of satisfactions.[24]

This point may apply to correspondence as much as to autobiographies; and it is consistent that, from all one knows of Susan Anthony's family background, it was far more serene and conflict-free than Elizabeth's.

Susan Anthony's parents were happily married, and her father was a strong and beloved figure throughout her life . He was a strong supporter of temperance and antislavery, even at the risk of financial penalty to himself. He took an active role in the rearing and education of his children, with consistent encouragement of their independence and initiative, and drew no distinction in such matters between sons and daughters. He supported the girls in any desire to acquire skills, believing that every girl should be trained to be self-supporting—a view the Anthony neighbors clearly did not share. Susan's first biographer and friend, Ida Harper, suggests that Daniel Anthony saw in Susan

> an ability of a high order and that same courage, persistence and aggres- siveness which entered into his own character. He encouraged her desire to go into the reforms which were demanding attention, gave her financial backing when necessary, moral support upon all occasions and was ever her most interested friend and faithful ally. [25]

While many parents of the early woman's movement leaders shared commit- ments to temperance and abolition, few were full supporters of the woman's rights movement. Susan's family was exceptional in this regard; her parents and sister

attended the earliest convention on woman's rights in Rochester and were among those signing petitions in support of the convention resolutions.

Drive, executive ability, and a single-mindedness of purpose became enduring characteristics of Susan Anthony. She was impatient with whatever did not contribute directly to the battles she waged in her various campaigns for reform. She began as a teacher at the age of seventeen, and for many years she was a critical observer and then vigorous participant at teachers' association conventions. An early example of her courage and ability to press to the main point of an argument can be seen in her role at the 1853 state convention of schoolteachers. At this time women teachers could attend but could not speak at the convention meetings. Susan listened to a long discussion on why the profession of teaching was not as respected as those of law, medicine, and the ministry. When she could stand it no longer, she rose from her seat and called out, "Mr. President!" After much consternation about recognizing her, she was asked what she wished. When informed that she wished to speak to the question under discussion, a half-hour's debate and a close vote resulted in permission. Then she said:

> It seems to me, gentlemen, that none of you quite comprehend the cause of the disrespect of which you complain. Do you not see that so long as society says a woman is incompetent to be a lawyer, minister or doctor, but has ample ability to be a teacher, that every man of you who chooses this profession tacitly acknowledges that he has no more brains than a woman? And this, too, is the reason that teaching is a less lucrative profession, as here men must compete with the cheap labor of woman. Would you exalt your profession, exalt those who labor with you. Would you make it more lucrative, increase the salaries of the women engaged in the noble work of educating our future Presidents, Senators and Congressmen.[26]

Susan's point on the wage scale of occupations in which many women are employed is as pertinent today as it was in the 1850s. Equal pay for equal work continues to be seen as applying to equal pay for men and women in the same occupation, while the larger point of continuing relevance in our day is that some occupations have depressed wages because women are the chief employees. The former is a pattern of sex discrimination, the latter of institutionalized sexism.

Stanton and Anthony were of one mind on the issue of political rights for women, and this unanimity was at the core of their concerted organizational efforts during the long decades of the suffrage campaigns. Beyond this collaboration, however, they had complementary secondary interests. As a single woman and a Quaker, Susan was deeply concerned with opening the doors to women in the professions and with improving the pay scale of women workers. As a married woman and the more radical thinker of the two, Elizabeth was concerned with legislative reform of marriage, divorce, and property laws. There was much debate in the inner circle of woman's rights leaders in the 1850s on the expediency of pressing an issue such as

divorce at woman's rights conventions, for it triggered far more violent responses from the public and was more divisive within their associations than even the political rights issue. It was also the case that the early leaders were not in agreement among themselves on the importance of marriage and divorce law reform or the solutions to sex inequity in the family sphere.

To trace these women leaders' views on marriage and divorce issues over the years would constitute a fascinating analysis that must remain for future scholars. I suspect, though only as a hypothesis, that the long-range trend of the woman's rights movement toward a narrower focus on the single issue of the vote was partially rooted in the aging of the leaders. Not only did these early pioneers live to a very old age, but they retained leadership positions in the movement well into their seventies. With increasing age, they may have felt far less personal involvement in such issues as marriage, child care, divorce, employment, and household management than they did in questions of political rights. Lucy Stone and Elizabeth Stanton were most concerned to press the issue of a woman's right to her own body in the 1850s, when they were young enough to be personally concerned. Thirty years later, the issue was no longer of high priority to them either personally or politically.

Some suggestion of the link between personal age and family status on the one hand and views on sex and maternity on the other can be seen in the fol lowing excerpts from writings of Elizabeth Stanton at various moments during her life. Elizabeth's age is recorded in parentheses along with the year in which she made each statement.

1853 (38) [Letter to Susan Anthony].

Man in his lust has regulated long enough this whole question of sexual intercourse. Now let the mother of mankind, whose prerogative it is to set bounds to his indulgence rouse up and give this whole matter a thorough, fearless examination.... I feel, as never before, that this whole question of woman's rights turns on the pivot of the marriage relation, and, mark my word, sooner or later, it will be the topic for discussion. I would not hurry it on, nor would I avoid it.[27]

1860 (45) [Letter to Susan Anthony].

Woman's degradation is in man's idea of his sexual rights. Our religion, laws, customs are all founded on the belief that woman was made for man. Come what will my whole soul rejoices in the truth that I have uttered. One word of thanks from a suffering woman outweighs with me the howls of all Christendom. How this marriage question grows on me. It lies at the very foundation of all progress. I never read a thing on this subject until I had arrived at my present opinion. My own life, observation, thought , feeling, reason, brought me to the conclusion. So fear not that I shall falter. I shall not grow conservative with age.[28]

1870 (55) [Letter to Susan Anthony].

Not only have I finished my lecture on marriage and divorce, but I have delivered it Women respond to this divorce speech as they never did to suffrage. In a word, I have had grand meetings. Oh, how the women flock to me with their sorrows. Such experiences as I listen to, plantation never equaled.[29]

1883 (68) [Excerpt from Diary].

I have been reading *Leaves of Grass*. Walt Whitman seems to understand everything in nature but woman. In "There is a Woman Waiting for Me," he speaks as if the female must be forced to the creative act, apparently ignorant of the great natural fact that a healthy woman has as much passion as a man, that she needs nothing stronger than the law of attraction to draw her to the male."[30]

1890 (75) [Excerpt from Diary].

Our trouble is not our womanhood, but the artificial trammels of custom under false conditions. We are, as a sex, infinitely superior to men, and if we were free and developed, healthy in body and mind, as we should be under natural conditions, our motherhood would be our glory. That function gives women such wisdom and power as no male ever can possess. When women can support themselves have their entry to all the trades and professions , with a house of their own over their heads and a bank account, they will own their bodies and be dicta tors in the social realm.[31]

There is an interesting progression in Elizabeth's ideas over the forty years covered by these excerpts, reflecting, one feels sure, not only the continuing evolution of her thought but also the subtle impact of her changing age and family status. Let us go back over these excerpts and try to see a connection between her ideas and the developmental stage she had reached in her own personal life.

The first two excerpts focus on sex and the power of men to impose their sexual demands on women: these are years during which Elizabeth was herself sexually active, with two pregnancies still ahead of her at the time of the 1853 writing , and a last birth just a year before she wrote the second excerpt in 1860.

The growing concern she felt for divorce reform was particularly apparent in the 1860s, culminating in the speech she delivered on marriage and divorce laws at numerous Lyceum lectures in 1870: with her own children now ranging in age from eleven to twenty-eight, she herself may have emerged from her peak dependent years. Indeed, since she was fifty-five years old in 1870, she was probably postmenopausal. Marital stability and termination now absorb her.

By 1883 there is a sharp shift in emphasis, with an image of woman as possessing a healthy sexual passion to match that of men: despite her age—sixty eight—she had read and traveled widely and given much thought to the question

IN MEMORIAM
ELIZABETH CADY STANTON.

On Sunday, October 26th, at three o'clock in the afternoon, Elizabeth Cady Stanton "fell asleep."

The news of her death transpired just as this department went to press. Scarcely more than a fortnight before her death Mrs. Stanton was talking with the Editor, who was impressed by the wonderful clearness of her mind and the sprightliness of her manner. At this time was taken the photograph of Mrs. Stanton reproduced herewith. The article printed with the photograph had just been dictated by Mrs. Stanton to her secretary for this department. Her signature is reproduced from a copy of "The Woman's Bible," which she had just signed and presented to the Editor.

Had Mrs. Stanton lived till November 12th she would have celebrated her eighty-seventh birthday, with Susan B. Anthony as her guest. Miss Anthony had sent her birthday greeting to Mrs. Stanton for publication in this department. The beautiful sentiment expressed by Miss Anthony in the last paragraph of this greeting makes it a fitting *in memoriam* of the noble life of her lifelong friend.

MISS ANTHONY'S BIRTHDAY GREETING TO MRS. STANTON.

My Dear Mrs. Stanton :—

I shall indeed be happy to spend with you the day on which you round out your four score and seven, over four years ahead of me, but, in age as in all else, I follow you closely. It is fifty-

Elizabeth Cady Stanton. Her last photograph taken about two weeks before her death.

we met, and we have
every one of them,
to recognize the rights
we grow, the more
humiliation of dis-
the more vividly we
tages in every depart-
most of all in the

We little dreamed
contest, optimistic
buoyancy of youth,
laterwewould be com-
finish of the battle to
women. But our
joy to know that they
equipped with a col-
business experience,
mitted right to speak
which were denied to
They have practically
—the suffrage; we had
courageous, capable
take our place and
There is an army of
but a handful; ancient

one years since first
been busy through
stirring up the world
of women. The older
keenly we feel the
franchisement, and
realize its disadvan-
ment of life, and
labor market.
when we began this
with the hope and
that half a century
pelled to leave the
another generation of
hearts are filled with
enter upon this task
lege education, with
with the fully ad-
in public — all of
women fifty years ago.
but one point to gain
all. These strong,
young women will
complete our work.
them, where we were
prejudice has become

so softened, public sentiment so liberalized, and women have so thoroughly demonstrated their ability, as to leave not a shadow of doubt that they will carry our cause to victory.

And we, dear old friend, shall move on the next sphere of existence—higher and larger, we cannot fail to believe, and one where women will not be placed in an inferior position, but will be welcomed on a plane of perfect intellectual and spiritual equality.

Ever lovingly yours,

Susan B. Anthony

Following Elizabeth Cady Stanton's death in October 1902, *Pearson's Magazine* published a birthday greeting Susan B. Anthony had prepared for Stanton's "four score and seventh" birthday, recalling their long, productive friendship.

Elizabeth Miller NAWSA Scrapbooks, Library of Congress

of sexuality; but she no longer had any personal need to act upon them. She was now fully independent of her husband, seldom traveling with him, and perhaps learning a more modern view of sexuality from her own married children, Theodore and Harriot.

By 1890 the view of maternity had again shifted, and a strong positive view of women emerges: now she is no longer focusing on what women are deprived of by men or subjected to by men—a topic which had absorbed her as a younger woman; rather, she is taking pride in what women have that men do not have. Perhaps her own independence and the circumstance of married children who acknowledge her prominence and share her interests now permit her to see the power and privilege that flow from maternity at a more mature age. It may also be significant that by this date she is living in New York City, in an apartment overlooking the Hudson River, which she shared with her daughter Margaret and her youngest son, Robert. But it is also a tribute to the openness of her intellect at seventy-five that she could envisage the significance to women of an independent household and independent income, some thirty-five years before Virginia Woolf argued that "500 guineas" and a "room of one's own" were the symbols of what women needed to achieve real emancipation.[32]

Elizabeth and Susan began their lives in the same social and political climate of central New York State, absorbing the perspectives on benevolent reform that marked the region during the 1820s and 1830s. A critical difference between them was rooted in their families: Susan's family applied the lofty reformist values to their own personal lives, whereas Elizabeth's did not. Hence, when the two women turned to the cause of their own sex, it was a rebellious step for Elizabeth but an acting-out of parental values for Susan. This difference between the two women had consequences that showed throughout their lives. The more rebellious Elizabeth was in part motivated by the discord rankling within her as a result of the ambivalence in her relations with her parents and husband. She was driven to a search for a better vision of a better life, one grounded in cooperation and marked by domestic harmony. Her intellect was opened outward to the future, while her political action was held in check by the necessities of organization and the pressure of her far more conservative supporters. Since her past did not nourish her as Susan's did, the impulse to open inquiry and acceptance of change continued strong. For Susan the world looked rather different. She had no inner rebellious feelings rooted in her early family experiences, since she enjoyed the support and praise of the people important in her private life . She was therefore the executor of the reform ideas developed by her friend . But her mission was to make the system work, while Elizabeth was drawn to social innovation and more fundamental change in the system. From all the evidence available, Elizabeth seems to have been correct when she wrote, at the age of seventy-nine, that "I get more radical as I grow older, while she [Susan] seems to get more conservative."[33]

Notes

Reprinted from Alice S. Rossi, editor. *The Feminist Papers, From Adams to de Beauvoir,* Copyright 1973 by Alice S. Rossi. Reprinted with the permission of Northeastern University Press, Boston.

1. Theodore Stanton and Harriot Stanton Blatch, eds. *Elizabeth Cady Stanton as Revealed in Her Letters, Diary and Reminiscences,* 2 vols. (New York, 1922, 2: 125). This account of the friendship between Elizabeth Stanton and Susan Anthony is a partial one at best, and the interested reader can find more detail and a better chronology of their individual lives in several biographies (Ida H. Harper, *The Life and Work of Susan B. Anthony.* 3 vols. (Indianapolis, 1898); Katherine Anthony, *Susan B. Anthony: Her Personal History and Her Era.* (Garden City , N. Y., 1954); Alma Lutz, *Susan B. Anthony,* (Boston, 1959); see also, Alma Lutz, *Created Equal. A Biography of Elizabeth Cady Stanton.* (New York, 1940); and Stanton and Blatch, 1922) and memoirs by Elizabeth Stanton herself (E.C. Stanton, *Eighty Years and More: Reminiscences of Elizabeth Cady Stanton.* 2 vols. (New York, 1898). The best introduction to the political and organizational efforts of these two friends is in the volumes of the *History of Woman Suffrage* themselves.

2. Elizabeth Cady Stanton, Susan B. Anthony, and Matilda Joslyn Gage, eds., *History of Woman Suffrage,* (New York, 1881), 1:459. Hereafter *HWS.*

3. Stanton and Blatch, *Elizabeth Cady Stanton as Revealed in Her Letters ...,* 2: 64-66.

4. Ibid, 66 -67.

5. *HWS* 1:458-459. *The Una,* edited by Paulina Wright Davis, was one of the first women's rights newspapers. *The Liberator* was William Lloyd Garrison's antislavery newspaper in which he also supported women's rights.

6. Stanton and Blatch, *Elizabeth Cady Stanton as Revealed...,* 2: 45.

7. Ibid., 73-74.

8. Ibid., 41.

9. Ibid., 174 .

10. Ibid., 65. Editor's note: Lucy Stone had one child and another that lived only briefly; her sister-in-law Antoinette Brown Blackwell, a Congregational and (later) Unitarian minister, author and lecturer, had seven children, though two died in

infancy. Blackwell nevertheless managed to publish nine books over her long life including an attack on the antifeminist uses of Darwinism. She was the only one of the antebellum women's rights leaders who lived long enough to vote, at age ninety-five.

11. Stanton and Blatch, *Elizabeth Cady Stanton as Revealed...,* 2:67.

12. Sarah Gilson, *Antoinette Brown Blackwell: Biographical Sketch,* 1909, 223-224. Unpublished manuscript in the Blackwell Family Papers, Schlesinger Library, Radcliffe College, Cambridge, Mass.

13. Ibid., 225.

14. Ibid., 233.

15. Stanton and Blatch, *Elizabeth Cady Stanton as Revealed...,* 2:127.

16. *HWS* 1:459.

17. Stanton and Blatch, *Elizabeth Cady Stanton as Revealed...,* 2:61.

18. Ibid ., 59, 60.

19. Henry B. Stanton, *Random Recollections.* (New York, 1887), 68.

20. Stanton and Blatch, *Elizabeth Cady Stanton as Revealed...,* 136.

21. E.C. Stanton, *Eighty Years and More,* 399- 400 .

22. Henry Stanton, *Random Recollections,* 1887, 147.

23. Stanton and Blatch, *Elizabeth Cady Stanton as Revealed...,* 1:157.

24. Gordon W. Allport, *The Use of Personal Documents in Psychological Science,* Bulletin 49, (New York: Social Science Research Council), 78.

25. Harper, *The Life and Work of Susan B. Anthony,* 1:57, 58.

26. *HWS* 1:514.

27. Stanton and Blatch, *Elizabeth Cady Stanton as Revealed...,* 2:49 .

28. Ibid., 2:82, 83.

29. Ibid., 2:127. Editor's note: "plantation never equaled" presumably means that the problems of women needing divorces and unable to secure them exceeded even those of the slaves.

30. Ibid., 2:210.

31. Ibid. , 2:270.

31. Virginia Woolf, *A Room of One's Own,* (London, 1931).

32. Stanton and Blatch, *Elizabeth Cady Stanton as Revealed...,* 2:254.

Five

WHITE WOMEN'S RIGHTS, BLACK MEN'S WRONGS:

Free Love, Blackmail,
and the Formation of the
American Woman Suffrage Association

Andrea Moore Kerr

Editor's Introduction: In this article, Andrea Moore Kerr, author of *Lucy Stone: Speaking Out for Equality*, describes the dilemmas and difficulties the youthful suffrage movement encountered two decades after the Seneca Falls Convention. After a "golden age" of woman suffrage activity in the 1850s under the leadership of Elizabeth Cady Stanton, Susan B. Anthony, and Lucy Stone, the movement was temporarily suspended due to the Civil War. During Reconstruction, the suffragists hoped that the expansion of the electorate that had begun before the war (the extension of the vote to all White men) would continue, and that a reform-minded Congress dominated by the Republican Party would enact universal suffrage for all. But when opponents of Black suffrage appeared to be using woman suffrage for their own ends, and some who proposed an alliance with the woman suffrage movement were clearly hostile to Black suffrage, the suffragists faced difficult decisions. And when even former allies including Frederick Douglass asked the suffragists to accept exclusion from the postwar suffrage amendments rather than endanger the prospects of the newly freed Black men, the suffragists did not all resolve their dilemma in the same way.

In these troubled times, the movement was torn apart, and two rival suffrage organizations were formed, creating a schism in the movement that lasted from 1869 to 1890. Anthony and Stanton, who believed that the enfranchisement of Black and immigrant men would actually make it even *more difficult* for women to win the vote, formed the National Woman Suffrage Association (NWSA) opposing the Fifteenth Amendment and calling for a federal amendment for woman suffrage. Lucy Stone, also distressed by the failure to seek universal suffrage but unwilling to oppose the enfranchisement of the freedmen, led those who founded the American Woman Suffrage Association (AWSA)—supporting the Fifteenth Amendment but working assiduously for woman suffrage. Unlike some historians, Kerr insists that the issue of whether or not to support the Fifteenth Amendment was *the* issue leading to the great schism of 1869 and the creation of the rival suffrage associations and was recognized as such at the time. Andrea Kerr describes these years—

from the Civil War to the reunification of the AWSA and NWSA in 1890s—as very difficult ones for the movement, where support was limited and allies few. Yet accepting help from would-be allies sometimes proved to be very costly for the movement. Kerr argues that the NWSA's brief embrace of the notorious Victoria Woodhull tarnished the reputation of the entire movement despite the AWSA's attempts at "damage control." Kerr also argues for the importance of Lucy Stone and the AWSA during these years, insisting that the AWSA was larger and better organized than the NWSA during the 1870s, and that their strategy was later vindicated. Though the NWSA deprecated the AWSA's state-by-state approach and willingness to work for partial suffrage, by the 1880s they recognized that these steps were necessary in order to build enough support for woman suffrage that a federal amendment could finally be won.

In part because her rivals, Anthony and Stone, co-edited the *History of Woman Suffrage*, Stone is the lesser-known of the three pioneering suffragists. Many remember her primarily for her insistence on being known after her marriage to Henry Blackwell as "Lucy Stone only": shortly after her death in 1893 a Lucy Stone League, consisting of women who "kept their own names," was formed that continued into the 1970s. A charismatic and compelling orator, Stone had a talent for organization that greatly benefited the nineteenth-century suffrage movement.

★　★　★　★　★

AS THE WOMAN SUFFRAGE MOVEMENT entered its second decade of activity in the early 1860s, its leaders could look back on a period of extraordinary accomplishment. From its modest beginnings—an 1846 public debate on woman suffrage at Oberlin College, the first public address on the subject of woman's rights in 1847, the Seneca Falls woman's rights convention of 1848—the movement for women's rights entered a period of growth unprecedented in the annals of reform. By the time of the first national convention held in 1850 in Worcester, Massachusetts, woman's rights, including the right of suffrage, had swept the land. The reform attracted so much attention that in 1854, P.T. Barnum sought to duplicate his success with the tour of Swedish singer Jenny Lind by hiring Lucy Stone to take her series of woman's rights lectures on a national tour.[1]

Antebellum Suffrage Activity: The "Golden Age"

The decade following the Worcester convention comprises a "golden age" of woman suffrage activity. Though the movement's proximate roots were intertwined with the antislavery organization, by the 1850s, woman suffrage had assumed a distinct reform identity. Loosely organized under the leadership of Lucy Stone, Elizabeth Cady Stanton, and Susan B. Anthony, women raised funds and managed finances, organized conventions, developed strategies, delineated goals, and determined the direction of the movement. They planned and carried

out petition drives and scheduled legislative hearings. With funds collected at meetings supplemented by earnings from lectures, women paid for the printing and distribution of books, tracts, and proceedings of the many local and national conventions. Groups of women formed education cadres and small political action committees in cities, towns, and rural hamlets.

The momentum gained by the fledgling movement in the 1850s came to a halt when Fort Sumter was fired upon in April of 1861. Woman suffrage activity ended while the American Civil War raged. In the war's aftermath, the fortunes of woman suffrage and the tangled politics of Reconstruction combined in a web of events and circumstances that threatened to reverse suffrage advances of the 1850s, making the enfranchisement of women an ever-more-distant goal. Out of this postwar chaos, two woman suffrage societies arose—the American and the National. For more than two decades, the two organizations labored separately toward the same goal. The story of one wing of suffragists—the National Woman Suffrage Association—has been told in the *History of Woman Suffrage*. A comprehensive history of the other wing—the American Woman Suffrage Association—has yet to be written.

Attempts to make clear distinctions between the two organizations falter before the changing tactics and strategies that marked both organizations for two decades after the war. Both labored more or less consistently for suffrage by Constitutional amendment; both eventually agreed on the need for state, municipal, and presidential suffrage. Lacking political experience, unschooled in consensus building, without the education formed in board room and back room, woman suffragists had to learn how to gain political ground the hard way—through trial and error. The ideologically driven but politically unwise actions of one wing of suffragists caused the woman suffrage movement to all but founder in the 1870s; the other association's attempt at damage control could not stem the flight of members nor turn the tide of public opinion that threatened to reverse the gains of two decades.

A look at events leading up to the division into two separate societies raises provocative questions about the politics of race and class. When the rights of two groups—in this instance, Black males and White women—came into conflict, as they did in the post-Civil War period, present-day historians face a problem of interpretation that possesses many of the same features as the original dilemma. In the years immediately after the war, the rights of women Black and White, former slaves and free, came to be counterpoised against the rights of newly emancipated Black males and free Southern Black males. The reaction to this conflict posed serious problems for woman suffragists then, and for women's historians now. In casting the Reconstruction dispute as hinging on universal suffrage versus Black male suffrage, as some historians have done, we are at risk of replicating the mistakes of those whose political misalliances and poor judgment led to a brief-but-regrettable period of egregiously racist and elitist conduct. When a small splinter group of woman suffragists chose to lobby for educated suffrage and to campaign actively to prevent Black freedmen from voting, the issues raised by their

conduct transcend the theoretical. By casting this benighted campaign as a quest for universal rights, we risk perpetuating a means-and-ends argument that fails to take into account the political exigencies of a particular historical moment.[2]

The Competing Claims of Race and Sex

The first intimation of trouble arising from competing claims based upon race and sex came while the Civil War was still in progress. The war had occasioned a dramatic increase in both the size and scope of women's organized benevolent work. Seeking a wider political role for women, Elizabeth Cady Stanton and Susan B. Anthony issued a "call" in the spring of 1863 for a meeting of the "Loyal Women of the Nation." Its language both echoes Revolutionary-era notions of Republican Womanhood and rhetorically transforms them into ideas of women's full political equality. Drafted by Stanton, the call provoked women to think of themselves as equal political participants in the struggle: "Woman is equally interested and responsible with man in the final settlement of this problem of self-government; therefore let none stand idle spectators now.... [I]t is high time for the daughters of the revolution, in solemn council, to...lay hold of their birthright of freedom, and keep it a sacred trust for all coming generations."[3]

Lucy Stone presided over the gathering of leaders at the inaugural meeting of the Loyal Women. A series of resolutions committing women to an all-out effort to secure to all African Americans a full share of constitutional rights and privileges passed handily. The fifth resolution, calling for "no peace until the civil and political rights of all citizens of African descent and all women are practically established," provoked opposition from those who feared that adding woman's rights to antislavery would encumber the push for freedom and civil rights for slaves. Here was the first indication of future antagonism. Despite serious objections, the resolution passed.[4]

The women of the Loyal League, led principally by the efforts of Stanton and Anthony, eventually gathered four hundred thousand signatures on a petition urging Congress to pass a Thirteenth Amendment ending slavery. Their labors earned them praise and respect from reformers and politicians alike, but the small skirmish at the organizing convention was a bellwether of the larger conflict that would erupt over the inclusion of women in the push for civil rights at war's end. The history of events leading up to the 1869 split in the woman's rights movement furnishes a cautionary chapter on the perils of trying to compel the cart of ideology to pull the horse of politics.[5]

With the end of the war in sight in January, 1865, Stone and Anthony presented a resolution calling for combining woman's rights and antislavery organizations at a meeting of the New England Anti-Slavery Society. To their dismay, Wendell Phillips deferred action on their proposal until the May national meeting. In the months leading up to the May meeting, Stone and Anthony corresponded furiously with suffrage and antislavery leaders about the necessity for including woman suffrage in the press for Black suffrage.[6]

At the May meeting, Wendell Phillips, a longtime friend of woman suffrage, insisted that this was the "Negro's Hour," and women must wait. Where the suffragists saw the hour as propitious, Phillips believed that adding woman suffrage would doom prospects for passage of a Black suffrage amendment. The political situation of emancipated Blacks was steadily deteriorating due to the passage of harsh and punitive Black Codes in the South. Northern Republicans were also aware that counting non-voting emancipated slaves as full persons, (rather than the three-fifths status apportioned by the Constitution), would gain fifteen potentially Democratic seats in Congress for the South. By enfranchising freedmen, Republicans hoped to gain substantial voters, a prospect appealing to non-reform as well as reform Republicans. Given the urgency of the moment, Wendell Phillips and other Republican leaders believed that passage of a Black suffrage amendment was possible. They realized, however, that even if Congress were to pass the amendment, its ratification would be difficult, and they refused to endanger its passage by including women.[7]

Concerned that woman suffrage was to be abandoned in the push for Black male suffrage, Stone, Stanton, and Anthony circulated woman suffrage petitions, lobbied for universal suffrage in the District of Columbia and organized a Woman's Rights convention at which they planned to go forward with plans for an Equal Rights Association with or without the cooperation of the existing antislavery organization. At the May 1866 convention, the two groups voted to merge, and the American Equal Rights Association (AERA) was born.[8]

In June of 1866, Congress passed the Fourteenth Amendment, introducing the word "male" into the Constitution as a qualification for voting. This dashed any lingering hopes suffragists might still have nurtured regarding universal suffrage. At an AERA convention in Albany, New York, that autumn, Stanton made a speech denouncing Republicans and praising Democrats, whose support she had hoped to gain—a hope that would later prove vain. Frederick Douglass objected, pointing out that the Democratic Party was on record as opposing any move to give suffrage or civil rights to Blacks; their support for woman suffrage, warned Douglass, was but "a trick of the enemy" intended to split reformers on racial lines. Douglass begged suffragists to resist the ploy, but Stanton and Anthony ignored his warning.[9]

Following the Albany convention, Stone, Stanton, and Anthony embarked on a tour of New England and the Mid-Atlantic states. They set up AERA adjuncts, spearheaded petition drives and lobbied Republican legislators. Toward the end of January, the three suffragists were on board a train to New York when a blizzard stranded them for more than twenty-four hours. The snowbound train offered a captive audience of "doctors, lawyers, and legislators." Stanton, Stone, and Anthony "separated themselves far apart and each one gathered a crowd and talked and answered questions. They had a most merry time," an observer wrote, "and did a vast deal of good, I have no doubt."[10]

If suffragists gave the appearance of unity, differences were emerging. Though Stone protested "the poor half loaf of justice for the Negro, poisoned by its lack of justice for every woman in the land," she was growing more concerned about the deteriorating political condition of Southern Blacks. Matters came to a head in the Kansas campaign of 1867. The Kansas debacle began with a simple request to AERA headquarters from Sam Wood, a Kansas Republican. He asked if Lucy Stone and other woman suffrage workers would come to Kansas to campaign on behalf of a woman suffrage referendum. They agreed to his request.[11]

Kansas: Issues of Race and Sex Collide

Still bearing the scars of its recent bloody past, Kansas in 1867 was a hotbed of mistrust and malfeasance. The Republican-dominated legislature had ratified the Fourteenth Amendment; those who had labored since 1862 for Black suffrage then called for a November referendum on a proposal to strike the word "White" from the state's list of voter qualifications. Sam Wood, a legislator who had voted against Black suffrage every year since 1862, immediately proposed adding a referendum that would strike the word "male," thereby enfranchising women. Blacks accused Wood of deliberately trying to sabotage Black suffrage by linking it to woman suffrage.[12]

Into this political quagmire came Lucy Stone and her husband Henry Blackwell, brimming with optimism and armed with two hundred and fifty pounds of suffrage leaflets they would distribute throughout the state. Blackwell, brother to the pioneer physicians Elizabeth and Emily Blackwell, was an ebullient optimist. "This is a glorious country, Mrs. S., and a glorious people," he wrote Stanton soon after their arrival. Stone and Blackwell stayed first at the home of former governor Charles Robinson, a relative of Stone's by marriage and a Republican Party leader who warned them that Sam Wood's proposal was an attempt to defeat Black suffrage by splitting Republicans. Within weeks, it became clear that party unity was not going to withstand the test of woman suffrage. "I can not send you a telegraphic dispatch as you wish for just now there is a plot to get the Republican Party to ... agree to canvass *only* for [striking] the word 'White,'" Stone wrote Anthony in early May. Soon afterward, Republicans voted by a very narrow majority to campaign for Black suffrage only.[13]

Returning to New York, Stone took over the AERA office, while Stanton and Anthony went to Kansas to continue the campaign that was growing more and more bitterly divided along racial lines. Newspapers reported suffragist Olympia Brown as inveighing "against placing the dirty, immoral, degraded negro before a White woman." Sam Wood engaged in a nasty editorial exchange with Black leaders. Long-time Republican friends of woman suffrage questioned the political wisdom of continuing their support.[14] The situation worsened in late October when Stanton and Anthony joined forces with George Francis Train, a Copperhead (i.e. Northerner who sympathized with the South in the Civil War) and a self-

Lucy Stone, c. 1880
SOPHIA SMITH COLLECTION

Poster, 1867 Kansas campaign
SCHLESINGER LIBRARY, RADCLIFFE INSTITUTE,
HARVARD UNIVERSITY

proclaimed candidate for president. He described his purpose: "By talking woman suffrage the Democrats 'beat the Republicans.' By stumping for woman suffrage Train 'beats the Republicans.' Copperheads know that the Republicans can carry Kansas unless they are divided."[15]

Back East, suffragists were dismayed to see an AERA-funded announcement of Train's entry into their campaign. Stone begged Anthony not to use AERA funds to campaign against Black suffrage. Train was making woman suffrage "a laughingstock everywhere," she wrote, lamenting that Train's presence was "enough to condemn [woman suffrage] in the minds of all persons not already convinced." Anthony ignored her, and she and Train toured Kansas together, she speaking in favor of woman suffrage and denouncing the "rotten" Republican Party; he making derogatory and insulting remarks about Blacks and uttering demagogic pronouncements about the dangers of Black suffrage. "Carry negro suffrage," he warned, "and we shall see some White woman in a case of negro rape being tried by 12 negro jurymen." Train sent newspapers copies of his and Anthony's speeches and paid to publish and distribute booklets as well. Divisions within the Repub-lican Party in Kansas and Train's association with the suffrage leaders drew national press attention. Train's anti-

Black campaign put Republicans who had remained staunchly pro-woman suffrage into an untenable position.[16]

Both woman suffrage and Black suffrage proposals went down to defeat. Stanton and Anthony afterward publicly credited Train with delivering the 9,070 votes cast for woman suffrage, ignoring the evidence that showed that votes for woman suffrage came from heavily Republican counties. In the aftermath of the defeat, Republican Party leaders blamed the "side issue" of woman suffrage for the failure of Black suffrage, sounding the alarm for any future attempts to combine both measures at the polls.[17]

Following the Kansas campaign, Stanton and Anthony announced that Train was financing a tour in which he would share the speakers' platform with them in cities and towns throughout the Midwest and East. Abolitionist and longtime friend of woman suffrage, William Lloyd Garrison, wrote that he was "mortified and astonished beyond measure in seeing Elizabeth Cady Stanton and Susan B. Anthony traveling about the country with that harlequin and semi-lunatic George Francis Train ... denouncing Republicanism and lauding Copperheadism .... The colored people and their advocates have not a more abusive assailant than this same Train; especially when he ... delights to ring the charges upon the "nigger," "nigger," "nigger," *ad nauseum.*"[18]

Stanton and Anthony turned a deaf ear to Train's anti-Black invective, however. The connection did not end with the close of the speaking tour. Returning East, the two women accepted Train's offer to establish a newspaper that would jointly serve his political aims and the cause of woman suffrage. He named the paper *The Revolution.* "So long as Mr. Train speaks nobly for the woman," Anthony wrote, "why should we repudiate his services, even if he does ring the charges 'nigger, nigger, nigger'?" As Stanton explained, "All there is about [Train] is that he has made it possible for us to establish a paper. If the Devil himself had come up and said ladies I will help you establish a paper I should have said Amen!"[19]

Dissension Deepens, Conflict Erupts

At the May, 1868, meeting of the AERA, Olympia Brown, who had remained close to Stanton and Anthony, made a speech critical of the Republican Party. Frederick Douglass rose to object, characterizing Republicans as "largely in favor of enfranchising woman." He asked Brown: "Where is the Democrat who favors woman suffrage?" When a voice in the audience shouted "Train!" Douglass erupted: "Yes, he hates the negro, and that is what stimulates him to substitute the cry of emancipation for women." Following Douglass's speech, Anthony introduced a surprise resolution urging women to oppose the Fourteenth Amendment and to resolve to work for woman suffrage only. Her resolutions were defeated by the near-unanimous vote of all present. Immediately after the 1868 convention, Anthony set up a Woman Suffrage Society, with Stanton as president. [20]

In January 1869, Stone, Stanton, and Anthony were in Washington, where Congress was drafting the Fifteenth Amendment. The women unsuccessfully attempted to convince legislators, in particular Charles Sumner, to make it a universal suffrage amendment. Sumner apologized to the women, but he could see no political way to assure Black enfranchisement if women were to be included. On February 27, Congress passed the proposed amendment, forbidding voter discrimination on the basis of "race, color, or previous condition of servitude." Immediately afterward, on March 15, 1869, George Julian proposed a Sixteenth Amendment forbidding voter discrimination based upon sex.[21]

Throughout the spring, Stanton continued to publish anti-Fifteenth Amendment editorials in *The Revolution*. In mid-April, Anthony called an emergency meeting of the executive committee of the AERA at which she tried and failed to get the committee to pass resolutions opposing ratification of the Fifteenth Amendment. If the AERA was willing to do all in its power to obtain suffrage for women, it refused to work to prevent Black freedmen from voting. The stage was set for a major battle.[22]

"It is a pity that the cause of 'Equal Rights' should have been so disgraced by such a lawless scrabble for entrance tickets as occurred in the vestibule of the Hall last evening," said the Brooklyn *Daily Union*. "Men and women remorselessly crushing and tearing one another, and suffocating the solitary policeman who had the matter in charge." Indeed, throngs had besieged Steinway Hall, the site of the May 1869 AERA convention, hoping to witness the anticipated showdown.[23]

The opening salvo was fired by abolitionist Stephen Foster when he voiced objection to the nomination of Stanton to the vice presidency, because she had "publicly repudiated the principles of the society." Pressed by Stanton for particulars, Foster replied:

> These ladies stand at the head of a paper which has adopted as its motto "Educated Suffrage".... *The Revolution* lately had an article headed "That Infamous Fifteenth Amendment" .... I am not willing to take George Francis Train on this platform with his ridicule of the negro and opposition to his enfranchisement.

Anthony responded with an impassioned defense of Train in which she protested that he had been *"almost* sent by God to furnish funds for *The Revolution."* This was too much for Foster, who replied angrily: "If you choose to put officers here that ridicule the negro and pronounce the Fifteenth Amendment infamous, why I must retire." [24]

Frederick Douglass then came forward and denounced Stanton's insistence on characterizing Blacks as "Sambo" and "bootblacks" in *The Revolution*. He begged her to cease her anti-Fifteenth Amendment campaign. Anthony responded to his plea by laying a match to whatever oil remained on the troubled waters. If the "entire people" could not have suffrage, she said, then it must go "to the most intelligent first," for if "intelligence, justice, and morality, are to have precedence in

the Government, let the question of woman be brought up first and that of the negro last." Anthony proceeded to introduce resolutions opposing ratification of the Fifteenth Amendment and in favor of educated suffrage. Lucy Stone rose and urged Anthony to withdraw the offending resolutions, arguing:

> We are lost if we turn away from the middle principle and argue for one class.... I thank God for the Fifteenth Amendment, and hope that it will be adopted in every State. I will be thankful in my soul if *any* body can get out of the terrible pit."[25]

Stanton's response to Stone's plea for withdrawal of the anti-Black resolutions was to announce that she "did not believe in allowing ignorant negroes and foreigners to make laws for her to obey."[26]

Dissidents Form New Suffrage Organization

Put to the vote, both Anthony's anti-Fifteenth Amendment and the Educated Suffrage resolutions were defeated. Instead, the AERA body voted overwhelmingly to ratify resolutions favoring ratification of the Fifteenth Amendment and calling for adoption of a Sixteenth Amendment. They also passed a resolution calling for the establishment of a national woman suffrage organization comprising a network of state and local associations. Stanton and Anthony decided to pre-empt the AERA by forming a new "national" organization immediately, rather than after preliminary correspondence and meetings, as they had earlier agreed to do.[27]

The following week's *Revolution* noted that a national woman suffrage association had been formed in the parlor of the Woman's Bureau following the close of the AERA convention. The splinter group, calling itself the National Woman Suffrage Association, immediately passed a resolution opposing the proposed amendment. "All Wise Women Will Oppose the Fifteenth Amendment," editorialized Stanton. In the summer and fall of 1869, *The Revolution* stepped up its anti-Black rhetoric, making references to the "barbarism," "brute force," and "tyranny" of Black men.[28]

The majority of woman suffragists worried about the effect of Stanton and Anthony's campaign on the prospects for ratification of the Fifteenth Amendment. "Just arouse Mrs. Stanton's ire," wrote Stone, "and with her paper circulating largely in the doubtful Western States, she can defeat the 15th Amendment." An editorial in the *Woman's Advocate* of July 1869, called for "a National Organization," that would "be careful it deny no right, even to the most hapless or degraded of God's children." The organization must concentrate its efforts "on the proposed Sixteenth Amendment and such immediate legislation by Congress as may be obtained without any Amendment." At the next meeting of the New England Woman Suffrage Association, (NEWSA) members voted to work to form "an organization at once more comprehensive and more widely representative."[29]

Formation of the American Woman Suffrage Association

Writing to Elizabeth Buffum Chace, president of the Rhode Island Woman Suffrage Association, Stone explained the need for a new organization:

> I think it is a great pity to try and create or give currency to the idea that the Woman's Movement is opposed to the 15th Amendment.
>
> At every convention ... we have adopted resolutions heartily endorsing the 15th amendment.... It is not true that our movement is opposed to the negro. But it will be very easy to make it so, to the mutual harm of both causes....[30]

Modern-day historians who describe the differences between the two suffrage associations as lying in federal versus state suffrage work, or radical versus conservative ideologies, or who ascribe the division to "personal" factors ignore the clear and compelling reasons put forward at the time of the split.

Similarly, historians who conflate woman suffrage history in the decade after the Civil War with the National wing rather than with the larger American Woman Suffrage Association formed later that year at Cleveland, Ohio, ignore such critical factors as representation, size, membership, budget, tactics, and political impact. For more than a decade, the "National" organization consisted of small meetings held in New York City, its principal effort an annual January convention in Washington D.C. Mainstream suffragists—the great majority of those in attendance at the 1869 convention—had refused to be drawn into an either/or campaign to defeat Black male suffrage, nor would they campaign for educated suffrage as a way of putting White women's interests ahead of those of freedmen.[31]

The American Woman Suffrage Association (AWSA) declared its purpose as securing the ballot to women, based upon the belief that "suffrage for woman is the great key that will unlock to her the doors of social and political equality." In pursuit of its goals, the AWSA proposed to organize for suffrage state by state, and to "prepare and circulate petitions to State Legislatures, to Congress, or to constitutional conventions in behalf of the legal and political equality of women," as well as to publish and distribute tracts and documents at below cost, and "employ lecturers and agents" to expand the organization.[32]

The volume of publications alone was staggering: in a single year AWSA sent out almost 216,000 leaflets from its Boston headquarters. At times, the organization had as many as four paid field agents who lectured and set up state and local societies in cities, towns, and villages throughout the country. AWSA's delegate basis ensured that state and local organizations would be represented at conventions held in different regions of the country so as to obtain the widest possible representation.[33]

In its early years, AWSA gained membership and auxiliaries at a rapid rate. In 1870, Lucy Stone began publication of a new woman's rights newspaper, *The Woman's Journal*. "Woman Suffrage has made astonishing progress," its editors reported. It had been "established in Wyoming, adopted in Utah, and submitted to

the vote...in Vermont," while "Minnesota has passed a bill to submit it to the concurrent votes of men and women." The article enumerated those states where woman suffrage was under consideration.[34]

In May of 1870, there were two woman suffrage conventions in New York City. At the AWSA meeting, a large crowd approved resolutions promising to continue state organizational work while supporting adoption of a federal woman suffrage amendment. Across town, at the NWSA convention, Stanton delineated what she called the "essential issue" dividing the two associations. The American society wished to "carry the measure step by step, year by year through the states" thereby forcing "educated refined women ... to kneel at the feet of paupers, knaves, and drunkards." Stanton made clear her scorn for this approach, saying that "those who have the stomach for such work" could "canvass every state from Maine to California, and humbly ask Tom, Dick, and Harry, Patrick, Hans, Yung-Tung and Sambo, to recognize such women as Lucretia Mott, Ernestine Rose, Susan B. Anthony and Anna Dickinson as *their* political equals."[35]

The NWSA rejection of any state-by-state work held for almost a dozen years. The American wing, on the other hand, believed that intensive, state-by-state organization would lay the groundwork for eventual adoption and ratification of a federal amendment, should such an amendment prove constitutionally possible. The constitutionality of enfranchising women by federal amendment was brought into question by a number of court cases in the 1870s.[36]

Although partial forms of suffrage were problematic at best, they were nonetheless a factor in the final push for suffrage. When at last the Nineteenth Amendment was passed by Congress and sent to the state legislatures for ratification in June of 1919, its success was far from assured. Despite strong opposition, state legislators were aware that partial suffrage had made women's vote a force in national politics; women were able to vote for 339 of 531 presidential electors. The ratification margin was narrow, and in states where women could vote, the Nineteenth Amendment was ratified most easily.[37]

By the early 1880s, the National wing had come around to the American strategy. Anthony was quoted as saying, "I don't know the exact number of States we shall have to have... but I do know that there will come a day when that number will automatically and resistlessly act on the Congress of the United States to compel the submission of a federal suffrage amendment."[38]

The emphasis on state-by-state political organization, and the lobbying of legislators for various forms of partial suffrage was an arduous task. The slow but steady trickle of states and towns granting school suffrage, municipal suffrage, presidential suffrage, and occasionally, full voting rights to women kept suffragists' hopes alive, though the gains were painfully slow in coming, and losses often outnumbered gains.[39]

Suffrage campaigns and the weekly publication of a newspaper were costly. To raise funds, AWSA and *The Woman's Journal* editors staged a series of "bazaars" in

Boston. These were enormous undertakings, usually occupying all three major public auditoriums, where merchants, entertainers, craftsmen, and restaurateurs donated time, goods, and services. There were daily theatrical and musical offerings, booths displaying crafts and various kinds of merchandise. Cakes, containing gold rings and little china dolls, were sold by the slice. At large concessions, women could buy "cooking-stoves, clothes-reels, bed-blankets, washing machines, wringers, pianos, sewing-machines of every variety, flowers, boxes of dried fish, soap, starch.... An art gallery displayed donated works, and one entire building had been "floored over and transformed into a large dining-room and restaurant." Hundreds of workers volunteered their time, and profits, usually eight to ten thousand dollars, went back into the suffrage effort.[40]

Woman Suffrage Linked to Free Love, Blackmail

Unfortunately, many of these organizational gains were undone by another misalliance. The NWSA leaders' actions in 1871 landed suffragists in an ever widening net of scandal and intrigue that caused membership rolls to plummet and had hecklers shouting "Free Love!" at suffrage gatherings for decades to come. In January of 1871, Anthony welcomed Victoria Woodhull onto the NWSA platform in Washington following the latter's memorial before Congress claiming the right of suffrage for women based upon a Fourteenth Amendment argument. The possibility of a constitutional remedy for women's disfranchisement, accompanied by Woodhull's promise to donate ten thousand dollars to the NWSA won her acceptance among its leaders, a move they would bitterly regret.

Though only thirty-three at the time of her entrance into the woman suffrage movement, Victoria Woodhull had already led a full and remarkable life. She had worked variously as a prostitute, a mesmerist and spiritualist who claimed Demosthenes as her medium, a quack healer, blackmailer, extortionist, performance artist, stockbroker, journalist, and at the time of her entrance into the woman suffrage campaign, self-proclaimed candidate for president of the United States. Woodhull was simultaneously dubbed "Mrs. Satan" in a Nast cartoon, called "Queen of the Prostitutes" by the daily papers.[41]

Before she was eighteen, Woodhull had married, borne two children, and been charged along with other members of her family with numerous crimes. Following a "magnetic healing session" with millionaire financier Cornelius Vanderbilt, she and her sister, Tennie C. Claflin, suddenly came into enough money to purchase a stock brokerage on Wall Street and to begin publication of a newspaper, *Woodhull & Claflin's Weekly*. Both in her newspaper and in her public speeches, Woodhull championed "free love." News that Anthony had welcomed Woodhull onto the NWSA platform caused Stanton to write begging her not to "have another Train affair with Mrs. Woodhull." Stanton would come to embrace Woodhull too. The initial flurry of interest in Woodhull subsided, and for a brief period, calm reigned.[42]

The following May, Stone opened the AWSA meeting in New York City with an account of the year's progress: Woman suffrage proposals were under legislative consideration in nearly every Eastern, Northern, and Western state, and despite repeated defeats, they drew larger average votes each year. Women were enfranchised in both Utah and Wyoming. Over fifty new county societies and five new state societies had been organized in Massachusetts alone. Stone and Livermore had been accredited party delegates to the Republican convention; the December bazaar netted close to $8,000; the Sixteenth Amendment was reintroduced in Congress, and the bill to grant woman suffrage in the District of Columbia had made a good legislative showing. With the circulation of *The Woman's Journal* nearing five thousand, she told the assembled gathering, there was much to celebrate.

Had Stone seen that day's New York *Tribune* with its bold headline, "Woman Suffrage and Free Love," she might have been less sanguine. The reference was to the rival NWSA convention and "[t]he people who 'work with and for' Mrs. Woodhull, new leader of the Woman Suffrage party, Woman Suffrage candidate for the Presidency and editor of *Woodhull & Claflin's Weekly*."[43]

Following the NWSA "Woodhull Convention," as it came to be known, membership in Anthony's society fell off so drastically that for the duration of 1871 and 1872, its leaders were able to hold "only parlor meetings." Former members set up separate suffrage organizations. Most of the New York women reorganized as the New York Central Woman Suffrage Association. The Connecticut Woman Suffrage Association led by Olympia Brown severed its tie to the NWSA and declared itself an independent society resolving to work *"only* for the elective franchise." In Iowa, Pennsylvania, Maryland, and Washington, resolutions were passed disavowing any tie to the Woodhull organization. By the end of 1871, fourteen of fifteen state suffrage societies had voted to become auxiliary to AWSA.[44]

In Boston in 1871, an Anti-Suffrage Committee was formed, and it was quick to offer Victoria Woodhull as "proof" of the serious threat to the sanctity of the family posed by those who claimed for women the right of suffrage. Propriety, no matter how numerous or decorous its adherents, was not news; Woodhull was. Waging a desperate counter-campaign, the Massachusetts AWSA paid three lecture agents/ organizers to set up twenty to thirty meetings per week in cities and towns throughout New England, a prodigious political undertaking.[45]

Following a free-love speech by Victoria Woodhull, newspaper headlines proclaimed: "Died of Free Love, November 25th In Steinway Hall the Woman Suffrage Movement." Woodhull's association with the NWSA lasted little more than a year; by May of 1872, its leaders had severed all ties to her. The New York suffragists' final disenchantment grew out of Woodhull's extortion campaign that spring, followed by her attempt to use the NWSA platform to campaign for the presidency of the United States. Woodhull's extortion methods consisted of presenting her victims with dummy copies of the front page of *Woodhull &*

Claflin's Weekly that featured detailed, wholly spurious allegations of supposed sexual indiscretions. She then demanded $500 to keep the story out of print. Woodhull tried this with many suffragists, among them Elizabeth Phelps, Laura Curtis Bullard, Lillie Devereaux Blake, and even Susan B. Anthony herself.[46]

In May, Anthony learned that Woodhull intended to take over the 1872 NWSA convention and use it as a nominating meeting for her presidential candidacy. Cutting short a lecture trip, Anthony returned to New York and ordered the janitor to douse the gas lights as Woodhull mounted the stage, afterwards writing, "A sad day for me; all came near to being lost. Our ship was so nearly stranded by leaving the helm to others, that we rescued it only by a hair's breadth." The "ship" of suffrage was not yet stranded, but it was a vessel with a serious leak.[47]

Scandal Erupts

Woodhull's withdrawal in the summer of 1872 and a split in the ranks of Republicans resulted in a momentary political triumph for the suffragists. With Horace Greeley running as an independent candidate against them, Republicans were persuaded in the 1872 election to include in their platform a carefully worded and less-than-wholehearted woman suffrage plank—a promise of "respectful consideration" of the woman suffrage question.[48]

Buoyed by this political action and free of the Woodhull alliance, Anthony proposed having the two rival associations "cooperate and make a systematic campaign covering the whole ground." Stone, in the midst of an AWSA campaign to orchestrate demonstrations involving half a million Republican women throughout New England as a means of pressuring politicians to press their claim for suffrage after the election, ignored Anthony's peace overture.[49]

Days before the November election, *Woodhull & Claflin's Weekly* appeared on the newsstands. Its lead article accused Henry Ward Beecher, president of the AWSA and one of the most famous and respected clergymen in the nation, of having seduced a number of his female parishioners, among these women, suffragist Elizabeth Tilton. The entire first printing of the *Weekly* sold out within minutes. Copies commanded up to forty dollars apiece, and newsboys and carriages created gridlock on lower Broad Street as they awaited a second edition. Along with the allegations against Beecher, the paper accused Luther Challis, a wealthy Brooklyn stockbroker, of sexual misconduct in a story replete with lurid and sensational sexual details. Woodhull was arrested under the recently- enacted Comstock Law and thrown into the Ludlow Street jail; Challis promptly sued for libel.[50]

Any hopes the suffragists had of escaping the scandal were quickly dashed. The newspapers focused on the woman's rights connection. The accused adulterer, Beecher, was president of the AWSA; the presumably wronged husband, Theodore Tilton, had headed the NWSA, and the imprisoned Victoria Woodhull was calling herself the woman suffrage candidate for president of the United States. If the connection to woman suffrage was inevitable, the tarring of all suffragists with the

brush of immorality seemed an unduly harsh consequence. A Midwestern editorialist described the irrationality of the public response to the scandal, writing that he regretted the injustice to "hundreds of thousands of honest men and pure women earnestly in favor of the [suffrage] reform to say that they were following at the leadstring of the notorious female, Mrs. Wood hull...." Despite the "unreason" of linking the majority of suffragists to free love, "five out of six people think so, and cannot be led to think anything else." [51]

The Beecher-Tilton trial was the longest and most-publicized trial to have occurred up to its time. For more than six months, the testimony of its various witnesses occupied the front pages of newspapers across the country. Woman suffragists struggled unsuccessfully to keep the political question of suffrage separate from the public sensation. From Ohio, suffrage workers reported that "'free love' (whatever it may mean) is the most efficient agent employed to frighten people from our ranks." The *Des Moines Register* headlined its woman suffrage report "Halt in Progress of Woman Suffrage." Indeed, throughout the country, support at the state and local level evaporated rapidly. Formerly friendly legislators advised woman suffragists that in the "current free-love storm" it would be best to table woman suffrage legislation. [52]

Although a jury failed to convict Beecher, voting nine to three for his innocence, the damage had been done. The defection of formerly staunch supporters cut deeply into existing suffrage ranks and crippled the drive to recruit and organize new members. Meetings were canceled; proprietors refused to rent their halls to suffragists. Twenty years later, as suffragists tried to post notices of their meetings, it was not unusual to hear some man shout across the street to another, "Are you going to hear Woodhull tonight?" A Vermont suffragist insisted that the Woodhull matter "set the cause back twenty years," and that country people persisted in thinking as late as 1889 that women wanted suffrage "for free love." [53]

In the Wake of Disaster: Rebuilding Begins

Lucy Stone's anniversary address at the following spring's AWSA convention was the most negative she had ever given. Though she tried to sound upbeat, she had never felt less optimistic. Membership was falling off at such a rate that the Massachusetts Woman Suffrage Association was forced to lower the number required for a quorum at business meetings. Attendance at the May NEWSA anniversary had been down by more than a third.

As new women's organizations sprang up, leaders were careful to distance themselves from woman suffrage organizations. When the Association for the Advancement of Women was formed, newspapers characterized it as an attempt to "make a 'New Departure' from Woman Suffrage." When members tried to include woman suffrage as one of the aims of the new organization, their efforts went down to defeat.[54]

The Woodhull misalliance did incalculable harm. While present-day historians may sympathize with Woodhull's radical politics, it is nonetheless clear that

Stanton and Anthony's embrace of an exotic, blackmailing, free-love advocate in the 1870s was a political disaster for woman suffrage. While the Woodhull connection directly tarnished the image of suffragists, it indirectly controlled the direction and tactics of the AWSA from the early 1870s on, as the "other" wing struggled to counter the image of impropriety with a purity crusade. "We *need* every clean soul to help us, now when such a flood of what is fatal to the peace, and purity of the family, is rolled in on our question," Lucy Stone wrote to a suffrage supporter in the midst of the Woodhull imbroglio."[55]

Eventually, memory of the scandals faded. The AWSA, which had been the larger and stronger organization, began to lose ground to the NWSA in the early 1880s as Anthony led the latter organization in a strong campaign to "capture" New England suffrage societies. Declining membership rolls and a shift by the NWSA to both state and federal work made Stone more amenable to merging the two societies. In 1887, Lucy Stone and her daughter, Alice Stone Blackwell, met with Susan B. Anthony and her protégé, Rachel Foster. Together, they agreed upon a committee to effect a reconciliation between the two societies. It was February 1890, before the two societies would formally merge as the National American Woman Suffrage Association, (NAWSA) but the groundwork for rapprochement had been laid.

Because Stanton and Anthony wrote the history of the movement, modern historians appear to accept the authors' *ex post facto* characterization of the 1869 split as devolving from tactical differences. All parties at the time of the split understood the issue to be the acceptance or rejection of Stanton and Anthony's campaign to defeat the Fifteenth Amendment. Mainstream suffragists in the American wing—the overwhelming majority—found the anti-Fifteenth Amendment campaign not only politically unwise, but morally repugnant.[56] Marginalized by their unpopular actions, the National wing—effectively a splinter group for more than a decade—found itself involved in a series of costly misalliances. In the decades that followed, Stanton and Anthony did extraordinary work for the cause of woman's rights; nevertheless, the political consequences of their earlier actions furnish a cautionary tale to those who continue to work for full equality for women today. Consensus building, the choice of rhetoric, decisions about which issues to include or exclude, and other strategic questions are as problematic to feminists today as those that confronted our foremothers. Ignoring what is painful in woman suffrage history diminishes the capacity to build on its strengths by learning from past mistakes. Even as today's historians acknowledge early suffragists' failings, we honor their legacy of courage, brilliance, fury, and power.

Notes

1. Carrie Chapman Catt and Nettie Rogers Shuler, *Woman Suffrage and Politics: The Inner Story of the Suffrage Movement* (New York, 1923), 31; P.T. Barnum to Dr. Trall, February 11, 1854; April 27, 1854; NAWSA Collection, Library of Congress (hereafter NAWSA LC).

2. Ellen Carol DuBois in "Outgrowing the Compact of the Fathers: Equal Rights, Woman Suffrage, and the United States Constitution, 1820-1878," in *Journal of American History* 74 (December, 1987), 841, casts the dispute in these terms. In her recent introduction to the revised edition of *The Elizabeth Cady Stanton-Susan B. Anthony Reader* (Boston, 1992), DuBois admits to a "profound sense of what was lost" in the break of Stanton and Anthony with abolitionists and Republicans. In identifying the 1869 break as the "moment the case for woman suffrage became simultaneously more gender-based and more elitist and racist," (xvi), DuBois conflates the woman suffrage movement with the actions of Stanton and Anthony, whose position on the issue was very much a minority position among suffragists.

3. See Lori Ginzberg, *Women and the Work of Benevolence: Morality, Politics, and Class in the Nineteenth-Century United States* (New Haven, 1990), chpt. 5; Elizabeth Cady Stanton, with Susan B. Anthony, Ida Husted Harper, *History of Woman Suffrage*, (Rochester, N.Y., 1889), 2: 53, (hereafter *HWS*).

4. "The Loyal Women's National League" in *HWS*, Stanton, et. al., 2: 50-67.

5. Eleanor Flexner, *Century of Struggle: The Woman's Rights Movement in the United States* (Cambridge, Mass., 1959), 110-111.

6. 1865 letters in Blackwell Family Collection, Library of Congress, (hereafter B-LC).

7. *New York Times*, May 10, 1865; Ratification of the Fourteenth Amendment would take more than two years. Although Northern sympathy for former slaves ran high, support for black suffrage did not. See William Gillette, *The Right to Vote: Politics and Passage of the Fifteenth Amendment* (Baltimore, 1965), 25-27.

8. *Proceedings* of the 1866 Woman's Rights Convention, (New York, 1866).

9. Ida Husted Harper, *Life and Work of Susan B. Anthony*, 3 vols. (New York, 1969), 1: 261-64.

10. Train incident in Ralph V. Harlow, *Gerrit Smith: Philanthropist and Reformer* (New York, 1972), 471. General suffrage activity in *HWS* 2: 172-82.

11. Lucy Stone to Abby Kelley Foster, January 24, 1867, B-LC.

12. See Eugene Berwanger, *The West and Reconstruction* (Urbana, Ill., 1981), 164-175.

13. Henry Blackwell to Elizabeth Cady Stanton, April 21, 1867, in B-LC; Andrea Moore Kerr, *Lucy Stone: Speaking Out for Equality* (New Brunswick, N.J., 1992), 124; Lucy Stone to Susan B. Anthony, May 9, 1867, B-LC; Daniel Wilder, *Annals of Kansas* (Topeka, 1875), 456.

14. Berwanger, *West*, 171.

15. George Francis Train, *The Great Epigram Campaign of Kansas* (Leavenworth, 1867), 47.

16. Elinor Rice Hays, *Morning Star: A Biography of Lucy Stone, 1818-1897* (New York, 1961), 197; Train, *Epigram*, 48, 58; Gillette, *Right*, 32-33.

17. Charles Robinson to Olympia Brown, December 22, 1867, Olympia Brown Collection, Schlesinger Library, Radcliffe; *Emporia News*, November 15, 1857; Gillette, *Right*, 31-40.

18. William Lloyd Garrison to Alfred Love, December 18, 1867, in Boston Public Library.

19. *The Revolution*, January 29, 1868; Elizabeth Cady Stanton to Olympia Brown, January, 1868, in Olympia Brown Collection.

20. Harper, *Susan B. Anthony*, 1: 304; *HWS*, 2: 341.

21. George W. Julian, *Political Recollections, 1840 to 1879* (Westport, Conn., 1884), 324.

22. Lucy Stone to Samuel May, April 9, 1869, in B-LC.

23. Brooklyn *Daily Union*, May 15, 1869.

24. *The Revolution*, May 20, 1869.

25. Brooklyn *Daily Union*, May 15, 1869; *The New York Times*, May 15, 1869; *HWS* 2: 383-84.

26. *The Revolution*, May 27, 1869.

27. *HWS* 2: 391-92, 320.

28. *The Revolution*, June 3, June 10, October 21, 1869.

29. Lucy Stone to Elizabeth Buffum Chace, July 11, 1869, in NAWSA-LC; *Woman's Advocate*, 2 (July, 1869).

30. Lucy Stone to Elizabeth Buffum Chace, July 11, 1869, in NAWSA-LC.

31. To date, no in-depth organizational history of either association has been done. Records indicate, however, that the AWSA dominated the 1870s, while the NWSA gained ascendance in the 1880s.

32. AWSA Convention in *HWS* 2: 763-64.

33. Lois Bannister Merk, "Massachusetts and the Woman Suffrage Movement," Ph.D. diss., Harvard University, 1961, 198.

34. *The Woman's Journal*, April 9, 1870.

35. Merk, "Massachusetts," 63; *The Revolution*, May 19, 1870.

36. See Catt and Shuler, Woman Suffrage, 96; and DuBois, "Outgrowing the Compact of the Fathers," 857-60.

37. See Catt and Shuler, *Woman Suffrage*; also see Appendix 5, "Partial Suffrage Gains," and chpt. 6, "Campaigning State by State" by Maud Wood Park in NAWSA, *Victory: How Women Won It* (New York, 1940), 69-80.

38. Anthony quote in Catt and Shuler, *Woman Suffrage*, 227.

39. See Catt and Shuler, *Woman Suffrage*; see also appendix and chart in NAWSA, *Victory*.

40. *The Woman's Journal*, December 31, 1870.

41. Emanie Sachs Arling, *The Terrible Siren* (New York, 1928), 1-15.

42. Elizabeth Cady Stanton to Susan B. Anthony, January 31, 1871, ECS Collection, LC.

43. New York *Tribune*, May 10, 1871.

44. *The Woman's Journal*, August 19, 1871; Katherine Deveraux Blake, *Champion of Woman: The Life of Lillie Deveraux Blake*, (New York, 1943), 91. Olympia Brown, *Acquaintances Old and New Among Reformers* (Milwaukee, 1911), 91; Louise Noun in *Strong-Minded Women: The Emergence of the Woman-Suffrage Movement in Iowa* (Ames, Iowa, 1986), 177-197.

45. *The Woman's Journal*, March 11, 18, 25, 1871; Merk, "Massachusetts," chpt. 10.

46. Lancaster *Gazette*, November 25, 1871; Woodhull defended her use of blackmail in *Woodhull & Claflin's Weekly*, April 6, 1872; Accounts of the blackmail scheme (which in one case included a threat on the recipient's life if she did not pay up) in Arling, *Siren*, 164-65; NAWSA-LC; Blake, *Champion*, 90; Susan B. Anthony to Isabella Beecher Hooker, June 19, 24, 1872, in Stowe-Day Collection.

47. Harper, *Anthony*, 1: 413-15.

48. *The Woman's Journal*, June 15, 1872; *HWS* 2: 517-20.

49. *The Woman's Journal*, June 29, 1872; Susan B. Anthony to Lucy Stone, September 4, 1872, in NAWSA-LC.

50. Arling, *Siren*, 176; *Woodhull & Claflin's Weekly*, November 2, 1872; Challis case in New York *Herald*, November 3, 5, 6, 8, 10, 11, 19, 1872.

51. *The Woman's Journal*, November 30, 1872; Quote in Noun, *Strong-Minded*, 200.

52. *The Woman's Journal*, November 25, 1872; Register quote in Noun, 199. Blake, *Champion*, 91.

53. See Margaret Campbell to Lucy Stone, December 28, 1872; Alice Stone Blackwell to Mary Hunter, August 12, 1838; Alice Stone Blackwell to Lucy Stone, June 12, 1889. All in NAWSA-LC.

54. *The Woman's Journal*, October 25, 1873 and November 22, 1873.

55. Lucy Stone to John K. Wildman, November 7, 1871, in B-LC.

56. Although later accounts by Stanton and Anthony ascribed the split to different causes, (*HWS* 2: 400), there was no such confusion at the time of the formation of the new organization. Both *The Revolution* (May 20, 1869) and the *Woman's Advocate* (May 29, 1869) make it clear that it was the issue of support for or opposition to the Fifteenth Amendment that precipitated the formation of the splinter group.

Satire of Anthony, Stanton, and Anna Dickinson claiming the right to vote under the Fourteenth Amendment, 1875

TAKING THE LAW INTO OUR OWN HANDS:

Bradwell, Minor, and Suffrage Militance in the 1870s

Ellen Carol DuBois

Editor's Introduction: Ellen Carol DuBois, one of the most well-known and prolific scholars of the suffrage movement in the United States, describes the militant strategy pursued by the National Woman Suffrage Association (NWSA) between the schism of 1869 and the reunification of the two suffrage camps in 1890. In contrast with Andrea Kerr, DuBois presents the actions of the NWSA and its leaders as bold and principled. This includes their association with Victoria Woodhull, whom DuBois views as a courageous defender of women's right to control their own bodies as well as an articulate and intelligent advocate of woman suffrage.

DuBois sees Susan B. Anthony, Elizabeth Cady Stanton, and the NWSA as champions of political equality for all, demanding for women the protections afforded "citizens" in the Fourteenth and Fifteenth Amendments. Furious at their abandonment by former allies in the Republican Party, who insisted that the inclusion of woman suffrage would endanger the success of these two Reconstruction amendments, Stanton and Anthony initially protested the amendments even while they simultaneously called for a separate federal woman suffrage amendment. Yet, as DuBois explains in this essay, calling for a new amendment to the Constitution was not the only constitutional approach through which these suffragists tried to secure the vote in the 1870s.

After ratification of the Fourteenth and Fifteenth Amendments, NWSA leaders came up with a bold new strategy for winning the vote by claiming that the Fourteenth and Fifteenth Amendments actually *enfranchised* women. This approach, (also described in the previous essay by Linda Kerber), was known among the suffragists as the "New Departure." Initiated by Virginia and Francis Minor of St. Louis, who pursued it through the courts, it was the principal argument developed by Victoria Woodhull in her famous speech before Congress in 1871. It also inspired Myra Bradwell to claim the right to practice law as a *citizen's right.*

The New Departure emboldened many women including Susan B. Anthony to turn to "direct action," to go to the polls and claim their right to vote as citizens of

the United States. Anthony's subsequent trial for "knowingly, wrongfully, and unlawfully vot[ing]" was one of the most dramatic incidents in the history of the suffrage movement. The judge, in a statement prepared in advance of the trial, directed the jury to find Anthony guilty, and ordered her to pay a one hundred dollar fine that she, of course, refused to pay.

Rather than *plead* for the vote to be extended to them, the NWSA suffragists *demanded* a right that they insisted was already theirs. In the 1870s, however, the nation was in retreat from Reconstruction, and Congress and the courts were increasingly unwilling to protect even the newly established Black male suffrage. The suffragists' militant strategy did not succeed, and direct action to demand woman suffrage as a right rather than a privilege gave way to more conservative tactics—at least until militancy was revived during the last years of the suffrage movement.

However, drawing parallels to the equality-versus-difference debate among feminists in the 1980s and 1990s, DuBois argues that—before they began arguing for enfranchisement on the basis of woman's ability to contribute to politics owing to their differences from men—they first exhausted every possibility of gaining the right to vote as citizens of the United States entitled to equal rights under the United States Constitution. As DuBois so aptly phrases it: "They first attempted to march into power directly through the main political entrance, rather than indirectly, through the back door of the nursery or kitchen."

★　　★　　★　　★　　★

A MONG THE MOST CONTESTED ELEMENTS of the Constitution have been the Reconstruction amendments, and a crucial aspect of that contest has been the relation of the Fourteenth Amendment to women's rights. This essay addresses the early history of women's rights claims to the Fourteenth and Fifteenth Amendments. It explores the legal arguments with which woman suffragists approached the Reconstruction amendments, the popular support and militant activism they inspired, and the role that the defeat of women's rights claims played in the larger history of Reconstruction constitutionalism. This mid-nineteenth-century episode in women's rights history was extremely brief, but it reverberates richly with many important and perplexing issues facing feminist thinkers and activists today. At various moments during which I worked on this essay, I felt that this material provided the historical key to current debates within feminism over "equality," over "rights," and over "politics."

Here, in the post-Civil War years, we can see proponents of women's rights as they move from universal to particularistic arguments, providing us with the Gilded Age equivalent of the shift from "equality" to "difference" in the feminism of our own time. While many of my contemporaries emphasize the abstract and "male" character of such universalistic categories as "person" or "citizen," I have

chosen to stress the many costs to the women's rights tradition of moving away from such frameworks—however "hegemonic" they may seem to our postmodern consciousness—which have helped situate women's emancipation in the larger context of humanity's freedom.[1]

Here, too, we can trace the course of the demands of a disempowered group based on the venerable but problematic constitutional concept of "rights." Of late, "rights arguments" have been criticized, not only by conservatives but also by those on the left, for the assumption that entitlement inheres "naturally" in individuals, flourishing in a "private" realm that must be protected from interference, by others and by the state. Such a concept of "rights," it is argued, masks the workings of power and favors those already privileged by existing social and political structures—men, White people, and the propertied.[2] But this episode in women's rights, perhaps the entire tradition, treats rights quite differently: as something to be won and exercised collectively rather than individually; as the object of political struggle as much as of judicial resolution; as that which government affirmatively establishes rather than negatively shields; and above all as that which has greatest meaning not to the powerful, who already enjoy their entitlements, but to the powerless, who have yet to have their full place in society recognized.

Finally, this episode has implications for the character and place of the "political" in women's history. While women's historians have deepened our knowledge of the public activism of women, even—or especially—before their enfranchisement, much of this scholarship has followed what is called (in shorthand) "the separate spheres" model. Women, it is argued, have had—and may still have—their own political culture distinct from men's, and they have chosen to work for their own and society's betterment by embracing different institutions, following different rules, and adhering to different political values.[3] This essay suggests that to the degree that nineteenth-century women abandoned a political terrain also occupied by men—of partisan power and judicial contest— they were driven from it by defeat and forced to pursue politics by other, more indirect means. This essay considers women as they attempted to march into power directly, through the main political entrance, rather than indirectly, through the back door of the nursery or kitchen.

Introduction to the New Departure

Most histories of women's rights—my own included—have emphasized the initial rage of women's rights leaders at the Radical Republican authors of the Fourteenth and Fifteenth Amendments. In 1865 Elizabeth Cady Stanton was horrified to discover what she called "the word male" in proposals for a Fourteenth Amendment. The second section of the amendment defines the basis of congressional representation as "male persons over the age of twenty-one" and in doing so makes the first reference to sex anywhere in the Constitution. The passage of the Fifteenth Amendment in 1869, a much more powerful constitutional defense

of political equality, only deepened the anger of women's rights advocates because it did not include sex among its prohibited disfranchisements.[4]

In 1869 the crisis split suffragists into two camps—the National Woman Suffrage Association, which protested the omission of women from the Reconstruction amendments, and the American Woman Suffrage Association, which accepted the deferral of their claims. This part of the story is well known to students of woman suffrage, as is the National Association's concentration, through most of its twenty-one-year life (in 1890 it amalgamated with the American Association), on securing a separate amendment enfranchising women. Inasmuch as the form that federal woman suffrage ultimately took was precisely a separate constitutional amendment—the Nineteenth, ratified in 1920—this strategy is taken as the entirety of woman suffragists' constitutional claims. Yet, in the first few years after the passage of the Fourteenth and Fifteenth Amendments, suffragists in the National Association camp energetically pursued another constitutional approach. They proposed a broad and inclusive construction of the Fourteenth and Fifteenth Amendments, under which, they claimed, women were already enfranchised. This constitutional strategy, known at the time as the New Departure, laid the basis for the subsequent focus on a separate woman suffrage amendment, even as it embodied a radical democratic vision that the latter approach did not have.

The Fourteenth and Fifteenth Amendments

While the Fourteenth Amendment was in the process of being ratified, woman suffragists concentrated on its second clause, because of the offensive reference to "male persons." This phrase was included by the amendment's framers because in 1867 there was an active movement demanding the franchise for women, and it would no longer do to use such gender neutral terms as "person" to mean only men.[5] Yet such explicit exclusions of particular groups from the universal blessings of American democracy were not at all in the egalitarian spirit of the age. Perhaps it was for this reason that in writing the first section of the Fourteenth Amendment, which defines federal citizenship, the framers could not bring themselves to speak of races or sexes but instead relied on the abstractions of "persons" and "citizens." In other words, the universalities of the first section of the Fourteenth Amendment, where federal citizenship is established, run headlong into the sex-based restrictions of the second section, where voting rights are limited. Those Reconstruction Era feminists angered at the restrictive clause quickly recognized these contradictions and became determined to get women's rights demands included in the broadest possible construction of the terms "persons" and "citizens" in the first section, to use, in other words, the first section to defeat the second.

After the Fifteenth Amendment was finally ratified, the suffragists of the National Association therefore shifted from the claim that the Reconstruction amendments excluded women and began to argue instead that they were broad

enough to include women's rights along with those of the freedmen. This strategic turn, the New Departure,[6] was first outlined in October 1869 by a husband and wife team of Missouri suffragists, Francis and Virginia Minor. They offered an elaborate and elegant interpretation of the Constitution to demonstrate that women already had the right to vote. Their construction rested on a consistent perspective on the whole Constitution, but especially on a broad interpretation of the Fourteenth Amendment.[7]

The Minors' first premise was that popular sovereignty preceded and underlay constitutional authority. In exchange for creating government, the people expected protection of their preeminent and natural rights. This is a familiar element of revolutionary ideology. Their second premise was to equate the power of the *federal* government with the defense of individual rights, to regard federal power as positive.[8] Historically, the federal government had been regarded as the enemy of rights; the Bill of Rights protects individual rights by enjoining the federal government from infringing on them. In the wake of the devastating experience of secession, the Fourteenth Amendment reversed the order, relying on federal power to protect its citizens against the tyrannical action of the states. The Minors thus argued in good Radical Reconstruction fashion that national citizenship had finally been established as supreme by the first section of the Fourteenth Amendment: "the immunities and privileges of American citizenship, however defined, are national in character and paramount to all state authority."

A third element in the Minors' case was that the benefits of national citizenship were equally the rights of all. This too bore the mark of the Reconstruction Era. In the words of the amendment, "all persons born or naturalized in the United States" were equally entitled to the privileges and protections of national citizenship; there were no additional qualifications. In the battle for the rights of the Black man, the rights of all had been secured. The war had expanded the rights of "proud White man" to all those who had historically been deprived of them, or so these radical reconstructionists believed.[9] In other words, the historic claim of asserting *individual* rights was becoming the modern one of realizing *equal* rights, especially for the lowly.

Finally, the Minors argued that the right to vote was one of the basic privileges and immunities of national citizenship. This was both the most controversial and the most important part of the New Departure constitutional construction. Popular sovereignty had always included an implicit theory of political power. The Minors' New Departure argument took this article of popular faith, reinterpreted it in light of Reconstruction Era egalitarianism, and gave it constitutional expression to produce a theory of universal rights to the suffrage. The New Departure case for universal suffrage brought together the Fourteenth Amendment, which nationalized citizenship and linked it to federal power, and the Fifteenth Amendment, which shifted the responsibility for the suffrage from the state to the national government.[10] This theory of the suffrage underlay much of the case for

Black suffrage as well, but because the drive for Black suffrage was so intertwined with Republican partisan interest, it was woman suffrage, which had no such political thrust behind it, that generated the most formal constitutional expression of this Reconstruction Era faith in political equality.

Women Take the Vote

The New Departure was not simply a lawyer's exercise in constitutional exegesis. Reconstruction was an age of popular constitutionalism. Although presented in formal, constitutional terms, what the Minors had to say had much support among the rank and file of the women's rights movement. The underlying spirit of the Minors' constitutional arguments was militant and activist. The basic message was that the vote was already women's right; they merely had to take it. The New Departure took on meaning precisely because of this direct action element. Many women took the argument to heart and went to the polls, determined to vote. By 1871 hundreds of women were trying to register and vote in dozens of towns all over the country.[11] In 1871 in Philadelphia, to take one of many examples, Carrie Burnham, an unmarried tax-paying woman, got as far as having her name registered on the voting rolls. When her vote was refused, she formed the Citizens Suffrage Association of Philadelphia, dedicated not only to the defense of women's political rights but also to the greater truth that the right to vote was inherent, not bestowed. If the contrary were true, if the right to vote were a gift, this "implied a right lodged somewhere in society, which society had never acquired by any direct concession from the people." Such a theory of political power was patently tyrannical.[12]

That the first examples of women's direct action voting occurred in 1868 and 1869, before the Minors made their formal constitutional argument, suggests that the New Departure grew out of a genuinely popular political faith. In 1868 in the radical, spiritualist town of Vineland, New Jersey, almost two hundred women cast their votes into a separate ballot box and then tried to get them counted along with the men's. "The platform was crowded with earnest refined intellectual women, who feel it was good for them to be there," *The Revolution* reported. "One beautiful girl said 'I feel so much stronger for having voted.'"[13] The Vineland women repeated the effort for several years, and the ballot box eventually became an icon, which the local historical society still owns. From Vineland, the idea of women's voting spread to nearby towns, including Roseville, where, despite the American Association's official disinterest in the New Departure, Lucy Stone and her mother tried—but failed—to register their votes.

On the other side of the continent, Mary Olney Brown also decided she had the right to vote because the legislature of Washington Territory had passed an act giving "all White American citizens above the age of twenty-one years the right to vote." She wrote to other "prominent women urging them to go out and vote at the coming election ... [but] I was looked upon as a fanatic and the idea of woman

voting was regarded as an absurdity." "Many [women] wished to vote...," she decided, "[but] had not the courage to go to the polls in defiance of custom." Finally, in 1869, she went to the polls with her husband, daughter, and son-in-law. Election officials threatened that she would not be "treated as a lady."

> Summoning all my strength, I walked up to the desk behind which sat the august officers of election, and presented my vote.... I was pompously met with the assertion, "You are not an American citizen; hence not entitled to vote." ...I said... "I claim to be an American citizen, and a native-born citizen at that; and I wish to show you from the fourteenth amendment to the constitution of the United States, that women are not only citizens having the constitutional right to vote, but also that our territorial election law gives women the privilege of exercising that right."...I went on to show them that the...emancipation of the Southern slaves threw upon the country a class of people, who, like the women of the nation, owed allegiance to the government, but whose citizenship was not recognized. To settle this question, the fourteenth amendment was adopted.

Whereupon, the local election official, "with great dignity of manner and an immense display of ignorance," insisted "that the laws of congress don't extend over Washington territory" and refused her vote. When Brown was refused again, two years later, she concluded, "It amounts to this: the law gives women the right to vote in this territory, and you three men who have been appointed to receive our votes, sit here and arbitrarily refuse to take them, giving no reason why, only that you have decided not to take the women's votes. There is no law to sustain you in this usurpation of power."[14]

News of the efforts of women to register and vote spread through formal and informal means. Women's rights and mainstream journals reported on them, but information also might have been passed by word of mouth through networks of activists. Many sisters and friends, often in different states, turn up in the stories of New Departure voting women. In her account, Mary Olney Brown tells of her sister, who was inspired by her efforts to try to vote in a nearby town. Brown's sister took a different approach and was more successful. Eager to vote in a school election, she and her friends prepared a special dinner for election officials. "When the voting was resumed, the women, my sister being the first, handed in their ballots as if they had always been accustomed to voting. One lady, Mrs. Sargent, seventy-two years old, said she thanked the Lord that he had let her live until she could vote."[15]

The voting women of the 1870s often went to the polls in groups. They believed in the suffrage as an individual right but an individual right that would be achieved and experienced collectively. The most famous of these voting groups was the nearly fifty local activists, friends, and relatives who joined Susan B.

Anthony in attempting to vote in Rochester, New York, in 1872. Virginia Minor herself was swept up in this collective activism. When she and some of her friends, all suffrage activists and Republican partisans, tried to register in St. Louis and were refused, she sued.

The congressional passage of the Enforcement Act in May 1870 to strengthen the Fifteenth Amendment greatly accelerated women's direct action voting. The Enforcement Act was meant to enforce the freedmen's political rights by providing recourse to the federal courts and penalties against local election officials who refused the lawful votes of citizens. Women who wanted to vote saw the act as a way to use the power of the federal government for their own benefit. Benjamin Quarles reports that freedwomen in South Carolina were encouraged by Freedmen's Bureau officials to attempt to vote by appealing to the Enforcement Act.[16] Some election officials responded to the Enforcement Act by accepting women's votes. When Nanette Gardner went to vote in Detroit in 1871, the ward official in her district was sympathetic to her protest and accepted her vote. The same man accepted Gardner's vote again in 1872, and she presented him with "a beautiful banner of white satin, trimmed with gold fringe on which was inscribed...'To Peter Hill, Alderman of the Ninth Ward, Detroit.... By recognizing civil liberty and equality for woman, he has placed the last and brightest jewel on the brow of Michigan.'"[17]

Most local officials, however, refused to accept women's votes. While Nanette Gardner voted successfully in Detroit, her friend Catherine Stebbins (the daughter of one of the Rochester voters) was turned away in the next ward. When Mary Brown's vote was refused in Olympia, she concluded that politicians more powerful than the local committeemen had decided to resist women's direct action efforts to vote and that "money was pledged in case of prosecution." In Santa Cruz, California, when Ellen Van Valkenberg was similarly turned back at the polls, she became the first woman to sue an election official under the Enforcement Act for refusing her vote.[18] By 1871 numerous New Departure woman suffrage cases were making their way through the federal courts.

Victoria Woodhull and the New Departure

Meanwhile, the New Departure gained an advocate who moved it from the local level into national politics: Victoria Woodhull. In January of 1871 Woodhull appeared before the House Judiciary Committee to make the constitutional case for women's right to vote. No woman had ever before been invited to address a committee of the United States Congress. Her appearance was sponsored by Massachusetts Republican Benjamin Butler, who may have helped her outline her constitutional case. The deeply felt conviction about women's rights underlying her argument was undoubtedly her own, however. Her memorial asked Congress to pass legislation clarifying the right of all women to vote under the new Reconstruction amendments.[19] The major difference

between Woodhull and the Minors was tactical; she urged women to turn to Congress to resolve the question, while they relied on the courts.

Like all New Departure advocates, Woodhull embraced the premise that popular sovereignty was absolute: "the sovereign power of this country is perpetual in the politically-organized people of the United States, and can neither be relinquished nor abandoned by any portion of them." Her case for woman suffrage was simple and, from a radical Reconstruction perspective, virtually unassailable: inasmuch as the first section of the Fourteenth Amendment made no reference to sex, women along with men were citizens of the United States, and foremost among the "privileges and immunities" of national citizenship was the right to vote.[20] Like the Minors, Woodhull argued that the Fourteenth Amendment established the supremacy of national over state citizenship and the obligation of the federal government to protect the rights of all citizens equally.

Victoria Claflin Woodhull, c. 1870
MATHEW BRADY

Woodhull also argued from the Fifteenth Amendment, which she interpreted broadly, that voting is "a Right, not a privilege of citizens of the United States."[21] She directly confronted the most obvious objection to this interpretation, that the Fifteenth Amendment specifically prohibits only disfranchisements by race, color, and previous condition. First, she argued, the amendment's wording does not bestow the right to vote but assumes it to be preexisting. Although it explicitly prohibited certain disfranchisements, Woodhull argued that it could not be read to implicitly permit others. Second, the Fifteenth Amendment forbids disfranchisement "under three distinct conditions, in all of which," Woodhull argued, "woman is distinctly embraced." In other words, "a race comprises all the people, male and female." Woodhull here seems to grasp what many modern White feminists are still struggling to understand, that counterpoising the discriminations of race and sex obscures the experience of those who suffer both, that is, Black women. Finally, Woodhull argued for her broad construction of the right of suffrage on the grounds of what she called "the blending of [the Constitution's] various parts," that is, the relation between the Fourteenth Amendment, which nationalizes citizenship and links it to the power of the federal government, and the Fifteenth Amendment, which shifts the responsibility for the suffrage from the state to the national government.[22]

The first official reaction to the New Departure came in response to Woodhull's memorial. The House Judiciary Committee issued two conflicting reports on the constitutional issues she raised.[23] Here we begin to see that debate over the feminists' particular constitutional arguments was inseparable from questions of the larger meaning of the Reconstruction amendments. The Majority Report rejected Woodhull's claims. Its author was John Bingham, one of the framers of the Fourteenth Amendment. Although Bingham conceded that women enjoyed the privileges of United States citizenship along with men, he disagreed that the Fourteenth Amendment added anything new to the content of national citizenship or altered the relationship between national and state citizenship. The Minority Report, signed by William Loughridge of Iowa and Benjamin Butler of Massachusetts, supported Woodhull's memorial and the generous and radical interpretation of the amendments on which it relied. The Minority Report interpreted the Fourteenth Amendment broadly, arguing that it was intended "to secure the natural rights of citizens as well as their equal capacities before the law." The Majority Report rejected Woodhull's argument that the Fifteenth Amendment shifted responsibility for the suffrage from the state to the national level, while the Minority Report agreed that the Fifteenth Amendment "clearly recognizes the right to vote, as one of the rights of a citizen of the United States."[24] "Thus it can be seen," Woodhull observed archly, "that equally able men differ upon a simple point of Constitutional Law."[25]

The mere fact of a congressional hearing was a victory for woman suffrage leaders, and the language of constitutional principle was an improvement over the semi-sexual innuendo with which their claims were often met.[26] The favorable Minority Report meant that some of the leaders of the Republican Party supported women's rights claims on the Constitution. In 1871 two committee rooms in the Capitol were put at the disposal of the suffragists to facilitate their lobbying efforts.[27] "Could you feel the atmosphere of...Congress, to-day, you would not doubt what the end must be, nor that it will be very soon," Isabella Beecher Hooker wrote.[28] The National Woman Suffrage Association urged women to put pressure on their congressmen to support the Butler Report, as well as to continue trying to vote and to work through the courts.[29]

Free Love and the Moral Divide

It was in this context, as Republicans struggled over the claims of the New Departure and suffragists grew hopeful, that the issue of "free love" was raised. The sexual discourse that soon surrounded the New Departure played a role in shaping the political context and therefore the constitutional outcome. Woodhull is generally remembered in the history books not for her powerful constitutional arguments but for her shady sexual reputation. These sexual issues, however, were introduced not by Woodhull but by her opponents, who saw in them a way to divert attention from the constitutional arguments she made. Republican

newspapers, notably the *New York Tribune,* accused Woodhull of multiple marriages, bigamy, and the advocacy of free love.[30] Suffrage leaders allied with Woodhull were either accused of sharing her "free love" sentiments or warned against the consequences of associating with disreputable women. As in other times, when politicians cannot face the genuine issues before them, the importance of "character" was asserted. "Men judge men's conventions not more by the formal platform they present than by...the character of those who are prominent in the proceedings," a New York periodical solemnly warned.[31]

Rather than react defensively to the attacks on her, Woodhull embraced the "free love" opprobrium with which she was charged. To her, the principles at the heart of sexual life were the same as those at the heart of political life, and the true basis of marriage was the same as the true basis of republican government: individual rights. Groping for a way to express her conviction that women, whether married or unmarried, must have unqualified control over their own reproductive and sexual lives, she used the language of Reconstruction constitutionalism to proclaim the doctrine of rights to and over one's own person. "Yes I am a Free lover," Woodhull responded to a heckler at one of her speeches. "I have an *inalienable, constitutional* and *natural* right to love whom I may,...to *change* that love *every day* if I please,...and it is your *duty* not only to *accord* [me my right], but, as a community, to see that I am protected in it."[32]

Such sex radicalism was not the predominant strain in nineteenth-century feminist circles. Most of the New Departure leaders (with the significant exception of Elizabeth Cady Stanton) were closer to the Victorian stereotype than Woodhull was, and they believed that the sex impulse must be tamed, not constitutionally secured. Nonetheless, even these "pious" women defended their alliance with Woodhull and rejected the conventional moral divide that separated "good" women from "bad." "God has raised up Woodhull to embody all questions of fellowship in political work [among] women irrespective of character," declared Isabella Beecher Hooker.[33] Instead of joining in a crusade against the immorality of women, New Departure suffrists began to attack the "hypocrisy" of men. Woodhull had been "raised up of God," suffragist and moral reformer Paulina Wright Davis claimed, to expose the perfidy of "a class that no one dares touch," men who said one thing and did another, men in power.[34] They shifted accusations of immorality not only from women to men but also from sexuality to politics. The true prostitutes, Woodhull asserted, were Republican leaders, who sold out principles for party power and wealth.[35]

The *Bradwell* Case

In late 1871, in the midst of this increasingly sexualized political context, the first New Departure cases began to reach the dockets of the federal courts. One was the case of Sara Spencer and seventy other women from the District of Columbia, who sued election officials under the Enforcement Act for refusing to permit them to

vote. The District of Columbia was a deliberate choice for testing the New Departure argument. There, as advocates of Black suffrage had first realized in 1867, the power of the federal government over the suffrage was not complicated by questions of dual sovereignty and states' rights.[36]

In October Judge Cartter of the Supreme Court of the District of Columbia ruled against Spencer. Cartter conceded that the Fourteenth Amendment included women along with men in the privileges and immunities of national citizenship; however, he rejected the democratic theory of suffrage on which the case rested. To concede that voting was a right was, in his opinion, to open the door to anarchy and would "involve the destruction of civil government." "The right of all men to vote is as fully recognized in the population of our large centres and cities as can well be done," wrote Cartter. "The result...is political profligacy and violence verging upon anarchy."[37] The larger context of the opinion, therefore, was anxiety about democratic politics, and Cartter's concern for the proper position of women in society was secondary. This was true of the entire New Departure debate (and perhaps of judicial disposition of women's rights claims more generally); it was conducted primarily in terms of "rights," not woman's sphere. What was claimed or denied for women was claimed or denied for all citizens, especially those previously excluded from rights due them. Whether this was because the question of women's place was subsumed in a more general struggle for political democracy or because sex-prejudice was still unspeakable in constitutional terms, the consequence was the same: denying women the rights they claimed under general provisions weakened those provisions in general.

The observation that general questions of constitutional rights had overtaken the specific discourse on woman's place is even clearer in the next major New Departure decision, *Bradwell v. Illinois* (1873). *Bradwell* was the first case touching on the New Departure to reach the Supreme Court. In 1869 Myra Bradwell, a Chicago feminist and pioneering woman lawyer, was refused admission to the Illinois bar. The grounds on which the state supreme court refused her application, along with the initial brief that Bradwell submitted in response, were concerned entirely with coverture, that is, with the question of the disabilities of married women before the law. By the time Bradwell brought her case before the United States Supreme Court in October 1871, she had changed the terms radically. Her case was no longer about coverture but had been reformulated in entirely New Departure terms. Her brief argued that her right to practice law was a citizen's right and that Illinois's action in refusing her was prohibited by the Fourteenth Amendment. As for coverture, she asserted that "the great innovation of the XIV Amendment...sweeps away the principles of the common law," so that even reforms of married women's property rights were no longer necessary. The *Bradwell* case is one of the few concerning women's rights commonly included in the history of constitutional law, but in my opinion it is not correctly situated, since it is usually cited to illustrate judicial assumptions about

woman's place rather than the con-stitutional issues of citizenship on which it was actually argued and decided.[38]

Bradwell's case was closely watched by suffragists as an indication of how much support to expect from the Republican Party. Bradwell was represented before the Supreme Court by Senator Matthew Carpenter, one of the major second-generation leaders of the Republican Party. While Carpenter took up Bradwell's case and argued it in strong Fourteenth Amendment terms, he prefaced his case with an equally strong argument about why the right to vote was not covered by the Reconstruction amendments. He

Myra Bradwell, 1870
LIBRARY OF CONGRESS

insisted, in other words, on a distinction between civil and political rights. While the federal government protected civil rights, women's as well as men's, Carpenter argued, the suffrage remained under the control of the states, beyond the lawful interference of federal power.[39]

Suffragists were understandably confused by the way Carpenter argued Bradwell's case. Was it an indication that Republican leaders were in favor of the New Departure or against it? Stanton allowed herself to be encouraged; if women were covered along with men under the Fourteenth Amendment, wasn't the fundamental point of equal rights won?[40] Victoria Woodhull, however, saw it differently; she argued that women might be admitted to the benefits of the postwar amendments only to find those amendments so narrowed that they bestowed virtually nothing at all, certainly not political rights. She charged that Republicans, "frightened by the grandeur and the extent" of the amendments they had enacted, had retreated to the enemies' doctrine of states' rights, where their own greatest achievements would ultimately be undone.[41]

The Supreme Court held back its decision on *Bradwell* until after the election. To trace the final judicial disposition of the suffragists' constitutional arguments, we have to understand what was at stake in this election and what a Republican victory would mean. The election of 1872 was a crisis for the Republicans.[42] In June 1872 an important group of reformers split off from regular Republicans to run an independent presidential campaign. These political rebels, the Liberal Republicans,

based their revolt on the old opposition between central government and individual rights. From the perspective of feminists, who were also looking for a political alternative to the regular Republicans, the terms of the bolt were particularly disappointing. Feminists had learned from freedmen to see the federal government not as a threat to their rights but as the agency for winning them.

To add insult to injury, the Liberal Republicans picked as their candidate Horace Greeley, a man who had made his opposition to woman suffrage clear many years before. Infuriated by the nomination of Greeley, many New Departure suffragists campaigned actively for Ulysses Grant in 1872.[43] The regular Republicans cultivated their support, sending them about the country on official speaking tours and inserting a timid little reference to "additional rights" for women in their platform, a plank so insignificant that suffragists called it a "splinter." Holding off a decision on *Bradwell* was consistent with this temporary friendliness. Anthony expected that if Republicans won, they would reward women with the suffrage by recognizing the New Departure claims. She was so sure that when she came home from her last speaking tour on election day, she gathered together friends and relatives and went down to her local polling place to submit her vote for Grant. Although the local Republican official accepted the votes of fifteen of the demonstrators, including Anthony,[44] a few weeks later a United States marshall came to her house and arrested her for violation of federal law—the Enforcement Act.

Anthony's arrest was a signal that the Republicans were ready to dispose of the New Departure. Because she was the most famous woman suffragist in the nation, there is good reason to suspect her arrest had been authorized at the highest level of government. The conduct of her trial several months later reinforces this suspicion. The trial was moved from her home county, where she had lectured extensively to educate potential jurors, to another venue. The judge, Ward Hunt, was no small-town jurist but a recent appointee to the United States Supreme Court. He refused to submit the case to the jury, instead directing a guilty verdict from the bench, a practice that was later found unconstitutional. Years later, Anthony's lawyer observed, "There never was a trial in the country with one half the importance of Miss Anthony's.... If Anthony had won her case on the merit it would have revolutionized the suffrage of the country.... There was a prearranged determination to convict her. A jury trial was dangerous and so the Constitution was deliberately and openly violated." Anthony was not even permitted to appeal.[45]

In general, the outcome of the election cleared the way for the Republican Party to retreat from the radical implications of the postwar amendments. There is a link between the judicial dismissal of the feminists' New Departure and the larger repudiation of the postwar amendments. It is embodied in the fact that the Supreme Court's opinions on *Bradwell* and on the *Slaughterhouse* cases were delivered on the same day in 1873. *Slaughterhouse* is generally considered the fundamental Fourteenth Amendment Supreme Court decision. The case involved a group of Louisiana butchers who challenged a state law regulating their

occupation on the grounds that it violated their rights as federal citizens (to practice their vocation—the same issue as *Bradwell*) and that the Fourteenth Amendment established the supremacy of national over state citizenship.[46]

Six months after the election, the Court delivered negative opinions in both cases, interpreting the Fourteenth Amendment very narrowly and finding it inapplicable in both cases. The case that the Court lingered over was *Slaughterhouse.*[47] By a bare majority, it ruled that the amendment's intent was only to ensure "the freedom of the slave race" and that it did not transfer the jurisdiction over fundamental civil rights from state to federal government. The opinion in *Bradwell* covered much less territory but did so by a larger majority. The Court merely rejected the claim that the right to practice law was one of the privileges and immunities of federal citizenship protected by the amendment. Beyond that, the Court simply commented that "the opinion just delivered in the *Slaughterhouse* Cases... renders elaborate argument in the present case unnecessary."[48] We should not be misled by this preemptory dismissal, however. The very interpretation under which the *Slaughterhouse* cases had been decided, that the Fourteenth Amendment was limited to matters of race and did not elevate national over state citizenship, had first been articulated in 1871 in the Majority Report of the House Judiciary Committee, rejecting Victoria Woodhull's claim that the Fourteenth Amendment guaranteed her right to vote.

The *Minor* Case

The Supreme Court ruled conclusively against the New Departure two years later, in 1875. The case in which it did so was *Minor v. Happersett*, brought, appropriately enough, by Virginia Minor, the woman who had first argued that as a citizen of the United States, she was constitutionally protected in her right to vote. Like Anthony, Minor had tried to vote in the 1872 election, but when her vote was refused, she brought suit under the Enforcement Act. The Missouri courts ruled against her, and she appealed to the United States Supreme Court on the grounds that constitutional protections of the citizen's right to vote invalidated any state regulations to the contrary. The Court ruled unanimously against her. Since the *Slaughterhouse* and *Bradwell* cases had disposed of the first element of the New Departure, that the Fourteenth Amendment established the supremacy of national citizenship, the decision in *Minor* concentrated on the second assertion, that suffrage was a right of citizenship. On this, the Court ruled starkly that "the Constitution of the United States does not confer the right of suffrage upon any one."[49]

Here, too, there was an intimate link between the fate of woman suffragists' constitutional claims and that of the Reconstruction amendments in general. The day after the Court delivered its opinion in *Minor*, it heard arguments in *United States v. Cruikshank*. In this case and in the *United States v. Reese*, Black men for the first time brought suit under the Enforcement Act for protection of their political rights under the Fourteenth and Fifteenth Amend-ments, and the Court ruled

Virginia Louise Minor

J.A. Scholten & J.C. Buttre

against them. In the process of ruling against the plaintiffs, the Court found the Enforcement Act, under which both feminists and freedmen had sought protection, unconstitutional. Citing the recent decision in *Minor,* the Court ruled that inasmuch as the Constitution did not bestow the suffrage on anyone, the federal courts were outside their jurisdiction in protecting the freedmen's political rights.

The rejection of woman suffrage arguments on the grounds that the Fifteenth Amendment was only intended to forbid disfran-chisement by race paved the way for a reading of the Fifteenth Amendment that was so narrow it did not even protect the freedmen themselves. In its decision in *United States v. Reese,* the Court argued that the plaintiff, although a Black man, had not proved that his vote was denied on the grounds of race and so was not covered by constitutional protections. Eventually, of course, the freedmen were effectively disfranchised on grounds of income, residence, and education, all surrogates for race. Anthony had anticipated this connection. At her own trial, she predicted that the general narrowing of the Reconstruction amendments would follow on the heels of the repudiation of women's claims of equal rights under them. "If we once establish the false principle, that United States citizenship does not carry with it the right to vote in every state in this Union," she said, "there is no end to the petty freaks and cunning devices that will be resorted to exclude one and another class of citizens from the right of suffrage." [50]

Three years after the *Minor* defeat, suffragists began their pursuit of a separate constitutional amendment to prohibit disfranchisement on account of sex. At many levels, this was a less radical strategy. With the defeat of the New Departure, winning the vote for women was no longer tied to an overall democratic interpretation of the Constitution. To the degree that the struggle for women's votes was not strategically linked to the general defense of political democracy, that its goal was "woman suffrage" not "universal suffrage," elitist and racist tendencies faced fewer barriers, had freer reign, and imparted a more conservative character to suffragism over the next half-century.

Yet, despite this very important strategic shift, the New Departure period left a deep mark on the history of feminism. From time to time, some suffragist would

see possibilities in the existing propositions of the Constitution and propose some clever legal mechanism for exploiting them.[51] Even direct action voting never completely died away. Twenty years after the *Minor* decision, Elizabeth Grannis of New York City made her eighth attempt to register to vote.[52] Certainly the larger spirit of militant direct action resurfaced in a spectacular way in the last decade of the American suffrage movement. The deepest mark of the New Departure, however, was to make women's rights and political equality indelibly constitutional issues. As Susan B. Anthony wrote, she "had learned... through the passage of the Fourteenth and Fifteenth amendments

Elizabeth B. Grannis, 1894

that it had been possible to amend [the Constitution] in such a way as to enfranchise an entire new class of voters."[53] The *Minor* case, the historian Norma Basch has observed, "drew the inferiority of women's status out of the grooves of common law assumptions and state provisions and thrust it into the maelstrom of constitutional conflict. The demand for woman suffrage...acquired a contentious national life."[54]

Notes

1. This essay is a reprint (with abbreviated notes) of an essay that first appeared in *Visible Women: New Essays on American Activism,* Nancy A. Hewitt and Suzanne Lebsock, eds., published in 1993 by the University of Illinois Press. It is reprinted here with permission of the press.
  The literature generated by the feminist debate on equality versus difference is enormous. Two excellent analyses by historians are Linda Gordon, "On Difference," *Genders* 10 (Spring 1991): 91-111; and Joan Scott, "Reconstructing Equality-versus-Difference; or the Uses of Poststructuralist Theory for Feminism," *Feminist Studies* 14 (Spring 1988): 33-50.
2. For a sampling of critical legal studies scholarship on the limitations of rights thinking, see Mark Tushnet, "An Essay on Rights," *Texas Law Review* 62 (May 1984): 1386; and Peter Gabel, "The Phenomenology of Rights Consciousness and the Pact of Withdrawn Selves," ibid., 1563-99.
3. Paula Baker made this argument most forcefully for the pre-1920 period; see "The Domestication of Politics: Women and American Political Society, 1780-1920," *American Historical Review* 89 (June 1984): 620-47.
4. Ellen Carol DuBois, *Feminism and Suffrage: The Emergence of an Independent Women's Movement in America, 1848-1869,* (Ithaca, N.Y., 1978); Elizabeth Cady Stanton, *Eighty Years and More: Reminiscences, 1815-1897,* ed. Ellen Carol DuBois (1898; Boston, 1993), 242.
5. Stanton, *Eighty Years and More,* 242.
6. Elizabeth Cady Stanton, Susan B. Anthony, and Matilda J. Gage, eds., *History of Woman Suffrage,* Vol. 2 (Rochester, N.Y., 1881), 407-520; Ida Husted Harper, ed., *Life and Work of Susan B. Anthony,* (Indianapolis, 1899), 1: 409-48.
7. *HWS* 2: 407-10; on the Minors, see Louise R. Noun, *Strong Minded Women: The Emergence of the Woman Suffrage Movement in Iowa* (Ames, 1986), 168-69.
8. David Montgomery notes the importance of this Reconstruction Era shift in attitude to the positive state in *Beyond Equality: Labor and the Radical Republicans* (New York, 1967), 80-81.

9. On this aspect of Reconstruction Era constitutional thought, see Judith A. Baer, *Equality Under the Constitution: Reclaiming the Fourteenth Amendment* (Ithaca, N.Y., 1983).
10. While the Fifteenth Amendment was still pending, the Minors found an alternative constitutional basis for their claim that suffrage was a natural right in the frequently cited 1820 case *Corfield v. Coryell,* which included the franchise as one of the privileges and immunities protected in Article 4.
11. In New Hampshire in 1870, Matilda Ricker tried to vote (*HWS* 2: 586-87). In New York in 1871, Matilda Joslyn Cage tried to vote in Fayetteville, and a group of women, led by Louise Mansfield, tried to vote in Nyack (Elizabeth Cady Stanton, Susan B. Anthony, and Matilda Joslyn Gage, eds., *History of Woman Suffrage,* [Rochester, N.Y., 1887], 3: 406; Isabelle K. Savelle, *Ladies' Lib: How Rockland Women Got the Vote* (New York, 1979), 13-16; in New York City, Victoria Woodhull and Tennessee Claflin tried to vote (Johanna Johnston, *Mrs. Satan* [New York, 1967], 110).
12. *HWS* 3: 461-62, and *HWS* 2: 600-601.
13. Eleanor Flexner, *Century of Struggle: The Women's Rights Movement in the United States* (Cambridge, Mass., 1959), 168, citing *The Revolution,* November 19, 1868, 307.
14. *HWS* 3: 780-86.
15. Ibid., 784.
16. Benjamin Quarles, "Frederick Douglass and the Woman's Rights Movement," *Journal of Negro History* 25 (June 1940): 35.
17. *HWS* 3: 523-24.
18. Ibid., 766.
19. Ibid., 2: 443-48.
20. Ibid., 445.
21. Victoria C. Woodhull, *Constitutional Equality: A Lecture Delivered at Lincoln Hall, Washington, D.C., February 16, 1871* (New York, 1871).
22. *HWS* 2: 445-46. The comment on "blending" was made in Woodhull's arguments in support of her congressional memorial. The comments are available in Victoria Woodhull, *The Argument for Woman's Electoral Rights under Amendment XIV and XV of the Constitution of the United States* (London, 1887), 44.

23. Both reports can be found in *HWS* 2: 461-82.

24. Ibid., 469, 478. In support of their interpretation, they cited the federal district court's decision in what was called the *Crescent City* case, later renamed the *Slaughterhouse* cases.

25. Woodhull, *Constitutional Equality*, 4.

26. Martha Wright complained to Elizabeth Stanton about a congressman who "said rudely to Mrs. Davis & Mrs. Griffing, 'You just call on us because you like to,'" to which Mrs. Griffing answered "'We call on you, because it is the only way known to us, to present our appeal to you,' & Mrs. Davis said 'You must remember that we are your constituents.'" Wright to Stanton, December 29, 1870, Garrison Family Collection, Smith College, Northampton, Mass.

27. *HWS* 2: 489.

28. Isabella Beecher Hooker to the Editor, *Independent*, February 11, 1871, reprinted in *Woodhull and Claflin's Weekly*, March 4, 1871, 10.

29. Ibid.; *An Appeal to the Women of the United States by the National Woman Suffrage and Educational Committee* (Hartford, Conn., April 19, 1871).

30. Woodhull's response to the charges can be found in the *New York World*, May 22, 1871, 3.

31. "The Voice of Apollo Hall," *Every Saturday*, June 17, 1871, 554.

32. Victoria C. Woodhull, *The Principles of Social Freedom, Delivered in New York City, November 20, 1871* (New York, 1871), 23-24.

33. Isabella Beecher Hooker to Anna E. Dickenson, April 22, (1871), box 9 Dickenson Papers, Library of Congress, Washington, D.C.

34. Paulina Wright Davis to Woodhull, May 29, 1871, Victoria Woodhull Martin Collection, Southern Illinois University, Carbondale.

35. Victoria C. Woodhull, "The Speech of Victoria C. Woodhull before the National Woman's Suffrage Convention at Apollo Hall, May 11, 1871," reprinted in Woodhull, *The Argument for Women's Electoral Rights*, 137.

36. *HWS* 2: 587-99.

37. Ibid., 598.

38. Ibid., 622. The opinion in Bradwell that is usually cited is not the terse dismissal of the Fourteenth Amendment argument that settled the case, but an individual concurring opinion by Justice Bradley that addressed the coverture issues that Bradwell had removed from her argument.

39. *HWS* 2: 618.

40. Elizabeth Cady Stanton, "Argument before the Senate Judiciary Committee," January 11, 1872, reprinted in *Woodhull and Claflin's Weekly*, January 27, 1872, 7; see also Stanton to Woodhull, December 29, [1872], Stanton Miscellaneous Papers, New York Public Library, New York.

41. Victoria Woodhull, *Carpenter and Cartter Reviewed: A Speech before the National Suffrage Association at Lincoln Hall, Washington, D.C, January 10, 1872* (New York, 1872), 20.

42. Montgomery, *Beyond Equality*, 379-86.

43. Anthony to Stanton, July 10, 1872, box 38, NAWSA Papers, Library of Congress.

44. Nancy A. Hewitt, *Women's Activism and Social Change: Rochester, New York, 1822-1872* (Ithaca, N.Y., 1984), 211. Anthony to Stanton, November 5, 1872, Harper Papers, Huntington Library, San Marino, California.

45. Harper, ed., *The Life and Work of Susan B. Anthony*, 1: 423-53; Charles Fairman, *History of the Supreme Court*, (New York, 1987), 7: 224.

46. Fairman, *History of the Supreme Court*, 285. Carpenter's argument in *Slaughterhouse* can be found in 21 Court Reporters Lawyers Edition, 399-401 (1872).

47. 16 Wall. 36 (1873).

48. 16 Wall. 130 (1873).

49. *HWS* 2: 734-42.

50. Ibid., 641.

51. The most important of these was Catherine McCullough's successful argument that the Constitution permitted states legislatively to enfranchise voters for presidential electors. In 1914 Illinois passed a "presidential suffrage" law, giving women votes in the 1916 presidential election. See Steven W. Buechler, *The Transformation of the Woman Suffrage Movement: The Case of Illinois, 1850-1920* (New Brunswick, N.J., 1986), 174-76.

52. Unidentified clipping, v. 12, 75, Susan B. Anthony Memorial Library Collection, Huntington Library, San Marino, Calif.

53. Susan B. Anthony and Ida Husted Harper, eds., *History of Woman Suffrage*, (Rochester, N.Y., 1902), 4: 10.

54. Norma Basch, "Reconstructing Female Citizenship" (Paper delivered at Women and the Constitution Conference, American University and the Smithsonian, October 1987).

HOW THE WEST WAS WON FOR WOMAN SUFFRAGE

Beverly Beeton

Editor's Introduction: In 1869 and 1870, as Eastern suffrage forces were in disarray following the failure of the Reconstruction amendments to establish universal suffrage for all, the territories of Wyoming and Utah stunned the nation by announcing the enfranchisement of women. Later, as they entered the Union as states, Wyoming (1890) and Utah (1896) insisted on retaining woman suffrage despite considerable opposition from Congress. They were joined as suffrage states by Colorado (1893) and Idaho (1896), which enfranchised women through state constitutional amendments. These were the only four states to enfranchise women in the nineteenth century.

In this essay, historian Beverly Beeton answers the question students of the suffrage movement have always pondered: what was behind this pioneering embrace of woman suffrage? Why was it that the West was far ahead of the rest of the nation in enfranchising women? Beeton, the author of the book *Women Vote in the West: The Woman Suffrage Movement, 1869-1896* and numerous articles on woman suffrage in the West, explains that there were many factors contributing to the early victories in the West, and that each of the four territories/states has its unique story. She emphasizes, however, that practical politics rather than advanced ideology explain the West's precociousness in adopting woman suffrage. While most Eastern and Southern politicians saw woman suffrage as worthy of scorn or ridicule and unpopular with their constituents, Western politicians embraced it as politically expedient for a fascinating variety of purposes. As Beeton explains, there *were* Western men who wanted women enfranchised out of a sense of justice. But the votes necessary for passage of suffrage bills were there because woman suffrage served practical needs ranging from attracting women settlers (using woman suffrage as an advertising gimmick) to protecting polygamy.

Beeton also discusses the relationship between the Eastern and Western suffrage movements, a relationship of mutual influence. Some Eastern proponents—including Congressmen—saw the territories as a good place to test this controversial new idea of woman suffrage. National suffrage leaders, including Lucy Stone, Elizabeth Cady Stanton, Susan B. Anthony, Anna Howard Shaw, and Carrie Chapman Catt, assisted with Western suffrage campaigns, beginning with the unsuccessful Kansas campaign of 1867. But they benefited from the opportunity to test and develop strategies and tactics in the West that were later used elsewhere.

One fascinating aspect of the Western story told by Beeton is the relationship between Mormon suffragists and Eastern suffrage leaders who tried to welcome and support the Mormon women while avoiding the appearance of condoning polygamy. In the wake of the Victoria Woodhull affair, the public was prepared to believe the worst regarding suffragists and unconventional ideas about sex and marriage, and the National Woman Suffrage Association (NWSA) particularly was hurt by its defense of Mormon suffragists. Beeton also explains that in the West, as in the rest of the nation, racism and ethnic tensions played a role in the suffrage movement, and that in this region the controversy over voting rights involved Chinese and Native Americans as well as African Americans.

The early victories in the West were of tremendous importance in the history of the American woman suffrage movement. As Beeton notes, suffragists and anti-suffragists alike gathered data and published studies on the effects of woman suffrage on Western society and politics, with each side insisting that the Western experience proved *them* right. Of greater significance, however, was the inspiration these Rocky Mountain states provided to suffragists in other regions of the United States.

★   ★   ★   ★   ★

A HALF-CENTURY prior to the 1920 ratification of the Nineteenth Amendment women voted in the Rocky Mountain West. In December 1869, Wyoming women were granted the right to vote, and two months later in February of 1870, their sisters across the mountains in Utah gained access to polling places. In both cases, women were enfranchised through woman suffrage bills adopted by their territorial legislatures and signed by the territorial governors. As a result of an 1893 referendum women in Colorado were also enfranchised, and a state constitutional amendment in Idaho in 1896 provided woman suffrage there. Thus, Wyoming, Utah, Colorado, and Idaho were the *only* states where women were enfranchised in the nineteenth century.[1]

Why were women in the Rocky Mountain West the first to vote? There is no one simple answer. An examination of events in the four nineteenth-century suffrage states reveals a variety of motives that together caused a sufficient number of male legislators and voters to support woman suffrage. There *were* liberal-minded men who believed voting rights were an inherent right of citizenship; but pragmatic objectives, usually political ones, were necessary for enough men to vote for woman suffrage for it to become a reality. In short, women were enfranchised in the American West primarily as a matter of expediency, not ideology.

Move West and Vote

In the West, woman suffrage was often seen as a means to advertise a region in hopes of attracting settlers or investors. Sometimes it was proposed as a device to embarrass political opponents if they voted against it or vetoed it. Often, territorial

residents saw it as a way to recruit Eastern support for their bids for statehood. When Black men, American-born Chinese men, and some Indian men voted, arguments for educated, property-owning, White women to have the same privilege appealed to many peoples' racial prejudices. Since the Rocky Mountain West was in the process of forming governments during the last quarter of the nineteenth century, the electorate had to be defined in the new laws and constitutions. Consequently, Westerners were forced to think about and debate the issue of who would be allowed to vote.

The fact that there was no significant, organized opposition in the four states (as there was from liquor interests in the states of Washington and California) made passage of legislation and referenda easier. Another contributing factor was the completion of the transcontinental railroad in 1869 that facilitated the quick transportation of people and ideas. Eastern lecture-bureau circuit riders, many of whom addressed women's issues, immediately toured the West, and Westerners traveled to the East more frequently and received news in a more timely fashion—including reports on Eastern debates regarding political rights for former slaves and women.

The existence of a post-Civil War woman suffrage movement also contributed to the early enfranchisement of Western women because Eastern suffragists kept the discussion of women's rights alive. It was in response to lobbyists' pressure for passage of a woman suffrage constitutional amendment that some Eastern newspapers and politicians proposed testing woman suffrage in the territories. Also, when campaigns were waged in the West, Eastern suffrage associations provided money and organizational expertise. Conversely, the suffrage movement as a whole benefited when strategies and campaign techniques were developed and tested in the Western states.

In 1867, when the Fourteenth Amendment defining national citizenship to include Black men was being ratified, a number of campaigns to amend state and territorial constitutions to provide for woman suffrage took place in the American West. The most vigorous effort was staged in Kansas where two amendments were proposed: one enfranchising Black men and one enfranchising women. Initially, the prospects appeared to be good because the 1861 Kansas constitution included school suffrage for women.[2]

Representing the American Equal Rights Association, the postwar organization advocating universal suffrage, Lucy Stone and her husband, Henry Blackwell, campaigned for a month in Kansas, and returned to Boston with optimistic reports that the Republicans had launched an irreversible movement for equal rights. However, this optimism proved premature. As the debate intensified, editors of national and local Republican and reform newspapers supported political privileges for Black men but failed to endorse equal rights for women. In the words of Horace Greeley, chair of the American Equal Rights Association, the extension of the franchise to women would be too revolutionary for public acceptance.

As the sunflowers blossomed in the late summer of 1867, Susan B. Anthony and Elizabeth Cady Stanton toured Kansas and found sentiment against woman suffrage growing. A month before the vote on the amendments, they were joined by George Francis Train, an avid Democrat and railroad financier, who brought money to the campaign. But association with Train caused abolitionists and Republicans to criticize severely Anthony and Stanton because Train used White supremacy arguments overtly to advance the women's cause. Responding to Republican critics, Anthony exclaimed: "Your test of faithfulness is the Negro, ours is the woman." [3]

Belatedly, many national newspaper editors tried to convince Kansas voters that the question was one of universal suffrage. Even Horace Greeley grudgingly acknowledged in his *New York Tribune* that while he regarded woman suffrage with distrust, he was willing to see it pioneered in Kansas.[4] Nevertheless, when the votes were tallied, both propositions failed. Neither women nor Black men were enfranchised as a result of the Kansas campaign in 1867.

Following the Kansas campaign, however, the woman suffrage movement adopted sunflower yellow as its campaign color, and the movement began to assume the form that it would take for the next quarter century. Feeling betrayed by the male equal rights reformers they had worked with for years before and after the Civil War, Stanton and Anthony launched a new organization in 1869 dedicated to woman suffrage, the National Woman Suffrage Association (NWSA), with headquarters in New York. They also founded a woman suffrage newspaper, *The Revolution*, which they used to oppose the Fourteenth and Fifteenth Amendments, advocating instead for suffrage for the educated, irrespective of sex or color. Immediate enfranchisement of all women through a federal constitutional amendment was their major focus. That same year, led by Lucy Stone, Henry Blackwell, and Julia Ward Howe, more moderate suffragists rallied to the banner of the American Woman Suffrage Association (AWSA) based in Boston. This group, which supported the Fourteenth and Fifteenth Amendments, endorsed the constitutional amendment for woman suffrage, but emphasized building support for woman suffrage in the states. This schism on goals and methods persisted until 1890 when the two factions merged into the National American Woman Suffrage Association (NAWSA).

Meanwhile, Congressmen continued to consider the idea of enfranchising women in the territories as an experiment. During the Kansas campaign, Hamilton Willcox, a representative of the New York Universal Franchise Association, proposed that women in *all* the territories be enfranchised, and *The New York Times* publicized this scheme for testing woman suffrage. Given legislative form by George Washington Julian, Republican Congressman from Indiana, the idea of women voting in the territories was appealing because it appeared to be safe from a political point of view.[5] Neither the political stability of

the established states nor the national political scene would be seriously altered (since territorial residents were not allowed to vote for their own governors or the president), and the definition of the electorate could be reexamined by Congress when the territories applied for admission to the Union as states. Moreover, since Congress controlled the territories, the experiment could be halted if it went awry. And the possible defeminizing impact that politics might have on women and the impact women would have on politics could be tested safely.

In addition, Willcox and others predicted that woman suffrage would be advantageous in relieving the problem of "surplus women" in the East (more women than men available for marriage as a result of the Civil War casualties, a problem exacerbated by male migration to the West). The adoption of woman suffrage in the West, they believed, would encourage Eastern women to move to the frontier.[6] These men also predicted that woman suffrage would lead to the elimination of polygamy—the Utah Mormon practice of men marrying multiple wives.

Of course, population redistribution and Mormon plural marriage were not the primary concerns of women's rights advocates who insisted that women had inherent natural rights and demanded a constitutional amendment protecting women's political rights as the proposed Fifteenth Amendment protected the rights of freedmen. Yet, as the Fifteenth Amendment was approved, the proposed woman suffrage amendment and the proposal to test woman suffrage in the territories languished. Representative Julian's bill on woman suffrage in the territories was now limited to Utah Territory where the bill's sponsors hoped woman suffrage could eradicate polygamy—a "relic of barbarism."

While Eastern suffragists divided over the best means of attaining the vote and Eastern politicians contemplated the theoretical consequences of woman suffrage, however, women in the Rocky Mountain West were voting.

Women's Rights in Wyoming

In December of 1869, the Wyoming territorial legislature surprised the nation by passing a bill enfranchising women. While there was no organized suffrage campaign in this new territory with fewer than nine thousand residents of which only slightly more than one thousand were women of voting age, the arguments for woman suffrage were well known. Traveling on the newly completed transcontinental railroad, the lyceum bureau's stellar speaker, Anna Dickinson, visited Wyoming on her Western tour. And Redelia Bates, a woman suffrage lecturer from St. Louis, spoke to the Wyoming territorial legislature. In addition, Eastern debates over women's rights were covered by local newspapers. Yet, though there were individuals in Wyoming such as the suffrage bill's introducer, William H. Bright, who believed in women's right to vote as a matter of citizenship, the bill passed because lawmakers believed woman suffrage was a way to advertize

Women voting in Wyoming,
November 1888

LIBRARY OF CONGRESS

the territory to potential investors and settlers. Some Democrats thought it would embarrass the Republican governor, John A. Campbell, who would (they presumed) veto it, but he surprised them by quickly signing the law that even went beyond suffrage to allow women to serve on juries and hold public office.

A jubilant Susan B. Anthony reported the news of the enfranchisement of women in Wyoming to the suffragists assembled for the first NWSA convention. She urged women "to emigrate to Wyoming and make a model State of it by sending a woman Senator to the National Capital,"[7] though she planned to stay home and work for a federal constitutional amendment enfranchising all women. While Eastern women did not heed the call to go West, they did use the Wyoming example to urge their own state legislatures to extend equal rights to them and to encourage Congress to amend the Constitution.

In the summer of 1871, Stanton and Anthony went West to "the land of freedom," as they called Wyoming, where they were warmly greeted by government officials and leading citizens. Returning east in December, Anthony learned that some Wyoming Democrats, unhappy about the election of several Republicans, were trying to repeal the woman suffrage law. However, Governor Campbell vetoed the repeal act, saying, "No legislature has the right to disfranchise its own constituents."[8] When an attempt was made to overturn his veto, the members of the Council and the House divided along party lines defeating the measure by one vote.

As the first and only place where women voted and sat on juries, Wyoming was an object of curiosity. Easterners were eager to question travelers and Wyoming residents to determine what impact woman suffrage had on women and on society. Two years after passage of the law, Edward M. Lee (who reportedly had been removed as Secretary of Wyoming Territory for public drunkenness and enjoying the company of a prostitute known as "the Circassian Girl") told *The Galaxy* magazine that the powers of the ballot had not caused women to abandon any of their womanly or wifely qualities. As he saw it, the time-honored ordinance of marriage seemed to be as everlasting as the mountains; moreover, there were no signs of that "pestiferous freelove doctrine" that seemed to be gaining converts in

the East.[9] At the 1874 NWSA convention, Aaron Sargent, a Congressman from California, praised woman suffrage in Wyoming "where women hold office, where they vote, where they have the most orderly society of any of the Territories."[10]

While Sargent was applauding the results of Wyoming women's new-found freedoms, however, a number of newspaper editors were questioning the experiment. When the *New York Independent* charged that only twenty-five women had voted in the last election, the AWSA investigated and its newspaper *The Woman's Journal* countered with assurances from citizens of Wyoming that women's participation in elections had "become a matter of course." Having observed women voting for four years, Governor Campbell testified he was convinced of the justice and wisdom of the measure. In 1888, the NWSA expressed its confidence in its convention banner proclaiming: "The vote of women transformed Wyoming from barbarism to civilization."

A year later, over one hundred Wyoming women demanded that woman suffrage be affirmed in the statehood constitution. Few convention delegates openly opposed woman suffrage, but nearly a third subscribed to the idea of separate submission (of woman suffrage and statehood) arguing that the citizens of Wyoming had not had an opportunity to vote on the proposition because voting rights had been granted to women by the territorial legislature. However, when the debates ended, woman suffrage was included, and two-thirds of the voters registered their support for the constitution. When Congress was about to reject Wyoming's admission into the Union because of the clause enfranchising women, Wyoming legislators telegraphed Congress saying they would remain out of the Union a hundred years rather than join without woman suffrage. Finally, the constitution was approved by a narrow margin with the controversial clause intact, and Wyoming became the first state to allow its female citizens to vote.

Utah Suffrage a Vote for Mormons

Two months after the 1869 passage of the initial woman suffrage bill in Wyoming, the Utah territorial legislature enfranchised Utah women. This move received considerable national attention because it admitted nearly forty times as many women to the polling places as had the Wyoming action; moreover, most of these women were members of the Mormon church that practiced plural marriage. Arguing that polygamy only existed where women were degraded, reformers predicted the ballot would be used to eradicate the practice. Even the NWSA proclaimed its confidence that the enfranchisement of women in Utah was the one safe, sure, and swift means to abolish polygamy. Reformers refrained, however, from claiming the vote would cause women to migrate to the territory because the Mormons promoted their marital system as a means to deal with "surplus women."

Generally, the national concern about Utah women amused the Mormons. Assuring readers that Utah women could vote "without running wild or becoming unsexed," George Q. Cannon, editor of the Mormon-controlled

newspaper, the *Deseret News*, expressed pleasure in the opportunity to be an example to the world.[11]

The Mormons, of course, expected that woman suffrage would reinforce rather than undermine Mormon traditions. In fact, enfranchisement of women in Utah was primarily an effort by the Mormons to counter the image painted by lecture-bureau circuit riders of Mormon women as downtrodden slaves and to stop national efforts to eliminate polygamy. Furthermore, in 1870, just before the territorial legislature acted, reports arrived in Salt Lake City that Congress was considering a variety of threatening legislation ranging from schemes to partition Utah and give segments to the surrounding territories and states, to proposals to disfranchise the Mormons, disqualify them from holding public office and sitting on juries, and deprive them of the right to homestead or preempt public lands, or disinherit their children. Mormons were also concerned about new threats to polygamy; when enforcement of the anti-polygamy law of 1862 seemed imminent, five thousand women gathered in the Mormon Tabernacle on Temple Square for a "great indignation meeting" to decry the "mean, foul" legislation.

It was against this background that the Utah legislature passed the bill extending the ballot to women, and on February 12, 1870, the non-Mormon, Territorial Secretary S.A. Mann, serving as acting governor, signed the bill into law. Responding to a resolution of appreciation from a delegation of Utah women, Mann penned a letter philosophizing about the intelligent use of the ballot. Mormon faithful, William Clayton, was less philosophical when he noted, "The poor, enslaved downtrodden!!! women of Utah can now act for themselves and take revenge on the men of Israel." Then he gleefully exclaimed that those who expected Mormon women to use the vote against polygamy would "gnash their teeth with rage" and "foam worse than ever," for "there are not many women here but will sustain all the measures of the authorities [of the church] better than some of the men do."[12]

There were individuals in Utah in 1870 who advocated woman suffrage for liberal, human rights reasons, and there was some concern about non-Mormons coming into the territory now that the transcontinental railroad was completed. But the compelling reasons for passage of the legislation were related to polygamy and statehood. "Bah!" was the *Salt Lake Herald's* response to the accusation that the Mormon-dominated legislature gave the vote to women to strengthen Mormon political power against non-Mormons. With a total population of 87,000 of which only about 4,500 were non-Mormons, doubling the Mormon voting power was not necessary.[13]

Ironically, now that Mormon women had proven to be supporters of polygamy, Congress began to try to strip them of the franchise. During the 1870s and 1880s, Utah repeatedly petitioned for statehood as Congress continually proposed legislation designed to take voting privileges from Utah women as part of the anti-polygamy effort. And Mormons repeatedly reminded Congress that the idea of enfranchising women in Utah was being considered in the East when the Utah territorial legislature acted.

Using the church's women's auxiliary, the Relief Society, as the communications network, Mormon women became skilled at holding "mass meetings" and producing "mammoth petitions" in opposition to hostile legislation or in support of statehood. Utah women and the territory's delegate to Congress were in regular communication with national suffrage leaders and were able to solicit suffragists to lobby Congress on Utah's behalf.

In 1883, when Congress was considering a number of measures to "elevate" the women of Utah and "relieve" them from their "bondage" by repealing the territorial act conferring the vote, the Washington, D.C., attorney, suffragist, and soon-to-be presidential candidate, Belva Lockwood, launched an aggressive campaign against the legislation saying: "It is not only a fight for `Mormon' female votes—it is a contest for woman's equal rights in principle." Persuading the NWSA to adopt a resolution against the legislation, Lockwood declared: "Only a fool or a knave would deny" the bill is a direct blow at woman suffrage.[14]

When suffragists were accused by anti-polygamists of being in "an attitude not unfriendly to polygamy" and anti-polygamy societies reported that Mormon women voted as instructed by the church hierarchy, national suffrage leaders realized their image was being tarnished by identification with Utah women. Thus, Anthony went to great lengths to clarify that the NWSA's only interest in Utah was woman suffrage. As the concern with polygamy intensified in Congress, suffrage leaders continued their support of Utah women's voting rights while trying to distance themselves from polygamy.

Reverend Anna Howard Shaw, Henry Blackwell, and Mary A. Hunt presented the arguments of the AWSA to the House Committee on Territories, objecting to the proposed disfranchisement of Utah women. Instead, they petitioned for a law to give women equal suffrage in all the territories. In 1887, the NWSA urged President Grover Cleveland to veto the Edmunds-Tucker Bill that proposed to take the vote from Utah women. He responded by allowing the bill to become law without his signature.[15] And the national suffrage cause was set back further when Congress once again refused to pass the Anthony Amendment.

The suffrage movement and the NWSA in particular were greatly weakened by identification with the Mormons and their marital system. Belva Lockwood's defense of the Mormons brought the wrath of society down on the NWSA and the cause. In the 1870s, society had a similar negative reaction to feminist Victoria Woodhull who was opposed to legal and clerical marriage and instead advocated "free love" with the assumption that each woman had the right to decide whether, when, and with whom to become sexually active.[16] Women's rights advocates could no longer be critical of the institution of marriage without being accused of favoring polygamy. It was now necessary for feminists to shun all criticisms of marital and family relations and pledge their belief in the sanctity of monogamous marriage.

Elizabeth Cady Stanton and Susan B. Anthony's methods and philosophy lost credibility after 1887, and American feminism took a conservative turn. The

state-by-state approach to gaining enfranchisement dominated the movement until 1914, and feminist critiques of marriage and women's roles in society were set aside as priority was given to securing the ballot. Susan B. Anthony continued to be revered, but a new and more conservative generation of suffragists emerged, and temperance was accepted as part of the movement in spite of warnings that it would rally liquor interests to work against woman suffrage. When the NWSA and the AWSA merged in 1890, only the women of Wyoming were enfranchised, because Utah women had lost the vote by Congressional action, and Washington women had, for the second time, seen their suffrage law declared invalid by that territory's supreme court.

While the relationship between women's rights leaders and the Mormons was strained, suffragists continued to visit Utah. In the spring of 1895, Anthony and Anna Howard Shaw led a three-day Rocky Mountain Suffrage Conference in Salt Lake City attended by women from Wyoming, Utah, and Colorado. National suffragists also assisted Utah women with the development of a territorial suffrage association—a step that seemed necessary because many Utah men were willing to abandon woman suffrage now that it could no longer be used to protect polygamy or advance the statehood cause. This became evident when Utah made a new bid for admission into the Union (still unsuccessful) with a constitution

Rocky Mountain Suffrage Conference, May 1895.
In the front row are Margaret N. Caine *(far right)* and Susan B. Anthony *(third from right)*. In the second row are Zina D. H. Young *(second from right)*, Emmeline B. Wells *(third from right)*, Sarah M. Kimball *(fourth from right)*, and Anna Howard Shaw *(fifth from right)*. In the third row are Mary C.C. Bradford *(far right)* and Estelle Kesl *(third from right)*. Theresa A. Jenkins is in the fourth row, *(third from right)*. In the back row are Mattie Hughes Cannon *(far left)*, Emily S. Richards *(fourth from left)*, and Ellis Meredith Stansbury *(fifth from left)*.

prohibiting polygamy and limiting suffrage to adult men.

The Utah feminist, Charlotte Ives Cobb Godbe Kirby, who was known for her radical rhetoric calling for women of the world to unite, wrote numerous articles and letters on behalf of the Utah Territory Woman Suffrage Association and sometimes vied with Emmeline B. Wells for the leadership role in the Utah woman suffrage movement.[17] Active on the local and nation-

Emmeline B. Wells

al scenes, Kirby and Wells were both involved in the discussion about woman suffrage in 1895 when the territory prepared to make a new bid for statehood and debated the provisions of the proposed state constitution.[18] However, two Mormon men, both of whom were historians and members of the Democratic party, led the convention debate over inclusion of women in the electorate. Brigham H. Roberts argued that women could not act independently because of relationships in the family; besides, he said, women are sufficiently represented in politics by husbands, fathers, sons, or brothers.[19] Orson F. Whitney, who compared Roberts to a bull standing in front of a train attempting to prevent it from passing ("I admire your courage but d__n your judgement"), insisted, "it is woman's destiny to have a voice in the affairs of government. She was designed for it. She has a right to it."[20]

Finally, Utah approved a constitution containing woman suffrage in 1895. Since the Mormon Church had officially abandoned polygamy in 1890, Congress approved the constitution with little protest about the enfranchisement of women, and President Cleveland did not raise the issue when he issued the proclamation admitting the territory of Utah as a state on January 4, 1896.

Colorado Suffrage, a Matter of Race

While polygamy was the major issue tied to woman suffrage in Utah, across the Rockies in Colorado racial concerns were predominant. The territorial legislature and newspapers had been discussing woman suffrage since the late 1860s, and Governor Edward M. McCook had called for Colorado to join its sister territory, Wyoming, as a leader in the cause of universal suffrage. Advocates argued it was taxation without representation when women were prohibited from voting. Opponents warned: women do not want to vote; involvement in politics might destroy "the symmetry of women's character"; only the class that goes to war

should be allowed to vote; and the enfranchisement of women at this time is premature. But race was the major issue.[21]

Representative M.S. Taylor warned Colorado territorial legislators in 1870 that Black women, as well Chinese women, will vote if the woman suffrage bill passes.[22] After studying the legislation, a house committee chaired by Representative A.H. DeFrance urged passage and argued it was unfair for uneducated, non-property-holding Black men to vote on matters concerning the property of White women who were not allowed to vote. He went on to suggest that women's presence in politics would have a "purifying influence" on society and politics. It was in response to DeFrance that Taylor warned of the folly of allowing "Negro wenches" and Chinese women to vote.

Unmoved by petitions from women requesting suffrage, lawmakers refused to approve the legislation. Thus, DeFrance sought a compromise by proposing that the suffrage bill be submitted to the qualified electorate of the territory, including women, for ratification or rejection.[23] After considerable parliamentary maneuvering by the friends and foes of woman suffrage, Taylor moved for postponement, and the house effectively killed the bill by voting fifteen to ten to delay action.

Even though the legislative measure was dead, the debate was kept alive in the newspapers and was periodically enlivened by the visit of a suffrage speaker. In July of 1870, the Eastern actress and lecturer Olive Logan spoke in Denver, and one year later, Stanton and Anthony lectured to a responsive crowd in the Denver Theater. As Colorado drafted a constitution in preparation for admission as the Centennial State, woman suffrage was a major issue. Fearing rejection by the Colorado electorate or the national Congress, constitutional convention delegates limited women's involvement in the political process to school district elections, but provided for a vote on woman suffrage in the first general election after statehood.

Consequently, in 1877 a major campaign began to persuade the Colorado male electorate to fully enfranchise women. The Colorado Suffrage Association coordinated speaking tours throughout the state that included local advocates such as William H. Bright, who had initiated the suffrage bill in Wyoming and was now living in Denver, and many Eastern headliners. Susan B. Anthony stumped mining towns and outlying communities speaking in saloons, in hotel dining rooms, at railroad stations, and on a soapbox in front of a courthouse.

While newspapers in Denver generally supported the referendum, Pueblo's *Colorado Chieftain* editorialized against suffragists. Denver's Catholic Bishop Machebeuf continued his pulpit campaign against woman suffrage and was soon joined by the Presbyterian Reverend Bliss, who referred to suffragists as "bawling, ranting women, bristling for their rights." If women vote, he told parishioners, married women will live in endless bickering with their husbands and single women will never marry. On election day when Reverend Bliss encountered women handing out fliers urging men to vote in the affirmative, he identified himself and

reiterated his objections to women voting. The AWSA's Lucy Stone countered, and a loud exchange ensued. Yet, when the day ended, Reverend Bliss's point of view was victorious; woman suffrage was defeated by a vote of two to one.[24]

Sixteen years passed before Colorado suffragists were once again able to get a referendum on the ballot in 1893—thanks to the support of Populist legislators and the Populist governor, David H. Waite. Colorado suffragists concentrated on converting male voters through newspapers and political parties. While they organized local suffrage leagues throughout the state, they limited the number of Eastern speakers invited to the state. When suffragists pledged their support of silver as a currency basis along with gold, miners and unionized workers seemed willing to support the referendum, and victory came within grasp when the Republican, Prohibitionist, and Populist parties endorsed equal suffrage. With strong support and little opposition the referendum passed.

National suffragists quickly seized Colorado as an attractive example because it had a large population and an urban center where the impact of women voting could be closely observed. Unlike Wyoming, Colorado did not have a reputation as a wild frontier with a high crime rate, and it was not tainted by polygamy as was Utah. Moreover, Colorado was unique as the first state to grant woman suffrage by referendum. The aggressive campaign methods used by Colorado suffragists with organizational and financial support from Eastern suffrage associations became the model for other states. The strategies of converting the male electorate through speeches, political parties, and public demonstrations, which were developed in Colorado under the guidance of NAWSA leader Carrie Chapman Catt, would be employed in other states, notably California and Idaho.

Idaho, Suffrage in Snake River Country

One year after women were enfranchised in Wyoming and Utah, Dr. Joseph William Morgan, a Democratic representative from Oneida County, announced that women in Idaho should enjoy the same rights and introduced a woman suffrage bill in the territorial legislature. However, Republican W.H. Van Slyke appealed to Blackstone's theory of the legal and political merger of the woman with the man upon marriage and warned, "that to give her the ballot would work an entire social revolution, disrupting the family tie, and bringing a conflict of sexes in the land."[25] When lawmakers put the issue to a vote, it resulted in a tie. Thus, Idaho's first woman suffrage bill died.

Occasionally, an Idaho suffragist would lecture or Abigail Scott Duniway,[26] the Oregon suffrage leader and editor of *The New Northwest* suffrage newsletter, would tour the territory speaking and soliciting subscribers, but for a decade and a half there was only limited discussion of woman suffrage in Idaho. Immigration, Mormons, prohibition, and woman suffrage were intertwined in a complex way in Idaho. One-fourth of the residents were Mormons, most of whom lived in Dr. Morgan's Southeastern part of the state along the Utah-Idaho border, and there

Abigail Scott Duniway
LIBRARY OF CONGRESS

were fears woman suffrage would give Mormons disproportionate political power because there were large numbers of women in Mormon settlements. Fearing voting rights for women might encourage more Mormons to move to Idaho some people reported: "The impression was getting abroad that Idaho was controlled by the leading Mormons in Salt Lake, and that this impression would tend to discourage [non-Mormon] immigration."[27] The underlying cause of most of this anxiety was political; at the time, most Mormons voted Democratic.

Concerns about prohibition posed a bigger problem for woman suffrage advocates in Idaho; Duniway and some other suffragists blamed the Woman's Christian Temperence Union (WCTU's) efforts to stop liquor traffic for a woman suffrage law being declared unconstitutional in Washington territory. Consequently, in 1889—when the constitutional convention was being lobbied to include woman suffrage and a clause prohibiting the sale of liquor—Duniway rushed to Boise. Arguing temperance and woman suffrage were not inexorably tied, she assured statehood constitution writers that women would not vote away beer and whiskey. However, delegates were more concerned that the document would not be accepted if Idaho was associated with the Mormons and woman suffrage than they were that women would use the ballot to bring about prohibition. Thus, both women and Mormon men were denied political rights and the opportunity to vote on the constitution that was submitted to the Idaho electorate and the United States Congress in 1890.

Abigail Scott Duniway, who now spent part of her time in Custer County, Idaho, where her sons had a homestead claim, thought woman suffrage would be submitted to the Idaho electorate in the first election after statehood as had been the case in Colorado. This did not happen, however. While Duniway, temperance advocates, and Mormon women worked in their own ways to advance the cause, six years passed before a woman suffrage amendment received the required two-thirds vote in the Idaho legislature. Anticipating that a major campaign was needed to persuade the electorate to support the amendment, Anthony told Duniway to leave suffrage in Idaho to the Eastern managers and to confine her activities to Oregon.[28] Thus, Emma Smith DeVoe of Illinois went to Idaho to manage the campaign, and Mell Woods, an active suffrage worker from Wallace, Idaho, (the daughter of the Utah's Mormon suffragist Emmeline B. Wells), was assigned to assist DeVoe.

Organizing local suffrage clubs as she traveled, DeVoe toured Idaho giving suffrage lectures. In November of 1895, delegates from these suffrage clubs converged in Boise to found the Idaho Equal Suffrage Association. Having just returned to her home in Buffalo, New York from California where she had worked

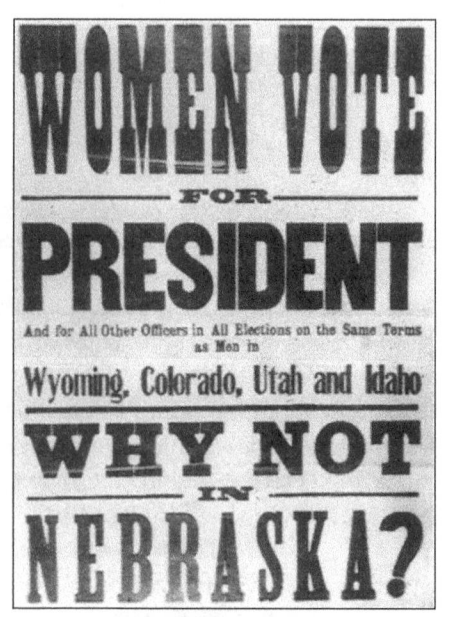

Flag with four stars representing states
where women could vote, c. 1900
SMITHSONIAN INSTITUTION

Poster from the
1911 Nebraska campaign
NEBRASKA STATE HISTORICAL SOCIETY

on that state's unsuccessful suffrage campaign, Anthony sent a telegram to Idaho suffrage conventioneers saying, "Women speakers can not reach them [male voters]."[29] Instead she advised Idaho suffragists to educate voters through political party newspapers and public meetings. Heeding Anthony's advice, Idaho suffragists organized for the upcoming campaign. In the spring of 1896, Laura M. Johns, a campaign organizer from Kansas, was coordinating activities in the Southwest part of the state. Helen Young, a lawyer from Wallace, Idaho, was in charge of the Northern part of the state, and Blanche Whitman of Montpelier was responsible for rallying the predominantly Mormon communities in the Southeast region, where Mormon men were now allowed to vote.

This approach minimized regional tensions and allowed suffragists to focus on gaining support for political rights for women. In their resolutions urging support for the amendment, Idaho suffragists pointed to the examples of women voting in the neighboring states, and called forth the principle of no taxation without representation. Appealing to racial biases, suffragists argued that White, native-born American women should be at least equal in political rights with Chinese men, who if born in the United States were allowed to vote, and Indian men, who under the the 1887 Dawes Act [dividing Western Indian reservations into individually owned land] were allowed citizenship and voting rights. In her Fourth of July speech, suffragist Laura M. Johns referred to the enfranchisement of Nez Pierce Indian men and said she believed, "Women were as much entitled to

privileges of citizenship as those savages."[30] NAWSA organizer Carrie Chapman Catt, who had refined campaign strategies in Colorado, came to Idaho during the summer to assist the Idaho association's advisory board with the preparation of instructions to the local suffrage clubs. As the election approached, most of the state's newspapers declared their support, and all four political parties—Populists, Democrats, Republicans, and Silver Republicans—endorsed the amendment.

On election day men cast 12,126 votes in support and 6,282 against. However, before celebrations proclaiming Idaho the fourth woman suffrage state could be staged, the board of canvassers ruled the measure was defeated because it had not received a majority of all votes cast in the election, just a majority cast on the amendment. Determined, the Idaho suffrage association commissioned lawyers, William E. Borah and James H. Hawley, who would eventually become Idaho's senator and governor, to carry the issue to the Idaho Supreme Court where the ruling was favorable. Idaho now joined the ranks of suffrage states.

Woman suffrage was realized in Idaho in 1896 because the political parties (especially the Populists) as well as the Mormons and the WCTU supported it, and there was no significant organized opposition from liquor interests as there was in the Pacific Coast states. Idaho suffragists perfected campaign techniques developed in Colorado that proved to be the major strategies of the women's movement for the next quarter century. In 1897, Catt instructed the NAWSA conventioneers to study the Idaho methods and improve them, for: "Until we do this kind of house-to-house work we can never expect to carry any of the states in which there are large cities."[31]

Four Experiments Examined

Idaho was the last and the least famous of the nineteenth-century woman suffrage states. The Wyoming experience was the best known and the longest tested. While the Utah example was considered anomalous by some as a result of the association of polygamy, Colorado—with its large population and urban center—was considered the most reliable test of suffrage strategies and suffrage itself.

Suffragists gathered data on the four states in an attempt to demonstrate the positive impact of woman suffrage. They concluded from their findings that women's involvement in politics had resulted in calmer and more orderly polling places, in the selection of candidates of higher moral character, in better schools, in more moral and sanitary legislation, and in making "intemperance and other bad habits unpopular."[32] More colorful, but less positive conclusions appeared in popular publications. The well-known Western novelist William Macleod Raine reported access to polling booths had not "unsexed" women, and they had not "regenerated the world" with their ballots.[33] Examining the experiences in the Rocky Mountain states, the editor of the Utah *Deseret News* found the promised purification of politics had "not panned out to any very extraordinary extent";

"The Awakening" is a well-known illustration by artist Henry Mayer. Lady Liberty strides across the Western states where women already had the vote, toward the East, where women are reaching out to her. Mayer's illustration was the centerfold of a special suffrage issue of *Puck* magazine, guest-edited in 1915 by New York suffrage groups.   LIBRARY OF CONGRESS

moreover, partisanship had "taken hold of the lady voter with equal if not greater force than" it had the men.[34] As one Colorado woman phrased it: "They vote with men, and for men, and just about like men."[35] A writer for *Pearson's Magazine* concluded women had used the ballot to do "nothing revolutionary, startling, uplifting, or sensational."[36]

Woman suffrage is usually viewed by historians as a middle-class reform movement; this view holds in the early experiences in the West. Most leaders and supporters of the movement in the four Rocky Mountain states were White, Protestant, protectors of the community. There was some identification of woman suffrage with temperance and Populism, but generally woman suffrage in the American West was not led by people who sought to overthrow or even radically reform the established social, economic systems. Even in the cases where the Populist Party was a prime force in bringing about their enfranchisement, after a year or two, women tended to vote for the more conventional political parties. Most Western suffragists held conservative political views and defended tradition, especially the role of wife and mother.

Arguments for and against political rights for women were often based on racist assumptions in the last quarter of the nineteenth century, in the West as elsewhere in the nation. Since White women were generally better educated and often owned property, it was argued, they should not be the political inferiors of Black, Chinese, or Indian men. The emotional appeals of equal rights workers and politicians that "my wife" or "my mother" is surely as good as a Black man were provocative, and

the cry of White women's superiority to Indians and Chinese had a special appeal in the American West. On the other hand, an often-heard condemnation of woman suffrage was that Black women, Chinese women, and Indian women could not be kept out of the voting booths if women were enfranchised. These arguments were frequently used by Westerners and by Eastern politicians and suffragists who kept woman suffrage alive on the national scene.

The fact that a national suffrage movement existed in the East and that governments were in a formative stage in the West also contributed to the establishment of women's rights during the last three decades of the nineteenth century. The West was a dynamic, evolving region. Railroads ended the isolation, the frontier was closing, and territorial status was being traded for statehood. In those days of boosterism, Westerners were promoters; so it was natural for them to seize on a non-threatening scheme such as woman suffrage as a means to publicize their regions and hopefully attract settlers, investors, and support for their admission to the Union as states.

The fact that Wyoming and Utah were territories in 1869 and 1870 allowed for quick enactment of woman suffrage. Once a territorial legislature approved a bill, only the governor's signature was needed for it to become law. Moreover, when Westerners were writing statehood constitutions and preparing themselves for self-government, they had to think through and vote consciously on a form of government including a definition of the electorate.

Certainly, there were liberal, egalitarian-minded individuals in the West who supported woman suffrage for human rights reasons, but enfranchisement became a reality as a result of expediency. The motives of the legislators and governors responsible for enfranchising women were usually conservative and political rather than progressive, ideological, and egalitarian. These men were not afraid that Western women would use the ballot to reform society or seize political power; after all, with the exception of Utah, there were not many women.[37] Moreover, in these four regions, women had not formed significant social reform movements. Even the WCTU was not considered a serious threat.

Fourteen Years to Light the Other Forty-Four States

After the 1896 amendment of the Idaho constitution, however, it was fourteen years before Wyoming, Utah, Colorado, and Idaho, were joined by another suffrage state and a new star was added to the woman suffrage flag displayed annually at the national suffrage meeting. Yet, when at last the woman suffrage movement emerged from its string of defeats and began to win battles in the states, the first victories *again* were in the American West. In 1910, Washington added its star to the suffrage flag, followed by California in 1911, Oregon, Arizona, and Kansas in 1912, the Territory of Alaska in 1913, and Montana and Nevada in 1914. Thus, at the beginning of World War I, woman suffrage existed in eleven Western states and the territory of Alaska. It would be seven more years before the Nineteenth Amendment would be ratified in 1920.

Notes

1. This essay is based on Beverly Beeton's book *Women Vote in the West: The Woman Suffrage Movement, 1869-1896*, published in the American Legal and Constitutional History series, edited by Harold Hyman and Stuart Bruchey, Garland Publishing, New York, 1986.

2. Ellen Carol DuBois, *Feminism and Suffrage: The Emergence of an Independent Woman's Movement in America, 1848-1869* (Ithaca, 1978).

3. Elizabeth Cady Stanton, Susan B. Anthony, Matilda J. Gage and Ida H. Harper, eds. *History of Woman Suffrage*, 6 vols. 1881-1922. (Reprint edition, New York: Arno, 1969), 2: 264, (hereafter, *HWS*).

4. *New York Tribune*, October 1, 1867.

5. *HWS* 2: 324-325.

6. In the post-Civil War years there was a great deal of concern about what the newspapers called the "surplus women" problem. Yet census data for 1890 reveals that there were 32,067,880 men in the nation and only 30,554,370 women. It seems to have been a problem more of perception than reality; to the extent that a marriage gap existed, it was a matter of age and geographical distribution, not of actual numbers.

7. As quoted in Katharine Anthony, *Susan B. Anthony: Her Personal History and Her Era* (New York, 1954), 248.

8. Hamilton Willcox, pamphlet, "Wyoming: The True Cause and Splendid Fruits of Woman Suffrage There from Official Records and Personal Knowledge correcting the errors of Horace Plunkett and Professor Bryce and supplying omissions in the *History of Woman Suffrage* by Mrs. Stanton, Mrs. Gage, and Miss Anthony, and in the *History of Wyoming* by Hubert Howe Bancroft with other information about the state." (New York: November 1890), 17, Bancroft Library, Berkeley, Calif.

9. Extract from *The Galaxy* article, 13 (June 1872): n.p., located in the Susa Young Gates papers, Widtsoe Collection at the Utah State Historical Society, Salt Lake City, Utah.

10. *HWS* 2: 545.

11. *Deseret News*, February 15, 1870.

12. William Clayton to Brother Jesse, and Clayton to Brother East, February 13, 1870. Clayton Letterbooks, Bancroft Library.

13. In *The Puritan Ethic and Woman Suffrage* (New York, 1967), Alan P. Grimes, employing status anxiety techniques similar to those developed by Richard Hofstadter, argues that "the constituency granting woman suffrage was composed of those who also supported prohibition and immigration restriction and felt woman suffrage would further their enactment." Grimes errs in his analysis when he reads backwards into history. The issues of prohibition and immigration restriction were not significant factors in Wyoming, Utah, Colorado, and Idaho when woman suffrage was enacted there.

14. Belva A. Lockwood's speech before the NWSA, January 24, 1883, as printed in the *Ogden Daily Herald*, June 9, 1883.

15. *Salt Lake Herald*, January 29, 1887; and *Deseret News*, March 4, 1887.

16. In *Everyone Was Brave: The Rise and Fall of Feminism* (Chicago, 1969), William L. O'Neil argues that suffragists' identification with Victoria Woodhull and her views on monogamy made it impossible for women's rights advocates to be critical of the institution of marriage without being accused of favoring free love. The same thesis is valid when applied to Lockwood and the identification with polygamy.

17. Beverly Beeton, "'I Am an American Woman': Charlotte Ives Cobb Godbe Kirby," *Journal of the American West*, 27 (April 1988): 13-19.

18. See Jean Bickmore White article, *Utah Historical Quarterly*, 42 (Fall 1974): 344-69.

19. Brigham Henry Roberts autobiography, copy of manuscript at Utah State Historical Society, Salt Lake City, Utah, 117-78.

20. O.F. Whitney speech, March 30, 1895, *Men and Woman* (May 14, 1895): 10-12.

21. William B. Faherty, "Regional Minorities and the Woman Suffrage Struggle," *Colorado Magazine* (July 1956), 1.

22. "Speech of M.S. Taylor on Suffrage," *Colorado Transcript*, January 26, 1870.

23. Billie Barnes Jensen, "Woman Suffrage in Colorado," M.A. thesis, University of Colorado, 1959, 20-21.

24. *HWS* 3: 723.

25. *Idaho Statesman*, January 10, 1871; also see the January 5, 1871 issue.

26. Abigail Scott Duniway's *Path Breaking: An Autobiographical History of the Equal Suffrage Movement in Pacific Coast States* (Portland, Oregon, 1914) is a detailed record of events in Idaho; however, Duniway had her prejudices and made herself and her point of view most important in her narration of events. *HWS* 4: 589-97 has a chapter on the suffrage campaign in Idaho written by two participants—Eunice Pond Athey and William Balderston, editor of the *Idaho Statesman*.

27. An article from the *Avalanche* as cited in the *Idaho Democrat*, a Mormon newspaper published in Southern Idaho, March 24, 1883.

28. T.A. Larson, "Woman's Rights in Idaho," *Idaho Yesterdays* 16 (Spring 1972): 2-15, 9. Larson published numerous articles on woman suffrage in the West. The most detailed version is "Emancipating the West's Dolls, Vassals and Hopeless Drudges: The Origins of Woman Suffrage in the West," in Roger Daniels, editor, *Essays in Western History in Honor of T.A. Larson*, v. 37 (Laramie: University of Wyoming Publications, 1971).

29. As quoted in *Idaho Statesman*, November 21, 1895; also see, Anthony Diary, November 18, 1895, in the Library of Congress, Manuscript Division, Washington, D.C.

30. *Caldwell Tribune*, July 4, 1896; also see, "Equal Suffragists' Desires," in the Equal Suffrage Association of Idaho file, Idaho State Historical Society, Boise, Idaho.

31. *HWS* 4: 293.

32. For detailed information on the impact of woman suffrage in the four states see Beeton, *Women Vote in the West*, 136-156.

33. As quoted in *Deseret News*, February 13, 1902.

34. *Deseret News* editorial, October 12, 1906.

35. Priscilla Leonard, "Woman Suffrage in Colorado," *Outlook*, 55 (March 2, 1897): 791.

36. Ike Russell, "What Women Have Done with Votes," *Pearson's Magazine*, n.d., 538, clipping in The Church Archives, Historical Department of the Church of Jesus Christ of Latter-day Saints, Salt Lake City, Utah.

37. The census data for 1870 indicates that when woman suffrage was being considered in the four territories the population was approximately 9,000 in Wyoming, 87,000 in Utah, 40,000 in Colorado, and 15,000 in Idaho. Utah was the only place where women represented nearly half of the total; in the other territories women composed one-fourth, or less, of the population.

Eight

FRANCES WILLARD
and the Woman's Christian
Temperance Union's Conversion
to Woman Suffrage

Carolyn De Swarte Gifford

Editor's Introduction: In the early 1880s, the woman suffrage movement received one of the most important endorsements in its history when the new president of the Woman's Christian Temperance Union (WCTU), Frances Willard, "converted" the WCTU to the suffrage cause. Willard thus brought into the movement large numbers of moderate women who were activists and would labor mightily for the "Home Protection Ballot"—women who otherwise might have avoided association with woman suffrage in an era when its national leaders were considered by many to be radical if not disreputable.

Carolyn De Swarte Gifford, editor of *"Writing Out My Heart": Selections from the Journal of Frances E. Willard, 1855-1896* and author of several articles on Willard and the WCTU, explains here that converting the WCTU to woman suffrage meant redefining the influential image of the "True Christian Woman." It meant convincing women that their God-given duty was to use their moral influence for good in the larger society—not just in the home as tradition required.

This was no easy task in late nineteenth-century America. Several generations of women had been influenced by a flood of prescriptive literature defining the "True Woman" as (in the words of historian Barbara Welter), "pure," "pious," "submissive," and "domestic." Most American women and men assumed that women were innately more religious than men and morally obligated to exercise influence for good in the world—but only through woman's "indirect influence" over husbands and children in the home. It was widely believed that participation in public affairs, particularly in the disreputable world of politics, would rob women of that very innocence and ignorance of evil that so inspired men to rule wisely for their sakes.

As early as the 1870s and 1880s, however, the women of the WCTU experienced the disillusionment with "indirect influence" that later converted many women reformers to the suffrage cause during the Progressive Era, which began around 1900. The WCTU women were convinced that their crusade would not succeed until women were enfranchised; and they insisted that if women were (as most

people believed) morally superior to men, it was their *solemn duty* to enter the political arena and clean it up—if only to protect the home.

Thus many evangelical Christian women were "converted" to woman suffrage, and convinced—like Frances Willard—that God had called them to serve the cause of woman suffrage as well as temperance. Through the WCTU, the influential concept of the True Woman was revised and expanded to include, as Gifford writes, the "public space" beyond the home. The WCTU, which in the late nineteenth century was the largest woman's organization yet in existence, had branches in twenty-one countries, and opened new doors for countless women. This was true even in the South, a stronghold of evangelical Christianity and conservatism, where resistance to expansion of woman's role was strong. Not every woman in the WCTU became a suffragist; but hundreds of thousands responded to Willard's message that it was not only *acceptable* to work for woman suffrage—it was their Christian duty.

The endorsement of woman suffrage by the WCTU was a mixed blessing for the cause, however, as it attracted a formidable opponent, the liquor industry. The so-called "whisky interest," composed of brewers, distillers, distributors, and saloon keepers, often combined forces with other industries that felt threatened by woman suffrage and spent heavily to defeat it. Carrie Chapman Catt and Nettie Rogers Shuler, in their 1923 retrospective *Woman Suffrage and Politics: The Inner Story of the Suffrage Movement,* devoted an entire chapter to the "corrupt manipulations" of American politics by the liquor industry. The industry, claimed Catt and Shuler, "dictat[ed] terms to parties and politicians," "kept Legislatures from submitting suffrage amendments," "organized droves of ignorant men to vote against suffrage amendments at the polls," and "restrained both dominant parties from endorsing woman suffrage,"—an "invisible and invincible power that for forty years kept suffragists waiting for the woman's hour." The "forty years" to which Catt and Shuler referred were the years between 1880, when the WCTU endorsed woman suffrage, to 1920 when suffragists were at last victorious.

★　★　★　★　★

THE SIXTH ANNUAL CONVENTION of the Woman's Christian Temperance Union in November 1879 promised fresh direction for the organization. Its newly elected leader, Frances E. Willard, a young, vigorous educator from the West, advocated woman suffrage as the means necessary to insure prohibition. The choice of Willard as president indicated that many WCTU leaders supported her suffrage position, a stance well known to them (and to her opposition within the organization) since she had been speaking about it publicly for several years. The WCTU could expect to enter the new decade of the 1880s faced with a difficult task: convincing its rapidly growing membership of mainly evangelical Christian women that woman suffrage was not a radical idea espoused by women whose behavior was at least questionable, if not outrageous. The vote for women must be

made acceptable, respectable, and in fact a part of woman's duty as a Christian. For this to occur the image of the True Christian Woman had to be redefined and broadened to include enfranchisement. This redefinition began for many WCTU members through a religious experience that they described as a conversion to woman suffrage. They claimed that God called them to work for the vote for women. Increasingly during the 1880s, evangelical women entered the struggle for woman suffrage, convinced that it was God's will that they do so.

Redefining True Womanhood

In 1880 the WCTU suffrage goal must have appeared as a vision far off in the future. Nevertheless, WCTU leaders began a campaign for woman suffrage throughout the country. Willard and other WCTU organizers traveled thousands of miles by rail and horse-drawn wagons stumping for the twin aims of prohibition and the vote for women. As they tirelessly crisscrossed the United States with their message, *Our Union* (after 1882 *The Union Signal*), the official organ of the WCTU, began to print a barrage of articles, editorials, columns, and letters, pushing woman suffrage from every angle that might appeal to its readership. Through the decade of the 1880s the organization labored to persuade its members that woman's sphere should be widened to include numerous activities believed by most Americans to be the prerogative of men.

Frances Willard announced the widening of woman's sphere in what became a favorite motto of the WCTU: "Woman will bless and brighten every place she enters, and she will enter every place."[1] The first half of the motto was not particularly alarming since "brightening every place she enters" had been woman's traditional duty and, moreover, her greatest pleasure, if one could believe the volumes of prescriptive literature written for and by women throughout the nineteenth century. The second half of the motto might prove disconcerting, however, if one grasped its full import. It boldly stated that women intended to move from the private, domestic sphere into the public world. Although the motto was constructed in the declarative rather than the imperative mode, as befitted a ladylike statement, Willard meant what she said. She was to spend her many years as WCTU president working out with determination her conviction that women belonged in every place, whether it be in the pulpit and in delegations to national church conferences or in the voting booth and in the conventions of national political parties. She envisioned a limitless space for women's abilities and talents.

Willard faced a dilemma in the 1880s: how was she to encourage and enable others to share in her vision for women? How would she inspire WCTU women to examine and reinterpret prescriptive images of woman that had shaped their lives? What motivation would compel evangelical women to work slowly and at times painfully toward a redefinition of the Christian woman?

There is power for change as well as for proscription inherent in symbols and images since they are, by their very nature, capable of revealing new depths of

meaning and lending themselves to nuances of interpretation. Particular persons and specific historical contexts may shape and alter traditional symbols and images, reinvesting them with further content and renewed vigor. Such a process of change occurred in the image of the True Christian Woman during the decades of the 1870s and 1880s. Certainly it had begun earlier in the century, but the women and men who initiated the task were often isolated from one another or involved in reform goals other than that of re-visioning woman's image. Other more radical women's rights reformers such as Elizabeth Cady Stanton and Susan B. Anthony, failed to evoke images of woman that appealed to the majority of mainstream evangelical Protestant women who were more timid and loath to challenge the status quo, than Stanton and Anthony.

Frances Willard
LIBRARY OF CONGRESS

In order to understand how vast numbers of WCTU women accepted a redefinition of the True Woman image that included enfranchisement, it is necessary to follow several lines of investigation. First, one must examine the image of woman current in the evangelical milieu from which most of the WCTU women came. Second, one must determine how closely the image or ideal of Christian womanhood conformed to the realities of women's lives. Third, one must assess the ways in which influential leaders such as Frances Willard were able to infuse ideals and images with new possibilities of content and meaning. Finally, one must seek to discover what other forces were at work in the last third of the nineteenth century, in both the church and the larger world, which might call forth or allow for enlarged roles for women. In short, one must try to recreate the historical moment in which the image of woman was opened up to dimensions previously unthinkable and thus unattainable for the majority of American evangelical Protestant women during the nineteenth century.

The Traditional Meaning of True Womanhood

These evangelical Protestant women who filled the ranks of the "white ribbon army" of the WCTU proudly displayed the tiny emblem of their membership on respectable, drab-colored, high-collared dresses. The simple grosgrain ribbons, in white to symbolize the purity of the True Woman, identified those who wore them as sisters battling for prohibition, but also for the elevation of women in all areas of

their lives. Quite often the white ribbon was entwined with a yellow ribbon signifying woman suffrage.[2] Both colors were worn proudly and in many cases with more than a hint of defiance. And no wonder, since these women were daring to stand up to the mighty weight of centuries of Christian tradition which taught that women were subordinate to men and to be governed by them, and therefore women had no justification for demanding the enfranchisement of their sex.

The authority of scripture was unquestionable for evangelical woman. They had grown up hearing, reading, and believing that the Bible, the word of God, decreed the dominant/subordinate male/female relationship. God had created it so, and Eve's rebellious refusal to obey God's word served to emphasize woman's fundamental irresponsibility with the corresponding necessity for male governance. The Pauline Epistles elaborated on woman's subordinate status, enjoining wives to submit to their husbands and ordering all women to keep silent in church. Along with the biblical injunctions came enormous numbers of sermons, homilies, home Bible study groups, and advice books based on biblical texts, which commented further on the attitudes and activities proper to the True Christian Woman. Often these commentaries included warnings to women who overstepped the bounds of woman's sphere, putting themselves in danger of becoming "unwomanly."

The editorial page of the February 1880 issue of *Our Union* featured an article containing such a warning, which was reprinted from an Indianapolis newspaper. The first paragraph of the article quoted from a Sunday evening sermon given November 2, 1879, by the Reverend J. Saunders Reed, priest of St. Paul's Episcopal Cathedral in Indianapolis. Reed had delivered his message just as the National WCTU, meeting in the same city, decided to embrace the goal of woman suffrage. He was obviously disturbed by the public behavior of women.

> It worries, it angers, it disheartens me to see women thrusting themselves into men's places and clamoring to be heard in our halls and churches. A woman-man I have always nauseated and loathed; but, oh, from a man-woman I would make haste to get me away as from a monstrosity of nature, a subverter of society, the cave of despair, the head of Medusa, a bird of ill-omen, a hideous specter, a travesty of all that is sacred and divine.[3]

Here was an example of a vicious verbal assault on women who ventured beyond their proper place. Why would the editors of *Our Union* choose to print such a diatribe, one invoking symbols and images that had served for centuries to proscribe women's activities and confine them to a restricted sphere?

Reed attacked women who entered the public arena, that "male territory" of church pulpit and lecture hall, and probably the city council and state legislature as well, since WCTU members had already appeared before these bodies seeking the passage of prohibition legislation. He accused women who acted in this manner of breaking down sanctified gender expectations, assuming male

prerogatives, and thereby becoming masculinized. Such an accusation could not be shrugged off lightly by a generation of women who had been socialized to understand that women and men were created by God for different though complementary tasks and spheres. Usurping a role of the opposite sex was deviant behavior as Reed so clearly charged. The woman who stepped out of her space was unnatural, even monstrous. She risked destroying the social order; worse, in committing "a travesty of all that is sacred and divine" she sinned willfully against God's plan for creation.

Reed's rhetoric played upon the powerful prescriptive symbol of the woman as Other—shameful, sinful, and, finally, less than fully human. In an age that was familiar with classical Greek mythology, he called up the horrible image of Medusa with her grotesque face surrounded by ringlets of writhing serpents, a monster turning those who looked upon her to stone. He might as effectively have chosen a biblical symbol of woman as Other—Eve, Mary Magdalene, Jezebel—whose mere mention would have served the same purpose as the name of Medusa, suggesting to his listeners woman's potential for unnaturalness and wickedness. Moreover, the priest was not alone in his opinion of woman's proper sphere and the qualities of those who overstepped its bounds. Undoubtedly the majority of Americans agreed with him. Even as late as 1879 few women had the courage to challenge the men (and women as well) who employed such evocative symbols of deviance and evil to keep women in their place.[4] Wouldn't the editors of *Our Union* have been wiser to leave this attack on "the public woman" out of the WCTU paper? Why not downplay such virulent criticism by ignoring it? But the editors of *Our Union* were neither stupid nor naive; rather, they were quite shrewd. They had an excellent reason for printing Reed's thoughts on the "man-woman."

The sermon excerpt had originally appeared as the lead paragraph in an article by a reporter covering the WCTU national convention for the *Indianapolis Journal*. The entire piece was printed in *Our Union*. In it, the *Journal* reporter took Reed to task for his statements and ridiculed him for being "angered, disheartened and worried" by such women as J. Ellen Foster, Mary Livermore, Mary T. Lathrop, Annie Wittenmyer, and Frances E. Willard, the convention's leaders. These women and others, according to the reporter, were the equals of any minister in an Indianapolis pulpit: "They were logical, forcible and concise, and held the attention of an audience from their first utterance to the close. They were conservative and sensible—much more so than a like number of men have usually been when convened on a similar occasion."[5] The writer thus captured in a paragraph the tone and demeanor that the WCTU as an organization would assume throughout the 1880s. He went on to accuse Reed and those who held similar opinions about woman's sphere, of being "many generations behind the age." The article closed with a veiled challenge: "The men have not all the brains, nor all the morals, nor all the religion, and should not be afraid to compete with the women in any place they can fill with equal ability and propriety."[6]

The interplay of Reed's attack and its vigorous rebuttal by a newspaper completely independent of the WCTU served an important strategic function. The points made in the article, though thoroughly endorsed by the union, did not appear to be special pleading by a self-interested group. The newspaper labeled as old-fashioned those who conformed to the prevalent attitude toward women and pronounced a rallying cry for WCTU women in the 1880s. Although this particular challenge came from the *Indianapolis Journal*, it was in fact similar to many such challenges and exhortations from the WCTU leaders to the membership that were regularly printed in *Our Union* and *The Union Signal*. Through its national newspaper as well as through its leaders' speeches, the WCTU directly confronted the issue with which nineteenth-century American women struggled: the binding force of the American religious-cultural tradition whose institutions interlocked to uphold the image of the ideal woman as pious, pure, domestic, and submissive, shut up in the private sphere of the home and its extension, the church.[7]

Many of the women who joined the WCTU spent all their time in their homes and their churches. These two areas were literally their lives. Even as late as the 1870s only a few exceptional women had rebelled against this pleasant prison, woman's sphere. Indeed, many enjoyed and took pride in their womanly tasks. Nothing could be more satisfying they felt, than providing a haven of peace and rest from the cares of the world for the True Man, counterpart of the True Woman. If the True Woman was to be dependent, passive, yielding, the True Man, her complement, was to be independent, aggressive, and a good provider for his family.

The earliest issues of *Our Union* abounded with descriptions of the gentle wife as the "soul force" of the home, welcoming her weary husband back to his domestic retreat and comforting him after his day of battle with the bustling economic enterprises of the nation. In this shelter she was also to nurture her children in a pure, protected environment. The frequency of these cloying portrayals moved Mary A. Livermore, Massachusetts WCTU leader and woman suffrage worker, to dismiss the contents of the paper as "pious blarney."[8] Yet alongside these glorifications of the home as haven, *Our Union* printed gruesome cautionary tales depicting the disintegration of families and homes through the drunkenness of husbands and fathers. It ran true stories, contributed by readers, about young boys eight or nine years old "led down the road to ruin" by saloon keepers who tempted them with liquor-filled candies and free lunches. Always the tales included descriptions of helpless wives and mothers wringing their hands and weeping but unable to do anything to stop their men and boys from the onslaught of "Demon Rum." The apparently naive and unintended juxtaposition of the ideal of True Man and True Woman with the stark reality of women's actual experience pointed out the failure of many families to live up to the expectations generated by powerful ideal images.

Clearly a terrible tension had developed between the ideal and the real. Such tension had always existed, but events during the 1870s brought many women

to the point of admitting the strain they felt themselves or observed in other women's lives. Male alcoholism was a key factor in creating this tension. Men who were drunkards often did not support their families and thus did not live up to the responsibilities of the True Man. Indeed, they were apt to abandon their families for long periods of time while they went on "binges," a pattern that one contemporary historian has described as a uniquely American phenomenon.[9] Women were unprepared to support their families economically and were thus in dire circumstances if the family wage earner disappeared or became disabled through chronic alcoholism. Excessive alcohol consumption had long been an American characteristic. Alcohol consumption had fallen in the decades just before the Civil War, partly through the efforts of the temperance movement. But it rose again rapidly during and after the war, and the number of saloons per capita grew as well. Faced with an intolerable situation, women acted in protest. In the winter of 1873-74 occurred the Ohio Women's Crusade, a spontaneous series of praying demonstrations by women aimed at forcing saloon keepers to shut down their establishments. In a welcoming address to the Fifth Annual Convention of the California WCTU in 1884, a member reminded the delegates of the crucial significance of the crusade as the start of a consciousness-raising process for women. As the news of the praying bands of women spread rapidly by telegraph throughout the nation:

> Men read and laughed and sneered; women, busy women stopped their work, read the strange lines, thought and lifted up their hearts to God in prayer. Had the time come for women to take the forefront in the battle against intemperance? Was it right? Had she not learned, and learned at her mother's knee that home is woman's sphere? Home her only safe abiding place?
>
> But on the other hand, had she not through long years been the sufferer? It was her frame that blighted and withered under the curse of this vile traffic. No wonder she was ready for acting. No wonder she sprang to the front.[10]

What had been implicit earlier in the pages of *Our Union*—the discontinuity between the ideal of the True Woman in her home and the awful reality of many women's lives—became explicit. Woman was not "safe" in her home. The lessons about womanhood that generations of mothers had taught their daughters were being seriously questioned. Woman was not necessarily the "queen" of the domestic realm; she was, in far too many cases, its victim. The corrupt world that she had attempted to shut out of the home invaded her supposedly pure, inviolate space, often through the saloon and its influence. Saloons were not a part of most women's experience. For many they epitomized male and thus public territory. The decision to move from the private to the

public sphere, to assail the enemy on his own ground, was a tremendous and frightening one for women. Yet clearly, as the quote suggests, they were fed up with their situation. And just as clearly, they believed they were being called by God out of their homes into active temperance agitation.[11]

The Traditional Meaning Loses Its Power

The women of Ohio were temporarily successful in achieving their goals. Some saloon keepers actually closed their businesses and took up other lines of work or moved West, at times assisted by crusade women who provided them with small sums of money to make a new start. During the crusade, however, women discovered to their dismay how powerless they really were. They had been taught that the moral and spiritual influence they exerted over men was enormous though indirect, and thus consistent with their subordinate status. While women provided pure home life and noble Christian example, men would somehow carry that atmosphere with them into the halls of government and law and guide public life accordingly. Believing this, the Ohio Crusade women, going to court on behalf of wives who were beaten and abandoned by drunken husbands, expected to find a sympathetic hearing. When they attempted to prosecute liquor dealers under statutes that made dealers responsible for selling liquor to known drunkards, they found that the male-run judicial system figuratively (and often literally) laughed in their faces. Occasionally, at the local level where a woman did wield some influence through her husband's position, a guilty verdict was brought against a liquor dealer. But it was swiftly appealed and thrown out in appellate court.[12] When women appeared before city councils and state legislatures all over the country lobbying for various prohibition measures, they encountered male reactions ranging from polite boredom to sarcastic ridicule to open hostility. In fact Reed's sermon, quoted earlier, was typical of the hostile reactions women provoked.

At first the women were merely puzzled. They had been told that they were the guardians of morality. Sometimes it was even suggested that women were spiritually and ethically superior to men, and yet they were ignored, ridiculed, or verbally attacked by men when they attempted to raise ethical issues in saloons, courtrooms, and legislatures. Some WCTU women discovered that men found it convenient to let women attend to morality while they attended to business, law, and politics. There was, in effect, a double standard of morality in regard to the public and private spheres.

Women became painfully aware that they and their spiritual, moral influence were not welcome in men's public life. Many husbands instructed their wives, politely and no doubt gently, to stay where they belonged—at home. There women could be as pious and pure as they pleased. And men could get on with the work of the public world, where the values of home and woman seemed not to operate. Many women sensed that a deep ethical split had occurred between the public and private spheres. Different moral systems prevailed in the two separated sectors.

Drusilla Wilson, president of the Kansas WCTU, addressed herself to the conflict that had developed between women's private and men's public values, as she spoke about her leadership of Lawrence, Kansas women who knelt on the floors of saloons, fervently praying that saloon keepers would stop selling liquor.

> Indelibly stamped upon some of our minds during the Crusade was the need of Prohibition, for then some of us learned that the [liquor] traffic was a child of the law. Woman saw it was inconsistent for our fathers and brothers and husbands to make laws protecting [liquor traffic] and the women follow in the wake pleading with men thus licensed [to sell liquor] to quit the business. A change must be brought about.[13]

Obviously, what many women viewed as moral—temperance, in this instance—did not accord with what the men in their own households believed to be in the interests of good business.

Wilson also emphasized what would become increasingly evident to the WCTU organization during its first decade (1874-84): "following in the wake pleading" was not an effective long-term strategy for reform. Women questioned both the dignity and the efficacy of such tactics. Drusilla Wilson, in her reserved Quaker manner, had described the methods as "inconsistent." Other women were humiliated and extremely angered by the failure of praying and pleading, typical women's tactics, to move men to support temperance reform measures. Their humiliation reflected their recognition of women's total powerlessness in the public sphere. It also reflected women's consternation in the face of the breakdown of the ideal complementary relationship of True Man and True Woman in the ethical realm.

Additionally, women began to perceive that although they were placed on a pedestal in much male rhetoric and there honored, adored, and cared for, men showed little actual sympathy for women who were victims of their dependent status, left without ways to support themselves and their children when men abandoned them. Nor did men really seem to take seriously women's ethical concerns, women's thoughts, women's activities, or women in general. It was a cruel hoax to be placed on a pedestal and dismissed with laughter, and women did not like it. Again and again in their accounts of temperance work, references appear to the indignation women felt when men found their public appearances, both praying and pleading, occasions of humorous diversion. Apparently the True Woman image functioned for many men only as a way to keep women from meddling in the male world. It was no longer an ideal they believed in but a convenient mechanism to put women in their place and out of men's way.

If this were the case, women would not be able to accomplish their temperance goals. They had to depend on male cooperation with their reform efforts, since these efforts increasingly involved legislative measures for prohibition. With few exceptions, in the 1870s and 1880s women could not vote and were not members

of legislative bodies. If they were not able to persuade men to vote for prohibition they could pray and plead, but to no effect. Definitely, as Drusilla Wilson maintained, a change must be brought about.

Woman suffrage was the change for which Wilson and other WCTU leaders called…. Furthermore, as evangelical Christians they had to be able to justify their political and suffrage activity religiously. It was absolutely essential for them to believe that their behavior sprang from an experience that convinced them that God wanted them, indeed called them, to vote.

God Calls WCTU Women to Vote

During the nineteenth century, the individual conversion—a personal experience of God's saving power and will for one's life—was a weighty source of authority for religious behavior. Revivals centering on such conversions were a fundamental characteristic of American evangelical Protestant life. Within such a religious climate, if one claimed to receive a changed, reinterpreted image of woman as the content of the conversion experience, the claim would be difficult for another to challenge, particularly if the challenger shared a belief in the possibility of individual conversion. Many WCTU women came from a background of revivalism. The Ohio Women's Crusade, which came to be looked upon as the formative event for the WCTU, had strong revivalistic features, including the participants' testimony that they received a pouring out of the Holy Spirit upon them, a fresh baptism of power renewing and deepening the baptism they had previously received upon entry into the Christian faith.

Frances Willard herself claimed to have experienced God's call to advocate woman suffrage. As she traveled through Ohio in the winter of 1876 organizing for the WCTU, she took time out from her hectic schedule for Bible study and prayer on Sunday morning:

> Upon my knees alone, in the room of my hostess who was a veteran Crusader, there was borne in upon my mind, as I believe from loftier regions, the declaration, "You are to speak for woman's ballot as a weapon of protection to her home and tempted loved ones from the tyranny of drink."[14]

Not only did Willard hear God's will that she work for what she labeled "The Ballot for Home Protection," she also received "a complete line of argument and illustration"[15] for her first speech on Home Protection which she delivered later in the year at the Woman's Congress in Philadelphia and at the National WCTU Annual Meeting in Newark.

An intense wave of revivalism led by Dwight L. Moody was sweeping through America's large Eastern and Mid-western cities during the 1870s. Willard worked with Moody in Boston for a short time during the winter of 1877 but left his revival circuit to devote her energy to her own methods of temperance reform. In a letter to

Moody's wife explaining why she was leaving, Willard set forth her differences with Moody's approach to the temperance aspect of his revivals. He expected and sought individual regeneration with an accompanying pledge by the saved person to drink no more. Willard noted sharply in her letter that Moody emphasized the regeneration of men and that she as a woman found his approach inadequate. She advocated the WCTU goals of prevention through education and legislation especially, she wrote, "putting the ballot in woman's hand for the protection of her little ones and her home."[16] Willard saw no distinction as Moody did between the religious activity of revival and the political activity of securing temperance legislation. A Christian, she felt, should work through any and every means available and consonant with her faith to reform the world and its institutions as well as individual believers. She understood no separation between the public and private spheres; both were arenas for reform and they overlapped. Women must strive for the reform of society in all its aspects and one of the most powerful means toward this aim was woman suffrage. In order to be effective reformers, women must have the ballot. After all, had not God himself validated this means of reform in Willard's personal religious experience "on her knees in prayer"?

For the next two years Willard "evangelized" for her belief in woman suffrage, managing to persuade a significant number of WCTU leaders and a portion of the membership of the rightness of her position. She became president in November 1879, an event that signaled the beginning of the National WCTU campaign for endorsement of a suffrage position among its member state organizations.

On January 1, 1880, *Our Union* featured the story of "One Woman's Experience." It was nothing less than a paradigmatic example of a conversion, that form of religious experience so prevalent in American Protestant life. However, its content was quite unusual. The anonymous writer claimed a conversion to woman suffrage:

> It would sound very strange and far-fetched to many ears, even absurd, that a woman should be morally and religiously converted to Home Protection. I feel I was actually converted by the Lord's Spirit, and led to a deeper feeling, if not a deeper knowledge of the truth.[17]

She described her attendance at a WCTU Annual Meeting, where, for the first time, she had the opportunity to see and hear the "consecrated women" who led the organization. She was convinced of the sincerity of their efforts in temperance reform and of their selfless dedication to the cause.

She contrasted their demeanor with her impressions of others who advocated woman suffrage. She had come to the convention believing that suffragists were "party aspirants and women who were always howling over the wrongs of woman, and the Lord had been so good to me I did not think women had such a hard time after all; nor in fact, do I now."[18] Her attitude toward suffragists was typical of that

of many WCTU women. They saw them as self-serving power seekers whose activities went beyond the bounds of propriety and who thus did not conform to the image of True Womanhood.

WCTU women were not iconoclastic. They had not abandoned or destroyed the ideal of True Woman but were in the process of dealing with some of its negative, prescriptive aspects and seeking to broaden and re-vision its possibilities. Thus they were frightened of radical suffragists who seemed to go too far, to act too boldly, and to take anticlerical, antireligious positions. Historians Nancy F. Cott and Ellen Carol DuBois have created a phrase to describe the change in religious attitude more radical suffragists underwent: "de-conversion," meaning "ideological disengagement from the convincing power of evangelical Protestantism (or inability to accept the whole of it)."[19] In contrast, one might call the experience of many WCTU women "re-conversion," an intense conviction that God demanded yet more from women, further consecration that would lead them toward places and forms of activity formerly thought off limits. "One Woman's Experience" continues with a vivid description of just such a "re-conversion."

> I had thought I had consecrated myself to the Lord, to work for Him both in the Church and in Temperance work; I thought I was willing to use any weapon for truth, justice and virtue He should place in my hand. But when I came into convention, the conviction kept forcing itself upon me that I was not wholly consecrated to His service: I was not willing to do anything and everything for Him. There was that fearful ballot woman "unsexing herself," etc., etc., according to Dr. Bushnell, whose arguments you know, and of which every letter I have hitherto endorsed.[20]

"De-conversion" implies a sharp breaking away, a definite denial of one's former tradition; "re-conversion" indicates not a rupture, but rather a deepening or re-dedication of one's life to God's service in new ways.

The Dr. Bushnell to whom the anonymous writer referred was the Reverend Horace Bushnell, a leading nineteenth-century evangelical theologian, dead for three years by the time this article was written, but whose thought obviously still wielded tremendous influence over American churchgoers. He had written a book, *Woman Suffrage: The Reform against Nature*,[21] which developed the argument that man was to govern, woman to be governed, and thus that woman could not vote since voting was governing. His views on woman's unsexing herself by the act of voting (woman as unnatural, as other) were so well known that the writer assumed she did not have to elaborate on them for her readers. And yet she was able to defy such a powerful theological figure on the strength of her personal experience of God's call to vote.

Her conversion did not come easily. She mentioned nights of "waking and weeping," during which God allowed her to "gather up her prejudices [against

woman suffrage] as a bundle and lay them aside." She felt her conversion as an easing of heart and conscience, accompanying her decision to work for woman's vote as an expression of God's will for her. Historian Donald M. Scott, in his article, "Abolition as a Sacred Vocation," describes the conversion to a reform, using as his example the position of Immediatism held by radical abolitionists. "Immediatism," Scott writes, "was less a program of what to do about slavery than, in evangelical terms, a 'disposition,' a state of being in which the heart and will were irrevocably set against slavery.... Immediatism became a sign of whether or not one was a saved Christian in abolition circles." [22] Although the reform is different, the "disposition" of the convert is very similar to that described in "One Woman's Experience." Belief in woman suffrage for Home Protection signified for a large number of WCTU members the deepest commitment to temperance and to woman. The belief in temperance was assumed, but support for woman suffrage became the mark of a truly consecrated worker.

Testimonies of conversion to woman suffrage multiplied on the pages of *Our Union* as WCTU women throughout the country felt a clear call from God to support the ballot for women as a means of Home Protection. A "Home Protection" column, running throughout the 1880s in *Our Union* and *The Union Signal*, carried reports of state and local efforts for woman's vote in school, municipal, state, and territorial elections and referenda. Each new gain was celebrated on the pages of the WCTU paper and announced in meetings where it was greeted with a restrained but enthusiastic waving of handkerchiefs and the singing of the "Temperance Doxology." A Boston prayer meeting in January 1880 with several hundred women and men present was described as exceeding the great revivals of Moody in the felt presence of the Holy Spirit.[23] At the end of a long day of prayer women left the church with petitions in their hands, determined to canvass Boston for woman's limited right to vote on the single issue of prohibition.

Mary A. Livermore wrote one of the more dramatic accounts of a conversion to woman suffrage in a memorial eulogy for a Massachusetts WCTU leader. Livermore quoted a letter written in the woman's last illness and addressed to the membership of the Massachusetts Union.

> Standing on the threshold of the better land, I see more clearly. I would like to urge the dear workers in our great cause to acquaint themselves more fully with the evil that destroys the beauty and glory of our nation. The desire comes strongly to me to entreat them to put aside all narrowness and prejudice in their methods of work. Dear sisters, hold yourselves open to conviction! If the ballot were in the hands of women as a temperance measure, it would be powerful for the overthrow of the liquor traffic. *Then do not fight against the movement to give the ballot to woman "lest haply you be found fighting against God."* [24]

The women of the Massachusetts WCTU were not noted at that time for their enthusiastic support of woman suffrage. But surely the deathbed pleading of one of their own would make them reexamine their "prejudices," particularly when their dying sister strongly hinted that they might be defying God by not supporting the ballot for Home Protection.

The True Woman as Voter

WCTU women were beginning to reverse the arguments used against them by those who warned that woman's voting would be an act of rebellion against God. With the strength and validation they gained from personal experience of God's will for them, the women were able to stand up to persons who cited the authority of scripture against woman's moving outside her sphere. Writings and speeches began to include many references to women of the Old and New Testaments who served God through entering the public sphere and engaging in the religious and political processes of their times. Deborah, judge of the people of Israel and leader of its armies, was a great favorite. Zerelda Wallace from Indiana, head of the WCTU franchise [suffrage] department during the 1880s and an outspoken supporter of woman suffrage, was fondly referred to as "the Deborah of the franchise movement." [25] Biblical women served as models of courage and power for WCTU women who were attempting to initiate new modes of behavior. They did not intend to question the authority of scripture but to enlist the weight of scripture in support of what they had experienced as the will of God for them. In doing so, they launched upon an extensive hermeneutical task as they pored over scriptural passages for fresh insight into their meaning.

WCTU speakers and writers began to place Galatians 3:28 ("There is neither Jew nor Greek, there is neither bond nor free, there is neither male nor female: for ye are all one in Christ Jesus" [KJV]) alongside Paul's more restrictive passages in recognition that the Bible lent itself to differing interpretations and emphases. Jesus was hailed as the friend of woman and, more boldly, as her Emancipator.[26] The WCTU had a number of excellent preachers in its membership, and these women filled pulpits across the nation speaking on temperance and other issues of concern to women. Wherever the National WCTU Annual Meeting was held, arrangements were made so that WCTU women spoke in as many churches as would receive them. Often over fifty women preached both Sunday morning and evening to packed sanctuaries. In their sermons they delivered powerful alternative understandings of scripture that inspired their listeners to re-vision woman's possibilities.

Thus the image of the True Woman went through a process of extensive reinterpretation in the 1880s. As more and more WCTU women experienced a "re-conversion" to woman suffrage, they could imagine the True Woman as a voter and her sphere as extending out from her home to include the public space beyond. The WCTU encouraged its members to try out their newly claimed power

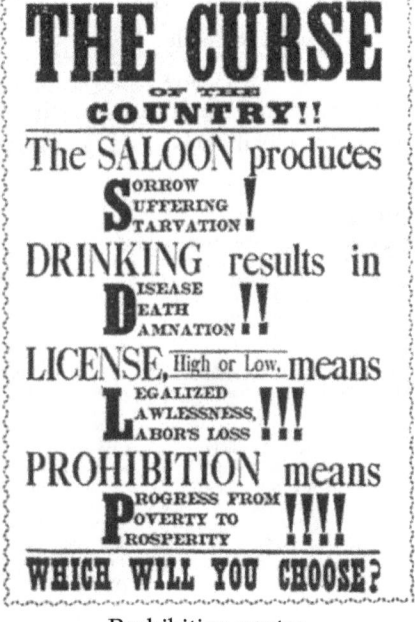

Frances Willard
FRANCES WILLARD MEMORIAL LIBRARY

Prohibition poster
WOMAN SUFFRAGE MEDIA COLLECTION

and define new roles for themselves. The WCTU functioned, historian Estelle Freedman notes, as "a strong public female sphere…mobiliz[ing] women [to gain] political leverage in the larger society."[27] As such it became far more than a temperance organization….

Frances Willard and other leaders repeatedly emphasized that the WCTU was a sisterhood that brought together women from all areas of the nation, as well as an educational endeavor that prepared them for intelligent and responsible participation in public life. As Willard declared in 1885:

> Our WCTU is a school, not founded in that thought or for that purpose, but sure to fit us for the sacred duties of patriots in the realm that lies just beyond the horizon of the coming century. Here [at the close of the nineteenth century] we try our wings that yonder [in the twentieth century] our flight may be strong and steady. Here we prove our capacity for great deeds. There we shall perform them.[28]

In this "school" WCTU members would be "educated up to the level of the equal suffrage movement" where there would be "no sex in citizenship."[29]

…The WCTU had struggled for nearly two decades reinterpreting the traditional image of woman…. The WCTU women were not discouraged from their suffrage goals by suggestions of unnaturalness or accusations of unwomanly behavior, as

they had been earlier. Their deep conviction that God called them to work for the vote for women enabled thousands of WCTU members to accept wholeheartedly Frances Willard's challenging statement to them: "Woman will bless and brighten every place she enters, and she will enter every place." For the WCTU in 1890, this was a vision in the process of becoming a reality.

Notes

This is a shortened version of Gifford's original article entitled "Home Protection: The WTCU's Conversion to Woman Suffrage," that appeared in *Gender, Ideology, and Action: Historical Perspectives on Women's Public Lives,* Janet Sharistanian, ed., (Greenwood Press, 1986), 95-120, and is reprinted with permission of Greenwood Publishing Group, Inc., Westport, CT.

1. Frances E. Willard, "Work of the W.C.T.U.," in Annie Nathan Meyer, *Woman's Work in America* (New York, 1891), 410. Also see Frances E. Willard, annual address at St. Louis NWCTU Convention, in *The Union Signal,* October 30, 1884, 2.

2. In "Politics and Culture in Women's History: A Symposium," *Feminist Studies* 6, no. 1 (Spring 1980): 26-64, Ellen DuBois and Mari Jo Buhle referred to the WCTU as a key organization for understanding the nineteenth-century woman's movement. Buhle identified the twenty-year period from 1870 to 1890 as an important gap which historians needed to fill in from a feminist historical approach. Subsequent scholarship on the WCTU included: See Ruth Bordin, *Woman and Temperance: The Quest for Power and Liberty, 1873-1900* (Philadelphia, 1982); Barbara Leslie Epstein, *The Politics of Domesticity: Women, Evangelism and Temperance in Nineteenth Century America* (Middletown, Conn., 1981); and, Jack S. Blocker Jr., *"Give to the Winds Thy Fears": The Women's Temperance Crusade, 1873-1874* (Westport, Conn., 1985).

3. "They Say: From Four Standpoints," *Our Union,* February 1, 1880, 1.

4. Ellen Carol Dubois, in *Feminism and Suffrage: The Emergence of an Independent Women's Movement in America, 1848-1869* (Ithaca, 1978), mentions Elizabeth Cady Stanton's 1869 meeting with Bloomington, Ill., women who had been reminded by a clergyman of their inferiority to men. Stanton reports (in *History of Woman Suffrage,* 2: 372) that she had to moderate her usually radical stance in the face of the women's resulting demoralization. Over a decade later, the situation had not much changed.

5. "They Say: From Four Standpoints," *Our Union,* February 1, 1880, 1.

6. Ibid.

7. Barbara Welter, *Dimity Convictions: The American Woman in the Nineteenth Century* (Athens, Ohio, 1976); Nancy F. Cott, *The Bonds of Womanhood: "Woman's Sphere" in New England, 1750-1835* (New Haven, 1977); and Kathryn Kish Sklar, *Catharine Beecher: A Study in American Domesticity* (New York, 1976) on the antebellum cult of True Womanhood and women like Catharine Beecher who sought to make of woman's sphere a shaping force for American society. See Carolyn De Swarte Gifford, "For God and Home and Native Land: The WCTU's Image of Woman in the Late Nineteenth Century," in Hilah F. Thomas and Rosemary Skinner Keller, eds., *Women in New Worlds: Historical Perspectives on the Wesleyan Tradition* (Nashville, 1981): 310-27.

8. Mary A. Livermore to Frances E. Willard, November 21, 1876. WCTU National Headquarters Historical Files (joint Ohio Historical Society-Michigan Historical Collections), WCTU microfilm edition, roll 11.

9. William J. Rorabaugh, *The Alcoholic Republic: An American Tradition* (New York, 1979), 163-68. See also Jacquie Jessup, "The Liquor Issue in American History: A Bibliography," in Jack S. Blocker, Jr., ed., *Alcohol, Reform and Society: The Liquor Question in Social Context* (Westport, Conn., 1979): 259-79; and Bordin, *Women and Temperance,* intro., chpts. 1 and 2.

10. "News from the Field," *The Union Signal,* October 2, 1884, 11.

11. Gifford, "For God and Home and Native Land," 8, 9, 15.

12. See Eliza Daniel Stewart, *Memories of the Crusade: A Thrilling Account of the Great Uprising of the Women of Ohio in 1873, against the Liquor Crime,* (Columbus, Ohio, 1889).

13. *Minutes of the Fourth Annual Meeting held at Burlingame, Kansas, September 27, 28, 29, 1882, State Woman's Christian Temperance Union of Kansas,* (Burlingame, Kans., 1882), 11.

14. Frances E. Willard, *Glimpses of Fifty Years: The Autobiography of an American Woman* (Chicago, 1892), 351.

15. Ibid.

16. Ibid., 360.

17. "One Woman's Experience," *Our Union,* January 1, 1880, 3.

18. Ibid.

19. Cott, *Bonds of Womanhood,* 204, n. 10.

20. "One Woman's Experience," 3.

21. Horace Bushnell, *Woman Suffrage: The Reform against Nature,* (New York, 1869).

22. Donald M. Scott, "Abolition as a Sacred Vocation," in Lewis Perry and Michael Feldman, eds., *Antislavery Reconsidered: New Perspectives on the Abolitionists* (Baton Rouge, 1979), 53, 54, 72.

23. "Home Protection," *Our Union,* February 1, 1880, 3.

24. "In Memoriam" by Mary A. Livermore. For Mrs. Lucinda B. Barrett of the Massachusetts WCTU in *The Union Signal,* July 3, 1884, 2. Emphasis added. The phrase "Lest haply you be found fighting against God" paraphrases Acts 5: 39 (KJV).

25. "Annual Convention," *Our Messenger,* December 1887, 4.

26. In *Our Messenger,* September 1887, the Wichita, Kans. WCTU announced that it was sending Rev. Hana's leaflet "Jesus Christ, the Emancipator of Women" to every minister in town.

27. Estelle Freedman, "Separatism as Strategy: Female Institution Building and American Feminism, 1870-1930," in *Feminist Studies* 5, 3 (Fall 1979): 513.

28. Frances E. Willard, Address to the Woman's Congress at Des Moines, Iowa, 1885, as quoted in Annie Nathan Meyer, *Woman's Work in America,* 408.

29. Ibid., 404. "No sectarian in religion, no sectionalism in politics, no sex in citizenship" was a popular slogan of the WCTU.

Nine

BRINGING IN THE SOUTH:

Southern Ladies, White Supremacy, and States' Rights in the Fight for Woman Suffrage

Marjorie J. Spruill

Editor's Introduction: There were distinct regional patterns in the history of the woman suffrage movement. It developed in the Northeast, an offshoot of the antislavery movement. The West provided the movement's crucial first victories. However, the South was notorious in the history of the woman suffrage movement as the region where the movement encountered the most resistance and experienced the least success.

In this essay, Marjorie J. Spruill, one of the first historians to focus on the Southern suffrage movement and place it in a national context, describes how and why an organized woman suffrage movement developed in such an inhospitable cultural and political climate, and why it failed to thrive, almost costing suffragists a national victory.

In the 1890s, a newly unified National American Woman Suffrage Association (NAWSA), committed to winning enough states that victory for a federal woman suffrage amendment was not only possible but inevitable, turned its attention to the South. NAWSA leaders understood that they faced a major challenge. To the elite White Southern men then seeking to restore White political supremacy in the region, Southern White womanhood—the symbol of racial purity whom Southern White men were bound to honor and defend—belonged on a pedestal and not in politics. Moreover, the suffrage movement was anathema owing to its antislavery roots.

There had been suffrage societies in the South during Reconstruction—the work of both White and African American women—that sent delegates to national suffrage conventions. The fact that these earliest suffrage groups in the region were the work of White "carpetbaggers" and "scalawags" in Virginia, and Black women active in Reconstruction-era politics in South Carolina, however, had only strengthened White conservative Southerners' disdain for the suffrage movement and reinforced their idea that advocacy of women's rights and the rights of African Americans were connected.

White Southern conservatives who perceived the Fifteenth Amendment as having been forced upon them during Reconstruction were infuriated in 1878 when suffragists from the Northeast demanded a similarly-worded Sixteenth

Amendment calling for federal protection of the voting rights of women. A few "respectable" White women of the South had dared speak out in favor of female enfranchisement in the 1870s and 1880s, but as the 1890s began, there was no organized suffrage movement in the region.

Beginning in 1892, however, a regional suffrage movement developed as a small number of White Southern women stepped up and assumed leadership of this unpopular cause. Working together, these Southern suffragists and national leaders developed a strategy they believed would succeed even in the inhospitable South.

In the first phase of the Southern suffrage movement from 1892 to 1903, most of its leaders were elite White women who sought enfranchisement primarily through amendments to state constitutions or through the new state constitutions adopted during that era. Later, between 1909 and 1916, a much larger and more diverse contingent of Southern suffragists took up the fight for enfranchisement through state action. When all of these efforts failed, most, but not all of these women, joined national leaders in supporting a federal suffrage amendment.

However, regional hostility to the suffrage movement frustrated Southern suffragists in their efforts to become enfranchised through either state or federal action. Before ratification of the Nineteenth Amendment in 1920, Southern women did not gain full enfranchisement in even one Southern state and gained partial suffrage in only four. In Congress, Southern politicians managed to block passage of the federal suffrage amendment for many years and after it was submitted to the states, made a concerted effort to prevent ratification—despite the pleas of regional favorite son President Woodrow Wilson to support the amendment for the sake of the National Democratic Party.

When victory ultimately came in 1920 through the Nineteenth Amendment, it was won with the support of four Southern states that broke ranks with the otherwise "Solid South": Kentucky, Texas, Arkansas, and the crucial thirty-sixth state, Tennessee, that ratified the amendment by just one vote. Nine of the ten states that refused to ratify were South of the Mason-Dixon line. Several Southern states passed "rejection resolutions" denouncing the federal amendment variously as "unwarranted," "unnecessary," "undemocratic," and "dangerous."

The struggle for woman suffrage in the South has received far less attention than the history of the movement in other regions. Yet, as Spruill makes clear, a full understanding of the suffrage movement in the United States requires examining its history in the region where it was least successful. In this essay, she explains why the South was so hostile to the suffrage movement, why certain Southern women signed on to lead this unpopular fight, and why and how they thought they could win it. She also explores the profound impact of race and states' rights issues, which rendered state victories in the region difficult if not impossible, and nearly prevented ratification of the Nineteenth Amendment in 1920.

★　★　★　★　★

I N 1892, KENTUCKY SUFFRAGIST Laura Clay issued a stern warning to the leaders of the National American Woman Suffrage Association (NAWSA): "Since we claim to be national let us never forget that the South cannot be left out of our calculations. You have worked for forty years and you will work for forty years more and do nothing unless you bring in the South."[1]

The woman suffrage movement, Clay realized, had begun in the Northeast and had spread to other sections of the nation. But in 1892, most White Southerners remained hostile to the movement as a product of an inferior Northern culture that, anti-suffragists insisted, had no place in the sunny South, the land of chivalry and devoted respect for women. Yet, as Clay said, the NAWSA would need support from all regions of the United States if it wanted to achieve a "national" victory. A woman suffrage amendment to the Constitution would have to be approved by two-thirds of each house of Congress and three-fourths of the states.

Laura Clay
LIBRARY OF CONGRESS

With this in mind, NAWSA leaders took Clay's advice to "launch their bark in the Southern sea." The NAWSA's "Southern Committee" headed by Clay, brought together a handful of Southern women already known to be suffrage sympathizers and recruited many more, especially seeking Southern White women with prestige and influence. The committee solicited and distributed funds, circulated suffrage literature, and dispatched NAWSA organizers into the region. By 1895, they had organized every Southern state. Together, Southern suffragists and their NAWSA allies launched a suffrage campaign designed to succeed in the South's exceedingly inhospitable political climate where the "Southern Lady," White supremacy, and state sovereignty were sacrosanct and perceived to be under attack.[2]

Why the South Was Last and Least

The unyielding opposition of the majority of White Southerners to the woman suffrage movement resulted from several interrelated cultural, political, and economic factors. The Southern suffrage movement took place from 1890 to 1920, a time when most White Southerners were devoted to preserving what they saw as a distinct and superior "Southern Civilization." They often spoke of defending the values of "the Lost Cause," those for which they claimed Confederate soldiers had fought in "the War Between the States"—most notably White supremacy and states' rights. As one regionally prominent minister put it, they were eager that the "victory over Southern arms" not be followed by "a victory over Southern opinions."[3]

A key element of this Southern Civilization most White Southerners wished to preserve was a dualistic conception of the natures and responsibilities of the

sexes that precluded the participation of women in politics and cast "the Southern Lady" as the guardian and symbol of Southern virtue. Charged with transmitting Southern culture to future generations as well as inspiring current statesmen to serve as their noble defenders, Southern womanhood had a vital role to play in preserving the values of the Lost Cause. A leading Lost Cause minister, Albert Bledsoe, urged Southern women to shun the fruit offered by the women's rights movement and take as their "mission" not to "imitate a Washington, or a Lee, or a Jackson," but to "rear, and train, and educate, and mould the future Washingtons, and Lees, and Jacksons of the South, to protect and preserve the sacred rights of woman as well as of man." In addition, leaders of burgeoning industries of the New South, particularly the textile industry, wanted Southern women to confine their beneficent influence to the home rather than vote for child labor legislation and other encumbrances that would adversely affect business growth and profits.[4]

In the eyes of White Southerners, the cornerstone of Southern Civilization was White supremacy, and their determination to restore White domination of politics—and then defend the state sovereignty thought necessary to preserve it— also presented a tremendous obstacle to the Southern suffrage movement. Most viewed the women's rights movement as yet another unfortunate product of an inferior Northern culture that they were trying to resist—one led by Northern women with the abolitionists' "naive" and dangerous belief in equality. Southern suffragists were scolded for playing into the hands of social "levelers" who had no understanding of the crucial social distinctions of gender and race that accounted for the superiority of Southern Civilization, and for unwittingly complicating ongoing efforts to restore and protect White supremacy. Southern anti-suffragists charged that suffragists failed to recognize that the proposed federal woman suffrage amendment was nothing more than a "reaffirmation of the Fifteenth Amendment" and that its ratification would not only signal acceptance of Black suffrage, but also concede the right of the federal government to determine suffrage qualifications in the states.[5] In 1919, during the ratification battle, a leading anti-suffragist, James Callaway, editor of the *Macon (Georgia) Telegraph*, clearly articulated these sentiments:

> May our Southern women remain on the pedestal, forever preserve that distinctive deference which is theirs so long as they remain as they are—our highest ideals of the true, the beautiful and the good.... Deference to its womankind has always been a distinguished characteristic of the Southern people. Southern men would perpetuate it. But foreign forces have invaded us, established branches over the South of a huge National Woman's Association whose ideals are not our ideals; whose women are not like our Southern women. They are women of a different clay, and are of different mould. Should these

foreign crusaders succeed, pervert the tastes of our women, persuade them to abandon their old ideals and descend into the arena of politics… woe is the day for Southern civilization.[6]

Even after President Woodrow Wilson became convinced that woman suffrage was inevitable and that the Democrats must not allow the Republicans to claim credit for the victory, he could not convince most Southern congressmen or state legislators to support woman suffrage. Surrender of principle in anticipation of defeat was not an acceptable alternative to these children of the Confederacy who had grown up amidst tales of the heroic sacrifices of their ancestors. The majority of Southern politicians believed that their constituents required them to fight to the last ditch and then some.[7]

The Making of Southern Suffragists

The Southern women willing to embrace woman suffrage, indeed to become leaders of such an unpopular cause, were formidable individuals. In their 1923 reflective, *Woman Suffrage and Politics*, Carrie Chapman Catt and Nettie Shuler observed, "No stronger characters did the long struggle produce than these great-souled Southern suffragists. They had need to be great of soul."[8] Catt and Shuler meant, of course, that advocacy of woman suffrage in such an inhospitable climate was character-building; but the leaders of the woman suffrage movement in the Southern states had to have unusual self-confidence and determination in order to take up this cause in the first place.

It was no coincidence that the most prominent leaders of the Southern suffrage movement were the descendants of the region's social and political elite. This pattern contrasted with suffrage leaders in other parts of the nation who were more often from middle-class backgrounds. In addition to Laura Clay, the so-called "Susan B. Anthony of the South," a crucial intermediary between Northern and Southern suffragists, there were other prominent Southern women who enlisted. Among them were the Gordon sisters, Kate and Jean, "silk-stockinged reformers" from New Orleans; Nellie Nugent Somerville, daughter of one of Mississippi's most prominent attorneys who was revered by Whites for his role in restoring "home rule" and ending Reconstruction; Lila Meade Valentine of Richmond, one of the "First Families of Virginia" (FFV); Mary Johnston, also of Virginia, descendent of Confederate heroes and nationally famous as a novelist; Rebecca Latimer Felton, whose husband served several terms in the Georgia legislature and in the United States Congress; Madeline McDowell Breckinridge of Kentucky, granddaughter of Henry Clay and wife of Desha Breckinridge, son of a congressman and editor of the *Lexington Herald*; and Pattie Ruffner Jacobs of Alabama, wife of a wealthy Birmingham industrialist.[9]

These women enjoyed more opportunities for education than most Southern women of their era as well as opportunities for travel outside the region that helped undermine provincial attitudes about woman's role. Wealth gave them the leisure

and the means to assume leadership roles in the suffrage movement. A few Southern leaders were members of families that were experiencing financial distress, including Mississippi's Belle Kearney, who wrote of taking in sewing for former slaves one day and the next day dancing as a debutante in the governor's mansion. There was also Tennessee's suffrage leader, Sue Shelton White, who supported herself as a court reporter. Most, however, were daughters of wealth and privilege who could hire maids, cooks, and baby tenders as well as personally finance most of the suffrage work in the South. Southern suffrage leaders generally assumed that that they should fund their own activities and sometimes expressed disdain for Mississippi's Kearney for requesting payment for her suffrage lectures in order to pay her bills.[10]

Exalted social position facilitated the work of Southern suffrage leaders, giving them familiarity and access to the political process and a degree of immunity from criticism—or at least social ostracism—not enjoyed by Southern women of lesser social standing. Well aware of the particular importance of social position in the South, national suffrage leaders sought to recruit Southern women from prominent families, women who had, as New Orleans suffragist Kate Gordon phrased it, "names to conjure with." These women could demand and receive a respectful hearing, even as Southern anti-suffragists denounced Northern suffragists in no uncertain terms. When Louisville Courier-Journal editor Henry Watterson dared criticize the suffragists of Kentucky, led by the women of the Breckinridge and Clay families, Lexington Herald editor Desha Breckinridge chastised him for assailing the reputations of these women, "the hems of whose garments he was not fit to touch."[11]

As leaders of an unpopular movement, these Southern women displayed remarkable self-confidence, in part the product of exalted social position. They were members of families that were accustomed to guiding public opinion, rather than simply being guided by it. Kate Gordon wrote, "Review every advance, moral or otherwise. Have the majority ever desired the advance? The great earnest minority always shapes thought and leads the van."[12]

Nellie Nugent Somerville and her associates in Greenville, Mississippi, signaled their attitude toward public opinion when they named their literary society after Hypatia, a learned woman stoned to death by a mob in ancient Egypt. Somerville also derived confidence from her religious convictions, and both Laura Clay and Belle Kearney felt that God had called them to serve the cause of women's rights. Still others revealed, through diaries and private correspondence, a mischievous desire to be different, deriving pleasure from going against the grain.[13]

The decisions of these suffrage leaders to take up this cause resulted from a combination of personal characteristics and experiences that made them receptive to feminism. The attitudes and actions of family members were crucial in shaping these women's views. For example, Laura Clay's family background—which would have converted almost anyone to feminism—certainly had that effect on Clay, her mother,

NEW
SOUTHERN
CITIZEN

OFFICIAL ORGAN OF
SOUTHERN STATES WOMAN'S SUFFRAGE CONFERENCE

Vol. 1. No. 1.   OCTOBER 1914

Votes for Women a Success

The Map Proves It

Make the Southern States White

PRICE 5 Cents   NEW ORLEANS, LA.   50 Cents PER YEAR

Kate Gordon, President of the Southern States Woman Suffrage Conference, left. In the organization's newspaper, the *New Southern Citizen,* Gordon used racist and states' rights appeals to attempt to persuade Southern White politicians to support woman suffrage.   LIBRARY OF CONGRESS

and all her sisters. After President Abraham Lincoln appointed Laura's father, Cassius Marcellus Clay as ambassador to Russia, he took his family with him to St. Petersburg. However, when living with six children and in the style expected of an ambassador proved too costly, he sent them back home. His wife, Mary Jane Clay, was somehow able to get her family back to Kentucky despite the hazards of travel in the midst of the Civil War, and managed the family plantation and a multitude of children by herself for eight years. She even remodeled and expanded their plantation and provided her daughters with a formal education despite her husband's objections. Meanwhile, Cassius Clay became involved in a well-publicized scandal involving a notorious St. Petersburg courtesan and then returned to Kentucky with a son whom he legally adopted. Advanced in his thinking when it suited his purposes, Clay divorced his wife who lost the plantation she had tended so carefully. As a result, Mary Jane Clay and her four daughters *all* became suffragists and advocates of expanded political and legal rights for women in Kentucky and the South.[14]

Positive attitudes toward women and feminism on the part of family members also played a role in the making of Southern suffrage leaders. Sue White and the Gordon sisters all had mothers who inspired them to adopt an expanded view of woman's role. Nellie Somerville's father saw to it that she received the best education available to a Southern woman and even invited his daughter to read for the law in his office, an offer she declined.[15]

Several suffrage leaders had sisters who supported them in their work. Anna Howard Shaw, president of the National American Woman Suffrage Association (NAWSA) once quipped, in reference to the Clays, the Gordons, the Johnstons, the Howards of Georgia, and the Finnegans of Texas, "If there was a failure to organize any state in the South…it must be due to the fact that no family there had three sisters to start the movement." Madeline Breckinridge, Pattie Jacobs, and Lila Meade Valentine all enjoyed the enthusiastic support of their husbands in their suffrage work. Contacts with suffragists from the North, the West, from other countries, as well as with suffragists from other Southern states, were also crucial in these key Southern women's decisions to become advocates of women's rights. And once recruited, they interested scores of other Southern women in the cause. Like all reformers, Southern suffragists came to see themselves as part of a supportive subculture and to judge themselves according to the precepts of that group, rather than those of the larger society they were trying to reform.[16]

Southern Ladies and Maternalism

The White women leading the Southern suffrage movement were reform-minded on some subjects, but nonetheless they identified strongly with the South and shared many of the attitudes of the men of their race and class. While seeking expanded rights and privileges for themselves and their gender, they nonetheless took pride in their heritage as Southern Ladies, embracing the traditional duties if not the restrictions that role entailed. Opponents called them "unconscious agents" of Northern saboteurs, but they fully understood what they were doing and why. For the most part, they considered their movement to be supportive rather than destructive of "Southern Civilization." Yet, they were clearly weary of women's indirect, limited role in politics, which they had concluded not only denied their individuality but also had proven to be inadequate for the protection of their interests or that of their "constituency," the "unprivileged" of the South—particularly women and children.[17]

In the 1890s, women who led the Southern suffrage movement fully supported the campaign led by elite Southern White men to return government to the so-called "best people." They took it for granted that it was the duty of the "most qualified" to guide and protect the rest, but they believed themselves to be among the best qualified. Indeed, their goal in fighting for suffrage was to add *maternalism* to paternalism, to carry the traditional role of the Southern Lady into politics and offer their services and unique feminine insights to the governing of their region. They sought, in fact, to restore and preserve elements they believed had once been integral in Southern politics, but were missing in the politics of the New South: morality, integrity, and the tradition of *noblesse oblige*.[18]

One important characteristic shared by these elite White Southern women that inspired them to take up this unpopular cause and continue working for it despite so many defeats, was their low opinion of the current management of the New

South. While all of the Southern suffrage leaders had friends or relatives in public office, they believed that Southern politics since the Civil War had degenerated to the point that too few honest and intelligent men were willing to serve. For example, Nellie Nugent Somerville contrasted the "boys" of the Confederacy, who "gave up prospects of material advancement to fight for principle," with the politicians of the present, who spoke of the rampant chaos and corruption in government as "practical politics," which if deplorable was nonetheless inevitable. She insisted that if "good men" continued to say "no man can go into politics and maintain his integrity and therefore hold themselves aloof and do not even vote," women would have to step in where men feared to tread. At the time of her conversion to the suffrage cause (1897), Somerville was furious about the overt bribery and coercion of voters employed by the "wets" in her county—those who opposed prohibition—with the knowledge and cooperation of local officials.[19]

A series of political murders in 1899 and 1900, including the shooting of a gubernatorial candidate by a member of a rival "gang" in the yard of the Kentucky state capitol, first prompted Madeline McDowell Breckinridge to become involved in politics. Shocked by what she considered a general atmosphere of lawlessness in her state, she organized a women's committee that pledged itself to "make every effort in our power for the overthrow of lawlessness and crime, and for the establishment of that social and political purity of righteousness which makes for good citizens and exalteth a nation."[20]

Rebecca Latimer Felton's long struggle for prohibition and against the convict lease system convinced her that women must be enfranchised; she was well aware of the "Liquor Interest's" eagerness to contain women's influence. When criticized for meddling in politics, she insisted that men's failure to give "sober homes to women and children" made it necessary for women to get involved. Although she was a member of the United Daughters of the Confederacy, she blasted Georgia politicians for invoking their war records and "waving the Bloody Shirt" to perpetuate their power and thereby extend their opportunities to fleece the public.[21]

Involvement in charitable work and reform societies led these women to a greater knowledge of social ills and a conviction that many of the social and economic problems that were formerly addressed by the private sector now required governmental attention. Yet, it seemed clear to the suffragists that Southern male politicians either failed to understand the crucial need for reforms, such as improved public education and health care, temperance, and legislation to protect women and children, or they simply preferred to use public office to line their own pockets. Indeed, the suffragists believed that in their eagerness to promote economic development, the leaders of the New South were willing to offer up the South's working class for Northern exploitation. Breckinridge accused Southern boosters of trading "ideals of the past" for material prosperity, and she expressed disgust at attempts to attract Northern manufacturers by advertising "that we have not only the cotton and the fuel ... but the cheap child labor as well."[22]

To the suffragists, this failure to live up to their responsibilities in keeping with the concept of *noblesse oblige* meant that the legislators needed women to assist them in fulfilling their moral obligations.

Inadequacy of "Indirect Influence"

Obviously, many Southern women of the same race and class, including other women attempting to influence public policy through voluntary associations, chose to rely strictly upon the traditional "weapon" of the Southern Lady—the highly touted "indirect influence." Some lacked the courage to defy public opinion; others had no desire for the vote and thought it foolish for women to insult men by demanding it. Still others insisted they had no need for the vote. For example, the president of the Georgia Federation of Women's Clubs testified that the state's women's clubs had "no difficulty getting their measures passed by the legislature" using powers of persuasion, that they were "the power behind the throne now, and would lose, not gain, by a change."[23]

It was true that Southern women lobbying their legislators through voluntary associations did achieve some successes. Suffrage clubs often worked together with traditional women's clubs and succeeded in bringing about a number of significant changes in women's status and opportunities, including the admission of women to colleges and professional schools, establishing women's right to serve on governmental commissions and boards and to work as factory inspectors in some states, and securing legal reforms regarding inheritance and custody, to name a few. But the women who became suffragists grew increasingly convinced that moral suasion was ineffective. Kentucky suffragist Madeline Breckinridge applauded the accomplishments of the women's clubs in her state, but she observed ruefully, "When one remembers that it is the result of twenty-five years of work of a group of able and determined women, it is seen to be small."[24]

To Southern suffragists, their own indirect influence seemed negligible compared to that exercised by the brewers, the "cotton men," the railroad barons, and other industrialists who regularly managed to influence politicians' decisions. As they grew increasingly frustrated by legislative resistance to the reforms they supported, the suffragists grew increasingly cynical about the celebrated chivalry of Southern men and denounced the Southern woman's enforced reliance upon indirect influence as degrading, as well as inefficient.[25]

Many Southern women were converted to what Jean Gordon called "a belief in the potency of the ballot beyond that of 'woman's influence'" after the defeat of child labor legislation. Gordon recalled that the failure of a child labor bill strongly supported by New Orleans clubwomen—including the wives of many legislators—caused many of the women to question the efficacy of indirect influence. We learned, Gordon observed, "what we had suspected," that "the much-boasted influence of the wife over the husband in matters political was one of the many theories which melt before the sun of experience."[26]

The suffragists in the South were disgusted by the way Southern politicians insisted on "chivalrously" shouldering the burden of politics for women by invoking chivalry as a reason for denying women direct influence, while refusing to offer women and children genuine legal protection. They were frustrated by the slow pace of reform as they sought to open up educational institutions to women and revise outdated guardianship and inheritance laws. Suffragists were indignant that legislators who so celebrated the influence of the mother, refused to change existing laws that gave the father full legal rights to their children, even the power to appoint a guardian for his unborn child. Breckinridge found it ironic that a society allegedly intent on protecting women clung to antiquated property and inheritance laws that left a married woman totally dependent on her husband's decency and his survival. "It was one of the anomalies of the old common law," she pointed out, "that it seemed to feel that a man left with children to support and without a wife, needed three times as much as a wife left with children and no husband."[27]

After observing the effects of the passage of woman suffrage in Colorado, Breckinridge noted that in the states where women were already enfranchised, the "age of consent" laws [laws specifying the age at which a person is able to voluntarily consent to sexual intercourse] ranged from eighteen to twenty-one, while in the South the "age of consent" ranged from ten to sixteen. Breckinridge asked, "Do Southern men protect Southern women at all comparably to the way Western women, granted the right to do it, protect their own sex?"[28]

Southern suffragists clearly saw that indirect influence was still their only weapon with which to pry suffrage from a reluctant South, so they tried to make their demand for power as unthreatening as possible. They did invoke "natural rights" arguments, insisting that, as Georgia suffragist Rebecca Latimer Felton put it, "I pay taxes and obey the laws, and I know the right belongs to me to assist in selecting those who rule over me."[29]

Somerville denied a statement by a Mississippi newspaper editor who asserted that the suffragists' chief argument was that enfranchised womanhood would "bring about great reforms." She wrote, "The orthodox suffragists do not base their claims on any such argument. We stand upon the Declaration of Independence, 'governments derive their just powers from the consent of the governed.' Any argument based on results is merely incidental and not fundamental."[30]

Yet, like many suffragists outside the South, the White women who led the Southern suffrage movement often argued for equal partnership in governing with the men of their race and class by emphasizing the differences in the interests and responsibilities of the sexes. This was a nice and less challenging way of saying that the interests of women and children would never be adequately represented as long as women were relying upon men to protect them. "Men have done remarkably well to battle so many foes of the human race and its progress," said

Pattie Jacobs, but as some "for-sighted [sic] men" now realize, woman's "highly developed moral nature and intimate knowledge of conditions governing the welfare of women and children... would ultimately result in great good to the state, the nation, and the race." Virginia suffragist Mary Johnston wrote in a similar vein: "Men have their minds too much fixed on the large political issues, and there are a multitude of details that slip through their fingers, so to speak, and which women can better attend to [including]... legislation concerning schools and children."[31]

Southern suffragists took care to look and act like ladies, avoided *additional* unpopular causes, issued press releases celebrating the beauty, femininity, and domesticity of their leaders, and sometimes addressed their legislators in such a fashion that Northern coworkers were shocked and dismayed at their "honey-tongued charm." In the last decade of the suffrage movement, most Southern suffragists strenuously avoided association with the National Woman's Party (NWP), publicly denouncing their "un-seemly," "fanatical," and "misguided" tactics, including suffragists picketing the White House and burning Woodrow Wilson's speeches in Lafayette Square. Virginia suffrage leader Lila Meade Valentine begged the public not to "condemn the suffrage cause as a whole because of the folly of a handful of women" and urged her state's suffragists to avoid all "spectacular tactics."[32]

Southern suffragists greatly resented having to stoop to wheedling and coddling male egos, however. Mary Johnston deplored the fact that society still encouraged—indeed required—women to rely upon this "sinuous, indirect way of approaching and of obtaining the object or the end which they desire...just as when they were the cowering mates of savages half as strong again as they." Johnston, a friend and admirer of author Charlotte Perkins Gilman, echoed Gilman's message that female dignity could only be won through economic independence and that marriage was somewhat akin to prostitution. She predicted that the phrase "indirect influence" would, in the near future, become "most distasteful to a naturally self-respecting and straightforward woman ... *It means, make me comfortable, and I will see what I can do about it.*"[33]

Clearly, these women recognized the contrast between rhetoric and reality when it came to discussions of woman's role in Southern society. Nellie Nugent Somerville wrote in a 1914 article:

> It is quite common for men to say...that women should not vote because they are too good and must not be degraded to the level of men.... Now the facts in the case are that there is not a word of truth in this proposition. It is exasperating because it is short-sighted, unreasonably and historically false.... Exclusion from the right to vote is a degradation—always has been, always will be, never was intended as anything else, cannot be sugarcoated into anything else. The age-long cause of all of these things [discrimination against women in education, in industry, in property

rights and political rights] has been the theory that women were too bad and too incompetent.[34]

Somerville and her associates in the suffrage movement demanded that men—Southern White men who surpassed all others in extolling the goodness and virtue of woman—accept woman's help in governing Southern society. These Southern ladies gladly accepted their role as soul and conscience of the South, but wanted to be in a position to actually carry out that role. They did not object to the vote being restricted so much as they wanted to be among the elect.

To them, the vote was a badge of honor as well as a tool. As Alabama suffragist Pattie Jacobs wrote, "We of all people understand the symbolism of the ballot… [as we live] in states where its use is restricted and professedly based upon virtue and intelligence."[35]

Indeed, it was largely the perception that *they*—moral, God-fearing, intelligent, educated, women whose families had been largely responsible for settling and guiding the South—were being denied the right to vote, even as inferior men were not only voting, but governing the region that fueled their activism. They wanted and believed that *they, if not all women,* deserved, in Mary Johnston's words, "the dignity of citizenship."[36]

Southern Suffragists and "The Negro Problem"

On race relations, the elite White women who took on leadership of the Southern suffrage movement were little different from the men of their race and class. White Southern suffragists, who spoke eloquently of the inalienable right of women as citizens to self-government, nevertheless advocated—or at least acquiesced in—the restoration of White political supremacy that took place contemporaneously with the Southern woman suffrage movement.

Like most elite White Southerners and a growing number of White, native-born Americans nationwide in the late nineteenth century, most Southern suffragists believed that voting was *not* a right of all citizens but the privilege and duty of those best qualified to exercise it. Indeed, to White Southern suffragists the contemporary meaning of the frequently used phrase "the negro problem" was not the use of the race issue against their cause—though this concerned them greatly—but the enfranchisement after the Civil War of several million African Americans whom Southern White conservatives considered to be ignorant, purchasable, and unfit for political participation.[37]

White Southern suffragists believed they were better qualified to participate in politics than most White men; they did not doubt that they and other White women were more desirable as voters than the African American men who had been enfranchised by the Fifteenth Amendment. Like many other elite Southerners, these privileged Southern women saw themselves as advocates for, and protectors of, Blacks. They paternalistically (or maternalistically) defended African

Woman Suffrage and White Supremacy in the South

The Federal Suffrage Amendment will not affect the negro situation in the South.
It sets aside no qualification for voting except the sex qualification. It simply eliminates the word "male". The same qualifications will apply to negro women as now apply to negro men. (See Constitution of North Carolina, Article 6, Section 4.)

The Census Report of the U. S. Government Tells the Story

1910—Population of North Carolina was upwards of	2,200,000
1920—At normal rate of increase population will now be upwards of	2,800,000
The rule is one adult male to every five persons, which gives us as adult males	560,000
There are fully as many adult females	560,000
Total adult males and females	1,120,000

As the ratio in North Carolina by the census is 70% white and 30% negro, it follows that the negro adults, male and female, are 336,000 and the white adults, male and female, are 784,000. One half (392,000) of these last are, of course, white females, making 56,000 more adult white women than the 336,000 negro men and negro women combined.

IF white domination is threatened in the South, it is, therefore, DOUBLY EXPEDIENT TO ENFRANCHISE THE WOMEN QUICKLY IN ORDER THAT IT BE PRESERVED.

U. S. Senator Simmons, who waged the successful fight for White Supremacy in North Carolina in 1898, advocates ratification of the Federal Suffrage Amendment by the Legislature of North Carolina.

The Democratic State Convention asked that the Legislature ratify this Amendment.
Woodrow Wilson urges every Democratic State to ratify.
Secretary of the Navy, Josephus Daniels is eager for North Carolina to ratify.
Chief Justice John M. Anderson, of Alabama, says: "This is the most important Amendment ever proposed to the Federal Constitution; indeed, more important than any original section of that instrument, as it seeks an interpretation of that part of the Bill of Rights which proclaims that all men are born equal by interpolating therein the word WOMAN".
Chief Justice Clark, of North Carolina, says: "No matter how bad a character a man has, if he can only keep out of the penitentiary and the insane asylum we permit him to vote and to take a share in the Government, but we are afraid to trust our mothers, wives, and daughters to give us the aid of their intelligence and clear insight".

Would these representative men of the South ask that a measure be passed which would endanger the civilization of the South?

EQUAL SUFFRAGE ASSOCIATION OF NORTH CAROLINA—RALEIGH

Circular distributed by North Carolina suffragists to quiet fears that a federal amendment for woman suffrage would imperil White Democrats' dominance of state politics and to argue that it could even help to preserve White supremacy in the state.

Americans' rights to public education and social services, and they expressed disgust at the mistreatment of Blacks by lower-class Whites. However, political rights were another matter. Indeed, these suffragists were highly indignant that Black men had become the political superiors of "the best White women of the South."[38]

Still, there was a range of opinion within this group of Southern suffrage leaders that in part reflected the area of the South in which they lived, as well as their age. On one end were negrophobes, including older suffragists like Rebecca Latimer Felton of Georgia, Kate Gordon of Louisiana, and Belle Kearney of Mississippi who spoke of African Americans as though speaking of another, inferior species. Felton was openly and unapologetically racist in her demand for woman suffrage, declaring in a 1915 speech:

> Freedom belongs to the white woman as her inherent right. Whatever belongs to the freeman of these United States belongs to the white woman. Her Anglo--Saxon forefathers, fleeing from English tyranny won this country from savage tribes and again from English bayonets, by the expenditure of blood and treasure. Whatever was won by these noble men of the Revolution was inherited alike by sons and daughters. Fifty years from now this country will hold up hands in holy horror that... any man or set of men in America should assume to themselves the authority to deny to free white women of America the ballot which is the badge and synonym of freedom.[40]

On the other end of the scale, there was Madeline McDowell Breckinridge, a "second generation" suffragist from Kentucky and a progressive reformer. She spoke of White supremacy in politics as a temporary necessity until "undesirable" voters became "desirable" through education and gradual social progress that Whites were morally obligated to support *noblesse oblige* and believed that meanwhile, "qualified" Blacks should be allowed to vote.[41] And there was Mary Johnston of Virginia, who disdained the use of racist tactics by suffragists like Gordon and warned against it. In a 1913 letter to Lila Meade Valentine, she wrote: "I think that as women we should be most prayerfully careful lest, in the future, that women—whether colored women or White women who are merely poor, should be able to say that we had betrayed their interests and excluded them from freedom."[42]

Still, most Southern suffragists employed racist arguments to promote woman suffrage—some aggressively and enthusiastically, and others defensively and reluctantly. While there were African American women supporting women's enfranchisement from inside the South, they were systematically excluded from all White-led suffrage organizations and meetings as the suffragists sought to distance their movement from its historic association with advocacy of the rights of Black Americans.[43]

The Rise and Fall of the Suffragists' "Southern Strategy"

White Southern conservatives' devotion to White supremacy was not only a prime obstacle to the suffragists' success in the region, it was also a major *causative* factor in the development of the Southern suffrage movement in the 1890s—not in causing Southern women to *want* suffrage, but in giving them a *reason to expect that they could win it*. An organized regional movement with strong national support came into existence in the 1890s because many leading suffragists—both Southern and Northern—believed the determination of White Southern politicians to restore White supremacy might be the key to female enfranchisement.[44]

It is one of history's many ironies that this strategy was originally conceived by leading suffragist and abolitionist Lucy Stone's husband, Henry Blackwell, an antislavery activist who once risked his life to rescue an enslaved girl from her master. He began presenting his idea to Southern politicians in 1867 and managed to persuade delegates to the Mississippi Constitutional Convention of 1890 (the first of several such conventions) to give it serious consideration. This impressed Laura Clay, whose pleas for woman suffrage as "justice" were falling upon deaf ears, and she promoted the idea to other leaders of the NAWSA.[45]

They launched a major campaign based on Blackwell's Southern strategy, investing considerable time and resources. Carrie Chapman Catt and Susan B. Anthony went on separate speaking tours, sweeping through the region. In addition, the NAWSA took the unusual step of holding national conventions in Atlanta and New Orleans. Eager to avoid offending their Southern hosts at the 1895 convention in Atlanta, NAWSA leaders even asked their aging hero Frederick Douglass—an honored participant in women's rights conventions elsewhere in the nation—to stay away.[46] At the New Orleans convention, delegates formally endorsed a "states' rights" measure accepting each state suffrage organization's right to determine its own goals, tactics, and membership requirements, Some, notably Anthony, showed signs that they felt bad about these concessions to Southern racism. While in New Orleans, Anthony met separately with African American members of the Phillis Wheatley Club, and on the way home, stopped in Alabama at the Tuskegee Institute, established by Booker T. Washington for African American students, where she shook the hand of every female student. But many national suffrage leaders, including Catt and Anna Howard Shaw, shared the indignation of these elite, White Southern women that their social "inferiors"—whether African Americans in the South or immigrants in the North—had become their political "superiors."[47]

Late-nineteenth-century suffragists found it quite difficult to believe that the federal government would—as it did— abandon the defense of Black suffrage and allow the South to solve its "negro problem" by disfranchising African American men. Even after Mississippi in1890 and South Carolina in 1895 led the South in adopting measures such as "understanding clauses" and poll taxes to "legally" keep Blacks from voting—instead of the usual fraud and violence

employed for decades—suffragists who supported this Southern strategy for gaining woman suffrage insisted that the federal government would not allow these measures to stand.[48]

Southern suffragists such as Clay and Kearney warned that Congress would invoke the Fifteenth Amendment's enforcement clause, or the Supreme Court would rule the states' disfranchisement provisions unconstitutional. Yet, solving "the negro problem" by *extending* the franchise to *women* with education or property," they argued, would ensure that the vast majority of new voters would be White and still be seen as a *liberalization,* rather than a restriction of suffrage. Thus, White political supremacy could be permanently restored without risking congressional retribution or an unfavorable Supreme Court ruling.[49]

Throughout the 1890s, many Southern suffragists believed that as the men of their class cast about for a means of countering the effects of Black suffrage, they might accept woman suffrage as a solution—just as politicians in Western states had used woman suffrage to consolidate their political position. By 1903, however, it was clear to most suffragists that Southern politicians had managed to restore White supremacy by disfranchising Black men and that they were going to be allowed to get away with it. NAWSA initiatives in the South ended and, except in states such as Kentucky and Louisiana where there were exceptionally committed suffragist leaders, the Southern suffrage movement foundered.[50]

Out of desperation, in 1906 and 1907 a few Southern suffragists initiated still more blatantly racist campaigns. Belle Kearney called for a new Southern campaign explicitly asking for woman suffrage "as a solution of the race problem," and Kate Gordon initiated a scheme to get a "White women only" amendment added to the Mississippi constitution. However, the NAWSA refused to give its endorsement to either scheme. NAWSA president, Anna Howard Shaw, wrote in a letter to suffragist Laura Clay of Kentucky, "It must appeal to you as to every fair-minded woman that such a call could not be sanctioned by the National Suffrage Association." It is "contrary to the spirit of our organization" and would "re-act against ourselves" by suggesting "that we really don't believe in the justice of suffrage, but simply that certain classes or races should dominate the government."[51]

Other national suffrage leaders, notably Henry Blackwell and his daughter Alice Stone Blackwell, pleaded with advocates of the "Whites only" amendment to abandon it. Alice explained that any measure that allowed Whites to vote, "no matter how ignorant or bad in character," and shut out every Black, "no matter how intelligent or how good," was "regarded everywhere outside the Southern States as an unmitigated iniquity."[52]

Though the NAWSA had for years sought to exploit the South's "negro problem" to bring in the inhospitable South, rejection of these explicitly racist schemes indicated that there was, after all, a limit to the racism the organization would support. NAWSA leaders feared an explicitly Whites-only campaign would weigh against the woman suffrage movement in the North and in the West—the region where suffragists would

finally achieve the crucial breakthroughs that gave momentum to the suffrage campaign and lead to the passage of the federal amendment.[53]

Most Southern suffrage clubs dissolved or lay dormant until approximately 1910. In the second stage of the suffrage movement in the South, 1910 to 1920, White suffragists rarely raised the race issue and were almost exclusively on the defensive in regard to race. As anti-suffragists used rabidly racist rhetoric to fight women's enfranchisement, especially by federal amendment, White suffragists now insisted that the race issue was irrelevant to the woman suffrage issue, a "non-issue" trumped up by their opponents. Even Mary Johnston denied that state suffrage amendments would enfranchise large numbers of African American women, insisting that only "a few educated, property-owning coloured women will vote, but not the mass of coloured women." Nellie Nugent Somerville brushed aside the question, "How would woman suffrage apply to the American negress?" saying, "I answer, just as it applies to the American negro."[54]

Divisions Over States' Rights

On the race issue, White Southern suffragists presented a united front. Those who questioned the use of racist tactics or disapproved of the wholesale exclusion of Blacks from the electorate, generally kept such sentiments to themselves or at least out of the public arena. They had no desire to confirm the widespread suspicion that White suffragists favored Black suffrage.[55] However, there was no such consensus or show of solidarity regarding the states' rights issue.

In the last decade of the suffrage movement, as the federal suffrage amendment gained momentum elsewhere in the nation, differences of opinion over the state sovereignty issue divided Southern suffragists into warring camps. The National American Woman Suffrage Association (NAWSA), the newly formed National Woman's Party (NWP), and a new Southern organization, the Southern States Woman Suffrage Conference (SSWSC) each followed separate strategies and competed for the loyalty of Southern suffragists. The controversy over different strategies strained, and in some cases, severed long-standing friendships and added to the difficulties the woman suffrage movement faced in the South.[56]

Southern White women who became suffragists generally identified strongly with their region and with their states. This was true even of those quite critical of the region and its institutions, such as Mary Johnston, who wrote in 1905: "In spite of all reason and [owing to] merely an ingrained and hereditary matter... Virginia (and incidentally the entire South) is my country, and not the stars and stripes but the stars and bars is my flag."[57]

In fact, reverence for their states and the South made Southern White suffragists determined to reform them. Thus, winning the suffrage battle at home was paramount. Even the suffragists with no theoretical objection to a federal amendment—those who were not states' rights devotees—longed for suffrage victories on the state level that would proclaim an acceptance of

women's equality and the triumph of a new progressive spirit. This filial attachment to their states and region, together with expediency (they were well aware of the regional reverence for state sovereignty, particularly in regard to the franchise), led them to seek enfranchisement only through state action until all hope of such action was lost.

A minority of Southern suffragists could not bring themselves to support a federal suffrage amendment, however. When in 1913, the NAWSA—prodded into action by Alice Paul and her associates—renewed its campaign for a federal suffrage amendment, Kate Gordon decided it was time that Southern suffragists go their own way. Gordon, a disgruntled former NAWSA officer and a committed states' rights advocate, led in the establishment of the Southern States Woman Suffrage Conference (SSWSC).[58]

Gordon and her followers insisted that Southern states would never allow a federal amendment to be passed by Congress. By promoting a federal solution, Gordon charged, the NAWSA was just wasting its time and money, and making things even more difficult for Southern suffragists to win state victories. In her view, Southern suffragists—who must gain their rights from Southern Democrats—must never even appear to favor a federal amendment. Gordon demanded that all Southern suffragists support the SSWSC and insisted that the NAWSA turn over the South to her leadership.[59]

Most Southern suffragists, however, did not follow Kate Gordon's lead. Few were willing to renounce federal suffrage when it might be their only means of gaining enfranchisement. In fact, after one of Gordon's tirades against NAWSA leaders, state suffrage organizations in Tennessee and Alabama formally rebuked Gordon and her attempts to lead a Southern revolt against the NAWSA and the federal amendment. Tennessee's resolution declared that "the Convention of the Tennessee Equal Suffrage Association go on record as disapproving the action of Miss Kate M. Gordon in undertaking to dictate to the NAWSA or its Congressional Committee in regard to its policy, methods, or plans... and in her presuming to speak for the women of the South."[60]

As Gordon and her tactics alienated nearly all of the prominent Southern suffrage leaders, the SSWSC ceased to exist except in name only. Of the leading suffragists, only Clay and Kate and Jean Gordon were so committed to the concept of state sovereignty that they ultimately refused to support, and indeed, opposed the federal suffrage amendment.[61]

After 1916 when many pleas for state suffrage amendments had been made and rejected throughout the South, and the NAWSA was fully committed to securing enfranchisement through federal action, most Southern suffragists campaigned actively for the proposed amendment. Some, including Nellie Nugent Somerville, set aside her own reservations about federal overreach and labored to convince fellow Southerners that the amendment held "no menace for the institutions of any State or any group of States." Others had no such reservations to overcome. Anne

Dallas Dudley of Tennessee insisted that "the spirit of the New South has been misunderstood by our representatives in Congress" who so long blocked the amendment, and that Southerners were "glad and proud to acclaim ourselves loyally an integral part of our nation today."[62]

Sue Shelton White, also of Tennessee, warned that rather than expect suffragists to uphold state sovereignty, the Democrats would be well advised to modify their doctrines in order to keep the loyalty of Southern women: "Moss-backed traditions of political parties will no longer be accepted as an excuse for withholding democracy from women," she wrote. "There are suffragists born Democrats who have hoped to live and die in the political faith of their fathers who can no longer accept such an excuse."[63]

Most Southern suffragists rallied behind NAWSA President Catt when she announced her "Winning Plan" to coordinate state suffrage work through a nationwide strategy to finally secure a federal amendment. Catt's plan, however, was not satisfactory to all the NAWSA supporters in the South, partly because it largely wrote off the region until time for ratification. The NAWSA fully supported and contributed generously to state suffrage campaigns in critical states such as New York where there was a good chance of victory. But fearing that failed state suffrage campaigns would blunt momentum, Catt demanded that NAWSA affiliates in states she considered poor prospects suspend efforts at winning full suffrage through state amendment and seek only partial suffrage. Yet, to the chagrin of some Southern suffragists, especially Madeline McDowell Breckinridge who believed victory in Kentucky was quite likely, Catt's list of poor prospects included *all* Southern states.[64]

When in June 1919 Congress finally submitted the proposed Nineteenth Amendment to the states for ratification, the leaders of the woman suffrage movement in the Southern states found themselves fighting one another as well as the antis—a situation that did nothing to help the cause. In Virginia, there was open hostility between NAWSA loyalists led by Lila Meade Valentine and the state's chapter of the NWP. In Mississippi, Somerville and her associates endured the bitter experience of sitting in the gallery of the capitol while Kate Gordon denounced the federal amendment as a threat to state sovereignty and the Constitution. In Louisiana, the Gordons and other advocates of woman suffrage through state action combated both federal amendment supporters *and* the anti-suffragists, creating a three-way struggle in which no form of woman suffrage was adopted. During the final, bitter battle which took place in Nashville, Tennessee, both Gordon sisters and Laura Clay actually campaigned against ratification of "this hideous amendment" though Clay expressed "a great distaste" at being publicly associated with the despised antis.[65]

As the end of the long struggle for woman suffrage approached, those Southern suffragists who opposed the Nineteenth Amendment were bitter, disappointed in their fellow suffragists, and dismayed that the success of woman suffrage for

which they had worked for so many years helped undermine another cherished political ideal—state sovereignty. Most Southern suffragists, however, were jubilant when ratification came at last and grateful to Tennessee for, in the words of Virginia suffragists, "redeeming the honor of the country."[66]

Still, their celebration was dampened by the fact that so many women had to be enfranchised "courtesy of Uncle Sam." Madeline McDowell Breckinridge, whose state was one of the four Southern states that ratified the Nineteenth Amendment, was joking when she told the NAWSA's "Jubilee Convention" in Chicago in 1920:

> We'll get all our rights with the help of Uncle Sam,
> For the way that they come, we don't give a _ _ _ _.[67]

Breckinridge fully understood the disappointment of those suffragists in the states that failed to ratify—or worse, adopted "rejection resolutions."

Pattie Ruffner Jacobs of Alabama, speaking for the "defeated" suffragists at the Jubilee Convention, observed: "It only remains for the outward and visible sign of our freedom to be put in the hands of Southern women by the generous men of other states, a situation which hurts our pride and to which we submit with deep regret but not apology."[68] Having hoped to win from their home states and region a public endorsement of woman's political equality, these Southern women—like African American men—had instead gained the right to vote over the strenuous objections of political leaders in their states.

The analogy was not lost on the suffragists. Jacobs acknowledged, "It is acutely distasteful to Southern suffragists not to be enfranchised by Southern men, for we of all people understand the symbolism of the ballot."[69] Yet, these White suffragists *would be allowed to exercise this privilege* granted them by the "generous men of other states." Most African American women in the region would not be so fortunate.[70]

Conclusion: Intractable as Well as Inhospitable

White Southern suffragists, with their elite cadre of leaders who shared many of the ideas of other Southerners of their race and class, offered no thorough-going indictment of their society. They did not challenge the idea that many within the region needed the "guardianship" of the more enlightened citizenry: they only objected to the idea that *they* needed such guidance and protection.[71] These suffragists were "radical" for their region only as advocates of reforms in laws and customs that would advance women's status in Southern society.

None of these reforms, however, were as threatening to the social order as woman suffrage; reforms short of suffrage could still be seen as evidence of male protection of women and children, secured through "indirect influence." The request for the vote, on the other hand, was interpreted as a challenge to the fundamentally hierarchical and paternalistic political structure of the region as well as to the White supremacy and the sovereignty of the states. However nicely the suffragists tried to put it, demanding the power to represent their own interests

constituted an indirect accusation of failure that White Southern male politicians understood and resented.

The South was never, as Laura Clay hoped, fully "brought in" to the suffrage fold, even though the defection of four states from the otherwise solid South allowed the Nineteenth Amendment to be ratified. In rejecting woman suffrage, Southern politicians made it clear that they still found much about the old pattern of relations between the sexes quite attractive.

As for African American women of the South, it would take half a century and a mass movement before Congress adopted the Voting Rights Act of 1965, which allowed them to take full advantage of the right bestowed through the Nineteenth Amendment. Then, between 1972 and 1982, the South again proved to be intractable in the battle over the proposed Equal Rights Amendment, which fell short of ratification by three states. Once again, most "unratified states" were Southern states.[72]

After 1920, women still had a long way to go in their quest for equality in the South.

Notes

This is a revised and expanded version of an essay that appeared in Marjorie Spruill (Wheeler), ed. *VOTES FOR WOMEN: The Woman Suffrage Movement in Tennessee, the South, and the Nation* (Knoxville: University of Tennessee Press, 1995).

1. Clipping, *Woman's Journal*, Laura Clay Scrapbook, Laura Clay Papers, Special Collections and Archives, Margaret I. King Library, University of Kentucky.

2. Spruill (Wheeler), *New Women of the New South: The Leaders of the Woman Suffrage Movement in the Southern States* (Oxford University Press, 1993), 115–18.

3. Charles Reagan Wilson, *Baptized in Blood: The Religion of the Lost Cause, 1865-1920* (Athens, Ga; University of Georgia Press, 1980); Gaines M. Foster, *Ghosts of the Confederacy: Defeat, the Lost Cause, and the Emergence of the New South, 1865 to 1913* (New York: Oxford University Press, 1988); Karen L. Cox, *Dixie's Daughters: The United Daughters of the Confederacy and the Preservation of Confederate Culture* (Gainesville, Fla: Univ. Press of Florida, 2003).

4. Quotation from Albert Taylor Bledsoe, "The Mission of Woman," *The Southern Review*, October 1871, 923–43; Spruill (Wheeler), *New Women of the New South*, 8–13.

5. Ibid., 4-9, 13–19.

6. Quotation from anti-suffrage pamphlet, Clay Papers.

7. Spruill (Wheeler), *New Women of the New South*, 29–37.

8. Carrie Chapman Catt and Nettie Rogers Shuler, *Woman Suffrage and Politics: The Inner Story of the Suffrage Movement* (Seattle & London: University of Washington Press, 1923), 88-89.

9. Spruill (Wheeler), *New Women of the New South*, 38-71.

10. Belle Kearney, *A Slaveholder's Daughter* (Abbey Press, 1900); James P. Louis, "Sue Shelton White," in *Notable American Women: A Biographical Dictionary Completing the Twentieth Century* (Harvard University Press, 1971); Kate Gordon to Henry Blackwell, Oct. 1, 1907, Clay Papers.

11. Quotation from Kate Gordon to Catherine Waugh McCulloch, June 1, 1915, McCulloch Papers, Schlesinger Library, Harvard University; Desha Breckinridge to Madeline McDowell Breckinridge, May 3, 1913, Madeline McDowell Breckinridge Papers in the Breckinridge Family Papers, Manuscripts Division, Library of Congress, hereafter MMB Papers.

12. Spruill (Wheeler), *New Women of the New South*, 58-60.

13. Ibid.

14. Paul E. Fuller, *Laura Clay and the Woman's Rights Movement*

(Lexington, KY: University Press of Kentucky, 1992), 1-29.

15. Spruill (Wheeler), *New Women of the New South*, 61-62.

16. Ibid., 61-65; Quotation, Anna Howard Shaw, *Story of a Pioneer*, (New York: Harper & Bros., 1915), 309.

17. Spruill (Wheeler), *New Women of the New South*, 50-57, 65-71.

18. Madeline McDowell Breckinridge, "The Prospects for Woman Suffrage in the South," address to the NAWSA convention of 1911, MMB Papers.

19. Spruill (Wheeler), *New Women of the New South*, 65-71; Nellie Nugent Somerville, "Christian Citizenship," 1898, and Somerville, "Presidential Address to First Mississippi Woman Suffrage Association," March 28, Somerville-Howorth Family Papers, Schlesinger Library, Harvard University.

20. Sophonisba P. Breckinridge, *Madeline McDowell Breckinridge: A Leader in the New South* (Chicago, IL: Univ. of Chicago Press, 1921), 34–42, quot. 41–42.

21. Spruill (Wheeler), *New Women of the New South*, 66-67; Rebecca Felton, "The Subjection of Women and the Enfranchisement of Women," No. 2, "Rebecca Latimer Felton Papers" (n.d.), Special Collections Division, Hargrett Rare Book and Manuscript Library, University of Georgia; Josephine Bone Floyd, "Rebecca Latimer Felton: Champion of Women's Rights," *Georgia Historical Quarterly* 30, no. June 1946 (n.d.): 81–104; Josephine Bone Floyd, "Rebecca Latimer Felton: Political Independent," *Georgia Historical Quarterly* 30, no. March 1946 (n.d.): 14–34; Rebecca Latimer Felton, *Country Life in Georgia in the Days of My Youth* (Atlanta, Ga, 1919).

22. Madeline Breckinridge, "Public Schools and Southern Development" (n.d.), MMB Papers.

23. A. Elizabeth Taylor, "Last Phase of the Woman Suffrage Movement in Georgia," *Georgia Historical Quarterly* 43, March 1959: 11–28, quotation, 14.

24. Madeline Breckinridge, "Direct Versus Indirect Influence in Kentucky," written for the *New York Evening Post*, February 3, 1914, MMB Papers.

25. Spruill (Wheeler), *New Women of the New South*, 65-69

26. Jean Gordon, "New Louisiana Child Labor Law," *Charities*, January 26, 1908, 481.

27. M. Breckinridge, "Direct Versus Indirect Influence in Kentucky."

28. Melba Porter Hay, "Madeline McDowell Breckinridge: Kentucky Suffragist and Progressive Reformer," (Dissertation, University of Kentucky, 1980), 139–40.

29. Floyd, "Rebecca Latimer Felton," 86.

30. Nellie Nugent Somerville to the editor of a Greenville, Miss. newspaper, 16 May ?, Scrapbook, Somerville-Howorth Family Papers.

31. Pattie Ruffner Jacobs to the editor, Birmingham Ledger, Feb. 12, 1912, Jacobs Scrapbook, Pattie Ruffner Jacobs Papers, Birmingham Public Library, Birmingham, Alabama; "Sentimental Idea Hurts Suffrage," Woman's Journal, Apr. 12, 1913, Mary Johnston Papers, University of Virginia, Charlottesville.

32. Spruill (Wheeler), New Women of the New South, 74-78; Northern suffragists' reaction described in Anne Firor Scott, The Southern Lady: From Pedestal to Politics: 1830-1930 (Chicago: Univ. of Chicago Press, 1970), 183, 184.

33. Mary Johnston, "Speech, Woman's Club Alumnae, May 31," [emphasis hers],1910-11 suffrage speeches, Johnston Papers.

34. Nellie Nugent Somerville, "Are Women Too Good to Vote?" clipping, ca 1914, Somerville-Howorth Family Papers.

35. Pattie Ruffner Jacobs, "Tradition Vs. Justice," speech at the 1920 NAWSA "Jubilee Convention" in Chicago, Clay Papers.

36. Pattie Ruffner Jacobs, "The Pulse of the South, How the South Really Feels About Woman Suffrage," clipping, Clay Papers; Mary Johnston, draft of a speech to be given in Philadelphia.

37. Spruill (Wheeler), New Women of the New South, 100–112; Marjorie Spruill (Wheeler), "Race, Reform, and Reaction at the Turn of the Century: Southern Suffragists, the NAWSA, and the 'Southern Strategy' in Context," in Votes for Women: The Struggle for Suffrage Revisited, ed. Jean H Baker (New York: Oxford Univ. Press, 2002), 102–17.

38. Spruill (Wheeler), New Women of the New South, 101.

39. Kearney, A Slaveholder's Daughter, 62–64, 92, and 97;

40. Felton, "The Subjection of Women."

41. M. Breckinridge to Miss Mary Winser, Jan. 1, 1912, Clay Papers; Historian Suzanne Lebsock states that the racism exhibited by Southern white suffragists should be considered in light of the extreme racism of anti-suffragists. White suffragists in Virginia, she wrote, "negotiated a middling course," neither "disavowing white supremacy" nor engaging in the "poisonous polemics" of the antis. Suzanne Lebsock, "Woman Suffrage and White Supremacy: A Virginia Case Study," in Visible Women: New Essays on American Activism, ed. Nancy A. Hewitt and Suzanne Lebsock (Urbana and Chicago: University of Illinois Press, 1993), 62–100; Spruill (Wheeler), New Women of the New South, 100-132.

42. Mary Johnston to Lila Meade Valentine, Jan. 5, 1913, and Oct ? 1915, Lila Meade Valentine Papers, Virginia Historical Society, Richmond.

43. Glenda Elizabeth Gilmore, Gender and Jim Crow: Women and the Politics of White Supremacy in North Carolina, 1896-1920 (University of North Carolina Press, 1996); Adele Logan Alexander, Princess of the Hither Isles: A Black Suffragist's Story from the Jim Crow South (Yale University Press, 2019); Adele Logan Alexander, "Adella Hunt Logan, the Tuskegee Woman's Club, and African Americans in the Suffrage Movement," in Marjorie Spruill (Wheeler), Votes for Women!: The Woman Suffrage Movement in Tennessee, the South, and the Nation (Knoxville: University of Tennessee Press, 1995): 71-104.

44. Spruill (Wheeler), New Women of the New South, 100–132; Spruill (Wheeler), "Race, Reform, and Reaction at the Turn of the Century.".

45. Spruill (Wheeler), New Women of the New South, 113-15.

46. Ibid., 116-120; Henry Blackwell, "What the South Can Do (1867)," in Up from the Pedestal: Selected Writings in the History of American Feminism (New York: Quadrangle Books, 1968), 253–

57; Henry Blackwell to Laura Clay, Nov. 21, 1885, Clay Papers; Fuller, Laura Clay, 54–56; A. Elizabeth Taylor, "The Woman Suffrage Movement in Mississippi, 1890–1920," Journal of Mississippi History 30, Feb. 1968 (1994): 1–34; Nellie Nugent Somerville, "President's Address, 1898, MWSA."

47. Alexander, "Adella Hunt Logan," 89; Spruill (Wheeler), New Women of the New South, 21, 118.

48. Ibid., 116-19.

49. Ibid.; Blackwell, "What the South Can Do (1867)"; Fuller, Laura Clay, 66–70; Belle Kearney, "Address to the 1903 NAWSA Convention," Belle Kearney Papers, Mississippi Department of Archives and History; Spruill (Wheeler), "Race, Reform, and Reaction"; Beverly Beeton, "How the West Was Won for Woman Suffrage," in this volume.

50. Spruill (Wheeler), New Women of the New South, 120.

51. Ibid., 120.

52. Ibid., 123.

53. Ibid.

54. Ibid., 125–32; Lebsock, "Virginia Women and White Supremacy."

55. For example, Mary Johnston wrote to Lila Meade Valentine that she was disgusted by Kate Gordon's racist "utterings" and refused the role of honorary vice-president of Gordon's Southern States Woman Suffrage Conference, but did so privately. Mary Johnston to Lila Meade Valentine, Jan. 5, 1913, Valentine Papers.

56. Spruill (Wheeler), New Women of the New South, 133–86.

57. Johnston quotation appears in Anne Goodwyn Jones, Tomorrow Is Another Day: The Woman Writer in the South, 1859-1936 (Baton Rouge: Louisiana State University Press, 1981), 186.

58. Spruill (Wheeler), New Women of the New South, 135-41.

59. Ibid., 133-70.

60. Ibid., 154–57; See "Resolution adopted by the 1915 state convention of Tennessee suffragists, Jackson," Sue Shelton White Papers, Schlesinger Library, Harvard University.

61. Spruill (Wheeler), New Women of the New South, 156–80.

62. Somerville quoted in Kenneth R. Johnston, "Kate Gordon and the Woman Suffrage Movement in the South," Journal of Southern History 38, Aug. 1972 (n.d.): 381; Anne Dallas Dudley to Mrs. John South, KERA president, Jan. 2, 1919, Clay Papers.

63. Clipping n.d., "Democratic Party May Lose Support, "White Papers."

64. On Catt's "Winning Plan," see Robert Booth Fowler's essay in this volume; Carrie Chapman Catt to Southern presidents, Jan. 11, 1916, Clay Papers; Madeline Breckinridge, "Kentucky Chapter Woman Suffrage History: 1900-1930," MMB Papers.

65. Spruill (Wheeler), New Women of the New South, 172–80; Laura Clay to Kate Gordon, July 31, 1920, Clay Papers; Fuller, Laura Clay, 160.

66. Richmond-Times Dispatch, Aug. 19, 1920.

67. S. Breckinridge, Madeline McDowell Breckinridge, 236, 237.

68. Pattie Ruffner Jacobs, "Tradition Vs. Justice."

69. Ibid.

70. As predicted, after 1920 the restrictions that prevented black men from voting were used against black women. See essay by Rosalyn Terborg-Penn in this volume.

71. See for example, Jacobs, "Tradition Vs. Justice."

72. Marjorie J. Spruill, Divided We Stand: The Battle Over Women's Rights and Family Values That Polarized American Politics (Bloomsbury, 2017).

Mary Church Terrell (center), and her two sisters,
Annette (left) and Sarah Church

MOORLAND-SPINGARN RESEARCH CENTER, HOWARD UNIVERSITY

AFRICAN AMERICAN WOMEN AND THE WOMAN SUFFRAGE MOVEMENT

Rosalyn Terborg-Penn

Editor's Introduction: This essay by renowned historian Rosalyn Terborg-Penn, the pioneering scholar in the study of African American women in the suffrage movement, provides an overview of their involvement in the movement's long and complex history. African American suffragists played an active role in the fight for female enfranchisement despite many obstacles. These included obstacles placed in their path by other suffragists—White women—who were willing, in many cases, to win their own enfranchisement at the expense of leaving their African American sisters behind.

The women's rights movement and the movement for justice for African Americans had a close, albeit erratic, relationship throughout American history. Women—Black and White—played an active role in the fight to abolish slavery. Yet discrimination against women who took on a highly visible role in the fight led antislavery feminists to begin an enduring movement for women's rights. Just after the Civil War, supporters of the rights of Blacks and women worked together—for *universal* suffrage—in the American Equal Rights Association founded in 1866. However, they divided rancorously in 1869 over the exclusion of women from enfranchisement through the Fourteenth and Fifteenth Amendments. As Terborg-Penn reminds us, supporters of woman suffrage broke into two woman suffrage organizations over this issue, with some suffragists refusing to accept the idea that this was "the Negro's Hour" and that women must wait their turn.

The situation was drastically different in the last three decades of the woman suffrage movement when the historic connection between women's rights and the rights of African Americans became a distinct liability for advocates of *woman* suffrage. The 1890s and early 1900s was an era in which the vast majority of Southern Black men were disfranchised through legislation and constitutional amendments—unchallenged by the federal government. In addition, Jim Crow laws were adopted establishing segregation in nearly every aspect of life, resulting in one of the worst periods in the history of American race relations. At this time, many national suffrage leaders, working with White Southern suffragists, tried unsuccessfully to

promote woman suffrage by saying that the enfranchisement of women—with educational requirements that would effectively limit the vote to White women—would actually help restore White supremacy in Southern politics. In the last decade of the suffrage movement, after disfranchisement had been completed, White suffragists insisted that woman suffrage and Black suffrage were *unrelated* issues. They countered anti-suffragists' claims that state or federal suffrage amendments threatened White supremacy by insisting that the same discriminatory provisions that kept Black men from voting would apply to Black women.

Victims of both racism and sexism and eager to fight against both, African American women were in a difficult position as relations between these two great social movements fluctuated. Not enfranchised along with the men of their race in the Reconstruction amendments, African American women faced a cruel dilemma when asked to wait patiently for their own enfranchisement. Their predicament worsened in the late nineteenth and early twentieth centuries. Black women who were eager to participate in the woman suffrage movement often found it difficult to do so, as White suffragists not only embraced racist tactics but excluded Black women from membership in suffrage organizations. When at last the long-awaited "woman's hour" seemed to be at hand, White suffragists deliberately avoided any action that might alarm White racists and endanger the suffrage cause—and *again* African American women were expected to understand.

As Terborg-Penn explains, African American women nevertheless played an active role in every stage of the suffrage movement from the antebellum period through the suffrage victory in 1920, working sometimes with White suffragists and sometimes in separate African American women's clubs. Among American suffragists, Black women were, perhaps, the most unwavering advocates of universal suffrage for all. Yet, as Terborg-Penn argues, they also understood and proclaimed publicly that the vote was essential for their own protection, the protection of their children, and the progress of their race.

African American suffragists did *not* understand or accept their exclusion from White suffrage organizations or the racist tactics employed by White suffragists. Neither did they accept the efforts of Southern state governments to exclude them from voting after the victory of the Nineteenth Amendment or the failure of White women's organizations to assist them in claiming that right. Though some African American women were able to register and vote even in the South, the vast majority remained disfranchised. Not until 1965 would Black women—and Black men—be fully enfranchised, after a new suffrage movement in which African American women *again* played a leading role. Only then was America, at last, a nation in which there was universal suffrage.

★　　★　　★　　★　　★

FRICAN AMERICAN WOMEN participated in the woman suffrage movement from the antebellum period through to the passage of the Nineteenth Amendment. Legal status, class, region of residence, gender, and racial identification determined the degree to which Black women could participate in the movement. Multiple forms of oppression, primarily slavery and then poverty, restricted many Black women from working to gain women's right to vote in the nineteenth century. Nevertheless, African American women resisted the many barriers put against their political participation. Similar categories bound all American women, and most African American men, all of whom were also disfranchised. However, during the seventy-two years of the movement, limitations on these groups were never as restricting as those set by the society for Black women.

Throughout the history of the movement, but particularly in the nineteenth century, Black women had little opportunity to participate in organized woman suffrage activities. During the antebellum period, only the relatively small number of legally free African American women were privileged enough to lobby for the right to vote. After emancipation during the post-Civil War years, impoverished Southern Black women seeking work, fleeing physical threats to their lives, and struggling with survival strategies for their families, could little afford to make the organized woman suffrage movement a priority. At this time, the large majority of Black women fell into this category. Nonetheless, there were always African American woman suffragists and as the century turned, more and more Black women, inside and outside of the South, began to flex their political muscles and demand the right to vote.

Although Blacks and Whites developed similar suffrage strategies and formed coalitions, differing experiences among the races and conflicts between the two groups resulted. The disfranchised all agreed that rational individuals could not argue against the ideas of freedom and justice for all adult citizens, though some educated White suffragists attempted to exclude immigrant women who did not speak English from qualifying to vote. Nonetheless, by the late nineteenth century an anti-Black woman suffrage strategy, more insidious than the anti-immigrant woman agenda, reinforced differences among African American and White woman suffragists, some of whom hoped to exclude Black women from gaining the right to vote. This anti-woman suffrage agenda further divided Black and White woman suffragists.

Class was another factor that influenced women's participation in the organized woman suffrage movement. Just as the majority of White women who actively participated in the organized movement were of the middle class, the majority of Black women suffragists appeared to have enjoyed higher status than the masses of women of their race. Because many of the activities of African American women participants were not recorded in the official histories of the movement, it is difficult to be sure that more middle-class Black women were suffragists than those of the working class. The changing status of African

American women during the duration of the movement—from slave to free, from rural to urban, from illiterate to literate—can be seen as factors which encouraged Black strategies to achieve women's enfranchisement. One thing is certain: for various reasons more and more Black women, like White women, joined the ranks of suffragists as the movement progressed in the twentieth century. This survey of African American women in the woman suffrage movement focuses on their reasons for supporting the "Votes for Women" campaign, but also on the obstacles they met along the way to enfranchisement.

Nineteenth-Century Black Woman Suffragists

There were two fundamental reasons why African Americans supported the woman suffrage movement during the nineteenth century. At mid-century their argument was based upon the belief, which was also held by White woman suffragists, that women were second-class citizens who needed the vote to improve their status in society. However, by the late nineteenth and early twentieth centuries, the rationale had grown to include the argument that Black women needed the vote in order to help uplift the race and to obtain their own rights. A discussion of the activities and views of Black female suffragists from the antebellum period to the turn of the century reveals that woman suffrage, to them, was a just and a practical cause.[1]

Although Black women participated throughout the nineteenth-century woman suffrage campaign, their views were seldom recorded during the antebellum period. During these years, most of the African Americans commonly associated with the leadership of the struggle were men. Nonetheless, several African American women were among the ranks of antebellum woman's rights advocates. The most renowned among them was Sojourner Truth, who attended several woman's rights meetings beginning with the Worcester, Massachusetts Convention of 1850. Ironically, she was quite unlike the other African American suffragists of her time. She was an emancipated slave who was illiterate and labored in various menial capacities for her keep. Her African American sisters in the movement were literate, privileged women who had been born free. Truth is known to the movement because the White leadership recorded her outspoken sentiments, often citing them as anomalous to those of the other women in the movement. In 1851, for example, at Akron, Ohio, Truth gave a remarkable address that made her famous in the annals of the movement, despite the attempts of some White feminists to thwart her efforts to be heard. From that time on, Truth's views on women's rights and woman suffrage, spoken in folk dialect, were highly publicized. At the New York City convention held in 1853, for example, Truth commented publicly about White prejudice against her, when she said: "I know that it feels a kind O'hissin' like to see a colored woman get up and tell you about things, and Woman's Rights."[2]

Unlike those of Sojourner Truth, the words of suffragists Harriet Forten Purvis and her sister, Margaretta Forten, were not recorded. Both women were founding members of the Philadelphia Female Anti-Slavery Society and daughters of the wealthy reformer James Forten, Sr. The sisters helped to lay the groundwork for the

first National Woman's Rights Convention ever held, in October 1854. Another early Black female suffragist was abolitionist lecturer Sarah Remond from Salem, Massachusetts. She was honored in 1858, when she spoke at the Ninth National Woman's Rights Convention held at New York City, but her remarks were not recorded. According to the recollections of Susan B. Anthony, journalist and militant abolitionist Mary Ann Shadd Cary began her support of woman's rights during the late 1850s. However, it appears that none of her statements on woman suffrage during the antebellum period have survived.[3]

After the Civil War, these Black female abolitionists and feminists were joined by Hattie Purvis, who was Harriet Purvis's daughter, and by abolitionist and poet Frances Ellen Watkins Harper. Both women participated in the American Equal Rights Association (AERA). In an effort to campaign for universal suffrage, this organization of men and women was founded in 1866 during a woman's rights convention. Frances Harper spoke at the convention and also served on the financial committee, but there appears to be no record of her remarks. Aside from her participation as a committee member, during this period, little is known about her reasons for supporting woman suffrage. Nevertheless, during the years in which the AERA functioned, from 1866 through 1869, Black women served on committees and contributed financial as well as moral support.[4]

If Sojourner Truth is best remembered for her folk words of wisdom, Harriet and Hattie Purvis can be remembered for their consistent service in a variety of roles in the AERA. In 1866 Harriet and Black abolitionist William Still were elected to the Executive Committee. In 1867 she and Black abolitionist Charles Lenox Remond appeared as the Blacks elected to the Finance Committee. In 1868, Hattie Purvis was elected recording secretary, along with Henry Blackwell. Both were reelected the following year.[5]

By 1869, differences in ideology among suffragists in the AERA over the proposed Fifteenth Amendment split the membership. Although the association members all supported the goal of universal suffrage, they disagreed on the means by which this goal was to be achieved. Some felt that a just amendment should include all disfranchised Americans, despite widespread public opposition to woman suffrage. Others believed that universal suffrage would have to be achieved in stages and that the most politically advantageous means was to enfranchise Black men first, the campaign for which was called "Negro suffrage." As a result of this controversy, the AERA ceased to function. Elizabeth Cady Stanton, Susan B. Anthony, and their supporters abandoned the AERA and formed the National Woman Suffrage Association (NWSA) in May 1869 and divorced themselves from the "Negro suffrage" issue. Although men were allowed to participate in the NWSA, they were excluded from official positions. By November 1869, Lucy Stone and Henry Ward Beecher had led their followers into the American Woman Suffrage Association (AWSA), which supported the Fifteenth Amendment and allowed males to hold office in the AWSA.[6]

Black suffragists, both males and females, became involved in this ideological dispute. Mary Ann Cary, for example, disagreed with the final form of the Fifteenth Amendment because it did not enfranchise women. On the other hand, Frances Harper, although committed to woman suffrage, felt that it was politically expedient to fight first to enfranchise Black men despite the setback to the woman suffrage cause.[7] Divisions among female suffragists affected Black affiliation in the resulting suffrage associations. Hattie Purvis attended NWSA meetings, as did Cary. Harper affiliated with the AWSA. Sojourner Truth attended meetings of both groups.[8]

During the 1870s, the AWSA attracted several additional Black women. Among them was Caroline Remond Putman of the crusading Remond family of Salem, Massachusetts, whose members actively lectured against slavery. In 1870 she helped to found the Massachusetts Woman Suffrage Association under the auspices of the AWSA.[9] Josephine St. Pierre Ruffin was another Massachusetts Black woman suffragist. She has been described as having played a leading role in every movement to emancipate Black women. Ruffin began her suffrage activities during 1875 as a member of the Massachusetts Woman Suffrage Association. A Bostonian, she affiliated with the group as a result of the welcome she received from Lucy Stone, Julia Ward Howe, and other pioneers in the Massachusetts movement.[10] Perhaps Ruffin's positive assessment of these prominent AWSA leaders gives clues as to why more African American women appear to have affiliated with the AWSA rather than the NWSA.

Mary Ann Shadd Cary
NATIONAL ARCHIVES OF CANADA

The first South Carolina delegate to a woman suffrage convention was a Black woman, Charlotte Rollin (known as Lottie) of Charleston. Along with her sisters, Frances, Louisa, and Kate, the Rollin sisters were influential in Reconstruction politics during the late 1860s and 1870s. Frances Rollin worked for and later married William J. Whipper who, as a delegate to the South Carolina Constitutional Convention of 1868, pleaded for the enfranchisement of women as well as Black men. Lottie Rollin worked for Black congressman Robert Brown Elliott. Rollin spoke on the floor of the South Carolina House of Representatives in 1869 to urge support of universal suffrage. By 1870, she chaired the founding meeting of the South Carolina Woman's Rights Association and was elected secretary. In 1871 her sister Louisa led a meeting at the state capital to

Frances Rollin, c. 1870 - 1879
NEW YORK PUBLIC LIBRARY

promote woman suffrage. The following year Kate Rollin was elected treasurer of the association, and Lottie Rollin represented South Carolina as an ex-officio member of the Executive Committee of the AWSA, which met in New York City that year.[11]

Not until the 1870s do we find Black female arguments on behalf of woman suffrage preserved in written form—other than those attributed to Sojourner Truth. At this time, Lottie Rollin addressed the chairman of the South Carolina Woman's Rights Convention in 1870 and said: "We ask suffrage not as a favor, not as a privilege, but as a right based on the ground that we are human beings, and as such entitled to all human rights."[12] The Rollin rationale on behalf of woman suffrage reflected the contemporary rhetoric that women were second-class citizens who needed the vote to improve their status in society.

One strategy used by Blacks as well as Whites to obtain the ballot for women was an appeal for female enfranchisement based on the Fifteenth Amendment. In 1872, White suffragist Mary Olney Brown of Washington State wrote a letter to Frederick Douglass, editor of the Black newspaper, *The New National Era* (Washington). Offering an emotional plea for Black male support of the vote for Black women, Brown argued that the Fifteenth Amendment, which had enfranchised Black men in 1870, should be applied to the enfranchisement of women because it did not exclude them in the definition of citizenship. Douglass printed the letter, wherein Brown encouraged voting Black men to support her strategy. This appears to be the first in many efforts made by White suffragists to reestablish the political coalition they had severed with African American men.[13]

Brown's strategy to demand suffrage as woman's legal right, a strategy frequently employed in the 1870s, could very well have come from journalist Mary Ann Cary, who had argued on behalf of the ballot for Black women in the 1860s and became one of the few women during this period who successfully registered to vote. She did this in 1871 in the District of Columbia, although like Susan B. Anthony and others, Cary was prohibited from voting. Cary is an example of the women historian Ellen DuBois calls radical feminists, who emerged in the 1870s as independent suffragists.[14] Cary attended the NWSA Convention that met in Washington in January of 1871 while she was a student in the Howard University Law School, and supported the memorial that Victoria Woodhull presented before the House Judiciary Committee the previous December. Woodhull had argued, like Mary Olney Brown, that the proposed Sixteenth Amendment to enfranchise women was not necessary, for as citizens, women had the right to vote under the Fourteenth and Fifteenth Amendments. She appealed to Congress merely to pass a declaratory resolution to that effect since the Constitution made no distinction between citizens based on gender.[15]

In support of this strategy, Cary prepared a testimony for the Judiciary Committee of the House of Representatives about the need for Black women to vote in the District of Columbia. She noted that she was a taxpayer with the same obligations as the Black male taxpayers of the city. Cary felt, therefore, that suffrage should be her right just as it was theirs. She noted that many women of her race in

the nation's capital supported the other women of the nation who demanded not only the vote, but the striking of the word "male" from the Constitution.[16]

Supporting her claim about Black female support for woman suffrage, Cary wrote the NWSA in 1876 on behalf of ninety-four Black women from the District of Columbia. Her letter requested that their names be enrolled in the July 4, 1876 centennial autograph book, as signers of the NWSA's Woman's Declaration of Rights. This declaration called for the immediate enfranchisement of American women.[17]

Cary and Mary Olney Brown were not alone in identifying woman suffrage as a potential source of strength to Black women during the Reconstruction years. Frances Harper argued similarly. In 1873, she attended the AWSA Convention at the Cooper Union in New York City. In making the closing speech, Harper declared that "as much as White women need the ballot, colored women need it more." She indicted what she called the "ignorant and often degraded men" who subjected Black women in the South to arbitrary legal authority. Acknowledging the progress already made by women of her race, Harper pleaded for equal rights and equal education for the African American women of the nation.[18]

The post-Civil War years were not only an era of change for White woman suffragists, they marked a time for expanding the rationale for woman suffrage among African American women. Even though Black women continued to express the original argument in support of woman suffrage—women are second-class citizens who need the vote—by the late nineteenth and early twentieth centuries, the rationale began to reflect more specifically needs of African American women. For example, in 1880 Cary organized the Colored Women's Progressive Franchise Association in the District of Columbia. Among the purposes of the group was what Cary called "an aggressive stand against the assumption that men only may begin and conduct industrial and other things." This idea was in keeping with the radical feminist belief that women, like men, should take leadership roles in developing industrial sectors in the economy. Cary even made plans to start a newspaper to support the rights and interests of women and to establish a joint stock company in which women were to have the controlling official power. There is no evidence, however, that she was ever able to accomplish these goals.[19]

Cary was not the only Black female journalist to favor woman suffrage in the 1880s. Gertrude Bustill Mossell of Philadelphia, like Cary, was from a prominent antebellum free-Negro family of reformers. Mossell initiated a woman's column in T. Thomas Fortune's first newspaper, *The New York Freeman*, a nationally oriented Black newspaper. In her first article, entitled "Woman Suffrage" published in 1885, she encouraged Blacks to read the *History of Woman Suffrage*, the *New Era*, the essays of John Stuart Mill, and other works about woman's rights to familiarize them with the woman suffrage movement and perhaps change the minds of those who opposed it. Mossell argued also that despite the anti-suffragists' charges to the contrary, most housewives supported woman suffrage.[20]

Other veteran suffragists continued their activities in the movement during the 1880s. Hattie Purvis was actively involved in the Pennsylvania Woman Suffrage

Mary McCurdy, 1897   Josephine St. Pierre Ruffin, 1902

Association. Frances Harper was a director of the Women's Congress, and by 1887 she was the Superintendent of Work Among Colored People for the Woman's Christian Temperance Union (WCTU), a national body quite supportive of woman suffrage. Josephine St. Pierre Ruffin was a member of the first board of the Massachusetts School Suffrage Association, which was founded in 1880.[21]

In the last decade of the nineteenth century, more and more African American women began to organize, raising their voices in support of woman suffrage. One of the reasons for this was the rising number of educated Blacks who emerged during the first generation out of slavery. With this new freedom, Black women, like White women, actively developed the women's club movement as a vehicle for change.

The first fifty-two delegates who met to organize the National Federation of Afro-American Women at Boston in August of 1895, were eager supporters of woman suffrage. The women cheered suffragist William Lloyd Garrison, Jr., who spoke of the need for political equality for women. Among the members of the Federation were veteran suffragists Frances Harper and Josephine Ruffin, who had made the initial call for an organization representative of African American women throughout the nation. Among the younger members destined to become prime movers among the Black woman suffragists of the twentieth century was Washington, D.C. educator Mary Church Terrell, a native of Memphis and an Oberlin graduate.[22]

In 1896 the National Federation of Afro-American Women merged with the National League of Colored Women to form the National Association of Colored Women (NACW). Mary Church Terrell was elected the first president. She and several other newly emerging Black female leaders included woman suffrage in their campaign to lead the nation's Black women toward self-help and racial uplift. Among this group was journalist Ida B. Wells-Barnett, who had been driven out of Memphis in 1892 because of her anti-lynching crusade. She later married, had a family, and settled in Chicago. Margaret Murray Washington, principal of the secondary school at Tuskegee Institute in Alabama and Booker T. Washington's

wife, was also among this group. By 1900, Susan B. Anthony listed these three women among the prominent advocates of woman suffrage.[23]

A lesser-known Southern Black woman of the 1890s was Mary McCurdy, a temperance leader and advocate of woman suffrage whose views echoed the changing rationale for woman suffrage exemplified by racial and gender identification. She personified the growing number of Southern women, educated during Reconstruction, who sought political means to solve the social ills of Black communities. While living in Rome, Georgia, McCurdy was president of the local Black woman's temperance union and an official in the state temperance organization. She also edited the *National Presbyterian*, a temperance paper published in 1890. A firm believer in woman suffrage, McCurdy saw the franchise as the means to prohibit the liquor traffic, a major vehicle for political corruption. Not only did she blame White men for keeping the ballot from the women of the nation, she also blamed them for the political corruption in the South. McCurdy felt that the majority of African American men who had voted in the South after the Fifteenth Amendment enfranchised them had either been robbed of that right, or had allowed their ballot to be purchased. African American women, she predicted, would never allow their votes to be bought.[24]

While touring the South during the Reconstruction years, Frances Harper observed the results of political corruption. She echoed McCurdy's opinion when she expressed her sentiments against corruption, published in a poem of 1896. Harper spoke in dialect through "Aunt Chloe," who said:

> And this buying up each other
>   Is something worse than mean.
> Though I think a heap of voting,
>   I go for voting clean.[25]

Although White women complained about political corruption in the South and in immigrant communities in the Northeast, they were usually on the offensive with their criticism of others. African American women were always on the defensive, defending their race as well as criticizing the ills that kept many former slaves powerless. Mary Church Terrell responded to White women's criticism of the purchase of the "Negro vote" at the National American Woman Suffrage Association (NAWSA) meeting that she attended in Washington in 1904. By then a national figure, she felt that Black men were being unduly condemned for selling their votes and she said: "They never sold their vote til they found that it made no difference how they cast them." Terrell noted also that there were many cases of Black men who were tempted, yet never sold their right to the ballot. Furthermore, she suggested that the White suffragists should aid rather than merely condemn Black voters: "My sisters of the dominant race, stand up not only for the oppressed sex, but also for the oppressed race!"[26]

At the turn of the century, Terrell, like other Black suffragists before her, admonished America for violating the principle "government of the people, for the people and by the people," by denying women the right to the ballot. As a

"Woman to the Rescue," a pro-suffrage cartoon from *The Crisis*, May 1916
WOMAN SUFFRAGE MEDIA COLLECTION

result of male-dominated politics, she asserted, women were held in subjugation by men, many of whom she called "illiterate, debauched, and vicious."[27] The Terrell rationale for support of woman suffrage included both themes—suffrage as the right of women as citizens and woman suffrage as a means to uplifting African Americans.

Twentieth-Century Black Woman Suffragists

By the first decade of the twentieth century, more Black women began to speak out about how important their right to vote could be to Black people as a whole and to Black women in particular. Yet, as growing numbers of African American women supported and joined the organized woman suffrage movement, their potential

political influence stimulated the creation of greater obstacles blocking their attempts to achieve the right to vote.[28]

With the creation of the "colored" women's club movement, more and more resourceful women had a means of spreading the word about strategies for uplifting themselves and their race. Adella Hunt Logan was one of them. She was the only Alabama woman, Black or White, listed in 1900 by the NAWSA as a life member. A native of Georgia who joined the Tuskegee Institute faculty in 1883 as principal of the training school, Logan wrote one of the most comprehensive arguments in support of woman suffrage. In 1905, she argued similarly to Terrell: "Government of the people, for the people and by the people is but partially realized so long as woman has no vote."[29] She could not understand why women were treated as citizens in other aspects of American life, but not when it came to the exercise of the franchise. Her words were similar to those of Cary, who had indicted America for imposing taxation without representation upon the majority of women of the nation. Noting the suffrage victories for women in various Western states, Logan argued that as a result of woman suffrage in those states, civic affairs had improved.[30]

Logan rejected the argument of anti-suffragists who alleged that women did not need the ballot because they were not interested in politics. She opposed the view that woman suffrage would bring women into politics and, as a result, cause them to neglect the home. Logan went further and also dismissed the theory that exercising the franchise was a complicated process that women could not understand. She concluded, as did Terrell, that the right of suffrage was withheld from women for political reasons by those she called "ignorant and vicious men." Finally, like Cary, Truth, Harper and other Black women of the nineteenth century, Logan argued that if White women needed the vote in order to acquire advantages as well as protection of their rights, then Black women needed the ballot even more, because they carried the double burden of racism and sexism.[31] Numerous African American women followed in this tradition, formulating arguments that emphasized why Black women, specifically, needed the vote.

When given the opportunity, African American women exercised the right to vote. For instance, Black women voted in Colorado at the turn of the century. Their political activities were noted by Helen Woodbury, who in 1909 published a study of the equal suffrage movement in Colorado. She commented that Black women were interested in politics because in 1901 there was a "colored woman's" Republican club in Denver. In addition, she found that 1,373 Blacks voted in Denver during the 1906 election, of whom 45.2 percent were women. From Woodbury's overall statistics, she concluded that a larger percentage of Black women than White women voted in that Denver election.[32] Needless to say, reports like Woodbury's sent up red flags in front of those who feared the potential power of Black women voters, especially the power of Black club women.

Woodbury's findings are not surprising because, during the last quarter of the nineteenth century, the woman's club movement had expanded dramatically,

usually with clubs developing membership and reform strategies along racially separate lines. Perhaps one reason for this separate development lay in the unique needs of Black women during the period. Native-born White women had no need to defend their dignity against widespread assumptions that they were wanton, immoral, and socially inferior. White women did not have the severe problems of racial discrimination that compounded Black women's plight in employment and education. Moreover, race consciousness was evident among African Americans in general as growing numbers of race-specific civil rights organizations, business groups, and self-help societies emerged at the century's end.[33]

Racism in the Suffrage Movement

Another reason for the development of racially separate women's groups was the exclusion of Black women from most White female clubs. Despite the differences between the two groups, there were some common causes and attempts at unity on local levels. Journalist Paula Giddings refers to the women who made these attempts as "radical interracialists"—Black women who were determined to enter the mainstream.[34] Nevertheless, doing so was not easy, for this was the era of "Jim Crow" nationwide. African American women were involved in temperance work, suffrage groups, and club work. The experiences of many of their leaders indicated the pervasiveness of White female prejudice and discrimination against Black females in women's groups, even those who were part of the woman suffrage coalition.[35]

Throughout the 1890s, Josephine St. Pierre Ruffin had challenged White women to unite with Blacks for the benefit of humanity, but her words went virtually unheeded outside of Massachusetts. She was discriminated against personally when attending the General Federation of Women's Clubs, which met in Wisconsin in 1900. Disillusioned by the incident, the Black woman's club she represented, The Woman's Era Club, made an official statement which included the view "that colored women should confine themselves to their clubs and the large field of work open to them there."[36]

At the same convention of the General Federation of Women's Clubs, Mary Church Terrell, representing the NACW, was refused permission to bring the group greetings on behalf of her association because the Southern clubs objected, threatening resignation. Despite this rebuff, Terrell was invited to speak before other White groups during the early years of the twentieth century. At the Minneapolis Convention of Women in 1900 she addressed the group not only about the needs of Black women, but also about the prejudice and lack of sympathy on the part of White women. Terrell indicted them for not extending a helping hand to African Americans whose aims were similar to their own. The same year, she made a similar speech at the NAWSA meeting in the District of Columbia.[37]

Ida B. Wells-Barnett reported how Fannie Barrier Williams, an African American club woman in Chicago, attempted to join the Chicago Woman's

Club in 1894. The all-White group split over the controversy created by those who wanted a Black member and those who did not. After fourteen months of controversy, Williams was admitted. At the turn of the century, Wells-Barnett noted that the issue was still significant in Illinois when the State Federation of Women's Clubs membership made it impossible for African American clubs to become members. Nonetheless, Black women's clubs were so numerous that by the second decade of the twentieth century a large federation of "colored" women's clubs was active in Black communities throughout Illinois. By 1914, Wells-Barnett helped to organize the Alpha Suffrage Club of African American women, who were influential later in electing a Black man to Congress, Oscar DePriest.[38]

The experiences of Ruffin, Terrell, Williams, and Wells-Barnett were not unique. During the same period, the woman suffrage campaign gained momentum, but the national leadership emulated the racial attitudes of White women's clubs around the nation. As historian Aileen Kraditor has observed, White supremacy was an influential factor in the strategy of the suffragists as the need developed for Southern support for a woman suffrage amendment. As early as the 1890s, Susan B. Anthony realized the potential to the woman suffrage cause in wooing Southern White women. She chose expedience over loyalty and justice when she asked veteran feminist Frederick Douglass not to attend the 1895 NAWSA Convention scheduled in Atlanta. Anthony explained to Wells-Barnett that Douglass's presence on the stage with the honored guests, his usual place at these conventions, would have offended the Southern hosts. Wells-Barnett, however, admonished Anthony for giving in to racial prejudice.[39]

By the 1903 NAWSA Convention in New Orleans, the board of officers prepared a statement endorsing the organization's position to allow states the right to develop their own woman suffrage positions, which was tantamount to an endorsement of White supremacy in most states, particularly in the South. The statement was signed by Susan B. Anthony, Carrie C. Catt, Anna Howard Shaw, Kate N. Gordon, Alice Stone Blackwell, Harriet Taylor Upton, Laura Clay, and Mary Coggeshall. During the convention week, Susan B. Anthony visited the Black Phillis Wheatley Club in New Orleans. In presenting flowers to Anthony on the occasion, Sylvanie Williams, president of the club, indicated that Black women were painfully aware of their "down trotten" [sic] position among White suffragists.[40]

Fear of offending Southern White suffragists in Atlanta and in New Orleans is one thing, but how can the prejudice against African American club women in Wisconsin, and in Chicago be explained? There was a nationwide, not just a Southern prejudice against African American women. It appears that White women outside of the South used Southern White women's overt prejudice as an excuse for the NAWSA's discriminatory policies, while hiding their own similar feelings about Black women, although they shared many of the Black women's goals for reform and women's political equity. African American woman suffragists

were quite aware of their position, and they were determined to move beyond the attempts to keep them disfranchised.

Black suffragists knew that although those national suffrage leaders who courted Black support endorsed equal suffrage among the races while in African American circles, their public actions and statements to the mainstream society often contradicted their professed egalitarianism. For example, Alice Paul, organizer of the National Woman's Party (NWP) and the suffrage parade in front of the White House in 1913, had expressed her sympathy for Black woman's enfranchisement. Yet before the parade the leaders asked Wells-Barnett, who was representing the Alpha Suffrage Club, not to march with the White Chicago delegates. Again the rationale was fear of offending White Southern women. Terrell marched in the parade with African American women from Howard University, assembled in the section reserved for Black women—at the end of the line. By 1919, she confided her feelings about Paul to Walter White of the National Association for the Advancement of Colored People (NAACP). Both questioned Paul's loyalty to Black women, concluding that if she and other White suffragist leaders could get the amendment through without enfranchising African American women they would.[41]

Why this suspicion among African American leaders on the eve of the passage of the Nineteenth Amendment? By this time, nearly all the major White suffrage leaders had compromised their support of Black woman suffrage. For example, despite endorsing Black suffrage, Anna Howard Shaw had been accused of refusing to allow an African American delegate at the Louisville NAWSA convention of 1911 to propose an anti-discrimination resolution. As president of the NAWSA from 1910 to 1915, Shaw avoided offending White, Southern suffragists, and supported the states' rights position of the association.[42]

The strength of the states' rights strategy among Southern, White suffragists can be observed as early as the 1890s, when, they sought suffrage for White women through new state constitutions, which had been drafted to disenfranchise Black men. Historian Marjorie Spruill confirms that White suffragists believed votes for White women could be used as a way of countering the "Negro vote" in the South. The dynamics of this Southern woman suffrage strategy can be seen in looking at the similar positions of two leaders of the Southern movement. Laura Clay came from Kentucky, a state with a small Black population—which could hardly have affected the balance of political power in the state—whereas Kate Gordon came from Louisiana, a state where the Black population was very large, and had held considerable political influence in the state during the Reconstruction Era. By 1906, however, Clay had come to agree with Gordon that Southern suffragists should campaign for state suffrage amendments containing "Whites-only" clauses.[43]

African American leaders directed their displeasure upon Southern suffragists like Clay. For example, NAACP officials noted that at the Jubilee Convention of the NAWSA in 1919, Clay proposed "that certain sections [of the proposed amendment] be amended with particular reference to those parts that would

permit the enfranchisement of Negro women in the South."[44] It appears that as the success of a non-restrictive woman suffrage amendment became apparent, some Southern leaders feared the potential threat to the status quo that an active and fast-growing Black woman suffrage movement would have in states such as Tennessee and Kentucky.

By 1919 a united front began to develop among African American suffragists nationwide, as Black women feared the growing alliance between national woman suffrage leaders and those who hoped to eliminate Blacks from the so-called Anthony Amendment being debated in Congress. As the amendment was debated in the Senate, several Southern senators attempted to alter it in ways that would either restrict the vote to White women, or restrict implementation to the states. For example, in 1918 Mississippi Senator John Sharp Williams proposed to amend the resolution to make it read, "The right of White citizens to vote shall not be denied."[45] However, the vote was laid on the table. Again in 1919, Mississippi Senator Pat Harrison attempted unsuccessfully to have the word "White" placed in the original amendment, while Louisiana Senator Edward J. Gay called for an amendment providing the states instead of the Congress the power to enforce it.[46]

Throughout the Congressional debates, the NAACP, representing Black and White supporters of enfranchising African American women, lobbied for the defeat of such efforts. In addition, the NACW took action by encouraging African American women in states where Black men still retained the franchise to pressure the NAWSA and the NWP to oppose any changes to the Anthony Amendment. In the meantime, NACW leaders knew that White woman suffragists, despite their reluctance to enfranchise Black women, needed the votes of Black men outside of the South. These African American women developed a strategy designed to expose the hypocrisy of the White suffrage leadership. In 1918, the leaders of the Northeastern Federation of Women's Clubs, which represented six thousand Black women from nine states, applied for NAWSA membership.[47] Carrie Chapman Catt, who was president of the NAWSA at the time, asked Ida Husted Harper, editor of the *History of Woman Suffrage* and a long-time friend of the late Susan B. Anthony, to discourage the Northeastern Federation from applying for membership. Both women felt NAWSA membership for the Black group would offend the White Southern organizations and hamper passage of the Anthony Amendment. Both Catt and Harper had argued in favor of Black woman suffrage in the past and apparently thought the Federation would understand their position and not be offended by their request.[48]

However, African American club women understood what White club women did not. Blacks were seeking more than NAWSA membership; they were seeking NAWSA support for the enfranchisement of African American women. Elizabeth C. Carter, president of the Federation, admonished Harper for her arrogance and patronizing testimony, which presumed that African American women were not politically sophisticated enough to use NAWSA membership as a strategy to gain

the vote.[49] Fortunately amendments seeking to enfranchise White women only failed with the close of the Sixty-Fifth Congress and the Anthony Amendment was passed by Congress in June 1919. However, African Americans understood how vulnerable their women were as the amendment made the rounds in the states toward ratification.

By the summer of 1920, only one state was needed for ratification and President Wilson successfully appealed to the governor of Tennessee for a special legislative session to consider the amendment. Tennessee appeared to be the only hope, but even in this state the legislature could not resolve the stalemate. Once again, the White suffrage leaders realized that African Americans may be needed to break the deadlock. Alice Paul turned to the NAACP for help. At this point, NAACP leaders lent their support by urging Black voting men in Tennessee to lobby their state legislators to support the amendment, but not before taking the opportunity to remind Paul how White women had either worked against Black political leaders who were males, or ignored the plight of Black suffragists who were females. Nonetheless, these women had no compunction about asking Black people for their help.[50]

Fortunately for woman suffragists, the Tennessee deadlock ended positively for the Nineteenth Amendment, which was ratified in August 1920. Despite the White suffragists' record of discrimination, most African American leaders, both men and women, welcomed woman suffrage. Naively, they hoped that Black women could help uplift the standards of their race through exercising the franchise. Like many White woman suffragists, Blacks believed the vote to be the panacea to their social problems.

The Disfranchising of Black Women in the South

African American hopes for political equity were quickly dashed as the majority of Black women who still lived in the South were quickly disfranchised. In addition, the Black Republican women and men outside the South began to lose their political influence within a decade after the passage of the Nineteenth Amendment.

Disfranchisement had been predicted by several White Southern suffragists. Kentucky's Madeline McDowell Breckinridge, for one, considered herself a liberal on racial issues, but did not believe African American women should be voters until they could be properly educated. Breckinridge advocated educational requirements at the state level that would eliminate most potential Black voters. Nonetheless, she opposed the blatantly racist statements made by Southern suffragists like Louisiana's Kate Gordon and Mississippi's Belle Kearney. Of the two, Gordon opposed a federal amendment, saying it invited Northern intervention in the affairs of the states that would endanger White supremacy. However, by the eve of the Nineteenth Amendment's ratification, Kearney attempted to change Gordon's mind about opposing the amendment, arguing that the South need not fear Northern intervention on behalf of disfranchised Black women. Kearney had

been convinced that Northerners were sympathetic with the South's "negro problem."[51] Indeed, she was correct.

African Americans, nonetheless, rallied nationwide to the woman suffrage victory. The enthusiastic responses of Black women may have seemed astonishing when one realizes that woman suffrage was a predominantly middle-class movement among native-born White women and that the Black middle class remained very small during the early twentieth century. Furthermore, the heyday of the woman suffrage movement embraced an era that historian Rayford Logan called "the nadir" in African American history, characterized by racial segregation, defamation of the character of Black women, and lynching of Black Americans, both men and women. It is a wonder that African American women dared to dream a White woman's dream—the right to enfranchisement.[52]

Apprehensions from discontented Black leaders about the inclusion of Black women as voters, especially in the South, had been evident throughout the second decade of the twentieth century. African American fears went beyond misgivings about White women in states like New York and Texas, where women gained the franchise before the ratification of the Nineteenth Amendment. In 1917, while the New York State woman suffrage referendum was pending in the legislature, Black suffragists in the state had complained of discrimination against their organizations by White suffragists during the state-wide convention at Saratoga. White suffrage leaders assured Black women that they were welcome in the movement. Although the majority of the African American delegates were conciliated, a vocal minority remained disillusioned. In 1918 the Black editors of the *Houston Observer* responded to Black disillusionment when they called upon the men and women of their race to register to vote in spite of the poll tax, which was designed especially to exclude Texas's African American voters.[53] Black women, nevertheless, were discriminated against. Six of them were refused the right to vote at Fort Worth on the grounds that the primaries were open to White Democrats only. Efforts to disfranchise Black women in Houston failed, however, when the women took legal action against the registrar who attempted to apply the Texas woman suffrage law to White women only. A similar attempt to disqualify African American women in Waxahachie, Texas failed also.[54]

After the ratification of the federal amendment, Black women registered in large numbers throughout the South, especially in Georgia and Louisiana, despite major obstacles placed against them by the White supremacists. In defense, African American women often turned to the NAACP for assistance. Field Secretary William Pickens was sent to investigate the numerous charges and recorded several incidents that he either witnessed personally or about which he received reports. In Columbia, South Carolina, for example, a requirement that a voter pay taxes on property valued at three hundred dollars or more was made mandatory for Black women. If they passed that test, the women were required to read from and to interpret the state or the federal constitutions. No such tests were required of White women.

Although the *Columbia State,* a local newspaper, reported disinterest in registering among African American women, Pickens testified to the contrary. By the end of the registration period, twenty Columbia Black women had signed an affidavit against the registrars who had disqualified them. In the surrounding Richland County, African American women were disqualified when they attempted to register to vote. As a result, several of them made plans to appeal the ruling.[55]

Many cases like these were handled by the NAACP, and after the registration periods ended in the South, its board of directors presented the evidence to Congress. The NAACP officials and others testified at a 1920 congressional hearing in support of the proposed Tinkham Bill that would have reduced representation in Congress from states where there was restriction of woman suffrage and thus protected African American women from disfranchisement. Belle Kearney's prediction was right, however. The North did not intervene in the Southern "negro problem." White supremacy prevailed, as Southern congressmen successfully claimed that Blacks were not disfranchised, just disinterested in voting. Despite the massive evidence produced by the NAACP, the Tinkham Bill failed to pass.[56]

White Southern apprehensions of a viable Black female electorate were not illusionary. "Colored women voter's leagues" were growing throughout the South, where the task of the leagues was to give Black women seeking to qualify to vote instructions for countering White opposition. Leagues could be found in Alabama, Georgia, Tennessee, and Texas. These groups were feared also by White supremacists because the women sought to qualify Black men as voters as well.[57]

African American women organize to vote in Georgia, 1920
SCHOMBURG CENTER, NEW YORK PUBLIC LIBRARY

During the November 1920 elections, Southern Whites also expected Black women to vote in larger numbers than White women. If this happened, they feared, the ballot would soon be returned to African American men. Black suffrage, it was believed, would also result in the return of the two-party system in the South, because African Americans would consistently vote Republican. These apprehensions were realized in Florida after the election. Black women in Jacksonville had registered and voted in greater numbers than White women. In reaction, the Woman Suffrage League of Jacksonville was reorganized into the Duval County League of Democratic Women Voters. The members were dedicated to maintain White supremacy and pledged to register White women voters.[58]

The inability of Congress and the NAACP to protect the rights of Black women voters led the women to seek help from national woman suffrage leaders. Not surprisingly, these attempts failed also. In 1919, anticipating victory, the NAWSA had changed its name to the League of Women Voters (LWV), a non-partisan organization designed to maintain women's political participation on national and local levels. At the 1921 national LWV convention held at Cleveland, African American women brought their complaints about disfranchisement before the LWV. The White Southern delegates at the convention threatened to walk out if the "negro problem" was debated. In typical League fashion, a compromise resulted, wherein African American women were allowed to speak before the body, but no action was taken by the organization.[59]

When the African American women suffragists sought assistance from the National Woman's Party, they were rebuffed totally. The NWP leadership position was that since Black women were discriminated against in the same ways as Black men, their problems were not woman's rights issues, but race issues. Therefore, the NWP felt no obligation to defend the right of African American women as voters.[60]

Abandonment by White women suffragists in 1920 really came as no surprise to most Black women leaders. The preceding decade of woman suffrage politics had reminded them of the assertions of Black woman suffrage supporters of the past. Frederick Douglass had declared in 1868 that Black women were victimized mainly because they were Blacks, not because they were women. Frances Ellen Watkins Harper answered in 1869 that for White women the priority in the struggle for human rights was sex, not race. By 1920 the situation had changed very little, and many African American suffragists had been thoroughly disillusioned by the racism of the White feminists they had encountered.[61]

A significant number of Black women and Black women's organizations had not only supported woman suffrage on the eve of the passage of the Nineteenth Amendment, but attempted to exercise their rights to vote in the elections immediately following the amendment's ratification in 1920. Unfortunately for them, African American women confronted racial discrimination in their efforts to support the amendment and to win the vote. Consequently, discontented Black feminists anticipated the disillusionment that their White counterparts

encountered within a decade following amendment ratification, as women's votes did not become the panacea to social problems of the larger society.

Notes

1. Rosalyn Terborg-Penn, "Nineteenth Century Black Women and Woman Suffrage," *The Potomac Review* 7 (Spring/ Summer 1977): 13-24, 13.

2. Elizabeth Cady Stanton, Susan B. Anthony, and Matilda J. Gage, eds., *History of Woman Suffrage*, 6 vols., (New York, 1969), Vol. 1: 115, 546, 567, hereafter *HWS*.

3. Ibid., 386, 668; *HWS* 3: 72.

4. *HWS* 2: 168, 222.

5. Ibid., 191, 221, 378-79; *HWS* 3: 457.

6. *HWS* 2: 400, 406.

7. Speech to the Judiciary Committee, Mary Ann Shadd Cary Papers, Folder No. 2, Moorland-Spingarn Research Center, Howard University, Washington, D.C.; *HWS* 2: 215, 391-92; *HWS* 3: 346-47, 358.

8. See the proceedings for the NWSA and the AWSA for 1869 to 1876 in *HWS* 2.

9. *HWS* 3: 268-69.

10. *The Crisis*, 10 (August 1915), 188; Booker T. Washington, ed., *A New Negro for a New Century* (Chicago, 1900), 392.

11. *HWS* 3: 821, 827-28; Carole Ione, *Pride of Family: Four Generations of American Women of Color* (New York, 1991), 74-75; Joel Williamson, *After Slavery: The Negro in South Carolina During Reconstruction, 1861-1877* (New York, 1975), 338; Nearly three decades later, in *HWS* 4 (1900), Virginia D. Young, president of the South Carolina suffragists, dated the beginning of the suffrage movement in her state as 1890, the year her association was founded, completely ignoring the activities of the interracial woman's rights association founded twenty years before. Terborg-Penn, "Nineteenth Century Black Women and Woman Suffrage," 16.

12. *HWS* 3: 828.

13. Terborg-Penn, "Nineteenth Century Black Women and Woman Suffrage," 17.

14. Ellen Carol DuBois, *Feminism and Suffrage: The Emergence of an Independent Women's Movement in America, 1848-1869* (Ithaca, 1978), 201-02.

15. Speech of A.G. Riddle to the NWSA Anniversary Meeting, January 11, 1871, Washington, D.C., Cary Papers, Folder No. 7A.

16. Speech to the Judiciary Committee, Cary Papers, Folder No. 2.

17. *HWS* 3: 31, 72, 955.

18. *HWS* 3: 828, 833-834; Terborg-Penn, "Nineteenth Century Black Women and Woman Suffrage," 18.

19. Statement of Purpose, Colored Women's Progressive Franchise Association, Cary Papers, Folder No. 5.

20. Gertrude Mossell, "Woman Suffrage," *The New York Freeman*, December 26, 1885.

21. *HWS* 4, (reprint, New York, 1969), 898, 1104; F.E.W. Harper, "A Factor in Human Progress," *AME Church Review* 2 (1885), 14; *HWS*, 3: 273.

22. T. Thomas Fortune, "The New Afro-American Woman," *The New York Sun*, August 7, 1895; *The Woman's Era* (Boston), July 1896; Terborg-Penn, "Nineteenth Century Black Women and Woman Suffrage," 19.

23. Terborg-Penn, "Nineteenth Century Black Women and Woman Suffrage," 19.

24. M.A. McCurdy, "Duty of the State to the Negro," *Afro-American Encyclopedia*, ed. James T. Haley (Nashville, 1895), 141-45.

25. Frances E. Harper, *Sketches of Southern Life* (Philadelphia, 1896), 16.

26. Ida H. Harper, *History of Woman Suffrage*, vols. 5 and 6, (New York, 1900-1920), 105-06.

27. *HWS* 4: 358-59.

28. Rosalyn Terborg-Penn, "Discrimination Against Afro-American Women in the Woman's Movement, 1830-1920," 17-27, in *The Afro-American Woman: Struggles and Images*, Sharon Harley and Rosalyn Terborg-Penn, eds. (Port Washington, N.Y., 1978), 24-27.

29. Adella Logan, "Woman Suffrage," *The Colored American Magazine*, 9 (September 1905), 487.

30. Ibid., 488.

31. Ibid., 489.

32. Helen Laura Sumner Woodbury, *Equal Suffrage: The Results of an Investigation in Colorado Made for the Collegiate Equal Suffrage League of New York State* (New York, 1909), 70, 114-17.

33. Terborg-Penn, "Discrimination Against Afro-American Women," 21.

34. Paula Giddings, *When and Where I Enter: The Impact of Black Women on Race and Sex in America* (New York, 1984), 154.

35. Terborg-Penn, "Discrimination Against Afro-American Women," 21.

36. J.W. Gibson and W.H. Crogman, *Progress of a Race, Or the Remarkable Advancement of the Colored American* (Naperville, Ill., 1902, 1912), 216-20.

37. *Minneapolis Journal*, November 1900, Mary Church Terrell Papers, Manuscript Division, Library of Congress, Washington, D.C.; *HWS* 4: 358-59.

38. Ida B. Wells-Barnett, *Crusade for Justice: The Autobiography of Ida B. Wells-Barnett*, Alfreda Duster, ed. (Chicago, 1970), 345-47.

39. Aileen Kraditor, *The Ideas of the Woman Suffrage Movement, 1890-1920* (Garden City, N.Y., 1971), 213-14: Wells-Barnett, *Crusade for Justice*, 229-30.

40. *HWS* 5: 55, 59, 60 n. 1.

41. Walter White to Mary Church Terrell, March 14, 1919, Terrell Papers.

42. Terborg-Penn, "Discrimination Against Afro-American Women," 25.

43. Kraditor, 144-154; Marjorie Spruill (Wheeler), *New Women of the New South: The Leaders of the Woman Suffrage Movement in the Southern States* (New York, 1993), 101-102, 104, 110, 113-125.

44. *The Crisis* 17 (June 1919), 103.

45. *HWS* 5: 640.

46. *HWS* 5: 645-46.

47. Terborg-Penn, "Discrimination Against Afro-American Women," 25-26; *New York World*, March 1, 1919, Suffrage File, NAACP Papers, Manuscript Division, Library of Congress, Washington, D.C.

48. Terborg-Penn, "Discrimination Against Afro-American Women," 26.

49. Elizabeth C. Carter to Ida Husted Harper, April 10, 1919, Suffrage File, NAACP Papers.

50. *HWS* 6: 617; Giddings, 164.

51. Spruill (Wheeler), *New Women of the New South*, 100-105, 143.

52. See Rayford W. Logan, *The Negro in the United States* (Princeton, 1957).

53. Rosalyn Terborg-Penn, "Afro-Americans in the Struggle for Woman Suffrage," Ph.D. diss., Howard University, 1977, 295-96.

54. Ibid, 301-02.

55. William Pickens, "The Woman Voter Hits the Color Line," *Nation* 3 (October 6, 1920): 372-73.

56. *Eleventh Annual Report of the NAACP for the Year 1920* (New York, 1921), 15, 25-30; Terborg-Penn, "Discontented Black Feminists," 267.

57. *The Crisis* 19 (November 1920), 23-25; *Negro Year Book*, 1921, 40.

58. Kenneth R. Johnson, "White Racial Attitudes as a Factor in the Arguments Against the Nineteenth Amendment," *Phylon* 31 (Spring 1970): 31-32, 35-37.

59. Giddings, 166.

60. Rosalyn Terborg-Penn, "Discontented Black Feminists: Prelude and Postscript to the Passage of the Nineteenth Amendment," 261-78, in *Decades of Discontent: The Women's Movement, 1920-1940*, edited by Lois Scharf and Joan M. Jenson (Westport, Conn., 1983), 267.

61. Ibid., 261, 267.

THE INTERNATIONAL HISTORY OF THE U.S. SUFFRAGE MOVEMENT

Katherine M. Marino

Editor's Introduction: The woman suffrage movement in the United States did not occur in isolation. As historian Katherine M. Marino explains in this essay, it was part of a global struggle for women's rights.

While suffragists in the United States were engaged in their long battle, women were fighting for enfranchisement in many other countries. The first victory came in New Zealand in 1893, followed within a decade by Australia, Finland, and Norway. During World War I, the vote was extended to women in Denmark, Iceland, and Canada, and by the end of 1918, in many more countries on both sides of the conflict, in part as recognition of their wartime contributions. Suffragists in the United States finally persuaded President Woodrow Wilson to support a federal suffrage amendment in part by embarrassing him before the world, reminding him that he had declared the war a crusade to save democracy while half of American adults remained voteless.

Katherine Marino helps readers discover the connections between suffrage struggles worldwide. Suffragists from the United States both inspired, and were inspired, by their counterparts abroad with whom they collaborated, sometimes through formal international organizations and publications. Leading suffragists in the United States were, in many cases, prominent leaders in international organizations as well. Marino also points out that women from abroad—including immigrants and refugees—played important roles in promoting women's rights in the United States. African American women traveling abroad were inspired by the reception they received. Some used the world stage to expose racism in their home country, as well as calling out Anglo-American condescension and dominance in the international suffrage movement.

In its last two decades, the suffrage movement in the United States was influenced by the development of a more modern, militant spirit abroad. Socialism inspired many European women workers who, in turn, inspired many U.S. suffragists.

Marino also points out that after ratification of the Nineteenth Amendment, women from the United States continued to be involved in a global drive for women's rights. African American women who were denied their right to vote now joined other women of color in a new wave of international activism against racism and colonialism, and for women's political autonomy. Veterans of the U.S.

woman suffrage movement kept up the fight for women's rights, working with activists in Europe and Latin America. However, women's rights advocates from Latin America resisted the efforts of U.S. women to dominate the movement and took the lead in getting women's rights included as goals of the United Nations as well as winning the vote for women in their own countries.

After World War II, women gained the right to vote in newly decolonized nations such as India, Malaysia, and Iran. Latin American women and women from other areas of the Global South continued to be leaders in an increasingly successful international women's movement in which women's rights activists from the United States, notably First Lady Eleanor Roosevelt, also played important roles.

★　★　★　★　★

THE HISTORY OF THE WOMAN SUFFRAGE MOVEMENT in the United States is usually told as a national one. It begins with the 1848 Seneca Falls convention; follows numerous state campaigns, court battles, and petitions to Congress; and culminates in the marches and protests that led to the Nineteenth Amendment. This narrative, however, overlooks how profoundly international the struggle was from the start. Suffragists from the United States and other parts of the world collaborated across national borders. They wrote to each other, shared strategies and encouragement, and spearheaded international organizations, conferences, and publications that in turn spread information and ideas. Many suffragists were *internationalist*, understanding the right to vote as a global goal.

Enlightenment concepts, socialism, and the abolitionist movement helped U.S. suffragists universalize women's rights long before Seneca Falls. They drew their inspiration not only from the American Revolution, but from the French and Haitian Revolutions, and later from the Mexican and Russian Revolutions. Many suffragists were immigrants who brought ideas from their homelands. Others capitalized on the Spanish-American War and the First World War to underscore contradictions between the United States' growing global power and its denial of woman suffrage. A number of women of color used the international stage to challenge U.S. claims to democracy, not only in terms of women's rights but also in terms of racism in the United States and in the suffrage movement itself. The complex international connections and strategies that suffragists cultivated reveal tensions in feminist organizing that reverberated in later movements and are instructive today.

These multiple, and sometimes conflicting, international strands worked in synergy, bolstering the suffrage cause and expanding the women's rights agenda. The resources that women shared with each other across national borders allowed suffrage movements to overcome political marginalization and hostility in their own countries.[1] A radical challenge to power, the U.S. movement for women's voting rights required transnational support to thrive.

Abolitionism and the Transnational Origins of Women's Rights

Although the American Revolution and U.S. circulation of Mary Wollstonecraft's *Vindication of the Rights of Woman* (1792) activated discussion of women's rights, it was the transatlantic crucible of abolitionism that truly galvanized the U.S. women's rights movement. The antislavery movement, which Frederick Douglass called "peculiarly woman's cause," provided broad ideals of "liberty" as well as key political strategies that suffragists would use for the next fifty years—the mass petition, public speaking, and the boycott.[2] Transatlantic networks of organizations, conferences, and publications drove abolitionism. Women in the United States looked to their British sisters, who in 1826 made the first formal demand for an immediate, rather than gradual, end to slavery.

Boston reformer and African American abolitionist Maria Stewart, one of the first U.S. women to publicly call for women's rights before a mixed-race and mixed-sex audience, embraced a diasporic vision of freedom when she asked in 1832, "How long shall the fair daughters of Africa be compelled to bury their minds and talents beneath a load of iron pots and kettles?"[3] Her vision of rights for African American women, specifically, in the face of economic marginalization, segregation, and slavery, drew upon universal rights that she found expressed not only in the U.S. Constitution and Declaration of Independence but in the French Declaration of the Rights of Man and the Haitian Revolution, the largest slave uprising, from 1791 to 1804.[4]

The hostility that Stewart and other female abolitionists faced for overstepping boundaries of female propriety by speaking out in public threw into sharp relief that, as U.S. abolitionist Angelina Grimké put it, "the manumission of the slave and the elevation of the woman" should be indivisible goals.[5] At the 1837 First Anti-Slavery Convention of American Women, an interracial group of two hundred women called for women's rights. When Quaker minister and abolitionist Lucretia Mott and other female delegates were excluded from the 1840 World Anti-Slavery Convention in London, Mott and Elizabeth Cady Stanton hatched the idea for a separate women's rights convention.

The resulting 1848 Seneca Falls Convention and its demands for women's rights were only possible because of abolitionists' groundwork and the broad meanings of emancipation flourishing in the United States and in Europe, where revolutions had broken out that year. Stanton's idea to include the right to vote in the convention's Declaration of Sentiments was directly inspired by calls for universal suffrage made by British Chartists, the first mass working-class movement in England.[6] Lucretia Mott explicitly connected the Declaration to the 1848 abolition of slavery in the French West Indies, opposition to the U.S. war with Mexico, and and defense of Native American rights. Mott and Stanton also found models in the matrilineal communities of the Seneca people, in which women held political power.[7] The right to vote proved to be the convention's most controversial demand, and abolitionist Frederick Douglass was one of its most avid proponents.

The right to vote became key to the many U.S. women's rights conventions that Seneca Falls set into motion, inspiring and drawing on the support of women in Europe and elsewhere, including immigrant women in the United States. In 1851, from Paris jail cells, revolutionary women's rights activists cheered U.S. women's activism. In March 1852, German immigrant and socialist Mathilde Anneke started the first women's rights journal in the United States published by a woman, the *Deutsche Frauen-Zeitung*. After the Prussian victory over Germany she had fled to the United States, where she became a friend of Stanton and Susan B. Anthony.[8] Polish-born immigrant and abolitionist Ernestine Rose expressed her global vision for suffrage in 1851: "We are not contending for the rights of women in New England, or of old England, but of the world."[9]

Sarah Parker Remond
THE PEABODY ESSEX MUSEUM

Such ideas resonated with Sarah Parker Remond, whose life reflects the overlapping transnational abolitionist and woman suffrage movements. In 1832 she helped found the first female antislavery group in Salem, Massachusetts. In 1859, while on an antislavery speaking tour in England, Remond reported, "I have been received here as a sister by White women for the first time in my life…. I have received a sympathy I never was offered before."[10] For Remond, transnational connections became a concrete way to escape racism in the United States. She settled permanently in Italy, where she became a physician. In 1866, Remond affixed her name to John Stuart Mill's petition to the British Parliament for woman suffrage.[11]

Internationalism was also key to African American abolitionist and suffragist Mary Ann Shadd Cary, who moved to Canada after the 1850 Fugitive Slave Act for fear it would endanger free Blacks like herself and enslaved people. She knit connections between her work for Black civil rights in Ontario, abolitionism, and the U.S. woman suffrage movement, founding one of the first suffrage organizations for Black women in the United States.[12]

Transnational Organizing and "Global Sisterhood"

Transnational connections initiated by the nineteenth-century abolitionist movement only grew in the following decades. After construction of the first transatlantic telegraph lines in the 1860s, communications, travel, and transnational print culture helped produce the first international organizations for women's

rights that drew significantly on U.S. women. They included the World's Woman's Christian Temperance Union (WCTU), founded in 1884 by U.S. temperance leader Frances Willard; the International Council of Women (ICW), founded in 1888 by Stanton and Anthony; the International Woman Suffrage Alliance (IWSA), later renamed the International Alliance of Women, founded in 1904 and presided over by Carrie Chapman Catt (then president of the National American Woman Suffrage Association); and the Women's International League for Peace and Freedom (WILPF), founded in part by U.S. social settlement worker Jane Addams in 1915.[13]

Alongside each organization's particular focus—international arbitration, universal disarmament, temperance, married women's civil rights, anti-trafficking of women, equal pay for equal work, among others—a global goal of women's political equality drove them.[14] These organizations connected women across the lines of nation, culture, and language, and had overlapping memberships.[15] They hosted international conferences and they helped spearhead publications such as the IAW's *Jus Sufffragii* and the ICW's *Bulletin*, which shared information about suffrage organizing in Asia, Latin America, Europe, and other parts of the world.

Of the four, the WCTU inspired the most dramatic grassroots suffrage activism, becoming the largest women's organization in the world, with over forty national affiliates. Like members of the WCTU in the United States, WCTU members in many nations argued that women could use their vote to promote temperance and end men's alcohol-infused violence. The organization transformed the goal of woman suffrage into a clear and compelling one for large numbers of women.[16] Spearheading the first organized suffrage efforts in the White British colonies of South Africa, New Zealand, and South Australia, the WCTU was responsible for the world's first national suffrage victory in New Zealand in 1893, and in Australia in 1902.[17]

Although these groups spoke of "global sisterhood," their memberships were predominantly Anglo American and European, and their publications usually only published in French, English, and German, in spite of demands to expand beyond these languages from women in Spanish-speaking countries and other parts of the world.[18] These international groups generally marginalized or excluded women of color, and in the U.S. WCTU's case the organization segregated them.

These groups often reflected what historians have called "imperial feminism"—a belief that White, Western women will "uplift" women in "uncivilized" parts of the world.[19] This logic went hand in hand with some suffrage efforts. WCTU missionaries in Hawaii who sought to secure woman suffrage there in the 1890s, allied with White U.S. business and military interests, establishing imperial control over the island.[20] Suffragists also demanded the vote in the Philippines and Puerto Rico, U.S. imperial acquisitions from the 1898 Spanish-American War, both as part of a civilizing mission and to force discussion of a federal suffrage amendment in the United States.[21] Meanwhile, as they celebrated early suffrage victories within the western United States in the same period, most White suffragists overlooked

the fact that these states denied the right to vote accorded native-born women to many Asian American, Mexican American, and Native American women.[22]

African American suffragists powerfully critiqued Anglo American dominance on the international stage and within the U.S. suffrage movement, even as they made important contributions to it. They also continued to connect global ideals of "freedom" with local women's rights issues, expanding the international agenda to address such goals as universal suffrage for men and women, anti-lynching laws, and education. Former abolitionist Frances Ellen Watkins Harper, a pivotal African American civil rights and women's rights leader, spoke at the 1888 founding of the ICW in Washington, D.C. and oversaw the formation of many "colored WCTU" groups that contributed to school suffrage victories in several states in the 1890s.[23] On a speaking tour in England, the anti-lynching activist Ida B. Wells-Barnett brought global attention to WCTU president Frances Willard's failure to defend African American men lynched on false rape accusations.[24] Wells-Barnett went on to found the most vital African American woman suffrage group in the country, the Alpha Suffrage Club in Chicago. At the 1913 suffrage march in Washington, D.C., Wells-Barnett refused to be relegated to the back of the procession reserved for African American women, and instead, marched with the Illinois delegation. In 1904, Mary Church Terrell, the first president of the National Association of Colored Women (NACW), spoke in fluent German at the International Council of Women (ICW) meeting in Berlin, pointing out that a global women's rights agenda must include attention to Black women's unequal access to many rights, including education and employment. Newspapers in Germany, France, Norway, and Austria lauded her speech.[25]

International Influences on the Modern Suffrage Movement

At the end of the nineteenth century, a more modern and militant suffrage internationalism emerged. A growing embrace of the term "feminism"—implying a movement that demanded women's full autonomy—along with working women's strong public presence, international socialism, and the Russian Revolution, contributed to the idea of a new womanhood breaking free from old constraints.[26]

International socialism had long upheld universal, direct, and equal suffrage as a demand, but in the 1890s, German socialist firebrand Clara Zetkin revived the goal, spearheading the inclusion of woman suffrage in the 1889 Second International in Paris. This gathering of socialist and labor parties from twenty countries in turn fostered vigorous women's movements in Germany, France, and elsewhere in Europe. In Finland, socialist feminists and the Social Democratic Party were critical to the country's woman suffrage victory in 1906, Europe's first.[27]

Socialism, and the growing numbers of working women it inspired, breathed new life into the U.S. suffrage movement. In 1909, women workers in New York demanded women's right to vote, launching what became International Women's

Teresa Villarreal
ARTE PÚBLICO PRESS,
UNIVERSITY OF HOUSTON

Day. Over the next six years, working women exploded in labor militancy, viewing the vote as a tool against unjust working conditions and for what Polish-born labor organizer and suffragist Rose Schneiderman called "bread and roses." The 1911 Triangle Shirtwaist Factory fire that claimed the lives of 145 workers, most of whom were young, immigrant women, made suffrage more urgent.[28] Collaborations with middle-class reformers helped spread many of the tactics that suffragists later employed on a wider scale; mass meetings, marches, and open-air street speaking.[29]

Immigrants and women from through-out the Americas were key to these efforts and to connecting suffrage to broad social justice goals. In cigar factories in Tampa, Florida, the Puerto Rican anti-imperialist, anarchist, and feminist Luisa Capetillo inspired African American, Cuban American, and Italian American women workers with calls for woman suffrage, and for free love, workers' rights, and vegetarianism.[30] From Texas, Mexican-born feminist Teresa Villarreal, who had fled the dictatorship of Porfirio Díaz, supported the Mexican Revolution, the Socialist Party, and woman suffrage. She and her sister Andrea Villarreal published the state's first feminist newspaper, *La Mujer Moderna* (*The Modern Woman*) in 1910, starting the publication *El Obrero* (*The Worker*) the same year.[31] In 1911, after the First Mexican Congress in Laredo, Texas, journalist Jovita Idár praised woman suffrage in *La Crónica* (*The Chronicle*), connecting it to her longstanding demands for Mexican American civil rights.[32]

Socialist, working-class suffrage militancy in England also galvanized the British Women's Social and Political Union (WSPU), founded in 1903 by Emmeline Pankhurst. This group broke away from the larger, more moderate National Union of Women's Suffrage Societies led by Millicent Garrett Fawcett and became the driving force in the British suffrage movement for nearly two decades, influencing militant activism around the world, including in China.[33]

After the U.S. suffragist Alice Paul, one of Pankhurst's followers, was arrested in London in 1912, she helped organize the 1913 suffrage march in Washington, D.C., and founded the Congressional Union for Woman Suffrage, later renamed the National Woman's Party (NWP). Paul and the NWP focused on a federal

constitutional suffrage amendment. Its confrontational suffrage strategies of civil disobedience and picketing government buildings were inspired in large part by the WSPU, although Paul, a Quaker, rejected the violence of British activism. The NWP sash of purple, white, and yellow was modeled on the WSPU purple, white, and green one. Though U.S. suffragists generally called themselves "suffragists," a few even took on the British term "suffragette"—a term coined by the British *Daily Mail* as an epithet—to signal their radicalism.[34]

Jovita Idár at family printing press
GEORGIA STATE UNIVERSITY LIBRARY

The First World War and a wave of suffrage legislation in Europe further accelerated the U.S. suffrage movement.[35] In the five years after 1914, woman suffrage was adopted in Denmark, Iceland, Russia, Canada, Austria, Germany, Poland, and England. Although the NWP had already been picketing the White House for several months, it was only when they embarrassed President Woodrow Wilson in front of a visiting Russian delegation, whose wartime cooperation he was trying to secure, that the first six suffragists were arrested.[36] These women, jailed on charges of obstructing traffic, were immediately followed by a long line of U.S. women imprisoned for suffrage activism. The violence suffragists faced on the picket line for holding signs saying "Kaiser Wilson" amid rabid anti-German sentiment, and in jail with forced feedings during hunger strikes, became international news.[37]

International pressure, including the fact that women in Germany had been enfranchised before those in the United States, helped compel Wilson's January 1918 announcement of support for suffrage, as he promoted the United States as a beacon of democracy. By this time, the House of Representatives had already passed the suffrage amendment, but the Senate still voted against it. Wilson's endorsement was significant to U.S. and international public opinion. In Uruguay, suffragists utilized Wilson's support to push their legislators toward suffrage.[38]

Two more years of federal and state lobbying and organizing led to ratification of the Nineteenth Amendment in August 1920. For Crystal Eastman, a pacifist, enthusiast of the Russian Revolution, and cofounder of the American Civil Liberties Union (ACLU), this accomplishment represented not an end, but a new beginning—one with international significance: "Now [feminists] can say what

they are really after," she announced, "and what they are after, in common with all the rest of the struggling world, is freedom."[39]

The International Afterlives of the U.S. Suffrage Movement

Struggles for women's voting rights did not end with ratification of the Nineteenth Amendment. Though African American women in other parts of the United States became voters, those living in the South faced the same obstacles—residency requirements, poll taxes, and literacy tests backed up by threatened or actual violence—that Southern states had adopted to counter the Fifteenth Amendment. It would take another major struggle for full enfranchisement—one that was a vital part of the civil rights movement in the 1960s—before Congress passed the Voting Rights Act of 1965 that made real the promises of the Fifteen and Nineteenth Amendments.[40]

For many African American women, deprival of their rights in the United States drove new transnational activism. In the 1920s and 1930s, they collaborated with women from Africa, the Caribbean, and around the globe in the International Council of Women of the Darker Races (1922) and in Pan Africanist and leftist organizing that connected demands for women's political autonomy with those for antiracism, anticolonialism, and Black nationalism, specifically viewing Black women's self-determination as critical to broad and transformative social justice.[41]

The involvement of women from the United States in European and Pan-American feminism was also an outgrowth of the U.S. suffrage movement. It reflected the differences in approach between the moderate and more radical U.S. suffragists that persisted beyond ratification of the Nineteenth Amendment in 1920. Carrie Chapman Catt was no longer the president of the National American Woman Suffrage Association (NAWSA)—which with the suffrage victory transformed itself into the League of Women Voters (LWV)—but she continued as president of the International Woman Suffrage Alliance (IWSA) until she retired in 1923. The National Woman's Party (NWP) continued under the leadership of Alice Paul who created an International Advisory Council to the NWP in 1925. Both the IWSA and the NWP aimed to support the efforts of suffragists in what the IWSA termed the "non-emancipated" countries where women still did not have the vote, and to aid in expanding women's rights in areas where woman suffrage had been established.[42]

However, divisions that had emerged between moderate and more radical suffragists only grew after the NWP introduced the Equal Rights Amendment (ERA) in 1923. Many progressive women's organizations and labor groups opposed the ERA for fear that requiring identical laws for women and men would eliminate hard-won labor legislation for working women. Nationally, the LWV took the lead in this opposition. Internationally, women's rights advocates were also divided over the issue of special legislation versus equal rights, and the IWSA had members on both sides. But in 1926, when the NWP applied for membership in the IWSA, and the LWV vigorously opposed it, the IWSA rejected the NWP application.[43]

The NWP thus turned its attention toward Latin America where a Pan-American feminist movement was growing. The IWSA was also interested in Latin America: between 1920 and 1923 Catt toured six countries in South America assessing the prospects for woman suffrage. And in 1922, the LWV hosted a Pan American Conference of Women in Baltimore, Maryland that brought a number of Latin American feminists to the United States. At the suggestion of the Latin American feminists, the Pan American Association for the Advancement of Women (PAAAW) emerged from the Baltimore conference and for a time played a role in knitting together leaders from throughout the Americas and providing a crucial apparatus for further development of a feminist movement in Latin America.

Many of the delegates from Latin America returned home and launched new feminist organizations in their own countries that were affiliated with the PAAAW. But Catt's negative assessment of the state of feminism and feminists in Latin America, along with her waning interest in the Pan American realm, alienated many Latin American suffragists. When NWP leaders became leaders of another new organization, the Inter-American Commission of Women (IACW), the NWP had more direct achievement in the Pan American arena.[44]

The IACW was created in 1928 by NWP members and Cuban feminists. It was the first intergovernmental organization that promoted women's rights in the world. Initially led by veteran NWP leader Doris Stevens, the commission forced international treaties for women's civil and political equal rights into Pan American and League of Nations congresses. These efforts led to League of Nations debates on married women's independent nationality rights and to a League of Nations sponsored commission on the legal status of women around the world.[45] In the Pan American realm, their efforts led to the passage of the Equal Nationality Treaty. Many countries in the Western Hemisphere ratified this treaty, including the United States in 1934, which led to a legislative act granting married women's equal nationality rights.[46]

Within the inter-American movement, however, a heterogeneous group of Latin American feminists also recognized continuing efforts of U.S. women to dominate, and developed a distinctive anti-imperialist, Pan-Hispanic feminism that included gaining the vote, but did not focus exclusively on suffrage. Asserting their own leadership over Pan-American feminism, they called for *derechos humanos*, which implied women's political, civil, social, and economic rights alongside anti-imperialism and anti-fascism. At the 1945 San Francisco meeting that created the United Nations (U.N.), Latin American female delegates, led by Brazilian feminist Bertha Lutz, drew on this movement to push women's rights into the U.N. Charter and proposed what became the U.N. Commission on the Status of Women. In the wake of these events, numerous Latin American countries passed woman suffrage.[47]

Women from the Global South continued to be pioneers on the international feminist stage in the postwar years, pushing for inclusion of women's rights in human rights treaties. Hansa Mehta from India, one of the two women on the

At this January 24, 1928, gathering of 200 women at the *Asociación de Reporteros* in Havana, Cuba, five U.S. National Woman's Party members joined suffragists from Cuba, Dominican Republic, Puerto Rico, and Costa Rica to successfully plan to inject women's rights into the 6th International Conference of American States meeting in Havana.

COURTESY OF THE SCHLESINGER LIBRARY, RADCLIFFE INSTITUTE, HARVARD UNIVERSITY

commission drafting the 1948 United Nations Universal Declaration of Human Rights with Eleanor Roosevelt, was responsible for Article 1 reading "All human beings are born free and equal" rather than "All men are born free and equal."[48]

After the Second World War, U.S. women's groups continued to connect with women throughout the world internationally, both through longstanding groups like the International Alliance of Women (IAW) and the Women's International League for Peace and Freedom (WILPF), as well as through new organs like the U.N. Commission on the Status of Women.

In the Cold War years, old tensions around feminist strategy were compounded by the Red Scare in the United States. In 1948, the Congress of American Women, a U.S. affiliate of the global leftist feminist group founded in 1946, the Women's International Democratic Federation (WIDF), was branded a communist front organization by the House Un-American Activities Committee, and it was dissolved in 1950. Meanwhile, the WIDF continued to be a major transnational feminist hub throughout the world, even after it was temporarily suspended from its consultative status with the United Nations. The WIDF merged demands for anticolonialism and antiracism with women's equality and political rights, and was linked to women's activism in decolonization struggles throughout Africa, Asia, the Middle East, and Latin America.[49]

In these years, suffrage for women spread throughout newly decolonized countries in India (1950), Malaysia (1957), Algeria (1962), Iran and Morocco (1963), Libya (1964), Bangladesh (1972) and elsewhere. In 1975, WIDF and the U.N.

Commission on the Status of Women were both responsible for the 1975 U.N. World Conference on Women in Mexico City. This conference sparked the United Nations Decade for Women from 1975 to 1985, a period that saw a profusion of new international feminist organizations, events, and activism.[50] One of its outcomes was the Convention on the Elimination of All Forms of Discrimination against Women (CEDAW), an international treaty on women's rights, adopted in 1979 by the U.N. General Assembly. Article 3 demands basic human rights and fundamental freedoms for women "on a basis of equality with men" in "political, social, economic, and cultural fields."[51] Since its institution in 1981, the treaty has been ratified by 189 countries, although not by the United States.

U.S. women's global activism, however, has never abated, and the transnational legacies of the suffrage movement are evident in U.S. women's ongoing quests for full citizenship today. Then, as now, fights for women's rights are connected to global movements for human rights—for immigrant, racial, labor, and feminist justice. The internationalist history of the woman suffrage movement shows us that activists and movements outside the United States, along with a broad range of diverse, international goals, were critical to organizing for that right deemed so quintessentially American—the right to vote. It reminds us how much we in the United States have to learn from feminist struggles around the world.

Notes

This article originally appeared as "The International History of the US Suffrage Movement" in the series, *19th Amendment and Women's Access to the Vote Across America*, edited by Tamara Gaskell and published online in 2019 by the U.S. National Park Service in cooperation with the National Conference of State Historic Preservation Officers.

1. Ellen Carol DuBois, "Woman Suffrage around the World," in *Suffrage and Beyond: International Feminist Perspectives*, ed. Caroline Daley and Melanie Nolan (New York: New York University Press, 1994), 254.

2. The full quote is "When the true history of the antislavery cause shall be written, women will occupy a large space in its pages; for the cause of the slave has been peculiarly woman's cause." Frederick Douglass, *Life and Times of Frederick Douglass* (Hartford, CT: Park Publishing, 1883), 570. On Wollstonecraft, see Estelle B. Freedman, *No Turning Back: The History of Feminism and the Future of Women* (New York: Ballantine Books, 2002), 51–52.

3. Maria W. Stewart, "Religion and the Pure Principles of Morality, the Sure Foundation on Which We Must Build. Productions from the Pen of Mrs. Maria W. Steward [*sic*], Widow of the Late James W. Steward, of Boston," reprinted in *Maria W. Stewart, America's First Black Woman Political Writer: Essays and Speeches*, ed. Marilyn Richardson (Bloomington: Indiana University Press, 1987), 38; Martha S. Jones, *All Bound Up Together: The Woman Question in African American Political Culture, 1830–1900* (Chapel Hill: University of North Carolina Press, 2007), 23–29.

4. On the significance of the Haitian Revolution to US abolitionists and debate about slavery, see Robin Blackburn, *The American Crucible: Slavery, Emancipation, and Human Rights* (London: Verso, 2011), and Manisha Sinha, *The Slave's Cause: A History of Abolition* (New Haven, CT: Yale University Press, 2016), 177–78, 245–50, 454–55. On female abolitionists' engagement with the Haitian Revolution, see Marlene L. Daut, *Tropics of Haiti: Race and Literary History of the Haitian Revolution in the Atlantic World, 1789–1865* (Liverpool: Liverpool University Press, 2015), and Carla L. Peterson, "Literary Transnationalism and Diasporic History: Frances Watkins Harper's 'Fancy Sketches,' 1859–60," in *Women's Rights and Transatlantic Slavery in the Era of Emancipation*, ed. Kathryn Kish Sklar and James Brewer Stewart (New Haven, CT: Yale University Press, 2007), 189–210.

5. Angelina Grimké to Sarah Douglass, February 25, 1838, quoted in Annelise Orleck, *Rethinking American Women's Activism* (New York: Routledge, 2016), 4; Sarah M. Grimké, "Letters on the Equality of the Sexes in Freedman (United States, 1837)," in *The Essential Feminist Reader*, ed. Estelle B. Freedman (New York: Modern Library, 2007), 47.

6. Ellen Carol DuBois, "Woman Suffrage and the Left: An International Socialist-Feminist Perspective," in *Woman Suffrage and Women's Rights*, ed. Ellen Carol DuBois (New York: New York University Press, 1998), 254.

7. Nancy A. Hewitt, "From Seneca Falls to Suffrage? Reimagining a 'Master' Narrative in U.S. Women's History," in *No Permanent Waves: Recasting Histories of U.S. Feminism*, ed. Nancy A. Hewitt (New Brunswick, NJ: Rutgers University Press, 2010), 24–25; Sally Roesch Wagner and Jeanne Shenandoah, *Sisters in Spirit: Haudenosaunee (Iroquois) Influence on Early American Feminists* (Summertown, TN: Native Voices, 2001).

8. Michaela Bank, *Women of Two Countries: German-American Women, Women's Rights and Nativism, 1848–1890* (New York: Berghahn Books, 2012), chap. 2. Her book also sheds light on the important work of German American suffragist Clara Neymann.

9. Quote from Freedman, *No Turning Back*, 54. Rose was instrumental in gaining married women's property rights in New York state. See Bonnie S. Anderson, *The Rabbi's Atheist Daughter: Ernestine Rose, International Feminist Pioneer* (New York: Oxford University Press, 2017). She also explained on the 1853 anniversary of West Indian emancipation, "I go for the recognition of human rights, without distinction of sect, party, sex, or color." Quote from Ellen Carol DuBois, "Ernestine Rose's Jewish Origins and the Varieties of Euro-American Emancipation in 1848," in Sklar and Stewart, *Women's Rights and Transatlantic Slavery in the Era of Emancipation*, 280.

10. Sarah Parker Remond, "Lecture at the Lion Hotel, Warrington (1859)," in *Documenting First Wave Feminisms*, vol. 1, *Transnational Collaborations and Crosscurrents*, ed. Maureen Moynagh and Nancy Forestell (Toronto: University of Toronto Press, 2012), 46.

11. Kenneth Salzer, "Great Exhibitions: Ellen Craft on the British Abolitionist Stage," in *Transatlantic Women: Nineteenth-Century American Women Writers and Great Britain*, ed. Beth Lynne Lueck, Brigitte Bailey, and Lucinda L. Damon-Bach (Durham: University

of New Hampshire Press, 2012), 147; Angela Y. Davis, *Women, Race, and Class* (New York: Random House, 1981), 65; Sirpa Salenius, *An Abolitionist Abroad: Sarah Parker Remond in Cosmopolitan Europe* (Amherst: University of Massachusetts Press, 2016); Elizabeth Crawford, *Suffrage Centenary: A Brief History: The Diversity of the Suffrage Movement* (London: Fawcett Society, 2017), fawcettsociety.org.uk / Handlers / Download. ashx?IDMF=7f935e2e-7d93-4fd3-98e8-41e37b588674. On John Stuart Mill and Harriet Taylor see Freedman, *No Turning Back*, 52–54.

12. Rosalyn Terborg-Penn, *African American Women in the Struggle for the Vote, 1850–1920* (Bloomington: Indiana University Press, 1999), 39.

13. On the importance of the telegraph in materially connecting nineteenth-century women's rights reformers, see Margaret H. McFadden, *Golden Cables of Sympathy: The Transatlantic Sources of Nineteenth-Century Feminism* (Lexington: University Press of Kentucky, 1999), 1–3. On the ICW, IWSA, and WILPF, see Leila J. Rupp, *Worlds of Women: The Making of an International Women's Movement* (Princeton, NJ: Princeton University Press, 1998). On the founding of the ICW in 1888 by Stanton and Anthony, see Lisa Tetrault, *The Myth of Seneca Falls: Memory and the Women's Suffrage Movement, 1848–1898* (Chapel Hill: University of North Carolina Press, 2014), chap. 5. These groups were preceded by Swiss leader Marie Goegg-Pouchoulin's 1868 founding of one of the first international women's organizations, the International Association of Women (*Association internationale des femmes*), whose goal was to organize women of all classes so they could enjoy the same rights as men within their own countries. Although this group included women from the United States, it was short-lived. Bob Reinalda, *Routledge History of International Organizations: From 1815 to the Present Day* (New York: Routledge, 2009), 150. Women from the United States also played a role in the formation of the *Congrès International du Droit des Femmes* in Paris in 1878. However, at this conference, discussion of suffrage was banned. Rupp, *Worlds of Women*, 14. In these years, the NAWSA used these groups to connect with other movements internationally, but Elizabeth Cady Stanton also worked independently of these groups to carve out important transatlantic networks. See Sandra Stanley Holton, "'To Educate Women into Rebellion': Elizabeth Cady Stanton and the Creation of a Transatlantic Network of Radical Suffragists," *American Historical Review* 99, no. 4 (October 1994): 1112–36.

14. During the First World War, Addams and 1,150 other women from the United States and Europe gathered in The Hague to demand international peace and founded the WILPF; their declaration urged that "the exclusion of women from citizenship is contrary to the principles of civilization and human right" and as contrary to permanent peace. Jane Addams, Emily G. Balch, and Alice Hamilton, *Women at The Hague: The International Congress of Women and Its Results*, ed. Harriet Hyman Alonso (Urbana: University of Illinois Press, 2003), 64. The original resolutions from the women at The Hague were praised by President Wilson and may have shaped his Fourteen Points in 1918. Their internationalist position was unpopular in the United States at the time, and one of the leaders, Emily Greene Balch, later winner of the Nobel Peace Prize, was fired from her position as a professor at Wellesley College in 1918. Interconnected, international goals were what the IWSA had in mind when it announced in 1909, "We have been baptized in that spirit of the twentieth century which the world calls internationalism." Quoted in Nitza Berkovitch, *From Motherhood to Citizenship: Women's Rights and International Organizations* (Baltimore: Johns Hopkins University Press, 1999), 18.

15. The ICW claimed to represent four to five million women by 1907. The IWSA attained twenty-six national affiliates by 1913. Rupp, *Worlds of Women*, 22, 70. They also sprang from each other. Although Stanton and Anthony founded the ICW to promote suffrage, when the organization turned away from the vote soon after its creation, German suffragists Lida Gustava Heymann and Anita Augspurg helped found the IWSA with Catt, committed to "secur[ing] the enfranchisement of the women of all nations." Rupp, *Worlds of Women*, 21–22. Both the ICW and IWSA would inspire national suffrage organizing in Brazil, Argentina, Uruguay, and other countries in the world. Katherine Marino, *Feminism for the Americas: The Making of an International Human Rights Movement* (Chapel Hill: University of North Carolina Press,

2019), chap. 1.

16. DuBois, "Woman Suffrage around the World," 256.

17. Ian Tyrrell, *Woman's World, Woman's Empire: The Woman's Christian Temperance Union in International Perspective, 1880–1930* (Chapel Hill: University of North Carolina Press, 1991), chap. 10.

18. Marino, *Feminism for the Americas*, 24. These organizations increasingly included representatives from countries outside of Western Europe from the 1920s through '40s. Maire Sandell, *The Rise of Women's Transnational Activism: Identity and Sisterhood between the World Wars* (London: I. B. Tauris, 2015).

19. On imperial feminism in these groups, see Antoinette Burton, *Burdens of History: British Feminists, Indian Women, and Imperial Culture, 1865–1915* (Chapel Hill: University of North Carolina Press, 1994); Margot Badran, *Feminism, Islam, and Nation: Gender and the Making of Modern Egypt* (Princeton, NJ: Princeton University Press, 1995), 108–10, 232–38; Charlotte Weber, "Unveiling Scheherazade: Feminist Orientalism in the International Alliance of Women, 1911–1950," *Feminist Studies* 27, no. 1 (Spring 2001): 125–57.

20. These suffrage efforts were ultimately unsuccessful. Patricia Grimshaw, "'Settler Anxieties, Indigenous Peoples, and Women's Suffrage in the Colonies of Australia, New Zealand, and Hawai'i, 1888–1902," in *Women's Suffrage in Asia: Gender, Nationalism, and Democracy*, ed. Louise Edwards and Mina Roces (London: RoutledgeCurzon, 2004), 220–39; Rumi Yasutake, "Re-Franchising Women of Hawai'i, 1912–1920: The Politics of Gender, Sovereignty, Race, and Rank at the Crossroads of the Pacific," in *Gendering the Trans-Pacific World*, ed. Catherine Ceniza Choy and Judy Tzu-Chun Wu (Leiden: Brill, 2017), 114–39. As Ian Tyrrell has pointed out, the WCTU's promotion of a "benign American civilization" included the "benevolent assimilation" of Native Americans, overlooking the violence of Wounded Knee–the massacre that killed over 150 men, women, and children of the Lakota on the heels of the forced removal of thousands. Tyrrell, *Woman's World, Woman's Empire*, 181.

21. Allison L. Sneider, *Suffragists in an Imperial Age: U.S. Expansion and the Woman Question, 1870–1929* (New York: Oxford University Press, 2008).

22. Rosalyn Terborg-Penn also connects US imperial feminism in Puerto Rico and St. Thomas to racism within the suffrage movement in "Enfranchising Women of Color: Woman Suffragists as Agents of Imperialism," in *Nation, Empire, Colony: Historicizing Gender and Race*, ed. Ruth Roach Pierson and Nupur Chaudhuri (Bloomington: Indiana University Press, 1998), 41–56.

23. Terborg-Penn, *African American Women in the Struggle for the Vote*, 86; Noaquia N. Callahan, "A Rare Colored Bird: Mary Church Terrell, *Die Fortschritte der Farbigen Frauen*, and the International Council of Women's Congress in Berlin, Germany, 1904," *German Historical Institute Bulletin Supplement* 13 (2017): 97; Michelle M. Rief, "Thinking Locally, Acting Globally: The International Agenda of African American Clubwomen, 1880–1940," *Journal of African American History* 89, no. 3 (Summer 2004): 203–4. For more on Frances Ellen Watkins Harper, see Jones, *All Bound Up Together*, and the new edition of Harper's *Iola Leroy, Or, Shadows Uplifted*, ed. Koritha Mitchell (Ontario: Broadview Editions, 2018).

24. Patricia Ann Schecter, *Ida B. Wells-Barnett and American Reform, 1888–1930* (Chapel Hill: University of North Carolina Press, 2001), 110–11; Mia Bay, *To Tell the Truth Freely: The Life of Ida B. Wells* (New York: Hill and Wang, 2010), 185–89, 206–17. Also, as Callahan explains, Wells's pamphlet *The Reason Why the Colored American Is Not in the World's Colombian Exposition* (1893), which criticized the exclusion of African Americans from the Columbian Exposition, "sparked international debate about the limits of American citizenship when it came to race and gender." Callahan, "Rare Colored Bird," 100–102. On the work of the Alpha Suffrage Club, see Wanda A. Hendricks, "Ida B. Wells-Barnett and the Alpha Suffrage Club of Chicago," Chapter 17 in this volume; Susan Ware, *Why They Marched: Untold Stories of the Women Who Fought for the Right to Vote* (Cambridge, MA: Harvard University Press, 2019), Chapter 7.

25. Fluent in German, French, Latin, and Greek in addition to her native English, Terrell overheard German women talking about how eagerly they awaited "die Negierin" (the Negress). Later Terrell recounted, "I represented not only the colored woman in my own country but, since I was the only woman taking part in the International Congress who had a drop of African blood in her

veins, I represented the whole continent of Africa as well." Brittney C. Cooper, *Beyond Respectability: The Intellectual Thought of Race Women* (Urbana: University of Illinois Press, 2018), 78–80; Callahan, "Rare Colored Bird."

26. The term *feminisme* had first been used in its modern sense by French suffragist Hubertine Auclert in the 1878 International Congress for the Rights of Women in Paris (*Congrès International du Droit des Femmes*), although that conference did not endorse woman suffrage itself. After 1882, she used the term in her newspaper *La citoyenne*. "Transatlantic Networks for Legal Feminism, 1888–1912," *German Historical Institute Bulletin Supplement* 13 (2017): 56; Karen Offen, *European Feminisms, 1700–1950: A Political History* (Stanford, CA: Stanford University Press, 2000), 19–20; Karen Offen, "On the French Origins of the Words *feminism* and *feminist*," *Feminist Issues* 8, no. 2 (June 1988): 45–51. For an excellent account of how the Russian Revolution infused modern suffragism, see Julia Mickenberg, "Suffragettes and Soviets: American Feminists and the Specter of Revolutionary Russia," *Journal of American History* 100, no. 4 (March 2014): 1021–51.

27. DuBois, "Woman Suffrage around the World," 265; Clara Zetkin, "From Women's Right to Vote," 1907, A Resolution Introduced at the International Socialist Congress," in Moynagh and Forestell, *Documenting First Wave Feminisms*, 1:137–43.

28. Annelise Orleck, *Common Sense and a Little Fire: Women and Working-Class Politics in the United States, 1900–1965* (Chapel Hill: University of North Carolina Press, 1995), chap. 3. Women workers demanded maternity legislation, child care, protective labor laws, and equal representation in unions. DuBois, "Woman Suffrage and the Left," 259.

29. On collaborations with the WTUL, see Orleck, *Common Sense and a Little Fire*. On the work of Stanton's daughter Harriot Stanton Blatch's suffrage organizing with working women in New York, see Ellen Carol DuBois, *Harriot Stanton Blatch and the Winning of Woman Suffrage* (New Haven, CT: Yale University Press, 1997).

30. Vicki L. Ruiz, "Class Acts: Latina Feminist Traditions, 1900–1930," *American Historical Review* 121, no. 1 (February 2016): 1–16; Nancy A. Hewitt, "In Pursuit of Power: The Political Economy of Women's Activism in Twentieth-Century Tampa," in *Visible Women: New Essays on Women's Activism*, ed. Nancy A. Hewitt and Suzanne Lebsock (Urbana: University of Illinois Press, 1993), 199–222.

31. Vicki L. Ruiz, *From Out of the Shadows: Mexican Women in Twentieth-Century America* (New York: Oxford University Press, 2008), 99. This was the first feminist newspaper in Texas. Leonor Villegas de Magnón, *The Rebel* (Houston: Arte Público Press, 1994), xv. For more on Teresa Villarreal and her sister Andrea, see Maylei Blackwell, *¡Chicana Power! Contested Histories of Feminism in the Chicano Movement* (Austin: University of Texas Press, 2011), 107–9. Emma Pérez, *The Decolonial Imaginary: Writing Chicanas into History* (Bloomington: Indiana University Press, 1999), 67–69; Nicolás Kanellos, "Envisioning the Re-visioning the Nation: Latino Intellectual Traditions," American Latino Theme Study, National Park Services website, home.nps.gov/ latinoheritageinitiatives/latino/latinothemestudy/intellectual traditions.htm.

32. Jovita Idár, a journalist and civil rights leader from Laredo, Texas, founded the League of Mexican Women, which promoted woman suffrage, educated poor children, promoted the Spanish language, and spoke out against discrimination and violence against Mexican Americans. Gabriela González, "Jovita Idár: The Ideological Origins of a Transnational Advocate for La Raza," in *Texas Women: Their Histories, Their Lives*, ed. Elizabeth Haynes Turner, Stephanie Cole, and Rebecca Sharpless (Athens: University of Georgia Press, 2015), 225–48. For more on her and Villarreal, see Gabriela González, *Redeeming la Raza: Transborder Modernity, Race, Respectability, and Rights* (New York: Oxford University Press, 2018), 21, 24–26, 37, 41–42.

33. DuBois, "Woman Suffrage and the Left," 266. The working-class based suffrage movement of Lancashire textile workers in the 1890s helped inspire the militant tactics and public agitation of the middle-class women. Pankhurst's group was founded in Manchester and moved to London in 1906. On suffrage activism in China, see Louise Edwards, Gender, Politics, and Democracy in China, *Women's Suffrage in China* (Stanford, CA: Stanford University Press, 2008) and Louise Edwards, "Chinese Women's Campaigns for Suffrage: Nationalism, Confucianism, and Political Agency," in Edwards and Roces, *Women's Suffrage in Asia*, 59–78.

34. Orleck, *Common Sense and a Little Fire*, 94. See "Suffragette" in Edwards and Roces, *Women's Suffrage in Asia*, 59–78.

35. For an excellent history of the way the war accelerated the phenomenon of the "new woman" and suffrage debate, and on connections between women's war work and suffrage, see Lynn Dumenil, *The Second Line of Defense: American Women and World War I* (Chapel Hill: University of North Carolina Press, 2017), especially chap. 1.

36. Mickenberg, "Suffragettes and Soviets," 1021.

37. Nancy F. Cott, *The Grounding of Modern Feminism* (New Haven, CT: Yale University Press, 1987), 59.

38. Marino, *Feminism for the Americas*, 247 n35; Paulina Luisi, *Movimiento sufragista: Conferencia leída en el Augusteo de Buenos Aires, el 21 de febrero 1919, a petido de la Unión Feminista Nacional* (Montevideo, Urug.: "El Siglo Ilustrado," de Gregorio V. Mariño, 1919). In 1917, Uruguayans had already supported a constitution that included a mechanism for enacting woman suffrage, before a federal amendment was in the offing in the United States. As historian Francesca Miller has noted, this made Uruguay "in theory, the first of all Western Hemisphere nations to recognize female suffrage," though suffrage did not pass there until 1934. Francesca Miller, *Latin American Women and the Search for Social Justice* (Hanover, NH: University Press of New England, 1991), 98.

39. Quoted in Mickenberg, "Suffragettes and Soviets," 1048.

40. In addition, as Nancy Hewitt has written, "millions of Asian and Mexican Americans in the West and American Indians across the country were denied suffrage until the 1940s, and some waited until the Voting Rights Act and its extension in 1970 addressed the bilingual needs of Spanish-speaking citizens." Hewitt, "From Seneca Falls to Suffrage?," 11.

41. Rief, "Thinking Locally, Acting Globally," and Michelle M. Rief, "Banded Close Together': An Afrocentric Study of African American Women's International Activism, 1850–1940, and the International Council of Women of the Darker Races" (PhD diss., Temple University, 2003); Keisha N. Blair, *Set the World on Fire: Black Nationalist Women and the Global Struggle for Freedom* (Philadelphia: University of Pennsylvania Press, 2018); Erik S. McDuffie, *Sojourning for Freedom: Black Women, American Communism, and the Making of Black Left Feminism* (Durham, NC: Duke University Press, 2011); Dayo Gore, *Radicalism at the Crossroads: African American Women Activists in the Cold War* (New York: New York University Press, 2011); Brandy Thomas Wells, "'She Pieced and Stitched and Quilted, Never Wavering nor Doubting': A Historical Tapestry of African American Women's Journeys and the Construction of Cross-Ethnic Racial Identity" (PhD diss., Ohio State University, 2015); and Lisa G. Materson, "African American Women's Global Internationalism, 1890s–1960s," *Women's Studies International Forum* 32, no. 1 (January–February 2009): 35–42.

42. Marino, *Feminism for the Americas*.

43. Rachel Adams, *Women and the Universal Declaration of Human Rights* (New York: Routledge, 2019).

44. Francisca de Haan, "Eugene Cotton, Park Chong-ae, and Claudia Jones, Rethinking Transnational Feminism and International Politics," *Journal of Women's History* 25, no. 4 (Winter 2013): 174–89.

45. Jocelyn Olcott, *International Women's Year: The Greatest Consciousness-Raising Event in History* (New York: Oxford University Press, 2017); Kristen Ghodsee, *Second World, Second Sex: Socialist Women's Activism and Global Solidarity during the Cold War* (Duke University Press, 2018).

46. U.N. General Assembly, Convention on the Elimination of All Forms of Discrimination Against Women, 18 December 1979, United Nations, Treaty Series, vol. 1249, p. 13, available at: refworld.org/docid/3ae6b3970.html [accessed 19 December 2019].

Dr. Anna Howard Shaw served as president of the
National American Woman Suffrage Association for eleven years.

THE SUFFRAGE RENAISSANCE:

A New Image for a New Century
1896—1910

Sara Hunter Graham

Editor's Introduction: One of the clearest and most fascinating examples in this volume of "rediscovering the woman suffrage movement" is this essay by historian Sara Hunter Graham, challenging long-accepted ideas about the woman suffrage movement at the turn of the century.

As the end of the nineteenth century approached, American suffragists were at last united in a single organization. The National Woman Suffrage Association and the American Woman Suffrage Association had come together to form the National American Woman Suffrage Association (NAWSA) in 1890. Susan B. Anthony quickly emerged as the organization's principal leader, serving as president from 1892 to 1900. Lucy Stone died in 1893, and Elizabeth Cady Stanton became somewhat estranged from the suffrage movement after the publication in 1895 of *The Woman's Bible* in which Stanton indicted Christianity for contributing to the subordination of women. Anthony, setting aside the militant tactics of the 1870s, now urged suffragists to avoid controversy and focus exclusively on gaining the vote. The NAWSA dedicated itself to building support throughout the nation and securing enough state victories that a federal amendment could be won.

The NAWSA leaders assisted suffragists throughout the nation in their efforts to obtain state suffrage amendments. The four thrilling victories in the Rocky Mountain states, however, stood out in contrast to countless defeats. The NAWSA's vigorous campaign in the South, an attempt to gain woman suffrage through the new state constitutions adopted during the 1890s, was unsuccessful. In fact, after the victories in Utah and Idaho in 1896, not a single state fell into the suffrage column until 1910.

The suffrage movement entered a stage that historian Eleanor Flexner in 1959—and suffrage historians ever since—describe as "the doldrums." As Flexner noted in her influential study, *Century of Struggle: The Woman's Rights Movement in the United States,* between 1896 and 1910 only six state referenda were held, and three of these were in Oregon. All of these failed, and the federal suffrage amendment "appeared moribund." Anthony retired from leadership, and her promising successor, Carrie Chapman Catt, rose to the presidency in 1900 only to be forced into retirement four years later due to the illness of her husband. Dr. Anna Howard Shaw, who served as NAWSA president from 1904 to 1915, is generally regarded by

historians as an extraordinary orator—less talented as an administrator—who presided over a de-centralized and ineffective NAWSA.

In this essay, however, Sara Hunter Graham offers a revisionist view of this era. Rather than a period of indecision and inactivity, Graham sees the period from 1896 to 1910 as one of careful and successful rebuilding, in which the leaders of the NAWSA deliberately reshaped the image of their movement. They also expanded their ranks in ways that greatly enhanced the prestige and effectiveness of the suffrage movement, recruiting wealthy and socially prominent women as well as a new generation of energetic and talented college-educated women.

The leadership for this "suffrage renaissance" came largely from Carrie Chapman Catt who, before having to resign as president, strengthened the NAWSA in many ways. This included the introduction at the national level of the "society plan," tested earlier in Colorado, that brought women of wealth, prestige, and influence into the suffrage movement—and made it quite difficult for anti-suffragists to stigmatize suffragists as fanatics.

Graham also informs us that determination to create a new and more saleable image led NAWSA leaders to rewrite the history of the woman suffrage movement, de-emphasizing controversial aspects of its past and virtually canonizing early leaders, particularly Anthony. They emphasized the progress women had made in terms of educational, professional, and legal reforms and pictured suffrage as the next logical step. Through new rituals, symbols and rhetoric, they promoted solidarity throughout an enlarged and diverse constituency united only by the desire to gain the vote for women. They also, Graham concludes, brought women into the movement by creating a new political culture based on membership in a single-interest pressure group that was far more attractive to women than the male political culture of saloons and smoke-filled rooms.

Thus, writes Graham, "the visionary cause of the pioneers" was transformed into "an eminently safe program" acceptable to middle-class club women and the social elite—a development NAWSA leaders regarded as "a necessary precondition that would eventually win the vote." As we will see in subsequent essays, other women who were not of the nation's elite would also be an important part of the massive and diverse coalition amassing in support of woman suffrage in the first two decades of the twentieth century; but as Graham makes clear, the NAWSA's successful efforts to make the movement attractive to women with leisure, funds, and influence to contribute to the cause played a crucial role in the success of the woman suffrage movement.

★　★　★　★　★

SUFFRAGISM IN THE EARLY 1900S was burdened with an image arising from its history that was in many respects a hindrance to further progress. Suffragists' advocacy of divorce reform, experimental dress, and feminist interpretations of the Bible had given the nineteenth-century movement a reputation of radicalism that

was exploited by the enemies of suffrage to dissuade more conventional women from participating in the movement. Consequently, during the years 1896 to 1910 suffragists made little tangible progress in state referenda or federal amendment campaigns. No new states were won for suffrage and, in Congress, the federal amendment lay dormant in committee, prompting one historian to label the period "the doldrums."[1]

Despite the poor record generated by state suffrage campaigns, however, the "doldrums" were in reality an important period of growth and renewal for the movement. So significant were these years of regeneration that the period might more appropriately be called "the suffrage renaissance." Aware of the movement's negative image but unwilling to disavow the contributions of the pioneers, the suffragists of the National American Woman Suffrage Association (NAWSA) sought to create a tradition that could reconcile their heroic and somewhat controversial past with the association's pragmatic plans for the future. Developing a reinterpreted, sanitized version of the past, coupled with a sincere celebration of the heroism of pioneer suffragists, NAWSA leaders forged a link between the heroic age of confrontational politics and the new organizational approach to reform that appealed to mainstream American women.

The Referendum of 1895: An Anti-suffrage Victory

A turning point for the woman suffrage movement came on election day, 1895, when the Massachusetts State Legislature held a mock, or nonbinding, suffrage referendum. The State Legislature had been besieged for years by both suffragists and their opponents to act on the issue. In an effort to determine public opinion on the question, the legislature ruled that both women and men would vote in the mock referendum. In a singularly odd twist, both suffragists and anti-suffragists opposed the contest. The former objected to the nonbinding status of the vote, while the latter expressed disgust at being forced to cast a vote in order to demonstrate their aversion to voting. Anti-suffragists resolved their dilemma, however, by clever strategy, good organization, and effective propaganda.[2]

The Massachusetts Association Opposed to Further Extension of the Suffrage to Women (MAOFESW), founded in 1882 by Mrs. Henry O. Houghton and revitalized several months before the November 1895 referendum, attempted to persuade women to abstain from voting on the issue. Arguing that a low female voter turnout would indicate the wishes of Massachusetts women far more convincingly than a large "no" vote, anti-suffragists solicited contributions from well-wishers and embarked on a house-to-house canvass of Boston in order to bring their message to the people. Aiding the MAOFESW workers was a group of prominent Boston men who formed the Man Suffrage Association (MSA). Boasting a membership that included two ex-governors of the state, the president of Harvard University, noted religious leaders, professors, business men and attorneys, the MSA raised over $3,600 in less than two months at a time when the combined expenditures of all suffrage advocates was a mere $1,300.[3]

In contrast to the wealthy and prestigious individuals that opposed woman suffrage, suffragists relied on reformers such as Henry Blackwell, his daughter Alice Stone Blackwell, Julia Ward Howe, and Thomas Wentworth Higginson for leadership and support. Blackwell and Higginson had served together in the abolition movement, and along with Julia Ward Howe, were among the pioneers of the nineteenth-century woman's rights crusade. In addition to the aging but able reformers, Senator George F. Hoar agreed to preside over the Suffrage Referendum State Committee, formed in July 1895, to coordinate the suffrage forces. Unfortunately, most suffragists continued their long-time practice of suspending suffrage work during the summer months. By the time the committee reassembled in October, its members faced a well-organized and active opposition. The anti-suffragists had used the summer to their advantage, circularizing each ward, publicizing their position in the press, and plastering walls and fences with huge placards bearing the message, "Men and Women, Vote No!"[4]

More effective than these publicity measures, however, was the anti-suffrage strategy that encouraged women to abstain from voting. On November 5, antis gleefully pointed to the low female turnout as proof that the vast majority of Massachusetts women did not want the vote. Of approximately 612,000 women eligible to register only 42,676 did so, and of those, only 23,065 actually cast a vote. Although women voters supported the measure 22,204 to 861, not a single female vote was cast in forty-four towns. Of the 273,946 male votes cast, a resounding 186,976 men voted against the measure.[5] By shifting attention away from the actual female vote in the mock referendum and emphasizing instead the percentage of the female population that stayed away from the polls, the anti-suffragists managed to interpret the referendum as an overwhelming victory for their position.

The 1895 referendum cast a long shadow: never again would suffragists call for a test of strength if that test was to include the disfranchised members of their own sex, and never again would anti-suffragists believe that the majority of women favored woman suffrage. Although suffrage leaders continued to maintain that a large latent sentiment for their reform existed, the strategic course that they pursued as the new century unfolded revealed a pragmatic acceptance of the weakness of their position. There was little doubt among suffragists that the majority of Americans accepted the idea of a separate domestic sphere for women. Moreover, in taking the position of defending the status quo and opposing any change in the status of women, the anti-suffragists had occupied the high ground in the coming battle for the vote.

During the Massachusetts referendum campaign, MAOFESW had demonstrated its ability to mobilize an influential constituency, utilize modern advertising methods, and raise large sums of money to finance their work. The suffragists, although dedicated to their cause, were unable to compete with the superior funding and efficiency of their opponents. Moreover, the anti-suffragists had effectively turned the referendum into a demonstration of indifference on the

part of Massachusetts women, and had placed the suffrage forces in the defensive position of supporting a democratic reform that the majority of women did not desire. In the aftermath of the contest, many Massachusetts suffrage clubs lost members or disbanded completely, while MAOFESW and other anti-suffrage organizations grew in size and strength. The referendum of 1895, repeatedly cited in national periodicals and in anti-suffrage tracts as proof of female indifference to woman suffrage, shaped the opposition to suffrage for years to come.

More immediately, however, the 1895 Massachusetts referendum forced suffragists to reassess the strengths and weaknesses of their organization. The lesson of 1895 seemed to point toward a continuation of the NAWSA policy of educating the public to the benefits of woman suffrage, but with a new emphasis on effective organization and strong financial support. In addition, suffragists slowly began to recognize the need for a new public image. In response to anti-suffrage propaganda that characterized them as fanatics, and in an effort to attract a larger, more stable membership, suffragists in the first decade of the twentieth century attempted to win respect for their cause and legitimize their organization through a variety of tactics. Their efforts demonstrated a new awareness of the importance of public opinion and marked a turning point in the movement itself. Suffragism of old, shaped by the dedication of a few faithful friends, was to become the movement of the masses, and as such, had to be packaged in a form more attractive to a wider audience.

The Society Plan

Most suffragists believed that the greatest obstacle to woman suffrage was not anti-suffrage opposition or male recalcitrance but rather the indifference of American women. Doubtless many agreed with one anti-suffragist's diagnosis of the problem her opponents faced. "What [the suffrage movement] has to overcome," she explained, "is not an argument but a feeling."[6] Even when this "feeling" manifested itself in overt hostility to the movement, suffrage leaders remained convinced that their foremost task was to exorcise the demon of indifference by converting the apathetic masses to the idea of distaff democracy. And in an age that saw the proliferation of female associations and voluntary societies, it is not surprising that suffrage advocates turned to women's clubs for their organizational model and to society women for the talisman of respectability.

The active recruitment of prominent women by NAWSA officials was not an innovation at the turn of the century; pioneer suffragists had made repeated efforts along those lines throughout the Gilded Age. One of the first successful attempts, however, came in 1893, when Lucy Stone and Carrie Catt attempted to organize the prominent women of Denver, Colorado, according to the "society plan." Although the Colorado Equal Suffrage Association claimed a small but dedicated number of "respectable middle class women," Stone believed that an untapped reservoir of suffrage support existed among wealthy Denver clubwomen. Stone wrote to Den-

Carrie Chapman Catt, c. 1890
UNIVERSITY OF ROCHESTER

ver civic leader Mrs. John R. Hanna, imploring her to make Catt's acquaintance and help her protégée organize the city's leading citizens for suffrage. Hanna duly asked the young suffragist to dinner, and after a long discussion, the two embarked upon an ambitious plan to recruit the city's society women for woman suffrage. Within weeks of their initial meeting, the Denver Equal Suffrage League was formed, composed almost entirely of wealthy clubwomen and socialites. One of the League's first functions, a large public meeting ostensibly in honor of Catt, featured a long list of distinguished speakers from Denver's political and financial circles and was attended by what local suffragists considered the city's "best people." "A most marked result," wrote one Denver suffragist, "was that not one paper in Denver said a word of ridicule or even mild amusement concerning suffragists," and went on to attribute the press's favorable coverage to the presence for the first time of prominent citizens among the suffrage ranks.[7] Moreover, Catt's "society plan" was hailed as the crucial factor in the suffrage referendum in 1893, when Colorado joined Wyoming as the second woman suffrage state.

With her election to the NAWSA presidency in 1900, Catt laid plans to recruit prestigious women of wealth to the suffrage fold at the national level. Initially, most of the NAWSA leadership agreed with Catt's "society plan." Susan B. Anthony, for example, endorsed the idea, and urged NAWSA Corresponding Secretary Rachel Foster Avery to include in the annual convention program a list of all delegates and alternates in order to display prominently the names and addresses of prestigious converts to the cause.[8] Moreover, Catt asked Business Committee members to compile lists of influential clubwomen, ministers and politicians from which to solicit new members, and included well-heeled men as well as society women in her recruitment scheme. Suffragists also sought to win over influential labor and agricultural leaders, and drew up lists of union officials and Grangers for postal propaganda.[9]

In 1904, the Association acknowledged the "society plan" at the annual convention, when the official plan of work for the year recommended that suffragists become active in civic, charitable, or educational work in their communities.[10] Through local clubs and organizations, suffrage advocates could recruit wealthy women with both time and money to devote to the cause. Experience gained in club

work could be turned to account in suffrage societies, enabling suffrage leaders to draw on a ready-made constituency already trained in parliamentary procedure, public speaking and fund-raising. Notably missing in the list of organizations to recruit, however, was the burgeoning Black women's club movement. The unspoken assumption of NAWSA leaders was that the "society plan" was for Whites only.

In addition to recruiting from White civic or charitable organizations, suffragists sought new members through parlor meetings, the traditional form of middle-class female assembly. Held in the privacy of the home, parlor meetings were deemed respectable by even the most modest Victorian women, and served to attract a conservative set that would have blanched at attending a public lecture or rally. One suffrage advocate described her role as a parlor meeting speaker in St. Paul:

> You had these little afternoon gatherings of women, maybe six or eight women. You had a cup of tea. A little social gathering. While we were drinking tea, I gave them a little talk and they asked questions about what was going on.... It was alot [sic] better, I thought at the time, than to have a lecture. Because a lot of them wouldn't go to a lecture. And it was what I could do.[11]

Occasionally, professional suffrage speakers would address parlor gatherings in the afternoon before a major nighttime suffrage rally. In this way advocates could reach both the timid and the bold; suffragists believed that through gradual education, encouragement, and attention to individual sensibilities, even the most timid souls could be transformed into "new women."

Although the days of ridicule experienced by nineteenth-century female reformers had passed, speaking in a public forum remained unthinkable for many women. Through the parlor meeting, elite women could gather in a non-threatening environment to discuss a wide range of topics. Woman suffrage, birth control, municipal reform, and labor conditions found their way into parlor conversations, along with the more traditional subjects of literature, history, and religion. Some women, like those who attended the Monday Club of Richburg, New York, combined the new with the old: on alternating weeks, club members turned their attention from New York history and bird-watching to the history of women and pro-suffrage arguments.[12] The growing interest in nontraditional subjects was reflected in other conservative women's groups like the General Federation of Women's Clubs (GFWC), an organization that refused to endorse woman suffrage until the second decade of the twentieth century. Evidence of this trend was demonstrated by the newly elected president of the GFWC when she informed the biennial convention that:

> Dante is dead. He has been dead for several centuries, and I think it is time that we dropped the study of his Inferno and turned our attention to our own.[13]

NAWSA headquarters in Warren, Ohio, c. 1900 was moved to a new
headquarters on Fifth Avenue in New York City, 1909,
thanks to wealthy patrons who supported suffrage.

FRANK CORBELL COLLECTION (LEFT) AND POSTCARD COLLECTION, LIBRARY OF CONGRESS

By concentrating their efforts on prosperous though conservative women, NAWSA suffragists sought to take advantage of the awakened interest in public affairs manifested by the GFWC and other women's organizations.

Initially, the "society plan" drew applause from many suffragists who had labored unsuccessfully to recruit new members in the past. Active recruitment in the woman suffrage state of Colorado, for example, drew influential women into the crusade and provided workers in non-suffrage states with ammunition with which to refute the negative stereotypes that had plagued the movement. One suffragist told congressmen at the 1904 Judiciary Hearing on Woman Suffrage that a leading anti-suffragist, when introduced to several prominent Colorado women, expressed admiration of their ability and dedication. "As social leaders, as philanthropists, as club women and church women, she had swallowed them whole and found them delicious," the suffragist testified. They only disagreed with her after she knew them also to be suffragists."[14]

While many society women limited their involvement in the suffrage crusade to timely financial support, others played a more important part in the movement. Wealthy New York socialite Mrs. Clarence Mackay, for example, organized her own suffrage league, contributed large sums to the cause, and recruited many of that state's most influential women into the suffrage camp.[15] Virginia's Equal Suffrage League included prominent Virginia writers Ellen Glasgow and Mary Johnston, as well as the great-granddaughters of Thomas Jefferson and George Mason.[16] Name

recognition, handsome contributions, and social prestige were welcome boons to an organization that had borne the stigma of fanaticism for decades.

Though few NAWSA members questioned the strategy that brought such bounty, the "society plan" led a minority to protest. To some suffragists the "society plan" smacked of impropriety and elitism. "I could not help wondering what Lucy Stone would have thought to have seen the Special representative of the cause she gave her life to, promenading in low neck and arms bare to the shoulders at the Governor's reception," one elderly suffragist wrote in despair. "Mrs. [Evelyn H.] Belden worked bravely...according to her ideas of the right way—*the Society Way*—but there are some old workers who do not think that some of the methods tended to elevate the cause."[17] Others, like Harriot Stanton Blatch, chafed under the yoke of gradualism. Blatch characterized the suffrage movement at the turn of the century as "in a rut worn deep and ever deeper," and in 1907 founded the League of Self-Supporting Women in an effort to escape the tedium and elitism embodied in the NAWSA's "society plan."[18] New York Socialists like Ida Crouch Hazlett viewed with apprehension the new emphasis on upper-class status, and spoke out against mainstream suffragists' "snobbish truckling to the women of influence and social position."[19] So pronounced was the effort to woo socialites that one popular periodical labeled the suffrage crusade a "gilt-chair movement" in reference to suffragists' swank gatherings.[20]

Creating a Suffrage Tradition

Though the "gilt-chair movement" offended some, most suffragists believed that their newly won sense of respectability more than compensated for what little criticism the "society plan" generated. And in keeping with the new emphasis on image at the expense of ideological unity, NAWSA leaders took steps to legitimize their organization through the creation of a formal suffrage historical tradition. On a simple level, tradition may be used to legitimize events, groups, or causes by associating them with the rhetoric, rituals, or personalities of an historic past. A political party, for example, may employ tradition to establish a link between its heroic past and its present platform, as in the recurrent allusions to "The Great Emancipator" made by Republicans trolling for Black votes. Used in this way, tradition may represent a series of unspoken assumptions and loyalties, and serve as a symbol of organizational unity.

At a deeper level, however, tradition may mask the varied ideological perspectives of a diverse constituency with what one historian has called its "undefined universality."[21] The trappings of tradition allow leaders to de-emphasize conflicting opinions and ideals by focusing attention on non-controversial rituals and rhetoric. Moreover, the creation or reinterpretation of traditions may help to steer a group or movement away from an unsavory past or a discarded ideology without the discussion or disagreement engendered by the democratic process. A salient characteristic of tradition is that, for all its presumed

foundation in the past, it can be manipulated with singular ease to suit the purposes of the present.

The chief components of the "new" suffrage tradition were a mixture of established, or genuine, rituals, and reinterpreted symbols, rhetoric, and practices that had been customized over time to suit the changing nature of the movement. One of the oldest and most important elements of suffrage tradition was an authorized history of women, with suffrage activism as its focal point. Suffragists had long insisted on the place of women in history. In this regard, nineteenth-century suffrage associations may be considered to have been the first American organizations to promote actively women's history as a discipline. The monumental *History of Woman Suffrage,* begun by Elizabeth Cady Stanton, Susan B. Anthony, and Matilda Joslyn Gage in 1881, was more than propaganda for the cause; to suffrage advocates it filled the void in history textbooks left by the omission of American women.[22] The multi-volume history was continued until the passage of the Nineteenth Amendment in 1920, and remains a testimony to the suffragists' conviction that the women's rights movement deserved a permanent place in history. One of Susan B. Anthony's last acts was to arrange for shipment of the unsold volumes, totaling over ten tons in weight, to NAWSA headquarters, from which the books were distributed to every major library in the country.[23]

The NAWSA showed a commitment to women's history by its efforts to disseminate works on or by women. Beginning in 1902, provisions were made to establish circulating suffrage libraries. These libraries gave women access to the major works on feminist theory and literature, as well as to biographies of famous women and histories of the women's rights movement. The 1903 NAWSA Plan of Work included the compilation of a catalog of woman suffrage literature, to be donated to libraries to encourage the use of such materials. Carrie Chapman Catt showed great enthusiasm for both the catalog and suffrage libraries, and urged each NAWSA suffrage league to appoint a committee on libraries to keep women's history before the public. "Perhaps someday we shall have in the Congressional Library in Washington a story of the work of women...," Catt mused to her friend Alice Stone Blackwell. "We must keep a careful record of our progress for the story is an important one."[24]

Many suffragists shared Catt's vision of the long-term significance of their cause, and despaired over the omission of women from traditional American histories of the period. "There never was another nation with as many parents as we have had," one suffragist wrote in disgust, "but they have all been fathers—Pilgrim Fathers, Plymouth Fathers, Forefathers, Revolutionary Fathers, City Fathers, Church Fathers—fathers of every description but no mothers!"[25] In response to such discontent, Pauline Steinem, chairman of NAWSA's Committee of Education, conducted a rudimentary investigation in 1909 of history and civics textbooks used in the public schools. Steinem wrote to four hundred school superintendents and twenty-six textbook publishing

companies in an attempt to survey educators and publishers on the extent of female representation in history books. Although some responses pointed to a handful of famous women like Martha Washington and Betsy Ross who had found their way into the schoolbooks, most of those surveyed replied that they had never considered the problem at all. Steinem attributed lack of recognition to the "masculine point of view which has dominated civilization," and vehemently protested against the impression conveyed by textbooks "that this world has been made by men and for men."[26]

Steinem's findings, coupled with a growing frustration with "the masculine point of view" as it related to suffragism, led NAWSA officials to take their message directly into the schools in 1910. One plan of attack was the idea of suffrage debates to be held in classrooms across America. The NAWSA initially furnished a packet of debate material at a modest price, including citations for both pro- and anti-suffrage works, but by 1912 debaters could turn to the latest volume in the Debaters Handbook Series, *Selected Articles on Woman Suffrage.*[27] School debates offered an opportunity to educate the young on the role of women in history, as well as attracting free publicity for the movement. As one suffragist pointed out, "get the young people involved and you [also] catch mothers!"[28] The injection of women's history or woman suffrage into the schools, while applauded by suffrage advocates, outraged anti-suffragists. "The woman suffrage question has no place in the schools," one anti-suffrage press release maintained, and went on to insist that as long as parents were divided on the issue, school boards should refrain from tampering with textbooks.[29]

Evolution of American Women

Suffragists' efforts to place women's history, and particularly suffrage history, in classrooms and public libraries reflects the NAWSA's belief in the importance of suffrage recruitment. On the one hand, suffragists' enthusiasm for women's history could be interpreted as the natural desire for self-gratification and glory that a heroic history can bestow upon its participants. Legendary feats and heroine-worship can help to sustain an organization in the face of adversity, and so it was with the suffrage movement. But beyond its capacity to distract and sustain a troubled membership, suffragists used the idea of women's history to provide justification for their cause while simultaneously shaping that history to fit the needs of their movement. In a sense, the suffragists created a "great woman" history that ran parallel to the contemporary historical works that excluded them. And throughout that history runs the recurrent theme of the steady evolution of women toward a egalitarian, if distant, utopia.

Advocates of suffrage did not question the belief that women were subject to the forces of evolution and were making progress throughout the ages. This sense of progress marked the rhetoric of suffrage orators like Anna Howard Shaw, who made repeated references in her speeches to the gains that women had won through

Ida Husted Harper
LIBRARY OF CONGRESS

decades of sacrifice. Shaw told one audience:

> The real reformer does not judge of the reform from the day or of an hour, but traces its progress from the beginning, and no human being with the eye of faith can fail to see traversing the whole progress of our movement a divinity shaping our ends... and that divinity is the gospel of democracy.[30]

Others, like writer Ida Husted Harper, drew on the theory of female evolution in widely circulated articles and pamphlets. In a *North American Review* article, for example, Harper first traced the history of the franchise in America, and pointed out that religious, property, educational, and racial qualifications had all been abandoned for male Americans. She then cited the changing status of women from colonial times to the twentieth century that resulted from hard-won legal reforms and educational advancements. In the area of education Harper found the most conclusive evidence of progress: in 1902, for example, there were more girls than boys enrolled in high, normal, and manual-training schools, and over a third of all college students were female. Moreover, of the total number of college degrees conferred in 1902, almost half went to female graduates. Coupled with statistics on the dramatic rise in the number of women entering the professions, Harper's findings documented the evolution of American women to an audience eager to believe in progress.[31]

From an unenlightened past into a clean, well-lighted future, the women of an unwritten history were made to march, and their suffragist creators made the most of their progress. "Women [of the past] lived in a twilight life, a half-life apart, and looked out and saw men as shadows walking," wrote M. Carey Thomas, president of Bryn Mawr and ardent suffragist:

> Now women have won the right to higher education and to economic independence. The right to become citizens of the State is the next and inevitable consequence of education and work outside the home. We have gone so far; we must go farther. We cannot go back.[32]

If evolution of women and the inevitability of their progress provided the philosophical foundation of early women's history, accounts of educational, legal, and professional advances served as testimonials to the doctrine of female progress.

Women's history as seen by suffragists was comprised of a factual body shaped by an ideologically informed philosophy, or in other words, a content and meaning that were intricately entwined and mutually supportive.

History of this sort was important to the suffrage movement in several ways. First, NAWSA leaders drew from women's, and particularly suffrage, history a tradition of leadership handed down from pioneer suffragists and women's rights activists, canonized in the *History of Woman Suffrage* and hagiographic accounts of the movement's early workers, and imbued with the legacy of a century of heroic struggle. As the lineal successors of Anthony, Stanton, and Stone, twentieth-century leaders found legitimation for their position through the celebration of, and association with, what might be called the "founding mothers" of their organization.

The Creation of Consensus

For the NAWSA rank and file the reinterpreted suffrage tradition bridged the gap between the content and meaning of their history. NAWSA membership rolls contained the names of radical feminists, timid society women, socialists, moderates, and states' rights Southerners; the old adage that "politics makes strange bedfellows" was especially true of the suffrage movement at the turn of the century. Suffragist leaders used both genuine and reinterpreted traditions to bind this diverse constituency together and to create what may be called a movement psychology. Through ritual and pageantry, selected events and individuals were molded into a form of popular history that encapsulated both the pasteurized version of the past and a diluted dose of suffrage ideology.

Perhaps the most revered of all NAWSA traditions centered on the veneration of selected suffrage pioneers. Since the formation of the NAWSA in 1890, a generous part of every convention was dedicated to the movement's early adherents. This celebration of the pioneers took several forms, including memorials for deceased workers, greetings from those too old or too infirm to attend, and tributes from younger members who recognized the contributions of their predecessors. During her years as president, Susan B. Anthony often spoke of the pioneers' achievements, using the time between speakers to recognize informally members of the audience who had served the cause for years. Moreover, her stories of what one suffragist called "the cabbage and rotten-egg days" served to immerse converts in a kind of "living suffrage history," providing both role models and a heroic legacy to inspire the new recruits.[33] Formal recognition for the movement's early advocates was also included in convention programs in the form of "Evenings with the Pioneers," and in 1910, a "Decoration Day for our Heroines" became a permanent suffrage tradition.[34]

NAWSA leaders' interpretation of the suffrage pioneers, however, was strangely reticent about some of their predecessors' more controversial actions. Retaining the philosophy of female progress and the legend of heroism and self-sacrifice,

NAWSA leaders presented to their constituents a sanitized version of the past that robbed the pioneers of much of their color, complexity, and principles. Issues such as divorce reform, racial equality, and feminist religious reinterpretations were quietly dropped from the suffrage liturgy in an effort to pasteurize the pioneer experience. Most notable in this reinterpreted history of the movement was the disappearance from the suffrage canon of none other than Elizabeth Cady Stanton, one of the founders of the Seneca Falls Convention and, with Anthony, a dynamic force in the nineteenth-century suffrage crusade. Although both women worked together for decades and shared many of the same ideas and goals for the movement, Anthony's vision of the cause was more pragmatic and in some ways more limited than that of Stanton. For Anthony, the primary goal of the suffrage crusade was unity with other women's groups to form a broad-based constituency for the vote for women. As time passed, Anthony became convinced that rather than addressing working women's issues in order to bring them into the suffrage fold, it was easier to recruit elite women to the cause. Moreover, their advocacy of suffrage would provoke less hostility among the public and the press.

Stanton shared Anthony's vision of unity, but envisioned the movement as an open platform for any issue that concerned women. Rather than narrowing the focus of the NAWSA to elites, Stanton urged suffragists to "stir up a whole group of new victims from time to time, by turning our guns on new strongholds."[35] True to her word, she had over the years endorsed a variety of reforms considered radical for the time. Divorce reform, feminist revision of the Bible, dress reform, separation of church and state—all were subjects for her pen. Stanton's writings and speeches constantly put forward the notion that once women had the vote, they would use their ballots to enact an explicit political agenda including these and other reforms. Her radicalism can best be seen in her belief that all movements for freedom were linked inextricably, and that suffrage was part and parcel of that radical tradition. Stanton's radicalism, however, was on a collision course with the NAWSA's growing conservatism. By the time of her death in 1902, she was largely eclipsed in suffrage hagiography by the less-threatening image of her old friend Anthony. More importantly, the NAWSA's disavowal of Stanton signaled the narrowing of the movement's goals and constituency that was to be a crucial component of the twentieth-century campaign for the vote.[36]

Building a Suffrage Constituency

A second and equally important suffrage tradition, although similar in some respects to that of the pioneers, was in fact the creation of twentieth-century suffragists. Beginning in 1906, NAWSA conventions regularly featured "College Evenings," events designed to appeal to the young, well-educated recruits who increasingly flocked to suffrage functions. Active recruitment of college women was the brainchild of Boston suffragists Maud Wood Park and Inez Haynes Gillmore. While students at Radcliffe, Park and Gillmore had been initiated into the

The College Evening

OF THE

**Fortieth Annual Convention
of the National American Woman
Suffrage Association**

The College Evening will be held under the
auspices of the Council of the College Equal
Suffrage League, Saturday, October 17, at
8 o'clock. The subject of the evening will be
the claims of equal suffrage on college women

ADDRESSES WILL BE MADE BY

MRS. MAUD MAY WOOD PARK
Graduate of Radcliffe College
and Founder of the League

MISS SOPHRONISBA P. BRECKENRIDGE
Dean of Junior Women's College of
The University of Chicago

MISS CAROLINE LEXOW
Graduate of Barnard College and President of
the New York Branch of the League

MRS. FRANCES SQUIRE POTTER
Professor of English, in the
University of Minnesota

MISS RAY COSTELLOE OF OXFORD, ENGLAND
Graduate of Newnham College
On Equal Suffrage Among English
University Women

MISS M. CAREY THOMAS
President of Bryn Mawr College

Maud Wood Park, 1898	College Days, 1908
LIBRARY OF CONGRESS	LIBRARY OF CONGRESS

suffrage ranks by Massachusetts Woman Suffrage Association (MWSA) president Alice Stone Blackwell. With Blackwell's encouragement, Park and Gillmore founded the Massachusetts College Equal Suffrage League in 1900.[37] Their efforts were so successful that at the NAWSA annual convention in 1906, delegates overwhelmingly voted to establish a national College Equal Suffrage League.

The delegates' enthusiasm for the new organization was in part a result of the first of many NAWSA "College Evenings," held at the Lyric Theater in Baltimore on February 8, 1906. Susan B. Anthony, M. Carey Thomas, and Mary E. Garrett had conceived the idea of such an evening in the fall of 1905, when Anthony, worried that the suffrage convention would not be well received in conservative Baltimore, urged her two co-workers to do what they could "to make [the convention] respectable."[38] The three women planned the event both to involve new workers in the convention program and to "illustrate distinctly the new type of womanhood— the College Woman" as an integral part of their movement. Together they incorporated the disparate yet vital elements of heroism, respectability, and progress into a suffrage tradition that symbolized the new membership, methods, and image of twentieth-century suffragism.

The president of The Johns Hopkins University presided over the 1906 "College Evening," and area college women clad in cap and gown served as ushers for the event. With pioneer suffragists Clara Barton and Julia Ward Howe seated on the podium, an array of college presidents, professors, and deans spoke on the topic, "What has been accomplished for the higher education of women by Susan B. Anthony and other woman suffragists." One by one, the distinguished guests

reminded the audience of the pioneers' achievements, and lauded their efforts to open the doors of higher education for women. "We are indebted to [the pioneer women]," Vassar historian Lucy M. Salmon told the audience, "for making it possible for us to spend our lives in fruitful work rather than in idle tears."[39] Others singled out Susan B. Anthony for special praise. "The women of today," one speaker maintained, "may well feel that it is Miss Anthony who has made life possible for them."[40] By linking the advancement of women's education to the pioneers, and in particular, to pioneer suffragists, College Evening dignitaries firmly bound a new generation of women to the historical continuum of the movement. Moreover, by presenting carefully selected early suffragists in a light that was clearly attractive to a college audience, College Evening speakers attributed to them an inflated influence on a development that was both respectable and popular.

In the years that followed the first College Evening, NAWSA leaders increasingly exploited this pioneer/college connection, and in doing so further steered clear of the radicalism of the movement's origins. According to Maud Wood Park, the purpose of the College Equal Suffrage League was to help college women "realize their debt to the women who worked so hard for them, and to make them understand that one way to pay that debt is to fight the battle in the quarter of the field in which it is still to be won, to make them realize the obligation of opportunity."[41] The "debt to the pioneers" became a kind of suffrage slogan, and was even adopted as the title of a 1907 Boston program to honor long-time suffrage workers. At that event, Park listed in her concluding remarks the names of women's rights activists including Frances Wright, Margaret Fuller, Ernestine Rose, and the Grimké sisters and the dates that they began their agitation, pointing out that many women's colleges were founded at the same time. "It seems to me," Park concluded, "that the so-called higher education, along with many other improvements in the standing of women, owes a heavy debt to the movement which advocated equal rights."[42] The debt to the pioneers would also resurface yearly at NAWSA conventions, as College Evening took its place beside such regular traditions as pioneer memorials and the president's address.

The Suffrage Saint

A third and final suffrage tradition grew out of both College Evening and pioneer memorials, and served as the touchstone of twentieth-century suffrage ideology, rhetoric, and ritual. The creation of this potent symbol occurred over a number of years, but reached fruition in March 1906, with the death of Susan B. Anthony. As past president of the NAWSA and as a representative of pioneer activism, Anthony had attained celebrity status within the movement long before her death. NAWSA conventions were carefully scheduled to coincide with the aging reformer's birthday, and convention-goers could count on lavish celebrations, emotional speeches, and a personal word or two from the celebrity herself. In addition to her appearances at the annual conventions, Anthony had travelled extensively for years

and was well-known to suffragists throughout America, who increasingly viewed her as the living embodiment of their cause. Local fund-raisers often took the form of "Susan B. Anthony Day," and state suffrage convention badges and programs routinely bore her picture.[43] Such was her stature in the movement that during her later years she often witnessed her own apotheosis. In 1903, for example, while dining on bluefish and "diplomate pudding" with a Brooklyn, New York, suffrage league, she heard a series of speeches presented on the topic "Susan B. Anthony: Lessons and Inspirations from Her Life."[44]

Susan B. Anthony

Ida Husted Harper was in part responsible for Anthony's transformation from reviled fanatic to adored leader. Her two-volume biography of the reformer was published in 1898, and provided readers with the day-to-day occurrences of her subject's life in almost Boswellian detail. A third volume, added after Anthony's death, extended the work to more than sixteen hundred pages and included excerpts from over a hundred highly favorable editorials on Anthony that appeared after her death.[45] In addition to her work as a hagiographer, Harper proved to be unsurpassed as a nascent press agent. In keeping with the NAWSA's new emphasis on respectability, she composed an article in 1903 for *Pearson's Magazine* entitled "Miss Anthony at Home" that portrayed the aging suffragist as "domestic in every fiber of her body."[46] With an eye to her prospective female audience, Harper cloaked her subject in the rhetoric of domesticity with such "feminine" attributes as neatness, hospitality, self-sacrifice, patience, and loyalty. According to the article, "Aunt Susan" sat down at the breakfast table looking "like a lovely grandmother," to a meal "strictly of the feminine order." Later she embarked upon a day of womanly pursuits that included cooking, cleaning, and sewing. "Miss Anthony," concluded the article, "never has suggested ways for repairing the damages of society with one-half the skill she employed in teaching her nieces her wonderful method of darning rents in garments and household linens."[47] Through her literary efforts, Harper helped to replace the stereotypical image of masculinized fanatic with a non-threatening feminine heroine imbued with domestic virtues.

The sanctification of Susan B. Anthony, however, was not completed until her death in 1906. At the NAWSA convention of that year, the aging reformer appeared before her devoted disciples for the last time. Her health gone, she exhorted the delegates in a faltering voice to continue in the great work begun at Seneca Falls,

and closed her remarks with the words, "Failure is impossible!" After the convention closed, she traveled to Washington to attend the annual Congressional Hearings but was too ill to leave her bed. Returning for the last time to her home in Rochester, New York, Anthony was attended by her niece and sister, and in her final hours, by Anna Howard Shaw. Profoundly shaken by the loss of her closest friend, Shaw would help to create the most enduring and vital of suffrage traditions: the suffrage saint.[48]

Like Harper, Anna Howard Shaw was uniquely fitted to the role of hagiographer. She met Anthony at a suffrage meeting in 1888, and a lifelong friendship had ensued. Shaw clearly worshipped the older woman. One of her favorite stories featured the seventy-year-old Anthony, wrapped in a dressing gown and talking until dawn, "foreseeing everything, forgetting nothing, and sweeping me with her in her flight toward our common goal until I...experienced an almost dizzy sense of exhilaration."[49] Such was Shaw's devotion that, in her 1915 autobiography, Anthony figures almost as prominently as does the author herself. As both president of the NAWSA and an Anthony disciple, Shaw hurried to Rochester when word came that the end was near. What followed would provide an important source of inspiration for the cult of personality that adopted Anthony as its patron saint.

Deathbed scenes were a popular literary device for turn-of-the-century novelists, and it is therefore not surprising that Shaw chose to record the scene she witnessed in both the periodical press and in her autobiography. Indeed, her vivid description of Anthony's pale visage and prophetic words lend credence to the expression, "life imitates art." Two passages in particular express the motif Shaw sought to capture. On the last afternoon of her life, Anthony suddenly began to recite the names of the women as this "final roll-call...seemed to file past her dying eyes that day in an endless, shadowy review," Shaw wrote, and she quoted Anthony as saying "I know the sacrifices they have made, but it has all been worth while!" With this benediction, Anthony lapsed into silence for a time, but rallied once more in order to assure Shaw that, after death, she would continue to be an active force in the woman suffrage movement. "Who knows?" Anthony speculated, "Perhaps I may be able to do more for the Cause after I am gone than while I am here."[50]

In a sense she was right. Anthony's vision (or Shaw's invention?) of "the shadowy review," coupled with her prophecy of a kind of mystic activism beyond the grave, suggests a type of secular sanctification well-known to readers of sentimental fiction of the period. The theme of suffrage saint was also conspicuous in a selection of poems written about Anthony and published after her death in Volume Three of Harper's biography. "She is not dead but more alive/ than in her fairest earthly days," one poet proclaimed, while another pictured her "with eyes that looked beyond the gates of death" and crowned by a "halo of her venerable age."[51] Perhaps the most explicit example of sanctification was by John Russell Hayes, who poetically recorded Anthony's entry into a supernatural suffrage procession:

And then my vision faded,
And a lordly melody rolled
As down celestial vistas
The saintly company strolled.
But the face of that latest comer
I longest kept in sight—
So ardent with consecration,
So lit with angelic light...
Crowned is she and sainted
In heavenly halls above
Who freely gave for her sisters
A life of boundless love.[52]

On March 15, 1906, the suffrage saint was buried in Rochester, New York. The mayor of Rochester, the president of Rochester University, and other local dignitaries were present, in addition to suffrage and temperance leaders, aging abolitionists, college women, friends, and family members. Despite a heavy snowfall, an estimated crowd of ten thousand assembled outside the church, pressing against the doors and windows in order to hear Anna Howard Shaw's eulogy. Touching briefly upon Anthony's "womanly attributes," she then described her subject's heroism and devotion to the cause. "There is no death for such as she," Shaw concluded, and predicted that "the ages will come to revere her name."[53] When the church doors were opened at the close of the service, crowds of mourners streamed past the body. One mourner in particular caught the attention of some reporters: an elderly Black woman, covered with snow and leaning heavily on a crutch, paused by the coffin and sobbed aloud into a frost-covered handkerchief. Other journalists chose to feature an aged Black man, also limping, who took as a *memento mori* a single leaf from the funeral wreath. The heroic eulogies, patriotic rhetoric and weeping Black spectators reminded some witnesses of another fallen emancipator. Describing the long line of mourners who filed past the body, one observer called them "the plain people, the people Susan B. Anthony and Abraham Lincoln loved." After the long procession had passed, a female honor guard from the university escorted the coffin past houses draped in black to the grave site where Shaw delivered the final words.[54]

In the days that followed, friends worked to ensure a lasting memory for their patron saint. Rochester educators named an elementary school after Susan B. Anthony, a local church commissioned a stained-glass window bearing her likeness, and women's clubs, temperance groups, and civic organizations honored her with memorials. Ida Husted Harper collected over a thousand editorials that eulogized Anthony, including one from the anti-suffrage *New York Times* lauding "the tender, womanly loveliness of the great reformer."[55]

Suffragists across the nation held memorial services similar to the one conducted by the Kentucky Equal Rights Association a week after Anthony's death. Mary Clay, a long-time suffragist and descendant of Henry Clay, "The Great Compromiser," presided over the service that took place in the Clay family home. In the center of the parlor draped in yellow satin and black crepe stood a large picture of Susan B. Anthony, flanked by a small candle in a pink candlestick, a souvenir from the suffrage leader's eightieth birthday celebration. On a nearby table was a smaller portrait of the reformer, surrounded by photographs of Lucy Stone, Elizabeth Cady Stanton, and Isabella Beecher Hooker. After a roll call of pioneer suffragists and a sketch of the reformer's work for women's rights, the assembly heard a series of elegies and a dramatic reading based on Anthony's final days. Following a rosary and benediction, the women sang "Nearer, My God, To Thee" and adjourned for refreshments.[56]

The nature of the Kentucky memorial service closely followed the form routinely employed by literary, church, or civic gatherings of women, but with a suffrage theme. Within this structure, songs, poems, and dramatic readings provided a thread of continuity between old forms and new meanings. The intimate atmosphere of the parlor meeting encouraged participation by women who would have shied away from speaking to a larger audience. Overtones of religious ritual endowed the service with both familiarity and stately respectability in accord with the tastes of the times. The parlor decor approached ecclesiastical parody with its makeshift altar and display of icons. In addition, the service followed a quasi-liturgical pattern, employing both poetic and prose readings and ending with the litany of the rosary and the benediction.

Kentucky suffragists also shaped the memorial service to suit the private agenda of their movement. Tradition played an important role: the veneration of the pioneers, the idea of a parallel women's history, and the philosophy of female progress were all incorporated into the ceremony. In her posthumous role, Susan B. Anthony became what no living woman could be: a universally shared symbol of the cause whose very name could conjure a constellation of images and sentiment. Across the nation clubwomen and suffragists met for similar services.[57] Within a decade Anthony had become, like Lincoln and Altgeld before her, part of the common mental property of Progressive Americans. Her picture was hung beside those of the Founding Fathers' in schoolrooms across America, her memory achieving a measure of the vague immortality accorded to the heroes of American democracy. In 1917, for example, Eugene V. Debs characterized her as "synonymous with the cause of human freedom and equal rights,…a moral heroine, an apostle of progress, a herald of the coming day."[58]

The Formation of a Female Political Culture

Mary Clay's memorial service, with its quaint sentimentality and solemn naiveté, summons up a lost world of women, conceived within the pages of

popular fiction of the period, adorned with the trappings of Victorian respectability, and bound by parlor walls. Although trivial when compared to the larger course of world affairs, it reminds us that political participation for women at the turn of the century was not accomplished merely by the conversion of Congress or the ratification of an amendment. Instead, women entered the political arena through a lengthy process that included such seemingly apolitical institutions as historical biography, sentimental fiction and parlor meetings, as well as more familiar processes of state referenda campaigns, lobbyist activity, and direct political coercion. It would be unjust to downplay the early efforts of women's political organization. Given the high degree of female participation in Progressive Era movements like temperance, child-labor reform, and civic betterment crusades, the timid parlor meetings of the 1900 to 1910 period should be seen as the training ground for many Progressive activists.

Thus by 1910 the visionary cause of the pioneers had been transformed into an eminently safe program for middle-class club meetings. This stage of development, which first brought a wealthy, "respectable" class of women into comfortable participation in suffrage, was seen by NAWSA leaders as a necessary precondition of the movement that would eventually win the vote. For better or worse, these middle-class leaders could not conceive of conducting a successful campaign without the approval and the financial support of the social elite.

NAWSA benefactor Alva Vanderbilt Belmont often hosted gatherings of suffragists at Marble House, her opulent "summer house" in Newport, RI, 1914.
RECORDS OF THE NATIONAL WOMAN'S PARTY, LIBRARY OF CONGRESS

As tangible proof of the wisdom of their strategy, leaders of the NAWSA could point to a dramatic increase in support for their reform. Membership rolls soared from about 12,000 in 1906, the year of Anthony's death, to over 117,000 in 1910. After 1910, a widescale organizational scheme was put into effect, and a corps of dedicated organizers largely drawn from the ranks of college-educated women was active throughout the country. Moreover, by 1914 a professional lobby was at work to push the federal amendment through Congress. This expanded effort was fueled by an ample treasury; in 1916, for example, the NAWSA's operational budget stood at $100,000 annually. The suffrage political strategy, based on the precondition of a respectable image, had paid high dividends and was the foundation of their victory in 1920.

In a few years' time, NAWSA leaders had built a solid political base for suffrage by attracting into the movement large numbers of women who previously were uninvolved in politics. They had accomplished this by giving a political meaning to traditional forms of female assembly, organization, and entertainment. For the women involved, the familiar surroundings and rituals legitimized and demystified the alien world of political action. Anti-suffrage propaganda and the unflattering stereotype of nineteenth-century suffragists had hammered home the proposition that femininity and politics could never mix. In the first decade of the new century, however, a generation of women drew a different message from what they soon would call the "suffrage ideal." Women who had always been excluded from political participation were drawn, not to party affiliations, bosses, and smoke-filled rooms, but rather to a new kind of political activity: active membership in a reform or single-interest pressure group. Scholars who lament the decline of popular political participation in the Progressive Era fail to take into account this shift from party affiliation to interest group loyalty. In fact, movements like suffrage, temperance, child-labor reform, and other Progressive causes involved and included vast numbers of people who had had no part in the political process during the hey day of the parties, yet were involved in a popular politics of their own making.

In the first decade of the twentieth century, suffrage leaders set out to create a new image for their movement. Their basic goal was to forge a notion of women's history and female progress that could be accepted as consonant with the wider aspirations of mainstream society. In a sense they banished the radical past, turned their back on nonconformity, and in the process captured the support of quietly influential groups of women. Gone was the taint of extremism that suffragists believed had haunted the movement for decades; the parlor meeting had adopted "Aunt Susan" as its patron saint, and suffragism had come of age.

Notes

This article is drawn from the author's book, *Woman Suffrage and the New Democracy*, published posthumously by Yale University Press in 1996.

1. Eleanor Flexner, *Century of Struggle: The Woman's Rights Movement in the United States*, (1959; Cambridge, Mass., 1975), 256.

2. Ibid., 230.

3. James J. Kenneally, "Woman Suffrage and the Massachusetts Referendum of 1895," *The Historian* 30 (August, 1968): 620-623.

4. Susan B. Anthony and Ida Husted Harper, eds., *History of Woman Suffrage*, vol. 4 (1883-1900; reprint, New York, 1969), 735-737 (hereafter cited as *HWS*); and Kenneally, "Woman Suffrage and the Massachusetts Referendum of 1895," 625.

5. Ibid., 630. In *HWS*, Alice Stone Blackwell's account of the 1895 referendum emphasizes the positive aspects of the contest.

6. Priscilla Leonard, "The Ladies Battle," *Current Literature* 36 (April, 1904): 386-389.

7. Minnie Reynolds to Alice Stone Blackwell, December 12, 1930, National American Woman Suffrage Association Papers (hereafter cited as NAWSA), Reel 17, Library of Congress (hereafter cited as LC).

8. Susan B. Anthony to Rachel Foster Avery, January 22, 1900, Papers of Susan B. Anthony, Reel 1, LC.

9. Carrie Chapman Catt to Catherine Waugh McCullough, August 8, 1900, Dillon Collection, Box 9, Schlesinger Library, Radcliffe College, (hereafter cited as SL).

10. *Proceedings of the Thirty-Sixth Annual Convention of the National American Woman Suffrage Association, 1904*, 14-15; *Current Literature* 36 (April, 1904): 386-389.

11. Sherna Gluck, ed. *From Parlor To Prison: Five American Suffragists Talk About Their Lives* (New York, 1976); Calendar for 1912, NAWSA, Reel 48, LC.

12. Monday Club of Richburg, New York, Calendar for 1912, NAWSA, Reel 48, LC.

13. Quoted in Gluck, *From Parlor To Prison*, 12-13.

14. House Committee on the Judiciary Hearing on Woman Suffrage, February 16, 1904, Statement of Mary C.C. Bradford, Women's Rights Collection, Folder 42, SL.

15. Carrie Chapman Catt to Mrs. Millicent Garrett Fawcett, October 19, 1909, Carrie Chapman Catt Papers, Reel 3, LC.

16. See Dorothy Scura, "Ellen Glasgow and Women's Suffrage," *Research in Action* 6 (Spring 1982): 12-15. For Mary Johnston, see Elizabeth D. Coleman, "Penwoman of Virginia's Feminists," *Virginia Cavalcade* 6 (Winter 1956): 8-11; and Marjorie Spruill (Wheeler), "Mary Johnston, Suffragist," *Virginia Magazine of History and Biography* 100 (January 1992): 99-118.

17. Margaret Campbell to Henry B. Blackwell, May 14, 1900, NAWSA Reel 5, LC.

18. Harriot Stanton Blatch and Alma Lutz, *Challenging Years: The Memoirs of Harriot Stanton Blatch*, (New York, 1940), 91-92.

19. *New York Call*, March 11, 1917. Quoted in Mari Jo Buhle, *Women and American Socialism, 1870-1920* (Urbana, Ill., 1983), 225.

20. *Literary Digest* 36 (February 29, 1908): 290-292.

21. For a detailed discussion of tradition and its uses, see Eric Hobsbawm and Terence Ranger, eds., *The Invention of Tradition* (Cambridge, 1983), 1-12.

22. Ida Husted Harper, *History of Woman Suffrage* vol. 5 (Reprint, New York, 1969): 228.

23. *HWS* 5: 204-206. Anthony's interest in placing the work is documented in Ida Husted Harper, *The Life and Work of Susan B. Anthony*, 3 vols., (Indianapolis, 1898 and 1908), 1278-1279.

24. Carrie Chapman Catt to Alice Stone Blackwell, November 6, 1908, Carrie Chapman Catt Papers, Reel 2, LC.

25. Speech by Anna Howard Shaw, "The Fate of the Republic," (1892) Dillon Collection, Folder 499, SL. "That is where the weakness of every Republic lies," Shaw continued, "they have been fathered to death."

26. *HWS* 5: 263.

27. Edith M. Phelps, ed., *Selected Articles on Woman Suffrage, Debaters Handbook Series*, (Minneapolis, 1912).

28. Mary Gray Peck, Report of the Headquarters Secretary, quoted in *HWS* 5: 266-268.

29. Press Release, "Anti Suffrage News and Comment" (n.d.), issued by New York State Association Opposed Women's Suffrage, Folder 2, SL.

30. Speech by Anna Howard Shaw to the NAWSA Convention, April 14, 1910, Women's Rights Collection, Folder 514, SL.

31. Ida Husted Harper, "Why Women Cannot Vote in the United States," *North American Review* 179 (July, 1904): 30-35.

32. Pamphlet by M. Carey Thomas, "A New Fashioned Argument for Woman Suffrage," (October 17, 1908) Women's Rights Collection, Folder 730, SL.

33. Volume 5 of *HWS* devotes ample coverage to the pioneers in its chapters on the annual conventions. For the quotation, see *HWS* 5: 123.

34. Anna Howard Shaw, Letter to "Progress," (March, 1910) Dillon Collection, Box 22, SL. For examples of pioneer celebrations, see *HWS* 5: 30-31 and 219-220.

35. Ellen Carol DuBois, *Elizabeth Cady Stanton/Susan B. Anthony: Correspondence, Writings, Speeches* (New York, 1981), 226.

36. Not only were Stanton's more radical activities omitted from the suffrage pioneer tradition, but her role in founding the American women's rights movement was also forgotten. According to historian Ellen DuBois, Stanton's papers were not collected and she found no biographer until 1940. See DuBois, *Elizabeth Cady Stanton/Susan B. Anthony…*, 191-192.

37. Maud Wood Park, "The College Equal Suffrage League: Introductory notes," (1942), Women's Rights Collection, Folder 696, SL; *HWS* 5: 660-662.

38. *HWS* 5: 167; and Anna Howard Shaw, *The Story of a Pioneer* (New York, 1915), 221-223.

39. *HWS* 5: 170.

40. Ibid., 171.

41. Maud Wood Park, "Address to the 28th Annual Convention of NAWSA, College Night," February 8, 1906, Women's Rights Collection, Folder 855, SL.

42. Typescript of *Woman's Journal* article, "Debt to the Pioneers," March 30, 1907, Women's Rights Collection, Folder 855, SL. For examples of this theme, see *HWS* 5: 173 and 226.

43. *HWS* 5: 1373; *Life and Work of Susan B. Anthony*, 1355.

44. Program, Kings County Political Equality League, Brooklyn, New York, February 14, 1903, NAWSA, Reel 26, LC.

45. Harper, *The Life and Work of Susan B. Anthony*.

46. *Pearson's Magazine* March, 1903. Excerpts from this article also appear in Harper, *Life and Work of Susan B. Anthony*, 1298-1304.

47. Ibid., 1295-1304.

48. Ellen DuBois used the term "suffrage saint" in reference to Anthony in a conversation with the author in 1986.

49. Anna Howard Shaw, *The Story of a Pioneer*, 189-190.

50. Ibid., 232-234.

51. Harper, *Life and Work of Susan B. Anthony*, 1604 and 1606-1607.

52. Ibid., 1607-1610.

53. Anna Howard Shaw, "Address at Memorial Service for Susan B. Anthony," March 15, 1906, Dillon Collection, Box 22, SL.

54. Accounts of the Anthony funeral are drawn from Shaw, *Story of a Pioneer*, 235-238; and Harper, *Life and Work of Susan B. Anthony*, 1429-1444.

55. *New York Times*, March 18, 1906. Clipping in the Breckinridge Family Papers, Box 700, LC.

56. Notes from KERA Memorial Service for Susan B. Anthony by Mary Clay, March 22, 1906, NAWSA, Reel 5, LC.

57. For example, see Program, ERA Club Memorial Service for Susan B. Anthony, May 8, 1906, NAWSA, Reel 26, LC.; and Program, "A Meeting of Appreciation of the Life and Work of Susan B. Anthony," Interurban Political Equality Council of Greater New York, April 1, 1906, NAWSA, Reel 26, LC.

58. Eugene V. Debs, "Susan B. Anthony: Pioneer of Freedom," *Pearson's Magazine* (July, 1917). Copy in NAWSA, Reel 26, LC.

Jane Addams, c. 1896

By this time, the famed Progressive reformer had founded Hull House, a settlement house in a working-class immigrant neighborhood in Chicago, where she and other middle-class reformers lived along with the people they sought to aid. As Jane Addams explained later, they sought to "provide a center for a higher civic and social life, to institute and maintain educational and philanthropic enterprises, and to investigate and improve the conditions in the industrial districts in Chicago."– Addams, *Twenty Years at Hull-House*.

Thirteen

JANE ADDAMS, PROGRESSIVISM, AND WOMAN SUFFRAGE:

An Introduction to
"Why Women Should Vote"
Victoria Bissell Brown

"Why Women Should Vote"
Jane Addams

Editor's Introduction: In the passage that follows, historian Victoria Bissell Brown illuminates for us one of the most popular and influential pro-suffrage documents written during the long campaign for woman suffrage, Jane Addams's "Why Women Should Vote." Brown, author of *The Education of Jane Addams,* a biography of the revered Progressive reformer and suffragist, discusses the popularity of Addams's essay and analyzes it in the context of Progressive reform philosophy and pro-suffrage rhetoric.

An understanding of the Progressive movement and its relationship to woman suffrage as explained by one of the movement's luminaries is crucial to our understanding of the success of the woman suffrage movement. For of all the factors leading to the victory in 1920, the emergence around 1900 of this new era of reform—the "Progressive Era"—is one of the most important.

Progressivism, which energized American politics until World War I, began at the grassroots level and strongly affected American politics at all levels—including both major political parties. Indeed, in 1912, Progressives in the Republican Party bolted and formed the "Progressive Party" with Theodore Roosevelt as their candidate, after the Republicans chose to back President William Howard Taft for re-election. Roosevelt and Taft then lost to Woodrow Wilson, the Progressive politician nominated by the Democrats.

This reform zeal arose in response to the many ills that plagued American society in the last half of the nineteenth century as a result of massive industrialization, urbanization, and immigration. Progressives insisted that the hands-off, non-interventionist style of government demanded by conservatives, while appropriate, perhaps, for a rural, agrarian society, was no longer adequate in a new era in which an individual's pursuit of happiness brought him or her

constantly into conflict with others, when large corporations ran roughshod over smaller businesses and exploited workers without restraint, and large numbers of people lived in close proximity in cities without adequate provision for sanitation, disease control, or recreation. Progressives demanded that government—from municipal to federal—*take action* on a variety of fronts, including (to name a few): regulating corporations to protect workers and consumers; safeguarding public health; banning child labor; establishing compulsory education, juvenile courts and public playgrounds; and reforming government to make it more responsible, accountable, and free of corruption.

The Progressive coalition included a diverse group of people determined to remedy the social evils produced by unrestrained capitalism but not always in agreement about solutions. In fact, Progressivism was riddled with contradictions. For example, Progressives generally supported democratic reforms including the secret ballot, the nomination of candidates by primaries rather than meetings in "smoke-filled rooms," and the direct election of United States Senators by the voters rather than the state legislatures. But some Progressives, believing that corrupt urban political machines were manipulating the "ignorant immigrant vote," favored undemocratic reforms such as literacy tests to eliminate the uneducated from the electorate. Most Progressives were middle class, and many patronizingly believed that the working class needed to be protected more than empowered: they believed that citizens like themselves should shape social policy out of a sense of noblesse oblige.

Progressivism aided the woman suffrage movement in several ways. New ideas about the functions of government were more in line with old ideas about woman's nature and abilities: a government that was expected to nurture and protect and arbitrate conflicts rather than focus exclusively on national defense and economic development might benefit from woman's presumably innate characteristics and domestic experience. In addition, public support for woman suffrage grew as a result of the widespread belief that women—if enfranchised—would support Progressive reforms because they were more moral, compassionate, and nurturing than men. People also assumed that woman suffrage would be a boon to Progressivism because hundreds of thousands of women were clearly demonstrating their support for Progressive reform as lobbyists and political activists. Indeed, many of these reform-minded women were converted to the suffrage movement out of frustration when politicians failed to take their lobbying seriously and/or opposed the reforms they supported. Like the women of the WCTU before them, women Progressives—and their male supporters—believed that they would be much more effective if women were able to vote rather than rely exclusively upon "indirect influence."

Suffragists recognized the advantages offered by this political climate. As the previous essay by Sara Hunter Graham demonstrates, early twentieth-century suffragists were eager to avoid the taint of radicalism, to counter the anti-suffragists'

claim that suffrage was unwomanly, and to link their movement with popular ideas. Indeed, though suffragists never ceased to argue for woman suffrage on the grounds that it was *right* and *just* and due to them as citizens of the United States, they were at all times searching for ways to persuade politicians that enfranchising women was politically *expedient.*

In the Progressive Era, rather than arguing against the idea of separate spheres, suffragists typically proclaimed that woman suffrage was completely compatible with woman's traditional duties. They often argued that, as a result of industrialization and urbanization, women were no longer able to protect their homes and children without the vote! Some suffragists, either believing in women's innate differences from men or pandering to this popular supposition, insisted that women would *naturally* support the new nurturing role many believed government should adopt. As one widely used suffrage poster stated: "Women are by nature and training housekeepers. Let them help in the city housekeeping. They will introduce an occasional spring cleaning."

As Victoria Brown explains, Jane Addams's "Why Women Should Vote" is in some ways consistent with and in other ways different from the prevailing usage of Progressive ideology in pro-suffrage rhetoric. Addams's essay is extremely important as one of the strongest statements of the argument that changed conditions *require* women to vote in order to continue to fulfill their traditional functions. Publishing this powerful endorsement of woman suffrage as inextricably linked to Progressivism was of inestimable value to the suffrage cause—the seal of approval from America's best-loved Progressive.

Brown insists, however, that Addams—though a leading suffragist—was not necessarily typical of suffragists and did not focus her political energies primarily on this cause. In fact, she presented woman suffrage as of crucial importance primarily as an *implement* through which women could more effectively reach their political goals, a way for women to assert their political values while still fulfilling their traditional functions.

Brown defends Addams against charges that have been leveled against her by some historians, accusations that she pandered to popular ideas and prejudices. For example, Brown rejects the idea that Addams "grounded her suffrage reasoning in biological essentialism." Rather, Brown insists, Addams believed that whatever differences existed in the political values of men and women were attributable to women's *experience,* not innate habits or instincts. Furthermore, Addams did not employ the nativist, elitist, or racist arguments embraced by some suffragists. Brown insists that Addams was a woman of principle, and that this essay is a sincere statement of her Progressive reform philosophy—not mere suffrage propaganda.

Still, Brown concedes that Jane Addams was a brilliant strategist and a habitual diplomat, owing to her desire to avoid conflict and promote harmony. In this and other works, writes Brown, Addams astutely presented woman suffrage as

inevitable given the new focus of government in the Progressive Era. Many a suffragist would follow her lead, presenting suffrage as something women were *compelled* to embrace given changed historical circumstances rather than the result of woman's desire for equality and power. "If there was any guile in Addams's pro-suffrage position," writes Brown, "this was surely it."

Yet Brown's emphasis here is on the sincerity of Addams's essay. The power of the essay, she argues, was in the neat fit between Addams's focus on the connection between suffrage and reform and the appeal of Progressivism. That the essay was so popular was a testimony to Addams's "unusual ability" to weave her Progressive concerns "into a pro-suffrage argument that appealed to mainstream sensibilities without bowing to mainstream prejudices."

★   ★   ★   ★   ★

IN THE YEARS between 1900 and 1915, close to two hundred articles appeared in popular American magazines concerning American woman suffrage. In the year 1910 alone, the interested American reader could sample some twenty-five articles on the subject. Perched at the top of this stack of articles for and against and about woman suffrage sits Jane Addams's editorial, "Why Women Should Vote," published in the January 1910 edition of *The Ladies' Home Journal*. Of all the popular articles on suffrage that appeared in these years, Addams's has probably been reprinted the most often, quoted the most regularly, cited the most frequently. The modern reader must ask, has this pro-suffrage essay received such attention over the years simply because it was written by the most famous woman of her day or because it best reflects the era's pro-suffrage ideology? Are the arguments Addams put forth in *The Ladies' Home Journal* unique to her or representative of the dozens of pro-suffrage articles Americans were reading in these years?

The answers to all of those questions are "yes." The article has, of course, received special attention because of Jane Addams's fame. But Addams's fame was due in no small part to her ability to craft popular articles that resonated with strong currents in public opinion while still marking out a unique philosophical position. Scholars have not always appreciated this particular talent in Jane Addams, nor have they always looked favorably on Addams's position in "Why Women Should Vote" that women "need this implement in order to preserve the home."

Back in the 1970s, when scholars of women were measuring every text by the single ideological yardstick of "liberal" feminism, Jane Addams's pro-suffrage argument appeared to fall short because she did not put the classical liberal emphasis on women's individual right to the vote. At that time, it was thought that her embrace of women's traditional domestic role in this *Ladies' Home Journal* essay, along with her focus on the social good women could perform with the vote, consti-tuted an accommodation to, even a pandering to, popular gender politics.[1] Current scholarship, however, allows for a new reading of "Why Women Should Vote." This

scholarship reminds us that women's progress depends as much on "republican" commitments to the common good as on "liberal" rights and individual autonomy. Read in the light of contemporary research on female culture and moral values, Addams's assumption that women speak "in a different voice" appears to be more a positive assertion of the need for that particular ideological voice in politics than a capitulation to existing notions of women's innate moral nature.[2] Read, too, in light of the work of current historical research on women reformers in the Progressive Era, Jane Addams's focus on women's collective duty to reform (rather than their individual right to autonomy) in "Why Women Should Vote" appears to be more a reflection of the political climate unique to the Progressive Era, and more a function of the very particular emphasis Addams placed on economic democracy, than an accommodation to conservative nostalgia for selfless womanhood.[3]

Understanding "Why Women Should Vote" requires understanding that Jane Addams's central political goal was the legislative enactment of a Progressive social agenda, including protective labor legislation, health and welfare programs, educational reform, and legal equity for Blacks and immigrants. When she said that woman suffrage was an "implement" women needed to "preserve the home," she was saying that she regarded the achievement of the Progressive agenda as essential to the preservation of the homes of millions of poor and working-class Americans. Further, she was saying that woman suffrage was crucial to enacting that agenda because women occupied the homes that needed preserving and, therefore, were most likely to support Progressive reform. It was this set of assumptions that motivated her active support for woman suffrage and that shaped the arguments she crafted for woman suffrage.

Placed alongside the other pro-suffrage articles published at the time, "Why Women Should Vote" thus appears to be quite representative of the pro-reform, "Progressive" mood dominant in American political life in 1910. And in being representative of Progressives, Addams appears unique among suffrage leaders. Her devotion to improving the lives of the working class by creating an interdependent polity as responsive to domestic as to commercial needs meant that questions of women's particular situation were subordinated, in her writing, to questions of women's duty to demand expansion of the nation's entire political agenda. Whatever readers today may think of this approach, its popularity at the time may be detected in the fact that a year after this essay appeared in *The Ladies' Home Journal*, Addams was elected to a vice presidency in the National American Woman Suffrage Association (NAWSA).

Close inspection of "Why Women Should Vote" suggests that Jane Addams's popularity derived not only from her Progressive concern for economic and political democracy, but from her unusual ability to weave that concern with her own mediating temperament, diplomatic style, and genuine respect for domesticity into a pro-suffrage argument that appealed to mainstream sensibilities without bowing to mainstream prejudices. "Why Women Should Vote," is, first and

foremost then, a statement of Jane Addams's Progressive reform philosophy. As such, the essay serves to inform our understanding of the ways in which woman suffrage and Progressivism were mutually reinforcing movements in the early twentieth century and the role Addams played in linking the success of one movement to the success of the other.

Jane Addams and Progressive Era Reform

When Jane Addams wrote "Why Women Should Vote" in 1910, she was fifty years old and enjoying a decade, 1905-1915, that would mark the peak of her power and influence in America. Four years before her pro-suffrage essay appeared in *The Ladies' Home Journal*, an article on Addams in *Current Literature* was published with the title, "The Only Saint America Has Produced." And in the year following her *Ladies' Home Journal* essay, when *The Independent* asked its readers to name "the most useful Americans," Addams was ranked second, behind Thomas Edison but ahead of Andrew Carnegie. Indeed, when *The Ladies' Home Journal* invited Addams to write "Why Women Should Vote," the magazine itself was on record in opposition to woman suffrage. Still, it gave Addams space to make a case for suffrage that was bound to be very appealing to *Journal* readers, and, three years later, hired her to write a monthly column on civic matters. The *Journal* introduced that column with the claim that "no woman in America today is so closely in touch with those great social and economic movements that are outside the home and yet vitally touch the home as Jane Addams." [4]

Addams had launched her reform career by opening, in 1889, the second, and by far the most famous, social settlement house in the United States, Hull House on Halstead Street in Chicago. The settlement began as one building, but by 1910 it comprised thirteen buildings encircling an entire square block of a working-class, immigrant neighborhood on Chicago's west side. Addams's settlement served as a meeting place for political activists, workers, students, immigrants, women's groups, unionists, artists and reformers, children and teenagers. It served as well as a catalyst for social legislation, political reform, social science theory, and labor organizing at the city, state, and national levels. Until her death in 1935, Jane Addams presided as the calm center of the storm that was Hull House, attracting extraordinarily gifted, innovative people around her and adroitly leading them in the development of all the sorts of social service programs and legislative agendas that have come to typify the "Progressive Era" of the 1890s and early 1900s.

Because of her close ties to the University of Chicago during that institution's glory years around the turn of the century, Addams is often called the founder of the academic discipline of social work. She was by nature more a sociologist than a social worker, however, and with the eye of a sociologist—and the voice of a kind and tactful but brutally honest aunt—she delivered thousands of speeches both in the United States and around the world, wrote over a dozen books, and published over five hundred articles for magazines and journals ranging from *The Ladies' Home*

Journal to the *Annals of the American Academy of Political and Social Sciences*. She was active with labor unions in strike mediation and labor legislation, was a founding member of the NAACP, served on the Chicago School Board, was the paid garbage inspector for her ward (the only paid position she ever held), staged unsuccessful political campaigns against corrupt ward bosses, worked on state programs for the criminal and the insane, was president of the National Conference of Charities and Corrections, and, as noted, served as a vice president of the National American Woman Suffrage Association from 1911 until 1914. Addams was a leading figure in Teddy Roosevelt's Progressive Party, becoming in 1912 the first American woman to give a nominating speech at a presidential political convention. In the course of her career, she traveled to every continent as a distinguished visitor, sat on countless boards and advisory committees, and counseled presidents, governors, mayors, senators, and congressmen as well as leaders of anarchist, socialist, feminist, immigrant, African American, and labor organizations.

Finally, Jane Addams was a peace activist who held out against supporting America's participation in World War I and formed, in protest, the Women's International League for Peace and Freedom. This unpopular political stance, the only political stance she ever adopted that was completely out of sync with her times, transformed Addams from a beloved American icon into public enemy number one. Almost fifteen years after the war was over, however, in 1931, Addams's on-going peace activism was vindicated when she became the first American woman to win the Nobel Peace Prize. But during the interim years, when she was vilified as a dangerous subversive, her critics published elaborate "spider web" charts on which they demonstrated that Jane Addams was the secret link connecting every reform and radical group in the country. Whatever we may now think of her critics' politics, we have to concede to the accuracy of their claim: Jane Addams was the secret link connecting every reform and radical group in the country in the years between 1890 and her death in 1935.[5]

The Appeal of Jane Addams

There were myriad reasons for Addams's enduring stature, not the least among them her ability to write about contentious public issues like woman suffrage in a persuasive but non-argumentative voice. Her argument for woman suffrage in *The Ladies' Home Journal* of 1910 is an excellent example of her unique stylistic ability to disarm opponents by gliding past fundamental disagreements, presuming shared goals, focusing almost entirely on the great good to be gained, and ignoring the position that was to be defeated. Though she herself would detest a military analogy, the contemporary reader cannot help but picture Addams striding untouched through battlefields where her comrades were engaged in bloody combat, always pointing to the hill that was to be captured and paying little heed to the enemy all around. Indeed, she was a master at occupying the enemy's ground. Her argument in "Why Women Should Vote" that the suffrage would help, not

hurt, the home was not unusual; plenty of other suffragists made the same case. But other suffragists made this, and other arguments, in a contentious way, directly attacking the antis' claim that woman suffrage would destroy the home. Addams, by contrast, never once mentioned that opponents of woman suffrage claimed to be preserving the home. She simply refused to contend that point and thus rose above the fray. This was vintage Addams.

A non-confrontational style is not the only feature distinguishing Jane Addams's approach in "Why Women Should Vote." There is, as well, her targeted deployment of woman suffrage as part of the Progressive assault on Gilded Age greed in politics and the economy, and there is her careful derivation of female values from history and experience, not biology and intuition. But in order to appreciate fully Addams's idiosyncratic handling of these issues and their relationship to woman suffrage, it is perhaps useful to examine first some of the popular magazine articles on suffrage appearing contemporaneously with "Why Women Should Vote."

Popular Suffrage Arguments of the Day

A chronological survey of articles published between 1900 and 1915 makes several points quite clear: first, that pro-suffrage arguments were one half of an active, national debate with anti-suffrage arguments, and both sides in that debate were shaped by the other. Second, suffragists and anti-suffragists alike had, by 1900, moved away from the broad philosophical debates over women's "rights" and "female nature" that typified the latter half of the nineteenth century. The debate after 1900 centered on more prosaic discussions of whether the majority of women actually wanted the vote and whether women's votes would actually bring about the benefits to Progressive reform that suffragists claimed. It is here that another point comes clear, and that is the extent to which woman suffrage had become linked in the public mind with the Progressive movement for political and economic reform, but also the degree to which it was easier for conservatives to attack woman suffrage than to attack Progressive reform. Anti-suffragists never openly opposed woman suffrage on the grounds that women voters would enact reform; rather, they tried to argue that woman suffrage was irrelevant to reform. This development in the debate was partially rooted in the peculiarities of United States suffrage history, which was distinguished by women's state-by-state, city-by-city acquisition of voting rights. The discussion of suffrage in popular magazines was, thus, not occurring in a political vacuum; it was all being conducted while women were actually going to the polls and voting in an increasing number of states and in dozens of municipalities. As the aged reformer Julia Ward Howe pointed out in 1909, concrete events meant that the whole question of woman suffrage had become entirely practical.[6]

Given the gradual accretion of women's voting rights in the United States, it is hardly surprising to find that over a third of the fifty articles surveyed for this essay were devoted to descriptions of woman suffrage campaigns, debates over whether

woman suffrage in Colorado or Wyoming or Idaho or Utah had achieved the Progressive benefits suffragists predicted, and arguments over whether women were actually going to the polls. By the first decade of the twentieth century, the time for philosophical debates about female nature and women's rights had pretty much passed.

This is not to say that the suffragists never mounted a principled argument for their position in popular magazines. On the contrary, the magazine evidence strongly supports the claim by historian Paula Baker that "the suffragists made every conceivable argument, from equal rights to home protection to the need for an intelligent electorate."[7] But what is interesting here is not that one pro-suffrage article would argue for equal rights while another would argue for home protection. The most striking characteristic of the popular pro-suffrage literature of the day is that within a single article could be found the whole array of justifications possible for woman suffrage.

So we find suffragists like Frank Parsons arguing on one page of *The Arena* in 1908 that "sex has nothing to do with the reasons on which the suffrage rests," and arguing two pages later that "women have a higher regard for principle than men...their gentleness, sympathy, refinement and incorruptibility are sadly needed in our politics." Or Rosamond Sutherland, another pro-suffrage writer, arguing in a 1910 issue of *North American Review* that "the emancipation of women is a natural evolution which can no more be stopped than the tides of the sea," while at the same time arguing that "woman is instinctively a home-maker," and the vote would not wash away that apparently non-evolving fact. Or the editors of *The Independent* asserting in 1915 that "partial suffrage—the suffrage of men alone—is a denial of democracy. Democracy will never be full and complete until every individual in the community has an equal right to determine how the affairs of the community shall be managed," and, in the same article, also asserting that "women, by the very nature of their being,...are experts on certain vital subjects.... Women have different qualities of mind from men. Men are...reasoning beings. Women are creatures of intuition."[8]

None of the authors of these articles worried about the inconsistencies now detectable in their positions; they slipped and slid easily from democratic principle to practical politics to biological determinism. As Julia Ward Howe said in 1909, "the fundamental argument for woman suffrage, of course, is its justice; and this would be enough were there no other. But a powerful argument can also be made for it from the standpoint of expediency."[9]

This "flexibility" in the pro-suffrage position allowed considerable room for volleying with the anti-suffragists. When the antis argued that women should rely on men for protection, not the ballot, the wealthy widow and suffrage militant Alva Belmont retorted that experience proved women could most definitely not rely on men for protection. When the antis argued that politics was a dirty, bloody battlefield that would soil and injure women, the suffrage

movement's most prodigious publicist Ida Husted Harper said that politics should be a cooperative effort, not a bloody battle. And in mock sympathy for the adversarial mess she said men had made of civic life, the attorney and suffragist Florida Pier offered women's help with the cleanup. (This was the sort of help, said Pier, that any human being would offer to another who was in a "pickle.") When the antis said that women's domesticity had made them too narrow-minded to vote, the suffragists responded that the vote would expand women's horizons. When the antis said that the majority of women did not wish to vote, Sutherland responded that in matters of principle, numbers were irrelevant. When the antis said that ignorant, immoral, and immigrant women would vote, some suffragists retorted that citizens in a democracy should have more faith in the common folk and others argued that women would double the "respectable" vote and out-poll the already-enfranchised unfit men. Finally, and most importantly, when the antis—skirting the knotty question of biology—argued that woman's social function as a mother was far too demanding and far too important to afford them the time and energy for civic activities, the suffragists turned that argument right on its head, insisting that it was precisely because their maternal duties were so vital to national life that they needed a voice in government. "Woman has a right to this most effective means of transforming the social environment into greater fitness for herself and all her loved ones," wrote Frank Parsons in 1908.[10] This, as it turned out, was the suffragists' most unassailable argument. And it was this argument that Jane Addams made most eloquently in her pro-suffrage writings.

Jane Addams's Progressive Suffrage Argument

The Ladies' Home Journal essay was one of dozens of speeches and articles Addams penned on woman suffrage in the years between 1897 and 1920. Comparing the *Journal* piece to her other writings makes clear that "Why Women Should Vote" was typical of her approach to woman suffrage and illuminates how her approach was both similar to and different from that of the other popular arguments being made at the time. Addams's writings on woman suffrage are distinctive because they do not "make every conceivable argument"; she did not blend a biological argument with a human rights argument with an elitist argument with a utilitarian argument. Like the proverbial hedgehog, Addams knew one thing, she knew it well, and she repeated it often: "Only when all the people become the governing class can the collective resources and organizations [of the society] be consistently utilized for the common weal."[11] As has already been noted, in applying this overarching Progressive philosophy to the question of woman suffrage, Addams was unique among suffrage advocates. Unlike other suffrage leaders, Addams subordinated women's particular gender-based situation to the broader, class-based concerns of the Progressive program. In addition, she was uniquely consistent, single-minded, even redundant, in not mixing her fierce

commitment to democracy and practical results with abstract liberalism. In "Pragmatism and Politics," written for *The Survey* in 1912, Addams declared:

> The American voter is not content with the 18th century formulae of liberty and equality, high-flown as they are, for they do not apply to the situation. Liberty has come to be a guarantee of equal opportunity to play our parts well in primary relations, and the elemental processes of birth, growth, nutrition, death are the great levellers that remind us of the essential equality of human life. No talk of liberty or equality "goes" that does not reckon with these.[12]

The pro-suffrage arguments Addams made must be viewed within the very particular political and historical context of the Progressive Era's assertion of collective over individual interests. Considered in terms of her outrage at Gilded-Age selfishness gone wild, Addams's focus on women's vote as a potential tool in the service of community interests makes all the sense in the world.

"Why Women Should Vote" requires no apology for its lack of attention to individual rights. In Jane Addams's world, individual rights had created the urban, industrial problems she and her neighbors battled every day. Her emphasis on the community good that housewives could enact with the vote does not make her a sellout to comfortable, bourgeois domesticity. Rather, it marks her as a fully engaged, Progressive Era reformer whose daily life was consumed with solving serious urban problems evident in every household in her neighborhood. From where Addams sat in Chicago's crowded, dirty Nineteenth Ward, living with other college-educated women who had joined her Hull-House settlement in order to use their privileges on behalf of the working poor, it was not gender per se that distinguished the disadvantaged in American society, it was class. And the remedy for that disadvantage was not, in Addams's experience, more individualism. Whatever "personal ambition" might have accomplished in the past, said Addams in 1912, "it is certainly too archaic to accomplish anything now. Our thoughts, at least for this generation, cannot be too much directed from mutual relationships and responsibilities."[13]

Contrary to what her critics have suggested, Addams did not focus on the collective utility of woman suffrage in order to take the sting out of female independence. Her focus derived honestly out of her political priorities; she was intent on eradicating the evils of economic inequality in American society and believed collective action was the only means to that end. She did not emphasize women's domestic role because she wished to placate the patriarchs or because she did not understand the power of patriarchy to manipulate women's traditional work to its own ends. She assigned great significance to female domesticity because her daily experience taught her that domesticity was no bourgeois ideal but a utilitarian reality for her working-class neighbors, and one that could be powerful if deployed in the political arena against America's individualistic patriarchs.

Addams never openly argued with the antis' claims that the mass of women were too weak or passive or uninterested to vote. Instead, she silently smothered those claims with her argument that the vote would make women stronger, more responsible, and more civic-minded. Note that the editorial for *The Ladies' Home Journal* is not titled "Why Women Should HAVE the Vote," but, rather, "Why Women Should Vote." She was not arguing constitutional principles here; she was talking about the pragmatic effect—on women and on men—of the act of voting.

Jane Addams, Biology, and Elitism

If all Jane Addams had cared about was the attractiveness of her pro-suffrage arguments to middle-class audiences, she would have done what so many of her peers in the movement did; she would have "made every conceivable argument." The fact that she did not, the fact that editorials like "Why Women Should Vote" made such a consistent and relatively narrow set of democratic and utilitarian arguments, deserves notice. Examination of her pro-suffrage language makes clear, for example, that Addams did not ground her suffrage reasoning in biological essentialism. Despite what some critics have charged, she did not claim that women were innately, "essentially," more moral than men.[14] Nor did she say that women were biologically destined for domesticity. In the opening paragraph of "Why Women Should Vote" Addams states that she regards women's domesticity as a product of history that could only be ended by "social change." She speaks of "tradition" in this and other pro-suffrage writings, and she speaks of women's "different experience." But this most careful of writers did not speak of biology determining women's nature or women's role. Yes, she does refer in *The Ladies' Home Journal* to "those affairs which naturally and historically belong to women," but readers familiar with Addams's phrasing as well as her psychology will agree that she used the word "naturally" in all sorts of arguments. It was, for her, a synonym for "logically," and served her need to sweep past opponents, leaving them with the burden of proving that she was not merely stating the obvious.

Back in the early 1970s, the historian Jill Conway claimed that Addams "accepted [the] idea of biologically determined masculine and feminine temperaments," and argued that Addams was incapable of "seeing men and women as moral equals."[15] But these claims are not supported by the language in Addams's own texts. Her argument in *The Ladies' Home Journal* against women influencing men's votes rests on the assumption that a man's "point of view" was "quite as honest and valuable" as a woman's. Indeed, in her first public address on woman suffrage in 1897, speaking before the Chicago Political Equality League, Addams stated:

> I am not one of those who believe—broadly speaking—that women are better than men. We have not wrecked railroads, nor corrupted Legislatures, nor done many unholy things that men have done; but then we must remember that we have not had the chance. But my

understanding of the matter is that woman should have the ballot because without this responsibility she cannot best develop her moral courage. As Mazzini once said…we have no right to call our country a country until every man has a vote, and surely no logical mind can stop at sex in granting suffrage.[16]

Seventeen years later, writing for the *Annals of the American Academy of Political and Social Science,* Addams would still claim, "good government is not a matter of sex when it means…defending little children."[17] She did believe, and recent historical research has borne Addams out on this, that women's daily experience made them more likely than men to place human welfare and aesthetics above concerns with profit—but she rooted that difference in nurture, not nature.[18]

The one possible exception to this general rule can be found in *The Ladies' Home Journal* for June of 1913 when Addams wrote an atypically ironic essay titled, "If Men Were Seeking the Franchise." There, in tones suggesting the influence of radical feminist philosopher Charlotte Perkins Gilman, Addams showed what women's objections to men voting would be if women controlled the government. Some of her arguments there—that men might not be good voters because they are "always so eager to make money," are "so reckless," think "so little of dust," and "are so fond of fighting…you always have been since you were little boys"—could be read as a biological, essentialist view of masculine and feminine nature. But it seems just as likely that Addams was trying to show the absurdity of essentialist claims. Certainly her concluding remarks for that article indicate that "such talk" was not serious, that "as far as the guardianship of the State is concerned there is no distinction between the powers of men and women save those which custom has made."[19] It would not be until the masculine carnage of World War I had seared her soul that Addams's language would begin to imply that female nature had any corner on morality. This was not her approach during the woman suffrage campaign.[20]

Just as she did not join other suffragists in making biological claims for women's right to the vote, so, too, Addams did not join the chorus of elitists, racists, and nativists who tried to argue that woman suffrage would double the "respectable," White, native-born vote more than it would expand the votes of the rabble. "Why Women Should Vote" is an excellent example of her view that working women and immigrant women and poor women not only needed the vote in order to protect their own interests and those of their families, but also wanted the vote in order to be responsible, active agents in their communities. By telling her largely White, largely middle-class readership that Scandinavian women were accustomed to the vote, that Jewish women had "covered markets" in Russia and Poland, and that Italian women saw no distinction between voting in school board elections to protect the education of older children and voting in state or federal elections to protect the milk drunk by younger children, Addams was slyly shaming those who had been surprised by the suffrage

enthusiasm among these groups of women. True, she did romanticize her neighbors by implying that ethnic women's naivete gave them an organic grasp of political common sense, but in the context of the era's ethnocentric elitism, Addams's romanticism looks more like protection than pandering.

Had Addams been purely a strategist, she would have brushed past her working-class women's suffrage enthusiasm in the way she brushed past other potentially controversial points. But Addams calculated where to earn and where to spend her political capital. She ignored questions of women's individual rights precisely because she did not want to ignore the political aspirations of the women in her neighborhood. It was her concern for their collective need to improve their lives, rather than her concern for her own individual right to vote, that fueled Addams's suffrage energies in the first place. To say that she fashioned a palatable domestic argument for woman suffrage in order to make female voters less threatening completely overlooks the very real political risk she took by predicting that working-class, immigrant women would, as voters, actively demand services and legislative protections from federal, state, and municipal governments. This was hardly a neutral stance to take during the Progressive Era, and it speaks volumes about the class-oriented nature of Addams's political activism.

The Strategic Power of Addams's Argument

The modern feminist may well cringe at the link Addams made between women's traditional domestic duties and the vote. But that reaction should not blind us to the sincerity of her argument—or to the strategic value of her argument.

While it took political risks, Addams's "spin" on suffrage was also strategically brilliant. In her hands, suffrage advocates became steadfast defenders of women's right to care for home and family, not the destroyers of domesticity depicted in anti-suffrage lore. In her hands, the feminine powers of "persuasion" which anti-suffragists preferred in place of voting became dishonest tools of manipulation, just as unworthy of women as they were unfair to men. Finally, and most interestingly, in Addams's hands, it was historical inevitability that required women to move their caregiving into the public sector, not some feminist scheme to alter the course of history. With a curious but very characteristic mix of assertiveness and self-effacement, Addams trumpeted women's ability to rise to history's challenge while sliding right past the role women reformers like herself had played in changing history by placing women's traditional concerns on the political agenda.

In "Votes for Women and Other Votes," which appeared in *The Survey* in 1912, Addams expanded on the argument for historical inevitability implicit in "Why Women Should Vote" and downplayed the role of historical agents like herself. Addams claimed in this article that history is "merely a record of new human interests" becoming "the subjects of governmental action and the incorporation into government itself of those classes who represented new interests." As government became involved in commerce, merchants became voters; as

Jane Addams, c. 1914	Woman suffrage leaflet, c. 1915
LIBRARY OF CONGRESS	SMITHSONIAN INSTITUTION

government became involved in industrial affairs, workers became voters. The campaign for woman suffrage, reasoned Addams, was the inevitable, sensible result of contemporary government's involvement with "the basic human interests with which women have been traditionally concerned." Thus skirting the female activism that had placed these "basic human interests" on the Progressive Era's political agenda, Addams argued that these new public duties had fallen to women simply through the natural unfolding of history. Pushing this argument even further, Addams claimed that women were only demanding a new household tool—the vote—"because they insist that they will not cease to perform their traditional duties, simply because these duties have been taken over by existing governments." [21]

If there was any guile in Addams's pro-suffrage position, this was surely it. According to her construction, the link between Progressive Era reforms and woman suffrage had arisen organically. Women's political activism was a result, not a cause, of the Progressive Era, and women's need for the vote was a result, not a cause, of historical change. Addams knew different, of course, but this approach satisfied her political and temperamental need to soothe the nerves of those dizzied by the explosion of Progressivism's government activism and women's connection to that activism. Rather than pandering to Americans' elitism or their nativism or their affection for biological essentialism, Addams instead insisted on democracy—economic, social, and legal—and then played to Americans' comfort with historical inevitability and with women's role as dutiful servants to posterity.

Conclusion

As one of America's most revered public figures, Jane Addams played an important role in the campaign for woman suffrage. Since her fame and stature did not reside in the woman suffrage movement, and since Americans perceived her as sincerely committed to the common good, her arguments for woman suffrage as a tool of reform carried special weight. It is doubtful that the majority of the readers of "Why Women Should Vote" in 1910 shared Addams's deep convictions about economic democracy, the dignity of immigrants and workers, or the historical (rather than biological) roots of female domesticity. But it is likely that they were sympathetic to her view that enfranchised women would strengthen contemporary efforts to clean up the factories and the cities, reduce poverty, and improve education and public health. And while Addams fashioned an emphasis on domesticity out of her desire to show the interdependence of the public and the private in modern life, it is also likely that readers found in Addams's domestic emphasis a comforting reassurance that woman suffrage would not destroy the traditional family. In this way, then, Addams maintained her own principles while still achieving popular appeal. The argument here is that Jane Addams's particular approach to woman suffrage, specifically her lack of attention to women's individual rights, arose less from political timidity about gender than from overriding, firm convictions about social and economic reform. As it happened, this focus on the link between suffrage and reform intersected sufficiently with the Progressive attitudes of many Americans to be attractive—despite the fact that Addams was more democratic in her goals than the majority of her readers.

Women's rights were always an avenue to matters of class for Addams; they were never the final destination on her political journey. "Why Women Should Vote" is just one piece of evidence that Addams's support for woman suffrage was rooted in her primary commitment to economic democracy, but it is a very strong piece of evidence. In addition, her writing in this essay, as in so many others, makes clear that, just as Addams always felt more comfortable privileging class issues over gender issues, so, too, she always felt more comfortable arguing for her causes in non-argumentative language. Over the course of her life, consciously and unconsciously, Addams trained the stream of her thinking to flow in elegantly diplomatic channels. Her personal recoil from conflict, coupled with her conviction that all conflict should be mediated, meant that she always presented her case in terms of ultimate harmony, not ultimate victory; this was no more or less true of her suffrage writings than of her writings about labor or militarism.

"Why Women Should Vote," like all of Jane Addams's contributions to the suffrage cause, is thus an exquisitely clever, carefully phrased, determinedly practical, democratic argument. One need not agree with it in order to appreciate its brilliance and its sincerity.

WHY WOMEN SHOULD VOTE

by Jane Addams, of Hull-House, Chicago

For many generations it has been believed that woman's place is within the walls of her home, and it is indeed impossible to imagine the time when her duty there shall be ended or to forecast any social change which shall release her from that paramount obligation.

This paper is an attempt to show that many women today are failing to discharge their duties to their own households properly simply because they do not perceive that as society grows more complicated it is necessary that woman shall extend her sense of responsibility to many things outside of her own home if she would continue to preserve the home in its entirety. One could illustrate in many ways. A woman's simplest duty, one would say, is to keep her house clean and wholesome and to feed her children properly. Yet if she lives in a tenement house, as so many of my neighbors do, she cannot fulfill these simple obligations by her own efforts because she is utterly dependent upon the city administration for the conditions which render decent living possible. Her basement will not be dry, her stairways will not be fireproof, her house will not be provided with sufficient windows to give light and air, nor will it be equipped with sanitary plumbing, unless the Public Works Department sends inspectors who constantly insist that these elementary decencies be provided. Women who live in the country sweep their own dooryards and may either feed the refuse of the table to a flock of chickens or allow it innocently to decay in the open air and sunshine. In a crowded city quarter, however, if the street is not cleaned by the city authorities no amount of private sweeping will keep the tenement free from grime; if the garbage is not properly collected and destroyed a tenement-house mother may see her children sicken and die of diseases from which she alone is powerless to shield them, although her tenderness and devotion are unbounded. She cannot even secure untainted meat for her household, she cannot provide fresh fruit, unless the meat has been inspected by city officials, and the decayed fruit, which is so often placed upon sale in the tenement districts, has been destroyed in the interests of public health. In short, if woman would keep on with her old business of caring for her house and rearing her children she will have to have some conscience in regard to public affairs lying quite outside of her immediate household. The individual conscience and devotion are no longer effective.

Chicago one spring had a spreading contagion of scarlet fever just at the time the school nurses had been discontinued because business men had pronounced them too expensive. If the women who sent their children to the schools had been sufficiently public-spirited and had been provided with an implement through which to express that public spirit they would have insisted that the schools be supplied with nurses in order that their own children might be protected from

contagion. In other words, if women would effectively continue their old avocations they must take part in the slow upbuilding of that code of legislation which is alone sufficient to protect the home from the dangers incident to modern life. One might instance the many deaths of children from contagious diseases the germs of which had been carried in tailored clothing. Country doctors testify as to the outbreak of scarlet fever in remote neighborhoods each autumn, after the children have begun to wear the winter overcoats and cloaks which have been sent from infected city sweatshops. That their mothers mend their stockings and guard them from "taking cold" is not a sufficient protection when the tailoring of the family is done in a distant city under conditions which the mother cannot possibly control. The sanitary regulation of sweatshops by city officials is all that can be depended upon to prevent such needless destruction. Who shall say that women are not concerned in the enactment and enforcement of such legislation if they would preserve their homes?

Even women who take no part in public affairs in order that they may give themselves entirely to their own families, sometimes going so far as to despise those other women who are endeavoring to secure protective legislation, may illustrate this point. The Hull-House neighborhood was at one time suffering from a typhoid epidemic. A careful investigation was made by which we were able to establish a very close connection between the typhoid and a mode of plumbing which made it most probable that the infection had been carried by flies. Among the people who been exposed to the infection was a widow who had lived in the ward for a number of years, in a comfortable little house which she owned. Although the Italian immigrants were closing in all around her she was not willing to sell her property and to move away until she had finished the education of her children. In the mean time she held herself quite aloof from her Italian neighbors and could never be drawn into any of the public efforts to protect them by securing a better code of tenement-house sanitation. Her two daughters were sent to an Eastern college; one June, when one of them had graduated and the other still had two years before she took her degree, they came to the spotless little house and to their self-sacrificing mother for the summer's holiday. They both fell ill, not because their own home was not clean, not because their mother was not devoted, but because next door to them and also in the rear were wretched tenements, and because the mother's utmost efforts could not keep the infection out of her own house. One daughter died and one recovered but was an invalid for two years following. This is, perhaps, a fair illustration of the futility of the individual conscience when woman insists upon isolating her family from the rest of the community and its interests. The result is sure to be a pitiful failure.

One of the interesting experiences in the Chicago campaign for inducing the members of the Charter Convention to recommend municipal franchise for women in the provisions of the new charter was the unexpected enthusiasm and help which came from large groups of foreign-born women. The Scandinavian

women represented in many Lutheran Church societies said quite simply that in the old country they had had the municipal franchise upon the same basis as men since the seventeenth century; all the women formerly living under the British Government, in England, Australia or Canada, pointed out that Chicago women were asking now for what the British women had long had. But the most unexpected response came from the foreign colonies in which women had never heard such problems discussed and took the prospect of the municipal ballot as a simple device—which it is—to aid them in their daily struggle with adverse city conditions. The Italian women said that the men engaged in railroad construction were away all summer and did not know anything about their household difficulties. Some of them came to Hull-House one day to talk over the possibility of a public wash-house. They do not like to wash in their own tenements, they have never seen a washing-tub until they came to America, and find it very difficult to use it in the restricted space of their little kitchens and to hang the clothes within the house to dry. They say that in the Italian villages the women all go to the streams together; in the town they go to the public wash-house; and washing, instead of being lonely and disagreeable, is made pleasant by cheerful conversation. It is asking a great deal of these women to change suddenly all their habits of living, and their contention that the tenement-house kitchen is too small for laundry-work is well taken. If women in Chicago knew the needs of the Italian colony they would realize that any change bringing cleanliness and fresh clothing into the Italian household would be a very sensible and hygienic measure. It is, perhaps, asking a great deal that the members of the City Council should understand this, but surely a comprehension of the needs of these women and efforts toward ameliorating their lot might be regarded as matters of municipal obligation on the part of voting women.

The same thing is true of the Jewish women in their desire for covered markets which have always been a municipal provision in Russia and Poland. The vegetables piled high upon the wagons standing in the open markets of Chicago become covered with dust and soot. It seems to these women a violation of the most rudimentary decencies and they sometimes say quite simply: "If women had anything to say about it they would change all that."

...The duty of a woman toward the schools which her children attend is so obvious that it is not necessary to dwell upon it. But even this simple obligation cannot be effectively carried out without some form of social organization as the mothers' school clubs and mothers' congresses testify, and to which the most conservative women belong because they feel the need of wider reading and discussion concerning the many problems of childhood. It is, therefore, perhaps natural that the public should have been more willing to accord a vote to women in school matters than in any other, and yet women have never been members of a Board of Education in sufficient numbers to influence largely actual school curriculi. If they had been kindergartens, domestic science courses and school

playgrounds would be far more numerous than they are. More than one woman has been convinced of the need of the ballot by the futility of her efforts in persuading a business man that young children need nurture in something besides the three r's. Perhaps, too, only women realize the influence which the school might exert upon the home if a proper adaptation to actual needs were considered. An Italian girl who has had lessons in cooking at the public school will help her mother to connect the entire family with American food and household habits. That the mother has never baked bread in Italy—only mixed it in her own house and then taken it out to the village oven—makes it all the more necessary that her daughter should understand the complication of a cooking-stove. The same thing is true of the girl who learns to sew in the public school, and more than anything else, perhaps, of the girl who receives the first simple instruction in the care of little children, that skillful care which every tenement-house baby requires if he is to be pulled through his second summer. The only time, to my knowledge, that lessons in the care of children were given in the public schools of Chicago was one summer when the vacation schools were being managed by a volunteer body of women. The instruction was eagerly received by the Italian girls, who had been "little mothers" to younger children ever since they could remember.

As a result of this teaching I recall a young girl who carefully explained to her Italian mother that the reason the babies in Italy were so healthy and the babies in Chicago were so sickly was not, as her mother had always firmly insisted, because her babies in Italy had goat's milk and her babies in America had cow's milk, but because the milk in Italy was clean and the milk in Chicago was dirty…. She also informed her mother that the "City Hall wanted to fix up the milk so that it couldn't make the baby sick, but that they hadn't quite enough votes for it yet." The Italian mother believed what her child had been taught in the big school; it seemed to her quite as natural that the city should be concerned in providing pure milk for her younger children as it should provide big schools and teachers for her older children. She reached this naïve conclusion because she had never heard those arguments which make it seem reasonable that a woman should be given the school franchise but no other.

But women are also beginning to realize that children need attention outside of school hours; that much of the petty vice in cities is merely the love of pleasure gone wrong, the overrestrained boy or girl seeking improper recreation and excitement. It is obvious that a little study of the needs of children, a sympathetic understanding of the conditions under which they go astray, might save hundreds of them. Women traditionally have had an opportunity to observe the plays of children and the needs of youth, and yet in Chicago, at least, they had done singularly little in this vexed problem of juvenile delinquency until they helped to inaugurate the Juvenile Court movement a dozen years ago. The Juvenile Court Committee, made up largely of women, paid the salaries of the probation officers connected with the

court for the first six years of its existence, and after the salaries were cared for by the county the same organization turned itself into a Juvenile Protective League, and through a score of paid officers are doing valiant service in minimizing some of the dangers of city life which boys and girls encounter....

The more extensively the modern city endeavors on the one hand to control and on the other hand to provide recreational facilities for its young people the more necessary it is that women should assist in their direction and extension. After all, a care for wholesome and innocent amusement is what women have for many years assumed. When the reaction comes on the part of taxpayers women's votes may be necessary to keep the city to its beneficent obligations toward its own young people.

...Ever since steam power has been applied to the processes of weaving and spinning woman's traditional work has been carried on largely outside of the home. The clothing and household linen are not only spun and woven, but also usually sewed, by machinery; the preparation of many foods has also passed into the factory and necessarily a certain number of women have been obliged to follow their work there, although it is doubtful, in spite of the large numbers of factory girls, whether women now are doing as large a proportion of the world's work as they used to do. Because many thousands of those working in factories and shops are girls between the ages of fourteen and twenty-two there is a necessity that older women should be interested in the conditions of industry. The very fact that these girls are not going to remain in industry permanently makes it more important that some one should see to it that they shall not be incapacitated for their future family life because they work for exhausting hours and under insanitary [sic] conditions.

If woman's sense of obligation had enlarged as the industrial conditions changed she might naturally and almost imperceptibly have inaugurated the movements for social amelioration in the line of factory legislation and shop sanitation. That she has not done so is doubtless due to the fact that her conscience is slow to recognize any obligation outside of her own family circle, and because she was so absorbed in her own household that she failed to see what the conditions outside actually were. It would be interesting to know how far the consciousness that she had no vote and could not change matters operated in this direction. After all, we see only those things to which our attention has been drawn, we feel responsibility for those things which are brought to us as matters of responsibility. If conscientious women were convinced that it was a civic duty to be informed in regard to these grave industrial affairs, and then to express the conclusions which they had reached by depositing a piece of paper in a ballot box, one cannot imagine that they would shirk simply because the action ran counter to old traditions.

To those of my readers who would admit that although woman has no right to shirk her old obligations, that all of these measures could be secured more easily through her influence upon the men of her family than through the direct use of the ballot; I should like to tell a little story. I have a friend in Chicago who is the

mother of four sons and the grandmother of twelve grandsons who are voters. She is a woman of wealth, of secured social position, of sterling character and clear intelligence, and may, therefore, quite fairly be cited as a "woman of influence".... I happened to call at her house on the day that Mr. McKinley was elected President against Mr. Bryan for the first time. I found my friend much disturbed. She said somewhat bitterly that she had at last discovered what the much-vaunted influence of woman was worth; that she had implored each one of her sons and grandsons, had entered into endless arguments and moral appeals to induce one of them to represent her convictions by voting for Bryan! That, although sincerely devoted to her, each one had assured her that his convictions forced him to vote the Republican ticket.... I contended that a woman had no right to persuade a man to vote against his own convictions; that I respected the men of her family for following their own judgement regardless of the appeal which the honored head of the house had made to their chivalric devotion. To this she replied that she would agree with that point of view when a woman had the same opportunity as a man to register her convictions by vote. I believed then as I do now, that nothing is gained when independence of judgement is assailed by "influence," sentimental or otherwise, and that we test advancing civilization somewhat by our power to respect differences and by our tolerance of another's honest conviction.

This is, perhaps, the attitude of many busy women who would be glad to use the ballot to further public measures in which they are interested and for which they have been working for years. It offends the taste of such a woman to be obliged to use "indirect influence" when she is accustomed to well-bred, open action in other affairs, and she very much resents the time spent in persuading a voter to take her point of view, and possibly to give up his own, quite as honest and valuable as hers, although different because resulting from a totally different experience. Public-spirited women who wish to use the ballot, as I know them, do not wish to do the work of men nor to take over men's affairs. They simply want an opportunity to do their own work and to take care of those affairs which naturally and historically belong to women, but which are constantly being overlooked and slighted in our political institutions....

To turn the administration of our civic affairs wholly over to men may mean that the American city will continue to push forward in its commercial and industrial development, and continue to lag behind in those things which make a city healthful and beautiful. After all, woman's traditional function has been to make her dwelling-place both clean and fair. Is that dreariness in city life, that lack of domesticity which the humblest farm dwelling presents, due to a withdrawal of one of the naturally cooperating forces? If women have in any sense been responsible for the gentler side of life which softens and blurs some of its harsher conditions, may they not have a duty to perform in our American cities?

In closing, may I recapitulate that if woman would fulfill her traditional responsibility to her own children; if she would educate and protect from danger factory children who must find their recreation on the street; if she would bring the cultural forces to bear upon our materialistic civilization; and if she would do it all with the dignity and directness fitting one who carries on her immemorial duties, then she must bring herself to the use of the ballot—that latest implement for self government. May we not fairly say that American women need this implement in order to preserve the home?

Notes

The article, "Why Women Should Vote," was first published in *The Ladies Home Journal*, 27, (January 1910): 21-22.

1. For examples of this critical view of Addams, see: Jill Conway, "Women Reformers and American Culture, 1870-1930," *Journal of Social History* 5 (Winter, 1971-72): 164-177; Jill Conway, "Stereotypes of Femininity in a Theory of Sexual Evolution," *Victorian Studies* 14 (September, 1970): 47-62; Judith Lacerte, "If Only Jane Addams Had Been a Feminist," *Social Casework* 57 (December, 1976): 656-660; William O'Neill, *Everyone was Brave: A History of Feminism in America* (Chicago, 1971), 120; Aileen Kraditor, *The Ideas of the Woman Suffrage Movement* (New York, 1965).

2. Carol Gilligan, *In a Different Voice: Psychological Theory and Women's Development* (Cambridge, Mass., 1982); Joan Tronto, "Beyond Gender Difference Toward a Theory of Care," *Signs* 12 (Summer, 1987): 644-663; Jean Bethke Elshtain, "Antigone's Daughters," *Democracy* 2 (April, 1982): 46-59; Mary Dietz, "Context is All: Feminism and Theories of Citizenship," *Daedalus* (1987): 1-24; Kathleen B. Jones, "Citizenship in a Woman-Friendly Polity," *Signs* 15 (Summer, 1990).

3. Paula Baker, "The Domestication of Politics: Women and American Political Society, 1780-1920," *American Historical Review* 89 (June, 1984): 620-647. Kathryn Kish Sklar, "Hull House in the 1890's: A Community of Women Reformers," *Signs* 10 (Summer, 1985): 658-677; and "The Historical Foundations of Women's Power in the Creation of the American Welfare State, 1830-1930," 43-93 and Eileen Boris, "The Power of Motherhood: Black and White Activist Women Redefine the 'Political,'" both in *Mothers of the New World: Maternalist Politics and the Origins of Welfare States*, Seth Koven and Sonya Michel, eds. (New York, 1993), 213-245.

4. "The Only Saint America Has Produced," *Current Literature* 40 (April, 1906); "The Most Useful Americans," *The Independent* 74 (May 1, 1913): 956-957; Editor's introduction to Addams's 1913 column, *The Ladies' Home Journal*, 30 (January, 1913): 25.

5. Allen F. Davis, *American Heroine: The Life and Legend of Jane Addams* (New York, 1973). Davis includes a copy of a "spider web" chart on p. 265.

6. Julia Ward Howe, "The Case for Woman Suffrage," *The Outlook* 91 (April 3, 1909): 780.

7. Baker, "The Domestication of Politics," 642.

8. Frank Parsons, "Shall Our Mothers, Wives and Sisters Be Our Equals or Our Subjects?" *The Arena* 40 (July, 1908): 92-94; Rosamond Sutherland, "The Appeal of Politics to Woman," *The North American Review* 191 (January, 1910): 82, 85; "The Justice and Desirability of Woman Suffrage," *The Independent* 82 (April 5, 1915): 3-4.

9. Howe, "The Case for Woman Suffrage," 781.

10. Alva P. Belmont, "Woman's Right to Govern Herself," *The North American Review* 190 (November, 1909): 664-674; Florida Pier, "The Delightfully Quaint Antis," *Harper's Weekly* 53 (December 11, 1909): 34; Harper, "Would Woman Suffrage Benefit the State, and Woman Herself?" 374; Sutherland, "The Appeal of Politics to Woman," 82; "Margaret vs. Bridget," *The Independent* 67 (1909): 1394; Parsons, "Shall Our Mothers, Wives and Sisters Be Our Equals or Our Subjects?" 93; Molly Warren, "The Housekeeper's Need of the Ballot," *The World Today* 12 (January-June, 1907): 418-421. For examples of anti-suffrage arguments in popular magazines in these years, see: "Concerning Woman's Suffrage," *The Outlook* 64 (March 10, 1900); Lyman Abbott, "Why Women Do Not Wish the Suffrage," *The Atlantic Monthly* 92 (September, 1903); Elizabeth McCracken, "The Women of America: Woman's Suffrage in Colorado," *The Outlook* 75 (November 28, 1903): 737-744; Annie Nathan Meyer, "Woman's Assumption of Sex Superiority," *North American Review* 178 (January, 1904): 103-109; Lyman Abbott, "The Assault on Womanhood," *The Outlook* 91 (April 3, 1909): 784-788; "Do Women Wish to Vote?" *The Outlook* 94 (February 19, 1910): 375-377; Molly Elliot Seawell, "The Ladies' Battle," *The Atlantic Monthly* 106 (September, 1910): 289-303; Jessie Atkinson McGriff, "Before the American Woman Votes," *The Ladies' Home Journal* 27 (April, 1910): 56.

11. Jane Addams, "Votes for Women and Other Votes," *The Survey* 29 (June 1, 1912): 368.

12. Jane Addams, "Pragmatism in Politics," *The Survey* 29 (October 5, 1912): 12.

13. Jane Addams, "A Modern Lear," *The Survey* 29 (November 2, 1912): 137.

14. Conway, "Women Reformers," and "Stereotypes of Femininity"; Davis, *American Heroine*, 187, 316.

15. Conway, "Women Reformers," 174, and "Stereotypes of Femininity," 58.

16. Jane Addams, "The Working Woman's Need of the Ballot," *The Woman's Journal* (November 20, 1897).

17. Jane Addams, "The Larger Aspects of the Woman's Movement," *Annals of the American Academy of Political and Social Science* 56 (November, 1914): 6.

18. See, for example, Maureen Flanagan, "Gender and Urban Political Reform: The City Club and the Woman's Club of Chicago in the Progressive Era," *American Historical Review* 95 (October, 1990): 1032-1050.

19. Jane Addams, "If Men Were Seeking the Franchise," *The Ladies' Home Journal* 30 (June, 1913): 21.

20. Jane Addams, "Women, War, and Suffrage," *The Survey* 35 (November 6, 1915): 148-149. This article indicates that Addams did not, in the years before 1920, rest her claims for women's role in international relations on biological essentialism.

21. Addams, "Votes for Women and Other Votes," 367-368.

"The New Woman —Wash Day." Suffrage opponents encouraged the idea that woman suffrage threatened to overturn traditional gender roles and the domestic division of labor in images like this from the 1890s.

Fourteen

"BETTER CITIZENS WITHOUT THE BALLOT":

American Anti-suffrage Women and Their Rationale During the Progressive Era

Manuela Thurner

Editor's Introduction: In this fascinating essay, Manuela Thurner discusses the women who organized to *oppose* woman suffrage, the anti-suffrage women popularly known as the "Antis." Thurner insists that these women are often misunderstood—when they are discussed at all—by historians who have accepted without sufficient examination the suffragists' characterization of their despised female adversaries as: "puppets of more powerful male forces"; selfish, pampered socialites, motivated by a desire to maintain their own highly privileged status; and reactionaries with an extremely narrow view of woman's proper role. Misunderstanding of the anti-suffrage women also stems from the fact that historians have at times generalized about anti-suffragists after studying only the writings of anti-suffrage men—who, in many cases, *were* reactionaries disturbed by the increasing public activity of women, or claimed that woman suffrage would "ruin women" and "destroy the home" out of fear that it would threaten their economic interests.

Thurner's own study, focusing particularly on Antis in the Northeast between 1900 and 1920 and based on the writings of anti-suffrage women and major Anti periodicals, avoids both of these pitfalls—and offers very different conclusions about anti-suffrage women. Thurner rejects the idea that the Antis were controlled by male anti-suffragists, and downplays the socio-economic differences between anti-suffragists and suffragists.

Most significantly, Thurner challenges prevailing assumptions about the *ideology* of the female anti-suffragists, who "portrayed themselves as very much in line with and in favor of turn-of-the-century Progressive reform and female activism." According to Thurner, the Antis *urged* women to play an active role in public affairs, but believed that this could best be done "without the ballot" by disinterested, nonpartisan women. They opposed woman's entry into politics believing that political activity—like participation in the woman suffrage movement itself—would diffuse women's energies and lessen their effectiveness by diverting them away from all-female clubs and organizations through which

women had already proven to be very influential. And they argued (like some feminists and scholars today) that female separatism might be more effective in achieving reforms women desire than the dilution of women's efforts in gender-integrated political organizations.

Indeed, Thurner insists that this set of ideas regarding women's participation in public affairs was one of the reasons the Antis were initially successful and able to forestall the suffrage victory as long as they did. She implies that, had Progressive-Era Antis insisted on women remaining completely in the domestic sphere—like some suffrage opponents who denounced public activism on the part of women as unwomanly and ungodly—they might have been less convincing. This in itself is strong testimony concerning the degree of change that had taken place in the late nineteenth century in ideas about woman's sphere.

★   ★   ★   ★   ★

"WILL HISTORY REMEMBER the heroines of feminism...? It will not." Thus anti-suffragist Florence R. Hall expressed her optimism about her opponents' fate in the September 1915 issue of *The Woman's Protest*, the official publication of the National Association Opposed to Woman Suffrage (NAOWS).[1] Seventy-five years after the passage of the Nineteenth Amendment, and after three decades of feminist scholarship, which has produced a huge body of literature on exactly those "heroines of feminism," Hall's assertion sounds peculiar, if not outright absurd. Yet, in the fall of 1915, this assessment on the part of an anti-suffrage woman was by no means far-fetched or unrealistic. The "Antis"—as the female anti-suffragists came to be known—accurately predicted victories for their cause in the November state suffrage referenda of New York, New Jersey, Massachusetts, and Pennsylvania. Coming, as they did, after a host of preceding suffrage defeats throughout the country, the Antis' triumphs in those four Eastern states constituted their latest and most promising success. That very same year, they could also point to the fact that suffrage amendments had been lost in twenty state legislatures. It was not until New York State finally adopted woman suffrage in November of 1917 and the House of Representatives voted in favor of a federal amendment, in the year following, that signs of disillusion and resignation began to show within the ranks of the organized anti-suffragists. Ultimately defeated in 1920 when Tennessee cast the necessary thirty-sixth vote to ratify the Nineteenth Amendment, anti-suffragists disappeared from the public stage—and from the subsequent historical record. Now, it was the suffragists' turn to invoke the dictum that "[v]ictorious movements record their history, vanquished ones rarely do."[2]

Historians and the Anti-suffrage Movement

Feminist scholarship has indeed recounted women's collective endeavors and triumphs more extensively than the manifold conflicts and tensions among women

of different ethnic, racial, religious, political, and class backgrounds. Women's historians all too often uncritically adopt feminist perspectives and judgments when they set out to write women into history. In the historiography of the woman suffrage movement, this point of view has led to various misconceptions about the women who opposed their own enfranchisement. Reiterating the assessments of prominent suffragists, later historians of the suffrage movement have dismissed the female antis as insignificant and have elaborated instead on the male liquor, business, political, and Southern states' rights interests as the more important and potent anti-suffrage forces.[3] The small body of secondary literature focusing on the anti-suffragists does little to modify these interpretations or to dispel the myths. While minutely exploring the organizational history and makeup of the more important anti-suffrage associations, it does not, surprisingly, take much care to investigate more fully those women's motivations for opposing their enfranchisement.[4]

The majority of scholars have accepted the "woman's place is in the home" argument as the fundamental and most frequently invoked rationale of the Antis. For the most part, historians have depicted the opponents of woman suffrage as late Victorians who, married with children, were not ready or willing to accommodate themselves to the individualistic tendencies and altered social and gender relations of the modern era, and whose adherence to an ideology of domesticity was doomed to failure in an era of widespread Progressive reform and public activism. However, an analysis of the female anti-suffragists' major periodicals and writings of the first two decades of the twentieth century, the most active and successful phase of the organized Antis' short history, reveals the relative insignificance of this argument. Instead, the Antis not only actually but also ideologically ventured considerably beyond the domestic sphere in their effort to forestall women's enfranchisement. They, in fact, portrayed themselves as very much in line with and in favor of turn-of-the-century Progressive reform and female activism. This may not only help to explain the fact that the Antis were able to prolong the suffrage fight considerably; it also promises an analysis of their arguments in terms that are of relevance to current debates about women's relationship to the public and political realms.

Women as Anti-suffrage Theorists and Activists

The organized anti-suffrage movement started in 1882 with the founding of the Massachusetts Association Opposed to the Further Extension of Suffrage to Women (MAOFESW). By 1900, there were female anti-suffrage associations in New York, Illinois, California, South Dakota, Washington, and Oregon. In 1911, the National Association Opposed to Woman Suffrage (NAOWS) opened its headquarters in New York City, from which it moved to Washington, D.C. in 1917. Due to the NAOWS's vigorous recruitment efforts, twenty-five state associations with combined membership estimated at 200,000 subscribed to the anti-suffrage cause by 1915.[5] Yet it is of minor significance to recollect the exact founding dates,

membership figures, and organizational structures of the twenty-odd anti-suffrage associations (the data offered on those counts by both contemporary observers and historians are incomplete and often contradictory) or to remember the names of the participating states (which varied from year to year). The crucial point is to realize that the movement was commonly understood to be founded, staffed, and led by women. Although men's anti-suffrage organizations existed, they did not issue their own periodicals or engage in the kind of sustained publicity work that became the hallmark of the older and more seasoned female organizations. In keeping with their avowed philosophy to steer clear of politics and to concentrate instead on educating the public about their beliefs, female antis occasionally voiced their resolve to "leav[e] the political end entirely to men."[6] Yet, in practice, it was usually representatives of female anti-suffrage organizations who appeared before congressional committees or other political forums to speak out against women's enfranchisement.

Women also came to be the most prolific theorists of the anti-suffrage movement. Not only did the bulk of articles and essays in the anti-suffrage periodical press stem from the pen of female contributors; women also authored the more elaborate treatises and tracts delineating a rationale for opposing women's enfranchisement. When Helen Kendrick Johnson's *Woman and the Republic* was first published in 1897, reviews across the nation were full of praise. *The St. Paul Pioneer-Press* termed it the "most temperate, concise, and well-conducted argument against woman suffrage which has yet appeared in book form."[7] One newspaper declared: "If the woman suffrage movement is ever to be finally defeated, it will be by women themselves, and by arguments and considerations like those so ably stated in this remarkable book."[8] Heartened by the press's generally favorable attitude towards their cause, other female anti-suffragists followed in Johnson's footsteps. Virginian Molly Elliot Seawell's *The Ladies' Battle* (1911); journalist Ida Tarbell's *The Business of Being a Woman* (1912); Grace Duffield Goodwin's *Anti-Suffrage: Ten Good Reasons* (1915), a booklet written by the president of the Washington, D.C. anti-suffrage association; and Annie Riley Hale's *The Eden Sphinx* (1916) were other well-received books that more or less forcefully advanced a coherent rationale for opposing women's enfranchisement.[9] Though none of these works achieved the popularity or critical acclaim of Johnson's treatise, their mere existence and wide circulation nevertheless testified to the fact that women not only worked but wrote to thwart their own enfranchisement.

Who were these women? In addressing this question, one encounters a host of stereotypes and clichés that have been transmitted through the suffragist record. "A little band of rich, ultra society women," "the candied fruit of a generation characterized by 'frenzied finance,'" "butterflies of fashion" who "move in a limited though most unimpeachable circle" were only a few of many unflattering epithets the suffragists held in store for their opponents.[10] Some sociologists and historians have in fact argued that the female anti-suffragists were mostly upper-class women whose primary motivation for their vehement opposition to the ballot

was their fear of a decline in status. According to this interpretation, the Antis were most of all wary of the democraticizing tendencies of suffragist politics and thus eager to safeguard their class privileges.[11]

However, the class-related differences between the proponents and the opponents of women's enfranchisement should not be overemphasized. To be sure, many of the female Antis came from old and well-established families whose names were often known well beyond their native states' boundaries for the social, political, and economic clout they had carried for decades or even centuries. It is also true that the organized leadership's particular makeup did not facilitate or encourage the participation of women of non-White, non-Protestant backgrounds. African American, immigrant, and working-class women may very well have harbored anti-suffrage sentiments, but they were not represented in the movement's front ranks or on the editorial boards of the anti-suffrage periodicals. Yet the suffrage movement, too, especially in its later phase, counted a fair number of socially prominent women among its activists and, moreover, had its own share of elitist, nativist, and racist rhetoric.

Most importantly, a college education, professional employment, and a life without a husband and children were not infallible indicators of a woman's pro-suffrage stance. Indeed, most anti-suffragists would have had no difficulty in embracing the label of the "New Woman" as appropriate designation for them-selves. Alike in many biographical particulars, pro- and anti-suffrage women shared above all one crucial conviction: both groups declared themselves to be deeply committed to women's public activism and social reform.

The Anti-suffragist as "New Woman"

In March 1909, *The Anti-Suffragist*, a publication of the New York State Associa-tion Opposed to Woman Suffrage (NYSAOWS), reprinted a comment by well-known suffragist Florence Kelley, general secretary of the National Consumers League, in which she branded the Antis as "shirks," "lazy, comfortable, sheltered creatures, caring nothing for the miseries of the poor."[12] Few other accusations could have struck more to the heart of the anti-suffrage women's self-definition and could have provoked a more indignant reaction. Addressing the Judiciary Committee of the House of Representatives in 1914, Massachusetts Anti Mrs. Henry Preston (Sarah C.) White took pains to refute such claims. Listing a long catalog of the MAOFESW members' and leaders' manifold philanthropic, charitable, educational, and civic activities, White asserted that the anti-suffragists, all widely publicized stereotypes to the contrary, were "disinterested, public-spirited citizens who give their time and service to questions of public service without the hope of political reward or preference."[13]

Similar assertions resounded throughout the anti-suffrage literature of the first two decades of the twentieth century. In a prefatory chapter to a collection of anti-suffrage essays by Massachusetts women, published on the occasion of the defeat

of the state's 1915 suffrage referendum, Mrs. John (Katharine Torbert) Balch, then president of the MAOFESW, emphasized that its members represented a fair cross section of the population, comprising women of every "class or type." Even more importantly, she asserted that she "could fill pages with the record" of the Antis' "public welfare activities."[14] As if to underscore that claim, every one of the seventeen anti-suffrage essays following Balch's introduction was prefaced by a roster of the various public activities of their respective authors—activities that included work in educational associations, municipal, health, consumer, and trade union leagues, women's clubs, settlement houses, state boards of charity, prison, playground, and child reform organizations.[15]

The public activities or the professional experiences of an anti-suffrage woman were often cited as if they conferred upon her the very legitimacy and authority to speak out in opposition to women's enfranchisement and to make her opinion one of particular interest and value to the female population of America. When addressing themselves to the public, whether in the form of legislative committees or a more general audience, Antis emphatically underscored their public commitment and thus took pains to dissociate themselves from the image of sheltered, domestic creatures foisted upon them by their opponents. Yet references to civic activities did more than boost the Antis' stature in public. The anti-suffragists' involvement in all kinds of reform and associational endeavors was reflected by and shaped the rationale of the women opposed to their enfranchisement. I want to argue that the arguments turn-of-the-century Antis most frequently invoked against women's enfranchisement had less to do with woman's place in the home than with her appropriate role in the public realm.

A Woman's Place Is in Public

Just as the Antis rejected their image as idle, elitist, "bridge-playing" socialites,[16] they steadfastly sought to refute the suffragists' assertions that the domestic sphere was the only one they allegedly considered appropriate for women. They continually pointed out that they did *not* "make a fetish of the home as a place, nor of woman in the home, merely because she happens to be there."[17] On the contrary. Turn-of-the-century anti-suffrage leaders constantly urged women to leave the household to engage in a multitude of extra-domestic activities. In what came to be the unofficial creed of NAOWS, reiterated time and again in *The Woman's Protest*, president Mrs. Arthur M. (Josephine) Dodge stated at the organization's fourth annual meeting in January 1916:

> We believe that women according to their leisure, opportunities, and experience should take part increasingly in civic and municipal affairs as they always have done in charitable, philanthropic and educational activities and we believe that this can best be done without the ballot by women, as a non-partisan body of disinterested workers.[18]

Another Anti put it even more forcefully: "Do not mistake me. No woman should spend all her time at home. Public needs and social duties must be attended to."[19] In an attempt to clarify the Antis' position on this issue, Mrs. J.B. Gilfillan, president of the Minnesota Association Opposed to Woman Suffrage, announced that:

> Anti-Suffragists are opposed to women in political life, opposed to women in politics. This is often interpreted to mean opposition to women in public life, which is a profound mistake. We believe in women in all the usual phases of public life, except political life. Wherever woman's influence, counsel or work is needed by the community, there you will find her, so far with little thought of political beliefs.... The pedestals they are said to stand upon move them into all the demands of the community.[20]

In keeping with their own public activism and visibility, anti-suffrage leaders, speakers, and authors thus saw women's legitimate sphere of action not reduced to or circumscribed by domestic concerns. Rather, they stimulated women to venture beyond the home dutifully to shoulder their responsibilities in the public realm of reform and civic activities.

Given their obvious advocacy of women's presence in public life, both in theory and in practice, the question becomes *why* the anti-suffragists shied away so vehemently from the political realm. What explains the resolute stance of New York journalist Jeanette L. Gilder who wrote: "Give woman everything she wants, but not the ballot. Open every field of learning, every avenue of industry to her, but keep her out of politics"?[21] What made the vote so unpalatable to those women who otherwise embraced a host of public duties and responsibilities?

Anti-suffragists of the Progressive Era provided two answers. Some, by far the minority among them, argued that women were already overburdened, "with the demands of society, the calls of charity, the church, and philanthropy constantly increasing."[22] They thus could not possibly take on other, i.e. political duties, which would include not only casting the ballot, but also serving on juries or running for office. A further diffusion of women's energies would not increase their positive effect on society, as the suffragists argued, but entail a lessening of female influence as women would be forced to sacrifice quality for quantity in their attempt to add another weighty task to their already packed agenda.

More often, however, the Antis' rejection of the vote reflected not so much their dread of overwork and exhaustion, as it was based on a more sophisticated and recommendable rationale. "For me, the vital argument against suffrage for women is that it would hamper them in their more effective work in social and political lines," social worker Mary Ella Swift wrote in the lead article of a 1913 issue of *The Woman's Protest*.[23] Most Antis would certainly have agreed with this observation. Swift and other anti-suffragists insisted that political beliefs and the ballot would not only be of little value to the female reformer, but would in fact constitute a serious handicap in her work for the social good. Since casting the ballot would

necessitate a woman's alignment with a political party, to become a voter would rob her of her political neutrality and non-partisanship. This in turn would diminish her influence with legislative or other governmental authorities that had so far been responsive to women's requests on the very grounds of their political disinterestedness.[24] Standing "apart from and beyond party politics," unenfranchised women, the Antis argued, were especially effective in addressing social problems and bringing about much-needed reform legislation.[25] "Outside the political machinery," *The Anti-Suffragist* announced in its December 1908 issue, "there is a world...where all reform begins."[26] "The more reform movements are separated from politics the better for them," the journal declared again in April 1912.[27]

It was largely for this reason that the powerful umbrella organization of the nation's myriad female literary and educational groups, the General Federation of Women's Clubs, did not officially endorse woman suffrage until 1914. When it did, this came as a serious blow to the Antis. For years, they had tried to prevent this development by insisting that the collective work of the women's clubs was "more potent" than women's individual exercise of political privileges, which would only splinter female solidarity along party lines.[28] Likewise, the Antis considered trade unions, not political organizations, the better representatives of working women's interests and the more effective agents in providing good working conditions and propagating fair labor legislation.[29] To alleviate and remedy all kinds of social ills, concerning all classes and segments of society, anti-suffragists preferred non-partisan to partisan bodies, and politically neutral women to male voters whose reform intentions they found to be inevitably compromised by their affiliations to a political party.

Far from supposedly urging women to stay in or retreat into a narrowly circumscribed domestic realm and to "shirk" their public responsibilities, the female anti-suffragists advanced arguments that derived from and reflected their sincere efforts to discharge those responsibilities with the best possible results. In their opinion, it was the advocates of woman suffrage who egotistically dodged all civic obligations, attending suffrage meetings instead of "giv[ing] hours, days, thought and energy to quiet, persistent, unheralded work toward the amelioration of the condition of women, children, and the unfortunate."[30] When the suffragists announced that they would stop contributing to civic and philanthropic causes until they were given the vote, the Antis uttered a collective cry of indignation. Taking this as further example of the suffragists' selfishness and unscrupulousness, they grasped the opportunity to portray themselves as the truly reform-oriented and caring social force of the two.

Nonpartisan Women, Society, and the State

The fight for woman suffrage, at least during the Progressive Era, was not a conflict between women who were active in public and those who advocated that a woman's place was in the home. Rather, it was two different notions of women's

relationship to the public and the political realm that were at odds in the debates concerning women's enfranchisement. In an essay entitled "Woman's Civic Work Better Done Without Suffrage," Anti Elizabeth McCracken summarized the controversy's underlying issue as follows:

> [O]ur position, as Anti-Suffragists, is not negative, but positive. We are not so much opposing the policy of the Suffragists as we are presenting a policy of our own. The Suffragists have one conception of the relation of women to good government—and we Anti-Suffragists have another—which seems to us better. Just as fervently as the Suffragists, do the Anti-Suffragists desire to be citizens, and intend to be citizens.... We Anti-Suffragists feel that we not only can be and are citizens without the ballot, but that we shall remain better citizens without it than with it.[31]

Mrs. Andrew J. (Alice N.) George, a principal secretary of both the Massachusetts and the National Association Opposed to Woman Suffrage, also asserted that "[w]oman's citizenship is as real as man's. The question we must answer is one of social efficiency."[32] Thus, the issue at stake was not, as many historians have argued implicitly or explicitly, one of anti-suffragists pitting their private female sphere of domestic concerns against a male public sphere of political affairs in a vestigial Victorian scenario. Rather, in the social and political context of the Progressive Era, Antis tried to hold on to what they considered to be a distinctive female public realm, different from the male realm of politics in its functions, but equal or even superior in its societal ramifications.

In order to bring women's positive influence to bear even more successfully upon public life, anti-suffragists believed that the boundaries between men's and women's public activities should not be erased, but rendered even more distinct. Such was the gist of a lecture Mrs. Barclay Hazard held before the New York State Federation of Women's Clubs in 1907:

> [W]e must accept partisanship, political trickery and office-seeking as necessary evils inseparable from modern conditions, and the question arises what can be done to palliate the situation. To our minds, the solution has been found by the entrance of women into public life. Standing in an absolutely independent position, freed from all party affiliations, untrammeled by any political obligations, the intelligent, self-sacrificing women of to-day are serving the State (though many of them hardly realize it) as a third party whose disinterestedness none can doubt.[33]

The successful continuation of women's disinterested work, "untainted by political ambition" and motives, would only be ensured, according to the anti-suffragists, by keeping men and women in their separate public spheres and by recognizing their respective promises as well as limitations.[34]

In the eyes of the anti-suffragists, the vote threatened to divest women of their public power. By forcibly redirecting women's attention and energies to politics, the proponents of women's enfranchisement were about to undermine the non-partisan foundation of the all-female clubs, societies, and associations, i.e., women's citadels of public power. Seeing the suffragists' demand for the vote as an indication of their willingness to sacrifice women's social activism in the arena of male electoral politics, the Antis were upset by this apparent denial of the efficiency and validity of women's public influence as manifested through channels other than electoral politics. Women's strength in the public sphere, the Antis argued, could be more fully developed if they remembered their difference, not their sameness with male political actors. What was at stake for the Antis in the debates about woman suffrage was not women's domesticity, but women's effectiveness as non-voting, yet public-spirited citizens and agents of social change.

In order to show that their claims about the reform successes and social efficiency of unenfranchised women were not just sheer hypotheses or wishful thinking on their part, the Antis cited a variety of evidence in their favor. Their preferred strategy was to enlist the testimony of a host of female social workers, reformers, and activists who maintained that they would have never accomplished what they did if they had been entitled to cast the ballot and thereby been asked to abdicate their political neutrality. Furthermore, the anti-suffragists buttressed their assertions with "empirical evidence" from the states that had already granted the franchise to their female populations. Charts unfavorably comparing the reform legislation as well as the laws pertaining to women in Colorado, the Antis' exemplary suffrage state, to those of the Eastern non-suffrage states filled the pages of the anti-suffrage periodicals.[35] Such legal documentation also constituted the basis for Minnie Bronson's influential anti-suffrage tract, "The Wage-Earning Woman and the State," reprinted annually in the early 1910s, which tried to disprove contentions about working women's need for the ballot.[36] Finally, the Antis cited statistical as well as impressionistic evidence to announce the numerical decline of women's civic and reform associations in the suffrage states.

The years during World War I seemed to be an especially propitious time for the Antis to advance their argument of the efficiency of politically neutral women carrying out disinterested relief service in the name of peace and patriotism. While some suffragists proclaimed that they ranked their efforts to win the vote above the country's commitment to win the war, the Antis instead never tired of highlighting their self-sacrificing and loyal stance towards the nation. In fact, they channeled much of their associational, human, and financial resources into war relief work, which was extensively documented in the war-year issues of *The Woman's Protest*. Asserting that the "importance of nonpolitical women to the state [was] greater than ever before," the anti-suffragists saw the global conflict as an opportunity to put an end to allegations about their idleness and to demonstrate the validity and relevance, not to mention the patriotic implications, of their rationale against

Headquarters of the National Association Opposed to Woman Suffrage
in New York City

women's enfranchisement.[37] Ironically, what had looked like a perfect opportunity
to underscore the logic of the Anti position turned out to be one of the major
determining factors in their ultimate defeat. In recognition of the invaluable aid
and service women had rendered to their country during this time of crisis, many
formerly undecided legislators finally acceded to the Nineteenth Amendment,
granting women the vote in 1920.

Anti-suffragism, Female Activism, and Progressive Reform

The emergence, in the 1890s and the first two decades of the 1900s, of an anti-
suffrage rationale that centered on the public activities rather than the domestic
"nature" and destiny of American women reflected and drew upon certain
historical developments and circumstances that made the argument both timely
and persuasive. This is not to say that *all* female or, for that matter, male, opponents
of women's suffrage espoused the reasoning outlined in this essay. Nor do I want to
argue that this has been the dominant anti-suffrage rationale ever since women
first demanded their enfranchisement. Rather, it was an argument particularly
suited to the Progressive Era. In that particular period of American history, which
was characterized by a near-universal preoccupation with reform and enthusiasm
for progress, women gained new visibility and clout. Women founded and

WHY WE DO NOT APPROVE
—OF—
WOMAN SUFFRAGE

BECAUSE: We feel that the ballot makes absolutely no difference in the economic status of woman. Whether she votes or not, her charities, great and small, will continue, professions will extend diplomas to her intelligence, and trade will grant recompense to her ability. As for the protection of the ballot to working women, it will protect them no farther than it protects men who, in spite of their voting power, find themselves unable to cope with labor conditions by legislation and form themselves into unions outside of law and law making.

BECAUSE: Our hospital Boards, our social and civic service work, our child welfare committees and countless other clubs and industries for the general welfare and uplift need women who can give non-partisan and unselfish service, the worth of which service would be greatly lessened by political affiliations.

BECAUSE: Behind law there must always be force to make it effective. If legislation was shaped by a majority of women over men we should soon have, not government, but chaos.

BECAUSE: It is an attested fact that politics degrade women more than women purify politics.

BECAUSE: We believe that American men would speedily remedy all conditions needing reform if urged with half the force now brought to bear in favor of suffrage.

BECAUSE: We believe that the interests of all women are as safe in the hands of men as in those of other women.

BECAUSE: Thorough investigation of the laws of suffrage states shows that non-suffrage states have by far the better and more humane laws, and that all laws are more strictly enforced than in suffrage states.

BECAUSE: We believe that if franchise for women would better general conditions, there would be some evidence of that betterment in states where it has been exercised for twenty and up to forty-four years.

BECAUSE: Women make little use of suffrage when it is given them. School suffrage has been a lamentable failure, the women vote averaging scarcely two per cent in any state.

BECAUSE: The energies of women are engrossed by their present duties and interests, from which men cannot relieve them, and there is great need of better performance of their present work rather than diversion to new fields of activity.

BECAUSE: The suffrage movement develops sex hatred which is a menace to society.

BECAUSE: Of the alliance of suffrage with socialism which advocates free love and institutional life for children.

BECAUSE: The greatest menace to the morals of today lies in the efforts of suffragists to convince the world that vice is predominant. In the mad rush for the ballot and the consequent advertisement of immorality, reverence has been dethroned and reticence annihilated. It is high time for the right thinking, purity-loving women to arise and undo the terrific impress made on the public mind by the preachments of these pursuers of vice.

BECAUSE: The great majority of intelligent, refined and educated women do not want enfranchisement. They realize no sense of injustice such as expressed by the small minority of suffragists. They have all the rights and freedom they desire, and consider their present trusts most sacred and important. They feel that the duties which naturally must ever revert to their sex are such that none but themselves can perform and that political responsibilities could not be borne by them without the sacrifice of the highest interests of their families and of society.

 Nebraska Association Opposed to Woman Suffrage.

Anti-suffrage leaflet, c. 1914

participated in a variety of associations, organizations, clubs, and societies; they entered many educational institutions that had formerly been the exclusive preserve of men; and they were newly visible in the public as clerical workers, department store employees, professionals, and social reformers.[38] Contrary to common historical wisdom, the female Antis were not opposed to but actively involved in such and similar developments. Their associational and sometimes (semi-)professional experiences did not only provide them with the expertise and the know-how to establish an organized anti-suffrage movement; they also became an integral part of their anti-suffrage rationale. Far from divorcing themselves from the activist and reformist traditions and tendencies of the past and the present, the anti-suffrage women eagerly stressed their indebtedness to nineteenth-century female reformers and emphasized their firm commitment to the reform agenda of the Progressive Era.

As a matter of fact, early twentieth-century Antis cited the female notables of the preceding century as fitting exemplars of women whose fame and reputation rested upon a host of extraordinary achievements, all of which had been possible without the ballot. The Antis were not at a loss to find distinguished nineteenth-century women who had combined public activism with a resolute anti-suffrage stance. English relief worker Octavia Hill was occasionally introduced as the prototypical woman whose distinctive and invaluable contribution was not that of a "politician," but of "a disinterested factor working to render public service uncolored by political motives."[39] Closer to home, educators Catharine Beecher, Emma Willard, and Civil War nurse Dorothea Dix, "the Florence Nightingale of this country," led the throng of influential women whom the American Antis took to be their sisters in spirit and action as well as the truly progressive forces in society.[40]

Claiming to be the rightful descendants of this distinctively female tradition of public activism, the anti-suffragists aligned themselves with the "true woman" ideology that they saw as the driving force behind all major reform achievements of the nineteenth and early twentieth centuries.[41] Anti Lilian Bayard Taylor Kiliani cited the entrance of women into institutions of higher education, industry, and the professions as well as the profusion of female reform associations and movements as irrefutable proof of how much women were able to achieve, "without going to the polls or becoming involved in party politics."[42] Helen Kendrick Johnson, in particular, made it her avowed objective to wrest praise for women's progress and manifold accomplishments from the suffragists. She asserted that "'Movement' and 'Progress' [were] not synonymous terms," but with regard to woman suffrage virtually irreconcilable opposites. In her *Woman and the Republic,* she argued that wherever advocates of woman suffrage had meddled in matters of major national concern—be it abolitionism, temperance, or woman's rights—they had only caused delays, dissensions, and serious disturbances, which had frustrated a more prompt and efficient approach to these affairs.[43]

Aware that "next to being unpopular, to be unprogressive, is the worst thing that can be said of an American, male or female,"[44] Antis were especially sensitive to criticism of that kind and went to great lengths to refute allegations about their aversion to change. New York Anti Annie Nathan Meyer, one of the driving forces behind the foundation of Barnard College and an associate editor of the anti-suffrage, anti-feminist, anti-socialist *The Woman's Patriot*, was especially insistent in refuting the widespread assumption that the "movement to obtain the ballot for women is identical with and not to be separated from all other movements for women's progress." In the spring of 1910, she indignantly wrote:

Anti-suffragist Annie Nathan Meyer. She and her sister, Maud Nathan, were leaders of opposite sides of the woman suffrage movement.

THE BARNARD ARCHIVES AND SPECIAL COLLECTIONS

The suffragists have battled for suffrage the past forty years in America—on the whole with rather conspicuous unsuccess. Some of them—fewer by far than is claimed—also incidentally battled for other reform, but never without the help and enthusiasm of convinced anti-suffragists.... The women who really blazed the paths of education and reform in this country were either outspoken antisuffragists or at best lukewarm suffragists who were too busy doing their work to bother about imaginary wrongs. This confusion of the suffrage movement with every movement that made for advance goes merrily on, and few take the trouble to stop it.[45]

Turning the tables on the suffragists, the Antis characterized the votes-for-women movement as "fifty years behind the time," calling it a "movement backward towards men and mastodons, the miocene hipparion and eocene anchitherium."[46] In comparison, the average female anti-suffragist was seen as standing "in the very front rank of progress for she [was] a preventive philanthropist," she was "the newest new woman...at work at home and in public."[47]

Because it allowed them to combine their rejection of women's enfranchisement with an unequivocal affirmation of the ideas of social progress and women's advancement, such reasoning understandably attracted many women to the anti-suffrage cause. The appeal of this particular argumentation could largely be explained by the fact that it built on and embraced several assumptions that were shared by most

women—and men—during the Progressive Era, regardless of their stance on the question of suffrage.

In fact, agreement on women's public influence and the need for social reform often brought opponents and proponents of woman suffrage alike together in their common concern for the public good. In 1891, Annie Nathan Meyer edited a book called *Woman's Work in America,* a collection of essays on women's manifold contributions to education, literature, journalism, medicine, ministry, law, industry, philanthropy, and the state.[48] Ironically, and significantly, most of the contributors to this volume, which was compiled by an ardent anti-suffragist, professed to be in favor of women's enfranchisement; the preface, for example, was written by well-known Bostonian suffragist Julia Ward Howe.

Suffragists were in fact willing to acknowledge the successes and positive changes in social work that women had wrought without the vote. In an essay entitled "The Legislative Influence of Unenfranchised Women," historian and activist Mary Ritter Beard conceded that "other influences than those of the ballot box operate on" legislators and state representatives.[49] Elaborating on this point, Beard in 1915 published her *Woman's Work in Municipalities,* an impressive compendium of the various types of women's activities on the local and communal levels—paying no heed to those women's opinion on the suffrage issue.[50]

While anti-suffragists most probably wholeheartedly welcomed Beard's observations, they could not assent to her suggestion that women's influence would reach even further if they were given the vote. For the Antis, it was the very fact of their disfranchisement and concomitant disinterestedness that had made women such efficient reformers. Looking back on women's multitudinous accomplishments over the past decades, they saw no reason to believe that the continuing success and expansion of women's charitable, philanthropic, and civic reform activities depended on the ballot. It was at this crucial juncture where anti- and pro-suffrage women's opinions took different turns. While the demand for the vote, in some instances, served as a unifying cause for many women of different backgrounds and interests, it became the divisive issue for many female activists who otherwise found themselves in general accord on matters concerning women's prominent role in turn-of-the-century social reform.[51] Agreeing on social reform as the desirable objective of women's public involvement, Antis and suffragists differed on which way was the better and more efficient to that end.

Conclusion

Such findings not only correct or modify traditional accounts concerning the female anti-suffragists' makeup and motives, but also carry with them implications that are relevant to larger debates in the field of women's history. It would not be an exaggeration to claim that women's involvement in reform associations, institutions, and movements is probably the most widely studied area of American women's history. Much of the secondary literature has focused on the

"O SAVE US, SENATORS, FROM OURSELVES!"

Cover of *Harper's Weekly,*
February 23, 1907

question of whether or to what extent women's manifold organizational activities foreshadowed and/or constituted the necessary prerequisites of suffragism and feminism. For the most part, historians have tried to establish a continuum between early- and mid-nineteenth-century women's participation in a variety of reform movements and turn-of-the-century women's espousal of suffrage and feminist principles. Earlier abolitionist, moral reform, temperance, and other largely single-sex reform societies have been seen as consciousness-raising training-grounds for later avid suffragists. Similarly, historians have argued that nineteenth-century women's activism gave them an incentive to expand their sphere of influence and provided them with a rationale to demand the vote to that end.[52]

The example of the female anti-suffragists, however, calls for a more complex interpretation. As their case demonstrates, women's public activities have not always been put to feminist ends nor have they necessarily bred ideas critical of the patriarchal organization of the state as women, so the story goes, came to realize their powerlessness and ineffectiveness in the political arena.[53] The Antis, as discussed in this essay, opposed women's enfranchisement not in spite of, but *because of* their involvement and experiences in a huge number of extra-domestic organizations, which they came to look upon as their bulwarks of public power and influence. The majority of organized Antis were women who occupied many public positions and offices and who brought their experiences and expertise in the public realm to bear on their anti-suffrage labor. While they saw suffragism and feminism as dangerous to the progress of society, they, at the same time, had no difficulty proclaiming their affinities with various pioneering women activists of the nineteenth century, or welcoming every possible development that they perceived as furthering women's progress. Both the Antis' own activism and their interpretations of women's historical and social mission combined to generate strong anti-feminist, defined as anti-suffrage, beliefs and convictions.

Yet, strangely and ironically, anti-suffrage women have something to tell the late twentieth-century feminist historian and theorist. Although the turn-of-the-century Antis' own definition of politics as a male, partisan enterprise was a very narrow one, which did not encompass their reform activities, this fact should not and cannot prevent us from regarding women's public activism in the realm of social reform legislation as highly political. Recent feminist scholarship has expanded traditional definition of politics so as to incorporate many areas, activities, and actors that have generally been excluded by political theory. Some scholars have even gone so far as to suggest that there were times, the Progressive Era prominent among them, when women's distinctive contributions to society had more far-reaching social and political implications than men's exercise of their voting privileges.[54] Emphasizing the integrity and importance of a distinctively female tradition of public activism and asserting that women's citizenship did not, for its valuation, depend on the vote, the turn-of-the-century anti-suffrage women styled themselves as champions and defenders of an area and of ideas that are of increasing interest to feminist political theorists who are trying to introduce an "alternative concept of public life" deriving its force from non-electoral, non-partisan forms of political participation.[55] Once historians and political theorists start to examine more closely the workings and the concerns of the female public culture of the past to gain insights for the present and the future, they cannot afford to ignore the voices of the women who opposed woman suffrage.

Notes

This essay is a revised version of an article originally published in the *Journal of Women's History* 5, no. 1 (Spring 1993), 33-60, and appears here with the permission of the journal.

1. Florence R. Hall, "Disinterested, Appealing to All Humanity," *The Woman's Protest* 7, no. 5 (September 1915), 6.

2. Carrie Chapman Catt and Nettie Rogers Shuler, *Woman Suffrage and Politics: The Inner Story of the Suffrage Movement* (1923; reprint, Seattle, 1969), 132.

3. See Eleanor Flexner, *Century of Struggle: The Woman's Rights Movement in the United States* (Cambridge, 1968), 294-305; Alan P. Grimes, *The Puritan Ethic and Woman Suffrage* (New York, 1967), 78-98; Aileen S. Kraditor, *The Ideas of the Woman Suffrage Movement, 1890-1920* (New York, 1965), 14-42; William L. O'Neill, *Feminism in America: A History* (New Brunswick, 1969), 55-64; and Carl N. Degler, *At Odds: Women and the Family in America from the Revolution to the Present* (New York, 1980), 349-355.

4. See, Jane Jerome Camhi, "Women Against Women: American Anti-Suffragism, 1880-1920," Ph.D. diss., Tufts University, 1973; Thomas J. Jablonsky, "Duty, Nature, and Stability: The Female Anti-Suffragists in the U.S., 1894-1920," Ph.D. diss., University of Southern California, 1978; See also Mara Mayor, "Fears and Fantasies of the Anti-Suffragists," *Connecticut Review* 7, no. 2 (April 1974): 64-74; Catherine Cole Mambretti, "The Battle Against the Ballot: Illinois Woman Antisuffragists," *Chicago History* 9, no. 3 (Fall 1980): 168-177; and Louise L. Stevenson, "Women Antisuffragists in the 1915 Massachusetts Campaign," *New England Quarterly* 52, no. 1 (March 1979): 80-93.

5. For more information see, Camhi, "Women Against Women," and Jablonsky, "Duty, Nature, and Stability."

6. *The Woman's Protest* 7, no. 1 (May 1915): 16.

7. *The St. Paul Pioneer-Press*, cited in Helen Kendrick Johnson, *Woman and the Republic: A Survey of the Woman-Suffrage Movement in the United States and a Discussion of the Claims and Arguments of Its Foremost Advocates* (1897; New York, 1913), 364, 367, 368.

8. *The Brooklyn Standard-Union*, quoted in Rossiter Johnson, *Helen Kendrick Johnson: The Story of Her Varied Activities* (New York, 1917), 51.

9. Molly Elliot Seawell, *The Ladies' Battle* (New York, 1911); Ida Tarbell, *The Business of Being a Woman* (New York, 1912); Grace Duffield Goodwin, *Anti-Suffrage: Ten Good Reasons* (New York, 1915); and Annie Riley Hale, *The Eden Sphinx* (New York, 1916).

10. Quotes are taken from *The Woman's Standard* (May 1906): 3, ibid. (February 1905): 1, cited in Jablonsky, "Duty, Nature, and Stability," 10; *The Woman's Protest* 8, no. 5 (March 1916): 13; and Susan B. Anthony and Ida Husted Harper, *History of Woman Suffrage* 4 (New York, 1969), 716.

11. Susan E. Marshall, "In Defense of Separate Spheres: Class and Status Politics in the Antisuffrage Movement," *Social Forces* 65, no. 2 (December 1986): 327-351; and Susan E. Marshall and Anthony M. Orum, "Opposition Then and Now: Countering Feminism in the Twentieth Century," in *Research in Politics and Society: A Research Annual; Vol. 2: Women and Politics: Activism, Attitudes and Office-Holding*, eds. Gwen Moore and Glenna Spitze (Greenwich, Conn., 1986), 23.

12. Florence Kelley, quoted in *The Anti-Suffragist* 1, no. 3 (March 1909): 2.

13. Mrs. Henry White, "Who Are the Anti-Suffragists—And Why," *The Woman's Protest* 4, no. 6 (April 1914): 5, 6.

14. See Mrs. John Balch, "Who the Massachusetts Anti-Suffragists Are," in *Anti-Suffrage Essays by Massachusetts Women*, ed. Ernest Bernbaum (Boston: Forum Publications, 1916), 21-23.

15. That this self-representation on the part of the Antis did indeed correspond with their actual experiences and

employments is corroborated by a look at the 1914-1915 edition of the *Woman's Who's Who of America*. In this biographical dictionary of American and Canadian women who "are leading in or contributing to women's larger participation in the good causes and higher endeavors of our time," one finds a great number of women who, while actively engaged in a host of leagues, clubs, societies, and voluntary organizations, declared themselves opposed to or undecided with regard to woman suffrage; see John William Leonard, ed., *Women's Who's Who of America: A Biographical Dictionary of Contemporary Women of the United States and Canada, 1914-1915* (New York, 1914), 22.

16. Laura Fay-Smith, quoted in Marshall, "In Defense of Separate Spheres," 341.

17. *The Woman's Protest* 5, no. 6 (October 1914): 14.

18. Mrs. Arthur M. Dodge, "The Report of the President," *The Woman's Protest* 8, no. 3 (January 1916): 6.

19. Mrs. Charles Burton Gulick, "The Imperative Demand Upon Women in the Home," in *Anti-Suffrage Essays by Massachusetts Women*, 133.

20. Mrs. J.B. Gilfillan, "Work and the Home," *The Woman's Protest* 7, no. 1 (May 1915): 17.

21. Jeanette L. Gilder, "Why I am Opposed to Woman Suffrage," pamphlet, 1894, MAOFESW, Mudd Library, Yale University (hereafter cited as Mudd).

22. Quoted in Kraditor, *The Ideas of the Woman Suffrage Movement*, 27-28; also *The Anti-Suffragist* 1, no. 1 (July 1908): 4; and Emily Bissell, "A Talk to Women on the Suffrage Question," pamphlet, 1909, 2, NYSAOWS, Mudd.

23. Mary Ella Swift, "Suffrage for Women a Handicap in Civic Work," *The Woman's Protest* 3, no. 4 (August 1913): 3.

24. See *The Anti-Suffragist* 1, no. 2 (December 1908): 11, 13; 2, no. 1 (September 1909): 5; 3, no. 3 (March 1911): 3; 3, no. 4 (June 1911): 8; 4 no. 2 (April 1912): 2; *The Woman's Protest* 1, no. 4 (August 1912): 12; 6, no. 3 (January 1915): 9; and 7, no. 5 (September 1915): 19. See also the contributions of Mrs. A.J. George, Monica Foley, Dorothy Godfrey Wayman, and Margaret C. Robinson in *Anti-Suffrage Essays by Massachusetts Women*.

25. *The Anti-Suffragist* 1, no. 2 (December 1908): 11.

26. *The Anti-Suffragist* 1, no. 2 (December 1908): 13.

27. *The Anti-Suffragist* 4, no. 2 (April 1912): 2.

28. Anon., "Women's Clubs More Potent Than the Ballot," *The Woman's Protest* 5, no. 3 (July 1914): 5.

29. See Anon., "Working Women and Suffrage," *The Anti-Suffragist* 2, no. 2 (December 1909): 1; and Adeline Knapp, "Do Working Women Need the Ballot?—An Address to the Senate and Assembly Judiciary Committee of the New York Legislature," NAOWS, Mudd.

30. Anon., "Missing the Opportunities," *The Woman's Protest* 1, no. 5 (September 1912): 4.

31. Elizabeth McCracken, "Woman's Civic Work Better Done Without Suffrage," *The Woman's Protest* 4, no. 3 (Jan 1914): 16.

32. Mrs. A.J. George, "Efficiency the Real Test of Woman Suffrage," *The Woman's Protest* 8, no. 6 (April 1916): 5.

33. Mrs. Barclay Hazard, "How Women Can Best Serve the State" (Chicago: Illinois Association Opposed to the Extension of Suffrage to Women; reprinted by courtesy of the NYSAOWS, n.d.), 2, Mudd.

34. *The Woman's Protest* 2, no. 2 (December 1912): 6; see also Annah Robinson Watson, "The Attitude of Southern Women on the Suffrage Question," *The Arena* 11 (February 1895): 366.

35. See Eliza D. Armstrong, "Non-Partisan Woman Wins Where Voters Fail," *The Woman's Protest* 4, no. 3 (December 1913): 21; Mrs. Rowland G. Hazard, "Some Reasons Why We Oppose Suffrage; Its Effect on the State," pamphlet, 1911, Rhode Island Association Opposed to Woman's Suffrage, Mudd; Ellen Mudge Burrill, "Some Practical Aspects of the Question"; and Catherine Robinson, "Massachusetts Compared With Suffrage States," in *Anti-Suffrage Essays by Massachusetts Women*, 43-52, 62-66.

36. Minnie Bronson, "The Wage-Earning Woman and the State," 1912, 1913, 1914, NAOWS, Mudd.

37. *The Woman's Protest* 7, no. 4 (August 1915): 7-8.

38. For an excellent overview of this period, see Sara M. Evans, *Born for Liberty: A History of Women in America* (New York, 1989), 145-173.

39. Mrs. Arthur M. Dodge, "Woman Suffrage Opposed to Woman's Rights," in *Women in Public Life*, ed. James P. Lichtenberger, *The Annals of the American Academy of Political and Social Science* 56 (November 1914), 104.

40. *The Woman's Protest* 8, no. 5 (March 1916): 19.

41. Mrs. Herbert Lyman, "The Anti-Suffrage Ideal," in *Anti-Suffrage Essays by Massachusetts Women*, 121; *The Woman's Protest* 5, no. 2 (June 1914): 10.

42. Lilian Bayard Taylor Kiliani, "Women Without Ballot Do Greater Work," *The Woman's Protest* 3, no. 2 (June 1913): 8.

43. See especially the introduction and the chapter on "Woman Suffrage and Philanthropy" in Johnson, *Woman and the Republic*, 5-9, 104-155; quotation on 104.

44. Mrs. Robert McVickar, "What is an Anti-Suffragist?," undated pamphlet, NAOWS, Mudd.

45. Annie Nathan Meyer, "Miss Johnston and Woman Suffrage," *The Bookman* 31 (May 1910): 314.

46. Alice Hill Chittenden, "The Inexpediency of Granting the Suffrage to American Women—An Address at the Tenth Biennial of the General Federation of Women's Clubs, Cincinnati, May 14, 1910," pamphlet, NAOWS, Mudd; Anon., "A Movement Toward Mastodons," *The Woman's Protest* 4, no. 1 (November 1913): 14.

47. Margaret H. Freeman, "The Voice of the Majority," *The Anti-Suffragist* 2, no. 1 (September 1909): 3; and Margaret Doane Gardiner, "A Mining Experiment," *The Anti-Suffragist* 3, no. 1 (September 1910): 3.

48. Annie Nathan Meyer, ed., *Woman's Work in America* (New York, 1972).

49. Mary Ritter Beard, "The Legislative Influence of Un-enfranchised Women," in *Women in Public Life*, 54, 60.

50. Mary Ritter Beard, *Woman's Work in Municipalities* (1915; New York, 1972).

51. See Lucy Jeanne Price, "Lessons Learned From the Campaign," *The Woman's Protest* 8, no. 1 (November 1915): 5-6.

52. See especially Keith Melder, "Ladies Bountiful: Organized Women's Benevolence in Early Nineteenth-Century America," *New York History* 48, no. 3 (July 1967): 231-255; Alice Rossi, "Social Roots of the Woman's Movement in America," in *The Feminist Papers*, ed. Alice Rossi, (New York, 1973), 241-281; Barbara Berg, *The Remembered Gate: Origins of American Feminism. The Woman and the City, 1800-1860* (New York, 1978); and Lori Ginzberg, "'Moral Suasion is Moral Balderdash': Women, Politics, and Social Activism in the 1850s," *Journal of American History* 73, no. 3 (December 1986): 601-622.

53. Studies that have acknowledged the anti-feminist potential of women's associations include: Mary Ryan, "The Power of Women's Networks: A Case Study of Female Moral Reform in Antebellum America," *Feminist Studies* 5, no. 1 (Spring 1979): 66-85; Nancy Cott, *The Bonds of Womanhood: "Woman's Sphere" in New England, 1780-1835* (New Haven, 1977); and Nancy A. Hewitt, *Women's Activism and Social Change: Rochester, N.Y., 1822-1872* (Ithaca, 1984).

54. See Estelle Freedman, "Separatism As Strategy: Female Institution Building and American Feminism, 1870-1930," *Feminist Studies* 5, no. 3 (Fall 1979): 512-529; Paula Baker, "The Domestication of Politics: Women and American Political Society, 1780-1920," *American Historical Review* 89, no.2 (June 1984): 620-647; idem., *The Moral Frameworks of Public Life: Gender, Politics, and the State in Rural New York, 1870-1930* (New York, 1991); and Maureen A. Flanagan, "Gender and Urban Political Reform: The City Club and the Woman's City Club of Chicago in the Progressive Era," *American Historical Review* 95 (October 1990): 1032-1050.

55. Sara M. Evans, "Women's History and Political Theory: Towards a Feminist Approach to Public Life," in *Visible Women: New Essays on American Activism*, Nancy A. Hewitt and Suzanne Lebsock, eds. (Urbana, 1993), 121.

Fifteen

WORKING WOMEN, CLASS RELATIONS, AND SUFFRAGE MILITANCE:

Harriot Stanton Blatch and the
New York Woman Suffrage Movement,
1894—1909

Ellen Carol DuBois

Editor's Introduction: Rediscovering the woman suffrage movement means revising a number of widely held but inaccurate ideas about the movement and its history. One of these misconceptions is that the woman suffrage movement in America was a "middle-class movement." Though it is true that many suffragists and suffrage leaders were middle-class, characterizing the movement as such, as Ellen Carol DuBois explains, "homogenizes" the movement. It distorts the picture by ignoring the presence in, and the contributions to, the suffrage movement of women from both ends of the economic scale.

As DuBois makes clear in this essay, elite women and working-class women were increasingly involved in the suffrage movement around the turn of the century. And in New York, a coalition of these women headed by Harriot Stanton Blatch, Elizabeth Cady Stanton's daughter, created a new tradition of class relations among women—one on which, writes DuBois, a "thriving, modern woman suffrage movement could be built." DuBois, author of *Harriot Stanton Blatch and the Winning of Woman Suffrage*, describes Blatch as a born politician with the "combination of suffrage convictions and class awareness to lead New York suffragists through that transition." After a fascinating discussion of the attitudes of the wealthy suffragists who became prominent in the movement in the 1890s, DuBois explains how Blatch rejected the pattern of class relations favored by many elite suffragists and pointed the way to a new and far more productive working relationship between women from both ends of the socioeconomic spectrum that would transform and invigorate the entire suffrage campaign.

Though from an elite background, Blatch rejected the maternalistic attitudes toward working-class women held by many elite suffragists who presumed that working-class women should defer to their leadership in return for their protection. And she emphatically denounced the idea endorsed by some suffrage leaders in the

1890s (including Elizabeth Cady Stanton) that suffragists should call for woman suffrage with an educational qualification that would curtail the number of working-class women who would be enfranchised. A college-educated woman with B.A. and M.A. degrees from Vassar, Blatch's view of work as the key to women's independence, dignity, and freedom was similar to that of her contemporary, the feminist intellectual, Charlotte Perkins Gilman. Indeed, Blatch saw working-class women more as exemplars for women like herself rather than "victims to be succored."

Blatch, like Jane Addams, was convinced that working-class women not only understood their own interests but needed the vote in order to represent those interests and support reform. Impressed by the successful efforts of some British suffragists to organize across class lines (Blatch had married an Englishman and lived in Great Britain from 1882 to 1902), and by the partnership created between working-class and wealthy women in the Women's Trade Union League, she was also convinced that working-class women were able co-workers in the fight for woman suffrage.

Blatch urged established suffrage societies "to recognize the importance of the vote to wage-earning women and the importance of wage-earning women to winning the vote." However, writes DuBois, when existing groups failed to respond, Blatch formed her own society, the "Equality League of Self-Supporting Women." This organization, which harnessed the talents of educated professionals and the power and political sagacity of trade-union women, provided the medium for introducing a new and aggressive—indeed militant—style of activism into the suffrage movement.

Indeed, DuBois helps us rediscover the suffrage movement in yet another very important way as she demonstrates that the militant tactics embraced by American suffragists in the twentieth century were not entirely imported, but partly home grown—a contribution of working-class suffragists. Their involvement in the movement "broaden[ed] the class basis and the outlook of American suffragism" and thus prepared the way for American women "to respond to the heroism of the British militants."

Following a 1907 visit to New York by a leader of the British militants, Blatch and other "new" suffrage leaders introduced their tactics into the American movement. Some New York suffragists even adopted the name "suffragette"—a term embraced by the British militants, but generally shunned by moderate or conservative American suffragists precisely because it associated them with the British militants and was used by American anti-suffragists to belittle or denigrate suffrage advocates. But the embrace of the term by some New York suffragists—as well as their participation in public demonstrations—suggested just how willing these suffragists had become to part with genteel tradition.

Militant tactics, including parades and open-air (as opposed to parlor) meetings, and other such attention-getting tactics, would soon be embraced by the mainstream suffrage movement all over the nation (though the NAWSA continued

to shun picketing and civil disobedience). These tactics proved to be extremely important to the cause, as they made it impossible for the press to continue to ignore the movement as they seemed determined to do. And, as Blatch shrewdly comprehended, participation in these public acts by women who had been taught to shun publicity was in itself good for the cause, in that it forced a re-examination of assumptions about definitions of femininity and cemented the participants' commitment to the cause.

★   ★   ★   ★   ★

THE POLITICS of Harriot Stanton Blatch illuminates the origin and nature of the woman suffrage movement in the Progressive Era. Blatch was the daughter of Elizabeth Cady Stanton, the founding mother of political feminism. Beginning in the early twentieth century, she was a leader in her own right, initially in New York, later nationally. As early as 1903, when politics was still considered something that disreputable men did, like spitting tobacco, Blatch proclaimed: "There are born politicians just as there are born artists, writers, painters. I confess that I should be a politician, that I am not interested in machine politics, but that the devotion to the public cause...rather than the individual, appeals to me."[1]

Just as her zest for politics marked Blatch as a new kind of suffragist, so did her efforts to fuse women of different classes into a revitalized suffrage movement. Blatch's emphasis on class was by no means unique; she shared it with other women reformers of her generation. Many historians have treated the theme of class by labeling the organized women's reform movement in the early twentieth century "middle-class." By contrast, I have tried to keep open the question of the class character of women's reform in the Progressive Era by rigorously avoiding the term. Characterizing the early twentieth-century suffrage movement as "middle-class" obscures its most striking element, the new interest in the vote among women at both ends of the class structure. Furthermore, it tends to homogenize the movement. The very term "middle-class" is contradictory, alternatively characterized as people who are not poor, and people who work for a living. By contrast, I have emphasized distinctions between classes and organized my analysis around the relations between them.

Class Complexities and Progressive Era Suffragism

No doubt there is some distortion in this framework, particularly for suffragists who worked in occupations like teaching. But there is far greater distortion in using the term "middle class" to describe women like Blatch or Carrie Chapman Catt or Jane Addams. For example, it makes more sense to characterize an unmarried woman with an independent income who was not under financial compulsion to work for her living as "elite," rather than "middle class." The question is not just one

of social stratification, but of the place of women in a whole system of class relations. For these new style suffragists, as for contemporary feminists who write about them, the complex relationship between paid labor, marital status, and women's place in the class structure was a fundamental puzzle. The concept of "middle class" emerged among early twentieth-century reformers, but may ultimately prove more useful in describing a set of relations between classes that was coming into being in those years, than in designating a segment of the social structure.

Blatch, examined as a political strategist and a critic of class relations, is important less as a unique figure than as a representative leader, through whose career the historical forces transforming twentieth-century suffragism can be traced. The scope of her leadership offers clues to the larger movement: She was one of the first to open up suffrage campaigns to working-class women, even as she worked closely with wealthy and influential upper-class women; she pioneered militant street tactics and backroom political lobbying at the same time. Blatch's political evolution reveals close ties between other stirrings among American women in the Progressive Era and the rejuvenated suffrage movement. Many of her ideas paralleled Charlotte Perkins Gilman's influential reformulation of women's emancipation in economic terms. Many of Blatch's innovations as a suffragist drew on her prior experience in the Women's Trade Union League. Overall, Blatch's activities suggest that early twentieth-century changes in the American suffrage movement, often traced to the example of militant British suffragettes, had deep, indigenous roots. Among them were the growth of trade unionism among working-class women and professionalism among the elite, changing relations between these classes, and the growing involvement of women of all sorts in political reform.

Wealthy Women and Suffragism in the 1890s

The suffrage revival began in New York in 1893-1894, as part of a general political reform movement. In the 1890s New York's political reformers were largely upper-class men concerned about political "corruption" which they blamed partly on city Democratic machines and the bosses who ran them, partly on the masses of voting men, ignorant, immigrant, and ripe for political manipulation. Their concern about political corruption and about the consequences of uncontrolled political democracy became the focus of New York's 1894 constitutional convention, which addressed itself largely to "governmental procedures: the rules for filling offices, locating authority and organizing the different branches."[2]

The New York woman suffrage movement, led by Susan B. Anthony, recognized a great opportunity in the constitutional convention of 1894. Focusing on political corruption, Anthony and her allies argued that women were the political reformers' best allies. For while men were already voters and vulnerable to the ethic of partisan loyalty—indeed a man without a party affiliation in the

1890s was damned close to unsexed—everyone knew that women were naturally nonpartisan. Enfranchising women was therefore the solution to the power of party bosses. Suffragists began by trying to get women elected to the constitutional convention itself. Failing this, they worked to convince the convention delegates to include woman suffrage among the proposed amendments.[3]

Anthony planned a house-to-house canvass to collect signatures on a mammoth woman suffrage petition. For the $50,000 she wanted to fund this effort, she approached wealthy women in New York City, including physician Mary Putnam Jacobi, society

Harriot Stanton Blatch, 1911

leader Catherine Palmer (Mrs. Robert) Abbe, social reformer Josephine Shaw Lowell, and philanthropist Olivia (Mrs. Russell) Sage. Several of them were already associated with efforts for the amelioration of working-class women, notably in the recently formed Consumers League, and Anthony had reason to think they might be ready to advocate woman suffrage.[4]

The elite women were interested in woman suffrage, but they had their own ideas about how to work for it. Instead of funding Anthony's campaign, they formed their own organization. At parlor meetings in the homes of wealthy women, they tried to strike a genteel note, emphasizing that enfranchisement would *not* take women out of their proper sphere and would *not* increase the political power of the lower classes. Eighty-year-old Elizabeth Stanton, observing the campaign from her armchair, thought that "men and women of the conservative stamp of the Sages can aid us greatly at this stage of our movement."[5]

Why did wealthy women first take an active and prominent part in the suffrage movement in the 1890s? In part they shared the perspective of men of their class that the influence of the wealthy in government had to be strengthened; they believed that with the vote they could increase the political power of their class. In a representative argument before the constitutional convention, Jacobi proposed woman suffrage as a response to "the shifting of political power from privileged classes to the masses of men." The disfranchisement of women contributed to this shift because it made all women, "no matter how well born, how well educated, how intelligent, how rich, how serviceable to the State," the political inferiors of all men, "no matter how base-born, how poverty stricken, how ignorant, how vicious, how brutal." Olivia Sage presented woman suffrage as an antidote to the growing and dangerous "idleness" of elite women, who had forgotten their responsibility to set the moral tone for society.[6]

Yet, the new elite converts also supported woman suffrage on the grounds of changes taking place in women's status, especially within their own class. Jacobi argued that the educational advancement of elite women "and the new activities into which they have been led by it—in the work of charities, in the professions, and in the direction of public education—naturally and logically tend toward the same result, their political equality." She argued that elite women, who had aided the community through organized charity and benevolent activities, should have the same "opportunity to serve the State nobly." Sage was willing to advocate woman suffrage because of women's recent "strides...in the acquirement of business methods, in the management of their affairs, in the effective interest they have evinced in civic affairs."[7]

Suffragists like Jacobi and Sage characteristically conflated their class perspective with the role they saw for themselves as women, contending for political leadership not so much on the grounds of their wealth, as of their womanliness. Women, they argued, had the characteristics needed in politics—benevolence, morality, selflessness, and industry; conveniently, they believed that elite women most fully embodied these virtues. Indeed, they liked to believe that women like themselves were elite *because* they were virtuous, not because they were wealthy. The confusion of class and gender coincided with a more general elite ideology that identified the fundamental division in American society not between rich and poor, but between industrious and idle, virtuous and vicious, community-minded and selfish. On these grounds Sage found the purposeless leisure of wealthy women dangerous to the body politic. She believed firmly that the elite, women included, should provide moral—and ultimately political—leadership, but it was important to her that they earn the right to lead.[8]

The problem for elite suffragists was that woman suffrage meant the enfranchisement of working-class, as well as elite, women. Jacobi described a prominent woman who "had interested herself nobly and effectively in public affairs,...but preferred not to claim the right [of suffrage] for herself, lest its concession entail the enfranchisement of ignorant and irresponsible women." An elite anti-suffrage organization committed to such views was active in the 1894 campaign as well, led by women of the same class, with many of the same beliefs, as the pro-suffrage movement. As Stanton wrote, "The fashionable women are about equally divided between two camps." The antis included prominent society figures Abby Hamlin (Mrs. Lyman) Abbott and Josephine Jewell (Mrs. Arthur) Dodge, as well as Annie Nathan Meyer, founder of Barnard College and member of the Consumers League. Like the elite suffragists, upperclass antis wanted to insure greater elite influence in politics; but they argued that woman suffrage would decrease elite influence, rather than enhance it.[9]

Elite suffragists' willingness to support woman suffrage rested on their confidence that their class would provide political leadership for all women once

they had the vote. Because they expected working-class women to defer to them, they believed that class relations among women would be more cooperative and less antagonistic than among men. Elite women, Jacobi argued before the 1894 convention, would "so guide ignorant women voters that they could be made to counterbalance, when necessary, the votes of ignorant and interested men." Such suffragists assumed that working-class women were too weak, timid, and disorganized to make their own demands. Since early in the nineteenth century, elite women had claimed social and religious authority on the grounds of their responsibility for the women and children of the poor. They had begun to adapt this tradition to the new conditions of an industrial age, notably in the Consumers League, formed in response to the pleas of women wage earners for improvement in their working conditions. In fact, elite antis also asserted that they spoke for working-class women, but they contended that working-class women neither needed nor wanted the vote.[10]

From an exclusively elite perspective, the anti-suffrage argument was more consistent than the pro-suffrage one; woman suffrage undoubtedly meant greater political democracy, which the political reform movement of the 1890s most fundamentally feared. Elite suffragists found themselves organizing their own arguments around weak refutations of the antis' objections.[11] The ideological weakness had political implications. Woman suffrage got no serious hearing in the constitutional convention, and the 1894 constitutional revisions designed to "clean up government" ignored women's plea for political equality.

The episode revealed dilemmas, especially with respect to class relations among women, that a successful suffrage movement would have to address. Elite women had begun to aspire to political roles that led them to support woman suffrage, and the resources they commanded would be crucial to the future success of suffrage efforts. But their attraction to woman suffrage rested on a portrait of working-class women and a system of class relations that had become problematic to a modern industrial society. Could elite women sponsor the entrance of working-class women into politics without risking their influence over them, and perhaps their position of leadership? Might not working-class women assume a newly active, politically autonomous role? The tradition of class relations among women had to be transformed before a thriving and modern woman suffrage movement could be built. Harriot Stanton Blatch had the combination of suffrage convictions and class awareness to lead New York suffragists through that transition.

Bringing Working Women Into Suffragism

The 1894 campaign, which confronted suffragists with the issue of class, also drew Blatch actively into the American woman suffrage movement. She had come back from England, where she had lived for many years, to receive a master's degree from Vassar College for her study of the English rural poor. A powerful orator, she was "immediately pressed into service...speaking every day" at parlor

suffrage meetings, often to replace her aged mother.[12] Like her mother, Blatch was comfortable in upper-class circles; she had married into a wealthy British family. She generally shared the elite perspective of the campaign, assuming that "educated women" would lead their sex. But she disliked the implication that politics could ever become too democratic and, virtually alone among the suffragists, criticized all "those little anti-republican things I hear so often here in America, this talk of the quality of votes." And while other elite suffragists discussed working-class women as domestic servants and shop clerks, Blatch understood the centrality of industrial workers, although her knowledge of them was still primarily academic.[13]

Blatch's disagreements with the elite suffrage framework were highlighted a few months after the constitutional convention in an extraordinary public debate with her mother. In *The Woman's Journal,* Stanton urged that the suffrage movement incorporate an educational restriction into its demand, to respond to "the greatest block in the way of woman's enfranchisement...the fear of the 'ignorant vote' being doubled." Her justification for this position, so at odds with the principles of a lifetime, was that the enfranchisement of "educated women" best supplied "the imperative need at the time...woman's influence in public life." From England, Blatch wrote a powerful dissent. Challenging the authority of her venerated mother was a dramatic act that—perhaps deliberately—marked the end of her political daughterhood. She defended both the need and the capacity of the working class to engage in democratic politics. On important questions, "for example...the housing of the poor," their opinion was more informed than that of the elite. She also argued that since "the conditions of the poor are so much harder...every working man needs the suffrage more than I do." And finally, she insisted on the claims of a group her mother had ignored, working women.[14]

The debate between mother and daughter elegantly symbolizes the degree to which class threatened the continued vitality of the republican tradition of suffragism. Blatch was able to adapt the republican faith to modern class relations, while Stanton was not, partly because of Blatch's participation in the British social democratic movement known as Fabianism. As a Fabian, Blatch had gained an appreciation for the political intelligence and power of the working class very rare among elite reformers in the United States. When she insisted that the spirit of democracy was more alive in England than in the United States, she was undoubtedly thinking of the development of a working-class political movement there.[15]

Over the next few years, Blatch explored basic assumptions of the woman suffrage faith she had inherited in the context of modern class relations. In the process, like other women reformers of her era, such as Charlotte Perkins Gilman, Florence Kelley, Jane Addams, and numerous settlement house residents and supporters of organized labor, she focused on the relation of women and work. She emphasized the productive labor that women performed, both as it contributed to the larger social good and as it created the conditions of freedom and equality for women themselves.

Women had always worked, she insisted. The new factor was the shift of women's work from the home to the factory and the office, and from the status of unpaid to paid labor. Sometimes she stressed that women's unpaid domestic labor made an important contribution to society; at other times she stressed that such unpaid work was not valued, but always she emphasized the historical development that was taking women's labor out of the home and into the commercial economy. The question for modern society was not whether women should work, but under what conditions, and with what consequences for their own lives.[16]

Although Blatch was troubled by the wages and working conditions of the laboring poor, her emphasis on work as a means to emancipation led her to regard wage-earning women less as victims to be succored, than as exemplars to their sex. She vigorously denied that women ideally hovered somewhere above the world of work. She had no respect for the "handful of rich women who have no employment other than organizing servants, social functions and charities." Upper-class women, she believed, should also "work," should make an individualized contribution to the public good, and where possible should have the value of their labor recognized by being paid for it.[17] As a member of the first generation of college-educated women she believed that education and professional achievement, rather than wealth and refinement, fitted a woman for social leadership.

Turning away from nineteenth-century definitions of the unity of women that emphasized their place in the home, their motherhood, and their exclusion from the economy, and emphasizing instead the unity that productive work provided for all women, Blatch rewrote feminism in its essentially modern form, around

A New York City suffrage parade, c. 1912

work. She tended to see women's work, including homemaking and child rearing, as a mammoth portion of the world's productive labor, which women collectively accomplished. Thus she retained the concept of "women's work" for the sex as a whole, while vigorously discarding it on the individual level, explicitly challenging the notion that all women had the same tastes and talents.[18]

Her approach to "women's work" led Blatch to believe that the interconnection of women's labor fundamentally shaped relations among them. Here were the most critical aspects of her thought. Much as she admired professional women, she insisted that they recognize the degree to which their success rested on the labor of other women, who cared for their homes and their children. "Whatever merit [their homes] possess," Blatch wrote, "is largely due to the fact that the actress when on the stage, the doctor when by her patient's side, the writer when at her desk, has a Bridget to do the homebuilding for her." The problem was that the professional woman's labor brought her so much more freedom than the housemaid's labor brought her. "Side by side with the marked improvement in the condition of the well-to-do or educated woman," Blatch observed, "our century shows little or no progress in the condition of the woman of the people." Like her friend Gilman, Blatch urged that professional standards of work—good pay, an emphasis on expertise, the assumption of a lifelong career—be extended to the nurserymaid and the dressmaker, as well as to the lawyer and the journalist. Until such time, the "movement for the emancipation of women [would] remain…a well-dressed movement."[19]

But professional training and better wages alone would not give labor an emancipatory power in the lives of working-class women. Blatch recognized the core of the problem of women's work, especially for working-class women: "How can the duties of mother and wage earner be reconciled?" She believed that wage-earning women had the same desire as professional women to continue to enjoy careers and independence after marriage. "It may be perverse in lowly wage earners to show individuality as if they were rich," Blatch wrote, "but apparently we shall have to accept the fact that all women do not prefer domestic work to all other kinds." But the problem of balancing a career and a homelife was "insoluble—under present conditions—for the women of the people." "The pivotal question for women," she wrote, "is how to organize their work as home-builders and race-builders, how to get that work paid for not in so called protection, but in the currency of the state."[20]

As the female labor force grew in the late nineteenth century, so did the number of married women workers and demands that they be driven from the labor force. The suffrage movement had traditionally avoided the conflict between work and motherhood by pinning the demand for economic equality on the existence of unmarried women, who had no men to support them. Blatch confronted the problem of work and motherhood more directly. In a 1905 article, she drew from the utopian ideas of William Morris to recommend that married women work in small, worker-owned manufacturing shops where they could have more control

over their hours and could bring their children with them. Elsewhere, she argued that the workplace should be reorganized around women's needs, rather than assume the male worker's standards, but she did not specify what that would mean. She never solved the riddle of work and children for women—nor have we—but she knew that the solution could not be to force women to choose between the two nor to banish mothers from the labor force.[21]

Blatch's vision of women in industrial society was democratic—all must work and all must be recognized and rewarded for their work—but it was not an egalitarian approach nor one that recognized most working women's material concerns. According to Blatch, women worked for psychological and ethical reasons, as much as for monetary ones. "As human beings we must have work," she wrote; "we rust out if we have not an opportunity to function on something." She emphasized the common promises and problems work raised in women's lives, not the differences in how they worked, how much individual choice they had, and especially in how much they were paid. She was relatively unconcerned with the way work enabled women to earn their livings. No doubt, her own experience partially explains this. As a young woman fresh out of college in the 1870s, she had dared to imagine that her desire for meaningful work and a role in the world need not deprive her of marriage and motherhood, and it did not. Despite her marriage, the birth of two children, and the death of one, she never interrupted her political and intellectual labors. But she also never earned her own living, depending instead on the income from her husband's family's business. In later years, she joked about the fact that she was the only "parasite" in the organization of self-supporting women she headed.[22]

But the contradictions in her analysis of the problem of work and women reflected more than her personal situation. There were two problems of work and women: the long-standing exploitation of laboring women of the working classes and the newly expanding place of paid labor in the lives of all women in bourgeois society. While the two processes were not the same, they were related, and women thinkers and activists of the Progressive period struggled to understand how. As more women worked for pay and outside of the home, how would the meaning of "womanhood" change? What would be the difference between "woman" and "man" when as many women as men were paid workers? And what would be the class differences between women if all of them worked? Indeed, would there be any difference between the classes at all, once the woman of leisure no longer existed? Virtually all the efforts to link the gender and class problems of work for woman were incomplete.

Blatch rethought the principles of political equality in the light of her emphasis on women's work. At an 1898 congressional hearing, Blatch hailed "the most convincing argument upon which our future claims must rest—the growing recognition of the economic value of the work of women."[23] Whereas her mother had based her suffragism on the nineteenth-century argument for natural rights

and on the individual, Blatch based hers on women's economic contribution and their significance as a group.

The contradictions in Blatch's approach to women and work also emerged in her attempts to link work and the vote. On the one hand, she approached women's political rights as she did their economic emancipation, democratically: Just as all sorts of women must work, all needed the vote. Wealthy women needed the vote because they were taxpayers and had the right to see that their money was not squandered; women industrial workers needed it because their jobs and factories were subject to laws, which they had the right to shape. On the other hand, she recognized the strategic centrality of the enormous class of industrial workers, whose economic role was so important and whose political power was potentially so great. "It is the women of the industrial class," she explained, "the wage-earners, reckoned by the hundreds of thousands,...the women whose work has been submitted to a money test, who have been the means of bringing about the altered attitude of public opinion toward woman's work in every sphere of life." [24]

New York City and Political Reform

Blatch returned to New York for several extended visits after 1894, and she moved back for good in 1902. She had two purposes. Elizabeth Stanton was dying, and Blatch had come to be with her. Blatch also intended to take a leading role in the New York City suffrage movement. On her deathbed in 1902, Stanton asked Anthony to aid Blatch. However, hampered by Anthony's determination to keep control of the movement, Blatch was not able to make her bid for suffrage leadership until Anthony died, four years later. [25]

Meanwhile, Blatch was excited by other reform efforts, which were beginning to provide the resources for a new kind of suffrage movement. During the first years of the twentieth century two movements contributed to Blatch's political education—a broadened, less socially exclusive campaign against political corruption and a democratized movement for the welfare of working women. By 1907, her combined experience in these two movements enabled her to put her ideas about women and work into practice within the suffrage movement itself.

Women had become more active in the campaign against political corruption after 1894. In New York City Josephine Shaw Lowell and Mary Putnam Jacobi formed the Woman's Municipal League, which concentrated on educating the public about corruption, in particular the links between the police and organized prostitution. Women were conspicuous in the reform campaigns of Seth Low, who was elected mayor in 1901. [26]

By the early 1900s, moreover, the spirit of political reform in New York City had spread beyond the elite. A left wing of the political reform movement had developed that charged that "Wall Street" was more responsible for political corruption than "the Bowery." Women were active in this wing, and there were

women's political organizations with links to the Democratic party and the labor movement, a Women's Henry George Society, and a female wing of William Randolph Hearst's Independence League. The non-elite women in these groups were as politically enthusiastic as the members of the Woman's Municipal League, and considerably less ambivalent about enlarging the electorate. Many of them strongly supported woman suffrage. Beginning in 1905, a group of them organized an Equal Rights League to sponsor mock polling places for women to register their political opinions on election day.[27]

Through the 1900s Blatch dutifully attended suffrage meetings, and without much excitement advocated the municipal suffrage for propertied women favored by the New York movement's leaders after their 1894 defeat. Like many other politically minded women, however, she found her enthusiasm caught by the movement for municipal political reform. She supported Low for mayor in 1901 and believed that his victory demonstrated "how strong woman's power really was when it was aroused." By 1903 she suggested to the National American Woman Suffrage Association (NAWSA) that it set aside agitation for the vote, so that "the women of the organization should use it for one year, nationally and locally, to pursue and punish corruption in politics." She supported the increasing attention given to "the laboring man" in reform political coalitions, but she pointedly observed that "the working woman was never considered."[28]

However, working-class women were emerging as active factors in other women's reform organizations. The crucial arena for this development was the Women's Trade Union League (WTUL), formed in 1902 by a coalition of working-class and elite women to draw wage-earning women into trade unions. The New York chapter was formed in 1905, and Blatch was one of the first elite women to join. The WTUL represented a significant move away from the tradition of elite, ameliorative sisterhood at work in the 1894 campaign for woman suffrage. Like the Consumers League, it had been formed in response to the request of women wage earners for aid from elite women, but it was an organization of both classes working together. Blatch had never been attracted to the strictly ameliorative tradition of women's reform, and the shift toward a partnership of upper-class and working-class women paralleled her own thinking about the relation between the classes and the role of work in women's lives. She and other elite women in the WTUL found themselves laboring not for working-class women, but with them, and toward a goal of forming unions that did not merely "uplift" working-class women, but empowered them. Instead of being working-class women's protectors, they were their "allies." Instead of speaking on behalf of poor women, they began to hear them speak for themselves. Within the organization wage earners were frequently in conflict with allies. Nonetheless, the league provided them an arena to articulate a working-class feminism related to, but distinct from, that of elite women.[29]

Rose Schneiderman speaking
at a union rally, c. 1910s

Although prominent as a suffragist, Blatch participated in the WTUL on its own terms, rather than as a colonizer for suffrage. She and two other members assigned to the millinery trade conducted investigations into conditions and organized mass meetings to interest women workers in unions. She sat on the Executive Council from 1906 through 1909 and was often called on to stand in for President Mary Dreier. Her academic knowledge of "the industrial woman" was replaced by direct knowledge of wage-earning women and their working conditions. She was impressed with what she saw of trade unionism, especially its unrelenting "militance." Perhaps most important, she developed working relations with politically sophisticated working-class women, notably Leonora O'Reilly and Rose Schneiderman. Increasingly she believed that the organized power of labor and the enfranchisement of women were closely allied.[30]

Working-class feminists in the league were drawn to ideas like Blatch's—to conceptions of dignity and equality for women in the workplace and to the ethic of self-support and lifelong independence; they wanted to upgrade the condition of wage-earning women so that they, too, could enjoy personal independence on the basis of their labor. On the one hand, they understood why most working-class women would want to leave their hateful jobs upon marriage; on the other, they knew that women as a group, if not the individual worker, were a permanent factor in the modern labor force. Mary Kenney O'Sullivan of Boston, one of the league's founders, believed that "self support" was a goal for working-class women, but that only trade unions would give the masses of working women the "courage, independence, and self respect" they needed to improve their conditions. She expected "women of opportunity" to help in organizing women workers, because they "owed much to workers who give them a large part of what they have and enjoy," and because "the time has passed when women of opportunity can be self respecting and work *for* others."[31]

Initially, the demand for the vote was less important to such working-class feminists than to the allies. Still, as they began to participate in the organized women's movement on a more equal basis, wage-earning women began to receive serious attention within the woman suffrage movement as well. Beginning about 1905, advocates of trade unionism and the vote for women linked the demands. At the 1906 suffrage convention WTUL member Gertrude Barnum pointed out that "our hope as suffragists lies with these strong working women." Kelley and

Addams wrote about the working woman's need for the vote to improve her own conditions. In New York, Blatch called on the established suffrage societies to recognize the importance of the vote to wage-earning women and the importance of wage-earning women to winning the vote. When she realized that existing groups could not adapt to the new challenges, she moved to form her own society.[32]

The Equality League of Self-Supporting Women

In January 1907 Blatch declared the formation of a new suffrage organization, the Equality League of Self-Supporting Women. The *New York Times* reported that the two hundred women present at the first meeting included "doctors, lawyers, milliners and shirtmakers."[33] Blatch's decision to establish a suffrage organization that emphasized female "Self-support"—lifelong economic independence—grew out of her ideas about work as the basis of women's claim on the state, the leadership role that she envisioned for educated professionals, and her discovery of the power and political capacity of trade-union women. The Equality League provided the medium for introducing a new and aggressive style of activism into the suffrage movement—a version of the "militance" Blatch admired among trade unionists.

Initially, Blatch envisioned the Equality League of Self-Supporting Women as the political wing of the Women's Trade Union League. All the industrial workers she recruited were WTUL activists, including O'Reilly, the Equality League's first vice president, and Schneiderman, its most popular speaker. To welcome working-class women, the Equality League virtually abolished membership fees; the policy had the added advantage of allowing Blatch to claim every woman who ever attended a league meeting in her estimate of its membership. She also claimed the members of the several trade unions affiliated with the Equality League, such as the bookbinders, overall makers, and cap makers, so that when she went before the New York legislature to demand the vote, she could say that the Equality League represented thousands of wage-earning women.[34]

Blatch wanted the Equality League to connect industrial workers, not with "club women" (her phrase), but with educated, professional workers, who should, she thought, replace benevolent ladies as the leaders of their sex. Such professionals—college educated and often women pioneers in their professions—formed the bulk of the Equality League's active membership. Many were lawyers, for instance, Ida Rauh, Helen Hoy, Madeleine Doty, Jessie Ashley, Adelma Burd, and Bertha Rembaugh. Others were social welfare workers, for instance the Equality League's treasurer, Kate Claghorn, a tenement housing inspector and the highest paid female employee of the New York City government. Blatch's own daughter, Nora, the first woman graduate civil engineer in the United States, worked in the New York City Department of Public Works. Many of these women had inherited incomes and did not work out of economic need, but out of a desire to give serious, public substance to their lives and to make an impact on society. Many of them expressed the determination to maintain economic independence after they married.[35]

Although Blatch brought together trade-union women and college-educated professionals in the Equality League, there were tensions between the classes. The first correspondence between O'Reilly and Barnard graduate Caroline Lexow was full of class suspicion and mutual recrimination. More generally, there were real differences in how and why the two classes of working women demanded the vote. Trade-union feminists wanted the vote so that women industrial workers would have power over the labor laws that directly affected their working lives. Many of the college-educated self-supporters were the designers and administrators of this labor legislation. Several of them were, or aspired to be, government employees, and political power affected their jobs through party patronage. The occupation that might have bridged the differences was teaching. As in other cities, women teachers in New York organized for greater power and equal pay. The Equality League frequently offered aid, but the New York teachers' leaders were relatively conservative and kept their distance from the suffrage movement.[36]

Blatch's special contribution was her understanding of the bonds and common interests uniting industrial and professional women workers. The industrial women admired the professional ethic, if not the striving careerism, of the educated working women, and the professionals admired the matter-of-fact way wage-earning women went out to work. The fate of the professional woman was closely tied to that of the industrial worker; the cultural regard in which all working women were held affected both. Blatch dramatized that tie when she was refused service at a restaurant because she was unescorted by a man (that is, because she was eating with a woman). The management claimed that its policy aimed to protect "respectable" women, like Blatch, from "objectionable" women, like the common woman worker who went about on her own, whose morals were therefore questionable. Blatch rejected the division between respectable women and working women, pointing out that "there are five million women earning their livelihood in this country, and it seems strange that feudal customs should still exist here."[37]

The dilemma of economically dependent married women was crucial to the future of both classes of working women. Blatch believed that if work was to free women, they could not leave it for dependence on men in marriage. The professional and working-class members of the Equality League shared this belief, one of the distinguishing convictions of their new approach to suffragism. In 1908, Blatch and Mary Dreier chaired a debate about the housewife, sponsored by the WTUL and attended by many Equality League members. Charlotte Perkins Gilman took the Equality League position, that the unemployed wife was a "parasite" on her husband, and that all women, married as well as unmarried, should work, "like every other self-respecting being." Anna Howard Shaw argued that women's domestic labor was valuable, even if unpaid, and that the husband was dependent on his wife. A large audience attended, and although they "warmly applauded" Gilman, they preferred Shaw's sentimental construction of the economics of marriage.[38]

A month after the Equality League was formed, Blatch arranged for trade-union women to testify before the New York legislature on behalf of woman suffrage, the first working-class women ever to do so. The New York Woman Suffrage Association was still concentrating on the limited, property-based form of municipal suffrage; in lethargic testimony its leaders admitted that they had "no new arguments to present." Everyone at the hearing agreed that the antis had the better of the argument. The Equality League testimony the next day was in sharp contrast. Clara Silver and Mary Duffy, WTUL activists and organizers in the garment industry, supported full suffrage for all New York women. The very presence of these women before the legislature, and their dignity and intelligence, countered the antis' dire predictions about enfranchising the unfit. Both linked suffrage to their trade-union efforts: While they struggled for equality in unions and in industry, "the state" undermined them, by teaching the lesson of female inferiority to male unionists and bosses. "To be left out by the State just sets up a prejudice against us," Silver explained. "Bosses think and women come to think themselves that they don't count for so much as men."[39]

The formation of the Equality League and its appearance before the New York legislature awakened enthusiasm. Lillie Devereux Blake, whose own suffrage group had tried "one whole Winter…to [interest] the working women" but found that they were "so overworked and so poor that they can do little for us," congratulated Blatch on her apparent success. Helen Marot, organizing secretary for the New York WTUL, praised the Equality League for "realizing the increasing necessity of including working women in the suffrage movement." Blatch, O'Reilly, and Schneiderman were the star speakers at the 1907 New York suffrage convention. "We realize that probably it will not be the educated workers, the college women, the men's association for equal suffrage, but the people who are fighting for industrial freedom who will be our vital force at the finish," proclaimed the newsletter of the NAWSA.[40]

Militance for American Suffragists

The unique class character of the Equality League encouraged the development of a new style of agitation, more radical than anything practiced in the suffrage movement since…since Elizabeth Stanton's prime. The immediate source of the change was the Women's Social and Political Union of England (WSPU), led by Blatch's comrade from her Fabian days, Emmeline Pankhurst. Members of the WSPU were just beginning to be arrested for their suffrage protests. At the end of the Equality League's first year, Blatch invited one of the first WSPU prisoners, Anne Cobden-Sanderson, daughter of Richard Cobden, to the United States to tell about her experiences, scoring a coup for the Equality League. By emphasizing Cobden-Sanderson's connection with the British Labour party and distributing free platform tickets to trade-union leaders, Blatch was able to get an overflow crowd at Cooper Union, Manhattan's labor temple, two-thirds of them men, many of them trade unionists.[41]

A crowd gathers to hear speeches from a group of New York suffragists who
admired the British militants and adopted the name "American Suffragettes."
LIBRARY OF CONGRESS

The Equality League's meeting for Cobden-Sanderson offered American
audiences their first account of the new radicalism of English suffragists, or as they
were beginning to be called, suffragettes. Cobden-Sanderson emphasized the
suffragettes' working-class origins. She attributed the revival of the British suffrage
movement to Lancashire factory workers; the heroic figure in her account was the
working-class suffragette, Annie Kenney, while Christabel Pankhurst, later
canonized as the Joan of Arc of British militancy went unnamed. After women
factory workers were arrested for trying to see the prime minister, Cobden-
Sanderson and other privileged women, who felt they "had not so much to lose as
[the workers] had," decided to join them and get arrested. She spent almost two
months in jail, living the life of a common prisoner and coming to a new awareness
of the poor and suffering women she saw there. Her simple but moving account
conveyed the transcendent impact of the experience.[42]

Cobden-Sanderson's visit to New York catalyzed a great outburst of suffrage
energy; in its wake, Blatch and a handful of other new leaders introduced the
WSPU tactics into the American movement, and the word suffragette became as
common in New York as in London. The "militants" became an increasingly
distinct wing of the movement in New York and other American cities. But it would
be too simple to say that the British example caused the new, more militant phase in
the American movement. The developments that were broadening the class basis
and the outlook of American suffragism had prepared American women to
respond to the heroism of the British militants.[43]

The development of militance in the American suffrage movement was marked by new aggressive tactics practiced by the WSPU, especially open-air meetings and outdoor parades. At this stage in the development of British militance American suffragists generally admired the heroism of the WSPU martyrs. Therefore, although the press emphasized dissent within the suffrage movement—it always organized its coverage of suffrage around female rivalries of some sort—the new militant activities were well received throughout the movement. And, conversely, even the most daring American suffragettes believed in an American exceptionalism that made it unnecessary to contemplate going to prison, to suffer as did the British militants.[44]

Despite Blatch's later claims, she did not actually introduce the new tactics in New York City. The first open-air meetings were organized immediately after the Cobden-Sanderson visit by a group called the American Suffragettes. Initiated by Bettina Borrmann Wells, a visiting member of the WSPU, most of the American Suffragettes' membership came from the Equal Rights League, the left-wing municipal reform group that had organized mock polling places in New York since 1905. Feminist egalitarians with radical cultural leanings, its members were actresses, artists, writers, teachers, and social welfare workers—less wealthy versions of the professional self-supporters in the Equality League. Their local leader was a librarian, Maud Malone, whose role in encouraging new suffrage tactics was almost as important as, although less recognized than, Blatch's own.[45]

The American Suffragettes held their first open-air meeting in Madison Square on New Year's Eve, 1907. After that they met in the open at least once a week. Six weeks later, they announced they would hold New York's first all-woman parade. Denied a police permit, they determined to march anyway. The twenty-three women in the "parade" were many times outnumbered by the onlookers, mostly working-class men. In a public school to which they adjourned to make speeches, the American Suffragettes told a sympathetic audience that "the woman who works is the underdog of the world"; thus she needed the vote to defend herself. Socialists and working women rose from the floor to support them. Two years later the Equality League organized a much more successful suffrage parade in New York. Several hundred suffragettes, organized by occupation, marched from Fifty-ninth Street to Union Square. O'Reilly, the featured speaker, made "a tearful plea on behalf of the working girl that drew the first big demonstration of applause from the street crowd."[46]

Perhaps because the American Suffragettes were so active in New York City, Blatch held the Equality League's first open-air meetings in May 1908 upstate. Accompanied by Maud Malone, she organized an inventive "trolley car campaign" between Syracuse and Albany, using the interurban trolleys to go from town to town. The audiences expressed the complex class character of the suffrage movement at that moment. In Syracuse Blatch had her wealthy friend Dora Hazard arrange a meeting among the workers at her husband's factory. She also held a successful outdoor meeting in Troy, home of the Laundry Workers'

Union, one of the oldest and most militant independent women's trade unions in the country. Albany was an anti-suffrage stronghold, and its mayor tried to prevent the meeting; but Blatch outwitted him. The highlight of the tour was in Poughkeepsie, where Blatch and Inez Milholland, then a student at Vassar College, organized a legendary meeting. Since Vassar's male president forbade any woman suffrage activities on college grounds, Blatch and Milholland defiantly announced they would meet students in a cemetery. Charlotte Perkins Gilman, who was extremely popular among college women, spoke, but it was the passionate trade-union feminist, Rose Schneiderman, who was the star.[47]

Blatch believed that the first function of militant tactics was to gain much-needed publicity for the movement. The mainstream press had long ignored suffrage activities. If an occasional meeting was reported, it was usually buried in a small back-page article, focusing on the absurdity and incompetence of women's efforts to organize a political campaign. Gilded Age suffragists themselves accepted the Victorian convention that respectable women did not court public attention. The Equality League's emphasis on the importance of paid labor for women of all classes struck at the heart of that convention. Blatch understood "the value of publicity or rather the harm of the lack of it." She encouraged open-air meetings and trolley car campaigns because they generated much publicity, which no longer held the conventional horror for her followers.[48]

Militant tactics broke through the "press boycott" by violating standards of respectable femininity, making the cause newsworthy, and embracing the subsequent ridicule and attention. "We...believe in standing on street corners and fighting our way to recognition, forcing the men to think about us," an *American Suffragette* manifesto proclaimed. "We glory...that we are theatrical." The militant pursuit of publicity was an instant success: Newspaper coverage increased immediately; by 1908 even the sneering *New York Times* reported regularly on suffrage. The more outrageous or controversial the event, the more prominent the coverage. Blatch was often pictured and quoted.[49]

The new methods had a second function; they intensified women's commitment to the movement. Militants expected that overstepping the boundary of respectability would etch suffrage beliefs on women's souls, beyond retraction or modification. Blatch caught the psychology of this process. "Society has taught women self sacrifice and now this force is to be drawn upon in the arduous campaign for their own emancipation," she wrote. "The new methods of agitation, in that they are difficult and disagreeable, lay hold of the imagination and devotion of women, wherein lies the strength of the new appeal, the certainty of victory." Borrmann Wells spoke of the "divine spirit of self-sacrifice" which underlay the suffragette's transgressions against respectability and was the source of the "true inwardness of the movement."[50]

If suffrage militants had a general goal beyond getting the vote, it was to challenge existing standards of femininity. "We must eliminate that abominable

Margaret Hinchey, head of the Laundry Workers Union of N.Y., leads union women in parade, 1914. Library of Congress

word ladylike from our vocabularies," Borrmann Wells proclaimed. "We must get out and fight." The new definition of femininity the militants were evolving drew, on the one hand, on traditionally male behaviors, like aggression, fighting, provocation, and rebelliousness. Blatch was particularly drawn to the "virile" world of politics, which she characterized as a male "sport" she was sure she could master. On the other hand, they undertook a spirited defense of female sexuality, denying that it need be forfeited by women who participated vigorously in public life. "Women are no longer to be considered little tootsey wootseys who have nothing to do but look pretty," suffragette Lydia Commander declared. "They are determined to take an active part in the community and look pretty too." A member of a slightly older generation, Blatch never adopted the modern sexual ethic of the new woman, but she constantly emphasized the fact that women had distinct concerns that had to be accommodated in politics and industry. These two notes— the difference of the sexes and the repressed ability of women for manly activities— existed side by side in the thought of all the suffrage insurgents.[51]

The militant methods, taking suffrage out of the parlors and into the streets, indicated the new significance of working-class women in several ways. Blatch pointed out that the new methods—open-air meetings, newspaper publicity— suited a movement whose members had little money and therefore could not afford to rent halls or publish a newspaper. As a style of protest, "militance" was an import from the labor movement; WTUL organizers had been speaking from street corners for several years. And disrespect for the standards of ladylike respectability showed at least an impatience with rigid standards of class distinction, at most the influence of class-conscious wage-earning women.[52]

Working-class feminists were eager to speak from the militants' platform, as were many Socialists. A Socialist cadre, Dr. Anna Mercy, organized a branch of the

American Suffragettes on the Lower East Side, which issued the first suffrage leaflets ever published in Yiddish. Militants also prepared propaganda in German and Italian and, in general, pursued working-class audiences. "Our relation to the State will be determined by the vote of the average man," Blatch asserted. "None but the converted...will come to us. We must seek on the highways the unconverted."[53]

Shoulder to Shoulder for Woman Suffrage

However, it would be a mistake to confuse the suffragettes' radicalism with the radicalism of a working-class movement. The ultimate goal of the suffragettes was not a single-class movement, but a universal one, "the union of women of all shades of political thought and of all ranks of society on the single issue of their political enfranchisement." While the Equality League's 1907 hearing before the state legislature highlighted trade-union suffragists, at the 1908 hearing the league also featured elite speakers, in effect de-emphasizing the working-class perspective.[54] Militants could neither repudiate the Socialist support they were attracting, and alienate working-class women, nor associate too closely with Socialists and lose access to the wealthy. Blatch—who actually became a Socialist after the suffrage was won—would not arrange for the Socialist party leader Morris Hillquit to join other pro-suffrage speakers at the 1908 legislative hearing. Similarly, the American Suffragettes allowed individual Socialists on their platform but barred Socialist propaganda. Speaking for Socialist women who found the "idea of a 'radical' suffrage movement...very alluring," Josephine Conger Kaneko admitted that the suffragettes left her confused.[55]

Moreover, the militant challenge to femininity and the emphasis on publicity introduced a distinctly elite bias; a society matron on an open-air platform made page one while a working girl did not, because society women were obliged by conventions and could outrage by flouting them. In their very desire to redefine femininity, the militants were anxious to stake their claim to it, and it was upper-class women who determined femininity. In Elizabeth Robin's drama about the rise of militance in the British suffrage movement, *The Convert*, the heroine of the title was a beautiful aristocratic woman who became radical when she realized the emptiness of her ladylike existence and the contempt for women obscured by gentlemen's chivalrous gestures. The Equality League brought *The Convert* to New York in 1908 as its first large fund-raising effort; working-class women, as well as elite women, made up the audience. Malone was one of the few militants to recognize and to protest against excessive solicitousness for the elite convert. She resigned from the American Suffragettes when she concluded that they had become interested in attracting "a well-dressed crowd, not the rabble."[56]

Blatch's perspective and associations had always been fundamentally elite. The most well connected of the new militant leaders, she played a major role in bringing the new suffrage propaganda to the attention of upper-class women. She presided over street meetings in fashionable neighborhoods, where reporters commented

on the "smart" crowds and described the speakers' outfits in society-page detail. Blatch's first important ally from New York's social leaders (the "Four Hundred") was Katherine Duer Mackay, wife of the founder of the International Telephone and Telegraph Company and a famous society beauty. Mackay's suffragism was very ladylike, but other members of her set who followed her into the movement were more drawn to militancy. Alva Belmont, a veritable mistress of flamboyance, began her suffrage career as Mackay's protégée. The elitist subtext of militance was a minor theme in 1908 and 1909. But by 1910 becoming a suffragette was proving "fashionable," and upper-class women began to identify with the new suffrage style in significant numbers. By the time suffragette militance became a national movement, its working-class origins and trade-union associations had been submerged, and it was in the hands of women of wealth.[57]

From the beginning, though, class was the contradiction at the suffrage movement's heart. In the campaign of 1894, elite women began to pursue more power for themselves by advocating the suffrage in the name of all women. When Cobden-Sanderson spoke for the Equality League at Cooper Union in 1907, she criticized "idle women of wealth" as the enemies of woman suffrage, and she was wildly applauded. But what did her charge mean? Were all rich women under indictment, or only those who stayed aloof from social responsibility and political activism? Were the militants calling for working-class leadership of the suffrage movement or for cultural changes in bourgeois definitions of womanhood? This ambiguity paralleled the mixed meanings in Blatch's emphasis on working women; it coincided with an implicit tension between the older, elite women's reform traditions and the newer trade-union politics they had helped to usher in; and it was related to a lurking confusion about whether feminism's object was the superfluity of wealthy women or the exploitation of the poor. It would continue to plague suffragism in its final decade, and feminism afterwards, into our own time.

Notes

This essay is an abridged version of the essay by the same title that appeared in the *Journal of American History*, 74 (1987), 34-58, and is printed here with the permission of the journal. The author wishes to thank the Papers of Elizabeth Cady Stanton and Susan B. Anthony, University of Massachusetts, Amherst, for providing generous research assistance.

1. "Mrs. Blatch's Address," clipping, 1903, Women's Club of Orange, N.J., Scrapbooks, v. 4 (New Jersey Historical Society, Trenton). Thanks to Gail Malmgreen for this citation.
2. Richard L. McCormick, *From Realignment to Reform: Political Change in New York State, 1893-1910*, (Ithaca, 1979), 53.
3. Susan B. Anthony and Ida Husted Harper, eds., *History of Woman Suffrage* (Rochester, 1902), 4: 847-52; New York State Woman Suffrage Party, *Record of the New York Campaign of 1894* (New York, 1895); Ida Husted Harper, *The Life and Work of Susan B. Anthony* 3 vols. (Indianapolis, 1898-1908), 2: 758-76, esp. 759.
4. Mary Putnam Jacobi, "Report of the Volunteer Committee in New York City," in *Record of the New York Campaign*, 217-20; Maud Nathan, *The Story of an Epoch-Making Movement* (Garden City, 1926); William Rhinelander Stewart, ed., *The Philanthropic Work of Josephine Shaw Lowell* (New York, 1911), 334-56.
5. *New York Times*, April 14, 1894, 2; ibid., April 15, 1894, 5 Suffrage scrapbooks, Mrs. Robert Abbe Collection (Manuscript

Division, New York Public Library). Theodore Stanton and Harriot Stanton Blatch, eds., *Elizabeth Cady Stanton As Revealed in Her Letters, Diary and Reminiscences*, 2 vols. (New York, 1922), 2: 299.
6. Mary Putnam Jacobi, "Address Delivered at the New York City Hearing," in *Record of the New York Campaign*, 17-26; Olivia Slocum Sage, "Opportunities and Responsibilities of Leisured Women," *North American Review*, 181 (Nov. 1905): 712-21.
7. Ibid.
8. Ibid.
9. Jacobi, "Report of the Volunteer Committee," 217; Stanton and Blatch, eds., *Elizabeth Cady Stanton*, 2: 305; *New York Times*, May 3, 1894, 9.
10. Jacobi, "Address Delivered at the New York City Hearing," 22; *New York Times*, April 12, 1894, 5.
11. *Woman's Journal*, May 12, 1894, 147.
12. Ibid., May 19, 1894. The study, patterned after Charles Booth and Mary Booth's investigation of the London poor, on which Blatch worked, was published as Harriot Stanton Blatch, "Another View of Village Life," *Westminster Review*, 140 (Sept. 1893): 318-24.
13. Stanton and Blatch, *Elizabeth Cady Stanton*, 11, 304: unidentified clipping, April 25, 1894, Scrapbook 20, Susan B.

Anthony Collection (Manuscript Division, Library of Congress); *New York Times*, April 25, 1894, 5; ibid., May 3, 1894, 9; *New York Sun*, April 15, 1894, n.p.

14. *Woman's Journal*, Nov. 3, 1894, 348-49; ibid., Dec. 22, 1894, 402; Ibid., Jan. 5, 1895, 1. Blatch wrote that her mother's position "pained" her but there is no evidence of any personal conflict between them at this time. Ibid., Dec. 22, 1894, 402.

15. Harriot Stanton Blatch and Alma Lutz, *Challenging Years: The Memoirs of Harriot Stanton Blatch* (New York, 1940), 77. *Woman's Journal*, Jan. 18, 1896, 18.

16. *Woman's Journal*, May 12, 1900, 146-47. Along with Blatch and Charlotte Perkins Gilman, Florence Kelley and Jane Addams were the most important figures to focus on women and class. See Charlotte Perkins Gilman, *Women and Economics: A Study of the Economic Relation between Men and Women as a Factor in Social Evolution* (Boston, 1898).

17. Harriot Stanton Blatch, "Specialization of Function in Women: *Gunton's Magazine* 10 (May 1896): 349-56, esp. 350.

18. Ibid.

19. Ibid., 354-55.

20. Blatch, "Specialization of Function in Women," 350, 353.

21. Harriot Stanton Blatch, "Weaving in a Westchester Farmhouse," *International Studio*, 26 (Oct. 1905): 102-5: *Woman's Journal*, Jan. 21, 1905; Ibid., Dec. 31, 1904, 423.

22. Blatch, "Weaving in a Westchester Farmhouse," 104; Blatch and Lutz, *Challenging Years*, 70-86; Rhoda Barney Jenkins interview by Ellen Carol DuBois, June 10, 1982 (in DuBois's possession); Ellen DuBois, "Spanning Two Centuries: The Autobiography of Nora Stanton Barney," *History Workshop*, no. 22 (Fall 1986), 131-52, esp. 149.

23. *HWS* 4: 311.

24. "Mrs. Blatch's Address," Women's Club of Orange, N.J., Scrapbooks; *HWS* 4: 311.

25. Harriot Stanton Blatch to Susan B. Anthony, Sept. 26, 1902, in *Epistolary Autobiography*, Theodore Stanton Collection (Douglass College Library, Rutgers University, New Brunswick, N.J.).

26. Oswald Garrison Villard, "Women in New York Municipal Campaign," *Woman's Journal*, March 8, 1902.

27. *New York Times*, Jan. 14, 1901, 7.

28. *HWS* 4: 861; Ida Husted Harper, ed., *History of Woman Suffrage*, (New York, 1922), 6: 454; *New York Times*, March 2, 1902, 8; *Woman's Tribune*, April 25, 1903, 49.

29. Minutes, March 29, 1906, reel 1, New York WTUL Papers (New York State Library, New York).

30. Nancy Schrom Dye, *As Equals and As Sisters: Feminism, the Labor Movement, and the Women's Trade Union of New York* (Columbia, 1980), 63; Minutes, April 26, Aug. 23, 1906, New York WTUL Papers; *New York Times*, April 11, 1907, 8.

31. Mary Kenney O'Sullivan, "The Need of Organization among Working Women (1905)," Margaret Dreier Robins Papers (University of Florida Library, Gainesville).

32. *Woman's Journal*, March 17, 1906, 43; Kelley, *Woman Suffrage*; Jane Addams, *Utilization of Women in Government*, in *Jane Addams: A Centennial Reader* (New York, 1960), 117-18; *Woman's Journal*, Dec. 31, 1904, 423; "Mrs. Blatch's Address," Women's Club of Orange, N.J., Scrapbooks.

33. *New York Times*, Jan. 3, 1907, 6; *Woman's Journal*, Jan. 12, 1907, 8.

34. *Progress*, June 1907. Carrie Chapman Catt to Millicent Garrett Fawcett, Oct. 19, 1909, container 5, Papers of Carrie Chapman Catt (Manuscript Division, Library of Congress).

35. *Woman's Journal*, Aug. 17, 1907, 129. On Nora Blatch (who later called herself Nora Stanton Barney), see DuBois, "'Spanning Two Centuries,'" 131-52. Those self-supporters who, I believe, had independent incomes include Nora Blatch, Caroline Lexow, Lavinia Dock, Ida Rauh, Gertrude Barnum, Elizabeth Finnegan, and Alice Clark.

36. Caroline Lexow to Leonora O'Reilly, Jan. 3, 1908, reel 4, Leonora O'Reilly Papers (Schlesinger Library, Radcliffe College, Cambridge, Mass.); O'Reilly to Lexow, Jan. 5, 1908, ibid; Robert Doherty, "Tempest on the Hudson: The Struggle for Equal Pay for Equal Work in the New York City Public Schools, 1907-1911," *Harvard Educational Quarterly* 19 (Winter 1979): 413-39. The role of teachers in the twentieth-century suffrage movement is a promising area for research. For information on teachers' organizations in the Buffalo New York, suffrage movement, I am indebted to Eve S. Faber, Swarthmore College, "Suffrage in

Buffalo, 1898-1913" (unpublished paper in DuBois's possession).

37. *New York Times*, June 6, 1907, 1.

38. On self-support for women after marriage, see *New York World*, July 26, 1908, 3; and Lydia Kingsmill Commander, "The Self Supporting Woman and the Family," *American Journal of Sociology*, 14 (March 1909), 752-57. On the debate, see *New York Times*, Jan. 7, 1909, 9.

39. *New York Times*, Feb. 6. 1907, 6.; Harriot Stanton Blatch, ed., *Two Speeches by Industrial Women* (New York, 1907), esp. 8.

40. *Woman's Tribune*, Feb. 9, 1907, 12; Minutes, April 27, 1909, New York WTUL Papers; *Progress*, Nov. 1907.

41. Blatch and Lutz, *Challenging Years*, 100-101; *Progress*, Jan. 1908.

42. *Woman's Journal*, Dec. 28, 1907, 205, 206-7.

43. By 1908, there was a racehorse named "Suffragette," *New York Evening Telegram*, Sept. 16, 1908. Blatch noted that once she left England in the late 1890s, she and Emmeline Pankhurst did not communicate until 1907, after they had both taken their respective countries' suffrage movements in newly militant directions. Blatch to Christabel Pankhurst, in Christabel Pankhurst, *Unshackled: How We Won the Vote* (London, 1959), 30.

44. The first American arrests were not until 1917. For American suffragists' early response to the WSPU, see *Woman's Journal*, May 30, 1908, 87. Even Carrie Chapman Catt praised the British militants at first. *Woman's Journal*, Dec. 12, 1908, 199. For an example of divisive coverage by the mainstream press, see "Suffragist or Suffragettes," *New York Times*, Feb. 29, 1908, 6.

45. On Bettina Borrmann Wells, see A.J.R., ed., *Suffrage Annual and Women's Who's Who* (London, 1913), 390. Thanks to David Doughan of the Fawcett Library for this reference. The American Suffragettes found a predecessor and benefactor in seventy-five-year-old Lady Cook, formerly Tennessee Claflin, in 1909 the wife of a titled Englishman. "Our Cook Day," *American Suffragette* I (Nov. 1909): 1.

46. On the first open air meeting, see *New York Times*, Jan. 1, 1908, 16. On the parade, see ibid., Feb. 17, 1908, 7; there is also an account in Dorr, *What Eight Million Women Want*, 298-99; *New York Evening Journal*, May 21, 1910.

47. Equality League of Self-Supporting Women, *Report for Year 1908-1909* (New York, 1909), 2; Blatch and Lutz, *Challenging Years*, 107-9. On Vassar, see also *New York American*, June 10, 1908.

48. Harriot Stanton Blatch, "Radical Move in Two Years," clipping, Nov. 8, 1908, suffrage scrapbooks, Abbe Collection. Blatch "starred" in a pro-suffrage movie, *What Eight Million Women Want*, produced in 1912. Kay Sloan, "Sexual Warfare in the Silent Cinema: Comedies and Melodramas of Woman Suffragism," *American Quarterly* 33 (Fall 1981): 412-36. She was also very interested in the propaganda possibilities of commercial radio, according to Lee de Forest, a pioneer of the industry who was briefly married to her daughter. Lee de Forest, *Father of Radio: The Autobiography of Lee de Forest* (Chicago, 1950), 248-49.

49. Mary Tyng, "Self Denial Week," *American Suffragette*, 1 (Aug. 1909); *New York Herald*, Dec. 19, 1908.

50. Blatch, "Radical Move in Two Years"; Mrs. B. Borrmann Wells, "The Militant Movement for Woman Suffrage," *Independent*, April 23, 1908, 901-3.

51. "Suffragettes Bar Word Ladylike," clipping, Jan. 13, 1909, Suffrage scrapbooks, Abbe Collection; Blatch and Lutz, *Challenging Years*, 91-242; *New York Herald*, March 8, 1908.

52. Blatch and Lutz, *Challenging Years*, 107; Dye, *As Equals and As Sisters*, 47.

53. *Woman's Journal*, May 30, 1908, 87; Blatch, "Radical Move in Two Years."

54. Borrmann Wells, "Militant Movement for Woman Suffrage," 901, *Woman's Journal*, Feb. 29, 1908, 34.

55. *New York Times*, Feb. 11, 1908, 6; [Josephine C. Kaneko], "To Join, or Not to Join," *Socialist Woman*, 1 (May 1908): 6.

56. On *The Convert*, see Equality League, *Report for 1908-1909*, 4; Jane Marcus, "Introduction," in *The Convert* (London, 1980), v-xvi; *New York Call*, Dec. 9, 1908, 6; and Minutes, Dec. 22, 1908, New York WTUL Papers.

57. *New York Times*, May 14, 1909, 5. On Mackay and her Equal Franchise Society, see *New York Times*, Feb. 21, 1909, part 5, 2. On Blatch's relation to Mackay, see Blatch and Lutz, *Challenging Years*, 118.

A POLITICS OF COALITION:

Socialist Women and the
California Suffrage Movement,
1900—1911

Sherry J. Katz

Editor's Introduction: In this study of the California suffrage movement, Sherry J. Katz illustrates the increasing diversity of the early twentieth-century suffrage movement as she highlights the contributions of socialist women to the successful California suffrage campaign of 1911. Socialist women, Katz explains, had an unusual degree of prominence and influence among California's suffragists. Though socialist women were active in state suffrage movements elsewhere, "mainstream suffragists" in the Northeast, Midwest, and South tended to marginalize or shun socialist women—even before World War I when socialists were persecuted for alleged disloyalty and subversiveness.

Socialist women had been active in the first attempt to gain a state suffrage amendment in California, the failed referendum of 1896. As the state's suffrage movement revived in the early 1900s, socialist women contributed to the revival. Particularly after 1907, writes Katz, California socialist women made a deliberate effort to broaden the perspective and the constituency of what they perceived to be a "bourgeois movement." From middle-class or stable working-class families, often well-educated and employed in professional or clerical positions, these socialist suffragists proved to be crucial intermediaries between the middle-class and elite suffragists and the working class. They were highly effective in recruiting working-class women into the movement and winning support from the labor movement and working-class men. After the success of California's state suffrage campaign in 1911—the second in a new round of twentieth-century victories that helped breathe new life into the national suffrage movement—mainstream suffragists in the state freely acknowledged the crucial role of the socialist suffragists.

Like the working-class suffragists in New York described by Ellen Carol DuBois, these suffragists introduced new arguments and modern tactics that contributed to the success of the suffrage movement. Though many of the arguments used by the socialists were similar to those of other suffragists, including the idea that women's "social housekeeping" talents would be useful in politics, the socialist suffragists emphasized that women were entitled to political

rights because of their economic contributions. "The heart of their argument," writes Katz, was "the idea that women's labor, inside and outside the home, had always contributed to 'social wealth' and that women, as social producers, deserved the ballot." California's socialist women employed some of the modern tactics used to attract publicity by working-class suffragists and their allies in New York, but they also invented new tactics—from door-to-door canvassing to the use of electric signs—that would become common during the movement's last decade. Significantly, the socialist suffragists' innovative tactics included printing campaign literature and conducting suffrage rallies in foreign languages, indicating a desire to attract the support of new immigrants. Yet even these women were affected by the racism that was so common among White suffragists in the early twentieth century.

The 1911 campaign seemed to socialist women to be a fulfillment of their dream of a cross-class sisterhood, writes Katz. After the victory, however, the level of unity and cooperation that marked the state suffrage campaign declined to a degree. Still, socialist and "mainstream" women's groups continued to work together and to achieve much. Indeed, Katz concludes, "socialist women's influence on the legislative proposals advocated by mainstream women's groups helps explain why California was at the forefront of social welfare legislation for women during the Progressive Era."

★　★　★　★　★

D URING THE EARLY TWENTIETH CENTURY the woman suffrage movement experienced a revitalization and expansion, becoming for the first time a mass coalition utilizing militant tactics and modern methods. The California suffrage campaign provides an illuminating case study of the political and social diversity of this mass movement, and sheds light on the process and success of coalition-building. Although socialist women in many regions of the country joined suffrage organizations or campaigned for suffrage through the Socialist Party, California socialist women achieved an apparently unprecedented level of integration, leadership, and influence. Their prominence depended, in part, on California's congenial political and social context, and on an effective strategy that socialist women devised to forge an influential left-wing constituency within the larger movement.

This case study demonstrates the critical role that socialists played in expanding the boundaries of the suffrage coalition, contributions less visible in states where they participated as individuals or achieved less prominence as an organized subgroup. By spearheading efforts to recruit wage-earning women, win the support of organized labor, and court the working-class vote, socialist women broadened the suffrage movement's base. In providing leadership and strategies for class-bridging, they emphasized new arguments for women's enfranchisement

and introduced modern methods of suffrage agitation, including militant and flamboyant street tactics. Socialist women's vigorous grassroots campaigns in urban, working-class communities, especially in Los Angeles, proved critical to the success of California's 1911 suffrage referendum. Socialist women made California, along with New York, a center of working-class coalition building and experimentation in militant strategies that influenced the trajectory of both state and national campaigns after 1911.

Socialism and Woman Suffrage: Linkages and Chasms

From 1890 to 1920, powerful international socialist and feminist movements helped to reinvigorate the woman suffrage demand and to create mass, militant, and modern suffrage movements. In the United States, the activism of both independent feminists sympathetic to socialism and female members of the Socialist Party of America helped to transform the suffrage movement into a broad and diverse coalition in the early twentieth century. Although the Second Socialist International instructed socialist women in 1907 to reject collaboration with mainstream suffragists and to conduct separate campaigns under party auspices, only party leaders in New York City adopted this policy. Everywhere else, Socialist Party women and independent left suffragists joined mainstream organizations, and, where feasible, built their own groups to represent working-class interests in the larger suffrage movement. Often working in close collaboration, they spearheaded the recruitment of working-class women, gained the support of organized labor, and introduced a new level of tactical militance. They played particularly forceful and effective roles in suffrage campaigns in the Western states, as well as in Wisconsin, and New York.[1]

Despite their vital contributions to the revitalization and expansion of the suffrage movement, socialists often faced marginalization by mainstream suffragists seeking to distance themselves from radical and working-class politics. Attempts to downplay the socialist contribution were most pronounced in the industrial Northeast and Midwest, where the predominantly native-born, elite leadership feared association with the immigrant masses, and after the onset of World War I, when socialism became identified with disloyalty and subversion. In the Southern states, social conservatism prompted the suffragists with socialist and trade union sympathies to avoid making public connections between radicalism and the suffrage cause.[2]

California's Fertile Ground for Political Experimentation

California socialist women achieved an apparently unprecedented level of integration, leadership, and influence in the suffrage coalition. The construction of their substantial left-wing presence depended, in part, on the fertile ground of the state's political climate and social context. During the late nineteenth century, the

state provided space for the growth of numerous indigenous protest movements, such as Bellamy Nationalism and Populism, that sought to combat the harsh consequences of corporate capitalism. California's speedy economic development, accompanied by glaring economic inequalities, nurtured an openness to radical ideas and political alternatives. This climate of political experimentation gave rise to a sizeable and well-organized socialist women's movement that flourished in California from the 1890s until World War I. Beginning in the 1890s, several generations of radical women active in suffrage and temperance crusades found in socialism the basis for an egalitarian society guaranteeing women's freedom. In the early 1900s, local activists built a network of autonomous socialist women's clubs, under the umbrella of the Woman's Socialist Union of California (WSU), and worked within both the male-dominated socialist movement and the mainstream woman's movement.[3]

The Woman's Socialist Union represented hundreds of the most active socialist-feminists in the state. A number of like-minded radical women remained independent, but developed close ties to their sisters in the WSU. Information gathered on thirty-five state and local leaders of the WSU suggests a social portrait of the leadership cadre of the socialist women's movement. Most were born in the United States in the 1860s and 1870s, attained either stable working-class or middle-class status, and came to the socialist women's movement through participation in

Votes for Women

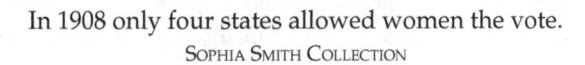

Equal Suffrage Map of the United States, 1908

Men and women vote on equal terms for all officers, even for presidential electors, in four of the United States. In twenty-seven other states, women have partial suffrage.

California women have no votes

Copies of this map may be obtained at California Equal Suffrage Headquarters
2419 California Street, San Francisco

Price one cent each

In 1908 only four states allowed women the vote.

SOPHIA SMITH COLLECTION

the woman and left movements of the 1890s. Many of these activists had been raised in Protestant households, had married and borne one or two children, and were surrounded by socialist family members. Relatively well educated, these women worked in professional or clerical occupations, particularly in teaching and newspaper work, for at least part of their adult lives. They were joined by a number of veteran activists born in the United States between the 1820s and the 1840s who had had formative political experiences in abolitionism, early women's rights, and spiritualism. A younger generation of women born in the United States in 1880s and 1890s joined the socialist women's movement around 1910.[4]

The same climate of openness to political alternatives that nurtured a vigorous socialist women's movement also enabled socialists to establish a strong presence within California's suffrage movement from its inception. In fact, prominent radical women founded the suffrage movement in Northern California in the 1870s and in Southern California a decade later. A favorable social context undergirded their leadership and eased their early efforts to expand the movement's base of support along the lines of class and culture. In Southern California, socialist women and their working-class allies largely shared the native-born, Protestant backgrounds of mainstream suffragists, which meant that radicalism did not suffer from association with "foreignness." In Northern California, where Northern European immigrants and their children comprised a majority of the urban working class, socialism appeared somewhat more threatening to mainstream suffragists. As the suffrage demand moved from the margins to the center of organized White womanhood's political agenda in the late 1880s and 1890s, socialist women remained at the forefront of the movement, especially in the southern part of the state.[5]

Cross-Class Coalition Building, 1900—1910

The founding of the Woman's Socialist Union in 1902 coincided with, and contributed to, the revival of the state suffrage movement and the creation of a diverse suffrage coalition. After the defeat of a state suffrage amendment in 1896, suffrage activism declined as many demoralized participants left the movement. But during the first decade of the century, California women, like their counterparts across the nation, created new voluntary associations and social movements, through which they exerted an enormous collective influence on public policy and pursued woman suffrage. As the membership of mainstream suffrage clubs associated with the California Equal Suffrage Association (CESA) expanded from 100 to over 50,000, White clubwomen, college-educated reformers, working-class labor activists, African American clubwomen, as well as socialists, established their own organizations dedicated to the suffrage cause.[6] The demand for suffrage unified women in the early twentieth century because it encompassed their sense of commonality as well as their differences. Disfranchisement was a powerful symbol of women's socially constructed unity and an indicator of their common oppression in

male-dominated society. Conceptualized as a tool of group interests, as well as a means of individual self-expression, the ballot also came to be understood as a means of achieving the goals considered important to different subgroups of women. The demand for suffrage constituted a "capacious umbrella" under which a large diversity of women, organizations, and beliefs, could temporarily stand. A genuine mass movement for women's enfranchisement emerged for the first time, one that embodied the widest spectrum of ideas and opinion, as well as participants, in its long history.[7]

As the suffrage coalition expanded after 1900, socialist women increased their numbers and their visibility as a distinctive left-wing entity within the movement. By 1907, WSU leader Josephine Cole celebrated the fact that every "Socialist woman [she knew] in this part of the country [was] a suffragist and almost every one of them [was] in a suffrage club." While Cole may have exaggerated, many WSU activists, female party members, and independent socialist-feminists joined mainstream suffrage groups. Although neither local suffrage clubs nor the CESA maintained good records, we know from scattered newspaper accounts that at least thirty-six socialists led local suffrage organizations and that most of them also served as delegates to or officers of the CESA. At least one socialist, and more often two or three, held important posts on the CESA's executive committee from 1903 to 1911. Under WSU guidance, socialist women exerted a strong, collective presence at state and local CESA conventions and in the Pacific Coast's suffrage press.[8]

Although few in-depth analyses of state suffrage movements are now available, in no other state did socialist women appear to gain so much prominence within the mainstream suffrage movement. Socialist women became leaders of the CESA based on their own dedication and commitment and because mainstream suffragists welcomed and acknowledged the participation of the left. This openness developed from the history of radical women's leadership in California suffrage, the context of political experimentation in California politics, and the public support offered by the state Socialist Party after its founding in 1902. Prominent suffragist Sarah M. Severance maintained in 1910 that "Socialists have [long] been our consistent friends" and she thanked them for their "just attitude" and "consistent record on woman's suffrage."[9]

Equally important in helping socialist women become "an acknowledged factor" in the state suffrage movement from 1902 to 1911 was the dual strategy of autonomous collaboration and full integration they devised to expand their influence. Rooted in their experience as participants in multiple and overlapping movements, dual strategy allowed them to collaborate with mainstream suffragists without losing their independent identity and separate base of power. "One woman lifting up her voice is not so well listened to as when she represents a body of women," WSU president Ethel Whitehead reasoned. The leaders of the WSU believed that socialist women's voices would carry greater weight when associated with independent organizations of radical suffragists.[10]

Socialist women self-consciously attempted to expand the boundaries of the suffrage coalition as leaders of the CESA and local mainstream organizations who remained based in, and coordinated their actions with, the WSU and other independent socialist suffrage groups. They believed that their "special mission... in the woman-suffrage field" involved enlarging the movement's constituency and political vision. The WSU leaders made the recruitment and integration of working-class women a major priority, arguing that no group was "better fitted" for the task. Socialist women also dedicated themselves to providing an "entering wedge" for the "Socialist thought" that would undergird a "more progressive, more democratic" movement. They hoped to convince non-socialists that women's emancipation depended upon economic independence, as well as political rights, and that such independence could be achieved only through a major restructuring of class relations and social resources. Likewise they sought to demonstrate that the social problems female reformers frequently attacked—child labor, prostitution, and poverty—could be eliminated only if women used their ballots to undermine capitalism. They envisioned the construction of an inclusive woman's movement dedicated to the emancipation of both women and the working class.[11]

In WSU affiliates, socialist women refined their arguments for enfranchisement. Many of their arguments paralleled those utilized by their non-socialist comrades. Both "sameness" and "difference" arguments appeared often in early twentieth-century suffrage literature. Suffragists argued that to the extent women were the same as men they deserved the ballot as a matter of justice, and to the extent they possessed special qualities, they needed a direct means of affecting public decision making.[12] Members of the WSU asserted that women deserved the ballot based on their inherent equality with men and their right to represent themselves. Most WSU activists also maintained that women's distinctive qualities—their socially constructed moral, maternal, and altruistic sensibilities—were desperately needed in the public sphere where male competitiveness and self-interest had been unable to combat the harsh social consequences of capitalist development. In combining these two strands of suffrage thought, Josephine Cole insisted that "possession of the ballot" would allow woman "the opportunity to alter many existing conditions which bear cruelty upon her, to her own injury and that of the race, but which...receive little attention from male legislators, be they Socialist or otherwise."[13]

Socialists also generated several new and distinctive arguments for suffrage shaped by their understandings of modern transformations in women's labor and the relation of women's work to women's emancipation. As socialist women pioneered these arguments in California, other members of a new generation of suffrage activists, many of them middle-class, college-educated reformers influenced by and sympathetic to radicalism, popularized them in New York and introduced them to the National American Woman Suffrage Association. Proponents of these new arguments drew upon the contributions of Charlotte Perkins Gilman, the most influential feminist theorist of their time, who insisted that gender equality depended

Charlotte Perkins Gilman, 1900

FRANCES B. JOHNSTON

upon women's economic independence achieved through wage labor outside the home and the socialization of housework and child rearing. Interestingly, Gilman developed her "sexuo-economic" theory of social relations in the early 1890s when she began her public career as a member of California's emerging socialist-feminist community.[14]

Socialist women proposed that women's economic contributions entitled them to political rights. The heart of their argument rested on the idea that women's labor, inside and outside the home, had always contributed to "social wealth" and that women, as social producers, deserved the ballot. But they highlighted the ways in which women's increasing involvement in the paid labor force provided a new rationale for suffrage. As women's "field of labor" shifted from the home to the factory, they became, in the words of Josephine Cole, permanent "financial factor[s]" who would "necessarily" be regarded as independent human beings and citizens rather than as "helpless dependents." Indeed the WSU's Jennie Arnott believed that because women's paid employment "forced their recognition as social units," it had "done more than any one thing to make the voters of the country see their need of the ballot." Ultimately, this wage-earners' suffragism not only provided a new rationale for women's entitlement to political rights, but helped socialist women draw working-class women into the suffrage coalition.[15]

A strong identification with working-class women undergirded socialist women's distinctive emphasis on wage-earning women's need of the ballot. Suffrage would provide wage-earning women with an important tool for their own advancement and self-protection, as well as for the empowerment of working-class communities. "That army of women who labor with their hands," WSU leader Mary Garbutt reminded her fellow suffragists, are the ones "whose hard experiences in life, long hours, poor pay and unsanitary conditions...really demand...the ballot for their protection against such untoward conditions."[16]

Wage-earning women never assumed the same importance in the arguments and literature of most mainstream suffragists in California. Socialist and trade-union activists generated most of the materials utilized by suffrage forces to attract such women. In this regard, independent socialist-feminist Alice Locke Park, a longtime ally of the WSU, played a key role as a prominent leader of the CESA's literature committee from 1906 to 1911. She issued several CESA leaflets directed towards working-class and wage-earning women, highlighted socialist and trade

union endorsements, and helped her colleagues in the WSU and union movement produce their own literature.[17]

Park's work on the literature committee was only part of an intensive effort on the part of socialist women, networked through the WSU, to broaden the arguments and constituency of the suffrage movement. At CESA conventions in 1906 and 1907, substantial and well-organized socialist delegations, in concert with Progressive suffragists sympathetic to working women, advocated the recruitment of wage-earning women, outreach to working-class communities, and efforts to obtain greater support from organized labor. The 1906 convention featured a discussion devoted to securing the "interest and co-operation of the wage-earning women" led by WSU leader Anna Ferry Smith, a veteran feminist labor activist, and several other socialist and trade union women. They advised suffragists to meet with the leaders of women's unions, as the Los Angeles county suffrage organization had recently done. In 1907, a proposal drafted by the socialist-dominated resolutions committee pledged the CESA to widen the "scope of the suffrage movement by enlisting in its service the tremendous force of the women who work for wages and bringing to bear the pressure which organized labor can exert." The resolution invited trade union women to join the suffrage movement, stressing that their "struggle for better economic conditions" was hampered by their lack of political power.[18]

The approval of this resolution solidified the commitment of mainstream suffragists to working-class recruitment. Pragmatism, as well as socialist organizing within the CESA, underlay this strategic shift. Suffrage leaders saw in the rise of Progressivism a political climate conducive to social reform and women's enfranchisement. But they also believed that a suffrage victory depended on a new and enlarged base of suffrage activists, the backing of male-dominated institutions, better organization, and coordinated legislative lobbying. Whether sympathetic to organized labor or not, mainstream suffragists understood by 1906 that unions had become a powerful force in state politics and that the passage of a constitutional amendment depended on working-class votes.[19]

The success of working-class outreach and integration differed by city and region. Social context and socialist leadership proved critical factors in coalition-building efforts. In Southern California, and particularly in Los Angeles, relative ethnic homogeneity among Whites and longstanding socialist leadership within organized womanhood facilitated class-bridging. But even as mainstream suffragists relied on their socialist comrades and supported the recruitment of wage-earning women, they felt uneasy in working-class environs. Socialist sympathizer Helen Bary recalled that elite and middle-class suffragists in Los Angeles thought her "very brave" to visit the Labor Temple, located in a downtown working-class district. In general, mainstream suffragists left the work of class-bridging to socialist women and their labor-identified allies.[20]

From 1906 to 1911, the Los Angeles WSU, a member of the local suffrage coalition, began to sponsor class-bridging activities in the form of meetings, conferences,

Frances Nacke Noel (right)
HUNTINGTON LIBRARY

and actions that brought mainstream suffragists and union women together. In 1908, Socialist Party member and WSU supporter Frances Nacke Noel emerged as the most prominent and effective organizer of class-bridging efforts. Under Noel's guidance, the California branch of the Woman's International Union Label League, an organization that promoted the consumption of union-made goods, became an important champion of female unionization, protective labor legislation, and woman suffrage.[21]

Label League activists drawn from the WSU's and the Socialist Party helped the organization become the grassroots, working-class component of the suffrage coalition in Southern California from 1908 to 1911. In Los Angeles, San Diego, and elsewhere, socialist women arranged joint meetings for label leaguers and mainstream suffragists in which they shared their thoughts on suffrage strategies and social reform proposals. In the winter of 1910, Los Angeles' Label League, Votes for Women Club, and WSU also collaborated on a Christmas benefit for the wives and children of local striking workers.[22] These activities culminated in the short-lived Woman's Conference of Los Angeles County, which Noel and her socialist comrades envisioned as a permanent cross-class umbrella organization devoted to advancing the welfare of women and children, particularly those from the laboring classes. Called by the Label League and women's unions, the conference attracted over one hundred delegates to its first meeting in January 1911, many of them from mainstream women's organizations. After demanding that the legislature place a constitutional amendment for woman suffrage on the ballot, the conference conducted investigations of housing, industrial working conditions, and protective labor legislation. The conference disbanded in March 1911 as many of its constituent groups found a more pressing collaborative venture in the upcoming suffrage amendment campaign.[23]

Modern Methods and Militant Tactics in the 1911 Campaign

In February 1911, shortly after the California legislature voted to place a suffrage amendment on the October ballot, CESA leaders approved a plan to coordinate suffrage activism during the campaign that lay ahead. Led by Elizabeth Lowe Watson, a longtime socialist ally, the CESA called for collaboration among the

thousands of suffragists in the state, including members of the California Federation of Women's Clubs (CFWC), the Woman's Christian Temperance Union (WCTU), women's trade unions, socialist organizations, and independent suffrage groups. The commitment to cooperation among diverse "kinds of suffrag[ists]," and the inclusion of radical and trade union organizations, rested on the preceding decade of socialist leadership and class-bridging efforts in the state association, as well as on the practical notion that a broad and well-organized suffrage coalition had the best chance of success. Although the Cooperative Council faced difficulty in "dove-tailing" precinct work and nurturing "new methods of propaganda and [an] exchange of talent" on the state level, regional coordinating bodies, especially in Southern California, facilitated cooperation among the many groups that comprised the suffrage coalition in 1911.[24]

Across California, and particularly in the southern part of the state, socialist women pioneered some of the most innovative tactics of the first state-level campaign to demonstrate the modern, militant, and often flamboyant methods characteristic of the suffrage movement's final decade. California suffragists perfected door-to-door canvassing and precinct organization, engaged in street speaking and car campaigning, coordinated press work, designed "modern" literature for mass distribution featuring concise arguments and catchy slogans, developed billboard ads and electric signs, staged plays and pageants, and held outdoor meetings and rallies. Socialist women helped to make press work and door-to-door canvassing—two modern tools of organization first introduced in the 1890s—more systematic and widespread. But they contributed most by experimenting with new styles of protest. Suffrage militance involved taking suffrage agitation aggressively into the streets. First employed to gain working-class support, militant methods became an effective means of acquiring widespread publicity because they challenged the bourgeois notions of female respectability that had mitigated against women's vigorous participation in public life. First in New York and then in California, socialists and working-class feminists helped popularize and expand the use of these militant methods nationwide.[25]

California Suffrage Poster designed by Bertha Boye, 1911

As the CESA formulated its plans for the suffrage campaign, WSU leaders prepared to mobilize their troops and the

Leaflet in Spanish from the
1911 California campaign

SOPHIA SMITH COLLECTION

state Socialist Party. They were overjoyed by the party's pledge to work actively for suffrage, a commitment they had attempted to secure for nearly a decade, and formed a State Woman's Committee to coordinate the party's effort. Committee chairs Mary Garbutt and Georgia Kotsch quickly realized, however, that the state party's commitment consisted primarily of generous use of its weekly newspaper, the *California Social-Democrat*. While few party locals developed sustained campaigns, socialist women in all regions stepped up their suffrage activism in mainstream organizations and autonomous groups. Through WSU branches, socialist suffrage clubs, wage-earners' suffrage leagues, and Socialist Party locals, they worked to gain the support of organized labor and working-class voters, often collaborating with mainstream suffrage organizations and regional coordinating committees in which their comrades exercised influence.[26]

In Los Angeles County, socialist women played a highly visible role in the regional campaign that achieved the greatest success in constructing a diverse, cross-class coalition. As the campaign began, socialist women occupied leadership positions in all of the county's major suffrage organizations—the Political Equality League, the Votes for Women Club, and the WCTU. Although socialists and other labor-identified suffragists secured commitments for outreach to immigrant and working-class communities, these organizations remained focused on gaining the support of middle-class women and men.[27] In order to conduct an intensive campaign among the county's working-class population, WSU veterans and their allies founded two new suffrage groups: the Socialist Suffrage Club (SSC) and the Wage Earners' Suffrage League (WESL). Delegates from the SSC, WESL, and several mainstream groups represented the socialist/labor forces on the county's Equal Suffrage Central Committee, which loosely coordinated the overall campaign and facilitated an extraordinary interchange of personnel among its constituent groups.[28]

Under the direction of Mary Garbutt, Ethel Whitehead, and Frances Noel, the SSC and the WESL developed distinctive, but complementary, niches in the campaign. The Socialist Suffrage Club, founded in March 1911 and led by WSU veterans, organized public meetings and conducted house-to-house canvasses in working-class communities throughout the county.[29] The WESL, initiated by Frances Noel in May 1911, attracted labor as well as socialist activists, especially working-class homemakers from the label leagues and members of the garment workers union. Modeled after a similar organization founded by elite labor reformer Maud Younger in San Francisco in 1908, the WESL focused on mobilizing the support of the county's trade unions. The WESL maintained a visible presence at the Labor Temple, distributed literature to union members, and brought street

speaking and outdoor meetings to neighborhoods in which union members resided. Both groups sought to empower working-class women, as well as to gain the support of working-class men.[30]

The actions of the SSC and the WESL reveal both the breadth and the limits of socialist women's conceptions of community and coalition, and the boundaries that circumscribed their political vision. Although their efforts focused on the predominantly White and native-born sector of Los Angeles' working-class community and labor movement, socialists campaigned in immigrant communities. In August, Noel promoted the suffrage cause in German at

Maud Younger, c.1919
LIBRARY OF CONGRESS

one of the first foreign-language meetings in the county. Similar meetings may have been held at the party's Jewish, Hungarian, Finnish, Latvian, and Mexican branches, and socialists probably distributed more foreign-language materials than any other sector of the county suffrage coalition. But many socialist women excluded Asian immigrants from their conception of the working class, despite a theoretical commitment to international solidarity. Socialists active in the labor movement internalized the hostility towards Asians that had ironically helped to unify California's White workers since the 1860s. Although their own suffrage materials were implicitly inclusive, socialist women widely distributed Maud Younger's "Why Wage-Earning Women Should Vote," first reproduced by Alice Park for the CESA in 1908, which decried the fact that native-born "Mongolians" (men) could vote and (White) women could not. In addition, socialist women apparently failed to challenge the exclusion of African American suffragists from mainstream suffrage groups and the county coordinating committee, even though their party had a small African American branch. Although socialist women clearly

included ethnic and immigrant Euro-Americans and Latinos in their "imagined communities," the constructions of racial difference shared by most White reformers in California during the Progressive Era impoverished the vision of female solidarity they possessed and the diversity of the suffrage coalition they worked to build.[31]

Through the SSC and the WESL, socialist suffragists experimented with modern methods of suffrage organization, many of which challenged the Victorian notion that respectable women should not seek public attention. An extensive use of the socialist and labor press reflected the suffrage movement's growing emphasis on the importance of systematic and sustained publicity. Leaders of the SSC and the WESL coordinated the publication of a steady stream of suffrage propaganda in the *Citizen*, the newspaper of the Los Angeles labor movement, and the *California Social-Democrat*. The September 29, 1911 "Votes for Women" issue of the *Citizen* featured seventeen articles on the subject.[32]

In July and September, the SSC organized forty neighborhood suffrage meetings held in socialist halls throughout the city, in order to reach systematically a predominantly White, native-born working-class population that comprised more than fifty percent of the residents of all but one of Los Angeles' wards, and more than seventy percent in East Side wards.[33] The SSC also conducted a house-to-house canvass that sent pairs of socialist suffragists into selected precincts in order to speak personally with female homemakers and registered male voters about the suffrage cause. The club's canvass appears to have dovetailed with that of the Political Equality League (PEL), the largest and most powerful suffrage organization in the county. While the PEL focused on the middle-class and elite West Side, socialists concentrated on the precincts with large populations of working people and socialist voters (primarily in central and eastern Los Angeles). Although canvassing has not been regarded by historians as a particularly militant method of suffrage organizing, WSU leaders Ethel Whitehead and Georgia Kotsch argued that it was an effective strategy in part because of the curiosity and interest that women's presence in the streets engendered about their new public roles. Kotsch reported that many women treated her as an "amusing creature" and welcomed the "break" from the "monotony [of] their lives" that her presence offered. Whitehead, who encountered more hostility, relished the excitement of "assailing the enemy on his own doorstep," as the embodiment of the modern woman fully engaged in public life.[34]

The WESL focused on gaining grassroots labor support through equally modern methods. The WESL sent a circular letter to hundreds of labor organizations in the county and throughout the state. The San Francisco WESL, the key working-class suffrage organization in the Bay Area, published the letter in the newspaper of the San Francisco Labor Council and mailed it to local unions that could not be personally contacted. Maud Younger believed that the letter "brought endorsements that otherwise might not have been forthcoming," increased

agitation among new converts, and garnered attention in the press. An innovative tear-off informed the WESL that the targeted organization had endorsed the suffrage amendment.[35]

As part of their effort to mobilize working-class support, socialist women pioneered the use of the most aggressively militant street tactics employed by California suffragists. Street tactics were certainly familiar to socialist women, since most had participated in the street demonstrations common to American labor and socialist protest. Socialist leaders of the CESA, including Alice Park and Jennie Arnott, had also been impressed with the militance of British suffragists since 1908.[36]

The WESL sponsored the first open-air meeting of the Southern California campaign on July 13 in Hollenbeck Park, located in an ethnically mixed, working-class neighborhood on Los Angeles' East Side. This move showed daring, not only because open-air meetings had not been part of conventional suffrage organizing, but also because the WESL had to find a way to circumvent a city ordinance prohibiting political speeches in public parks. Instead of speaking, the hundred suffrage supporters in attendance sang their arguments for the ballot and informally discussed the issue around picnic tables where coffee and doughnuts were served. Excellent press coverage in papers across the state emphasized the innovativeness of the outdoor gathering and the courage displayed in challenging local police. Good coverage, in turn, encouraged many suffrage groups to sponsor outdoor meetings in other areas of the county and state.[37]

The WESL also "broke the way for street speaking, going into the highways and byways to talk to the men who would not come to [them]." During the last three weeks of the campaign, the league conducted daily street speaking in working-class wards of central and eastern Los Angeles. Before street meetings held near the Labor Temple, WESL speakers would drive about the neighborhood "with votes for women banners flying in the breeze" in order to draw a larger crowd.[38] Many mainstream suffragists in Los Angeles and elsewhere found the courage to speak on the streets with the example and encouragement of socialists. Alice Park reported that by September street speaking had become so popular that many suffragists were engaging in it who had "no idea three months ago they would ever do such a thing."[39]

Victory and Its Aftermath

The broad, militant, and well-organized suffrage campaign, waged in the context of popular enthusiasm for "direct democracy" and Progressive reform, resulted in the enfranchisement of California women on October 10, 1911. But the suffrage amendment remained one of the most contested of all ballot measures in 1911, approved by the state's voters by a narrow margin of 3,587 out of 246,487 votes cast. The amendment won in Southern California and in most of the rural regions of the state, but it lost in San Francisco and Oakland. A complex set of demographic and political factors contributed to these regional differences. In San Francisco, a largely

Teacher Emma Tom Leung (left) and Clara Elizabeth Chan Lee of Oakland, California register to vote in 1911 as their husbands look on. They became the first Chinese American women to become eligible to vote in the United States.

OAKLAND TRIBUNE

German and Irish Catholic population associated woman suffrage with temperance activists and moral reformers who appeared to threaten their traditional social customs. The union movement remained ambivalent or opposed, Progressive political forces failed to make suffrage a priority, and a well-organized opposition funded by liquor interests campaigned vigorously against the amendment. Although mainstream suffragists went after the working-class and immigrant vote, an undercurrent of nativism and anti-union sentiment informed their campaign and strained relations with working-class suffragists. In the southern cities and rural counties, the population tended to be native-born and Protestant, and hence theoretically more favorable to temperance and suffrage. In Los Angeles, Progressive reformers, organized labor, and a popular Socialist Party endorsed suffrage with more fervor. And the opposition, aligned with the anti-reform and anti-union Merchants and Manufacturers Association, may have actually increased support for the amendment among both working-class and middle-class voters. The suffrage coalition, with socialist women serving as an important class-bridging force, more successfully united women from divergent backgrounds.[40]

It is difficult to assess the precise impact of socialist women on the outcome of the suffrage campaign. In many cities, their contributions cannot be separated from those of their non-socialist sisters, although they no doubt took the lead in agitating in working-class communities and in the streets.[41] In Los Angeles, however, socialist women clearly made a difference, playing a major role in

securing a victory for suffrage in working-class neighborhoods and therefore in the city overall. Of Los Angeles' seven assembly districts, five supported the amendment, and four of those contained working-class majorities. Contemporary accounts suggest that working-class precincts provided greater margins of victory than the middle-class and elite precincts that favored the amendment. The voters most likely to reject the amendment lived on the "respectable, stylish West Side" and in the downtown neighborhoods that housed the city's most transient and impoverished residents. The precinct surrounding the Labor Temple, in which many union members lived, carried the amendment by a two-to-one margin.[42]

Mainstream suffragists freely acknowledged the critical importance of working-class and socialist support and praised socialist suffragists for their activism. The *Western Woman Voter*, the organ of the West Coast suffrage movement, credited the victory in Southern California to the fact that "the labor unions and the Socialists there…[had] actively lined up in favor of the amendment." Progressive suffragist Helen Bary considered the campaign to get out the labor and socialist vote conducted by the WESL and the SSC more "productive" than the "whole elaborate campaign" devised by mainstream groups to gain support among the elite and middle classes.[43]

For socialist women, the 1911 campaign seemed to represent the fulfillment of their "dream of solidarity among women," of a sisterhood that crossed the boundaries of class, political ideology, and organizational affiliation. Tensions between mainstream and socialist activists surfaced periodically in the post-suffrage period, however, especially during partisan elections. But overall, enfranchisement contributed to greater collaboration among socialist and mainstream women on a wider variety of political projects, rather than to a fragmentation of the woman's movement. Socialist women, in alliance with a small group of labor-oriented Progressive clubwomen, continued to comprise a left-wing of the woman's movement from 1911 to 1917. During this period, radical women became the leading proponents of labor legislation and unionization, the most outspoken advocates of a redistributive social welfare state, and the earliest supporters of birth control. In fact, socialist women's influence on the legislative proposals advocated by mainstream women's groups helps explain why California was at the forefront of social welfare legislation for women during the Progressive Era. Socialist women's activism appears to offer an important reason why California devised better protection for women workers than most other states and debated more comprehensive and less oppressive mothers' pension programs than were considered elsewhere.[44]

The activism of Josephine Cole and her comrades highlights the ways in which socialist women reinvigorated and expanded the suffrage movement in the early twentieth-century United States. An influential sector of California's suffrage coalition, socialist women broadened its boundaries by recruiting working-class women, emphasizing new arguments, and introducing militant methods. They also demonstrated a fruitful strategy for coalition-building, one that made them a

distinctive and independent tendency within the larger movement. Their grassroots activism in working-class communities contributed to a critical suffrage victory that, following on the heels of the successful Washington State campaign in 1910, ignited expectations nationwide. As the California campaign served to emphasize the importance of collaborative and class-bridging efforts, innovative methods, and working-class support, the socialist suffragists of the state helped shape the course of the national suffrage movement.

Notes

1. Ellen Carol DuBois, "Woman Suffrage and the Left: An International Socialist-Feminist Perspective," *New Left Review*, no. 186 (March/April 1991), 29-45; Mari Jo Buhle, *Women and American Socialism, 1870-1920* (Urbana, 1981), chpt. 6; Nancy F. Cott, *The Grounding of Modern Feminism* (New Haven, 1987), chpt. 1.; John D. Buenker, "The Politics of Mutual Frustration: Socialists and Suffragists in New York and Wisconsin," in Sally M. Miller, *Flawed Liberation: Socialism and Feminism* (Westport, Conn., 1981), 113-144.

2. Buhle, *Socialism*, 231-238; Buenker, "Politics," 113-144; Marjorie Spruill (Wheeler), *New Women of the New South: The Leaders of the Woman Suffrage Movement in the Southern States* (New York, 1993), 74-75, 184.

3. Michael Kazin, "The Great Exception Revisited: Organized Labor and Politics in San Francisco and Los Angeles, 1870-1940," *Pacific Historical Review* 55 (August 1986), 381-388; Sherry Jeanne Katz, "Dual Commitments: Feminism, Socialism, and Women's Political Activism in California, 1890-1920," (Ph.D. diss., University of California, Los Angeles, 1991), chpts. 1-3.

4. Katz, "Dual Commitments," 106-112; and Sherry Katz, "Socialist Women and Progressive Reform," in William Deverell and Tom Sitton, eds., *California Progressivism Revisited* (Berkeley, 1994), 119.

5. Gayle Ann Gullett, "Feminism, Politics, and Voluntary Groups: Organized Womanhood in California, 1886-1896," (Ph.D. diss., University of California, Riverside, 1983), esp. 19-21, 144-150, 176-184, 196-201, 297-313; Susan L. Englander, "The San Francisco Wage Earners' Suffrage League: Class Conflict and Class Coalition in the California Woman Suffrage Movement, 1907-1912," (M.A. thesis, San Francisco State University, 1989), 54-80; Katz, "Dual Commitments," 54-69.

6. Donald Waller Rodes, "The California Woman Suffrage Campaign of 1911," (M.A. thesis, California State University, Hayward, 1974), 10-11, 33-31; Ronald Schaffer, "The Problem of Consciousness in the Woman Suffrage Movement: A California Perspective," *Pacific Historical Review* 45 (Nov. 1976), 469-493; Douglas Flamming, "African-Americans and the Politics of Race in Progressive-Era Los Angeles," in Deverell and Sitton, eds., *California Progressivism*, 206-208; Bess Marjory Munn, "Activity of the Suffragette," *Citizen* (Los Angeles), Sept. 29, 1911.

7. Nancy F. Cott, "Feminist Theory and Feminist Movements: The Past Before Us," in Juliet Mitchell and Ann Oakley, eds., *What Is Feminism?* (New York, 1986), 52-54.

8. Josephine R. Cole, "In Defense of Woman Suffrage," *Common Sense* (Los Angeles), March 30, 1907; Katz, "Dual Commitments," 259-277.

9. Katz, "Dual Commitments," 263-264; n. 47-48, 317-320; "For Political Equality," *People's Paper* (Los Angeles), September 24, 1910.

10. M[ary] E. G[arbutt], "Notes from the Convention of the Socialist Women's Union of California," *Los Angeles Socialist*, Oct. 4, 1902; Ethel Whitehead, "Woman and the Socialist Movement," *People's Paper*, Oct. 28, 1910; Ethel Whitehead, "The Woman's Movement in California," *Progressive Woman* 2 (May 1909), 7.

11. Josephine R. Cole, "Women's Unions," *Appeal to Reason*, June 13, 1903; report by M[ary] E. G[arbutt], *Los Angeles Socialist*, Jan. 3, 1903; Josephine R. Cole, "A Reply to Mrs. Corbin," *Los Angeles Socialist*, June 20, 1903; Agnes Halpin Downing, "Woman's Needs," *Socialist Woman* 1 (March 1908), 2; Whitehead, "Woman and the Socialist Movement."

12. Cott, "Feminist Theory," 50-54; Cott, *Grounding*, 19-21, 29-30.

13. Sallie E. Bowman, "Why Women Should Have the Ballot," *Citizen*, March 5, 1909; Georgia Kotsch, "The Mission of the Socialist Woman," *Progressive Woman* 5 (Aug. 11), 13-14; J[osephine] R. Cole, "Political Power for Women," *Los Angeles Socialist*, April 4, 1903.

14. Ellen Carol DuBois, "Working Women, Class Relations, and Suffrage Militance: Harriot Stanton Blatch and the New York Woman Suffrage Movement," in this volume; Cott, *Grounding*, 24-25, 41-42; Ann J. Lane, *To "Herland" and Beyond: The Life and Works of Charlotte Perkins Gilman* (New York, 1990), chpts. 6-10.

15. Josephine R. Cole, "The Economic Cause of Woman's Advancement," *Yellow Ribbon* 1 (Feb. 1907), 1-3; Jennie Arnott, "Forces Which Are Working For Suffrage," *Yellow Ribbon* 1 (Jan. 1907), 1.

16. [Mary Garbutt], *Los Angeles Socialist*, Feb. 28, 1903.

17. Alice Park, "The Ballot," *Yellow Ribbon* 1 (Oct. 1906), 3; CESA leaflet, "Woman Suffrage Endorsed by California Conventions," [1906], box 4, Keith-McHenry-Pond Family Papers, Bancroft Library, University of California, Berkeley; "California Literature," *Woman's Journal*, April 29, 1911; [Alice] Park to [Agnes] Downing, March 8, 1911, box 3, Alice Locke Park Collection, Huntington Library, (hereafter cited as Park Coll., HL.)

18. M[able] C[raft] D[eering], "Annual Convention of California Equal Suffrage Association," *Yellow Ribbon* 1 (Nov. 1906), 1-2; *San Francisco Call*, Oct. 6, 1907; CESA convention program, *Western Woman* 1 (Oct. 1907), 12.

19. Report of the San Francisco Equal Suffrage League, *Yellow Ribbon* 1 (Dec. 1906), 1; Rodes, "Woman Suffrage Campaign," 23-57; Englander, "San Francisco Wage Earners' League," 81-86.

20. Helen Valeska Bary, "Labor Administration and Social Security: A Woman's Life," interview by Jacqueline K. Parker, 1972-1973, Regional Oral History Office, Bancroft Library, 1974, 20-21, (hereafter cited as Bary OH, BL).

21. Georgia Kotsch, "State Conference of the Women's Socialist Union," *World*, May 22, 1909; Mary E. Garbutt to Mrs. [Mary] Wilshire, May 20, 1909, in *Wilshire's Magazine* 13 (Aug. 1909), 18; Katz, "Dual Commitments," 273, n. 70, 329-330, 578-580, n. 28, 614-615.

22. "San Diego Women Study Laws for Women," *Citizen*, March 4, 1910; "The Union Label and Votes For Women," *Citizen*, Dec. 9, 1910; "Christmas for Strikers' Children," *People's Paper*, Dec. 23, 1910.

23. See recruitment letters and Noel's "The Woman's Conference of Los Angeles County: It's Aim and Object," folder 12, box 4, Frances Noel Papers, Department of Special Collections, University Research Library, UCLA, (hereafter cited as Noel Papers, UCLA); "Council of Women Formed," *Citizen*, Jan. 20, 1911; "Woman's Conference of L.A. County," *Citizen*, Feb. 24, 1911.

24. Elizabeth Lowe Watson, "To the Members of the California Equal Suffrage Association and friends who favor Votes for Women, throughout the State of California," March 2, 1911, box 227, John Randolph Haynes Papers, Special Collections, University Research Library, UCLA (hereafter cited as Haynes Papers, UCLA); "Denver Woman Will Conduct Local Battle," San Francisco Call, Sept. 19, 1911; list, Equal Suffrage Campaign Committee, n.d., [1911], box 10, Elizabeth Morrison (Boynton) Harbert Collection, Huntington Library (hereafter cited as Harbert Coll., HL).

25. Buhle, Socialism, 230; Cott, Grounding, 24-29; DuBois, Woman Suffrage and the Left," 35-41; DuBois, "Suffrage Militance," 52-58.

26. "Official Bulletin of the Socialist Party of California," California Social-Democrat (Los Angeles), Sept. 9, 1911; State Woman's Committee, "Suffrage Amendment Must Be Carried at the Polls," California Social-Democrat, July 22, 1911; Agnes H. Downing, "Woman Suffrage in California," Progressive Woman 5 (Sept. 1911), 1; Katz, "Dual Commitments," 279-296.

27. Katz, "Dual Commitments," 287-288, n. 106, 346-347; Bary, OH, BL, 17-22, 24; Helen V. Bary to Adela M. Parker, Nov. 23, 1911, box 3, Park Coll., HL.

28. Downing, "Woman Suffrage in California"; list, Equal Suffrage Central Committee, [1911], and Lloyd Galpin to "Dear Madam," Aug. 30, 1911, box 10, Harbert Coll., HL; California Social-Democrat, Sept. 9, 1911.

29. "Socialists Open Woman Suffrage Campaign," Citizen, June 2, 1911; Ethel Whitehead, "The Socialists' Fight," California Social-Democrat, Sept. 9, 1911.

30. "Wage-Earners' Suffrage Rally," Citizen, June 2, 1911, WESL circular letter, "To All Union Men of California," [1911] and Estelle Lawton Lindsey, "The Wage-Earners Suffrage League Plans Great Educational Campaign," Los Angeles Record, n.d., folders 7 and 14, box 1, Noel Papers, UCLA.

31. "Next Municipal Election May Be Open to Women," n.p., n.d., Woman's Suffrage Scrapbook, compiled by Mrs. M.A. Holmes, Pasadena Historical Society, Pasadena, California (hereafter cited as Suffrage Scrapbook, PHS); Leonard Pitt, "Red Flag Over City Hall? The Socialist Labor Ticket in the Los Angeles Mayoral Election of 1911," (Paper delivered at AHA Convention, 1989), n. 12, 29; Bary, OH, 20-22; Bary to Parker, Nov. 23, 1911, box 3, Park Coll., HL; "Report on Publicity of the Political Equality League of Southern California," box 227, Haynes Papers, UCLA; Kazin, "Great Exception," 378-380, 384, 389-392; and Maud Younger, "Why Wage-Earning Women Should Vote," folder 1, box 1, Noel Papers, UCLA; Flamming, "Politics of Race," 207-210.

32. On the increased use of publicity among suffragists, see DuBois, "Suffrage Militance."

33. People's Paper, July 1, 1911; Citizen, July 14, Sept. 8, 1911; Whitehead, "The Socialists' Fight"; California Social-Democrat, July 22, Sept. 9, 1911; Downing, "Woman Suffrage in California"; Pitt, "Red Flag?" 14-18.

34. "Workers are Wanted," People's Paper, July 1, 1911; report from Mary Garbutt, Citizen, July 21, 1911; Woman's Journal, April 15, June 17, 1911; Whitehead, "The Socialists' Fight"; Georgia Kotsch, "Through Battle's Smoke," Citizen, Oct. 20, 1911.

35. Citizen, July 28, 1911; WESL circular letter; "Wage Earners' Suffrage League," Labor Clarion (San Francisco), Sept. 1, 1911; Maud Younger to [Frances] Noel, Oct. 24, 1911, Knox Mellon Collection (a collection of Frances Nacke Noel materials held privately by historian Knox Noel Mellon, hereafter cited as Mellon Coll.).

36. Woman's Journal, Oct. 10, 1908; Sofia M. Loebinger to Alice Park, Aug. 4, 1909 and Alice Park, American Suffragette, n.p., n.d., box 2, Park Coll., HL.

37. "Suffrage Battle Hymn Swells in City Park," Los Angeles Herald, July 14, 1911; "Musical Pleas for Votes By Women Thwart Police," San Francisco Call, July 15, 1911, 1911 clippings, Suffrage Scrapbook, PHS; Woman's Journal, Aug. 26, 1911.

38. "Behold the Advent of the Woman Orator," Los Angeles Tribune, Oct. 20, 1911; Citizen, Sept. 15, 1911; [Frances Noel] to Ethel Duppy Turner] Oct. 19, 1911, Mellon Coll.; "Suffrage Message Carried to Men in Territory Before Neglected," n.p., n.d., Suffrage Scrapbook, PHS.

39. Letter from Elizabeth Lowe Watson, Woman's Journal, Aug. 12, 1911; Alice Park, "The California Campaign," Western Woman Voter 1 (Oct.-Nov. 1911).

40. Katz, "Dual Commitments," 277-297, n. 140, 356-358.

41. Ibid., 283-287.

42. Pitt, "Red Flag?" 19-20; California Social-Democrat, Oct. 14, 1911; Bary OH, BL, 18-24, esp. 24; "At Los Angeles," Progressive Woman 5 (Dec. 1911); 5; Citizen, Oct. 13, 1911.

43. Western Woman Voter 1 (Oct.-Nov. 1911), 1; Bary to Parker, Nov. 23, 1911, box 3, Park Coll., HL.

44. Bary to Parker, Nov. 23, 1911, box 3, Park Coll., HL; Katz, "Dual Commitments," 299-301; Katz, "Socialist Women and Progressive Reform," 117-143.

Ida B. Wells-Barnett and her children, 1909.
From left: Charles Aked; Ida B. Wells, Jr.; Alfreda Marguerita;
and Herman Kohlsaat

Seventeen

IDA B. WELLS-BARNETT AND THE ALPHA SUFFRAGE CLUB OF CHICAGO

Wanda A. Hendricks

Editor's Introduction: Wanda A. Hendricks's article on Ida B. Wells-Barnett and the first African American woman suffrage club in Chicago, like the articles by Ellen DuBois and Sherry Katz that precede it, underscores the diversity of the suffrage movement in the early twentieth century. Though Black women encountered much discrimination from White suffragists, they were active participants in the movement nonetheless. One of the most famous of the African American suffragists was the indomitable Ida B. Wells-Barnett, under whose leadership Black women in Chicago not only worked for suffrage but played a significant role in the city's politics.

Beginning with her refusal to move from the "ladies car" to the "colored car" on a train in Mississippi in 1884, Ida B. Wells-Barnett did not allow anyone to deny her or her race their rights without a challenge—and the National American Woman Suffrage Association (NAWSA) was no exception. The famous incident Hendricks describes below, in which Wells-Barnett refused to obey the NAWSA's instructions to march with an all-Black contingent at the end of the 1913 suffrage parade in Washington, D.C. rather than with the Illinois delegation, would have come as no surprise to those who knew her. She was well known for her opposition to accommodation and gradualism and for her fearless advocacy of justice and equality.

Wells-Barnett was convinced that the vote was crucial for Black Americans—including as a weapon in the crusade against lynching to which she devoted much of her life—and thus she fought *against* the disfranchisement of African American men and *for* the enfranchisement of African American women. And through the Alpha Suffrage Club, the first and most important of several Black suffrage clubs in Chicago, she helped African American women and Chicago politicians realize that Black women could play a decisive role in city elections.

The fact that in 1913 Illinois gave women the right to vote in presidential and municipal elections (the first state east of the Mississippi River to do so), meant that Illinois suffragists had the opportunity to be politically active and influential— even while working for *full* suffrage. As Wanda Hendricks clearly demonstrates,

these African American suffragists took full advantage of this opportunity. The women of the Alpha Suffrage Club worked hard and successfully to get more Black women and men to register and vote in Chicago elections, thus encouraging African Americans to run for office. Their support was a decisive factor in the election of Oscar DePriest, the first Black alderman in Chicago's history, who later (1928) made history as the first Northern Black to be elected to Congress and the first Black congressman since the disfranchisement of Southern Blacks in the 1890s.

★ ★ ★ ★ ★

IDA BELL WELLS-BARNETT played an important role in the municipal politics of Chicago during the second decade of the twentieth century. She sought civic representation for the masses of Black women and men who fled the South seeking economic, social, and political opportunity. In defense of the rights of African Americans and women, she had by 1915 formed the largest Black women's suffrage club in Illinois, defied the National American Woman Suffrage Association's ban on allowing African American women to march under their state banners alongside their White counterparts at the landmark 1913 suffrage parade in Washington, and played a crucial role in the election of the first African American alderman in Chicago.

Like most African Americans growing up in the Jim Crow South, Wells's early life was wrought with strife and conflict. She was the eldest of eight children, born in Holly Springs, Mississippi, on July 16, 1862 to a former slave from Virginia named Lizzie Warrenton and Jim Wells, the son of his master.[1] Despite the ravages of segregated Mississippi, the Wells educated their children at Shaw University in Holly Springs, later renamed Rust College. A community activist, Jim Wells became a trustee at Shaw while Lizzie Wells accompanied her children to classes so that she could learn to read and write.[2]

In 1878, the yellow fever epidemic that swept through the area drastically changed Ida Wells's life. Her father, mother, and a nine-month-old sibling, died in the epidemic, leaving sixteen-year-old Ida to care for the other children.[3] Financially responsible for the family, she passed the teachers' exam for the county schools and gained employment at a school six miles from her home that paid a monthly salary of $25. A year later, invited by her mother's sister in Memphis, Tennessee, Wells left Holly Springs. She took the two younger girls with her and left a sister and two brothers with relatives. Another brother had died several years earlier of spinal meningitis.[4]

Post-Reconstruction Memphis, like much of the South, began a program built on the usurpation of African American rights. With the aid of the Supreme Court, Southern states implemented a pervasive system of Jim Crow rules. The Court, in a series of cases, had by 1883 upheld the right of Southern states to enforce laws that violated the civil rights gained by African Americans in the post-Civil War era.

Deeply disturbed over the events leading to the restoration of White supremacy, Wells challenged the legality of the system. In May 1884, twenty-two-year-old Wells boarded a train owned by Chesapeake and Ohio Railroad and chose a seat in the "ladies" coach. Though informed by the conductor that as a Black woman she could not sit in the car reserved for White females, Wells stood her ground and refused to move to the all-Black Jim Crow car. Rather than allow Wells to remain seated, the conductor attempted forcefully to remove her. In retaliation, she bit his hand. Refusing to be outdone, the conductor sought the aid of the baggage man who assisted in dragging Wells from the coach.

Seeking justice, Wells hired a lawyer, and sued the railroad. Though she was initially victorious, the settlement of $500 was bittersweet. The state supreme court reversed the ruling of the lower court. Though disappointed, she understood that hers' "was the first case in which a colored plaintiff in the South had appealed to a state court since the repeal of the Civil Rights Bill by the United States Supreme Court," and if she had won, it "would have set a precedent which others would doubtless have followed."[5] The case and its subsequent reversal served as a springboard for her career to fight racism and discrimination. Over the years Wells pushed the system to its limit by persistently defending her rights as an African American woman. She advocated protest, demanded equality, and sought redress for crimes committed against the race.

One of the media Wells used to publicize her message was the newspaper. Before she reached thirty years of age, she had been co-owner of the *Memphis Free Speech and Headlight* and contributed articles to local and national publications such as the *Memphis Watchman* and the *Living Way*, the *New York Age*, and the *Indianapolis World*.[6] Many of the articles centered on the lynchings of African American men. The deaths of three colleagues, Thomas Moss, Calvin McDowell, and Henry Stewart by a lynch mob on March 9, 1892 in Memphis prompted these writings.

The three successfully managed the People's Grocery in a heavily populated Black section just outside Memphis. Accompanied by a police deputy, a competing White grocery store owner whose business was failing, harassed two of the African American owners. In the ensuing altercation, McDowell knocked the White grocer down and confiscated his gun. Stewart and McDowell were charged with assault and battery and arrested. McDowell later posted bond and they were released. The following Saturday night, the White grocer accompanied by a mob of White men entered the back door of People's Grocery. Fear compelled the African American men inside to fire several shots. Three of the White men were wounded. Chaos erupted when several Black men were dragged from their homes and questioned or incarcerated. Eventually, Moss, McDowell, and Stewart were indicted and thrown in jail. During the night they were removed from the county jail, shot, mutilated, and hanged.[7]

The African American community responded in several ways. The *Free Speech*

ran an editorial that indicted the entire White community for the deaths of the three men and encouraged Blacks to leave the city. Pushed by fear, many Black Memphis residents heeded the call of the *Free Speech* and migrated to Oklahoma. So many departed that Black ridership on the City Railway Company's trains rapidly deteriorated. Reduced profits for the owners of the railway company and other businesses heavily trafficked by African Americans resulted. Concern over the massive out-migration forced mainstream White newspapers to discourage such moves and declare Oklahoma to be a major disappointment and plagued by hardships.

Wells refused to bow to pressure from White business owners to join them in their efforts to terminate the movement. Lost profits, she believed, were such a small price to pay for the lives of three responsible citizens. She even visited several Black churches and urged members "to keep on staying off the [railway] cars." Too, she quietly "rejoiced" when many more Blacks sought refuge in Oklahoma.[8]

Wells also decided to do her own investigation of the murders. The fates of Moss, McDowell, and Stewart forced her to question the rationale of White mob action and rethink her own ideas about the reasons for lynchings. Like most Americans, Black and White, she had been heavily influenced by White myths that suggested that lynchings happened to accused rapists; that is, Black men raping White women. The men brutally murdered in Memphis, however, did not fall into that category. They were outstanding community citizens whose only crime involved competing with a White grocer. The realization compelled Wells to examine previous lynching cases. After extensive research, she concluded that more often than not, the cry of rape masqueraded as a legitimate device for White men to eliminate African American competitors.

Subsequently, she wrote a scathing editorial: "Eight Negroes lynched since last issue of the *Free Speech*. Three were charged with killing White men and five with raping White women. Nobody in this section believes the old thread-bare lie that Negro men assault White women. If Southern men are not careful they will overreach themselves and a conclusion will be reached which will be very damaging to the moral reputation of their women."[9] The editorial attacked Southern White male honor and suggested that White women could be attracted to Black men. And, it infuriated the White community.

Fortunately, when the editorial appeared, Wells was en route to Philadelphia to attend the African Methodist Episcopal General Church Conference. Warnings from an enraged White mob persuaded the co-owner of the paper to flee. The mob destroyed the newspaper office and in their rage threatened Wells's life should she dare return to Memphis. Exiled from her home, she went to New York, joined the staff of the *New York Age* and continued her exposé on lynchings.[10]

Ida B. Wells had met the editor of the *New York Age*, Timothy Thomas Fortune, in the summer of 1888 and maintained her contact with him. When Fortune called for the formation of the National Afro-American League, she supported him. Through

Ida B. Wells' pamphlet, *Southern Horrors,*written in 1892, and her portrait, 1893
LIBRARY OF CONGRESS & NATIONAL PORTRAIT MUSEUM

the *Age* and the encouragement of Fortune, Americans were alerted to the inherent problems of disfranchisement, lynching, inequitable distribution of educational funding, the convict lease system, and Jim Crow.[11]

Wells's research on lynching culminated in the pamphlet *Southern Horrors: Lynch Law In All Its Phases.* Published in October 1892, Wells prefaced it with "Somebody must show that the Afro-American race is sinned against [rather] than sinning, and it seems to have fallen upon me to do so." She was determined to prove that Blacks were not a "bestial race" and to "arouse the conscience of the American people to a demand for justice to every citizen."[12]

Creating the Alpha Suffrage Club

By the time Wells married newspaper publisher and attorney Ferdinand Barnett in 1895, she had visited England twice, caused an uproar at the Columbian Exposition of 1893 held in Chicago by publishing and handing out the pamphlet *The Reason Why The Colored American is not in the World's Columbian Exposition,* and become an active club woman by establishing the Ida B. Wells Club. Marriage to Barnett brought part ownership in his newspaper, the *Conservator,* two step-children and four of her own. Domestic duties as a wife and mother did not deter Wells from public life. She joined the National Association of Colored Women, organized in 1896, actively pursued the

suffrage cause for both disenfranchised African American men and all women, and heeded the call for the development of the National Association for the Advancement of Colored People (NAACP) in the aftermath of the 1908 Springfield, Illinois, race riot. She also continued her exposés on lynching. In 1910 she wrote "How Enfranchisement Stops Lynching," for *Original Rights Magazine*.[13]

The Barnetts resided on the South Side of Chicago in the Second Ward. By the second decade of the twentieth century, the largest majority of African Americans in the city also lived in the area. In 1910 African Americans comprised twenty-five percent of the 42,801 population in the Ward and by 1915 represented nearly forty percent of the 63,342 residents.[14] Voting-age women in the ward developed a keen interest in the electoral process, particularly because of the pending female suffrage bill in the state legislature. They founded several suffrage clubs, developed voter education classes and held mass rallies.[15]

One of the most important and the first African American suffrage club in the city was the Alpha Suffrage Club. Wells-Barnett and a White colleague, Belle Squire, established the organization in January 1913.[16] Ida B. Wells-Barnett used the Suffrage Club as a basis to demonstrate the significance of the ballot to the masses of Black women in Chicago. During her early years in Chicago she toured the state for the Women's State Central Committee encouraging women to organize and develop political knowledge. She found on one of these trips that "in only a few instances did I see any of my own people." From this she concluded that "if the White women were backward in political matters, our own women were even more so."[17]

Lacking the skills to understand the political process, Wells-Barnett concluded, hindered African American women from full participation in civic matters. The necessity for the suffrage club took on new urgency when it became clear "that we were likely to have a restricted suffrage, and the White women of the organization [Women's Suffrage Association] were working like beavers to bring it about."[18]

To generate interest in the Suffrage Club and the ballot, she pooled her meager resources, organized meetings and insisted that the club hold membership in national, state, and local organizations such as the National Federation of Colored Women, the State Federation of Colored Women's Club, the Illinois Federation of Colored Women's Clubs and the City Federation of Colored Women's Clubs. The Club's goals included showing Black women how to use their "vote for the advantage of ourselves and our race" and acting as a liaison to the city, state, and national organizations. Within less than three years of its founding two hundred women claimed membership. Ida B. Wells-Barnett was elected president.[19]

Racism in the Suffrage Movement

One of Wells-Barnett's first official duties as president was to attend the March 1913 parade sponsored by the National American Woman Suffrage Association in the nation's capital. Carrying banners representing almost every state in the union, the parade marchers highlighted the demand for universal female enfranchisement.

But because of racist attitudes, African American women were relegated to the back of the line regardless of state residency. Sixty-five enthusiastic delegates from Illinois prepared for the march along Pennsylvania Avenue. As they lined up, Grace Wilbur Trout, president of the Illinois Equal Suffrage Associa-

Ida B. Wells-Barnett at 1913 NAWSA suffrage parade
Chicago Daily Tribune

tion and chairperson of the Illinois delegation, informed the Illinois group that the NAWSA advised them "to keep our delegation entirely white" because many women, especially those from the South, resented the presence of a Black woman in the Illinois ranks. They would not march, Trout concluded, if Wells-Barnett remained in the Illinois line. They expected her to march with the Black women's contingent at the end of the procession.

Fear of antagonizing Southern White women, whose support was worth more to the NAWSA's cause than that of African American women, prompted state colleagues to deny Wells-Barnett's opportunity to march with them. Viewing Black women as a threat to White supremacy, White Southern women rejected the legitimacy of Black female state delegates marching with White state delegates. Historian Steven Buechler argues that the NAWSA became the vehicle for Southern White women to "maximize White women's votes, minimize Black women's votes, and leave restrictions on Black male voters intact." The desire of Southern White suffragists to assure the public and their state legislatures that African American suffrage and woman suffrage were unconnected pushed them to devise the Jim Crow strategy and to petition for the assistance of the NAWSA.[20] The NAWSA's acquiescence made it blatantly clear that the organization took advantage of the racist agenda, especially when it proved expedient. Ida B. Wells-Barnett's inclusion in the state delegation in the 1913 parade threatened to impede that tactic by stripping away the veil of Jim Crow and opening the door to other African American women.

When Trout pleaded with Wells-Barnett to march with the Black delegates at the back of the procession, she refused; she insisted that "the Southern women have tried to evade the question time and again by giving some excuse or other every time it has been brought up. If the Illinois women do not take a stand now in this great democratic parade then the colored women are lost."[21] But, Wells-Barnett's plea fell on deaf ears just as an earlier appeal from Virginia Brooks, a White woman from West Hammond, had. If "[w]e have come down here to march for equal rights," then, "[i]t would be autocratic to exclude men or women of any color,"

Brooks told the contingent. Furthermore, she continued, "I think that we should allow Mrs. Barnett to walk in our delegation. If the women of other states lack moral courage, we should show them that we are not afraid of public opinion. We should stand by our principles. If we do not the parade will be a farce."[22] The state delegates refused to reconsider and acquiesced to the demands of Southern White women. Black women could march only if they maintained a very low profile and stayed in their place—at the back of the line.

Angry at the blatant disregard for her right as a woman and an Illinois resident to take part, Wells-Barnett told delegates that "I shall not march at all unless I can march under the Illinois banner" because "[w]hen I was asked to come down here I was asked to march with the other women of our state, and I intend to do so or not take part in the parade at all." One member of the group retorted "If I were a colored woman, I should be willing to march with the other women of my race." Wells-Barnett replied "there is a difference,...which you probably do not see.... I shall not march with the colored women. Either I go with you or not at all. I am not taking this stand because I personally wish for recognition. I am doing it for the future benefit of my whole race."[23]

After this debate Wells-Barnett disappeared from the parade site. Illinois delegates probably assumed that she had relented and decided to march with the Black contingent. But, as the delegates began marching down Pennsylvania Avenue, she quietly stepped out from the crowd of spectators and joined the only White Illinois colleagues sympathetic to her cause, Belle Squires and Virginia Brooks. So important was the event that a photograph of her, flanked by Squires and Brooks, appeared in *The Chicago Daily Tribune* giving the event and its participants local and national exposure.[24] As the marchers proceeded, Southerners did not defect. This may be in part because they did not learn of Wells-Barnett's inclusion until after the parade ended. At any rate, the press coverage reassured many Black women of their own tenuous place in the suffrage movement and probably convinced many Whites, despite the NAWSA's insistence, that the "Negro question" and female suffrage were not separate issues.

The staunch refusal by Wells-Barnett to march with the Black contingent impeded the White female prerogative of discriminating against African American women on racial grounds while simultaneously embracing them along gender lines. Racial xenophobia rather than gender inclusion guided their principles. The endorsement of Jim Crow segregation blinded White participants to the fact that unlike the requirement for their African American counterpart, they did not have to separate their Whiteness from their femaleness. Indeed, they could embrace the White, middle-class, nativist, racist sentiments prevalent during the Progressive Era under the guise of expediency. Ultimately, White women could express the desire for the enfranchisement of women while ignoring African American women.

But, Wells-Barnett frustrated their plans. She defined the battle for African American women by intertwining her state citizenship, her African American-ness,

and her femaleness. She affirmed African American women's place in the fight for the ballot by confronting White women. For women and for the race, she rejected the notion that she did not belong among her state delegates.

Electing a Black Man as Alderman

On May 7 of that same year, the Illinois Senate passed the Presidential and Municipal Suffrage Bill and on June 11 the House approved the measure. Before the month ended, the legislature ratified the bill that granted partial suffrage to female citizens twenty-one years or older. Illinois became the first state east of the Mississippi River to enfranchise its women.[25] More importantly, for the first time in the city's history, African American females could cast their ballots in the race for alderman of the Second Ward. Mobilizing their forces quickly and instituting a large grassroots campaign, Black women became powerful political allies to voting-age African American men.

The Alpha Suffrage Club increased its activism in communities with large percentages of African Americans, especially since the aldermanic primary was less than a year away. Under Wells-Barnett's leadership, the Club implemented a block system to canvass neighborhoods. In addition, once-a-week meeting sessions were established as learning centers on the rights and duties of citizens. Women worked as clerks in the voter registration process and provided the necessary civic education.[26]

In the 1914 aldermanic primary the club endorsed the Independent candidate, William Randolph Cowan, a prominent Black real estate businessman, against the incumbent machine candidate, Hugh Norris.[27] While Black politicians championed the new gender-integrated electorate, several other ward men challenged female entry into their domain. As members of the Alpha Suffrage Club marshalled their forces and canvassed the Black community, registering women for the February 1914 primary, some men "jeered at them and told them they ought to be at home taking care of the babies." Other male hecklers accused them of "trying to take the place of men and wear the trousers."[28] The jeers made an impact on these Victorian ladies. Discouraged and unsure of their own place in politics, many of the women questioned the legitimacy of their role in the faction-riddled arena. Reassuring members that their efforts were important, Wells-Barnett refused to allow Black women to bow to male pressure. She urged each of the workers to return to the neighborhoods and continue registering women. Under her tutelage, most of the women stuck by their convictions, continued the registration efforts, and, in the process realized the importance of their participation in politics.

Some 7,290 female and 16,327 male potential voters registered during this campaign.[29] Though the club was not solely responsible for the number of registrants, it does suggest that the members aroused considerable interest and probably increased the potential number of African American voters. Ida B. Wells-Barnett proudly proclaimed that due to the impressive demonstration of women,

"our men politicians were surprised," especially "because not one of them even our ministers, had said one word to influence women to take advantage of the suffrage opportunity Illinois had given to her daughters."[30]

The Black weekly, the *Chicago Defender*, captured the sentiments of many women in its sensational headlines for February 21, 1914: "Women To Show Loyalty By Casting First Ballot For Cowan For Alderman"; "Second Ward Women Determine to Use Their Power to Better Themselves and Strengthen the Race"; "Asserted Men Needed Their Assistance"; and "Garbage Question, Children's Playgrounds, Ventilation in Public Places, Supervision of 'Movies' Important Matters to Them." The paper triumphantly predicted that Black women would become "the balance of power" in the aldermanic campaign and would "see their first vote make race history in Chicago."[31]

On primary day, almost 3,000 women cast ballots in the Second Ward. Still, William Cowan lost the election. Though disappointed with the outcome, the Suffrage Club women consoled themselves with the knowledge that they had played a significant role in attracting forty-five percent of the women who voted for Cowan to the polls. For the *Defender*, this showed that Black women understood better than the men the interconnection between duty and politics because "they were actuated by principal in politics just as they are in everything else." Moreover, the newspaper article stated that "The women's vote was a revelation to everyone, and after analysis shows them still actuated by the sense of duty to do more" and that because of female votes "Traitorous leaders are to be relegated to the background and citizens of strength and character are to take their places." The *Defender* vigorously promoted both Victorian ideals and female access to the electoral process.[32]

The female vote even compelled another weekly, the *Broad Ax,* to acknowledge that "Cowan and his followers woke things up...for he received 2,700 votes more than one thousand of that number being cast by the ladies." The vote "plainly brought to the front one thing and that is that within the next two or four years at the longest a high class popular solid Colored man of affairs can and will be elected to the city council from that ward." For if only three hundred of the Black votes to Norris had been transferred to Cowan, the paper concluded, "nothing could have prevented him from breaking into the city council."[33]

The Alpha Suffrage Club's role generated the most attention. Within a few days after Cowan's defeat, two members of the Republican Party visited the Alpha Suffrage Club. A Black Republican and contractor, Oscar DePriest, joined the president of the ward organization, Samuel Ettelson, in an appeal for the women to campaign and vote for the machine candidate in the next election.[34] The two men urged the women not to support an Independent candidate for alderman as they had in the Cowan primary, because if they did so, the Black vote would split and the Democratic candidate might win. In turn, the Republican Party "having realized that there was now a demand for a colored man, would itself nominate one at the next vacancy." The next vacancy, they were told would probably be in

1915. In November, 1914, George Harding, a Second Ward alderman, was elected state senator. Keeping its promise, the organization pushed DePriest to the forefront by endorsing him as their Black candidate for alderman.[35]

Despite the Chicago political machine's endorsement of DePriest, his candidacy was contested. As a matter of fact, his nomination opened the door for other African American candidates seeking the coveted post of alderman. For the first time in Chicago's political history, three Black candidates campaigned for alderman in the primary. Joining DePriest were Louis Anderson, a former journalist from Washington, D.C., and Charles Griffin, an insurance and real estate broker.[36]

With battle lines drawn, the candidates began seeking votes. One of the first forums for the three politicians was at the Alpha Suffrage Club's headquarters. They presented their political platform and entertained questions. The Club decided to "endorse" the Republican ticket and "our young giant Oscar DePriest for alderman of the Second Ward." They pledged "to leave no stone unturned" for his election because "we realize that in no other way can we safeguard our own rights than by holding up the hands of those who fight our battles."[37]

On February 27, 1915, DePriest won the Republican primary. After the victory DePriest appealed to those who did not vote for him. "[A]s all good Republicans," he wrote, I hope that they "give me in my coming fight for election their heartiest loyalty and support."[38] But despite his plea dissenters lingered. For example, Edward Wright, disgruntled over DePriest's victory and his own failed bids for alderman, requested that the Political Equality League endorse William Cowan as an independent candidate against DePriest. As a member of the League and on behalf of the Alpha Suffrage Club, Wells-Barnett recoiled from the appeal. She argued that this scheme was conjured up by "this nameless white man" who "had not been prompted by the desire to secure a better man for nomination. It simply was to get two colored men to fight against each other, and the result would be that neither one of them would secure the place." The League agreed and the Wright-Cowan challenge ended.[39]

The contest between DePriest and three White candidates drew thousands of African Americans in the Second Ward to the polls to cast their ballots. When the votes were tabulated, DePriest was the clear winner—and became the first Black alderman of Chicago. The final count was: DePriest, 10,599 (Republican); Al Russell, 6,893 (Democrat); Simon P. Gary, 3,697 (Progressive); Samuel Block, 433 (Socialist).[40]

Oscar DePriest's victory inspired public discussion of the significance of the female electorate. The woman's vote was a decisive factor and without it, DePriest would not have been the first Black alderman. Women's ballots accounted for more than one third of the ballots cast for DePriest. The nearly 4,000 remaining votes went to the other candidates.[41] More than one third of the total votes cast came from women.

DePriest acknowledged his debt to Second Ward women. Soon after the election, he asserted in the national Black journal, *The Crisis*, "I favor extension of the right of suffrage to women" because the women in Chicago "cast as intelligent a vote as the men." Although there was a certain degree of "timidity" during "the first campaign

in which women voted in Chicago," women educated themselves. And in the 1914 and 1915 campaigns, "the work of the women was as earnest and the interest as keen as that of the men and in some instances the partisanship was almost bitter." Moreover, DePriest asserted that during

> the campaign of 1915 when colored men were primary candidates for alderman, the women of the race seemed to realize fully what was expected of them, and, with the men, rolled up a very large and significant vote for the colored candidates; and they were consistent at the election, contributing to a plurality of over 3,000 votes for the successful colored candidate in a field of five. Personally, I am more than thankful for their work and as electors believe they have every necessary qualification that the men possess.[42]

The Legacy

A year after the election, the Alpha Club elected new officers and continued its suffrage work. Ida B. Wells-Barnett retained the presidency.[43] In addition to the Second Ward, the Club also canvassed the Sixth, Fourteenth, and Thirtieth Wards in Chicago because each had high concentrations of African Americans. The lure of jobs opened by America's involvement in World War I and the fear of the continued deterioration

Ida B. Wells-Barnett, c. 1917-1919, wearing "Martyred Negro Soldiers" button

UNIVERSITY OF CHICAGO LIBRARY

of race relations in the South prompted a mass exodus from Southern states to large urban areas like Chicago. By 1920, the Second Ward African American population was 47,647 or sixty-nine percent of the residents. Voting-age women accounted for 17,144, while men numbered 19,894.[44] This united force challenged political leaders, elected African Americans to the aldermanic post, and commanded some of the spoils from patronage politics.

Little is known about the Alpha Suffrage Club during those late teen years. It is likely that African American women in the Second Ward and other heavily populated Black wards continued canvassing and voting in large numbers, in part because of the preceding labor by Suffrage Club members. Despite the passage of the Nineteenth Amendment in 1920 granting suffrage to all women, the political necessity of a united African American constituency remained. For that reason Wells-Barnett continued to press for Black women to vote by making speeches and canvassing throughout Chicago and the state. In 1930 she ran for the Illinois Senate as an Independent candidate. Though she lost, her zeal for political involvement continued.[45]

The year after her political bid for the senate Wells-Barnett died of a kidney

disease.[46] She left a legacy of activism in social and civic endeavors. Courageously, she exposed the horrors of lynching to a national audience, inspired the growth of the Black female club movement in the state, encouraged African Americans to become a part of the political process, and inspired hundreds of women to enter into the public domain of politics.

Notes

1. Alfreda Duster, ed. *Crusade For Justice: The Autobiography of Ida B. Wells* (Chicago, 1970), 7-8; See also Neil R. McMillen, *Dark Journey: Black Mississippians In The Age of Jim Crow* (Urbana, 1989) for discussion of African American life in Mississippi in the post-Civil War era.
2. Duster, *Crusade*, 8-9.
3. Ibid., 9-17; Monroe A. Majors, *Noted Negro Women Their Triumphs And Activities* (Chicago, 1893; reprint ed., Nashville, Tenn., 1971), 187-188.
4. Duster, *Crusade*, 15-18.
5. Ibid., xvii, 18-20; Mildred Thompson, "Ida B. Wells-Barnett: An Exploratory Study of An American Black Woman, 1893-1930," (Ph.D. diss., George Washington University, 1979), 26-28.
6. Duster, *Crusade*, 22-24, 69, 71; Thompson, "Ida B. Wells Barnett: An Exploratory Study of An American Black Woman, 1893-1930," 29-31; Majors, *Noted Negro Women*, 189.
7. Duster, *Crusade*, 47-51; Ida B. Wells, *Southern Horrors: Lynch Law In all Its Phases* in *On Lynchings* (New York, 1892; reprint ed., New York, 1969), 18-19; David M. Tucker, "Miss Ida B. Wells and Memphis Lynching," *Phylon* 32 (1971): 115-116.
8. Duster, *Crusade*, 53-58.
9. Ibid., 65-66.
10. Ibid., 61-67.
11. Ibid., 71, 77; Thompson "Ida B. Wells Barnett: An Exploratory Study of An American Black Woman, 1893-1930," 36-37, 58; Emma Lou Thornbrough, "The National Afro-American League, 1887-1908," *Journal of Southern History* 27 (1961): 504.
12. Wells, *Southern Horrors*, preface.
13. Duster, *Crusade*, xxiii, 239, 321-327; Ida B. Wells, *The Reason Why The Colored American is Not in the World's Columbian Exposition* (Chicago, 1893); Elizabeth Lindsay Davis, *The Story of The Illinois Federation of Colored Women's Clubs* (Chicago, 1922), 26-28, 56; Ida B. Wells-Barnett, "How Enfranchisement Stops Lynching," *Original Rights Magazine* (June 1910), 42-53.
14. *Thirteenth Census Of The United States, 1910: Population*, v. 2: The breakdown of the population was Native White, native parentage = 11,642; Native White, foreign or mixed = 11,225; Foreign-Born White = 9,118; Negro = 10,709; Indian, Chinese, Japanese, and all other = 107. Yearly census data for the area was kept by the *Chicago Daily News*. Corrections and updates can be found in James Langland, M.A. Compiler, *The Chicago Daily News Almanac And Year-Book For 1916* (Chicago, 1916), 585, 586. Also see Allan H. Spear, *Black Chicago: The Making Of A Negro Ghetto 1890-1920* (Chicago, 1967) 15 and 122 for population data from 1915.
15. *Chicago Defender*, February 21, 1914; Also see listing in Ford S. Black, *Black's Blue Book Directory Of Chicago's Active Colored People And Guide To Their Activities* (Chicago, Ill., 1916), 55, Illinois State Historical Library, Springfield, Ill.
16. Katherine E. Williams, "The Alpha Suffrage Club," *The Half Century Magazine* (September 1916): 12.
17. Duster, *Crusade*, 244-245.
18. Ibid., 345.
19. Williams, "The Alpha Suffrage Club," 12; *Alpha Suffrage Record*, 18 March 1914 [1915], Ida B. Wells-Barnett Papers, University of Chicago. Other officers included: Mary Jackson, Viola Hill, Vera Wesley Green, Sadie L. Adams, and K.J. Bills. There is not an "official" roster of members.
20. Carrie Chapman Catt and Nettie Rogers Shuler, *Woman Suffrage and Politics: The Inner Story of the Suffrage Movement* (1923; reprint, Seattle, 1969), 241-242; Rosalyn Terborg-Penn, "Discrimination Against Afro-American Women in the Woman's Movement, 1830-1920," in *The Afro-American Woman: Struggles And Images*, eds. Sharon Harley and Rosalyn Terborg-Penn (New York, 1978), 24-25; Aileen S. Kraditor, *The Ideas of the*

Woman Suffrage Movement, 1890-1920 (1965; reprint New York, 1981), 212-218; Steven Buechler, *The Transformation of The Woman Suffrage Movement: The Case of Illinois, 1850-1920* (New Jersey, 1986), 149-150, 226; Adade Mitchell Wheeler, "Conflict in the Illinois Woman Suffrage Movement of 1913," *Journal of the Illinois State Historical Society* 76 (Summer 1983): 106; Marjorie Spruill (Wheeler), *New Women Of The New South: The Leaders of the Woman Suffrage Movement in the Southern States* (New York, 1993); *The Chicago Daily Tribune*, March 3 and 4, 1913.
21. *The Chicago Daily Tribune*, March 4, 1913.
22. Ibid.
23. Ibid.
24. Ibid.
25. John D. Buenker, "Illinois and the Four Progressive-Era Amendments to the United States Constitution," *Illinois Historical Journal* 80 (Winter 1987): 210-227; Wheeler, "Conflict in the Illinois Woman Suffrage Movement of 1913," 65-114; Anne Firor Scott and Andrew MacKay Scott, *One Half the People: The Fight for Woman Suffrage* (1975; reprint, Urbana, Ill., 1982), 116-121.
26. Williams, "The Alpha Suffrage Club," 12.
27. *Broad Ax*, January 17, 1914; Gosnell, *Negro Politicians*, 74.
28. Duster, *Crusade*, 346.
29. *The Chicago Daily News Almanac And Year-Book For 1915* (Chicago, 1914), 632, Chicago Municipal Library, Chicago, Ill.; Also, the *Chicago Defender*, February 21, 1914, mentions the Alpha Political Club and Josephine Crawford as active in the political process as well.
30. Duster, *Crusade*, 346.
31. *Chicago Defender*, February 21, 1914.
32. Spear, *Black Chicago*, 81-82; *Chicago Defender*, March 28, 1914.
33. *The Chicago Daily News Almanac And Year-Book For 1915*, 632. Spear, *Black Chicago*, 123; *Chicago Defender*, February 21, 1914; *Broad Ax*, February 28, 1914.
34. Duster, *Crusade*, 346.
35. Duster, *Crusade*, 346-348; Gosnell, *Negro Politicians*, 170.
36. Gosnell, *Negro Politicians*, 30, 70, 104-105; Pinderhughes, *Race and Ethnicity*, 77-78.
37. *Suffrage Record*, March 18, 1914 [1915].
38. *Chicago Defender*, February 27, 1915; *The Chicago Daily News Almanac And Year-Book For 1916* (Chicago, 1916), 567.
39. Duster, *Crusade*, 348.
40. *The Chicago Daily News Almanac And Year-Book For 1916*, 567, 591; Gosnell, *Negro Politicians*, 171.
41. *The Chicago Daily News Almanac And Year-Book For 1916*, 567, 591; Gosnell, *Negro Politicians*, 171.
42. Oscar DePriest, "Chicago and Woman's Suffrage," *The Crisis* 10 (August 1915): 179.
43. Williams, "The Alpha Suffrage Club," 12. Other officers were: Sadie L. Adams, E.D. Wyatt, J.E. Hughes, W.N. Mills, and Laura Beasley.
44. *Fourteenth Census of the United States*, 274.
45. See Wanda Hendricks, "Ida Bell Wells-Barnett," In Darlene Clark Hine, ed. *Black Women In America: An Historical Encyclopedia*, v. 2, s.v. (New York, 1993), 1245.
46. Ibid., 1246.

Alice Paul celebrating the victory of the ratification of the
Nineteenth Amendment, 1920

Eighteen

ALICE PAUL AND THE TRIUMPH OF MILITANCY

Linda G. Ford

Editor's Introduction: As historian Linda G. Ford so clearly illustrates in this article, the spirit of militancy that had been evident in the early stages of the woman suffrage movement was rekindled near its end. This militant spirit inspired women to bold and dramatic acts that made it impossible for the public or the politicians to ignore the movement or fail to perceive the determination of suffragists to bring the long battle to a victorious conclusion.

As the movement entered its last decade, a new mood was developing among American suffragists: there was a growing impatience with the slow progress and a sense that victory should have come long ago. Indeed, to a generation of women who had come of age in an era of greater educational and employment opportunities for women and who witnessed the political activism of women in the Progressive Era, the denial of the vote to women seemed like an anachronism that must be swiftly rejected—along with the concept of separate spheres upon which that denial was based. This new generation of suffragists, together with many veterans of the movement who had buried one revered suffrage leader after another while politicians still denied them their rights, were responsible for the new wave of suffrage militancy. Militant tactics, as we have seen, were increasingly evident, including in the states of New York and California. Suffrage militants were incensed that women were forced to plead and cajole and to devise arguments as to why woman suffrage was good for society. Equal suffrage was their right, they declared, and they would *take* it.

Alice Paul soon emerged as the leader of the American militants. Paul had returned from Great Britain in 1910, but for two years devoted herself to the completion of her doctoral degree, earning a Ph.D. in sociology from the University of Pennsylvania. During her three years in Great Britain (where she was a caseworker for a settlement house), Paul had been inspired by Emmeline Pankhurst and the militant Women's Social and Political Union (WSPU). Radicalized by participation in the bold and defiant British suffrage movement, Paul was disturbed by the relative docility of the National American Woman Suffrage Association (NAWSA) under President Anna Howard Shaw, and appalled that the entire

energies of American suffragists were absorbed by state suffrage campaigns while the federal amendment remained on the back burner.

Working at first through the NAWSA's Congressional Committee and later the NAWSA-affiliated Congressional Union (CU), Paul tried to refocus the attention of suffragists on the federal amendment and revitalize—and publicize—the national suffrage movement. Paul masterminded the dramatic suffrage parade in 1913 during Woodrow Wilson's inauguration, a grand and dramatic display of the strength of the national movement that became even more sensational when the largely hostile crowd attacked the marchers—provoking massive press coverage and a Congressional investigation, commanding the attention of the nation.

As explained in this essay by Linda Ford and the subsequent essay by Robert Booth Fowler, Alice Paul and the CU soon parted company with the NAWSA (in 1914), largely over the issue of tactics. Influenced by the strategy of the British suffragists, Paul introduced her famous plan of holding the party in power responsible for the failure to enfranchise women. Rather than beg for enfranchisement, Paul sought to direct the full power of the women already enfranchised in Western states against President Wilson and the Democrats (who had a majority in Congress), hoping to force the president and his party to abandon their traditional insistence on states' rights and to secure the passage of the federal woman suffrage amendment. Paul's approach violated the NAWSA's traditional nonpartisan strategy, and led to a new schism in suffrage ranks. For the rest of the movement's history, the NAWSA and the militants would be involved in a public dispute over strategy and tactics.

It is interesting to note that one point of disagreement between the two groups was the *name* of the federal amendment. Soon after the CU became an independent organization, its members began referring to the proposed amendment as "The Susan B. Anthony Amendment"—over the objections of the NAWSA and some CU members, including Harriot Stanton Blatch, who believed it was inappropriate to single out any one of the nineteenth-century pioneers for this recognition.

The CU continued to exist as a separate organization and was renamed the National Woman's Party (NWP) when it merged with its Western affiliate (the Woman's Party) in 1917. As Ford describes, the NWP gradually but steadily became more militant, engaging in acts of non-violent civil disobedience that provoked a stern—even violent—response from the Wilson administration. But the harsh and unjust treatment the suffragists received only cemented their determination. Women became the first in the United States to picket the White House, a form of protest that lasted nearly three years before the Nineteenth Amendment was ratified. During this time hundreds of suffragists were arrested illegally and jailed, with some organizing hunger strikes while in jail, and facing forced feedings by prison officials. These actions, and more, continued to focus the public's and the politicians' attention on woman suffrage.

Militancy, Ford insists, was a success. Not only did suffrage militancy successfully focus attention on woman suffrage and reawaken the "slumbering issue of a national woman suffrage amendment," it "made the government and politicians acutely aware of women's potential political power." Though reviled by many politicians—and suffragists—the militants "created a situation in which something had to be done." The violent reaction to their uncompromising demand for political equality solidified their determination to win the vote and also to wipe out all vestiges of discrimination against American women. It was this group that drafted and introduced the Equal Rights Amendment in 1923—an amendment they called the "Lucretia Mott Amendment."

★   ★   ★   ★   ★

THE STRONG, FEMINIST MILITANCY of the National Woman's Party (NWP) evolved as a logical response to the intransigence of male-centered government in the first decades of this century. Feminist militancy, which I define as the readiness to resist governmental authorities and break the law for the cause of women's rights, developed gradually from men's (non)reaction to women's political claims to equal citizenship. Woman militants for suffrage were not shy about critiquing the male monopoly on power, and, in turn, male authorities responded to the perceived threat, describing the suffragists as "unnatural, iron-jawed" females—even "revolutionaries." Militant suffragists were *feminist* revolutionaries, "striking the blow" themselves to secure drastic political change for women, and with that, change in women's social role, status and image.

Women's New Independence

In the early twentieth century, angry women—potential militants—were beginning actively to change their lives. Time and time again, in autobiographies of women of this period, there emerges a strong sense of impatient resentment and desire for independence. A growing number of women wanted independence from the nineteenth-century concept of a stiffly corseted, rigidly role-stereotyped woman. These women wanted freedom from centuries of having to depend on men for identity, sustenance, and decision-making.

In the twentieth century, cultural and economic change would slowly make a difference in the social role a woman could play. Virginia Woolf wrote that if a woman had the means to support herself, all sorts of possibilities arose; she might even be able to do something with her anger. The American feminist theorist Charlotte Perkins Gilman echoed Woolf, arguing that the time had come for women to be completely independent, especially economically, of men. In the early twentieth-century, women were a rapidly growing presence in the labor force, in offices and factories, and even in "male" professions such as law and medicine. In addition, these women's expectations were growing.[1]

In the United States, the women who joined Alice Paul in a new militant suffrage movement were, as Paul put it, not of any particular class, but shared a "feeling of loyalty to our own sex and an enthusiasm to have every degradation that was put upon our sex removed." *The Suffragist*, the militants' weekly journal, was decidedly feminist in tone and subject matter. These new suffrage leaders saw revolutionary social implications in their struggle for political rights, and they were not the only ones to see them. A 1916 *New York Times* editorial called the "threat of sex vs. sex" carried out by the suffragists:

> political blackmail...an ugly portent, whose possibilities of damage are not limited to politics, but may extend to other parts of the social structure. These [women] leaders have justified to the extent of their powers the worst that has ever been said about the danger of giving votes to women.

That same year a Georgia woman wrote Western suffrage leader Anne Martin: "A female creature, queer and quaint, Who longs to be just what she ain't/ We cannot efface—we can't forget her—We love her still—the stiller the better."[2] Suffrage militants were not at all within the bounds of proper womanhood.

American and English Suffragists

"Improper" woman suffragists revealed their impatience with passive roles in both England and the United States. There was a very direct relation between the arch-militant Women's Social and Political Union (WSPU) of England and the National Woman's Party of the United States. Women who were very important to the woman suffrage movement had long traveled the Atlantic to inspire and inform each other. Many of them advocated a new sort of independence for women featuring a determination to act—strike their own blows—to take matters into their own hands. The feminism of mid-nineteenth century reformer Elizabeth Cady Stanton was directly inspired by English women like Mary Wollstonecraft, author of the 1792 *A Vindication of the Rights of Woman*, and Frances Wright, who spoke out for women's rights when she came to America in the 1820s. *The Revolution*, published by Stanton and feminist reformer Susan B. Anthony, kept close track of the English scene.[3]

By 1887 the American/English Women's Franchise League included among its members the British Emmeline Pankhurst, along with Stanton and her daughter, Harriot Stanton Blatch (who had married an Englishman). Both the Pankhursts and the Stantons advocated a certain aggressive style of seeking reform. According to both Emmeline and her daughter Christabel Pankhurst, when Susan B. Anthony visited London in 1901, she was a great inspiration for British feminists. Realizing that Anthony would die without gaining the franchise for women, Christabel Pankhurst decided that "deeds, not words" should be the motto of the WSPU's organized fight for woman suffrage.[4]

American graduate student Alice Paul was "extremely thrilled" when she joined the parliamentary deputations of the WSPU while in England. Alice Paul, like her

Alice Paul in academic robes, 1913
LIBRARY OF CONGRESS

Alice Paul started *The Suffragist* in 1913 along with NAWSA's Congressional Union.

idol Susan B. Anthony before her, had a feminist philosophy that demanded full equality for women and a belief that moral principles should be committed to action. Paul was born in 1885 in the Quaker community of Moorestown, New Jersey, and was brought up with the Quaker maxim that women were equal before God and were entitled, even obliged, to address social problems. Paul had a serious-minded childhood, during which she developed a strong sense of right and wrong, and the belief that any life without a cause was empty. For Paul, although trained as a social worker, that cause would single-mindedly be women's rights.

Although not without hesitation and much trepidation, Paul first became involved in women's rights advocacy in England by interrupting the speeches of Foreign Secretary Edward Grey and Home Secretary Winston Churchill. In addition, she went to Scotland to organize and rabble-rouse—traveling with fellow American Lucy Burns and Emmeline Pankhurst herself. It was while working with the WSPU in England that Paul and Burns first felt a "blazing" feminist anger, both at the rough treatment they received at the hands of male police and jailers—including forced feeding in jail—*and* at the continued indifference of male political authorities.[5]

Their militant experiences in England gave Paul and Burns a notoriety of sorts and a credibility with American suffragists upon their return to the United States in 1910. Their English experiences also left Paul and Burns with a lasting adulation for the Pankhursts and the WSPU, although they never did use the Pankhurst's "violent" tactics such as destroying property. After their deputations

to Parliament were repeatedly dispersed with violence, and after suffering harsh jail terms, the women of the WSPU reasoned that the violent actions against them demonstrated that property—not human life—was most important to the English government. The British authorities unleashed a tremendously hostile counterattack and in the process spurred a large portion of public opinion to shift to the WSPU side. Only World War I would put an end to the war between the WSPU and the British government.[6] What Alice Paul learned from her participation in the British movement was a resentment of male domination, a desire for full equality, and a determination to organize women to act aggressively on their demands—to *take* their rights.

A Militant Approach in America

The fame they gained in England culminated in an invitation for Alice Paul and Lucy Burns to speak to the National American Woman Suffrage Association (NAWSA) in 1910. Two years later, through the auspices of social reform paragon Jane Addams, Paul and Burns were asked to chair a "congressional committee" for the NAWSA that would work for a federal woman suffrage amendment in Washington. The two young militants brought a new excitement—an aggressive spirit—to what had become a lethargic woman suffrage movement in America.

The flamboyance of the militants' new committee was directed toward overcoming indifference to women's issues in the United States. In time, their concerted militant actions generated hostility and violence—directed at them as "unnatural" women. How would a movement to energize the campaign for the middle-class, Progressive reform of woman suffrage come to be considered a dangerously militant, antigovernment conspiracy? The coming of World War I certainly helped shape events, but Woman's Party policy—a direct reaction to government non-action—went through gradual, increasingly militant stages, leading to the women's arrest and imprisonment.

The Congressional Committee was defiant and aggressive from the beginning. That brand of impatient, militant feminism, coupled with competition over NAWSA-held suffrage territory and money, soon offended the NAWSA's deliberately moderate leaders. The Congressional Committee evolved into the Congressional Union (CU), a more independent and stronger group. The CU approach of strong feminism and militant-spirited strategies—obviously influenced by the British—became a liability and an embarrassment to a NAWSA leadership determined not to erode the legislative and public support they had painstakingly won for suffrage. NAWSA officers were sure that the aggressive CU was doing damage by pushing too hard, alienating President Woodrow Wilson and antagonizing the public with their incessant, unladylike lobbying. The CU promoted militancy, an aggressive, unapologetically egalitarian, militant style, which the more moderate NAWSA members could not countenance. In 1914, Paul and Burns' group was expelled from the NAWSA for being "too British."[7]

A billboard in Denver goes up in 1916, part of the NWP's strategy to harness the voting power of Western women to pressure the national Democratic Party to support a woman suffrage amendment.

LIBRARY OF CONGRESS

As an independent organization, the CU used increasingly militant methods between 1914 and 1917, trying to force the Wilson administration to secure the passage of woman suffrage. They began with "heckling" Wilson—interrupting speeches and asking pointed questions—and combined that with strenuous speaking and petitioning campaigns for suffrage. A small but dedicated new suffrage organization, the CU was particularly well-known for the British-inspired tactic of organizing women voters in the West to vote against recalcitrant Democrats in 1914 and again in 1916. In the 1916 elections, under a strict "party responsibility" policy, the Democrats were held responsible for non-action on the newly formed Western Woman's Party's one and only plank, "the enfranchisement of the women of America through a Federal Amendment." Through the efforts of traveling organizers and helped by their own increasingly popular journal, *The Suffragist*, the militants did their best to convince women in the Western states, many of whom had had the vote for years, to vote "Republican, Socialist, Prohibitionist or Progressive—anything but Democratic." Although studies have shown that the Woman's Party did affect those elections with their appeals to Western women to "help their sisters in the East," the Wilson administration was not impressed enough to pass the suffrage amendment. However, a few years later, Wilson *was* persuaded to favor woman suffrage due to a shift in public opinion. Unquestionably this change of heart was influenced by the NWP pressure and propaganda, yet personally Wilson remained "repelled" by women who, by speaking in public, "reversed the social order."[8]

Organizing the National Woman's Party

When the assertive policy of holding the party in power responsible did not secure woman suffrage, the Woman's Party began overt acts of militancy in defiance of authority and the law. This group of militant women decided in March of 1917 that in order to further a united, politically powerful campaign, they needed to merge the Western campaign's Woman's Party with the Washington-based CU, and to call themselves the National Woman's Party (NWP). The militants' tactics, including their shrewd use of women's existing political power and their obvious courage and iron-willed determination, continued to reflect their belief that women were worthy of political power. Increasingly resentful of the men who held power over them, NWP suffragists used progressively more militant actions against an unyielding government. At the same time, they sharpened their feminist critique. They slowly shifted from just insisting on a greater democracy that included women, to a condemnation of an oppressive, "autocratic," patriarchal society, including their effort to show that the "women's" militancy—picketing and civil disobedience—was different from and highly superior to, the current manifestation of "men's" militancy—war. Paradoxically, the NWP used the weapon of nonviolence very effectively to illustrate their enormous strength as women. Furious that the war-harried Wilson decided to receive no more NWP suffragist delegations, the militant women, in the first stage of their open militancy, began a perpetual delegation of White House pickets in January 1917, continuing almost daily pickets even after the United States entered the war in April.

The first stage of outright militancy was characterized by beautifully staged and deliberately peaceful, nonviolent demonstrations—consisting of banner-holding suffragists arranged outside the White House—protesting the Wilson government's inaction on suffrage. The NWP's suffrage strategy is a classic example of nonviolent resistance against a government, with the intent to defy and coerce authorities to act. A typical NWP banner mocked the president by using his own lofty moral rhetoric. One example of this was the use of Wilson's war message: "We shall fight for the things which we have always held nearest our hearts—for democracy, for the right of those who submit to authority to have a voice in their own government."[9] The peaceful and perfectly legal picketing method was adopted from several sources, including labor activists as well as the British militant suffragists. The tactic also in part reflected Alice Paul's adherence to a tradition of Quaker civil disobedience. To some NWP leaders, such demonstrations were particularly appropriate for women, "peace-loving by nature," to show that "woman's" militancy was brave and defiant, but peaceful, whereas "male" militancy, in 1917, was violent and destructive. Paul said it was clear that "women were the peace-loving half of the world and that by giving power to women we would diminish the possibilities of war."[10] Whether they thought women naturally more peaceful or not, all NWP pickets demanded that Wilson act on woman suffrage immediately, and give women a voice in decisions on war.

Suffragists Arrested

The first mob attacks, arrests, and jailings began the second stage of open militancy in June 1917. The government began to regard the women as more than a nuisance when the pickets raised new banners that were sharply critical of the Wilson government, proclaiming that America, fighting a war for freedom in Europe, was not as democratic as "free Russia," which had enfranchised its women. Banners lambasted "Kaiser Wilson" and his "dictatorial and oppressive" policies toward women. The Wilson administration's violent reaction, including jailing many of the protesters and exposing them to harsh treatment and terrible conditions, brought the NWP to the third stage of open militancy—the October demands for political prisoner status in the face of what the women called "administration terrorism" against their members.

The abusive treatment meted out to the NWP demonstrators was suffered by rich and poor, old and young suffragists alike. Co-leaders Alice Paul and Lucy Burns—both from very comfortable backgrounds, highly educated and progressive "New Women" professionals (one an educator, the other a social worker/scholar) initially attracted other impatient feminists of similar backgrounds. The core membership of the NWP in the suffrage period, 1912-1920, tended to be of two types: the state and local officers, either mature (over forty) social reformer/ clubwomen, inspired to greater militancy; or speaker/organizers, young college-educated "New Women," with very liberal, modern ideas of women's equality and economic independence. There was, therefore, conflict within the NWP over race and class issues and over how inclusive their "united sisterhood" should be. But to all NWP suffrage leaders and organizers, the defiant stance against the Wilson administration, as part of the battle against sexism, always came first.

Other groups of antigovernment dissenters directed their protests directly against war itself, or against the capitalist system which made a war of "imperialist

Police arrest suffrage pickets, Washington, D.C., 1917
WOMAN SUFFRAGE MEDIA COLLECTION

aggression" possible. The antigovernment, feminist demonstrators of the NWP also wanted to change the system, but their vision was one in which women should be included, not just in government, but in full equality in all aspects of American society. Some NWP feminists stressed women's "superior" qualities, evolved over centuries of being "other directed," but many others stressed that all women must be given the opportunity to participate fully in their culture, whatever qualities they did or did not possess.[11] National Woman's Party feminists shared a radical vision of completely equal opportunity, and were not willing to wait for their goal. In fact, they were more than willing to act, to fight against their opponent, the Wilson government.

Political Prisoners

The government started jailing militant suffragists in June 1917. But the sentences were not more than a few days in length until mid-August and the "Kaiser" banners, when sixty-day sentences at Occoquan Workhouse in Virginia began to be meted out. By mid-September, sympathetic socialist women began to be more apparent among the arrested, including newspaper writer Peggy Baird Johns, one of the first to suggest demanding political prisoner status. The women at Occoquan, including Lucy Burns, readily assented to the plan, agreeing that they were not "traffic obstructors," as charged, but in reality, political offenders. The women drafted a letter to the district commissioners in Washington demanding political prisoner privileges and protesting their unjust and erratic sentences that ranged from a suspended sentence to sixty days for the same offense.[12] Their letter went unanswered, but the women continued to demand recognition as political prisoners.

Helena Hill Weed jailed for picketing in 1917
LIBRARY OF CONGRESS

Government and prison authorities had little patience for the women's demands and showed their growing irritation in late October by giving Alice Paul a seven-month sentence for picketing. Paul was placed in a psychopathic ward and force-fed after she decided to go on a hunger strike along with socialist Rose Winslow. Alice Paul and Winslow decided to go on hunger strikes in order to get political prisoner status "in accordance with the plan started by the sixty-day group"—the group led by Peggy Baird Johns and arrested back in September. Paul had not wanted other NWP suffragists to hunger strike, but only wanted to take the sacrifice on herself. As she wrote national board member Dora Lewis, "Things took a more serious turn than I had planned, but it's happened rather well because we'll have ammunition against the Administration, and the more harsh and repressive

Dora Lewis arriving at NWP Headquarters after five days of a hunger strike in prison in 1918. Lewis, a member of a prominent Philadelphia family, was the oldest suffragist to be imprisoned, and endured repeated jail sentences, a hunger strike, forcible feeding, and during the "night of terror," was knocked unconscious. Still, she persisted in supporting the cause.

DORIS STEVENS, *Jailed for Freedom*, LIBRARY OF CONGRESS

they seem the better."[13] The administration's reaction to her hunger strike was to forcibly feed her in order to "save" her. Lewis protested to District Commissioner Gwynne Gardener, insisting that Paul and the other prisoners be given political offender status as "government enemies."[14]

The Night of Terror and Forced Feedings

On November 14, thirty-three NWP women, arrested for picketing the White House in protest against the treatment of Alice Paul, suffered Superintendent Raymond Whittaker's infamous "night of terror." The terror began immediately when two soldiers attacked the picketing Boston matron Agnes Morey, jabbing her broken, splintered banner pole between her eyes. Philadelphia grandmother Dora Lewis, always in the forefront, was knocked about by three youths. All the arrested suffrage militants regarded themselves as political prisoners of the Wilson administration, and were quite willing to undergo whatever was necessary to have prison and government authorities recognize them as such. After the women were taken to Occoquan Workhouse, their demands for political offender status were not even delivered to prison superintendent Whittaker before his men seized Lewis. The guards seemed in a frenzy of rage. After Louisiana suffragist Alice Cosu was clubbed into her cell, Whittaker told her that "in her work she could stand anything." Cosu later wrote that she "was completely unnerved....I was sick all

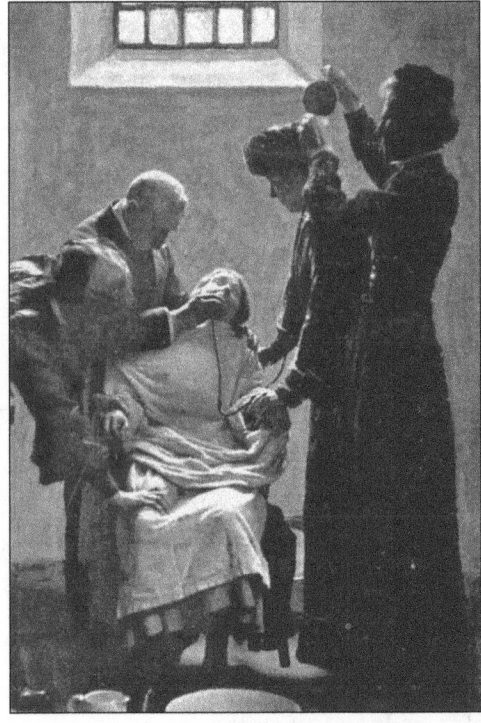

This image shows a suffragist being force fed; taken from U.K. suffragist Sylvia Pankhurst's book, *The Suffragette: The History of the Women's Militant Suffrage Movement, 1905–1910.*

night long from this treatment." When the other women suspected Cosu had had a heart attack, their cries to Whittaker's guards for help were ignored. NWP vice president Lucy Burns, a vocal leader at Occoquan, was singled out for especially rough treatment. When she resisted being hauled away, she was beaten and then eventually had her wrists handcuffed high on her cell door. A young suffrage organizer, Julia Emory, stood in the same position as Burns in sympathy. Dorothy Day (founder of the Catholic Workers' Movement) said she "naturally... tried to pull away" from the guards, so they responded by pinching her arms, twisting her wrists, then wrestling her down over an iron bench, bruising her back and shoulders. One man had his hand at her throat. By morning, Day was "in an hysterical and sick condition." No one treated Day's or anyone else's injuries; they were not even allowed to use a toilet. This was true although most of the women reported later they were at least bruised and shaken, and felt "terrorized." [15]

Their night of terror ended, but the women did not relinquish their insistence on being considered Wilson's political prisoners. The only practical resistance seemed to be to use the hunger strike, just as the British had, to secure public sympathy and move the government to act on woman suffrage. But the hunger strike had its own horrors. It was met by the counterforce of "forcible feeding," ostensibly done to save lives, but a harsh and cruel procedure. Feeding was done with tubing forced down the mouth or nostrils, and the suffragists faced it stoically but with dread. Rose Winslow, who experienced forcible feeding three times a day during her imprisonment, smuggled out notes saying:

> I had a nervous time of it, gasping a long time afterward, and my stomach rejecting during the process.... The poor soul who fed me got liberally besprinkled during the process. I heard myself making the most hideous sounds.... One feels so forsaken when one lies prone and people shove a

pipe down one's stomach…. Yesterday was a bad day for me in feeding. I was vomiting continually during the process. The tube had developed an irritation somewhere that is painful…. The same doctor feeds both Alice Paul and me. Don't let them tell you we take this well…. We think of the coming feeding all day. It is horrible.

Besides using forcible feeding, doctors and matrons tried to "persuade, bully and threaten" the women out of "sticking to their purpose, hunger striking to gain political offender status." But on November 23, 1917, Judge Edmund Waddill decided the suffragists had been illegally committed to Occoquan, and should be remanded to the District Jail; all were released on November 27 and 28.[16]

The Wilson Administration Versus the Militants

The violence of the night of November 14, 1917, and the trauma of forcible feedings that NWP suffragists endured, were all endured for a cause about which they were deadly serious. The women insisted that the Wilson government was oppressing and discriminating against American women, while hypocritically fighting a war for democracy in Europe. The government considered the suffragists' on-going, defiant presence near the White House to be a threat to national security, and therefore did not stop mob abuse of the pickets and freely arrested demonstrators for "obstructing traffic."

In March of 1918, the Federal Court of Appeals decided that the women arrested in 1917, some serving several months in jail, had been tried and imprisoned under no existing law.[17] The pickets had been caught up in a wave of war hysteria. (They might arguably have been tried under the Sedition Act on expressing "scurrilous" opinions of the administration, but that act was not passed until May of 1918.) The militant suffragists were deprived of their civil liberties in the same way numerous others would soon be, from high school teachers and ministers with antiwar opinions to radical socialists. The suffragists had been arrested for obstructing traffic, a misdemeanor, but their lengthy sentences were far from appropriate punishment for such a crime. The sentences backfired as a deterrent however, since the jail experience thoroughly radicalized the suffragists in terms of their feminism and sense of solidarity with all women, as well as in terms of their disillusionment with the government, leading to still further acts of militancy.

In the highest circles of government, NWP suffragists had made themselves very unpopular since their 1914 presidential heckling. Between 1914 and 1917 President Wilson had become more and more respectful and attentive to the moderate NAWSA, as he became more convinced that NWP women were unreasonable radicals. In October of 1917 he had written NAWSA President Carrie Chapman Catt, saying that he realized her group should not be associated with the militants, who had "laid themselves open to serious criticism." Wilson was convinced "the treatment of the woman picketeers [sic] has been grossly exaggerated" and there had been "an extraordinary

Lucy G. Branham, an organizer for the NWP, protesting treatment of jailed suffragists. LIBRARY OF CONGRESS

amount of lying about the thing." He also wrote his secretary, Joseph Tumulty, on November 16, stating that the United States had no political prisoners, but the militant suffragists "offended against an ordinance of the District and are undergoing the punishment appropriate in the circumstances."[18] Wilson apparently thought that the misdemeanor of disobeying a traffic regulation required a punishment of harsh treatment at the workhouse with some sentenced to six months or more.

The Wilson administration had also tried to thwart the militants in other ways besides imprisonment. The NWP militancy was designed to reach the public through the media; its effectiveness depended on public support, sympathy and outrage. Therefore, the administration thought press control of the suffragists' activities might be an effective curb. In July of 1917, Tumulty suggested to the president a press blackout of NWP stories. Wilson thought that "bare, colorless chronicles" might be better, but many papers, particularly the Washington *Times, Star,* and *Post,* eventually adopted a policy of rarely covering NWP activities, or covering them in an unfavorable light.[19] The NWP organizers testified time and again that the lack of coverage by the press became a problem. Also, after the June "Russian" banner appeared, contrasting Russia's franchise for women with "democratic" America's lack of one, the government's brand-new Secret Service kept tabs on the NWP all across the country. Western NWP leader Anne Martin was especially plagued by agents in October and November of 1917, with several of them usually in attendance at her suffrage rallies; she even found one listening at her hotel door. One reason for such vigilance may have been Martin's proclivity for making statements like "Russia fears the world war is only a capitalistic war" because the United States' "democracy" jails its women. In Los Angeles, a government agent informed her that she would not hold a meeting. In response, she told him America had guarantees of freedom of speech and assembly, and he could come arrest her if she said something "seditious." Martin wrote to NWP activist Pauline Clarke: "The hand of the administration is certainly reaching out after us. The prison story gets the women and they fear it." Martin argued strongly that criticizing

Wilson's blocking of woman suffrage was not treason.[20] Obviously, the Wilson government disagreed.

A week after the "night of terror," the *New York Tribune* accused the NWP of having incriminating links with radical socialists and "anarchists." From 1917 to 1919 the militants would be accused of "bolshevism," charges they would usually not even bother to answer. The Wilson administration and the public considered the NWP's feminist views and their militant actions "radical," and many (leftist) political radicals agreed. The socialist *Liberator* reported in early 1918, "Alice Paul and her young army of militants are one of the leading radical forces in American politics in the near future."[21] Beginning in 1917, socialist women joined the NWP in droves to demonstrate against the Wilson government. "Laboring women,"

KAISER WILSON

HAVE YOU FORGOTTEN YOUR SYMPATHY WITH THE POOR GERMANS BECAUSE THEY WERE NOT SELF-GOVERNED?

20.000.000 AMERICAN WOMEN ARE NOT SELF-GOVERNED.

TAKE THE BEAM OUT OF YOUR OWN EYE.

Virginia Arnold holding the infamous banner that enraged soldiers and sailors who attacked the NWP pickets in August 1917

NATIONAL WOMAN'S PARTY RECORDS, LIBRARY OF CONGRESS

particularly Connecticut munitions workers protesting their lack of suffrage as workers and as women, also joined the fray.[22] Obviously, many NWP members did not wholeheartedly embrace the anticapitalist stance of the socialists, but at least for a time they were united with socialists in feeling left out of American society and in their grievances against the Wilson government for suppressing their rights to free speech, and for sustaining a war in which they felt they had had no say.

Fighting Hypocrisy

The violence that NWP suffragists suffered at the hands of the Wilson administration, beyond showing that the government perceived the NWP as a threat to national security along with other dissenters, served to radicalize further and to disillusion the largely middle-class and relatively sheltered woman suffragists. The jail experience made the NWP feel alienated from their own government. However, it strengthened their radical feminism and identification with other women; for some of them this identification extended even to the poor and Black women in prison. The suffragists all recoiled in disbelief from the way in which the government had had them punished, simply for fighting for women's

rights. In essence, the Woman's Party suffragists were angry at the hypocrisy of the Wilson government in fighting for democracy in Europe while denying American women the right to vote—or even the right to free speech.

When Alice Paul and Lucy Burns first founded the NWP, they staunchly believed, as good Progressive reformers, in the promise of American democracy. They also expected a superior generosity of American men as compared to the unyielding British political system and brutish "bobbies" who had put down the Pankhurst rebellion. By 1917 the NWP saw the promise of American liberty as empty. Upon being released after the November terrors, Paul asked how "people fail to see our fight as part of the great American struggle for democracy? We are bearing on the American tradition, living up to the American spirit."[23]

It would be difficult for women jailed by their society for exercising their rights of free speech to look upon that society in the same way ever again. Perhaps because they were middle-class reformers, the NWP suffragists reacted to their brutal treatment with incredulity and anger. The Occoquan prisoners felt desolate, alienated, and very bitter. New York suffragist, Kathryn Lincoln, who participated

In 1917, the day after the police announced that future suffrage pickets would be given a limit of six months in prison, Alice Paul led a picket line with a banner reading: "The time has come to conquer or submit for there is but one choice – we have made it." Paul is followed by Dora Lewis leaving the National Woman Party's headquarters.

LIBRARY OF CONGRESS

in the hunger strike, said the days in jail were "an eternity." She would throw herself on her bed sobbing, feeling that she was "gradually losing my hold upon life." Buffalo newspaper columnist Ada Davenport Kendall testified that Occoquan was "a place of chicanery, sinister horror, brutality and dread" from which "no one could come out without just resentment against any government which could maintain such an institution."[24] These women reformers had come to a conclusion similar to that of socialists and other radical dissidents—that there was no justice, no real democracy in America in 1917.

The NWP suffragists blamed the government, and Wilson in particular, for their harsh treatment, for the suppression of their rights, and for their continued political powerlessness as women. As Boston NWP leader Agnes Morey wrote: "So far as democracy and liberalism goes it is for men—that politicians speak—women are outside their cosmos."[25] Inasmuch as the government ignored their claims as women, the militants felt their grievance as feminists more pointedly. Perceived common oppression increased the "bonds of sisterhood." Many imprisoned suffragists saw life in prison as a microcosm, in extreme form, of women's situation in American society. They experienced utter powerlessness and violent attacks at the hands of male authorities.

In prison, the women saw more clearly the particular injustice of women's vulnerable position vis-à-vis men, a view amplified by a new knowledge of the condition of their fellow women, especially Black women, prisoners. As Estelle Freedman wrote in *Their Sisters' Keepers*, under the control of male jail keepers, woman prisoners represent "an extreme case of sexual powerlessness," symbolizing the constraints placed on all women by authoritarian institutions. Many of the guards at Occoquan seemed to carry out their duties with relish. Linda Gordon, author of *Woman's Body, Woman's Right: A Social History of Birth Control in America*, has argued that guards were "hostile and violent" to women imprisoned for working for birth control, because they seemed to "violate every male fantasy about what women should be like."[26] Militant suffragists were regarded as unnatural members of their sex by those outside the prison, from the mobs in the streets to the President of the United States. They were also perceived as unwomanly within prison walls and treated accordingly.

For most Woman's Party activists, harsh treatment by prison guards did not dampen their feminist ardor, but only intensified it. As Texas suffragist Lucille Shields explained: "In jail as one empty hour succeeds another, you realize more keenly the years that women have struggled to be free and the tasks that they have been forced to leave undone for lack of power to do them." Or note Massachusetts NWP leader Katharine Fisher's statement: "In prison or out, American women are not free....Disfranchisement is the prison of women's power and spirit." If disillusion and anger at injustice was one effect of jail, inspiration and renewed faith in their fellow women and in their cause, was another. Although, as mentioned above, she had at first despaired in prison, Kathryn Lincoln testified upon her

Watchfire outside of the White House was maintained by
National Woman's Party pickets, 1919.

NATIONAL ARCHIVES

release in late November 1917: "Prison bars mean only freedom....The cause of women must advance."[27] Many of the released prisoners insisted the government had not daunted their spirit, and their continued militancy made that clear.

In spite of physical injury and illness, and of deeply felt disillusion and anger, most suffrage prisoners came out of jail renewed in purpose. As middle-class Progressive reformers, which most of them were, they had first believed in the process of American democracy, although they went well beyond the bounds of Progressive reformism with their militancy. When the Wilson government cracked down on the pickets, unleashing mob and police attacks and leaving the imprisoned suffragists to the vagaries of Occoquan Superintendent Whittaker and his guards, the radical suffragists' militancy and determination only increased. As established feminist radicals in 1918 and 1919, they would persist with demonstrations pointedly critical of the Wilson administration and would continue to be jailed.

More Militant Action

The National Woman's Party did not shrink from further acts of militancy when woman suffrage was still not won in 1918. In January, President Wilson finally endorsed woman suffrage by federal action and the House passed the suffrage amendment. According to the NWP all this political progress was made as a direct result of the Woman's Party's actions.[28] But by the fall of 1918, the Senate had not yet passed the amendment, lacking two votes. This necessitated further militancy by the NWP. Picketing and arrests began again. In early 1919,

Doris Stevens (center) standing with Alice Paul (right). Stevens was imprisoned many times and wrote *Jailed for Freedom*, documenting suffragists' experiences.
LIBRARY OF CONGRESS

the demonstrations were intent upon forcing the Wilson administration's hand. With World War I over, Wilson was triumphant on the world stage; but to frustrated suffrage militants, the battle was not yet won. The NWP kept "watchfires" burning in front of the White House, fueling the flames with Wilson's hypocritical words as well as with his effigy. In February 1919, a "welcome party" of protesting NWP women met Wilson in Boston, upon his return from the peace talks in Europe. Using nonviolent resistance against the Boston police, a line of silent pickets held banners calling for the president's aid. Women also gathered on Boston Common and burned the parts of Wilson's Boston speech that spoke of democracy and liberty. Additionally a group of Woman's Party luminaries—women who had been (as NWP leader Doris Stevens wrote) "jailed for freedom"—toured on a "Prison Special" train, wearing replicas of their prison uniforms and taking the cause to cities throughout the country.[29] The men of the Senate remained unmoved.

What turned out to be the NWP's last militant protest provoked the harshest response from authorities and bystanders yet. It was held outside the New York Metropolitan Opera House in March of 1919. On March 3, Congress had adjourned without a Senate vote. When President Wilson stopped in New York to speak at the Opera House, Alice Paul planned to burn immediately a copy of anything he said about democracy. Bearing banners protesting Wilson's "autocracy" at home, a picket line of twenty-five women marched toward the Opera House, but were soon met by two hundred policemen in close formation. The police were joined by a crowd made up of mostly soldiers and sailors, rushed the pickets, and the ensuing battle went on for hours. Doris Stevens, a participant, wrote:

> Not a word was spoken by a single officer of the 200 policemen in the attack to indicate the nature of our offense. Clubs were raised and lowered and the women beaten back with such cruelty as none of us had ever witnessed before.... Women were knocked down and trampled under foot, some of them almost unconscious, others bleeding from the hands and face; arms were bruised and twisted; pocket-books were snatched and wrist-watches stolen.

Called a "bunch of cannibals and Bolsheviks" by the police, the militants were charged with "disorderly conduct" and "assaulting the police," and arrested, but then released.[30]

Until victory was finally achieved, the NWP moved from one action to another, continually keeping the pressure on the authorities. By late spring 1919, victory was finally in sight for the militant suffragists. In May, the House passed the amendment again, and in June, Wilson secured the last Senate votes for passage. After another long and arduous lobbying campaign, including picketing the Republican convention, the Susan B. Anthony Woman Suffrage Amendment was finally ratified by a sufficient number of states in August 1920. The National Woman's Party took full credit for the victory, saying the Wilson administration had "yielded under the gunfire" of the NWP.[31]

The Woman's Party was certainly instrumental in moving the "center" of the woman suffrage movement toward greater activity by its own radical actions. The militants demanded attention for the cause of woman suffrage and got it. They reawakened the slumbering issue of a national woman suffrage amendment, revitalized the entire movement and made the government and politicians acutely aware of women's potential political power. The militants' stubborn protests, however reviled they may have been, created a situation in which something had to be done. Each act of open militancy was followed by government action: feminist militancy worked.

In the process, feminist militancy—which insisted on the vital importance of a woman's right to participate in the political life of her society—transformed the suffragists themselves. Feminist militancy was a tactic, but it was also a state of mind. Doris Stevens wrote that the militants' campaign compelled women to "stop being such good and willing slaves." In June of 1919 Alice Paul declared that, "Freedom has come not as a gift but as a triumph, and it is therefore a spiritual as well as a political freedom which women receive."[32]

And the NWP emphasized that winning suffrage was only the first step in "woman's emancipation." As *The Suffragist* observed just after the victory: "The ballot is the symbol of a new status in human society, it is the greatest possible single step forward in the progress of women, but it does not in itself complete their freedom." For the members of the NWP, then, the struggle did not end with gaining the vote. They knew there was much more to do to secure women's

equality in all facets of American society. In a press release just after the ratification was announced, Alice Paul stated her determination to use the vote as "the tool with which [women] must end completely all discriminations against them." "Our victory," she said, "cannot be a signal for rest."[33] Thus began the fight for the Equal Rights Amendment, spearheaded by the NWP, and first introduced in Congress only three years after ratification of the Nineteenth Amendment.[34]

Notes

This essay is drawn largely from Linda Ford's *Iron-Jawed Angels: The Suffrage Militancy of the National Woman's Party, 1912-1920* (Lanham, Md.: University Press of America, Inc., 1991), and appears here with the permission of the publisher.

1. See George Dangerfield, *The Strange Death of Liberal England* (London, 1936); Marian Ramelson, *Petticoat Rebellion: A Century of Struggle for Women's Rights* (London, 1967); Charlotte Perkins Gilman, *Women and Economics* (Boston, 1900).

2. *New York Times*, July 14, 1916, 10; Nelly Gordon to Anne Martin, Feb. 4, 1916, Reel 23 of the National Woman's Party Papers, Suffrage Years, on microfilm, Microfilming Corporation of America, 1981, hereafter referred to as NWPP.

3. On militancy in the American suffrage movement before Alice Paul, see Ellen DuBois, "Taking the Law into Our Own Hands: Bradwell, Minor, and Suffrage Militance in the 1870s," and "Working Women, Class Relations, and Suffrage Militance: Harriot Stanton Blatch and the New York Woman Suffrage Movement, 1894-1909," in this volume.

4. Harriot Stanton Blatch and Alma Lutz, *Challenging Years: The Memoirs of Harriot Stanton Blatch* (New York, 1940), 73; Emmeline Pankhurst, *My Own Story*, (New York, 1917), 19-30, 33-40; Andrew Rosen, *Rise Up, Women! The Militant Campaign of the WSPU, 1903-1914* (London, 1974), 80-85; Katharine Anthony, *Susan B. Anthony: Her Personal History and Her Era* (Garden City, N.Y., 1954), 366, 484.

5. Katharine Anthony, *Susan B. Anthony*, Amelia Fry, interview with Alice Paul in 1972-73, "Woman Suffrage and the Equal Rights Amendment," Bancroft Library Suffragists Oral History Project, University of California at Berkeley; Sylvia Pankhurst, *The Suffragettes: The History of the Women's Militant Suffrage Movement, 1905-1910* (New York, 1912), 416-417.

6. Pankhurst, extended accounts in *My Own Story*; Rosen, *Rise Up!*, 80-85.

7. See NAWSA's Mary Ware Dennett to Paul, Oct. 30, 1913, Reel 5, NWPP; Robert Gallagher's interview with Alice Paul, "I Was Arrested, Of Course," *American Heritage*, Feb. 1974, 17-24; 92-94; *New York Times*, Jan. 5, 1914, 3. On the "too British" accusation, see Shaw to Burns, Nov. 29, 1913, Reel 5, NWPP.

8. Inez Irwin, *Alice Paul and the National Woman's Party*, (1921: Fairfax, Va., 1964), 158-160; Sidney Bland, "'Never Quite as Committed as We'd Like': The Suffrage Militancy of Lucy Burns," *Journal of Long Island History*, (Summer/Fall 1981): 12-13; Meredith Snapp, "Defeat the Democrats: The Congressional Union for Woman Suffrage in Arizona, 1914 and 1916," *Journal of the West*, (1975): 131-138; Edwin A. Weinstein, *Woodrow Wilson; A Medical and Psychological Biography* (Princeton, 1981), 83.

9. Banner is quoted in Irwin, *Paul and the NWP*, 214.

10. Fry interview with Paul, 551.

11. NWP activist Rheta Childe Dorr wrote for *The Suffragist* (April 1920, 36) that if women voted as a group on social and political problems, improvements would occur. However, Mabel Vernon argued that women had a right to vote, no matter their views or qualities. Fry interview with Vernon, "Mabel Vernon: Speaker for Suffrage and Petitioner for Peace," Bancroft Project 1976, 164.

12. See Sherna Gluck, ed., *Parlor to Prison: Five American Suffragists Talk About Their Lives* (New York, 1976), 228, 242-243; Doris Stevens, *Jailed For Freedom* (1920: New York, 1976), 177.

13. Alice Paul to Dora Lewis, Nov. 1917, Reel 53, NWPP.

14. Dora Lewis to Gwynne Gardener, Nov. 7, 1917, Reel 52, NWPP.

15. Papers of Camilla Whitcomb, Schlesinger Library, Radcliffe, n.d., *Worcester Telegram* article; Cosu affidavit, Nov. 28, 1917, Reel 53; Emory affidavit, Nov. 1917, Reel 53; Burns's Nov. 1917 statement, Reel 52; Day affidavit, Nov. 28, 1917, Reel 53; Nolan affidavit, Nov. 23, 1917, Reel 52, NWPP.

16. Rose Winslow quotation from Doris Stevens, *Jailed for Freedom*, (1920: Troutdale, Ore., 1995), 118-119; Day, *The Long Loneliness*, (New York, 1952), 89-90; NWP Press Release, Nov. 27, 1917, Reel 92, NWPP.

17. In 1918 and 1919 the NWP protesters would receive sentences of up to fifteen days, first for holding public meetings without a permit and climbing on a public statue, and then for building fires. Stevens, *Jailed*, 229; Irwin, *Paul and the NWP*, 273, 418.

18. Wilson to Catt, Oct. 13, 1917, Reel 210; Wilson to Tumulty, Nov. 12, 1917; Wilson to "WFJ, Secretary," Nov. 16, 1917, Reel 210, Wilson Papers, Library of Congress.

19. A. Brisbane to Joseph Tumulty, July 20, 1917; Tumulty to Wilson, July 21, 1917; Wilson to Tumulty, July 21, 1917, Reel 210, Wilson Papers.

20. Author's interview with Rebecca Hourwich Reyher, April 23, 1983; Anne Martin to Pauline Clarke, Oct. 31, 1917, Reel 51 and Nov. 19, 1917, Reel 51; Martin to a Eugene, Oregon editor, Nov. 1, 1917, Reel 51, NWPP.

21. *New York Tribune*, Nov. 22, 23, 1917, Reel 95, NWPP; *Suffragist*, March 2, 1918.

22. See NWP Press Releases, Jan. 19 and 23, 1918, Reel 92, NWPP.

23. NWP Press Release, Nov. 27, 1917, Reel 91, NWPP.

24. Lincoln affidavit, Nov. 28, 1917, Reel 53; Kendall affidavit, Nov. 2, 1920, Reel 83, NWPP.

25. Morey to Mabel Vernon, May 3, 1917, Reel 42, NWPP.

26. *Their Sisters' Keepers: Woman's Prison Reform in America, 1830-1930* (Ann Arbor, 1981), 1; Gordon, *Woman's Body, Woman's Right: A Social History of Birth Control in America* (New York, 1974), 233.

27. Shields, NWP Press Release, Jan. 18, 1919, Reel 92, NWPP; Stevens, *Jailed*, 156; Lincoln affidavit, Nov. 28, 1917, Reel 53, NWPP.

28. Irwin, *Paul and the NWP*, 344-345, 349; Stevens, *Jailed*, 248.

29. Stevens, *Jailed*.

30. Stevens, *Jailed*, 331-332; *New York Times*, March 5, 1919, 3, 10; *Suffragist*, March 15, 1919, 4-5.

31. *Suffragist*, June 4, 1919, 10-11; Sept. 1920, 191; NWP Press Release, March 20, 1920, Reel 92, NWPP.

32. Stevens, "Militant Campaign," Stevens Papers, Schlesinger Library, Radcliffe, Cambridge, Mass.; *Suffragist*, March 29, 1919, 8.

33. NWP Press Release, 1920, in Folder 24, Anna Kelton Wiley Papers, Radcliffe.

34. *The Suffragist*, Sept. 1920, 191.

Carrie Chapman Catt, 1909
National American Woman Suffrage President
1900-1904 and 1915-1920

Nineteen

CARRIE CHAPMAN CATT, STRATEGIST

Robert Booth Fowler

Editor's Introduction: Political scientist Robert Booth Fowler discusses the strategic decisions made by Carrie Chapman Catt, president of the National American Woman Suffrage Association (NAWSA). Catt's decisions were of vital importance for the woman suffrage movement, and as president of the NAWSA twice—from 1900 to 1904 and from 1915 to 1920—she had a major influence on the strategy pursued by the organization in both periods. In this essay, a chapter from his book *Carrie Catt: Feminist Politician,* Fowler focuses primarily on Catt's second presidency, analyzing her decisions that he claims were crucial to the success of the federal suffrage amendment in 1920.

Fowler emphasizes that, though Catt cared deeply about other reforms and political issues, during the last years of the suffrage battle she focused her energies on woman suffrage alone. Like Susan B. Anthony with whom she had worked closely in the 1890s, Catt was determined not to allow other issues to divide suffragists, dispel their energy, or alienate potential supporters. Continuing the strategy of making woman suffrage appear respectable and in keeping with widely shared American values and goals, she was particularly eager to distance the movement from unpopular causes or radical tactics that could undermine the steady growth in support for woman suffrage between 1910 and 1920. This strategy disappointed many within the movement as well as would-be allies outside the movement. Fowler insists, however, that Catt's pragmatism was strategically sound, even if it seems—then and now—cynical or unethical. As a single-issue campaign, the woman suffrage movement was more efficient, united, and less vulnerable to its critics.

A dramatic example of Catt's implementation of this policy was her decision to put aside her own strong antiwar sentiments and shun an alliance between the woman suffrage and peace movements during World War I. As public opinion shifted rapidly from an insistence upon American neutrality to an overwhelming prowar fervor that tolerated no dissent, Catt aligned the NAWSA and its leaders first with "preparedness" and then the war effort. Though some suffragists, notably peace advocate Jane Addams, were dismayed by this turn of events, Fowler argues that this decision saved Catt and the NAWSA from the extreme hostility and loss of influence that Addams and other peace advocates endured during the war, and

aided the suffrage cause significantly with Wilson and the public—creating the impression that women deserved the vote as a reward for war service.

A second example of Catt's pragmatic strategy discussed by Fowler is "The Plan" that Catt devised soon after she returned to the NAWSA presidency late in 1915. "The Plan" was approved by NAWSA members at an "Emergency Convention" in Atlantic City in September 1916. Often called "The Winning Plan," this strategy was designed to centralize authority within the massive but disorganized NAWSA, and coordinate the efforts of suffragists nationwide in a final campaign that would at last secure the adoption of the federal amendment. It is interesting to note that, as Fowler observes, this decision does not seem at all controversial today; indeed, both Catt and Alice Paul are celebrated for their role in finally returning the suffrage movement to an emphasis on the federal approach to winning woman suffrage. Yet in 1916, this decision was far more controversial than Catt's alignment of the suffrage movement with the war effort.

Catt's "Winning Plan," was a significant departure from the policy of her predecessor Anna Howard Shaw, whose highly decentralized administration had given scant attention to the federal amendment. Shaw was influenced to an extent by Southern suffragists including Laura Clay and Kate Gordon who served for years as self-appointed "watch-dogs" for the South on the NAWSA Executive Board and who opposed suffrage by federal amendment. Catt, however, had no difficulty finding other Southern women to work with such as Madeline McDowell Breckinridge, Pattie Ruffner Jacobs, Anne Dallas Dudley, and Minnie Fisher Cunningham who, frustrated by repeated rejections of state suffrage initiatives in the South, enthusiastically supported the federal amendment. As Fowler explains, Catt believed that the state approach would never enfranchise *all* American women, and that the national approach was more in keeping with "women's dignity," allowing suffragists to bypass at least some of the state-by-state pleading that, even back in the 1870s, Elizabeth Cady Stanton and Susan B. Anthony rejected as demeaning.

Fowler also analyzes Catt's dealings with the militant suffragists, emphasizing that while Catt agreed with Paul on the need to refocus on the federal amendment, she objected strenuously to the tactics employed by Alice Paul and the National Woman's Party and believed that Paul lacked the "pragmatic sense" essential in a leader. Catt was particularly critical of Paul and the NWP for engaging in partisanship and picketing, believing that they were alienating Democrats in Congress whose votes were so desperately needed—not to mention President Wilson himself. Catt was convinced that the NAWSA's lobbying campaign directed by Maud Wood Park and Helen Gardener between 1917 and 1919—dignified, diplomatic, non-partisan, non-threatening and nicknamed by the press the "Front Door Lobby"—was the only way of persuading Congressmen to approve the federal amendment.

Historians *still* debate this issue—the strategic effectiveness of both Paul and Catt's tactics—as we try to explain why the woman suffrage amendment was finally adopted and assess the relative contributions of the NAWSA and the NWP

to that victory. Most would agree with Fowler that both groups played a positive role and that "the Woman's Party's tactical radicalism helped enormously to legitimate the NAWSA."

Catt's "Winning Plan" was clearly a major factor in the final victory. Historian Eleanor Flexner described Catt as bringing "order out of chaos and victory out of apparent stagnation," and a genius at uniting all of the disparate elements within the massive NAWSA into a "potent political force." Instead of allowing suffragists in the various states to adopt whatever policy they wished and launch campaigns as they chose, Catt assigned a role to each state and demanded that state suffrage leaders adhere to an over-arching national strategy. As Maud Wood Park later explained in her 1960 autobiography *Front Door Lobby*, Catt divided the states into four categories and "assigned a particular form of legislative work" to each. First, she directed suffrage organizations in the equal suffrage states and in Illinois (which had presidential and municipal suffrage) to obtain from their legislatures resolutions requesting that Congress approve the federal amendment and send it to the states. Second, Catt identified several states including the key state of New York where she believed there was a good chance of winning a state suffrage amendment, and urged workers from those states to prepare at once for a new campaign. Third, she advised the remaining states to try for presidential suffrage, as this could be granted by legislatures without having to be approved by the voters in referenda. Last, Catt advised suffragists in the Southern, one-party states to try for "primary suffrage," which could also be granted by the legislatures. Much to the disappointment of suffragists in states such as Kentucky, in which local women were far more optimistic than Catt about the chances of successful state amendment campaigns, the NAWSA president demanded that they defer to her judgment, and play their assigned part in "The Plan."

Catt's plan, then, did not abandon state campaigns, but coordinated them with unprecedented care to insure that a series of victories would together build momentum for the federal amendment, and that defeats in states she considered "hopeless" would be avoided. The Plan was not announced to the public. Swearing everyone to secrecy, Maud Wood Park recalled Catt explained that these initiatives would be launched at the beginning of legislative sessions the following January (1917), catching the opposition off-guard, and requiring the anti-suffragists to fight on "many fronts at once." Catt presented a "compact" to be signed by suffragists representing at least thirty-six states—the number needed for ratification. As the signing ceremony ended, wrote Park, "I felt like Moses on the mountain top after the Promised Land had been shown to him and he knew the long years of wandering in the Wilderness were soon to end. For the first time I saw our goal as possible of attainment in the near future." Park concluded:

> Often since then, remembering how hard it was at best to win our vote in the Congress and the subsequent ratification by thirty-six states, I have

speculated as to what would have happened if Mrs. Catt's plan had not been presented on that sultry afternoon in 1916. Undoubtedly a woman suffrage amendment would have been adopted at some time, even if Mrs. Catt had never been born; but, if success had not come when it did, the cause might easily have been caught in a period of postwar reaction, and victory postponed for another half-century. That women all over the United States were able to vote in 1920 is due, I believe, to the carrying out of the plan prepared and presented by an incomparable leader.

★   ★   ★   ★   ★

A NYONE WHO KNOWS the story of the struggle for the enfranchisement of women in the 1915-1920 period knows that Carrie Catt's strategic decisions were of fateful importance. Their pragmatic wisdom is clear, though their ethical wisdom is now, as it was then, a good deal more controversial.

Catt's Progressive agenda was wide-ranging, and suffrage for her was in large part a *means* to realize other reform objectives. Nevertheless, during the suffrage fight Catt focused all her energies on that issue. Her conscious strategy was to allow no other cause to enter the NAWSA's agenda: "As a matter of fact we do not care a ginger snap about anything but that Federal Amendment."[1] She did not object when the NAWSA Convention adopted all sorts of resolutions favoring a number of this or that measures to assist women in economic, professional, and legal realms. But she insisted that the NAWSA would be doing nothing about them. She did not think it could and at the same time promote women's enfranchisement: "we cannot...until the Federal Amendment is through, spare any force for the support of any bill...we haven't the power to do anything but merely pass a resolution. It is of no avail."[2]

Catt made sure her wishes were followed as she fashioned her version of that very contemporary phenomenon, the single-issue pressure group. Her rationale was simple, one goal would mobilize women and the NAWSA's resources in a focused direction. It was efficient and—equally valuable—it freed the NAWSA of the conflicts and attacks that involvement with other causes inevitably generated.

This was not a self-evident strategic choice, however, and it drew opponents. On the one hand, some earlier feminist leaders, such as Elizabeth Cady Stanton, objected to this approach as too narrow. On the other, some groups, especially the WCTU, the Anti-Saloon League, and, later, peace groups sought alliance with Catt and the NAWSA and were not happy when they did not get it. But Catt pushed all such complaints aside, arguing that even hints of such links were a formula for disaster.[3]

Woman Suffrage and World War I

A remarkable illustration of Carrie Catt's willingness to pursue this strategy—even at the cost of compromise with other of her values—came in her much disputed strategic moves before and during World War I. All her life, Catt proudly identified with efforts to end war. In the decades after 1920 this became her principal field of public activity. However, when the First World War began in Europe, Catt was caught between her antiwar inclinations and her suspicion that suffragist peace activity could adversely affect the struggle for women's enfranchisement. Catt calculated even before the United States became a direct belligerent in the Great War that the situation was out of control and suffragists' efforts would be a costly venture for nothing. Concerned women, led by Jane Addams, might try, but the unleashed forces of war could not be stopped by their necessarily "puny effort." She doubted that anything could stop "these men in whom the furious beast" had been unchained.[4] Trying to stop them was "like throwing a violet at a stone wall." "There is no power on earth that is going to stop that war until there has been perhaps the most terrible battle that the world has ever seen."[5]

At first Catt tried to have it both ways. While accounts differ as to whom credit belongs for initiating organized opposition to the war among women, in 1914 Catt and Addams worked together in this cause. In general, Catt worked behind the scenes lest she create the kind of backlash toward suffrage that so worried her. She specifically refused to accept a public leadership post. On the other hand, Catt did

U.S. delegates to the Women's Peace Conference in The Hague, aboard the *MS Noordam*, April 1915. Jane Addams is third from left.

LIBRARY OF CONGRESS

not avoid public appearances altogether, and her participation with Addams and others undoubtedly lent peace forces prestige without which its modest endeavor might have collapsed even sooner than it did. Catt did, for example, go to the White House on several occasions in 1914 to urge American neutrality to Woodrow Wilson and to Secretary of State William Jennings Bryan. She felt that she took a great risk in such public actions. That risk certainly did not diminish when Catt continued, albeit as quietly as possible, to support Addams when she founded the Woman's Peace Party.[6]

Nonetheless, Catt's heart was not in the Woman's Peace Party or any other part of the active but tiny women's peace movement in the United States from 1914 to 1917. She insisted she had to be concerned about votes for women above all else. She observed with dismay the barrage of attacks on her and woman suffrage by anti-suffragist publications once war broke out in Europe. She feared that if she were more active in the peace cause she might confirm their propaganda that the woman's movement was a harbor for pacifists at best and for disloyal American women at worst. Most of the main organs of the anti-suffragists were early on the bandwagon of United States preparedness and outspoken hostility to Germany and they ridiculed every effort of peace groups and every peace plan. Such ideas, they challenged, were dangerous and had a large part in encouraging the weakness that led to war in the first place. Moreover, as time went on, anti-suffragists lost the distinction between pacifist "disloyalty" and outright support for Germany and the Kaiser. It all became rather ugly and the charges specifically toward Catt were as ugly as the rest.[7]

As war approached for the United States, Catt moved with the tide. She had no intention of allowing enemies of her crusade to get away with their antiwar, pro-German charges and thus damage it. In February 1917, Catt convened the NAWSA, recognizing that war for the United States was imminent. It was necessary for the NAWSA to get its house in order because "The future of our movement depends upon the right action being taken now."[8] What Catt wanted was a willingness on the part of the NAWSA to support national war readiness. She got it, successfully steering past both extremist doves and hawks. In her terms the convention was a great success also because it attracted favorable publicity from the growing prowar segments in American society and brought the NAWSA into contact with such influential government notables as Secretary of War Newton Baker and Secretary of the Navy Josephus Daniels.

When the United States did declare war on Germany and the contest she had long expected (and dreaded) began in earnest, Catt quickly offered her personal endorsement; she made sure that the NAWSA was in line with national war policy in every way; and she repudiated suffragists who disagreed, notably Montana Congresswoman Jeannette Rankin, who voted against the war.[9]

These actions led to Catt's ejection from the Woman's Peace Party and a good many hard feelings between her and its small cohort of pacifists. Her decision could not have come as a surprise to them, but it still led to some bitter denuncia-

tions. They did not really bother her because she had absolutely no hesitation about paying this price. For her, opposition to the war, once the United States had entered it, was courting martyrdom and taking the suffrage movement down in the process. And so Carrie Catt began her war work, publicly working to get women involved in the Red Cross, canteen service, food production, and the like. She campaigned in Liberty Loan drives, and she accepted appointment to the Woman's Committee of the Council of National Defense (under Anna Howard Shaw's leadership).[10]

These activities, especially service on the Woman's Committee of the Council of National Defense, were not easy. Catt hated war and now she found herself busy supporting one, albeit one she eventually con-

Dr. Anna Howard Shaw receiving the Distinguished Service Medal from Secretary of War Newton D. Baker, May 1919, in recognition of her coordination of women's contributions during World War I.

vinced herself was legitimate. Equally difficult was the treatment Catt, along with the other members of the committee (especially Shaw), received from the male leaders of the Council of National Defense and assorted government agencies. They found themselves, once again, treated as second-class citizens, bossed, patronized, or ignored. The situation was often acutely frustrating, but Catt remained convinced that working for the war was vital to the suffrage cause.[11]

There clearly were a great many enemies waiting to pounce. Once the United States entered the war, they crossed the already thin line between criticism of suffragists and wild, even frenzied accusations. Without any shame, critics called suffragists disloyal and pro-German. "Woman suffrage is proving of more potent assistance to the Kaiser than his wonderful army." In addition, anti-suffragists repeatedly tried to tar them with the brush of socialism, bolshevism, and just about anything that might make suffragists seem anti-American in what became a time of unpleasant xenophobia.[12]

Once again, the anti-suffragists singled out Catt for special charges and smears. How intensely the anti-suffragists, now garbed in the most patriotic of uniforms,

hated Catt is difficult to comprehend unless one actually reads the flood of denunciatory articles on her in their press during World War I. In their portrait Catt was a knowing opponent of the war, a virtual traitor who continued to criticize her government in disgusting fashion during wartime. Her work for the war was a sham, hiding her conspiratorial actions for woman suffrage, and often for the Germans. In at least one article deportation was suggested as the way to deal with Catt.[13]

It is only in this context that Catt's own strategy can be understood. And it is only in this context, despite the loud cries of the anti-suffragists, that its success can be understood. For, despite the cries of the anti-suffragists, Catt's strategy regarding World War I worked. All over the country she gained praise as a patriot actively behind the war effort. Though publicly abused, Catt and the NAWSA escaped the almost unbelievable hostility that befell some others, Jane Addams in particular, which undercut their political influence for a time. When charges of disloyalty and other ugly words flew, Catt could and did reply with her war record and that of the NAWSA.

It would be wrong, however, to portray Catt's strategic purposes in World War I, as only defensive. She looked in this direction, but she also realized that there was another, much more positive side to her strategy. Patriotic service could create "opportunity" for the cause of women's enfranchisement. It could greatly increase the respectability of suffragists and their cause, and thus advance the cause, which is exactly what happened both with the public at large and with many Washington decision-makers including Woodrow Wilson. It happened in part because Catt made sure every contribution by the NAWSA and prominent members of the NAWSA received as much publicity as possible. The not very subtle point was that the vote for women was American, was patriotic. Meanwhile, Catt sought to foster the impression that women, while they gave their service freely, nonetheless deserved something in return, and that something of course, was the vote.[14]

Catt did not hesitate to make sure that people got the point that suffragist war service deserved repayment with enfranchisement. In fact, Catt relentlessly kept up the pressure for woman suffrage throughout the war. A frequent argument was that women's enfranchisement was needed "as a war measure."[15] Her argument that, if it was to fight a war for democracy, the United States should advance democracy at home by making women full citizens was effective—just how effective is indicated by the outrage it provoked from anti-suffragists. They stormed at Catt, accusing her of being a monomaniac, pursuing her cause at all costs, and thus threatening American democracy when such divisive matters ought to be laid aside in the name of wartime unity.[16]

Catt paid no attention. Just as she spurned those who expected her peace concern would lead her to oppose the war, so she rejected those who urged she drop the cause of the vote during the war. For her the central issue never changed.

Overall, Catt was proud of her strategy during the Great War, though she hoped

it would never be required again and dreamed that once women got the vote they might well end all wars. But questions were raised then—and have been since. Shouldn't she of all people have known the shortsightedness of her strategy? After all, from her own perspective, war corrupted progressive impulses in history. Some historians agree, regarding World War I.[17] But this analysis does not apply to votes for women. World War I hardly killed the chance for enfranchisement.

The uneasiness over Catt's strategy mostly derives from a sense that it was cynical. Cynical it was, but Catt did not see it this way. She never had any interest in a politics of purity in the impure world. To her the fact was that she could not stop the war, but the NAWSA's opposition to war could seriously delay women's enfranchisement. And her belief was that she was called to help women. Her devotion in subsequent decades of her public life to the cause of world peace was not an act of expiation. It was rather a resumption of the peace mission, which she had never lost sight of. But it was a long-range goal and she had no intention of losing momentum for women's enfranchisement because of it.

The Winning Plan

Much less controversial in retrospect, but much more so at the time, was the adoption of "The Plan," in 1916, to push for congressional passage of the Anthony Amendment to the United States Constitution, giving women the right to vote. Catt had long looked toward the Anthony Amendment as a way of overcoming the slow and cumbersome process of achieving women's enfranchisement state-by-state.[18] But by 1915-1916, she was sure it was absolutely necessary to concentrate NAWSA resources on this strategy, a major shift in NAWSA focus.

"The Plan" was adopted in 1916 at an emergency meeting of the NAWSA which Catt had called at Atlantic City, New Jersey.[19] Catt was by

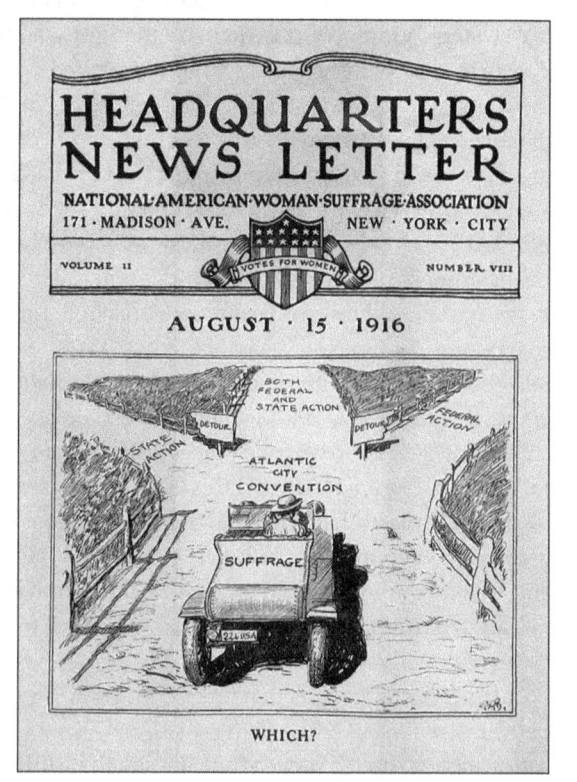

Cartoon illustrating the choices of strategy Carrie Chapman Catt confronted as she again became NAWSA president in 1915.
LIBRARY OF CONGRESS.

then president of the NAWSA, and she reflected dissatisfaction with the NAWSA's drift during Shaw's long reign towards (unsuccessful) campaigning for the extension of suffrage at the state level, including support for the Shafroth-Palmer constitutional amendment intended to encourage opportunities for state electorates to vote on woman suffrage. The Shafroth-Palmer proposal would have required any state to hold a vote on woman suffrage where eight percent of the voters in the previous presidential election petitioned for such a referendum.

The drift during the Shaw years towards action on the state level was the result of several factors. One was fealty to those in the NAWSA, including Catt, who had been struggling for success state-by-state. Another was the necessity of placating Southern members of the NAWSA who were states' rights oriented and strongly against the Anthony Amendment. A third was anger at Alice Paul and her supporters, who were committed exclusively to the federal strategy—a knee-jerk resistance on the NAWSA's part to whatever Paul and her faction favored.[20]

But by 1916 Catt was convinced that reversal of strategy was essential. She based her strategic judgment on what she thought was the practical situation. The old approach now seemed what Catt frankly called "negative—not positive."[21] It simply was not working, certainly not fast enough. No doubt, the memory of the loss of the suffrage referendum in New York State in 1915 was a painful factor in this assessment. As she looked ahead, moreover, Catt increasingly doubted the state approach alone could ever work. Its chances in many states were nearly hopeless. State election laws and constitutional provisions often made state constitutional revision almost impossible. Even worse, Catt doubted whether there was a majority of men in many states who would soon vote for women's enfranchisement if they got the chance. She continued to be haunted by "the others," the "groups of recently naturalized and even unnationalized foreigners, Indians, Negroes, large numbers of illiterates, ne'er-do-wells, and drunken loafers," who she felt resisted women's enfranchisement.[22] Catt also worried that even if she was wrong, and some states did begin to approve enfranchisement, this might represent a victory of distinctly mixed blessings. Concern with national enfranchisement might decline in every state that granted women the vote. Valuable energy and talent might be lost to the NAWSA; and "disintegration" would increase.[23] Thus, from every angle it seemed imperative to Catt to redirect attention to the national effort to obtain congressional passage of the Anthony Amendment.

Catt's expectation was that Congress would prove more cooperative than many of the resistant states. She understood that this was a gamble and intended to keep some pressure on the states while hoping that suffrage states and those with strong pro-suffrage forces would help by pressuring Congress. Pressure from the states was needed, after all, to impress Congress that there was popular support for woman suffrage. Moreover, the states could not be ignored because, when Congress finally capitulated, the Anthony Amendment would need approval by three-

fourths of the state legislatures. Yet Catt was convinced emphasis had to shift to the federal level. Victory there would lead to victory everywhere.[24]

Catt also argued that the national approach best fit her long-run ideal for women. It acknowledged women's dignity, she insisted, because it took them seriously. It made the issue of woman suffrage a national matter, as it should be, and it left behind the image of women pleading state-by-state for something that was basic to democracy and human rights.[25]

At the Atlantic City convention Catt pushed her strategy through largely on the force of her personal and political leadership. In a mood for strong leadership and attracted by her effective plea for her strategic gamble, the convention swung behind "The Plan" with an enthusiasm that overcame earlier positions and earlier doubts.[26]

Undoubtedly, Catt was aided in her coup by the decision of Anna Howard Shaw to back her plan fully (except for moving the national headquarters [from New York] to Washington). While Shaw had lost much respect within the NAWSA during her presidency, she was still, second only to Catt, the most formidable force to be reckoned with. Her enthusiasm for "The Plan" was strong. She helped arrange the special Atlantic City meeting, in fact, and thereafter repeatedly backed its decisions, probably in part because she thought it would undermine the appeal of the Woman's Party.[27]

On the other hand, there were costs. There were personal costs: Catt drove herself night and day as she built support within the NAWSA for her shift in strategy. There were organizational costs: there was serious opposition to "The Plan" from significant Southern voices in the NAWSA. Kate Gordon, of Louisiana, and Laura Clay, of Kentucky, both prominent during the Shaw presidency, argued that suffrage could (and should) have appeal in the South only if it did not remind Southerners of earlier national attempts to change the South at the behest of federal edicts. And they feared that if a national effort were successful in this instance a similar attempt to dictate to the South on the subject of race might follow.

Moreover opponents of several stripes felt that Catt bulldozed her plan through in Atlantic City with precious little concern for them or for a diverse NAWSA. From their perspective, they were quite right. But Catt wanted action in response to the strategic imperative at hand. They had had their way for a long time; now their day was over. Indeed, Catt believed it should have ended long before, since an honest evaluation would have revealed that the "littleness of the view, which our states' rights' plan has stimulated for a hundred years, is the greatest enemy of woman suffrage."[28]

Privately, Catt had arranged to resign if "The Plan" was not adopted by the NAWSA. She insisted there just was no point in continuing the struggle in the old, humiliating, and ineffective fashion. This issue went beyond compromise or temporizing. But Catt won in Atlantic City and she used "The Plan" as her vehicle towards victory, defending it as she went.[29]

Dealing with Divisiveness

Catt's strategic analysis is further illuminated by her attitude towards and dealings with "the Militants" in the later suffrage movement. The first major sign of division in the suffrage crusade occurred in 1907 when Harriot Stanton Blatch, daughter of Elizabeth Cady Stanton, turned against the NAWSA. Influenced by the more active and more militant movement in Great Britain, Blatch founded a more radical

Alice Paul, 1915
LIBRARY OF CONGRESS

organization in 1907, which became the Women's Political Union in 1910. While Blatch's tiny splinter movement played a minor role, it was a harbinger of the future.

A far more serious split in the suffrage forces became apparent in 1913 with the emergence of the remarkable Alice Paul. Paul's first serious work for votes for women began in England, where she associated with the British militants and went to prison for her militancy.[30] With this background, the young Alice Paul arrived in Washington in 1913 and went to work for the NAWSA's Congressional Committee. Through the force of her charismatic personality, Paul soon transformed the committee. She changed it from the inactive, sleepy arena it had been under Anna Howard Shaw's regime into a permanent committee that was a busy lobbying center determined to push the Susan B. Anthony Amendment through Congress. In spite of the changes, Paul became dissatisfied with the unwieldy committee, linked as it was to the "conservative" NAWSA and its multileveled strategies. As an alternative, Paul set up the Congressional Union to concentrate exclusively on the Anthony Amendment, ignoring state efforts for suffrage and efforts to get Congress to encourage enfranchisement of women by the states. At first Paul acted within the NAWSA and with the approval of President Shaw, but Paul's focus and her sometimes brash style soon aroused opposition within NAWSA circles. Moreover, as the Congressional Union took on the unmistakable appearance of a separate and independent organization, still others within the NAWSA became uncomfortable. Aware of the criticisms by the end of 1913, Paul defended herself by claiming that the Congressional Union existed only to assist the Congressional Committee.

In reality, however, the Congressional Union was an almost separate organization—empire, critics charged—which used NAWSA stationery to raise money and

recruit membership while not accepting direction from the NAWSA board. Indeed, as Anna Howard Shaw eventually argued, it pursued policies never approved by the NAWSA. Not surprisingly, the NAWSA board sought to force Paul to do its bidding. The result was that in 1914 Paul was asked to resign as head of the Congressional Committee. She did so and she soon took the Congressional Union with her, feeling very much that she had been rejected and forced to secede. While in later years Paul

conceded that she had erred in not communicating along the way with the NAWSA leadership, she doubted at the time that compromise was possible—and it was not, in fact.[31]

Paul did not act alone. She had support from others who had tired of the NAWSA's largely fruitless pursuit of votes for women via state referenda. They wanted to get the Anthony constitutional amendment passed, and they wanted to move fast. Among them were Blatch, whose Women's Political Union fused with the Congressional Union in 1916, and Alva Belmont, who contributed a great deal of her considerable wealth to the cause. By 1916 the Woman's Party had emerged, with Anne Martin as first chair. Martin

Dr. Anna Howard Shaw, 1914

was a former NAWSA board member from Nevada who, like a number of others from Western states where woman suffrage was a reality, was impatient with the slow progress of the NAWSA towards national enfranchisement of women. Finally, in 1917 the National Woman's Party was founded with Alice Paul as its acknowledged leader.[32]

It was Anna Howard Shaw who took the role of chief and consistent opponent and who rallied those within the NAWSA seeking to control Paul. Shaw detested Paul. "I wish something would happen to Miss Paul," she wrote, and one senses she did not mean something pleasant.[33] But her larger complaint went to Paul's followers, who were "blank fools"[34] and who, Shaw insisted, hurt the suffrage cause by their divisiveness, disloyalty, and tactical militance.

Shaw blamed herself for not attacking Paul's tendency to go her own way from the first, stopping her before she was in a position to make a cause célèbre out of the affair. Shaw suspected that would have ended the entire affair, since in her judgment it was not at bottom a fight over tactics or policy but a matter of willful ambition on the part of Paul and her coworker Lucy Burns.[35]

Alice Stone Blackwell
LIBRARY OF CONGRESS

Shaw's opinion was widely shared among other suffragists. One of the most important, and most hostile, was Alice Stone Blackwell, [editor of *The Woman's Journal* and daughter of Lucy Stone and Henry Blackwell], who was still denouncing the Woman's Party in the late 1920s. She would not forgive them for the divisions she felt they had brought to the suffrage cause, and she thought it incredible that they blithely took credit for the passage of the Anthony Amendment. And yet even Blackwell acknowledged their appeal. They might be "pestiferous," but they had "cleverness and enthusiasm"—which made them continually "dangerous."[36]

In 1913 and 1914, while Catt shared Shaw's doubts about the organizational loyalty of the Paul group, Catt did not join President Shaw in her assault on them.[37] Nor did she share the antagonism that some in the NAWSA felt toward Paul and her allies because they wished to push Congress to adopt the Anthony Amendment. Indeed, Catt favored the same approach. This fact explains why informed critics of the NAWSA did not single out Catt nearly as much as they did Shaw as a major cause of the split.[38]

1915 was a decisive year in Catt's relations with the Alice Paul group, by then gone from the NAWSA. On the one hand, Catt made efforts to heal the wounds between the NAWSA and Paul. She met with Paul, despite Shaw's intense disapproval and fear,[39] though to no good result.[40] And she moved rapidly, upon her election to the presidency of the NAWSA in 1915, towards adoption of a national strategy for women's enfranchisement (which Paul had supported with no success within the NAWSA), a goal she accomplished when "The Plan" was approved in 1916.

By then, however, the split was too deep, too personal, and too institutionalized for the two groups to get back together. Moreover, new conflicts arose that sealed a split between Catt and her NAWSA and Paul and her associates. As a consequence, while all of Catt's contacts with Woman's Party supporters did not dissolve,[41] Catt made her decision. Alice Paul and her group—soon to be the National Woman's Party—were a destructive influence on the cause, and the NAWSA must keep free from them. While never denying that they sometimes were "doing some good work," Catt concluded that there was a fundamental split and all suffragists had to choose: "No one can carry water on both shoulders."[42] At the same time Catt unrealistically hoped to avoid open warfare. A choice had to be made but that did not mean each group should continually waste energy "battling each other when they should be more concerned to help the big cause on."[43]

The source of conflict between Catt and Paul concerned tactics, and whether Paul and her allies had a realistic understanding of practical politics. The question

Alva Belmont (left) c. 1914 and Anne Martin, c. 1916, joined Alice Paul to establish the National Woman's Party. Martin became the party's first chair.
LIBRARY OF CONGRESS

Catt asked of any strategy or tactic was: will it help the cause, will it maximize votes in referenda and in Congress? In Catt's judgment this pragmatic sense was missing among people such as Alice Paul. A "sharp tongue," radical pronouncements, radical actions did not produce votes. They were the products of those who chose self-indulgence over practicality.[44]

In the suffrage fight two tactics of the Paul group drew Catt's opposition, partisanship and picketing. The militants' eagerness to abandon nonpartisan-ship, enter the world of party and electoral politics, and campaign against political enemies appealed to some women activists more than nonpartisanship did.[45] Catt claimed to appreciate the appeal of activism by recognizing that nonpartisanship "lacks the avenger's satisfaction."[46] She could also agree with those such as Rose Young who thought more in terms of positive action and wondered if using a "big stick" such as electoral politics might not speed progress by striking fear into politicians.[47]

But Catt thought this was a dangerous idea, a judgment undoubtedly encouraged by her natural suspicion of partisan politics in every situation. Catt insisted, first, that alliances for or against a political party invariably proved costly in terms of independence. In this case, she feared that suffrage would be swallowed up by other party concerns and the compromising, self-promoting ethic of all parties. Second, even if one were to enter party politics to the extent of endorsing candidates—which was too much involvement to begin with—the endorsements had to cross party lines or else one would find oneself saddled with a partisan label and the bitter opposition of at least one political party.

Catt's position was faithful to the long-time gospel of the women's movement, especially the ideas of Susan B. Anthony. Had there been a party prepared to

endorse "Freedom to Women" on its banner, Anthony and, later, Catt would have rallied to it. In the meantime, Catt was prepared to follow Anthony's classic advice to appeal to both parties and to serve as "a balance of power" when possible, never accepting a marriage to one party or a crusade against another.[48] It was incredible to her that Paul and her allies sought to go after all Democrats in the 1914 and 1916 elections, blaming Democratic President Wilson and all congressional Democrats for the failure of Congress to pass the Anthony Amendment. The policy of nonpartisanship failed to distinguish between Democrats who favored suffrage and those who did not. Moreover, it was bound to alienate desperately needed Democrats in Congress where the Anthony Amendment had to gain a two-thirds majority if it were to start its way to final enactment.

It was also bound to alienate President Wilson, whose support was needed, especially to persuade reluctant Southern Democrats in Congress to give their support. Nor was it the way to promote success in state referenda. As she wrote Jane Addams, any crusade against the Democrats was "exceedingly distasteful to most of us because it committed the stupendous stupidity of making an anti-democratic campaign when the suffrage question was pending in eleven states and depending for success upon Democratic votes."[49]

Instead, Catt preferred to work closely with friends in both parties while exerting pressure in all legal (but nonelectoral) ways on senators, members of the House, and the president. She gave full support to Maud Wood Park's direct lobbying work on Capitol Hill and kept in close lobbying touch with Park's "Front Door" effort, the joint strategy sessions, and "machinations," which were (and are) part of the game there. She worked the White House personally, convinced that dignified lobbying was the way to get results.[50]

Yet Catt did not object only because she considered entering partisan, electoral politics a strategic mistake. The Woman's Party's strategy also offended her ideals. It was natural for her to skate away from playing partisan electoral politics. Such a strategy clashed with her nonpartisan ideal for a democracy and activated her substantial ambivalence about politics in general and party politics in particular. The Woman's Party was guilty of a tactical blunder, in her mind, but it also seriously offended Catt's dream for a politics without politics. Catt fought for her perspective with all her energy, challenging Charles A. Beard when he defended the Woman's Party's partisanship in that bosom of Progressivism, the *New Republic*. And she fought back against other critics. A lot was at stake for her that went beyond strategy, though her replies invariably stressed her claim that only her approach would work—and was working. And Catt had the considerable satisfaction (if that is the word) of watching the radicals' adventures into partisan electoral politics fail in both 1914 and 1916.[51]

Nonpartisanship remained a fixed star in her belief, but by 1918 Catt became open to the idea of bringing women's muscle to bear on congressional opponents of women's enfranchisement through the electoral process. Her impatience with the manifest dilatoriness of Congress from 1915 to 1917 had

grown. She began to issue unmistakable warnings that votes for women was an idea that would "not perish," but "the party which opposed it may," and she told the 1917 convention to expect to take action against individual senators who were up for re-election in 1918 if they opposed woman suffrage.[52] When the 1918 campaign came, Catt led the NAWSA into a carefully circumscribed, nonpartisan battle to defeat four recalcitrant senators (three Republicans and one Democrat), and was delighted by the defeat of one of them in November. Of course—though not for the first time—this move reflected the adoption of a part of Paul's strategy, yet it did so only within Catt's nonpartisan strategic constraints, which, she asserted once again, preserved the NAWSA's freedom while advancing its effectiveness.[53]

A far more rigid position was adopted by the head of the NAWSA towards the other major "radical" tactic of the Woman's Party, the aggressive picketing of the president which began in 1917. Women picketers caused a sensation and, in many circles including within the NAWSA, they created a scandal. Nor were the Woman's Party picketers necessarily modest and sedate. As time went on they became more aggressive in pursuit of their mission, refusing to cooperate when police arrested them.[54]

Once again the issue here was not solely a matter of strategic effectiveness. Catt put it this way. So did her opponents. Interminable arguments followed over whether militant picketing and what became civil disobedience were, or ever could be, effective. Catt was convinced that suffrage was past its strictly agitational phase. What it needed now was male support, and especially the support of the male who was president of the United States. Picketing could not accomplish this goal. It was better to work mostly on education, particularly during the war, as that would produce more male acquiescence or support.[55]

Though Catt and everybody else treated the matter in these terms, the enormous national controversy over a few picketers suggested much more was at stake. The fight over the picketers actually involved an intense and significant dispute over the definition of a good woman. Were women pushing for suffrage always to be proper ladies and law-abiding citizens? Or was it appropriate for free women in control of their lives to break convention and law in pursuit of the vote? Most of the leadership and members of the NAWSA were outraged at the tactics of the picketers, in part because they seemed brash and unfeminine—and thus were detrimental to their cause.

Carrie Chapman Catt, however, was not among those who joined the assault on the picketers as unladylike women. Given Catt's resentment over undignified treatment of women, indeed their daily humiliation, it is no surprise that she had more than a sneaking sympathy with the picketers' tactical militance—especially when they were safely located in Great Britain. At home the problem for Catt, as always, concerned their political effectiveness.[56] She knew the public reaction would be negative—as it was. She also observed the picketers' negative effects on Congress.

Carrie Chapman Catt on April 6, 1916 christening the *Golden Flyer*. Alice Burke and Nell Richardson are in the car about to began a journey across the United States to promote women's right to vote.   LIBRARY OF CONGRESS

As a result, Catt publicly appealed in 1917 for the Woman's Party to stop damaging the chances for passage of the Anthony constitutional amendment by its picketing. She privately wrote Alice Paul deploring the "futile annoyance to the members of Congress."[57] She worried too about picketing as "an insult to President Wilson," which could alienate his needed support. (She tried to compensate by quietly notifying the White House of planned embarrassments to Wilson, which her friends in the Woman's Party leaked to her.) Finally, Catt saw only unfortunate effects on the state level also, since she was certain that "the picket party" had hurt the 1917 New York campaign for the enfranchisement of women.[58]

Everywhere she heard opponents denouncing the picketing. They charged it showed the danger of women in politics and the foolishness of granting women the vote. They insisted that to give women the ballot while they were picketing would reward tactics that should have no place in American politics. At another, lower level, anti-suffragists consciously used the uproar over the picketers as an opportunity to denounce the suffragists as exemplars of "fanaticism," and as "freaks" and "spoiled" children undeserving of suffrage. Moreover, intent on destroying all suffragists through public disapproval of the picketers, they worked as hard as they could to collapse any distinction between them and Catt and the NAWSA. Over and over they asserted that Catt and the NAWSA were in league with the militants, equally deserving of popular condemnation.[59]

Throughout much of 1917 and thereafter, Catt tried to repair the continuing damage she believed the picketers caused the movement. Her private assistance to

the White House was an illustration of this, but mostly Catt did her work in public. She succeeded in getting the NAWSA to disavow the picketing tactic and she led the NAWSA to publish its objections in some 350 newspapers across the country. She spoke out personally, arguing that all suffragists should not be judged by what she correctly insisted was a tiny minority. She was especially anxious to establish that suffragists were not against Wilson (and thus not unpatriotic) in what was wartime.

Catt's course offended (and still does) those who contended that Catt should have embraced the picketers as fellow participants in the struggle who were determined to get action quickly. Such judgments did not impress Catt. Her constant refrain was that one had to be practical, to make trade-offs, and to ask about the consequences of tactics. Catt thought she, and not the Woman's Party, recognized how to play politics. And those who did not know its rules had to be neutralized because, though naive, they could hurt the work of those who did. The danger was always that the Woman's Party might become the tail that wagged the suffrage dog, that the work of two million women might be lost in the actions of a group that never was larger than 50,000.[60]

Pragmatism was not the only root of Catt's objections to the picketers, however. She may not have found their "unladylike" activities offensive to her ideal of womanhood, but their actions did clash with her ideal of the kind of politics she wanted suffragists to model for society at large. When Carrie Catt looked at the Woman's Party, she saw individuals who had already proven themselves "untrustworthy and extremely disloyal."[61] They operated by churning up dark forces of emotion and conflict, not at all the kind of politics she wanted anything to do with. After all, Catt was to devote almost as many years of her life to world peace as to woman suffrage. She could not see how promoting "warfare" in any realm for any reason was acceptable. In this Catt's thought was identical to that of Jane Addams and many other Progressives. Conflict was their enemy. It could not and did not facilitate a harmonious democracy or a peaceful world. In effect, Catt's complaint was that the militants were merely reflecting the world in their tactical moves. They did not represent change and were not reformers at all. They had surrendered to the world and were trying to beat men at their own game.

Of course, Catt respected toughness and employed military language often enough that she had no business being too self-righteous in condemning the Woman's Party. Moreover, all along she suspected that emotional appeals could at times be more effective than rational ones. Yet none of these things were quite to the point in Catt's calculations. To her, the Woman's Party gloried in confrontation and seemed to operate under the illusion that conflictual emotionalism was somehow laudatory. It would not work, nor, she thought, should it work if the woman suffrage movement was to herald the new politics of Catt's Progressive dreams.[62]

Another factor that alienated Catt from the radicals was clashing temperaments. It cannot be neatly separated from more straightforward issues. We know Catt

loved order and organization; that inclination automatically recoiled from the milieu of Alice Paul and the Woman's Party, which Catt believed housed a good many unconventional souls, organizational arrangements, and, of course, tactics. Even the NAWSA sometimes attracted what Catt saw as strange people, but Catt was pleased that they rarely stayed long. She felt they were welcome in the Woman's Party, where disorder was a way of life.

Catt misunderstood how the Woman's Party actually functioned. It may have been unconventional in many ways, but it was not disorganized. In practice Alice Paul commanded it in a remote but far tighter fashion than Catt ever dreamed of doing with the NAWSA. Moreover, the picketers were extremely disciplined generally. But to Catt the Woman's Party was another part of America out of control in a country already blighted by too many other instances of the same thing.[63]

Eventually Peck and Catt conceded that both the NAWSA and the Woman's Party had contributed to the success of the suffrage crusade. While it was true that "an icy gulf existed" between the two groups, "the two organizations worked side by side" in effect.[64] Each had done so by compensating for the limitations of the other. The limitations of the NAWSA spurred the creation of the Woman's Party as a home for militants who could not work for suffrage elsewhere and provided a base for the development of more radical and experimental tactics and strategies. For instance, the Woman's Party and its predecessors created the idea of the suffrage parade and it argued for the federal amendment strategy, both of which Catt's NAWSA adopted. Above all, the Woman's Party's tactical radicalism helped enormously to legitimate the NAWSA: it turned the NAWSA into a respectable vehicle for reform and increased its effectiveness both in attracting women and the public at large. Catt went a bit far in later years when she pretended that "there was no serious quarrel between the two." She was more convincing in her perception that each organization had nothing to apologize for in its respective endeavors.[65] By her lights neither organization was flawless, neither was totally "right," and neither deserved full credit for the adoption of the suffrage amendment.[66]

Conclusion

In reflecting on Carrie Catt as a strategist, we can see how much strategy mattered to her and how much she was involved in its formation and defense. Thinking strategically was natural to her, integral to Catt's very being. No one can have a sense of her as a politician, or recognize her as one, without understanding that strategy was foremost on her mind. This is what it means to say she had an intensely political mind. She had goals, of course, and they meant a lot to her, but she never visualized them apart from strategy. It was not just that she did not approve of "unrealistic" or "unstrategic" idealists. She was totally different from such people just as, in turn, her Progressive form of idealism prevented her from being merely another politician.

Her single-minded pursuit of woman suffrage led Catt to be flexible in strategy and tactics, so flexible indeed that she sometimes seemed to compromise far too much, as in her response to World War I or her tolerance of racism. But she insisted that being practical in this fashion was being moral. It was not the whole of morality, but without it moral idealism was more a self-righteous pose than a relevant program to change the world.

Notes

This essay was originally published as "Strategy," Chapter Nine of Robert Booth Fowler's *Carrie Catt: Feminist Politician* (Boston: Northeastern University Press, 1986), and appears here with the permission of the publisher.

1. C.C. Catt to Ethel M. Smith (Aug. 3, 1917), Carrie Chapman Catt Papers, Library of Congress, Washington, D.C., (hereafter designated as Catt Papers), box 8.

2. C.C. Catt in "Proceedings," 1919 NAWSA Convention, 418, National American Woman Suffrage Association Papers, Library of Congress, Washington, D.C. (hereafter designated as NAWSA Papers), box 84.

3. As they often were. See, for example, Abigail Duniway to Alice Stone Blackwell (Dec. 12, 1913), NAWSA Papers, box 10.

4. C.C. Catt to Jane Addams (Dec. 14, 1914), Catt Papers, box 4; Loretta E. Zimmerman, "Alice Paul and the National Woman's Party," Ph.D. diss., Tulane University, 1964, 245.

5. C.C. Catt to Jane Addams (Nov. 12, 1915), Catt Papers, box 4.

6. Robert E. Riegel, *American Women: A Story of Social Change*, (Rutherford, N.J., 1970), 290; Marie Louise Degen, *The History of the Woman's Peace Party* (1939: New York, 1974), 36, 30; Mercedes M. Randall, *Improper Bostonian: Emily Greene Balch* (New York, 1964), 162, 138; Barbara J. Steinson, *American Women's Activism in World War I* (New York, 1982), chpts. 1 and 3; also see Steinson for "Minutes of the Peace Parade Committee" (Aug. 12, 1914), 10; William L. O'Neill, *Everyone Was Brave: The Rise and Fall of Feminism in America* (Chicago, 1969), 174.

7. "The Flag," *Woman's Protest* 9 (Oct. 1916): 3; "The Suffragist Peace Fiasco," *Woman's Protest* 7 (July 1915): 6-7; "Peace of Politics," *Woman's Protest* 6 (March 1915): 4; "For Woman's Service or Woman Suffrage?" *Woman's Protest* 10 (March 1917): 8; Alice Hill Chittendon, "Our Duty to the State," *Woman's Protest* 10 (April 1917): 3; "Questions for Mrs. Catt To Answer," *Woman's Protest* 11 (Sept. 1917): 16; Grace D. Goodwin, *Anti-Suffrage: Ten Good Reasons* (New York, 1912), 142.

8. C.C. Catt to Executive Council, (Feb. 5, 1917), NAWSA Papers, box 82.

9. Ida Husted Harper, *History of Woman Suffrage*, (New York, 1922), vol. 5: 722-730 and 517; C.C. Catt, "Organized Womanhood," *Woman Voter* 8 (April 1917): 9; J. Stanley Lemons, "The New Woman in the New Era: The Woman Movement From the Great War to the Great Depression," Ph.D. diss., University of Missouri, 1967, 27-28.

10. Steinson, *American Women's Activism*, 237-240 and 308-312; "Third Liberty Loan Drive," *Woman Citizen* 2 (March 30, 1918): 355; also see Mary Summer Boyd, "The Menace to War Workers," *Woman Citizen* 1 (June 9, 1917): 31, for a characteristic expression of concern for mobilized women.

11. "Mrs. Catt Urges Big Drive For More Food," *Woman's Journal* 48 (April 14, 1917): 85-86; Lemons, "The New Woman," 26; Mary G. Peck, *Carrie Chapman Catt* (New York, 1944), 270-272; Ida Tarbell, *All In The Days Work* (New York, 1939), 320-327; David Howard Katz, "Carrie Chapman Catt and the Struggle for Peace," Ph.D. diss., Syracuse University, 1973, 41, 44-45; Steinson, *American Women's Activism*, 313-315.

12. Margaret Robinson, "Woman Suffrage and Pacifism," *Woman Patriot* 1 (April 27, 1918): 3; Margaret Robinson, "Germany's Strongest Allies," *Woman Patriot* 1 (July 6, 1918): 4; "Woman's Suffrage To Please Germans Is Now Urged By Suffrage Leaders," *Woman Patriot* 1 (Oct. 26, 1918): 3; "How Pro-Germans and Pacifists Carried Suffrage In New York," *Woman's Protest* 11 (Nov. 1917): 4-5.

13. "Mrs. Catt and the Schwimmer Peace Plan," *Woman's Protest* 11 (Oct. 1917): 10-11; "Suffragists Have No Part in This War," *Woman Patriot* 1 (July 13, 1918): 4; "Mrs. Catt's Defamation of Her Country," *Woman Patriot* 4 (June 19, 1920): 6; "War Record of Mrs. Carrie Chapman Catt," *Woman Patriot* 1 (Nov. 16, 1918): 3, 5; "Unscrupulous Suffrage Leaders Playing Politics Without Stint Limit with Council of Defense," *Woman Patriot* 1 (Oct. 12, 1918): 1; "Mrs. Catt Again Attacks the Government," *Woman Patriot* 3 (Dec. 27, 1919): 3.

14. C.C. Catt to Maud Wood Park (April 13, 1918), Catt Papers, box P80-5453; *HWS* 5: 736; Steinson, *American Women's Activism*, 319-320.

15. C.C. Catt, speech, "Woman Suffrage As A War Measure," *Woman Citizen* 3 (June 1918), and other speeches on the same theme, see NAWSA Papers, box 83.

16. "Suffrage As A War Measure," *Remonstrance* (Oct. 1917): 7; "Is Suffrage A War Measure?" *Woman Patriot* 1 (Sept. 28, 1918): 4; "Suffrage vs. Patriotism," *Woman's Protest* 11 (May 1917): 5.

17. Richard Hofstadter, *The Age of Reform: From Bryan to F.D.R.* (1955; New York, 1960), 275.

18. For example, C.C. Catt, statement, Committee on Judiciary, House of Representatives (1904), 19, Catt Collection, Box 1, folder 13, Sophia Smith Library, Smith College.

19. "The Plan" was in Catt's "Report: Campaign and Survey Committee" (1916), NAWSA Papers, box 82.

20. David Morgan, *Suffragists and Democrats: The Politics of Woman Suffrage in America* (East Lansing, Mich., 1972), chpts. 6 and 7.

21. C.C. Catt, "Report: Campaign and Survey Committee" (1916), 32, NAWSA Papers, box 82.

22. Ibid., 1-2 and passim; C.C. Catt, editor, *Woman Suffrage by Federal Constitutional Amendment* (New York, 1917), 6-7, 35, and passim; C.C. Catt, speech, "The Crisis" (Sept. 7, 1916), "Suffrage: U.S." Catt Collection, Box 6, folder 117.

23. C.C. Catt, "Report: Campaign and Survey Committee" (1916), 34-35, NAWSA Papers, box 82.

24. Morgan, *Suffragists and Democrats*, 112; C.C. Catt to Ida H. Harper (Oct. 14, 1921), Catt Papers, box 5; Inez Haynes Irwin, *Angels and Amazons: A Hundred Years of American Women*, (1933; New York, 1974), 372; Mari Jo Buhle and Paul Buhle, eds. *The Concise History of Woman Suffrage* (Urbana, Ill., 1978), 38; also see Alice Blackwell's report on Catt's calculations in the Blackwell Papers, Library of Congress, box 36.

25. C.C. Catt, *An Address to the Legislature of the United States* (New York, 1919), 19-22; C.C. Catt, *An Address to the Congress of the United States* (New York, 1917), 8, 17, 19.

26. See "Handbook" and "Proceedings," 1916 Convention.

27. See, for example, Anna Howard Shaw to C.C. Catt, (July 1916 [two letters], Sept. 1916, and Jan. 4, 1916, NAWSA Papers, box 27.

28. C.C. Catt to Sue White (May 16, 1918), Sue White Collection, Box 2, folder 21, Schlesinger Library, Radcliffe College; Aileen S. Kraditor, *Ideas of the Woman Suffrage Movement: 1890-1920*, (New York, 1965), 173; Paul E. Fuller, *Laura Clay and the Woman's Rights Movement*, (Lexington, 1975), chpt. 9, and the 1919 NAWSA Convention "Proceedings," 13-27, NAWSA Papers, box 84; also see Dewey W. Grantham, *Southern Progressivism: The Reconciliation of Progress and Tradition* (Knoxville, 1983), 200-217.

29. C.C. Catt, *An Address to the Legislature*, 1-23.

30. Amelia R. Fry, interviewer, *Conversations with Alice Paul: Woman Suffrage and the Equal Rights Amendment*, (Berkeley, 1976), section I, Schlesinger Library, Radcliffe College.

31. Ibid., 96 and 106-107.

32. Robert McHenry, *Liberty's Women*, (Springfield, Mass., 1980), 28, 37-38, 272, 319-320; Zimmerman, "Alice Paul and the National Woman's Party," 40; Caroline Katzenstein, *Lifting the Curtain*, (Philadelphia, 1955), 165-200; Inez Haynes Irwin, *The Story of the Woman's Party*, (1921; New York, 1971), 12 and Part 1, chpt. 5; *HWS* 5: 380-381; Penelope P.B. Huse, "Appeals to Congress," in NAWSA, *Victory: How Women Won It*, (New York, 1940), 103; Anna H. Shaw, "Tells of the Stand of the Union," *Woman's Journal* 45 (Feb. 14, 1914): 54; also see *Woman's Journal* throughout 1913 and 1914 (vols. 44-45) on the Congressional Union; Andrew Sinclair, *The Better Half: The Emancipation of the American Woman*, (New York, 1965), 300-304; Irwin, *Angels and Amazons*, 357; Carrie Chapman Catt and Nettie Rogers Shuler, *Woman Suffrage and Politics: The Inner Story of the Suffrage Movement*, (1923; Seattle, 1970), 255; Inez H. Irwin to Maud Wood Park (March 14, 1921), NAWSA Papers, box 17.

33. Anna Howard Shaw to Harriet Laidlaw (Aug. 16, 1917), Laidlaw Collection, Box 8, folder 137, Schlesinger Library, Radcliffe College.

34. Ibid.

35. See, for example, Anna H. Shaw to Rosamond Danielson (March 11, 1914) and Anna H. Shaw to C.C. Catt (Oct. 14, 1916, and March 12, 1916), all in NAWSA Papers, box 27.

36. Alice Stone Blackwell to C.C. Catt (Sept. 4, 1929), Blackwell Papers, box 12; by the 1930s, however, Blackwell and Alice Paul were corresponding fairly regularly; see NAWSA Papers, box 23.

37. Fry, *Conversations with Alice Paul*, 96-98.

38. Zimmerman, "Alice Paul and the National Woman's Party," chpt. 3 and, 65; Sinclair, *Better Half*, 303-304; C.C. Catt to Harriet Laidlaw (May 23, 1912), Laidlaw Collection, Box 7, folder 101; Fry, *Conversations with Alice Paul*, 324.

39. Anna Howard Shaw to Harriet Laidlaw (June 5, 1915), Laidlaw Collection, Box 7, folder 101.

40. Paul claimed that Catt announced no compromise was possible; Fry, *Conversations with Alice Paul*, 202-203.

41. For example, Sue White to C.C. Catt (April 27, 1918; May 9, 1918; and May 16, 1918), Sue White Collection, Box 2, folder 21.

42. C.C. Catt to Mrs. Leslie Warner (April 24, 1918), Sue White Collection, Box 2, folder 21; C.C. Catt to Maud Wood Park (Dec. 11, 1918), Carrie Chapman Catt Collection, Box 4, folder 33, Schlesinger Library, Radcliffe College.

43. C.C. Catt to Sue White (July 20, 1918), Sue White Collection, Box 2, folder 21.

44. C.C. Catt to Clara Hyde (May 29, 1911), Catt Papers, box 6: Eleanor Flexner, *Century of Struggle: The Woman's Rights Movement in the United States*, (1959; New York, 1973), 287; C.C. Catt, "Their First Convention" (1920), Catt Papers, box P80-5456; Sinclair, *Better Half*, 330.

45. C.C. Catt to Sue White (May 6, 1918), Sue White Collection, Box 2, folder 21.

46. Catt, "Report: Campaign and Survey Committee" (1916), 30.

47. Rose Young to C.C. Catt (Aug. 8, 1916), Blackwell Papers, box 36.

48. Susan B. Anthony to Alice Stone Blackwell (June 14, 1872), Blackwell Papers, box 9, in which she enunciates the classic position that Catt followed.

49. C.C. Catt to Jane Addams (Jan. 4, 1915), Catt Papers, box 4.

50. C.C. Catt to Joseph Tumulty (Jan. 19, 1917), Catt Papers, box 9; Catt and Shuler, *Woman Suffrage and Politics*, chpt. 11; *HWS* 5: 714; C.C. Catt to Joseph Tumulty (May 3, 1918), Catt Papers, box 9; C.C. Catt, statement (May 21, 1915), Catt Papers, box P80-5459; Morgan, *Suffragists and Democrats*, chpts. 9 and 10; Grace Sample McClure to Alda Wilson (March 20, 1947), Catt Papers, box 9; Maud Wood Park, *Front Door Lobby* (Boston, 1960), is the fullest account.

51. C.C. Catt, "The Suffrage Platform," *Woman's Journal* 46 (June 12, 1915): 184; C.C. Catt, "If We Win in New York," *Woman's Journal* 46 (Oct. 30, 1915): 345; C.C. Catt, "Opening of the Convention," *Woman Citizen* 2 (Dec. 15, 1917): 54.

52. C.C. Catt, "Opening of the Convention," 54.

53. C.C. Catt, "What Every Senator Knows," *Woman Citizen* 2 (March 2, 1918): 263; C.C. Catt to Maud Wood Park (April 18, 1933), Catt Papers, box 7; Catt and Shuler, *Woman Suffrage and Politics*, 327-328.

54. Fry, *Conversations with Alice Paul*, 209-241.

55. C.C. Catt, "Why We Did Not Picket the White House," *Good Housekeeping* 66 (March 1918): 32.

56. C.C. Catt to Mary G. Peck (April 20, 1913), quoted in Peck, *Carrie Chapman Catt*, 210.

57. C.C. Catt to Alice Paul, quoted in Zimmerman, "Alice Paul and the National Woman's Party," 238-239.

58. C.C. Catt, "Excuses Only," *Woman Citizen* 1 (Aug. 11, 1917): 179.

59. "Militant Methods In Action," *Woman's Protest* 10 (Nov. 1916): 5-6; "Organized Obtrusion for a Campaign of Clamor," *Woman's Protest* 9 (July 1916): 3; "Pickets Determine to Persecute President," *Woman Patriot* 1 (Aug. 3, 1918): 1; "Recent Militant Freaks," *Remonstrance* (Oct. 1913): 1; "More Proof that 'Pickets and Conservative' Suffragists Have a 'Mutual Working Agreement,'" *Woman Patriot* 2 (Jan. 4, 1918): 8; "Do American Suffragists Favor Militancy?" *Woman Patriot* 4 (Dec. 1913): 12; "Picketing and 'Pestering,'" *Woman Patriot* 1 (Aug. 24, 1918): 8.

60. See, for example, C.C. Catt, "Pickets Are Behind the Times," *Woman Citizen* 1 (Nov. 1917): 470; Zimmerman, "Alice Paul and the National Woman's Party," 243; 50,000 is undoubtedly too high a figure for the Woman's Party; so is two million for the NAWSA. But the proportions are roughly correct.

61. C.C. Catt to Sue White (May 6, 1918), Sue White Collection, Box 2, folder 21.

62. C.C. Catt to Millicent G. Fawcett (Oct. 19, 1909), Catt Papers, box 5; C.C. Catt to E. Garrison (Aug. 1, 1914), quoted in Riegel, *American Feminists*, 178; "Mrs. Catt's International Address," *Woman's Journal* 39 (June 27, 1908): 101-103; C.C. Catt, "Their First Convention" (1920), Catt Papers, box P80-5456; Harriot Stanton Blatch and Alma Lutz, *Challenging Years: The Memoirs of Harriot Stanton Blatch*, (New York, 1940), 129, 203.

63. Susan D. Becker, *The Origins of the Equal Rights Amendment: American Feminism Between the Wars*, (Westport, Conn., 1981), 89; C.C. Catt to Millicent G. Fawcett (Oct., 19, 1909), Catt Papers, box 5; Shaw, "Tells of the Stand of the Union," *Woman's Journal* 45 (Feb. 14, 1914): 54; Zimmerman, "Alice Paul and the National Woman's Party," 97.

64. Mary G. Peck, "Changing the Mind of a Nation: The Story of Carrie Chapman Catt," *World Tomorrow* 13 (Sept. 1930): 358-361.

65. C.C. Catt to Eileen Morrissey (March 4, 1933), Catt Papers, box P80-5458; on NAWSA borrowings, see, for example, Rheta Childe Dorr, *A Woman of Fifty*, (New York, 1924), 222.

66. Others agree: Morgan, *Suffragists and Democrats*, 186; Blatch and Lutz, *Challenging Years*, 131, 199; Buhle, *Concise History*, 38; Irwin, *Angels and Amazons*, 392-393; Sinclair, *Better Half*, 304.

MINNIE FISHER CUNNINGHAM'S BACK DOOR LOBBY IN TEXAS:
Political Maneuvering in a One-Party State

Judith N. McArthur

Editor's Introduction: In this essay, Judith McArthur tells the fascinating story of the Texas suffragists who, shrewdly exploiting a rift within the state's Democratic Party, achieved something that had long seemed impossible: they made it politically expedient to support woman suffrage in a Southern state. In keeping with Carrie Chapman Catt's "Winning Plan," Texas suffragists in 1918 sought and won primary suffrage, the right to vote in the state-wide elections through which the political parties selected their candidates—an important gain in a one-party state. More significantly, this victory was a major breakthrough in the virtually "Solid South," setting the stage for ratification in Texas, which became one of the few Southern states to approve the Nineteenth Amendment. If the South had remained solidly opposed to ratification, the amendment would have failed.

This victory did not come easily. Texas suffragists were opposed by anti-suffrage forces that were powerful and entrenched, and amply funded by the liquor industry. Their implacable enemy, Governor James E. Ferguson, a well-known "wet" (opponent of prohibition), had led the anti-suffrage forces at the 1916 National Democratic Convention. Driven from office in 1917 in a scandal, he was down but not out—and he was determined to return to office.

Texas suffrage leader Minnie Fisher Cunningham and her supporters, however, outfoxed even the wily Ferguson, beating him at his own game of political maneuvering. By 1918, suffragists had long since learned that, if they were to win, they would have to convince politicians that it was in their interest to support woman suffrage. But this was particularly difficult to accomplish in the South where there was such hostility to woman suffrage and (in most Southern states) no two-party competition to exploit. Yet Cunningham and her associates found a way to convince politicians it was expedient to assist them by skillfully playing one faction within the Democratic Party against another, and making it clear that women voters would support a politician who welcomed them into the political fold. Cunningham and the Texas suffragists also demonstrated their ability—and willingness—to exploit ethnic tensions and war-time anxieties and cater to racial prejudice, as did the male politicians. But in the process, they prevented the

re-election of James Ferguson, who, if victorious, would have been in office at the time of the ratification campaign and, in all likelihood, prevented Texas from ratifying the Nineteenth Amendment.

This essay is a vivid reminder of the fact that suffragists did not win the battle in 1920 by appealing to politicians' sense of justice alone. As McArthur clearly illustrates, "front door lobbying" was aided and abetted by "back door lobbying." To win, suffragists found it necessary to master the intricacies of partisan politics and, at times, embrace demagogic tactics—as unsavory as it might seem. Some suffragists found political maneuvering distasteful; others found it exciting. Some, including Minnie Fisher Cunningham, found that they were quite good at it.

Impressed with her success in Texas, Carrie Chapman Catt called Cunningham to Washington to be the Secretary for the NAWSA's Congressional Committee headed by Maud Wood Park. Thus Cunningham became part of the core group of suffragist-politicians that successfully lobbied Congress for the passage of the Nineteenth Amendment.

★　★　★　★　★

I N THE SPRING OF 1893, thirty-nine women and nine men met in Dallas to form the Texas Equal Rights Association, the state's first suffrage organization. One of the most outspoken feminists in the small group, Dr. Grace Danforth, M.D., warned that hard work and justice alone would probably not bring success. "Every concession of right or suffrage that has ever been made to the people has proceeded from the need of the powers that be for the votes of the people," she pointed out. Danforth then made a perceptive prediction: "The Republican party needed the votes of the negroes and the negroes were enfranchised. It will not be long until some party will need the votes of the women, and then we will be granted the right of suffrage."[1]

Grace Danforth's observation was optimistic as well as cynical, for in the 1890s it appeared that Southern Democrats might be receptive to votes for women—White women—as the "solution" to Negro suffrage that the Republican Party had imposed after the Civil War. As Southern legislatures pondered ways to restore White supremacy, the National American Woman Suffrage Association (NAWSA) created a special Southern Committee to launch an organizing effort in the former Confederacy. Money from the Southern Committee helped bring the Texas Equal Rights Association and other Southern suffrage societies into being, but their aspirations were thwarted as state legislatures and local vigilantes invented ways to reestablish White supremacy without sacrificing patriarchy. Legal restrictions—especially the poll tax (which Texas approved in 1902) and the literacy test—now supplanted violence, fraud, and intimidation in disfranchising the majority of Blacks. Many lower-class Whites who had been attracted to the Populist Party's challenge to conservative Democratic rule in the 1890s were also winnowed out of the electorate in the process.[2]

The result was one-party government that, in combination with deeply rooted cultural obstacles, made the South barren ground for suffragists. Anti-feminism, negrophobia, and the gospel of states' rights created formidable obstacles to the suffrage movement. The lack of viable Republican opposition in most of the Southern states made it impossible for suffragists to exploit party competition, a strategy that helped advance the cause in the North. Consequently, most suffrage campaigns below the Mason-Dixon line met repeated failure. None of the Southern states gave women full suffrage, and the opposition of their Senators and Congressmen killed, year after year, the federal bill that eventually became the Nineteenth Amendment. When it finally passed in 1919, seventy percent of Southern congressional representatives voted in opposition.[3]

Minnie Fisher Cunningham, 1900
LIBRARY OF CONGRESS

By that time, however, Southern suffragists had won three partial victories that were to have important consequences nationally: the right to vote in primary elections in Arkansas (1917) and Texas (1918); and in presidential elections in Tennessee (1919). The NAWSA still needed to persuade thirty-six state legislatures to ratify the amendment, and some of those votes would have to be found in the South. Southern Democratic opponents of ratification, led by Governor Ruffin Pleasant of Louisiana, called upon the thirteen Southern state legislatures to unite to defeat the amendment, and several of them passed rejection resolutions.[4] The three partial-suffrage states, however, helped clinch the victory in just fourteen months by providing the only ratifying votes from the former Confederacy.

What accounts for these isolated successes in the most anti-suffrage region in the country? In the case of Texas, the victory was the result of skillful political maneuvering by state suffrage leaders, who found a way to exploit political rivalry even in the absence of a two-party system. The women and their male allies left a paper trail that clearly contradicts the legislators' public professions that primary suffrage was a reward for women's patriotic work on the homefront during World War I. Although Grace Danforth did not live to see it, the supposedly impossible came to pass in a one-party Southern state: women were enfranchised because politicians needed their votes.

In 1918 the Texas Democratic Party was temporarily rent by issues that divided it into bitterly feuding factions. The president of the Texas Equal Suffrage

Association shrewdly exploited the rift by back door lobbying; she invited collusion with a group of legislators who had self-interested motives for helping the cause. Facing a hotly contested primary election that it appeared likely to lose, the Progressive-prohibitionist wing of the party made a quiet bargain with suffrage leaders. It pushed a bill permitting women to vote in primary elections through the legislature in return for a promise that they would turn out en masse to vote for its gubernatorial candidate.

Early Failures

Until 1918 the Texas suffrage movement shared the same history of discouragement and defeat as its counterparts in the rest of the South. Like the other Southern societies that the NAWSA helped establish in the 1890s, the Texas Equal Rights Association had a short, unproductive life. Still tainted in Southern eyes by its abolitionist origins, woman suffrage evoked little positive response among women whose conservative culture idealized retiring, refined ladyhood "protected" by chivalrous manhood. One by one, the Southern suffrage associations disbanded, lapsed into dormancy, or ceased to be more than sporadically active. Unsuccessful in recruiting members and raising money, the Texas Equal Rights Association had stopped holding meetings by 1896. Another organizing attempt in 1903 produced the Texas Woman Suffrage Association that expired in all but name two years later when its president moved to New York.

In the 1910s, as increasing numbers of women were drawn into the Progressive movement and discovered the ballot's potential usefulness as a weapon for social reform, the Southern suffrage movement was reborn and revitalized. New associations were founded and dormant ones like the Texas Woman Suffrage Association revived; it was reactivated in 1913 and within three years had eighty local affiliates.[5] Yet the second generation of Southern suffrage leaders, enthusiastic, hard-working, and backed by state associations that now counted membership in the thousands, faced the familiar pattern of defeat as they lobbied state legislatures for constitutional amendments to enfranchise women. The experience of the Texas organization, which changed its name to Texas Equal Suffrage Association (TESA) in 1916, was typical: constitutional amendments were voted down decisively in the biennial legislative sessions of 1915 and 1917. The margin of defeat was even larger in 1917 than in 1915, and alternative bills for primary and presidential suffrage failed to come to a vote.[6]

Discouraging results like these in every part of the nation helped convince NAWSA president Carrie Chapman Catt to devise a new strategy, the famous "Winning Plan" adopted in 1916. Thereafter the NAWSA gave priority to securing a federal amendment and continued state work selectively, mounting campaigns only where there was a strong likelihood of success. State presidents in the unpromising South were instructed to focus on partial enfranchisement—primary or presidential suffrage.[7] Legislators could grant these partial measures as

amendments to existing election laws without the public referenda required for constitutional amendments, which had often been expensive failures. And since "white primary" laws restricted Black participation, primary suffrage would circumvent the conservative argument that woman suffrage would bring huge numbers of Black women to the polls. (This reality unfortunately proved no obstacle to anti-suffragists determined to manipulate debate on the "negro problem.") When Texas suffragists failed again in 1917, it appeared that the state would remain part of the "Solid South" against woman suffrage.

Suffragists Versus Governor Ferguson

In the months that followed, the governor of Texas, James E. Ferguson, and the president of the TESA, Minnie Fisher Cunningham of Galveston, emerged as protagonists in a political drama that unexpectedly made Texas women voters. Both were strong personalities and they first clashed publicly at the Democratic National Convention in 1916 in St. Louis, where suffragists were demonstrating for a plank supporting suffrage by federal amendment. The convention's compromise endorsement of suffrage on a state-by-state basis merely stiffened the conservatives' determination to keep it out of their own states. Governor Ferguson, leading the Texas delegation, infuriated the women by presenting the dissenting minority report in a theatrical speech studded with injunctions about "woman's place." A member of the Resolutions Committee who defended the suffrage plank was howled down by the Texas delegation. Minnie Fisher Cunningham, who had a flair for political theater herself, retorted by leading the state suffrage delegation in a counter demonstration: the Texas suffragists carried a Lone Star Flag draped with mourning that Cunningham improvised by cutting up a black crepe dress.[8]

Both Cunningham and Ferguson shared a common allegiance to the Democratic party, but their political supporters came from different ends of the socio-economic spectrum. Suffragists were disproportionately urban women from the middle and upper classes, the wives and daughters of professional men. Minnie Fisher Cunningham, who in 1901 had become one of the first women to earn a pharmacy degree from the University of Texas, was married to an attorney and belonged to the selective Woman's Wednesday Club of Galveston and the Woman's Health Protective Association, a citywide coalition of activists and reformers. Although Cunningham's interest in suffrage far exceeded her rather nominal involvement in voluntary associations, many TESA women were active in club-inspired civic work and often at odds with entrenched political interests over social reform issues.[9]

Governor Ferguson had started out as a struggling farm youth, but after several years of drifting and manual labor he had studied law, married well, and opened a bank. He had promoted himself for governor as a successful self-made businessman and a populist who sympathized with farmers' problems, especially the high rate of tenancy (in excess of fifty percent) and the poor quality of rural schools. Ferguson's studied platform image of folksy but shrewd "Farmer Jim" won him a

large following among native-born rural Whites. He made education a focal point of his populism, denouncing the University of Texas as an elitist institution where rich men's sons were educated with the tax dollars of struggling farmers and workers. When he tried to purge the university of half a dozen professors whose politics he disliked and vetoed its appropriation in 1917, organized women were prominent in the coalition that rallied to its defense. An Austin suffragist, fuming in her diary, expressed the common opinion of elite women: the governor was "an ignorant, common personage." Stronger adjectives tempted her, "—but not having the vocabulary of a sea captain...I can't express what I think of Jim Ferguson."[10]

Elite women particularly disliked Ferguson because he enjoyed strong support among opponents of prohibition, including the state's substantial populations of German, Czech, and Mexican immigrants. Prohibition had been the dominant political issue in Texas for a decade, splitting the Democratic party into "wet" and "dry" camps. More than a moral question or a social problem, prohibition took center stage as an issue of political corruption and the power of special interests. Since most organized women sympathized with the drys, anti-prohibitionism went hand in hand with anti-suffragism. The politically strong brewing interests helped fund the "Texas Business Men's Association," a powerful and underhanded lobbying organization that distributed anti-suffrage and anti-prohibition boilerplate to hundreds of county newspapers. Brewery money, raised by a sixty-cents-per-barrel-sold assessment, and the organized ethnic vote helped put Ferguson in office and regularly elected anti-prohibition, anti-suffrage majorities in the Texas Legislature.[11]

Consequently, Cunningham and the TESA rejoiced when the governor's enemies began scrutinizing his questionable administrative expenditures and flexible ethics in the summer of 1917. Suffrage activity was put on hold while they quietly assisted the legislative investigation against Ferguson and publicized his misdeeds.[12] When he was impeached in August 1917 on multiple counts of misusing public funds and barred from again seeking public office, the Democratic Party was left bitterly divided in Texas and the political future unpredictable.

A New Governor Hesitates

Governor Ferguson's departure elevated the young lieutenant governor, William P. Hobby, to the governorship. A thirty-nine-year-old newspaper publisher nurtured in the party's conservative inner circle, Hobby, like Ferguson, had been elected as an anti-prohibitionist; the influential conservatives who backed him also opposed woman suffrage. Hobby himself took no public stand on the issue, but Cunningham knew from his response to a legislative questionnaire sent out by her predecessor that he was privately receptive. This and the post-impeachment political climate encouraged her to seek the NAWSA's approval for another attempt to secure primary suffrage. The revelations of the legislative investigation had lent credence to the demand for the woman's ballot to "clean house" in political affairs.

"It has been a full six weeks since I have found any man with the temerity to look us in the eye and say he opposed women's voting in the face of the outrageous condition that has been proven to prevail in our state government," Cunningham reported to Carrie Chapman Catt that fall.[13]

Cunningham pinned her hopes on the near certainty that Hobby would have to call the Thirty-fifth Legislature back into special session to deal with problems caused by the Ferguson impeachment and mobilization for the First World War. But she had no illusions that women could succeed solely on the claim of morality and political housecleaning unless they could make these issues seem more compelling than in the past. The fact that the state constitution disfranchised men in uniform while permitting resident aliens, many of whom were German-born, to vote after applying for their preliminary citizenship papers seemed to Cunningham to open a window of opportunity for a suffrage bill. Women's votes could be presented as a way of compensating for those of husbands and brothers in the army, offsetting the ballots of unnaturalized aliens, who were known to be "wet" and pro-Ferguson and suspected of being disloyal. The TESA hoped to arouse public sentiment against the fact that "enemy aliens" could vote, while loyal American women were disfranchised. If the legislators held a fourth special session, Cunningham told Catt, "Perhaps we can prove to them that they need us even if they do not want us!"[14]

Cunningham could not make the case to the legislators, however, unless Hobby summoned them back to Austin, and he deliberately delayed. War mobilization was inflaming the divisive prohibition question, and a special session would make it a front-page issue. Hobby would have to run for the gubernatorial nomination in his own right in the July 1918 primary and feared that any position he took on the liquor question would cost votes. It would be safer not to convene another session until after the election, by which time Congress would probably have passed a prohibition amendment and resolved the issue. Governor Hobby took the same approach to suffrage, putting off the TESA representatives as they repeatedly tried to extract a promise that primary suffrage would be part of the agenda of any special session.[15]

Pressure from the Progressive spokesmen in the party, and increasing public and War Department concern over reports of free-flowing liquor and open prostitution near Texas's numerous army training camps and military airfields, eventually persuaded Hobby to capitulate and call the special session. Popular sentiment was increasing for prohibition as a war measure, and Hobby himself was beginning to think it might be justifiable.[16] But he remained immovable on woman suffrage; there was no reason to think that it would pass the same legislature that had already rejected three different bills, and endorsement would cost him votes among the anti-prohibitionists. His message to the legislature did not mention suffrage or even amending the election laws, which would have opened the door for a primary suffrage bill. Since a special session could not consider any measures except those submitted by the governor, the TESA's options once again appeared to have been foreclosed.

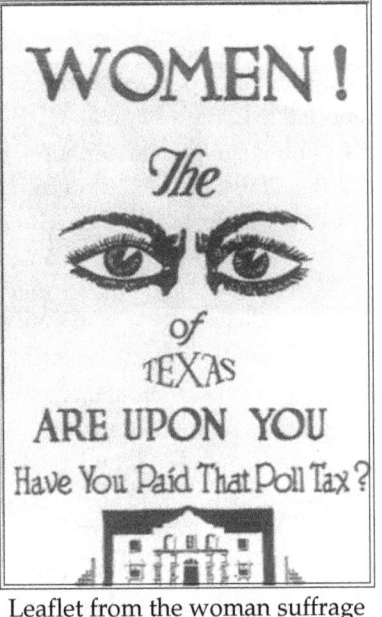

Minnie Fisher Cunningham
AUSTIN PUBLIC LIBRARY

Leaflet from the woman suffrage
campaign in Texas
AUSTIN PUBLIC LIBRARY

The Back Door Lobby

A potential friend had failed the Texas suffragists, but a confirmed enemy would inadvertently be their salvation. The impeached James Ferguson had declared himself a candidate for governor in 1918, contending that the legal ban against him was invalid because he had resigned from office before the senate voted for conviction. A peerless stump speaker, Ferguson had the backing of the powerful brewing interests, and he stood a good chance of winning a plurality in the primary. His political resurrection worried the Progressive-prohibitionist wing of the Democratic Party, who knew he would get the wet vote, especially the manipulated Hispanic portion of it along the Mexican border, where political bosses ruled. James Ferguson's candidacy also worried the old-line conservatives, who shared Ferguson's aversion to prohibition and woman suffrage but feared his strong appeal to tenant farmers and the working class. When the suffragists called on Governor Hobby late in January 1918, Cunningham reported, "We found him somewhat exercised over Mr. Ferguson's activity, and we left him more so. We had nothing cheerful to tell him along that line."[17]

However, Cunningham was an astute politician, and as Ferguson's star rose she quietly began to negotiate a back door approach to suffrage. She knew that Representative Charles Metcalfe of San Angelo, a friend of the TESA, was actively supporting Hobby's campaign and that he had a son in the army. Before the date for the special session had even been announced, Cunningham asked Metcalfe by letter to help persuade Hobby to submit a primary suffrage bill. She offered two

reasons: the necessity to support the troops overseas by electing a loyal American government and not one chosen by "a solid pro-German vote"; and the very real possibility that a divided vote among the prohibitionists would allow Ferguson to win the governor's race by a plurality. She hinted broadly that it would be in Hobby's own best interest to submit the suffrage bill: "A large number of new and grateful voters would be his salvation, I should think!"[18]

Representative Metcalfe ignored the reference to the "German menace" and took the hint, as Cunningham had hoped, about the real danger to his candidate. The prohibitionists had lost the gubernatorial election in 1910 by fielding multiple candidates who split the dry vote. They had lost again in 1914 (to Ferguson) by offering a weak candidate with doubtful prohibition credentials (like Hobby) who had failed to rally the drys. Several prohibitionists had already announced their interest in running for governor, and as Ferguson's campaign gathered momentum, it appeared that the Progressives were once again poised to snatch defeat from the jaws of victory. Metcalfe asked Cunningham if she could truly guarantee to deliver the woman vote for Hobby. He cautioned her to keep their discussion confidential:

> Please write me at once saying how the women of the state to your knowledge would vote in the Governors [sic] race if they have the ballot: not officially—but so I can use your letter if I wish to do so, not for publication, but as I see fit otherwise. It seems to me very probable if you know they will vote right, that…a bill may be passed….

He added bluntly that success would also depend on the suffragists' maintaining a low profile, that he did not want to be pestered by "the old maids and *masterful* women, or *militants*. They get in the way & tire me and the others."[19]

Immediately, Cunningham furnished the "unofficial" letter for Metcalfe to circulate. In it she explained that at the last TESA board meeting the suffrage leaders had passed a resolution to support Hobby's candidacy if he submitted their primary suffrage bill with a recommendation for passage. Some of the other candidates were strong friends of suffrage, but their chances of winning were slim. It was better strategy to back the incumbent and persuade him to adopt suffrage convictions. Knowing full well what cards the other political players were holding, Cunningham laid her aces on the table:

> …vote in hand we will quite naturally concentrate on the man who enfranchised us. And with the Pro's divided, with the purchasable, corrupt, ignorant, pro-German vote going to Ferguson, whomsoever the women of Texas concentrate on in the July primaries, that man is just as good as elected. But without us, it is Ferguson with a plurality,…[20]

Representative Metcalfe had worked with the suffragists long enough to know that they had amassed complete political profiles of every representative and senator. He asked Cunningham for a breakdown of legislators according to their

views on suffrage—supportive, opposed, or undecided—for his "confidential use" so that he could begin "all the lining up possible" before the lawmakers assembled in Austin at the end of February.[21] Although Metcalfe felt certain that women's ballots could offset the wet vote that Hobby would lose by supporting suffrage, the young acting governor was not inclined to take the risk. His promise to support dry zones around the military cantonment towns, which he could justify to wets by pleading pressure from the War Department, prompted the dry candidates to withdraw and throw him their support. Expecting to draw votes from both sides with his "win the war" platform, Hobby avoided the controversial suffrage issue like a virus. When the suffragists urged him to reconsider, he replied that he would ask to have the election laws brought up *only* if presented with a petition signed by a majority of both houses of the legislature.

It was a clever response: whether they succeeded or failed, he would be absolved of responsibility. If Hobby anticipated failure he underestimated the determination of women like Nonie B. Mahoney, of the TESA's Dallas chapter, who helped staff the special suffrage headquarters set up during the called session. An anti-suffrage Dallas representative told Mahoney that he would not believe women really wanted the vote unless five thousand of his townswomen petitioned for it; four days later Mahoney lugged a suitcase to the speaker's rostrum and presented the petition—with *ten* thousand signatures. When the suffragists had succeeded "after many hours of labor" in collecting signatures from two-thirds of the legislators, prompting the necessary action from Hobby's office at last, Metcalfe and several co-sponsors immediately introduced a primary suffrage amendment.[22]

Since the deadline for paying the poll tax had passed, Metcalfe and company were careful to specify that women would be exempted for the current year. Fear of Ferguson pushed wet anti-suffrage conservatives into a reluctant alliance with the Progressive-prohibitionist faction, and the bill moved through the legislature quickly. Within four days after it was introduced on March 12 the bill had been passed to its third reading and cleared the House with seventy-one percent of the vote. Less than a week later, the Senate gave it an even larger majority.[23] Governor Hobby signed the bill on March 26, four months before the primary election.

Sidestepping the "Negro Problem"

As Cunningham had foreseen, woman suffrage passed in Texas in 1918 because it was a subtle and effective way of outflanking Ferguson.[24] Restricting women to primary suffrage secured the benefit of their votes without subjecting legislators to accusations of betraying the White race. A provision requiring each woman to fill out her registration blank in her own hand was added as a de facto literacy test to keep out the "illiterate negro women and the Mexican women along the border" who would be likely to vote for Ferguson. Minnie Fisher Cunningham was personally opposed to this restriction but conceded

that it was necessary to appease influential conservatives like the senate's Rienzi M. Johnston. Editor and part owner of the *Houston Post,* Johnston was Hobby's political and journalistic mentor and a spokesman for the party's conservative wing. The edition of the *Post* that announced the bill's passage carried Johnston's dire warning that allowing Black women to vote would bring Black men into the primaries and put an end to the state's political sovereignty. The paper refrained from mentioning that Johnston, like other conservatives torn between personal conviction and political necessity, had quietly cast an affirmative vote.[25]

Like other Southern suffragists of this era, Cunningham countered that the "negro problem" was a smoke screen; the majority of Blacks had long been disfranchised. In Texas some 100,000 Black men had voted in the 1890s; by the early twentieth century the poll tax and the White primary had reduced the number to about 5,000. Anti-suffragists nevertheless thundered about the danger of "placing the ballot in the hands of 300,000 negro women and prostitutes." Rienzi Johnston claimed that 10,000 Northern women were prodding the federal government to enforce the Fifteenth Amendment in the South.[26]

The TESA's decision not to admit African American members needs to be judged within this context. Perpetually on the defensive and unable to puncture this emotional negrophobic rhetoric with logic and facts, Cunningham and her followers had no realistic hope of succeeding unless they distanced themselves from Black women. Consequently, the suffrage leadership was taken aback when, in the midst of the post-victory registration campaign to enroll the new women voters, a Black women's club applied for TESA membership. In the letters they exchanged pondering the dilemma none of the White suffragists expressed any personal objection to admitting the Black women; the issue was their enemies' potential reaction. What the legislature had given it could take away, and conservatives would have raised an angry cry that they had been right all along: Black women were flocking to the polls.

Ultimately, the TESA officers made the politically expedient decision. Minnie Fisher Cunningham followed Carrie Chapman Catt's advice to tell the Black women "that you will be able to get the vote for women more easily if they do not embarrass you by asking for membership." On her own, she added resourcefully that since the application was without precedent it would require a convention vote and the next convention would not meet until 1919, by which time she hoped that the federal amendment enfranchising all women would have passed.[27]

Suffragists Keep Their Promise

The more immediate concern for Cunningham was fulfilling her part of the political bargain that had brought the suffragists' victory. Representative Metcalfe urged a massive registration campaign, reminding her of the danger that many women would not want to vote, and some country women would even vote for

Ferguson. "I hope tho [sic] to be vindicated in my statements that they *will vote* and for the *right men*," Metcalfe reminded Cunningham. The NAWSA was equally concerned. If Ferguson regained control of the statehouse, Texas would vote against ratifying the federal suffrage amendment that was almost certain to pass within the next year. Carrie Chapman Catt quietly diverted a thousand dollars to the Texas suffragists, with instructions to use it to get out the anti-Ferguson vote.[28]

Characteristically, Cunningham had an inspiration of her own: a woman candidate on the ticket to help draw women to the polls. At its convention in May, the TESA unanimously adopted a resolution urging Annie Webb Blanton, a professor of English at North Texas State Normal College to run for state superintendent of public instruction. Since public education was conceded to be woman's domain and several other states had already elected female superintendents, a woman candidate was unlikely to arouse significant male criticism. In Blanton the suffragists also had a proven candidate: she had just completed a term as the first woman president of the Texas State Teachers' Association. As a professional, she could also be expected to appeal strongly to educated urban women, the ones most likely to vote for Hobby.[29]

Once Blanton had been persuaded to make the race, Cunningham channeled all of the TESA's energy and resources into signing up as many women as possible during the seventeen-day registration period that had been substituted for the poll tax. Local equal franchise societies transformed themselves into precinct committees and "suffrage schools" that taught women how to mark ballots. "Women's Hobby Clubs" chauffeured women without transportation to the courthouse and volunteered as hostesses at the registration booths; in the larger cities suffragists persuaded officials to authorize registration substations in popular department stores, permitting women the easy option of registering while they did their errands. "Hobby Club" women stood on downtown street corners to hand out campaign literature and urge registration; they distributed yellow badges, signifying intention to vote, for women to pin on their street clothes.[30]

The suffragists astutely linked registration and voting to war patriotism, stressing women's "duty" to take the place of their absent husbands and brothers at the polls, and urged every woman to turn out in defense of her home and not be a "slacker." Since some 100,000 men were away in the army, it was possible that a large female turnout might decide the election, which added news interest to the registration drive. The large metropolitan newspapers published running tallies of local registrations and speculated that between seventy-five to ninety percent of these women would vote for Hobby. Some 386,000 women ultimately signed up, and Cunningham exulted that "the registration figures are enough to make Ferguson sick."[31]

Faced with an apparent groundswell of female support for Hobby, "Farmer Jim" worked to divide women along rural-urban lines, appealing to country women to vote against "an aristocracy that doesn't care anything more about you than a hog

does for a side-pocket." He urged farm wives not to be influenced by the "pink tea and poodle dog nursing women" of the cities.[32] Ferguson was justly feared for the effectiveness of such rhetoric, and suffragists met it with action. Although residents of towns under 10,000 in population were not legally required to register, suffragists organized Hobby Clubs and registration drives in country precincts to draw out rural women. While Ferguson mounted a populist assault, suffrage leaders countered with a cross-class appeal for gender solidarity by presenting Hobby as the "woman's" candidate.

First, they emphasized how much Hobby's tenure in office had benefitted the female sex. Speakers stressed that a Ferguson victory would mean the repeal of primary suffrage: "If your first vote is not cast for the man who made it possible for you to have a vote, you may never cast a second vote." To engage women who had not actively sought suffrage, they promoted the connection between the candidate and the unprecedented reform legislation or "Hobby laws" passed during the special session: liquor and prostitution outlawed within ten miles of military training camps; the age of consent for girls raised from fifteen to eighteen years of age; and statutory prohibition for the entire state. All were reforms for which women's voluntary associations had lobbied. Campaign flyers addressed "To the Women of Texas" stressed women's indebtedness to Hobby for the realization of their legislative goals. One signed by five women's organizations, including the Woman's Christian Temperance Union, the Federation of Women's Clubs, and the Congress of Mothers, exhorted women to elect "by an OVERWHELMING MAJORITY OUR SPLENDID YOUNG GOVERNOR who speaks through deeds rather than words."[33]

Second, the suffragists made political capital from the old tradition of separate spheres and cultural assumptions about female moral superiority, appealing to women across divisions of class and geography to help save the state. Governor Hobby and his advisors were accusing Ferguson of ties to the German-American Alliance, which had admitted during a United States Senate investigation to having taken an "interest" in his 1914 gubernatorial race. There was also the matter of $156,000 that Ferguson had once borrowed to cover a business debt from friends whose names he refused to reveal; speculation ranged from the brewing interests to the Kaiser himself. The suffragists helped the Hobby forces invert Ferguson's populism and define the contest as a struggle against brewery-manipulated, special-interest politics by urging women to stand together for good government and morality. The cards they distributed for Hobby proclaimed him to be "The Man Whom Good Women Want."[34]

Ferguson on the Defensive

So successful were Cunningham and the suffrage leadership in mobilizing vocal female support for Hobby and helping shape public debate that they made the unimaginable happen in a Southern state: it actually became politically expedient to be *for* suffrage rather than against it. The once reluctant Hobby began

to cultivate his new female constituency and to embrace the pro-woman image that the suffragists had manufactured for him. He urged women to help make Texas safe for democracy by going to the polls and even promised to recommend a constitutional amendment for full suffrage to the next legislature.[35]

Noting the direction of the prevailing political wind, Ferguson abruptly switched tactics and made his own pitch for the female vote. He claimed he had never opposed the *principle* of suffrage for women, only the idea of forcing them to become voters without their consent. His weekly paper, the *Ferguson Forum*, played up the occasional endorsement from a prominent woman, the formation of women's Ferguson clubs, and supportive letters from female readers. By June the *Ferguson Forum* was regularly running long pieces supposedly by "Sally Jane Spottswood," represented as a school teacher in mythical Pine Hollow, Texas, who addressed women directly. Lauding Ferguson as "the proven friend of every mother in the state," she urged country women to register. "Follow your intuition and you can't go wrong," Sally Jane exhorted. "Intuitively you will vote for Ferguson!"[36]

The Ferguson camp repeatedly tried to make an issue of the fact that Hobby's recently acquired enthusiasm for woman suffrage and prohibition was an eleventh-hour conversion for political advantage. The claim that Hobby had given women the vote was "sheer political buncombe," Ferguson jeered. He offered a new hat to any woman who could show that the governor had ever done anything to assist suffrage except sign the bill. A two-part article in the *Ferguson Forum* by "One Who Was There" described how the primary suffrage bill had passed without any assistance from "our young Christian governor and reformed anti-prohibitionist for political reasons." "After this year they are going to charge you good women $1.75 [in poll taxes] to vote," Ferguson pointed out, "but this year you can vote for Hobby for free. Instead of wanting to do something for the women, he wants you to do something for him."[37]

The charge was perfectly true, but it failed to stick. The superheated passions of wartime provided the suffragists with the same kind of political cover that their enemies had so long exploited with the "negro problem." Now the "German menace" made women's enfranchisement appear not only necessary but patriotic. The Progressives who had persuaded Hobby to change his position on the liquor issue had astutely predicted that it could be pulled off with "a show of patriotism" that would smother charges of "flopping to the pros overnight." The same strategy worked for suffrage, as Southern-bred Woodrow Wilson had already demonstrated by taking up the NAWSA's claim that women deserved the vote as a reward for their war work. Using the TESA's variation of this rationale, Hobby, who turned out to be better than anticipated on the hustings, claimed that women had been admitted to the primaries "to offset the votes of those whose carcasses are in this country but whose souls are in Germany." Former governor Tom Campbell hit the campaign trail declaring that "every slacker and every pro-German will vote for James E. Ferguson for Governor and it is up to the good women of this State to kill those votes."[38]

Women Clench Hobby's Victory

When the ballots were counted, both Hobby and Annie Webb Blanton won enormous victories. "'Hurrah for the women!'" R.M. Dudley, who had won nomination to the state senate, wrote jubilantly to Cunningham. "We probably would have elected Hobby anyway, but we know the women clenched it and nailed it down." Governor Hobby's total was more than twice as large as Ferguson's; Blanton won nearly 70,000 more votes than the incumbent superintendent of public instruction and a minor third candidate combined and carried every county except one. About the voters themselves, only anecdotal evidence exists. A Hobby chairman in East Texas, a Ferguson stronghold, reported during registration that many women were saying that they planned to vote for Hobby even though their husbands supported Ferguson. They may well have done so. Ferguson had predicted that he would win only twenty percent of the urban women but that eighty percent of the country women would support him; afterward he admitted that women had apparently voted ten to one for Hobby. Analysis of the election returns for San Antonio, where the newspaper published the candidates' total votes by precinct as well as a numerical breakdown of men and women registered in each precinct, indicates that at least eighty percent of women voters cast their ballots for Hobby for governor and eighty-six percent voted for Blanton as superintendent of public instruction.[39]

This impressive show of "voting right" notwithstanding, Cunningham soon discovered that her allies of convenience had not altered their underlying convictions. Rienzi Johnston's *Houston Post*, for years the anti-suffrage foil of the Progressive *Houston Chronicle*, had done a sharp editorial about-face after the suffrage bill passed. During the registration campaign it monitored the rising totals in a regular front page feature, urging the city toward a goal of 15,000 enrolled women. Rienzi Johnston abruptly ceased agitating the race issue and became so indifferent to the Black women who signed up that the *Post* did not even bother to tally them beyond round numbers. In the end, Black women made up less than eight percent of the female registrants in Houston, home to the state's largest Black community, and surrounding Harris County. The *Post* celebrated Hobby's victory by declaring that "the hand that rocks the cradle is the hand that rules the ballot box."[40] But when Cunningham asked Hobby for a resolution endorsing the federal suffrage amendment on the eve of the state Democratic convention six weeks later, he declined because his mentor, Johnston (who would be acting governor later that month while Hobby was out of the state), was adamantly opposed.

Minnie Fisher Cunningham "still feeling a little pert," as she later said, from the election victory, promptly declared that she would organize a women's floor fight for the resolution and was reproached for threatening to embarrass a young governor with "a fine political future." "If he doesn't support this amendment, he doesn't *have* any future," Cunningham retorted. Weeks before, Cunningham had been named to chair the convention as a reward for the women's campaign, but on

the opening day she coolly rose and declined the honor. Her only purpose as a delegate was to secure endorsement for the federal suffrage amendment, she announced, and she reserved the right to speak on the subject if the committee report was unsatisfactory. "We really did organize a fine floor fight; it's a pity we didn't have to have it," she recollected forty years later. "We would have shown them something in termagants they had never seen." The opposition backed down and the convention endorsed the federal amendment, virtually guaranteeing the NAWSA a vote for ratification when the Nineteenth Amendment passed the following summer.[41]

Only two years earlier, in 1916, Cunningham and two other TESA suffragists had appeared before the state Democratic convention to ask for suffrage and been rebuffed; James Ferguson, fresh from his performance in St. Louis, had been in control. Nothing then seemed less likely than that the suffragists' implacable enemy would soon be their means to victory. As historian Aileen Kraditor noted long ago, political considerations often override personal convictions when legislators vote, and a reform movement has the best chance of succeeding if its leadership is "politically sophisticated" and has "something to offer the potential ally,... something to trade." The lack of such opportunities in the one-party South, she pointed out, doomed suffragists there to failure.[42] In 1918 Texas suffragists unexpectedly found themselves possessed of precisely those essentials for success: [intra-] party competition, something to trade, and a leader politically shrewd enough to recognize it.

Prudently, Cunningham and her inner circle kept the details of their legislative bargain to themselves. Political trading did not fit the self-image suffragists projected as earnest pleaders for simple justice, a "front door lobby" that shunned back room deals and politicking. It appeared that hardworking women had persevered until fair-minded men had seen the light of reason, when in fact temporary political expediency camouflaged in patriotic rhetoric had secured the suffrage victory. Years later, in a letter to one of her closest associates, Cunningham neatly summed up in words what they had earlier demonstrated in deed: "At the moment, we were the smartest group of politicians in the state."[43]

Notes

1. Grace Danforth, "Struggling for Freedom," *Dallas Morning News*, May 11, 1893. On the founding of the Texas Equal Rights Association, see Ruthe Winegarten and Judith N. McArthur, eds., *Citizens at Last: The Woman Suffrage Movement in Texas* (Austin, Tex., 1987), 87-93.

2. Marjorie Spruill (Wheeler), *New Women of the New South: The Leaders of the Woman Suffrage Movement in the Southern States* (New York, 1993), 13-14, 113-116; *Proceedings of the Twenty-sixth Annual Convention of the National American Woman Suffrage Association, February 15-20, 1894*, edited by Harriet Taylor Upton (Warren, Ohio, [1894]), 47-49.

3. On the "Solid South" see Carrie Chapman Catt and Nettie Rogers Shuler, *Woman Suffrage and Politics: The Inner Story of the Suffrage Movement* (1926; reprint, Seattle, 1969), 323-26; Eleanor

Flexner, *Century of Struggle: The Woman's Rights Movement in the United States* (1959; reprint, New York, 1974), 302-305; and David Morgan, *Suffragists and Democrats: The Politics of Woman Suffrage in America* (East Lansing, 1972), 122-23, 155-56, 165-77. Anne Firor Scott, *The Southern Lady: From Pedestal to Politics, 1830-1930* (Chicago, 1970), chpt. 7, and Spruill (Wheeler), *New Women of the New South*, chpt. 1, analyze the difficulties of Southern suffragists.

4. Spruill (Wheeler), *New Women of the New South*, 37. Kentucky, which was not part of the former Confederacy, is sometimes mentioned as the fourth Southern state that ratified.

5. For the history of the Texas suffrage movement, see A. Elizabeth Taylor, "The Woman Suffrage Movement in Texas" *Journal of Southern History*, 27 (May 1951): 194-215.

6. 63 percent of the Texas House of Representatives voted for the amendment in 1915; 59 percent did in 1917. In both sessions the amendment failed to come to a vote in the Senate. Calculated from tallies in Taylor, "The Woman Suffrage Movement in Texas," 208-212.

7. Spruill (Wheeler), *New Women of the New South*, 160-62.

8. Catt and Shuler, *Woman Suffrage and Politics*, 255-56; Jane Y. McCallum, "Activities of Women in Texas Politics," in *Texas Democracy: A Centennial History of Politics and Personalities of the Democratic Party, 1836-1936*, 2 vols., Frank Carter Adams, ed. (Austin, 1937), 1: 470-74; *Dallas Times-Herald*, June 16, 1916; Maud Wood Park, *Front Door Lobby*, Edna Lamprey Stantial, ed., (Boston, 1960), 14-15.

9. Elizabeth Hayes Turner, "'White-Gloved Ladies' and 'New Women' in the Texas Woman Suffrage Movement," in *Southern Women: Histories and Identities*, Virginia Bernhard et al, eds. (Columbia, Mo., 1992), 129-156.

10. Lewis L. Gould, *Progressives and Prohibitionists: Texas Democrats in the Wilson Era* (Austin, 1973), 130-32, 185-221, and Gould, "The War with Jim Ferguson," *Southwestern Historical Quarterly*, 86 (Oct. 1982): 255-76; Janet Humphrey, ed., *A Texas Suffragist: Diaries and Writings of Jane Y. McCallum* (Austin, 1988), quotations 64, 80-81.

11. "Brewing Propaganda," *New Republic*, Aug. 21, 1915, 62-64; Anti-Saloon League, *The Brewers and Texas Politics*, 2 vols. (San Antonio, 1916), 1: 109-112. Catt and Shuler, *Woman Suffrage and Politics*, list Texas as one of the eight states where the "organized German-liquor vote was hurled into woman suffrage referenda campaigns with the unerring accuracy claimed for it," 148.

12. See Judith N. McArthur, "Motherhood and Reform in the New South: Texas Women's Political Culture in the Progressive Era," (Ph.D. diss., University of Texas at Austin, 1992), 479-490.

13. Minnie Fisher Cunningham to Carrie Chapman Catt, Sept. 26, 1917, box 1, folder 8, Minnie Fisher Cunningham Papers, Houston Metropolitan Research Center, Houston Public Library.

14. Cunningham to Catt, July 31 (quotation), Aug. 27, 1917, ibid.

15. Hobby to Thomas B. Love, Oct. 22, Nov. 16, Dec. 31, 1917; Feb. 9, 1918, Thomas B. Love Papers, Dallas Historical Society. Cunningham to Hortense Ward, Sept. 27, 1917; Ward to Cunningham, Dec. 7, 22, 1917, box 13, folder 193, Cunningham Papers; Cunningham to Carrie Chapman Catt, Jan. 25, 1918, box 1, folder 9, ibid.

16. Gould, *Progressives and Prohibitionists*, 227-33; Hobby to Thomas B. Love, Dec. 31, 1917; Feb. 9, 1918, Love Papers.

17. Cunningham to Tom Finty, Jan. 28, 1918, box 4, folder 3, Jane McCallum Family Papers (Part I), Austin History Center, Austin Public Library.

18. Cunningham to C.B. Metcalfe, Jan. 28, 1918, box 14, folder 213, Cunningham Papers.

19. Metcalfe to Cunningham, Feb. 10, 1918, ibid.

20. Cunningham to Metcalfe, Feb. 13, 1918, ibid.

21. Metcalfe to Cunningham, Feb. 18, 13, 1918, ibid.

22. McCallum, "Activities of Women in Texas Politics," 481.

23. Texas Legislature, *House Journal*, 35th Leg., 4th Called Sess., (Austin, 1918), 264, 328-36. Final vote appears in *Senate Journal*, 355. Only the previous summer sentiment against suffrage had been so strong that Cunningham had not dared to attempt a second try at bringing a primary suffrage bill to a vote before the third special session ended. See Cunningham to Hortense Ward, Sept. 5, 1917, box 13, folder 193, Cunningham Papers.

24. The primary suffrage bill was only one of several election law changes passed during the special session in an attempt to keep Ferguson from winning. See Robert Maxwell, "Texas in the Progressive Era," in *Texas: A Sesquicentennial Celebration* (Austin, 1984), 191-92; Gould, *Progressives and Prohibitionists*, 234; and *Austin American*, March 19, 24, 1918.

25. *Austin American*, March 21, 1918 (quotation); Cunningham to Catt, March 25, 1918, box 1, folder 9, Cunningham Papers; *Houston Post*, March 21, 1918; *Farm and Ranch*, April 6, 1918.

26. Alwyn Barr, *Black Texans: A History of Negroes in Texas, 1528-1971* (Austin, 1981), 79-80; *Houston Post*, April 11, 1915, March 21, 1918.

27. Mrs. E. Sampson to Mrs. [Maud Wood] Park, June 1918; Belle C. Critchett to Edith Hinkle League, July 1, 1918; League to Ruth White, July 8, 1918, and White to League, July 12, 1918; Catt to League July 17, 1918; Cunningham to Sampson, Aug. 31, 1918. All in box 3, folder 4, McCallum Papers, (Part I).

28. Metcalfe to Cunningham, April 12, 1918, box 14, folder 213, Cunningham Papers; "Minutes of Special Meeting of Executive Board of the Leslie Woman Suffrage Commission, Inc., Held June 20, 1918," Mrs. Percy V. Pennybacker Papers, Center for American History, University of Texas at Austin; Carrie Chapman Catt to Minnie Fisher Cunningham, June 20, 1918, box 18, folder 5, McCallum Papers (Part II).

29. Debbie Mauldin Cottrell, *Pioneer Woman Educator: The Progressive Spirit of Annie Webb Blanton* (College Station, Tex., 1993), 53-55.

30. *Austin American*, *Dallas Morning News*, *Fort Worth Star-Telegram*, *Houston Post*, and *San Antonio Express*, June 26 through July 12, 1918,.

31. McCallum, "Activities of Women in Texas Politics," 482; Cunningham to T.N. Jones, July 13, 1918, box 3, folder 4, McCallum Papers (Part I).

32. *Dallas Morning News*, July 27, 1918, July 19, 1918.

33. Humphrey, ed., *A Texas Suffragist*, 18, "To the Women of Texas," campaign flyer, box 19, folder 279, Cunningham Papers.

34. *Home and State*, June 1, 1918; "Vote for HOBBY for Governor," box 15, folder 234, Cunningham Papers.

35. *Austin American*, May 30, 1918.

36. "Extract from speech by James E. Ferguson, at City Auditorium, Houston, Texas, May 22, 1918—stenographic report by J.A. Lord," typescript, box 15, folder 227, Cunningham Papers; *Ferguson Forum*, March 28, April 25, 1918; July 11, 1918, June 20, 1918.

37. *Dallas Morning News*, June 27, 1918, July 19, 1918; *Ferguson Forum*, April 18, 1918, May 21, 1918.

38. M.M. Crane to Hobby, Feb. 2, 1918, box 3N98, folder 4, Martin McNulty Crane Papers, Center for American History, University of Texas at Austin; Thomas B. Love to Hobby, Jan. 26, 1918, Love Papers; *Dallas Morning News*, July 3, 1918, June 30, 1918.

39. R.M. Dudley to Cunningham, July 31, 1918, box 14, folder 206, Cunningham Papers; Seth Shepard McKay, *Texas Politics, 1906-1944* (Lubbock, Tex., 1952), 82; Cottrell, *Pioneer Woman Educator*, 61; Blanton to Anna Pennybacker, Aug. 9, 1918, Pennybacker Papers; M.M. Crane to Walter Crawford, July 12, 1918, box 3N98, Crane Papers; *Ferguson Forum*, July 18, Aug. 1, 1918; McArthur, "Motherhood and Reform in the New South," 554-556; Hobby received 461,479 votes to Ferguson's 217,012. Ferguson carried only 22 counties of 245, including 6 of the 9 "German" counties in the central part of the state.

40. *Houston Post*, July 4, 9, 12, 13, 29 (quotation), 1918. In Harris County black women were allowed to register at a separate table in the courthouse after the NAACP filed a protest. *The Houston Post*, on July 13, 1918, reported a final total of 14,400 white and 1,200 Negro women who registered. The 1920 census recorded 25,528 Negroes age 21 and over in the county; 1,200 is less than ten percent of the female half. Newspaper reports indicate in Texas black women were permitted to register in some counties, turned away in others, and in still others permitted to register but told that they would not be allowed to vote.

41. "Spanning the Old to the New South," *Texas Observer*, Nov. 21, 1958 (Cunningham quotations).

42. McCallum, "Activities of Women in Texas Politics," 206; Gould, *Progressives and Prohibitionists*, 170-73; Aileen S. Kraditor, "Tactical Problems of the Woman Suffrage Movement in the South," *Louisiana Studies*, 4 (Winter 1966): 295, 300 (quotations).

43. Cunningham to Jane Y. McCallum, April 5 [ca. 1939], box 7, folder 3, McCallum Papers (Part I).

Nina Pinckard, a Confederate veteran, and Josephine Pearson at the Anti-ratification Headquarters, Hermitage Hotel, Nashville. The caption, handwritten by Pearson on the original photograph, reflects Southern antis' equation of the fight against the federal woman suffrage amendment with the Confederates' unsuccessful battle to protect states' rights during the Civil War. The caption reads verbatim:

"'Truth Crushed to the Earth will rise again"—is illustrated in this lovely picture of Mrs. Jas. S. Pinckard, president general of the Southern Woman's League for the Rejection of the Susan B. Anthony Amendment, who as grand-niece of John C. Calhoun-unfurls the Confederate flag as emblematic of Southerners' States Rights fight for the defeat of the Federal Amendment; to her left sits the Veteran who 'fought and bled' for Tennessee's States Rights; standing to his left, holding the flag of the Union, is Miss Josephine A. Pearson, Pres. Of the Tenn. Division of the Southern Women's Rejection League for the Rejection of the Susan B. Anthony Amendment, who led the fight in Tennessee which became the Battle Ground of the Nation, August 1920."

Twenty-One

ARMAGEDDON IN TENNESSEE:
The Final Battle Over the
Nineteenth Amendment

Anastatia Sims

Editor's Introduction: In 1917, with the adoption of a suffrage amendment by the influential state of New York, the suffrage bandwagon seemed to be gaining momentum. As the list of "suffrage states" grew and the numbers of Congressmen accountable to women voters rose, the prospects for passage of the federal suffrage amendment brightened. In 1918 President Wilson finally endorsed the measure and urged Democrats on Capitol Hill to give it their support. To the great delight of the suffragists, the House of Representatives approved the amendment in January 1918. But, despite a personal plea from Wilson, the Senate failed to give it the two-thirds vote required for adoption. Before Congress met again, the National American Woman Suffrage Association and the National Woman's Party—joined by national political leaders well aware of the electoral votes now controlled by suffrage states—sought desperately to gain the two votes yet needed for Senate approval. In May of 1919, the House of Representatives again overwhelmingly approved the amendment, and this time the Senate concurred. On June 4, 1919, the Congress of the United States finally approved the woman suffrage amendment.

Even as they celebrated, however, suffragists were all too aware of the challenge that remained: getting three-fourths of the states (thirty-six) to ratify the amendment. The task did indeed prove to be difficult, and seemed to grow more difficult as it neared completion. As historian Anastatia Sims tells us in this dramatic and colorful essay, the battle for the thirty-sixth state was a virtual "Armageddon," in which suffragists fought opponents whose determination and willingness to resort to any means necessary to defeat the amendment astounded even seasoned veterans of the suffrage movement including Carrie Chapman Catt.

By mid-June 1920, a year after Congress had sent the amendment to the states for approval, thirty-five states had ratified. Needing only one more state, suffragists were extremely frustrated when Delaware unexpectedly defeated the amendment—the only state north of the Mason-Dixon line to do so—and no other state was slated to hold a legislative session before the November 1920 presidential election. Polls of the Republican-dominated legislatures in Connecticut and

Vermont indicated that they would ratify if called into special session, but the anti-suffrage, anti-Prohibition governors of the two states refused to do so—despite frantic efforts by local and national suffragists to persuade them. Woodrow Wilson was able to convince Democratic governors in North Carolina and Tennessee to call special sessions, but North Carolina legislators defeated the amendment—and urged Tennessee to follow their example. Wilson exhorted these predominantly Democratic legislatures to ratify for the sake of the national Democratic Party, but North Carolina anti-suffrage legislators declared that "they were not going to sacrifice their honor upon the fickle altar of supposed political expediency" and urged their counterparts in Tennessee to "fight to the last ditch, and then some." The Tennessee anti-suffragists did exactly that.

As both sides mobilized for the fight, writes Sims, suffragists had reason to be encouraged. In keeping with Catt's "Winning Plan," Tennessee suffragists had persuaded these legislators to enact presidential and municipal suffrage for women in 1919, and many powerful political leaders, businessmen, and newspaper editors were pro-suffrage. However, as Catt warned, the anti-suffragists would spare no tactic or expense to dissuade legislators from supporting the amendment.

Anti-suffragists made use of anti-feminist arguments now nauseatingly familiar to the suffragists, including the idea that woman suffrage would ruin women and destroy the home. And familiar corporate opponents—particularly the liquor industry—were clearly operating in Tennessee. Sims describes the liquor industry, allied with the railroads and the cotton textile industry, as playing a leading role in the struggle.

That this final battle took place in the South clearly added to the difficulties of the suffragists, as anti-suffragists used race and states' rights arguments lavishly to arouse public sentiment against the amendment. Since the 1890s, Southern suffragists had struggled against anti-suffragists who denounced the suffrage movement as anathema to Southern values including White supremacy, state sovereignty, and reverence for traditional womanhood, and the antis now presented the fight over ratification as a battle to save "Southern Civilization." Earlier in the year, when Mississippi rejected the amendment, the Jackson *Clarion-Ledger* proclaimed (inaccurately) that "the vile old thing is as dead as its author [Susan B. Anthony], the old advocate of social equality and intermarriage of the races, and Mississippi will never be annoyed with it again." The leader of the Tennessee Division of the Southern Women's League for the Rejection of the Susan B. Anthony Amendment, Josephine Pearson, declared to her followers that Tennessee "could not fail in this most crucial test of Southern rights and honor, when Tennessee became the pivotal battle-ground of the Nation!" Ironically, two Southern suffragists and former NAWSA officers, Laura Clay and Kate Gordon, agreeing that the federal amendment was a threat to states' rights, actually came to Nashville and lobbied against ratification—though Clay hated being associated with the antis.

Leaders from both sides of the suffrage battle flocked to the state to assist their allies in Tennessee. Anti-suffrage leaders including Anne Pleasant, the wife of the Louisiana governor who had attempted to unite the South against the amendment, was there, for example, as was Charlotte Rowe of the National Association Opposed to Woman Suffrage. From the NAWSA, Marjorie Shuler, and finally President Carrie Chapman Catt herself, came to Nashville to assist Tennessee suffrage leaders, including Nashville socialite and former NAWSA Vice President Anne Dallas Dudley who had played a leading role in the NAWSA's lobbying of Congress. Alice Paul of the NWP did not come, but lobbied actively from a distance and dispatched capable assistants to the state. This was a wise decision: leading Tennessee Democrats greatly resented the NWP's campaign against their party and the picketing of President Wilson, and NWP orators on a 1917 speaking tour in the state had difficulty even obtaining a lecture hall. However, Paul was well represented by Sue Shelton White, formerly editor of the NWP's national organ *The Suffragist* and chair of the NWP in Tennessee, who worked well with all suffrage factions.

As the long, hot, summer progressed, suffragists struggled to retain their supporters and win new ones, but the anti-suffragists nearly succeeded in their dogged and unscrupulous fight to block ratification. It is amazing but true, as Sims explains, that after the seventy-two-year-long struggle for woman suffrage, the outcome was determined by an elderly mother in the Tennessee mountains who instructed her son (from an anti-suffrage district) to vote for woman suffrage if it became necessary. May her name live in the annals of the movement: Febb King Ensminger Burn, mother of twenty-four-year-old Harry Burn whose vote for ratification saved the woman suffrage amendment from defeat.

The anti-suffragists believed that, had they been able to prevent ratification of the suffrage amendment until after the November 1920 national elections, this "fad" that Wilson had promoted as a war measure would lose momentum and they might be able to block it permanently. They may have been right. As Catt and Shuler reported in *Woman Suffrage and Politics*, there was only one other ratification between that of Tennessee and the November election: in September, the Connecticut legislature was called into session to make provisions for registering women and took the occasion to ratify the Nineteenth Amendment—against the instructions of their anti-suffrage governor. This put the Nineteenth Amendment on firmer ground—since, as Sims describes below, anti-suffragists were *still* contesting the validity of Tennessee's ratification. However, the Connecticut legislature would not have had the *opportunity* to ratify had it not been for Tennessee's action. Without Tennessee's ratification, it is possible that in the conservative climate of the 1920s, the amendment would have failed—a scenario that seems more plausible after the failure of the Equal Rights Amendment in more recent times.

Suffragists, however, celebrated August 26, 1920, the day Tennessee's ratification reached Washington and was signed by the Secretary of State, as the day of their

great victory. As the news spread, bells rang and whistles blew, and politicians of many stamps offered congratulations and attempted to take credit for enfranchising women. Carrie Chapman Catt returned to Washington to a giant victory celebration, and went on to New York for another. Alice Paul sewed the last star—the thirty-sixth—on a suffrage banner and hung it from the balcony of the NWP headquarters in Washington. In Seneca Falls a flag was draped over the tablet that marked the site where it had all begun.

★　★　★　★　★

IN JUNE 1919 Congress passed the Nineteenth Amendment and sent it on to the states. By the summer of 1920 thirty-five states had ratified it. If suffragists could win the approval of just one more state, they would, at long last, achieve their goal. When the Delaware legislature unexpectedly defeated the amendment in early June, women pinned their hopes on Tennessee. During a steamy Southern summer, Nashville, the "Athens of the South," became the site of one of the most fiercely fought contests in American political history. For the amendment's friends and foes alike it was Armageddon—the final battle in the long, bitter struggle that had, in the words of one observer, pitted "powers that pray" against "powers that prey."[1]

Suffragists were by no means certain of victory. Tennessee, like the rest of the South, had a history of hostility toward women's rights. In 1908, for example, Governor Malcolm R. Patterson offered this comment on woman suffrage: "Let the women pray and the men vote."[2] Twelve years later many Tennesseans—male and female alike—still agreed with the governor. Woman's place was at home, in church, in the schoolroom or even in the factory—but not at the polls.

At the same time, there appeared to be reasons for cautious optimism. In 1919, just two months before Congress submitted the Nineteenth Amendment to the states, the Tennessee General Assembly had passed a law giving women the right to vote in presidential and municipal elections, and the same men would consider the amendment. The state Democratic party had endorsed woman suffrage, and so had most of the state's major newspapers.

As suffragists knew from past experience, however, appearances could be deceiving, and close examination revealed a grim picture in Tennessee. The first obstacle was a section of the state constitution that prohibited ratification by a legislature elected before Congress submitted an amendment to the states. (Members of the current legislature had been elected in 1918.) When the United States Supreme Court handed down a decision that nullified that provision, suffragists immediately began clamoring for a special session. Sue Shelton White, chair of the National Woman's Party (NWP) in Tennessee, requested the session in a letter to Governor Albert H. Roberts on June 19. Two days later, Catherine Talty Kenny and Kate Burch Warner of the Tennessee Equal Suffrage Association (an

affiliate of the National American Woman Suffrage Association) led a delegation of women who urged the governor to call the session in time for women to vote in the state primaries August 5. At the request of the Tennessee League of Women Voters and the NAWSA, pro-suffrage politicians from Tennessee and elsewhere wrote the governor. The United States attorney general, the state attorney general and other prominent jurists assured Roberts that such a session would be legal. Even President Woodrow Wilson bowed to the suffragists' pleas, and telegraphed his support.[3]

Sue Shelton White
LIBRARY OF CONGRESS

But the governor stalled. During his campaign two years earlier Roberts had spoken out against woman suffrage. According to Catherine Kenny, he had signed the presidential and municipal suffrage bill only because he believed it was unconstitutional. Subsequently, he had blocked women's attempts to expand their political power further when he refused to call a special session to give women the right to vote in party primaries.[4]

Roberts had good reason to want to keep women out of politics. There were persistent rumors that his highly paid private secretary, who had been working for him on the state payroll since 1915, was a woman of questionable reputation. He was firmly allied with the "wet" [anti-prohibition] wing of the Democratic Party, and his advisers were hostile to votes for women. As a candidate, he was unlikely to appeal to women voters.[5]

And it was his appeal as a candidate that was foremost in A.H. Roberts's mind in the summer of 1920. He was embroiled in a bitter fight for renomination. He confronted challengers within his own party, as well as strong Republican opposition. His tax reform program had alienated farmers, while his support for management during the strikes of 1919 turned industrial workers against him. Opponents accused him of raising taxes and increasing the state's debt.[6]

With his political career hanging in the balance, Governor Roberts faced a seemingly impossible choice. If he endorsed woman suffrage, perhaps women

would forgive his other transgressions, and maybe their support would offset disillusioned farmers and workers. On the other hand, if women voted (as suffragists predicted they would) on moral issues alone, he might be ensuring his own defeat. Whatever women did, Roberts was under increasing pressure from his own party. Democratic leaders at the national level, including President Wilson himself, were staking the party's honor (and chances for victory in the November elections) on their ability to ratify the Nineteenth Amendment and enfranchise women who, they presumed, would then express their gratitude by voting the Democratic ticket. Uncertain of his own chances for reelection, Roberts could not afford to repudiate the national platform. Within Tennessee, however, he drew his support from men likely to oppose votes for women. If he followed Wilson's lead, he risked offending some of his staunchest friends. Finally, however, the governor capitulated. On June 25 he announced that he would convene the legislature later in the summer—*after* the Democratic primary August 5.

The Battle Begins

The governor's announcement set off one of the most heated political fights ever witnessed in Tennessee, a state hardly known for political tranquility. Professor Edwin Mims observed that "The Battle of Nashville in 1864 was a five o'clock tea in comparison with this one." Writing fifty years after the fact, journalist Joe Hatcher described the special session as "the bitterest, bare-fisted, name-calling, back-biting session in the state's history." The stakes were high, and both sides were hard at work long before the session opened.[7]

Suffragists initiated their campaign by recruiting a Men's Ratification Committee composed of some of the most prominent men in the state. With former governor Tom Rye as chair, the committee included newspaper publishers (George Fort Milton of the *Chattanooga News*, Edward B. Stahlman of the *Nashville Banner* and Luke Lea of the *Nashville Tennessean*), politicians (speaker of the Tennessee house Seth Walker, Memphis political boss Edward H. Crump, United States Senator Kenneth D. McKellar, former Republican Governor Ben Hooper, and Republican gubernatorial candidate Alfred A. Taylor) and businessmen (Guilford Dudley, among others). It was an eclectic coalition, representing diverse political factions and economic interests. Such strange bedfellows were unlikely to rest easily together. Before the end of the summer, some of the men who had allowed themselves to be named to the Ratification Committee had joined the opposition, and the committee itself played only a limited role in the campaign.[8]

Suffragists expected that in Tennessee, as elsewhere, they would lead the fight to win votes for women. Accordingly Abby Crawford Milton, president of the Tennessee League of Women Voters, appointed a Women's Ratification Committee, with Catherine Kenny as chair. To their dismay, Governor Roberts decided to form his own Women's Ratification Committee. He named as its head Kate Warner, "a lady of culture and refinement," and a lady who, unlike Milton and Kenny, was

firmly aligned with the Roberts camp.[9] Abby Milton's husband edited the *Chattanooga News,* which had endorsed Roberts's rival for the Democratic gubernatorial nomination. Catherine Kenny was a friend of Luke Lea, publisher of the anti-Roberts, pro-suffrage *Nashville Tennessean,* and arch-rival of Major Edward B. Stahlman, one of Roberts's strongest supporters. Factionalism was the keynote of Tennessee politics; factionalism had earlier torn apart the suffrage movement in Tennessee. "You know we Tennesseans and Kentuckians are rather strong on 'feuds,'" Catherine Kenny wrote the NAWSA president Carrie Chapman Catt. "Sorter [sic] drunk it in with our mother's milk." Now factionalism jeopardized the ratification of the Nineteenth Amendment.

Anne Dallas Dudley
LIBRARY OF CONGRESS

"I don't believe there's a ghost of a chance of ratification in either Tennessee or North Carolina," Catt told Nashville suffragist Anne Dallas Dudley on July 12. "Tennessee has always been torn by factions in all men's and women's work, and it was these factions which defeated us in Delaware."[10]

The existence of two "official" women's ratification committees implied that there was disagreement among the suffragists themselves (and, in fact, the two groups were not always in harmony). Suffrage leaders recognized that the appearance of disunity could seriously damage their cause. The NAWSA's representative in Nashville, Marjorie Shuler, negotiated a compromise, persuading Governor Roberts, the League of Women Voters, and the NAWSA to recognize both committees. Through letters, telegrams, and telephone calls Shuler kept in close touch with Carrie Chapman Catt in New York. In mid-July, Catt decided the situation required her personal attention. She arrived in Nashville on July 17, expecting to stay only a few days. Instead, she remained more than a month.[11]

Upon her arrival Catt told reporters, "I have no definite plan of action for my stay in Nashville." At least one reporter knew better. After describing her "pleasing personality," "kindly but animated face," and "soft, musical voice," he added, "yet there is about her expression something that strongly suggests that she can be firm when the occasion requires, and, if need be, aggressive."[12] Catt had worked for suffrage for thirty years. She was an intelligent woman, and a shrewd politician. She came to Tennessee determined to win the final victory.

Catt had been coordinating the campaign from New York long before she set foot in Nashville. In June she instructed Tennessee suffragists to begin polling the legislators

National Woman's Party Headquarters in Nashville, Tenn. where the
campaign for ratification of the suffrage amendment was centered.
LIBRARY OF CONGRESS

to determine how they would vote on the amendment. They should not rely on
hearsay, she warned; they should accept only the word of "bona fide" suffrage
workers. She urged volunteers to get firm commitments, but cautioned them that
these might not be binding. At the same time the women undertook to poll the
legislators, they conducted another survey to find out which lawmakers might be
susceptible to bribes. Catt was a seasoned politician, with few illusions about the
political process. "[N]o matter how well the women may work or how effective their
results may be," she wrote Catherine Kenny, "ratification in Tennessee will go through
the work and actions of men, and the great motive that will finally put it through will
be political and nothing else. We have long since recovered from our previous faith in
the action of men based upon a love of justice. That is an animal that doesn't exist."[13]

The Anti-suffragists

While suffragists organized, their opponents also went into action. On the same
day that Carrie Chapman Catt arrived in Nashville, Josephine Anderson Pearson,
an educator from east Tennessee who had been tapped to lead the fight against suffrage in 1917, was entertaining guests in her mountain home when she received a
telegram summoning her to Nashville to fight the *"invasion by foreign forces."* She
caught the train to the capital city that afternoon. That night she checked into the

cheapest room available at the Hermitage Hotel, and reserved assembly rooms on the mezzanine and the first floor for the Tennessee branch of the Southern Women's Rejection League (full name: Southern Women's League for the Rejection of the Susan B. Anthony Amendment). For the next six weeks the Hermitage Hotel would be her home, and anti-suffrage headquarters.[14]

Although the anti-suffragists (or antis) criticized suffragists for bringing in "foreign forces" they did not hesitate to call in their own reinforcements. Mrs. James Pinckard of Alabama, Mrs. Ruffin Pleasant of Louisiana, and Miss Charlotte Rowe of New York were among the women who came to Nashville to fight the Nine-teenth Amendment. These women were not really outsiders, Josephine Pearson declared, because "Tennessee considers no influence as 'outside' that is Southern, or invited to this state by united Southern sentiment for the preservation of our state constitution and white civilization."[15] Like the suffragists, female anti-suffragists recognized that this confrontation was crucial, and, like the suffragists, they believed they acted for the good of women and of society.

"A few women representatives of the National Association Opposed to Woman Suffrage are in Nashville," Marjorie Shuler reported in early August, "but far more deadly is the corps of men who have quietly stolen into the state and whose work is evident in the wavering of certain legislators and in the organization of a Tennessee Constitutional League." The League, a subsidiary of the American Constitutional League and the anti-suffrage counterpart to the Men's Ratification Committee, was dedicated to the defeat of the Susan B. Anthony Amendment. It included "prominent lawyers and business men," men who would use their wealth and influence in their attempt to block ratification in Tennessee.[16]

Suffragists faced formidable adversaries. They believed that "sinister forces" were working against them, and they set out to discredit their opponents. In late July, Carrie Chapman Catt and Abby Crawford Milton embarked on a statewide speaking tour, to convince the public that the "whiskey lobby, manufacturers' lobby, and the railroad lobby" were united against "the women of Tennessee."[17] After the fight was over, Catt declared: "Never in the history of politics has there been such a nefarious lobby as labored to block ratification in Nashville." Other participants and observers agreed with Catt's assessment. George Fort Milton described the antis as "insidious," and "a well-organized and unscrupulous opposition." The *Christian Science Monitor* compared the anti lobbyists to "a horde of locusts," and characterized the battle over ratification as "justice against vested influence." Writing four months after the suffragists had won, Abby Crawford Milton insisted that the devil himself had been at work in Tennessee in the summer of 1920, collaborating with the antis to keep the ballot from women.[18]

"Nefarious." "Insidious." "Unscrupulous." These are strong words, even when hurled in the wake of a feverish political contest. Were the suffragists prone to hyperbole, or were their accusations on target? Certainly by 1920 the suffragists were skilled publicists for their own cause, and they recognized the advantages of

portraying themselves as defenseless women fighting ruthless political machines and heartless corporate giants. The portrait was an effective piece of public relations. It was also rooted in fact. Across the nation distillers, brewers, and manufacturers (particularly those who employed large numbers of women and children) subsidized campaigns against state suffrage referenda and against the federal woman suffrage amendment, although they worked, for the most part, in secrecy. A Senate investigation of the United States Brewers' Association in 1918 revealed that that organization had actively tried to defeat woman suffrage in several states.[19] In some states textile manufacturers joined with liquor interests. Walter Clark, Chief Justice of the North Carolina Supreme Court, believed that "the Whiskey Interests and the Cotton Mill owners of the South" underwrote anti-suffrage campaigns. Clark was one of the South's leading Progressive reformers, but his son, David, edited the *Southern Textile Bulletin*, mouthpiece of the region's cotton industry.[20]

These forces had been evident on the political scene in Tennessee for years, and it is likely that they were in Nashville in the summer of 1920. Prohibition had been the central issue of Tennessee politics during the first fifteen years of the twentieth century, and distillers and brewers had mobilized to protect their businesses. The Manufacturers' Association was also active politically, opposing bills to regulate child labor, set minimum wages, and establish employers' responsibility for workers' safety on the job. Finally, the Louisville and Nashville Railroad (L&N) had been involved in Tennessee politics since the 1880s. The L&N's generosity in distributing free passes to legislators in 1913 (while the General Assembly was considering a railroad bill) led to an Interstate Commerce Committee investigation in 1916. Woman suffrage—with its promise to deliver women's votes for the enforcement of Prohibition, regulation of child labor, and reforms to end political corruption—threatened vital interests of all three of these powerful lobbies.[21]

Suffragists charged that these groups "paid the bills" for the antis in 1920. There is no concrete evidence to confirm or refute their accusations. We do know that some of the men who led the fight against the Nineteenth Amendment in Tennessee were affiliated with the businesses that had opposed woman suffrage elsewhere. For example, John Vertrees, one of the best-known opponents of suffrage, was also associated with the liquor industry. Although he denied being part of the "whiskey ring," he represented at least one executive of George A. Dickel and Company in both personal and business matters, and was closely identified with liquor interests.[22] Garnett Andrews, one of the founding members of the Tennessee Constitutional League, was involved with several knitting and hosiery mills, and, according to John Trotwood Moore, was "one of the most prominent representatives of the knitting industry in the South."[23] Mr. and Mrs. George A. Washington both participated in the fight against woman suffrage; Mr. Washington was a director of the L&N.[24]

Finally there was Edward Bushrod Stahlman, "the Major," publisher of the *Nashville Banner* and one of the most colorful (and powerful) figures in Tennessee

politics. Stahlman had come to the United States from Germany before the Civil War. He got a job with the L&N in 1863, and worked his way up to a vice presidency. In 1884 he led a successful attempt to abolish the state railroad commission, established only two years earlier. During that debate Stahlman not only presented the L&N's case to the General Assembly, he also attempted to curry favor with Nashville newspapers. His attempts failed. By the time the fight was over, all the papers in the capital city were hostile to the railroad, a situation that could weaken the L&N in future legislative contests. In 1885, Stahlman bought the Banner. He left the L&N in 1890 to become commissioner of the Southern Railway and Steamship Association, a post he held until 1895. After that he devoted his attention to his family, the *Banner,* and Tennessee politics.[25] Although he officially severed his ties with the railroad industry, his critics (notably Luke Lea) suspected that he continued to represent the L&N's interests in Nashville. In 1914 Lea's *Nashville Tennessean* ran an editorial cartoon with the following caption: "Tennessee is governed by [Republican Governor Ben] Hooper; Hooper is manipulated by Stahlman; Stahlman is dominated by L&N; find the real ruler of Tennessee."[26] Stahlman dismissed Lea's accusation as "a malicious lie"; nevertheless, some Tennesseans continued to regard the *Banner* publisher as an agent of the L&N. In the summer of 1920, Stahlman waffled on woman suffrage. After being named to the Men's Ratification Committee, he changed his mind, and, through the pages of the *Banner* as well as in public addresses, became an outspoken opponent of votes for women.[27]

The influential men who fought the Nineteenth Amendment may have acted from conviction instead of (or in addition to) self-interest. Many antis sincerely believed that women had no business in politics, and that enfranchising them would only create problems. But connections between prominent antis and liquor, textile, and railroad companies convinced the suffragists that these men represented larger interests. Events like Stahlman's change of heart and what Marjorie Shuler described as "the wavering of certain legislators" persuaded the women that their enemies were employing underhanded tactics. As the special session drew near, more and more lawmakers who had pledged themselves to suffrage switched sides. Two days before the legislature was to meet, suffragists lost one of their most valuable allies, Seth Walker, Speaker of the House of Representatives. Just a week earlier, a newspaper had announced that Walker was firmly committed to ratification. He had even promised to introduce the resolution. His defection, according to *The Suffragist,* official journal of the NWP, was a "sure indication of the strength of the opposition forces at work."[28] Support for the amendment eroded steadily. By the time the session opened, suffragists who earlier in the summer had been confident of victory were worried. "All that we can say at this writing," reported the NAWSA's *Woman Citizen,* "is that the signs are favorable, but that the opposition is massed as it was never massed before." Before the final vote on the amendment, every single legislator who the suffragists had identified as bribable moved from the pro column to the anti list.[29]

The Battle Intensifies

At the same time that both sides worked behind the scenes to influence lawmakers, they also waged massive publicity campaigns to sway public opinion. Anti-suffragists took the offensive with assertions that representatives and senators who voted for the amendment would violate their oath of office. Attempting to circumvent the Supreme Court decision, they maintained that legislators pledged to uphold the state constitution as it was written, not as it was interpreted by the United States Supreme Court. Suffragists countered with numerous opinions from legal authorities within Tennessee and throughout the United States.[30]

Anti-suffragists also relied on arguments that had been used ever since the idea of woman suffrage was introduced in 1848. They predicted that female enfranchisement would result in nothing less than the end of civilization. It would destroy the home and the family. Wives would divorce their husbands when they disagreed about politics. Mothers, preoccupied with their new status as voters, would neglect their children. Women would become "masculinized" and men "feminized." One anti-suffrage leaflet warned men: "A Vote for Federal Suffrage is a Vote for Organized Female Nagging Forever."[31]

Suffragists quickly responded to the anti attack. They affirmed their loyalty to domesticity and motherhood. A widely circulated photograph showed Anne Dallas Dudley, a Tennessee suffrage activist with an impeccable pedigree, reading to her children. Suffragists argued that circumstances of modern life required housewives to get involved in politics, because politics affected family life. The vote would not make women forsake their home duties, suffragists insisted. Instead, it would enable them to fulfill their domestic obligations more effectively.[32]

At the beginning of the campaign, Carrie Chapman Catt warned Tennessee suffragists that "The anti suffragists will flood Tennessee with the most outrageous literature it has ever been your lot to read…. It will be extremely harmful, and the 'nigger question' will be put forth in ways to arouse the greatest possible prejudice."[33] Catt was right. For many Southern opponents of suffrage, the central issue in 1920 was race. Josephine Pearson identified "three deadly principles" in the Nineteenth Amendment: "1st, surrender of state sovereignty. 2nd, Negro woman suffrage. 3rd, Race equality."[34] A leaflet addressed to the "Men of the South" reminded voters of the similarity between the Fifteenth and Nineteenth Amendments, and predicted that ratification would lead to "another period of Reconstruction horrors," when African American men and "female carpetbaggers" would rule. Anti leaders informed White Southerners that Congress had three "force bills" ready for consideration, bills similar to those used during Reconstruction.[35] A broadside entitled "Woman Suffrage, A Menace to the South" warned that the Nineteenth Amendment would destroy state sovereignty and increase the number of African American voters in the South because it would enable Black women to vote.[36] Anti-suffrage propaganda quoted feminists and African American leaders who favored

social equality between Blacks and Whites, and concluded that woman suffrage would lead to interracial marriage. Again and again Southern antis declared that woman suffrage would result in the downfall of White supremacy, which, they implied, would leave White Southern women vulnerable to assaults by Black men. According to Mrs. Ruffin Pleasant of Louisiana, "the passage of the Nineteenth Amendment would embolden both the negro [sic] woman and the negro man to give us even greater trouble than they are doing now."[37]

To counter the anti assault, suffragists pledged to uphold White supremacy, and argued that the same measures that disfranchised African American men would also disqualify African American women. Privately, some suffragists defended the contributions Black women could make to politics. Because of the presidential and municipal suffrage bill enacted in 1919, African American women had already begun to vote in Tennessee. In January, 1920, Catherine Kenny told Carrie Chapman Catt that the record of Black women voters in Nashville was "one of which every Southern suffragist may not only feel proud but hopeful for the future." In July she repeated her endorsement: "[I]n every instance…they voted with the best White women thereby eliminating any political prejudice." After the ratification fight was over, Kenny wrote in the Tennessee chapter of the *History of Woman Suffrage* that African American woman suffrage "was anything but the 'bugaboo' politicians had tried to show it would be and in some instances it was a contributing factor to good government." In Tennessee, as in other Southern states, Black women had joined in the campaign for woman suffrage, working in segregated organizations.[38]

The special session was scheduled to open on Monday, August 9. Lawmakers began arriving in Nashville on Saturday, and they, along with suffragists and antis, converged on the Hermitage Hotel. There were others at the Hermitage, too, "mysterious men," whom the suffragists did not recognize, but who clearly had a stake in the outcome of the vote. Suffragists observed these unidentified men escorting legislators to a room on the eighth floor, a room where liquor flowed freely. By late in the evening, Carrie Chapman Catt recalled, "legislators, both suffrage and anti-suffrage men, were reeling through the hall in a state of advanced intoxication." Horrified suffragists asked officials to enforce the Prohibition laws. They were told that this was the "Tennessee way," and that "in Tennessee, whiskey and legislation go hand in hand."[39]

Armageddon: The Final Showdown

The legislature convened at noon on Monday, August 9. The Senate was solidly pro-suffrage. The ratification resolution was introduced on August 10, and referred to the committee on constitutional amendments the following day. On Friday, August 13, the committee recommended its adoption. "National woman's suffrage is at hand," the majority report stated; "it may be delayed but it cannot be defeated,

and we covet for Tennessee the signal honor of being the thirty-sixth and last State necessary to consummate this great reform." That same day, the Senate passed the resolution by a vote of 25 to 4.[40]

With the question settled in the Senate, suffragists and their opponents focused their attention on the House. The antis immediately invoked a number of delaying tactics, and continued their efforts to win over lawmakers. Each side accused the other of foul play. Carrie Chapman Catt claimed that anti-suffrage men tapped phones, listened at transoms, and intercepted telegrams in order to anticipate the suffragists' plans. According to Catt, they used liquor, loans, bribes, promises of high office and "every other device which old hands at illicit politics could conceive or remember"[41] to get legislators to vote their way. On August 12 a newspaper reported that "Nashville looks like a real oasis in the dry desert. Moonshine corn whiskey is flowing freely."[42]

The suffragists, meanwhile, allegedly employed tactics that were more subtle but no less persuasive. "Automobile rides, hugs, kisses, even the absurdity of powdering the members' noses and rouging their cheeks in the assembly hall were frequently witnessed," *The Lookout* of Chattanooga told its readers. The suffragists were testing the boundaries of ladylike behavior with their aggressive tactics, the journal implied, and *The Lookout* clearly disapproved. According to *The Lookout's* vigilant observer, one suffragist—"a very pretty lady"—eager to convert a dubious legislator "grabbed his tie…and held him in a grip that one would suppose invincible." As the woman kept talking, the man pulled a knife out of his pocket, cut himself loose, and walked away, leaving the startled suffragist holding the remnants of his tie. "Just keep it," he remarked as he strolled away.[43]

In the House, as in the Senate, a ratification resolution had been introduced on August 10. But day after day passed; the House took no action. On August 17, the committee on constitutional convention and amendments issued a favorable report. Dismissing the arguments that ratification would be unconstitutional or a violation of the oath of office, the committee agreed with its Senate counterpart that it would be "an honor" for Tennessee to be the final state to ratify the amendment, "giving to our mothers, wives, daughters, sisters and sweethearts a precious right which they have so long been unjustly denied."[44]

The debate began. In an impassioned speech, Seth Walker urged his colleagues to vote against the ratification resolution on states' rights grounds. He also defended his reputation. He resented the charge that he had changed his mind on the issue because of pressure from "a certain railroad," he declared. But, as Marjorie Shuler noted, he "made no specific denial." Speaking for the suffragists, Joe Hanover of Memphis condemned the interference of antis from other states, and denounced the tactics of Tennessee's own anti-suffragists. "What is a greater crime," he demanded, "than for certain newspapers connected with the opposition to threaten you as they have been doing for the last ten days?" The debate continued for several hours, but the House adjourned without voting.[45]

That night was a long one for suffragists. They patrolled the corridors of the Hermitage Hotel and stationed sentries at the train station to prevent the untimely departure of any of the men still pledged to support them. They met in Carrie Chapman Catt's room for yet another strategy session. But this time even Catt had exhausted her political resources. "There is one more thing we can do—only one," she said. "We can pray."[46] After all the careful organization, the years of winning over public opinion, the arduous task of wooing legislators, the women were still left to pray while the men voted.

The galleries were packed when House Speaker Seth Walker called the session to order on August 18. The atmosphere was tense; both sides knew the vote was too close to call. An anti motion to table the ratification resolution ended in a tie.[47] It was a victory for suffragists, but the real test lay ahead.

"The hour has come!" Seth Walker shouted. The roll call began. There were two votes for, followed by four against. The seventh name on the list was Harry Burn. At twenty-four, he was the youngest man in the legislature, a Republican from McMinn County in east Tennessee. Suffrage polls listed him as undecided. He had voted with the antis on the motion to table. Although Burn had promised suffrage leaders he would vote with them if they needed his vote to ratify, suffragists feared he would continue to side with the antis. They knew that political leaders in his home district opposed the Nineteenth Amendment. But they did not know that in his pocket was a letter from his mother telling him to "be a good boy" and vote for ratification. When his name was called, Harry Burn voted yes.[48]

It took a few moments for the suffragists to absorb what had happened, but before the roll call was over they realized that Harry Burn had given them the last vote they needed. The antis realized it, too. As soon as the clerk announced the vote—49 to 47—Seth Walker changed his vote from no to aye, and introduced a motion to reconsider. (Under House rules, only a representative voting with the winning side could move to reconsider). That parliamentary maneuver did not diminish the suffragists' joy. "Emancipated at last!" some exclaimed. That night, Carrie Chapman Catt sent a telegram to North Carolina suffragist Gertrude Weil: "The thirty-sixth state is won."[49]

The story should have ended there, but it continued. For two days Walker refused to bring up the motion to reconsider, while he and the antis tried to round up enough votes to defeat the measure on the second vote. They sent telegrams to pro-suffrage representatives, reproaching them for their votes. Two legislators, T.O. Simpson and S.F. Stovall, complained that they "were called up every half hour day and night so that they had no sleep." Assemblyman Simpson received threats that he would lose his teaching job if he did not change sides. But the pro-suffrage majority held firm. Late on the night of August 20, thirty-eight anti-suffrage representatives fled to Decatur, Alabama, on an L&N train ("very suitably indeed in their choice of conveyance" was Marjorie Shuler's caustic comment). Members of the "Red Rose Brigade" (named after the anti-suffrage emblem, the red rose;

Harry Burn

Febb King Ensminger Burn

suffragists adopted the yellow rose) hoped that their absence would break the quorum, and prevent further action on the amendment.[50]

Meanwhile, antis appealed to public opinion. On August 19, they held a mass meeting at Ryman Auditorium "to save the South." E.B. Stahlman was the featured speaker. Antis organized similar rallies throughout the state later in the month. Observers disagreed on the response to the meetings. "Indignation Spreads Over Whole State" declared a headline in the anti-suffrage *Chattanooga Daily Times,* while the pro-suffrage *Nashville Tennessean* reported "Little Interest Manifested in Mass Meetings."[51] Antis all over the nation condemned the Tennessee legislators who voted with the suffragists. Martin Lee Calhoun of Selma, Alabama, compared them to "assassins of the night who have stabbed the heart of the South and its traditions to the core."[52]

Antis directed much of their outrage at Harry Burn. Josephine Pearson labelled him a "traitor to manhood's honor," while anti newspapers reported that Joe Hanover paid him $10,000 to change his vote.[53] In response to the antis' attacks on his integrity, Burn inserted a personal statement in the House journal, explaining that he cast his vote for morality, justice, his mother, and the glory of the Republican party. Charges of bribery did not stick to Harry Burn, but they persisted against the antis. In September, a grand jury investigated the activities of lobbyists during the campaign. It returned no indictments against either side.[54]

House custom gave the representative who introduced a motion to reconsider three days to bring the motion before the floor; after that, any member could call the

question. Pro-suffrage legislators were determined to resolve the issue once and for all on August 21; if Walker did not call for a vote on his motion, they would. The legislature convened, with all the suffrage men in their places, and women occupying the desks of the absent members, sitting in silent protest against the retreat of the Red Rose Brigade. Fifty-eight members of the legislature were present that morning—forty-nine suffrage men and nine antis. T.K. Riddick, one of the amendment's strongest supporters, moved to reconsider the ratification resolution. Speaker Walker ruled him out of order. There was no quorum, he said. Besides, he announced, just that morning antis had won an injunction to prohibit the governor from certifying Tennessee's ratification. Riddick appealed the Speaker's decision to the members of the House. They

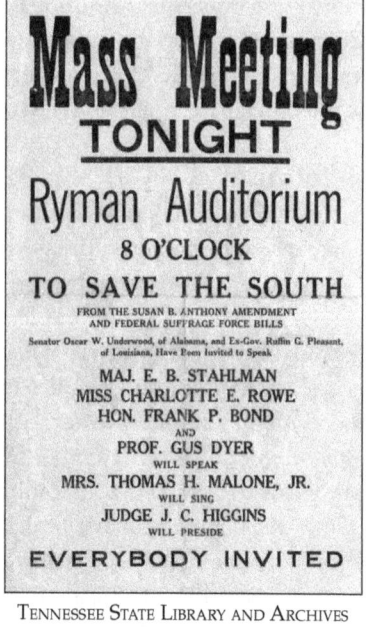

voted 49 to 8 to overturn Walker's ruling (Walker abstained) then went on to table the motion to reconsider. Walker's procedural ploy had failed.[55]

On August 23, the Tennessee Supreme Court overturned the injunction against the governor. Governor Roberts signed the certificate of ratification on August 24 and sent it on to Washington. On the morning of August 26, Secretary of State Bainbridge Colby issued a proclamation declaring the Nineteenth Amendment ratified and part of the United States Constitution.[56]

Still the antis refused to surrender. When members of the Red Rose Brigade returned to the House August 31, they moved to expunge the activities of August 21 from the record. The motion carried, largely because pro-suffrage members refused to vote. "I consider that the Nineteenth Amendment has been legally adopted," one stated, "and that any other action by this House would be a farce." Having erased August 21 from history, anti legislators went on to reconsider the Nineteenth Amendment, and vote it down. Most pro-suffrage representatives were recorded as present and not voting.[57]

Anne Dallas Dudley found it highly amusing. "Tennessee enacted a little farce to add to the gayety [sic] of the nation today," she wired Carrie Chapman Catt. A day later she was not laughing. "Find out from Washington if action yesterday seriously injures our case," her next telegram read. "Lawyers here differ. Must know at once."[58] She had no reason to worry. Ratification was secure, despite Tennessee's attempt to rescind its approval, and despite Seth Walker's ongoing efforts to prevent the amendment from taking effect. In September, he and other antis went first to Washington, to persuade Secretary of State Colby that Tennessee's

ratification was unconstitutional (the Secretary was not convinced) then on to Connecticut, where the legislature was considering ratification. There, as well, too few men heeded their pleas. Connecticut ratified in mid-September, and American women's right to vote was at last assured.[59]

Aftermath

The antis were no more gracious in defeat than they had been during the battle. Unable to stop woman suffrage, in the fall of 1920 they encouraged women voters to vote against the men who had enfranchised them. In Tennessee, they set their sights on Harry Burn and A.H. Roberts. Roberts was particularly vulnerable. Already unpopular because of his tax program and hostility to organized labor, he had alienated his political allies with his stand on suffrage. The special session of the General Assembly, after acceding to his request to ratify the Nineteenth Amendment by the narrowest of margins, proceeded to turn down every other proposal he submitted. E.B. Stahlman's *Nashville Banner,* which had supported him in the Democratic primary, now turned against him. The *Chattanooga Daily Times* even demanded that he be removed from the ticket.[60]

Suffragists rallied to the aid of their champions. Abby Crawford Milton traveled around the state, defending Burn and organizing women for Roberts. In Nashville, Catherine Kenny appealed to working women to support the governor. Still, suffragists recognized that Roberts's campaign was in serious trouble. In early October, a member of the women's committee of the state Democratic Party turned to Carrie Chapman Catt for help. "This is private and confidential and TNT," she began. "The Antis have concentrated their campaign against Governor Roberts and intend to defeat him at any cost." She pleaded with Catt to use her influence to raise money for the governor's campaign, and concluded: "If I knew anyway to make this appeal stronger I would do it. I shall feel forever disgraced if Roberts is repudiated. This is a woman's fight and we can't afford to lose."[61]

But they did lose. "Election Returns Prove Strength of Anti-Suffragists" proclaimed the *Woman Patriot,* official newspaper of the National Association Opposed to Woman Suffrage. Harry Burn won reelection, but A.H. Roberts went down to defeat, and Republican presidential candidate Warren G. Harding carried Tennessee. Female anti-suffragists—women who had not wanted the vote in the first place—now claimed that they had used the franchise to drive their enemies from office.[62] Democratic politicians blamed women for the defeat as well—Black women, who, they said, had turned out in large numbers and voted Republican. The day after the election, Edward H. Crump of Memphis wrote: "I was never so certain in all my life as I was that with woman suffrage and no poll tax provision it would be harmful to the Democratic party in Tennessee."[63]

The outcome of the election troubled suffragists, and they, too, cast about for scapegoats. Catherine Kenny attributed Roberts's loss to labor, farmers, and the Democrats themselves. The state party made only feeble attempts to turn out White

women's votes, she reported, while Republicans actively recruited Black female voters. She conceded, too, that the governor was an unattractive candidate. "He was pathetic," she told Carrie Chapman Catt, and unable to overcome the scandals that had tainted his reputation.[64]

Catherine Talty Kenny

Woman suffrage undoubtedly played a crucial role in Roberts' loss. The large turnout of both men and women in Republican east Tennessee meant a strong anti-Democratic vote.[65] The governor's half-hearted support of suffrage, along with the rumors surrounding him and his secretary, alienated potential women voters. Most important, when he called the special session and endorsed ratification of the Nineteenth Amendment, he turned many of his own allies against him. Roberts was an unpopular incumbent facing a beloved Republican opponent. When powerful friends like E.B. Stahlman deserted him because of his stand on woman suffrage, Roberts' candidacy was doomed.

Suffragists had staked their honor on a Roberts victory, and his loss hurt them. In January 1921, Catherine Kenny forecast a cold political season for women voters. "I believe the effect of our successful fight here in Tennessee will be to nullify any real power or influence of the women in either party," she told Carrie Chapman Catt. The newly elected legislators—"about 70% [sic] new men, inexperienced, and not even up to the usual poor standard"—seemed uniformly hostile to any measures of interest to women. Antis continued their efforts to dilute women's political strength. They introduced a bill to abolish primaries. Since women had little influence within party organizations, if the proposal succeeded it would, in the words of Abby Crawford Milton, "about disfranchise the women of Tennessee." Although the General Assembly voted to retain the primary, women's political prospects remained bleak. "Just now in Sunny Tennessee, we are certainly 'dead ones,'" Kenny concluded.[66]

Woman suffrage had, for the moment, failed to live up to its promise. But Kenny, Milton, and other suffragists never abandoned their faith in their cause and, in spite of their disappointments, they continued to believe that the prize was worth the price. "I shall never be as thrilled by the turn of any event as I was at that moment when the roll call that settled the citizenship of American women was heard," Abby Crawford Milton declared. "It seemed too dramatic to happen in real life, with the real thrill of history making, not the excitement of the stage or movies. Personally, I had rather have had a share in the battle for woman suffrage than any other world event."[67] It was, indeed, an historic occasion. The women and men

who secured the ratification of the Nineteenth Amendment acknowledged the truth of the message suffragists had been spreading since 1848: that women and men *were* equal, with the same rights, privileges, and responsibilities. In that hot Nashville August, suffragists faced their Armageddon and emerged victorious; "powers that pray" vanquished "powers that prey." They demonstrated once and for all that, when it came to politics, women were capable of far more than prayer, and they moved the nation one step closer to realizing its ideal of equality.

Notes

This essay is drawn from, "'Powers That Pray and Powers That Prey': Tennessee and the Fight for Woman Suffrage," *Tennessee Historical Quarterly* 50(4), 1991, and is reprinted with permission of the journal.

1. "Why?," newspaper clipping, *Nashville Tennessean*, Aug. 22, 1920, Harry T. Burn Scrapbook, Manuscripts Department, Special Collections, University of Tennessee Library, Knoxville; [For further information on the ratification struggle in Tennessee, including reprints of many of the pro- and anti-suffrage documents mentioned in this article, see Marjorie Spruill (Wheeler), ed. *Votes for Women! The Woman Suffrage Movement in Tennessee, the South, and the Nation,* (Knoxville, 1995)].

2. Quoted in Wilma Dykeman, *Tennessee Women, Past and Present,* Narrative by Wilma Dykeman with selected additional material edited by Carol Lynn Yellin (Memphis, Nashville, 1977), 25.

3. Carrie Chapman Catt and Nettie Rogers Shuler, *Woman Suffrage and Politics: The Inner Story of the Suffrage Movement* (New York, 1923), 424-28; Sue Shelton White to Gov. Albert H. Roberts, June 19, 1920, box 26, folder 4, Albert H. Roberts Papers, Tennessee State Library and Archives, Nashville (hereafter cited as TSLA); "Special Session in Tennessee!" *The Suffragist* 8 (July 1920): 121-22; Catherine Talty Kenny to Rose Young, June 21, 1920, box 1, folder 13; Charles Evans Hughes to Mary Garrett Hay, June 25, 1920, box 1, folder 10; Catherine Kenny to Carrie Chapman Catt, July 11, 1920, box 1, folder 14, all in Carrie Chapman Catt Papers, TSLA; "What's The Matter With Tennessee?" *Woman Citizen* 5 (July 3, 1920): 125.

4. Catherine T. Kenny to Ida Husted Harper, Dec. 16, 1919, box 1, folder 13; Catherine T. Kenny to Carrie Chapman Catt, Jan. 5, 1920, box 1, folder 13; Catherine T. Kenny to Mrs. Shuler, June 28, 1920, box 1, folder 14; Catt Papers; Albert H. Roberts, March 11, 1920, box 36, folder 1, Roberts Papers.

5. Catherine T. Kenny to Mrs. Shuler, June 28, 1920; Sue Shelton White, "The Tennessee Campaign at Close Range," *The Suffragist* 8 (Aug. 1920): 164; Gary W. Reichard, "The Defeat of Governor Roberts," *Tennessee Historical Quarterly* 30 (1971): 94-110.

6. Reichard, "Defeat of Governor Roberts"; "How Leading Democratic Newspapers Size Up Gov. Roberts and His Administration," (Nashville, [1920]), pamphlet, TSLA. See also Kenneth S. Braden, "The Wizard of Overton: Governor A.H. Roberts," *Tennessee Historical Quarterly* 43 (1984): 273-94.

7. Edwin Mims, *The Advancing South: Stories of Progress and Reaction* (1926; reprint, Port Washington, N.Y., 1969), 238; Joe Hatcher, "1920: Amendment and a Perfect 36," *Nashville Tennessean*, March 26, 1972, Vertical File—Woman Suffrage, TSLA.

8. Taylor, *Woman Suffrage Movement in Tennessee,* 108, n. 140.

9. Albert H. Roberts to Carrie Chapman Catt, July 10, 1920, box 1, folder 18, Catt Papers.

10. Catherine T. Kenny to Carrie Chapman Catt, July 11, 1920; Carrie Chapman Catt to Mrs. Guilford Dudley, July 12, 1920, box 1, folder 6, Catt Papers.

11. Catt and Shuler, *Woman Suffrage and Politics,* 432-33; Taylor, *Woman Suffrage Movement in Tennessee,* 109.

12. "Mrs. Carrie C. Catt Arrives in City," clipping, n.p., n.d., Vertical File—Woman Suffrage, TSLA.

13. Carrie Chapman Catt to Mrs. John M. [Catherine Talty] Kenny, June 29, 1920, box 1, folder 6, Catt Papers; Catt and Shuler, *Woman Suffrage and Politics,* 435-37; "Tennessee—The 36th," *The Suffragist* 9 (Sept. 1920): 199.

14. Josephine Anderson Pearson, "My Story!" 1, 19, box 1, folder 17, Josephine Anderson Pearson Papers, TSLA.

15. "Antis Gather New Strength," clipping, *Chattanooga Daily Times,* Aug. 9, 1920, box 2, folder 6, Catt Papers.

16. Marjorie Shuler, "Outside Influences Fight Suffrage in Tennessee," clipping, *Public Ledger,* Philadelphia, Pa., Aug. 8, 1920, box 2, folder 4; "Anti-suffrage Faction Busy," clipping, *Chattanooga Daily Times,* July 30, 1920, box 2, folder 5, both in Catt Papers.

17. Ida Husted Harper, ed., *History of Woman Suffrage,* (New York, 1922), vol. 6: 620; NAWSA, *VICTORY: How Women Won It: A Centennial Symposium, 1840-1940* (New York, 1940), 149.

18. *HWS* 6: 621 n.; G.F. Milton, "Editorial Correspondence," clipping, *Chattanooga News,* Aug. 19, 1920, Burn Scrapbook; "Winning the Vote in Tennessee," clipping, *Christian Science Monitor,* Sept. 4, 1920, Burn Scrapbook; Abby Crawford Milton to Carrie Chapman Catt, Jan. 13, 1921.

19. Catt and Shuler, *Woman Suffrage and Politics,* 135-38.

20. Walter Clark to Henry Watterson, April 12, 1919, in Aubrey Lee Brooks and Hugh Talmage Lefler, eds., *The Papers of Walter Clark* (Chapel Hill, 1950) 2: 396. See also David Morgan, *Suffragists and Democrats: The Politics of Woman Suffrage in America* (East Lansing, Mich., 1972), 157-77, and Jane Jerome Camhi, "Women Against Women: American Antisuffragism, 1880-1920," (Ph.D. diss., Tufts University, 1974), 183-94.

21. See Joe Michael Shahan, "Reform and Politics in Tennessee, 1906-1914," (Ph.D. diss., Vanderbilt University, 1981); Paul E. Isaac, *Prohibition and Politics: Turbulent Decades in Tennessee 1885-1920* (Knoxville, 1965); and Maury Klein, *History of the Louisville and Nashville Railroad* (New York, 1972), 368-94.

22. Paul E. Isaac, historian of the prohibition movement in Tennessee, identified Vertrees as "an attorney for liquor concerns"; see Isaac, *Prohibition and Politics,* 46.

23. John Trotwood Moore, *Tennessee: The Volunteer State 1769-1923* (Chicago, Nashville, 1923), 4: 650-51.

24. "Speaker Walker Lauded From Many States," *Woman Patriot* 4 (Aug. 28, 1920): 1.

25. Will T. Hale and Dixon C. Merritt, *A History of Tennessee and Tennesseans: The Leaders and Representative Men in Commerce, Industry and Modern Activities* (Chicago, New York, 1913) 5: 1401-02; Dumas Malone, ed., *Dictionary of American Biography* (New York, 1936) 9: 493-94; *National Cyclopedia of American Biography* (New York, 1898) 8: 224; Klein, *History of the Louisville and Nashville Railroad,* 376-78.

26. "The Power Behind the Throne," clipping, *Nashville Tennessean,* July 11, 1914, box 1, folder 3, Edwin A. Price Scrapbook, TSLA.

27. Clipping, *Nashville Banner*, July 11, 1914, box 1, folder 3, Price Scrapbook; Catt and Shuler, *Woman Suffrage and Politics*, 443.

28. Marjorie Shuler, "From the Tennessee Firing Line," *Woman Citizen* 5 (Aug. 28, 1920): 331; "Tennessee—The 36th," 200.

29. Quotation, "The Crisis," *Woman Citizen* 5 (Aug. 14, 1920): 277; Catt and Shuler, *Woman Suffrage and Politics*, 441, 446.

30. "Supreme Law of Tennessee Prohibits Ratification," broadside, box 1, folder 4; "Foster V. Brown, Champion of Suffrage, Declares That Ratification is Violation," broadside, box 1, folder 4; "The Federal Suffrage Amendment WILL NEVER BE RATIFIED If The People of Tennessee Guard Their Rights," broadside, box 1, folder 4; "Can The Present Legislature Act?" pamphlet, box 1, folder 5; Josephine A. Pearson to "Dear Sir or Madam," box 1, folder 7, all in Pearson Papers; "Vertrees Says There is No Excuse for Ratification," *Woman Patriot* 4 (Aug. 7, 1920): 1-2; Shuler, "Outside Influences Fight Suffrage in Tennessee"; "History of the Bitter Struggle to Ratify Suffrage," clipping, *Nashville Tennessean*, Aug. 29, 1920, Burn Scrapbook; Catherine T. Kenny to Carrie Chapman Catt, July 11, 1920; Catt and Shuler, *Woman Suffrage and Politics*, 434-36, 440; NAWSA, *VICTORY: How Women Won It*, 149.

31. "America When Feminized," broadside, box 1, folder 4, Pearson Papers. For other examples see broadsides in box 1, folder 4, and pamphlets in box 1, folder 3, Pearson Papers.

32. The photograph of Mrs. Dudley and her children is reprinted in John Egerton, *Nashville: The Faces of Two Centuries*, (Nashville, 1979), 184.

33. Carrie Chapman Catt to Mrs. John M. [Catherine T.] Kenny, June 29, 1920, box 1, folder 6, Catt Papers.

34. Josephine Pearson to "Dear [blank]," form letter, Aug. 9, 1920, box 1, folder 18, Pearson Papers.

35. "Beware!" broadside, box 1, folder 4. See also "That Deadly Parallel," "Can Anybody Terrorize Tennessee Manhood," and other leaflets and broadsides, folders 3, 4, and 5; "Three Federal Suffrage Force Bills in Congress," press release, May 15, 1920, *Woman Patriot*, all in Pearson Papers.

36. "Woman Suffrage, A Menace to the South. A Protest Against Its Imposition Through Federal Authority," pamphlet, box 1, folder 3, Pearson Papers.

37. Quotation from "Statement of Mrs. R.C. Pleasant, Leader of Anti-Federal Suffrage Ratification Forces of Louisiana," Burn Scrapbook.

38. Catherine T. Kenny to Carrie Chapman Catt, Jan. 5, 1920; Kenny to Catt, July 11, 1920; *HWS* 6: 606.

39. Catt and Shuler, *Woman Suffrage and Politics*, 442.

40. *House and Senate Journals of the Extraordinary Session of the Sixty-First General Assembly of the State of Tennessee*, (Nashville, 1920), 254, 263, 292-96; quotation, 293.

41. *HWS* 6: 621 n.; Catt and Shuler, *Woman Suffrage and Politics*, 445-46.

42. "Tennessee Likely To Vote Suffrage in Next Few Days," clipping, Aug. 12, 1920, n.p., box 2, folder 7, Catt Papers.

43. "The People Against the Politicians," *The Lookout: A Journal of Southern Society* 25 (Aug. 24, 1920): 1, box 1, folder 8, Pearson Papers. Carol Lynn Yellin identified the suffragist and the solon as Anne Dallas Dudley and Senator Lon McFarland; see Carol Lynn Yellin, "Countdown in Tennessee, 1920" *American Heritage* 30 (1978): 29-30.

44. *House Journal*, 33, 86-88; quotation, 87.

45. Quotations, Marjorie Shuler, "From the Tennessee Firing Line," 331. See also "Winning the Vote In Tennessee"; *House Journal*, 89; *HWS* 6: 623; Catt and Shuler, *Woman Suffrage and Politics*, 447.

46. Catt and Shuler, *Woman Suffrage and Politics*, 447.

47. *House Journal*, 91; Catt and Shuler, *Woman Suffrage and Politics*, 448-49.

48. Shuler, "From the Tennessee Firing Line," 331; Catt and Shuler, *Woman Suffrage and Politics*, 449; *HWS* 6: 623; "Suffrage Amendment Adopted By House," clipping, *Nashville Tennessean*, Aug. 19, 1920; G.F. Milton, "Burn Vote Was Influenced By His Mother's Views," clipping, *Chattanooga News*, Aug. 19, 1920; "Burn Changed Vote On Advice of His Mother," clipping, *Nashville Tennessean*, Aug. 20, 1920; Zoe Beckley, "Mother Proud of Boy Who Cinched Suffrage Victory," clipping, *Memphis Press*, Aug. 31, 1920; all in Burn Scrapbook.

49. Quotations from "Shouts of Joy and Groans of Dismay Greet News of Action of Legislature on Suffrage," clipping, *Knoxville Journal and Tribune*, Aug. 19, 1920, Burn Scrapbook, and telegram, Carrie Chapman Catt to Gertrude Weil, box 3, folder 4, Catt Papers; *House Journal*, 92-94; Catt and Shuler, *Woman Suffrage and Politics*, 449; "History of Bitter Struggle to Ratify Suffrage."

50. Quotations, Shuler, "On The Tennessee Firing Line," 332, 334. See also "Suffragists Inspired With House Victory," clipping, *Chattanooga News*, Aug. 20, 1920, Burn Scrapbook; Pearson, "My Story!" n.p.; *HWS* 6: 624; Catt and Shuler, *Woman Suffrage and Politics*, 450-54.

51. "MASS MEETING TONIGHT TO SAVE THE SOUTH," broadside, box 1, folder 2, Catt Papers; "Indignation Spreads Over Whole State," *Chattanooga Daily Times*, Aug. 26, 1920; "Little Interest Manifested in Mass Meetings," clipping, *Nashville Tennessean*, Aug. 29, 1920, box 1, folder 2, Price Scrapbook.

52. Martin Lee Calhoun, "God of Our Fathers Spare Us Yet!" *Woman Patriot* 4 (Sept. 11, 1920): 3.

53. Pearson, "My Story!" 13; "Burn Strongly Denies Charges" and "Nashville Papers Publish Affidavits Alleging Burn Was Approached on Subject," clippings, *Knoxville Sentinel*, Aug. 19, 1920, Burn Scrapbook; "The Truth About The Tennessee Campaign," *Woman Patriot* 4 (Sept. 11, 1920):6.

54. *House Journal*, 94-95; telegram, Carrie Chapman Catt to Frank J. Shuler, Aug. 20, 1920, box 3, folder 4, Catt Papers; "Reconsideration of Ratification Comes Up Today," clipping, *Nashville Tennessean*, Aug. 20, 1920, Burn Scrapbook; *HWS* 6, 621.

55. Catt and Shuler, *Woman Suffrage and Politics*, 450, 453-54; *House Journal*, 117-21; *HWS* 6: 624.

56. *HWS* 6: 624-25; Catt and Shuler, *Woman Suffrage and Politics*, 454-55.

57. *House Journal*, 130-35; quotation, 136-37.

58. Telegram, Anne Dallas Dudley to Carrie Chapman Catt, Aug. 31, 1920; telegram, Anne Dallas Dudley to Carrie Chapman Catt, Sept. 1, 1920, box 3, folder 5, Catt Papers.

59. Catt and Shuler, *Woman Suffrage and Politics*, 459-60.

60. "Anti-Suffrage Party Declares Bitter War," clipping, n.p., July 21 [1920], box 2, folder 4, Catt Papers; A.H. Roberts to Carrie Chapman Catt, Sept. 13, 1920, box 1, folder 18, Catt Papers; "Tennessee Antis Wage Campaign Against Roberts," *Woman Patriot* 4 (Oct. 16, 1920): 1-2; "The Truth About the Tennessee Campaign," 6; Braden, "The Wizard of Overton," 287-91; Reichard, "Defeat of Governor Roberts," 106-08.

61. Ellis Meredith to Carrie Chapman Catt, Oct. 5, 1920, box 1, folder 15, Catt Papers. See also Catherine T. Kenny to Carrie Chapman Catt, Sept. 10, 1920; Abby Crawford Milton to Carrie Chapman Catt, Sept. 1, 1920, box 1, folder 16, Catt Papers.

62. "Election Returns Prove Strength of Anti-Suffragists," *Woman Patriot* 4 (Nov. 6, 1920): 1; "Governors Who Forced Ratification Defeated," *Woman Patriot* 4 (Nov. 13, 1920): 6.

63. Edward H. Crump to Hill McAlister, Nov. 5, 1920, box 9, folder 5, Hill McAlister Papers, TSLA.

64. Catherine Talty Kenny to Carrie Chapman Catt, Nov. 16, 1920, box 1, folder 14, Catt Papers; "Where the Suffrage Issue Counted," *Woman Citizen* 5 (Nov. 20, 1920): 682.

65. Reichard, "Defeat of Governor Roberts," 108-09.

66. Catherine T. Kenny to Carrie Chapman Catt, Jan. 21, 1921, box 1, folder 14; Abby Crawford Milton to Carrie Chapman Catt, Feb. 5, 1921, box 1, folder 17, both in Catt Papers.

67. Abby Crawford Milton to Carrie Chapman Catt, Feb. 5, 1921, box 1, folder 17, Catt Papers.

ACROSS THE GREAT DIVIDE:
Women in Politics Before and After 1920

Nancy F. Cott

Editor's Introduction: In this thought-provoking essay, eminent historian Nancy F. Cott challenges widespread assumptions concerning women and politics "across the Great Divide." The passage of the Nineteenth Amendment in 1920 was unquestionably one of the great turning points in American history. However, as Cott argues, "too great a focus on the achievement of the Nineteenth Amendment obscures the similarities in women's political behavior before and after it and the relation of that behavior to broader political and social context."

In the immediate aftermath of the suffrage victory, political analysts and historians posited theories concerning the impact of the Nineteenth Amendment on American politics and women's political behavior that remained unchallenged for many decades. The often-told story went something like this: despite suffragists' claims that women would transform politics, many failed to vote, and those who voted did not vote as a "bloc." As a result, politicians quickly lost their new-found respect for women voters, and women were relegated to a minor role in party politics. Furthermore, the massive and cohesive women's movement, having lost—by winning—the issue that held it together, disintegrated, with many former suffragists becoming politically apathetic and the few that remained active locked in bitter combat with one another over the Equal Rights Amendment introduced in 1923. Such theories implied that woman suffrage was a failure, or, at best, a great victory that led (ironically) to a decline in women's political activism.

As Cott acknowledges, these widespread perceptions are correct in part. No significant "gender gap" emerged in the immediate aftermath of the Nineteenth Amendment. The massive National American Woman Suffrage Association (NAWSA) converted itself into the League of Women Voters (LWV), but the LWV retained only a small percentage of the giant suffrage organization's membership. The National Woman's Party (NWP), which continued under the same name, introduced the Equal Rights Amendment (ERA), hoping to wipe out all remaining legal discrimination against women. But this proposal alarmed the LWV and many women reformers who insisted that who insisted that working women desperately needed the laws that "discriminated" in their *favor*—the "protective legislation" for women that had been a primary accomplishment of the Progressive Era and that was under attack in the conservative climate of the 1920s.

However, as Cott explains (and readers of *One Woman, One Vote* are by now well aware), the woman suffrage movement was never a "unity"; there was diversity and factiousness in the women's movement *before* and *after* 1920. From the debate in the 1860s over whether or not to support the Fifteenth Amendment, to the dispute over the picketing of the White House as the movement neared an end, suffragists disagreed fervently over tactics—even as they agreed upon a goal. Furthermore, the suffrage coalition included women of diverse racial, ethnic, religious, regional, and class backgrounds, as well as party identifications, who could not reasonably be expected to fall into a solid "bloc" after enfranchisement. Indeed, as Cott suggests, those who lamented—or merely pointed out—the fact that enfranchised womanhood failed to "bloc vote" were quite unrealistic. Given the natural divisions among women (as among men), Cott considers the idea of a "woman's bloc" as an imaginary construct, "an interpretive fiction rather than a realistic expectation." Furthermore, re-examining the pronouncements of the suffragists on this subject, Cott makes it clear that "even when maintaining that women would exercise civic duties differently from men, suffragists rarely if ever portrayed a future voting 'bloc' of women." They spoke of issues about which they expected women voters to be concerned, such as children's health, political corruption, and the liquor traffic, but they "rarely specified by what means, exactly, the injection of women's votes into the polity was to bring about change."

Cott also objects strongly to the suggestion that 1920 ushered in a great decline in women's political and social activism. On the issue of voter turnout, she points out that women's political participation can only be understood when studied in the context of overall voter turnout—which *declined* in the 1920s. She also explains that both before and after 1920, women were involved in a range of political activities besides voting or even party politics. Cott is particularly disdainful, however, of the idea that women's participation in voluntary organizations declined sharply after 1920, and suggests that to measure women's political activity, as many have done, by comparing the size of the NAWSA and the dissimilar League of Women Voters is absurd. For a more accurate picture, Cott insists, one must examine (as she does in this essay) the broad range of women's voluntary associations from the Parents and Teachers Associations (PTA) to the Daughters of the American Revolution (DAR) to the American Birth Control League. Indeed, writes Cott, the years between the two world wars were marked by an extremely high level of political activity on the part of women, though they often were engaged in organizations with conflicting—or directly competing—agendas. The disagreement among feminists over the ERA in the 1920s was only one of many areas in which female activists of all persuasions exercised their right to pursue their diverse political goals. Indeed, it might be argued that, with its success, the Nineteenth Amendment freed women to disagree among themselves, as well as to work for a wide variety of causes other than suffrage, whether individually, in women's groups, or in mixed-gender organizations.

Cott's reminder about the diversity among politically active women before and after 1920 not only sets the record straight, but, combined with her point about the impossibility of a woman's bloc, it clearly demonstrates (in her words) "the unique power of disenfranchisement to bring diverse women into coalition." Millions of American women who became suffragists agreed on one point if nothing else: they were weary of a social and political system based on the idea of separate spheres and wanted full recognition of their individuality, equality, and right to participate fully and directly in making the laws under which they lived.

★   ★   ★   ★   ★

THE NINETEENTH AMENDMENT is the most obvious benchmark in the history of women in politics in the United States. To neglect the political watershed of 1920 when assessing the history of women's politics would be obtuse, since the sex barrier to the ballot was eliminated then and also the decades-long campaign for the vote, which had mobilized millions of women, ended. Yet too great a focus on the achievement of the Nineteenth Amendment obscures the similarities in women's political behavior before and after it and the relation of that behavior to broader political and social context.

There were striking continuities in women's political choices and actions on both sides of 1920. After women gained the ballot, they continued to engage in a range of politics broader than simply electoral activity. While it may be impossible to compare the influence women as a group had in politics before and after the Nineteenth Amendment, it is possible to consider more carefully suffragists' promises and their results. Women's voting must be put in the context of men's voting—that is, in the context of popular political participation in the period. Perhaps most important, the organizational and political roles of women's voluntary associations—which, far from declining, multiplied in membership—must be considered within rather than outside of politics.

The Suffrage Coalition — A Woman's Bloc?

Although historians have long presented the campaign for suffrage as a unity, in contrast to the disunity among women's groups of the 1920s, there is reason to see disunity among politically active women as typical of both the 1910s and 1920s. For instance, suffragists were opposed by female anti-suffragists; White suffragists raised racial bars to Blacks. In other matters great and small, from the conflicts between clubwomen and entertainers over the status and standards of dance halls to standoffs between pacifists and preparedness advocates during World War I, there were strategic, ideological, class-based and race-based differences among groups of women that were acted out in the public arena before as well as after 1920. From 1869 on, within the suffrage movement itself there were successive deep divisions over strategy and method. Intense internal conflicts over leadership,

finances, and tactics so racked the National American Woman Suffrage Association (NAWSA) in 1911 that longtime suffragist, the Reverend Olympia Brown, called her colleagues' "shallow false talk of love excellence harmony &c &c ...so false that it makes me vomit."[1] The bitter split between the National American Woman Suffrage Association and the Congressional Union (CU) leaderships beginning in 1913 was the latest but not the only such cleavage.

The way that suffragists built coalitions during the 1910s acknowledged that women had variant and perhaps clashing loyalties. Suffrage leaders purposely addressed defined groups (mothers, wage-earners, Black women, White women, professionals) with specifically designed instrumental appeals, tacitly acknowledging that not all women shared the same definition of self-interest. Even nonvoting women took on partisan affiliations, which mattered: In the final years of the suffrage campaign Maud Wood Park, head of Congressional lobbying for the NAWSA, was so aware of Republican and Democratic partisan loyalties clashing within her own Congressional Committee that she preferred to meet with its members individually. The women were so "inclined to be suspicious" of one another that full meetings of the committee were unproductive. Though distressed by the division, Park took it for granted that "party women could not be expected to free themselves from the prevailing currents of thought."[2]

Even when maintaining that women would exercise civic duties differently from men, suffragists rarely if ever portrayed a future voting "bloc" of women. It is striking that the one time that a small minority of suffragists *did* attempt to marshal women's votes into a voting bloc, they were condemned by the majority of their colleagues. That was in 1914 and 1916, when the Congressional Union (predecessor of the National Woman's Party) campaigned among enfranchised women of the Western states to defeat all Democrats. They intended to "punish the party in power" in Washington for failure to adopt a constitutional amendment for woman suffrage. Their effort to make women's power at the polls count on a single issue inspired horrified rejection from mainstream suffragist leaders and little agreement from women voters. Alice Paul, architect of the CU plan, had a definite conception of a single-issue feminist bloc—not a generalized "woman bloc"—operating in a two-party system to swing the balance: "To count in an election you do not have to be the biggest Party; you have to be simply an independent Party that will stand for one object and that cannot be diverted from that object."[3]

Very likely the CU strategy failed to evoke support from the bulk of suffragists not only because of its approach but because of its object—to unseat all Democrats, whether they as individuals supported woman suffrage or not. There was the thorn on the rose of any such proposal: a woman's bloc, to cohere and have an impact, had to make a single issue its clear priority, while candidates' positions on so-called women's issues would not stand alone but would combine with their positions on other questions that concerned women. The NAWSA's judgment that the CU was misguided gave more evidence that women had differing priorities

Women casting their ballots in New York City
LIBRARY OF CONGRESS

and tactics; perceiving that division, suffragists were unlikely to imagine women voting as one. When the National Woman's Party moved on to militant demonstrations, which the NAWSA also deplored, Maud Wood Park found nothing more exasperating than having to answer Congressmen's questions: "'Why don't you women get together? You can't expect us to vote for you if you can't agree among yourselves.'" She pointed out as "mildly" as possible "that men, even within the same party, were not without their differences. But sauce for the gander was rarely accepted as sauce for the goose." Lest we assume that suffragists were too naive to recognize the coalition nature of their association, they remind us, as Harriot Stanton Blatch reminded a colleague in 1918, "altho [sic] all sorts and conditions of women were united for suffrage...they are not at one in their attitude towards other questions in life."[4]

Suffragists spoke of issues—safeguarding children's health, eliminating political corruption, ending the liquor traffic, improving the economic leverage of women wage-earners—but rarely addressed exactly how or for whom women's votes would be collected, whether electing women to office was a high priority, or whether women's votes were adjuncts or substitutes for the established practice of lobbying and educational work by women's voluntary

associations. As much as suffragists talked about women's inclinations, duties, and contributions, they rarely specified by what means, exactly, the injection of women's votes into the polity was to bring about change. Suffragists usually made very general or else modest claims, and (interestingly) rarely touched on the subject of women in political office. True, there were some overarching retorts such as Anna Howard Shaw's to an anti-suffragist who objected that voting women would have little time for charity, "Thank God, there will not be so much need of charity and philanthropy!" There was rhetoric—equally vague— regarding women's inclination against war, such as the Congressional Union's claim that "A government responsible to all women, as well as all men, will be less likely to go to war, without real necessity." There were particular anticipations of women's efficacy, such as Florence Kelley's that "the enfranchisement of women is indispensable to the solution of the child labor problem." Typically, however, suffragists' proposals and predictions in the 1910s were locally relevant: it was claimed at the New York Woman Suffrage Party's 1910 convention, for instance, that women's votes would help to alleviate the evils of inadequate inspection of milk, high prices, overcrowded classrooms, crime, prostitution, and child labor; the ballot would enable women to preside as associate justices in children's court and women's night court. During the 1915 New York campaign, Carrie Chapman Catt even warned suffragist speakers against promising "what women will do with the vote."[5]

The idea that women's votes would line up in one direction certainly existed in an implicit imprecise form, in the views of both suffragists and their opponents. As prospective voters, women were often expected to punish candidates who did not show deference to women's organizations' aims and to embrace those who supported Prohibition and social legislation. There was some evidence in the 1910s (mainly from Scandinavia) that women were "conservative" voters and some claims (from New York City) that women swelled the "radical" vote. When Washington, Oregon, and Arizona each adopted Prohibition shortly after adopting woman suffrage, women's votes were presumed to have turned the tide. Since the Western states that enfranchised women early did not have extensive industries employing women and children, they gave little evidence whether women's ballots would decisively protect such vulnerable wage-earners. Shortly after New York women got the right to vote, however, four state legislators who had opposed minimum-wage legislation for women, child-labor laws, and other social legislation were unseated. Two of the four were replaced with assembly*women*. In Columbus, Ohio, in 1919, after women received municipal suffrage, their organizing and voter-registration work through voluntary associations succeeded in dumping the city boss who had been mayor for sixteen years, despite his organization's labeling them a "shrieking sisterhood." However, most big-city machine politicians had dropped objections to woman suffrage by the late 1910s after observing and reasoning that enfranchised women had *not* shown a habit of

voting together to oppose existing political organizations. Claims about the impact of women's votes were so speculative and contradictory by 1919, in fact, that social scientists William Ogburn and Inez Goltra, after studying "how women vote," could conclude only that there might be some significant sex differences *or* that "the enfranchisement of women will have no other effect than approximately to double the number of votes previously cast." With more evidence, a 1923 study drew the similarly ambivalent conclusion that women neither "merely vote the same as men" nor vote "with marked independence."[6]

Voter Turnout

The unspoken notion that adding women to the electorate should transform politics did prompt some suffragists to be disappointed at the lack of outcome in the 1920s, but they were not the only ones looking dourly at the scene. Both popular journalists and political scientists expressed a mood of skepticism, if not downright cynicism, about mass political participation. Social scientists stressed the irrational motivations driving individual political behavior, the inability of the mass public to make objective judgments in popular government, and the likelihood that politicians would manipulate these failings.[7] Observers' discouragement about democratic participation found corroboration in the deepening decline in voter participation, a trend continuous from 1896 and intensifying from the 1910s to the 1920s. Mean national turnout in the presidential election years 1920, 1924, and 1928 was just over half of the eligible electorate, as compared to an average of almost eighty percent in the late nineteenth century. In the off-year elections between 1922 and 1930, little more than a third of the electorate voted, whereas nearly two-thirds, on the average, had voted in the off-years between 1876 and 1896.[8]

The meaning of the decline in voter turnout is not absolutely clear, in great part because of the debatable meaning of early twentieth-century Progressive reform—that is, whether its intents and/or effects were democratic or elitist. In light of such reforms as direct election of senators, direct primaries, the initiative, referendum and recall, it seems ironic, even tragic, that the Progressive Era should have ushered in the decade of the lowest voter participation ever. But if Progressive reforms intended to keep the reins of the state in the hands of the expert or the economically powerful few—as some reforms more than others indicate—then the decline in voter turnout fulfilled rather than undid that aim. Voting "reforms" included the continuing disfranchisement of Blacks and Populist or Republican Whites in the South by means of poll taxes, literacy tests, and other bars to registration and balloting; more complicated and rigorous residency and registration requirements in Northern states which limited immigrant voting; and, at the municipal level, replacement of district voting with at-large elections, which predestined minority interest-group candidates to fail.

While Progressive reformers embraced the salutary aim to eliminate corrupt influence-peddling and substitute neutral and informed standards, their emphasis

on expert presence and management in the state also diverted control away from the populace, to an elite of professional and business-managerial experts. The results could be seen institutionalized in the 1920s in various forms, from city-manager rule in municipalities, to federal and state commissions, to such quasi-governmental institutions as the National Bureau of Economic Research. "It is a misfortune for the woman's movement," mordantly commented Suzanne La Follette, a feminist and pacifist of anti-statist leanings, in 1926, "that it has succeeded in securing political rights for women at the very period when political rights are worth less than they have been at any time since the eighteenth century." The most persuasive explanations of downsliding voter turnout from 1896 to the 1920s also have to do with the entrenchment of the Democratic Party's hold on the South and the Republican Party's domination of the North and West (and thus of the national government) to the extent that the interest of voters in partisan contest, and voter sense of efficacy, collapsed. The portrait of increasingly dispirited voters does not account for the vigor of third parties during the period, but it does account for the overall trend.[9]

Analyses in the 1920s pinned much of the blame for the contemporary drop in voter turnout on newly eligible women. Just before the presidential election in 1924, journalists and political scientists turned the spotlight on the "failure" of women to flock to the polls, although dependable data on voting behavior were very scarce.[10] Votes were not counted by sex except in the state of Illinois. In the 1920 national elections, slightly less than half of the eligible women in Illinois cast a ballot, while three-quarters of the eligible men did. Early discussions based on that evidence generalized only downward, on the reasoning that Illinois women were more likely than most to vote since they had had the ballot since 1913.

Women's voting participation actually varied greatly from place to place, group to group, and issue to issue. Fewer women than men voted, but the difference in their voting behavior was not as stark as initial extrapolations from the Illinois data established. Analysis via regression techniques have now made it clear that the 1920s low in turnout was not due to women's behavior alone, but also to male voters' sinking interest. Hull House leader Jane Addams was on the mark when to a magazine's 1924 question, "Is Woman Suffrage Failing?" she responded that the question ought to be "is suffrage failing?"[11]

Voting Women and Their Organizations

As Addams noted, the context in which to look at women's voting behavior in the 1920s is that of declining voter participation overall. A few vigorous female voices, such as that of former National Woman's Party leader Anne Martin of Nevada, urged women to enter the electoral arena in force and move directly to claim "woman's share, woman's *half* in man-controlled government."[12] The much more general trend—and one deplored by Martin as merely "indirect influence"— was women's reliance on voluntary associations rather than the electoral arena for

League of Women Voters members encouraging voter registration, August 1920.
LIBRARY OF CONGRESS

political efficacy. Since the early nineteenth century, women had influenced what took place in electoral and legislative halls from outside, not only by seeking suffrage but by inquiring about a range of health, safety, moral, and welfare issues. They had built a tradition of exercising political influence (one admittedly hard to measure), which continued vigorously once the vote was gained. Women's organizations' lobbying route should be seen as pioneering in the modern mode of exerting political force—that is, interest-group politics. This voluntarist mode, with its use of lobbying to effect political influence, and the kinds of interests pursued (i.e., health, safety, moral, and welfare issues), prevailed in women's political participation both before and after 1920.[13]

From recent histories one might gain the impression that women's voluntary organizations waned after 1920, but nothing is further from the truth. In her 1933 history of women, author and former NWP suffragist Inez Haynes Irwin observed that women were, if anything, *over*organized in voluntary associations during the 1920s and 1930s. She closed her book with a staggering list, from professional to civic to patriotic to social welfare to charitable to ethnic and religious women's organizations.[14] Although historians often cite as evidence of decimation in activism the contrast between the two million women in the NAWSA in the 1910s and the tiny fraction of that membership—probably five percent—who joined in the NAWSA's successor group, the National League of Women Voters (LWV), the two figures are not really comparable. The two organizations differed widely in form and intent: the first was a federation that pursued one specific goal, made few demands on its local members, imposed no homogeneity upon affiliates, and used all volunteer labor; the subsequent organization stated many aims (including civic

reform, citizenship education, international peace, and women's rights), made strenuous demands on its local members, attempted standardized national procedure, and employed professional staff.

Quickly evolving into a "good government" rather than a feminist organization, its premise being to ready women for political life, the LWV found itself, ironically, competing with women's partisan activity as much as preparing women for it. When all women became fair game for party organizations, Republican and Democratic women's divisions vied with the nonpartisan League for the time and loyalty of women interested in politics. Some leading NAWSA suffragists went directly into party organizations instead of into the League. Lillian Feickert, for example, a prominent New Jersey suffragist who was named vice-chairman of the Republican state committee in 1920, built the New Jersey Women's Republican Club on the grassroots model of the New Jersey Woman Suffrage Association. Feickert claimed that three-quarters of the suffragists joined; by the spring of 1922 the club claimed 60,000 members. Women's divisions in state and national party committees should be seen, as logically as the League, as successor organizations to the NAWSA.[15]

More generally, where one large or vital pre-1920 women's organization declined or ended, more than one other arose to take its space, if not its exact task. While the General Federation of Women's Clubs seemed to decline in vigor (although not clearly in membership), the National Congress of Parents and Teachers Associations (PTA) rose into a mass membership whose local units took up efforts similar to those of many unnamed women's clubs of the earlier generation, working to establish playgrounds, libraries, and health clinics, as well as lobbying at the national level, on issues from film standards to international peace. More than quintupling during the 1920s, the membership of the PTA reached over a million and a half by 1931. Its color bar led (in effect) to the founding in 1926 of a National Colored Parent-Teachers Association, which had at least the cooperation of the older group.[16]

The two national organizations that had labored most avidly on behalf of wage-earning women in the pre-World War I era did show drastic reductions in membership and resources in the 1920s. These were the National Consumers League (NCL)—not strictly but for the most part a women's group—and the National Women's Trade Union League (WTUL). Although both had set out auspicious programs in 1919, neither gained members nor momentum, their experience more like that of labor unions than of women's associations. Both the WTUL's and the NCL's efforts had informed public consciousness to the extent that unions themselves and agencies of government took up the concerns raised by those voluntary associations. As pressure from women's voluntary organizations was instrumental in making local public health and school departments assume some responsibilities for sanitation and for children's safety, and in inducing states to institute social welfare and protective labor legislation and the federal

government to establish pure food and drug laws, likewise it was pressure from the WTUL and NCL (and other women's groups) that led to establishing the Women's Bureau in the United States Department of Labor. The Women's Bureau's mandate was to investigate the conditions and protect the interests of wage-earning women; it also took on the WTUL's aim to educate the public, and, in alliance with the WTUL, staunchly defended sex-based protective legislation.[17]

The WTUL's intention to raise the trade-union consciousness of industrially employed women as well as sweeten their lives through association was seized by Industrial Clubs formed by the YWCA. In 1926, the YWCA stopped requiring that members be Protestant Christians, and membership grew; by 1930 the organization boasted over 600,000 members, 55,000 volunteer advisors, and a dispersed professional staff of almost 3,500. The YWCA Industrial Clubs educated and helped to organize both Black and White women workers in Southern textile mills, and brought them to testify before legislatures about industrial conditions. These clubs also served as recruitment grounds for summer schools for women workers. The summer schools themselves, founded during the 1920s by labor reformers and academics, formed a sequel to the WTUL cross-class efforts earlier in the century.[18]

The YWCA was also instrumental in bringing together white-collar women workers. The founding in 1919 of the National Federation of Business and Professional Women's Clubs (BPW) resulted from a conference of businesswomen called by the YWCA during World War I. Lena Madesin Phillips, a Kentucky-born lawyer who was drafted from her wartime YWCA position to become the first executive secretary of the National Federation, warmed to the subject of encouraging business and professional women's teamwork, courage, risk-taking, and self-reliance. The slogan the federation used to develop hundreds of local educational fundraising efforts during the 1920s, "at least a high school education for every business girl," indicated its orientation toward ordinary white-collar workers. Lawyers, teachers, and independent entrepreneurs also formed an important part of its membership. The clubs affiliated with the federation (required to have three-quarters of their members actively employed) numbered 1,100 by 1931, including about 56,000 individuals. Scores of new associations of women professionals were also founded between 1915 and 1930, as were two more federations of such clubs, called Zonta International and Quota International.[19]

The alliance with professionals—social workers, social researchers, college and university professors—so noticeably important in efforts on behalf of women workers and in the YWCA in the 1920s was also apparent in the birth control movement. In 1919 Margaret Sanger, leader in the American Birth Control League, left behind her former socialist politics, along with her purposeful lawbreaking and agitation in working-class communities and her emphasis on women's control of their own bodies. Sanger thenceforward emphasized eugenic reasoning about better babies. The American Birth Control League organized and educated the public and lobbied for the legalization of birth control on the

First Convention of the Montana Federation of Negro Women's Clubs,
Butte, Montana, August 3, 1921

premise of allowing "doctors only" to provide information and methods. Women who saw the virtues of that approach and volunteered their time for birth control in the 1920s were mainly middle-class matrons, more socially and politically conservative than the birth control advocates of the 1910s, and also more numerous. The American Birth Control League claimed over 37,000 members in 1926, almost ninety percent female. Fewer women followed the approach of civil libertarian Mary Ware Dennett, founder of the Voluntary Parenthood League, which stood on First Amendment rights and aimed to decriminalize birth control by removing it from federal obscenity statutes.[20]

While major women's organizations founded earlier, such as the Woman's Christian Temperance Union (WCTU), persisted, a host of organizations that women could and did join in the 1920s were new ones, founded during or after World War I. The American Association of University Women (AAUW), whose members had to be graduates of accredited collegiate institutions, evolved from the Association of Collegiate Alumnae into a truly national operation in 1921 under the new name and a decade later had 36,818 members in 551 branches. Black collegiate alumnae, excluded by the spirit if not the letter of the AAUW, founded their own national association in 1924, not only to promote mutual benefit, educational standards, and scholarship among their own race, but also to work toward "better conditions of contact" between White and Black college women. In 1932 it had eight branches and almost 300 members.[21]

Group consciousness among minority-group women was a major source of new organizations. Both Jewish women and Catholic women founded numerous voluntary associations during the 1920s and 1930s.[22] Black women continued the National Association of Colored Women (NACW), the organizational hub that had been

central to Black suffragist efforts and had linked Black clubwomen in communities across the nation. Its umbrella covered between 150,000 and 200,000 members in forty-one states in the mid-1920s. Many of its leaders also pursued their aims of racial uplift through male-dominated Black organizations, especially the NAACP, the Urban League, and the Commission on Interracial Cooperation. All through the decade, Black women campaigned vigorously against lynching and for the federal anti-lynching bill languishing in the Southern-dominated United States Senate—their numbers far beyond Ida B. Wells-Barnett's lone crusade in an earlier generation. Despite (or, perhaps, because of) the way that the NACW had brought women into political activism, its numbers declined by the end of the decade to about 50,000. Civil rights and welfare organizations of men and women were conducting the kinds of activities the NACW had begun, and they had more benefit of White financial support. Lacking resources, in 1930 the NACW cut its departments from thirty-eight to two: the home, and women in industry. But five years later Mary McLeod Bethune, a former president of the NACW and longtime laborer in the Black struggle for freedom, led the way in establishing a new national clearinghouse, the National Council of Negro Women. She was emphatic that neither organizations dominated by Black men nor by White women had given Black women sufficient voice.[23]

Other new organizations women joined in the 1920s were patriotic, security-minded societies formed in the wake of World War I, including the American War Mothers and the American Legion Auxiliary, which grew from an initial 131,000 to over 400,000 members after ten years. The American Legion Auxiliary often worked in concert with the longer-established Daughters of the American Revolution (DAR), which more than doubled in size between 1910 and 1932, reaching 2,463 chapters and almost 170,000 members by the latter date. During the 1920s and 1930s these women's organizations—loudly anti-communist and enthusiastic in red-baiting—advocated military preparedness.[24] They positioned themselves against women's peace organizations, for international peace was *the* major item of concern among organized women in the 1920s.

In an unprecedented tide of public concern, a range of peace groups from the conservative and nationalistic American Peace Society, through Protestant church agencies, to the left-wing pacifist War Resisters League formed during and after the war. In the 1920s they proposed competing alternatives, including the League of Nations, the World Court, international arbitration conferences, disarmament, and noncooperation with the military. Women could follow a number of avenues instigated and dominated by men; they appeared in all the peace societies, but clustered in their own organizations. Two groups were founded in 1919: the Women's International League for Peace and Freedom, whose American section included such luminaries of social reform as Jane Addams, Lillian Wald, and Alice Hamilton, and the much smaller, more extremely nonresistant Women's Peace Society. The foundings of the Women's Peace Union of the Western Hemisphere, and the Women's Committee for World Disarmament, followed in 1921. In

addition, the major women's organizations—the LWV, the AAUW, the WCTU, the BPW, and the PTA—all put international peace prominently on their agendas. In 1925 Carrie Chapman Catt, the former general of NAWSA, assembled from the memberships of the major women's organizations with peace departments the National Committee on the Cause and Cure of War (NCCCW). That collectivity met annually for many years and formed a basis for peace lobbying; it claimed cumulative membership over five million at the start and eight million—or one out of five adult women in the United States—by the 1930s.[25]

The Politics of Women's Voluntary Associations

The level of organization among American women after 1920 thus appears to compare very favorably to that before, even considering that voluntary memberships would have to increase by slightly more than a fifth to keep up with the growth in the adult female population. The number of women in organizations is compelling although memberships in the various organizations could and often did overlap, as had been no less true of the pre-war generation. Repeated foundings and aggregate memberships make it clear that women were still joining women's organizations, as they had for generations. By their very constitution of specialized memberships (professional women, religious women, mothers, women of a particular political bent) and purposes (birth control, education, anti-lynching, peace, and so on), such organizations were as likely to sustain or even to rigidify the differentiations and diversities among women according to racial, ethnic, class, and political grounds, however, as to make women feel a common cause. The more purposive and specialized a women's organization was, the more likely it was to be instrumentally allied with professional expertise and involved with the bureaucratic machinery of institutions, commissions, and conferences that developed rapidly in and outside government during the 1920s. It was also more likely to be working in concert with male-dominated organizations pursuing similar purposes. These women's organizations were not purporting to emanate from or to operate in a separate sphere, as had many of their forebears in the nineteenth century. Consequently, there was an omnipresent potential for the groups working on issues not peculiar to women—peace, for example—to self-destruct by routing their members toward male-dominated organizations that had more funds and thus seemed more effective (as it happened with the NACW).

Carrying on the voluntarist legacy of pre-war (unenfranchised) women's groups, women's organizations in the 1920s and 1930s had the benefit of the ballot and the ethos that women were full citizens. Such organizations benefitted from the much increased rate of high school and college education among women and the lower birth rate, which together meant that there were many more women knowledgeable about social issues and not entirely occupied with child care. At the same time, three-quarters of all adult women were not gainfully employed. These factors created the pool of enfranchised women who peopled voluntary associations in the

First Board of the LWV at the Chicago Victory Convention, February 1920. First row, from left; Maud Wood Park, Grace Wilbur Trout; Carrie Chapman Catt. Standing, from left; Katharine Ludington, Marie Stuart Edwards, Della Dortch, Edna Fischel Gellhorn, Mabeth Hurd Paige, Euphemia "Effie" Comstock Simmons, Pattie Ruffner Jacobs. LIBRARY OF CONGRESS

era between the two world wars, very probably the highest proportion of women so engaged in the whole history of American women.

Not all women's organizations entered politics, but most of the national organizations did. They adopted the mode of pressure politics rather than fielding their own candidates: that is, they aimed to educate the public and lobbied for specific bills as they had during the suffrage campaign. As the first president of the LWV, Maud Wood Park took the lead in 1920 in forming among ten women's organizations a Capitol Hill lobbying clearinghouse, the Women's Joint Congressional Committee (WJCC). The National League of Women Voters, the General Federation of Women's Clubs, the Woman's Christian Temperance Union, the National Congress of Parents and Teachers, the National Federation of Business and Professional Women's Clubs, were all charter members. The WJCC promised to establish a lobbying committee on behalf of any item that at least five of its constituent members wished to forward, and it immediately started working on two different attempts, one for federal funds for maternity and infancy health protection (realized in 1921 in the Sheppard-Towner Act), the other for removal of citizenship discrimination against American women who married aliens (partially realized in the Cable Act of 1922).

Describing the WJCC in 1924, by which time it included twenty-one organizations, Mary Anderson, Director of the United States Women's Bureau,

asserted with pride that "American women are organized, highly organized, and by the millions. They are organized to carry out programs of social and political action." She called the WJCC the "cooperative mouthpiece" of American women, conveying its members' opinions to Washington and bringing back to them news of legislators' doings. Women's organizations operated from motives and resources different from those of men's chambers of commerce, fraternal organizations, manufacturers' associations and so on, in Anderson's view. Where men's pressure groups relied on economic power in politics and looked for commercial or financial advantage or professional gain, women's organizations were working without self-interest, for the public good, for social welfare, on largely volunteer talent, relying on their influence on public opinion and "upon their voting strength for their success."[26] Anderson's commentary highlighted how far women leaders such as she persisted in assumptions formed before suffrage about women citizens' salutary disinterestedness. It also, unintentionally, explained why women's organizations (lobby as they might, and did) commanded only a weak position. Women could marshal only votes (in an era of widespread voter resignation) and public opinion. Men had the economic clout.

Voluntary Conflicts

The considerable unity of method among women's organizations contrasted with the diversity—often acrimony—among their specific goals.[27] Although women formed groups of probably greater number and variety in the 1920s than ever before, that did not necessarily mean they could work together nor could any particular group claim—without being countered—to speak politically for women. Differences among women's groups were at least as characteristic as their techniques of pressure politics. The controversy over the Equal Rights Amendment in the 1920s is well known: when the National Woman's Party had introduced into Congress in December 1923 an amendment to the Constitution reading "Men and women shall have equal rights throughout the United States and every place subject to its jurisdiction," it was immediately—and for decades after—opposed by the LWV and most other major women's organizations, which supported sex-based protective labor legislation, presumed to be put at risk by an ERA.[28] What is not so well recognized are the other equally important divisions among politically active women, and the fact that these divisions might cross-cut. Partisan loyalty has been wrongly slighted in historians' assessments of women's political behavior in the 1920s: women loyal to one party not only conflicted with women loyal to another, but also, importantly, partisan women conflicted with women who wanted to organize nonpartisan alliances.[29]

On the peace issue—where at first glance women seemed most wholeheartedly united—women's groups urging disarmament were opposed by patriotic women's organizations who boosted military preparedness. To counter the antimilitarist impact that the Women's International League for Peace and Freedom (WILPF) was making, the DAR and allied groups in 1924 formed a National Patriotic

Council. When WILPF speakers testified in Congress in 1928 against the naval building program, for instance, members of the DAR and the Dames of the Loyal Legion were also present, and Mrs. Noble Newport Potts, president of the National Patriotic Council, outspokenly warned the House Naval Affairs Committee Chairman about Dorothy Detzer, executive secretary of the WILPF, "That's a dangerous woman you've been talking to!" In that particular instance WILPF and other antimilitarists had the desired effect, and the House Committee, deluged by adverse mail, cut their authorization from seventy-one to sixteen naval vessels. Still, confidence that antimilitarism was "women's" stance was shattered.[30]

The impact that women activists made on one side or another of the pacifism/militarism question proved, ironically, the absence rather than the substance of gender solidarity. Right-wing women's confrontation and red-baiting of women pacifists and antimilitarists also led Carrie Chapman Catt, who intended to be moderate and mainstream, to leave out the WILPF and the Women's Peace Union when she organized the National Committee on the Cause and Cure of War. Regardless, ultra-patriotic women's organizations tarred Catt with the same brush that they used on the pacifists.[31]

On Prohibition—generally presumed in the 1910s to command women's support—the late 1920s revealed another crevasse. Pauline Morton Sabin recalled being motivated to found the Women's Organization for National Prohibition Reform (WONPR) when she heard Ella Boole, president of the WCTU, announce to the Congress, "I represent the women of America!" Sabin felt, "Well, lady, here's one woman you don't represent." A New Yorker born to wealth and elite social position, Sabin was president of the Women's National Republican Club, an active Republican fund-raiser and director of Eastern women's activities for the Coolidge and Hoover presidential campaigns. Sabin first brought together women of her own class and acquaintance, but after she launched her organization formally in Chicago in 1929 with a national advisory council of 125 women from twenty-six states, it gathered much broader middle-class membership. Its numbers grew to 300,000 by mid-1931 and doubled that a year later, vastly exceeding the membership of the longer-established men's Association Against the Prohibition Amendment and surpassing the membership claimed by the WCTU. The WONPR actively challenged the stereotype that women supported Prohibition. For instance, it disputed the WCTU's public assurance that the three million women under the aegis of the General Federation of Women's Clubs endorsed the Eighteenth Amendment. After WONPR leaders dared the GFWC to poll its membership on Prohibition—emphasizing that WONPR members also belonged to GFWC clubs—the WCTU no longer made that assertion.[32]

The Fiction of a Woman's Bloc

"The woman 'bloc' does not tend to become more and more solidified but tends to become more and more disintegrated," journalist William Hard observed in 1923.[33] The quantity of evidence that women arrayed themselves on opposing political sides (even if they used gender-dependent justifications to do

Rally of the Women's Organization for National Prohibition Reform, 1932
HAGLEY MUSEUM AND LIBRARY

so) calls into question the very possibility of a woman bloc. Given the divisions among women and given the nature of the political system, a women's voting bloc—or, even the possibility of a lobbying bloc representing *all* women—must be considered an interpretive fiction rather than a realistic expectation, useful perhaps to some minds, but requiring a willing suspension of disbelief.

In the 1920s most politically active women (and the LWV as an organization) eschewed the notion of a women's voting bloc in favor of women's diverse individuality. In her early leadership of the LWV, Carrie Chapman Catt made clear that it was not a woman's party intending to mobilize women's votes but a group dedicated to guiding women into the male-dominated political process and parties where change could be effected from the inside. Only a very few spokeswomen pointedly disagreed: Anne Martin, for instance, excoriated the decision to "train women for citizenship," saying that it handed women over to the Republican and Democratic parties "exactly where men political leaders wanted them, bound, gagged, divided, and delivered." The head of the Republican Women's Division believed, however, that voting women "do not want to differ from men on lines of sex distinction" and predicted that women would never vote for female candidates because of their sex alone but would choose the most qualified individuals. Grace Abbott, head of the Children's Bureau, said that women's voting record by 1925 showed that they were "trying hard to vote as citizens rather than as women, measuring a party or candidate in terms of their judgment on general community needs." Cornelia Bryce Pinchot, a leading Pennsylvania Republican, believed that women should enter politics to improve the position of their sex; nonetheless, as a

candidate for Congress she found it counterproductive to isolate women as such in politics. She wanted to be listened to as an individual with views on many issues. Freda Kirchwey, influential left-leaning writer for *The Nation*, emphasized that "women are going to vote according to the dictates of class interest and personal interest as well as sex interest." To urge women otherwise, she contended, was to make them "forget they are human beings."[34]

Such remarks suggest that feminist impulses might scuttle the notion of a woman's bloc as reasonably as champion it. The fiction that women were unified in the political arena laid a foundation for feminist action, but also involved risks— most pointedly, the risks of denying women's diversity and individuality or prescribing a "woman's sphere" in politics. As much as suffragist rhetoric had stressed women's need to represent themselves and women's duty to become voters because their interests and expertise differed from men's, it had also stressed that women and men were equally citizens and individuals in relation to the state. A *New York Times* editorialist heard the suffragists' clarion to be that "women are people—human beings sharing certain fundamental human interests, aspirations, and duties with men." That very important strand of suffragist rationale was renewed in the 1910s along with rationales stressing women's differences from men; it justified and anticipated women's integration into men's political associations rather than the formation of a woman bloc.[35]

There were also strategically defensive reasons why most women active in politics did not pursue nor speak of their goals in terms of mobilizing a woman bloc. The notion of a woman bloc was portrayed as the deployment of destructive sex antagonism and was condemned in the harshest terms by mainstream male politicians as well as by right-wing ideologues. Once when the fledgling LWV did try to marshal a women's voting bloc—in New York in 1920, trying to unseat Republican Senator James Wadsworth, an intransigent opponent of woman suffrage whose wife headed the National Association Opposed to Woman Suffrage—the organization was violently condemned by New York's Republican governor as *"a menace to our free institutions and to representative government."* In the two-party system, Governor Nathan Miller said, "there is no proper place for a *league of women voters,* precisely as I should say there was no proper place for a *league of men voters."* His attack differed only in degree rather than in kind from the blast of *The Woman Patriot,* a right-wing hyper-patriotic "news"-sheet published during the 1920s by former anti-suffragists, which trumpeted that women's organizations on Capitol Hill formed an "interlocking lobby dictatorship" bent on "organizing women for class and sex war." *The New York Times,* too, censured the forming of a political organization by women, claiming that such formation presupposed that women were "a class, a group, something apart,…a class which apparently hates and distrusts men." In *The New York Times'* editorialist's view, such thinking not only signaled a "revival of sex-antagonism" but even amounted to a "socialist" theory, of "a world divided into hostile classes."[36]

Anne Martin of Nevada, in the front passenger seat, on the campaign trail, 1920
NEVADA HISTORICAL SOCIETY

Although rarely proposed or envisioned by women leaders as desirable or likely, the notion of a woman bloc was denigrated, repressed and ridiculed by defenders of "politics as usual" as fiercely as if it threatened them. Although the woman bloc could only have been an interpretive fiction, it was, curiously, a large enough looming specter for male politicians to slay it again and again. Those who have imagined that women entering politics in the 1920s should have or could have constituted a bloc of women voters similar to the coalition formed on behalf of woman suffrage have underestimated how profoundly at cross purposes to the existing party system such a proposition really was. Yet how else could women lobbyists, without economic resources to speak of (as Mary Anderson admitted) swing any weight? Women leaders in the political arena faced a classic double bind: damned outright for attempting to form a woman bloc, damned (in effect) by male politicians' indifference or scorn for failing to form one. There was the dilemma for women who intended to make it clear that politics was no longer a man's world.

Conclusion

An improved view across the great divide of 1920 clarifies the accomplishments of women in American politics and the limits to those accomplishments. A more continuous view highlights not only the immense organizational implications of women's lack of the ballot until the early twentieth century but also the unique power of disenfranchisement to bring diverse women into coalition. By taking fuller account of women's political efforts (including voluntary associations and lobbying

as well as candidacies and voting), and by acknowledging that political efforts by various subsets of women may be mutually counterpoised, we might move the focus of inquiry after 1920 from the "woman bloc" to the possibility of a feminist bloc—the latter admittedly a grouping by politics and ideology rather than by sex.

Notes

This is a revised version of Cott's article by the same title that appeared in Women, Politics, and of Change, Louise A. Tilly and Patricia Gurin, eds., published by the Russell Sage Foundation, 1990 and is printed here with permission of the Russell Sage Foundation.

1. Olympia Brown to Catharine Waugh McCulloch, June 25, 1911, folder 236, Dillon Collection, Schlesinger Library, Radcliffe College; Rosalyn Terborg-Penn, "African American Women and the Woman Suffrage Movement," in this volume, One Woman, One Vote; Gayle Gullett, "City Mothers, City Daughters, and the Limits of Female Political Power in San Francisco, 1913," in Barbara J. Harris and JoAnn McNamara, eds., Women and the Structure of Society (Durham, N.C., 1984), 149-159; Barbara Stinson, American Women's Activism in World War I (New York, 1982).

2. Maud Wood Park, Front Door Lobby, Edna Stantial, ed. (Boston, 1960).

3. Paul's statement, from 1916, is quoted in Inez Haynes Irwin, The Story of the Woman's Party (New York, 1921), 151. On the CU, see Eleanor Flexner, Century of Struggle (Cambridge, Mass., 1968), 261-70; 275-77, 282-89; Nancy F. Cott, The Grounding of Modern Feminism (New Haven, 1987), 53-59; Christine A. Lunardini, From Equal Suffrage to Equal Rights: Alice Paul and the National Woman's Party, 1913-1928 (New York, 1986).

4. Park, Front Door Lobby, 23; Harriet Stanton Blatch to Anne Martin, May 14, [1918], Anne Martin Collection, Bancroft Library, University of California, Berkeley; On the mixed nature of the suffrage coalition, see Cott, Grounding, 24-33.

5. Quotations from Shaw, CU, and Kraditor cited by Aileen S. Kraditor, The Ideas of the Woman Suffrage Movement, 1890-1920 (New York, 1971); 50; Ronald Schaffer, "The New York City Woman Suffrage Party, 1910-1919," New York History 43 (1962): 273; Catt quotation, Doris Daniels, "Building a Winning Coalition: The Suffrage Fight in New York State," New York History 60 (1979):71.

6. J. Stanley Lemons, The Woman Citizen: Social Feminism in the 1920s (Urbana, Ill., 1973), 92-93; John D. Buenker, "The Urban Political Machine and Woman Suffrage," The Historian 33 (1970-71): 264-79; William Ogburn and Inez Goltra, "How Women Vote: A Study of An Election in Portland, Oregon," Political Science Quarterly 34 (1919): 413-33; Stuart A. Rice and Malcolm M. Willey, "American Women's Ineffective Use of the Vote," Current History 20 (1924): 641-47.

7. See Edward A. Purcell, Jr. The Crisis of Democratic Theory (Lexington, Ky., 1973), 95-114, on political scientists.

8. Walter Dean Burnham, "The Changing Shape of the American Political Universe," American Political Science Review, 59 (1965): 10; see also E.E. Schnattschneider, The Semisovereign People (Hinsdale, Ill., 1960).

9. See Schattschneider, Burnham, "Changing Shape"; Samuel P. Hays, "The Politics of Reform in Municipal Government in the Progressive Era," Pacific Northwest Quarterly, 55 (1964): 157-69; James Weinstein, The Corporate Ideal in the Liberal State, 1900-1918 (Boston, 1968), esp. 92-116; J. Morgan Kousser, The Shaping of Southern Politics (New Haven, 1974); David W. Eakins, "The Origins of Corporate Liberal Policy Research, 1916-1922: The Political Economic Expert and the Decline of Public Debate," in Jerry Israel, ed., Building the Organizational Society: Essays on Associational Activities in Modern America (New York, 1972), 163-179, 288-291. Quotation from Suzanne LaFollette, Concerning Women (New York, 1926), 268.

10. Susan Bourque and Jean Grossholz, "Politics an Unnatural Practice: Political Science Looks at Female Participation," Politics and Society, (1974): 225-266, very effectively shows that early 1920s analyses of female non-voting—especially Charles Meriam and Harold Gosnell, NonVoting: Causes and Methods of Control (Chicago, 1923) were still being repeated in political science texts of the 1960s.

11. Addams quoted in "Is Woman Suffrage Failing?" Woman Citizen, n.s. 8 (April 19, 1924): 14-16; Early analyses are Stuart A. Rice and Malcolm M. Willey, "American Women's Ineffective Use of the Vote," Current History, 20 (1924): 641-47; and Hugh L. Keenleyside, "The American Political Revolution of 1924," Current History, 21 (1925): 833-40; see also Meriam and Gosnell, Non-Voting. Recent treatments are Paul Kleppner, "Were Women to Blame? Female Suffrage and Voter Turnout," Journal of Interdisciplinary History 12 (1982): 621-643; and Sara Alpern and Dale Baum, "Female Ballots: The Impact of the Nineteenth Amendment," Journal of Interdisciplinary History 16 (1985): 43-67.

12. Anne Martin, "Woman's Vote and Woman's Chains," Sunset Magazine, April 1922, 14; see also Anne Martin, "Feminists and Future Political Action," Nation, 115 (Feb. 18, 1925) 161-166; Frances Kellor, "Women in British and American Politics," Current History, 17 (Feb. 1923): 831-35.

13. Viz. Edward B. Logan, "Lobbying," Annals AAPSS 144 supplement, (1929), 32; Dorothy Johnson, "Organized Women as Lobbyists in the 1920s," Capital Studies, 1 (1972): 41-58; Paula Baker, "The Domestication of Politics: Women and American Political Society, 1780-1920," American Historical Review, 89 (1984): 620-48; Anne Firor Scott, Making the Invisible Woman Visible (Urbana, Ill., 1984), 259-294, have stressed the voluntarist political tradition among women in the nineteenth century, but its continuity after 1920 has received little attention, except very recently in the N.J. study by Felice D. Gordon, After Winning: The Legacy of the New Jersey Suffragists, 1920-1947, (New Brunswick, N.J., 1986).

14. Inez Haynes Irwin, Angels and Amazons (Garden City, N.Y, 1933).

15. The League had branches in 45 states in 1931, with total membership probably under 100,000; see Sophonisba Breckinridge, Women in the Twentieth Century: A Study of their Political, Social and Economic Activities (New York, 1933), 66-68. On the LWV program, Lemons, Woman Citizen, 49-55; on Feickert, Gordon, After Winning, 79.

16. On GFWC, see Margaret Gibbons Wilson, American Woman in Transition: The Urban Influence 1870-1920 (Westport, Conn., 1979), 98, 100-101, 107 n. 26; William P. O'Neill, Everyone Was Brave: A History of Feminism in America (Chicago, 1969), 256-62; Breckinridge, Women, 39; on Parent-Teacher Associations, 53-54, 79-80.

17. Allis Wolfe, "Women, Consumerism, and the National Consumers League in the Progressive Era, 1900-23," Labor History, 16 (1975): 378-92; Nancy Schrom Dye, As Equals and As Sisters: Feminism, Unionism, and the Women's Trade Union League of N.Y. (Columbia, Mo., 1980); Lemons, Woman Citizen, 25-30, 122-49.

18. Breckinridge, Women, 56-57; Alice Kessler-Harris, Out to Work: A History of Wage-Earning Women in the U.S. (New York, 1982); Theresa Wolfson, "Trade Union Activities of Women," Annals AAPSS, 143 (1929): 130-131; Mary Frederickson, "The Southern Summer School for Women Workers," Southern Exposure, 4 (1977): 70-75; Mary Frederickson, "'I know which side I'm on': Southern Women in the Labor Movement in the Twentieth Century," in Ruth Milkman, ed., Women, Work and Protest (Boston, 1985), 169-171; Dolores Janiewski, Sisterhood Denied: Race, Gender and Class in a New South Community (Philadelphia, 1985), 83, 151; Rita Heller, "The Bryn Mawr Workers' Summer School, 1921-1933: A Surprising Alliance," History of Higher Education Annual, (1981), 110-31.

19. Lemons, Woman Citizen, 58-59 n.8; Breckinridge, Women, 63-64.

20. See Linda Gordon, Woman's Body, Woman's Right (New York,

1976), 295-98; Joan Jensen, "The Evolution of Margaret Sanger's Family *Limitation Pamphlet*, 1914-21," *Signs* 6 (1981): 548-67; Ellen Chesler, *Woman of Valor* (New York, 1992).

21. Breckinridge, *Women*, 54-55, 79.

22. Breckinridge, *Women*, 49-51, 58-59; June Sochen, *Consecrate Each Day: The Public Lives of Jewish American Women 1880-1980* (Albany, 1981); Norma Fain Pratt, "Transitions in Judaism: The Jewish American Woman Through the 1930s," in Janet James, ed., *Women in American Religion* (Philadelphia, 1978), 222.

23. Breckinridge, *Women*, 77-79; Rosalyn Terborg-Penn, "Discontented Black Feminists: Prelude and Postscript to the Passage of the Nineteenth Amendment," in Lois Scharf and Joan Jensen, eds., *Decades of Discontent* (Westport, Conn., 1983), 269-70, 272-73; Paula Giddings, *When and Where I Enter: The Impact of Black Women on Race and Sex in America* (New York, 1984), 177, 183-185, 203-204. On Southern white women's anti-lynching efforts, see Jacqueline Dowd Hall, *Revolt Against Chivalry: Jessie Daniel Ames and the Women's Campaign against Lynching* (New York, 1979).

24. Breckinridge, *Women*, 43-49, 58.

25. Charles De Benedetti, *Origins of the Modern American Peace Movement, 1915-1929* (Millwood, N.Y., 1978), esp. 90-97; Charles Chatfield, *For Peace and Justice: Pacifism in America, 1914-1941* (Knoxville, Tenn., 1971); Florence Brewer Boeckel, "Women in International Affairs," *Annals AAPSS*, 143 (1929): 231-32; Joan Jensen, "All Pink Sisters: the War Department and the Feminist Movement in the 1920s," in Scharf and Jensen, eds., *Decades of Discontent*; Breckinridge, *Women*, 85-87.

26. [Mary Anderson,] "Organized Women and their Program," typescript, c. 1924, folder 84, Mary Anderson Collection, Schlesinger Library.

27. See Kay Lehman Schlozman, "Representing Women in Washington: Sisterhood and Pressure Politics," in Tilly and Gurin, eds., *Women, Politics, and Change*, 339-382.

28. In 1943 the NWP changed the wording of the ERA to its current reading. On the controversy between women's organizations over the ERA see O'Neill, *Everyone*, 274-94; William Chafe, *The American Woman: Her Changing Political, Social and Economic Roles, 1920-1970* (New York, 1972), 112-32; Lemons, *Woman Citizen*, 184-99; Sheila Rothman, *Woman's Proper Place* (New York, 1978), 153-65; Kessler-Harris, *Out to Work*, 205-12; Susan Becker, *The Origins of the Equal Rights Amendment: American Feminism between the Wars* (Westport, Conn., 1981), 121-51; Lunardini, *From Equal Suffrage*; Cott, *Grounding*, 115-42.

29. Partisan/nonpartisan controversies bulked large in the first year or two of the LWV; see Lemons, *Woman Citizen*, 49-53, and Gordon, *After Winning*, 34-39.

30. Carrie Foster-Hayes, "The Women and the Warriors: Dorothy Detzer and the WILPF," Ph.D. diss., University of Denver, 1984, 318-21.

31. See Jensen, "All Pink Sisters," and Cott, *Grounding*, 244-61.

32. David Kyvig, "Women Against Prohibition," *American Quarterly*, 28 (1976): 465-82, and *Repealing National Prohibition* (Chicago, 1979), 118-127.

33. William Hard, quoted in "What the American Man Thinks," *Woman Citizen*, Sept. 8, 1923, cited by O'Neill, *Everyone*, 264.

34. On Catt, see Lemons, *Woman Citizen*, 90-91; Anne Martin, "Feminists," 185; on Pinchot, John Furlow, "Cornelia Bryce Pinchot: Feminism in the Post-Suffrage Era," *Pennsylvania History*, 95 (1976): 329-346; all other quotations are cited from Alpern and Baum, "Female Ballots," 60-62.

35. *New York Times*, Nov. 30, 1918, 16. See Cott, *Grounding*, 29-30, 37-38.

36. Lemons, *Woman Citizen*, 98-100; "Are Women a Menace?" *Nation*, 112 (Feb. 9, 1921): 198; "The Interlocking Lobby Dictatorship," *The Woman Patriot*, 6 (Dec. 1, 1922); "Organizing Women for Class and Sex War," *The Woman Patriot*, 7 (April 15, 1923); *New York Times*, Nov. 30, 1918, 16.

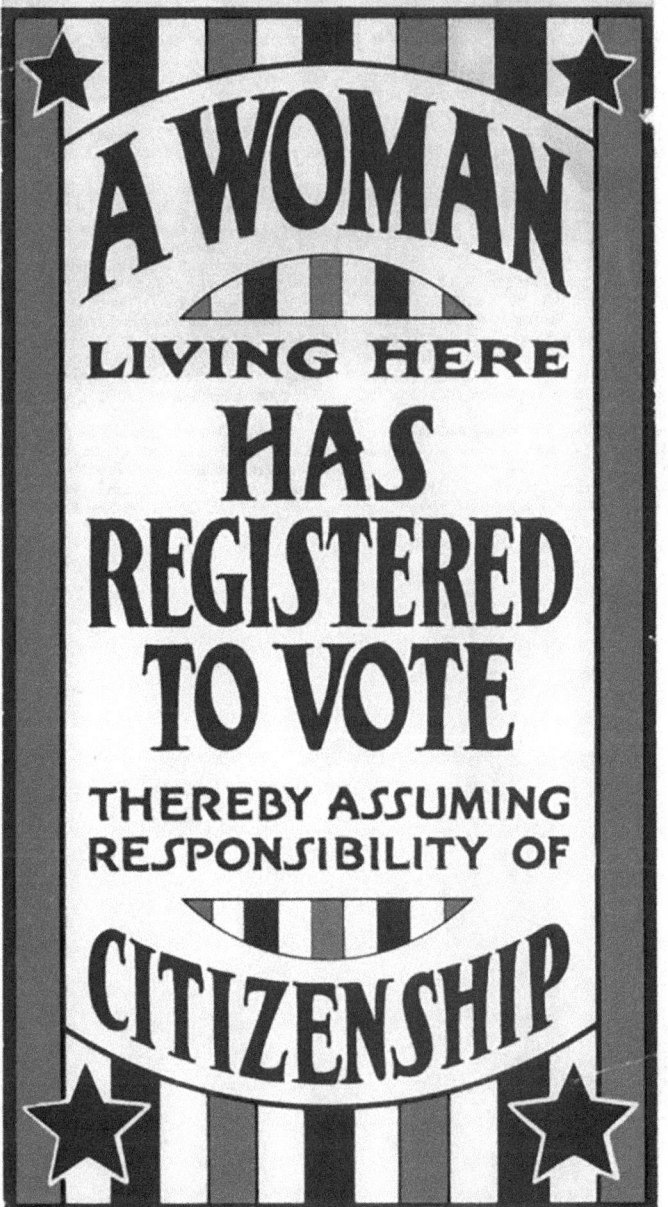

In 1920, fliers like this were widely displayed in windows of homes to honor new women voters and to encourage other women to register to vote.

A CENTURY OF WOMAN SUFFRAGE
Marjorie J. Spruill

Editor's Introduction: The ratification of the Nineteenth Amendment on August 26, 1920 was one of the most important events in the history of the United States—not only because it added more than twenty-seven million new voters to the electorate. It empowered women to participate in the making of the laws that governed them. Implicitly, it recognized women as individuals entitled to direct influence, rather than female auxiliaries to male decision makers, reliant on indirect influence. Ratification of the Nineteenth Amendment was also a crucial step toward women gaining access to power through elected office and full equality in the laws of the land, though over the past century those ongoing battles have proven to be as long and as frustrating as the suffrage battle itself.

The success of the Nineteenth Amendment was both a reflection of changing attitudes about women and gender roles and a factor that encouraged further change. Henceforth, women who organized to advocate for or against a political issue would be backed by the weight of their votes.

One hundred years after women were enfranchised through the Nineteenth Amendment, the women's vote is recognized as massive and highly influential in the outcomes of elections. Politicians are keenly aware that women turn out to vote at a higher rate than men and that there are significant differences in the voting patterns of the sexes. In the 2012, 2016, and 2020 presidential elections, women outvoted men by millions of ballots and were more likely than men to vote for the Democratic candidate—trends that were first noticeable in the 1980 election. However, these two trends were slow to appear. It took many decades for women to vote at the same rate as men, or for the "gender gap" to emerge.

In 1920, and for many years thereafter, there were cultural obstacles as well as deliberately constructed barriers that kept many women away from the polls. The deeply entrenched ideas about gender roles that led so many to oppose woman suffrage did not immediately disappear upon ratification of the Nineteenth Amendment. Despite the fact that the enfranchisement of women led election officials to relocate polling places from saloons and livery stables to schools, libraries, and city halls, the idea that politics was a nasty and complicated business, inappropriate for respectable women, was slow to die. As a result, many women shied away from politics and voting.

At the same time, many women who were eager to vote were kept away from the polls. In the Southern states, the majority of African American women were prevented

from voting through an array of laws and policies adopted by state governments determined to preserve White supremacy in politics. While turnout among White women increased gradually after 1920, turnout among African American women increased dramatically only after Congress passed the Voting Rights Act of 1965. Meanwhile, federal policy regarding immigration and naturalization also kept many women who were living in the United States and its territories—women who were then barred from becoming citizens—from becoming voters.

For much of the first century of woman suffrage, women who chose to vote and were permitted to do so, voted like similarly situated men. Despite persistent assumptions that gender would shape their political preferences, women voters tended to make their voting choices in much the same way as men, influenced by their class, race, ethnicity, religion, and region, as well as the party preferences of their families and communities. It would take another major voting rights movement, followed closely by a new wave of the women's rights movement, for women to turn out to vote at higher rates than men and for the gender gap to develop.

Yet, even as women became more politically active, they were as divided as ever in their ideas about what was best for women, families, and society. The new wave of the American women's rights movement profoundly altered American society as feminists succeeded in changing many laws and customs to correspond to new realities of women's lives and broke down barriers that had long prevented women from full and equal participation in society and politics. But the movement's success inspired a new wave of activism by socially conservative women deeply invested in traditional ideas about women's nature and social roles and determined to roll back feminist gains. The competition for influence between the two groups heightened women's political activism as both sides sought to apply the weight of their votes.

As the centennial of the Nineteenth Amendment approached, the "woman's vote" was widely recognized as large and influential, though divided. Women turned out to vote at higher rates than men and were active in both parties and a wide range of political organizations. But despite important gains, women remained severely under-represented in elected office, especially at the highest levels of government, and they were more determined than ever to change that.

Ironically, the approaching celebration of women's long struggle to gain the vote coincided with major efforts to suppress voting, especially voting by people of color. There was a new appreciation of the fact that voting rights are not only hard to win but, once gained, must be defended. Over the years, women, especially African American women, had emerged as leaders in registering and mobilizing voters, and in 2020 those efforts would have national impact as women of color led successful campaigns against voter suppression.

In 2020, women were determined that their votes were counted and their voices were heard. After a century of voting, they were determined to gain their share of political power. In 2018 and 2020, women ran for office in record numbers and record numbers of them won, many of them women of color. As the first century of

woman suffrage came to an end, there were more women in Congress than ever before. And for the first time in U.S. history, a woman—a woman of color—was elected Vice President of the United States.

★ ★ ★ ★ ★

THE IMMEDIATE AFTERMATH of ratification of the Nineteenth Amendment was a time of great excitement and high anxiety. Former suffragists went right to work to leverage the power of their votes, eager to capitalize on their victory. In towns and cities across the nation, the League of Women Voters (LWV), successor to the National American Woman Suffrage Association (NAWSA), ran "citizenship schools" to educate the new voters about procedures for registering and voting. With so little time between the August 1920 ratification of the Nineteenth Amendment and the November elections, there was no time to lose. The LWV sponsored registration drives, conducted house-to-house canvassing, and provided information to prospective voters. State fairs in many places featured mock voting booths where women could practice filling out ballots or pulling voting machine levers; in some cities, civic-minded merchants featured department store windows with women mannequins standing in line to vote.1 The Nineteenth Amendment had enfranchised more than twenty-seven million women. Previously, women had voted in fifteen states, but now women would have full voting rights in every state, including the ten states that had refused to ratify the amendment. Politicians were understandably anxious about this tremendous expansion of the electorate and quickly sprang into action to court women's votes.

Democrats and Republicans were singing the same tune: one political cartoonist, paraphrasing a popular song, portrayed a donkey and an elephant singing in unison, "How Dear to My Heart are the Sweet Lady Voters, the Coming Election Reveals Them to View," with the caption, "Strange to Say, the Feeling Seems to Be Unanimous." The Democratic Party doubled the size of its national committees to include a woman as well as a man from each state. The Republican Party created a "Women's Division" to attract and integrate women into the party. Both parties seated far more women as convention delegates. And both claimed credit for having "given" women the vote. Democrats reminded women voters that the Nineteenth Amendment had been adopted under the Woodrow Wilson administration. Republicans replied that it had won congressional approval only because of overwhelming support from the GOP, and that twenty-nine of the thirty-six ratifying states were controlled by Republicans.2

Great Expectations

Politicians speculated endlessly about the strength and nature of the women's vote. Many people assumed that women would vote similarly, differently from men, and that a "woman's bloc" would emerge. They believed that owing to

woman's nature and responsibilities as wives and mothers, women had common sensibilities, needs, and concerns, and required different political appeals. Some politicians worried that women did not have a man's concept of party loyalty and never would: they predicted the parties would have to scramble to attract women voters, asserting that party labels meant nothing to women, but instead, issues such as health, education, maternity, and infant protection were paramount. Republican and Democratic Party leaders were rattled by the creation of the non-partisan League of Women Voters and feared women might eschew party politics and create a party of their own. Moreover, politicians were keenly aware that many proponents as well as opponents of women's enfranchisement had predicted woman suffrage would clean up politics. Who knew what that might mean? And what if they chose to run for office themselves?[3]

Some women did just that. The number of women announcing their candidacy increased steadily throughout the decade, especially at the state and local levels. Between 1920 and 1923, at least twenty-two women won races for mayor in towns from Washington to Georgia. By 1929, there were 149 women serving in state legislatures in 38 states, and by 1931, only Louisiana had failed to elect a female legislator. At the federal level, party nominations for seats in Congress were so coveted that male politicians were rarely willing to sacrifice them. A few women, including former suffrage leader Ruth Hanna McCormick of Illinois, were elected to Congress, but most women who served in Congress in the 1920s filled seats previously held by their late husbands. Women's primary gains at the federal level were to appointed positions. By 1929, women had entered nearly every aspect of the U.S. government, many of them reformers seeking to carry out their reform objectives.[4]

Many politicians expected that since the suffrage movement had ridden to victory on the wave of the Progressive Movement, former suffragists would press hard for reform. They did not disappoint. Maud Wood Park, formerly the coordinator of the National American Woman Suffrage Association's (NAWSA) "Front Door Lobby" and in 1920, the first national president of the League of Women Voters (LWV), presented the Democratic and Republican conventions with what the LWV called "The First Woman's Platform." The fifteen planks endorsed restrictions on child labor, a minimum wage for working women, government programs to aid pregnant women and children, and improvements in public health and education, as well as other reforms. The Democratic Party and the Republican Party endorsed several of the LWV's recommended planks, and Republican presidential nominee Warren Harding—who won the 1920 presidential election in part because of women's votes—endorsed them all.[5]

In Washington, the LWV took the lead in organizing the Women's Joint Congressional Committee (WJCC), representing ten major women's groups that collectively claimed ten million members. The WJCC included a variety of organizations that had worked for woman suffrage, among them the General Federation of Women's Clubs (GFWC), the Women's Trade Union League (WTUL),

Leaders of the National LWV display the "First Woman's Platform" that the new organization promoted at the 1920 Democratic Convention. Seated: (left) Della Dortch, Marie Stuart Edwards. Standing: (from left) Mary McDowell, Adah Bush, Pattie Ruffner Jacobs, Maud Wood Park, Effie Simmons, Mabeth Hurd Paige
LIBRARY OF CONGRESS

the Woman's Christian Temperance Union (WCTU), and the Daughters of the American Revolution (DAR). The WJCC's purpose was to coordinate lobbying efforts, and as a result, measures it backed passed with surprising regularity. Each year from 1921 to 1924, the WJCC made gains regarding consumer protection and protection of women and children, including passage of a child labor amendment. Congress seemed to view the WJCC as the lobbyist for an energized womanhood, backed by an amorphous feminine threat the strength of which was yet to be determined—the women's vote.[6]

The most dramatic victory came right away. In 1921, Congress passed the Sheppard-Towner Maternity and Infancy Protection Act, which appropriated money for states to run maternal and infant care clinics. This was an effort to curb the United States' appallingly high infant mortality rates. Significantly, it was the first bill providing federal funds for a social welfare purpose. Privately, many politicians who voted for the Sheppard-Towner Act regarded it as outrageous government overreach, but they feared being punished at the polls. One supporter observed, "If the members could have voted in the cloakroom it would have been killed." Instead, the progressive measure passed by overwhelming margins with bipartisan support. One historian called it "the first major dividend of the full enfranchisement of women."[7]

Former suffragists also sought to use their votes to expand women's rights at the state and federal levels. In many states, women led successful campaigns for women to have the right to serve on juries. By 1922, twenty state legislatures had complied. At the national level, women reformers were eager to establish "independent citizenship" for married women, and again, Congress was responsive. At their urging, Congress passed The Cable Act of 1922, repealing a previous immigration law that had denied an American woman her U.S. citizenship—and thus her right to vote—if she married an "alien," a law that had not applied to male U.S. citizens who married foreign women. With all these victories, some historians called the early twenties a "honeymoon" for women reformers.[8]

By the end of the 1920s, however, former suffragists were keenly disappointed as it became clear that many women did not vote. Though no separate records were kept and there were no exit polls, in the early 1920s voter turnout was low generally and most contemporaries blamed the newly enfranchised women. Twenty-first century political scientists confirm that in 1920 only one third of women turned out to vote. Former adversaries gloated that perhaps women had not wanted to vote after all and those who did vote did not all favor reform. But the "failure" to vote as a bloc should not have been surprising.[9]

In retrospect, a "woman's bloc" was an imaginative construct. Political scientists assert that women vote much like others in their immediate communities: factors including class, race, ethnicity, region, and religion—all of which influence party preferences—shape their political opinions. And though women's shared experiences and concerns do have some impact on their voting preferences, gender identity affects their vote far less than these other factors.[10]

Furthermore, given the great diversity of the suffrage movement at its height, it was unreasonable and unrealistic to expect that once enfranchised, all former supporters of woman suffrage would have the same political goals. To win a federal woman suffrage amendment, suffragists had to bring into the movement women of diverse backgrounds, ethnicities, and ideologies who agreed with one another on a single goal: gaining the right to vote. The ratification of the Nineteenth Amendment freed women to disagree and to use their new political power however they saw fit.[11]

And they did. Women pursued their political goals through both the Democratic and Republican parties, as well as through a great variety of voluntary organizations across the political spectrum that, at times, pitted them against one another. Some, like Ruth Hanna McCormick, urged women to enter the political arena solely through the parties. McCormick was a staunch Republican, as were Mary Church Terrell and Hallie Q. Brown, who worked to turn out the African American vote for "the party of Lincoln." McCormick hired Terrell to head the Colored Division of her campaign when she ran for the Senate in 1929. Nannie Burroughs was a cofounder and first president of the National League of Republican Colored Women, established in 1924. Throughout the 1920s, Burroughs traveled as a representative of the Republican Party's national speakers bureau.[12]

In turn, Emily Newell Blair, a Missouri writer not previously affiliated with a party, in 1920 became head of the Democrat's new Women's Division and traveled the country, giving hundreds of speeches urging women to become Democrats. In 1923, the party rewarded Blair by making her a Vice Chairman of the Democratic National Committee, a position she held throughout the decade. Social reformer Belle Moskowitz, considered one of the most powerful women in the Democratic party, was said to be the "right arm" of Al Smith, the New York mayor Democrats nominated for president in 1928.[13]

Miss NANNIE H. BURROUGHS PRESIDENT NAT'L LEAGUE OF REP. COLORED WOMEN

LIBRARY OF CONGRESS

Some worried that the non-partisan LWV was competing with the parties for women's time. Carrie Chapman Catt insisted women should join the LWV *and* a political party, saying, "We are not going to be such quitters to stay on the outside and let all the reactionaries have it their way." In her view, woman suffrage was only one round in the fight for women's progress; having won the vote, women should work through the parties to advance the women's movement. Catt emphasized that the LWV was not a party, but it should show parties the way forward on this and other issues. "If the League of Women Voters hasn't the power and the vision to see what is coming, and what ought to come, and to be five years ahead of the political parties," she insisted, "then our work is of no value."[14]

Anne Martin, a former University of Nevada history professor who had been jailed for working for suffrage both in the United Kingdom and the United States, the leader of the successful Nevada suffrage campaign in 1914, was one of those urging women to enter partisan politics in force. The daughter of a Nevada state senator, Martin ran unsuccessfully for the U.S. Senate in 1918 and 1920. She discouraged women's continued reliance on nonpartisan voluntary organizations for political efficacy. However, after ratification of the Nineteenth Amendment, large numbers of women continued to be involved in women's groups, old and new, inspired by the belief that their lobbying efforts were now backed by the power of women's votes. The decades following women's enfranchisement saw a remarkably high level of political activity on the part of women, often in organizations with conflicting or competing agendas. For instance, many women were active in pacifist groups while others were involved in organizations advocating military preparedness.[15]

In the 1920s, some groups that had been part of the suffrage coalition continued to work for progressive reform; others moved sharply to the right—even attacking women reformers as dangerous radicals. For example, the DAR, which had joined the WJCC and backed the Sheppard-Towner Act, changed dramatically during the

Even before drafting a constitutional amendment to establish women's equality, fifty prominent members of the National Woman's Party met with President Warren Harding in April 1921 asking for his support in passing an "Equal Rights Bill" for women in the next Congress.

RECORDS OF THE NATIONAL WOMAN'S PARTY, LIBRARY OF CONGRESS

1920s. By the end of the decade, the DAR denounced the Sheppard-Towner Act as Bolshevism and joined far-right organizations in red-baiting, even accusing many Progressive reformers of being communist sympathizers.[16]

The Equal Rights Amendment

Even former suffragists who agreed on the need to press forward on women's rights and to advance the status of women in America were divided about the best way to do so. One of the most passionate and public disputes between political activists in the 1920s was the fight between the League of Women Voters (LWV) and its Women's Joint Congressional Committee (WJCC) allies on one side of the fight, and the National Woman's Party (NWP) on the other side. The battle, as intense as the conflicts between the National American Woman Suffrage Association (NAWSA) and the NWP in the previous decade, was over the NWP's bold new proposal, the Equal Rights Amendment (ERA).[17]

After ratification of the Nineteenth Amendment, the NWP, still led by Alice Paul, chose as its new goal the establishment of complete equality for women and removal of the legal disabilities they still faced. Unlike most former suffragists, NWP members embraced the term "feminist," a term originating in Europe that caught on in the United States after 1910 among women interested not only in better treatment of

women by society but women's equality and autonomy.[18] NWP surveys of state and federal statutes identified over a thousand state laws that restricted women's activities and discriminated against them regarding property ownership, inheritance, guardianship of children, and ability to serve on juries and as elected or appointed offices. In 1923, the NWP proposed an additional constitutional amendment calling for equal rights for men and women throughout the United States and its jurisdictions. Unveiling the Equal Rights Amendment at ceremonies at Seneca Falls, and initially calling it the "Lucretia Mott Amendment," the NWP presented the ERA as a means of fulfilling suffragists' unfinished goals. It was introduced in Congress in December 1923 by Susan B. Anthony's nephew, Daniel Anthony.[19]

If added to the U.S. Constitution, the ERA would prohibit sex-specific legislation. For that reason, the LWV and its allies, including labor unions, bitterly opposed it. They viewed the ERA as a threat to hard-won protective legislation such as minimum wage and maximum hour laws—strongly opposed by conservatives—that reformers had been able to gain for women but not for men. To a certain extent, the ERA was a partisan issue; some business-friendly Republicans—including many NWP members—favored the ERA *because* it would end protective legislation. Democrats—including many women reformers—were generally opposed.[20]

Florence Kelley, a member of the NWP's National Council who was also head of the National Consumers Union, parted ways with the NWP over the ERA; she insisted women workers in hazardous occupations that employed mostly women needed special legislation that would be wiped out if the ERA was adopted, and that the privileged NWP members were blind to the needs of women industrial workers. Throughout the 1920s and for decades thereafter, the LWV and its allies strenuously opposed the ERA, which got nowhere in Congress. Meanwhile, the NWP vigorously opposed protective legislation for women, and when courts struck down minimum wage and maximum hour laws, the NWP celebrated it as a victory. These very public battles over how best to aid women and advance the cause of

After "unveiling" the ERA at Seneca Falls, New York, in July 1923, Alice Paul (right) and Anita Pollitzer visited Susan B. Anthony's gravesite in nearby Rochester.

women's rights thoroughly undermined the idea that women were united in their political goals.[21]

Woman Suffrage a Failure?

By the mid-1920s, politicians recognized that there was no unified "woman's vote" to fear. In Washington, D.C., the honeymoon for women reformers was over. Congress became far less receptive to the Women's Joint Congressional Committee (WJCC) and much of the reformers' attention had to shift to a rear-guard action to defend gains already made. The Supreme Court undercut reformers' previous victories in rulings against a federal child labor law and a minimum wage for women, and the child labor bill failed when it was not ratified by a sufficient number of states. The women's campaign to gain jury service, so successful in the early 1920s, ground to a halt, and in some states the League of Women Voters (LWV) had to fight to prevent cutbacks in women's jury participation. At the end of the decade, the Sheppard-Towner Act—which symbolized politicians' desire to court women voters right after ratification of the Nineteenth Amendment when there was great uncertainty about its impact—was not renewed, and it expired in June 1929.[22]

By 1925, observers were already assessing the impact of woman suffrage. It was common for newspapers and popular magazines to question its success, such as *Harper's* 1925 article, "Are Women a Failure in Politics?" and *The Century's* 1924 essay, "Is Woman Suffrage a Failure?" Some claimed that this tremendous innovation in American politics had made little difference, and that woman suffrage had failed to live up to its promise to improve society. Others suggested that suffragists had promised too much and raised expectations too high, especially near the end of the long movement.[23]

The tenth anniversary of the Nineteenth Amendment brought a groundswell of such articles, some from former suffragists expressing their disappointment about the results of woman suffrage and others who rose in its defense. Alice Paul, who always insisted that woman suffrage was a woman's right no matter what she chose to do with it, roundly rejected the question. She countered, "Why not ask if this country is better off because men have voted for the last four years, the last forty years or a hundred years?" Carrie Chapman Catt also shrugged off assertions that woman suffrage had failed, but for a different reason: She insisted that no adequate appraisal of its impact could be made after just ten years and that women's influence had grown even though no woman's bloc had appeared.[24]

For decades thereafter, many scholars who analyzed the effects of woman suffrage concluded that with low turnout and no bloc vote, woman suffrage had little impact. As one eminent historian writing in the 1950s put it, "women's suffrage had few consequences, good or evil," and though millions of women voted and some held office, "the new electorate caused scarcely a ripple in American political life."[25] Others, however, including historians who deplored the

conservative turn in the United States in the 1920s, offered a more positive assessment of women's impact on politics after 1920. They credited women reformers for keeping progressive ideas alive through an era of retrenchment until the 1930s when many of the policies they had supported in the 1920s were carried out and on a much larger scale.[26] Frances Perkins, the former suffragist appointed in 1933 as Secretary of Labor by President Franklin Roosevelt—making her the first woman to serve in a Presidential Cabinet—was instrumental in the development and implementation of the New Deal's fair labor laws, including the forty-hour work week, abolishing child labor under age sixteen, the nation's first minimum wage, and Social Security.[27]

Newer research on the impact of the Nineteenth Amendment, which focused more on state and local results of women's voting than on the impact on national politics, also found positive results. Scholars have suggested that woman suffrage led to increases in spending on charities and hospitals as well as on social programs and public education. Moreover, across the nation—even in the South—women used "the weight of their votes" effectively, lobbying state legislators for policy changes and threatening them with defeat if their demands were ignored. Furthermore, scholars have pointed out that the establishment of woman suffrage opened paths toward office-holding and party activism.[28]

An Incomplete Victory

Recent research not only questions the idea that woman suffrage had little impact, it also emphasizes the tremendous obstacles to women's participation in elections and the impact of voter suppression, which continues to be a problem in the United States.[29] There were many reasons, cultural and political, for the low voter turnout in the 1920s and for the subsequent slow rate of increase. Any analysis of the impact of the Nineteenth Amendment that fails to take these factors into account is as incomplete as the 1920 suffrage victory itself.

In their 1923 book, *Woman Suffrage and Politics: The Inner Story of the Suffrage Movement*, Carrie Chapman Catt and Nettie Rogers Shuler noted that victory had "been virtually wrung from hesitant and often resentful leaders." Even after ratification, some of those resentful politicians refused to surrender. A small, hardcore faction of anti-suffragists continued to challenge the validity of the Nineteenth Amendment, taking the issue all the way to the Supreme Court. In one court case, the American Constitutional League (ACL) argued that forcing states that had not ratified the amendment to allow women to vote was a violation of the states' constitutional rights, stating as an aside that the almost identical Fifteenth Amendment, a product of military force during a time "when civil war overrode all constitutional guarantees," was thus, a dead letter. In 1922, the Supreme Court ruled against the ACL, finally putting the challenges to rest.[30]

Still, the resentment of political leaders in the states that refused to ratify the Nineteenth Amendment was evident in the sluggish way it was implemented.

Georgia and Mississippi did not allow any women to vote in 1920, refusing to hold the special legislative sessions necessary to set up the mechanism for female participation in the November 1920 elections. Florida did so only under court order.[31]

Even for many White women who were free to vote if they wished, it took a while to get past the norms against women's participation in politics in the states where political leaders had resisted woman suffrage "to the last ditch, and then some," comparing themselves to their ancestors who had fought for the Confederacy. Southern anti-suffragists had denigrated suffragists as unfeminine as well as ungrateful. After 1920, many White men—and women—continued to see politics as a dirty business outside the sphere of a respectable woman. However, far more significant for understanding Southern women's relatively low voter turnout—as well as the grim politics of the "Solid South" in the four decades following adoption of the Nineteenth Amendment—were the successful efforts to suppress the vote conducted by conservative White officials in Southern states.[32]

Obstacles to the African American Vote

Unlike many countries that initially enfranchised White women while denying the vote to women of color or indigenous people, the United States did extend the franchise to all women citizens in 1920.[33] However, states erected many obstacles, including residency requirements, educational or literacy tests, and poll taxes that deprived vast numbers of women—especially women of color and the poor—of their voting rights. And for a half century, the federal government did little to stop this flagrant voter suppression. The effect on African Americans was devastating.

Outside the South, Black women registered and voted. For instance, members of Ida B. Wells-Barnett's Alpha Suffrage Club in Chicago had been voting since 1913 when Illinois extended the vote to women in presidential and municipal elections, and they were influential in city politics. In the early 1920s, the Republican Party still valued and courted African American votes, for example engaging Mary Church Terrell as its director of "Work Among Colored Women in the East." However, when the Nineteenth Amendment took effect, the vast majority of African American women lived in the Southern states. And though they sought to register and vote in large numbers, most were blocked by state governments that quickly applied the same or similar measures used for decades to deprive Black men of the vote.[34]

Recent scholarship emphasizes the heroic efforts of African American women as they tried to register and vote in the South and the tremendous resistance they encountered. At first, some state election officials were caught off guard and registered African American women. For instance, in North Carolina approximately one thousand Black women registered in Charlotte, Greensboro, Asheville, Salisbury, Southport, New Bern, and elsewhere. In Atlanta, Georgia, 6,400 African American women registered. Often, these results were the product of collective efforts to

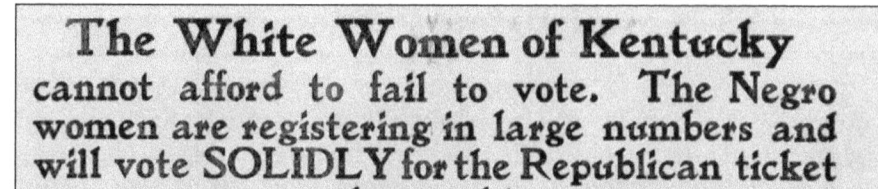

The White Women of Kentucky

cannot afford to fail to vote. The Negro women are registering in large numbers and will vote SOLIDLY for the Republican ticket thus making

A Negro Vote of 150,000

and theirs will be the deciding vote in this election if the White Women Do Not Register and Vote The Straight Democratic Ticket

STAMP Under The  ROOSTER

VOTE THIS WAY ⓧ UNDER THE ROOSTER

A broadside urging "The White Women of Kentucky" to vote and offset the Republican bloc of African Americans who had already registered for the vote

LIBRARY OF CONGRESS

mobilize voters. Since there was safety in numbers, sometimes large groups of African American women appeared together to confront hostile registrars.[35]

Soon, on their own or under orders from government officials, White registrars began taking action to rebuff these applicants. In Columbia, South Carolina, twenty-eight Black women reported that the local registrar required them to take literacy tests that were different from the one mandated by the state. The African American women protested that "white women were not required to go through this illegal routine."[36]

The high turnout of African American women registering to vote in many places alarmed White politicians, especially when it exceeded the turnout by White women. In either case, the White press rallied to protect White supremacy, raising bogus alarms about the threat of "Negro domination." A Fulton County, Georgia newspaper stated that "the registration of negro women has been at least ten to one heavier than the registration of White women." The registrar also reported there were "automobiles hauling negro women to the courthouse Tuesday morning when he closed the books." In Americus, Georgia, the registrar would personally "hide the book or himself" when African American women approached his office.[37]

The fact that many African American women were initially successful—before registrars figured out just how to exclude them—inspired some Black men, including servicemen returning from the war in Europe, to renew efforts to claim the vote. This, in turn, fueled the fears of White Southern politicians about the survival of White supremacy and the Democratic Party's dominance of the region.

As a result, they not only applied to African American women the legal barriers used to deter Black male voters, at times they resorted to intimidation and violence.[38]

After reports of heavy Black registration in Jacksonville, Florida, White supremacists organized in opposition. A Republican campaign official reported that a thousand members of a revived Ku Klux Klan paraded the streets just days before the November 1920 election. In the town of Ocoee, Florida, African Americans' attempts to vote led to a pogrom in which a mob organized by the Klan attacked the Black community, killing many and leaving the town in ashes.[39]

At the same time, Mary McLeod Bethune, founder of Daytona Normal and Industrial Institute for Negro Girls in Daytona Beach, Florida and a member of the Equal Suffrage League, an offshoot of the National Association of Colored Women (NACW), led a group of one hundred African American women and men to the polls. Beforehand, she had knocked on doors to raise funds to pay for poll taxes and held special night classes on how to pass the tests required to register. When the Klan heard about Bethune's activities, they threatened to burn down her school on the night before the election. Determined to vote, Bethune met the Klan at the front

Leaders of the Southeastern Federation of Colored Women's Clubs. Front row, left to right; Margaret Murray Washington, Mary McLeod Bethune, Lucy Craft Laney, Mary Jackson McCrorey. Second row, left to right; Janie Porter Barrett, M.L. Crosthwaite, Charlotte Hawkins Brown, Eugenia Burns Hope

of the campus "with arms folded and head held high." The Klan members backed down, and though Bethune and her group were forced to wait all day before being allowed to cast their ballots, they voted. That year, Bethune helped create the Southeastern Federation of Colored Women's Clubs, which galvanized African American women across the region to fight to vote. Not long thereafter, she became president of the NACW.[40]

After the November 1920 election, African American women worked with the National Association for the Advancement of Colored People (NAACP) to gather evidence documenting the flagrant violation of the Nineteenth and Fifteenth Amendments to present to Congress. In December 1920, NAACP leaders testified at a hearing on the Tinkham Bill proposed by Massachusetts Congressman George H. Tinkham. The bill called for reducing the size of Congressional delegations from Southern states that were preventing African Americans from voting—punishment mandated by the Fourteenth Amendment. Former suffragist Mary B. Talbert, then president of the National Association of Colored Women (NACW) and a NAACP vice president, was one of those who testified. Archibald Henry Grimké also testified; a nephew of women's rights and antislavery pioneers, Sarah and Angelina Grimké, he was a former U.S. consul to the Dominican Republic, in 1920 serving as the head of the District of Columbia branch of the NAACP. Despite this, White Southern Democrats still insisted that African Americans in their states were simply not interested in voting and Congress refused to intervene.[41]

African American women then appealed to the League of Women Voters (LWV) and the National Woman's Party (NWP) for assistance, but without success. When they brought their complaints about disfranchisement to the LWV national convention in Cleveland, Ohio in 1921, White women delegates from the South threatened to walk out if the "Negro problem" was debated. In a compromise, the LWV allowed the African American women to present their case, but in the end, the organization took no action other than forming a "Special Committee on Negro Problems" to study the issue. Prominent White LWV members, including Minnie Fisher Cunningham of Texas and Adele Clark of Virginia, served as chairs of the committee, but it accomplished nothing, largely because too few White Southern LWV members were willing to serve on it, some resenting the committee's very existence.[42]

As the 1921 conference of the NWP approached, African American women wishing to appeal for support were denied a hearing. In response, a delegation of sixty women from Black women's organizations in fourteen states appeared at Alice Paul's office a few days before the conference, demanding an interview. They presented Paul with verified evidence of African American women being denied the vote, along with a "memorial" praising pioneers of the woman suffrage movement who believed not only "in the inherent rights of women, but of humanity at large, and gave themselves to the fight against slavery in the United States." The African American delegation also praised the NWP for being "in the

forefront of the organizations that have undergone all the pains of travail to bring into existence the Nineteenth Amendment." Then they stated:

> We can not then believe that you will permit this amendment to be so distorted in its interpretation that it shall lose its power and effectiveness. Five million women in the United States can not be denied their rights without all the women of the United States feeling the effect of that denial. No women are free until all are free.[43]

The African American delegation requested that Paul use her influence "to have the convention of the National Woman's Party appoint a special committee to ask Congress for an investigation of the violations of the Susan B. Anthony Amendment in the election of 1920." Paul replied that since the discriminatory laws in the South applied to both sexes, this was a racial problem rather than a gender problem and therefore, outside the NWP's mission. Freda Kirchwey, a White NWP member and an associate editor of *The Nation*, bitterly protested this incident in her journal, calling Paul's rebuff "of the representatives of the colored women" a "tragic chapter" of the NWP's story. Meanwhile, both the LWV and NWP were actively assisting women in other countries in gaining the vote, particularly in Europe and Latin American, and in some cases, in U.S. overseas territories.[44]

Women Left Without the Vote

Though African American women, as American citizens, were enfranchised by the Nineteenth Amendment, many Native American women and immigrant women were ineligible to vote because they lacked citizenship status. In 1920, this was the case for at least one third of Native American adults who were considered wards of the U.S. government. After Congress passed the Indian Citizenship Act of 1924, all Native Americans could become citizens with full voting rights. Still, especially in the West, many faced barriers that were similar to those used to suppress the African American vote in the South.[45]

Zitkála-Šá, "Red Bird," 1898
GERTRUDE STANTON KÄSEBIER

One of those most influential in advocating for the Indian Citizenship Act was Native American suffragist Zitkála-Šá (Red Bird), a Yankton Dakota Sioux writer, educator, musician, and activist, also known as Gertrude Simmons Bonnin. A member of the Society of American Indians since 1913, she promoted suffrage for women and Native Americans, traveling nationwide giving speeches as well as writing to legislators and testifying at congressional hearings. Like the African American women who sought Alice Paul's aid in 1921, Zitkála-Šá appealed to the National Woman's Party (NWP) without success. However, at Zitkála-Šá's urging, the General Federation of Women's Clubs (GFWC) created a Department of Indian Welfare and hired her to travel the country as an investigator and speaker, urging White women to use their votes to enfranchise Native people. In 1926, Zitkála-Šá co-founded and began serving as president of the National Council of American Indians, working to expand and protect Native Americans' voting rights and other civil rights.[46]

Asian American women born in the United States were enfranchised in 1920, but those who had been born abroad were ineligible to become U.S. citizens and vote, no matter how long they had lived in the United States. Mabel Ping-Hua Lee, Ph.D., who as a young woman had worked for suffrage, even leading a New York City suffrage parade, hoped that her support for suffrage—and that of other Chinese American women—might help change U.S. policy toward Asians. But in 1924, Congress passed the Johnson-Reed Immigration Act that further restricted immigration from China and broadened the policy to apply to all Asian countries.[47]

These anti-Asian policies did not begin to change until the 1940s, after China fought as an ally of the United States in World War II. The first major change came in 1943 when Chinese immigrants were allowed to naturalize. Laws allowing Japanese, Filipino, and East Indian immigrants to become citizens with full voting rights soon followed.

Woman Suffrage in U.S. Territories

The Nineteenth Amendment did not mention the U.S. territories when it prohibited the states from denying the vote to American citizens "on account of sex." Thus, the issue of women's enfranchisement had to be resolved territory by territory and in different ways, depending upon local circumstances and each territory's unique and evolving relationship with the U.S. government. In 1920, the United States possessed six territories: Alaska, purchased in 1867; Hawai'i, annexed in 1898; the Philippines, Puerto Rico, and Guam that came under U.S. control in 1898 after war

Mabel Ping-Hua Lee
RECORDS OF THE INS/
NATIONAL ARCHIVES

with Spain; and the U.S. Virgin Islands, purchased from Denmark in 1916.[48]

In some cases, the "organic acts" —laws passed by Congress to organize each territorial government—left decisions about suffrage requirements to the territorial legislatures. In other cases, Congress expressly forbid the territorial legislature from enfranchising women. This occurred despite the efforts of Susan B. Anthony and other mainland suffragists who fought to keep the word "male" out of the various organic acts and territorial constitutions that Congress devised—efforts reminiscent of their unsuccessful quest to keep the word "male" out of the Fourteenth Amendment. Thus, policies regarding women's eligibility to vote in the territories changed gradually as suffragists secured the vote by a different means in each U.S. territory. In each case, women played an active role in their own enfranchisement, and in some instances sought and received support from mainland suffragists.[49]

Alaska

By 1920, one U.S. territory, Alaska, had already settled the issue. In 1912, Congress authorized Alaska to form a territorial legislature and empowered the legislature to extend the right to vote to women, if it so chose. Alaska legislators were ready, having been lobbied extensively by Alaskan women who were aided by the National American Woman Suffrage Association (NAWSA).[50]

The first bill they passed extended the vote to women citizens on the same basis as men. However, indigenous women of the territory remained disfranchised. Few Alaska Natives were citizens: territorial law allowed citizenship only for Alaska Natives willing to go through a complicated process to prove abandonment of tribal relationships and customs. Even after Congress passed the Indian Citizenship Act of 1924, Alaska's indigenous people continued to face obstacles. In 1925, the Alaska legislature passed the Alaska Voters Literacy Act to prevent voting by people who did not read or speak English, further limiting the numbers of Alaska Natives able to vote. Alaska became a state in 1949.[51]

Hawai'i

A U.S. territory since 1898, Hawai'i had a government organized by Congress, much like other U.S. territories destined for eventual statehood. However, despite Hawai'i's long history of women leaders—the last Hawai'ian monarch, deposed in a revolt instigated by Americans, had been Queen Lili'uokalani—the U.S. Congress *still* prohibited Hawai'i from enfranchising women. Susan B. Anthony was furious and called on all other suffragists to "raise your voices in protest against the impending crime of this Nation upon the Islands it has clutched from other folks." And Carrie Chapman Catt demanded that Congress omit the word male, arguing that "the declared intention of the United States in annexing the Hawai'ian Islands [was] to give them the benefits of the most advanced civilization."[52]

Thus, by 1920 Hawai'ian women had been working for years to remove that ban on their enfranchisement. Mainland suffragists saw an opportunity to promote

woman suffrage by federal action by assisting the suffrage effort in Hawai'i, so they provided aid and encouragement. In 1912, Catt met with suffragists in both Hawai'i and the Philippines while on a world tour as president of the International Woman Suffrage Association (IWSA). When Catt arrived in Honolulu, she knew little about Hawai'ian culture and was surprised to be greeted by Native Hawai'ian women who were the officers of the Women's Equal Suffrage Association of Hawai'i (WESAH). The leader, Wilhelmina Kekelaokalaninul Widemann Dowsett, was a Native Hawai'ian whose father was a German planter and her mother a Native Hawai'ian of the chiefess rank. Catt was impressed by the Hawai'ian suffragists and in 1918 returned to the islands to provide assistance and encouragement.[53]

Queen Lili'uokalani, 1891
HAWAI'I STATE ARCHIVES

Congress's Hawai'ian Organic Act of 1900 had enfranchised male citizens as long as they were literate in English or Hawai'ian, but excluded foreign-born Asians, a group ineligible for citizenship under U.S. law until 1943. Thus, Native Hawai'ian men constituted the majority of voters. Native Hawai'ian women were the principal force in the islands' woman suffrage movement, joined by a smaller number of "white-settler" women.[54]

At the urging of the WESAH, in 1915 the territorial legislature requested that its delegate to the U.S. House of Representatives, Prince Kūhiō, beseech Congress to amend the Organic Act for Hawai'i to extend suffrage to women. Congress took no action, but in 1918 under pressure from mainland suffragists, Congress relegated to the territorial legislature the authority to decide the issue. Hawai'ian suffragists

Wilhelmine Kekelaokalaninul
Widemann Dowsett, 1918
HAWAI'I STATE ARCHIVES

assumed their legislature would enfranchise them. However, for two years the leg-islature delayed a decision as they debated how and when to extend the vote to women, and what restrictions should be applied.[55]

In 1919, after the Hawai'ian Senate approved the woman suffrage bill, but the Hawai'ian House of Representatives resisted, Wilhelmina Dowsett organized a protest with more than five hundred women of all ages and nationalities who marched to the state capitol, demanding enfranchisement, but to no avail. After several more demonstrations, Dowsett and her associates began lobbying the U.S. Congress directly all the while confidently preparing women across the islands for the time when they would finally win the vote.[56]

When the Nineteenth Amendment was ratified in 1920, it was taken as granting suffrage to women who were citizens of Hawai'i. Thus, when Hawai'i became a state in 1949, Hawai'ian women had been voting for twenty-nine years.[57]

Philippines

The path to woman suffrage was much more challenging in the Philippines and Puerto Rico, territories that had not been designated as on track to become states and where residents were not considered citizens of the United States. The U.S. Supreme Court's decision in the Insular Cases (1901) declared that the Philippines and Puerto Rico were not *part of* the United States, but rather *belonged* to the United States. The women and men of these "appurtenant territories" were, correspond-ingly, deemed subjects, not citizens of the republic.[58]

Many, if not most Filipinas, did not wish to become U.S. citizens, but supported Philippine independence. After Spain ceded the Philippines, along with Puerto Rico and Guam, to the United States in 1898, Filipino nationalist forces kept up a costly fight for independence, which was defeated by U.S. military forces in 1902. Proclaiming its intent to "civilize" the Filipinos and prepare them for self-government, Congress then established a territorial government with a Governor General and an upper house appointed by the U.S. Congress and a lower house to be elected by male Filipino voters. However, suffrage was severely restricted by literacy, property, and language requirements, to the point that less than two percent of the total population—men and women—were able to vote.[59]

The United States governed the Philippines like a colony until granting the country independence in 1946. Many Filipinas sought to participate in the limited self-government granted to male residents, simultaneously participating in campaigns for woman suffrage and independence. For example, Filipina suffragist Clemencia López traveled for two years in the United States seeking to build support for Philippine independence, and at one point testifying before Congress. In 1902, when addressing the New England Woman Suffrage Association in Boston, López declared, "I believe that we are both striving for much the same object—you for the right to take part in national life; we for the right to have a national life to take part in."[60]

The first woman suffrage bill in the territory was put forth in the Philippine Assembly in 1907, encouraged by Pura Villanueva Kalaw, a women's rights pioneer and founder of the *Asociacion Feminista Ilonga* (Association of Ilonga Feminists) created in 1906. Throughout the decade a core group of Filipina women's rights supporters, including Kalaw, López, and Sofia Reyes de Veyra, pushed for women's enfranchisement through several different organizations.[61]

Clemencia López

After meeting with Carrie Chapman Catt in 1912, they established the Society for the Advancement of Women (SAW), later renamed *Club Damas de Manila* or Women's Club of Manila (CDM), to take up the suffrage cause.[62] In 1917, de Veyra worked with mainland suffragists after coming to Washington, D.C. with her husband who was the Resident Commissioner of the Philippines to the House of Representatives. Upon returning home, de Veyra continued her work for woman suffrage together with other educated clubwomen and writers, allied with Rosario Lam and other working women.[63]

The Filipino women's fight for woman suffrage continued through the 1920s and into the 1930s. In 1922, María Paz Guanzón, M.D., organized *Liga Nacional de Damas Filipinas* (National League of Filipino Women), to work for suffrage, as well as for better working conditions in factories and for Philippine independence.[64]

Oddly, Filipinas won the vote, then lost it, then regained it, which meant they had to reassemble a suffrage movement after briefly attaining their goal. In 1933, the Philippine Legislature passed a law granting women suffrage, but in 1934 the U.S. Congress passed an act establishing the Philippine Commonwealth, which did not secure woman's suffrage, and the previous Philippine legislation was swept away before it took effect.[65]

The new constitution that Filipinos adopted called for a plebiscite of women voters to determine if they wanted to be enfranchised. In 1937, Filipina women overwhelmingly reaffirmed their desire for the vote, and the vote was granted. Still, suffrage in the Philippines was limited to a privileged few; at the end of the American period only fourteen percent of Filipinos could vote. Universal adult suffrage did not exist until 1946 when the Philippine Republic was established.[66]

Puerto Rico

It took almost as long for women to win the vote in Puerto Rico where, as in the Philippines, residents were initially considered subjects rather than citizens of the

First Lady Florence Harding (center) welcomes to the White House the wives of a Philippine delegation seeking independence, presented by Sofia Reyes de Veyra, second from right, 1922.
LIBRARY OF CONGRESS

United States. In 1917, Congress granted Puerto Ricans citizenship—some claimed so that the men could be called to serve in World War I—but left it as an "unincorporated territory" of the United States, not slated for future statehood. Beginning in 1900, Puerto Ricans were governed by a presidentially appointed upper house and a lower house of representatives consisting of members elected by male residents of the territory. The territorial government had the authority to set the requirements for voting but did not enfranchise women.[67]

Ana Roqué de Duprey, an educator, writer, and journalist was one of the territory's earliest women's rights advocates and suffragists. She began publishing the territory's first feminist newspaper, *La Mujer*, in 1894, and helped found the University of Puerto Rico in 1903. Duprey also enlisted others in the cause of woman suffrage, including many of the teachers who graduated from the university. In 1917, Puerto Ricans gained U.S. citizenship, but since women were still unable to vote, Duprey helped establish one of the first suffrage organizations in her country, the *Liga Femínea Puertorriqueña* (Puerto Rican Feminist League).[68]

Another Puerto Rican advocate of women's enfranchisement was Luisa Capetillo, a leading labor organizer, writer, and anarchist who worked for gender equality and

Luisa Capetillo

Milagros Benet de Mewton
LIBRARY OF CONGRESS

class emancipation throughout her life. Capetillo believed in the inseparable tie between class struggle and woman suffrage. She promoted the woman's vote as a part of her work for radical reform in Puerto Rico, and at times, in Florida where she worked with Hispanic U.S. labor leaders while employed as a *lectora* (a reader hired by the workers to inform and entertain them) in cigar factories. In 1911, Capetillo published Puerto Rico's earliest feminist treatise in which she promoted radical ideas such as equal education for all and "free love." She is also remembered for being among the first women to wear pants in public, an act of defiance for which she was arrested more than once. Capetillo's radicalism set her apart from most Puerto Rican suffragists, as did her advocacy of suffrage for all. Many working-class Puerto Rican women supported suffrage, often through the Socialist Party, which began pressing for woman suffrage when it was founded in 1915. Women workers' strong support for suffrage made conservative male lawmakers fear that enfranchising women would strengthen socialism in Puerto Rico.[69]

Middle-class and upper-class suffragists in Puerto Rico organized separately. One of the most prominent, Milagros Benet de Mewton, a teacher and activist, was born to a liberal, intellectual family with family members who were elected officials and politically influential. In 1917, de Mewton became active in the *Liga Femínea Puertorriqueña*, later renamed *La Liga Social Sufragista* (Suffragist Social League) to reflect an expansion of goals beyond suffrage to include a woman's right to hold public office.[70]

After 1920, both working-class and middle-class suffragists sought to get the Nineteenth Amendment applied in Puerto Rico. Within a few weeks after the amendment was ratified, Genara Pagán, a labor activist, tested the political waters in Puerto Rico by seeking to register to vote. When denied, she filed a complaint

that led the governor of Puerto Rico to request a ruling from the U.S. federal government, which stated the Nineteenth Amendment had no bearing on the case of Puerto Rican women. De Mewton and several other women filed lawsuits challenging the right of the Puerto Rican officials to refuse to register women on the grounds that they were U.S. citizens, but the territorial supreme court ruled against them in each case. They also pressed the territorial legislature to enfranchise women, but suffrage bills failed repeatedly.[71]

Puerto Rican suffragists also traveled to Washington, D.C. seeking support. De Mewton personally lobbied Presidents Calvin Coolidge and Herbert Hoover for woman suffrage. In addition, Puerto Rican suffragists sought support from mainland women's rights advocates, including the National Woman's Party (NWP), which took up their cause and successfully lobbied Congress on their behalf. In 1928, the U.S. House passed a bill enfranchising all Puerto Rican women and the Senate was about to do the same, when the Puerto Rican legislature pre-empted universal suffrage for Puerto Rican women by passing a bill extending voting rights only to women who were literate. The U.S. Congress did not intervene and thus, in 1929, only a minority of Puerto Rican women who could read and write gained the vote. Finally, in 1935 the Puerto Rican legislature allowed *all* women in the territory to vote.[72]

Virgin Islands

Another U.S. territory where women had to fight for woman suffrage long after 1920 was the U.S. Virgin Islands (St. Croix, St. John, St. Thomas, and several smaller islands). At the time the Nineteenth Amendment was ratified, the Virgin Islands had only recently become part of the United States, purchased from Denmark in 1917. The islands were administered by the U.S. Navy until 1931. After that, civilian governors appointed by the U.S. president administered the islands. In 1932, the U.S. Congress granted U.S. citizenship to all Virgin Islanders, however, women were not allowed to vote.[73]

Gaining women's enfranchisement took years of strategic activism by women of the Islands, with teachers at the heart of the struggle. The St. Thomas Teachers Association, a network of teachers, students, and working women founded by Edith Williams, known as the "Mother of Education" for her lifelong work on behalf of students in St. Thomas, played a crucial role. Williams was one of the founding members of the Suffragist League, established in 1932 by St. Thomas entrepreneur Ella Gifft. Other suffragists included Anna Vessup and Eulalie Stevens; like Williams, they were teachers who had spent time in African American communities on the mainland United States and had witnessed the use of judicial power in relationship to voting rights.[74]

In 1935, these Virgin Islands suffragists seized a promising opportunity presented by the appointment of Federal Judge Albert Levitt to St. Thomas District Court. Levitt was married to Elsie Hill, a former chair of the National Woman's Party who

Virgin Islands suffrage leaders
Edith WIlliams, Anna Vessup, and Eulalie Stevens, 1930s.
LIBRARY OF CONGRESS

soon joined the local women's groups and became a key advocate for the women of St. Thomas, helping them acquire a lawyer. After Edith Williams applied to become a registered voter, twenty-three more women also filed, but the St. Thomas electoral board rejected their applications. Hill, Stevens, and Vessup then filed a petition, seeking a court order to be added as voters. A few days later, Judge Levitt issued a judgment, ruling that the three women were "herewith adjudged to be duly and properly qualified voters," and allowing all women of the Virgin Islands to vote in local elections. In 1936, the Organic Act of the Virgin Islands established a "civil government" for the territorial domain and prohibited "any discrimination in qualification [for voting rights] be made or based upon difference in race, color, sex, or religious belief."[75]

Guam

The United States acquired the small, western Pacific island of Guam in 1898 at the outbreak of the Spanish-American War in a bloodless takeover of the territory. As part of its strategy to overtake the Philippines from Spain, the United States considered Guam to be a strategic acquisition. It was not until 1950 that the U.S. government passed the Guam Organic Act, which established a government in Guam. The Act also declared those born in Guam to be U.S. citizens. Subsequent amendments to the Guam Organic Act applied several U.S. constitutional amendments to Guam, including the Nineteenth Amendment. However,

Guamanians still cannot vote for U.S. president, and similar to other U.S. territories, they have no voting representatives in Congress.[76]

Samoa

American Samoa became a U.S. territory in 1900 after establishing treaties with local island chiefs, Great Britain, and Germany. Acquired for strategic purposes, Samoa was administered by the U.S. Navy until transferred to the U.S. Department of the Interior in 1951. American Samoans are still not citizens of the United States and people born in the territory are considered U.S. nationals. The Nineteenth Amendment and many other provisions of the U.S. Constitution do not apply in American Samoa, but the American Samoan Constitution, established in 1967, enfranchised "every person" age eighteen and older. In 1977, for the first time Samoans elected their own governor and legislature. In 1981, American Samoans elected the territory's first delegate to the U.S. House of Representatives, however, this is a nonvoting position, except in congressional committees where the delegate is a member.[77]

Gaining the vote in all of these overseas territories was a limited victory. As of 2020, residents *still* cannot vote in presidential elections and are allowed only one, non-voting representative in the House of Representatives.

Washington, D.C.

Strange but true, women (and men) with full U.S. citizenship but living in the nation's capital, Washington, D.C., have faced—and still face as of 2020—a struggle for full enfranchisement. For a brief period after Congress established the city in 1790, residents could vote as residents of Maryland or Virginia. But when Congress adopted the District of Columbia Organic Act of 1801, it took full control of governing the city and as a result, residents lost their right to vote in federal elections.[78]

In 1961, the Twenty-third Amendment to the U.S. Constitution extended the right to vote in presidential elections to D.C. residents. Still, until 1973 when they were permitted to elect their own city officials, they were governed by Congress. In 1971, Congress began allowing D.C. residents to elect a non-voting "Delegate to the United States House of Representatives." As of 2020, the District is led by two African American women; Muriel Bowser who has served the district as mayor since 2015, and Eleanor Holmes Norton, a nationally prominent civil rights and women's rights leader, who has served as the district's delegate to Congress since 1991. Both support a goal long held by many D.C. residents—statehood.[79]

Some who oppose the District of Columbia becoming a state, insist it would require amending the U.S. Constitution. Every year since 1991, Delegate Norton has proposed a congressional bill that would by-pass this formidable obstacle. While not eliminating the "seat of government" that the Constitution called for, the bill would

shrink the national capital to a small complex of federal buildings and allow the rest of the district to become the 51st state. The name proposed for the new state, "State of Washington, Douglass Commonwealth," would maintain the "D.C." abbreviation while paying homage to the famous African American leader and long-time D.C. resident, Frederick Douglass. If adopted, the 700,000 Americans living in the District of Columbia would gain full voting rights and representation in the House and the Senate. However, the bill faces formidable obstacles owing to partisanship. Since most D.C. residents are Democrats, Republicans strongly oppose it.[80]

The Voting Rights Movement of the 1960s

For a half century after ratification of the Nineteenth Amendment, the woman's vote gradually increased, but the two major trends that were much discussed in the 1920s continued: a lower turnout of women voters compared to men, and the absence of a woman's voting bloc. Women continued to vote much like the men in their families and communities. It was rare for either women or men to engage in crossover voting, breaking with their parties even temporarily. During rare instances of re-alignment, including African Americans' shift from the Republican to the Democratic Party during the New Deal in the 1930s, and White Southerners' shift from the Democratic to the Republican Party in the 1960s through the 1980s, women moved in the same direction as similarly situated men.[81]

The wholesale suppression of the African American vote in the South continued with little change. However, in the 1960s and 1970s, major political and social movements led to changes in women's voting patterns that had major consequences for the nation. In the 1960s, a mass movement for voting rights in which African American women played leading roles compelled the federal government to remove the barriers that so thoroughly suppressed the African American vote in the South. Leaders in the movement for voting rights included remarkable women such as Ella Josephine Baker, Septima Poinsette Clark, and Fannie Lou Hamer.

Ella Baker, born in Virginia and reared in North Carolina, grew up determined to work for social justice, in part from hearing her grandmother's stories about being enslaved. After college, Baker moved to New York City where she began her career as an activist for race, gender, and economic justice. After working as a field secretary for the National Association for the Advancement of Colored People (NAACP), she helped Martin Luther King, Jr. organize a new organization, the Southern Christian Leadership Conference (SCLC) and ran a voter registration campaign called the Crusade for Citizenship.[82]

After African American students began spontaneous sit-ins and demanding service in restaurants and stores, Baker left the SCLC to guide this emerging youth movement, helping to establish the Student Nonviolent Coordinating Committee (SNCC). In 1960, Baker brought the students together at Shaw University in Raleigh, North Carolina, and invited Vanderbilt University theology student,

James Lawson, to address them on the philosophy and strategy of promoting justice through non-violent direct action. Lawson had been influenced by Mahatma Gandhi, who as a young man visiting London was inspired by the courage and methods of the militant suffragists. Their example aided him in developing his non-violent mass movement through which India had won independence.[83]

The SNCC was also devoted to registering voters, and in 1964 it helped create Freedom Summer in which brave volunteers—White and Black young people from across the United States—spread out in towns and rural areas through the state, encouraging and assisting people eager to become voters. Baker worked largely behind the scenes for more than five decades, inspiring and guiding other civil rights activists, particularly young people. She always insisted that voting was a key to freedom.[84]

South Carolinian Septima Poinsette Clark was an educator who became an organizer with the NAACP and the SCLC, pioneering the link between education and political organizing aimed at gaining the right to vote. Her own experiences with racism fueled her activism, and she was a major advocate for teachers, working with Thurgood Marshall for equal pay for Black teachers in South Carolina. She left the state after the South Carolina legislature prohibited state

Septima Clark (center) poses with Rosa Parks (left) and Parks's mother, Leona Mc-Cauley, a rural teacher, in 1956 at the Highlander Folk School in Tennessee, known for its work in developing leadership training for civil rights leaders.

LIBRARY OF CONGRESS

employees from involvement in civil rights organizations, and soon became the director of education and teaching for the SCLC. Eventually, Clark was responsible for establishing nearly 900 adult "citizenship schools" throughout the South, which focused on empowering and enfranchising African Americans. The schools made it possible for many African Americans in the South, especially previously uneducated people in rural areas, to navigate the challenges to voting that Southern states had adopted to suppress the Black vote, including literacy tests and "understanding" tests that required interpreting portions of the Constitution.[85]

Fannie Lou Hamer, who grew up in poverty in rural Mississippi, the youngest of twenty children, became a courageous and inspiring advocate for voting rights for African Americans and an advocate of economic and gender justice. After eighteen years working as a sharecropper and timekeeper on a Sunflower County plantation, in 1962 she attended her first mass meeting where representatives of the SNCC and the SCLC emphasized the importance of voting.[86]

Inspired by the speeches, Hamer volunteered to be part of a group going to the county courthouse to register to vote, becoming the group's leader. Returning home, her boss demanded she withdraw the application and when Hamer refused, she was fired and ordered off the plantation. After several attempts, she managed to register, but then was unable to vote because of the poll tax. During this time, Hamer and her family were continuously harassed by local authorities and shot at from speeding cars. Undaunted, Hamer became active in the civil rights movement, serving as a field secretary for SNCC, helping develop welfare programs for needy Black families, and all the while working to get more African Americans registered to vote.[87]

Fannie Lou Hamer
LIBRARY OF CONGRESS

Between 1960 and 1964, the extensive voter registration drives in the Southern states led to the most dramatic increase in the African American vote of any four-year period since Reconstruction. Still, registration rates of Black voters remained low, due to poll taxes, tests designed to suppress the Black vote, and violence or threats of violence against African Americans who wanted to vote. In early 1965, the registration rate for voting-age African Americans was less than twenty percent in Alabama and less than seven percent in Mississippi.[88]

For lower income people of all races, it was a big step forward when the Twenty-fourth Amendment, ratified in 1964, abolished poll taxes. However, it was a big disappointment that during Freedom Summer of 1964, when African Americans in

Marchers on the Edmund Pettus Bridge during the
Selma to Montgomery March in 1965. Alabama Dept. of Archives and History

Mississippi launched a major voting rights effort that was countered by massive white violence, the federal government *still* failed to protect African Americans' voting rights.[89]

In 1964, Hamer was a co-founder of the Mississippi Freedom Democratic Party (MFDP), which promoted voter registration while also challenging the legitimacy of the all-White "Mississippi Regulars." The official Democratic Party in the state, the Regulars protested the national party's support for the civil rights movement and barred African Americans from its activities.[90]

Hamer was frustrated and "sick and tired of being sick and tired" about Mississippi's continued efforts to oppress African Americans and disenfranchise Black voters. When the state Democratic Party sent its usual all-White Democratic delegation to the party's national convention in Atlantic City, New Jersey in 1964, Hamer and sixty other representatives of the MFDP traveled to Atlantic City, insisting that the Mississippi Regulars' segregated delegate selection process had violated party rules and demanded that the party seat *them* instead of the all-White state delegation.[91]

National Democratic Party leadership, fearful of losing the Southern White vote, offered the MFDP an insulting compromise of two seats, which they rejected and walked out. Before leaving, Hamer gave a fiery speech, covered on national television, iconic in the history of the voting rights movement in the United States. She told of the brutal beatings and assassination attempts she had endured in Mississippi as a result of simply claiming her right to vote—a right she did not even know she had until she was in her forties.[92]

Brutalizing marchers on "Bloody Sunday." The late Georgia Congressman John Lewis, then a young SNCC leader (on the ground, center) is severely beaten.

LIBRARY OF CONGRESS

The Voting Rights Act of 1965

The following year, Alabama police shocked the nation by brutally attacking hundreds of non-violent demonstrators peacefully marching from Selma to Montgomery in support of the voting rights of African Americans. Martin Luther King, Jr., John Lewis, and other civil rights leaders had chosen Selma, Alabama as the center of the campaign for voting rights because only two percent of eligible African Americans in that city were registered to vote, despite the concerted efforts of local people. The police responded violently and after a protestor was shot and killed, the activists set out to march to Montgomery, the state capital, fifty-four miles away, to publicize the worsening situation for African Americans and demand the vote.[93]

On March 7, 1965, with John Lewis of the Student Nonviolent Coordinating Committee (SNCC) and Reverend Hosea Williams of the Southern Christian Leadership Conference (SCLC) in the lead, about 600 marchers began walking across the Edmund Pettus Bridge, only to be blocked by state troopers and local policemen who viciously attacked the crowd with clubs, whips, and tear gas as White onlookers cheered.

National television coverage of what became known as "Bloody Sunday" sparked national outrage; two days later, about two thousand marchers, including large numbers of clergy, poured into Alabama to join King and other civil rights leaders to complete the march across the bridge and to the state capitol. This time, federalized Alabama National Guardsmen and agents of the Federal Bureau of Investigation (FBI) protected the marchers.[94]

The public outcry over the brutality in Selma forced President Lyndon Johnson to encourage Congress to pass the Voting Rights Act of 1965, one of the most consequential laws in U.S. history. The Voting Rights Act of 1965 banned election-related practices, including literacy tests, that states used to keep African American women and men away from the polls. The Voting Rights Act directed the Department of Justice to monitor voter registration in Southern counties where less than half of African American residents were registered. It also required counties and states with a history of discrimination against African American enfranchisement to get advance approval ("pre-clearance") from the Department of Justice before applying any new voting regulations.[95]

The results were dramatic. By the end of 1965, some 250,000 new African American voters had registered to vote, a third of them registered by federal examiners. Within two years, Black voter registration rates in Mississippi increased to around sixty percent. Before the Voting Rights Act of 1965, an estimated twenty-three percent of African Americans of voting age were registered nationally, but by 1969, sixty-one percent had registered. Not surprising, while many Southern White Democrats left the party to become Republicans, African American allegiance to the Democratic Party solidified. Over time, African American women would prove to be the Democratic party's most loyal supporters, turning out in large numbers for every election.[96]

For the rest of the century, the federal government continued to take action to expand voter eligibility and to facilitate registration and voting. In 1971, the Twenty-sixth Amendment lowered the voting age to eighteen years. In the 1990s, Congress passed the Americans with Disabilities Act (ADA) requiring states to ensure that people with disabilities could vote. In 1993, Congress adopted the National Voter Registration Act ("Motor Voter") to make voter registration easier and to encourage turnout. And in 2009, through the Military and Overseas Empowerment Act, Congress mandated reforms to facilitate military troops voting while serving overseas, as well as voting by expatriates.[97]

Congress also expanded or extended the Voting Rights Act of 1965 several times under both Democratic and Republican administrations. In 1975, it added provisions requiring bilingual election materials in areas of the nation with a significant number of "language minority" voters. As a result, Native Americans, Asian Americans, Alaskan Natives, and Spanish-speaking voters gained protection against discrimination at the polls.[98]

A Surge in Women's Political Activism

Like the civil rights movement, a renewed movement for women's rights that began in the 1960s brought about a major increase in voter turnout. Often called the "Second Wave" of the women's movement, relative to the "First Wave," which fought for women's enfranchisement, it heightened women's group consciousness and interest in politics. The Second Wave led to increased political activism among

both women's rights activists—who during this time generally embraced the term "feminist"—and later, conservative women who in the 1970s launched what they called the "pro-family" movement in opposition.[99]

The amorphous Second Wave began in the early 1960s and grew rapidly. It was initially spearheaded by older, politically moderate women who served on federal and state commissions that identified laws negatively impacting women and recommended reforms. Many were White, but women of color also played crucial roles as the movement got underway. Operating in a completely different political climate regarding race than the suffragists who fought for the vote in the late nineteenth and early twentieth centuries, Second Wave feminists did not avoid association with the civil rights movement and its leaders. Rather, many women's rights activists of the 1960s supported both movements and borrowed many tactics and strategies from the civil rights movement, which was then experiencing considerable success.[100]

One of the feminists' earliest and most important victories came as an addendum to a major civil rights bill. Title VII of the Civil Rights Act of 1964 extended the Act's ban on race-based discrimination in employment to prohibit sex-based discrimination as well. Ironically, Virginia Senator Howard Smith, a White Southern conservative who adamantly opposed the civil rights movement, introduced Title VII, and at first, Smith presented it in Congress as if it were a joke. Many thought he added the provision banning sex discrimination as a poison pill to kill the bill.[101]

In fact, Smith acted at the behest of Alice Paul and other aging members of the National Woman's Party (NWP) who had for years urged him to support the Equal Rights Amendment (ERA) and other measures to enhance women's equality. In the 1960s, NWP members were still working with scant success for passage of the ERA, which they had first introduced in 1923. They perceived an opportunity to promote equal rights for women by attaching the Title VII clause to the civil rights measure. With strong support from Congresswoman Martha Griffiths, a Democrat from Michigan, and Senator Margaret Chase Smith, a Republican from Maine, Congress adopted Title VII. At first, the Equal Employment Opportunity Commission (EEOC) created to enforce the Civil Rights Act of 1964, ignored complaints based on sex discrimination. But in time, Title VII proved to be one of the most important pieces of legislation in advancing gender equality and the basis for many feminist victories.[102]

In 1966, feminists disturbed by the EEOC ignoring Title VII and wanting to lobby more effectively for the reforms recommended by the state and federal women's commissions, created a new non-government organization modeled somewhat after the National Association for the Advancement of Colored People (NAACP). The National Organization for Women (NOW) was dedicated to promoting women's equality in all aspects of American society—public and private. Betty Friedan was one of NOW's founders and its first president. Friedan, a journalist, was the author of the 1963 best-seller, *The Feminine Mystique*, which articulated the frustrations of many White middle-class women and brought many of them to feminism. Friedan's fame helped attract thousands to the new feminist organization.[103]

Pauli Murray, an African American lawyer and civil rights activist, also played a leading role in the founding of NOW, and co-authored with Friedan NOW's eloquent and comprehensive "Statement of Purpose." It began with the declaration:

> We, men and women who hereby constitute ourselves as the National Organization for Women, believe that the time has come for a new movement toward true equality for all women in America, and toward a fully equal partnership of the sexes, as part of the world-wide revolution of human rights now taking place within and beyond our national borders.
>
> The purpose of NOW is to take action to bring women into full participation in the mainstream of American society now, exercising all the privileges and responsibilities thereof in truly equal partnership with men.[104]

Aileen Hernandez, an African American activist and union organizer who succeeded Friedan as NOW president in 1970, worked to make NOW more inclusive and to focus attention on issues facing women of color. The women's movement grew rapidly as thousands of women, mostly younger and more radical who had come from the civil rights movement and the anti-Vietnam War movement, joined the fight for women's rights.[105]

In 1967, NOW adopted the ERA as one of its key goals, much to the delight of Alice Paul and other NWP members who had pursued this goal for so long and with so few allies. They were thrilled to see younger women become excited over the amendment. Soon thereafter, NOW also voted to work for legalization of abortion—and in the early 1970s, for protection of the rights of lesbians.[106]

By 1970, the fiftieth anniversary of the Nineteenth Amendment, the women's rights movement was vast, vocal, and highly visible. On August 26, 1970, feminists took to the streets to celebrate the suffrage victory and to press for more change.

Across the nation, there were huge demonstrations and parades sponsored by NOW that had challenged women to take the day off in a "Women's Strike for

"Women's Strike for Equality" marchers, August 26, 1970, the Fiftieth Anniversary of the Nineteenth Amendment. LIBRARY OF CONGRESS

Equality." The largest and most spectacular march was along New York's Fifth Avenue with an estimated fifty thousand marchers, which exceeded even the largest suffrage marches in the city a half a century earlier. Elsewhere in the city where public monuments to famous females were conspicuously absent, women erected temporary statues to honor suffragists and other famous women. On that day, women participated in many moving tributes to their feminist forebears. A caravan of women visited graves of famous suffragists, ending at Seneca Falls where the governor of New York proclaimed August 26 a state holiday.[107]

Promoting Women in Politics

The creation of the National Women's Political Caucus (NWPC) a year later underscored feminists' awareness of women's severe underrepresentation in elected office and their determination to increase women's political power. The organization was founded after Betty Friedan reached out to prominent women in politics who were eager to move more women and women's issues to the forefront of American politics.

In 1971, Friedan and Bella Abzug, a newly-elected Democratic Congresswoman from New York, along with Congresswoman Shirley Chisholm of New York, the first African American woman in Congress, and Congresswoman Patsy Takemoto Mink of Hawai'i, the first Asian American woman in Congress, brought together a diverse group of women that established the NWPC. Other prominent women in the organization included journalist Gloria Steinem, editor of the new feminist magazine *Ms.*; Dorothy Height, president of the National Council of Negro Women; Eleanor Holmes Norton, attorney; Fannie Lou Hamer, civil rights movement leader; LaDonna Harris, Comanche Leader and founder of Americans for Indian Opportunity; Lupe Anguiano, Mexican-American civil rights activist; Margaret Heckler, Republican Congresswoman from Massachusetts; and Jill Ruckelshaus, who worked within the Nixon and Ford administrations to promote women's equality. Through the NWPC, feminists from both political parties worked together to boost women's influence in political parties, promote feminist legislation, and get more women elected to office. In addition, as the NWPC statement of purpose made clear, they sought action "against sexism, racism, institutional violence, and poverty."[108]

In 1972, more women ran for Congress than ever before. There were dramatic successes, including Barbara Jordan, a feminist Democrat from Texas, who became the first African American women to be elected to Congress from a Southern state. That same year, Congresswoman Shirley Chisholm launched a campaign for president of the United States. As she announced her candidacy, Chisholm declared: I am not the candidate of Black America, although I am Black and proud. I am not the candidate of the women's movement of this country, although I am a woman, and I am equally proud of that.... I am the candidate of the people of America. And my presence before you now symbolizes a new era in American political history." Though not successful in gaining the Democratic nomination, Chisholm stayed in the race all

Shirley Chisholm, 1972

the way to the national convention, running on the same slogan that had helped her win her seat in Congress, "Unbought and Unbossed." It would be several decades more before women made sizable breakthroughs in politics, and still more before winning the highest offices in the land. But women and women's issues were now at the forefront of national politics and so they would remain. It *was* a new era.[109]

All of this activity, together with public opinion polls that showed widespread support for women's equality, caught the attention of lawmakers in both parties. This resulted in a second honeymoon for women reformers, reminiscent of the early 1920s. In the early 1970s, even politicians who were not fans of feminism were supportive. All three branches of the federal government took action that advanced the feminist agenda. This included legislation to end sex discrimination in jobs and education, aid for women and families, and a new cause for the women's movement: protection of a woman's right to control her own body—what feminists called "reproductive freedom." In 1973, the Supreme Court issued a landmark decision for women, *Roe v. Wade*, legalizing abortion.[110]

In the 1971-1972 session, Congress passed more women's rights bills than in all previous legislative sessions combined. The greatest indicator of congressional support for the women's rights movement was its approval of the Equal Rights Amendment (ERA) by overwhelming majorities. Since the 1920s, the ERA had languished in Congress despite support from Republicans. Democrats had remained opposed to the ERA because women reformers and organized labor objected. But by the early 1970s, protective legislation for workers had been extended to men as well as women and these groups dropped their objections. At last, the League of Women Voters (LWV) and the National Woman's Party (NWP) were on the same page regarding the ERA. In 1972, the opposition would come from an entirely different source.[111]

Conservative Women Organize

After Congress sent the Equal Rights Amendment (ERA) to the states for their consideration in March 1972, many states rushed to ratify it, and it appeared the amendment would soon be added to the U.S. Constitution. Within a year, thirty of the

required thirty-eight states had ratified. However, conservative women organized in opposition, seeking to prevent further ratification and to persuade states that had ratified to rescind even though legal precedents suggest rescission is invalid. Though Congress extended the ratification period from seven to ten years, only five more states ratified before the 1982 deadline and five states voted to rescind.[112]

Phyllis Schlafly of Illinois, an experienced political activist from the Republican Party's right wing, together with conservative women activists from across the nation, mobilized thousands of women in a powerful anti-ERA movement. Most of their recruits were politically inexperienced women from a variety of conservative religious groups that saw the ERA as a threat to the traditional patriarchal family. Lottie Beth Hobbs of Texas, a leader among women in the Church of Christ, brought many of these women into the anti-ERA movement through an organization she founded, Women Who Want to be Women (WWWW). The anti-ERA coalition included conservative Catholics, Mormons, evangelical and fundamentalist Protestants, and Orthodox Jews—groups previously hostile to one another but now united against the ERA and feminism.[113]

The anti-ERA coalition also included old-line political conservatives such as the John Birch Society and a number of prominent Southern senators who had fought against the civil rights movement and now applied the politics of backlash and obstruction to the fight against the women's movement. In the South, many women who had actively resisted racial integration now worked to oppose the ERA and feminism. As in the case of the Nineteenth Amendment, most states that refused to ratify the ERA were in the South.[114]

Outside the White House, Phyllis Schlafly protests First Lady Rosalynn Carter's advocacy of the ERA, January 21, 1977. LIBRARY OF CONGRESS

Through the rest of the 1970s until the ERA deadline of 1982, American women became even more polarized and politicized as the two women's movements competed to influence politicians and policies. Tensions accelerated in 1977 as feminists and conservative women faced off during a series of state and federal conferences sponsored by Congress. The United Nations had declared 1975 to 1985 "The Decade of Women" and sponsored a 1975 International Women's Year conference in Mexico City where a "World Plan of Action" was adopted. Inspired by the conference, U.S. feminist leaders had suggested these conferences so American women could elect delegates and produce a "National Plan of Action" to guide future federal policy on women's issues.[115]

After fierce battles for control of the state conferences—which feminists won—the elected delegates and thousands of observers gathered in Houston, Texas for a culminating National Women's Conference. Feminists had worked hard to encourage the participation of women from diverse racial, ethnic, and economic groups, including veterans of the civil rights movement, hoping to unite them all in an even more powerful women's rights movement. The National Plan of Action the feminist majority adopted to send to Congress called for ratifying the ERA, protecting minority rights, and supporting reproductive rights, including publicly funded abortion. The delegates shocked many Americans by supporting lesbian and gay rights—then a new issue in American politics.[116]

However, the conservatives had expanded their ranks and strengthened their coalition during the year as anti-ERA and anti-abortion groups joined forces. During the National Women's Conference, they organized a massive "Pro-Life, Pro-Family Rally," also in Houston, and wholeheartedly denounced the National Plan of Action and federal support for feminism. Announcing the start of a "pro-family" movement, conservatives vowed to remain politically active, to roll back the gains of the feminists, and to take back their country from the moderate and liberal politicians who supported feminism. The 1977 IWY conferences—a major turning point in U.S. history—had further polarized American women and made them more politically active as both sides mobilized more supporters and clarified their political agendas.[117]

The battle between advocates of women's rights and their conservative opponents had a major impact on American political culture, making it clear to politicians that women had become a force to be reckoned with, though bitterly divided in their goals. In 1980, while Democrats continued to support the women's rights movement, the Republican Party chose to side with the conservative women's movement. Abandoning the ERA, which the party had supported for many decades, and embracing a strong pro-life position, the Republican Party cast itself as the party of "family values."[118]

Watershed Election in 1980

By 1980, the successful drive to gain federal protection of voting rights had led to dramatic increases in African American voters in the South. This, along with two

decades of feminist activism and almost a decade of conflict between advocates of women's rights and family values, led far more women to turn out to vote. In the 1980 election in which President Jimmy Carter lost to Ronald Reagan, women voted at a higher rate than men for the first time in the history of the United States. This proved to be the start of an enduring trend.[119] By 2000, even African American and White women of the South, whose voter turnout had previously lagged behind women from other regions of the United States and behind Southern men, voted at levels that approached women in other regions and at a higher rate than Southern men.[120]

There was still no "woman's bloc." The 1980 presidential election, however, saw the emergence of a differential between women's and men's voting preferences in which women tended to be more supportive of Democrats and men more supportive of Republicans, which also proved to be an enduring trend.[121] Feminists, including National Organization for Women (NOW) leader Eleanor Smeal and former Congresswoman Bella Abzug, moved quickly to identify and name this differential the "gender gap," hoping it would enhance their political clout, especially within the Democratic Party. In any case, the gender gap attracted considerable attention from the press, pundits, and political strategists—all seeking to explain it. Many attributed the gender gap to the women's movement, which had taught women to see their own values in political terms. Women who embraced the movement generally embraced the Democratic Party as the party more amenable to political action on behalf of women's equality.[122]

On the defensive, Republicans were quick to point out that the gender gap could also be read as men's declining support for the Democrats. This is supported by political scientists who note that men are less likely than women to favor the social welfare programs as well as the civil rights positions that the Democratic Party has advocated increasingly since the 1960s. Republicans also pointed out, correctly, that White married women tended to vote for their party while women of color and single women of all races favored the Democrats. Republican strategists insisted that the gender gap was really a "racial gap" or a "marriage gap." Thus, while GOP leaders understood the enhanced importance of women's votes, they would try to win them, not by increased support for feminism but by symbolic appointments and gestures, and by fidelity to policies that appealed to their pro-family base.[123]

Two Parties, Two "Women's Blocs"

Over the next several decades, Republicans continued to court pro-family voters, becoming increasingly reliant upon them, and alienating many moderate voters in the process. Republican feminists largely vanished from the party. At the same time, the GOP continued to attract large numbers of disaffected White Democrats from the South, becoming more uniformly conservative as well as racially homogenous. In fact, in the South, anti-feminism became a crucial part of the GOP's "Southern Strategy" to grow the party—quite useful in an era when overt racism

had become increasingly unacceptable. Many leaders of the anti-ERA effort in the South had earlier battled the civil rights movement, which suggested a sizable overlap between White supremacist and anti-feminist constituencies in the region. White Southern conservatives became a crucial part of the Republican base and Southern White women consistently demonstrated great party loyalty when casting their votes.[124]

Democrats continued to support women's rights along with civil rights for minorities, and became increasingly supportive of gay rights. Barack Obama, a Democrat, a feminist, and the nation's first African American president, was elected in 2008 with a seven-point gender gap; four years later, he was re-elected with an even larger gender gap of ten points. As president, Obama also became a champion of LGBT rights and eventually, same-sex marriage. During his presidency in *Obergefell v. Hodges* (2015), the Supreme Court ruled that married same-sex couples are entitled to be treated equally under the law. In celebration of this landmark decision, President Obama had the White House illuminated in rainbow colors, the symbol of LGBT pride and solidarity. A great many voters who identify as racial and ethnic minorities, including African Americans and Latinos, continue to support the Democratic Party in all elections.[125]

In the twenty-first century, the differences of opinion on women's and gender issues that divided American women in the 1970s, continue to divide the two major political parties and the nation: Democrats are still firmly aligned with women's rights advocates, while Republicans still cater to their traditional pro-family base.[126]

There continue to be dramatic differences in party identification related to race. According to one study, African American voters' overwhelming support for Democratic candidates in presidential elections is "stunning," especially among Black women who consistently cast less than ten percent of their votes for Republican candidates. The unified "woman's bloc" that many predicted as women gained the vote in 1920 never materialized. Instead, the United States has two women's blocs; a racially diverse feminist bloc closely aligned with the Democratic Party, and a largely White conservative bloc closely aligned with the GOP.[127]

Gutting the Voting Rights Act

The ever-expanding differences between the Democratic and Republican Parties in their racial composition and race-related policies had a negative effect on state and national policies regarding voting rights. After decades of expanding and enforcing voting laws, eliminating barriers that suppressed turnout especially of African Americans, and adopting new measures to encourage participation in elections, in 2013 the United States took a major step backward. In *Shelby County v. Holder*, the Supreme Court ruled unconstitutional a crucial section of the Voting Rights Act of 1965, the "pre-clearance" section. As a result, states were free to make

changes to voter qualifications without having to first prove that the new voting rules did not discriminate on the basis of race.[128]

Almost immediately, the legislatures in many states adopted new laws and procedures regarding voting, including restrictive photo I.D. requirements, purges of registration lists, cuts to early voting, and relocating or closing polling places. These changes have disqualified countless numbers of women and men who are unaware of, or unable to satisfy, the new voting requirements. Most advocates of these new voting restrictions are Republicans who promote these changes as a means of preventing election fraud—despite neutral studies that show that such fraud is extremely rare. Critics, mostly Democrats, insist that the measures are intended to suppress voter registration and participation by minorities and the poor—and they have had that effect. Research has shown that some of these voter requirements are particularly hard on women.[129]

As of 2021, equal suffrage advocates are demanding that Congress restore the power of the Voting Rights Act while also fighting to stop voter suppression at the state level.[130] Clearly, in the United States equal voting rights are not only hard to acquire, but difficult to keep. It appears that the suffrage battle never ends.

Almost the First Woman President

The two trends that first became visible in 1980—women turning out to vote in greater numbers than men and, as a group, being more likely than men to support Democratic candidates—have accelerated in recent elections. In addition, women's and gender issues continue to play a crucial role in national politics.

In the 2016 election, the major party platforms indicated that the tendency of Republicans to promote conservative family values and of Democrats to support women's rights, was stronger than ever.[131] The two parties took diametrically opposing positions on the issue of abortion, and both presidential candidates appealed for support by reminding voters of the importance of future Supreme Court appointments. For many conservative women and men, that issue was paramount. Still, pundits predicted that the majority of women—including Republicans—would vote to elect Democrat Hillary Rodham Clinton who had served previously as a Secretary of State, a Senator from New York, and a First Lady. In a contest between a woman with extensive experience in government and a strong record of supporting women's rights, and a man with no political experience who proudly opposed feminism, pundits reasoned there was a strong possibility that the first woman president would be the result.[132]

On election day 2016, large numbers of women voters visited Susan B. Anthony's grave in homage, leaving their "I voted" stickers, fully expecting to witness the election of the first woman president of the United States. Clinton won the popular vote by 2.9 million more votes than the Republican candidate, Donald J. Trump, but Trump's electoral college victory made him president of the United States.[133]

Hillary Rodham Clinton accepts the Democratic Party's
nomination for president, 2016. LIBRARY OF CONGRESS

Clinton benefitted only slightly from crossover voting. For the most part, in the 2016 presidential election the persistent pattern of voters remaining loyal to their parties held. As a Pew Research Center report stated, "Voter Choice and party affiliation were nearly synonymous." Over ninety percent of women who identified as Republicans voted for Trump, the same rate as Republican men. Democrats also voted overwhelmingly for their party's nominee with ninety-four percent supporting Clinton. The roughly one-third of the electorate, thirty-four percent, who identified as "independents" divided their votes almost evenly between the two candidates or voted for a third-party candidate.[134]

Hillary Clinton did win the women's vote by a sizable margin: over-all fifty-four percent of women voted for Clinton compared to forty-one percent for Trump. Exit polls also estimated that among her voters, women outnumbered men by thirteen percent—a thirteen-point gender gap. However, as before, the Democrats' advantage with women was largely due to solid support from women of color. Nearly one hundred percent of African American women voted for Clinton, along with a large majority of Latinas and other women of color. Across the board, women of color voted Democratic to a far greater extent than the men in their communities, though the men also voted heavily for Democrats. Most White voters, both male and female, voted for Trump, although far more college-educated White voters (fifty-five percent) supported Clinton. Non-college Whites were a majority of Trump's voters (sixty-four percent).[135]

After the election, pundits and the press expressed shock that, according to exit

polls, most White women (fifty-two percent) had voted for Trump. Later, more accurate analysis put the figure at forty-seven percent for Trump, and fifty-five percent for Clinton, a plurality but a statistical tie. The expression of shock revealed the persistence of the enduring but inaccurate expectation that women's gender is the main determinant of women's politics.[136]

Analysts seeking to explain White women's support for Trump emphasized that the majority of college-educated White women voted for Clinton. However, nearly all failed to point out that that there were strong regional differences in women's choices. Most White women living outside the South supported Clinton; fifty-two percent of them voted for her compared to the forty-eight percent who voted for Trump. But he won the votes of White women living in the South by a margin of sixty-four percent to thirty-six percent. That many White women residing in Southern states shared Trump's anti-feminist views made a huge difference in his election.[137]

In post-election analysis, much of the narrative explaining Trump's victory focused on economic displacement and anxiety as motivating factors among his supporters, especially non-college-educated Whites. However, research shows that Trump's advantage with these voters, usually attributed to differences in education, was more the result of sexist and racist attitudes, and that men do not have a monopoly on either. When White women are asked to respond to statements such as "women are taking privilege and power away from men," or "gender bias is not a real problem or not as much of a problem as many women make it out to be," or "women need to be protected," many of them agreed. And those beliefs had a powerful impact on their vote choices in 2016. Many women as well as men who voted for Trump strongly disliked Hillary Clinton's feminism.[138]

Younger voters were significantly more supportive of Clinton. Notably, voters under age thirty—just thirteen percent of the voters—reported voting for Clinton over Trump by a margin of fifty-eight percent to twenty-eight percent. Voters between thirty to forty-nine years old favored Clinton by a fifty-one percent to forty percent margin. However, the majority of voters over fifty years old went for Trump.[139]

Women March, Resist, Organize, Run, and Win

Clinton's defeat set off an immediate chain reaction culminating in massive public protests led by women, many of them young women, both White women and women of color. The result was the largest public protest in U.S. history. The Women's March on Washington, held on January 21, 2017, the day after Trump's inauguration, was accompanied by more than five hundred marches nationwide with an estimated turnout of between three-and-a-half million and five million marchers. The Washington March alone drew more than 450,000 participants to the nation's capital. The U.S. marchers were joined by women-led marches in more than a hundred cities around the world.[140]

Women who had supported Hillary Clinton were fired up after the defeat. Across the country, women formed new grassroots "resistance" organizations and

besieged their Republican representatives. The largest of these groups founded in response to Trump's election, Indivisible, reported that three-quarters of its members were female. Many women decided to seek office themselves, leading to a record number of women filing to run for office at every level of governance—from school boards to state offices to the U.S. Senate.[141]

There had been other periods in U.S. history when women's outrage with their government led to surges in the number of women seeking power to right wrongs through political action. Most notably, in 1992, anger over White male senators' dismissive treatment of Anita Hill, an African American law professor who denounced Supreme Court nominee, Clarence Thomas, for sexual harassment, prompted a spike in women's candidacies that resulted in many victories, especially by Democrats. Five women senators were elected and the number of women in the House of Representatives doubled—but only to forty-seven. But after that, the number of women in Congress had inched up gradually and only slightly. In 2016, Congress remained still less than twenty percent female.[142]

Trump's election inspired many more women to run for public office. As one political analyst explained, "It was if a switch had been flipped.... Suddenly, women were eager to run, as if they'd realized that the men were screwing everything up and they were going to have to do the job themselves." After Trump's victory, EMILY's List (an acronym for "Early Money Is Like Yeast"), founded in 1985 to fund campaigns for pro-choice Democratic women, was contacted by an astounding forty-two thousand women interested in running for everything from school board to Congress.[143]

Women's March, Washington, D.C., January 21, 2017

In the 2018, mid-term election—which attracted the highest voter turnout in a midterm election in at least forty years—a record number of women emerged victorious. Women's high turnout played a major role in producing a "blue wave" that turned the House of Representatives back to a Democratic majority, led by House Speaker Nancy Pelosi. In the House,102 women won election, including forty-three women of color; in the Senate, fourteen women were elected or re-elected; and for state governorships, nine women won.[144]

In one of the most publicized races of 2018, Stacey Y. Abrams, a lawyer, voting rights activist, and the minority leader in the Georgia legislature, was narrowly defeated in the state election for governor. Georgia's election was marred by major controversy over apparent attempts to suppress the minority vote. Abrams was the first African American female nominated by a major party to run as a gubernatorial nominee in the United States. Her opponent was a White male Trump supporter, Bryan Kemp, who was serving as Georgia's Secretary of State during the election, and thus, in charge of safeguarding the state's elections. From the beginning, there were problems. In the months leading up to election day, Kemp oversaw highly suspicious purges of some 300,000 voters from the rolls in a contested but court-sanctioned move claimed to be "list maintenance" that disfranchised a large number of African Americans who supported Abrams. On election day, voters encountered poll closures, long lines, and malfunctioning voting equipment, especially in largely minority areas.[145]

Similar to 2016 when defeat inspired action, Abrams's loss in 2018 set off yet another major, woman-led political battle that focused on the issue of voting rights. Abrams launched a national voter protection program, Fair Fight, focusing on twenty battleground states. The ongoing goal of Fair Fight is to end systematic voter suppression, and to press for free and fair elections.[146]

Woman Suffrage at 100

In 2020, the United States celebrated the centennial of the passage of the Nineteenth Amendment. As the year began, there were festivals, symposia, and countless new books, documentaries, and films about the long and dramatic struggle American women waged to gain the right to vote. The participation of African American women and other women of color in the struggle received long overdue acknowledgment. Historians, museum curators, and the media alike more fully documented the discrimination

Stacey Y. Abrams

Black women and women of color faced within the woman suffrage movement and their post-1920 fight against disfranchisement by Southern states.[147]

In Washington, D.C., the Smithsonian, the Library of Congress, the National Archives, and the National Portrait Gallery all featured major exhibits commemorating the fight for woman suffrage and the ratification of the Nineteenth Amendment. The congressionally appointed Women's Suffrage Centennial Commission (WSCC) sponsored numerous events, including the "Forward Into Light Campaign" in which buildings and landmarks across the nation were lit up in the suffrage colors purple and gold on August 26, 2020. That week the WSCC also sponsored a massive mosaic of Ida B. Wells-Barnett on the floor of Washington, D.C.'s Union Station, a mosaic created from thousands of small photos of women who fought for the vote. The U.S. Mint issued the 2020 Women's Suffrage Centennial Coin and the U.S. Postal Service issued a commemorative stamp.[148]

In January 2020, House Speaker Nancy Pelosi, the most powerful woman in the federal government, along with many congresswomen, honored the suffragists who fought so hard for the vote by wearing white to the State of the Union Address. Also in January, Virginia made history by becoming the thirty-eighth state to ratify the Equal Rights Amendment (ERA) as women in suffrage banners cheered from the gallery of the state house after witnessing this historic vote. Whether or not the ERA can become law, given that the deadline Congress had set for ratification was 1982, remained unclear.[149]

Beyond Washington, D.C., state governments as well as local historical societies throughout the nation also hosted exhibits on woman suffrage. Many states

House Speaker Nancy P. Pelosi

and cities celebrated by erecting new statues, in particular Tennessee, which took special pride in its role as "The Perfect Thirty-Six" and began its commemoration of the Nineteenth Amendment early. In addition to the Women's Suffrage Memorial dedicated in 2006, Knoxville dedicated a statue in 2018 in honor of Harry T. Burn and his mother, Febb Ensminger Burn, who, together played a pivotal role at the end of the long suffrage saga. In August 2020, two more statues went up in the state; the Tennessee Triumph Women's Suffrage Monument in Clarksville and the Tennessee Woman Suffrage Monument in Nashville's Centennial Park.[150]

In Virginia, a nonprofit, volunteer organization, The Turning Point Suffragist

Memorial Association, worked to complete a national memorial to American suffragists on the site of the Occoquan Workhouse where suffragists were once imprisoned for picketing the White House. This new museum and memorial, the Turning
Point Suffragist Memorial, will provide an overview of the suffrage movement and
include bronze statues donated by the National Suffrage Center Commission, honoring three suffrage leaders: Alice Paul, co-founder of the National Woman's Party
and author of the Equal Rights Amendment; Mary Church Terrell, co-founder of
the National Association of Colored Women (NACW) and the National Association for the Advancement of Colored People (NAACP) who was also a NWP member who had picketed the White House for woman suffrage; and Carrie Chapman
Catt, President of the National American Woman Suffrage Association (NAWSA),
founder and president of the International Woman Suffrage Association (IWSA),
and founder of the League of Women Voters (LWV).[151]

On the fiftieth anniversary of the Nineteenth Amendment, feminists had set up
temporary statues in New York City's Central Park to call attention to the absence
of statues honoring *actual* women—rather than fictional or allegorical figures. For
the centennial of the Nineteenth Amendment, Monumental Women, a volunteer
nonprofit organization, installed a *permanent* statue of suffragists. The group had
been at work on the project since 2014, determined to break the "bronze ceiling"
and create "the first-ever statue honoring real women in the 167-year history of
New York City's Central Park."[152]

On August 26, 2020, Monumental Women unveiled the Women's Rights Pioneers
Monument, a statue of Susan B. Anthony, Elizabeth Cady Stanton, and Sojourner
Truth created by noted sculptor Meredith Bergmann. Hillary Rodham Clinton

Women's Rights Pioneers Monument, Central Park
NYC PARKS/DANIEL AVILA

spoke at the dedication, saying: "There is nothing more important to honor the women portrayed in this statue than to vote" and that "a century later, the struggle to enforce the right to vote continues."[153]

The Pandemic of 2020

In March 2020, all commemorative events for the Nineteenth Amendment suddenly had to be postponed, canceled, or conducted online because of a new and deadly virus, COVID-19, which spread rapidly around the world and by the end of the year, killed more than 350,000 Americans.[154] The pandemic forced people in the United States and worldwide to isolate themselves in their homes. Ironically, the 2020 pandemic brought new attention to a little-known part of the woman suffrage story; how suffrage activities were disrupted by the deadly influenza pandemic that began in 1918 and killed between twenty million and fifty million worldwide.[155]

The 2020 pandemic affected all parts of life in the United States, including voting, leading to bitter partisan debates about how to safely conduct elections in the midst of an epidemic. Many called for national voting by mail, while others insisted that would lead to voter fraud. By the summer, election officials and voting-rights experts who had earlier predicted a high level of participation in the November 2020 election, expressed concern that the "Pandemic Threatens Monster Turnout in November."[156]

However, several events during the summer, and the fact that an extremely controversial president was seeking re-election, led voters in 2020—especially women and people of color—to be highly motivated, despite the pandemic.

Events Inspire Massive Voter Registration

A series of killings of African Americans, mostly by police officers, inspired a national outpouring of support for racial justice. In late May and early June, millions of women and men from all walks of life—all ages, races, and religions— took to the streets despite the pandemic to demonstrate in support of the Black Lives Matter movement. The protests peaked on June 6, 2020 when over half a million people turned out for demonstrations in more than five hundred sites across the United States. Analysts estimated that about fifteen million to twenty-six million people participated in Black Lives Matter marches over a period of weeks— in some cities, months—becoming the largest protests in the nation's history.[157]

The massive marches were accompanied by voter registration drives. In the midst of the protests, Congressman John Lewis, who had nearly been killed in 1965 marching for voting rights, died on July 17, 2020. After the civil rights icon's death, voting registration efforts surged, as did calls to restore the pre-clearance part of the Voting Rights Act of 1965, and to name the bill in Lewis's honor.[158]

That some of the marches were also accompanied by riots, arson, and violence— much of it by right-wing saboteurs—alienated many conservatives. This reaction was compounded by protestors' calls for "defunding the police" and removing

statues of Confederate heroes. President Trump responded by demanding "law and order" and sending unmarked federal police to restrain mostly peaceful demonstrators. When White supremacist groups engaged in counter protests and acts of violence, the president insisted that they were acting in self-defense. All of this galvanized many conservatives and led to efforts to bolster conservative turnout in the coming election.[159]

Many voters, especially critics of the Trump administration, were also angered by numerous efforts to undermine public trust in the voting process and to suppress the vote. These included attacks instigated by the U.S. President on the U.S. Postal Service and its ability to handle massive voting by mail, casting doubt on the credibility of the election itself. Trump predicted massive voter fraud would result from mailed-in ballots and encouraged his supporters to volunteer as "poll watchers," which was largely interpreted as the latest version of voter intimidation and disfranchisement. Ultimately, Trump shocked the nation with his unprecedented refusal to commit to a peaceful transfer of power if defeated. Many feared that the very survival of the United States as a democracy was in danger.[160]

After Democrats nominated former Vice President Joseph R. Biden as their candidate for president, he announced his intention to select a woman as his running mate. In August, Biden announced his choice for vice president, California Senator Kamala Devi Harris, the daughter of immigrants from India and Jamaica. This nomination energized women and people of color to get behind the Democratic ticket. This was a major step forward for women. Democrats had nominated Congresswoman Geraldine Ferraro in 1982 and Republicans had nominated Governor Sarah Palin in 2008, both unsuccessful. Harris became the third woman—and the first woman of color—to be nominated for vice president by a major political party.[161]

In late September, Supreme Court Justice Ruth Bader Ginsburg, who had served on the high court for twenty-seven years and solidified the court's liberal block, died. She was a beloved champion and icon of equal rights for women, racial minorities, and the LGBTQ community. Immediately, supporters of women's reproductive rights understood the implications of Ginsburg's passing for *Roe v. Wade,* the Supreme Court decision of 1973 that had legalized abortion. Within days of her death, Trump and Senate Majority Leader Mitch McConnell, a Republican, made clear their intention to quickly replace Justice Ginsburg with a woman who was conservative and pro-life. Suddenly, the issue of abortion and the protection of women's rights loomed even larger as factors in the presidential election.[162]

Trump's choice, Judge Amy Coney Barrett, pleased many conservatives who admired her legal credentials and judicial philosophy, and expected her to be a solid defender of conservatism on the Court for many decades to come. But the choice *thrilled* White Christian conservative women, who saw in her a new kind of

Speaker Nancy Pelosi and other Congresswomen, wearing white because of the suffrage centennial and masks due to the Covid 19 pandemic, pay tribute to the late Supreme Court Justice Ruth Bader Ginsburg, October 2020.

icon, one who reached the heights of her profession while unabashedly religious and who openly prioritized her conservative Catholic faith and her family, which included seven children, among them two children adopted from Haiti and a young son with Down syndrome. Trump's choice of Barrett enthused not only Catholics but conservative evangelical Protestants, as she was part of an ecumenical Christian community whose worship practices and ideas were similar to some Protestant traditions, including the authority of the husband in the family. The Eagle Forum, founded by Phyllis Schlafly in 1975, was jubilant; The headline in its newsletter declared, "Finally, a Woman of Faith and Family on Supreme Court."[163]

With no historic understanding of woman suffrage or sense of the irony involved, Trump courted conservative women by pardoning suffrage icon Susan B. Anthony for voting illegally in 1872—a radical act of civil disobedience Anthony hoped would lead to arrest and conviction so she could take her case to the higher courts. Representatives of the Susan B. Anthony List, a conservative group whose mission is to end abortion rights by electing pro-life national leaders, surrounded Trump in the Oval Office as he ceremoniously signed Anthony's pardon on the anniversary of Tennessee's ratification of the Nineteenth Amendment. Feminists had long rejected the Susan B. Anthony List's claim that Anthony was anti-abortion and were quick to denounce this symbolic pardon that Anthony would never have sought or accepted.[164]

Trump also made overtures to women in the suburbs, a group that had supported him heavily in 2016 but, according to polls, were turning away from him in droves. At rallies, he appealed to suburban women: "Please, Please Like

Me," and rather ham-fistedly referred to them as "housewives" whose husbands' jobs he protected. And assuming falsely that suburban women were all White and racist as well as married, he also boasted of "saving the suburbs" from destruction by opposing Democratic proposals for low-income housing that Trump claimed would invite crime and ruin their neighborhoods.[165]

President Trump's handling of the Coronavirus crisis also roiled women voters. As women navigated careers and taking care of families, or in so many cases, were on the frontlines as healthcare personnel or teachers, the president downplayed the seriousness of the illness. He flouted the guidance of public health experts and urged "reopening" the country. He also persisted in holding large campaign rallies, defying many states' recommendations against large gatherings and for mask wearing in public. Eventually, Trump contracted the virus, along with several family members, numerous staff members, Secret Service agents, and politicians who followed his lead. Yet, he seemed to have learned nothing from his illness, continuing to hold large public gatherings and generally downplaying the seriousness of the pandemic as casualty rates soared to unimagined heights.[166]

Many predicted that Trump's reckless approach to the pandemic would cause many women supporters to abandon him, and pundits predicted the largest gender gap in U.S. history. However, while it alienated many women, Trump loyalists defended him, agreeing that reopening the country was important for saving jobs and keeping children in school.[167]

Women Vote, Women Win in 2020

The November 2020 election saw the largest voter turnout in a century. Again, women cast far more ballots than men, but both sexes voted in record numbers. There was an unprecedented amount of absentee voting and mail-in-voting, as well as early, in-person voting that resulted in long lines of voters—most wearing masks to avoid the deadly virus—daily for weeks before the election.

Results were not clear on election day, but within a week, Joseph R. Biden and Kamala D. Harris were declared President and Vice President Elect of the United States. But while the Democrats fared well in the presidential race, in other elections across the nation Republicans held their own. The results were a clear rejection of President Trump and his leadership. Biden defeated Trump by more than seven million votes, receiving more than eighty-one million votes, the highest number of votes ever cast for a presidential candidate in U.S. history. However, about seventy-four million cast votes for Trump, the second highest number of votes for a presidential candidate.[168]

Early reports of the results in this record-shattering election indicated that trends regarding women's voting that had been in place for decades persisted. The gender gap, which had averaged about eight points in the past ten presidential elections, was approximately the same with a nine-point difference

between the percentages of women and men that favored Biden and Harris over Trump and Vice President Mike Pence.[169]

Women were crucial to the Biden/Harris win, and African American women played an even greater role in Democratic success than usual. The Democratic ticket received ninety-three percent of African American women who turned out to vote in large numbers.[170] In addition, they took the lead in mobilizing large numbers of other Democratic voters, including many who were previously unregistered. Some of the fervor African American women demonstrated in the election was inspired by Biden's choice of Harris as his running mate. Like Melanie Campbell, head of the Black Women's Roundtable and president of the National Coalition on Black Civic Participation, many African American women interpreted Harris's nomination as a sign that the Democratic Party had finally come to realize and appreciate their essential contributions as the most consistent part of its voting and organizing base.[171]

African American women's most celebrated contributions were in Georgia where the Democratic presidential candidate won for the first time in twenty-eight years. The victory astonished many Americans, including Trump, who refused to accept the results in Georgia as legally cast votes. He quickly filed numerous lawsuits challenging election results in some other key states where Democrats had prevailed. Trump relentlessly pressured Republican election officials to overturn the results and flip electoral votes into Trump's column. His attempts to overturn election results and to convince supporters that the election had been stolen eventually led to Trump's second impeachment after he incited his supporters to storm the Capitol and "Stop the Steal" by interrupting the Senate's final certification of the electoral votes on January 6, 2021.[172]

The Biden/Harris victory in Georgia was the result of years of work by Stacey Abrams and two organizations she founded, along with several other women-led groups that together beat back efforts at voter suppression and registered hundreds of thousands of new voters, including disengaged voters of color and many young people. This vast number of first-time voters put the Biden/Harris ticket over the top, and within a few months delivered the Democrats control of the U.S. Senate by helping elect two new senators, Rev. Raphael Warnock, an African American pastor at Martin Luther King, Jr.'s historic church in Atlanta, and Jon Ossof, Georgia's first Jewish senator who began his political career as an aide to voting rights champion John Lewis.[173]

The Democratic victory in Georgia owed much to the votes of suburban women—a group that is varied in terms of race, ethnicity, marital status, and occupation. But the Democrats narrowly lost to Trump among White women, largely due to Trump's support from White women in rural areas. Trump won handily among White women without college degrees, garnering support from about sixty percent of this group. Biden got thirty-nine percent of the votes of

non-college White woman, but won the votes of White women with college degrees by about sixty percent.[174]

One of the most significant demographic changes from the 2016 presidential election to the 2020 election was the number of men who switched their preferences from Trump to Biden. Exit polls indicated that forty-six percent of all men supported Biden, while in 2016, forty-one percent had supported Democrat Hillary Rodham Clinton. Some analysts, including Eleanor Smeal, a former president of the National Organization for Women (NOW) and head of the organization Feminist Majority, interpreted this outcome as the result of some men's discomfort—or misogynist attitudes—in relation to Clinton.[175]

Women made major gains in Congress in the 2020 elections. Overall, a record number of women—at least 141—serve in the 117th Congress, including 105 Democrats and thirty-six Republicans, breaking the record of 127 women lawmakers in the 116th Congress. The new Congress in 2021 also has a record number of women of color, including three Native American women, the most in U.S. history.[176]

In sharp contrast to the 2018 mid-term election, the surprise was the number (eighteen) of Republican women who were elected to the House of Representatives. All are opposed to abortion, prompting Marjorie Dannenfelser, president of the pro-life political action group, the Susan B. Anthony List, to celebrate their victories and the re-election of two pro-life Republican women senators as "breathtaking progress, something that Republican insiders and even some staunch pro-lifers doubted could be done." Since the 1970s, far fewer Republican women than Democratic women have run for office and been elected. The Republican Party historically has a poor record of recruiting and supporting women candidates compared to the Democrats. However, after losing so many seats to a diverse group of Democratic women candidates in the 2018 midterm elections, Republican leaders had come to see female candidates as an asset. In 2020, they put aside their disdain for "identity politics," at least temporarily, and actively recruited a diverse group of Republican women to run.[177]

The election of these Republican women more than doubled the number of GOP congresswomen, though at twenty-eight their numbers are still fall far short of the number of Democratic congresswomen, which numbers eighty-eight in the 117th Congress. The record-breaking diversity of the new Congress was also due largely to the Democrats: of the fifty-one women of color elected, forty-six are Democrats. The Georgia runoff victories meant that Democrats would control the Senate. As the two Independent senators normally caucused with the Democrats, the two parties would had equal numbers of votes, with Vice President Harris playing a crucial role as the "tie breaker" when the Senate votes were evenly split. This also meant that when President Biden nominated the most diverse cabinet in history, including twelve women, eight of them women of color—including Biden's pick of the first Native American cabinet member, Representative Deb Haaland of New Mexico as Secretary of the Interior—their chances of confirmation were high.[178]

However, the major gain for women—all women—was the historic, glass-ceiling-shattering election of Kamala Devi Harris as Vice President of the United States. She is not only the first woman to reach the second-highest office in the nation, she is the first person of color. It had taken a century for women to reach the top tier of American elections.[179]

A Beacon of Achievement

On August 26, 1920, the day the Nineteenth Amendment was ratified, Carrie Chapman Catt, president of the National American Women Suffrage Association (NAWSA), addressed the "women of America" in a victory speech. She reminded them of the years of struggle by generations of suffragists, and the many sacrifices made so that "you and your daughters might inherit political freedom."[180]

One hundred years later, on November 7, 2020, the night the Biden/Harris victory was declared, Vice President-Elect Kamala Devi Harris reminded the nation of that heritage. Wearing White in honor of the suffragists, she gave an acceptance speech in which she thanked "all the women who worked to secure and protect the right to vote for over a century: a hundred years ago with the Nineteenth Amendment, fifty-five years ago with the Voting Rights Act and now, in 2020, with a new generation of women in our country who cast their ballots and continued the fight for their fundamental right to vote and be heard."[181]

As Harris paid homage to her late mother, Shymala Gopalan Harris, who left India for the United States at age nineteen, she offered special praise to the countless African American, Latina, and Native American women "throughout our nation's history who have paved the way for this moment tonight."[182]

Harris was also mindful of the impact of her election on children, including the starstruck girls in her vast television audience. "Every little girl watching tonight sees that this is a country of possibilities." As Harris concluded, she declared, "While I may be the first woman in this office, I will not be the last."[183]

Kamala D. Harris giving her acceptance speech as Vice President elect

In her remarks and in her choice of colors, Vice President-Elect Harris sent a message to the nation and the world. As one *New York Times* reporter observed, dressing in white—which suffragist Alice Paul said symbolized "the quality of our purpose"—had been a celebrated symbol of women's rights for decades. Over the last four years, the reporter noted, wearing white had "taken on even more potency and power." Now, finally, it was "transformed into a beacon of achievement."[184]

Kamala D. Harris taking oath for vice presidency,
January 20, 2021. "I stand on the shoulders of
those who came before."

A new Vice President, a woman, now stood before the world, embodying and celebrating the achievements of American women as a century of woman suffrage concluded and a new one began.

Notes

1 Louise Merwin Young, and Ralph A. Young, *In the Public Interest: The League of Women Voters, 1920-1970* (Greenwood Press, 1989), 33-38; Meilan Solly, "What the First Women Voters Experienced When Registering for the 1920 Election," *Smithsonian Magazine*, July 30, 2020; Lorraine Gates Schuyler, *The Weight of Their Votes: Southern Women and Political Leverage in the 1920s* (University of North Carolina Press, 2006).

2 Jo Freeman, *A Room at a Time: How Women Entered Party Politics* (Rowman & Littlefield, 2000), 81-85; Catherine E. Rymph, *Republican Women: Feminism and Conservatism from Suffrage*

Through the Rise of the New Right (University of North Carolina Press, 2006),14-29; J. Stanley Lemons, *The Woman Citizen: Social Feminism in the 1920s* (University of Illinois Press, 1973), 85-89; Cartoon from the *Philadelphia Inquirer*, in Marjorie Spruill (Wheeler), ed., *Votes for Women: The Woman Suffrage Movement in Tennessee, the South, and the Nation* (University of Tennessee Press, 1995), 319.

3 Freeman, *A Room at a Time*,124-29; Rymph, *Republican Women*,16-22; Young and Young, *In the Public Interest*, 33-38; Nancy F, Cott, "Across the Great Divide: Women in Politics

Before and After 1920," Chapter Twenty-two, in Marjorie J. Spruill, ed., *One Woman, One Vote: Rediscovering the Woman Suffrage Movement*, Second Edition (NewSage Press, 2021).

4 Liette Gidlow, "Beyond 1920: The Legacies of Woman Suffrage," National Park Service Series: The 19th Amendment and Women's Access to the Vote Across America, nps.gov/articles/beyond-1920-the-legacies-of-woman-suffrage.htm; Lemons, *The Woman Citizen*, 73-81, 103-108; Elisabeth Israels Perry, "Women in Action: Rebels and Reformers, 1920-1980," League of Women Voters Educational Fund, 1995, 6; Freeman, *A Room at a Time*, 230-32.

5 Ibid.; 203; Christina Wolbrecht and J. Kevin Corder, *A Century of Votes for Women: American Elections since Suffrage* (Cambridge University Press, 2020), 1-2; Rymph, *Republican Women*, 23.

6 Lemons, *The Woman Citizen*, 55-58, 151-76.

7 William H. Chafe, *The Paradox of Change* (Oxford University Press), 1972,1991), quotation, 27; Lemons, *The Woman Citizen*, 153-76. Lemons quotation,153.

8 Ibid., 63-68, 72-73.

9 Cott, Chapter Twenty-two; Wolbrecht and Corder, *A Century of Votes for Women*, 2; J. Kevin Corder and Christina Wolbrecht, *Counting Women's Ballots: Female Voters from Suffrage Through the New Deal* (Cambridge University Press, 2016); In the 1920 presidential election, approximately 36 percent of eligible women and sixty-eight percent of eligible men voted, compared to sixty-three percent of women and fifty-nine percent of men in the 1920 presidential election. Solly, "What the First Women Voters Experienced."

10 Ibid., 3-5; Cott, Chapter Twenty-two.

11 Ibid.

12 Alison M. Parker, *Unceasing Militant: The Life of Mary Church Terrell* (University of North Carolina Press, 2021), 160-78; Rymph, *Republican Women*, 34-35, 46, 52-60; Freeman, *A Room at a Time*, 99.

13 Ibid., 85-89; Elisabeth Israels Perry, *Belle Moskowitz: Feminine Politics and the Exercise of Power in the Age of Alfred E. Smith* (Routledge, 2018).

14 Lemons, *The Woman Citizen*, 85-112, quotation, 90; Cott, Chapter Twenty-two.

15 Ibid.; Anne Bail Howard, *The Long Campaign: A Biography of Anne Martin* (University of Nevada Press, 1985); Lemons, *The Woman Citizen*, 41-62.

16 Ibid, 123-24,172-73; Gidlow, "Beyond 1920."

17 Lemons, *The Woman Citizen*, 181-204; Christine A. Lunardini, *From Equal Suffrage to Equal Rights: Alice Paul and the National Woman's Party, 1910-1928* (New York University Press, 1986), 150-68; Kathryn Kish Sklar, "Why Were Most Politically Active Women Opposed to the ERA in the 1920s?" in Kathryn Kish Sklar and Thomas Dublin, eds., *Women and Power in American History*, Vol. 2 (Prentice Hall, 2002): 154-161.

18 Susan Ware, *Why They Marched: Untold Stories of the Women Who Fought for the Right to Vote* (Harvard University Press, 2019), 75-76; Freeman, *A Room at a Time*, 57-58.

19 Lunardini, *From Equal Suffrage to Equal Rights*,164-65.

20 Ibid.,150-68.

21 Ibid.; Freeman, *A Room at a Time*,129-30,135-38, 203-205; Lemons, *The Woman Citizen*,142-44,181-204, 238-39.

22 Ibid.

23 Ibid., 233-34; J. Kevin Corder and Christina Wolbrecht, "For Women's Equality Day, Here's the Key Question: Was Women's Suffrage a Failure?" *Washington Post*, Aug. 26, 2017.

24 Lemons, *The Woman Citizen*, 234.

25 Estelle B. Friedman, "The New Woman: Changing Views of Women in the 1920s," *Journal of American History* 61, no.2 (1974): 372-93 Quotation from William Leuchtenburg, *Perils of Prosperity: 1914-32* (University of Chicago Press,1958), 160.

26 Cott, Chapter Twenty-two; Chafe, *The Paradox of Change*; For examples of scholars asserting that women reformers kept Progressivism alive through the 1920s, see Clarke A. Chambers, *Seedtime of Reform: American Social Service and Social Action, 1918-1933* (University of Minnesota Press, 1963); Anne Firor Scott, "After Suffrage: Southern Women in the Twenties," *Journal of Southern History*, XXX (Aug. 1964): 298-318; Lemons, *The Woman Citizen*; Perry, "Women in Action."

27 Perkins was also Secretary of Labor under President Harry Truman. Serving from 1933 to1945, to date she remains the longest serving Secretary of Labor. Kirsten Downey, *The Woman Behind the New Deal: The Life of Frances Perkins, FDR's Secretary of Labor and His Moral Conscience* (Anchor, 2009); On women "New Dealers," see Susan Ware, *Beyond Suffrage: Women in the New Deal* (Harvard University Press, 1987).

28 For examples of the recent emphasis on the positive impact of woman suffrage, see Alia Wong, "How Women's Suffrage Improved Education for a Whole Generation of Children," Aug. 28, 2018, *The Atlantic*, theatlantic.com/education/archive/2018/08/womens-suffrage-educational-improvement/568726/; Schuyler, *The Weight of Their Votes*; Gidlow, "Beyond 1920."

29 See for example Liette Gidlow, "Resistance after Ratification: The Nineteenth Amendment, African American Women, and the Problem of Female Disfranchisement after 1920," in *Women and Social Movements in the U.S., 1600-2000* (Alexandria, VA: Alexander Street, 2017), womhist.alexanderstreet.com/index.htm.

30 Carrie Chapman Catt and Nettie Rogers Shuler, *Woman Suffrage and Politics: The Inner Story of the Suffrage Movement* (Charles Scribner's Sons, 1923), 5; The Supreme Court ruled against the challenge to the Nineteenth Amendment in 1922 in *Fairchild v. Hughes* and *Leser v. Garnett*, Lemons, *The Woman Citizen*,14.

31 Marjorie Spruill (Wheeler), *New Women of the New South: The Leaders of the Woman Suffrage Movement in the Southern States* (Oxford University Press, 1993),181. Florida called a special session only after a state supreme court justice reminded the governor that if the state failed to put the amendment into effect, the enforcement clause of the Nineteenth Amendment and perhaps of the Fifteenth Amendment might be invoked.; Gidlow, "Resistance after Ratification."

32 Marjorie J. Spruill, "Bringing in the South: Southern Ladies, White Supremacy, and State's Rights in the Fight for Woman Suffrage," Chapter Nine, and Rosalyn Terborg-Penn, "African American Women and the Woman Suffrage Movement," Chapter Ten, in Spruill, *One Woman, One Vote*, Second Edition; Schuyler, *The Weight of Their Votes*; Gidlow, "Resistance after Ratification."

33 Examples: Australia enfranchised white women in 1902 but did not extend the vote to aboriginal people of either sex until 1962. Canada enfranchised white women in 1918 but no "First Canadians" of either sex could vote until 1960. Chinese Canadians of both sexes were enfranchised in 1947. In 1919 Kenya and Rhodesia enfranchised only white women: in 1956 Kenya extended the vote to African women and men with educational and property requirements that were abolished in 1963; Rhodesia (which became Zimbabwe in 1980) adopted universal suffrage without regard for race in 1987. Mart Martin, *The Almanac of Women and Minorities in World Politics* (Westview Press, 2000); Jad Adams, *Women and the Vote: A World History* (Oxford University Press, 2014).

34 Wanda A. Hendricks, "Ida B. Wells-Barnett and the Alpha Suffrage Club of Chicago," Chapter Seventeen, and Terborg-Penn, Chapter Ten, in Spruill, *One Woman, One Vote*, Second Edition; Parker, *Unceasing Militant*.

35 Gidlow, "Resistance after Ratification"; Schuyler, *The Weight of Their Votes*; Martha S. Jones, *Vanguard: How Black Women Broke Barriers, Won the Vote, and Insisted on Equality for All* (Basic Books, 2020); On North Carolina see Glenda Elizabeth Gilmore, *Gender and Jim Crow: Women and the Politics of White Supremacy in North Carolina, 1896-1920* (University of North Carolina Press, 1996), 220-24.

36 Ibid.; on Columbia, see Schuyler, *The Weight of Their Votes*, 48-49; quotation, Gidlow, "Resistance after Ratification."

37 Gilmore, *Gender and Jim Crow*, 218; quotations, Gidlow, "Resistance after Ratification."

38 Ibid.

39 Ibid.

40 Ida E. Jones, "Mary McLeod Bethune, True Democracy, and the Fight for Universal Suffrage," *Yellow Rose Journal*, Women's Vote Centennial Commission, nps.gov/articles/000/mary-mcleod-bethune-true-democracy-and-the-fight-for-universal-suffrage.htm; "Mary McLeod Bethune," Turning Point Suffragist Memorial, suffragistmemorial.org/mary-mcleod-bethune-1875-1955/.

41 Terborg-Penn, Chapter Ten; Terborg-Penn, *African American Women in the Struggle for the Vote* (Indiana University Press,

1998),154-55; Archibald Grimké and his two brothers were the sons of Sarah Grimké's and Angelina Grimké Weld's brother Henry and Nancy Weston, enslaved by the Grimké family. In the 1860s, the Grimké Sisters first learned of the brothers and welcomed them as family members, providing financial support for their education. Archibald graduated from Harvard Law School. He named his daughter Angelina Weld Grimké, a poet and writer, for her aunt.; Dickson D. Bruce, Jr., *Archibald Grimké: Portrait of a Black Independent* (Louisiana State University Press, 1993); Schuyler, *The Weight of the Votes*, 52-56.

42 Carolyn Jefferson-Jenkins, *The Untold Story of Women of Color in the League of Women Voters*, (Praeger, 2020), 88-115; Terborg-Penn, Chapter Ten.

43 Freda Kirchwey, "Alice Paul Pulls the Strings," *The Nation*, March 2, 1921, 332-33. In "How Did the National Woman's Party Address the Issue of the Enfranchisement of Black Women, 1919-1924?" by Kathryn Kish Sklar and Jill Dias, in *Women and Social Movements of the United States,1600-2000* (Alexandria, VA: Alexander Street), documents.alexanderstreet.com.

44 Ibid.; Terborg-Penn, Chapter Ten, and Katherine M. Marino, "The International History of the U.S. Suffrage Movement Chapter," Chapter Eleven, in Spruill, *One Woman, One Vote*, Second Edition.

45 Cathleen D. Cahill, *Recasting the Vote: How Women of Color Transformed the Suffrage Movement* (University of North Carolina Press, 2020).

46 Ibid.

47 Ibid.; The American-born children of Chinese immigrants had citizenship rights after 1898, when the U.S. Supreme Court ruled that a person born in the United States to Chinese immigrant parents was a U.S. citizen at birth, a decision based on the Fourteenth Amendment. *United States v. Wong Kim Ark*, 169 U.S. 649 (1898).

48 Laura Prieto, "Votes for Colonized Women," *Process: A Blog for American History*, Organization of American Historians, May 28, 2020, processhistory.org/prieto-votes-colonized/.

49 Ibid.; Allison L. Sneider, *Suffragists in an Imperial Age: U.S. Expansion and the Woman Question, 1870-1929* (Oxford University Press, 2008).

50 "Alaska's Suffrage Star: Alaska Women And The Vote in the 1910s and 1920s," Alaska State Libraries and Archives and Museum, lam.alaska.gov/suffrage-star.

51 Ibid.

52 Sneider, *Suffragists in an Imperial Age*, quotation, 106; Jason Daley, "Five Things To Know About Lili'uokalani, the Last Queen of Hawai'i," *Smithsonian Magazine*, Nov. 10, 2017; Rumi Yasutake, "Women in Hawai'i and the Nineteenth Amendment," *Journal of Women's History*, Vol. 32, No.1, Spring 2020, 32-40.

53 Ibid.; Shawn Gilbert, "Suffragists You Need to Meet: Wilhelmina Dowsett (1861-1929)," League of Women Voters of Diablo Valley, my.lwv.org/california/diablo-valley/article/suffragists-you-need-meet-wilhelmina-dowsett-1861-1929.

54 Yasutake, "Women in Hawai'i and the Nineteenth Amendment."

55 Ibid.

56 Gilbert, "Suffragists You Need to Meet: Wilhelmina Dowsett."

57 Yasutake, "Women in Hawai'i and the Nineteenth Amendment"; Sneider, *Suffragists in an Imperial Age*, 128.

58 Prieto, "Votes for Colonized Women"; Juan R. Torruella, "Ruling America's Colonies: *The Insular Cases*," *Yale Law & Policy Review*.

59 Sneider, *Suffragists in an Imperial Age*,123-24; Eva-Lotta E. Hedman and John T. Sidel, *Politics and Society in the Twentieth Century: Colonial Legacies, Post-Colonial Trajectories* (Routledge, 2000), 14-15.

60 Sneider, *Suffragists in an Imperial Age*, quotation 124.

61 Leonora C. Angeles, "Philippines Suffragist Movement," *Woman Suffrage and Beyond*, Feb. 22, 2012.

62 Ibid.

63 Prieto, "Votes for Colonized Women"; "More to the Movement," Library of Congress, loc.gov/exhibitions/women-fight-for-the-vote/about-this-exhibition/more-to-the-movement/?st=gallery.

64 Angeles, "Philippines Suffragist Movement."

65 Prieto, "Votes for Colonized Women."

66 Ibid.; Hedman and Sidel, *Politics and Society in the Twentieth Century*, 15.

67 Sneider, *Suffragists in an Imperial Age*, 114-17.

68 Prieto, "Votes for Colonized Women"; G. Jiménez Mu oz, "Deconstructing Colonialist Discourse: Links Between the Women's Suffrage Movement in the United States and Puerto Rico," *Phoebe: An Interdisciplinary Journal of Feminist Scholarship, Theory, and Aesthetics*, 5 (Spring 1993), 9–34; Frances R. Grant, "Porto Rican Women Out for Reform," *Brooklyn Eagle Magazine* (Brooklyn, NY), Oct. 2, 1932, 89.

69 Hahna Cho, "Luisa Capetillo: Feminism and Labor In Puerto Rico," *Backstory*, Sept. 7, 2018, backstoryradio.org/blog/luisa-capetillo-feminism-and-labor-in-puerto-rico/; Taru Spiegel, "Luisa Capetillo: Puerto Rican Changemaker," Library of Congress, blogs.loc.gov/international-collections/2019/11/luisa-capetillo-puerto-rican-changemaker/; Prieto, "Votes for Colonized Women."

70 Ibid.; Milagros Benet de Newton, "More to the Movement," Library of Congress; Grant, "Porto Rican Women Out for Reform"; María de Barceló-Miller, "Halfhearted Solidarity: Women Workers and the Women's Suffrage Movement in Puerto Rico During the 1920s," in Felix Matos-Rodriguez, and Linda Delgado, Linda eds., *Puerto Rican Women's History: New Perspectives* (Routledge 2015):126–142.

71 Anne S. Macpherson, "The 19th Amendment Didn't Grant Puerto Rican Women Suffrage," *Washington Post*, Aug. 26, 2020.

72 Ibid.; On the NWP's aid to Puerto Rican suffragists, see Sneider, *Suffragists in an Imperial Age*, 117-34.

73 Jennifer Johnson, "After the 19th Amendment: Women in the US Virgin Islands Secure the Vote," National Archives, rediscovering-black-history.blogs.archives.gov/2020/12/16/virgin-islands-secure-the-vote/.

74 Ibid.; Prieto, "Votes for Colonized Women."

75 Ibid.; Johnson, "After the 19th Amendment."

76 Prieto, "Votes for Colonized Women"; "Guam and the 19th Amendment," National Park Service, nps.gov/articles/guam-and-the-19th-amendment.htm; Becky Little, "How the United States Ended Up With Guam," history.com/news/how-the-united-states-ended-up-with-guam.

77 "American Samoa and the 19th Amendment," National Park Service, nps.gov/articles/american-samoa-and-the-19th-amendment.htm; Ann M. Simmons, "American Samoans Aren't Actually U.S. Citizens. Does That Violate the Constitution?" *Los Angeles Times*, April 6, 2018.

78 Meagan Flynn and Teddy Amenabar, "Could D.C. Become a State? Explaining the Hurdles to Statehood, *Washington Post*, Jan. 8, 2021.

79 Ibid.

80 Ibid.

81 Wolbrecht and Corder, *A Century of Votes for Women*.

82 Barbara Ransby, *Ella Baker and The Black Freedom Movement: A Radical Democratic Vision* (University of North Carolina Press, 2005).

83 Ibid.; Ramachandra Guha, "How the Suffragettes influenced Mahatma Gandhi," *Hindustan Times*, New Delhi, India, Feb. 24, 2018.

84 Ransby, *Ella Baker*.

85 Katherine Mellen Charron, *Freedom's Teacher: The Life of Septima Clark* (University of North Carolina Press, 2012).

86 Chana Kai Lee, *For Freedom's Sake: The Life of Fannie Lou Hamer* (University of Illinois Press, 2000).

87 Ibid.

88 "Introduction: The Origins and Evolution of the Voting Rights Act," in *50 Years of the Voting Rights Act*, Joint Center for Political and Economic Studies, jointcenter.org/wp-content/uploads/2019/11/VRA-report-3.5.15-1130-amupdated.pdf.

89 In 1964, five states had a poll tax: Alabama, Arkansas, Mississippi, Texas, and Virginia. The amendment applied only to federal elections. In 1966, a Supreme Court decision, *Harper v. Virginia Board of Elections*, made poll taxes unconstitutional in elections at any level, not only federal. *Harper v. Virginia Board of Elections*, 383 U.S. 663 (1966); John Dittmer, *Local People: The Struggle for Civil Rights in Mississippi* (University of Illinois Press, 1995).

90 Bettye Collier-Thomas and V. P. Franklin, *Sisters in the Struggle: African American Women in the Civil Rights-Black Power*

Movement (New York University Press, 2001); Vicky L. Craw-ford, Jacqueline Anne Rouse, and Barbara Woods, Women in the Civil Rights Movement: Trailblazers and Torchbearers, 1941-1965 (Indiana University Press, 1993).

91 Keisha N. Blain, "'God Is Not Going to Put It in Your Lap,' What Made Fannie Lou Hamer's Message on Civil Rights So Radical—And So Enduring," Time, Oct. 4, 2019.

92 Ibid.

93 Robert A. Pratt, Selma's Bloody Sunday: Protest, Voting Rights, and the Struggle for Racial Equality (Johns Hopkins University Press, 2017).

94 Jon Meacham, His Truth Is Marching On: John Lewis and the Power of Hope (Random House, 2020).

95 John Lewis, Walking with the Wind: A Memoir of the Movement (Simon & Schuster, 2015); German Lopez, "How the Voting Rights Act Transformed Black Voting Rights in the South," Vox, vox.com/2015/3/6/8182219/voting-rights-act-1965.

96 ACLU, "Voting Rights Act: Major Dates in History," aclu.org/voting-rights-act-major-dates-history; Lopez, "How the Voting Rights Act Transformed Black Voting Rights in the South"; Library of Congress, "Voting Rights for African Americans"; Jo Freeman, "Gender Gaps in Presidential Elections," Political Science and Politics, Vol. 32, No. 2, June 1999, 191-92; Wolbrecht and Corder, A Century of Votes for Women, 236-37.

97 Carnegie Corporation, "Voting Rights: A Short History."

98 Rosen, "Give Us the Ballot." In 1982 the Voting Rights Act was extended for another twenty-five years. In 2006 it was extended for an additional twenty-five-year period. Carnegie Corporation, "Voting Rights: A Short History."

99 Marjorie J. Spruill, Divided We Stand: The Battle Over Women's Rights and Family Values That Polarized American Politics (New York: Bloomsbury, 2017), 14-29; Historian Cynthia Harrison noted that most women's rights advocates in the 1940s through mid-1960s strenuously avoided the word "feminist" which some people associated with "selfish" and "strident" women, and that even National Woman's Party members "employed the word feminism cautiously, generally restricting its usage en famille." Furthermore, "not until the appearance in 1966 of the National Organization for Women...did women fighting on behalf of women reclaim the word." Cynthia Harrison, On Account of Sex: The Politics of Women's Issues 1945-1968 (University of California Press, 1988), xi.

100 Spruill, Divided We Stand,14-29; On the origins and development of the modern women's rights movement, see Harrison, On Account of Sex; Ruth Rosen, The World Split Open: How the Modern Women's Movement Changed America (Penguin, 2003); Sara M. Evans, Tidal Wave: How Women Changed America at Century's End (Free Press, 2003); Susan M. Hartmann, From Margin to Mainstream: American Women and Politics Since 1960 (Knopf, 1989); Dorothy Sue Cobble, Linda Gordon, and Astrid Henry, Feminism Unfinished: A Short, Surprising History of American Women's Movements (W.W. Norton & Company, 2014).

101 Spruill, Divided We Stand, 17-18; Harrison, On Account of Sex,176-82.

102 Jo Freeman, "How 'Sex' Got into Title VII: Persistent Opportunism as a Maker of Public Policy," in Freeman, We Will be Heard: Women's Struggle for Political Power in the United States (Rowan and Littlefield, 2008),171-90.

103 Flora Davis, Moving the Mountain: The Women's Movement in America since 1960 (University of Illinois Press, 1991, 1999), 14-93; Daniel Horowitz, Betty Friedan and the Making of "The Feminine Mystique": The American Left, the Cold War, and Modern Feminism (University of Massachusetts Press, 1998); Spruill, Divided We Stand, 14-41.

104 "NOW Statement of Purpose, 1966," now.org/about/history/statement-of-purpose/.

105 "Aileen Hernandez, 90, Ex-NOW President and Feminist Trailblazer Dies," New York Times, Feb. 28, 2017; "NOW Mourns the Loss of Aileen Hernandez," NOW press release, Feb. 27, 2017, now.org/media-center/press-release/now-mourns-the-loss-of-aileen-hernandez/; On women coming to the feminist movement from the civil rights movement and the New Left, see Sara M. Evans, Personal Politics: The Roots of Women's Liberation in the Civil Rights Movement and the New Left (Vintage Books, 1980); Alice Echols, Daring to Be Bad: Radical Feminism in America, 1967-1975 (University of Minnesota Press, 1997).

106 Davis, Moving the Mountain, 66-68; Spruill, Divided We Stand, 20.

107 Ibid., 21-22; Friedan, It Changed My Life; Writings on the Women's Movement, 184-92 (Harvard University Press, 1998); Rosen, The World Split Open, 92-93.

108 Ibid.,14-15, 20, 25-29; Liz Carpenter, Getting Better All the Time (Simon and Schuster, 1987),121-128; Barbara Winslow, Shirley Chisholm: Catalyst for Change (Routledge, 2018); Friedan, It Changed My Life, 208-32; Tanya Melich, The Republican War Against Women: An Insider's Report from Behind the Lines (Bantam Books, 1998); Leandra Ruth Zarnow, Battling Bella: The Protest Politics of Bella Abzug (Harvard University Press, 2019).

109 Spruill, Divided We Stand, 28-29; Max Sherman, Barbara Jordan: Speaking the Truth with Eloquent Thunder (University of Texas Press, 2007); Barbara Winslow, Shirley Chisholm: Catalyst for Change (Westview Press, 2014).

110 In Roe v. Wade (1973), the U.S. Supreme Court declared that a woman is legally entitled to have an abortion until the end of the first trimester of pregnancy and that a state could not proscribe abortion until after the fetus became viable. Spruill, Divided We Stand, 29-30, 32-50.

111 Ibid., 29-32.

112 Jone Johnson Lewis, "Which States Have Ratified the Equal Rights Amendment," ThoughtCo, Aug. 26, 2020, thoughtco.com/which-states-ratified-the-era-3528872; Jane J. Mansbridge, Why We Lost the ERA (University of Chicago Press, 1986).

113 Ibid.; Spruill, Divided We Stand, 71-113; Ruth Murray Brown, For a "Christian America": A History of the Religious Right (Prometheus Books, 2002); Donald T. Critchlow, Phyllis Schlafly and Grassroots Conservatism: A Woman's Crusade (Princeton University Press, 2008).

114 Spruill, Divided We Stand, 32, 84-85, 95, 187-88, 306, 127. 201-202; Donald G. Mathews and Jane Sherron De Hart, Sex, Gender, and the Politics of ERA: A State and the Nation (Oxford University Press, 1990).

115 Spruill, Divided We Stand.

116 Ibid., The Spirit of Houston: The First National Women's Conference: An Official Report to the President, the Congress and the People of the United States (U.S. Government Printing Office, 1978).

117 Spruill, Divided We Stand; For a first-person account from the conservative perspective, see Rosemary Thomson, The Price of Liberty (Creation House, 1978).

118 Spruill, Divided We Stand, Chapters 13 and 14; Melich, The Republican War against Women.

119 Spruill, Divided We Stand, 316-17.

120 Wolbrecht and Corder, A Century of Votes for Women, 236-37.

121 Ibid. Though women split their votes almost equally between Reagan (46%) and Carter (45), men favored Reagan by a large margin. Exit polls showed that men gave 54% of their votes for Reagan, creating an unprecedented eight-percentage-point difference between women's and men's choices. news.gallup.com/poll/135588/gender-gap-2012-vote-largest-gallup-history.aspx.

122 Wolbrecht and Corder, A Century of Votes for Women, 7-8; When referring to the "gender gap," most scholars and pundits mean the difference in the percentage of women and men who support a given candidate, usually the winning candidate, not the gap within a gender. Carroll, "The Gender Gap as a Tool for Women's Political Empowerment: The Formative Years, 1980-84," in Angie Maxwell and Todd Shields, eds. The Legacy of Second Wave Feminism in American Politics (Cham Palgrave Macmillan, 2018); J. Ryan-Hume, "The National Organization for Women and the Democratic Party in Reagan's America," The Historical Journal, 1-23, doi:10.1017/S00182463200175.

123 Ibid.; Wolbrecht and Corder, A Century of Votes for Women, Spruill, Divided We Stand, 316-318.

124 Spruill, Divided We Stand, 316-17, 325; Melich, The Republican War against Women," Spruill, "Feminism, Antifeminism, and the New Southern Strategy," in Maxwell and Shields, The Legacy of Second Wave Feminism in American Politics; Angie Maxwell and Todd G. Shields, The Long Southern Strategy: How Chasing White Voters in the South Changed American Politics (Oxford University Press, 2019).

125 CAWP 2017 Fact Sheet, "The Gender Gap," Voting Choices

in Presidential Elections," cawp.rutgers.edu/sites/default/files/resources/ggpresvote.pdf; Juliet Eilperin, "For Obama, Rainbow White House Was 'A Moment Worth Savoring,'" *Washington Post*, June 30, 2015.

126 Spruill, *Divided We Stand*, 325-44.

127 Ibid.; Wolbrecht and Corder, *A Century of Votes for Women*, 216.

128 Rosen, "'Give Us the Ballot'"; Carnegie Corporation, "Voting Rights: A Short History"; ACLU: "Voting Rights Act: Major Dates in History."

129 Ibid.; Lisa Rab, "Why Republicans Can't Find the Big Voter Fraud Conspiracy," *Politico*, April 2, 2017; Andrew Gumbel, "Election Fraud and the Myths of American Democracy," *Social Research* 75, no. 4 (2008): 1109-134. jstor.org/stable/40972109; Rosen, "'Give Us the Ballot'"; LWV, "How Voter ID Laws Disproportionately Impact Women – And What We're Doing About It." lwv.org/blog/how-voter-id-laws-disproportionately-impact-women-and-what-were-doing-about-it; Danyelle Solomon and Connor Maxwell, "Women of Color: A Collective Powerhouse in the U.S. Electorate," Center for American Progress, Nov.19, 2019 americanprogress.org/issues/race/reports/2019/11/19/477309/women-color-collective-powerhouse-u-s-electorate/.

130 Luke Broadwater, "After Death of John Lewis, Democrats Renew Push for Voting Rights Law," *New York Times*, July 21, 2020.

131 Editorial, The Most Extreme Republican Platform in Memory," *New York Times*, July 18, 2016; Editorial, "The Democratic Platform is Far More Liberal than Four Years Ago. Here's Why That Matters," *Washington Post*, July 7, 2016.

132 Spruill *Divided We Stand*, 334-43; Wolbrecht and Corder, *A Century of Votes for Women*, 228-229.

133 Cleve Wootson, "Susan B. Anthony's Tombstone Covered in 'I Voted' Stickers, *Washington Post*, Nov. 8, 2016; Drew DeSilver, "Trump's Victory Another Example of How Electoral College Wins are Bigger Than Popular Vote Ones," Dec. 20, 2016, Pew Research Center, pewresearch.org/facttank/2016/12/20/why-electoral-college-landslides-are-easier-to-win-than-popular-vote-ones/.

134 Wolbrecht and Corder, *A Century of Votes for Women*, 230-31; Of independents, the vote was 43 percent Trump, 42 percent Clinton. Pew Research Center, "An Examination of the 2016 Electorate, Based on Validated Voters August 9, 2018," pewresearch.org/politics/2018/08/09/an-examination-of-the-2016-electorate-based-on-validated-voters/.

135 Ibid. In 2018, the Pew Research Center estimated the 2016 presidential election gender gap was 13 percent, based on validated voters. Exit polls conducted in 2016 by Edison Research had reported an eleven-point gender gap. CAWP 2017 Fact Sheet, "The Gender Gap: Voting Choices in Presidential Elections"; Wolbrecht and Corder, *A Century of Votes for Women*, 230-31.

136 Ibid., 228-33; Pew Research Center, "An Examination of the 2016 Electorate, Based on Validated Voters August 9, 2018"; Molly Ball, "Donald Trump Didn't Really Win 52% of White Women in 2016," *Time*, Oct. 18, 2018.

137 Angie Maxwell, "What We Get Wrong about the Southern Strategy," *Washington Post*, July 26, 2019; Angie Maxwell, "Why Southern White Women Vote against Feminism," *Washington Post*, Sept. 11, 2019; Maxwell and Shields, *The Long Southern Strategy*.

138 Wolbrecht and Corder, *A Century of Votes for Women*, 229-30, 235.

139 Trump had a fourteen-point advantage with voters from fifty to six-four and an eleven-point lead among voters sixty-five and older. Pew Research Center, "An Examination of the 2016 Electorate."

140 On the action inspired by women's outrage over the 2026 election, see Rebecca Traister, *Good and Mad: The Revolutionary Power of Women* (Simon and Schuster, 2019); Michael Hais and Morley Winograd, "The Future is Female," Feb.19, 2020. Brookings Institute, brookings.edu/blog/fixgov/2020/02/19/the-future-is-female-how-the-growing-political-power-of-women-will-remake-american-politics/; Anemona Hartocollis and Yamiche Alcindor, "Women's March Highlights as Huge Crowds Protest Trump: 'We're Not Going Away,'" *New York Times*, Jan. 21, 2017; Kaveh Waddell, "The Exhausting Work of

Tallying America's Largest Protest," *The Atlantic*, Jan. 23, 2017, theatlantic.com/technology/archive/2017/01/womens-march-protest-count/514166/.

141 Ball, *Pelosi* (Henry Holt and Company, 2020), 258-60.

142 Ibid.; Traister, *Good and Mad*; Spruill, *Divided We Stand*, 322.

143 Ibid; Ball, *Pelosi*, quotations, page 259; Traister, *Good and Mad*.

144 Politico: The WOMEN Candidate Tracker, A Collaboration with the Center for American Women and Politics at Rutgers and the Women in Public Service Project at The Wilson Center, Nov. 28, 2018, politico.com/interactives/2018/women-rule-candidate-tracker/; Jens Manuel Krogstad, Luis Noe-Bustamante, and Antonio Flores, Pew Research Center, "Historic Highs in 2018 Voter Turnout Extended Across Racial and Ethnic Groups," pewresearch.org/fact-tank/2019/05/01/historic-highs-in-2018-voter-turnout-extended-across-racial-and-ethnic-groups/.

145 Reis Thebault and Hannah Knowles, "Georgia Purged 309,000 Voters from Its Rolls," *Washington Post*, Dec. 17, 2019; Adam Edelman and Dartunorro Clark, "Democrat Stacey Abrams Ends Bid for Georgia Governor, Accuses Waiver of Voter Suppression," NBC News, Nov. 16, 2018, nbcnews.com/politics/elections/democrat-stacey-abrams-ends-candidacy-georgia-governor-race-blasts-process-n937356.

146 Vanessa Williams, "Stacey Abrams Chooses Building a National Voter Protection Program Over Running for President in 2020," *Washington Post*, Aug.13, 2019; Stacey Abrams, *Lead from the Outside: How to Build Your Future and Make Real Change* (Henry Holt and Company, 2018); Stacey Abrams, *Our Time is Now: Purpose, and the Fight for a Fair America* (Henry Holt and Company, 2020).

147 For examples, see: Martha S. Jones, *Vanguard: How Black Women Broke Barriers, Won the Vote, and Insisted on Equality for All* (New Basic Books, 2020); Cathleen D. Cahill, *Recasting the Vote: How Women of Color Transformed the Suffrage Movement* (University of North Carolina Press, 2020); Library of Congress, "More to the Movement," loc.gov/exhibitions/women-fight-for-the-vote/about-this-exhibition/more-to-the-movement/?st=gallery; National Portrait Gallery "Votes for Women: A Portrait of Persistence," npg.si.edu/exhibition/votes-for-women?utm_source=siedu&utm_medium=referral&utm_campaign=spotlight.

148 Women's Vote Centennial, womensvote100.org/ and ourstory100.com/; DeNeen L. Brown, "Ida B. Wells Gets Her Due as a Black Suffragist Who Rejected Movement's Racism," *Washington Post*, Aug. 25, 2020; United States Mint Announces Design for 2020 Women's Suffrage Centennial Silver Medal, usmint.gov/news/press-releases/united-states-mint-announces-design-for-2020-womens-suffrage-centennial-silver-medal; "Forever Stamp Honors Centennial of Women's Suffrage," Aug.14, 2020, about.usps.com/newsroom/national-releases/2020/0814ma-forever-stamp-honors-centennial-of-women-suffrage.htm.

149 For a review of ERA history since 1972, including the "three states strategy" and twenty-first century efforts to complete ratification, see Lewis, "Which States Have Ratified the Equal Rights Amendment?"; "Why Democratic Congresswomen Wore White Again to Send a Message at the State of the Union," *Time*, time.com/5777514/women-wearing-white-state-of-the-union/; Veronica Stracqualursi, CNN, "Virginia General Assembly Passes Resolutions Ratifying ERA," Jan.15, 2020, cnn.com/2020/01/15/politics/virginia-general-assembly-equal-rights-amendment/index.html.

150 Kylie Hubbard, "Suffrage Coalition to Unveil Burn Memorial on Saturday," *Knox News*, June 7, 2018, knoxnews.com/story/news/2018/06/07/suffrage-coalition-unveil-harry-burn-memorial-downtown-market-square/677044002/;Tennessee Triumph Women's Suffrage Monument, artsandheritage.us/tn-triumph-womens-suffrage-statue/; Tennessee Woman Suffrage Monument in Centennial Park," / tnsuffragemonument.org/.

151 Mary Tyler March, "Virginia Gets New Museum Honoring Suffragists," wamu.org/story/20/01/24/virginia-gets-new-museum-honoring-suffragists-100-years-after-women-got-the-right-to-vote/; Turning Point Suffragist Memorial, suffragistmemorial.org/memorial-dedication-postponed/.

152 Monumental Women, monumentalwomen.org.

153 Sarah Cascone, "Hillary Clinton Urged Americans to Vote During the Unveiling of a New Monument to Suffragists in Central Park," Aug. 26, 2020, *Artnet News*, news.artnet.com/art-world/central-park-womens-rights-pioneers-monument-1904271.

154 Amy Harmon, "The Number of People with the Virus Who Died in the U.S. Passes 300,000," *New York Times*, Dec. 14, 2020; according to the Center for Disease Control Covid Date Tracker, by January 5, there had been 352,464 deaths, covid.cdc.gov/covid-data-tracker/#cases_casesper100klast7days.

155 Ellen Carol DuBois, "A Pandemic Nearly Derailed the Women's Suffrage Movement," *National Geographic*, April 20, 2020.

156 Zach Montellaro, "Pandemic Threatens Monster Turnout in November," *Politico*, March 21, 2020, politico.com/news/2020/03/31/states-struggle-voting-pandemic-155700.

157 Larry Buchanan, Quoctrung Bui and Jugal K. Patel, "Black Lives Matter May Be the Largest Movement in U.S. History," *New York Times*, July 3, 2020.

158 Luke Broadwater, "After Death of John Lewis, Democrats Renew Push for Voting Rights Law," *New York Times*, July 21, 2020; David Greenberg, "A Civil Rights Legend Who Saw Humanity in His Oppressors," Dec. 26, 2020, *Politico*, politico.com/news/magazine/2020/12/26/john-lewis-civil-rights-legend-obituary-2020-445135.

159 Eugene Scott, "Democrats are Avoiding 'Defund the Police,' While Republicans Harp On It," *Washington Post*, June 11, 2020; Aimee Ortiz and Johnny Diaz, "George Floyd Protests Reignite Debate Over Confederate Statues," *New York Times*, June 3, 2020; Michelle Mark and Connor Perrett, "Trump Said He Intends to Declare Antifa as a Terrorist Organization. Here's What We Know about the Decades-old, Leaderless Group," *Business Insider*, June 2, 2020, businessinsider.com/what-is-antifa-movement-charlottesville-va-trump-news-2017-8.

160 Jane C. Timm, "GOP Recruits Army of Poll Watchers to Fight Voter Fraud No One Can Prove Exists," NBC News, nbcnews.com/politics/donald-trump/gop-recruits-army-poll-watchers-fight-voter-fraud-no-can-n1217391; Allan Rappeport, "Postal Service Pick With Ties to Trump Raises Concerns Ahead of 2020 Election," *New York Times*, May 7, 2020.

161 Alexander Burns, "Joe Biden's Vice-Presidential Pick: Kamala Harris," *New York Times*, Aug. 11, 2020.

162 Peter Baker and Maggie Haberman, "McConnell Vows Vote on Ginsburg Replacement as Her Death Upends the 2020 Race," *New York Times*, Sept. 18, 2020.

163 Ruth Graham, "For Conservative Christian Women, Amy Coney Barrett's Success Is Personal," *New York Times*, Sept. 28, 2020; Eagle Forum, Oct. 26, 2020, eagleforum.org/publications/press-releases/amy-coney-barretts-confirmation-to-the-supreme-court.html.

164 Samantha Schmidt, "Susan B. Anthony Was Arrested for Voting When Women Couldn't. Now Trump Will Pardon Her," *Washington Post*, Aug. 18, 2020; Ellen Carol DuBois, "Taking the Law into Our Own Hands: *Bradwell, Minor*, and Suffrage Militance in the 1870s," Chapter Six in Spruill, *One Woman, One Vote*, Second Edition.

165 Lisa Lerer, "'Please Like Me,' Trump Begged. For Many Women, It's Way Too Late," *New York Times*, Oct. 17, 2020; Christina Wolbrecht and Erin Cassese, "President Trump's Appeals to Women Show That the More Things Change, the More They Stay the Same," Center for American Women and Politics (CAWP), Nov. 2, 2020, cawp.rutgers.edu/election-analysis/trump-appeals-suburban-women.

166 Erin Haines, "The Pandemic is Political—and Women are Angry at the President, *USA Today*, Oct. 16, 2020.

167 Ibid.; Courtney Subramanian, "Trump Campaign's Pitch to Women Voters: Let's Get Back to Pre-pandemic 'Normal,'" *USA Today*, Oct. 10, 2020.

168 Domenico Montanaro, "The 2020 Election Was a Good One for Republicans Not Named Trump," NPR, Nov. 11, 2020, npr.org/2020/11/11/933435840/the-2020-election-was-a-good-one-for-republicans-not-named-trump; Kate Sullivan and Jennifer Agiesta, "Biden's Popular Vote Margin over Trump Tops 7 Million," CNN Politics, Dec. 4, 2020, cnn.com/2020/12/04/politics/biden-popular-vote-margin-7-million/index.html.

169 These statistics about the election come from VoteCast.

Jocelyn Noveck, "Women Crucial to Biden's Win, Even as Gender Gap Held Steady," *AP News*, Nov. 16, 2020 apnews.com/article/election-2020-joe-biden-donald-trump-voting-rights-elections-84ef3db79532c0029894ff25a316370b.

170 Ibid.

171 Astead W. Herndon, "Georgia Was a Big Win for Democrats. Black Women Did the Groundwork," *New York Times*, Dec. 5, 2020.

172 Amber Phillips and Peter W. Stevenson, "What Happens Next in Trump's Impeachment?" *Washington Post*, Feb. 12, 2021.

173 Ibid.; Eric Lipton, "Trump Call to Georgia Official Might Violate State and Federal Law," *New York Times*, Jan. 3, 2021; Joan Walsh, "Democrats Did What They Had To Do: Beat Back Voter Suppression and Keep Voter Turnout High," *The Nation*, Jan. 22, 2021.

174 Jocelyn Noveck, "Women Crucial to Biden's Win."

175 Ibid.

176 Deena Zaru, Kiara Brantley-Jones , and Arielle Mitropoulos, "Record Gain for Women in Congress Highlights Lack of Diversity among Republicans," ABC News, Dec. 5, 2020, abcnews.go.com/Politics/record-gain-women-congress-highlights-lack-diversity-republicans/story?id=74023373.

177 Ibid.; Marjorie Dannenfelse," Election of Pro-Life Women Shows Tide Is Turning," *RealClear Politics*, realclearpolitics.com/articles/2020/11/18/election_of_pro-life_women_shows_tide_is_turning_144687.html#!; Erin Delmore, NBC, "Inside the Movement that Swept Republican Women into Congress," Nov. 20, 2020, nbcnews.com/know-your-value/feature/inside-movement-swept-republican-women-congress-ncna1248394; Rachael Bade, "GOP Women's Record-Breaking Success Reflects Party's Major Shift on Recruiting and Supporting Female Candidates, *Washington Post*, Dec. 7, 2020; Swanee Hunt, "Republican Women in the House Could Change Everything," CNN Opinion, Jan. 2, 2021, cnn.com/2021/01/02/opinions/republican-women-117th-congress-hunt/index.html.

178 Zaru, Brantley-Jones, and Mitropoulos, "Record Gain for Women in Congress Highlights Lack of Diversity among Republicans"; Alexa Mikhail, "Women Are at the Table: Biden Nominates a Record Number of Women for His Cabinet," *The 19th*, Jan. 22, 2021, 19thnews.org/2021/01/biden-women-cabinet-nominations/?utm_campaign=19th-social&utm_source=-facebook&utm_medium=social&fbclid=IwAR3d-ZQkwhmYOChNF6JN4kVg5RZkbOt8HNfN8gouCqHtpgNsZWFDGhMX6dTY.

179 Vanessa Friedman, "Kamala Harris in a White Suit, Dressing for History: This Wasn't about Fashion, It Was about Politics, Past and Future," *New York Times*, Nov.8, 2020.

180 Quotation from *The Woman Citizen*, Sept. 4, 1920; Barbara Stuhler, *For the Public Record: A Documentary History of the League of Women Voters* (Greenwood Publishing Group, 2000), 26.

181 Sarah Maisey, "Why Kamala Harris's Suffragette White Suit is a Beacon of Hope for the Future," *The National*, Nov. 9, 2020, thenationalnews.com/about-us.

182 Ibid.

183 Ibid.

184 Friedman, "Kamala Harris in a White Suit."

Life

October 28, 1920

Vol. 76.   Copyright, 1920, Life Publishing Company   No. 1982

Price 15 Cents

"*Congratulations*"

Appendix I

THE ELECTORAL THERMOMETER

Woman Suffrage Won by State
Constitutional Amendments and
Legislative Acts Before the Proclamation
of the Nineteenth Amendment

		Electoral Vote
1890	Wyoming was admitted to statehood with woman suffrage, having had it as a territory since 1869.	3
1893	Colorado adopted a constitutional amendment after defeat in 1877.	6
1896	Idaho adopted a constitutional amendment on its first submission.	4
1896	Utah, having had woman suffrage as a territory since 1870, was deprived of it by Congress in 1887. It was reinstated by constitutional referendum when admitted to statehood.	4
1910	Washington adopted a constitutional amendment after defeats in 1889 and 1898. The territorial legislature twice enacted woman suffrage, but lost it by court decisions.	7
1911	California adopted a constitutional amendment after defeat in 1896.	13
1912	Oregon adopted a constitutional amendment after defeats in 1884, 1900, 1906, 1908, 1910.	5
1912	Kansas adopted a constitutional amendment after defeats in 1867 and 1893.	10
1912	Arizona adopted a constitutional amendment submitted as a result of referendum petitions.	3
1913	Illinois was the first state to get presidential suffrage by legislative enactment.	29
1914	Montana adopted a constitutional amendment on its first submission.	4
1914	Nevada adopted a constitutional amendment on its first submission.	3
1917	North Dakota secured presidential suffrage by legislative enactment, after defeat of a constitutional amendment in 1914.	5
1917	Nebraska secured presidential suffrage by legislative enactment after defeats of a constitutional amendment in 1882 and 1914.	8

1917	Rhode Island secured presidential suffrage by legislative enactment after defeat of a constitutional amendment in 1887.	5
1917	New York adopted a constitutional amendment after defeat in 1915.	45
1917	Arkansas secured primary suffrage by legislative enactment.	9
1918	Michigan adopted a constitutional amendment after defeats in 1874, 1912, and 1913. Secured presidential suffrage by legislative enactment in 1917.	15
1918	Texas secured primary suffrage by legislative enactment.	20
1918	South Dakota adopted a constitutional amendment after six prior campaigns for suffrage had been defeated, each time by a mobilization of the alien vote by American-born political manipulators. In that state, as in nine others in 1918, the foreign-born could vote on their "first papers" and citizenship was not a qualification for the vote. The last defeat, in 1916, had been so definitely proved to have been caused by the vote of German-Russians in nine counties that public sentiment, in addition to the war spirit, aroused a desire to make a change in the law that resulted in victory.	5
1918	Oklahoma adopted a constitutional amendment after defeat in 1910.	10
1919	Indiana secured presidential suffrage by legislative enactment in 1917. Rendered doubtful by a court decision, the law was re-enacted with but six dissenting votes.	15
1919	Maine secured presidential suffrage by legislative enactment after defeat of a constitutional amendment in 1917.	6
1919	Missouri secured presidential suffrage by legislative enactment after defeat of a constitutional amendment in 1914.	18
1919	Iowa secured presidential suffrage by legislative enactment after defeat of a constitutional amendment in 1916.	13
1919	Minnesota secured presidential suffrage by legislative enactment.	12
1919	Ohio secured presidential suffrage by legislative enactment after defeat of referendum on the law in 1917 and of a constitutional amendment in 1912 and 1914.	24
1919	Wisconsin secured presidential suffrage by legislative enactment after defeat of a constitutional amendment in 1912.	13
1919	Tennessee secured presidential suffrage by legislative enactment.	12
1920	Kentucky secured presidential suffrage by legislative enactment.	13

Total of presidential electors for whom women were entitled to vote before the Nineteenth Amendment was adopted, 339.
(Full number 531).

In 1913 the territory of Alaska had adopted woman suffrage.
It was the first bill approved by the governor.

From: The National American Woman Suffrage Association, *VICTORY: How Women Won It* (New York: H.W. Wilson Company, 1940), Appendix 4, 161-164.

Appendix II

CHRONOLOGY OF CONGRESSIONAL ACTION

1868   Passage of the Fourteenth Amendment, which introduced the word male into the Constitution.

1869   First woman suffrage bill introduced into the House.

1869   Hearing on woman suffrage.

1878   Introduction by Senator Sargent of the Woman Suffrage Amendment in its final form.

1887   January 25, first vote in the Senate, yeas 16, nays 34, 50 voting.

1914   March 19, second vote in the Senate, yeas 35, nays 34, 69 voting.

1915   January 12, first vote in the House, yeas 174, nays 204, 378 voting.

1917   September 24, creation of Woman Suffrage Committee in the House.

1918   January 10, second vote in the House, yeas 274, nays 136, 410 voting.

1918   October 1, third vote in the Senate, yeas, including pairs, 62,

1919   February 10, fourth vote in the Senate, yeas, including pairs, 63, nays 33.

1919   May 21, third vote in the House, yeas 304, nays 89.

1919   June 4, fifth vote in the Senate, yeas, including pairs, 66, nays 30.

1920   August 26, proclamation by the Secretary of State of the Nineteenth Amendment.

From: The National American Woman Suffrage Association. *VICTORY: How Women Won It* (New York: H.W. Wilson Company, 1940), Appendix 8, 172.

Appendix III
RECORD OF ACTION ON NATIONAL SUFFRAGE AMENDMENT IN THE STATES 1919-1920

	STATE	DATE OF RATIFICATION	VOTE SENATE	VOTE HOUSE	PARTY OF GOVERNOR	PARTY CONTROLLING LEGISLATURE
1	Wisconsin	June 10, 1919	24-1	54-2	Rep.	Rep.
2	*Michigan	June 10, 1919	Unan.	Unan.	Rep.	Rep.
3	*Kansas	June 16, 1919	Unan.	Unan.	Rep.	Rep.
4	*Ohio	June 16, 1919	27-3	73-6	Dem.	Rep.
5	*New York	June 16, 1919	Unan.	Unan.	Dem.	Rep.
6	Illinois	June 17, 1919	Unan.	133-4	Rep.	Rep.
7	Pennsylvania	June 24, 1919	32-6	153-44	Rep.	Rep.
8	Massachusetts	June 25, 1919	34-5	184-77	Rep.	Rep.
9	*Texas	June 29, 1919	Unan.	96-21	Dem.	Dem.
10	*Iowa	July 2, 1919	Unan.	95-5	Rep.	Rep.
11	*Missouri	July 3, 1919	28-3	125-4	Dem.	Div'd
12	*Arkansas	July 20, 1919	20-2	76-17	Dem.	Dem.
13	*Montana	July 30, 1919	38-1	Unan.	Dem.	Rep.
14	*Nebraska	Aug. 2, 1919	Unan.	Unan.	Rep.	Rep.
15	*Minnesota	Sept. 8, 1919	60-5	120-6	Rep.	Rep.
16	*New Hampshire	Sept. 10, 1919	14-10	212-143	Rep.	Rep.
17	*Utah	Sept. 30, 1919	Unan.	Unan.	Dem.	Dem.
18	*California	Nov. 1, 1919	Unan.	73-2	Rep.	Rep.
19	*Maine	Nov. 5, 1919	24-5	72-68	Rep.	Rep.
20	*North Dakota	Dec. 1, 1919	38-4	103-6	Rep.	Rep.
21	*South Dakota	Dec. 4, 1919	Unan.	Unan.	Rep.	Rep.
22	*Colorado	Dec. 12, 1919	Unan.	Unan.	Rep.	Rep.
23	Rhode Island	Jan. 6, 1920	37-1	89-3	Rep.	Rep.
24	Kentucky	Jan. 6, 1920	30-8	72-25	Rep.	Div'd
25	*Oregon	Jan. 12, 1920	Unan.	Unan.	Rep.	Rep.
26	*Indiana	Jan. 16, 1920	43-3	Unan.	Rep.	Rep.
27	*Wyoming	Jan. 27, 1920	Unan.	Unan.	Rep.	Rep.
28	*Nevada	Feb. 7, 1920	Unan.	Unan.	Dem	Div'd

Appendix III *(cont)*
RECORD OF ACTION ON NATIONAL SUFFRAGE AMENDMENT IN THE STATES 1919 -1920

	STATE	DATE OF RATIFICATION	VOTE SENATE	VOTE HOUSE	PARTY OF GOVERNOR	PARTY CONTROLLING LEGISLATURE
29	New Jersey	Feb. 10, 1920	18-2	34-24	Dem.	Rep.
30	*Idaho	Feb. 11, 1920	29-6	Unan.	Rep.	Rep.
31	*Arizona	Feb. 12, 1920	Unan.	Unan.	Rep.	Dem.
32	*New Mexico	Feb. 19, 1920	17-5	36-10	Rep.	Rep.
33	*Oklahoma	Feb. 27, 1920	24-15	84-12	Dem.	Dem.
34	*West Virginia	Mar. 10, 1920	15-14	47-40	Dem.	Rep.
35	*Washington	Mar. 22, 1920	Unan.	Unan.	Rep.	Rep.
36	*Tennessee	Aug. 18, 1920	25-4	49-47	Dem.	Dem.

From: Doris Stevens, *The Story of the Militant American Suffragist Movement,*
(New York: Boni and Liveright, 1920), Appendix 1.

About the Suffragists on the Book Cover

Marie Louise Bottineau Baldwin, Chippewa attorney and advocate for Native American and woman suffrage

Fannie Barrier Williams, educator and activist for African American and women's rights, and the first Black woman to become a member of the Chicago Woman's Club

Mabel Ping-Hua Lee, Chinese-born immigrant who worked for U.S. woman suffrage though unable to naturalize and vote herself

Susan B. Anthony *(center),* leader of the woman suffrage movement from the 1850s through the early 1900s

Dora Lewis, National Woman's Party leader, one of the oldest suffragists jailed for picketing the White House

Rose Winslow, also known as Wenclawska, Polish-American factory worker and union organizer who endured hunger strikes and forced feedings for the cause of woman suffrage

Nannie Helen Burroughs, educator, religious leader and activist for African American and women's rights

All photos from the Library of Congress, except Anthony's photo, which is from Elizabeth Cady Stanton's book, *Eighty Years and More,*1898

Contributors

BEVERLY BEETON was well known for her scholarship on the woman suffrage movement in the Western United States. Her books on the subject include the influential *Women Vote in the West: The Woman Suffrage Movement 1869-1896* (Garland Publishing, 1986). She also published numerous articles on the Western suffrage movement, including "Susan B. Anthony's Woman Suffrage Crusade in the American West," (with co-author G. Thomas Edwards) in *Journal of the West* (1982). Beeton obtained her Ph.D. from the University of Utah. She was a university administrator and history professor for twenty-five years, serving at four different universities in Utah, Illinois, and Alaska. She retired as Provost and Vice Chancellor for Academic Affairs at the University of Alaska Anchorage. After retirement she continued to write and speak on women's history, including on woman suffrage and the 1918 influenza pandemic. After moving to Seattle, Washington in 2010 she wrote a family history about the development of Northern Utah through the lives of her ancestors who were among the first homesteaders. Beeton died in 2020.

VICTORIA BISSELL BROWN is Professor Emerita of History at Grinnell College where she taught for twenty-five years. She received her Ph.D. from the University of California, San Diego. Her scholarship has focused on the Progressive Era, particularly Jane Addams and Woodrow Wilson. Brown is the author of a biographical study of Addams, *The Education of Jane Addams: Politics and Culture in Modern America* (University of Pennsylvania Press, 2003, 2004, 2007), and editor of an edition of Jane Addams's memoir, *Twenty Years at Hull-House* (Bedford /St. Martin's,1999, Second Edition 2018). She has also published articles on Woodrow Wilson's gender politics and appeared in the PBS "American Experience" documentary on Wilson. Her current research is on the history of the American grandmother in the twentieth century. Brown resides near Philadelphia, Pennsylvania.

NANCY F. COTT is the Jonathan Trumbull Research Professor of American History at Harvard University. After earning her Ph.D. from Brandeis University, she went on to write extensively on American culture, focusing on women's history. Cott is one of the founders of the field of U.S. Women's History. Her publications range widely over questions concerning women, gender, marriage, feminism, citizenship, and sexuality from the eighteenth century to the contemporary United States. She explored a new area in her most recent book, *Fighting Words: The Bold American Journalists Who Brought the World Home between the Wars* (Basic Books, 2020). Her other books include *The Bonds of Womanhood: "Woman's Sphere" in New England, 1780–1835* (Yale University Press, 1977), *The Grounding of Modern Feminism* (Yale University Press, 1987), and *Public Vows: A History of Marriage and the Nation* (Harvard University Press, 2000). Cott served as president of the Organization of American Historians in 2016-17, and she is an elected member of the American Academy of Arts and Sciences. She lives in Cambridge, Massachusetts.

ELLEN CAROL DUBOIS is the author of numerous works on the woman suffrage movement, including *Suffrage: Women's Long Battle for the Vote* (Simon and Schuster, 2020). Among her other works on suffrage are *Feminism and Suffrage: The Emergence of an Independent Woman Suffrage Movement, 1848-1869* (Cornell University Press, 1978); *Harriot Stanton Blatch and the Winning of Woman Suffrage* (Yale University Press, 1997); and *The Elizabeth Cady Stanton-Susan B. Anthony Reader: Correspondence, Writings, Speeches* (McFarland Press, 2022; first published 1987). She is the co-author, along with Brenda Stevenson of the sixth edition of the leading textbook on U.S. women's history, *Through Women's Eyes: An American History with Documents* (Bedford/St. Martin's, 2022), and was the original co-editor, with Vicki L. Ruiz, of *Unequal Sisters: An Inclusive Reader in U.S. Women's History* (Routledge; 4th edition,

2008). Her current project is a comprehensive biography of Elizabeth Cady Stanton, with Basic Books. Du Bois received her Ph.D. from Northwestern University. After teaching at the University of Buffalo, she taught for thirty years at the University of California, Los Angeles (UCLA) where she is now a Distinguished Research Professor in the History Department.

LINDA G. FORD is the author of three books on women's history, including *Iron-Jawed Angels: The Suffrage Militancy of the National Woman Party* (University Press of America,1991), which won the Gustavus Myers Award for human rights. She also authored *Lady Hoopsters: A History of Women's Basketball in America* (Half-Moon Books, 2001), and *Women Politicals in America: Jailed Dissidents from Mother Jones to Lynne Stewart* (2018). After receiving her Ph.D. from Syracuse University, she taught at Keene State College in New Hampshire and at Colgate University in New York. Ford, a feminist activist, is also the author of numerous articles on feminist history and issues of the left, particularly in the publications *Counterpunch* and *Dissident Voice*.

ROBERT BOOTH FOWLER is Professor Emeritus in the Political Science Department at the University of Wisconsin, Madison. He received his Ph.D. from Harvard University. Fowler is the author of *Carrie Catt: Feminist Politician* (Northeastern University Press, 1986) as well as numerous articles about Catt as the National American Woman Suffrage Association leader. He has published numerous books and articles in his areas of specialty, political thought and religion, and American politics. He lives in Madison, Wisconsin and Tucson, Arizona

CAROLYN DE SWARTE GIFFORD is an authority on American women's religious experience and social reform activity. She earned her Ph.D. in Religion from Northwestern University. She has published numerous books and articles on Frances Willard and the WCTU. Among her books are *Writing Out My Heart: Selections from the Journal of Frances E. Willard, 1855-1896* (University of Illinois Press, 1995); *Let Something Good Be Said: Speeches and Writings of Frances E. Willard,* co-edited with Amy R. Slagell (University of Illinois Press, 2007); *Women in American Protestant Religion, 1800 to 1930* (Garland, 1987); and *Gender and the Social Gospel,* co-edited with Wendy Deichmann (University of Illinois Press, 2007). Gifford served as an associate editor of both *Past and Promise: Lives of New Jersey Women* (The Scarecrow Press, 1990) and *Women Building Chicago 1790-1990: A Biographical Dictionary* (Indiana University Press, 2001). She resides in Reno, Nevada.

SARA HUNTER GRAHAM was an associate professor at Louisiana State University and a specialist in women's history and political history. She received her Ph.D. from the University of Texas, Austin. Her highly acclaimed book, *Woman Suffrage and the New Democracy* (Yale University Press, 1996), was published posthumously, shortly after her death in 1996. Her work on the woman suffrage movement also included "Woman Suffrage in Virginia: The Equal Suffrage League and Pressure-Group Politics, 1909-1920," published in *The Virginia Magazine of History and Biography.*

WANDA A. HENDRICKS is a Distinguished Professor Emerita at the University of South Carolina. She received her Ph.D. from Purdue University. Hendricks is the author of *Gender, Race, and Politics: Black Club Women in Illinois* (Indiana University Press, 1998); senior editor of the three-volume *Black Women in America: Second Edition* (Oxford University Press, 2005); and an editor of the *Women, Gender, and Sexuality in American History Series* at the University of Illinois Press. Her many published articles and essays include, "On the Margins: Creating a Space and Place in the Academy," which appeared in *Telling Histories: Black Women Historians in the Ivory Tower* (University of North Carolina Press, 2008). Hendricks's most recent book, *Fannie Barrier Williams: Crossing the Borders of Region and Race* (University of Illinois Press, 2014) was awarded the Letitia Woods Brown prize by the Association of Black Women Historians for the best book by a senior scholar in African American Women's

History. Hendricks's current book on the transnational activism of Madie Hall Xuma, the African American wife of South African and African National Congress president Alfred Bitini Xuma, will be published by the University of Illinois Press. Hendricks resides in Columbia, South Carolina.

SHERRY J. KATZ has taught U.S. women's and gender history and other courses for over twenty years in the Department of History at San Francisco State University. She received her Ph.D. in History from the University of California, Los Angeles (UCLA) in 1991. Katz has written extensively on early twentieth century socialist feminist activists in California and their coalition-building work for woman suffrage, protective labor and social welfare legislation, birth control legalization, and equality in partisan politics. She has published a number of essays and articles, including "'Researching Around Our Subjects': Excavating Radical Women," *Journal of Women's History* (Spring 2008). Katz co-edited a collection of essays on women's history methodologies, *Contesting Archives: Finding Women in the Sources* (University of Illinois Press, 2010), which won the Western Association of Women Historians' Barbara "Penny" Kanner Prize. Her most recent publications include biographical sketches of socialist feminists for the "Online Biographical Dictionary of the Woman Suffrage Movement in the U.S." Katz is currently writing on socialist feminist Estelle Lawton Lindsey, the first city councilwoman elected in a major U.S. city (Los Angeles, 1915).

LINDA K. KERBER is the May Brodbeck Professor in Liberal Arts & Sciences and Professor of History Emerita at the University of Iowa, as well as a Lecturer in the College of Law. She received the A.B. from Barnard College in 1960 and the Ph.D. in history from Columbia University in 1968. She has served as President of the American Studies Association, the Organization of American Historians, and the American Historical Association. In 2006-2007 she was Harmsworth Professor of American History at Oxford University. Kerber is an elected member of the American Philosophical Society and a Fellow of the American Academy of Arts and Sciences. In 2020, she offered the Charles Homer Haskins Prize Lecture "A Life of Learning" for the American Council of Learned Societies. In her writing and teaching, Kerber has emphasized the history of citizenship, gender, and authority. Her book *No Constitutional Right to Be Ladies: Women and the Obligations of Citizenship* (Hill and Wang, 1998) won best book in women's history and in legal history (both prizes awarded by the American Historical Association). Among Kerber's other books are *Toward an Intellectual History of Women* (University of North Carolina Press, 1997, 2001); *Women of the Republic: Intellect and Ideology in Revolutionary America* (University of North Carolina Press, 1980-2014); and *Federalists in Dissent: Imagery and Ideology in Jeffersonian America* (Cornell University Press, 1970, 1980, 2018). Kerber also co-edited *Women's America: Refocusing the Past* (Oxford University Press, ninth edition 2020); and *U.S. History as Women's History: New Feminist Essays* (University of North Carolina Press, 1995).

ANDREA MOORE KERR, a women's historian and independent scholar in Washington, D.C., earned her Ph.D. from the University of Maryland. She was the author of *Lucy Stone: Speaking Out for Equality* (Rutgers University Press, 1992). Kerr served on the board of directors of the Humanities Council District of Columbia, the Eastern Market Preservation Corporation, Washington, and on the steering committee of Washington Women Historians. Kerr died on December 1, 2018.

KATHERINE M. MARINO is an Associate Professor of History at the University of California, Los Angeles. She obtained her Ph.D. from Stanford University in 2013. Her research and teaching explore histories of women, gender, and sexuality in the United States and Latin America, as well as human rights and transnational feminism. Her book *Feminism for the Americas: The Making of an International Human Rights Movement* (University of North

Carolina Press, 2019) received the Latin American Studies Association Luciano Tomassini Latin American International Relations Book Award, the Western Association of Women Historians (WAWH) Barbara "Penny" Kanner Award, and co-won the Ida Blom-Karen Offen Prize in Transnational Women's and Gender History. It also received Honorable Mentions for the Organization of American Historians Mary Jurich Nickliss Prize in U.S. Women's and/or Gender History and for the WAWH Frances Richardson Keller-Sierra Prize. Her articles have been published in the *Journal of Women's History* and *Gender & History, Frontiers: A Journal of Women's Studies*, as well as in several news media outlets, including the *Washington Post*. Marino lives in Los Angeles, California.

JUDITH N. MCARTHUR received her Ph.D. from the University of Texas at Austin and taught at the University of Houston-Victoria. She is the author of *Creating the New Woman: The Rise of Southern Women's Progressive Culture in Texas, 1893-1918* (University of Illinois Press, 1998). She is co-author (with Orville Vernon Burton) of *A Gentleman and an Officer: A Military and Social History of James B. Griffin's Civil War* (Oxford University Press, 1996); and co-author (with Harold L. Smith) of *Minnie Fisher Cunningham: A Suffragist's Life in Politics*, and of *Texas Through Women's Eyes: The Twentieth-Century Experience* (Oxford University Press, 2003). McArthur is the co-editor (with Ruthe Winegarten) of *Citizens at Last: The Woman Suffrage Movement in Texas* (Texas A&M University Press, Reissue edition 2015), and (with Angela Boswell) of *Women Shaping the South: Creating and Confronting Change* (University of Missouri, 2006). Her essays include, "A. Elizabeth Taylor: Searching for Southern Suffragists," published in *Reading Southern History: Essays on Interpreters and Interpretations* (ed. Glenn Feldman); and "Maternity Wars: Gender, Race, and the Sheppard-Towner Act in Texas," published in *Texas Women: Their Histories, Their Lives* (ed. Elizabeth Hayes Turner, Stephanie Cole, and Rebecca Sharpless.) McArthur lives in Fort Collins, Colorado.

ALICE S. ROSSI, a leading scholar and activist, was the Harriet Martineau Professor of Sociology Emerita at the University of Massachusetts, Amherst. She received her Ph.D. from Columbia University. Rossi was a founder of the National Organization for Women (NOW) and a member of NOW's original governing board. She was president of the American Sociological Association and the first president of Sociologists for Women in Society. Rossi also served as Vice President of the American Association of University Professors, Chair of the Social Science Research Council, and a member of the Advisory Council for the National Institute on Aging. Appointed by President Jimmy Carter, Rossi served on the National Commission for the Observance of International Women's Year (1977) and then published a scholarly analysis of it, *Feminists in Politics: A Panel Analysis of the First National Women's Conference* (Academic Press, 1982). Her extensive publications also include *Sexuality Across the Life Course* (University of Chicago Press, 1994); *Caring and Doing for Others: Social Responsibility in the Domains of Family, Work and Community* (University of Chicago Press, 2001). Rossi was the editor of four books, including the classic anthology, *The Feminist Papers: From Adams to de Beauvoir*, first published in 1973. Alice Rossi died on November 3, 2009.

ANASTATIA SIMS is Professor Emerita of History at Georgia Southern University. She received her Ph.D. from the University of North Carolina at Chapel Hill. Sims wrote *The Power of Femininity in the New South: Women's Organizations and Politics in North Carolina, 1880-1930* (University of South Carolina Press, 1997); and co-edited *Negotiating the Boundaries of Southern Womanhood: Dealing with the Powers That Be* (University of Missouri Press, 2000). She has also authored several articles on women's organizations and woman suffrage in journals and anthologies. Sims is currently working on a biography of Juliette Gordon Low, founder of the Girl Scouts of the United States. She lives in Statesboro, Georgia.

MARJORIE J. SPRUILL is Distinguished Professor Emerita of History at the University of South Carolina. She received a B.A. from the University of North Carolina, Chapel Hill, an M.A.T. from Duke University, and an M.A. and Ph.D. from the University of Virginia. In addition to *One Woman, One Vote: Rediscovering the Woman Suffrage Movement* (NewSage Press, 1995; Second Edition, 2021), she is the author or editor of five books on woman suffrage, including *New Women of the New South: The Woman Suffrage Movement in the Southern States* (Oxford University Press, 1993), and *Votes for Women! The Woman Suffrage Movement in Tennessee, the South, and the Nation* (University of Tennessee Press, 1995). Spruill also co-edited a two-volume textbook on the history of the American South and two multi-volume anthologies about the "lives and times" of women in South Carolina and Mississippi. Her most recent book is *Divided We Stand: The Battle Over Women's Rights and Family Values That Polarized American Politics* (Bloomsbury 2017). During her career, Spruill was a professor at the University of Southern Mississippi; Vanderbilt University, where she was an Associate Provost; and at the University of South Carolina. She served as President of the Southern Association for Women Historians (SAWH), as well as on the Executive Council of the Southern Historical Association, (SHA), and on the editorial boards of the SHA *Journal of Southern History* and the British Association for American Studies (BAAS) *Journal of American Studies*. In 2018, Spruill was inducted into the Society of American Historians. She currently serves on the Scholar's Advisory Council of the National Women's History Museum and on the South Carolina Archives and History Commission. Spruill lives in Folly Beach, South Carolina.

ROSALYN TERBORG-PENN earned her Ph.D. at Howard University and was a professor of history at Morgan State University in Baltimore for more than three decades. Terborg-Penn published extensively on topics in African American women's history, and edited (with Sharon Harley) a groundbreaking book, *The Afro-American Woman: Struggles and Images* (Kennikat Press, 1978). At a time when many scholars failed to recognize the important role of African American women in the suffrage movement, Terborg-Penn persevered in highlighting and celebrating their work, as well as focusing attention on racism among White suffragists. Terborg-Penn first wrote about African American suffragists in a well-known dissertation that evolved into a highly recognized article and later, into her seminal book *African American Women in the Struggle for the Vote, 1850-1920* (Indiana University Press, 1998). Another major contribution was Terborg-Penn's anthology, *Women in Africa and the African Diaspora: A Reader*, which was co-edited with Sharon Harley and Andrea Benton Rushing, published in 1987, and revised and expanded in 1996. The volume grew out of the first national symposium held by a new organization that she co-founded, The Association of Black Women Historians. Terborg-Penn was also one of the editors of *Black Women in America: An Historical Encyclopedia* (Carlson, 1993). In 2000, Terborg-Penn became a founding member of the Association for the Study of the Worldwide African Diaspora. Her most recent work focused on writings on race and race relations in Suriname. Terborg-Penn died on December 25, 2018.

MANUELA THURNER is an editor, translator, and writer. She received her Ph.D. in American Studies from Yale University with a doctoral thesis on *Girlkultur* and *Kulturfeminismus*: Gender and Americanism in Weimar Germany, 1918-1933. Her other publications include an essay, "Subject to Change: Theories and Paradigms of U.S. Feminist History," published in the *Journal of Women's History* in 1997 and anthologized in *Major Problems in American Women's History*, edited by Mary Beth Norton and Ruth M. Alexander (Houghton Mifflin Co., 2003). Thurner lives in Munich, Germany.

Acknowledgments

I would like to thank several people who were essential to the development and production of this second edition of *One Woman, One Vote: Rediscovering the Woman Suffrage Movement*. The first edition, published in 1995, was originally designed as the companion book to the PBS "American Experience" documentary *One Woman, One Vote*, produced by the Educational Film Center (EFC). In particular, I am grateful to Steve Rabin, who was EFC President at the time, and to Ruth Pollak, the writer and producer of the documentary, for inviting me to design and edit the companion book. I will always be grateful for the support EFC provided for the first edition.

None of this would have been possible, however, without the dedication and skill of the publisher of NewSage Press, Maureen R. Michelson, who moved mountains to produce the first edition of the book in record time for the 75th anniversary of the Nineteenth Amendment in 1995. Twenty-five years later, we have worked together again in close partnership to bring out this new and expanded edition for the 100th anniversary.

As the 2020 suffrage centennial approached, Maureen and I were inspired to produce a new and expanded edition of *One Woman, One Vote*. Our goal was to add new chapters that incorporate the latest scholarship, offer new material on the role of race and region, and further diversify the cast of characters in this account of how women won the right to vote. We also wanted to place the story of the U.S. suffrage movement in an international context, and to bring the story of women and the vote up to the present.

The original plan was to release the book in 2020. However, there were extraordinary events in that year in which women played essential roles as voters and as organizers and candidates. In addition, voting rights were once again under attack, proving to be so relevant and important to the story that we decided to remain at work throughout the year. We were eager to provide a fuller account of the long suffrage struggle, which has proven to be never ending

Maureen has gone far beyond the usual role of a publisher, encouraging me to take as long as necessary to make the story complete and timely, skillfully editing all new material. In addition, we worked together to add more than a hundred new photographs that greatly enrich the book. For both of us, it has been a labor of love.

Maureen's dedication to publishing work by and about women, specifically the second edition of *One Woman, One Vote*, was recognized by the writing organization Soapstone as the recipient of its 2021 "Soapstone Bread and Roses Award." The award traditionally honors a woman whose work has sustained the writing community and includes a generous donation, which was used toward the production of this book. I congratulate Maureen and thank Soapstone for honoring her and supporting *One Woman, One Vote*.

Special thanks to the book designer, Sherry Wachter, for her great work in designing this book—expertly and patiently working with us through several drafts. Sherry, too, is a woman of tremendous talent and dedication to quality.

She has gone above and beyond the duties of a designer, putting in countless hours to help bring the suffrage story to readers in a visually inspiring format. On several occasions, Sherry went the extra mile, telling us she wanted the book to be the best it can be. Thank you, Sherry!

I also thank Angie Maxwell, Anastatia Sims, and Christina Wolbrecht for their assistance with fact checking, and Carole Bucy, Connie Lester, and Corinne Porter for aid in locating and identifying photos. I am grateful to Adele Logan Alexander for allowing me to include the photo of her grandmother, Adella Hunt Logan, and to Pam Elam, President of Monumental Women, for the photo of the Women's Rights Pioneers Monument.

I extend a heartfelt thanks to the eighteen authors of the essays, distinguished scholars who tailored their essays to make them accessible and inviting to a general audience. I offer a special tribute to Rosalyn Terborg-Penn, the first historian to capture the story of African American women in the suffrage movement, who inspired others to follow in her footsteps. Her unexpected passing on the eve of the suffrage centennial was greatly mourned by the entire community of suffrage scholars.

During the production of this second volume, pioneering scholar of the Western suffrage movement, Beverly Beeton, died. Still earlier, authors Sara Hunter Graham, Alice Rossi, and Andrea Kerr, passed away. I have been proud to work with these scholars, and with all the authors of essays in *One Woman, One Vote*. I am deeply grateful for their contributions. This book is dedicated to them, and to generations of scholars, past, present, and future, of the woman suffrage movement and the struggle for equal voting rights in the United States.

Finally, I would like to thank my historian husband Don H. Doyle for his help with editorial and technical support, and for his constant encouragement.

—*Marjorie J. Spruill*

About the Editor

Marjorie J. Spruill, Distinguished Professor Emerita, University of South Carolina, is the author or editor of numerous books on the woman suffrage movement. Recently retired from a career of teaching and writing women's history, she is a frequent speaker on woman suffrage nationally and abroad, as well as a media consultant and an advisor for documentaries, films, and museum exhibits on suffrage and the larger subject of women's history and politics.

Spruill was an advisor to the National Archives for its centennial exhibit, "Rightfully Hers," and was commissioned to participate in several projects sponsored by the Women's Suffrage

Marjorie J. Spruill

Centennial Commission. As an authority on the American South, she worked with Nashville Public Television on the recent documentary *By One Vote: Woman Suffrage in the South,* and with South Carolina Educational Television on *Sisterhood: SC Suffragists.* Earlier, she was the historical advisor for the 2004 HBO film, *Iron Jawed Angels.* Spruill currently serves on the Scholar's Advisory Council of the National Women's History Museum and on the South Carolina Archives and History Commission.

As editor of the Second Edition of *One Woman, One Vote,* Spruill has continued the story of women and the vote up through the 2020 election, bringing to the task her expertise on modern feminism and anti-feminism. Her publications in those areas include *Divided We Stand: The Battle Over Women's Rights* and *Family Values That Polarized American Politics* (Bloomsbury 2017) in which she described the rise of the modern women's rights movement, the mobilization of conservative women in opposition, their competition for influence on federal policy, and the role this played in the development of modern American political culture. Spruill's work has been supported by the Radcliffe Institute for Advanced Study, Harvard University; the Woodrow Wilson International Center for Scholars; the National Endowment for the Humanities; the National Humanities Center; the Gerald R. Ford Presidential Foundation; and the American Association of University Women.

Spruill lives in Folly Beach, South Carolina, where she continues to research, write, and consult about women's history.

Other Books by Marjorie J. Spruill

Divided We Stand: Women's Rights, Family Values, and the Polarization of American Politics. Bloomsbury.

New Women of the New South: The Leaders of the Woman Suffrage Movement in the Southern States. Oxford University Press.

VOTES FOR WOMEN! The Woman Suffrage Movement in Tennessee, the South, and the Nation, editor. University of Tennessee Press.

Jailed for Freedom, memoir by suffragist Doris Stevens, first published in 1920. Editor. Lakeside Classics, R.R. Donnelley & Sons.

Hagar, pro-suffrage novel by Mary Johnston, first published in1913. Editor. University Press of Virginia.

South Carolina Women: Their Lives and Times. Co-edited with Valinda W. Littlefield and Joan Marie Johnson. University of Georgia Press, Volumes 1-3.

Mississippi Women: Their Histories, Their Lives. Co-edited with Martha Swain and Elizabeth Payne. University of Georgia Press, Volumes 1-2.

The South in the History of the Nation: A Reader. Co-edited with William A. Link, Bedford/St. Martin's, Volumes 1-2.

Index

Page references for illustrations are in italics.

CPSIA information can be obtained
at www.ICGtesting.com
Printed in the USA
JSHW031430020721
16546JS00002B/8

CHAPTER
Aspen
ONE

"**I** FEEL LIKE I'm forgetting something," Aurora says as she thumbs through her wedding binder. When she finally set an official wedding date, it didn't take us long to fill that thing up. It's a good thing my sister is very decisive on what she wants for her wedding. And Grant, he just wants Aurora to have the wedding of her dreams. Big or small, he doesn't care, as long as at the end of the day she's his wife. He's a goner for my big sister.

"Sweetheart." Mom places her hand over Aurora's. "We've been through everything. It's all been handled. Just take a breath," she says, pulling in a deep breath and slowly exhaling as if my sister needs a visual to understand her request.

I think we're all a little overstimulated with wedding planning. We managed to hire two new employees at Warm Delights to cover while we're gone for the wedding. Aurora is stressing out about this. That's not all we did. We planned a small intimate wedding at the Riggins's family cabin in the Smoky Mountains, and every detail is perfect. All of this was done in a matter of a few months. To say we are exhausted is an understatement.

"Rory." I wait for her to look at me. "We've got this. McKenzie and Gloria are both doing amazing at the bakery. They can handle it. And all this" —I point to the binder she's clutching to her chest— "we've all got you covered. This wedding is going to go off without a hitch, and you and Grant are going to be in wedded bliss, working on a house full of little Riggins babies." I immediately cover my mouth and glance over at Lena Riggins, Grant's mom. "Sorry," I say sheepishly.

She waves me off. "Please, I'm ready for the house full of little Riggins babies," she assures me with a kind smile. She then turns her gaze to my sister. "It's all going to be perfect. It's going to be the day that you've imagined and planned it to be. We'll make sure of it." Something passes in her eyes. I've seen that same look in all five of her sons. Determination. Lena Riggins is going to make damn sure that my sister's wedding to her middle son is executed with precision.

"It's going to be a day to remember," Mom says, wiping at her eyes.

"Mom," Aurora whines, dragging out the word. "Please don't do that. You're going to make me cry."

"And I have a rule, no one cries in front of me alone," Lena says, dabbing at the corner of her eyes with a tissue.

"I love you, Rory. Take a deep breath. It's all going to be fine. I'll personally drive up early to make sure of it," I offer.

"Really? You'd do that?"

"Hello, sister, best friend, and maid of honor, of course, I'll do that. I'll be there to coordinate deliveries and decorators, and it's all going to be perfect." I watch as her posture visibly relaxes, and the worry lines across her forehead diminish.

"Thank you, Aspen."

I wave my hand in the air. "It's nothing you wouldn't do for me. I can take your dress with me too. This way, you can ride to the cabin with Grant with no worries of him seeing your dress."

A smile breaks out across her face. "That's a great idea."

Just the idea that she gets to ride with him to the cabin has her smiling like a kid in a candy store. Grant Riggins has worked his Riggins voodoo magic on my sister, but if it keeps that smile on her face, I'm good with it. That doesn't mean I believe in the "magic" hype that they all talk about. I'm skeptical, but Aurora, Sawyer, and Layla are all believers. I guess love does that to you. It makes you believe in things that aren't real, like magic.

"Now," Mom says, clapping her hands together, "all that's left is the honeymoon cabin." A slight blush coats her cheeks, which makes me grin.

"Wh-What about it?" Aurora stammers.

I chance a glance at Lena, and she's smirking. After raising five boys, nothing fazes her. My smile grows as I prepare to embarrass both my mom and my sister. "I'll take care of the condoms and lube," I say, writing said items on my notebook, giving it all of my attention.

"Aspen!" Mom gasps.

I hear laughter and look up to find Lena with one hand clamped over her mouth and the other holding her stomach as her amusement shakes her entire body.

"You doing all right there, Momma Riggins?" I wink.

"I-I'm sorry," she sputters. "I just—" She shakes her head, taking a deep breath. "I was just thinking that if any of the boys were here, that's exactly what they would have said."

"I'll take that as a compliment. However, my main goal was to embarrass these two." I point over to Mom and Aurora, and both of their cheeks are rosy, making me feel as though I did my job effectively. "But in all seriousness, I'll take care of the honeymoon cabin as well."

"Are you sure?" Aurora asks. "You're already driving up early."

"Positive. It's just down the road, right?" I look to Lena for confirmation.

"Yes. Some friends of ours. It's about a mile up the road."

"Easy peasy," I tell them. "I've got this. Aurora, make me a list, and I'll text Grant as well to make sure all of his demands are also met."

"Demands?" Aurora chuckles. "It's not prison."

"No, but your future husband may have plans for you." I wag my eyebrows, and instead of blushing, she throws her head back in laughter. "I hope so." The blush comes with her words, making me laugh just as hard.

"Aurora!" Mom scolds.

"She started it." Aurora points at me with wide eyes.

Mom looks over at Lena. "I apologize for my daughters. I raised them better than this."

Lena waves her off. "You've met my sons."

"Okay, ladies. I think we have a plan. Aurora, anything else you can think of?" Mom asks.

"No." Aurora shakes her head.

"Perfect. In two weeks, you're going to have the wedding of your dreams, and you'll be Mrs. Grant Riggins." Mom's grin is infectious.

"Finally," Lena says dramatically, sitting back in her seat. "Three down and two to go."

"In a hurry to marry them off, are ya?" I ask her.

"I want more grandbabies. A house full. I also want my sons to meet the loves of their lives. I want them to know how it feels to have that one person, your soul mate, to navigate life with. I just need Conrad and Marshall to find their magic."

"The magic," I repeat her words. These Riggins sure do believe in the hype of the magic of finding love.

"Well, I need to get back to the house. Layla is supposed to be dropping Carter off for some mamaw and papaw time." The smile on Lena's face is one filled with love for her grandson.

"I want one of those," Mom tells Aurora.

"Give me time to get down the aisle, and I'll see what I can do."

What Aurora doesn't tell our mother is that she and Grant are also ready to start a family. If Grant had his way, they would already be pregnant or at least trying. Seeing the light that he brings to my sister's eyes after the hell she's been through is a welcome sight. Grant brought her back to life, and I'll forever be grateful to him for it.

After a round of hugs for Mom and Lena, I stand to go as well. "You're leaving?" Aurora asks.

"Yeah. Grant will be here soon, and I don't need to be here for all that." I pretend to gag, and she pushes at my arm.

"Stop. We're not that bad."

"I know. I'm just giving you a hard time. I need to get some laundry done, and I'm going to get a head start on packing since I'm leaving earlier than everyone else."

"Are you sure you're okay with that? Driving there and staying on that mountain all alone?"

"Rory, it's the Smoky Mountains, and there is civilization just down the road, and at the bottom of the mountain. It's not like I'm going to no man's land."

"I know, but I just worry about you."

"I'll be fine, big sister. You just worry about keeping yourself stress-free for this wedding."

"I love you, Aspen." Her voice cracks.

"I love you too. I'll see you in the morning."

"See you."

"Do you have your cell charger?" Aurora asks.

"Yes, Mom." I fight the urge to roll my eyes.

"And you have cash on hand, right?" The look on her face tells me that she's going through her mental checklist.

"Aurora, it's a three-and-a-half-hour drive. I'm not driving across the country," I remind her.

"Hush. I just worry. You're doing this for me." She shrugs like that explains her constant nagging questions she's been giving me all morning.

"I'll be fine. I'll call you when I get there. I have my phone charger, plus my phone is fully charged. I have the address in my GPS and the printed direction you gave me just in case I lose reception."

"I packed a cooler of drinks and snacks. It's already in the passenger seat of your SUV."

"Thank you." I don't remind her again that the drive is only a few hours. She's entitled to a little obsessive-compulsive tendency. She is getting married in six days.

"And my dress is hanging up in the back seat."

"I'll take good care of it."

"I know you will. Aspen, I can't thank you enough for this. Knowing that you're going to be there to handle everything is a huge stress relief for me."

"A few days in the mountains on my own isn't a hardship. I have my e-reader full of new books, and to be honest, I'm looking forward to sleeping in for a few days in a row."

"Me too," she agrees. "Okay. Drive safe. I love you and can't thank you enough."

"I will. I love you too, and when the day comes that I get married and become full of nervous energy, you can repay me the favor."

"I'm not full of nervous energy," she denies as she rubs her hands together.

Reaching out, I place my hands over hers. "Breathe, Aurora." It's then that I wonder if it's really just nervous energy. "Are you having second thoughts?"

"What? No. Never. I love him, and I can't wait to be his wife. I just—I want it all to be perfect."

"Perfect is overrated," I tell her. "Just roll with it. I promise you it's all going to turn out the way that it's supposed to. Now, I'm going to get on the road. I'll call you when I get there." We both move to step outside, and I pull my coat tight around me. I'll be taking it off as soon as I get in the car. I don't want to drive all that way feeling like a snowman.

"Love you." She wraps her arms around me in a hug.

"I love you too. I'll see you in four days."

"See you then." She steps back and allows me room to remove my coat.

I toss it into the passenger seat, climb behind the wheel, and offer her a wave before putting the SUV in Drive. I'm looking forward to a road trip where I can crank up the radio, maybe listen to an audiobook, and just enjoy some me-time. And tomorrow, this girl is sleeping in.

CHAPTER
Conrad
TWO

I T'S SATURDAY NIGHT, and I'm sitting home alone on my couch. It's balls cold outside, and I'm just not in the mood to go out. Next week is going to be a crazy one as we leave for our family's cabin in the Smoky Mountains on Wednesday for Grant and Aurora's wedding. I need to pack and do laundry, which is another reason I'm sitting home alone on a Saturday night.

I'm scrolling through the channels trying to find something to watch, with a cold beer in my hand. My phone rings, giving me a break from the mindless options. "Hey, can you tell me why I pay for a billion channels and can't find one damn thing to watch?" I ask my oldest brother, Royce.

His laughter greets me. "You need to spend more time at home, then maybe you would have a couple of shows to watch."

I grumble in reply. "What's up?" I ask, before taking a drink of my beer.

"What's your week look like?" he asks.

"It's light. I have nothing scheduled, just in case. My department is running like a well-oiled machine." Not that I need to. Royce stays on top of everything that involves Riggins Enterprises. As the CEO, that's his job, and out of the five of us, I'm glad it was him. What I'm really glad about is him meeting his wife, Sawyer. He's no longer growly Royce. Well, sometimes, but that smile on his face since he finally gave in to his feelings for Sawyer seems as though it's going to be a permanent fixture. Add in the fact that they're expecting their first baby, and his level of happiness and contentment with his life is off the charts. "Why?"

"Not sure yet. Mom called me about twenty minutes ago and said she needed some help with something. She wanted to know if you or Marsh were free to help her this week."

"Why didn't she just call us?" I ask him.

"My guess is she wanted the facts before she called either of you, so you jokers couldn't try to weasel your way out of helping."

"I'd say you're right. What's she need help with?" I might pretend that I didn't want to do whatever task she asks, but let's be honest, if my mother needs a favor from me, I'm going to make it happen. I know Marshall and the rest of my brothers feel the same way. "And why just me and Marshall?"

"She said I had to be with Sawyer, and Owen needed to be with Layla and Carter. Grant's getting married, so his head won't be on whatever task she has planned, so that leaves you and Marsh."

"Makes sense. What's Marsh got going on?"

"You were my first call."

"Don't bother calling him. I know he's been working on the new campaign that's going to launch next month. I'll call Mom and take care of whatever it is."

"You sure?"

"Yeah. I'm just sitting here scrolling through mindless TV anyway."

"Thanks, Con. I'll see you tomorrow at Sunday dinner."

"I'll be there," I assure him before ending the call and

immediately dialing my mom's number. "Hey, Mom," I greet her when she answers.

"Conrad, are you home on a Saturday night? Two weeks in a row?" she asks.

I cringe. I forgot that I stayed in last week as well. I ran into my mom at the grocery store. If I'm honest, it's been weeks since I've been out. When it was my brothers and me, it was a good time. Now they're all married off or will be — except for Marshall and me — it's just not the same. I know Marsh is feeling it too. He's been working crazy hours on this new marketing campaign. At least he has an excuse. Me? I'm just over the going out every weekend scene. I, however, won't be confessing that detail to my mother.

"It finally wore you down, huh?" Mom asks.

"What?" I shake out of my thoughts. I need to pay attention to the conversation.

"My baby boy is growing up."

"I'm a man, Momma," I remind her. "Anyway," I quickly change the subject, "Royce called and said you needed help with something."

"I do. Are you my volunteer?"

"Yep." I take another swig of my beer.

"Thank you. I feel so much better."

"What am I doing exactly?" I ask skeptically. She's way too happy for me to just be doing her a favor.

"Well, I need you to drive up to the cabin early. Just to make sure everything gets done."

"Okay, but I thought Aspen was driving up early?"

"Oh, she is. She's leaving tomorrow."

"All right, so what, you want me to go up Tuesday?" I ask, knowing that all of us are supposed to drive up on Wednesday. Taking off a day early won't be an issue.

"Well, I was hoping you could drive up tomorrow."

"Tomorrow? Why?"

"Well, I worry about Aspen staying up in that cabin all alone. And what if she needs help? No one will be there to support her."

"Mom, Aspen is an adult. I'm sure she can figure it out."

"Conrad Riggins." My name rolls off her tongue in her "mom" voice, and I know I'm going to be leaving for the mountains tomorrow.

"I guess I need to get off here and start packing."

"Thank you, son." The relief in her voice is palpable, which tells me she really was worried about Aspen staying at the cabin all alone. To be honest, her staying there alone is probably not the best idea, and spending time with the youngest Steele sister won't be the worst thing. She's sexy as hell, and she's fun to be around.

"Both of those girls are family," Mom adds.

"Is there anything specific that I need to do while I'm there?" I ask as I stand to toss my empty beer bottle in the trash and swap out the laundry.

"No. Just be there to help her. She's coordinating the schedule of the decorators and caterers, and while I don't think there will be much to do, I'd feel better knowing she's not staying in that big old cabin by herself all week."

"Sure, thing. I'll call Royce and let him know."

"Thank you, Conrad. Stop by the house, and I'll pack you up some snacks for the road. In fact, just come here for breakfast. I'm sure you'll want to get an early start."

"So no Sunday dinner?" I sound like a whiney child, even to my own ears. I love Sunday dinners with the family and getting time with my nephew, Carter. I also enjoy getting my brothers riled up with pretending to hit on their wives. Good times I tell you.

"I'll be sure to make it worth your while," she assures me.

"All right, I'll see you in the morning."

"Love you, Con."

"Love you too, Mom." I end the call and call my brother back. "Royce," I say when he answers.

"What did she rope you into?"

"Well, she wants me to leave for the cabin early. She's worried about Aspen being up there all alone."

"Hmm, not a bad plan, really. I'm sure that will make Aurora feel better to know you're going to be there too."

"She wants me to leave tomorrow since that's when Aspen is leaving."

"Anything I need to handle for you this week at the office?"

"Nah, I had an easy week. I'll take my laptop and can work remotely if needed. I'll be able to keep up on emails and anything else that arises from the cabin." Now that I think about it, this is going to be nice. A few days away from the office sounds like just what the doctor ordered.

"All right, brother. I guess I'll see you later this week."

"See you then." I end the call, and even though I want another beer, I pass instead and detour to my bedroom to start packing.

"I'll be sure to bring your suit," Mom tells me. "Oh, and here." She hands me a cooler.

"What's this?"

"Snacks for the trip as promised. There's another one in the back seat. I had Dad load it when you got here."

"How did I miss that?" I ask with a shake of my head. This woman never ceases to amaze me.

"I have my ways. If there is anything you forgot, just call me, and I'll make sure to bring it with us on Wednesday."

"I think I'm good but will let you know." I pull her into a hug and kiss her cheek. "See you in a few days." With a handshake for Dad and another hug from Mom, I'm pulling out of their driveway for my impromptu road trip.

The sky is gray, and from the looks of it, it could bring a winter storm. I'm kicking myself in the ass for not driving my truck. The weather wasn't even a factor, and it should have been.

"Perfect. Here comes the snow," I murmur to myself a little more than three hours into the trip. Huge flakes are falling from the sky, and from the temperatures and the size, I know it's going to stick. I just hope I can make it to the cabin before the roads are too treacherous to drive on.

"Damn." In a matter of minutes, I've driven into an all-out snowstorm. Both hands grip the wheel so tightly my knuckles are white. Reaching over, I turn down the radio and can't help but laugh. My mom used to do the same thing when I was a kid like it was going to make her a better driver or something. We would always give her a hard time, and here I am acting just like her. I don't want the music to be a distraction. I need to stay focused on the road. I also keep my eyes peeled for Aspen's SUV. I'm not sure what time she was leaving. I hope she missed this or at least caught the tail end of it before arriving at the cabin.

"Maybe I should call her," I say to myself as I go to reach for my phone. My car spins, and in my haste to put both hands back on the wheel, I drop my phone. Thankfully, I have Bluetooth. I hit the button on my steering wheel, and it pops up on my screen that there's no phone connected. Damn it. My phone battery has been draining quickly, and I've been turning off my Bluetooth to save battery life. I didn't even realize it wasn't connected when I started out earlier.

The snow is falling so hard I can hardly see the road, and I'm worried that if I pull off, I won't be getting back on the interstate. The GPS on the dash says I'm about thirty minutes away from the cabin. I can't really tell from this whiteout I'm driving through. I just hope Aspen is there and she's safe.

Thirty minutes turns into an hour, but I'm finally pulling into the driveway of my family's cabin. Aspen's silver SUV is parked in the drive. Her window is covered in snow, and there are no tire tracks, which tells me that she's been here for a while. I feel my shoulders ease from the knowledge and the fact that my drive is over. We are definitely hunkering down for the evening.

Pulling the hood of my sweatshirt up to ward off the cold, I climb out and feel around on the floorboard for my cell phone. I find it wedged up under the seat. Slamming the door, I start to head to the front porch when I remember Mom saying she packed extra snacks. I don't know how prepared Aspen is, but we're definitely not going back out in this mess tonight. Retracing my steps, I grab my suitcase, as well as my laptop bag. I'll have to make a second trip for the cooler. It's just one suitcase, but this cooler is a full-size cooler, and it's heavy as hell. It's hard to tell what Mom has sent with me. One thing's for sure; I know it's going to be good, and I'm starving. The small bag of snacks she sent disappeared an hour into the trip.

Arms loaded down, I make my way up the steps of the porch and manage to open the door without setting anything down. My feet haven't even passed the threshold when a blood-curdling scream pierces my ears. I stand frozen, letting the cold air and snow seep into the heated cabin. My legs are frozen in place, but it has nothing to do with the cold.

It's her.

Aspen Steele.

She's standing in the living room in nothing but a small white towel wrapped around her body. Her hair is hanging in wet tendrils down her face, and she's shivering. That's what kicks me into gear as I tear my eyes away from her creamy skin.

"Aspen, it's me. Conrad."

"C-Co-Con," she sputters out through her shivers.

"What's going on?" I drop my bags and slam the door closed. In a few long strides, I'm standing in front of her. The smell of lavender washes over me, and my dick takes notice. He and I are on the same page. How could we not? She's a goddess, an almost naked, standing in front of me, soaking wet and freezing goddess.

"The heat is out, so I took a hot shower to warm up. I didn't realize that the hot water would be out too. The water was warm, and then it wasn't."

"Shit. Where are your clothes?"

"In my car. I w-was so c-cold I forgot that I hadn't brought in both of my bags yet. Just my toiletries."

Reaching around her, I pull the thick blanket from the back of the couch and wrap it around her. She's still shivering, so I do the only other thing I can think of at the moment to warm her up. I tear off my sweatshirt and T-shirt all in one go, open the blanket, and pull her into my arms.

CHAPTER

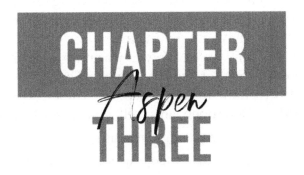

Aspen

THREE

CONRAD WRAPS HIS arms around me, and I melt into him. My teeth are still chattering, but I'm still able to release a sigh as the warmth of his bare chest and the blanket surround me. His hands are roaming over my back. I know he's just trying to help me, and he is, but he's not just warming me from the cold. He's turning me on. Conrad Riggins has been hiding a perfect six-pack under all those suits he wears, and even on the verge of hypothermia, I can appreciate how damn sexy he is.

"Better?" he asks when my body stops shaking.

I don't want to say yes, because I'm not ready for him to pull away. It's been way too long since a man has held me in his arms, even if it's for survival purposes. "Yes," I eventually say. I go to pull away, but he tightens his hold on me.

"Let's go have a seat." He manages to lead us to the couch, where he sits and pulls me into his lap, wrapping the blanket around both of us. "Tell me what happened."

"By the time I reached town, the snow was falling hard. When I got here, I had to use the restroom, so I grabbed one small bag, my phone, and purse and made my way inside. The cabin was freezing, still is freezing." I shiver. "Anyway, I couldn't get the thermostat to work. So I thought I would make a fire, then call Aurora and Grant to see what I was doing wrong. All the firewood is covered in snow. I went outside to grab some anyway to bring it in and thaw out. By the time I was done, I was frozen to the bone. The only way I knew to warm up was a hot shower. The hot water ran out not long after I got in. So, I got out and came in search of my phone to call someone to come and help. That's when I heard the door open, and well, you know the rest."

"Shit," he mumbles as he tightens his grip.

"What?" I try to sit up to look at him, but his hold on me is strong. I don't fight him and keep my head resting on his shoulder.

"The thermostat isn't broken. It's locked."

"Seriously?" I ask. "Why in the hell is it locked?"

"That's my fault. Do you remember when me and my brothers came up here for the weekend back in September to go fishing?"

"Yeah. Aurora had to practically force Grant to go."

"So did Sawyer and Layla." He chuckles. "Anyway, it was cooler weather outside because of the wind, so we had to bundle up—nothing we're not used to. When we got back to the cabin, we had a few beers, and Marshall was whining that he was hot. He still had on all of his layers and a few beers in him. He kept trying to mess with the thermostat to turn on the air, which me and the others agreed that we did not need, so I locked it."

"You locked it?" This time when I try to sit up, he lets me. He has an apologetic frown on his face. "How did you lock it?"

"IT guy, remember?" He shrugs.

"So, it's not broken?"

"No." He reaches into his pocket and pulls out his phone. He holds the screen so that I can watch him. He taps a thermostat icon and turns up the heat. The furnace immediately kicks on. "We have it, so we can program it from anywhere. We do that so that we can maintain the temperature before we come up, and keep it high enough in the winter that the pipes don't freeze, and also not cost us a fortune to heat it when there is no one staying here."

"No one thought to turn it up since I was driving up early?"

"I'm sorry."

"And the water heater?"

"Just a freak coincidence. I'll take a look. I don't know that we've ever replaced it. I'll call Dad to verify. My guess is that it's just broken and we'll need to get someone here to install a new one. I didn't bring my truck, or I could go pick one up and install it myself."

"You know how to do that?"

"Yes." His eyes are locked on mine as he lifts his hand and palms my cheek. "I'm so sorry, Aspen. I hate the thought of you here alone and freezing."

"Speaking of alone, what are you doing here?"

"Mom wanted me to be here in case you needed help with anything. Well, not me specifically. Me or Marshall since she knew getting the others away from their wives would be impossible."

"You drew the short stick?" I hate the thought of Conrad or Marshall, either one feeling as though they need to be here to babysit me. Despite the situation he walked in on, I am perfectly capable of taking care of myself.

"No. I volunteered." Something passes in his eyes, something I can't name, but it makes my insides all gooey and me very aware I'm still sitting on his lap in nothing but a towel with wet hair, and he's shirtless with his tattoos that he keeps hidden behind those button-up shirts on display.

"I should, um, go get dressed."

"Yeah. Let me go grab your bags. Where are your keys?"

"On the table by the door." Pulling the cover away, I stand from his lap and instantly miss the heat of his body against mine. The room is warmer, but there's still a chill in the air. I step back and watch as Conrad stands and slips back into his T-shirt and sweatshirt before grabbing my keys and stepping outside.

I can't believe he saw me like this. Grabbing the blanket, I wrap myself back up in it so when he comes in with my bag, I'll at least have all my skin covered, that is unless he's a foot man, and I seriously doubt it.

I've barely got the blanket around me when the door pushes open, bringing Conrad, some snow, the cold air, and my bags. "It's really coming down out there. My tracks are already covered."

"I didn't think it was supposed to snow," I say lamely. Have I really resorted to talking to the sexy man in front of me about the weather? Pathetic.

"You know how it is this time of year. The weather is unpredictable. Which room are you staying in?" he asks.

"Oh, end of the hall, last door on the right."

He grins. "I guess that means I finally got one of the Steele sisters into my bed." He winks, and I almost choke at his words.

"That's your room?" I try to think back to when we stayed here over the Fourth of July weekend, and that's the room my parents stayed in.

"Yep," he says, popping the *p*. The grin on his face grows wider.

"I-I can switch."

"Nah, I like the thought of you sleeping in my bed." His eyes roam over my body, and even though I'm covered with the blanket, I feel as if he can see right through it.

"You sure?"

"Positive. I'll take this upstairs for you."

"Thanks, Conrad." He nods and walks around me to go upstairs. I follow after him, admiring the view of his ass in those jeans on the way up. I'm so distracted that I trip on the last step. I let out a screech, dropping the blanket and preparing myself for the impact that never comes. At least not with the floor. No, strong arms wrap around my naked body. Naked body! I dropped the towel when I dropped the blanket. His hands grip my bare waist.

"You all right?" His voice is husky, his grip tight.

"Y-Yes. I'm so sorry." I pull away, and he lets me as I scramble to gather the blanket and haphazardly wrap it around me. My knees quiver as I take my bag from his hands, and move past him to my room, correction, his room, to get dressed.

As soon as the door is closed, I lean my back against it, closing my eyes and taking a deep breath. My heart is racing like I just ran a marathon, or how I imagine it would feel to run a marathon. I'm not a runner. I pull in deep, even breaths to try to regulate my breathing. I need to get a grip. Conrad is just a man. He's going to be my sister's brother-in-law. So what if he saw me naked. It's not like it's something he's not seen before.

Spying my bags on the bed, I move and pull out my clothes, quickly getting dressed. Once I've slid on some leggings and a sweatshirt, I sit to tug on my socks. That's when I remember what he said—that he likes the thought of me sleeping in his bed. I would have chalked the statement up to teasing that the Riggins brothers are notorious for, but the look in his eyes and the huskiness of his voice tells me he wasn't teasing.

Standing from the bed, my shoulders back, I open the door and make my way back downstairs. Conrad has a fire roaring in the fireplace, and the room is warm and cozy, a stark contrast to how it was when I got here earlier today.

"Hey," he says when he sees me. "I called a local plumber. They're supposed to be here tomorrow, weather permitting, to replace the water heater. In the meantime, we can just warm up water on the stove and use the tub in one of the bedrooms down here, so we don't have to carry the water upstairs."

"Sounds like a plan. Thanks for the fire. It's nice."

"Come here." He holds his hand out for me, and I don't know what to expect, but it doesn't stop me from walking to him and placing my hand in his. "Let me show you this." He moves to the left side of the fireplace and pulls on the bookcase. It opens, and behind it is a small room filled with dry firewood.

"That would have been good to know."

"Yeah, sorry. You should have been better prepared for the visit. That has to be why Mom wanted someone here with you. Anyway, she didn't want the wood in the house since it's messy, so Dad made this room to cover it up. You can access it from the outside as well."

"Any other secrets I should know about?" I ask. I'm not upset, just frustrated Conrad had to save me, and more than once in the short amount of time that he's been here.

"No secrets, but Mom sent me with a ton of food. It's actually still out in my car. I wanted to get the fire going before I went out to get it."

"That was a good call on her part. With this weather, going to the store to stock up isn't going to happen. Not tonight."

"Agreed. I'll be right back." He gives my hand a gentle squeeze before letting go.

I watch him as he slips into a coat he wasn't wearing when he got here. He disappears outside, and I watch him go. When the door closes, I jolt out of my Conrad fog and go to the kitchen to see what our options are. There are some canned foods, but other than that, it's slim pickings. Thankfully, Lena Riggins was prepared, like I should have been.

Lesson learned.

CHAPTER

Conrad

FOUR

T HE COLD SNOW pelts my face, but I welcome the sting. I need
something to smack my ass out of this Aspen fog I've suddenly
found myself in. I've always thought she was beautiful. Both of
the Steele sisters are lookers. I've been around her multiple times,
but I've never had this reaction to her. You know, the "toss her
over my shoulder, take her to my room, and bury myself inside of
her until we can't figure out where she ends and I begin" one.

I'm in trouble.

Grant will hand my ass to me if I do something to upset her,
but the heat in her eyes isn't helping me stay away from her. And
her skin... her skin is so fucking soft, and she smells like heaven.
Fuck, I need to stop this.

Making it to the car, I jerk open the back door and grab the
cooler that Mom packed for the trip. I wouldn't put it past her to
have known about the weather. She's always prepared for any
and all situations. She claims to have learned that raising five
rowdy boys. Did she know we would get snowed in? She had no

way of knowing that the water heater would go out and that the beautiful Aspen would greet me in nothing but a towel. A very tiny white towel that barely covered her. She also had no way of knowing she would trip on the stairs and fall naked into my arms. Fuck, I can still feel her skin beneath the palm of my hands.

Silky.

Smooth.

Sexy.

How am I supposed to forget seeing her like that? I'll tell you how. I'm not. I can't. It's not possible. The memory of her soft naked body in my arms will forever be burned into my brain. Basically, I'm fucked.

Closing the car door, I make my way through the snow back to the cabin. "Aspen," I call out when I enter.

"In the kitchen," she calls back.

"I don't know what she put in here, but it's heavy," I tell her, hefting the cooler up on the counter.

"We're stocked." She opens the door to the industrial refrigerator Mom insisted on since she was feeding a small army.

"Mom must have arranged that. I wonder what's in here?" I point to the cooler before opening the lid.

"What did she send?" Aspen bounces over to stand next to me, standing on her tiptoes to peer into the cooler.

Inside there are a few containers. I pull the first one out and see that it's two pieces of chocolate cake. "She knows this is my favorite."

"I see Grant's not the only Riggins brother with a sweet tooth," Aspen teases.

"We all have one but Grant's on another level. Just another reason Aurora is perfect for him," I tell her, reaching into the cooler for another container.

"What's that?" Aspen asks.

Pulling off the lid, I see a pan of baked spaghetti. "Mom's baked spaghetti."

"Oh, God," Aspen moans, and the sound has my cock twitching in my pants. "I love your mom's baked spaghetti."

"My guess is that there's garlic bread in the other container. And this." I pull out a smaller lunch box that feels as though it weighs a ton. Reaching inside, I pull out two rolls of cookie dough.

"That explains all of the sprinkles and frosting in the cabinets," Aspen muses. "Why didn't she just add the cookie dough to the grocery delivery?"

"These are homemade."

"Really?"

"Yep. Mom's famous sugar cookies. To buy them store-bought is a crime in our house," I tell her. "This was my great-grandma's recipe."

"Wait! Are these the sugar cookies she had at Christmas?"

"That would be them."

"We have to make these. Forget the spaghetti." She reaches for the container of cookie dough, but I hold it over her head.

"Now, now, you know you have to eat all of your dinner before dessert."

Her hazel eyes fill with heat as they roam over my body. "Right." She coughs. "Dinner. I'll grab some plates, and we can heat this up." She's quick to step away and start rummaging through the cabinets, pulling out two plates. In the drawer next to the stove, she finds a spoon for dipping and a couple of forks.

"Here." I hand her the first plate when it comes out of the microwave.

"Thanks, I'm starving. I don't really know how. I had all kinds of snacks on the way here."

"Snacks don't really fill you up, though. They satisfy the hunger, but you never really feel full. At least I don't."

"Facts! And it's the same way at the bakery. I can graze on our treats all day, and I'm still starving by the time we close up shop." She takes a hefty bite of her spaghetti, and my eyes are trained on her lips as they close around the fork.

It's erotic, watching her eat. I've never thought that in my entire life. I don't even know why I'm thinking it now, but it's true. Her lips sliding across the stainless steel utensil has me wishing it was something else in her mouth — something of mine. The beeping of the microwave pulls me out of my dirty thoughts.

"So, what's on the agenda? What do we need to do while we're here?" I ask. I'm trying to get us on an even playing ground, and I need to stop thinking about her in any way other than my brother's future sister-in-law. She's always just been Aspen before now. Gorgeous, fun, friendly Aspen. Today, she's more than that. She's all smooth skin and luscious lips.

Fuck. Stop. Thinking. About. Her.

"Nothing major," she replies. She's completely unaware of my thoughts and what sitting here with her like this is doing to me. "The caterers are supposed to deliver supplies on Tuesday and will be back on Saturday for the wedding to set up. There's a decorating crew that's supposed to do the same. I think Aurora just wanted me here, just in case, you know? She's worried something is going to go wrong."

"Grant won't let that happen. Trust me. It won't matter what he has to do. He's going to make sure that this wedding is exactly what she wants it to be."

"What about him?"

I shrug. "Like my brothers who've taken the leap before him, he just wants her to be happy. It's not where, when, or how they get married. It's that they get married. He wants her to be his wife, change her last name, and make babies."

"What about you? Is that what you want?"

"Yeah, I mean, isn't that the goal?"

"I don't know. You don't seem too eager to settle down."

"It's not that I don't want to settle down. It's that I've yet to meet someone I want to settle with. Every day of forever is a long-ass time. I want to know that the woman I choose is just as invested as I am."

"You don't think you've met her?"

"No. Everyone I meet knows who we are. They know I'm a Riggins, and they see dollar signs. My brothers have been lucky enough to find women who love them for who they are. Sawyer, Layla, and Aurora don't give a fuck about our money. They just want them. That's what I'm waiting for."

"And when you find her?"

"I'm never going to let go." Settling down isn't at the top of my list of priorities, but I will admit watching my three older brothers, and seeing how happy they are, does appeal to me. As I venture into the later side of my twenties, the random nights out aren't as fun as they used to be. I guess that means I'm getting old.

"Wow," she breathes.

"What?"

She shakes her head. "I just wasn't expecting that kind of reply from you. I guess I've never seen you this serious."

"I can be serious when I need to be. I take my job seriously, and I take my position as a son, brother, brother-in-law, and uncle very seriously."

"Still competing for that favorite uncle title?" She chuckles.

"Yep. I was at the top of the leader board until last weekend when Grant and Aurora brought Carter cookies." My confession makes her laugh. Not just any laugh. This one is from somewhere deep inside her. Her head is thrown back, and the sound of pure glee surrounds us. It's intoxicating.

So is she.

The conversation is easy as we finish our meal. "Ready to make cookies?" I ask as she pushes her empty plate away from her.

"Yes, but no. I'm stuffed. I ate so much. I don't think I can move," she groans, placing her hands over her toned flat belly. I know this because of the towel incident at the top of the stairs that's still burned in my brain. It's a moment I will never in my life forget.

"Okay, no cookies," I concede. "How about a movie?" I stand to gather our plates and place them in the dishwasher.

"Perfect. Now, if you could just carry me to wherever this event is happening, that would be great."

Visions of the two of us lying naked in my bed, watching TV, flashes through my mind. It's so clear it almost brings me to my knees. "I can arrange that." I stand and lift her into my arms bridal style. She yelps out in surprise but doesn't hesitate to link her arms around my neck and hold on. Her scent, that same lavender from earlier, assaults me. "Where to?" My voice is thick.

"Um, what are our options?"

"Basement, theater, living room, or either of our bedrooms. All four have TVs."

"Y-You decide," she replies, almost breathless.

I head toward the stairs, but I make a quick right to the basement instead. If I take her to either of our rooms, I know she will be impossible for me to resist. So, basement theater it is. There are recliners down there and a huge couch, with a chaise lounge big enough for me and all four of my brothers. That's the perfect spot for the two of us to snuggle. *Snuggle?* I'm losing my damn mind. I don't snuggle.

The grip she has around my neck tightens as we descend the stairs into the basement. I manage to turn on the lights with my elbow before carrying her to the chaise lounge and gently setting her down. I miss the feel of her in my arms instantly, and that is not something that's ever happened to me before.

Walking over to a big trunk, I pull out a soft blanket and toss it to her. She smiles and wastes no time snuggling underneath it. Grabbing the remote for the projection screen, I power it on and kill the lights, bathing the room in darkness, nothing but the glow of the screen to light my path back to her.

I don't ask her if it's okay if I sit next to her. I don't ask her if it's okay if we share a blanket. Instead, I take the seat and pull the covers over me. "What do you want to watch?" I pull up the streaming app and begin to scroll through the options.

"Oh, I'll have to watch that one when you're asleep," she says when I land on a chick flick.

"Why not watch it now?"

"It's a romance." She says it like I'm crazy for even suggesting it.

"And? Am I not allowed to enjoy a good romance?"

"Do you?"

"My mom loved these movies. It didn't matter that there were six males living in the house with her. We watched them with her. As long as it's got a good plot, I'm all in."

"Really?" Her eyes light up. "I've been dying to watch it, but I've been pulling extra time training the new staff and helping Rory with the wedding planning."

"Well, tonight is your lucky night." I hit Play for the movie, tossing the remote beside me on the lounge, and without a thought, I put my arm around her shoulders and pull her close to me.

"What's this?" she asks, resting her hand against my chest.

"Shh, the movie's starting." I avoid her question because I don't know the answer. All I know is that she's close, and she needs to be in my arms. I can't give her or myself any other explanation than that.

CHAPTER
Aspen
FIVE

I DON'T KNOW what's going on. His arm is around me, and my head is resting against his chest. A movie I've been dying to watch is playing on the massive projection screen, and all I can focus on is how good he smells and how warm he is. I snuggle a little closer, and his grip tightens on my shoulder.

It's been too long since I've been held like this. Not since moving to Nashville. To be honest, watching what Aurora went through with her ex had me running scared from relationships. I've been on a few dates, but nothing serious or long term. More of dinner, maybe some dancing, and then we go our separate ways.

When the Riggins brothers waltzed into our lives, I knew the minute I saw Grant and Aurora together that they were meant to be. Instant attraction, and the way they look at each other, talk about couple goals. They have what I want someday. However, I've yet to find a man who holds my attention for longer than an evening out.

As for tonight, Conrad Riggins has my full attention. I know I should pull away, but what's the harm in a little snuggling while we watch a movie? It's not like there are any witnesses to this one small indiscretion.

So, instead of doing what I know that I should, I remain where I am, with my cheek pressed to his chest, soaking up his warmth. I'm more comfortable than I have been in I don't know how long. I don't know if it's this massive couch that I'm sure was crazy expensive or if it's the man. My last thought before drifting off to sleep is that it's both.

Definitely both.

My bladder is screaming to be emptied, but I'm warm. So damn warm and comfortable that I don't want to move, but my bladder demands attention. Forcing my eyes open, I blink a few times taking in my surroundings, and that's when I remember where I am. I'm at the Riggins's family cabin with Conrad. Conrad, the fourth Riggins brother, and the man who has his arms wrapped tight around me, breathing softly against my neck.

Conrad Riggins.

I don't want to lose this moment, the feeling of his arms wrapped around me, but I need to pee, or I'm going to embarrass myself. Reluctantly and as careful as I can, I slide out from underneath his hold and tiptoe to the bathroom. After taking care of business and washing my hands, I crave the warmth of his arms. I know I shouldn't, but it is what it is. Softly, I walk back to the couch to see if he's still sleeping.

"Come back to bed," he says groggily.

"We're not in a bed." I try to talk to the half-sleeping Adonis of a man. I take a step closer to get a better look at him.

"Then come back to me."

My movement halts. Is he asleep? Does he know what he's saying? Who he's talking to? "Aspen?" I jump when he says my name. My eyes find his that are now half-open. "Come back to me," he says. His voice is deep from sleep, but there is a sincerity there I can't ignore. His words tug at the strings of my heart. With a nod, I take my place next to him on the chaise lounge. He lifts the covers over us and pulls me back into his arms. My body is stiff. I can't seem to relax. My mind is racing. What does this mean? Does it even mean anything? Maybe he's just tired and doesn't want to worry about me roaming around the cabin on my own? I can't seem to shut it all out, that is until I hear him release a heavy sigh, and his body molds around mine. Oddly enough, it relaxes me too. So much so that I drift off to sleep in his warm embrace.

"I can feel you staring at me, creeper." I keep my eyes closed, not wanting to see his as he watches me. I can only imagine what he's thinking. I know what I look like first thing in the morning with my hair all a mess. He's seeing me in all my glory—sleep lines, messy hair, no makeup, all of it.

"You're cute when you sleep."

His words have me peeling one eye open to look at him. "Did aliens abduct you while we slept?" I'm teasing, my tone light, but this isn't the teasing flirting Conrad I'm used to. This is a serious, soft, and sweet Conrad. Forcing the other eye to open, I take him in. His hair is mussed, and he, too, has sleep lines on his face.

"No." He smiles, reaching out and tucking a loose strand of hair behind my ear. "No aliens, but I didn't peg you for a runner?"

"Me? I'm not."

"Then why did I have to coax you back to bed last night."

"This isn't a bed." It's the best I've got. I can't tell him that I wanted to be next to him, to feel his body wrapped around mine. That would have us crossing lines that we shouldn't cross. Sure, it wouldn't be the end of the world, but I am not doing a single thing to mess with my sister's wedding. I think she would be happy for me, for us, but it's not worth the risk. Maybe one day…. What am I saying? No. I'm letting one night and a naked incident cloud my mind. It was just a thing. Two adults falling asleep on the couch. So we cuddled? Big deal.

"Well, it was warm with you lying there with me."

"I didn't peg you for a cuddler," I counter before I can think better of it.

"I'm not." He gives me a dazzling smile that I'm sure has hearts breaking and panties dropping all over Tennessee.

"Come on, lazybones. I've been waiting for you to wake up for almost an hour. Let's go make some breakfast." He tosses off the covers and climbs to his feet. Reaching out, he offers me his hand and pulls me to mine as well.

"Are you making breakfast?" I ask him.

"Yep."

"Huh," I say, following him up the stairs.

"Huh? What do you mean, huh? I know how to cook. I'm damn good at it if I do say so myself."

"Your momma raised you right."

"She did. I remember growing up she used to tell us that our future wives would thank her one day."

"Smart woman, that Lena Riggins." I smile as I perch my behind on a stool at the kitchen island. "So, fancy pants, what are we having?"

He opens the fridge and peruses his options. "How about scrambled eggs and bacon, with some toast?"

"Perfect. What can I do to help?"

"Nothing. Just keep me company."

"I'll start the coffee." I slide off the stool and get busy starting the coffee pot. When I go to fill the pot with water, I look outside and gasp. "Oh my gosh. Did you see how much snow is out there?" I ask, staring out the window at the blanket of white that's covering the ground.

I feel his body as he slides up behind me and looks over my head out the window. "No," his deep voice says next to my ear. "That's a lot, and it's still coming down. Good thing Mom thought ahead and ordered supplies to be delivered."

"How did she do that anyway?" I ask, hitting Start on the coffee pot.

"She has a service company she uses. They take care of maintaining the place when we're not here. We used to come up a lot as kids, not so much now that all five of us kids are working at the company. Adult life keeps us from having as much downtime."

"That's good that you have someone who helps maintain it. It's not so good that you don't get to spend as much time here. I love this place."

"Yeah, me too," he says wistfully. "All right." He claps his hands. "Sit back and watch the master at work."

I do as he says, taking my seat at the island, and watch as he prepares us breakfast. "Is this snow going to affect the wedding?"

"I don't know. I don't think they were calling for this much snow. I'm surprised we haven't heard from anyone at home asking about it." He turns off the stove and plates our food. "We have a company we use to clear the drive, but we can't call them until it stops snowing. Removing the snow now won't do a bit of good with it still coming down like it is." He places a plate of scrambled eggs, toast, and bacon in front of me. "Eat up, and we'll get some warm clothes on and go check it out."

Not needing to be told twice, I dive into my food, Conrad doing the same as we clear our plates. "I don't know if I brought warm enough clothes for all of that." I point out the kitchen window after I finish washing the dishes. It was only fair since he cooked. Besides, he stood next to me the entire time and dried as I washed.

"Mom has this place stocked for the winter. Come on. I'm sure we can find something that will fit you." He grabs my hand and pulls me to a room off the back of the kitchen. There he opens a door that leads to a huge closet that's more like a bedroom than a closet. The walls are lined with shoe racks and closet organizers. "Told you." He chuckles. "Mom likes to be prepared. We have winter gear on this wall and summer gear on this one." He points at each wall as he tells me what they hold.

"Your mom is a superhero. I want to be like her when I grow up." My words cause his chuckle to turn into all-out laughter.

"Come on, crazy girl. Let's find you something to wear." We

shuffle through the winter racks, and within fifteen minutes, I'm in snow pants, a jacket that makes me feel like the abominable snowman, and snow boots that fit like a glove.

"Now, we need a scarf and some gloves. What about a hat? Are you good with the one on the coat?" he asks.

"Yes. This should be fine. I'm actually burning up. Can you get with the program?" I tease.

"Hush it, woman. I'm making sure you don't freeze to death."

"We're just going to check out the snow."

"Oh, no, we're doing more than that. It's been too damn long since I've had a snow day with snow like this. We're making the best of it."

"I'm afraid to ask what that means." He grins at my comment and winks. "Get dressed," I tell him. What I don't say is that I'm excited to spend the day with him frolicking in the snow. It's been ages. I was a kid the last time I've done anything like this.

Ten minutes later, we're on the front porch looking at all the snow. It's still falling hard, and I send up a silent prayer that this doesn't stop my sister's wedding.

"What are you waiting for?" Conrad asks.

I pull my attention to him, and he's now standing at the bottom of the porch, his deep footprints in the snow that comes to his knees. "How tall are you?"

He tilts his head to the side. "Six three."

"I'm five-three."

"Okay?"

"I'm a foot shorter than you, and the snow is to your knees. I can't walk in that. And how did this happen? How did the weatherman not know this was coming? Aurora is going to freak the hell out when she finds out about this."

"I think you're doing enough of that for the both of you. It's Mother Nature, Aspen. It happens. I promise you this won't stop the wedding. As long as it stops," he adds. "And as far as the snow, you'll be fine, and I'll be right here with you. I'll go grab the shovel and make a path for you, but we are going in that." He points to the side of the cabin. "And we are going to build a snowman. Hell, we might even build an igloo with all of this snow. My brothers and I did that plenty of times growing up." His eyes light up with happiness at the memory.

"Yeah, Aurora and I did too. It's been years since we've had this much snow."

"And we're making the best of what we are given. We can't do anything else, not until the snow stops, so we might as well have fun and enjoy it." He points to me. "You stay there. I'm going to grab the shovel."

I watch him walk away, and even bundled up, he's easy on the eyes. Maybe a day in the snow to distract me is exactly what I need. I can't be fantasizing about him if my entire body is too frozen to function.

CHAPTER
Conrad
SIX

WHEN I WAS growing up, Dad used to tell us that the heat was in the tools. We would gripe and complain about shoveling the sidewalks when, in reality, we were thrilled to be outside in the snow. As an adult, I get it. He was telling us if we move, we'd stay warm. However, what dear old Dad forgot to mention is that the gaze of a beautiful woman also brings the heat and lust, desire, want, and need. I could go on, but I'm trying like hell not to think about it. Not to think about her, even though I can feel her watching my every move.

I don't get it. I've known Aspen for a while now. She's been to countless Sunday dinners with my family, and we've hung out a fair amount of times. Our siblings are getting married; that's to be expected. I've never had this kind of reaction to her before. Sure, I've always thought she was beautiful; so is her sister. So are Sawyer and Layla, for that matter. My brothers have chosen well for their wives, and they're all three lucky bastards. I just wish I could understand why now? Is it because it's only the two of us? I don't think that's it.

Whatever it is, it's pushing me to my limits. I crave to have my hands on her.

"You need some help?" Aspen asks when I glance up at her.

"As a matter of fact, I do. You and I are going to build a snowman." Her eyes light up, and it does something to me. It's like my heart misses a beat or something, but that doesn't make sense. Right? I don't understand what's happening here, but I know that I want more time with her. I know that I'm going to give my mother the biggest fucking hug on earth for sending me here early. Did she know? No, how could she have known?

"Hey." I feel her hand on my arm. I can literally feel the heat through her gloves and my layers of clothing. "You okay?"

"Fine. Just thinking about our next move." *My* next move is more like it, but I'm not going to tell her that. I just want to enjoy spending time with her, and we'll see where it goes. I still have her all to myself today and tomorrow. Surely, whatever this attraction is will be settled by then.

"I think I was like twelve the last time I built a snowman," she states as she smiles up at me.

"Yeah? Well, today we're breaking that streak." Grabbing the snow shovel with one hand, I capture hers with the other and lead her to the side of the house. "Okay, I'm going to shovel a circle for you so that you won't get lost in the snow."

"Hey!" She smacks at my arm. "Is that a short joke?" From the expression on her face, she's trying to act as if she's offended, but I can see the hint of a smile tilting her lips.

"Nope. You're the one who said it would bury you."

"Not exactly, but thank you. You're my hero." She bats her long eyelashes, and I want nothing more than to bend my head and press my lips to hers. Instead, I grip the shovel and get to work, making her an area that she can walk comfortably.

Fifteen minutes later, I'm sweating despite the cold temperatures, but Aspen is smiling, and when she wraps her arms around me in a hug as a thank-you, I don't hesitate to hug her back. I'll take anything and everything she's willing to give me. I'm also not going to try and decipher why that is.

"Yay! I'm so excited. Let's get started." She wastes no time getting to work on our snowman. Tossing the shovel to the side, I join her in her efforts.

I'm placing the final piece of our snowman, the head on top of his layers of body, when I feel something hit my back. The giggle that follows has me turning to see Aspen with a snowball in her hands, ready to fire.

"Oops." She shrugs.

"Oops? Did that snowball just fall out of your hands?" I ask. Bending down, I grab my own pile of snow and pack it tight in my hands, forming a perfect ball. "Is that how you're going to play it?" I toss the ball up gently and smirk.

"It was an accident." She takes a step back.

"Why don't I believe you?" I take a step forward. Raising my arm, I aim and fire. The snowball hits her right in the chest. She stands still, looks down at the snow on her coat, then fires one back. Back and forth, we throw handfuls of snow at one another. I chase her around the snowman, and although she's fast, I'm faster. Snaking my arm around her waist, I swing her around and fall back into the snow, with her landing on top of me.

We're both laughing and breathing heavily. Reaching up, I move her hair out of her eyes. "Hey." I smile up at her. She moves to sit up, which has her sitting on my hard cock. Even through our layers, I know she can feel it. I open my mouth to say something smooth, but I can't for the life of me think of anything. Me, Conrad Riggins, can't find the words to say to a beautiful woman who's straddling his lap. I open my mouth to try again but don't get the chance because Aspen does it for me, smashing a handful of snow on top of my head.

"Oh, it's like that." I grab my own handful of snow, which has her scrambling from my lap, and the chase begins. She rushes up the front steps, but before she can get the door open, I grab her around the waist and turn her to face me. I hold my handful of snow over her head.

"Uncle," she says with a laugh. The sound warms me from my head to my toes.

"I don't know. I think it's payback time."

"Conrad, please." Those hazel eyes of hers stare up at me, and I know that I could never deny her anything.

Instead, I step forward, causing her back to press against the side of the cabin. Dropping the snow, I place my hands flat on the cabin over her head. She tilts her head back to look at me. She's so fucking beautiful; she takes my breath away. I lean in, not really thinking about the consequences. All I know at this moment is that I need to kiss her. I need to taste those soft lips. Her tongue peeks out and licks her lips, and I lean in a little closer. I'm going for it. It's a kiss. What's the harm in a kiss?

Our lips are a breath apart when her cell phone rings. I watch as she blinks hard three times, and just like that, the spell is broken. Dropping my hands, I take a step back, giving her the space she needs to dig her cell phone out of her pocket.

"Hey," she answers breathlessly. "No. Conrad and I just built a snowman." I assume she's talking to Aurora. "Let me call you back. We're heading in now. Let me get out of all of these clothes." She nods even though the caller can't see her. "Great. Give me ten." She ends the call. "That was Aurora. She was calling to check on things. I have to tell her about all this snow. Look, the path you shoveled is already covered again."

"Let's get you inside and warmed up, and I'll pull up the weather report."

"What good is that going to do us? They didn't call for this." I can hear the frustration in her tone.

"Surely by now, they know what's up. Come on." Lacing her fingers with mine, I push open the door and lead her inside. Together we peel out of our clothes, and I stoke the fire, adding wood. "I'll make us some hot chocolate."

"Thanks, Con," she says, taking a seat on the couch, covering her lap with a blanket. "Hey, Rory." I hear her say before I disappear into the kitchen.

I can tell she's talking, but with the noise I'm making, I can't hear what she's saying. The cabin is huge, and the distance between us is what we need, what I need. I almost kissed her. I almost crossed a line that we wouldn't be able to uncross. I don't know what the hell has gotten into me. Grabbing the can of whipped cream from the fridge, I add a healthy amount to both mugs and carry them into the living room.

"Hey, Con's here, hold on. I'll put you on speaker."

I hand her a mug as she places her phone on speaker, setting it on the couch. I take the other cushion. "Who we talking to?" I ask, taking a sip of my hot chocolate.

"Hey, brother," Grant says.

"What's up?"

"How's the weather?"

"Shit. It's still snowing. We have about two feet out there now." There's no use in hiding it from him.

"Oh, no," Aurora says.

"I haven't checked the details, but I'm sure it's going to be fine."

"We're here, and we're going to stay on top of it. Hopefully, it stops soon, and the roads can be cleared," Aspen tells them.

"Have you seen any trucks?" Grant asks.

Aspen looks at me and bites her lip. She knows the answer. "No. Not yet. Ours isn't passable. But you know, as soon as the snow stops, they'll be all over it. They always are."

"Yeah," Grant agrees. He knows this is how things go, but I get it. He's getting married to the love of his life, and he wants it all to go off without a hitch. It's just immediate family, and I have no doubt my parents and brothers will do whatever it takes to get Aspen and Aurora's parents here as well as the rest of the family. We will have a wedding. It just might look a little different than they originally had planned.

"Too early to stress just yet," I tell them.

"Keep me posted?" Grant asks.

"You know it."

"Thanks, brother. Aspen, thanks for being there. Both of you. We appreciate you taking care of things."

"Not much we can do right now."

"But you're there," Aurora tells her. "We know firsthand what's going on. That means so much to us. Thank you both."

"We'll keep you posted." After a round of goodbyes and promises to keep them updated, we end the call.

"Is this wedding going to happen?" Aspen asks, biting down on her bottom lip.

"Yeah, it's going to happen. We might not have the caterers and the decorators to do their job, but I promise everyone will be here, and we will have a wedding."

"How are you so sure?"

I sigh. "This is going to sound conceited, but it's the truth. Money. My family has the means to get everyone here, even if we need to do it by chopper. The wedding will go on. It just won't be the one they planned."

"Oh, thank God." She's genuinely relieved. Not a single flinch when I mentioned our family's money. That does nothing for my need to kiss her. She's different from anyone I've ever met. Most women's eyes light up when I mention my family and money. Not Aspen. She's just worried about her sister getting the wedding of her dreams.

"I'm going to go see if I can figure out what's wrong with the water heater."

"You need me to come with you?" she offers.

"I should be fine. Be right back." Making my way to the basement, I open the door for the mechanical room. Reaching for the light, I flip the switch but it doesn't come on. Pulling my phone out of my pocket to use as a flashlight, I look around. I don't see any water on the floor, so I don't think there's a leak. I know last time this happened, the breaker had tripped from a power surge. On the other side of the room, I reach the circuit panel and flip the breaker. The lights come on and the water heater makes a gurgling sound. Hopefully, we will have hot water soon.

"How did it go?" Aspen asks once I'm back upstairs.

"Good. I'm pretty sure the circuit breaker was tripped. Should have hot water soon."

"You're a rockstar." She smiles at me, and I feel like I'm ten feet tall.

"Hungry?" I ask her.

"Not right now. How about a movie?" she suggests.

"You pick." Grabbing the remote from the table, I toss it to her. She scrolls through and picks an action film. It's one I've seen before. There's a good plot and a love story. Something for both of us. Grabbing another blanket from the back of the couch, I pull it over us as we sit on opposite ends and watch a movie while the snow continues to fall heavily outside. I try not to think about the woman sitting at the opposite end of the couch. I try not to think about the way those hazel eyes of hers were staring up at me with need earlier today.

My efforts are useless. She's all that I can think about.

I'm in trouble.

So much trouble.

CHAPTER
Aspen
SEVEN

THE CREDITS ROLL, and I'm glad I've seen this movie before. I couldn't concentrate on anything but the fact Conrad was sitting so close yet so far away. I don't know why it took just the two of us coming to this cabin for me to see him differently. So much so I know I'm just seconds away from making a fool of myself and kissing him. Speaking of kisses, I was sure he was going to kiss me earlier, and I was here for it. I wouldn't have stopped him. In fact, I wish I would have leaned in a little sooner.

"I'm starving," Conrad announces. He throws his cover off his lap and stands. "You?"

"I could eat." Or I could settle for making out here on the couch.

"Come on." He holds his hand out for me, and I don't hesitate to feel his skin against mine, even with just the simple act of him pulling me from the couch. "Feed me, woman." He laughs once I'm on my feet.

"You need to feed me." I give him a look that says his macho man stuff isn't working on me.

"How about we feed each other?" His eyes heat, and I have to fight the urge to jump him. Images of all the ways we could "feed each other" roll through my mind like a movie reel.

What the hell is wrong with me? This is Conrad. My sister's future brother-in-law. I can't be having these feelings for him. I can't complicate the relationship my sister has with Grant's brother. I won't do that. I need to just keep my hormones in check for a couple more days, and when everyone else finally gets here, all of this sexual tension will fade away. It's just the two of us being snowed in together. It has to be.

"We'll cook together. Maybe I can teach you a thing or two," he teases.

"You do know I work at a bakery, right?" I ask, following along behind him to the kitchen like a lost puppy.

"You do know that Lena Riggins is my mother, right?" he fires back with a smirk.

"Touché." I laugh. "So what are we making?"

"Let's see what we've got." He drops my hand, and I miss the contact immediately.

I watch as he rummages through the cabinets and then the refrigerator and freezer before he turns to face me. "Well, Chef Riggins, what's it going to be?"

"How about… drum roll, please." He waits for me to tap my hands against the counter before announcing. "Hamburger Helper."

I throw my head back in laughter. "You had me thinking we were going to have a big four-course meal, and the best you can come up with is Hamburger Helper?"

"What? I love this stuff, and it's easy to make," he defends.

"I'm not dissing Hamburger Helper. What are our options?"

"We have…" He clears his throat and turns back to the cabinet. "Cheeseburger macaroni, or three-cheese lasagna."

"Hmm." I tap my index finger against my chin, pretending to ponder my options when really there is no contest. The lasagna wins hands down every time. "Do we have any garlic bread?"

He nods, opens the freezer, and produces a box of frozen garlic bread. "It's breadsticks, which is better," he says, holding up the box.

"Perfect. Three-cheese lasagna it is."

He gives me a boyish grin that tugs at something in my chest. "A woman after my own heart." He winks and gets to work, pulling out a pan and a pound of hamburger from the freezer.

"Where are the baking sheets?" I ask, holding up the box of breadsticks.

"That cabinet over there." He points to a lower cabinet next to the refrigerator.

After reaching into the cabinet, I pull out the baking sheet and busy myself placing the breadsticks evenly spaced apart. "Do you cook a lot?" I ask.

"I've started to cook more meals at home than I used to. It used to be me, and one or more of my brothers would grab dinner and a few drinks, or we would end up at Mom and Dad's. Now that Royce, Owen, and Grant are coupled up, we do less of that. Marshall and I still do from time to time, but it gets old after a while. It used to be a way to just hang out with my brothers, now it's the same, but with just Marsh and me, we don't do it as often."

"Do the others never join you?"

"No, they do, just not as often as they used to. It's fine. I get it. If I had a woman waiting for me at home, knowing I got to fall asleep next to her, I'd be the same way."

"Any prospects?" I ask before I can think better of it.

"Nah, just me and my lonely boxed dinners." He holds up the box of Hamburger Helper. "What about you? Do you cook a lot?"

"Not really. We bake all day, and when Aurora still lived with me, we cooked more. Now that it's just me, I find myself eating bagels, cereal, and even peanut butter and jelly for dinner."

"Grape or strawberry?"

"What?"

"Grape or strawberry jelly? You can tell a lot about a person with the flavor of their jelly."

"Well, when it comes to jelly, I'm a grape girl. However, when it comes to other things like candy, I always go for strawberry over grape."

"Interesting." He grins.

"So what does that tell you about me?" I ask, intrigued.

He shrugs. "It tells me you like grape jelly."

It's not funny, not really, but I find myself throwing my head back with laughter anyway. "You're ridiculous," I say through my laughter.

"Well, I might be ridiculous, but I made you laugh, and you're beautiful when you laugh."

I sputter on my laughter as it turns into a cough of surprise at his confession. "What else can I do?" I ask, deciding to ignore his comment. Well, internally, my body is all warm and fuzzy, knowing that he thinks I'm beautiful. On the outside, however, I don't let him see that his words affect me.

"I think I've got it from here. Should be ready in about twenty minutes or so."

I nod. "Okay. I think I'm going to take a hot shower. I'll be quick." I rush out of the kitchen like my ass is on fire. I need a minute. Knowing that he thinks I'm beautiful just heightens my desire for him. It's stupid and superficial, but I can't help the way that I feel. I can't stop how his words affect me, no matter how bad I wish that I could.

Upstairs, I grab some clothes and head across the hall to the bathroom. Reaching into the shower, I turn the water to hot and then strip, waiting for it to warm up. Reaching into the closet, I grab a towel and hang it up just outside of the shower before step under the hot spray. The hot water is warm and inviting and just what I needed. My toes were still a little chilled from being outside earlier. I stand still, letting the water rain down as I soak up all the warmth it provides.

Knowing dinner will be ready soon, I reach for the shampoo when something on the ceiling catches my eye. Lifting my head, I see a huge black spider and let out a loud scream, and scramble to get out of the shower. I hate spiders, and this one was looking right at me. I know I need to turn off the water and do something about the bathroom intruder, but I need to let my heart rate settle just a little before I attempt to do anything.

"Aspen!" Fists pound against the bathroom door. I open my mouth to reply when the door bursts open. Standing in the doorway is a frazzled Conrad, fists balled tight. "What is it? What happened?" He looks around the room, and then his eyes land on me.

I'm holding the towel I laid out in front of me, and I'm dripping wet, and my body is chilled, missing the heat that the water was providing. "Sp-Spider," I say, pointing to the ceiling of the shower.

I'm calm enough that I notice his shoulders visibly relax. "Spider," he repeats, taking a step toward me. I don't know what I expected, but it's not him pulling my naked wet body into his chest, holding me tight. "I thought something happened, that maybe somebody was in here with you." His words are a whispered confession, and I can hear the relief in his voice.

He was worried about me.

He pulls away slightly, and his brown eyes study me. His hand cups my cheek, and I lean into his touch. "So beautiful," he whispers. His touch sends a current racing through my veins.

I think he's going to kiss me. I want him to kiss me. My heart is pounding in my chest, and I can practically already feel his lips pressed to mine. He leans in, and I will him to do it. To kiss me. To put us both out of this constant "will he or will she back and forth" we've been playing.

Instead, he pulls away all too soon. I slump back against the counter as I watch him grab some toilet paper off the roll and step into the shower, grabbing the spider from its spot on the ceiling and flushing it down the toilet.

"You okay?" he asks, his voice husky.

"Y-Yeah." My voice is thick with my want for him.

"I'll see you downstairs." He swallows hard and raises his hand. I think he's going to touch me again, but he quickly drops it to his side and leaves me alone.

I stand still and listen to his footsteps as they pound down the stairs, the sound the same rhythm as the beat of my heart in my chest. When I can no longer hear his footsteps, I move to get dressed. My hands tremble as I finish drying off and pull on my clothes. I don't know if I'm cold or if it's my body's reaction to his touch. Either way, I know that I need to be near him. I don't think about what that means or what I'm going to do about it. I rush through, brushing out my hair before tying it up wet and rushing down the steps to see him.

"Thanks for that," I say when I make it to the kitchen.

"I'll be sure to add spider slayer to my résumé," he teases. "Ready to eat?" he asks, pulling the baking sheet of bread sticks from the oven.

"Starving," I tell him honestly. What I don't tell him is that even though my stomach is growling, I'd pass up the opportunity of food for one taste of his lips pressed to mine. I watch as he makes us both a plate.

"Are we eating in here or in the living room?"

"Another movie?" I ask.

"You pick. I'll be right in with drinks."

Taking our plates I set his on the table while I settle on the couch with mine. Reaching for the remote, I scroll through our options, pulling up a series I've never seen before.

"Have you seen this?" he asks from behind me. Walking around the couch, he hands me a beer and sets one for himself on the end table.

"No."

"Me either. I say we go for it."

I shrug and hit Play. Together we eat in silence as we allow ourselves to get lost in the series. It's really good, and by the third episode, we're both addicted. By the fourth episode, my head is in his lap, his hands are running through my hair, my hair tie I used to put it up earlier today, long since forgotten, and I have a blanket thrown over me. Conrad Riggins and his touch are quickly becoming my addiction.

CHAPTER
Conrad
EIGHT

THE BATHROOM DOOR closing down the hall wakes me from sleep. My cock is already hard from the dream I was having about her. *Aspen*. Now to know that she's just down the hall, naked and wet, I'm so hard it's painful.

I carried her to bed again last night. I wanted her to ask me to stay. I wanted to crawl under the covers and hold her against me all night long. That's not me. That's never been who I am. I never bring women back to my place so I can get away. I usually blame it on work or need to help one of my brothers, but I always find an excuse not to stay.

Now here I am with Aspen, and all I want is to stay. Stay with her. My mind takes me back to last night when I heard her scream. I couldn't climb the stairs fast enough to get to her. My heart stalled in my chest until I laid eyes on her and could see she was okay. I held her mostly naked body next to mine, and it took every ounce of effort I possessed to pull away from her. I don't know how much longer I can resist her. Hell, I don't even know if I want to resist her anymore.

My phone rings, and I see Grant's goofy face smiling at me. "What's up, brother?" I answer.

"How are things there? Is it still snowing?"

"Honestly, I'm not sure. I'm still in bed. Give me a second." Tossing off the covers, I climb to my feet and make my way to the window. "It finally stopped. Let's hope they can get to the roads today." I can hear him exhale with relief through the line.

"The roads are the least of my worries. We can get that taken care of." He doesn't say it, but I know what he's thinking. We can hire a private contractor who has a snowplow and dump truck for salt to treat the road. That won't stop us from having this wedding. "Why are you still in bed?"

"Aspen and I started this series last night, and we watched like five episodes before we both dropped to exhaustion."

"How are things going?"

"Good. Fine. Good."

"That's a lot of fine and good, little brother."

I sigh into the line. "I think it's just cabin fever."

"Are the two of you not getting along?" There's concern in his voice.

"No. We're getting along fine." Too fine, I think to myself.

"Fine," he repeats. "What's going on, Con?"

"Nothing. Everything is fine. We've been watching movies, and yesterday we even built a snowman."

"Good. We're all still driving there tomorrow. We're not leaving here until noon-ish, so we should be there around dinner time. Hopefully, the road is good by then. If not, we'll just rent a room in town, and then get on the phone and get it handled."

"I can do that today," I offer.

"Nah. Let's give it time and see what happens. I've been watching the forecast, and no more snow is supposed to be headed that way until next week. You'll all be back in Nashville by then, and my wife and I will be on our way to the Bahamas."

"I can hear you smiling," I tell him with a smile of my own that he can't see.

"Been a long time coming."

"It's been a little over a year."

"Too damn long," Grant replies.

"I hear ya. Just don't start spouting all that magic shit."

"Trust me. It's magic. When it hits you, you'll know. You'll find the right woman, and suddenly she's all that matters to you. I'm telling you, Conrad, you'll never be the same after you meet her." Aspen is the first image to pop into my head, but I ignore it.

"I think Dad has you brainwashed."

"What about Royce and Owen?" he calls me out.

"Them too. Marshall and I are the babies. He likes us best." His roar of laughter filters through the phone, and I can't help but grin.

"I can't wait until I get to say I told you so," he tells me.

"Yeah, yeah. I'll see you tomorrow."

"We'll be there. Thanks for being there, Conrad. I appreciate it."

"Anytime, brother," I say, ending the call, only for it to ring again. Glancing at the screen, I see it's my dad. "Hey, Pop."

"Conrad. How are things?"

"Better. It finally stopped snowing. I'm hoping by the time y'all get here, the roads will be passable."

"That's good to hear. Your mom has been worrying herself sick over the weather. She just wants this wedding to be everything your brother and Aurora want it to be."

"We all do. Aspen and I are staying on top of things here," I assure him.

"How is Aspen?" he asks.

"She's good. Great. We've been hanging out, built a snowman, had a snowball fight, just trying to keep ourselves occupied since we're stuck here."

"Ah," he says like he knows the answer to world peace.

"Ah? What does *ah* mean?"

"Nothing."

"Come on, old man. Don't start holding out on me now."

"You like her."

"Sure, I mean, I guess. She's cool, and she's going to be a part of our family, so yeah."

"Not technically. Just in our eyes. We've adopted her as Aurora's sister to be one of us, but she's not family, son."

"That doesn't sound like you. What would Mom say if she caught you talking like that?" I told him. There is more heat in my tone than necessary, but it pisses me off he would say that about Aspen. She's one of us.

"Don't go getting yourself all twisted. You misunderstood where I was going with that. It was simply a reminder to you that Aspen is of no relation to you. So, if you were interested in her, there would be nothing wrong with that."

"What's Mom been feeding you?" I ask, trying to hide the fact that I jumped to her defense when I know my parents both love Aspen and consider her family. I let my feelings blind my view of the discussion.

My feelings?

Do I have feelings for Aspen?

No. She's hot as hell, but I don't have feelings for her. I couldn't, she's... not family.

Fuck me.

"There it is," Dad says.

"What are you talking about?"

"Nothing. Nothing at all. We're leaving around noon tomorrow. We should be there around dinner time."

"That's what Grant told me earlier."

"Good. Is there anything you forgot that you need me to bring?"

I think about it for a few minutes just to make sure there isn't anything that I need. "No. I'm good. Thanks, Dad."

"All right, we'll see you tomorrow, son. Oh, and, Conrad?"

"Yeah?"

"Let it happen."

"You feeling okay?" I ask him. He's acting weird.

"Fine as frog hair. See you soon."

"Drive safe."

"Always."

Ending the call, I toss my phone on the bed and hear the bathroom door open. At least my family distracted me from the fact that Aspen was wet and naked. My cock twitches, ready to go at just the thought of her. "Not going to happen," I mumble turning away from the window. Grabbing some clothes, I rush down the hall to the bathroom to take a long, hot shower. As soon as I step into the bathroom, I'm surrounded by her smell. She's everywhere, and my cock takes notice. After turning the water on, I strip down and make sure the door is locked. Stepping under the spray, I close my eyes and think about last night. About holding her mostly naked, wet body next to me. The fear I felt when I thought something might be wrong, and the way I felt empty when I had to let her go.

I can't stop thinking about her, and I need relief. Seeing her naked two days in a row is more than what any man can handle. Feeling her body pressed to mine both of those times, well, the memory of that is what has me reaching for my cock. Bracing one arm on the shower wall, I close my eyes and bow my head as the memories of my time with Aspen these last two days filter through my mind.

I stroke from root to tip, hard and fast. My spine stiffens, and my body is tight, and I pump faster. Within minutes I'm exploding into the shower, and although the orgasm gave me some relief, I still want her, and my cock knows the difference between my hand and Aspen. With a heavy sigh, which I'm not sure is relief or disappointment, I wash and turn off the water.

Fifteen minutes later, the smell of bacon and eggs leads me to the kitchen. "Morning," I greet Aspen. She's wearing black tights or leggings or whatever they're called, and an old sweatshirt. After closer inspection, I see it's mine. She must have taken it from my closet. "That looks familiar," I say, pulling at the hood as I pass her to grab a cup of coffee. Once I have my cup poured, I lean back against the counter, crossing my legs at the ankles so I can get a better look at her.

"Sorry," she says sheepishly. "I was freezing, and it looked so warm."

"I don't mind." She has no idea what it does to me to see her in my clothes. Girls in college would steal my clothes all the time. They'd wear them to a party to try to get a reaction out of me and nothing. I felt *nothing*. Maybe less if it was one of my favorites, but nothing like this. I have an overwhelming need to beat on my chest and scream to the world she's mine. Right after I kiss the hell out of her, that is.

"Hungry?" She holds up a plate filled with bacon, eggs, and toast.

"Thank you." I take the plate and sit on one of the stools at the island. She tops off her cup of coffee and joins me.

"So, what's on the agenda today?" she asks before taking a bite of eggs.

You and me in bed all day. "More of the same. The snow finally stopped, so hopefully, they will get up here to the roads."

"They won't be here until around dinner time tomorrow. I talked to Aurora this morning," she explains.

"Yeah, I talked to Dad and Grant, and they said the same thing. Hopefully, the road is good to go by then."

"If not, we have a plan. Well, Grant has a plan." I go on to explain hiring a private company to clear the road to the cabin.

"I have no doubt he will do whatever needs to be done to marry my sister. He's one of the good ones."

I nod. She's right, he is. All of my brothers are. I'd like to think that I can include myself in that assessment as well. However, I've never really cared if a woman thought I was one of the good ones. Not until now, and I'm not sure why I do. I just know I want her to think that about me.

"So, when the road clears, this place is going to be hopping with activity. The decorators will need to get in here, and then the caterers wanted to set up prior as well. That's why I'm here early."

"Yeah, we'll make it happen. Don't worry."

"What if the caterer and whoever she hired to decorate can't do it with the delay? Then what?"

"Then we take over. I promise you that your sister and my brother are getting married on Saturday."

"I know. I have no doubts about you and your family. I just worry, you know? She's been through so much, and she deserves to be happy. I want that for her more than anything."

I nod. I do know. Aurora's ex did a number on her, but Grant is working hard to turn that all around. I think he's well on his way. "What about your parents?" I ask to keep the conversation flowing. If I don't, my mind will go to her soft, plump lips, at least I think they're soft. I'd love to find out for myself.

"Oh, they're already in Nashville. They came a few days early to start looking for a place. I guess now Aurora is getting married, they want to make sure they're close by when the grandkids start to arrive."

"Do you know something I don't know?" I raise my eyebrows in question.

"No. At least, I don't think so. Mom and Dad know we're happy in Nashville, and now that Aurora and hopefully me one day will start our own families, or at least settle down, they want to be close."

"You want to settle down, do you?" It's a question I would *never* ask, but I *want* the answer from her as much as I want to kiss her.

"Yes." There is no hesitation in her reply. "However, I don't want to settle if that makes sense. I want a partner in life. Someone I know will love me unconditionally, like Grant and Aurora.

There isn't a single doubt in my mind that your brother isn't one hundred percent devoted, head over heels in love with my sister. And her with him."

"So you want to marry Grant?" I tease.

"No!" She smacks playfully at my arm. "I just want someone who looks at me the way he looks at Aurora."

"I get it. All three of my brothers have been lucky to find great partners in life."

"And you're still looking?" she questions.

"Yep. I'm just waiting for the right woman."

"And what is your idea of the right woman?"

You. "Someone who is with me for me, and all my quirks, and not my family's money."

"That has to be hard."

I shrug. "We're used to it. All five of us had to deal with it, and Royce's first wife pretty much married him because of it. That's why he fought his feelings for Sawyer so hard. He didn't trust himself to choose again, and right this time."

"I'd say he did well for himself. Sawyer is great."

"She really is. So, what do you want to do today?" I change the subject. Talking about this just makes me want to kiss her even more. Who am I kidding? Everything Aspen does makes me want to kiss her. It doesn't matter what we're talking about.

"Cookies. I saw the dough in the fridge, and it needs to be made so it doesn't go to waste. How are your cookie decorating skills, Riggins?"

"I know my way around a cookie." I smirk, and her face turns beet red.

"You!" She shakes her head. "Dishes. I cooked. I'm going to run upstairs and… make sure I unplugged the hairdryer. I'll be right back." She races out of the room like her ass is on fire, but that's okay because I saw those hazel eyes, and they were filled with desire. Desire for me. Today is going to be another great day.

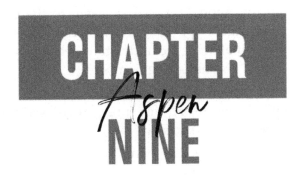

CHAPTER *Aspen* NINE

"**I** CAN'T BELIEVE your mom thought of all of this," I tell Conrad as I cut out another heart-shaped cookie to place on the baking sheet.

"She's always been one for details," he says, adding his own cut-out version of Xs and Os onto the sheet.

"Perfect." Picking up the sheet, I place our final batch in the oven and set the timer. "Now, it's time to drag out all the decorating supplies." I busy myself doing just that. When I turn around, I find Conrad watching me intently. "Thanks for this," I say, holding up my hands that are full of icing and sprinkles.

"That was all Mom."

"No. I mean, thank you for humoring me and making cookies. I'm sure this isn't your idea of fun."

"Is it yours?" His gaze is intense as he waits for my answer.

"Yeah, I mean, I know I do it every day, but I enjoy it. And this is for fun, and well, you're here," I add on without thinking.

"I'm glad I'm here with you to bake and decorate cookies."

I watch as he pulls his phone out of his pocket and taps the screen. When the music begins to play from somewhere other than his phone, I look around for a speaker. "Where is that coming from?"

"Oh, we have a Bluetooth system throughout the cabin. I can control it from my phone. So we can listen to the same music throughout, or change it up." He holds his phone up so that I can see the screen as if that helps me understand what he's saying. "IT guy"—he points at his chest—"remember?"

"I'm sure there's a good story behind that. I mean, you blocked Marshall from the thermostat. I'm sure you've used this to your advantage at one point or another."

"Who me?" He places his hand over his heart as if he's offended. "Maybe," he confesses. I raise my eyebrows and give him an "I don't believe you" look. "Okay," he admits with a laugh. "One night, Royce had this sappy depressing song on repeat. He was annoying the hell out of all of us. It was right after he and his first wife split. Anyway, this song was sad as hell, and we were all over it, but his drunk ass insisted that's what we listen to on repeat. So, when he went to bed, I might have piped 'You Are My Sunshine' into his room while he slept."

"You did not. Was he mad?"

"I set it to turn off at around 6:00 a.m. He was surprisingly happy the next day."

"Subliminal message. Nice." I hold my fist out to him, and we bump. The timer dings, and I set the tray on top of the stove to cool. "Now we decorate." I grin at Conrad.

"Let's do it."

Side by side, we begin to ice and decorate the cookies. I'm glad that everyone will be here tomorrow. If the two of us were to eat all of these, they'd have to roll us out of here. I'm focused on dropping sprinkles on the outline of the heart I'm decorating, which is the only reason I don't see his finger coming until it's too late. I yell out in surprise as Conrad swipes icing down my cheek. "No, you didn't." I laugh, grabbing a towel and wiping at my face.

Swiping my index finger through the bowl of icing, I hold it up so he can see it. "Payback." I grin and step around the counter. He retreats, which means I have to chase after him. He takes off toward the living room with me hot on his trail. He moves around the couch, and I jump over the back to get to him. It would have worked too, but he's much bigger and stronger than I am. While I was gaining my footing, he had his arms wrapped around me from behind and my finger with the dollop of icing in his mouth.

When his lips wrap around my finger, and his tongue goes to work, removing the icing, every single nerve in my body is awakened. I stop squirming and lean against him. His grip tightens as he pulls me closer to his chest. The heat of him sears my back even through his sweatshirt that I'm wearing.

"Delicious," he whispers huskily after letting my finger drop from his mouth. I feel his hot breath against my neck, and I will him to kiss me.

Anywhere.

Everywhere.

My breath stalls in my lungs as I wait to see what he's going to do. The song changes to WALK THE MOON's "Shut Up and Dance," and I feel his lips next to my ear. His hot breath sending tingles down my spine.

"Dance with me." His words are whispered, but they are not a request. They're a command as he takes my hand in his and spins me out from his chest. Laughter bubbles up inside of me, and when he pulls me back in so we are now chest to chest, I can't help but smile up at him. "Show me what you got, Steele," he murmurs.

Something Conrad might not know about me is that I love to dance. Not one to ever turn down the opportunity to do something I love, I begin to sway my hips. His hands guide me as we move to the beat. He dips me low over his arm and spins me around before releasing me and going into the sprinkler. I'm laughing so hard it steals the breath from my lungs, but I keep on dancing as I gasp for air, watching him and his impressive moves.

"Is that the best you've got, Riggins?" I break out in the

running man and watch in fascination as he throws his head back and roars with laughter. One song leads to another as we go back and forth, trying to one-up each other with our ridiculous over-the-top dance moves. It's the most fun I've had in years, if not ever with a man.

When Brantley Gilbert's "Let it Ride" comes on, the atmosphere changes. We're no longer dancing to silly fast songs, and this one slows things down. I take a step back to put some space between us, but Conrad has other ideas. His arms snake around my waist, and he pulls me close to his chest, his hands resting low on my back, just above my ass. Neither one of us says a word as Brantley croons about being caught up in the moment and letting it ride. I couldn't have chosen the lyrics better if I had written them myself.

Without conscious thought, I rest my head against his chest, and his arms hold me close. I listen to the lyrics of the song as it plays out how I'm feeling at this moment. It's like fate knows we're both fighting this attraction between us. I'm not blind. Even though I've been pretending that I don't see it, I know he's feeling the same desire I am. I see it in his eyes.

When I feel his lips press to the top of my head, I move from my position resting against his chest, and peer up at him. His hands that were holding me close move to cradle my face in the palm of his hands. His brown eyes are intense as they take me in. He looks to my lips and then back to my eyes. I recognize his intentions, and if he's waiting for me to stop him, he's going to be waiting a long time. I want this. I'll think about the consequences later. Besides, it's just a kiss.

Conrad leans in, and I want him to know I want this, so I stand on my tiptoes and bring us even closer together. His eyes darken, and I close my eyes, waiting for the press of his lips against mine.

He doesn't disappoint me.

When our lips finally touch, it's a feeling I've never experienced, almost as if I'm home. His lips are familiar and new all at the same time. My hands snake up around his neck and run through his hair. I give it a gentle tug, and he moans, deepening the kiss as his tongue slides past my lips.

He's taller than me, so we're at an awkward angle, and I wish I were taller. Conrad either feels my struggle or needs me closer too. Either way, the end result is him gripping my ass and lifting me in the air. Without being told, I wrap my arms and legs around him like a spider monkey, and the thought that I never want to let go filters through my mind.

I'm so distracted from our kiss that I don't realize we are moving until he sets me on the kitchen counter. Keeping my legs locked around his waist, I use them as leverage and pull him as close to me as I can get him. He's wearing lounge pants, and I'm in leggings, so I can feel him—every inch of him between my thighs. His lips trail down my neck, and the hussy that I am for him, I tilt my head to the side, giving him all the access he needs. He doesn't get far due to his sweatshirt, and I'm cursing my idea to wear it today.

It doesn't seem to deter him as his lips once again capture mine, and our tongues dance to the beat of the song. My hands roam over his back as his slide under his sweatshirt I'm wearing. His hands are warm and sure as they trail over my stomach to cup my breasts. I moan from somewhere deep inside, and I can't find it in me to be ashamed. It's been too damn long since I've had a man's hands on me, and this isn't just any man. This is Conrad Riggins, and if I wasn't willing to admit it before, I have no choice now.

I'm falling for him.

Reaching for the hem of the shirt I'm wearing, I'm ready to tear it from my body so I can feel his skin against mine. However, before I get that far, my cell phone starts to ring. Conrad slows our kiss and eventually stopping altogether as he rests his forehead against mine.

"We don't have to answer that," he tells me as he labors to catch his breath. The ringing stops, and he grins. "They read my mind." He moves in for another kiss, only for my phone to ring again. He sighs, presses a chaste kiss to my lips, and steps out of my hold to retrieve my phone from the island. "Your mom," he says, handing me the phone.

With shaking hands, I accept the call, placing the phone to my ear. "Hey, Mom."

"Aspen, how are you holding up?"

"Fine. We're snowed in, but Conrad is hopeful that the snowplows will get us dug out today. It finally stopped snowing."

"That's what your sister just told me. Your dad and I are on our way to Nashville now. Is there anything that you need us to do at the bakery or bring with us?"

"I'm sure everything is fine, Mom."

"Your sister is there, and she's nervous about leaving the new staff, but I've assured her that between the two of you, they're trained and ready."

"They are. You know Aurora, she's a worrier."

Conrad steps between my legs and assists me with wrapping them back around his waist. I give him a questioning look, and he just grins at me. His eyes find mine, and he smirks before moving in and pressing a kiss just under my ear that's not listening to my mother.

"Aspen, can you hear me?" Mom asks, pulling me away from Conrad and back to the conversation.

"Yes. Sorry, we're baking cookies, and I got distracted." It's not a complete lie.

"Oh, that sounds fun. I'm glad Conrad is there with you. I wasn't thrilled about you being up there in that cabin all alone."

If she could only see us now. "Mom, I'm an adult and am perfectly capable of taking care of myself."

"I can take care of you," Conrad whispers low enough for only me to hear. My body quivers from his words.

"I know you can. I just worry. That's my job as your mother. Just wait. One day when you have children, you'll understand."

"I know. I love you for it, but I promise you I'm fine. We're fine."

"Yes, you are," Conrad says, his voice low and husky in my ear.

"Well, I'll let you get back to what you were doing. Love you, Aspen."

"Love you too, Mom. I'll see you tomorrow." Ending the call, I drop my phone to the counter and sigh as Conrad continues to kiss on my neck.

His hands slide back up my shirt, and I'm ready for whatever he's willing to give when this time it's his phone that interrupts us. "Fuck," he mumbles.

"I think the universe is working against us here." I chuckle.

"Me too, babe." He kisses me sweetly, then steps away to answer his phone. This time he doesn't come back. Instead, he sits at the island and talks to what sounds like one of his brothers.

Composing myself, I hop off the counter and take my seat next to him, and start again on decorating the remaining cookies. When Conrad finishes his call, he helps me with the last remaining few, and together we clean up the mess that we made.

Neither one of us mention the kisses, and that's okay. We're better off to pretend it never happened. Our siblings are getting married, and if this… whatever it was didn't work out, that would wreck the dynamics of both of our worlds. It doesn't matter how much I crave his touch. It's not something I can have.

CHAPTER
Conrad
TEN

"I'M IMPRESSED."

I turn to see Aspen walk into the kitchen and perch on a stool at the island. "Woman, did you doubt me?" I ask her.

"No." She shakes her head. "However, I wasn't sure what to expect either. That looks great." She points to where I'm standing at the stove, slicing the homemade pizza I made us for dinner.

"Don't get too excited. It's just cheese and hamburger. I didn't see anything else to use as toppings."

"It sounds and smells delicious," she assures me.

I finish cutting it and add a couple of slices to a plate for each of us and carry them to the island. "Here you go, my dear." I place the plate in front of her and press a kiss to her lips.

"Thank you." Her smile is bright, just as it has been all damn day.

I've snuck more kisses today than I have with a woman in my entire life, and it still doesn't feel like enough. I could spend hours just kissing her, and even then, I don't know if it would be enough.

Neither one of us mentioned this new dynamic between us. Dancing with Aspen and holding her close, I couldn't resist. One thing led to another, and my hands and my mouth were all over her until we kept getting interrupted. She seemed fine, and I'm glad I didn't upset her. It wasn't until we came into the living room to watch more of the series we started that I tried again. I pulled her into my arms and kissed the breath from her lungs before she had time to hit Play. Then I held her the entire time. This day has not sucked. Not at all.

"So good," she says, covering her mouth with her hand.

"Just call me Chef Conrad," I joke.

"You're going to spoil me. I'm used to cooking for one and eating alone. Now that it's just me."

"Aw, sweets, are you trying to say that you're going to miss me?" I tease.

"Maybe." Her confession is followed by a smile that lights up my entire fucking universe.

"Well, I'll have to make sure to cook for you when we get home too." I toss the idea out there. She doesn't dispute it, just nods her agreement.

"So, everyone gets here tomorrow?" she asks.

"Yeah. My contact at the city assured me they would be working on our road tomorrow. They had to get the main roads taken care of first."

"How exactly do you have a contact at the city?" she muses.

"Funny story. My brothers and I were here one weekend fishing. Josh, that's the contact's name, he was at the lake. We all got to shooting the shit and drinking a few beers."

"I'm guessing there was more beer drinking than fishing going on."

"You know it. That's man code for drinking a few with my buddies. Anyway," I say dramatically, "turns out, Josh works for the city, and he's over at road maintenance."

"Does everything come easy to you and your brothers?"

"No."

"Name one thing that you've struggled with?"

"Being used for my last name and bank account."

"Other than that."

"It's a struggle to sit next to you and not have my hands on you," I tell her honestly.

"Come on." She laughs. "Be serious."

"Oh, I'm serious."

"What's stopping you?"

I ponder her question. "I don't want to assume or push you."

"You've been stealing kisses and touches all day."

"And?"

"And what?"

"How do you feel about that?"

"Did I protest?"

"No."

"There's your answer."

"It's more complicated than that."

"I know."

"And?"

"How do you feel about that?" She sighs. "I feel like we're talking in circles here, Conrad."

"I know. I'm sorry. I know it's complicated, but I never thought I'd have these feelings for you."

"It's not me."

"What do you mean it's not you?"

"It's our situation. We're stranded here. We're attracted to one another, and that's heightened since it's just the two of us."

"I think it's more than that."

"That's the situation too. We're not thinking clearly. Once the others get there, there will be more of a buffer, and that will all change."

"You seem certain." What I don't say is that I call bullshit. This thing between us isn't just some act of boredom, at least not for me. I'm into this girl. Really into her. I can't stop thinking about her, and the taste of her lips, or the smell of her hair.

"That's really the only answer. We've been around each other countless times in a group setting, and we've never felt... this, whatever this is between us."

I don't argue with her because I don't know if she's right. My gut tells me she's not. That this is more, maybe it's because it's never been just the two of us. We've never really had the chance to get to know one another and explore more. Whatever it is, I'm dreading leaving her on Sunday.

"Look at this." I hand Aspen my phone. "Owen just sent me that."

"Aw, look at Carter. He's hamming it up for the camera." She hands the phone back to me.

"It's still surreal to see Owen as a father. Out of all of my brothers, I was certain he would be the last to fall."

"Fall?"

"Head over ass in love."

"Is that what you call it?" She laughs.

"You know what I mean. He was always the quiet, stoic one. Hell, I don't even ever remember him dating anyone. I mean, obviously he did, but he was discreet about it. Now here he is announcing his love for his wife to anyone who will listen, and his son—" I shake my head. "He's such a good father, not that I didn't think he would be. It's just surreal to see him as a dad."

"Royce will be there with him soon," she reminds me.

"Yeah." I nod. "I'm sure Grant will be as well, if he has his say."

"I'd say you're right. I know Aurora wants kids. And I know she told him she wanted to be married before they started trying. It won't surprise me if she gets pregnant right away."

"Grant would be thrilled."

"Rory would be too."

"Have you ever done that?" I nod to my phone. "Built a fort?"

"Yeah. Haven't you?"

"Sure, we did it all the time as kids, but it's been years. And isn't Carter a little young to enjoy it?" I ask her.

"I don't think that's the point. It's more for the memories of it, you know? Owen and Layla will remember it, and they'll have pictures to show Carter of his first homemade fort in the living room."

"We should build one."

"What?" She looks at me as if I might be losing my mind. Maybe I am, but I want this memory of my time with her.

"Let's do it. It's just us, so we don't have to worry about disturbing anyone else, and Mom has a shit-ton of pillows and blankets. Lena Riggins is nothing if not prepared."

"Are you being serious?" This time there is a light in her eyes and hope in her voice.

"Very. I'll grab some supplies from the hall closet. You work on thinking out our design. I'll be right back." I kiss her quickly because I can, and she has yet to tell me not to and rush off to gather blankets and pillows.

"This will get us started," I say a few minutes later. Dropping the pile of pillows and blankets to the floor, I help Aspen start moving furniture.

"I think we should push the couch and the loveseat together. We can use that corner for lots of pillows and a base of sorts to lean against."

"Look at you, my little fort building pro," I tease.

"This is not my first time, Conrad Riggins." She winks, and the action has my cock twitching, taking notice of her words and their double meaning.

"Sounds like I could learn a thing or two from you."

Something flashes in her eyes, but she quickly masks it when she tosses a pillow at my head. "Watch and learn," she tells me.

Doing as I'm told, I watch her grab a blanket and drape it over the couch and then the coffee table, setting pillows on top to hold it in place. "You need some help?" I ask when the blanket keeps slipping off the end of the table before she can get the pillow there to hold it down. "I mean, as much as I'm enjoying the master at work, I hate to watch you struggle."

She blows out a breath, making her hair fly all around her face. "Yes, please," she concedes.

Over the next hour, we build a fort worthy of a king. We managed to make it high enough that when we're lying inside, we can still have a clear view of the fireplace. We even moved the TV to the floor so we could continue to watch our series from our new fort.

"Do you think we need more blankets?" Aspen asks.

"We have what, three layers?"

"Yeah, but it's nothing but the hardwood floor underneath. I want to be comfy."

"You can lay on me," I tell her without thinking.

"I'll go grab another blanket." She rushes off. As her footfalls sound at the steps, I can't help but feel excited about today—about my time with her and what tonight could bring. The fort is not very big, so we're going to be close, and if there is anything to make my night, it's snuggling up with Aspen.

"Look at this one," she says, pulling me from my thoughts. "I think it weighs like twenty pounds; it's so thick. This is exactly what we needed." She drops the blanket at the edge of the fort and then falls to her knees to get busy spreading it out on top of the other three.

As for me, I stand back and watch the show of her ass in the air in those leggings that she wears. I don't know who invented them, but it must have been a man. Sure, they look like they're comfortable, but no way would a woman create them knowing how crazy it would make the male population. Then again, maybe it was a woman. Regardless, I'm thankful to those involved. Aspen's ass in those things is life-changing.

"There," she says, backing out of the fort and climbing to her feet. "It's perfect. However, there is one thing we still need." She skips off to the kitchen, and like the puppy I am when it comes to her, I follow behind.

"What are you looking for?" I ask as I stand back and watch her opening the cabinets.

"Popcorn." She digs in a few more cabinets and pauses with a smile. "Jackpot." She holds up a box of microwave movie theater butter popcorn.

"I'll make us some hot chocolate and grab a couple of bottles of water too," I say, getting busy. We work side by side in the kitchen, just like we have the entire time we've been here. I like it. It feels natural. Everything with Aspen feels that way. Nothing is forced or fake. It's just us, and I love that a hell of a lot more than I ever thought I would.

"Ready?" she asks, holding a massive bowl of popcorn.

"Let's do this." Together we make our way to the living room. "I'm glad you suggested the small end table under there, so we have somewhere safe to set these." I hold up the two mugs of hot chocolate. "How about you set the popcorn down, and I climb in? I'll hand you everything."

"I'm so excited," she says, the sparkle in her hazel eyes glimmering.

I wait for her to settle in the fort and carefully hand her one mug at a time, the two bottles of water, and the bowl of popcorn. "I'm going to get the lights," I tell her. Making my way through the downstairs, turning off lights, and checking the door. We haven't been outside today, but I still check it to make sure it's locked. I could have done it all from the app on my phone, but I'm not taking any chances of something not being locked up. Not with Aspen. Moving back to the living room, I spy both of our phones on the mantel and grab those, as well as an additional blanket to cover up with.

"Another blanket?" she asks, taking our phones when I hand them to her and placing them on the small end table.

"Yeah, we have a cushion, but nothing to cover up with."

"Damn. I can't believe I forgot that."

"That's why we make a great team." I mean that in more ways than one, but I don't know if she's ready to hear that just yet. Hell, I'm not sure I'm prepared to say it out loud.

"All right, you ready?" I ask her.

"Yep." I settle next to her, setting the bowl of popcorn between us, and hit Play on the remote. The night is just starting, and it's already the best one I can ever remember having.

CHAPTER
Aspen
ELEVEN

WHY IS IT that sitting next to him eating popcorn turns me into my teenage self? Case in point, every time both of our hands enter the bowl of popcorn, and we touch, I get all giddy inside. I'm a grown woman. I should have more control than this, but I'm discovering there are different rules when it comes to Conrad Riggins.

As if I need more validity of my point, we're currently watching a steamy scene in this series we've been binging, and I'm squirming all over the damn place. Why is it that I can watch this a thousand times and sit perfectly still, no matter how hot the scene, but watching it with him is about to send me into orbit, and he's not even touching me?

The universe hates me. That's why.

"You all right?" Conrad asks. His lips are next to my ear, and although I knew we were sitting close, I didn't realize we were that close.

"Yes. Good. Fine," I assure him like a bumbling idiot fumbling over my words.

"Come here." His arm slides around my shoulders.

Snuggling into his chest, I try to concentrate on the show, but it's hard when he's running his fingers through my hair. If I thought I was turned on before, it's tenfold now. I try my hardest not to squirm, but it's useless as I rub my thighs together.

"Aspen." Conrad's voice is husky, and I'm half afraid to look at him. I know I won't be able to resist him. The simple touches, the kisses all day today, it's been a version of extended foreplay, and I'm about to combust.

Holding strong, I ignore him and keep my eyes glued to the television, even though I haven't any idea of what's happening on the screen.

"Hey," he whispers. No longer able to ignore him, I lift my head to find him watching me intently. "So beautiful," he whispers.

Resting my hand against his cheek, I relish in the feel of his beard beneath my palm. I've never been into men with this much facial hair, but as with everything else, that rule doesn't seem to apply with Conrad.

When his head lowers, I close my eyes and just feel. The press of his lips is soft yet firm. He doesn't seem to be hurried as he lazily strokes his tongue against my own. When he nips at my bottom lip with his teeth, I know I need to be closer. Climbing to my knees, I straddle his lap. Conrad wastes no time sliding his hand behind my neck and deepening the kiss.

"So sweet," he murmurs against my lips.

The hussy in me is strong when it comes to him. I grind my hips against his erection, which has us both grappling for the other. "More," I say, holding his face in the palm of my hands and kissing him with everything I have.

No words are passed between us when he slides his hands under his sweatshirt and unclasps my bra. Lifting my arms up over my head as far as I can without destroying the fort ceiling, together, we manage to wrangle his sweatshirt off me. His touch is sure as he slides the straps of my bra over my shoulders.

"Damn," he murmurs once my bra is discarded. When his hands cup my breasts, I tilt my head back and let the feel of his thumbs brushing over my nipples wash over me. At this point, I'm certain there is nothing he could do to me that I wouldn't enjoy.

"Aspen, look at me. Please." There is a hint of pleading in his tone. Lifting my head, I stare into his eyes. Thanks to the soft glow of the fire and the TV, I can see him perfectly. "I need to taste them." His thumbs make another pass on my breasts.

"Are you asking for permission?" He nods, swallowing hard. Leaning in close, our mouths barely a breath apart, I whisper, "Permission granted." I kiss him, but he's having none of that. He pulls away and moves us to where I'm lying on the mountain of blankets with him hovering over me.

When his mouth closes around my nipple and his tongue takes over, I can do nothing but grip his forearms and hold on for the ride. With an audible pop, he releases one breast only to feast on the other with his lips, tongue, and teeth.

"Please." I'm fully aware I'm begging, and I'm good with that as long as he doesn't stop.

"Please what?" There's desire and humor in his voice.

"Don't stop."

"Wasn't planning on it." His lips trail down my stomach until he reaches my leggings. This time he doesn't stop to ask for permission. He sits back on his knees and pulls the fabric from my body. "Matching." He grins when he sees my panties. The purple lace does indeed match my purple lace bra that he removed.

I shrug, the best I can lying down, and smile up at him. What I don't tell him is that I've been thanking my lucky stars that I packed all matching sets, and when I've gotten dressed since being here, I think about him. This morning I wondered if he liked the color purple.

He moves next to me, his strong hands roaming over my body. "Even though it would kill me, you still have time to stop this."

"Wh-What?"

"I've already had a taste of you. If I were to have more…" His hand lightly traces over the waistband of my panties. "I don't know if I'll be able to stop."

"I don't want you to stop."

"You sure?"

Instead of using my words to answer him, I grab his hand and guide it beneath the lace fabric to where I need his touch the most.

"Fuck, you're so wet." That little nudge is all it takes for him to take over. My hands grip the sheets as his fingers work their magic on me. Closing my eyes, I just feel and memorize every second of his hands. Every single touch.

When I feel his lips press just above my pelvic bone, my eyes spring open to find him peering up at me. "I'm drunk on you, Aspen."

I don't know what to say to that, so I don't say anything. What can I say? That I'm drunk on him too? I'm way past drunk. I'm highly intoxicated. We're talking way over the legal limit here.

"These need to go." He pulls on my panties, and I lift my hips, making it easier for him. "There she is," he murmurs. "All of you." He runs his fingers through my folds. Bending his head, he captures a nipple in his mouth, and suddenly my senses are on overload. He's everywhere, and yet I need more of him. The rhythm of his tongue against my breast matches the steady thrum of his fingers inside me, and I lose all control. My cry is one of relief and uninhibited desire as my orgasm races through my veins, causing my back to arch off our bed of blankets.

"Hey." He smiles down at me once I'm able to pry open my eyes and look at him. "Nice to have you back," he teases.

"My turn." Reaching out, I slide my hand beneath his lounge pants and stroke his hard length over his boxer briefs.

"Fuck, Aspen. You're killing me here, sweetheart."

"Not until I get this," I say, squeezing his cock.

"You sure?"

"Less talking. More fucking, Riggins."

"Yes, ma'am." He manages to strip in record time in our little fort and settles between my thighs. He leans in, his hard cock rubbing against the wetness of my orgasm. "Shit," he mutters, resting his forehead against mine.

"What? What shit? You can't back out now, Conrad Riggins." My tone is half scolding, half accusing.

"No. I'm not. It's just that I don't have protection."

"You're a Riggins."

"What the hell does that mean?" He laughs.

"I mean that isn't this your thing? Hooking up? Were you not a boy scout?" I add, making him laugh harder.

"Hooking up is not my thing. I've hooked up, but it's not a thing. I don't have a new woman in my bed every night, and no, I wasn't a boy scout. None of us were."

"Huh," I muse, and he shakes his head in amusement. "So that means this is a no go?"

"I'm afraid so." There's disappointment in his tone, and I feel it deep in my soul.

"What if I told you I was on the pill?"

"I'd tell you that I'm going to need more information than that."

"Like what?"

"Like what are you saying, Aspen? You want me to be inside of you bare?" He chokes back the final word.

"I'm clean."

"I never doubted that you weren't."

"I've only slept with two other people. Both were in relationships."

"I don't need your dating history."

"Then what do you need?"

"A minute."

"A minute?"

"Yes, beautiful. I need a minute. The sexiest woman I've ever seen, ever had the privilege to have my hands on has just told me I can have her bare. I'm trying to get my shit under control."

"You don't have to—I mean, no pressure."

"Aspen." He leans in close. His cock rests against my belly, and his eyes bore into mine. "I want you. I want to. It's just a first for me, and I know as soon as I slide inside you, I'm going to lose control."

"You already took care of me."

"That's not how this works, babe. You come before me and with me. Always."

"That's not possible, Conrad. Be reasonable."

He quirks a brow, daring me to argue his point. "So, how do we fix this?"

"You're sure you want me bare?"

The way he asks has me wanting to reach between us and guide him inside me right this second. "I'm sure. We're protected."

He nods. "I'll take it from there." His lips press to mine, and then he's gone. I miss the heat of his body, and I'm too focused on the loss of his heat to realize his plan until I feel his hands grip my thighs and his mouth cover my clit.

"Conrad!" I call out in both surprise and lust. He doesn't stop. He devours me like a man who hasn't eaten in days. When he pushes one digit inside me, my body convulses around his finger. "Sensitive," I pant.

"Mmm," he moans, and I feel the sound from my head to my toes.

My hands are buried in his hair as I hold him to me. I need more. I need all he's willing to give me. I'm ready to beg for… I'm not sure what, but I hold steady, letting him have control. He's doing a stellar job without my instruction. My grip tightens on his hair, and I realize that I may be hurting him, so I force myself to release my hold on his locks and grip the sheets instead. He sucks harder at my clit, and I feel the tell-tale signs that my second orgasm of the night is close, when all of a sudden, he's gone. His mouth. His hands, all gone.

"Con—" I don't get to finish when he pushes inside me. Full. I feel so full, deliciously so. My hands that were gripping the sheets bury into his back as I lock my legs around his waist and hold on for the ride.

CHAPTER
Conrad
TWELVE

F UCK ME.

I knew she would feel like heaven. However, I was in no way prepared for the actual experience—the feel of her heat, the silky smoothness of her body gripping mine like a vise. I'm buried as deep as I can go, and I'm afraid to move. I can't move. I'm sure I'll come with one more stroke. I need to breathe.

Just breathe, Riggins.

Closing my eyes, I tilt my head back to the ceiling of our fort and take a deep breath, slowly exhaling. That helped—a little. Lowering my head, I open my eyes, and what I see has me gritting my teeth. Aspen beneath me, her hair mussed, her lips swollen from our kisses. Her body flushed from her release, perky tits just begging for my mouth.

Her hands move from where they're buried in my back to frame my face. "You with me?"

I'm more than with you, baby. "I'm right here," I assure her.

She pulls me into a kiss. "Move, Con," she whispers against my lips.

Never one to disappoint, I pull out and push back in. I fight to keep my eyes from rolling into the back of my head. Never has a woman ever felt this good. Never. I want this to last forever, but I know the way my cock is throbbing inside her that it's not going to, no matter how hard I try to make it happen. If you can't beat them, you join them, right?

"Hold on to me," I instruct, and she does exactly as she's told, her hands gripping my back. Her nails dig in, and that only lights the fire inside me to flame even higher. "You're perfect." I drop a kiss to her lips and pull out, then push back in. This time I don't stop as I set a steady pace of my hips rocking with her as I slide my cock in and out of her over and over.

My spine starts to tingle. That, mixed with the sting from the dig of her nails against my back and the vise that is her pussy is too much. With one more long, deep stroke, I still, spilling over inside her. She calls out my name. At the same time, hers falls from my lips.

Heaven.

This has to be what heaven feels like. Aspen's pussy is heaven. That's the only explanation. Knowing I need to separate us so she can clean up, I begrudgingly slide out of her and lie next to her, pulling her into my embrace.

"You're incredible," I declare, kissing her temple.

She taps her hands against my chest. "That," she says, still groggy from her orgasm.

I know we need to get cleaned up, but I need just a few more minutes with her in my arms. I don't know what will happen when we break this trance we're in, and I need this. I need her. That's a shocking realization. I've never needed a woman in my life. Never liked one enough to think about keeping her around. Aspen has changed that.

"Babe, I need to go grab something to clean you up with."

"Shower."

"The only way you're going to shower is if I'm in there with you. I need you close right now."

"I can't walk, my legs are shaking, but I really do want a shower." She looks up at me with those hazel eyes.

"Come on." Reluctantly, I let her go and crawl buck-ass naked out of our fort, and help her stand before lifting her into my arms and carrying her upstairs. We take a shower, and although there's a lot of touching and kissing, that's as far as it goes. It's the most intimate I've ever been with a woman. Sure, sex is intimate, but this.... We're both naked, and it's about the touch of my skin against hers and the sated look in her eyes. A look that's also full of heat when her eyes find mine. It's more than sex. It was us, and whatever this is between us burning bright. Touch by touch, we learned one another.

"I say we sleep in the fort tonight," she says as we make our way back downstairs.

"We can do that."

"Really?" She turns to look at me, her eyes bright.

"Sure. We worked hard on that fort. Besides, it holds some memories."

"That it does," she agrees.

We make our way back to the living room, and I turn off the TV before climbing back into our fort and pulling her into my arms. We spend the next hour making out like teenagers, my hands memorizing her, which leads to making love to her again before she drifts off to sleep.

I didn't sleep a wink last night. I didn't know what the light of day would bring, and I couldn't bear to miss a second with her sleeping peacefully in my arms. Her naked body pressed close to mine.

I lost track of the number of times I've replayed last night over and over in my mind. I know part of what made it so incredible was the lack of barrier between us, but it was more than that. It was magical.

Magic.

Maybe the old man isn't crazy after all.

Every time she would wake up and reach for me, it did something to me. Something I can't explain. Hands down, last night was the most incredible night of my life.

Now I just need to figure out what to do about it. Things can't go back to the way they were. I can't see her and pretend she didn't single-handedly change me as a man. I don't know how she's feeling or what she thinks, but I intend to find out. Today. Before our families arrive, I need her to know that last night wasn't just a night of fun for me. It meant something. *She* means something. She means everything. In the span of a few days, she's suddenly everything.

I need to get up and add some wood to the fire, and it's starting to get chilly down here on the floor. It would help if we put clothes on, but trust me, you wouldn't be dressed either if you were me. Not to mention, I need her again. She slept so peacefully I couldn't bear to wake her up. I need her again before we have the talk about what this means and where we go from here.

My phone rings and I clamber to answer it. I manage to grab it from the end table and see Marshall's name on the screen. "Hey, Marsh." Aspen cuddles closer, and I can tell that she's now awake.

"Con, you ready for the family to descend?"

I look down at the beauty in my arms. I'm not ready, but we will be by this evening. That gives us all day to talk. "Yeah."

"Good. We're about an hour out."

"What?" I still. "What do you mean an hour out?"

"Grant got a call from Josh letting him know that they took care of the road to the cabin last night. Everyone decided to come earlier to make sure it's all hands on deck."

"Good deal. Listen, Marsh, I need to shower. I'll see you when you get here."

"Yeah, I've heard that one before. I thought you might appreciate the heads-up. I'm leading the pack, so I'll make a stop. Buy you some time."

"Not necessary," I tell him.

"Conrad, I can tell by the sound of your voice. Kick whatever random woman you have in your bed, wake up Aspen, and get your ass in gear. Ninety minutes, brother, that's the best that I can do." He ends the call without saying goodbye.

"What's going on?" Aspen asks.

I lean in and kiss her slow and deep. Regardless of the fact that we need to get this place in order and ourselves, I need to kiss her good morning. Nothing would keep me from that. Not even our families. "The roads are clear. Josh called Grant. They left early. They're about an hour and a half away."

"Shit!" She scrambles out of the fort, bringing some of it down with her. "We have to clean this place up. Shit. Shit. Shit."

"Hey." I grab her arm, stopping her movements. "We need to talk about last night."

"We will. I promise, but not right now. Get moving, Riggins!" She pulls my sweatshirt over her head and starts picking up blankets and pillows.

I stand frozen as I watch the nest we created be torn to pieces, and something in my chest tightens. "Conrad!" She stomps her foot.

"Sorry, I'm moving. Why don't you go on up and shower, and I'll get the living room back in order?"

"We need to wash the blankets." Her face turns red.

"I'll start a load."

"They're going to ask why."

"We'll tell them that I made love to you, and they needed washing."

"No! Are you crazy? We can't tell them that. No. Nope." She shakes her head. "Okay. I'll just tell them I was trying to freshen them up since no one has stayed here for a couple of months."

"Fine," I grumble. "Go, so we can talk."

She gives me a look I can't decipher before grabbing an arm full of pillows and rushing up the stairs. The thick blanket that we slept on and the one we covered up with should be sufficient as far as washing them. The one on top was thick, and well, I came inside her. My cock twitches at the memory.

Aspen takes the world's fastest shower and is back downstairs in less than thirty minutes, just as I'm moving the first load to the dryer. I did a quick cycle to speed up the process. "Hey, go grab something to eat. I have everything down here handled."

"You sure?" Her eyes scan the room, and when her shoulders relax, I know she sees that I do indeed have the downstairs back in order. No one will ever know about the night we shared in our fort by the fire. No one but us, and I promise it's a night I will never forget.

"We have an hour," she says, looking at her phone. "That's good. Go shower, and I'll make us some breakfast."

"Thanks, babe." I lean in for a kiss, and she flinches. "Aspen."

"Sorry, I'm just... nervous, I guess. Last night and now they're going to be here soon, and it's just a lot to process. We'll talk. Okay. Go, shower." She waves her hand in the air. I lean in again for a kiss. This time she lets me, but she's stiff and the first to pull away.

My heart sinks. No way am I letting her push me away after what we shared. Her touch is branded on my skin, and I can't just forget something like that.

I rush through a shower, hoping to have some time with her to discuss us while we eat. In ten minutes flat, I'm back at the kitchen island just in time for her to plate up some eggs and toast.

"Quick and easy today." She smiles, but the smile doesn't reach her eyes.

"Aspen?"

"I'm sorry. It's been the two of us in this bubble we've been in the past few days, and that bubble's about to be burst. I'm just feeling... off." She smiles again, and although it's not forced, it still lacks the brightness I'm used to from her.

"Come here." I hold out my hand, and she takes it, allowing me to pull her between my legs and hug her tight. "It will all work out. We're in this together. It took both of us," I tell her.

"Yeah," she agrees. "Eat up." She moves out of my hold and digs into her food.

I wait until she's finished to try again, but I'm stopped when the front door to the cabin opens. "I'm getting married!" Aurora cheers as she makes a beeline for her sister.

"Hey, bro." Grant laughs. "She's all kinds of excited that the roads were cleared early."

"Of course, she is. Your wedding day is a big deal."

"You good?" he asks.

"Yeah. I stayed up late reading over a new code for the security system," I lie.

Grant holds his hand up to stop me. "Say no more."

The rest of our families file into the cabin. There are handshakes, hugs, and between Mom, Aspen, and Aurora's mom, Sheila, orders are given out. I'm instructed to help my brothers salt the sidewalks and driveway. I should have already had it done, but spending time with Aspen was more important. There are five of us. We can knock this out in no time, same as we did as kids. I don't know when, but I'll find time in the chaos of this wedding to talk to my girl.

CHAPTER
Aspen
THIRTEEN

EVERYONE IS IN wedding mode. Thankfully, they're all too preoccupied to notice I'm distracted. The past few days are replaying in my mind over and over again, with last night as the highlight reel. I feel... different. I couldn't explain it even if I tried.

I've never had a man touch me so reverently and have the touch feel as though it was reaching my soul. It sounds crazy even thinking about it, but it's the best way I know how to describe it. Being with Conrad was an out-of-body experience, one I'd happily relive every day for the rest of my life. However, I know that's not possible. I'll have the memories forever. That will have to do.

"Aspen, what do you think?" Mom asks.

"Oh, yeah." I nod. I have no idea what she just asked me, but I'm going with it.

"Me too," Aurora agrees.

Dodged a bullet. "So, what's left?" I ask.

"I think that's it. The decorators are coming at three, and the caterers are confirmed. They're dropping off tables tomorrow," Lena explains just as the dryer dings.

"I'll get it," Conrad says, walking into the kitchen to get to the laundry room.

"You're doing laundry? Did you not bring enough clothes?" Lena questions. "I thought your dad asked if you needed anything?"

"That's my fault." I'm quick to come to his defense. "I was drinking hot chocolate and spilled a little on the blanket. Conrad threw it in the wash for me. I'm sorry." The apology is for the lie that I'm going to hell for telling, but I can't tell her that.

"Nonsense." Lena waves me off.

Conrad's eyes find mine, and the look he gives me tells a story. One of passion and risks and yearning. I recognize it because it's exactly how I feel when I look at him. What we did was risky. I've never once thought of having sex without a condom, but there was no way I could have stopped.

The passion and yearning go hand in hand. Last night was explosive and unlike any other experience I've ever had with a man. The yearning, well, I long to have him again. To have his hands on me, his mouth, to know that his touch is all mine. That he's all mine.

"That was sweet of you," Mom tells Conrad, breaking our gaze. He simply nods and continues on to the laundry room.

"Aspen, will you come up to my room with me? I want to go over my hair and makeup plan." My sister nods her head toward the stairs. The look on her face tells me it's not her hair she wants to talk about.

"We've practiced," I remind her.

When she asked me to do her hair for her wedding, I thought she was crazy, but we've done a few trial runs, and we're ready. She wants curls, nothing fancy, just lots of curls in her long locks. We practiced with her short veil, which comes with a jeweled headband. She's going to be a beautiful bride. Grant's not going to know what hit him when he sees her walk down the stairs to him on Saturday.

"I know, but I want to go over it again. Mom, Lena, do you need us?"

"No," they reply in unison.

"Come on." Aurora grabs my hand, and I have no choice but to follow her up to the room she's sharing with Grant. His only requirement for the wedding. He refused to sleep in separate rooms, and my sister happily obliged him.

"Where's the fire?" I ask as Aurora pulls me into her room and shuts the door, turning the lock.

"What. Was. That?" Her hands settle on her hips, and she gives me a look that I imagine will have her future children singing like canaries. I, on the other hand, hold strong.

"What are you talking about?"

"That—" She points to the floor. "Down there in the kitchen. Spill it, sister."

"Wedding planning? Maybe you should lie down. I think the stress is getting to you."

"Aspen!" She stomps her foot. I have to bite down on my lip to keep from laughing. I love riling her up.

"Aurora!" I stomp my foot, mocking her.

"Stop it. What did I miss?"

"Lots of snow."

"Damn it, Aspen."

"Nothing. You didn't miss anything. I don't even know what you're talking about." Lies. All lies.

"Conrad. What was that? He looked at you like he wanted to eat you for dinner."

Damn it. She had to go there. I feel my face heat. "There might have been a kiss or two." Or fifty.

"And I'm just now finding out about this?"

"When was I supposed to tell you, Rory? While Mom and Lena were in full swing wedding planning? Or how about when Mom and Dad gave me a hug hello? It was nothing. We were here all cooped up alone. It happens. It's done."

"That look he gave you, the one you returned, that wasn't nothing."

"It is if I say." I'm aware I sound like a toddler, but she's backed me into a corner, and we both know it.

"You can tell me," she urges.

"I just did. A few kisses, that's it. It's done."

"Aspen." Her tone is softer, and I can't handle that. I don't know what we are. We didn't talk about it, and I know that's my fault. I'm not sure what it meant, if anything, and I'm giving him an easy out.

"Aurora. This is your weekend. You're getting married in a few days to the love of your life. Let's focus on that."

She studies me for far too long, and I'm worried I'm going to have to think of another way to leave this alone. "For now. After the wedding, we're talking about this."

"You'll be on your honeymoon. Talking to me will be the last of your priorities." I start to sing the lyrics of "I Just Had Sex," and we both fall into a fit of laughter. "Come on, future Mrs. Riggins. Let's go back downstairs and see what else we can do."

Arm in arm, we do just that. I don't know how I'm going to manage to avoid Conrad for the next few days, but if I'm anything, I'm resourceful. I'll make it happen one way or another. We are not letting this, whatever this might be, ruin our siblings' wedding.

I don't know how, but I've managed to avoid Conrad the entire day. Until now. My dad and Stanley ran into town and brought back pizza. Everyone grabbed a chair around the table, and wouldn't you know it, the spot closest to me is open. I focus on the pepperoni and cheese on my plate and pretend I don't notice Conrad is not sitting at the table. I thought I might get lucky, but when I see him come around the corner with his plate of pizza in one hand and a bottle of beer in the other, I know my time is up.

I pretend to ignore him as he takes his seat next to me. It's not until his hand finds its way to my thigh under the table, and I feel his hot breath next to my ear, that I realize I'm kidding myself thinking I could pretend he's not sitting next to me.

"Missed you today," he whispers in my ear. His hand falls away as he begins to eat.

As for me, well, I strike up a conversation with Lena, who is on the other side of me. We talk about the memories of her boys growing up here in the cabin, and I love that my sister and her children are going to be able to have similar memories.

"Aspen?" I feel a hand on my shoulder. It's with that simple touch that I know it's Conrad before I even turn to look. "What do you say?"

"Sorry. I missed what you were saying."

"We're going to go night sledding. You're going with us," Aurora tells me.

"Who is we?"

"Me and Grant and you and Conrad. Sawyer can't go because she's pregnant, and Royce won't leave her. Owen and Layla want to get Carter down for the night, and Marshall"—she looks over at her future brother-in-law—"is just a wimp."

"Hey!" Marshall tosses a napkin at her. "I'm not a wimp. I'm just not in the mood to freeze my balls off."

"Marshall Riggins!" Lena scolds him, and the entire table erupts in laughter. "I swear you'd think you boys were raised in a barn."

"What? It's the truth. It's too cold out there."

"Getting soft in your old age?" Grant teases him.

"Not soft. Smart." Marshall grins. "Aren't you worried about being banged up for your wedding night?" he asks.

"Wedding day," Grant corrects him.

"Nope. The wedding night, you know when the extracurriculars take place." Marshall wags his eyebrows.

"Marshall!" Aurora sputters with laughter.

I glance around the table and see us all as one big happy family. My parents, as well as Lena and Stanley, only seem amused with our conversation. It's wonderful how well we all get along and fit together. I love that for my sister and her future husband.

"Well?" Conrad asks.

I search for a good excuse, and I don't have one. Conrad already knows that I enjoy being outside despite the cold. I'm worried it's going to be awkward. How could it be with Grant and Aurora there as a buffer, right? "Sure. I'm in." Conrad's eyes light up, and you would have thought I just gave him the world with my agreement.

Aurora and I help clean up while the guys dig out the sleds and some winter gear. "You up for this?" Aurora asks me once we're upstairs to add some layers of clothes.

"I agreed to go, didn't I?"

"Yeah, but you looked like it was going to kill you to come with us."

It just might. "That's silly. I love the snow, and it's been ages since I've been sledding."

"But you and Conrad built that snowman I saw when we pulled up?"

"You know that we did. I told you that."

"I know." She grins. No matter what she says, I still think that all this wedding stuff is getting to her.

"Come on, crazy girl. We have hills to slide down." Arm in arm, we make our way downstairs to find Grant and Conrad waiting on us. As soon as we reach them, Grant tugs Aurora from my arms to his with a sly grin on his face. He slides his arm around her shoulders and kisses her temple.

"Ready, baby?" he asks.

"Yes!" Aurora's excitement is infectious.

That's my excuse for not realizing that Conrad was moving in and sliding his arm around my shoulders. "Ready, baby?" he asks. I know he's mocking his brother. However, with the look in his eyes and the way my body responds to his nearness, we both know it's not just mocking Grant. He's asking for himself.

"Yes!" I exaggerate Aurora's reply, which has her sticking her tongue out at me while Grant and Conrad laugh. I expect him to release his hold on me, but he doesn't. Instead, he leaves his arm around my shoulders as the four of us head outside.

"Where are we going?" I ask, ducking out from under his arm.

"Just around the back. There's a pretty decent hill there that won't kill us to walk back up."

"I say we team up," my traitor of a sister suggests.

"Perfect." Conrad is quick to agree. Grant is none the wiser, but my sister, on the other hand, she's on to us.

"We'll go first," Aurora says.

Conrad and I stand back while they situate themselves on their sled, with Aurora sitting in front of Grant between his legs. I know she did this on purpose, so Conrad and I would follow their lead. She thinks she's sneaky when she's anything but.

"Con, give us a push," Grant says, his arms clasped tight around my sister.

Conrad does as he asks, and they go soaring down the hill, their laughter following them the entire way.

"You ready for this?" Conrad claps his hands together gleefully.

"Do I have a choice?"

"Nope." He gives me that boyish grin. "Come on. You get settled first, and I'll climb on behind you."

"What are you waiting for?" Grant calls up the hill.

Knowing there's no way of getting out of this, I settle on the front of the sled and wait for Conrad to take his place behind me. With his arm around my waist, he pulls me back against his chest. "That's better."

"They're watching," I warn him.

"Let them watch, Aspen."

"Can we not do this right now? Not during their wedding?"

"Fine. But we are going to talk about it. About us."

"There is no us, Conrad."

"Oh, baby, there is most definitely an us. Now, hold on." His grip grows tight as he rocks back and forth to get the sled to move. The movement reminds me of last night, and I'm suddenly overheated despite the freezing temperatures. We start moving, and the cold wind against my face is much-needed to cool me down. By the time we reach the bottom, we're both laughing as the sled flips into the snow in order for us to stop. We're a pile of sled, snow, arms, and legs. It's perfect.

Just another moment to add to my long list of my time with him.

CHAPTER
Conrad
FOURTEEN

SHE'S CUTE. I don't have another word to describe her right now. Aspen, Aurora, Layla, and Sawyer with her baby belly are trying to one-up each other with crazy dance moves, much like Aspen and I did two nights ago. The same night we spent in each other's arms in our homemade fort. That night she was sexy and silly. Tonight, she's downright adorable. Huh, I guess I do have another word that describes her.

Forcing myself to stop staring at her, I look around at my brothers. Royce has his eyes glued to his wife as Sawyer holds her hands on her baby bump and attempts the running man. His lips are quirked to one side as he looks at her adoringly, and I can only imagine what he's thinking.

Owen pretty much has the same look of adoration as he watches Layla. Their son, Carter, is sleeping peacefully against his chest, amongst the chaos that is his parents and his aunts and uncles. He looks content and happy. The stoic, quiet brother I've always known is still there, but his wife and son bring out a new side of him, one we are all more than happy to see each and every day.

Grant is watching Aurora, but his gaze is half predatory, half infatuation. They're still in the honeymoon phase, so to speak, and it shows. Don't get me wrong, he adores her as much as my two older brothers do their wives, but Grant and Aurora are getting married in two days. My guess is he's thinking about finally making love to his wife. Last week that wouldn't have even crossed my mind. Okay, maybe it would have, but I would have said fucking her as his wife. My time here with Aspen has changed my outlook.

I have a theory of my own. Whatever this feeling is, it's not magic. It's magic pussy. It has to be. That's a small detail my dad and brothers left out. There is no other explanation for the thoughts in my head and how I go out of my way to brush up against her and rush to the table to sit next to her. This isn't me, but then again, it is. It's me when it comes to Aspen.

Marshall stands and begins to dance around with the girls. He makes sure to dance up close to each of them. It's innocent. We all know that. He's trying to get a rise out of us, but it's not going to work. We might not like seeing another man around our women, yes, *our* women, but this is Marsh. We know he would never go after any of them. His efforts are a waste, but at least it's entertaining. They're having a good time, and I want nothing more than to be out there with them. With her.

That about sums up my current situation. I'm nursing a beer and watching Aspen shake her ass on the makeshift dance floor delegated by the ladies in the basement of my parents' cabin. I'd rather her be shaking her ass on me, maybe sitting on my lap? However, as an alternative, this doesn't suck. Not at all.

Something passes between Aurora and Aspen. Whatever it is causes Aspen's posture to stiffen. I sit up from where I'm lounging on the couch, ready to go to her, when Aurora announces, "Time for Truth or Dare."

Aspen looks worried, but me, I'm ready. Bring it on. I'm not going to hide the way I'm feeling. I've tried talking to her, but she keeps putting me off. If a game of Truth or Dare is what it takes to get her to admit that there is something between us, so be it. I couldn't care less who knows.

Each of the women in my life go to the brother of mine that they're attached to. Marshall pulls up a bean bag and sits on the floor facing the huge sectional couch where we're all sitting, and by the look on her face, Aspen begrudgingly takes the last open seat next to me.

Where she belongs.

"I'll go first." Marshall rubs his hands together in glee.

"Why do you get to go first?" Aurora pouts.

"I'm the youngest." Marshall winks at her. "Being the lastborn Riggins brother often comes in handy."

"That was Mom's rule when we were kids, so we wouldn't leave you out," Royce counters.

"Well, I say the rule applies." He taps his chin. "Owen, truth or dare?"

"Truth."

"How long until you knock her up again?" Marshall laughs and points at Layla.

"As soon as she's ready," Owen replies without missing a beat.

"Come on," Grant chides him. "We all already knew the answer to that one."

"We're just warming up," Marshall replies. He stands and grabs another round of beers for everyone except for Sawyer. She gets water. "Your turn, O," Marshall says, taking his seat on the beanbag.

"Royce, truth or dare?"

"Truth," Royce replies.

"Marriage and babies are making you all boring," Marshall comments.

"You might want to think about your truth question and see how the boring title applies to you." Royce laughs.

"Are you hoping for a boy or a girl?" He points to Sawyer's baby belly that Royce is resting his hand on.

"Healthy." Royce is quick to reply.

"I still can't believe you all are waiting until the baby gets here to find out the sex," Aspen says. "Not knowing would drive me insane."

"Oh, it's driving us crazy too, but there's excitement in waiting to find out."

"How do you shop?" Layla asks. "We knew Carter was a boy, and we had the nursery and everything all set up."

"We're going with greens and yellows and neutral tones," Sawyer explains.

"All right, my turn," Royce says. "Marsh, truth or dare?"

"Dare."

Royce looks around the room. "Eat a bowl of popcorn covered in ketchup."

"Pft." Marshall climbs to his feet. "Surely, you can do better than that, brother." Marshall stands and makes his way to the small kitchen in the basement. "We're in luck," he says, holding a half-empty bottle of ketchup in the air. Reaching into the cabinet, he grabs a paper bowl and comes over to the couch, holding it out for Sawyer. "Fill me up, sis," he tells her.

Sawyer laughs as she fills the smaller bowl full of popcorn from one of the many bowls we've been eating out of tonight. "I get to add the ketchup too. You might need a spoon or something," she tells him. Marsh hands her the bottle of ketchup and skips, yes skips, back to the kitchen to grab a spoon, and then skipping back. "Here you go." Sawyer grins when she hands him the ketchup-drenched popcorn. Marsh takes it from her and eats it like a starving man.

"Done." He grins, grabs his beer, and downs the rest of it. "Anyone else need another?" he asks. With a round of nos, he grabs himself another, tosses the bowl, and takes his seat again. "Let's see, Aspen, truth or dare?" he asks.

I feel her stiffen beside me. "Truth."

"Who here has the nicest ass?"

"That's easy." She shrugs.

"Well, let's hear it," he coaxes her.

"Carter," she says with a straight face.

"Ooh!" Owen laughs. "She got you there."

"You said here, that does include Carter, doesn't it?" She laughs. The sound wraps around me like an embrace.

"I'll get you." Marshall grins and points his index finger at her in a warning.

"Aurora." Aspen grins. "Truth or dare?"

"Dare," Aurora replies confidently.

Aspen gazes around the room, much like Royce did for his turn. Her eyes light up, and I know she's found her dare. "I dare you to eat a banana with no hands."

"Elementary, my dear." Aurora laughs.

"I'll get it." Aspen is up and in the kitchen, grabbing a banana from the basket on the counter.

Mom always has fruit lying around. She says it's with hope, that with all the junk we consumed as kids, we would get a little bit of healthy too. She still does it to this day. I guess habits are hard to break.

After pulling a paper towel off the roll, Aspen hands it and the banana to her sister. "Eat up."

"So, how does this work?" Grant asks.

"She's going to need someone to hold it for her. The only rule is that she can't use her hands."

"Fuck." Grant shifts his position. Every man in this room is thinking exactly the same thought that just ran through his mind. Fuck is the perfect response to the images I'm sure we're all seeing.

"Will you hold it for me?" Aurora asks, and I know I do not imagine the drop in her tone of voice. It's almost sultry. From the hard swallow Grant performs, I know I didn't. Aurora makes a show of peeling the banana slowly, and dropping the peel onto the paper towel, and handing the banana to Grant.

She's my future sister-in-law, which means she's my sister, and a year ago, I never could have imagined her agreeing to this. Grant is good for her. They're good for each other. With that being said, I'm a man, and I can't look away as she leans in, her hands clasped behind her back, and takes her first bite. But it's not any bite. She makes sure to make it as provocative as possible, licking the tip of the banana and moaning before taking a bite.

"Son of a bitch," Grant hisses. He moves the banana and takes a huge bite. "All done," he says, his mouth full. The room erupts in laughter, and my brother, well, he's flushed, and the look he gives his fiancée tells me her little performance isn't over. He has plans for her. It's written all over their faces.

"Okay… uh, Rory, it's your turn," Marshall says, tilting his beer to his lips and taking a long pull. I do the same. I think we all need a drink after that.

Aurora throws her head back and laughs. All the women seem to be amused. "Conrad," Aurora calls me out. "Truth or dare?"

I see a look pass between the sisters. "Truth," I reply and feel Aspen's shoulders relax.

"Let's see. What is your ultimate sexual fantasy?"

"I need to clarify that in order for this to be the 'ultimate sexual fantasy,' it needs to be with someone I care about." I don't look at Aspen, but I do press my thigh into hers, letting her know this is all about her. "Finding someone you care about, someone who wants you for the man that you are and not your name or money. Someone who is also your best friend."

"Get to the good stuff," Marshall chides.

"It's going to disappoint you," I tell Marshall. Then I make eye contact with each of my three older brothers. "You three will get it." No one says anything, so I keep going. "Something intimate yet informal. Like maybe building a fire, and hell, I don't know building a fort, you know, like we did when we were kids? I'd imagine that making love to someone you care about in that kind of situation would be the ultimate fantasy. You get to be silly and romantic, all at once with your best friend." I shrug like it's no big deal, but my heart is racing as our night together flashes in my mind. It's a night I know I will never forget.

"Wow," Layla breathes. "That's… wow."

"I second that," Sawyer chimes in.

"Damn, Con." Aurora fans herself.

"That wasn't even hot. He said making love. I was expecting leather and chains and shit," Marshall jokes.

"Nah, it's about the intimacy, little brother."

"Who are you and what have you done with my brother? Wait!" Marshall points at me, giving me a pointed look. "Don't tell me you've fallen down the rabbit hole too? Damn it, Conrad," he scolds me. "We were supposed to be the last two holdouts." He sounds defeated.

"You find your magic, brother?" Royce asks.

I don't hesitate to answer him. "Yeah. I found my magic." My confession has my three older brothers nodding, and even though I know they want to ask me, they let it slide. I'm certain the first opportunity they have, they'll corner me.

"This one needs to be put down." Owen looks over at his wife and stands. "See you all in the morning."

Royce and Sawyer agree, as do Grant and Aurora. We all know what they're rushing off to bed for. "You two bailing on me too?" Marshall asks, moving to the couch.

"Want to watch a movie?" Aspen asks him.

"Hit the lights!" Marshall calls after our siblings and scrolls through, finding a movie to watch. He doesn't ask us our opinion, and really, I don't care. I'm not going to be paying attention anyway. Instead, I pull a cover off the couch and cover Aspen with it, sliding my hand under the covers and lacing my fingers with hers. I'm acting like a teenager, but I don't give a fuck. It's my skin against hers, and I'll take it.

Not twenty minutes into the movie, and her head falls to my shoulder. Knowing she's asleep, I press my lips to the top of her head.

"It's like that, huh?" Marshall whispers.

I almost forgot he was here. Almost. "It's like that," I admit.

"She know?"

"She knows."

"You happy?"

"Yeah, Marsh. I'm happy."

"Is she?"

"I think so. We have a lot to talk about. Everyone arriving early threw a wrench in that. No one knows, so can you keep it between us until she and I have had a chance to talk?"

"You plan on keeping her a secret?"

"No. Fuck that. I want everyone to know, but she and I need to talk first."

"I can keep a secret," he assures me.

"I hope it won't be a secret for long."

"Your fantasy?" Marshall asks.

"Yep."

"Damn," he breathes.

"Yeah." I kiss the top of her head again and know that I need to get her upstairs. I'd love nothing more than to hold her here all night, but I know Aspen, and waking up with me and my little brother in the basement will not be something that she's excited about, especially since she's been ignoring me. "I'm going to take her to her room. I'll be right back."

"You sure about that?" he teases.

"I'll be back," I assure him. Standing, I carefully lift her into my arms.

"Conrad?" she asks sleepily.

"It's me, baby."

"I miss you," she replies groggily.

"You have no idea." My reply falls on deaf ears as she falls back to sleep. Luckily I'm able to carry her up both flights of steps without running into anyone. When I lay her on her bed, her eyes open.

"I wish you could stay with me."

"I can if that's what you want. I'll stay."

"You can't."

"Why not?"

"Because it was a one-time thing."

That noise you heard? That was my heart cracking. "No. It wasn't."

"You don't do serious."

"I do now."

"You expect me to believe that?"

"Have I given you reason not to?"

"Only every minute since I've known you."

"And our time here? Does that not count for something?" I want to strip her out of her clothes and remind her how good we are together. Surely, she hasn't forgotten.

"It was the circumstances, Conrad. You and I both know that."

"No." I lean in close so she is sure to see me. I want her to look into my eyes. "What I know is I've never felt about anyone the way I feel about you. What I know is that our time here has changed me. Our night together altered my universe. I want you." I finish speaking and place the palm of my hand against her cheek. My touch seems to have her melting into the mattress. That tells me all I need to know.

"Goodnight, Conrad."

Dismissed.

I want to scream and yell and fight for her. Fight for us, but this isn't the time or the place. We'll get through this wedding, and then I'll show her. I'll prove to her that she's changed me, and there is no one on this earth better for me than her. Leaning in, I press a gentle kiss to her lips. "This isn't over." I kiss her again and stand. "Night, baby."

I force myself to leave her room. In my mind, I'm already formulating a plan to win the girl. Touch by touch, I'll prove to her that we're meant to be. She is my magic, after all.

CHAPTER
FIFTEEN

Aspen

"**Y**OU'RE BEAUTIFUL," I tell my sister. I'm trying like hell not to cry and ruin my makeup. However, seeing her in her wedding dress, knowing that in less than ten minutes, she'll marry the love of her life, it's got me all up in my feels. While I know that we will forever be the Steele sisters, she's also going to be a Riggins. I'm happy for her. She deserves nothing but the happiness that Grant and his family have brought into her life.

"Stop." She fans her face with her hands, trying not to cry.

"Knock, knock." Layla sticks her head in the door. "Aspen, we're ready for you," she tells us. "Oh, and your dad is here for you, Aurora."

"Thanks, Lay." She smiles. "Give us just a second." Aurora opens her arms wide, and I step into her embrace. "I love you, Aspen. Thank you for being here with me."

"I love you too. Now, it's time to get this party started." I pull away, dab at my eyes, and turn for the door. I give Dad a hug and make my way to the top of the stairs, taking my spot.

Grant has four brothers, and they're all close. However, it's just Aurora and me, and when she asked me to be her maid of honor, that made the choice easier for Grant. He wanted Royce and Owen to walk in with their wives. That left Marshall and Conrad. Marshall called dibs on Carter, saying that chicks dig a man with a baby. That was before he knew it was going to be a small, intimate wedding. That left Conrad and me as maid of honor and best man.

Five months ago, when this was all decided, I was good with it. I didn't care who I walked in with. All I cared about was being here for my sister on her big day. Life, however, had other plans, and as I reach the end of the hall on shaking legs, I try like hell not to make eye contact with Conrad.

I was able to avoid him the majority of yesterday. The cabin was a flurry of wedding activities, which helped. I'm a coward, and I know that. I'll own it. I refuse to let any drama between the two of us interfere with my sister's wedding.

"There she is." Conrad smiles when I join the group.

"Is she ready?" Sawyer asks.

"More than ready." I walk to the front and take my place next to Conrad.

He leans in close. "You take my breath away."

My heart hammers in my chest at his words. I want so badly to believe him. I want the fantasy world we've been living in the past week to be real. However, I've known Conrad for a while now, and he's all about the fun, and nothing about him has ever said to me that he's ready to settle down. I want what my sister has, and I refuse to settle for anything less.

"Shall we?" He offers me his arm. I take it and slide my arm through his. He rests his hand over mine, and it feels so natural to be standing here with him like this. Together, we start down the open staircase to where the living room has been transformed for today's ceremony.

When we reach the arch of flowers where Grant is standing, I have to let go of him, and I feel the action in my soul. I want to keep him for me. I want this past week to be our normal, and I know that it won't be. I swallow hard at the emotions clogging my throat. I hadn't figured I would find a man who turns me inside out, and he's emotionally unavailable. He thinks he wants me, wants what we had here, but once we're back home and our everyday lives resume, he's going to be seeing things more clearly. It hurts now. I can't imagine the pain of him changing his mind.

No, thank you.

Self-preservation is in full effect.

Royce and Sawyer, Owen and Layla, and finally Marshall, who's holding Carter in his little suit, follow in beside Conrad and me. When the music changes, I don't turn to look for my father and my sister. Instead, I turn my gaze toward Grant. His face lights up the minute he sees my sister. I watch as his eyes well with tears. The smile pulling at his lips tells me all I need to know. Aurora has given her heart to a good man with a loving, supporting family, and I couldn't be happier for her.

"I love you," Grant says loud and clear as soon as Aurora is standing next to him.

I wipe at my cheeks as my eyes, on their own accord, stray from the happy couple to Conrad. He's watching me intently. What I wouldn't give to be able to read his mind. With extreme effort, I pull my gaze from his and focus on my sister and his brother. Today is their day, one I have no doubt will be the start of a beautiful life together.

When a hand lands on my shoulder, I know it's him. How is it that in just a short amount of time, my body knows his touch? "Dance with me?" His lips brush against my cheek.

Quickly my eyes dart around to see if anyone is watching. I shouldn't worry. Not a single person is paying us an ounce of attention. "I'm not sure that's a good idea."

"Come on. We've already had one dance tonight."

He's right. We have. As soon as the ceremony was over, the

men in the Riggins family, along with the help of my father, moved the tables that were set at the edge of the room and moved the chairs around them. That gave a place for everyone to sit and left the remaining open floor space for the dance floor. Somehow, Conrad was able to set up a tablet to be the DJ, and we can even punch in song requests, and the music is piped through to the entire first floor of the cabin.

Aurora went on and on about how cool it was and that he had it all worked out to just tap the button for each event. Such as when the bride entered the room, the first dance as husband and wife, father-daughter, and mother-son dances. She raved about his tech skills, and it took everything I had not to tell her that he's skilled in more than just computer technology. However, I was able to bite my lip and nod at her as she sang his praises.

"Aspen," he whispers my name.

I can't deny him. I know that I need to protect myself and my heart, but I can't. Just one more dance. We all head home tomorrow, and things will go back to normal. This is my last chance to be in his arms. It's an opportunity I know I should pass, but I just can't.

With a nod, I scoot back in my chair and stand. He offers me his hand to lead me to the dance floor, and I take it. I crave his touch, and the realization that this could be the last time I ever experience it has hot tears pricking the back of my eyes. Swallowing hard, I smile at him as he settles his hands on my hips and pulls me into his embrace. Sawyer and Royce, Owen and Layla, Grant and Aurora, and Lena and Stanley are already dancing.

My eyes scan the room to find Marshall and my mom joining us on the dance floor while my father tosses a laughing Carter into the air over and over. He's going to be a wonderful grandpa. Sadness washes over me. Will I ever find true love? Will I ever be able to give them grandkids?

"Hey." Conrad places his index finger under my chin and assists me with lifting my chin so we are looking eye to eye. "What's going through that pretty head of yours?"

"Nothing. I'm fine."

"Aspen, baby, you can talk to me."

I want to. I want more than anything to tell him that in a matter of a few days, he's made me fall for him, but I don't. "I'm good," I assure him.

"I missed you yesterday and today. I feel like I've barely gotten to see you."

"It's been a busy few days."

"I'll be glad when we get home and can spend some more time together."

"Conrad—" I start just as the song changes. Brantley Gilbert's "Let it Ride" flows through the speakers, and I give him an accusing glare.

"I might have had something to do with the song selection," he confesses. I didn't think it was possible, but he pulls me closer, holding me tighter. "This is our song," he says as he proceeds to sing the lyrics low, his lips next to my ear.

I feel the meaning. It's us, and we both know it. We are most definitely caught up in the moment, and just as Brantley suggests, we're letting it ride. I feel myself start to get choked up. I really like him. No, it's more than that. I care about him, and the thought of not having more moments like this is enough to cause an ache inside of me that I'm not sure will ever be cured.

"Let me show you, Aspen. Let me show you how great we will be together."

"Conrad, you're caught up in the moment. You're blinded by the events of the past week."

"No. I'm blinded by your beauty. I'm blinded by how perfect you fit in my arms. I'm caught up in your hazel eyes and the feel of your skin against mine. I'm lost in the fact that all I want to do is touch you. I don't care if it's holding your hand, sitting with my hand on your lap at dinner, spinning you around on the dance floor, or making love to you. I crave you and your touch."

"Con—" My voice cracks, and I feel his lips press against my temple. I'm very aware that our families are in the same room with us and could see him kissing me. They can see him holding me as if I'm his. I pull out of his arms and stare up at him. "I can't do this." Turning, I walk out of the living room and close myself into the bathroom at the end of the hall. Tears well in my eyes.

I want so badly to believe him. I want to believe that our circumstances are not what's fueling his confessions, but I know better. Or do I? Can someone really change just like that? Is it possible that everything he says is true? Looking at myself in the mirror, I say a silent prayer that the universe leads us back together. Only time will tell how serious he is. I vow to keep an open mind. When we get home, we'll see if he changes his mind.

Opening the door, I find Marshall leaning against the wall. "You good?"

"Y-Yes," I stammer.

He throws his arm over my shoulders and leads me back out to the living room. "I know my brother can be an ass, and take it from a man who's already watched three of them fall ass over head in love. He's into you."

"Wh-What do you mean?"

"Come on, Aspen. Only a blind man would miss the tension between the two of you." He must read the panic on my face. "Don't worry. Everyone here is wrapped up in their significant other. I, on the other hand, have had a lot of time to people watch. Just promise me you'll think about giving my big brother a chance."

"Did Conrad put you up to this?"

"Hell no. As the youngest, only unattached Riggins brother, I have a reputation to uphold." He laughs. "I just see the way he looks at you, and that's exactly how the rest of them look at their wives." With that, he gives me a hug and makes a beeline for his parents, stealing Carter from their mom. He takes him to the dance floor and starts spinning him around, and Carter's laughter echoes through the room over the music.

For the second time in a matter of minutes, I'm sending up a silent prayer. "Please let him be right," I whisper.

CHAPTER
Conrad
SIXTEEN

I SLEPT LIKE shit last night. I got home from the cabin around five and texted Aspen, asking her to come over. She declined. Not that I expected her to actually accept the offer, but it still put me in a bad mood. I lie awake all night trying to think of ways to show her that what I feel for her isn't just some random idea from the time we spent together. The best I can come up with is to just stay consistent. To let her see that I want her in my life. No, I need her in my life. Not as my brother's sister-in-law but as my... everything. Whatever the two of us decide that looks like is okay with me.

She just needs to be mine.

It's a little after 5:00 a.m., and going to sleep now would be a disaster considering I have to be at the office at eight. Instead, I drag my tired ass out of bed and text Marshall.

Me: Gym?

Marshall: You think you can keep up, old man?

Me: Probably not. No sleep. See you there.

I don't wait for his reply. Instead, I dress in clothes for the gym, grab my phone and keys, and head out. I'll come back here to shower and get ready for work, and maybe grab some breakfast. On second thought, stopping at Warm Delights for breakfast sounds like a better plan. I know my girl will be there. Suddenly, regardless of my lack of sleep, I'm looking forward to the day. At least the beginning of the day. If I'm lucky, she'll agree to dinner, and I can look forward to the ending too.

"You look like hell," Marshall greets me.

"Fuck off."

He throws his head back in laughter. "Trouble in paradise?"

I glare at him. "Spot me," I say, going to the weight bench.

"What are you going to do about it?" he asks, standing behind the bench to spot me.

"What am I going to do about what?" We both know that I know what he's talking about. I choose to ignore the fact.

"How are you going to get the girl?"

"That is the million-dollar question. I've been up all night, and nothing I can come up with seems to be enough. How do you convince a woman you spent a few magical days with that you want her forever?"

"There you go using that magic shit. You can't tell me that you buy into that."

"I didn't, no. Now, I absolutely do."

"And forever? Really, Con? That's a long-ass time."

"Not long enough."

He whistles. "Aspen has you by the balls." I don't confirm or deny. Not that he needs confirmation. He knows me well enough to read between the lines.

We work out in silence for maybe ten minutes when he blurts, "Flowers."

"What?"

"Flowers. You win her over with flowers."

"Come on, man, you have to know I need more than flowers to prove to her that I'm in this."

"Women love flowers," he defends.

"I'm not disputing that. However, flowers are not going to say, hey, this guy wants to be with me."

"Have you ever tried it?"

"No."

"Then, don't shoot it down. I'm telling you. Flowers is where it's at." He taps his temple and grins.

"Fine, I'll send her flowers, but you need to put that thinking cap of yours back on. It's going to take more than that to convince her."

"What did you do?" he asks accusingly.

"What do you mean? I didn't do anything. Unless you count falling for her."

"So, why is she resisting so much?"

"She thinks I'm not the settling down type."

"Well, yeah, but look at our brothers. They weren't either. I mean Royce was, then he wasn't, but now he is again."

"Apparently, she feels as though I was wrapped up in our circumstances."

"Were you?"

"No. Yes. Yes, I was wrapped up in our circumstances, but not the way she thinks. I was wrapped up in her. I only want to be wrapped up in her. It was our circumstances that gave me the time to see that she's special, but it's not only our circumstances that have me feeling this way."

"I feel like we're talking in riddles." He laughs.

"I feel like I'm living in one. Seriously, Marsh, I need something to wow her. To show her I'm in this. That she's who I want." It's painfully obvious that she needs more than words. I've never regretted the way I lived my life. I've owned my nights out and the random hook-ups, but it's finally catching up with me. I need her to understand that she's the only one for me. She's all I see.

"Maybe you should take some time to think about it. She thinks your feelings were circumstantial. Take some time to see if she was right."

"I hate to admit it, but you might be right." I never thought I would be saying those words to my little brother. "I can't just walk away, though."

"Don't. Be there. Hell, be everywhere. Let her see that you're not resorting to your old Conrad ways, going out and never settling. In the meantime, maintain some distance. Let her see. What is it that they say? Actions speak louder than words."

"I guess you're right, but fuck me, it's going to be hard to sit on the sidelines."

"Not forever. Just long enough for her to see. And you won't be on the sidelines per se. Think of it as being the back-up quarterback. You're there to support the team, but you don't get called into the game until the time is right."

"There is never a right time for a back-up quarterback."

He laughs. "You know what I mean. Stay close, send flowers, call her, text her, keep yourself in the front of her mind, but give her time to see you."

"Who are you, and what have you done with my little brother?"

"Hey, I'm more than just a pretty face. I've watched my now four older brothers fall into the trap that is love. I've learned a thing or two along the way."

"Right. You know you're not fooling anyone, right? You're probably the most soft-hearted out of all of us."

"I resent that statement." He laughs.

"Resembles is more like it."

"Regardless, you know I'm right. Give her some time to see you. The real you. Not the one people think they know. Let her see Conrad Riggins. The brother, the son, the uncle, and one of the best guys I know."

I swallow hard, taking in his words. "Did we just have a moment? I feel like we had a moment." I tease him to lighten the heaviness of the conversation.

"Fuck off," he says with a laugh. "Get your ass up and spot me."

At exactly seven thirty, I'm walking through the doors of Warm Delights. There's already a line, which I expected. That's fine. I don't mind. It gives me time to watch my girl in action. She's great with the customers, and she always has a smile on her face. Her smile lights up the room. It always has. I was just too blind to see before now.

"Can I help you?" she asks as she finishes her last transaction. I don't say anything, waiting for her to look up. "Oh." She pats at her hair. "Conrad. How are you?"

"Better. How's your day going?"

"I'm tired as hell. I should have stayed on my early to rise, early to sleep regimen while we were gone."

"You have to give yourself a break now and then."

"What can I get you?"

You. "What's today's special?"

"Cinnamon rolls."

"Great. Give me a dozen. I might as well take some back to the office." It's not lost on me that Grant brought a box from Warm Delights almost daily since he met Aurora. Now with me trying to win over her sister, we're all bound to gain a few pounds. I need to make sure I keep hitting the gym.

"Sure thing." She busies herself, packaging my dozen cinnamon rolls while I busy myself watching her. "Here you go." She slides the box across the counter, and I hand her my card. I make sure our fingers touch, and the way she pulls her arm back, I know she feels the electricity between us. It's there. She feels it. I feel it. I just need her to accept it.

"How about you let me take you to dinner tonight? I know you're exhausted."

"I'm going to be going to bed early," she assures me.

"An early dinner then."

"Conrad...." She sighs.

I hear Marshall's voice telling me to let her see me but not to push her. I can't believe I'm taking love advice from my younger, very single brother. "Another time then."

"Have a great day. Tell everyone I said hello."

Leaning over the counter, I make sure I have her full attention. "You too, baby." Her breath hitches, and that little sound will be what gets me through the day.

"Morning, sis," I greet Layla.

"Oh, what do you have for me?" she asks, standing from her chair. She reaches for the box, and I happily hand it over. "Oh, these look so good," she says, opening the box and peering inside.

"What looks good?" Royce appears from his office.

"Conrad brought cinnamon rolls." She manages to tell him before taking a huge bite of the one she chose.

"Thanks, Con," Royce says, helping himself to a roll.

"I smell something good," Marshall says, exiting the elevator. "I was certain with Grant being out of the office, this was going to be a long boring week without treats. It appears I was wrong." He winks at me, and it's obvious as hell.

"What's that about?" Royce points to Marshall.

"Nothing." I'm quick to reply, and I see the question in his eyes.

"Hey, Layla, I have—" Sawyer stops in her tracks when she sees us. "I see how you are. Trying to hide the goods." She moves to stand next to Layla and grabs a cinnamon roll, taking a huge bite much like the rest of us.

"Who's harassing my wife?" Owen asks.

"No one is harassing your wife," Marshall tells him. "But you're late to the party."

"Nothing new." Owen grabs a roll, kisses Layla, and takes a bite.

"What was up with the look and the wink?" Royce isn't going to let this go.

"Nothing."

"Oh, it's something. It appears that our brother here has found himself in somewhat of a pickle."

"A pickle? Really, Marsh?" He shrugs and grins around his cinnamon roll.

"What's going on?" Owen asks, his tone serious. My two older brothers and their wives stare at me with concern while Marshall smirks, watching it go down. He knows he has me between a rock and a hard place. I never lie to my brothers. Never.

"Do we have to do this here?" I ask.

"Yes," all five of them say at the same time.

"Fine. Can we at least move this to the conference room?"

Layla grabs her sign, welcoming any guests, telling them to have a seat in the small waiting area and that someone will be right with them. "Ready." She smiles at me.

Great. Sisters are coming too. Perfect. "Big mouth," I say to Marshall as I pass by him to go to the conference room.

"I'll bring the cinnamon rolls," he calls after us. I can only imagine how much he's enjoying this.

In the conference room, I wait for everyone to take a seat. I open my mouth to tell them, but I don't really know what to say.

"Con's in looove," Marshall says, stretching out the word. I glare at him, and he just grins.

"What?" Royce asks.

"Who is she?" Owen asks.

"Aspen," Sawyer and Layla say at the same time.

"Yes. No. I mean, yes, It's Aspen, but I'm not in love. I just... I really like her."

"Aw." Another simultaneous reply from my sisters.

"When did this happen?"

"At the cabin. Look, I don't want to say too much. However, I will admit that yes, I am interested in Aspen."

"And is she interested in you?" Owen asks.

"Yes."

"So, what's the issue? Are you worried about Grant and Aurora? I can't see either of them having an issue with this."

"No. It's not that." I rake my hands through my hair. My brothers know me better than anyone. None of us hid our need for fun and random women. That sounds worse than it is. I've not been with a laundry list, but I've never had a serious relationship either.

"She thinks he's a player."

"No. She didn't say I was a player." I go on to tell them what she did say, which is very little. Just enough for me to know she thinks I'm not into her and that I'll change my mind.

I won't.

"So what are you going to do?" Layla asks.

"Flowers," Marshall answers for me. "I told him to send her flowers. I also told him to chill and just let her see that he's all about her and no one else."

"Good idea. Try text messages telling her to have a good day, and good morning, goodnight, things like that," Sawyer adds.

"Are you serious about her? You know that she's family now."

"Of course, he is," the girls chime in.

"Didn't you see the way they were looking at each other? Oh, and the dance at the wedding." Layla fans herself.

"I'm serious." Never been more serious.

"All right!" Royce claps his hands together. "Operation Win Aspen Over is in full force."

"What? No. No. No. No. I can handle this on my own."

"Clearly not if you went to Marsh for advice," Owen retorts.

"Hey!" Marshall furrows his brow.

"Thanks, guys, but I don't need help. Not yet anyway. Just give me some time to try and figure this out." The five of them nod, but it doesn't look very damn convincing to me. Who knows, maybe I need to rally the troops to convince her. I'm not marking the idea off the list just yet.

CHAPTER
Aspen
SEVENTEEN

T ODAY WAS EXHAUSTING. I didn't sleep well last night. I couldn't seem to turn my mind off. I kept replaying my time with Conrad at the cabin. There's an ache in my chest that I don't understand. How can I miss him? We spent a few short days together, but it felt like it was a lifetime.

Stepping out of the shower, I barely have my hair in a towel when I hear someone knocking on the door. Rushing to slip into my fluffy winter robe, I pad through the small apartment I used to share with my sister above our bakery, Warm Delights, and answer the door.

"Fuck," Conrad murmurs. His eyes roam over my body. He can't see anything, but we both know I'm naked under this robe, and the heat in his eyes tells me he's imagining that very thing.

"Conrad, what are you doing here?" I pull at the robe to make sure I'm covered. Not that it matters, he's seen all of me.

My question seems to pull him out of his stupor, and he raises his eyes to mine and holds up a bag of Chinese. "I brought you dinner."

"You didn't have to do that."

"I know, but you were tired, and you had to get up early, and I wanted to see you." His hand holding the bag drops to his side as he waits for me to invite him in.

I shouldn't. It's only going to prolong this... whatever this is, and then my heart will be the collateral damage at the end of it all. "Come on in," I say, ignoring my own mental pep talk. The grin he gives me is one of victory, and I fight the urge to roll my eyes. "I need to put some clothes on."

"Not on my account." He winks.

"I'll be right back." After scurrying down the hall to my room, I slam the door, and for the first time, I engage the lock. I've never needed to before, but my resistance when it comes to him is weak, and I think the barrier will help.

Luckily for me, he's a gentleman, and by the time I'm dressed and have my hair brushed, hanging wet down my back, I find him in the small kitchen, at the tiny dining table with our dinner laid out for us.

"I wasn't sure what you liked, so I just bought a variety." He motions toward the small table that is covered with Chinese takeout containers.

"Thank you. You really didn't have to do this. You don't need to feel guilty or obligated or whatever," I ramble. I can feel my face heat from embarrassment, but I felt like the words needed to be said.

"Aspen." The way he says my name affects me more than it should. "Babe?"

No longer able to resist, I look up at him. "Conrad."

He grins. "I want to be here. I don't feel obligated in any way to spend time with you. I wanted to bring you dinner, and I wanted to see you."

I nod. I don't have words. I'm glad he's here, as I've missed him, which is crazy. However, there is still the fact that he's

Conrad Riggins. I've known him now for more than a year, and I've never seen him serious about dating. In fact, I've heard him give his brothers a hard time, so much so, I am convinced this isn't what he wants. He's still caught up in the adventure of being snowed in together for a few days. That's all this is. We've been home what? Twenty-four hours? He's still back in that cabin.

"Conrad—" I start, but when he places his hand over mine, I freeze.

"Eat, Aspen. You've had a long day, and you're exhausted. Eat your dinner, let me enjoy your company, and I'll get out of your hair so you can get some rest." The look in his eyes is soft, and his tone gentle.

I'm starving, and it's nice to not have to worry about dinner after the long day I've had. "Thank you," I concede.

He nods, takes a bite, and I do the same. "So, how was your day?" he asks.

Holding up my index finger, asking him to give me a minute, I finish chewing. "Busy. But I missed it. Don't get me wrong, it was nice to get some time away, but I really do love the bakery."

"It was Aurora's dream, though, right?" he asks before taking another bite.

"Yeah, she's always wanted to own her own bakery. I was working at a dead-end job that I hated, and when she said she was moving to Nashville, I jumped at the chance to come with her."

"She's lucky to have you."

"I'm lucky to have her. Her dream saved me too. Now I'm doing something I love and could never imagine doing anything else." I take a bite of my food, and it's delicious. It's definitely hitting the spot. I watch him as he does the same while his eyes dart around the tiny apartment.

"What about living above the bakery? How's that?"

"Fine." I shrug. "The commute to and from work is nice." I laugh.

"That helps with the crazy early hours you keep. Are you scared about living here alone?"

"No. The neighborhood is safe, and we have a security system."

"Well, I don't live far from here, so if you ever need me…." He lets the offer hang between us.

"Thank you, but I'm sure I'll be fine. I've been staying here for months on my own."

He nods. "I know, but I—Just know that you can call me for anything." There's something in his gaze that I can't name.

"Got it. Call Conrad when the trash needs taking out," I tease.

"That too." He smiles, the heaviness of the mood-lifting. "I mean, I have to use these guns for something." He smirks as he flexes his arms. He's still wearing the long-sleeve dress shirt he wore to work today, but I know what's hiding under those white sleeves of his.

"You better roll your pants up, Con. Shit's starting to get deep in here." I grin at him, taking a huge bite of rice.

"I could take them off, you know, to make sure I don't get shit on them."

"The pants must stay on." I point at him and give him a stern look.

"Party-pooper," he grumbles good-naturedly.

We spend the next thirty minutes eating, talking, and laughing like old friends. The tension from our time at the cabin disappears. Well, I'm hiding it, but the atmosphere is light, and it's nice. He's a good guy. I know he is. I just don't think he's good for my heart. I've heard him pick on his brothers and give them a hard time about the magic their family believes in when it comes to love and how he doesn't believe in it.

Here's the thing. I believe in it. I watched it work for my sister. I was certain she would remain single after what her dick of an ex did to her. He tore her down, ripped her spirit and her soul to shreds. I was convinced she was done with relationships. That is until Grant Riggins walked into Warm Delights, and instantly there were sparks flying between the two of them. Grant fought for them, for her.

Conrad called bullshit. So did Marshall. Sure, all the brothers claim to not have believed in it, but three out of the five have fallen hard. Conrad and Marshall both still insisted it was crazy talk.

I want the magic.

"Thank you for dinner," I say, pushing away from the table. "I ate so much. I don't think I can move."

He, too, pushes back from the table, only he stands. I yelp out in surprise when he lifts me into his arms and carries me to the couch. "You sit. I'll clean up."

"You don't have to do that," I tell him. He ignores me and walks the short distance back to the small kitchen area and begins to close containers and toss the trash.

"I'll leave these in the fridge. You can have them for lunch tomorrow."

"Why not breakfast?" I fire back just to mess with him.

"When you make treats as good as yours, you don't eat Chinese for breakfast." He tosses the trash and makes his way back to take a seat next to me on the couch.

"Maybe that's why I want to eat it for breakfast. I didn't make it."

"I'll make you breakfast any day. You just say the word."

"Right." I chuckle. "I'm up and in the bakery no later than 4:00 a.m. every day. You're still snoozing while I'm working my life away."

"I'll have you know I was up and at the gym by five this morning."

"I was up at three thirty."

"I was up most of the night," he counters.

I don't ask him why. I don't want to hear the answer. I cover my yawn before I can think of a reply. I'm exhausted, and with a full belly, it's going to be lights out for me soon.

"Come on." He stands and once again lifts me into his arms as if I weigh nothing.

"You know, my legs do work."

"I'm aware of that. But you're exhausted, and I like you in my arms." It's a simple statement, but I feel it deep in my core. "Which one?" he asks.

"This one." I point to my bedroom door.

He pushes inside and places me on the bed. "I'll be sure to lock up when I leave. You can set the alarm from your phone, yeah?" he asks.

"Yes."

"Let me go grab it. I'll be right back." He disappears, and I'm thankful as I suck in a deep breath to try to calm my nerves. "Here you go. I'll make sure everything is locked, and I'll text you once I'm outside." He leans over, and I lick my lips, thinking he's going to kiss me, and I know without a doubt that I'm going to let him. There is nothing better than this man's lips when they are pressed against mine.

However, his lips don't land on mine. Instead, they press to my forehead. "Night, beautiful," he whispers. His voice is low and husky and hot as fuck.

"N-Night," I stammer.

Gripping my phone tightly in my hand, I listen as his footsteps retreat. I hear the sound of the door closing, but I don't move a muscle. I wait, gripping my phone like a lifeline. When it pings, alerting me to a message, I'm quick to swipe at the screen.

Conrad: All locked up. Set the alarm.

Me: Thanks for dinner.

Conrad: Anytime. Get some rest.

Closing out of the messaging app, I pull up the one for the security system and set the alarm. I'm not scared to stay here on my own, but I do like the added security that the system provides. Plugging my phone in, I place it on the nightstand and close my eyes. It doesn't take long for me to fall asleep, Conrad the last thing on my mind.

CHAPTER
Conrad
EIGHTEEN

"**C**ONRAD, HOW ARE things?" Sawyer asks. She's sitting on the couch with a paper plate filled with pizza resting on her baby belly.

"Living the dream," I tell her, taking a drink of my sweet tea. My pizza has long since been devoured. I was starving.

"Come on now, you know we want all the details," Layla chides me from her place in the rocking chair. My nephew sleeps peacefully on her chest. He was cranky as hell and only wanted his momma. Once she cradled him against her chest and began to rock, he was sound asleep. Layla is a natural, as I'm sure Sawyer will be too.

"There are no details. I showed up at her place Monday night and brought her dinner. We ate, and I left. I've been to the bakery every morning, as you all already know from the goodies I've been bringing to work with me."

"I must say that you and Grant are keeping the office stocked with yummy treats," Layla comments.

"More like keeping them in business," Marshall jokes.

"Hey." I glare at him. "I'll have you know the business is thriving. They don't need Grant or me to keep them afloat."

"Sorry." Marshall holds up his hands in defense.

"Nothing? You have nothing to report?" Sawyer asks, and is that disappointment I hear in her voice?

"Sorry, sis." I finish off my glass of tea just to give me something to do. I wish Carter was awake so I could use him as a buffer.

"Did you send her flowers, as I told you to?" Marshall asks.

"No."

"There—" He points at me. "That's why you have nothing to report. You didn't listen."

"What do you know about relationship advice?" Owen laughs.

"Hey, I have a way with the ladies." Marshall puffs out his chest, and even I'm laughing at my little brother's antics.

"A way of scaring them off," Royce teases. "However, the flowers aren't a bad idea."

"All women like to get flowers," Layla agrees.

"This one"—I point to Marshall—"told me to just lay low. To be there but not be all in her face about dating me."

"And you listened to him?" Sawyer questions.

"I don't know what else to do. She thinks this is just some fling that I want to extend."

"Have you told her otherwise?" Layla inquires.

"I've tried. She's shutting me down at every turn." I know I haven't tried as hard as I could, but the last thing I want to do is make her feel pressured and push her even further away. That's why I took Marsh's advice.

"I can't believe I'm going to say this, but I think Marshall might be onto something," Owen admits. "She claims you want this fling extended. Show her she's wrong. That is assuming that you're done with clubs and random women?" He gives me a pointed look.

"Over it." I am. I'm not just saying that, and I know that my family believes me. I can see it in every single one of their faces. They're on my side.

"We're going to help you," Layla announces. She glances at Sawyer, who gives her a nod and a smile.

"Ladies, I can do this. I have to do this. She needs to see it from me." I just wish I knew how to do it and if the current method of being there but don't pressure her is working. Just my fucking luck, I'm going to get friend-zoned. Just the thought pisses me off.

"You do you," Sawyer tells me. "But trust us. She needs to hear it from other people too. Leave it to your sisters. We've got this."

"What are you going to do?" I'm almost afraid for her to tell me.

"Nothing. Not really. Layla and I can casually bring up how you're no longer going out on the weekends and that we think you've met someone."

"No! Don't tell her I've met someone. That's the opposite of what I need her to think."

"You didn't let me finish," Sawyer scolds. She looks over at Layla and grins. "You know, Lay, Conrad hasn't been his usual self lately."

"Oh, how so?" Layla jumps right into the conversation, and I feel as though I'm at a tennis match looking between the two of them.

"Royce said he's been staying home on the weekends."

"Really? He loves the club life."

"I know."

"How long has this been going on? Should I have Owen talk to him?" Layla replies.

"He said since the wedding." Sawyer turns to her side, where no one is sitting. "Have either of you noticed anything different about him?" she asks the air.

That's when I get it. They're going to talk me up without really talking me up. I look over at my two older brothers, who are sitting next to one another. "You two are lucky bastards. You know that?"

"We know," they reply, nodding.

"Conrad, we've got your back. You do your thing. Call her, text her, take her dinner, whatever, and yes, send flowers." Sawyer nods at Marshall. "We'll do what's best on our end as well."

"Grant and Aurora have no idea."

"When they see this side of you"—Royce points to me—"once they see how serious you are, you're not going to have an issue."

"We're going to help you get the girl." Sawyer slowly stands and comes over to give me a hug. "Come on, Layla, let's go talk strategy." They disappear into the kitchen, leaving me with my brothers.

I love my family, and knowing they're here for me makes all the difference.

It's Friday morning, and I'm on my way to Warm Delights to see Aspen and pick up an order of whatever today's special is. Marshall and I have met at the gym every morning this week, and I'm glad. Coming to her work has been the only time I've been able to see her this week. If I keep buying boxes full of goodies every day, I'm going to have to move into the gym. I now understand why Grant installed a home gym. He wants to be where Aurora is, and her career isn't good for the waistline.

Monday night, I brought her dinner, and every other night she's blown me off, or I've worked late. Tuesday, she claimed she and a couple of the girls from the bakery were going shopping and to dinner. We had a server issue on Wednesday that kept me at the office late. Last night, we were all at Royce's to help assemble furniture for the nursery. I was standing in Sawyer's office when she called her and personally invited her to join us. She claimed she needed to do laundry and clean. I was at her place Monday night, and it was spotless. I know it's an excuse, but there's not much I can do about it.

Shaking out of my thoughts, I push open the door to Warm

Delights. "Good morning, Conrad," Gloria, one of the new hires, greets me.

"Morning, Gloria. How are you today?"

She grins. "I'm good, but we both know you're not here to ask about my day."

I smile because I've been here for Aspen once since our time together. That tells me that they've been talking about me. Suddenly my day just got a little brighter. "Of course, I am."

"Uh-huh, she's in the back." She points to the swinging door that leads to the kitchen and office area.

"Thanks." I wink and move around the counter, pushing through the doors that lead me to the back of the bakery. Aspen is pulling a large tray of muffins out of the oven. "Are those for me?"

She turns and looks over her shoulder, offering me a smile. "Good morning to you too. And yes, these are today's special. I assume that's why you're here."

I'm here for you. "That, among other things." I'm trying to take the advice of my little brother, because let's be honest. It's the best I've got right now. That is until my sisters-in-law have their little performance. Grant and Aurora come home tomorrow. Hopefully, that means that it will be soon. However, first, I need to tell Grant and Aurora that I want to be with Aspen. I can only imagine what they're going to say when they find out about what happened between us.

I can foresee a lecture from Grant to not hurt her and only to pursue her if I'm serious, much like Royce and Owen warned me. And Aurora, well, I'm not sure. I'd like to think she knows I'm a good man and that she would be happy for us, but only time will tell.

I smell the air. "Are those banana nut?"

"Yes!" She smiles. "These are my favorite. Aurora has this recipe perfected."

"Loves banana nut. Noted." I wink.

"I love lots of things, Conrad Riggins."

Could you love me? "Oh, yeah? Maybe we should have dinner tonight, and you can tell me all about them."

"Con—" She starts to turn me down; I can tell by the tone of her voice.

"You have to eat, right? Besides, you skipped out on us last night."

"I didn't skip out on you. I had to clean and do laundry. I still hadn't done laundry since being at the cabin." Her face heats at the mention of the cabin.

"Well, now that's done, we should have dinner."

"I really shouldn't. I have to be up early tomorrow." She bites down on her bottom lip, and my dick twitches. Does she know how sexy she is when she does that?

"Come on, Aspen. I'll pick up takeout. You can go upstairs and shower, and I'll bring dinner. You can go to bed with a full belly." I'm begging, but I don't care. Just a little time spent with her is worth any amount of begging and pleading that I might need to do to make it happen.

"Sorry to interrupt." Gloria sticks her head around the door. "Aspen, do you have more of those muffins? They're a hit," she says and disappears back upfront as quickly as she appeared.

"Shit. Sorry, Gloria." Just as she reaches for the tray, the timer on the oven goes off. "Damn it."

I feel bad that I'm distracting her. "You get the timer. I'm not a baker. I'll take these up front."

"Thank you," she says, relieved, rushing to the oven to pull out another batch of muffins.

"Order up," I say, walking the tray of fresh muffins out to the front counter.

"Does he come with the muffins?" I hear a woman ask.

I look up at her and smile. "Sorry, I'm taken."

"I don't see a ring," she says bluntly.

"Yeah, well, I have to convince her to marry me first." I'm teasing her, but I realize that I wouldn't mind a ring on my finger.

Not if that ring attached me to Aspen. It's a shocking revelation, one I'll dissect further, but now is not that time. Gloria gives me a wide smile, and I retreat to the kitchen.

"Thanks, Conrad. You saved me there."

"Anytime. So, what do you say? Dinner?"

"I really shouldn't. Thank you for the offer. I really do want to get to bed early and get a head start here tomorrow. Things are going well, but I want to do some bookwork before Aurora gets in tomorrow."

"You've done an amazing job while she's been gone."

"Thanks." She blushes. "However, I don't want her coming back and being stressed, so I'm going to catch up on the books for her."

"I can help."

"No. Thanks. It's a one-person job." She reaches for a white box. "Here, these are on the house."

"I can pay for them."

"No. Please take them. I'll see you," she says, turning her back to me, effectively dismissing me.

Not wanting to press my luck, I take my box and head back to the front counter. I stop at the tip jar that I know they all split and drop a one-hundred-dollar bill into the jar. Gloria gasps, but I can't even find it in me to offer her a wink. Instead, I keep walking as if I didn't hear her and head to work. I know I'm going to have to be patient, but that's hard when you want something as bad as I want her.

CHAPTER
Aspen
NINETEEN

I T'S SATURDAY, AND the lovebirds come home from their honeymoon today. Aurora called me as soon as their plane landed and asked me to meet them at their place. She claimed she had so much to tell me. I told her we could wait. This is her first day home, but she insisted I be there. So, here I am, driving to their place. I know it's not just what she has to tell me. It's my sister finally getting answers for what she thinks she saw when we were at the cabin.

Today's special was magic bars, and I know how much Grant loves them. I also remember it was his first purchase and what might have started his obsession with my sister. Okay, I know that's not it, but I thought it was fitting, so I grabbed a dozen and set them back since I knew I was coming to their place this afternoon.

Pulling into their driveway, I'm surprised to see the garage door is up, and my sister's SUV is inside. Grabbing the box of magic bars and my phone, I make my way to the door. I don't even get to knock before it's flung open, and my sister is hugging me.

"I missed you!"

"I missed you too, Rory."

"Babe, let her in the house. It's cold as balls out there." Grant laughs.

"Thanks. For that, you get these," I say, handing him the box once my sister releases me.

"Aw, sis, you love me." Grant opens the box and swallows hard. "You do this on purpose?" he asks me.

"Nope. That's all your wife. She plans out the daily special."

"You plan this?" he asks Aurora.

"No. Not intentionally, but it's fitting."

"I thought so," I agree with her.

"Love you." He leans in and kisses her a lot longer and deeper than he should be since they're standing in front of company.

"I'm gonna go." I take a step back. Aurora pulls out of the kiss and grabs my wrist.

"No, you're not. We have so much to catch up on. My husband is going to go eat his magic bars while we do."

"My wife is right. These are calling my name. They brought me my magic already." He kisses her again and walks away.

"Come on in." Aurora tugs on my arm.

"Hold on, let me get my shoes off." I laugh. After kicking off my shoes and hanging my coat up in the hall closet, I follow her into the living room. "So, how's married life?" I ask, sitting next to her on the couch. We're both sitting sideways, facing one another.

"Bliss." She smiles, and it's blinding. "I don't know how else to explain it. I mean, nothing is really different between us."

"Your last name!" Grant calls from the kitchen.

"Except that." Aurora grins. "And our titles."

"And the honeymoon?"

"Perfect. We went snorkeling and just laid around on the beach most of the time."

"I'm surprised Grant let you out of the house you rented."

"It was a private beach," she confesses, and her face turns beet red.

"Ahh, say no more." I laugh.

"Enough about me. I'm an old married woman." She smiles. "Tell me about you. How's the bakery, and what was that at the cabin?"

"There it is." I shake my head, a smile tilting my lips. "I knew it."

"What? I told you when I got back we were going to get to the bottom of whatever it was. I'm back. Let's have it."

Grant walks in at that time and hands us each a plate with a magic bar and two cups of coffee. "I thought you could use a snack."

"Were you ever a waiter?" I ask him.

"Nope. I'm just that good, little sister."

"Oh, so now I'm a little sister?" I tease.

He shrugs. "You are younger than me."

"Thank you for the snack and the coffee. I'm going to need it for your wife's interrogation."

"Damn, babe. I thought you would have had it out of her by now."

"You told him?" I say, my voice raising an octave.

"No. I didn't tell him. He asked. We all saw it, Aspen. So spill. What's going on?" Aurora reaches over and places her hand over mine.

"We spent that time together." I know she's not going to let me get away with that explanation, but it's buying me some time.

"You want me to go?" Grant asks.

"No." I shake my head. "I'm sure he'll tell you. I know you all are close."

Grant nods and pulls my sister from the couch, takes her seat, and tugs her back to his lap. "Did he hurt you?" Grant asks. His tone is serious, and I know I have to tell them. I can't have him thinking Conrad, in any way, did something I didn't want him to do.

"No. No way. He wouldn't do that."

"I know he wouldn't physically. But in here." Grant taps his chest.

I smile at my brother-in-law. He's such an amazing man. "No, he didn't hurt my heart. I knew what I was doing. I was a willing participant."

"Can you stop hinting around and tell me already?" Aurora pleads.

"Fine. It all started that first day. I didn't know he was coming." I go on to tell them everything. From the minute he walked into the cabin until yesterday when he came in and asked me to go to dinner. "There, you have it," I tell them.

"It's the magic." Grant grins at me. "I can guarantee you that's what it is."

"Come on, Riggins," I tease. "I bought into all that because you love my sister, but let's be realistic here."

"I don't know, Aspen. Have you talked to Layla and Sawyer? They're the ones who convinced me it's real."

"He's not a settling down kind of guy. We all know this."

"Love changes you." Grant's looking at my sister when he says this. "I was content with life. Sure, I knew I wanted to settle down and have a couple of kids one day, but the minute I laid eyes on your sister, I knew she was different. I wish I could explain it to you, Aspen, but to be honest, I don't know that you would believe me if I could. What I do know is that from my grandpa to my dad, to my two older brothers, and then me. It's all happened that way. We meet the woman who is to be our wife, and we just know."

"Conrad isn't proposing marriage. Hell, I don't know what he's proposing. Dinner? More sex? I just don't know."

"Have you tried asking him?" Aurora suggests.

"No. I've been blowing him off." I take a deep breath. "Here's the deal. You two have to keep this between us. Got it?" I wait for each of them to give me their word. "I really like him. Like, really *really* like him. It's all kinds of complicated. I'm her sister. He's your brother," I tell Grant. "If we let this… whatever it is keep going, and then it dies a painful death, then what? How awkward would that be? Family dinners? Holidays? It would make things way too complicated." I pause, collecting my thoughts. "I know my heart would be broken, and I also know I wouldn't be able to stand by and watch him move on to someone else or multiple someone elses. At least this way, I know I can be around him. Sure, it will be awkward at first, and seeing him with someone else will still bother me, but that would be so much worse if I were to let myself fall harder."

"You're falling in love with him," Aurora says. It's not a question but a statement.

"What? No."

"Yes." She points at my face. "You are."

"That's crazy talk," I scoff. I'm not in love with him. We had a magical, no not magical, fucking magic…. We had a few great days together, where we enjoyed each other's company. Sure, I wasn't ready for it to end, but all good things must come to an end.

"It's not crazy talk. I know you. If you're not in love with him, you're close."

"I care about him, but I cared about him before. He's your brother-in-law," I remind her.

"Aspen," Grant says, waiting for my full attention. "I'll talk to him. I'll find out where his head is at, but I can promise you, my brother doesn't play games. None of us ever have. That's not how we roll. We're all straight shooters. If he says he wants to spend time with you, then he means it."

"But I can't just have this 'benefits' relationship. I'm not cut out for it. I'll catch feelings, and then when he's done, I'll be left," I confess.

"Sis, maybe he's catching feelings too?" Grant says softly.

"It was just a few days."

"I get that. I do. But it only took one look for me to know that your sister was going to be significant in my life."

"I've known Conrad for over a year. Nothing in that time between us. Friends. Nothing more, nothing less from either of us. Then he walks into that cabin, and something I can't even describe happens, and here I am." I shrug, defeated.

"Just don't close yourself off yet," Aurora pleads. "Let Grant talk to him and find out where his head is at."

"You can't tell him I told you. You can't tell him any of this," I beg.

"Hey." Grant grabs my hand. "I promise I won't tell him, but I do want to hear his side now that I've heard yours."

"You two can't possibly be okay with this?"

"Why not? There's no law that says sisters can't marry brothers from the same family," Aurora counters.

"Incest is illegal, Rory," I joke.

"Stop it. You know what I meant."

"I mean, my mom and the rest of my family already dubbed you an honorary Riggins, so this way you'll get the name to go with the title." He smirks.

"Whoa, back up the cookie truck. No one is talking about marriage and changing names."

"It's worth it. You should try it," Aurora tells me.

"You two"—I point at the two of them—"are in this love bubble and want everyone to have your happiness."

"Is that so wrong? You're my sister, and I love you. I want you to find a good man to spend your life with. How do we know that's not Conrad?"

"How did this conversation go from possibly dating to marriage?"

"It's the magic," Grant says, deadpan.

He really does believe in all of this magic of finding love stuff.

I don't know what I believe. I know Conrad is constantly on my mind. I know I've spent more time replaying my time with him in the cabin than anything else this past week. I know every time he comes into the bakery, I question my decision and wonder if any time spent with him would be worth the heartache.

"Hey, Mom," Grant says, pulling me out of my thoughts. "We're home. Aspen is here." He pauses. "We'll be there. Okay. I'll tell her." Another pause. "My wife is perfect. We'll be there, Mom. Love you," he says, ending the call.

"Mom wanted to make sure we could make it to Sunday dinner."

"Our first one as husband and wife." My sister sounds so happy it brings tears to my eyes.

Grant leans in and presses his lips to hers. "Our first of many." He pulls away and pins his gaze on me. "Mom also insisted you be there."

"I don't think that's such a good idea," I say as my phone rings. Grabbing it from the table, I see Lena Riggins's name flash across my screen. "Hi, Lena," I greet her, and both my sister and brother-in-law grin like fools. "I appreciate the invite." I listen as she tells me that she's not taking no for an answer. "Okay. Thank you. I'll be there." She tells me I better be, or she's sending one of the boys to get me before ending the call.

"She knew you would try to decline."

"How?"

"I told you. We could all see the tension between the two of you. Not to mention the dance and the way Conrad's eyes would follow you no matter where you were in that cabin." Aurora smiles at me.

"I think I've had enough of the love matchmaking for today. I'm beat. I'm going to head home and get some sleep."

"Be safe. We love you." Aurora stands to give me a hug, Grant doing the same.

"I'll talk to him. We're going to get to the bottom of this."

"There is nothing to get to the bottom of." It's a lie, and we both know it. After another round of hugs and the promise to see them tomorrow, I head back to my place above the bakery. The entire drive home, I'm thinking about what they said. Is there a chance that Conrad really does want more?

Once in my apartment, I kick off my shoes and plop down on the couch. I am exhausted. I haven't been sleeping well. In fact, that last full night's sleep I got was that night I spent in his arms.

My phone rings, and it's Conrad. Taking a deep breath, I place the phone next to my ear. "Hello."

"It's good to hear your voice," Conrad greets me.

"Hey." I don't know what to say to that. His words have my heart tripping over in my chest.

"What are you doing?"

"I actually just got home. I went to see Aurora and Grant."

"How are the newlyweds?"

"Definitely in the honeymoon phase." I laugh softly.

"I love that sound."

"What sound?"

"Your laugh."

What do I say to that? I ignore him instead of trying to find a reply. "What are you getting into tonight?"

"Holding down the couch."

"Really?" I'm surprised he's not at a club.

"Yep. My girl has a job where she gets up really early, and she's been blowing me off a lot lately. So, it's just me tonight."

"You're dating?" My heart feels as though it's stuck in my throat.

"Depends."

"O-On what?" I croak. I don't want to know, but I need to hear him say it. To confirm that I was right.

"Are you ready to say yes?"

"Wh-What?" I'm a stuttering fool when it comes to this conversation.

"You're the only one I want, Aspen." His voice is low and deep.

"Conrad." I sigh.

"I know I need to prove it to you, and I'm going to. I told myself that I would give you more time before I told you about my plan, but I can't wait anymore. I'm going to prove to you that I want you. That you're the only one I want."

"Say you do. Then what?"

"Come on, baby, you know how the story ends. Then we live happily ever after."

I clamp my hand over my mouth to stop the sob. I want that. I want him and all he's offering, but it's only been a week. He's still caught up in our time at the cabin. He needs more time to make sure this is what he wants. Without a doubt, he is who I want. I know that. We have led two very different lives up to this point. He's been wild and carefree. That's a big deal to give that up.

"Will you come to Sunday dinner with me tomorrow?" he asks.

"Your mom called me earlier and invited me."

"Did you tell her you'd be there?"

"I did."

"Can I pick you up?"

"I'll be there."

"I'll take it. You sound exhausted. Get some rest. I'll see you tomorrow."

"Night, Con," I whisper.

"Night, beautiful."

The line goes dead, and I'm both giddy and fearful at the same time. Every interaction with him, I fall a little harder. That only confirms what I already knew. I would never survive losing him if he was mine.

CHAPTER

Conrad
TWENTY

WHEN I WAS in high school, there was this girl, Lucy Anderson, new to our high school, and all the guys wanted her. Even me. She agreed to sit with me at the basketball game, and the night before, I didn't sleep well. It took forever to fall asleep, and I woke up hours before I needed to. I was excited that she picked me.

That was my past.

My present looks similar. Only this time, it's more than just excitement to have the new, prettiest girl in my grade choose me. This is deeper. This is Aspen agreeing to come to Sunday dinner. This is Aspen not telling me we can't be together when I told her I would prove to her that I know without a doubt she's it for me.

Aspen is different.

She's my future.

The clock reads 6:00 a.m. on the dot. I don't have to be at my parents' until five this afternoon. That's when we eat. I have all damn day to occupy my time, and all I want to do is lie here and think about her. No, what I want to do is go to her place and hold her. I just need to touch her soft skin. Fuck, but do I miss the feel of her skin pressed to mine.

I debate on calling Marshall, asking him to go to the gym with me, but I know he went out last night. He's not going to be interested in the gym. Not today. Instead, I grab my phone and scroll through social media. An advertisement for a local realtor pops up, and it's for a house I recognize. It's not far from Grant's. Clicking on the ad, I look through the pictures. This place has been completely renovated, and it's nice. Really nice.

I like my condo. I do. It's close to downtown and the nightlife. Something Marsh and I have taken full advantage of over the years. His condo is on the other side of town. Depending on where we are, determines whose place we would end up at the end of the night.

Those days are over.

Even if I never convince Aspen to give me more of her, I can't go back to that life. I want more. She's made me want more. I refuse to think about what might happen if I can't convince her.

After hitting the Contact Me button, I place the phone to my ear. It's now just after seven in the morning and probably too damn early to be calling a realtor on a Sunday, but I want to see that house.

"This is Dan," a man answers on the third ring.

"Hi, Dan, my name is Conrad Riggins." I know our family is well known. "I'm calling about the listing." I go on to tell him which house I'm looking at, and he asks me a few questions about what I'm looking for. "I wasn't, to be honest. I just happened to see the listing, and it's near one of my brothers."

"Well, I can meet you there at your earliest convenience. It's vacant and was just listed yesterday."

"I can meet you there in thirty minutes."

"Um, okay. Mr. Riggins. I'll see you there."

Throwing off the covers, I make my way to the kitchen to start a pot of coffee before rushing through a shower. I don't know where this sudden urgency is coming from, but the location is perfect. Besides, what better way to show Aspen that I'm serious than to give up the bachelor pad in the heart of downtown Nashville?

Driving down the road, I'm getting excited. This is a great area, and Grant and Aurora literally live maybe two miles from here. The location is perfect. I pull into the drive behind, who I assume, is the realtor. A man with salt and pepper hair steps out of the black sedan. "Mr. Riggins?" he asks.

"Conrad." I offer him my hand. "Thanks for meeting me on such short notice, Dan."

"That's my job. You want to start inside or outside?"

"Let's go inside. I drive here all the time on the way to my brother's place. I'm familiar with the area."

"Great. Just so you know, I'm not sure if you read through the entire listing. There is a total of eleven acres, and two of that is a pond."

"I did see that. Thanks," I say, following him into the house.

"I'm going to hang out here and give you time to walk through. Since it's vacant, I don't need to be with you."

"Thanks."

"You're welcome. Take your time. I have calls and emails to keep me company." He chuckles, and I like him immediately. He's not a pushy salesman.

Taking my time, I walk through every room, and it's easy for me to imagine myself living here. The house has been completely remodeled, and it's stunning. Exactly what I would have done had I built it on my own. The master bedroom is huge, and the bathroom has a large walk-in shower, a soaker tub, his and her sinks, as well as his and her closets. There are three additional bedrooms upstairs and a fully finished basement.

It's entirely too much house for a single guy, but I hope to not be single for long. And, if I am, it's still a great place to have my family over. I can imagine my nieces and nephews here running and playing in the backyard, having pool parties. I know we have

Mom and Dad's land for fishing but having my own pond is nice too. There isn't a single solitary thing I can find that I don't like about it.

"I'll take it," I tell Dan, joining him in the living room.

"All right. We can write an offer up now. What—" he starts, but I stop him.

"Full asking. This place is brand-new, and the price is good."

"The owners bought it, spent all the time and money to remodel, and his job was relocated. They need to move it."

"Good. Let's write it up." We spend the next thirty minutes writing up the offer. I agree to stop by his office in the morning and drop off the earnest check. I didn't bring my checkbook. I didn't think I'd be buying a house today, but damn, this place feels like home.

"Thank you, Conrad. If you need help selling your current home, please let me know. I'd love to assist you with that."

"Yes. Let's get it on the market. How about you just stop by in the morning? I can give you my check, and we can get it listed."

"Perfect. I'll see you then."

I stand in the driveway and look at my new home. It feels right. I fight the urge to call Aspen and tell her what I did, but she'll find out soon enough. Instead, I climb back into my car and head to my brother's. I time the drive, and it takes me three and a half minutes to get to his place.

When I pull into Grant and Aurora's driveway, I can't contain my smile as I climb out of the car and jog to the front door. My hand is raised to knock when Grant opens the door. "Hey." I smile.

"What's up? Come on in." He steps back, allowing me room to pass.

"I did a thing, and since I was closest to your place, you're the first to know," I tell him, barely able to hold in my excitement. With each minute that passes, I get more and more excited.

"First, to know what?" Aurora asks.

I smile at her and notice the similarities she and Aspen share. "I have news."

"Oh, yeah?" Her eyes sparkle. "Come on in and fill us in."

"Wait, how was the honeymoon?"

"Too short," Grant replies.

"Wonderful." Aurora beams.

"Glad to have you home."

"Yeah, yeah." Aurora waves me off. "What's this news you've been yammering on about? The suspense is killing me here."

"Well, I bought a house."

Both of their mouths drop open in surprise. "You did what now?" Grant asks.

"I bought a house."

"That is not what I was expecting you to say," Aurora admits.

"Where? When? Were you looking?" my brother fires off a round of questions.

"No, I wasn't looking. However, it popped up on my phone this morning, and it caught my eye. I called the realtor, just looked at it, and put in an offer."

"That's... wow. Where is it?"

"We're going to be neighbors. I bought the two-story brick just down the road. I timed it. We're three and a half minutes apart."

"For real? That's a nice place. They've been working on remodeling from the trucks that have been there."

"They did. The entire place is brand-new inside. Eleven acres, with a two-acre pond, in-ground pool." I continue to name off all the attributes that I loved about the place, which is everything.

"And you bought it? Just like that?" Aurora asks.

"Yep."

"What about your condo?" Grant asks.

"Selling it. The realtor is coming over Monday morning to list it."

"You're giving up the bachelor pad? You were stoked to find that place."

"Yep."

"You feeling all right?"

"Never better." Well, one thing that would make it better would be for Aspen to be mine, but I'm working on that.

"What brought all this on?" Aurora asks.

Here goes. I look her in the eye and make sure she can see how serious I am. "Your sister."

"My sister?" she asks, confused.

"She's my magic." I shrug.

"Son of a bitch," Grant huffs out a laugh.

"What? Why is that funny?"

"Told you so." He grins, pulling Aurora into a hug.

"I'm going to need some more information. Come on." Aurora slides out from underneath Grant's arm and grabs my hand, pulling me into the living room. "Sit." She points to the couch, and I do as I'm told. "Tell me all the things." Her smile is wide, and her eyes are focused on me.

"We spent time together at the cabin. She's... amazing, and I want to spend more time with her."

"Have you told her that?"

"I have. She seems to think that our time together was circumstantial. That's fine, though. I get it. I've preached the entire time that she's known me that the magic wasn't real, and it was an excuse the oldest Riggins men used to be pussy-whipped. I understand why she feels that way. So, I'm going to show her."

"So, you bought a house?" Grant clarifies.

"I'm over the party life. It was fun, but I've grown out of it. I'd slowed down a lot even before my week with her at the cabin. Now, I have no desire to go back."

"You love your condo."

"Yeah, I did. It was convenient after a night out, but that's not me. I want a home."

"Wow," they say together.

"I promise you I'm not playing games with her."

"I believe you," they say again at the same time.

"This newlywed finishing each other's sentences stuff is creepy as fuck."

Grant throws his head back in laughter while Aurora giggles. "Just wait, brother."

"If that's what it means to have her in my life, bring it." I didn't really plan to just come out with it like that, but I'm not hiding how I feel for her, not from her and not from my family. She needs to see that I've changed, that I mean what I say. I'll give her not only the actions but the words too.

"Listen, can you all keep this between us? I want to make sure the offer goes through and all that before I tell her or the rest of the family. You all were close, and well, I needed to tell someone."

"We'll keep your secret," Aurora assures me. "I'm excited for you and for my sister. I hope the two of you can work things out."

"Me too, sis, me too. All right, I need to get home and tidy up my place a little, so I don't have to do it tonight. I'll see you all later at Mom and Dad's." With a hug to both of them, I let myself out.

I take my time driving by the house and pull in to take a few pictures on my phone. Life is changing, and I'm excited about it. I just hope this house isn't the only change coming soon. I hope my relationship status changes as well.

CHAPTER
Aspen
TWENTY ONE

ALL DAY LONG, I've racked my brain, trying to come up with an excuse not to go to Sunday dinner at Lena and Stanley Riggins's house this evening. The only excuses I could come up with are lies, and that's not me. So, here I am, standing in front of my closet, looking for something to wear. I don't want to look frumpy, and well, I don't want it to look like I tried too hard either. However, I need to choose something soon, or I'm going to be late.

It's February in Tennessee, so I can't go wrong with black leggings and a long steel-gray sweater. I'll wear my black Sperry boots and call it good. My hair is in loose curls falling over my shoulders, and my makeup is light.

Making sure I have my phone and keys, I head to the bakery before leaving. I need to grab the box of leftover goodies from yesterday. I hate tossing them, and I know the guys love everything we have to offer. I figure it's as good a place as any to take them. I sent Gloria and McKenzie home with a box as well.

Anything leftover on Saturdays is donated. We usually drop off boxes to local businesses, hotels, nursing homes, bars, and the boxes are always labeled with the Warm Delights logo. It's a good form of marketing, and I really do feel like we've gained a lot of exposure and business from it. However, this week, it's the staff who got the treats. I had planned to drop some boxes off today, but when Lena called, and I knew I couldn't get out of it, I combined them all in one.

The traffic this evening is light, so I get to the Riggins's in record time. However, from the cars in the driveway, I'm the last to arrive. Climbing out of my car, I grab my phone and then reach into the back seat to retrieve the box of goodies.

"Hey, babe, let me help with that." Conrad takes the box from my hands. "I have been waiting to lay eyes on you all weekend," he says, grinning. "Come on, let's get you inside where it's warm."

I follow him inside and stop at the foyer to take off my boots and coat. By the time I'm sliding off my last boot, he's back and pulling me into a hug. "I missed you."

"Conrad, you saw me yesterday."

Pulling out of the hug, he laces his fingers through mine and pulls me down the hall and into the laundry room. "That was at the bakery. It's been over a week since I've held you."

"Conrad, we're not together." I say the words, but I don't want them to be true.

"We are. You just haven't admitted it yet. Come here." He pulls me back into his arms, and I'm too weak to resist him. I let him hug me tightly and end up wrapping my arms around him in return. As soon as I do, he exhales and squeezes me a little tighter.

His warmth wraps around me, and it brings tears to my eyes. I've missed him more than I was willing to admit to myself. It's been a week, and here I am, hidden in his parents' laundry room, stealing hugs.

"Come on before they notice we're missing."

I hate that my heart sinks. I hate that I'm questioning if he's hiding for my benefit or for his. I hate that I won't take the risk of getting my heart smashed beyond repair to be with him. After watching what Aurora went through with her ex, I promised myself I wouldn't settle. That I would hold out for a man who loved me. I want more than anything for Conrad to be that man. The problem is I'm too afraid to find out.

With his hand on the small of my back, Conrad leads me out of the laundry room, and we make our way to the kitchen. Just before we reach the door, he drops his hand, and I miss his touch. I miss the warmth of his touch and the comfort that it brings me.

"There she is." Marshall cheers when we walk into the room.

"Hey." I wave and offer him a smile.

"Thanks for these." Stanley holds up a cookie from where he stands at the counter in front of the Warm Delights box.

"You're welcome."

"Everyone grab a plate. It's ready," Lena says, pulling the last of three large pans of baked spaghetti out of the oven.

I turn my head to find Conrad watching me. He shrugs, and I can't help but wonder if he requested his mom make baked spaghetti. The same meal we had the first night in the cabin. Was that really just a week ago? It feels as if a lifetime has passed.

Everyone grabs a plate and lines up, leaving Conrad and me at the back of the line. His hand that's closest to the counter rests on my hip, where no one can see. I want to turn and tell him to stop, that someone might see, but it's him and me while the others fill their plates in front of us. It might also feel nice to have his hands on me. I crave his touch.

Lena and Stanley are the last to filter out of the room, leaving Conrad and me to fill our plates. "I love Mom's spaghetti, but I wish we were back in the cabin, just the two of us," Conrad says, keeping his voice low.

"I'm sure you can think of better things to do." I keep my eyes on my plate as I add a scoop of spaghetti and begin to add salad.

"The only thing that would be better would be you being with me now. Here."

His words cause me to freeze. Slowly, I turn to look at him. "You can't say things like that."

"I say what I mean, Aspen. Something happened in that cabin. I know you feel it." He reaches out and places his hand on my cheek. "I miss you like fucking crazy," he says huskily. "All I do is think about you."

"Conrad—" I start but find myself freezing again when he leans in and places his lips on my forehead. "Let me show you, Aspen. Let me show you what I feel when it comes to you."

"We need to go," I say, turning and walking into the dining room. There are two empty seats right when you walk in. There are others around the table, but none of them are next to my sister, so it would appear odd if I were to take them. Instead, I sit, knowing Conrad will take the seat next to me.

I've barely got my chair pushed in when he indeed takes a seat next to me. I ignore him the best that I can, but having him so close and pretending he's not there is almost impossible.

"Now, tell us all about it. How was the honeymoon?" Lena asks.

"Mom, I don't really want to hear about all the details," Marshall whines. "She's our sister, and yeah, no." He shakes his head, and we all laugh.

"Oh, hush." She waves him off. "I hope you enjoyed yourselves," Lena tries again.

"It was everything we hoped it would be," Aurora answers. She looks at Grant, and so much love passes between them in a single glance.

"Wonderful. Welcome home," Stanley says.

Carter shoves a noodle into his mouth and giggles, capturing our attention. Owen and Layla praise him as conversations filter around the table. I keep to myself and focus on eating and ignoring Conrad.

"Aspen, how was the bakery this week? I was expecting a phone call," Lena says.

"It was good. Busy, but the new help we hired is doing an outstanding job."

"I was hoping to get some man time in with my boy Carter, but you never called," Stanley says dramatically. "This one is a baby hog, so you calling her away would have given us some man time."

"Stop." Lena pushes at his arms, smiling warmly. "I'm glad you had a good week," she tells me.

More conversation with great food and good company. My sister is beaming with happiness, and I'm thrilled for her that she has this new extended family who so graciously brought not only her but me into their fold.

"Well, boys, it's time to get on the dishes," Stanley says, after all of our plates have been cleared.

"I can help." I stand, but Conrad does at the same time, placing his hand on mine.

"It's fine, babe. We've got this. Go gossip with the rest of the women." My breath hitches at the term of endearment.

"Hey!" Sawyer calls out. "We do not gossip."

"Yeah, it's called catching up," Layla defends.

"Fine. Go catch up." Conrad chuckles.

Nodding, I pull my hand from under his and follow my sister, and her new sisters-in-law, and mother-in-law into the living room. As soon as we're seated, Sawyer surprises me.

"He's been acting different," she says.

"Who?" Aurora asks.

"Conrad."

"I've noticed that too," Lena agrees.

"Me too," Layla announces.

All eyes turn to me. "I-I haven't noticed."

"He stayed home last night," Lena tells them. "He called me around nine, and he was at home. It's been that way for a couple of months now."

All eyes turn to me. "What?"

"Well, you were with him for a few days up in the cabin. Did he say anything to you?" Lena asks.

I'm a terrible liar. Terrible as in I can't do it. "We kissed," I blurt and quickly cover my face. I cannot believe that I just told his mom that of all people.

His. Mom.

"I knew it!" Lena scoots to the edge of her seat. "I thought I saw some sparks between the two of you. Is he treating you good?" she asks.

I find my sister's eyes from across the room. "We're uh… we're not dating."

"Well, why not?" she asks.

"Yeah, babe, why not?" I hear Conrad ask from behind me.

"Can we not do this right now?"

He sits on the floor in front of me, resting his back between my legs. His hand rests on my calf, and even through my leggings, the heat of his touch scorches my skin. "Take all the time you need," he says once he's settled.

"All the time she needs for what?" Stanley asks.

"I'm trying to convince Aspen to go out with me, Dad," Conrad tells him. "She needs more time."

"Make him work for it, sweetheart." Stanley winks. "These boys need to know what it's like to put in the work."

"Hey, I put in work," Royce objects.

"So did I," Owen adds.

"I think we can all agree that I worked the hardest," Grant chimes in.

"And you have wonderful wives because of it. If it's not worth fighting for, it's not worth it."

"She's worth it," Conrad says. The conviction in his voice brings tears to my eyes.

"Enough of that," Lena says. I have a feeling she can sense I'm on the verge of tears. "Sawyer, how have you been feeling?"

Conrad stays seated on the floor next to me, just as his brothers do with their wives the remainder of the night. And when I announce I need to head home, he's on his feet, helping me into my coat and walking me to the door.

"Shit, I didn't know it was snowing. I'll follow you home," he says as we make our way outside.

"I know how to drive in the snow."

"I know, but I'd feel better if I drove you."

"I can handle it."

"Will you at least call me and let me know you made it home safely?"

"I can do that."

"Thank you." He reaches for my door, pulling it open. "Drive safe."

"Night," I say, climbing behind the wheel. As I pull out of the driveway, I try not to let the disappointment take over that he didn't kiss me goodbye. I need to get my head on straight. I have to decide once and for all how I'm going to handle him and this thing between us. If I'm not willing to give him… give *us* a chance, then I need to keep my distance for a while.

Before I know it, I'm pulling into the back lot of the bakery. Thankfully, it's well lit, something our father insisted on when we moved here. Still, I pull my keys from the ignition and place my finger on my mace, just to be safe.

Once I'm inside with the door locked, I call Conrad like I promised. "I made it home," I say as soon as he answers.

"Thank you."

"Night, Con."

"Night, baby."

I head straight to my room to change and climb into bed. I have to be up early tomorrow, and I'm exhausted. Luckily, exhaustion takes over, and I fall fast asleep.

CHAPTER
Conrad
TWENTY TWO

T HIS IS THE fourth Monday since we've been back from the cabin that I've started my week by stopping at Warm Delights. I now have Gloria, McKenzie, and Aurora on my side, and Aspen, well, I can see it in her eyes that she's warming up to the idea of us. I can feel it.

Today is also the third Monday in a row that I've delivered flowers on my own. Sure, there's something to be said for the florist delivering them, but then they're the ones who get to see her smile and the way her eyes light up. I'm a selfish bastard when it comes to Aspen Steele, and I want it all. So I've arranged for early pick up of a different bouquet for the past three weeks, and it's been more than worth it.

The bell chimes, alerting the staff that they have a customer. McKenzie is behind the counter this morning, and she smiles brightly. "Morning, Conrad."

"McKenzie." I nod. "She in the back?"

"Not today. She's actually upstairs. She's not feeling well."

My steps falter. The thought of her not feeling well twists something inside me. "Thanks." I push through the swinging kitchen door to find my brother and his wife's lips locked. Normally I would come off with a smart-aleck comment, but today, I have bigger issues. "Aspen's sick?" I ask as they pull apart.

"Yeah. She was up all night with a head cold. She couldn't sleep because she couldn't breathe and she was coughing her head off. I had to force her to take the day off."

"Why didn't you call me?" I ask.

"Because she's a grown woman who can take care of herself."

"But what if she needs something?" She shouldn't be alone if she's sick.

"She's fine, and I'm right downstairs if she needs something."

"I'm going up," I tell her. I don't ask or wait for permission. My feet take the stairs two at a time until I reach their apartment door. Trying the handle, I find it unlocked, so I let myself in. As quiet as I can, I make my way to her bedroom and push open the door. She's in bed with a mound of pillows propping up her head. Stepping into the room, I set her flowers down on top of her dresser and smile when I see the other two sitting there as well.

I can see it in her eyes that my efforts are having an impact on her.

Kneeling beside the bed, I gently take her hand in mine, bringing it to my lips. Her eyes flutter open, and she gives me a small smile. "What are you doing here?" she asks, her voice gravelly.

"Aurora told me you were sick."

"Ugh," she groans. "Just kill me now." She pulls her hand from mine. "I don't want you to get it." She coughs.

Reaching up, I take it back. "I don't care. Can I get you anything?" I search her face, looking for I'm not really sure what. I can tell her throat is sore, and from the cough and stuffy nose, I'm sure she's miserable.

"Looks like you already brought the patient flowers."

"Of course, I did. Are you hungry?"

"No." Another cough.

I don't know what to do for her. I'm racking my brain when I get an idea. Pulling my phone out of my pocket, I swipe at the screen, and dial my mom. "Hey, Mom. Aspen isn't feeling well. What should I do for her?" I say as soon as she answers.

"Good morning to you too." She laughs. "What are her symptoms?"

"Baby, what are your symptoms?" Her eyes soften at my term of endearment. She rattles off that she has a stuffy nose, sinus pressure, a cough, and a sore throat. "You hear all that?" I ask my mom.

"Yes. Has she taken anything?"

"Have you taken anything?" I feel like an ass. I should have already asked her that.

"Nyquil."

I repeat her reply to my mom. "That's good. She's going to need something for the daytime too. Dayquil will work. Make sure she's drinking and staying hydrated, and it will help to put a vaporizer in her room, to help moisten the air. That will help with the chest congestion and her cough."

"Thanks, Mom."

"You're welcome, dear. Let me know if I can do anything."

"Will do. Love you." I end the call, sliding the phone back into my pocket. "I'm going to run out and get you some more medicine and a vaporizer."

"You d-don't have to do that," she says over another cough.

"Hey." I stand and lean over her. "I'm taking care of you." Closing the distance, I press my lips to her forehead. "I'll be back. Is there anything else you'd like to have?"

"Cough drops."

"Done. I'll be back as soon as I can." Closing her bedroom door behind me, I head back downstairs to the bakery. Grant is still there, talking to his wife. "Hey, I'm not going to be in today. I'm heading to get a vaporizer and some other stuff Mom suggested for Aspen. I'll call Layla on my way and tell her to cancel my day."

"I'm here, Conrad. You don't have to miss work," Aurora assures me.

I give her a look that tells her I don't care who's here. I'm going to be here too. "I'll be back. Can you think of anything else she might want or need?"

"She only likes the red Halls cough drops, and maybe some Sprite? Oh, and since you're going out, grab some tissues. The box she was using last night was halfway empty."

"Got it. I'll be back." I wave to them and head out. In my car, I call the office, and Layla answers. "Hey, Layla."

"Morning, Conrad."

"Aspen isn't feeling well, so I'm going to take the day off. I had one meeting this afternoon with a new vendor who's trying to get us to switch servers. Can you call and move them to wherever next week?"

"Sure. Is she okay?"

"Yeah, just a cold. I'm on my way to pick up a few things and take them back to her."

"Aw, well, take good care of her. We'll handle things here."

"Thanks, Layla."

"You're welcome."

I hit End on my steering wheel just as I pull into the parking lot of the pharmacy.

Thirty minutes later, after parking in the back of the bakery next to Aspen, I'm walking through the back door with my arms loaded down with bags.

"What in the world?" Aurora says when she sees me.

"I wanted to make sure she had options." I shrug and start my trek up the stairs.

"Conrad." I hear Aurora call up the steps. Turning, I look down the stairs, giving her my attention. "She's lucky to have you."

"I'm the lucky one." Turning back around, I manage to turn the knob and open the door without dropping any of the bags. Setting them on the small kitchen table, I begin to unpack them. First things first, I grab the medicine, the tissues, the cough drops, the vapor rub, and a bottle of water, and head back to her room.

"What's all of that?" Aspen asks weakly when I enter her room.

I kneel at the side of her bed. "Can you sit up for me? You need to take some medicine."

She groans and coughs a deep barky cough but manages to sit up. I hand her two tablets and the bottle of water, and she takes them without complaint. "Now, cough drop?"

"Yes. Thank you." She unwraps it, then pops it into her mouth.

"This will help with the congestion. You can put it under your nose and on your chest. That's what the pharmacist told me. My mom used this stuff on us when we were kids, and it's a miracle worker. It smells bad, but it works."

"We used that too."

"Do you want me to put some on you?"

"Please." She nods and eases back down on her mound of pillows.

After opening the jar, I place a tiny bit on the tip of my index finger and rub it along the top of her lip under her nose. "Want some on your chest?" I ask.

"Might as well," she says over a cough.

This time I use two fingers to swipe through the container, getting a bigger glob. Pulling back the covers, I lift her shirt and begin to gently rub the salve onto her chest. She's wearing nothing but cotton panties and a T-shirt. I know she's sick, and thinking about her in any other way than to take care of her is a dick move, but she takes my breath away. I've missed the feel of her smooth skin beneath my fingers.

"There," I croak. "I'm going to go wash my hands, and then I'll set up the vaporizer."

"Conrad." She rasps my name when I get to the door.

"Yeah?"

"Thank you for taking care of me."

"There's nowhere else I'd rather be."

After washing my hands, I put the Sprite, 7UP, and orange juice I brought in the fridge. Opening the three-pack of tissues, I pull out a box and take them back to her. Next, I tackle the vaporizer. Unpacking it from the box, I take a seat on the chair to read the instructions. It's not complicated, but I don't want to mess it up. Filling it to the appropriate line with water, I add the liquid-vapor and head back to her room. She's resting, so I try to set it up on the nightstand, being as quiet as I can.

"You think that will help?" she asks.

"I'm not really sure. My mom says it will, and I remember her using one for us as kids when we were sick."

"My mom did too."

"Can I get you anything?" I ask, sitting on the edge of the bed once the vaporizer is running.

"You've already done too much."

I smooth her hair back out of her eyes. "I'll be in the living room if you need me. Just yell for me, or your phone is on the nightstand."

"You're not going to work?"

"No. I'm going to be right here in case you need anything."

"Conrad, it's just a cold."

I nod. "I know, but I want to take care of you."

Her eyes well with tears. "Will you lie with me?" she asks. "I-I miss you." Her whispered confession in her scratchy voice is like music to my ears.

Standing from her bed, I kick off my shoes and slip out of my suit jacket, shirt, and tie, then drape them over the chair in the corner of her room. Next, I remove my pants and socks, place them over the rest of my clothes before rounding the bed and sliding under the covers. I pull her into my arms, and as soon as our bodies touch, it's as if two pieces of a puzzle are finally in the right places.

"I missed you. I missed this," I confess, kissing the top of her head.

"I'm weak."

"I know, babe. A few days and you'll feel good as new."

"No. Well, that too, but I meant I'm weak when it comes to you."

"You've been putting up a pretty good fight."

"I don't want to resist you anymore."

"Then don't."

She turns to face me. "Don't break my heart, Conrad Riggins."

"Never." I hold her close as she rests her head on my chest and falls back to sleep. I don't know if it's the cold medicine, the cold, or maybe a little of both that was talking, but I can't help but hope that it was her. That I've finally proven to Aspen that she's the only woman for me. With her in my arms, I too drift off to sleep.

CHAPTER
Aspen
TWENTY THREE

T HIS HAS BEEN the longest week. I hate being sick, but I must admit that having Conrad take such good care of me has been a perk. He stayed with me Monday. We lay in bed all day until Aurora came up to check on us when the bakery closed. She came with a huge pot of homemade chicken noodle soup that Lena dropped off. Aurora offered to stay, but Conrad ushered her out the door. We ate soup and went back to bed.

He stayed with me all night. I didn't need him to. It was a head cold, but I also didn't want him to leave. It's been pure hell turning him down day after day, and when he dropped everything to take care of me, and buy me half of the pharmacy, suddenly my fears were not that big. Sure, I know he can break my heart, but that's a risk I'm taking.

He just doesn't know it yet.

After my whispered confession, neither of us brought it up again. I know he thinks it was the cold medicine talking, but it was more than that. The minute he wrapped his arms around me,

I knew. It doesn't matter how many times I turn him away. It's his touch that I'll crave. Over the last month, he's found little ways to touch me, a brush of his hand against mine, his hand on the small of my back, and a hug whenever he gets the chance. Each one chipped away at my resolve. However, when he climbed into bed with me, knowing I was sick, and his arms held me tight, there was no more resistance left in me.

Touch by touch, he's captured my heart.

Tuesday morning, I had to force him to go home and shower and go to work. I missed him, but he texted and called often to check on me. That night, and every other night this week, he's brought dinner to my place, but he's not stayed again. I miss him more now than ever, and I've spent more time with him this week. Conrad Riggins is my weakness.

The bell chimes, and I look up to see him walking in. "Hey." I smile.

"You look like you're feeling better."

"Much better. Grant already stopped in and took a box full of stuff to the office."

"That's fine. I'm not here for that anyway. I wanted to see you."

His words have me melting on the inside. "That's sweet of you. I really am feeling better."

"Good enough to have dinner out with me tonight?"

I stare at him for a few heartbeats, and the look on his face tells me he might be hopeful, but he expects me to turn him down again. "Pick me up at six?" I ask.

His mouth falls open and closes a few times before a slow, sexy grin pulls at his lips. Bracing his hands on the counter, he leans over and presses his lips to mine. "I'll see you at six," he murmurs against my lips.

Pulling away, he walks backward until he reaches the door— his sexy grin on full display. "Have a great day, baby," he says from the door. Everyone in the bakery stops to look at him and then me. He laughs before pushing out the door.

"What was that about?" Aurora asks. "And did I see him kiss you?"

"I'm not really sure, and yes, he kissed me."

"And you let him?"

"We're going on a date tonight."

"What?" she shrieks. "You're finally letting him in?"

"Looks like it."

"That was him staking his claim," she tells me.

"What are you talking about?"

"That little 'have a great day, baby,'"—she deepens her voice to sound like him—"was him staking his claim on you."

"That's crazy," I defend, but to be honest, it kind of seemed like it to me as well.

"You do realize that now you've said yes, he's going to pull out all the stops, right?"

I nod. I do know this, and I'm okay with it. In fact, I'm looking forward to it. Fighting him made us both miserable. This week spending time with him has been incredible. I can't wait to see what tonight holds.

At ten minutes until six, there's a knock at my door. I expected him to be early, and thankfully, I'm ready. When I pull open the door, he's standing with his hands over his head, braced on the frame. He's wearing a pair of dark jeans and a long-sleeve black button-down. He's sexy and looking at me like I hung the moon.

"Where's your coat? You're going to freeze to death."

"Babe, it's April in Tennessee. I'm not going to freeze to death." Dropping his hands, he slides them around my waist and pulls me into him. "You take my breath away."

"Am I dressed okay?" I'm wearing a long-sleeve black dress that hits just above my knee, with black knee-high boots.

"You're perfect, Aspen." His lips land on mine. It's just a quick peck that leaves us both wanting more. "We need to go now. Because if we stand here a minute longer, I'm canceling our plans and taking you to bed."

"I am tired," I tease.

"Come on, funny girl." He releases his hold on me.

"Let me grab my phone and my coat." Turning, I grab my coat and my purse, double-checking that my phone is in my purse and that I have my house keys. "Ready." I make sure to lock the apartment as well as the back-entry door. "So, where are we going?" I ask once we're in his car and on the road.

"It's a surprise," he tells me.

"Are you really not going to tell me?" I ask.

"You'll see. How are you feeling?" he asks, reaching over the console and resting his hand on my knee.

"Much better. I still have a lingering cough every now and then."

"Good. I hate you being sick."

We make small talk the rest of the short drive until we pull into the Gaylord Hotel. "You're taking me to a hotel?"

"They have an incredible steakhouse, and the inside offers a lot of things to see and do. There's shopping and a waterfall. We can even take a romantic boat ride."

"In a hotel?"

"Yes, in a hotel. Stay put." He climbs out of the car and rushes around to open my door. Hand in hand, we make our way inside and to the steakhouse. "Reservation for Riggins," he tells the lady.

We're seated at a back table, with low lighting, and it's very romantic. "Wow, how did I not know about this place? It's like an indoor village out there," I say, referring to the interior of the hotel.

"It really is. This place attracts a lot of tourists. Then again, Nashville, in general, attracts a lot of tourists." He laughs.

"It's the music. I admit it's a fun city to live in. That's why you live downtown, right? To be in the center of the action?"

Something passes in his eyes. "Initially." He doesn't get the chance to say more as our waiter approaches. We both order sweet tea to drink and an appetizer. "You're not drinking?" he asks.

"No. I'm still taking cold medicine, and I don't want to mix the two. Besides, I want to remember this night. What about you?"

"I'm driving."

"One glass of wine won't hurt."

"You're right, but I would never put you in that situation."

"A gentleman."

"Only when it comes to you." He winks.

"You've got me here. You don't have to keep trying," I tease him.

"This is me, Aspen. This is me with you. I'm not trying, just speaking the truth."

I ignore him and the impact his words have deep inside. "What are you getting?" I ask, opening my menu.

"Steak."

"What kind of steak?" I chuckle.

"I'm thinking the New York strip. You?" He glances at me over his menu.

"This barbecue chicken sounds good," I say just as the waiter approaches. We place our order and fall into an easy conversation. That's the thing with Conrad. It's always easy. He's easy to talk to, easy on the eyes, and easy to fall for. The only thing not easy about him is trying to push him away. I failed miserably at that.

"I'm stuffed," I tell him as we exit the restaurant.

"You feel like walking around?"

"Definitely." He takes my hand in his, and we begin to stroll. "I can't believe I've lived here as long as I have and have never been here."

"Over there." He nods toward a waterfall. We head in that direction and take the steps. "We have to document this moment," he says, pulling out his phone. He settles in behind me and presses his lips to my temple. "There." He checks his phone and the picture he just took.

"Send me that." I can feel myself wavering. If nothing else, I'll have the picture to look back on.

"Thank you for agreeing to come out with me tonight," he says as we walk along the path of the lazy river.

"I was exhausted trying to push you away," I say as we stop at a bench. Conrad points, and I take a seat.

"Why were you? Pushing me away, I mean?"

"Because you made me feel too much. I've never met a man who can reduce me to goo from just a simple touch of his hand."

"I do that to you?"

I nod. "I know that when this ends, my heart will be broken. I also know I won't ever recover."

"Who says it has to end?"

I ignore his question. "Part of the reason I pushed you away is that from the day I met you, you've been all about going out to the clubs and meeting new people—meeting new women. You've constantly given your brothers a hard time for settling down. To me, that told me you and I don't want the same things."

"That's the thing. I'd already been distancing myself from that lifestyle before that weekend. It wasn't fun for me anymore. I may have been giving my brothers shit, but I was envious of what they've found in their wives. As far as the women, I liked to meet new people, have some drinks, but I didn't sleep with all of them."

"That's none of my business."

"You're wrong, Aspen." His hand cradles my cheek. "It is your business. You're the one I want. Not just for a night or two, but for all of my nights moving forward. I'm an open book for you."

"Just like that?"

"As I said, I was already distancing myself and envious of my brothers. Then our week at the cabin happened. You showed me what I was missing. What it really means to be with one woman for more than just a night of fun. In a few short days, you captured all of my attention."

"Please don't break me," I whisper.

"Baby, don't you see? It's you who has the power to break me."

"Is this the part where you kiss me?"

"Fucking, finally." He smirks, and then his lips are on mine. The kiss is slow and sensual as our tongues battle with one another. His hands cradle my cheeks, and it's hands down the greatest kiss of my life. I don't know if it's because I've tried so hard to convince myself it would never happen or if I missed him that much. I think it's a little bit of both.

"Come on. We have a boat ride to take."

We take a ride on the lazy river, cuddled next to one another. My heart is happy. I'm happy. Conrad Riggins is the one for me. I'm still worried he'll break my heart, but he looked me in the eye, and I could see it—his determination and the truth in his words. It's been a month since our time at the cabin, and not once has he stopped telling me I'm who he wants. Maybe with a little luck, we too will get our happily ever after.

CHAPTER
Conrad
TWENTY FOUR

I CLOSED ON my house today. The house that only my brother Grant and his wife, Aurora, know about. I don't know why I've kept it a secret, but I do know the first person I want to show it to.

Aspen.

I took the day off. My brothers didn't even ask what was up. I'm sure they assume it has something to do with my girl. Yep, she's my girl. It's official. After our date night, last Friday night, I took her home and locked that shit down. I made sure she knew that we were exclusive, and there was no one else for me. She confessed the same.

This week with her has been nothing short of amazing. We've had dinner every night this week, and I stop to see her every day on my way to the office. She missed Sunday dinner but claimed she was behind on laundry. I know she was sick last week, so I brought her leftovers and sat with her watching movies while she did her laundry.

I've yet to stay over again, and that's okay. I haven't had her at my place because it sold, and I've been packing a little each night before bed. There are boxes everywhere, and until I tell her about the house, I didn't want her to see it.

That all changes today. I called Aurora and asked her if she could spare her sister. When I told her I closed on the house and I wanted to show Aspen, she practically begged me to come and pick Aspen up.

That brings me to now. I walk through the bakery doors to find Aspen standing behind the counter. "Hey, I didn't expect to see you in the middle of the day." I watch her as her eyes take me in. I'm in jeans and a long-sleeve T-shirt. Not something I would wear to the office. "I thought you had a meeting this morning."

"I did." I told her last night I wouldn't be in this morning because of my meeting. It wasn't a lie. The closing was scheduled for seven so the owners could make their flight home.

"What's going on, Conrad?"

"I have something I want to show you."

"Now?" she asks, raising her eyebrows.

"Yes, now." I smile at her.

"Go on," Aurora says, joining the conversation.

"I'm working."

"And now you're not." Aurora grins. "Go. The man has something to show you."

"Are you in on this?" Aspen narrows her eyes at her sister.

"No. I'm not, but he did call me and tell me he was on his way and wanted to swoop you away for the rest of the day."

"Are you sure?"

"Yes. It's after nine, and our morning rush is pretty much over. Go with your man. Let him show you whatever it is he needs to show you."

"You know what it is, don't you?" Aspen asks, placing her hands on her hips.

"Maybe, but he's the only one who can tell you."

"Come on, baby. I want to take you somewhere."

"You two." Aspen points between the two of us. "I'm not sure how I feel about you teaming up on me." She steps out from around the counter and comes to me, wrapping her arms around my waist. "Let me grab my purse." On her tiptoes, she presses her lips to mine, and then she's gone, disappearing behind the swinging door.

"If you smile any bigger, your face might crack," Aurora teases.

"She's finally mine, sis."

She nods. "Take care of her, Conrad."

"Always."

"Okay," Aspen says, coming back out front with her purse, phone, and jacket in hand. "Let's see what you've got, Riggins."

My cock jumps, thinking about showing her exactly what I've got. I ignore him and take my girl's hand in mine. "Later, Aurora," I call over my shoulder, leading Aspen out of the bakery.

"So, where are we headed?" she asks once we're both buckled in.

"I have something I want to show you."

"I don't even get a hint?"

"It's a new beginning," I say vaguely.

"New beginning? That's cryptic. I thought we were your new beginning." She laughs.

"We are. You are, but this is too. Hold your horses, woman. We'll be there in fifteen minutes."

"Did you really have a meeting today?"

"Yes."

"You wore that?"

"Yes."

"To the office?"

"No."

"Conrad," she half whines, half laughs.

"Patience, beautiful," I say, giving her thigh a gentle squeeze.

She's quiet for the rest of the ride—I'm sure trying to figure out in her mind where we're going and what I'm so excited to show her. "Are we going to Aurora's?" she asks when we turn on my road.

My. Road.

I can't believe I bought this place with only my brother and Aspen's sister knowing. I hope she loves it as much as I do. When I bought it, I thought of her living here with me. I hope that one day that's not just a dream but a reality.

"No. We're going here," I say, turning on my turn signal and turning into the drive.

"Wow, this place is beautiful. Who lives here?"

"No one." It's not a complete lie. I'm not living here yet.

"What are we doing here?"

"I wanted you to see it."

"Oh, okay," she says, confused, but takes off her seat belt and climbs out of the car. "I love the front porch."

"Yeah?" I ask her.

"It's so inviting." She follows me up onto the front porch and gasps when I pull keys out of my pocket. "Do you know the owner?"

"I do." Pushing open the door, I step back, allowing her room to pass me.

"Wow," she breathes. "Look at these floors. I love this color," she says of the gray hardwood floors.

"Come on. I'll take you for a tour." We spend the next half hour or so going from room to room, and in each one, she comments on something that she loves about the place. It's the same exact reaction I had.

"This place feels like a home. I know that sounds crazy, but it's just... homey," she says, twirling in circles in the kitchen. "Why did your friends ever move from here?"

"Well, I didn't know the previous owners, but it just sold, and I know the new owner."

"I bet they're excited to move in."

"I am." I let my confession hang. It takes her a minute to register what I've just said. I can tell the minute she gets it. She stops and slowly turns to face me.

"Did you just say I am?"

"Yep."

"You own this place?"

"Yep."

"Can you give me more than yep?" she asks.

"I closed on it this morning."

"You bought a house? A huge, gorgeous house?"

"Yep." I smirk.

"When? Why didn't you say anything? Why? You love your condo." She fires off questions.

"I put in an offer about a month ago. We had to wait for appraisal, inspections, and the owners to find time to fly in from California to close. That happened this morning. I did love my condo, but it was more of the convenience to downtown. I don't live that life anymore."

"I don't understand."

"I wanted to show you I was serious about leaving all of that behind. I was scrolling through social media one morning and found an ad for this place. I called the realtor and put in an offer that day."

"Did anyone know?"

"Your sister and my brother. And before you get mad that they didn't tell you, I asked them not to."

"I'm not mad, I'm just... processing, I guess. Wow. Congratulations." She walks toward me and wraps her arms around my waist.

"Thank you. Do you think you could ever see yourself living here?"

"Who couldn't?"

"Aspen, answer the question."

She tilts her head back and looks up at me. "I could."

"When you're ready, you let me know." I bend down and kiss the tip of her nose.

"When I'm ready?"

"To move in."

"Are you asking me to move in with you?"

"Yes. When you're ready, when I've proved to you we're the real deal, I'd love nothing more than for you to live here with me. To be able to fall asleep with you in my arms and wake up the same way."

"Y-You're serious?"

"Never been more serious about anything."

"Living together is a big step, Conrad."

"One I'm ready to take."

"I—" She starts, but I kiss her to stop her.

"When you're ready, baby. No rush on my end. Although, I will be moving in starting today, and I was hoping I could get your help decorating. This place is a hell of a lot bigger than my condo."

"I'd love to."

"Perfect. As much as I wish we could stay here, we can't. We have to get to my place. The moving truck will be there soon."

"Are you packed?"

"Yep."

She rolls her beautiful hazel eyes. "I guess that's why you haven't asked me to your place?"

"I didn't want to spoil the surprise."

"You really bought this place?"

"I really did. And I was hoping you would stay here with me tonight. You know, a new house and all the new noises. I might get scared."

"Well, we can't have that now, can we?" She laughs. "I'd love to. I'm so excited for you."

"Thank you. Now, come on, we need to go." Together, we lock up and head back to my car. "Reach into the glove box," I say, backing out of the drive.

"What am I looking for?" she asks, opening the glove box.

"A set of keys."

"These?" she asks, holding up the keys.

"Yep. Those are yours."

"These aren't mine." I can tell she's a little defensive, thinking I maybe mixed her up with someone else.

"They are now. That's your set of keys to the new house."

"Conrad—" She stops. "I don't know what to say to this."

"You don't say anything. You put them in your purse and know that anytime you want to use them, they're there for when you're ready. The first bay in the garage is yours. Here is the garage door opener for your car." I pick it up from the cupholder and hand it to her.

"This feels like I'm moving in."

"It's me giving my girlfriend full access to me and my home. It's me telling you that I want you in my life, and I'm willing to take any part of yours that you're willing to give."

"I don't know what to say."

"Don't say anything. Just take the keys and the door opener and promise me that you'll use them."

"Okay," she whispers, sliding the keys and the garage door opener into her purse. This time she's the one who reaches over the console and laces our fingers together.

I need to call my family and tell them what I've done, but today, I just want to spend some time with her. We'll meet the movers, then follow them back here to instruct them where to unload, and the first order of business is setting up my bed. After that, we'll call my family, and maybe even invite them over. We can order pizza or something. All I know is tonight will be my first night in my new house, and Aspen will be in my bed next to me. There's nothing more in this world I want.

CHAPTER

TWENTY FIVE

HE'S MOVING. HE bought a house to prove to me he's serious about us. Talk about a grand gesture. It's not just a house. It's a beautiful house—huge and perfect. It's my dream house. The moving truck just loaded the last of the boxes and the furniture.

"I still have a few things to pack, but we can come back and get that. I need to meet them there to let them in," Conrad tells me.

"Why don't you drop me off at my place? I'll grab some clothes for tomorrow and pick up lunch."

"That sounds perfect. I'm starving. I'm going to call my parents and my brothers on the way. What do you think about having them over tonight for pizza? I know they're going to want to see the place."

"That's up to you."

"Yeah, but you're a part of this."

"Conrad, I love your family."

"Good. They love you too. I'll set it up for later, maybe seven? That gives the movers time to unload and for us to have some time together."

"Okay. I'll stop at the store on my way and grab some drinks, and paper plates, things like that."

"Here." He reaches into his pocket and pulls out his wallet. He hands me a one-hundred-dollar bill.

"I'm not taking your money."

"It's for my family."

"Who has told me multiple times that I'm one of them. I have money, Conrad."

"Aspen," he warns.

"Take it or leave it. Either I pay, or I just stay at my place."

"You wouldn't."

"Try me."

He stares at me for a few seconds, but I can tell he's going to concede. "Fine," he grumbles, shoving the money back in his wallet. "You win this time."

"Come on. We need to get a move on. The movers are going to be waiting on you."

"They get paid by the hour."

"That doesn't mean you waste time and money. Come on, slowpoke." I pull him out the door and to his car. He drops me off at my place with a quick kiss to my lips and a promise from me that I'll be right behind him.

When I walk into the bakery, Aurora is all smiles. "Well?"

"You already know."

"But I haven't seen the inside. How is it? Is it as pretty on the inside as it is on the outside?"

"It's gorgeous."

"Are you moving in with him?"

Reaching into my purse, I pull out the keys and the garage door opener he gave me. "He said these are mine to use as I see fit. He also says that as soon as I decide that I'm ready to move in that he's ready."

"Well?"

"We just started dating."

"So? You've known him forever."

"A little over a year is hardly forever."

She waves me off. "He's in love with you."

My heart stalls in my chest. "Did he tell you that?"

"No, but he didn't have to. You can see it the way he looks at you, and he bought a freaking house, Aspen. A house for you."

"He bought it for him."

"For both of you."

"Well, I'm not moving in. I did tell him I would stay with him tonight, but I'm not moving in." Not yet. It's too soon, right? We've been official for a week. We need to slow this train a little.

"It's been longer than a week. The minute you two got snowed in at the cabin, this started, so it's been over a month." My sister sticks her tongue out at me.

Before I can fire back a reply, her phone rings. "Hello, husband." She smiles. She's quiet while she listens. "Sure, sounds good to me. I'll whip up something to bring with us. See you at home. Love you," she says, ending the call. "That was Grant. It seems his little brother is having a small gathering at his new house tonight."

"I was getting to that," I tell her.

"I'm going to make something to take. Any requests?"

"Nope. You know they'll eat anything you make. I'm going to run to the store and grab some drinks, and paper plates, and napkins before heading over there."

"I assume you're helping him pack this weekend?"

"He's mostly packed. We just met the movers at his place, and they took all the boxes he had packed and all of his furniture."

"Damn. He's not messing around."

"No. No, he's not. You good here? Need any help?"

"Nope. We've got it. Gloria and McKenzie are finishing up lunch. I'll go back and make something when they get back."

"Love you, Rory."

"Love you too, little sister."

"Marshall is picking up the pizza," Conrad tells me.

"That's nice of him. I have the drinks in the fridge, and Aurora is bringing a dessert."

"And they're all coming at seven. That gives us three hours to take a nap. I'm exhausted."

"I can't believe all the furniture is placed and put back together. Hiring movers is definitely the way to go."

"We'll do that when you move in too. It makes it nice to not have to do all of the heavy lifting."

"You sure you don't want to unpack some more?"

"No. I want to go down the hall to the master bedroom and lie in bed with my girlfriend, and take a nap. The work will be here tomorrow."

"Okay," I say, covering a yawn.

"Come with me." With his fingers laced with mine, he leads me to his bedroom. It's weird that his bed is all set up, and his dressers are all placed. This all happened so fast. "We have to make the bed first."

"Um, do you know where the sheets are?"

"No clue." He laughs.

"Did you mark the box?"

"Yeah, it should say bed shit."

"Eloquent," I tease him.

"Hey, it's done. That's all that matters."

We begin to look at the boxes in the bedroom when I finally find the one that reads *master bedroom shit – clean* and one that reads *master bedroom shit – dirty*. "Look at you being all organized."

"I had an ulterior motive. I was afraid you wouldn't want to nap with me on dirty sheets." He shrugs. "I packed that one this morning." He lifts the box onto the bed and pulls out a clean set of sheets and a soft, fuzzy blanket.

"Is that yours?" I ask.

"Yes. Mom bought us all one a few years ago for Christmas."

"It's so soft."

"We can use it all the time when you move in if that's what it takes."

"Conrad, I can't move in with you."

"Why not?"

"We've been dating a week."

"So? When you know, you know."

"Stop." I chuckle. "Help me make this bed. You promised me a nap."

In no time at all, we have the bed made and are cuddled up with one another under the super-soft blanket. "This moment right here, this is one I'll never forget."

"Why this one?"

"Because you're mine," he says over a yawn.

I don't comment. We're both too exhausted. Instead, I close my eyes and let the security of his embrace lull me to sleep.

"It's a nice place you have here, son," Stanley tells Conrad.

"Thanks, Dad."

"I can't believe you kept this from us," Lena comments. She doesn't sound angry, just surprised.

"It all happened kind of fast." His hand that's resting on my shoulder gives a soft squeeze.

"Well, you've chosen well," his mom tells him.

"Which room is mine?" Marshall asks, shoving the last bite of pizza from his plate into his mouth.

"You have your own place," Conrad answers.

"Yeah, but this place is huge. You can't stay here all by yourself. You'll get lonely," he teases.

"I won't be as soon as Aspen decides she's ready to move in." He says the words with such confidence and assurance.

"Oh, that's wonderful," Lena praises.

"I'm not moving in," I tell him.

"Why not?" Sawyer asks, holding her belly.

"Are you okay?" I ask her.

"I'm fine." She waves me off. "It's these stupid Braxton Hicks. I'm ready to meet this little one." She smiles softly.

"How long have you been having them?" Lena asks.

"A couple of days now."

"I have the bags in the car and the car seat. Maybe we should go to the hospital?" Royce suggests. He looks haggard and worried about his wife and unborn child.

"I'm fine, Royce. This is all a part of being pregnant."

"You were due yesterday," Layla reminds her.

"I know, but sometimes with the first baby, you go over."

"And sometimes you can be in labor and be too stubborn to realize it," Royce grumbles.

"Royce, my water hasn't even broken. I'm not in labor. I was just at the doctor yesterday, and they checked me. There was no change from the week before."

"These things can happen fast," Lena says worriedly.

Royce kneels next to his wife. "Please, let me take you to get checked out."

"We can't run to the hospital every five minutes."

"They're getting worse. That's a change from yesterday. At least let me call the doctor."

"Fine. You can call, but I'm telling you I'm fine." Sawyer stands from the recliner and freezes. Her eyes go wide. "Oh, shit. I think I'm in labor," she says, looking down at the wetness between her legs.

"Damn it," Royce growls. "Somebody get the door." He scoops her into his arms, and there's a flurry of activity as everyone follows after them.

"We're right behind you," Stanley tells him.

"I'm driving." Marshall takes the keys from Royce and climbs behind the wheel.

"All right then, I guess we're moving this party to the hospital." Conrad laughs. "You all go on. We're going to clean up here." He winces, and I know he's thinking about the mess on the floor. "We'll be right behind you."

Everyone says goodbye and rushes to the hospital. "So, do we know where the cleaning supplies are?" I ask Conrad with a smile.

"Somewhere in the kitchen boxes." Together we find the cleaning supplies and get the living room floor cleaned up. "It's hell, isn't it? What women have to go through to have a family?"

"Not hell, but it's not without pain either."

"How many do you want?"

"How many what?" I ask, playing dumb.

"Kids? How many do you want?"

"At least two, maybe more."

"Two." He nods. "I think I can do this two more times."

"Not every woman's water breaks like that. And who says it's me you have kids with?" I'm only teasing. The thought of having his babies makes me feel all warm and fuzzy inside.

"If there is a man that's going to have part of him growing inside you, Aspen Steele, it's going to be me." He kisses me hard. "Now, grab your shoes. We have a nephew to meet."

I don't correct him that this baby isn't related to me. I also don't correct him when he says nephew. Royce and Sawyer wanted to be surprised. Instead, I grab my shoes, my phone, and purse and follow him out to the garage. Ready to meet the newest member of the Riggins family.

CHAPTER
Conrad
TWENTY SIX

WATCHING MY BROTHER hold his son is surreal. The smile on his face looks as if it will be permanent. The same goes for Sawyer. Royce has always wanted a family. He's never been one to party a lot and sleep around. When his first wife cheated on him, he became jaded and gave up on love.

That is until he met a gorgeous woman on a plane. Sawyer is perfect for him, and I love seeing him happy. However, now that he's holding their son, it's an all-new level of happiness I see in his eyes. I want what he has.

My eyes turn to Aspen, who is sitting next to me. Her eyes are soft, a smile tilting her lips as she watches my brother and his family. How did I not see her before our time at the cabin? How did I not realize how incredible she is and that she's the one for me? They say everything happens for a reason, and I believe the universe knew I needed to pull my head out of my ass and see the woman who has been in front of me, in my life for the last year. I needed the push to see her, to really see her, and now that I have, I want her all to myself.

If this is what the men in my family refer to as the magic, I'm pissed I didn't get to experience it sooner. Then again, when I first met her, I was still happily unattached. As each of my older brothers fell for their wives, I began to see the appeal of having someone to share my life with, not random faces in a club night after night.

"He's beautiful," Aspen says, pulling me from my thoughts.

"He is, isn't he?" Sawyer beams with pride. Her labor was quick. Only three short hours after they arrived at the hospital, she delivered a healthy baby boy.

"Do we have a name?" I ask them, glancing at the time on my watch. We've already been warned no more than two visitors at a time. We're a large family, and everyone was excited to meet the little guy, but we're playing nice and taking turns.

"Yeah. Roan Gibson Riggins," Sawyer says with tears in her eyes. "Royce thought, giving him my maiden name for his middle name was a cool idea, and I readily agreed."

"I love that idea," Aspen tells her.

"You plan on letting us hold him before our time is up?" I ask Royce.

"Fine," he grumbles good-naturedly. I get ready, sitting up straighter, but he stops at Aspen, who is sitting next to me but closest to him. "Roan, this is your aunt Aspen," Royce says softly, handing over his son.

Aunt Aspen.

Those two words have me all up in my feels, and I don't hate it. Not one single bit. In fact, I want to make it happen. I want her to be a member of our family, and not just because her sister married my brother. I want her to be mine. I want us to share a moment like this where we introduce our baby to our family. The reality of what that means has me swallowing hard.

She's everything.

"Hey, sweet boy," she coos at my nephew.

Watching her hold him, it moves something in my chest. It's as if I can see a flash of my future with her and our kids, and I like it. I like it a whole hell of a lot.

"He's so tiny." She looks over at me and smiles.

That smile, the joy on her face is something I want to give her. Something I want us to share together. I'm getting ahead of myself here, but for me, she's the one. I just need to make her see that. I know it's going to take time, but this right here, this is my end game.

"Hey, Roan." I reach over and run my index finger down his cheek. He's currently wrapped up like a burrito, and he's snoozing away. I remember when Carter was born, he slept a lot.

"You need one," Royce says out of the blue.

Turning my head, I see him sitting on the side of the bed with his arm around his wife, and both of their eyes are on us. He thinks he's calling me out. Little does he know I've already come to that conclusion. "Whenever she's ready," I answer, pulling my gaze back to my nephew.

Aspen's eyes snap to mine, and I shrug. Royce lets out a belly laugh. I'm sure at her reaction. "If you were going for the shock factor, it worked." He chuckles.

"When can we do it again?" Sawyer asks, turning the heat from us to them.

"Whenever you're ready," Royce tells her—spinning my words to answer his wife.

"Aspen, who would have thought a tiny human could bring these Riggins men to their knees?" She laughs.

"Not just the tiny humans, their mommas too, or future mommas," I tell my sister-in-law before Aspen can reply. My hand rests on her knee, and I give it a gentle squeeze, hoping she gets the meaning. I'm talking about her. She's the future momma I'm referring to. I've shocked her by the look on her face, but that's okay. I'm just now realizing this is what I want too. The only difference is, to me, we're a done deal. She has to catch up to where I am.

My phone rings, and it's Grant. "Hey," I greet him. "You're on speaker."

"Are you done yet? You've been in there forever," he whines, making us all snigger.

"Yeah, we're about done. Let me steal him from Aspen to get my fix, and we'll be right out."

"Baby hog," he mutters as we end the call.

"Here." Aspen transfers Roan into my arms. "I could hold him all day."

"So, what you're saying is if we need a sitter, you're the one to call?" Sawyer asks.

"Definitely. No way am I passing up baby snuggles," Aspen tells her.

Staring down at my nephew, I decide I need to start my campaign. "All right, little man, we need to have a serious talk. I'm the favorite uncle. Remember that when those others come in here and try to take my title," I tell the sleeping baby.

Aspen giggles, and I can't not look at her. "You're crazy."

"Hey, we take the favorite uncle title very seriously in this family."

"I think we need more babies to even it out. Five babies, five uncles, everyone wins." Sawyer laughs.

"You might be onto something, sis," I tell her. "All right, buddy. Uncle Grant is eager to meet you, so we need to go." Standing, I hand him back to Royce. "Here you go, Daddy."

Royce's eyes mist with tears as he takes his son into his arms. He looks down at Roan, then to Sawyer. "Thank you for him. For loving me when I fought against it, for this life that we share. I love you." He leans down and kisses her, and that's our cue to go. We don't bother saying goodbye, instead choosing to sneak out of the room.

"Finally," Grant says when he sees us in the waiting room.

"Hey, blame Mom and Dad. They were in there longer than us," I defend.

"Ready, babe?" he asks Aurora.

"For baby snuggles? Yes, please."

"He's so cute and tiny," Aspen tells her.

"We're heading out," I tell my brother. "We're going to grab some sleep. We'll be back later."

"Check in with Mom. She was talking about bringing food by."

"Sounds good." Taking Aspen's hand in mine, I lead her out of the hospital and to my car. As soon as we're on the road, my cell rings through the car speakers. "Hey, O, you're on speaker with Aspen."

"How's the baby?"

"Good. Cute and tiny." I laugh.

"You on your way home?"

"Yeah, Grant and Aurora are in with them now."

"You need me to watch Carter so you can go?"

"Maybe in a few hours. You need to get some sleep, and we don't want to wake him up to bring him out."

"I can come to you," I offer. I love my nephew and don't mind helping, but what I really want to do is go home and curl up with Aspen in my arms and catch a few hours of sleep.

"Why are you up in the middle of the night?" I ask him.

He chuckles. "Little man was fussy. I got up to rock him a little."

"Aw," Aspen says.

"Call me in the morning if you want me to watch him."

"Will do. Drive safe, oh, and, Aspen?"

"Yeah?"

"Keep his ass in line, will you?" Owen says before ending the call.

"I love your family," Aspen comments.

"They love you too." Reaching over, I take her hand in mine.

"I'm so tired, but it was worth it." Glancing at the clock on the dash, it's just after one in the morning.

"Me too, but you're right, it was worth it." The rest of the drive to my place is quiet, and I think she's fallen asleep until I pull into the garage and she opens her door. Placing my hand on the small of her back, I lead her inside. "You hungry? Thirsty?" I ask her.

"Just sleep," she says, covering a yawn.

"I'm glad we made the bed earlier," I say, leading her down the hall to my room. It's weird being here, in this new house. This isn't how I thought this night would turn out, but I wouldn't change it. Roan is here and healthy, Sawyer is doing great, and my big brother, well, he's beside himself with love for his family. I'd say the night ended better than I could have imagined. I have a new nephew, and Aspen is here with me. I couldn't ask for more.

In my room, she digs into the bag she packed and disappears into the bathroom without a word. A few minutes later, she's opening the door in a pair of pajamas, and her hair is tied up on her head.

"Climb in bed. I'm going to change." I kiss the corner of her mouth as we pass one another on my way to the bathroom. I rush through changing and brushing my teeth before turning off the light and blindly making my way to the bed. "Ouch," I curse when I stub my toe on a box.

"You okay?" her sleepy voice asks.

"Sorry. Yeah, I need to unpack these boxes."

"I told you so," she says. I can hear the smirk in her voice.

Finally reaching the bed, I feel around and realize it's the side of the bed that she chose. It will forever, from this point on, be her side of the bed. "I'm coming in," I say, climbing over her and snuggling up to her back.

"Am I on your side?"

"No. I don't have a side. I sleep alone. This is now your side of the bed."

"You sure? I don't mind moving."

"You're not moving. I finally got you where I want you." I kiss her shoulder. "Night, babe."

"Goodnight," she whispers.

Within no time, we're both sound asleep. How could I not be? She's here in my arms, where she belongs.

CHAPTER
TWENTY SEVEN
Aspen

CONRAD'S THUMB LAZILY strokes my belly. He thinks I'm asleep, and I would have been had it not been for his touch. The feel of his skin against mine is too real, and I knew it wasn't a dream. No, this is the real thing. I'm here in his new house, in his bed, relishing his touch.

"Morning," I say sleepily. I glance over my shoulder to find him watching me.

"I love that you're here."

"Me too," I confess before tossing off the covers.

"Where are you going?"

"I have to pee."

"You're coming back to bed, right?"

"Do you want me to?" I ask, moving toward the bathroom door.

"If I had my way, you'd be living here, and I wouldn't have to worry about you leaving me anytime soon."

"Baby steps, Riggins," I say, closing the bathroom door. Quickly, I take care of business and wash my hands and brush my teeth. As I brace my hands on the counter, I let his words filter through my mind. He wants me to live here. It's crazy and too soon. However, if I've learned anything about Conrad these past six weeks, it's that once he's made up his mind, that's it. He's all in. What's even crazier than him asking me to move in with him is that I want to. I want to be in his arms every night.

Opening the door, I find him leaning against the wall, his legs crossed at the ankles. "My turn, but I'm not done snuggling you." He gives me a pointed look, which tells me I'm to get back in bed. He's not going to get any complaints out of me. It's still early, and snuggling with Conrad is something that I can easily become addicted to.

I'm barely back under the covers when Conrad climbs over the top of me and slides under the covers. His arms wrap around me, holding me close. "I missed being able to touch you. The feel of your skin," he says as he slides his hand under my shirt. I hate sleeping in a bra, so he has easy access to my breasts, which he takes full advantage of. His thumb traces over the peak of one nipple, then the next, and that simple action has me desperate for more.

"How is it that one simple touch from you is all it takes to make me a pile of goo in your arms?"

"It's the magic." He smiles down at me from where he's resting his weight on his elbow. "I didn't believe in it until my time with you in the cabin."

"The magic," I repeat.

"Yeah, I was actually thinking about that last night at the hospital. How were you in my life for so long, and I failed to see what you could mean to me?"

"Circumstances." We'd never really spent any time alone. It was always in a group setting. That's what I was worried about when we started this. That our time together at the cabin was due to being snowed in. However, here we are six weeks later, and he's still interested.

"Maybe," he muses. The featherlight touch of his thumb on my nipple causes me to rub my thighs together. He seems to be completely unaffected. "Maybe we just weren't ready, you know? Maybe it just wasn't our time."

"And you think now is?"

He nods. "I know it is. You're all I think about. I can't seem to focus, and I sleep like shit. Last night is the first good night's sleep I've had since the night I made love to you and held you in my arms at the cabin."

"Not sex?" It felt as though he was making love to me that night, but I assumed it was my love-struck heart.

"Yeah, I mean, it's sex, but it was more than that, right? I've never felt that kind of connection with anyone before."

"It scared me. Still does," I confess.

"Hey." He waits for me to roll over and give him my full attention. "You think I'm not scared?"

I shake my head. "You're so confident."

"I'm not scared of you. I'm afraid of not having you in my life. I wish I could tell you how or explain it, but my time there with you changed me. I'm fearful of my world if you're not a part of it."

I don't have words. I don't know what to say, and I'm not sure I could find my voice to say them anyway. Instead, I place my palm against his cheek and kiss him. This time, I hold nothing back. I don't let my fear of a broken heart keep me from showing him how he makes me feel.

We're a tangle of limbs as we move to undress one another. Clothes fly through the air and land somewhere in the room. I can't seem to find it in me to care. Not when his hands roam over my body, his tongue traces my lips, and he settles between my thighs.

His touch lights me on fire. Skin to skin, so close, not even air can come between us. This is where I want to be. Today, tomorrow, and always. He does this move where he swivels his hips, and his hard cock presses against my core. I moan, closing my eyes, getting lost in his touch.

"Aspen." His voice is husky. "Babe, we have to stop." My eyes pop open, and my heart plummets. "Condom," he explains. "I don't have one. Well, I might, but I wouldn't begin to know where to look for them." He smiles sheepishly.

"My purse."

His eyes light up. "Where did we leave it?"

"I think it might be in the living room." I try to think back to last night, or early this morning, rather, and I can't remember. "Maybe we left it in the car."

"Do." Kiss. "Not." Kiss. "Move." Kiss. He climbs off the bed and disappears down the hall.

I miss the heat of his touch immediately, which has me reaching for the covers, pulling them up to my chin. I hear him rummaging around the house, and then his footsteps grow louder as they reach his room. He holds up my purse, and it would be comical if I weren't so turned on. He's naked as the day he was born, his hard cock resting against his belly, holding my purse up in the air like a trophy.

"There's a new small box in there," I tell him.

He fumbles with my purse, digging around inside for a condom. The funny thing is, I almost didn't have one either. I stopped at the pharmacy to grab a card for Gloria earlier this week for her birthday. I just happened to walk past the condoms. I wanted to be prepared just in case. I didn't know if I would need them, but I didn't want to be in a situation where we needed them and didn't have them. I guess it worked out.

I see it the minute that he finds the box. His eyes sparkle with mischief, and he drops my purse to the floor. "Were you hoping to get lucky, baby?" he teases.

"I was a girl scout," I tell him with a straight face. It's true, I was, but they didn't teach us to keep condoms on hand.

"Funny girl." He smiles, tearing open the box, pulling out the three-pack of condoms, and letting the packaging drop to the floor.

"You think you're going to need all of those?" I ask him.

"Maybe not today, but yeah, we're going to need them."

All right then. I watch in fascination as he tears open the small package and slides it over his length. He takes a step toward the bed, and I hold up the covers, allowing him to take it and slide back under the covers. He settles between my thighs, and suddenly all is right in my world.

"Full disclosure?" he asks, smoothing my hair from my face. I nod. "This is going to be quick."

A slow smile spreads across my face. "They have pills for that," I tease.

"I might have to look into that." He kisses me lightly. "I've craved the feeling of being inside you since the moment I pulled out the first time. I know me, and I know how bad I want you." He gives a slight shrug.

"Is this a one-time thing?"

"Hell no."

I mimic his shrug. "Then it doesn't matter. I mean, if we need to practice for your stamina, I could get on board with that. You know, taking one for the team and all that." I can barely contain my laughter, that is until he pushes inside me.

"What's wrong, babe?" he chides.

I shake my head. "Perfect."

"You're perfect." Bending his head, he presses his lips to mine. All laughter and conversation are lost as we lose ourselves in one another. His lips never leave mine. Not when his hands clasp tightly onto mine, holding them over our heads, and not when I feel my orgasm crash through my body like a hurricane. It's not until we're both spent and sated that his lips leave mine.

"You're incredible, Aspen," he whispers, his lips next to my ear.

I can't speak, not yet. He's stolen my ability to form words, so I do all that I can, and that's hold him close. My grip is tight, and I can't help but think that I never want to let him go.

Never.

"This kitchen is insane," I say about an hour later. I'm sitting on the island in one of his T-shirts while he makes us bacon and eggs for breakfast. "Thank you for making me breakfast. A girl could get used to this."

He steps to the island and kisses me softly. "Thankfully, you were thinking ahead and picked up some groceries when you bought drinks last night. Otherwise, I'd be feeding you leftover pizza for breakfast."

"Nothing wrong with pizza for breakfast," I tell him.

"No. But I like that I'm cooking for you after our first night here." He plates up our bacon and eggs just as there's a knock at the door.

Panicked, I look down at my bare legs as I'm in nothing but his T-shirt. "I should go change," I say, but he stops me.

"No. This is our home, you stay. I'll see who it is."

"Conrad, I'm in nothing but your T-shirt. I don't even have a bra on!" I exclaim.

"Exactly how I want you. Here." He reaches for his hoodie that he had on yesterday and tosses it to me. "You can put this on too, but don't move." He points at me and grins.

I don't know why, but I stay put, my ass perched on the counter, and slide the sweatshirt over my head.

"We're just eating breakfast. Are you all hungry?" I hear him ask.

I'm going to kill him.

"Come on in," he says, and I hear the door shut. "Babe, our siblings are here," he calls out, giving me a heads-up.

I tug on the sweatshirt, and it covers me, but I still feel uncomfortable. At least they can't tell I'm not wearing a bra or panties. Don't judge.

"Hey, sis." Aurora smiles.

"Hi." I wave awkwardly.

Conrad walks in behind them and comes to stand between my

legs. He picks up his plate and begins to eat. "I can make more if you're hungry," he tells them.

"Nah, we just ate." Grant grins. "We just wanted to stop in and see if you all planned to go back to the hospital today. We're headed there now."

"We haven't talked about it," Conrad tells him.

Aurora has her nose buried in her phone while the brothers talk while I sit awkwardly on the island, staring at Conrad's bare chest. It's not until I hear my sister that I pull my eyes to her. Her grin is huge, and I know without a doubt she's up to something.

"Aspen, I have a song I want you to hear," she tells me. It's then that "I Just Had Sex" by Lonely Island plays from her phone. She bobs her head to the beat and starts singing the lyrics. Conrad and Grant are cracking up laughing. I try my hardest to keep a straight face, but I can't, and I end up joining them.

"You earned that one," Grant tells me with a smile.

"I'm sorry." Aurora beams. "I had to do it."

"We're even," I tell her.

"We'll see." She chuckles.

Conrad, who is already finished with his breakfast, while my plate remains untouched, places his hands on my thighs. "You want to go back to the hospital?" he asks me.

"Sure."

"Mom's bringing food. Anything we need to do?"

"Nah, she's got it all handled. You know Mom, she lives for feeding her family."

I can't help but think I'd be the same way with my kids. "I still have the magic bars from last night that we never got to eat. I'll bring those," I tell them.

"Sounds like a plan," Grant agrees.

"Wait, who has Carter?" Conrad asks.

"They dropped him off at Mom and Dad's. They're going to visit early."

"We can watch him," I tell Conrad.

"We offered too," Aurora tells me. "Owen insisted they wouldn't stay long. Besides, I can guarantee we get kicked out at one point or another. There is a lot of us." She smiles warmly at her husband.

"We'll see you there?" Grant asks Conrad.

"Yeah, we'll get a shower and head over." With a wave, my sister and her husband turn and head for the front door.

"Oh, Aspen." Aurora stops and turns to look at me.

"Yeah?"

"Don't forget to wipe down the counter." She winks, and then they're gone.

"Remind me to never let you answer the door again. Not unless I'm fully dressed," I tell Conrad.

He smiles and hands me my plate. "Does that mean you plan on sleeping here more often?"

I ignore him, taking a big bite of my eggs. He throws his head back in laughter. The sound fills my heart and my soul. We both know he's worn me down. I'm tired of fighting, and I can't resist him. Not even if I really wanted to.

CHAPTER
Conrad
TWENTY EIGHT

"**D**O YOU HAVE to go home?" Conrad asks.

We're sitting on the couch at his new place. He's lived here for a week, and every day he's asked me when I'm moving in. "Yes. I have so much laundry to do, and I need to clean out my refrigerator. I've been spending so much time here, all the food is expired, and I need to toss it before it starts to stink."

"Okay, so I come with you. You grab your clothes while I clean out the fridge, and then we come back here."

"Con, I don't live here."

"Why not?" he asks.

"We've been dating a hot minute."

"Do you want to be here?" he asks.

"That's not the point. Of course, I love spending time with you, but I have responsibilities."

"Bring your responsibilities here," he counters.

"It will be good for us to spend a night apart." I say the words, even though I'm dreading it just as much as he is. I've stayed here every night since his first night here last weekend. I need to go home and process all of this. Not to mention, I really do need to catch up on laundry and clean out the fridge.

"I don't think I'll survive it," he says dramatically.

"Stop." I laugh. "I think you'll be just fine."

"I don't like it," he grumbles.

"It's hard to live out of an overnight bag." As soon as the words are out of my mouth, I know he's going to turn them around on me.

"Then don't." He moves to the floor from his seat on the couch, and on his knees, he wraps his arms around my waist. "I want you here. With me. All the time. Please, move in with me." He bats his long eyelashes, and I almost cave.

Almost.

"I'll come back one night this week, and we can make dinner together." That's something I've discovered about Conrad. He's hands-on. If we're making dinner, he's right there next to me.

"How about I come home with you, and we stay at your place tonight?" he offers.

"Con, it's one night."

"But I'll miss you."

"Absence makes the heart grow fonder."

"My heart is full as fuck with fondness for you, babe," he says, sighing loudly. "Fine. Go home. I don't want to pressure you. Well, I do want to pressure you because I want you here, but I get it. Will you call me when you get there?"

"Yes." Bracing my hands on his face, I run my fingers through his beard. "I'll call you when I get there, and I'll call before I go to sleep."

"Oh, God, I can't sleep when you're not here."

"How do you know?" I counter. "You've never had to."

"I know, trust me. I slept like shit without you after our time at the cabin, and I've had you here now for over a week. It's going to suck."

"You'll be fine." I kiss him softly. When I pull out of the kiss, he stands and leads me to his room so I can pack my clothes.

"You know you could just leave those here. I'll toss them in the wash with mine. That way, you don't have to pack them back and forth." He sounds so hopeful I hate to disappoint him.

"Fine, but I still have a pile of laundry at home that needs to be done."

"Come on. I'll walk you out." Hand in hand, he leads me to the garage. He hits the button on the wall to raise the door for the first bay, the one he declared as mine. "Drive safe," he says, kissing me soundly.

"I'll call you when I get there," I assure him. He nods and closes my door, standing with his legs spread apart, arms crossed over his chest, watching me as I drive away.

I'm barely at the end of the road when my phone rings. Hitting Accept on my steering wheel, I answer, "Hello?"

"I miss you already."

My smile is blinding. "I miss you too, but I can't neglect my responsibilities."

"You wouldn't have to if you moved in with me. We could take care of all of it together."

"I'll think about it."

"I don't like it. You're supposed to be here with me. Not in that apartment all alone."

"I'm a big girl. I'll be fine."

"You'd be better in my arms." He pouts.

"Why don't you call Marshall and see if he wants to hang out or go to the gym?"

"Yeah," he agrees half-heartedly. "I need to set up the home gym here in the basement."

"There you go. He can help you do that."

"I need to order the equipment."

"He can give you his opinion."

"Fine," he grumbles. "I'll call Marsh."

"See, you won't even notice I'm gone."

"You know that's not true."

I admit the fact he wants me there so badly warms my heart. I went from thinking the time we shared all those weeks ago was just a fling, when in fact, it's turned into so much more. Conrad has proven to me that he's in this for the long haul. This week with him has been incredible. It's taken everything I have not to tell him that I'm going to pack up everything that will fit in my car and be back there later tonight, but I hold strong.

"I'm pulling into the bakery now. Call Marshall. Spend some time with your brother. I bet he misses you."

"Yeah. Okay. Call me later?"

"I promise."

"Aspen, I—" He stops. "I'll talk to you soon."

"Bye." I end the call in time to unlock the bakery door, making sure I lock it behind me before heading up the stairs to the apartment.

Two hours later, I hear keys in the door. I freeze until I see Aurora step into the room. "Hey, what are you doing here?"

"Your boyfriend stole my husband." She chuckles. "Poor guy, he called and sounded so sad. He recruited all of his brothers to come over and help him plan out the home gym in the basement."

"All of them?"

"Yep. Sawyer and Layla both forced their husbands out of the house, and Marshall gave Conrad a hard time telling him that he felt neglected."

"I can't even imagine. I'm glad you're here. I've missed you."

"Me too. Conrad said you were doing laundry and cleaning, so I thought I'd stop by and help."

"I'm all done. Well, I'm just waiting to swap out the washer and dryer." I pat the couch next to me. "Sit. How's married life?"

"I fall more in love with him every day."

"I'm so happy for you." She has a glow about her, and her smile is wide. I study her for a few minutes, and there's something I'm missing. "What else aren't you telling me? What's Conrad planning?" At this point, I'm not sure whatever it is would surprise me.

"It's not Con, not this time." She laughs.

"Well, spill."

"You can't say anything. We agreed to wait, but I have to tell you." Her eyes well with tears, and if it were not for the smile on her face, I'd be freaked out right now. Hell, who am I kidding? I'm still freaked out.

"Rory!" I can't take it.

"I'm pregnant," she blurts.

"What?" I launch myself at her, pulling her into a fierce hug. "I didn't know that you were trying."

"We're not. I mean, we weren't not trying, if that makes sense. I stopped taking my birth control the week of our wedding. From what I've read, it was supposed to take some time, but here we are."

"How did Grant take the news?"

"He's ecstatic. We both are. I'm going to be a mom, Aspen. You're going to be an aunt."

Hot tears prick my eyes as I process my sister's news. I can't begin to explain how happy I am for her. "Mom and Dad are going to freak," I tell her.

"I know! We agreed to wait a little while before telling anyone, but I had to tell you. Besides, I can't imagine him having all four of his brothers together and him not telling them."

We spend the next couple of hours talking about everything and just catching up. I didn't realize how much I missed my time with my sister until today.

At just before eight, I make sure the door is locked and the alarm is set, and make my way to my room. I get settled into bed before calling Conrad, as I promised.

"Are you on your way here?" he greets me.

"No. I'm lying in bed. How was your afternoon?"

"Good. All four of my brothers came over, and we mapped out the home gym."

"See." I smile.

"I didn't say I didn't miss you."

"I know you did. I missed you too, but Aurora showed up, and we had some time together too. I miss my sister."

"Yeah, as much as I hate to admit it, you were right. I miss hanging out with my brothers too. Now that we're all married, well except for Marshall, and they're having babies, the time just isn't there."

"We're not married." I'm smiling because I already know what he's going to say.

"We might as well be."

"Did Grant happen to have any news?"

He laughs. "Yep. I'm taking it that Aurora did as well?"

"Yeah. I'm so excited for them. And I'm going to be an aunt."

"You're already an aunt."

"Not really."

"Well, you will be once you agree to marry me."

"Whoa. I thought we were talking about moving in together first?"

"Yeah, but you have to know that I want to marry you. You do know that, don't you?"

He's not wrong. He drops hints all the time. My only holdback is that neither one of us has dropped that little four-letter word yet. I know I love him. I know he's the only man for me, and he tells me the same, but we have both yet to say the words.

"Aspen, I—" He starts, but I stop him.

"Don't, not over the phone."

"If you were here, I could tell you to your face. I could show you with my touch what you mean to me. I could hold you in my arms and taste your lips. I could do all of that all the time if you lived here with me."

I'll admit he's starting to wear me down. Part of that is coming back to my apartment over the bakery after staying at his place for a week. It's lonely here without him. "I miss you."

"Baby, you have no idea. Let me come to you."

"That's silly. I'll come over tomorrow when you get home from work."

"Come over as soon as you're done at the bakery."

"You won't even be there."

"I know, but I want to come home to you."

Last week, I would come to my place, change and tidy up a little, or work on the next day prep in the bakery until he got off and we would both get to his place at the same time. I have yet to use the keys that he gave me. "Okay," I agree.

"Want me to bring home dinner?"

"Nah, I say we make something."

"You spending the night?"

"Yes." I don't even have to think about my answer. I want to be where he is.

"I'll see you in the morning. Night, baby."

"Night, Con." I end the call, and surprisingly, I fall right to sleep.

CHAPTER
Conrad
TWENTY NINE

I T FEELS AS though I've just finally fallen asleep when my phone wakes me with a jolt. I smack around on the nightstand until I find it, seeing that it's Royce calling. I also notice that it's two in the morning. Something's wrong.

"Brother," I greet him.

"Con—" His voice cracks.

"What's wrong?" I sit farther up in bed.

"Listen, man. Marshall is on his way to your house. I need you to be dressed and ready. Can you do that?"

"Royce? What the fuck is going on?"

"Just do as I ask. Get dressed and be ready. Stay on the line with me. As soon as you're with Marsh, I'll tell you more."

"Is it Mom and Dad?" I ask, standing to pull on some sweats.

"Fuck," he mutters. "Conrad. Just fucking do as you're told." There is more pain in his voice than heat.

"I'm up. I'm getting dressed." I put the phone on speaker and toss it on the bed while I grab the hoodie I wore yesterday and pull it on. I ignore the tremble in my hands. Something is wrong, and I need to know what the fuck it is. "Royce?"

"Yeah?"

"Where's Sawyer and the baby?" My stomach sinks. Please, God, please don't let it be Sawyer or the baby. Fuck, don't let it be anyone we love.

"They're with me."

I pull in a deep breath. I need answers, but I know he's not going to give them to me. Not yet. My mind races with what could be going on. "Why Marshall?" I ask.

"He was already en route to you."

"Just tell me, Royce. What. Is. Going. On?" My tone is both pleading and demanding.

Racing to the living room, I pull on my tennis shoes just as headlights shine through the windows. "Marshall's here."

"Good." He sounds relieved.

Grabbing my keys, I rush out the front door, tugging and locking it behind me. Pulling open the door to Marshall's SUV, I climb in. "I'm with Marshall. What's going on?" I still have him on speaker, so I set the phone in the cupholder.

I look over at my little brother for some guidance, and his face is grim, and he looks like he's on the verge of losing his shit. "Buckle in," Marshall tells me.

"Fuck. Fine, I'm buckling in. Can the two of you please tell me what the fuck is going on?"

"Marshall?" Royce asks.

"We're en route," Marshall says, more serious than I think I've ever seen him.

"Conrad, I need you to listen to me." He pauses. From the croak in his voice, I'm not sure if it's for his benefit or mine. "There was a fire."

"A fire?" My heart is beating wildly in my chest. Someone is hurt. My mind swirls as I start to put the pieces together. Everyone is keeping me in the dark, that can only mean one thing.

Aspen.

Oh, fuck no. "Where? Spit it fucking out, Royce!" I slam my hand against the dash.

"The bakery. There was a fire." His voice breaks on a sob, and my heart stops. Making a fist, I have to pound against my chest to force myself to breathe. This can't be happening. Not her. I just found her.

"No. No. No. No. Aspen?" I ask him. "Where is Aspen? Where the fuck is she?" I shout.

Marshall reaches over and places his hand on my shoulder. I don't have the energy to throw him off. There is so much left we need to share. Marriage, kids, and the next sixty years. I can't lose her. I won't survive losing her.

"R-Royce—" I feel the first hot tear slide across my cheek. "Wh-Where is my girl? Tell me she's okay. Say it, damn it! Tell me she's okay." I turn wild eyes to Marshall. He, too, has tracks of his own tears on his cheeks. "Marsh." I can barely form words from the tightness in my throat. "Where is she?"

Royce clears his throat. "They took her to the hospital. That's all that we know," he says quietly.

"No! That's not good enough. I need you to call them now. Right now. Royce, you have to call them. Tell them we have money. We don't care what it costs. They need to take care of her. They need to tell her that I'm on my way. I need her!" I yell into the car.

"Marsh?" Royce's voice is pained.

"Y-Yeah? We're almost there," he replies.

That's when I notice we're speeding. No, we're flying through the streets of downtown Nashville weaving in and out of traffic as my little brother races to get me to my love. That woman is my fucking heart. My soul. I can't live this life without her. I can't. I can't do it.

"Please," I cry. "Please, God, please let her be okay. Please. Please. Please." I close my eyes and rest my head back against the seat. I hear Marshall sniff, and if I'm not mistaken, a sob comes from my phone.

My brothers are torn up over this, which means it's bad. *Fuck. Fuck. Fuck.* Running my fingers through my hair, I try to get my shit together, but it's no use. I'm a basket case, and I will be until I can lay eyes on her. Until I can feel her skin against mine.

I just need to touch her. That's how connected we are. I know that my touch will pull her through this. My love. Fuck me. I still haven't told her that I love her. I started to last night on the phone. She stopped me, and even though my gut told me I needed to tell her, I didn't. I stopped, and now she might not ever know.

"We're here," Marshall says.

"Good. Grant and Aurora are in the waiting room, so are Mom and Dad," Royce says.

As soon as the car comes to a stop, I'm out and running as fast as I can to the emergency room doors. I rush to the receptionist's desk, breathing heavily, bracing my hands on the counter for support. "Aspen Steele. I need to see her."

"I'm sorry, are you family?" the receptionist asks.

"Fuck! Am I family? She lives right fucking here." I slam my fist over my heart. "I need to see her."

"Con?" I turn to find Aurora standing behind me. Her eyes are red-rimmed from tears, and her face is pale.

I don't think. I just pull her into my arms, crushing her to me. "Is she okay?" I ask Aurora.

"We're still waiting," she says, stepping out of my hold. She then turns to the receptionist. "This is her fiancé. Conrad Riggins. He'll need to be on the list."

"Of course," the receptionist replies, typing on her computer. I assume giving me access to Aspen. "Please have a seat, and someone will be out to speak with you soon."

"No." I shake my head. "No. I won't sit out here and wait. I need to see her."

"Sir, I'm sorry, but the medical staff is with her. They need time to assess her injuries. I promise they will be with you soon."

"Come on, son." I feel my dad's hand on my shoulder as he guides me to the corner of the waiting room where my family is holding vigil.

"Tell me? How did this happen? How is she? Somebody needs to tell me something," I say, pacing back and forth in front of the chairs where my family is sitting.

"Conrad," Mom says softly. "Please sit, and we'll tell you what we know."

"How am I supposed to sit when my heart is somewhere in this fucking hospital, and no one will tell me how she is?"

"Conrad." Aurora stands and comes to me. She wraps her arms around my waist, and I hold her. Aspen is her sister. If anyone is going to begin to understand how I feel, it's her. "I can't lose her, sis. I can't." My voice breaks. I hold her tightly and let the tears fall.

I break.

My legs feel weak, but I needn't worry because I feel the arms of my family wrap around me. Grant comes first, then Marsh, and our parents. I soak up every ounce of love and support they have to give because I know we all need to be strong for her. When I finally feel as though I can stay calm, I break away and take a seat. My hand is clasped tightly around Aurora's, and thankfully, my brother lets it ride. I need to be close to her right now.

"Tell me," I whisper, my voice gravelly.

"At around one thirty, Rory got a call from the security company telling her that there were indications of a fire and that the appropriate personnel were en route," Grant explains solemnly.

"I tried to call her," Aurora says through her tears. "I tried over and over again, and we couldn't get through."

"We got in the car and drove over. I called Mom and Dad on the way. They called everyone else."

"I was awake," Marshall adds. "When Dad called, I was awake, so I told him I would come and get you."

"Royce and Owen have the little ones, so we told them to stay home until we know more. Royce wanted to be the one to call you," Mom explains.

That sounds like my big brother. He's always looking out for us, and I know that phone call was hard on him. I could hear it in his voice, but that's the bond of brothers. He needed me to know he was there for me.

"How is she?" I look away from Mom to find Owen and Royce standing in the waiting room. They left their families to come and support me.

A sob rattles my chest as I stand and rush to my brothers. I grip Royce in a hug so fierce I'm surprised either of us can breathe. I move to Owen and give him the same treatment. I fucking love my family, and I know without a shadow of a doubt I would be losing my shit right now if I didn't have them here with me.

Royce, Owen, and I take a seat, and I nod at Grant. "When we got there, the flames—" He shakes his head, swallowing hard. "It was bad, Con. Luckily, when the alarm company called, we were able to tell them Aspen was inside. We told them which room was hers, and when we got there, they were placing her on a stretcher and loading her into the back of an ambulance."

"Was sh-she okay?" I ask. It's a stupid fucking question. Of course, she wasn't okay, but I know that he knows what I meant.

"I don't know. The ambulance was racing off before we could get answers. All they would tell us is that they were bringing her here."

"The family of Aspen Steele," a nurse calls out.

I stand and rush to her. "Conrad Riggins," I announce. "How is she?"

"How are you related to Ms. Steele?" she asks.

"I'm her sister, Aurora. Conrad is her fiancé," Aurora says, coming to stand next to me. "And they"—she points behind her—"are our family too."

"Oh my. Okay, let me see if I can find a private waiting area that will accommodate everyone." She turns to leave.

"Wait!" I call out. "How is she?"

"I'm sorry, I don't have an update. The doctor asked me to get the family." She gives me a sad smile and walks away.

We go back to our seats. I can't sit still. My legs are bouncing up and down. My heart feels as though it could thump right out of my chest. I need answers. I need to see her.

"Family of Aspen Steele," the same nurse calls out about five minutes later.

We all stand and follow her down a long hallway to a small waiting room that reads *Private*. It's barely large enough to hold all of us, but we make it work. "The doctor will be right with you."

I open my mouth to bitch about having to wait yet again when the door opens, and a tall, older gentleman in a white coat steps into the room. "Hello, I'm Dr. Black. Are you all here for Aspen Steele?" he asks, glancing down at the tablet in his hand.

"Yes. I'm her sister, and this is her fiancé, Conrad," Aurora answers.

He nods. "She's stable. When they found her, she was unconscious, so they intubated her to make sure she had a clear airway. I've just reviewed her X-rays, and her lungs look clear."

"Is she awake?" Aurora asks.

"No." He shakes his head. "We'll need to leave her intubated for several hours. We need to watch her for flash pulmonary edema. We're working on getting her admitted to a room."

"Doc." My voice cracks. "Is she going to be okay?"

"Like I said, she's stable. Her vitals are good and her lungs are clear. The next few hours will be the test to see if she develops FPD. We'll monitor her closely over the next several hours and then do another X-ray. If that comes back normal, we can begin to extubate and bring her out of sedation."

"I need to see her." I don't ask for permission.

He nods. "One at a time."

I look at Aurora, and her eyes are soft. She looks over at Grant and then back to me. "Please tell her I love her," she says through her fresh tears.

"When we get her settled into a room, we can do two visitors at a time," the doctor adds, having sensed our dilemma.

"A-Are you sure?" I ask Aurora. I feel like a dick. She's her sister, but I can't breathe without Aspen.

"I'm sure. I'll see her when they get her into a room."

I wrap my arms around Aurora and hold her close. "I love her, sis. I love her so fucking much."

"I know you do," she says when I release her. "Go. She needs you."

Grant steps up behind her and wraps her in his embrace, and I know she understands. The bond they share is much like the one I share with Aspen. In fact, I'm sure if I was in her shoes, I'd let her go first also. I love my brothers, but Aspen, she's my everything.

Our footsteps echo off the walls as I follow the doctor. The noises around me fade away, and I feel as though I'm walking through a tunnel. I don't know what to expect when I see Aspen. I don't know how I'm going to react. I just know she needs me. I know if I can just touch her, if I can tell her how much I love her, she'll come back to me.

The doctor stops just outside of a room with a closed door. "A nurse will be in to check on both of you in a minute." The doctor pats my shoulder and walks away.

Taking a deep breath, I grip the handle, turn, and push. I keep my eyes on the floor as I close the door and make my way to the side of her bed. Lifting my gaze, I take in my love. My knees feel weak, which has me gripping the rails of her bed to remain standing.

She has a tube down her throat and IVs in her arms. Her face is pale with smudges of black, and the smell of smoke is overwhelming. I don't attempt to stop the tears as they fall from my eyes. "Baby," I whisper.

"Just checking her vitals," a nurse says softly, entering the room.

I grab the chair next to the wall and move it close to the bed before falling into it. Carefully, I pick up Aspen's hand to hold it in mine, my thumb softly tracing her knuckles. "Can I clean her up?" I ask when I bring her hand to my lips for a kiss.

"Sure, I'll grab some supplies. We can have the nursing staff do that when she's admitted upstairs," she offers.

"No." I shake my head. "I want to do it."

Her eyes soften. "I'm sorry, we don't allow that. However, I promise to take good care of her."

The door closes softly behind her, and I place my attention back on Aspen. "Aspen." My voice breaks. I bring her hand to my lips and kiss her palm. "I don't know if you can hear me right now, but if you can, I need you to listen. Can you do that, baby?" I pause, swallowing hard. "I need you. I need you to fight this. I need to tell you how much I love you. I need to see those pretty hazel eyes when I tell you that I plan to love the fuck out of you for the rest of our lives. I want to marry you and have babies with you. I want to watch our babies have babies. With. You," I emphasize. Resting my forehead against the mattress, I keep her hand held in mine as my tears fall freely.

"Please, God," I whisper. "Please don't take her from me."

The door opens again, and I wipe at my cheeks with the sleeve of my sweatshirt. "She's been assigned a room," the nurse, who was just in here checking her vitals, informs me. "She's going to be on the third floor, room 3098."

"Are you moving her now?"

"Yes. If you want to inform your family and head up that way. There's a large waiting room just across the hall from her room." She smiles softly.

"Thank you." Standing, I lean over the bed and place my lips against her forehead. "I love you. They're taking you to a new room. I'll meet you up there." I don't know if she can hear me, but I hope so. I hope she hears my pleas for her to come back to me. I need her to hear me so I can tell her I love her. So I can look into her eyes and tell her what she means to me. I vow to never let a single day pass by that I don't tell her how much I love her.

My feet are heavy as I make my way back to the waiting room to give our family an update. As soon as they see me, they're all on their feet. All eyes are on me as I approach them.

"She's... I don't know if she can hear me," I say, defeated, my eyes cast to the floor. Hot tears begin to build behind my eyes. "I told her that I love her, but I don't know if she can hear me." I look up at our family to find they all have the same look of grief and misty eyes as well. "I've never said the words to her. I wanted to, but I didn't want to scare her away. I tried to last night, on the phone, and I think she knew, but she stopped me. I get it. You don't tell the love of your life over the phone for the first time that you love them, but I felt this urgency to tell her. Now, what if I never get the chance? How will I live with myself if she doesn't come out of this and she never knew that she lived right here?" I place my hand, palm flat against my chest.

"She knows," Aurora cries. "She knows, and she loves you too."

"She has to wake up, Rory. She has to. I need her to wake up." I know I'm being irrational. The doctors have assured me that they are keeping her asleep with sedation. However, I still have this deep-rooted fear that she might not wake up. What if decreasing the medicine doesn't work? What if I never get to look into her eyes and tell her I love her?

My dad steps forward and places his hands on my shoulders. "You fight for her, Conrad Riggins. Do you hear me? You fight for her. You hold onto the magic that is your love for her, and you fucking fight." Dad's voice is stern, but there is an underlying sadness to his words. "She needs you to be strong. She needs you to be her strength in all of this."

Wiping at my eyes, I nod. "They're uh, they're putting her in a room. Third floor, room 3098. The nurse said there's a waiting room just across the hall."

"Come on, let's get up there so when she's settled, we can all take our turn going in to see her," Mom instructs.

That's when it hits me. I turn to look at Aurora. "Your parents?"

"They're on their way," Grant answers for his wife.

"Good." With that, I turn and make my way to the elevator. I don't bother looking to see if my family is behind me. I know they are. Just like they always have been and always will be. She has the Riggins clan in her corner, her sister, and her parents. We are her family, and we will fight for her. Fight with her, to see her through this. There is no other option.

CHAPTER
Aspen
THIRTY

CAN HEAR Conrad, but I can't see him. I feel the press of his lips to my forehead and his whispered words of love, but I can't see his face. I want to see him, but my eyelids feel heavy, and I'm just too sleepy to try any harder. I need to tell him I love him too. I need him to know I'm done running. I'm done fighting our love. I just want to wake up and be in his arms. I want to tell him I'll move in with him. I want to tell him he's my magic. I need to tell him he made me a believer.

I just want to open my eyes.

I need to tell him.

I'm fighting, Conrad.

I love you too.

CHAPTER

Conrad

THIRTY ONE

FIVE HOURS. THAT'S how long I've been sitting in this chair, praying that when they bring her out of sedation she comes back to me. I'm terrified the doctors are wrong, and I'll never get to see her open her eyes again. I refuse to leave her side. I can't. What if she wakes up and I'm not here? The doctor said it would take a little while for the sedation to wear off once it's been stopped. Our limit is two at a time, but we've been pushing that to three. I refuse to leave, and her parents, mine, as well as my brothers and their wives, have all taken turns coming to see her. Marshall is sitting with me now; I can feel his stare, but I don't take my eyes off Aspen.

"You really believe in the magic?" he asks.

"I didn't use to," I confess.

"How did you know?"

"Know she was my magic? Know that I loved her? What are we talking here, Marshall?" I ask, turning to look at him.

He shrugs. "All of it."

"You meet someone?"

"Nah, but I'm the last holdout, and it seems as though I'm the one missing out."

I nod. "You are."

"One woman for the rest of your life," he says.

"The right woman. It makes all the difference. I wish I could explain it to you. It's as if nothing is bright unless I can share it with her. She's the first thing I think about when I open my eyes and the last before I close them at night. Hanging with her watching television is more fun than any night out at a club." I shake my head, smiling. My eyes go back to Aspen. "My heart isn't my own anymore. She has her hands around it, and I hope she never lets go."

"Damn," he mutters.

"One day, Marshall, you're going to find a woman who will bring you to your knees, and then you'll understand. It's not something I can explain to you. It's something you have to feel. That you have to experience all on your own."

"Knock, knock," a man's voice says. Glancing up, I see Dr. Haroldson, the doctor who took over for Dr. Black and has been taking care of her since she was admitted. He looks to Marshall and then back to me. "May I speak freely?"

"Yes, this is my brother Marshall."

The doctor nods. "The radiologist just read her most recent X-rays, and her lungs still look good. We're going to extubate her and start to bring her back from sedation."

"What does that mean?"

"That means that we're going to wake her up. Her vitals are strong, and despite the smoke, her lungs look great. She's going to have a sore throat and possibly a cough. I have full reason to believe she will make a complete recovery."

My shoulders relax, and I feel as though a thousand-pound weight has been lifted. She's going to be okay. Pulling her hand to my lips, I kiss her palm. "You're going to be okay," I tell her. "I love you," I say, feeling my throat get tight.

She's going to be okay.

"Now," Dr. Haroldson says, "I'm going to have Dr. Connor come up and do an ultrasound to check on the baby. However, with Aspen's vitals and recovery, her lungs being clear, we have full reason to believe that your baby is safe, and she should be able to carry to full term."

Wait.

What?

"Baby?"

"Yes, it says here that Aspen is expecting."

"Are you sure?"

Dr. Haroldson looks up from his tablet in his hands. "I'm sorry, were you not aware?"

I shake my head—a baby. We're having a baby. Standing, I lean over the bed and place my lips next to her ear. "Aspen, we're having a baby. I don't know if you knew that or not. If not, I wanted to be the one to tell you. I love you. I love you both so much." I press a kiss to her temple.

"Right, well, I'll send Dr. Connor up right away," the doctor says, and then he's gone.

"Did you hear that, Marsh?" I ask my little brother. Reaching out, I gently place my hand on Aspen's belly. "I'm having a baby. I'm going to be a father."

Marshall is on his feet and pulling me into a hug. "Happy for you, brother."

"Thanks," I say, getting choked up this time from happiness, not fear. "Listen, can you not tell the others? I don't think she knows, and I want her to find out first. Then we can tell everyone together." I glance down at my future wife. The mother of my child. "When she wakes up, we'll tell them together." No way would she have known about this and not told me. I feel that deep in my soul. She would have told me.

The last two hours have been a flurry of activity. I sent Marshall to the waiting room to give our families an update about her progress, minus the baby. I had him tell them that there were no visitors allowed while they were extubating her, other than me—they knew I refused to leave. It's true. No way am I leaving her, but it bought me some time for the OBGYN to come in and see her and our baby.

They brought an ultrasound machine, and I was able to see our baby for the first time. The flicker of his or her little heartbeat was flashing on the screen. The doctor assured me the baby was perfectly healthy, and there's no reason to be concerned.

I hate she missed this moment. The tech who was assisting the doctor printed me lots of pictures and even handed me a DVD, which had me tearing up. Now, not only can I show Aspen, but our family too.

I'm going to be a father.

"I love you," I say from my spot next to her bed. The tube is out of her throat, and she's doing well, breathing on her own. Her vitals look good, and now we just need her to wake up. "I never got to tell you that." My eyes are glued to her belly, where our child grows. "I was so afraid you would run if I did. This taught me a valuable lesson. Say today what you might not get to tomorrow. Never again will I go a single day without telling you how much I love you. How much I love our baby."

"Baby?" a raspy voice asks.

My head jerks to her, and I blink hard. Once, twice, three times to make sure I'm not seeing things that aren't really happening. She's awake. "I missed you," I say, leaning in and pressing my lips to hers. Pulling back, I offer her a sip of water.

She drinks greedily. "You said baby."

I nod. "Did you know you were pregnant?" I ask.

Tears well in her eyes. "No. Is—" She stops, getting choked up.

"The baby is fine. You're going to be fine. Do you remember what happened?"

"I woke up to the smoke alarm and lots of smoke. I couldn't see, and the heat..." She shivers.

"You're safe." I lean in and kiss her again. "You and our baby are safe."

"Conrad, I-I didn't know."

"Now we do. Starting today, we focus on our forever."

"I could feel you. I could hear you, but I couldn't say anything back." She swallows hard, and I offer her another drink of water. "I focused on the feeling of your hand in mine."

"I need to call the doctor and let them know you're awake, but first." I reach into the bedside table and pull out the ultrasound pictures. "This is our baby," I say, pointing out the heartbeat. "They said you're about seven weeks along. So, our night together at the cabin."

"I'm on the pill, and we used protection. I don't understand?" *Except that one time.*

"It's the magic, baby. It doesn't matter how or why. All that matters is what is. We're going to have a baby."

"I love you," she whispers.

"I love you."

Reaching over her head, I call the doctor to come and check on her before our families come in. "I'm going to text Aurora and tell her that you're awake. I didn't tell anyone about the baby except for Marshall. He was in here when the doctor told me."

"Can we tell them all at the same time?"

I think about the two people at a time rule that we've been breaking all day and decide I don't give a fuck. The worse that they can do is kick everyone back to the waiting room. I'll never deny her anything. "Yeah. I'll make that happen."

For the first time since she was admitted, I step out of her room and across the hall to the waiting room. All eyes land on me, and I smile. I can see the tension leave every single one of them from that simple act alone.

"She's awake. They just checked her out, and she's doing well. They're going to keep her overnight, just as a precaution."

"Can we see her?" her mom asks.

"Actually, I'm going to need all of you to sneak across the hall as quietly as you can." I glance around. Layla and Sawyer aren't here, but that's okay. They're where they should be at home with their babies. I'll be sure to have Royce and Owen call them before we make our announcement. I don't want them to miss out on this.

The tiny room is packed with all ten of us, eleven counting Aspen. She's sitting up in bed, and I take a seat next to her. "Owen, Royce, I'm going to need you to call your wives and put them on speaker."

They give me a quizzical look but do as I ask. Once Sawyer and Layla are on the line and can hear me, I look over at Aspen and nod. We decided she would be the one to tell our families that we're having a baby.

Her eyes zero in on her sister, and she smiles. "Conrad and I have something to tell you."

Aurora gasps, having already figured it out in that weird way siblings do. Grant looks down at her and back at me, and the slow grin that tilts his lips tells me he did as well.

"What was that?" Sawyer asks. "What did I miss?"

"Yeah, what's going on?"

"Nothing." I laugh. "We're getting ready to tell you."

"Well, get on with it," Layla says.

"Babe." I nod toward Aspen.

She looks at me with so much love in her eyes that it's a good thing I'm sitting, or it would bring me to my knees. "Conrad and I are having a baby." Her voice is strong, although still a little gruff. That's okay. From the commotion around the room, our friends and family hear her just fine.

There are lots of tears, smiles, hugs, and congratulations, and of course, the nurse stops in and tells us that we're breaking the rules. After kissing Aspen on the head, I leave her, letting her have time with her sister and her parents while Marshall and I grab something to eat in the cafeteria. This day started out as my worst nightmare and ended with me being a father. It could have been so much worse, and I thank God, as I will every day, for keeping my family safe.

CHAPTER
THIRTY TWO

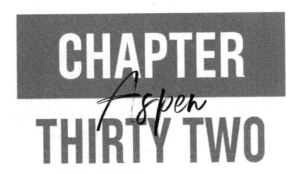

C ONRAD KISSES ME softly before promising to be back in a little while. I watch him leave before turning my eyes back to my parents and my sister.

"He loves you," Dad says with confidence.

"I love him too."

"And you're having a baby." Mom sniffles, trying and failing miserably to hide her tears.

"We were certain Aurora would give us our first grandchild." Dad smiles at my sister.

I hold out my hand, and Aurora takes the seat next to me on the bed that Conrad just vacated. "About that," she says, gripping my hand tightly.

"No," Mom gasps, covering her mouth with her hand.

Aurora smiles, tears welling in her eyes. "I went to the doctor on Friday. I'm six weeks along."

My parents look at me, and I know by the look in their eyes what they're asking. "Seven weeks," I tell them.

I watch as my father pulls my mother into his arms and kisses her forehead. "Two grandbabies a week apart." Dad smiles. He looks down at Mom. "Sheila, I think it's time we make that move."

"Yes," Mom agrees emphatically.

The four of us sit and talk about what's to come. I'm so excited to be going through this pregnancy journey with my sister. She's my best friend, like our kids—cousins—I'm sure will be as well.

Aurora yawns for the fourth time, and I know I need to assure them that I'm fine so they can all go home and get some rest. "I'm good," I tell her. "You need your rest." I glance from her to my parents, who also look exhausted. "Go home, get some rest. You know Conrad isn't going to leave here without me. I'll call you if there are any changes, but I'm going to be okay."

They finally relent after a little more coaxing, and with the room quiet, I close my eyes and drift off to sleep.

I wake a little while later to a dark room. Turning my head to the window, I see that my room is not the only darkness. Glancing around the room, I find Conrad sleeping in the chair. His head is tilted forward, and his arms are crossed over his chest. I'm not surprised to find him here. I knew he wouldn't leave me.

His voice and his touch are what pulled me through all of this. I know that sounds crazy, even to my own ears, but it's the truth. I wanted to scream at him that I loved him too, but I couldn't. Now that I can, I want to tell him over and over and over again.

My eyes dart to my still flat stomach. A baby. I'm going to be a mom. Aurora and I are having babies at the same time, and I couldn't be happier. I will never forget the look in Conrad's eyes when he told me. His eyes held nothing but love for me and our unborn child. I'm excited and scared, but that's to be expected with the unknown. What I'm not is worried about doing this alone. I know he's going to be there with me every step of the way.

I lie still, watching him sleep. This man, the love of my life, the father of my unborn child, he's everything I could ever want and more than I ever could have hoped for.

"I feel you watching me," he says, stretching.

"Come lie with me."

Not needing further invitation, he kicks off his shoes, and I move over to one side of the bed. Carefully, he climbs into the bed next to me, pulling me into his arms. "I love you so much," he says softly. "I thought I lost you, babe. I was so angry at myself for not telling you sooner. I was scared as hell that I was going to lose you without ever having the opportunity to look into your beautiful hazel eyes and tell you what you mean to me."

"I'm right here."

"I missed you."

I smile. "I love you, Conrad Riggins. Or maybe I should call you baby daddy."

"Daddy," he muses. "Don't think I'm losing my mind or anything, but, Aspen, I love this baby so much. Already. How is that possible? How can I love this tiny living human inside you who I've never met?"

My heart melts at his words. I place my hand on his cheek, relishing the feel of his beard beneath my palm as I stare into his eyes. "Because he or she is a part of you. Conceived out of love."

His lips press to mine, and just like that, all is right in my world. Sure, I'm in a hospital bed, but I'm okay. Our baby is okay. This man, he loves me with an intensity that fills my soul. I get lost in his kiss, sore throat be damned.

"Will you move in with me?" he asks, breaking the kiss.

"Yes."

His smile lights up his eyes. "Just like that?"

"Just like that. I don't want to fight this anymore. Life is too short. I used to be worried that you would decide you didn't want me, but I see it in your eyes. I feel it in your touch. Our souls are one."

"You and this baby, you're everything to me." He goes quiet.

"I don't know what kind of shape the bakery is in. In fact, I didn't even ask. I know that it's terrible you and your sister lost your business, you lost your home, but all of that can be replaced. I could never replace you."

"You're stuck with me, Riggins."

"Bring it, baby momma." He grins. "Bring it." He sits up and moves from the bed. "Come on. Aurora brought you some clothes. Let's get you a shower."

"Oh my God, did they say I could shower?"

"Yes. They're releasing you in the morning." He points to my hand. "The nurse stopped the IV, but they have to leave it in just in case. It's hospital protocol, but you're no longer hooked up to anything."

"Will you shower with me?" I ask him.

"I thought I heard you yell that you needed help washing your hair." He winks. I watch him as he grabs a small bag and carries it to the bathroom. "No lock," he tells me, checking the door.

"I guess we'll just have to take our chances."

"I guess we will. Come on, you." He helps me stand and walks next to me into the bathroom. "They brought me clean clothes as well." He points to the bag.

"We're lucky to have so much support."

"We are. We're going to need it when this little one comes." He presses his hand over my still-flat belly.

Together we shower. He's very attentive, taking extreme caution with me, all while making sure any remnants of smoke from the fire are washed away from my hair and skin. His hands roam over my body, and I not only feel cherished, but I feel safe — safe in his arms, safe by his touch.

By the time we're finished, I'm exhausted. Together we curl up in our clean clothes in my bed and drift off to sleep in each other's arms.

EPILOGUE
Conrad

SHE'S RADIANT. ASPEN'S smile lights up the entire room. We're at my parents' house, having a joint baby shower for both Aspen and Aurora. It's been four months since the fire, and I thank God every day for saving her.

A lot has happened in those four months. Hank and Sheila are now living in Nashville. With both of their daughters expecting grandbabies a week apart, they felt it was time. I'm thrilled to have them closer. I know that Aspen and Aurora are as well. It will be nice for our kids to have two sets of grandparents to spoil them.

The bakery was a complete loss. The first time I went to see it after Aspen was released from the hospital, I got sick. Tossed my cookies right there on the sidewalk. I don't know how they got her out safely, but I made sure to make a hefty donation to the local fire and EMS. Those men and women risk their lives to save ours, and that doesn't go unnoticed. Not by me.

Since the girls are both pregnant, and they are still dealing with insurance for the bakery, they've decided not to rebuild just yet. I know for a fact that Grant and I are both thrilled with this idea. I never want to clip her wings, and if they one day want to reopen,

I will be their biggest cheerleader, Grant too, but until then, they've got a more important job, taking care of themselves and our babies.

"You getting excited?" Grant asks from beside me.

"I am. You?"

"I can't fucking wait. I love Roan and Carter, but to know that in just a few months, we're going to be holding our own kids—" He shakes his head in disbelief. "It's surreal, man."

"I love that all our kids are going to be growing up together, close in age like the five of us."

"Well, maybe. We don't know what Marshall has going on." Grant laughs.

"I think he knows he's missing out," I confess, thinking about the conversation I had with him when Aspen was in the hospital.

"And the other thing?" Grant asks.

I pat my shorts pocket. "I'm good to go."

"When are you going to do it?"

"See that little green bag?" I point to the gift table next to Aspen.

"Yeah."

"Keep your eye on that one."

"Are you going to make me look bad?" He points to the gift table next to Aurora. "That little yellow one is mine."

"Depends. What's in yours?"

"A gift card for a mommy spa day. What's in yours?"

"Oh, I got her one of those too. But that little bag, that one holds the best gift."

"What is it?"

"You're about to find out." When Sawyer hands Aspen the little green bag, I step forward and kneel next to her. She takes my breath away.

EPILOGUE
Aspen

"**H**EY, YOU." CONRAD kneels in front of me. "You doing all right?"

"Yes. Have you been watching? Have you seen all of these cute gifts? And the clothes, they're so tiny."

He places his hand on my belly. "I've been watching. This baby is loved, that's for sure." He leans in and presses a kiss to my belly.

I've long since stopped blushing at his public displays of affection. Much like his brothers with their wives, Conrad couldn't care less who sees him kissing or touching me. Well, within reason.

"Open this one." He nudges the little green bag in my lap.

Pushing aside the tissue paper, I reach into the bag and pull out some type of clothing. I swear these outfits are so small. It's hard to believe in a few months, Conrad and I are going to be responsible for a tiny human that will fit into these clothes.

Unfolding the onesie, I hold it up so that I can read what it says. I read the words and then read them again—tears welling in my eyes.

Will you marry my daddy?

"Well, what does it say?" my sister asks from her seat next to mine. I turn it so that everyone can read it.

I drop the onesie in my lap to look at Conrad to find him holding up a small black box. "Oh," I gasp, my hands flying over my mouth as tears threaten to fall.

"Aspen Steele. You, beautiful, are the love of my life. The mother of my child. The keeper of my soul. Would you do me the incredible honor of becoming my wife?" He opens the box, and the most beautiful princess cut ring surrounded by a band of diamonds sparkles back at me.

I stare at the ring and then back to Conrad. He looks nervous, and that makes me smile. He has to know there is nothing I want more than to be his wife. To share this life that we're building together until we are old and gray.

"Uh, Aspen," Marshall calls out. "You need me to pull the getaway car around?" he teases, making everyone laugh.

"Baby?" Conrad whispers.

"Yes. Yes. Yes. I'll marry you."

His lips press to mine, and he kisses me as if his life depends on it. The room erupts with cheers and catcalls as he breaks away from this kiss. My hands are still resting on his cheeks, and I keep them there to ensure I have his full attention.

"You are the love of my life. Touch by touch, you showed me the kind of man you are. You showed me I was your first choice. You, Conrad Riggins, are my first choice. I love you."

"I love you too, future Mrs. Riggins."

Thank you for taking the time to read Touch by Touch. Are you ready for more of the Riggins brothers? Marshall's story is next in Beat by Beat.

Never miss a new release:
http://bit.ly/2UW5Xzm

More about Kaylee's books:
http://bit.ly/2S6clWe

Facebook:
http://bit.ly/2C5DgdF

Instagram:
http://bit.ly/2reBkrV

Reader Group:
http://bit.ly/2o0yWDx

Goodreads:
http://bit.ly/2HodJvx

BookBub:
http://bit.ly/2KulVvH

Website:
www.kayleeryan.com

OTHER WORKS by KAYLEE RYAN

With You Series:
Anywhere With You | More With You | Everything With You

Soul Serenade Series:
Emphatic | Assured | Definite | Insistent

Southern Heart Series:
Southern Pleasure | Southern Desire
Southern Attraction | Southern Devotion

Unexpected Arrivals Series:
Unexpected Reality | Unexpected Fight
Unexpected Fall | Unexpected Bond | Unexpected Odds

Standalone Titles:
Tempting Tatum | Unwrapping Tatum | Levitate
Just Say When | I Just Want You
Reminding Avery | Hey, Whiskey | When Sparks Collide
Pull You Through | Beyond the Bases
Remedy | The Difference
Trust the Push

OTHER WORKS *by* **KAYLEE RYAN**

Entangled Hearts Duet
Agony | Bliss

Co-written with Lacey Black:
It's Not Over | Just Getting Started | Can't Fight It

Cocky Hero Club:
Lucky Bastard

Riggins Brothers Series:
Play by Play | Layer by Layer
Piece by Piece | Kiss by Kiss
Touch by Touch

ACKNOWLEDGEMENTS

To my family:
I love you. I could not do this without your love and support. Thank you for everything.

Wander Aguiar:
It's always a pleasure working with you. You and Andrey always go above and beyond to help me find the perfect image. Thank you for your talent behind the lens and bringing Conrad's story to life.

Mason Mostajo:
Thank you for doing what you do. You brought Conrad to life. Best of luck to you in all of your future endeavors.

Tami Integrity Formatting:
Thank you for making the paperbacks beautiful. You're amazing and I cannot thank you enough for all that you do.

Lori Jackson:
You nailed it. You were patient with me, and worked your photoshop magic. Thank you for another amazing cover. It has been my pleasure working with you.

Lacey Black:
My dear friend. Thank you for always being there with life, and work. I value our friendship, and our working relationship more than you will ever know. I can't wait to see where our co-writing journey takes us.

My beta team:

Jamie, Stacy, Lauren, Erica, and Franci I would be lost without you. You read my words as much as I do, and I can't tell you what your input and all the time you give means to me. Countless messages and bouncing idea, you ladies keep me sane with the characters are being anything but. Thank you from the bottom of my heart for taking this wild ride with me.

Give Me Books:

With every release, your team works diligently to get my book in the hands of bloggers. I cannot tell you how thankful I am for your services.

Tempting Illustrations:

Thank you for everything. I would be lost without you.

Julie Deaton:

Thank you for giving this book a set of fresh final eyes.

Lia Fairchild:

Thank you for being my second set of fresh final eyes.

Becky Johnson:

I could not do this without you. Thank you for pushing me, and making me work for it.

Marisa Corvisiero:

Thank you for all that you do. I know I'm not the easiest client. I'm blessed to have you on this journey with me.

Kimberly Ann:

Thank you for organizing and tracking the ARC team. I couldn't do it without you.

Brittany Holland:

Thank you for your assistance with the blurb. You saved me!

Bloggers:

Thank you, doesn't seem like enough. You don't get paid to do what you do. It's from the kindness of your heart and your love of reading that fuels you. Without you, without your pages, your voice, your reviews, spreading the word it would be so much harder if not impossible to get my words in reader's hands. I can't tell you how much your never-ending support means to me. Thank you for being you, thank you for all that you do.

To my Kick Ass Crew:

The name of the group speaks for itself. You ladies truly do KICK ASS! I'm honored to have you on this journey with me. Thank you for reading, sharing, commenting, suggesting, the teasers, the messages all of it. Thank you from the bottom of my heart for all that you do. Your support is everything!

With Love,

Kaylee Ryan
AUTHOR